The
OFFICIAL
ENCYCLOPEDIA
of
BASEBALL

TENTH REVISED EDITION

The
OFFICIAL
ENCYCLOPEDIA
of
BASEBALL

TENTH REVISED EDITION

by

Hy TURKIN and S. C. THOMPSON

Revisions by Pete Palmer

DOLPHIN BOOKS
DOUBLEDAY & COMPANY, INC.
GARDEN CITY, NEW YORK
1979

THE OFFICIAL ENCYCLOPEDIA OF BASEBALL was originally published by
A. S. Barnes and Company, Inc., in 1951. The Dolphin Edition is
published by arrangement with A. S. Barnes and Company, Inc.

Dolphin Edition, 1979

ISBN: 0-385-15092-X

Library of Congress Catalog Card Number: 78-20725

© 1951, 1956 by Hy Turkin and S. C. Thompson

© 1959, 1962, 1963 by Florence Kerr Turkin, as Administratrix
of the Estate of Hy Turkin and S. C. Thompson

© 1968, 1970, 1972, 1974, 1976, 1977, 1979 by A. S. Barnes and Company, Inc.

CONTENTS

PREFACE

It took an earthquake to start this book.

One evening in September, 1944, Hy Turkin felt his chair shake and saw his living-room pictures sway. To an abstemious sportswriter the deduction was simple: an earthly tremor. So he phoned his paper, the *New York Daily News*. His report was included in a Page Two story of the major earthquake that had rocked the Atlantic seaboard.

Next morning, S. C. Thompson read the account, complete with name and address. Discovering therefrom that Turkin lived only about a fungo-hit from his home, Thompson decided to go around the corner and introduce himself to his sports-minded neighbor. "I'd like you to visit my house sometime, Hy, and look over my baseball collection. I know you'll find it interesting."

Interesting? It proved to be overwhelming. His profession as a musician in Broadway shows provided "Tommy" with spare time and money. These he parlayed with an unquenchable thirst for big league data to amass one of the most exhaustive files in baseball history.

Almost 20 years had gone into the collection of this statistical "diamond" treasure. But it took less than 20 minutes to fully appreciate the immensity of his compilation. Thus began a paired project dedicated to presenting sports fans the most complete baseball compendium ever attempted. Thompson, in several years at his sideline job as statistician in the Al Munro Elias Baseball Bureau, had perfected his technique of collecting and collating data. Turkin burrowed through musty ledgers in Health Departments of distant cities, and interviewed the ever-thinning legion of 19th century heroes of the game, seeking vital data of the more obscure players of bygone years.

The entire project was slanted toward publication in baseball's Jubilee Year, 1951.

This all-time register offered the fascinating challenge of a private-detective job. Every clue had to be tracked down. For instance, a yellowed newspaper in the public library dated 1892, carried an agate line about a certain rookie being signed by a National League team after pitching three shutouts for the University of Maryland. Needed—full name, birthplace and birthdate of this player. Next step—a wire sent to the registrar of the college.

Came the reply: "No school record for such a name. However, it might interest you to know that before 1895 it was not necessary for a boy to be enrolled at this college in order to play for its baseball team!"

A better source proved to be the obituary columns. It's boring and slightly ghoulish to snoop through death notices in the newspapers 365 days a year, but any item involving an old ballplayer was quickly followed up by a letter

to the Board of Health in the city where the player died, enclosing a dollar for a photostatic copy of the death certificate. The return document bore the authentic full name, age and birthplace. It also invariably revealed the man to be one to four years older than his "baseball age." The latter is a stock-in-trade fib every player uses to attract pro scouts in the beginning and to shield time's true toll from managers toward the end of an active career.

So some leads died. But others, which literally led to the graveyard, brought rewards of vital information. Thompson trekked to four cemeteries in Philadelphia to copy data directly off the tombstones of former major leaguers. Turkin visited the Indian reservation burial grounds of Chief Sockalexis and learned the famous outfielder's true birthdate from a plaque placed there by the Penobscot tribe.

The project continued to grow, with years of interviewing baseball officials and players . . . of searching through private collections . . . of comparing notes with assorted amateur statisticians . . . of chasing all over the country for original box scores that would help reconstruct season averages of the very first professional league, the National Association 1871-75, all of whose official records were destroyed in a fire . . . of bringing compass and steel tape to ballparks to plot the playing area and measure the height of every fence . . . of pumping league publicity directors . . . of writing and rewriting and editing.

To pour such oceans of effort into a job, long before any sign of financial backing or official endorsement, proves it was a labor of love. Writing baseball history is never as much fun as playing it, watching it or even reading it. The authors will therefore be ever grateful for encouragement early and late, from such experts as Ernest J. Lanigan, Frank G. Marcellus, Thomas P. Shea, Lee Allen, Phil Redelheim and Harry Simmons who made possible The Jubilee Edition.

Fifty thousand copies of the Jubilee Edition were sold and it was obvious that a new edition would have to be placed in print before too long. Work started on the Revised Edition directly after the Jubilee Edition was issued, and five years later, in 1956, the First Revised Edition, greatly expanded, was published.

It was expected that another five years would be permitted to pass before issuing still another revised work. But the face of baseball was altered with the shifts of two franchises to the West Coast; the major league audience was now spread from border to border, and the ever-increasing televising of games created additional interest and new fans. As a result work on a Second Revised Edition was speeded and many more facts had to be added, rechecked and verified for the ever-growing All-Time Register of Players and Managers. Many had to be called to help, and among them were George S. Hipp of Indianapolis, Indiana, Robert McConnell of Wilmington, Delaware, Joseph M. Overfield of Buffalo, New York, Ralph E. Lin Weber of Toledo ,Ohio, Robert A. Styer of Seattle, Washington, and Clarence Blasco

of Kirkwood, Missouri. Their contributions were enormous in helping the Fourth Revised Edition arrive on schedule.

Following the deaths of Mr. Turkin and Mr. Thompson, after publication of the Third Edition, Roger Treat, author-editor of *The Official Encyclopedia of Baseball,* was chosen to prepare the Fourth Edition. Mr. Treat died in 1969 and the Fifth and Sixth Editions were edited by his daughter-in-law, and assistant, Mrs. Peter Rowe Treat. Pete Palmer, currently the editor of *The All-Time Rosters of Major League Baseball Clubs,* was selected to edit the Seventh Edition.

Special gratitude must be recorded for the help received from the National and American League offices, John Phillips of the Howe News Bureau, Don Harrison of Naugatuck, Connecticut, and Bill Haber of New York City.

For contributions originally made to the Eighth Revised Edition, continued thanks go to George Hipp, who uncovered many missing vital statistics, Bob McConnell, who prepared a comprehensive list of switch hitters included in the player register, and Bill Haber, who provided missing data on recent players and also contributed greatly to the Baseball Hall of Fame project of locating information on all former major leaguers. Material from this study, directed by Cliff Kachline and supported by the Society for American Baseball Research, was made available to the Encyclopedia. In addition, Ron Liebman of Flushing, New York provided information on various record performances and Mrs. Rose Thompson of Middleton, Connecticut contributed previously unpublished data compiled by her husband, the late S. C. Thompson.

The Tenth Revised Edition contains a great deal of material concerning player names, births and deaths supplied by Bill Haber. This material represents data found in the period between the death of S. C. Thompson and the beginning of the Baseball Hall of Fame research bulletins. The Hall of Fame/Society for American Baseball Research project is continuing. Members of the committee are Cliff Kachline, Joe Simenic, Bill Haber, Tom Hufford, Bill Gustafson, Tom Shea, Rich Malatzky, Ralph Winnie, Bob McConnell, Dan Ginsburg, Craig Carter and Bob Davids.

I EVOLUTION OF BASEBALL

Historical Origin

Just when, where, and by whom baseball was introduced in its most primitive form has made historians dig as far back as the early days of civilization to supply some evidence of the origin of a game which is now perhaps one of the most highly-specialized of all team skills.

No matter the amount of scientific probing into its earlier beginnings the game has been placed in various birthplaces . . . France . . . England . . . the United States, and some have even drawn strong hints that the first bat-and-ball activity can be traced to the era of the caveman. Then there is that school of diamond thought which insists all evolution should be traced from 1884, many years after the first recorded activity, since that is the year overhand pitching was first introduced. Others are just as certain that a form of the game which bears some facsimile to the present-day sport was in vogue many centuries ago.

However, most of the unbiased probers have come to accept the version unearthed by Robert William Henderson in his book, *Ball, Bat and Bishop* (Rockport Press, 1947). Henderson, as the librarian of the Racquet and Tennis Club of New York, had an abiding interest in bat-and-ball games. Also, his role as supervisory chief of the main reading room in the New York Public Library and his 35 years of research on game origins come through this volume as clear-cut, complete and convincing.

Quoting eminent anthropologists, Henderson repeatedly proves that all modern ball games are derived from religious rites of ancient times, with fertility (of crops or people) as the main theme. He places the first recorded "batting contest" in Egypt some 5,000 years ago.

Stick-wielding worshippers of the Egyptian god of agriculture, Osiris, would place his image on a cart and try to rush it into the Temple of Papremis. An army of priests, also wielding wooden clubs, would line up just outside the Temple and try to fight them back. Though many heads were split in this annual affair, it was only mock combat and more of a traditional drama around crop-planting-time.

As for games with a ball, these sprang up not as natural amusement but also as an offshoot of rituals. Egyptian king-gods and high priests used a ball as the central symbol of Springtime ceremonies. Authorities disagree as to whether the ball represented the sun (which is the source of life) or the mummified head of Osiris (symbol of growth and fertility). But in either case it is an object of potency, and so ball-tossing "games" or "rituals" became common among women. Archaeologists have found pictures of semi-nude women playing ball, carved into the tomb of Beni Hasan, which was built before 2,000 B.C.

Ancient Greeks and Romans played ball. The Romans built "ball rooms" in their bath houses. But in these cultures ball-playing was strictly for conditioning, much as the medicine ball is used in our modern gymnasium. The ball games that climaxed religious rites spread from the Egyptians to the Arabs and finally into southern Europe by way of the invading Moors.

11

Noticing how tremendously popular were the pagan fertility rites, the Christian church decided to adopt it in their Easter ceremony. Islamic customs had reached southwestern France, and records show that early in the 12th century, in the high church of Vienna, the Archbishop would pass a ball back and forth with clerics lined up for the processional. After the services, the Archbishop threw the ball among the assembled people, who followed the Moorish custom of splitting into "teams."

The popular custom spread throughout France and Spain. Even the Cathedral of Rheims wound up Easter services with a ball game. Contending teams developed two different styles of propelling the ball: either they kicked it (leading eventually to modern soccer and football) or they swatted it with a stick (leading to games like lacrosse, golf and . . . eventually . . . baseball!). The French called these early mass games "la soule."

When the ball-playing phase of the medieval Easter festival crossed the English Channel, the British soon developed a variation nearer the modern game of baseball, called stoolball. It first was played in a churchyard, with a pitcher trying to throw the ball against an upturned stool and an opponent trying to punch or bat the ball away before it reached the "home" stool.

The game soon spread over the countryside. Milkmaids added a second stool, then a third, fourth and more "bases" to be circled after striking the ball. When players added the rule that a runner could be put out by being hit with a thrown ball, this led into the more familiar British youngsters' game of rounders . . . the French game of "poison ball" . . . and our own "Massachusetts game" of baseball in the 1800's. In rounders, the stools were replaced by wooden posts driven into the ground. These posts or "bases" were sometimes called "goals," so that researcher Henderson found 18th-century references to "goal ball" and "base ball" in Britain.

American Development

English immigrants brought the game of rounders to these shores. When there weren't enough boys to make up two full teams, they would play variations so commonly known to sandlot youngsters of today: One Old Cat, Two Old Cat, etc. In One Old Cat, only one base is used, and the game requires only three players: pitcher, catcher and batter. More men, more bases, higher "Old Cats."

Sometimes called rounders, other times baseball, a game closely resembling our present national pastime was played in the United States long before its supposed invention by Doubleday in 1839. Dr. Oliver Wendell Holmes told of playing baseball while at Harvard in 1829. Henderson's scholarly volume mentions other similar evidence.

Helping prove his contention that the American game of baseball is derived directly from the British game of rounders, Henderson reveals that the first U. S. book to deal with baseball was Robin Carver's *Book of Sports,* printed in 1834 in Boston. In the preface, Carver admits being "indebted" to a London book published six years earlier, *The Boy's Own Book.* The latter explains in detail the game of rounders, including a lettered diagram for placing the posts (bases) in the shape of a diamond.

Carver's book copies the rules for rounders almost verbatim—yet the Bostonian calls this game "base, or goal ball." Carver's book is notable in another respect: it printed the first American picture of the game.

Baseball was still a waddling infant with uncertain step when a bewhiskered surveyor named Alexander J. Cartwright put it on a solid footing in 1845. For several years, he had been playing the game with fellow New Yorkers of high

social standing. Tired of haphazard games, he proposed a regular organization and proceeded to sign enough men to make a formal ball club, the first in history.

Cartwright headed a committee to frame a standard set of rules. Drawing heavily upon the popular Carver's *Book of Sports* and exercising excellent judgment in using the best phases of play in the community, Cartwright proposed, a list of rules which was adopted September 23, 1845. Much of that original code still is in force today. Here are some of the more interesting provisions (with the authors' comments appended in parentheses) :

(1) Bases shall be from home to second, and first to third, 42 paces equidistant. (Remember, a pace is three feet, making that home-to-second distance 126 feet as compared with the present 127 feet, 3⅜ inches. Also, the infield was made square, not an elongated diamond.)

(2) The game is to consist of 21 counts or aces, but at the conclusion an equal number of hands must be played. (An ace meant a run, hand was an out.)

(3) The ball must be pitched, not thrown for the bat. (This meant underhand pitching only.)

(4) A ball knocked outside the range of first or third base is foul.

(5) Three balls being struck at and missed, and the last one caught is a hand out; if not caught is considered fair and the striker bound to run.

(6) A ball being struck or tipped, and caught either flying or on the first bound, is a hand out.

(7) A player running the bases shall be out if the ball is in the hands of an adversary on the base and the runner is touched by it before he makes his base; it being understood, however, that in no instance is a ball to be thrown at him. (This put it out of the rounders class.)

(8) A player running, who shall prevent an adversary from catching or getting the ball before making his base, is a hand out.

(9) Three hands out, all out.

(10) No ace or base can be made on a foul strike.

(11) But one base allowed when the ball bounds out of the field when struck.

Since the Knickerbockers were about to lose their playing field, in midtown Manhattan, a committee went looking for a new site. They took the ferry across the Hudson River and ended their hunt at the Elysian Fields, Hoboken, New Jersey. That was the home field for the elegant Knickerbockers the next year when they accepted a challenge from a group called the New York Nine.

Though all teams in those days were amateur, this first ·recorded match in history was for the side bet of a dinner per player. On this ill-starred afternoon of June 19, 1846, the Knickerbockers suffered just about the worst defeat in their 37-year career—23 to 1 in four innings. One of the New York players named Davis was fined six cents for swearing at the umpire, who was Cartwright himself.

Though the Knickerbockers didn't play a match game again for five years, their rules were universally adopted by many other clubs which sprang up in this period. The Elysian Fields drew clubs like the Gothams, Eagles, Empires and Mutuals. The Baltics played in Harlem, the Unions in the Bronx and the Atlantic, Excelsior, Putnam and Eckford clubs in Brooklyn.

In Philadelphia, an organization named the Olympic Club antedated the Knickerbockers, but played town ball from 1833 on and didn't switch to baseball until 1860. In New England, teams still "soaked" the runner with the ball, but the game grew rapidly there after the Olympic Club of Boston became the first to organize in that area.

By May of 1857 there were so many clubs in the field that the Knickerbockers begrudgingly called a convention in New York. They accomplished little beyond

Here is where it all began, the Elysian Fields in Hoboken, N. J., on June 19, 1846 where the first game under the Cartwright rules was played. No admission was charged to see the New York team rout the Knickerbockers, 23-1.

fixing the rules for the coming season: the complete Knickerbocker set, with the one important exception that nine innings, not 21 runs, constituted a game.

Three delegates from each of 25 different clubs flocked to the next convention, March 10, 1858. This time they formed the game's first league, the National Association of Base Ball Players. Their rules gained nationwide prestige, and the game was on its way to becoming the national pastime, though still amateur.

In its first season of operation, the new league capitalized on the natural Brooklyn-New York rivalry by staging a series of All-Star Games between teams from those cities. Because of the cost of fixing up the Fashion Race Course on Long Island for the opening game on July 20, 1858, an admission fee of 50 cents was charged. This is the first time fans were ever asked to pay at the gate. For the record, a crowd of 1,500 saw New York beat Brooklyn, 22 to 18.

The year 1860 saw the first tour by an organized baseball club. The Excelsiors of Brooklyn visited central and western New York and thumped all opposition. Later they traveled to Philadelphia and Baltimore to beat picked teams. The triumphal tour was heralded throughout the sports world, and more and more baseball teams began springing up all over the country.

Baseball suffered a sharp readjustment from 1861–65. In those years of Civil War, the number of clubs in and around New York City dwindled from 62 to 28. The championship went to the Atlantic Club of Brooklyn in 1861, 1864–65, but the Eckfords of New York finished first in 1862 and repeated with an unbeaten slate in 1863.

While the grade of league ball deteriorated during the war, the game's gospel was spread so effectively through intermingling of the troops from far-separated states that valuable groundwork was laid for post-war expansion. In Army camps and prison stockades, soldiers from both sides were teaching and learning this popular game.

Post-Civil War Highlights

Veterans coming home from the Civil War found baseball changed in one important aspect—an 1864 rule abolished the "out" for a fair hit caught on one bounce. There were even bigger surprises in store, for the game was headed for a record post-war boom, just as it was to flourish immediately after later wars.

The league's annual convention in 1866 drew representatives from more than 100 clubs. The next year the number rose to 237, including over 100 from states as far west as Ohio, Wisconsin, Illinois and Indiana.

Increasing interest in the midwest built up a natural rivalry between sections of the country. However, since all clubs were supposedly 100 per cent amateur at this time, no one could afford an extended trip till a group of government clerks and college students representing the Nationals of Washington, D. C., started out in July, 1867 for a 3,000-mile tour of the west. The club bore all its own expenses. Since the Nationals did not share in any of the gate receipts, the trip cost $5,000.

Washington won every game of that memorable trip but one—losing to the Forest City Club of Rockford, Illinois. Pitching for the winners that day was a 17-year-old-boy named A. G. Spalding, who had learned the game from an invalided Civil War veteran in his home town.

Spalding, who later became a great player, famous clubowner and successful sporting goods dealer, also figured in the first eastern trip taken by an amateur western team. Early in 1870, a group of businessmen in Rockford pooled $7,000

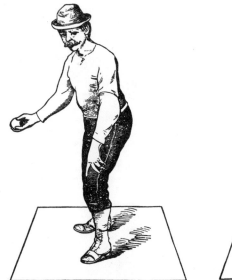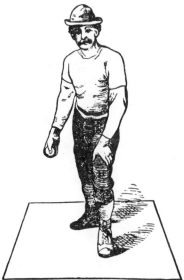

Pitching deliveries—improper and legal—under the game's earliest rules. A pitch (left) was illegal if delivered from above the hip line. A legal delivery was made with an underhand toss to the plate.

to underwrite their hometown heroes' junket. The trip was highly successful, including Spalding victories over the Atlantics and Nationals.

Though baseball was booming, its lone league was steadily waning. Heavy betting surrounded each game, and soon some players were blatantly "throwing" games in return for bribes. The league was powerless . . . or at least it didn't choose to use any disciplinary powers it had.

By the late 1860's, amateurism was a sham. Star players either were being paid sub rosa or with semipro inducements like sinecure jobs with local merchants. Al Reach, who like Spalding later became a wealthy sporting goods manufacturer and publisher of the annual baseball guide, was the first admittedly pro player, drawing a regular salary from the Philadelphia club in 1864.

The straw that really broke the amateur association's back was Cincinnati's determination to organize an out-and-out pro club in 1869. Harry Wright, captain and center fielder, drew $1,200, and lured his brother George, a brilliant shortstop, from the Unions club by paying him $1,400. Pitcher Asa Brainard drew $1,100 and third baseman Fred Waterman an even thousand. The rest got $800 each: Doug Allison, C; Charles Gould, 1B; Charles Sweazy, 2B; Andy Leonard, LF; Cal McVey, RF, and Dick Hurley, substitute. That made a total payroll of $9,500.

Playing every prominent club between California and Massachusetts, the legendary Red Stockings never lost a game all season. They won 65 and drew one—when the Haymakers of Troy, New York, pulled their team off the field in the sixth inning because of an argument over a foul tip with the score 17 to 17. The club traveled 11,877 miles and played before 200,000 people, and upon their triumphal return "home" (Gould was the only actual Cincinnatian) were greeted by club president Aaron Champion who exulted at the victory banquet, "I'd rather be president of the Cincinnati Reds than of the United States!"

The winning streak carried over into the next season, including a triumphant tour of the deep south. However, the historic string was snapped at 92 when the Atlantics of Brooklyn pulled the tremendous upset on the Capitoline Grounds. The date: June 14, 1870. The Atlantics were ready to quit when the score stood 5 to 5 at the end of nine innings, but Harry Wright insisted that the rules called for extra innings. The argument was brought to the attention of official scorer Henry Chadwick, pioneer baseball writer who later framed many of baseball's official rules and edited the game's guides for half a century.

Chadwick decreed that the game should go on. Cincinnati scored twice in the 11th, but lost when the home team came back with three. Some accounts of that final rally report that a fan climbed on outfielder Cal McVey while he was chasing Joe Start's fly, which went for a triple.

Despite this heartbreaking defeat . . . and another to the Atlantics later in the season . . . the Red Stockings succeeded in transforming the entire baseball picture of America. Purely amateur clubs couldn't hope to keep up with finished professionals like Cincinnati. At first, rival clubs tried proselyting, scouting and semipro-type bonuses. By the end of 1870 halfway measures were proven too weak, and the time was ripe for formation of the first professional league in history.

II MAJOR LEAGUE HISTORY

National Association

The diamond success of the Cincinnati Red Stockings spurred other cities in the midwest to seek the same national publicity which a baseball team had brought to the Rhineland.

"Why can't we attain similar status?" was the cry of civic leaders through the west and the east. Cincinnati had showed them how a successful baseball team can bring fame to a metropolis, and civic pride more than profit provided the impetus toward the formation of baseball's first professional league.

If smart business operators had taken time to examine the financial ledgers of the Cincinnati Baseball Club of the day they would have shied away from such a speculative venture. The Red Stockings, although the most artistic success of their time, were a profound financial failure even if their statements were marked in black ink.

Baseball's No. 1 attraction, which had awakened a spirit of sport among promoters in other cities, showed a net profit of ONE DOLLAR AND THIRTY-NINE CENTS the preceding year, scarcely a sum to excite industrial giants to get on the baseball bandwagon.

The figures were not deceiving. The Red Stocking gate receipts amounted to $29,726.26; salaries and expenses in maintaining the club totalled $29,724.87. Net profit: $1.39. Yet Harry Wright's red-hued heroes had reaped so much glory for the Rhineland City that almost all the other leading clubs were turning professional, too.

With the amateur National Association withering away from sheer impotence, Father Chadwick campaigned in his *New York Clipper* columns for formation of a professional group. Al Wright echoed this in his *Philadelphia Mercury*. Another powerful advocate was Nick Young, secretary of the Washington club, who was later to become secretary of the National Association and president of the National League.

Ten club delegates held a preliminary parley on March, 4, 1871. Two weeks later, on St. Patrick's Day, they met again in Collier's Cafe, on New York's Broadway and 13th Street. There, in a smoky gaslit hallroom adjoining the Cafe (saloon), pro baseball suffered its real birth pangs, for that meeting established the National Association of Professional Base-Ball Players.

After electing James N. Kerns of Troy, New York, as president, they drew up a set of championship rules, but no fixed schedule. Every club was to play each of the others a best three-out-of-five series, and the team with the best record at the end of the season was entitld to fly the championship streamer (also called the "whip pennant") at its ballpark for a year. The entry fee was fixed at $10 per club.

Brooklyn's Eckfords thought the organization too loosely knit to survive. They wouldn't risk the $10 fee for a chance to be recognized as champions of the United States. So the NAPBBP (generally shortened to NA) started the season with the remaining nine clubs represented at that meeting: Athletics, of Philadelphia; Bostons, of Boston; White Stockings, of Chicago; Haymakers, of Troy;

Olympics, of Washington; Forest City, of Rockford, Illinois; Kekiongas, of Fort Wayne, Indiana; Mutuals, of New York, and Forest City, of Cleveland.

When the Kekionga franchise wilted in August, the Eckfords belatedly decided that professional league baseball was here to stay, so they paid their $10 and replaced Kekionga. But a special post-season convention nullified their games because of the late entry, and they were stricken from the league standings.

It is ironic that the Kekionga club, the only one not to weather the season, won the opening game by 2 to 0. Not only was this noteworthy as the first pro league game of record, but it was also the lowest- scoring game in the first four years of the league. Here are the highlights of that historic inaugural:

The Kekiongas won the toss and sent Forest City to bat. Bobby Mathews threw the first pitch, a ball. James (Deacon) White was the first batter and he led off with the first major league hit, a double. Gene Kimball followed with a fly to second, but when White took too long a lead, Tom Carey pulled an un-assisted double play.

There were several other "famous firsts" in that game. In the second inning, Art Allison struck out. However, Jim Lennon missed the third strike, and Allison reached base safely. Lennon atoned for his error in the home half of the inning by scoring the first run, which also proved to be the winning run. He doubled and came in on Joe McDermott's single. Kekionga had the game clinched by the ninth, but was ready to take its last batting turn anyway when a sudden rainfall caused umpire Boake to call a halt.

FOREST CITY (Cleveland) at KEKIONGA (Fort Wayne)

May 4, 1871

CLEVELAND	AB	R	H	O	A		FORT WAYNE	AB	R	H	O	A
J. White, c	4	0	3	9	0		Williams, rf	4	0	0	4	0
Kimball, 2b	4	0	0	3	4		Mathews, p	4	0	0	1	0
Pabor, cf	4	0	0	0	0		Foran, 3b	3	0	1	2	0
Allison, rf	4	0	1	2	0		Goldsmith, 2b	3	0	0	3	1
E. White, lf	3	0	0	1	0		Lennon, c	3	1	1	9	1
Pratt, p	3	0	0	1	0		Carey, ss	3	0	0	3	1
Sutton, 3b	3	0	1	0	0		Mincher, lf	3	0	0	2	0
Carleton, 1b	3	0	0	6	0		McDermott, cf	3	0	1	0	1
Bass, ss	3	0	0	2	3		Kelly, 1b	3	1	1	3	0
Totals	31	0	5	24	7		Totals	29	2	4	27	4

Cleveland	000	000	000	---	0
Fort Wayne	010	010	00x	---	2

(Called, in 9th: rain)

First base by errors—Cleveland 4, Fort Wayne 0. Two base hits—J. White, Lennon. Double play—Carey (unassisted). Walks, by—Mathews, 1, Pratt 1. Strikeouts, by—Mathews 6. Passed balls—J. White 2, Lennon 1. Umpire—J. L. Boake. Time—2 hours.

Chicago quickly displaced Kekionga as league leader by winning its first seven straight games. Unbeaten, the White Stockings invaded New York on June 5 to meet the Mutuals, owned by the notorious political potentate, Boss Tweed. Despite the 50-cent admission fee, a record 6,000 crowd jammed the

stands, and 3,000 others watched from beyond the fences, perched on neighboring roofs or wagons. Pushcart owners charged 10 cents for standing room on their vehicles.

The Mutuals brought great joy to Gotham fans by beating Chicago, 8 to 5. The New Yorkers continued on a winning streak of their own that soon put them in first place. Incidentally, though at first they refused to share their gate receipts, the Mutuals finally agreed to grant the visiting club one-third of the gross.

New York fortunes sagged in July. George Zettlein proceeded to pitch Chicago back into the league lead. However, the most destructive cow of all time, Mrs. O'Leary's bovine villain, ruined more than a good part of the city of Chicago by kicking over that fateful kerosene lamp in a barn on October 8. Rockford players entering the city that day saw the colossal blaze that seared the lakefront grounds as well as millions of dollars of other property. No ballpark . . . no game . . . and, as it turned out, no pennant.

The demoralized White Stockings had to play their remaining games on the road, where they lost the last three straight and the flag. In the game that decided the championship, October 30, Chicago was "home team" at the Union Grounds, Brooklyn, where the Athletics took a 4–1 decision behind the fine efforts of the league's ace pitcher, ex-cricketeer Dick McBride, and the batting champion, Long Levi Meyerle (.403).

Still, it took a post-season decision by the NA's championship committee to determine the whip-pennant winner. Two games which the Athletics had lost to Rockford were declared forfeited to the Philadelphia team because Rockford had used an ineligible player, W. Scott Hastings.

Boston's failure to finish on top, due to an untimely series of player injuries, upset the experts of the day. The Beaneaters had taken over more than the Red Stocking nickname of the old invincible Cincinnati club. They had the four key players: the Wright brothers, McVey and Gould. They also bore the same "professional" stamp of competence as their famed predecessors. There was less gambling and swearing and fighting in Boston games than anywhere else in the circuit, so Harry Wright's team was respected.

Even more brilliant an organizer and leader than a player, bewhiskered Harry Wright bolstered his Red Stocking nucleus in Boston by proselyting A. G. Spalding, destined to become the NA's greatest pitcher, Ross Barnes and Fred Cone from the 1870 Rockfords.

In 1872, it was decided to name a player as NA president. The honor went to Bob Ferguson, famed captain-third baseman of Brooklyn's Atlantics. Chicago, not sufficiently recovered from the big fire, dropped out of pro ball for two years. Rockford quit, and its best player, Adrian Constantine (Cap) Anson, switched to the Athletics to continue a big league career that lasted 27 years, an all-time record.

Four new clubs swelled the NA to 11 teams in '72. A vital new rule allowed pitchers to use snap and jerk deliveries, though still restricted to underhand serves, thereby opening the door to curve ball pitching. Spalding never threw a curve in his life. The rugged Westerner relied on contol and change of pace, and these proved enough to carry Boston to four straight pennants, by steadily wider margins, from 1872–75. Boston added two more diamond immortals to its rolls in '73, Deacon White and James (Orator) O'Rourke.

The monotony of Boston triumphs (one local paper gloated that Boston Conquers All with this headline in Latin: "BOSTON OMNIA VINCIT") was only a minor factor in the demise of the NA. Gamblers infested the ranks so badly that the public was fast losing confidence in pro games.

Boston, scourge of the first league, took NA titles from 1872 through '75. Standing (l. to r.): McVey, Spalding, White, Barnes. Seated: O'Rourke, Leonard, George Wright, Harry Wright, Hall, Schaefer, Beals.

Open pool-selling on the day's results used to take place right in the park. As much as $20,000 would be bet on a game, with the expected consequence of widespread bribery and open intimidation of umpires and players. Toughs who had come to the park mainly to bet would pour profanity at a player whose error or strikeout hurt the club they were backing. Compounded with this were growing evils such as liquor-selling on the premises, contract-jumping and player desertions.

Small wonder the NA proved a pushover for the logical reform wave leading to the formation of the National League in 1876.

National League

When William A. Hulbert of Chicago died in 1882, the National League passed a resolution "that to him alone is due the credit of having founded the National League, and to his able leadership, sound judgment and impartial management is the success of the league chiefly due."

True enough. Yet if Hulbert had been able to hear his eulogy, the walrus-mustached pioneer would have insisted that A. G. Spalding be credited with an "assist" in the founding of baseball's first indestructible league.

The Hulbert-Spalding saga goes back to 1875. Early that year, owners of the weak Chicago franchise offered the club presidency to Hulbert, a successful businessman who was a die-hard rooter for the die-easy White Stockings team of his home city. He asked for a few weeks to consider the offer.

The next time the champion Bostons came to Chicago, Hulbert visited their star pitcher, Spalding himself, and told how thousands of Chicago fans were wild for a winning team but couldn't get one because of constant player piracy on the part of Eastern clubs, which dominated professional baseball. He emphasized the other growing evils in the sport, including gambling, and

Spalding nodded sympathetically. Finally Hulbert spoke of his own proffered job and urged in earnest tones:

"Spalding, you've no business playing in Boston. You're a Western boy and you belong right here. If you come to Chicago to play and manage next season, I'll accept the presidency of this club, and we'll give those fellows a fight for their lives."

Promise of a handsome contract dispelled any remaining doubt in Spalding's mind. Shaking hands to seal the deal, he promised to bring Chicago a real contender for 1876. In June of 1875, Hulbert visited Boston, where Spalding helped him sign teammates Ross Barnes, Cal McVey and Deacon Jim White. Then they went to Philadelphia, where they secretly signed Cap Anson and Ezra Sutton, who had been recruited earlier by Spalding. Sutton later backed out because of pressure from the Athletics' fans and officials.

Every effort was made to keep the signings a secret till the end of the season, since a man contracting in midseason to play with a different club the next year was subject to automatic expulsion by the NA . . . though this threat was rarely invoked. Chicagoans were bursting with too much pride and joy to keep the coup quiet for more than a few weeks. When the entire story came to light in a Chicago newspaper, tremors were felt throughout the league.

Bostonians felt bitter over the defection of their Big Four. Boys followed them on the street, hooting, "Oh, you seceders! Your White Stockings will get dirty." With the country still feeling the scourge of post-Civil War reconstruction, the term "seceder" was still as vile an epithet as a New Englander could summon.

Stung by criticism, the Big Four leaned over backward to prove their integrity. Spalding led the league's pitchers, Barnes paced the batters. Boston never lost a game all year on home grounds. Their season's won-lost of 71–8 meant a winning percentage of .899, which never has been matched in major league history.

Worried over rumors of his expulsion at the next NA convention, Spalding visited Hulbert's home at the end of the season. Chicago's enterprising president reassured him, "Why, they can't expel you. They wouldn't dare. In the eyes of the public, you six players are stronger than the whole Association."

Hulbert put Spalding further at ease by vowing that regardless of any action by the Association, the newly signed players would be paid for the entire 1876 season. Then the wavy-haired, silver-tongued executive became engrossed in deep thought. Suddenly he jumped up and said, "Spalding, I have a new scheme. Let us anticipate the Eastern cusses and organize a new association before their March meeting. Then we'll see who'll do the expelling!"

They held daily conferences thereafter. In one of these, Hulbert suggested, "Let us get away from the old, wornout title, 'National Association of Base Ball Players,' and call it 'The National League of Professional Base Ball Clubs.'" His idea here was to organize reform on a responsible business basis of clubs rather than depend on a flabby federation of players.

When they had determined most of the principles of their projected league, Hulbert and Spalding had Judge Orrick C. Bishop of St. Louis draw up a formal constitution. The jurist also framed a standard form of player's contract designed to end the evil of "revolving" (jumping).

In January of 1876, Hulbert summoned officials of the Cincinnati, St. Louis and Louisville clubs to a secret meeting in Louisville. The downtrodden Westerners gave Hulbert an enthusiastic vote of confidence. Most important, they assigned power of attorney to him and Charles A. Fowles of St. Louis in dealing with Eastern clubs.

Hulbert and Fowles sent a circular letter to the remaining NA teams, asking for a conference "on matters of interest to the game at large, with special reference

Charley Comiskey, St. Louis leader of AA days; first owner of the Chicago (AL) White Sox.

John Montgomery Ward, brilliant all-around performer; he won 84 games in 1879 and '80.

Hoss Radbourn, Providence pitching great of the 80s.

Pop Anson, NA pioneer; he played the longest, 27 years.

to reformation of existing abuses." Time: 12 noon, Wednesday, February 2, 1876. Place: Hulbert's suite in the Grand Central Hotel, Broadway at Third Street, New York City.

Impelled by curiosity, caution and common sense, the Eastern club presidents all came—G. W. Thompson of Philadelphia, N. T. Appolonio of Boston, M. G. Bulkeley of Hartford and W. H. Cammeyer of the New York Mutuals. According to Spalding's historical volume, *America's National Game*, Hulbert locked the door of his room, put the key in his pocket, turned to the puzzled magnates and said, "Gentlemen, you have no occasion for uneasiness. I locked the door simply to prevent any intrusions from without . . . and incidentally to make it impossible for any of you to leave until I have finished what I have to say. I promise not to take more than an hour."

In that historic hour, Hulbert expertly outlined all the evils that were demoralizing the players and fans. He proved that the NA was either unable or unwilling to correct the abuses. He climaxed his remarks by producing a copy of the model constitution for a new National League. Chicago's spellbinder won their support on the spot, and the NL was born right then and there.

One of the first steps taken by the new league was to raise the franchise fee from $10 to $100. To insure sizeable gate receipts, so that payrolls could be met, membership was limited to cities of at least 75,000 population. Bookmaking and liquor selling were banned on league ball-grounds. Players found guilty of betting or taking bribes were to be expelled from professional baseball.

When it came to election of officers, Hulbert diplomatically appeased the uneasy Easterners by plumping for "one of their own" for the presidency of

the league, Hartford's esteemed Morgan G. Bulkeley. Backed unanimously, Bulkeley accepted. Never more than a league figurehead, he quit a year later to pursue a political career that saw him elected Mayor of Hartford, Governor of Connecticut and U. S. Senator. Hulbert succeeded Bulkeley and ruled the league with an iron hand until his death in 1882.

For that inaugural season of 1876, the NL decided on five home games and five road games round-robin style between the charter member clubs—New York, Boston, Hartford, Philadelphia, Chicago, St. Louis, Cincinnati and Louisville. They played three times a week, making 70 games for each team. Admission was pegged at 50 cents, though tickets were sold for a dime after the third inning had been played.

With rain delaying the other openers, the first game in NL history was played at Philadelphia on Saturday, April 22, 1876. Boston won by a score of 6 to 5. Jim (Orator) O'Rourke of the winners made the first hit, and teammate Tom McGinley the first run, while Ezra Sutton, who had changed his mind about jumping to Chicago with Spalding, committed the first error. The full box score follows:

BOSTON (6)	AB	R	H	PO	A	E	PHILADELPHIA (5)	AB	R	H	PO	A	E
G. Wright, ss	4	2	1	2	2	0	Force, ss	5	0	1	0	4	1
Leonard, 2b	4	0	2	0	4	1	Eggler, cf	5	0	0	4	1	1
O'Rourke, cf	5	1	2	0	0	0	Fisler, 1b	5	1	3	13	0	1
Murnane, 1b	6	1	2	8	0	0	Meyerle, 2b	5	1	1	3	2	0
Schafer, 3b	5	1	1	1	0	1	Sutton, 3b	5	0	0	1	0	2
McGinley, c	5	1	0	8	0	3	Coons, c	4	2	2	1	2	3
Manning, rf	4	0	0	4	0	0	Hall, lf	4	0	2	1	0	0
Parks, lf	4	0	0	3	0	1	Fouser, rf	4	0	0	3	1	1
Borden, p	3	0	0	1	1	1	Knight, p	4	1	1	1	3	2
Totals	40	6	8	27	7	7	Totals	41	5	10	27	13	11

Boston	012	010	002	---	6	
Philadelphia	010	003	001	---	5	

Earned runs—Boston 1, Philadelphia 2. Total bases on hits—Boston 9, Philadelphia 12. First base on errors—Boston 6, Philadelphia 3. Left on bases—Boston 7, Philadelphia 9. Double plays—Eggler-Coons, Force-Fouser-Fisler. Umpire—Mr. William McLean. Time—2:05. Attendance—3,000.

As the season rolled on, gambling and drinking were markedly reduced, though not wiped out completely. Hulbert's dream of conquest came true in that very first year as his beloved Chicagos, bolstered by Boston's Big Four and Cap Anson, romped off with the pennant. However, Hulbert's brainchild league was threatened in midseason when the Philadelphia and New York clubs, fearing they would lose money on long road trips, refused to play their return games in the West.

Boasting the bulk of the NL's population, the Philadelphia and New York franchises announced, "The league needs us more than we need them." They were counting on the old practice of the NA, which condoned such offenses. But when Hulbert ascended to the league presidency at the December, 1876, meetings, he saw to it that both clubs were expelled.

There was further trial-by-fire the next year, but Hulbert had the courage and conviction to guide the league according to its avowed principles. Cincinnati, disheartened by a last-place finish in 1876, failed to pay its dues the next year. Though the league was already reduced to six members, Hulbert insisted

They started it all, William A. Hulbert and Ban Johnson. Through their efforts, the National and American Leagues were organized. Hulbert was the NL's second president; Johnson was the first in the AL.

Cincinnati be dropped, too. This season of 1877 also saw a prearranged league schedule, another Hulbert innovation, instead of the old plan whereby it was left to club secretaries to arrange series with other league teams.

With Spalding retiring from the mound in 1877, Tommy Bond of Boston became the hotshot pitcher of the season, leading his club to the pennant. But the Beaneaters' return to glory was vitiated by the game's worst scandal of the 19th century. Embarking on a road trip late in the season with the pennant practically clinched, Louisville proceeded to lose games with such regularity that the club's vice-president, Charles E. Chase, initiated an investigation.

Struck by the great number of telegrams received daily by Louisville's substitute player, Al Nichols, Chase asked him for a written authorization to open all his wires, since he was one of the players suspected of dealing with gamblers. Nichols refused.

"Your refusal is an admission of guilt," Chase insisted. "That means you're barred for life."

"All right, then," muttered Nichols. "Open them."

Damning, damaging evidence was brought to light. Several of the Grays players had been taking bribes from Eastern gamblers, telegraphing the code word "sash" for games that they agreed to throw. Faced with the wires, George Hall and Jim Devlin confessed, implicating Nichols and Bill Craver. Devlin had been the team's star pitcher. Outfielder Hall was the team captain and the league's first home run king, with five for the 1876 season.

Chase suspended the four players for life. Though Devlin was a personal friend of his, league president Hulbert sustained the decision, and none of the four ever played professional baseball again. Devlin visited every annual league meeting thereafter, humbly repenting and begging for reinstatement. It never

was granted. Ironically, he ended his days enforcing law and order as a member of the Philadelphia city police force.

Though expulsion of the crooked players insured the league of a stronger footing in the country's estimation, it caused several immediate headaches. Bereft of its star players, Louisville dropped out of the league. So did St. Louis, which had secretly negotiated for the ill-fated four to join them the following season . . . until the gambling scandal broke. Hartford couldn't draw at home, and had to give up the ghost.

Cincinnati was reinstated for 1878. Indianapolis, Milwaukee and Providence were rounded up by Hulbert, to make the NL a six-club circuit again. Indianapolis and Milwaukee had to quit after one season, but the Providence team prospered for eight years, never finishing worse than third. These were the halcyon days in Rhode Island, which toasted the Wright brothers, George and Harry, and the immortal pitcher, Charles Radbourn.

The 1879 season was distinguished for several reasons. It saw the institution of the reserve rule by the Boston club's thrifty president, Arthur H. Soden, allowing each club exclusive bargaining rights with a designated five of its players for the following season. The number of reserve players rapidly increased, finally reaching the 100 per cent figure under which all professional sports operate in America today.

In 1879, too, Hulbert expanded the NL to eight teams. This is the number of clubs it has fielded until 1962; except for the turbulent 90's when the collapse of two rival leagues caused the league to expand to an even dozen clubs.

From 1880–82, Cap Anson's Chicago White Stockings ran roughshod over the league. Featuring such colorful stars as King Kelly, Silver Flint, Ed Williamson and Larry Corcoran, the flamboyant Westerners rang up three straight pennants. Club president Hulbert and secretary Spalding decked the team out in expensive uniforms, put them up at the best hotels and had the White Stockings ride to the ballpark in open barouches drawn by white horses.

The NL faced a series of crises in 1882. Hulbert died of heart failure that April. Soden presided over the league strictly as a fill-in. It was not until December that a capable successor was found in Abraham G. Mills, former Civil War soldier and brilliant lawyer who had played and served as club president for the old Washington Olympics. Also, that year, Dick Higham became the first (and last) umpire convicted of collusion with gamblers, and was instantly fired.

But the sharpest threat of all came from a newly-founded major league, the American Association, which charged only half the NL's admission fee and played Sunday ball (which was expressly forbidden in the NL constitution). The popular AA ran franchises in large cities which had dropped out of the NL for one reason or another. And it weathered player piracy by the senior circuit. The NL monopoly of professional baseball was at an end.

Mills set to work realistically. Rather than embark on a suicidal war with the AA, the new NL president formulated a live-and-let-live National Agreement. Under this historic document, all organized major and minor leagues agreed to honor existing player contracts. The AA and NL clubs were each allowed to bind 14 players via reserve clause. Blacklists of dishonest players were to be mutually recognized.

With interleague peace came prosperity in 1883. Attendances boomed. Gearing his league for full-blown competition with the AA, Mills made two small fading franchises, Troy and Worcester, transfer their players to the great cities of New York and Philadelphia. He also adopted the AA's plan of hiring a staff of league

umpires, free from all club control, and paying them on a yearly basis. To bolster the league further, he reinstated 15 players who had been suspended for minor offenses.

A scant year later, war thundered across baseball's plains again. St. Louis realtor Henry V. Lucas organized the Union Association in 1884 specifically to fight the "outrageous" reserve rule. His UA stole players wholesale from the AA and NL, though the latter circuits pitched into a secret cash pool to pay bonuses to would-be jumpers from their leagues.

Soon after Charlie Sweeney of Providence NL had struck out 19 batters in one game for a new record, the star-struck UA plucked him with a heavily-moneyed hand. That left poor Providence with only one able-bodied pitcher, Radbourn . . . who happened to be under temporary suspension for insubordination. Manager Frank Bancroft raised the ban. The 30-year-old right-hander proceeded to earn his nickname of Old Hoss by pitching the last 38 consecutive games. Radbourn won 60 games that season, the last 18 in a row, against only 12 defeats. He not only clinched the pennant but added a World Series fillip with three straight victories to sweep the interleague playoffs.

With three major leagues and 34 clubs operating in 1884, there simply were not enough cash customers to go around. The UA sank in a sea of red ink. NL president Mills, who had temporized with the AA, felt no mercy toward the insurgent UA.

Over Mills' bitter objection, UA founder Lucas was admitted into the NL as head of a new St. Louis franchise in 1885. When the league over-rode his decision to blacklist the contract-jumping players, welcoming them back instead upon payment of a fine, Mills resigned in protest. Nick Young, a conciliatory Washingtonian who had served as league secretary continuously since 1876, was elevated to the presidency, and he held the post for 18 years.

Baseball pioneers were Henry Chadwick (left), who designed the rules changes in the 19th century, and Branch Rickey, who created the game's 'farm' system which supplied an endless stream of minor league players to the majors.

Now owner and president of the Chicago NL club, Spalding exulted in two more league pennants, 1885–86. But when his team blew the winner-take-all World Series to the underdog St. Louis Browns in '86, he angrily sold his league batting champion, King Kelly, to Boston for the record price of $10,000. The next year he shipped Kelly's batterymate, pitcher John Clarkson, to the same team for the same fabulous fee. Having won five times in seven years, Chicago now entered an era of NL pennant drought that lasted 20 years . . . so the lucrative sales turned out to be poor deals indeed.

Another major player deal of that period involved the end of Buffalo's franchise in the NL. Detroit bought Buffalo's "Big Four" of Dan Brouthers, Deacon White (who had been a member of the original "Big Four" in Boston a decade earlier), Hardy Richardson and Jack Rowe for $8,500, and entered the league in 1886. These four sluggers made Detroit a strong contender the first year, world champions the next.

Stovepipe-hatted Jim Mutrie lorded it when his Giants brought New York the flag in 1888 and '89, abetted by the fearless backstopping of Buck Ewing, the blazing pitching of Tim Keefe and the classic shortstopping of John Montgomery Ward. However, around this time the lesser-clarioned classification rule came to life . . . a veritable bombshell that exploded into another three-league war in 1890.

John T. Brush, president of the Indianapolis club, fathered the classification rule, designed to clamp a ceiling on ever-growing player salaries. Players were to be graded according to ability from class A to E, corresponding salaries to range from $2,500 down to $1,500.

This unjust and unworkable harness was slipped over the players at a time when John Montgomery Ward, leader of their benevolent organization (called the Brotherhood), was out of the country on a world tour with Spalding's squads. As brilliant a lawyer as he was a shortstop, Ward approached the magnates upon his return to protest, but was brushed off with the statement, "There is nothing to discuss." It was too late to organize any resistance for the 1889 season, but the next year Ward obtained financial backing for a Players' League, which drew most of the best players from the AA and NL.

The 1890 season was disastrous for all. Aggregate deficit for the three leagues ran close to a million dollars. Brooklyn was represented in all three leagues, but was proudest of its NL team which won the 1890 pennant.

Though they outdrew their rivals, the PL had to surrender at the close of 1890. But this peaceful settlement quickly touched off a disastrous battle destined to doom the AA, as the surviving leagues squabbled over the player spoils.

Somehow, the Athletics AA team forgot to include their PL jumpers, Louis Bierbauer and Harry Stovey, on their reserve list. Bierbauer (father of musical comedy star Elsie Janis) was claimed by Pittsburgh NL, and irate Philadelphians shouted "Pirates!", a nickname that stuck to Pittsburgh. Boston NL claimed Stovey, former home-run and base-stealing king. When the board of arbitration deprived the A's of both their straying stars, the entire junior circuit angrily rebelled by withdrawing from the National Agreement.

The cold war between the former friendly enemies lasted just one year. The AA began to raid the NL's players in the fall of 1891 . . . but the senior league meanwhile maneuvered a series of deals that brought over four of the best franchises from the AA. That spelled finis for the AA.

From 1892–1900, the NL reigned alone. It listed a dozen clubs, shrinking to eight in the depression following the Spanish-American War. During the Gay Nineties, Frank Selee managed five pennant winners and Ned Hanlon the other five. Selee's star in Boston was Charles (Kid) Nichols, who notched at least

20 victories in each of his first 10 seasons. Hanlon led the boisterous, brainy Baltimore Orioles to 1894-95-96 flags, thanks to the brillance of Wee Willie Keeler, John McGraw, Hughie Jennings, et al. Hanlon switched to Brooklyn in '99 and brought along most of his Oriole prodigies, a combination that rang up two quick pennants.

But the new century brought new woes to the NL. The public now was ready for a second major league. Not so the NL. It fought the inevitable trend with its worst weapon: smugness. Far worse, the league was wracked internally by a secret plot to reorganize baseball's entire structure on a syndicate basis. Behind all this was Andrew Freedman, subway contractor who owned the New York franchise.

First of the vital challenges which the NL bungled developed when a zealous ex-sportswriter named Ban Johnson came to the league meeting, hat in hand, to discuss Eastern franchises for his soundly-organized American League in 1901. Instead of hearing his proposition, the NL sneaked an adjournment and left Johnson standing foolishly in the foyer.

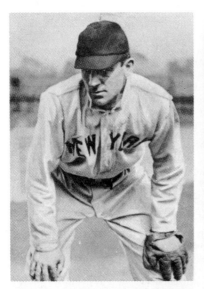 

Smallest but mightiest New York Giant was John McGraw, a fiery third baseman, a crafty manager. He created an early Polo Grounds dynasty.

This spelled "war," and Ban waged it brilliantly. First, he pulled out of the National Agreement with the NL. Then he raided the haughty enemy's ranks with devastating sweeps. Star players of the NL were practically "sitting ducks" for Johnson the hunter, since the old league was still operating under a player salary limit of $2,400. Of 182 AL players that first season, 111 came directly from the NL, including Cy Young, Nap Lajoie, Jimmy Collins and Clark Griffith.

In the summer of 1901, the NL made its next mistake. To patch up its riddled ranks it abrogated the National Agreement and thereby made all minor leaguers

fair game. New suggestions of truce with the AL were immediately squashed by the Freedman faction.

Prior to the league's winter meetings of 1901, Freedman gathered his fellow conspirators from the Cincinnati, Boston and St. Louis clubs. At a parley on his estate at Red Bank, New Jersey, they worked out a master plan to syndicate the league, issuing preferred stock to the league "trust" and common stock among the clubs, with Freedman's henchmen to get the lion's share.

With the four remaining clubs solidly opposed to syndicate baseball, the matter came to a showdown at the annual meeting in December. Freedman's group wanted Nick Young as league president again. The opposition put up Spalding, by now a million-dollar sporting goods dealer, who still bore tremendous prestige as a constant crusader for the sport. Twenty-five times they balloted. Twenty-five times the vote was 4 to 4.

When the Freedman clique finally left the room, Spalding was elected "Unanimously." Spalding seized league papers and records, but had to resign the following March when a New York court granted a permanent injunction against him. Instead of a league president, the circuit was ruled by a three-man "compromise board" the rest of the season.

In April of that tumultuous 1902 campaign, the Pennsylvania Supreme Court granted an injunction against Lajoie, who had jumped from Philadelphia NL. to the A's, and ordered his return to the NL club. Johnson's antidote was to switch Lajoie to Cleveland and keep him out of the state of Pennsylvania. It was a hollow victory for the NL.

Three months later, the new league suffered a real jolt when John McGraw deserted Baltimore to manage the Giants under Freedman's banner. It was to

Tinker (left) to Evers (right) to Chance, the fabulous trio which carried the Chicago Cubs to early 20th century glory in the National League. All three were simultaneously placed in the Hall of Fame.

be Freedman's last triumph. He sold out his baseball holdings at the year's end to John T. Brush, opening the avenue to NL settlement on a sensible candidate for president, young Harry C. Pulliam.

When Pulliam initiated truce talks with the AL early in 1903, Brush sought to employ the injunction weapon his predecessor had used successfully against Spalding. Brush bristled at the AL for moving the Baltimore franchise, which wilted after McGraw's flight, to New York, not far from his Polo Grounds. However, Brush was persuaded to drop the court action, and by August full-scale peace reigned with the signing of a new National Agreement. The AL-NL olive branch became a tangible reality that fall when their teams tangled in the first modern World Series.

On the field of battle, a bowlegged "Flying Dutchman" called Honus Wagner performed daily miracles at shortstop and wielded a murderous bat to bring Pittsburgh pennants in 1901–02–03. Christy Mathewson's pitching genius featured Giant victories the next two years. But the Cubs dominated the NL for the rest of that dead-ball decade. The Tinker-Evers-Chance combination came out on top in 1906–07–08 and '10, with a 104-games-won second-place team to show for that one-year gap.

Chicago's 1906 array set an all-time mark by winning 116 games. But the '08 team roused its fandom most. That was the year Chicago, New York and Pittsburgh all came down the stretch neck-and-neck. In the last Cub visit to New York, the last game of the series was tied with two out in the ninth, with Moose McCormick on third and Fred Merkle on first, when Al Bridwell lashed a clean hit to center. McCormick scampered in with the "winning" run, and the joyous crowd swarmed on the field. But . . .

The big "but" centered around the actions of Merkle, then a 19-year-old substitute first baseman. Noticing Bridwell's drive landing safely, and McCormick scampering home with ease, Merkle veered away on his run toward second and headed for the clubhouse in centerfield instead.

The throw from the outfield landed near third base, and amid the confusion of people streaming on the field, Giant coach Joe McGinnity grabbed the ball and threw it into the stands. Floyd Kroh, Cub pitcher not in the game, retrieved it, and second baseman Johnny Evers was credited with putting out Merkle for the inning-ending force out at second base. As umpire Hank O'Day was led off the field by police, he kept shouting, "The man is out. The game has got to go on." By now there were too many people on the field to resume play, so O'Day called the game on account of darkness.

At first the game went into the books as a Giant victory. If this result had remained, the New Yorkers would have won the flag by a full game from Chicago and Pittsburgh. However, after considerable official delay, the league board of directors ordered the game replayed. On October 8, one day after the scheduled close of the season, the teams tangled at the Polo Grounds. Heroic Matty, who had won 37 games that season for the Giants, lost this crucial one to his lifelong rival, Mordecai (Three-Fingered) Brown, 4 to 2.

The modern era of offensive baseball unfolded when the leagues sanctioned the use of a cork-center ball in 1911. The AL placed 35 hitters in the .300 circle that season. Over in the NL, Frank (Wildfire) Schulte of the Cubs broke all home-run records with a total of 21. Apparently a master of offense as well as defense, McGraw led the Giants to successive pennants in 1911–12–13; but the Little Napoleon met his Waterloo in the World Series each of those years.

Assassination of an archduke in far off Serbia touched off a world war in 1914. Baseball faced virtual assassination around the same time, as the newly-formed Federal League sued to have the entire structure of organized ball invalidated

by the courts. Time proved a valuable ally for the old leagues. The lawsuit languished. On the field, the inexperienced Feds failed to find the gold mine they had envisioned. With the world situation steadily worsening in 1916, FL ring-leaders surrendered to generous settlement terms by the NL and AL . . . ending the last major league "war" after over-all losses totalling perhaps $10,000,000.

In the two troubled years of FL activity, the NL sprang two of the most surprising winners of all. Boston's "Miracle Team" rose from last place on July 19, 1914, to a breathtaking pennant finish and a sweep of the World Series. The next year, Philadelphia took its first NL championship as Grover Alexander notched 31 victories.

Congress declared war just before the baseball season opened in 1917. Catcher Hank Gowdy of the Braves was the first to enlist, but the bulk of hundreds of major leaguers who joined the armed forces did not leave until the following season. McGraw won another pennant with his Giants in '17.

Baseball had tougher going in 1918. Army drafting claimed many star players. "Work or fight" was the national slogan, with orders from Washington curtailing the season to Labor Day.

The post-war boom took most magnates by surprise. Attendance records were set in many parks in 1919. The World Series drew almost a quarter of a million dollars more than the previous all-time high, the half-million dollar Series of 1912. Amidst such prosperity, baseball suffered a near-fatal blow upon the revelation that the infamous Chicago "Black Sox" had thrown the 1919 Series to Cincinnati.

Between its sturdy new Commissioner, Judge Landis, and its astounding new home-run hero, Babe Ruth, baseball recaptured public confidence and enthusiasm. The game headed for unprecedented prosperity. Sunday baseball was legalized in New York in 1920, and the Gotham crowds were rewarded with topnotch teams in both leagues. Quite a bit more portly, but not a mite mellower than in his firebreathing Oriole days, McGraw rose to the apex of his managerial career by conquering all NL rivals with his Giants of 1921-22-23-24, the longest unbroken reign in league history.

McGraw now had 10 flags in 21 years. He never won another. But a bright new dynasty was about to dawn: nine flags in the next 21 years for the St. Louis Cardinals. Guiding genius behind this plethora of pennants was Branch Rickey, who had a versatile background as country schoolmaster, college football coach, lawyer, big league catcher, major league scout, manager in both major leagues, etc. Rickey finally found his perfect niche in baseball as a general manager.

Joining the impoverished Cards in 1919, Rickey hit upon a brilliant scheme. It was the only way his team could become a contender in a league where rich clubs like McGraw's Giants regularly paid outlandish prices for star players of rival teams. "Let's grow our own talent," Rickey told St. Louis clubowner Sam Breadon. "We can round up promising young prospects and develop them on our own minor league clubs."

It was simple enough to find minor clubs as a framework for a "farm system." The critical test was to discover enough diamond nuggets in-the-rough. Rickey himself had a matchless gift for evaluating the baseball potential of even the most callow teen-ager . . . "putting a dollar sign on a muscle," his admirers termed it. But he couldn't transmit such talent to his scouts, so he told them this rule-of-thumb to use on a prospect: "Can he run? Can he throw? Can he hit?"

It's World Series time, and here's part of stylishly-attired crowd which attended 1905 classic between Athletics and Giants. Derby hats and milady's best bonnet add to the festive atmosphere.

In 1926, the first of a long string of home-grown Cardinal champions hit the headlines. Player-manager Rogers Hornsby spurred them on to trample seven league rivals, and they went on to whip the vaunted Yankees in the Series. It was the beginning of a familiar pattern of St. Louis pennants—Bill McKechnie's Cards of '28; Gabby Street's crew of 1930 and '31; Frankie Frisch's Gashouse Gang of 1934; Billy Southworth's lean-and-hungry kids from '42 through '44, and Eddie Dyer, the slow-speaking and quick-thinking Texan, led the Redbirds to a tight victory over the slam-bang Red Sox in 1946.

Rickey was gone from St. Louis when the Cards registered pennants in 1943 and 1946, but those title teams were still mainly his farm products. When he switched to Brooklyn in 1943, the Dodgers already were blessed with a widespread farm system established by one of the many Rickey proteges in major league front offices, Larry MacPhail. Flatbush farmhands fashioned two more flags under Rickey, 1947 and 1949.

In between Card pennant winners, the NL turned up other worthy titlists. Big Poison and Little Poison, those deadly-hitting Waner brothers, brought Pittsburg home in front in 1927. Two years later, a former minor league infielder named Joe McCarthy managed the Cubs for the first of his nine big league pennants.

Replacing Rogers Hornsby as Cub manager on August 2, 1932, first baseman Charlie Grimm drove his team to the top in the two remaining months. That depression year also saw probably the greatest manager of all time, John McGraw, retire in ill health. The sulphuric-tongued, trigger-brained taskmaster's last official move was typically brilliant. Passing over more popular candidates, he hand-picked as successor his coldly efficient first baseman, Bill Terry, who proceeded to win the world championship in his first full season at the helm, 1933. Terry and the Giants repeated as pennant winners in 1936–37.

Terry's pacemakers of 1934 were overtaken on the last day of the race by the

fantastic Gashouse Gang of St. Louis. This was the most colorful club since the old Orioles. They had Pepper Martin, who used his chest to slide on or to stop hard-hit grounders; Dizzy Dean, 30-game winner who outdid his lurid boasts; fun-loving Rip Collins on first base; Lippy Durocher, literally a howling success at shortstop, and similar characters. But manager Frankie Frisch, still the old "Fordham Flash" at second base, could match any of his charges for verve, nerve and deeds of derring-do. These were worthy world champions.

A month after the 1934 World Series, John A. Heydler retired as league president after 18 years of distinguished service in that post. He was followed by Ford C. Frick, former Hoosier schoolmaster, front-line baseball writer and radio sportscaster, who had joined the league as service bureau director the preceding year. Frick's blend of tact, intelligence and devotion to the game earned him continuous re-election, and eventually the post as commissioner.

The same 1934 meetings that elected Frick also voted to allow Leland Stanford (Larry) MacPhail to institute night baseball in his Cincinnati ball-park, and the first game was played on May 24, 1935 when the Reds beat the Phillies, 4 to 1. It proved an instant success. Chicago took the pennant in 1935, and also won in 1938, but increasing night ball revenue enabled general manager MacPhail to plow funds into a farm system that developed pennant winners at Cincinnati in 1939–40.

Redhaired MacPhail was gone from the Reds by the time his farm talent matured into title winners. The boldly imaginative "Barnum" went to work reviving the arid Dodger franchise, and by 1941 he had fashioned a flag for Flatbush. However, Larry suffered his bitterest disappointment just before entering war service in the Fall of 1942, for his star-studded Dodgers frittered

Judge Kenesaw Mountain Landis signs contract which makes him baseball's first commissioner. Club owners gathered at the historic scene are (l. to r.) Phil Ball, Browns; Barney Dreyfuss, Pirates; Connie Mack, Athletics; Clark Griffith, Senators; Jacob Ruppert, Yankees; Frank Navin, Tigers; Sam Breadon, Cardinals; Charles Ebbets, Dodgers; James C. Dunn, Indians; Charles Stoneham, Giants; Garry Herrmann, Reds; Harry Frazee, Red Sox; William Veeck, Cubs; Bob Quinn, Braves. Partially hidden from view are William F. Baker, Phillies, standing behind Ebbets, and Charles A. Comiskey, White Sox, standing behind Dunn.

away a 10½-game lead in August to the Cardinal youngsters. St. Louis repeated as rulers the next two years, which saw hundreds of big leaguers doff playing flannels to don military uniforms.

Baseball weathered World War II, despite severe travel restrictions, thanks to a heartening "green light" letter from President Franklin D. Roosevelt, who lauded the game's contribution to the nation's morale.

Bolstered by the effective pitching of Hank Borowy, a $100,000 waiver "cast-off" from the Yankees, the Cubs captured the 1945 pennant. That year was also notable for the signing of Jackie Robinson, first Negro in modern pro baseball, by the Dodgers' farm club of Montreal.

Baseball's new Commissioner, former U. S. Senator Albert B. (Happy) Chandler, was hardly in office a year when the Mexican League raided the major rosters heavily in the spring of 1946. Chandler warned all contract jumpers that they would be banned from organized baseball for five years, but dozens of them ignored the warning to scoop up the free-flowing pesos south of the border.

Despite the loss of its star pitcher, Max Lanier, and two others who went along on the "Mexican hayride," St. Louis spurted in the last week and finished the season in a tie with Brooklyn, the first deadlock in league history. The Cards swept the two-game playoff and went on to greater glory by outhustling the heavily-favored Red Sox in the Series.

Between the Mexican League threat and a near-successful attempt at player unionization by a Boston lawyer named Bob Murphy, the perturbed clubowners made many important concessions in 1946. The players organized a permanent committee, which had no trouble gaining beneficent terms like a $5,000 salary minimum; pension fund to be bolstered by club payments; limitation of salary cuts to 25 per cent in one season and a shortened spring training season.

Brooklyn's "Peck's Bad Boy," Leo Durocher, climaxed a series of run-ins with baseball's top brass by popping off during the spring training exhibition season of 1947 against his former boss, Yankee general manager MacPhail. Commissioner Chandler clamped down with a year's suspension for the Dodger manager. Called out of semi-retirement to lead the Flock, Burt Shotton succeeded in winning the flag, thanks to the spark of a flock of Rickey farm products, notably Jackie Robinson, who won the base-stealing title in his rookie season.

Billy Southworth skillfully piloted a collection of oldsters in Boston uniform to first place in 1948. The next year, with Shotton replacing Durocher in mid-season, Brooklyn won another flag, bolstered by batting-king Robinson. The game was jolted early in 1949 when stranded Mexican Leaguers brought lawsuits for being blacklisted by pro baseball. Commissioner Chandler wisely declared a general amnesty in June of that year, and later made an out-of-court settlement with the last challenger of the legality of the reserve clause, Danny Gardella.

Bonuses boomed in post-war years. Half a dozen prospects collected more than $50,000 each to sign with pro teams. One of the heaviest investors in this costly market was a young Delaware millionaire, Bob Carpenter, who owned the lowly Phillies. The policy paid off. Fashioned mainly by general manager Herb Pennock, who unfortunately died of a heart attack before his handiwork blossomed into Philadelphia's first pennant in 35 years, the Phillie Whiz Kids won all the NL marbles in 1950. It took a 10th-inning homer on the last day of the season by Dick Sisler, son of the first base immortal, to bring the Phils the decision over Brooklyn's fast finishers. Serving as chief Dodger scout at the time, George Sisler sat in the stands on that final day and watched his son's homer kayo the pennant hopes of the club he was working for.

The league lost a president when Frick was named Commissioner of Baseball, replacing Chandler who resigned July 15, 1951 when he learned his con-

tract wouldn't be renewed. Frick was handed a three-year pact at $65,000 a year and brought in his manager of the service bureau, Charley Segar, to serve as secretary-treasurer.

Warren C. Giles, head of the Cincinnati Reds, was elected to Frick's vacant post and Dave Grote, who handled the publicity of the Rhinelanders, was appointed manager of the service bureau.

Perhaps the most historic dash toward a pennant since the run of Boston's Miracle Braves in 1914, occurred in 1951 when the New York Giants, after being 13½ games behind Brooklyn in mid-August, finally caught the Dodgers, but only after the two clubs finished the season in a dead tie upon conclusion of the regular playing schedule. The stage was now set for the second league playoff in five years.

The Giants, after winning the first of the best-of-three-game playoff series, 3 to 1, lost the second clash 10 to 0. What followed provided perhaps the most dramatic climax recorded in the league's history.

Leading 4 to 1 entering the ninth inning of the final clash, the Dodgers needed but three outs to win the pennant. But they were to get only one. With one run in and runners on second and third base for the Giants, Dodger manager Chuck Dressen replaced starting pitcher Don Newcombe with Ralph Branca. Bobby Thomson was at the plate, and he represented the winning run. After Branca threw one strike, Thomson swung on the next pitch and lofted it into the left field stands for a home run, a 5-4 Giant victory and the league flag.

The Dodgers were winners in 1952 and '53, the latter year a notable one since it marked the first franchise shift in 53 years.

The shift was made March 18, 1953 when the Perini brothers, Lou and Charles, announced the transfer of their Boston Braves to Milwaukee. Sagging attendance figures and apathy on the part of the fans to adequately support the Braves were the reasons given by the Perinis for the switch.

Milwaukee proved a gold lode. In the first 13 home dates at the beer capital the Braves drew a total of 302,667, more than had flocked through the portals of Braves' Field for all of their 1952 home dates. A season attendance mark of 1,826,397 was a new league standard.

Milwaukee continued to prosper in 1954 when 2,131,388 paid to watch the third place Braves. The financial success of the Braves started baseball owners thinking of new diamond horizons, where television could be controlled in an intelligent manner and people would pay to see their heroes in the flesh instead of watching them from their own living room.

The Giants were 1954 champions, sweeping Cleveland in the Series, and the Dodgers bounced back to win in 1955 and '56. In both these seasons the Milwaukee attendance continued above the two million mark and these high figures evidently began to start a couple of clubowners wondering just how they could also increase their own gate receipts. Brooklyn president Walter O'Malley made a significant move in '56 when he took his Brooklyn team to Jersey City, New Jersey where the Dodgers played seven "home" games, one with each league rival. This started the speculation that the Dodgers would soon depart from Brooklyn permanently.

The Dodgers again played seven games in Jersey City in 1957, the year Milwaukee drew a record attendance of 2,215,404—the fourth straight season the Braves topped the two-million mark. On the field, the Braves rewarded their faithful with their first pennant, climaxed by a World Series victory over the Yankees.

The most historic events of the year—in fact in the history of baseball—

were the announcements, first by the New York Giants, then by the Brooklyn Dodgers, that their teams were leaving the vast metropolitan New York area for the West Coast. On August 19, Horace Stoneham, president of the Giants, announced that his club would leave New York at the end of the season and move to San Francisco. Brooklyn's O'Malley made it official on October 8 when he stated the Dodgers would be transferred to Los Angeles. Both owners cited old parks and limited parking facilities as main reasons for the shifts, but the unlimited possibilities of pay-television and the opportunity to acquire vast real estate properties were other vital factors in the move to the West.

Milwaukee repeated as pennant winners in 1958, the year the league took on a coast-to-coast "new look." The Dodgers, who were unable to get immediate approval for construction of a new stadium in the Chavez Ravine area of Los Angeles, played their games in the vast Los Angeles Memorial Coliseum, a field constructed specifically for football, and drew 1,845,556 fans. The Giants moved into much-smaller Seals' Stadium, where they attracted 1,272,625 fans.

These attendance figures represented an increase over the previous season when both teams were located in the East. However the Dodgers became involved in legal battles and delays over the construction of their new playing area; the Giants had little trouble in obtaining permission to start construction on a new park which was scheduled to be ready for the 1960 season.

Los Angeles set a new single-day league attendance mark on April 18 when 78,672 fans saw the Dodgers play the Giants in the first major league game ever to be played on the Pacific Coast.

A proposed third major league, headed by Branch Rickey and Congressional hearings into the laws governing organized baseball, overshadowed the events on the playing field to a considerable extent in 1959. When Congress failed to pass the Kefauver bill and the game's status remained unchanged Rickey's embryo Continental League was dealt a body blow from which it never recovered. The successful move to the West Coast by the Dodgers and Giants created a demand for expansion which was discussed in great detail by both leagues without reaching an agreement.

On the playing field the Dodgers, participating in their third play-off, defeated the Braves and went on to win the World Championship from the White Sox in a Series that shattered the former attendance mark of 86,288 set at Cleveland in 1948. Playing in the huge Los Angeles Coliseum the Dodgers bettered that record in all three home games. The first game drew 92,394 fans, the second was witnessed by 92,650 while the third game saw the largest crowd in World Series history—92,796—a record topped only by the Campanella benefit exhibition against the Yankees which drew 93,103, largest turnout in Major League history.

Definite expansion plans for both major leagues after the demise of Branch Rickey's proposed Continental League marked 1960 as a year of dramatic development. First, the National, then the American edged into the lead in the expansion race with President Cronin's American League finally emerging as the winner by voting to expand to ten clubs in 1961, while the more conservative National decided to withhold their plans until 1962.

On the field the swash-buckling Pirates landed Pittsburgh its first pennant since 1927. Their specialty was coming from behind to win games apparently hopelessly lost. They won 23 games during the season in their final turn at bat— 12 of these after two were out. Warren Spahn of the Braves won 21 games. It was the eleventh time in his major league career in which he had won 20 or more games per season. Established as preseason favorites, the Giants folded completely after the sudden discharge of Skipper Bill Rigney on June 18th. The

Cubs tried a novel but unsuccessful move when Manager Charlie Grimm and radio announcer Lou Boudreau switched jobs. Boudreau, however, had no more success than "Jolly Chollie" and the club finished a bad seventh, just one game ahead of the perpetual cellar-dwelling Phillies.

The underdog Reds surprised all of the experts by winning the 1961 flag despite the presence of some slightly "shopworn" players. In the race all of the way, they finished four games ahead of the favored Los Angeles Dodgers. It was the first Cincinnati pennant since 1940. On August 16th their double header with the Dodgers at the Coliseum in Los Angeles set a National League record for double headers when 72,140 fans witnessed the twin bill. The Pirates, winners in 1960, collapsed completely and finished a poor 6th. Phil Wrigley's innovation of installing a staff of coaches rather than a single manager failed miserably to improve the Cubs who finished a poor 7th just ahead of the perennial cellar-dwellers, the Phils, who rounded out their 4th consecutive year trailing the pack. Starting on July 23rd, they lost 28 out of 29 games setting a 20th century record of 23 losses in a row.

The 1962 National League season was marked by the Senior Circuit's expansion into a ten-club league, the first time the league has had more than the conventional 8 clubs since 1899. The clubs were poorly balanced and the result, while tense with the Giants, Dodgers and Reds fighting for the pennant, was just another season for the rest of the league. The Giants and Dodgers had to go into a play-off as they finished in a dead heat at the end of the regular season, the Giants winning two of the three play-off games. The Dodgers opened the season in their magnificent new Chavez Ravine Stadium. Maury Wills of the Dodgers was the toast of the league when he stole 104 bases, surpassing the immortal Ty Cobb's 1915 record of 96. Stan (The Man) Musial added a few more records to his already bulging collection when he passed Honus Wagner for the most total hits in National League history and moved past Tris Speaker in the all-time hit total where he is surpassed only by the great Ty Cobb. On the debit side of the ledger was the extremely poor showing of the New York Mets under Casey Stengel who set a new record for losses in a single season by dropping 120 decisions while the floundering Cubs lost 100 games for the first time in their National League history.

The Dodgers bounced back in 1963, taking the flag behind a superlative pitching staff headed by Sandy Koufax. Wild and inconsistent as a youngster, the Dodger southpaw's fast ball now was complemented by gilt-edge control. Sandy won 25 of 30 decisions, struck out a modern league record of 306 and tossed 11 shutouts in firmly establishing himself as baseball's premier pitcher. The Cardinals made a great bid in late season, winning 19 of 20 games to move within one game of the Dodgers, but Los Angeles terminated the streak and ended the Red Birds' flag hopes by sweeping a three-game series in St. Louis. Musial, who had announced his retirement at the club's annual summer picnic, was honored by the home fans on the season's final day and The Man wrote an appropriate ending to his fabulous success story by hitting singles in his final two at bats. Stan closed out his illustrious career with 3,630 hits and a host of records.

With Musial in his first year as a Cardinal vice-president, the Red Birds overhauled the Phillies on the final day to win the 1964 pennant. Philadelphia, which seemed to have an insurmountable lead with two weeks left, proceeded to drop 10 straight games and a one-team race became a four-team affair as the Cards, Reds and Giants surged into late contention. With only three days to go, all four had a chance, and the Giants didn't fall by the wayside until the next-to-last-day. St. Louis wrapped it up on the final day by whipping the lowly

Mets, 11–5, after losing to them the two previous days. Had the Cards lost the finale, the race would have ended in a three-way tie. Perhaps more startling than the Cards' triumph was the resignation of their pilot, Johnny Keane, one day after their World Series victory over the Yankees. And more surprising still was that Keane succeeded Yogi Berra at the Yankee helm. Berra was fired the same day that Keane quit the Cards. The year also marked the opening of the Mets' magnificent new home, Shea Stadium, named after William Shea, the New York attorney who was instrumental in returning National League ball to New York. The Phils' ace, Jim Bunning, gave the new park a proper christening by pitching a perfect game there June 21. Koufax also tossed a 1964 no-hitter, the third of his career, tying him with Bob Feller, Cy Young and Larry Corcoran. Houston's Ken Johnson also had a hitless gem, but his came in a losing cause. Cincinnati scored a ninth-inning run on two errors—one by Johnson—to win, 1–0.

Koufax, Don Drysdale, newcomer Claude Osteen and a marvelous bullpen brought the pennant flag to Los Angeles in 1965 and '66. Sandy smashed all modern strikeout marks with 382 in '65 and also won 26 games, including a record fourth no-hitter, which happened to be a perfect game. The peerless Dodger southpaw reached a high of 27 victories and fanned 317 batters in '66. Both years presented ding-dong pennant races, too, with the Giants challenging strongly both times and the Pirates, boasting a wrecking crew second to none, figuring prominently in '66. Houston had its new stadium, the $20,500,000 Astrodome, ready for the 1965 season and both St. Louis and Atlanta had new playing areas in 1966. Atlanta also had a new ball team, the Milwaukee Braves shifting operations to the Georgia capital that year after an abortive attempt the year before.

The 1965 season was marred by an incident at San Francisco August 22 when the Giants' mound star, Juan Marichal, struck Dodger catcher John Roseboro over the head with a bat. Marichal drew a $1,750 fine and a nine-day suspension for his "unprovoked and obnoxious" assault.

Although only 30 years old, Koufax announced his retirement in November, 1966, saying his aching left arm could endure no more pain. With Koufax gone, the Dodgers fell into the second division and the Cardinals, now managed by Red Schoendienst, a long time Red Bird star, climbed to the top led by the slugging of Orlando Cepeda, the running of Lou Brock and a well-balanced mound staff. Pittsburgh's Roberto Clemente continued to win more laurels, capturing his fourth batting crown with a career high of .357. Only Musial, Hornsby and Wagner won more often. At the winter meetings in Mexico City the league voted to expand to 12 clubs and began accepting franchise applications.

The Cardinals again breezed to the pennant in 1968. Bob Gibson led the Cards by setting a new league E.R.A. mark of 1.12. The league expanded to 12 teams in 1969, adding the Montreal Expos, the first major league team outside the United States, and the San Diego Padres. Two divisions were established, the East with Chicago, Montreal, New York, Philadelphia, Pittsburgh and St. Louis, and the West with Atlanta, Cincinnati, Houston, Los Angeles, San Diego and San Francisco.

The amazing New York Mets ran away with the championship, winning 27 more games than the previous season. Gil Hodges made good use of his entire roster. He relied mainly on a solid pitching staff, led by Tom Seaver, Jerry Koosman and Tug McGraw, and hitting topped by Cleon Jones. The Atlanta Braves won the West in a close race, but were swept aside by the Mets in the playoff. In December of 1969, Charles (Chub) Feeney was elected president of the National League, succeeding the retiring Warren Giles.

The next three years resulted in a battle between the Pittsburgh Pirates and

the Cincinnati Reds, with only one close division race. That was in 1971, when the Reds had an off year, and the Giants edged the Dodgers by a game on the final day. The Reds easily whipped the Pirates in the playoff of 1970, and the Pirates returned the favor to the Giants the following year. 1972 marked the first close championship series, as the Reds nipped the Bucs in five games. The Mets bounced back in 1973 to win the East title in the closest race in major league history. With only two days remaining, a five-way tie was still possible. New York went on to edge the Reds in five games in the playoff. The Mets made the miracle Braves' feat in 1914 look like a cinch. The New Yorkers were in last place on August 31st, then went on to pass five clubs in a month. The Braves had been in last place on July 19th, but moved up to fourth on July 21st and were second on August 31st.

Tom Seaver was the top performer for the Mets over the period, winning the Cy Young award in 1969, 1973 and 1975. Steve Carlton had the best individual season mark, winning 27 games for the lowly Phillies in 1972. Ferguson Jenkins of the Cubs strung six 20-win seasons in a row through 1972. Willie McCovey was the number one hitter for the three years through 1970, but was then hobbled by injuries. Pete Rose won three batting titles and led the Reds to their playoff victory in 1972. Johnny Bench, winner of two MVP awards, along with Joe Morgan, Tony Perez and Dave Concepcion were large contributors to the Reds' success, while Gary Nolan, when healthy, and Don Gullett were their most effective pitchers.

The leader of the Pirates was Roberto Clemente, whose tragic death in an airplane crash in 1972 shocked the baseball world. Clemente was aided by slugger Willie Stargell and hurler Steve Blass. Willie Mays ended his glorious career in 1973 after 22 years, while Hank Aaron just kept rolling along, setting a new league record for fewest at-bats per home run in 1973 and finally breaking Babe Ruth's lifetime homer record in 1974. Hank moved to the AL in 1975, and when he retired after 1976, he had set new lifetime marks for games, at-bats, total bases and runs batted in as well. Lou Brock set an all-time stolen base mark with 118 in 1974.

The Reds and Pirates moved into new stadiums in 1970, as did the Phils a year later. This left only the Cubs with a park built before 1960. Artificial turf was installed in six of the fields.

The Dodgers won in 1974, beating out Cincinnati in a close race and whipping Pittsburgh in the playoffs. But the Reds came back in 1975 to win 108 games, the best record in over twenty years. Again the Pirates bit the dust in the championship series.

In 1976, the Reds took the West for the fifth time in seven years and won their second straight World Series. This was the first time since 1922 that an NL team had performed the feat. The Phils won the East, but were swept aside by Cincinnati, who became the first team to win seven post-season games in a row. Bill Madlock won his second straight batting title, while Randy Jones won at least twenty games two years in a row for lowly San Diego. Mike Schmidt led in homers for the third successive year and hammered out four in one game as well.

The Dodgers moved ahead of the Reds to take the league title in both 1977 and 1978, beating the Phils each time in the playoffs. Major contributors for Los Angeles were Steve Garvey, Reggie Smith and Don Sutton. Pete Rose of the Reds went over 3000 hits and also tied Willie Keeler's 44-game hitting streak in 1978. San Diego was the only club to load up on free agents, and their performance was not improved.

American League

The groundwork for the formation of the American League actually was started nine years before its official beginning in 1901. Byron (Ban) Johnson, a minister's son, and Charles Albert Comiskey, player-manager of the Cincinnati team in the unwieldy National League, began their dreams of secession and a new diamond empire in the beer parlors of the Rhineland, as early as 1892.

The 27-year-old Johnson, who conducted a no-holds barred baseball column for the *Cincinnati Gazette,* held no particular affection for John T. Brush, club-owner of the local nine. But, for Comiskey, Johnson had nothing but admiration. Brush, a clothing magnate, was the target of some of Ban's choicest and most sulphuric adjectives, and was severely criticized for what Johnson claimed were "stingy tactics" which he said were harming the local franchise.

Comiskey, recognizing in Johnson an alert and imaginative mind who envisioned greater horizons for baseball, soon convinced clubowners anxious to reform the old Western Association that Ban was their man to head the league. Johnson, who went to the league's convention as a reporter, returned as its new president, mainly because Commy was so lavish in his praise of the sports writer.

Comiskey himself left Cincinnati at the close of the 1894 season to take a managerial post with Sioux City, where he started on a club-owning career which was to make him one of the game's most powerful and influential figures.

Johnson tackled his new assignment in typical fashion, hard-hitting and hard-working, and his eyes were cocked continuously at major-league status. He was especially alert for defections in the NL ranks and kept his ears close to the ground for rumblings of discontent.

Ban made his initial move in 1896, after Connie Mack had been fired as Pittsburgh pilot for making caustic comments against the second-guessing of a critical front office. Ban snapped up Mack for his league, offering the lean catcher-manager a bonus which consisted of part-interest in the Milwaukee club. Three years later, a series of bold and shrewd moves by Ban convinced him that his dreams of an American League were not too far removed from reality.

When the NL dropped four of its dozen clubs after the 1899 season, Johnson persuaded Charles Somers, Great Lakes shipping tycoon, to take over the vacated Cleveland franchise. Somers "steered" the league in its roughest period, over the next two years. Ban also set up a club in Buffalo. It took Commy's engineering, though, before Jim Hart, owner of the Chicago NL team, allowed Comiskey to switch his St. Paul team to Chicago's South Side. Hart never thought fans would tolerate the stockyard smells to see a ball game in that rundown district of town.

At this point, prestige-wise Johnson announced that his circuit was changing its name from the Western to the American League. Commy's team won the 1900 pennant after a prosperous season for the league in general. Johnson was now ready for the master stroke. Using as a pretext the rumored re-organization of the old American Association as a direct threat against his league, Ban sought NL permission to expand into Baltimore, Washington and Philadelphia. Unable to obtain even the courtesy of an audience with the haughty Nationals, Johnson launched open warfare.

First, Ban scrapped the National Agreement, so that all players became fair game in the eyes of rival leagues. He forestalled an AA-inspired plan to move into Boston by sending Connie Mack to the Hub to lease a plot for a ballpark (using Somers' bankroll). Somers, who had loaned Comiskey money to build a park in Chicago, also had a financial finger in the Philadelphia club, as well as his own titular Cleveland franchise.

The AL's expansion to the East proved popular, and the dissension-ridden rival league lost customers. Johnson's full-fledged major league began official operations on Wednesday, April 24, 1901. Other teams were rained out that day, but there was a gala inaugural in Chicago, which was destined to win the flag with Clark Griffith as manager and Comiskey now in the front office. The first American League box score:

CLEVELAND (2)	AB	R	H	PO	A	E	CHICAGO (8)	AB	R	H	PO	A	E
Pickering, rf	4	0	1	0	0	0	Hoy, cf	5	0	1	3	0	0
McCarthy, lf	4	0	2	4	0	0	Jones, rf	2	2	1	4	0	0
Genins, cf	4	0	0	1	0	0	Mertes, lf	3	2	1	4	0	0
LaChance, 1b	4	1	1	13	0	1	Shugart, ss	2	2	0	4	4	0
Bradley, 3b	4	0	0	2	5	0	Isbell, 1b	3	1	1	8	0	0
Beck, 2b	2	0	2	0	4	0	Hartman, 3b	4	0	1	0	5	1
Hallman, ss	3	1	0	1	3	1	Brain, 2b	4	0	0	1	3	0
Wood, c	4	0	1	2	2	0	Sullivan, c	4	1	2	2	0	0
Hoffer, p	4	0	0	1	0	0	Patterson, p	4	0	0	1	1	0
Totals	33	2	7	24	14	2	Totals	31	8	7	27	13	1

Cleveland	000	100	100	---	2
Chicago	250	000	10x	---	8

Left on base—Chicago 5, Cleveland 3. Two base hit—Beck. Double plays—Shugart-Isbell, Hoffer-Hallman-LaChance. Struck out—by Hoffer 1. Bases on balls—off Patterson 2, Hoffer 6. Umpire—Connolly. Time—1:30. Attendance—14,500.

Johnson's platform of "clean baseball and more 25-cent seats" drew increasing patronage. Star players kept streaming toward the better-paying AL. Ban backed his umpires religiously, even though it brought him head-on against such personal friends as Clark Griffith. Griff took the censure in good grace. Not so John McGraw, who couldn't shed his "Old Orioles" stripe. In midseason of 1902, irascible McGraw sold out his Baltimore holdings and jumped back to the NL. Johnson's answer was to move the Baltimore franchise to New York for 1903— despite politicians' threats to run city streets through his ballpark—and the AL finally had an eight-club alignment.

Connie Mack's A's were hard hit by an injunction that cost them the services of Nap Lajoie and other NL "jumpers." But an erratic southpaw named Rube Waddell came in from the Coast to strong-arm Mack's team to the 1902 pennant.

By now, the NL knew it had had enough. At a peace meeting in January of 1903, the old circuit tried the old stratagem that worked against the AA— offering to absorb the stronger teams of the rival circuit. Johnson and his fellow delegates snapped out of their seats, reached for their hats and stomped out of the conference. Four days later, there was a different tone at the interleague meeting. The NL asked only that Johnson promise not to invade Pittsburgh. Ban nodded. They shook hands, signed a preliminary agreement that established the dual-major league principle and finally set up a joint committee to settle ownership of disputed players.

Cy Young, still a 28-game winner at the age of 36, led Boston to the 1903 pennant. Teammate Bill Dinneen, who won 21, beat the Pirates three times in the ensuing World Series.

Hairbreadth finishes featured AL races the next few years. Of these, none brought greater satisfaction to Johnson than the 1906 campaign. Ban exulted along with his crony, Commy, whose Chicago "Hitless Wonders" put together 19 straight victories at one stage to finish on top of the heap. Then they deflated the mighty Cubs in baseball's first intracity World Series.

From 1907–09, it was all Detroit. Hughie Jennings managed this triumphant

Tiger pack. As one of the "Old Orioles," Hughie was used to blood-and-thunder aggressiveness on the field. But he had to admit none of his former teammates could approach the fierce, flaming will-to-win of his young outfielder, a tight-lipped Georgian named Ty Cobb. A basepath terror and batting wonder, Cobb captured the hitting crown all three of these pennant-winning seasons . . . and nine times afterward. His lifetime average over 24 years was a stratospheric .367, just one of the dozens of records still held by the "Georgia Peach."

Connie Mack's A's ruled the roost for four of the first five years after the cork ball came into use. Boasting the "Hundred thousand dollar infield" of McInnis-Collins-Barry-Baker, and the iron-armed pitching trio of Bender-Plank-Coombs, the White Elephants trumpeted triumphantly in 1910–11, 1913–14.

Boston's Red Sox, with a famed outfield trio of Speaker-Hooper-Lewis, also bagged four flags around that time: 1912, 1915–16, 1918. Comiskey's club in Chicago won the other pair of pennants in the second decade of this century. League overlord Johnson chortled as his clubs of this period posted four Series successes over the Giants of McGraw, his despised enemy ever since the 1902 desertion of Baltimore.

The Damon-Pythias bond between Johnson and Comiskey was strained when the AL chief suspended a White Sox outfielder for three days. Returning from a fishing trip that week, Ban sent Commy his best catch. Back came a bitter wire: "Do you think I can play that fish in left field?" The rift widened into an angry feud when Commy's infamous "Black Sox" were exposed for throwing the 1919 World Series.

Tris Speaker and his world champion Clevelands of 1920 were overshadowed by the eruption of the Sox scandal. Along came Babe Ruth, to fire the imagination with his wondrous homers, and Judge K. M. Landis, to restore faith in the game, and baseball was back on the glory road of sportsdom's Golden Era.

Ruth already had gained fame as a Red Sox pitching star and a part-time outfielder who could practically knock the cover off the ball. But his light shone brightest after his sale to the Yankees, who had never won a pennant. Babe helped dispel the title famine by whacking the unbelievable total of 59 homers in 1921. His howitzer at the plate enabled New York to stay on top in 1922 and 1923. In the latter year, his team moved from the National League's Polo Grounds into its own million dollar ballpark, Yankee Stadium, which was suitably tagged "The House that Ruth Built."

After 17 seasons with a trailing team, old faithful Walter Johnson, greatest pitcher in AL history, broke into two World Series when his Senators won in 1924–25. Manager Bucky Harris was the "Boy Wonder" at the helm each time.

The next phase of league history featured the "Murderers' Row" Yankee champions of 1926–27–28. Beer baron Col. Jacob Ruppert made a fetish of success, and the Yankee owner had the right men to insure it—richly experienced Edward G. Barrow as general manager, clever little Miller Huggins as field pilot and Babe Ruth backboning a lineup of "window breakers" like Lou Gehrig, Bob Meusel, Tony Lazzeri, et al. Babe hit 60 homers in 1927, the all-time record.

Even as these awe-inspiring Yanks enjoyed the spotlight, other real titans were bowing out in the wings. Ty Cobb and Tris Speaker closed their active careers after spending the 1928 season side by side in the A's outfield. Walter Johnson and Ban Johnson quit in 1927, the former after winning more than 400 games and the latter after broken-heartedly losing his long vendetta against the all-powerful Commissioner.

Ban Johnson's successor as AL president was Cleveland's chief executive, Ernest S. Barnard. Johnson and Barnard both died suddenly in 1931, as did

Comiskey. Gentlemanly Will Harridge rose to the presidency after 20 years in the league office as secretary.

Coincident with the cataclysmic Wall Street crash of 1929 was Connie Mack's return to baseball prosperity. Buoyant as ever in his late 60's, the league's managerial dean paraded to three straight pennants from 1929–31. Four of his aces came from Jack Dunn's Baltimore club, which had spawned Babe Ruth earlier. Dunn received upwards of $150,000 for Lefty Grove, George Earnshaw, Max Bishop and Joe Boley. Mack's fame finally transcended baseball's halls, and he received the Bok Award in 1929 for distinguished service to the city of Philadelphia.

An NL managerial castoff, Joe McCarthy, came to the Yankees to restore the regal sway of the Bronx Bombers. Holdovers from the Huggins regime helped him nail the flag in 1932. A frustrated runnerup each of the next three years, McCarthy finally hit his stride in 1936 for seven pennants in the next eight seasons and four straight world championships.

The renewed dynasty started in the rookie season of Joe DiMaggio, a fisherman's son grown into a graceful outfielder second only to Ruth in New York annals. It continued unabated as the farm chain, master-minded by Barrow and George Weiss, developed a string of summa cum laude graduates—Joe Gordon, Charlie Keller, Spud Chandler, Phil Rizzuto, Hank Borowy, et al. These youngsters were balanced with ageless veterans of topnotch caliber, like Lefty Gomez, Bill Dickey, Red Ruffing and Frank Crosetti. Tommy Henrich was a free-agent bargain at $20,000 in 1937.

Detroit's slow but slugging club of 1940 interrupted the Yank pennant monopoly. Cries of "Break up the Yankees" were often raised, but it took the tail end of World War II to do it. After the Yankees won in 1941, '42 and '43 the lowly Browns, under Luke Sewell, won their only AL title in 1944. Detroit, with slim Hal Newhouser and bespectacled Dizzy Trout as the 1–2 mound punch, won in 1945. The next year was the payoff for long-suffering Tom Yawkey, who had poured millions into the Red Sox for more than a decade before finally realizing a pennant. It was powered by batting king Ted Williams, baseball's most feared slugger since Babe Ruth.

With diamond dynamo Larry MacPhail operating as one-third owner of the Yanks in 1947, world championship days were back in the Bronx. Larry brought Bucky Harris back from the managerial boneyard to guide this club.

Cleveland interrupted a new Yankee era of domination in 1948, beating Boston in the league's first post-season playoff after the Indians and the Red Sox had concluded the regular season with identical records. Lou Boudreau, manager-shortstop, paced the Tribe down the stretch with his great hitting and fielding, and it was his momentum which enabled Cleveland to down Boston in an unprecedented one-game, sudden-death playoff battle in the Hub's Fenway Park.

The Yankees resumed their old position at the top of the heap for the next five years (1949–53), Casey Stengel leading a new group of Bombers to five straight world championships, a new record in the annals of the game. This was the same Stengel who had been found deficient as a manager of the Boston and Brooklyn entries of the NL.

It was Cleveland again which temporarily halted the fantastic Yankee pennant pushes. Al Lopez, who once played for Stengel in the NL, whipped his teacher in 1954. The Indians rolled up an impressive total of 111 victories—an all-time AL season high—but were humiliated in the Series when they dropped four straight to the New York Giants. It was the first AL post-season defeat in eight years.

During the Indians' drive they established another record, this for attendance for a single day when 84,587 stormed Municipal Stadium on September 12 to see the Tribe belt the Yankees in a doubleheader.

The Korean conflict, during the '50s, claimed several players who previously had served in the forces during World War II. Ted Williams, who held a reserve commission in the Marine Air Corps, was recalled to active duty soon after the start of the '52 year, not to return until the '53 campaign was well under way.

Perhaps the most startling developments of the early '50s were the franchise shifts which left St. Louis and Philadelphia bereft of AL representation for the first time since Ban Johnson organized the loop.

The St. Louis Browns were transferred to Baltimore on September 29, 1953 for a total reported to be $2,475,000. The Philadelphia Athletics were to go one year later, being bought by Arnold Johnson and associates for the sum of approximately three and one half million dollars. Both clubs drew well in their initial season, the Orioles pulling 1,060,910 through the gates in '54 and the Athletics, despite a sixth-place finish, attracting 1,393,054 in '55.

It was the same old AL story as the 1950s drew to a close—too much Yankee dominance. The greatest baseball dynasty ever created won pennants from 1955 through '58, but only got an even break in Series competition, losing the '55 and '57 sets to Brooklyn and Milwaukee. For manager Stengel it made nine pennants in 10 years.

Ted Williams remained the game's most provocative personality, and in 1956 created some sort of history by getting stung with a record-equaling fine of $5,000. The Boston thumper was penalized this amount by his club when he spat in the direction of the stands after the fans in his home park booed for desultory play.

Although the Yankees had the vast Metropolitan area to themselves in 1958 their attendance dropped some 68,000 over their 1957 total. Many theories were advanced for this fall-off, but there was no doubt that the day and night televising of games was beginning to take its toll of the attendance.

Will Harridge, president of the AL since 1931, startled the mid-winter league 1958 meeting when he announced his retirement. He gave no reasons for his decision but many believed that Harridge was bowing out due to the many problems baseball would be forced to face in the next few years. Talk of a third league, a demand by the players for 20 per cent of all gate, concession and television monies and constant discussion on the problems of television and how it should be regulated were some of the factors which, many believed, decided to make the 72-year-old Harridge announce his retirement. Joe Cronin, former star shortstop and manager of Boston and Washington, Hall-of-Famer, and general manager of the Red Sox, was named as his successor.

Picked to win their fifth straight pennant in 1959 the Yankees suddenly found themselves in the unfamiliar surroundings of the cellar where they landed on May 20th. From there they waged an up-hill battle but they were never able to regain their former prestige winding up in third place, 15 games behind the pennant-winning White Sox. Early Wynn of the White Sox was the biggest winner in the majors with 22 victories. Meanwhile the magnates were experiencing "growing pains." Expansion fever was at a high pitch due to the threat of Branch Rickey's Continental League. Suddenly the American League voted to study the request of Minneapolis-St. Paul for a spot in the junior circuit. Cronin's loop proposed expansion to nine clubs for each league by taking a franchise in Minneapolis-St. Paul and granting the National a club in New York. The National rejected this plan claiming they were "not interested" in expansion at the time.

With the Continental League on the ropes due to the pigeon-holing of the Kefauver bill in 1960, the American League once more discussed expansion and decided to go into action as soon as the National advised them of similar word. Meeting in Chicago on July 18th the National League cast a solid vote in favor of the move. When the senior circuit voted to add Houston and New York to the loop in 1962 the American League broke all speed records by boosting their league to 10 clubs. They authorized Calvin Griffith of the Washington club to make his move to Minneapolis-St. Paul, approved a new franchise for Washington to a syndicate headed by General Elwood Quesada, head of the FAA, and awarded a Los Angeles franchise to a group led by cowboy singer Gene Autry and TV tycoon Bob Reynolds. Starting from scratch it was a herculean task to field two brand new major league clubs in less than four months and the result was the wildest talent scramble in major league history.

The year also witnessed the dissolution of the game's most successful managerial team when both General Manager George Weiss and Manager Casey Stengel, of the New York Yankees, were relieved of their posts. This pair had guided the Yanks to ten pennants and seven World Championships in the last twelve years. Another unusual managerial shift occurred in 1960 when Jimmie Dykes of the Tigers and Joe Gordon of the Indians switched jobs. The American League launched the 1961 season with the first 10-club league in its history and also embarked on a marathon 162-games schedule. The new clubs, Minneapolis and Los Angeles, had rough going finishing 7th and 8th respectively. The Yankees, as usual, topheavy favorites did not disappoint their followers and repeated for their 12th pennant in 15 years. Under a new manager, Ralph Houk who assumed the helm after the departure of Casey Stengel, they did not lose their stride and not only copped the flag but continued on to take the Reds four games to one in the World Series. The big guns were Roger Maris who topped the famous Bambino's Home Run record by clouting 61, Mickey Mantle who was right behind him with 54 and pitcher Ed Ford who copped 25 decisions while losing only 4. In winning the pennant on his first try, manager Houk joined three of freshman managers, namely Bucky Harris, Joe Cronin, and Eddie Dyer. The Tigers under Bob Scheffing proved to be the surprise club of the year setting the pace for the first half of the season. Unfortunately the Tigers lacked the pitching depth necessary to stay in front but they were topped only by the Yanks in batting. Norm Cash won the batting crown with an average of .361 while Al Kaline and Rocky Colavito helped the cause with Kaline hitting .324 and Rocky clubbing 45 homers. The newly-born Angels surprised their followers by winning a respectable 70 victories.

It was the old, old story again in 1962 when the Yanks won their 10th flag in the past 12 years. However, they faced unexpected opposition from the two new clubs, the Minnesota Twins and the Los Angeles Angels who finished second and third respectively and gave the Yanks a run for their money, in fact, the Yanks could not find the magic wand until the final two weeks of the season when the Twins and Angels ran out of gas. General manager Fred Haney, the man of the hour in the Angels' set-up made some astounding deals which kept the club in the running until the very end. It was the most surprising club in the history of the game. Early Wynn was one of the tragic figures of the campaign. Trying hard for his 300th victory, he missed on several occasions and had to wait until the middle of the 1963 season to achieve the magic 300. Freshman Bo Belinsky, Earl Wilson and Bill Monbouquette of the Bosox and Jack Kralick of the Minnesota Twins all pitched no-hit games while 20-game winners included Dick Donovan, Ralph Terry, Ray Herbert and Camilo Pascual.

The Yankees continued their dynasty into 1963 and '64, winning two more

pennants to extend their streak to five. The only other club to win five consecutive flags was the Yankees of 1949–53. They won in '63 with their two big sluggers, Micky Mantle and Roger Maris, incapacitated much of the way; they won in '64 under a freshman manager, Yogi Berra, who succeeded Ralph Houk when the latter moved up to general manager. The Bombers won in a breeze in '63, finishing 10½ games in front of Chicago. But the 1964 race was a three-team affair between New York, Chicago and Baltimore, and the Bombers didn't clinch their 29th American League pennant until the next-to-last day.

Berra was fired the day after the World Series ended, despite his success during the season and extending the Cardinals to seven games in the Series. He was replaced by Johnny Keane, his opposite number on the Cards, who had resigned the same day Berra got the ax. The major change in the Yankee structure, however, took place in August when Dan Topping and Del Webb sold 80 per cent of their stock to the Columbia Broadcasting System. Webb sold his remaining 10 per cent to CBS six months later.

Minnesota rookie outfielder Tony Oliva burst onto the scene in 1964 and won the batting title with a .323 average and ranked first in several other batting departments. He repeated in 1965 with a .321 figure, helping the Twins to their first flag. Minnesota was a power club led by all-round shortstop Zoilo Versalles, who did everything well enough to earn the Most Valuable Player award. The Yankees surprised everybody by dropping to sixth place, their lowest finish since 1925 when they wound up seventh.

The Baltimore Orioles, bolstered by the acquisition of Frank Robinson in an inter-league trade with Cincinnati, captured the 1966 flag handily, finishing nine games ahead of the defending champion Twins. Robby won the Triple Crown with a .316 average, 49 home runs and 122 runs batted in and also was instrumental in the Birds' four-game sweep of the Dodgers in the World Series. Nothing much to talk about during the regular season, the Baltimore pitching staff held Los Angeles to a record low of two runs. The Angels' new park in Anaheim was unveiled, a triple-decked structure built in less than two years at a cost of $24,000,000. The Yankees continued their plunge downward and wound up in the league basement, only the third time in their proud 64-year history that they finished so poorly. There were other developments in Gotham, too. Keane was let out as manager on May 7 and replaced by Houk, who relinquished his front office duties. And then, in mid-September, Dan Topping sold his remaining stock in the club to CBS and Michael Burke, 50, a network vice-president and a former football player at the University of Pennsylvania, was named president. A month later, Lee MacPhail, son of the old baseball magnate, was added to the front office team as general manager.

The Boston Red Sox, ninth in 1966 and a study in futility for most of the post-Korean War era, produced one of the biggest surprises in history by winning the 1967 pennant, and on the final day, too. Their kingpin was Carl Yastrzemski, the sometimes moody leftfielder, who won the Triple Crown in even more heroic fashion than had Frank Robinson. Yaz seemed to hit game-winning homers or throw out runners at the plate nearly every day as he tied the Twins' Harmon Killebrew in homers with 44 and led in RBI's (121) and batting (.326). Boston had to withstand a furious four-team race to win, though, a race in which Minnesota, Detroit, Chicago and the Red Sox took turns holding the lead. Chicago, which had a woeful batting attack, was the first to drop out, two days before the end, but the others hung on until the final day.

Boston defeated Minnesota twice, on the final Saturday and Sunday, to assure itself of at least a tie, and then had to await the outcome of the Tigers' double-

header with the Angels. Detroit won the opener, but California spoiled the Tigers' pennant plans by taking the nightcap.

Charlie O. Finley, the controversial owner of the Kansas City Athletics, obtained permission to move the club to Oakland when the league met in October. The AL owners considered Finley's shift and expansion in one package. What came out of it was the Oakland Athletics and new franchises in Kansas City and Seattle, the latter two to begin operation in 1969.

Denny McLain led the Detroit Tigers to a comfortable twelve-game margin in the 1968 pennant race. McLain (31–6) was the first 30-game winner since Dizzy Dean in 1934. He also led in winning percentage, complete games and innings pitched. Jim (Catfish) Hunter of Oakland pitched the first regular season perfect game in 46 years.

With the expansion to 12 teams in 1969, the league was split into two divisions, East and West. Baltimore, Boston, Cleveland, Detroit, New York and Washington made up the East, while California, Chicago, Minnesota, Oakland and the two new teams, Kansas City and Seattle, made up the West. The Championship Series, a three-of-five clash between division winners to determine the league World Series representative, was also adopted.

The Baltimore Orioles, sparked by Frank Robinson, ran roughshod over the other clubs for the first three years, and also won nine straight playoff games. Manager Earl Weaver had essentially the same lineup for these years, including Brooks Robinson, "Boog" Powell, Paul Blair, Mark Belanger and pitchers Dave McNally, Jim Palmer and Mike Cuellar. The Birds topped the Twins in 1969 and 1970 as well as Oakland in 1971.

Detroit came back to win the East Crown in 1972. This was one of the closest races in league history, with four clubs still alive in the final week. The Tigers won the crucial first game of the final series of two with Boston to beat the Red Sox by half a game. The player strike had shortened the season by a week, leaving Detroit with one more game than Boston.

Meanwhile, in the West, the Oakland Athletics were beginning to move. Their manager was Dick Williams, who had guided the Red Sox to the 1967 pennant. In his third year at Oakland (1971) the A's became the first team in three years to come within ten games of the Orioles, but lost the playoff in three straight. In 1972 Oakland fought off the White Sox in the West and then nipped Detroit in the championship series in five games. Oakland continued its winning ways in 1973, gaining revenge over the Orioles in the playoff three games to two. Each team had won its division easily.

Reggie Jackson, Sal Bando, Joe Rudi, Bert Campaneris, Gene Tenace and pitchers Jim Hunter, Ken Holtzman, Vida Blue and Rollie Fingers formed the nucleus of the team which took over from Baltimore as the league's best. Oakland won again in 1974, beating the Orioles in the playoffs. They then went on to take their third straight World Series, the first time this feat had been accomplished in over twenty years. The Athletics led the Western Division once more in 1975, but were denied a chance at their fourth world championship by the rejuvenated Boston Red Sox. The Sox benefited from the play of super rookie Fred Lynn, who became the first player in history to win both MVP and rookie awards the same year.

Carl Yastrzemski won his third batting title in 1968 and lost out by less than a point in 1970. Rod Carew won five batting titles, leading in 1969 and 1972 through 1975. Harmon Killebrew topped the league in homers for the sixth time in 1969. Nolan Ryan of California set a new major league strikeout record in 1973 and also threw four no-hitters. Wilbur Wood of the White Sox,

once the league's best relief pitcher, won 20 games as a starter in 1974, giving 90 wins in four years.

After only one season, the Seattle club was switched to Milwaukee for 1970. Milwaukee made another move in 1972—to the East Division, as Bob Short moved his Washington club to Texas and the West.

The AL had their best season for attendance in history in 1973, aided by the new designated hitter rule which allowed a permanent pinch-hitter for the pitcher. It was announced in October that Joe Cronin would move from league president to chairman of the board, and that Lee MacPhail would take over as president for 1974.

A great deal of news continued to be made off the field. Hank Aaron came over from the NL in 1975 to finish his career with Milwaukee. Cleveland made news when they hired Frank Robinson, who became the first black manager in the majors, also in 1975. The biggest story concerned Jim "Catfish" Hunter. Relieved of his obligation to Oakland due to a breach of contract by Athletics owner Charles O. Finley, the Catfish went on the open market and was able to sell his services to the Yankees for a reported three-plus million dollars.

The Yankees were back on top in 1976 for the first time in twelve years, with the help of the Catfish and Thurman Munson. Kansas City won a close race from Oakland in the West and extended the Yanks to five games in the championship series. The Royals became the first expansion AL team to manage a first place finish. The usual fireworks occurred in Oakland. Faced with the likely defection through free agent status of several more of his stars, Finley tried to sell Vida Blue to New York and Joe Rudi and Rollie Fingers to Boston. Commissioner Kuhn voided the sales, stating that it was not in the best interests of baseball. Detroit's newcomer, Mark "The Bird" Fidrych regularly attracted crowds of 50,000 with his fine pitching and unique style of enthusiasm.

The Yankees and Royals continued their rivalry through 1978, with the New Yorkers winning each time, and also taking the World Series twice. The free agent rule, which allowed any player to sell himself to the highest bidder after six years, permitted the Yanks to beef up their squad with Reggie Jackson, Rich Gossage and Don Gullett. Texas and California also signed a number of free agents, with little improvement, while Minnesota and Oakland lost several players. The league expanded to 14 teams in 1977, adding Toronto and Seattle. Charles Finley almost sold his club to Denver interests in 1978, but the deal fell apart at the last minute. Rod Carew won two more battling titles, bringing his total to seven, swatting .388 in 1977, while Jim Rice led in almost everything the following year, Ron Guidry dominated pitching with the best season in many years in 1978, going 25 and 3 with a 1.74 earned run average. Guidry was the winning pitcher in the first playoff game in thirty years, as the Yankees beat the Boston Red Sox 5-4 for the Eastern Division title.

American Association

In the earlier years of the National League many of the mid-western cities were envious of the financial inroads the league had made, especially in hinterland towns which were not of major league status. Touring Easterners from the NL drew heavy gates in exhibitions played in Western areas, and the West soon started to sound out several cities as prospective entries in a new major circuit.

H. D. (Denny) Knight of Pittsburgh and Justus Thorner of Cincinnati rounded up a half dozen clubs and went into the field in 1882, avowed rivals of the NL. The newly-founded American Association was now in business.

With prideful, suspicious Soden acting as NL president, Eastern reception was openly hostile, extending to bold player raids and the coining of a favorite epithet. "Beer and Whiskey League," they termed the AA, deriding the fact that financial backers of the new circuit mainly derived their income from alcohol.

On the other side of the fence, name-calling consisted of tagging the NL the "rich man's league." To court the "plain workingmen" clientele, the AA slashed the admission price to half its rival's 50-cent standard, featured Sunday baseball (then expressly forbidden in the NL under threat of expulsion) and dispensed beer in the stands.

Cincinnati won the first AA flag behind the pitching of bespectacled Will White. The novelty of good baseball in fertile cities, bringing a host of new Western heroes into the diamond limelight, resulted in a prosperous inaugural season. The AA added two more franchises for 1883. Thanks to newly-elected president A. G. Mills, the NL wisely made peace with its lusty young rival, and under the National Agreement they operated as dual major leagues.

The most fabulous figure in AA history was not any of its new playing heroes, but a bulbous-nosed German immigrant named Chris Von der Ahe. Owner of a pleasure resort in the St. Louis suburbs, the hearty and generous "sport" became interested in baseball as a means of attracting customers to his place. But he was smart enough to know how ignorant he was of the game's intricacies, so Chris relied on the judgment of Alfred H. Spink, a zealous baseball writer and guiding spirit of the game in early St. Louis days.

Another colorful character who helped develop the Browns was Ted Sullivan, railroad concessionaire who sponsored a powerful team in Dubuque, Iowa. Ted brought the newly-formed Browns his best men, including first baseman Charlie Comiskey. St. Louis finished a close second to the pennant-winning Athletics in 1883, slumped in '84, and the next year, with Commy at the helm, started a streak of four straight pennants.

Though Al Spink, who founded *The Sporting News* soon afterward, and Comiskey, who revolutionized first base play, were the guiding geniuses behind the Browns' dynasty, expansive Von der Ahe swaggered under such sustained success and unabashedly proclaimed himself "the smartest feller in baseball." On the contrary, Chris' petulant orders to dispose of several important players after his crushing World Series loss to Detroit in 1887 proved costly. Commy repeated the flag in '88, but was nipped in quest of a fifth straight pennant by a Brooklyn team that had bought the standout players who incurred the displeasure of the St. Louis baron.

War with the Players' League in 1890 crippled the AA. Unable to meet budgets on a 25-cent-admission plank, several key clubs deserted to the NL. A year later, the AA withdrew from the National Agreement . . . only to lose the "cold war" when more clubowners secretly capitulated to the NL.

Despite its inglorious finish, the AA played a valuable role in baseball history. It pioneered reforms which the NL eventually adopted, like league control of umpires, Sunday baseball and the percentage system of determining pennant winners. Healthy competition also forced the NL to draft a National Agreement that served as a basis for present-day pacts guiding major and minor league operations.

Union Association

Insisting that the reserve rule "reserves all that is good for the owners, leaving the remainder for the players," St. Louis millionaire Henry V. Lucas embarked on a one-man crusade to end the players' "bondage." He organized the Union Association as a third major league in 1884. George Wright, given the concession of manufacturing the official ball for the circuit, agreed to run the Boston franchise. Thorner came in with his Cincinnati club after the AA founder thought he had received short shrift in his circuit.

Widely-traveled Ted Sullivan was dispatched to round up players willing to ignore the reserve clause binding them to the AA or NL. Before the season started, the Unions had about 50 of these. But most of the recruits suddenly repented and stayed with their old clubs. As owner of the St. Louis Maroons franchise, Lucas was able to ante up extra bonus money to keep his reserve-clause jumpers in line, so the UA's "angel" wound up with an overpowering pennant-winner that won its first 20 games and quickly killed interest in the "race." Only five clubs finished the season, though a dozen participated.

Unwilling to draw any distinction between breaking a current contract or the holdover clause, both the AA and NL raided UA ranks in the early months, and kidnapped many players who had drawn heavy advances in salary. On July 1, the UA declared open warfare and started to induce the stars of rival leagues to jump in mid-season, too.

The three-way war was too costly all around. Weaker clubs in the UA folded in profusion. Only in St. Louis, where Lucas unstintingly gave his fans the best in players and accommodations—including dozens of caged canaries strewn about the stands—was there any sustained prosperity.

When the UA expired at the end of the season, Lucas opportunistically snapped up the Cleveland NL franchise (which he had helped ruin by mid-season player raids) for $2,500. As part of his price for peace, Lucas insisted on moving into the NL. He transferred his Cleveland holding to St. Louis, paid Von der Ahe $5,000 for territorial privileges and ungraciously absented himself from the UA's dissolution meeting in order to concentrate on his new NL interest.

Players' League

The one-year stand of the Players' League (1890) was actually a movement motivated by players who were members of the National Brotherhood of Professional Players. This was a benevolent organization which used dues of five dollars a month from its members to aid its sick and needy.

After the 1885 season, the NL and AA magnates set a ceiling on players salaries and forbade any cash advances during the off-season. John Montgomery Ward, later a successful attorney, served as the Brotherhood's spokesman in protesting the salary scale of $2,000. Although the salary limit never was enforced, though kept on the books, additional grievances were fought successfully by the Brotherhood which demanded, and received, official recognition in 1887.

While Ward was away on a world tour, the magnates instituted the unfair

Classification System of scaling players' salaries. Upon his return, the brilliant Giant shortstop couldn't even get an audience with the NL. Declaring lack of good faith on the part of the league, the Brotherhood published a Declaration of Independence on November 4, 1889, and lined up financial support for a Players' League in 1890.

Players in the new circuit signed three-year contracts at their 1889 figure, which could be raised at the discretion of the club, but not slashed. Even more interesting, the PL abandoned the reserve rule by allowing players to switch clubs at will at the close of the season. However, the latter plan never got a trial, since the league lived only one year.

The secession movement was populer. Four out of five NL regulars jumped to the PL. Though forced to operate with makeshift lineups, the NL magnates boldly took on the insurgents by scheduling and re-scheduling games in order to conflict with PL contests in the same city. In New York, only a wall separated games played simultaneously by the rival leagues.

Spalding, appointed head of a "war committee" of the NL, offered King Kelly a $10,000 bribe plus a three-year League contract "at any figure you want to write in" to skip back. But the colorful "King Kel" couldn't go back on his Brotherhood mates and turned down the offer. Kelly went on to pilot the PL pennant-winners in Boston.

Rainy weather in the late stages of the race hurt PL attendances, and inexperienced magnates quickly lost heart at the reverses. A few sold out to eager NL rivals, and the Brotherhood collapsed. All contract-jumpers were restored to their original clubs without penalty.

Federal League

Unlike the Union Association and Players' League, which became third major leagues principally on "reform" platforms, the Federal League moved into the baseball picture strictly in the spirit of a capital investment. When coal magnate James A. Gilmore became president of the FL in September, 1913, it was still a sectional minor league operating in the Midwest.

Gilmore had the gift of gab, and soon sold a group of businessmen on the wisdom of backing a third major league. Glib Jim painted a rosy financial picture, dipping heavily into the figure of the "Half million dollar World Series" of 1912, which netted each of the competing clubs almost $150,000. As a clincher, he accented the advertising value of owning a ball club which daily made nation-wide headlines.

The spellbinder convinced the Ward baking brothers, who took the Brooklyn franchise; Charles Weeghman, who owned a chain of Chicago restaurants; Harry Sinclair, oil tycoon who took the Newark Club; Phil Ball, St. Louis ice king; Otto Stifel, wealthy brewer, and others.

Gilmore then went to work on the players. His first conquest was Joe Tinker of Cub fame, who was hired to manage the Chicago Whales. Other established stars followed. Even though they didn't fall for the greenback bait, such standouts as Ty Cobb and Tris Speaker had their salaries doubled to keep them from joining the "outlaw league."

Eight new ballparks were built within three months, including the Chicago plant that is now known as Wrigley Field. Indianapolis nosed out Chicago in a close race in 1914, while Chicago shaded St. Louis by one percentage point the next year. Only the imminence of American entry into the World War persuaded the FL magnates to listen to peace feelers from the AL and NL.

The price of peace came high. First, the Feds insisted that their rivals assume

the $385,000 worth of FL player contracts. Weeghman was permitted to buy the Cubs and Ball the Browns. Payments spread over five to 20 years were to reimburse the Ward interests, Sinclair and Pittsburgh backers. Of the many Fed players sold back to the majors, the highest price went for Benny Kauff, the "Ty Cobb of the Feds," whom the Giants snapped up for $35,000.

The settlement made no provision for the Baltimore club, which thereupon instituted an anti-trust suit against organized baseball that went all the way to the U. S. Supreme Court before Justice Holmes finally ruled in 1922 the sport was not "interstate commerce."

CLUB STANDINGS YEAR BY YEAR

CLUB STANDINGS YEAR-BY-YEAR
F indicates where club finished at end of season. x indicates did not finish season. t indicates finished in a tie for this position. p indicates playoff used to break tie at end of scheduled season.

1871—NATIONAL ASSOCIATION

CLUB	F	W	L	PCT	MGR
ATH	1	22	7	.759	Hayhurst
CHI	2	20	9	.690	Foley
BOS	3	22	10	.688	Wright
OLY	4	16	15	.516	Young
HAY	5	15	15	500	Pike / Craver
MUT	6	16	18	.471	Ferguson
CLE	7	10	19	.345	Pabor
KEK	8x	7	21	.250	Deane / Lennon
ROK	9	6	20	.231	Waldo

1872—NATIONAL ASSOCIATION

CLUB	F	W	L	PCT	MGR
BOS	1	38	8	.826	Wright
ATH	2	31	15	.674	Hayhurst
L BAL	3	35	19	.648	Henderson
MUT	4	35	21	.625	Pearce
HAY	5x	15	10	.600	Wood
CLE	6x	6	15	.286	Hastings
ATL	7	9	28	.243	Ferguson
OLY	8x	2	7	.222	Young
MAN	9x	5	19	.208	Putnam
ECK	10	3	26	.103	Clinton / Wood
NAT	11x	0	11	.000	Miller

1873—NATIONAL ASSOCIATION

CLUB	F	W	L	PCT	MGR
BOS	1	43	16	.729	Wright
PHI	2	36	16	.692	Young, G.
L BAL	3	34	22	.607	Henderson
ATH	4	28	23	.549	Hayhurst
MUT	5	29	25	.537	Cammeyer
ATL	6	17	37	.315	Ferguson
NAT	7	8	31	.205	Young, N.
RES	8x	2	21	.087	Benjamin
MAR	9x	0	6	.000	Smith

1874—NATIONAL ASSOCIATION

CLUB	F	W	L	PCT	MGR
BOS	1	52	18	.743	Wright
MUT	2	42	23	.646	Higham
ATH	3	33	22	.600	Hayhurst
PHI	4	29	29	.500	Ferguson
CHI	5	28	31	.475	Young, N.
ATL	6	23	32	.418	Ferguson
HAR	7	15	38	.283	Pike
L BAL	8	9	38	.191	Henderson

1875—NATIONAL ASSOCIATION

CLUB	F	W	L	PCT	MGR
BOS	1	71	8	.899	Wright
ATH	2	53	20	.726	Hayhurst
HAR	3	54	28	.659	Ferguson
ST.L	4	37	28	.569	Graffen
PHI	5	37	31	.544	Young, G
MUT	6	31	38	.449	Hicks
CHI	7	30	37	.448	Wood
RS	8x	4	15	.211	Sweazy
NAT	9x	5	23	.179	Childs
N H	10	7	40	.149	Gould
CEN	11x	2	12	.143	Craver
WES	12x	1	12	.077	Trimble
ATL	13	2	42	.045	Pabor

1876—NATIONAL LEAGUE

CLUB	F	W	L	PCT	MGR
CHI	1	52	14	.788	Spalding
St. L	2	45	19	.703	Graffen
HAR	3	47	21	.691	Ferguson
BOS	4	39	31	.557	Wright, W.
LOU	5	30	36	.455	Fulmer
MUT	6	21	35	.375	Cammeyer
ATH	7	14	45	.237	Wright, A.
CIN	8	9	56	.135	Gould

1877—NATIONAL LEAGUE

CLUB	F	W	L	PCT	MGR
BOS	1	42	18	.700	Wright
LOU	2	35	25	.583	Chapman
HAR	3	31	27	.534	Ferguson
ST.L	4	28	32	.467	Lucas / McManus
CHI	5	26	33	.441	Spalding
CIN	6	15	42	.263	Pike / Addy

1878—NATIONAL LEAGUE

CLUB	F	W	L	PCT	MGR
BOS	1	41	19	.683	Wright
CIN	2	37	23	.617	McVey
PRO	3	33	27	.550	Ware
CHI	4	30	30	.500	Ferguson
IND	5	24	36	.400	Clapp
MIL	6	15	45	.250	Chapman

1879—NATIONAL LEAGUE

CLUB	F	W	L	PCT	MGR
PRO	1	55	23	.705	Wright, G.
BOS	2	49	29	.628	Wright, W.
BUF	3t	44	32	.579	McGunnigle
CHI	3t	44	32	.579	Anson
CIN	5	38	36	.514	White, J. L. / McVey
SYR	6x	15	27	.357	Smith
CLE	7	24	53	.312	McCormick
TRO	8	19	56	.253	Clapp

1880—NATIONAL LEAGUE

CLUB	F	W	L	PCT	MGR
CHI	1	67	17	.798	Anson
PRO	2	52	32	.619	Bullock
CLE	3	47	37	.559	McCormick
TRO	4	41	42	.494	Ferguson
WOR	5	40	43	.482	Bancroft / Brown
BOS	6	40	44	.476	Wright, W
BUF	7	24	58	.293	McGunningle / Crane
CIN	8	21	59	.263	Clapp

1881—NATIONAL LEAGUE

CLUB	F	W	L	PCT	MGR
CHI	1	56	28	.667	Anson
PRO	2	47	37	.559	Bullock / Morrow
BUF	3	45	38	.542	O'Rourke
DET	4	41	43	.488	Bancroft
TRO	5	39	45	.464	Ferguson
BOS	6	38	45	.458	Wright, W
CLE	7	36	48	.429	McCormick
WOR	8	32	50	.390	Brown

1882—NATIONAL LEAGUE

CLUB	F	W	L	PCT	MGR
CHI	1	55	29	.655	Anson
PRO	2	52	32	.619	Wright, W
BOS	3t	45	39	.536	Morrill
BUF	3t	45	39	.536	O'Rourke
CLE	5	42	40	.512	Evans
DET	6	42	41	.506	Bancroft
TRO	7	35	48	.422	Ferguson
WOR	8	18	66	.214	Brown / Bond / Chapman

1882—AMERICAN ASSOCIATION

CLUB	F	W	L	PCT	MGR
CIN	1	54	26	.675	Fulmer
ECL	2	44	35	.557	Dyler / Reccius / Maskrey
ATH	3	40	35	.533	Sharsig / Mason
ALL	4	39	39	.500	Pratt
ST.L	5	36	43	.456	Cuthbert / Sullivan
BAL	6	19	54	.260	Myers

1883—NATIONAL LEAGUE

CLUB	F	W	L	PCT	MGR
BOS	1	63	35	.643	Burdock / Morrill
CHI	2	59	39	.602	Anson
PRO	3	58	40	.592	Wright, W
CLE	4	55	42	.567	Bancroft
BUF	5	52	45	.536	O'Rourke
N Y	6	46	50	.479	Clapp
DET	7	40	58	.408	Chapman
PHI	8	17	81	.173	Ferguson

1883—AMERICAN ASSOCIATION

CLUB	F	W	L	PCT	MGR
ATH	1	66	32	.673	Knight / Mason / Sharsig
St. L	2	65	33	.663	Sullivan / Comiskey
CIN	3	62	36	.633	Snyder
MET	4	54	42	.563	Mutrie
ECL	5	52	45	.536	Reccius / Maskrey / Gerhardt
COL	6	32	65	.330	Phillips
ALL	7	30	68	.306	Pratt / Butler / Battin
BAL	8	28	68	.292	Barnie

1884—NATIONAL LEAGUE

CLUB	F	W	L	PCT	MGR
PRO	1	84	28	.750	Bancroft
BOS	2	73	38	.658	Morrill
BUF	3	64	47	.577	O'Rourke
CHI	4t	62	50	.554	Anson
N Y	4t	62	50	.554	Price
PHI	6	39	73	.348	Wright, W
CLE	7	35	77	.313	Hackett
DET	8	28	84	.250	Chapman

1884—AMERICAN ASSOCIATION

CLUB	F	W	L	PCT	MGR
MET	1	75	32	.701	Mutrie
COL	2	69	39	.639	Schmelz
ECL	3	68	40	.630	Gerhardt / Walsh
St. L	4	67	40	.626	Williams / Von der Ahe
CIN	5	68	41	.624	Snyder / White
BAL	6	63	43	.594	Barnie
ATH	7	61	46	.570	Mason / Sharsig
TOL	8	46	58	.442	Morton
BRO	9	40	64	.385	Taylor
VIR	10	12	30	.286	Moses
ALL	11	30	78	.278	Battin / Creamer / Ferguson / McKnight / Phillips
IND	12	29	78	.271	Gifford / Watkins
NAT	13x	12	51	.190	Hollingshead

1884—UNION ASSOCIATION

CLUB	F	W	L	PCT	MGR
St. L	1	91	16	.850	Sullivan
					Dunlap
MIL	2x	8	3	.727	McKee
CIN	3	68	35	.660	O'Leary
					Crane
BAL	4	56	48	.538	Levis
					Henderson
BOS	5	58	51	.532	Murnane
					Furniss
					Morse
CHI	6x	33	35	.485	Hengle
NAT	7	47	66	.416	Scanlon
PIT	8x	7	10	.412	Battin
					Ellick
KEY	9x	21	46	.313	Malone
					Pratt
St. P	10	2	6	.250	Thompson
ALT	11x	6	19	.240	Curtis
K C	12	14	63	.182	Sullivan
WIL	13x	2	15	.118	Simmons

1885—NATIONAL LEAGUE

CLUB	F	W	L	PCT	MGR
CHI	1	87	25	.776	Anson
N Y	2	85	27	.758	Mutrie
PHI	3	56	54	.509	Wright, W
PRO	4	53	57	.481	Bancroft
BOS	5	46	66	.410	Morrill
DET	6	41	67	.379	Morton
					Watkins
BUF	7	38	74	.339	Chapman
					Hughson
					Galvin
St. L	8	36	72	.333	Dunlap
					Fine
					Lucas

1885—AMERICAN ASSOCIATION

CLUB	F	W	L	PCT	MGR
St. L	1	79	33	.705	Comiskey
CIN	2	63	49	.563	Caylor
ALL	3	56	55	.505	Phillips
ATH	4	55	57	.491	Knight
					Mason
					Sharsig
BRO	5t	53	59	.473	Doyle
					Hackett
					Byrne
ECL	5t	53	59	.473	Hart
MET	7	44	64	.407	Gifford
BAL	8	41	68	.376	Barnie

1886—NATIONAL LEAGUE

CLUB	F	W	L	PCT	MGR
CHI	1	90	34	.725	Anson
DET	2	87	36	.707	Watkins
N Y	3	75	44	.630	Mutrie
PHI	4	71	43	.622	Wright, W
BOS	5	56	61	.478	Morrill
St. L	6	43	79	.352	Schmelz
K C	7	30	91	.247	Rowe
WAS	8	28	92	.233	Scanlon
					Gaffney

1886—AMERICAN ASSOCIATION

CLUB	F	W	L	PCT	MGR
ST.L	1	93	46	.669	Comiskey
ALL	2	80	57	.584	Phillips
BRO	3	76	61	.555	Byrne
ECL	4	66	70	.485	Hart
CIN	5	65	72	.471	Caylor
ATH	6	63	73	.467	Simmons
					Mason
					Sharsig
MET	7	53	82	.393	Gifford
					Ferguson
BAL	8	48	83	.366	Barnie

1887—NATIONAL LEAGUE

CLUB	F	W	L	PCT	MGR
DET	1	79	45	.637	Watkins
PHI	2	75	48	.610	Wright, W
CHI	3	71	50	.587	Anson
N Y	4	68	55	.553	Mutrie
BOS	5	61	60	.504	Morrill
PIT	6	55	69	.444	Phillips
WAS	7	46	76	.377	Gaffney
					Dennis
IND	8	37	89	.294	Fogel
					Burnham
					Thomas

1887—AMERICAN ASSOCIATION

CLUB	F	W	L	PCT	MGR
ST.L	1	95	40	.704	Comiskey
CIN	2	81	54	.600	Schmelz
BAL	3	77	58	.570	Barnie
ECL	4	76	60	.559	Kelly
ATH	5	64	69	.481	Bancroft
					Mason
					Sharsig
BRO	6	60	74	.448	Byrne
MET	7	44	89	.331	Ferguson
					Caylor
					Orr
CLE	8	39	92	.298	Williams

1888—NATIONAL LEAGUE

CLUB	F	W	L	PCT	MGR
N Y	1	84	47	.641	Mutrie
CHI	2	77	58	.578	Anson
PHI	3	69	61	.531	Wright, W
BOS	4	70	64	.522	Morrill
DET	5	68	63	.519	Watkins
					Leadley
PIT	6	66	68	.493	Phillips
IND	7	50	85	.370	Spence
WAS	8	48	86	.358	Hewitt
					Sullivan
					Whitney

1888—AMERICAN ASSOCIATION

CLUB	F	W	L	PCT	MGR
ST.L	1	92	43	.681	Comiskey
BRO	2	88	52	.629	McGunnigle
ATH	3	81	52	.609	Sharsig
CIN	4	80	54	.597	Schmelz
BAL	5	57	80	.416	Barnie
CLE	6	50	82	.378	Williams
					Loftus
ECL	7	48	87	.360	Kerins
					Davidson
K C	8	43	89	.326	Rowe
					Barkley
					Watkins

1889—NATIONAL LEAGUE

CLUB	F	W	L	PCT	MGR
N Y	1	83	43	.659	Mutrie
BOS	2	83	45	.648	Hart
CHI	3	67	65	.508	Anson
PHI	4	63	64	.496	Wright, W
PIT	5	61	71	.462	Phillips
					Dunlap
					Hanlon
CLE	6	61	72	.459	Loftus
IND	7	59	75	.440	Bancroft
					Glasscock
WAS	8	41	83	.331	Morrill
					Irwin

1889—AMERICAN ASSOCIATION

CLUB	F	W	L	PCT	MGR
BRO	1	93	44	.679	McGunnigle
ST.L	2	90	45	.667	Comiskey
ATH	3	75	58	.564	Sharsig
CIN	4	76	63	.547	Schmelz
BAL	5	70	65	.519	Barnie
COL	6	60	78	.435	Buckenberger
					(Continued)

1889—American Association (Cont.)

		W	L	PCT	MGR
K C	7	55	82	.401	Watkins
					Manning
ECL	8	27	111	.195	Davidson
					Brown
					Means
					McKinney
					Shannon
					Wolf
					Chapman

1890—NATIONAL LEAGUE

CLUB	F	W	L	PCT	MGR
BRO	1	86	43	.667	McGunnigle
CHI	2	83	53	.610	Anson
PHI	3	78	53	.595	Wright, W
CIN	4	78	55	.586	Loftus
BOS	5	76	57	.571	Selee
N Y	6	63	68	.481	Mutrie
CLE	7	44	88	.333	Schmelz
					Leadley
PIT	8	23	114	.168	Hecker

1890—AMERICAN ASSOCIATION

CLUB	F	W	L	PCT	MGR
ECL	1	88	44	.667	Chapman
COL	2	79	55	.590	Buckenberger
					Sullivan
					Schmelz
ST.L	3	78	58	.574	McCarthy
					Roseman
					Campau
TOL	4	68	64	.515	Morton
ROC	5	63	63	.500	Powers
BAL	6	15	19	.441	Barnie
SYR	7	55	72	.433	Fessenden
					Frazer
ATH	8	54	78	.409	Sharsig
BRO	9x	26	73	.263	Kennedy

1890—PLAYERS' LEAGUE

CLUB	F	W	L	PCT	MGR
BOS	1	81	48	.628	Kelly
BRO	2	76	56	.576	Ward
N Y	3	74	57	.565	Ewing
CHI	4	75	62	.547	Comiskey
PHI	5	68	63	.519	Hilt
					Fogarty
					Buffinton
PIT	6	60	68	.469	Hanlon
CLE	7	55	75	.423	Faatz
					Larkin
					Tebeau
BUF	8	36	96	.273	Rowe

1891—NATIONAL LEAGUE

CLUB	F	W	L	PCT	MGR
BOS	1	87	51	.630	Selee
CHI	2	82	53	.607	Anson
N Y	3	71	61	.538	Mutrie
PHI	4	68	69	.496	Wright, W
CLE	5	65	74	.468	Leadley
					Tebeau
BRO	6	61	76	.445	Ward
CIN	7	56	81	.409	Latham
PIT	8	55	80	.407	Hanlon
					McGunnigle

1891—AMERICAN ASSOCIATION

CLUB	F	W	L	PCT	MGR
BOS	1	93	42	.689	Irwin
ST.L	2	86	52	.623	Comiskey
MIL	3	21	15	.583	Cushman
BAL	4	71	64	.526	Barnie
					Van Haltren
ATH	5	73	66	.525	Sharsig
					Wood
					Barnie
COL	6	61	76	.445	Schmelz
CIN	7x	43	57	.430	Kelly
ECL	8	55	84	.396	Chapman
WAS	9	44	91	.326	Trott
					Snyder
					Shannon
					Griffin

1892—NATIONAL LEAGUE

CLUB	F	W	L	PCT	MGR
BOS	1	102	48	.680	Selee
CLE	2	93	56	.624	Tebeau
BRO	3	95	59	.617	Ward
PHI	4	87	66	.569	Wright, W
CIN	5	82	68	.547	Comiskey
PIT	6	80	73	.523	Burns / Buckenberger
CHI	7	70	76	.479	Anson
N Y	8	71	80	.470	Powers
LOU	9	63	89	.414	Pfeffer / Chapman
WAS	10	58	93	.384	Barnie / Irwin / Richardson / Wagner
ST.L	11	56	94	.373	Von der Ahe / Waltz / Hanlon
BAL	12	46	101	.313	Van Haltren

1893—NATIONAL LEAGUE

CLUB	F	W	L	PCT	MGR
BOS	1	86	44	.662	Selee
PIT	2	81	48	.628	Buckenberger
CLE	3	73	55	.570	Tebeau
PHI	4	72	57	.558	Wright, W
N Y	5	68	64	.515	Ward
BRO	6t	65	63	.508	Foutz
CIN	6t	65	63	.508	Comiskey
BAL	8	60	70	.462	Hanlon
CHI	9	57	71	.445	Anson
ST.L	10	57	75	.432	Watkins
LOU	11	50	75	.400	Barnie
WAS	12	40	89	.310	Wagner / O'Rourke

1894—NATIONAL LEAGUE

CLUB	F	W	L	PCT	MGR
BAL	1	89	39	.695	Hanlon
N Y	2	88	44	.667	Ward
BOS	3	83	49	.629	Selee
PHI	4	71	56	.559	Irwin
BRO	5	70	61	.534	Foutz
CLE	6	68	61	.527	Tebeau
PIT	7	65	65	.500	Buckenberger / Mac't
CHI	8	57	75	.432	Anson
ST.L	9	56	76	.424	Miller
CIN	10	54	75	.419	Comiskey
WAS	11	45	87	.341	Schmelz
LOU	12	36	94	.277	Barnie

1895—NATIONAL LEAGUE

CLUB	F	W	L	PCT	MGR
BAL	1	87	43	.669	Hanlon
CLE	2	84	46	.646	Tebeau
PHI	3	78	53	.595	Irwin
CHI	4	72	58	.554	Anson
BOS	5t	71	60	.542	Selee
BRO	5t	71	60	.542	Foutz
PIT	7	71	61	.538	Mack
CIN	8	66	64	.508	Ewing
N Y	9	66	65	.504	Davis / Doyle / Watkins
WAS	10	43	85	.336	Schmelz
ST.L	11	39	92	.298	Buckenberger / Quinn / Phelan / Von der Ahe
LOU	12	35	96	.267	McCloskey

1896—NATIONAL LEAGUE

CLUB	F	W	L	PCT	MGR
BAL	1	90	39	.698	Hanlon
CLE	2	80	48	.625	Tebeau
CIN	3	77	50	.606	Ewing
BOS	4	74	57	.565	Selee
CHI	5	71	57	.555	Anson
PIT	6	66	63	.512	Mack
N Y	7	64	67	.489	Foutz / Joyce

(Continued)

1896-National League (Cont.)

CLUB	F	W	L	PCT	MGR
PHI	8	62	68	.477	Nash
BRO	9t	58	73	.443	Foutz
WAS	9t	58	73	.443	Schmelz
ST.L	11	40	90	.306	Diddlebock / Latham / Conner / Dowd
LOU	12	38	93	.290	McCloskey / McGunnigle

1897—NATIONAL LEAGUE

CLUB	F	W	L	PCT	MGR
BOS	1	93	39	.705	Selee
BAL	2	90	40	.693	Hanlon
N Y	3	83	48	.634	Joyce
CIN	4	76	56	.576	Ewing
CLE	5	69	62	.527	Tebeau
BRO	6t	61	71	.462	Barnie
WAS	6t	61	71	.462	Schmelz / Brown
PIT	8	60	71	.458	Donovan
CHI	9	59	73	.447	Anson
PHI	10	55	77	.417	Stallings / Clarke
LOU	11	52	78	.400	Rogers
ST.L	12	29	102	.221	Dowd / Nicol / Hallman / Von der Ahe

1898—NATIONAL LEAGUE

CLUB	F	W	L	PCT	MGR
BOS	1	102	47	.685	Selee
BAL	2	96	53	.644	Hanlon
CIN	3	92	60	.605	Ewing
CHI	4	85	65	.567	Burns
CLE	5	81	68	.544	Tebeau
PHI	6	78	71	.523	Stallings / Shettsline
N Y	7	77	73	.513	Joyce / Anson
PIT	8	72	76	.486	Watkins
LOU	9	70	81	.464	Clarke
BRO	10	54	91	.372	Barnie / Griffin / Ebbets
WAS	11	51	101	.336	Brown / Doyle / McGuire / Irwin
ST.L	12	39	111	.260	Hurst

1899—NATIONAL LEAGUE

CLUB	F	W	L	PCT	MGR
BRO	1	88	42	.677	Hanlon
BOS	2	95	57	.625	Selee
PHI	3	94	58	.618	Shettsline
BAL	4	84	58	.592	McGraw
ST.L	5	84	67	.557	Tebeau
CIN	6	83	67	.553	Ewing
PIT	7	76	73	.510	Watkins / Donovan
CHI	8	75	73	.507	Burns
LOU	9	75	77	.493	Clarke
N Y	10	60	86	.411	Day / Hoey
WAS	11	53	95	.358	Irwin
CLE	12	20	134	.129	Cross / Quinn

1900—NATIONAL LEAGUE

CLUB	F	W	L	PCT	MGR
BRO	1	82	54	.603	Hanlon
PIT	2	79	60	.568	Clarke
PHI	3	75	63	.543	Shettsline
BOS	4	66	72	.478	Selee
CHI	5t	65	75	.464	Loftus
ST.L	5t	65	75	.464	Tebeau / Heilbroner
CIN	7	62	77	.446	Allen
N Y	8	60	78	.435	Ewing / Davis

1901—NATIONAL LEAGUE

CLUB	F	W	L	PCT	MGR
PIT	1	90	49	.647	Clarke
PHI	2	83	57	.593	Shettsline
BRO	3	79	57	.581	Hanlon
ST.L	4	76	64	.543	Donovan
BOS	5	69	69	.500	Selee
CHI	6	53	86	.381	Loftus
N Y	7	52	85	.380	Davis
CIN	8	52	87	.374	McPhee

1901—AMERICAN LEAGUE

CLUB	F	W	L	PCT	MGR
CHI	1	83	53	.610	Griffith
BOS	2	79	57	.581	Collins
DET	3	74	61	.548	Stallings
PHI	4	74	62	.544	Mack
BAL	5	68	65	.511	McGraw
WAS	6	61	72	.459	Manning
CLE	7	54	82	.397	McAleer
MIL	8	48	89	.350	Duffy

1902—NATIONAL LEAGUE

CLUB	F	W	L	PCT	MGR
PIT	1	103	36	.741	Clarke
BRO	2	75	63	.543	Hanlon
BOS	3	73	64	.533	Buckenberger
CIN	4	70	70	.500	McPhee / Bancroft / Kelley
CHI	5	68	69	.496	Selee
ST.L	6	56	78	.418	Donovan
PHI	7	56	81	.409	Shettsline
N Y	8	48	88	.353	Fogel / Smith / McGraw

1902—AMERICAN LEAGUE

CLUB	F	W	L	PCT	MGR
PHI	1	83	53	.610	Mack
ST.L	2	78	58	.574	McAleer
BOS	3	77	60	.562	Collins
CHI	4	74	60	.552	Griffith
CLE	5	69	67	.507	Armour
WAS	6	61	75	.449	Loftus
DET	7	52	83	.385	Dwyer
BAL	8	50	88	.362	McGraw / Robinson

1903—NATIONAL LEAGUE

CLUB	F	W	L	PCT	MGR
PIT	1	91	49	.650	Clarke
N Y	2	84	55	.604	McGraw
CHI	3	82	56	.594	Selee
CIN	4	74	65	.532	Kelley
BRO	5	70	66	.515	Hanlon
BOS	6	58	80	.420	Buckenberger
PHI	7	49	86	.363	Zimmer
ST.L	8	43	94	.314	Donovan

1903—AMERICAN LEAGUE

CLUB	F	W	L	PCT	MGR
BOS	1	91	47	.659	Collins
PHI	2	75	60	.556	Mack
CLE	3	77	63	.550	Armour
N Y	4	72	62	.537	Griffith
DET	5	65	71	.478	Barrow
ST.L	6	65	74	.468	McAleer
CHI	7	60	77	.438	Callahan
WAS	8	43	94	.314	Loftus

1904—NATIONAL LEAGUE

CLUB	F	W	L	PCT	MGR
N Y	1	106	47	.693	McGraw
CHI	2	93	60	.608	Selee
CIN	3	88	65	.575	Kelley
PIT	4	87	66	.569	Clarke
ST.L	5	75	79	.487	Nichols
BRO	6	56	97	.366	Hanlon
BOS	7	55	98	.360	Buckenberger
PHI	8	52	100	.342	Duffy

1904—AMERICAN LEAGUE

CLUB	F	W	L	PCT	MGR
BOS	1	95	59	.617	Collins
N Y	2	92	59	.609	Griffith
CHI	3	89	65	.578	{Callahan / Jones
CLE	4	86	65	.570	Armour
PHI	5	81	70	.536	Mack
ST.L	6	65	87	.428	McAleer
DET	7	62	90	.408	{Barrow / Lowe
WAS	8	38	113	.251	{Kittredge / Donovan

1905—NATIONAL LEAGUE

CLUB	F	W	L	PCT	MGR
N Y	1	105	48	.686	McGraw
PIT	2	96	57	.627	Clarke
CHI	3	92	61	.601	{Selee / Chance
PHI	4	83	69	.546	Duffy
CIN	5	79	74	.516	Kelley
ST.L	6	58	96	.377	{Nichols / Burke / Robison
BOS	7	51	103	.331	Tenney
BRO	8	48	104	.316	Hanlon

1905—AMERICAN LEAGUE

CLUB	F	W	L	PCT	MGR
PHI	1	92	56	.621	Mack
CHI	2	92	60	.605	Jones
DET	3	79	74	.516	Armour
BOS	4	78	74	.513	Collins
CLE	5	76	78	.494	Lajoie
N Y	6	71	78	.477	Griffith
WAS	7	64	87	.421	Stahl
ST.L	8	54	99	.354	McAleer

1906—NATIONAL LEAGUE

CLUB	F	W	L	PCT	MGR
CHI	1	116	36	.763	Chance
N Y	2	96	56	.632	McGraw
PIT	3	93	60	.608	Clarke
PHI	4	71	82	.464	Duffy
BRO	5	66	86	.434	Donovan
CIN	6	64	87	.424	Hanlon
ST.L	7	52	98	.347	McCloskey
BOS	8	49	102	.324	Tenney

1906—AMERICAN LEAGUE

CLUB	F	W	L	PCT	MGR
CHI	1	93	58	.616	Jones
N Y	2	90	61	.596	Griffith
CLE	3	89	64	.582	Lajoie
PHI	4	78	67	.538	Mack
ST.L	5	76	73	.510	McAleer
DET	6	71	78	.477	Armour
WAS	7	55	95	.367	Stahl, G.
BOS	8	49	105	.318	{Collins / Stahl,C.

1907—NATIONAL LEAGUE

CLUB	F	W	L	PCT	MGR
CHI	1	107	45	.704	Chance
PIT	2	91	63	.591	Clarke
PHI	3	83	64	.566	Murray
N Y	4	82	71	.536	McGraw
BRO	5	65	83	.439	Donovan
CIN	6	66	87	.431	Hanlon
BOS	7	58	90	.392	Tenney
ST.L	8	52	101	.340	McCloskey

1907—AMERICAN LEAGUE

CLUB	F	W	L	PCT	MGR
DET	1	92	58	.613	Jennings
PHI	2	88	57	.607	Mack
CHI	3	87	64	.576	Jones
CLE	4	85	67	.559	Lajoie
N Y	5	70	78	.473	Griffith

(Continued)

1907-American League (Cont.)

ST.L	6	69	83	.454	McAleer
BOS	7	59	90	.396	{Young / Huff / Unglaub / McGuire
WAS	8	49	102	.325	Cantillon

1908—NATIONAL LEAGUE

CLUB	F	W	L	PCT	MGR
CHI	1	99	55	.643	Chance
N Y	2t	98	56	.636	McGraw
PIT	2t	98	56	.636	Clarke
PHI	4	83	71	.539	Murray
CIN	5	73	81	.474	Ganzel
BOS	6	63	91	.409	Kelley
BRO	7	53	101	.344	Donovan
ST.L	8	49	105	.318	McCloskey

1908—AMERICAN LEAGUE

CLUB	F	W	L	PCT	MGR
DET	1	90	63	.588	Jennings
CLE	2	90	64	.584	Lajoie
CHI	3	88	64	.579	Jones
ST.L	4	83	69	.546	McAleer
BOS	5	75	79	.487	{McGuire / Lake
PHI	6	68	85	.444	Mack
WAS	7	67	85	.441	Cantillon
N Y	8	51	103	.331	{Griffith / Elberfeld

1909—NATIONAL LEAGUE

CLUB	F	W	L	PCT	MGR
PIT	1	110	42	.724	Clarke
CHI	2	104	49	.680	Chance
N Y	3	92	61	.601	McGraw
CIN	4	77	76	.504	Griffith
PHI	5	74	79	.484	Murray
BRO	6	55	98	.359	Lumley
ST.L	7	54	98	.355	Bresnahan
BOS	8	45	108	.294	{Bowerman / Smith

1909—AMERICAN LEAGUE

CLUB	F	W	L	PCT	MGR
DET	1	98	54	.645	Jennings
PHI	2	95	58	.621	Mack
BOS	3	88	63	.583	Lake
CHI	4	78	74	.513	Sullivan
N Y	5	74	77	.490	Stallings
CLE	6	71	82	.464	{Lajoie / McGuire
ST.L	7	61	89	.407	{McAleer / O'Connor
WAS	8	42	110	.276	Cantillon

1910—NATIONAL LEAGUE

CLUB	F	W	L	PCT	MGR
CHI	1	104	50	.676	Chance
N Y	2	91	63	.591	McGraw
PIT	3	86	67	.562	Clarke
PHI	4	78	75	.510	Dooin
CIN	5	75	79	.487	Griffith
BRO	6	64	90	.416	Dahlen
ST.L	7	63	90	.412	Bresnahan
BOS	8	53	100	.346	Lake

1910—AMERICAN LEAGUE

CLUB	F	W	L	PCT	MGR
PHI	1	102	48	.680	Mack
N Y	2	88	63	.583	{Stallings / Chase
DET	3	86	68	.558	Jennings
BOS	4	81	72	.529	Donovan
CLE	5	71	81	.467	McGuire
CHI	6	68	85	.444	Duffy
WAS	7	66	85	.437	McAleer
ST.L	8	47	107	.305	O'Connor

1911—NATIONAL LEAGUE

CLUB	F	W	L	PCT	MGR
N Y	1	99	54	.647	McGraw
CHI	2	92	62	.597	Chance
PIT	3	85	69	.552	Clarke
PHI	4	79	73	.520	Dooin
ST L	5	75	74	.503	Bresnahan
CIN	6	70	83	.458	Griffith
BRO	7	64	86	.427	Dahlen
BOS	8	44	107	.291	Tenney

1911—AMERICAN LEAGUE

CLUB	F	W	L	PCT	MGR
PHI	1	101	50	.669	Mack
DET	2	89	65	.578	Jennings
CLE	3	80	73	.523	{McGuire / Stovall
CHI	4	77	74	.5099	Duffy
BOS	5	78	75	.5098	Donovan
N Y	6	76	76	.500	Chase
WAS	7	64	90	.416	McAleer
ST.L	8	45	107	.296	Wallace

1912—NATIONAL LEAGUE

CLUB	F	W	L	PCT	MGR
N Y	1	103	48	.682	McGraw
PIT	2	93	58	.616	Clarke
CHI	3	91	59	.607	Chance
CIN	4	75	78	.490	O'Day
PHI	5	73	79	.480	Dooin
ST.L	6	63	90	.412	Bresnahan
BRO	7	58	95	.379	Dahlen
BOS	8	52	101	.340	Kling

1912—AMERICAN LEAGUE

CLUB	F	W	L	PCT	MGR
BOS	1	105	47	.691	Stahl
WAS	2	91	61	.599	Griffith
PHI	3	90	62	.592	Mack
CHI	4	78	76	.506	Callahan
CLE	5	75	78	.490	{Davis / Birmingham
DET	6	69	84	.451	Jennings
ST.L	7	53	101	.344	{Wallace / Stovall
N Y	8	50	102	.329	Wolverton

1913—NATIONAL LEAGUE

CLUB	F	W	L	PCT	MGR
N Y	1	101	51	.664	McGraw
PHI	2	88	63	.583	Dooin
CHI	3	88	65	.575	Evers
PIT	4	78	71	.523	Clarke
BOS	5	69	82	.457	Stallings
BRO	6	65	84	.436	Dahlen
CIN	7	64	89	.418	Tinker
ST.L	8	51	99	.340	Huggins

1913—AMERICAN LEAGUE

CLUB	F	W	L	PCT	MGR
PHI	1	96	57	.627	Mack
WAS	2	90	64	.584	Griffith
CLE	3	86	66	.566	Birmingham
BOS	4	79	71	.527	{Stahl / Carrigan
CHI	5	78	74	.513	Callahan
DET	6	66	87	.431	Jennings
N Y	7	57	94	.377	Chance
ST.L	8	57	96	.373	{Stovall / Austin / Rickey

1914—NATIONAL LEAGUE

CLUB	F	W	L	PCT	MGR
BOS	1	94	59	.614	Stallings
N Y	2	84	70	.545	McGraw
ST.L	3	81	72	.529	Huggins
CHI	4	78	76	.506	O'Day
BRO	5	75	79	.487	Robinson
PHI	6	74	80	.481	Dooin
PIT	7	69	85	.448	Clarke
CIN	8	60	94	.390	Herzog

1914—AMERICAN LEAGUE

CLUB	F	W	L	PCT	MGR
PHI	1	99	53	.651	Mack
BOS	2	91	62	.595	Carrigan
WAS	3	81	73	.526	Griffith
DET	4	80	73	.523	Jennings
ST.L	5	71	82	.464	Rickey
CHI	6t	70	84	.455	Callahan
N Y	6t	70	84	.455	Chance/Peckinpaugh
CLE	8	51	102	.333	Birmingham

1914—FEDERAL LEAGUE

CLUB	F	W	L	PCT	MGR
IND	1	88	65	.575	Phillips
CHI	2	87	67	.565	Tinker
BAL	3	84	69	.549	Knabe
BUF	4	80	71	.530	Schlafly
BRO	5	77	77	.500	Bradley
K C	6	69	84	.451	Stovall
PIT	7	64	88	.421	Gessler/Oakes
ST.L	8	61	89	.407	Brown/Jones

1915—NATIONAL LEAGUE

CLUB	F	W	L	PCT	MGR
PHI	1	90	62	.592	Moran
BOS	2	83	69	.546	Stallings
BRO	3	80	72	.527	Robinson
CHI	4	73	80	.477	Bresnahan
PIT	5	73	81	.474	Clarke
ST.L	6	72	81	.471	Huggins
CIN	7	71	83	.461	Herzog
N Y	8	69	83	.454	McGraw

1915—AMERICAN LEAGUE

CLUB	F	W	L	PCT	MGR
BOS	1	101	50	.669	Carrigan
DET	2	100	54	.649	Jennings
CHI	3	93	61	.604	Rowland
WAS	4	85	68	.556	Griffith
N Y	5	69	83	.454	Donovan
ST.L	6	63	91	.409	Rickey
CLE	7	57	95	.375	Birmingham/Fohl
PHI	8	43	109	.283	Mack

1915—FEDERAL LEAGUE

CLUB	F	W	L	PCT	MGR
CHI	1	86	66	.566	Tinker
ST.L	2	87	67	.565	Jones
PIT	3	86	67	.562	Oakes
K C	4	81	72	.533	Stovall
NEW	5	80	72	.526	Phillips/McKechnie
BUF	6	74	78	.487	Schlafly/Blair/Lord
BRO	7	70	82	.461	Magee/Ganzel
BAL	8	47	107	.305	Knabe

1916—NATIONAL LEAGUE

CLUB	F	W	L	PCT	MGR
BRO	1	94	60	.610	Robinson
PHI	2	91	62	.595	Moran
BOS	3	89	63	.586	Stallings
N Y	4	86	66	.566	McGraw
CHI	5	67	86	.438	Tinker
PIT	6	65	89	.422	Callahan
CIN	7t	60	93	.392	Herzog/Wingo/Mathewson
ST.L	7t	60	93	.392	Huggins

1916—AMERICAN LEAGUE

CLUB	F	W	L	PCT	MGR
BOS	1	91	63	.591	Carrigan
CHI	2	89	65	.578	Rowland
DET	3	87	67	.565	Jennings
N Y	4	80	74	.519	Donovan
ST.L	5	79	75	.513	Jones
CLE	6	77	77	.500	Fohl
WAS	7	76	77	.497	Griffith
PHI	8	36	117	.235	Mack

1917—NATIONAL LEAGUE

CLUB	F	W	L	PCT	MGR
N Y	1	98	56	.636	McGraw
PHI	2	87	65	.572	Moran
ST.L	3	82	70	.539	Huggins
CIN	4	78	76	.506	Mathewson
CHI	5	74	80	.481	Mitchell
BOS	6	72	81	.471	Stallings
BRO	7	70	81	.464	Robinson
PIT	8	51	103	.331	Callahan/Wagner/Bezdek

1917—AMERICAN LEAGUE

CLUB	F	W	L	PCT	MGR
CHI	1	100	54	.649	Rowland
BOS	2	90	62	.592	Barry
CLE	3	88	66	.571	Fohl
DET	4	78	75	.510	Jennings
WAS	5	74	79	.484	Griffith
N Y	6	71	82	.464	Donovan
ST.L	7	57	97	.370	Jones
PHI	8	55	98	.359	Mack

1918—NATIONAL LEAGUE

CLUB	F	W	L	PCT	MGR
CHI	1	84	45	.651	Mitchell
N Y	2	71	53	.573	McGraw
CIN	3	68	60	.531	Mathewson/Groh
PIT	4	65	60	.520	Bezdek
BRO	5	57	69	.452	Robinson
PHI	6	55	68	.447	Moran
BOS	7	53	71	.427	Stallings
ST.L	8	51	78	.395	Hendricks

1918—AMERICAN LEAGUE

CLUB	F	W	L	PCT	MGR
BOS	1	75	51	.595	Barrow
CLE	2	73	54	.575	Fohl
WAS	3	72	56	.563	Griffith
N Y	4	60	63	.488	Huggins
ST.L	5	58	64	.475	Jones/Austin/Burke
CHI	6	57	67	.460	Rowland
DET	7	55	71	.437	Jennings
PHI	8	52	76	.402	Mack

1919—NATIONAL LEAGUE

CLUB	F	W	L	PCT	MGR
CIN	1	96	44	.686	Moran
N Y	2	87	53	.621	McGraw
CHI	3	75	65	.536	Mitchell
PIT	4	71	68	.511	Bezdek
BRO	5	69	71	.493	Robinson
BOS	6	57	82	.410	Stallings
ST.L	7	54	83	.394	Rickey
PHI	8	47	90	.343	Coombs/Cravath

1919—AMERICAN LEAGUE

CLUB	F	W	L	PCT	MGR
CHI	1	88	52	.629	Gleason
CLE	2	84	55	.604	Fohl/Speaker
N Y	3	80	59	.576	Huggins
DET	4	80	60	.571	Jennings
ST.L	5	67	72	.482	Burke
BOS	6	66	71	.4817	Barrow
WAS	7	56	84	.400	Griffith
PHI	8	36	104	.257	Mack

1920—NATIONAL LEAGUE

CLUB	F	W	L	PCT	MGR
BRO	1	93	61	.604	Robinson
N Y	2	86	68	.558	McGraw
CIN	3	82	71	.536	Moran
PIT	4	79	75	.513	Gibson
CHI	5t	75	79	.487	Mitchell
ST.L	5t	75	79	.487	Rickey
BOS	7	62	90	.408	Stallings
PHI	8	62	91	.405	Cravath

1920—AMERICAN LEAGUE

CLUB	F	W	L	PCT	MGR
CLE	1	98	56	.636	Speaker
CHI	2	96	58	.623	Gleason
N Y	3	95	59	.617	Huggins
ST.L	4	76	77	.497	Burke
BOS	5	72	81	.471	Barrow
WAS	6	68	84	.447	Griffith
DET	7	61	93	.396	Jennings
PHI	8	48	106	.312	Mack

1921—NATIONAL LEAGUE

CLUB	F	W	L	PCT	MGR
N Y	1	94	59	.614	McGraw
PIT	2	90	63	.588	Gibson
ST.L	3	87	66	.569	Rickey
BOS	4	79	74	.516	Mitchell
BRO	5	77	75	.507	Robinson
CIN	6	70	83	.458	Moran
CHI	7	64	89	.418	Evers/Killefer
PHI	8	51	103	.331	Donovan/Wilhelm

1921—AMERICAN LEAGUE

CLUB	F	W	L	PCT	MGR
N Y	1	98	55	.641	Huggins
CLE	2	94	60	.610	Speaker
ST.L	3	81	73	.526	Fohl
WAS	4	80	73	.523	McBride
BOS	5	75	79	.487	Duffy
DET	6	71	82	.464	Cobb
CHI	7	62	92	.403	Gleason
PHI	8	53	100	.346	Mack

1922—NATIONAL LEAGUE

CLUB	F	W	L	PCT	MGR
N Y	1	93	61	.604	McGraw
CIN	2	86	68	.558	Moran
PIT	3t	85	69	.552	Gibson/McKechnie
ST.L	3t	85	69	.552	Rickey
CHI	5	80	74	.520	Killefer
BRO	6	76	78	.494	Robinson
PHI	7	57	96	.373	Wilhelm
BOS	8	53	100	.346	Mitchell

1922—AMERICAN LEAGUE

CLUB	F	W	L	PCT	MGR
N Y	1	94	60	.610	Huggins
ST.L	2	93	61	.604	Fohl
DET	3	79	75	.513	Cobb
CLE	4	78	76	.507	Speaker
CHI	5	77	77	.500	Gleason
WAS	6	69	85	.448	Milan
PHI	7	65	89	.422	Mack
BOS	8	61	93	.396	Duffy

1923—NATIONAL LEAGUE

CLUB	F	W	L	PCT	MGR
N Y	1	95	58	.621	McGraw
CIN	2	91	63	.591	Moran
PIT	3	87	67	.565	McKechnie
CHI	4	83	71	.539	Killefer
ST.L	5	79	74	.516	Rickey
BRO	6	76	78	.494	Robinson
BOS	7	54	100	.351	Mitchell
PHI	8	50	104	.325	Fletcher

1923—AMERICAN LEAGUE

CLUB	F	W	L	PCT	MGR
N Y	1	98	54	.645	Huggins
DET	2	83	71	.539	Cobb
CLE	3	82	71	.536	Speaker
WAS	4	75	78	.490	Bush
ST.L	5	74	78	.487	Fohl / Austin
PHI	6	69	83	.454	Mack
CHI	7	69	85	.448	Gleason
BOS	8	61	91	.401	Chance

1924—NATIONAL LEAGUE

CLUB	F	W	L	PCT	MGR
N Y	1	93	60	.608	McGraw
BRO	2	92	62	.597	Robinson
PIT	3	90	63	.588	McKechnie
CIN	4	83	70	.542	Hendricks
CHI	5	81	72	.530	Killefer
ST.L	6	65	89	.422	Rickey
PHI	7	55	96	.364	Fletcher
BOS	8	53	100	.346	Bancroft

1924—AMERICAN LEAGUE

CLUB	F	W	L	PCT	MGR
WAS	1	92	62	.597	Harris
N Y	2	89	63	.586	Huggins
DET	3	86	68	.558	Cobb
ST.L	4	74	78	.487	Sisler
PHI	5	71	81	.467	Mack
CLE	6	67	86	.438	Speaker
BOS	7	67	87	.435	Fohl
CHI	8	66	87	.431	Evers

1925—NATIONAL LEAGUE

CLUB	F	W	L	PCT	MGR
PIT	1	95	58	.621	McKechnie
N Y	2	86	66	.566	McGraw
CIN	3	80	73	.523	Hendricks
ST.L	4	77	76	.503	Rickey / Hornsby
BOS	5	70	83	.458	Bancroft
BRO	6t	68	85	.444	Robinson
PHI	6t	68	85	.444	Fletcher
CHI	8	68	86	.442	Killefer / Maranville / Gibson

1925—AMERICAN LEAGUE

CLUB	F	W	L	PCT	MGR
WAS	1	96	55	.636	Harris
PHI	2	88	64	.579	Mack
ST.L	3	82	71	.536	Sisler
DET	4	81	73	.526	Cobb
CHI	5	79	75	.513	Collins
CLE	6	70	84	.455	Speaker
N Y	7	69	85	.448	Huggins
BOS	8	47	105	.309	Fohl

1926—NATIONAL LEAGUE

CLUB	F	W	L	PCT	MGR
ST.L	1	89	65	.578	Hornsby
CIN	2	87	67	.565	Hendricks
PIT	3	84	69	.549	McKechnie
CHI	4	82	72	.532	McCarthy
N Y	5	74	77	.490	McGraw
BRO	6	71	82	.464	Robinson
BOS	7	66	86	.434	Bancroft
PHI	8	58	93	.384	Fletcher

1926—AMERICAN LEAGUE

CLUB	F	W	L	PCT	MGR
N Y	1	91	63	.591	Huggins
CLE	2	88	66	.571	Speaker
PHI	3	83	67	.553	Mack
WAS	4	81	69	.540	Harris
CHI	5	81	72	.529	Collins
DET	6	79	75	.513	Cobb
ST.L	7	62	92	.403	Sisler
BOS	8	46	107	.301	Fohl

1927—NATIONAL LEAGUE

CLUB	F	W	L	PCT	MGR
PIT	1	94	60	.610	Bush
ST.L	2	92	61	.601	O'Farrell
N Y	3	92	62	.597	McGraw
CHI	4	85	68	.556	McCarthy
CIN	5	75	78	.490	Hendricks
BRO	6	65	88	.425	Robinson
BOS	7	60	94	.390	Bancroft
PHI	8	51	103	.331	McInnis

1927—AMERICAN LEAGUE

CLUB	F	W	L	PCT	MGR
N Y	1	110	44	.714	Huggins
PHI	2	91	63	.591	Mack
WAS	3	85	69	.552	Harris
DET	4	82	71	.536	Moriarty
CHI	5	70	83	.458	Schalk
CLE	6	66	87	.431	McCallister
ST.L	7	59	94	.386	Howley
BOS	8	51	103	.331	Carrigan

1928—NATIONAL LEAGUE

CLUB	F	W	L	PCT	MGR
ST.L	1	95	59	.617	McKechnie
N Y	2	93	61	.604	McGraw
CHI	3	91	63	.591	McCarthy
PIT	4	85	67	.559	Bush
CIN	5	78	74	.513	Hendricks
BRO	6	77	76	.503	Robinson
BOS	7	50	103	.327	Slattery / Hornsby
PHI	8	43	109	.283	Shotton

1928—AMERICAN LEAGUE

CLUB	F	W	L	PCT	MGR
N Y	1	101	53	.656	Huggins
PHI	2	98	55	.641	Mack
ST.L	3	82	72	.532	Howley
WAS	4	75	79	.487	Harris
CHI	5	72	82	.468	Schalk / Blackburne
DET	6	68	86	.442	Moriarty
CLE	7	62	92	.403	Peckinpaugh
BOS	8	57	96	.373	Carrigan

1929—NATIONAL LEAGUE

CLUB	F	W	L	PCT	MGR
CHI	1	98	54	.645	McCarthy
PIT	2	88	65	.575	Bush / Ens
N Y	3	84	67	.556	McGraw
ST.L	4	78	74	.513	McKechnie / Southworth
PHI	5	71	82	.464	Shotton
BRO	6	70	83	.458	Robinson
CIN	7	66	88	.429	Hendricks
BOS	8	56	98	.364	Fuchs / Evers

1929—AMERICAN LEAGUE

CLUB	F	W	L	PCT	MGR
PHI	1	104	46	.693	Mack
N Y	2	88	66	.571	Huggins / Fletcher
CLE	3	81	71	.533	Peckinpaugh
ST.L	4	79	73	.520	Howley
WAS	5	71	81	.467	Johnson
DET	6	70	84	.455	Harris
CHI	7	59	93	.388	Blackburne
BOS	8	58	96	.377	Carrigan

1930—NATIONAL LEAGUE

CLUB	F	W	L	PCT	MGR
ST.L	1	92	62	.597	Street
CHI	2	90	64	.584	McCarthy / Hornsby
N Y	3	87	67	.565	McGraw
BRO	4	86	68	.558	Robinson
PIT	5	80	74	.519	Ens
BOS	6	70	84	.455	McKechnie
CIN	7	59	95	.383	Howley
PHI	8	52	102	.338	Shotton

1930—AMERICAN LEAGUE

CLUB	F	W	L	PCT	MGR
PHI	1	102	52	.662	Mack
WAS	2	94	60	.610	Johnson
N Y	3	86	68	.558	Shawkey
CLE	4	81	73	.526	Peckinpaugh
DET	5	75	79	.487	Harris
ST.L	6	64	90	.416	Killefer
CHI	7	62	92	.403	Bush
BOS	8	52	102	.338	Wagner

1931—NATIONAL LEAGUE

CLUB	F	W	L	PCT	MGR
ST.L	1	101	53	.656	Street
N Y	2	87	65	.572	McGraw
CHI	3	84	70	.545	Hornsby
BRO	4	79	73	.520	Robinson
PIT	5	75	79	.487	Ens
PHI	6	66	88	.429	Shotton
BOS	7	64	90	.416	McKechnie
CIN	8	58	96	.377	Howley

1931—AMERICAN LEAGUE

CLUB	F	W	L	PCT	MGR
PHI	1	107	45	.704	Mack
N Y	2	94	59	.614	McCarthy
WAS	3	92	62	.597	Johnson
CLE	4	78	76	.506	Peckinpaugh
ST.L	5	63	91	.409	Killefer
BOS	6	62	90	.408	Collins
DET	7	61	93	.396	Harris
CHI	8	56	97	.366	Bush

1932—NATIONAL LEAGUE

CLUB	F	W	L	PCT	MGR
CHI	1	90	64	.584	Hornsby / Grimm
PIT	2	86	68	.558	Gibson
BRO	3	81	73	.526	Carey
PHI	4	78	76	.506	Shotton
BOS	5	77	77	.500	McKechnie
N Y	6t	72	82	.468	McGraw / Terry
ST.L	6t	72	82	.468	Street
CIN	8	60	94	.390	Howley

1932—AMERICAN LEAGUE

CLUB	F	W	L	PCT	MGR
N Y	1	107	47	.695	McCarthy
PHI	2	94	60	.610	Mack
WAS	3	93	61	.604	Johnson
CLE	4	87	65	.572	Peckinpaugh
DET	5	76	75	.503	Harris
ST.L	6	63	91	.409	Killefer
CHI	7	49	102	.325	Fonseca
BOS	8	43	111	.279	Collins / McManus

1933—NATIONAL LEAGUE

CLUB	F	W	L	PCT	MGR
N Y	1	91	61	.599	Terry
PIT	2	87	67	.565	Gibson
CHI	3	86	68	.558	Grimm
BOS	4	83	71	.539	McKechnie
ST.L	5	82	71	.536	Street / Frisch
BRO	6	65	88	.425	Carey
PHI	7	60	92	.395	Shotton
CIN	8	58	94	.382	Bush

1933—AMERICAN LEAGUE

CLUB	F	W	L	PCT	MGR
WAS	1	99	53	.651	Cronin
N Y	2	91	59	.607	McCarthy
PHI	3	79	72	.523	Mack
CLE	4	75	76	.497	Peckinpaugh / Johnson
DET	5	75	79	.487	Harris / Baker

(Continued)

1933-American League (Cont.)

CHI	6	67	83	.447	Fonseca
BOS	7	63	86	.423	McManus
ST.L	8	55	96	.364	Killefer / Sothoron / Hornsby

1934—NATIONAL LEAGUE

CLUB	F	W	L	PCT	MGR
ST.L	1	95	58	.621	Frisch
N Y	2	93	60	.608	Terry
CHI	3	86	65	.570	Grimm
BOS	4	78	73	.517	McKechnie
PIT	5	74	76	.493	Gibson / Traynor
BRO	6	71	81	.467	Stengel
PHI	7	56	93	.376	Wilson
CIN	8	52	99	.344	O'Farrell / Shotton / Dressen

1934—AMERICAN LEAGUE

CLUB	F	W	L	PCT	MGR
DET	1	101	53	.656	Cochrane
N Y	2	94	60	.610	McCarthy
CLE	3	85	69	.552	Johnson
BOS	4	76	76	.500	Harris
PHI	5	68	82	.453	Mack
ST.L	6	67	85	.441	Hornsby
WAS	7	66	86	.434	Cronin
CHI	8	53	99	.349	Fonseca / Dykes

1935—NATIONAL LEAGUE

CLUB	F	W	L	PCT	MGR
CHI	1	100	54	.649	Grimm
ST.L	2	96	58	.623	Frisch
N Y	3	91	62	.595	Terry
PIT	4	86	67	.562	Traynor
BRO	5	70	83	.458	Stengel
CIN	6	68	85	.444	Dressen
PHI	7	64	89	.418	Wilson
BOS	8	38	115	.248	McKechnie

1935—AMERICAN LEAGUE

CLUB	F	W	L	PCT	MGR
DET	1	93	58	.616	Cochrane
N Y	2	89	60	.597	McCarthy
CLE	3	82	71	.536	Johnson / O'Neill
BOS	4	78	75	.510	Cronin
CHI	5	74	78	.487	Dykes
WAS	6	67	86	.438	Harris
ST.L	7	65	87	.428	Hornsby
PHI	8	58	91	.389	Mack

1936—NATIONAL LEAGUE

CLUB	F	W	L	PCT	MGR
N Y	1	92	62	.597	Terry
CHI	2t	87	67	.565	Grimm
ST.L	2t	87	67	.565	Frisch
PIT	4	84	70	.545	Traynor
CIN	5	74	80	.481	Dressen
BOS	6	71	83	.461	McKechnie
BRO	7	67	87	.435	Stengel
PHI	8	54	100	.351	Wilson

1936—AMERICAN LEAGUE

CLUB	F	W	L	PCT	MGR
N Y	1	102	51	.667	McCarthy
DET	2	83	71	.539	Cochrane
CHI	3	81	70	.5364	Dykes
WAS	4	82	71	.5359	Harris
CLE	5	80	74	.519	O'Neill
BOS	6	74	80	.481	Cronin
ST.L	7	57	95	.375	Hornsby
PHI	8	53	100	.346	Mack

1937—NATIONAL LEAGUE

CLUB	F	W	L	PCT	MGR
N Y	1	95	57	.625	Terry
CHI	2	93	61	.604	Grimm
PIT	3	86	68	.558	Traynor
ST.L	4	81	73	.526	Frisch
BOS	5	79	73	.520	McKechnie
BRO	6	62	91	.405	Grimes
PHI	7	61	92	.399	Wilson
CIN	8	56	98	.364	Dressen / Wallace

1937—AMERICAN LEAGUE

CLUB	F	W	L	PCT	MGR
N Y	1	102	52	.662	McCarthy
DET	2	89	65	.578	Cochrane
CHI	3	86	68	.558	Dykes
CLE	4	83	71	.539	O'Neill
BOS	5	80	72	.526	Cronin
WAS	6	73	80	.477	Harris
PHI	7	54	97	.358	Mack
ST.L	8	46	108	.299	Hornsby / Bottomley

1938—NATIONAL LEAGUE

CLUB	F	W	L	PCT	MGR
CHI	1	89	63	.586	Grimm / Hartnett
PIT	2	86	64	.573	Traynor
N Y	3	83	67	.553	Terry
CIN	4	82	68	.547	McKechnie
BOS	5	77	75	.507	Stengel
ST.L	6	71	80	.470	Frisch / Gonzales
BRO	7	69	80	.463	Grimes
PHI	8	45	105	.300	Wilson / Lobert

1938—AMERICAN LEAGUE

CLUB	F	W	L	PCT	MGR
N Y	1	99	53	.651	McCarthy
BOS	2	88	61	.591	Cronin
CLE	3	86	66	.566	Vitt
DET	4	84	70	.545	Cochrane / Baker
WAS	5	75	76	.497	Harris
CHI	6	65	83	.439	Dykes
ST.L	7	55	97	.362	Street / Melillo
PHI	8	53	99	.349	Mack

1939—NATIONAL LEAGUE

CLUB	F	W	L	PCT	MGR
CIN	1	97	57	.630	McKechnie
ST.L	2	92	61	.601	Blades
BRO	3	84	69	.549	Durocher
CHI	4	84	70	.545	Hartnett
N Y	5	77	74	.510	Terry
PIT	6	68	85	.444	Traynor
BOS	7	63	88	.417	Stengel
PHI	8	45	106	.298	Prothro

1939—AMERICAN LEAGUE

CLUB	F	W	L	PCT	MGR
N Y	1	106	45	.702	McCarthy
BOS	2	89	62	.589	Cronin
CLE	3	87	67	.565	Vitt
CHI	4	85	69	.552	Dykes
DET	5	81	73	.526	Baker
WAS	6	65	87	.428	Harris
PHI	7	55	97	.362	Mack
ST.L	8	43	111	.279	Haney

1940—NATIONAL LEAGUE

CLUB	F	W	L	PCT	MGR
CIN	1	100	53	.654	McKechnie
BRO	2	88	65	.575	Durocher
ST.L	3	84	69	.549	Blades / Gonzales / Southworth (Continued)

1940-National League (Cont.)

PIT	4	78	76	.506	Frisch
CHI	5	75	79	.487	Hartnett
N Y	6	72	80	.474	Terry
BOS	7	65	87	.428	Stengel
PHI	8	50	103	.327	Prothro

1940—AMERICAN LEAGUE

CLUB	F	W	L	PCT	MGR
DET	1	90	64	.584	Baker
CLE	2	89	65	.578	Vitt
N Y	3	88	66	.571	McCarthy
BOS	4t	82	72	.532	Cronin
CHI	4t	82	72	.532	Dykes
ST.L	6	67	87	.435	Haney
WAS	7	64	90	.416	Harris
PHI	8	54	100	.351	Mack

1941—NATIONAL LEAGUE

CLUB	F	W	L	PCT	MGR
BRO	1	100	54	.649	Durocher
ST.L	2	97	56	.634	Southworth
CIN	3	88	66	.571	McKechnie
PIT	4	81	73	.526	Frisch
N Y	5	74	79	.484	Terry
CHI	6	70	84	.455	Wilson
BOS	7	62	92	.403	Stengel
PHI	8	43	111	.279	Prothro

1941—AMERICAN LEAGUE

CLUB	F	W	L	PCT	MGR
N Y	1	101	53	.656	McCarthy
BOS	2	84	70	.545	Cronin
CHI	3	77	77	.500	Dykes
CLE	4t	75	79	.487	Peckinpaugh
DET	4t	75	79	.487	Baker
ST.L	6t	70	84	.455	Haney / Sewell
WAS	6t	70	84	.455	Harris
PHI	8	64	90	.416	Mack

1942—NATIONAL LEAGUE

CLUB	F	W	L	PCT	MGR
ST.L	1	106	48	.688	Southworth
BRO	2	104	50	.675	Durocher
N Y	3	85	67	.559	Ott
CIN	4	76	76	.500	McKechnie
PIT	5	66	81	.449	Frisch
CHI	6	68	86	.442	Wilson
BOS	7	59	89	.399	Stengel
PHI	8	42	109	.278	Lobert

1942—AMERICAN LEAGUE

CLUB	F	W	L	PCT	MGR
N Y	1	103	51	.669	McCarthy
BOS	2	93	59	.612	Cronin
ST.L	3	82	69	.543	Sewell
CLE	4	75	79	.487	Boudreau
DET	5	73	81	.474	Baker
CHI	6	66	82	.446	Dykes
WAS	7	62	89	.411	Harris
PHI	8	55	99	.357	Mack

1943—NATIONAL LEAGUE

CLUB	F	W	L	PCT	MGR
ST.L	1	105	49	.682	Southworth
CIN	2	87	67	.565	McKechnie
BRO	3	81	72	.529	Durocher
PIT	4	80	74	.519	Frisch
CHI	5	74	79	.484	Wilson
BOS	6	68	85	.444	Stengel
PHI	7	64	90	.416	Harris / Fitzsimmons
N Y	8	55	98	.359	Ott

1943—AMERICAN LEAGUE

CLUB	F	W	L	PCT	MGR
N Y	1	98	56	.636	McCarthy
WAS	2	84	69	.549	Bluege
CLE	3	82	71	.536	Boudreau
CHI	4	82	72	.532	Dykes
DET	5	78	76	.506	O'Neill
ST.L	6	72	80	.474	Sewell
BOS	7	68	84	.447	Cronin
PHI	8	49	105	.318	Mack

1944—NATIONAL LEAGUE

CLUB	F	W	L	PCT	MGR
ST.L	1	105	49	.682	Southworth
PIT	2	90	63	.588	Frisch
CIN	3	89	65	.578	McKechnie
CHI	4	75	79	.487	Wilson / Johnson / Grimm
N Y	5	67	87	.435	Ott
BOS	6	65	89	.422	Coleman
BRO	7	63	91	.409	Durocher
PHI	8	61	92	.399	Fitzsimmons

1944—AMERICAN LEAGUE

CLUB	F	W	L	PCT	MGR
ST.L	1	89	65	.578	Sewell
DET	2	88	66	.571	O'Neill
N Y	3	83	71	.539	McCarthy
BOS	4	77	77	.500	Cronin
CLE	5t	72	82	.468	Boudreau
PHI	5t	72	82	.468	Mack
CHI	7	71	83	.461	Dykes
WAS	8	64	90	.416	Bluege

1945—NATIONAL LEAGUE

CLUB	F	W	L	PCT	MGR
CHI	1	98	56	.636	Grimm
ST.L	2	95	59	.617	Southworth
BRO	3	87	67	.565	Durocher
PIT	4	82	72	.532	Frisch
N Y	5	78	74	.513	Ott
BOS	6	67	85	.441	Coleman / Bissonette
CIN	7	61	93	.396	McKechnie
PHI	8	46	108	.299	Fitzsimmons / Chapman

1945—AMERICAN LEAGUE

CLUB	F	W	L	PCT	MGR
DET	1	88	65	.575	O'Neill
WAS	2	87	67	.565	Bluege
ST.L	3	81	70	.536	Sewell
N Y	4	81	71	.533	McCarthy
CLE	5	73	72	.503	Boudreau
CHI	6	71	78	.477	Dykes
BOS	7	71	83	.461	Cronin
PHI	8	52	98	.347	Mack

1946—NATIONAL LEAGUE

CLUB	F	W	L	PCT	MGR
ST.L	1p	98	58	.628	Dyer
BRO	2p	96	60	.615	Durocher
CHI	3	82	71	.536	Grimm
BOS	4	81	72	.529	Southworth
PHI	5	69	85	.448	Chapman
CIN	6	67	87	.435	McKechnie / Gowdy
PIT	7	63	91	.409	Frisch / Davis
N Y	8	61	93	.396	Ott

1946—AMERICAN LEAGUE

CLUB	F	W	L	PCT	MGR
BOS	1	104	50	.675	Cronin
DET	2	92	62	.597	O'Neill
N Y	3	87	67	.565	McCarthy / Dickey / Neun
WAS	4	76	78	.494	Bluege

(Continued)

1946-American League (Cont.)

CHI	5	74	80	.481	Dykes / Lyons
CLE	6	68	86	.442	Boudreau
ST.L	7	66	88	.429	Sewell / Taylor
PHI	8	49	105	.318	Mack

1947—NATIONAL LEAGUE

CLUB	F	W	L	PCT	MGR
BRO	1	94	60	.610	Sukeforth / Shotton
ST.L	2	89	65	.578	Dyer
BOS	3	86	68	.558	Southworth
N Y	4	81	73	.526	Ott
CIN	5	73	81	.474	Neun
CHI	6	69	85	.448	Grimm
PHI	7t	62	92	.403	Chapman
PIT	7t	62	92	.403	Herman / Burwell

1947—AMERICAN LEAGUE

CLUB	F	W	L	PCT	MGR
N Y	1	97	57	.630	Harris
DET	2	85	69	.552	O'Neill
BOS	3	83	71	.539	Cronin
CLE	4	80	74	.519	Boudreau
PHI	5	78	76	.506	Mack
CHI	6	70	84	.455	Lyons
WAS	7	64	90	.416	Bluege
ST.L	8	59	95	.383	Ruel

1948—NATIONAL LEAGUE

CLUB	F	W	L	PCT	MGR
BOS	1	91	62	.595	Southworth
ST.L	2	85	69	.552	Dyer
BRO	3	84	70	.545	Durocher / Shotton
PIT	4	83	71	.539	Meyer
N Y	5	78	76	.506	Ott / Durocher
PHI	6	66	88	.429	Chapman / Cooke / Sawyer
CIN	7	64	89	.418	Neun / Walters
CHI	8	64	90	.416	Grimm

1948—AMERICAN LEAGUE

CLUB	F	W	L	PCT	MGR
CLE	1p	97	58	.626	Boudreau
BOS	2p	96	59	.619	McCarthy
N Y	3	94	60	.610	Harris
PHI	4	84	70	.545	Mack
DET	5	78	76	.506	O'Neill
ST.L	6	59	94	.386	Taylor
WAS	7	56	97	.366	Kuhel
CHI	8	51	101	.336	Lyons

1949—NATIONAL LEAGUE

CLUB	F	W	L	PCT	MGR
BRO	1	97	57	.630	Shotton
ST.L	2	96	58	.623	Dyer
PHI	3	81	73	.526	Sawyer
BOS	4	75	79	.487	Southworth / Cooney
N Y	5	73	81	.474	Durocher
PIT	6	71	83	.461	Meyer
CIN	7	62	92	.403	Walters / Sewell
CHI	8	61	93	.396	Grimm / Frisch

1949—AMERICAN LEAGUE

CLUB	F	W	L	PCT	MGR
N Y	1	97	57	.630	Stengel
BOS	2	96	58	.623	McCarthy
CLE	3	89	65	.578	Boudreau
DET	4	87	67	.565	Rolfe
PHI	5	81	73	.526	Mack
CHI	6	63	91	.409	Onslow
ST.L	7	53	101	.344	Taylor
WAS	8	50	104	.324	Kuhel

1950—NATIONAL LEAGUE

CLUB	F	W	L	PCT	MGR
PHI	1	91	63	.591	Sawyer
BRO	2	89	65	.578	Shotton
N Y	3	86	68	.558	Durocher
BOS	4	83	71	.539	Southworth
ST.L	5	78	75	.510	Dyer
CIN	6	66	87	.431	Sewell
CHI	7	64	89	.418	Frisch
PIT	8	57	96	.373	Meyer

1950—AMERICAN LEAGUE

CLUB	F	W	L	PCT	MGR
N Y	1	98	56	.636	Stengel
DET	2	95	59	.617	Rolfe
BOS	3	94	60	.610	McCarthy / O'Neill
CLE	4	92	62	.597	Boudreau
WAS	5	67	87	.435	Harris
CHI	6	60	94	.390	Onslow / Corriden
ST.L	7	58	96	.377	Taylor
PHI	8	52	102	.338	Mack

1951—NATIONAL LEAGUE

CLUB	F	W	L	PCT	MGR
N Y	1p	98	59	.624	Durocher
BRO	2p	97	60	.618	Dressen
ST.L	3	81	73	.526	Marion
BOS	4	76	78	.494	Southworth / Holmes
PHI	5	73	81	.474	Sawyer
CIN	6	68	86	.442	Sewell
PIT	7	64	90	.416	Meyer
CHI	8	62	92	.403	Frisch / Cavarretta

1951—AMERICAN LEAGUE

CLUB	F	W	L	PCT	MGR
N Y	1	98	56	.636	Stengel
CLE	2	93	61	.604	Lopez
BOS	3	87	67	.565	O'Neill
CHI	4	81	73	.526	Richards
DET	5	73	81	.474	Rolfe
PHI	6	70	84	.455	Dykes
WAS	7	62	92	.403	Harris
ST.L	8	52	102	.338	Taylor

1952—NATIONAL LEAGUE

CLUB	F	W	L	PCT	MGR
BRO	1	96	57	.627	Dressen
N Y	2	92	62	.597	Durocher
ST.L	3	88	66	.571	Stanky
PHI	4	87	67	.565	Sawyer / O'Neill
CHI	5	77	77	.500	Cavarretta
CIN	6	69	85	.448	Sewell / Hornsby
BOS	7	64	89	.418	Holmes / Grimm
PIT	8	42	112	.273	Meyer

1952—AMERICAN LEAGUE

CLUB	F	W	L	PCT	MGR
N Y	1	95	59	.617	Stengel
CLE	2	93	61	.604	Lopez
CHI	3	81	73	.526	Richards
PHI	4	79	75	.513	Dykes
WAS	5	78	76	.506	Harris
BOS	6	76	78	.494	Boudreau
ST.L	7	64	90	.416	Hornsby / Marion
DET	8	50	104	.325	Rolfe / Hutchinson

1953—NATIONAL LEAGUE

CLUB	F	W	L	PCT.	MGR
BRO	1	105	49	.682	Dressen
MIL	2	92	62	.597	Grimm
PHI	3t	83	71	.539	O'Neill
St.L	3t	83	71	.539	Stanky
N Y	5	70	84	.455	Durocher
CTN	6	68	86	.442	Hornsby, Mills
CHI	7	65	89	.422	Cavarretta
PIT	8	50	104	.325	Haney

1953—AMERICAN LEAGUE

CLUB	F	W	L	PCT.	MGR
N Y	1	99	52	.656	Stengel
CLE	2	92	62	.597	Lopez
CHI	3	89	65	.578	Richards
BOS	4	84	69	.549	Boudrenu
WAS	5	76	76	.500	Harris
DET	6	60	94	.390	Hutchinson
PHI	7	59	95	.383	Dykes
St.L	8	54	100	.351	Marion

1954—NATIONAL LEAGUE

CLUB	F	W	L	PCT.	MGR
N Y	1	97	57	.630	Durocher
BRO	2	92	62	.597	Alston
MIL	3	89	65	.578	Grimm
PHI	4	75	79	.487	O'Neill, Moore
CIN	5	74	80	.481	Tebbetts
St.L	6	72	82	.468	Stanky
CHI	7	64	90	.416	Hack
PIT	8	53	101	.344	Haney

1954—AMERICAN LEAGUE

CLUB	F	W	L	PCT.	MGR
CLE	1	111	43	.721	Lopez
N Y	2	103	51	.669	Stengel
CHI	3	94	60	.610	Richards, Marion
BOS	4	69	85	.448	Boudreau
DET	5	68	86	.442	Hutchinson
WAS	6	66	88	.429	Harris
BAL	7	54	100	.351	Dykes
PHI	8	51	103	.331	Joost

1955—NATIONAL LEAGUE

CLUB	F	W	L	PCT.	MGR
BRO	1	98	55	.641	Alston
MIL	2	85	69	.552	Grimm
N Y	3	80	74	.519	Durocher
PHI	4	77	77	.500	Smith
CIN	5	75	79	.487	Tebbetts
CHI	6	72	81	.471	Hack
St.L	7	68	86	.442	Stanky, Walker
PIT	8	60	94	.390	Haney

1955—AMERICAN LEAGUE

CLUB	F	W	L	PCT.	MGR
N Y	1	96	58	.623	Stengel
CLE	2	93	61	.604	Lopez
CHI	3	91	63	.591	Marion
BOS	4	84	70	.545	Higgins
DET	5	79	75	.513	Harris
K C	6	63	91	.409	Boudreau
BAL	7	57	97	.370	Richards
WAS	8	53	101	.344	Dressen

1956—NATIONAL LEAGUE

CLUB	F	W	L	PCT.	MGR
BRO	1	93	61	.604	Alston
MIL	2	92	62	.597	Grimm, Haney
CIN	3	91	63	.591	Tebbetts
St.L	4	76	78	.494	Hutchinson
PHI	5	71	83	.461	Smith
N Y	6	67	87	.435	Rigney
PIT	7	66	88	.429	Bragan
CHI	8	60	94	.390	Hack

1956—AMERICAN LEAGUE

CLUB	F	W	L	PCT.	MGR
N Y	1	97	57	.630	Stengel
CLE	2	88	66	.571	Lopez
CHI	3	85	69	.552	Marion
BOS	4	84	70	.545	Higgins
DET	5	82	72	.532	Harris
BAL	6	69	85	.448	Richards
WAS	7	59	95	.383	Dressen
K C	8	52	102	.338	Boudreau

1957—NATIONAL LEAGUE

CLUB	F	W	L	PCT.	MGR
MIL	1	95	59	.617	Haney
St.L	2	87	67	.565	Hutchinson
BRO	3	84	70	.545	Alston
CIN	4	80	74	.519	Tebbetts
PHI	5	77	77	.500	Smith
N Y	6	69	85	.448	Rigney
CHI t	7t	62	92	.403	Scheffing
PIT t	7t	62	92	.403	Bragan, Murtaugh

1957—AMERICAN LEAGUE

CLUB	F	W	L	PCT.	MGR
N Y	1	98	56	.636	Stengel
CHI	2	90	64	.584	Lopez
BOS	3	82	72	.532	Higgins
DET	4	78	76	.506	Tighe
BAL	5	76	76	.500	Richards
CLE	6	76	77	.497	Farrell
K C	7	59	94	.386	Boudreau, Craft
WAS	8	55	99	.357	Dressen, Lavagetto

1958—NATIONAL LEAGUE

CLUB	F	W	L	PCT.	MGR
MIL	1	92	62	.597	Haney
PIT	2	84	70	.545	Murtaugh
S F	3	80	74	.519	Rigney
CIN	4	76	78	.494	Tebbetts, Dykes
St.L	5t	72	82	.468	Hutchinson, Hack
CHI	5t	72	82	.468	Scheffing
L A	7	71	83	.461	Alston
PHI	8	69	85	.448	Smith, Sawyer

1958—AMERICAN LEAGUE

CLUB	F	W	L	PCT.	MGR
N Y	1	92	62	.597	Stengel
CHI	2	82	72	.532	Lopez
BOS	3	79	75	.513	Higgins
CLE	4	77	76	.503	Bragan, Gordon
DET	5	77	77	.500	Tighe, Norman
BAL	6	74	79	.484	Richards
K C	7	73	81	.474	Craft
WAS	8	61	93	.396	Lavagetto

1959—NATIONAL LEAGUE

CLUB	F	W	L	PCT.	MGR
L A	1p	88	68	.564	Alston
MIL	2p	86	70	.551	Haney
S F	3	83	71	.539	Rigney
PIT	4	78	76	.506	Murtaugh
CHI	5t	74	80	.481	Scheffing
CIN	5t	74	80	.481	Smith, Hutchinson
St.L	7	71	83	.461	Hemus
PHI	8	64	90	.416	Sawyer

1959—AMERICAN LEAGUE

CLUB	F	W	L	PCT.	MGR.
CHI	1	94	60	.610	Lopez
CLE	2	89	65	.578	Gordon
N Y	3	79	75	.513	Stengel
DET	4	76	78	.494	Norman, Dykes, Higgins
BOS	5	75	79	.487	York, Jurges
BAL	6	74	80	.481	Richards
K C	7	66	88	.429	Craft
WAS	8	63	91	.409	Lavagetto

1960—NATIONAL LEAGUE

CLUB	F	W	L	PCT.	MGR
PIT	1	95	59	.617	Murtaugh
MIL	2	88	66	.571	Dressen
St.L	3	86	68	.558	Hemus
L A	4	82	72	.532	Alston
S F	5	79	75	.513	Rigney, Sheehan
CIN	6	67	87	.435	Hutchinson
CHI	7	60	94	.390	Grimm, Boudreau
PHI	8	59	95	.383	Sawyer, Mauch

1960—AMERICAN LEAGUE

CLUB	F	W	L	PCT.	MGR
N Y	1	97	57	.630	Stengel
BAL	2	89	65	.578	Richards
CHI	3	87	67	.565	Lopez
CLE	4	76	78	.494	Gordon, White, Dykes
WAS	5	73	81	.474	Lavagetto
DET	6	71	83	.461	Dykes, Hitchcock, Gordon
BOS	7	65	89	.422	Jurges, Higgins
K C	8	58	96	.377	Elliott

1961—NATIONAL LEAGUE

CLUB	F	W	L	PCT.	MGR
CIN	1	93	61	.604	Hutchinson
L A	2	89	65	.578	Alston
S F	3	85	69	.552	Dark
MIL	4	83	71	.539	Dressen, Tebbetts
St.L	5	80	74	.519	Hemus, Keane
PIT	6	75	79	.487	Murtaugh
CHI	7	64	90	.416	Himsl, Craft, Tappe, Klein
PHI	8	47	107	.305	Mauch

1961—AMERICAN LEAGUE

CLUB	F	W	L	PCT.	MGR
N Y	1	109	53	.673	Houk
DET	2	101	61	.623	Scheffing
BAL	3	95	67	.586	Richards, Harris
CHI	4	86	76	.531	Hitchcock
CLE	5	78	83	.484	Dykes, Harder
BOS	6	76	86	.469	Higgins
MIN	7	70	90	.438	Lavagetto, Mele
L A	8	70	91	.435	Rigney
K C	9t	61	100	.379	Gordon, Bauer
WAS	9t	61	100	.379	Vernon

1962—NATIONAL LEAGUE

CLUB	F	W	L	PCT.	MGR
S F	1p	103	62	.624	Dark
L A	2p	102	63	.618	Alston
CIN	3	98	64	.605	Hutchinson
PIT	4	93	68	.578	Murtaugh
MIL	5	86	76	.531	Tebbetts
St.L	6	84	78	.519	Keane
PHI	7	81	80	.503	Mauch
HOU	8	64	96	.400	Craft
CHI	9	59	103	.364	Tappe, Klein, Metro
N Y	10	40	120	.250	Stengel

1962—AMERICAN LEAGUE

CLUB	F	W	L	PCT.	MGR
N Y	1	96	66	.593	Houk
MIN	2	91	71	.562	Mele
L A	3	86	76	.531	Rigney
DET	4	85	76	.528	Scheffing
CHI	5	85	77	.525	Lopez
CLE	6	80	82	.494	McGaha
BAL	7	77	85	.475	Hitchcock
BOS	8	76	84	.475	Higgins
K C	9	72	90	.444	Bauer
WAS	10	60	101	.373	Vernon

1963—NATIONAL LEAGUE

CLUB	F	W	L	PCT.	MGR
L A	1	99	63	.611	Alston
St.L	2	93	69	.574	Keane
S F	3	88	74	.543	Dark
PHI	4	87	75	.537	Mauch
CIN	5	86	76	.531	Hutchinson
MIL	6	84	78	.516	Bragan
CHI	7	82	80	.506	Kennedy
PIT	8	74	88	.457	Murtaugh
HOU	9	66	96	.407	Craft
N Y	10	51	111	.315	Stengel

1963—AMERICAN LEAGUE

CLUB	F	W	L	PCT.	MGR
N Y	1	104	57	.646	Houk
CHI	2	94	68	.580	Lopez
MIN	3	91	70	.565	Mele
BAL	4	86	76	.531	Hitchcock
CLE	5t	79	83	.488	Tebbetts
DET	5t	79	83	.488	{Scheffing, Dressen
BOS	7	76	85	.472	Pesky
K C	8	73	89	.451	Lopat
L A	9	70	91	.435	Rigney
WAS	10	56	106	.346	{Vernon, Hodges

1964—NATIONAL LEAGUE

CLUB	F	W	L	PCT.	MGR
St.L	1	93	69	.574	Keane
CIN	2t	92	70	.568	Hutchinson
PHI	2t	92	70	.568	Mauch
S F	4	90	72	.556	Dark
MIL	5	88	74	.543	Bragan
L A	6t	80	82	.494	Alston
PIT	6t	80	82	.494	Murtaugh
CHI	8	76	86	.469	Kennedy
HOU	9	66	96	.407	{Craft, Harris
N Y	10	53	109	.327	Stengel

1964—AMERICAN LEAGUE

CLUB	F	W	L	PCT.	MGR
N Y	1	99	63	.611	Berra
CHI	2	98	64	.605	Lopez
BAL	3	97	65	.599	Bauer
DET	4	85	77	.525	Dressen
L A	5	82	80	.506	Rigney
CLE	6t	79	83	.488	Tebbetts
MIN	6t	79	83	.488	Mele
BOS	8	72	90	.444	{Pesky, Herman
WAS	9	62	100	.388	Hodges
K C	10	57	105	.352	{Lopat, McGaha

1965—NATIONAL LEAGUE

CLUB	F	W	L	PCT.	MGR
L A	1	97	65	.599	Alston
S F	2	95	67	.586	Franks
PIT	3	90	72	.556	Walker
CIN	4	89	73	.549	Sisler
MIL	5	86	76	.531	Bragan
PHI	6	85	76	.528	Mauch
St.L	7	80	81	.497	Schoendienst
CHI	8	72	90	.444	{Kennedy, Klein
HOU	9	65	97	.401	Harris
N Y	10	50	112	.309	{Stengel, Westrum

1965—AMERICAN LEAGUE

CLUB	F	W	L	PCT.	MGR
MIN	1	102	60	.630	Mele
CHI	2	95	67	.586	Lopez
BAL	3	94	68	.580	Bauer
DET	4	89	73	.549	Dressen
CLE	5	87	75	.537	Tebbetts
N Y	6	77	85	.475	Keane
CAL	7	75	87	.463	Rigney
WAS	8	70	92	.432	Hodges
BOS	9	62	100	.383	Herman
K C	10	59	103	.364	{McGaha, Sullivan

1966—NATIONAL LEAGUE

CLUB	F	W	L	PCT.	MGR
L A	1	95	67	.586	Alston
S F	2	93	68	.578	Franks
PIT	3	92	70	.568	Walker
PHI	4	87	75	.537	Mauch
ATL	5	85	77	.525	{Bragan, Hitchcock
St.L	6	83	79	.512	Schoendienst
CIN	7	76	84	.495	{Heffner, Bristol
HOU	8	72	90	.444	Hatton
N Y	9	66	95	.410	Westrum
CHI	10	59	103	.364	Durocher

1966—AMERICAN LEAGUE

CLUB	F	W	L	PCT.	MGR
BAL	1	97	63	.606	Bauer
MIN	2	89	73	.549	Mele
DET	3	88	74	.543	{Dressen, Swift, Skaff
CHI	4	83	79	.512	Stanky
CLE	5	81	81	.500	{Tebbetts, Strickland
CAL	6	80	82	.494	Rigney
K C	7	74	86	.463	Dark
WAS	8	71	88	.447	Hodges
BOS	9	72	90	.444	{Herman, Runnels
N Y	10	70	89	.440	{Keane, Houk

1967—NATIONAL LEAGUE

CLUB	F	W	L	PCT.	MGR
St.L	1	101	60	.627	Schoendienst
S F	2	91	71	.562	F·anks
CHI	3	87	74	.540	Durocher
CIN	4	87	75	.537	Bristol
PHI	5	82	80	.506	Mauch
PIT	6	81	81	.500	{Walker, Murtaugh
ATL	7	77	85	.475	{Hitchcock, Silvestri
L A	8	73	89	.451	Alston
HOU	9	69	93	.426	Hatton
N Y	10	61	101	.377	{Westrum, Parker

1967—AMERICAN LEAGUE

CLUB	F	W	L	PCT.	MGR
BOS	1	92	70	.568	Williams
DET	2t	91	71	.562	Smith
MIN	2t	91	71	.562	{Mele, Ermer
CHI	4	89	73	.549	Stanky
CAL	5	84	77	.522	Rigney
BAL	6t	76	85	.472	Bauer
WAS	6t	76	85	.472	Hodges
CLE	8	75	87	.463	Adcock
N Y	9	72	90	.444	Houk
K C	10	62	99	.385	{Dark, Appling

1968—NATIONAL LEAGUE

CLUB	F	W	L	PCT.	MGR
St.L	1	97	65	.599	Schoendienst
S F	2	88	74	.543	Franks
CHI	3	84	78	.519	Durocher
CIN	4	83	79	.512	Bristol
ATL	5	81	81	.500	Harris
PIT	6	80	82	.494	Shepard
L A	7t	76	86	.469	Alston
PHI	7t	76	86	.469	{Mauch, Myatt, Skinner
N Y	9	73	89	.451	Hodges
HOU	10	72	90	.444	{Hatton, Walker

1968—AMERICAN LEAGUE

CLUB	F	W	L	PCT.	MGR
DET	1	103	59	.636	Smith
BAL	2	91	71	.562	{Bauer, Weaver
CLE	3	86	75	.534	Dark
BOS	4	86	76	.531	Williams
N Y	5	83	79	.512	Houk
OAK	6	82	80	.506	Bob Kennedy
MIN	7	79	83	.488	Ermer
CAL	8t	67	95	.414	Rigney
CHI	8t	67	95	.414	{Stanky, Moss, Lopez
WAS	10	65	96	.404	Lemon

1969—NATIONAL LEAGUE EASTERN DIVISION

CLUB	F	W	L	PCT.	MGR
N Y	1	100	62	.617	Hodges
CHI	2	92	70	.568	Durocher
PIT	3	88	74	.543	{Shepard, Grammas
St.L	4	87	75	.537	Schoendienst
PHI	5	63	99	.389	{Skinner, Myatt
MON	6	52	110	.321	Mauch

1969—NATIONAL LEAGUE WESTERN DIVISION

CLUB	F	W	L	PCT.	MGR
ATL	1	93	69	.574	Harris
S F	2	90	72	.556	King
CIN	3	89	73	.549	Bristol
L A	4	85	77	.525	Alston
HOU	5	81	81	.500	Walker
S D	6	52	110	.321	Gomez

1969—AMERICAN LEAGUE EASTERN DIVISION

CLUB	F	W	L	PCT.	MGR
BAL	1	109	53	.673	Weaver
DET	2	90	72	.556	Smith
BOS	3	87	75	.537	{R. Williams, Popowski
WAS	4	86	76	.531	T. Williams
N Y	5	80	81	.497	Houk
CLE	6	62	99	.385	Dark

1969—AMERICAN LEAGUE WESTERN DIVISION

CLUB	F	W	L	PCT.	MGR
MIN	1	97	65	.599	Martin
OAK	2	88	74	.543	{Bauer, McNamara
CAL	3	71	91	.438	{Rigney, Phillips
K C	4	69	93	.426	Gordon
CHI	5	68	94	.420	{Lopez, Gutteridge
SEA	6	64	98	.395	Schultz

1970—NATIONAL LEAGUE EASTERN DIVISION

CLUB	F	W	L	PCT.	MGR
PIT	1	89	73	.549	Murtaugh
CHI	2	84	78	.519	Durocher
N Y	3	83	79	.512	Hodges
St.L	4	76	86	.469	Schoendienst
PHI	5	73	88	.453	Lucchesi
MON	6	73	89	.451	Mauch

1970—NATIONAL LEAGUE WESTERN DIVISION

CLUB	F	W	L	PCT.	MGR
CIN	1	102	60	.630	Anderson
LA	2	87	74	.540	Alston
SF	3	86	76	.531	{King, Fox
HOU	4	79	83	.488	Walker
ATL	5	76	86	.469	Harris
SD	6	63	99	.389	Gomez

1970—AMERICAN LEAGUE EASTERN DIVISION

CLUB	F	W	L	PCT.	MGR
BAL	1	108	54	.667	Weaver
NY	2	93	69	.574	Houk
BOS	3	87	75	.537	Kasko
DET	4	79	83	.488	Smith
CLE	5	76	86	.469	Dark
WAS	6	70	92	.432	T. Williams

1970—AMERICAN LEAGUE WESTERN DIVISION

CLUB	F	W	L	PCT.	MGR
MIN	1	98	64	.605	Rigney
OAK	2	89	73	.549	McNamara
CAL	3	86	76	.531	Phillips
KC	4t	65	97	.401	Metro, Lemon
MIL	4t	65	97	.401	Bristol
CHI	6	56	106	.346	Gutteridge, Adair, Tanner

1971—NATIONAL LEAGUE EASTERN DIVISION

CLUB	F	W	L	PCT.	MGR
PIT	1	97	65	.599	Murtaugh
StL	2	90	72	.556	Schoendienst
CHI	3t	83	79	.512	Durocher
NY	3t	83	79	.512	Hodges
MON	5	71	90	.441	Mauch
PHI	6	67	95	.414	Lucchesi

1971—NATIONAL LEAGUE WESTERN DIVISION

CLUB	F	W	L	PCT.	MGR
SF	1	90	72	.556	Fox
LA	2	89	73	.549	Alston
ATL	3	82	80	.506	Harris
HOU	4t	79	83	.488	Walker
CIN	4t	79	83	.488	Anderson
SD	6	61	100	.379	Gomez

1971—AMERICAN LEAGUE EASTERN DIVISION

CLUB	F	W	L	PCT.	MGR
BAL	1	101	60	.627	Weaver
DET	2	91	71	.562	Martin
BOS	3	85	77	.525	Kasko
NY	4	82	80	.506	Houk
WAS	5	63	96	.396	T. Williams
CLE	6	60	102	.370	Dark, Lipon

1971—AMERICAN LEAGUE WESTERN DIVISION

CLUB	F	W	L	PCT.	MGR
OAK	1	101	60	.627	R. Williams
KC	2	85	76	.528	Lemon
CHI	3	79	83	.488	Tanner
CAL	4	76	86	.469	Phillips
MIN	5	74	86	.463	Rigney
MIL	6	69	92	.429	Bristol

1972—NATIONAL LEAGUE EASTERN DIVISION

CLUB	F	W	L	PCT.	MGR
PIT	1	96	59	.619	Virdon
CHI	2	85	70	.548	Durocher, Lockman
NY	3	83	73	.532	Berra
StL	4	75	81	.481	Schoendienst
MON	5	70	86	.449	Mauch
PHI	6	59	97	.378	Lucchesi, Owens

1972—NATIONAL LEAGUE WESTERN DIVISION

CLUB	F	W	L	PCT.	MGR
CIN	1	95	59	.617	Anderson
HOU	2	84	69	.549	Walker, Parker, Durocher
LA	3	85	70	.548	Alston
ATL	4	70	84	.455	Harris, Mathews
SF	5	69	86	.445	Fox
SD	6	58	95	.379	Gomez, Zimmer

1972—AMERICAN LEAGUE EASTERN DIVISION

CLUB	F	W	L	PCT.	MGR
DET	1	86	70	.551	Martin
BOS	2	85	70	.548	Kasko
BAL	3	80	74	.519	Weaver
NY	4	79	76	.510	Houk
CLE	5	72	84	.462	Aspromonte
MIL	6	65	91	.417	Bristol, McMillan, Crandall

1972—AMERICAN LEAGUE WESTERN DIVISION

CLUB	F	W	L	PCT.	MGR
OAK	1	93	62	.600	R. Williams
CHI	2	87	67	.565	Tanner
MIN	3	77	77	.500	Rigney, Quilici
KC	4	76	78	.494	Lemon
CAL	5	75	80	.484	Rice
TEX	6	54	100	.351	T. Williams

1973—NATIONAL LEAGUE EASTERN DIVISION

CLUB	F	W	L	PCT.	MGR
NY	1	82	79	.509	Berra
St.L	2	81	81	.500	Schoendienst
PIT	3	80	82	.494	Virdon, Murtaugh
MON	4	79	83	.488	Mauch
CHI	5	77	84	.478	Lockman
PHI	6	71	91	.438	Ozark

1973—NATIONAL LEAGUE WESTERN DIVISION

CLUB	F	W	L	PCT.	MGR
CIN	1	99	63	.611	Anderson
LA	2	95	66	.590	Alston
SF	3	88	74	.543	Fox
HOU	4	82	80	.506	Durocher
ATL	5	76	85	.472	Mathews
SD	6	60	102	.370	Zimmer

1973—AMERICAN LEAGUE EASTERN DIVISION

CLUB	F	W	L	PCT.	MGR
BAL	1	97	65	.599	Weaver
BOS	2	89	73	.549	Kasko, Popowski
DET	3	85	77	.525	Martin, Schultz
NY	4	80	82	.494	Houk
MIL	5	74	88	.457	Crandall
CLE	6	71	91	.438	Aspromonte

1973—AMERICAN LEAGUE WESTERN DIVISION

CLUB	F	W	L	PCT.	MGR
OAK	1	94	68	.580	Williams
KC	2	88	74	.543	McKeon
MIN	3	81	81	.500	Quilici
CAL	4	79	83	.488	Winkles
CHI	5	77	85	.475	Tanner
TEX	6	57	105	.352	Herzog, Wilber, Martin

1974—NATIONAL LEAGUE EASTERN DIVISION

CLUB	F	W	L	PCT.	MGR
PIT	1	88	74	.543	Murtaugh
St. L	2	86	75	.534	Schoendienst
PHI	3	80	82	.494	Ozark
MON	4	79	82	.491	Mauch
NY	5	71	91	.438	Berra
CHI	6	66	96	.407	Lockman, Marshall

1974—NATIONAL LEAGUE WESTERN DIVISION

CLUB	F	W	L	PCT.	MGR
LA	1	102	60	.630	Alston
CIN	2	98	64	.605	Anderson
ATL	3	88	74	.543	Mathews, King
HOU	4	81	81	.500	Gomez
SF	5	72	90	.444	Fox, Westrum
SD	6	60	102	.370	McNamara

1974—AMERICAN LEAGUE EASTERN DIVISION

CLUB	F	W	L	PCT.	MGR
BAL	1	91	71	.562	Weaver
NY	2	89	73	.549	Virdon
BOS	3	84	78	.519	Johnson
CLE	4	77	85	.475	Aspromonte
MIL	5	76	86	.469	Crandall
DET	6	72	90	.444	Houk

1974—AMERICAN LEAGUE WESTERN DIVISION

CLUB	F	W	L	PCT.	MGR
OAK	1	90	72	.556	Dark
TEX	2	84	76	.525	Martin
MIN	3	82	80	.506	Quilici
CHI	4	80	80	.500	Tanner
KC	5	77	85	.475	McKeon
CAL	6	68	94	.420	Winkles, Herzog, Williams

1975—NATIONAL LEAGUE EASTERN DIVISION

CLUB	F	W	L	PCT.	MGR
PIT	1	92	69	.571	Murtaugh
PHI	2	86	76	.531	Ozark
NY	3t	82	80	.506	Berra, McMillan
St. L	3t	82	80	.506	Schoendienst
CHI	5t	75	87	.463	Marshall
MON	5t	75	87	.463	Mauch

1975—NATIONAL LEAGUE WESTERN DIVISION

CLUB	F	W	L	PCT.	MGR
CIN	1	108	54	.667	Anderson
LA	2	88	74	.543	Alston
SF	3	80	81	.497	Westrum
SD	4	71	91	.438	McNamara
ATL	5	67	94	.416	King
HOU	6	64	97	.398	Gomez, Virdon

1975—AMERICAN LEAGUE EASTERN DIVISION

CLUB	F	W	L	PCT.	MGR
BOS	1	95	65	.594	Johnson
BAL	2	90	69	.566	Weaver
NY	3	83	77	.519	Virdon, Martin
CLE	4	79	80	.497	Robinson
MIL	5	68	94	.420	Crandall, Kuenn
DET	6	57	102	.358	Houk

1975—AMERICAN LEAGUE WESTERN DIVISION

CLUB	F	W	L	PCT.	MGR
OAK	1	98	64	.605	Dark
KC	2	91	71	.562	McKeon, Herzog
TEX	3	79	83	.488	Martin, Lucchesi
MIN	4	76	83	.478	Quilici
CHI	5	75	86	.466	Tanner
CAL	6	72	89	.447	Williams

1976—NATIONAL LEAGUE EASTERN DIVISION

CLUB	F	W	L	PCT.	MGR
PHI	1	101	61	.623	Ozark
PIT	2	92	70	.568	Murtaugh
N Y	3	86	76	.531	Frazier
CHI	4	75	87	.463	Marshall
St.L	5	72	90	.444	Schoendienst
MON	6	55	107	.340	Kuehl, Fox

1976—NATIONAL LEAGUE WESTERN DIVISION

CLUB	F	W	L	PCT.	MGR
CIN	1	102	60	.630	Anderson
L A	2	92	70	.568	Alston, Lasorda
HOU	3	80	82	.494	Virdon
S F	4	74	88	.457	Rigney
S D	5	73	89	.451	McNamara
ATL	6	70	92	.432	Bristol

1976—AMERICAN LEAGUE EASTERN DIVISION

CLUB	F	W	L	PCT.	MGR
N Y	1	97	62	.610	Martin
BAL	2	88	74	.543	Weaver
BOS	3	83	79	.512	Johnson, Zimmer
CLE	4	81	78	.509	Robinson
DET	5	74	87	.460	Houk
MIL	6	66	95	.410	Grammas

1976—AMERICAN LEAGUE WESTERN DIVISION

CLUB	F	W	L	PCT.	MGR
K C	1	90	72	.556	Herzog
OAK	2	87	74	.540	Tanner
MIN	3	85	77	.525	Mauch
CAL	4t	76	86	.469	Williams, Sherry
TEX	4t	76	86	.469	Lucchesi
CHI	6	64	97	.398	Richards

1977—NATIONAL LEAGUE EASTERN DIVISION

CLUB	F	W	L	PCT.	MGR
PHI	1	101	61	.623	Ozark
PIT	2	96	66	.593	Tanner
St. L	3	83	79	.512	Rapp
CHI	4	81	81	.500	Franks
MON	5	75	87	.463	Williams
N Y	6	64	98	.395	Frazier, Torre

1977—NATIONAL LEAGUE WESTERN DIVISION

CLUB	F	W	L	PCT.	MGR
L A	1	98	64	.605	Lasorda
CIN	2	88	74	.543	Anderson
HOU	3	81	81	.500	Virdon
S F	4	75	87	.463	Altobelli
S D	5	69	93	.426	McNamara, Skinner, Dark
ATL	6	61	101	.377	Bristol, Turner, Bristol

1977—AMERICAN LEAGUE EASTERN DIVISION

CLUB	F	W	L	PCT.	MGR
N Y	1	100	62	.617	Martin
BAL	2t	97	64	.602	Weaver
BOS	2t	97	64	.602	Zimmer
DET	4	74	88	.457	Houk
CLE	5	71	90	.441	Torborg
MIL	6	67	95	.414	Grammas
TOR	7	54	107	.335	Hartsfield

1977—AMERICAN LEAGUE WESTERN DIVISION

CLUB	F	W	L	PCT.	MGR
K C	1	102	60	.630	Herzog
TEX	2	94	68	.580	Lucchesi, Stanky, Hunter
CHI	3	90	72	.556	Lemon
MIN	4	84	77	.522	Mauch
CAL	5	74	88	.457	Sherry, Garcia
SEA	6	64	98	.395	Johnson
OAK	7	63	98	.391	McKeon, Winkles

1978—NATIONAL LEAGUE EASTERN DIVISION

CLUB	F	W	L	PCT.	MGR
PHI	1	90	72	.556	Ozark
PIT	2	88	73	.547	Tanner
CHI	3	78	83	.488	Franks
MON	4	76	86	.469	Williams
St. L	5	69	93	.426	Rapp, Krol, Boyer
N Y	6	66	96	.407	Torre

1978—NATIONAL LEAGUE WESTERN DIVISION

CLUB	F	W	L	PCT.	MGR
L A	1	95	67	.586	Lasorda
CIN	2	92	69	.571	Anderson
S F	3	89	73	.549	Altobelli
S D	4	84	78	.519	Craig
HOU	5	74	88	.457	Virdon
ATL	6	69	93	.426	Cox

1978—AMERICAN LEAGUE EASTERN DIVISION

CLUB	F	W	L	PCT.	MGR
N Y	1p	100	63	.613	Martin, Howser, Lemon
BOS	2p	99	64	.607	Zimmer
MIL	3	93	69	.574	Bamberger
BAL	4	90	71	.559	Weaver
DET	5	86	76	.531	Houk
CLE	6	69	90	.434	Torborg
TOR	7	59	102	.366	Hartsfield

1978—AMERICAN LEAGUE WESTERN DIVISION

CLUB	F	W	L	PCT.	MGR
K C	1	92	70	.568	Herzog
CAL	2t	87	75	.537	Garcia, Fregosi
TEX	2t	87	75	.537	Hunter, Corrales
MIN	4	73	89	.451	Mauch
CHI	5	71	90	.441	Lemon, Doby
OAK	6	69	93	.426	Winkles, McKeon
SEA	7	56	104	.350	Johnson

CHAMPIONSHIP SERIES

Beginning in 1969, the American and National Leagues were split into two six-club divisions, East and West. As a result, a post season best-of-five series was initiated to determine each league's representative in the World Series.

1969 — NATIONAL LEAGUE

New York (East) 3 games vs. Atlanta (West) 0 games

Oct. 4	at Atlanta	New York 9, Atlanta 5
Oct. 5	at Atlanta	New York 11, Atlanta 6
Oct. 6	at New York	New York 7, Atlanta 4

1969 —— AMERICAN LEAGUE

Baltimore (East) 3 games vs. Minnesota (West) 0 games
Oct. 4   at Baltimore   Baltimore 4, Minnesota 3
Oct. 5   at Baltimore   Baltimore 1, Minnesota 0
Oct. 6   at Minnesota   Baltimore 11, Minnesota 2

1970 — NATIONAL LEAGUE

Cincinnati (West) 3 games vs. Pittsburgh (East) 0 games
Oct. 3   at Pittsburgh   Cincinnati 3, Pittsburgh 0
Oct. 4   at Pittsburgh   Cincinnati 3, Pittsburgh 1
Oct. 5   at Cincinnati   Cincinnati 3, Pittsburgh 2

1970 — AMERICAN LEAGUE

Baltimore (East) 3 games vs. Minnesota (West) 0 games
Oct. 3   at Minnesota   Baltimore 10, Minnesota 6
Oct. 4   at Minnesota   Baltimore 11, Minnesota 3
Oct. 5   at Baltimore   Baltimore 6, Minnesota 1

1971 — NATIONAL LEAGUE

Pittsburgh (East) 3 games vs. San Francisco (West) 1 game
Oct. 2   at San Francisco   San Francisco 5, Pittsburgh 4
Oct. 3   at San Francisco   Pittsburgh 9, San Francisco 4
Oct. 5   at Pittsburgh   Pittsburgh 2, San Francisco 1
Oct. 6   at Pittsburgh   Pittsburgh 9, San Francisco 5

1971 — AMERICAN LEAGUE

Baltimore (East) 3 games vs. Oakland (West) 0 games
Oct. 3   at Baltimore   Baltimore 5, Oakland 3
Oct. 4   at Baltimore   Baltimore 5, Oakland 1
Oct. 5   at Oakland   Baltimore 5. Oakland 3

1972 — NATIONAL LEAGUE

Cincinnati (West) 3 games vs. Pittsburgh (East) 2 games
Oct. 7   at Pittsburgh   Pittsburgh 5, Cincinnati 1
Oct. 8   at Pittsburgh   Cincinnati 5, Pittsburgh 3
Oct. 9   at Cincinnati   Pittsburgh 3, Cincinnati 2
Oct. 10   at Cincinnati   Cincinnati 7, Pittsburgh 1
Oct. 11   at Cincinnati   Cincinnati 4, Pittsburgh 3

1972 — AMERICAN LEAGUE

Oakland (West) 3 games vs. Detroit (East) 2 games
Oct. 7   at Oakland   Oakland 3, Detroit 2
Oct. 8   at Oakland   Oakland 5, Detroit 0
Oct. 10   at Detroit   Detroit 3, Oakland 0
Oct. 11   at Detroit   Detroit 4, Oakland 3
Oct. 12   at Detroit   Oakland 2, Detroit 1

1973 — NATIONAL LEAGUE

New York (East) 3 games vs. Cincinnati (West) 2 games
Oct. 6   at Cincinnati   Cincinnati 2, New York 1
Oct. 7   at Cincinnati   New York 5, Cincinnati 0
Oct. 8   at New York   New York 9, Cincinnati 2
Oct. 9   at New York   Cincinnati 2, New York 1
Oct. 10   at New York   New York 7, Cincinnati 2

1973 — AMERICAN LEAGUE

Oakland (West) 3 games vs. Baltimore (East) 2 games
Oct. 6   at Baltimore   Baltimore 6, Oakland 0
Oct. 7   at Baltimore   Oakland 6, Baltimore 3
Oct. 9   at Oakland   Oakland 2, Baltimore 1
Oct. 10   at Oakland   Baltimore 5, Oakland 4
Oct. 11   at Oakland   Oakland 3, Baltimore 0

1974 — NATIONAL LEAGUE

Los Angeles (West) 3 games vs. Pittsburgh (East) 1 game
Oct. 5   at Pittsburgh   Los Angeles 3, Pittsburgh 0
Oct. 6   at Pittsburgh   Los Angeles 5, Pittsburgh 2
Oct. 8   at Los Angeles   Pittsburgh 7, Los Angeles 0
Oct. 9   at Los Angeles   Los Angeles 12, Pittsburgh 1

1974 —— AMERICAN LEAGUE

Oakland (West) 3 games vs. Baltimore (East) 1 game
Oct. 5   at Oakland   Baltimore 6, Oakland 3
Oct. 6   at Oakland   Oakland 5, Baltimore 0
Oct. 8   at Baltimore   Oakland 1, Baltimore 0
Oct. 9   at Baltimore   Oakland 2, Baltimore 1

1975 — NATIONAL LEAGUE

Cincinnati (West) 3 games vs. Pittsburgh (East) 0 games

Oct.	4	at Cincinnati	Cincinnati 8, Pittsburgh 3
Oct.	5	at Cincinnati	Cincinnati 6, Pittsburgh 1
Oct.	7	at Pittsburgh	Cincinnati 5, Pittsburgh 3

1975 — AMERICAN LEAGUE

Boston (East) 3 games vs. Oakland (West) 0 games

Oct.	4	at Boston	Boston 7, Oakland 1
Oct.	5	at Boston	Boston 6, Oakland 3
Oct.	7	at Oakland	Boston 5, Oakland 3

1976 — NATIONAL LEAGUE

Cincinnati (West) 3 games vs. Philadelphia (East) 0 games

Oct.	9	at Philadelphia	Cincinnati 6, Philadelphia 3
Oct.	10	at Philadelphia	Cincinnati 6, Philadelphia 2
Oct.	12	at Cincinnati	Cincinnati 7, Philadelphia 6

1976 — AMERICAN LEAGUE

New York (East) 3 games vs. Kansas City (West) 2 games

Oct.	9	at Kansas City	New York 4, Kansas City 1
Oct.	10	at Kansas City	Kansas City 7, New York 3
Oct.	12	at New York	New York 5, Kansas City 3
Oct.	13	at New York	Kansas City 7, New York 4
Oct.	14	at New York	New York 7, Kansas City 6

1977 — NATIONAL LEAGUE

Los Angeles (West) 3 games vs. Philadelphia (East) 1 game

Oct.	4	at Los Angeles	Philadelphia 7, Los Angeles 5
Oct.	5	at Los Angeles	Los Angeles 7, Philadelphia 1
Oct.	7	at Philadelphia	Los Angeles 6, Philadelphia 5
Oct.	8	at Philadelphia	Los Angeles 4, Philadelphia 1

1977 — AMERICAN LEAGUE

New York (East) 3 games vs. Kansas City (West) 2 games

Oct.	5	at New York	Kansas City 7, New York 2
Oct.	6	at New York	New York 6, Kansas City 2
Oct.	7	at Kansas City	Kansas City 6, New York 2
Oct.	8	at Kansas City	New York 6, Kansas City 4
Oct.	9	at Kansas City	New York 5, Kansas City 3

1978 — NATIONAL LEAGUE
Los Angeles (West) 3 games vs. Philadelphia (East) 1 game

Oct.	4	at Philadelphia	Los Angeles 9, Philadelphia 5
Oct.	5	at Philadelphia	Los Angeles 4, Philadelphia 0
Oct.	6	at Los Angeles	Philadelphia 9, Los Angeles 4
Oct.	7	at Los Angeles	Los Angeles 4, Philadelphia 3

1978 — AMERICAN LEAGUE
New York (East) 3 games vs. Kansas City (West) 1 game

Oct.	3	at Kansas City	New York 7, Kansas City 1
Oct.	4	at Kansas City	Kansas City 10, New York 4
Oct.	6	at New York	New York 6, Kansas City 5
Oct.	7	at New York	New York 2, Kansas City 1

EVOLUTION OF MAJOR LEAGUE CITIES
(alphabetically)

The letters in parenthesis indicate the league. (n) National Association; (N) National League; (a) American Association; (U) Union Association; (p) Players League; (A) American League; (F) Federal League.

ALTOONA: (U) 1884.

ATLANTA: (N) 1966 to date.

BALTIMORE: (n) 1872–74, listed as Lord Baltimore in club standings; also had second club in league in 1873, listed as Marylands in club standings; (a) 1882–91; (U) 1884; (N) 1892–99; (A) 1901–02; 1954 to date; (F) 1914–15.

BOSTON: (n) 1871–75; (N) 1876–1952; (U) 1884; (p) 1890; (a) 1891; (A) 1901 to date.

BROOKLYN: (n) 1872–75, listed as Atlantics in club standings; also had second club in league in 1872, listed as Eckfords in club standings; (a) 1884–90; (p) 1890; (N) 1890–1957; (F) 1914–15.

BUFFALO: (N) 1879–85; (p) 1890; (F) 1914–15.

CALIFORNIA: (A) 1965 to date.

CHICAGO: (n) 1871, 1874–75; (N) 1876 to date; (U) 1884; (p) 1890; (A) 1901 to date; (F) 1914–15.

CINCINNATI: (N) 1876–80, 1890 to date; (a) 1882–89, 1891; (U) 1884.

CLEVELAND: (n) 1871–72; (N) 1879–84, 1889–99; (a) 1887–88; (p) 1890; (A) 1901 to date.

COLUMBUS: (a) 1883–84, 1889–91.

DETROIT: (N) 1881–88; (A) 1901 to date.

ELIZABETH: (n) 1873, listed as Resolutes in club standings.

FT. WAYNE: (n) 1871, listed as Kekiongas in club standings.

HARTFORD: (n) 1874–75; (N) 1876–77.

HOUSTON: (N) 1962 to date.

INDIANAPOLIS: (N) 1878, 1887–89; (a) 1884; (F) 1914.

KANSAS CITY: (U) 1884; (N) 1886; (a) 1888–89; (F) 1914–15; (A) 1955–67, 1969 to date.

KEOKUK: (n) 1875, listed as Westerns in club standings.

LOS ANGELES: (N) 1958 to date; (A) 1961–64.

LOUISVILLE: (N) 1876–77; 1892–99; (a) 1882–91, listed as Eclipse in club standings.

MIDDLETOWN: (n) 1872, listed as Mansfields in club standings.

MILWAUKEE: (N) 1878, 1953–65; (U) 1884; (a) 1891; (A) 1901, 1970 to date.

MINNESOTA: (A) 1961 to date (Minneapolis-St. Paul).

MONTREAL: (N) 1969 to date.

NEWARK: (F) 1915.

NEW HAVEN: (n) 1875.

NEW YORK: (n) 1871–75, listed as Mutuals in club standings; (N) 1876, listed as Mutuals in club standings; 1883–1957, 1962–date; (a) 1883–87, listed as Metropolitans in club standings; (p) 1890; (A) 1903 to date.

OAKLAND: (A) 1968 to date.

PHILADELPHIA: (n) 1871–75, listed as Athletics in club standings; also had second club in league, 1873–75; also had third club in league in 1875, listed as Centennials in club standings; (N) 1876, listed as Athletics in club standings;

1883 to date; (a) 1882–91, listed as Athletics in club standings; (U) 1884, listed as Keystone in club standings; (p) 1890; (A) 1901–54.

PITTSBURGH: (a) 1882–86, listed as Allegheny in club standings; (U) 1884; (N) 1887 to date; (p) 1890; (F) 1914–15.

PROVIDENCE: (N) 1878–85.

RICHMOND: (a) 1884, listed as Virginia in club standings.

ROCKFORD: (n) 1871.

ROCHESTER: (a) 1890.

ST. LOUIS: (n) 1875, listed as Red Stockings in club standings; also had second club in league; (N) 1876–77, 1885–86, 1892 to date; (a) 1882–91; (U) 1884; (A) 1902–53; (F) 1914–15.

ST. PAUL: (U) 1884.

SAN DIEGO: (N) 1969 to date.

SAN FRANCISCO: (N) 1958 to date.

SEATTLE: (A) 1969, 1977 to date

SYRACUSE: (N) 1879; (a) 1890.

TEXAS: (A) 1972–date.

TOLEDO: (a) 1884, 1890.

TORONTO: (A) 1977 to date

TROY: (n) 1871–72, listed as Haymakers in club standings; (N) 1879–82.

WASHINGTON: (n) 1871, listed as Olympics in club standings; in 1872 had two clubs in league, listed as Olympics and Nationals in club standings; 1873, 1875, listed as Nationals in club standings; (a) 1884, listed as Nationals in club standings; 1891; (U) 1884, listed as Nationals in club standings; (N) 1886–89; 1892–99; (A) 1901–71.

WILMINGTON: (U) 1884.

WORCESTER: (N) 1880–82.

NATIONAL LEAGUE

ANNUAL ATTENDANCE

1901 — 1,920,031	1940 — 4,389,693
1902 — 1,683,012	1941 — 4,777,647
1903 — 2,390,362	1942 — 4,353,353
1904 — 2,664,271	1943 — 3,769,342
1905 — 2,734,310	1944 — 3,974,588
1906 — 2,781,213	1945 — 5,260,703
1907 — 2,640,220	1946 — 8,902,107
1908 — 3,512,108	1947 — 10,388,470
1909 — 3,496,420	1948 — 9,770,743
1910 — 3,494,544	1949 — 9,484,718
1911 — 3,231,768	1950 — 8,320,616
1912 — 2,735,759	1951 — 7,244.002
1913 — 2,831,531	1952 — 6,339,148
1914 — 1,707,397	1953 — 7,419,721
1915 — 2,430,142	1954 — 8,013,519
1916 — 3,051,634	1955 — 7,674,412
1917 — 2,361,136	1956 — 8,649,567
1918 — 1,372,127	1957 — 8,819,601
1919 — 2,878,203	1958 — 10,164,596
1920 — 4,036,575	1959 — 9,994,525
1921 — 3,986,984	1960 — 10,684,963
1922 — 3,941,820	1961 — 8,731,502
1923 — 4,069,817	1962 — 11,360,159
1924 — 4,340,644	1963 — 11,382,227
1925 — 4,353,704	1964 — 12,045,190
1926 — 4,920,399	1965 — 13,581,136
1927 — 5,309,917	1966 — 15,015,471
1928 — 4,881,097	1967 — 12,971,430
1929 — 4,925,713	1968 — 11,785,358
1930 — 5,446,532	1969 — 15,094,946
1931 — 4,583,815	1970 — 16,662,198
1932 — 3,841,334	1971 — 17,324,857
1933 — 3,162,821	1972 — 15,529,730
1934 — 3,200,105	1973 — 16,675,322
1935 — 3,657,309	1974 — 16,978,314
1936 — 3,903,691	1975 — 16,600,490
1937 — 4,204,228	1976 — 16,660,529
1938 — 4,560,837	1977 — 19,070,228
1939 — 4,707,177	1978 — 20,106,649

AMERICAN LEAGUE

ANNUAL ATTENDANCE

1901 — 1,683,584	1940 — 5,433,791
1902 — 2,206,454	1941 — 4,911,956
1903 — 2,344,888	1942 — 4,200,216
1904 — 3,024,028	1943 — 3,696,569
1905 — 3,120,752	1944 — 4,798,158
1906 — 2,938,076	1945 — 5,580,420
1907 — 3,398,764	1946 — 9,621,182
1908 — 3,611,366	1947 — 9,486,069
1909 — 3,739,570	1948 — 11,150,099
1910 — 3,270,689	1949 — 10,730,647
1911 — 3,339,514	1950 — 9,142,361
1912 — 3,263,631	1951 — 8,882,674
1913 — 3,526,805	1952 — 8,293,896
1914 — 2,747,591	1953 — 6,964,076
1915 — 2,434,684	1954 — 7,922,364
1916 — 3,451,885	1955 — 8,942,971
1917 — 2,858,858	1956 — 7,893,683
1918 — 1,707,999	1957 — 8,196,218
1919 — 3,654,236	1958 — 7,296,034
1920 — 5,084,300	1959 — 9,149,454
1921 — 4,620,328	1960 — 9,226,526
1922 — 4,874,355	1961 — 10,163,016
1923 — 4,602,589	1962 — 10,015,056
1924 — 5,255,439	1963 — 9,094,847
1925 — 5,186,851	1964 — 9,235,151
1926 — 4,912,583	1965 — 8,860,764
1927 — 4,612,951	1966 — 10,166,738
1928 — 4,221,188	1967 — 11,336,923
1929 — 4,662,470	1968 — 11,317,387
1930 — 4,685,730	1969 — 12,134,745
1931 — 3,883,292	1970 — 12,085,135
1932 — 3,133,232	1971 — 11,868,560
1933 — 2,926,210	1972 — 11,438,538
1934 — 3,763,606	1973 — 13,433,604
1935 — 3,688,007	1974 — 13,047,294
1936 — 4,178,922	1975 — 13,189,423
1937 — 4,735,835	1976 — 14,657,802
1938 — 4,445,684	1977 — 19,639,551
1939 — 4,270,602	1978 — 20,529,965

NATIONAL LEAGUE SINGLE GAME ATTENDANCE

Atlanta	53,775	(vs. L.A., Apr. 8, 1974) *
Chicago	46,572	(vs. Bro., May 18, 1947)
Cincinnati	53,390	(vs. Hou., Apr. 11, 1976)
Houston	50,908	(vs. L.A., June 22, 1966) *
Los Angeles	78,672	(vs. S.F., Apr. 18, 1958)
Montreal	57,592	(vs. Phi., Apr. 15, 1977)
New York	56,738	(vs. L.A., June 23, 1968)
Philadelphia	63,283	(vs. N.Y., July 4, 1977)
Pittsburgh	51,695	(vs. St.L., Apr. 6, 1973)
St. Louis	50,548	(vs. N.Y., Sept. 14, 1975)
San Diego	50,569	(vs. St. L., Apr. 24, 1976) *
San Francisco	47,273	(vs. L.A., Apr. 17, 1977)

* Night Game

AMERICAN LEAGUE SINGLE GAME ATTENDANCE

Baltimore	51,798	(vs. Bos., Sept. 18, 1977)
Boston	36,350	(vs. N.Y., Aug. 7, 1956)
California	53,591	(vs. N.Y., July 13, 1962) *
Chicago	53,940	(vs. N.Y., June 8, 1951) *
Cleveland	78,382	(vs. Chi., Aug. 20, 1948) *
Detroit	57,888	(vs. Cle., Sept. 26, 1948)
Kansas City	40,502	(vs. Bos., Aug. 20, 1977) *
Milwaukee	55,120	(vs. Balt., Apr. 12, 1977)
Minnesota	46,463	(vs. Chi., June 26, 1977)
New York	74,747	(vs. Bos., May 26, 1947) *
Oakland	48,758	(vs. Det., June 6, 1970)
Seattle	57,762	(vs. Cal., Apr. 6, 1977) *
Texas	40,854	(vs. Cal., May 21, 1976) *
Toronto	44,649	(vs. Chi., Apr. 7, 1977)

* Night Game

III   ALL-TIME REGISTER
OF
PLAYERS AND MANAGERS

This All-Time Register intends to cover every man who ever appeared in a regularly scheduled major league game since the birth of professional league play in 1871. There are gaps, but they have been plugged considerably since publication of the initial edition of the *Encyclopedia*, many by readers who were willing to supply the pegs which fitted holes; others by former players or members of their families.

This historic compilation consists of an alphabetical listing of all players and managers in the majors from 1871 through 1978. Information is arranged as follows:

Last name, followed by first and middle names, then nickname in parentheses, ONLY if the information is available. Birthplace, birthdate, death date. Year-by-year playing record, including club, league, positions played, total number of games played and playing performance. The last line carries the bats and throws of the player and his lifetime batting average or his won-lost lifetime total if a pitcher, or both.

73

KEY TO ABBREVIATIONS

Teams:
ALL (Allegheny) ; ALT (Altoona) ; ATH (Athletics) ; ATL (Braves) ; BAL (Baltimore) ; BOS (Boston) ; BRO (Brooklyn) ; BUF (Buffalo) ; CAL (California) ; CEN (Centennials) ; CHI (Chicago) ; CIN (Cincinnati) ; CLE (Cleveland) ; COL (Columbus) ; DET (Detroit) ; ECK (Eckford) ; ECL (Eclipse) ; HAR (Hartford) ; HOU (Houston) ; IND (Indianapolis) ; KC (Kansas City) ; KEK (Kekiongas) ; KEO (Keokuk) ; KEY (Keystone) ; LA (Los Angeles) ; LB (Lord Baltimore) ; LOU (Louisville) ; MAN (Mansfield) ; MAR (Maryland) ; MET (Metropolitans) ; MIL (Milwaukee) ; MINN (Minnesota) ; MON (Montreal) ; MUT (Mutuals) ; NAT (Nationals) ; NEW (Newark) ; NH (New Haven) ; NY (New York) ; OAK (Oakland) ; OLY (Olympics) ; PHI (Philadelphia) ; PIT (Pittsburgh) ; PRO (Providence) ; RES (Resolutes) ; RIC (Richmond) ; ROC (Rochester) ; ROK (Rockford) ; RS (Red Stockings) ; St.L (St. Louis; SD (San Diego) ; SEA (Seattle) ; SF (San Francisco) ; SYR (Syracuse) ; TEX (Texas) ; TOL (Toledo) ; TOR (Toronto) ; TRO (Troy) ; VIR (Virginia) ; WAS (Washington) ; WIL (Wilmington) ; WOR (Worcester) .

LEAGUES

NA—National Association
N—National League
AA—American Association
U—Union Association
P—Players League
A—American League
F—Federal League

A dash indicates no record available
(Used for batting average before 1876)

BL—bats left
BR—bats right
BB—bats both

POSITIONS

C—Catcher
P—Pitcher
1—First base
2—Second base
S—Shortstop
3—Third base
O—Outfield
H—Pinch hitter
R—pinch runner
M—Manager
D—Designated hitter
ALL—Played all positions

TL—throws left
TR—throws right

Note: Prior to 1965, positions are listed in the same order (P-C-1-2-S-3-O) without regard to games played. Beginning in 1965, positions are listed in order of games played. An asterisk indicates at least 100 games at the position. All positions to the right of a slash are the result of less than ten games played at that position.

ALL-TIME REGISTER

NOTE:

Certain Latin-American players who include their mother's maiden name in parentheses after their own last name are so indicated. Nicknames are shown in quotation marks for all players who are usually called by any name other than their own given first name. Games pitched are shown in the GP column for any player who appeared as a pitcher in fewer games than his total for any season. Total games pitched are also shown in the GP column for lifetime if less than the total number of games played lifetime. Players who appeared in ten or more games as the designated hitter for American League teams beginning in 1973 show the symbol 'D' in the position column.

```
YR   CL LEA POS      GP    G     REC

AARON, HENRY LOUIS (HANK)
OR (HAMMERIN' HANK)
B.FEB.5,1934 MOBILE,ALA.
1954 MIL N  O           122   .280
1955 MIL N  2-O         153   .314
1956 MIL N  O           153   .328
1957 MIL N  O           151   .322
1958 MIL N  O           153   .326
1959 MIL N  3-O         154   .355
1960 MIL N  2-O         153   .292
1961 MIL N  3-O         155   .327
1962 MIL N  1-O         156   .323
1963 MIL N  O           161   .319
1964 MIL N  2-O         145   .328
1965 MIL N  *O          150   .318
1966 ATL N  *O/2        158   .279
1967 ATL N  *O/2        155   .307
1968 ATL N  *O-1        160   .287
1969 ATL N  *O/1        147   .300
1970 ATL N  *O-1        150   .298
1971 ATL N  1-O         139   .327
1972 ATL N  *1-O        129   .265
1973 ATL N  *O          120   .301
1974 ATL N  O           112   .268
1975 MIL A  *D/O        137   .234
1976 MIL A  D/O          85   .229
            BRTR        3298  .305

AARON, TOMMIE LEE
B.AUG.5,1939 MOBILE,ALA.
1962 MIL N  1-2-3-O     141   .231
1963 MIL N  1-2-3-O      72   .200
1965 MIL N  /1            8   .188
1968 ATL N  O-1/3        98   .244
1969 ATL N  1/O          49   .250
1970 ATL N  1-O          44   .206
1971 ATL N  1/3          25   .226
            BRTR        437   .229

AASE, DONALD WILLIAM (DON)
B.SEPT.8,1954 ORANGE,CAL.
1977 BOS A  P       13   6- 2
1978 CAL A  P       29  11- 8
            BRTR    42  17-10

ABADIE, JOHN
B.NOV.4,1858 PHILADELPHIA,PA.
D.MAY 17,1905
1875 CEN NA 1           11    -
     ATL NA 1            1    -
                        12    -

ABBATICCHIO, EDWARD JAMES (BATTY)
B.APR.15,1877 LATROBE,PA.
D.JAN.6,1957 FT.LAUDERDALE,FLA.
1897 PHI N  2            3   .300
1898 PHI N  3           20   .262
1903 BOS N  2-S        133   .227
1904 BOS N  S          154   .256
1905 BOS N  S          153   .279
1907 PIT N  2          147   .262
1908 PIT N  2          144   .250
1909 PIT N  S           23   .230
1910 PIT N  S            1   .000
     BOS N  S           47   .247
                       825   .255

ABBEY, BERT WOOD
B.NOV.29,1869 ESSEX,VT.
D.JUNE 11,1962 ESSEX JUNCTION,VT.
1892 WAS N  P       21   6-15
1893 CHI N  P        8   3- 5
1894 CHI N  P       11   2- 7
1895 CHI N  P        2   0- 1
     BRO N  P        8   4- 3
1896 BRO N  P       19   8- 8
            BRTR    69  23-39


ABBEY, CHARLES S.
B.1867 FALLS CITY,NEB.
1893 WAS N  O           31   .277
1894 WAS N  O          129   .318
1895 WAS N  O          133   .275
1896 WAS N  O           75   .255
1897 WAS N  O           78   .264
                       446   .283

ABBOTT, FREDERICK HARRY
[REAL NAME
HARRY FREDERICK WINBIGLER]
B.OCT.22,1874 VERSAILLES,OHIO
D.JUNE 11,1935 LOS ANGELES,CAL.
1903 CLE A  C           76   .271
1904 CLE A  C           42   .168
1905 PHI N  C           39   .195
            BRTR       157   .226

ABBOTT, LEANDER FRANKLIN (BIG DAN)
B.MAR.16,1862 PORTAGE,OHIO
D.FEB.13,1930 OTTAWA LAKE,MICH.
1890 TOL AA P        3   1- 2
     TR

ABBOTT, ODY CLEON
B.SEPT.5,1888 NEW EAGLE,PA.
D.APR.13,1933 WASHINGTON,D.C.
1910 STL N  O           21   .186
            BRTR

ABBOTT, WILLIAM GLENN (GLENN)
B.FEB.16,1951 LITTLE ROCK,ARK.
1973 OAK A  /P       5   1- 0
1974 OAK A  P       19   5- 7
1975 OAK A  P       30   5- 5
1976 OAK A  P       19   2- 4
1977 SEA A  P       36  12-13
1978 SEA A  P       29   7-15
            BRTR   138  32-44

ABER, ALBERT JULIUS (LEFTY)
B.JULY 31,1927 CLEVELAND,OHIO
1950 CLE A  P        1   1- 0
1953 CLE A  P        6   1- 1
     DET A  P       17   4- 3
1954 DET A  P       32   5-11
1955 DET A  P       39   6- 3
1956 DET A  P       42   4- 4
1957 DET A  P       28   3- 3
     KC  A  P        3   0- 0
            BLTL   168  24-25

ABERCROMBIE, DAVID
B.1840 FALKIRK,SCOTLAND
D.SEPT.2,1916
1871 TRO NA S           1   .000

ABERNATHIE, WILLIAM EDWARD
B.JAN.30,1929 TORRANCE,CAL.
1952 CLE A  P        1   0- 0
            BRTR

ABERNATHY, TALMADGE LAFAYETTE (TED)
B.OCT.30,1921 BYNUM,N.C.
1942 PHI A  P        1   0- 0
1943 PHI A  P        5   0- 3
1944 PHI A  P        1   0- 0
            BRTL     7   0- 3


ABERNATHY, THEODORE WADE (TED)
B.MAR.6,1933 STANLEY,N.C.
1955 WAS A  P       40   5- 9
1956 WAS A  P        5   1- 3
1957 WAS A  P       26   2-10
1960 WAS A  P        2   0- 0
1963 CLE A  P       43   7- 2
1964 CLE A  P       53   2- 6
1965 CHI N  P       84   4- 6
1966 CHI N  P       20   1- 3
     ATL N  P       38   4- 4
1967 CIN N  P       70   6- 3
1968 CIN N  P       78  10- 7
1969 CHI N  P       56   4- 3
1970 CHI N  P       11   0- 0
     STL N  P       11   1- 0
     KC  A  P       36   9- 3
1971 KC  A  P       63   4- 6
1972 KC  A  P       45   3- 4
            BRTR   681  63-69

ABERNATHY, VIRGIL WOODROW (WOODY)
B.FEB.1,1915 FOREST CITY,N.C.
1946 NY  N  P       15   1- 1
1947 NY  N  P        1   0- 0
            BLTL    16   1- 1

ABERSON, CLIFFORD ALEXANDER (KIP)
B.AUG.26,1921 CHICAGO,ILL.
D.JUNE 23,1973 VALLEJO,CAL.
1947 CHI N  O           47   .279
1948 CHI N  O           12   .188
1949 CHI N  O            4   .000
            BRTR        63   .251

ABLES, HARRY TERRELL (HANS)
B.OCT.4,1884 TERRELL,TEX.
D.FEB.8,1951 SAN ANTONIO,TEX.
1905 STL A  P        6   0- 3
1909 CLE A  P        6   1- 1
1911 NY  A  P        3   0- 1
            BRTL    15   1- 5

ABRAMS, CALVIN ROSS
B.MAR.2,1924 PHILADELPHIA,PA.
1949 BRO N  O            8   .083
1950 BRO N  O           38   .205
1951 BRO N  O           67   .280
1952 BRO N  O           10   .200
     CIN N  O           71   .278
1953 PIT N  O          119   .286
1954 PIT N  O           17   .143
     BAL A  O          115   .293
1955 BAL A  1-O        118   .243
1956 CHI A  O            4   .333
            BLTL       567   .269

ABRAMS, GEORGE ALLEN
B.NOV.9,1899 SEATTLE,WASH.
1923 CIN N  P        3   0- 0
            BRTR

ABREU, JOSEPH LAWRENCE
B.MAY 24,1916 OAKLAND,CAL.
1942 CIN N  2-3          9   .214
            BRTR

ABSTEIN, WILLIAM HENRY (BIG BILL)
B.FEB.2,1883 ST.LOUIS,MO.
D.APR.8,1940 ST.LOUIS,MO.
1906 PIT N  O            8   .200
1909 PIT N  1          135   .260
1910 STL A  1           25   .149
            BRTR       168   .242

ACEVEDO, ARNULFO [ESPINOSA]
[SEE ARNULFO ACEVEDO ESPINOSA]
```

ACHENBACH, CHARLES SHUH
[PLAYED UNDER NAME OF
RAYMOND CHARLES]

ACKER, THOMAS JAMES (TOM)
B.MAR.7,1930 PATERSON,N.J.

YR	CL	LEA	POS	GP	G	REC
1956	CIN	N	P		29	4- 3
1957	CIN	N	P		49	10- 5
1958	CIN	N	P		38	4- 3
1959	CIN	N	P		37	1- 2
	BRTR				153	19-13

ACKLEY, FLORIAN FREDERICK (FRITZ)
B.APR.10,1937 HAYWARD,WIS.

1963	CHI	A	P		2	1- 0
1964	CHI	A	P		3	0- 0
	BLTR				5	1- 0

ACOSTA, BALMADERO PEDRO (MERITO)
B.MAY 19,1896 HAVANA,CUBA
D.NOV.17,1963 MIAMI,FLA.

1913	WAS	A	O		12	.250
1914	WAS	A	O		38	.257
1915	WAS	A	O		72	.209
1916	WAS	A	O		5	.125
1918	WAS	A	O		3	.000
	PHI	A	O		49	.302
	BLTL				179	.252

ACOSTA, CECILIO [MIRANDA] (CY)
B.NOV.22,1946 SABINO,MEXICO

1972	CHI	A	P		26	3- 0
1973	CHI	A	P		48	10- 6
1974	CHI	A	P		27	0- 3
1975	CHI	N	/P		6	0- 0
	BRTR				107	13- 9

ACOSTA, EDUARDO ELIXBET (ED)
B.MAR.9,1944 BOQUETE,PANAMA

1970	PIT	N	/P		3	0- 0
1971	SD	N	/P		8	3- 3
1972	SD	N	P		46	3- 6
	BBTR				57	6- 9
	BR 1970					

ACOSTA, JOSE (ACOSTICA)
B.MAR.4,1891 SAN ANTONIO DEL
RIO BLANCO,CUBA

1920	WAS	A	P		17	5- 4
1921	WAS	A	P		33	5- 4
1922	CHI	A	P		5	0- 2
	BRTR				55	10-10
	BB 1920					

ADAIR, JAMES AUDREY (CHOPPY)
B.JAN.25,1907 WAXAHACHAIE,TEX.

1931	CHI	N	S		18	.276
	BRTR					

ADAIR, KENNETH JERRY (JERRY)
B.DEC.17,1936 SAND SPRINGS,OKLA.

1958	BAL	A	2-S		11	.105
1959	BAL	A	2-S		12	.314
1960	BAL	A	2		3	.200
1961	BAL	A	2-S-3		133	.264
1962	BAL	A	2-S-3		139	.284
1963	BAL	A	2		109	.228
1964	BAL	A	2		155	.248
1965	BAL	A	+2		157	.259
1966	BAL	A	2		17	.288
	CHI	A	S-2		105	.243
1967	CHI	A	2		28	.204
	BOS	A	3-S-2		89	.291
1968	BOS	A	S-2/3-1		74	.216
1969	KC	A	*2/S-3		126	.250
1970	KC	A	/2		7	.148
	BRTR				1165	.254

ADAIR, MARION DANNE (BILL)
B.FEB.10,1913 MOBILE,ALA.
NON-PLAYING MANAGER
CHI[A] 1970 [INTERIM]

ADAMS, ACE TOWNSEND
B.MAR.2,1912 WILLOWS,CAL.

1941	NY	N	P		38	4- 1
1942	NY	N	P		61	7- 4
1943	NY	N	P		70	11- 7
1944	NY	N	P		65	8-11
1945	NY	N	P		65	11- 9
1946	NY	N	P		3	0- 1
	BRTR				302	41-33

ADAMS, CHARLES BENJAMIN (BABE)
B.MAY 18,1882 TIPTON,IND.
D.JULY 27,1968 SILVER SPRING,MD

1906	STL	N	P		1	0- 1
1907	PIT	N	P		4	2- 2
1909	PIT	N	P		25	12- 3
1910	PIT	N	P		34	18- 9
1911	PIT	N	P		40	22-12
1912	PIT	N	P		28	11- 8
1913	PIT	N	P		43	21-10
1914	PIT	N	P		40	13-16
1915	PIT	N	P		40	14-14
1916	PIT	N	P		16	2- 9
1918	PIT	N	P		3	1- 1
1919	PIT	N	P		34	17-10
1920	PIT	N	P		35	17-13
1921	PIT	N	P		25	14- 5
1922	PIT	N	P		27	8-11
1923	PIT	N	P		26	13- 7
1924	PIT	N	P		9	3- 1
1925	PIT	N	P		3	6- 5
1926	PIT	N	P		19	2- 3
	BLTR				482	196-140

ADAMS, CHARLES DWIGHT (RED)
B.OCT.7,1921 PARLIER,CAL.

1946	CHI	N	P		8	0- 1
	BRTR					

ADAMS, DANIEL LESLIE
B.JUNE 19,1889 ST.LOUIS,MO.
D.OCT.6,1964 ST.LOUIS,MO.

1914	KC	F	P		36	4- 9
1915	KC	F	P		11	0- 2
	BRTR				47	4-11

ADAMS, EARL JOHN (SPARKY)
B.AUG.26,1894 NEWTOWN,PA.

1922	CHI	N	2		11	.250
1923	CHI	N	S-O		95	.289
1924	CHI	N	2-S		117	.280
1925	CHI	N	2-S		149	.287
1926	CHI	N	2-3		154	.309
1927	CHI	N	2-S-3		146	.292
1928	PIT	N	2-S		135	.276
1929	PIT	N	2-S-3		74	.260
1930	STL	N	2-3		137	.314
1931	STL	N	3		143	.293
1932	STL	N	3		31	.276
1933	STL	N	S-3		8	.167
	CIN	N	S-3		137	.262
1934	CIN	N	2-3		87	.252
	BRTR				1424	.286

ADAMS, ELVIN CLARK (BUSTER)
B.JUNE 24,1915 TRINIDAD,COL.

1939	STL	N	H		2	.000
1943	STL	N	O		8	.091
	PHI	N	O		111	.256
1944	PHI	N	O		151	.283
1945	PHI	N	O		14	.232
	STL	N	O		140	.292
1946	STL	N	O		81	.185
1947	PHI	N	O		69	.247
	BRTR				576	.266

ADAMS, GEORGE
B.GRAFTON,MASS.

1879	SYR	N	1-O		4	.214

ADAMS, GLENN CHARLES
B.OCT.4,1947 NORTHBRIDGE,MASS.

1975	SF	N	O		61	.300
1976	SF	N	/O		69	.243
1977	MIN	A	D-O		95	.338
1978	MIN	A	*D/O		116	.258
	BLTR				341	.291

ADAMS, HAROLD DOUGLAS (DOUG)
B.JAN.27,1943 BLUE RIVER,WIS.

1969	CHI	A	/C		8	.214
	BLTR					

ADAMS, HERBERT LOREN (HERB)
B.APR.14,1928 HOLLYWOOD,CAL.

1948	CHI	A	O		8	.273
1949	CHI	A	O		56	.293
1950	CHI	A	O		34	.203
	BLTL				95	.261

ADAMS, JAMES IRVIN (WILLIE)
B.SEPT.27,1890 CLEARFIELD,PA.
D.JUNE 18,1937 ALBANY,N.Y.

1912	STL	A	P		13	2- 3
1913	STL	A	P		4	0- 1
1914	PIT	F	P		15	1- 1
1918	PHI	A	P		32	5-12
1919	PHI	A	P		1	0- 0
	BRTR				65	8-17

ADAMS, JAMES J.
B.1868 E.ST.LOUIS,ILL.

1890	STL	AA	C		1	.250

ADAMS, JOHN BERTRAM
B.JUNE 21,1891 WHARTON,TEX.
D.JUNE 24,1940 LOS ANGELES,CAL.

1910	CLE	A	C		5	.230
1911	CLE	A	C		2	.250
1912	CLE	A	C		20	.204
1915	PHI	N	C		24	.111
1916	PHI	N	C		11	.231
1917	PHI	N	C		43	.206
1918	PHI	N	C		84	.176
1919	PHI	N	C-1		78	.233
	BBTR				267	.202

ADAMS, JOSEPH EDWARD
B.OCT.28,1877 COWDEN,ILL.
D.OCT.8,1952 MONTGOMERY CITY,MO

1902	STL	N	P		1	0- 0
	TL					

ADAMS, KARL TUTWILER (REBEL)
B.AUG.11,1891 COLUMBUS,GA.
D.SEPT.17,1967 EVERETT,WASH.

1914	CIN	N	P		4	0- 0
1915	CHI	N	P		26	1- 9
	BRTR				30	1- 9

ADAMS, REUBEN ALEXANDER
B.DEC.23,1878 PARIS,TEX.
D.MAR.10,1955 PARIS,TEX.

1905	WAS	A	P		8	2- 6
	BLTL					

ADAMS, RICHARD LEROY
B.APR.8,1920 TUOLOMNE,CAL.

1947	PHI	A	1-O		37	.202
	BRTL					

ADAMS, ROBERT ANDREW
B.JAN.20,1907 BIRMINGHAM,ALA.
D.MAR.6,1970 JACKSONVILLE,FLA.

1931	PHI	N	P		1	0- 1
1932	PHI	N	P		4	0- 0
	BRTR				5	0- 1

ADAMS, ROBERT BURDETTE
B.JULY 24,1901 HOLYOKE,MASS.

1925	BOS	A	P		2	0- 0
	BRTR					

ADAMS, ROBERT HENRY (BOBBY)
B.DEC.14,1921 TUOLUMNE,CAL.

1946	CIN	N	2-3-0		94	.244
1947	CIN	N	2		81	.272
1948	CIN	N	2-3		87	.298
1949	CIN	N	2-3		107	.253
1950	CIN	N	2-3		115	.282
1951	CIN	N	2-3-0		125	.266
1952	CIN	N	3		154	.283
1953	CIN	N	3		150	.275
1954	CIN	N	2-3		110	.269
1955	CIN	N	2-3		64	.273
	CHI	A	2-3		28	.095
1956	BAL	A	2-3		41	.225
1957	CHI	N	2-3		60	.251
1958	CHI	N	1-2-3		62	.281
1959	CHI	N	1		3	.000
	BRTR				1281	.269

ADAMS, ROBERT MELVIN (BOB)
B.JAN.6,1952 PITTSBURGH,PA.

1977	DET	A	/1-C		15	.250
	BRTR					

ADAMS, ROBERT MICHAEL (MIKE)
B.JULY 24,1948 CINCINNATI,OHIO

1972	MIN	A	/O		3	.333
1973	MIN	A	/O		55	.212
1976	CHI	N	/O-3-2		25	.138
1977	CHI	N	/O		2	.000
1978	OAK	A	/2-3		15	.200
	BRTR				100	.195

ADAMS, SPENCER DEWEY
B.JUNE 21,1898 LAYTON,UTAH
D.NOV.24,1970 SALT LAKE CITY,UT

1923	PIT	N	2-S		25	.250
1925	WAS	A	2-S-3		39	.272
1926	NY	A	2		28	.120
1927	STL	A	2-3		88	.256
	BLTR				180	.256

ADAMSON, JOHN MICHAEL (MIKE)
B.SEP.13,1947 SAN DIEGO,CAL.

1967	BAL	A	/P		3	0- 1
1968	BAL	A	/P		2	0- 2
1969	BAL	A	/P		6	0- 1
	BRTR				11	0- 4

YR	CL LEA POS	GP	G	REC

ADCOCK, JOSEPH WILBUR (JOE)
B.OCT.30,1927 COUSHATTA,LA.

1950	CIN N 1-0	102	.293	
1951	CIN N O	113	.243	
1952	CIN N 1-0	117	.278	
1953	MIL N 1	157	.285	
1954	MIL N 1	133	.308	
1955	MIL N 1	84	.264	
1956	MIL N 1	137	.291	
1957	MIL N 1	65	.287	
1958	MIL N 1-0	105	.275	
1959	MIL N 1-0	115	.292	
1960	MIL N 1	138	.298	
1961	MIL N 1	152	.285	
1962	MIL N 1	121	.248	
1963	CLE A 1	97	.251	
1964	LA A 1	118	.268	
1965	CAL A 1	122	.241	
1966	CAL A 1	83	.273	
	BRTR	1959	.277	

NON-PLAYING MANAGER CLE(A) 1967

ADDIS, ROBERT GORDON (BOB)
B.NOV.6,1925 MINERAL,OHIO

1950	BOS N O	16	.250	
1951	BOS N O	85	.276	
1952	CHI N O	93	.295	
1953	CHI N O	10	.167	
	PIT N H	4	.000	
	BLTR	208	.281	

ADDY, ROBERT EDWARD (MAGNET)
B.1838 ROCHESTER,N.Y.
D.APR.10,1910 POCATELLO,IDAHO

1871	ROK NA 2-0	24	-	
1873	PHI NA 2	10	-	
	HAR NA O	31	-	
1874	HAR NA 2-S-3	50	-	
1875	PHI NA 2-0	69	.263	
1876	CHI N O	33	.272	
1877	CIN N M-O	57	.278	
	BLTL	274	-	

ADERHOLT, MORRIS WOODROW
B.SEPT.13,1915 MT.OLIVE,N.C.
D.MAR.18,1955 SARASOTA,FLA.

1939	WAS A 2	7	.200	
1940	WAS A 2	1	.000	
1941	WAS A 2-3	11	.143	
1944	BRO N O	17	.271	
1945	BRO N O	39	.217	
	BOS N 2-0	31	.333	
	BLTR	106	.267	

ADKINS, GRADY EMMETT (BUTCHER BOY)
B.JUNE 29,1897 JACKSONVILLE,ARK
D.MAR.31,1966 LITTLE ROCK,ARK.

1928	CHI A P	36	39	10-16
1929	CHI A P	31	37	2-11
	BRTR	67	76	12-27

ADKINS, JOHN DEWEY
B.MAY 11,1918 NORCATUR,KAN.

1942	WAS A P	1	0- 0	
1943	WAS A P	7	0- 0	
1949	CHI N P	30	2- 4	
	BRTR	38	2- 4	

ADKINS, MERLE THERON (DOC)
B.AUG.5,1872 TROY,WIS.
D.FEB.21,1934 DURHAM,N.C.

1902	BOS A P	4	1- 1	
1903	NY A P	2	0- 1	
	TR	6	1- 2	

ADKINS, RICHARD EARL
B.MAR.3,1920 ELECTRA,TEX.
D.SEPT.12,1955 ELECTRA,TEX.

1942	PHI A S	3	.143	
	BRTR			

ADKINSON, HENRY MAGEE
B.SEPT.1,1874 CHICAGO,ILL.
D.MAY 1,1923 SALT LAKE CITY,UT.

1895	STL N O	1	.400	

ADLESH, DAVID GEORGE (DAVE)
B.JULY 15,1943 LONG BEACH,CAL.

1963	HOU N C	6	.000	
1964	HOU N C	3	.200	
1965	HOU N /C	15	.147	
1966	HOU N /C	3	.000	
1967	HOU N C	39	.181	
1968	HOU N C	40	.183	
	BRTR	106	.168	

AGEE, TOMMIE LEE
B.AUG.9,1942 MAGNOLIA,ALA.

1962	CLE A O	5	.214	
1963	CLE A O	13	.148	
1964	CLE A O	13	.167	
1965	CHI A /O	10	.158	
1966	CHI A *O	160	.273	
1967	CHI A *O	158	.234	
1968	NY N *O	132	.217	
1969	NY N *O	149	.271	
1970	NY N *O	153	.286	
1971	NY N *O	113	.285	
1972	NY N *O	114	.227	
1973	HOU N O	83	.235	
1973	STL N O	26	.177	
	BRTR	1129	.255	

AGGANIS, HARRY (GREEK)
B.APR.30,1930 LYNN,MASS.
D.JUNE 27,1955 CAMBRIDGE,MASS.

1954	BOS A 1	132	.251	
1955	BOS A 1	25	.313	
	BLTL	157	.261	

AGLER, JOSEPH ABRAM
B.JUNE 12,1887 COSHOCTON,OHIO
D.APR.26,1971 MASSILLON,OHIO

1912	WAS A 1	2	.000	
1914	BUF F 1-0	135	.272	
1915	BUF F 1	25	.178	
	BAL F 1-2	70	.214	
	BLTL	232	.246	

AGNEW, SAMUEL LESTER (SLAM)
B.APR.12,1887 FARMINGTON,MO.
D.JULY 19,1951 SONOMA,CAL.

1913	STL A C	104	.208	
1914	STL A C	113	.212	
1915	STL A C	104	.203	
1916	BOS A C	40	.209	
1917	BOS A C	85	.208	
1918	BOS A C	72	.166	
1919	WAS A C	42	.235	
	BRTR	560	.204	

AGUILERA, SILVIO ANTONIO [CHEVEZ]
[PLAYED UNDER NAME OF SILVIO ANTONIO CHEVEZ]

AGUIRRE, HENRY JOHN (HANK)
B.JAN.31,1932 AZUSA,CAL.

1955	CLE A P	4	2- 0	
1956	CLE A P	16	3- 5	
1957	CLE A P	10	1- 1	
1958	DET A P	44	3- 4	
1959	DET A P	3	0- 0	
1960	DET A P	37	5- 3	
1961	DET A P	45	4- 4	
1962	DET A P	42	16- 8	
1963	DET A P	38	14-15	
1964	DET A P	32	5-10	
1965	DET A P	32	14-10	
1966	DET A P	30	3- 9	
1967	DET A P	31	0- 1	
1968	LA N P	25	1- 2	
1969	CHI N P	41	1- 0	
1970	CHI N P	17	3- 0	
	BBTL	447	75-72	
	BR 1955-64			

AHEARN, CHARLES
B.TROY,N.Y.

1880	TRO N C	1	.250	

AIKENS, WILLIE MAYS
B.OCT.14,1954 SENECA,S.C.

1977	CAL A 1-0	42	.198	
	BLTR			

AINSMITH, EDWARD WILBUR (DORF)
B.FEB.4,1892 CAMBRIDGE,MASS.

1910	WAS A C	33	.192	
1911	WAS A C	61	.222	
1912	WAS A C	60	.226	
1913	WAS A C	77	.210	
1914	WAS A C	58	.225	
1915	WAS A C	47	.200	
1916	WAS A C	51	.170	
1917	WAS A C	125	.191	
1918	WAS A C	96	.212	
1919	DET A C	114	.272	
1920	DET A C	69	.231	
1921	DET A C	35	.276	
	STL N C	27	.290	
1922	STL N C	119	.293	
1923	STL N C	82	.213	
	BRO N C	2	.200	
1924	NY N C	10	.600	
	BRTR	1066	.232	

AITCHISON, RALEIGH LEONIDAS
B.DEC.5,1887 TYNDALL,S.D.
D.SEPT.26,1958 COLUMBUS,KAN.

1911	BRO N P	1	0- 1	
1914	BRO N P	26	12- 7	
1915	BRO N P	7	0- 4	
	BRTL	34	12-12	

AITON, GEORGE WILSON
B.DEC.29,1890 KINGMAN,KAN.
D.AUG.16,1976 VAN NUYS,CAL.

1912	STL A O	10	.235	
	BBTR			

AKE, JOHN LECKIE
B.AUG.29,1861 ALTOONA,PA.
D.MAY 11,1887 LA CROSSE,WIS.

1884	BAL AA S-3-0	13	.208	

AKER, JACKIE DELANE (JACK)
B.JULY 13,1940 TULARE,CAL.

1964	KC A P	9	10	0- 1
1965	KC A P	34	4- 3	
1966	KC A P	66	8- 4	
1967	KC A P	57	3- 8	
1968	OAK A P	54	4- 4	
1969	SEA A P	15	0- 2	
	NY A P	38	8- 4	
1970	NY A P	41	4- 2	
1971	NY A P	41	4- 4	
1972	NY A P	4	0- 0	
	CHI N P	48	6- 6	
1973	CHI N P	47	4- 5	
1974	ATL N P	17	0- 1	
	NY N P	24	2- 1	
	BRTR	495	496	47-45

AKERS, ALBERT EARL
B.NOV.1,1887 SHELBYVILLE,IND.

1912	WAS A P	5	0- 0	
	BRTR			

AKERS, WILLIAM G. (BILL) OR (BUMP)
B.DEC.25,1904 CHATTANOOGA,TENN.
D.APR.13,1962 CHATTANOOGA,TENN.

1929	DET A S	24	.265	
1930	DET A S-3	85	.278	
1931	DET A S	29	.197	
1932	BOS N 3	36	.258	
	BRTR	174	.261	

ALBANESE, JOSEPH PETER (JOE)
B.JUNE 26,1933 NEW YORK,N.Y.

1958	WAS A P	6	0- 0	
	BRTR			

ALBERTS, AUGUSTUS PETER
B.1861 READING,PA.
D.MAY 7,1912 IDAHO SPRINGS,COLO

1884	PIT AA S	2	.200	
	WAS U S	4	.250	
1888	CLE AA S-3	101	.192	
1891	MIL A 3	12	.100	
	BRTR	119	.186	

ALBERTS, FRANCIS BURT (BUTCH)
B.MAY 4,1950 WILLIAMSPORT,PA.

1978	TOR A /H	6	.278	
	BRTR			

ALBERTS, FREDERICK JOSEPH (CY)
B.JAN.14,1882 GRAND RAPIDS,MICH
D.AUG.27,1917 FORT WAYNE,IND.

1910	STL N P	4	1- 2	

ALBERTS, JAMES
[PLAYED UNDER NAME OF ALVIN JAMES DOLAN]

ALBOSTA, EDWARD JOHN (RUBE)
B.OCT.27,1918 SAGINAW,MICH.

1941	BRO N P	2	0- 2	
1946	PIT N P	17	0- 6	
	BRTR	19	0- 8	

ALBRECHT, EDWARD ARTHUR
B.FEB.28,1929 ST. LOUIS CO.,MO.

1949	STL A P	1	1- 0	
1950	STL A P	2	0- 1	
	BRTR	3	1- 1	

ALBRIGHT, HAROLD JOHN (JACK)
B.JUNE 30,1921 ST.PETERSBURG,FL

1947	PHI N S	41	.232	

ALBURY, VICTOR (VIC)
B.MAY 12,1947 KEY WEST,FLA.

1973	MIN A P	14	1- 0	
1974	MIN A P	32	8- 9	
1975	MIN A P	32	6- 7	
1976	MIN A P	23	3- 1	
	BLTL	101	102	18-17

ALCALA, SANTO
[REAL NAME SANTO ANIBAL [ALCALA]]
B.DEC.23,1952 SAN PEDRO DE MACORIS,D.R.

1976	CIN N P	30	11- 4	
1977	CIN N /P	7	1- 1	
	MON N P	31	2- 6	
	BRTR	68	14-11	

YR	CL LEA POS	GP	G	REC

ALCARAZ, ANGEL LUIS [ACOSTA] (LUIS)
B.JUNE 20,1941 HUMACAO,P.R.
1967	LA N 2		17	.233
1968	LA N 2-3/S		41	.151
1969	KC A 2/3-S		22	.253
1970	KC A 2		35	.167
	BRTR		115	.192

ALCOCK, JOHN FORBES (SCOTTY)
B.NOV.29,1885 WOOSTER,OHIO
D.JAN.30,1973 WOOSTER,OHIO
| 1914 | CHI A 3 | | 54 | .173 |
| | BRTR | | | |

ALDERSON, DALE LEONARD
B.MAR.8,1918 BELDEN,NEB.
1943	CHI N P		4	0- 1
1944	CHI N P		12	0- 0
	BRTR		16	0- 1

ALDRIDGE, VICTOR EDDINGTON
B.OCT.25,1893 INDIAN SPRGS.,IND
D.APR.17,1973 TERRE HAUTE,IND.
1917	CHI N P		30	6- 6
1918	CHI N P		3	0- 1
1922	CHI N P		36	16-15
1923	CHI N P		30	16- 9
1924	CHI N P		32	15-12
1925	PIT N P		30	15- 7
1926	PIT N P		30	10-13
1927	PIT N P		35	15-10
1928	NY N P		22	4- 7
	BRTR		248	97-80

ALENO, CHARLES (CHUCK)
B.FEB.19,1917 ST.LOUIS,MO.
1941	CIN N 1-3		54	.243
1942	CIN N 2-3		7	.143
1943	CIN N O		7	.300
1944	CIN N 1-S-3		50	.165
	BRTR		118	.209

ALEXANDER, DAVID DALE (MOOSE)
B.APR.26,1903 GREENVILLE,TENN.
1929	DET A 1		155	.343
1930	DET A 1		154	.326
1931	DET A 1		135	.325
1932	DET A 1		23	.250
	BOS A 1		101	.372
1933	BOS A 1		94	.281
	BRTR		662	.331

ALEXANDER, DOYLE LAFAYETTE
B.SEP.4,1950 CORDOVA,ALA.
1971	LA N P		17	6- 6
1972	BAL A P		35	6- 8
1973	BAL A P		29	12- 8
1974	BAL A P		30	6- 9
1975	BAL A P		32	8- 8
1976	BAL A P		11	3- 4
	NY A P		19	10- 5
1977	TEX A P		34	17-11
1978	TEX A P		31	9-10
	BRTR		238	77-69

ALEXANDER, GARY WAYNE
B.MAR.27,1953 LOS ANGELES,CAL.
1975	SF N /C		3	.000
1976	SF N C		23	.178
1977	SF N C/O		51	.303
1978	OAK A D/O-C-1		58	.207
	CLE A C-D		90	.235
	BRTR		225	.232

ALEXANDER, GROVER CLEVELAND (PETE)
B.FEB.26,1887 ELBA,NEB.
D.NOV.4,1950 ST.PAUL,NEB.
1911	PHI N P		48	28-13
1912	PHI N P		46	19-17
1913	PHI N P		47	22- 8
1914	PHI N P	46	48	27-15
1915	PHI N P		49	31-10
1916	PHI N P	48	49	33-12
1917	PHI N P	45	47	30-13
1918	CHI N P		3	2- 1
1919	CHI N P		30	16-11
1920	CHI N P		46	27-14
1921	CHI N P		31	15-13
1922	CHI N P		33	16-13
1923	CHI N P		39	22-12
1924	CHI N P		21	12- 5
1925	CHI N P		32	15-11
1926	CHI N P		7	3- 3
	STL N P		23	9- 7
1927	STL N P		37	21-10
1928	STL N P		34	16- 9
1929	STL N P		22	9- 8
1930	PHI N P		9	0- 3
	BRTR	696	701	373-208

ALEXANDER, HUGH
B.JULY 10,1917 BUFFALO,MO.
| 1937 | CLE A P | | 7 | .091 |
| | BRTR | | | |

ALEXANDER, MATTHEW (MATT)
B.JAN.30,1947 SHREVEPORT,LA.
1973	CHI N /O		12	.200
1974	CHI N 3/O-2		45	.204
1975	OAK A R-D-O/2-3		63	.100
1976	OAK A O-R		61	.033
1977	OAK A O-S-O/2-3		90	.238
1978	PIT N R		7	.000
	BBTR		278	.170

ALEXANDER, ROBERT SOMERVILLE
B.AUG.7,1922 VANCOUVER,B.C.,CAN
1955	BAL A P		4	1- 0
1957	CLE A P		5	0- 1
	BRTR		9	1- 1

ALEXANDER, WALTER ERNEST
B.MAR.5,1891 ATLANTA,GA.
1912	STL A C		37	.175
1913	STL A C		42	.141
1915	STL A C		1	.000
	NY A C		25	.250
1916	NY A C		36	.256
1917	NY A C		20	.137
	BRTR		161	.189

ALEXANDER, WILLIAM HENRY (NIN)
B.NOV.24,1858 PANA,ILL.
D.DEC.22,1933 PANA,ILL.
1884	KC U C-S-O		19	.127
	STL AA C-O		1	.000
			20	.119

ALLEN, ARTEMUS WARD (NICK)
B.SEPT.14,1888 NORTON,KAN.
D.OCT.16,1939 HINES,ILL.
1914	BUF F C		31	.235
1915	BUF F C		83	.205
1916	CHI N C		5	.063
1918	CHI N C		37	.260
1919	CIN N C		15	.320
1920	CIN N C		43	.271
	BRTR		214	.231

ALLEN, BERNARD KEITH (BERNIE)
B.APR.16,1939 E. LIVERPOOL,O.
1962	MIN A 2		159	.269
1963	MIN A 2		139	.240
1964	MIN A 2		74	.214
1965	MIN A 2/3		19	.231
1966	MIN A 2/3		101	.238
1967	WAS A 2		87	.193
1968	WAS A *2/3		120	.241
1969	WAS A *2/3		122	.247
1970	WAS A 2-3		104	.234
1971	WAS A 2-3		97	.266
1972	NY A 3-2		84	.227
1973	NY A 2		17	.228
	MON N /2-3		16	.180
	BLTR		1139	.239

ALLEN, CYRUS ALBAN (JACK)
B.OCT.2,1855 WOODSTOCK,ILL.
D.APR.21,1915 GIRARD,PA.
1879	SYR N 3-O		11	.184
	CLE N 3-O		16	.117
			27	.165

ALLEN, ETHAN NATHAN
B.JAN.1,1904 CINCINNATI,OHIO
1926	CIN N O		18	.308
1927	CIN N O		111	.295
1928	CIN N O		129	.305
1929	CIN N O		143	.292
1930	CIN N O		21	.271
	NY N O		76	.307
1931	NY N O		94	.329
1932	NY N O		54	.175
1933	STL N O		91	.241
1934	PHI N O		145	.330
1935	PHI N O		156	.307
1936	PHI N O		30	.296
	CHI N O		91	.295
1937	STL A O		103	.316
1938	STL A O		19	.303
	BRTR		1281	.300

ALLEN, FLETCHER MANSON (SLED)
B.AUG.23,1886 WEST PLAINS,MO.
D.OCT.16,1959 LUBBOCK,TEX.
| 1910 | STL A C | | 14 | .095 |
| | TR | | | |

ALLEN, FRANK LEON
B.AUG.26,1889 NEWBERN,ALA.
D.JULY 30,1933 GAINESVILLE,ALA.
1912	BRO N P		20	3- 9
1913	BRO N P		34	4-18
1914	BRO N P	36	37	8-14
	PIT F P		1	1- 0
1915	PIT F P		41	23-13
1916	BOS N P		19	8- 2
1917	BOS N P		29	3-11
	BRTL	180	181	50-67

ALLEN, HAROLD ANDREW (HANK)
B.JULY 23,1940 WAMPUM,PA.
1966	WAS A /O		9	.387
1967	WAS A O		116	.233
1968	WAS A O-3-2		68	.219
1969	WAS A O/3-2		109	.277
1970	WAS A O		22	.211
	MIL A O/2-1		28	.236
1972	CHI A /3		9	.143
1973	CHI A /3-1-O-C-2		28	.103
	BRTR		389	.241

ALLEN, HEZEKIAH (HAM)
B.1862 NORWALK,CONN.
1872	MAN NA S-O		16	.169
1884	PHI N C		1	.667
			17	.189

ALLEN, HORACE TANNER (PUG)
B.JUNE 11,1899 DELAND,FLA.
| 1919 | BRO N O | | 4 | .000 |
| | BLTR | | | |

ALLEN, JESSE HALL (PETE)
B.APR.1,1868 COLUMBIANA,OHIO
D.APR.16,1946 PHILADELPHIA,PA.
| 1893 | CLE N C | | 1 | .000 |
| | BRTR | | | |

ALLEN, JOHN MARSHALL
B.OCT.27,189C BERKELEY SPRINGS,W.VA.
D.SEPT.24,1967 HAGERSTOWN,MD.
| 1914 | BAL F P | | 1 | 0- 0 |
| | BRTR | | | |

ALLEN, JOHN THOMAS
B.SEPT.30,1905 LENOIR,N.C.
D.MAR.29,1959 ST.PETERSBURG,FLA
1932	NY A P		33	17- 4
1933	NY A P		25	15- 7
1934	NY A P		13	5- 2
1935	NY A P		23	13- 6
1936	CLE A P	36	37	20-10
1937	CLE A P		24	15- 1
1938	CLE A P		30	14- 8
1939	CLE A P	28	34	9- 7
1940	CLE A P		32	9- 8
1941	STL A P		20	2- 5
	BRO N P		11	3- 0
1942	BRO N P		27	10- 6
1943	BRO N P		17	5- 1
	NY N P		15	1- 3
1944	NY N P	18	24	4- 7
	BRTR	352	365	142-75

ALLEN, LLOYD CECIL
B.MAY 8,1950 MERCED,CAL.
1969	CAL A /P		4	0- 1
1970	CAL A /P		8	1- 1
1971	CAL A P		54	4- 6
1972	CAL A P		42	3- 7
1973	CAL A /P		5	0- 0
	TEX A P		23	0- 6
1974	TEX A P		14	0- 1
	CHI A /P		6	0- 1
1975	CHI A /P		3	0- 2
	BRTR		159	8-25

ALLEN, MYRON SMITH (ZEKE)
B.MAR.22,1854 KINGSTON,N.Y.
D.MAR.8,1924 KINGSTON,N.Y.
1883	NY N P		1	0- 1
1886	BOS N 1		2	.000
1887	CLE AA O		117	.330
1888	KC AA O		37	.215
		1	157	0- 1
				.304

ALLEN, RICHARD ANTHONY (DICK)
B.MAR.8,1942 WAMPUM,PA.
1963	PHI N 3-O		10	.292
1964	PHI N 3		162	.316
1965	PHI N *3/S		161	.302
1966	PHI N 3-O		141	.317
1967	PHI N *3/2-S		122	.307
1968	PHI N *O-3		152	.263
1969	PHI N *1		118	.288
1970	STL N 1-3/O		122	.279
1971	LA N 3-O-1		155	.295
1972	CHI A *1/3		148	.308
1973	CHI A 1/2		72	.316
1974	CHI A *1/2		128	.301
1975	PHI N *1		119	.233
1976	PHI N 1		85	.268
1977	OAK A 1		54	.240
	BRTR		1749	.292

ALLEN, ROBERT
B.1896
| 1919 | PHI A O | | 11 | .094 |
| | BRTR | | | |

ALLEN, ROBERT EARL (THIN MAN)
B.JULY 2,1914 SMITHVILLE,TENN.
| 1937 | PHI N P | | 3 | 0- 1 |
| | BRTR | | | |

YR	CL	LEA	POS	GP	G	REC

ALLEN, ROBERT GILMAN
B.JULY 10,1867 MARION,OHIO
D.MAY 14,1943 LITTLE ROCK,ARK.

YR	CL	LEA	POS	G	REC
1890	PHI	N	S	133	.225
1891	PHI	N	S	117	.227
1892	PHI	N	S	148	.229
1893	PHI	N	S	123	.283
1894	PHI	N	S	40	.233
1897	BOS	N	S	33	.309
1900	CIN	N	M-S	5	.179
	BRTR			599	.246

ALLEN, ROBERT GRAY (BOB)
B.OCT.23,1937 TATUM,TEX.

YR	CL	LEA	POS	G	REC
1961	CLE	A	P	48	3- 2
1962	CLE	A	P	30	1- 1
1963	CLE	A	P	43	1- 2
1966	CLE	A	P	36	2- 2
1967	CLE	A	P	47	0- 5
	BLTL			204	7-12

ALLEN, RONALD FREDRICK (RON)
B.DEC.23,1943 WAMPUM,PA.

YR	CL	LEA	POS	G	REC
1972	STL	N	/1	7	.091
	BBTR				

ALLEY, LEONARD EUGENE (GENE)
B.JULY 10,1940 RICHMOND,VA.

YR	CL	LEA	POS	G	REC
1963	PIT	N	2-S-3	17	.216
1964	PIT	N	2-S-3	81	.211
1965	PIT	N	*S-2/3	153	.252
1966	PIT	N	*S	147	.299
1967	PIT	N	*S	152	.287
1968	PIT	N	*S-2	133	.245
1969	PIT	N	2-S/3	82	.246
1970	PIT	N	*S/2-3	121	.244
1971	PIT	N	*S/3	114	.227
1972	PIT	N	S/3	119	.248
1973	PIT	N	S/3	76	.203
	BRTR			1195	.254

ALLIE, GAIR ROOSEVELT
B.OCT.26,1931 STATESVILLE,N.C.

YR	CL	LEA	POS	G	REC
1954	PIT	N	S-3	121	.199
	BRTR				

ALLIETTA, ROBERT GEORGE (BOB)
B.MAY 14,1952 NEW BEDFORD,MASS.

YR	CL	LEA	POS	G	REC
1975	CAL	A	C	21	.178
	BRTR				

ALLISON, ANDREW K.
B.1848 NEW YORK,N.Y.

YR	CL	LEA	POS	G	REC
1872	ECK	NA	1-0	25	.140

ALLISON, ARTHUR ALGERNON
B.JAN.29,1849 PHILADELPHIA,PA.
D.FEB.25,1916 WASHINGTON,D.C.

YR	CL	LEA	POS	G	REC
1871	CLE	NA	O	29	-
1872	CLE	NA	O	18	.261
1873	RES	NA	C-1-0	22	-
1875	NAT	NA	C-1-0	25	-
	HAR	NA	2-0	35	-
1876	LOU	N	1-0	31	.205
				160	-

ALLISON, DOUGLAS (DOUG)
B.1846 PHILADELPHIA,PA.
D.DEC.19,1916 WASHINGTON,D.C.

YR	CL	LEA	POS	G	REC
1871	OLY	NA	C	27	-
1872	TRO	NA	C-S	23	.319
	ECK	NA	C	18	.299
1873	RES	NA	C	17	-
	MUT	NA	C	11	-
1874	MUT	NA	C-0	65	-
1875	HAR	NA	C-1	60	-
1876	HAR	N	C	43	.256
1877	HAR	N	C	29	.148
1878	PRO	N	C	18	.267
1879	PRO	N	C	1	.000
1883	BAL	AA	C	1	.500
	BRTR			313	-

ALLISON, MACK PENDLETON
B.JAN.23,1887 OWENSBORO,KY.
D.MAR.13,1964 ST.JOSEPH,MO.

YR	CL	LEA	POS	G	REC
1911	STL	A	P	3	2- 1
1912	STL	A	P	31	6-17
1913	STL	A	P	11	1- 2
	BRTR			45	9-20

ALLISON, MILO HENRY
B.OCT.16,1890 ELK RAPIDS,MICH.
D.JUNE 18,1957 KENOSHA,WIS.

YR	CL	LEA	POS	G	REC
1913	CHI	N	O	2	.333
1914	CHI	N	O	1	1.000
1916	CLE	A	O	14	.263
1917	CLE	A	O	32	.143
	BLTR			49	.213

ALLISON, WILLIAM ANDREW
B.SEPT.18,1848 PHILADELPHIA,PA.
D.JUNE 12,1923

YR	CL	LEA	POS	G	REC
1872	ECK	NA	2-0	3	.182

ALLISON, WILLIAM ROBERT (BOB)
B.JULY 11,1934 RAYTOWN,MO.

YR	CL	LEA	POS	G	REC
1958	WAS	A	O	11	.200
1959	WAS	A	O	130	.261
1960	WAS	A	1-0	144	.251
1961	MIN	A	1-0	159	.245
1962	MIN	A	O	149	.266
1963	MIN	A	O	148	.271
1964	MIN	A	1-0	149	.287
1965	MIN	A	*0/1	135	.233
1966	MIN	A	O	70	.220
1967	MIN	A	*0	153	.258
1968	MIN	A	*0-1	145	.247
1969	MIN	A	0/1	81	.228
1970	MIN	A	0/1	47	.208
	BRTR			1541	.255

ALMADA, MELO BALDOMERO (MEL)
B.FEB.7,1913 HWATABAMPO,SONORA,
MEXICO

YR	CL	LEA	POS	G	REC
1933	BOS	A	O	14	.341
1934	BOS	A	O	23	.233
1935	BOS	A	1-0	151	.290
1936	BOS	A	O	96	.253
1937	BOS	A	O	32	.236
	WAS	A	O	100	.309
1938	WAS	A	O	47	.244
	STL	A	O	102	.342
1939	STL	A	O	42	.239
	BRO	N	O	39	.214
	BLTL			646	.284

ALMEIDA, RAFAEL D. (MIKE)
B.JULY 30,1887 HAVANA,CUBA
D.MAR.1,1968 HAVANA,CUBA

YR	CL	LEA	POS	G	REC
1911	CIN	N	3	29	.313
1912	CIN	N	3	16	.220
1913	CIN	N	3	50	.262
	BRTR			95	.270

ALMON, WILLIAM FRANCIS (BILL)
B.NOV.21,1952 PROVIDENCE,R.I.

YR	CL	LEA	POS	G	REC
1974	SD	N	S	16	.316
1975	SD	N	/S	6	.400
1976	SD	N	S	14	.246
1977	SD	N	*S	155	.261
1978	SD	N	*3-S/2	138	.252
	BRTR			329	.260

ALOMA, LUIS [BARBA] (WITTO)
B.JULY 23,1923 HAVANA, CUBA

YR	CL	LEA	POS	G	REC
1950	CHI	A	P	42	7- 2
1951	CHI	A	P	25	6- 0
1952	CHI	A	P	25	3- 1
1953	CHI	A	P	24	2- 0
	BRTR			116	18- 3

ALOMAR, SANTOS [CONDE] (SANDY)
B.OCT.19,1943 SALINAS,P.R.

YR	CL	LEA	POS	G	REC
1964	MIL	N	S	19	.245
1965	MIL	N	S-2	67	.241
1966	ATL	N	2/S	31	.091
1967	NY	N	S/3-2	15	.000
	CHI	A	/S-2	12	.200
1968	CHI	A	2-3/S-0	133	.253
1969	CHI	A	2	22	.224
	CAL	A	*2	134	.250
1970	CAL	A	*2-S/3	162	.251
1971	CAL	A	*2-S	162	.260
1972	CAL	A	*2/S	155	.239
1973	CAL	A	*2-S	136	.238
1974	CAL	A	S-2/3-0	46	.222
	NY	A	2	76	.269
1975	NY	A	*2/S	151	.239
1976	NY	A	2/S-3-1-0	67	.239
1977	TEX	A	0-2/S-0-1-3	69	.265
1978	TEX	A	/1-2-3-S	24	.207
	BRTR			1481	.245
	BR 1964 (PART),65-66				

ALOU, FELIPE ROJAS
[REAL NAME FELIPE ROJAS (ALOU)]
B.MAY 12,1935 HAINA,D.R.

YR	CL	LEA	POS	G	REC
1958	SF	N	O	75	.253
1959	SF	N	O	95	.275
1960	SF	N	O	106	.264
1961	SF	N	O	132	.289
1962	SF	N	O	154	.316
1963	SF	N	O	157	.281
1964	MIL	N	1-0	121	.253
1965	MIL	N	1-0/3-S	143	.297
1966	ATL	N	1-0/3-S	154	.327
1967	ATL	N	1-0	140	.274
1968	ATL	N	*0	160	.317
1969	ATL	N	*0	123	.282
1970	OAK	A	*0/1	154	.271
1971	OAK	A	/O	2	.250
	NY	A	0-1	131	.289
1972	NY	A	1-0	120	.278
1973	NY	A	1-0	93	.236
	MON	N	0/1	19	.208
1974	MIL	A	/O	3	.000
	BRTR			2082	.286

ALOU, JESUS MARIA ROJAS
[REAL NAME
JESUS MARIA ROJAS (ALOU)]
B.MAR.24,1942 HAINA,D.R.

YR	CL	LEA	POS	G	REC
1963	SF	N	O	16	.250
1964	SF	N	O	115	.274
1965	SF	N	*0	143	.298
1966	SF	N	*0	110	.259
1967	SF	N	*0	129	.292
1968	SF	N	*0	120	.263
1969	HOU	N	*0	115	.248
1970	HOU	N	*0	117	.306
1971	HOU	N	*0	122	.279
1972	HOU	N	O	52	.312
1973	HOU	N	O	28	.236
	OAK	A	O	36	.306
1974	OAK	A	D-0	96	.268
1975	NY	N	O	62	.265
1978	HOU	N	O	77	.324
	BRTR			1338	.280

ALOU, MATEO ROJAS (MATTY)
[REAL NAME MATEO ROJAS (ALOU)]
B.DEC.22,1938 HAINA,D.R.

YR	CL	LEA	POS	GP	G	REC
1960	SF	N	O		4	.333
1961	SF	N	O		81	.310
1962	SF	N	O		78	.292
1963	SF	N	O		63	.145
1964	SF	N	O		110	.264
1965	SF	N	*0/P	1	117	0- 0
						.231
1966	PIT	N	*0		141	.342
1967	PIT	N	*0/1		139	.338
1968	PIT	N	*0		146	.332
1969	PIT	N	*0		162	.331
1970	PIT	N	*0		155	.297
1971	STL	N	0-1		149	.315
1972	STL	N	1-0		108	.314
	OAK	A	0/1		32	.281
1973	NY	A	0-1		123	.296
	STL	N	/1-0		11	.273
1974	SD	N	0/1		48	.198
	BLTL			1	1667	0- 0
						.307

ALPERMAN, CHARLES AUGUSTUS (WHITEY)
B.NOV.11,1879 ETNA,PA.
D.DEC.25,1942 PITTSBURGH,PA.

YR	CL	LEA	POS	G	REC
1906	BRO	N	2-S	127	.252
1907	BRO	N	2	138	.233
1908	BRO	N	2	57	.197
1909	BRO	N	2	108	.248
	BRTR			430	.237

ALSTON, WENDELL (DELL)
B.SEPT.22,1952 VALHALLA,N.Y.

YR	CL	LEA	POS	G	REC
1977	NY	A	O	22	.325
1978	NY	A	/H	3	.000
	OAK	A	0/1	58	.208
	BLTR			83	.227

ALSTON, THOMAS EDISON (TOM)
B.JAN.31,1931 GREENSBORO,N.C.

YR	CL	LEA	POS	G	REC
1954	STL	N	1	66	.246
1955	STL	N	1	13	.125
1956	STL	N	1	3	.000
1957	STL	N	1	9	.294
	BRTR			91	.244

ALSTON, WALTER EMMONS (SMOKEY)
B.DEC.1,1911 VENICE,OHIO

YR	CL	LEA	POS	G	REC
1936	STL	N	1	1	.000
	BRTR				

NON-PLAYING MANAGER
BRO[N] 1954-57, LA[N] 1958-76

ALTEN, ERNEST MATTHIAS (LEFTY)
B.DEC.1,1894 AVON,OHIO

YR	CL	LEA	POS	G	REC
1920	DET	A	P	14	0- 1
	BRTL				

ALTENBURG, JESSE HOWARD
B.JAN.2,1893 ASHLEY,MICH.
D.MAR.12,1973 LANSING,MICH.

YR	CL	LEA	POS	G	REC
1916	PIT	N	O	8	.429
1917	PIT	N	O	11	.176
	BLTR			19	.290

ALTIZER, DAVID TILDEN (FILIPINO)
B.NOV.6,1876 PEARL,ILL.
D.MAY 14,1964 PLEASANT HILL,ILL

YR	CL	LEA	POS	G	REC
1906	WAS	A	S	115	.256
1907	WAS	A	1-S-0	147	.269
1908	WAS	A	O	66	.218
	CLE	A	S-0	30	.227
1909	CHI	A	S-0	116	.233
1910	CIN	N	S	3	.600
1911	CIN	N	S	26	.227
	BLTR			503	.250

ALTMAN, GEORGE LEE
B.MAR.20,1933 GOLDSBORO,N.C.

YR	CL	LEA	POS	GP	G	REC
1959	CHI	N	O		135	.245
1960	CHI	N	1-O		119	.266
1961	CHI	N	1-O		138	.303
1962	CHI	N	1-O		147	.318
1963	STL	N	O		135	.274
1964	NY	N	O		124	.230
1965	CHI	N	O/1		90	.235
1966	CHI	N	O/1		88	.222
1967	CHI	N	/O-1		15	.111
		BLTR			991	.269

ALTOBELLI, JOSEPH (JOE)
B.MAY 26,1932 DETROIT,MICH.

1955	CLE	A	1		42	.200
1957	CLE	A	1-O		83	.207
1961	MIN	A	1-O		41	.221
		BLTL			166	.210

NON-PLAYING MANAGER SF[N] 1977-78

ALTROCK, NICHOLAS (NICK)
B.SEPT.15,1876 CINCINNATI,OHIO
D.JAN.20,1965 WASHINGTON,D.C.

1898	LOU	N	P		11	3- 4
1902	BOS	A	P		3	1- 2
1903	BOS	A	P		3	0- 3
	CHI	A	P		11	4- 2
1904	CHI	A	P		38	21-13
1905	CHI	A	P	40	41	21-10
1906	CHI	A	P		38	20-13
1907	CHI	A	P		30	8-12
1908	CHI	A	P		23	3- 7
1909	CHI	A	P		5	1- 4
	WAS	A	P-O	9	12	1- 3
						.350
1912	WAS	A	P		1	0- 0
1913	WAS	A	P		4	0- 0
1914	WAS	A	P		1	0- 0
1915	WAS	A	P		1	0- 0
1918	WAS	A	P		6	1- 2
1919	WAS	A	P		1	0- 0
1924	WAS	A	P		1	0- 0
1929	WAS	A	O		1	1.000
1931	WAS	A	H		1	.000
1933	WAS	A	H		1	.000
		BBTL		226	233	84-75
						.178

ALUSIK, GEORGE JOSEPH
B.FEB.11,1935 ASHLEY,PA.

1958	DET	A	O		2	.000
1961	DET	A	O		15	.143
1962	DET	A	H		2	.000
	KC	A	1-O		90	.273
1963	KC	A	O		87	.267
1964	KC	A	1-O		102	.240
		BRTR			298	.256

ALVARADO, LUIS CESAR [MARTINEZ]
B.JAN.15,1949 LA JAS,P.R.

1968	BOS	A	S		11	.100
1969	BOS	A	/S		6	.000
1970	BOS	A	3-S		59	.224
1971	CHI	A	S-2		99	.216
1972	CHI	A	S-2/3		103	.213
1973	CHI	A	S-2-3		80	.232
1974	CHI	A	/S-2-3		8	.100
	STL	N	S		17	.130
	CLE	A	2/S		61	.219
1976	DET	N	2		16	.286
1977	NY	N	/2		1	.000
	DET	A	/3		2	.000
		BRTR			463	.214

ALVAREZ, JESUS MANUEL ORLANDO [MONGE] (ORLANDO)
B.FEB.28,1952 RIO GRANDE,P.R.

1973	LA	N	/H		2	.250
1974	LA	N	/O		2	.000
1975	LA	N	/H		4	.000
1976	CAL	A	O		15	.167
		BRTR			25	.157

ALVAREZ, OSWALDO [GONZALEZ]
B.OCT.19,1933 MATANZAS,CUBA

1958	WAS	A	2-S-3		87	.209
1959	DET	A	H		8	.500
		BRTR			95	.212

ALVAREZ, ROGELIO [FERNANDEZ]
B.APR.18,1938 PINAR DEL RIO,CUBA

1960	CIN	N	1		3	.111
1962	CIN	N	1		14	.214
		BRTR			17	.189

ALVIS, ROY MAXWELL (MAX)
B.FEB.2,1938 JASPER,TEX.

1962	CLE	A	3		12	.216
1963	CLE	A	3		158	.274
1964	CLE	A	3		107	.252
1965	CLE	A	*3		159	.247
1966	CLE	A	*3		157	.245
1967	CLE	A	*3		161	.256
1968	CLE	A	*3		131	.223
1969	CLE	A	3/S		66	.225
1970	MIL	A	3		62	.183
		BRTR			1013	.247

ALVORD, WILLIAM C. (UNCLE BILL)
B.ST.LOUIS,MO.

1885	STL	N	3		2	.000
1889	KC	AA	3		50	.221
1890	TOL	AA	3		120	.283
1891	CLE	N	3		13	.282
	WAS	AA	3		81	.235
1893	CLE	N	3		3	.250
					269	.256

ALYEA, GARRABRANT RYERSON (BRANT)
B.DEC.8,1940 PASSAIC,N.J.

1965	WAS	A	/1-O		8	.231
1968	WAS	A	O		53	.267
1969	WAS	A	O/1		104	.249
1970	MIN	A	O		94	.291
1971	MIN	A	O		79	.177
1972	OAK	A	/O		20	.194
	STL	N	/O		13	.158
		BRTR			371	.247

AMALFITANO, JOHN JOSEPH (JOEY)
B.JAN.23,1934 SAN PEDRO,CAL.

1954	NY	N	2-3		9	.000
1955	NY	N	S-3		36	.227
1960	SF	N	2-S-3-O		106	.277
1961	SF	N	2-3		109	.255
1962	HOU	N	2-3		117	.237
1963	SF	N	2-3		54	.175
1964	CHI	N	1-2-S		100	.241
1965	CHI	N	2/S		67	.271
1966	CHI	N	2/3-S		41	.158
1967	CHI	N	/H		4	.000
		BRTR			643	.244

AMARO, RUBEN [MORA]
B.JAN.6,1936 VERA CRUZ,MEXICO

1958	STL	N	2-S		40	.224
1960	PHI	N	S		92	.231
1961	PHI	N	1-2-S		135	.257
1962	PHI	N	1-S		79	.243
1963	PHI	N	1-S-3		115	.217
1964	PHI	N	1-2-S-3-O		129	.264
1965	PHI	N	1-S/2		118	.212
1966	PHI	N	A S		14	.217
1967	NY	A	*S/3-1		130	.223
1968	NY	A	S-1		47	.122
1969	CAL	A	1/2-S-3		41	.222
		BRTR			940	.234

AMBLER, WAYNE HARPER
B.NOV.9,1915 ABINGTON,PA.

1937	PHI	A	2		56	.216
1938	PHI	A	S		120	.234
1939	PHI	A	2-S		95	.211
		BRTR			271	.224

AMES, LEON KESSLING (RED)
B.AUG.2,1882 WARREN,OHIO
D.OCT.8,1936 WARREN,OHIO

1903	NY	N	P		2	2- 0
1904	NY	N	P		16	4- 0
1905	NY	N	P		34	19- 7
1906	NY	N	P		31	12-10
1907	NY	N	P		39	10-12
1908	NY	N	P		18	7- 4
1909	NY	N	P		34	15-10
1910	NY	N	P		33	12-11
1911	NY	N	P		34	11-10
1912	NY	N	P		33	11- 5
1913	NY	N	P		8	2- 1
	CIN	N	P		31	11-13
1914	CIN	N	P		47	15-23
1915	CIN	N	P		17	2- 4
	STL	N	P		15	9- 3
1916	STL	N	P		45	11-10
1917	STL	N	P		43	15-10
1918	STL	N	P		27	9-14
1919	STL	N	P		23	3- 5
	PHI	N	P		3	0- 2
		BBTR			533	180-166

AMOLE, MORRIS GEORGE (DOC)
B.JULY 5,1878 COATESVILLE,PA.
D.MAR.7,1912

1897	BAL	N	P		10	4- 4
1898	WAS	N	P		7	0- 6
					17	4-10

AMOR, VICENTE [ALVAREZ]
B.AUG.6,1932 HAVANA,CUBA

1955	CIN	N	P		4	0- 1
1957	CIN	N	P		9	1- 2
		BRTR			13	1- 3

AMOROS, EDMUNDO ISASI (SANDY)
B.JAN.30,1930 HAVANA,CUBA

1952	BRO	N	O		20	.250
1954	BRO	N	O		79	.274
1955	BRO	N	O		119	.247
1956	BRO	N	O		114	.260
1957	BRO	N	O		106	.277
1959	LA	N	H		9	.200
1960	LA	N	O		9	.143
	DET	A	O		65	.149
		BLTL			517	.255

ANCKER, WALTER
B.APR.10,1894 NEW YORK,N.Y.
D.FEB.13,1954 ENGLEWOOD,N.J.

1915	PHI	A	P		4	0- 1
		BRTR				

ANDERSEN, LARRY EUGENE
B.MAY 6,1953 PORTLAND,ORE.

1975	CLE	A	/P		3	0- 0
1977	CLE	A	P		11	0- 1
		BRTR			14	0- 1

ANDERSON, ALFRED WALTON
B.JAN.28,1914 GAINESVILLE,GA.

1941	PIT	N	S		70	.215
1942	PIT	N	S		54	.271
1946	PIT	N	H		2	.000
		BRTR			126	.238

ANDERSON, ANDY HOLM
B.NOV.13,1922 BREMERTON,WASH.

1948	STL	A	1-2-S		70	.276
1949	STL	A	2-S-3		71	.125
		BRTR			122	.184

ANDERSON, ARNOLD REVOLA (RED)
B.JUNE 19,1912 LAWTON,IOWA
D.AUG.7,1972 SIOUX CITY,IOWA

1937	WAS	A	P		2	0- 1
1940	WAS	A	P		2	1- 1
1941	WAS	A	P		32	4- 6
		BRTR			36	5- 8

ANDERSON, DAVID S. (DAVE)
B.OCT.10,1868 CHESTER,PA.
D.MAR.22,1897 CHESTER,PA.

1889	PHI	N	P		3	0- 2
1890	PHI	N	P		6	1- 2
	PIT	N	P		13	2-11
					22	3-15

ANDERSON, DWAIN CLEAVEN
B.NOV.23,1947 OAKLAND,CAL.

1971	OAK	A	S/2-3		16	.270
1972	OAK	A	/S-3		3	.000
	STL	N	S-3/2		57	.267
1973	STL	N	/S-O		18	.118
	SD	N	S/3		53	.121
1974	CLE	A	/2		2	.333
		BRTR			149	.203

ANDERSON, EDWARD JOHN (GOAT)
B.JAN.13,1880 CLEVELAND,OHIO
D.MAR.15,1923 SOUTH BEND,IND.

1907	PIT	N	O		121	.206
		TR				

ANDERSON, FERRELL JACK (ANDY)
B.JAN.9,1918 MAPLE CITY,KAN.
D.MAR.12,1978 JOPLIN,MO.

1946	BRO	N	C		79	.245
1953	STL	N	C		18	.286
		BRTR			97	.261

ANDERSON, GEORGE JENDRUS (ANDY)
[BORN GEORGE ANDREW JENDRUS]
B.SEPT.20,1889 CLEVELAND,OHIO
D.MAY 28,1962 CLEVELAND,OHIO

1914	BRO	F	O		97	.310
1915	BRO	F	O		134	.259
1918	STL	N	O		35	.295
		BLTR			266	.282

ANDERSON, GEORGE LEE (SPARKY)
B.FEB.22,1934 BRIDGEWATER,S.DAK

1959	PHI	N	2		152	.218
		BRTR				

NON-PLAYING MANAGER CIN[N] 1970-78

ANDERSON, HAROLD
B.FEB.10,1904 ST.LOUIS,MO.
D.MAY 1,1974 ST.LOUIS,MO.

1932	CHI	A	O		9	.250
		BRTR				

ANDERSON, HARRY WALTER
B.SEPT.10,1931 NORTH EAST,MD.

1957	PHI	N	O		118	.268
1958	PHI	N	1-O		140	.301
1959	PHI	N	O		142	.240
1960	PHI	N	1-O		38	.247
	CIN	N	1-O		42	.167
1961	CIN	N	H		4	.250
		BLTR			484	.264

ANDERSON, JAMES LEA (JIM)
B.FEB.23,1957 LOS ANGELES,CAL.

1978	CAL	A	S/2		48	.194
		BRTR				

ANDERSON, JOHN CHARLES
B.NOV.23,1932 ST.PAUL,MINN.

1958	PHI	N	P		5	0- 0
1960	BAL	A	P		4	0- 0
1962	STL	N	P		5	0- 0
	HOU	N	P		10	0- 0
		BRTR			24	0-0

YR	CL LEA POS	GP	G	REC

ANDERSON, JOHN FREDERICK (FRED)
B.DEC.11,1885 CALAHAN,N.C.
D.NOV.8,1957 WINSTON-SALEM,N.C.
1909	BOS A P	1		0- 0
1913	BOS A P	10		0- 6
1914	BUF F P	38		13-15
1915	BUF F P	36		19-13
1916	NY N P	38		9-13
1917	NY N P	38		8- 8
1918	NY N P	18		4- 2
	BRTR	179		53-57

ANDERSON, JOHN JOSEPH (HONEST JOHN)
B.DEC.14,1873 SASBOURG,NORWAY
D.JULY 23,1949 WORCESTER,MASS.
1894	BRO N O	16		.301
1895	BRO N O	103		.296
1896	BRO N 1-O	104		.314
1897	BRO N O	116		.332
1898	BRO N O	6		.138
	WAS N O	108		.305
	BRO N 1-O	19		.275
1899	BRO N 1-O	112		.274
1901	MIL A 1	138		.339
1902	STL A 1-O	126		.284
1903	STL A 1	139		.285
1904	NY A 1-O	143		.281
1905	NY A O	25		.212
	WAS A O	100		.295
1906	WAS A O	151		.271
1907	WAS A 1-O	87		.288
1908	CHI A O	123		.262
	BBTR	1616		.293

ANDERSON, LAWRENCE DENNIS (LARRY)
B.DEC.3,1952 MAYWOOD,CAL.
1974	MIL A /P	2		0- 0
1975	MIL A P	8		1- 0
1977	CHI A /P	6		1- 3
	BRTR	16		2- 3

ANDERSON, MICHAEL ALLEN (MIKE)
B.JUNE 22,1951 FLORENCE,S.C.
1971	PHI N O	26		.247
1972	PHI N O	36		.194
1973	PHI N O	87		.254
1974	PHI N *O/1	145		.251
1975	PHI N *O/1	115		.259
1976	STL N O/1	86		.291
1977	STL N O	94		.221
1978	BAL A O	53		.094
	BRTR	642		.247

ANDERSON, NORMAN CRAIG (CRAIG)
B.JULY 1,1938 WASHINGTON,D.C.
1961	STL N P	25		4- 3
1962	NY N P	50		3-17
1963	NY N P	3		0- 2
1964	NY N P	4		0- 1
	BRTR	82		7-23

ANDERSON, ROBERT CARL (BOB)
B.SEP.29,1935 E. CHICAGO,IND.
1957	CHI N P	8		0- 1
1958	CHI N P	17		3- 3
1959	CHI N P	37		12-13
1960	CHI N P	38	39	9-11
1961	CHI N P	57		7-10
1962	CHI N P	57		2- 7
1963	DET A P	32		3- 1
	BRTR	246	247	36-46

ANDERSON, VARNEY SAMUEL (VARN)
B.JUNE 18,1866 GENEVA,ILL.
D.NOV.5,1941 ROCKFORD,ILL.
1889	IND N P	1		0- 1
1894	WAS N P	2		0- 2
1895	WAS N P	26		9-16
1896	WAS N P	2		0- 1
	BRTR	31		9-20

ANDERSON, WALTER CARL (LEFTY)
B.SEP.25,1897 GRAND RAPIDS,MICH
1917	PHI A P	14		0- 0
1919	PHI A P	3		1- 1
	BLTL	17		1- 1

ANDERSON, WILLIAM
B.TAYLORSVILLE,KY.
| 1889 | LOU AA P | 1 | | 0- 1 |

ANDERSON, WILLIAM EDWARD (LEFTY)
B.DEC.3,1895 BOSTON,MASS.
| 1925 | BOS N P | 2 | | 0- 0 |
| | BRTL | | | |

ANDERSON, WINGO CHARLIE
B.AUG.13,1886 ALVARADO,TEX.
D.DEC.19,1950 FORT WORTH,TEX.
| 1910 | CIN N P | 7 | | 0- 0 |
| | BLTL | | | |

ANDRE, JOHN EDWARD
B.JAN.8,1923 BROCKTON,MASS.
| 1955 | CHI N P | 22 | | 0- 1 |
| | BLTR | | | |

ANDRES, ERNEST HENRY (JUNIE)
B.JAN.11,1918 JEFFERSONVILLE,IND.
| 1946 | BOS A 3 | 15 | | .098 |

ANDREW, KIM DARRELL
B.NOV.14,1953 GLENDALE,CAL.
| 1975 | BOS A /2 | 2 | | .500 |
| | BRTR | | | |

ANDREWS, ELBERT DEVORE
B.DEC.11,1901 GREENWOOD,S.C.
| 1925 | PHI A P | 6 | | 0- 0 |
| | BLTR | | | |

ANDREWS, FRED
B.MAY 4,1952 LAFAYETTE,LA.
1976	PHI N /2	4		.667
1977	PHI N /2	12		.174
	BRTR	16		.276

ANDREWS, GEORGE EDWARD (ED)
B.APR.5,1859 PAINESVILLE,OHIO
D.AUG.12,1934 W.PALM BEACH,FLA.
1884	PHI N 2	108		.221
1885	PHI N 2-O	103		.266
1886	PHI N O	106		.249
1887	PHI N O	103		.354
1888	PHI N O	123		.238
1889	PHI N 2-O	10		.282
	IND N O	40		.306
1890	BRO P O	95		.258
1891	CIN AA O	83		.210
	BRTR	771		.263

ANDREWS, HERBERT CARL (HUB)
B.AUG.31,1922 BURBANK,OKLA.
1947	NY N P	7		0- 0
1948	NY N P	1		0- 0
	BRTR	8		0- 0

ANDREWS, IVY PAUL (POISON)
B.MAY 6,1907 DORA,ALA.
D.NOV.24,1970 BIRMINGHAM,ALA.
1931	NY A P	7		2- 0
1932	NY A P	4		2- 1
	BOS A P	25	27	8- 6
1933	BOS A P	34	35	7-13
1934	STL A P	43		4-11
1935	STL A P	50		13- 7
1936	STL A P	36		7-12
1937	CLE A P	20		3- 4
	NY A P	11		3- 2
1938	NY A P	19		1- 3
	BRTR	249	253	50-59

ANDREWS, JAMES PRATT
B.JUNE 6,1865 SHELBURNE FALLS,MASS.
| 1890 | PIT N O | 53 | | .188 |

ANDREWS, JOHN RICHARD
B.FEB.9,1949 MONTEREY PARK,CAL.
| 1973 | STL N P | 16 | | 1- 1 |
| | BLTL | | | |

ANDREWS, MICHAEL JAY (MIKE)
B.JULY 9,1943 LOS ANGELES,CAL.
1966	BOS A /2	5		.167
1967	BOS A *2/S	142		.263
1968	BOS A *2/S-3	147		.271
1969	BOS A *2	121		.293
1970	BOS A *2	151		.253
1971	CHI A 2-1	109		.282
1972	CHI A *2/1	148		.220
1973	OAK A 0/1-2-3	52		.201
	OAK A D/1-2-3	18		.190
	BRTR	893		.258

ANDREWS, NATHAN HARDY (NATE)
B.SEPT.30,1913 PEMBROKE,N.C.
1937	STL N P	4		0- 0
1939	STL N P	11		1- 2
1940	CLE A P	6		0- 1
1941	CLE A P	2		0- 0
1943	BOS N P	36		14-20
1944	BOS N P	37		16-15
1945	BOS N P	21	22	7-12
1946	CIN N P	7		2- 4
	NY N P	3		1- 0
	BRTR	127	128	41-54

ANDREWS, ROBERT PATRICK (ROB)
B.DEC.11,1952 SANTA MONICA,CAL.
1975	HOU N 2/S	103		.238
1976	HOU N *2/S	109		.256
1977	SF N *2	127		.264
1978	SF N 2/S	79		.220
	BRTR	418		.250

ANDREWS, STANLEY JOSEPH (POLO)
[REAL NAME STANLEY JOSEPH
ANDRUSKEWICZ]
B.APR.17,1917 LYNN,MASS.
1939	BOS N C	13		.231
1940	BOS N C	19		.182
1944	BRO N C	4		.125
1945	BRO N C	21		.163
	PHI N C	13		.333
	BRTR	70		.215

ANDREWS, WILLIAM WALTER (WALLY)
B.SEPT.18,1859 PHILADELPHIA,PA.
D.JAN.20,1940 INDIANAPOLIS,IND.
1884	LOU AA 1	15		.185
1885	PRO N 3	1		.000
1888	LOU AA 1	27		.202
		43		.191

ANDRUS, FREDERICK HOTHAM
B.AUG.23,1850 WASHINGTON,MICH.
D.NOV.10,1937 DETROIT,MICH.
1876	CHI N O	8		.306
1884	CHI N P	1		0- 0
	BRTR	9		0- 0
				.286

ANDRUS, WILLIAM MORGAN (ANDY)
B.JULY 25,1907 BEAUMONT,TEX.
1931	WAS A 3	3		.000
1937	PHI N 3	3		.000
	BRTR	6		.000

ANDRUSKEWICZ, STANLEY JOSEPH
[PLAYED UNDER NAME OF
STANLEY JOSEPH ANDREWS]

ANDUJAR, JOAQUIN
B.DEC.12,1952 SAN PEDRO DE
MACORIS,D.R.
1976	HOU N P	28		9-10
1977	HOU N P	26		11- 8
1978	HOU N P	35	36	5- 7
	BBTR	89	90	25-25

ANGELINI, NORMAN STANLEY (NORM)
B.SEP.24,1947 SAN FRANCISCO,CAL.
1972	KC A P	21		2- 1
1973	KC A /P	7		0- 1
	BLTL	28		2- 1

ANGLEY, THOMAS SAMUEL
B.OCT.2,1904 BALTIMORE,MD.
D.OCT.26,1952 WICHITA,KAN.
| 1929 | CHI N C | 5 | | .250 |
| | BLTR | | | |

ANIBAL, SANTO (ALCALA)
[SEE SANTO ALCALA]

ANKENMAN, FREDERICK NORMAN (PAT)
B.DEC.23,1912 HOUSTON,TEX.
1936	STL N S	1		.000
1943	BRO N S	1		.500
1944	BRO N 2-S	13		.250
	BRTR	15		.241

ANNIS, WILLIAM PERLEY
B.MAY 24,1857 STONEHAM,MASS.
D.NOV.17,1917
| 1884 | BOS N O | 26 | | .184 |

ANSON, ADRIAN CONSTANTINE (CAP)
B.APR.11,1852 MARSHALLTOWN,IOWA
D.APR.14,1922 CHICAGO,ILL.
1871	ROK NA C-2-3		24	.352
1872	ATH NA 3		45	.381
1873	ATH NA C-1-2-3-O		50	.353
1874	ATH NA 1-S-3-O		54	.367
1875	ATH NA C-1-3-O		69	.318
1876	CHI N 3		66	.343
1877	CHI N C-3		59	.337
1878	CHI N 2-O		59	.336
1879	CHI N M-1		49	.407
1880	CHI N M-1-2-S-3		84	.338
1881	CHI N M-C-1-S		84	.399
1882	CHI N M-C-1		82	.362
1883	CHI N M-P-	2	98	0- 0
	C-1			.307
1884	CHI N M-1	1	111	0- 0
	C-1-S			.337
1885	CHI N M-C-1		112	.310
1886	CHI N M-1		125	.371
1887	CHI N M-1		122	.421
1888	CHI N M-1		134	.343
1889	CHI N M-1		134	.341
1890	CHI N M-1		139	.311
1891	CHI N M-1-2		136	.294
1892	CHI N M-1		147	.274
1893	CHI N M-1		101	.322
1894	CHI N M-1		83	.394
1895	CHI N M-1		122	.338
1896	CHI N M-1		106	.335
1897	CHI N M-1		112	.302
	BRTR	3	2507	0- 0
				.341

NON-PLAYING MANAGER NY[N] 1898

ANTOLICK, JOSEPH
B.APR.11,1916 HOKENDAUQUA,PA.
| 1944 | PHI N C | 4 | | .333 |
| | BRTR | | | |

ANTONELLI, JOHN AUGUST (JOHNNY)
B.APR.12,1930 ROCHESTER,N.Y.

YR	CL	LEA	POS	GP	G	REC
1948	BOS	N	P		6	0- 0
1949	BOS	N	P		22	3- 7
1950	BOS	N	P		20	2- 3
1953	MIL	N	P		31	12-12
1954	NY	N	P		39	21- 7
1955	NY	N	P		38	14-16
1956	NY	N	P	41	49	20-13
1957	NY	N	P	40	47	12-18
1958	SF	N	P	41	47	16-13
1959	SF	N	P	40	43	19-10
1960	SF	N	P	41	42	6- 7
1961	CLE	A	P	11	12	0- 4
	MIL	N	P		9	1- 0
		BLTL		377	403	126-110

ANTONELLI, JOHN LAWRENCE
B.JULY 15 1915 MEMPHIS,TENN.

YR	CL	LEA	POS	G	REC
1944	STL	N	1-2-3	8	.190
1945	STL	N	3	2	.000
	PHI	N	1-2-S-3	125	.256
		BRTR		135	.252

ANTONELLI, WILLIAM JAMES (BILL)
B.MAY 19,1927 BROOKLYN,N.Y.

YR	CL	LEA	POS	G	REC
1953	BRO	N	O	40	.163
		BRTR			

APARICIO, LUIS ERNESTO (MONTIEL)
B.APR.29,1934 MARACAIBO,VENEZ.

YR	CL	LEA	POS	G	REC
1956	CHI	A	S	152	.266
1957	CHI	A	S	143	.257
1958	CHI	A	S	145	.266
1959	CHI	A	S	152	.257
1960	CHI	A	S	153	.277
1961	CHI	A	S	156	.272
1962	CHI	A	S	153	.241
1963	BAL	A	S	146	.250
1964	BAL	A	S	146	.266
1965	BAL	A	*S	144	.225
1966	BAL	A	*S	151	.276
1967	BAL	A	*S	134	.233
1968	CHI	A	*S	155	.264
1969	CHI	A	*S	156	.280
1970	CHI	A	*S	146	.313
1971	BOS	A	*S	125	.232
1972	BOS	A	*S	110	.257
1973	BOS	A	*S	132	.271
		BRTR		2599	.262

APODACA, ROBERT JOHN (BOB)
B.JAN.31,1950 LOS ANGELES,CAL.

YR	CL	LEA	POS	G	REC
1973	NY	N	/P	1	0- 0
1974	NY	N	P	35	6- 6
1975	NY	N	P	46	3- 4
1976	NY	N	P	43	3- 7
1977	NY	N	P	59	4- 8
		BRTR		184	16-25

APPLEGATE, FREDERICK ROMAINE
B.MAY 9,1879 WILLIAMSPORT,PA.
D.APR.21,1968 WILLIAMSPORT,PA.

YR	CL	LEA	POS	G	REC
1904	PHI	A	P	3	1- 2
		BRTR			

APPLETON, EDWARD SAMUEL (WHITEY)
B.FEB.29,1892 ARLINGTON,TEX.
D.JAN.27,1932 ARLINGTON,TEX.

YR	CL	LEA	POS	G	REC
1915	BRO	N	P	34	4-10
1916	BRO	N	P	14	1- 2
		BRTR		48	5-12

APPLETON, PETER WILLIAM (JAKE)
[PLAYED UNDER NAME OF
PETER WILLIAM JABLONOWSKI IN
1927-33, REST OF CAREER UNDER
NAME OF PETER WILLIAM APPLETON,
AFTER CHANGING NAME LEGALLY]
B.MAY 20,1904 TERRYVILLE,CONN.
D.JAN.18,1974 TRENTON,N.J.

YR	CL	LEA	POS	GP	G	REC
1927	CIN	N	P		6	2- 1
1928	CIN	N	P-O	31	32	3- 4
						.323
1930	CLE	A	P		39	8- 7
1931	CLE	A	P	29	30	4- 4
1932	CLE	A	P		4	0- 0
	BOS	A	P		11	0- 3
1933	NY	A	P		1	0- 0
1936	WAS	A	P		38	14- 9
1937	WAS	A	P		35	8-15
1938	WAS	A	P		43	7- 9
1939	WAS	A	P		40	5-10
1940	CHI	A	P		25	4- 0
1941	CHI	A	P		13	0- 3
1942	CHI	A	P		4	0- 0
	STL	A	P		14	1- 1
1945	STL	A	P		2	0- 0
	WAS	A	P		6	1- 0
		BRTR		341	343	57-66
						.233

APPLING, LUCIUS BENJAMIN (LUKE)
B.APR.2,1909 HIGH POINT,N.C.

YR	CL	LEA	POS	G	REC
1930	CHI	A	S	6	.308
1931	CHI	A	S	96	.232
1932	CHI	A	2-S-3	139	.274
1933	CHI	A	S	151	.322
1934	CHI	A	S	118	.303
1935	CHI	A	S	153	.307
1936	CHI	A	S	138	.388
1937	CHI	A	S	154	.317
1938	CHI	A	S	81	.303
1939	CHI	A	S	148	.314
1940	CHI	A	S	150	.348
1941	CHI	A	S	154	.314
1942	CHI	A	S	142	.262
1943	CHI	A	S	155	.328
1945	CHI	A	S	18	.362
1946	CHI	A	S	149	.309
1947	CHI	A	S-3	139	.306
1948	CHI	A	S-3	139	.314
1949	CHI	A	S	142	.301
1950	CHI	A	1-2-S	100	.234
		BRTR		2422	.310

NON-PLAYING MANAGER KC[A] 1967

ARAGON, ANGEL VALDES JR. (JACK)
B.NOV.20,1915 HAVANA,CUBA

YR	CL	LEA	POS	G	REC
1941	NY	N	H	1	.000
		BRTR			

ARAGON, ANGEL VALDES SR. (PETE)
B.AUG.2,1893 HAVANA,CUBA
D.JAN.24,1952 NEW YORK,N.Y.

YR	CL	LEA	POS	G	REC
1914	NY	A	O	6	.142
1916	NY	A	3-O	12	.208
1917	NY	A	S-3-O	14	.067
		BRTR		32	.123

ARCHDEACON, MAURICE JOHN (FLASH)
B.DEC.14,1898 ST.LOUIS,MO.
D.SEPT.5,1954 ST.LOUIS,MO.

YR	CL	LEA	POS	G	REC
1923	CHI	A	O	22	.402
1924	CHI	A	O	95	.319
1925	CHI	A	O	10	.111
		BLTL		127	.333

ARCHER, FREDERICK MARVIN (LEFTY)
B.MAR.7,1910 JOHNSON CITY,TENN.

YR	CL	LEA	POS	G	REC
1936	PHI	A	P	6	2- 3
1937	PHI	A	P	1	0- 0
		BLTL		7	2- 3

ARCHER, JAMES PATRICK
B.MAY 13,1883 DUBLIN,IRELAND
D.MAR.29,1958 MILWAUKEE,WIS.

YR	CL	LEA	POS	G	REC
1904	PIT	N	C	7	.157
1907	DET	A	C	18	.119
1909	CHI	N	C	80	.230
1910	CHI	N	C-1	89	.259
1911	CHI	N	C	112	.252
1912	CHI	N	C	120	.283
1913	CHI	N	C	111	.266
1914	CHI	N	C	79	.258
1915	CHI	N	C	97	.243
1916	CHI	N	C	77	.220
1917	CHI	N	C	2	.000
1918	PIT	N	C-1	24	.155
	BRO	N	C	9	.273
	CIN	N	C-1-O	9	.269
		BRTR		854	.250

ARCHER, JAMES WILLIAM (JIM)
B.MAY 25,1932 MAX MEADOWS,VA.

YR	CL	LEA	POS	G	REC
1961	KC	A	P	39	9-15
1962	KC	A	P	18	0- 1
		BRTL		57	9-16

ARCHIE, GEORGE ALBERT
B.APR.27,1914 NASHVILLE,TENN.

YR	CL	LEA	POS	G	REC
1938	DET	A	H	3	.000
1941	WAS	A	1-3	105	.269
	STL	A	1	9	.379
1946	STL	A	1	4	.182
		BRTR		121	.273

AKCIA, JOSE RAIMUNDO (ORTA)
B.AUG.22,1943 HAVANA,CUBA

YR	CL	LEA	POS	G	REC
1968	CHI	N	O-2/S-3	59	.190
1969	SD	N	2-S/3-O-1	120	.215
1970	SD	N	S-2/3-O	114	.223
		BRTR		293	.215

ARDELL, DANIEL MIERS
B.MAY 27,1941 SEATTLE,WASH.

YR	CL	LEA	POS	G	REC
1961	LA	A	1	7	.250
		BLTL			

ARDIZOLA, RINALDO JOSEPH (RUGGER)
B.NOV.20,1919 OLEGGIO,ITALY

YR	CL	LEA	POS	G	REC
1947	NY	N	P	1	0- 0
		BRTR			

ARDNER, JOSEPH A. (OLD HOSS)
B.FEB.27,1858 MT.VERNON,OHIO
D.SEPT.15,1935 CLEVELAND,OHIO

YR	CL	LEA	POS	G	REC
1884	CLE	N	2	26	.174
1890	CLE	N	2	84	.223
		BRTR		110	.212

ARELLANES, FRANK JULIAN
B.JAN.28,1882 SANTA CRUZ,CAL.
D.DEC.13,1918 SAN JOSE,CAL.

YR	CL	LEA	POS	GP	G	REC
1908	BOS	A	P		12	4- 3
1909	BOS	A	P	45	46	16-12
1910	BOS	A	P		18	4- 7
		BRTR		75	76	24-22

ARFT, HENRY IRVEN (BOW WOW)
B.JAN.28,1922 MANCHESTER,MO.

YR	CL	LEA	POS	G	REC
1948	STL	A	1	69	.238
1949	STL	A	H	6	.200
1950	STL	A	1	98	.268
1951	STL	A	1	112	.261
1952	STL	A	1	15	.143
		BLTL		300	.253

ARIAS, RODOLFO [MARTINEZ] (RUDY)
B.JUNE 6,1931 LAS VILLAS,CUBA

YR	CL	LEA	POS	G	REC
1959	CHI	A	P	34	2- 0
		BLTL			

ARLETT, RUSSELL LORIS (BUZZ)
B.JAN.3,1899 ELMHURST,CAL.
D.MAY 16,1964 MINNEAPOLIS,MINN.

YR	CL	LEA	POS	G	REC
1931	PHI	N	1-O	121	.313
		BBTR			

ARLICH, DONALD LOUIS (DON)
B.FEB.15,1943 WAYNE,MICH.

YR	CL	LEA	POS	G	REC
1965	HOU	N	/P	1	0- 0
1966	HOU	N	/P	7	0- 1
		BLTL		8	0- 1

ARLIN, STEPHEN RALPH (STEVE)
B.SEP.25,1945 SEATTLE,WASH.

YR	CL	LEA	POS	G	REC
1969	SD	N	/P	4	0- 1
1970	SD	N	/P	2	1- 0
1971	SD	N	P	36	9-19
1972	SD	N	P	38	10-21
1973	SD	N	P	34	11-14
1974	SD	N	P	16	1- 7
	CLE	A	P	11	2- 5
		BRTR		141	34-67

ARMAS, ANTONIO RAFAEL (MACHADO)
(TONY)
B.JULY 12,1953 ANZOATEGUI,VENEZ.

YR	CL	LEA	POS	G	REC
1976	PIT	N	/O	4	.333
1977	OAK	A	*O/S	118	.240
1978	OAK	A	O	91	.213
		BRTR		213	.230

ARMBRISTER, EDISON ROSANDA (ED)
B.JULY 4,1948 NASSAU,BAHAMAS

YR	CL	LEA	POS	G	REC
1973	CIN	N	O	18	.216
1974	CIN	N	/O	9	.286
1975	CIN	N	O	59	.185
1976	CIN	N	O	73	.295
1977	CIN	N	O	65	.256
		BRTR		224	.245

ARMBRUST, ORVILLE MARTIN
B.MAR.2,1910 BEIRNE,ARK.
D.OCT.2,1967 MOBILE,ALA.

YR	CL	LEA	POS	G	REC
1934	WAS	A	P	3	1- 0
		BRTR			

ARMBRUSTER, CHARLES A.
B.AUG.30,1880 CINCINNATI,OHIO
D.OCT.7,1964 GRANTS PASS,ORE.

YR	CL	LEA	POS	G	REC
1905	BOS	A	C	35	.198
1906	BOS	A	C	72	.144
1907	BOS	A	C	23	.100
	CHI	A	C	1	.000
		TR		131	.149

ARMBRUSTER, HARRY (ARMY)
B.MAR.20,1882 CINCINNATI,OHIO
D.DEC.10,1953 CINCINNATI,OHIO

YR	CL	LEA	POS	G	REC
1906	PHI	A	O	91	.238
		BLTL			

ARMOUR, WILLIAM R.
B.SEPT.3,1869 HOMESTEAD,PA.
D.DEC.2,1922 MINNEAPOLIS,MINN.
NON-PLAYING MANAGER
CLE[A] 1902-04, DET[A] 1905-06

ARMSTRONG, GEORGE NOBLE (DODO)
B.JUNE 3,1924 ORANGE,N.J.

YR	CL	LEA	POS	G	REC
1946	PHI	A	C	8	.167
		BRTR			

ARMSTRONG, HOWARD ELMER
B.DEC.2,1889 E.CLARIDON,OHIO
D.MAR.8,1926 CANISTEO,N.Y.

YR	CL	LEA	POS	G	REC
1911	PHI	N	P	1	0- 1
		TR			

ARMSTRONG, SAMUEL
B.FT.WAYNE,IND.

YR	CL	LEA	POS	G	REC
1871	KEK	NA	O	13	-

```
YR  CL LEA POS      GP   G   REC          YR  CL LEA POS      GP   G   REC          YR  CL LEA POS      GP   G   REC

ARNDT, HARRY J.                           ASBJORNSON, ROBERT ANTHONY (CASPER)       ASTROTH, JOSEPH HENRY (JOE)
B.FEB.12,1879 SOUTH BEND,IND.             [NAME CHANGED TO ASBY]                    B.SEPT.1,1922 EAST ALTON,ILL.
D.MAR.24,1921 SOUTH BEND,IND.             B.JUNE 19,1909 CONCORD,MASS.             1945 PHI A  C          10   .059
1902 DET A 1-0        10   .135           D.JAN.21,1970 WILLIAMSPORT,PA.           1946 PHI A  C           4   .143
     BAL A 2-S-3-0    67   .257           1928 BOS A  C          6   .187           1949 PHI A  C          55   .243
1905 STL N 2         111   .243           1929 BOS A  C         17   .103           1950 PHI A  C          39   .327
1906 STL N 3          67   .270           1931 CIN N  C         45   .305           1951 PHI A  C          64   .246
1907 STL N 1           9   .130           1932 CIN N  C         29   .172           1952 PHI A  C         104   .249
          TR         264  .248                       BRTR       97   .235           1953 PHI A  C          82   .296
                                                                                    1954 PHI A  C          77   .221
ARNOLD, CHRISTOPHER PAUL (CHRIS)          ASH, KENNETH LOWTHER                      1955 KC  A  C         101   .252
B.NOV.6,1947 LONG BEACH,CAL.              B.SEPT.16,1901 ANMOORE,W.VA.             1956 KC  A  C           8   .077
1971 SF  N /2          6   .231           1925 CHI A  P          2   0- 0                      BRTR      544   .254
1972 SF  N 3/2-S      51   .226           1928 CIN N  P          9   3- 3
1973 SF  N /C-2-3     49   .296           1929 CIN N  P-O   29  30   1- 5           ATHERTON, CHARLES MORGAN
1974 SF  N /2-3       78   .241                                      .143           HERBERT (PREXY)
1975 SF  N /2-0       29   .195           1930 CIN N  P     16  17   2- 0           B.OCT.19,1873 NEW BRUNSWICK,N.J
1976 SF  N /2-3-1-S   60   .217                      BRTR   56  58   6- 8           D.DEC.19,1934 VIENNA,AUSTRIA
          BRTR       273   .237                                      .133           1899 WAS N  3          63   .240

ARNOLD, WILLIS S. (BILLY)                 ASHBURN, DON RICHIE                       ATKINS, FRANCIS MONTGOMERY (TOMMY)
B.MAR.2,1851 MIDDLETOWN,CONN.             (RICHIE) OR (WHITEY)                      B.DEC.9,1887 PONCA,NEB.
D.JAN.17,1899                             B.MAR.19,1927 TILDEN,NEB.                 D.MAY 7,1956 CLEVELAND,OHIO
1872 MAN NA M-O        2   .125           1948 PHI N  O        117   .333           1909 PHI A  P           1   0- 0
                                          1949 PHI N  O        154   .284           1910 PHI A  P          15   3- 2
ARNOVICH, MORRIS (SNOOKER)                1950 PHI N  O        151   .303                      BLTL       16   3- 2
B.NOV.16,1910 SUPERIOR,WIS.               1951 PHI N  O        154   .344
D.JULY 20,1959 SUPERIOR,WIS.              1952 PHI N  O        154   .282           ATKINS, JAMES CURTIS
1936 PHI N  O         13   .313           1953 PHI N  O        156   .330           B.MAR.10,1921 BIRMINGHAM,ALA.
1937 PHI N  O        117   .290           1954 PHI N  O        153   .313           1950 BOS A  P           1   0- 0
1938 PHI N  O        139   .275           1955 PHI N  O        140   .338           1952 BOS A  P           3   0- 1
1939 PHI N  O        134   .324           1956 PHI N  O        154   .303                      BLTR        4   0- 1
1940 PHI N  O         39   .199           1957 PHI N  O        156   .297
     CIN N  O         62   .284           1958 PHI N  O        152   .350           ATKINSON, ALBERT W.
1941 NY  N  O         85   .280           1959 PHI N  O        153   .266           B.MAR.9,1861 CLINTON,ILL.
1946 NY  N  O          1   .000           1960 CHI N  O        151   .291           D.JUNE 17,1952 ELKHORN TOWNSHIP MO.
          BRTR       590   .287           1961 CHI N  O        109   .257           1884 ATH AA P          22  11-11
                                          1962 NY  N  2-O      135   .306                CHI U  P          12   5- 7
ARNTZEN, ORIE EDGAR (OLD FOLKS)                     BLTR      2189   .308                                      .278
B.OCT.18,1909 BEVERLY,ILL.                                                               PIT U  P-O    8   9   2- 6
D.JAN.28,1970 CEDAR RAPIDS,IOWA           ASHBY, ALAN DEAN                                                    .121
1943 PHI A  P         32   4-13           B.JULY 8,1951 LONG BEACH,CAL.             1886 ATH AA P          43  25-17
          BRTR                            1973 CLE A  C         11   .172           1887 ATH AA P          16   5- 9
                                          1974 CLE A /C         10   .143                             109 110  51-55
ARRIGO, GERALD WILLIAM (GERRY)            1975 CLE A  C/1-3     90   .224                                      .183
B.JUNE 12,1941 CHICAGO,ILL.               1976 CLE A  C/1-3     89   .239
1961 MIN A  P          7   0- 1           1977 TOR A *C        124   .210           ATKINSON, EDWARD
1962 MIN A  P          1   0- 0           1978 TOR A  C         81   .261           B.BALTIMORE,MD.
1963 MIN A  P          5   1- 2                      BBTR      405   .229           1873 NAT NA O           2   .000
1964 MIN A  P         41   7- 4                      BL 1976
1965 CIN N  P     27  28   2- 4                                                     ATKINSON, HUBERT BERLEY (LEFTY)
1966 CIN N /P          3   0- 0           ASHFORD, THOMAS STEVEN (TUCKER)           B.JUNE 4,1904 CHICAGO,ILL.
     NY  N  P         17   3- 3           B.JUNE 15,1954 MEMPHIS,TENN.             D.FEB.12,1961 CHICAGO,ILL.
1967 CIN N  P         32   6- 6           1976 SD  N /3          4   .000           1927 WAS A  H           1   .000
1968 CIN N  P         36  12-10           1977 SD  N  3-S/2     81   .217
1969 CIN N  P         20   4- 7           1978 SD  N  3-2-1     75   .245           ATKINSON, WILLIAM CECIL GLENN (BILL)
1970 CHI A /P          5   0- 3                      BRTR      160   .232           B.OCT.4,1954 CHATHAM,ONT.,CAN.
          BLTL  194 195  35-4C                                                      1976 MON N  P           4   0- 0
                                          ASMUSSEN, THOMAS WILLIAM                  1977 MON N  P     55  56   7- 2
ARROYO, FERNANDO                          B.SEPT.26,1876 CHICAGO,ILL.              1978 MON N  P          29   2- 2
B.MAR.21,1952 SACRAMENTO,CAL.             D.AUG.21,1963 ARLINGTON HEIGHTS ILL.               BLTR       88  89   9- 4
1975 DET A  P         14   2- 1           1907 BOS N  C          2   .000
1977 DET A  P         38   8-18                      TR                            ATTREAU, RICHARD GILBERT
1978 DET A /P          2   0- 0                                                     B.APR.8,1897 CHICAGO,ILL.
          BRTR        54  10-19           ASPROMONTE, KENNETH JOSEPH (KEN)          D.JULY 5,1964 CHICAGO,ILL.
                                          B.SEP.22,1931 BROOKLYN,N.Y.              1926 PHI N  1          17   .230
ARROYO, LUIS ENRIQUE                      1957 BOS A  2         24   .269           1927 PHI N  1          44   .205
B.FEB.18,1927 PENUELAS,P.R.               1958 BOS A  2          6   .125                      BLTR       61   .215
1955 STL N  P         35  11- 8                WAS A  2-S-3     92   .225
1956 PIT N  P         18   3- 3           1959 WAS A  1-2-S-O   70   .244           ATWELL, MAURICE DAILEY (TOBY)
1957 PIT N  P     54  56   3-11           1960 WAS A  H          4   .000           B.MAR.8,1924 LEESBURG,VA.
1959 CIN N  P         10   1- 0                CLE A  2-3      117   .290           1952 CHI N  C         107   .290
1960 NY  A  P         29   5- 1           1961 LA  A  2         66   .223           1953 CHI N  C          24   .230
1961 NY  A  P         65  15- 5                LA  A  2         22   .229                PIT N  C          53   .245
1962 NY  A  P         27   1- 3           1962 CLE A  2-3       20   .143           1954 PIT N  C          96   .289
1963 NY  A  P          6   1- 1                MIL N  2-3       34   .291           1955 PIT N  C          71   .213
          BLTL  244 246  40-32            1963 CHI N  1-2       20   .147           1956 PIT N  C          12   .111
                                                     BRTR      475   .249                MIL N  C          15   .167
ARROYO, RUDOLPH (RUDY)                    NON-PLAYING MANAGER CLE[A] 1972-74                   BRTR      378   .260
B.JUNE 19,1950 NEW YORK,N.Y.
1971 STL N /P          9   0- 1           ASPROMONTE, ROBERT THOMAS (BOB)          ATWOOD, WILLIAM FRANKLIN
          BLTR                            B.JUNE 19,1938 BROOKLYN,N.Y.             B.SEPT.25,1911 ROME,GA.
                                          1956 BRO N  H          1   .000           1936 PHI N  C          71   .302
ARUNDEL, HARRY                            1960 LA  N  S-3       21   .182           1937 PHI N  C          87   .244
B.1894 PHILADELPHIA,PA.                   1961 LA  N  2-S-3     47   .241           1938 PHI N  C         102   .196
D.MAR.25,1904 CLEVELAND,OHIO              1962 HOU N  2-S-3    149   .266           1939 PHI N  C           4   .000
1875 ATL NA O          1   .000           1963 HOU N  1-3      136   .214           1940 PHI N  C          78   .192
1882 PIT AA P-S       14   4-10           1964 HOU N  3        157   .280                      BRTR      342   .229
                           .192           1965 HOU N *3/1-S    152   .263
1884 PRO N  P          1   1- 0           1966 HOU N *3/1-S    152   .252           ATZ, JACOB HENRY
                      16   5-10           1967 HOU N *3        137   .294           B.JULY 1,1879 WASHINGTON,D.C.
                           .183           1968 HOU N  3-0/1-S  124   .225           D.MAY 22,1945 NEW ORLEANS,LA.
                                          1969 ATL N  0-3-S/2   82   .253           1902 WAS A  2           3   .100
ARUNDEL, JOHN THOMAS (TUG)                1970 ATL N  3/S-1-0   62   .213           1907 CHI A  3           4   .125
B.JUNE 30,1862 AUBURN,N.Y.                1971 NY  N  3        104   .225           1908 CHI A  2          83   .194
D.SEPT.5,1912 AUBURN,N.Y.                            BRTR     1324   .252           1909 CHI A  2         119   .236
1882 ATH AA C-O        1   .000                                                                BRTR      209   .218
1884 TOL AA C         14   .087           ASSELSTINE, BRIAN HANLY
1887 IND N  C         43   .236           B.SEPT.23,1953 SANTA BARBARA,CAL          AUBREY, HARRY HERBERT (CHUB)
1888 WAS N  C         16   .196           1976 ATL N /O         11   .212           B.JULY 5,1880 ST.JOSEPH,MO.
                      74   .199           1977 ATL N  O         83   .210           D.SEPT.18,1953 BALTIMORE,MD.
                                          1978 ATL N  O         39   .272           1903 BOS N  S          94   .212
ASBELL, JAMES MARION (BIG TRAIN)                     BLTR      133   .235                      TR
B.JUNE 22,1914 DALLAS TEX.
D.JULY 6,1967 SAN MATEO,CAL.
1938 CHI N  O         17   .162
          BRTR
```

```
YR   CL LEA POS      GP    G    REC
```

AUERBACH, FREDERICK STEVEN (RICK)
B.FEB.15,1950 WOODLAND HILLS,CAL
```
1971 MIL A  S              79   .203
1972 MIL A *S             153   .218
1973 MIL A /S               6   .100
1974 LA  N  S-2/3          45   .342
1975 LA  N  S/2-3          85   .224
1976 LA  N  S/3-2          36   .128
1977 CIN N  2-S            33   .156
1978 CIN N  S-2/3          63   .327
        BRTR              500   .222
```

AUGUSTINE, DAVID RALPH (DAVE)
B.NOV.28,1949 FOLLANSBEE,W.VA.
```
1973 PIT N /O              11   .286
1974 PIT N  O              18   .182
        BRTR               29   .207
```

AUGUSTINE, GERALD LEE (JERRY)
B.JULY 24,1952 KEWAUNEE,WIS.
```
1975 MIL A /P               5   2- 0
1976 MIL A  P              39   9-12
1977 MIL A  P              33  12-18
1978 MIL A  P              35  13-12
        BLTL              112  36-42
```

AUKER, ELDON LEROY (SUBMARINE)
B.SEPT.21,1910 NORCATUR,KAN.
```
1933 DET A  P         15   3- 3
1934 DET A  P         43  15- 7
1935 DET A  P         36  18- 7
1936 DET A  P         35  13-16
1937 DET A  P     39  43  17- 9
1938 DET A  P         27  11-10
1939 BOS A  P         31   9-10
1940 STL A  P         38  16-11
1941 STL A  P     34  37  14-15
1942 STL A  P     35  51  14-13
        BRTR   333 356 130-101
```

AULDS, LEYCESTER DOYLE (TEX)
B.DEC.28,1920 FARMERVILLE,LA.
```
1947 BOS A  C          3   .250
        BRTR
```

AULT, DOUGLAS REAGAN (DOUG)
B.MAR.9,1950 BEAUMONT,TEX.
```
1976 TEX A /1          9   .300
1977 TOR A *1        129   .245
1978 TOR A  1/O       54   .240
        BRTL        192   .246
```

AUST, DENNIS KAY
B.NOV.23,1940 TECUMSEH,NEB.
```
1965 STL N /P          6   0- 0
1966 STL N /P          9   0- 1
        BRTR          15   0- 1
```

AUSTIN, HENRY C.
B.1844 BROOKLYN,N.Y.
D.SEPT.3,1895
```
1873 RES NA O         22     -
```

AUSTIN, JAMES PHILIP (PEPPER)
B.DEC.8,1879 SWANSEA,WALES
D.MAR.6,1965 LAGUNA BEACH,CAL.
```
1909 NY  A  S-3      136   .231
1910 NY  A  3        133   .218
1911 STL A  3        148   .261
1912 STL A  3        149   .252
1913 STL A  M-3      142   .273
1914 STL A  3        130   .238
1915 STL A  3        141   .266
1916 STL A  3        129   .207
1917 STL A  3        127   .239
1918 STL A  M-S-3    110   .264
1919 STL A  3        106   .237
1920 STL A  3         83   .271
1921 STL A  S         27   .273
1922 STL A  3         15   .290
1923 STL A  M-H        1   .000
1925 STL A  3          1   .000
1926 STL A  3          1   .500
1929 STL A  3          1   .000
        BBTR       1580   .247
```

AUSTIN, RICK GERALD
B.OCT.27,1946 SEATTLE,WAS.
```
1970 CLE A  P         31   2- 5
1971 CLE A  P         23   0- 0
1975 MIL A  P         32   2- 3
1976 MIL A /P          3   0- 0
        BRTL          89   4- 8
```

AUTRY, ALBERT (AL)
B.FEB.29,1952 MODESTO,CAL.
```
1976 ATL N /P          1   1- 0
        BRTR
```

AUTRY, MARTIN GORDON (CHICK)
B.MAR.5,1903 MARTINDALE,TEX.
D.JAN.26,1950 SAVANNAH,GA.
```
1924 NY  A  C          2   .000
1926 CLE A  C          3   .143
1927 CLE A  C         16   .255
1928 CLE A  C         22   .300
1929 CHI A  C         43   .208
1930 CHI A  C         34   .253
        BRTR        120   .245
```

AUTRY, WILLIAM ASKEW (CHICK)
B.JAN.2,1885 HUMBOLDT,TENN.
D.JAN.16,1976 SANTA ROSA,CAL.
```
1907 CIN N  O          7   .200
1909 CIN N  1          9   .182
     BOS N  1         61   .196
        BLTL          77   .199
```

AVERILL, EARL DOUGLAS
B.SEP.9,1931 CLEVELAND,O.
```
1956 CLE A  O         42   .237
1958 CLE A  3         17   .182
1959 CHI N  C-2-3-O   74   .237
1960 CHI N  C-3-O     52   .235
     CHI A  C         10   .214
1961 LA  A  C-2-O    119   .266
1962 LA  A  C-O       92   .219
1963 PHI N  C-1-3-O   47   .268
        BRTR        449   .242
```

AVERILL, HOWARD EARL (ROCK)
B.MAY 21,1902 SNOHOMISH,WASH.
```
1929 CLE A  O        152   .330
1930 CLE A  O        139   .339
1931 CLE A  O        155   .333
1932 CLE A  O        153   .314
1933 CLE A  O        151   .301
1934 CLE A  O        154   .313
1935 CLE A  O        140   .288
1936 CLE A  O        152   .378
1937 CLE A  O        156   .299
1938 CLE A  O        134   .330
1939 CLE A  O         24   .273
     DET A  O         87   .262
1940 DET A  O         64   .280
1941 BOS N  O          8   .118
        BLTR       1669   .316
```

AVILA, ROBERTO FRANCISCO
(GONZALEZ) (BOBBY)
B.APR.2,1924 VERA CRUZ,MEXICO
```
1949 CLE A  2         31   .214
1950 CLE A  2-S       80   .299
1951 CLE A  2        141   .305
1952 CLE A  2        150   .300
1953 CLE A  2        141   .286
1954 CLE A  2-S      143   .341
1955 CLE A  2        141   .272
1956 CLE A  2        138   .224
1957 CLE A  2-3      129   .268
1958 CLE A  2-3      113   .253
1959 BAL A  2-3-O     20   .170
     BOS A  2         22   .244
     MIL N  2         51   .238
        BRTR       1300   .281
```

AVILES, RAMON ANTONIO [MIRANDA]
B.JAN.22,1952 MANATI,P.R.
```
1977 BOS A /2          1   .000
        BRTR
```

AVREA, JAMES EPHERIUM (JAY)
B.JULY 6,1920 CLEBURNE,TEX.
```
1950 CIN N  P          2   0- 0
        BRTR
```

AYALA, BENIGNO [FELIX] (BENNY)
B.FEB.7,1951 YAUCO,P.R.
```
1974 NY  N  O         23   .235
1976 NY  N /O         22   .115
1977 STL N /O          1   .333
        BRTR          46   .206
```

AYDELOTTE, JACOB S.
B.1865 MARION,IND.
```
1884 IND AA P-O       12   5- 7
                           .114
1886 ATH AA P          2   0- 2
                      14   5- 9
                           .098
```

AYERS, WILLIAM OSCAR
B.AUG.27,1918 NEWNAN,GA.
```
1947 NY  N  P         13   0- 3
        BRTR
```

AYERS, YANCY WYATT (DOC)
B.MAY 20,1890 FANCY GAP,VA.
D.MAY 26,1968 PULASKI,VA.
```
1913 WAS A  P          4   2- 1
1914 WAS A  P         49  12-16
1915 WAS A  P         40  15- 9
1916 WAS A  P         43   5- 9
1917 WAS A  P         40  11-10
1918 WAS A  P         40  10-12
1919 WAS A  P         12   2- 6
     DET A  P         23   4- 3
1920 DET A  P         46   7-14
1921 DET A  P          2   0- 0
        BRTR        299  68-80
```

AYLWARD, RICHARD JOHN (DANDY)
B.JUNE 4,1925 BALTIMORE,MD.
```
1953 CLE A  P          4   .000
        BRTR
```

AZCUE, JOSE JOAQUIN [LOPEZ] (JOE)
B.AUG.18,1939 CIENFUEGOS,CUBA
```
1960 CIN N  C         14   .097
1962 KC  A  C         72   .229
1963 KC  A  C          2   .000
     CLE A  C         94   .284
1964 CLE A  C         83   .273
1965 CLE A *C        111   .230
1966 CLE A  C         98   .275
1967 CLE A  C         86   .251
1968 CLE A  C        115   .280
1969 CLE A /C          7   .292
     BOS A  C         19   .216
     CAL A  C         80   .218
1970 CAL A *C        114   .242
1972 CAL A /C          3   .000
     MIL A /C         11   .143
        BRTR        909   .252
```

BABB, CHARLES AMOS
B.FEB.20,1873 MILWAUKIE,ORE.
D.MAR.20,1954 PORTLAND,ORE.
```
1903 NY  N  S        121   .248
1904 BRO N  S        151   .265
1905 BRO N  1-S       74   .187
        BRTR        346   .243
```

BABE, LOREN ROLLAND
(LOREN) OR (BEE BEE)
B.JAN.11,1928 PISGAH,IOWA
```
1952 NY  A  3         12   .095
1953 NY  A  3          5   .333
     PHI A  S-3      103   .224
        BLTR        120   .223
```

BABICH, JOHN CHARLES
B.MAY 14,1913 ALBION,CAL.
```
1934 BRO N  P         25   7-11
1935 BRO N  P         37   7-14
1936 BOS N  P          3   0- C
1940 PHI A  P         31  14-13
1941 PHI A  P         16   2- 7
        BRTR        112  30-45
```

BABINGTON, CHARLES PERCY
B.MAY 4,1895 CRANSTON,R.I.
D.MAR.22,1957 PROVIDENCE,R.I.
```
1915 NY  N  O         28   .242
```

BACKMAN, LESTER JOHN
B.MAR.20,1888 CLEVES,OHIO
D.NOV.8,1975 CINCINNATI,OHIO
```
1909 STL N  P         21   3-11
1910 STL N  P         26   6- 7
             TR       47   9-18
```

BACON, EDGAR SUTER
B.APR.8,1895 FRANKLIN CO.,,KY.
D.OCT.2,1963 FRANKFURT,KY.
```
1917 PHI A  P          4   0- 0
```

BACSIK, MICHAEL JAMES (MIKE)
B.APR.1,1952 DALLAS,TEX.
```
1975 TEX A /P          7   1- 2
1976 TEX A  P         23   3- 2
1977 TEX A /P          2   0- 0
        BRTR          32   4- 4
```

BACZEWSKI, FREDERIC JOHN
(FRED) OR (LEFTY)
B.MAY 15,1926 ST.PAUL,MINN.
D.NOV.14,1976 CULVER CITY,CAL.
```
1953 CHI N  P          9   0- 0
     CIN N  P         24  11- 4
1954 CIN N  P         29   6- 6
1955 CIN N  P          1   0- 0
        BLTL          63  17-10
```

BADER, ARTHUR HERMAN
B.SEPT.21,1886 ST.LOUIS,MO.
D.APR.5,1957 ST.LOUIS,MO.
```
1904 STL A  O          2   .000
```

BADER, LORE VERNE (KING)
B.APR.27,1888 BADER,ILL.
D.JUNE 2,1973 LE ROY,KAN.
```
1912 NY  N  P          2   2- 0
1917 BOS A  P         15   2- 0
1918 BOS A  P          5   1- 3
        BLTR          22   5- 3
```

BADGRO, MORRIS HIRAM (RED)
B.DEC.1,1902 ORILLA,WASH.
```
1929 STL A  O         54   .284
1930 STL A  O         89   .239
        BLTR        143   .257
```

BAECHT, EDWARD JOSEPH
B.MAY 15,1907 BADEN,OKLA.
D.AUG.15,1957 QUARRY TOWNSHIP,ILL.
```
1926 PHI N  P         28   2- 0
1927 PHI N  P          1   0- 1
1928 PHI N  P          9   1- 1
1931 CHI N  P         22   2- 4
1932 CHI N  P          1   0- 0
1937 STL A  P          3   0- 0
        BRTR          64   5- 6
```

```
YR   CL LEA POS     GP    G    REC
```

BAERWALD, RUDOLPH FRED
[PLAYED UNDER NAME OF JOHN BELL]

BAEZ, JOSE ANTONIO
(REAL NAME
JOSE ANTONIO MOTA [BAEZ])
B.DEC.31,1953 SAN CRISTOBAL,D.R.
```
1977 SEA A 2/3         91   .259
1978 SEA A 2/3         23   .160
        BRTR          114   .245
```

BAGBY, JAMES CHARLES JACOB JR.
B.SEPT.8,1916 CLEVELAND,OHIO
```
1938 BOS A  P    43   45  15-11
1939 BOS A  P         21   5- 5
1940 BOS A  P-O  36   44  10-16
                          .203
1941 CLE A  P    33   35   9-15
1942 CLE A  P    38   39  17- 9
1943 CLE A  P-S  36   41  17-14
                          .268
1944 CLE A  P    13   14   4- 5
1945 CLE A  P         25   8-11
1946 BOS A  P         21   7- 6
1947 PIT N  P         37   5- 4
        BRTR    303  322  97-96
                          .226
```

BAGBY, JAMES CHARLES JACOB SR.
(SARGE)
B.OCT.5,1889 BARNETT,GA.
D.JULY 28,1954 MARIETTA,GA.
```
1912 CIN N  P          5   2- 0
1916 CLE A  P    48   51  16-15
1917 CLE A  P         49  23-13
1918 CLE A  P    45   47  17-16
1919 CLE A  P    35   37  17-11
1920 CLE A  P    48   49  31-12
1921 CLE A  P    40   41  14-12
1922 CLE A  P         25   4- 5
1923 PIT N  P         21   3- 2
        BBTR    316  325 127-86
```

BAGLEY, EDWARD N.
[PLAYED UNDER NAME OF
EDWARD N. BEGLEY]

BAGWELL, WILLIAM MALLORY (BIG BILL)
B.FEB.24,1896 CHOUDRANT,LA.
D.OCT.5,1976 CHOUDRANT,LA.
```
1923 BOS N  O    56   .290
1925 PHI A  O    36   .300
        BLTL     92   .294
```

BAHNSEN, STANLEY RAYMOND (STAN)
B.OCT.15,1944 COUNCIL BLUFFS,IA.
```
1966 NY  A /P         4   1- 1
1968 NY  A  P        37  17-12
1969 NY  A  P        40   9-16
1970 NY  A  P        36  14-11
1971 NY  A  P        36  14-12
1972 CHI A  P    43  44  21-16
1973 CHI A  P        42  18-21
1974 CHI A  P        38  12-15
1975 CHI A  P        12   4- 6
     OAK A  P        21   6- 7
1976 OAK A  P        35   8- 7
1977 OAK A  P        11   1- 2
     MON N  P        23   8- 9
1978 MON N  P        44   1- 5
        BRTR    422  423 134-140
```

BAHR, EDSON GARFIELD
B.OCT.16,1919 ROULEAU,SASK.,CANADA
```
1946 PIT N  P    27   29   8- 6
1947 PIT N  P    19   21   3- 5
        BRTR     46   50  11-11
```

BAHRET, FRANK J.
```
1884 BAL U  O     1   .000
     IND AA C-O   5   .071
                  6   .056
```

BAICHLEY, GROVER CLEVELAND
B.JAN 7,1890 TOLEDO,ILL.
D.JUNE 30,1956 SAN JOSE,CAL.
```
1914 STL A  P     4   0- 0
        BRTR
```

BAILEY, ABRAHAM LINCOLN (SWEETBREAD)
B.FEB.12,1895 JOLIET,ILL.
D.SEPT.27,1939 JOLIET,ILL.
```
1919 CHI N  P    21   3- 5
1920 CHI N  P    21   1- 2
1921 CHI N  P     3   0- 0
     BRO N  P     7   0- 0
        BRO      52   4- 7
```

BAILEY, ARTHUR EUGENE (GENE)
B.NOV.25,1893 PEARSALL,TEX.
D.NOV.14,1973 HOUSTON,TEX.
```
1917 PHI A  O     5   .083
1919 BOS N  O     4   .333
1920 BOS N  O    13   .083
     BOS A  O    46   .230
1923 BRO N  1-O 127   .265
1924 BRO N  O    18   .239
        BRTR    213   .247
```

BAILEY, FREDERICK MIDDLETON (PENNY)
B.AUG.16,1895 MT.HOPE,W.VA.
D.AUG.16,1972 HUNTINGTON,W.VA.
```
1916 BOS N  O     6   .100
1917 BOS N  O    50   .191
1918 BOS N  O.    9   .250
        BLTL     65   .185
```

BAILEY, HARRY LEWIS
B.NOV.19,1881 SHAWNEE,OHIO
D.OCT.27,1967 SEATTLE,WASH.
```
1911 NY  A  O     9   .111
        BLTR
```

BAILEY, HARVEY FRANCIS
B.NOV.24,1876 ADRIAN,MICH.
D.JULY 22,1922 TOLEDO,OHIO
```
1899 BOS N  P    12   6- 4
1900 BOS N  P     4   0- 1
        TL       16   6- 5
```

BAILEY, JAMES HOPKINS
B.DEC.16,1934 STRAWBERRY
PLAINS, TENN.
```
1959 CIN N  P     3   0- 1
        BBTL
```

BAILEY, LEMUEL (KING)
B.CINCINNATI,OHIO
D.JUNE 2,1952
```
1895 CIN N  P     1   1- 0
        BLTL
```

BAILEY, LONAS EDGAR (ED)
B.APR.15,1931 STRAWBERRY
PLAINS,TENN.
```
1953 CIN N  C      2   .375
1954 CIN N  C     73   .197
1955 CIN N  C     21   .205
1956 CIN N  C    118   .300
1957 CIN N  C    122   .261
1958 CIN N  C    112   .250
1959 CIN N  C    121   .264
1960 CIN N  C    133   .261
1961 CIN N  C     12   .302
     SF  N  C-O  107   .238
1962 SF  N  C     96   .232
1963 SF  N  C    105   .263
1964 MIL N  C     93   .262
1965 SF  N  C/1   24   .107
     CHI N  C/1   66   .253
1966 CAL A  /H     5   .000
        BLTR    1212   .256
```

BAILEY, ROBERT SHERWOOD (BOB)
B.OCT.13,1942 LONG BEACH,CAL.
```
1962 PIT N  3      14   .167
1963 PIT N  S-3   154   .228
1964 PIT N  S-3-0 143   .281
1965 PIT N *3-0   159   .256
1966 PIT N  3-0/1 126   .279
1967 LA  N  3/S-0 116   .227
1968 LA  N  3/S-0 105   .227
1969 MON N  1-0/3 111   .265
1970 MON N  3-0/1 131   .287
1971 MON N *3-0/1 157   .251
1972 MON N *3/0/1 143   .233
1973 MON N *3/0  151   .273
1974 MON N  0-3  152   .280
1975 MON N  0/3  106   .273
1976 CIN N  0-3   69   .298
1977 CIN N  /O    49   .253
     BOS A  /H     2   .000
1978 BOS A  0/3-0  43  .191
        BRTR    1931   .257
```

BAILEY, STEVEN JOHN (STEVE)
B.FEB.12,1942 BRONX,N.Y.
```
1967 CLE A  P    32   2- 5
1968 CLE A  /P    2   0- 1
        BRTR     34   2- 6
```

BAILEY, WILLIAM F.
B.APR.12,1889 FT.SMITH,ARK.
D.NOV.2,1926 HOUSTON,TEX.
```
1907 STL A  P         6   4- 1
1908 STL A  P        22   3- 5
1909 STL A  P    31  38   9-11
1910 STL A  P        34   3-18
1911 STL A  P         5   0- 4
1912 STL A  P         3   0- 0
1914 BAL F  P        19   7- 9
1915 BAL F  P        30   4-15
     CHI F  P        11   6- 5
1918 DET A  P         8   1- 2
1921 STL N  P        19   2- 5
1922 STL N  P        12   0- 2
        BLTL    200  207  39-77
```

BAILOR, ROBERT MICHAEL (BOB)
B.MAR.10,1951 CONNELLSVILLE,PA.
```
1975 BAL A /S-2    5   .143
1976 BAL A /S      9   .333
1977 TOR A  0-S  122   .310
1978 TOR A *0-3/S 154  .264
        BRTR     290   .284
```

BAIN, HERBERT LOREN
B.JULY 4,1922 STAPLES,MINN.
```
1945 NY  N  P     3   0- 0
        BRTR
```

BAIR, CHARLES DOUGLAS (DOUG)
B.AUG.22,1949 DEFIANCE,OHIO
```
1976 PIT N /P     4   0- 0
1977 OAK A  P    45   4- 6
1978 CIN N  P    70   7- 6
        BRTR    119  11-12
```

BAIRD, ALBERT WELLS
B.JUNE 2,1895 CLEBURNE,TEX.
D.NOV.27,1976 SHREVEPORT,LA.
```
1917 NY  N  2     10   .292
1919 NY  N  2-S-3  38   .241
        BRTR      48   .251
```

BAIRD, HOWARD DOUGLAS (DOUG)
B.SEPT.27,1891 ST.CHARLES,MO.
D.JUNE 13,1967 THOMASVILLE,GA.
```
1915 PIT N  3-0   145   .219
1916 PIT N  2-3-0 128   .216
1917 PIT N  3      43   .259
     STL N  3     104   .253
1918 STL N  3      82   .247
1919 PHI N  3      66   .260
     STL N  2-3-0  16   .260
1920 BRO N  H       6   .333
     NY  N  3       7   .125
        BRTR     617   .234
```

BAIRD, ROBERT ALLEN (BOB)
B.JAN.16,1940 KNOXVILLE,TENN.
D.APR.11,1974 CHATTANOOGA,TENN.
```
1962 WAS A  P     3   0- 1
1963 WAS A  P     5   0- 3
        BLTL      8   0- 4
```

BAKELY, EDWARD ENOCH
[REAL NAME EDWARD ENOCH BAKLEY]
B.APR.17,1864 BLACKWOOD,N.J.
D.FEB.17,1915
```
1883 ATH AA P-0        9   5- 4
                          .139
1884 KEY U  P-1-  39  43  14-24
                          .134
     WIL U  P           2   0- 2
     KC  U  P-0    5   6   2- 2
                          .167
1888 CLE AA P         60  25-33
1889 CLE N  P         34  12-22
1890 CLE P  P         44  13-26
1891 WAS AA P         12   2-10
     BAL AA P         13   4- 2
        BRTR    218  223  77-125
                          .154
```

BAKENHASTER, DAVID LEE (DAVE)
B.MAR.5,1945 COLUMBUS,O.
```
1964 STL N  P     2   0- 0
        BRTR
```

BAKER, ALBERT JONES
B.FEB.28,1906 BATESVILLE,MISS.
```
1938 BOS A  P     3   0- 0
        BRTR
```

BAKER, CHARLES
B.HUDSON,MASS.
```
1884 CHI U  2-S-0  11   .167
     PIT U  O       3   .083
                   14   .148
```

BAKER, CHARLES (SMILING BOCK)
B.JULY 17,1878 TROY,N.Y.
```
1901 CLE A  P     1   0- 1
     PHI A  P     1   0- 1
                  2   0- 2
```

BAKER, CHARLES JOSEPH (HUCK)
B.DEC.6,1952 SEATTLE,WASH.
```
1978 MON N  2-S  44   .207
        BRTR
```

BAKER, DELMER DAVID
B.MAY 3,1892 SHERWOOD,ORE.
D.SEP.11,1973 SAN ANTONIO,TEX.
```
1914 DET A  C    43   .214
1915 DET A  C    68   .246
1916 DET A  C    61   .153
        BRTR    172   .209
```
NON-PLAYING MANAGER
DET(A) 1933,38-42

BAKER, EARNEST GOULD
B.AUG.8,1875 CONCORD,MICH.
D.OCT.25,1945 HOMER,MICH.
```
1905 CIN N  P     1   0- 0
```

YR	CL	LEA	POS	GP	G	REC

BAKER, EUGENE WALTER (GENE)
B.JUNE 15,1925 DAVENPORT,IOWA

YR	CL	LEA	POS	GP	G	REC
1953	CHI	N	2		7	.227
1954	CHI	N	2		135	.275
1955	CHI	N	2		154	.268
1956	CHI	N	2		140	.258
1957	CHI	N	2		12	.250
	PIT	N	2-S-3		111	.266
1958	PIT	N	2-3		29	.250
1960	PIT	N	2-3		33	.243
1961	PIT	N	3		9	.100
	BRTR				630	.265

BAKER, FLOYD WILSON
B.OCT.10,1916 LURAY,VA.

YR	CL	LEA	POS	GP	G	REC
1943	STL	A	S-3		22	.174
1944	STL	A	2-S		44	.175
1945	CHI	A	2-3		82	.250
1946	CHI	A	3		9	.250
1947	CHI	A	2-3		105	.264
1948	CHI	A	2-S-3		104	.215
1949	CHI	A	2-S-3		125	.260
1950	CHI	A	2-3-0		83	.317
1951	CHI	A	2-S-3		82	.263
1952	WAS	A	2-S-3		79	.262
1953	WAS	A	3		9	.000
	BOS	A	2-3		81	.273
1954	BOS	A	2-3		21	.200
	PHI	N	2-3		23	.227
1955	PHI	N	3		5	.000
	BLTR				874	.251

BAKER, FRANK
B.JAN.11,1944 BARTOW,FLA.

YR	CL	LEA	POS	GP	G	REC
1969	CLE	A	0		52	.256
1971	CLE	A	0		73	.210
	BLTR				125	.232

BAKER, FRANK WATTS
B.OCT.29,1946 MERIDIAN,MISS.

YR	CL	LEA	POS	GP	G	REC
1970	NY	A	S		33	.231
1971	NY	A	S		43	.139
1973	BAL	A	S/2-1-3		44	.190
1974	BAL	A	S/2-3		24	.172
	BLTR				146	.191

BAKER, GEORGE F.
B.1859 ST.LOUIS,MO.

YR	CL	LEA	POS	GP	G	REC
1883	BAL	AA	C-S		6	.227
1884	STL	U	C		64	.171
1885	KC	N	C-2-3-0		39	.122
1886	KC	N	C		1	.250
					110	.159

BAKER, HOWARD FRANCIS
B.MAR.1,1888 BRIDGEPORT,CONN.
D.JAN.16,1964 BRIDGEPORT,CONN.

YR	CL	LEA	POS	GP	G	REC
1912	CLE	A	3		11	.167
1914	CHI	A	3		15	.277
1915	CHI	A	H		2	.000
	NY	N	3		1	.000
	BRTR				29	.220

BAKER, JACK EDWARD
B.MAY 4,1950 BIRMINGHAM,ALA.

YR	CL	LEA	POS	GP	G	REC
1976	BOS	A	/1		2	.130
1977	BOS	A	/1		12	.000
	BRTR				14	.115

BAKER, JESSE
[REAL NAME MICHAEL SILVERMAN]
B.1896

YR	CL	LEA	POS	GP	G	REC
1919	WAS	A	S		1	.000

BAKER, JESSE ORMOND
B.JUNE 3,1888 ANDERSON ISLAND,WASH.
D.SEPT.26,1972 TACOMA,WASH.

YR	CL	LEA	POS	GP	G	REC
1911	CHI	A	P		22	2- 7
	BLTL					

BAKER, JOHN FRANKLIN
(FRANK) OR (HOME RUN)
B.MAR.13,1886 TRAPPE,MD.
D.JUNE 28,1963 TRAPPE,MD.

YR	CL	LEA	POS	GP	G	REC
1908	PHI	A	3		9	.290
1909	PHI	A	3		148	.305
1910	PHI	A	3		146	.283
1911	PHI	A	3		148	.334
1912	PHI	A	3		149	.347
1913	PHI	A	3		149	.336
1914	PHI	A	3		150	.319
1916	NY	A	3		100	.269
1917	NY	A	3		146	.282
1918	NY	A	3		126	.306
1919	NY	A	3		141	.293
1921	NY	A	3		94	.294
1922	NY	A	3		69	.277
	BLTR				1575	.307

BAKER, JOHNY B (DUSTY)
B.JUNE 15,1949 RIVERSIDE,CAL.

YR	CL	LEA	POS	GP	G	REC
1968	ATL	N	/0		6	.400
1969	ATL	N	/0		3	.000
1970	ATL	N	0		13	.292
1971	ATL	N	0		29	.226
1972	ATL	N	*0		127	.321
1973	ATL	N	*0		159	.288
1974	ATL	N	*0		149	.256
1975	ATL	N	*0		142	.261
1976	LA	N	*0		112	.242
1977	LA	N	*0		153	.291
1978	LA	N	*0		149	.262
	BRTR				1042	.274

BAKER, KIRTLY
B.JAN 24,1869 AURORA,IND.
D.APR.15,1927 LAWRENCEBURG,IND.

YR	CL	LEA	POS	GP	G	REC
1890	PIT	N	P		23	2-19
1893	BAL	N	P		19	3-10
1898	WAS	N	P		2	0- 0
1898	WAS	N	P		6	1- 3
1899	WAS	N	P		12	1- 8
					62	7-40

BAKER, NEAL VERNON
B.APR.30,1904 LAPORTE,TEX.

YR	CL	LEA	POS	GP	G	REC
1927	PHI	A	P		5	0- 0
	BRTR					

BAKER, NORMAN LESLIE
B.OCT.14,1862 PHILADELPHIA,PA.

YR	CL	LEA	POS	GP	G	REC
1883	PIT	AA	P-0	3	4	0- 2
						.000
1885	LOU	AA	P		25	13-12
1890	BAL	AA	P		2	1- 1
				30	31	14-15
						.143

BAKER, PHILIP
B.SEPT.19,1856 PHILADELPHIA,PA.
D.JUNE 4,1940 WASHINGTON,D.C.

YR	CL	LEA	POS	GP	G	REC
1883	BAL	AA	C-S-0		27	.280
1884	WAS	U	C-1		83	.282
1886	WAS	N	1-0		81	.221
					191	.257

BAKER, STEVEN BYRNE (STEVE)
B.AUG.30,1956 EUGENE,ORE.

YR	CL	LEA	POS	GP	G	REC
1978	DET	A	P		15	2- 4

BAKER, THOMAS CALVIN (RATTLESNAKE)
B.JUNE 11,1913 NURSERY,TEX.

YR	CL	LEA	POS	GP	G	REC
1935	BRO	N	P		11	1- 0
1936	BRO	N	P		37	1- 8
1937	BRO	N	P		7	0- 1
	NY	N	P		13	1- 0
1938	NY	N	P		2	0- 0
	BRTR				70	3- 9

BAKER, THOMAS HENRY (TOM)
B.MAY 6,1934 PORT TOWNSEND,WASH.

YR	CL	LEA	POS	GP	G	REC
1963	CHI	N	P		10	0- 1
	BLTL					

BAKER, TRACY LEE
B.NOV.7,1891 PENDLETON,ORE.
D.MAR.14,1975 PLACERVILLE,CAL.

YR	CL	LEA	POS	GP	G	REC
1911	BOS	A	1		1	.000
	BRTR					

BAKER, WILLIAM PRESLEY
B.FEB.22,1911 PAW CREEK,N.C.

YR	CL	LEA	POS	GP	G	REC
1940	CIN	N	C		27	.217
1941	CIN	N	C		2	.000
	PIT	N	C		35	.224
1942	PIT	N	C		18	.118
1943	PIT	N	C		63	.273
1946	PIT	N	C-1		53	.239
1948	STL	N	C		45	.294
1949	STL	N	C		20	.133
	BRTR				263	.253

BAKLEY, EDWARD ENOCH
[PLAYED UNDER NAME OF
EDWARD ENOCH BAKELY]

BALAS, MITCHELL FRANCIS (MIKE)
[REAL NAME MITCHELL FRANCIS BALASKI]
B.MAY 17,1910 LOWELL,MASS.

YR	CL	LEA	POS	GP	G	REC
1938	BOS	N	P		1	0- 0
	BRTR					

BALASKI, MITCHELL FRANCIS
[PLAYED UNDER NAME OF
MITCHELL FRANCIS BALAS]

BALAZ, JOHN LAWRENCE
B.NOV.24,1950 TORONTO,ONT.,CAN.

YR	CL	LEA	POS	GP	G	REC
1974	CAL	A	0		14	.238
1975	CAL	A	0-0		45	.242
	BRTR				59	.241

BALCENA, ROBERT RUDOLPH (BOBBY)
B.AUG.1,1928 SAN PEDRO,CAL.

YR	CL	LEA	POS	GP	G	REC
1956	CIN	N	0		7	.000
	BRTL					

BALDSCHUN, JACK EDWARD
B.OCT.16,1936 GREENVILLE,O.

YR	CL	LEA	POS	GP	G	REC
1961	PHI	N	P		65	5- 3
1962	PHI	N	P		67	12- 7
1963	PHI	N	P		65	11- 7
1964	PHI	N	P		71	6- 9
1965	PHI	N	P		65	5- 8
1966	CIN	N	P		42	1- 5
1967	CIN	N	/P		9	0- 0
1969	SD	N	P		61	7- 2
1970	SD	N	P		12	1- 0
	BRTR				457	48-41

BALDWIN, CHARLES BUSTED (LADY)
B.APR.8,1859 ORMEL,N.Y.
D.MAR.7,1937 HASTINGS,MICH.

YR	CL	LEA	POS	GP	G	REC
1884	MIL	U	P-0	2	7	1- 1
						.214
1885	DET	N	P-0	20	31	11- 9
						.241
1886	DET	N	P	56	57	42-13
1887	DET	N	P		24	13-10
1888	DET	N	P		6	3- 3
1890	BRO	N	P		2	1- 0
	BUF	P	P		7	2- 5
	BLTL			117	134	73-41
						.226

BALDWIN, CLARENCE GEOGHAN (KID)
B.NOV.1,1864 NEWPORT,KY.
D.JULY 12,1897 CINCINNATI,OHIO

YR	CL	LEA	POS	GP	G	REC
1884	KC	U	C-2-3-0		49	.202
	CHI	U	C		1	1.000
1885	CIN	AA	P-C-	2	26	0- 0
			2-3-0			.147
1886	CIN	AA	C-0		86	.238
1887	CIN	AA	C-0		96	.262
1888	CIN	AA	C-1-0		66	.220
1889	CIN	AA	C-1-3-0		60	.246
1890	CIN	N	0		21	.153
	ATH	AA	C		24	.239
	BRTR			2	429	0- 0
						.227

BALDWIN, DAVID GEORGE (DAVE)
B.MAR.30,1938 TUCSON,ARIZ.

YR	CL	LEA	POS	GP	G	REC
1966	WAS	A	/P		4	0- 0
1967	WAS	A	P		58	2- 4
1968	WAS	A	P		40	0- 2
1969	WAS	A	P		43	2- 4
1970	MIL	A	P		28	2- 1
1973	CHI	A	/P		3	0- 0
	BRTR				176	6-11

BALDWIN, FRANK DE WITT
B.DEC.25,1928 HIGH BRIDGE,N.J.

YR	CL	LEA	POS	GP	G	REC
1953	CIN	N	C		16	.100
	BRTR					

BALDWIN, HENRY CLAY (TED)
B.JUNE 13,1894 CHADDS FORD,PA.
D.FEB.24,1964 WEST CHESTER,PA.

YR	CL	LEA	POS	GP	G	REC
1927	PHI	N	S-3		6	.313
	BRTR					

BALDWIN, HOWARD EDWARD (HARRY)
B.JUNE 3,1900 BALTIMORE,MD.
D.JAN.23,1958 BALTIMORE,MD.

YR	CL	LEA	POS	GP	G	REC
1924	NY	N	P	10	11	3- 1
1925	NY	N	P		1	0- 0
	BRTR			11	12	3- 1

BALDWIN, MARCUS ELMORE (FIDO)
B.OCT.29,1863 PITTSBURGH,PA.
D.NOV.10,1929 PITTSBURGH,PA.

YR	CL	LEA	POS	GP	G	REC
1887	CHI	N	P	38	40	19-17
1888	CHI	N	P	28	30	13-15
1889	COL	AA	P	63	64	26-34
1890	CHI	P	P		58	32-21
1891	PIT	N	P		54	20-28
1892	PIT	N	P		57	25-27
1893	PIT	N	P		5	1- 1
	NY	N	P		35	12-19
	BRTR			338	343	148-162

BALDWIN, O. F.
B.YOUNGSTOWN,OHIO

YR	CL	LEA	POS	GP	G	REC
1908	STL	N	P		4	1- 3

BALDWIN, REGINALD CONRAD (REGGIE)
B.AUG.19,1954 RIVER ROUGE,MICH.

YR	CL	LEA	POS	GP	G	REC
1978	HOU	N	C		38	.254
	BRTR					

BALDWIN, RICKEY ALAN (RICK)
B.JUNE 1,1953 FRESNO,CAL.

YR	CL	LEA	POS	GP	G	REC
1975	NY	N	P		54	3- 5
1976	NY	N	P		11	0- 0
1977	NY	N	P		40	1- 2
	BLTR				105	4- 7

BALDWIN, ROBERT HARVEY (BILLY)
B.JUNE 9,1951 TAZEWELL,VA.

YR	CL	LEA	POS	GP	G	REC
1975	DET	A	0		30	.221
1976	NY	N	/0		9	.273
	BLTL				39	.231

YR	CL	LEA	POS	GP	G	REC

BALENTI, MICHAEL RICHARD
B.JULY 3,1886 CALUMET,OKLA.
D.AUG.4,1955 ALTUS,OKLA.
1911	CIN	N	S		7	.250
1913	STL	A	S		70	.181
			BRTR		77	.183

BALES, WESLEY OWEN (LEE)
B.DEC.4,1944 LOS ANGELES,CAL.
1966	ATL	N	/2-3		12	.063
1967	HOU	N	/2-S		19	.111
					31	.093

BALL, ARTHUR
B.1874 CHICAGO,ILL.
D.DEC.26,1919 CHICAGO,ILL.
1894	PHI	N	S		1	.333
1898	BAL	N	3		25	.175
					26	.181

BALL, CORNELIUS (NEAL)
B.APR.22,1881 GRAND HAVEN,MICH.
D.OCT.15,1957 BRIDGEPORT,CONN.
1907	NY	A	S		15	.205
1908	NY	A	S		132	.247
1909	NY	A	S		8	.214
			CLE	A	S	96	.255
1910	CLE	A	S		53	.210
1911	CLE	A	2-3		116	.296
1912	CLE	A	2		38	.233
		BOS	A	2		17	.182
1913	BOS	A	2		21	.172
			BRTR		496	.251

BALL, EUGENE J.
[PLAYED UNDER NAME OF
EDWARD J. HENDERSON]

BALL, JAMES CHANDLER
B.1885 HARFORD,COUNTY,MD.
1907	BOS	N	C		11	.150
1908	BOS	N	C		6	.133
			TR		17	.145

BALLENGER, PELHAM ASHBY
B.FEB.6,1894 GILREATH MILL,S.C.
D.DEC.8,1948 W.GANTT TOWNSHIP,S.C.
| 1928 | WAS | A | 2-3 | | 3 | .111 |
| | | | BRTR | | | |

BALLINGER, MARK ALAN
B.JAN.3,1949 GLENDALE,CAL.
| 1971 | CLE | A | P | | 18 | 1- 2 |
| | | | BRTR | | | |

BALLOU, NOBLE WINFIELD (WIN)
B.NOV.30,1897 MOUNT MORGAN,KY.
D.JAN.30,1963 SAN FRANCISCO,CAL.
1925	WAS	A	P		10	1- 1
1926	STL	A	P		43	10-10
1927	STL	A	P		21	5- 6
1929	BRO	N	P		25	2- 3
			BRTL		99	18-20

BALSAMO, ANTHONY FRED
B.NOV.21,1937 BROOKLYN,N.Y.
| 1962 | CHI | N | P | | 18 | 0- 1 |
| | | | BRTR | | | |

BAMBERGER, GEORGE IRVIN
B.AUG.1,1925 STATEN ISLAND,N.Y.
1951	NY	N	P		2	0- 0
1952	NY	N	P	5	6	0- 0
1959	BAL	A	P		3	0- 0
			BRTR	10	11	0- 0
NON-PLAYING MANAGER MIL[A] 1978

BAMBERGER, HAROLD EARL (DUTCH)
B.OCT.29,1924 LEBANON,PA.
| 1948 | NY | N | O | | 7 | .083 |
| | | | BLTR | | | |

BANCROFT, DAVID JAMES (BEAUTY)
B.APR.20,1891 SIOUX CITY,IOWA
D.OCT.9,1972 SUPERIOR,WIS.
1915	PHI	N	S		153	.254
1916	PHI	N	S		142	.212
1917	PHI	N	S		127	.243
1918	PHI	N	S		125	.265
1919	PHI	N	S		92	.272
1920	PHI	N	S		42	.276
		NY	N	S		108	.308
1921	NY	N	S		153	.319
1922	NY	N	S		156	.321
1923	NY	N	2-S		107	.304
1924	BOS	N	M-S		79	.279
1925	BOS	N	M-S		128	.319
1926	BOS	N	M-S		127	.311
1927	BOS	N	M-S		111	.243
1928	BRO	N	S		149	.247
1929	BRO	N	P		104	.277
1930	NY	N	S		10	.059
			BBTR		1913	.279

BANCROFT, FRANK CARTER
B.MAY 9,1846 LANCASTER,MASS.
D.MAR.31,1921 CINCINNATI,OHIO
NON-PLAYING MANAGER
WOR[N] 1880s DET[N] 1881-82,
CLE[N] 1883, PRO[N] 1884-85,
ATH[AA] 1887, IND[N] 1889
AND CIN[N] 1902.

BANDO, SALVATORE LEONARD (SAL)
B.FEB.13,1944 CLEVELAND,O.
1966	KC	A	/3		11	.292
1967	KC	A	3		47	.192
1968	OAK	A	*3/O		162	.251
1969	OAK	A	*3		162	.281
1970	OAK	A	*3		155	.263
1971	OAK	A	*3		153	.271
1972	OAK	A	*3/2		152	.236
1973	OAK	A	*3		162	.287
1974	OAK	A	*3		146	.243
1975	OAK	A	*3		160	.230
1976	OAK	A	*3/S		158	.240
1977	MIL	A	*3-O/2-S		159	.250
1978	MIL	A	*3-O/1		152	.285
			BRTR		1779	.257

BANE, EDWARD NORMAN (EDDIE)
B.MAR.22,1952 CHICAGO,ILL.
1973	MIN	A	P		23	0- 5
1975	MIN	A	/P		4	3- 1
1976	MIN	A	P	17	18	4- 7
			BRTL	44	45	7-13

BANEY, RICHARD LEE (DICK)
B.NOV.1,1946 FULLERTON,CAL.
1969	SEA	A	/P		9	1- 0
1973	CIN	N	P		11	2- 1
1974	CIN	N	P		22	1- 0
			BRTR		42	4- 1

BANKHEAD, DANIEL ROBERT (DAN)
B.MAY 3,1920 EMPIRE,ALA.
D.MAY 2,1976 HOUSTON,TEX.
1947	BRO	N	P		4	0- 0
1950	BRO	N	P		41	9- 4
1951	BRO	N	P	7	15	0- 1
			BRTR	52	62	9- 5

BANKS, ERNEST (ERNIE)
B.JAN.31,1931 DALLAS,TEX.
1953	CHI	N	S		10	.314
1954	CHI	N	S		154	.275
1955	CHI	N	S		154	.295
1956	CHI	N	S		139	.297
1957	CHI	N	S-3		156	.285
1958	CHI	N	S		154	.313
1959	CHI	N	S		155	.304
1960	CHI	N	S		156	.271
1961	CHI	N	1-S-O		138	.278
1962	CHI	N	1-3		154	.269
1963	CHI	N	1		130	.227
1964	CHI	N	1		157	.264
1965	CHI	N	*1		163	.265
1966	CHI	N	*1/3		141	.272
1967	CHI	N	*1		151	.276
1968	CHI	N	*1		150	.246
1969	CHI	N	*1		155	.253
1970	CHI	N	1		72	.252
1971	CHI	N	1		39	.193
			BRTR		2528	.274

BANKS, GEORGE EDWARD
B.SEP.24,1938 PACOLET MILLS,S.C.
1962	MIN	A	3-O		63	.252
1963	MIN	A	3		25	.155
1964	MIN	A	H		1	.000
		CLE	A	2-3-O		9	.294
1965	CLE	A	/3		4	.200
1966	CLE	A	/H		4	.250
			BRTR		106	.219

BANKS, WILLIAM JOHN
[REAL NAME WILLIAM JOHN YERRICK]
B.FEB.26,1874 DANVILLE,PA.
D.SEPT.8,1936 DANVILLE,PA.
1895	BOS	N	P		1	1- 0
1896	BOS	N	P		4	0- 3
					5	1- 3

BANKSTON, WILBORN EVERETT
B.MAY 25,1893 BARNESVILLE,GA.
D.FEB.26,1970 GRIFFIN,GA.
| 1915 | PHI | A | O | | 11 | .142 |
| | | | BLTR | | | |

BANNING, JAMES M.
B.1866 NEW YORK,N.Y.
1888	WAS	N	C		1	.000
1889	WAS	N	C		2	.000
			BLTR		3	.000

BANNISTER, ALAN
B.SEPT.3,1951 MONTEBELLO,CAL.
1974	PHI	N	/O-S		26	.120
1975	PHI	N	O/2-S		24	.262
1976	CHI	A	O-S/2-3		73	.248
1977	CHI	A	*S/2-O		139	.275
1978	CHI	A	O-O/S-2		49	.224
			BRTR		311	.259

BANNISTER, FLOYD FRANKLIN
B.JUNE 10,1955 PIERRE,S.D.
1977	HOU	N	P		24	8- 9
1978	HOU	N	P		28	3- 9
			BLTL		52	11-18

BANNOCK
1871	CHI	NA	3		3	-
1875	CHI	NA	3		2	.000
					5	-

BANNON, JAMES HENRY (FOXY GRANDPA)
B.MAY 5,1871 AMESBURY,MASS.
D.MAR.24,1948 GLEN ROCK,N.J.
1893	STL	N	P-O	2	23	0- 1
						.363
1894	BOS	N	O		127	.336
1895	BOS	N	O		121	.339
1896	BOS	N	O		87	.256
			BR	2	358	0- 1
						.320

BANNON, THOMAS EDWARD (WARD SIX)
B.MAY 8,1869 S.GROVELAND,MASS.
D.JAN.26,1950 LYNN,MASS.
1895	NY	N	O		37	.266
1896	NY	N	O		2	.143
					39	.267

BANTA, JOHN KAY (JACK)
B.JUNE 24,1925 HUTCHINSON,KAN.
1947	BRO	N	P		3	0- 1
1948	BRO	N	P		2	0- 1
1949	BRO	N	P		48	10- 6
1950	BRO	N	P		16	4- 4
			BLTR		69	14-12

BAPTIST, ALFREDO CLAUDINO
(GRIFFIN)
[SEE ALFREDO CLAUDINO GRIFFIN]

BARBARE, WALTER LAWRENCE (DINTY)
B.AUG.11,1891 GREENVILLE,S.C.
D.OCT.28,1965 GREENVILLE,S.C.
1914	CLE	A	S		15	.308
1915	CLE	A	3		77	.191
1916	CLE	A	3		13	.229
1918	BOS	A	3		13	.172
1919	PIT	N	2-3		85	.273
1920	PIT	N	S		57	.274
1921	BOS	N	S		134	.302
1922	BOS	N	1-2-3		106	.231
					500	.260

BARBARY, DONALD ODELL (RED)
B.JUNE 20,1920 SIMPSONVILLE,S.C
| 1943 | WAS | A | H | | 1 | .000 |
| | | | BRTR | | | |

BARBEAU, WILLIAM JOSEPH (JAP)
B.JUNE 10,1882 NEW YORK,N.Y.
D.SEPT.10,1969 MILWAUKEE,WIS.
1905	CLE	A	3		12	.237
1906	CLE	A	3		42	.194
1909	PIT	N	3		85	.220
		STL	N	3		44	.251
1910	STL	N	2-3-O		7	.227
			BRTR		190	.224

BARBEE, DAVID MONROE
B.MAY 7,1905 GREENSBORO,N.C.
D.JULY 1,1968 ALBERMARLE,N.C.
1926	PHI	A	O		19	.173
1932	PIT	N	O		97	.257
			BRTR		116	.246

BARBER, CHARLES D.
B.1854 MARTINSBURG,PA.
D.NOV.23,1914 PHILADELPHIA,PA.
| 1884 | CIN | U | 2 | | 48 | .190 |
| | | | BR | | | |

BARBER, STEPHEN DAVID (STEVE)
B.FEB.22,1939 TAKOMA PARK,MD.
1960	BAL	A	P		36	10- 7
1961	BAL	A	P		37	18-12
1962	BAL	A	P		28	9- 6
1963	BAL	A	P		39	20-13
1964	BAL	A	P		36	9-13
1965	BAL	A	P		37	15-10
1966	BAL	A	P		25	10- 5
1967	BAL	A	P		15	4- 9
		NY	A	P		17	6- 9
1968	NY	A	P		20	6- 5
1969	SEA	A	P		25	4- 7
1970	CHI	N	/P		5	0- 1
		ATL	N	/P		5	0- 1
1971	ATL	N	P		39	3- 1
1972	ATL	N	/P		5	0- 0
		CAL	A	P		34	4- 4
1973	CAL	A	P		50	3- 2
1974	SF	N	P		13	0- 1
			BLTL		466	121-106

BARBER, STEVEN LEE (STEVE)
B.MAR.13,1948 GRAND RAPIDS,MICH.
1970	MIN	A	/P	18	19	0- 0
1971	MIN	A	/P	4	6	1- 0
			BRTR	22	25	1- 0

YR	CL	LEA	POS	GP	G	REC

BARBER, TYRUS TURNER (TURNER)
B.JULY 9,1893 LAVINIA,TENN.
D.OCT.20,1968 MILAN,TENN.

YR	CL	LEA	POS	GP	G	REC
1915	WAS	A	O		20	.302
1916	WAS	A	O		15	.212
1917	CHI	N	O		7	.214
1918	CHI	N	1-O		55	.236
1919	CHI	N	O		76	.313
1920	CHI	N	1-O		94	.265
1921	CHI	N	O		127	.314
1922	CHI	N	1-O		84	.309
1923	BRO	N	O		13	.217
	BLTR				491	.289

BARBERICH, FRANK FREDERICK
B.FEB.3,1882 NEW TOWN,N.Y.
D.MAY 1,1965 OCALA,FLA.

1907	BOS	N	P		2	1- 0
1910	BOS	A	P		2	0- 0
	BBTR				4	1- 0

BARBIERI, JAMES PATRICK (JIM)
B.SEP.15,1941 SCHENECTADY,N.Y.

| 1966 | LA | N | O | | 39 | .280 |
| | BLTR | | | | | |

BARCLAY, CURTIS CORDELL (CURT)
B.AUG.22,1931 CHICAGO,ILL.

1957	NY	N	P		37	9- 9
1958	SF	N	P		6	1- 0
1959	SF	N	P		1	0- 0
	BRTR				44	10- 9

BARCLAY, GEORGE OLIVER (DEERFOOT)
B.MAY 16,1876 MILLVILLE,PA.
D.APR.3,1909 PHILADELPHIA,PA.

1902	STL	N	O		137	.301
1903	STL	N	O		107	.248
1904	STL	N	O		103	.200
	BOS	N	O		24	.226
1905	BOS	N	O		28	.176
	TR				399	.249

BARE, RAYMOND DOUGLAS (RAY)
B.APR.15,1949 MIAMI,FLA.

1972	STL	N	P		14	0- 1
1974	STL	N	P		10	1- 2
1975	DET	A	P		29	8-13
1976	DET	A	P		30	7- 8
1977	DET	A	/P		5	0- 2
	BRTR				88	16-26

BARFOOT, CLYDE RAYMOND (FOOTS)
B.JULY 8,1891 RICHMOND,VA.
D.MAR.11,1971 HIGHLAND PARK,CAL

1922	STL	N	P		42	4- 5
1923	STL	N	P	33	37	3- 3
1926	DET	A	P		11	1- 2
	BRTR			86	90	8-10

BARGER, EROS BOLIVAR (CY)
B.MAY 18,1885 JAMESTOWN,KY.
D.SEPT.23,1964 COLUMBIA,KY.

1906	NY	A	P		2	0- 0
1907	NY	A	P		1	0- 0
1910	BRO	N	P		35	15-15
1911	BRO	N	P	30	42	11-15
1912	BRO	N	P	16	17	1- 9
1914	PIT	F	P		33	10-16
1915	PIT	F	P		34	9- 8
	BLTR			151	164	46-63

BARKER, ALFRED
B.JAN.18,1839 ROCKFO-D,ILL.
D.SEPT.15,1912

| 1871 | ROK | NA | O | | 1 | - |

BARKER, LEONARD HAROLD (LEN)
B.JULY 7,1955 FORT KNOX,KY.

1976	TEX	A	P		2	1- 0
1977	TEX	A	P		15	4- 1
1978	TEX	A	P		29	1- 5
	BRTR				46	6- 6

BARKER, RAYMOND HERRELL
(RAY) OR (BUDDY)
B.MAR.12,1936 MARTINSBURG,W.VA.

1960	BAL	A	O		5	.000
1965	CLE	A	/1		11	.000
	NY	A	1/3		98	.254
1966	NY	A	1		61	.187
1967	NY	A	1		17	.077
	BLTR				192	.214

BARKLEY, JOHN DUNCAN (RED)
B.SEPT.19,1913 CHILDRESS,TEX.

1937	STL	A	2		31	.267
1939	BOS	N	S-3		12	.000
1943	BRO	N	S		20	.314
	BRTR				63	.264

BARKLEY, SAMUEL WILSON
B.MAY 19,1859 WHEELING,W.VA.
D.APR.20,1912 WHEELING,W.VA.

1884	TOL	AA	2		104	.300
1885	STL	AA	1-2		96	.179
1886	PIT	AA	2		122	.269
1887	PIT	N	1-2		90	.286
1888	KC	AA	M-2		116	.220
1889	KC	AA	2		45	.277
	TR				573	.279

BARLOW, MICHAEL ROSWELL (MIKE)
B.APR.30,1948 STAMFORD,N.Y.

1975	STL	N	/P		9	0- 0
1976	HOU	N	P		16	2- 2
1977	CAL	A	P		20	4- 2
1978	CAL	A	/P		1	0- 0
	BLTR				46	6- 4

BARLOW, THOMAS H.

1872	ATL	NA	C-S		35	.276
1873	ATL	NA	C		23	-
	MUT	NA	C		1	-
	ATL	NA	C		31	-
1874	HAR	NA	S		32	-
1875	NH	NA	S		1	-
	ATL	NA	2		1	.000
					124	-

BARMES, BRUCE RAYMOND (SQUEAKY)
B.OCT.23,1929 VINCENNES,IND.

| 1953 | WAS | A | O | | 5 | .200 |
| | BLTR | | | | | |

BARNA, HERBERT PAUL (BABE)
B.MAR.2,1915 CLARKSBURG,W.VA.
D.MAY 18,1972 CHARLESTON,W.VA.

1937	PHI	A	H		14	.389
1938	PHI	A	O		9	.133
1941	NY	N	O		10	.214
1942	NY	N	O		104	.257
1943	NY	N	O		40	.204
	BOS	A	O		30	.170
	BLTR				207	.232

BARNABE, CHARLES EDWARD
B.JUNE 12,1900 RUSSELL GULCH,COLO.
D.AUG.16,1977 WACO,TEX.

1927	CHI	A	P	17	18	0- 5
1928	CHI	A	P	7	11	0- 2
	BLTL			24	29	0- 7

BARNES, EMILE DEERING (RED)
B.DEC.25,1903 SUGGSVILLE,ALA.
D.JULY 3,1959 MOBILE,ALA.

1927	WAS	A	O		3	.364
1928	WAS	A	O		114	.305
1929	WAS	A	O		72	.200
1930	WAS	A	O		12	.167
	CHI	A	O		85	.248
	BLTR				286	.269

BARNES, EVERETT DUANE (EPPIE)
B.DEC.1,1900 OSSINING,N.Y.

1923	PIT	N	1		2	.500
1924	PIT	N	1		2	.000
	BLTL				4	.143

BARNES, FRANK
B.AUG.26,1928 LONGWOOD,MISS.

1957	STL	N	P	3	4	0- 1
1958	STL	N	P	8	13	1- 1
1960	STL	N	P		4	0- 1
	BRTR			15	21	1- 3

BARNES, FRANK SAMUEL (LEFTY)
B.JAN.9,1900 DALLAS,TEX.
D.SEPT.27,1967 HOUSTON,TEX.

1929	DET	A	P		4	0- 1
1930	NY	A	P		3	0- 1
	BLTL				7	0- 2

BARNES, JESSE LAWRENCE
(JESS) OR (NUBBY)
B.AUG.26,1892 PERKINS,OKLA.
D.SEPT.9,1961 SANTA ROSA,N.MEX.

1915	BOS	N	P		9	3- 0
1916	BOS	N	P		33	6-14
1917	BOS	N	P	50	53	13-21
1918	NY	N	P		9	6- 1
1919	NY	N	P	38	46	25- 9
1920	NY	N	P	43	45	20-15
1921	NY	N	P		42	15- 9
1922	NY	N	P		37	13- 8
1923	NY	N	P		12	3- 1
	BOS	N	P		31	10-14
1924	BOS	N	P		37	15-20
1925	BOS	N	P		32	11-16
1926	BRO	N	P		31	10-11
1927	BRO	N	P		18	2-10
	BLTR			422	435	152-149

BARNES, JOHN FRANCIS (HONEY)
B.JAN.31,1900 FULTON,N.Y.

| 1926 | NY | A | C | | 1 | .000 |
| | BLTR | | | | | |

BARNES, JUNIE SHOAF (LEFTY)
B.DEC.1,1911 LINWOOD,N.C.
D.DEC.31,1963 JACKSONVILLE,N.C.

| 1934 | CIN | N | P | | 2 | 0- 0 |
| | BLTL | | | | | |

BARNES, LUTHER OWENS (LUTE)
B.APR.28,1947 FOREST CITY,IOWA

1972	NY	N	2/S		24	.236
1973	NY	N	/H		3	.500
	BRTR				27	.243

BARNES, ROBERT AVERY (LEFTY)
B.JAN.6,1902 WASHBURN,ILL.

| 1924 | CHI | A | P | | 2 | 0- 0 |
| | BLTL | | | | | |

BARNES, ROSCOE CONKLING (ROSS)
B.MAY 8,1850 MT.MORRIS,N.Y.
D.FEB.5,1915 CHICAGO,ILL.

1871	BOS	NA	2-S		33	.374
1872	BOS	NA	2		45	.404
1873	BOS	NA	2-3		60	.406
1874	BOS	NA	2		52	.353
1875	BOS	NA	2-O		78	.372
1876	CHI	N	2		66	.404
1877	CHI	N	2		22	.272
1879	CIN	N	2-S		76	.256
1881	BOS	N	2-S		69	.271
	BRTR				501	.350

BARNES, SAMUEL THOMAS
B.DEC.18,1899 SUGGSVILLE,ALA.

| 1921 | DET | A | 2 | | 7 | .182 |

BARNES, VIRGIL JENNINGS (ZEKE)
B.MAR.5,1897 ONTARIO,KAN.
D.JULY 24,1958 WICHITA,KAN.

1919	NY	N	P		1	0- 0
1920	NY	N	P		1	0- 1
1922	NY	N	P		22	1- 0
1923	NY	N	P		22	2- 3
1924	NY	N	P		35	16-10
1925	NY	N	P		32	15-11
1926	NY	N	P		31	8-13
1927	NY	N	P		35	14-11
1928	NY	N	P		10	3- 3
	BOS	N	P		16	2- 7
	BRTR				205	61-59

BARNES, WILLIAM H.
B.INDIANAPOLIS,IND.

| 1884 | STP | U | C | | 8 | .161 |

BARNEY, EDMUND J.
B.JAN.23,1890 AMERY,WIS.
D.OCT.4,1967 RICE LAKE,WIS.

1915	NY	A	O		11	.191
	PIT	N	O		32	.273
1916	PIT	N	O		45	.197
	BLTR				88	.224

BARNEY, REX EDWARD
B.DEC.19,1924 OMAHA,NEB.

1943	BRO	N	P		9	2- 2
1946	BRO	N	P		16	2- 5
1947	BRO	N	P		28	5- 2
1948	BRO	N	P		44	15-13
1949	BRO	N	P		38	9- 8
1950	BRO	N	P		20	2- 1
	BRTR				155	35-31

BARNHART, CLYDE LEE (POOCH)
B.DEC.29,1895 BUCK VALLEY,PA.

1920	PIT	N	3		12	.326
1921	PIT	N	3		124	.258
1922	PIT	N	3-O		75	.330
1923	PIT	N	O		114	.324
1924	PIT	N	O		102	.276
1925	PIT	N	O		142	.325
1926	PIT	N	O		76	.192
1927	PIT	N	O		108	.319
1928	PIT	N	O		61	.296
	BRTR				814	.295

BARNHART, EDGAR VERNON
B.SEPT.16,1904 PROVIDENCE,MO.

| 1924 | STL | A | P | | 1 | 0- 0 |
| | BLTR | | | | | |

BARNHART, LESLIE EARL (BARNEY)
B.FEB.23,1905 HOXIE,KAN.
D.OCT.7,1971 SCOTTSDALE,ARIZ.

1928	CLE	A	P		2	0- 1
1930	CLE	A	P		1	1- 0
	BRTR				3	1- 1

BARNHART, VICTOR DEE
B.SEPT.1,1922 HAGERSTOWN,MD.

1944	PIT	N	S		1	.500
1945	PIT	N	S-3		71	.269
1946	PIT	N	H		2	.000
	BRTR				74	.270

YR	CL LEA POS	GP	G	REC

BARNICLE, GEORGE BERNARD (BARNEY)
B.AUG.26,1917 FITCHBURG,MASS.
1939 BOS N P		6	2- 2
1940 BOS N P		13	1- 0
1941 BOS N P		1	0- 1
BRTR		20	3- 3

BARNIE, WILLIAM HARRISON (BALD BILLY)
B.JAN.26,1853 NEW YORK,N.Y.
D.JULY 15,1900 HARTFORD,CONN.
1874 HAR NA C-S-O	44	-
1875 WES NA C-O	10	-
MUT NA C-O	10	-
1883 BAL AA M-C-S-O	17	.200
	81	-

NON-PLAYING MANAGER
BAL[AA] 1884-91, ATH[AA] 1891,
WAS(N) 1892, LOU(N) 1893-94
AND BRO(N) 1897-98.

BARNOWSKI, EDWARD ANTHONY (ED)
B.AUG.23,1943 SCRANTON,PA.
1965 BAL A /P		4	0- 0
1966 BAL A /P		2	0- 0
BRTR		6	0- 0

BARONE, RICHARD ANTHONY (DICK)
B.OCT.3,1932 SAN JOSE,CAL.
| 1960 PIT N S | | 3 | .000 |
| BRTR | | | |

BARR, HYDER EDWARD (SCOTTY)
B.OCT.6,1886 BRISTOL,TENN.
D.DEC.2,1934 FT.WORTH,TEX.
1908 PHI A 2	19	.143
1909 PHI A O	22	.079
BRTR	41	.112

BARR, JAMES LELAND (JIM)
B.FEB.10,1948 LYNWOOD,CAL.
1971 SF N P		17	1- 1
1972 SF N P		44	8-10
1973 SF N P		41	11-17
1974 SF N P	44	56	13- 9
1975 SF N P	35	38	13-14
1976 SF N P	37	41	15-12
1977 SF N P	38	44	12-16
1978 SF N P	32	34	8-11
BRTR	288	315	81-90

BARR, ROBERT ALEXANDER
B.MAR.12,1908 NEWTON,MASS.
| 1935 BRO N P | | 2 | 0- 0 |
| BRTR | | | |

BARR, ROBERT MC CLELLAND
B.1856 WASHINGTON,D.C.
D.MAR.11,1930 WASHINGTON,D.C.
1883 PIT AA P-1-	24	28	6-18
O			.230
1884 WAS AA P-1-	33	39	9-24
O			.152
IND AA P-O	16	18	3-11
			.188
1886 WAS N P		22	4-18
1890 ROC AA P		57	28-25
1891 NY N P		5	0- 3
	157	169	50-99
			.204

BARR, STEVEN CHARLES (STEVE)
B.SEPT.8,1951 ST.LOUIS,MO.
1974 BOS A /P		1	1- 0
1975 BOS A /P		3	0- 1
1976 TEX A P		20	2- 6
BLTL		24	3- 7

BARRAGAN, FACUNDO (CUNO)NY
B.JUNE 20,1932 SACRAMENTO,CAL.
1961 CHI N C	10	.214
1962 CHI N C	58	.201
1963 CHI N C	1	.000
BRTR	69	.202

BARRETT, CHARLES HENRY (RED)
B.FEB.14,1915 SANTA BARBARA,CAL
1937 CIN N P		1	0- 0
1938 CIN N P		6	2- 0
1939 CIN N P		2	0- 0
1940 CIN N P		3	1- 0
1943 BOS N P		38	12-18
1944 BOS N P		42	9-16
1945 BOS N P		9	2- 3
STL N P		36	21- 9
1946 STL N P		23	3- 2
1947 BOS N P		36	11-12
1948 BOS N P		34	7- 8
1949 BOS N P		23	1- 1
BRTR		253	69-69

BARRETT, FRANCIS JOSEPH (FRANK) OR (RED)
B.JULY 1,1913 FT.LAUDERDALE,FLA
1939 STL N P		1	0- 1
1944 BOS A P		38	8- 7
1945 BOS A P		37	4- 3
1946 BOS N P		23	2- 4
1950 PIT N P		5	1- 2
BRTR		104	15-17

BARRETT, JAMES ERIGENA
B.MAR.28,1875 ATHOL,MASS.
D.OCT.24,1921 DETROIT,MICH.
1899 CIN N O	26	.374
1900 CIN N O	138	.316
1901 DET A O	136	.294
1902 DET A O	136	.304
1903 DET A O	136	.315
1904 DET A O	162	.269
1905 DET A O	18	.254
1906 CIN N O	5	.000
1907 BOS A O	106	.243
1908 BOS A O	3	.125
BLTR	866	.291

BARRETT, JOHN JOSEPH (JACK)
B.DEC.18,1915 LOWELL,MASS.
D.AUG.17,1974 SEABROOK BEACH,N.H.
1942 PIT N O	111	.247
1943 PIT N O	130	.231
1944 PIT N O	149	.269
1945 PIT N O	142	.256
1946 PIT N O	32	.169
BOS N O	24	.233
BLTL	588	.251

BARRETT, MARTIN
B.CENTRAL FALLS,R.I.
| 1884 BOS N C | 3 | .000 |
| BRTR | | |

**BARRETT, RICHARD OLIVER
[SEE TRACY SOUTER BARRETT]**

BARRETT, ROBERT SCHLEY (JUMBO)
B.JAN.27,1899 ATLANTA,GA.
1923 CHI N H	3	.333
1924 CHI N 1-2-3	54	.241
1925 CHI N 2-3	14	.313
BRO N H	1	.000
1927 BRO N H	99	.259
1929 BOS A 3	68	.270
BRTR	239	.260

**BARRETT, TRACY SOUTER (KEWPIE)
[ALSO PLAYED UNDER NAMES OF
RICHARD OLIVER, 1933 AND
RICHARD OLIVER BARRETT 1934-43]**
B.SEPT.28,1906 MONTOURSVILLE,PA
D.OCT.30,1966 SEATTLE,WASH.
1933 PHI A P		15	4- 4
1934 BOS N P		15	1- 3
1943 CHI N P		15	0- 4
PHI N P		23	10- 9
1944 PHI N P		37	12-18
1945 PHI N P		36	8-20
BRTR		141	35-58

BARRETT, WILLIAM
B.WASHINGTON,D.C.
1871 KEK NA C	1	-
1872 OLY NA C	1	.000
ATL NA O	7	.267
1873 BAL NA O	1	-
	10	-

BARRETT, WILLIAM JOSEPH (WHISPERING BILL)
B.MAY 28,1900 CAMBRIDGE,MASS.
D.JAN.26,1951 CAMBRIDGE,MASS.
1921 PHI A P	4	14	1- 0
1923 CHI A O	44	.271
1924 CHI A S-O	119	.271
1925 CHI A 2-S-3-O	81	.363
1926 CHI A O	111	.307
1927 CHI A O	147	.286
1928 CHI A 2-O	76	.277
1929 CHI A O	3	.000
BOS A O	111	.270
1930 BOS A O	6	.176
WAS A H	6	.000
BRTR	4	718	1- 0
			.288

BARRIOS, FRANCISCO JAVIER [JIMENEZ]
B.JUNE 10,1953 HERMOSILLO,MEX.
1974 CHI A /P		2	0- 0
1976 CHI A P		35	5- 9
1977 CHI A P		33	14- 7
1978 CHI A P		33	9-15
BRTR		103	28-31

BARRON, DAVID IRENUS (RED)
B.JUNE 21,1900 CLARKSVILLE,GA.
| 1929 BOS N O | 10 | .190 |
| BRTR | | |

BARRON, FRANK JOHN
B.AUG.6,1890 ST.MARY S,W.VA.
D.SEPT.18,1964 ST.MARY S,W.VA.
| 1914 WAS A P | | 1 | 0- 0 |
| BLTL | | | |

BARROW, EDWARD GRANT (COUSIN ED)
B.MAY 10,1868 SPRINGFIELD,ILL.
D.DEC.15,1953 PORT CHESTER,N.Y.
NON-PLAYING MANAGER
DET[A] 1903-04, BOS[A] 1918-20.

BARROWS, FRANK LEWIS
B.BOSTON,MASS.
D.SEPT.24,1901
1871 BOS NA 2-O	20	-
1874 BAL NA O	16	-
	36	-

BARROWS, ROLAND (CUKE)
B.OCT.20,1883 GRAY,MAINE
D.FEB.10,1955 GORHAM,MAINE
1909 CHI A O	4	.150
1910 CHI A O	6	.200
1911 CHI A O	13	.195
1912 CHI A O	8	.231
BLTR	31	.190

BARRY, EDWARD (JUMBO)
B.FREEPORT,IND.
1905 BOS A P		7	1- 2
1906 BOS A P		3	0- 3
1907 BOS A P		2	0- 1
TL		12	1- 6

BARRY, HARDIN (FINN)
B.MAR.26,1891 SUSANVILLE,CAL.
D.NOV.5,1969 CARSON CITY,NEV.
| 1912 PHI A P | | 3 | 0- 0 |
| BRTR | | | |

BARRY, JOHN C. (SHAD)
B.SEPT.28,1876 NEWBURGH,N.Y.
D.NOV.27,1936 LOS ANGELES,CAL.
1899 WAS N O	75	.303
1900 BOS N 2-S-O	66	.261
1901 BOS N O	11	.179
PHI N 3-O	63	.245
1902 PHI N 1-O	138	.302
1903 PHI N 1-O	138	.276
1904 PHI N 1-O	33	.205
CIN N 1-O	72	.262
1905 CIN N 1	26	.212
CIN N 1	126	.324
1906 CIN N 1-O	73	.287
STL N 1-O	62	.249
1907 STL N O	81	.248
1908 STL N O	71	.228
NY N O	31	.149
BRTR	1066	.270

BARRY, JOHN JOSEPH (JACK)
B.APR.26,1887 MERIDEN,CONN.
D.APR.23,1961 SHREWSBURY,MASS.
1908 PHI A 2	40	.222
1909 PHI A S	124	.215
1910 PHI A S	145	.259
1911 PHI A S	127	.265
1912 PHI A S	139	.261
1913 PHI A S	135	.275
1914 PHI A S	140	.242
1915 PHI A S	54	.218
BOS A 2	78	.265
1916 BOS A 2	94	.203
1917 BOS A M-2	116	.214
1919 BOS A 2	31	.241
BRTR	1223	.243

BARRY, RICHARD DONOVAN (RICH)
B.SEP.12,1940 BERKELEY,CAL.
| 1969 PHI N /O | 20 | .188 |
| BRTR | | |

BARRY, THOMAS ARTHUR
B.APR.10,1879 ST.LOUIS,MO.
D.JUNE 4,1946 ST.LOUIS,MO.
| 1904 PHI N P | | 1 | 0- 1 |

YR	CL	LEA	POS	GP	G	REC

BARTELL, RICHARD WILLIAM
(DICK) OR (ROWDY RICHARD)
B.NOV.22,1907 CHICAGO,ILL.

YR	CL	LEA	POS	GP	G	REC
1927	PIT	N	S	1		.000
1928	PIT	N	2-S	72		.305
1929	PIT	N	2-S	143		.302
1930	PIT	N	S	129		.320
1931	PHI	N	S	135		.289
1932	PHI	N	S	154		.308
1933	PHI	N	S	152		.271
1934	PHI	N	S	146		.310
1935	NY	N	S	137		.262
1936	NY	N	S	145		.298
1937	NY	N	S	128		.306
1938	NY	N	S	127		.262
1939	CHI	N	S	105		.238
1940	DET	A	S	139		.233
1941	DET	A	S	5		.167
	NY	N	S-3	104		.303
1942	NY	N	S-3	90		.244
1943	NY	N	S-3	99		.270
1946	NY	N	2-3	5		.000
			BRTR	2016		.284

BARTHELSON, ROBERT EDWARD
B.JULY 15,1924 NEW HAVEN,CONN.

| 1944 | NY | N | P | 7 | | 1- 1 |
| | | | BRTR | | | |

BARTHOLD, JOHN FRANCIS (HANS)
B.APR.14,1882 PHILADELPHIA,PA.
D.NOV.4,1946 FAIRVIEW VILLAGE,PA.

| 1904 | PHI | A | P | 4 | | 0- 1 |
| | | | BBTR | | | |

BARTHOLOMEW, LESTER JUSTIN
B.APR.4,1903 MADISON,WIS.
D.SEPT.19,1972 BARRINGTON,ILL.

1928	PIT	N	P	6		0- 0
1932	CHI	A	P	3		0- 0
			BRTL	9		0-0

BARTIROME, ANTHONY JOSEPH
B.MAY 9,1932 PITTSBURGH,PA.

| 1952 | PIT | N | 1 | 124 | | .220 |
| | | | BLTL | | | |

BARTLEY, BOYD OWEN
B.FEB.11,1920 CHICAGO,ILL.

| 1943 | BRO | N | S | 9 | | .048 |
| | | | BRTR | | | |

BARTLEY, WILLIAM JACKSON
B.JAN.8,1885 CINCINNATI,OHIO
D.MAY 17,1965 CINCINNATI,OHIO

1903	NY	N	P	1		0- 0
1906	PHI	A	P	3		0- 0
1907	PHI	A	P	15		0- 0
			BRTR	19		0- 0

BARTLING, IRVING HENRY
B.JUNE 27,1914 BAY CITY,MICH.
D.JUNE 12,1973 WESTLAND,MICH.

| 1938 | PHI | A | S | 14 | | .174 |

BARTON, HARRY LAMB
B.JAN.20,1875 CHESTER,PA.
D.JAN.25,1955 UPLAND,PA.

| 1905 | PHI | A | C | 18 | | .167 |
| | | | BBTR | | | |

BARTON, ROBERT WILBUR (BOB)
B.JULY 30,1941 NORWOOD,O.

1965	SF	N	/C	4		.571
1966	SF	N	C	43		.176
1967	SF	N	/C	7		.211
1968	SF	N	C	46		.261
1969	SF	N	C	49		.170
1970	SD	N	C	61		.218
1971	SD	N	*C	121		.250
1972	SD	N	C	29		.193
1973	CIN	N	/C	3		.000
1974	SD	N	C	30		.235
			BRTR	393		.226

BARTON, VINCENT DAVID
B.FEB.1,1908 EDMONTON,ALBERTA,CANADA
D.SEPT.13,1973 TORONTO,ONT.,CAN

1931	CHI	N	O	66		.238
1932	CHI	N	O	36		.224
			BLTR	102		.233

BARTOSCH, DAVID ROBERT
B.MAR.24,1917 ST.LOUIS,MO.

| 1945 | STL | N | O | 24 | | .255 |
| | | | BRTR | | | |

BARTSON, CHARLES FRANKLIN
B.MAR.13,1865 PEORIA,ILL.
D.JUNE 9,1936 PEORIA,ILL.

| 1890 | CHI | P | P | 26 | | 9-14 |

BASGALL, ROMANUS (MONTY)
B.FEB.8,1922 PFEIFER,KAN.

1948	PIT	N	2	38		.216
1949	PIT	N	2-3	107		.218
1951	PIT	N	2	55		.209
			BRTR	200		.215

BASHANG, ALBERT C.
B.AUG.22,1888 CINCINNATI,OHIO
D.JUNE 23,1967 CINCINNATI,OHIO

1912	DET	A	O	6		.167
1918	BRO	N	O	2		.200
			BBTR	8		.174

BASHORE, WALTER FRANKLIN
B.OCT.6,1909 HARRISBURG,PA.

| 1936 | PHI | N | O | 10 | | .200 |

BASINSKI, EDWIN FRANK
(BAZOOKA) OR (FIDDLER)
B.NOV.4,1922 BUFFALO,N.Y.

1944	BRO	N	2-S	39		.257
1945	BRO	N	2-S	108		.262
1947	PIT	N	2	56		.199
			BBTR	203		.244

BASKETTE, JAMES BLAINE (BIG JIM)
B.DEC.10,1887 ATHENS,TENN.
D.JULY 30,1942 ATHENS,TENN.

1911	CLE	A	P	4		1- 2
1912	CLE	A	P	29		8- 4
1913	CLE	A	P	2		0- 0
			BRTR	35		9- 6

BASS, JOHN E.
B.1850 BALTIMORE,MD.

1871	CLE	NA	3	23		-
1872	ATL	NA	O	1		.250
1877	HAR	N	O	1		.250
				25		-

BASS, NORMAN DELANEY (NORM)
B.JAN.21,1939 LAUREL,MISS.

1961	KC	A	P	40	41	11-11
1962	KC	A	P	22	2- 6
1963	KC	A	P	3		0- 0
			BRTR	65	66	13-17

BASS, RANDY WILLIAM
B.MAR.13,1954 LAWTON,OKLA.

1977	MIN	A	/H	9		.105
1978	KC	A	/H	2		.000
			BLTR	11		.95

BASS, RICHARD WILLIAM
B.JULY 7,1906 ROGERSVILLE,TENN.

| 1939 | WAS | A | P | 1 | | 0- 1 |
| | | | BRTR | | | |

BASS, WILLIAM C. (DOC)
B.CINCINNATI,OHIO

| 1918 | BOS | N | O | 1 | | 1.000 |

BASSETT, CHARLES EDWIN
B.FEB.9,1863 CENTRAL FALLS,R.I.
D.MAY 28,1942 PAWTUCKET,R.I.

1884	PRO	N	2-S-3-O	21		.144
1885	PRO	N	2-S-3-O	81		.143
1886	KC	N	S	90		.260
1887	IND	N	2	119		.270
1888	IND	N	2	128		.241
1889	IND	N	2	126		.253
1890	NY	N	2	100		.239
1891	NY	N	3	130		.266
1892	NY	N	2-3	34		.185
	LOU	N	2-3	78		.213
			BRTR	907		.237

BASSLER, JOHN LANDIS
B.JUNE 3,1895 LANCASTER,PA.

1913	CLE	A	C	1		.000
1914	CLE	A	C	43		.182
1921	DET	A	C	119		.307
1922	DET	A	C	121		.323
1923	DET	A	C	135		.298
1924	DET	A	C	124		.346
1925	DET	A	C	121		.279
1926	DET	A	C	66		.305
1927	DET	A	C	81		.285
			BLTR	811		.304

BASTIAN, CHARLES J.
B.JULY 4,1860 PHILADELPHIA,PA.
D.JAN.18,1932 MERCHANTVILLE,N.J

1884	WIL	U	P-2-S	1	17	0- 0
						.200
	KC	U	2		11	.255
1885	PHI	N	S	104		.167
1886	PHI	N	2	104		.217
1887	PHI	N	2-S	60		.275
1888	PHI	N	2	80		.192
1889	CHI	N	S	46		.135
1890	CHI	P	2-S	80		.186
1891	CIN	AA	2	1		.000
	PHI	N	S	1		.000
			BRTR	1	504	0- 0
						.198

BATCH, EMIL (HEINIE) OR (ACE)
B.JAN.21,1880 BROOKLYN,N.Y.
D.AUG.23,1926 BROOKLYN,N.Y.

1904	BRO	N	3	28		.255
1905	BRO	N	3	145		.252
1906	BRO	N	O	52		.256
1907	BRO	N	O	106		.247
			BRTR	331		.251

BATCHELDER, JOSEPH EDMUND (WIN)
B.JULY 11,1898 WENHAM,MASS.

1923	BOS	N	P	4		1- 0
1924	BOS	N	P	3		0- 0
1925	BOS	N	P	4		0- 0
			BRTL	11		1- 0

BATEMAN, JOHN ALVIN
B.JULY 21,1942 KILLEEN,TEX.

1963	HOU	N	C	128		.210
1964	HOU	N	C	74		.190
1965	HOU	N	C	45		.197
1966	HOU	N	*C	131		.279
1967	HOU	N	C	76		.190
1968	HOU	N	*C	111		.249
1969	MON	N	C	74		.209
1970	MON	N	*C	139		.237
1971	MON	N	*C	139		.242
1972	MON	N	/C	18		.241
	PHI	N	C	82		.222
			BRTR	1017		.230

BATES, BUSH

| 1889 | KC | AA | P | 1 | | 0- 1 |

BATES, CHARLES RICHARD (DICK)
B.OCT.7,1945 MCARTHUR,O.

| 1969 | SEA | A | /P | 1 | | 0- 0 |
| | | | BLTR | | | |

BATES, CHARLES WILLIAM
B.SEPT.17,1905 PHILADELPHIA,PA.

| 1927 | PHI | A | O | 9 | | .237 |
| | | | BRTR | | | |

BATES, DELBERT OAKLEY (DEL)
B.JUNE 12,1940 SEATTLE,WASH.

| 1970 | PHI | N | C | 22 | | .133 |

BATES, FRANK CHARLES
B.CHATTANOOGA,TENN.

1898	CLE	N	P	4		2- 1
1899	STL	N	P	4		0- 0
	CLE	N	P	20		1-19
				28		3-20

BATES, HUBERT EDGAR (BUD)
B.MAR.16,1912 LOS ANGELES,CAL.

| 1939 | PHI | N | O | 15 | | .259 |
| | | | BRTR | | | |

BATES, JOHN WILLIAM
B.AUG.21,1882 STEUBENVILLE,OHIO
D.FEB.10,1949 STEUBENVILLE,OHIO

1906	BOS	N	O	140		.252
1907	BOS	N	O	119		.260
1908	BOS	N	O	117		.258
1909	BOS	N	O	60		.268
	PHI	N	O	73		.293
1910	PHI	N	O	131		.305
1911	CIN	N	O	147		.292
1912	CIN	N	O	81		.289
1913	CIN	N	O	131		.276
1914	CIN	N	O	58		.252
	CHI	N	O	9		.125
	BAL	F	O	59		.307
			BLTL	1125		.278

BATES, RAYMOND
B.FEB.9,1890 PATERSON,N.J.
D.AUG.15,1970 TUCSON,ARIZ.

1913	CLE	A	3	20		.167
1917	PHI	A	3	127		.237
			BRTR	147		.233

BATISTA, RAFAEL
[REAL NAME RAFAEL ROBLE (BATISTA)]
B.NOV.21,1945 INGENIO CONSUELO,P.R.

1973	HOU	N	/1	12		.267
1975	HOU	N	H	10		.300
			BLTL	22		.280

BATSCH, WILLIAM MC KINLEY
B.MAY 18,1892 MINGO JUNCTION,O.
D.DEC.31,1963 CANTON,OHIO

| 1916 | PIT | N | H | 1 | | .000 |
| | | | BRTR | | | |

BATTAM, LAWRENCE
B.MAY 1,1878 BROOKLYN,N.Y.
D.JAN.27,1938 BROOKLYN,N.Y.

| 1895 | NY | N | 3 | 2 | | .250 |

BATTEN, GEORGE BURNETT
B.OCT.7,1891 HADDONFIELD,N.J.
D.AUG.4,1972 NEW PORT RICHEY,FLA.

| 1912 | NY | A | 2 | 1 | | .000 |
| | | | BRTR | | | |

YR	CL LEA POS	GP	G	REC

BATTEY, EARL JESSE
B.JAN.5,1935 LOS ANGELES,CAL.
1955	CHI A C		5	.286
1956	CHI A C		4	.250
1957	CHI A C		48	.174
1958	CHI A C		68	.226
1959	CHI A C		26	.219
1960	WAS A C		137	.270
1961	MIN A C		133	.302
1962	MIN A C		148	.280
1963	MIN A C		147	.285
1964	MIN A C		131	.272
1965	MIN A *C		131	.297
1966	MIN A *C		115	.255
1967	MIN A C		48	.165
	BRTR		1141	.270

BATTIN, JOSEPH V.
B.NOV.11,1851 PHILADELPHIA,PA.
D.DEC.10,1937 AKRON,OHIO
1871	CLE NA O		1	-
1873	ATH NA O		1	-
1874	ATH NA 2-S-O		51	-
1875	STL NA 2-3		63	.263
1876	STL N 3		64	.294
1877	STL N P-2-	1	57	0- 0
	3-O			.199
1882	PIT AA 3		28	.207
1883	PIT AA M-P-3	1	96	0- 0
				.202
1884	PIT AA M-3		43	.178
	PIT U M-3		18	.197
	BAL U 2-3		17	.086
1890	SYR AA 3		29	.194
	BRTR	2	468	0- 0
				-

BATTLE, JAMES MILTON
B.MAR.26,1901 BAILEY,TEX.
D.SEPT.30,1965 CHICO,CAL.
| 1927 | CHI A S-3 | | 6 | .375 |
| | BRTR | | | |

BATTON, CHRISTOPHER SEAN (CHRIS)
B.AUG.24,1954 LOS ANGELES,CAL.
| 1976 | OAK A /P | | 2 | 0- 0 |
| | BRTR | | | |

BATTS, MATTHEW DANIEL (MATT)
B.OCT.16,1921 SAN ANTONIO,TEX.
1947	BOS A C		7	.500
1948	BOS A C		46	.314
1949	BOS A C		60	.242
1950	BOS A C		75	.273
1951	BOS A C		11	.136
	STL A C		79	.302
1952	DET A C		56	.237
1953	DET A C		116	.278
1954	DET A C		12	.286
	CHI A C		55	.228
1955	CIN N C		26	.254
1956	CIN N H		3	.000
	BRTR		546	.269

BAUCKER, JOHN (STUD)
B.PHILADELPHIA,PA.
| 1875 | NH NA C-2-S-3 | | 19 | - |

BAUER, HENRY ALBERT (HANK)
B.JULY 31,1922 E.ST.LOUIS,ILL.
1948	NY A O		19	.180
1949	NY A O		103	.272
1950	NY A O		113	.320
1951	NY A O		118	.296
1952	NY A O		141	.293
1953	NY A O		133	.304
1954	NY A O		114	.294
1955	NY A C-O		139	.278
1956	NY A O		147	.241
1957	NY A O		137	.259
1958	NY A O		128	.268
1959	NY A O		114	.238
1960	KC A O		95	.275
1961	KC A M-O		43	.264
	BRTR		1944	.277
NON-PLAYING MANAGER
KC[A] 1962, BAL[A] 1964-68,
OAK[A] 1969

BAUER, LOUIS WALTER
B.NOV.30,1898 EGG HARBOR CITY,N.J.
| 1918 | PHI A P | | 1 | 0- 0 |

BAUERS, ALBERT J.
B.1850 COLUMBUS,OHIO
D.SEPT.6,1913
1884	COL AA P		3	1- 2
1886	STL N P		4	0- 4
	TL		7	1- 6

BAUERS, RUSSELL LEE
B.MAY 10,1914 TOWNSEND,WIS.
1936	PIT N P		1	0- 0
1937	PIT N P		34	13- 6
1938	PIT N P		40	13-14
1939	PIT N P		15	2- 4
1940	PIT N P		15	0- 2
1941	PIT N P		8	1- 3
1946	CHI N P		15	2- 1
1950	STL A P		1	0- 0
	BLTR		129	31-30

BAUMANN, CHARLES JOHN (PADDY)
B.DEC.20,1885 INDIANAPOLIS,IND.
D.NOV.20,1969 INDIANAPOLIS,IND.
1911	DET A 2		26	.256
1912	DET A 3-O		13	.262
1913	DET A 2		49	.298
1914	DET A 2		3	.000
1915	NY A 2-3		76	.292
1916	NY A 3-O		79	.287
1917	NY A 2		49	.218
			295	.268

BAUMANN, FRANK MATT
(FRANK) OR (THE BEAU)
B.JULY 1,1933 ST.LOUIS,MO.
1955	BOS A P		7	2- 1
1956	BOS A P		7	2- 1
1957	BOS A P		4	1- 0
1958	BOS A P		10	2- 2
1959	BOS A P		26	6- 4
1960	CHI A P		47	13- 6
1961	CHI A P	53	55	10-13
1962	CHI A P		40	7- 6
1963	CHI A P		24	2- 1
1964	CHI A P		22	0- 3
1965	CHI N /P		4	0- 1
	BLTL		244 246	45-38

BAUMER, JAMES SLOAN (JIM)
B.JAN.29,1931 TULSA,OKLA.
1949	CHI A S		8	.400
1961	CIN N 2		10	.125
	BRTR		18	.206

BAUMGARDNER, GEORGE WASHINGTON
B.JULY 22,1891 BARBOURSVILLE,W.VA.
D.DEC.13,1970 BARBOURSVILLE,W.VA.
1912	STL A P		30	11-14
1913	STL A P		38	10-19
1914	STL A P		45	14-13
1915	STL A P		7	0- 2
1916	STL A P		4	1- 0
	BLTR		124	36-48

BAUMGARTEN, ROSS
B.MAY 27,1955 HIGHLAND PARK,ILL.
| 1978 | CHI A /P | | 7 | 2- 2 |
| | BLTL | | | |

BAUMGARTNER, HARRY E.
B.OCT.6,1892 S.PITTSBURG,TENN.
D.DEC.3,1930 AUGUSTA,GA.
| 1920 | DET A P | | 9 | 0- 1 |
| | BL | | | |

BAUMGARTNER, JOHN EDWARD
B.MAY 29,1931 BIRMINGHAM,ALA.
| 1953 | DET A 3 | | 7 | .185 |
| | BRTR | | | |

BAUMGARTNER, STANWOOD FULTON
B.DEC.14,1894 HOUSTON,TEX.
D.OCT.4,1955 PHILADELPHIA,PA.
1914	PHI N P		15	2- 2
1915	PHI N P		16	0- 2
1916	PHI N P		1	0- 0
1921	PHI N P	22	31	3- 6
1922	PHI N P		6	1- 1
1924	PHI A P		36	13- 6
1925	PHI A P		37	6- 3
1926	PHI A P		10	1- 1
	BLTL	143 152		26-21

BAUMHOLTZ, FRANK CONRAD
B.OCT.7,1918 MIDVALE,OHIO
1947	CIN N O		151	.283
1948	CIN N O		128	.296
1949	CIN N O		27	.235
	CHI N O		58	.226
1951	CHI N O		146	.284
1952	CHI N O		103	.325
1953	CHI N O		133	.306
1954	CHI N O		90	.297
1955	CHI N O		105	.289
1956	PHI N O		76	.270
1957	PHI N H		2	.000
	BLTL		1019	.293

BAUSEWINE, GEORGE
B.MAR.22,1869 PHILADELPHIA,PA.
D.JULY 29,1947 NORRISTOWN,PA.
| 1889 | ATH AA P | | 7 | 1- 4 |

BAUTA, EDUARDO [GALVEZ] (ED)
B.JAN.6,1935 FLORIDA CAMAGUEY,CUBA
1960	STL N P		9	0- 0
1961	STL N P		13	2- 0
1962	STL N P		20	1- 0
1963	STL N P		38	3- 4
	NY N P		9	0- 0
1964	NY N P		8	0- 2
	BRTR		97	6- 6

BAXES, DIMITRIOS S.
B.JULY 5,1928 SAN FRANCISCO,CAL
1959	LA N 3		11	.303
	CLE A 2-3		77	.239
	BRTR		88	.246

BAXES, MICHAEL (MIKE)
B.DEC.18,1930 SAN FRANCISCO,CAL
1956	KC A 2-S		73	.226
1958	KC A 2-S		73	.212
	BRTR		146	.217

BAXTER, JOHN
B.SPOKANE,WASH.
| 1907 | STL N 1 | | 6 | .190 |

BAY, HARRY ELBERT (DEERFOOT)
B.JAN.17,1878 PONTIAC,ILL.
D.MAR.20,1952 PEORIA,ILL.
1901	CIN N O		34	.205
1902	CIN N O		6	.375
	CLE A O		108	.287
1903	CLE A O		141	.310
1904	CLE A O		132	.260
1905	CLE A O		143	.298
1906	CLE A O		68	.275
1907	CLE A O		34	.179
1908	CLE A H		2	.000
	BLTL		668	.280

BAYER, CHRISTOPHER A.
[PLAYED UNDER NAME OF BURLEY BYERS]

BAYLESS, HARRY OWEN (DICK)
B.SEPT.6,1893 JOPLIN,MO.
D.DEC.16,1920 SANTA RITA,N.M.
| 1908 | CIN N O | | 19 | .225 |

BAYLOR, DON EDWARD
B.JUNE 28,1949 AUSTIN,TEX.
1970	BAL A /O		8	.235
1971	BAL A /O		1	.000
1972	BAL A O/1		102	.253
1973	BAL A *O/1		118	.286
1974	BAL A *O/1		137	.272
1975	BAL A *O/1		145	.282
1976	OAK A O-1-D		157	.247
1977	CAL A O-D-1		154	.251
1978	CAL A O-D-1		158	.255
	BRTR		980	.263

BAYNE, WILLIAM LEAR (BEVERLY)
B.APR.18,1899 PITTSBURGH,PA.
1919	STL A P		2	1- 1
1920	STL A P		18	5- 6
1921	STL A P		47	11- 5
1922	STL A P		26	4- 5
1923	STL A P		19	2- 2
1924	STL A P		22	1- 3
1928	CLE A P		37	2- 5
1929	BOS A P		27	5- 5
1930	BOS A P		1	0- 0
	BLTL		199	31-32

BEACH, STONEWALL JACKSON (JACK)
B.1862 ALEXANDRIA,VA.
| 1884 | WAS AA O | | 8 | .094 |

BEALL, JOHN WOOLF
B.MAR.12,1882 BELTSVILLE,MD.
D.JUNE 14,1926 BELTSVILLE,MD.
1913	CLE A H		6	.167
	CHI A O		17	.267
1915	CIN N O		10	.232
1916	CIN N O		6	.333
1918	STL N O		19	.224
	BLTR		58	.257

BEALL, ROBERT BROOKS (BOB)
B.APR.24,1948 PORTLAND,ORE.
1975	ATL N /1		20	.226
1978	ATL N 1/O		108	.243
	BBTL		128	.241

BEALL, WALTER ESAU
B.JULY 29,1899 WASHINGTON,D.C.
D.JAN.28,1959 SUITLAND,MD.
1924	NY A P		4	2- 0
1925	NY A P		8	0- 1
1926	NY A P		20	2- 4
1927	NY A P		1	0- 0
1929	WAS A P		3	1- 0
	BRTR		36	5- 5

BEALS, THOMAS L.
[PLAYED UNDER NAME OF
W.THOMAS IN 1871 AND 1873]
B.NOV.9,1911

YR	CL	LEA	POS	GP	G	REC
1871	OLY	NA	2-O		10	.194
1872	OLY	NA	2-S-O		9	.282
1873	NAT	NA	C-2-O		37	-
1874	BOS	NA	1-2-O		19	.204
1875	BOS	NA	2-O		35	.293
1880	CHI	N	2-O		13	.149
					123	-

BEAM, ALEXANDER RODGER
B.NOV.21,1870 JOHNSTOWN,PA.
D.APR.17,1938 NOGALES,ARIZ.

YR	CL	LEA	POS	GP	G	REC
1889	PIT	N	P		2	1- 1

BEAM, ERNEST J.
B.1867 MANSFIELD,OHIO
D.SEPT.13,1918 MANSFIELD,OHIO

YR	CL	LEA	POS	GP	G	REC
1895	PHI	N	P		9	0- 2

BEAMON, CHARLES ALFONZO JR. (CHARLIE)
B.DEC.4,1953 OAKLAND,CAL.

YR	CL	LEA	POS	GP	G	REC
1978	SEA	A	/1		10	.182
BLTL						

BEAMON, CHARLES ALFONZO SR.
B.DEC.25,1934 OAKLAND,CAL.

YR	CL	LEA	POS	GP	G	REC
1956	BAL	A	P		2	2- 0
1957	BAL	A	P		4	0- 0
1958	BAL	A	P	21	22	1- 3
	BRTR			27	28	3- 3

BEAN, BEVERIC BENTON (BILL)
B.APR.23,1905 MULLIN,TEX.

YR	CL	LEA	POS	GP	G	REC
1930	CLE	A	P		23	3- 3
1931	CLE	A	P		4	0- 1
1933	CLE	A	P		27	1- 2
1934	CLE	A	P		21	5- 1
1935	CLE	A	P		1	0- 0
	WAS	A	P		10	2- 0
	BRTR				86	11- 7

BEAN, JOSEPH WILLIAM
B.MAR.18,1874 BOSTON,MASS.
D.FEB.15,1961 ATLANTA,GA.

YR	CL	LEA	POS	GP	G	REC
1902	NY	N	S		50	.235
	TR					

BEARD, CRAMER THEODORE (TED)
B.JAN.7,1921 WOODSBORO,MD.

YR	CL	LEA	POS	GP	G	REC
1948	PIT	N	O		25	.198
1949	PIT	N	O		14	.083
1950	PIT	N	O		61	.232
1951	PIT	N	O		22	.188
1952	PIT	N	O		15	.182
1957	CHI	A	O		18	.205
1958	CHI	A	O		19	.091
	BLTL				194	.198

BEARD, MICHAEL RICHARD (MIKE)
B.JUNE 23,1950 LITTLE ROCK,ARK.

YR	CL	LEA	POS	GP	G	REC
1974	ATL	N	/P		6	0- 0
1975	ATL	N	P		34	4- 0
1976	ATL	N	P		30	0- 2
1977	ATL	N	/P		4	0- 0
	BLTL				74	4- 2

BEARD, OLIVER PERRY
B.MAY 2,1862 LEXINGTON,KY.
D.APR 28,1929 CINCINNATI,OHIO

YR	CL	LEA	POS	GP	G	REC
1889	CIN	AA	S		141	.293
1890	CIN	N	S		122	.268
1891	LOU	AA	2		68	.247
	BRTR				331	.273

BEARD, RALPH WILLIAM
B.FEB.11,1929 CINCINNATI,OHIO

YR	CL	LEA	POS	GP	G	REC
1954	STL	N	P		13	0- 4
	BRTR					

BEARDEN, HENRY EUGENE (GENE)
B.SEPT.5,1920 LEXA,ARK.

YR	CL	LEA	POS	GP	G	REC
1947	CLE	A	P		1	0- 0
1948	CLE	A	P		37	20- 7
1949	CLE	A	P		32	8- 8
1950	CLE	A	P		14	1- 3
	WAS	A	P-1	12	14	3- 5
						.227
1951	WAS	A	P		1	0- 0
	DET	A	P		37	3- 4
1952	STL	A	P	34	45	7- 8
1953	CHI	A	P	25	31	3- 3
	BLTL			193	212	45-38
						.236

BEARE, GARY RAY
B.AUG.22,1952 SAN DIEGO,CAL.

YR	CL	LEA	POS	GP	G	REC
1976	MIL	A	/P		6	2- 3
1977	MIL	A	P		17	3- 3
	BRTR				23	5- 6

BEARNARTH, LAWRENCE DONALD (LARRY)
B.SEP.11,1941 NEW YORK,N.Y.

YR	CL	LEA	POS	GP	G	REC
1963	NY	N	P		58	3- 8
1964	NY	N	P		44	5- 5
1965	NY	N	P		40	3- 5
1966	NY	N	P		29	2- 3
1971	MIL	A	P		2	0- 0
	BRTR				173	13-21

BEASLEY, LEWIS PAIGE (LEW)
B.AUG.27,1948 SPARTA,VA.

YR	CL	LEA	POS	GP	G	REC
1977	TEX	A	O/S		25	.219
	BLTR					

BEATIN, EBENEZER AMBROSE
B.AUG.10,1866 BALTIMORE,MD.
D.MAY 9,1925 BALTIMORE,MD.

YR	CL	LEA	POS	GP	G	REC
1887	DET	N	P		2	1- 1
1888	DET	N	P		16	5- 7
1889	CLE	N	P		37	20-14
1890	CLE	N	P		53	22-31
1891	CLE	N	P		5	1- 4
	BBTL				113	49-57

BEATLE, DAVID
B.1861 NEW YORK,N.Y.

YR	CL	LEA	POS	GP	G	REC
1884	DET	N	C-O		1	.000

BEATTIE, JAMES LOUIS (JIM)
B.JULY 4,1954 HAMPTON,VA.

YR	CL	LEA	POS	GP	G	REC
1978	NY	A	P		25	6- 9
	BRTR					

BEATTY, ALOYSIUS DESMOND (DESPERATE)
B.APR.7,1893 BALTIMORE,MD.
D.OCT.6,1969 NORWAY,MAINE

YR	CL	LEA	POS	GP	G	REC
1914	NY	N	3		1	.000
	BRTR					

BEAUCHAMP, JAMES EDWARD (JIM)
B.AUG.21,1939 VINITA,OKLA.

YR	CL	LEA	POS	GP	G	REC
1963	STL	N	H		4	.000
1964	HOU	N	1-O		23	.164
1965	HOU	N	/O-1		24	.189
	MIL	N	/1		4	.000
1967	ATL	N	/H		4	.000
1968	CIN	N	O/1		31	.263
1969	CIN	N	/O-1		43	.250
1970	HOU	N	O		31	.192
	STL	N	O/1		44	.259
1971	STL	N	1/O		77	.235
1972	NY	N	1/O		58	.242
1973	NY	N	1		50	.279
	BRTR				393	.231

BEAUMONT, CLARENCE HOWETH (GINGER)
B.JULY 23,1876 ROCHESTER,WIS.
D.APR.10,1956 BURLINGTON,WIS.

YR	CL	LEA	POS	GP	G	REC
1899	PIT	N	O		104	.350
1900	PIT	N	O		138	.282
1901	PIT	N	O		132	.328
1902	PIT	N	O		131	.357
1903	PIT	N	O		141	.341
1904	PIT	N	O		153	.301
1905	PIT	N	O		97	.328
1906	PIT	N	O		78	.265
1907	BOS	N	O		149	.322
1908	BOS	N	O		121	.267
1909	BOS	N	O		111	.263
1910	CHI	N	O		56	.267
	BLTR				1411	.311

BEAZLEY, JOHN ANDREW (NIG)
B.MAY 25,1918 NASHVILLE,TENN.

YR	CL	LEA	POS	GP	G	REC
1941	STL	N	P		1	1- 0
1942	STL	N	P		43	21- 6
1946	STL	N	P		19	7- 5
1947	BOS	N	P		9	2- 0
1948	BOS	N	P		3	0- 1
1949	BOS	N	P		1	0- 0
	BRTR				76	31-12

BECANNON, JAMES MELVIN (BUCK)
B.AUG.22,1859 NEW YORK,N.Y.
D.NOV.5,1923 NEW YORK,N.Y.

YR	CL	LEA	POS	GP	G	REC
1884	MET	AA	P		1	1- 0
1885	MET	AA	P		10	2- 8
1887	NY	N	3		1	.000
				11	12	3- 8
						.238

BECHTEL, GEORGE A.
B.1848 PHILADELPHIA,PA.

YR	CL	LEA	POS	GP	G	REC
1871	ATH	NA	P-3-	3	21	1- 2
			O			.360
1872	MUT	NA	1-O		52	.302
1873	PHI	NA	P-O	3	52	1- 2
						-
1874	PHI	NA	P-O	4	31	1- 3
						2- 0
1875	CEN	NA	P		14	2-12
	ATH	NA	P	4	34	3- 1
						-
1876	LOU	N	O		14	.182
	MUT	N	O		2	.273
				28	220	8-20
						-

BECK, CLYDE EUGENE (JERSEY)
B.JAN.6,1902 BASSETT,CAL.

YR	CL	LEA	POS	GP	G	REC
1926	CHI	N	2		30	.198
1927	CHI	N	2-3		117	.258
1928	CHI	N	S-3		131	.257
1929	CHI	N	S-3		54	.211
1930	CHI	N	2-S		83	.213
1931	CIN	N	S-3		53	.154
	BRTR				468	.232

BECK, ERWIN THOMAS (DUTCH)
B.JULY 19,1878 TOLEDO,OHIO
D.DEC.22,1916 TOLEDO,OHIO

YR	CL	LEA	POS	GP	G	REC
1899	BRO	N	S		7	.158
1901	CLE	A	2		135	.283
1902	CIN	N	1-2-O		43	.305
	DET	A	1-O		41	.304
	BRTR				226	.298

BECK, FRANK J.
B.1862 POUGHKEEPSIE,N.Y.

YR	CL	LEA	POS	GP	G	REC
1884	PIT	AA	P		3	0- 3
	BAL	U	P-O	2	6	0- 2
						.208
	TR			5	9	0- 5
						.257

BECK, FREDERICK THOMAS
B.NOV.17,1886 HAVANNA,ILL.
D.MAR.12,1962 HAVANNA,ILL.

YR	CL	LEA	POS	GP	G	REC
1909	BOS	N	1-O		88	.198
1910	BOS	N	1-O		153	.275
1911	CIN	N	O		41	.184
	PHI	N	O		64	.281
1914	CHI	F	1		158	.279
1915	CHI	F	1		121	.219
	BLTL				625	.251

BECK, GEORGE F.
B.1889 MOLINE,ILL.

YR	CL	LEA	POS	GP	G	REC
1914	CLE	A	P		1	0- 0
	BRTR					

BECK, RICHARD HENRY (RICH)
B.JAN.21,1941 PASCO,WASH.

YR	CL	LEA	POS	GP	G	REC
1965	NY	A	/P		3	2- 1
	BBTR					

BECK, WALTER WILLIAM (BOOM-BOOM)
B.OCT.16,1904 DECATUR,ILL.

YR	CL	LEA	POS	GP	G	REC
1924	STL	A	P		1	0- 0
1927	STL	A	P		3	1- 0
1928	STL	A	P		16	2- 3
1933	BRO	N	P		43	12-20
1934	BRO	N	P		22	2- 6
1939	PHI	N	P		34	7-14
1940	PHI	N	P		29	4- 9
1941	PHI	N	P		34	1- 9
1942	PHI	N	P	26	27	0- 1
1943	PHI	N	P		4	0- 0
1944	DET	A	P		28	1- 2
1945	CIN	N	P		11	2- 4
	PIT	N	P		14	6- 1
	BRTR			265	266	38-69

BECK, ZINN BERTRAM
B.SEPT.30,1885 STEUBENVILLE,O.

YR	CL	LEA	POS	GP	G	REC
1913	STL	N	3		10	.218
1914	STL	N	S-3		137	.232
1915	STL	N	3		70	.223
1916	STL	N	3		62	.223
1918	NY	A	1		11	.600
	BRTR				290	.227

BECKENDORF, HENRY WARD (HEINE)
B.JUNE 15,1884 NEW YORK,N.Y.
D.SEPT.15,1949 JACKSON HEIGHTS,N.Y.

YR	CL	LEA	POS	GP	G	REC
1909	DET	A	C		15	.259
1910	DET	A	C		3	.429
	WAS	A	C		37	.146
	BRTR				55	.182

BECKER, CHARLES S. (BUCK)
B.OCT.14,1888 WASHINGTON,D.C.
D.JULY 30,1928 WASHINGTON,D.C.

YR	CL	LEA	POS	GP	G	REC
1911	WAS	A	P		11	3- 5
1912	WAS	A	P		4	0- 0
	BLTL				15	3- 5

BECKER, DAVID BEALS (BEALS)
B.JULY 5,1886 EL DORADO,KAN.
D.AUG.16,1943 HUNTINGTON PARK,CAL.

YR	CL	LEA	POS	GP	G	REC
1908	PIT	N	O		17	.154
	BOS	N	O		43	.275
1909	BOS	N	O		152	.245
1910	NY	N	O		46	.286
1911	NY	N	O		55	.262
1912	NY	N	O		125	.264
1913	CIN	N	O		30	.296
	PHI	N	O		88	.324
1914	PHI	N	O		138	.325
1915	PHI	N	O		112	.246
	BLTL				806	.276

| YR | CL LEA POS | GP | G | REC |

BECKER, HEINZ REINHARD (DUTCH)
B.AUG.26,1915 BERLIN,GERMANY
1943 CHI N 1   24   .145
1945 CHI N 1   67   .286
1946 CHI N H   9   .286
     CLE A 1   50   .299
1947 CLE A H   2   .000
            BBTR   152   .263
            BL 1946

BECKER, JOSEPH EDWARD
B.JUNE 25,1908 ST.LOUIS,MO.
1936 CLE A C   22   .180
1937 CLE A C   18   .333
            BRTR   40   .241

BECKER, MARTIN HENRY
B.DEC.22,1893 TIFFIN,OHIO
D.SEPT.25,1957 CINCINNATI,OHIO
1915 NY N 0   17   .250
            BBTL

BECKER, ROBERT CHARLES
B.AUG.15,1875 SYRACUSE,N.Y.
D.OCT.11,1951 SYRACUSE,N.Y.
1897 PHI N P   5   0- 2
1898 PHI N P   1   0- 0
                      6   0- 2

BECKERT, GLENN ALFRED
B.OCT.12,1940 PITTSBURGH,PA.
1965 CHI N *2   154   .239
1966 CHI N *2/S   153   .287
1967 CHI N *2   146   .280
1968 CHI N *2   155   .294
1969 CHI N *2   131   .291
1970 CHI N *2/0   143   .288
1971 CHI N *2   131   .342
1972 CHI N *2   120   .270
1973 CHI N 2   114   .255
1974 SD N 2/3   64   .256
1975 SD N /3   9   .375
            BRTR   1320   .283

BECKLEY, JACOB PETER
(JAKE) OR (EAGLE EYE)
B.AUG.4,1867 HANNIBAL,MO.
D.JUNE 25,1918 KANSAS CITY,MO.
1888 PIT N 1   71   .342
1889 PIT N 1   121   .300
1890 PIT P 1   121   .325
1891 PIT N 1   129   .291
1892 PIT N 1   152   .250
1893 PIT N 1   131   .324
1894 PIT N 1   132   .324
1895 PIT N 1   131   .324
1896 PIT N 1   54   .244
     NY N 1   45   .297
1897 NY N 1   18   .268
     CIN N 1   96   .336
1898 CIN N 1   116   .299
1899 CIN N 1   135   .333
1900 CIN N 1   138   .343
1901 CIN N 1   140   .300
1902 CIN N P-1   1 129   0- 1
                            .331
1903 CIN N 1   119   .327
1904 STL N 1   142   .325
1905 STL N 1   134   .286
1906 STL N 1   85   .247
1907 STL N 1   32   .209
            BLTL   1 2373   0- 1
                            .309

BECKMAN, JAMES JOSEPH
B.MAR.1,1905 CINCINNATI,OHIO
1927 CIN N P   4   0- 1
1928 CIN N P   6   0- 1
            BRTR   10   0- 2

BECKMANN, WILLIAM ALOYSIUS
B.DEC.8,1907 CLAYTON,MO.
1939 PHI A P   27   7-11
1940 PHI A P   34   8- 4
1941 PHI A P   22   5- 9
1942 PHI A P   5   0- 1
     STL N P   2   1- 0
            BRTR   90   21-25

BECQUER, JULIO (VILLEGAS)
B.DEC.20,1931 HAVANA,CUBA
1955 WAS A 1   10   .214
1957 WAS A 1   105   .226
1958 WAS A 1-0   86   .238
1959 WAS A 1   108   .268
1960 WAS A P-1   1 110   0- 0
                            .252
1961 LA A 1   11   .000
     MIN A P-1-0   1 57   0- 0
                            .238
1963 MIN A H   1   .000
            BLTL   2 488   0- 0
                            .244

BEDELL, HOWARD WILLIAM (HOWIE)
B.SEP.29,1935 CLEARFIELD,PA.
1962 MIL N O   58   .196
1968 PHI N /H   9   .143
            BLTR   67   .193

BEDFORD, JAMES ELDRED
B.MAR.26,1904 HUDSON,N.Y.
D.JUNE 27,1962 POUGHKEEPSIE,N.Y
1925 CLE A 2   2   .000
            TR

BEDGOOD, PHILLIP BURLETTE
B.MAR.6,1898 HARRISON,GA.
D.NOV.8,1927 FORT PIERCE,FLA.
1922 CLE A P   1   1- 0
1923 CLE A P   9   0- 2
            BRTR   10   1- 2

BEDIENT, HUGH CARPENTER
B.OCT.23,1889 GERRY,N.Y.
D.JULY 21,1965 JAMESTOWN,N.Y.
1912 BOS A P   41   20-10
1913 BOS A P   43   15-14
1914 BOS A P   42   8-12
1915 BUF F P   53   16-18
            BRTR   179   59-54

BEDNAR, ANDREW JACKSON
B.AUG.16,1908 STREATOR,ILL.
D.NOV.26,1937 GRAHAM,TEX.
1930 PIT N P   2   0- 0
1931 PIT N P   3   0- 0
                      5   0- 0

BEEBE, FREDERICK LEONARD
B.DEC.31,1880 LINCOLN,NEB.
D.OCT.30,1957 ELGIN,ILL.
1906 CHI N P   14   6- 1
     STL N P   20   9- 9
1907 STL N P   31   7-19
1908 STL N P   29   5-13
1909 STL N P   44   15-21
1910 CIN N P   35   12-14
1911 PHI N P   9   3- 3
1916 CLE A P   21   5- 3
            BRTR   203   62-83

BEECHER, EDWARD (SCRAP IRON)
B.AUG.27,1873
1897 STL N O   3   .333
1898 CLE N O   8   .200
                     11   .257

BEECHER, EDWARD H.
B.JULY 2,1860 GUILFORD,CONN.
D.SEPT.12,1935 HARTFORD,CONN.
1887 PIT N O   40   .272
1889 WAS N O   41   .296
1890 BUF P P-O   1 126   0- 1
                            .357
1891 WAS AA O   56   .233
     ATH AA O   16   .205
            BL   1 279   0- 1
                            .299

BEECHER, LEROY (COLONEL)
B.MAY 10,1884 SWANTON,OHIO
D.OCT.11,1952 TOLEDO,OHIO
1907 NY N P   2   0- 2
1908 NY N P   2   0- 0
            BLTR   4   0- 2

BEELER, JOSEPH SAM (JODIE)
B.NOV.26,1921 DALLAS,TEX.
1944 CIN N 2-3   3   .000
            BRTR

BEENE, FREDDY RAY (FRED)
B.NOV.24,1942 ANGLETON,TEX.
1968 BAL A /P   1   0- 0
1969 BAL A /P   2   0- 0
1970 BAL A /P   4   0- 0
1972 NY A P   29   30 1- 3
1973 NY A P   19   6- 0
1974 NY A /P   6   0- 0
     CLE A P   32   33 4- 4
1975 CLE A P   19   20 1- 0
            BBTR   112   115 12- 7
            BR 1974

BEERS, CLARENCE SCOTT
B.DEC.9,1918 EL DORADO,KAN.
1948 STL N P   1   0- 0
            BRTR

BEGGS, JOSEPH STANLEY (FIREMAN)
B.NOV.4,1910 RANKIN,PA.
1938 NY A P   14   3- 2
1940 CIN N P   37   12- 3
1941 CIN N P   37   4- 3
1942 CIN N P   38   6- 5
1943 CIN N P   39   7- 6
1944 CIN N P   1   1- 0
1946 CIN N P   28   12-10
1947 CIN N P   11   0- 3
     NY N P   32   3- 3
1948 CIN N P   1   0- 0
            BRTR   238   48-35

BEGLEY, EDWARD N.
[REAL NAME EDWARD N. BAGLEY]
B.1863 NEW YORK,N.Y.
D.JULY 24,1919 WATERBURY,CONN.
1884 NY N P-O   31   32 12-18
                            .181
1885 MET AA P-O   15   4- 9
                            .173
                     46   47 16-27
                            .179

BEGLEY, EUGENE I.
B.1863 BROOKLYN,N.Y.
1886 NY N C   3   .111

BEGLEY, JAMES LAWRENCE (IMP)
B.SEPT.19,1902 SAN FRANCISCO,CAL.
D.FEB.20,1957 SAN FRANCISCO,CAL
1924 CIN N 2   2   .200
            BRTR

BEHAN, CHARLES FREDERICK (PETE)
B.DEC.11,1887 DALLAS CITY,PA.
D.JAN.22,1957 BRADFORD,PA.
1921 PHI N P   2   0- 1
1922 PHI N P   7   4- 2
1923 PHI N P   30   34 3-12
            BRTR   39   43 7-15

BEHEL, STEPHEN ARNOLD DOUGLAS
B.ROCKFORD,ILL.
1884 MIL U O   9   .222
1886 MET AA O   59   .208
                     68   .211

BEHNEY, MELVIN BRIAN (MEL)
B.SEP.2,1947 NEWARK,N.J.
1970 CIN N /P   5   0- 2
            BLTL

BEHRMAN, HENRY BERNARD (HANK)
B.JUNE 27,1921 BROOKLYN,N.Y.
1946 BRO N P   47   11- 5
1947 BRO N P   40   5- 3
     PIT N P   10   0- 2
1948 BRO N P   34   5- 4
1949 NY N P   43   3- 3
            BRTR   174   24-17

BEJMA, ALOYSIUS FRANK (OLLIE)
B.SEPT.12,1907 SOUTH BEND,IND.
1934 STL A 2-S-3-0 95   .271
1935 STL A 2-S-3   64   .192
1936 STL A 2   67   .259
1939 CHI A 2   90   .251
            BRTR   316   .245

BELANGER, MARK HENRY
B.JUNE 8,1944 PITTSFIELD,MASS.
1965 BAL A /S   11   .333
1966 BAL A /S   8   .158
1967 BAL A S-2/3   69   .174
1968 BAL A *S   145   .208
1969 BAL A *S   150   .287
1970 BAL A *S   145   .218
1971 BAL A *S   150   .266
1972 BAL A *S   113   .186
1973 BAL A *S   154   .226
1974 BAL A *S   155   .225
1975 BAL A *S   152   .226
1976 BAL A *S   153   .270
1977 BAL A *S   144   .206
1978 BAL A *S   134   .213
            BRTR   1683   .231

BELANGIO, PROSPER ALBERT
[PLAYED UNDER NAME OF
PROSBY ALBERT BLANCHE]

BELARDI, CARROLL WAYNE
B.SEPT.5,1930 CALISTOGA,CAL.
1950 BRO N 1   10   .000
1951 BRO N H   3   .333
1953 BRO N 1   69   .239
1954 BRO N H   11   .222
     DET A 1   88   .232
1955 DET A H   3   .000
1956 DET A 1-0   79   .279
            BLTL   263   .242

BELDEN, IRA ALLISON
B.APR.16,1874 CLEVELAND,OHIO
D.JULY 15,1916 LAKEWOOD,OHIO
1897 CLE N O   8   .250

BELINSKY, ROBERT (BO)
B.DEC.7,1936 NEW YORK,N.Y.
1962 LA A P   33   34 10-11
1963 LA A P   13   2- 9
1964 LA A P   23   9- 8
1965 PHI N P   30   31 4- 9
1966 PHI N /P   9   0- 2
1967 HOU N P   27   3- 9
1969 PIT N /P   8   0- 3
1970 CIN N /P   3   0- 0
            BLTL   146   148 28-51

YR	CL LEA POS	GP	G	REC

BELL, CHARLES C.
B.AUG.12,1868 CINCINNATI,OHIO
D.FEB.7,1937 CINCINNATI,OHIO

1889	KC AA P		1	1- 0
1891	LOU AA P		11	3- 8
	CIN AA P		4	1- 0
			16	5- 8

BELL, DAVID GUS (BUDDY)
B.AUG.27,1951 PITTSBURGH,PA.

1972	CLE A *O/3		132	.255
1973	CLE A *3/O		156	.268
1974	CLE A *3		116	.262
1975	CLE A *3		153	.271
1976	CLE A *3/1		159	.281
1977	CLE A *3-O		129	.292
1978	CLE A *3		142	.282
	BRTR		987	.274

BELL, DAVID RUSSELL (GUS)
B.NOV.15,1928 LOUISVILLE,KY.

1950	PIT N O		111	.282
1951	PIT N O		149	.278
1952	PIT N O		131	.250
1953	CIN N O		151	.300
1954	CIN N O		153	.299
1955	CIN N O		154	.308
1956	CIN N O		150	.292
1957	CIN N O		121	.292
1958	CIN N O		112	.252
1959	CIN N O		148	.293
1960	CIN N O		143	.262
1961	CIN N O		103	.255
1962	NY N O		30	.149
	MIL N O		79	.285
1963	MIL N H		3	.333
1964	MIL N H		3	.000
	BRTR		1741	.281

BELL, FERN LEE (DANNY)
B.JAN.21,1913 ADA,OKLA.

1939	PIT N O		83	.286
1940	PIT N H		6	.000
	BRTR		89	.283

BELL, FRANK GUSTAV
B.1863 CINCINNATI,OHIO
D.APR.14,1891 CINCINNATI,OHIO

1885	BRO AA C-3-O		10	.167

BELL, GARY
B.NOV.17,1936 SAN ANTONIO,TEX.

1958	CLE A P		33	12-10
1959	CLE A P		44	16-11
1960	CLE A P	28	30	9-10
1961	CLE A P		34	12-16
1962	CLE A P		57	10- 9
1963	CLE A P		58	8- 5
1964	CLE A P		56	8- 6
1965	CLE A P		60	6- 5
1966	CLE A P		40	14-15
1967	CLE A /P		9	1- 5
	BOS A P		29	12- 8
1968	BOS A P		35	11-11
1969	SEA A P		13	2- 6
	CHI A P		23	0- 0
	BRTR		519	521 121-117

BELL, GEORGE GLENN (FARMER)
B.NOV.2,1874 GREENWOOD,N.Y.
D.DEC.25,1941 NEW YORK,N.Y.

1907	BRO N P		35	8-16
1908	BRO N P		29	4-15
1909	BRO N P		33	16-15
1910	BRO N P		44	10-27
1911	BRO N P		19	5- 6
	BRTR		160	43-79

BELL, HERMAN S (HI)
B.JULY 16,1897 MT.SHERMAN,KY.
D.JUNE 7,1949 GLENDALE,CAL.

1924	STL N P		28	3- 8
1926	STL N P		27	6- 6
1927	STL N P		25	1- 3
1929	STL N P		7	0- 2
1930	STL N P		39	4- 3
1932	NY N P		35	8- 4
1933	NY N P		38	6- 5
1934	NY N P		22	4- 3
	BRTR		221	32-34

BELL, JERRY HOUSTON
B.OCT.6,1947 MADISON,TENN.

1971	MIL A /P		8	2- 1
1972	MIL A P		25	5- 1
1973	MIL A P		31	9- 9
1974	MIL A /P		5	1- 0
	BBTR		69	17-11

BELL, JOHN
[REAL NAME RUDOLPH FRED BAERWALD]
B.JAN.1,1881 WAUSAU,WIS.
D.JULY 28,1955 ALBUQUERQUE,N.M.

1907	NY A O		17	.212
	BRTR			

BELL, KEVIN ROBERT
B.JULY 13,1955 LOS ANGELES,CAL.

1976	CHI A 3		68	.248
1977	CHI A /S-3-O		9	.179
1978	CHI A 3		54	.191
	BRTR		131	.230

BELL, LESTER ROWLAND
B.DEC.14,1901 HARRISBURG,PA.

1923	STL N S		15	.373
1924	STL N S		17	.246
1925	STL N S-3		153	.285
1926	STL N 3		155	.325
1927	STL N S-3		115	.259
1928	BOS N 3		153	.277
1929	BOS N 3		139	.298
1930	CHI N 3		74	.278
1931	CHI N 3		75	.282
	BRTR		896	.290

BELL, RALPH ALBERT (LEFTY)
B.NOV.6,1890 KOHOKA,MO.
D.OCT.18,1959 BURLINGTON,IOWA

1912	CHI A P		2	0- 0
	BLTL			

BELL, ROY CHESTER (BEAU)
B.AUG.20,1907 BELLVILLE,TEX.
D.SEPT.14,1977 COLLEGE STATION,TEX.

1935	STL A 1-3-O		76	.250
1936	STL A 1-O		155	.344
1937	STL A 1-O		156	.340
1938	STL A O		147	.262
1939	STL A O		11	.219
	DET A O		54	.239
1940	CLE A 1-O		120	.279
1941	CLE A 1-O		48	.192
	BRTR		767	.297

BELL, WILLIAM SAMUEL
(BILL) OR (DING DONG)
B.OCT.24,1933 GOLDSBORO,N.C.
D.OCT.11,1962 DURHAM,N.C.

1952	PIT N P		4	0- 1
1955	PIT N P		1	0- 0
	BRTR		5	0- 1

BELLA, JOHN (ZEKE)
B.AUG.23,1930 GREENWICH,CONN.

1957	NY A O		5	.100
1959	KC A 1-O		47	.207
	BRTL		52	.196

BELLAN, ESTEBAN ENRIQUE
B.1850 CUBA
D.AUG.8,1932

1871	TRO NA S-3		29	.213
1872	TRO NA S-3-O		23	.243
1873	MUT NA 3		7	-
			59	-

BELLMAN, JOHN CHARLES
B.LOUISVILLE,KY.

1889	STL AA C		1	.500

BELLOIR, ROBERT EDWARD (ROB)
B.JULY 13,1948 HEIDELBERG,GER.

1975	ATL N S/2		43	.219
1976	ATL N S-3/2		30	.200
1977	ATL N /S		6	.000
1978	ATL N /S-3		2	1.000
	BRTR		81	.216

BEMIS, HARRY PARKER
B.FEB.1,1874 FARMINGTON,N.H.
D.MAY 23,1947 CLEVELAND,OHIO

1902	CLE A C-2-O		93	.311
1903	CLE A C		93	.258
1904	CLE A C		95	.225
1905	CLE A C		69	.292
1906	CLE A C		93	.274
1907	CLE A C		65	.250
1908	CLE A C		91	.224
1909	CLE A C		42	.187
1910	CLE A C		61	.215
	BRTR		702	.254

BENCH, JOHNNY LEE
B.DEC.7,1947 OKLAHOMA CITY,OKLA.

1967	CIN N C		26	.163
1968	CIN N *C		154	.275
1969	CIN N *C		148	.293
1970	CIN N *C-O-1/3		158	.293
1971	CIN N *C-1-O/3		149	.238
1972	CIN N *C-O/1-3		147	.270
1973	CIN N *C-O/1-3		152	.253
1974	CIN N *C-3/1		160	.280
1975	CIN N *C-O/1		142	.283
1976	CIN N *C/O-1		135	.234
1977	CIN N *C/O-1-3		142	.275
1978	CIN N *C-1/O		120	.260
	BRTR		1633	.268

BENDER, CHARLES ALBERT (CHIEF)
B.MAY 5,1883 BRAINERD,MINN.
D.MAY 22,1954 PHILADELPHIA,PA.

1903	PHI A P		36	43 17-15
1904	PHI A P	28	29	7-14
1905	PHI A P		35	15-10
1906	PHI A P	37	44	15-10
1907	PHI A P	33	45	16- 8
1908	PHI A P		20	8- 9
1909	PHI A P	34	40	18- 8
1910	PHI A P	30	36	23- 5
1911	PHI A P	31	32	17- 5
1912	PHI A P		27	13- 8
1913	PHI A P		48	19- 9
1914	PHI A P		28	17- 3
1915	BAL F P		26	4-16
1916	PHI N P	27	28	7- 7
1917	PHI N P		20	8- 2
1925	CHI A P		1	0- 0
	BRTR	461	502	204-129

BENEDICT, ARTHUR M.
B.MAR.31,1862 CORNWALL,ILL.
D.JAN.20,1948 BLUE RAPIOS,KAN.

1883	PHI N 2		3	.267
	BRTR			

BENEDICT, BRUCE EDWIN
B.AUG.18,1955 BIRMINGHAM,ALA.

1978	ATL N C		22	.250
	BRTR			

BENES, JOSEPH ANTHONY (BANANAS)
B.JAN.8,1901 LONG ISLAND CITY,N.Y.

1931	STL N 2-S-3		10	.167
	BRTR			

BENGE, RAYMOND ADELPHIA (RAY)
B.APR.22,1902 JACKSONVILLE,TEX.

1925	PHI N P		2	1- 0
1926	CLE A P		8	1- 0
1928	PHI N P	40	42	8-18
1929	PHI N P	38	43	11-15
1930	PHI N P		38	11-15
1931	PHI N P		38	14-18
1932	PHI N P		41	13-12
1933	BRO N P		37	10-17
1934	BRO N P		36	14-12
1935	BRO N P		23	6- 9
1936	BOS N P		21	7- 9
	PHI N P		15	1- 4
1938	CIN N P		9	1- 1
	BRTR	346	353	101-130

BENGOUGH, BERNARD OLIVER (BENNY)
B.JULY 27,1898 NIAGARA FALLS,N.Y.
D.DEC.22,1968 PHILADELPHIA,PA.

1923	NY A C		19	.132
1924	NY A C		11	.312
1925	NY A C		95	.258
1926	NY A C		36	.381
1927	NY A C		31	.247
1928	NY A C		58	.267
1929	NY A C		23	.194
1930	STL A C		44	.235
1931	STL A C		40	.250
1932	STL A C		54	.252
	BRTR		411	.255

BENIQUEZ, JUAN JOSE (TORRES)
B.MAY 13,1950 SAN SEBASTIAN,P.R.

1971	BOS A S		16	.298
1972	BOS A S		33	.242
1974	BOS A O		106	.267
1975	BOS A O-O-3		78	.291
1976	TEX A *O/2		145	.255
1977	TEX A *O		123	.269
1978	TEX A *O		127	.260
	BRTR		628	.266

BENJAMIN, ALFRED STANLEY (STAN)
B.MAY 20,1914 FRAMINGHAM,MASS.

1939	PHI N 3-O		12	.140
1940	PHI N O		8	.222
1941	PHI N 1-2-3-O		129	.235
1942	PHI N 1-O		78	.224
1945	CLE A O		14	.333
	BRTR		241	.229

BENJAMIN, JOHN W.
B.1837 ELIZABETH,N.J.
D.NOV.14,1895 ELIZABETH,N.J.
NON-PLAYING MANAGER RES[NA]1873

BENN, HENRY OMER
B.JAN.25,1890 VIOLA,WIS.
D.JUNE 4,1967 MADISON,WIS.

1914	CHI N P		1	0- 0
	BRTR			

BENNERS, ISAAC B. (IKE)
B.PHILADELPHIA,PA.

1884	BRO AA O		49	.209
	WIL U O		6	.045
			55	.191

```
YR  CL LEA POS      GP    G   REC

BENNETT, CHARLES WESLEY
B.NOV.21,1854 NEW CASTLE,PA.
D.FEB.24,1927 DETROIT,MICH.
1878 MIL N C-O          48  .246
1880 WOR N C-O          50  .223
1881 DET N C-O          76  .301
1882 DET N C-1-2-3      80  .304
1883 DET N C-2-O        89  .301
1884 DET N C-1-2-S-O    88  .264
1885 DET N C-3-O        91  .269
1886 DET N C            69  .242
1887 DET N C            46  .363
1888 DET N C            72  .263
1889 BOS N C            80  .230
1890 BOS N C            85  .213
1891 BOS N C            74  .215
1892 BOS N C            32  .201
1893 BOS N C            58  .218
        BRTR          1038  .262

BENNETT, DAVID HANS (DAVE)
B.NOV.7,1945 BERKELEY,CAL.
1964 PHI N P             1   0- 0
        BRTR

BENNETT, DENNIS JOHN
B.OCT.5,1939 OAKLAND,CAL.
1962 PHI N P            31   9- 9
1963 PHI N P            23   9- 5
1964 PHI N P            41  12-14
1965 BOS A P            34   5- 7
1966 BOS A P            16   3- 3
1967 BOS A P            13   4- 3
     NY  N /P            8   1- 1
1968 CAL A P            16   0- 5
        BLTL           182  43-47

BENNETT, FRANCIS ALLEN (CHIP)
B.OCT.27,1904 MARDELA SPRINGS,MD.
D.MAR.18,1966 NEW CASTLE,DEL.
1927 BOS A P             4   0- 1
1928 BOS A P             1   0- 0
        BRTR             5   0- 1

BENNETT, HERSCHEL EMMETT
B.SEPT.21,1896 ELWOOD,MO.
D.SEPT.9,1964 SPRINGFIELD,MO.
1923 STL A O             5  .000
1924 STL A O            41  .330
1925 STL A O            93  .279
1926 STL A O            80  .266
1927 STL A O            93  .266
        BLTR           312  .276

BENNETT, JAMES FRED (RED)
B.MAR.15,1902 ATKINS,ARK.
D.MAY 12,1957 ATKINS,ARK.
1928 STL A O             7  .250
1931 PIT N O            32  .281
        BRTR            39  .278

BENNETT, JOSEPH HARLEY (BUGS)
[SEE JOSEPH HARLEY MORRIS]

BENNETT, JOSEPH ROSENBLUM
B.JULY 2,1900 NEW YORK,N.Y.
1923 PHI N 3             1  .000
        BRTR

BENNETT, JUSTIN TITUS (PUG)
B.FEB.20,1874 PONCA,NEB.
D.SEPT.12,1935 KIRKLAND,WASH.
1906 STL N 2           153  .262
1907 STL N 2            86  .222
        TR             239  .248

BENSON, ALLEN WILBERT (BULLET BEN)
B.JULY 12,1908 HURLEY,S.DAK.
1934 WAS A P             2   0- 1
        BRTR

BENSON, VERNON ADAIR
B.SEPT.19,1924 GRANITE QUARRY,N.C.
1943 PHI A H             2  .000
1946 PHI A O             7  .000
1951 STL N 3-O          13  .261
1952 STL N 3            20  .191
1953 STL N H            13  .000
        BLTR            55  .202

BENTLEY, CYRUS G.
B.WATERBURY,CONN.
1872 MAN NA P-O    16   23   2-14
                              .239

BENTLEY, JOHN NEEDLES (JACK)
B.MAR.8,1895 SANDY SPRING,MD.
D.OCT.24,1969 OLNEY,MD.
1913 WAS A P             3   0- 0
1914 WAS A P            30   5- 7
1915 WAS A P             4   0- 2
1916 WAS A P             2   0- 0
1923 NY  N P       31   52  13- 8
1924 NY  N P       28   46  16- 5
1925 NY  N P-1-    29   64  11- 9
         O                    .303
1926 PHI N P-1      7   75   0- 2
                              .258
     NY  N P        1    3   0- 0
1927 NY  N P             8   0- 0
        BLTL      143  287  45-33
                              .291

BENTON, ALFRED LEE (BUTCH)
B.AUG.24,1957 TAMPA,FLA.
1978 NY  N /C            4  .500
        BRTR

BENTON, JOHN ALTON (AL)
B.MAR.13,1911 NOBLE,OKLA.
D.APR.14,1968 LYNWOOD,CAL.
1934 PHI A P            32   7- 9
1935 PHI A P            27   3- 4
1938 DET A P            19   5- 3
1939 DET A P            37   6- 8
1940 DET A P            42   6-10
1941 DET A P            38  15- 6
1942 DET A P            35   7-13
1945 DET A P            31  13- 8
1946 DET A P            28  11- 7
1947 DET A P            36   6- 7
1948 DET A P            30   2- 2
1949 CLE A P            40   9- 6
1950 CLE A P            36   4- 2
1952 BOS A P            24   4- 3
        BRTR           455  98-88

BENTON, JOHN CLEBON (RUBE)
B.JUNE 27,1887 CLINTON,N.C.
D.DEC.12,1937 DOTHAN,ALA.
1910 CIN N P            12   0- 1
1911 CIN N P             6   3- 3
1912 CIN N P            50  18-20
1913 CIN N P            23  11- 7
1914 CIN N P            41  16-18
1915 CIN N P            34   6-13
     PIT N P             1   0- 0
     NY  N P            10   3- 5
1916 NY  N P            38  16- 8
1917 NY  N P            35  15- 9
1918 NY  N P             3   1- 2
1919 NY  N P            33  17-11
1920 NY  N P            33   9-16
1921 NY  N P            18   5- 2
1923 CIN N P            33  14-10
1924 CIN N P            32   7- 9
1925 CIN N P            33   9-10
        BLTL           437 150-144

BENTON, LAWRENCE JAMES
B.NOV.20,1897 ST.LOUIS,MO.
D.APR.3,1953 AMBERLY VILLAGE,O.
1923 BOS N P            35   5- 9
1924 BOS N P            30   5- 7
1925 BOS N P       31   32  14- 7
1926 BOS N P       43   45  14-14
1927 BOS N P            11   4- 2
     NY  N P            31  13- 5
1928 NY  N P            42  25- 9
1929 NY  N P       39   41  11-17
1930 NY  N P             8   1- 3
     CIN N P            35   7-12
1931 CIN N P            38  10-15
1932 CIN N P            35   6-13
1933 CIN N P            34  10-11
1934 CIN N P            16   0- 1
1935 BOS N P            29   2- 3
        BRTR      455  462 127-128

BENTON, SIDNEY WRIGHT
B.AUG.4,1895 BUCKNER,ARK.
D.MAR.8,1977 FAYETTEVILLE,ARK.
1922 STL N P             1   0- 0
        BRTR

BENTON, STANLEY W. (RABBIT)
B.SEPT.29,1901 CANAL CITY,KY.
1922 PHI N 2             6  .211
        BRTR

BENZ, JOSEPH LOUIS (JOE)
(BLITZEN) OR (BUTCHER BOY)
B.JAN.21,1886 NEW ALSACE,IND.
D.APR.22,1957 CHICAGO,ILL.
1911 CHI A P            12   3- 2
1912 CHI A P            41  13-17
1913 CHI A P            33   7-10
1914 CHI A P            48  14-19
1915 CHI A P            39  15-11
1916 CHI A P            28   9- 9
1917 CHI A P            19   7- 3
1918 CHI A P            29   7- 8
1919 CHI A P             1   0- 0
        BRTR           250  75-75

BERARDINO, JOHN (BERNIE)
B.MAY 1,1917 LOS ANGELES,CAL.
1939 STL A 2           126  .256
1940 STL A 2-S-3       142  .258
1941 STL A S-3         128  .271
1942 STL A 1-2-S-3      29  .284
1946 STL A 2        2  144  .265
1947 STL A 2            90  .261
1948 CLE A 1-2-S-3      66  .190
1949 CLE A 2-S-3        50  .191
1950 CLE A 2-3           4  .400
     PIT N 2-3          40  .206
1951 STL A 1-2-3-O      39  .227
1952 CLE A 1-2-S-3      35  .094
     PIT N 2            19  .143
        BRTR           912  .249

BERBERET, LOUIS JOSEPH
B.NOV.20,1929 LONG BEACH,CAL.
1954 NY  A C             5  .400
1955 NY  A C             2  .400
1956 WAS A C            95  .261
1957 WAS A C            99  .261
1958 WAS A C             5  .167
     BOS A C            57  .210
1959 DET A C           100  .216
1960 DET A C            85  .194
        BLTR           448  .230

BERENGUER, JUAN BAUTISTA
B.NOV.30,1954 AGUADULCE,PAN.
1978 NY  N /P            5   0- 2
        BRTR

BERG, MORRIS (MOE)
B.MAR.2,1902 NEW YORK,N.Y.
D.MAY 29,1972 BELLEVILLE,N.J.
1923 BRO N 2-S          49  .186
1926 CHI A S            41  .221
1927 CHI A C-2          35  .247
1928 CHI A C            76  .246
1929 CHI A C           107  .287
1930 CHI A C            20  .115
1931 CLE A C            10  .077
1932 WAS A C            75  .236
1933 WAS A C            40  .185
1934 WAS A C            33  .244
     CLE A C            29  .258
1935 BOS A C            38  .286
1936 BOS A C            39  .240
1937 BOS A C            47  .255
1938 BOS A C            10  .333
1939 BOS A C            14  .273
        BRTR           663  .243

BERGAMO, AUGUST SAMUEL
B.FEB.14,1917 DETROIT,MICH.
D.AUG.19,1974 GROSSE POINTE
CITY,MICH.
1944 STL N 1-O          80  .286
1945 STL N 1-O          94  .316
        BLTL           174  .305

BERGEN, MARTIN
B.OCT.25,1871 N.BROOKFIELD,MASS
D.JAN.19,1900 N.BROOKFIELD,MASS
1896 BOS N C            62  .267
1897 BOS N C            83  .247
1898 BOS N C           120  .269
1899 BOS N C            71  .257
        TR             336  .268

BERGEN, WILLIAM ALOYSIUS
B.JUNE 13,1873 N.BROOKFIELD,MASS.
D.DEC.19,1943 WORCESTER,MASS.
1901 CIN N C            82  .172
1902 CIN N C            89  .181
1903 CIN N C            58  .227
1904 BRO N C            94  .182
1905 BRO N C            76  .190
1906 BRO N C           103  .161
1907 BRO N C            51  .159
1908 BRO N C            99  .175
1909 BRO N C           112  .139
1910 BRO N C            89  .161
1911 BRO N C            84  .132
        BRTR           937  .170

BERGER, CHARLES (HEINIE)
B.JAN.7,1882 LASALLE,ILL.
D.FEB.10,1954 LAKEWOOD,OHIO
1907 CLE A P            14   3- 3
1908 CLE A P            29  13- 8
1909 CLE A P            34  13-14
1910 CLE A P            13   3- 4
        TR              90  32-29

BERGER, CLARENCE EDWARD
B.NOV.1,1894 E.CLEVELAND,OHIO
D.JUNE 30,1959 WASHINGTON,D.C.
1914 PIT N O             5  .083
        BLTR

BERGER, JOHN HENNE
B.AUG.27,1901 PHILADELPHIA,PA.
1922 PHI A C             2 1.000
1927 WAS A C             9  .267
        BRTR            11  .353
```

YR	CL LEA POS	GP	G	REC

BERGER, JOHN HENRY (TUN)
B.DEC.6,1867 PITTSBURGH,PA.
D.JUNE 10,1907 PITTSBURGH,PA.

1890 PIT	N C-S-O	104		.266
1891 PIT	N C-2	37		.240
1892 WAS	N S	25		.142
		166		.241

BERGER, JOSEPH AUGUST (FATS)
B.DEC.20,1886 ST.LOUIS,MO.
D.MAR.6,1956 ROCK ISLAND,ILL.

1913 CHI	A 2	77		.215
1914 CHI	A S	47		.155
	BRTR	124		.191

BERGER, LOUIS WILLIAM (BOZE)
B.MAY 13,1910 BALTIMORE,MD.

1932 CLE	A S	1		.000
1935 CLE	A 1-2-S-S-3	124		.258
1936 CLE	A 1-2-S-S-3	28		.173
1937 CHI	A 3	52		.238
1938 CHI	A 2-S	118		.217
1939 BOS	A S	20		.300
	BRTR	343		.236

BERGER, WALTER ANTONE
B.OCT.10,1905 CHICAGO,ILL.

1930 BOS	N O	151		.310
1931 BOS	N O	156		.323
1932 BOS	N 1-O	145		.307
1933 BOS	N O	137		.313
1934 BOS	N O	150		.298
1935 BOS	N O	150		.295
1936 BOS	N O	138		.288
1937 BOS	N O	30		.274
	NY N O	59		.291
1938 NY	N O	16		.188
	CIN N O	99		.307
1939 CIN	N O	97		.258
1940 CIN	N H	2		.000
	PHI N 1-O	20		.317
	BRTR	1350		.300

BERGH, JOHN BAPTIST
B.OCT.8,1857 BOSTON,MASS.
D.APR.16,1883 BOSTON,MASS.

1876 ATH	N C	1		.000
1880 BOS	N C	11		.167
		12		.152

BERGHAMMER, MARTIN ANDREW (PEPPER)
B.JUNE 18,1888 ELLIOTT,PA.
D.DEC.21,1957 PITTSBURGH,PA.

1911 CHI	A 2	2		.000
1913 CIN	N S	74		.218
1914 CIN	N S	77		.223
1915 PIT	F S	132		.238
	BLTR	285		.230

BERGMAN, ALFRED HENRY (DUTCH)
B.SEPT.27,1890 PERU,IND.
D.JUNE 20,1961 FORT WAYNE,IND.

| 1916 CLE | A 2 | 7 | | .214 |
| | BRTR | | | |

BERGMAN, DAVID BRUCE (DAVE)
B.JUNE 6,1953 EVANSTON,ILL.

1975 NY	A /O	7		.000
1977 NY	A /O-1	5		.250
1978 HOU	N 1-O	104		.231
	BLTL	116		.213

BERKELBACH, FRANK P.
B.PHILADELPHIA,PA.

| 1884 CIN | AA O | 6 | | .231 |

BERKENSTOCK, NATHAN
B.1883 PENNSYLVANIA
D.FEB.23,1900

| 1871 ATH | NA O | 1 | | .000 |

BERLY, JOHN CHAMBERS
B.MAY 24,1903 NATCHITOCHES,LA.
D.JUNE 26,1977 HOUSTON,TEX.

1924 STL	N P	4		0- 0
1931 NY	N P	27		7- 8
1932 PHI	N P	21		1- 2
1933 PHI	N P	13		2- 3
	BRTR	65		10-13

BERMAN, ROBERT LEON
B.JAN.24,1899 NEW YORK,N.Y.

| 1918 WAS | A C | 2 | | .000 |
| | BRTR | | | |

BERNAL, VICTOR HUGO
B.OCT.6,1953 LOS ANGELES,CAL.

| 1977 SD | N P | 15 | | 1- 1 |
| | BRTR | | | |

BERNARD, CURTIS HENRY
B.FEB.18,1878 PARKERSBURG,W.VA.
D.APR.10,1955 CULVER CITY,CAL.

1900 NY	N O	19		.243
1901 NY	N O	19		.192
	BLTR	38		.217

BERNARD, DWIGHT VERN
B.MAY 31,1952 MT.VERNON,ILL.

| 1978 NY | N P | 30 | | 1- 4 |
| | BRTR | | | |

BERNARD, JOSEPH

| 1909 STL | N P | 1 | | 0- 0 |

BERNHARD, WILLIAM HENRY
(STRAWBERRY BILL)
B.MAR.16,1871 CLARENCE,N.Y.
D.MAR.30,1949 SAN DIEGO,CAL.

1899 PHI	N P	17		6- 5
1900 PHI	N P	28		14-11
1901 PHI	N P	30	31	17-11
1902 PHI	A P	1		1- 0
	CLE A P	27		17- 6
1903 CLE	A P	20		14- 5
1904 CLE	A P	38		21-13
1905 CLE	A P	22		6-14
1906 CLE	A P	31		16-15
1907 CLE	A P	8		0- 1
	BBTR	222	223	112-81

BERNHARDT, JUAN RAMON (CORADIN)
B.AUG.31,1953 SAN PEDRO DE
MACORIS,D.R.

1976 NY	A /O-3	10		.190
1977 SEA	A O-3/1	89		.243
1978 SEA	A 1-3	54		.230
	BRTR	153		.236

BERNHARDT, WALTER JACOB
B.MAY 20,1893 PLEASANT VILLAGE,PA.
D.JULY 26,1958 WATERTOWN,N.Y.

| 1918 NY | A P | 1 | | 0- 0 |
| | BRTR | | | |

BERNIER, CARLOS (RODRIGUEZ)
B.JAN.28,1929 JUANA DIAZ,P.R.

| 1953 PIT | N O | 105 | | .213 |
| | BRTR | | | |

BERO, JOHN GEROGE
B.DEC.22,1922 GARY,W.VA.

1948 DET	A 2	4		.000
1951 STL	A 2-S	61		.213
		65		.201

BEKRA, DALE ANTHONY
B.DEC.13,1956 RIDGEWOOD,N.J.

1977 PIT	N 3	17		.175
1978 PIT	N 3/S	56		.207
	BRTR	73		.200

BERRA, LAWRENCE PETER (YOGI)
B.MAY 12,1925 ST.LOUIS,MO.

1946 NY	A C	7		.364
1947 NY	A C-O	83		.280
1948 NY	A C-O	125		.305
1949 NY	A C	116		.277
1950 NY	A C	151		.322
1951 NY	A C	141		.294
1952 NY	A C	142		.273
1953 NY	A C	137		.296
1954 NY	A C-3	151		.307
1955 NY	A C	147		.272
1956 NY	A C-O	140		.298
1957 NY	A C-O	134		.251
1958 NY	A C-1-O	122		.266
1959 NY	A C-O	131		.284
1960 NY	A C-O	120		.276
1961 NY	A C-O	119		.271
1962 NY	A C-O	86		.224
1963 NY	A C	64		.293
1965 NY	A /C	4		.222
	BLTR	2120		.285

NON-PLAYING MANAGER
NY(A) 1964; NY(N) 1972-75

BERRENS, JOSEPH

| 1912 CHI | A O | 2 | | .250 |

BERRES, RAYMOND FREDERICK (RAY)
B.AUG.31,1907 KENOSHA,WIS.

1934 BRO	N C	39		.215
1936 BRO	N C	105		.240
1937 PIT	N C	2		.167
1938 PIT	N C	40		.230
1939 PIT	N C	81		.229
1940 PIT	N C	21		.188
	BOS N C	85		.192
1941 BOS	N C	120		.201
1942 NY	N C	12		.188
1943 NY	N C	20		.143
1944 NY	N C	16		.471
1945 NY	N C	20		.167
		561		.216

BERRY, ALLEN KENT (KEN)
B.MAY 10,1941 KANSAS CITY,MO.

1962 CHI	A O	3		.333
1963 CHI	A 2-O	4		.200
1964 CHI	A O	12		.375
1965 CHI	A *O	157		.218
1966 CHI	A *O	147		.271
1967 CHI	A *O	147		.241
1968 CHI	A *O	153		.252
1969 CHI	A *O	130		.232
1970 CHI	A *O	141		.276
1971 CAL	A *O	111		.221
1972 CAL	A *O	119		.289
1973 CAL	A *O	136		.284
1974 MIL	A O-D	98		.240
1975 CLE	A O	25		.200
	BRTR	1383		.255

BERRY, CHARLES FRANCIS
B.OCT.18,1902 PHILIPSBURG,N.J.
D.SEPT.6,1972 EVANSTON,ILL.

1925 PHI	A C	10		.214
1928 BOS	A C	80		.260
1929 BOS	A C	77		.242
1930 BOS	A C	88		.289
1931 BOS	A C	111		.283
1932 BOS	A C	10		.188
	CHI A C	72		.305
1933 CHI	A C	86		.259
1934 PHI	A C	99		.268
1935 PHI	A C	62		.253
1936 PHI	A C	13		.059
1938 PHI	A C	1		.000
	BRTR	709		.267

BERRY, CHARLES JOSEPH
B.SEPT.6,1860 ELIZABETH,N.J.
D.FEB.16,1940 PHILLIPSBURG,N.J.

1884 ALT	U 2	7		.269
	KC U 2-3-O	29		.267
	CHI U 2	5		.118
	PIT U 2	2		.100
	BRTR	43		.243

BERRY, CLAUDE ELZY (ADMIRAL)
B.FEB.14,1880 LOSANTVILLE,IND.
D.FEB.1,1974 RICHMOND,IND.

1904 CHI	A C	3		.000
1906 PHI	A C	10		.226
1907 PHI	A C	8		.291
1914 PIT	F C	124		.243
1915 PIT	F C	99		.192
	BRTR	244		.224

BERRY, CORNELIUS JOHN (NEIL)
B.JAN.11,1922 KALAMAZOO,MICH.

1948 DET	A 2-S	87		.266
1949 DET	A 2-S	109		.237
1950 DET	A 2-S-3	38		.256
1951 DET	A 2-S-3	67		.229
1952 DET	A S-3	73		.226
1953 STL	A 2-S-3	57		.283
	CHI A 2	5		.125
1954 BAL	A S	5		.111
	BRTR	441		.244

BERRY, JONAS ARTHUR (JITTERY JOE)
B.DEC.16,1904 HUNTSVILLE,ARK.
D.SEPT.27,1958 ANAHEIM,CAL.

1942 CHI	N P	2		0- 0
1944 PHI	A P	53		10- 8
1945 PHI	A P	52		8- 7
1946 PHI	A P	5		0- 1
	CLE A P	21		3- 6
	BLTR	133		21-22

BERRY, JOSEPH HOWARD JR. (NIG)
B.DEC.31,1894 PHILADELPHIA,PA.
D.APR.29,1976 PHILADELPHIA,PA.

1921 NY	N 2	9		.333
1922 NY	N H	6		.000
	BBTR	15		.333

BERRY, JOSEPH HOWARD SR (HODGE)
B.SEPT.10,1872 WHEELING,W.VA.
D.MAR.13,1961 ALLENWOOD,N.J.

| 1902 PHI | N C | 1 | | .250 |
| | BBTR | | | |

BERRY, THOMAS HANEY
B.DEC.31,1842 CHESTER,PA.
D.JUNE 15,1915

| 1871 ATH | NA O | 1 | | .250 |

BERTAINA, FRANK LOUIS
B.APR.14,1944 SAN FRANCISCO,CAL.

1964 BAL	A P	6		1- 0
1965 BAL	A /P	2		0- 0
1966 BAL	A P	16		2- 5
1967 BAL	A /P	5		1- 1
	WAS A P	18	19	6- 5
1968 WAS	A P	27		7-13
1969 WAS	A P	14		1- 3
	BAL A /P	3		0- 0
1970 STL	N /P	8		1- 2
	BLTL	99	100	19-29

YR	CL LEA POS	GP	G	REC

BERTE, HARRY
B.MAY 10,1872 COVINGTON,KY.
1903 STL N 2-S   4 .357
          TR

BERTELL, RICHARD GEORGE (DICK)
B.NOV.21,1935 OAK PARK,ILL.
1960 CHI N C   5 .133
1961 CHI N C   92 .273
1962 CHI N C   77 .302
1963 CHI N C   100 .233
1964 CHI N C   112 .238
1965 CHI N C   34 .214
     SF N C   22 .188
1967 CHI N /C   2 .167
          BRTR   444 .250

BERTHRONG, HENRY W. (HARRY)
B.JAN.1,1844 MUMFORD,N.Y.
D.APR.28,1928 CHELSEA,MASS.
1871 OLY NA 2-3-0   17 .244
          TR

BERTOIA, RENO PETER
B.JAN.8,1935 ST.VITO UDINE,ITALY
1953 DET A 2   1 .000
1954 DET A 2-S-3   54 .162
1955 DET A S-3   38 .206
1956 DET A 2-3   22 .182
1957 DET A 2-S-3   97 .275
1958 DET A S-3-0   86 .233
1959 WAS A 2-S-3   90 .237
1960 WAS A 2-3   121 .265
1961 MIN A 3   35 .212
     KC A 2-3   39 .242
     DET A 2-S-3   24 .217
1962 DET A 2-S-3   5 .000
          BRTR   612 .244

BERTRAND, ROMAN MATHIAS (LEFTY)
B.FEB.28,1909 COBDEN,MINN.
1936 PHI N P   1 0- 0
          BRTL

BESANA, FREDERICK CYRIL (FRED)
B.APR.5,1931 LINCOLN,CAL.
1956 BAL A P   7 1- 0
          BRTL

BESCHER, ROBERT HENRY
B.FEB.25,1884 LONDON,OHIO
D.NOV.29,1942 LONDON,OHIO
1908 CIN N O   32 .272
1909 CIN N O   117 .240
1910 CIN N O   150 .250
1911 CIN N O   153 .275
1912 CIN N O   145 .281
1913 CIN N O   141 .258
1914 NY N O   135 .270
1915 STL N O   130 .263
1916 STL N O   151 .235
1917 STL N O   42 .155
1918 CLE A O   25 .333
          BBTL   1221 .258

BESSE, HERMAN A.
B.AUG.16,1911 ST.LOUIS,MO.
D.AUG.13,1972 LOS ANGELES,CAL.
1940 PHI A P   17 0- 3
1941 PHI A P   6 2- 6
1942 PHI A P   30 34 2- 9
1943 PHI A P   5   7 1- 1
1946 PHI A P   7 0- 2
          BLTL   65 71 5-15

BESSENT, FRED DONALD (DON)
B.MAR.13,1931 JACKSONVILLE,FLA.
1955 BRO N P   24 8- 1
1956 BRO N P   38 4- 3
1957 BRO N P   27 1- 3
1958 LA N P   19 1- 0
          BRTR   108 14- 7

BESTICK
1872 ECK NA C   4 .214

BESWICK, JAMES WILLIAM (JIM)
B.FEB.12,1958 WILKINSBURG,PA.
1978 SD N /O   17 .050
          BBTR

BETCHER, FRANKLIN LYLE
[REAL NAME FRANKLIN LYLE BETTGER]
B.FEB.15,1888 PHILADELPHIA,PA.
1910 STL N S   27 .202
          BBTR

BETHEA, WILLIAM LAMAR
(BILL) OR (SPOT)
B.JAN.1,1942 HOUSTON,TEX.
1964 MIN A 2-S   10 .167
          BRTR

BETHKE, JAMES CHARLES (JIM)
B.NOV.5,1946 FALLS CITY,NEB.
1965 NY N P   25 2- 0
          BRTR

BETTENCOURT, LAWRENCE JOSEPH
B.SEPT.22,1905 NEWARK,CAL.
D.SEPT.15,1978 NEW ORLEANS,LA.
1928 STL A 3   67 .283
1931 STL A O   74 .257
1932 STL A 3-0   27 .133
          BRTR   168 .258

BETTGER, FRANKLIN LYLE
[PLAYED UNDER NAME OF
FRANKLIN LYLE BETCHER]

BETTS, HAROLD MATTHEW (HARRY)
(CHUBBY) OR (GINGER)
B.JUNE 19,1881 ALLIANCE,OHIO
D.MAY 22,1946 SAN ANTONIO,TEX.
1903 STL N P   1 0- 1
1913 CIN N P   1 0- 0
          BRTR   2 0- 1

BETTS, WALTER MARTIN (HUCK)
B.FEB.18,1897 MILLSBORO,DEL.
1920 PHI N P   27 1- 1
1921 PHI N P   32 3- 7
1922 PHI N P   7 1- 0
1923 PHI N P   19 20 2- 4
1924 PHI N P   37 38 7-10
1925 PHI N P   35 37 4- 5
1932 BOS N P   31 13-11
1933 BOS N P   35 11-11
1934 BOS N P   40 17-10
1935 BOS N P   44 2- 9
          BRTR   307 311 61-68

BETZEL, CHRISTIAN FREDERICK
ALBERT JOHN HENRY DAVID (BRUNO)
B.DEC.6,1894 CHATTANOOGA,OHIO
D.FEB.7,1965 W.HOLLYWOOD,FLA.
1914 STL N 2-3   7 .000
1915 STL N 3   117 .251
1916 STL N 2-3   142 .233
1917 STL N 2-0   106 .217
1918 STL N 2-3-0   76 .222
          BRTR   448 .231

BEVACQUA, KURT ANTHONY
B.JAN.23,1947 MIAMI BEACH,FLA.
1971 CLE A 2/O-3-S   55 .204
1972 CLE A O/3   19 .114
1973 KC A 3-2-0-0/1 99 .257
1974 PIT N /3-0   18 .114
1975 MIL A 3-2/S-1   39 .211
     MIL A 3-2/S-1 104 .229
1976 MIL A /2   12 .143
1977 TEX A O-3/1-2   39 .333
1978 TEX A 3-0-2/1   90 .222
          BRTR   475 .231

BEVAN, JOSEPH HAROLD (HAL)
B.NOV.15,1930 NEW ORLEANS,LA.
D.OCT.5,1968 NEW ORLEANS,LA.
1952 BOS A 3   1 .000
     PHI A 3   8 .353
1955 KC A 3   3 .000
1961 CIN N H   3 .333
          BRTR   15 .292

BEVANS, E. P.
B.1848 NEW YORK
1871 TRO NA 2   3 .333
1872 ATL NA 2-S-0   10 .205
          TR   13 .237

BEVENS, FLOYD CLIFFORD (BILL)
B.OCT.21,1916 HUBBARD,ORE.
1944 NY A P   8 4- 1
1945 NY A P   29 13- 9
1946 NY A P   31 16-13
1947 NY A P   28 7-13
          BRTR   96 40-36

BEVIL, LOUIS EUGENE
[REAL NAME LOUIS EUGENE BEVILACQUA]
B.NOV.27,1922 NELSON,ILL.
O.FEB.1,1973 DIXON,ILL.
1942 WAS A P   4 0- 1

BEVILACQUA, LOUIS EUGENE
[PLAYED UNDER NAME OF
LOUIS EUGENE BEVIL]

BEVILLE, CLARENCE BENJAMIN (BEN)
B.AUG.28,1877 COLUSA,CAL.
D.JAN.5,1937 YOUNTVILLE,CAL.
1901 BOS A P   3 0- 2

BEVILLE, HENRY MONTE
B.FEB.24,1875 DUBLIN,IND.
D.JAN.24,1955 GRAND RAPIDS,MICH
1903 NY A C   82 .194
1904 NY A C-1   9 .273
     DET A C   53 .225
          BLTR   144 .210

BEZDEK, HUGO FRANK
B.APR.1,1884 PRAGUE,CZECH KIA
D.SEPT.19,1952 ATLANTIC CITY,N.J.
NON-PLAYING MANAGER PIT [N] 1917-19

BIANCO, THOMAS ANTHONY (TOMMY)
B.DEC.16,1952 ROCKVILLE CNTR,N.Y
1975 MIL A /3-1   18 .176
          BBTR

BIASATTI, HENRY ARCADO (HANK)
B.JAN.14,1922 BEANO,ITALY
1949 PHI A 1   21 .083
          BLTL

BIBBY, JAMES BLAIR (JIM)
B.OCT.29,1944 FRANKLINTON,N.C.
1972 STL N /P   6 1- 3
1973 STL N /P   6 0- 2
     TEX A P   26 27 9-10
1974 TEX A P   41 19-19
1975 TEX A P   12 2- 6
     CLE A P   24 5- 9
1976 CLE A P   34 13- 7
1977 CLE A P   37 12-13
1978 PIT N P   34 8- 7
          BRTR   220 221 69-76

BICKFORD, VERNON EDGELL (VERN)
B.AUG.17,1920 HELLIER,KY.
D.MAY 6,1960 CONCORD,VA.
1948 BOS N P   33 11- 5
1949 BOS N P   37 16-11
1950 BOS N P   40 19-14
1951 BOS N P   25 11- 9
1952 BOS N P   26 7-12
1953 MIL N P   20 2- 5
1954 BAL A P   1 0- 1
          BRTR   182 66-57

BICKHAM, DANIEL DENISON
B.OCT.31,1864 DAYTON,OHIO
D.MAR.3,1951 DAYTON,OHIO
1886 CIN AA P   1 1- 0

BICKNELL, CHARLES STEPHEN (BUD)
B.JULY 27,1928 PLAINFIELD,N.J.
1948 PHI N P   17 0- 1
1949 PHI N P   13 0- 0
          BRTR   30 0- 1

BIELASKI, OSCAR
B.MAR.21,1847 WASHINGTON,D.C.
D.NOV.8,1911 WASHINGTON,D.C.
1872 NAT NA O   10 .170
1873 NAT NA O   38   -
1874 BAL NA 1-2-0   25   -
1875 CHI NA O   52   -
1876 CHI N O   31 .206
          BRTR   156   -

BIEMILLER, HARRY LEE
B.OCT.9,1897 BALTIMORE,MD.
D.MAY 25,1965 ORLANDO,FLA.
1920 WAS A P   5 1- 0
1925 CIN N P   23 0- 1
          BRTR   28 1- 1

BIERBAUER, LOUIS W.
B.SEPT.23,1865 ERIE,PA.
D.JAN.31,1926 ERIE,PA.
1886 ATH AA 2   137 .244
1887 ATH AA 2   126 .302
1889 ATH AA 2   130 .313
1888 ATH AA 2   134 .279
1890 BRO P 2   132 .319
1891 PIT N 2   117 .202
1892 PIT N 2   153 .240
1893 PIT N 2   128 .298
1894 PIT N 2   131 .301
1895 PIT N 2   119 .255
1896 PIT N 2   57 .277
1897 STL N 2   12 .217
1898 STL N 2   4 .000
          BLTR   1380 .275

BIERMAN, CHARLES S.
B.1845 HOBOKEN,N.J.
D.AUG.4,1879 HOBOKEN,N.J.
1871 KEK NA 1   1 .000

BIGBEE, CARSON LEE (SKEETER)
B.MAR.31,1895 WATERLOO,ORE.
D.OCT.17,1964 PORTLAND,ORE.
1916 PIT N 2-O   43 .250
1917 PIT N 2-O   133 .239
1918 PIT N O   92 .255
1919 PIT N O   125 .276
1920 PIT N O   137 .280
1921 PIT N O   147 .323
1922 PIT N O   150 .350
1923 PIT N O   123 .299
1924 PIT N O   69 .262
1925 PIT N O   66 .238
1926 PIT N O   42 .221
          BLTR   1147 .287

BIGBEE, LYLE RANDOLPH (AL)
B.AUG.22,1893 SWEET HOME,ORE.
D.AUG.5,1942 PORTLAND,ORE.
1920 PHI A P   12 37 0- 3
1921 PIT N P   5 0- 0
          BLTR   17 42 0- 3

YR	CL LEA POS	GP	G	REC

**BIGELOW, ELLIOT ALLARDICE
(BABE) OR (GILLY)**
B.OCT.13,1897 TARPON SPRINGS,FLA.
D.AUG.10,1933 TAMPA,FLA.

| 1929 BOS A | O | 100 | .285 |
| | BLTL | | |

BIGGS, CHARLES ORVAL
B.SEPT.15,1906 FRENCH LICK,IND.
D.MAY 24,1954 FRENCH LICK,IND.

| 1932 CHI A | P | 6 | 1- 1 |
| | BRTR | | |

BIGNELL, GEORGE WILLIAM
B.JULY 18,1858 TAUNTON,MASS.
D.JAN.16,1925 PROVIDENCE,R.I.

| 1884 MIL U | C | 4 | .222 |

BIITTNER, LAWRENCE DAVID (LARRY)
B.JULY 27,1945 POCAHONTAS,IA.

1970 WAS A	/H	2	.000
1971 WAS A	O/1	66	.257
1972 TEX A	1-O	137	.259
1973 TEX A	O-1	83	.252
1974 MON N	/O	18	.269
1975 MON N	O	121	.315
1976 MON N	/O	11	.188
CHI N	1-O	78	.245
1977 CHI N	1-O/P	1	138	0- 0
				.298
1978 CHI N	1-O	120	.257
	BLTL	1	774	0- 0
				.273

BILBREY, JAMES MELVIN
D.APR.24,1924 RICKMAN,TENN.

| 1949 STL A | P | 1 | 0- 0 |
| | BRTR | | |

BILDILLI, EMIL (HILL BILLY)
D.SEPT.16,1912 DIAMOND,IND.
D.SEPT.16,1946 HARTFORD CITY,IND.

1937 STL A	P	4	0- 1
1938 STL A	P	5	1- 2
1939 STL A	P	2	1- 1
1940 STL A	P	28	2- 4
1941 STL A	P	2	0- 0
	BRTL	41	42	4- 8

BILKO, STEPHEN THOMAS (STEVE)
B.NOV.13,1928 NANTICOKE,PA.
D.MAR.7,1978 WILKES-BARRE,PA.

1949 STL N	1	6	.294
1950 STL N	1	10	.182
1951 STL N	1	21	.222
1952 STL N	1	20	.264
1953 STL N	1	154	.251
1954 STL N	1	8	.143
CHI N	1	47	.239
1958 CIN N	1	31	.264
LA N	1	47	.208
1960 DET A	1	78	.207
1961 LA A	1-O	114	.279
1962 LA A	1	64	.287
	BRTR	600	.249

BILLIARD, HARRY PREE (PRE)
B.NOV.11,1883 MONROE,IND.
D.JUNE 3,1923 WOOSTER,OHIO

1908 NY A	P	6	0- 0
1914 IND F	P	32	8- 7
1915 NEW F	P	14	0- 1
	BRTR	52	8- 8

BILLINGHAM, JOHN EUGENE (JACK)
B.FEB.21,1943 ORLANDO,FLA.

1968 LA N	P	50	3- 0
1969 HOU N	P	52	6- 7
1970 HOU N	P	46	13- 9
1971 HOU N	P	33	10-16
1972 CIN N	P	36	12-12
1973 CIN N	P	40	19-10
1974 CIN N	P	36	19-11
1975 CIN N	P	33	15-10
1976 CIN N	P	34	12-10
1977 CIN N	P	36	10-10
1978 DET A	P	30	15- 8
	BRTR	426	134-103

BILLINGS, HASKELL CLARK (JOSH)
B.SEPT.27,1907 NEW YORK,N.Y.

1927 DET A	P	10	5- 4
1928 DET A	P	21	5-10
1929 DET A	P	8	0- 1
	BRTR	39	10-15

BILLINGS, JOHN AUGUSTUS (JOSH)
B.NOV.30,1891 GRANTVILLE,KAN.

1913 CLE A	C	1	.000
1914 CLE A	C	10	.250
1915 CLE A	C	7	.266
1916 CLE A	C	22	.160
1917 CLE A	C	66	.178
1918 CLE A	C	2	.333
1919 STL A	C	38	.198
1920 STL A	C	66	.278
1921 STL A	C	20	.217
1922 STL A	C	5	.429
1923 STL A	C	4	.000
	BRTR	241	.217

BILLINGS, RICHARD ARLIN (DICK)
B.DEC.4,1942 DETROIT,MICH.

1968 WAS A	/O-3	12	.182
1969 WAS A	/O-3	27	.135
1970 WAS A	/C	11	.250
1971 WAS A	C-O/3	116	.246
1972 TEX A	C-O/3-1	133	.254
1973 TEX A	C/O-1	81	.179
1974 TEX A	C/O	16	.226
STL N	/C	1	.000
1975 STL N	/H	3	.000
	BRTR	400	.227

**BINKOWSKI, GEORGE ALVIN
(PLAYED UNDER NAME OF
GEORGE EUGENE BINKS)**

**BINKS, GEORGE ALVIN (BINGO)
(REAL NAME GEORGE ALVIN BINKOWSKI)**
B.JULY 11,1916 CHICAGO,ILL.

1944 WAS A	O	5	.250
1945 WAS A	1 -O	145	.278
1946 WAS A	O	65	.194
1947 PHI A	1-O	104	.258
1948 PHI A	O	17	.098
STL A	1-O	15	.217
	BLTL	351	.254

BIRAS, STEPHEN ALEXANDER
B.FEB.26,1922 E.ST.LOUIS,ILL.
D.APR.21,1965 ST.LOUIS,MO.

| 1944 CLE A | 2 | 2 | 1.000 |
| | BRTR | | |

BIRCHALL, A. JUDSON (JUD)
B.1858 GERMANTOWN,PA.
D.DEC.22,1887 PHILADELPHIA,PA.

1882 ATH AA 2-O	75	.263
1883 ATH AA O	95	.230
1884 ATH AA O	53	.262
	223	.256

BIRD, FRANK ZEPHERIN (DODO)
D.MAR.10,1869 SPENCER,MASS.
D.MAY 20,1958 WORCESTER,MASS.

| 1892 STL N | C | 17 | .196 |
| | BRTR | | |

BIRD, GEORGE R.
B.JUNE 23,1850 STILMAN VALLEY,ILL.
D.NOV.9,1940

| 1871 ROK NA O | 25 | - |

BIRD, JAMES DOUGLAS (DOUG)
B.MAR.5,1950 CORONA,CAL.

1973 KC A	P	54	4- 4
1974 KC A	P	55	7- 6
1975 KC A	P	51	9- 6
1976 KC A	P	39	12-10
1977 KC A	P	53	11- 4
1978 KC A	P	40	6- 6
	BRTR	292	49-36

BIRD, JAMES EDWARD (RED)
B.APR.25,1890 STEPHENVILLE,TEX.
D.MAR.23,1972 MURFREESBORO,ARK.

| 1921 WAS A | P | 1 | 0- 0 |
| | BLTL | | |

BIRDSALL, DAVID SOLOMON
B.JULY 16,1839 NEW YORK,N.Y.
D.JAN.30,1896

1871 BOS NA C-O	31	-
1872 BOS NA C-O	14	.179
1873 BOS NA O	3	-
	BRTR	48	-

BIRKOFER, RALPH JOSEPH (LEFTY)
B.NOV.5,1908 CINCINNATI,OHIO
D.MAR.16,1971 CINCINNATI,OHIO

1933 PIT N	P	9	4- 2
1934 PIT N	P	41	11-12
1935 PIT N	P	37	38	9- 7
1936 PIT N	P	34	7- 5
1937 BRO N	P	11	12	0- 2
	BLTL	132	134	31-28

BIRMINGHAM, JOSEPH LEO (DODE)
B.AUG.6,1884 ELMIRA,N.Y.
D.APR.24,1946 TAMPICO,MEXICO

1906 CLE A	O	10	.275
1907 CLE A	O	136	.235
1908 CLE A	O	122	.213
1909 CLE A	O	100	.289
1910 CLE A	O	104	.229
1911 CLE A	3-O	125	.304
1912 CLE A	M-O	107	.255
1913 CLE A	M-O	47	.282
1914 CLE A	M-O	19	.128
	BRTR	770	.253

NON-PLAYING MANAGER CLE(A) 1915

BIRRER, WERNER JOSEPH (BABE)
B.JULY 4,1928 BUFFALO,N.Y.

1955 DET A	P	36	4- 3
1956 BAL A	P	4	0- 0
1958 LA N	P	16	0- 0
	BRTR	56	4- 3

BISCAN, FRANK STEPHEN (PORKY)
B.MAR.13,1920 MT.OLIVE,ILL.
D.MAY 22,1959 ST.LOUIS,MO.

1942 STL A	P	11	0- 1
1946 STL A	P	16	1- 1
1948 STL A	P	47	6- 7
	BLTL	74	7- 9

BISCHOFF, JOHN GEORGE (SMILEY)
B.OCT.28,1894 GRANITE CITY,ILL.

1925 CHI A	C	7	.091
BOS A	C	41	.278
1926 BOS A	C	59	.260
	BRTR	107	.262

BISHOP, CHARLES TULLER
B.JAN.11,1924 ATLANTA,GA.

1952 PHI A	P	6	2- 2
1953 PHI A	P	39	40	3-14
1954 PHI A	P	20	22	4- 6
1955 KC A	P	4	1- 0
	BRTR	69	72	10-22

BISHOP, FRANK
B.CHICAGO,ILL.

| 1884 CHI U | S-3 | 4 | .200 |

BISHOP, JAMES MORTON
B.JAN.28,1898 MONTGOMERY CITY,MO.
D.SEPT.20,1973 MONTGOMERY CITY,MO.

1923 PHI N	P	15	0- 3
1924 PHI N	P	7	0- 1
	BRTR	22	0- 4

BISHOP, LLOYD CLIFTON
B.APR.25,1890 CONWAY SPRINGS,KAN.
D.JUNE 18,1968 WICHITA,KAN.

| 1914 CLE A | P | 3 | 0- 1 |
| | BRTR | | |

**BISHOP, MAX FREDERICK (MAX)
(TILLY) OR (CAMERA EYE)**
B.SEPT.5,1899 WAYNESBORO,PA.
D.FEB.24,1962 WAYNESBORO,PA.

1924 PHI A	2	91	.255
1925 PHI A	2	105	.280
1926 PHI A	2	122	.265
1927 PHI A	2	117	.277
1928 PHI A	2	126	.316
1929 PHI A	2	129	.232
1930 PHI A	2	130	.252
1931 PHI A	2	130	.294
1932 PHI A	2	114	.294
1933 PHI A	2	117	.294
1934 BOS A	1-2	97	.261
1935 BOS A	1-2-S	60	.230
	BLTL	1338	.271

BISHOP, WILLIAM HENRY (LEFTY)
B.OCT.22,1900 HOUTZDALE,PA.
D.FEB.11,1956 ST.JOSEPH,MO.

| 1921 PHI A | P | 2 | 0- 0 |
| | BLTL | | |

BISHOP, WILLIAM ROBINSON
B.DEC.27,1869 ADAMSBURG,PA.
D.DEC.15,1932 PITTSBURGH,PA.

1886 PIT AA P	2	0- 1
1887 PIT N	P	4	0- 4
1889 CHI N	P	2	0- 0
		8	0- 5

BISLAND, RIVINGTON MARTIN
B.FEB.17,1890 NEW YORK,N.Y.
D.JAN.11,1973 SALZBURG,AUSTRIA

1912 PIT N	H	1	.000
1913 STL A	S	12	.136
1914 CLE A	S	16	.105
	BRTR	31	.117

YR   CL LEA POS   GP   G   REC

BISSONETTE, DELPHIA LOUIS (DEL)
B.SEPT.6,1899 WINTHROP,ME.
D.JUNE 9,1972 AUGUSTA,MAINE
1928 BRO N 1   155   .320
1929 BRO N 1   116   .281
1930 BRO N 1   144   .336
1931 BRO N 1   192   .290
1933 BRO N 1   35   .246
          BLTL   604   .305
NON-PLAYING MANAGER BOS[N] 1945

BITHORN, HIRAM GABRIEL (HI)
B.MAR.18,1916 SANTURCE,P.R.
D.JAN.1,1952 EL MANTE,MEX.
1942 CHI N P   38   9-14
1943 CHI N P   39 18-12
1946 CHI N P   26   6- 5
1947 CHI A P   2   1- 0
          BRTR   105 34-31

BITTMAN, HENRY (RED)
B.CINCINNATI,OHIO
1889 KC AA 2   4   .286

BIVIN, JAMES NATHANIEL
B.DEC.11,1909 JACKSON,MISS.
1935 PHI N P   47   2- 9
          BRTR

BLACK, DAVID
B.APR.19,1892 CHICAGO,ILL.
D.OCT.27,1936 PITTSBURGH,PA.
1914 CHI F P   9   1- 0
1915 CHI F P   21   3- 2
         BAL F P   12   4- 8
1923 BOS A P   2   0- 0
          TR   44   8-10

BLACK, DONALD PAUL (DON)
B.JULY 20,1916 SALIX,IOWA
D.APR.21,1959 CUYAHOGA FALLS,O.
1943 PHI A P   33   6-16
1944 PHI A P   29 10-12
1945 PHI A P   26   5-11
1946 CLE A P   18   1- 2
1947 CLE A P   30 10-12
1948 CLE A P   18   2- 2
          BRTR   154 34-55

BLACK, JOHN FALCNOR (JACK)
[REAL NAME JOHN FALCNOR HADDOW]
B.FEB.23,1890 COVINGTON,KY.
D.MAR.20,1962 RUTHERFORD,N.J.
1911 STL A 1   54   .150
          BRTR

BLACK, JOHN WILLIAM (JIGGER)
B.AUG.12,1899 PHILADELPHIA,PA.
D.JAN.14,1968 PHILADELPHIA,PA.
1924 CHI A 2   6   .200
          BLTR

BLACK, JOSEPH (JOE)
B.FEB.8,1924 PLAINFIELD,N.J.
1952 BRO N P   56   57 15- 4
1953 BRO N P   34   6- 3
1954 BRO N P   5   0- 0
1955 BRO N P   6   1- 0
         CIN N P   32   5- 2
1956 CIN N P   32   34   3- 2
1957 WAS A P   7   0- 1
          BRTR   172 175 30-12

BLACK, ROBERT BENJAMIN (BOB)
B.DEC.10,1862 CINCINNATI,OHIO
D.MAR.21,1933 SIOUX CITY,IOWA
1884 KC U P-2-   16   38   3- 9
            S-O   .245

BLACK, WILLIAM CARROLL (BUD)
B.JULY 9,1932 ST.LOUIS,MO.
1952 DET A P   2   0- 1
1955 DET A P   3   1- 1
1956 DET A P   5   1- 1
          BRTR   10   2- 1

BLACKABY, ETHAN ALLEN
B.JULY 24,1940 CINCINNATI,O.
1962 MIL N O   6   .154
1964 MIL N O   9   .083
          BLTL   15   .120

BLACKBURN, EARL STUART
B.NOV.1,1892 LEESVILLE,OHIO
D.AUG.3,1966 MANSFIELD,OHIO
1912 PIT N C   1   .000
         CIN N C   1   .000
1913 CIN N C   17   .259
1915 BOS N C   3   .167
1916 BOS N C   47   .273
1917 CHI N C   2   .000
          BRTR   71   .262

BLACKBURN, FOSTER EDWIN (BABE)
B.JAN.6,1895 CHICAGO,ILL.
1915 KC F P   7   0- 1
1921 CHI A P   1   0- 0
                            8   0- 1

BLACKBURN, GEORGE W.
(SMILING GEORGE)
B.SEPT.2,1871 OZARK,MO.
1897 BAL N P   5   2- 2

BLACKBURN, JAMES RAY
(JIM) OR (BONES)
B.JUNE 19,1924 WARSAW,KY.
D.OCT.26,1969 CINCINNATI,OHIO
1946 CIN N P   16   0- 2
1951 CIN N P   2   0- 0
          BRTR   18   0- 2

BLACKBURN, RONALD HAMILTON
B.APR.23,1935 MT.AIRY,N.C.
1958 PIT N P   38   2- 1
1959 PIT N P   26   1- 1
          BRTR   64   3- 2

BLACKBURNE, RUSSELL AUBREY
(LENA) OR (SLATS)
B.OCT.23,1886 CLIFTON HEIGHTS,PA.
D.FEB.29,1968 RIVERSIDE,N.J.
1910 CHI A S   75   .174
1912 CHI A S   5   .000
1914 CHI A 2   144   .222
1915 CHI A 3   96   .216
1918 CIN N S   125   .228
1919 BOS N 1-2-S-3   31   .272
         PHI N 1-3   72   .197
1927 CHI A H   1 1.000
1929 CHI A M-P   1   0- 0
                      1 550   0- 0
                                .214
NON-PLAYING MANAGER CHI[A] 1928

BLACKERBY, GEORGE FRANKLIN
B.NOV.10,1903 GLUTHER,OKLA.
1928 CHI A O   30   .253
          BRTR

BLACKSTONE, ROBERT J.
[PLAYED UNDER NAME OF
ROBERT J. BLAKISTON]

BLACKWELL, EWELL (THE WHIP)
B.OCT.23,1922 FRESNO,CAL.
1942 CIN N P   2   0- 0
1946 CIN N P   33   9-13
1947 CIN N P   33 22- 8
1948 CIN N P   22   7- 9
1949 CIN N P   30   5- 5
1950 CIN N P   40 17-15
1951 CIN N P   38   39 16-15
1952 CIN N P   23   3-12
         NY A P   5   1- 0
1953 NY A P   8   2- 0
1955 KC A P   2   0- 1
          BRTR   236 237 82-78

BLACKWELL, FREDRICK WILLIAM (BLACKY)
B.SEPT.7,1891 BOWLING GREEN,KY.
D.DEC.8,1975 MORGANTOWN,KY.
1917 PIT N C   3   .000
1918 PIT N C   8   .153
1919 PIT N C   24   .215
          BLTR   35   .205

BLACKWELL, TIMOTHY P #TIM#
B.AUG.19,1952 SAN DIEGO,CAL.
1974 BOS A C   44   .246
1975 BOS A C   59   .197
1976 PHI N /C   4   .250
1977 PHI N /C   1   .000
         MON N C   16   .091
1978 MON N C   49   .223
          BBTR   173   .214

BLADES, FRANCIS RAYMOND (RAY)
B.AUG.6,1896 MT.VERNON,ILL.
1922 STL N S-3-O   37   .300
1923 STL N 3-O   98   .246
1924 STL N 2-3-O   131   .311
1925 STL N 3-O   122   .342
1926 STL N O   107   .305
1927 STL N O   61   .317
1928 STL N O   51   .233
1930 STL N O   45   .396
1931 STL N O   35   .284
1932 STL N O   80   .229
          BRTR   767   .301
NON-PLAYING MANAGER
ST.LOUIS[N] 1939-40

BLADT, RICHARD ALAN (RICK)
B.DEC.9,1946 SANTA CRUZ,CAL.
1969 CHI N /O   10   .154
1975 NY A O   52   .222
          BRTR   62   .215

BLAEHOLDER, GEORGE FRANKLIN
B.JAN.26,1904 ORANGE,CAL.
D.DEC.29,1947 GARDEN GROVE,CAL.
1925 STL A P   2   0- 0
1927 STL A P   1   0- 1
1928 STL A P   38 10-15
1929 STL A P   42 14-15
1930 STL A P   37 11-13
1931 STL A P   35 11-15
1932 STL A P   42 14-14
1933 STL A P   38 15-19
1934 STL A P   39 14-18
1935 STL A P   6   1- 1
         PHI A P   23   6-10
1936 CLE A P   35   8- 4
          BRTR   338 104-125

BLAEMIRE, RAE BERTRAM
B.FEB.8,1911 GARY,IND.
1941 NY N C   2   .400
          BRTR

BLAIR, CLARENCE VICK (FOOTSIE)
B.JULY 13,1903 PRYOR,OKL.
1929 CHI N 1-2-3   26   .319
1930 CHI N 2-3   134   .273
1931 CHI N 1-2   86   .258
          BLTR   246   .273

BLAIR, DENNIS HERMAN
B.JUNE 5,1954 MIDDLETOWN,OHIO
1974 MON N P   22 11- 7
1975 MON N P   30   8-15
1976 MON N /P   5   0- 2
          BRTR   57 19-24

BLAIR, LOUIS NATHAN (BUDDY)
B.SEPT.10,1910 COLUMBIA,MISS.
1942 PHI A 3   137   .279
          BLTR

BLAIR, PAUL L D
B.FEB.1,1944 CUSHING,OKLA.
1964 BAL A O   8   .000
1965 BAL A O   119   .234
1966 BAL A *O   133   .277
1967 BAL A *O   151   .293
1968 BAL A *O/3   141   .211
1969 BAL A *O   150   .285
1970 BAL A *O/3   133   .267
1971 BAL A *O   141   .262
1972 BAL A *O   142   .233
1973 BAL A *O   146   .280
1974 BAL A *O   151   .261
1975 BAL A *O/1   140   .218
1976 BAL A *O   145   .197
1977 NY A O   83   .262
1978 NY A O/2-S-3   74   .176
          BRTR   1857   .253
          BB 1971 (PART)

BLAIR, WALTER ALLEN (HEAVY)
B.OCT.13,1883 LANDRUS,PA.
D.AUG.20,1948 LEWISBURG,PA.
1907 NY A C   7   .173
1908 NY A C   76   .190
1909 NY A C   42   .209
1910 NY A C   6   .227
1911 NY A C   85   .194
1914 BUF F C   127   .239
1915 BUF F M-C   98   .224
          BRTR   441   .215

BLAIR, WILLIAM ELLSWORTH
B.SEPT.17,1863 PITTSBURGH,PA.
D.FEB.22,1890 PITTSBURGH,PA.
1888 ATH AA P   5   1- 4
          TL

BLAISDELL, HOWARD CARLETON (DICK)
B.JUNE 18,1862 BRADFORD,MASS.
D.AUG.20,1886 MALDEN,MASS.
1884 KC U P-O   3   4   0- 3
                                 .295

BLAKE, EDWARD JAMES
B.DEC.23,1925 E.ST.LOUIS,ILL.
1951 CIN N P   3   0- 0
1952 CIN N P   2   0- 0
1953 CIN N P   1   0- 0
1957 KC A P   2   0- 0
          BRTR   8   0- 0

BLAKE, HARRY COOPER
B.JUNE 16,1874 PORTSMOUTH,OHIO
D.OCT.14,1919 CHICAGO,ILL.
1894 CLE N O   73   .286
1895 CLE N O   83   .280
1896 CLE N O   102   .242
1897 CLE N O   31   .256
1898 CLE N O   137   .245
1899 STL N O   94   .238
                          520   .257

```
YR   CL LEA POS      GP   G   REC

BLAKE, JOHN FREDERICK (SHERIFF)
B.SEPT.17,1899 ANSTED,W.VA.
1920 PIT N P              6   0- 0
1924 CHI N P             29   6- 6
1925 CHI N P             36  10-18
1926 CHI N P             39  11-12
1927 CHI N P             32  13-14
1928 CHI N P        34   35  17-11
1929 CHI N P        35   38  14-13
1930 CHI N P        34   36  10-14
1931 CHI N P             16   0- 4
     PHI N P              4   4- 5
1937 STL A P             15   2- 2
     STL N P             14   0- 3
     BBTR          304  310  87-102

BLAKELY, LINCOLN HOWARD (LINC)
B.FEB.12,1912 OAKLAND,CAL.
D.SEPT.28,1976 OAKLAND,CAL.
1934 CIN N O             34   .225
     BRTR

BLAKISTON, ROBERT J.
[REAL NAME ROBERT J. BLACKSTONE]
B.OCT.2,1855 SAN FRANCISCO,CAL.
D.DEC.25,1918 SAN FRANCISCO,CAL
1882 ATH AA 2-3-O        72   .242
1883 ATH AA 1-3-O        40   .249
1884 ATH AA 1-2-S-3-O    33   .266
     IND AA 1-O           0   .000
                        151   .248

BLANCHARD, JOHN EDWIN (JOHNNY)
B.FEB.26,1933 MINNEAPOLIS,MINN.
1955 NY  A C              1   .000
1959 NY  A C-1-O         49   .169
1960 NY  A C             53   .242
1961 NY  A C-O           93   .305
1962 NY  A C-1-O         93   .232
1963 NY  A O             76   .223
1964 NY  A C-1-O         77   .255
1965 NY  A C             12   .147
     KC  A O-C           52   .200
     MIL N /O            10   .100
     BLTR          516        .239

BLANCO, DAMASO (CARIPE)
B.DEC.11,1941 CURIEPE,VENEZ.
1972 SF  N 3/S-2         39   .350
1973 SF  N /3-S-2        28   .000
1974 SF  N /H             5   .000
     BRTR           72        .212

BLANCO, GILBERT HENRY (GIL)
B.DEC.15,1945 PHOENIX,ARIZ.
1965 NY  A P             17   1- 1
1966 KC  A P             11   2- 4
     BLTL           28        3- 5

BLANCO, OSWALDO C. [DIAZ] (OSSIE)
[BORN CARLOS OSVALDO BLANCO]
B.SEP.8,1945 CARACAS,VENEZ.
1970 CHI A 1/O           34   .197
1974 CLE A 1             18   .194
     BBTR           52        .196

BLANDING, FREDERICK JAMES (FRITZ)
B.FEB.8,1888 REDLANDS,CAL.
D.JULY 16,1950 SALEM,VA.
1910 CLE A P              6   2- 2
1911 CLE A P        29   30   7-11
1912 CLE A P             39  18-14
1913 CLE A P             41  15-10
1914 CLE A P        29   30   3- 9
     BRTR          144  146  45-46

BLANK, FRANK IGNATZ (COONIE)
B.OCT.18,1892 ST.LOUIS,MO.
D.DEC.8,1961 ST.LOUIS,MO.
1909 STL N C              1   .000

BLANK, FREDERICK AUGUST
B.JUNE 18,1874 DESOTO,MO.
D.FEB.5,1936 ST.LOUIS,MO.
1894 CIN N P              1   0- 1
     BLTL

BLANKENSHIP, CLIFFORD DOUGLAS
B.APR.10,1880 COLUMBUS,GA.
D.APR.26,1956 OAKLAND,CAL.
1905 CIN N 1             15   .196
1907 WAS A C             37   .225
1909 WAS A C             39   .250
     BRTR           91        .225

BLANKENSHIP, HOMER (SI)
B.AUG.4,1902 BONHAM,TEX.
D.JUNE 22,1974 LONGVIEW,TEX.
1922 CHI A P              4   0- 0
1923 CHI A P              4   1- 1
1928 PIT N P              5   0- 2
     BRTR           13        1- 3


BLANKENSHIP, THEODORE
B.MAY 10,1901 BONHAM,TEX.
D.JAN.14,1945 ATOKA,OKLA.
1922 CHI A P             24   8-10
1923 CHI A P             44   9-14
1924 CHI A P             25   7- 6
1925 CHI A P             40  17- 8
1926 CHI A P             29  13-10
1927 CHI A P             38  12-17
1928 CHI A P             27   9-11
1929 CHI A P              8   0- 2
1930 CHI A P              7   2- 1
     BRTR          242       77-79

BLANKS, LARVELL
B.JAN.28,1950 DEL RIO,TEX.
1972 ATL N 2/S-3         33   .329
1973 ATL N /3-2-S        17   .222
1974 ATL N /3             3   .250
1975 ATL N *S-2         141   .234
1976 CLE A S-2/3        104   .280
1977 CLE A S-2/3        105   .286
1978 CLE A S-2/3         70   .254
     BRTR          473        .265

BLANTON, DARRELL ELIJAH (CY)
B.JULY 6,1908 WAURIKA,OKLA.
D.SEPT.13,1945 NORMAN,OKLA.
1934 PIT N P              1   0- 1
1935 PIT N P             35  18-13
1936 PIT N P             44  13-15
1937 PIT N P             36  14-12
1938 PIT N P             29  11- 7
1939 PIT N P             10   2- 3
1940 PHI N P             13   4- 3
1941 PHI N P             28   6-13
1942 PHI N P              6   0- 4
     BLTR          202       68-71

BLASINGAME, DON LEE
B.MAR.16,1932 CORINTH,MISS.
1955 STL N 2-S            5   .375
1956 STL N 2-S-3        150   .261
1957 STL N 2            154   .271
1958 STL N 2            143   .274
1959 STL N 2            150   .289
1960 SF  N 2            136   .235
1961 SF  N H              3   .000
     CIN N 2            123   .222
1962 CIN N 2            141   .281
1963 CIN N 2*3           18   .161
     WAS A 2             69   .256
1964 WAS A 2            143   .267
1965 WAS A *2           129   .223
1966 WAS A 2/S           68   .215
     KC  A /2            12   .158
     BLTR         1444        .258

BLASINGAME, WADE ALLEN
B.NOV.22,1943 DEMING,N.MEX.
1963 MIL N P              2   0- 0
1964 MIL N P        28   29   9- 5
1965 MIL N P             38  16-10
1966 ATL N P        16   18   3- 7
1967 ATL N P             10   1- 0
     HOU N P        15   16   4- 7
1968 HOU N P             22   1- 2
1969 HOU N P        26   27   0- 5
1970 HOU N P             13   3- 3
1971 HOU N P             30   9-11
1972 HOU N P             10   0- 0
     NY  A P             12   0- 1
     BLTL          222  227  46-51

BLASS, STEPHEN ROBERT (STEVE)
B.APR.18,1942 CANAAN,CONN.
1964 PIT N P             24   5- 8
1966 PIT N P             34  11- 7
1967 PIT N P             32   6- 8
1968 PIT N P/O      33   35  18- 6
                              .138
1969 PIT N P        38   44  16-10
1970 PIT N P        31   32  10-12
1971 PIT N P        33   34  15- 8
1972 PIT N P        33   35  19- 8
1973 PIT N P        23   24   3- 9
1974 PIT N /P             1   0- 0
     BRTR          282  295 103-76
                              .172

BLATERIC, STEPHEN LAWRENCE (STEVE)
B.MAR.20,1944 DENVER,COLO.
1971 CIN N /P             2   0- 0
1972 NY  A /P             1   0- 0
1975 CAL A /P             2   0- 0
     BRTR            5        0- 0

BLATNIK, JOHN LOUIS (JOHNNY)
B.MAR.10,1921 BRIDGEPORT,OHIO
1948 PHI N O            121   .260
1949 PHI N O              6   .125
1950 PHI N O              4   .250
     STL N O              7   .150
     BRTR          138        .253


BLATTNER, ROBERT GARNETT (BUDDY)
B.FEB.8,1920 ST.LOUIS,MO.
1942 STL N 2-S           19   .043
1946 NY  N 1-2          126   .255
1947 NY  N 2-3           55   .261
1948 NY  N 2              8   .200
1949 PHI N 2-S-3         64   .247
     BRTR          272        .247

BLAUVELT, HENRY R.
B.ROCHESTER,N.Y.
1890 ROC AA P             2   0- 1

BLAYLOCK, GARY NELSON
B.OCT.11,1931 CLARKTON,MO.
1959 STL N P        26   31   4- 5
     NY  A P             15   0- 1
     BRTR           41   46   4- 6

BLAYLOCK, MARVIN EDWARD (MARV)
B.SEPT.30,1929 FT.SMITH,ARK.
1950 NY  N H              1   .000
1955 PHI N 1-O          113   .208
1956 PHI N 1-O          136   .254
1957 PHI N 1-O           37   .154
     BLTL          287        .235

BLAYLOCK, ROBERT EDWARD (BOB)
B.JUNE 28,1935 CHATTANOOGA,OKLA
1956 STL N P             14   1- 6
1959 STL N P              3   0- 1
     BRTR           17        1- 7

BLEFARY, CURTIS LEROY (CURT)
B.JULY 5,1943 BROOKLYN,N.Y.
1965 BAL A *O           144   .260
1966 BAL A *O-1         131   .255
1967 BAL A *O-1         155   .242
1968 BAL A O-C-1        137   .200
1969 HOU N *1/O         155   .253
1970 NY  A O/1           90   .212
1971 NY  A O/1-S         21   .194
     OAK A C-O/3-2       50   .218
1972 OAK A /1-2-O         8   .455
     SD  N C/1-3-O       74   .196
     BLTR          974        .237

BLEMKER, RAY
B.AUG.9,1937 HUNTINGBURG,IND.
1960 KC  A P              1   0- 0
     BRTL

BLESSITT, ISAIAH (IKE)
B.SEP.30,1949 DETROIT,MICH.
1972 DET A /O             4   .000
     BRTR

BLETHEN, CLARENCE WALDO (CLIMAX)
B.JULY 11,1893 DOVER-FOXCROFT,MAINE
D.APR.11,1973 FREDERICK,MD.
1923 BOS A P              5   0- 0
1929 BRO N P              2   0- 0
     BLTR            7        0- 0

BLEWETT, ROBERT LAWRENCE
B.JUNE 28,1877 FOND DU LAC,WIS.
D.MAR.17,1958 SEDRO WOOLLEY,WASH.
1902 NY  N P              5   0- 2
     BLTL

BLIGH, EDWIN FORREST (NED)
B.JUNE 30,1864 BROOKLYN,N.Y.
D.APR.16,1892 BROOKLYN,N.Y.
1886 BAL AA C             3   .000
1888 CLE AA C-O           3   .000
1889 COL AA C            27   .126
1890 COL AA C             8   .214
     LOU AA C            24   .154
     BRTR           65        .151

BLISS, ELMER WARD
B.MAR.9,1875 PENFIELD,PA.
D.MAR.18,1962 BRADFORD,PA.
1903 NY  A P              1   1- 0
1904 NY  A P              1   0- 0
     BLTR            2        1- 0

BLISS, FRANK E.
B.MILWAUKEE,WIS.
1878 MIL N 3-O            2   .125

BLISS, JOHN JOSEPH ALBERT (JACK)
B.JAN.9,1882 VANCOUVER,WASH.
D.OCT.23,1968 TEMPLE CITY,CAL.
1908 STL N C             43   .213
1909 STL N C             32   .221
1910 STL N C             16   .063
1911 STL N C             85   .229
1912 STL N C             49   .246
     BRTR          225        .219

BLOCHOWICZ, JAMES JOHN
[PLAYED UNDER NAME OF
JAMES JOHN BLOCK]
```

YR	CL	LEA	POS	GP	G	REC

BLOCK, JAMES JOHN (BRUNO)
[REAL NAME JAMES JOHN BLOCHOWICZ]
B.MAR.13,1885 WISCONSIN RAPIDS,WIS.
D.AUG.6,1937 S.MILWAUKEE,WIS.
1907 WAS A C   24 .140
1910 CHI A C   55 .210
1911 CHI A C   39 .304
1912 CHI A C   46 .257
1914 CHI F C   45 .212
        BRTR   209 .234

BLOCK, SEYMOUR (CY)
B.MAY 4,1919 BROOKLYN,N.Y.
1942 CHI N 2-3   9 .364
1945 CHI N 2-3   2 .143
1946 CHI N 3   6 .231
        BRTR   17 .302

BLOGG, WESLEY C.
B.1855 NORFOLK,VA.
D.MAR 10,1897
1883 PIT AA C-1-O   9 .147

**BLOMBERG, RONALD MARK
(RON) OR (BOOMER)**
B.AUG.23,1948 ATLANTA,GA.
1969 NY A /O   4 .500
1971 NY A O   64 .322
1972 NY A 1   107 .268
1973 NY A O-1   100 .329
1974 NY A O-0   90 .311
1975 NY A D/O   34 .255
1976 NY A /H   1 .000
1978 CHI A D/1   61 .231
        BLTR   461 .293

BLONG, JOSEPH MYLES
B.SEPT.17,1853 ST.LOUIS,MO.
D.SEPT.22,1892 ST.LOUIS,MO.
1875 RS NA P-O   13 16 3-10
                             -
1876 STL N O   62 .233
1877 STL N P-2-   25 58 10- 9
            O   .216
        BRTR   38 136 13-19
                             -

BLOODWORTH, JAMES HENRY (JIMMY)
B.JULY 26,1917 TALLAHASSEE,FLA.
1937 WAS A 2   15 .220
1939 WAS A 2   83 .289
1940 WAS A 1-2-3   119 .245
1941 WAS A 2-S-3   142 .245
1942 DET A 2-S   137 .242
1943 DET A 2   129 .241
1946 DET A 2   76 .245
1947 PIT N 2   88 .250
1949 CIN N 1-2-3   134 .261
1950 CIN N 2   4 .214
        PHI N 1-2-3   54 .229
1951 PHI N 1-2   21 .143
        BRTR   1002 .248

BLOOMFIELD, CLYDE STALCUP (BUD)
B.JAN.5,1936 OKLAHOMA CITY,OKLA.
1963 STL N 3   1 .000
1964 MIN N 2-S   7 .143
        BRTR   8 .143

BLOTT, JOHN LEONARD (JACK)
B.AUG.24,1902 GIRARD,OHIO
D.JUNE 11,1964 ANN ARBOR,MICH.
1924 CIN N C   2 .000
        BRTR

BLUE, BIRD WAYNE (BERT)
B.DEC.14,1876 BETTSVILLE,OHIO
D.DEC.11,1928 DETROIT,MICH.
1908 STL A C   11 .375
        PHI A C   6 .167
            TR   17 .286

BLUE, LUZERNE ATWELL (LU)
B.MAR.5,1897 WASHINGTON,D.C.
D.JULY 28,1958 ALEXANDRIA,VA.
1921 DET A 1   153 .308
1922 DET A 1   145 .300
1923 DET A 1   129 .284
1924 DET A 1   108 .311
1925 DET A 1   150 .307
1926 DET A 1   128 .287
1927 DET A 1   112 .260
1928 STL A 1   154 .281
1929 STL A 1   151 .293
1930 STL A 1   117 .235
1931 CHI A 1   155 .304
1932 CHI A 1   112 .249
1933 BRO N 1   1 .000
        BBTL   1615 .287

BLUE, VIDA ROCHELLE
B.JULY 28,1949 MANSFIELD,LA.
1969 OAK A P   12 1- 1
1970 OAK A /P   6 2- 0
1971 OAK A P   39 24- 8
1972 OAK A P   25 27 6-10
1973 OAK A P   37 38 20- 9
1974 OAK A P   40 17-15
1975 OAK A P   39 22-11
1976 OAK A P   37 18-13
1977 OAK A P   38 14-19
1978 SF N P   35 18-10
        BBTL   308 311 142-96
        BL 1969

BLUEGE, OSWALD LOUIS (OSSIE)
B.OCT.24,1900 CHICAGO,ILL.
1922 WAS A 3   19 .197
1923 WAS A 3   109 .245
1924 WAS A 3   117 .281
1925 WAS A S-3   145 .287
1926 WAS A 3   139 .271
1927 WAS A 3   146 .274
1928 WAS A 3   146 .297
1929 WAS A 2-S-3   64 .295
1930 WAS A 3   134 .290
1931 WAS A 3   152 .272
1932 WAS A 3   149 .258
1933 WAS A 3   140 .261
1934 WAS A S-3-O   99 .246
1935 WAS A 2-S-3   100 .263
1936 WAS A 2-S-3   90 .288
1937 WAS A S   42 .283
1938 WAS A 2-S   58 .261
1939 WAS A 1   18 .153
        BRTR   1867 .272
NON-PLAYING MANAGER WAS[A] 1943-47

BLUEGE, OTTO ADAM (SQUEAKY)
B.JULY 20,1909 CHICAGO,ILL.
D.JUNE 28,1977 CHICAGO,ILL.
1932 CIN N H   1 .000
1933 CIN N 2-S-3   108 .213
        BRTR   109 .213

BLUEJACKET, JAMES
[REAL NAME JAMES SMITH]
B.JULY 8,1887 ADAIR,OKLA.
D.MAR.26,1947 PEKIN,ILL.
1914 BRO F P   17 4- 4
1915 BRO F P   24 10-11
1916 CIN N P   3 0- 1
        BRTR   44 14-16

BLUHM, HARVEY FRED (RED)
D.JUNE 27,1894 CLEVELAND,OHIO
D.MAY 7,1952 FLINT,MICH.
1918 BOS A H   1 .000
        BRTR

BLUME, CLINTON WILLIS
B.OCT.17,1898 BROOKLYN,N.Y.
D.JUNE 12,1973 ISLIP,L.I.,N.Y.
1922 NY N P   1 1- 0
1923 NY N P   12 2- 0
        BRTR   13 3- 0

BLYLEVEN, RIK AALBERT (BERT)
B.APR.6,1951 ZEIST,HOLLAND
1970 MIN A P   27 10- 9
1971 MIN A P   38 16-15
1972 MIN A P   39 17-17
1973 MIN A P   40 20-17
1974 MIN A P   37 17-17
1975 MIN A P   35 15-10
1976 MIN A P   12 4- 5
        TEX A P   24 9-11
1977 TEX A P   30 14-12
1978 PIT N P   34 37 14-10
        BRTR   316 319 136-123

BLYZKA, MICHAEL JOHN (MIKE)
B.DEC.25,1928 HAMTRAMCK,MICH.
1953 STL A P   33 2- 6
1954 BAL A P   37 1- 5
        BRTR   70 3-11

BOAK, CHESTER ROBERT (CHET)
B.JUNE 19,1935 NEW CASTLE,PA.
1960 KC A 2   5 .154
1961 WAS A 2   5 .000
        BRTR   10 .100

BOARDMAN, CHARLES LOUIS
B.APR.27,1893 SENECA FALLS,N.Y.
D.AUG.10,1968 SACRAMENTO,CAL.
1913 PHI A P   2 0- 2
1914 PHI A P   2 0- 0
1915 STL N P   3 1- 0
        BLTL   7 1- 2

BOARDMAN, FREDERICK
B.CHICAGO,ILL.
1874 BAL NA O   1   -

BOBB, MARK RANDALL (RANDY)
B.JAN.1,1948 LOS ANGELES,CAL.
1968 CHI N /C   7 .125
1969 CHI N /C   3 .000
        BRTR   10 .100

BOCCABELLA, JOHN DOMINIC
B.JUNE 29,1941 SAN FRANCISCO,CAL
1963 CHI N 1   24 .189
1964 CHI N 1-O   9 .391
1965 CHI N /1-O   6 .333
1966 CHI N O-1/C   75 .228
1967 CHI N /O-1-C   25 .171
1968 CHI N /C-O   7 .071
1969 MON N C   40 .105
1970 MON N 1-C/3   61 .269
1971 MON N C-1/3   74 .220
1972 MON N C/1-3   83 .227
1973 MON N C/1   118 .233
1974 SF N C   29 .138
        BRTR   551 .229

BOCEK, MILTON FRANK
B.JULY 16,1912 CHICAGO,ILL.
1933 CHI N O   11 .364
1934 CHI N O   19 .211
        BRTR   30 .267

BOCHTE, BRUCE ANTON
B.NOV.12,1950 PASADENA,CAL.
1974 CAL A O-1   57 .270
1975 CAL A #1   107 .285
1976 CAL A O-1   146 .258
1977 CAL A O   25 .290
        CLE A O-1   112 .304
1978 SEA A O-D/1   140 .263
        BLTL   587 .276

BOCHY, BRUCE DOUGLAS
B.APR.16,1955 LANDES DE BUSSAC,
FRANCE
1978 HOU N C   54 .266
        BRTR

BOCKMAN, JOSEPH EDWARD (EDDIE)
B.JULY 26,1920 SANTA ANA,CAL.
1946 NY A 3   4 .083
1947 CLE A 2-S-3   46 .258
1948 PIT N 2-3   70 .239
1949 PIT N 2-3   79 .223
        BRTR   199 .230

BODIE, FRANK STEPHAN (PING)
[REAL NAME
FRANCESCO STEPHANO PEZZOLO]
B.OCT.8,1887 SAN FRANCISCO,CAL.
D.DEC.17,1961 SAN FRANCISCO,CAL
1911 CHI A 2-O   145 .288
1912 CHI A O   137 .294
1913 CHI A O   127 .265
1914 CHI A O   107 .229
1917 PHI A O   148 .291
1918 NY A O   91 .256
1919 NY A O   134 .278
1920 NY A O   129 .295
1921 NY A O   31 .172
        BRTR   1049 .276

BOECKEL, NORMAN DOXIE (TONY)
B.AUG.25,1892 LOS ANGELES,CAL.
D.FEB.16,1924 SAN DIEGO,CAL.
1917 PIT N 3   64 .265
1919 PIT N 3   45 .250
        BOS N 3   95 .249
1920 BOS N 3   153 .268
1921 BOS N 3   153 .313
1922 BOS N 3   119 .289
1923 BOS N S-3   148 .298
        BRTR   777 .282

BOEHLER, GEORGE HENRY
B.JAN.2,1892 LAWRENCEBURG,IND.
D.JUNE 23,1958 LAWRENCEBURG,IND
1912 DET A P   4 1- 2
1913 DET A P   1 0- 1
1915 DET A P   9 1- 1
1916 DET A P   5 1- 1
1920 STL A P   3 0- 1
1921 STL A P   1 0- 0
1923 PIT N P   10 1- 3
1926 BRO N P   26 11 1- 0
1914 DET A P   18 2- 3
        BRTR   61 62 7-12

BOEHLING, JOHN JOSEPH (JOE)
B.MAR.20,1891 RICHMOND,VA.
D.SEPT.8,1941 RICHMOND,VA.
1912 WAS A P   3 0- 0
1913 WAS A P   38 17- 7
1914 WAS A P   27 12- 8
1915 WAS A P   41 13-13
1916 WAS A P   28 9-10
        CLE A P   11 2- 4
1917 CLE A P   14 1- 6
1920 CLE A P   3 0- 1
        BLTL   165 54-49

```
YR   CL LEA POS        GP   G   REC
```

BOEHMER, LEONARD JOSEPH STEPHEN (LEN)
B.JUNE 28,1941 FLINT HILL,MO.
```
1967 CIN N /2          2       .000
1969 NY  A 1/3-2-S    45       .176
1971 NY  A /3          3       .000
          BRTR        50       .164
```

BOERNER, LAWRENCE HYER
B.JAN.21,1905 STAUNTON,VA.
D.OCT.16,1969 STAUNTON,VA.
```
1932 BOS A  P         21      0- 4
          BRTR
```

BOGART, JOHN RENZIE (BIG JOHN)
B.SEPT.21,1900 BLOOMSBURG,PA.
```
1920 DET A  P          4      2- 1
          BRTR
```

BOGGS, RAYMOND JOSEPH (LEFTY)
B.DEC.12,1904 REAMSVILLE,KAN.
```
1928 BOS N  P          4      0- 0
          BLTL
```

BOGGS, THOMAS WINTON (TOMMY)
B.OCT.25,1955 POUGHKEEPSIE,N.Y.
```
1976 TEX A  P         13      1- 7
1977 TEX A /P          6      0- 3
1978 ATL N  P         16      2- 8
          BRTR        35      3-18
```

BOGLE, WARREN FREDERICK
B.OCT.19,1946 PASSAIC,N.J.
```
1968 OAK A  P         16      0- 0
          BLTL
```

BOHEN, LEO IGNATIUS (PAT)
B.OCT.20,1891 NAPA,CAL.
D.APR.9,1942 NAPA,CAL.
```
1913 PHI A  P          1      0- 1
1914 PIT N  P          1      0- 0
          BRTR         2      0- 1
```

BOHN, CHARLES
B.1857 CLEVELAND,OHIO
D.AUG.1,1903 CLEVELAND,OHIO
```
1882 LOU AA P-O    2   4      1- 1
                              .154
```

BOHNE, SAMUEL ARTHUR
[REAL NAME SAMUEL ARTHUR COHEN]
B.OCT.22,1896 SAN FRANCISCO,CAL.
D.MAY 23,1977 PALO ALTO,CAL.
```
1916 STL N  S         14      .237
1921 CIN N  2-3      153      .285
1922 CIN N  2-S      112      .274
1923 CIN N  1-2-S-3  139      .252
1924 CIN N  2-S-3    100      .255
1925 CIN N  1-2-S-3-O 73      .257
1926 CIN N  2         25      .204
     BRO N  S-3       47      .200
          BRTR       663      .261
```

BOISCLAIR, BRUCE ARMAND
B.DEC.9,1952 PUTNAM,CONN.
```
1974 NY  N /O          7      .250
1976 NY  N  O        110      .287
1977 NY  A O/1       127      .293
1978 NY  N O/1       107      .224
          BLTL       351      .272
```

BOITANO, DANNY JON (DAN)
B.MAR.22,1953 SACRAMENTO,CAL.
```
1978 PHI N /P          1      0- 0
          BRTR
```

BOKELMANN, RICHARD WERNER
B.OCT.26,1926 ARLINGTON HEIGHTS,ILL.
```
1951 STL N  P         20      3- 3
1952 STL N  P         11      0- 1
1953 STL N  P          3      0- 0
          BRTR        34      3- 4
```

BOKEN, ROBERT ANTHONY
B.FEB.23,1908 MARYVILLE,ILL.
```
1933 WAS A  2-S-3     55      .278
1934 WAS A  2         11      .222
     CHI A  2-S       81      .236
          BRTR       147      .247
```

BOKINA, JOSEPH
B.APR.4,1910 NORTHAMPTON,MASS.
```
1936 WAS A  P          5      0- 2
          BRTR
```

BOLAND
```
1875 ATL NA O          1       -
```

BOLAND, BERNARD ANTHONY
B.JAN.21,1892 ROCHESTER,N.Y.
D.SEPT.12,1973 DETROIT,MICH.
```
1915 DET A  P         47     13- 6
1916 DET A  P     47  49     10- 3
1917 DET A  P     43  45     16-11
1918 DET A  P         29     14-10
1919 DET A  P         35     14-16
1920 DET A  P          4      0- 2
1921 STL A  P          8      1- 4
          BRTR   213 217     68-52
```

BOLAND, EDWARD JOHN
B.APR.18,1908 LONG ISLAND CITY,N.Y.
```
1934 PHI N  O          8      .300
1935 PHI N  O         30      .213
1944 WAS A  O         19      .271
          BLTL        57      .257
```

BOLD, CHARLES DICKENS (DUTCH)
B.OCT.27,1894 KARLSKRONA,SWEDEN
```
1914 STL A  1          2      .000
          BRTR
```

BOLDEN, WILLIAM HORACE (BIG BILL)
B.MAY 9,1893 DANDRIDGE,TENN.
D.DEC.8,1966 JEFFERSON CITY,TENN.
```
1919 STL N  P          3      0- 1
          BRTR
```

BOLEN, STEWART O NEAL
B.OCT.12,1902 JACKSON,ALA.
D.AUG.30,1969 MOBILE,ALA.
```
1926 STL A  P          5      0- 0
1927 STL A  P          3      0- 1
1931 PHI N  P         28      3-12
1932 PHI N  P          5      0- 0
          BLTL        41      3-13
```

BOLES, CARL THEODORE
B.OCT.31,1934 CENTER POINT,ARK.
```
1962 SF  N  O         19      .375
          BRTR
```

BOLEY, JOHN PETER (JOE)
[REAL NAME JOHN PETER BOLINSKY]
B.JULY 19,1896 MAHANOY CITY,PA.
D.DEC.30,1962 MAHANOY CITY,PA.
```
1927 PHI A  S        118      .311
1928 PHI A  S        132      .264
1929 PHI A  S         91      .251
1930 PHI A  S        121      .276
1931 PHI A  S         67      .228
1932 PHI A  S         10      .206
     CLE A  S          1      .250
          BRTR       540      .269
```

BOLGER, JAMES CYRIL (DUTCH)
B.FEB.23,1932 CINCINNATI,OHIO
```
1950 CIN N  O          2      .000
1951 CIN N  H          2      .000
1954 CIN N  O          5      .333
1955 CHI N  O         64      .206
1957 CHI N  3-O      112      .275
1958 CHI N  O         84      .225
1959 CLE A  H          8      .000
     PHI N  O         35      .083
          BRTR       312      .229
```

BOLIN, BOBBY DONALD
B.JAN.29,1939 HICKORY GROVE,S.C.
```
1961 SF  N  P         37      2- 2
1962 SF  N  P         41      7- 3
1963 SF  N  P         47     10- 6
1964 SF  N  P     38  39      6- 9
1965 SF  N  P         45     14- 6
1966 SF  N  P         36     11-10
1967 SF  N  P         37      6- 8
1968 SF  N  P         34     10- 5
1969 SF  N  P         30      7- 7
1970 MIL A  P         32      5-11
     BOS A /P          6      2- 0
1971 BOS A  P         52      5- 3
1972 BOS A  P         21      0- 1
1973 BOS A  P         39      3- 4
          BRTR   495 496     88-75
```

BOLINSKY, JOHN PETER
[PLAYED UNDER NAME OF.
JOHN PETER BOLEY]

BOLLING, FRANK ELMORE
B.NOV.16,1931 MOBILE,ALA.
```
1954 DET A  2        117      .236
1956 DET A  2        102      .281
1957 DET A  2        146      .269
1958 DET A  2        154      .269
1959 DET A  2        127      .266
1960 DET A  2        139      .254
1961 MIL N  2        148      .262
1962 MIL N  2        122      .271
1963 MIL N  2        142      .244
1964 MIL N  2        120      .199
1965 MIL N *2        148      .264
1966 ATL N  2         75      .211
          BRTR      1540      .254
```

BOLLING, JOHN EDWARD
B.FEB.20,1917 MOBILE,ALA.
```
1939 PHI N  1         69      .289
1944 BRO N  1         56      .351
          BLTL       125      .313
```

BOLLING, MILTON JOSEPH (MILT)
B.AUG.9,1930 MISSISSIPPI CITY,MISS.
```
1952 BOS A  S         11      .222
1953 BOS A  S        109      .263
1954 BOS A  S-3      113      .249
1955 BOS A  S          6      .200
1956 BOS A  2-S-3     45      .212
1957 BOS A  H          1      .000
     WAS A  2-S-3     91      .227
1958 DET A  2-S-3     24      .194
          BRTR       400      .241
```

BOLLO, GREGORY GENE (GREG)
B.NOV.16,1943 DETROIT,MICH.
```
1965 CHI A  P         15      0- 0
1966 CHI A /P          3      0- 1
          BRTR        18      0- 1
```

BOLLWEG, DONALD RAYMOND (DON)
B.FEB.12,1921 WHEATON,ILL.
```
1950 STL N  1          4      .182
1951 STL N  1          6      .111
1953 NY  A  1-O       70      .297
1954 PHI A  1        103      .224
1955 KC  A  1         12      .111
          BLTL       195      .243
```

BOLTON, CECIL GLENFORD (GLENN)
B.FEB.13,1904 BOONEVILLE,MISS.
```
1928 CLE A  1          4      .154
          BLTR
```

BOLTON, WILLIAM CLIFTON (CLIFF)
B.APR.10,1907 HIGH POINT,N.C.
```
1931 WAS A  C         23      .255
1933 WAS A  C-O       33      .410
1934 WAS A  C         42      .270
1935 WAS A  C        110      .304
1936 WAS A  C         86      .291
1937 DET A  C         27      .263
1941 WAS A  C         14      .000
          BLTR       335      .291
```

BOMBACK, MARK VINCENT
B.APR.14,1953 PORTSMOUTH,VA.
```
1978 MIL A /P          2      0- 0
          BRTR
```

BOND, THOMAS HENRY
B.APR.2,1856 GRANARD,IRELAND
D.JAN.24,1941 BOSTON,MASS.
```
1874 ATL NA P         55     23-31
1875 HAR NA P-1-  39  71     19-16
                2-O            -
1876 HAR N  P         45     32-13
1877 BOS N  P-O   58  61     40-17
                              .228
1878 BOS N  P         59     40-19
1879 BOS N  P     62  65     42-19
1880 BOS N  P-1-  56  74     26-29
                O             .216
1881 BOS N  P          3      0- 3
1882 WOR N  M-P-   2   8      0- 0
                O             .125
1884 BOS U  P-3-  23  36     12- 9
                O             .291
     IND AA P-O    5   7      0- 5
                              .186
          BRTR   407 484    234-161
```

BOND, WALTER FRANKLIN (WALT)
B.OCT.19,1937 DENMARK,TENN.
D.SEP.14,1967 HOUSTON,TEX.
```
1960 CLE A  O         40      .221
1961 CLE A  O         38      .173
1962 CLE A  O         12      .380
1964 HOU N  1-O      148      .254
1965 HOU N  1-O      117      .263
1967 MIN A /O         10      .313
          BLTR       365      .256
```

BONDS, BOBBY LEE
B.MAR.15,1946 RIVERSIDE,CAL.
```
1968 SF  N  O         81      .254
1969 SF  N *O        158      .259
1970 SF  N *O        157      .302
1971 SF  N *O        155      .288
1972 SF  N *O        153      .259
1973 SF  N *O        160      .283
1974 SF  N *O        150      .256
1975 NY  A *O-O      145      .270
1976 CAL A  O         99      .265
1977 CAL A *O-O      158      .264
1978 CHI A  O         26      .278
     TEX A *O-O      130      .265
          BRTR      1572      .271
```

BONE, GEORGE DRUMMOND
B.AUG.28,1876 NEW HAVEN,CONN.
D.MAY 26,1918 WEST HAVEN,CONN.
```
1901 MIL A  S         12      .292
          BBTR
```

```
YR  CL LEA POS     GP   G   REC        YR  CL LEA POS     GP   G   REC        YR  CL LEA POS     GP   G   REC

BONETTI, JULIO G.                      BOOKER, RICHARD LEE (BUDDY)            BOOTH, EDWARD H.
B.JULY 14,1911 GENOA,ITALY             B.MAY 28,1942 LYNCHBURG,VA.           B.BROOKLYN,N.Y.
D.JUNE 17,1952 BELMONT,CAL.            1966 CLE A C       18     .214        1872 MAN NA 2-O     24     .336
1937 STL A P       28     4-11         1968 CHI A /C       5     .000             ATL NA 2-O     14     .250
1938 STL A P       17     2- 3              BLTR          23     .182        1873 RES NA 2-O     18      -
1940 CHI N P        1     0- 0                                                    ATL NA O       13      -
     BRTR          46     6-14         BOOL, ALBERT J.                       1874 ATL NA O       44      -
                                       B.AUG.24,1897 LINCOLN,NEB.            1875 MUT NA 2-O     68      -
BONEY, HENRY TATE (HANEY)              1928 WAS A C        2     .143        1876 MUT N  O       57     .213
B.OCT.28,1903 WALLACE,N.C.             1930 PIT N         78     .259                           238      -
1927 NY  N P        3     0- 0         1931 BOS N         49     .188
     BRTR                                   BRTR         129     .237        BOOZER, JOHN MORGAN
                                                                             B.JULY 6,1938 COLUMBIA,S.C.
BONGIOVANNI, ANTHONY THOMAS (NINO)     BOOLES, SEABRON JESSE (RED)           1962 PHI N P        9     0- 0
B.DEC.21,1911 PIKE S PEAK,CAL.         B.JULY 14,1880 BERNICE,LA.            1963 PHI N P       26     3- 4
1938 CIN N O        2     .286         D.MAR.16,1955 MONROE,LA.              1964 PHI N P    22 23     3- 4
1939 CIN N O       66     .258         1909 CLE A P        4     0- 1        1965 PHI N /P       2     0- 0
     BLTL          68     .259              BLTL                             1966 PHI N /P       2     0- 0
                                                                             1967 PHI N P       28     5- 4
BONHAM, ERNEST EDWARD (TINY)           BOONE, GEORGE M.                      1968 PHI N P       38     2- 2
B.AUG.16,1913 IONE,CAL.                B.LOUISVILLE,KY.                      1969 PHI N P       46     1- 2
D.SEPT.15,1949 PITTSBURGH,PA.          1891 LOU AA P       4     1- 0             BRTR       171 172   14-16
1940 NY  A P       12     9- 3
1941 NY  A P       23     9- 6         BOONE, ISAAC MORGAN (IKE)             BORBON, PEDRO (RODRIGUEZ)
1942 NY  A P       28    21- 5         B.FEB.17,1897 SAMANTHA,ALA.           B.DEC.2,1946 VALVERDE,MAO,D.R.
1943 NY  A P       28    15- 8         D.AUG.1,1958 NORTHPORT,ALA.           1969 CAL A P       22     2- 3
1944 NY  A P       26    12- 9         1922 NY  N O        2     .500        1970 CIN N P       12     0- 2
1945 NY  A P       23     8-11         1923 BOS A O        5     .267        1971 CIN N /P       3     0- 0
1946 NY  A P       18     5- 8         1924 BOS A O      128     .333        1972 CIN N P       62     8- 3
1947 PIT N P       33    11- 8         1925 BOS A O      133     .330        1973 CIN N P       80    11- 4
1948 PIT N P       22     6-10         1927 CHI A O       29     .226        1974 CIN N P       73    10- 7
1949 PIT N P       18     7- 4         1930 BRO N O       40     .297        1975 CIN N P       67     9- 5
     BRTR         231   103-72         1931 BRO N H        6     .200        1976 CIN N P       69     4- 3
                                       1932 BRO N H       13     .143        1977 CIN N P       73    10- 5
BONHAM, WILLIAM GORDON (BILL)               BLTR         356     .319        1978 CIN N P       62     8- 2
B.OCT.1,1948 GLENDALE,CAL.                                                        BRTR         523    62-34
1971 CHI N P       33     2- 1         BOONE, JAMES ALBERT (DAN)
1972 CHI N P       19     1- 1         B.JAN.19,1895 SAMANTHA,ALA.           BORCHERS, GEORGE BENARD (CHIEF)
1973 CHI N P       44     7- 5         D.MAY 11,1968 TUSCALOOSA,ALA.         B.APR.18,1869 SACRAMENTO,CAL.
1974 CHI N P    44 48    11-22         1919 PHI A P        3     0- 1        D.OCT.24,1938 SACRAMENTO,CAL.
1975 CHI N P    38 40    13-15         1921 DET A P        1     0- 0        1888 CHI N P       10     4- 5
1976 CHI N P       32     9-13         1922 CLE A P       11     4- 6        1895 LOU N P        1     0- 1
1977 CHI N P    34 35    10-13         1923 CLE A P       27     4- 6             BBTR          11     4- 6
1978 CIN N P       23    11- 5              BRTR          42     8-13
     BRTR       267 274   64-75                                              BORDAGARAY, STANLEY GEORGE (FRENCHY)
                                       BOONE, LUTE JOSEPH (LUKE) OR (DANNY)  B.JAN.3,1912 COALINGA,CAL.
BONIKOWSKI, JOSEPH PETER               B.MAY 6,1890 PITTSBURGH,PA.           1934 CHI N O       29     .322
B.JAN.16,1941 PHILADELPHIA,PA.         1913 NY  A S        6     .250        1935 BRO N O      120     .282
1962 MIN A P       30     5- 7         1914 NY  A 2      106     .222        1936 BRO N 2-O    125     .315
     BRTR                              1915 NY  A 2      130     .204        1937 STL N 3-O     96     .293
                                       1916 NY  A 2       46     .185        1938 STL N O       81     .282
BONIN, ERNEST LUTHER (BONNIE)          1918 PIT N 2-S     27     .198        1939 CIN N 2-O     63     .197
B.JAN.13,1888 GREEN HILL,IND.               BRTR         315     .208        1941 NY  A O        6     .260
D.AUG.3,1965 SYCAMORE,OHIO                                                   1942 BRO N O       36     .241
1913 STL A H        1     .000         BOONE, RAYMOND OTIS (IKE)             1943 BRO N 3-O     89     .302
1914 BUF F O       21     .173         B.JULY 27,1923 SAN DIEGO,CAL.         1944 BRO N 3-O    130     .281
     BLTR          22     .171         1948 CLE A S        6     .400        1945 BRO N 3-O    113     .256
                                       1949 CLE A S       86     .252             BRTR         930     .283
BONNELL, ROBERT BARRY (BARRY)          1950 CLE A S      109     .301
B.OCT.27,1953 CLERMONT COUNTY,O.       1951 CLE A S      151     .233        BORDEN, JOSEPH EMLEY
1977 ATL N O-3    100     .300         1952 CLE A 2-S-3  103     .263        [PLAYED UNDER NAME OF
1978 ATL N *O-3   117     .240         1953 CLE A S       34     .241        JOSEPH EMLEY JOSEPH IN 1875]
     BRTR         217     .273              DET A S-3     101     .312        B.MAY 9,1854 JACOBSTOWN,N.J.
                                       1954 DET A S-3     148     .295        D.OCT.14,1929 YEADON,PA.
BONNER, FRANK J.                       1955 DET A 3       135     .284        1875 PHI NA P        7     2- 4
B.AUG.20,1869 LOWELL,MASS.             1956 DET A 3       131     .308        1876 BOS N P-O   24 32    12-12
D.DEC.31,1905 KANSAS CITY,MO.          1957 DET A 1-3     129     .273                                  .202
1894 BAL N 2       27     .301         1958 DET A 1        39     .237             BRTR        31 39    14-16
1895 BAL N 3       11     .249              CHI A 1        77     .244
     STL N S       14     .132         1959 CHI A 1         9     .238        BORDETZKI, ANTONIO
1896 BRO N 2        7     .185              KC  A 1-3       61     .273        [PLAYED UNDER NAME OF
1899 WAS N 2       85     .276              MIL N 1        13     .200        ANTHONY VINCENT BRIEF]
1902 CLE A 2       34     .278         1960 MIL N 1         7     .250
     PHI A 2       11     .182              BOS A 1        34     .205        BORGMANN, GLENN DENNIS
1903 BOS N 2-S     46     .220              BRTR        1373     .275        B.MAY 25,1950 PATERSON,N.J.
     TR          235     .254                                                1972 MIN A C       56     .234
                                       BOONE, ROBERT RAYMOND (BOB)           1973 MIN A C       12     .265
BONNESS, WILLIAM JOHN (LEFTY)          B.NOV.19,1947 SAN DIEGO,CAL.          1974 MIN A *C     128     .252
B.DEC.15,1923 CLEVELAND,OHIO           1972 PHI N C       16     .275        1975 MIN A *C     125     .207
1944 CLE A P        2     0- 1         1973 PHI N *C      145     .261        1976 MIN A C       24     .246
     BRTL                              1974 PHI N *C      146     .242        1977 MIN A C       17     .256
                                       1975 PHI N C/3      97     .246        1978 MIN A C       49     .211
BONO, ADLAI WENDELL (GUS)              1976 PHI N *C/1    121     .271             BRTR         411     .231
B.AUG.29,1894 DOE RUN,MO.              1977 PHI N *C/3    132     .284
D.DEC.3,1948 DEARBORN,MICH.            1978 PHI N *C/1-0  132     .283        BORK, FRANK BERNARD
1920 WAS A P        4     0- 2              BRTR         789     .265        B.JULY 13,1940 BUFFALO,N.Y.
     BRTR                                                                    1964 PIT N P       33     2- 2
                                       BOOTH, AMOS SMITH (DARLING)                BRTL
BONURA, HENRY JOHN (ZEKE)              B.SEPT.4,1852 CINCINNATI,OHIO
B.SEPT.20,1908 NEW ORLEANS,LA.         D.JULY 1,1921 MIAMISBURG,OHIO         BORKOWSKI, ROBERT VILARIAN
1934 CHI A 1      127     .302         1876 CIN N P-C-    1    63    0- 1     B.JAN.27,1926 DAYTON,OHIO
1935 CHI A 1      138     .295                    S-3                .293     1950 CHI N 1-O     85     .273
1936 CHI A 1      148     .330         1877 CIN N P-C-   12    43    1- 7     1951 CHI N O       58     .157
1937 CHI A 1      116     .345                  2-S-3-O             .170     1952 CIN N 1-O    126     .252
1938 WAS A 1      137     .289         1880 CIN N O             1    .000     1953 CIN N O       94     .269
1939 NY  N 1      123     .321         1882 BAL AA 3           1    .000     1954 CIN N 1-O     73     .265
1940 WAS A 1       79     .273              LOU AA 2          1    .000     1955 CIN N 1-O     25     .167
     CHI N 1       49     .264              BRTR         13   109    1- 8          BRO N O        9     .105
                 917     .307                                       .219          BRTR         470     .251

BOOE, EVERETT LITTLE                                                         BORLAND, THOMAS BRUCE
B.SEPT.28,1891 MOCKSVILLE,N.C.                                               (TOM) OR (SPIKE)
D.MAY 21,1969 KENEDY,TEX.                                                    B.FEB.14,1933 EL DORADO,KAN.
1913 PIT N O       29     .200                                               1960 BOS A P       26     0- 4
1914 IND F O       19     .233                                               1961 BOS A P        1     0- 0
     BUF F O       73     .220                                                    BLTL          27     0- 4
     BLTR         121     .217
```

BOROM, EDWARD JONES (RED)
B.OCT.30,1915 SPARTANBURG,S.C.

YR	CL	LEA	POS	GP	G	REC
1944	DET	A	2		7	.071
1945	DET	A	2-S-3		55	.269
		BLTR			62	.250

BORDS, STEPHEN (STEVE)
B.SEP.3,1936 FLINT,MICH.

YR	CL	LEA	POS	GP	G	REC
1957	DET	A	S-3		24	.146
1958	DET	A	2		6	.000
1961	DET	A	3		116	.270
1962	DET	A	2-3		116	.228
1963	CHI	N	1-0		41	.211
1964	CIN	N	3		117	.257
1965	CIN	N	/3		2	.000
		BRTR			422	.245

BOROWY, HENRY LUDWIG (HANK)
B.MAY 12,1916 BLOOMFIELD,N.J.

YR	CL	LEA	POS	GP	G	REC
1942	NY	A	P		25	15- 4
1943	NY	A	P		29	14- 9
1944	NY	A	P		35	17-12
1945	NY	A	P		18	10- 5
	CHI	N	P		15	11- 2
1946	CHI	N	P	32	33	12-10
1947	CHI	N	P	40	41	8-12
1948	CHI	N	P		39	5-10
1949	PHI	N	P		28	12-12
1950	PHI	N	P		3	0- 0
	PIT	N	P		11	1- 3
	DET	A	P		13	1- 1
1951	DET	A	P		26	2- 2
		BRTR		314	316	108-82

BORTON, WILLIAM BAKER (BABE)
B.AUG.14,1888 MARION,ILL.
D.JULY 29,1954 BERKELEY,CAL.

YR	CL	LEA	POS	GP	G	REC
1912	CHI	A	1		31	.371
1913	CHI	A	1		28	.275
	NY	A	1		33	.121
1915	STL	F	1		159	.289
1916	STL	A	1		66	.225
		BLTR			317	.271

BOSCH, DONALD JOHN (DON)
B.JULY 15,1942 SAN FRANCISCO,CAL

YR	CL	LEA	POS	GP	G	REC
1966	PIT	N	/O		3	.000
1967	NY	N	O		44	.140
1968	NY	N	O		50	.171
1969	MON	N	O		49	.179
		BBTR			146	.164

BOSETTI, RICHARD ALAN (RICK)
B.AUG.5,1953 REDDING,CAL.

YR	CL	LEA	POS	GP	G	REC
1976	PHI	N	/O		13	.278
1977	STL	N	O		41	.232
1978	TOR	A	/O		136	.259
		BRTR			190	.256

BOSLEY, THADDIS (THAD)
B.SEPT.17,1956 OCEANSIDE,CAL.

YR	CL	LEA	POS	GP	G	REC
1977	CAL	A	O		58	.297
1978	CHI	A	O		66	.269
		BLTL			124	.283

BOSMAN, RICHARD ALLEN (DICK)
B.FEB.17,1944 KENOSHA,WIS.

YR	CL	LEA	POS	GP	G	REC
1966	WAS	A	P		13	2- 6
1967	WAS	A	/P	7	8	3- 1
1968	WAS	A	P		46	2- 9
1969	WAS	A	P	31	32	14- 5
1970	WAS	A	P		36	16-12
1971	WAS	A	P		35	12-16
1972	TEX	A	P		29	8-10
1973	TEX	A	/P		7	2- 5
	CLE	A	P		22	1- 8
1974	CLE	A	P		25	7- 5
1975	CLE	A	/P		6	0- 2
	OAK	A	P		22	11- 4
1976	OAK	A	P		27	4- 2
		BRTR		306	308	82-85

BOSS, ELMER HARLEY (LEFFY)
B.NOV.19,1908 HODGE,LA.
D.MAY 15,1964 NASHVILLE,TENN.

YR	CL	LEA	POS	GP	G	REC
1928	WAS	A	1		16	.250
1929	WAS	A	1		28	.273
1930	WAS	A	1		3	.000
1933	CLE	A	1		112	.269
		BLTL			155	.268

BOSSER, MELVIN EDWARD
B.FEB.8,1920 JOHNSTOWN,PA.

YR	CL	LEA	POS	GP	G	REC
1945	CIN	N	P		7	2- 0

BOSTICK, HENRY LANDERS
[REAL NAME HENRY LANDERS LIFSITT]
B.JAN.12,1895 BOSTON,MASS.

YR	CL	LEA	POS	GP	G	REC
1915	PHI	A	3		2	.000
		BRTR				

BOSTOCK, LYMAN WESLEY
B.NOV.22,1950 BIRMINGHAM,ALA.
D.SEPT.23,1978 GARY,IND.

YR	CL	LEA	POS	GP	G	REC
1975	MIN	A	O		98	.282
1976	MIN	A	*O		128	.323
1977	MIN	A	*O		153	.336
1978	CAL	A	*O		147	.296
		BLTR			526	.311

BOSWELL, ANDREW COTTRELL
B.SEPT.5,1874 NEW GRETNA,N.J.
D.FEB.3,1936 OCEAN CITY,N.J.

YR	CL	LEA	POS	GP	G	REC
1895	NY	N	P		5	2- 2
	WAS	N	P-1	6	7	1- 3
						.231
				11	12	3- 5
						.200

BOSWELL, DAVID WILSON (DAVE)
B.JAN.20,1945 BALTIMORE,MD.

YR	CL	LEA	POS	GP	G	REC
1964	MIN	A	P		4	2- 0
1965	MIN	A	P	27	36	6- 5
1966	MIN	A	P	28	32	12- 5
1967	MIN	A	P	37	44	14-12
1968	MIN	A	P	34	37	10-13
1969	MIN	A	P	39	40	20-12
1970	MIN	A	P	18	20	3- 7
1971	DET	A	/P		3	0- 0
	BAL	A	P		15	1- 2
		BRTR		205	231	68-56

BOSWELL, KENNETH GEORGE (KEN)
B.FEB.23,1946 AUSTIN,TEX.

YR	CL	LEA	POS	GP	G	REC
1967	NY	N	/2-3		11	.225
1968	NY	N	2		75	.261
1969	NY	N	2		102	.279
1970	NY	N	*2		105	.254
1971	NY	N	*2		116	.273
1972	NY	N	2		100	.211
1973	NY	N	3/2		76	.227
1974	NY	N	2-3/0		96	.216
1975	HOU	N	3/2-0		91	.262
1976	HOU	N	2-3		86	.242
1977	HOU	N	2/3		72	.216
		BLTR			930	.248

BOTTARINI, JOHN CHARLES
B.SEPT.14,1908 CROCKETT,CAL.

YR	CL	LEA	POS	GP	G	REC
1937	CHI	N	C		26	.275
		BRTR				

BOTTOMLEY, JAMES LEROY (SUNNY JIM)
B.APR.23,1900 OGLESBY,ILL.
D.DEC.11,1959 ST.LOUIS,MO.

YR	CL	LEA	POS	GP	G	REC
1922	STL	N	1		37	.325
1923	STL	N	1		134	.371
1924	STL	N	1-2		137	.316
1925	STL	N	1		153	.367
1926	STL	N	1		154	.299
1927	STL	N	1		152	.303
1928	STL	N	1		149	.325
1929	STL	N	1		146	.314
1930	STL	N	1		131	.304
1931	STL	N	1		108	.348
1932	STL	N	1		91	.296
1933	CIN	N	1		145	.250
1934	CIN	N	1		142	.284
1935	CIN	N	1		107	.258
1936	STL	A	1		140	.298
1937	STL	A	M-1		65	.239
		BLTL			1991	.309

BOTZ, ROBERT ALLEN
B.APR.28,1935 MILWAUKEE,WIS.

YR	CL	LEA	POS	GP	G	REC
1962	LA	A	P		35	2- 1
		BRTR				

BOUCHEE, EDWARD FRANCIS (ED)
B.MAR.7,1933 LIVINGSTON,MONT.

YR	CL	LEA	POS	GP	G	REC
1956	PHI	N	1		9	.273
1957	PHI	N	1		154	.293
1958	PHI	N	1		89	.257
1959	PHI	N	1		136	.285
1960	PHI	N	1		22	.262
	CHI	N	1		98	.237
1961	CHI	N	1		112	.248
1962	NY	N	1		50	.161
		BLTL			670	.265

BOUCHER, ALEXANDER FRANCIS (BO)
B.NOV.13,1881 FRANKLIN,MASS.
D.JUNE 23,1974 TORRANCE,CAL.

YR	CL	LEA	POS	GP	G	REC
1914	STL	F	3		147	.232
		BRTR				

BOUCHER, MEDRIC T.
B.1889

YR	CL	LEA	POS	GP	G	REC
1914	BAL	F	C		14	.235
	PIT	F	C		1	.000
		BRTR			15	.235

BOUDREAU, LOUIS (LOU)
B.JULY 17,1917 HARVEY,ILL.

YR	CL	LEA	POS	GP	G	REC
1938	CLE	A	3		1	.000
1939	CLE	A	S		53	.258
1940	CLE	A	S		155	.295
1941	CLE	A	S		148	.257
1942	CLE	A	M-S		147	.283
1943	CLE	A	M-C-S		152	.286
1944	CLE	A	M-C-S		150	.327
1945	CLE	A	M-S		97	.306
1946	CLE	A	M-S		140	.293
1947	CLE	A	M-S		150	.307
1948	CLE	A	M-C-S		152	.355
1949	CLE	A	M-1-2-S-3		134	.284
1950	CLE	A	M-1-2-S-3		81	.269
1951	BOS	A	1-S-3		82	.267
1952	BOS	A	M-S-3		4	.000
		BRTR			1646	.295

NON-PLAYING MANAGER
BOS[A] 1953-54, KCC[A] 1955-57,
CHI[N] 1960

BOULDIN, CARL EDWARD
B.SEP.7,1939 GERMANTOWN,KY.

YR	CL	LEA	POS	GP	G	REC
1961	WAS	A	P		2	0- 1
1962	WAS	A	P	6	7	1- 2
1963	WAS	A	P		10	2- 2
1964	WAS	A	P	9	10	0- 3
		BBTR		27	29	3- 8
		BL 1961				

BOULTES, JAKE JOHN
B.AUG.6,1884 ST.LOUIS,MO.
D.DEC.24,1959 ST.LOUIS,MO.

YR	CL	LEA	POS	GP	G	REC
1907	BOS	N	P	24	29	5- 9
1908	BOS	N	P		17	3- 5
1909	BOS	N	P		1	0- 0
		TR		42	47	8-14

BOURQUE, PATRICK DANIEL (PAT)
B.MAR.23,1947 WORCESTER,MASS.

YR	CL	LEA	POS	GP	G	REC
1971	CHI	N	1		14	.189
1972	CHI	N	/1		11	.259
1973	CHI	N	1		57	.209
	OAK	A	D/0		23	.190
1974	OAK	A	1		73	.229
	MIN	A	1		23	.219
		BLTR			201	.215

BOUTHILLIER, ARTHUR E.
[PLAYED UNDER NAME OF
ARTHUR E. BUTLER]

BOUTON, JAMES ALAN (JIM)
B.MAR.8,1939 NEWARK,N.J.

YR	CL	LEA	POS	GP	G	REC
1962	NY	A	P	36	38	7- 7
1963	NY	A	P		40	21- 7
1964	NY	A	P		36	18-13
1965	NY	A	P	30	31	4-15
1966	NY	A	P		24	3- 8
1967	NY	A	P		17	1- 0
1968	NY	A	P		12	1- 1
1969	SEA	A	P		57	2- 1
	HOU	N	P		16	0- 2
1970	HOU	N	P		29	4- 6
1978	ATL	N	/P		5	1- 3
		BRTR		304	307	62-63

BOWA, LAWRENCE ROBERT (LARRY)
B.DEC.6,1945 SACRAMENTO,CAL.

YR	CL	LEA	POS	GP	G	REC
1970	PHI	N	*S/2		145	.250
1971	PHI	N	*S		159	.249
1972	PHI	N	*S		152	.250
1973	PHI	N	*S		122	.211
1974	PHI	N	*S		162	.275
1975	PHI	N	*S		136	.305
1976	PHI	N	*S		156	.248
1977	PHI	N	*S		154	.280
1978	PHI	N	*S		156	.294
		BBTR			1342	.265

BOWCOCK, BENJAMIN JAMES (BENNY)
B.OCT.28,1879 FALL RIVER,MASS.
D.JUNE 16,1961 NEW BEDFORD,MASS.

YR	CL	LEA	POS	GP	G	REC
1903	STL	A	2		14	.300
		BRTR				

BOWDEN, DAVID TIMON (TIM)
B.AUG.15,1891 MCDONOUGH,GA.
D.OCT.25,1949 EMORY UNIVERSITY,GA.

YR	CL	LEA	POS	GP	G	REC
1914	STL	N	0		6	.285
		BLTR				

BOWEN, EMMONS JOSEPH (CHICK)
B.JULY 26,1897 NEW HAVEN,CONN.
D.AUG.9,1948 NEW HAVEN,CONN.

YR	CL	LEA	POS	GP	G	REC
1919	NY	N	0		3	.200
		BRTR				

BOWEN, SAMUEL THOMAS (SAM)
B.SEPT.18,1952 BRUNSWICK,GA.

YR	CL	LEA	POS	GP	G	REC
1977	BOS	A	/0		3	.000
1978	BOS	A	/0		6	.143
		BRTR			9	.111

YR	CL LEA POS	GP	G	REC

BOWEN, SUTHERLAND MC COY
B.FEB.17,1871 KINGSTON,IND.
D.JAN.25,1925 GREENSBURG,IND.

| 1896 NY | N P | | 2 | 0- 1 |
| | BRTR | | | |

BOWENS, SAMUEL EDWARD (SAM)
B.MAR.23,1939 WILMINGTON,N.C.

1963 BAL A	O		15	.333
1964 BAL A	O	139		.263
1965 BAL A	O	84		.163
1966 BAL A	O	89		.210
1967 BAL A	O	62		.183
1968 WAS A	O	57		.191
1969 WAS A	O	33		.193
	BRTR	479		.223

BOWERMAN, FRANK EUGENE (MIKE)
B.DEC.5,1868 ROMEO,MICH.
D.NOV.30,1948 ROMEO,MICH.

1895 BAL	N C		1	.000
1896 BAL	N C		4	.125
1897 BAL	N C	33		.323
1898 BAL	N C		5	.438
	PIT N C	62		.278
1899 PIT	N C-1	107		.269
1900 NY	N C	73		.260
1901 NY	N C	52		.217
1902 NY	N C-1	99		.253
1903 NY	N C	59		.276
1904 NY	N C	90		.232
1905 NY	N C-1	90		.269
1906 NY	N C-1	67		.228
1907 NY	N C-1	90		.260
1908 BOS	N C	74		.228
1909 BOS	N M-C	27		.212
	BRTR	953		.255

BOWERS, GROVER BILL (BILLY)
B.MAR.25,1923 PARKIN,ARK.

| 1949 CHI A | O | | 26 | .192 |
| | BLTR | | | |

BOWERS, STEWART COLE (DOC)
B.FEB.24,1915 NEW FREEDOM,PA.

1935 BOS A	P	10	11	2- 1
1936 BOS A	P		6	0- 0
1937 BOS A	P		1	0- 0
	BRTR	17	18	2- 1

BOWES, FRANK C.
B.1865 BATH,N.Y.
D.JAN.21,1895 BROOKLYN,N.Y

| 1890 BRO AA C | | | 62 | .207 |
| | TR | | | |

BOWLER, GRANT TIERNEY (MOOSE)
B.OCT.24,1907 DENVER,COL.
D.JUNE 25,1968 DENVER,COLO.

1931 CHI A	P		13	0- 1
1932 CHI A	P		4	0- 0
	BRTR		17	0- 1

BOWLES, CHARLES JAMES
B.MAR.15,1917 NORWOOD,MASS.

1943 PHI A	P	2	3	1- 1
1945 PHI A	P	8	13	0- 3
	BRTR	10	16	1- 4

BOWLES, EMMETT JEROME (CHIEF)
B.AUG.2,1848 WANETTE,OKLA.
D.SEPT.3,1959 FLAGSTAFF,ARIZ.

| 1922 CHI A | P | | 1 | 0- 0 |
| | BRTR | | | |

BOWLIN, LOIS WELDON
(WELDON) OR (HOSS)
B.DEC.10,1940 PARAGOULD,ARK.

| 1967 KC | A /3 | | 2 | .200 |
| | BRTR | | | |

BOWLING, STEPHEN SHADDON (STEVE)
B.JUNE 26,1952 TULSA,OKLA.

1976 MIL A	O		14	.167
1977 TOR A	O		89	.206
		103		.199

BOWMAN, ALVAH EDSON (ABE)
B.JAN.25,1893 GREENUP,ILL.

1914 CLE A	P	22		2- 7
1915 CLE A	P	2		0- 1
	BRTR	24		2- 8

BOWMAN, ELMARI WILHELM (BIG BOW)
B.MAR.19,1897 PROCTOR,VT.

| 1920 WAS A | H | | 2 | .000 |
| | BRTR | | | |

BOWMAN, ERNEST FERRELL (ERNIE)
B.JULY 28,1935 JOHNSON CITY,TENN.

1961 SF	N 2-S-3	38		.211
1962 SF	N 2-S-3	46		.190
1963 SF	N 2-S-3	81		.184
	BRTR	165		.190

BOWMAN, JOSEPH EMIL
B.JUNE 17,1910 ARGENTINE,KAN.

1932 PHI A	P		7	0- 1
1934 NY	N P	30	31	5- 4
1935 PHI	N P-0	33	49	7-10
				.194
1936 PHI	N P	40	44	9-20
1937 PIT	N P	30	35	8- 8
1938 PIT	N P	17	18	3- 4
1939 PIT	N P	37	70	10-14
1940 PIT	N P	32	57	9-10
1941 PIT	N P	18	22	3- 2
1944 BOS	A P	26	59	12- 8
1945 BOS	A P	3	9	0- 2
	CIN N P	25	29	11-13
	BLTR	298	430	77-96
				.221

BOWMAN, ROBERT JAMES
B.OCT.3,1910 KEYSTONE,W.VA.
D.SEPT.4,1972 BLUEFIELD,W.VA.

1939 STL	N P	51		13- 5
1940 STL	N P	28		7- 5
1941 NY	N P	29		6- 7
1942 CHI	N P		1	0- 0
	BRTR	109		26-17

BOWMAN, ROBERT LEROY (BOB)
B.MAY 10,1931 LAYTONVILLE,CAL.

1955 PHI	N O		3	.000
1956 PHI	N O		6	.188
1957 PHI	N O	99		.266
1958 PHI	N O	91		.288
1959 PHI	N P-O	5	57	0- 1
				.127
	BRTR	5	256	0- 1
				.249

BOWMAN, ROGER CLINTON
B.AUG.18,1927 AMSTERDAM,N.Y.

1949 NY	N P		2	0- 0
1951 NY	N P		9	2- 4
1952 NY	N P		2	0- 0
1953 PIT	N P	30		0- 4
1955 PIT	N P		7	0- 3
	BRTL	50		2-11

BOWMAN, SUMNER SALLADE
B.FEB.9,1867 MILLERSBURG,PA.
D.JAN.11,1954 MILLERSBURG,PA.

1890 PHI	N P		4	1- 0
	PIT N P		10	2- 7
1891 ATH	AA P-0	8	14	2- 5
				.215
	TL	22	28	5-12
				.258

BOWMAN, WILLIAM G.
B.CHICAGO,ILL.

| 1891 CHI | N C | | 15 | .088 |

BOWSER, JAMES H. (RED)
B.GREENSBURG,PA.

| 1910 CHI | A O | | 1 | .000 |

BOWSFIELD, EDWARD OLIVER (TED)
B.JAN.10,1935 VERNON,B.C.,CANADA

1958 BOS A	P	16	17	4- 2
1959 BOS A	P		5	0- 1
1960 BOS A	P		17	1- 2
	CLE A P		11	3- 4
1961 LA	A P	41	46	11- 8
1962 LA	A P	34	44	9- 8
1963 KC	A P	41	43	5- 7
1964 KC	A P	50	52	4- 7
	BRTL	215	235	37-39

BOYD, JACOB HENRY (JAKE)
B.1874 MARTINSBURG,W.VA.

1894 WAS N P			6	0- 3
1895 WAS N P-O		14	46	1- 7
				.284
1896 WAS N P			4	1- 2
	TL	32	56	2-12
				.257

BOYD, FRANK JAY
B.APR.2,1868 WEST MIDDLETOWN,PA
D.DEC.16,1937 OIL CITY,PA.

| 1893 CLE | N C | | 1 | .200 |
| | BRTR | | | |

BOYD, GARY LEE
B.AUG.22,1946 PASADENA,CAL.

| 1969 CLE | N /P | | 8 | 0- 2 |
| | BRTR | | | |

BOYD, RAYMOND C.
B.FEB.11,1887 HORTONVILLE,IND.
D.FEB.11,1920 FRANKFORT,IND.

1910 STL A	P		3	0- 2
1911 CIN N P			7	3- 3
	BRTR		10	3- 5

BOYD, ROBERT RICHARD
(BOB) OR (THE ROPE)
B.OCT.1,1926 POTTS CAMP,MISS.

1951 CHI A	1		12	.167
1953 CHI A	1-0		55	.297
1954 CHI A	1-0		29	.179
1956 BAL A	1-0		70	.311
1957 BAL A	1-0	141		.318
1958 BAL A	1	125		.309
1959 BAL A	1	128		.265
1960 BAL A	1	71		.317
1961 KC	A 1	26		.229
	MIL N 1	36		.244
	BLTL	693		.293

BOYD, WILLIAM J.

1872 MUT NA S-3-O			35	.254
1873 ATL NA 3-O			48	-
1874 HAR NA 3-O			26	-
1875 ATL NA 1-2-3-O			36	-
			145	-

BOYER, CLETIS LEROY (CLETE)
B.FEB.9,1937 CASSVILLE,MO.

1955 KC	A 2-S-3	47		.241
1956 KC	A 2-3	67		.217
1957 KC	A 2-3	10		.000
1959 NY	A S-3	47		.175
1960 NY	A S-3	124		.242
1961 NY	A S-3-O	148		.224
1962 NY	A 3	158		.272
1963 NY	A 2-S-3	152		.251
1964 NY	A S-3	147		.218
1965 NY	A *3/S	148		.251
1966 NY	A 3-S	144		.240
1967 ATL	N *3/S	154		.245
1968 ATL	N 3	71		.227
1969 ATL	N *3	144		.250
1970 ATL	N *3/S	134		.246
1971 ATL	N 3/S	30		.245
	BRTR	1725		.242

BOYER, CLOYD VICTOR (JUNIOR)
B.SEPT.1,1927 ALBA,MO.

1949 STL N P			4	0- 0
1950 STL N P			36	7- 7
1951 STL N P			19	2- 5
1952 STL N P		23	24	6- 6
1955 KC	A P		30	5- 5
	BRTR	112	113	20-23

BOYER, KENTON LLOYD (KEN)
B.MAY 20,1931 LIBERTY,MO.

1955 STL N 3		147		.264
1956 STL N 3		150		.306
1957 STL N 3-O		142		.265
1958 STL N S-3-O		150		.307
1959 STL N S-3		149		.309
1960 STL N 3		151		.304
1961 STL N 3		153		.329
1962 STL N 3		160		.291
1963 STL N 3		159		.285
1964 STL N 3		162		.295
1965 STL N *3		144		.260
1966 NY	N *3/1	136		.266
1967 NY	N 3/1	56		.235
	CHI A 3-1	57		.261
1968 CHI A /3-1		10		.125
	LA N 3-1	83		.271
1969 LA	N /1	25		.206
	BRTR	2034		.287
NON-PLAYING MANAGER STL[N] 1978

BOYLAND, DORIAN SCOTT (DOE)
B.JAN.6,1955 CHICAGO,ILL.

| 1978 PIT N /1 | | | 6 | .250 |
| | BLTL | | | |

BOYLE, EDWARD J.
B.MAY 8,1874 CINCINNATI,OHIO
D.FEB.8,1941 CINCINNATI,OHIO

1896 LOU N C			3	.111
	PIT N C		2	.000
			5	.071

BOYLE, HENRY J. (HANDSOME HENRY)
B.SEPT.20,1860 PHILADELPHIA,PA.

1884 STL U P-O	18	49	16- 2
				.260
1885 STL N P-2-	42	72	15-25
	O			.201
1886 STL N P		30	9-15
1887 IND N P		41	13-24
1888 IND N P		37	15-22
1889 IND N P		44	20-23
	TR	203	273	88-111
				.224

BOYLE, JAMES JOHN
B.JAN.19,1904 CINCINNATI,OHIO
D.DEC.24,1958 CINCINNATI,OHIO

| 1926 NY | N C | | 1 | .000 |
| | BRTR | | | |

YR	CL	LEA	POS	GP	G	REC

BOYLE, JOHN ANTHONY (HONEST JACK)
B.MAR.22,1866 CINCINNATI,OHIO
D.JAN.7,1913 CINCINNATI,OHIO
1886 CIN AA C — 1 .250
1887 STL AA C — 88 .240
1888 STL AA C — 71 .245
1889 STL AA C — 99 .250
1890 CHI P C-S-3 100 .257
1891 STL AA C-S 120 .280
1892 NY N C-1 116 .201
1893 PHI N 1 117 .305
1894 PHI N 1 116 .291
1895 PHI N 1 133 .254
1896 PHI N C 39 .288
1897 PHI N C-1 73 .259
1898 PHI N C-1 6 .091
  BRTR 1079 .259

BOYLE, JOHN BELLEW
B.JULY 9,1869 MORRIS,ILL.
D.APR.3,1971 FT.LAUDERDALE,FLA.
1912 PHI N S-3 15 .280
  BLTR

BOYLE, RALPH FRANCIS (BUZZ)
B.FEB.9,1908 CINCINNATI,OHIO
D.NOV.12,1978 CINCINNATI,OHIO
1929 BOS N O 17 .263
1930 BOS N O 1 .000
1933 BRO N O 93 .299
1934 BRO N O 128 .305
1935 BRO N O 127 .272
  BLTL 366 .293

BOYLES, HARRY (STRETCH)
B.NOV.29,1911 GRANITE CITY,ILL.
1938 CHI A P 9 0-4
1939 CHI A P 2 0-0
  BRTR 11 0-4

BRABENDER, EUGENE MATHEW (GENE)
B.AUG.16,1941 MADISON,WIS.
1966 BAL A P 31 4-3
1967 BAL A P 14 6-4
1968 BAL A P 37 6-7
1969 SEA A P 40 41 13-14
1970 MIL A P 29 6-15
  BRTR 151 152 35-43

BRACK, GILBERT HERMAN (GIBBY)
B.MAR.29,1908 CHICAGO,ILL.
D.JAN.20,1960 GREENVILLE,TEX.
1937 BRO N O 112 .274
1938 BRO N O 40 .214
  PHI N O 72 .287
1939 PHI N 1-O 91 .289
  BRTR 315 .279

BRACKEN, JOHN JAMES
B.APR.14,1881 CLEVELAND,OHIO
D.JULY 16,1954 HIGHLAND PARK,MICH.
1901 CLE A P 12 4-8

BRACKENRIDGE, JOHN GIVLER
B.DEC.24,1880 HARRISBURG,PA.
D.MAR.20,1953 HARRISBURG,PA.
1904 PHI N P 7 0-2
  BRTR

BRADEY, DONALD EUGENE (DON)
B.OCT.4,1934 CHARLOTTE,N.C.
1964 HOU N P 3 0-2
  BRTR

BRADFORD, CHARLES WILLIAM (BUDDY)
B.JULY 25,1944 MOBILE,ALA.
1966 CHI A /O 14 .143
1967 CHI A O 24 .100
1968 CHI A O 103 .217
1969 CHI A O 93 .256
1970 CHI A O 32 .187
  CLE A O/3 75 .196
1971 CLE A O 20 .158
  CIN N O 79 .200
1972 CHI A O 35 .271
1973 CHI A O 53 .238
1974 CHI A O 39 .333
1975 CHI A O 25 .155
  STL N O 50 .272
1976 CHI A O 55 .219
  BRTR 697 .226

BRADFORD, HENRY VICTOR (VIC)
B.MAR.5,1915 BROWNSVILLE,TENN.
1943 NY N P 6 .200

BRADFORD, LARRY
B.DEC.21,1951 CHICAGO,ILL.
1977 ATL N /P 2 0-0
  BRTL

BRADFORD, WILLIAM D
B.AUG.28,1921 CHOCTAW,ARK.
1956 KC A P 1 0-0
  BRTR

BRADLEY, FRED LANGDON
B.JULY 31,1920 PARSONS,KAN.
1948 CHI A P 8 0-0
1949 CHI A P 1 0-0
  BRTR 9 0-0

BRADLEY, GEORGE H. (FOGHORN)
B.1853 MILFORD,MASS.
D.APR.3,1900 PHILADELPHIA,PA.
1876 BOS N P 22 11-9
  BRTR

BRADLEY, GEORGE WASHINGTON (GRIN)
B.JULY 13,1852 READING,PA.
D.OCT.2,1931 PHILADELPHIA,PA.
1875 STL NA P-3 58 31-25
1876 STL N P 64 45-19
1877 CHI N P-1- 50 59 19-23
  3-O .243
1879 TRO N P 61 13-40
1880 PRO N P-1- 22 78 12-9
  3-O .226
1881 DET N S 1 .000
  CLE N P-S- 7 61 3-4
  3-O .252
1882 CLE N P-1- 17 29 7-10
  3-O .183
1883 CLE N S 4 .313
  ATH AA P-1- 27 77 17-7
  3-O .238
1884 CIN U P-S 34 52 21-13
  .202
1886 CLE N S 13 .149
1888 BAL AA S 1 .000
  BRTR 332 554 168-150
  .229

BRADLEY, GEORGE WASHINGTON
B.APR.1,1914 GREENWOOD,ARK.
1946 STL A O 4 .167
  BRTR

BRADLEY, HERBERT THEODORE
B.JAN.3,1903 AGENDA,KAN.
D.OCT.16,1959 CLAY CENTER,KAN.
1927 BOS A P 6 1-1
1928 BOS A P 15 0-3
1929 BOS A P 3 0-0
  BRTR 24 1-4

BRADLEY, HUGH FREDERICK (CORNS)
B.MAY 23,1885 GRAFTON,MASS.
D.JAN.26,1949 WORCESTER,MASS.
1910 BOS A 1 32 .169
1911 BOS A 1 12 .300
1912 BOS A 1 40 .190
1914 PIT F 1 118 .302
1915 PIT F 1 26 .288
  BRO F 1 37 .246
  NEW F 1 12 .094
  BRTR 277 .257

BRADLEY, J. NICHOLAS (NICK)
B.ALTOONA,PA.
D.JAN.16,1889
1884 WAS U O 1 .000

BRADLEY, JOHN THOMAS (JACK)
B.SEPT.20,1893 DENVER,COLO.
D.MAR.18,1969 TULSA,OKLA.
1916 CLE A C 2 .667
  BRTR

BRADLEY, THOMAS WILLIAM (TOM)
B.MAR.16,1947 ASHEVILLE,N.C.
1969 CAL A /P 3 0-1
1970 CAL A P 17 2-5
1971 CHI A P 45 48 15-15
1972 CHI A P 40 43 15-14
1973 SF N P 35 13-12
1974 SF N P 30 8-11
1975 SF N P 13 2-3
  BRTR 183 189 55-61

BRADLEY, WILLIAM JOSEPH (BILL)
B.FEB.13,1878 CLEVELAND,OHIO
D.MAR.11,1954 CLEVELAND,OHIO
1899 CHI N 3 35 .307
1900 CHI N 1-3 120 .288
1901 CLE A 3 136 .296
1902 CLE A 3 136 .341
1903 CLE A 3 137 .315
1904 CLE A 3 154 .300
1905 CLE A 3 145 .268
1906 CLE A 3 82 .275
1907 CLE A 3 139 .223
1908 CLE A S-3 148 .243
1909 CLE A 3 95 .186
1910 CLE A 3 61 .196
1914 BRO F M-H 7 .500
1915 KC F 3 66 .192
  BRTR 1458 .272

BRADSHAW, DALLAS CARL (WINDY)
B.NOV.23,1895 WOLF CREEK,ILL.
D.DEC.11,1939 HERRIN,ILL.
1917 PHI A 2 2 .000
  BLTR

BRADSHAW, GEORGE THOMAS
B.SEPT.12,1924 SALISBURY,N.C.
1952 WAS A C 10 .217
  BRTR

BRADSHAW, JOE SIAH
B.AUG.17,1897 ROELLEN,TENN.
1929 BRO N P 2 0-0
  BRTR

BRADY, CLIFFORD FRANCIS
B.MAR.6,1897 ST.LOUIS,MO.
D.SEPT.25,1974 BELLEVILLE,ILL.
1920 BOS A 2 53 .228
  BRTR

BRADY, CORNELIUS JOSEPH (NEAL)
B.MAR.4,1897 COVINGTON,KY.
D.JUNE 19,1947 FORT MITCHELL,KY
1915 NY A P 2 0-0
1917 NY A P 2 1-0
1925 CIN N P 20 1-3
  BRTR 24 2-3

BRADY, FREDERICK
[SEE WILLIAM LORENZ KOPF]

BRADY, JAMES JOSEPH
(JIM) OR (DIAMOND JIM)
B.MAR.2,1936 JERSEY CITY,N.J.
1956 DET A P 6 0-0
  BLTL

BRADY, JAMES WARD (KING)
B.MAY 28,1881 ELMER,N.J.
D.AUG.21,1947 ALBANY,N.Y.
1905 PHI N P 2 1-1
1906 PIT N P 3 1-1
1907 DET N P 1 0-0
1908 BOS A P 1 1-0
1912 BOS N P 1 0-0
  BRTR 8 3-2

BRADY, ROBERT JAY
B.NOV.8,1922 LEWISTOWN,PA.
1946 BOS N C 3 .200
1947 BOS N H 1 .000
  BLTR 4 .167

BRADY, STEPHEN A.
B.JULY 14,1851 WORCESTER,MASS.
D.NOV.2,1917 HARTFORD,CONN.
1874 HAR NA 3-O 25 —
1875 HAR NA 1-2-O 18 —
  CHI NA O 1 —
1883 MET AA 1-O 97 .280
1884 MET AA O 112 .269
1885 MET AA O 108 .296
1886 MET AA O 123 .234
  484 —

BRADY, THOMAS
B.HARTFORD,CONN.
1875 HAR NA O 1 .000

BRADY, WILLIAM A. (KING)
B.1888
D.APR.12,1917
1912 BOS N P 1 0-0
  TR

BRAGAN, ROBERT RANDALL (NIG)
B.OCT.30,1915 BIRMINGHAM,ALA.
1940 PHI N S-3 132 .222
1941 PHI N 2-S-3 154 .251
1942 PHI N C-2-S-3 109 .218
1943 BRO N C-3 74 .264
1944 BRO N C-2-S-3 94 .267
1947 BRO N C 25 .194
1948 BRO N C 9 .167
  BRTR 597 .240
NON-PLAYING MANAGER
PIT(N) 1956-57, CLE(A) 1958,
MIL(N) 1963-65, ATL(N) 1966

BRAGGINS, RICHARD REALF
B.DEC.25,1879 MERCER,PA.
D.AUG.16,1963 LAKE WALES,FLA.
1901 CLE A P 4 1-2
  BRTR

BRAIN, DAVID LEONARD
B.JAN.24,1879 HEREFORD,ENGLAND
D.MAY 25,1959 LOS ANGELES,CAL.
1901 CHI A 2 5 .350
1903 STL N S-3 118 .231
1904 STL N S-3-O 125 .266
1905 STL N S-3 41 .226
  PIT N S-3 82 .257
1906 BOS N 3 139 .250
1907 BOS N 3 133 .279
1908 CIN N O 16 .190
  NY N O 9 .076
  BRTR 668 .254

YR	CL	LEA	POS	GP	G	REC

BRAINARD, ASA (COUNT)
B.1841 ALBANY,N.Y.
D.DEC.10,1888

YR	CL	LEA	POS	GP	G	REC
1871	OLY	NA	P		30	13-15
1872	OLY	NA	P		9	2- 7
1872	MAN	NA	P-2	3	9	0- 3
						.161
1873	BAL	NA	P-O	13	15	5- 7
						-
1874	BAL	NA	P-2-O	28	46	5-23
		TR		83	107	25-55
						-

BRAINERD, FREDERICK F.
B.FEB.17,1892 CHAMPAIGN,ILL.
D.APR.19,1960 GALVESTON,TEX.

YR	CL	LEA	POS	G	REC
1914	NY	N	2	2	.500
1915	NY	N	1-3	91	.201
1916	NY	N	3	2	.000
		BRTR		95	.202

BRAITHWOOD, ALFRED
B.FEB.15,1892 BRACEVILLE,ILL.
D.NOV.24,1960 ROWLESBURG,W.VA.

YR	CL	LEA	POS	G	REC
1915	PIT	F	P	1	0- 0

BRAME, ERVIN BECKHAM
B.OCT.12,1901 BIG ROCK,TENN.
D.NOV.22,1949 HOPKINSVILLE,KY.

YR	CL	LEA	POS	GP	G	REC
1928	PIT	N	P	24	35	7- 4
1929	PIT	N	P	37	59	16-11
1930	PIT	N	P	32	50	17- 8
1931	PIT	N	P	26	48	9-13
1932	PIT	N	P	23	26	3- 1
		BLTR		142	218	52-37

BRAMHALL, ARTHUR WASHINGTON
B.FEB.22,1909 CHICAGO,ILL.

YR	CL	LEA	POS	G	REC
1935	PHI	N	S-3	2	.000
		BRTR			

BRANCA, RALPH THEODORE JOSEPH (HAWK)
B.JAN.6,1926 MT.VERNON,N.Y.

YR	CL	LEA	POS	G	REC
1944	BRO	N	P	21	0- 2
1945	BRO	N	P	16	5- 6
1946	BRO	N	P	24	3- 1
1947	BRO	N	P	43	21-12
1948	BRO	N	P	36	14- 9
1949	BRO	N	P	34	13- 5
1950	BRO	N	P	43	7- 9
1951	BRO	N	P	42	13-12
1952	BRO	N	P	16	4- 2
1953	BRO	N	P	7	0- 0
	DET	A	P	17	4- 7
1954	DET	A	P	17	3- 3
	NY	A	P	5	1- 0
1956	BRO	N	P	1	0- 0
		BRTR		322	88-68

BRANCATO, ALBERT (BRONK)
B.MAY 29,1919 PHILADELPHIA,PA.

YR	CL	LEA	POS	G	REC
1939	PHI	A	3	21	.206
1940	PHI	A	S-3	107	.191
1941	PHI	A	S-3	144	.234
1945	PHI	A	S	10	.118
		BRTR		282	.214

BRANCH, HARVEY ALFRED
B.FEB.8,1939 MEMPHIS,TENN.

YR	CL	LEA	POS	G	REC
1962	STL	N	P	1	0- 1
		BRTL			

BRANCH, NORMAN DOWNS (RED)
B.MAR.22,1915 SPOKANE,WASH.

YR	CL	LEA	POS	G	REC
1941	NY	A	P	27	5- 1
1942	NY	A	P	10	0- 1
		BRTR		37	5- 2

BRAND, RONALD GEORGE (RON)
B.JAN.13,1940 LOS ANGELES,CAL.

YR	CL	LEA	POS	G	REC
1963	PIT	N	C-2-3	46	.288
1965	HOU	N	*C/3-0	117	.235
1966	HOU	N	C/2-0-3	56	.244
1967	HOU	N	C/2-0	84	.242
1968	HOU	N	C/3-0	43	.160
1969	MON	N	C/O	103	.258
1970	MON	N	S-3/C-0-2	72	.238
1971	MON	N	S/3-0-C-2	47	.214
		BRTR		568	.239

BRANDOM, CHESTER MILTON (CHICK)
B.MAR.31,1887 COLDWATER,KAN.
D.OCT.7,1958 SANTA ANA,CAL.

YR	CL	LEA	POS	G	REC
1908	PIT	N	P	7	1- 0
1909	PIT	N	P	13	1- 0
1915	NEW	F	P	16	1- 1
		TR		32	3- 1

BRANDON, DARRELL G (BUCKY)
B.JULY 8,1940 NACOGDOCHES,TEX.

YR	CL	LEA	POS	GP	G	REC
1966	BOS	A	P	40	41	8- 8
1967	BOS	A	/P		39	5-11
1968	BOS	A	/P		8	0- 0
1969	SEA	A	/P		8	0- 1
	MIN	A	/P		3	0- 0
1971	PHI	N	P		52	6- 6
1972	PHI	N	P		42	7- 7
1973	PHI	N	P		36	2- 4
		BRTR		228	229	28-37

BRANDT, EDWARD ARTHUR (BIG ED)
B.FEB.17,1905 SPOKANE,WASH.
D.NOV.1,1944 SPOKANE,WASH.

YR	CL	LEA	POS	GP	G	REC
1928	BOS	N	P	38	39	9-21
1929	BOS	N	P	26	29	8-13
1930	BOS	N	P		18	0- 0
1931	BOS	N	P	33	34	18-11
1932	BOS	N	P		35	16-16
1933	BOS	N	P	41	47	18-14
1934	BOS	N	P	40	48	16-14
1935	BOS	N	P	29	31	5-19
1936	BRO	N	P	38	43	11-13
1937	PIT	N	P		33	11-10
1938	PIT	N	P		24	5- 4
		BLTL		378	404	121-146

BRANDT, JOHN GEORGE (JACKIE)
B.APR.28,1934 OMAHA,NEB.

YR	CL	LEA	POS	G	REC
1956	STL	N	O	27	.286
	NY	N	O	98	.299
1958	SF	N	O	18	.250
1959	SF	N	1-2-3-0	137	.270
1960	BAL	A	1-3-0	145	.254
1961	BAL	A	3-0	139	.297
1962	BAL	A	3-0	143	.255
1963	BAL	A	3-0	142	.248
1964	BAL	A	O	137	.243
1965	BAL	A	O	96	.243
1966	PHI	N	O	82	.250
1967	PHI	N	/O	16	.105
	HOU	N	1/0-3	41	.236
		BRTR		1221	.262

BRANDT, WILLIAM GEORGE
B.MAR.21,1915 AURORA,IND.
D.MAY 16,1968 FORT WAYNE,IND.

YR	CL	LEA	POS	G	REC
1941	PIT	N	P	2	0- 1
1942	PIT	N	P	3	1- 1
1943	PIT	N	P	29	4- 1
		BRTR		34	5- 3

BRANNAN, OTIS OWEN
B.MAR.13,1899 GREENBRIER,ARK.
D.JUNE 6,1967 LITTLE ROCK,ARK.

YR	CL	LEA	POS	G	REC
1928	STL	A	2	135	.244
1929	STL	A	2	23	.294
		BRTR		158	.249

BRANOM, EDGAR DUDLEY (DUD)
B.NOV.30,1897 SULPHUR SPRINGS,TEX.

YR	CL	LEA	POS	G	REC
1927	PHI	A	1	30	.234
		BLTL			

BRANSFIELD, WILLIAM EDWARD (KITTY)
B.JAN.7,1875 WORCESTER,MASS.
D.MAY 1,1947 WORCESTER,MASS.

YR	CL	LEA	POS	G	REC
1898	BOS	N	C	5	.222
1901	PIT	N	1	139	.274
1902	PIT	N	1	100	.308
1903	PIT	N	1	127	.265
1904	PIT	N	1	139	.223
1905	PHI	N	1	151	.259
1906	PHI	N	1	139	.275
1907	PHI	N	1	92	.233
1908	PHI	N	1	143	.304
1909	PHI	N	1	138	.292
1910	PHI	N	1	110	.239
1911	PHI	N	1	23	.256
	CHI	N	1	3	.400
		BRTR		1309	.270

BRASHEAR, NORMAN C. (KITTY)
B.AUG.27,1877 MANSFIELD,OHIO
D.DEC.22,1934 LOS ANGELES,CAL.

YR	CL	LEA	POS	G	REC
1902	STL	N	1-2-S-0	106	.284

BRASHEAR, ROY PARKS
B.JAN.3,1874 ASHTABULA,OHIO
D.APR.20,1951 LOS ANGELES,CAL.

YR	CL	LEA	POS	G	REC
1899	LOU	N	P	3	1- 0
1903	PHI	N	2	20	.227
		TR		23	1- 0
					.231

BRATCHER, JOSEPH WARLICK (GOOBERS)
B.JULY 22,1898 GRAND SALINE,TEX

YR	CL	LEA	POS	G	REC
1924	STL	N	O	4	.000
		BLTR			

BRATSCHI, FREDERICK OSCAR (FRITZ)
B.JAN.16,1892 ALLIANCE,OHIO
D.JAN.10,1962 MASSILLON,OHIO

YR	CL	LEA	POS	G	REC
1921	CHI	A	O	16	.286
1926	BOS	A	O	72	.275
1927	BOS	A	H	1	.000
		BRTR		89	.276

BRAUN, JOHN PAUL
B.DEC.26,1939 MADISON,WIS.

YR	CL	LEA	POS	G	REC
1964	MIL	N	P	1	0- 0
		BRTR			

BRAUN, STEPHEN RUSSELL (STEVE)
B.MAY 8,1948 TRENTON,N.J.

YR	CL	LEA	POS	G	REC
1971	MIN	A	3-2-S/0	128	.254
1972	MIN	A	3-2-S/0	121	.289
1973	MIN	A	*3/0	115	.283
1974	MIN	A	*0-3	129	.280
1975	MIN	A	*O/1-3-2	136	.302
1976	MIN	A	D-0-3	122	.288
1977	SEA	A	*0-0/3	139	.235
1978	SEA	A	D/0	32	.230
	KC	A	D-0-3	64	.263
		BLTR		986	.274

BRAVO, ANGEL ALFONSO [URDANETA]
B.AUG.4,1942 MARACAIBO,VENEZ.

YR	CL	LEA	POS	G	REC
1969	CHI	A	O	27	.289
1970	CIN	N	O	65	.277
1971	CIN	N	/H	5	.200
	SD	N	/O	52	.155
		BLTL		149	.248

BRAXTON, EDGAR GARLAND
B.JUNE 10,1900 SNOW CAMP,N.C.
D.FEB.25,1966 NORFOLK,VA.

YR	CL	LEA	POS	G	REC
1921	BOS	N	P	17	1- 3
1922	BOS	N	P	25	1- 2
1925	NY	A	P	3	1- 1
1926	NY	A	P	37	5- 1
1927	WAS	A	P	58	10- 9
1928	WAS	A	P	38	13-11
1929	WAS	A	P	37	12-10
1930	WAS	A	P	15	3- 2
	CHI	A	P	19	4-10
1931	CHI	A	P	17	0- 3
	STL	A	P	11	0- 0
1933	STL	A	P	5	0- 1
		BBTL		282	50-53

BRAY, CLARENCE WILBUR (BUSTER)
B.APR.1,1913 BIRMINGHAM,ALA.

YR	CL	LEA	POS	G	REC
1941	BOS	N	O	4	.091
		BLTL			

BRAZILL, FRANK LEO
B.AUG.11,1899 SPANGLER,PA.
D.NOV.3,1976 OAKLAND,CAL.

YR	CL	LEA	POS	G	REC
1921	PHI	A	1	66	.271
1922	PHI	A	3	6	.077
		BLTR		72	.258

BRAZLE, ALPHA EUGENE (COTTON)
B.OCT.19,1913 LOYAL,OKLA.
D.OCT.24,1973 GRAND JUNCTION,COLO.

YR	CL	LEA	POS	GP	G	REC
1943	STL	N	P		13	8- 2
1946	STL	N	P		37	11-10
1947	STL	N	P		44	14- 8
1948	STL	N	P	42		10- 6
1949	STL	N	P		39	14- 8
1950	STL	N	P	46	47	11- 9
1951	STL	N	P		56	6- 5
1952	STL	N	P		46	12- 5
1953	STL	N	P		60	6- 7
1954	STL	N	P		58	5- 4
		BLTL		441	445	97-64

BREAZEALE, JAMES LEO (JIM)
B.OCT.3,1949 HOUSTON,TEX.

YR	CL	LEA	POS	G	REC
1969	ATL	N	/1	2	.000
1971	ATL	N	/1	10	.190
1972	ATL	N	1/3	52	.247
1978	CHI	A	1	25	.208
		BRTR		89	.223

BRECHEEN, HARRY DAVID (THE CAT)
B.OCT.14,1914 BROKEN BOW,OKLA.

YR	CL	LEA	POS	GP	G	REC
1940	STL	N	P		3	0- 0
1943	STL	N	P		29	9- 6
1944	STL	N	P	30	31	16- 5
1945	STL	N	P		24	15- 4
1946	STL	N	P	36	37	15-15
1947	STL	N	P		29	16-11
1948	STL	N	P		33	20- 7
1949	STL	N	P		32	14-11
1950	STL	N	P		27	8-11
1951	STL	N	P		24	8- 4
1952	STL	N	P		25	7- 5
1953	STL	A	P	26		5-13
		BLTL		318	321	133-92

BRECKINRIDGE, WILLIAM ROBERTSON
B.OCT.27,1905 TULSA,OKLA.
D.AUG.23,1958 TULSA,OKLA.

YR	CL	LEA	POS	G	REC
1929	PHI	A	P	3	0- 0
		BRTR			

BREEDEN, DANNY RICHARD
B.JUNE 27,1942 ALBANY,GA.

YR	CL	LEA	POS	G	REC
1969	CHI	N	/C	3	.125
1971	CHI	N	/C	25	.154
		BRTR		28	.151

YR	CL	LEA	POS	GP	G	REC

BREEDEN, HAROLD NOEL (HAL)
B.JUNE 26,1944 ALBANY,GA.

1971	CHI	N	/1		23	.139
1972	MON	N	1/0		42	.230
1973	MON	N	1		105	.275
1974	MON	N	1		79	.247
1975	MON	N	1		24	.135
			BRTL		273	.243

BREEDING, MARVIN EUGENE (MARV)
B.MAR.8,1934 DECATUR,ALA.

1960	BAL	A	2		152	.267
1961	BAL	A	2		90	.209
1962	BAL	A	2-S-3		95	.246
1963	BAL	A	2-S-3		58	.274
	LA	N	2-S-3		20	.167
			BRTR		415	.250

BREITENSTEIN, ALONZO
B.NOV.9,1857 UTICA,N.Y.
D.JUNE 19,1932 UTICA,N.Y.

| 1883 | PHI | N | P | | 1 | 0- 1 |

BREITENSTEIN, THEODORE P. (THEO)
B.JUNE 1,1869 ST.LOUIS,MO.
D.MAY 3,1935 ST.LOUIS,MO.

1891	STL	AA	P		5	0- 1
1892	STL	N	P	34	38	14-20
1893	STL	N	P		41	19-20
1894	STL	N	P		53	27-25
1895	STL	N	P	51	66	18-30
1896	STL	N	P	43	48	17-26
1897	CIN	N	P	35	39	23-12
1898	CIN	N	P	36	39	21-14
1899	CIN	N	P	24	33	14-10
1900	CIN	N	P	22	33	10-10
1901	STL	N	P		3	0- 3
			BLTL	347	398	163-171

BREMER, HERBERT FREDERICK
B.OCT.25,1913 CHICAGO,ILL.

1937	STL	N	C		11	.212
1938	STL	N	C		50	.219
1939	STL	N	C		9	.111
			BRTR		70	.212

BRENEGAN, OLAF SELMAR
B.SEPT.1,1890 GALESVILLE,WIS.
D.APR.20,1956 GALESVILLE,WIS.

| 1914 | PIT | N | C | | 1 | .000 |
| | | | BLTR | | | |

BRENNAN, ADDISON FOSTER (AD)
B.JULY 18,1881 LAHARPE,KAN.
D.JAN.7,1962 KANSAS CITY,MO.

1910	PHI	N	P	19	21	2- 0
1911	PHI	N	P		5	3- 1
1912	PHI	N	P		27	11- 9
1913	PHI	N	P		40	14-12
1914	CHI	F	P		16	5- 5
1915	CHI	F	P		19	3- 9
1918	WAS	A	P		2	0- 0
	CLE	A	P		1	0- 0
			BLTL	129	131	38-36

BRENNAN, JAMES A.
B.1862 ST.LOUIS,MO.
D.OCT.18,1904 PHILADELPHIA,PA.

1884	STL	U	C-O		45	.210
1885	STL	N	3-O		3	.100
1888	KC	AA	C		34	.174
1889	ATH	AA	C		31	.214
1890	CLE	P	C-3		59	.251
					172	.217

BRENNAN, JAMES DONALD (DON)
B.DEC.2,1903 AUGUSTA,MAINE
D.APR.26,1953 BOSTON,MASS.

1933	NY	A	P		18	5- 1
1934	CIN	N	P		28	4- 3
1935	CIN	N	P		38	5- 5
1936	CIN	N	P		41	5- 2
1937	CIN	N	P		10	1- 1
	NY	N	P		6	1- 0
			BRTR		141	21-12

BRENNEMAN, JAMES LEROY (JIM)
B.FEB.13,1941 SAN DIEGO,CAL.

| 1965 | NY | A | /P | | 3 | 0- 0 |
| | | | BRTR | | | |

**BRENNER, DELBERT HENRY
(BERT) OR (DUTCH)**
B.JULY 18,1887 MINNEAPOLIS,MINN
D.APR.11,1971 ST.LOUIS PARK,MINN.

| 1912 | CLE | N | P | | 2 | 1- 0 |
| | | | BRTR | | | |

BRENTON, LYNN DAVIS (BUCK) OR (HERB)
B.OCT.7,1890 PEORIA,ILL.
D.OCT.14,1968 LOS ANGELES,CAL.

1913	CLE	A	P		1	0- 0
1915	CLE	A	P		11	2- 3
1920	CIN	N	P		5	2- 1
1921	CIN	N	P		17	1- 8
			BRTR		34	5-12

BRENZEL, WILLIAM RICHARD
B.MAR.3,1910 OAKLAND,CAL.

1932	PIT	N	C		9	.042
1934	CLE	A	C		15	.216
1935	CLE	A	C		52	.218
			BRTR		76	.198

**BRESNAHAN, ROGER PHILIP (DUKE)
OR (THE DUKE OF TRALEE)**
B.JUNE 11,1879 TOLEDO,OHIO
D.DEC.4,1944 TOLEDO,OHIO

1897	WAS	N	P		7	4- 1
1900	CHI	N	C		1	.000
1901	BAL	A	P-C	1	86	0- 0
						.262
1902	BAL	A	C-3-O		66	.273
	NY	N	C-1-S-3-O		50	.292
1903	NY	N	O		111	.350
1904	NY	N	O		107	.284
1905	NY	N	C		95	.302
1906	NY	N	C-O		124	.281
1907	NY	N	C		104	.253
1908	NY	N	C		139	.283
1909	STL	N	M-C		69	.244
1910	STL	N	M-C		78	.278
1911	STL	N	M-C		78	.278
1912	STL	N	M-C		48	.333
1913	CHI	N	C		69	.228
1914	CHI	N	C		101	.278
1915	CHI	N	M-C		77	.204
			BRTR	8	1410	4- 1
						.279

BRESSLER, RAYMOND BLOOM (RUBE)
B.OCT.23,1894 CODER,PA.
D.NOV.7,1966 CINCINNATI,OHIO

1914	PHI	A	P		29	10- 4
1915	PHI	A	P	32	33	4-17
1916	PHI	A	P		4	0- 3
1917	CIN	N	P		3	0- 0
1918	CIN	N	P-O	17	23	8- 5
						.274
1919	CIN	N	P-O	13	61	2- 4
						.206
1920	CIN	N	P-1	10	21	2- 0
						.267
1921	CIN	N	O		109	.307
1922	CIN	N	1-O		52	.264
1923	CIN	N	1-O		54	.277
1924	CIN	N	1-O		115	.347
1925	CIN	N	1-O		97	.348
1926	CIN	N	1-O		86	.357
1927	CIN	N	O		124	.291
1928	BRO	N	O		145	.295
1929	BRO	N	O		136	.318
1930	BRO	N	O		109	.299
1931	BRO	N	O		67	.281
1932	PHI	N	O		27	.229
	STL	N	O		10	.158
			BRTL	108	1305	26-33
						.302

BRESSOUD, EDWARD FRANCIS (EDDIE)
B.MAY 2,1932 LOS ANGELES,CAL.

1956	NY	N	S		49	.227
1957	NY	N	S-3		49	.268
1958	SF	N	2-S-3		66	.263
1959	SF	N	1-2-S-3		104	.251
1960	SF	N	S		116	.225
1961	SF	N	2-S-3		59	.211
1962	BOS	A	S		153	.277
1963	BOS	A	S		140	.260
1964	BOS	A	S		158	.293
1965	BOS	A	S/3-O		107	.226
1966	NY	N	S-3/1-2		133	.225
1967	STL	N	S/3		52	.134
			BRTR		1186	.252

BRETON, JOHN FREDERICK (JIM)
B.JULY 15,1891 CHICAGO,ILL.
D.MAY 30,1973 BELOIT,WIS.

1913	CHI	A	3		12	.173
1914	CHI	A	3		81	.212
1915	CHI	A	3		16	.139
			BRTR		109	.202

BRETT, GEORGE HOWARD
B.MAY 15,1953 WHEELING,W.VA.

1973	KC	A	3		13	.125
1974	KC	A	*3/S		133	.282
1975	KC	A	*3/S		159	.308
1976	KC	A	*3/S		159	.333
1977	KC	A	*3/S		139	.312
1978	KC	A	*3/S		128	.294
			BLTR		731	.305

BRETT, HERBERT JAMES (DUKE)
B.MAY 23,1900 LAWRENCEVILLE,VA.
D.NOV.25,1974 ST.PETERSBURG,FLA

1924	CHI	N	P		1	0- 0
1925	CHI	N	P		10	1- 1
			BRTR		11	1- 1

BRETT, KENNETH ALVEN (KEN)
B.SEP.18,1948 BROOKLYN,N.Y.

1967	BOS	A	/P		1	0- 0
1969	BOS	A	/P		8	2- 3
1970	BOS	A	P		41	8- 9
1971	BOS	A	P		29	0- 3
1972	MIL	A	P	26	31	7-12
1973	PHI	N	P	31	37	13- 9
1974	PIT	N	P	27	43	13- 9
1975	PIT	N	P	23	26	9- 5
1976	NY	A	/P		2	0- 0
	CHI	A	P	27	33	10-12
1977	CHI	A	P		13	6- 4
	CAL	A	P	21	22	7-10
1978	CAL	A	P		31	3- 5
			BLTL	280	317	78-81

BREUER, MARVIN HOWARD (BABY FACE)
B.APR.29,1914 ROLLA,MO.

1939	NY	A	P		1	0- 0
1940	NY	A	P		27	8- 9
1941	NY	A	P		26	9- 7
1942	NY	A	P		27	8- 9
1943	NY	A	P		5	0- 1
			BRTR		86	25-26

BREWER, JAMES THOMAS (JIM)
B.NOV.17,1937 MERCED,CAL.

1960	CHI	N	P	5	6	0- 3
1961	CHI	N	P		36	1- 7
1962	CHI	N	P		6	0- 1
1963	CHI	N	P		29	3- 2
1964	LA	N	P		34	4- 3
1965	LA	N	P	19	20	3- 2
1966	LA	N	P		13	0- 2
1967	LA	N	P		30	5- 4
1968	LA	N	P		54	8- 3
1969	LA	N	P		59	7- 6
1970	LA	N	P		58	7- 6
1971	LA	N	P		55	6- 5
1972	LA	N	P		51	8- 7
1973	LA	N	P		56	6- 8
1974	LA	N	P		24	4- 4
1975	LA	N	P		21	3- 1
	CAL	A	P		21	1- 0
1976	CAL	A	P		13	3- 1
			BLTL	584	586	69-65

**BREWER, JOHN HERNDON
(JACK) OR (BUDDY)**
B.JULY 21,1919 LOS ANGELES,CAL.

1944	NY	N	P		14	1- 4
1945	NY	N	P		28	8- 6
1946	NY	N	P		1	0- 0
			BRTR		43	9-10

BREWER, THOMAS AUSTIN (TOM)
B.SEPT.3,1931 WADESBORO,S.C.

1954	BOS	A	P	33	37	10- 9
1955	BOS	A	P	31	33	11-10
1956	BOS	A	P	32	38	19- 9
1957	BOS	A	P	32	45	16-13
1958	BOS	A	P	33	42	12-12
1959	BOS	A	P	36	47	10-12
1960	BOS	A	P	34	43	10-15
1961	BOS	A	P	10	18	3- 2
			BRTR	241	305	91-82

BREWSTER, CHARLES LAWRENCE
B.DEC.27,1916 MARTHAVILLE,LA.

1943	CIN	N	2-S		7	.125
	PHI	N	S		49	.220
1944	CHI	N	S		10	.250
1946	CLE	A	S		3	.000
			BRTR		69	.221

BRICE, ALAN HEALEY
B.OCT.1,1937 NEW YORK,N.Y.

| 1961 | CHI | A | P | | 3 | 0- 1 |
| | | | BRTR | | | |

BRICKELL, FRITZ DARRELL
B.MAR.19,1935 WICHITA,KAN.
D.OCT.15,1965 WICHITA,KAN.

1958	NY	A	2		2	.000
1959	NY	A	2-S		18	.256
1961	LA	A	S		21	.122
			BRTR		41	.182

BRICKELL, GEORGE FREDERICK (FRED)
B.APR.8,1906 SAFFORDVILLE,KAN.
D.OCT.1,1961 WICHITA,KAN.

1926	PIT	N	O		24	.345
1927	PIT	N	O		32	.286
1928	PIT	N	O		81	.322
1929	PIT	N	O		60	.314
1930	PIT	N	O		68	.297
	PHI	N	O		53	.246
1931	PHI	N	O		130	.253
1932	PHI	N	O		45	.333
1933	PHI	N	O		8	.308
			BLTR		501	.281

BRICKLEY, GEORGE VINCENT
B.JULY 19,1894 EVERETT,MASS.
D.FEB.23,1947 EVERETT,MASS.

| 1913 | PHI | A | O | | 5 | .166 |
| | | | BRTR | | | |

```
YR  CL LEA POS    GP    G   REC
```

BRICKNER, RALPH HAROLD
(RALPH) OR (BRICK)
B.MAY 2,1925 CINCINNATI,OHIO
```
1952 BOS A  P       14        3- 1
        BRTR
```

BRIDEWESER, JAMES EHRENFELD
B.FEB.13,1927 LANCASTER,OHIO
```
1951 NY  A  S        2       .375
1952 NY  A  2-S-3   42       .263
1953 NY  A  S        7     1.000
1954 BAL A  2-S     73       .265
1955 CHI A  2-S-3   34       .207
1956 CHI A  S       10       .182
     DET A  2-S-3   70       .268
1957 BAL A  2-S-3   91       .268
        BRTR       329       .252
```

BRIDGES, EVERETT LAMAR (ROCKY)
B.AUG.7,1927 REFUGIO,TEX.
```
1951 BRO N  2-S-3   63       .254
1952 BRO N  2-S-3   51       .196
1953 CIN N  2-S-3  122       .227
1954 CIN N  2-S-3   53       .231
1955 CIN N  2-S-3   95       .286
1956 CIN N  2-S-3-0 71       .211
1957 CIN N  2-S-3    5       .000
     WAS A  2-S-3  120       .228
1958 WAS A  2-S-3  116       .263
1959 DET A  2-S    116       .268
1960 DET A  S-3     10       .200
     CLE A  S-3     10       .333
     STL N  2        3       .000
1961 LA  A  2-S-3   84       .240
        BRTR       919       .247
```

BRIDGES, MARSHALL
(MARSHALL) OR (SHERIFF)
B.JUNE 2,1931 JACKSON,MISS.
```
1959 STL N  P       27        6- 3
1960 STL N  P       20        2- 2
     CIN N  P       14        4- 0
1961 CIN N  P       13        0- 1
1962 NY  A  P       52        8- 4
1963 NY  A  P       23        2- 0
1964 NY  A  P       17        0- 3
1965 WAS A  P       40        1- 2
        BBTL      206       23-15
     BR 1962-65
```

BRIDGES, THOMAS JEFFERSON DAVIS
B.DEC.28,1906 GORDONSVILLE,TENN
D.APR.19,1968 NASHVILLE,TENN.
```
1930 DET A  P        8        3- 2
1931 DET A  P       35        8-16
1932 DET A  P       34       14-12
1933 DET A  P       33       14-12
1934 DET A  P       36       22-11
1935 DET A  P       36       21-10
1936 DET A  P       39       23-11
1937 DET A  P       34       15-12
1938 DET A  P       25       13- 9
1939 DET A  P       29       17- 7
1940 DET A  P       29       12- 9
1941 DET A  P       25        9-12
1942 DET A  P       23        9- 7
1943 DET A  P       25       12- 7
1945 DET A  P        4        1- 0
1946 DET A  P        9        1- 1
        BRTR      424      194-138
```

BRIDWELL, ALBERT HENRY
B.JAN.4,1884 FRIENDSHIP,OHIO
D.JAN.23,1969 PORTSMOUTH,OHIO
```
1905 CIN N  3-0     74       .252
1906 BOS N  S      120       .227
1907 BOS N  S      140       .218
1908 NY  N  S      147       .285
1909 NY  N  S      145       .294
1910 NY  N  S      141       .276
1911 NY  N  S       76       .270
     BOS N         51       .291
1912 BOS N  S       31       .236
1913 CHI N  S      136       .240
1914 STL F  S      117       .234
1915 STL F  2-3     63       .226
        BLTR      1241       .255
```

BRIEF, ANTHONY VINCENT (BUNNY)
[REAL NAME ANTONIO BORDETZKI]
B.JULY 3,1892 REMUS,MICH.
D.FEB.10,1963 MILWAUKEE,WIS.
```
1912 STL A  1-0     15       .310
1913 STL A  1       84       .217
1915 CHI A  1       48       .214
1917 PIT N  1       36       .217
        BRTR      183       .223
```

BRIGGS, CHARLES R.
```
1884 CHI U  2-0     50       .171
```

BRIGGS, DAN LEE
B.NOV.18,1952 SCOTIA,CAL.
```
1975 CAL A  /1-0    13       .226
1976 CAL A  1       77       .214
1977 CAL A  1-0     59       .162
1978 CLE A  O       15       .163
        BLTL      164       .199
```

BRIGGS, GRANT
B.PHILADELPHIA,PA.
```
1890 SYR AA C       86       .179
1891 LOU AA C        1       .250
1892 STL N  C-O     23       .070
1895 LOU N  C        1       .000
                  111       .163
```

BRIGGS, HERBERT THEODORE (BUTTONS)
B.JULY 19,1875 POUGHKEEPSIE,N.Y.
D.FEB.18,1911 CLEVELAND,OHIO
```
1896 CHI N  P       22       12- 8
1897 CHI N  P       22        5-17
1898 CHI N  P        5        1- 4
1904 CHI N  P       34       19-11
1905 CHI N  P       20        9-10
        BRTR      103       46-50
```

BRIGGS, JOHN EDWARD
B.MAR.10,1944 PATERSON,N.J.
```
1964 PHI N  1-0     61       .258
1965 PHI N  O       93       .236
1966 PHI N  O       81       .282
1967 PHI N  O      106       .232
1968 PHI N  O-1    110       .254
1969 PHI N  *O/1   124       .238
1971 PHI N  /O      10       .182
     MIL A  O-1    125       .264
1972 MIL A  *O-1   135       .266
1973 MIL A  *O     142       .246
1974 MIL A  *O     154       .253
1975 MIL A  O       87       .231
        BLTL     1366       .253
```

BRIGGS, JONATHAN TIFT (JOHN)
B.JAN.24,1934 NATOMA,CAL.
```
1956 CHI N  P        3        0- 0
1957 CHI N  P        3        0- 1
1958 CHI N  P       20        5- 5
1959 CLE A  P        4        0- 1
1960 CLE A  P       21        4- 2
     KC  A  P        8        0- 2
        BRTR       59        9-11
```

BRIGHT, HARRY JAMES
B.SEP.22,1929 KANSAS CITY,MO.
```
1958 PIT N  3       15       .250
1959 PIT N  2-3-0   40       .250
1960 PIT N  P        4       .000
1961 WAS A  C-2-3   72       .240
1962 WAS A  C-1-3  113       .273
1963 CIN N  1        1       .000
     NY  A  1-3     60       .274
1964 NY  A  1        4       .200
1965 CHI N  H       27       .280
        BRTR      336       .255
```

BRILES, NELSON KELLEY
B.AUG.5,1943 DORRIS,CAL.
```
1965 STL N  P       37        3- 3
1966 STL N  P       49        4-15
1967 STL N  P       49       14- 5
1968 STL N  P       33       19-11
1969 STL N  P       36       15-13
1970 STL N  P       30        6- 7
1971 PIT N  P       37        8- 4
1972 PIT N  P       28       14-11
1973 PIT N  P       33       14-13
1974 KC  A  P       18        5- 7
1975 KC  A  P       24        6- 6
1976 TEX A  P       32       11- 9
1977 TEX A  P       28        6- 4
     BAL A  /P       2        0- 0
1978 BAL A  P       16        4- 4
        BRTR      452      129-112
```

BRILL, JOHN E
B.ASTORIA,N.Y.
```
1884 DET N  P-O   12   13     2-10
                              .130
```

BRILLHEART, JAMES BENSON
B.SEPT.28,1903 DUBLIN,VA.
D.SEPT.2,1972 RADFORD,VA.
```
1922 WAS A  P       31        4- 6
1923 WAS A  P       12        0- 1
1927 CHI N  P       32        4- 2
1931 BOS A  P       11        0- 0
        BRTL       86        8- 9
```

BRINKER, WILLIAM HUTCHINSON (DODE)
B.AUG.30,1883 WARRENSBURG,MO.
D.FEB.5,1965 ARCADIA,CAL.
```
1912 PHI N  3=0      9       .222
        BBTR
```

BRINKMAN, CHARLES ERNEST (CHUCK)
B.SEP.16,1944 CINCINNATI,O.
```
1969 CHI A  C       14       .067
1970 CHI A  /C       9       .250
1971 CHI A  C       15       .200
1972 CHI A  C       35       .135
1973 CHI A  C       63       .137
1974 CHI A  /C       8       .143
     PIT N  /C       4       .143
        BRTR      148       .172
```

BRINKMAN, EDWIN ALBERT (ED)
B.DEC.8,1941 CINCINNATI,O.
```
1961 WAS A  3        4       .091
1962 WAS A  S-3     54       .165
1963 WAS A  S      145       .228
1964 WAS A  S      132       .224
1965 WAS A  *S     154       .185
1966 WAS A  *S     158       .229
1967 WAS A  *S     109       .188
1968 WAS A  S/2-0   77       .187
1969 WAS A  *S     151       .266
1970 WAS A  *S     158       .262
1971 DET A  *S     159       .228
1972 DET A  *S     156       .203
1973 DET A  *S     162       .237
1974 DET A  *S/3   153       .221
1975 STL N  S       28       .240
     TEX A /3        1       .000
     NY  A  S/2-3   44       .175
        BRTR     1845       .224
```

BRINKOPF, LEON CLARENCE
B.OCT.20,1926 CAPE GIRARDEAU,MO
```
1952 CHI N  S        9       .182
        BRTR
```

BRIODY, CHARLES F. (ALDERMAN)
B.AUG.13,1858 TROY,N.Y.
```
1880 TRO N  C        1       .000
1882 CLE N  C       52       .263
1883 CLE N  C-1-2-3 39       .232
1884 CLE N  C-0     43       .169
     CIN U  C       23       .326
1885 STL N  C-2-3   61       .195
1886 KC  N  C       55       .237
1887 DET N  C       32       .277
1888 KC  AA C       13       .208
                  319       .234
```

BRISSIE, LELAND VICTOR (LOU)
B.JUNE 5,1924 ANDERSON,S.C.
```
1947 PHI A  P        1        0- 1
1948 PHI A  P       39       14-10
1949 PHI A  P       34       16-11
1950 PHI A  P       46        7-19
1951 PHI A  P        2        0- 2
     CLE A  P       54        4- 3
1952 CLE A  P       42        3- 2
1953 CLE A  P       16        0- 0
        BLTL      234       44-48
```

BRISTOL, JAMES DAVID (DAVE)
B.JUNE 23,1933 MACON,GA.
NON-PLAYING MANAGER
CIN(N) 1966-69; MIL(A) 1970-72;
ATL(N) 1976-77

BRISTOW, GEORGE T.
B.1871 PAWPAW,ILL.
```
1899 CLE N  O        3       .125
```

BRITT, JAMES E.
```
1872 ATL NA P       35        8-27
1873 ATL NA P       23        9-14
     MUT NA P        1        0- 1
     ATL NA P       30        7-22
                   89       24-64
```

BRITTAIN, AUGUST SCHUSTER
B.NOV.29,1909 WILMINGTON,N.C.
D.FEB.16,1974 WILMINGTON,N.C.
```
1937 CIN N  C        3       .167
        BRTR
```

BRITTIN, JOHN ALBERT (JACK)
B.MAR.4,1924 ATHENS,ILL.
```
1950 PHI N  P        3        0- 0
1951 PHI N  P        3        0- 0
        BRTR        6        0- 0
```

BRITTON, JAMES ALLAN (JIM)
B.MAR.25,1944 N.TONAWANDA,N.Y.
```
1967 ATL N  /P       2        0- 2
1968 ATL N  P       34        4- 6
1969 ATL N  P       24        7- 5
1971 MON N  P       16        2- 3
        BRTR       76       13-16
```

BRITTON, STEPHEN GILBERT (GIL)
B.SEPT.21,1891 PARSONS,KAN.
```
1913 PIT N  S        3       .000
        BRTR
```

BROACA, JOHN JOSEPH
B.OCT.3,1909 LAWRENCE,MASS.
```
1934 NY  A  P       26       12- 9
1935 NY  A  P       29       15- 7
1936 NY  A  P       37       12- 7
1937 NY  A  P        7        1- 4
1939 CLE A  P       22        4- 2
        BRTR      121       44-29
```

```
YR  CL LEA POS      GP   G   REC
```

BROBERG, PETER SVEN (PETE)
B.MAR.2,1940 WEST PALM BEACH,FLA
```
1971 WAS A  P            18   5- 9
1972 TEX A  P            39   5-12
1973 TEX A  P       22   23   5- 9
1974 TEX A  P            12   0- 4
1975 MIL A  P            38  14-16
1976 MIL A  P            20   1- 7
1977 CHI N  P            22   1- 2
1978 OAK A  P            35  10-12
         BRTR      206  207  41-71
```

BROCK, JOHN ROY
B.OCT.16,1896 HAMILTON,ILL.
D.OCT.27,1951 CLAYTON,MO.
```
1917 STL N  C             7   .400
1918 STL N  C-O          27   .212
         BRTR            34   .263
```

BROCK, LOUIS CLARK (LOU)
B.JUNE 18,1939 EL DORADO,ARK.
```
1961 CHI N  O             4   .091
1962 CHI N  O           123   .263
1963 CHI N  O           148   .258
1964 CHI N  O            52   .251
     STL N  O           103   .348
1965 STL N  *O          155   .288
1966 STL N  *O          156   .285
1967 STL N  *O          159   .299
1968 STL N  *O          159   .279
1969 STL N  *O          157   .298
1970 STL N  *O          155   .304
1971 STL N  *O          157   .313
1972 STL N  *O          153   .311
1973 STL N  *O          160   .297
1974 STL N  *O          153   .306
1975 STL N  *O          136   .309
1976 STL N  *O          133   .301
1977 STL N  *O          141   .272
1978 STL N   O           92   .221
         BLTL          2496   .292
```

BROCKETT, LEWIS ALBERT (KING)
B.JULY 23,1880 BROWNSVILLE,ILL.
D.SEPT.19,1960 NORRIS CITY,ILL.
```
1907 NY  A  P            10   1- 3
1909 NY  A  P            26  10- 8
1911 NY  A  P       17   19   2- 4
         TR        53   55  13-15
```

BRODERICK, MATTHEW T.
B.DEC.2,1876 LATTIMER MINES,PA.
D.FEB.22,1941 FREELAND,PA.
```
1903 BRO N  2             2   .000
         TR
```

BRODIE, WALTER SCOTT (STEVE)
B.SEPT.11,1868 WARRENTON,VA.
D.OCT.30,1935 BALTIMORE,MD.
```
1890 BOS N  O           132   .295
1891 BOS N  O           134   .266
1892 STL N  2-O         154   .256
1893 STL N  O           107   .336
     BAL N  O            25   .372
1894 BAL N  O           129   .369
1895 BAL N  O           130   .305
1896 BAL N  O           132   .294
1897 PIT N  O           100   .298
1898 PIT N  O            42   .274
     BAL N  O            23   .286
1899 BAL N  O           138   .309
1901 BAL A  O            84   .310
1902 NY  N  O           109   .281
         BL           1439   .308
```

BRODOWSKI, RICHARD STANLEY (DICK)
B.JULY 26,1932 BAYONNE,N.J.
```
1952 BOS A  P            20   5- 5
1955 BOS A  P            16   1- 0
1956 WAS A  P             7   0- 3
1957 WAS A  P             6   0- 1
1958 CLE A  P             5   1- 0
1959 CLE A  P            18   2- 2
         BRTR            72   9-11
```

BROGLIO, ERNEST GILBERT (ERNIE)
B.AUG.27,1935 BERKELEY,CAL.
```
1959 STL N  P            35   7-12
1960 STL N  P            52  21- 9
1961 STL N  P            29   9-12
1962 STL N  P            34  12- 9
1963 STL N  P            39  18- 8
1964 STL N  P            11   3- 5
     CHI N  P            18   4- 7
1965 CHI N  P            26   1- 6
1966 CHI N  P            15   2- 6
         BRTR           259  77-74
```

BROHAMER, JOHN ANTHONY (JACK)
B.FEB.26,1950 MAYWOOD,CAL.
```
1972 CLE A  *2/3        136   .233
1973 CLE A  2           102   .220
1974 CLE A  2           101   .270
1975 CLE A  2            69   .244
1976 CHI A  *2/3        119   .251
1977 CHI A  3-2          59   .257
1978 BOS A  3-0-2        81   .234
         BLTR           667   .243
         BB 1972 (PART)
```

BRONDELL, KENNETH LEROY
B.OCT.17,1921 BRADSHAW,NEB.
```
1944 NY  N  P        7    8   0- 1
         BRTR
```

BRONKIE, HERMAN CHARLES (DUTCH)
B.MAR.31,1885 S.MANCHESTER,CONN
D.MAY 27,1968 SOMERS,CONN.
```
1910 CLE A  S-3           5   .181
1911 CLE A  3             2   .167
1912 CLE A  3             6   .000
1914 CHI N  3             1  1.000
1918 STL N  3            18   .221
1919 STL N  2-3          67   .255
1922 STL N  3            23   .281
         BRTR           122   .240
```

BRONSTAD, JAMES WARREN (JIM)
B.JUNE 22,1936 FT.WORTH,TEX.
```
1959 NY  A  P            16   0- 3
1963 WAS A  P       25   27   1- 3
1964 WAS A  P             4   0- 1
         BRTR      45   47   1- 7
```

BROOKENS, EDWARD DWAIN (IKE)
B.JAN.3,1949 CHAMBERSBURG,PA.
```
1975 DET A  /P            3   0- 0
         BRTR
```

BROOKS, HARRY F.
B.PHILADELPHIA,PA.
```
1886 MET AA P            1   0- 1
```

BROOKS, JONATHAN JOSEPH (MANDY)
(REAL NAME JONATHAN JOSEPH BROZEK)
B.AUG.16,1898 MILWAUKEE,WIS.
D.JUNE 17,1962 KIRKWOOD,MO.
```
1925 CHI N  O            90   .281
1926 CHI N  O            26   .186
         BRTR           116   .270
```

BROOKS, ROBERT (BOBBY)
B.NOV.1,1945 LOS ANGELES,CAL.
```
1969 OAK A  O            29   .241
1970 OAK A  /O            7   .333
1972 OAK A  O            15   .179
1973 CAL A  /O            4   .143
         BRTR            55   .231
```

BROSKIE, SIGMUND THEODORE
(SIG) OR (CHOPS)
B.MAR.23,1911 ISELIN,PA.
D.MAY 17,1975 CANTON,OHIO
```
1940 BOS N  C            11   .273
         BRTR
```

BROSNAN, JAMES PATRICK (JIM)
B.OCT.24,1929 CINCINNATI,O.
```
1954 CHI N  P            18   1- 0
1956 CHI N  P            30   5- 9
1957 CHI N  P            41   5- 5
1958 CHI N  P             8   3- 4
     STL N  P            33   8- 4
1959 STL N  P            20   1- 3
     CIN N  P            26   8- 3
1960 CIN N  P            57   7- 2
1961 CIN N  P            53  10- 4
1962 CIN N  P            48   4- 4
1963 CIN N  P             6   0- 1
     CHI A  P            45   3- 8
         BRTR           385  55-47
```

BROSSEAU, FRANKLIN LEE (FRANK)
B.JULY 31,1944 DRAYTON,N.D.
```
1969 PIT N  /P            2   0- 0
1971 PIT N  /P            1   0- 0
         BRTR             3   0- 0
```

BROTTEM, ANTON CHRISTIAN (TONY)
B.APR.30,1892 HALSTEAD,MINN.
D.AUG.5,1929 CHICAGO,ILL.
```
1916 STL N  C-O          26   .182
1918 STL N  1             2   .000
1921 WAS A  C             4   .147
     PIT N  C            30   .242
         BRTR            62   .218
```

BROUGHTON, CECIL CALVERT (CAL)
B.DEC.28,1860 MAGNOLIA,WIS.
D.MAR.15,1939 EVANSVILLE,WIS.
```
1883 CLE N  C             4   .167
1884 MIL U  C-O           9   .188
1885 STL AA C             3   .083
     MET AA C            12   .356
1888 DET N  C             1   .000
         BRTR            40   .257
```

BROUTHERS, ARTHUR H.
B.NOV.25,1882 MONTGOMERY,ALA.
D.SEPT.28,1959 CHARLESTON,S.C.
```
1906 PHI A  3            36   .208
         TR
```

BROTHERS, DENNIS JOSEPH
(DAN) OR (BIG DAN)
B.MAY 3,1858 SYLVAN LAKE,N.Y.
D.AUG.3,1932 E.ORANGE,N.J.
```
1879 TRO N  P-1      2   39   0- 2
                              .273
1880 TRO N  1             3   .154
1881 BUF N  1-O          65   .318
1882 BUF N  1            84   .367
1883 BRO N  P-1-3    2   97   0- 0
                              .371
1884 BUF N  1-3          90   .325
1885 BUF N  1            98   .358
1886 DET N  1           121   .370
1887 DET N  1           122   .419
1888 DET N  1           129   .306
1889 BOS N  1           126   .373
1890 BOS P  1           123   .345
1891 BOS AA 1           130   .352
1892 BRO N  1           152   .335
1893 BRO N  1            75   .348
1894 BAL N  1           123   .344
1895 BAL N  1             5   .261
1896 PHI N  1            24   .296
1904 NY  N  1             2   .000
         BLTL      4 1665   0- 2
                              .348
```

BROVIA, JOSEPH JOHN (JOE) OR (OX)
B.FEB.18,1922 DAVENPORT,CAL.
```
1955 CIN N  H            21   .111
         BLTR
```

BROWER, FRANK WILLARD (TURKEYFOOT)
B.MAR.26,1893 GAINESVILLE,VA.
D.NOV.20,1960 BALTIMORE,MD.
```
1920 WAS A  O            36   .311
1921 WAS A  O            83   .261
1922 WAS A  O           139   .293
1923 CLE A  O           126   .285
1924 CLE A  P-1-O    1   66   0- 0
                              .280
         BLTR      1  450   0- 0
                              .286
```

BROWER, LOUIS LESTER
B.JULY 1,1900 CLEVELAND,OHIO
```
1931 DET A  S            21   .161
         BRTR
```

BROWN, ALTON LEO (DEACON)
B.APR.16,1925 NORFOLK,VA.
```
1951 WAS A  P             7   0- 0
         BRTR
```

BROWN, CARROLL WILLIAM (BOARDWALK)
B.FEB.20,1887 WOODBURY,N.J.
D.FEB.8,1977 BURLINGTON,N.J.
```
1911 PHI A  P             2   0- 1
1912 PHI A  P            35  13-11
1913 PHI A  P            44  18-11
1914 PHI A  P            15   1- 6
     NY  A  P            20   5- 5
1915 NY  A  P       19   21   3- 5
         BRTR      135  137  40-39
```

BROWN, CHARLES E.
B.1878 BALTIMORE,MD.
```
1897 CLE N  P             4   1- 3
         TL
```

BROWN, CHARLES EDWARD (BUSTER)
B.AUG.31,1881 BOONE,IOWA
D.FEB.9,1914 SIOUX CITY,IOWA
```
1905 STL N  P            23   8-11
1906 STL N  P            32   8-16
1907 STL N  P             9   2- 7
     PHI N  P            21   8- 5
1908 PHI N  P             4   0- 0
1909 PHI N  P             7   0- 0
     BOS N  P            18   4- 8
1910 BOS N  P            46   9-23
1911 BOS N  P            42   8-18
1912 BOS N  P            31   4-15
1913 BOS N  P             2   0- 0
         BRTR           235  51-103
```

BROWN, CHARLES ROY (CURLY OR)LEFTY(
B.DEC.9,1888 SPRING HILL,KAN.
D.JUNE 10,1968 SPRING HILL,KAN.
```
1911 STL A  P             3   0- 2
1912 STL A  P            16   1- 3
1913 STL A  P             2   1- 1
1915 CIN N  P             9   0- 2
         BLTL            30   2- 8
```

YR CL LEA POS   GP   G   REC

BROWN, CLINTON HAROLD (CLINT)
B.JULY 8,1903 BLACKASH,PA.
D.DEC.31,1955 ROCKY RIVER,OHIO

YR	CL	LEA	POS	GP	G	REC
1928	CLE	A	P		2	0- 1
1929	CLE	A	P		3	0- 2
1930	CLE	A	P		35	11-13
1931	CLE	A	P		39	11-15
1932	CLE	A	P	37	39	15-12
1933	CLE	A	P	33	34	11-12
1934	CLE	A	P		17	4- 3
1935	CLE	A	P		23	4- 3
1936	CHI	A	P		38	6- 2
1937	CHI	A	P		53	7- 7
1938	CHI	A	P		8	1- 3
1939	CHI	A	P		61	11-10
1940	CHI	A	P		37	4- 6
1941	CLE	A	P		41	3- 3
1942	CLE	A	P		7	1- 1
	BLTR			434	437	89-93

BROWN, CURTIS
B.SEP.14,1945 SACRAMENTO,CAL.
| 1973 | MON | N | /O | | 1 | .000 |
| | BRTR | | | | | |

BROWN, DELOS HIGHT
B.OCT.4,1892 ANNA,ILL.
D.DEC.21,1964 CARBONDALE,ILL.
| 1914 | CHI | A | H | | 1 | .000 |
| | BRTR | | | | | |

BROWN, DRUMMOND NICHOLS
B.JAN.31,1885 TAFT,CAL.
D.JAN.24,1927 PARKVILLE,MO.
1913	BOS	N	C		15	.324
1914	KC	F	C		30	.207
1915	KC	F	C		77	.263
	BRTR				122	.242

BROWN, EDWARD P.
B.CHICAGO,ILL.
1882	STL	AA	P-2-O	1	17	0- 0
						.177
1884	TOL	AA	3		42	.174
	TR			1	59	0- 0
						.175

BROWN, EDWARD WILLIAM (EDDIE)
OR (GLASS ARM EDDIE)
B.JULY 17,1891 MILLIGAN,NEB.
D.SEPT.10,1956 VALLEJO,CAL.
1920	NY	N	O		3	.125
1921	NY	N	O		70	.281
1924	BRO	N	O		114	.308
1925	BRO	N	O		153	.306
1926	BOS	N	O		153	.328
1927	BOS	N	O		155	.306
1928	BOS	N	O		142	.268
	BRTR				790	.303

BROWN, EDWIN RANDOLPH (RANDY)
B.AUG.29,1944 LEESBURG,FLA.
1969	CAL	A	C/O		13	.160
1970	CAL	A	/C		5	.000
	BLTR				18	.138

BROWN, ELMER YOUNG (SHOOK)
B.MAR.25,1883 SOUTHPORT,IND.
D.JAN.23,1955 INDIANAPOLIS,IND.
1911	STL	A	P		5	2- 1
1912	STL	A	P		23	4- 8
1913	BRO	N	P		3	0- 0
1914	BRO	N	P		11	1- 2
1915	BRO	N	P		1	0- 0
	BLTR				43	7-11

BROWN, FRED HERBERT
B.APR.12,1879 OSSIPEE,N.H.
D.FEB.3,1955 SOMERSWORTH,N.H.
1901	BOS	N	O		7	.125
1902	BOS	N	O		1	.000
	BRTR				8	.111

BROWN, FREEMAN
B.JAN.31,1845 HUBBARDSTOWN,MASS
D.DEC.27,1916 WORCESTER,MASS.
NON-PLAYING MANAGER WOR[N] 1880-82

BROWN, HECTOR HAROLD
(HAL) OR (SKINNY)
B.DEC.11,1924 GREENSBORO,N.C.
1951	CHI	A	P	3	4	0- 0
1952	CHI	A	P	24	51	2- 3
1953	CHI	A	P		30	11- 6
1954	BOS	A	P		40	1- 8
1955	BOS	A	P		2	1- 0
	BAL	A	P	15	25	0- 4
1956	BAL	A	P	35	42	9- 7
1957	BAL	A	P	25	30	7- 8
1958	BAL	A	P-3	19	21	7- 5
						.148
1959	BAL	A	P		31	11- 9
1960	BAL	A	P		30	12- 5
1961	BAL	A	P		27	10- 6
1962	BAL	A	P		22	6- 4
	NY	A	P		2	0- 1
1963	HOU	N	P		26	5-11
1964	HOU	N	P		27	3-15
	BRTR			358	410	85-92
						.169

BROWN, ISAAC (IKE)
B.APR.13,1942 MEMPHIS,TENN.
1969	DET	A	2-3/O-S		70	.229
1970	DET	A	2/O-3		56	.287
1971	DET	A	1/O-2-3-S		59	.255
1972	DET	A	O-1/2-S-3		51	.250
1973	DET	A	1-O/3		42	.289
1974	DET	A	/3		2	.000
	BRTR				280	.256

BROWN, JACKIE GENE
B.MAY 31,1943 HOLDENVILLE,OKLA.
1970	WAS	A	P		24	2- 2
1971	WAS	A	P		14	3- 4
1973	TEX	A	P		25	5- 5
1974	TEX	A	P		35	13-12
1975	TEX	A	P		17	5- 5
	CLE	A	P		25	1- 2
1976	CLE	A	P		32	9-11
1977	MON	N	P		42	9-12
	BRTR				214	47-53

BROWN, JAMES DONALDSON
(DON) OR (MOOSE)
B.MAR.31,1897 LAUREL,IND.
1915	STL	N	O		1	.500
1916	PHI	A	O		14	.233
	BRTR				15	.244

BROWN, JAMES ROBERSON
B.APR.25,1910 JAMESVILLE,N.C.
D.DEC.29,1977 BATH,N.C.
1937	STL	N	2-S		138	.276
1938	STL	N	2-S-3		108	.301
1939	STL	N	2-S		147	.298
1940	STL	N	2-S-3		107	.280
1941	STL	N	2-O		132	.306
1942	STL	N	2-S-3		145	.256
1943	STL	N	2-S-3		34	.182
1946	PIT	N	2-S-3		79	.241
	BRTR				890	.279

BROWN, JAMES W. M.
B.DEC.12,1860 CLINTON CO.,PA.
D.APR.6,1908 WILLIAMSPORT,PA.
1884	ALT	U	P-O	11	21	2- 9
						.239
	NY	N	P		1	0- 1
	STP	U	P-1-O		6	1- 3
						.313
1886	ATH	AA	P		1	0- 1
				19	29	3-14
						.237

BROWN, JERALD RAY (JAKE)
B.MAR.3,1948 SUMRALL,MISS.
| 1975 | SF | N | O | | 41 | .209 |
| | BRTR | | | | | |

BROWN, JOHN J. (AD)
B.TRENTON,N.J.
| 1897 | BRO | N | P | | 2 | 0- 2 |

BROWN, JOHN LINDSAY
(LINDSAY) OR (RED)
B.JULY 22,1911 MASON,TEX.
D.JAN.1,1967 SAN ANTONIO,TEX.
| 1937 | BRO | N | S | | 48 | .270 |
| | BRTR | | | | | |

BROWN, JOPHERY CLIFFORD
B.JAN.22,1945 GRAMBLING,LA.
| 1968 | CHI | N | /P | | 1 | 0- 0 |
| | BLTR | | | | | |

BROWN, JOSEPH E.
B.APR.4,1859 WARREN,PA.
D.JUNE 28,1888 WARREN,PA.
1884	CHI	N	P-C-	7	15	3- 2
			1-O			.220
1885	BAL	AA	P-2	4	5	0- 4
						.158
				11	20	3- 6
						.205

BROWN, JOSEPH HENRY
B.JULY 3,1900 LITTLE ROCK,ARK.
D.MAR.7,1950 LOS ANGELES,CAL.
| 1927 | CHI | A | P | | 1 | 0- 0 |
| | BRTR | | | | | |

BROWN, LARRY LESLIE
B.MAR.1,1940 SHINNSTON,W.VA.
1963	CLE	A	2-S		74	.255
1964	CLE	A	2-S		115	.230
1965	CLE	A	S-2		124	.253
1966	CLE	A	S-2		105	.229
1967	CLE	A	*S		152	.227
1968	CLE	A	*S		154	.234
1969	CLE	A	*S-3/2		132	.239
1970	CLE	A	S-3-2		72	.258
1971	CLE	A	S		13	.220
	OAK	A	S-2-3		70	.196
1972	OAK	A	2/3		47	.183
1973	BAL	A	3/2		17	.250
1974	TEX	A	3/2-S		54	.197
	BRTR				1129	.233

BROWN, LEON
B.NOV.16,1949 SACRAMENTO,CAL.
| 1976 | NY | N | O | | 64 | .214 |
| | BBTR | | | | | |

BROWN, LEWIS J. (BLOWER)
B.FEB.1,1858 LEOMINSTER,MASS.
D.JAN.16,1889 BOSTON,MASS.
1877	BOS	N	C		45	.207
1878	BOS	N	C-1		58	.253
1878	PRO	N	P-C-	1	57	0- 0
			1-O			.315
1879	PRO	N	C-O		51	.262
	CHI	N	1		6	.273
1881	DET	N	1		27	.243
	PRO	N	1-O		18	.228
1883	BOS	N	1		14	.236
	LOU	AA	C-1		14	.197
1884	BOS	U	P-C-	1	84	1- 0
			1-O			.236
	BRTR			2	374	1- 0
						.252

BROWN, LLOYD ANDREW
(LLOYD) OR (GIMPY)
B.DEC.25,1904 BEEVILLE,TEX.
D.JAN.14,1974 OPALOCKA,FLA.
1925	BRO	N	P		17	0- 3
1928	WAS	A	P		27	4- 4
1929	WAS	A	P		40	8- 7
1930	WAS	A	P		38	16-12
1931	WAS	A	P		42	15-14
1932	WAS	A	P		46	15-12
1933	STL	A	P		8	1- 6
	BOS	A	P		33	8-11
1934	CLE	A	P		38	5-10
1935	CLE	A	P		42	8- 7
1936	CLE	A	P		24	8-10
1937	CLE	A	P		31	2- 6
1940	PHI	N	P		18	1- 3
	BLTL				404	91-105

BROWN, MACE STANLEY
B.MAY 21,1909 NORTH ENGLISH,IA.
1935	PIT	N	P		18	4- 1
1936	PIT	N	P		47	10-11
1937	PIT	N	P		50	7- 2
1938	PIT	N	P		51	15- 9
1939	PIT	N	P		47	9-13
1940	PIT	N	P		48	10- 9
1941	PIT	N	P		1	0- 0
	BRO	N	P		24	3- 2
1942	BOS	A	P		34	9- 3
1943	BOS	A	P		49	6- 6
1946	BOS	A	P		18	3- 1
	BRTR				387	76-57

BROWN, MORDECAI PETER CENTENNIAL
(THREE FINGER) OR (MINER)
B.OCT.19,1876 NYESVILLE,IND.
D.FEB.14,1948 TERRE HAUTE,IND.
1903	STL	N	P		26	9-13
1904	CHI	N	P		27	15- 9
1905	CHI	N	P		30	17- 9
1906	CHI	N	P		36	26- 6
1907	CHI	N	P	34	35	20- 6
1908	CHI	N	P		44	29- 9
1909	CHI	N	P		50	27- 9
1910	CHI	N	P		46	25-14
1911	CHI	N	P		53	21-11
1912	CHI	N	P	15	16	5- 6
1913	CIN	N	P		39	11-12
1914	STL	F	M-P		26	11- 5
	BRO	F	P		9	3- 6
1915	CHI	F	P		35	17- 8
1916	CHI	N	P		12	2- 3
	BBTR			482	484	238-126

BROWN, MYRL LINCOLN
B.OCT.10,1894 WAYNESBORO,PA.
| 1922 | PIT | N | P | | 7 | 3- 1 |
| | BRTR | | | | | |

BROWN, NORMAN
B.FEB.1,1919 EVERGREEN,N.C.

YR	CL	LEA	POS	GP	G	REC
1943	PHI	A	P		1	0- 0
1946	PHI	A	P		4	0- 1
	BBTR				5	0- 1

BROWN, OLIVER S.
B.1849 BROOKLYN,N.Y.
D.SEPT.23,1932 BROOKLYN,N.Y.

YR	CL	LEA	POS	GP	G	REC
1872	ATL	NA	O		4	.059
1874	BAL	NA	S		1	.000
1875	ATL	NA	1-O		3	.000
					8	.036

BROWN, OLLIE LEE
(OLLIE) OR (DOWNTOWN)
B.FEB.11,1944 TUSCALOOSA,ALA.

YR	CL	LEA	POS	GP	G	REC
1965	SF	N	/O		6	.200
1966	SF	N	*O		115	.233
1967	SF	N	*O		120	.267
1968	SF	N	O		40	.232
1969	SD	N	*O		151	.292
1970	SD	N	*O		139	.292
1971	SD	N	*O		145	.273
1972	SD	N	O		23	.171
	OAK	A	O		20	.241
	MIL	A	O/3		66	.279
1973	MIL	A	D/O		97	.280
1974	HOU	N	O		27	.217
	PHI	N	O		43	.242
1975	PHI	N	O		84	.303
1976	PHI	N	O		92	.254
1977	PHI	N	O		53	.243
	BRTR				1221	.265

BROWN, OSCAR LEE
B.FEB.8,1946 LONG BEACH,CAL.

YR	CL	LEA	POS	GP	G	REC
1969	ATL	N	/O		7	.250
1970	ATL	N	O		28	.383
1971	ATL	N	O		27	.209
1972	ATL	N	O		76	.226
1973	ATL	N	O		22	.207
	BRTR				160	.244

BROWN, PAUL DWAYNE
B.JUNE 10,1941 FT.SMITH,ARK.

YR	CL	LEA	POS	GP	G	REC
1961	PHI	N	P		5	0- 1
1962	PHI	N	P		23	0- 6
1963	PHI	N	P		6	0- 1
1968	PHI	N	/P		2	0- 0
	BRTR				36	0- 8

BROWN, PAUL PERCIVAL (RAY)
B.JAN.31,1889 CHICAGO,ILL.
D.MAY 29,1955 LOS ANGELES,CAL.

YR	CL	LEA	POS	GP	G	REC
1909	CHI	N	P		1	1- 0

BROWN, RICHARD ERNEST (DICK)
B.JAN.17,1935 SHINNSTON,W.VA.
D.APR.17,1970 BALTIMORE,MD.

YR	CL	LEA	POS	GP	G	REC
1957	CLE	A	C		34	.263
1958	CLE	A	C		68	.237
1959	CLE	A	C		48	.220
1960	CHI	A	C		16	.163
1961	DET	A	C		93	.266
1962	DET	A	C		134	.241
1963	BAL	A	C		59	.246
1964	BAL	A	C		88	.257
1965	BAL	A	C		96	.231
	BRTR				636	.244

BROWN, RICHARD P. (STUB)
B.AUG.3,1870 BALTIMORE,MD.
D.MAR.11,1948 BALTIMORE,MD.

YR	CL	LEA	POS	GP	G	REC
1893	BAL	N	P		11	0- 0
1894	BAL	N	P		9	4- 2
1897	CIN	N	P		2	0- 2
	TL				22	4- 4

BROWN, ROBERT M.
NON-PLAYING MANAGER LOU[AA]1889

BROWN, ROBERT M.
B.1891

YR	CL	LEA	POS	GP	G	REC
1914	BUF	F	P		15	0- 0
	BRTR					

BROWN, ROBERT MURRAY
B.APR.1,1911 DORCHESTER,MASS.

YR	CL	LEA	POS	GP	G	REC
1930	BOS	N	P		3	0- 0
1931	BOS	N	P		3	0- 1
1932	BOS	N	P		35	14- 7
1933	BOS	N	P		6	0- 0
1934	BOS	N	P		16	1- 3
1935	BOS	N	P	15	16	1- 8
1936	BOS	N	P		2	0- 2
	BRTR			80	81	16-21

BROWN, ROBERT WILLIAM (DOC)
B.OCT.25,1924 SEATTLE,WASH.

YR	CL	LEA	POS	GP	G	REC
1946	NY	A	S-3		7	.333
1947	NY	A	S-3-O		69	.300
1948	NY	A	2-S-3-O		113	.300
1949	NY	A	3-O		104	.283
1950	NY	A	3		95	.267
1951	NY	A	3		103	.268
1952	NY	A	3		29	.247
1954	NY	A	3		28	.217
	BLTR				548	.279

BROWN, SAMUEL WAKEFIELD
B.MAY 21,1878 WEBSTER,PA.
D.NOV.8,1931 TRAUGER,PA.

YR	CL	LEA	POS	GP	G	REC
1906	BOS	N	C		65	.208
1907	BOS	N	C		66	.190
	BRTR				131	.199

BROWN, THOMAS DALE (TOM)
B.AUG.10,1949 LAFAYETTE,LA.

YR	CL	LEA	POS	GP	G	REC
1978	SEA	A	/P		6	0- 0
	BRTR					

BROWN, THOMAS MICHAEL
(TOMMY) OR (BUCKSHOT)
B.DEC.6,1927 BROOKLYN,N.Y.

YR	CL	LEA	POS	GP	G	REC
1944	BRO	N	S		46	.164
1945	BRO	N	S-O		57	.245
1947	BRO	N	S-3-O		15	.235
1948	BRO	N	1-3		54	.241
1949	BRO	N	O		41	.303
1950	BRO	N	O		48	.291
1951	BRO	N	O		11	.160
	PHI	N	1-2-3-O		78	.219
1952	PHI	N	1-O		18	.160
	CHI	N	1-2-S		61	.320
1953	CHI	N	S-O		65	.196
	BRTR				494	.241

BROWN, THOMAS T.
B.SEP.21,1860 LIVERPOOL,ENGLAND
D.OCT.27,1927 WASHINGTON,D.C.

YR	CL	LEA	POS	GP	G	REC
1882	BAL	AA	P-O	2	46	0- 0
						.293
1883	COL	AA	P-S-O	2	97	.276
1884	COL	AA	P-O	2	107	1- 1
						.275
1885	PIT	AA	O		108	.304
1886	PIT	AA	O		114	.280
1887	PIT	N	O		46	.284
	IND	N	O		36	.223
1888	BOS	N	O		107	.247
1889	BOS	N	O		88	.232
1890	BOS	P	O		127	.277
1891	BOS	AA	O		137	.323
1892	LOU	N	O		153	.232
1893	LOU	N	O		121	.253
1894	LOU	N	O		130	.251
1895	STL	N	O		87	.226
	WAS	N	O		31	.227
1896	WAS	N	O		113	.299
1897	WAS	N	M-O		116	.287
1898	WAS	N	M-O		15	.164
	BLTR			6	1779	1- 3
						.269

BROWN, THOMAS WILLIAM (TOM)
B.DEC.12,1940 LAURELDALE,PA.

YR	CL	LEA	POS	GP	G	REC
1963	WAS	A	1-O		61	.147
	BBTL					

BROWN, WALTER GEORGE (JUMBO)
B.APR.30,1907 GREENE,R.I.
D.OCT.2,1966 FREEPORT,N.Y.

YR	CL	LEA	POS	GP	G	REC
1925	CHI	N	P		2	0- 0
1927	CLE	A	P		8	0- 2
1928	CLE	A	P		5	0- 1
1932	NY	A	P		19	5- 2
1933	NY	A	P		21	7- 5
1935	NY	A	P		20	6- 5
1936	NY	A	P		20	1- 4
1937	CIN	N	P		4	1- 0
	NY	N	P		4	1- 0
1938	NY	N	P		43	5- 3
1939	NY	N	P		31	4- 0
1940	NY	N	P		41	2- 4
1941	NY	N	P		31	1- 5
	BRTR				249	33-31

BROWN, WALTER IRVING
B.APR.23,1915 JAMESTOWN,N.Y.

YR	CL	LEA	POS	GP	G	REC
1947	STL	A	P		19	1- 0
	BRTR					

BROWN, WILLARD
(BIG BILL) OR (CALIFORNIA)
B.1866 SAN FRANCISCO,CAL.
D.DEC.20,1897 SAN FRANCISCO,CAL

YR	CL	LEA	POS	GP	G	REC
1887	NY	N	C		46	.261
1888	NY	N	C		17	.271
1889	NY	N	C		33	.259
1890	NY	P	C-1		59	.274
1891	PHI	N	1		112	.242
1893	BAL	N	1		7	.129
	LOU	N	1		111	.320
1894	LOU	N	1		13	.192
	STL	N	1		17	.257
					416	.268

BROWN, WILLARD JESSIE
B.JUNE 26,1915 SHREVEPORT,LA.

YR	CL	LEA	POS	GP	G	REC
1947	STL	A	O		21	.179
	BRTR					

BROWN, WILLIAM JAMES (GATES)
B.MAY 2,1939 CRESTLINE,O.

YR	CL	LEA	POS	GP	G	REC
1963	DET	A	O		55	.268
1964	DET	A	O		123	.272
1965	DET	A	O		96	.256
1966	DET	A	O		88	.266
1967	DET	A	O		51	.187
1968	DET	A	O/1		67	.370
1969	DET	A	O		60	.204
1970	DET	A	O		81	.226
1971	DET	A	O		82	.338
1972	DET	A	O		103	.230
1973	DET	A	*D/O		125	.236
1974	DET	A	O		73	.242
1975	DET	A	H		47	.171
	BLTR				1051	.257

BROWN, WILLIAM VERNA (BROWNIE)
B.JULY 8,1893 COLEMAN,TEX.
D.MAY 13,1965 LUBBOCK,TEX.

YR	CL	LEA	POS	GP	G	REC
1912	STL	A	O		9	.200
	BLTL					

BROWNE, BYRON ELLIS
B.DEC.27,1942 ST.JOSEPH,MO.

YR	CL	LEA	POS	GP	G	REC
1965	CHI	N	/O		4	.000
1966	CHI	N	*O		120	.243
1967	CHI	N	O		10	.158
1968	HOU	N	/O		10	.231
1969	STL	N	O		22	.226
1970	PHI	N	O		104	.248
1971	PHI	N	O		58	.206
1972	PHI	N	/O		21	.190
	BRTR				349	.236

BROWNE, GEORGE EDWARD
B.JAN.12,1876 RICHMOND,VA.
D.DEC.9,1920 HYDE PARK,N.Y.

YR	CL	LEA	POS	GP	G	REC
1901	PHI	N	O		8	.192
1902	PHI	N	O		68	.237
	NY	N	O		95	.348
1903	NY	N	O		141	.313
1904	NY	N	O		149	.283
1905	NY	N	O		127	.293
1906	NY	N	O		121	.264
1907	NY	N	O		121	.260
1908	BOS	N	O		138	.228
1909	CHI	N	O		12	.200
	WAS	A	O		103	.272
1910	WAS	A	O		7	.182
	CHI	A	O		30	.241
1911	BRO	N	O		7	.333
1912	PHI	N	H		6	.200
	BLTR				1093	.274

BROWN, EARL JAMES (SNITZ)
B.*1911 LOUISVILLE,KY.

YR	CL	LEA	POS	GP	G	REC
1935	PIT	N	1		9	.250
1936	PIT	N	1-O		8	.304
1937	PHI	N	1-O		105	.292
1938	PHI	N	1		21	.257
	BLTL				143	.283

BROWNE, PRENTICE ALMONT (PIDGE)
B.MAR.21,1929 PEEKSKILL,N.Y.
D.MAR.21,1929 PEEKSKILL,N.Y.

YR	CL	LEA	POS	GP	G	REC
1962	HOU	N	1		65	.210
	BLTL					

BROWNING, CALVIN DUANE
B.MAR.16,1938 BURNS FLAT,OKLA.

YR	CL	LEA	POS	GP	G	REC
1960	STL	N	P		1	0- 0
	BLTL					

BROWNING, FRANK (DUTCH)
B.OCT.29,1882 FALMOUTH,KY.
D.MAY 19,1948 SAN ANTONIO,TEX.

YR	CL	LEA	POS	GP	G	REC
1910	DET	A	P		11	2- 2
	BRTR					

BROWNING, LOUIS ROGERS
(PETE) OR (THE GLADIATOR)
B.JULY 17,1858 LOUISVILLE,KY.
D.SEPT.10,1905 LOUISVILLE,KY.

YR	CL	LEA	POS	GP	G	REC
1882	LOU	AA	2-S-3		69	.382
1883	LOU	AA	1-2-S-3-O		83	.349
1884	LOU	AA	P-1-3-O	1	105	0- 1
						.341
1885	LOU	AA	O		113	.367
1886	LOU	AA	O		112	.339
1887	LOU	AA	O		134	.471
1888	LOU	AA	O		99	.313
1889	LOU	AA	O		83	.253
1890	CLE	P	O		118	.391
1891	PIT	N	O		50	.287
	CIN	N	O		51	.362
1892	LOU	N	O		21	.260
	CIN	N	O		81	.300
1893	LOU	N	O		57	.371
1894	LOU	N	O		2	.143
	BRO	N	O		1	1.000
	BRTR			1	1179	0- 1
						.355

BROZEK, JONATHAN JOSEPH
[PLAYED UNDER NAME OF
JONATHAN JOSEPH BROOKS]

```
YR  CL LEA POS      GP   G    REC
```

BRUBAKER, BRUCE ELLSWORTH
B.DEC.29,1941 HARRISBURG,PA.
```
1967 LA  N /P         1        0- 0
1970 MIL A /P         1        0- 0
           BRTR       2        0- 0
```

BRUBAKER, WILBUR LEE (BILL)
B.NOV.7,1910 CLEVELAND,OHIO
```
1932 PIT N  3         7        .417
1933 PIT N  3         2        .000
1934 PIT N  3         3        .333
1935 PIT N  3         6        .000
1936 PIT N  3       145        .289
1937 PIT N  3       120        .254
1938 PIT N  3        45        .295
1939 PIT N  2-3     100        .282
1940 PIT N  1-5-3    38        .192
1943 BOS N  1-3      13        .421
           BRTR     479        .264
```

BRUCE, LOUIS R.
B.JAN.16,1877 ST.REGIS,N.Y.
D.FEB.9,1968 ILION,N.Y.
```
1904 PHI A  P-O       1   30   0- 0
                                .277
           BLTR
```

BRUCE, ROBERT JAMES (BOB)
B.MAY 16,1933 DETROIT,MICH.
```
1959 DET A  P         2        0- 1
1960 DET A  P        34        4- 7
1961 DET A  P        14        1- 2
1962 HOU N  P        32       10- 9
1963 HOU N  P    30  32        5- 9
1964 HOU N  P    35  37       15- 9
1965 HOU N  P        35        9-18
1966 HOU N  P        25        3-13
1967 ATL N  P        12        2- 3
           BRTR  219 223       49-71
```

BRUCKBAUER, FREDERICK JOHN
B.MAY 27,1938 NEW ULM,MINN.
```
1961 MIN A  P         1        0- 0
           BRTR
```

BRUCKER, EARLE FRANCIS JR.
B.AUG.29,1925 LOS ANGELES,CAL.
```
1948 PHI A  C         2        .167
           BLTR
```

BRUCKER, EARLE FRANCIS SR.
B.MAY 6,1901 ALBANY,N.Y.
```
1937 PHI A  C       102        .259
1938 PHI A  C        53        .374
1939 PHI A  C        62        .291
1940 PHI A  C        23        .196
1943 PHI A  H         1        .000
           BRTR     241        .290
```

BRUCKMILLER, ANDREW
D.JAN.1,1882 MC KEESPORT,PA.
D.JAN.12,1970 MC KEESPORT,PA.
```
1905 DET A  P         1        0- 0
           BRTR
```

BRUGGY, FRANK LEO
B.MAY 4,1891 ELIZABETH,N.J.
D.APR.5,1959 ELIZABETH,N.J.
```
1921 PHI N  C        96        .310
1922 PHI A  C        53        .279
1923 PHI A  C        54        .210
1924 PHI A  C        50        .265
1925 CIN N  C         6        .214
           BRTR     259        .277
```

BRUHERT, MICHAEL EDWIN (MIKE)
B.JUNE 24,1951 JAMAICA,N.Y.
```
1978 NY  N  P        27        4-11
           BRTR
```

BRUMLEY, TONY MIKE (MIKE)
B.JULY 10,1938 GRANITE,OKLA.
```
1964 WAS A  C       136        .244
1965 WAS A  C        79        .208
1966 WAS A /C         9        .111
           BLTR     224        .229
```

BRUNER, JACK RAYMOND
B.JULY 1,1924 WATERLOO,IOWA
```
1949 CHI A  P         4        1- 2
1950 CHI A  P         9        0- 0
     STL A  P        13        1- 2
           BLTL      26        2- 4
```

BRUNER, WALTER ROY
B.FEB.10,1917 CECILIA,KY.
```
1939 PHI N  P         4        0- 4
1940 PHI N  P         2        0- 0
1941 PHI N  P        13        0- 3
           BRTR      19        0- 7
```

BRUNET, GEORGE STUART
(GEORGE) OR (LEFTY)
B.JUNE 8,1935 HOUGHTON,MICH.
```
1956 KC  A  P         6        0- 0
1957 KC  A  P         4        0- 1
1959 KC  A  P         2        0- 0
1960 KC  A  P         3        0- 2
     MIL N  P        17        2- 0
1961 MIL N  P         5        0- 0
1962 HOU N  P        17        2- 4
1963 HOU N  P         5        0- 3
     BAL A  P        16        0- 1
1964 LA  A  P        10        2- 2
1965 CAL A  P        41        9-11
1966 CAL A  P        41       13-13
1967 CAL A  P        40       11-19
1968 CAL A  P        39       13-17
1969 CAL A  P        23        6- 7
     SEA A  P        12        2- 5
1970 WAS A  P        24        8- 6
     PIT N  P        12        1- 2
1971 STL N /P         7        0- 1
           BRTL     324       69-93
```

BRUNO, THOMAS MICHAEL (TOM)
B.JAN.26,1953 CHICAGO,ILL.
```
1976 KC  A  P        12        1- 0
1977 TOR A  P        12        0- 1
1978 STL N  P        18        4- 3
           BRTR      42        5- 4
```

BRUNSBERG, ARLO ADOLPH
B.AUG.15,1940 FERTILE,MINN.
```
1966 DET A /C         2        .333
           BLTR
```

BRUSH, ROBERT
B.MAR.8,1875 OSAGE,IOWA
D.APR.2,1944 SAN BERNADINO,CAL.
```
1907 BOS N  1         2        .000
```

BRUSSTAR, WARREN SCOTT
B.FEB.2,1952 OAKLAND,CAL.
```
1977 PHI N  P        46        7- 2
1978 PHI N  P        58        6- 3
           BRTR     104       13- 5
```

BRUTON, WILLIAM HARON (BILL)
B.DEC.22,1925 PANOLA,ALA.
```
1953 MIL N  O       151        .250
1954 MIL N  O       142        .284
1955 MIL N  O       149        .275
1956 MIL N  O       147        .272
1957 MIL N  O        79        .278
1958 MIL N  O       100        .280
1959 MIL N  O       133        .289
1960 MIL N  O       151        .286
1961 DET A  O       160        .257
1962 DET A  O       147        .278
1963 DET A  O       145        .256
1964 DET A  O       106        .277
           BLTR    1610        .273
```

BRUYETTE, EDWARD T.
B.AUG.31,1874 WANAWA,WIS.
```
1901 MIL A  O        28        .180
           TR
```

BRYAN, WILLIAM RONALD (BILLY)
B.DEC.4,1938 MORGAN,GA.
```
1961 KC  A  C         9        .158
1962 KC  A  C        25        .149
1963 KC  A  C        24        .169
1964 KC  A  C        93        .241
1965 KC  A  C       108        .252
1966 KC  A  C/1      32        .132
     NY  A  C/1      27        .217
1967 NY  A /C        16        .167
1968 WAS A  C        40        .204
           BLTR     374        .216
```

BRYANT, CLAIBORNE HENRY (CLAY)
B.NOV.16,1911 MADISON HEIGHTS,VA.
```
1935 CHI N  P         9   12   1- 2
1936 CHI N  P        26   32   1- 2
1937 CHI N  P        38   47   9- 3
1938 CHI N  P        44   50  19-11
1939 CHI N  P         4   28   2- 1
1940 CHI N  P         8   16   0- 1
           BRTR     129  185  32-20
```

BRYANT, DONALD RAY (DON)
B.JULY 13,1941 JASPER,FLA.
```
1966 HOU N  C        13        .308
1969 HOU N  C        31        .186
1970 HOU N  C        15        .208
           BRTR      59        .220
```

BRYANT, G.
```
1885 DET N  2         1        .000
```

BRYANT, RONALD RAYMOND (RON)
B.NOV.12,1947 REDLANDS,CAL.
```
1967 SF  N /P         1        0- 0
1969 SF  N  P        16        4- 3
1970 SF  N  P        34        5- 8
1971 SF  N  P        27        7-10
1972 SF  N  P        35       14- 7
1973 SF  N  P    41  42       24-12
1974 SF  N  P        41        3-15
1975 STL N  P        10        0- 1
           BBTL     205 206   57-56
```

BRYE, STEPHEN ROBERT (STEVE)
B.FEB.4,1949 ALAMEDA,CAL.
```
1970 MIN A /O         9        .182
1971 MIN A  O        28        .224
1972 MIN A  O       100        .241
1973 MIN A  O        92        .263
1974 MIN A *O       135        .283
1975 MIN A  O        86        .252
1976 MIN A  O        87        .264
1977 MIL A  O        94        .249
1978 PIT N  O        66        .235
           BRTR     697        .258
```

BRYNAN, CHARLES R.
B.PHILADELPHIA,PA.
```
1888 CHI N  P         3        2- 1
1891 BOS N  P         1        0- 0
           BRTR       4        2- 1
```

BUBSER, HAROLD FRED
B.SEPT.28,1895 CHICAGO,ILL.
```
1922 CHI A  H         3        .000
           BRTR
```

BUCHA, JOHN GEORGE
B.JAN.22,1925 ALLENTOWN,PA.
```
1948 STL N  C         2        .000
1950 STL N  C        22        .139
1953 DET A  C        60        .222
           BRTR      84        .205
```

BUCHANAN, JAMES FORREST
B.JULY 1,1876 CHATHAM HILL,VA.
D.JUNE 15,1949 RANDOLPH,NEB.
```
1905 STL A  P        22        7- 9
           BLTR
```

BUCHEK, GERALD PETER (JERRY)
B.MAY 9,1942 ST.LOUIS,MO.
```
1961 STL N  S        31        .133
1963 STL N  S         3        .250
1964 STL N  2-S-3    35        .200
1965 STL N  2-S/3    55        .247
1966 STL N  2-S/3   100        .236
1967 NY  N  2-3/S   124        .236
1968 NY  N  3-2/O    73        .182
           BRTR     421        .220
```

BUCHER, JAMES QUINTER
B.MAR.11,1911 MANASSAS,VA.
```
1934 BRO N  2        47        .226
1935 BRO N  2-3-O   123        .302
1936 BRO N  2-3-O   110        .251
1937 BRO N  2-3     125        .253
1938 STL N  2        17        .226
1944 BOS A  2-3      80        .274
1945 BOS A  2-3      52        .225
           BLTR     554        .265
```

BUCKENBERGER, ALBERT C.
B.JAN.31,1861 DETROIT,MICH.
D.JULY 1,1917 SYRACUSE,N.Y.
NON-PLATING MANAGER
COL[AA] 188.-90; PIT[N] 1892-94
STL[N] 1895 AND BOS[N] 1902-04

BUCKEYE, GARLAND MAIERS (GOB)
B.OCT.16,1897 HERON LAKE,MINN.
D.NOV.14,1975 STONE LAKE,WIS.
```
1918 WAS A  P         1        0- 0
1925 CLE A  P        30       13- 8
1926 CLE A  P        32        6- 9
1927 CLE A  P        35       10-17
1928 CLE A  P         9        1- 5
     NY  N  P         1        0- 0
           BBTL     108       30-39
```

BUCKINGHAM, EDWARD TAYLOR
B.MAY 12,1874 METUCHEN,N.J.
D.JULY 30,1942 BRIDGEPORT,CONN.
```
1895 WAS N  P         1        0- 1
```

BUCKLES, JESSE ROBERT
(JESS) OR (JIM)
B.MAY 20,1890 LA VERNE,CAL.
D.AUG.2,1975 WESTMINSTER,CAL.
```
1916 NY  A  P         2        0- 0
           BLTL
```

BUCKLEY, JOHN EDWARD
B.MAR.20,1870 MARLBORO,MASS.
D.MAY 3,1942 WESTBOROUGH,MASS.
```
1890 BUF P  P         4        1- 3
```

YR CL LEA POS / GP / G / REC

BUCKLEY, RICHARD D.
B.SEPT.21,1858 TROY,N.Y.
D.DEC.12,1929 PITTSBURGH,PA.

YR	CL	LEA	POS	GP	G	REC
1888	IND	N	C-3		71	.273
1889	IND	N	C		65	.258
1890	NY	N	C		70	.255
1891	NY	N	C		67	.211
1892	STL	N	C		106	.220
1893	STL	N	C		7	.057
1894	STL	N	C		28	.169
	PHI	N	C		39	.302
1895	PHI	N	C		29	.255
	TR				482	.243

BUCKNER, WILLIAM JOSEPH (BILL)
B.DEC.14,1949 VALLEJO,CAL.

YR	CL	LEA	POS	GP	G	REC
1969	LA	N	/H		1	.000
1970	LA	N	O/1		28	.191
1971	LA	N	O-1		108	.277
1972	LA	N	O-1		105	.319
1973	LA	N	1-0		140	.275
1974	LA	N	*O/1		145	.314
1975	LA	N	O		92	.243
1976	LA	N	*O/1		154	.301
1977	CHI	N	1		122	.284
1978	CHI	N	*1		117	.323
	BLTL				1012	.293

BUDASKA, MARK DAVID
B.DEC.27,1952 SHARON,PA.

YR	CL	LEA	POS	GP	G	REC
1978	OAK	A	/O		4	.250
	BBTL					

BUDD

YR	CL	LEA	POS	GP	G	REC
1890	CLE	P	O		1	.000

BUDDIN, DONALD THOMAS
B.MAY 5,1934 TURBEVILLE,S.C.

YR	CL	LEA	POS	GP	G	REC
1956	BOS	A	S		114	.239
1958	BOS	A	S		136	.237
1959	BOS	A	S		151	.241
1960	BOS	A	S		124	.245
1961	BOS	A	S		115	.263
1962	HOU	N	S-3		40	.163
	DET	A	2-S-3		31	.229
	BRTR				711	.241

BUDNICK, MICHAEL JOE
B.SEPT.15,1919 ASTORIA,ORE.

YR	CL	LEA	POS	GP	G	REC
1946	NY	N	P		35	2- 3
1947	NY	N	P		7	0- 0
	BRTR				42	2- 3

BUELOW, CHARLES JOHN
B.JAN.12,1877 DUBUQUE,IOWA
D.MAY 4,1951 DUBUQUE,IOWA

YR	CL	LEA	POS	GP	G	REC
1901	NY	N	3		19	.112
	BRTR					

BUELOW, FREDERICK WILLIAM (FRITZ)
B.FEB.13,1876 BERLIN,GERMANY
D.DEC.27,1933 DETROIT,MICH.

YR	CL	LEA	POS	GP	G	REC
1899	STL	N	C		7	.285
1900	STL	N	C		7	.235
1901	DET	A	C		69	.229
1902	DET	A	C-1		64	.223
1903	DET	A	C		90	.222
1904	DET	A	C		42	.115
	CLE	A	C		42	.180
1905	CLE	A	C		74	.174
1906	CLE	A	C		34	.163
1907	STL	A	C		26	.147
	BRTR				455	.182

BUES, ARTHUR FREDERICK
B.MAR.3,1888 MILWAUKEE,WIS.
D.NOV.7,1954 WHITEFISH BAY,WIS.

YR	CL	LEA	POS	GP	G	REC
1913	BOS	N	3		2	.000
1914	CHI	N	2-3		14	.227
	BRTR				16	.222

BUFFINTON, CHARLES G.
B.JUNE 14,1861 FALL RIVER,MASS.
D.SEPT.23,1907 FALL RIVER,MASS.

YR	CL	LEA	POS	GP	G	REC
1882	BOS	N	P-1-O	6	15	2- 3
						.250
1883	BOS	N	P-1-O	37	86	24-13
						.237
1884	BOS	N	P-1-O	65	84	47-14
						.263
1885	BOS	N	P-1-O	50	82	23-27
						.239
1886	BOS	N	P-1	17	44	7-10
						.289
1887	PHI	N	P-O	38	66	21-17
						.296
1888	PHI	N	P		44	28-15
1889	PHI	N	P		43	26-17
1890	PHI	N	M-P		41	19-13
1891	BOS	AA	P	46	56	27- 9
1892	BAL	N	P		13	5- 8
	BRTR			400	574	229-146
						.253

BUFORD, DONALD ALVIN (DON)
B.FEB.2,1937 LINDEN,TEX.

YR	CL	LEA	POS	GP	G	REC
1963	CHI	A	2-3		12	.286
1964	CHI	A	2-3		135	.262
1965	CHI	A	*2-3		155	.283
1966	CHI	A	*3-2-0		163	.244
1967	CHI	A	*3-2/O		156	.241
1968	BAL	A	O-2/3		130	.282
1969	BAL	A	*O-2/3		144	.291
1970	BAL	A	*O/2-3		144	.272
1971	BAL	A	*O		122	.290
1972	BAL	A	*O		125	.206
	BBTR				1286	.264

BUHL, ROBERT RAY (BOB)
B.AUG.12,1928 SAGINAW,MICH.

YR	CL	LEA	POS	GP	G	REC
1953	MIL	N	P		30	13- 8
1954	MIL	N	P		31	2- 7
1955	MIL	N	P		38	13-11
1956	MIL	N	P		38	18- 8
1957	MIL	N	P		34	18- 7
1958	MIL	N	P		11	5- 2
1959	MIL	N	P		31	15- 9
1960	MIL	N	P		36	16- 9
1961	MIL	N	P		32	9-10
1962	MIL	N	P		1	0- 1
	CHI	N	P		34	12-13
1963	CHI	N	P		37	11-14
1964	CHI	N	P		36	15-14
1965	CHI	N	P		32	13-11
1966	CHI	N	/P		1	0- 0
	PHI	N	P		32	6- 8
1967	PHI	N	/P		3	0- 0
	BRTR				457	166-132
	BB 1958-60, 66					

BUKER, CYRIL OWEN
B.FEB.5,1919 GREENWOOD,WIS.

YR	CL	LEA	POS	GP	G	REC
1945	BRO	N	P		42	7- 2
	BLTR					

BUKER, HARRY L. (HAPPY)

YR	CL	LEA	POS	GP	G	REC
1884	DET	N	S-O		30	.136

BULLARD, GEORGE DONALD (CURLY)
B.OCT.24,1928 LYNN,MASS.

YR	CL	LEA	POS	GP	G	REC
1954	DET	A	S		4	.000
	BRTR					

BULLING, TERRY CHARLES
B.DEC.15,1952 LYNWOOD,CAL.

YR	CL	LEA	POS	GP	G	REC
1977	MIN	N	C		15	.156
	BRTR					

BULLAS, SIMEON EDWARD (SIM)
B.APR.10,1861 CLEVELAND,OHIO
D.JAN.14,1908 CLEVELAND,OHIO

YR	CL	LEA	POS	GP	G	REC
1884	TOL	AA	C-O		13	.067

BULLOCK, JAMES LEONARD
B.JAN.13,1845 BRISTOL,R.I.
D.AUG.12,1912
NON-PLAYING MANAGER PRO[N] 1880-81

BULLOCK, MALTON JOSEPH (RED)
B.OCT.12,1912 BILOXI,MISS.

YR	CL	LEA	POS	GP	G	REC
1936	PHI	A	P		12	0- 2
	BLTL					

BUMBRY, ALONZA BENJAMIN (AL)
B.APR.21,1947 FREDERICKSBURG,VA.

YR	CL	LEA	POS	GP	G	REC
1972	BAL	A	/O		9	.364
1973	BAL	A	O		110	.337
1974	BAL	A	O		94	.233
1975	BAL	A	O-O/3		114	.269
1976	BAL	A	*O-O		133	.251
1977	BAL	A	*O		133	.317
1978	BAL	A	O		33	.237
	BLTR				626	.283

BUNCE, JOSHUA
B.BROOKLYN,N.Y.

YR	CL	LEA	POS	GP	G	REC
1877	HAR	N	O		1	.000

BUNKER, WALLACE EDWARD (WALLY)
B.JAN.25,1945 SEATTLE,WASH.

YR	CL	LEA	POS	GP	G	REC
1963	BAL	A	P		1	0- 1
1964	BAL	A	P		29	19- 5
1965	BAL	A	P		34	10- 8
1966	BAL	A	P	29	30	10- 6
1967	BAL	A	P		29	3- 7
1968	BAL	A	P		18	2- 0
1969	KC	A	P		35	12-11
1970	KC	A	P		24	2-11
1971	KC	A	/P		7	2- 3
	BRTR			206	207	60-52

BUNNING, JAMES PAUL DAVID (JIM)
B.OCT.23,1931 SOUTHGATE,KY.

YR	CL	LEA	POS	GP	G	REC
1955	DET	A	P		15	3- 5
1956	DET	A	P		15	5- 1
1957	DET	A	P		45	20- 8
1958	DET	A	P	35	36	14-12
1959	DET	A	P		40	17-13
1960	DET	A	P	36	38	11-14
1961	DET	A	P		38	17-11
1962	DET	A	P	41	43	19-10
1963	DET	A	P	39	41	12-13
1964	PHI	N	P		41	19- 8
1965	PHI	N	P		39	19- 9
1966	PHI	N	P		43	19-14
1967	PHI	N	P		40	17-15
1968	PIT	N	P		27	4-14
1969	PIT	N	P		25	10- 9
	LA	N	/P		9	3- 1
1970	PHI	N	P	34	35	10-15
1971	PHI	N	P	29	31	5-12
	BRTR			591	601	224-184

BURBACH, WILLIAM DAVID (BILL)
B.AUG.22,1947 DICKEYVILLE,WIS.

YR	CL	LEA	POS	GP	G	REC
1969	NY	A	P		31	6- 8
1970	NY	A	/P		4	0- 2
1971	NY	A	/P		2	0- 1
	BRTR				37	6-11

BURBRINK, NELSON EDWARD
B.DEC.28,1921 CINCINNATI,OHIO

YR	CL	LEA	POS	GP	G	REC
1955	STL	N	C		58	.276
	BRTR					

BURCH, ALBERT WILLIAM
B.OCT.7,1883 ALBANY,N.Y.
D.OCT.5,1926 BROOKLYN,N.Y.

YR	CL	LEA	POS	GP	G	REC
1906	STL	N	O		91	.266
1907	STL	N	O		48	.227
	BRO	N	O		36	.292
1908	BRO	N	O		116	.243
1909	BRO	N	O		152	.271
1910	BRO	N	O		83	.236
1911	BRO	N	O		46	.228
	BLTR				572	.254

BURCH, ERNEST W.
B.1858 DEKALB CO.,ILL.

YR	CL	LEA	POS	GP	G	REC
1884	CLE	N	O		31	.201
1886	BRO	AA	O		114	.253
1887	BRO	AA	O		48	.400
	BL				193	.285

BURCHART, LARRY WAYNE
B.FEB.8,1940 TULSA,OKLA.

YR	CL	LEA	POS	GP	G	REC
1969	CLE	A	P		29	0- 2
	BRTR					

BURCHELL, FREDERICK DUFF
B.JULY 14,1879 PERTH AMBOY,N.J.
D.NOV.20,1951 JORDAN,N.Y.

YR	CL	LEA	POS	GP	G	REC
1903	PHI	N	P		6	0- 3
1907	BOS	A	P		2	0- 1
1908	BOS	A	P	31	32	10- 8
1909	BOS	A	P		10	3- 3
	BRTL				50	13-15

BURDA, EDWARD ROBERT (BOB)
B.JULY 16,1938 ST.LOUIS,MO.

YR	CL	LEA	POS	GP	G	REC
1962	STL	N	O		7	.071
1965	SF	N	1/O		31	.111
1966	SF	N	/1-O		37	.163
1969	SF	N	1-O		97	.230
1970	SF	N	/1-O		28	.261
	MIL	A	O/1		78	.248
1971	STL	N	1/O		65	.296
1972	BOS	A	1/O		45	.104
	BLTL				388	.224

BURDETTE, FREDDIE THOMASON
B.SEP.15,1936 MOULTRIE,GA.

YR	CL	LEA	POS	GP	G	REC
1962	CHI	N	P		8	0- 0
1963	CHI	N	P		4	0- 0
1964	CHI	N	P		18	1- 0
	BRTR				30	1- 0

YR CL LEA POS GP G REC

BURDETTE, SELVA LEWIS (LEW)
B.NOV.22,1926 NITRO,W.VA.
1950 NY A P 2 0- 0
1951 BOS N P 3 0- 0
1952 BOS N P 45 6-11
1953 MIL N P 46 15- 5
1954 MIL N P 38 39 15-14
1955 MIL N P 42 45 13- 8
1956 MIL N P 39 45 19-10
1957 MIL N P 37 41 17- 9
1958 MIL N P 40 47 20-10
1959 MIL N P 41 52 21-15
1960 MIL N P 45 46 19-13
1961 MIL N P 40 42 18-11
1962 MIL N P 37 39 10- 9
1963 MIL N P 15 17 6- 5
STL N P 21 3- 8
1964 STL N P 8 1- 0
CHI N P 28 9- 9
1965 CHI N /P 7 8 0- 2
PHI N P 19 3- 3
1966 CAL A P 54 7- 2
1967 CAL A P 19 1- 0
BRTR 626 666 203-144

BURDICK, WILLIAM B.
B.1862 JANESVILLE,WIS.
1888 IND N P 21 10-10
1889 IND N P 9 0- 3
BRTR 30 10-13

BURDOCK, JOHN JOSEPH (BLACK JACK)
B.1851 BROOKLYN,N.Y.
D.NOV.28,1931 BROOKLYN,N.Y.
1872 ATL NA C-2-S 35 .250
1873 ATL NA C-2 55 -
1874 MUT NA 3 61 -
1875 HAR NA 2-3 74 -
1876 HAR N 2 69 .248
1877 HAR N 2-3 58 .260
1878 BOS N 2 60 .260
1879 BOS N 2 84 .240
1880 BOS N 2 84 .256
1881 BOS N 2-S 73 .237
1882 BOS N 2 82 .239
1883 BOS N M-2 96 .330
1884 BOS N 2 84 .267
1885 BOS N 2 45 .142
1886 BOS N 2 59 .217
1887 BOS N 2 64 .305
1888 BOS N 2 21 .202
BRO AA 2 69 .125
1891 BRO N 2 3 .083
BRTR 1176 -

BURG, JOSEPH PETER (PETE)
B.JUNE 4,1882 CHICAGO,ILL.
D.APR.28,1969 JOLIET,ILL.
1910 BOS N S-3 13 .348
TR

BURGESS, FORREST HARRILL (SMOKY)
B.FEB.6,1927 CAROLEEN,N.C.
1949 CHI N C 46 .268
1951 CHI N C 94 .251
1952 PHI N C 110 .296
1953 PHI N C 102 .292
1954 PHI N C 108 .368
1955 PHI N C 7 .190
CIN N C 116 .306
1956 CIN N C 90 .275
1957 CIN N C 90 .283
1958 CIN N C 99 .283
1959 PIT N C 114 .297
1960 PIT N C 110 .294
1961 PIT N C 100 .303
1962 PIT N C 103 .328
1963 PIT N C 91 .280
1964 PIT N C 68 .246
CHI A H 7 .200
1965 CHI A /C 80 .286
1966 CHI A /C 79 .313
1967 CHI A H 77 .133
BLTR 1691 .295

BURGESS, THOMAS ROLAND
B.SEPT.1,1927 LONDON,ONT.,CAN.
1954 STL N O 17 .048
1962 LA A 1-O 87 .196
BLTL 104 .177

BURGMEIER, THOMAS HENRY (TOM)
B.AUG.2,1943 ST.PAUL,MINN.
1968 CAL A P/O 56 71 1- 4
.000
1969 KC A P/O 31 47 3- 1
.167
1970 KC A P 41 42 6- 6
1971 KC A P 67 68 9- 7
1972 KC A P 51 6- 2
1973 KC A /P 6 0- 0
1974 MIN A P 50 51 5- 3
1975 MIN A P 46 47 5- 8
1976 MIN A P 57 8- 1
1977 MIN A P 61 6- 4
1978 BOS A P 35 2- 1
BLTL 501 536 51-37
.212

BURGO, WILLIAM ROSS
B.NOV.5,1919 JOHNSTOWN,PA.
1943 PHI A O 17 .371
1944 PHI A O 27 .239
BRTR 44 .297

BURICH, WILLIAM MAX
B.MAY 29,1918 CALUMET,MICH.
1942 PHI N S-3 25 .288
1946 PHI N 3 2 .000
BRTR 27 .284

BURK, CHARLES SANFORD (SANDY)
B.APR.22,1887 COLUMBUS,OHIO
D.OCT.11,1934 BROOKLYN,N.Y.
1910 BRO N P 4 0- 3
1911 BRO N P 13 1- 3
1912 BRO N P 2 0- 0
STL N P 12 1- 3
1913 STL N P 19 0- 2
1915 PIT F P 2 0- 0
BRTR 52 2-11

BURK, MACK EDWIN
B.APR.21,1935 NACOGDOCHES,TEX.
1956 PHI N C 15 1.000
1958 PHI N H 1 .000
BRTR 16 .500

BURKAM, CHAUNCEY DE PEW (CHRIS)
B.OCT.13,1892 BENTON HARBOR,MICH.
D.MAY 9,1964 KALAMAZOO,MICH.
1915 STL A H 1 .000
BLTR

BURKART, ELMER ROBERT (SWEDE)
B.FEB.1,1917 TORRESDALE,PA.
1936 PHI N P 2 0- 0
1937 PHI N P 7 0- 0
1938 PHI N P 2 0- 1
1939 PHI N P 5 1- 0
BRTR 16 1- 1

BURKE, DANIEL L.
B.MAR.1869 WHITMAN,MASS.
D.MAR.20,1933 TAUNTON,MASS.
1890 ROC AA O 30 .286
SYR AA C 9 .000
1892 BOS N C 1 .000
40 .204

BURKE, EDWARD D.
B.OCT.6,1866 NORTHUMBERLAND,PA.
D.NOV.26,1907 UTICA,N.Y.
1890 PHI N O 100 .280
PIT N O 32 .225
1891 MIL AA O 34 .224
1892 CIN N 2-O 14 .139
NY N 2-O 83 .266
1893 NY N O 135 .289
1894 NY N O 138 .299
1895 NY N O 39 .256
CIN N O 56 .279
1896 CIN N O 122 .342
1897 CIN N O 94 .269
BRTR 847 .284

BURKE, FRANK ALOYSIUS
B.FEB.16,1880 CARBON,CO.,PA.
D.SEPT.17,1946 LOS ANGELES,CAL.
1906 NY N O 8 .222
1907 BOS N O 36 .178
TR 44 .181

BURKE, GLENN LAWRENCE
B.NOV.16,1952 OAKLAND,CAL.
1976 LA N O 25 .239
1977 LA N O 83 .254
1978 LA N O 16 .211
OAK A O/1 78 .235
BRTR 202 .242

BURKE, JAMES TIMOTHY (SUNSET JIMMY)
B.OCT.12,1874 ST.LOUIS,MO.
D.MAR.26,1942 ST.LOUIS,MO.
1898 CLE N 3 13 .111
1899 STL N 2 2 .333
1901 MIL A S-3 64 .207
CHI A 3 41 .248
PIT N 3 34 .211
1902 PIT N 2-S-3-O 55 .296
1903 STL N 2-3 113 .285
1904 STL N 3 118 .227
1905 STL N M-3 122 .225
BRTR 562 .243
NON-PLAYING MANAGER STL[A] 1918-20

BURKE, JOHN PATRICK
B.JAN.27,1877 HAZELTON,PA.
D.AUG.4,1950 JERSEY CITY,N.J.
1902 NY N P-O 2 4 0- 1
.153
BRTR

BURKE, JOSEPH M.
B.CINCINNATI,OHIO
D.DEC.29,1896
1890 STL AA 3 2 .571
1891 CIN AA 2 1 .250
3 .455

BURKE, LEO PATRICK
B.MAY 6,1934 HAGERSTOWN,MD.
1958 BAL A 3-O 7 .455
1959 BAL A 2-3 5 .200
1961 LA A H 6 .000
1962 LA A S-3-O 19 .266
1963 STL N 3-O 30 .204
CHI N 1-2 27 .184
1964 CHI N C-1-2-3-O 59 .262
1965 CHI N /C-O 12 .200
BRTR 165 .239

BURKE, LESLIE KINGSTON (BUCK)
B.DEC.18,1902 LYNN,MASS.
D.MAY 6,1975 DANVERS,MASS.
1923 DET A 2-3 9 .090
1924 DET A 2 72 .253
1925 DET A 2 77 .289
1926 DET A 2 38 .227
BLTR 196 .258

BURKE, MICHAEL E.
B.CINCINNATI,OHIO
D.JUNE 6,1889
1879 CIN N S-3-O 29 .222
BRTR

BURKE, PATRICK EDWARD
B.MAY 13,1901 ST.LOUIS,MO.
D.JULY 7,1965 ST.LOUIS,MO.
1924 STL A 3 1 .000
BRTR

BURKE, ROBERT JAMES
B.JAN.23,1907 JOLIET,ILL.
D.FEB.8,1971 JOLIET,ILL.
1927 WAS A P 36 3- 2
1928 WAS A P 26 2- 4
1929 WAS A P 37 6- 8
1930 WAS A P 24 3- 4
1931 WAS A P 30 8- 3
1932 WAS A P 22 23 3- 6
1933 WAS A P 25 4- 3
1934 WAS A P 37 41 8- 8
1935 WAS A P 15 16 1- 8
1937 PHI N P 2 0- 0
BLTL 254 260 38-46

BURKE, STEVEN MICHAEL (STEVE)
B.MAR.5,1955 STOCKTON,CAL.
1977 SEA A /P 6 0- 1
1978 SEA A P 18 0- 1
BBTR 24 0- 2

BURKE, WALTER R.
B.CALIFORNIA
D.MAR.3,1911 MEMPHIS,TENN.
1882 BUF N P-O 1 0- 1
.000
1883 BUF N P-O 1 0- 0
.200
1884 BOS U P-O 39 45 19-15
.212
1887 DET N P 2 0- 1
43 49 19-17
.209

BURKE, WILLIAM IGNATIUS
B.JULY 11,1889 CLINTON,MASS.
D.FEB.9,1967 WORCESTER,MASS.
1910 BOS N P 19 20 1- 0
1911 BOS N P 2 0- 1
BLTL 21 22 1- 1

BURKETT, JESSE CAIL (CRAB)
B.DEC.4,1868 WHEELING,W.VA.
D.MAY 27,1953 WORCESTER,MASS.
1890 NY N P-O 14 101 3-11
.306
1891 CLE N O 40 .271
1892 CLE N O 145 .277
1893 CLE N O 124 .372
1894 CLE N O 124 .357
1895 CLE N O 132 .423
1896 CLE N O 133 .410
1897 CLE N O 128 .383
1898 CLE N O 148 .345
1899 STL N O 138 .402
1900 STL N O 142 .360
1901 STL N O 142 .382
1902 STL A P-S- 1 137 0- 1
3-O .306
1903 STL A O 133 .296
1904 STL A O 147 .273
1905 BOS A O 149 .257
BLTL 15 2063 3-12
.342

BURKHARDT, KENNETH WILLIAM
[PLAYED UNDER NAME OF
KENNETH WILLIAM BURKHART]

YR	CL	LEA	POS	GP	G	REC

BURKHART, KENNETH WILLIAM (KEN)
[REAL NAME
KENNETH WILLIAM BURKHARDT]
B.NOV.18,1916 KNOXVILLE,TENN.

1945	STL	N	P		42	18- 8
1946	STL	N	P		25	6- 3
1947	STL	N	P		34	3- 6
1948	STL	N	P	20	21	0- 0
	CIN	N	P		16	0- 3
1949	CIN	N	P		11	0- 0
		BRTR		148	149	27-20

**BURLESON, RICHARD PAUL
(RICK) OR (ROOSTER)**
B.APR.29,1951 LYNWOOD,CAL.

1974	BOS	A	S-2/3		114	.284
1975	BOS	A	*S		158	.252
1976	BOS	A	*S		152	.291
1977	BOS	A	*S		154	.293
1978	BOS	A	*S		145	.248
		BRTR			723	.272

BURNETT, HERCULES 4.
B.AUG.13,1869 LOUISVILLE,KY.

1888	LOU	AA	O		1	.000
1895	LOU	N	O		5	.411
					6	.333

BURNETT, JOHN HENDERSON
B.NOV.1,1904 BARTOW,FLA.
D.AUG.13,1959 TAMPA,FLA.

1927	CLE	A	2		17	.000
1928	CLE	A	S		3	.500
1929	CLE	A	S		19	.152
1930	CLE	A	S-3		54	.312
1931	CLE	A	2-S-3		111	.300
1932	CLE	A	2-S		129	.297
1933	CLE	A	2-S-3		83	.272
1934	CLE	A	3-S-0		72	.293
1935	STL	A	2-S-3		70	.223
		BLTR			558	.283

BURNETT, JOHN P.

| 1907 | STL | N | O | | 59 | .238 |

BURNETTE, WALLACE HARPER
B.JUNE 26,1929 BLAIRS,VA.

1956	KC	A	P		18	6- 8
1957	KC	A	P		38	7-11
1958	KC	A	P		12	1- 1
		BRTR			68	14-20

BURNHAM, GEORGE WALTER (WATCH)
B.MAY 20,1860 ALBION,MICH.
D.NOV.18,1902 DETROIT,MICH.
NON-PLAYING MANAGER IND[N] 1887

BURNS, DENNIS
B.MAY 24,1898 TIFF CITY,MO.
D.MAY 21,1969 TULSA,OKLA.

1923	PHI	A	P		3	2- 1
1924	PHI	A	P		37	6- 8
		BRTR			40	8- 9

BURNS, EDWARD JAMES
B.OCT.31,1888 SAN FRANCISCO,CAL
D.JUNE 1,1942 MONTEREY,CAL.

1912	STL	N	C		1	.000
1913	PHI	N	C		17	.260
1914	PHI	N	C		70	.259
1915	PHI	N	C		67	.241
1916	PHI	N	C		78	.233
1917	PHI	N	C		20	.204
1918	PHI	N	C		68	.207
		BRTR			321	.229

BURNS, GEORGE HENRY (TIOGA GEORGE)
B.JAN.31,1893 NILES,OHIO
D.JAN.7,1978 KIRKLAND,WASH.

1914	DET	A	1		137	.291
1915	DET	A	1		105	.253
1916	DET	A	1		135	.286
1917	DET	A	1		119	.226
1918	PHI	A	1		130	.352
1919	PHI	A	1-0		126	.296
1920	PHI	A	1		21	.259
	CLE	A	1-0		45	.242
1921	CLE	A	1		84	.361
1922	BOS	A	1		147	.306
1923	BOS	A	1		146	.328
1924	CLE	A	1		129	.310
1925	CLE	A	1		127	.336
1926	CLE	A	1		151	.358
1927	CLE	A	1		140	.319
1928	CLE	A	1		82	.249
	NY	A	1		4	.500
1929	NY	A	1		9	.000
	PHI	A	1		29	.265
		BRTR			1866	.307

BURNS, GEORGE JOSEPH
B.NOV.24,1889 UTICA,N.Y.
D.AUG.15,1966 GLOVERSVILLE,N.Y.

1911	NY	N	O		6	.059
1912	NY	N	O		29	.294
1913	NY	N	O		150	.286
1914	NY	N	O		154	.303
1915	NY	N	O		155	.272
1916	NY	N	O		155	.279
1917	NY	N	O		152	.302
1918	NY	N	O		119	.290
1919	NY	N	O		139	.303
1920	NY	N	O		154	.287
1921	NY	N	O		149	.299
1922	CIN	N	O		156	.285
1923	CIN	N	O		154	.274
1924	CIN	N	O		93	.256
1925	PHI	N	O		88	.292
		BRTR			1853	.287

BURNS, JAMES (FARMER) OR (SLAB)
B.ASHTABULA,OHIO

| 1901 | STL | N | P | | 1 | 0- 0 |
| | | TR | | | | |

BURNS, JAMES M.
B.QUINCY,ILL.

1888	KC	AA	O		19	.273
1889	KC	AA	O		133	.303
1891	WAS	AA	O		20	.313
					168	.303

BURNS, JOHN IRVING (JACK) OR (SLUG)
B.AUG.31,1907 CAMBRIDGE,MASS.
D.APR.18,1975 BRIGHTON,MASS.

1930	STL	A	1		8	.300
1931	STL	A	1		144	.260
1932	STL	A	1		150	.305
1933	STL	A	1		144	.288
1934	STL	A	1		154	.257
1935	STL	A	1		143	.286
1936	STL	A	1		9	.214
	DET	A	1		138	.283
		BLTL			890	.280

BURNS, JOHN JOSEPH (JACK)
B.MAY 13,1877 MOOSIC,PA.
D.JUNE 24,1957 PLEASURE BEACH,CONN.

1903	DET	A	2		10	.256
1904	DET	A	2		4	.125
		BRTR			14	.211

BURNS, JOSEPH FRANCIS
B.MAR.26,1889 IPSWICH,MASS.

1910	CIN	N	H		1	1.000
1913	DET	A	O		4	.309
		BLTL			5	.357

BURNS, JOSEPH FRANCIS
B.FEB.25,1900 TRENTON,N.J.

| 1924 | PHI | A | C | | 8 | .105 |
| | | BRTR | | | | |

BURNS, JOSEPH JAMES
B.JUNE 17,1916 BRYN MAWR,PA.
D.JUNE 24,1974 BRYN MAWR,PA.

1943	BOS	N	3-0		52	.208
1944	PHI	A	2-3		28	.240
1945	PHI	A	1-3-0		31	.256
		BRTR			111	.230

BURNS, PATRICK

1884	BAL	AA	1		6	.154
	BAL	U	1		1	.500
					7	.200

BURNS, RICHARD SIMON
B.DEC.26,1863 HOLYOKE,MASS.
D.NOV.11,1937 HOLYOKE,MASS.

1883	DET	N	P-0	15	36	2-12
						.192
1884	CIN	U	P-0	41	68	25-16
						.315
1885	STL	N	P-0	1	14	0- 0
						.218
		BL		57	118	27-28
						.271

BURNS, ROBERT BRITT (BRITT)
B.JUNE 8,1959 HOUSTON,TEX.

| 1978 | CHI | A | /P | | 2 | 0- 2 |
| | | BLTL | | | | |

BURNS, THOMAS EVERETT
B.MAR.30,1857 HONESDALE,PA.
D.MAR.19,1902 JERSEY CITY,N.J.

1880	CHI	N	P-C-	1	82	0- 0
			S-3			.309
1881	CHI	N	2-S-3		84	.277
1882	CHI	N	2-S		84	.247
1883	CHI	N	2-S-0		97	.293
1884	CHI	N	S-3		82	.245
1885	CHI	N	2-S		111	.271
1886	CHI	N	3		111	.276
1887	CHI	N	3		115	.317
1888	CHI	N	3		134	.238
1889	CHI	N	3		136	.257
1890	CHI	N	3		139	.277
1891	CHI	N	3		57	.231
1892	PIT	N	M-3-0		12	.210
		BRTR		1	1244	0- 0
						.271

NON-PLAYING MANAGER CHI[N] 1898-99

BURNS, THOMAS P. (OYSTER)
B.SEPT.6,1864 PHILADELPHIA,PA.
D.NOV.11,1928 BROOKLYN,N.Y.

1884	WIL	U	S		2	.143
	BAL	AA	P-2-	2	36	0- 0
			3-0			.304
1885	BAL	AA	P-2-	11	76	7- 4
			S-0			.229
1887	BAL	AA	S-3		140	.401
1888	BAL	AA	S-0		77	.308
	BRO	AA	2-S-0		52	.286
1889	BRO	AA	O		132	.316
1890	BRO	N	O		119	.284
1891	BRO	N	O		122	.281
1892	BRO	N	O		139	.310
1893	BRO	N	O		107	.279
1894	BRO	N	O		126	.358
1895	BRO	N	O		17	.192
	NY	N	O		33	.298
		BRTR		13	1178	7- 4
						.310

BURNS, WILLIAM
B.HAGERSTOWN,MD.

| 1902 | BAL | A | H | | 1 | 1.000 |

BURNS, WILLIAM THOMAS (SLEEPY BILL)
B.JAN.29,1880 SAN SABA,TEX.
D.JUME 6,1953 RAMONA,CAL.

1908	WAS	A	P		23	6-11
1909	WAS	A	P		6	2- 0
	CHI	A	P		20	7-13
1910	CHI	A	P		1	0- 0
	CIN	N	P		31	8-13
1911	CIN	N	P		6	0- 0
	PHI	N	P		21	3- 7
1912	DET	A	P		6	1- 4
		BBTL			114	27-48

BURNSIDE, PETER WILLITS (PETE)
B.JULY 2,193C EVANSTON,ILL.

1955	NY	N	P		2	1- 0
1957	NY	N	P		10	1- 4
1958	SF	N	P		6	0- 0
1959	DET	A	P		30	1- 3
1960	DET	A	P		31	7- 7
1961	WAS	A	P		33	4- 9
1962	WAS	A	P		40	5-11
1963	BAL	A	P		6	0- 1
	WAS	A	P		38	0- 1
		BRTL			196	19-36

BURNSIDE, SHELDON JOHN
B.DEC.22,1954 SOUTH BEND,IND.

| 1978 | DET | A | /P | | 2 | 0- 0 |
| | | BRTL | | | | |

BURPO, GEORGE HARVIE
B.JUNE 19,1922 JENKINS,KY.

| 1946 | CIN | N | P | | 2 | 0- 0 |
| | | BRTL | | | | |

BURR, ALEXANDER THOMSON
B.NOV.1,1893 CHICAGO,ILL.
D.NOV.11,1918 FRANCE

| 1914 | NY | A | O | | 1 | .000 |
| | | BRTR | | | | |

BURRELL, FRANK ANDREW (BUSTER)
B.DEC.22,1866 E.WEYMOUTH,MASS.
D.MAY 8,1962 S.WEYMOUTH,MASS.

1891	NY	N	C		15	.075
1895	BRO	N	C		10	.160
1896	BRO	N	C		58	.307
1897	BRO	N	C		31	.238
		BRTR			114	.243

BURRELL, HARRY J.
B.1866 E.WEYMOUTH,MASS.
D.DEC.11,1914 OMAHA,NEB.

| 1891 | STL | AA | P | | 9 | 3- 2 |

YR	CL	LEA	POS	GP	G	REC

BURRIGHT, LARRY ALLEN
(LARRY) OR (POSSUM)
B.JULY 10,1937 ROSEVILLE,ILL.

1962	LA	N	2-S	115		.205
1963	NY	N	2-S-3	41		.220
1964	NY	N	2	3		.000
		BRTR		159		.205

BURRIS, ALVA BURTON
B.JAN.28,1874 WARWICK,MD.
D.MAR.24,1938 SALISBURY,MD.

| 1894 | PHI | N | P | | 1 | 0- 0 |
| | | BRTR | | | | |

BURRIS, BERTRAM RAY (RAY)
B.AUG.22,1950 IDABEL,OKLA.

1973	CHI	N	P		31	1- 1
1974	CHI	N	P	40	41	3- 5
1975	CHI	N	P	36	38	15-10
1976	CHI	N	P	37	39	15-13
1977	CHI	N	P	39	40	14-16
1978	CHI	N	P	40	41	7-13
		BRTR		223	230	55-58

BURRIS, PAUL ROBERT
B.JULY 21,1923 HICKORY,N.C.

1948	BOS	N	C		2	.500
1950	BOS	N	C		10	.174
1952	BOS	N	C		55	.220
1953	MIL	N	C		2	.000
		BRTR			69	.219

BURROUGHS, HENRY F.
B.1845 DETROIT,MICH.

1871	OLY	NA	3-O		12	.222
1872	OLY	NA	O		2	.125
					14	.211

BURROUGHS, JEFFREY ALAN (JEFF)
B.MAR.7,1951 LONG BEACH,CAL.

1970	WAS	A	/O		6	.167
1971	WAS	A	O		59	.232
1972	TEX	A	O/1		22	.185
1973	TEX	A	*O/1	151		.279
1974	TEX	A	*O	152		.301
1975	TEX	A	*O	152		.226
1976	TEX	A	*O	158		.237
1977	ATL	N	*O	154		.271
1978	ATL	N	*O	153		.301
		BRTR		1007		.264

BURROWS, JOHN
B.OCT.30,1913 WINNFIELD,LA.

1943	PHI	N	P		4	0- 1
	CHI	N	P		23	0- 2
1944	CHI	N	P		3	0- 0
		BRTL			30	0- 3

BURRUS, MAURICE LENNON (DICK)
B.JAN.29,1898 HATTERAS,N.C.
D.FEB.2,1972 ELIZABETH CITY,N.C.

1919	PHI	A	1		70	.258
1920	PHI	A	1		71	.185
1925	BOS	N	1	152		.340
1926	BOS	N	1	131		.270
1927	BOS	N	1		72	.318
1928	BOS	N	1		64	.270
		BLTL		560		.291

BURT, FRANK J.
B.CAMDEN,N.J.

| 1882 | BAL | AA | O | | 10 | .108 |

BURTON, ELLIS NARRINGTON
B.AUG.12,1936 LOS ANGELES,CAL.

1958	STL	N	O		8	.233
1960	STL	N	O		29	.214
1963	CLE	A	O		26	.194
	CHI	N	O		93	.230
1964	CHI	N	O		42	.190
1965	CHI	N	O		17	.175
		BBTR		215		.216

BURTON, JIM SCOTT
B.OCT.27,1949 ROYAL OAK,MICH.

1975	BOS	A	P		29	1- 2
1977	BOS	A	/P		1	0- 0
		BRTL			30	1- 2

BURTSCHY, EDWARD FRANK (MOE)
B.APR.18,1922 CINCINNATI,OHIO

1950	PHI	A	P		9	0- 1
1951	PHI	A	P		7	0- 0
1954	PHI	A	P		46	5- 4
1955	KC	A	P		7	2- 0
1956	KC	A	P		21	3- 1
		BRTR			90	10- 6

BURWELL, RICHARD MATTHEW
B.JAN.23,1940 ALTON,ILL.

1960	CHI	N	P		3	0- 0
1961	CHI	N	P		2	0- 0
		BRTR			5	0- 0

BURWELL, WILLIAM EDWIN
B.MAR.27,1895 JARBALO,KAN.
D.JUNE 11,1973 ORMOND BEACH,FLA

1920	STL	A	P	33	35	6- 4
1921	STL	A	P		33	2- 4
1928	PIT	N	P		4	1- 0
		BLTR		70	72	9- 8
NON-PLAYING MANAGER PIT[N] 1947

BUSBY, JAMES FRANKLIN (JIM)
B.JAN.8,1927 KENEDY,TEX.

1950	CHI	A	O		18	.208
1951	CHI	A	O		143	.283
1952	CHI	A	O		16	.128
	WAS	A	O		129	.244
1953	WAS	A	O		150	.312
1954	WAS	A	O		155	.298
1955	WAS	A	O		47	.230
	CHI	A	O		99	.243
1956	CLE	A	O		135	.239
1957	CLE	A	O		30	.189
	BAL	A	O		86	.250
1958	BAL	A	3-O		113	.237
1959	BOS	A	O		61	.225
1960	BOS	A	O		1	.000
	BAL	A	O		79	.258
1961	BAL	A	O		75	.258
1962	HOU	N	C-O		15	.182
		BRTR		1352		.263

BUSBY, PAUL MILLER (RED)
B.AUG.25,1918 WAYNESBORO,MISS.

1941	PHI	N	O		10	.313
1943	PHI	N	O		26	.250
		BLTR			36	.268

BUSBY, STEVEN LEE (STEVE)
B.SEP.29,1949 BURBANK,CAL.

1972	KC	A	/P		5	3- 1
1973	KC	A	P		37	16-15
1974	KC	A	P		38	22-14
1975	KC	A	P		34	18-12
1976	KC	A	P		13	3- 3
1978	KC	A	/P		7	1- 0
		BRTR		134		63-45

BUSCH, EDGAR JOHN
B.NOV.16,1917 LEBANON,ILL.

1943	PHI	A	S		4	.294
1944	PHI	A	2-S-3	140		.271
1945	PHI	A	1-2-S-3	126		.250
		BRTR		270		.262

BUSCHHORN, DONALD LEE (DON)
B.APR.29,1946 INDEPENDENCE,MO.

| 1965 | KC | A | P | 12 | 13 | 0- 1 |
| | | BRTR | | | | |

BUSH, GUY TERRELL (GUY)
OR (THE MISSISSIPPI MUDCAT)
B.AUG.23,1901 ABERDEEN,MISS.

1923	CHI	N	P		1	0- 0
1924	CHI	N	P		16	2- 5
1925	CHI	N	P		42	6-13
1926	CHI	N	P		35	13- 9
1927	CHI	N	P		36	10-10
1928	CHI	N	P		42	15- 6
1929	CHI	N	P		50	18- 7
1930	CHI	N	P		46	15-10
1931	CHI	N	P		39	16- 8
1932	CHI	N	P		40	19-11
1933	CHI	N	P		41	20-12
1934	CHI	N	P	40	41	18-10
1935	PIT	N	P		41	11-11
1936	PIT	N	P		16	1- 3
	BOS	N	P		19	4- 5
1937	BOS	N	P	32	33	8-15
1938	STL	N	P		6	0- 1
1945	CIN	N	P		4	0- 0
		BRTR		542	544	176-136

BUSH, LESLIE AMBROSE (BULLET JOE)
B.NOV.27,1892 BRAINERD,MINN.
D.NOV.1,1974 FT.LAUDERDALE,FLA.

1912	PHI	A	P		1	0- 0
1913	PHI	A	P		39	13- 7
1914	PHI	A	P		38	16-12
1915	PHI	A	P		25	5-15
1916	PHI	A	P	40	41	15-22
1917	PHI	A	P		37	11-17
1918	BOS	A	P		36	15-15
1919	BOS	A	P		5	0- 0
1920	BOS	A	P	35	45	15-15
1921	BOS	A	P	36	51	16- 9
1922	NY	A	P		39	26- 7
1923	NY	A	P	37	38	19-15
1924	NY	A	P	39	60	17-16
1925	STL	A	P-O	33	57	14-14
						.254
1926	WAS	A	P	12	17	1- 8
	PIT	N	P	19	28	6- 6
1927	PIT	N	P		5	10	1- 2
	NY	N	P		3	1- 1
1928	PHI	A	P	11	15	2- 1
		BRTR		490	585	193-182
						.242

BUSH, OWEN JOSEPH (DONIE)
B.OCT.8,1887 INDIANAPOLIS,IND.
D.MAR.28,1972 INDIANAPOLIS,IND.

1908	DET	A	S		20	.294
1909	DET	A	S		157	.273
1910	DET	A	S		142	.262
1911	DET	A	S		150	.232
1912	DET	A	S		144	.231
1913	DET	A	S		152	.251
1914	DET	A	S		157	.252
1915	DET	A	S		155	.228
1916	DET	A	S		145	.225
1917	DET	A	S		147	.281
1918	DET	A	S		128	.234
1919	DET	A	S		129	.244
1920	DET	A	S		141	.263
1921	DET	A	2-S		104	.279
	WAS	A	S		23	.238
1922	WAS	A	3		41	.238
1923	WAS	A	M-2-3		10	.409
		BBTR		1945		.250
NON-PLAYING MANAGER
PIT[N] 1927-29, CHI[A] 1930-31,
AND CIN[N] 1933

BUSHELMAN, JOHN FRANCIS (JACK)
B.AUG.29,1885 CINCINNATI,OHIO
D.OCT.26,1955 ROANOKE,VA.

1909	CIN	N	P		1	0- 1
1911	BOS	A	P		3	0- 1
1912	BOS	A	P		3	1- 0
		BRTR			7	1- 2

BUSHEY, FRANCIS CLYDE
B.AUG.1,1906 WHEATON,KAN.
D.MAR.18,1972 TOPEKA,KAN.

1927	BOS	A	P		1	0- 0
1930	BOS	A	P		11	0- 1
		BRTR			12	0- 1

BUSHONG, ALBERT JOHN (DOC)
B.SEPT.15,1856 PHILADELPHIA,PA.
D.AUG.19,1908 BROOKLYN,N.Y.

1875	NA	N	C		1	.600
1876	ATH	N	C		5	.048
1880	WOR	N	C-O		37	.163
1881	WOR	N	C		75	.229
1882	WOR	N	C		69	.152
1883	CLE	N	C		61	.172
1884	CLE	N	C		60	.231
1885	STL	AA	C		85	.265
1886	STL	AA	C		107	.229
1887	STL	AA	C		53	.295
1888	BRO	AA	C		69	.220
1889	BRO	AA	C		25	.163
1890	BRO	N	C		16	.234
		BRTR			663	.219

BUSKEY, JOSEPH HENRY (JAZZBOW)
B.DEC.18,1902 CUMBERLAND,MD.
D.APR.11,1949 CUMBERLAND,MD.

| 1926 | PIT | N | S | | 5 | .000 |
| | | BRTR | | | | |

BUSKEY, MICHAEL THOMAS (MIKE)
B.JAN.13,1949 SAN FRANCISCO,CAL.

| 1977 | PHI | N | /S | | 6 | .286 |

BUSKEY, THOMAS WILLIAM (TOM)
B.FEB.20,1947 HARRISBURG,PA.

1973	NY	A	/P		8	0- 1
1974	NY	A	P		51	2- 6
	CLE	A	P		51	2- 6
1975	CLE	A	P		50	5- 3
1976	CLE	A	P		39	5- 4
1977	CLE	A	P		21	0- 0
1978	TOR	A	/P		8	0- 1
		BRTR		181		12-16

BUSSE, RAYMOND EDWARD (RAY)
B.SEP.25,1948 DAYTONA BEACH,FLA.

1971	HOU	N	/S-3		10	.147
1973	STL	N	S		24	.143
	HOU	N	/S-3		15	.059
1974	HOU	N	/3		19	.206
		BRTR			68	.148

BUTCHER, ALBERT MAXWELL (MAX)
B.SEPT.21,1910 HOLDEN,W.VA.
D.SEPT.15,1957 MAN,W.VA.

1936	BRO	N	P	38	42	6- 6
1937	BRO	N	P	39	40	11-15
1938	BRO	N	P	24	25	5- 4
	PHI	N	P		12	4- 8
1939	PHI	N	P		19	2-13
	PIT	N	P		14	4- 4
1940	PIT	N	P	35		36	8- 9
1941	PIT	N	P		33	17-12
1942	PIT	N	P		24	5- 8
1943	PIT	N	P		30	10- 8
1944	PIT	N	P	35	36	13-11
1945	PIT	N	P		28	10- 8
		BRTR		334	342	95-106

BUTCHER, HENRY JOSEPH
B.JULY 12,1886 CHICAGO,ILL.

YR	CL	LEA	POS	GP	G	REC
1911	CLE	A	O		38	.240
1912	CLE	A	O		24	.195
	BRTR				62	.223

BUTKA, EDWARD LUKE (BABE)
B.JAN.7,1916 CANONSBURG,PA.

YR	CL	LEA	POS	GP	G	REC
1943	WAS	A	1		3	.333
1944	WAS	A	1		15	.195
	BRTR				18	.220

BUTLAND, WILBURN RUE (BILL)
B.MAR.22,1918 TERRE HAUTE,IND.

YR	CL	LEA	POS	GP	G	REC
1940	BOS	A	P		3	1- 2
1942	BOS	A	P		23	7- 1
1946	BOS	A	P		5	1- 0
1947	BOS	A	P		1	0- 0
	BRTL				32	9- 3

BUTLER, ARTHUR EDWARD
(REAL NAME
ARTHUR EDWARD BOUTHILLIER)
B.DEC.19,1887 FALL RIVER,MASS.

YR	CL	LEA	POS	GP	G	REC
1911	BOS	N	3		19	.176
1912	PIT	N	2		43	.273
1913	PIT	N	2-S		82	.280
1914	STL	N	S		86	.201
1915	STL	N	S		130	.254
1916	STL	N	O		86	.209
	BRTR				446	.241

BUTLER, CECIL DEAN
(CECIL) OR (SLEWFOOT)
B.OCT.23,1937 DALLAS,GA.

YR	CL	LEA	POS	GP	G	REC
1962	MIL	N	P		9	2- 0
1964	MIL	N	P		2	0- 0
	BRTR				11	2- 0

BUTLER, CHARLES THOMAS
B.MAY 12,1906 GREEN COVE
SPRINGS,FLA.
D.MAY 10,1964 ST.SIMON S ISLAND,GA.

YR	CL	LEA	POS	GP	G	REC
1933	PHI	N	P		1	0- 0
	BRTL					

BUTLER, FRANK DEAN
(STUFFY) OR (GOLDBRICK)
B.JULY 18,1860 SAVANNAH,GA.
D.JULY 10,1945 JACKSONVILLE,FLA

YR	CL	LEA	POS	GP	G	REC
1895	NY	N	O		5	.272
	BLTL					

BUTLER, FRANK E. (KID)
B.1862 BOSTON,MASS.
D.APR.9,1921 S.BOSTON,MASS.

YR	CL	LEA	POS	GP	G	REC
1884	BOS	U	O		70	.160

BUTLER, ISAAC BURR
B.AUG.22,1873 LANGSTON,MICH.
D.MAR.17,1948 OAKLAND,CAL.

YR	CL	LEA	POS	GP	G	REC
1902	BAL	A	P-O	15	18	2-11
						.115
	TR					

BUTLER, JOHN ALBERT
(PLAYED UNDER NAME OF
FREDERICK KING IN 1901)
B.JULY 26,1879 BOSTON,MASS.
D.FEB.8,1949 BOSTON,MASS.

YR	CL	LEA	POS	GP	G	REC
1901	MIL	A	C		1	.500
1904	STL	N	C		12	.167
1906	BRO	N	C		1	.000
1907	BRO	N	C		29	.127
	BRTR				43	.145

BUTLER, JOHN STEPHEN (TROLLEY LINE)
B.MAR.20,1893 FALL RIVER,KAN.
D.APR.29,1967 SEAL BEACH,CAL.

YR	CL	LEA	POS	GP	G	REC
1926	BRO	N	S-3		147	.269
1927	BRO	N	S-3		149	.238
1928	CHI	N	3		62	.270
1929	STL	N	S-3		17	.164
	BRTR				375	.252

BUTLER, ORMOND HOOK
B.NOV.1854 WEST VIRGINIA
D.SEPT.12,1915 MT.HOPE,MD.
NON-PLAYING MANAGER PIT[AA]1883

BUTLER, RICHARD H.
B.BROOKLYN,N.Y.

YR	CL	LEA	POS	GP	G	REC
1897	LOU	N	C		10	.184
1899	WAS	N	C		12	.263
					22	.224

BUTLER, W. J. (BILL)
B.1861 NEW ORLEANS,LA.

YR	CL	LEA	POS	GP	G	REC
1884	IND	AA	O		9	.206

BUTLER, WILLIAM FRANKLIN (BILL)
B.MAR.12,1947 HYATTSVILLE,MD.

YR	CL	LEA	POS	GP	G	REC
1969	KC	A	P		34	9-10
1970	KC	A	P		25	4-12
1971	KC	A	P		14	1- 2
1972	CLE	A	/P		6	0- 0
1974	MIN	A	P		26	4- 6
1975	MIN	A	P		23	5- 4
1977	MIN	A	/P		6	0- 1
	BLTL				134	23-35

BUTLER, WILLIS EVERETT (KID)
D.FEB.22,1964 RICHMOND,CAL.

YR	CL	LEA	POS	GP	G	REC
1907	STL	A	3		20	.220
	BRTR					

BUTTERS, THOMAS ARDEN (TOM)
B.APR.8,1938 DELAWARE,O.

YR	CL	LEA	POS	GP	G	REC
1962	PIT	N	P		4	0- 0
1963	PIT	N	P		6	0- 0
1964	PIT	N	P		28	2- 2
1965	PIT	N	P		5	0- 1
	BRTR				43	2- 3

BUTTERY, FRANK
B.JUNE 16,1851 NORWALK,CONN.
D.DEC.16,1902 SILVER MINE,CONN.

YR	CL	LEA	POS	GP	G	REC
1872	MAN	NA	P-3=	6	17	3- 2
			O			.295

BUXTON, RALPH STANLEY (BUCK)
B.JUNE 7,1911 WEYBURN,SASK.,CAN

YR	CL	LEA	POS	GP	G	REC
1938	PHI	A	P		5	0- 1
1949	NY	A	P		14	0- 1
	BRTR				19	0- 2

BUZAS, JOSEPH JOHN
B.OCT.2,1919 ALPHA,N.J.

YR	CL	LEA	POS	GP	G	REC
1945	NY	A	S		30	.262
	BRTR					

BUZHARDT, JOHN WILLIAM
B.AUG.17,1936 PROSPERITY,S.C.

YR	CL	LEA	POS	GP	G	REC
1958	CHI	N	P		6	3- 0
1959	CHI	N	P		31	4- 5
1960	PHI	N	P	30	32	5-16
1961	PHI	N	P		41	6-18
1962	CHI	A	P		28	8-12
1963	CHI	A	P	19	20	9- 4
1964	CHI	A	P		31	10- 8
1965	CHI	A	P	32	34	13- 8
1966	CHI	A	P	33	34	6-11
1967	CHI	A	P		28	3- 9
	BAL	A	/P		7	0- 1
	HOU	N	/P		1	0- 0
1968	HOU	N	P		39	4- 4
	BRTR			326	332	71-96

BYERLY, ELDRED WILLIAM (BUD)
B.OCT.26,1920 WEBSTER GROVES,MO

YR	CL	LEA	POS	GP	G	REC
1943	STL	N	P		2	1- 0
1944	STL	N	P		9	2- 2
1945	STL	N	P		33	4- 5
1950	CIN	N	P		4	0- 1
1951	CIN	N	P	40	41	2- 1
1952	CIN	N	P		12	0- 1
1956	WAS	A	P		25	2- 4
1957	WAS	A	P		47	6- 6
1958	WAS	A	P		17	2- 0
	BOS	A	P		18	1- 2
1959	SF	N	P		11	1- 0
1960	SF	N	P		19	1- 0
	BRTR			237	238	22-22

BYERS, BURLEY
(REAL NAME CHRISTOPHER A. BAYER)
B.DEC.19,1875 LOUISVILLE,KY.
D.MAY 30,1933 LOUISVILLE,KY.

YR	CL	LEA	POS	GP	G	REC
1899	LOU	N	S		1	.000

BYERS, JAMES WILLIAM (BILL)
B.OCT.3,1877 BRIDGETON,IND.
D.SEPT.8,1948 BALTIMORE,MD.

YR	CL	LEA	POS	GP	G	REC
1904	STL	N	C		17	.217
	TR					

BYRD, HARRY GLADWIN
B.FEB.3,1925 DARLINGTON,S.C.

YR	CL	LEA	POS	GP	G	REC
1950	PHI	A	P		6	0- 0
1952	PHI	A	P		37	15-15
1953	PHI	A	P		40	11-20
1954	NY	A	P		25	9- 7
1955	BAL	A	P		14	3- 2
	CHI	A	P		25	4- 6
1956	CHI	A	P		3	0- 1
1957	DET	A	P		37	4- 3
	BRTR				187	46-54
	BB 1955					

BYRD, JEFFREY ALAN (JEFF)
B.NOV.11,1956 LA MESA,CAL.

YR	CL	LEA	POS	GP	G	REC
1977	TOR	A	P		17	2-13
	BRTR					

BYRD, SAMUEL DEWEY (SAMMY)
OR (BABE RUTH S LEGS)
B.OCT.15,1907 BREMEN,GA.

YR	CL	LEA	POS	GP	G	REC
1929	NY	A	O		62	.312
1930	NY	A	O		92	.284
1931	NY	A	O		115	.270
1932	NY	A	O		105	.297
1933	NY	A	O		85	.280
1934	NY	A	O		106	.246
1935	CIN	N	O		121	.262
1936	CIN	N	O		59	.248
	BRTR				745	.274

BYRNE, CHARLES H.
B.SEPT.1843 NEW YORK,N.Y.
D.JAN.4,1898 NEW YORK,N.Y.
NON-PLAYING MANAGER BRO[AA] 1885-87

BYRNE, GERALD WILFORD (JERRY)
B.FEB.2,1907 PARNELL,MICH.
D.AUG.11,1955 LANSING,MICH.

YR	CL	LEA	POS	GP	G	REC
1929	CHI	A	P		3	0- 1
	BRTR					

BYRNE, JOHN K.
(PLAYED UNDER NAME OF
JOHN K. O BRIEN)

BYRNE, ROBERT MATTHEW
B.DEC.31,1884 ST.LOUIS,MO.
D.DEC.31,1964 WAYNE,PA.

YR	CL	LEA	POS	GP	G	REC
1907	STL	N	3		149	.256
1908	STL	N	3		126	.191
1909	STL	N	3		105	.214
	PIT	N	3		46	.256
1910	PIT	N	3		148	.296
1911	PIT	N	3		152	.259
1912	PIT	N	3		130	.288
1913	PIT	N	3		113	.270
	PHI	N	3		19	.224
1914	PHI	N	2-3		126	.272
1915	PHI	N	2-3		105	.209
1916	PHI	N	3		48	.234
1917	PHI	N	2-3		13	.357
	CHI	A	2		1	.000
	BRTR				1281	.253

BYRNE, THOMAS JOSEPH (TOMMY)
B.DEC.31,1919 BALTIMORE,MD.

YR	CL	LEA	POS	GP	G	REC
1943	NY	A	P	11	13	2- 1
1946	NY	A	P	4	14	0- 1
1947	NY	A	P		4	0- 0
1948	NY	A	P		31	8- 5
1949	NY	A	P	32	35	15- 7
1950	NY	A	P	31	34	15- 9
1951	NY	A	P		9	2- 1
	STL	A	P	19	34	4-10
1952	STL	A	P	29	40	7-14
1953	CHI	A	P	6	18	2- 0
	WAS	A	P	6	14	0- 5
1954	NY	A	P	5	7	3- 2
1955	NY	A	P	27	45	16- 5
1956	NY	A	P	37	44	7- 3
1957	NY	A	P	30	35	4- 6
	BLTL			261	377	85-69

BYRNES, JAMES JOSEPH
B.JAN.5,1880 SAN FRANCISCO,CAL.
D.JULY 31,1941 SAN FRANCISCO,CAL

YR	CL	LEA	POS	GP	G	REC
1906	PHI	A	C		10	.167
	BRTR					

BYRNES, MILTON JOHN (SKIPPY)
B.NOV.15,1916 ST.LOUIS,MO.

YR	CL	LEA	POS	GP	G	REC
1943	STL	A	O		129	.280
1944	STL	A	O		128	.295
1945	STL	A	1-O		133	.249
	BLTL				390	.274

CABALLERO, RALPH JOSEPH (PUTSY)
B.NOV.5,1927 NEW ORLEANS,LA.

YR	CL	LEA	POS	GP	G	REC
1944	PHI	N	3		4	.000
1945	PHI	N	3		9	.000
1947	PHI	N	2-3		2	.143
1948	PHI	N	2-3		113	.245
1949	PHI	N	2-5		29	.279
1950	PHI	N	2-5-3		46	.167
1951	PHI	N	2-5-3		84	.186
1952	PHI	N	2-5-3		35	.238
	BRTR				322	.228

CABELL, ENOS MILTON
B.OCT.8,1949 FORT RILEY,KAN.

YR	CL	LEA	POS	GP	G	REC
1972	BAL	A	/1		3	.000
1973	BAL	A	1/3		32	.213
1974	BAL	A	1-0-3/2		80	.241
1975	HOU	N	O-1-3		117	.264
1976	HOU	N	*3/1		144	.273
1977	HOU	N	*3/1-S		150	.282
1978	HOU	N	*3-1/S		162	.295
	BRTR				688	.276

CABRERA, ALFREDO A.
B.1883 CANARY ISLANDS
D.HAVANA,CUBA

YR	CL	LEA	POS	GP	G	REC
1913	STL	N	S		1	.000
	TR					

YR CL LEA POS   GP   G   REC

CACEK, CRAIG THOMAS
B.SEPT.10,1954 HOLLYWOOD,CAL.
1977 HOU N /1   7   .050
        BRTR

CADORE, LEON JOSEPH (CADDY)
B.NOV.20,1890 CHICAGO,ILL.
D.MAR.16,1958 SPOKANE,WASH.
1915 BRO N P   7   0-2
1916 BRO N P   1   0-0
1917 BRO N P   37   13-13
1918 BRO N P   2   1-0
1919 BRO N P   35   37   14-12
1920 BRO N P   35   15-14
1921 BRO N P   35   13-14
1922 BRO N P   29   8-15
1923 BRO N P   8   9   4-1
        CHI A P   1   0-1
1924 NY N P   2   0-0
        BRTR 192   195   68-72

CADREAU, WILLIAM
[PLAYED UNDER NAME OF
WILLIAM CHOUNEAU]

CADY, CHARLES B.
B.CHICAGO,ILL.
1883 CLE N P   1   3   0-1
                            .000
1884 CHI U P-O 4   6   2-0
                            .695
        KC U 2   1   .000
        5   10   2-1
                            .056

CADY, FORREST LEROY (HICK)
B.JAN.26,1886 BISHOP HILL,ILL.
D.MAR.3,1946 CEDAR RAPIDS,IOWA
1912 BOS A C   47   .259
1913 BOS A C   39   .242
1914 BOS A C   61   .258
1915 BOS A C   78   .278
1916 BOS A C   78   .191
1917 BOS A C   17   .152
1918 CLE A H   1   .000
1919 PHI N   34   .214
        BRTR   355   .239

CAFEGO, THOMAS
B.AUG.21,1911 WHIPPLE,W.VA.
D.OCT.29,1961 DETROIT,MICH.
1937 STL A O   4   .000
        BLTR

CAFFIE, JOSEPH CLIFFORD
(JOE) OR (RABBIT)
B.FEB.14,1931 RAMER,ALA.
1956 CLE A O   12   .342
1957 CLE A O   32   .270
        BLTR   44   .291

CAFFYN, BENJAMIN THOMAS
B.FEB.10,1880 PEORIA,ILL.
D.NOV.22,1942 PEORIA,ILL.
1906 CLE A O   30   .194

CAGE, WAYNE LEVELL
B.NOV.23,1951 MONROE,LA.
1978 CLE A D-1   36   .245
        BLTL

CAHILL, JOHN FRANCIS (PATSY)
B.PHILADELPHIA,PA.
D.NOV.1,1901 PLEASANTON,CAL.
1884 COL AA P-O 1   59   1-0
                            .210
1886 STL N O   125   .198
1887 IND N O   68   .231
        BRTR   1   252   1-0
                            .211

CAHILL, THOMAS H.
B.OCT.1868 FALL RIVER,MASS.
D.DEC.25,1894 SCRANTON,PA.
1891 LOU AA P-C- 1 119   0-1
        S   .263

CAIN, LESLIE (LES)
B.JAN.13,1948 SAN LUIS OBISPO,CAL.
1968 DET A /P   8   1-0
1970 DET A P   29   12-7
1971 DET A P   26   27   10-9
1972 DET A /P   5   0-3
        BLTL 68   69   23-19

CAIN, MERRITT PATRICK (SUGAR)
B.APR.5,1907 NACON,GA.
D.APR.3,1975 ATLANTA,GA.
1932 PHI A P   10   3-4
1933 PHI A P   38   39   13-12
1934 PHI A P   36   9-17
1935 PHI A P   6   0-5
        STL A P 30   31   9-8
1936 STL A P   4   1-1
        CHI A P   31   14-10
1937 CHI A P   18   4-2
1938 CHI A P   5   0-1
        BLTR 178   180   53-60
        BB 1932-33

CAIN, ROBERT MAX (BOB) OR (SUGAR)
B.OCT.16,1924 LONGFORD,KAN.
1949 CHI A P   6   0-0
1950 CHI A P   34   35   9-12
1951 CHI A P   4   1-2
        DET A P   35   11-10
1952 STL A P   29   35   12-10
1953 STL A P   32   34   4-10
1954 CHI A N   1   .000
        BLTL 140   150   37-44
                            .196

CAITHAMER, GEORGE THEODORE (SIDEL)
B.JULY 22,1910 CHICAGO,ILL.
D.JUNE 1,1954 CHICAGO,ILL.
1934 CHI A C   5   .316
        BRTR

CALDERONE, SAMUEL FRANCIS (SAM)
B.FEB.6,1926 BEVERLY,N.J.
1950 NY N C   34   .299
1953 NY N C   35   .222
1954 MIL N C   22   .379
        BRTR   91   .291

CALDWELL, BRUCE
B.FEB.8,1906 ASHTON,R.I.
D.FEB.15,1959 WEST HAVEN,CONN.
1928 CLE A O   18   .222
1932 BRO N 1   7   .091
        BRTR   25   .184

CALDWELL, CHARLES WILLIAM (CHUCK)
B.AUG.2,1901 BRISTOL,VA.
D.NOV.1,1957 PRINCETON,N.J.
1925 NY A P   3   0-0
        BRTR

CALDWELL, EARL WELTON (TEACH)
B.APR.9,1905 SPARKS,TEX.
1928 PHI N P   5   1-4
1935 STL A P   6   3-2
1936 STL A P   41   7-16
1937 STL A P   9   0-0
1945 CHI A P   27   6-7
1946 CHI A P   39   13-4
1947 CHI A P   40   1-4
1948 CHI A P   25   1-5
        BOS A P   8   1-1
        BRTR   200   33-43

CALDWELL, RALPH GRANT (LEFTY)
B.JAN.18,1884 PHILADELPHIA,PA.
D.AUG.5,1969 W.TRENTON,N.J.
1904 PHI N P   6   3-3
1905 PHI N P   7   1-1
        BLTL   13   4-4

CALDWELL, RALPH MICHAEL (MIKE)
B.JAN.22,1949 TARBORO,N.C.
1971 SD N /P   6   1-0
1972 SD N P   42   7-11
1973 SD N P   55   56   5-14
1974 SF N P   31   14-5
1975 SF N P   38   7-13
1976 SF N P   50   1-7
1977 CIN N P   14   0-0
        MIL A P   21   5-8
1978 MIL A P   37   22-9
        BRTL 294   295   62-67

CALDWELL, RAYMOND BENJAMIN
(RAY), (RUBE) OR (SUM)
B.APR.26,1888 CORYDON,PA.
D.AUG.17,1967 SALAMANCA,N.Y.
1910 NY A P   6   1-0
1911 NY A P   41   59   14-14
1912 NY A P   30   39   8-16
1913 NY A P   27   51   9-8
1914 NY A P   31   58   17-9
1915 NY A P   37   72   19-16
1916 NY A P   20   45   5-12
1917 NY A P   36   63   13-16
1918 NY A P-O 24   65   9-8
                            .291
1919 BOS A P   17   31   5-4
        CLE A P   63   7-1
1920 CLE A P   34   41   20-10
1921 CLE A P   37   6-6
        BLTR 347   575 133-120
                            .248

CALHOUN, JOHN CHARLES
(JACK) OR (RED)
B.DEC.14,1879 PITTSBURGH,PA.
D.FEB.27,1947 CINCINNATI,OHIO
1902 STL N 1-3-0   17   .156
        BRTR

CALHOUN, WILLIAM DAVITTE (MARY)
B.JUNE 23,1890 ROCKMART,GA.
D.FEB.11,1955 SANDERSVILLE,GA.
1913 BOS N 1   6   .076
        BLTL

CALIGIURI, FREDERICK JOHN
B.OCT.22,1918 W.HICKORY,PA.
1941 PHI A P   5   2-2
1942 PHI A P   13   0-3
        BRTR   18   2-5

CALIHAN, WILLIAM T.
B.1869 ROCHESTER,N.Y.
D.DEC.20,1917 ROCHESTER,N.Y.
1890 ROC AA P 37   48   18-13
1891 ATH AA P   16   5-7
        53   64   23-20

CALLAGHAN, MARTIN FRANCIS
B.JUNE 9,1900 NORWOOD,MASS.
D.JUNE 23,1975 NORFOLK,MASS.
1922 CHI N O   74   .257
1923 CHI N O   61   .225
1928 CIN N O   81   .290
1930 CIN N O   79   .276
        BLTL   295   .270

CALLAHAN, DAVID JOSEPH
B.JULY 20,1888 OTTAWA,ILL.
D.OCT.28,1969 OTTAWA,ILL.
1910 CLE A O   13   .181
1911 CLE A O   6   .250
        BLTR   19   .194

CALLAHAN, EDWARD J.
B.BOSTON,MASS.
1884 STL U S   1   .000
        KC U S   1   .250
        BOS U   4   .357
        6   .286

CALLAHAN, JAMES J.
B.PHILADELPHIA,PA.
1902 NY N O   1   .000

CALLAHAN, JAMES JOSEPH
B.MAR.18,1874 FITCHBURG,MASS.
D.OCT.4,1934 BOSTON,MASS.
1894 PHI N P   9   2-3
1897 CHI N P-2- 23   90   13-10
        S-O   .308
1898 CHI N P   31   42   20-11
1899 CHI N P   35   45   21-12
1900 CHI N P   33   12-16
1901 CHI A P   27   45   15-7
1902 CHI A P-S- 34   68   16-14
        O   .239
1903 CHI A M-P-3 3 118   1-2
                            .290
1904 CHI A M-2-O   132   .263
1905 CHI A O   96   .272
1911 CHI A O   120   .281
1912 CHI A M-O   111   .272
1913 CHI A M-O   6   .222
        BRTR 195   915 100-75
                            .275

NON-PLAYING MANAGER
CHI(A) 1914 AND PIT(N) 1916-17

CALLAHAN, JAMES W.
B.MOBERLY,MO.
1898 STL N P   2   0-2

CALLAHAN, JOSEPH THOMAS
B.OCT.8,1916 E.BOSTON,MASS.
D.MAY 24,1949 S.BOSTON,MASS.
1939 BOS N P   4   1-0
1940 BOS N P   6   0-2
        BRTR   10   1-2

CALLAHAN, LEO DAVID
B.AUG.9,1890 BOSTON,MASS.
1913 BRO N O   33   .171
1919 PHI N O   81   .230
        BLTL   114   .221

CALLAHAN, PATRICK HENRY
B.OCT.15,1866 CLEVELAND,OHIO
D.FEB.4,1940 LOUISVILLE,KY.
1884 IND AA 3   61   .263

CALLAHAN, RAYMOND JAMES (PAT)
B.AUG.29,1891 ASHLAND,WIS.
D.JAN.23,1973 OLYMPIA,WASH.
1915 CIN N P   3   0-0
        BLTL

CALLAHAN, WESLEY LEROY
B.JULY 3,1888 LYONS,IND.
D.SEPT.13,1953 DAYTON,OHIO
1913 STL N S   7   .285
        TR

CALLAWAY, FRANK BURNETT
B.FEB.26,1898 KNOXVILLE,TENN.
1921 PHI A   14   .240
1922 PHI A 2   29   .270
        BRTR   43   .255

YR	CL	LEA	POS	GP	G	REC

CALLISON, JOHN WESLEY (JOHNNY)
B.MAR.12,1939 QUALLS,OKLA.
1958	CHI	A	O		18	.297
1959	CHI	A	O		49	.173
1960	PHI	N	O		99	.260
1961	PHI	N	O		138	.266
1962	PHI	N	O		157	.300
1963	PHI	N	O		157	.284
1964	PHI	N	O		162	.274
1965	PHI	N	*O		160	.262
1966	PHI	N	*O		155	.276
1967	PHI	N	*O		149	.261
1968	PHI	N	*O		121	.244
1969	PHI	N	*O		134	.265
1970	CHI	N	*O		147	.264
1971	CHI	N	O		103	.210
1972	NY	A	O		92	.258
1973	NY	A	O-D		45	.176
			BLTR		1886	.264

CALMUS, RICHARD LEE (DICK)
B.JAN.7,1944 LOS ANGELES,CAL.
1963	LA	N	P		21	3- 1
1967	CHI	N	/P		1	0- 0
			BRTR		22	3- 1

CALVERT, PAUL LEO EMILE (PAUL)
B.OCT.6,1917 MONTREAL,QUE.,CAN.
1942	CLE	A	P		1	0- 0
1943	CLE	A	P		5	0- 0
1944	CLE	A	P		35	1- 3
1945	CLE	A	P		1	0- 0
1949	WAS	A	P	34	35	6-17
1950	DET	A	P		32	2- 2
1951	DET	A	P		1	0- 0
			BRTR	109	110	9-22

CALVO, JACINTO [GONZALEZ] (JACK)
[BORN JACINTO DEL CALVO]
B.JUNE 11,1894 HAVANA,CUBA
D.JUNE 15,1965 MIAMI,FLA.
1913	WAS	A	O		16	.242
1920	WAS	A	O		17	.043
			BLTL		33	.161

CAMBRIA, FREDERICK DENNIS (FRED)
B.JAN.22,1948 CAMBRIA HEIGHTS,N.Y.
| 1970 | PIT | N | /P | | 6 | 1- 2 |
| | | | BRTR | | | |

CAMELLI, HENRY RICHARD (HANK)
B.DEC.12,1914 GLOUCESTER,MASS.
1943	PIT	N	C		1	.000
1944	PIT	N	C		63	.296
1945	PIT	N	C		1	.000
1946	PIT	N	C		42	.208
1947	BOS	N	C		52	.193
			BRTR		159	.229

CAMERON, JOHN WILLIAM (HAPPY JACK)
B.1885 BOSTON,MASS.
| 1906 | BOS | N | P-O | 2 | 18 | 0- 0 |
| | | | | | | .180 |

CAMILLI, ADOLPH LOUIS (DOLPH)
B.APR.23,1907 SAN FRANCISCO,CAL
1933	CHI	N	1		16	.224
1934	CHI	N	1		32	.275
	PHI	N	1		102	.212
1935	PHI	N	1		156	.261
1936	PHI	N	1		151	.315
1937	PHI	N	1		131	.339
1938	BRO	N	1		146	.251
1939	BRO	N	1		157	.290
1940	BRO	N	1		142	.287
1941	BRO	N	1		149	.285
1942	BRO	N	1		150	.252
1943	BRO	N	1		95	.246
1945	BOS	A	1		63	.212
			BLTL		1490	.277

CAMILLI, DOUGLAS JOSEPH (DOUG)
B.SEP.22,1936 PHILADELPHIA,PA.
1960	LA	N	C		6	.333
1961	LA	N	C		13	.133
1962	LA	N	C		45	.284
1963	LA	N	C		49	.162
1964	LA	N	C		50	.179
1965	WAS	A	C		75	.192
1966	WAS	A	C		44	.206
1967	WAS	A	C		30	.183
1969	WAS	A	/C		1	.333
			BRTR		313	.199

CAMILLI, LOUIS STEVEN (LOU)
B.SEP.24,1946 EL PASO,TEX.
1969	CLE	A	3		13	.000
1970	CLE	A	/S-2-3		16	.000
1971	CLE	A	S-2		39	.198
1972	CLE	A	/S-2		39	.146
			BBTR		107	.146

CAMMEYER, WILLIAM HENRY
B.MAR.20,1821 NEW YORK,N.Y.
D.SEPT.4,1898 NEW YORK,N.Y.
NON-PLAYING MANAGER
MUT[NA] 1873 AND MUT[N] 1876

CAMNITZ, HENRY RICHARDSON
B.OCT.26,1884 MC KINNEY,KY.
D.JAN.6,1951 LOUISVILLE,KY.
1909	PIT	N	P		1	0- 0
1911	STL	N	P		2	1- 0
			BRTR		3	1- 0

CAMNITZ, SAMUEL HOWARD
(HOWIE) OR (RED)
B.AUG.22,1881 COVINGTON,KY.
D.MAR.2,1960 LOUISVILLE,KY.
1904	PIT	N	P		10	1- 2
1906	PIT	N	P		2	1- 0
1907	PIT	N	P		31	13- 8
1908	PIT	N	P		38	16- 9
1909	PIT	N	P		41	25- 6
1910	PIT	N	P		38	12-13
1911	PIT	N	P		40	20-15
1912	PIT	N	P		41	22-12
1913	PIT	N	P		36	6-17
	PHI	N	P		9	3- 3
1914	PIT	F	P		36	14-19
1915	PIT	F	P		4	0- 0
			BRTR		326	133-104

CAMP, HOWARD LEE (RED)
B.JULY 1,1893 MUMFORD,ALA.
D.MAY 8,1960 EASTABOGA,ALA.
| 1917 | NY | A | O | | 5 | .286 |
| | | | BLTR | | | |

CAMP, LLEWELLYN ROBERT (LEW)
B.FEB.22,1868 COLUMBUS,OHIO
D.OCT.1,1948 OMAHA,NEB.
1892	STL	N	3		43	.204
1893	CHI	N	3		38	.268
1894	CHI	N	2		8	.156
			BRTR		89	.229

CAMP, RICK LAMAR
B.JUNE 10,1953 TRION,GA.
1976	ATL	N	/P		5	0- 1
1977	ATL	N	P		54	6- 3
1978	ATL	N	P		42	2- 4
			BRTR		101	8- 8

CAMP, WINFIELD SCOTT (KID)
B.1870 COLUMBUS,OHIO
D.MAR.2,1895 OMAHA,NEB.
1892	PIT	N	P		4	0- 2
1894	CHI	N	P		3	0- 1
					7	0- 3

CAMPANELLA, ROY
B.NOV.19,1921 PHILADELPHIA,PA.
1948	BRO	N	C		83	.258
1949	BRO	N	C		130	.287
1950	BRO	N	C		126	.281
1951	BRO	N	C		143	.325
1952	BRO	N	C		128	.269
1953	BRO	N	C		144	.312
1954	BRO	N	C		111	.207
1955	BRO	N	C		123	.318
1956	BRO	N	C		124	.219
1957	BRO	N	C		103	.242
			BRTR		1215	.276

CAMPANERIA, DAGOBERTO [BLANCO]
[PLAYED UNDER NAME OF
DAGOBERTO CAMPANERIS [BLANCO]]

CAMPANERIS, DAGOBERTO [BLANCO]
(BERT) OR (CAMPY)
[REAL NAME
DAGOBERTO CAMPANERIA [BLANCO]]
B.MAR.9,1942 PUEBLO NUEVO,CUBA
1964	KC	A	S-3-O		67	.257
1965	KC	A	/P-	1	144	0- 0
			*S-O/C-1-2-3			.270
1966	KC	A	*S		142	.267
1967	KC	A	*S		147	.248
1968	OAK	A	*S/O		159	.276
1969	OAK	A	*S		135	.260
1970	OAK	A	*S		147	.279
1971	OAK	A	*S		134	.251
1972	OAK	A	*S		149	.240
1973	OAK	A	*S		151	.250
1974	OAK	A	*S		134	.290
1975	OAK	A	*S		137	.265
1976	OAK	A	*S		149	.256
1977	TEX	A	*S		150	.254
1978	TEX	A	S		98	.186
				1	2043	0- 0
						.259

CAMPANIS, ALEXANDER SEBASTIAN
B.NOV.2,1916 COS,GREECE
| 1943 | BRO | N | 2 | | 7 | .100 |
| | | | BBTR | | | |

CAMPANIS, JAMES ALEXANDER (JIM)
B.FEB.9,1944 NEW YORK,N.Y.
1966	LA	N	/C		1	.000
1967	LA	N	C		41	.161
1968	LA	N	/C		4	.091
1969	KC	A	C		30	.157
1970	KC	A	C/O		31	.130
1973	PIT	N	/H		6	.167
			BRTR		113	.147

CAMPAU, CHARLES C. (COUNT)
B.OCT.17,1863 DETROIT,MICH.
D.APR.3,1938 NEW ORLEANS,LA.
1888	DET	N	O		70	.203
1890	STL	AA	M-O		74	.274
1894	WAS	N	O		2	.142
					146	.245

CAMPBELL, ARCHIBALD STEWART
(ARCHIE) OR (IRON MAN)
B.OCT.20,1903 MAPLEWOOD,N.J.
1928	NY	A	P		13	0- 1
1929	WAS	A	P		4	0- 1
1930	CIN	N	P		23	2- 4
			BRTR		40	2- 6

CAMPBELL, ARTHUR VINCENT (VIN)
B.JAN.30,1888 ST.LOUIS,MO.
D.NOV.16,1969 TOWSON,MD.
1908	CHI	N	O		1	.000
1910	PIT	N	O		74	.326
1911	PIT	N	O		21	.312
1912	BOS	N	O		145	.296
1914	IND	F	O		133	.315
1915	NEW	F	O		127	.314
			BLTR		501	.310

CAMPBELL, BRUCE DOUGLAS
B.OCT.20,1909 CHICAGO,ILL.
1930	CHI	A	O		5	.500
1931	CHI	A	O		4	.412
1932	CHI	A	O		7	.222
	STL	A	O		139	.285
1933	CHI	A	O		148	.277
1934	CLE	A	O		138	.279
1935	CLE	A	O		80	.325
1936	CLE	A	O		76	.372
1937	CLE	A	O		134	.301
1938	CLE	A	O		133	.290
1939	CLE	A	O		130	.287
1940	DET	A	O		103	.283
1941	DET	A	O		141	.275
1942	WAS	A	O		122	.278
			BLTR		1360	.290

CAMPBELL, CLARENCE (SOUP)
B.MAR.7,1915 SPARTA,VA.
1940	CLE	A	O		35	.226
1941	CLE	A	O		104	.250
			BLTR		139	.246

CAMPBELL, DAVID ALAN (DAVE)
B.SEPT.3,1951 PRINCETON,IND.
1977	ATL	N	P		65	0- 6
1978	ATL	N	P		53	4- 4
			BRTR		118	4-10

CAMPBELL, DAVID WILSON (DAVE)
B.JAN.14,1942 MANISTEE,MICH.
1967	DET	A	/1		2	.000
1968	DET	A	/2		9	.125
1969	DET	A	1/2-3		32	.103
1970	SD	N	*2		154	.219
1971	SD	N	2-3/S-1-O		108	.227
1972	SD	N	3/2		33	.240
1973	SD	N	2/1-3		33	.229
	STL	N	/2		13	.000
	HOU	N	/3-1-O		9	.267
1974	HOU	N	/2-1-3-O		35	.206
			BRTR		428	.213

CAMPBELL, HUGH F.
D.1881
| 1873 | RES | NA | P-2- | 17 | 19 | 2-15 |
| | | | O | | | - |

CAMPBELL, JAMES ROBERT (JIM)
B.JUNE 24,1937 PALO ALTO,CAL.
1962	HOU	N	C		27	.221
1963	HOU	N	C		55	.222
			BRTR		82	.221

CAMPBELL, JAMES ROBERT (JIM)
B.JAN.10,1943 HARTSVILLE,S.C.
| 1970 | STL | N | H | | 13 | .231 |
| | | | BLTR | | | |

CAMPBELL, JOHN MILLARD
B.SEPT.13,1907 WASHINGTON,D.C.
| 1933 | WAS | A | P | | 1 | 0- 0 |
| | | | BRTR | | | |

CAMPBELL, JOSEPH EARL (JOE)
B.MAR.10,1944 LOUISVILLE,KY.
| 1967 | CHI | N | /O | | 1 | .000 |
| | | | BRTR | | | |

CAMPBELL, MARC THADDEUS
B.NOV.29,1884 PUNXSUTAWNEY,PA.
D.FEB.13,1946 NEW BETHLEHEM,PA.
| 1907 | PIT | N | S | | 2 | .250 |
| | | | BLTR | | | |

CAMPBELL, MICHAEL
B.NEW JERSEY
| 1873 | RES | NA | 1-S-O | | 20 | |

YR	CL LEA POS	GP	G	REC

CAMPBELL, PAUL MC LAUGHLIN
B.SEPT.1,1917 PAW CREEK,N.C.
1941 BOS A H		1	.000
1942 BOS A D	26		.067
1946 BOS A 1	28		.115
1948 DET A 1	59		.265
1949 DET A 1	87		.278
1950 DET A H		3	.000
BLTL	204		.255

CAMPBELL, RONALD THOMAS (RON)
B.APR.5,1940 CHATTANOOGA,TENN.
1964 CHI N 2	26		.272
1965 CHI N /H		2	.000
1966 CHI N S/3	24		.217
BRTR	52		.247

CAMPBELL, SAMUEL
B.PHILADELPHIA,PA.
| 1890 ATH AA 2 | | 2 | .000 |

CAMPBELL, WILLIAM GILTHORPE (GILLY)
B.FEB.13,1908 KANSAS CITY,KAN.
D.FEB.21,1973 LOS ANGELES,CAL.
1933 CHI N C	46		.281
1935 CIN N C-1-D	88		.257
1936 CIN N C-1	89		.268
1937 CIN N C	18		.275
1938 BRO N C	54		.246
BLTR	295		.263

CAMPBELL, WILLIAM JAMES (BILL)
B.NOV.5,1873 PITTSBURGH,PA.
D.OCT.6,1957 CINCINNATI,OHIO
1905 STL N P		2	1- 1
1907 CIN N P		3	2- 0
1908 CIN N P	35		12-13
1909 CIN N P	30		7-11
BLTL	70		22-25

CAMPBELL, WILLIAM RICHARD (BILL)
B.AUG.9,1948 HIGHLAND PARK,ILL.
1973 MIN A P	28		3- 3
1974 MIN A P	63		8- 7
1975 MIN A P	47		4- 6
1976 MIN A P	78		17- 5
1977 BOS A P	69		13- 9
1978 BOS A P	29		7- 5
BLTR	314		52-35

CAMPER, CARDELL
B.JULY 6,1952 BOLEY,OKLA.
| 1977 CLE A /P | | 3 | 1- 0 |
| BRTR | | | |

CAMPFIELD, WILLIAM HOLTON (SAL)
B.FEB.19,1868 MEADVILLE,PA.
D.MAY 16,1952 MEADVILLE,PA.
| 1896 NY N P | | 6 | 0- 1 |
| BRTR | | | |

CAMPISI, SALVATORE JOHN (SAL)
B.AUG.11,1942 BROOKLYN,N.Y.
1969 STL N /P		7	1- 0
1970 STL N P	37		2- 2
1971 MIN A /P		6	0- 0
BRTR	50		3- 2

CAMPOS, FRANCISCO JOSE (LOPEZ) (FRANK)
B.MAY 11,1924 HAVANA,CUBA
1951 WAS A O		8	.423
1952 WAS A O	53		.259
1953 WAS A H	10		.111
BLTL	71		.279

CANAVAN, HUGH EDWARD (HUGO)
B.MAY 13,1897 WORCESTER,MASS.
D.SEPT.4,1967 BOSTON,MASS.
| 1918 BOS N P | 16 | | 0- 4 |
| BLTL | | | |

CANAVAN, JAMES EDWARD
B.NOV.26,1866 NEW BEDFORD,MASS.
D.MAY 27,1949 NEW BEDFORD,MASS.
1891 CIN AA S	91		.253
MIL AA 2-S	34		.268
1892 CHI N 2	118		.166
1893 CIN N O	118		.238
1894 BRO N O	100		.293
1897 BRO N 2	63		.222
BRTR	524		.231

CANDELARIA, JOHN ROBERT (JOHN) OR (CANDY MAN)
B.NOV.6,1953 NEW YORK,N.Y.
1975 PIT N P		18	8- 6
1976 PIT N P	32		16- 7
1977 PIT N P	33		20- 5
1978 PIT N P	30	31	12-11
BLTL	113	114	56-29

CANDINI, MARIO CAIN (MILO)
B.AUG.3,1917 MANTECA,CAL.
1943 WAS A P		28	11- 7
1944 WAS A P	28		6- 7
1946 WAS A P		9	2- 0
1947 WAS A P	38		3- 4
1948 WAS A P	35		2- 3
1949 WAS A P		3	0- 0
1950 PHI N P		18	1- 0
1951 PHI N P		15	1- 0
BRTR	174		26-21

CANEIRA, JOHN CASCAES
B.OCT.7,1952 WATERBURY,CONN.
1977 CAL A /P		6	2- 2
1978 CAL A /P		2	0- 0
BRTR		8	2- 2

CANNELL, VIRGIN WIRT (RIP)
B.JAN.23,1880 S.BRIDGTON,MAINE
D.AUG.26,1948 BRIDGTON,MAINE
1904 BOS N O		93	.234
1905 BOS N O	154		.247
BLTR	247		.242

CANNIZZARO, CHRISTOPHER JOHN (CHRIS)
B.MAY 3,1938 OAKLAND,CAL.
1960 STL N C		7	.222
1961 STL N C		6	.500
1962 NY N C-O	59		.241
1963 NY N C		16	.242
1964 NY N C	60		.311
1965 NY N *C	114		.183
1968 PIT N C	25		.241
1969 SD N *C	134		.220
1970 SD N *C	111		.279
1971 SD N C	21		.190
CHI N C	71		.213
1972 LA N C	73		.240
1973 LA N C	17		.190
1974 SD N C	26		.183
BRTR	740		.235

CANNON, JOSEPH JEROME (JOE)
B.JULY 13,1953 CAMP LEJEUNE,N.C.
1977 HOU N /O		9	.118
1978 HOU N /O		8	.222
BLTR		17	.171

CANTILLON, JOSEPH D. (PONGO)
B.AUG.19,1861 JANESVILLE,WIS.
D.JAN.31,1930 HICKMAN,KY.
NON-PLAYING MANAGER WAS(A) 1907-09

CANTRELL, GUY DEWEY (GUNNER)
B.APR.9,1904 CLARITA,OKLA.
D.JAN.31,1961 MC ALESTER,OKLA.
1925 BRO N P		14	1- 0
1927 BRO N P		6	0- 0
PHI A P		2	0- 2
1930 DET A P	16		1- 5
BRTR	38		2- 7

CANTWELL, BENJAMIN CALDWELL
B.APR.13,1902 MILAN,TENN.
D.DEC.4,1962 SALEM,MO.
1927 NY N P		5	1- 1
1928 NY N P		7	1- 0
BOS N P	22		3- 3
1929 BGS N P	27		4-13
1930 BOS N P	31	34	9-15
1931 BOS N P	33	40	7- 9
1932 BOS N P	37		13-11
1933 BOS N P	40	49	20-10
1934 BOS N P	27	29	5-11
1935 BOS N P	39	41	4-25
1936 BOS N P	34	35	9- 9
1937 NY N P		1	0- 1
BRO N P		13	0- 0
BRTR	316	340	76-108

CANTWELL, MICHAEL JOSEPH
B.JAN.15,1896 WASHINGTON,D.C.
D.JAN.5,1953 OTEEN,N.C.
1916 NY A P		1	0- 0
1919 PHI N P		5	1- 3
1920 PHI N P		5	0- 3
BLTL		11	1- 6

CANTWELL, THOMAS ALOYSIUS
B.DEC.23,1888 WASHINGTON,D.C.
D.APR.1,1968 WASHINGTON,D.C.
1909 CIN N P		6	1- 0
1910 CIN N P		2	0- 0
BLTR		8	1- 0

CANTZ, BARTHOLOMEW L.
B.JAN.29,1860 PHILADELPHIA,PA.
D.FEB.12,1943 PHILADELPHIA,PA.
1888 BAL AA C	37		.165
1889 BAL AA C	21		.158
1890 ATH AA C		5	.096
	63		.157

CAPILLA, DOUGLAS EDMUND (DOUG)
B.JAN.7,1952 HONOLULU,HAWAII
1976 STL N P		7	1- 0
1977 STL N /P		2	0- 0
CIN N P	22		7- 8
1978 CIN N /P	6	7	0- 1
BLTL	37	38	8- 9

CAPRA, LEE WILLIAM (BUZZ)
B.OCT.1,1947 CHICAGO,ILL.
1971 NY N /P		3	0- 1
1972 NY N P	14		3- 2
1973 NY N P	24		2- 7
1974 ATL N P	39		16- 8
1975 ATL N P	12		4- 7
1976 ATL N /P		5	0- 1
1977 ATL N P	45		6-11
BRTR	142		31-37

CAPRI, PATRICK NICHOLAS
B.NOV.27,1918 NEW YORK,N.Y.
| 1944 BOS N 2 | | 7 | .000 |
| BRTR | | | |

CAPRON, RALPH EARL
B.MAR.11,1893 MINNEAPOLIS,MINN.
1912 PIT N O		1	.000
1913 PHI N O		5	.000
BLTR		6	.000

CARAWAY, CECIL BRADFORD PATRICK (PAT)
B.SEPT.26,1905 ERATH CO.,TEX.
D.JUNE 9,1974 EL PASO,TEX.
1930 CHI A P		38	10-10
1931 CHI A P	51	52	10-24
1932 CHI A P		19	2- 6
BLTR	108	109	22-40

CARBINE, JOHN C.
B.OCT.12,1855 SYRACUSE,N.Y.
D.SEPT.1,1915 CHICAGO,ILL.
1875 WES NA 1		10	-
1876 LOU N 1		6	.150
		16	-

CARBO, BERNARDO (BERNIE)
B.AUG.5,1947 DETROIT,MICH.
1969 CIN N /H		4	.000
1970 CIN N *O	125		.310
1971 CIN N O	106		.219
1972 CIN N /O		19	.143
STL N O/3	99		.258
1973 STL N O	111		.286
1974 BOS A O-D	117		.249
1975 BOS A O-D	107		.257
1976 BOS A D/O		17	.236
MIL A D-O	69		.235
1977 BOS A O	86		.289
1978 BOS A /O		17	.261
CLE A D/O	60		.287
BLTR	937		.264

CARDEN, JOHN BRUTON
B.MAY 19,1921 KILLEEN,TEX.
D.FEB.8,1949 MEXIA,TEX.
| 1946 NY N P | | 1 | 0- 0 |
| BRTR | | | |

CARDENAL, JOSE ROSARIO DOMEC [REAL NAME JOSE ROSARIO DOMEC [CARDENAL]]
B.OCT.7,1943 MATANZAS,CUBA
1963 SF N O		9	.200
1964 SF N O		20	.000
1965 CAL A *O-S/2	134		.250
1966 CAL A *O	154		.276
1967 CAL A *O	108		.236
1968 CLE A *O	157		.257
1969 CLE A *O/3	146		.257
1970 STL N *O	148		.293
1971 STL N O	69		.243
MIL A O	53		.258
1972 CHI N *O	143		.291
1973 CHI N *O	145		.303
1974 CHI N *O	143		.293
1975 CHI N *O	154		.317
1976 CHI N *O	136		.299
1977 CHI N O/2-S	100		.239
1978 PHI N 1-O	87		.249
BRTR	1926		.275

YR	CL LEA POS	GP	G	REC

CARDENAS, LEONARDO LAZARO
[ALFONSO] (LEO) OR (CHICO)
B.DEC.17,1938 MATANZAS,CUBA

YR	CL LEA POS	GP	G	REC
1960	CIN N S		48	.232
1961	CIN N S		74	.308
1962	CIN N S		153	.294
1963	CIN N S		158	.235
1964	CIN N S		163	.251
1965	CIN N *S		156	.287
1966	CIN N *S		160	.255
1967	CIN N *S		108	.256
1968	CIN N *S		137	.235
1969	MIN A *S		160	.280
1970	MIN A *S		160	.247
1971	MIN A *S		153	.264
1972	CAL A *S		150	.223
1973	CLE A S/3		72	.215
1974	TEX A 3-S		34	.242
1975	TEX A 3/S-2		55	.235
	BRTR		1941	.257

CARDINAL, CONRAD SETH
B.MAR.3,1942 BROOKLYN,N.Y.

YR	CL LEA POS	GP	G	REC
1963	HOU N P		6	0- 1
	BRTR			

CARDONI, ARMAND JOSEPH (BIG BEN)
B.AUG.21,1920 JESSUP,PA.
D.APR.2,1969 JESSUP,PA.

YR	CL LEA POS	GP	G	REC
1943	BOS N P		11	0- 0
1944	BOS N P	22	29	0- 6
1945	BOS N P		3	0- 0
	BRTR	36	43	0- 6

CARDWELL, DONALD EUGENE (DON)
B.DEC.7,1935 WINSTON-SALEM,N.C.

YR	CL LEA POS	GP	G	REC
1957	PHI N P		30	4- 8
1958	PHI N P		16	3- 6
1959	PHI N P	25	26	9-10
1960	PHI N P		5	1- 2
	CHI N P	31	33	8-14
1961	CHI N P	39	40	15-14
1962	CHI N P		41	7-16
1963	PIT N P		33	13-15
1964	PIT N P		4	1- 2
1965	PIT N P		37	13-10
1966	PIT N P		32	6- 6
1967	NY N P	26	27	5- 9
1968	NY N P	29	30	7-13
1969	NY N P		30	8-10
1970	NY N P		16	0- 2
	ATL N P		16	2- 1
	BRTR	410	416	102-138

CAREW, RODNEY CLINE (ROD)
B.OCT.1,1945 GATUN,PANAMA

YR	CL LEA POS	GP	G	REC
1967	MIN A *2		137	.292
1968	MIN A *2/S		127	.273
1969	MIN A *2		123	.332
1970	MIN A 2/1		51	.366
1971	MIN A *2/3		147	.307
1972	MIN A *2		142	.318
1973	MIN A *2		149	.350
1974	MIN A *2		153	.364
1975	MIN A *2-1		143	.359
1976	MIN A *1/2		156	.331
1977	MIN A *1/2		155	.388
1978	MIN A *1/2-0		152	.333
	BLTR		1635	.334

CAREY, ANDREW ARTHUR (ANDY)
[REAL NAME ANDREW ARTHUR NORDSTROM]
B.OCT.18,1931 OAKLAND,CAL.

YR	CL LEA POS	GP	G	REC
1952	NY A S-3		16	.150
1953	NY A 2-S-3		51	.321
1954	NY A 3		122	.302
1955	NY A 3		135	.257
1956	NY A 3		132	.237
1957	NY A 3		85	.255
1958	NY A 3		102	.286
1959	NY A 3		41	.257
1960	NY A 3-0		4	.333
	KC A 3		102	.233
1961	KC A 3		39	.244
	CHI A 3		56	.266
1962	LA N 3		53	.234
	BRTR		938	.260

CAREY, GEORGE C. (SCOOPS)
B.OCT.4,1870 E.LIVERPOOL,OHIO
D.DEC.17,1916 E.LIVERPOOL,OHIO

YR	CL LEA POS	GP	G	REC
1895	BAL N 1		123	.271
1898	LOU N 1		8	.187
1902	WAS A 1		120	.316
1903	WAS A 1		48	.198
	BRTR		299	.275

CAREY, MAX GEORGE (MAX) OR (SCOOPS)
[REAL NAME MAXIMILIAN CARNARIUS]
B.JAN.11,1890 TERRE HAUTE,IND.
D.MAY 30,1976 MIAMI,FLA.

YR	CL LEA POS	GP	G	REC
1910	PIT N O		2	.500
1911	PIT N O		122	.258
1912	PIT N O		150	.302
1913	PIT N O		154	.277
1914	PIT N O		156	.243
1915	PIT N O		140	.254
1916	PIT N O		154	.264
1917	PIT N O		155	.296
1918	PIT N O		126	.274
1919	PIT N O		66	.307
1920	PIT N O		130	.289
1921	PIT N O		140	.309
1922	PIT N O		155	.329
1923	PIT N O		153	.308
1924	PIT N O		149	.297
1925	PIT N O		133	.343
1926	PIT N O		86	.222
	BRO N O		27	.260
1927	BRO N O		144	.266
1928	BRO N O		108	.247
1929	BRO N O		19	.304
	BBTR		2469	.285

NON-PLAYING MANAGER BRO(N) 1932-33

CAREY, THOMAS FRANCIS ALOYSIUS
(SCOOPS)
B.OCT.11,1906 HOBOKEN,N.J.
D.FEB.21,1970 ROCHESTER,N.Y.

YR	CL LEA POS	GP	G	REC
1935	STL A 2		76	.291
1936	STL A 2		134	.273
1937	STL A 2-S		130	.275
1939	BOS A 2-S		54	.242
1940	BOS A 2-S-3		43	.323
1941	BOS A 2-S		24	.200
1942	BOS A 2		1	1.000
1946	BOS A 2		3	.200
	BRTR		465	.275

CAREY, THOMAS JOHN
[REAL NAME J. J. NORTON]
B.1849 BROOKLYN,N.J.
D.FEB.13,1899 LOS ANGELES,CAL.

YR	CL LEA POS	GP	G	REC
1871	KEK NA 2		19	-
1872	BAL NA 1-2-S-3-0		41	.296
1873	BAL NA 2-S-3		55	-
1874	MUT NA 2-S		64	-
1875	HAR NA S		85	-
1876	HAR N S		68	.301
1877	HAR N S		60	.255
1878	PRO N S		59	.251
1879	CLE N S		80	.238
	TR		531	-

CARGO, ROBERT J. (BOBBY) OR (CHIC)
B.1871 PITTSBURGH,PA.
D.APR.27,1904 ATLANTA,GA.

YR	CL LEA POS	GP	G	REC
1892	PIT N S		2	.200
	BRTR			

CARISCH, FREDERICK BEHLMER
B.NOV.14,1881 FOUNTAIN CITY,WIS
D.APR.19,1977 SAN GABRIEL,CAL.

YR	CL LEA POS	GP	G	REC
1903	PIT N C		5	.352
1904	PIT N C-1		36	.248
1905	PIT N C		30	.206
1906	PIT N C		4	.083
1912	CLE A C		81	.216
1913	CLE A C		81	.216
1914	CLE A C		40	.216
1923	DET A C		2	.000
	BRTR		222	.228

CARL, FREDERICK E.
B.1858 BALTIMORE,MD.
D.JULY 30,1897

YR	CL LEA POS	GP	G	REC
1889	LOU AA 2-0		25	.202

CARL, LEWIS
B.BALTIMORE,MD.

YR	CL LEA POS	GP	G	REC
1874	BAL NA C		1	.000

CARLETON, JAMES
B.1849 NEW YORK

YR	CL LEA POS	GP	G	REC
1871	CLE NA 1		29	-
1872	CLE NA 1		7	.316
			36	-

CARLETON, JAMES OTTO (TEX)
B.AUG.19,1906 COMANCHE,TEX.
D.JAN.11,1977 FORT WORTH,TEX.

YR	CL LEA POS	GP	G	REC
1932	STL N P		44	10-13
1933	STL N P	44	46	17-11
1934	STL N P	40	41	16-11
1935	CHI N P		31	11- 8
1936	CHI N P		35	14-10
1937	CHI N P	32	34	16- 8
1938	CHI N P		33	10- 9
1940	BRO N P		34	6- 6
	BBTR		293 298	100-76

CARLIN, JAMES ARTHUR
B.FEB.23,1918 WYLAM,ALA.

YR	CL LEA POS	GP	G	REC
1941	PHI N 3-0		16	.143
	BRTR			

CARLISLE, WALTER G. (ROSY)
B.JULY 6,1883 YEADON,ENGLAND
D.MAY 27,1945 HOLLYWOOD,CAL.

YR	CL LEA POS	GP	G	REC
1908	BOS A O		3	.100
	BBTR			

CARLOS, FRANCISCO MANUEL (CISCO)
B.SEP.17,1940 MONROVIA,CAL.

YR	CL LEA POS	GP	G	REC
1967	CHI A /P		8	2- 0
1968	CHI A P		29	4-14
1969	CHI A P		25	4- 3
	WAS A /P		6	1- 1
1970	WAS A /P		5	0- 0
	BRTR		73	11-18

CARLSEN, DONALD HERBERT (DON)
B.OCT.15,1926 CHICAGO,ILL.

YR	CL LEA POS	GP	G	REC
1948	CHI N P		1	0- 0
1951	PIT N P		7	2- 3
1952	PIT N P		5	0- 1
	BRTR		13	2- 4

CARLSON, HAROLD GUST
B.MAY 17,1892 ROCKFORD,ILL.
D.MAY 28,1930 CHICAGO,ILL.

YR	CL LEA POS	GP	G	REC
1917	PIT N P		34	7-11
1918	PIT N P		3	0- 1
1919	PIT N P		22	8-10
1920	PIT N P		39	14-13
1921	PIT N P		31	4- 8
1922	PIT N P		39	9-12
1923	PIT N P		4	0- 0
1924	PHI N P	38	39	8-17
1925	PHI N P	35	38	13-14
1926	PHI N P	35	38	17-12
1927	PHI N P	11	12	4- 5
	CHI N P		27	12- 8
1928	CHI N P		20	3- 2
1929	CHI N P		31	11- 5
1930	CHI N P		8	4- 2
	BRTR	377	385	114-120

CARLSON, JOSEPH MARTIN NAPOLEON
[PLAYED UNDER NAME OF
JOSEPH MARTIN NAPOLEON MUNSON]

CARLSON, LEON ALTON (SWEDE)
B.FEB.17,1895 JAMESTOWN,N.Y.
D.SEPT.15,1961 JAMESTOWN,N.Y.

YR	CL LEA POS	GP	G	REC
1920	WAS A P		3	0- 0
	BRTR			

CARLSTROM, ALBIN OSCAR (SWEDE)
B.OCT.26,1886 ELIZABETH,N.J.
D.APR.28,1935 ELIZABETH,N.J.

YR	CL LEA POS	GP	G	REC
1911	BOS A S		2	.167
	BRTR			

CARLTON, STEVEN NORMAN
(STEVE) OR (LEFTY)
B.DEC.22,1944 MIAMI,FLA.

YR	CL LEA POS	GP	G	REC
1965	STL N P		15	0- 0
1966	STL N /P		9	3- 3
1967	STL N P		30	14- 9
1968	STL N P	34	35	13-11
1969	STL N P	31	32	17-11
1970	STL N P		34	10-19
1971	STL N P		37	20- 9
1972	PHI N P		41	27-10
1973	PHI N P		40	13-20
1974	PHI N P		39	16-13
1975	PHI N P		37	15-14
1976	PHI N P		35	20- 7
1977	PHI N P		36	23-10
1978	PHI N P		34	16-13
	BLTL		452 454	207-149

CARLYLE, HIRAM CLEO
B.SEPT.7,1902 FAIRBURN,GA.
D.NOV.12,1967 LOS ANGELES,CAL.

YR	CL LEA POS	GP	G	REC
1927	BOS A O		95	.234
	BLTR			

CARLYLE, ROY EDWARD (DIZZY)
B.DEC.10,1900 BUFORD,GA.
D.NOV.22,1956 NORCROSS,GA.

YR	CL LEA POS	GP	G	REC
1925	WAS A O		1	.000
	BOS A O		93	.326
1926	BOS A O		45	.285
	NY A O		35	.385
	BLTR		174	.318

CARMEL, LEON JAMES (DUKE)
B.APR.23,1937 NEW YORK,N.Y.

YR	CL LEA POS	GP	G	REC
1959	STL N O		10	.130
1960	STL N 1-0		4	.000
1963	STL N 1-0		57	.227
	NY N 1-0		47	.235
1965	NY A /1		6	.000
	BLTL		124	.211

CARMEN, GEORGE W.
B.DOYLESTOWN,PA.

YR	CL LEA POS	GP	G	REC
1890	ATH AA S		25	.151

CARMICHAEL, CHESTER KELLER
B.JAN.9,1888 EATON,IND.
D.AUG.23,1960 ROCHESTER,N.Y.

YR	CL	LEA	POS	GP	G	REC
1909	CIN	N	P		2	0- 0
	BRTR					

CARNARIUS, MAXIMILIAN
[PLAYED UNDER NAME OF
MAX GEORGE CAREY]

CARNETT, EDWIN ELLIOTT (LEFTY)
B.OCT.21,1916 SPRINGFIELD,MO.

YR	CL	LEA	POS	GP	G	REC
1941	BOS	N	P		2	0- 0
1944	CHI	A	P-1-O	2	126	0- 0
						.276
1945	CLE	A	P-O	2	30	0- 0
						.219
	BLTL			6	158	0- 0
						.268

CARNEY, JOHN JOSEPH (HANDSOME JACK)
B.NOV.10,1866 SALEM,MASS.
D.OCT.19,1925 LITCHFIELD,N.H.

YR	CL	LEA	POS	G	REC
1889	WAS	N	1-O	69	.230
1890	BUF	P	1	28	.262
	CLE	P	O	25	.344
1891	CIN	AA	1	91	.276
	MIL	AA	1	30	.291
	BRTR			243	.270

CARNEY, PATRICK JOSEPH (DOC)
B.AUG.7,1876 HOLYOKE,MASS.
D.JAN.9,1953 WORCESTER,MASS.

YR	CL	LEA	POS	GP	G	REC
1901	BOS	N	O		13	.302
1902	BOS	N	P-O	2	137	0- 1
						.266
1903	BOS	N	P-O	10	102	6- 4
						.240
1904	BOS	N	P-O	5	76	0- 2
						.204
	BLTL			17	328	4- 7
						.245

CARNEY, WILLIAM JOHN
B.MAR.25,1874 ST.PAUL,MINN.
D.JULY 31,1938 HOPKINS,MINN.

YR	CL	LEA	POS	G	REC
1904	CHI	N	O	2	.000

CARPENTER, LEWIS EMMETT
B.AUG.16,1913 WOODSTOCK,GA.

YR	CL	LEA	POS	G	REC
1943	WAS	A	P	4	0- 0
	BRTR				

CARPENTER, PAUL CALVIN
B.AUG.12,1894 GRANVILLE,OHIO
D.MAR.14,1968 NEWARK,OHIO

YR	CL	LEA	POS	G	REC
1916	PIT	N	P	5	0- 0
	BRTR				

CARPENTER, ROBERT LOUIS
B.DEC.12,1917 CHICAGO,ILL.

YR	CL	LEA	POS	G	REC
1940	NY	N	P	5	2- 0
1941	NY	N	P	29	11- 6
1942	NY	N	P	28	11-10
1946	NY	N	P	12	1- 3
1947	NY	N	P	2	0- 0
	CHI	N	P	4	0- 1
	BRTR			80	25-20

CARPENTER, WARREN WILLIAM (HICK)
B.AUG.16,1855 GRAFTON,MASS.
D.APR.18,1937 SAN DIEGO,CAL.

YR	CL	LEA	POS	G	REC
1879	SYR	N	1-3-O	63	.201
1880	CIN	N	1-3	76	.243
1881	WOR	N	3	82	.209
1882	CIN	AA	3	80	.354
1883	CIN	AA	3	94	.308
1884	CIN	AA	3-O	109	.265
1885	CIN	AA	3	112	.291
1886	CIN	AA	3	111	.221
1887	CIN	AA	3	127	.269
1888	CIN	AA	3	135	.269
1889	CIN	AA	1-3	123	.257
1892	STL	N	3	1	.333
	BRTL			1113	.264

CARPIN, FRANK DOMINIC
B.SEP.14,1938 BROOKLYN,N.Y.

YR	CL	LEA	POS	G	REC
1965	PIT	N	P	39	3- 1
1966	HOU	N	P	10	1- 0
	BLTL			49	4- 1

CARR, CHARLES CARBITT
B.DEC.27,1876 COATESVILLE,PA.
D.NOV.25,1932 MEMPHIS,TENN.

YR	CL	LEA	POS	G	REC
1898	WAS	N	1	20	.197
1901	PHI	A	1	2	.125
1903	DET	A	1	135	.262
1904	DET	A	1	91	.270
	CLE	A	1	32	.223
1905	CLE	A	1	89	.235
1906	CIN	N	1	22	.191
1914	IND	F	1	115	.292
	BRTR			506	.251

CARR, LEWIS SMITH
B.AUG.15,1872 UNION SPRINGS,N.Y
D.JUNE 15,1954 MORAVIA,N.Y.

YR	CL	LEA	POS	G	REC
1901	PIT	N	S	9	.233
	TR				

**CARRASQUEL, ALEJANDRO APARICIO
ELROY (ALEX)**
[REAL NAME
ALEJANDRO CARRASQUEL ELROY]
D.AUG.19,1969 CARACAS,VENEZ.

YR	CL	LEA	POS	G	REC
1939	WAS	A	P	40	5- 9
1940	WAS	A	P	28	6- 2
1941	WAS	A	P	35	6- 2
1942	WAS	A	P	35	7- 7
1943	WAS	A	P	39	11- 7
1944	WAS	A	P	43	8- 7
1945	WAS	A	P	35	7- 5
1949	CHI	A	P	3	0- 0
	BRTR			258	50-39

CARRASQUEL, ALFONSO [COLON] (CHICO)
B.JAN.23,1928 CARACAS,VENEZ.

YR	CL	LEA	POS	G	REC
1950	CHI	A	S	141	.282
1951	CHI	A	S	147	.264
1952	CHI	A	S	100	.248
1953	CHI	A	S	149	.279
1954	CHI	A	S	135	.255
1955	CHI	A	S	145	.256
1956	CLE	A	S-3	141	.243
1957	CLE	A	S	125	.276
1958	CLE	A	S-3	49	.256
	KC	A	S-3	59	.213
1959	BAL	A	1-2-S-3	114	.223
	BRTR			1325	.258

CARREON, CAMILO [GARCIA] (CAM)
B.AUG.6,1937 COLTON,CAL.

YR	CL	LEA	POS	G	REC
1959	CHI	A	C	1	.000
1960	CHI	A	C	8	.235
1961	CHI	A	C	78	.271
1962	CHI	A	C	106	.256
1963	CHI	A	C	101	.274
1964	CHI	A	C	37	.274
1965	CLE	A	C	19	.231
1966	BAL	A	/C	4	.222
	BRTR			354	.264

**CARRICK, WILLIAM MARTIN
(DOUGHNUT BILL)**
B.SEPT.5,1873 ERIE,PA.
D.MAR.7,1932 PHILADELPHIA,PA.

YR	CL	LEA	POS	GP	G	REC
1898	NY	N	P		5	3- 1
1899	NY	N	P		44	16-25
1900	NY	N	P		42	19-21
1901	WAS	A	P		42	15-22
1902	WAS	A	P-O	31	33	12-17
						.187
	TR			164	166	65-86
						.161

CARRIGAN, WILLIAM FRANCIS (ROUGH)
B.OCT.22,1883 LEWISTON,ME.
D.JULY 8,1969 LEWISTON,ME.

YR	CL	LEA	POS	G	REC
1906	BOS	A	C	37	.211
1908	BOS	A	C	57	.235
1909	BOS	A	C	94	.296
1910	BOS	A	C	114	.249
1911	BOS	A	C	87	.289
1912	BOS	A	C	87	.263
1913	BOS	A	M-C	85	.242
1914	BOS	A	M-C	81	.253
1915	BOS	A	M-C	46	.200
1916	BOS	A	M-C	33	.270
	BRTR			706	.257

NON-PLAYING MANAGER BOS[A] 1927-29

CARRITHERS, DONALD GEORGE (DON)
B.SEP.15,1949 LYNWOOD,CAL.

YR	CL	LEA	POS	GP	G	REC
1970	SF	N	P		11	2- 1
1971	SF	N	P		22	5- 3
1972	SF	N	P	25	26	4- 8
1973	SF	N	P	25	28	1- 2
1974	MON	N	P		22	5- 2
1975	MON	N	P		19	5- 3
1976	MON	N	P	34	35	6-12
1977	MIN	A	/P		7	0- 1
	BRTR			165	170	28-32

**CARROLL, CLAY PALMER
(CLAY) OR (HAWK)**
B.MAY 2,1941 CLANTON,ALA.

YR	CL	LEA	POS	G	REC
1964	MIL	N	P	11	2- 0
1965	MIL	N	P	19	0- 1
1966	ATL	N	P	73	8- 7
1967	ATL	N	P	42	6-12
1968	ATL	N	P	10	0- 1
	CIN	N	P	58	7- 7
1969	CIN	N	P	71	12- 6
1970	CIN	N	P	65	9- 4
1971	CIN	N	P	61	10- 4
1972	CIN	N	P	65	6- 4
1973	CIN	N	P	93	8- 8
1974	CIN	N	P	57	12- 5
1975	CIN	N	P	56	7- 5
1976	CHI	A	P	29	4- 4
1977	STL	N	P	51	4- 2
	CHI	A	/P	8	1- 3
1978	PIT	N	/P	2	0- 0
	BRTR			731	96-73

CARROLL, DORSEY LEE (DIXIE)
B.MAY 9,1891 PADUCAH,KY.

YR	CL	LEA	POS	G	REC
1919	BOS	N	O	15	.275
	BLTR				

CARROLL, E. (CHICK)
B.CHICAGO,ILL.

YR	CL	LEA	POS	G	REC
1884	WAS	U	O	4	.200

CARROLL, EDGAR FLEISCHER
B.JULY 27,1907 BALTIMORE,MD.

YR	CL	LEA	POS	G	REC
1929	BOS	A	P	24	1- 0
	BRTR				

CARROLL, FREDERICK HERBERT
B.JULY 2,1864 SACRAMENTO,CAL.
D.NOV.7,1904 SAN RAFAEL,CAL.

YR	CL	LEA	POS	G	REC
1884	COL	AA	C-O	69	.283
1885	PIT	AA	C	69	.263
1886	PIT	AA	C-1	122	.292
1887	PIT	N	C-1-O	101	.380
1888	PIT	N	C-O	96	.243
1889	PIT	N	C-O	90	.330
1890	PIT	P	C-O	111	.302
1891	PIT	N	O	87	.228
	BRTR			745	.295

CARROLL, JOHN E. (SCRAPPY)
B.AUG.27,1860 BUFFALO,N.Y.
D.NOV.14,1942 BUFFALO,N.Y.

YR	CL	LEA	POS	G	REC
1884	STP	U	3-O	9	.083
1885	BUF	N	2-O	12	.056
1887	CLE	AA	O	57	.252
1892	CHI	N	3	1	.000
				79	

CARROLL, OWEN THOMAS (OWNIE)
B.NOV.11,1902 KEARNY,N.J.
D.JUNE 8,1975 ORANGE,N.J.

YR	CL	LEA	POS	GP	G	REC
1925	DET	A	P-O	10	11	2- 2
						.375
1927	DET	A	P	31	37	10- 6
1928	DET	A	P	34	43	16-12
1929	DET	A	P	34	37	9-17
1930	DET	A	P		6	0- 5
	NY	A	P	10	11	0- 1
	CIN	N	P		3	0- 1
1931	CIN	N	P	29	30	3- 9
1932	CIN	N	P	32	35	10-19
1933	BRO	N	P	33	34	13-15
1934	BRO	N	P	26	28	1- 3
	BRTR			248	275	64-90
						.200

CARROLL, PATRICK
B.PHILADELPHIA,PA.
D.FEB.14,1916 PHILADELPHIA,PA.

YR	CL	LEA	POS	G	REC
1884	ALT	U	C-O	11	.255
	KEY	U	C	5	.158
				16	.229

CARROLL, RALPH ARTHUR (DOC) OR (RED)
B.DEC.28,1891 WORCESTER,MASS.

YR	CL	LEA	POS	G	REC
1916	PHI	A	C	10	.091
	BRTR				

CARROLL, RICHARD THOMAS (SHADOW)
B.JULY 21,1884 CLEVELAND,OHIO
D.NOV.22,1945 CLEVELAND,OHIO

YR	CL	LEA	POS	G	REC
1909	NY	A	P	2	0- 0
	BRTR				

CARROLL, SAMUEL CLIFFORD (CLIFF)
B.OCT.18,1859 CLAY GROVE,IOWA
D.JUNE 12,1923 PORTLAND,ORE.

YR	CL	LEA	POS	G	REC
1882	PRO	N	O	10	.121
1883	PRO	N	O	58	.264
1884	PRO	N	O	112	.261
1885	PRO	N	O	104	.232
1886	WAS	N	O	111	.228
1887	WAS	N	O	101	.276
1888	PIT	N	O	7	.107
1890	CHI	N	O	136	.285
1891	CHI	N	O	130	.255
1892	STL	N	O	100	.273
1893	BOS	N	O	120	.234
	BB			989	.256

YR CL LEA POS   GP   G   REC

CARROLL, THOMAS EDWARD (TOM)
B.SEPT.17,1936 JAMAICA,N.Y.
```
1955 NY  A  S         14  .333
1956 NY  A  S-3       36  .353
1959 KC  A  S-3       14  .143
          BRTR        64  .300
```

CARROLL, THOMAS MICHAEL (TOM)
B.NOV.5,1952 ORISKANY,N.Y.
```
1974 CIN N  P         16  4- 3
1975 CIN N  P         12  4- 1
          BLTR        28  8- 4
```

CASEY, WILFRED (KID)
B.OCT.22,1870 NEW YORK,N.Y.
D.MAR.29,1960 MIAMI,FLA.
```
1891 WAS AA P     53  59  14-33
1892 PHI N  P         35  19-16
1893 PHI N  P     35  36  22-12
1894 PHI N  P     31  32  16-14
1895 PHI N  P         41  24-17
1896 PHI N  P         24  11-13
1897 PHI N  P          6  4- 2
     STL N  P     12  13  1- 7
1898 STL N  P     17  33  1-12
1899 CLE N  P          9  1- 8
     WAS N  P          7  1- 2
     NY  N  S-3        5  .333
1901 BRO N  P          2  1- 0
              272 302 115-136
                         .212
```

CARSON, ALEXANDER JAMES (SOLDIER)
B.MAY 1,1881 NEW JERSEY
D.AUG.18,1954 LOS ANGELES,CAL.
```
1910 CHI N  P          2  0- 0
          TR
```

CARSON, WALTER LLOYD (KIT)
B.NOV.15,1912 COLTON,CAL.
```
1934 CLE A  O          5  .278
1935 CLE A  O         16  .227
          BLTL        21  .250
```

CARSWELL, FRANK WILLIS
(TEX) OR (WHEELS)
B.NOV.6,1919 PALESTINE,TEX.
```
1953 DET A  O         16  .267
          BRTR
```

CARTER, ARNOLD LEE (HOOK) OR (LEFTY)
B.MAR.14,1918 RAINELLE,W.VA.
```
1944 CIN N  P     33  37  11- 7
1945 CIN N  P     13  19  2- 4
          BLTL    46  56  13-11
```

CARTER, CONRAD POWELL (NICK)
B.MAY 19,1879 OATLANDS,VA.
D.NOV.23,1961 GRASONVILLE,MO.
```
1908 PHI A  P         17  2- 5
          TR
```

CARTER, GARY EDMUND
B.APR.8,1954 CULVER CITY,CAL.
```
1974 MON N  /C-O       9  .407
1975 MON N  O-C/3    144  .270
1976 MON N  C         91  .219
1977 MON N  *C/O     154  .284
1978 MON N  *C/1     157  .255
          BRTR       555  .263
```

CARTER, JOHN HOWARD (HOWIE)
B.OCT.13,1904 NEW YORK,N.Y.
```
1926 CIN N  2-S        5  .000
          BRTR
```

CARTER, OTIS LEONARD (BLACKIE)
B.SEPT.30,1902 LANGLEY,S.C.
```
1925 NY  N  O          1  .000
1926 NY  N  O          5  .235
          BRTR         6  .190
```

CARTER, PAUL WARREN (NICK)
B.MAY.1,1894 LAKE PARK,GA.
```
1914 CLE A  P          5  1- 3
1915 CLE A  P     11  12  1- 2
1916 CHI N  P          8  2- 2
1917 CHI N  P         23  5- 8
1918 CHI N  P         21  3- 2
1919 CHI N  P     28  29  5- 4
1920 CHI N  P         31  3- 6
          BLTR   127 129  20-27
```

CARTER, SOLOMON MOBLEY (BUCK)
B.DEC.23,1908 PICAYUNE,MISS.
```
1931 PHI A  P          2  0- 0
          BRTR
```

CARTWRIGHT, EDWARD CHARLES (JUMBO)
B.OCT.6,1859 JOHNSTOWN,PA.
D.1924 FLORIDA
```
1890 STL AA 1         75  .281
1894 WAS N  1        132  .292
1895 WAS N  1        121  .327
1896 WAS N  1        131  .274
1897 WAS N  1         33  .250
          BRTR       492  .292
```

CARTY, RICARDO ADOLFO JACOBO (RICO)
[REAL NAME
RICARDO ADOLFO JACOBO (CARTY)]
B.SEP.1,1939 SAN PEDRO DE
MACORIS,D.R.
```
1963 MIL N  H          2  .000
1964 MIL N  O        133  .330
1965 MIL N  O         83  .310
1966 ATL N  *O-C/1-3 151  .326
1967 ATL N  *O/1     134  .255
1969 ATL N  O        104  .342
1970 ATL N  *O       136  .366
1972 ATL N  O         86  .277
1973 TEX A  O-O       86  .232
     CHI N  O         22  .214
     OAK A  /H         7  .250
1974 CLE A  O/1       33  .363
1975 CLE A  O-1-O    118  .308
1976 CLE A  *O-1/O   152  .310
1977 CLE A  *O/1     127  .280
1978 TOR A  *O       104  .284
     OAK A  O         41  .277
          BRTR      1519  .303
```

CARUTHERS, ROBERT LEE (PARISIAN BOB)
B.JAN.5,1864 MEMPHIS,TENN.
D.AUG.5,1911 PEORIA,ILL.
```
1884 STL A  P-O   13  23  7- 2
                         .253
1885 STL AA P         60  40-13
1886 STL AA P-O   45  86  30-14
                         .342
1887 STL AA P-O   38  98  29- 9
                         .459
1888 BRO AA P-O   45  94  29-15
                         .230
1889 BRO AA P     55  57  40-12
1890 BRO N  P-O   34  71  22-11
                         .265
1891 BRO N  P     34  47  17-17
1892 STL N  P-O   10 142  2- 8
                         .277
1893 CHI N  P          1  0- 0
     CIN N  O         13  .286
          BLTR   335 692 216-101
                         .301
```

CARY, SCOTT RUSSELL (RED)
B.APR.11,1923 KENDALLVILLE,IND.
```
1947 WAS A  P         23  3- 1
          BLTL
```

CASALE, JERRY JOSEPH
B.SEPT.27,1933 BROOKLYN,N.Y.
```
1958 BOS A  P          2  0- 0
1959 BOS A  P         31  13- 8
1960 BOS A  P         29  2- 9
1961 LA  A  P         13  1- 5
     DET A  P          3  0- 0
1962 DET A  P         18  1- 2
          BRTR        96  17-24
```

CASANOVA, PAULINO [ORTIZ] (PAUL)
B.DEC.21,1941 COLON,MATANZAS,CUBA
```
1965 WAS A  /C          5  .308
1966 WAS A  *C        122  .254
1967 WAS A  *C        141  .248
1968 WAS A  C          96  .196
1969 WAS A  *C        124  .216
1970 WAS A  *C        104  .229
1971 WAS A  C          94  .203
1972 ATL N  C          49  .206
1973 ATL N  C          82  .216
1974 ATL N  C          42  .202
          BRTR        859  .225
```

CASCARELLA, JOSEPH THOMAS
(JOE) OR (CROONING JOE)
B.JUNE 29,1907 PHILADELPHIA,PA.
```
1934 PHI A  P         42  12-15
1935 PHI A  P          9  1- 6
     BOS A  P          6  0- 3
1936 BOS A  P         10  0- 2
     WAS A  P         22  9- 8
1937 WAS A  P         10  0- 5
     CIN N  P         11  1- 2
1938 CIN N  P         33  4- 7
          BRTR       143  27-48
```

CASE, CHARLES EMMETT
B.SEPT.7,1879 RURAL,OHIO
D.APR.16,1964 CLAIRMONT,OHIO
```
1901 CIN N  P          3  1- 2
1904 PIT N  P         18  10- 5
1905 PIT N  P         31  12-10
1906 PIT N  P          2  1- 1
                      54  24-18
```

CASE, GEORGE WASHINGTON
B.NOV.11,1915 TRENTON,N.J.
```
1937 WAS A  O         22  .289
1938 WAS A  O        107  .305
1939 WAS A  O        128  .302
1940 WAS A  O        154  .293
1941 WAS A  O        153  .271
1942 WAS A  O        125  .320
1943 WAS A  O        141  .294
1944 WAS A  O        119  .249
1945 WAS A  O        123  .294
1946 CLE A  O        118  .225
1947 WAS A  O         36  .150
          BRTR      1226  .282
```

CASEY, DANIEL MAURICE
B.NOV.20,1862 BINGHAMTON,N.Y.
D.FEB.8,1943 WASHINGTON,D.C.
```
1884 WIL U  P          2  1- 1
1885 DET N  P         12  4- 8
1886 PHI N  P         44  25-19
1887 PHI N  P         44  28-13
1888 PHI N  P         33  14-19
1889 PHI N  P         18  8-10
1890 SYR AA P         48  20-22
          BRTL       201  100-92
```

CASEY, DENNIS PATRICK
B.MAR.30,1858 BINGHAMTON,N.Y.
D.JAN.19,1909 BINGHAMTON,N.Y.
```
1884 WIL U  O          2  .167
     BAL AA O         38  .274
1885 BAL AA O         64  .282
1887 NY  N  2          1  .000
          BLTR       105  .275
```

CASEY, HUGH THOMAS
B.OCT.14,1913 ATLANTA,GA.
D.JULY 3,1951 ATLANTA,GA.
```
1935 CHI N  P         13  0- 0
1939 BRO N  P         40  15-10
1940 BRO N  P     44  45  11- 8
1941 BRO N  P         45  14-11
1942 BRO N  P         50  6- 3
1946 BRO N  P         46  11- 5
1947 BRO N  P         46  10- 4
1948 BRO N  P         22  3- 0
1949 PIT N  P         33  4- 1
     NY  A  P          4  1- 0
          BRTR   343 344  75-42
```

CASEY, JAMES PATRICK (DOC)
B.MAR.15,1870 LAWRENCE,MASS.
D.DEC.31,1936 DETROIT,MICH.
```
1898 WAS N  3         28  .270
1899 WAS N  3          9  .118
     BRO N  3        136  .267
1900 BRO N  3          1  .333
1901 DET A  3        131  .280
1902 DET A  3        132  .275
1903 CHI N  3        112  .290
1904 CHI N  3        136  .268
1905 CHI N  3        142  .232
1906 BRO N  3        149  .233
1907 BRO N  3        138  .231
          BLTR      1114  .253
```

CASEY, JOSEPH FELIX
B.AUG.15,1887 BOSTON,MASS.
D.JUNE 2,1966 MELROSE,MASS.
```
1909 DET A  C          3  .200
1910 DET A  C         23  .164
1911 DET A  C         15  .152
1918 WAS A  C          8  .235
          BRTR        49  .188
```

CASEY, O. ROBINSON
B.1859 CANADA
```
1882 DET N  2-3        9  .231
```

CASEY, WILLIAM B.
B.ST.LOUIS,MO.
```
1887 ATH AA P          1  0- 0
```

CASH, DAVID (DAVE)
B.JUNE 11,1948 UTICA,N.Y.
```
1969 PIT N  2         18  .279
1970 PIT N  2         64  .314
1971 PIT N  *2-3/S   123  .289
1972 PIT N  2         99  .282
1973 PIT N  2-3      116  .271
1974 PHI N  *2       162  .300
1975 PHI N  *2       162  .305
1976 PHI N  *2       160  .284
1977 MON N  *2       153  .289
1978 MON N  *2       159  .252
          BRTR      1216  .286
```

YR	CL LEA POS	GP	G	REC

CASH, NORMAN DALTON (NORM)
B.NOV.10,1934 JUSTICEBURG,TEX.
1958 CHI A O			13	.250
1959 CHI A 1			58	.240
1960 DET A 1-O			121	.286
1961 DET A 1			159	.361
1962 DET A 1-O			148	.243
1963 DET A 1			147	.270
1964 DET A 1			144	.257
1965 DET A *1			142	.266
1966 DET A *1			160	.279
1967 DET A *1			152	.242
1968 DET A *1			127	.263
1969 DET A *1			142	.280
1970 DET A *1			130	.259
1971 DET A *1			135	.283
1972 DET A *1			137	.259
1973 DET A *1			121	.262
1974 DET A 1			53	.228
BLTL			2089	.271

CASH, RONALD FORREST (RON)
B.NOV.20,1949 ATLANTA,GA.
1973 DET A /O-3			14	.410
1974 DET A 1/3			20	.226
BRTR			34	.297

CASHION, JAY CARL (CARL)
B.JUNE 16,1891 MECKLENBURG,N.C.
D.NOV.17,1935 LAKE MILLICENT,WIS.
1911 WAS A P	11	21	2- 3	
1912 WAS A P	26	42	11- 6	
1913 WAS A P-O	3	9	1- 2	
				.294
1914 WAS A P		2	0- 1	
				0- 1
BLTR	42	74	14-12	
				.247

CASKEY, CRAIG DOUGLAS
B.DEC.11,1949 VISALIA,CAL.
| 1973 MON N /P | | 9 | 0- 0 | |
| BRTL | | | | |

CASKIN, EDWARD JAMES
B.DEC.30,1851 DANVERS,MASS.
D.OCT.9,1924 DANVERS,MASS.
1879 TRO N C-S			67	.259
1880 TRO N C-S			82	.231
1881 TRO N S			62	.226
1883 NY N 2-S			93	.238
1884 NY N C-S			97	.232
1885 STL N C-S-3			70	.179
1886 NY N S			1	.500
TR			472	.230

CASSADY, HARRY D.
B.JULY 20,1880 BELLEFLOWER,ILL.
1904 PIT N O			11	.214
1905 WAS A O			10	.128
			21	.181

CASSIAN, EDWIN
B.CONNECTICUT
1891 PHI N P		6	1- 3	
WAS AA P		7	0- 0	
		13	1- 3	

CASSIDY, JOHN P.
B.1855 BROOKLYN,N.Y.
D.JULY 3,1891 BROOKLYN,N.Y.
1875 ATL NA P-1-	25	40	1-24	
	2-O			-
NH NA 1		6	-	
1876 HAR N O		12	.271	
1877 HAR N P-O	2	60	1- 1	
				.378
1878 CHI N O			60	.261
1879 TRO N 1-O			8	.176
1880 TRO N 2-O			83	.253
1881 TRO N O			84	.219
1882 TRO N 3-O			28	.176
1883 PRO N 1-2-O			89	.237
1884 BRO AA O			106	.211
1885 BRO AA O			54	.211
TL	27	630	2-25	
				-

CASSIDY, JOSEPH PHILLIP
B.FEB.8,1883 CHESTER,PA.
D.MAR.25,1906 CHESTER,PA.
1904 WAS A S-3-O			152	.234
1905 WAS A S			151	.215
BRTR			303	.225

CASSIDY, PETER FRANCIS
B.APR.8,1873 WILMINGTON,DEL.
D.JULY 9,1929 WILMINGTON,DEL.
1896 LOU N 1			48	.221
1899 BRO N S-3			6	.150
WAS N 1			45	.315
BRTR			99	.261

**CASSINI, JACK DEMPSEY (JACK)
(GABBY) OR (SCAT)**
B.OCT.26,1919 DEARBORN,MICH.
| 1949 PIT N H | | 8 | .000 | |

CASTER, GEORGE JASPER (UG)
B.AUG.4,1907 COLTON,CAL.
D.DEC.18,1955 LAKEWOOD,CAL.
1934 PHI A P		5	3- 2	
1935 PHI A P	25	26	1- 4	
1937 PHI A P	34	37	12-19	
1938 PHI A P		42	16-20	
1939 PHI A P		28	9- 9	
1940 PHI A P		36	4-19	
1941 STL A P		32	3- 7	
1942 STL A P		39	8- 2	
1943 STL A P		39	6- 8	
1944 STL A P		42	6- 6	
1945 STL A P		10	1- 2	
DET A P		22	5- 1	
1946 STL A P		26	2- 1	
BRTR	376	380	76-100	

CASTIGLIA, JAMES VINCENT
B.SEPT.30,1918 PASSAIC,N.J.
| 1942 PHI A C | | 16 | .389 | |
| BLTR | | | | |

CASTIGLIONE, PETER PAUL (PETE)
B.FEB.13,1921 GREENWICH,CONN.
1947 PIT N S			13	.280
1948 PIT N S			4	.000
1949 PIT N S-3-O			118	.268
1950 PIT N 1-2-S-3			94	.259
1951 PIT N S-3			132	.261
1952 PIT N 1-3-O			67	.266
1953 PIT N 3			45	.208
STL N S-3			67	.173
1954 STL N 3			5	.000
BRTR			545	.255

CASTILLO, ANTHONY (TONY)
B.JUNE 14,1957 SAN JOSE,CAL.
| 1978 SD N /C | | 5 | .125 | |
| BRTR | | | | |

CASTILLO, ROBERT ERNIE
B.APR.18,1955 LOS ANGELES,CAL.
1977 LA N /P		6	1- 0	
1978 LA N P		18	0- 4	
BRTR			24	1- 4

CASTINO, VINCENT CHARLES
B.OCT.11,1917 WILLISVILLE,ILL.
D.MAR.6,1967 SACRAMENTO,CAL.
1943 CHI A C			33	.228
1944 CHI A C			29	.231
1945 CHI A C			26	.216
BRTR			88	.227

CASTLE, DONALD HARDY (DON)
B.FEB.1,1950 KOKOMO,IND.
| 1973 TEX A /H | | 4 | .308 | |
| BLTL | | | | |

CASTLE, JOHN FRANCIS
B.JUNE 1,1883 HONEY BROOK,PA.
D.APR.15,1929 PHILADELPHIA,PA.
| 1910 PHI N O | | 2 | .250 | |

CASTLEMAN, CLYDELL (SLICK)
B.SEPT.8,1913 DONELSON,TENN.
1934 NY N P		7	1- 0	
1935 NY N P	29	15- 6		
1936 NY N P	29	30	4- 7	
1937 NY N P		23	11- 6	
1938 NY N P	21	22	4- 5	
1939 NY N P		12	1- 2	
BRTR	121	123	36-26	

CASTLEMAN, FOSTER EPHRAIM
B.JAN.1,1931 NASHVILLE,TENN.
1954 NY N O			13	.250
1955 NY N 2-3			15	.214
1956 NY N 2-S-3			124	.226
1957 NY N 2-S-3			18	.162
1958 BAL A 2-S-3-O			98	.170
BRTR			268	.205

CASTLETON, ROYAL EUGENE (ROY)
B.JULY 26,1885 SALT LAKE CITY,UTAH
D.JUNE 24,1967 LOS ANGELES,CAL.
1907 NY A P		3	1- 1	
1909 CIN N P		4	1- 1	
1910 CIN N P		4	1- 2	
BRTL		11	3- 4	

CASTNER, PAUL HENRY (LEFTY)
B.FEB.16,1897 ST.PAUL,MINN.
| 1923 CHI A P | | 6 | 0- 0 | |
| BLTL | | | | |

CASTRO, LOUIS M. (JUD)
B.1877 COLUMBIA,SOUTH AMERICA
D.VENEZUELA
| 1902 PHI A 2-S-3-O | | | 41 | .248 |
| TR | | | | |

**CASTRO, WILLIAM RADHAMES (CHECO)
(BILL)**
B.DEC.13,1953 SANTIAGO,D.R.
1974 MIL A /P		8	0- 0	
1975 MIL A P		18	3- 2	
1976 MIL A P		39	4- 6	
1977 MIL A P		51	8- 6	
1978 MIL A P		42	5- 4	
BRTR		158	20-18	

CATER, DANNY ANDERSON
B.FEB.25,1940 AUSTIN,TEX.
1964 PHI N 1-3-O			60	.296
1965 CHI A *O-3/1			142	.270
1966 CHI A O			21	.183
KC A 1-3-O			116	.292
1967 KC A 3-O-1			142	.270
1968 OAK A *1-O/2			147	.290
1969 OAK A *1-O/2			152	.262
1970 NY A *1+3/O			155	.301
1971 NY A 1-3			121	.276
1972 BOS A 1			92	.237
1973 BOS A 1-3			63	.313
1974 BOS A 1-O			56	.246
1975 STL N 1			22	.229
BRTR			1289	.276

CATES, ELI ELDO
B.JAN.26,1877 GREENSFORK,IND.
D.MAY 29,1964 RICHMOND,IND.
| 1908 WAS A P | | 40 | 4- 8 | |
| BRTR | | | | |

CATHER, THEODORE P
B.MAY 20,1889 CHESTER,PA.
D.APR.9,1945 ELKTON,MD.
1912 STL N O		5	.421	
1913 PIT N P-1-	1	67	0- 0	
O				.213
1914 STL N O		39	.273	
BOS N O		50	.296	
1915 BOS N O		40	.206	
BRTR	1	201	0- 0	
				.252

CATHEY, HARDIN (ABNER)
B.JULY 6,1919 BURNS,TENN.
| 1942 WAS A P | | 12 | 1- 1 | |
| BRTR | | | | |

**CATON, JAMES HOWARD
(HOWDY) OR (BUSTER)**
B.JULY 16,1896 ZANESVILLE,OHIO
D.JAN.8,1948 ZANESVILLE,OHIO
1917 PIT N S			14	.211
1918 PIT N S			80	.234
1919 PIT N S-3-O			39	.176
1920 PIT N S			98	.236
BRTR			231	.226

CATTANACH, JOHN LECKIE
B.MAY 10,1863 PROVIDENCE,R.I.
D.NOV.11,1926 PROVIDENCE,R.I.
1884 PRO N P-O		1	0- 1	
				.000
STL U P		2	1- 1	
		3	1- 2	
				.000

CATTERSON, THOMAS HENRY
B.AUG.25,1884 WARWICK,R.I.
D.FEB.5,1920 PORTLAND,MAINE
1908 BRO N O			18	.191
1909 BRO N O			9	.222
BL			27	.200

CAULFIELD, JOHN JOSEPH (JAKE)
B.NOV.23,1918 LOS ANGELES,CAL.
| 1946 PHI A S-3 | | 44 | .277 | |
| BRTR | | | | |

CAUSEY, CECIL ALGERNON (RED)
B.AUG.11,1893 GEORGETOWN,FLA.
D.NOV.11,1960 AVON PARK,FLA.
1918 NY N P		29	11- 6	
1919 NY N P	19	21	9- 3	
BOS N P		10	4- 5	
1920 PHI N P		35	44	7-14
1921 PHI N P	7	8	3- 3	
NY N P		7	9	1- 1
1922 NY N P		24	25	4- 3
BRTR	131	146	39-35	

```
YR  CL LEA POS    GP    G    REC        YR  CL LEA POS    GP    G    REC        YR  CL LEA POS    GP    G    REC

CAUSEY, JAMES WAYNE (WAYNE)             CEPEDA, ORLANDO MANUEL (PENNE)          CHAKALES, ROBERT EDWARD (CHICK)
B.DEC.26,1936 RUSTON,LA.               (BABY BULL) OR (CHA CHA)                B.AUG.10,1927 ASHEVILLE,N.C.
1955 BAL A  2-S-3     68   .194        B.SEP.17,1937 PONCE,P.R.                1951 CLE A  P          17    3- 4
1956 BAL A  2-3       53   .170        1958 SF  N  1          148   .312       1952 CLE A  P           5    1- 2
1957 BAL A  2-3       14   .200        1959 SF  N  1-3-O      151   .317       1953 CLE A  P           7    0- 2
1961 KC  A  2-S-3    104   .276        1960 SF  N  1-O        151   .297       1954 CLE A  P           3    2- 0
1962 KC  A  2-S-3    117   .252        1961 SF  N  1-O        152   .311            BAL A  P          38    3- 7
1963 KC  A  S-3      139   .280        1962 SF  N  1-O        162   .306       1955 CHI A  P           7    0- 0
1964 KC  A  2-S-3    157   .281        1963 SF  N  1-O        156   .316            WAS A  P          29    2- 3
1965 KC  A  S-2-3    144   .261        1964 SF  N  1-O        142   .304       1956 WAS A  P          43    4- 4
1966 KC  A  3-S       28   .228        1965 SF  N  /1-O        33   .176       1957 WAS A  P           4    0- 1
     CHI A  2/S-3     78   .244        1966 SF  N  /O-1        19   .286            BOS A  P          18    0- 2
1967 CHI A  2/S      124   .226        1967 STL N  *1         123   .303            BRTR            171   15-25
1968 CHI A  2         59   .180        1968 STL N  *1         157   .325
     CAL A  /2         4   .000        1969 ATL N  *1         154   .257       CHALK, DAVID LEE (DAVE)
     ATL N  /2-S-3    16   .108        1970 ATL N  *1         148   .305       B.AUG.30,1950 DEL RIO,TEX.
     BLTR           1105   .252        1971 ATL N  1           71   .276       1973 CAL A  S-3         24   .232
                                       1972 ATL N  1           28   .298       1974 CAL A  S-3        133   .252
CAVANAUGH, PATRICK JOHN                 1973 BOS A  *O        142   .289       1975 CAL A  *3         149   .273
B.1900 READING,PA.                     1974 KC  A  D           33   .215       1976 CAL A  *S-3       142   .217
1919 PHI N  3          1   .000             BRTR            2124   .297       1977 CAL A  *3/2-S      149   .277
                                                                              1978 CAL A  S-2-3      135   .253
CAVARETTA, PHILIP JOSEPH (PHIL)         CERMAK, EDWARD HUGO                          BRTR            732   .255
B.JULY 19,1916 CHICAGO,ILL.            D.NOV.22,1911 CLEVELAND,OHIO
1934 CHI N  1          7   .381        B.MAR.10,1882 CLEVELAND,OHIO            CHALMERS, GEORGE W. (DUT)
1935 CHI N  1        146   .275        1901 CLE A  O           1   .000        B.JUNE 7,1888 EDINBURGH,SCOT.
1936 CHI N  1        124   .273             BRTR                               D.AUG.5,1940 BRONX,N.Y.
1937 CHI N  1-O      106   .286                                               1910 PHI N  P           4    1- 1
1938 CHI N  1-O       92   .239        CERONE, RICHARD ALDO (RICK)            1911 PHI N  P          38   13-10
1939 CHI N  1         22   .273        B.MAY 19,1954 NEWARK,N.J.              1912 PHI N  P          12    3- 4
1940 CHI N  1         65   .280        1975 CLE A  /C          7   .250        1913 PHI N  P          26    3-10
1941 CHI N  1-O      107   .286        1976 CLE A  /C          7   .125        1914 PHI N  P           3    0- 3
1942 CHI N  1-O      136   .270        1977 TOR A  C          31   .200        1915 PHI N  P          26    8- 9
1943 CHI N  1-O      143   .291        1978 TOR A  C          88   .223        1916 PHI N  P          12    1- 1
1944 CHI N  1-O      152   .321             BRTR            133   .215              BRTR            121   29-41
1945 CHI N  1-O      132   .355
1946 CHI N  1-O      139   .294        CERV, ROBERT HENRY (BOB)                CHAMBERLAIN, JOSEPH JEREMIAH
1947 CHI N  1-O      127   .314        B.MAY 5,1926 WESTON,NEB.               B.MAY 10,1910 SAN FRANCISCO,CAL
1948 CHI N  1-O      111   .279        1951 NY  A  O          12   .214        1934 CHI A  S-3        43   .241
1949 CHI N  1-O      105   .294        1952 NY  A  O          36   .241
1950 CHI N  1-O       82   .273        1953 NY  A  H           3   .000        CHAMBERLAIN, WILLIAM VINCENT
1951 CHI N  M-1       89   .311        1954 NY  A  O          56   .260        B.APR.21,1909 STOUGHTON,MASS.
1952 CHI N  M-1       41   .238        1955 NY  A  O          55   .341        1932 CHI A  P          12    0- 5
1953 CHI N  M-H       27   .286        1956 NY  A  O          54   .304             BRTL
1954 CHI A  1-O       71   .316        1957 KC  A  O         124   .272
1955 CHI A  1          6   .000        1958 KC  A  O         141   .305        CHAMBERLIN, ELTON P. (ICEBERG)
     BLTL           2030   .293        1959 KC  A  O         125   .285        B.NOV.5,1867 BUFFALO,N.Y.
                                       1960 KC  A  O          23   .256        D.SEPT.22,1929 BALTIMORE,MD.
CAVENEY, JAMES CHRISTOPHER (IKE)             NY  A  1-O       87   .250        D.MAY 11,1977 PALATKA,FLA.
B.DEC.10,1894 SAN FRANCISCO,CAL        1961 LA  A  O          18   .158        1886 LOU AA P-O         4    6    0- 3
D.JULY 6,1949 SAN FRANCISCO,CAL              NY  A  1-O       57   .271                                         .150
1922 CIN N  S        118   .238        1962 NY  A  O          14   .118        1887 LOU AA P          37   18-16
1923 CIN N  S        138   .277             HOU N  O          19   .226        1888 LOU AA P          26    9- 8
1924 CIN N  2-S       95   .273             BRTR            829   .276              STL AA P-O        20   11- 2
1925 CIN N  S        115   .249                                                                              .080
     BRTR            466   .260        CEY, RONALD CHARLES (RON)               1889 STL AA P          53   35-15
                                       B.FEB.15,1948 TACOMA,WASH.             1890 STL AA P           5    2- 3
CAVET, TILLER H. (PUG)                 1971 LA  N  /3          2   .000        1891 ATH AA P          28   13- 7
B.DEC.24,1889 MCGREGOR,TEX.            1972 LA  N  3          11   .270            ATH AA P      51   54   21-22
D.AUG.6,1966 SAN LUIS OBISPO,CAL.      1973 LA  N  *3        152   .245        1892 CIN N  P          44   19-23
1911 DET A  P          1   0- 0        1974 LA  N  *3        159   .262        1893 CIN N  P          27   14- 9
1914 DET A  P         31   7- 7        1975 LA  N  *3        158   .283        1894 CIN N  P          20    9-11
1915 DET A  P         17   4- 3        1976 LA  N  *3        145   .277        1896 CLE N  P           2    0- 1
     TL             49  11-10          1977 LA  N  *3        153   .241              BRTR            317  322 151-120
                                       1978 LA  N  *3        159   .270                                         .195
CAYLOR, OLIVER PERRY                         BRTR            939   .263
B.OCT.7,1849 NEAR DAYTON,OHIO                                                 CHAMBERS, CLIFFORD DAY (LEFTY)
D.OCT.19,1897 WINONA,MINN.             CHACON, ELIO [RODRIGUEZ]                B.JAN.10,1922 PORTLAND,ORE.
NON-PLAYING MANAGER                    B.OCT.26,1936 CARACAS,VENEZ.            1948 CHI N  P           2    2- 9
CIN[AA]1885-86 and MET[AA]1887         1960 CIN N  2-O        49   .181        1949 PIT N  P          34   13- 7
                                       1961 CIN N  2-O        61   .265        1950 PIT N  P          37   12-15
CECCARELLI, ARTHUR EDWARD              1962 NY  A  2-S       118   .236        1951 PIT N  P          10    3- 6
(ART) OR (CHIC)                             BRTR            228   .232              STL N  P          21   11- 6
B.APR.2,1930 NEW HAVEN,CONN.                                                   1952 STL N  P          26    4- 4
1955 KC  A  P         31   4- 7        CHADBOURNE, CHESTER JAMES (POP)         1953 STL N  P          32    3- 6
1956 KC  A  P          3   0- 1        B.OCT.26,1884 PARKMAN,ME.                    BLTL            189   48-53
1957 BAL A  P         20   0- 5        D.JUNE 23,1943 LOS ANGELES,CAL.
1959 CHI N  P         18   5- 5        1906 BOS A  2          11   .302        CHAMBERS, JOHNNIE MONROE
1960 CHI N  P          7   0- 0        1907 BOS A  O          10   .289        B.SEPT.10,1911 COPPER HILL,TENN
     BRTL             79   9-18        1914 KC  F  O         147   .275        1937 STL N  P           2    0- 0
     BB 1957                           1915 KC  F  O         152   .224             BLTR
                                       1918 BOS N  O          27   .260
CECIL, REX ROLSTON                          BLTR            347   .255        CHAMBERS, ROME J.
B.OCT.8,1916 LINDSAY,OKLA.                                                    B.KERNERSVILLE,N.C.
D.OCT.30,1966 LONG BEACH,CAL.          CHAGNON, LEON WILBUR (SHAG)             1900 BOS N  P           1    0- 0
1944 BOS A  P         11   4- 5        B.SEPT.28,1902 PITTSFIELD,N.H.               BLTL
1945 BOS A  P          7   2- 5        D.JULY 30,1953 AMESBURY,MASS.
     BLTR             18   6-10        1929 PIT N  P           1    0- 0        CHAMBERS, WILLIAM CHRISTOPHER
                                       1930 PIT N  P          18   0- 3        B.SEPT.13,1889 CAMERON,W.VA.
CEDENO, CESAR [ENCARNACION]            1932 PIT N  P          30   9- 6        D.MAR.27,1962 FORT WAYNE,IND.
B.FEB.25,1951 SANTO DOMINGO,D.R.       1933 PIT N  P          39   6- 4        1910 STL N  P           1    0- 0
1970 HOU N  O          90   .310       1934 PIT N  P          33   4- 1
1971 HOU N  *O/1      161   .264       1935 NY  N  P          14   0- 2        CHAMBLISS, CARROLL CHRISTOPHER
1972 HOU N  *O        139   .320             BRTR            135  19-16        (CHRIS)
1973 HOU N  *O        139   .320                                              B.DEC.26,1948 DAYTON,O.
1974 HOU N  *O        160   .269                                              1971 CLE A  *1         111   .275
1975 HOU N  *O        131   .288                                              1972 CLE A  1          121   .292
1976 HOU N  *O        150   .297                                              1973 CLE A  *1         155   .273
1977 HOU N  *O        141   .279                                              1974 CLE A  1           17   .328
1978 HOU N  O          50   .281                                                   NY  A  *1         110   .243
     BRTR           1161   .291                                               1975 NY  A  *1         150   .304
                                                                              1976 NY  A  *1         156   .293
CENTER, MARVIN EARL (PETE)                                                    1977 NY  A  *1         157   .287
B.APR.22,1912 HAZEL GREEN,KY.                                                 1978 NY  A  *1         162   .274
1942 CLE A  P          1   0- 0                                                    BLTR            1139   .282
1943 CLE A  P         24   1- 2
1945 CLE A  P         31   6- 3
1946 CLE A  P         21   0- 2
     BRTR             77   7- 7
```

CHAMPION, BUFORD BILLY (BILL)
B.SEP.18,1947 SHELBY,N.C.

YR	CL	LEA	POS	GP	G	REC
1969	PHI	N	P		23	5-10
1970	PHI	N	/P		7	0- 2
1971	PHI	N	P		37	3- 5
1972	PHI	N	P	30	32	4-14
1973	MIL	A	P		37	5- 8
1974	MIL	A	P		31	11- 4
1975	MIL	A	P		27	6- 6
1976	MIL	A	P		10	0- 1
			BRTR	202	204	34-50

CHAMPION, ROBERT MICHAEL (MIKE)
B.FEB.10,1955 MONTGOMERY,ALA.

YR	CL	LEA	POS	GP	G	REC
1976	SD	N	2		11	.237
1977	SD	N	*2		150	.229
1978	SD	N	2/3		32	.226
			BRTR		193	.229

CHANCE, FRANK LEROY (HUSK)
OR (THE PEERLESS LEADER)
B.SEPT.9,1877 FRESNO,CAL.
D.SEPT.15,1924 LOS ANGELES,CAL.

YR	CL	LEA	POS	GP	G	REC
1898	CHI	N	C-O		42	.288
1899	CHI	N	C		57	.289
1900	CHI	N	C		48	.304
1901	CHI	N	O		63	.289
1902	CHI	N	C-1-O		67	.284
1903	CHI	N	1		123	.327
1904	CHI	N	1		124	.310
1905	CHI	N	M-1		115	.316
1906	CHI	N	M-1		136	.319
1907	CHI	N	M-1		109	.293
1908	CHI	N	M-1		126	.272
1909	CHI	N	M-1		92	.271
1910	CHI	N	M-1		87	.298
1911	CHI	N	M-1		29	.239
1912	CHI	N	M-1		2	.200
1913	NY	A	M-1		11	.208
1914	NY	A	M-1		1	.000
			BRTR		1232	.297

NON-PLAYING MANAGER BOS[A] 1923

CHANCE, ROBERT (BOB)
B.SEPT.10,1940 STATESBORO,GA.

YR	CL	LEA	POS	GP	G	REC
1963	CLE	A	O		16	.288
1964	CLE	A	1-O		120	.279
1965	WAS	A	1/O		72	.256
1966	WAS	A	1		37	.175
1967	WAS	A	1		27	.214
1969	CAL	A	/1		5	.143
			BLTR		277	.261

CHANCE, WILMER DEAN (DEAN)
B.JUNE 1,1941 WAYNE,O.

YR	CL	LEA	POS	GP	G	REC
1961	LA	A	P		5	0- 2
1962	LA	A	P		50	14-10
1963	LA	A	P		45	13-18
1964	LA	A	P		46	20- 9
1965	CAL	A	P		36	15-10
1966	CAL	A	P		41	12-17
1967	MIN	A	P		41	20-14
1968	MIN	A	P		43	16-16
1969	MIN	A	P		20	5- 4
1970	CLE	A	P		45	9- 8
	NY	N	/P		3	0- 1
1971	DET	A	P		31	4- 6
			BRTR		406	128-115

CHANDLER, EDWARD OLIVER
B.FEB.17,1922 PINSON,ALA.

YR	CL	LEA	POS	GP	G	REC
1947	BRO	N	P		15	0- 1
			BRTR			

CHANDLER, SPURGEON FERDINAND (SPUD)
B.SEPT.12,1907 COMMERCE,GA.

YR	CL	LEA	POS	GP	G	REC
1937	NY	A	P		12	7- 4
1938	NY	A	P		23	14- 5
1939	NY	A	P		11	3- 0
1940	NY	A	P		27	8- 7
1941	NY	A	P		28	10- 4
1942	NY	A	P		24	16- 5
1943	NY	A	P		30	20- 4
1944	NY	A	P		1	0- 0
1945	NY	A	P		4	2- 1
1946	NY	A	P		34	20- 8
1947	NY	A	P		17	9- 5
			BRTR		211	109-43

CHANEY, DARREL LEE
B.MAR.9,1948 HAMMOND,IND.

YR	CL	LEA	POS	GP	G	REC
1969	CIN	N	S		93	.191
1970	CIN	N	S-2/3		57	.232
1971	CIN	N	/S-2-3		10	.125
1972	CIN	N	S-2-3		83	.250
1973	CIN	N	S-2-3		105	.181
1974	CIN	N	3-2-S		117	.200
1975	CIN	N	S-2-3		71	.219
1976	ATL	N	*S/2-3		153	.252
1977	ATL	N	S-2		74	.201
1978	ATL	N	S/3-2		89	.224
			BBTR		852	.220

BL 1973 (PART), 74-75

CHANEY, ESTY CLYON
B.JAN.29,1891 HADLEY,PA.
D.FEB.5,1952 CLEVELAND,OHIO

YR	CL	LEA	POS	GP	G	REC
1913	BOS	A	P		1	0- 0
1914	BRO	F	P		1	0- 0
			BRTR		2	0- 0

CHANNELL, LESTER CLARK
(GOAT) OR (GINT)
B.MAR.3,1886 CRESTLINE,OHIO
D.MAY 8,1954 DENVER,COLO.

YR	CL	LEA	POS	GP	G	REC
1910	NY	A	O		6	.263
1914	NY	A	O		1	1.000
			BLTL		7	.300

CHANT, CHARLES JOSEPH (CHARLIE)
B.AUG.7,1951 BELL,CAL.

YR	CL	LEA	POS	GP	G	REC
1975	OAK	A	/O		5	.000
1976	STL	N	O		15	.143
			BRTR		20	.105

CHAPLIN, BERT EDGAR
[REAL NAME BERT EDGAR CHAPMAN]
B.SEPT.25,1893 PELZER,S.C.
D.AUG.15,1978 SANFORD,FLA.

YR	CL	LEA	POS	GP	G	REC
1920	BOS	A	C		4	.250
1921	BOS	A	C		3	.000
1922	BOS	A	C		28	.189
			BLTR		35	.182

CHAPLIN, JAMES BAILEY (TINY)
B.JULY 13,1905 LOS ANGELES,CAL.
D.MAR.25,1939 NATIONAL CITY,CAL

YR	CL	LEA	POS	GP	G	REC
1928	NY	N	P		12	0- 2
1930	NY	N	P		19	2- 6
1931	NY	N	P		16	3- 0
1936	BOS	N	P		40	10-15
			BRTR		87	15-23

CHAPMAN, BERT EDGAR
[PLAYED UNDER NAME OF
BERT EDGAR CHAPLIN]

CHAPMAN, CALVIN LOUIS
B.DEC.20,1910 COURTLAND,MISS.

YR	CL	LEA	POS	GP	G	REC
1935	CIN	N	2-S		15	.340
1936	CIN	N	2-O		96	.247
			BLTR		111	.265

CHAPMAN, EDWIN VOLNEY
B.NOV.28,1905 COURTLAND,MISS.

YR	CL	LEA	POS	GP	G	REC
1933	WAS	A	P		6	0- 0
			BBTR			

CHAPMAN, FREDERICK JOSEPH
B.NOV.24,1872 LITTLE COOLEY,PA.
D.DEC.14,1957 UNION CITY,PA.

YR	CL	LEA	POS	GP	G	REC
1887	ATH	AA	P		1	1- 0
			BRTR			

CHAPMAN, GLENN JUSTICE (PETE)
B.JAN.21,1906 CAMBRIDGE CITY,IND.

YR	CL	LEA	POS	GP	G	REC
1934	BRO	N	2-O		67	.280
			BRTR			

CHAPMAN, HARRY E.
B.OCT.26,1887 SEVERANCE,KAN.
D.OCT.21,1918 NEVADA,MO.

YR	CL	LEA	POS	GP	G	REC
1912	CHI	N	C		1	.250
1913	CIN	N	C		2	.500
1914	STL	F	C		59	.209
1915	STL	F	C		62	.198
1916	STL	A	C		18	.097
			BRTR		142	.195

CHAPMAN, JOHN CURTIS
B.MAY 8,1843 BROOKLYN,N.Y.
D.JUNE 10,1916 BROOKLYN,N.Y.

YR	CL	LEA	POS	GP	G	REC
1874	ATL	NA	1-O		53	-
1875	STL	NA	O		41	.246
1876	LOU	N	O		17	.235
			TR		111	-

NON-PLAYING MANAGER
LOU[N] 1877, MIL[N] 1878,
WOR(N) 1882, DET(N) 1883-84,
BUF(N) 1885, LOU(AA) 1889-91
AND LOU(N) 1892

CHAPMAN, JOHN JOSEPH
B.OCT.15,1899 CENTRALIA,PA.
D.NOV.3,1953 PHILADELPHIA,PA.

YR	CL	LEA	POS	GP	G	REC
1924	PHI	A	S		19	.282
			BRTR			

CHAPMAN, RAYMOND JOHNSON (RAY)
B.JAN.15,1891 BEAVER DAM,KY.
D.AUG.17,1920 NEW YORK,N.Y.

YR	CL	LEA	POS	GP	G	REC
1912	CLE	A	S		31	.312
1913	CLE	A	S		140	.254
1914	CLE	A	2-S		106	.275
1915	CLE	A	S		154	.270
1916	CLE	A	2-S-3		109	.231
1917	CLE	A	S		156	.302
1918	CLE	A	S		128	.267
1919	CLE	A	S		115	.300
1920	CLE	A	S		111	.303
			BRTR		1050	.278

CHAPMAN, SAMUEL BLAKE (SAM)
B.APR.11,1916 TIBURON,CAL.

YR	CL	LEA	POS	GP	G	REC
1938	PHI	A	O		114	.259
1939	PHI	A	1-O		140	.269
1940	PHI	A	O		134	.276
1941	PHI	A	O		143	.322
1945	PHI	A	O		9	.200
1946	PHI	A	O		146	.261
1947	PHI	A	O		149	.252
1948	PHI	A	O		123	.258
1949	PHI	A	O		154	.278
1950	PHI	A	O		144	.251
1951	PHI	A	O		18	.169
	CLE	A	1-O		94	.228
			BRTR		1368	.266

CHAPMAN, WILLIAM BENJAMIN (BEN)
B.DEC.25,1908 NASHVILLE,TENN.

YR	CL	LEA	POS	GP	G	REC
1930	NY	A	2-3		138	.316
1931	NY	A	2-O		149	.315
1932	NY	A	O		151	.299
1933	NY	A	O		147	.312
1934	NY	A	O		149	.308
1935	NY	A	O		140	.289
1936	NY	A	O		36	.266
	WAS	A	O		97	.332
1937	WAS	A	O		35	.262
	BOS	A	O		113	.307
1938	BOS	A	O		127	.340
1939	CLE	A	O		149	.290
1940	CLE	A	O		143	.286
1941	WAS	A	O		28	.255
	CHI	A	O		57	.226
1944	BRO	N	P	11	20	5- 3
1945	BRO	N	P	10	13	3- 3
	PHI	N	M-P-3-O	3	24	0- 0 .314
1946	PHI	N	M-P		1	0- 0
			BRTR	25	1717	8- 6 .302

CHAPMAN, WILLIAM FRED (CHAPPIE)
B.JULY 17,1916 LIBERTY,S.C.

YR	CL	LEA	POS	GP	G	REC
1939	PHI	A	SS		15	.286
1940	PHI	A	SS		26	.159
1941	PHI	A	2-S-3		35	.159
			BRTR		76	.193

NON-PLAYING MANAGER PHI[N] 1947-48

CHAPPAS, HARRY PERRY
B.OCT.26,1957 MT.RANIER,MD.

YR	CL	LEA	POS	GP	G	REC
1978	CHI	A	S		20	.267
			BBTR			

CHAPPELL, LA VERNE ASHFORD (LARRY)
B.FEB.19,1890 MC CLUSKY,ILL.
D.NOV.8,1918 SAN FRANCISCO,CAL.

YR	CL	LEA	POS	GP	G	REC
1913	CHI	A	O		60	.229
1914	CHI	A	O		21	.231
1915	CHI	A	H		1	.000
1916	CLE	A	O		3	.000
	BOS	N	O		20	.226
1917	BOS	N	O		3	.000
			BLTR		108	.225

CHAPPELLE, WILLIAM HOGAN (BIG BILL)
B.MAR.22,1884 WATERLOO,N.Y.
D.DEC.31,1944 MINEOLA,N.Y.

YR	CL	LEA	POS	GP	G	REC
1908	BOS	N	P		13	2- 4
1909	BOS	N	P		5	1- 1
	CIN	N	P		1	0- 0
1914	BRO	F	P		16	4- 2
			BRTR		35	7- 7

CHARLES, EDWIN DOUGLAS (ED)
B.APR.29,1933 DAYTONA BEACH,FLA.

YR	CL	LEA	POS	GP	G	REC
1962	KC	A	2-3		147	.288
1963	KC	A	3		158	.267
1964	KC	A	3		150	.241
1965	KC	A	*3/2-S		134	.269
1966	KC	A	*3/1-O		118	.286
1967	KC	A	3		19	.246
	NY	N	3		101	.238
1968	NY	N	*3/1		117	.276
1969	NY	N	3		61	.207
			BRTR		1005	.263

CHARLES, RAYMOND (CHAPPY)
[REAL NAME CHARLES SHUH ACHENBACH]
B.MAR.25,1881 PHILLIPSBURG,N.J.
D.AUG.4,1959 BETHLEHEM,PA.

YR	CL	LEA	POS	GP	G	REC
1908	STL	N	2-S-3		119	.205
1909	STL	N	2-S		99	.236
	CIN	N	2-S		13	.256
1910	CIN	N	S		4	.133
			BRTR		235	.219

CHARTAK, MICHAEL GEORGE (SHOTGUN)
B.APR.28,1916 BROOKLYN,N.Y.
D.JULY 25,1967 CEDAR RAPIDS,IA.

YR	CL	LEA	POS	GP	G	REC
1940	NY	A	O		11	.133
1942	NY	A	O		5	.000
	WAS	A	O		24	.217
	STL	A	O		73	.249
1943	STL	A	1-O		108	.256
1944	STL	A	1-O		35	.236
			BLTL		256	.243

YR	CL LEA POS	GP	G	REC

CHARTON, FRANK LANE (PETE)
B.DEC.21,1942 JACKSON,TENN.
1964 BOS A P   25   0- 2
      BLTR

CHASE, HAROLD HOMER (PRINCE HAL)
B.FEB.13,1883 LOS GATOS,CAL.
D.MAY 18,1947 COLUSA,CAL.
1905 NY A 1   126 .249
1906 NY A 1   151 .323
1907 NY A 1   125 .287
1908 NY A 1   106 .257
1909 NY A 1   118 .283
1910 NY A M-1   130 .290
1911 NY A M-1   133 .315
1912 NY A 1   131 .274
1913 NY A 1-2-O   39 .228
      CHI A 1   102 .281
1914 CHI A 1   58 .267
      BUF F 1   75 .354
1915 BUF F 1   145 .284
1916 CIN N 1-2-O 142 .339
1917 CIN N 1   152 .277
1918 CIN N 1-O   74 .301
1919 NY N 1   110 .284
      BRTL   1917 .291

CHASE, KENDALL FAY (LEFTY)
B.OCT.6,1913 ONEONTA,N.Y.
1936 WAS A P   1   0- 0
1937 WAS A P   14   4- 3
1938 WAS A P   32   9-10
1939 WAS A P   32 10-19
1940 WAS A P   35 15-17
1941 WAS A P   33   6-18
1942 BOS A P   13   5- 1
1943 BOS A P   7   0- 4
      NY N P   21   23   4-12
      BLTL   188 190 53-84

CHATHAM, CHARLES L (BUSTER)
B.DEC.25,1901 WEST,TEX.
D.DEC.15,1975 WACO,TEX.
1930 BOS N S-3   112 .267
1931 BOS N S-3   17 .227

CHATTERTON, JAMES M.
B.OCT.14,1864 BROOKLYN,N.Y.
D.DEC.15,1944 TEWKSBURY,MASS.
1884 KC U P-1-   1   4   0- 1
        O   .125

CHAVARRIA, OSVALDO [QUIJANO] (OSSIE)
B.AUG.5,1940 COLON,PANAMA
1966 KC A O-S-2/1-3   8b .241
1967 KC A 2/3-O-S   38 .102
      BRTR   124 .208

CHAVEZ, NESTOR ISAIAS [SILVA]
B.JULY 6,1947 CHACAO,VENEZ.
D.MAR.16,1969 MARACAIBO,VENEZ.
1967 SF N /P   2   1- 0
      BRTR

CHEADLE, DAVID BAIRD (DAVE)
B.FEB.19,1952 GREENSBORO,N.C.
1973 ATL N /P   2   0- 1
      BLTL

CHECH, CHARLES WILLIAM
B.APR.27,1878 MADISON,WIS.
D.JAN.31,1938 LOS ANGELES,CAL.
1905 CIN N P   39 13-13
1906 CIN N P   11   1- 4
1908 CLE A P   27 11- 7
1909 BOS A P   17   7- 6
      BRTR   94 32-30

CHEEK, HARRY G.
B.KANSAS CITY,MO.
1910 PHI N C   2   .500
      TR

CHEEVES, VIRGIL EARL (CHIEF)
B.FEB.12,1901 OKLAHOMA CITY,OKLA.
1920 CHI N P   5   0- 0
1921 CHI N P   37 11-12
1922 CHI N P   39 12-11
1923 CHI N P   19   3- 4
1924 CLE A P   8   0- 0
1927 NY N P   3   0- 0
      BRTR   111 26-27

CHELINI, ITALO VINCENT
(CHILLY) OR (LEFTY)
B.OCT.10,1914 SAN FRANCISCO,CAL
D.AUG.25,1972 SAN FRANCISCO,CAL
1935 CHI A P   2   0- 0
1936 CHI A P   18   4- 3
1937 CHI A P   4   0- 1
      BLTL   24   4- 4

CHENEY, LAURANCE RUSSELL (LARRY)
B.MAY 2,1886 BELLEVILLE,KAN.
D.JAN.6,1969 DAYTONA BEACH,FLA.
1911 CHI N P   19   6- 9
1912 CHI N P   42 26-10
1913 CHI N P   54 56 21-14
1914 CHI N P   50 20-18
1915 CHI N P   25   8- 9
1915 BRO N P   5   0- 2
1916 BRO N P   41 18-12
1917 BRO N P   35   8-12
1918 BRO N P   32 33 11-13
1919 BRO N P   9   1- 3
      BOS N P   8   0- 2
      PHI N P   9   2- 5
      BRTR   313 316 116-100

CHENEY, THOMAS EDGAR (TOM)
B.OCT.14,1934 MORGAN,GA.
1957 STL N P   4   0- 1
1959 STL N P   11   0- 1
1960 PIT N P   11   2- 2
1961 PIT N P   1   0- 0
      WAS A P   10 13   1- 3
1962 WAS A P   37   7- 9
1963 WAS A P   23 26   8- 9
1964 WAS A P   15   1- 3
1966 WAS A /P   3   0- 1
      BRTR   115 121 19-29

CHERVINKO, PAUL
B.JULY 28,1910 TRAUGER,PA.
D.JUNE 3,1976 DANVILLE,ILL.
1937 BRO N C   30 .146
1938 BRO N C   12 .148
      BRTR   42 .147

CHESBRO, JOHN DWIGHT (HAPPY JACK)
B.JUNE 5,1874 N.ADAMS,MASS.
D.NOV.6,1931 CONWAY,MASS.
1899 PIT N P   19   6- 9
1900 PIT N P   29 15-13
1901 PIT N P   33 21- 9
1902 PIT N P   34 27- 6
1903 NY A P   40 21-15
1904 NY A P   55 41-13
1905 NY A P   38 20-13
1906 NY A P   48 24-16
1907 NY A P   29   9-10
1908 NY A P   44 14-20
1909 NY A P   8   0- 3
      BOS A P   2   0- 2
      BRTR   382 198-129

CHESLEY, HARRY STEPHEN PATRICK
[PLAYED UNDER NAME OF
HARRY STEPHEN PATRICK CHILD]

CHESNES, ROBERT VINCENT (BOB)
B.MAY 9,1921 OAKLAND,CAL.
1948 PIT N P   25   39 14- 6
1949 PIT N P   27   42   7-13
1950 PIT N P   9   3- 3
      BBTR   61   90 24-22

CHETKOVICH, MITCHELL
B.JULY 21,1917 FAIRPOINT,OHIO
D.AUG.24,1971 GRASS VALLEY,CAL.
1945 PHI N P   4   0- 0
      BRTR

CHEVEZ, SILVIO ANTONIO (TONY)
[REAL NAME SILVIO ANTONIO
AGUILERA (CHEVEZ)]
B.JUNE 20,1954 TELICA,NICARAGUA
1977 BAL A /P   4   0- 0
      BRTR

CHILD, HARRY STEPHEN PATRICK
[REAL NAME
HARRY STEPHEN PATRICK CHESLEY]
B.MAY 23,1905 BALTIMORE,MD.
D.NOV.8,1972 ALEXANDRIA,VA.
1930 WAS A P   9   0- 0
      BBTR

CHILDERS
B.ST.LOUIS,MO.
1895 LOU N P   1   0- 0

CHILDS, A. F.
NON-PLAYING MANAGER NAT[NA]1875

CHILDS, CLARENCE ALGERNON (CUPID)
B.AUG.8,1867 CALVERT CO.,MO.
D.NOV.8,1912 BALTIMORE,MD.
1888 PHI N 2   2   .000
1890 SYR AA 2   136 .344
1891 CLE N 2   141 .295
1892 CLE N 2   144 .335
1893 CLE N 2   122 .332
1894 CLE N 2   117 .365
1895 CLE N 2   120 .312
1896 CLE N 2   132 .348
1897 CLE N 2   114 .336
1898 CLE N 2   109 .289
1899 STL N 2   125 .266
1900 STL N 2   138 .243
1901 CHI N 2   63 .257
      BLTR   1463 .313

CHILDS, GEORGE PETER (PETE)
B.NOV.15,1871 PHILADELPHIA,PA.
D.FEB.15,1922 PHILADELPHIA,PA.
1901 STL N 2   8   .609
      CHI N 2   60 .221
1902 PHI N 2   120 .192
      TR   188 .217

CHILES, PEARCE NUGET
(WHAT S THE USE)
B.MAY 28,1867 DEEPWATER,MO.
1899 PHI N 1-O   81 .329
1900 PHI N 1-O   28 .220
                  109 .301

CHILES, RICHARD FRANCIS (RICH)
B.NOV.22,1949 SACRAMENTO,CAL.
1971 HOU N O   67 .227
1972 HOU N /O   9 .273
1973 NY N /O   8 .120
1976 HOU N /O   5 .500
1977 MIN A O-O   108 .264
1978 MIN A O   87 .268
      BLTL   284 .254

CHIOZZA, DINO JOSEPH (DYNAMO)
B.JUNE 30,1912 MEMPHIS,TENN.
D.APR.23,1972 MEMPHIS,TENN.
1935 PHI N S   2   .000
      BLTR

CHIOZZA, LOUIS PEO
B.MAY 17,1910 TALLULAH,LA.
D.FEB.28,1971 MEMPHIS,TENN.
1934 PHI N 2-3-O   134 .304
1935 PHI N 2-3   124 .284
1936 PHI N 2-3-O   144 .297
1937 NY N 3-O   117 .232
1938 NY N 2-O   57 .235
1939 NY N 3   40 .268
      BLTR   616 .277

CHIPMAN, ROBERT HOWARD
(BOB) OR (MR. CHIPS)
B.OCT.11,1918 BROOKLYN,N.Y.
D.NOV.8,1973 HUNTINGTON,N.Y.
1941 BRO N P   1   1- 0
1942 BRO N P   2   0- 0
1943 BRO N P   1   1- 0
1944 BRO N P   11   3- 1
      CHI N P   26   9- 9
1945 CHI N P   25   4- 5
1946 CHI N P   34   6- 5
1947 CHI N P   32 33   7- 6
1948 CHI N P   34   2- 1
1949 CHI N P   38   7- 8
1950 BOS N P   27   7- 7
1951 BOS N P   33   4- 3
1952 BOS N P   29   1- 1
      BLTL   293 294 51-46

CHIPPLE, WALTER JOHN
[REAL NAME WALTER JOHN CHLIPALA]
B.SEPT.26,1918 UTICA,N.Y.
1945 WAS A O   18   .136
      BRTR

CHITI, HARRY
B.NOV.16,1932 KINCAID,ILL.
1950 CHI N C   3   .333
1951 CHI N C   9   .355
1952 CHI N C   32   .274
1955 CHI N C   113   .231
1956 CHI N C   72   .212
1958 KC A C   103   .268
1959 KC A C   55   .272
1960 KC A C   58   .221
      DET A C   37   .163
1961 DET A C   5   .083
1962 NY N C   15   .195
      BRTR   502   .238

CHITTUM, NELSON BOYD
B.MAR.25,1933 HARRISONBURG,VA.
1958 STL N P   13   0- 1
1959 BOS A P   21   3- 0
1960 BOS A P   6   0- 0
      BRTR   40   3- 1

YR	CL LEA POS	GP	G	REC

CHLIPALA, WALTER JOHN
[PLAYED UNDER NAME OF
WALTER JOHN CHIPPLE]

CHLUPSA, ROBERT JOSEPH (BOB)
B.SEP.16,1945 NEW YORK,N.Y.
1970 STL N P 14 0- 2
1971 STL N /P 1 0- 0
BRTR 15 0- 2

CHOATE, DONALD LEON
B.JULY 2,1938 POTOSI,MO.
1960 SF N P 4 0- 0
BRTR

CHOUINARD, FELIX GEORGE
B.OCT.5,1887 HINES,ILL.
D.APR.28,1955 HINES,ILL.
1910 CHI A O 24 .195
1911 CHI A 2-O 14 .157
1914 PIT F 2-O 5 .440
BRO F 2-O 15 .366
BAL F 2-O 26 .217
1915 BRO F 2-O 4 .500
BLTR 88 .244

CHOUNEAU, WILLIAM (CHIEF)
[REAL NAME WILLIAM CADREAU]
B.SEPT.2,1889 CLOQUET,MINN.
D.SEPT.17,1948 CLOQUET,MINN.
1910 CHI A P 1 0- 0
TR

CHOZEN, HARRY KENNETH
B.SEPT.27,1915 WINNEBAGO,MINN.
1937 CIN N C 1 .250
BRTR

CHRISLEY, BARBRA O NEIL (NEIL)
B.DEC.16,1931 CALHOUN FALLS,S.C
1957 WAS A O 26 .197
1958 WAS A 3-O 105 .215
1959 DET A O 65 .132
1960 DET A 1-O 96 .255
1961 MIL N H 10 .222
BLTR 302 .210

CHRISTENBURY, LLOYD REID (LOW)
B.OCT.19,1893 MECKLENBURG CO.,N.C.
D.DEC.13,1944 BIRMINGHAM,ALA.
1919 BOS N O 7 .290
1920 BOS N 2-S-O 65 .208
1921 BOS N 2 62 .352
1922 BOS N 2-3-O 71 .250
BLTR 205 .271

CHRISTENSEN, BRUCE RAY
B.FEB.22,1948 MADISON,WIS.
1971 CAL A S 29 .270
BLTR

CHRISTENSEN, WALTER NIELS
(SEACAP) OR (CUCKOO)
B.OCT.24,1899 SAN FRANCISCO,CAL
1926 CIN N O 114 .350
1927 CIN N O 57 .254
BLTL 171 .315

CHRISTENSON, LARRY RICHARD
B.NOV.10,1953 EVERETT,WASH.
1973 PHI N P 10 1- 4
1974 PHI N P 10 1- 1
1975 PHI N P 29 11- 6
1976 PHI N P 32 13- 8
1977 PHI N P 34 19- 6
1978 PHI N P 33 13-14
BRTR 148 58-39

CHRISTIAN, ROBERT CHARLES (BOB)
B.OCT.17,1945 CHICAGO,ILL.
D.FEB.20,1974 SAN DIEGO,CAL.
1368 DET A /1-O 3 .333
1969 CHI A O 39 .217
1970 CHI A /O 12 .267
54 .224

CHRISTMAN, H. B.
B.DAYTON,OHIO
1888 KC AA C 1 .250

CHRISTMAN, MARQUETTE JOSEPH (MARK)
B.OCT.21,1913 MAPLEWOOD,MO.
D.OCT.9,1976 ST.LOUIS,MO.
1938 DET A S-3 95 .248
1939 DET A S 6 .250
STL A S 79 .216
1943 STL A 1-2-S-3 98 .271
1944 STL A 1-3 148 .271
1945 STL A 3 78 .277
1946 STL A S-3 128 .258
1947 WAS A 2-S 110 .223
1948 WAS A 2-S-3 120 .259
1949 WAS A 1-2-S-3 49 .214
BRTR 911 .253

CHRISTOPHER, JOSEPH O NEAL (JOE)
B.DEC.13,1935 FREDERIKSTED,V.I.
1959 PIT N O 15 .000
1960 PIT N O 50 .232
1961 PIT N O 76 .263
1962 NY N O 119 .244
1963 NY N O 64 .221
1964 NY N O 154 .300
1965 NY N *O 148 .249
1966 BOS A /O 12 .077
BRTR 638 .260

CHRISTOPHER, LOYD EUGENE
B.DEC.31,1919 RICHMOND,CAL.
1945 BOS A O 8 .286
CHI N O 1 .000
1947 CHI A O 7 .217
BRTR 16 .243

CHRISTOPHER, RUSSELL ORMAND
B.SEPT.12,1907 RICHMOND,CAL.
D.DEC.5,1954 RICHMOND,CAL.
1942 PHI A P 30 4-13
1943 PHI A P 24 5- 8
1944 PHI A P 35 14-14
1945 PHI A P 33 34 13-13
1946 PHI A P 30 9- 7
1947 PHI A P 44 10- 7
1948 CLE A P 45 3- 2
BRTR 241 242 54-64

CHURCH, EMORY NICHOLAS (BUBBA)
B.SEPT.12,1924 BIRMINGHAM,ALA.
1950 PHI N P 31 39 8- 6
1951 PHI N P 38 39 15-11
1952 PHI N P 2 0- 0
CIN N P 29 32 5- 9
1953 CIN N P 11 12 3- 3
CHI N P 27 4- 5
1954 CHI N P 8 1- 3
1955 CHI N P 3 0- 0
BRTR 147 162 36-37

CHURCH, HIRAM LINCOLN
B.CENTRAL SQUARE,N.Y.
1890 BRO AAO 3 .125

CHURCH, LEONARD (LEN)
B.MAR.21,1942 CHICAGO,ILL.
1966 CHI N /P 4 0- 1
BBTR

CHURN, CLARENCE NOTTINGHAM (CHUCK)
B.FEB.1,1930 BRIDGETOWN,VA.
1957 PIT N P 5 0- 0
1958 CLE A P 6 0- 0
1959 LA N P 14 3- 2
BRTR 25 3- 2

CHURRY, JOHN
B.NOV.26,1900 JOHNSTOWN,PA.
D.FEB.8,1970 ZANESVILLE,OHIO
1924 CHI N C 6 .143
1925 CHI N C 3 .500
1926 CHI N C 2 .000
1927 CHI N C 1 1.000
BRTR 12 .278

CIAFFONE, LAWRENCE THOMAS
(SYMPHONY LARRY)
B.AUG.17,1924 BROOKLYN,N.Y.
1951 STL N O 5 .000
BRTR

CICERO, JOSEPH FRANCIS (DODE)
B.NOV.18,1910 ATLANTIC CITY,N.J
1929 BOS A O 10 .313
1930 BOS A 3-O 18 .167
1945 PHI A 3-O 12 .158
BRTR 40 .222

CICOTTE, ALVA WARREN (AL) OR (BOZO)
B.DEC.23,1929 MELVINDALE,MICH.
1957 NY A P 20 2- 2
1958 WAS A P 8 0- 3
DET A P 14 15 3- 1
1959 CLE A P 26 3- 1
1961 STL N P 29 2- 6
1962 HOU N P 5 0- 0
BRTR 102 104 10-13

CICOTTE, EDWARD VICTOR (KNUCKLES)
B.JUNE 19,1884 DETROIT,MICH.
D.MAY 5,1969 DETROIT,MICH.
1905 DET A P 4 4- 0
1908 BOS A P 38 39 11-12
1909 BOS A P 26 13- 5
1910 BOS A P 36 15-11
1911 BOS A P 35 11-14
1912 BOS A P 9 1- 2
CHI A P 20 9- 8
1913 CHI A P 41 18-12
1914 CHI A P 45 11-16
1915 CHI A P 39 40 13-11
1916 CHI A P 44 15- 7
1917 CHI A P 49 28-12
1918 CHI A P 38 12-19
1919 CHI A P 40 29- 7
1920 CHI A P 37 21-10
BBTR 501 503 211-146

CIESLAK, THADDEUS WALTER (TED)
B.NOV.22,1916 MILWAUKEE,WIS.
1944 PHI N 3-O 85 .245
BRTR

CIHOCKI, ALBERT JOSEPH
B.MAY 7,1924 NANTICOKE,PA.
1945 CLE A 2-S-3 92 .212
BRTR

CIHOCKI, EDWARD JOSEPH (CY)
B.MAY 9,1907 WILMINGTON,DEL.
1932 PHI A O 1 .000
1933 PHI A S 33 .144
BRTR 34 .143

CIMINO, PETER WILLIAM (PETE)
B.OCT.17,1942 PHILADELPHIA,PA.
1965 MIN A /P 1 0- 0
1966 MIN A P 35 2- 5
1967 CAL A P 46 3- 3
1968 CAL A /P 4 0- 0
BRTR 86 5- 8

CIMOLI, GINO NICHOLAS
B.DEC.18,1929 SAN FRANCISCO,CAL.
1956 BRO N O 73 .111
1957 BRO N O 142 .293
1958 LA N O 109 .246
1959 STL N O 143 .279
1960 PIT N O 101 .267
1961 PIT N O 21 .299
MIL N O 37 .197
1962 KC A O 152 .275
1963 KC A O 145 .263
1964 KC A O 4 .000
BAL A O 38 .138
1965 CAL A /O 4 .000
BRTR 969 .265

CIOLA, LOUIS ALEXANDER
B.SEPT.6,1922 NORFOLK,VA.
1943 PHI A P 12 1- 3
BRTR

CIPRIANI, FRANK DOMINICK
B.APR.14,1941 BUFFALO,N.Y.
1961 KC A O 13 .250
BRTR

CISAR, GEORGE JOSEPH
B.AUG.25,1912 CHICAGO,ILL.
1937 BRO N P 20 .207
BRTR

CISCO, GALEN BERNARD
B.MAR.7,1936 ST MARY S,OHIO
1961 BOS A P 17 18 2- 4
1962 BOS A P 23 4- 7
NY N P 4 1- 1
1963 NY N P 51 7-15
1964 NY N P 36 6-19
1965 NY N P 35 4- 8
1967 BOS A P 10 0- 1
1969 KC A P 15 1- 1
BRTR 192 193 25-56

CISSELL, CHALMER WILLIAM (BILL)
B.JAN.3,1904 PERRYVILLE,MO.
D.MAR.15,1949 CHICAGO,ILL.
1928 CHI A S 125 .260
1929 CHI A S 152 .280
1930 CHI A 2-S-3 141 .271
1931 CHI A 2-S 109 .220
1932 CHI A S 12 .296
CLE A 2-S 131 .320
1933 CLE A 2-S-3 112 .230
1934 BOS A 2 102 .267
1937 PHI A 2 34 .265
1938 NY N 2 38 .268
BRTR 956 .267

CLABAUGH, JOHN WILLIAM (MOOSE)
B.NOV.13,1901 ALBANY,MO.
1926 BRO N O 11 .071
BLTR

YR	CL	LEA	POS	GP	G	REC

CLACK, ROBERT S. (GENTLEMANLY BOB)
[REAL NAME ROBERT S. CLARK]
B.1851 BROOKLYN,N.Y.
D.OCT.22,1933 DANVERS,MASS.

YR	CL	LEA	POS	GP	G	REC
1874	ATL	NA	O		30	-
1875	ATL	NA	O		17	-
1876	CIN	N	P-1	1	31	0- 0
					2-3-0	.154
	BRTR			1	78	0- 0
						-

CLAIRE, DAVID MATTHEW
B.NOV.17,1897 LUDINGTON,MICH.
D.JAN.7,1956 LAS VEGAS,NEV.

1920	DET	A	S		3	.000
	BRTR					

CLANCEY, WILLIAM EDWARD
B.APR.12,1878 REDFIELD,N.Y.
D.FEB.10,1948 ORISKANY,N.Y.

1905	PIT	N	1		56	.229
	TR					

CLANCY, ALBERT HARRISON
B.AUG.14,1888 LAS CRUCES,N.MEX.
D.OCT.17,1951 LAS CRUCES,N.MEX.

1911	STL	A	3		3	.000
	BRTR					

CLANCY, JAMES (JIM)
B.DEC.18,1955 CHICAGO,ILL.

1977	TOR	A	P		13	4- 9
1978	TOR	A	P		31	10-12
	BRTR				44	14-21

CLANCY, JOHN WILLIAM (BUD)
B.SEPT.15,1900 ODELL,ILL.
D.SEPT.26,1968 OTTUMWA,IOWA

1924	CHI	A	1		13	.257
1925	CHI	A	1		4	.000
1926	CHI	A	1		12	.342
1927	CHI	A	1		130	.300
1928	CHI	A	1		130	.271
1929	CHI	A	1		92	.283
1930	CHI	A	1		68	.244
1932	BRO	N	1		53	.306
1934	PHI	N	1		20	.245
	BLTL				522	.281

CLANTON, EUCAL (UKE) OR (CAT)
B.FEB.19,1898 POWELL,MO.
D.FEB.24,1960 ANTLERS,OKLA.

1922	CLE	A	1		1	.000
	BLTL					

CLAPP, AARON BRONSON
B.JULY 1856 ITHACA,N.Y.
D.JAN.13,1914 SAYRE,PA.

1879	TRO	N	1-0		34	.272
	TR					

CLAPP, JOHN EDGAR
B.JULY 17,1851 ITHACA,N.Y.
D.DEC.18,1904 ITHACA,N.Y.

1872	MAN	NA	C		19	.306
1873	ATH	NA	C-2-S		43	-
1874	ATH	NA	C-S-0		39	-
1875	ATH	NA	C		59	.248
1876	STL	N	C		64	.298
1877	STL	N	C-1-0		60	.316
1878	IND	N	M-1-0		60	.296
1879	BUF	N	C		67	.265
1880	CIN	N	M-C-0		79	.253
1881	CLE	N	C-0		65	.253
1883	NY	N	M-C-0		19	.178
	BRTR				574	-

CLARE, DANIEL J. (DENNY)
B.BROOKLYN,N.Y.

1872	ATL	NA	2		2	.143

CLAREY, DOUGLAS WILLIAM (DOUG)
B.APR.20,1954 LOS ANGELES,CAL.

1976	STL	N	/2		9	.250
	BRTR					

CLARK, ALFRED ALOYSIUS (ALLIE)
B.JUNE 16,1923 S.AMBOY,N.J.

1947	NY	A	O		24	.373
1948	CLE	A	1-3-0		81	.310
1949	CLE	A	1-0		35	.176
1950	CLE	A	O		59	.215
1951	CLE	A	O		3	.300
	PHI	A	3-0		56	.248
1952	PHI	A	1-0		71	.274
1953	PHI	A	O		20	.203
	CHI	A	1-0		9	.067
	BRTR				358	.262

CLARK, ALFRED ROBERT (DAD) OR (FRED)
B.JUL.16,1873 SAN FRANCISCO,CAL
D.JULY 26,1956 OGDEN,UTAH

1902	CHI	N	1		12	.186
	BLTL					

CLARK, BAILEY EARL (EARL)
B.NOV.6,1907 WASHINGTON,D.C.
D.JAN.16,1938 WASHINGTON,D.C.

1927	BOS	N	O		13	.273
1928	BOS	N	O		28	.304
1929	BOS	N	O		84	.315
1930	BOS	N	O		82	.296
1931	BOS	N	O		16	.220
1932	BOS	N	O		50	.250
1933	BOS	N	O		7	.348
1934	STL	A	O		13	.171
	BRTR				293	.291

CLARK, DANIEL CURRAN
B.JAN.18,1894 MERIDIAN,MISS.
D.MAY 23,1937 MERIDIAN,MISS.

1922	DET	A	2		63	.292
1924	BOS	A	3		104	.277
1927	STL	N	O		58	.236
	BLTR				245	.277

CLARK, EDWARD C.
B.CINCINNATI,OHIO

1886	ATH	AA	P		1	0- 1
1891	COL	AA	P		5	1- 2
					6	1- 3

CLARK, GLEN ESTER
B.MAR.7,1941 AUSTIN,TEX.

1967	ATL	N	/H		4	.000
	BBTR					

CLARK, GEORGE MYRON
B.MAY 19,1891 SMITHLAND,IOWA
D.NOV.14,1940 SIOUX CITY,IOWA

1913	NY	A	P		11	0- 1
	BRTL					

CLARK, HARRY (PEP)
B.MAR.20,1883 UNION CITY,OHIO
D.JUNE 8,1965 MILWAUKEE,WIS.

1903	CHI	A	3		15	.308
	BRTR					

CLARK, HARVEY DANIEL (GINGER)
B.MAR.7,1879 WOOSTER,OHIO
D.MAY 10,1943 LAKE CHARLES,LA.

1902	CLE	A	P		1	1- 0
	BRTR					

CLARK, JACK ANTHONY
B.NOV.10,1955 NEW BRIGHTON,PA.

1975	SF	N	/O-3		8	.235
1976	SF	N	O		26	.225
1977	SF	N	*O		136	.252
1978	SF	N	*O		156	.306
	BRTR				326	.278

CLARK, JAMES
[REAL NAME JAMES PETROSKY]
B.SEPT.21,1927 BAGLEY,PA.

1948	WAS	A	S-3		9	.250
	BRTR					

CLARK, JAMES EDWARD (JIM)
B.APR.30,1947 KANSAS CITY,KAN.

1971	CLE	A	/O-1		13	.167
	BRTR					

CLARK, JAMES F.
B.DEC.26,1887 BROOKLYN,N.Y.

1911	STL	N	O		14	.176
1912	STL	N	O		2	.000
	BRTR				16	.125

CLARK, JOHN CARROL (CAP)
B.SEPT.19,1906 SNOW CAMP,N.C.
D.FEB.16,1957 FAYETTEVILLE,N.C.

1938	PHI	N	C		52	.257
	BLTR					

CLARK, MELVIN EARL (MEL)
B.JULY 7,1926 LETART,W.VA.

1951	PHI	N	O		10	.323
1952	PHI	N	3-0		47	.335
1953	PHI	N	O		60	.298
1954	PHI	N	O		83	.240
1955	PHI	N	O		10	.156
1957	DET	A	O		5	.000
	BRTR				215	.277

CLARK, MICHAEL JOHN (MIKE)
B.FEB.12,1922 CAMDEN,N.J.

1952	STL	N	P		12	2- 0
1953	STL	N	P		23	1- 0
	BRTR				35	3- 0

CLARK, OWEN F. (SPIDER)
B.SEPT.16,1867 BROOKLYN,N.Y.
D.FEB.8,1892 BROOKLYN,N.Y.

1889	WAS	N	C		37	.255
1890	BUF	N	C-2-0		69	.268
	TR				106	.259

CLARK, PHILIP JAMES (PHIL)
B.OCT.3,1932 ALBANY,GA.

1958	STL	N	P	7	8	0- 1
1959	STL	N	P	7	7	0- 1
	BRTR			14	15	0- 2

CLARK, RICKEY CHARLES
B.MAR.21,1946 MT.CLEMENS,MICH.

1967	CAL	A	P		32	12-11
1968	CAL	A	P		21	1-11
1969	CAL	A	/P		6	0- 0
1971	CAL	A	P		11	2- 1
1972	CAL	A	P	26	27	4- 4
	BRTR			96	97	19-32

CLARK, ROBERT H.
B.MAR.18,1863 COVINGTON,KY.
D.AUG.21,1919 COVINGTON,KY.

1886	BRO	AA	C		72	.228
1887	BRO	AA	C		47	.289
1888	BRO	AA	C		45	.245
1889	BRO	AA	C		53	.265
1890	BRO	N	C		43	.218
1891	CIN	N	C		15	.132
1893	LOU	N	C		11	.103
	BRTR				286	.239

CLARK, ROBERT S.
[PLAYED UNDER NAME OF
ROBERT S. CLACK]

CLARK, ROBERT WILLIAM
B.AUG.22,1897 NEWPORT,PA.
D.MAY 18,1944 CARLSBAD,N.MEX.

1920	CLE	A	P		11	1- 2
1921	CLE	A	P		5	0- 0
	BRTR				16	1- 2

CLARK, RONALD BRUCE (RON)
B.JAN.14,1943 FT.WORTH,TEX.

1966	MIN	A	/3		5	1.000
1967	MIN	A	3		20	.167
1968	MIN	A	3-S-2		104	.185
1969	MIN	A	/3		5	.125
	SEA	A	S-3/2-1		57	.196
1971	OAK	A	/H		2	.000
1972	OAK	A	2/3		14	.267
	MIL	A	2-3		22	.185
1975	PHI	N	/H		1	.000
	BRTR				230	.189

CLARK, ROY ELLIOTT (PEPPER)
B.MAY 11,1874 NEW HAVEN,CONN.
D.NOV.1,1925 BRIDGEPORT,CONN.

1902	NY	N	O		20	.139
	BLTR					

CLARK, WILLIAM H. (DAD)
B.JAN.7,1865 OSWEGO,N.Y.
D.JUNE 3,1911 LORAIN,OHIO

1888	CHI	N	P		3	2- 0
1891	COL	NA	P		5	0- 0
1894	NY	N	P		16	2- 4
1895	NY	N	P		32	18-14
1896	NY	N	P		43	16-27
1897	NY	N	P		6	0- 3
	LOU	N	P		7	3- 3
1898	LOU	N	P		1	0- 1
	BBTR				113	41-52

CLARK, WILLIAM OTIS (WEE WILLIE)
B.AUG.16,1872 PITTSBURGH,PA.
D.NOV.13,1932 PITTSBURGH,PA.

1895	NY	N	1		22	.261
1896	NY	N	1		65	.303
1897	NY	N	1		118	.282
1898	PIT	N	1		57	.310
1899	PIT	N	1		79	.282
					341	.289

CLARK, WILLIAM OTIS (OTIE)
B.MAY 22,1918 BOSCOBEL,WIS.

1945	BOS	A	P		12	4- 4
	BRTR					

CLARK, WILLIAM WATSON
(WATTY) OR (LEFTY)
B.MAY 16,1902 ST.JOSEPH,LA.
D.MAR.4,1972 CLEARWATER,FLA.

1924	CLE	A	P		12	1- 3
1927	BRO	N	P		77	7- 2
1928	BRO	N	P		40	12- 9
1929	BRO	N	P	41	42	16-19
1930	BRO	N	P		44	13-13
1931	BRO	N	P		34	14-10
1932	BRO	N	P		40	20-12
1933	BRO	N	P		11	2- 4
	NY	N	P		16	3- 4
1934	NY	N	P		5	1- 2
	BRO	N	P		17	2- 0
1935	BRO	N	P	33	34	13- 8
1936	BRO	N	P		33	7-11
1937	BRO	N	P		2	0- 0
	BLTL			359	357	111-97

CLARK, WILLIAM WINFIELD
B.APR.11,1875 CIRCLEVILLE,OHIO
D.APR.15,1959 LOS ANGELES,CAL.

1897	LOU	N	2		4	.176

YR	CL	LEA	POS	GP	G	REC

CLARKE, ALAN THOMAS (LEFTY)
B.MAR.8,1896 CLARKSVILLE,MD.
D.MAR.11,1975 CHEVERLY,MD.

| 1921 | CIN | N | P | | 1 | 0- 1 |
| | | | BBTL | | | |

CLARKE, ARTHUR FRANKLIN (ARTIE)
B.MAY 6,1865 PROVIDENCE,R.I.
D.NOV.14,1949 BROOKLINE,MASS.

1890	NY	N	C-2-3-0	101		.225
1891	NY	N	C	46		.188
			TR	147		.214

CLARKE, FRED CLIFFORD (FRED) OR (CAP)
B.OCT.3,1872 WINTERSET,IOWA
D.AUG.14,1960 WINFIELD,KAN.

1894	LOU	N	O		76	.275
1895	LOU	N	O	132		.354
1896	LOU	N	O	131		.327
1897	LOU	N	M-O	129		.406
1898	LOU	N	M-O	147		.318
1899	LOU	N	M-O	147		.348
1900	PIT	N	M-O	103		.281
1901	PIT	N	M-O	128		.316
1902	PIT	N	M-O	114		.321
1903	PIT	N	M-O	102		.351
1904	PIT	N	M-O	70		.306
1905	PIT	N	M-O	137		.299
1906	PIT	N	M-O	110		.309
1907	PIT	N	M-O	144		.289
1908	PIT	N	M-O	151		.265
1909	PIT	N	M-O	152		.287
1910	PIT	N	M-O	118		.263
1911	PIT	N	M-O	101		.324
1913	PIT	N	M-O	9		.077
1914	PIT	N	M-H	2		.000
1915	PIT	N	M-O	1		.500
			BLTR	2204		.315
NON-PLAYING MANAGER PIT[N] 1912

CLARKE, HARRY CORSON
B.1861
D.MAR.3,1923

| 1889 | WAS | N | O | | 1 | .000 |

CLARKE, HENRY TEFFT
B.AUG.28,1875 BELLEVUE,NEB.
D.MAR.28,1950 COLORADO SPRINGS,COLO.

1897	CLE	N	P		8	3- 5
1898	CHI	N	P		2	1- 0
			BRTR		10	4- 5

CLARKE, HORACE MEREDITH
B.JUNE 2,1940 FREDERIKSTED,
ST.CROIX,V.I.

1965	NY	A	3/2-S	51		.259
1966	NY	A	S-2/3	96		.266
1967	NY	A	*2	143		.272
1968	NY	A	*2	148		.230
1969	NY	A	*2	156		.285
1970	NY	A	*2	158		.251
1971	NY	A	*2	159		.250
1972	NY	A	*2	147		.241
1973	NY	A	*2	148		.263
1974	NY	A	2	24		.234
	SD	N	2	42		.189
			BBTR	1272		.256

CLARKE, JAY JUSTIN (NIG)
B.DEC.15,1882 AMHERSTBURG,ONT.,
CANADA
D.JUNE 15,1949 RIVER ROUGE,MICH

1905	CLE	A	C		6	.162
	DET	A	C		2	.400
	CLE	A	C	37		.202
1906	CLE	A	C	57		.358
1907	CLE	A	C	120		.269
1908	CLE	A	C	97		.241
1909	CLE	A	C	55		.274
1910	CLE	A	C	21		.155
1911	STL	A	C	82		.215
1919	PHI	N	C	26		.242
1920	PIT	N	C		3	.000
			BRTR	506		.254

CLARKE, JOSHUA BALDWIN (PEPPER)
B.MAR.8,1879 WINFIELD,KAN.
D.JULY 2,1962 VENTURA,CAL.

1898	LOU	N	O		6	.167
1905	STL	N	2-O		46	.247
1908	CLE	A	O	131		.242
1909	CLE	A	O		4	.000
1911	BOS	N	O		30	.233
			BLTR	217		.239

CLARKE, RICHARD GREY (GREY) OR (NOISY)
B.SEPT.26,1912 FULTON,ALA.

| 1944 | CHI | A | 3 | 63 | | .260 |
| | | | BRTR | | | |

CLARKE, RUFUS RIVERS
B.APR.13,1900 ESTILL,S.C.

1923	DET	A	P		5	1- 1
1924	DET	A	P		2	0- 0
			TR		7	1- 1

CLARKE, SUMPTER MILLS
B.OCT.18,1897 SAVANNAH,GA.
D.MAR.16,1962 KNOXVILLE,TENN.

1920	CHI	N	3		1	.333
1923	CLE	A	O		1	.000
1924	CLE	A	O	45		.227
			BRTR	47		.224

CLARKE, THOMAS ALOYSIUS (TOMMY)
B.MAY 9,1888 NEW YORK,N.Y.
D.AUG.14,1945 CORONA,N.Y.

1909	CIN	N	C	17		.250
1910	CIN	N	C	56		.278
1911	CIN	N	C	82		.241
1912	CIN	N	C	72		.281
1913	CIN	N	C	114		.264
1914	CIN	N	C	113		.262
1915	CIN	N	C	96		.288
1916	CIN	N	C	78		.237
1917	CIN	N	C	58		.291
1918	CHI	N	C		1	.000
			BRTR	687		.265

CLARKE, VIBERT ERNESTO (WEBBO)
B.JUNE 8,1928 COLON,PANAMA
D.JUNE 14,1970 CRISTOBAL,C.Z.

| 1955 | WAS | A | P | | 7 | 0- 0 |
| | | | BLTL | | | |

CLARKE, WILLIAM JONES (BOILERYARD)
B.OCT.18,1868 NEW YORK,N.Y.
D.JULY 29,1959 PRINCETON,N.J.

1893	BAL	N	C	47		.194
1894	BAL	N	C	27		.270
1895	BAL	N	C	60		.297
1896	BAL	N	C	77		.290
1897	BAL	N	C	63		.274
1898	BAL	N	C	77		.245
1899	BOS	N	C	60		.229
1900	BOS	N	C	71		.320
1901	WAS	A	C	109		.284
1902	WAS	A	C	87		.262
1903	WAS	A	C-1	126		.239
1904	WAS	A	C-1	85		.213
1905	NY	N	1	27		.180
			BRTR	916		.260

CLARKE, WILLIAM STUART (STU)
B.JAN.24,1906 SAN FRANCISCO,CAL
D.JUNE 13,1971 MILL VALLEY,CAL

1929	PIT	N	S-3	57		.264
1930	PIT	N	2		4	.444
			BRTR	61		.273

CLARKSON, ARTHUR HAMILTON (DAD)
B.AUG.31,1866 CAMBRIDGE,MASS.
D.FEB.6,1911 CAMBRIDGE,MASS.

1891	NY	N	P		5	1- 2
1892	BOS	N	P		1	0- 0
1893	STL	N	P	21		12- 9
1894	STL	N	P	27		9-18
1895	STL	N	P	11		1- 6
	BAL	N	P	17		13- 4
1896	BAL	N	P		7	3- 2
				89		39-41

CLARKSON, JAMES BUSTER (BUS)
B.MAR.13,1918 HOPKINS,S.C.

| 1952 | BOS | N | S-3 | 14 | | .200 |
| | | | BRTR | | | |

CLARKSON, JOHN GIBSON
B.JULY 1,1861 CAMBRIDGE,MASS.
D.FEB.4,1909 CAMBRIDGE,MASS.

1882	WOR	N	P-1		3	1- 1
						.364
1884	CHI	N	P-1-		20	10- 3
			3-O			.261
1885	CHI	N	P-3-	70	72	52-16
			O			.215
1886	CHI	N	P	53	55	35-17
1887	CHI	N	P	59	61	38-21
1888	BOS	N	P		54	33-20
1889	BOS	N	P		72	48-19
1890	BOS	N	P		44	26-18
1891	BOS	N	P		55	34-19
1892	BOS	N	P		16	9- 7
	CLE	N	P		27	17-10
1893	CLE	N	P		34	16-16
1894	CLE	N	P		16	8- 8
			BRTR	523	529	327-175
						.225

CLARKSON, WALTER HAMILTON
B.NOV.3,1878 CAMBRIDGE,MASS.
D.OCT.10,1946 CAMBRIDGE,MASS.

1904	NY	A	P	13		2- 2
1905	NY	A	P		8	2- 2
1906	NY	A	P	32		9- 4
1907	NY	A	P		6	0- 0
	CLE	A	P	16		5- 7
1908	CLE	A	P		2	0- 0
			TR	77		18-15

CLARKSON, WILLIAM HENRY (BLACKIE)
B.SEPT.27,1898 PORTSMOUTH,VA.
D.AUG.27,1971 RALEIGH,N.C.

1927	NY	N	P	26	28	3- 9
1928	NY	N	P		4	0- 0
	BOS	N	P		19	0- 2
1929	BOS	N	P		2	0- 1
			BRTR	51	53	3-12

CLARY, ELLIS (CAT)
B.SEPT.11,1916 VALDOSTA,GA.

1942	WAS	A	2	76		.275
1943	WAS	A	3	73		.296
	STL	A	2-S-3	23		.275
1944	STL	A	2-3	25		.265
1945	STL	A	2-3	26		.211
			BRTR	223		.263

CLASET, GOWELL SYLVESTER (LEFTY)
B.NOV.26,1907 BATTLE CREEK,MICH

| 1933 | PHI | A | P | | 8 | 2- 0 |
| | | | BBTL | | | |

CLAUSEN, FREDERICK WILLIAM (FRITZ)
B.APR.26,1869 NEW YORK,N.Y.
D.FEB.11,1960 MEMPHIS,TENN.

1892	LOU	N	P		24	9-13
1893	LOU	N	P		9	1- 3
	CHI	N	P		10	5- 3
1894	CHI	N	P		2	0- 1
1896	LOU	N	P		2	0- 1
			BRTL		47	15-21

CLAUSS, ALBERT STANLEY (LEFTY)
B.JUNE 24,1891 NEW HAVEN,CONN.
D.SEPT.13,1952 NEW HAVEN,CONN.

| 1913 | DET | A | P | | 4 | 0- 2 |
| | | | BRTL | | | |

CLAY, DAIN ELMER (DAIN) (SNIFFY) OR (DING-A-LING)
B.JULY 10,1919 HICKSVILLE,OHIO

1943	CIN	N	O		49	.269
1944	CIN	N	O		110	.250
1945	CIN	N	O		153	.280
1946	CIN	N	O		121	.228
			BRTR		433	.258

CLAY, FREDERICK C. (BILL)
B.NOV.23,1874 BALTIMORE,MD.
D.OCT.12,1917 YORK,PA.

| 1902 | PHI | N | O | | 3 | .250 |
| | | | TR | | | |

CLAY, KENNETH EARL (KEN)
B.APR.6,1954 LYNCHBURG,VA.

1977	NY	A	P	21		2- 3
1978	NY	A	P	28		3- 4
			BRTR	49		5- 7

CLEARY, JOSEPH CHRISTOPHER (FIRE)
B.DEC.3,1919 CORK CITY,EIRE,IRELAND

| 1945 | WAS | A | P | | 1 | 0- 0 |
| | | | BRTR | | | |

CLEMENS, CHESTER SPURGEON
B.MAY 10,1917 SAN FERNANDO,CAL.

1939	BOS	N	O		9	.217
1944	BOS	N	O		19	.176
			BRTR		28	.200

CLEMENS, CLEMENT LAMBERT (COUNT)
[REAL NAME
CLEMENT LAMBERT ULATOWSKI]
B.NOV.2,1886 CHICAGO,ILL.
D.NOV.2,1967 ST.PETERSBURG,FLA.

1914	CHI	F	C	12		.154
1915	CHI	F	C	11		.136
	CHI	N	C	10		.000
			BRTR	33		.111

CLEMENS, DOUGLAS HORACE (DOUG)
B.JUNE 9,1939 LEESPORT,PA.

1960	STL	N	O		1	.000
1961	STL	N	O		6	.167
1962	STL	N	O		4	.167
1963	STL	N	O		5	.167
1964	STL	N	O		33	.205
	CHI	N	O		54	.279
1965	CHI	N	*O	128		.221
1966	PHI	N	O/1	79		.256
1967	PHI	N	O		69	.178
1968	PHI	N	O		29	.211
			BLTR	452		.229

CLEMENS, ROBERT BAXTER
B.AUG.9,1886 MT.HEBRON,MO.
D.APR.5,1964 MARSHALL,MO.

| 1914 | STL | A | O | | 8 | .214 |
| | | | BRTR | | | |

CLEMENSEN, WILLIAM MELVILLE (BILL)
B.JUNE 20,1919 NEW BRUNSWICK,N.J.

1939	PIT	N	P		12	0- 1
1941	PIT	N	P		2	1- 0
1946	PIT	N	P		1	0- 0
			BRTR		15	1- 1

YR	CL LEA POS	GP	G	REC

CLEMENT, WALLACE OAKES
B.JULY 21,1881 AUBURN,ME.
D.NOV.1,1953 CORAL GABLES,FLA.

YR	CL LEA POS	GP	G	REC
1908 PIT N O		12	.242
1909 PHI N O		3	.000
BRO N O		88	.256
BLTR		103	.251

CLEMENTE, ROBERTO [WALKER]
(ROBERTO) OR (BOB)
B.AUG,18,1934 CAROLINA,P.R.
D.DEC.31,1972 SAN JUAN,P.R.

1955 PIT N O		124	.255
1956 PIT N 2-3-O		147	.311
1957 PIT N O		111	.253
1958 PIT N O		140	.289
1959 PIT N O		105	.296
1960 PIT N O		144	.314
1961 PIT N O		146	.351
1962 PIT N O		144	.312
1963 PIT N O		152	.320
1964 PIT N O		155	.339
1965 PIT N *O		152	.329
1966 PIT N *O		154	.317
1967 PIT N *O		147	.357
1968 PIT N *O		132	.291
1969 PIT N *O		138	.345
1970 PIT N *O		108	.352
1971 PIT N *O		132	.341
1972 PIT N *O		102	.312
BRTR		2433	.317

CLEMENTS, EDWARD
B.PHILADELPHIA,PA.

| 1890 PIT N S | | 1 | .000 |

CLEMENTS, JOHN J. (JACK)
B.JULY 24,1864 PHILADELPHIA,PA.
D.MAY 23,1941 NORRISTOWN,PA.

1884 KEY U C-S-O		41	.289
PHI N C		8	.240
1885 PHI N C-O		52	.191
1886 PHI N C		54	.205
1887 PHI N C		63	.306
1888 PHI N C		85	.247
1889 PHI N C		78	.284
1890 PHI N C		97	.315
1891 PHI N C		105	.305
1892 PHI N C		102	.270
1893 PHI N C		90	.290
1894 PHI N C		47	.343
1895 PHI N C		84	.389
1896 PHI N C		50	.362
1897 PHI N C		49	.239
1898 STL N C		85	.268
1899 CLE N C		4	.167
1900 BOS N C		16	.307
BLTL		1110	.288

CLEMONS, LANCE LEVIS
B.JULY 7,1947 PHILADELPHIA,PA.

1971 KC A P		10	1- 0
1972 STL N /P		3	1- 0
1974 BOS A /P		6	1- 0
BLTL		19	2- 1

CLEMONS, VERNE JAMES
(STINGER) OR (TUBBY)
B.SEPT.8,1891 CLEMONS,IOWA
D.MAY 5,1959 BAY PINES,FLA.

1916 STL N C		3	.000
1919 STL N C		88	.264
1920 STL N C		112	.281
1921 STL N C		117	.320
1922 STL N C		71	.256
1923 STL N C		57	.285
1924 STL N C		25	.321
BRTR		473	.287

CLENDENON, DONN ALVIN
B.JULY 15,1935 NEOSHO,MO.

1961 PIT N O		9	.314
1962 PIT N 1-O		80	.302
1963 PIT N 1		154	.275
1964 PIT N 1		133	.242
1965 PIT N *1		162	.301
1966 PIT N *1		155	.299
1967 PIT N *1		131	.249
1968 PIT N *1		158	.257
1969 MON N 1-O		38	.240
NY N 1/O		72	.252
1970 NY N *1		121	.288
1971 NY N 1		88	.247
1972 STL N 1		61	.191
BRTR		1362	.274

CLEVELAND, ELMER ELLSWORTH
B.SEPT.15,1862 WASHINGTON,D.C.
D.OCT.8,1913 ZIMMERMAN,O.

1884 CIN U 2		26	.281
1888 NY N 3		10	.270
PIT N 3		30	.204
1891 COL AA 3		12	.142
BRTR		78	.228

CLEVELAND, REGINALD LESLIE (REGGIE)
B.MAY 23,1948 SWIFT CURRENT,
SASK.,CANADA

1969 STL N /P		1	0- 0
1970 STL N P		16	0- 4
1971 STL N P		34	12-12
1972 STL N P		33	14-15
1973 STL N P		32	14-10
1974 BOS A P		41	12-14
1975 BOS A P		31	13- 9
1976 BOS A P		41	10- 9
1977 BOS A P		36	11- 8
1978 BOS A /P		1	0- 1
TEX A P		53	5- 7
BRTR		319	91-89

CLEVENGER, TRUMAN EUGENE (TEX)
B.JULY 9,1932 VISALIA,CAL.

YR	CL LEA POS	GP	G	REC
1954 BOS A P	23	25	2- 4
1956 WAS A P		20	0- 0
1957 WAS A P		52	7- 6
1958 WAS A P		55	9- 9
1959 WAS A P		50	8- 5
1960 WAS A P		53	5-11
1961 LA A P		12	2- 1
A P		21	1- 1
1962 NY A P	21	22	7- 4
BRTR	307	310	36-37

CLIFT, HARLOND BENTON (DARKIE)
B.AUG,12,1912 EL RENO,OKLA.

1934 STL A 3		147	.260
1935 STL A 2-3		137	.295
1936 STL A 3		152	.302
1937 STL A 3		155	.306
1938 STL A 3		149	.290
1939 STL A 3		151	.270
1940 STL A 3		150	.273
1941 STL A 3		154	.255
1942 STL A S-3		143	.274
1943 STL A 3		105	.232
WAS A 3		8	.100
1944 WAS A 3		12	.159
1945 WAS A 3		119	.211
BRTR		1582	.272

CLIFTON, HERMAN EARL (FLEA)
B.DEC,12,1909 CINCINNATI,OHIO

1934 DET A 2-3		16	.063
1935 DET A 2-S-3		43	.255
1936 DET A 2-S-3		13	.192
1937 DET A 2-S-3		15	.116
BRTR		87	.200

CLINE, JOHN (MONK)
B.LOUISVILLE,KY.

1882 BAL AA 2-S-3-O		45	.222
1884 LOU AA S-O		94	.287
1885 LOU AA 3-O		2	.222
1888 KC AA O		73	.243
1891 LOU AA O		19	.304
		233	.277

CLINE, TYRONE ALEXANDER (TY)
B.JUNE 15,1939 HAMPTON,S.C.

1960 CLE A O		7	.308
1961 CLE A O		12	.209
1962 CLE A O		118	.248
1963 MIL N O		72	.236
1964 MIL N 1-O		101	.302
1965 MIL N O/1		123	.191
1966 MIL N /O		7	.353
ATL N O/1		42	.254
1967 ATL N /O		10	.000
SF N O		64	.270
1968 SF N O-1		116	.223
1969 MON N O-1		101	.239
1970 MON N /H		2	.500
CIN N O		48	.270
1971 CIN N O/1		69	.196
BLTL		892	.238

CLINES, EUGENE ANTHONY (GENE)
B.OCT.6,1946 SAN PABLO,CAL.

1970 PIT N /O		31	.405
1971 PIT N O		97	.308
1972 PIT N O		107	.334
1973 PIT N O		110	.263
1974 PIT N O		107	.225
1975 NY N O		82	.227
1976 TEX A *O-D		116	.276
1977 CHI N O		101	.293
1978 CHI N O		109	.258
BRTR		860	.277

CLINGMAN, WILLIAM FREDERICK
B.NOV.21,1869 CINCINNATI,OHIO
D.MAY 14,1958 CINCINNATI,OHIO

1890 CIN N S		7	.258
1891 CIN AA 2		1	.200
1895 PIT N 3		108	.261
1896 LOU N 3		120	.230
1897 LOU N 3		115	.232
1898 LOU N S-3		154	.262
1899 LOU N 3		108	.267
1900 CHI N S		46	.201
1901 WAS A S		137	.245
1903 CLE A 2-S-3		21	.286
BBTR		817	.248

CLINTON, JAMES LAWRENCE (BIG JIM)
B.AUG.10,1850 NEW YORK,N.Y.
D.SEPT.3,1921 BROOKLYN,N.Y.

YR	CL LEA POS	GP	G	REC
1872 ECK NA M-2-S-3-O		24	.188
1873 RES NA 3-O		8	-
1874 ATL NA 1-2-O		4	-
1875 ATL NA P-1-	13	22	1-12
2-O			
1876 LOU N P-O	2	16	0- 1
			.338
1882 WOR N O		26	.163
1883 BAL AA 2-O		94	.305
1884 BAL AA O		105	.281
1885 CIN AA O		98	.239
1886 BAL AA O		23	.183
BRTR	15	420	1-13
			-

CLINTON, LUCIEN LOUIS (LOU)
B.OCT.13,1937 PONCA CITY,OKLA.

1960 BOS A O		96	.228
1961 BOS A O		17	.255
1962 BOS A O		114	.294
1963 BOS A O		148	.232
1964 BOS A O		37	.258
LA A O		91	.248
1965 CAL A O		89	.243
KC A /O		1	.000
CLE A /O		12	.176
1966 NY A O		80	.220
1967 NY A /O		6	.500
BRTR		691	.247

CLOLO, CARLOS
[PLAYED UNDER NAME OF
CHARLES LOUIS HALL]

CLONINGER, TONY LEE
B.AUG.13,1940 LINCOLN,N.C.

1961 MIL N P		19	7- 2
1962 MIL N P		24	8- 3
1963 MIL N P		41	9-11
1964 MIL N P		38	19-14
1965 MIL N P	40	46	24-11
1966 ATL N P	39	47	14-11
1967 ATL N P		16	4- 7
1968 ATL N /P		8	1- 3
CIN N P	17	21	4- 3
1969 CIN N P	35	36	11-17
1970 CIN N P		30	9- 7
1971 CIN N P		28	3- 6
1972 CIN N P		17	0- 2
BRTR	352	366	113-97

CLOSTER, ALAN EDWARD (AL)
B.JUNE 15,1943 CREIGHTON,NEB.

1966 WAS A /P		1	0- 0
1971 NY A P		14	2- 2
1972 NY A /P		2	0- 0
1973 ATL N /P		4	0- 0
BLTL		21	2- 2

CLOUGH, EDGAR GEORGE
(BIG ED) PR (SPEC)
B.OCT.28,1906 WICONISCO,PA.
D.JAN.30,1944 HARRISBURG,PA.

1924 STL N O		7	.071
1925 STL N P		3	0- 1
1926 STL N P		1	0- 0
BLTL	4	11	0- 1
			.111

CLOWERS, WILLIAM PERRY
B.AUG.14,1898 SAN MARCOS,TEX.
D.JAN.13,1978 SWEENY,TEX.

| 1926 BOS A P | | 2 | 0- 0 |
| BLTL | | | |

CLYDE, DAVID EUGENE
B.APR.22,1955 KANSAS CITY,KAN.

1973 TEX A P		18	4- 8
1974 TEX A P		28	3- 9
1975 TEX A /P		1	0- 1
1978 CLE A P	28	29	8-11
BLTL	75	76	15-29

CLYDE, THOMAS KNOX
B.AUG.17,1923 WACHAPREAGUE,VA.

| 1943 PHI A P | | 4 | 0- 0 |
| BRTR | | | |

CLYMER, OTIS EDGAR
B.JAN.27,1880 PINE GROVE,PA.
D.FEB.27,1926 ST.PAUL,MINN.

1905 PIT N O		90	.296
1906 PIT N O		11	.244
1907 PIT N O		16	.227
WAS A O		57	.316
1908 WAS A O		110	.253
1909 WAS A O		45	.196
1913 CHI N O		30	.229
BOS N O		14	.324
BLTR		373	.267

CLYMER, WILLIAM JOHNSTON
(DERBY DAY BILL)
B.DEC.18,1873 PHILADELPHIA,PA.
D.DEC.26,1936 PHILADELPHIA,PA.

| 1891 ATH AA S | | 3 | .000 |

```
YR  CL LEA POS    GP   G   REC        YR  CL LEA POS    GP   G   REC        YR  CL LEA POS    GP   G   REC
```

COAKLEY, ANDREW JAMES
[PLAYED UNDER NAME OF
JACK MC ALLISTER IN 1902]
B.NOV.20,1882 PROVIDENCE, R.I.
D.SEPT.27,1963 NEW YORK,N.Y.
```
1902 PHI A P         3       2-1
1903 PHI A P         6       0-3
1904 PHI A P        11       7-4
1905 PHI A P        34      20-8
1906 PHI A P        22       7-8
1907 CIN N P        37      17-16
1908 CIN N P        32       8-18
     CHI N P         4       2-0
1909 CHI N P         1       0-1
1911 NY  A P         2       0-1
     BLTR          152      63-66
```

COAN, GILBERT FITZGERALD (GIL)
B.MAY 18,1922 MONROE,N.C.
```
1946 WAS A O        59      .209
1947 WAS A O        11      .500
1948 WAS A O       138      .232
1949 WAS A O       111      .218
1950 WAS A O       104      .303
1951 WAS A O       135      .303
1952 WAS A O       107      .205
1953 WAS A O        68      .196
1954 BAL A O        94      .279
1955 BAL A O        61      .238
     CHI A O        17      .176
     NY  N O         9      .154
1956 NY  N H         4      .000
     BLTR          918      .254
```

COATES, JAMES ALTON (JIM)
B.AUG.4,1932 FARNHAM,VA.
```
1956 NY  A P         2       0-0
1959 NY  A P        37       6-1
1960 NY  A P        35      13-3
1961 NY  A P        43      11-5
1962 NY  A P        50       7-6
1963 WAS A P        20       2-4
     CIN N P         9       0-0
1965 CAL A P        17       2-0
1966 CAL A /P        9       1-1
1967 CAL A P        25       1-2
     BRTR          247      43-22
```

COBB, GEORGE WASHINGTON
B.SAN FRANCISCO,CAL.
```
1892 BAL N P        47  49   9-38
```

COBB, HERBERT EDWARD
B.AUG.6,1904 PINETOPS,N.C.
```
1929 STL A P         1       0-0
     BRTR
```

COBB, JOSEPH STANLEY
[REAL NAME JOSEPH STANLEY SERAFIN]
B.JAN.24,1895 HUDSON,PA.
D.DEC.24,1947 ALLENTOWN,PA.
```
1918 DET A C         1      .000
     BRTR
```

COBB, TYRUS RAYMOND (TY)
OR (THE GEORGIA PEACH)
B.DEC.18,1886 NARROWS,GA.
D.JULY 17,1961 ATLANTA,GA.
```
1905 DET A O        41      .240
1906 DET A O        97      .320
1907 DET A O       150      .350
1908 DET A O       150      .324
1909 DET A O       156      .377
1910 DET A O       140      .385
1911 DET A O       146      .420
1912 DET A O       140      .410
1913 DET A 2-O     122      .390
1914 DET A O        97      .368
1915 DET A O       156      .369
1916 DET A O       145      .371
1917 DET A O       152      .383
1918 DET A 1-O     111      .382
1919 DET A O       124      .384
1920 DET A O       112      .334
1921 DET A M-O     128      .389
1922 DET A M-O     137      .401
1923 DET A M-O     145      .340
1924 DET A M-O     155      .338
1925 DET A M-P-   1 121      0-0
             O             .378
1926 DET A M-O      79      .339
1927 PHI A O       134      .357
1928 PHI A O        95      .323
     BLTR       1 3033       0-0
                           .367
```

COBLE, DAVID LAMAR
B.DEC.24,1912 MONROE,N.C.
D.OCT.15,1971 ORLANDO,FLA.
```
1939 PHI N C        15      .280
     BRTR
```

COCHRAN, ALVAH JACKSON (GOAT)
B.JAN.31,1891 CONCORD,GA.
D.MAY 23,1947 ATLANTA,GA.
```
1915 CIN N P         1       0-0
     BRTR
```

COCHRAN, GEORGE LESLIE
B.FEB.12,1889 RUSK,TEX.
D.MAY 21,1960 HARBOR CITY,CAL.
```
1918 BOS A 3        25      .127
     TR
```

COCHRANE, GORDON STANLEY (MICKEY)
B.APR.6,1903 BRIDGEWATER,MASS.
D.JUNE 28,1962 LAKE FOREST,ILL.
```
1925 PHI A C       134      .331
1926 PHI A C       120      .273
1927 PHI A C       126      .338
1928 PHI A C       131      .293
1929 PHI A C       135      .331
1930 PHI A C       130      .357
1931 PHI A C       122      .349
1932 PHI A C       139      .293
1933 PHI A C       130      .322
1934 DET A M-C     129      .320
1935 DET A M-C     115      .319
1936 DET A M-C      44      .270
1937 DET A M-C      27      .306
     BLTR         1482      .320
```
NON-PLAYING MANAGER DET [A]1938

COCKMAN, JAMES
B.APR.26,1873 GUELPH,ONT.,CAN.
D.SEPT.28,1947 GUELPH,ONT.,CAN.
```
1905 NY A 3         13      .076
     BRTR
```

COCREHAM, EUGENE
B.NOV.14,1884 LULING,TEX.
D.DEC.27,1945 LULING,TEX.
```
1913 BOS N P         1       0-1
1914 BOS N P        15       3-4
1915 BOS N P         1       0-0
     BRTR           17       3-5
```

COFFEY, JOHN FRANCIS (JACK)
[REAL NAME JOHN JOSEPH SMITH]
B.JAN.28,1887 NEW YORK,N.Y.
D.FEB.14,1966 BRONX,N.Y.
```
1909 BOS N S        73      .186
1918 DET A 2        22      .209
     BOS A 2-3      15      .159
     BRTR          110      .188
```

COFFEY, JOHN JOSEPH
B.AUG.8,1893 OSWAYA,PA.
```
1912 DET A P         1      .000
     TR
```

COFFMAN, GEORGE DAVID (SLICK)
B.DEC.11,1910 VETO,ALA.
```
1937 DET A P        28       7-5
1938 DET A P        39       4-4
1939 DET A P        23       2-1
1940 STL A P     31 32       2-2
     BRTR        121 122    15-12
```

COFFMAN, SAMUEL RICHARD (DICK)
B.DEC.18,1906 VETO,ALA.
D.MAR.24,1972 ATHENS,ALA.
```
1927 WAS A P         5       0-1
1928 STL A P        29       4-5
1929 STL A P        27       1-1
1930 STL A P        38       8-18
1931 STL A P        32       9-13
1932 STL A P         9       5-3
     WAS A P        22       1-6
1933 STL A P        21       3-7
1934 STL A P        40       9-10
1935 STL A P        41       5-11
1936 NY  N P        42       7-5
1937 NY  N P        42       8-3
1938 NY  N P        51       8-4
1939 NY  N P        28       1-2
1940 BOS N P        31       1-5
1945 PHI N P        14       2-1
     BRTR          472      72-95
```

COGAN, RICHARD HENRY
B.DEC.5,1871 PATERSON,N.J.
D.MAY 2,1948 PATERSON,N.J.
```
1897 BAL N P         1       0-0
1899 CHI N P         8       2-3
1900 NY  N P         3       0-0
                    12       2-3
```

COGGINS, FRANKLIN (FRANK)
B.MAY.22,1944 GRIFFIN,GA.
```
1967 WAS A 2        19      .307
1968 WAS A 2        62      .175
1972 CHI N /H        6      .000
     BBTR           87      .215
```

COGGINS, RICHARD ALLEN (RICH)
B.DEC.7,1950 INDIANAPOLIS,IND.
```
1972 BAL A O        16      .333
1973 BAL A *O      110      .319
1974 BAL A *O      113      .243
1975 MON N O        13      .270
     NY  A O        51      .224
1976 NY  A /O        7      .250
     CHI A O        32      .156
     BLTL          342      .265
```

COGSWELL, EDWARD
B.FEB.25,1854 ENGLAND
D.JULY 27,1888 FITCHBURG,MASS.
```
1879 BOS N 1        49      .322
1880 TRO N 1        47      .301
1882 WOR N 1        13      .122
     BR            109      .291
```

COHEN, ALTA ALBERT (SCHOOLBOY)
B.DEC.25,1908 NEW YORK,N.Y.
```
1931 BRO N O         1      .667
1932 BRO N O         9      .156
1933 PHI N O        19      .188
     BLTL           29      .194
```

COHEN, ANDREW HOWARD
B.OCT.25,1904 BALTIMORE,MD.
```
1926 NY  N 2-S      32      .257
1928 NY  N 2       129      .274
1929 NY  N 2       101      .294
     BRTR          262      .281
```

COHEN, HARRY
[PLAYED UNDER NAME OF HARRY KANE]

COHEN, HYMAN
B.JAN.29,1931 BROOKLYN,N.Y.
```
1955 CHI N P         7       0-0
     BRTR
```

COHEN, REUBEN
[PLAYED UNDER NAME OF REUBEN EWING]

COHEN, SAMUEL ARTHUR
[PLAYED UNDER NAME OF
SAMUEL ARTHUR BOHNE]

COHEN, SYDNEY HARRY
B.MAY 7,1908 BALTIMORE,MD.
```
1934 WAS A P-O      3   4    1-1
                           .273
1936 WAS A P        19       0-2
1937 WAS A P        33       2-4
     BBTL          55  56    3-7
                           .152
```

COHN, PHILIP
[PLAYED UNDER NAME OF PHILIP COONEY]

COKER, JAMES GOODWIN (JIMMIE)
B.MAR.28,1936 HOLLY HILL,S.C.
```
1958 PHI N C         2      .167
1960 PHI N C        81      .214
1961 PHI N C        11      .400
1962 PHI N H         5      .000
1963 SF  N C         4      .200
1964 CIN N C        11      .313
1965 CIN N C        24      .246
1966 CIN N C/O      50      .252
1967 CIN N C        45      .186
     BRTR          233      .231
```

COLAVITO, ROCCO DOMENICO (ROCKY)
B.AUG.10,1933 NEW YORK,N.Y.
```
1955 CLE A O         5      .444
1956 CLE A O       101      .276
1957 CLE A O       134      .252
1958 CLE A P-1-O  1 143      0-0
                           .303
1959 CLE A O       154      .257
1960 DET A O       145      .249
1961 DET A O       163      .290
1962 DET A O       161      .273
1963 DET A O       160      .271
1964 KC  A O       160      .274
1965 CLE A *O      162      .287
1966 CLE A *O      151      .238
1967 CLE A O        63      .241
     CHI A O        60      .221
1968 LA  A O        40      .204
     NY  A O/P     1  39     1-0
                           .220
     BRTR        2 1841      1-0
                           .266
```

COLBERN, MICHAEL MALLOY (MIKE)
B.APR.19,1955 SANTA MONICA,CAL.
```
1978 CHI A C        48      .270
     BRTR
```

COLBERT, NATHAN (NATE)
B.APR.9,1946 ST.LOUIS,MO.
```
1966 HOU N H        19      .000
1968 HOU N O/1      20      .151
1969 SD  N *1      139      .255
1970 SD  N *1/3    156      .259
1971 SD  N *1      156      .264
1972 SD  N *1      151      .250
1973 SD  N *1      145      .270
1974 SD  N 1-O     119      .207
1975 DET A 1        45      .147
     MON N 1        38      .173
1976 MON N /O-1     14      .200
     OAK A /H        2      .000
     BRTR         1004      .243
```

```
YR  CL LEA POS     GP   G   REC
```

COLBERT, VINCENT NORMAN (VINCE)
B.DEC.20,1945 WASHINGTON,D.C.
```
1970 CLE A  P           23    1- 1
1971 CLE A  P      50   52    7- 6
1972 CLE A  P      22   23    1- 7
      BRTR        95   98    9-14
```

COLBORN, JAMES WILLIAM (JIM)
B.MAY 22,1946 SANTA PAULA,CAL.
```
1969 CHI N /P            6    1- 0
1970 CHI N  P           34    3- 1
1971 CHI N  P           14    0- 1
1972 MIL A  P           39    7- 7
1973 MIL A  P           43   20-12
1974 MIL A  P           33   10-13
1975 MIL A  P           36   11-13
1976 MIL A  P           32    9-15
1977 KC  A  P      36   37   18-14
1978 KC  A  /P           8    1- 2
      SEA A  P           20    3-10
      BRTR       301  302   83-88
```

COLCOLOUGH, THOMAS BERNARD
B.OCT.8,1870 CHARLESTON,S.C.
D.DEC.10,1919 CHARLESTON,S.C.
```
1893 PIT N  P            8    2- 0
1894 PIT N  P           19    7- 7
1895 PIT N  P            8    1- 1
1899 NY  N  P           14    4- 5
      BRTR        49   14-13
```

COLE, ALBERT GEORGE (BERT)
B.JULY 1,1896 SAN FRANCISCO,CAL
D.MAY 30,1975 SAN MATEO,CAL.
```
1921 DET A  P      20   30    7- 4
1922 DET A  P      24   27    1- 6
1923 DET A  P      52   58   13- 5
1924 DET A  P      28   33    3- 9
1925 DET A  P           14    2- 3
      CLE A             13    1- 1
1927 CHI A             27    1- 4
      BLTL       177  202   28-32
```

COLE, DAVID BRUCE (DAVE)
B.AUG.29,1930 WILLIAMSPORT,MD.
```
1950 BOS N  P            4    0- 1
1951 BOS N  P           23    2- 4
1952 BOS N  P           22    1- 1
1953 MIL N  P           10    0- 1
1954 CHI N  P      18   19    3- 8
1955 PHI N  P            7    0- 3
      BRTR        84   85    6-18
```

COLE, EDWARD WILLIAM
[REAL NAME
EDWARD WILLIAM KISLEAUSKAS]
B.MAR.22,1909 WILKES-BARRE,PA.
```
1938 STL A  P           36    1- 5
1939 STL A  P            6    0- 2
      BRTR        42    1- 7
```

COLE, LEONARD LESLIE (KING)
B.APR.15,1886 TOLEDO,IOWA
D.JAN.6,1916 BAY CITY,MICH.
```
1909 CHI N  P            1    1- 0
1910 CHI N  P           33   20- 4
1911 CHI N  P           32   18- 7
1912 CHI N  P            8    1- 2
      PIT N  P           12    2- 2
1914 NY  A  P           33   11- 9
1915 NY  A  P           10    2- 3
      BRTR       129   55-27
```

COLE, RICHARD ROY (DICK)
B.MAY 6,1926 LONG BEACH,CAL.
```
1951 STL N  2           15    .194
      PIT N  2-S        42    .238
1953 PIT N  1-2-S       97    .272
1954 PIT N  2-S-3      138    .270
1955 PIT N  2-S-3       77    .226
1956 PIT N  2-S-3       72    .212
1957 MIL N  1-2-3       15    .071
      BRTR       456    .249
```

COLE, WILLIS RUSSELL
B.JAN.6,1862 MILTON JUNCTION,WIS.
D.OCT.11,1965 MADISON,WIS.
```
1909 CHI A  O      46    .236
1910 CHI A  O      22    .175
      BRTR        68    .216
```

COLEMAN, CLARENCE (CHOO CHOO)
B.AUG.25,1937 ORLANDO,FLA.
```
1961 PHI N  C      34    .128
1962 NY  N  C      55    .250
1963 NY  N  C-O   106    .178
1966 NY  N  /C      6    .188
      BLTR       201    .197
```

COLEMAN, CURTIS HANCOCK
B.FEB.18,1887 SALEM,ORE.
```
1912 NY  A  3      12    .263
      BRTR
```

COLEMAN, DAVID LEE (DAVE)
B.OCT.26,1950 DAYTON,OHIO
```
1977 BOS A  /O     11    .000
      BRTR
```

COLEMAN, GERALD FRANCIS (JERRY)
B.SEPT.14,1924 SAN JOSE,CAL.
```
1949 NY  A  2-S       128    .275
1950 NY  A  2-S       153    .287
1951 NY  A  2-S       121    .249
1952 NY  A  2          11    .405
1953 NY  A  2-S         8    .200
1954 NY  A  2-S-3     107    .217
1955 NY  A  2-S-3      43    .229
1956 NY  A  2-S-3      80    .257
1957 NY  A  2-S-3      72    .268
      BRTR       723    .263
```

COLEMAN, GORDON CALVIN (GORDY)
B.JULY 5,1934 ROCKVILLE,MD.
```
1959 CLE A  1           6    .533
1960 CIN N  1          66    .271
1961 CIN N  1         150    .287
1962 CIN N  1         136    .277
1963 CIN N  1         123    .247
1964 CIN N  1          89    .242
1965 CIN N  1         168    .302
1966 CIN N  1          91    .251
1967 CIN N  /1          4    .000
      BLTR       773    .273
```

COLEMAN, JOHN
B.BRISTOL,PA.
```
1890 PHI N  P            1    0- 0
```

COLEMAN, JOHN
B.JEFFERSON CITY,MO.
```
1895 STL N  P            2    0- 1
```

COLEMAN, JOHN FRANCIS
B.MAR.6,1863 SARATOGA SPGS.,N.Y
D.MAY 31,1922 DETROIT,MICH.
```
1883 PHI N  P-O    63   89   13-48
                             .232
1884 PHI N  P-1-   19   43    5-14
            O                .245
      ATH AA P-O    3   30    0- 2
                             .196
1885 ATH AA P-O    4   97    1- 3
                             .309
1886 ATH AA P-O    2  122    1- 1
                             .252
      PIT AA O           10    .333
1887 PIT N  O          115    .334
1888 PIT N  1-O        115    .230
1889 ATH AA P            6    3- 2
1890 PIT N  P            9    3- 2
      BLTR       100  630   23-72
                             .267
      BB 1887
```

COLEMAN, JOSEPH HOWARD (JOE)
B.FEB.3,1947 BOSTON,MASS.
```
1965 WAS A  /P           2    2- 0
1966 WAS A  /P           1    1- 0
1967 WAS A  P           28    8- 9
1968 WAS A  P      33   34   12-16
1969 WAS A  P           40   12-13
1970 WAS A  P           39    8-12
1971 DET A  P           39   20- 9
1972 DET A  P           40   19-14
1973 DET A  P           40   23-15
1974 DET A  P           41   14-12
1975 DET A  P           31   10-18
1976 DET A  P           12    2- 5
      CHI N  P           39    2- 8
1977 OAK A  P           43    4- 4
1978 OAK A  P           10    3- 0
      TOR A  P           31    2- 0
      BRTR       469  470  142-135
```

COLEMAN, JOSEPH PATRICK (JOE)
B.JULY 30,1922 MEDFORD,MASS.
```
1942 PHI A  P            1    0- 1
1946 PHI A  P            4    0- 2
1947 PHI A  P           32    6-12
1948 PHI A  P           33   14-13
1949 PHI A  P           33   13-14
1950 PHI A  P           15    0- 5
1951 PHI A  P           28    1- 6
1953 PHI A  P           21    3- 4
1954 BAL A  P           33   13-17
1955 BAL A  P            2    0- 0
      DET A  P           17    2- 1
      BRTR       223   52-76
```

COLEMAN, PARKE EDWARD (ED)
B.DEC.1,1901 CANBY,ORE.
D.AUG.5,1964 OREGON CITY,ORE.
```
1932 PHI A  O          26    .342
1933 PHI A  O         102    .281
1934 PHI A  O         101    .280
1935 PHI A  O          10    .077
      STL A  O         108    .287
1936 STL A  O          92    .292
      BLTR       439    .285
```

COLEMAN, PIERCE D. (PERCY)
B.CINCINNATI,OHIO
```
1897 STL N  P           12    1- 5
1898 CIN N  P            1    0- 1
                        13    1- 6
```

COLEMAN, RAYMOND LEROY (RAY)
B.JUNE 4,1922 DUNSMUIR,CAL.
```
1947 STL A  O         116    .259
1948 STL A  O          17    .172
      PHI A  O          68    .243
1950 STL A  O         117    .271
1951 STL A  O          91    .282
      CHI A  O          51    .276
1952 CHI A  O          85    .215
      STL A  O          20    .196
      BLTR       559    .258
```

COLEMAN, ROBERT HUNTER
B.SEPT.26,1890 HUNTINGBURG,IND.
D.JULY 16,1959 BOSTON,MASS.
```
1913 PIT N  C          24    .180
1914 PIT N  C          73    .266
1916 CLE A  C          19    .214
      BRTR       116    .241
```
NON-PLAYING MANAGER BOS [N] 1944-45

COLEMAN, WALTER GARY (RIP)
B.JULY 31,1931 TROY,N.Y.
```
1955 NY  A  P           10    2- 1
1956 NY  A  P           29    3- 5
1957 KC  A  P           19    0- 7
1959 KC  A  P           29    2-10
1960 BAL A  P            3    0- 0
      BAL A              5    0- 2
      BLTL        95    7-25
```

COLES, CADWALLADER R. (CAD)
B.JAN.17,1889 ROCKHILL,S.C.
D.JUNE 30,1942 MIAMI,FLA.
```
1914 KC  F  O          77    .253
      BLTR
```

COLES, CHARLES EDWARD (CHUCK)
B.JUNE 27,1931 FREDERICKTOWN,PA
```
1958 CIN N  O           5    .182
      BLTL
```

COLETTA, CHRISTOPHER MICHAEL (CHRIS)
B.AUG.2,1944 BROOKLYN,N.Y.
```
1972 CAL A  /O         14    .300
      BLTR
```

COLGAN, WILLIAM H. (ED)
B.E.ST.LOUIS,ILL.
D.AUG.13,1895 GREAT FALLS,MONT.
```
1884 PIT AA C          48    .166
```

COLIVER, WILLIAM J.
B.1867 DETROIT,MICH.
D.MAR.24,1888 DETROIT,MICH.
```
1885 BOS N  O           1    .000
```

COLLAMORE, ALLAN EDWARD
B.JUNE 5,1887 WORCESTER,MASS.
```
1911 PHI A  P            2    0- 0
1914 CLE A  P           27    3- 7
1915 CLE A  P      11   13    2- 5
      BRTR        40   42    5-12
```

COLLARD, EARL CLINTON (HAP)
B.AUG.29,1898 WILLIAMS,ARIZ.
D.JULY 9,1968 JAMESTOWN,CAL.
```
1927 CLE A  P            4    0- 0
1928 CLE A  P            1    0- 0
1930 PHI N  P      30   31    6-12
      BRTR        35   36    6-12
```

COLLIER, ORLIN EDWARD
B.FEB.17,1907 E.PRAIRIE,MO.
D.SEPT.9,1944 MEMPHIS,TENN.
```
1931 DET A  P            2    0- 1
      BRTR
```

COLLIFLOWER, JAMES HARRY (COLLIE)
B.MAR.11,1869 PETERSVILLE,MD.
D.AUG.14,1961 WASHINGTON,D.C.
```
1899 CLE N  P           21    1-11
      BLTL
```

COLLINS, CHARLES (CHUB)
B.1862 DUNDAS,ONT.,CANADA
D.MAY 20,1914 DUNDAS,ONT.,CAN.
```
1884 BUF N  2-S        45    .177
      IND A 2          38    .229
1885 DET N  S          14    .179
                       97    .197
```

COLLINS, CYRIL WILSON (WILSON)
B.MAY 7,1889 PULASKI,TENN.
D.FEB.28,1941 KNOXVILLE,TENN.
```
1913 BOS N  O          16    .333
1914 BOS N  O          27    .257
      BRTR        43    .263
```

COLLINS, DANIEL THOMAS
B.JULY 12,1854
D.SEPT.21,1883 NEW ORLEANS,LA.
```
1874 CHI NA P-S    2    3    1- 1
1876 LOU N  O            7    .143
                   2   10    1- 1
```

YR	CL	LEA	POS	GP	G	REC

COLLINS, DAVID S #DAVE#
B.OCT.20,1952 RAPID CITY,S.D.
1975	CAL	A	O-D	93		.266
1976	CAL	A	O-D	99		.263
1977	SEA	A	O-D	120		.239
1978	CIN	N	O	102		.216
	BBTL			414		.252

COLLINS, DONALD EDWARD (DON)
B.SEPT.15,1952 LYONS,GA.
| 1977 | ATL | N | P | 40 | | 3- 9 |
| | BRTL | | | | | |

COLLINS, EDWARD TROWBRIDGE JR.
B.NOV.23,1916 LANSDOWNE,PA.
1939	PHI	A	O	32		.238
1941	PHI	A	O	80		.242
1942	PHI	A	O	20		.235
	BLTR			132		.241

COLLINS, EDWARD TROWBRIDGE SR.
[PLAYED UNDER NAME OF
EDWARD T. SULLIVAN IN 1906]
B.MAY 2,1887 MILLERTON,N.Y.
D.MAR.25,1951 BOSTON,MASS.
1906	PHI	A	3	6		.200
1907	PHI	A	3	14		.320
1908	PHI	A	2-S	102		.273
1909	PHI	A	2	153		.346
1910	PHI	A	2	153		.322
1911	PHI	A	2	132		.365
1912	PHI	A	2	153		.348
1913	PHI	A	2	148		.345
1914	PHI	A	2	152		.344
1915	CHI	A	2	155		.332
1916	CHI	A	2	155		.308
1917	CHI	A	2	156		.289
1918	CHI	A	2	97		.276
1919	CHI	A	2	140		.319
1920	CHI	A	2	153		.369
1921	CHI	A	2	139		.337
1922	CHI	A	2	154		.324
1923	CHI	A	2	145		.360
1924	CHI	A	2	152		.349
1925	CHI	A	M-2	118		.346
1926	CHI	A	M-2	106		.344
1927	PHI	A	2	95		.338
1928	PHI	A	S	36		.303
1929	PHI	A	H	9		.000
1930	PHI	A	H	3		.500
	BLTR			2826		.333

COLLINS, GEORGE HUBBERT (HUB)
B.APR.15,1864 LOUISVILLE,KY.
D.MAY 21,1892 BROOKLYN,N.Y.
1886	LOU	AA	O	27		.287
1887	LOU	AA	O	129		.349
1888	LOU	AA	2-O	114		.321
	BRO	AA	2	12		.295
1889	BRO	AA	2	138		.268
1890	BRO	N	2	129		.278
1891	BRO	N	2-O	107		.284
1892	BRO	N	O	20		.302
	BRTR			676		.300

COLLINS, HARRY WARREN (RIP)
B.FEB.26,1896 WEATHERFORD,TEX.
D.MAY 27,1968 BRYAN,TEX.
1920	NY	A	P	36		14- 8
1921	NY	A	P	28		11- 5
1922	BOS	A	P	32		14-11
1923	DET	A	P	17		3- 7
1924	DET	A	P	34	37	14- 7
1925	DET	A	P	26		6-11
1926	DET	A	P	30	31	8- 8
1927	DET	A	P	30		13- 7
1929	STL	A	P	26		11- 6
1930	STL	A	P	35		9- 7
1931	STL	A	P	17		5- 5
	BBTR	311		315		108-82
	BR 1924-31					

COLLINS, JAMES ANTHONY (RIP)
B.MAR.30,1904 ALTOONA,PA.
D.APR.15,1970 NEW HAVEN,CONN.
1931	STL	N	1	89		.301
1932	STL	N	1-O	149		.279
1933	STL	N	1	132		.310
1934	STL	N	1	154		.333
1935	STL	N	1	150		.313
1936	STL	N	1	103		.292
1937	CHI	N	1	115		.274
1938	CHI	N	1	143		.267
1941	PIT	N	1-O	49		.210
	BBTL			1084		.296

COLLINS, JAMES JOSEPH (JIMMY)
B.JAN.16,1870 BUFFALO,N.Y.
1895	BOS	N	3	11		.205
	LOU	N	3	93		.286
1896	BOS	N	3	83		.300
1897	BOS	N	3	133		.346
1898	BOS	N	3	152		.337
1899	BOS	N	3	151		.275
1900	BOS	N	3	142		.299
1901	BOS	A	M-3	138		.329
1902	BOS	A	M-3	105		.325
1903	BOS	A	M-3	130		.296
1904	BOS	A	M-3	156		.265
1905	BOS	A	M-3	131		.276
1906	BOS	A	M-3	37		.275
1907	BOS	A	3	41		.294
	PHI	A	3	100		.273
1908	PHI	A	3	115		.217
	BRTR			1718		.294

COLLINS, JOHN EDGAR (ZIP)
B.MAY 2,1892 BROOKLYN,N.Y.
1914	PIT	N	O	49		.242
1915	PIT	N	O	101		.293
	BOS	N	O	5		.308
1916	BOS	N	O	93		.209
1917	BOS	N	O	8		.148
1921	PHI	A	O	24		.282
	BLTL			280		.253

COLLINS, JOHN FRANCIS (SHANO)
B.DEC.4,1885 CHARLESTOWN,MASS.
D.SEPT.10,1955 NEWTON,MASS.
1910	CHI	A	1-O	97		.197
1911	CHI	A	1	106		.262
1912	CHI	A	O	153		.290
1913	CHI	A	O	148		.239
1914	CHI	A	O	154		.274
1915	CHI	A	1-O	153		.257
1916	CHI	A	O	143		.243
1917	CHI	A	O	82		.234
1918	CHI	A	O	103		.274
1919	CHI	A	O	63		.279
1920	CHI	A	1	133		.303
1921	BOS	A	O	141		.286
1922	BOS	A	O	135		.271
1923	BOS	A	O	97		.231
1924	BOS	A	1-O	89		.292
1925	BOS	A	O	2		.333
	BRTR			1799		.264
NON-PLAYING MANAGER
BOSTON [A] 1931-32

COLLINS, JOSEPH EDWARD (JOE)
[REAL NAME JOSEPH EDWARD KOLLONIGE]
B.DEC.3,1922 SCRANTON,PA.
1948	NY	A	H	5		.200
1949	NY	A	1	7		.100
1950	NY	A	1-O	108		.234
1951	NY	A	1-O	125		.286
1952	NY	A	1	122		.280
1953	NY	A	1-O	127		.269
1954	NY	A	1	130		.271
1955	NY	A	1-O	105		.234
1956	NY	A	1-O	100		.225
1957	NY	A	1-O	79		.201
	BLTL			908		.256

COLLINS, KEVIN MICHAEL
(KEVIN) OR (CASEY)
B.AUG.4,1946 SPRINGFIELD,MASS.
1965	NY	N	/3-S	11		.174
1967	NY	N	/2	4		.100
1968	NY	N	3/2-S	58		.201
1969	NY	N	3	16		.150
	MON	N	2-3	52		.240
1970	DET	A	/1	25		.208
1971	DET	A	/3-O-2	35		.268
	BRTR			201		.209

COLLINS, ORTH STEIN (BUCK)
B.APR.27,1880 LAFAYETTE,IND.
D.DEC.13,1949 FT.LAUDERDALE,FLA
1904	NY	A	O	5		.352
1909	WAS	N	P-O	1	8		0- 0
						.000
	BLTR			1	13		.250

COLLINS, PHILIP EUGENE
(FIDGETY PHIL)
B.AUG.27,1901 CHICAGO,ILL.
D.AUG.14,1948 CHICAGO,ILL.
1923	CHI	N	P	1		1- 0
1929	PHI	N	P	43	59	9- 7
1930	PHI	N	P	47	55	16-11
1931	PHI	N	P	42	44	12-16
1932	PHI	N	P	43		14-12
1933	PHI	N	P	42	43	8-13
1934	PHI	N	P	45	48	13-18
1935	PHI	N	P	3		0- 2
	STL	N	P	26		7- 6
	BRTR			292	322	80-85

COLLINS, RAYMOND WILLISTON
B.FEB.11,1887 COLCHESTER,VT.
D.JAN.9,1970 BURLINGTON,VT.
1909	BOS	A	P	12		4- 3
1910	BOS	A	P	35		13-11
1911	BOS	A	P	31		11-12
1912	BOS	A	P	27		14- 8
1913	BOS	A	P	30		19- 8
1914	BOS	A	P	39		20-13
1915	BOS	A	P	25		5- 7
	BLTL			199		86-62

COLLINS, ROBERT JOSEPH (RIP)
B.SEPT.18,1909 PITTSBURGH,PA.
D.APR.19,1969 PITTSBURGH,PA.
1940	CHI	N	C	47		.208
1944	NY	A	C	3		.333
	BRTR			50		.211

COLLINS, THARON PATRICK (PAT)
B.SEPT.13,1896 SWEET SPRGS.,MO.
D.MAY 20,1960 KANSAS CITY,KAN.
1919	STL	A	C	11		.143
1920	STL	A	C	23		.214
1921	STL	A	C	58		.243
1922	STL	A	C	63		.307
1923	STL	A	C	85		.177
1924	STL	A	C	32		.315
1926	NY	A	C	102		.286
1927	NY	A	C	92		.275
1928	NY	A	C	70		.220
1929	BOS	N	C	7		.000
	BRTR			543		.254

COLLINS, WILLIAM J.
B.1863 DUBLIN,IRELAND
D.JUNE 8,1893 NEW YORK,N.Y.
1887	MET	AA	C	1		.250
1889	ATH	AA	C	1		.200
1890	ATH	AA	C	1		.000
1891	CLE	N	C	2		.000
1892	STL	N	O	1		.000
	BR			6		.143

COLLINS, WILLIAM SHIRLEY
B.MAR.27,1882 CHESTERTON,IND.
D.JUNE 26,1961 SAN BERNADINO,CAL.
1910	BOS	N	O	151		.241
1911	BOS	N	O	17		.149
	CHI	N	O	7		.333
1913	BRO	N	O	32		.189
1914	BUF	F	O	20		.164
	BBTR			227		.224

COLLUM, JACK DEAN (JACKIE)
B.JUNE 21,1927 VICTOR,IA.
1951	STL	N	P	3		2- 1
1952	STL	N	P	2		0- 0
1953	STL	N	P	7		0- 0
	CIN	N	P	30		7-11
1954	CIN	N	P	36		7- 3
1955	CIN	N	P	32		9- 8
1956	CIN	N	P	38		6- 2
1957	CHI	N	P	9		1- 1
	BRO	N	P	3		0- 0
1958	LA	N	P	2		0- 0
1962	MIN	A	P	8		0- 2
	CLE	A	P	1		0- 0
	BLTL			171		32-28

COLMAN, FRANK LLOYD
B.MAR.2,1918 LONDON,ONT.,CANADA
1942	PIT	N	O	10		.135
1943	PIT	N	O	32		.271
1944	PIT	N	1-O	99		.270
1945	PIT	N	O	77		.209
1946	PIT	N	1-O	26		.170
	NY	A	O	5		.267
1947	NY	A	O	22		.107
	BLTL			271		.228

COLPAERT, RICHARD CHARLES (DICK)
B.JAN 3,1944 FRASER,MICH.
| 1970 | PIT | N | /P | 8 | | 1- 0 |
| | BRTR | | | | | |

COLSON, LOYD ALBERT
B.NOV.4,1947 WELLINGTON,TEX.
| 1970 | NY | A | /P | 1 | | 0- 0 |
| | BRTR | | | | | |

COLTON, LAWRENCE ROBERT (LARRY)
B.JUNE 8,1942 LOS ANGELES,CAL.
| 1968 | PHI | N | /P | 1 | | 0- 0 |
| | BLTR | | | | | |

COLUCCIO, ROBERT PASQUALI (BOB)
B.OCT.2,1951 CENTRALIA,WASH.
1973	MIL	A	*O-O	124		.224
1974	MIL	A	*O-O	138		.223
1975	MIL	A	O	22		.194
	CHI	A	O	61		.205
1977	CHI	A	O	20		.270
1978	STL	N	/O	5		.000
	BRTR			370		.220

YR CL LEA POS   GP   G   REC

COMBS, EARLE BRYAN (EARLE)
OR (THE KENTUCKY COLONEL)
B.MAY 14,1899 PEBWORTH,KY.
D.JULY 21,1976 RICHMOND,KY.
```
1924 NY A O         24  .400
1925 NY A O        150  .343
1926 NY A O        145  .299
1927 NY A O        152  .356
1928 NY A O        149  .310
1929 NY A O        142  .345
1930 NY A O        137  .344
1931 NY A O        138  .318
1932 NY A O        144  .321
1933 NY A O        122  .298
1934 NY A O         63  .319
1935 NY A O         89  .282
     BLTR         1455  .325
```

COMBS, MERRILL RUSSELL (MERL)
B.DEC.11,1919 LOS ANGELES,CAL.
```
1947 BOS A 3        17  .221
1949 BOS A S-3      14  .208
1950 BOS A H         1  .000
     WAS A S        37  .245
1951 CLE A S        19  .179
1952 CLE A 2-S      52  .165
     BLTR          140  .202
```

COMELLAS, JORGE (PANCHO)
B.DEC.7,1916 HAVANA,CUBA
```
1945 CHI N P         7  0- 2
     BRTR
```

COMER, HARRY WAYNE (WAYNE)
B.FEB.1,1944 SHENANDOAH,VA.
```
1967 DET A /O        4  .333
1968 DET A O/C      48  .125
1969 SEA A *O/C-3  147  .245
1970 MIL A /O       13  .059
     WAS A O/3      77  .233
1972 DET A O        27  .111
     BRTR          316  .229
```

COMER, STEVEN MICHAEL (STEVE)
B.JAN.13,1954 MINNEAPOLIS,MINN.
```
1978 TEX A P        30  11- 5
     BBTR
```

COMISKEY, CHARLES ALBERT
(COMMY) OR (THE OLD ROMAN)
B.AUG.15,1859 CHICAGO,ILL.
D.OCT.26,1931 EAGLE RIVER,WIS.
```
1882 STL AA P-1      1  78   0- 1
                             .244
1883 STL AA M-1-O   95  .290
1884 STL AA 1      108  .241
1885 STL AA M-1     83  .260
1886 STL AA M-1    131  .260
1887 STL AA M-1    125  .368
1888 STL AA M-1    137  .271
1889 STL AA M-1    137  .288
1890 CHI P  M-1     88  .248
1891 STL AA M-1    139  .257
1892 CIN N  M-1    140  .223
1893 CIN N  M-1     62  .225
1894 CIN N  M-1     59  .265
     BRTR        1 1382  0- 1
                        .269
```

COMMAND, JAMES DALTON
(JIM) OR (IGOR)
B.OCT.15,1928 GRAND RAPIDS,MICH
```
1954 PHI N 3         9  .222
1955 PHI N H         5  .000
     BLTR           14  .174
```

COMOROSKY, ADAM
B.DEC.9,1905 SWOYERSVILLE,PA.
D.MAR.2,1951 SWOYERSVILLE,PA.
```
1926 PIT N O         8  .267
1927 PIT N O        18  .230
1928 PIT N O        51  .295
1929 PIT N O       127  .321
1930 PIT N O       152  .313
1931 PIT N O        99  .243
1932 PIT N O       108  .286
1933 PIT N O        64  .264
1934 CIN N O       127  .258
1935 CIN N O        59  .246
     BRTR          813  .285
```

COMPTON, ANNA SEBASTIAN
(PETE) OR (BASH)
B.SEPT.28,1889 SAN MARCOS,TEX.
D.FEB.3,1978 KANSAS CITY,MO.
```
1911 STL A O        28  .272
1912 STL A O       100  .280
1913 STL A O        61  .180
1915 STL F O         2  .250
     BOS N O        39  .241
1916 BOS N O        34  .302
     PIT N O         5  .100
1918 NY  N O        21  .217
     BLTL          286  .239
```

COMPTON, HARRY LEROY (JACK)
B.MAR.9,1882 LANCASTER,OHIO
D.JULY 4,1974 LANCASTER,OHIO
```
1911 CIN N P         8  1- 1
     BRTR
```

COMPTON, MICHAEL LYNN (MIKE)
B.AUG.15,1944 STAMFORD,CONN.
```
1970 PHI N C        47  .164
     BRTR
```

COMPTON, ROBERT CLINTON (CLINT)
B.NOV.1,1950 MONTGOMERY,ALA.
```
1972 CHI N /P        1  0- 0
     BLTL
```

COMSTOCK, RALPH REMICK (COMMY)
B.NOV.24,1890 SYLVANIA,OHIO
D.SEPT.13,1966 TOLEDO,OHIO
```
1913 DET A P        10  2- 5
1915 BOS A P         3  1- 0
     PIT F P        12  3- 3
1918 PIT N P        15  5- 6
     BRTR           40  11-14
```

CONATSER, CLINTON ASTOR
(CLINT) OR (CONNIE)
B.JULY 24,1921 LOS ANGELES,CAL.
```
1948 BOS N O        90  .277
1949 BOS N O        53  .263
     BRTR          143  .271
```

CONCEPCION, DAVID ISMAEL
(BENITEZ) (DAVE)
B.JUNE 17,1948 ARAGUA,VENEZ.
```
1970 CIN N S/2     101  .260
1971 CIN N *S-2/3-O 130  .205
1972 CIN N *S/3-2  119  .209
1973 CIN N S/O      89  .287
1974 CIN N *S/O    160  .281
1975 CIN N *S/3    140  .274
1976 CIN N *S      152  .281
1977 CIN N *S      156  .271
1978 CIN N *S      153  .301
     BRTR         1200  .268
```

CONDE, RAMON LUIS (WITO)
B.DEC.29,1934 JUANA DIAZ,P.R.
```
1962 CHI A 3        14  .000
     BRTR
```

CONE, H. B.
B.TEXAS
```
1915 PHI A P         1  0- 0
```

CONE, JOSEPH FREDERICK
B.MAY 1848 ROCKFORD,ILL.
D.APR.13,1909
```
1871 BOS NA O       18   -
```

CONGALTON, WILLIAM MILLAR (BUNK)
B.JAN.24,1875 GUELPH,ONT.,CAN.
D.AUG.16,1937 CLEVELAND,OHIO
```
1902 CHI N O         7  .245
1905 CLE A O        12  .369
1906 CLE A O       117  .320
1907 CLE A O         9  .182
     BOS A O       124  .286
     BL            309  .293
```

CONGER, RICHARD
B.APR.3,1921 LOS ANGELES,CAL.
D.FEB.16,1970 LOS ANGELES,CAL.
```
1940 DET A P         2  1- 0
1941 PIT N P         2  0- 0
1942 PIT N P     2   3  0- 0
1943 PHI N P        13  2- 7
     BRTR       19  20  3- 7
```

CONIGLIARO, ANTHONY RICHARD (TONY)
B.JAN.7,1945 REVERE,MASS.
```
1964 BOS A O       111  .290
1965 BOS A *O      138  .269
1966 BOS A *O      150  .265
1967 BOS A O        95  .287
1969 BOS A *O      141  .255
1970 BOS A *O      146  .266
1971 CAL A O        74  .222
1975 BOS A O        21  .123
     BRTR          876  .264
```

CONIGLIARO, WILLIAM MICHAEL (BILLY)
B.AUG.15,1947 REVERE,MASS.
```
1969 BOS A O        32  .288
1970 BOS A *O      114  .271
1971 BOS A *O      101  .262
1972 MIL A O        52  .230
1973 OAK A O/2      48  .200
     BRTR          347  .256
```

CONKWRIGHT, ALLEN HOWARD (RED)
B.DEC.4,1896 SEDALIA,MO.
```
1920 DET A P         5  2- 1
     BRTR
```

CONLAN, JOHN BERTRAND (JOCKO)
B.DEC.6,1899 CHICAGO,ILL.
```
1934 CHI A O        63  .249
1935 CHI A O        65  .286
     BLTL          128  .263
```

CONLEY, DONALD EUGENE (GENE)
B.NOV.10,1930 MUSKOGEE,OKLA.
```
1952 BOS N P         4  0- 3
1954 MIL N P        28  14- 9
1955 MIL N P        22  11- 7
1956 MIL N P        31  8- 9
1957 MIL N P        35  9- 9
1958 MIL N P        26  0- 6
1959 PHI N P        25  12- 7
1960 PHI N P        29  8-14
1961 BOS A P        33  11-14
1962 BOS A P        34  15-14
1963 BOS A P         9  3- 4
     BRTR          276  91-96
```

CONLEY, EDWARD J.
B.JULY 10,1864 SANDWICH,MASS.
D.OCT.16,1894 CUMBERLAND,R.I.
```
1884 PRO N P         8  4- 4
```

CONLEY, JAMES PATRICK (SNIPE)
B.APR.25,1894 CRESSONA,PA.
D.JAN.7,1978 DE SOTO,TEX.
```
1914 BAL F P        35  4- 6
1915 BAL F P        25  1- 4
1918 CIN N P         5  2- 0
     BRTR           65  7-10
```

CONLEY, ROBERT BURNS
B.FEB.11,1934 KNOTT COUNTY,VA.
```
1958 PHI N P         2  0- 0
     BRTR
```

CONLAN, ARTHUR JOSEPH (JOCKO)
B.DEC.10,1897 WOBURN,MASS.
```
1923 BOS N 2-S-3    59  .218
```

CONN, ALBERT THOMAS (BERT)
B.SEPT.22,1879 PHILADELPHIA,PA.
D.NOV.2,1944 PHILADELPHIA,PA.
```
1898 PHI N P         1  0- 0
1900 PHI N P         6  0- 1
1901 PHI N P         5  .222
     TR         7  12  0- 1
                        .267
```

CONNALLY, GEORGE WALTER (SARGE)
B.AUG.31,1898 MCGREGOR,TEX.
D.JAN.27,1978 TEMPLE,TEX.
```
1921 CHI A P         5  0- 1
1923 CHI A P         3  0- 0
1924 CHI A P        44  7-13
1925 CHI A P        40  6- 7
1926 CHI A P        31  6- 5
1927 CHI A P        43  10-15
1928 CHI A P        28  2- 5
1929 CHI A P        11  0- 0
1931 CLE A P        17  5- 5
1932 CLE A P        35  8- 6
1933 CLE A P        41  5- 3
1934 CLE A P         5  0- 0
     BRTR          303  49-60
```

CONNASTER, BROADUS MILBURN (BRUCE)
B.SEPT.19,1902 SEVIERVILLE,TENN
D.JAN.27,1971 TERRE HAUTE,IND.
```
1931 CLE A 1        12  .286
1932 CLE A 1        23  .233
     BRTR           35  .257
```

CONNAUGHTON, FRANK H.
B.JAN.1,1869 CLINTON,MASS.
D.DEC.1,1942 BOSTON,MASS.
```
1894 BOS N S        38  .337
1896 NY  N S-O      83  .257
1906 BOS N 2-S      12  .205
     BRTR          133  .278
```

CONNELL, EUGENE JOSEPH
B.MAY 10,1906 HAZELTON,PA.
D.AUG.31,1937 WAVERLY,N.Y.
```
1931 PHI N C         6  .250
     BRTR
```

CONNELL, JOSEPH BERNARD
B.JAN.16,1902 BETHLEHEM,PA.
D.SEPT.21,1977 TREXLERTOWN,PA.
```
1926 NY  N H         2  .000
     BLTL
```

CONNELL, PETER J.
B.BROOKLYN,N.Y.
```
1886 MET AA 3        1  .000
```

CONNELLY, TERENCE G.
B.JUNE 17,1855 PHILADELPHIA,PA.
D.MAR.25,1924
```
1874 CHI NA C        1  .000
```

```
YR  CL LEA POS    GP   G   REC        YR  CL LEA POS    GP   G   REC        YR  CL LEA POS    GP   G   REC

CONNELLY, JOHN M. (RED)               CONNOR, ROGER                         CONSOLO, WILLIAM ANGELO (BILLY)
B.1857                                B.JULY 1,1857 WATERBURY,CONN.         B.AUG.18,1934 CLEVELAND,OHIO
D.MAR.1,1896 NEW YORK,N.Y.            D.JAN.4,1931 WATERBURY,CONN.          1953 BOS A  2-3        47    .215
1886 STL N  O           2    .000     1880 TRO N  3          83    .332      1954 BOS A  2-S-3      91    .227
                                      1881 TRO N  1          84    .288      1955 BOS A  2           8    .222
                                      1882 TRO N  1-3-O      79    .327      1956 BOS A  2          48    .182
CONNELLY, THOMAS MARTIN               1883 NY  N  1          96    .361      1957 BOS A  2-S-3      68    .270
B.OCT.20,1898 CHICAGO,ILL.            1884 NY  N  2-3-O     112    .316      1958 BOS A  2-S-3      46    .125
1920 NY  A  O           1    .000     1885 NY  N  1         110    .371      1959 BOS A  S          10    .214
1921 NY  A  O           4    .200     1886 NY  N  1         118    .354           WAS A  2-S        79    .213
      BLTR              5    .167     1887 NY  N  1         127    .382      1960 WAS A  2-S-3     100    .207
                                      1888 NY  N  1         134    .291      1961 MIN A  2-S-3      11    .000
                                      1889 NY  N  1         131    .316      1962 PHI N  H          13    .400
CONNELLY, WILLIAM WIRT (WILD BILL)    1890 NY  P  1         123    .372           LA  A  2-S-3      28    .100
B.JUNE 29,1925 ALBERTA,VA.            1891 NY  N  1         123    .293           KC  A  S          54    .240
1945 PHI A  P           2   1- 1      1892 PHI N  1         153    .285            BRTR            603    .221
1950 CHI A  P           2   0- 0      1893 NY  N  1         135    .322
     DET A  P           2   0- 0      1894 NY  N  1-O        22    .293
1952 NY  N  P          11   5- 0           STL N  1          99    .318      CONSTABLE, JIMMY LEE
1953 NY  N  P           8   0- 1      1895 STL N  1         104    .326      (JIM) OR (SHERIFF)
      BLTR             25   6- 2      1896 STL N  M-1       126    .282      B.JUNE 14,1933 JONESBORO,TENN.
                                      1897 STL N  1          22    .229      1956 NY  N  P           3   0- 0
                                            BLTL           1981    .327      1957 NY  N  P          16   1- 1
CONNOLLY, EDWARD JOSEPH JR. (ED)                                            1958 SF  N  P           9   1- 0
B.DEC.3,1939 BROOKLYN,N.Y.                                                       CLE A  P           6   0- 1
1964 BOS A  P          27   4-11      CONNORS, JEREMIAH                          WAS A  P          15   0- 1
1967 CLE A  P          15   2- 1      B.PHILADELPHIA,PA.                    1962 NIL N  P           3   1- 1
      BLTR             42   6-12      1892 PHI N  O           1    .000      1963 SF  N  P           4   0- 0
                                                                                  BBTL             56   3- 4
CONNOLLY, EDWARD JOSEPH SR (ED)       CONNORS, JOSEPH P.
B.JULY 17,1908 BROOKLYN,N.Y.          B.1850 NEW YORK                       CONSUEGRA, SANDALIO SIMEON
D.NOV.12,1963 PITTSFIELD,MASS.        1871 TRO NA 1-2-O       7    .182      (CASTELLON) (SANDY)
1929 BOS A  C           5    .000                                           B.SEPT.3,1920 POTRERILLO,CUBA
1930 BOS A  C          27    .188                                           1950 WAS A  P       21  24   7- 8
1931 BOS A  C          42    .075     CONNORS, JOSEPH P.                     1951 WAS A  P          40   7- 8
1932 BOS A  C          75    .225     B.PHILADELPHIA,PA.                     1952 WAS A  P          30   6- 0
      BRTR            149    .178     1884 ALT U  P-3-    1   3   0- 1      1953 WAS A  O           4   0- 0
                                                             .100                CHI A  P          29   7- 5
                                           KC  U  P-O    2   3   0- 1      1954 CHI A  P-3        39  16- 3
CONNOLLY, JOSEPH ALOYSIUS                                    .091                                    .229
B.FEB.12,1888 N.SMITHFIELD,R.I.                         3   6   0- 2      1955 CHI A  P          44   6- 5
D.SEPT.1,1943 SPRINGFIELD,R.I.                              .095            1956 CHI A  P          28   1- 2
1913 BOS N  O         126    .281                                               BAL A  P           4   1- 1
1914 BOS N  O         120    .306     CONNORS, KEVIN JOSEPH ALOYSIUS        1957 BAL A  P           5   0- 0
1915 BOS N  O         104    .298     (CHUCK)                                    NY  N  P           4   0- 0
1916 BOS N  O          62    .227     B.APR.10,1921 BROOKLYN,N.Y.                 BRTR           248 251  51-32
      BLTR            412    .288      1949 BRO N  H           1    .000                               .170
                                      1951 CHI N  1          66    .239
CONNOLLY, JOSEPH GEORGE                      BLTL             67    .238      CONWAY, CHARLES CONNELL
(COASTER JOE)                                                               B.APR.28,1886 YOUNGSTOWN,OHIO
B.JUNE 4,1896 SAN FRANCISCO,CAL       CONNORS, MERVYN JAMES (MERV)          D.SEPT.12,1918 YOUNGSTOWN,OHIO
D.MAR.30,1960 SAN FRANCISCO,CAL       B.JAN.23,1914 BERKELEY,CAL.           1911 WAS A  O           2    .333
1921 NY  N  O           2    .000     1937 CHI A  3          28    .233            BRTR
1922 CLE A  O          12    .244     1938 CHI A  1          24    .355
1923 CLE A  O          52    .303            BRTR             52    .279      CONWAY, JACK CLEMENTS
1924 BOS A  O          14    .100                                           B.JULY 30,1919 BRYAN,TEX.
      BRTR             80    .268     CONNORS, WILLIAM JOSEPH (BILL)         1941 CLE A  S           2    .500
                                      B.NOV.2,1941 SCHENECTADY,N.Y.         1946 CLE A  2-S-3      68    .225
                                      1966 CHI N  P          11   0- 1      1947 CLE A  2-S-3      34    .180
CONNOLLY, MERVIN THOMAS               1967 NY  N  P           6   0- 0      1948 NY  N  2-S-3      24    .245
(BUD) OR (MIKE)                       1968 NY  N /P           9   0- 1            BRTR            128    .223
B.MAY 25,1901 SAN FRANCISCO,CAL             BRTR             26   0- 2
D.JUNE 12,1964 BERKELEY,CAL.                                                CONWAY, JAMES P.
1925 BOS A  S-3        43    .261     CONOVAR, THEODORE (HUCK)              B.CLIFTON,PA.
      BRTR                            B.MAR.10,1868 LEXINGTON,KY.           1884 BRO AA P-S-   13  14   3- 9
                                      D.JULY 27,1910 PARIS,KY.                                 O         .133
CONNOLLY, THOMAS FRANCIS              1889 CIN AA P           1   0- 0                      O        2   1- 1
(BLACKIE) OR (HAM)                                                                             .167
B.DEC.30,1892 BOSTON,MASS.            CONROY, BENJAMIN EDWARD               1885 ATH AA P-O         2   1- 1
D.MAY 14,1966 BOSTON,MASS.            B.1871 PHILADELPHIA,PA.                                    .167
1915 WAS A  3-O        50    .184     1890 ATH AA 2-S       116    .175      1889 KC  AA P          41  18-19
      BLTL                                                                         TR  56  57  22-29
                                      CONROY, TIMOTHY JAMES (TIM)                                .191
                                      B.APR.3,1960 MC KEESPORT,PA.
                                      1978 OAK A /P           2   0- 0      CONWAY, JEROME PATRICK
CONNOR, JAMES MATTHEW                                                       B.JUNE 7,1901 HOLYOKE,MASS.
(REAL NAME JAMES MATTHEW O CONNOR)    CONROY, WILLIAM EDWARD (WID)          1920 WAS A  P           1   0- 0
B.MAY 11,1863 PORT JERVIS,N.Y.        B.APR.5,1877 CAMDEN,N.J.                    BLTL
D.SEPT.3,1950 PROVIDENCE,R.I.         D.DEC.6,1959 MT.HOLLY,N.J.
1892 CHI N  2          10    .057     1901 MIL A  S         131    .269      CONWAY, OWEN SYLVESTER
1897 CHI N  2          77    .296     1902 PIT N  S-O        95    .241      B.OCT.23,1890 NEW YORK,N.Y.
1898 CHI N  2         136    .206     1903 NY  A  3         125    .277      D.MAR.13,1942 PHILADELPHIA,PA.
1899 CHI N  2-3        66    .206     1904 NY  A  S-3       140    .249      1915 PHI A  3           4    .067
      BRTR            289    .235     1905 NY  A  S-3-O     101    .273            TR
                                      1906 NY  A  S-O       148    .245
                                      1907 NY  A  S-O       140    .234      CONWAY, PETER J.
CONNOR, JOHN                          1908 NY  A  3         141    .237      B.OCT.30,1866 BURMONT,PA.
B.LASALLE,ILL.                        1909 WAS A  3         139    .244      D.JAN.14,1903 MEDIA,PA.
D.OCT.13,1932                         1910 WAS A  3-O       103    .254      1885 BUF N  P-1-   27  29  10-17
1884 BOS N  P           7   1- 4      1911 WAS A  3-O       106    .232                         S         .111
1885 BUF N  P           1   0- 1            BRTR           1369    .250      1886 KC  N  P-O    21  52   5-16
     LOU AA P           4   1- 3                                                                   .235
                       12   2- 8      CONROY, WILLIAM FREDERICK (PEP)            DET N  P           11   6- 5
                                      B.JAN.9,1899 CHICAGO,ILL.             1887 DET N  P      18  24   8-10
                                      D.JAN.23,1970 CHICAGO,ILL.            1888 DET N  P           45  31-14
CONNOR, JOSEPH FRANCIS                1923 WAS A  3          18    .133      1889 PIT N  P           3   2- 1
B.DEC.8,1874 WATERBURY,CONN.                                                     8R  125 164  62-63
D.NOV.6,1957 WATERBURY,CONN.          CONROY, WILLIAM GORDON (BILL)                                .227
1895 STL N  3           2    .000     B.FEB.26,1915 BLOOMINGTON,ILL.
1900 BOS N  C           7    .200     1935 PHI A  C           1    .250      CONWAY, RICHARD BUTLER
1901 MIL A  C-2-O      38    .272     1936 PHI A  C           1    .500      B.APR.25,1866 LOWELL,MASS.
     CLE A  C          38    .138     1937 PHI A  C          26    .200      D.SEPT.9,1926 LOWELL,MASS.
1905 NY  A  C-1         8    .271     1942 BOS A  C          83    .200      1886 BAL AA P           9   2- 7
      BRTR             93    .203     1943 BOS A  C          39    .180      1887 BOS N  P      25  39   9-15
                                      1944 BOS A  C          19    .213      1888 BOS N  P           6   4- 1
                                            BRTR            169    .199            BLTR             40  54  15-23

                                                                            CONWAY, RICHARD DANIEL (RIP)
                                                                            B.APR.18,1896 WHITE BEAR,MINN.
                                                                            D.DEC.3,1971 ST.PAUL,MINN.
                                                                            1918 BOS N  2          14    .167
```

```
YR   CL LEA POS      GP   G    REC
```

CONWAY, WILLIAM F.
B.NOV.28,1861 LOWELL,MASS.
D.DEC.28,1943 SOMERVILLE,MASS.
1884 PHI N C   1   .000
1886 BAL AA C   7   .142
                           8   .111

CONWELL, EDWARD JAMES (IRISH)
B.JAN.29,1890 CHICAGO,ILL.
1911 STL N 3   1   .000
     BRTR

CONYERS, HERBERT LEROY (HERB)
B.JAN.8,1921 COWGILL,MO.
D.SEPT.16,1964 CLEVELAND,OHIO
1950 CLE A 1   7   .333
     BLTR

CONZELMAN, JOSEPH HARRISON
B.JULY 14,1889 BRISTOL,CONN.
1913 PIT N P   2   0- 1
1914 PIT N P   33   5- 6
1915 PIT N P   18   1- 1
     BRTR   53   6- 8

COOGAN, DALE ROGER
B.AUG.14,1930 LOS ANGELES,CAL.
1950 PIT N 1   53   .240
     BLTL

COOGAN, DANIEL GEORGE
B.FEB.16,1875 PHILADELPHIA,PA.
D.OCT.28,1942 PHILADELPHIA,PA.
1895 WAS N S   21   .203

COOK, EARL DAVIS
B.DEC.10,1908 STOUFFVILLE,ONT.,
1941 DET A P   1   0- 0
     BRTR

COOK, FREDERICK RUSSELL
[PLAYED UNDER NAME OF
FREDERICK RUSSELL WINCHELL]

COOK, JAMES FITCHIE
B.NOV.10,1879 DUNDEE,ILL.
D.JUNE 17,1949 ST.LOUIS,MO.
1903 CHI N O   8   .120
     BRTR

COOK, LUTHER ALMUS (DOC)
B.JUNE 24,1886 WITT,TEX.
D.JUNE 30,1973 LAWRENCEBURG,TENN.
1913 NY A O   20   .264
1914 NY A O   131   .283
1915 NY A O   132   .271
1916 NY A O   4   .100
     BLTR   287   .274

COOK, PAUL
B.MAY 5,1863 CALEDONIA,N.Y.
D.MAY 26,1905
1884 PHI N C   3   .083
1886 LOU AA C-1   66   .205
1887 LOU AA C-1   63   .267
1888 LOU AA C   53   .200
1889 LOU AA C   81   .226
1890 BRO P C-1   59   .242
1891 LOU AA C   39   .232
     STL AA C   7   .179
     BRTR   373   .227

COOK, RAYMOND CLIFFORD (CLIFF)
B.AUG.20,1936 DALLAS,TEX.
1959 CIN N 3   9   .381
1960 CIN N 3-O   54   .208
1961 CIN N 3   4   .000
1962 CIN N 3   6   .000
     NY N 3-O   40   .232
1963 NY N 1-3-O   50   .142
     BRTR   163   .201

COOK, ROLLIN EDWARD
B.OCT.5,1890 TOLEDO,OHIO
D.AUG.11,1975 TOLEDO,OHIO
1915 STL A P   5   0- 0
     BRTR

COOK, RONALD WAYNE (RON)
B.JULY 11,1947 JEFFERSON,TEX.
1970 HOU N P   41   43   4- 4
1971 HOU N /P   5   6   0- 4
     BLTL   46   49   4- 8

COOKE, ALLEN LINDSEY (DUSTY)
B.JUNE 23,1907 SWEPSONVILLE,N.C
1930 NY A O   92   .255
1931 NY A O   27   .333
1932 NY A O   3   .000
1933 BOS A O   119   .291
1934 BOS A O   74   .244
1935 BOS A O   100   .306
1936 BOS A O   111   .273
1938 CIN N O   82   .275
     BLTR   608   .291
NON-PLAYING MANAGER PHI[N] 1948

COOKE, FREDERICK B.
B.PAULDING,OHIO
1897 CLE N O   5   .295

COOLEY, D. G. (DICK)
B.MAR.29,1873 LEAVENWORTH,KAN.
D.AUG.9,1937 DALLAS,TEX.
1893 STL N O   26   .359
1894 STL N O   52   .299
1895 STL N O   132   .340
1896 STL N O   40   .302
     PHI N O   64   .301
1897 PHI N O   131   .327
1898 PHI N O   148   .317
1899 PHI N 1   94   .280
1900 PIT N 1   65   .200
1901 BOS N O   60   .270
1902 BOS N 1-O   134   .289
1903 BOS N O   138   .289
1904 BOS N O   122   .272
1905 DET A O   97   .247
     BRTR   1303   .295

COOMBS, CECIL LYSANDER
B.MAR.18,1888 MOWEAQUA,ILL.
D.NOV.25,1975 FORT WORTH,TEX.
1914 CHI A O   7   .173
     BRTR

COOMBS, DANIEL BERNARD (DANNY)
B.MAR.23,1942 LINCOLN,ME.
1963 HOU N P   1   0- 0
1964 HOU N P   7   1- 1
1965 HOU N P   26   0- 2
1966 HOU N /P   2   0- 0
1967 HOU N /P   6   3- 0
1968 HOU N P   40   4- 3
1969 HOU N /P   8   0- 1
1970 SD N P   35   10-14
1971 SD N P   19   1- 6
     BRTL   144   19-27

COOMBS, JOHN WESLEY (COLBY JACK)
B.NOV.18,1882 LE GRAND,IOWA
D.APR.15,1957 PALESTINE,TEX.
1906 PHI A P   23   24   10-11
1907 PHI A P   23   24   6- 9
1908 PHI A P-O   26   78   7- 5
                               .255
1909 PHI A P   30   37   12-11
1910 PHI A P   45   46   31- 9
1911 PHI A P   47   52   28-12
1912 PHI A P   40   54   21-10
1913 PHI A P   1   0- 1
     PHI A P   5   0- 1
1915 BRO N P   29   15-10
1916 BRO N P   27   13- 8
1917 BRO N P   31   32   7-11
1918 BRO N P-O   27   46   8-14
                               .168
1920 DET A P   2   0- 0
     BBTR   356   457 158-111
                               .235
NON-PLAYING MANAGER PHI[N] 1919

COOMBS, RAYMOND FRANKLIN (BOBBY)
B.FEB.2,1908 GOODWINS MILLS,ME.
1933 PHI A P   21   0- 1
1943 NY N P   9   0- 1
     BRTR   30   0- 2

COON, WILLIAM K.
B.MAR.21,1855 PENNSYLVANIA
D.AUG.30,1915 BURLINGTON,N.J.
1875 ATH NA C   3   -
1876 ATH N C-O   54   .225
                          57   -

COONEY, JAMES EDWARD
(JIMMY) OR (SCOOPS)
B.AUG.24,1894 CRANSTON,R.I.
1917 BOS A 2   11   .222
1919 NY N S   5   .214
1924 STL N 2-S-3   110   .295
1925 STL N 2-S-O   54   .273
1926 CHI N S   141   .251
1927 CHI N S   33   .242
     PHI N S   76   .270
1928 BOS N S   18   .137
     BRTR   448   .262

COONEY, JAMES JOSEPH (JIMMY)
B.JULY 9,1865 CRANSTON,R.I.
D.JULY 1,1903 CRANSTON,R.I.
1890 CHI N S   135   .271
1891 CHI N S   118   .250
1892 CHI N S   84   .171
     WAS N S   6   .154
     BRTR   343   .243

COONEY, JOHN WALTER (JOHNNY)
B.MAR.18,1901 CRANSTON,R.I.
1921 BOS N P   8   0- 1
1922 BOS N P   4   1- 2
1923 BOS N P-1   23   42   3- 5
                 O
1924 BOS N P-1   34   55   8- 9
                 O   .254
1925 BOS N P-1   31   54   14-14
                 O   .320
1926 BOS N P-1   19   64   3- 3
                 O   .302
1927 BOS N H   10   .000
1928 BOS N P   24   33   3- 7
1929 BOS N P-O   14   41   2- 3
                               .319
1930 BOS N P   2   4   0- 0
1935 BRO N O   10   .310
1936 BRO N O   130   .282
1937 BRO N O   120   .293
1938 BOS N 1-O   120   .271
1939 BOS N O   118   .274
1940 BOS N 1-O   108   .318
1941 BOS N 1-O   123   .319
1942 BOS N 1-O   74   .207
1943 BRO N 1   37   .206
1944 BRO N O   7   .750
     NY A O   10   .125
     BRTL   159   1172   34-44
                               .286
NON-PLAYING MANAGER BOS[N] 1949

COONEY, PHILIP
[REAL NAME PHILIP COHN]
B.SEPT.14,1886 PATERSON,N.J.
1905 NY A 3   1   .000
     BRTR

COONEY, ROBERT DANIEL
B.JULY 12,1907 GLENS FALLS,N.Y.
D.MAY 9,1976 GLENS FALLS,N.Y.
1931 STL A P   5   0- 3
1932 STL A P   23   24   1- 2
     BRTR   28   29   1- 5

COONEY, WILLIAM A. (CUSH)
B.APR.4,1887 BOSTON,MASS.
D.NOV.6,1928 ROXBURY,MASS.
1909 BOS N P   5   0- 0
1910 BOS N P   8   0- 0
     TR   13   0- 0

COOPER, ARLEY WILBUR (WILBUR)
B.FEB.24,1892 BEARSVILLE,W.VA.
D.AUG.7,1973 ENCINO,CAL.
1912 PIT N P   6   3- 0
1913 PIT N P   30   5- 3
1914 PIT N P   40   16-15
1915 PIT N P   38   5-16
1916 PIT N P   44   12-11
1917 PIT N P   41   17-11
1918 PIT N P   38   19-14
1919 PIT N P   36   19-13
1920 PIT N P   44   24-15
1921 PIT N P   38   22-14
1922 PIT N P   41   23-14
1923 PIT N P   39   17-19
1924 PIT N P   38   20-14
1925 CHI N P   32   12-14
1926 CHI N P   8   2- 1
     DET A P   8   0- 4
     BRTL   521 216-178

COOPER, CALVIN ASA
B.AUG.11,1922 GREAT FALLS,S.C.
1948 WAS A P   1   0- 0
     BRTR

COOPER, CECIL CELESTER
B.DEC.20,1949 BRENHAM,TEX.
1971 BOS A 1   14   .310
1972 BOS A /1   12   .235
1973 BOS A 1   30   .238
1974 BOS A 1-O   121   .275
1975 BOS A O-1   106   .311
1976 BOS A 1-O   123   .282
1977 MIL A *1-O   160   .300
1978 MIL A 1-O   107   .312
     BLTL   673   .293

COOPER, CLAUDE WILLIAM
B.APR.1,1892 TROUPE,TEX.
D.JAN.21,1974 PLAINVIEW,TEX.
1913 NY N O   27   .300
1914 BRO F O   110   .239
1915 BRO F 1-O   152   .291
1916 PHI N O   56   .192
1917 PHI N O   24   .103
     BLTL   369   .258

COOPER, GUY EVANS (REBEL)
B.JAN.28,1893 ROME,GA.
D.AUG.2,1951 SANTA MONICA,CAL.
1914 NY A P   1   0- 0
     BOS A P   10   1- 1
1915 BOS A P   1   0- 0
     BBTR   12   1- 1

COOPER, MORTON CECIL (MORT)
B.MAR.2,1913 ATHERTON,MO.
D.NOV.17,1958 LITTLE ROCK,ARK.

YR	CL	LEA	POS	GP	G	REC
1938	STL	N	P		4	2- 1
1939	STL	N	P	45	47	12- 6
1940	STL	N	P		38	11-12
1941	STL	N	P		29	13- 9
1942	STL	N	P		37	22- 7
1943	STL	N	P		37	21- 8
1944	STL	N	P		34	22- 7
1945	STL	N	P		4	2- 0
	BOS	N	P		20	7- 4
1946	BOS	N	P		28	13-11
1947	BOS	N	P		10	2- 5
	NY	N	P		8	1- 5
1949	CHI	N	P		1	0- 0
		BRTR		295	297	128-75

COOPER, ORGE PATTERSON (PAT)
B.NOV.26,1917 ALBEMARLE,N.C.

YR	CL	LEA	POS	GP	G	REC
1946	PHI	A	P		1	0- 0
1947	PHI	A	1		13	.250
		BRTR		1	14	0- 0
						.250

COOPER, WILLIAM WALKER (WALK)
B.JAN.8,1915 ATHERTON,MO.

YR	CL	LEA	POS	GP	G	REC
1940	STL	N	C		6	.316
1941	STL	N	C		68	.245
1942	STL	N	C		125	.281
1943	STL	N	C		122	.319
1944	STL	N	C		112	.317
1945	STL	N	C		4	.389
1946	NY	N	C		87	.268
1947	NY	N	C		140	.305
1948	NY	N	C		91	.266
1949	NY	N	C		42	.211
	CIN	N	C		82	.280
1950	CIN	N	C		15	.191
	BOS	N	C		102	.329
1951	BOS	N	C		109	.313
1952	BOS	N	C		102	.235
1953	MIL	N	C		53	.219
1954	PIT	N	C		14	.200
	CHI	N	C		57	.310
1955	CHI	N	C		54	.279
1956	STL	N	C		40	.265
1957	STL	N	C		48	.269
		BRTR			1473	.285

COOPER, WILLIE G.
[PLAYED UNDE- NAME OF
WILLIAM G. NANCE]

COPELAND, MAYS
B.AUG.31,1913 MOUNTAIN VIEW,ARK

YR	CL	LEA	POS	GP	G	REC
1935	STL	N	P		1	0- 0
		BRTR				

COPPOLA, HENRY PETER
B.AUG.6,1912 E.DOUGLAS,MASS.

YR	CL	LEA	POS	GP	G	REC
1935	WAS	A	P		19	3- 4
1936	WAS	A	P		6	0- 0
		BRTR			25	3- 4

CORBETT, EUGENE LOUIS
B.OCT.25,1913 WINONA,MINN.

YR	CL	LEA	POS	GP	G	REC
1936	PHI	N	1		6	.143
1937	PHI	N	2-3		7	.333
1938	PHI	N	1		24	.080
		BLTR			37	.120

CORBETT, JOSEPH A.
B.DEC.4,1875 SAN FRANCISCO,CAL.
D.MAY 2,1945 SAN FRANCISCO,CAL.

YR	CL	LEA	POS	GP	G	REC
1895	WAS	N	P		8	0- 3
1896	BAL	N	P		8	3- 1
1897	BAL	N	P	35	36	24- 8
1904	STL	N	P		14	5- 9
		BRTR		65	66	32-21

CORBIN, ALTON RAY (RAY)
B.FEB.12,1949 LIVE OAK,FLA.

YR	CL	LEA	POS	GP	G	REC
1971	MIN	A	P		52	8-11
1972	MIN	A	P	31	34	8- 9
1973	MIN	A	P		51	8- 5
1974	MIN	A	P		29	7- 6
1975	MIN	A	P		18	5- 7
		BRTR		181	184	36-38

CORBITT, CLAUDE ELLIOTT
B.JULY 21,1915 SUNBURY,N.C.

YR	CL	LEA	POS	GP	G	REC
1945	BRO	N	3		2	.500
1946	CIN	N	S		82	.248
1948	CIN	N	2-S-3		87	.256
1949	CIN	N	2-S-3		44	.181
		BRTR			215	.243

CORCORAN, ARTHUR ANDREW (BUNNY)
B.NOV.23,1894 ROXBURY,MASS.
D.JULY 27,1958 CHELSEA,MASS.

YR	CL	LEA	POS	GP	G	REC
1915	PHI	A	3		1	.000
		TR				

CORCORAN, JOHN A.
B.1873 CINCINNATI,OHIO
D.NOV.1,1901 CINCINNATI,OHIO

YR	CL	LEA	POS	GP	G	REC
1895	PIT	N	S-3		6	.150

CORCORAN, JOHN H.
B.LOWELL,MASS.

YR	CL	LEA	POS	GP	G	REC
1884	BRO	AA	C		52	.215

CORCORAN, LAWRENCE J.
B.AUG.10,1859 BROOKLYN,N.Y.
D.OCT.14,1891 NEWARK,N.J.

YR	CL	LEA	POS	GP	G	REC
1880	CHI	N	P-S-	57	70	43-14
			O			.221
1881	CHI	N	P-S-	45	47	31-14
			O			.222
1882	CHI	N	P-3		41	27-13
						.207
1883	CHI	N	P-2-	52	66	31-21
			S-O			.207
1884	CHI	N	P-S-	59	63	35-23
			O			.230
1885	CHI	N	P-S		7	5- 2
						.227
	NY	N	P-O		2	1- 1
						.375
1886	NY	N	O		1	.000
	WAS	N	P-O	1	21	0- 1
						.185
1887	IND	N	P		3	0- 2
		TR		265	321	173-91
						.218

CORCORAN, MICHAEL
B.BROOKLYN,N.Y.

YR	CL	LEA	POS	GP	G	REC
1884	CHI	N	P		1	0- 1

CORCORAN, MICHAEL JOSEPH (MICKEY)
B.AUG.26,1882 BUFFALO,N.Y.
D.DEC.9,1950 BUFFALO,N.Y.

YR	CL	LEA	POS	GP	G	REC
1910	CIN	N	3		14	.217
		BRTR				

CORCORAN, THOMAS WILLIAM
(TOMMY) OR (CORKY)
B.JAN.4,1869 NEW HAVEN,CONN.
D.JUNE 25,1960 PLAINFIELD,CONN.

YR	CL	LEA	POS	GP	G	REC
1890	PIT	P	S		123	.219
1891	ATH	AA	S		132	.252
1892	BRO	N	S		151	.237
1893	BRO	N	S		115	.281
1894	BRO	N	S		129	.302
1895	BRO	N	S		128	.277
1896	BRO	N	S		132	.299
1897	CIN	N	2-S		108	.288
1898	CIN	N	S		153	.244
1899	CIN	N	S		135	.279
1900	CIN	N	S		128	.242
1901	CIN	N	S		30	.184
1902	CIN	N	2-S		137	.251
1903	CIN	N	S		115	.246
1904	CIN	N	S		150	.230
1905	CIN	N	S		151	.248
1906	CIN	N	S		117	.207
1907	NY	N	2		62	.265
		BRTR			2196	.257

CORCORAN, TIMOTHY MICHAEL (TIM)
B.MAR.19,1953 GLENDALE,CAL.

YR	CL	LEA	POS	GP	G	REC
1977	DET	A	O		55	.282
1978	DET	A	*O		116	.265
		BLTL			171	.269

COREY, EDWARD N.
B.APR.10,1900 CHICAGO,ILL.

YR	CL	LEA	POS	GP	G	REC
1918	CHI	A	P		1	0- 0
		BRTR				

COREY, FREDERICK HARRISON
B.1857 S.KINGSTON,R.I.
D.NOV.27,1912 PROVIDENCE,R.I.

YR	CL	LEA	POS	GP	G	REC
1878	PRO	N	P-1-	4	6	1- 3
			2			.125
1880	WOR	N	P-1-	24	41	9- 8
			S-O			.162
1881	WOR	N	P-S-	23	51	6-14
			O			.221
1882	WOR	N	P-1-	16	63	1-15
			S-3-O			.247
1883	ATH	AA	P-2-	20	71	9- 5
			S-3-O			.254
1884	ATH	AA	3		106	.273
1885	ATH	AA	P-3	1	95	1- 0
						.252
		BRTR		88	433	27-45
						.245

CORGAN, CHARLES HOWARD
B.DEC.4,1902 WAGONER,OKLA.
D.JUNE 13,1928 WAGONER,OKLA.

YR	CL	LEA	POS	GP	G	REC
1925	BRO	N	S		14	.170
1927	BRO	N	2		19	.263
		BLTR			33	.221

COLMAN, ROY GEORGE (IRISH)
B.OCT.21,1887 INDIANAPOLIS,IND.
D.NOV.24,1958 SAN FRANCISCO,CAL

YR	CL	LEA	POS	GP	G	REC
1911	CHI	A	S		43	.213
1916	STL	N	S		92	.210
		BRTR			135	.211

CORKHILL, JOHN STEWART (POP)
B.APR.11,1858 PARKESBURG,PA.
D.APR.4,1921 PENNSAUKEN,N.J.

YR	CL	LEA	POS	GP	G	REC
1883	CIN	AA	2-S-O		86	.222
1884	CIN	AA	P-1-	1	111	1- 0
			S-3-O			.276
1885	CIN	AA	P-1-	5	112	1- 4
			O			.291
1886	CIN	AA	P-1-	1	129	0- 0
			S-O			.283
1887	CIN	AA	P-O	5	127	0- 0
						.330
1888	CIN	AA	P-1-	1	118	0- 0
			2-O			.271
	BRO	AA	O		19	.386
1889	BRO	AA	O		138	.258
1890	BRO	N	O		51	.225
1891	ATH	AA	O		83	.211
	CIN	N	O		1	.000
	PIT	N	O		41	.231
1892	PIT	N	O		67	.191
		BLTR		13	1083	2- 4
						.265

CORKINS, MICHAEL PATRICK (MIKE)
B.MAY 25,1946 RIVERSIDE,CAL.

YR	CL	LEA	POS	GP	G	REC
1969	SD	N	/P		6	1- 3
1970	SD	N	P	24	25	5- 6
1971	SD	N	/P		8	0- 0
1972	SD	N	P		47	6- 9
1973	SD	N	P	47	48	5- 8
1974	SD	N	P	25	30	2- 2
		BRTR		157	164	19-28

CORNEJO, NIEVES MARDIE (MARDIE)
B.AUG.5,1951 WELLINGTON,KAN.

YR	CL	LEA	POS	GP	G	REC
1978	NY	N	P		25	4- 2
		BRTR				

CORNUTT, TERRY STANTON
B.OCT.2,1952 ROSEBURG,ORE.

YR	CL	LEA	POS	GP	G	REC
1977	SF	N	P		28	1- 2
1978	SF	N	/P		1	0- 0
		BRTR			29	1- 2

CORRALES, PATRICK (PAT)
B.MAR.20,1941 LOS ANGELES,CAL.

YR	CL	LEA	POS	GP	G	REC
1964	PHI	N	H		2	.000
1965	PHI	N	C		63	.224
1966	STL	N	C		28	.181
1968	CIN	N	C		20	.268
1969	CIN	N	C		29	.264
1970	CIN	N	C		43	.236
1971	CIN	N	C		40	.181
1972	CIN	N	/C		2	.000
	SD	N	C		44	.193
1973	SD	N	C		29	.208
		BRTR			300	.216

NON-PLAYING MANAGER
TEX[A] 1978 [INTERIM]

CORRELL, VICTOR CROSBY (VIC)
B.FEB.5,1946 WASHINGTON,D.C.

YR	CL	LEA	POS	GP	G	REC
1972	BOS	A	/C		1	.500
1974	ATL	N	C		73	.238
1975	ATL	N	C		103	.215
1976	ATL	N	C		69	.225
1977	ATL	N	C		54	.208
1978	CIN	N	C		52	.238
		BRTR			352	.224

CORRIDEN, JOHN MICHAEL JR.
B.OCT.6,1918 LOGANSPORT,IND.

YR	CL	LEA	POS	GP	G	REC
1946	BRO	N	H		1	.000
		BBTR				

CORRIDEN, JOHN MICHAEL SR. (RED)
B.SEPT.4,1887 LOGANSPORT,IND.
D.SEPT.28,1959 INDIANAPOLIS,IND

YR	CL	LEA	POS	GP	G	REC
1910	STL	A	S		26	.155
1912	DET	A	3		38	.203
1913	CHI	N	S		46	.175
1914	CHI	N	S		107	.230
1915	CHI	N	S		6	.000
		BRTR			223	.205

NON-PLAYING MANAGER CHI[A] 1950

CORRIDON, FRANK J. (FIDDLER)
B.NOV.25,1880 NEWPORT,R.I.
D.FEB.21,1941 SYRACUSE,N.Y.

YR	CL	LEA	POS	GP	G	REC
1904	CHI	N	P	12	19	5- 5
	PHI	N	P		12	6- 5
1905	PHI	N	P		35	11-13
1907	PHI	N	P	37	38	17-14
1908	PHI	N	P		27	14-10
1909	PHI	N	P		27	11- 7
1910	STL	N	P		30	6-14
		BRTR		180	188	70-68

CORRIGAN

YR	CL	LEA	POS	GP	G	REC
1884	CHI	U	2-O		2	.143

CORT, BARRY LEE
B.APR.15,1956 TORONTO,ONT.,CAN.

YR	CL	LEA	POS	GP	G	REC
1977	MIL	A	/P		7	1- 1
		BRTR				

YR	CL	LEA	POS	GP	G	REC

CORTAZZO, JOHN FRANCIS (JESS)
B.SEPT.26,1904 WILMERDING,PA.
D.MAR.4,1963 PITTSBURGH,PA.
| 1923 | CHI | A | H | | 1 | .000 |

BRTR

CORWIN, ELMER NATHAN (AL)
B.DEC.3,1926 NEWBURGH,N.Y.
1951	NY	N	P		15	5- 1
1952	NY	N	P	21	23	6- 1
1953	NY	N	P	48	54	6- 4
1954	NY	N	P	20	23	1- 3
1955	NY	N	P		13	0- 1

BRTR   117   128   18-10

COSCARART, JOSEPH MARVIN
B.NOV.18,1909 ESCONDIDO,CAL.
| 1935 | BOS | N | 2-S-3 | | 86 | .236 |
| 1936 | BOS | N | 3 | | 104 | .245 |

BRTR   190   .241

COSCARART, PETER JOSEPH
B.JUNE 16,1913 ESCONDIDO,CAL.
1938	BRO	N	2		32	.152
1939	BRO	N	2		115	.277
1940	BRO	N	2		143	.237
1941	BRO	N	2-S		43	.127
1942	PIT	N	2-S		133	.228
1943	PIT	N	2-S-3		133	.242
1944	PIT	N	2-S-3-0		139	.264
1945	PIT	N	2-S		123	.242
1946	PIT	N	S		3	.500

BRTR   864   .243

COSGROVE, MICHAEL JOHN (MIKE)
B.FEB.17,1951 PHOENIX,ARIZ.
1972	HOU	N	/P		7	0- 1
1973	HOU	N	P		13	1- 1
1974	HOU	N	P		45	7- 3
1975	HOU	N	P		32	1- 2
1976	HOU	N	P		22	3- 4

BRTL   119   12-11

COSMAN, JAMES HENRY (JIM)
B.FEB.19,1943 BROCKPORT,N.Y.
1966	STL	N	/P		1	1- 0
1967	STL	N	P		10	1- 0
1970	CHI	N	/P		1	0- 0

BRTR   12   2- 0

COSTELLO, DANIEL FRANCIS
(DASHING DAN)
B.SEPT.9,1891 JESSUP,PA.
D.MAR.26,1936 PITTSBURGH,PA.
1913	NY	A	H		2	.500
1914	PIT	N	O		21	.297
1915	PIT	N	O		71	.216
1916	PIT	N	O		60	.239

BRTR   154   .243

COSTELLO
[REAL NAME KENNETH LELAND NASH]

COTE, HENRY JOSEPH
B.FEB.19,1864 TROY,N.Y.
D.APR.28,1940 TROY,N.Y.
| 1894 | LOU | N | C | | 10 | .313 |
| 1895 | LOU | N | C | | 10 | .265 |

                            20   .288

COTE, WARREN PETER (PETE)
B.AUG.30,1902 CAMBRIDGE,MASS.
| 1926 | NY | N | H | | 2 | .000 |

BRTR

COTTER, DANIEL JOSEPH
B.APR.14,1867 BOSTON,MASS.
D.SEPT.14,1935 DORCHESTER,MASS.
| 1890 | BUF | P | P | | 1 | 0- 1 |

TR

COTTER, EDWARD CHRSITOPHER
B.JULY 4,1904 HARTFORD,CONN.
D.JUNE 14,1959 HARTFORD,CONN.
| 1926 | PHI | N | S-3 | | 17 | .308 |

BRTR

COTTER, HARVEY LOUIS (HOOKS)
B.MAY.22,1900 HOLDEN,MO.
D.AUG.6,1955 LOS ANGELES,CAL.
| 1922 | CHI | N | 1 | | 1 | 1.000 |
| 1924 | CHI | N | 1 | | 98 | .261 |

BLTL   99   .264

COTTER, RICHARD RAPHAEL
B.OCT.12,1889 MANCHESTER,N.H.
D.APR.4,1945 BROOKLYN,N.Y.
| 1911 | PHI | N | C | | 17 | .283 |
| 1912 | CHI | N | C | | 26 | .278 |

TR   43   .280

COTTER, THOMAS B.
B.SEPT.30,1866 WALTHAM,MASS.
D.NOV.22,1906 BROOKLINE,MASS.
| 1891 | BOS | AA | C | | 5 | .273 |

COTTIER, CHARLES KEITH (CHUCK)
B.JAN.8,1936 DELTA,COLO.
1959	MIL	N	2		10	.125
1960	MIL	N	2		95	.227
1961	DET	A	2-S		10	.286
			WAS	A	2	101	.234
1962	WAS	A	2		136	.242
1963	WAS	A	2-S-3		113	.205
1964	WAS	A	2-S-3		73	.168
1965	WAS	A	/H		7	.000
1968	CAL	A	3/2		33	.194
1969	CAL	A	/2		2	.000

BRTR   580   .220

COTTRELL, ENSIGN STOVER
B.AUG.29,1888 HOOSICK FALLS,N.Y.
D.FEB.27,1947 SYRACUSE,N.Y.
1911	PIT	N	P		1	0- 0
1912	CHI	N	P		1	0- 0
1913	PHI	A	P		1	0- 0
1914	BOS	N	P		1	0- 1
1915	NY	A	P		7	0- 1

BLTL   11   0- 2

COUCH, JOHN DANIEL
B.MAR.31,1891 VAUGHN,MONT.
D.DEC.8,1975 SAN MATEO,CAL.
1917	DET	A	P		3	0- 0
1922	CIN	N	P		43	16- 9
1923	CIN	N	P		19	2- 7
			PHI	N	P	11	12	2- 4
1924	PHI	N	P		37	4- 8
1925	PHI	N	P		34	5- 6

BLTR   147   148   29-34

COUGHLAN, EDWARD E.
B.HARTFORD, CONN.
| 1884 | BUF | N | P-O | | 2 | 0- 0 |
| | | | | | | .250 |

COUGHLIN, DENNIS F.
1872 NAT NA 2-S-3-0   8   .324

COUGHLIN, WILLIAM E. (ROSCOE)
B.MAR.15,1868 WALPOLE,MASS.
D.MAR.20,1951 CHELSEA,MASS.
| 1890 | CHI | N | P | | 11 | 4- 7 |
| 1891 | NY | N | P | | 8 | 3- 4 |

TR   19   7-11

COUGHLIN, WILLIAM PAUL
(SCRANTON BILL)
B.JULY 12,1878 SCRANTON,PA.
D.MAY 7,1943 SCRANTON,PA.
1899	WAS	N	3		5	.100
1901	WAS	A	3		137	.277
1902	WAS	A	2-S-3		121	.298
1903	WAS	A	3		125	.251
1904	WAS	A	3		64	.261
			DET	A	3		56	.355
1905	DET	A	3		138	.252
1906	DET	A	3		147	.235
1907	DET	A	3		134	.243
1908	DET	A	3		119	.215

BRTR   1046   .252

COUGHTRY, JAMES MARLAN (MARLAN)
B.SEPT.11,1934 HOLLYWOOD,CAL.
1960	BOS	A	2-3		15	.158
1962	LA	A	2-3		11	.182
			KC	A	3		6	.182
			CLE	A	H		3	.500

BLTR   35   .185

COULSON, ROBERT JACKSON
B.JUNE 17,1887 DONORA,PA.
D.SEPT.11,1953 WASHINGTON,PA.
1908	CIN	N	O		8	.333
1910	BRO	N	O		25	.247
1911	BRO	N	O		145	.234
1914	PIT	F	O		18	.203

BRTR   196   .233

COULTER, THOMAS LEE (TIM)
B.JUNE 5,1945 STEUBENVILLE,O.
| 1969 | STL | N | /2 | | 6 | .316 |

BBTR

COUMBE, FREDERICK NICHOLAS (FRITZ)
B.DEC.13,1889 ANTRIM,PA.
D.MAR.21,1978 PARADISE,CAL.
1914	BOS	A	P		17	1- 2
			CLE	A	P		15	1- 5
1915	CLE	A	P	31	35	4- 7
1916	CLE	A	P	29	31	7- 5
1917	CLE	A	P	34	35	8- 6
1918	CLE	A	P	30	32	13- 7
1919	CLE	A	P		8	1- 1
1920	CIN	N	P-O		5	0- 1
						.231
1921	CIN	N	P	28	31	3- 4

BLTL   197   209   38-38
                            .199

COURTNEY, CLINTON DAWSON
(SCRAP IRON)
B.MAR.16,1927 HALL SUMMIT,LA.
D.JUNE 16,1975 ROCHESTER,N.Y.
1951	NY	A	C		1	.000
1952	STL	A	C		119	.286
1953	STL	A	C		106	.251
1954	BAL	A	C		122	.270
1955	CHI	A	C		19	.378
			WAS	A	C		75	.298
1956	WAS	A	C		101	.300
1957	WAS	A	C		91	.267
1958	WAS	A	C		134	.251
1959	WAS	A	C		72	.233
1960	BAL	A	C		83	.227
1961	KC	A	C		1	.000
			BAL	A	C		22	.267

BLTR   946   .266

COURTNEY, ERNEST E.
B.JAN.20,1875 DES MOINES,IOWA
D.FEB.29,1920 BUFFALO,N.Y.
1902	BOS	N	S-O		40	.212
			BAL	A	3		1	.500
1903	NY	A	S		25	.241
			DET	A	3		23	.253
1905	PHI	N	3		155	.275
1906	PHI	N	3		112	.236
1907	PHI	N	1-3		130	.243
1908	PHI	N	3		42	.181

BLTR   528   .245

COURTNEY, HENRY SEYMOUR (HARRY)
B.NOV.19,1898 ASHEVILLE,N.C.
1919	WAS	A	P		4	3- 0
1920	WAS	A	P		37	8-11
1921	WAS	A	P	30	32	6- 9
1922	WAS	A	P		5	0- 1
			CHI	A	P		18	5- 6

BLTL   94   96   22-27

COUSINEAU, EDWARD THOMAS
B.DEC.16,1898 WATERTOWN,MASS.
D.JULY 14,1951 WATERTOWN,MASS.
1923	BOS	N	C		1	1.000
1924	BOS	N	C		3	.000
1925	BOS	N	C		1	.000

BRTR   5   .500

COVELESKI, HARRY FRANK
(GIANT KILLER)
[REAL NAME HARRY FRANK KOWALEWSKI]
B.APR.23,1886 SHAMOKIN,PA.
D.AUG.4,1950 SHAMOKIN,PA.
1907	PHI	N	P		4	1- 0
1908	PHI	N	P		6	4- 1
1909	PHI	N	P		24	6-10
1910	CIN	N	P		7	1- 1
1914	DET	A	P		44	22-12
1915	DET	A	P		50	23-13
1916	DET	A	P		44	21-10
1917	DET	A	P		16	4- 6
1918	DET	A	P		3	0- 1

BBTL   198   82-54

COVELESKI, STANLEY ANTHONY
[REAL NAME STANISLAUS KOWALEWSKI]
B.JULY 13,1889 SHAMOKIN,PA.
1912	PHI	A	P		3	2- 1
1916	CLE	A	P		44	15-12
1917	CLE	A	P	45	46	19-14
1918	CLE	A	P		38	22-13
1919	CLE	A	P		43	24-12
1920	CLE	A	P		41	24-14
1921	CLE	A	P		43	23-13
1922	CLE	A	P		35	17-14
1923	CLE	A	P		33	13-14
1924	CLE	A	P		37	15-16
1925	WAS	A	P		32	20- 5
1926	WAS	A	P		36	14-11
1927	WAS	A	P		5	2- 1
1928	NY	A	P		12	5- 1

BRTR   447   448   215-141

COVENEY, JOHN PATRICK (JACK)
B.JUNE 10,1880 S.NATICK,MASS.
D.MAR.28,1961 WAVERLY,MASS.
| 1903 | STL | N | C | | 3 | .200 |

TR

COVINGTON, CHESTER ROGERS
(CHET) OR (CHESTY)
B.NOV.6,1910 CAIRO,ILL.
D.JUNE 11,1976 PEMBROKE PARK,FLA.
| 1944 | PHI | N | P | | 19 | 1- 1 |

BBTL

COVINGTON, CLARENCE OTTO (SAM)
B.DEC.17,1892 HENRYVILLE,TENN.
D.JAN.4,1963 DENISON,TEX.
1913	STL	A	1		20	.150
1917	BOS	N	1		17	.197
1918	BOS	N	O		3	.333

BLTR   40   .178

YR	CL	LEA	POS	GP	G	REC

COVINGTON, JOHN WESLEY (WES)
B.MAR.27,1932 LAURINBURG,N.C.

1956	MIL	N	O		75	.283
1957	MIL	N	O		96	.284
1958	MIL	N	O		90	.330
1959	MIL	N	O		103	.279
1960	MIL	N	O		95	.249
1961	MIL	N	O		9	.190
	CHI	A	O		22	.288
	KC	A	O		17	.159
	PHI	N	O		57	.303
1962	PHI	N	O		116	.283
1963	PHI	N	O		119	.303
1964	PHI	N	O		129	.280
1965	PHI	N	O		101	.247
1966	PHI	N	/O		9	.091
	LA	N	/O		37	.121
	BLTR				1075	.279

COVINGTON, WILLIAM WILKES (TEX)
B.MAR.6,1887 HENRYVILLE,TENN.
D.DEC.10,1931 DENISON,TEX.

1911	DET	A	P	17		7- 1
1912	DET	A	P	14		3- 4
	BLTR			31		10- 5

COWAN, BILLY ROLAND
B.AUG.28,1938 CALHOUN CITY,MISS.

1963	CHI	N	O		14	.250
1964	CHI	N	O		139	.241
1965	NY	N	O/2-S		82	.179
	MIL	N			19	.185
1967	PHI	N	O/2-3		34	.153
1969	NY	A	O/1		32	.167
	CAL	A			28	.304
1970	CAL	A	O-1/3		68	.276
1971	CAL	A	O/1		74	.276
1972	CAL	A	/H		3	.000
	BRTR				493	.236

COWENS, ALFRED EDWARD (AL)
B.OCT.25,1951 LOS ANGELES,CAL.

1974	KC	A	*O/3		110	.242
1975	KC	A	*O		120	.277
1976	KC	A	*O		152	.265
1977	KC	A	*O		162	.312
1978	KC	A	*O/3		132	.274
	BRTR				676	.279

COX, ELMER JOSEPH (DICK)
B.SEPT.30,1897 PASADENA,CAL.
D.JUNE 1,1966 MORRO BAY,CAL.

1925	BRO	N	O		122	.329
1926	BRO	N	O		124	.296
	BRTR				246	.314

COX, ERNEST THOMPSON
B.FEB.5,1894 BIRMINGHAM,ALA.
D.APR.29,1974 BIRMINGHAM,ALA.

1922	CHI	A	P	1		0- 0
	BLTR					

COX, FRANK BERNHARDT (RUNT)
B.MAR.17,1858 WALTHAM,MASS.
D.1928

1884	DET	N	S		27	.127

COX, GEORGE MELVIN
B.NOV.15,1904 SHERMAN,TEX.

1928	CHI	A	P	26		1- 2
	BRTR					

COX, GLENN MELVIN
B.FEB.3,1931 MONTEBELLO,CAL.

1955	KC	A	P	2		0- 2
1956	KC	A	P	3		0- 2
1957	KC	A	P	10		1- 0
1958	KC	A	P	2		0- 0
	BRTR			17		1- 4

COX, JAMES CHARLES (JIM)
B.MAY 28,1950 BLOOMINGTON,ILL.

1973	MON	N	/2		9	.133
1974	MON	N	2		77	.220
1975	MON	N	2		11	.259
1976	MON	N	2		13	.172
	BRTR				110	.215

COX, JOSEPH CASEY (CASEY)
B.JULY 3,1941 LONG BEACH,CAL.

1966	WAS	A	P	66		4- 5
1967	WAS	A	P	54		7- 4
1968	WAS	A	/P	4		0- 1
1969	WAS	A	P	52		12- 7
1970	WAS	A	P	37		8-12
1971	WAS	A	P	54		5- 7
1972	TEX	A	P	35		3- 3
	NY	A	/P	5		0- 1
1973	NY	A	/P	1		0- 0
	BRTR			308		39-42

COX, LARRY EUGENE
B.SEP.11,1947 BLUFFTON,OHIO

1973	PHI	N	/C	1		.000
1974	PHI	N	C		30	.170
1975	PHI	N	C		11	.200
1977	SEA	N	C		35	.247
1978	CHI	N	C		59	.281
	BRTR				136	.246

COX, LESLIE WARREN
B.AUG.14,1905 JUNCTION,TEX.
D.OCT.14,1934 SAN ANGELO,TEX.

1926	CHI	A	P	2		0- 1
	BRTR					

COX, PLATEAU REX (RED)
B.FEB.16,1895 LAUREL SPRINGS,N.C.

1920	DET	A	P	3		0- 0
	BLTR					

COX, ROBERT JOE (BOBBY)
B.MAY 21,1941 TULSA,OKLA.

1968	NY	A	*3		135	.229
1969	NY	A	3/2		85	.215
	BRTR				220	.225

NON-PLAYING MANAGER ATL[N] 1978

COX, TERRY LEE
B.MAR.30,1949 ODESSA,TEX.

1970	CAL	A	/P	3		0- 0
	BRTR					

COX, WILLIAM DONALD
B.JUNE 23,1913 ASHMORE,ILL.

1936	STL	N	P	2		0- 0
1937	CHI	A	P	3		1- 0
1938	CHI	A	P	7		0- 2
	STL	A	P	22	24	1- 4
1939	STL	A	P	4		0- 2
1940	STL	A	P	12	13	0- 1
	BRTR			50	53	2- 9

COX, WILLIAM RICHARD (BILLY)
B.AUG.29,1919 NEWPORT,PA.
D.MAR.30,1978 HARRISBURG,PA.

1941	PIT	N	S		10	.270
1946	PIT	N	S		121	.290
1947	PIT	N	S		132	.274
1948	BRO	N	2-S-3		88	.249
1949	BRO	N	3		100	.234
1950	BRO	N	2-S-3		119	.257
1951	BRO	N	S-3		142	.279
1952	BRO	N	2-S-3		116	.259
1953	BRO	N	2-S-3		100	.291
1954	BRO	N	2-S-3		77	.235
1955	BAL	A	2-S-3		53	.211
	BRTR				1058	.262

COX, WILLIAM TED (TED)
B.JAN.24,1955 OKLAHOMA CITY,OKLA

1977	BOS	A	D		13	.362
1978	CLE	A	O-3-D/1-S		82	.233
	BRTR				95	.260

COYLE, WILLIAM CLAUDE
B.PITTSBURGH,PA.

1893	WAS	N	P	1		0- 1
	TR					

COYNE, (TOOTS)

1914	PHI	A	3	1		.000
	TR					

COZART, CHARLES RHUBIN
B.OCT.17,1919 LENOIR,N.C.

1945	BOS	N	P	5		1- 0
	BRTL					

CRABB, JAMES ROY (ROY)
B.AUG.23,1890 MONTICELLO,IOWA
D.MAR.30,1940 LEWISTON,MONT.

1912	CHI	A	P	2		0- 0
	PHI	A	P	7		2- 5
	BRTR			9		2- 5

CRABLE, GEORGE E.
B.1866 BROOKLYN,N.Y.

1910	BRO	N	P	2		0- 0
	BLTL					

CRABTREE, C. C.
(PLAYED UNDER NAME OF
CHARLES E. MC DONALD)

CRABTREE, ESTEL CRAYTON
(ESTEL) OR (CRABBY)
B.AUG.19,1903 CRABTREE,OHIO
D.JAN.4,1967 LOGAN,OHIO

1929	CIN	N	O	1		.000
1931	CIN	N	1-3-O		117	.269
1932	CIN	N	O		108	.274
1933	STL	N	O		23	.265
1941	STL	N	3-O		77	.341
1942	STL	N	H		10	.333
1943	CIN	N	O		95	.276
1944	CIN	N	1-O		58	.286
	BLTR				489	.281

CRADDOCK, WALTER ANDERSON
B.MAR.25,1932 PAX,W.VA.

1955	KC	A	P	4		0- 2
1956	KC	A	P	2		0- 2
1958	KC	A	P	23		0- 3
	BRTL			29		0- 7

CRAFT, HARRY FRANCIS (WILDFIRE)
B.APR.19,1915 ELLISVILLE,MISS.

1937	CIN	N	O		10	.310
1938	CIN	N	O		151	.270
1939	CIN	N	O		134	.257
1940	CIN	N	1-O		115	.244
1941	CIN	N	O		119	.249
1942	CIN	N	O		37	.177
	BRTR				566	.253

NON-PLAYING MANAGER
KC[A] 1957-59; CHI[N] 1961
HOU[N] 1962-64

CRAFT, MAURICE MONTAGUE (HOLLY)
B.NOV.28,1895 PORTSMOUTH,VA.

1916	WAS	A	P	3		0- 1
1917	WAS	A	P	8		0- 0
1918	WAS	A	P	3		0- 0
1919	WAS	A	P	16		0- 3
	BRTR			30		0- 4

CRAGHEAD, HOWARD OLIVER (JUDGE)
B.MAY 25,1908 SELMA,CAL.
D.JULY 15,1962 SAN ZIELOE,CAL.

1931	CLE	A	P	4		0- 0
1933	CLE	A	P	11		0- 0
	BRTR			15		0- 0

CRAIG, GEORGE MCCARTHY (LEFTY)
B.NOV.15,1887 PHILADELPHIA,PA.
D.APR.23,1911 INDIANAPOLIS,IND.

1907	PHI	A	P	2		0- 0
	TL					

CRAIG, PETER JOEL (PETE)
B.JULY 10,1940 LASALLE,ONT.,CAN.

1964	WAS	A	P	2		0- 0
1965	WAS	A	/P	3		0- 3
1966	WAS	A	/P	1		0- 0
	BLTR			6		0- 3

CRAIG, ROGER LEE
B.FEB.17,1931 DURHAM,N.C.

1955	BRO	N	P		21	5- 3
1956	BRO	N	P		35	12-11
1957	BRO	N	P		32	6- 9
1958	LA	N	P		9	2- 1
1959	LA	N	P		29	11- 5
1960	LA	N	P		40	5- 6
1961	LA	N	P		42	10-24
1962	NY	N	P		42	10-24
1963	NY	N	P		46	5-22
1964	STL	N	P		39	7- 9
1965	CIN	N	P		40	1- 4
1966	PHI	N	P		14	2- 1
	BRTR				368	74-98

NON-PLAYING MANAGER SD[N] 1978

CRAM, GERALD ALLEN
B.DEC.9,1947 LOS ANGELES,CAL.

1969	KC	A	/P	5		0- 1
1974	NY	N	P	10		0- 1
1975	NY	N	/P	4		0- 1
1976	KC	A	/P	4		0- 0
	BRTR			23		0- 3

CRAMER, ROGER MAXWELL
(DOC) OR (FLIT)
B.JULY 22,1905 BEACH HAVEN,N.J.

1929	PHI	A	O		2	.000
1930	PHI	A	O		30	.232
1931	PHI	A	O		65	.260
1932	PHI	A	O		92	.336
1933	PHI	A	O		152	.295
1934	PHI	A	O		153	.311
1935	PHI	A	O		149	.332
1936	BOS	A	O		154	.292
1937	BOS	A	O		133	.305
1938	BOS	A	P-O	1	148	0- 0
						.301
1939	BOS	A	O		137	.311
1940	BOS	A	O		150	.303
1941	WAS	A	O		154	.273
1942	DET	A	O		151	.263
1943	DET	A	O		140	.300
1944	DET	A	O		143	.292
1945	DET	A	O		141	.275
1946	DET	A	O		68	.294
1947	DET	A	O		73	.268
1948	DET	A	O		4	.000
	BLTR			1	2239	0- 0
						.296

CRAMER, WILLIAM B.
B.BROOKLYN,N.Y.
D.AUG.12,1885 CAMDEN,N.J.

1883	NY	N	O		2	.125

CRAMER, WILLIAM WENDELL
B.MAY 21,1891 BEDFORD,IND.
D.SEPT.11,1966 FORT WAYNE,IND.

1912	CIN	N	P	1		0- 0
	BRTR					

YR	CL	LEA	POS	GP	G	REC

CRANDALL, DELMAR WESLEY (DEL)
B.MAR.5,1930 ONTARIO,CAL.

YR	CL	LEA	POS	GP	G	REC
1949	BOS	N	C		67	.263
1950	BOS	N	C-1		79	.220
1953	MIL	N	C		116	.272
1954	MIL	N	C		138	.242
1955	MIL	N	C		133	.236
1956	MIL	N	C		112	.238
1957	MIL	N	C-1-0		118	.253
1958	MIL	N	C		131	.272
1959	MIL	N	C		150	.257
1960	MIL	N	C		142	.294
1961	MIL	N	C		15	.200
1962	MIL	N	C-1		107	.297
1963	MIL	N	C-1		86	.201
1964	SF	N	C		69	.231
1965	PIT	N	C		60	.214
1966	CLE	A	C		50	.231
			BRTR		1573	.254

NON-PLAYING MANAGER MIL[A] 1972-75

CRANDALL, JAMES OTIS (DOC)
B.OCT.8,1887 WADENA,MINN.
D.AUG.17,1951 BELL,CAL.

YR	CL	LEA	POS	GP	G	REC
1908	NY	N	P		32	12-12
1909	NY	N	P		30	6- 4
1910	NY	N	P	42	43	17- 4
1911	NY	N	P	41	50	15- 5
1912	NY	N	P	37	50	13- 7
1913	NY	N	P	24	31	4- 4
	STL	N	H		2	.000
	NY	N	P	11	15	0- 0
1914	STL	F	P-2	27	115	12- 9
						.312
1915	STL	F	P	51	81	21-15
1916	STL	A	P	2	16	0- 0
1918	BOS	N	P	5	14	1- 2
			BRTR	302	479	101-62
						.286

CRANE, EDWARD NICHOLAS (CANNON-BALL)
B.MAY 1862 BOSTON,MASS.
D.SEPT.19,1896 ROCHESTER,N.Y.

YR	CL	LEA	POS	GP	G	REC
1884	BOS	U	P-C-	2	99	0- 2
			O			.364
1885	PRO	N	P-O		1	0- 0
						.000
	BUF	N	O		13	.269
1886	BOS	N	P-O	10	80	2- 6
						.171
1888	NY	N	P		12	5- 6
1889	NY	N	P		28	14-10
1890	NY	P	P		44	16-23
1891	CIN	AA	P-O	32	34	14-17
						.145
	CIN	N			14	2-10
1892	NY	N	P		40	14-26
1893	NY	N	P		10	2- 4
	BRO	N	P		3	0- 2
			BRTR	196	378	69-106
						.236

CRANE, SAMUEL BYREN (LUCKY) OR (RED)
B.SEPT.13,1894 HARRISBURG,PA.
D.NOV.12,1955 PHILADELPHIA,PA.

YR	CL	LEA	POS	GP	G	REC
1914	PHI	A	S		4	.000
1915	PHI	A	S		8	.229
1916	PHI	A	S		2	.250
1917	WAS	A	S		32	.179
1920	CIN	N	S-2-S-3-O		54	.215
1921	CIN	N	S		73	.233
1922	BRO	N	S		3	.250
			BRTR		174	.208

CRANE, SAMUEL NEWHALL
B.JAN.2,1854 SPRINGFIELD,MASS.
D.JUNE 26,1925 NEW YORK,N.Y.

YR	CL	LEA	POS	GP	G	REC
1873	RES	NA	2		1	-
1875	ATL	NA	1-O		21	-
1880	BUF	N	M-2-O		10	.125
1883	MET	AA	2-O		97	.234
1884	CIN	U	M-2		68	.231
1885	DET	N	2		68	.191
1886	DET	N	2		49	.139
	STL	N	2		37	.175
1887	WAS	N	2		7	.312
1890	NY	N	1-O		2	.000
	PIT	N	2-S		22	.200
	NY	N	2		2	.000
			BRTR		384	-

CRAUSE, CLARENCE
[PLAYED UNDER NAME OF
CLARENCE CROSS]

CRAVATH, CLIFFORD CARLTON (GAVVY)
B.MAR.23,1881 ESCONDIDO,CAL.
D.MAY 23,1963 LAGUNA BEACH,CAL.

YR	CL	LEA	POS	GP	G	REC
1908	BOS	A	O		94	.256
1909	CHI	A	O		18	.061
	WAS	A	O		6	1.000
1912	PHI	N	O		130	.284
1913	PHI	N	O		147	.341
1914	PHI	N	O		149	.298
1915	PHI	N	O		150	.285
1916	PHI	N	O		137	.283
1917	PHI	N	O		120	.280
1918	PHI	N	O		121	.232
1919	PHI	N	M-O		83	.341
1920	PHI	N	M-O		46	.289
			BRTR		1219	.287

CRAVER, WILLIAM H.
B.1844 TROY,N.Y.
D.JUNE 17,1901 TROY,N.Y.

YR	CL	LEA	POS	GP	G	REC
1871	TRO	NA	M-C-1-2-S		27	.303
1872	BAL	NA	C-1-2-3-O		33	.278
1873	BAL	NA	C-1-2-S-O		38	-
1874	PHI	NA	M-C-2		55	-
1875	CEN	NA	M-1-2-S-3		14	-
	ATH	NA	C-2		55	.314
1876	MUT	N	C-2		56	.222
1877	LOU	N	S		57	.263
			BRTR		335	-

CRAWFORD, CHARLES LOWRIE (LARRY)
B.APR.27,1914 SWISSVALE,PA.

YR	CL	LEA	POS	GP	G	REC
1937	PHI	N	P		6	0- 0
			BLTL			

CRAWFORD, CLIFFORD RANKIN (PAT)
B.JAN.28,1902 SOCIETY HILL,S.C.

YR	CL	LEA	POS	GP	G	REC
1929	NY	N	1		65	.298
1930	NY	N	1-2		25	.276
	CIN	N	1-2		76	.290
1933	STL	N	1-2-3		91	.268
1934	STL	N	2-3		61	.271
			BLTR		318	.280

CRAWFORD, FORREST A.
B.MAY 10,1881 ROCKDALE,TEX.
D.MAR.27,1908 AUSTIN,TEX.

YR	CL	LEA	POS	GP	G	REC
1906	STL	N	S		45	.207
1907	STL	N	S		7	.227
	TR				52	.210

CRAWFORD, GEORGE

YR	CL	LEA	POS	GP	G	REC
1890	ATH	AA	O		5	.111

CRAWFORD, GLENN MARTIN (SHORTY)
B.DEC.2,1913 NORTH BRANCH,MICH.
D.JAN.2,1972 SAGINAW,MICH.

YR	CL	LEA	POS	GP	G	REC
1945	STL	N	O		4	.000
	PHI	N	2-S-O		82	.295
1946	PHI	N	H		1	.000
			BLTR		87	.291

**CRAWFORD, JAMES FREDERICK
(JIM) OR (CATFISH)**
B.SEP.29,1950 CHICAGO,ILL.

YR	CL	LEA	POS	GP	G	REC
1973	HOU	N	P		48	2- 4
1975	HOU	N	P		44	3- 5
1976	DET	A	P		32	1- 8
1977	DET	A	P		37	7- 8
1978	DET	A	P		20	2- 3
			BLTL		181	15-28

CRAWFORD, KENNETH DANIEL
B.OCT.31,1894 SOUTH BEND,IND.
D.NOV.11,1976 PITTSBURGH,PA.

YR	CL	LEA	POS	GP	G	REC
1915	BAL	F	1-O		23	.244
			BLTR			

CRAWFORD, RUFUS (JAKE)
B.MAR.20,1928 CAMPBELL,MO.

YR	CL	LEA	POS	GP	G	REC
1952	STL	A	O		7	.182
			BRTR			

CRAWFORD, SAMUEL EARL (WAHOO SAM)
B.APR.18,1880 WAHOO,NEB.
D.JUNE 15,1968 HOLLYWOOD,CAL.

YR	CL	LEA	POS	GP	G	REC
1899	CIN	N	O		31	.308
1900	CIN	N	O		96	.270
1901	CIN	N	O		124	.334
1902	CIN	N	O		140	.333
1903	DET	A	O		137	.332
1904	DET	A	O		150	.247
1905	DET	A	1-O		154	.297
1906	DET	A	1-O		145	.295
1907	DET	A	O		144	.323
1908	DET	A	1-O		152	.311
1909	DET	A	O		156	.314
1910	DET	A	O		154	.289
1911	DET	A	O		146	.378
1912	DET	A	O		149	.325
1913	DET	A	1-O		153	.316
1914	DET	A	O		157	.314
1915	DET	A	O		156	.299
1916	DET	A	O		100	.286
1917	DET	A	1-O		61	.173
			BLTL		2505	.309

CRAWFORD, WILLIE MURPHY
B.SEP.7,1946 LOS ANGELES,CAL.

YR	CL	LEA	POS	GP	G	REC
1964	LA	N	O		10	.313
1965	LA	N	/O		52	.148
1966	LA	N	R		6	.000
1967	LA	N	/O		4	.250
1968	LA	N	O		61	.251
1969	LA	N	*O		129	.250
1970	LA	N	O		109	.234
1971	LA	N	O		114	.281
1972	LA	N	O		96	.251
1973	LA	N	*O		145	.295
1974	LA	N	*O		139	.295
1975	LA	N	*O		124	.263
1976	STL	N	*O		120	.304
1977	HOU	N	O		42	.254
	OAK	A	O-O		59	.184
			BLTL		1210	.268

CREAMER, GEORGE W.
[REAL NAME GEORGE W. TRIEBEL]
B.1855 PHILADELPHIA,PA.
D.JUNE 27,1886 PHILADELPHIA,PA.

YR	CL	LEA	POS	GP	G	REC
1878	MIL	N	2-O		50	.212
1879	SYR	N	2-S-O		15	.213
1880	WOR	N	2		83	.202
1881	WOR	N	2		79	.209
1882	WOR	N	2		81	.228
1883	PIT	AA	2		89	.243
1884	PIT	AA	M-2		100	.185
			BRTR		497	.216

CREE, WILLIAM FRANKLIN (BIRDIE)
B.OCT.23,1882 KHEDIVE,PA.
D.NOV.8,1942 SUNBURY,PA.

YR	CL	LEA	POS	GP	G	REC
1908	NY	A	O		21	.269
1909	NY	A	O		104	.262
1910	NY	A	O		134	.287
1911	NY	A	O		137	.348
1912	NY	A	O		76	.290
1913	NY	A	O		147	.271
1914	NY	A	O		77	.309
1915	NY	A	O		74	.214
			BRTR		744	.292

CREEDEN, CORNELIUS STEPHEN
B.JULY 21,1915 DANVERS,MASS.
D.NOV.30,1969 SANTA ANA,CAL.

YR	CL	LEA	POS	GP	G	REC
1943	BOS	N	P		5	.250
			BLTL			

CREEDEN, PATRICK FRANCIS (WHOOPS)
B.MAY 23,1906 NEWBURYPORT,MASS.

YR	CL	LEA	POS	GP	G	REC
1931	BOS	A	2		5	.000
			BLTR			

CREEGAN, MARTIN
B.SAN FRANCISCO,CAL.

YR	CL	LEA	POS	GP	G	REC
1884	WAS	U	C-1-3-O		9	.152

CREEL, JACK DALTON (TEX)
B.APR.23,1916 KYLE,TEX.

YR	CL	LEA	POS	GP	G	REC
1945	STL	N	P	26	35	5- 4
			BRTR			

CREELY, AUGUST
B.1867 ST.LOUIS,MO.

YR	CL	LEA	POS	GP	G	REC
1890	STL	AA	S		4	.000

CREGAN, PETER JAMES (PEEKSKILL PETE)
B.APR.13,1875 KINGSTON,N.Y.
D.MAY 18,1945 NEW YORK,N.Y.

YR	CL	LEA	POS	GP	G	REC
1899	NY	N	O		1	.000
1903	CIN	N	O		6	.111
			BRTR		7	.095

CREGER, BERNARD ODELL
B.MAR.21,1927 WYTHEVILLE,VA.

YR	CL	LEA	POS	GP	G	REC
1947	STL	N	S		15	.188
			BRTR			

CREMINS, ROBERT ANTHONY (LEFTY)
B.FEB.15,1906 PELHAM MANOR,N.Y.

YR	CL	LEA	POS	GP	G	REC
1927	BOS	A	P		4	0- 0
			BLTL			

CRESPI, FRANK ANGELO JOSEPH (CREEPY)
B.FEB.16,1918 ST.LOUIS,MO.

YR	CL	LEA	POS	GP	G	REC
1938	STL	N	H		7	.263
1939	STL	N	H		15	.172
1940	STL	N	S-3		3	.273
1941	STL	N	2		146	.279
1942	STL	N	2-S		93	.243
			BRTR		264	.263

**CRESS, WALKER JAMES
(WALKER) OR (FOOTS)**
B.MAR.6,1917 BEN HUR,VA.

YR	CL	LEA	POS	GP	G	REC
1948	CIN	N	P	30	31	0- 1
1949	CIN	N	P		3	0- 0
			BRTR	33	34	0- 1

CRIDER, JERRY STEPHEN
B.SEP.2,1941 SIOUX FALLS,S.D.

YR	CL	LEA	POS	GP	G	REC
1969	MIN	A	P		21	1- 0
1970	CHI	A	P		32	4- 7
			BRTR		53	5- 7

YR CL LEA POS GP G REC

CRIGER, LOUIS
B.FEB.3,1872 ELKHART,IND.
D.MAY 14,1934 TUCSON,ARIZ.
1896 CLE N C 2 .000
1897 CLE N C 38 .230
1898 CLE N C 81 .273
1899 STL N C 75 .256
1900 STL N C 76 .266
1901 BOS A C 69 .240
1902 BOS A C-O 86 .259
1903 BOS A C 96 .197
1904 BOS A C 98 .217
1905 BOS A C 109 .198
1906 BOS A C 6 .214
1907 BOS A C 75 .181
1908 BOS A C 84 .190
1909 STL A C 74 .170
1910 NY A C 27 .189
1912 STL A C 1 .000
BRTR 997 .223

CRIMIAN JOHN MELVIN (JACK)
B.FEB.17,1926 PHILADELPHIA,PA.
1951 STL N P 11 1-0
1952 STL N P 5 0-0
1956 KC A P 54 55 4-8
1957 DET A P 4 0-1
BRTR 74 75 5-9

CRIPE, DAVID GORDON (DAVE)
B.APR.7,1951 ROMONA,CAL.
1978 KC A /3 7 .154
BRTR

CRISCIONE, DAVID GERALD (DAVE)
B.SEPT.2,1951 DUNKIRK,N.Y.
1977 BAL A /C 7 .333
BRTR

CRISCOLA, ANTHONY PAUL
B.JULY 9,1915 WALLA WALLA,WASH.
1942 STL A O 91 .297
1943 STL A O 29 .154
1944 CIN N O 64 .229
BLTR 184 .248

CRISHAM, PATRICK J.
B.JUNE 4,1877 AMESBURY,MASS.
D.JUNE 12,1915 SYRACUSE,N.Y.
1899 BAL N 1 44 .303

CRISP, JOSEPH SHELBY
B.JULY 8,1889 HIGGINSVILLE,MO.
D.FEB.7,1939 KANSAS CITY,MO.
1910 STL A C 1 .000
1911 STL A C 1 1.000
BRTR 2 .500

CRISS, DODE
B.MAR.12,1885 SHERMAN,MISS.
D.SEPT.8,1955 SHERMAN,MISS.
1908 STL A P-O 1 64 0-1
.341
1909 STL A P 10 35 1-4
1910 STL A P-O 3 70 2-1
.231
1911 STL A P-O 4 58 0-2
.253
BLTR 18 227 3-8
.276

CRISS, HARRY
[PLAYED UNDER NAME OF
HUGH IGNATIUS DAILY]

CRIST, CHESTER ARTHUR (SQUAK)
B.FEB.10,1882 COZADDALE,OHIO
D.JAN.7,1957 CINCINNATI,OHIO
1906 PHI N C 5 .000
TR

CRISTALL, WILLIAM ARTHUR (LEFTY)
B.SEPT.12,1878 ODESSA,RUSSIA
D.JAN.28,1939 BUFFALO,N.Y.
1901 CLE A P 6 1-4
BLTL

CRISTANTE, LEO DANTE
B.DEC.10,1926 DETROIT,MICH.
D.AUG.24,1977 DEARBORN,MICH.
1951 PHI N P 10 1-1
1955 DET A P 20 0-1
BRTR 30 1-2

CRITCHLEY, MORRIS ARTHUR
B.MAR.26,1850 NEW LONDON,CONN.
D.MAR.6,1910 PITTSBURGH,PA.
1882 PIT AA P 4 0-3
STL AA P 5 1-3

CRITZ, HUGH MELVILLE (HUGHIE)
B.SEPT.17,1900 STARKVILLE,MISS.
1924 CIN N 2-S 102 .322
1925 CIN N 2 144 .277
1926 CIN N 2 155 .270
1927 CIN N 2 113 .278
1928 CIN N 2 153 .296
1929 CIN N 2-S 107 .247
1930 CIN N 2 28 .231
1930 NY N 2 124 .265
1931 NY N 2 66 .290
1932 NY N 2 151 .276
1933 NY N 2 133 .246
1934 NY N 2 137 .242
1935 NY N 2 65 .187
BRTR 1478 .268

CROCKER, CLAUDE ARTHUR
B.JULY 20,1924 CAROLEEN,N.C.
1944 BRO N P 2 0-0
1945 BRO N P 1 0-0
BRTR 3 0-0

CROCKETT, DANIEL SOLOMON (DAVEY)
B.OCT.5,1875 ROANOKE,VA.
D.FEB.23,1961 CHARLOTTESVILLE,VA.
1901 DET A 1 28 .291
BLTR

CROFT, ARTHUR F.
B.JAN.23,1855 ST.LOUIS,MO.
D.MAR.16,1884 ST.LOUIS,MO.
1875 RS N A O 19 -
1877 STL N 1-2-O 54 .233
1876 IND N 1-O 57 .162
130 -

CROFT, HENRY T.
B.CHICAGO,ILL.
1899 LOU N O 1 .000
PHI N 2 2 .143
1901 CHI N O 3 .333
6 .250

CROLIUS, FRED JOSEPH
B.DEC.16,1876 JERSEY CITY,N.J.
D.AUG.25,1960 ORMOND BEACH,FLA.
1901 BOS N O 50 .238
1902 PIT N O 9 .263
59 .239

CROMARTIE, WARREN LIVINGSTON
B.SEPT.29,1953 MIAMI BEACH,FLA.
1974 MON N /O 8 .176
1976 MON N O 33 .210
1977 MON N *O 155 .282
1978 MON N *O/1 159 .297
BLTL 355 .283

CROMPTON, EDWARD (NED)
B.FEB.12,1889 LIVERPOOL,ENGLAND
D.SEPT.28,1950 ASPINWALL,PA.
1909 STL A O 17 .157
1910 CIN N O 1 .000
BLTL 18 .154

CROMPTON, HERBERT BRYAN (WORKHORSE)
B.NOV.7,1911 TAYLOR RIDGE,ILL.
D.AUG.5,1963 MOLINE,ILL.
1937 WAS A C 2 .333
1945 NY A C 36 .192
BKTR 38 .196

CRONE, RAYMOND HAYES (RAY)
B.AUG.7,1931 MEMPHIS,TENN.
1954 MIL N P 19 1-0
1955 MIL N P 33 10-9
1956 MIL N P 35 11-10
1957 MIL N P 11 3-1
NY N P 25 4-8
1958 SF N P 14 1-2
BRTR 137 30-30

CRONIN, DANIEL
B.1857 S.BOSTON,MASS.
D.NOV.30,1885 BOSTON,MASS.
1884 CHI U 2 1 .250
STL U O 1 .000
2 .111

CRONIN, JAMES JOHN
B.AUG.7,1905 RICHMOND,CAL.
1929 PHI A 2 25 .232
BBTR

CRONIN, JOHN J. (JACK)
B.MAY 26,1874 W.NEW BRIGHTON,
S.I.,N.Y.
D.JULY 12,1929 MIDDLETOWN,N.Y.
1895 BRO N P 2 0-0
1898 PIT N P 4 2-2
1899 CIN N P 5 2-2
1901 DET A P 31 12-16
1902 DET A P 4 1-0
BAL A P 9 2-5
NY N P-O 13 19 5-6
.167
1903 NY N P 20 6-4
1904 BRO N P 40 11-22
BRTR 128 134 41-57
.181

CRONIN, JOSEPH EDWARD (JOE)
B.OCT.12,1906 SAN FRANCISCO,CAL.
1926 PIT N 2-S 38 .265
1927 PIT N S 12 .227
1928 WAS A S 63 .243
1929 WAS A S 145 .282
1930 WAS A S 154 .346
1931 WAS A S 156 .306
1932 WAS A S 143 .318
1933 WAS A S 152 .309
1934 WAS A M-S 127 .284
1935 WAS A M-S 144 .295
1936 BOS A M-S-3 81 .281
1937 BOS A M-S 148 .307
1938 BOS A M-S 143 .325
1939 BOS A M-S 143 .308
1940 BOS A M-S-3 149 .285
1941 BOS A M-S-3-O 143 .311
1942 BOS A M-1-S-3 45 .304
1943 BOS A M-3 59 .312
1944 BOS A M-1 76 .241
1945 BOS A M-3 3 .375
BRTR 2124 .302
NON-PLAYING MANAGER
WAS[A] 1933-34, BOS[A] 1935-47

CRONIN, WILLIAM PATRICK (CRUNGY)
B.DEC.26,1902 W.NEWTON,MASS.
D.OCT.26,1966 NEWTON,MASS.
1928 BOS N C 3 .000
1929 BOS N C 6 .111
1930 BOS N C 66 .253
1931 BOS N C 51 .206
BRTR 126 .232

CROOKE, THOMAS A.
B.WASHINGTON,D.C.
D.APR.5,1929 QUANTICO,VA.
1909 WAS A 1 3 .286
1910 WAS A 1 8 .182
TR 11 .207

CROOKS, JOHN CHARLES
B.NOV.9,1866 ST.PAUL,MINN.
D.JAN.29,1918 ST.LOUIS,MO.
1889 COL AA 2 12 .323
1890 COL AA 2 135 .221
1891 COL AA 2 138 .240
1892 STL N 2-3 127 .213
1893 STL N 3 128 .251
1895 WAS N 2 118 .291
1896 WAS N 2-3 24 .280
LOU N 2 37 .232
1898 STL N 2 71 .238
790 .244

CROSBY, EDWARD CARLTON (ED)
B.MAY 26,1949 LONG BEACH,CAL.
1970 STL N S/3-2 38 .253
1972 STL N S-2-3 101 .217
1973 STL N /S-2-3 22 .128
CIN N S/2 36 .216
1974 CLE A 3-S/2 37 .209
1975 CLE A S-2-3 61 .234
1976 CLE A /3 2 .500
BLTR 297 .220

CROSBY, GEORGE W.
B.CHICAGO,ILL.
1884 CHI N P 3 1-2

CROSBY, KENNETH STEWART (KEN)
B.DEC.15,1947 NEW DENVER,B.C.,CANADA
1975 CHI N /P 9 1-0
1976 CHI N /P 7 0-0
BRTR 16 1-0

YR	CL	LEA	POS	GP	G	REC

CROSETTI, FRANK PETER JOSEPH (CROW)
B.OCT.4,1910 SAN FRANCISCO,CAL.

YR	CL	LEA	POS	GP	G	REC
1932	NY	A	S-3		116	.241
1933	NY	A	S		136	.253
1934	NY	A	S-3		138	.265
1935	NY	A	S		87	.056
1936	NY	A	S		151	.288
1937	NY	A	S		149	.234
1938	NY	A	S		157	.263
1939	NY	A	S		152	.233
1940	NY	A	S		145	.194
1941	NY	A	S-3		50	.223
1942	NY	A	2-S-3		74	.242
1943	NY	A	S		95	.233
1944	NY	A	S		55	.239
1945	NY	A	S		130	.238
1946	NY	A	S		28	.288
1947	NY	A	2-S		3	.000
1948	NY	A	2-S		17	.286
		BRTR			1683	.245

CROSS, AMOS C.
B.1861 CZECHOSLOVAKIA
D.JULY 16,1888 CLEVELAND,OHIO

1885	LOU	AA	C		35	.295
1886	LOU	AA	C-1		74	.276
1887	LOU	AA	C		9	.297
					118	.280

CROSS, CLARENCE
[REAL NAME CLARENCE CRAUSE]
B.MAR.4,1856 ST.LOUIS,MO.
D.JUNE 23,1931 SEATTLE,WASH.

1884	ALT	U	3		2	.572
	KEY	U	S		2	.143
	KC	U	S		25	.212
1887	MET	AA	S		16	.245
					45	.222

CROSS, FRANK ATWELL (MICKEY)
B.JAN.20,1873 CLEVELAND,OHIO
D.NOV.2,1932 GEAUGA LAKE,OHIO

| 1901 | CLE | A | O | | 1 | .600 |
| | | TR | | | | |

CROSS, GEORGE LEWIS (LEM)
B.JAN.9,1872 MANCHESTER,N.H.
D.OCT.9,1930 MANCHESTER,N.H.

1893	CIN	N	P		2	0- 2
1894	CIN	N	P		9	2- 4
					11	2- 6

CROSS, JOFFRE JAMES (JEFF)
B.AUG.28,1918 TULSA,OKLA.

1942	STL	N	S		1	.250
1946	STL	N	2-S-3		49	.217
1947	STL	N	2-S-3		51	.102
1948	STL	N	H		2	.000
	CHI	N	2-S		16	.100
		BRTR			119	.162

CROSS, LAFAYETTE NAPOLEON (LAVE)
B.MAY 12,1866 MILWAUKEE,WIS.
D.SEPT.6,1927 TOLEDO,OHIO

1887	LOU	AA	C		54	.327
1888	LOU	AA	C		47	.213
1889	ATH	AA	C		55	.226
1890	PHI	P	C		60	.299
1891	ATH	AA	C-3-O		109	.302
1892	PHI	N	C-3-O		134	.262
1893	PHI	N	C-3		94	.302
1894	PHI	N	3		120	.388
1895	PHI	N	3		124	.277
1896	PHI	N	S-3		106	.261
1897	PHI	N	2-3		88	.261
1898	STL	N	3		151	.319
1899	CLE	N	M-3		38	.263
	STL	N	3		103	.304
1900	STL	N	3		16	.300
	BRO	N	3		117	.292
1901	PHI	A	3		100	.331
1902	PHI	A	3		137	.339
1903	PHI	A	3		137	.292
1904	PHI	A	3		155	.290
1905	PHI	A	3		146	.266
1906	WAS	A	3		130	.263
1907	WAS	A	3		41	.199
		BRTR			2262	.293

CROSS, MONTFORD MONTGOMERY (MONTE)
B.AUG.31,1869 PHILADELPHIA,PA.
D.JUNE 21,1934 PHILADELPHIA,PA.

1892	BAL	N	S		15	.160
1894	PIT	N	S		13	.404
1895	PIT	N	S		108	.255
1896	STL	N	S		124	.264
1897	STL	N	S		130	.288
1898	PHI	N	S		149	.259
1899	PHI	N	S		153	.259
1900	PHI	N	S		130	.200
1901	PHI	N	S		139	.197
1902	PHI	N	S		137	.207
1903	PHI	N	S		138	.245
1904	PHI	A	S		153	.182
1905	PHI	A	S		78	.270
1906	PHI	A	S		134	.200
1907	PHI	A	S		77	.206
		BRTR			1678	.233

CROSSIN, FRANK PATRICK
B.JUNE 15,1891 AVONDALE,PA.
D.DEC.6,1965 KINGSTON,PA.

1912	STL	A	C		7	.277
1913	STL	A	C		3	.333
1914	STL	A	C		43	.122
		BRTR			53	.147

CROTHERS, DOUGLAS
B.ST.LOUIS,MO.

1884	KC	U	P	3	4	1- 2
1885	MET	AA	P	21	18	7-11
					22	8-13

CROTTY, JOSEPH
B.CINCINNATI,OHIO

1862	LOU	AA	C		5	.100
	STL	AA	C-O		8	.133
1884	CIN	U	C		20	.287
1885	LOU	AA	C		39	.172
1886	MET	AA	C		12	.205
		BR			84	.199

CROUCH, JACK ALBERT (ROXY)
B.JUNE 12,1903 SALISBURY,N.C.
D.AUG.25,1972 LEESBURG,FLA.

1930	STL	A	C		6	.143
1931	STL	A	C		8	.000
1933	STL	A	C		19	.167
	CIN	N	C		10	.125
		BRTR			43	.125

CROUCH, WILLIAM ELMER
B.AUG.20,1910 WILMINGTON,DEL.

1939	BRO	N	P		6	4- 0
1941	PHI	N	P		20	2- 3
	STL	N	P		18	1- 2
1945	STL	N	P		6	1- 0
		BBTR			50	8- 5

CROUCH, WILLIAM HENRY (SKIP)
B.DEC.3,1886 MARSHALLTON,DEL.
D.DEC.22,1945 HIGHLAND PARK,MICH.

| 1910 | STL | A | P | | 1 | 0- 0 |
| | | BLTL | | | | |

CROUCHER, FRANK DONALD (DINGLE)
B.JULY 23,1914 SAN ANTONIO,TEX.

1939	DET	A	S		97	.269
1940	DET	A	2-S-3		37	.105
1941	DET	A	S		136	.254
1942	WAS	A	2		26	.277
		BRTR			296	.251

CROUSE, CLYDE ELSWORTH (BUCK)
B.JAN.6,1897 ANDERSON,IND.

1923	CHI	A	C		23	.257
1924	CHI	A	C		94	.259
1925	CHI	A	C		54	.352
1926	CHI	A	C		49	.237
1927	CHI	A	C		85	.239
1928	CHI	A	C		78	.252
1929	CHI	A	C		45	.272
1930	CHI	A	C		42	.254
		BLTR			470	.262

CROWDER, ALVIN FLOYD (GENERAL)
B.JAN.11,1899 WINSTON-SALEM,N.C
D.APR.3,1972 WINSTON-SALEM,N.C.

1926	WAS	A	P		19	7- 4
1927	WAS	A	P		15	4- 7
	STL	A	P		21	3- 5
1928	STL	A	P		41	21- 5
1929	STL	A	P		40	17-15
1930	STL	A	P		13	3- 7
	WAS	A	P		27	15- 9
1931	WAS	A	P		44	18-11
1932	WAS	A	P	50	51	26-13
1933	WAS	A	P		52	24-15
1934	WAS	A	P		29	4-10
	DET	A	P		9	5- 1
1935	DET	A	P		33	16-10
1936	DET	A	P		9	4- 3
		BLTR		402	403	167-115

CROWE, GEORGE DANIEL (BIG GEORGE)
B.MAR.22,1923 WHITELAND,IND.

1952	BOS	N	1		73	.258
1953	MIL	N	1		47	.286
1955	MIL	N	1		104	.281
1956	CIN	N	1		77	.290
1957	CIN	N	1		133	.271
1958	CIN	N	1-2		111	.275
1959	STL	N	1		77	.301
1960	STL	N	1		73	.236
1961	STL	N	H		7	.143
		BLTL			702	.270

CROWELL, MINOT JOY (CAP)
B.SEPT.5,1892 ROXBURY,MASS.
D.SEPT.30,1962 CENTRAL FALLS,R.I.

1915	PHI	A	P		10	2- 6
1916	PHI	A	P		9	0- 5
		BRTR			19	2-11

CROWELL, WILLIAM THEODORE (BILLY)
B.NOV.6,1865 CINCINNATI,OHIO
D.JULY 24,1935 FT.WORTH,TEX.

1887	CLE	AA	P		45	13-32
1888	CLE	AA	P		18	0-12
1888	CLE	AA	P		7	5- 2
		BRTR			70	18-46

CROWLEY, EDGAR JEWEL
B.AUG.20,1906 WATKINSVILLE,GA.
D.APR.14,1970 BIRMINGHAM,ALA.

| 1928 | WAS | A | 3 | | 2 | .000 |
| | | BRTR | | | | |

CROWLEY, JOHN A.
B.JAN.12,1862 LAWRENCE,MASS.
D.SEPT.23,1896 LAWRENCE,MASS.

| 1884 | PHI | N | C | | 44 | .244 |

CROWLEY, TERRENCE MICHAEL (TERRY)
B.FEB.16,1947 STATEN ISLAND,N.Y.

1969	BAL	A	/1-O		7	.333
1970	BAL	A	/1		83	.257
1971	BAL	A	/O-1		18	.174
1972	BAL	A	O-1		97	.231
1973	BAL	A	D-O/1		54	.206
1974	CIN	N	O/1		84	.240
1975	CIN	N	/1-O		66	.288
1976	ATL	N	/H		7	.000
	BAL	A	D/1		33	.246
1977	BAL	A	/1		18	.364
1978	BAL	A	D/O-1		62	.253
		BLTL			529	.241

CROWLEY, WILLIAM MICHAEL
B.APR.8,1857 PHILADELPHIA,PA.
D.JULY 14,1891 GLOUCESTER,MASS.

1875	PHI	NA	1-2-3-O		9	-
1877	LOU	N	C-2-S-3-O		61	.281
1879	BUF	N	C-O		59	.282
1880	BUF	N	C-O		82	.261
1881	BOS	N	O		71	.254
1883	ATH	AA	1-O		24	.265
	CLE	N	O		11	.317
1884	BOS	N	O		103	.265
1885	BUF	N	O		92	.241
		BRTR			512	-

CROWSON, THOMAS WOODROW (WOODY)
B.SEPT.9,1918 FUQUAY SPRGS.,N.C
D.AUG.14,1947 MAYODAN,N.C.

| 1945 | PHI | A | P | | 1 | 0- 0 |

CRUISE, WALTON EDWIN
B.MAY 6,1890 CHILDERSBURG,ALA.
D.JAN.9,1975 SYLACAUGA,ALA.

1914	STL	N	O		95	.227
1916	STL	N	O		3	.667
1917	STL	N	O		153	.295
1918	STL	N	O		70	.271
1919	STL	N	1-O		9	.095
	BOS	N	O		73	.216
1920	BOS	N	O		91	.278
1921	BOS	N	O		108	.346
1922	BOS	N	1-O		104	.276
1923	BOS	N	O		21	.211
1924	BOS	N	O		9	.444
		BLTR			736	.277

CRUM, CALVIN N.
B.JULY 27,1890 COOKS MILLS,ILL.
D.DEC.7,1945 TULSA,OKLA.

1917	BOS	N	P		1	0- 0
1918	BOS	N	P		1	0- 1
		BRTR			2	0- 1

CRUMLING, EUGENE LEON
B.APR.5,1922 WRIGHTSVILLE,PA.

| 1945 | STL | N | C | | 6 | .083 |

CRUMP, ARTHUR ELLIOTT (BUDDY)
B.NOV.29,1901 NORFOLK,VA.
D.SEPT.7,1976 RALEIGH,N.C.

| 1924 | NY | N | O | | 1 | .000 |
| | | BLTL | | | | |

CRUMPLER, ROY MAXTON
B.JULY 8,1896 CLINTON,N.C.

1920	DET	A	P		4	1- 0
1925	PHI	N	P		3	0- 0
		BLTL			7	1- 0

CRUTCHER, RICHARD LOUIS
B.NOV.25,1889 FRANKFORT,KY.
D.JUNE 19,1952 FRANKFORT,KY.

1914	BOS	N	P		33	5- 6
1915	BOS	N	P		14	2- 2
		BRTR			47	7- 8

CRUTHERS, CHARLES PRESTON (PRESS)
B.SEPT.8,1890 MARSHALLTON,DEL.

1913	PHI	A	2		5	.235
1914	PHI	A	2		4	.200
		BRTR			9	.219

YR	CL LEA POS	GP	G	REC

CRUZ, CIRILO [DILAN] (TOMMY)
B.FEB.15,1951 ARROYO,P.R.
```
1973 STL N /O              3   .000
1977 CHI A /O              4   .000
        BLTL               7   .000
```

CRUZ, HECTOR LOUIS [DILAN] (HEITY)
B.APR.2,1953 ARROYO,P.R.
```
1973 STL N /O             11   .000
1975 STL N  3/O           23   .146
1976 STL N *3            151   .228
1977 STL N *O/3          118   .236
1978 CHI N  O/3           30   .237
     SF   N  O-3          79   .223
        BRTR             412   .225
```

CRUZ, HENRY [ACOSTA]
B.FEB.27,1952 CHRISTIANSTED,V.I.
```
1975 LA  N  O             53   .266
1976 LA  N  O             49   .182
1977 CHI A /O             16   .286
1978 CHI A  O             53   .221
        BLTL             171   .229
```

CRUZ, JOSE [DILAN]
B.AUG.8,1947 ARROYO,P.R.
```
1970 STL N /O              6   .353
1971 STL N  O             83   .274
1972 STL N *O            117   .235
1973 STL N *O            132   .227
1974 STL N  O/1          107   .261
1975 HOU N  O            120   .257
1976 HOU N *O            133   .303
1977 HOU N *O            157   .299
1978 HOU N *O/1          153   .315
        BLTL            1008   .278
```

CRUZ, JULIO LOUIS
B.DEC.2,1954 BROOKLYN,N.Y.
```
1977 SEA A  2             60   .256
1978 SEA A *2/S          147   .235
        BBTR             207   .240
```

CRUZ, TODD RUBEN
B.NOV.23,1955 HIGHLAND PARK,MICH
```
1978 PHI N /S              3   .500
        BRTR
```

CRUZ, VICTOR MANUEL
B.DEC.24,1957 RANCHO VIEJO
LA VEGA,D.R.
```
1978 TOR A  P             32   7- 3
        BRTR
```

CUBBAGE, MICHAEL LEE (MIKE)
B.JUL.21,1950 CHARLOTTESVILLE,VA
```
1974 TEX A /3-2            9   .000
1975 TEX A  2/3           58   .224
1976 TEX A /2-3           14   .219
     MIN A  3/2          104   .260
1977 MIN A *3            129   .264
1978 MIN A *3/2          125   .282
        BLTR             439   .260
```

CUCCINELLO, ALFRED EDWARD
B.NOV.26,1914 LONG ISLAND CITY,N.Y.
```
1935 NY  N  3             54   .248
        BRTR
```

CUCCINELLO, ANTHONY FRANCIS
(TONY), (COOCH) OR (CHICK)
B.NOV.8,1907 LONG ISLAND CITY,N.Y.
```
1930 CIN N  2-S-3        123   .312
1931 CIN N  2            154   .315
1932 BRO N  2            154   .281
1933 BRO N  2-3          134   .252
1934 BRO N  2-3          140   .261
1935 BRO N  2-3          102   .292
1936 BOS N  2            150   .308
1937 BOS N  2            152   .271
1938 BOS N  2            147   .265
1939 BOS N  2             81   .306
1940 BOS N  3             34   .270
     NY   N  2-3          88   .208
1942 BOS N  2-3           40   .202
1943 BOS N  2-S-3         13   .000
     CHI A  3             34   .272
1944 CHI A  2-3           38   .262
1945 CHI A  3            118   .308
        BRTR            1704   .280
```

CUCCURULLO, ARTHUR JOSEPH (COOKIE)
B.FEB.8,1918 ASBURY PARK,N.J.
```
1943 PIT N  P              1   0- 1
1944 PIT N  P         32  36   2- 1
1945 PIT N  P             29   1- 3
        BLTL          62  66   3- 5
```

CUDWORTH, JAMES ALARIC (CUDDY)
B.AUG.22,1858 FAIRHAVEN,MASS.
D.DEC.21,1943 MIDDLEBORO,MASS.
```
1884 KC  U  P-1        1  29   0- 0
        O                      .134
        BRTR
```

CUELLAR, JESUS PATRACIS (CHARLIE)
B.SEPT.24,1917 YBOR CITY,FLA.
```
1950 CHI A  P              2   0- 0
```

CUELLAR, MIGUEL ANGEL [SANTANA]
(MIKE)
B.MAY 8,1937 LAS VILLAS,CUBA
```
1959 CIN N  P              2   0- 0
1964 STL N  P             32   5- 5
1965 HOU N  P             25   1- 4
1966 HOU N  P             38  12-10
1967 HOU N  P         36  38  16-11
1968 HOU N  P             28   8-11
1969 BAL A  P             39  23-11
1970 BAL A  P         40  41  24- 8
1971 BAL A  P             38  20- 9
1972 BAL A  P             35  18-12
1973 BAL A  P             38  18-13
1974 BAL A  P             38  22-10
1975 BAL A  P             36  14-12
1976 BAL A  P             26   4-13
1977 CAL A /P              2   0- 1
        BLTL        453 456 185-130
```

CUELLAR, ROBERT (BOBBY)
B.AUG.20,1952 ALICE,TEX.
```
1977 TEX A /P              4   0- 0
        BRTR
```

CUETO, DAGOBERTO [CONCEPCION]
B.AUG.14,1937 SAN LUIS,PINAR,CUBA
```
1961 MIN A  P              7   1- 3
        BRTR
```

CUETO, MANUEL (POTATO)
B.FEB.8,1892 GUANAJAY,CUBA
D.JUNE 29,1942 REGLA,HAVANA,CUBA
```
1914 STL F  S-3           15   .100
1917 CIN N  C-2-O         56   .200
1918 CIN N  C-2-S-O       47   .296
1919 CIN N  3-O           29   .250
        BRTR             147   .229
```

CUFF, JOHN J.
B.JERSEY CITY,N.J.
```
1884 BAL U  C              3   .083
```

CULBERSON, DELBERT LEON
(LEON) OR (LEE)
B.AUG.6,1919 HALL S STATION,GA.
```
1943 BOS A  O             80   .272
1944 BOS A  O             75   .238
1945 BOS A  O             97   .275
1946 BOS A  3-O           59   .313
1947 BOS A  3-O           47   .238
1948 WAS A  O             12   .172
        BRTR             370   .266
```

CULLEN, JOHN J.
B.MARYSVILLE,CAL.
```
1884 WIL U  S-O            9   .194
```

CULLEN, JOHN PATRICK (JACK)
B.OCT.6,1939 NEWARK,N.J.
```
1962 NY  A  P              2   0- 0
1965 NY  A  P             12   3- 4
1966 NY  A /P              5   1- 0
        BRTR              19   4- 4
```

CULLEN, TIMOTHY LEO (TIM)
B.FEB.16,1942 SAN FRANCISCO,CAL.
```
1966 WAS A /3-2           18   .235
1967 WAS A  S-2-3/O      124   .236
1968 CHI A  2             72   .200
     WAS A  S-2/3         47   .272
1969 WAS A *2/S-3        119   .209
1970 WAS A *2/S          123   .214
1971 WAS A  2-S          129   .191
1972 OAK A  2/3-S         72   .261
        BRTR             700   .220
```

CULLENBINE, ROY JOSEPH
B.OCT.18,1915 NASHVILLE,TENN.
```
1938 DET A  O             25   .284
1939 DET A  O             75   .240
1940 BRO N  O             22   .180
     STL A  1-O           86   .230
1941 STL A  1-O          149   .317
1942 STL A  O             38   .193
     WAS A  O             64   .286
     NY   A  1-O          21   .364
1943 CLE A  1-O          138   .289
1944 CLE A  O            154   .284
1945 CLE A  3-O            8   .077
     DET A  O            146   .277
1946 DET A  1-O          113   .335
1947 DET A  1            142   .224
        BBTR            1181   .276
```

CULLER, RICHARD BROADUS (DICK)
B.JAN.15,1915 HIGH POINT,N.C.
D.JUNE 16,1964 CHAPEL HILL,N.C.
```
1936 PHI A  2-S            9   .237
1943 CHI A  2-S-3         53   .216
1944 BOS N  S              8   .071
1945 BOS N  S-3          136   .262
1946 BOS N  S            134   .255
1947 BOS N  S             77   .248
1948 CHI N  2-S           48   .169
1949 NY  N  S              7   .000
        BRTR             472   .244
```

CULLOP, HENRY NICHOLAS
(NICK) OR (TOMATO FACE)
B.OCT.16,1900 ST.LOUIS,MO.
D.DEC.1,1978 GAHANNA,OHIO
```
1926 NY  A  O              2   .500
1927 WAS A  O             15   .217
     CLE A  P-O        1  32   0- 0
                              .235
1929 BRO N  O             13   .195
1930 CIN N  O              7   .182
1931 CIN N  O            104   .263
        BRTR           1 173   0- 0
                              .249
```

CULLOP, NORMAN ANDREW (NICK)
B.SEPT.17,1887 CHILHOWIE,VA.
D.APR.15,1961 TAZEWELL,VA.
```
1913 CLE A  P             23   3- 7
1914 CLE A  P              1   0- 1
     KC   F  P            44  14-19
1915 KC   F  P            44  22-11
1916 NY  A  P             27  13- 6
1917 NY  A  P             30   5- 9
1921 STL A  P              4   0- 2
        BLTL             173  57-55
```

CULLOTON, BERNARD ALOYSIUS (BUD)
B.MAY 19,1896 KINGSTON,N.Y.
D.NOV.9,1976 KINGSTON,N.Y.
```
1925 PIT N  P              9   0- 1
1926 PIT N  P              4   0- 0
        BRTR              13   0- 1
```

CULP, BENJAMIN BALDY
B.JAN.19,1914 PHILADELPHIA,PA.
```
1942 PHI N  C              1   .000
1943 PHI N  C             10   .208
1944 PHI N  C              4   .000
        BRTR              15   .192
```

CULP, RAYMOND LEONARD (RAY)
B.AUG.6,1941 ELGIN,TEX.
```
1963 PHI N  P             34  14-11
1964 PHI N  P             30   8- 7
1965 PHI N  P             33  14-10
1966 PHI N  P             34   7- 4
1967 CHI N  P             30   8-11
1968 BOS A  P             35  16- 6
1969 BOS A  P             32  17- 8
1970 BOS A  P             33  17-14
1971 BOS A  P             35  14-16
1972 BOS A  P             16   5- 8
1973 BOS A  P             10   2- 6
        BRTR            322 122-101
```

CULP, WILLIAM EDWARD
B.JUNE 11,1887 BELLAIRE,OHIO
D.SEPT.3,1969 ARNOLD,PA.
```
1910 PHI N  P              4   0- 0
        BBTR
```

CULVER, GEORGE RAYMOND
B.JULY 8,1943 SALINAS,CAL.
```
1966 CLE A /P              5   0- 2
1967 CLE A  P             53   7- 3
1968 CIN N  P         42  49  11-16
1969 CIN N  P             32   5- 7
1970 STL N  P             11   3- 3
     HOU N  P             32   3- 3
1971 HOU N  P             59   5- 8
1972 HOU N  P             45   6- 2
1973 LA  N  P             28   4- 4
     PHI N  P             14   3- 1
1974 PHI N  P             14   1- 0
        BRTR          335 342 48-49
```

CUMBERLAND, JOHN SHELDON
B.MAY 10,1947 WESTBROOK,ME.
```
1968 NY  A /P              1   0- 0
1969 NY  A /P              2   0- 0
1970 NY  A  P             15   3- 4
     SF   N /P              7   2- 0
1971 SF   N  P             45   9- 6
1972 SF   N /P              9   0- 4
     STL N  P             14   1- 1
1974 CAL A  P             17   0- 1
        BRTL             110  15-16
```

CUMMINGS, JOHN WILLIAM (JACK)
B.APR.1,1904 PITTSBURGH,PA.
D.OCT.5,1962 W.MIFFLIN,PA.
```
1926 NY  N  C             27   .313
1927 NY  N  C             43   .363
1928 NY  N  C             33   .333
1929 NY  N  H              3   .333
     BOS N  H              3   .167
        BRTR              89   .338
```

YR	CL	LEA	POS	GP	G	REC

CUMMINGS, WILLIAM ARTHUR (CANDY)
B.OCT.18,1948 WARE,MASS.
D.MAY 16,1924 TOLEDO,OHIO

1872	MUT	NA	P	54	55	33-21
1873	BAL	NA	P-3		42	27-14
						-
1874	PHI	NA	P		54	28-26
1875	HAR	NA	P-O	47	52	35-12
1876	HAR	N	P		24	15- 8
1877	CIN	N	P-O		19	5-14
						.200
		BRTR		240	246	143-95
						-

CUNNINGHAM, BRUCE LEE
B.SEPT.29,1905 SAN FRANCISCO,CAL.

1929	BOS	N	P	17	19	4- 6
1930	BOS	N	P	36	37	5- 6
1931	BOS	N	P	33	34	3-12
1932	BOS	N	P		18	1- 0
		BRTR		104	108	13-24

CUNNINGHAM, ELLSWORTH ELMER (BERT)
B.NOV.25,1866 WILMINGTON,DEL.
D.MAY 14,1952 CRAGMERE,DEL.

1887	BRO	AA	P		3	0- 2
1888	BAL	AA	P	51	22-29
1889	BAL	AA	P	37	40	15-19
1890	PHI	P	P		15	3-10
	BUF	P	P		29	10-15
1891	BAL	AA	P		31	11-14
1895	LOU	N	P	28	31	11-16
1896	LOU	N	P	23	24	7-14
1897	LOU	N	P		30	15-14
1898	LOU	N	P		43	28-15
1899	LOU	N	P	37	43	18-16
1900	CHI	N	P		8	5- 3
1901	CHI	N	P		1	0- 1
		BRTR		336	349	145-168

CUNNINGHAM, GEORGE HAROLD
B.JULY 13,1894 STURGEON LAKE,MINN.
D.MAR.10,1972 CHATTANOOGA,TENN.

1916	DET	A	P		35	7-10
1917	DET	A	P		44	2- 7
1918	DET	A	P-O	27	56	6- 7
						.223
1919	DET	A	P	17	26	1- 1
1921	DET	A	P		1	.000
		BRTR		123	162	16-25
						.224

CUNNINGHAM, JOSEPH ROBERT (JOE)
B.AUG.27,1931 PATERSON,N.J.

1954	STL	N	1	85	.284
1956	STL	N	1	4	.000
1957	STL	N	1-O	122	.318
1958	STL	N	1-O	131	.312
1959	STL	N	1-O	144	.345
1960	STL	N	1-O	139	.280
1961	STL	N	1-O	113	.286
1962	CHI	A	1-O	149	.295
1963	CHI	A	1	67	.286
1964	CHI	A	1	40	.250
	WAS	A	1	49	.214
1965	WAS	A	1	95	.229
1966	WAS	A	/1	3	.125
		BLTL		1141	.291

CUNNINGHAM, RAYMOND LEE
B.JAN.17,1908 MESQUITE,TEX.

1931	STL	N	3	3	.000
1932	STL	N	2-3	11	.182
		BRTR		14	.154

CUNNINGHAM, RUDOLPH (MIKE)
B.KERSHAW,S.C.

| 1906 | PHI | A | P | 6 | 0- 0 |
| | | TR | | | |

CUNNINGHAM WILLIAM ALOYSIUS
B.JUL.30,1895 SAN FRANCISCO,CAL
D.SEPT.26,1953 COLUSA,CAL.

1921	NY	N	O	40	.276
1922	NY	N	3-O	85	.327
1923	NY	N	2-O	79	.271
1924	BOS	N	O	114	.272
		BRTR		318	.286

CUNNINGHAM, WILLIAM JAMES
B.JUNE 9,1888 SCHENECTADY,N.Y.
D.FEB.21,1946 SCHENECTADY,N.Y.

1910	WAS	A	2	22	.297
1911	WAS	A	2	94	.190
1912	WAS	A	2	8	.185
		BRTR		124	.208

CUPPY, GEORGE JOSEPH (NIG)
(REAL NAME GEORGE KOPPE)
B.JULY 3,1869 LOGANSPORT,IND.
D.JULY 27,1922 ELKHART,IND.

1892	CLE	N	P		43	27-16
1893	CLE	N	P		28	17-11
1894	CLE	N	P	40	41	21-16
1895	CLE	N	P		42	26-16
1896	CLE	N	P	40	41	25-15
1897	CLE	N	P		17	10- 6
1898	CLE	N	P		16	9- 7
1899	STL	N	P		21	10- 8
1900	BOS	N	P		17	8- 4
1901	BOS	A	P		17	4- 6
		TR		281	283	157-105

CURLEY, WALTER JAMES (DOC)
B.MAR.12,1874 UPTON,MASS.
D.SEPT.23,1920 FRAMINGHAM,MASS.

| 1899 | CHI | N | 2 | 10 | .105 |
| | | BRTR | | | |

CURRAN, SIMON FRANCIS (SAMMY)
B.OCT.30,1874 DORCHESTER,MASS.
D.MAY 19,1936 DORCHESTER,MASS.

| 1902 | BOS | N | P | 1 | 0- 0 |

CURREN, PETER
B.BALTIMORE,MD.

| 1876 | ATH | N | C-O | 3 | .333 |

CURRENCE, DELANCY LAFAYETTE
(LAFAYETTE)
B.DEC.3,1951 ROCK HILL,S.C.

| 1975 | MIL | A | /P | 8 | 0- 2 |
| | | BBTL | | | |

CURRIE, CLARENCE F.
B.DEC.30,1878 GLENCOE,ONT.,CAN.
D.JULY 15,1941 LITTLE CHUTE,WIS.

1902	CIN	N	P	10	3- 4
	STL	N	P	13	7- 5
1903	BRO	N	P	22	4-12
	CHI	N	P	6	1- 2
		BRTR		51	15-23

CURRIE, MURPHY ARCHIBALD
B.AUG.31,1893 FAYETTEVILLE,N.C.
D.JUNE 22,1939 ASHEBORO,N.C.

| 1916 | STL | N | P | 6 | 0- 0 |
| | | BRTR | | | |

CURRIE, WILLIAM CLEVELAND
B.NOV.29,1928 LEARY,GA.

| 1955 | WAS | A | P | 3 | 0- 0 |
| | | BRTR | | | |

CURRIN, PERRY GILMORE
B.SEPT.27,1928 WASHINGTON,D.C.

| 1947 | STL | A | S | 3 | .000 |
| | | BLTR | | | |

CURRY, GEORGE ANTHONY (TONY)
B.DEC.22,1938 NASSAU,BAHAMAS

1960	PHI	N	O	95	.261
1961	PHI	N	O	15	.194
1966	CLE	A	H	19	.125
		BLTL		129	.246

CURRY, GEORGE JAMES (SOLDIER BOY)
B.DEC.21,1888 BRIDGEPORT,CONN.
D.OCT.5,1963 STRATFORD,CONN.

| 1911 | STL | A | P | 3 | 0- 3 |
| | | BRTR | | | |

CURRY, JAMES E.
B.MAR.10,1893 CAMDEN,N.J.
D.AUG.2,1938 LAKELAND,N.J.

1909	PHI	A	2	1	.250
1911	NY	A	2	4	.182
1918	DET	A	2	5	.250
		BRTR		10	.229

CURRY, WESLEY
B.APR.1,1860 WILMINGTON,DEL.
D.MAY 19,1933 PHILADELPHIA,PA.

| 1884 | RIC | AA | P | 2 | 0- 2 |

CURTIS, CLIFTON GARFIELD
B.JULY 3,1883 DELAWARE,OHIO
D.APR.23,1943 NEWARK,OHIO

1909	BOS	N	P	10	4- 5
1910	BOS	N	P	43	6-24
1911	BOS	N	P	12	1- 8
	CHI	N	P	4	0- 2
	PHI	N	P	8	1- 1
1912	PHI	N	P	10	2- 5
	BRO	N	P	19	4- 7
1913	BRO	N	P	30	8- 9
		BRTR		136	28-61

CURTIS, EDWIN R.
NON-PLAYING MANAGER ALT(U) 1884

CURTIS, EUGENE HOLMES (EUDE)
B.MAY 5,1863 BETHANY,W.VA.
D.JAN.1,1919 STEUBENVILLE,OHIO

| 1903 | PIT | N | P | 5 | .421 |
| | | BRTR | | | |

CURTIS, FREDERICK MARION
B.OCT.30,1880 BEAVER LAKE,MICH.
D.APR.5,1939 MINNEAPOLIS,MINN.

| 1905 | NY | A | 1 | 2 | .222 |
| | | BRTR | | | |

CURTIS, HARRY ALBERT
B.FEB.19,1883 PORTLAND,MAINE
D.AUG.1,1951 CHICAGO,ILL.

| 1907 | NY | N | C | 6 | .222 |
| | | TR | | | |

CURTIS, JACK PATRICK
B.JAN.11,1937 RHODHISS,N.C.

1961	CHI	N	P	31	10-13
1962	CHI	N	P	4	0- 2
	MIL	N	P	30	4- 4
1963	CLE	A	P	4	0- 0
		BLTL		69	14-19

CURTIS, JOHN DUFFIELD (JACK)
B.MAR.9,1948 NEWTON,MASS.

1970	BOS	A	/P	1	0- 0
1971	BOS	A	/P	5	2- 2
1972	BOS	A	P	26	27	11- 8
1973	BOS	A	P		35	13-13
1974	STL	N	P	33	34	10-14
1975	STL	N	P		39	8- 9
1976	STL	N	P	37	38	6-11
1977	SF	N	P	43	44	3- 3
1978	SF	N	P		46	4- 3
		BLTL		265	269	57-63

CURTIS, VERNON EUGENE (TURK)
B.MAY 24,1920 CAIRO,ILL.

1943	WAS	A	P	2	0- 0
1944	WAS	A	P	3	0- 1
1946	WAS	A	P	11	0- 0
		BRTR		16	0- 1

CURTISS, IRVIN DUANE (TACKS)
B.DEC.27,1861 COLDWATER,MICH.
D.FEB.14,1945 NORTH ADAMS,MASS.

1891	CIN	N	O	27	.266
	WAS	AA	O	29	.252
	BL			56	.257

CURTWRIGHT, GUY PAXTON
B.OCT.18,1912 HOLLIDAY,MO.

1943	CHI	A	O	138	.291
1944	CHI	A	O	72	.253
1945	CHI	A	O	98	.281
1946	CHI	A	O	23	.200
		BRTR		331	.276

CUSHMAN, CHARLES H.
B.MAY 25,1850 NEW YORK,N.Y.
D.JUNE 29,1909 MILWAUKEE,WIS.
NON-PLAYING MANAGER MIL(AA)1891

CUSHMAN, EDGAR LEANDER
B.MAR.27,1852 EAGLESVILLE,OHIO
D.SEPT.26,1915 ERIE,PA.

1883	BUF	N	P-O	7	4- 3
						.200
1884	MIL	U	P	4	4- 0
1885	ATH	AA	P	10	3- 7
	MET	AA	P	22	8-14
1886	MET	AA	P	38	17-21
1887	MET	AA	P	26	11-14
1890	TOL	AA	P	39	17-20
		BRTL		146	64-79
						.177

CUSHMAN, HARVEY BARNES
B.JULY 10,1877 ROCKLAND,ME.
D.DEC.27,1920 EMSWORTH,PA.

| 1902 | PIT | N | P | 4 | 0- 4 |

CUSICK, ANTHONY DANIEL (ANDY)
B.1860 FALL RIVER,MASS.

1884	WIL	U	C-2-S-3-O	11	.147
	PHI	N	C	9	.143
1885	PHI	N	C-O	39	.177
1886	PHI	N	C	27	.221
1887	PHI	N	C	7	.358
				93	.196

CUSICK, JOHN PETER (JACK)
B.JUNE 12,1928 WEEHAWKEN,N.J.

1951	CHI	N	S	65	.177
1952	BOS	N	S-3	49	.167
		BRTR		114	.174

CUTHBERT, EDGAR EDWARD (NED)
B.JUNE 20,1845 PHILADELPHIA,PA.
D.FEB.6,1905 ST.LOUIS,MO.

1871	ATH	NA	C-O	28	.276
1872	ATH	NA	O	46	.328
1873	PHI	NA	O	50	-
1874	CHI	NA	C-O	58	-
1875	STL	NA	C-O	65	.266
1876	STL	N	O	62	.242
1877	CIN	N	O	12	.175
1882	STL	AA	M-O	60	.219
1883	STL	AA	1-O	21	.158
1884	BAL	U	O	42	.193
		BRTR		444	-

```
YR  CL LEA POS    GP    G   REC
```

CUTSHAW, GEORGE WILLIAM
(GEORGE) OR (CLANCY)
B.JULY 27,1887 WILMINGTON,ILL.
D.AUG.22,1973 SAN DIEGO,CAL.
```
1912 BRO N 2          102  .280
1913 BRO N 2          147  .267
1914 BRO N 2          153  .257
1915 BRO N 2          154  .246
1916 BRO N 2          154  .260
1917 BRO N 2          135  .259
1918 PIT N 2          126  .285
1919 PIT N 2          139  .242
1920 PIT N 2          131  .252
1921 PIT N 2           98  .340
1922 DET A 2          132  .267
1923 DET A 2           45  .223
        BRTR         1516  .265
```

CUYLER, HAZEN SHIRLEY (KIKI)
B.AUG.30,1899 HARRISVILLE,MICH.
D.FEB.11,1950 ANN ARBOR,MICH.
```
1921 PIT N O            1  .000
1922 PIT N H            1  .000
1923 PIT N O           11  .250
1924 PIT N O          117  .354
1925 PIT N O          153  .357
1926 PIT N O          157  .321
1927 PIT N O           85  .309
1928 CHI N O          133  .285
1929 CHI N O          139  .360
1930 CHI N O          156  .355
1931 CHI N O          154  .330
1932 CHI N O          110  .291
1933 CHI N O           70  .317
1934 CHI N O          142  .338
1935 CHI N O           45  .274
     CIN N O           62  .251
1936 CIN N O          144  .326
1937 CIN N O          117  .271
1938 BRO N O           82  .273
        BRTR         1879  .321
```

CVENGROS, MICHAEL JOHN
B.DEC.1,1901 PANA,ILL.
D.AUG.22,1970 HOT SPRINGS,ARK.
```
1922 NY  N P            1  0- 1
1923 CHI A P           41  12-13
1924 CHI A P           26  3-12
1925 CHI A P           22  3- 9
1927 PIT N P           23  2- 1
1929 CHI N P       32  33  5- 4
        BLTL     145 146  25-40
```

CYPERT, ALFRED BOYD (CY)
B.AUG.8,1889 LITTLE ROCK,ARK.
D.JAN.9,1973 WASHINGTON,D.C.
```
1914 CLE A 3            1  .000
        BRTR
```

D ACQUISTO, JOHN FRANCIS
B.DEC.24,1951 SAN DIEGO,CAL.
```
1973 SF  N /P           7  1- 1
1974 SF  N P       38  39  12- 4
1975 SF  N P           10  2- 4
1976 SF  N P            3  3- 8
1977 STL N /P          29  0- 0
1978 SD  N P           17  1- 2
1978 SD  N P           45  4- 3
        BRTR     148 149  23-32
```

DADE, LONNIE PAUL (PAUL)
B.DEC.7,1951 SEATTLE,WASH.
```
1975 CAL A /3-0        11  .200
1976 CAL A /0-2-3      13  .111
1977 CLE A 0-3/2      134  .291
1978 CLE A 0           93  .254
        BRTR          251  .271
```

DAGENHARD, JOHN DOUGLAS
B.APR.29,1917 MAGNOLIA,OHIO
```
1943 BOS N P            2  1- 0
        BRTR
```

DAGLIA, PETER GEORGE
B.FEB.28,1906 NAPA,CAL.
D.MAR.11,1952 WILLITS,CAL.
```
1932 CHI A P           12  2- 4
        BRTR
```

DAGRES, ANGELO GEORGE
(ANGELO) OR (JUNIOR)
B.AUG.22,1934 NEWBJRYPORT,MASS.
```
1955 BAL A O         8  .267
        BLTL
```

DAHL, JAY STEVEN
B.DEC.6,1945 SAN BERNARDINO,CAL.
D.JUNE 20,1965 SALISBURY,N.C.
```
1963 HOU N P            1  0- 1
        BBTL
```

DAHLEN, WILLIAM FREDERICK (BAD BILL)
B.JAN.5,1870 HELLISTON,N.Y.
D.DEC.5,1950 BROOKLYN,N.Y.
```
1891 CHI N S-3-0      135  .263
1892 CHI N S-3        143  .294
1893 CHI N S-0        115  .311
1894 CHI N S-3        121  .362
1895 CHI N S          131  .273
1896 CHI N S          125  .361
1897 CHI N S           75  .296
1898 CHI N S          141  .290
1899 BRO N S          122  .276
1900 BRO N S          134  .259
1901 BRO N S          130  .261
1902 BRO N S          136  .267
1903 BRO N S          138  .262
1904 NY  N S          145  .268
1905 NY  N S          148  .242
1906 NY  N S          143  .240
1907 NY  N S          143  .207
1908 BOS N S          144  .239
1909 BOS N S           57  .233
1910 BRO N M-M          3  .000
1911 BRO N M-S          1  .000
        BRTR         2430  .277
```
NON-PLAYING MANAGER BRO[N] 1912-13

DAHLGREN, ELLSWORTH TENNEY (BABE)
B.JUN.15,1912 SAN FRANCISCO,CAL
```
1935 BOS A 1          149  .263
1936 BOS A 1           16  .281
1937 NY  A H            1  .000
1938 NY  A 1-3         27  .186
1939 NY  A 1          144  .235
1940 NY  A 1          155  .264
1941 BOS N 1-3         44  .235
     CHI N 1           99  .281
1942 CHI N 1           17  .214
     STL A H            2  .000
     BRO N 1           17  .173
1943 PHI N C-1-S-3    136  .288
1944 PIT N 1          158  .289
1945 PIT N 1          144  .250
1946 STL A 1           28  .175
        BRTR         1137  .261
```

DAHLKE, JEROME ALEXANDER
(JERRY) OR (JOE)
B.JUNE 8,1930 MARATHON,WIS.
```
1956 CHI A P            5  0- 0
        BRTR
```

DAILEY, JOHN J.
B.BROOKLYN,N.Y.
D.JAN.8,1896
```
1875 NAT NA 2-S-3      25  -
     ATL NA 1-0         2  .125
                       27  -
```

DAILEY, SAMUEL LAURENCE
B.MAR.31,1904 OAKFORD,ILL.
```
1929 CHI N P           20  2- 2
        BLTR
```

DAILEY, VINCENT PERRY
B.DEC.25,1864 OSCEOLA,PA.
D.NOV.14,1919 HORNELL,N.Y.
```
1890 CLE N P           64  .288
```

DAILEY, WILLIAM GARLAND (BILL)
B.MAY 13,1935 ARLINGTON,VA.
```
1961 CLE A P           12  1- 0
1962 CLE A P           27  2- 2
1963 MIN A P           66  6- 3
1964 MIN A P           14  1- 2
        BRTR          119  10- 7
```

DAILY, CORNELIUS F. (CON)
B.SEPT.11,1864 BLACKSTONE,MASS.
D.JUNE 14,1928 BROOKLYN,N.Y.
```
1884 KEY U C            2  .000
1885 PRO N C-1-0       59  .260
1886 BOS N C           50  .239
1887 BOS N C           33  .217
1888 IND N C           57  .218
1889 IND N C           60  .251
1890 BRO P C-1         46  .253
1891 BRO N C           53  .294
1892 BRO N C           78  .243
1893 BRO N C           58  .286
1894 BRO N C           65  .269
1895 BRO N C           40  .233
1896 BRO N C            1  .000
     CHI N C            9  .075
                      611  .258
```

DAILY, EDWARD M.
B.SEPT.7,1862 PROVIDENCE,R.I.
D.OCT.21,1891 WASHINGTON,D.C.
```
1885 PHI N P-O         49  26-22
                          .206
1886 PHI N P-O    26  78  13- 9
                          .226
1887 PHI N P-O     6  25  0- 4
                          .306
     WAS N P-O     1  80  1- 1
                          .296
1888 WAS N P-O     8 110  2- 4
                          .225
1889 COL AA O        137  .254
1890 BRO AA P-O   30  93  9-15
                          .250
     NY  N P            4  2- 1
     LOU AA P-O   12  23  6- 2
                          .244
1891 LOU AA P-O   15  22  4- 8
                          .277
     WAS AA P-O    4  17  0- 0
                          .206
        BRTR     155 638  62-66
                          .250
```

DAILY, HUGH IGNATIUS
[REAL NAME HARRY CRISS]
B.1857 BALTIMORE,MO.
```
1882 BUF N P           29  15-14
1883 CLE N P-O         42  24-18
                          .109
1884 CHI U P-2-        47  22-25
           S-O            .235
     PIT U P           10  5- 4
     WAS U P            2  1- 1
1885 STL N P           11  3- 8
1886 WAS N P            6  0- 6
1887 CLE AA P          17  4-12
        BRTR          164  74-88
                          .155
```

DAISEY, GEORGE K.
```
1884 ALT U O            1  .000
```

DAL CANTON, JOHN BRUCE (BRUCE)
B.AUG.15,1942 CALIFORNIA,PA.
```
1967 PIT N /P           8  2- 1
1968 PIT N /P           7  1- 1
1969 PIT N P           57  8- 2
1970 PIT N P           41  9- 4
1971 KC  A P           25  8- 6
1972 KC  A P           35  6- 6
1973 KC  A P           32  4- 3
1974 KC  A P           31  8-10
1975 KC  A /P           4  0- 2
1976 ATL N P           26  2- 7
1977 CHI A /P           8  0- 2
        BRTR          316  51-49
```

DALE, EMMETT EUGENE (GENE)
B.JUNE 16,1889 ST.LOUIS,MO.
D.MAR.20,1958 ST.LOUIS,MO.
```
1911 STL N P            5  0- 2
1912 STL N P       19  20  0- 5
1915 CIN N P           49  18-17
1916 CIN N P           17  3- 4
        BRTR       90  91  21-28
```

DALEY, JOHN FRANCIS
B.MAY 25,1889 PITTSBURGH,PA.
```
1912 STL A S           17  .173
        BRTR
```

DALEY, JUDSON LAWRENCE (JUD)
B.MAR.14,1884 S.COVENTRY,CONN.
D.JAN.26,1967 GASDEN,ALA.
```
1911 BRO N O           16  .231
1912 BRO N O           61  .256
        BLTR           77  .250
```

DALEY, LEAVITT LEO (BUD)
B.OCT.7,1932 ORANGE,CAL.
```
1955 CLE A P            2  0- 1
1956 CLE A P           14  1- 0
1957 CLE A P           34  8- 8
1958 KC  A P           26  3- 2
1959 KC  A P           39  16-13
1960 KC  A P           37  16-16
1961 KC  A P           16  4- 8
     NY  A P           23  8- 9
1962 NY  A P           43  7- 5
1963 NY  A P            1  0- 0
1964 NY  A P           13  3- 2
        BLTL          248  60-64
```

DALEY, PETER HARVEY (PETE)
D.JAN.14,1930 GRASS VALLEY,CAL.
```
1955 BOS A C           17  .220
1956 BOS A C           59  .267
1957 BOS A C           78  .225
1958 BOS A C           27  .321
1959 BOS A C           65  .225
1960 KC  A C-O         73  .263
1961 WAS A C           72  .192
        BRTR          391  .239
```

YR CL LEA POS   GP   G   REC

DALEY, THOMAS FRANCIS (PETE)
B.NOV.13,1884 DUBOIS,PA.
D.DEC.2,1934 LOS ANGELES,CAL.
1908 CIN N O   13   .108
1913 PHI A O   59   .260
1914 PHI A O   28   .241
     NY A O   67   .258
1915 NY A O   10   .250
     BLTR   177   .243

DALEY, WILLIAM
B.JUNE 27,1868 POUGHKEEPSIE,N.Y
D.MAY 4,1922 POUGHKEEPSIE,N.Y.
1889 BOS N P   9   3- 3
1890 BOS P P   34 47   20-12
1891 BOS AA P   19 20   9- 5
     TL   62 76   32-20

**DALLESSANDRO, NICHOLAS DOMINIC
(DIM DOM)**
B.OCT.3,1913 READING,PA.
1937 BOS A O   68   .231
1940 CHI N O   107   .268
1941 CHI N O   140   .272
1942 CHI N O   96   .261
1943 CHI N O   87   .222
1944 CHI N O   117   .305
1946 CHI N O   65   .225
1947 CHI N O   66   .287
     BLTL   746   .267

DALRYMPLE, ABNER FRANK
B.SEPT.9,1857 WARREN,ILL.
D.JAN.25,1939 WARREN,ILL.
1878 MIL N O   60   .356
1879 CHI N O   87   .300
1880 CHI N O   84   .332
1881 CHI N O   81   .323
1882 CHI N O   84   .294
1883 CHI N O   80   .297
1884 CHI N O   110   .310
1885 CHI N O   113   .274
1886 CHI N O   82   .232
1887 PIT N O   92   .300
1888 PIT N O   56   .224
1891 MIL AA O   31   .315
     BLTL   940   .298

DALRYMPLE, CLAYTON ERROL (CLAY)
B.DEC.3,1936 CHICO,CAL.
1960 PHI N C   82   .272
1961 PHI N C   129   .220
1962 PHI N C   123   .276
1963 PHI N C   142   .252
1964 PHI N C   127   .238
1965 PHI N *C   103   .213
1966 PHI N *C   114   .245
1967 PHI N C   101   .172
1968 PHI N C   85   .207
1969 BAL A C   37   .238
1970 BAL A C   13   .219
1971 BAL A C   23   .204
     BLTR   1079   .233

DALRYMPLE, MICHAEL
B.ST.LOUIS,MO.
1915 STL A A   3   .000
     TR

DALTON, TALBOT PERCY (JACK)
B.JULY 3,1885 HENDERSON,TENN.
1910 BRO N O   72   .227
1914 BRO N O   128   .319
1915 BUF F O   132   .294
1916 DET A O   8   .182
     BRTR   340   .287

DALY, ALBERT JOSEPH (BERT)
B.APR.8,1881 BAYONNE,N.J.
D.SEPT.3,1952 BAYONNE,N.J.
1903 PHI A 2-S-3   10   .190
     BRTR

DALY, GEORGE JOSEPH (PECKS)
B.JULY 26,1887 BUFFALO,N.Y.
D.DEC.12,1957 BUFFALO,N.Y.
1909 NY N P   3   0- 3
     BRTR

DALY, JAMES J. (SUN)
B.JAN.6,1865 RUTLAND,VT.
D.APR.30,1938 ALBANY,N.Y.
1891 MIL AA O   1   .000
1892 BAL N O   13   .229
                        14   .216

DALY, JOSEPH JOHN
B.SEPT.21,1868 CONSHOHOCKEN,PA.
D.MAR.21,1943 PHILADELPHIA,PA.
1890 ATH AA P-C-   1 20   0- 1
                 O   .180
1891 CLE N O   1   .000
1892 BOS N C   1   .000
                     1 22   0- 1
                                  .175

DALY, THOMAS DANIEL
B.DEC.12,1891 ST.JOHN,N.B.,CAN.
D.NOV.7,1946 MEDFORD,MASS.
1913 CHI A C   1   .000
1914 CHI A O   61   .233
1915 CHI A C   29   .191
1916 CLE A C   31   .219
1918 CHI N C   1   .000
1919 CHI N C   25   .220
1920 CHI N C   44   .311
1921 CHI N C   51   .238
     BRTR   243   .239

DALY, THOMAS PETER (TIDO)
B.FEB.7,1866 PHILADELPHIA,PA.
D.OCT.29,1939 BROOKLYN,N.Y.
1887 CHI N C   74   .269
1888 CHI N C   65   .191
1889 WAS N C   69   .300
1890 BRO N C   82   .243
1891 BRO N C   61   .293
1892 BRO N C-3-O   120   .295
1893 BRO N 2-3   126   .306
1894 BRO N 2   123   .338
1895 BRO N 2   122   .289
1896 BRO N 2   64   .280
1898 BRO N 2   23   .329
1899 BRO N 2   143   .312
1900 BRO N 2   98   .313
1901 BRO N 2   132   .310
1902 CHI A 2   137   .231
1903 CHI A 2   45   .201
     CIN N 2   79   .293
     BBTR   1563   .284

DAM, ELBRIDGE RUST (BILL)
B.APR.4,1885 CAMBRIDGE,MASS.
D.JUNE 22,1930 QUINCY,MASS.
1909 BOS N O   1   .500

DAMASKA, JACK LLOYD
B.AUG.21,1937 BEAVER FALLS,PA.
1963 STL N 2-O   5   .200
     BRTR

DAMMAN, WILLIAM HENRY (WEE WILLIE)
B.AUG.9,1872 CHICAGO,ILL.
D.DEC.6,1948 LYNNHAVEN,VA.
1897 CIN N P   16   7- 5
1898 CIN N P   28   16- 8
1899 CIN N P   9   2- 1
     BLTR   53   25-14

**DAMRAU, HARRY ROBERT
(ALSO KNOWN AS ARTHUR LEE WHITEHORN)**
B.SEPT.11,1890 NEWBURGH,N.Y.
D.AUG.21,1957 STATEN ISLAND,N.Y
1915 PHI A 3   16   .196
     BRTR

DANEY, ARTHUR LEE
B.JULY 9,1904 TALIHINA,OKLA.
1928 PHI A P   1   0- 0
     BRTR

**DANFORTH, DAVID CHARLES
(DAVE) OR (DAUNTLESS DAVE)**
B.MAR.7,1890 GRANGER,TEX.
D.SEPT.19,1970 BALTIMORE,MD.
1911 PHI A P   14   5- 2
1912 PHI A P   3   0- 0
1916 CHI A P   28   6- 5
1917 CHI A P   50   11- 6
1918 CHI A P   39   6-15
1919 CHI A P   15   1- 2
1922 STL A P   20   5- 2
1923 STL A P   38   16-14
1924 STL A P   41   13-12
1925 STL A P   38   7- 9
     BLTR   286   72-67

DANIEL, CHARLES EDWARD (CHUCK)
B.SEPT.17,1933 BLUFFTON,ARK.
1957 DET A P   1   0- 0
     BRTR

DANIEL, HANDLEY JACOB (JAKE)
B.APR.22,1912 ROANOKE,ALA.
1937 BRO N 1   12   .185
     BLTL

DANIELS, BENNIE
B.JUNE 17,1932 TUSCALOOSA,ALA.
1957 PIT N P   1   0- 1
1958 PIT N P   8   0- 3
1959 PIT N P   34   36   7- 9
1960 PIT N P   10   1- 3
1961 WAS A P   32   12-11
1962 WAS A P   44   7-16
1963 WAS A P-O 35   36   5-10
                                  .152
1964 WAS A P   33   8-10
1965 WAS A P   33   5-13
     BLTR   230 233   45-76
                                  .170

DANIELS, BERNARD ELMER (BERT)
B.OCT.13,1882 DANVILLE,ILL.
D.JUNE 6,1958 CEDAR GROVE,N.J.
1910 NY A 1-3-O   95   .253
1911 NY A O   131   .286
1912 NY A O   133   .274
1913 NY A O   93   .216
1914 CIN N O   71   .219
     BRTR   523   .255

DANIELS, CHARLES L.
B.JULY 1,1861 ROXBURY,MASS.
1884 BOS U P-O   2   3   0- 2
                                  .273

DANIELS, FREDERICK CLINTON (TONY)
B.DEC.28,1924 GASTONIA,N.C.
1945 PHI N 2-3   76   .200
     BRTR

**DANIELS, HAROLD JACK
(JACK) OR (SOUR MASH JACK)**
B.DEC.21,1927 CHESTER,PA.
1952 BOS N O   106   .187
     BLTL

DANIELS, LAWRENCE LONG (LAW)
B.JULY 14,1862 NEWTON,MASS.
D.JAN.7,1929 WALTHAM,MASS.
1887 BAL AA C   47   .287
1888 KC AA C   61   .205
                       108   .240

DANIELS, PETER J. (SMILING PETE)
B.APR.8,1864 COUNTY CAVAN,IRELAND
D.FEB.13,1928 INDIANAPOLIS,IND.
1890 PIT N P   4   1- 2
1898 STL N P   10   1- 6
     BL   14   2- 8

DANNER, HENRY FREDERICK (BUCK)
B.JUNE 8,1891 DEDHAM,MASS.
D.SEPT.19,1949 BOSTON,MASS.
1915 PHI A S   3   .250
     BRTR

DANNING, HARRY (THE HORSE)
B.SEPT.6,1911 LOS ANGELES,CAL.
1933 NY N C   3   .000
1934 NY N C   53   .330
1935 NY N C   65   .243
1936 NY N C   32   .159
1937 NY N C   93   .288
1938 NY N C   120   .306
1939 NY N C   135   .313
1940 NY N C   140   .300
1941 NY N C-1   130   .244
1942 NY N C   119   .279
     BRTR   890   .285

DANNING, IKE
B.JAN.20,1905 LOS ANGELES,CAL.
1928 STL A C   2   .500
     BRTR

DANTONIO, JOHN JAMES (FATS)
B.DEC.31,1919 NEW ORLEANS,LA.
1944 BRO N C   3   .143
1945 BRO N C   47   .250
     BRTR   50   .244

DANZIG, HAROLD P. (BABE)
B.APR.30,1887 BINGHAMTON,N.Y.
D.JUL.14,1931 SAN FRANCISCO,CAL
1909 BOS A 1   6   .143
     BRTR

DAPPER, CLIFFORD ROLAND
B.JAN.2,1920 LOS ANGELES,CAL.
1942 BRO N C   8   .471

DARBY, GEORGE W. (DEACON)
B.1869 KANSAS CITY,MO.
1893 CIN N P   4   2- 1
     PHI N P   4   0- 0
     BLTR   8   2- 1

DARCY, PATRICK LEONARD (PAT)
B.MAY 12,1950 TROY,OHIO
1974 CIN N /P   6   1- 0
1975 CIN N P   27   11- 5
1976 CIN N P   11   2- 3
     BLTR   44   14- 8

DARINGER, CLIFFORD CLARENCE (SHANTY)
B.APR.10,1885 HAYDEN,IND.
D.DEC.26,1971 SACRAMENTO,CAL.
1914 KC F S-3   60   .247
     BLTR

DARINGER, ROLLA HARRISON
B.NOV.15,1888 N.VERNON,IND.
D.MAY 23,1974 SEYMOUR,IND.
1914 STL N S   2   .500
1915 STL N S   10   .087
     BLTR   12   .148

YR	CL LEA POS	GP	G	REC

DARK, ALVIN RALPH (BLACKIE)
B.JAN.7,1922 COMANCHE,OKLA.

YR	CL	LEA	POS	GP	G	REC
1946	BOS	N	S-0		15	.231
1948	BOS	N	S		137	.322
1949	BOS	N	S-3		130	.276
1950	NY	N	S		154	.279
1951	NY	N	S		156	.303
1952	NY	N	S		151	.301
1953	NY	N	P-2-	1	155	0- 0
			S-3-0			.300
1954	NY	N	S		154	.293
1955	NY	N	S		115	.282
1956	NY	N	S		48	.252
	STL	N	S		100	.286
1957	STL	N	S-3		140	.290
1958	STL	N	S-3		18	.297
	CHI	N	3		114	.295
1959	CHI	N	1-S-3		136	.264
1960	PHI	N	1-3		55	.242
	MIL	N	1-2-3-0		50	.298
			BRTR	1	1828	0- 0
						.289

NON-PLAYING MANAGER
SF(N) 1961-64, KC(A) 1966-67,
CLE(A) 1968-71, OAK(A) 1974-75
SD(N) 1977

DARLING, CONRAD (DELL)
B.DEC.21,1861 ERIE,PA.
D.NOV.20,1904

YR	CL	LEA	POS	G	REC
1883	BUF	N	C	5	.158
1887	CHI	N	C-0	38	.411
1888	CHI	N	C	20	.213
1889	CHI	N	C	35	.191
1890	CHI	P	C-1	58	.259
1891	STL	AA	C	17	.137
			BRTR	173	.266

DARNELL, ROBERT JACK
B.NOV.6,1930 WEWOKA,OKLA.

YR	CL	LEA	POS	G	REC
1954	BRO	N	P	6	0- 0
1956	BRO	N	P	1	0- 0
			BRTR	7	0- 0

DARR, MICHAEL EDWARD (MIKE)
B.MAR.23,1959 POMONA,CAL.

YR	CL	LEA	POS	G	REC
1977	TOR	A	/P	1	0- 1
			BRTR		

DARRAGH, JAMES S.
B.JULY 17,1866 EBENSBURG,PA.
D.AUG.12,1939 ROCHESTER,PA.

YR	CL	LEA	POS	G	REC
1891	LOU	AA	P	1	1- 0

DARROW, GEORGE OLIVER
B.JULY 12,1909 BELOIT,KAN.

YR	CL	LEA	POS	G	REC
1934	PHI	N	P	17	2- 6
			BLTL		

DARWIN, ARTHUR BOBBY LEE (BOBBY)
B.FEB.16,1943 LOS ANGELES,CAL.

YR	CL	LEA	POS	GP	G	REC
1962	LA	A	P		1	0- 1
1969	LA	N	/P	3	6	0- 0
1971	LA	N	/0		11	.250
1972	MIN	A	*0		145	.267
1973	MIN	A	*0		145	.252
1974	MIN	A	*0		152	.264
1975	MIN	A	0-0		48	.219
	MIL	A	0		55	.247
1976	MIL	A	0		25	.247
	BOS	A	0-0		43	.179
1977	BOS	A	/0		4	.222
	CHI	N	/0		11	.167
			BRTR	4	649	0- 1
						.251

DARWIN, DANNY WAYNE
B.OCT.25,1955 BONHAM,TEX.

YR	CL	LEA	POS	G	REC
1978	TEX	A	/P	3	1- 0
			BRTR		

DASHIELL, JOHN WALLACE (WALLY)
B.MAY 9,1902 JEWETT,TEX.
D.MAY 20,1972 PENSACOLA,FLA.

YR	CL	LEA	POS	G	REC
1924	CHI	A	S	1	.000

DASHNER, LEE CLAIRE (LEFTY)
B.APR.25,1887 RENAULT,ILL.
D.DEC.16,1959 EL DORADO,KAN.

YR	CL	LEA	POS	G	REC
1913	CLE	A	P	1	0- 0
			BBTL		

DASSO, FRANCIS JOSEPH NICHOLAS (FRANK)
B.AUG.31,1917 CHICAGO,ILL.

YR	CL	LEA	POS	G	REC
1945	CIN	N	P	16	4- 5
1946	CIN	N	P	2	0- 0
			BRTR	18	4- 5

DAUB, DANIEL WILLIAM (MICKEY)
B.JAN.12,1868 MIDDLETOWN,OHIO
D.MAR.25,1951 BRADENTON,FLA.

YR	CL	LEA	POS	G	REC
1892	CIN	N	P	5	1- 1
1893	BRO	N	P	12	6- 6
1894	BRO	N	P	28	10-15
1895	BRO	N	P	20	10-10
1896	BRO	N	P	27	14-11
1897	BRO	N	P	18	5-11
				110	46-54

DAUBERT, HARRY (JAKE)
B.JUNE 19,1892 COLUMBUS,OHIO
D.JAN.8,1944 DETROIT,MICH.

YR	CL	LEA	POS	G	REC
1915	PIT	N	S	1	.000
			BRTR		

DAUBERT, JACOB ELLSWORTH (JAKE)
B.APR.17,1884 SHAMOKIN,PA.
D.OCT.9,1924 CINCINNATI,OHIO

YR	CL	LEA	POS	G	REC
1910	BRO	N	1	144	.264
1911	BRO	N	1	149	.307
1912	BRO	N	1	145	.308
1913	BRO	N	1	139	.350
1914	BRO	N	1	126	.329
1915	BRO	N	1	150	.301
1916	BRO	N	1	127	.316
1917	BRO	N	1	125	.261
1918	BRO	N	1	108	.308
1919	CIN	N	1	140	.276
1920	CIN	N	1	142	.304
1921	CIN	N	1	136	.306
1922	CIN	N	1	156	.336
1923	CIN	N	1	125	.292
1924	CIN	N	1	102	.281
			BLTL	2014	.303

DAUER, RICHARD FREMONT (RICH)
B.JULY 27,1952 SAN BERNARDINO,CAL.

YR	CL	LEA	POS	G	REC
1976	BAL	A	2	11	.103
1977	BAL	A	2/3	96	.243
1978	BAL	A	2-3	133	.264
			BRTR	240	.248

DAUGHERTY, HAROLD RAY (DOC)
B.OCT.12,1927 PARIS,PA.

YR	CL	LEA	POS	G	REC
1951	DET	A	H	1	.000
			BRTR		

DAUGHTERS, ROBERT FRANCIS (RED)
B.AUG.5,1914 CINCINNATI,OHIO

YR	CL	LEA	POS	G	REC
1937	BOS	A	H	1	.000

DAUSS, GEORGE AUGUST (HOOKS)
B.SEPT.22,1889 INDIANAPOLIS,IND
D.JULY 27,1963 ST.LOUIS,MO.

YR	CL	LEA	POS	GP	G	REC
1912	DET	A	P		2	0- 1
1913	DET	A	P		33	13-12
1914	DET	A	P		45	18-15
1915	DET	A	P		46	23-13
1916	DET	A	P		39	18-12
1917	DET	A	P	37	38	17-14
1918	DET	A	P		33	13-16
1919	DET	A	P		34	21- 9
1920	DET	A	P		38	13-21
1921	DET	A	P		32	10-15
1922	DET	A	P		39	13-13
1923	DET	A	P		50	21-13
1924	DET	A	P		40	12-11
1925	DET	A	P		35	16-11
1926	DET	A	P		35	12- 7
			BRTR	538	539	220-181

DAVALILLO, POMPEYO ANTONIO (RODRIGUEZ) (YO-YO)
B.JUNE 30,1931 CARACAS,VENEZ.

YR	CL	LEA	POS	G	REC
1953	WAS	A	S	19	.293
			BRTR		

DAVALILLO, VICTOR JOSE (RODRIGUEZ) (VIC)
B.JULY 31,1936 CABIMAS,VENEZ.

YR	CL	LEA	POS	GP	G	REC
1963	CLE	A	0		90	.292
1964	CLE	A	0		150	.270
1965	CLE	A	*0		142	.301
1966	CLE	A	*0		121	.250
1967	CLE	A	*0		139	.287
1968	CLE	A	0		51	.239
	CAL	A	0		93	.298
1969	CAL	A	0/1		33	.155
	STL	N	0/P	2	63	0- 0
						.265
1970	STL	N	0		111	.311
1971	PIT	N	0-1		99	.285
1972	PIT	N	0/1		117	.318
1973	PIT	N	1-0		59	.181
	OAK	A	0/1		38	.188
1974	OAK	A	/0		17	.174
1977	LA	N	0		24	.313
1978	LA	N	0/1		75	.312
			BLTL	2	1422	0- 0
						.280

DA VANON, FRANK GERALD (JERRY)
B.AUG.21,1945 OCEANSIDE,CAL.

YR	CL	LEA	POS	G	REC
1969	SD	N	2/S	24	.136
	STL	N	S	16	.300
1970	STL	N	/3-2	11	.111
1971	BAL	A	2-S/3-1	38	.235
1973	CAL	A	S-2/3	41	.245
1974	STL	N	S/3-2-0	30	.150
1975	HOU	N	S/2-3	32	.278
1976	HOU	N	2-S/3	61	.290
1977	STL	N	/2	9	.000
			BRTR	262	.234

DAVENPORT, CLAUDE EDWIN (BIG DAVE)
B.MAY 28,1898 RUNGE,TEX.
D.JUNE 13,1976 CORPUS CHRISTI,TEX.

YR	CL	LEA	POS	G	REC
1920	NY	N	P	1	0- 0
			BRTR		

DAVENPORT, DAVID W. (DAVE)
B.FEB.20,1890 DE RIDDER,LA.
D.OCT.16,1954 EL DORADO,ARK.

YR	CL	LEA	POS	G	REC
1914	CIN	N	P	10	2- 2
	STL	F	P	33	10-15
1915	STL	F	P	55	22-18
1916	STL	A	P	59	12-11
1917	STL	A	P	47	17-17
1918	STL	A	P	31	10-11
1919	STL	A	P	24	2-11
			BRTR	259	75-85

DAVENPORT, JAMES HOUSTON (JIM)
B.AUG.17,1933 SILURIA,ALA.

YR	CL	LEA	POS	G	REC
1958	SF	N	S-3	134	.256
1959	SF	N	S-3	123	.258
1960	SF	N	S-3	112	.251
1961	SF	N	3	137	.278
1962	SF	N	3	144	.297
1963	SF	N	2-S-3	147	.252
1964	SF	N	2-S-3	116	.236
1965	SF	N	3-S-2	106	.251
1966	SF	N	S-3-2/1	111	.249
1967	SF	N	3-S-2	124	.275
1968	SF	N	3-S/2	113	.224
1969	SF	N	*3/1-S-0	112	.241
1970	SF	N	3	22	.243
			BRTR	1501	.258

DAVENPORT, JOUBERT LUM (LUM)
B.JUNE 27,1900 TUCSON,ARIZ.
D.APR.21,1961 DALLAS,TEX.

YR	CL	LEA	POS	GP	G	REC
1921	CHI	A	P	13	15	0- 3
1922	CHI	A	P	9	12	1- 1
1923	CHI	A	P		2	0- 0
1924	CHI	A	P		1	0- 0
			BLTL	25	30	1- 4

DAVEY, MICHAEL GERARD (MIKE)
B.JUNE 2,1952 SPOKANE,WASH.

YR	CL	LEA	POS	G	REC
1977	ATL	N	P	16	0- 0
1978	ATL	N	/P	3	0- 0
			BRTL	19	0- 0

DAVIAULT, RAYMOND JOSEPH ROBERT
B.MAY 27,1934 MONTREAL,QUE.,CAN

YR	CL	LEA	POS	G	REC
1962	NY	N	P	36	1- 5
			BRTR		

DAVIDSON, CLAUDE BOUCHER (DAVEY)
B.OCT.13,1896 ROXBURY,MASS.
D.APR.18,1964 WEYMOUTH,MASS.

YR	CL	LEA	POS	G	REC
1918	PHI	A	2	31	.185
1919	WAS	A	3	2	.375
			BLTR	33	.202

DAVIDSON, HOMER HURD (DIVVY)
B.OCT.14,1884 CLEVELAND,OHIO
D.JULY 26,1948 DETROIT,MICH.

YR	CL	LEA	POS	G	REC
1908	CLE	A	C-0	9	.000
			TR		

DAVIDSON, MORDECAI H.
B.NOV.30,1846 PORT WASHINGTON,O
D.SEPT.6,1940 LOUISVILLE,KY.
NON-PLAYING MANAGER LOU(AA) 1888-89

DAVIDSON, THOMAS EUGENE (TED)
B.OCT.4,1939 LAS VEGAS,NEV.

YR	CL	LEA	POS	G	REC
1965	CIN	N	P	24	4- 3
1966	CIN	N	P	54	5- 4
1967	CIN	N	/P	9	1- 0
1968	CIN	N	P	23	1- 0
	ATL	N	/P	4	0- 0
			BRTL	114	11- 7

DAVIDSON, WILLIAM
B.MAY 10,1887 LAFAYETTE,IND.

YR	CL	LEA	POS	G	REC
1909	CHI	N	0	2	.142
1910	BRO	N	0	131	.238
1911	BRO	N	0	74	.233
			BRTR	207	.235

DAVIE, GERALD LEE (JERRY)
B.FEB.10,1933 DETROIT,MICH.

YR	CL	LEA	POS	G	REC
1959	DET	A	P	11	2- 2
			BRTR		

DAVIES, GEORGE WASHINGTON
B.FEB.22,1868 COLUMBUS,WIS.
D.SEPT.22,1906

YR	CL	LEA	POS	GP	G	REC
1891	MIL	AA	P		12	7- 5
1892	CLE	N	P		25	10-15
1893	CLE	N	P		3	0- 1
	NY	N	P		4	1- 2
					44	18-23

DAVIES, LLOYD GARRISON (CHICK)
B.MAR.6,1897 PEABODY,MASS.
D.SEPT.5,1973 MIDDLETOWN,CONN.

YR	CL	LEA	POS	GP	G	REC
1914	PHI	A	P	1	19	1- 0
1915	PHI	A	P-O	4	56	0- 2
						.182
1925	NY	N	P-O	2	4	0- 0
						.000
1926	NY	N	P		38	2- 4
	BLTL			45	117	3- 6
						.196

DAVIS, ALFONZO DEFORD (LEFTY)
B.FEB.4,1875 NASHVILLE,TENN.
D.FEB.7,1919 COLLINS,N.Y.

YR	CL	LEA	POS	G	REC
1901	BRO	N	O	25	.209
	PIT	N	O	88	.308
1902	PIT	N	O	59	.291
1903	NY	A	O	108	.245
1907	CIN	N	O	70	.229
	BLTL			350	.264

DAVIS, ARTHUR WILLARD (BILL)
B.JUNE 6,1942 GRACEVILLE,MINN.

YR	CL	LEA	POS	G	REC
1965	CLE	A	H	10	.300
1966	CLE	A	/1	23	.158
1969	SD	N	1	31	.175
	BLTL			64	.181

DAVIS, BRYSHEAR BARNETT (BROCK)
B.OCT.19,1943 OAKLAND,CAL.

YR	CL	LEA	POS	G	REC
1963	HOU	N	O	34	.200
1964	HOU	N	O	1	.000
1966	HOU	N	/O	10	.148
1970	CHI	N	/O	6	.000
1971	CHI	N	O	106	.256
1972	MIL	A	O	85	.318
	BLTL			242	.260

DAVIS, CURTIS BENTON (COONSKIN)
B.SEPT.7,1903 GREENFIELD,MO.
D.OCT.13,1965 COVINA,CAL.

YR	CL	LEA	POS	GP	G	REC
1934	PHI	N	P		51	19-17
1935	PHI	N	P	44	46	16-14
1936	PHI	N	P	10	11	2- 4
					24	11- 9
1937	CHI	N	P		28	10- 5
1938	STL	N	P		40	12- 8
1939	PHI	N	P	49	63	22-16
1940	STL	N	P		14	0- 4
	BRO	N	P		22	8- 7
1941	BRO	N	P	28	31	13- 7
1942	BRO	N	P		32	15- 6
1943	BRO	N	P		31	10-13
1944	BRO	N	P		31	10-11
1945	BRO	N	P		24	10-10
1946	BRO	N	P		1	0- 0
	BRTR			429	449	158-131

DAVIS, FRANK TALMADGE (DIXIE)
B.OCT.12,1890 WILSON MILLS,N.C.
D.FEB.4,1944 RALEIGH,N.C.

YR	CL	LEA	POS	GP	G	REC
1912	CIN	N	P		7	0- 1
1915	CHI	A	P		2	0- 0
1918	PHI	N	P	17	18	0- 2
1920	STL	A	P		38	18-12
1921	STL	A	P		39	16-16
1922	STL	A	P		25	11- 6
1923	STL	A	P		19	4- 6
1924	STL	A	P		29	11-13
1925	STL	A	P		35	12- 7
1926	STL	A	P		27	4- 8
	BRTR			238	239	76-71

DAVIS, GEORGE ALLEN (IRON)
B.MAR.9,1890 LANCASTER,N.Y.
D.JUNE 4,1961 BUFFALO,N.Y.

YR	CL	LEA	POS	G	REC
1912	NY	A	P	10	1- 5
1913	BOS	N	P	2	0- 0
1914	BOS	N	P	9	3- 3
1915	BOS	N	P	15	3- 3
	BBTR			36	7-11

DAVIS, GEORGE STACEY
B.AUG.23,1870 COHOES,N.Y.
D.OCT.17,1940 PHILADELPHIA,PA.

YR	CL	LEA	POS	GP	G	REC
1890	CLE	N	O		134	.264
1891	CLE	N	P-3-	1	136	0- 0
			O			.292
1892	CLE	N	S-3-O		143	.253
1893	NY	N	3		133	.373
1894	NY	N	3		124	.345
1895	NY	N	M-3		110	.330
1896	NY	N	S-3		124	.315
1897	NY	N	S		131	.358
1898	NY	N	S		121	.306
1899	NY	N	S		111	.348
1900	NY	N	M-S		113	.325
1901	NY	N	M-S-3		130	.309
1902	CHI	A	1-S		132	.298
1903	NY	N	S		4	.250
1904	CHI	A	S		152	.256
1905	CHI	A	S		151	.278
1906	CHI	A	S		133	.277
1907	CHI	A	S		132	.238
1908	CHI	A	2-S		128	.217
1909	CHI	A	1		28	.132
	BBTR				2370	0- 0
						.297

DAVIS, GEORGE WILLIS (KIDDO)
B.FEB.12,1902 BRIDGEPORT,CONN.

YR	CL	LEA	POS	G	REC
1926	NY	A	O	1	.000
1932	PHI	N	O	137	.309
1933	NY	N	O	126	.258
1934	STL	N	O	16	.303
	PHI	N	O	100	.283
1935	NY	N	O	47	.264
1936	NY	N	O	47	.239
1937	NY	N	O	56	.263
	CIN	N	O	40	.257
1938	CIN	N	O	5	.278
	BRTR			575	.282

DAVIS, HARRY ALBERT (STINKY)
B.MAY 7,1908 SHREVEPORT,LA.

YR	CL	LEA	POS	G	REC
1932	DET	A	1	141	.269
1933	DET	A	1	66	.214
1937	STL	A	1	120	.276
	BLTL			327	.264

DAVIS, HARRY H (JASPER)
B.JULY 19,1873 PHILADELPHIA,PA.
D.AUG.11,1947 PHILADELPHIA,PA.

YR	CL	LEA	POS	G	REC
1895	NY	N	1	7	.333
1896	NY	N	1	64	.254
	PIT	N	1-O	43	.206
1897	PIT	N	1-3	107	.309
1898	PIT	N	1	58	.290
	LOU	N	1-2-O	36	.227
	WAS	N	1	1	.000
1899	WAS	N	1	18	.188
1901	PHI	A	1	117	.307
1902	PHI	A	1-O	132	.308
1903	PHI	A	1	101	.298
1904	PHI	A	1	102	.308
1905	PHI	A	1	149	.284
1906	PHI	A	1	145	.292
1907	PHI	A	1	149	.266
1908	PHI	A	1	147	.248
1909	PHI	A	1	149	.268
1910	PHI	A	1	139	.248
1911	PHI	A	1	57	.197
1912	CLE	A	M-1	2	.000
1913	PHI	A	C-1	8	.444
1914	PHI	A	1	7	.333
1915	PHI	A	1	5	.167
1916	PHI	A	O	4	.167
1917	PHI	A	H	1	.000
	BRTR			1748	.277

DAVIS, HERMAN THOMAS (TOMMY)
B.MAR.21,1939 BROOKLYN,N.Y.

YR	CL	LEA	POS	G	REC
1959	LA	N	H	1	.000
1960	LA	N	3-O	110	.276
1961	LA	N	3-O	132	.278
1962	LA	N	3-O	163	.346
1963	LA	N	3-O	146	.326
1964	LA	N	O	152	.275
1965	LA	N	O	17	.250
1966	LA	N	O/3	100	.313
1967	NY	N	*O/1	194	.302
1968	CHI	A	*O/1	132	.268
1969	SEA	A	*O/1	123	.271
	HOU	N	O	24	.241
1970	HOU	N	O	57	.282
	CHI	N	O	11	.262
	OAK	A	O/1	66	.290
1971	OAK	A	1-O/2-3	79	.324
1972	CHI	N	/1-O	15	.269
	BAL	A	D/1	26	.256
1973	BAL	A	*D/1	137	.306
1974	BAL	A	*D	158	.289
1975	BAL	A	*D	116	.283
1976	CAL	A	D/1	72	.265
	KC	A	/H	8	.263
	BRTR			1999	.294

DAVIS, ISAAC MARION (IKE)
B.JUNE 14,1895 PUEBLO,COL.

YR	CL	LEA	POS	G	REC
1919	WAS	A	S	7	.000
1924	CHI	A	S	10	.242
1925	CHI	A	S	146	.240
	BRTR			163	.235

DAVIS, J. IRA (SLATS)
B.JULY 8,1870 BROOKLYN,N.Y.
D.DEC.21,1942 BROOKLYN,N.Y.

YR	CL	LEA	POS	G	REC
1899	NY	N	1-S	6	.250

DAVIS, JACKE SYLVESTA
B.MAR.5,1936 CARTHAGE,TEX.

YR	CL	LEA	POS	G	REC
1962	PHI	N	O	48	.213

DAVIS, JAMES BENNETT
B.SEPT.15,1924 RED BLUFF,CAL.

YR	CL	LEA	POS	G	REC
1954	CHI	N	P	46	11- 7
1955	CHI	N	P	42	7-11
1956	CHI	N	P	46	5- 7
1957	STL	N	P	10	0- 1
	NY	N	P	10	1- 0
	BBTL			154	24-26

DAVIS, JAMES J. (JUMBO)
B.NEW YORK,N.Y.
D.FEB.1921

YR	CL	LEA	POS	G	REC
1884	KC	U	3	7	.222
1886	BAL	AA	3	59	.185
1887	BAL	AA	S-3	130	.345
1888	KC	AA	3	122	.266
1889	KC	AA	3	62	.258
	STL	AA	S-O	2	.000
1890	STL	AA	3	21	.250
	BRO	AA	3	37	.284
1891	WAS	AA	3	18	.250
	BLTR			458	.278

DAVIS, JOHN A. (DAISY)
B.MAY 17,1858 BOSTON,MASS.

YR	CL	LEA	POS	GP	G	REC
1884	STL	AA	P	23	28	11-12
	BOS	N	P-O		5	1- 3
						.050
1885	BOS	N	P		11	5- 6
				39	44	17-21
						.159

DAVIS, JOHN HUMPHREY (RED)
B.JULY 15,1915 LAUREL RUN,PA.

YR	CL	LEA	POS	G	REC
1941	NY	N	3	21	.214
	BRTR				

**DAVIS, JOHN WILBUR
(BUD) OR (COUNTRY)**
B.DEC.7,1896 MERRY POINT,VA.
D.MAY 26,1967 WILLIAMSBURG,VA.

YR	CL	LEA	POS	G	REC
1915	PHI	A	P	20	1- 2
	BLTR				

DAVIS, LAWRENCE COLUMBUS (CRASH)
B.JULY 14,1919 CANON,GA.

YR	CL	LEA	POS	G	REC
1940	PHI	A	2-S	23	.269
1941	PHI	A	1-2	39	.219
1942	PHI	A	1-2-S	86	.224
	BRTR			148	.230

DAVIS, OTIS ALLEN (SCAT)
B.SEPT.24,1920 CHARLESTON,ARK.

YR	CL	LEA	POS	G	REC
1946	BRO	N	H	1	.000
	BLTL				

DAVIS, RAY THOMAS (PEACHES)
B.MAY 31,1905 GLEN ROSE,TEX.

YR	CL	LEA	POS	G	REC
1936	CIN	N	P	26	8- 8
1937	CIN	N	P	42	11-13
1938	CIN	N	P	29	7-12
1939	CIN	N	P	20	1- 0
	BLTR			117	27-33

DAVIS, RICHARD EARL (DICK)
B.SEPT.25,1953 LONG BEACH,CAL.

YR	CL	LEA	POS	G	REC
1977	MIL	A	O	22	.275
1978	MIL	A	D-O	69	.248
	BRTR			91	.253

DAVIS, ROBERT BRANDON (BRANDY)
B.SEPT.10,1928 NEWARK,DEL.

YR	CL	LEA	POS	G	REC
1952	PIT	N	O	55	.179
1953	PIT	N	O	12	.205
	BRTR			67	.187

DAVIS, ROBERT EDWARD (BOB)
B.SEPT.11,1933 NEW YORK,N.Y.

YR	CL	LEA	POS	G	REC
1958	KC	A	P	8	0- 4
1960	KC	A	P	21	0- 0
	BRTR			29	0- 4

DAVIS, ROBERT JOHN EUGENE (BOB)
B.MAR.1,1952 PRYOR,OKLA.

YR	CL	LEA	POS	G	REC
1973	SD	N	/C	5	.091
1975	SD	N	C	43	.234
1976	SD	N	C	51	.205
1977	SD	N	C	48	.181
1978	SD	N	C	19	.200
	BRTR			166	.205

YR	CL LEA POS	GP	G	REC

DAVIS, RONALD EVERETTE (RON)
B.OCT.21,1941 ROANOKE RAPIDS,N.C
1962	HOU N O		6	.214
1966	HOU N O		48	.247
1967	HOU N O		94	.256
1968	HOU N O		52	.212
	STL N O		33	.177
1969	PIT N O		62	.234
	BRTR		295	.233

DAVIS, RONALD GENE (RON)
B.AUG.6,1955 HOUSTON,TEX.
| 1978 | NY A /P | | 4 | 0- 0 |
| | BRTR | | | |

DAVIS, THOMAS J.
| 1890 | CLE N O | | 6 | .214 |

DAVIS, THOMAS OSCAR (TOD)
B.JULY 24,1924 LOS ANGELES,CAL.
1949	PHI A 2-S-3		31	.267
1951	PHI A 2-3		11	.067
	BRTR		42	.233

DAVIS, VIRGIL LAWRENCE (SPUD)
B.DEC.20,1904 BIRMINGHAM,ALA.
1928	STL N C		2	.200
	PHI N C		67	.282
1929	PHI N C		98	.342
1930	PHI N C		106	.313
1931	PHI N C		120	.326
1932	PHI N C		125	.336
1933	PHI N C		141	.349
1934	STL N C		107	.300
1935	STL N C-1		102	.317
1936	STL N C		112	.273
1937	CIN N C		76	.268
1938	CIN N C		12	.167
	PHI N C		70	.247
1939	PHI N C		87	.307
1940	PIT N C		99	.326
1941	PIT N C		57	.252
1944	PIT N C		54	.301
1945	PIT N C		23	.242
	BRTR		1458	.308
NON-PLAYING MANAGER PIT(N) 1946

DAVIS, WILEY ANDERSON
B.AUG.1,1875 SEYMOUR,TENN.
D.SEPT.22,1942 DETROIT,MICH.
| 1896 | CIN N P | | 2 | 0- 0 |
| | BRTR | | | |

DAVIS, WILLIAM HENRY (WILLIE)
B.APR.15,1940 MINERAL SPRINGS,ARK.
1960	LA N O		22	.318
1961	LA N O		128	.254
1962	LA N O		157	.285
1963	LA N O		156	.245
1964	LA N O		157	.294
1965	LA N *O		142	.238
1966	LA N *O		153	.284
1967	LA N *O		143	.257
1968	LA N *O		160	.250
1969	LA N *O		129	.311
1970	LA N *O		146	.305
1971	LA N *O		158	.309
1972	LA N *O		149	.289
1973	LA N *O		152	.285
1974	MON N *O		153	.295
1975	TEX A O		42	.249
	STL N O		98	.291
1976	SD N *O		141	.268
	BLTL		2386	.279

DAVIS, WOODROW WILSON (BABE)
B.APR.25,1913 NICHOLLS,GA.
| 1938 | DET A P | | 2 | 0- 0 |
| | BRTR | | | |

DAVISON, MICHAEL LYNN (MIKE)
B.AUG.4,1945 GALESBURG,ILL.
1969	SF N /P		1	0- 0
1970	SF N P		31	3- 5
	BLTL		32	3- 5

DAWSON, ANDRE FERNANDO
B.JULY 10,1954 MIAMI,FLA.
1976	MON N O		24	.235
1977	MON N *O		139	.282
1978	MON N *O		157	.253
	BRTR		320	.264

DAWSON, RALPH FENTON (JOE)
B.MAR.9,1897 BOW,WASH.
D.JAN.4,1978 LONGVIEW,TEX.
1924	CLE A P		4	1- 2
1927	PIT N P		20	3- 7
1928	PIT N P		31	7- 7
1929	PIT N P		4	0- 1
	BRTR		59	11-17

DAWSON, REXFORD PAUL
B.FEB.10,1889 SKAGIT CO.,WASH.
D.OCT.20,1958 INDIANAPOLIS,IND.
| 1913 | WAS A P | | 1 | 0- 0 |
| | BLTR | | | |

YR	CL LEA POS	GP	G	REC

DAY, CHARLES FREDERICK (BOOTS)
B.AUG.31,1947 ILION,N.Y.
1969	STL N /O		11	.000
1970	CHI N /O		11	.250
	MON N O		41	.269
1971	MON N *O		127	.283
1972	MON N *O		128	.233
1973	MON N O		101	.275
1974	MON N O		52	.185
	BLTL		471	.256

DAY, CLYDE HENRY (PEA RIDGE)
B.AUG.26,1899 PEA RIDGE,ARK.
D.MAR.22,1934 KANSAS CITY,MO.
1924	STL N P		3	1- 1
1925	STL N P		17	2- 4
1926	CIN N P		4	0- 0
1931	BRO N P		22	2- 2
	BRTR		46	5- 7

DAY, JOHN B.
B.MAR.2,1847 PORTLAND,CONN.
D.JAN.25,1925 CLIFFSIDE,N.J.
NON-PLAYING MANAGER NY(N) 1899

DAY, WILLIAM
B.JULY 26,1867 WILMINGTON,DEL.
D.AUG.6,1923 WILMINGTON,DEL.
1889	PHI N P		3	0- 3
1890	PHI N P		4	1- 0
	PIT N P		7	0- 7
	TR		14	1-11

DEAGLE, LORENZO BURROUGHS (REN)
B.JUNE 26,1858 NEW YORK,N.Y.
D.DEC.24,1937 KANSAS CITY,MO.
1883	CIN N P-S		19	10- 8
				.130
1884	CIN AA P-S		3	2- 1
	LOU AA P-O		12	4- 6
				.114
	BRTR		34	16-15
				.109

DEAL, CHARLES ALBERT
B.OCT.30,1891 WILKINSBURG,PA.
1912	DET A 3		41	.225
1913	DET A 3		16	.220
	BOS N 3		10	.309
1914	BOS N 3		79	.210
1915	STL F 3		65	.314
1916	STL A 3		23	.135
	CHI N 3		2	.250
1917	CHI N 3		135	.254
1918	CHI N 3		119	.239
1919	CHI N 3		116	.289
1920	CHI N 3		129	.240
1921	CHI N 3		115	.289
	BRTR		850	.256

DEAL, ELLIS FERGASON (COT)
B.JAN.23,1923 ARAPAHO,OKLA.
1947	BOS A P		5	0- 1
1948	BOS A P		4	1- 0
1950	STL N P		3	0- 0
1954	STL N P		33	2- 3
	BRTR	45	46	3- 4
	BL 1947-48			

DEAL, FRED LINDSAY
B.SEPT.3,1911 LENOIR,N.C.
| 1939 | BRO N P | | 4 | .000 |
| | BLTR | | | |

DEAL, JOHN WESLEY (SNAKE)
B.JAN.21,1879 CONSHOHOCKEN,PA.
D.MAY 9,1944 HARRISBURG,PA.
| 1906 | CIN N 1 | | 65 | .208 |
| | BRTR | | | |

DEALEY, PATRICK E.
B.MOOSUP,CONN.
D.JAN.1925 BUFFALO,N.Y.
1884	STP U C-O		5	.143
1885	BOS N C-1-S-3		34	.230
1886	BOS N C		14	.333
1887	WAS N C-S		56	.286
1890	SYR AA P-C		1	18	0- 1
				.174
	BRTR		1	127	0- 1
				.256

YR	CL LEA POS	GP	G	REC

DEAN, ALFRED LOVILL (CHUBBY)
B.AUG.24,1916 MT.AIRY,N.C.
D.DEC.21,1970 RIVERSIDE,CAL.
1936	PHI A 1		111	.287
1937	PHI A P-1	2	104	1- 0
				.262
1938	PHI A P		6	16	2- 1
1939	PHI A P		54	80	5- 8
1940	PHI A P-1		30	67	6-13
				.289
1941	PHI A P		18	27	2- 4
				.237
	CLE A P-1		8	17	1- 4
				.167
1942	CLE A P		27	70	8-11
1943	CLE A P		17	41	5- 5
	BLTL		162	533	30-46
				.274

DEAN, CHARLES WILSON (DORY)
B.NOV.6,1852 CINCINNATI,OHIO
D.MAY 4,1935 NASHVILLE,TENN.
1874	BAL NA 2-O		47	-
1876	CIN N P-S-		30	34	4-26
	O				.257
	BRTR		30	81	4-26
				-

DEAN, JAMES HARRY
B.MAY 12,1915 ROCKMART,GA.
D.JUNE 1,1960 ROCKMART,GA.
| 1941 | WAS A P | | 2 | 0- 0 |
| | BRTR | | | |

DEAN, JAY HANNA (DIZZY)
B.JAN.16,1911 LUCAS,ARK.
D.JULY 17,1974 RENO,NEVADA
1930	STL N P		1	1- 0
1932	STL N P		46	47	18-15
1933	STL N P		48	51	20-18
1934	STL N P		50	51	30- 7
1935	STL N P		50	53	28-12
1936	STL N P		51	24-13
1937	STL N P		27	13-10
1938	CHI N P		13	7- 1
1939	CHI N P		19	6- 4
1940	CHI N P		10	3- 3
1941	CHI N P		1	0- 0
1947	STL A P		1	0- 0
	BRTR		317	325	150-83

DEAN, PAUL DEE (DAFFY)
B.AUG.14,1913 LUCAS,ARK.
1934	STL N P		39	19-11
1935	STL N P		46	19-12
1936	STL N P		17	5- 5
1937	STL N P		1	0- 0
1938	STL N P		5	3- 1
1939	STL N P		16	0- 1
1940	NY N P		27	4- 4
1941	NY N P		5	0- 0
1943	STL A P		3	0- 0
	BRTR		159	50-34

DEAN, TOMMY DOUGLAS
B.AUG.30,1945 IUKA,MISS.
1967	LA N S		12	.143
1969	SD N S/2		101	.176
1970	SD N S		61	.222
1971	SD N S-3/2		41	.114
	BRTR		215	.180

DEAN, WAYLAND OGDEN
B.JUNE 20,1902 RICHMOND,W.VA.
A.APR.10,1930 HUNTINGTON,W.VA.
1924	NY N P		26	6-12
1925	NY N P		33	10- 7
1926	PHI N P		33	63	8-16
1927	PHI N P		2	3	0- 1
	CHI N P		2	0- 0
	BBTR		96	127	24-36

DEANE, JOHN HENRY
B.MAY 6,1846 TRENTON,N.J.
D.MAY 31,1925.
| 1871 | KEK NA M-O | | 5 | - |

DEAR, PAUL STANFORD (BUDDY)
B.DEC.1,1905 NORFOLK,VA.
| 1927 | WAS A 2 | | 2 | .000 |
| | BRTR | | | |

DE ARMOND, CHARLES HOMMER (HUMMER)
B.FEB.13,1877 OKEANA,OHIO
D.DEC.17,1933 MORNING SUN,OHIO
| 1903 | CIN N 3 | | 11 | .297 |
| | BRTR | | | |

DEASLEY, JAMES (SACK)
B.PHILADELPHIA,PA.
1884	WAS U S		31	.216
	KC U S		13	.175
			44	.207

YR CL LEA POS GP G REC

DEASLEY, THOMAS H. (PAT)
B.NOV.17,1857 PHILADELPHIA,PA.
D.APR.1,1943 PHILADELPHIA,PA.
1881 BOS N C-1-S-O 43 .229
1882 BOS N C-S-O 66 .267
1883 STL AA C-O 53 .250
1884 STL AA C 73 .202
1885 NY N C-S 52 .256
1886 NY N C 38 .265
1887 NY N C 29 .362
1888 WAS N C 34 .157
BRTR 388 .246

DE BARR, DENNIS LEE
B.JAN.16,1953 CHEYENNE,WYO.
1977 TOR A P 14 0- 1
BLTL

DE BERRY, JOHN HERMAN (HANK)
B.DEC.29,1894 SAVANNAH,TENN.
D.SEPT.10,1951 SAVANNAH,TENN.
1916 CLE A C 15 .273
1917 CLE A C 25 .273
1922 BRO N C 85 .301
1923 BRO N C 78 .285
1924 BRO N C 77 .243
1925 BRO N C 67 .259
1926 BRO N C 48 .287
1927 BRO N C 68 .234
1928 BRO N C 82 .252
1929 BRO N C 68 .262
1930 BRO N C 35 .295
BRTR 648 .267

DE BERRY, JOSEPH GADDY
B.NOV.29,1896 MT.GILEAD,N.C.
D.OCT.9,1944 SOUTHERN PINES,N.C
1920 STL A P 10 2- 4
1921 STL A P 10 0- 1
BLTR 20 2- 5

DEBUS, ADAM JOSEPH
B.OCT.7,1892 CHICAGO,ILL.
D.MAY 13,1977 CHICAGO,ILL.
1917 PIT N S-3 38 .229
BRTR

DE BUSSCHERE, DAVID ALBERT (DAVE)
B.OCT.16,1940 DETROIT,MICH.
1962 CHI A P 12 0- 0
1963 CHI A P 24 3- 4
BRTR 36 3- 4

DECATUR, ARTHUR RUE
B.JAN.14,1894 CLEVELAND,OHIO
D.APR.25,1966 TALLADEGA,ALA.
1922 BRO N P 29 3- 4
1923 BRO N P 36 3- 3
1924 BRO N P 31 10- 9
1925 BRO N P 1 0- 0
PHI N P 25 4-13
1926 PHI N P 2 0- 0
1927 PHI N P 29 3- 5
BRTR 153 23-34

DE CINCES, DOUGLAS VERNON (DOUG)
B.AUG.29,1950 BURBANK,CAL.
1973 BAL A /3-2-S 10 .111
1974 BAL A /3 1 .000
1975 BAL A 3-S-2/1 61 .251
1976 BAL A *3-2-1/S 129 .234
1977 BAL A *3/1-2 150 .259
1978 BAL A *3-2 142 .286
BRTR 493 .258

DECKER, EDWARD HARRY
B.SEPT.3,1854 LOCKPORT,ILL.
1879 SYR N C-1-O 3 .100
1882 STL AA 2 2 .250
1884 IND AA C 4 .286
KC U C-O 23 .136
1886 DET N C-O 15 .203
WAS N C-3 6 .143
1889 PHI N C-2 11 .103
1890 PHI N C-1-O 5 .368
PIT N C 90 .273
BRTR 159 .236

DECKER, GEORGE A (GENTLEMAN GEORGE)
B.JUNE 1,1869 YORK,PA.
D.JUNE 9,1909 COMPTON,CAL.
1892 CHI N 2-O 79 .231
1893 CHI N 1-2-O 81 .276
1894 CHI N 1-O 89 .310
1895 CHI N O 70 .291
1896 CHI N 1-O 106 .281
1897 CHI N 1-O 109 .307
1898 STL N 1 64 .263
LOU N 1-O 42 .315
1899 LOU N 1 38 .234
WAS N 1-O 4 .000
682 .281

YR CL LEA POS GP G REC

DECKER, GEORGE HENRY (JOE)
B.JUNE 16,1947 STORM LAKE,IA.
1969 CHI N /P 4 1- 0
1970 CHI N P 24 2- 7
1971 CHI N P 21 22 3- 2
1972 CHI N /P 5 1- 0
1973 MIN A P 29 10-10
1974 MIN A P 37 16-14
1975 MIN A P 10 1- 3
1976 MIN A P 13 2- 7
BRTR 143 144 36-43

DEDE, ARTHUR RICHARD
B.JULY 12,1895 BROOKLYN,N.Y.
D.SEPT.6,1971 KEENE,N.H.
1916 BRO N C 1 .000
BRTR

DEDEAUX, RAOUL MARTIAL (ROD)
B.FEB.17,1915 NEW ORLEANS,LA.
1935 BRO N S 2 .250
BRTR

DEE, JAMES D.
B.BUFFALO,N.Y.
1884 PIT AA S 13 .136

DEE, MAURICE LEO (SHORTY)
B.OCT.4,1889 HALIFAX,N.S.,CAN.
D.AUG.12,1971 JAMACIA PLAIN,MASS.
1915 STL A S 1 .000
BRTR

DEEGAN, W. JOHN (DUMMY)
B.NEW YORK,N.Y.
1901 NY N P 2 0- 2

DEERING, JOHN THOMAS
B.JUNE 25,1878 LYNN,MASS.
D.FEB.15,1943 BEVERLY,MASS.
1903 DET A P 11 3- 8
NY A P 9 3- 1
TR 20 6- 9

DEES, CHARLES HENRY (CHARLIE)
B.JUNE 24,1935 BIRMINGHAM,ALA.
1963 LA A 1 60 .307
1964 LA A 1 26 .077
1965 CAL A /1 12 .156
BLTL 98 .265

DE FATE, CLYDE HERBERT (TONY)
B.FEB.22,1895 KANSAS CITY,MO.
D.SEPT.3,1963 NEW ORLEANS,LA.
1917 STL N S 14 .143
DET A 2 3 .000
BRTR 17 .133

DE FREITAS, ARTURO MARCELINO [SIMON]
B.APR.26,1953 SAN PEDRO DE MACORIS,D.R.
1978 CIN N /1 9 .211
BRTR

DEGERICK, MICHAEL ARTHUR (MIKE)
B.APR.1,1943 NEW YORK,N.Y.
1961 CHI A P 1 0- 0
1962 CHI A P 1 0- 0
BRTR 2 0- 0

DE GROFF, EDWARD ARTHUR (RUBE)
B.SEPT.2,1879 HYDE PARK,N.Y.
D.DEC.17,1955 POUGHKEEPSIE,N.Y.
1905 STL N O 15 .250
1906 STL N O 1 .000
16 .233

DEHLMAN, HERMAN J.
B.1850 CATASAQUA,PA.
D.MAR.13,1885 WILKES-BARRE,PA.
1872 ATL NA 1 35 .201
1873 ATL NA 1 54 -
1874 ATL NA 1 53 -
1875 STL NA 1 64 .215
1876 STL N 1 64 .178
1877 STL N 1-O 32 .185
302 -

DEIDEL, JAMES LAWRENCE (JIM)
B.JUNE 6,1949 DENVER,COL.
1974 NY A /C 2 .000
BRTR

DEININGER, OTTO CHARLES (PEP)
B.OCT.10,1877 WASSERALFINGEN,GERMANY
D.SEPT.25,1950 BOSTON,MASS.
1902 BOS A P 2 0- 1
1908 PHI N O 1 .000
1909 PHI N O 46 .260
BLTL 2 49 0- 1
.263

DEISEL, EDWARD (PAT)
B.APR.29,1876 RIPLEY,OHIO
D.APR.17,1948 CINCINNATI,OHIO
1902 BRO N C 1 .667
1903 CIN N C 2 .000
BRTR 3 .667

YR CL LEA POS GP G REC

DEITRICK, WILLIAM ALEXANDER
B.APR.20,1902 HANOVER CO.,VA.
D.MAY 6,1946 BETHESDA,MD.
1927 PHI N S 5 .167
1928 PHI N O 52 .200
BRTR 57 .198

DEJAN, MICHAEL DAN (MIKE)
B.JAN.13,1915 CLEVELAND,OHIO
D.FEB.2,1953 W.LOS ANGELES,CAL.
1940 CIN N O 12 .188
BLTL

DE JESUS, IVAN [ALVAREZ]
B.JAN.9,1953 SANTURCE,P.R.
1974 LA N /S 3 .333
1975 LA N S 63 .184
1976 LA N S/3 22 .171
1977 CHI N *S 155 .266
1978 CHI N *S 160 .278
BRTR 403 .263

DEKONING, WILLIAM CALLAHAN
B.DEC.19,1919 BROOKLYN,N.Y.
1945 NY N C 3 .000
BRTR

DE LA CRUZ, TOMAS
B.SEPT.18,1914 MARIANAO,CUBA
D.SEPT.6,1956 HAVANA,CUBA
1944 CIN N P 34 36 9- 9
BRTR

DELAHANTY, EDWARD JAMES (BIG ED)
B.OCT.30,1867 CLEVELAND,OHIO
D.JULY 2,1903 NIAGARA FALLS,N.Y
1888 PHI N 2 74 .227
1889 PHI N 2-O 54 .292
1890 CLE P 2-S-O 115 .296
1891 PHI N 1-O 128 .249
1892 PHI N O 120 .312
1893 PHI N O 132 .370
1894 PHI N O 114 .400
1895 PHI N O 116 .399
1896 PHI N 1-O 122 .394
1897 PHI N O 129 .377
1898 PHI N O 142 .334
1899 PHI N O 145 .408
1900 PHI N 1 130 .319
1901 PHI N 1-O 138 .357
1902 WAS A 1-O 123 .376
1903 WAS A O 43 .338
BRTR 1825 .346

DELAHANTY, FRANK GEORGE (PUDGIE)
B.JAN.29,1883 CLEVELAND,OHIO
D.JULY 22,1966 CLEVELAND,OHIO
1905 NY A 1-O 9 .240
1906 NY A O 92 .238
1907 CLE A O 15 .173
1908 NY A O 37 .256
1914 BUF F O 79 .212
PIT F O 42 .213
1915 PIT F O 14 .238
BRTR 288 .219

DELAHANTY, JAMES CHRISTOPHER
B.JUNE 20,1879 CLEVELAND,OHIO
D.OCT.17,1953 CLEVELAND,OHIO
1901 CHI N 3 16 .174
1902 NY N O 7 .231
1904 BOS N 2-3 138 .285
1905 BOS N O 124 .258
1906 CIN N 3 112 .280
1907 STL A 2-3 33 .219
WAS A 2-3 108 .293
1908 WAS A 2 82 .317
1909 WAS A 2 88 .221
DET A 2 48 .253
1910 DET A 2 106 .293
1911 DET A 1-2 144 .339
1912 DET A 2-3-O 78 .286
1914 BRO F 2 74 .284
1915 BRO F 1 16 .250
BRTR 1174 .283

DELAHANTY, JOSEPH NICHOLAS
B.OCT.18,1875 CLEVELAND,OHIO
D.JAN.9,1936 CLEVELAND,OHIO
1907 STL N O 6 .303
1908 STL N O 138 .255
1909 STL N 2-O 111 .214
BRTR 255 .238

DELAHANTY, THOMAS JAMES
B.MAR.9,1872 CLEVELAND,OHIO
D.JAN.10,1951 SANFORD,FLA.
1894 PHI N 2 1 .250
1896 CLE N 3 15 .216
PIT N S 1 .333
1897 LOU N 2 1 .333
BLTR 255 .238

YR	CL	LEA	POS	GP	G	REC

DE LA HOZ, MIGUEL ANGEL (MIKE)
B.OCT.2,1939 HAVANA,CUBA
1960	CLE	A	S-3		49	.256
1961	CLE	A	2-S-3		61	.260
1962	CLE	A	2		12	.083
1963	CLE	A	2-S-3-0		67	.267
1964	MIL	N	2-S-3		78	.291
1965	MIL	N	S-3-2/1		81	.295
1966	ATL	N	3/2-S		71	.218
1967	ATL	N	2-3/S		74	.203
1969	CIN	N	/H		1	.000
			BRTR		494	.251

DE LANCEY, WILLIAM PINKNEY
B.NOV.28,1911 GREENSBORO,N.C.
D.NOV.28,1946
1932	STL	N	C		8	.192
1934	STL	N	C		93	.316
1935	STL	N	C		103	.279
1940	STL	N	C		15	.222
			BLTR		219	.289

DE LANCY, WILLIAM L.
B.CINCINNATI,OHIO
| 1890 | CLE | N | 2 | | 36 | .189 |

DELANEY, ARTHUR DEWEY (SWEDE)
[REAL NAME ARTHUR DEWEY HELENIUS]
B.NOV.28,1901 GREENSBORO,N.C.
D.MAY 2,1970 HAYWARD,CAL.
1924	STL	N	P		8	1- 0
1928	BOS	N	P		39	9-17
1929	BOS	N	P		20	3- 5
			BRTR		67	13-22

DE LA ROSA, JESUS
B.JULY 28,1953 SANTO DOMINGO,D.R
| 1975 | HOU | N | /H | | 3 | .333 |
| | | | BRTR | | | |

DEL CALVO, JACINTO
[PLAYED UNDER NAME OF JACINTO CALVO]

DELGADO, LUIS FELIPE [ROBLES]
B.FEB.2,1954 HATILLO,P.R.
| 1977 | SEA | A | 0 | | 13 | .182 |
| | | | BBTL | | | |

DEL GRECO, ROBERT GEORGE (BOBBY)
B.APR.7,1933 PITTSBURGH,PA.
1952	PIT	N	0		99	.217
1956	PIT	N	3-0		14	.200
	STL	N	0		102	.215
1957	CHI	N	0		20	.200
	NY	A	0		8	.429
1958	NY	A	0		12	.200
1960	PHI	N	0		100	.237
1961	PHI	N	2-3-0		41	.259
	KC	A	0		74	.230
1962	KC	A	0		132	.254
1963	KC	A	3-0		121	.212
1965	PHI	N	/0		8	.000
			BRTR		731	.229

DELHI, LEE WILLIAM (FLAME)
B.NOV.5,1892 HARQUA HALA,ARIZ.
D.MAY 9,1966 SAN RAFAEL,CAL.
| 1912 | CHI | A | P | | 1 | 0- 0 |
| | | | BRTR | | | |

DELIS, JUAN FRANCISCO
B.FEB.27,1928 SANTIAGO,CUBA
| 1955 | WAS | A | 2-3-0 | | 54 | .189 |
| | | | BRTR | | | |

DELKER, EDWARD ALBERTS
B.APR.17,1907 DE ALTO,PA.
1929	STL	N	2-S-3		22	.150
1931	STL	N	3		1	.500
1932	STL	N	2		20	.119
	PHI	N	2		30	.161
1933	PHI	N	2-3		25	.171
			BRTR		98	.155

DELL, WILLIAM GEORGE (WHEEZER)
B.JUNE 11,1887 TUSCARORA,NEV.
D.AUG.24,1966 INDEPENDENCE,CAL.
1912	STL	N	P		3	0- 0
1915	BRO	N	P		40	11-10
1916	BRO	N	P		32	8- 9
1917	BRO	N	P		17	0- 4
			BRTR		92	19-23

DELMAS, ALBERT CHARLES (BERT)
B.MAY 20,1911 SAN FRANCISCO,CAL
| 1933 | BRO | N | 2 | | 12 | .250 |
| | | | BLTR | | | |

DELOCK, IVAN MARTIN (IKE)
B.NOV.11,1929 HIGHLAND PARK,MICH
1952	BOS	A	P		39	4- 9
1953	BOS	A	P		23	3- 1
1955	BOS	A	P		29	9- 7
1956	BOS	A	P		48	13- 7
1957	BOS	A	P		49	9- 8
1958	BOS	A	P		31	14- 8
1959	BOS	A	P		28	11- 6
1960	BOS	A	P		24	9-10
1961	BOS	A	P		28	6- 9
1962	BOS	A	P		17	4- 5
1963	BOS	A	P		6	1- 2
	BAL	A	P		7	1- 3
			BRTR		329	84-75

DE LOS SANTOS, RAMON [GENERO]
B.NOV.4,1949 SANTO DOMINGO,D.R.
| 1974 | HOU | N | P | | 12 | 1- 1 |
| | | | BLTL | | | |

DEL SAVIO, GARTON ORVILLE
B.NOV.26,1913 NEW YORK,N.Y.
| 1943 | PHI | N | S | | 4 | .091 |
| | | | BRTR | | | |

DELSING, JAMES HENRY (JIM)
B.NOV.13,1925 RUDOLPH,WIS.
1948	CHI	A	0		20	.190
1949	NY	A	0		9	.350
1950	NY	A	H		12	.400
	STL	A	0		69	.263
1951	STL	A	0		131	.249
1952	STL	A	0		93	.255
	DET	A	0		33	.274
1953	DET	A	0		138	.288
1954	DET	A	0		122	.248
1955	DET	A	0		114	.239
1956	DET	A	0		10	.000
	CHI	A	0		55	.122
1960	KC	A	0		16	.250
			BLTR		822	.255

DE MAESTRI, JOSEPH PAUL (OATS)
B.DEC.9,1928 SAN FRANCISCO,CAL.
1951	CHI	A	2-S-3		56	.203
1952	STL	A	S-3		81	.226
1953	PHI	A	S		111	.255
1954	PHI	A	2-S-3		146	.249
1955	KC	A	S		123	.249
1956	KC	A	2-S		133	.233
1957	KC	A	S		135	.245
1958	KC	A	S		139	.219
1959	KC	A	S		118	.244
1960	NY	A	2-S		49	.229
1961	NY	A	2-S-3		30	.146
			BRTR		1121	.236

DEMAREE, ALBERT WENTWORTH
B.SEPT.8,1884 QUINCY,ILL.
D.APR.30,1962 LOS ANGELES,CAL.
1912	NY	N	P		2	1- 0
1913	NY	N	P		31	13- 4
1914	NY	N	P		38	10-17
1915	NY	N	P		32	14-11
1916	PHI	N	P		39	19-14
1917	CHI	N	P		24	5- 9
	NY	N	P		15	4- 5
1918	NY	N	P		26	8- 6
1919	BOS	N	P		25	6- 6
			BLTR		232	80-72

DEMAREE, JOSEPH FRANKLIN (FRANK)
[REAL NAME JOSEPH FRANKLIN DIMARIA]
B.JUNE 10,1910 WINTERS,CAL.
D.AUG.30,1958 LOS ANGELES,CAL.
1932	CHI	N	0		23	.250
1933	CHI	N	0		134	.272
1935	CHI	N	0		107	.325
1936	CHI	N	0		154	.350
1937	CHI	N	0		154	.324
1938	CHI	N	0		129	.273
1939	NY	N	0		150	.304
1940	NY	N	0		121	.302
	BOS	N	0		16	.171
1941	NY	N	0		16	.171
	BOS	N	0		48	.230
1942	BOS	N	0		64	.225
1943	STL	N	0		39	.291
1944	STL	A	0		16	.255
			BRTR		1155	.299

DEMARRIS, FRED
B.1865 NASHUA,N.H.
| 1890 | CHI | N | P | | 1 | 0- 0 |
| | | | TR | | | |

DE MARS, WILLIAM LESTER (KID)
B.AUG.26,1925 BROOKLYN,N.Y.
1948	PHI	A	S-3		18	.172
1950	STL	A	S-3		61	.247
1951	STL	A	S		1	.250
			BRTR		80	.237

DE MERIT, JOHN STEPHEN
(JOHN) OR (THUMPER)
B.JAN.8,1936 WEST BEND,WIS.
1957	MIL	N	0		33	.147
1958	MIL	N	0		3	.667
1959	MIL	N	0		11	.200
1961	MIL	N	0		32	.162
1962	NY	N	0		14	.188
			BRTR		93	.174

DEMERY, LAWRENCE CALVIN (LARRY)
B.JUNE 4,1953 BAKERSFIELD,CAL.
1974	PIT	N	P		19	21	6- 6
1975	PIT	N	P		45	49	7- 5
1976	PIT	N	P		36	40	10- 7
1977	PIT	N	P		39	47	6- 5
			BRTR		139	157	29-23

DEMETER, DONALD LEE (DON)
B.JUNE 25,1935 OKLAHOMA CITY,OKLA
1956	BRO	N	0		3	.333
1958	LA	N	0		43	.189
1959	LA	N	0		139	.256
1960	LA	N	0		64	.274
1961	LA	N	0		15	.172
	PHI	N	1-0		106	.257
1962	PHI	N	1-3-0		153	.307
1963	PHI	N	1-3-0		154	.258
1964	DET	A	1-0		134	.256
1965	DET	A	0-1		122	.278
1966	DET	A	0/1		32	.212
	BOS	A	0/1		73	.292
1967	BOS	A	0/3		20	.279
	CLE	A	0/3		51	.207
			BRTR		1109	.265

DEMETER, STEPHEN (STEVE)
B.JAN.27,1935 HOMER CITY,PA.
1959	DET	A	3		11	.111
1960	CLE	A	3		4	.000
			BRTR		15	.087

DE MILLER, HARRY
B.NOV.12,1867 WOOSTER,OHIO
D.DEC.19,1928 SANTA ANA,CAL.
| 1892 | STL | N | S | | 1 | .000 |
| | | | BR | | | |

DEMMITT, CHARLES RAYMOND (RAY)
B.FEB.2,1884 ILLIOPOLIS,ILL.
D.FEB.19,1956 GLEN ELLYN,ILL.
1909	NY	A	0		119	.241
1910	STL	A	0		10	.173
1914	DET	A	0		3	.000
	CHI	A	0		145	.258
1915	CHI	A	0		9	.000
1917	STL	A	0		14	.283
1918	STL	A	0		116	.281
1919	STL	A	0		79	.238
			BLTR		493	.257

DE MOLA, DONALD JOHN (DON)
B.JULY 5,1952 GLEN COVE,N.Y.
1974	MON	N	P		25	1- 0
1975	MON	N	P		60	4- 7
			BRTR		85	5- 7

DE MONTREVILLE, EUGENE
B.MAR.26,1874 ST.PAUL,MINN.
D.FEB.18,1935 MEMPHIS,TENN.
1894	PIT	N	S		2	.250
1895	WAS	N	S		12	.227
1896	WAS	N	S		130	.349
1897	WAS	N	2-S		132	.349
1898	BAL	N	2-S		151	.325
1899	CHI	N	2		83	.286
	BAL	N	2		60	.276
1900	BRO	N	2		63	.250
1901	BOS	N	2-3		140	.305
1902	BOS	N	2-3		123	.269
1903	WAS	A	2		11	.292
1904	STL	A	2		4	.111
			BRTR		911	.308

DE MONTREVILLE, LEON (LEE)
B.SEPT.23,1879 ST.PAUL,MINN.
D.MAR.22,1962 PELHAM MANOR,N.Y.
| 1903 | STL | N | S | | 20 | .243 |
| | | | TR | | | |

DE MOTT, BENYEW HARRISON
B.APR.2,1889 GREEN VILLAGE,N.J.
D.JULY 5,1963 SOMERVILLE,N.J.
1910	CLE	A	P		9	0- 3
1911	CLE	A	P		2	0- 1
			BRTR		11	0- 4

DEMPSEY, CORNELIUS FRANCIS (CON)
B.SEP.16,1923 SAN FRANCISCO,CAL
| 1951 | PIT | N | P | | 3 | 0- 2 |
| | | | BRTR | | | |

YR	CL	LEA	POS	GP	G	REC

DEMPSEY, JOHN RIKARD (RICK)
B.SEP.13,1949 FAYETTEVILLE,TENN.
1969	MIN	A	/C		5	.500
1970	MIN	A	/C		5	.000
1971	MIN	A	/C		6	.308
1972	MIN	A	C		25	.200
1973	NY	A	/C		6	.182
1974	NY	A	C/O		43	.239
1975	NY	A	C-D/O-D		71	.262
1976	NY	A	/C-O		21	.119
	BAL	A	C/O		59	.213
1977	BAL	A	C		91	.226
1978	BAL	A	*C		136	.259
			BRTR		468	.237

DENEHY, WILLIAM FRANCIS (BILL)
B.MAR.31,1946 MIDDLETOWN,CONN.
1967	NY	N	P	15		1- 7
1968	WAS	A	/P	3		0- 0
1971	DET	A	P	31		0- 3
			BBTR	49		1-10
			BL 1971			

DENNEHY, THOMAS FRANCIS (TOD)
B.MAY 12,1899 PHILADELPHIA,PA.
| 1923 | PHI | N | O | | 9 | .250 |
| | | | BLTL | | | |

DENNING, OTTO GEORGE (DUTCH)
B.DEC.28,1912 HAYS,KAN.
1942	CLE	A	C-O		92	.210
1943	CLE	A	1		37	.240
			BRTR		129	.215

DENNIS, DONALD RAY (DON)
B.MAR.3,1942 UNIONTOWN,KAN.
1965	STL	N	P	41		2- 3
1966	STL	N	P	38		4- 2
			BRTR	79		6- 5

DENNIS, WALTER L.
B.1853 WASHINGTON,D.C.
D.SEPT.10,1889
NON-PLAYING MANAGER WAS[N] 1887

DENNY, JEREMIAH DENNIS (JERRY)
[REAL NAME JEREMIAH DENNIS ELDRIDGE]
B.MAR.16,1859 NEW YORK,N.Y.
D.AUG.16,1927 HOUSTON,TEX.
1881	PRO	N	3		84	.240
1882	PRO	N	3		84	.246
1883	PRO	N	3		98	.274
1884	PRO	N	C-1-2-3		108	.251
1885	PRO	N	3		83	.223
1886	STL	N	3		119	.257
1887	IND	N	3		122	.340
1888	IND	N	S-3		126	.261
1889	IND	N	3		133	.262
1890	NY	N	3		114	.212
1891	NY	N	3		4	.250
	CLE	N	3		36	.229
	PHI	N	1-3		19	.301
1893	LOU	N	S		44	.251
1894	LOU	N	3		60	.274
			BRTR		1234	.263

DENNY, JOHN ALLEN
B.NOV.8,1952 PRESCOTT,ARIZ.
1974	STL	N	/P	2		0- 0
1975	STL	N	P	25	26	10- 7
1976	STL	N	P		30	11- 9
1977	STL	N	P		26	8- 8
1978	STL	N	P		33	14-11
			BRTR	116	117	43-35

DENT, ELLIOTT ESTILL (EDDIE)
B.DEC.8,1867 BALTIMORE,MD.
D.NOV.25,1974 BIRMINGHAM,ALA.
1909	BRO	N	P	6		2- 4
1911	BRO	N	P	5		2- 1
1912	BRO	N	P	1		0- 0
				12		4- 5

DENT, RUSSELL EARL (BUCKY)
B.NOV.25,1951 SAVANNAH,GA.
1973	CHI	A	S/2-3		40	.248
1974	CHI	A	*S		154	.274
1975	CHI	A	*S		157	.264
1976	CHI	A	*S		158	.246
1977	NY	A	*S		158	.247
1978	NY	A	*S		123	.243
			BRTR		790	.255

DENTE, SAMUEL JOSEPH (BLACKIE)
B.APR.26,1922 HARRISON,N.J.
1947	BOS	A	3		46	.232
1948	STL	A	S		98	.270
1949	WAS	A	S		153	.273
1950	WAS	A	2-S		155	.239
1951	WAS	A	3-S		88	.238
1952	CHI	A	1-2-S-3-O		62	.221
1953	CHI	A	S		2	.000
1954	CLE	A	2-S		68	.266
1955	CLE	A	S-S-3		73	.257
			BRTR		749	.252

DENZER, ROGER (PEACEFUL VALLEY)
B.OCT.5,1871 LESEUR,MINN.
D.SEPT.18,1949 LESEUR,MINN.
1897	CIN	N	P	12		3- 6
1901	NY	N	P	11		2- 5
			TR	23		5-11

DE PHILLIPS, ANTHONY ANDREW
B.SEPT.20,1912 NEW YORK,N.Y.
| 1943 | CIN | N | C | | 35 | .100 |
| | | | BRTR | | | |

DERBY, EUGENE A.
B.TROY,N.Y.
| 1885 | BAL | AA | P-C- | 1 | 10 | 0- 1 |
| | | | | | | .129 |

DERBY, GEORGE H. (JONAH)
B.JULY 6,1857 WEBSTER,MASS.
D.JULY 4,1925 PHILADELPHIA,PA.
1881	DET	N	P-O	55	59	29-26
						.186
1882	DET	N	P-O	36	38	16-20
						.202
1883	BUF	N	P-O		15	3-11
						.237
			BLTR	106	112	48-57
						.199

DERRICK, CLAUD LESTER (DEEK)
B.JUNE 11,1886 BURTON,GA.
D.JULY 15,1974 CLAYTON,GA.
1910	PHI	A	S		2	.000
1911	PHI	A	2		36	.230
1912	PHI	A	S		21	.241
1913	NY	A	S		22	.292
1914	CIN	N	S		3	.333
	CHI	N	S		28	.219
			BRTR		112	.242

DERRICK, JAMES MICHAEL (MIKE)
B.SEPT.19,1943 COLUMBIA,S.C.
| 1970 | BOS | A | /O-1 | | 24 | .212 |
| | | | BLTR | | | |

DERRINGER, SAMUEL PAUL (DUKE)
B.OCT.17,1906 SPRINGFIELD,KY.
1931	STL	N	P		35	18- 8
1932	STL	N	P		39	11-14
1933	STL	N	P		3	0- 2
	CIN	N	P		33	7-25
1934	CIN	N	P		47	15-21
1935	CIN	N	P		45	22-13
1936	CIN	N	P		51	19-19
1937	CIN	N	P		43	10-14
1938	CIN	N	P		41	21-14
1939	CIN	N	P		38	25- 7
1940	CIN	N	P		37	20-12
1941	CIN	N	P		29	12-14
1942	CIN	N	P		29	10-11
1943	CHI	N	P		32	10-14
1944	CHI	N	P		42	7-13
1945	CHI	N	P		35	16-11
			BRTR		579	223-212

DERRINGTON, CHARLES JAMES
(JIM) OR (BLACKIE)
B.NOV.29,1939 COMPTON,CAL.
1956	CHI	A	P	1		0- 1
1957	CHI	A	P	20		0- 1
			BLTL	21		0- 2

DERRY, ALVA RUSSELL (RUSS)
B.OCT.7,1916 PRINCETON,MO.
1944	NY	A	O		38	.254
1945	NY	A	O		78	.225
1946	PHI	A	O		69	.207
1949	STL	N	H		2	.000
			BLTR		187	.224

DESAUTELS, EUGENE ABRAHAM (RED)
B.JUNE 13,1907 WORCESTER,MASS.
1930	DET	A	C		42	.190
1931	DET	A	C		3	.091
1932	DET	A	C		28	.236
1933	DET	A	C		30	.143
1937	BOS	A	C		96	.243
1938	BOS	A	C		108	.291
1939	BOS	A	C		76	.243
1940	BOS	A	C		71	.225
1941	CLE	A	C		66	.201
1942	CLE	A	C		62	.247
1943	CLE	A	C		68	.205
1945	CLE	A	C		10	.111
1946	PHI	A	C		52	.215
			BRTR		712	.233

DE SHONG, JAMES BROOKLYN
B.NOV.30,1909 HARRISBURG,PA.
1932	PHI	A	P	6		0- 0
1934	NY	A	P	31		6- 7
1935	NY	A	P	29		4- 1
1936	WAS	A	P	34	35	18-10
1937	WAS	A	P		37	14-15
1938	WAS	A	P		31	5- 8
1939	WAS	A	P		7	0- 3
			BRTR	175	176	47-44

DES JARDIEN, PAUL RAYMOND (SHORTY)
B.AUG.24,1893 COFFEYVILLE,KAN.
D.MAR.7,1956 MONROVIA,CAL.
| 1916 | CLE | A | P | 1 | | 0- 0 |
| | | | BRTR | | | |

DESSAU, FRANK ROLLAND (RUBE)
B.MAR.29,1883 NEW GALILEE,PA.
D.MAY 6,1952 YORK,PA.
1907	BOS	N	P		2	0- 1
1910	BRO	N	P		19	2- 3
			BBTR		21	2- 4

DETORE, GEORGE FRANCIS
B.NOV.11,1906 UTICA,N.Y.
1930	CLE	A	3		3	.167
1931	CLE	A	S-3		30	.267
			BRTR		33	.250

DETTORE, THOMAS ANTHONY (TOM)
B.NOV.17,1947 CANONSBURG,PA.
1973	PIT	N	P		12	0- 1
1974	CHI	N	P		16	3- 5
1975	CHI	N	P		36	5- 4
1976	CHI	N	/P		4	0- 1
			BLTR		68	8-11

DETWEILER, ROBERT STERLING (DUCKY)
B.FEB.15,1919 TRUMBAUERSVILLE,PA.
1942	BOS	N	3		12	.318
1946	BOS	N	H		1	.000
			BRTR		13	.311

DEUTSCH, MELVIN ELLIOTT
B.JULY 26,1915 CALDWELL,TEX.
| 1946 | BOS | A | P | | 3 | 0- 0 |
| | | | BRTR | | | |

DEVENS, CHARLES
B.JAN.1,1910 MILTON,MASS.
1932	NY	A	P		1	1- 0
1933	NY	A	P		14	3- 3
1934	NY	A	P		1	1- 0
			BRTR		16	5- 3

DEVINE, PAUL ADRIAN (ADRIAN)
B.DEC.2,1951 GALVESTON,TEX.
1973	ATL	N	P		24	2- 3
1975	ATL	N	/P		5	1- 0
1976	ATL	N	P		48	5- 6
1977	TEX	A	P		56	11- 6
1978	ATL	N	P		31	5- 4
			BRTR		164	24-19

DEVINE, WALTER JAMES (JIM)
B.OCT.5,1858 BROOKLYN,N.Y.
D.JAN.11,1905 SYRACUSE,N.Y.
1883	BAL	AA	P-O		2	1- 1
						.222
1886	NY	N	O		1	.000
			TL	2	3	1- 1
						.167

DEVINE, WILLIAM PATRICK (MICKEY)
B.MAY 9,1892 ALBANY,N.Y.
D.OCT.1,1937 ALBANY,N.Y.
1918	PHI	N	C		4	.125
1920	BOS	A	C		8	.201
1925	NY	N	C-3		21	.273
			BRTR		33	.226

DEVINEY, HAROLD J. (HAL)
B.APR.11,1893 NEWTON,MASS.
D.JAN.5,1933 WESTWOOD,MASS.
| 1920 | BOS | A | P | | 1 | 0- 0 |

DE VIVEIROS, BERNARD JOHN
B.APR.19,1901 OAKLAND,CAL.
1924	CHI	A	S		1	.000
1927	DET	A	S		24	.227
					25	.217

DEVLIN, ARTHUR MC ARTHUR
B.OCT.16,1879 WASHINGTON,D.C.
D.SEPT.18,1948 JERSEY CITY,N.J.
1904	NY	N	3		130	.281
1905	NY	N	3		153	.246
1906	NY	N	3		148	.299
1907	NY	N	3		143	.277
1908	NY	N	3		137	.253
1909	NY	N	3		143	.265
1910	NY	N	3		147	.260
1911	NY	N	3		95	.278
1912	BOS	N	1-5-3		124	.289
1913	BOS	N	3		73	.229
			BRTR		1313	.269

DEVLIN, JAMES ALEXANDER
B.1849 PHILADELPHIA,PA.
D.OCT.10,1883 PHILADELPHIA,PA.
1873	PHI	NA	1-5-3-O		21	-
1874	CHI	NA	1-3-O		44	-
1875	CHI	NA	P-1-	26	70	6-14
			O			-
1876	LOU	N	P		68	30-35
1877	LOU	N	P		61	35-25
			BRTR	155	264	71-74
						-

YR CL LEA POS   GP   G   REC

DEVLIN, JAMES H.
B.APR.16,1856 TROY,N.Y.
D.DEC.14,1900 TROY,N.Y.

YR	CL	LEA	POS	GP	G	REC
1886	NY	N	P		1	0- 0
1887	PHI	N	P		2	0- 2
1888	STL	AA	P		12	6- 5
1889	STL	AA	P		9	4- 2
	TL				24	10- 9

DEVLIN, JAMES RAYMOND
B.JAN.4,1922 PLAINS,PA.

YR	CL	LEA	POS	GP	G	REC
1944	CLE	A	C		1	.000
	BLTR					

DE VOGT, REX EUGENE
B.JAN.4,1888 CLARE,MICH.
D.NOV.9,1935 ALMA,MICH.

YR	CL	LEA	POS	GP	G	REC
1913	BOS	N	C		3	.000
	BRTR					

DEVORE, JOSHUA D. (JOSH)
B.NOV.13,1887 MURRAY CITY,OHIO
D.OCT.6,1954 CHILLICOTHE,OHIO

YR	CL	LEA	POS	GP	G	REC
1908	NY	N	O		5	.167
1909	NY	N	O		23	.160
1910	NY	N	O		130	.304
1911	NY	N	O		149	.280
1912	NY	N	O		106	.275
1913	NY	N	O		16	.190
	CIN	N	O		66	.267
	PHI	N	O		23	.282
1914	PHI	N	O		30	.302
	BOS	N	O		51	.227
	BLTL				599	.278

DE VORMER, ALBERT E.
B.AUG.19,1891 GRAND RAPIDS,MICH
D.AUG.29,1966 GRAND RAPIDS,MICH

YR	CL	LEA	POS	GP	G	REC
1918	CHI	A	C		8	.315
1921	NY	A	C		22	.347
1922	NY	A	C		24	.203
1923	BOS	A	C		74	.258
1927	NY	N	C		68	.248
	BRTR				196	.261

DEVOY, WALTER JOSEPH
B.MAR.14,1885 ST.LOUIS,MO.
D.DEC.17,1953 ST.LOUIS,MO.

YR	CL	LEA	POS	GP	G	REC
1909	STL	A	O		19	.247

DEWALD, CHARLES H.
B.1867 NEWARK,N.J.

YR	CL	LEA	POS	GP	G	REC
1890	CLE	P	P		2	2- 0
	TL					

DEXTER, CHARLES DANA
B.JUNE 15,1876 EVANSVILLE,IND.
D.JUNE 9,1934 CEDAR RAPIDS,IOWA

YR	CL	LEA	POS	GP	G	REC
1896	LOU	N	C-O		98	.284
1897	LOU	N	C-O		63	.292
1898	LOU	N	O		112	.311
1899	LOU	N	O		76	.262
1900	CHI	N	C		35	.201
1901	CHI	N	1-3-O		112	.278
1902	CHI	N	1-3-O		70	.227
	BOS	N	2-S-3-O		49	.257
1903	BOS	N	O		120	.223
	TR				735	.263

DIAZ, BAUDILIO JOSE [SEIJAS] (BO)
B.MAR.23,1953 CUA,VENEZUELA

YR	CL	LEA	POS	GP	G	REC
1977	BOS	A	/C		2	.000
1978	CLE	A	C		44	.236
	BRTR				46	.234

DIBUT, PEDRO
B.NOV.18,1892 CIENFUEGOS,CUBA
DECEASED

YR	CL	LEA	POS	GP	G	REC
1924	CIN	N	P		7	3- 0
1925	CIN	N	P		1	0- 0
	BRTR				8	3- 0

DICKEN, PAUL FRANKLIN
B.OCT.2,1943 DELAND,FLA.

YR	CL	LEA	POS	GP	G	REC
1964	CLE	A	H		11	.000
1966	CLE	A	/H		2	.000
	BRTR				13	.000

DICKERMAN, LEO LOUIS
B.OCT.31,1896 DE SOTO,MO.

YR	CL	LEA	POS	GP	G	REC
1923	BRO	N	P		35	8-12
1924	BRO	N	P		7	0- 0
	STL	N	P		18	7- 4
1925	STL	N	P		29	4-11
	BRTR				69	19-27

DICKERSON, GEORGE CLARK
B.DEC.1,1892 RENNER,TEX.
D.JULY 9,1938 LOS ANGELES,CAL.

YR	CL	LEA	POS	GP	G	REC
1917	CLE	A	P		1	0- 0
	BRTR					

DICKERSON, LEWIS PESSANO (BUTTERCUP)
B.OCT.1,1858 TYASKIN,MD.
D.JULY 23,1920 BALTIMORE,MD.

YR	CL	LEA	POS	GP	G	REC
1878	CIN	N	O		30	.309
1879	CIN	N	O		80	.294
1880	TRO	N	S-O		30	.189
	WOR	N	O		31	.316
1881	WOR	N	O		80	.316
1883	PIT	AA	2-S-O		80	.283
1884	STL	U	3-O		46	.357
	BAL	AA	O		13	.232
	LOU	AA	O		5	.138
1885	BUF	N	S-O		5	.048
	BLTR				403	.286

DICKEY, GEORGE WILLARD (SKEETS)
B.JULY 10,1915 KENSETT,ARK.
D.JUNE 16,1976 DEWITT,ARK.

YR	CL	LEA	POS	GP	G	REC
1935	BOS	A	C		5	.000
1936	BOS	A	C		10	.043
1941	CHI	A	C		32	.200
1942	CHI	A	C		59	.233
1946	CHI	A	C		37	.192
1947	CHI	A	C		83	.223
	BBTR				226	.204

DICKEY, WILLIAM MALCOLM (BILL)
B.JUNE 6,1907 BASTROP,LA.

YR	CL	LEA	POS	GP	G	REC
1928	NY	A	C		10	.200
1929	NY	A	C		130	.324
1930	NY	A	C		109	.339
1931	NY	A	C		130	.327
1932	NY	A	C		108	.310
1933	NY	A	C		130	.318
1934	NY	A	C		104	.322
1935	NY	A	C		120	.279
1936	NY	A	C		112	.362
1937	NY	A	C		140	.332
1938	NY	A	C		132	.313
1939	NY	A	C		128	.302
1940	NY	A	C		106	.247
1941	NY	A	C		109	.284
1942	NY	A	C		82	.295
1943	NY	A	C		85	.351
1946	NY	A	M-C		54	.261
	BLTR				1789	.313

DICKMAN, GEORGE EMERSON (EMERSON)
B.NOV.12,1914 BUFFALO,N.Y.

YR	CL	LEA	POS	GP	G	REC
1936	BOS	A	P		1	0- 0
1938	BOS	A	P		32	5- 5
1939	BOS	A	P		48	8- 3
1940	BOS	A	P		35	8- 6
1941	BOS	A	P		9	1- 1
	BRTR				125	22-15

DICKSHOT, JOHN OSCAR (UGLY)
(REAL NAME JOHN OSCAR DICKSUS)
B.JAN.24,1910 WAUKEGAN,ILL.

YR	CL	LEA	POS	GP	G	REC
1936	PIT	N	O		9	.222
1937	PIT	N	O		82	.254
1938	PIT	N	O		29	.229
1939	NY	N	O		10	.235
1944	CHI	A	O		62	.253
1945	CHI	A	O		130	.302
	BRTR				322	.276

DICKSON, JAMES EDWARD (JIM)
B.APR.20,1938 PORTLAND,ORE.

YR	CL	LEA	POS	GP	G	REC
1963	HOU	N	P		13	0- 1
1964	CIN	N	P		4	1- 0
1965	KC	A	P		68	3- 2
1966	KC	A	P		24	1- 0
	BLTR				109	5- 3

DICKSON, MURRY MONROE
B.AUG.21,1916 TRACY,MO.

YR	CL	LEA	POS	GP	G	REC
1939	STL	N	P		1	0- 0
1940	STL	N	P		1	0- 0
1942	STL	N	P		36	6- 3
1943	STL	N	P		31	8- 2
1946	STL	N	P		47	15- 6
1947	STL	N	P		47	13-16
1948	STL	N	P	42	43	12-16
1949	PIT	N	P		44	12-14
1950	PIT	N	P	51	52	10-15
1951	PIT	N	P	45	46	20-16
1952	PIT	N	P	43	47	14-21
1953	PIT	N	P		45	10-19
1954	PHI	N	P		40	10-20
1955	PHI	N	P		36	12-11
1956	PHI	N	P		9	0- 3
	STL	N	P	28	32	13- 8
1957	STL	N	P		14	
1958	KC	A	P	27	28	9- 5
1959	KC	A	P		14	0- 2
	NY	A	P		8	1- 2
	BRTR			625	638	172-181

DICKSON, WALTER R. (HICKORY)
B.DEC.3,1878 NEW SUMMERFIELD,TEX.
D.DEC.9,1918 ARDMORE,OKLA.

YR	CL	LEA	POS	GP	G	REC
1910	NY	N	P		12	1- 0
1912	BOS	N	P		36	3-19
1913	BOS	N	P		19	6- 7
1914	PIT	F	P		40	9-19
1915	PIT	F	F		27	7- 5
	BRTR				134	26-50

DICKSUS, JOHN OSCAR
(PLAYED UNDER NAME OF
JOHN OSCAR DICKSHOT)

DIDDLEBOCK, HENRY H.
B.JUNE 27,1854 PHILADELPHIA,PA.
D.FEB.5,1900 PHILADELPHIA,PA.
NON-PLAYING MANAGER STL[N] 1896

DIDIER, ROBERT DANIEL (BOB)
B.FEB.16,1949 HATTIESBURG,MISS.

YR	CL	LEA	POS	GP	G	REC
1969	ATL	N	*C		114	.256
1970	ATL	N	C		57	.149
1971	ATL	N	C		51	.219
1972	ATL	N	C		13	.300
1973	DET	A	/C		7	.455
1974	BOS	A	/C		5	.071
	BBTR				247	.229

DIEHL, ERNEST GUY
B.OCT.2,1877 CINCINNATI,OHIO
D.NOV.6,1958 MIAMI,FLA.

YR	CL	LEA	POS	GP	G	REC
1903	PIT	N	O		1	.333
1904	PIT	N	S-O		12	.162
1906	BOS	N	S		3	.545
1909	BOS	N	O		1	.500
	BRTR				17	.255

DIEHL, GEORGE KRAUSE
B.FEB.25,1918 ALLENTOWN,PA.

YR	CL	LEA	POS	GP	G	REC
1942	BOS	N	P		1	0- 0
1943	BOS	N	P		1	0- 0
	BRTR				2	0- 0

DIERING, CHARLES EDWARD ALLEN (CHUCK)
B.FEB.5,1923 ST.LOUIS,MO.

YR	CL	LEA	POS	GP	G	REC
1947	STL	N	O		105	.216
1948	STL	N	O		7	.000
1949	STL	N	O		131	.263
1950	STL	N	O		69	.250
1951	STL	N	O		64	.259
1952	NY	N	O		41	.174
1954	BAL	A	O		128	.258
1955	BAL	A	S-3-O		137	.256
1956	BAL	A	3-O		50	.186
	BRTR				752	.249

DIERKER, LAWRENCE EDWARD (LARRY)
B.SEP.22,1946 HOLLYWOOD,CAL.

YR	CL	LEA	POS	GP	G	REC
1964	HOU	N	P		3	0- 1
1965	HOU	N	P		26	7- 8
1966	HOU	N	P		29	10- 8
1967	HOU	N	P		15	6- 5
1968	HOU	N	P	32	33	12-15
1969	HOU	N	P		39	20-13
1970	HOU	N	P		37	16-12
1971	HOU	N	P		24	12- 6
1972	HOU	N	P		31	15- 8
1973	HOU	N	P		14	1- 1
1974	HOU	N	P		33	11-10
1975	HOU	N	P		34	14-16
1976	HOU	N	P		28	13-14
1977	STL	N	P		11	2- 6
	BRTR			356	357	139-123

DIETRICH, WILLIAM JOHN (BULLFROG)
B.MAR.29,1910 PHILADELPHIA,PA.
D.JUNE 20,1978 PHILADELPHIA,PA.

YR	CL	LEA	POS	GP	G	REC
1933	PHI	A	P		8	0- 1
1934	PHI	A	P	39	40	11-12
1935	PHI	A	P	43	44	7-13
1936	PHI	A	P		21	4- 6
	WAS	A	P		5	0- 1
	CHI	A	P		14	4- 4
1937	CHI	A	P		29	8-10
1938	CHI	A	P		8	2- 4
1939	CHI	A	P		25	7- 8
1940	CHI	A	P		23	10- 6
1941	CHI	A	P		19	5- 8
1942	CHI	A	P		26	6-11
1943	CHI	A	P		26	12-10
1944	CHI	A	P		36	16-17
1945	CHI	A	P		18	7-10
1946	CHI	A	P		11	3- 3
1947	PHI	A	P		11	5- 2
1948	PHI	A	P		4	1- 2
	BRTR			366	368	108-128

DIETZ, LLOYD ARTHUR (DUTCH)
B.FEB.9,1912 CINCINNATI,OHIO
D.OCT.29,1972 BEAUMONT,TEX.

YR	CL	LEA	POS	GP	G	REC
1940	PIT	N	P		4	0- 1
1941	PIT	N	P		33	7- 2
1942	PIT	N	P		40	6- 9
1943	PIT	N	P	8	10	0- 3
	PHI	N	P		21	1- 1
	BRTR			106	110	14-16

YR	CL	LEA	POS	GP	G	REC

DIETZ, RICHARD ALLEN (DICK)
B.SEP.18,1941 CRAWFORDSVILLE,IND.

YR	CL	LEA	POS	GP	G	REC
1966	SF	N	/C		13	.043
1967	SF	N	C		56	.225
1968	SF	N	C		98	.272
1969	SF	N	C		79	.230
1970	SF	N	*C		148	.300
1971	SF	N	*C		142	.252
1972	LA	N	C		27	.161
1973	ATL	N	1-C		83	.295
	BRTR				646	.261

DIETZEL, LEROY LOUIS (ROY)
B.JAN.9,1931 BALTIMORE,MD.

1954	WAS	A	2-3		9	.238
	BRTR					

DIFANI, CLARENCE JOSEPH (JAY)
B.DEC.21,1923 CRYSTAL CITY,MO.

1948	WAS	A	H		2	.000
1949	WAS	A	2		2	1.000
	BRTR				4	.333

DIGGS, REESE WILSON (DIGGSY)
B.SEPT.22,1915 MATHEWS,VA.

1934	WAS	A	P		4	1- 2
	BBTR					

DIGNAN, STEPHEN E.
B.MAY.16,1859 BOSTON,MASS.
D.JULY 11,1881 BOSTON,MASS.

1880	BOS	N	O		8	.324
	WOR	N	O		3	.300
					11	.318

DI LAURO, JACK EDWARD
B.MAR.3,1943 AKRON,OHIO

1969	NY	N	P		23	1- 4
1970	HOU	N	P	42	43	1- 3
	BBTL			65	66	2- 7

DILLARD, DAVID DONALD (DON)
B.JAN.8,1937 GREENVILLE,S.C.

1959	CLE	A	H		10	.400
1960	CLE	A	O		6	.143
1961	CLE	A	O		74	.272
1962	CLE	A	O		95	.230
1963	MIL	N	O		67	.225
1965	MIL	N	/O		20	.158
	BLTR				272	.244

DILLARD, ROBERT LEE (PAT)
B.JUNE 12,1874 CHATTANOOGA,TENN

D.JULY 22,1907 DENVER,COLO.

1900	STL	N	3-O		44	.237

DILLARD, STEPHEN BRADLEY (STEVE)
B.FEB.6,1951 MEMPHIS,TENN.

1975	BOS	A	/2		1	.400
1976	BOS	A	3-2-S		57	.275
1977	BOS	A	2/S		66	.241
1978	DET	A	2		56	.223
	BRTR				180	.251

DILLHOEFER, WILLIAM MARTIN (PICKLES)
B.OCT.13,1894 CLEVELAND,OHIO
D.FEB.22,1922 ST.LOUIS,MO.

1917	CHI	N	C		42	.126
1918	PHI	N	C		8	.090
1919	STL	N	C		45	.213
1920	STL	N	C		76	.263
1921	STL	N	C		76	.241
	BRTR				247	.223

**DILLINGER, HARLEY HUGH
(HOKE) OR (LEFTY)**
B.OCT.30,1894 POMEROY,OHIO
D.JAN.8,1959 CLEVELAND,OHIO

1914	CLE	A	P		10	0- 1
	BRTL					

DILLINGER, ROBERT BERNARD (DUKE)
B.SEPT.17,1918 GLENDALE,CAL.

1946	STL	A	S-3		83	.280
1947	STL	A	3		137	.294
1948	STL	A	3		153	.321
1949	STL	A	3		137	.324
1950	PHI	A	3		84	.309
	PIT	N	3		58	.288
1951	PIT	N	3		12	.233
	CHI	A	3		89	.301
	BRTR				753	.306

DILLMAN, WILLIAM HOWARD (BILL)
B.MAY 25,1945 TRENTON,N.J.

1967	BAL	A	P	32	33	5- 9
1970	MON	N	P		18	2- 3
	BRTR			50	51	7-12

DILLON, FRANK EDWARD (POP)
B.OCT.17,1873 NORMAL,ILL.
D.SEPT.12,1931 LOS ANGELES,CAL.

1899	PIT	N	1		30	.258
1900	PIT	N	1		5	.111
1901	DET	A	1		75	.298
1902	DET	A	1		66	.205
	BAL	A	1		2	.286
1904	BRO	N	1		134	.258
	BL				312	.255

DILLON, PACKARD ANDREW
B.ST.LOUIS,MO.
D.JAN.8,1890 GUELPH,ONT.,CANADA

1875	RS	NA	C		3	-

DILLON, STEPHEN EDWARD (STEVE)
B.MAR.20,1943 YONKERS,N.Y.

1963	NY	N	P		1	0- 0
1964	NY	N	P		2	0- 0
	BLTL				3	0- 0

DILONE, MIGUEL ANGEL [REYES]
B.NOV.1,1954 SANTIAGO,D.R.

1974	PIT	N	/O		12	.000
1975	PIT	N	/O		18	.000
1976	PIT	N	/O		16	.235
1977	PIT	N	O		29	.136
1978	OAK	A	O-O/3		135	.228
	BBTR				210	.210

**DI MAGGIO, DOMINIC PAUL (DOM)
OR (THE LITTLE PROFESSOR)**
B.FEB.12,1917 SAN FRANCISCO,CAL

1940	BOS	A	O		108	.301
1941	BOS	A	O		144	.283
1942	BOS	A	O		151	.286
1946	BOS	A	O		142	.316
1947	BOS	A	O		136	.283
1948	BOS	A	O		155	.285
1949	BOS	A	O		145	.307
1950	BOS	A	O		141	.328
1951	BOS	A	O		146	.296
1952	BOS	A	O		128	.294
1953	BOS	A	H		3	.333
	BRTR				1399	.298

**DI MAGGIO, JOSEPH PAUL (JOE)
(JOLTIN' JOE)
OR (THE YANKEE CLIPPER)**
B.NOV.25,1914 MARTINEZ,CAL.

1936	NY	A	O		138	.323
1937	NY	A	O		151	.346
1938	NY	A	O		145	.324
1939	NY	A	O		120	.381
1940	NY	A	O		132	.352
1941	NY	A	O		139	.357
1942	NY	A	O		154	.305
1946	NY	A	O		132	.290
1947	NY	A	O		141	.315
1948	NY	A	O		153	.320
1949	NY	A	O		76	.346
1950	NY	A	1-O		139	.301
1951	NY	A	O		116	.263
	BRTR				1736	.325

DI MAGGIO, VINCENT PAUL (VINCE)
B.SEPT.6,1912 MARTINEZ,CAL.

1937	BOS	N	O		132	.256
1938	BOS	N	O		150	.228
1939	CIN	N	O		8	.071
1940	CIN	N	O		2	.250
	PIT	N	O		110	.289
1941	PIT	N	O		151	.267
1942	PIT	N	O		143	.238
1943	PIT	N	S-O		157	.248
1944	PIT	N	3-O		109	.240
1945	PHI	N	O		127	.257
1946	PHI	N	O		6	.211
	NY	N	O		15	.000
	BRTR				1110	.249

**DIMARIA, JOSEPH FRANKLIN
[PLAYED UNDER NAME OF
JOSEPH FRANKLIN DEMAREE]**

**DIMITRIHOFF, DIMITRI IVANOVICH
[PLAYED UNDER NAME OF
ALEXANDER JOHN SCHAUER]**

DIMMEL, MICHAEL WAYNE (MIKE)
B.OCT.16,1954 ALBERT LEA,MINN.

1977	BAL	A	O		25	.000
1978	BAL	A	/O		8	.000
	BRTR				33	.000

DINEEN, KERRY MICHAEL
B.JULY 1,1952 ENGLEWOOD,N.J.

1975	NY	A	/O		7	.364
1976	NY	A	/O		4	.286
1978	NY	A	/O		5	.250
	BLTL				16	.324

DINGES, VANCE GEORGE
B.MAY 29,1915 ELIZABETH,N.J.

1945	PHI	N	1-O		109	.287
1946	PHI	N	1-O		50	.308
	BLTL				159	.291

DINNEEN, WILLIAM HENRY (BIG BILL)
B.APR.5,1876 SYRACUSE,N.Y.
D.JAN.13,1955 SYRACUSE,N.Y.

1898	WAS	N	P	26	27	9-16
1899	WAS	N	P		36	14-18
1900	BOS	N	P		37	21-16
1901	BOS	N	P		40	16-19
1902	BOS	A	P-O	42	44	21-20
						.134
1903	BOS	A	P		34	21-11
1904	BOS	A	P		39	24-15
1905	BOS	A	P		31	14-14
1906	BOS	A	P		28	8-19
1907	BOS	A	P		7	0- 4
	STL	A	P		22	7-11
1908	STL	A	P		27	14- 7
1909	STL	A	P		17	6- 7
	BRTR			386	389	175-177
						.193

DIORIO, RONALD MICHAEL (MIKE)
B.JULY 15,1946 WATERBURY,CONN.

1973	PHI	N	P		23	0- 0
1974	PHI	N	/P		2	0- 0
	BRTR				25	0- 0

DI PIETRO, ROBERT LOUIS PAUL
B.SEPT.1,1927 SAN FRANCISCO,CAL

1951	BOS	A	O		4	.091
	BRTR					

DISCH, GEORGE CHARLES
B.MAR.15,1879 LINCOLN,MO.
D.AUG.25,1950 RAPID CITY,S.D.

1905	DET	A	P		8	0- 2

DISTASO, ALEC JOHN
B.DEC.23,1948 LOS ANGELES,CAL.

1969	CHI	N	/P		2	0- 0
	BRTR					

DISTEL, GEORGE ADAM (DUTCH)
B.APR.15,1896 MADISON,IND.
D.FEB.12,1967 MADISON,IND.

1918	STL	N	2-S		8	.176
	BRTR					

DITMAR, ARTHUR JOHN (ART)
B.APR.3,1929 WINTHROP,MASS.

1954	PHI	A	P		14	1- 4
1955	KC	A	P		35	12-12
1956	KC	A	P		44	12-22
1957	NY	A	P		46	8- 3
1958	NY	A	P		38	9- 8
1959	NY	A	P		38	13- 9
1960	NY	A	P	34	36	15- 9
1961	NY	A	P		12	2- 3
	KC	A	P		20	0- 5
1962	KC	A	P		6	0- 2
	BRTR			287	289	72-77

DITTMER, JOHN DOUGLAS (JACK)
B.JAN.10,1928 ELKADER,IOWA

1952	BOS	N	2		93	.193
1953	MIL	N	2		138	.266
1954	MIL	N	2		66	.245
1955	MIL	N	2		38	.125
1956	MIL	N	2		44	.245
1957	DET	A	2-3		16	.227
	BLTR				395	.232

DIXON, JOHN CRAIG (SONNY)
B.NOV.5,1924 CHARLOTTE,N.C.

1953	WAS	A	P		43	5- 8
1954	WAS	A	P		16	1- 2
	PHI	A	P		38	5- 7
1955	KC	A	P		2	0- 0
1956	KC	A	P		3	0- 1
	BBTR				102	11-18

DIXON, LEO MICHAEL
B.SEPT.6,1896 CHICAGO,ILL.

1925	STL	A	C		76	.224
1926	STL	A	C		33	.191
1927	STL	A	C		36	.194
1929	CIN	N	C		14	.167
	BRTR				159	.206

DIXON, THOMAS EARL (TOM)
B.APR.23,1955 ORLANDO,FLA.

1977	HOU	N	P		9	1- 0
1978	HOU	N	P		30	7-11
	BRTR				39	8-11

```
YR  CL LEA POS   GP    G   REC
```

DOAK, WILLIAM LEOPOLD (SPITTIN' BILL)
B.JAN.28,1891 PITTSBURGH,PA.
D.NOV.26,1954 BRADENTON,FLA.
```
1912 CIN N P      1   0-0
1913 STL N P     15   2-8
1914 STL N P     36  19-6
1915 STL N P     38  16-18
1916 STL N P     29  12-8
1917 STL N P     44  16-20
1918 STL N P     31   9-15
1919 STL N P     31  13-14
1920 STL N P     39  20-12
1921 STL N P     32  15-6
1922 STL N P     37  11-13
1923 STL N P     30   8-13
1924 STL N P     11   2-1
     BRO N P     21  11-5
1927 BRO N P     27  11-8
1928 BRO N P     28   3-8
1929 STL N P      3   1-2
     BRTR       453 169-157
```

DOAN, WALTER RUDOLPH
B.MAR.12,1887 BELLEVUE,IDAHO
D.OCT.19,1935 W.BRANDYWINE,PA.
```
1909 CLE A P-0   1    4   0-1
                          .167
1910 CLE A P          6   0-1
     BLTR        7   10   0-1
                          .188
```

DOBB, JOHN KENNETH (LEFTY)
B.NOV.15,1901 MUSKEGON,MICH.
```
1924 CHI A P      2   0-0
     TL
```

DOBBEK, DANIEL JOHN (DAN)
B.DEC.6,1934 ONTONAGON,MICH.
```
1959 WAS A O     16  .250
1960 WAS A O    110  .218
1961 MIN A O     72  .168
     BLTR       198  .208
```

DOBBS, JOHN GORDON
B.JUNE 3,1876 CHATTANOOGA,TENN.
D.SEPT.9,1934 CHARLOTTE,N.C.
```
1901 CIN N O    108  .276
1902 CIN N O     63  .287
     CHI N O     59  .310
1903 CHI N O     16  .230
     BRO N O    110  .237
1904 BRO N O     95  .248
1905 BRO N O    123  .254
     BLTR       574  .263
```

DOBENS, RAYMOND JOSEPH (RAY) OR (LEFTY)
B.JULY 28,1906 NASHUA,N.H.
```
1929 BOS A P     11   0-0
     BLTL
```

DOBERNIC, ANDREW JOSEPH (JESS)
B.NOV.20,1917 MT.OLIVE,ILL.
```
1939 CHI N P      5   0-1
1948 CHI N P     54   7-2
1949 CHI N P      4   0-0
     CIN N P     14   0-0
     BRTR        76   7-3
```

DOBSON, CHARLES THOMAS (CHUCK)
B.JAN.10,1944 KANSAS CITY,MO.
```
1966 KC  A P     14   4-6
1967 KC  A P  32 33  10-10
1968 OAK A P     35  12-14
1969 OAK A P     35  15-13
1970 OAK A P     41  16-15
1971 OAK A P     30  15-5
1973 OAK A P      1   0-1
1974 CAL A /P     5   2-3
1975 CAL A /P     9   0-2
     BRTR    202 203  74-69
```

DOBSON, JOSEPH GORDON (JOE) OR (BURRHEAD)
B.JAN.20,1917 DURANT,OKLA.
```
1939 CLE A P     35   2-3
1940 CLE A P     40   3-7
1941 BOS A P     27  12-5
1942 BOS A P     30  11-9
1943 BOS A P     25   7-11
1944 BOS A P     32  13-7
1947 BOS A P     33  18-8
1948 BOS A P     38  16-10
1949 BOS A P     33  14-12
1950 BOS A P     39  15-10
1951 CHI A P     24   7-6
1952 CHI A P     29  14-10
1953 CHI A P     23   5-5
1954 BOS A P      2   0-0
     BRTR       414 137-103
```

DOBSON, PATRICK EDWARD (PAT)
B.FEB.12,1942 DEPEW,N.Y.
```
1967 DET A P     28   1-2
1968 DET A P     47   5-8
1969 DET A P     49   5-10
1970 SD  N P     40  14-15
1971 BAL A P     38  20-8
1972 BAL A P     38  16-18
1973 ATL N P     12   3-7
     NY  A P     22   9-8
1974 NY  A P     39  19-15
1975 NY  A P     33  11-14
1976 CLE A P     35  16-12
1977 CLE A P     33   3-12
     BRTR       414 122-129
```

DOBY, LAWRENCE EUGENE (LARRY)
B.DEC.13,1924 CAMDEN,S.C.
```
1947 CLE A 1-2-S   29  .156
1948 CLE A O      121  .301
1949 CLE A O      147  .280
1950 CLE A O      142  .326
1951 CLE A O      134  .295
1952 CLE A O      140  .276
1953 CLE A O      149  .263
1954 CLE A O      153  .272
1955 CLE A O      131  .291
1956 CHI A O      140  .268
1957 CHI A O      119  .288
1958 CLE A O       89  .283
1959 DET A O       18  .218
     CHI A 1-0     21  .241
     BLTR        1533  .283
```
NON-PLAYING MANAGER CHI[A] 1978

DOCKINS, GEORGE WOODROW (LEFTY)
B.MAY 5,1917 CLYDE,KAN.
```
1945 STL N P     31   8-6
1947 BRO N P      4   0-0
     BLTL        35   8-6
```

DODD, ONA MELVIN
B.OCT.14,1886 SPRINGTOWN,TEX.
D.MAR.31,1929 NEWPORT,ARK.
```
1912 PIT N 2      5  .000
     BRTR
```

DODGE, JOHN LEWIS
B.APR.27,1889 BOLIVAR,TENN.
D.JUNE 19,1916 MOBILE,ALA.
```
1912 PHI N 2-S-3   30  .120
1913 PHI N 3        9  .333
     CIN N 3       94  .243
     BRTR         127  .215
```

DODGE, SAMUEL EDWARD
B.DEC.19,1889 PHILADELPHIA,PA.
```
1921 BOS A P      2   0-0
1922 BOS A P      3   0-1
     BRTR         4   0-1
```

DOE, ALFRED GEORGE (FRED) OR (COUNT)
B.APR.18,1864 GLOUCESTER,MASS.
D.OCT.4,1938 QUINCY,MASS.
```
1890 BUF P P      1   0-1
     PIT P P      1   0-1
     BRTR         2   0-2
```

DOERR, ROBERT PERSHING (BOBBY)
B.APR.7,1918 LOS ANGELES,CAL.
```
1937 BOS A 2      55  .224
1938 BOS A 2     145  .289
1939 BOS A 2     127  .318
1940 BOS A 2     151  .291
1941 BOS A 2     132  .282
1942 BOS A 2     144  .290
1943 BOS A 2     155  .270
1944 BOS A 2     125  .325
1946 BOS A 2     151  .271
1947 BOS A 2     146  .258
1948 BOS A 2     140  .285
1949 BOS A 2     139  .309
1950 BOS A 2     149  .294
1951 BOS A 2     106  .289
     BRTR       1865  .288
```

DOHERTY, EDWARD R.
B.NOV.24,1874 NORTHFIELD,VT.
D.DEC.29,1916 WORCESTER,MASS.
```
1895 NY  N P      3   0-3
1896 NY  N P     17   7-7
1897 NY  N P     10   6-4
1898 NY  N P     35   8-19
1899 NY  N P     35  14-16
1900 NY  N P     18   4-14
1901 NY  N P      9   2-4
     PIT N P     11   6-3
1902 PIT N P     21  17-4
1903 PIT N P     27  16-8
     BLTL       179  80-82
```

DOHERTY, JOHN MICHAEL
B.AUG.22,1951 WOBURN,MASS.
```
1974 CAL A 1     74  .256
1975 CAL A 1     30  .202
     BLTL       104  .240
```

DOLAN, ALVIN JAMES (COZY)
[REAL NAME JAMES ALBERTS]
B.DEC.6,1882 OSKOSH,WIS.
D.DEC.10,1958 CHICAGO,ILL.
```
1909 CIN N 3       3  .167
1911 NY  A 3      19  .304
1912 NY  A 3      17  .200
     PHI N 3      11  .280
1913 PHI N 3      55  .262
     PIT N 3      35  .203
1914 STL N 3-0   126  .240
1915 STL N O     111  .280
1922 NY  N H       1  .000
     BRTR        378  .252
```

DOLAN, E. L. (BIDDY)
```
1914 IND F 1      31  .223
     BR
```

DOLAN, JOHN
B.SEPT.12,1867 NEWPORT,KY.
D.MAY 8,1948 SPRINGFIELD,OHIO
```
1890 CIN N P       2   1-1
1891 COL AA P  27 28  13-10
1893 STL N P       3   0-2
1895 CHI N P       2   0-1
     TR        34 35  14-14
```

DOLAN, JOSEPH
B.FEB.24,1873 BALTIMORE,MD.
D.MAR.24,1938 OMAHA,NEB.
```
1896 LOU N S      44  .219
1897 LOU N 2-S    35  .210
1899 PHI N 2      60  .256
1900 PHI N 2-3    70  .194
1901 PHI N 2       5  .071
     PHI A S-3    97  .219
     TR          311  .215
```

DOLAN, PATRICK HENRY (COZY)
B.DEC.3,1872 CAMBRIDGE,MASS.
D.MAR.29,1907 LOUISVILLE,KY.
```
1892 WAS N P       5   2-2
1895 BOS N P      23  11-9
1896 BOS N P       6   1-4
1900 CHI N O      13  .205
1901 CHI N O      43  .262
     BRO N O      62  .280
1902 BRO N O     140  .283
1903 CHI A 1      28  .250
     CIN N O      93  .288
1904 CIN N 1-0   126  .284
1905 CIN N 1      22  .234
     BOS N O     112  .275
1906 BOS N O     152  .248
     BLTL    34 825  14-15
                          .271
```

DOLAN, THOMAS J.
B.JAN.10,1859 NEW YORK,N.Y.
D.JAN.26,1913 ST.LOUIS,MO.
```
1879 CHI N C       1  .000
1882 BUF N C-2-O  22  .157
1883 STL AA P-C-   1  78  0-0
     O                    .222
1884 STL AA C     35  .263
     STL U  C-3-O  20  .194
1885 STL N C       3  .222
1886 STL N C      15  .250
     BAL AA C     37  .153
1888 STL AA C     11  .194
1891 STL AA C      1   0-0
     TR         1 223   0-0
                          .203
```

DOLE, W. C.
```
1875 NH NA O       1   -
```

DOLJACK, FRANK JOSEPH (DOLIE)
B.OCT.5,1907 CLEVELAND,OHIO
D.JAN.23,1948 CLEVELAND,OHIO
```
1930 DET A O      20  .257
1931 DET A O      63  .278
1932 DET A O       8  .385
1933 DET A O      42  .286
1934 DET A O      56  .233
1943 CLE A O       3  .000
     BRTR        192  .269
```

DOLL, ARTHUR JAMES (MOOSE)
B.MAY 7,1913 CHICAGO,ILL.
```
1935 BOS N C       3  .100
1936 BOS N P       1   0-0
1938 BOS N P       3   0-0
     BRTR          4   0-1
                          .154
```

DOMEC, JOSE ROSARIO [CARDENAL]
[SEE JOSE ROSARIO DOMEC CARDENAL]

DONAHUE, CHARLES MICHAEL (SHE)
B.JUNE 28,1877 OSWEGO,N.Y.
D.AUG.28,1914 NEW YORK,N.Y.
```
1904 STL N S       4  .267
     PHI N S-3    56  .215
     BRTR         60  .219
```

158   THE OFFICIAL ENCYCLOPEDIA OF BASEBALL

YR	CL	LEA	POS	GP	G	REC

DONAHUE, FRANCIS ROSTELL (RED)
B.JAN.23,1873 WATERBURY,CONN.
D.AUG.25,1913 PHILADELPHIA,PA.

YR	CL	LEA	POS	GP	G	REC
1893	NY	N	P		2	0- 1
1895	STL	N	P		1	0- 1
1896	STL	N	P		33	7-23
1897	STL	N	P		44	11-33
1898	PHI	N	P		34	17-16
1899	PHI	N	P		34	22- 7
1900	PHI	N	P		26	16-10
1901	PHI	N	P		35	20-13
1902	STL	A	P		35	22-11
1903	STL	A	P		14	6- 4
	CLE	A	P		19	6-13
1904	CLE	A	P		35	18-14
1905	CLE	A	P		20	6-11
1906	DET	A	P		29	13-14
	BRTR				361	164-171

DONAHUE, JAMES AUGUSTUS
B.JAN.6,1862 LOCKPORT,ILL.
D.APR.19,1935 LOCKPORT,ILL.

YR	CL	LEA	POS	GP	G	REC
1886	MET	AA	C-O		50	.201
1887	MET	AA	C		60	.345
1888	KC	AA	C		87	.241
1889	KC	AA	C		67	.238
1891	COL	AA	C		77	.217
	TR				341	.245

DONAHUE, JOHN AUGUSTUS (JIGGS)
B.JULY 13,1879 SPRINGFIELD,OHIO
D.JULY 19,1913 COLUMBUS,OHIO

YR	CL	LEA	POS	GP	G	REC
1900	PIT	N	C		3	.200
1901	PIT	N	C		2	.000
	MIL	A	C		37	.305
1902	STL	A	C-1		29	.250
1904	CHI	A	1		102	.251
1905	CHI	A	1		149	.287
1906	CHI	A	1		154	.257
1907	CHI	A	1		157	.259
1908	CHI	A	1		93	.204
1909	CHI	A	1		2	.000
	WAS	A	1		84	.237
	BLTL				812	.256

DONAHUE, JOHN FREDERICK (JIGGS)
B.APR.19,1894 ROXBURY,MASS.
D.OCT.3,1949 BOSTON,MASS.

YR	CL	LEA	POS	GP	G	REC
1923	BOS	A	O		10	.343
	BBTR					

DONAHUE, JOHN STEPHEN MICHAEL (DEACON)
B.JUNE 23,1920 CHICAGO,ILL.

YR	CL	LEA	POS	GP	G	REC
1943	PHI	N	P		2	0- 0
1944	PHI	N	P		6	0- 2
	BRTR				8	0- 2

DONAHUE, PATRICK WILLIAM
B.NOV.8,1884 SPRINGFIELD,OHIO
D.JAN.31,1966 SPRINGFIELD,OHIO

YR	CL	LEA	POS	GP	G	REC
1908	BOS	A	C		35	.198
1909	BOS	A	C		64	.209
1910	BOS	A	C		2	.000
	PHI	A	C		16	.143
	CLE	A	C		2	.167
	BRTR				119	.212

DONAHUE, TIMOTHY CORNELIUS (BRIDGET)
B.JUNE 8,1870 RAYNHAM,MASS.
D.JUNE 12,1902 TAUNTON,MASS.

YR	CL	LEA	POS	GP	G	REC
1891	BOS	AA	C		3	.000
1895	CHI	N	C		62	.271
1896	CHI	N	C		54	.226
1897	CHI	N	C		53	.234
1898	CHI	N	C		117	.236
1899	CHI	N	C		90	.250
1900	CHI	N	C		65	.239
1902	WAS	A	C		3	.250
	BLTR				447	.241

DONALD, RICHARD ATLEY (SWAMPY)
B.AUG.19,1910 MORTON,MISS.

YR	CL	LEA	POS	GP	G	REC
1938	NY	A	P		2	0- 1
1939	NY	A	P		24	13- 3
1940	NY	A	P		24	8- 3
1941	NY	A	P		22	9- 5
1942	NY	A	P		20	11- 3
1943	NY	A	P		22	8- 4
1944	NY	A	P		30	13-10
1945	NY	A	P		9	5- 4
	BLTR				153	65-33

DONALDS, EDWARD ALEXANDER (SKIPPER)
B.JUNE 22,1885 GALLIPOLIS,OHIO
D.JULY 3,1950 COLUMBUS,OHIO

YR	CL	LEA	POS	GP	G	REC
1912	CIN	N	P		1	1- 0
	BRTR					

DONALDSON, JOHN DAVID
B.MAY 5,1943 CHARLOTTE,N.C.

YR	CL	LEA	POS	GP	G	REC
1966	KC	A	/2		15	.133
1967	KC	A	*2/S		105	.276
1968	OAK	A	2/3-S		127	.220
1969	OAK	A	/2		12	.077
	SEA	A	2/3-S		95	.234
1970	OAK	A	2/5-3		41	.247
1974	OAK	A	/2-3		10	.133
	BLTR				405	.238

DONDERO, LEONARD PETER (MIKE)
B.SEPT.12,1903 NEWARK,CAL.

YR	CL	LEA	POS	GP	G	REC
1929	STL	A	3		19	.194
	BRTR					

DONLIN, MICHAEL JOSEPH (TURKEY MIKE)
B.MAY 30,1878 ERIE,PA.
D.SEPT.24,1933 HOLLYWOOD,CAL.

YR	CL	LEA	POS	GP	G	REC
1899	STL	N	P-O		1 67	0- 0
						.329
1900	STL	N	1		77	.327
1901	BAL	A	1-O		122	.340
1902	CIN	N	P-S-	1	33	0- 1
			O			.294
1903	CIN	N	O		124	.351
1904	CIN	N	O		59	.356
	NY	N	O		37	.280
1905	NY	N	O		150	.356
1906	NY	N	O		30	.314
1908	NY	N	O		155	.334
1911	NY	N	O		12	.333
	BOS	N	O		56	.318
1912	PIT	N	O		77	.316
1914	NY	N	O		35	.161
	BLTL				2 1034	0- 0
						.334

DONNELLY, EDWARD (BIG ED) OR (NED)
B.JULY 29,1880 HAMPTON,N.Y.
D.NOV.28,1957 RUTLAND,VT.
[REAL NAME EDWARD O DONNELL]

YR	CL	LEA	POS	GP	G	REC
1911	BOS	N	P		5	3- 2
1912	BOS	N	P	37	38	5-10
	BRTR			42	43	8-12

DONNELLY, EDWARD VINCENT
B.DEC.10,1934 ALLEN,MICH.

YR	CL	LEA	POS	GP	G	REC
1959	CHI	N	P		9	1- 1
	BRTR					

DONNELLY, FRANKLIN MARION
B.OCT.7,1869 TAMAROA,ILL.
D.FEB.8,1953 CANTON,ILL.

YR	CL	LEA	POS	GP	G	REC
1893	CHI	N	P		6	3- 1
1894	CHI	N	P		1	0- 0
					7	3- 1

DONNELLY, JAMES B.
B.JULY 19,1865 NEW HAVEN,CONN.
D.MAR.5,1915 NEW HAVEN,CONN.

YR	CL	LEA	POS	GP	G	REC
1884	KC	U	C-3		6	.130
	IND	AA	S-3		40	.249
1885	DET	N	1-3		55	.232
1886	KC	N	P-3	1	113	0- 1
						.201
1887	WAS	N	3		117	.229
1888	WAS	N	3		122	.201
1889	WAS	N	3		4	.154
1890	STL	AA	3		11	.344
1891	COL	AA	3		17	.241
1896	BAL	N	3		104	.330
1897	PIT	N	3		43	.177
	NY	N	3		23	.205
1898	STL	N	3		1	1.000
	BR			1	656	0- 1
						.234

DONNELLY, SYLVESTER URBAN (BLIX)
B.JAN.21,1914 OLIVIA,MINN.
D.JUNE 20,1976 OLIVIA,MINN.

YR	CL	LEA	POS	GP	G	REC
1944	STL	N	P		27	2- 1
1945	STL	N	P		31	8-10
1946	STL	N	P		13	1- 2
	PHI	N	P		12	3- 4
1947	PHI	N	P		38	4- 6
1948	PHI	N	P		26	5- 7
1949	PHI	N	P		23	2- 1
1950	PHI	N	P		14	2- 4
1951	BOS	N	P		6	0- 1
	BRTR				190	27-36

DONNELLY, T. J.

YR	CL	LEA	POS	GP	G	REC
1871	KEK	NA	3-O		9	.233
1873	NAT	NA	2-S-O		30	-
1874	PHI	NA	2-S-O		5	-
					44	-

DONOHUE, JAMES THOMAS (JIM)
B.OCT.31,1938 ST.LOUIS,MO.

YR	CL	LEA	POS	GP	G	REC
1961	DET	A	P		14	1- 1
	LA	A	P		38	4- 6
1962	LA	A	P		12	1- 0
	MIN	A	P		6	0- 1
	BRTR				70	6- 8

DONOHUE, JOSEPH F.
B.1869 SYRACUSE,N.Y.
D.NOV.12,1894

YR	CL	LEA	POS	GP	G	REC
1891	PHI	N	O		6	.317

DONOHUE, PETER JOSEPH
B.NOV.5,1900 ATHENS,TEX.

YR	CL	LEA	POS	GP	G	REC
1921	CIN	N	P		21	7- 6
1922	CIN	N	P		33	18- 9
1923	CIN	N	P		42	21-15
1924	CIN	N	P	35	36	16- 9
1925	CIN	N	P	42	43	21-14
1926	CIN	N	P		47	20-14
1927	CIN	N	P		33	6-16
1928	CIN	N	P		23	7-11
1929	CIN	N	P		32	10-13
1930	CIN	N	P		8	1- 3
	NY	N	P		18	7- 6
1931	NY	A	P		4	0- 1
	CLE	A	P		2	0- 0
1932	BOS	A	P		4	0- 1
	BRTR			344	346	134-118

DONOSO, LINO GALATA
B.SEPT.23,1922 HAVANA,CUBA

YR	CL	LEA	POS	GP	G	REC
1955	PIT	N	P		25	4- 6
1956	PIT	N	P		3	0- 0
	BLTL				28	4- 6

DONOVAN, FREDERICK M.
B.CLEVELAND,OHIO

YR	CL	LEA	POS	GP	G	REC
1895	CLE	N	C		3	.083

DONOVAN, JEREMIAH FRANCIS
B.SEPT.3,1876 LOCK HAVEN,PA.
D.JUNE 27,1938 ST.PETERSBURG,FLA.

YR	CL	LEA	POS	GP	G	REC
1906	PHI	N	P		53	.199
	BRTR					

DONOVAN, MICHAEL BERCHMAN
B.OCT.18,1881 BROOKLYN,N.Y.
D.FEB.3,1938 NEW YORK,N.Y.

YR	CL	LEA	POS	GP	G	REC
1904	CLE	A	S		2	.000
1908	NY	A	3		5	.157
	BRTR				7	.143

DONOVAN, PATRICK JOSEPH (PATSY)
B.MAR.16,1865 COUNTY CORK,IRELAND
D.DEC.25,1953 LAWRENCE,MASS.

YR	CL	LEA	POS	GP	G	REC
1890	BOS	N	O		32	.245
	BRO	N	O		26	.380
1891	LOU	AA	O		98	.319
	WAS	AA	O		17	.200
1892	WAS	N	O		40	.252
	PIT	N	O		88	.311
1893	PIT	N	O		110	.331
1894	PIT	N	O		133	.306
1895	PIT	N	O		126	.316
1896	PIT	N	O		129	.316
1897	PIT	N	M-O		120	.326
1898	PIT	N	O		147	.302
1899	PIT	N	M-O		123	.296
1900	STL	N	O		127	.324
1901	STL	N	M-O		129	.294
1902	STL	N	M-O		126	.309
1903	STL	N	M-O		105	.327
1904	WAS	A	M-O		125	.219
1906	BRO	N	M-O		7	.238
1907	BRO	N	M-O		1	.000
	BLTL				1809	.304

NON-PLAYING MANAGER BRO[N] 1908
BOS[A] 1910-11

DONOVAN, RICHARD EDWARD (DICK)
B.DEC.7,1927 BOSTON,MASS.

YR	CL	LEA	POS	GP	G	REC
1950	BOS	N	P		10	0- 2
1951	BOS	N	P		8	0- 0
1952	BOS	N	P		7	0- 2
1954	DET	A	P		2	0- 0
1955	CHI	A	P	29	40	15- 9
1956	CHI	A	P	34	44	12-10
1957	CHI	A	P	28	30	16- 6
1958	CHI	A	P		34	15-14
1959	CHI	A	P		31	9-10
1960	CHI	A	P		33	6- 1
1961	WAS	A	P	23	24	10-10
1962	CLE	A	P		34	20-10
1963	CLE	A	P	30	31	11-13
1964	CLE	A	P	30	31	7- 9
1965	CLE	A	P		12	1- 3
	BLTR			345	371	122-99

DONOVAN, THOMAS JOSEPH
B.JULY 7,1879 LOCK HAVEN,PA.
D.FEB.20,1955 WILLIAMSPORT,PA.

YR	CL	LEA	POS	GP	G	REC
1901	CLE	A	O		18	.253
	BRTR					

DONOVAN, WILLARD EARL
B.JULY 6,1916 MAYWOOD,ILL.

YR	CL	LEA	POS	GP	G	REC
1942	BOS	N	P		31	3- 6
1943	BOS	N	P		7	1- 0
	BRTL				38	4- 6

YR CL LEA POS   GP   G   REC

DONOVAN, WILLIAM EDWARD (WILD BILL)
B.OCT.13,1876 LAWRENCE,MASS.
D.DEC.9,1923 FORSYTH,N.Y.
```
1898 WAS N  P-O     11   30   1- 6
                                .178
1899 BRO N  P              4   1- 2
1900 BRO N  P              5   1- 2
1901 BRO N  P             41  25-15
1902 BRO N  P-1-    34   46  17-15
                    2-O            .169
1903 DET A  P       36   39  17-15
1904 DET A  P       34   44  17-16
1905 DET A  P       34   46  18-14
1906 DET A  P       25   28   9-15
1907 DET A  P       32   37  25- 4
1908 DET A  P       29   30  18- 7
1909 DET A  P       21   22   8- 7
1910 DET A  P            26  18- 7
1911 DET A  P       20   24  10- 9
1912 DET A  P             6   1- 0
1915 NY  A  M-P          10   0- 3
1916 NY  A  M-P           1   0- 0
1918 DET A  P             2   0- 0
          BRTR     369  441 186-137
                                .196
```
NON-PLAYING MANAGER NY[A] 1917
PHI[N] 1921

DOOIN, CHARLES SEBASTIAN (RED)
B.JUNE 12,1879 CINCINNATI,OHIO
D.MAY 14,1952 ROCHESTER,N.Y.
```
1902 PHI N  C-O     87   .228
1903 PHI N  C       53   .218
1904 PHI N  C      104   .242
1905 PHI N  C      108   .250
1906 PHI N  C      107   .245
1907 PHI N  C       96   .211
1908 PHI N  C      132   .248
1909 PHI N  C      140   .224
1910 PHI N  M-C     94   .242
1911 PHI N  M-C     74   .328
1912 PHI N  M-C     69   .234
1913 PHI N  M-C     55   .226
1914 PHI N  M-C     53   .178
1915 CIN N  C       10   .323
     NY  N  C       46   .218
1916 NY  N  C       15   .118
          BRTR    1243   .240
```

DOOLAN, MICHAEL JOSEPH
(MICKEY) OR (DOC)
[REAL NAME MICHAEL JOSEPH DOOLITTLE]
B.MAY 7,1880 ASHLAND,PA.
D.NOV.1,1951 ORLANDO,FLA.
```
1905 PHI N  S      135   .254
1906 PHI N  S      154   .230
1907 PHI N  S      145   .204
1908 PHI N  S      129   .234
1909 PHI N  S      147   .219
1910 PHI N  S      148   .263
1911 PHI N  S      145   .238
1912 PHI N  S      146   .258
1913 PHI N  S      151   .218
1914 BAL F  S      144   .245
1915 BAL F  S      119   .195
     CHI F  S       24   .256
1916 CHI N  S       28   .211
     NY  N  S       18   .240
1918 BRO N  2       92   .179
          BRTR    1725   .231
```

DOOLITTLE, MICHAEL JOSEPH
[PLAYED UNDER NAME OF
MICHAEL JOSEPH DOOLAN]

DOOMS, HARRY E. (JACK)
B.ST.LOUIS,MO.
D.DEC.1899 ST.LOUIS,MO.
```
1892 LOU N  O        1   .000
```

DORAN, JOHN F.
B.1869 NEW JERSEY
```
1891 LOU AA P       17   5- 9
```

DORAN, THOMAS J. (LONG TOM)
B.DEC.2,1880 WESTCHESTER CO.,N.Y.
D.JUNE 22,1910 NEW YORK,N.Y.
```
1904 BOS A  C        5   .000
1905 BOS A  C        3   .000
     DET A  C       29   .165
1906 BOS A  C        2   .000
          TR        39   .146
```

DORAN, WILLIAM JAMES
B.JUN.14,1900 SAN FRANCISCO,CAL
```
1922 CLE A  3        3   .500
          BLTR
```

DO REGO, ANTONE
[PLAYED UNDER NAME OF ANTONE REGO]

DORGAN, JEREMIAH F.
B.1856 MERIDEN,CONN.
D.JUNE 10,1891 NEW HAVEN,CONN.
```
1880 WOR N  C-O      9   .229
1882 ATH AA C-O     45   .287
1884 IND AA O       34   .294
     BRO AA C        4   .308
1885 DET N  O       39   .285
          TR       131   .286
```

DORGAN, MICHAEL CORNELIUS
B.OCT.2,1853 MIDDLETOWN,CONN.
D.APR.26,1909 SYRACUSE,N.Y.
```
1877 STL N  C-S-3-O     60   .308
1879 SYR N  1-3-O       59   .266
1880 PRO N  P-3-     1  76   0- 0
            O                .246
1881 WOR N  1-S-O       51   .254
     DET N  1-3-O        8   .229
1883 NY  N  P-C-     4  62   0- 1
            O                .235
1884 NY  N  P-2-    14  79   8- 6
            2-O              .276
1885 NY  N  O           88   .325
1886 NY  N  O          118   .292
1887 NY  N  O           71   .295
1890 SYR AA O           31   .219
          BRTR      19 703   8- 7
                             .273
```

DORISH, HARRY (FRITZ)
B.JULY 13,1921 SWOYERSVILLE,PA.
```
1947 BOS A  P       41   7- 8
1948 BOS A  P        9   0- 1
1949 BOS A  P        5   0- 0
1950 STL A  P   29  30   4- 9
1951 CHI A  P-3     32   5- 6
                         .258
1952 CHI A  P       39   8- 4
1953 CHI A  P       55  10- 6
1954 CHI A  P       37   6- 4
1955 CHI A  P       13   2- 0
     BAL A  P       35   3- 3
1956 BAL A  P       13   0- 0
     BOS A  P       15   0- 2
          BRTR     323 324  43-43
                             .157
```

DORMAN, CHARLES WILLIAM (SLATS)
B.APR.23,1898 SAN FRANCISCO,CAL
D.NOV.15,1928 SAN FRANCISCO,CAL
```
1923 CHI A  C        1   .500
          BRTR
```

DORMAN, DWIGHT DEXTER
(CURLEY) OR (RED)
B.OCT.3,1905 JACKSONVILLE,ILL.
D.DEC.7,1974 ANAHEIM,CAL.
```
1928 CLE A  P       25   .364
          BRTR
```

DORNER, AUGUSTUS (GUS)
B.AUG.18,1876 CHAMBERSBURG,PA.
D.MAY 4,1956 CHAMBERSBURG,PA.
```
1902 CLE A  P        4   3- 1
1903 CLE A  P       12   3- 5
1906 CIN N  P        2   0- 0
     BOS N  P       34   8-26
1907 BOS N  P       36  12-16
1908 BOS N  P       38   8-19
1909 BOS N  P        5   1- 2
          BRTR     131  35-69
```

DORR, CHARLES ALBERT (BERT)
B.FEB.2,1862 NEW YORK
D.JUNE 16,1914 DICKINSON TOWN,N.Y.
```
1882 STL AA P        8   3- 5
```

DORSETT, CALVIN LEAVELLE (PREACHER)
B.JUNE 10,1913 LONE OAK,TEX.
D.OCT.22,1970 ELK CITY,OKLA.
```
1940 CLE A  P        1   0- 0
1941 CLE A  P        5   0- 1
1947 CLE A  P        2   0- 0
          BRTR       8   0- 1
```

DORSEY, JEREMIAH
B.1885 OAKLAND,CAL.
```
1911 PIT N  O        2   .000
```

DORSEY, MICHAEL JEREMIAH (JERRY)
B.1854 CANADA
D.NOV.3,1938 AUBURN,N.Y.
```
1884 BAL U  P-O      2   0- 1
                         .000
```

DOSCHER, JOHN HENRY JR. (JACK)
B.JULY 27,1880 TROY,N.Y.
D.MAY 27,1971 PARK RIDGE,N.J.
```
1903 CHI N  P       10   0- 1
     BRO N  P        3   0- 0
1904 BRO N  P        2   0- 1
1905 BRO N  P       11   1- 5
1906 BRO N  P        2   0- 1
1908 CIN N  P        6   1- 3
          BLTL      25   2-11
```

DOSCHER, JOHN HENRY SR. (HERM)
B.DEC.20,1852 NEW YORK,N.Y.
D.MAR.20,1934 BUFFALO,N.Y.
```
1872 ATH NA O        6   .346
1873 ATH NA O        1    -
1875 NAT NA S-3     21    -
1879 TRO N  3       46   .223
1881 CLE N  3        5   .211
1882 CLE N  3-O     25   .240
          BRTR     104    -
```

DOTTER, GARY RICHARD
B.AUG.7,1942 ST.LOUIS,MO.
```
1961 MIN A  P        2   0- 0
1963 MIN A  P        2   0- 0
1964 MIN A  P        3   0- 0
          BLTL       7   0- 0
```

DOTTERER, HENRY JOHN (DUTCH)
B.NOV.11,1931 SYRACUSE,N.Y.
```
1957 CIN N  C        4   .083
1958 CIN N  C       11   .250
1959 CIN N  C       52   .267
1960 CIN N  C       33   .228
1961 WAS A  C        7   .263
          BRTR     107   .248
```

DOTY, ELMER L. (BABE)
B.DEC.17,1867 GENOA,OHIO
D.NOV.20,1929 TOLEDO,OHIO
```
1890 TOL AA P        1   1- 0
          BLTR
```

DOUGHERTY, CHARLES WILLIAM
B.FEB.7,1862 DARLINGTON,WIS.
D.FEB.18,1925
```
1884 ALT U  2-S-3-O     23   .259
```

DOUGHERTY, PATRICK HENRY (PATSY)
B.OCT.27,1876 ANDOVER,N.Y.
D.APR.30,1940 BOLIVAR,N.Y.
```
1902 BOS A  3-O        106   .335
1903 BOS A  O          139   .332
1904 BOS A  O           59   .268
     NY  A  O           96   .289
1905 NY  A  O          116   .263
1906 NY  A  O           12   .170
     CHI A  O           75   .238
1907 CHI A  O          148   .270
1908 CHI A  O          138   .278
1909 CHI A  O          139   .285
1910 CHI A  O          127   .248
1911 CHI A  O           76   .289
          BLTR        1231   .284
```

DOUGHERTY, THOMAS JAMES (SUGAR BOY)
B.MAY 30,1881 CHICAGO,ILL.
D.NOV.6,1953 MILWAUKEE,WIS.
```
1904 CHI A  P        1   0- 0
          BLTR
```

DOUGLAS, CHARLES WILLIAM (WHAMMY)
B.FEB.17,1935 CARRBORO,N.C.
```
1957 PIT N  P       11   3- 3
          BRTR
```

DOUGLAS, JOHN FRANKLIN
B.SEPT.14,1917 THAYER,W.VA.
```
1945 BRO N  1        5   .000
          BLTL
```

DOUGLAS, LAWRENCE HOWARD
B.JUNE 5,1890 JELLICO,TENN.
D.NOV.4,1949 JELLICO,TENN.
```
1915 BAL F  P        2   1- 0
```

DOUGLAS, PHILLIP BROOKS
(SHUFFLIN PHIL)
B.JUNE 17,1890 CEDARTOWN,GA.
D.AUG.1,1952 SEQUATCHIE VALLEY,TENN.
```
1912 CHI A  P        3   0- 1
1914 CIN N  P       45  11-18
1915 CIN N  P        8   1- 5
     BRO N  P       20   5- 5
     CHI N  P        4   1- 1
1917 CHI N  P       51  14-20
1918 CHI N  P       25  10- 9
1919 CHI N  P       25  10- 6
     NY  N  P        8   2- 4
1920 NY  N  P       46  14-10
1921 NY  N  P       40  15-10
1922 NY  N  P       24  11- 4
          BRTR     299  94-93
```

DOUGLASS, ASTYANAX SAUNDERS
B.SEPT.19,1899 COVINGTON,TEX.
D.JAN.26,1975 EL PASO,TEX.
```
1921 CIN N  C        4   .143
1925 CIN N  C        7   .176
          BLTR      11   .174
```

YR CL LEA POS   GP   G   REC

DOUGLASS, WILLIAM BINGHAM (KLONDIKE)
B.MAY 10,1872 BOSTON,PA.
D.DEC.13,1953 BEND,ORE.
```
1896 STL N O            79  .268
1897 STL N C-1-O       127  .327
1898 PHI N 1           146  .266
1899 PHI N C            72  .264
1900 PHI N C            45  .306
1901 PHI N C            47  .333
1902 PHI N C-1-O       107  .235
1903 PHI N 1            97  .255
1904 PHI N 1             3  .333
        BLTR          723  .278
```

DOUTHIT, TAYLOR LEE
B.APR.22,1901 LITTLE ROCK,ARK.
```
1923 STL N O             9  .185
1924 STL N O            53  .277
1925 STL N O            30  .274
1926 STL N O           139  .308
1927 STL N O           130  .262
1928 STL N O           154  .295
1929 STL N O           150  .336
1930 STL N O           154  .303
1931 STL N O            36  .331
     CIN N O            95  .262
1932 CIN N O            96  .243
1933 CIN N O             1  .000
     CHI N O            27  .225
        BRTR          1074  .291
```

DOW, CLARENCE G.
B.OCT.11,1854 CHARLESTOWN,MASS.
D.MAR.11,1893 SOMERVILLE,MASS.
```
1884 BOS U O             1  .333
```

DOWD, JAMES JOSEPH (KIP)
B.FEB.16,1889 HOLYOKE,MASS.
D.DEC.20,1960 HOLYOKE,MASS.
```
1910 PIT N P             1  0- 0
        BRTR
```

DOWD, JOHN LEO
B.JAN.3,1891 S.WEYMOUTH,MASS.
```
1912 NY  A S            10  .194
        BRTR
```

DOWD, RAYMOND BERNARD (SNOOKS)
B.DEC.20,1897 SPRINGFIELD,MASS.
D.APR.4,1962 SPRINGFIELD,MASS.
```
1919 DET A H             1  .000
     PHI A 2-S-3        13  .158
1926 BRO N 2             2  .060
        BRTR            16  .077
```

DOWD, THOMAS JEFFERSON
(BUTTERMILK TOMMY)
B.APR.20,1869 HOLYOKE,MASS.
D.JULY 2,1933 HOLYOKE,MASS.
```
1891 BOS AA O            4  .167
     WAS AA 2          105  .252
1892 WAS N 2-3-O       141  .246
1893 STL N O           131  .294
1894 STL N O           123  .267
1895 STL N O           127  .325
1896 STL N M-2-O       125  .266
1897 STL N M-2-O        35  .267
     PHI N O            90  .290
1898 STL N O           139  .243
1899 CLE N O           146  .275
1901 BOS A O           138  .270
        BRTR          1304  .272
```

DOWIE, JOSEPH E.
B.1866 NEW ORLEANS,LA.
D.SEPT.3,1893 NEW ORLEANS,LA.
```
1889 BAL AA O           20  .240
```

DOWLING, DAVID BARCLAY (DAVE)
B.AUG.23,1942 BATON ROUGE,LA.
```
1964 STL N P             1  0- 0
1966 CHI N /P            1  1- 0
        BRTL             2  1- 0
```

DOWLING, HENRY PETER (PETE)
B.KENTUCKY
D.JUNE 30,1905 HOT LAKE,ORE.
```
1897 LOU N P             4  1- 3
1898 LOU N P            35  13-17
1899 LOU N P            35  13-18
1901 MIL A P            10  3- 5
     CLE A P            34  8-15
        TL             118  38-58
```

DOWLING, RODNEY J.
[PLAYED UNDER NAME OF
ROBERT J. GLENALVIN]

DOWNEY, ALEXANDER CUMMINGS (RED)
B.FEB.6,1889 AURORA,IND.
D.JULY 10,1949 DETROIT,MICH.
```
1909 BRO N O            19  .256
        BLTL
```

DOWNEY, THOMAS EDWARD
B.JAN.1,1884 LEWISTON,ME.
D.AUG.3,1961 PASSAIC,N.J.
```
1909 CIN N O           119  .231
1910 CIN N S-3         109  .270
1911 CIN N S           106  .261
1912 PHI N 3            54  .292
     CHI N 3            13  .182
1914 BUF F 2-S         151  .223
1915 BUF F 2-3          90  .199
        BBTR           642  .241
```

DOWNING, ALPHONSO ERWIN (AL)
B.JUNE 28,1941 TRENTON,N.J.
```
1961 NY  A P             5  0- 1
1962 NY  A P             1  0- 0
1963 NY  A P            24  13- 5
1964 NY  A P       37   40  13- 8
1965 NY  A P       35   36  12-14
1966 NY  A P            30  10-11
1967 NY  A P            31  14-10
1968 NY  A P            15  3- 3
1969 NY  A P            30  7- 5
1970 OAK A P            10  3- 3
     MIL A P            17  2-10
1971 LA  N P            37  20- 9
1972 LA  N P            31  9- 9
1973 LA  N P            30  9- 9
1974 LA  N P            21  5- 6
1975 LA  N P            22  2- 1
1976 LA  N P            17  1- 2
1977 LA  N P            12  0- 1
        BRTL      405  493 123-107
```

DOWNING, BRIAN JAY
B.OCT.9,1950 LOS ANGELES,CAL.
```
1973 CHI A O-C/3        34  .178
1974 CHI A C-O         108  .225
1975 CHI A *C          138  .240
1976 CHI A C-O         104  .256
1977 CHI A C/O          69  .284
1978 CAL A *C          133  .255
        BRTR           586  .246
```

DOWNS, DAVID RALPH (DAVE)
B.JUNE 21,1952 LOGAN,UTAH
```
1972 PHI N /P            4  1- 1
        BRTR
```

DOWNS, JEROME WILLIS (RED)
B.AUG.23,1883 NEOLA,IOWA
D.OCT.12,1939 COUNCIL BLUFFS,IA
```
1907 DET A 2-O         105  .219
1908 DET A 2            84  .221
1912 BRO N 2             9  .250
     CHI N 2            43  .263
        BRTR           241  .227
```

DOWSE, THOMAS JOSEPH
B.AUG.12,1866 IRELAND
D.DEC.14,1946 RIVERSIDE,CAL.
```
1890 CLE N O            40  .207
1891 COL AA C          103  .173
1892 LOU N P-C      1   40  0- 1
                                 .173
     CIN N C             1  .000
     PHI N C            16  .170
     WAS N C-O           6  .243
        BRTR       1   158  0- 1
                                 .196
```

DOYLE, BRIAN REED
B.JAN.26,1955 GLASGOW,KY.
```
1978 NY  A 2/S-3        39  .192
        BLTR
```

DOYLE, CORNELIUS J.
B.1858 HOLYOKE,MASS.
D.JAN.18,1927 E.ORANGE,N.J.
```
1883 PHI N O            16  .203
1890 TOL AA 3            1  .000
                        17  .197
```

DOYLE, EDWARD H.
B.1853 ILLINOIS
D.FEB.6,1929 HAVRE,MONT.
```
1882 STL AA P            3  0- 3
```

DOYLE, HOWARD JAMES (DANNY)
B.JAN.24,1917 MCLOUD,OKLA.
```
1943 BOS A C            13  .209
        BBTR
```

DOYLE, JAMES FRANCIS
B.DEC.25,1881 SYRACUSE,N.Y.
D.FEB.1,1912 SYRACUSE,N.Y.
```
1910 CIN N 3             7  .191
1911 CIN N 3           127  .282
        BRTR           134  .277
```

DOYLE, JESSE HERBERT (JESS)
B.APR.14,1898 KNOXVILLE,TENN.
D.MAR.15,1961 BELLEVILLE,ILL.
```
1925 DET A P            45  4- 7
1926 DET A P             2  0- 0
1927 DET A P             7  0- 0
1931 STL A P             1  0- 0
        BRTR            55  4- 7
```

DOYLE, JOHN A.
B.NOVA SCOTIA,CANADA
```
1884 PIT AA O           23  .203
```

DOYLE, JOHN JOSEPH
(JACK) OR (DIRTY JACK)
B.OCT.25,1869 KILLORGIN,IRELAND
D.DEC.31,1958 HOLYOKE,MASS.
```
1889 COL AA C-2-O       11  .355
1890 COL AA P-C     1   76  1- 0
                                 .272
1891 CLE N C-3-O        64  .263
1892 CLE N C-1-O        22  .300
     NY  N C-2-O        86  .295
1893 NY  N C-O          80  .322
1894 NY  N 1           105  .369
1895 NY  N M-1          78  .316
1896 BAL N 1           118  .345
1897 BAL N 1           114  .356
1898 WAS N M-1-2        42  .285
     NY  N 1            79  .297
1899 NY  N 1           117  .308
1900 NY  N 1           130  .273
1901 CHI N 1            73  .241
1902 NY  N 1            50  .300
     WAS A C-1-2-O      78  .238
1903 BRO N 1           139  .313
1904 BRO N 1             8  .227
     PHI N 1            64  .220
1905 NY  A 1             1  .000
        BRTR       1 1535  1- 0
                                 .302
```

DOYLE, JOSEPH J.
B.APR.9,1838 NEW YORK,N.Y.
D.JAN.7,1906 WHITE PLAINS,N.Y.
NON-PLAYING MANAGER BRO[AA]1885

DOYLE, JOSEPH K.
B.CINCINNATI,OHIO
```
1872 NAT NA 2-S          8  .222
```

DOYLE, JUDD BRUCE (SLOW JOE)
B.SEPT.15,1881 CLAY CENTER,KAN.
D.NOV.21,1947 TANNERSVILLE,N.Y.
```
1906 NY  A P             9  2- 2
1907 NY  A P            29  11-11
1908 NY  A P            12  1- 1
1909 NY  A P            17  8- 6
1910 NY  A P             3  0- 2
     CIN N P             5  0- 0
        BRTR            75  22-22
```

DOYLE, LAWRENCE JOSEPH
(LAUGHING LARRY)
B.JULY 31,1886 CASEYVILLE,ILL.
D.MAR.1,1974 SARANAC LAKE,N.Y.
```
1907 NY  N 2             9  .260
1908 NY  N 2           102  .308
1909 NY  N 2           144  .302
1910 NY  N 2           151  .285
1911 NY  N 2           141  .310
1912 NY  N 2           143  .330
1913 NY  N 2           132  .280
1914 NY  N 2           145  .260
1915 NY  N 2           150  .320
1916 NY  N 2           115  .264
     CHI N 2             9  .436
1917 NY  N 2           135  .254
1918 NY  N 2            75  .261
1919 NY  N 2           113  .289
1920 NY  N 2           137  .285
        BLTR          1759  .290
```

DOYLE, PAUL SINNOTT
B.OCT.2,1939 PHILADELPHIA,PA.
```
1969 ATL N P            36  2- 0
1970 CAL A P            40  3- 1
     SD  N /P            9  0- 2
1972 CAL A /P            2  0- 0
        BLTL            87  5- 3
```

DOYLE, ROBERT DENNIS (DENNY)
B.JAN.17,1944 GLASGOW,KY.
```
1970 PHI N *2          112  .208
1971 PHI N 2            95  .231
1972 PHI N *2          123  .249
1973 PHI N *2          116  .273
1974 CAL A *2/S        147  .260
1975 CAL A /2-3          8  .067
     BOS A 2/3-S        89  .310
1976 BOS A *2          117  .250
1977 BOS A *2          137  .240
        BLTR           944  .250
```

DOYLE, WILLIAM CARL (CARL)
B.JULY 30,1912 KNOXVILLE,TENN.
D.SEPT.4,1951 KNOXVILLE,TENN.
```
1935 PHI A P            14  2- 7
1936 PHI A P             8  0- 3
1939 BRO N P             5  1- 2
1940 BRO N P             3  0- 0
     STL N P            21  3- 3
        BRTR            51  6-15
```

YR	CL	LEA	POS	GP	G	REC

DOZIER, WILLIAM JOSEPH (BUZZ)
B.AUG.31,1927 WACO,TEX.

YR	CL	LEA	POS	GP	G	REC
1947	WAS	A	P		2	0- 0
1949	WAS	A	P		2	0- 0
	BRTR				4	0- 0

DRABOWSKY, MYRON WALTER (MOE)
B.JULY 21,1935 OZANNA,POLAND

YR	CL	LEA	POS	GP	G	REC
1956	CHI	N	P		9	2- 4
1957	CHI	N	P		36	13-15
1958	CHI	N	P		22	9-11
1959	CHI	N	P		31	5-10
1960	CHI	N	P	32	33	3- 1
1961	MIL	N	P		16	0- 2
1962	CIN	N	P		23	2- 6
	KC	A	P		10	1- 1
1963	KC	A	P		26	7-13
1964	KC	A	P	53	54	5-13
1965	KC	A	P		14	1- 5
1966	BAL	A	P		44	6- 0
1967	BAL	A	P		43	7- 5
1968	BAL	A	P		45	4- 4
1969	KC	A	P		52	11- 9
1970	KC	A	P		24	1- 2
	BAL	A	P		21	4- 2
1971	STL	N	P		51	6- 1
1972	STL	N	P		30	1- 1
	CHI	A	/P		7	0- 0
	BRTR			589	591	88-105

DRAGO, RICHARD ANTHONY (DICK)
B.JUNE 25,1945 TOLEDO,OHIO

YR	CL	LEA	POS	GP	G	REC
1969	KC	A	P		41	11-13
1970	KC	A	P		35	9-15
1971	KC	A	P		35	17-11
1972	KC	A	P	34	35	12-17
1973	KC	A	P	37	38	12-14
1974	BOS	A	P		33	7-10
1975	BOS	A	P		40	2- 2
1976	CAL	A	P		43	7- 8
1977	CAL	A	P		13	0- 1
	BAL	A	P		36	6- 3
1978	BOS	A	P		37	4- 4
	BRTR			384	386	87-98

DRAKE

YR	CL	LEA	POS	GP	G	REC
1884	WAS	AA	O		2	.286

DRAKE, DELOS DANIEL
B.DEC.3,1886 GIRARD,OHIO
D.OCT.3,1965 FINDLAY,OHIO

YR	CL	LEA	POS	GP	G	REC
1911	DET	A	O		95	.279
1914	STL	F	1-O		138	.252
1915	STL	F	O		99	.265
	BRTR				332	.264

DRAKE, LARRY FRANCIS
B.MAY 4,1921 MC KINNEY,TEX.

YR	CL	LEA	POS	GP	G	REC
1945	PHI	A	O		1	.000
1948	WAS	A	O		4	.266
	BLTR				5	.222

DRAKE, LOGAN GAFFNEY (L.G.)
B.DEC.26,1900 SPARTANBURG,S.C.
D.JUNE 3,1940 COLUMBIA,S.C.

YR	CL	LEA	POS	GP	G	REC
1922	CLE	A	P		1	0- 0
1923	CLE	A	P		4	0- 0
1924	CLE	A	P		5	0- 1
	BRTR				10	0- 1

DRAKE, SAMUEL HARRISON (SAMMY)
B.OCT.7,1934 LITTLE ROCK,ARK.

YR	CL	LEA	POS	GP	G	REC
1960	CHI	N	2-3		15	.067
1961	CHI	N	O		13	.000
1962	NY	N	2		25	.192
	BBTR				53	.153

DRAKE, SOLOMON LOUIS (SOLLY)
B.OCT.23,1930 LITTLE ROCK,ARK.

YR	CL	LEA	POS	GP	G	REC
1956	CHI	N	O		65	.256
1959	LA	N	O		9	.250
	PHI	N	O		67	.145
	BBTR				141	.232

DRAKE, THOMAS KENDALL
B.AUG.7,1914 BIRMINGHAM,ALA.

YR	CL	LEA	POS	GP	G	REC
1939	CLE	A	P		8	0- 1
1941	BRO	N	P-O	10	11	1- 1
						.400
	BRTR			18	19	1- 2
						.286

DRAUBY, JACOB C.
B.1865 HARRISBURG,PA.

YR	CL	LEA	POS	GP	G	REC
1892	WAS	N	3		10	.205

DREESEN, WILLIAM RICHARD
B.JULY 29,1904 NEW YORK,N.Y.
D.NOV.9,1971 MT.VERNON,N.Y.

YR	CL	LEA	POS	GP	G	REC
1931	BOS	N	3		48	.222
	BLTR					

DREISEWERD, CLEMENT JOHN (STEAMBOAT)
B.JAN.24,1916 OLD MONROE,MO.

YR	CL	LEA	POS	GP	G	REC
1944	BOS	A	P		7	2- 4
1945	BOS	A	P		2	0- 1
1946	BOS	A	P		20	4- 1
1948	STL	A	P		13	0- 2
	NY	N	P		4	0- 0
	BLTL				46	6- 8

DRENNAN, K. JOHN

YR	CL	LEA	POS	GP	G	REC
1904	DET	A	1		1	.000

DRESCHER, WILLIAM CLAYTON (DUTCH)
B.MAY 23,1921 CONGERS,N.Y.
D.MAY 15,1968 HAMMERSTRAW,N.Y.

YR	CL	LEA	POS	GP	G	REC
1944	NY	A	C		4	.143
1945	NY	A	C		48	.270
1946	NY	A	C		5	.333
	BRTR				57	.266

DRESSEN, CHARLES WALTER (CHUCK)
B.SEPT.20,1898 DECATUR,ILL.
D.AUG.10,1966 DETROIT,MICH.

YR	CL	LEA	POS	GP	G	REC
1925	CIN	N	2-3-O		76	.274
1926	CIN	N	3-O		127	.266
1927	CIN	N	S=3		144	.292
1928	CIN	N	3		135	.291
1929	CIN	N	2-3		110	.244
1930	CIN	N	2-3		33	.211
1931	CIN	N	3		5	.067
1933	NY	N	3		16	.222
	BRTR				646	.272

NON-PLAYING MANAGER
CIN(N) 1934-37, BRO(N) 1951-53,
WAS(A) 1955-57, MIL(N) 1960-61
DET(A) 1963-66

DRESSEN, LEE AUGUST
B.JULY 23,1889 ELLINWOOD,KAN.
D.JUNE 30,1931 DILLER,NEB.

YR	CL	LEA	POS	GP	G	REC
1914	STL	N	1		46	.233
1918	DET	A	1		31	.178
	BLTL				77	.205

DRESSER, EDWARD

YR	CL	LEA	POS	GP	G	REC
1898	BRO	N	S		1	.250

DRESSER, ROBERT NICHOLSON
B.OCT.4,1878 NEWTON,MASS.
D.JULY 27,1924 DUXBURY,MASS.

YR	CL	LEA	POS	GP	G	REC
1902	BOS	N	P		1	0- 1
	TL					

DRESSLER, ROBERT ANTHONY (ROB)
B.FEB.2,1954 PORTLAND,ORE.

YR	CL	LEA	POS	GP	G	REC
1975	SF	N	/P		3	1- 0
1976	SF	N	P		25	3-10
1978	STL	N	/P		3	0- 1
	BRTR				31	4-11

DREW, DAVID

YR	CL	LEA	POS	GP	G	REC
1884	KEY	U	P-2	1	2	0- 0
						.444
	WAS	U	1-S-O		13	.327
				1	15	0- 0
						.344

DREWS, FRANK JOHN
B.MAY 25,1916 BUFFALO,N.Y.
D.APR.22,1972 BUFFALO,N.Y.

YR	CL	LEA	POS	GP	G	REC
1944	BOS	N	2		46	.206
1945	BOS	N	2		49	.204
	BRTR				95	.205

DREWS, KARL AUGUST
B.FEB.22,1920 STATEN ISLAND,N.Y
D.AUG.15,1963 DANIA,FLA.

YR	CL	LEA	POS	GP	G	REC
1946	NY	A	P		3	0- 1
1947	NY	A	P		30	6- 6
1948	NY	A	P		19	2- 3
	STL	A	P		20	3- 2
1949	STL	A	P		31	4-12
1951	PHI	N	P		5	1- 0
1952	PHI	N	P		33	14-15
1953	PHI	N	P		47	9-10
1954	PHI	N	P		8	1- 0
	CIN	N	P		22	4- 4
	BRTR				218	44-53

DRIESSEN, DANIEL (DAN)
B.JULY 29,1951 HILTON HEAD,S.C.

YR	CL	LEA	POS	GP	G	REC
1973	CIN	N	3-1/O		102	.301
1974	CIN	N	*3-1/O		150	.281
1975	CIN	N	1-O		88	.281
1976	CIN	N	1-O		98	.247
1977	CIN	N	*1		151	.300
1978	CIN	N	*1		153	.250
	BLTR				742	.278

DRILL, LEWIS L
B.MAY 9,1877 BROWERVILLE,MINN.
D.JULY 4,1969 ST.PAUL,MINN.

YR	CL	LEA	POS	GP	G	REC
1902	WAS	A	C-2-S-O		37	.272
	BAL	A	C-1		2	.250
	WAS	A	C-2-S-O		32	.250
1903	WAS	A	C		51	.252
1904	WAS	A	C		43	.394
	DET	A	C-1		51	.225
1905	DET	A	C		72	.261
	BRTR				288	.255

DRISCOLL, JAMES BERNARD (JIM)
B.MAY 14,1944 MEDFORD,MASS.

YR	CL	LEA	POS	GP	G	REC
1970	OAK	A	/2-S		21	.192
1972	TEX	A	/2-S		15	.000
	BLTR				36	.143

DRISCOLL, JOHN F. (DENNY)
B.NOV.19,1855 LOWELL,MASS.
D.JULY 11,1886 LOWELL,MASS.

YR	CL	LEA	POS	GP	G	REC
1880	BUF	N	P-O	6	18	1- 3
						.136
1882	PIT	AA	P		22	13- 9
1883	PIT	AA	P-C-	39	41	18-21
			3-O			.185
1884	LOU	AA	P-O		13	7- 6
						.167
1885	BUF	N	2		7	.158
				82	101	39-59
						.160

DRISCOLL, JOHN LEO (PADDY)
B.JAN.11,1895 EVANSTON,ILL.
D.JUNE 29,1968 CHICAGO,ILL.

YR	CL	LEA	POS	GP	G	REC
1917	CHI	N	2		13	.107
	BRTR					

DRISCOLL, MICHAEL COLUMBUS
B.OCT.19,1892 FOXBORO,MASS.
D.MAR.21,1953 FOXBORO,MASS.

YR	CL	LEA	POS	GP	G	REC
1916	PHI	A	P		1	0- 1
	BRTR					

DRISSEL, MICHAEL F. (MIKE)
B.DEC.19,1864 ST.LOUIS,MO.
D.FEB.26,1913 ST.LOUIS,MO.

YR	CL	LEA	POS	GP	G	REC
1885	STL	AA	C		6	.056
	BRTR					

DROHAN, DAVID
[PLAYED UNDER NAME OF DAVID ROWAN]

DROHAN, THOMAS F
B.AUG.26,1887 FALL RIVER,MASS.
D.SEPT.17,1926 KEWANEE,ILL.

YR	CL	LEA	POS	GP	G	REC
1913	WAS	A	P		2	0- 0
	BRTR					

DROPO, WALTER (MOOSE)
B.JAN 30,1923 MOOSUP,CONN.

YR	CL	LEA	POS	GP	G	REC
1949	BOS	A	1		11	.146
1950	BOS	A	1		136	.322
1951	BOS	A	1		99	.239
1952	BOS	A	1		37	.265
	DET	A	1		115	.279
1953	DET	A	1		152	.248
1954	DET	A	1		107	.281
1955	CHI	A	1		141	.280
1956	CHI	A	1		125	.266
1957	CHI	A	1		93	.256
1958	CHI	A	1		28	.192
	CIN	N	1		63	.290
1959	CIN	N	1		26	.103
	BAL	A	1-3		62	.278
1960	BAL	A	1-3		79	.268
1961	BAL	A	1		14	.259
	BRTR				1288	.270

DROTT, RICHARD FRED
(DICK) OR (HUMMER)
B.JULY 1,1936 CINCINNATI,OHIO

YR	CL	LEA	POS	GP	G	REC
1957	CHI	N	P		38	15-11
1958	CHI	N	P		39	7-11
1959	CHI	N	P		8	1- 2
1960	CHI	N	P		23	0- 6
1961	CHI	N	P		35	1- 4
1962	HOU	N	P		6	1- 0
1963	HOU	N	P		27	2-12
	BRTR				176	27-46

DRUCKE, LOUIS FRANK
B.DEC.3,1888 WACO,TEX.
D.SEPT.22,1955 WACO,TEX.

YR	CL	LEA	POS	GP	G	REC
1909	NY	N	P		3	2- 1
1910	NY	N	P		34	12-10
1911	NY	N	P		15	4- 4
1912	NY	N	P		1	0- 0
	TR				53	18-15

DRUHOT, CARL A. (COLLIE)
B.SEPT.1,1882 OHIO
D.FEB.11,1918 PORTLAND,ORE.

YR	CL	LEA	POS	GP	G	REC
1906	CIN	N	P		14	6- 8
	STL	N	P		5	2- 1
1907	STL	N	P		2	0- 2
	BLTL				21	8-11

YR CL LEA POS GP G REC

DRUMRIGHT, KEITH ALAN
B.OCT.21,1954 SPRINGFIELD,MO.
1978 HOU N 2 17 .164
BLTR

DRYSDALE, DONALD SCOTT (DON)
B.JULY 23,1936 VAN NUYS,CAL.
1956 BRO N P 25 26 5- 5
1957 BRO N P 34 37 17- 9
1958 LA N P 44 47 12-13
1959 LA N P 44 46 17-13
1960 LA N P 41 15-14
1961 LA N P 40 13-10
1962 LA N P 43 25- 9
1963 LA N P 42 19-17
1964 LA N P 40 18-16
1965 LA N P 44 58 23-12
1966 LA N P 40 46 13-16
1967 LA N P 38 13-16
1968 LA N P 31 14-12
1969 LA N P 12 5- 4
BRTR 518 547 209-166

DUBIEL, WALTER JOHN (MONK)
B.FEB.12,1919 HARTFORD,CONN.
D.OCT.23,1969 HARTFORD,CONN.
1944 NY A P 30 31 13-13
1945 NY A P 26 10- 9
1948 PHI N P 37 38 8-10
1949 CHI N P 32 33 6- 9
1950 CHI N P 39 6-10
1951 CHI N P 22 2- 2
1952 CHI N P 1 0- 0
BRTR 187 190 45-53

DUBUC, JEAN JOSEPH OCTAVE
ARTHUR (CHAUNCEY)
B.SEPT.15,1888 ST.JOHNSBURY,VT.
D.AUG.28,1958 FORT MYERS,FLA.
1908 CIN N P 16 5- 6
1909 CIN N P 19 2- 5
1912 DET A P 37 17-10
1913 DET A P 36 66 16-14
1914 DET A P 36 69 13-14
1915 DET A P 40 60 17-12
1916 DET A P 36 52 10- 8
1918 BOS A P 5 0- 1
1919 NY N P 36 37 6- 4
BRTR 261 360 86-74

DUCKWORTH, JAMES RAYMOND (JIM)
B.MAY 24,1939 NATIONAL CITY,CAL.
1963 WAS A P 37 4-12
1964 WAS A P 30 1- 6
1965 WAS A P 17 2- 2
1966 WAS A /P 5 0- 3
KC A /P 8 0- 2
BRTR 97 7-25

DUDLEY, ELZIE CLISE (CLISE)
B.AUG.8,1903 GRAHAM,N.C.
1929 BRO N P 35 36 6-14
1930 BRO N P 21 2- 4
1931 PHI N P 30 44 8-14
1932 PHI N P 13 23 1- 1
1933 PIT N P 1 0- 0
BLTR 100 125 17-33

DUDLEY, ERNEST
[PLAYED UNDER NAME OF
ERNEST DUDLEY LEE]

DUDRA, JOHN JOSEPH
B.MAY 27,1916 ASSUMPTION,ILL.
D.OCT.24,1965 PANA,ILL.
1941 BOS N 1-2-S-3 14 .360
BRTR

DUES, HAL JOSEPH
B.SEPT.22,1954 LA MARQUE,TEX.
1977 MON N /P 6 1- 1
1978 MON N P 25 5- 6
BRTR 31 6- 7

DUFF, CECIL ELBA (LARRY)
B.NOV.30,1897 RADERSBURG,MONT.
D.NOV.10,1969 BEND,ORE.
1922 CHI A P 3 1- 1
BLTR

DUFF, PATRICK HENRY
B.MAY 6,1875 PROVIDENCE,R.I.
D.SEPT.11,1925 PROVIDENCE,R.I.
1906 WAS A C 1 .000
TR

DUFFALO, JAMES FRANCIS (JIM)
B.NOV.25,1935 HELVETIA,PA.
1961 SF N P 24 25 5- 1
1962 SF N P 24 1- 2
1963 SF N P 34 4- 2
1964 SF N P 35 5- 1
1965 SF N /P 2 0- 1
CIN N P 22 0- 1
BRTR 141 142 15- 8

DUFFEE, CHARLES EDWARD (HOME RUN)
B.JAN.27,1866 MOBILE,ALA.
D.DEC.24,1894 MOBILE,ALA.
1889 STL AA O 137 .245
1890 STL AA O 98 .274
1891 COL AA O 137 .302
1892 WAS N O 129 .252
1893 CIN N O 4 .200
BR 505 .266

DUFFIE, JOHN BROWN
B.OCT.4,1945 GREENWOOD,S.C.
1967 LA N /P 2 0- 2
BRTR

DUFFY, BERNARD ALLEN
B.AUG.18,1893 VINSON,OKLA.
D.FEB.9,1962 ABILENE,TEX.
1913 PIT N P 3 0- 0
BRTR

DUFFY, EDWARD C.
B.1844 IRELAND
1871 CHI NA S-3 25 -

DUFFY, FRANK THOMAS
B.OCT.14,1946 OAKLAND,CAL.
1970 CIN N /S 6 .182
1971 CIN N S 13 .188
SF N /S-2-3 21 .179
1972 CLE A *S 130 .239
1973 CLE A *S 116 .263
1974 CLE A *S 158 .233
1975 CLE A *S 146 .243
1976 CLE A *S 133 .212
1977 CLE A *S 122 .201
1978 BOS A 3-S-2 64 .260
BRTR 909 .233

DUFFY, HUGH
B.NOV.26,1866 CRANSTON,R.I.
D.OCT.19,1954 BOSTON,MASS.
1888 CHI N O 71 .282
1889 CHI N O 136 .311
1890 CHI P O 137 .328
1891 BOS AA O 127 .340
1892 BOS N O 146 .302
1893 BOS N O 131 .378
1894 BOS N O 124 .438
1895 BOS N O 131 .352
1896 BOS N O 131 .302
1897 BOS N O 134 .341
1898 BOS N O 151 .319
1899 BOS N O 147 .279
1900 BOS N O 50 .298
1901 MIL A M-O 78 .308
1904 PHI N M-O 16 .261
1905 PHI N M-O 15 .307
1906 PHI N M-H 1 .000
BRTR 1726 .329
NON-PLAYING MANAGER
CHI[A] 1910-11, BOS[A] 1921-22

DUGAN, DANIEL PHILLIP
B.FEB.22,1907 PLAINFIELD,N.J.
D.JUNE 25,1968 GREEN BROOK,N.J.
1928 CHI A P 1 0- 0
1929 CHI A P 19 1- 4
BLTL 20 1- 4

DUGAN, EDWARD J.
B.1864 BROOKLYN,N.Y.
1884 RIC AA P-2 20 21 5-15
KC U O 3 .000
.114
20 24 5-15
.095

DUGAN, JOSEPH ANTHONY (JUMPING JOE)
B.MAY.12,1897 MAHANOY CITY,PA.
1917 PHI A S 43 .194
1918 PHI A 2-S 120 .195
1919 PHI A S 104 .271
1920 PHI A 2-S-3 123 .322
1921 PHI A 3 119 .295
1922 BOS A S-3 84 .281
NY A 3 60 .294
1923 NY A 3 146 .283
1924 NY A 3 148 .302
1925 NY A 3 102 .292
1926 NY A 3 123 .288
1927 NY A 3 112 .269
1928 NY A 3 94 .276
1929 BOS N 3 60 .304
1931 DET A 3 8 .235
BRTR 1446 .280

DUGAN, WILLIAM E.
B.1864 KINGSTON,N.Y.
1884 RIC AA C 8 .040

DUGAS, AUGUSTIN JOSEPH (GUS)
B.MAR.24,1907 ST.JEAN DEMATHA,
QUE.,CANADA
1930 PIT N O 9 .290
1932 PIT N O 55 .237
1933 PHI N 1-O 37 .169
1934 WAS A O 24 .053
BLTL 125 .209

DUGDALE, DANIEL EDWARD
B.OCT.28,1864 PEORIA,ILL.
D.MAR.9,1934 SEATTLE,WASH.
1886 KC N C 12 .175
1894 WAS N C 33 .217
45 .207

DUGEY, OSCAR JOSEPH (JAKE)
B.OCT.25,1887 PALESTINE,TEX.
D.JAN.1,1966 DALLAS,TEX.
1913 BOS N S-3 5 .250
1914 BOS N 2-O 58 .193
1915 PHI N 2 42 .154
1916 PHI N 2 41 .220
1917 PHI N 2 44 .194
1920 BOS N H 5 .000
BRTR 195 .194

DUGGAN, JAMES ELMER (MER)
B.JUNE 3,1884 WHITELAND,IND.
D.DEC.5,1951 INDIANAPOLIS,IND.
1911 STL A 1 1 .000
BLTL

DUGGLEBY, WILLIAM JAMES
(FROSTY BILL)
B.MAR.16,1874 UTICA,N.Y.
D.AUG.30,1944 REDFIELD,N.Y.
1898 PHI N P 9 3- 3
1901 PHI N P 33 19-12
1902 PHI A P 2 1- 1
PHI N P 31 11-17
1903 PHI N P 36 13-18
1904 PHI N P 32 12-14
1905 PHI N P 38 18-16
1906 PHI N P 42 13-19
1907 PHI N P 5 1- 2
PIT N P 9 0- 2
TR 237 91-104

DUKE, MARTIN F. (DUCK)
B.COLUMBUS,OHIO
D.DEC.31,1898 MINNEAPOLIS,MINN.
1891 WAS AA P 4 0- 4
TL

DUKES, NOBLE JAN (JAN)
B.AUG.16,1945 CHEYENNE,WYO.
1969 WAS A /P 8 0- 2
1970 WAS A /P 5 0- 0
1972 TEX A /P 3 0- 0
BLTL 16 0- 2

DUKES, THOMAS EARL (TOM)
B.AUG.31,1942 KNOXVILLE,TENN.
1967 HOU N P 17 0- 2
1968 HOU N P 43 2- 2
1969 SD N P 13 1- 0
1970 SD N P 53 1- 6
1971 BAL A P 28 1- 5
1972 CAL A /P 7 0- 1
BRTR 161 5-16

DULIBA, ROBERT JOHN (BOB)
B.JAN.9,1935 GLEN LYON,PA.
1959 STL N P 11 0- 1
1960 STL N P 27 4- 4
1962 STL N P 28 2- 0
1963 LA A P 6 1- 1
1964 LA A P 58 6- 4
1965 BOS A P 39 4- 2
1967 KC A /P 7 0- 0
BRTR 176 17-12

DUMONT, GEORGE HENRY (PEA SOUP)
B.NOV.13,1895 MINNEAPOLIS,MINN.
D.OCT.13,1956 MINNEAPOLIS,MINN.
1915 WAS A P 6 2- 1
1916 WAS A P 17 2- 2
1917 WAS A P 37 5-14
1918 WAS A P 4 1- 1
1919 BOS A P 13 0- 4
BRTR 77 10-22

DUMOULIN, DANIEL LYNN (DAN)
B.AUG.20,1953 KOKOMO,IND.
1977 CIN N /P 5 0- 0
1978 CIN N /P 3 1- 0
BRTR 8 1- 0

DUMOVICH, NICHOLAS
B.JAN.2,1902 SACRAMENTO,CAL.
1923 CHI N P 28 3- 5
BLTL

DUNCAN, DAVID EDWIN (DAVE)
B.SEP.26,1945 DALLAS,TEX.
1964 KC A C 25 .170
1967 KC A C 34 .188
1968 OAK A C 82 .191
1969 OAK A C 58 .126
1970 OAK A C 86 .259
1971 OAK A *C 103 .253
1972 OAK A *C 121 .218
1973 CLE A C 95 .233
1974 CLE A *C/1 136 .200
1975 BAL A C 96 .205
1976 BAL A C 93 .204
BRTR 929 .214

YR CL LEA POS   GP   G   REC

DUNCAN, JAMES WILLIAM (JIM)
B.JULY 1,1871 SALTSBURG,PA.
D.OCT.16,1901 FOXBURG,PA.
1899 WAS N C   15   .234
     CLE N C   30   .231
          BRTR   45   .232

DUNCAN, LOUIS BAIRD (PAT)
B.OCT.6,1893 COALTON,OHIO
D.JULY 17,1960 JACKSON,OHIO
1915 PIT N O   3   .200
1919 CIN N O   31   .244
1920 CIN N O   154   .295
1921 CIN N O   145   .308
1922 CIN N O   151   .327
1923 CIN N O   147   .327
1924 CIN N O   96   .270
          BRTR   727   .307

DUNCAN, TAYLOR MC DOWELL
B.MAY 12,1953 MEMPHIS,TENN.
1977 STL N /3   8   .333
1978 OAK N 3-2/S   104   .257
          BRTR   112   .260

DUNCAN, VERNON VAN DUKE
B.JAN.6,1890 CLAYTON,N.C.
D.JUNE 1,1954 DAYTONA BEACH,FLA
1913 PHI N O   8   .416
1914 BAL F O   157   .287
1915 BAL F 3-O   146   .269
          BLTR   3.1   .280

DUNDON, AUGUSTUS JOSEPH
B.JULY 10,1874 COLUMBUS,OHIO
D.SEPT.1,1940 PITTSBURGH,PA.
1904 CHI A 2   108   .234
1905 CHI A 2   106   .192
1906 CHI A 2   33   .135
          BRTR   247   .204

DUNDON, EDWARD JOSEPH (DUMMY)
B.JULY 10,1859 COLUMBUS,OHIO
D.AUG.18,1893 COLUMBUS,OHIO
1883 COL AA P-2=2   19   26   3-16
                 O   .161
1884 COL AA P-2   10   26   5- 4
                               .140
          TR   29   52   8-20
                               .151

DUNEGAN, JAMES WILLIAM (JIM)
B.AUG.6,1947 BURLINGTON,IOWA
1970 CHI N /P   7   10   0- 2
          BRTR

DUNGAN, SAMUEL MORRISON
B.JAN.29,1866 FERNDALE,CAL.
D.MAR.16,1939 SANTA ANA,CAL.
1892 CHI N O   113   .291
1893 CHI N O   107   .310
1894 CHI N O   10   .237
     LOU N O   8   .333
1900 CIN N O   6   .266
1901 WAS A 1-O   137   .324
          BR   361   .309

DUNHAM, HENRY HUSTON (WILEY)
B.JAN.30,1877 PIKETOWN,OHIO
D.JAN.16,1854 CLEVELAND,OHIO
1902 STL N P   7   2- 3

DUNHAM, LELAND HUFFIELD (LEE)
B.JUNE 9,1902 ATLANTA,ILL.
D.MAY 11,1961 ATLANTA,ILL.
1926 PHI N 1   5   .250
          BLTL

DUNKLE, EDWARD PERKS (DAVEY)
B.AUG.30,1872 PHILLIPSBURG,PA.
D.NOV.19,1941 LOCK HAVEN,PA.
1897 PHI N P   7   5- 2
1898 PHI N P   9   1- 5
1899 WAS N P   4   0- 2
1903 CHI A P   11   5- 8
     WAS A P   14   5- 8
1904 WAS A P   12 13   2- 9
          BBTR   57 58 18-31

DUNLAP, FREDERICK C. (SURE SHOT)
B.MAY 21,1859 PHILADELPHIA,PA.
D.DEC.1,1902 PHILADELPHIA,PA.
1880 CLE N 2   84   .273
1881 CLE N 2-3   78   .324
1882 CLE N 2   82   .278
1883 CLE N 2   90   .328
1884 STL U M-P-   1 81   0- 0
            2-O   .420
1885 STL N M-2   106   .269
1886 DET N M-2   73   .281
     DET N M-2   49   .284
1887 DET N M-2   64   .326
1888 PIT N M-2   81   .261
1889 PIT N M-2   121   .235
1890 PIT N 2   17   .172
     NY P 2   1   .000
1891 WAS AA 2   7   .200
          BRTR   1 934   0- 0
                               .295

DUNLAP, GRANT LESTER (SNAP)
B.DEC.20,1923 STOCKTON,CAL.
1953 STL N O   16   .353
          BRTR

DUNLAP, WILLIAM JAMES
B.MAY 1,1909 THREE RIVERS,MASS.
1929 BOS N O   10   .414
1930 BOS N O   16   .069
          BRTR   26   .241

DUNLEAVY, JOHN FRANCIS (JACK)
B.SEPT.14,1879 HARRISON,N.J.
D.APR.12,1944 S.NORWALK,CONN.
1903 STL N P-O   14 52   6- 8
                               .249
1904 STL N P-O   7 51   1- 4
                               .236
1905 STL N O   119   .241
                    21 222   7-12
                               .241

DUNLOP, GEORGE HENRY
B.JULY 19,1888 MERIDEN,CONN.
D.DEC.12,1972 MERIDEN,CONN.
1913 CLE A S-3   7   .222
1914 CLE A S   1   .000
          BRTR   8   .190

DUNN, JAMES WILLIAM (JIM) OR (BILL)
B.FEB.25,1931 VALDOSTA,GA.
1952 PIT N P   3   0- 0

DUNN, JOHN JOSEPH (JACK)
B.OCT.6,1872 MEADVILLE,PA.
D.OCT.22,1928 TOWSON,MD.
1897 BRO N P   25 34 16- 9
1898 BRO N P   37 45 15-21
1899 BRO N P   38 39 21-12
1900 BRO N P   8   3- 5
     PHI N P   10   4- 5
1901 PHI N P   2   0- 1
     BAL A P-S-   6 96   3- 3
            3   .247
1902 NY N P-2   3 96   C- 3
            S-3   .211
     S-3-O
1903 NY N 2-S-3   72   .241
1904 NY N P-3   1 55   0- 0
                               .309
          BRTR   130 457 62-59
                               .247

DUNN, JOSEPH EDWARD
B.MAR.11,1885 SPRINGFIELD,OHIO
D.MAR.19,1944 SPRINGFIELD,OHIO
1908 BRO N C   20   .172
1909 BRO N C   7   .160
          BRTR   27   .169

DUNN, RONALD RAY (RON)
B.JAN.24,1950 OKLAHOMA CITY,OKLA
1974 CHI N 2/3   23   .294
1975 CHI N 3/O-2   32   .159
          BRTR   55   .241

DUNN, STEPHEN
B.DEC.21,1858 LONDON,ONT.,CAN.
D.MAY 5,1933 LONDON,ONT.,CAN.
1884 STP U 1-2   9   .242

DUNNING, ANDREW J.
B.NEW YORK,N.Y.
1889 PIT N P   2   0- 2
1891 NY N P   1   0- 0
                        3   0- 2

DUNNING, STEVEN JOHN (STEVE)
B.MAY 15,1949 DENVER,COLO.
1970 CLE A P   19   4- 9
1971 CLE A P   31 32   8-14
1972 CLE A P   16 20   6- 4
1973 CLE A /P   4   0- 2
     TEX A P   23 27   2- 6
1974 TEX A /P   1   0- 0
1976 CAL A /P   4   0- 0
     MON N /P   32   2- 6
1977 OAK A /P   6   1- 0
          BRTR   136 145 23-41

DUPAUGHER, MICHAEL H.
B.SAN FRANCISCO,CAL.
1884 PHI N C   2   .250

DUPEE, FRANK OLIVER
B.APR.29,1877 MONKTON,VT.
D.AUG.14,1956 PORTLAND,ME.
1901 CHI A P   1   0- 0
          TR

DUPREE, MICHAEL DENNIS (MIKE)
B.MAY 29,1953 KANSAS CITY,KAN.
1976 SD N P   12   0- 0
          BRTR

DURBIN, BLAINE ALPHONSUS (KID)
B.SEPT.10,1886 KANSAS
D.SEPT.11,1943 KIRKWOOD,MO.
1907 CHI N P   5 10   0- 1
1908 CHI N O   14   .363
1909 CIN N H   6   .200
1909 PIT N H   1   .000
          BLTL   5 31   0- 1
                               .271

DUREN, RINOLD GEORGE (RYNE)
B.FEB.22,1929 CAZENOVIA,WIS.
1954 BAL A P   1   0- 0
1957 KC A P   14   0- 3
1958 NY A P   44   6- 4
1959 NY A P   41   3- 6
1960 NY A P   42   3- 4
1961 NY A P   4   0-11
     LA A P   40   6-12
1962 LA A P   42   2- 9
1963 PHI N P   33 34   6- 2
1964 PHI N P   2   0- 0
     CIN N P   26   0- 2
1965 PHI N /P   6   0- 0
     WAS A P   16   1- 1
          BRTR   311 312 27-44

DURHAM, DONALD GARY (DON)
B.MAR.21,1949 YOSEMITE,KY.
1972 STL N P   10 14   2- 7
1973 TEX A P   15 16   0- 4
          BRTR   25 30   2-11

DURHAM, EDWARD FANT (BULL)
B.AUG.17,1908 CHESTER,S.C.
D.APR.27,1976 CHESTER,S.C.
1929 BOS A P   14   1- 0
1930 BOS A P   33   4-15
1931 BOS A P   38 39   8-10
1932 BOS A P   34 35   6-13
1933 CHI A P   24 10- 6
          BLTR   143 145 29-44

DURHAM, JOHN GARFIELD
B.OCT.7,1881 DOUGLASS,KAN.
D.MAY 7,1949 COFFEYVILLE,KAN.
1902 CHI A P-O   3   5   1- 1
                               .066

DURHAM, JOSEPH VANN (JOE) OR (POP)
B.JULY 31,1931 NEWPORT NEWS,VA.
1954 BAL A O   10   .225
1957 BAL A O   77   .185
1959 STL N O   6   .000
          BRTR   93   .188

DURHAM, LOUIS G. (BULL)
B.1881 BOLIVAR,N.Y.
1904 BRO N P   2   1- 0
1907 WAS A P   2   0- 0
1908 NY N P   1   0- 0
1909 NY N P   4   0- 0
          TR   9   1- 0

DURNBAUGH, ROBERT EUGENE
(BOBBY) OR (SCROGGY)
B.JAN.15,1933 DAYTON,OHIO
1957 CIN N S   2   .000

DURNING, GEORGE WARREN
B.MAY 9,1898 PHILADELPHIA,PA.
1925 PHI N O   5   .357
          BRTR

DURNING, RICHARD KNOTT (RICH)
B.OCT.10,1892 LOUISVILLE,KY.
D.SEPT.23,1948 CASTLE POINT,N.Y
1917 BRO N P   1   0- 0
1918 BRO N P   1   0- 0
          BLTL   2   0- 0

DUROCHER, LEO ERNEST (LIPPY)
B.JULY 27,1905 W.SPRINGFIELD,MASS.
1925 NY A S   2   .000
1928 NY A 2-S   102   .270
1929 NY A 2-S   106   .246
1930 CIN N 2-S   119   .243
1931 CIN N S   121   .227
1932 CIN N S   143   .217
     STL N S   16   .216
     STL N S   123   .258
1934 STL N S   146   .260
1935 STL N S   143   .265
1936 STL N S   136   .286
1937 STL N S   135   .203
1938 BRO N S   141   .219
1939 BRO N M-S   116   .277
1940 BRO N M-2-S   62   .231
1941 BRO N M-2-S   18   .286
1943 BRO N M-S   6   .222
1945 BRO N M-2   2   .200
          BBTR   1637   .247
          88 1928-29
NON-PLAYING MANAGER
BRO(N) 1942, 1944, 1946, 1948,
NY(N) 1948-55, CHI(N) 1966-72,
HOU(N) 1972-73

YR	CL LEA POS	GP	G	REC

DURRETT, ELMER CHARLES (RED)
B.FEB.23,1921 SHERMAN,TEX.
1944	BRO N O		11	.156
1945	BRO N O		8	.125
	BLTL		19	.146

DURST, CEDRIC MONTGOMERY
B.AUG.23,1896 AUSTIN,TEX.
D.FEB.16,1971 SAN DIEGO,CAL.
1922	STL A O		15	.333
1923	STL A 1-O		45	.212
1926	STL A O		80	.237
1927	NY A O		65	.248
1928	NY A O		74	.252
1929	NY A O		92	.257
1930	NY A O		8	.188
	BOS A O		102	.243
	BLTL		481	.244

DURYEA, JAMES WHITNEY
(JESSE) OR (CYCLONE JIM)
B.SEPT.7,1862 OSAGE,IOWA
D.AUG.7,1942 ALGONA,IOWA
1889	CIN AA P-O	54	55	32-21
				.268
1890	CIN N P		32	17-13
1891	CIN N P		11	2- 8
	STL AA P		4	1- 3
1892	CIN N P-O		11	3- 5
				.111
	WAS N P		16	2-12
1893	WAS N P		17	5- 8
	BRTR	145	146	62-68
				.192

DUSAK, ERVIN FRANK (FOUR SACK)
B.JULY 29,1920 CHICAGO,ILL.
1941	STL N O		6	.143
1942	STL N 3-O		12	.185
1946	STL N 2-3-O		100	.240
1947	STL N 3-O		111	.284
1948	STL N P-2-	1	114	0- 0
	S-3-O			.209
1949	STL N H		1	.000
1950	STL N P-O	14	23	0- 2
				.083
1951	STL N P		5	0- 0
	PIT N P-2-	3	21	0- 1
	3-O			.008
1952	PIT N O		20	.222
	BRTR	23	413	0- 3
				.243

DUSER, CARL ROBERT
B.JULY 22,1932 HAZLETON,PA.
1956	KC A P		2	1- 1
1958	KC A P		1	0- 0
	BLTL		3	1- 1

DUSTAL, ROBERT ANDREW (BOB)
B.SEP.28,1935 SAYREVILLE,N.J.
| 1963 | DET A P | | 7 | 0- 1 |
| | BRTR | | | |

DUZEN, WILLIAM GEORGE
B.FEB.21,1870 BUFFALO,N.Y.
D.MAR.11,1944 BUFFALO,N.Y.
| 1890 | BUF P P | | 2 | 0- 2 |
| | BRTR | | | |

DWIGHT
B.CHICAGO,ILL.
| 1884 | KC U C-O | | 12 | .268 |

DWYER, JAMES EDWARD (JIM)
B.JAN.3,1950 EVERGREEN PARK,ILL.
1973	STL N O		28	.193
1974	STL N O/1		74	.279
1975	STL N /O		21	.194
	MON N O		60	.286
1976	MON N O		50	.185
	NY N /O		11	.154
1977	STL N O		13	.226
1978	STL N O		34	.215
	SF N O-1		73	.225
	BLTL		364	.235

DWYER, JOHN E.
| 1882 | CLE N C-O | | 1 | .000 |

DWYER, JOHN FRANCIS (FRANK)
B.MAR.25,1868 LEE,MASS.
D.FEB.4,1943 PITTSFIELD,MASS.
1888	CHI N P		5	4- 1
1889	CHI N P	29	33	16-12
1890	CHI P P		16	1- 7
1891	CIN AA P-2-	29	34	13-18
	O			.250
	MIL AA P		10	5- 4
1892	STL N P		14	2- 6
	CIN N P	33	46	20-10
1893	CIN N P		32	18-14
1894	CIN N P	39	49	18-19
1895	CIN N P		34	18-13
1896	CIN N P		35	25-10
1897	CIN N P	33	35	17-12
1898	CIN N P		29	16-10
1899	CIN N P		5	0- 5
	BRTR	347	377	173-141
				.233

NON-PLAYING MANAGER DET[A] 1902

DWYER, JOSEPH MICHAEL (DOUBLE JOE)
B.MAR.27,1901 ORANGE,N.J.
| 1937 | CIN N H | | 12 | .273 |
| | BLTL | | | |

DYCK, JAMES ROBERT (JIM)
B.FEB.3,1922 OMAHA,NEB.
1951	STL A 3		4	.067
1952	STL A 3-O		122	.269
1953	STL A 3-O		112	.213
1954	CLE A H		2	1.000
1955	BAL A 3-O		61	.279
1956	BAL A O		11	.217
	CIN N 1-3		18	.091
	BRTR		330	.245

DYER, BENJAMIN FRANKLIN
B.FEB.13,1893 CHICAGO,ILL.
D.AUG.7,1959 KENOSHA,WIS.
1914	NY N 2-S		7	.250
1915	NY N S-3		7	.211
1916	DET A S		4	.308
1917	DET A S		30	.209
1918	DET A O		13	0- 0
1919	DET A 3		44	.347
	BRTR		105	0- 0
				.238

DYER, DON ROBERT (DUFFY)
B.AUG.15,1945 DAYTON,OHIO
1968	NY N /C		1	.333
1969	NY N C		29	.257
1970	NY N C		59	.209
1971	NY N C		59	.231
1972	NY N C/O		94	.231
1973	NY N C		70	.185
1974	NY N C		83	.211
1975	PIT N C		48	.227
1976	PIT N C		69	.223
1977	PIT N C		94	.241
1978	PIT N C		58	.221
	BRTR		644	.223

DYER, EDWIN HAWLEY (EDDIE)
B.OCT.11,1900 MORGAN CITY,LA.
D.APR.20,1964 HOUSTON,TEX.
1922	STL N P		2	6	0- 0
1923	STL N P-O	4	35	2- 1
				.267
1924	STL N P-O	29	50	8-11
				.237
1925	STL N P		31	4- 3
1926	STL N P		6	1- 0
1927	STL N P		1	0- 0
	BLTL	73	129	15-15
				.223

NON-PLAYING MANAGER STL[N] 1946-50

DYGERT, JAMES HENRY (SUNNY JIM)
B.JULY 5,1884 UTICA,N.Y.
D.FEB.8,1936 NEW ORLEANS,LA.
1905	PHI A P		6	1- 3
1906	PHI A P		35	11-13
1907	PHI A P		42	20- 9
1908	PHI A P		41	11-15
1909	PHI A P		32	8- 5
1910	PHI A P		19	4- 4
	TR		175	55-49

DYKES, JAMES JOSEPH (JIMMY)
B.NOV.10,1896 PHILADELPHIA,PA.
D.JUNE 15,1976 PHILADELPHIA,PA.
1918	PHI A 2		59	.188
1919	PHI A 2		17	.184
1920	PHI A 2-3		142	.256
1921	PHI A 2		155	.274
1922	PHI A 3		145	.275
1923	PHI A 2-S		124	.252
1924	PHI A 2-3		110	.312
1925	PHI A 2-S-3		122	.325
1926	PHI A 3		124	.287
1927	PHI A P-1-	2	121	0- 0
	3			.324
1928	PHI A 2-S-3		85	.277
1929	PHI A 2-S-3		119	.327
1930	PHI A 3		125	.301
1931	PHI A S-3		101	.273
1932	PHI A S-3		153	.265
1933	CHI A 3		151	.260
1934	CHI A M-1-2-3		127	.268
1935	CHI A M-1-2-3		117	.288
1936	CHI A M-3		127	.267
1937	CHI A M-1-3		30	.306
1938	CHI A M-2		26	.303
1939	CHI A M-3		2	.000
	BRTR	2	2282	0- C
				.280

NON-PLAYING MANAGER
CHI[A] 1940-46, PHI[A] 1951-53,
BAL[A] 1954, CIN[N] 1958,
DET[A] 1959-60, CLE[A] 1960-61

DYLER, JOHN F.
B.LOUISVILLE,KY.
| 1882 | LOU AA M-O | | 1 | .000 |

EADDY, DONALD JOHNSON (DON)
B.FEB.16,1934 GRAND RAPIDS,MICH
| 1959 | CHI N 3 | | 15 | .000 |
| | BRTR | | | |

EAGAN, CHARLES EUGENE (TRUCK)
B.AUG.10,1877 SAN FRANCISCO,CAL
D.MAR.19,1949 SAN FRANCISCO,CAL
1901	PIT N S		4	.083
	CLE A 2-3		5	.176
			9	.138

EAGAN, WILLIAM (BAD BILL)
B.JUNE 1,1869 CAMDEN,N.J.
D.FEB.14,1905 DENVER,COLO.
1891	STL AA 2		81	.222
1893	CHI N 2		6	.300
1898	PIT N 2		16	.328
			103	.240

EAGLE, WILLIAM
B.ROCKVILLE,MD.
| 1898 | WAS N O | | 4 | .335 |

EAKLE, CHARLES EMORY
B.SEPT.27,1867 MARYLAND
D.JUNE 15,1959 BALTIMORE,MD.
| 1915 | BAL F 2 | | 2 | .286 |

EARL, HOWARD J.
B.FEB.25,1867 PALMYRA,N.Y.
D.DEC.23,1916 NORTH BAY,N.Y.
1890	CHI N 2-O		92	.247
1891	MIL AA O		30	.254
			122	.248

EARLE, WILLIAM MOFFAT (BILLY)
OR (THE LITTLE GLOBETROTTER)
B.NOV.10,1867 PHILADELPHIA,PA.
D.MAY 30,1946 OMAHA,NEB.
1889	CIN AA C-1-O		'53	.269
1890	STL AA C		23	.212
1892	PIT N C		5	.500
1893	PIT N C		26	.317
1894	LOU N C		19	.377
	BRO N C-2		14	.321
	BRTR		140	.297

EARLEY, ARNOLD CARL
B.JUNE ,1933 LINCOLN PARK,MICH.
1960	BOS A P		2	0- 1
1961	BOS A P		33	2- 4
1962	BOS A P		38	4- 5
1963	BOS A P		53	3- 7
1964	BOS A P		25	1- 1
1965	BOS A P		57	0- 1
1966	CHI N P		13	2- 1
1967	HOU N /P		2	0- 0
	BLTL		223	12-20

EARLEY, THOMAS FRANCIS ALOYSIUS
B.FEB.19,1917 ROXBURY,MASS.
1938	BOS N P		2	1- 0
1939	BOS N P		14	1- 4
1940	BOS N P		4	2- 0
1941	BOS N P	33	34	6- 8
1942	BOS N P		27	6-11
1945	BOS N P	11	13	2- 1
	BRTR	91	94	18-24

YR	CL LEA POS	GP	G	REC

EARLY, JACOB WILLARD (JAKE)
B.MAY 19,1915 KING S MOUNTAIN,N.C.

YR	CL LEA POS	GP	G	REC
1939 WAS A C		32	.262
1940 WAS A C		80	.257
1941 WAS A C		104	.287
1942 WAS A C		104	.204
1943 WAS A C		126	.258
1946 WAS A C		64	.201
1947 STL A C		87	.224
1948 WAS A C		97	.220
1949 WAS A C		53	.246
BLTR		747	.241

EARNSHAW, GEORGE LIVINGSTON (MOOSE)
B.FEB.15,1900 NEW YORK,N.Y.
D.DEC.1,1976 LITTLE ROCK,ARK.

YR	CL LEA POS	GP	G	REC
1928 PHI A P		26	7- 7
1929 PHI A P		44	24- 8
1930 PHI A P		49	22-13
1931 PHI A P		43	21- 7
1932 PHI A P		36	19-13
1933 PHI A P		21	5-10
1934 CHI A P		33	14-11
1935 CHI A P		3	1- 2
BRO N P		25	8-12
1936 BRO N P		19	4- 9
STL N P		20	2- 1
BRTR		319	127-93

EASLER, MICHAEL ANTHONY (MIKE)
B.NOV.29,1950 CLEVELAND,OHIO

YR	CL LEA POS	GP	G	REC
1973 HOU N /O		6	.000
1974 HOU N H		15	.067
1975 HOU N /H		5	.000
1976 CAL A O		21	.241
1977 PIT N /O		10	.444
BLTR		57	.222

EASON, MALCOLM WAYNE (KID)
B.MAR.13,1879 BROOKVILLE,PA.
D.APR.16,1970 DOUGLAS,ARIZ.

YR	CL LEA POS	GP	G	REC
1900 CHI N P		1	1- 0
1901 CHI N P		25	8-17
1902 CHI N P		6	1- 1
BOS N P		25	9-14
1903 DET A P		7	2- 4
1905 BRO N P	27	29	5-20
1906 BRO N P	34	36	10-17
TR	125	129	36-73

EAST, CARLTON WILLIAM
B.AUG.27,1894 ROME,GA.
D.JAN.15,1953 CLEM,GA.

YR	CL LEA POS	GP	G	REC
1915 STL A P		1	0- 0
1924 WAS A O		2	.333
BLTR	1	3	0- 0
			.286

EAST, GORDON HUGH
B.JULY 7,1919 BIRMINGHAM,ALA.

YR	CL LEA POS	GP	G	REC
1941 NY N P		2	1- 1
1942 NY N P		4	0- 2
1943 NY N P	13	17	1- 3
BRTR	19	23	2- 6

EAST, HENRY H. (HARRY)
B.ST.LOUIS,MO.

YR	CL LEA POS	GP	G	REC
1882 BAL AA 3		1	.000

EASTER, LUSCIOUS LUKE (LUKE)
B.AUG.4,1914 ST.LOUIS,MO.

YR	CL LEA POS	GP	G	REC
1949 CLE A O		21	.222
1950 CLE A 1-O		141	.280
1951 CLE A 1		128	.270
1952 CLE A 1		127	.263
1953 CLE A 1		68	.303
1954 CLE A H		6	.167
BLTR		491	.273

EASTERLING, PAUL
B.SEPT.28,1905 REIDSVILLE,GA.

YR	CL LEA POS	GP	G	REC
1928 DET A O		43	.325
1930 DET A O		29	.202
1938 PHI A O		4	.286
BRTR		76	.275

EASTERLY, JAMES MORRIS (JAMIE)
B.FEB.17,1953 HOUSTON,TEX.

YR	CL LEA POS	GP	G	REC
1974 ATL N /P		3	0- 0
1975 ATL N P		21	2- 9
1976 ATL N /P		4	1- 1
1977 ATL N P	22	23	2- 4
1978 ATL N P		37	3- 6
BBTL	87	88	6-20

EASTERLY, THEODORE HARRISON
B.APR.20,1885 LINCOLN,NEB.
D.JULY 6,1951 CLEAR LAKE HIGHLANDS,CAL.

YR	CL LEA POS	GP	G	REC
1909 CLE A C		98	.261
1910 CLE A C-O		110	.306
1911 CLE A C-O		99	.324
1912 CLE A C		65	.296
CHI A C		28	.304
1913 CHI A C		60	.235
1914 KC F C		134	.331
1915 KC F C		110	.267
BLTR		704	.299

EASTERWOOD, ROY CHARLES (SMAG)
B.JAN.12,1915 WAXAHACHIE,TEX.

YR	CL LEA POS	GP	G	REC
1944 CHI N C		17	.212
BRTR			

EASTON, JOHN DAVID (GOOSE)
B.MAR.4,1933 TRENTON,N.J.

YR	CL LEA POS	GP	G	REC
1955 PHI N H		1	.000
1959 PHI N H		3	.000
BRTR		4	.000

EASTON, JOHN S. (JACK)
B.FEB.28,.867 BRIDGEPORT,OHIO
D.NOV.1903 STEUBENVILLE,OHIO

YR	CL LEA POS	GP	G	REC
1889 COL AA P		4	1- 0
1890 COL AA P		37	14-13
1891 COL AA P		15	5-10
STL AA P		9	4- 3
COL AA P-O	3	6	0- 3
			.105
1892 STL N P		5	2- 3
1894 PIT N P		3	0- 1
	76	79	26-33
			.194

EASTWICK, RAWLINS JACKSON (RAWLY)
B.OCT.24,1950 CAMDEN,N.J.

YR	CL LEA POS	GP	G	REC
1974 CIN N /P		8	0- 0
1975 CIN N P		58	5- 3
1976 CIN N P		71	11- 5
1977 CIN N P		23	2- 2
STL N P		41	3- 7
1978 NY A /P		8	2- 1
PHI N P		22	2- 1
BRTR		231	25-19

EATON, ZEBULON VANCE (RED)
B.FEB.2,1920 COOLEEMEE,N.C.

YR	CL LEA POS	GP	G	REC
1944 DET A P		9	0- 0
1945 DET A P		26	4- 2
BRTR		35	4- 2

EAVES, VALLIE ENNIS (CHIEF)
B.SEPT.6,1911 ALLEN,OKLA.
D.APR.19,1960 NORMAN,OKLA.

YR	CL LEA POS	GP	G	REC
1935 PHI A P		3	1- 2
1939 CHI A P		2	0- 1
1940 CHI A P		5	0- 2
1941 CHI N P		12	3- 3
1942 CHI N P		2	0- 0
BRTR		24	4- 8

EAYRS, EDWIN
B.NOV.10,1890 BLACKSTONE,MASS.
D.NOV.30,1969 WARWICK,R.I.

YR	CL LEA POS	GP	G	REC
1913 PIT N P		4	0- 0
1920 BOS N P-O	7	87	1- 2
			.328
1921 BOS N P	2	15	0- 0
BRO N P		8	.167
BLTL	13	114	1- 2
			.306

EBBETS, CHARLES HERCULES
B.OCT.29,1859 NEW YORK,N.Y.
D.APR.18,1925
NON-PLAYING MANAGER BRO[N] 1898

EBRIGHT, HIRAM C. (BUCK)
B.JUNE 12,1859 LANCASTER CO.,PA
D.OCT.24,1916 MILWAUKEE,WIS.

YR	CL LEA POS	GP	G	REC
1889 WAS N 3		15	.254
BRTR			

ECCLES, HARRY JOSIAH (BUGS)
B.JULY 7,1893 KENNEDY,N.Y.
D.JUNE 22,1955 JAMESTOWN,N.Y.

YR	CL LEA POS	GP	G	REC
1915 PHI A P		5	0- 1
BLTL			

ECHOLS, JOHN GRESHAM
B.JAN.4,1917 ATLANTA,GA.
D.NOV.13,1972 ATLANTA,GA.

YR	CL LEA POS	GP	G	REC
1939 STL N 2		2	.000

ECKERSLEY, DENNIS LEE
B.OCT.3,1954 OAKLAND,CAL.

YR	CL LEA POS	GP	G	REC
1975 CLE A P		34	13- 7
1976 CLE A P		36	13-12
1977 CLE A P	33	34	14-13
1978 BOS A P		35	20- 8
BRTR	138	139	60-40

ECKERT, ALBERT GEORGE (OBBIE)
B.MAY 17,1906 MILWAUKEE,WIS.
D.APR.20,1974 MILWAUKEE,WIS.

YR	CL LEA POS	GP	G	REC
1930 CIN N P		2	0- 1
1931 CIN N P		14	0- 1
1935 STL N P		2	0- 0
BLTL		18	0- 2

ECKERT, CHARLES WILLIAM (BUZZ)
B.AUG.8,1897 PHILADELPHIA,PA.

YR	CL LEA POS	GP	G	REC
1919 PHI A P		2	0- 1
1920 PHI A P		2	0- 0
1922 PHI A P		21	0- 2
BRTR		25	0- 3

ECKHARDT, OSCAR GEORGE (OX)
B.DEC.23,1901 YORKTOWN,TEX.
D.APR.22,1951 YORKTOWN,TEX.

YR	CL LEA POS	GP	G	REC
1932 BOS N H		8	.250
1936 BRO N O		16	.182
BLTR		24	.192

EDDY, DONALD EUGENE (DON)
B.OCT.25,1946 MASON CITY,IOWA

YR	CL LEA POS	GP	G	REC
1970 CHI A /P		7	0- 0
1971 CHI A P		22	0- 2
BRTL		29	0- 2

EDELEN, EDWARD JOSEPH (DDC)
B.MAR.16,1912 BRYANTOWN,MD.

YR	CL LEA POS	GP	G	REC
1932 WAS A P		2	0- 0
BRTR			

EDELMAN, JOHN ROGERS
B.JULY 27,1935 PHILADELPHIA,PA.

YR	CL LEA POS	GP	G	REC
1955 MIL N P		5	0- 0
BRTR			

EDEN, CHARLES M.
B.JAN.18,1855 LEXINGTON,KY.
D.SEPT.17,1920 CINCINNATI,OHIO

YR	CL LEA POS	GP	G	REC
1877 CHI N O		15	.218
1879 CLE N O		81	.272
1884 PIT AA P-O	1	32	0- 1
			.305
1885 PIT AA P-O	3	98	1- 2
			.264
BRTR	4	226	1- 3
			.269

EDEN, EDWARD MICHAEL (MIKE)
B.MAY 22,1949 FORT CLAYTON, CANAL ZONE

YR	CL LEA POS	GP	G	REC
1976 ATL N /2		5	.000
1978 CHI A /S-2		10	.118
BBTR		15	.80

EDGERTON, WILLIAM ALBERT (BILL)
B.AUG.16,1941 SOUTH BEND,IND.

YR	CL LEA POS	GP	G	REC
1966 KC A /P		6	0- 1
1967 KC A /P		7	1- 0
1969 SEA A /P		4	0- 1
BLTL		17	1- 2

EDINGTON, JACOB FRANK (STUMP)
B.JULY 4,1891 ROLEEN,IND.
D.NOV.11,1969 BASTROP,LA.

YR	CL LEA POS	GP	G	REC
1912 PIT N O		15	.302
BLTL			

EDMONDSON, GEORGE HENDERSON
B.MAY 18,1896 WAXAHACHIE,TEX.
D.JULY 11,1973 WACO,TEX.

YR	CL LEA POS	GP	G	REC
1922 CLE A P		2	0- 0
1923 CLE A P		1	0- 0
1924 CLE A P		5	0- 0
BRTR		8	0- 0

EDMONDSON, PAUL MICHAEL
B.FEB.12,1943 KANSAS CITY,KAN.
D.FEB.13,1970 SANTA BARBARA,CAL.

YR	CL LEA POS	GP	G	REC
1969 CHI A P		14	1- 6
BRTR			

EDMONDSON, ROBERT E.
B.APR.30,1879 PARIS,KY.
D.AUG.14,1931 LAWRENCE,KAN.

YR	CL LEA POS	GP	G	REC
1906 WAS A P		3	0- 1
1908 WAS A O		26	.188
BRTR	3	29	0- 1
			.193

EDMONSON, EARL EDWARD (EDDIE)
B.NOV.20,1889 HOPEWELL,PA.
D.MAY 10,1971 LEESBURG,FLA.

YR	CL LEA POS	GP	G	REC
1913 CLE A 1-O		2	.000
BLTR			

EDMONSTON, SAMUEL SHERWOOD (BIG SAM)
B.AUG.30,1883 WASHINGTON,D.C.

YR	CL LEA POS	GP	G	REC
1907 WAS A P		1	0- 0
BLTL			

EDWARDS

YR	CL LEA POS	GP	G	REC
1875 ATL NA O		1	-

EDWARDS, ALBERT
B.1896 FREEPORT,L.I.,N.Y.

YR	CL LEA POS	GP	G	REC
1915 PHI A 2		2	.000
TR			

YR	CL LEA POS	GP	G	REC

EDWARDS, CHARLES BRUCE (BRUCE) OR (BULL)
B.JULY 15,1923 QUINCY,ILL.
D.APR.25,1975 SACRAMENTO,CAL.

YR	CL LEA POS	GP	G	REC
1946	BRO N C		92	.267
1947	BRO N C		130	.296
1948	BRO N C-1-3-O		96	.276
1949	BRO N C-3-O		64	.209
1950	BRO N C-1		50	.183
1951	BRO N C		17	.250
	CHI N C-1		51	.234
1952	CHI N C-2		50	.245
1954	CHI N H		4	.000
1955	WAS A C-3		30	.175
1956	CIN N C-2-3		7	.200
	BRTR		591	.256

EDWARDS, DAVID LEONARD (DAVE)
B.FEB.24,1954 LOS ANGELES,CAL.

1978	MIN A O		15	.250
	BRTR			

EDWARDS, FOSTER HAMILTON (EDDIE)
B.SEPT.1,1903 HOLSTEIN,IOWA

1925	BOS N P		1	0- 0
1926	BOS N P		3	2- 0
1927	BOS N P	29	33	2- 8
1928	BOS N P		21	2- 1
1930	NY A P		2	0- 0
	BRTR	56	60	6- 9

EDWARDS, HENRY ALBERT (HANK)
B.JAN.29,1919 ELMWOOD PLACE,O.

1941	CLE A O		16	.221
1942	CLE A O		13	.250
1943	CLE A O		92	.276
1946	CLE A O		124	.301
1947	CLE A O		108	.260
1948	CLE A O		55	.269
1949	CLE A O		5	.267
	CHI N O		58	.290
1950	CHI N O		41	.364
1951	BRO N H		35	.226
	CIN N O		41	.315
1952	CIN N O		74	.263
	CHI A O		8	.333
1953	STL A O		65	.198
	BLTL		735	.280

EDWARDS, HOWARD RODNEY (DOC)
B.DEC.10,1937 VARNEY,W.VA.

1962	CLE A C		53	.273
1963	CLE A C		10	.258
	KC A C		71	.250
1964	KC A C-1		97	.224
1965	KC A /C		6	.150
	NY A C		45	.190
1970	PHI N C		35	.269
	BRTR		317	.238

EDWARDS, JAMES CORBETTE (LITTLE JOE)
B.DEC.14,1894 BANNER,MISS.
D.JAN.19,1965 PONTOTOC,MISS.

1922	CLE A P		25	3- 8
1923	CLE A P		38	10-10
1924	CLE A P		10	4- 3
1925	CLE A P		13	0- 3
	CHI A P		9	1- 2
1926	CHI A P		32	6- 9
1928	CIN N P		18	2- 2
	BRTL		145	26-37

EDWARDS, JOHN ALBAN (JOHNNY)
B.JUNE 10,1938 COLUMBUS,OHIO

1961	CIN N C		52	.186
1962	CIN N C		133	.254
1963	CIN N C		148	.259
1964	CIN N C		126	.281
1965	CIN N *C		114	.267
1966	CIN N C		98	.191
1967	CIN N C		80	.206
1968	STL N C		85	.239
1969	HOU N *C		151	.232
1970	HOU N *C		140	.221
1971	HOU N *C		106	.233
1972	HOU N C		108	.268
1973	HOU N C		79	.244
1974	HOU N C		50	.222
	BLTR		1470	.242

EDWARDS, MICHAEL LEWIS (MIKE)
B.AUG.27,1952 FORT LEWIS,WASH.

1977	PIT N /2		7	.000
1978	OAK A *2/S		142	.274
	BRTR		149	.270

EDWARDS, SHERMAN STANLEY
B.JULY 25,1909 MT.IDA,ARK.

1934	CIN N P		1	0- 0
	BRTR			

EELLS, HARRY ARCHIBALD (SLIPPERY)
B.FEB.14,1881 IDA GROVE,IOWA
D.OCT.15,1940 LOS ANGELES,CAL.

1906	CLE A P		14	4- 5
	BRTR			

EGAN, ALOYSIUS JEROME (WISH)
B.JUNE 16,1881 EVART,MICH.
D.APR.13,1951 DETROIT,MICH.

1902	DET A P		3	1- 2
1905	STL N P		23	5-16
1906	STL N P		16	2- 9
			42	8-27

EGAN, ARTHUR AUGUSTUS (BEN)
B.NOV.20,1883 AUGUSTA,N.Y.
D.FEB.18,1968 SHERRILL,N.Y.

1908	PHI A C		2	.143
1912	PHI A C		48	.174
1914	CLE A C		29	.227
1915	CLE A C		42	.108
	BRTR		121	.164

EGAN, JAMES
B.1838 ANSONIA,CONN.
D.SEPT.26,1884 NEW HAVEN,CONN.

1882	TRO N P-C-	14	29	4- 6
	O			.181

EGAN, JOHN JOSEPH (RIP)
B.JULY 9,1871 PHILADELPHIA,PA.
D.DEC.22,1950 CRANSTON,R.I.

1894	WAS N P		1	0- 0

EGAN, RICHARD JOSEPH
B.JUNE 23,1884 PORTLAND,ORE.
D.JUNE 30,1947 OAKLAND,CAL.

1908	CIN N 2		18	.206
1909	CIN N 2		126	.275
1910	CIN N 2		134	.245
1911	CIN N 2		152	.249
1912	CIN N 2		149	.247
1913	CIN N 2-S		60	.282
1914	BRO N S		106	.226
1915	BRO N 2		3	.000
	BOS N 2-O		83	.264
1916	BOS N 2		83	.223
	BRTR		914	.250

EGAN, RICHARD WALLIS (DICK)
B.MAR.24,1937 BERKELEY,CAL.

1963	DET A P		20	0- 1
1964	DET A P		23	0- 0
1966	CAL A P		11	0- 0
1967	LA N P		20	1- 1
	BLTL		74	1- 2

EGAN, THOMAS PATRICK (TOM)
B.JUNE 9,1946 LOS ANGELES,CAL.

1965	CAL A C		18	.263
1966	CAL A /C		7	.000
1967	CAL A /C		1	.000
1968	CAL A C		16	.116
1969	CAL A C		46	.142
1970	CAL A C		79	.238
1971	CHI A C/1		85	.239
1972	CHI A C		50	.191
1974	CAL A C		43	.117
1975	CAL A C		28	.229
	BRTR		373	.200
	BB .1974 (PART), 75			

EGGERT, ELMER ALBERT (MOSE)
B.JAN.29,1902 ROCHESTER,N.Y.
D.APR.9,1971 ROCHESTER,N.Y.

1927	BOS A P		5	0- 0
	BRTR			

EGGLER, DAVID DANIEL
B.APR.30,1851 BROOKLYN,N.Y.
D.APR.5,1902 BUFFALO,N.Y.

1871	MUT NA O		33	-
1872	MUT NA O		56	.346
1873	MUT NA O		54	-
1874	PHI NA 2-O		58	-
1875	ATH NA O		66	.288
1876	ATH N O		39	.295
1877	CHI N O		33	.265
1879	BUF N O		77	.208
1883	BAL AA O		53	.194
	BUF N O		38	.245
1884	BUF N O		58	.198
1885	BUF N O		6	.083
	BRTR		571	-

EHMKE, HOWARD JONATHAN (HOWARD) OR (BOB)
B.APR.24,1894 SILVER CREEK,N.Y.
D.MAR.17,1959 PHILADELPHIA,PA.

1915	BUF F P		18	0- 2
1916	DET A P		5	3- 1
1917	DET A P		35	10-15
1919	DET A P		33	17-10
1920	DET A P		38	15-16
1921	DET A P		30	13-14
1922	DET A P		45	17-17
1923	BOS A P		43	20-17
1924	BOS A P	45	46	19-17
1925	BOS A P		34	9-20
1926	BOS A P		14	3-10
	PHI A P	20	21	12- 4
1927	PHI A P		30	12-10
1928	PHI A P		23	9- 8
1929	PHI A P		11	7- 2
1930	PHI A P		3	0- 1
	BRTR	427	429	166-166

EHRET, PHILIP SYDNEY (RED)
B.AUG.31,1868 LOUISVILLE,KY.
D.JULY 28,1940 CINCINNATI,OHIO

1888	KC AA P-O	7	16	4- 3
				.186
1889	LOU AA P	47	66	9-29
1890	LOU AA P		42	24-13
1891	LOU AA P		26	13-12
1892	PIT N P		40	18-19
1893	PIT N P		36	17-17
1894	PIT N P		41	18-22
1895	STL N P		31	6-20
1896	CIN N P		33	18-15
1897	CIN N P		27	10-10
1898	LOU N P		12	3- 7
	BRTR	342	370	140-167
				.220

EHRHARDT, WELTON CLAUDE (RUBE)
B.NOV.20,1894 BEECHER,ILL.

1924	BRO N P		15	5- 3
1925	BRO N P		36	10-14
1926	BRO N P		44	2- 5
1927	BRO N P		46	3- 7
1928	BRO N P		21	2- 3
1929	CIN N P		24	1- 2
	BRTR		193	22-34

EIBEL, HENRY HACK (HACK)
B.DEC.6,1893 BROOKLYN,N.Y.
D.OCT.16,1945 MACON,GA.

1912	CLE A O		1	.000
1920	BOS A P	3	29	0- 0
	BLTL	3	30	0- 0
				.174

EICHELBERGER, JUAN ROBERTO
B.OCT.21,1953 ST.LOUIS,MO.

1978	SD N /P		3	0- 0
	BRTR			

EICHRODT, FREDERICK GEORGE (IKE)
B.JAN.6,1903 CHICAGO,ILL.
D.JULY 14,1965 INDIANAPOLIS,IND

1925	CLE A O		15	.230
1926	CLE A O		37	.313
1927	CLE A O		85	.221
1931	CHI A O		34	.214
	BRTR		171	.234

EILERS, DAVID LOUIS (DAVE)
B.DEC.3,1936 OLDENBURG,TEX.

1964	MIL N P		6	0- 0
1965	MIL N /P		6	0- 0
	NY N P		11	1- 1
1966	NY N P		23	1- 1
1967	HOU N P		35	6- 4
	BRTR		81	8- 6

EISENHARDT, JACOB HENRY
B.OCT.3,1922 PERKASIE,PA.

1944	CIN N P		1	0- 0
	BLTL			

EISENSTAT, HARRY
B.OCT.10,1915 BROOKLYN,N.Y.

1935	BRO N P		2	0- 1
1936	BRO N P		5	1- 2
1937	BRO N P		13	3- 3
1938	DET A P		32	9- 6
1939	DET A P		10	2- 2
	CLE A P		26	6- 7
1940	CLE A P		27	1- 4
1941	CLE A P		21	1- 1
1942	CLE A P		29	2- 1
	BLTL		165	25-27

EITELJORG, EDWARD HENRY
B.MAR.14,1871 BERLIN,GERMANY
D.DEC.7,1942 GREENCASTLE,IND.

1890	CHI N P		1	0- 0
1891	WAS AA P		9	2- 6

YR	CL	LEA	POS	GP	G	REC

ELAND
1873 MAR NA O   1   .000

ELBERFELD, NORMAN ARTHUR (KID)
OR (THE TABASCO KID)
B.APR.13,1875 POMEROY,OHIO
D.JAN.13,1944 CHATTANOOGA,TENN.
1898	PHI	N	3		13	.228
1899	CIN	N	S		41	.259
1901	DET	A	S		122	.309
1902	DET	A	S		139	.265
1903	DET	A	S		35	.323
	NY	A	S		90	.290
1904	NY	A	S		122	.256
1905	NY	A	S		108	.262
1906	NY	A	S		99	.306
1907	NY	A	S		120	.271
1908	NY	A	M-S		19	.196
1909	NY	A	S-3		106	.237
1910	WAS	A	3		127	.250
1911	WAS	A	2-3		127	.272
1914	BRO	N			30	.226
		BRTR			1298	.270

ELDER, GEORGE REZIN
B.MAR.10,1921 LEBANON,KY.
| 1949 | STL | A | O | | 41 | .250 |
| | | BLTR | | | | |

ELDER, HENRY KNOX (HEINIE)
B.AUG.23,1890 SEATTLE,WASH.
D.NOV.13,1958 LONG BEACH,CAL.
| 1913 | DET | A | P | | 1 | 0- 0 |
| | | BLTL | | | | |

ELDRIDGE, JEREMIAH DENNIS
[PLAYED UNDER NAME OF
JEREMIAH DENNIS DENNY]

ELIA, LEE CONSTANTINE
B.JULY 16,1937 PHILADELPHIA,PA.
1966	CHI	A	S		80	.205
1968	CHI	N	/S-2-3		15	.176
		BKTR			95	.203

ELKO, PETER (PICCOLO PETE)
B.JUNE 17,1918 WILKES-BARRE,PA.
1943	CHI	N	3		9	.133
1944	CHI	N	3		7	.227
		BRTR			16	.173

ELLAM, ROY (WHITEY) OR (SLIPPERY)
B.FEB.8,1886 CONSHOHOCKEN,PA.
D.OCT.28,1948 CONSHOHOCKEN,PA.
1909	CIN	N	S		10	.190
1918	PIT	N	S		26	.130
		BRTR			36	.143

ELLER, HORACE OWEN (HOD)
B.JULY 5,1894 MUNCIE,IND.
D.JULY 18,1961 INDIANAPOLIS,IND
1917	CIN	N	P		37	10- 5
1918	CIN	N	P		37	16-12
1919	CIN	N	P		38	19- 9
1920	CIN	N	P-1-	35	38	13-12
			2			.253
1921	CIN	N	P		13	2- 2
		BRTR		160	163	60-40
						.221

ELLERBE, FRANCIS ROGERS
(FRANK) OR (GOVERNOR)
B.DEC.25,1895 MARION,S.C.
1919	WAS	A	S		28	.276
1920	WAS	A	S-3		101	.292
1921	WAS	A	S		10	.200
	STL	A	S		105	.288
1922	STL	A	S		91	.246
1923	STL	A	S		18	.184
1924	STL	A	S		21	.194
	CLE	A	S		46	.261
		BRTR			420	.268

ELLICK, JOSEPH J.
B.1856 CINCINNATI,OHIO
1875	RS	NA	S-3-O		7	-
1878	MIL	N	P-C-3		3	0- 0
						.154
1880	WOR	N	3		5	.053
1884	CHI	U	C-2-S-O		72	.253
	PIT	U	M-S		18	.167
	KC	U	2-O		2	.000
	BAL	U	S-O		7	.148
					114	0- 0
						-

ELLINGSEN, H. BRUCE
B.APR.26,1949 POCATELLO,IDAHO
| 1974 | CLE | A | P | | 16 | 1- 1 |
| | | BLTR | | | | |

ELLIOT, LAWRENCE LEE (LARRY)
B.MAR.5,1938 SAN DIEGO,CAL.
1962	PIT	N	O		8	.300
1963	PIT	N	H		4	.000
1964	NY	N	O		80	.228
1966	NY	N	O		65	.246
		BLTL			157	.236

ELLIOTT, ALLEN CLIFFORD (ACE)
B.DEC.25,1897 ST.LOUIS,MO.
1923	CHI	N	1		53	.250
1924	CHI	N	1		10	.143
		BLTR			63	.242

ELLIOTT, CARTER WARD
B.NOV.29,1893 ATCHISON,KAN.
D.MAY 21,1959 PALM SPRINGS,CAL.
| 1921 | CHI | N | S | | 12 | .250 |
| | | BLTR | | | | |

ELLIOTT, CLAUDE JUDSON
(CHAUCER) OR (OLD PARDEE)
B.NOV.17,1879 PARDEEVILLE,WIS.
D.JUNE 21,1923 PARDEEVILLE,WIS.
1904	CIN	N	P		10	4- 6
	NY	N	P		3	0- 1
1905	NY	N	P		10	2- 1
		BRTR			23	6- 8

ELLIOTT, EUGENE BIRMINGHOUSE
B.FEB.8,1889 FAYETTE CITY,PA.
D.JAN.5,1976 HUNTINGDON,PA.
| 1911 | NY | A | 3 | | 5 | .077 |
| | | BLTR | | | | |

ELLIOTT, HAROLD B. (ROWDY)
B.JULY 8,1890 BLOOMINGTON,ILL.
D.FEB.12,1934 SAN FRANCISCO,CAL
1910	BOS	N	C		1	.000
1916	CHI	N	C		23	.255
1917	CHI	N	C		85	.251
1918	CHI	N	C		5	.000
1920	BRO	N	C		41	.241
		BRTR			155	.241

ELLIOTT, HAROLD WILLIAM
B.MAY 29,1899 MT.CLEMENS,MICH.
D.APR.25,1963 HONOLULU,HAWAII
1929	PHI	N	P		40	3- 7
1930	PHI	N	P		48	6-11
1931	PHI	N	P		16	0- 2
1932	PHI	N	P		16	2- 4
		BRTR			120	11-24

ELLIOTT, HARRY LEWIS
B.DEC.30,1925 SAN FRANCISCO,CAL
1953	STL	N	O		24	.254
1955	STL	N	O		68	.256
		BRTR			92	.256

ELLIOTT, HERBERT GLENN
(GLENN) OR (LEFTY)
B.NOV.11,1919 SAPULPA,OKLA
D.JULY 27,1969 PORTLAND,ORE.
1947	BOS	N	P		11	0- 1
1948	BOS	N	P		1	0- 0
1949	BOS	N	P		22	3- 4
		BLTL			34	4- 5

ELLIOTT, JAMES THOMAS (JUMBO)
B.OCT.22,1900 ST.LOUIS,MO.
D.JAN.7,1970 TERRE HAUTE,IND.
1923	STL	A	P		1	0- 0
1925	BRO	N	P		3	0- 2
1927	BRO	N	P		30	6-13
1928	BRO	N	P		41	9-14
1929	BRO	N	P		6	1- 2
1930	BRO	N	P		35	10- 7
1931	PHI	N	P		52	19-14
1932	PHI	N	P		39	11-10
1933	PHI	N	P	35	36	6-10
1934	PHI	N	P		3	0- 1
	BOS	N	P		7	1- 1
		BRTL		252	253	63-74

ELLIOTT, RANDY LEE
B.JUNE 5,1951 OXNARD,CAL.
1972	SD	N	O		14	.204
1974	SD	N	O/1		13	.212
1977	SF	N	O		73	.240
		BRTR			100	.229

ELLIOTT, ROBERT IRVING
(BOB) OR (MR. TEAM)
B.NOV.26,1916 SAN FRANCISCO,CAL
D.MAY 4,1966 SAN DIEGO,CAL.
1939	PIT	N	O		32	.333
1940	PIT	N	O		148	.292
1941	PIT	N	O		141	.273
1942	PIT	N	3-O		143	.297
1943	PIT	N	2-S-3		156	.315
1944	PIT	N	S-3		143	.298
1945	PIT	N	3-O		144	.290
1946	PIT	N	3-O		140	.263
1947	BOS	N	3		150	.317
1948	BOS	N	3		151	.283
1949	BOS	N	3		139	.280
1950	BOS	N	3		142	.305
1951	BOS	N	3		136	.285
1952	NY	N	O		98	.228
1953	STL	A	3		48	.250
	CHI	A	3-O		67	.260
		BRTR			1978	.289
NON-PLAYING MANAGER KC[A] 1960

ELLIS, BENJAMIN F.
B.POTTSVILLE,PA.
| 1896 | PHI | N | S | | 4 | .063 |

ELLIS, DUCK PHILLIP
B.MAR.11,1945 LOS ANGELES,CAL.
1968	PIT	N	P		26	6- 5
1969	PIT	N	P		35	37	11-17
1970	PIT	N	P		30	38	13-10
1971	PIT	N	P		31	44	19- 9
1972	PIT	N	P		25	36	15- 7
1973	PIT	N	P		28	29	12-14
1974	PIT	N	P		26	30	12- 9
1975	PIT	N	P		27	30	8- 9
1976	NY	A	P		32	17- 8
1977	NY	A	/P		3	1- 1
	OAK	A	/P		7	1- 5
	TEX	A	P		23	10- 6
1978	TEX	A	P		22	9- 7
		BBTR		315	358	134-107

ELLIS, GEORGE WILLIAM (RUBE)
B.NOV.17,1885 DOWNEY,CAL.
D.MAR.13,1938 RIVERA,CAL.
1909	STL	N	O		145	.268
1910	STL	N	O		141	.258
1911	STL	N	O		148	.250
1912	STL	N	O		109	.269
		BLTL			543	.260

ELLIS, JAMES RUSSELL (JIM)
B.MAR.25,1945 TULARE,CAL.
1967	CHI	N	P		8	1- 1
1969	STL	N	P		2	0- 0
		BRTL			10	1- 1

ELLIS, JOHN CHARLES
B.AUG.21,1948 NEW LONDON,CONN.
1969	NY	A	C		22	.290
1970	NY	A	1/3-C		78	.248
1971	NY	A	1/C		83	.244
1972	NY	A	C/1		52	.294
1973	CLE	A	C-O-1		127	.270
1974	CLE	A	1-C-O		128	.285
1975	CLE	A	C/1		92	.230
1976	TEX	A	/C		11	.419
1977	TEX	A	C-O/1		49	.235
1978	TEX	A	C		34	.245
		BRTR			676	.264

ELLIS, ROBERT WALTER (ROB)
B.JULY 3,1950 GRAND RAPIDS,MICH.
1971	MIL	A	3-O		36	.198
1974	MIL	A	O/3		22	.292
1975	MIL	A	/O		6	.286
		BRTR			64	.229

ELLIS, SAMUEL JOSEPH (SAMMY)
B.FEB.11,1941 YOUNGSTOWN,OHIO
1962	CIN	N	P		8	2- 2
1964	CIN	N	P		52	10- 3
1965	CIN	N	P		44	22-10
1966	CIN	N	P	41	43	12-19
1967	CIN	N	P		32	8-11
1968	CAL	A	P		42	9-10
1969	CHI	A	P		10	0- 3
		BLTR		229	231	63-58

ELLISON, GEORGE RUSSELL
B.1897
| 1920 | CLE | A | P | | 1 | 0- 0 |
| | | BRTR | | | | |

ELLISON, HERBERT SPENCER (BERT)
B.NOV.15,1895 RUTLAND,ARK.
D.AUG.11,1955 SAN FRANCISCO,CAL
1916	DET	A	3		2	.125
1917	DET	A	1		9	.172
1918	DET	A	2		7	.260
1919	DET	A	2		56	.216
1920	DET	A	1		61	.219
		BRTR			135	.215

ELLSWORTH, RICHARD CLARK (DICK)
B.MAR.22,1940 LUSK,WYO.
1958	CHI	N	P		1	0- 1
1960	CHI	N	P		31	7-13
1961	CHI	N	P		37	10-11
1962	CHI	N	P		37	9-20
1963	CHI	N	P		37	22-10
1964	CHI	N	P		37	14-18
1965	CHI	N	P		36	14-15
1966	CHI	N	P		38	8-22
1967	PHI	N	P		32	6- 7
1968	BOS	A	P		31	16- 7
1969	BOS	A	/P		2	0- 0
	CLE	A	P		34	6- 9
1970	MIL	A	P		29	3- 3
	MIL	A	P		14	0- 0
1971	MIL	A	P		11	0- 1
		BLTL			407	115-137

ELMORE, VERDO WILSON (ELLIE)
B.DEC.10,1899 GORDO,ALA.
D.AUG.5,1969 BIRMINGHAM,ALA.
| 1924 | STL | A | O | | 7 | .176 |
| | | BLTR | | | | |

YR	CL	LEA	POS	GP	G	REC

ELROY, ALEJANDRO CARRASQUEL
[PLAYED UNDER NAME OF
ALEJANDRO CARRASQUEL]

ELSH, EUGENE ROY
B.MAR.1,1896 PENNSGROVE,N.J.

1923	CHI	A	O		81	.249
1924	CHI	A	O		60	.306
1925	CHI	A	1-O		32	.188
	BRTR				173	.262

ELSTON, DONALD RAY (DON)
B.APR.26,1929 CAMPBELLSTOWN,OHIO

1953	CHI	N	P		2	0- 1
1957	BRO	N	P		1	0- 0
	CHI	N	P		39	6- 7
1958	CHI	N	P		69	9- 8
1959	CHI	N	P		65	10- 8
1960	CHI	N	P		60	8- 9
1961	CHI	N	P		58	6- 7
1962	CHI	N	P		57	4- 8
1963	CHI	N	P		51	4- 1
1964	CHI	N	P		48	2- 5
	BRTR				450	49-54

ELY, FREDERICK WILLIAM (BONES)
B.JUNE 7,1863 GIRARD,PA.
D.JAN.10,1952 IMOLA,CAL.

1884	BUF	N	P-O		1	0- 1
						.000
1886	LOU	AA	P-O	5	10	0- 4
						.147
1890	SYR	AA	S-O		118	.263
1891	BRO	N	S		31	.171
1892	BAL	N	P		1	0- 1
1893	STL	N	S		44	.263
1894	STL	N	S		127	.305
1895	STL	N	S		118	.266
1896	PIT	N	S		126	.287
1897	PIT	N	S		133	.282
1898	PIT	N	S		148	.210
1899	PIT	N	S		138	.288
1900	PIT	N	S		130	.242
1901	PIT	N	S		62	.219
	PHI	A	S		45	.223
1902	WAS	A	S		105	.263
	BRTR			7	1337	0- 5
						.259

EMBREE, CHARLES WILLARD (RED)
B.AUG.30,1917 EL MONTE,CAL.

1941	CLE	A	P		1	0- 1
1942	CLE	A	P		19	3- 4
1944	CLE	A	P		3	0- 1
1945	CLE	A	P		8	4- 4
1946	CLE	A	P		28	8-12
1947	CLE	A	P	27	28	8-10
1948	NY	A	P		20	5- 3
1949	STL	A	P	35	40	3-13
	BRTR			141	147	31-48

EMBREY, CHARLES AKIN (SLIM)
B.AUG.17,1901 COLUMBIA,TENN.
D.OCT.10,1947 NASHVILLE,TENN.

1923	CHI	A	P		1	0- 0
	BRTR					

EMERSON, CHESTER ARTHUR (CHUCK)
B.OCT.27,1889 STOW,ME.
D.JULY 2,1971 AUGUSTA,ME.

1911	PHI	A	O		7	.222
1912	PHI	A	H		1	.000
	BLTR				8	.211

EMERY, CALVIN WAYNE (CAL)
B.JUNE 28,1937 CENTRE HALL,PA.

1963	PHI	N	1		16	.158
	BLTR					

EMERY, HERRICK SMITH (SPOKE)
B.DEC.10,1898 BAY CITY,MICH.
D.JUNE 2,1975 CAPE CANAVERAL,FLA.

1924	PHI	N	O		5	.667
	BRTR					

EMIG, CHARLES H.
B.BELLEVUE,KY.

1896	LOU	N	P		1	0- 1

EMMER, FRANK WILLIAM
B.FEB.17,1896 CRESTLINE,OHIO
D.OCT.18,1963 HOMESTEAD,FLA.

1916	CIN	N	2-S-3-O		42	.146
1926	CIN	N	S		60	.96
	BRTR				102	.162

EMMERICH, ROBERT G.
B.AUG.1,1897 NEW YORK,N.Y.
D.NOV.23,1948 BRIDGEPORT,CONN.

1923	BOS	N	O		13	.083
	BRTR					

EMMERICH, WILLIAM PETER (SLIM)
B.SEPT.29,1919 ALLENTOWN,PA.

1945	NY	N	P		31	4- 4
1946	NY	N	P		2	0- 0
	BRTR				33	4- 4

EMSLIE, ROBERT DANIEL
B.JAN.27,1859 GUELPH,ONT.,CAN.
D.APR.26,1943 ST.THOMAS,ONT.,CANADA

1883	BAL	AA	P-O		28	9-16
						.153
1884	BAL	AA	P	50	51	32-18
1885	BAL	AA	P		13	2-10
	ATH	AA	P-O		4	0- 3
						.083
	BRTR			95	96	43-47
						.187

ENDICOTT, WILLIAM FRANKLIN
B.SEPT.4,1918 ACORN,MO.

1946	STL	N	O		20	.200
	BLTL					

ENGEL, JOSEPH WILLIAM
B.MAR.12,1893 WASHINGTON,D.C.
D.JUNE 12,1969 CHATTANOOGA,TENN

1912	WAS	A	P		17	1- 5
1913	WAS	A	P		36	8- 9
1914	WAS	A	P		35	7- 5
1915	WAS	A	P		11	1- 3
1917	CIN	N	P		1	0- 1
1919	CLE	A	P		1	0- 0
1920	WAS	A	P		1	0- 0
	BRTL				102	17-23

**ENGLE, ARTHUR CLYDE
(CLYDE) OR (HACK)**
B.MAR.19,1884 DAYTON,OHIO
D.DEC.26,1939 BOSTON,MASS.

1909	NY	A	O		135	.278
1910	NY	A	3		6	.200
	BOS	A	3		105	.266
1911	BOS	A	1-3		146	.270
1912	BOS	A	1-2		57	.234
1913	BOS	A	1		143	.290
1914	BOS	A	1		55	.194
	BUF	F	3		32	.259
1915	BUF	F	2-3-O		141	.263
1916	CLE	A	3		11	.133
	BRTR				831	.266

ENGLE, CHARLES
B.AUG.27,1903 BROOKLYN,N.Y.

1925	PHI	A	S		1	.000
1926	PHI	A	S		19	.105
1930	PIT	N	2-S-3		67	.264
	BRTR				87	.251

ENGLISH, CHARLES DEWIE
B.APR.8,1910 DARLINGTON,S.C.

1932	CHI	A	3		24	.317
1933	CHI	A	2		3	.444
1936	NY	N	2		6	.000
1937	CIN	N	2-3		17	.238
	BRTR				50	.287

ENGLISH, ELWOOD GEORGE (WOODY)
B.MAR.2,1907 FREDONIA,OHIO

1927	CHI	N	S		87	.290
1928	CHI	N	S		116	.299
1929	CHI	N	S		144	.276
1930	CHI	N	S-3		156	.335
1931	CHI	N	S-3		156	.319
1932	CHI	N	S-3		127	.272
1933	CHI	N	S-3		105	.261
1934	CHI	N	S-3		109	.278
1935	CHI	N	S-3		34	.202
1936	CHI	N	S-3		64	.247
1937	BRO	N	2-S		129	.238
1938	BRO	N	3		34	.250
	BRTR				1261	.286

ENGLISH, GILBERT RAYMOND
B.JULY 2,1909 GLENOLA,N.C.

1931	NY	N	3		3	.000
1932	NY	N	S-3		59	.225
1936	DET	A	3		1	.000
1937	DET	A	2		18	.262
	BOS	N	3		79	.290
1938	BOS	N	3		53	.248
1944	BRO	N	2-S-3		27	.152
	BRTR				240	.245

ENNIS, DELMER (DEL)
B.JUNE 8,1925 PHILADELPHIA,PA.

1946	PHI	N	O		141	.313
1947	PHI	N	O		139	.275
1948	PHI	N	O		152	.290
1949	PHI	N	O		154	.302
1950	PHI	N	O		153	.311
1951	PHI	N	O		144	.267
1952	PHI	N	O		151	.289
1953	PHI	N	O		152	.285
1954	PHI	N	1-O		145	.261
1955	PHI	N	O		146	.296
1956	PHI	N	O		153	.260
1957	STL	N	O		136	.286
1958	STL	N	O		106	.261
1959	CIN	N	O		5	.333
	CHI	A	O		26	.219
	BRTR				1903	.284

ENNIS, RUSSELL ELWOOD (HACK)
B.MAR.10,1897 SUPERIOR,WIS.
D.JAN.21,1949 SUPERIOR,WIS.

1926	WAS	A	C		1	.000
	BRTR					

ENRIGHT, GEORGE ALBERT
B.MAY 9,1954 NEW BRITAIN,CONN.

1976	CHI	A	/C		2	.000
	BRTR					

ENRIGHT, JOHN PERCY
B.1896 FORT WORTH,TEX.

1917	NY	A	P		1	0- 1
	BRTR					

ENS, ANTON (MUTZ)
B.NOV.8,1884 ST.LOUIS,MO.
D.JUNE 28,1950 ST.LOUIS,MO.

1912	CHI	A	1		3	.600
	BLTL					

ENS, JEWEL WINKLEMEYER
B.AUG.24,1889 ST.LOUIS,MO.
D.JAN.17,1950 SYRACUSE,N.Y.

1922	PIT	N	1-2-S-3		47	.295
1923	PIT	N	1-3		12	.267
1924	PIT	N	1		5	.300
1925	PIT	N	1		3	.200
	BRTR				67	.290
NON-PLAYING MANAGER PIT[N] 1929-31

ENWRIGHT, CHARLES MICHAEL
B.OCT.6,1887 SACRAMENTO,CAL.
D.JAN.19,1917 SACRAMENTO,CAL.

1909	STL	N	P		3	.142
	BLTR					

ENYART, TERRY GENE
B.OCT.10,1950 IRONTON,OHIO

1974	MON	N	/P		2	0- 0
	BRTL					

ENZENROTH, CLARENCE HERMAN (JACK)
B.NOV.4,1885 MINERAL POINT,WIS.
D.FEB.21,1944 DETROIT,MICH.

1914	STL	A	C		3	.167
	KC	F	C		24	.168
1915	KC	F	C		14	.158
	BRTR				41	.165

ENZMANN, JOHN
B.MAR.4,1890 BROOKLYN,N.Y.

1914	BRO	N	P		7	1- 0
1918	CLE	A	P		30	5- 7
1919	CLE	A	P		14	1- 2
1920	PHI	N	P	16	17	2- 3
	BRTR			67	68	9-12

EPPERLY, ALBERT PAUL (TUB) OR (PARD)
B.MAY 7,1918 GLIDDEN,IOWA

1938	CHI	N	P		9	2- 0
1950	BRO	N	P		5	0- 0
	BLTR				14	2- 0

EPPS, AUBREY LEE (YO-YO)
B.MAR.3,1912 MEMPHIS,TENN.

1935	PIT	N	C		1	8750
	BRTR					

EPPS, HAROLD FRANKLIN
B.MAR.26,1914 ATHENS,GA.

1938	STL	N	O		17	.300
1940	STL	N	O		11	.200
1943	STL	N	O		8	.286
1944	STL	A	O		22	.177
	PHI	A	O		67	.262
	BLTL				125	.253

**EPSTEIN, MICHAEL PETER
(MIKE) OR (SUPERJEW)**
B.APR.4,1943 BRONX,N.Y.

1966	BAL	A	/1		6	.182
1967	BAL	A	/1		9	.154
	WAS	A	1		96	.229
1968	WAS	A	*1		123	.234
1969	WAS	A	*1		131	.278
1970	WAS	A	*1		140	.256
1971	WAS	A	1		24	.247
	OAK	A	1		104	.234
1972	OAK	A	*1		138	.270
1973	TEX	A	1		27	.188
	CAL	A	1		91	.215
1974	CAL	A	1		18	.161
	BLTL				907	.244

ERARDI, JOSEPH GREGORY (GREG)
B.MAY 31,1954 SYRACUSE,N.Y.

1977	SEA	A	/P		5	0- 1
	BRTR					

YR   CL LEA POS   GP   G   REC   YR   CL LEA POS   GP   G   REC   YR   CL LEA POS   GP   G   REC

ERAUTT, EDWARD LORENZ SEBASTIAN
(EDDIE)
B.SEPT.26,1924 PORTLAND,ORE.
1947 CIN N P   36   4- 9
1948 CIN N P   2   0- 0
1949 CIN N P   39   4-11
1950 CIN N P   33   4- 2
1951 CIN N P   30   0- 0
1953 CIN N P   4   0- 0
1953 STL N P   20   3- 1
        BRTR   164   15-23

ERAUTT, JOSEPH MICHAEL
(JOE) OR (STUBBY)
B.SEPT.1,1921 VIBANK,SASK.,CAN.
D.OCT.6,1976 PORTLAND,ORE.
1950 CHI A C   16   .222
1951 CHI A C   16   .160
        BRTR   32   .186

ERICKSON, DON LEE
B.DEC.13,1931 SPRINGFIELD,ILL.
1958 PHI N P   9   0- 1

ERICKSON, ERIC GEORGE ADOLPH
B.MAR.13,1895 GOTEBORG,SWEDEN
D.MAY 19,1965 JAMESTOWN,N.Y.
1914 NY N P   1   0- 1
1916 DET A P   7   0- 2
1918 DET A P   12   4- 5
1919 DET A P   3   0- 2
        WAS A P   20   5-10
1920 WAS A P   39   12-16
1921 WAS A P   32   8-10
1922 WAS A P   30   4-12
        BRTR   144   33-58

ERICKSON, HAROLD JAMES (HAL)
B.JULY 17,1919 PORTLAND,ORE.
1953 DET A P   18   0- 1
        BRTR

ERICKSON, HENRY NELS
(HANK) OR (POPEYE)
B.NOV.11,1907 CHICAGO,ILL.
D.DEC.13,1964 LOUISVILLE,KY.
1935 CIN N C   37   .261
        BRTR

ERICKSON, PAUL WALFORD (LI L ABNER)
B.DEC.14,1919 ZION,OHIO
1941 CHI N P   32   5- 7
1942 CHI N P   18   1- 6
1943 CHI N P   15   1- 3
1944 CHI N P   33   5- 9
1945 CHI N P   28   7- 4
1946 CHI N P   32   9- 7
1947 CHI N P   40   7-12
1948 CHI N P   3   0- 0
   '   PHI N P   4   2- 0
        NY N P   2   0- 0
        BRTR   207   37-48

ERICKSON, RALPH LIEF
B.JUNE 25,1904 DUBOIS,IDAHO
1929 PIT N P   1   0- 0
1930 PIT N P   7   1- 0
        BLTL   8   1- 0

ERICKSON, ROGER FARRELL
B.AUG.30,1956 SPRINGFIELD,ILL.
1978 MIN A P   37   14-13
        BRTR

ERMER, CALVIN COOLIDGE (CAL)
B.NOV.10,1923 BALTIMORE,MD.
1947 WAS A 2   1   .000
        BRTR
NON-PLAYING MANAGER MIN[A] 1967-68

ERNAGA, FRANK JOHN
B.AUG.22,1930 SUSANVILLE,CAL.
1957 CHI N O   20   .314
1958 CHI N H   9   .125
        BRTR   29   .279

ERRICKSON, RICHARD MERRIWELL (LIEF)
B.MAR.9,1914 VINELAND,N.J.
1938 BOS N P   34   9- 7
1939 BOS N P   28   6- 9
1940 BOS N P   34   12-13
1941 BOS N P   38   6-12
1942 BOS N P   21   2- 5
        CHI N P   13   1- 1
        BLTR   168   36-47

ERSKINE, CARL DANIEL
(CARL) OR (OISK)
B.DEC.13,1926 ANDERSON,IND.
1948 BRO N P   17   6- 3
1949 BRO N P   22   8- 1
1950 BRO N P   22   7- 6
1951 BRO N P   46   16-12
1952 BRO N P   33   14- 6
1953 BRO N P   39   20- 6
1954 BRO N P   38   11- 8
1955 BRO N P   31   11- 8
1956 BRO N P   31   13-11
1957 BRO N P   15   5- 3
1958 LA N P   31   4- 4
1959 LA N P   10   0- 3
        BRTR   335 360 122-78

ERSKINE, JAMES
[PLAYED UNDER NAME OF
ERSKINE JOHN MAYER]

ERSKINE, SAMUEL FRANKEL
[PLAYED UNDER NAME OF
SAMUEL FRANKEL MAYER]

ERWIN, ROSS EMIL (TEX)
B.DEC.22,1885 FORNEY,TEX.
D.APR.5,1953 ROCHESTER,N.Y.
1907 DET A C   4   .200
1910 BRO N C   68   .188
1911 BRO N C   74   .271
1912 BRO N C   59   .211
1913 BRO N C   20   .258
1914 BRO N C   7   .500
        CIN N C   14   .306
        BLTR   246   .237

ESCALERA, SATURNINO CUADRADO (NINO)
B.DEC.1,1929 SANTURCE,P.R.
1954 CIN N 1-S-O   73   .159
        BLTR

ESCHEN, JAMES GODRICH
B.AUG.21,1891 BROOKLYN,N.Y.
D.SEPT.27,1960 SLOATSBURG,N.Y.
1915 CLE A O   15   .239
        BRTR

ESCHEN, LAWRENCE EDWARD
B.SEPT.22,1920 SUFFERN,N.Y.
1942 PHI A 2-S   12   .000
        BRTR

ESMOND, JAMES J.
B.AUG.8,1889 ALBANY,N.Y.
D.JUNE 26,1948 TROY,N.Y.
1911 CIN N S   59   .273
1912 CIN N S   82   .195
1914 IND F S   150   .295
1915 New F S   155   .258
        BRTR   446   .264

ESPER, CHARLES H. (DUKE)
B.JULY 28,1868 SALEM,N.J.
D.AUG.31,1910 PHILADELPHIA,PA.
1890 ATH AA P   19   7- 8
        PIT N P   2   0- 2
        PHI N P   6   4- 0
1891 PHI N P   34   20-13
1892 PHI N P   26   13- 6
        PIT N P   4   1- 0
1893 WAS N P   40   12-26
1894 WAS N P   15   6- 9
        BAL N P   16   9- 2
1895 BAL N P   27   12-12
1896 BAL N P   19   14- 5
1897 STL N P   8   1- 6
1898 STL N P   10   3- 5
        TL   226 102-94

ESPINOSA, ARNULFO ACEVEDO (NINO)
[REAL NAME
ARNULFO ACEVEDO [ESPINOSA]]
B.AUG.15,1953 VILLIA ALTAGRACIA,
D.R.
1974 NY N /P   2   0- 0
1975 NY N /P   2   0- 1
1976 NY N P   12   4- 4
1977 NY N P   32   10-13
1978 NY N P   32   11-15
        BRTR   80   25-33

ESPOSITO, SAMUEL (SAMMY)
B.DEC.15,1931 CHICAGO,ILL.
1952 CHI A S   1   .250
1955 CHI A 3   3   .000
1956 CHI A 2-S-3   81   .228
1957 CHI A 2-S-3-O   94   .205
1958 CHI A 2-S-3-O   98   .247
1959 CHI A 2-S-3   69   .167
1960 CHI A 2-S-3   57   .182
1961 CHI A 2-S-3   63   .170
1962 CHI A 2-S-3   75   .235
1963 CHI A R   1   .000
        KC A 2-S-3   18   .200
        BRTR   560   .207

ESSEGIAN, CHARLES ABRAHAM (CHUCK)
B.AUG.9,1931 BOSTON,MASS.
1958 PHI N O   39   .246
1959 STL N O   17   .179
        LA N O   24   .304
1960 LA N O   52   .215
1961 BAL A H   1   .000
        KC A O   4   .333
        CLE A O   60   .289
1962 CLE A O   106   .274
1963 KC A O   101   .225
        BRTR   404   .255

ESSIAN, JAMES SARKIS (JIM)
B.JAN.2,1951 DETROIT,MICH.
1973 PHI N /C   2   .000
1974 PHI N /C   17   .100
1975 PHI N /C   2   1.000
1976 CHI A C/1-3   78   .246
1977 CHI A *C/3   114   .273
1978 OAK A *C/1-2   126   .223
        BRTR   339   .245

ESSICK, WILLIAM EARL (VINEGAR BILL)
B.DEC.18,1881 GRAND RIDGE,ILL.
D.OCT.11,1951 LOS ANGELES,CAL.
1906 CIN N P   6   1- 1
1907 CIN N P   3   0- 2
        TR   9   1- 3

ESTALELLA, ROBERTO [MENDEZ] (BOBBY)
B.APR.25,1911 CARDENAS,CUBA
1935 WAS A 3   15   .314
1936 WAS A H   13   .222
1939 WAS A O   82   .275
1941 STL A O   46   .241
1942 WAS A 3-O   133   .277
1943 PHI A O   117   .259
1944 PHI A 1-O   140   .298
1945 PHI A O   126   .299
1949 PHI A O   8   .250
        BRTR   680   .282

ESTELLE, RICHARD HENRY (DICK)
B.JAN.18,1942 LAKEWOOD,N.J.
1964 SF N P   6   1- 2
1965 SF N /P   6   0- 0
        BBTL   12   1- 2

ESTERBROOK, THOMAS JOHN (DUDE)
B.JUNE 20,1857 STATEN IS.,N.Y.
D.APR.30,1901 MIDDLETOWN,N.Y.
1880 BUF N C-1-2-S-O   63   .241
1882 CLE N 1-O   45   .246
1883 MET AA 1   41   .250
1884 MET AA 3   112   .408
1885 NY N 3-O   88   .256
1886 NY N 3   123   .264
1887 MET AA S   26   .224
1888 IND N 1   64   .219
        LOU AA 1   23   .226
1889 LOU AA 1   11   .309
1890 NY N 1   45   .289
1891 BRO N 2   3   .375
        BRTR   644   .278

ESTERDAY, HENRY
B.SEPT.16,1864 PHILADELPHIA,PA.
1884 KEY U S   28   .250
1888 KC AA S   114   .195
1889 COL AA S   105   .175
1890 COL AA S   52   .145
        ATH AA S   19   .154
        LOU AA S   7   .087
        BRTR   325   .177

ESTOCK, GEORGE JOHN
B.NOV.2,1924 STIRLING,N.J.
1951 BOS N P   37   0- 1
        BRTR

ESTRADA, CHARLES LEONARD (CHUCK)
B.FEB.15,1938 SAN LUIS OBISPO,CAL.
1960 BAL A P   36   18-11
1961 BAL A P   33   15- 9
1962 BAL A P   34   38   9-17
1963 BAL A P   8   3- 2
1964 BAL A P   17   18   3- 2
1966 CHI N /P   9   1- 1
1967 NY N /P   9   1- 2
        BRTR   146   151   50-44

ESTRADA, FRANCISCO [SOTO] (FRANK)
B.FEB.12,1948 NAVOJOA,SONORA,MEX
1971 NY N /C   1   .500
        BRTR

ESTRADA, OSCAR
B.FEB.15,1904 HAVANA,CUBA
D.JAN.2,1978 HAVANA,CUBA
1929 STL A P   1   0- 0
        BLTL

YR	CL LEA POS	GP	G	REC

ETCHEBARREN, ANDREW AUGUSTE (ANDY)
B.JUNE 20,1943 WHITTIER,CAL.

YR	CL LEA POS	GP	G	REC
1962	BAL A C		2	.333
1965	BAL A /C		5	.167
1966	BAL A *C		121	.221
1967	BAL A *C		112	.215
1968	BAL A C		74	.233
1969	BAL A C		73	.249
1970	BAL A C		78	.243
1971	BAL A C		70	.270
1972	BAL A C		71	.202
1973	BAL A C		54	.257
1974	BAL A C		62	.222
1975	BAL A /C		8	.200
	CAL A C		31	.280
1976	CAL A *C		103	.227
1977	CAL A C		80	.254
1978	MIL A /C		4	.400
	BRTR		948	.235

ETCHISON, CLARENCE HAMPTON (BUCK)
B.JAN.27,1915 BALTIMORE,MD.

YR	CL LEA POS	GP	G	REC
1943	BOS N 1		10	.316
1944	BOS N 1		109	.214
	BLTL		119	.220

ETHERIDGE, BOBBY LAMAR (BOBBY) OR (LUKE)
B.NOV.25,1942 GREENVILLE,MISS.

YR	CL LEA POS	GP	G	REC
1967	SF N 3		40	.226
1969	SF N 3/S		56	.260
	BRTR		96	.244

ETTEN, NICHOLAS RAYMOND THOMAS (NICK)
B.SEPT.19,1913 SPRING GROVE,ILL.

YR	CL LEA POS	GP	G	REC
1938	PHI A 1		22	.259
1939	PHI A 1		43	.252
1941	PHI N 1		151	.311
1942	PHI N 1		139	.264
1943	NY A 1		154	.271
1944	NY A 1		154	.293
1945	NY A 1		152	.285
1946	NY A 1		108	.232
1947	PHI N 1		14	.244
	BLTL		937	.277

EUBANK, JOHN FRANKLIN (HONEST JOHN)
B.SEPT.9,1872 SERVIA,IND.
D.NOV.3,1958 BELLEVUE,MICH.

YR	CL LEA POS	GP	G	REC
1905	DET A P		7	2- 0
1906	DET A P	23	26	4-10
1907	DET A P		15	2- 3
	BRTR	45	48	8-13

EUBANKS, UEL MELVIN (POSS)
B.FEB.14,1903 QUINLAN,TEX.
D.NOV.2,1954 DALLAS,TEX.

YR	CL LEA POS	GP	G	REC
1922	CHI N P		2	0- 0
	BRTR			

EUNICK, FERNANDAS BOWEN
B.APR.22,1892 BALTIMORE,MD.
D.DEC.4,1959 BALTIMORE,MD.

YR	CL LEA POS	GP	G	REC
1917	CLE A 3		1	.000
	BRTR			

EUSTACE, FRANK JOHN
B.NOV.7,1873 NEW YORK,N.Y.
D.OCT.20,1932 POTTSVILLE,PA.

YR	CL LEA POS	GP	G	REC
1896	LOU N S		25	.163

EVANS, ALFRED HUBERT (AL)
B.SEPT.28,1916 KENLY,N.C.

YR	CL LEA POS	GP	G	REC
1939	WAS A C		7	.333
1940	WAS A C		14	.320
1941	WAS A C		53	.277
1942	WAS A C		74	.229
1944	WAS A C		14	.091
1945	WAS A C		51	.260
1946	WAS A C		88	.254
1947	WAS A C		99	.241
1948	WAS A C		93	.259
1949	WAS A C		109	.271
1950	WAS A C		90	.235
1951	BOS N C		12	.125
	BRTR		704	.250

EVANS, BARRY STEVEN
B.NOV.30,1955 ATLANTA,GA.

YR	CL LEA POS	GP	G	REC
1978	SD N 3		24	.267
	BRTR			

EVANS, CHARLES FRANKLIN (CHICK)
B.OCT.15,1889 ARLINGTON,VT.
D.SEPT.26,1916 SCHENECTADY,N.Y.

YR	CL LEA POS	GP	G	REC
1909	BOS N P		4	0- 3
1910	BOS N P		13	1- 1
	BRTR		17	1- 4

EVANS, DARRELL WAYNE
B.MAY 26,1947 PASADENA,CAL.

YR	CL LEA POS	GP	G	REC
1969	ATL N /3		12	.231
1970	ATL N 3		12	.318
1971	ATL N 3/O		89	.242
1972	ATL N *3		125	.254
1973	ATL N *3-1		161	.281
1974	ATL N *3		160	.240
1975	ATL N *3/1		156	.243
1976	ATL N 1/3		44	.173
	SF N 1/3		92	.222
1977	SF N O-1-3		144	.254
1978	SF N *3		159	.243
	BLTR		1154	.248

EVANS, DWIGHT MICHAEL (DWIGHT) OR (DEWEY)
B.NOV.3,1951 SANTA MONICA,CAL.

YR	CL LEA POS	GP	G	REC
1972	BOS A O		18	.263
1973	BOS A *O		119	.223
1974	BOS A *O		133	.281
1975	BOS A *O		128	.274
1976	BOS A *O		146	.242
1977	BOS A O		73	.287
1978	BOS A *O		147	.247
	BRTR		764	.258

EVANS, J. FORD
B.DEC.15,1844 AKRON,OHIO
NON-PLAYING MANAGER CLE[N] 1882

EVANS, JACOB (BLOODY JAKE)
B.BALTIMORE,MD.
D.FEB.3,1907 BALTIMORE,MD.

YR	CL LEA POS	GP	G	REC
1875	NH NA O		1	-
1879	TRO N O		70	.230
1880	TRO N P-S-	1	47	0- 0
	O			.255
1881	TRO N O		81	.242
1882	WOR N P-2-	1	80	0- 1
	S-O			.212
1883	CLE N P-2-	1	89	0- 0
	3-O			.235
1884	CLE N 2-S-O		80	.258
1885	BAL AA O		20	.205
	TR	3	468	0- 1
				-

EVANS, JOSEPH PATTON (DOC)
B.MAY 15,1895 MERIDIAN,MISS.
D.AUG.9,1953 GULFPORT,MISS.

YR	CL LEA POS	GP	G	REC
1915	CLE A 3		42	.257
1916	CLE A 3		33	.146
1917	CLE A 3		132	.290
1918	CLE A 3		79	.263
1919	CLE A S		21	.071
1920	CLE A O		56	.349
1921	CLE A O		57	.333
1922	CLE A O		75	.269
1923	WAS A 3-O		106	.263
1924	STL A O		77	.254
1925	STL A O		55	.314
	BRTR		733	.259

EVANS, LE ROY
B.MAR.19,1874 KNOXVILLE,TENN.

YR	CL LEA POS	GP	G	REC
1897	STL N P		2	0- 1
	LOU N P		9	5- 4
1898	WAS N P		7	3- 3
1899	WAS N P		7	3- 2
1902	NY N P		19	8-11
1903	BRO N P		13	5- 6
	BRO N P		15	5- 9
	STL A P		7	1- 5
	BRTR		79	30-41

EVANS, LOUIS RICHARD (STEVE)
B.FEB.17,1885 CLEVELAND,OHIO
D.DEC.28,1943 CLEVELAND,OHIO

YR	CL LEA POS	GP	G	REC
1908	NY N O		2	.333
1909	STL N O		143	.259
1910	STL N O		151	.241
1911	STL N O		150	.294
1912	STL N O		135	.283
1913	STL N O		97	.249
1914	BRO F 1-O		145	.355
1915	BRO F O		63	.289
	BAL F O		87	.319
	BLTL		973	.288

EVANS, RUSSELL EARL (RED)
B.NOV.12,1906 CHICAGO,ILL.

YR	CL LEA POS	GP	G	REC
1936	CHI A P	17	18	0- 3
1939	BRO N P		24	1- 8
	BRTR	41	42	1-11

EVANS, WILLIAM ARTHUR
B.AUG.3,1911 ELVINS,MO.
D.JAN.8,1952 WICHITA,KAN.

YR	CL LEA POS	GP	G	REC
1932	CHI A P		7	0- 0
	BBTL			

EVANS, WILLIAM JAMES
B.FEB.10,1894 REIDSVILLE,N.C.
D.DEC.21,1946 BURLINGTON,N.C.

YR	CL LEA POS	GP	G	REC
1916	PIT N P		13	2- 5
1917	PIT N P		8	0- 4
1919	PIT N P		7	0- 4
	BRTR		28	2-13

EVANS, WILLIAM LAWRENCE (BILL)
B.MAR.25,1919 CHILDRESS,TEX.

YR	CL LEA POS	GP	G	REC
1949	CHI A P		4	0- 1
1951	BOS A P		9	0- 0
	BRTR		13	0- 1

EVERETT, WILLIAM L. (WILD BILL)
B.DEC.13,1868 FT.WAYNE,IND.
D.JAN.19,1938 DENVER,COLO.

YR	CL LEA POS	GP	G	REC
1895	CHI N 3		133	.356
1896	CHI N 3-O		131	.333
1897	CHI N 3		90	.314
1898	CHI N 1		149	.325
1899	CHI N 1		136	.309
1900	CHI N 1		23	.236
1901	WAS A 1		33	.189
	TR		695	.320

EVERITT, EDWARD LEON (LEON)
B.JAN.12,1947 MARSHALL,TEX.

YR	CL LEA POS	GP	G	REC
1969	SD N /P	5	6	0- 1
	BLTR			

EVERS, JOHN JOSEPH (JOHNNY) (CRAB) OR (TROJAN)
B.JULY 22,1883 TROY,N.Y.
D.MAR.28,1947 ALBANY,N.Y.

YR	CL LEA POS	GP	G	REC
1902	CHI N 2-S		25	.225
1903	CHI N 2		123	.293
1904	CHI N 2		152	.265
1905	CHI N 2		99	.276
1906	CHI N 2		154	.255
1907	CHI N 2		151	.250
1908	CHI N 2		123	.300
1909	CHI N 2		126	.263
1910	CHI N 2		125	.263
1911	CHI N 2		44	.226
1912	CHI N 2		143	.341
1913	CHI N M-2		136	.285
1914	BOS N 2		139	.279
1915	BOS N 2		83	.263
1916	BOS N 2		71	.216
1917	BOS N 2		24	.176
	PHI N 2		56	.231
1922	CHI A 2		1	.000
1929	BOS N M-2		1	.000
	BLTR		1776	.270
NON-PLAYING MANAGER
CHI[N] 1921, CHI[A] 1924

EVERS, JOSEPH FRANCIS
B.SEPT.10,1891 TROY,N.Y.
D.JAN.4,1949 ALBANY,N.Y.

YR	CL LEA POS	GP	G	REC
1913	NY N 3		1	.000
	BRTR			

EVERS, THOMAS FRANCIS
B.MAR.31,1892 TROY,N.Y.
D.MAR.23,1925 WASHINGTON,D.C.

YR	CL LEA POS	GP	G	REC
1882	BAL AA 2		1	.000
1884	WAS U 2		106	.234
			107	.232

EVERS, WALTER ARTHUR (HOOT)
B.FEB.8,1921 ST.LOUIS,MO.

YR	CL LEA POS	GP	G	REC
1941	DET A O		1	.000
1946	DET A O		81	.266
1947	DET A O		126	.296
1948	DET A O		139	.314
1949	DET A O		132	.303
1950	DET A O		143	.323
1951	DET A O		116	.224
1952	DET A H		1	1.000
	BOS A O		106	.262
1953	BOS A O		99	.240
1954	BOS A O		6	.000
	NY N O		12	.091
	DET A O		30	.183
1955	BAL A O		60	.238
	CLE A O		39	.288
1956	CLE A H		3	.000
	BAL A O		48	.241
	BRTR		1142	.278

EWELL
B.WASHINGTON,D.C.

YR	CL LEA POS	GP	G	REC
1871	CLE NA O		1	.000

EWING, GEORGE LEMUEL (LONG BOB)
B.APR.24,1873 NEW HAMPSHIRE,O.
D.JUNE 20,1947 WAPAKONETA,OHIO

YR	CL LEA POS	GP	G	REC
1902	CIN N P-O	15	19	5- 6
				.171
1903	CIN N P	29	31	14-13
1904	CIN N P	26	30	11-12
1905	CIN N P	40	42	21-12
1906	CIN N P		33	13- 4
1907	CIN N P	41	44	17-19
1908	CIN N P		37	17-15
1909	CIN N P		31	11-12
1910	PHI N P		34	16- 4
1911	PHI N P		6	0- 2
1912	STL N P		1	0- 0
	BKTR	291	306	125-119
				.195

YR	CL	LEA	POS	GP	G	REC

EWING, JOHN (LONG JOHN)
B.JUNE 1,1863 CINCINNATI,OHIO
D.APR.23,1895 DENVER,COLO.

YR	CL	LEA	POS	GP	G	REC
1883	STL	AA	O		1	.000
1884	CIN	U	O		1	.000
	WAS	U	O		1	.200
1888	LOU	AA	P		21	8-13
1889	LOU	AA	P	40	41	7-30
1890	NY	P	P		35	19-10
1891	NY	N	P		31	21-10
	TR			127	131	55-63
						.186

EWING, REUBEN
[REAL NAME REUBEN COHEN]
B.NOV.30,1899 ODESSA,RUSSIA
D.OCT.5,1970 W.HARTFORD,CONN.

YR	CL	LEA	POS	GP	G	REC
1921	STL	N	O		3	.000

EWING, SAMUEL JAMES (SAM)
B.APR.9,1949 LEWISBURG,TENN.

YR	CL	LEA	POS	GP	G	REC
1973	CHI	A	/1		11	.150
1976	CHI	A	D/1		19	.220
1977	TOR	A	D-O/1		97	.287
1978	TOR	A	/O		40	.179
	BLTL				167	.255

EWING, WILLIAM (BUCK)
B.OCT.17,1859 HOAGLANDS,OHIO
D.OCT.20,1906 CINCINNATI,OHIO

YR	CL	LEA	POS	GP	G	REC
1880	TRO	N	C-O		13	.152
1881	TRO	N	C-S-3-O		65	.243
1882	TRO	N	P-C-	1	72	0- 0
			3			.273
1883	NY	N	C-2-S-3		85	.306
1884	NY	N	P-C-	1	88	0- 1
			S-O			.278
1885	NY	N	P-C-	1	61	0- 1
			1-S-3-O			.304
1886	NY	N	C-O		70	.309
1887	NY	N	2-3		76	.365
1888	NY	N	C-3		103	.306
1889	NY	N	P-C	2	96	0- 0
						.326
1890	NY	P	M-P-	1	83	0- 1
			C			.349
1891	NY	N	C-2		14	.340
1892	NY	N	C-1		97	.319
1893	CLE	N	O		114	.371
1894	CLE	N	O		53	.255
1895	CIN	N	M-1		103	.316
1896	CIN	N	M-1		67	.282
1897	CIN	N	M-1		1	.000
	BRTR			6	1281	.311

NON-PLAYING MANAGER
CIN[N] 1898-99, NY[N] 1900

EWOLDT, ARTHUR LEE (SHERIFF)
B.JAN.8,1894 PAULLINA,IOWA

YR	CL	LEA	POS	GP	G	REC
1919	PHI	A	3		9	.233
	BRTR					

EYRICH, GEORGE LINCOLN
B.MAR.3,1925 READING,PA.

YR	CL	LEA	POS	GP	G	REC
1943	PHI	N	P		9	0- 0
	BRTR					

EZZELL, HOMER ESTELL
B.FEB.28,1896 VICTORIA,TEX.
D.AUG.31,1976 SAN ANTONIO,TEX.

YR	CL	LEA	POS	GP	G	REC
1923	PHI	A	3		88	.247
1924	BOS	A	S-3		90	.271
1925	BOS	A	2-3		58	.285
	BRTR				236	.265

FAATZ, JAYSON S. (JAY)
B.OCT.24,1860 WEEDSPORT,N.Y.
D.APR.10,1923 SYRACUSE,N.Y.

YR	CL	LEA	POS	GP	G	REC
1884	PIT	AA	1		29	.230
1888	CLE	AA	1		120	.264
1889	CLE	N	1		119	.230
1890	BUF	P	1		32	.200
	BRTR				296	.242

NON-PLAYING MANAGER CLE[N] 1890

FABER, URBAN CHARLES (RED)
B.SEPT.6,1888 CASCADE,IOWA
D.SEPT.25,1976 CHICAGO,ILL.

YR	CL	LEA	POS	GP	G	REC
1914	CHI	A	P		40	10- 9
1915	CHI	A	P		50	24-13
1916	CHI	A	P		35	17- 9
1917	CHI	A	P		41	16-13
1918	CHI	A	P		11	5- 1
1919	CHI	A	P		25	11- 9
1920	CHI	A	P		40	23-13
1921	CHI	A	P		43	25-15
1922	CHI	A	P		43	21-17
1923	CHI	A	P	32	33	14-11
1924	CHI	A	P		21	9-11
1925	CHI	A	P		34	12-11
1926	CHI	A	P		27	15- 8
1927	CHI	A	P		18	4- 7
1928	CHI	A	P		27	13- 9
1929	CHI	A	P		31	13-13
1930	CHI	A	P		29	8-13
1931	CHI	A	P		44	10-14
1932	CHI	A	P		42	2-11
1933	CHI	A	P		36	3- 4
	BBTR			669	670	255-211

FABRIQUE, ALBERT LA VERNE (BUNNY)
B.DEC.23,1887 CLINTON,MICH.
D.JAN.10,1960 ANN ARBOR,MICH.

YR	CL	LEA	POS	GP	G	REC
1916	BRO	N	S		2	.000
1917	BKO	N	S		25	.205
	BBTR				27	.200

FACE, ELROY LEON (ROY)
B.FEB.20,1928 STEPHENTOWN,N.Y.

YR	CL	LEA	POS	GP	G	REC
1953	PIT	N	P	41	43	6- 8
1955	PIT	N	P	42	43	5- 7
1956	PIT	N	P	68	69	12-13
1957	PIT	N	P		59	4- 6
1958	PIT	N	P		57	5- 2
1959	PIT	N	P	57	58	18- 1
1960	PIT	N	P		68	10- 8
1961	PIT	N	P		62	6-12
1962	PIT	N	P		63	8- 7
1963	PIT	N	P		56	3- 9
1964	PIT	N	P		55	3- 3
1965	PIT	N	P		16	5- 2
1966	PIT	N	P		54	6- 6
1967	PIT	N	P		61	7- 5
1968	PIT	N	P		43	2- 4
	DET	A	P		2	0- 0
1969	MON	N	P		44	4- 2
	BBTR			848	853	104-95
	BR 1953-59					

FAETH, ANTHONY JOSEPH
B.JULY 9,1893 ABERDEEN,S.D.

YR	CL	LEA	POS	GP	G	REC
1919	CLE	A	P		6	0- 0
1920	CLE	A	P		13	0- 0
	BRTR				19	0- 0

FAGAN, EVERETT JOSEPH
B.JAN.13,1918 POTTERSVILLE,N.J.

YR	CL	LEA	POS	GP	G	REC
1943	PHI	A	P		18	2- 6
1946	PHI	A	P		20	0- 1
	BRTR				38	2- 7

FAGAN, WILLIAM A. (CLINKERS)
B.FEB.15,1869 TROY,N.Y.
D.MAR.21,1930 TROY,N.Y.

YR	CL	LEA	POS	GP	G	REC
1887	MET	AA	P		6	1- 4
1888	KC	AA	P	17	18	6-11
				23	24	7-15

FAGIN, FREDERICK H.
B.CINCINNATI,OHIO

YR	CL	LEA	POS	GP	G	REC
1895	STL	N	C		1	.333

FAHEY, FRANCIS RAYMOND
B.JAN.22,1896 MILFORD,MASS.
D.MAR.19,1954 UXBRIDGE,MASS.

YR	CL	LEA	POS	GP	G	REC
1918	PHI	A	P		10	0- 0
	BBTR					

FAHEY, HOWARD SIMPSON (CAP) OR (KID)
B.JUNE 24,1892 MEDFORD,MASS.
D.OCT.24,1971 CLEARWATER,FLA.

YR	CL	LEA	POS	GP	G	REC
1912	PHI	A	S		5	.000
	BRTR					

FAHEY, WILLIAM ROGER (BILL)
B.JUNE 14,1950 DETROIT,MICH.

YR	CL	LEA	POS	GP	G	REC
1971	WAS	A	/C		2	.000
1972	TEX	A	C		39	.168
1974	TEX	A	/C		6	.250
1975	TEX	A	C		21	.249
1976	TEX	A	C		38	.250
1977	TEX	A	C		37	.221
	BLTR				143	.213

FAHR, GERALD WARREN (JERRY)
B.DEC.9,1924 MARMADUKE,ARK.

YR	CL	LEA	POS	GP	G	REC
1951	CLE	N	P		5	0- 0
	BRTR					

FAHRER, CLARENCE WILLIE (PETE)
B.MAR.10,1890 HOLGATE,OHIO
D.JUNE 10,1967 FREMONT,MICH.

YR	CL	LEA	POS	GP	G	REC
1914	CIN	N	P		5	0- 0
	TR					

FAIN, FERRIS ROY (BURRHEAD)
B.MAY 29,1921 SAN ANTONIO,TEX.

YR	CL	LEA	POS	GP	G	REC
1947	PHI	A	1		136	.291
1948	PHI	A	1		145	.281
1949	PHI	A	1		150	.263
1950	PHI	A	1		151	.282
1951	PHI	A	1-O		117	.344
1952	PHI	A	1		145	.327
1953	CHI	A	1		128	.256
1954	CHI	A	1		65	.302
1955	DET	A	1		58	.264
	CLE	A	1		56	.254
	BLTL				1151	.290

FAIRBANK, JAMES LEE (LEE) OR (SMOKY)
B.MAR.17,1881 DEANSBORO,N.Y.
D.DEC.27,1955 UTICA,N.Y.

YR	CL	LEA	POS	GP	G	REC
1903	PHI	A	P		1	0- 0
1904	PHI	A	P		3	0- 1
					4	0- 1

FAIRCLOTH, JAMES LAMAR (RAGS)
B.AUG.19,1892 KENTON,TENN.

YR	CL	LEA	POS	GP	G	REC
1919	PHI	N	P		2	0- 0
	BRTR					

FAIREY, JAMES BURKE (JIM)
B.SEP.22,1944 ORANGEBURG,S.C.

YR	CL	LEA	POS	GP	G	REC
1968	LA	N	O		99	.199
1969	MON	N	O		20	.286
1970	MON	N	O		92	.242
1971	MON	N	O		92	.245
1972	MON	N	O		86	.234
1973	LA	N	H		10	.222
	BLTL				399	.235

FAIRLY, RONALD RAY (RON)
B.JULY 12,1938 MACON,GA.

YR	CL	LEA	POS	GP	G	REC
1958	LA	N	O		15	.283
1959	LA	N	O		118	.238
1960	LA	N	O		14	.108
1961	LA	N	1-O		111	.322
1962	LA	N	1-O		147	.278
1963	LA	N	1-O		152	.271
1964	LA	N	1		150	.256
1965	LA	N	*O-1		158	.274
1966	LA	N	O-1		117	.288
1967	LA	N	O-1		153	.220
1968	LA	N	*O-1		141	.234
1969	LA	N	1-O		30	.219
	MON	N	1-O		70	.289
1970	MON	N	*1/O		119	.288
1971	MON	N	*1-O		146	.257
1972	MON	N	O-1		140	.278
1973	MON	N	*O/1		142	.298
1974	MON	N	1-O		101	.245
1975	STL	N	1-O		107	.301
1976	STL	N	1		73	.264
	OAK	A	1		15	.239
1977	TOR	A	O-1-O		132	.279
1978	CAL	A	1		91	.217
	BLTL				2442	.266

FALCH, ANTON

YR	CL	LEA	POS	GP	G	REC
1884	MIL	U	C-O		5	.471

FALCONE, PETER (PETE)
B.OCT.1,1953 BROOKLYN,N.Y.

YR	CL	LEA	POS	GP	G	REC
1975	SF	N	P		34	12-11
1976	STL	N	P		32	12-16
1977	STL	N	P		27	4- 8
1978	STL	N	P		19	2- 7
	BLTL				112	30-42

FALK, BIBB AUGUST (JOCKEY)
B.JAN.27,1899 AUSTIN,TEX.

YR	CL	LEA	POS	GP	G	REC
1920	CHI	A	O		7	.294
1921	CHI	A	O		152	.285
1922	CHI	A	O		131	.298
1923	CHI	A	O		87	.307
1924	CHI	A	O		138	.352
1925	CHI	A	O		154	.301
1926	CHI	A	O		155	.345
1927	CHI	A	O		145	.327
1928	CHI	A	O		98	.290
1929	CLE	A	O		126	.310
1930	CLE	A	O		82	.325
1931	CLE	A	O		79	.304
	BLTL				1354	.314

FALK, CHESTER EMANUEL (SPOT)
B.MAY.15,1905 AUSTIN,TEX.

YR	CL	LEA	POS	GP	G	REC
1925	STL	A	P	13	17	0- 0
1926	STL	A	P	18	19	4- 4
1927	STL	A	P		9	1- 0
	BLTL			40	45	5- 4

FALKENBERG, FREDERICK PETER (CY)
B.DEC.17,1880 CHICAGO,ILL.
D.APR.14,1961 SAN FRANCISCO,CAL

YR	CL	LEA	POS	GP	G	REC
1903	PIT	N	P		10	1- 5
1905	WAS	A	P		12	4- 4
1906	WAS	A	P		40	14-20
1907	WAS	A	P	32	33	5-18
1908	WAS	A	P		17	6- 1
	CLE	A	P		8	2- 5
1909	CLE	A	P		24	10- 9
1910	CLE	A	P		37	14-13
1911	CLE	A	P	15	16	8- 5
1913	CLE	A	P		39	23-10
1914	IND	F	P		49	25-16
1915	NEW	F	P		16	4- 6
	BRO	F	P		16	7- 8
1917	PHI	A	P		15	2- 6
			BRTR	330	332	125-126

FALLENSTEIN, EDWARD JOSEPH (JACK)
[REAL NAME EDWARD JOSEPH VALESTIN]
B.DEC.22,1908 NEWARK,N.J.
D.NOV.24,1971 ORANGE,N.J.

YR	CL	LEA	POS	GP	G	REC
1931	PHI	N	P		24	0- 0
1933	BOS	N	P	9	11	2- 1
			BRTR	33	35	2- 1

FALLON, GEORGE DECATUR (FLASH)
B.JULY 8,1916 JERSEY CITY,N.J.

YR	CL	LEA	POS	GP	G	REC
1937	BRO	N	2		4	.250
1943	STL	N	2		36	.231
1944	STL	N	2-S-3		69	.199
1945	STL	N	2-S		24	.236
			BRTR		133	.216

FALSEY, PETER JAMES
B.APR.24,1891 NEW HAVEN,CONN.

YR	CL	LEA	POS	GP	G	REC
1914	PIT	N	P		3	0- 0
			BLTL			

FANNIN, CLIFFORD BRYSON
(CLIFF) OR (MULE)
B.MAY 13,1924 LOUISA,KY.
D.DEC.11,1966 SANDUSKY,OHIO

YR	CL	LEA	POS	GP	G	REC
1945	STL	A	P		5	0- 0
1946	STL	A	P		27	5- 2
1947	STL	A	P		26	6- 8
1948	STL	A	P	34	48	10-14
1949	STL	A	P	30	37	8-14
1950	STL	A	P	25	33	5- 9
1951	STL	A	P	7	8	0- 2
1952	STL	A	P	10	11	0- 2
			BLTR	164	195	34-51

FANNING, JOHN JACOB
B.1863 S.ORANGE,N.J.
D.JUNE 10,1917 ABERDEEN,WASH.

YR	CL	LEA	POS	GP	G	REC
1889	IND	N	P		1	0- 1
1894	PHI	N	P		6	1- 3
					7	1- 4

FANNING, WILLIAM JAMES (JIM)
B.SEPT.14,1927 CHICAGO,ILL.

YR	CL	LEA	POS	GP	G	REC
1954	CHI	N	C		11	.184
1955	CHI	N	C		5	.000
1956	CHI	N	C		1	.250
1957	CHI	N	C		47	.180
			BRTR		64	.170

FANOK, HARRY MICHAEL (HARRY)
OR (THE FLAME THROWER)
B.MAY 11,1940 WHIPPANY,N.J.

YR	CL	LEA	POS	GP	G	REC
1963	STL	N	P		12	2- 1
1964	STL	N	P		4	0- 0
			BBTR		16	2- 1

FANOVICH, FRANK JOSEPH
(FRANK) OR (LEFTY)
B.JAN.11,1922 NEW YORK,N.Y.

YR	CL	LEA	POS	GP	G	REC
1949	CIN	N	P		29	0- 2
1953	PHI	A	P		26	0- 3
			BLTL		55	0- 5

FANWELL, HARRY CLAYTON
B.OCT.16,1886 PATAPSCO,MD.
D.JULY 15,1965 BALTIMORE,MD.

YR	CL	LEA	POS	GP	G	REC
1910	CLE	A	P		17	2- 9
			BBTR			

FANZONE, CARMEN RONALD
B.AUG.30,1943 DETROIT,MICH.

YR	CL	LEA	POS	GP	G	REC
1970	BOS	A	/3		10	.200
1971	CHI	N	/O-3-1		12	.186
1972	CHI	N	3-1-2/S-O		86	.225
1973	CHI	N	3-1/O		64	.273
1974	CHI	N	3-2/1-O		65	.190
			BRTR		237	.224

FARLEY, ROBERT JACOB (BOB)
B.NOV.15,1937 WATSONTOWN,PA.

YR	CL	LEA	POS	GP	G	REC
1961	SF	N	1-O		13	.100
1962	CHI	A	1		35	.189
	DET	A	1-O		36	.160
			BLTL		84	.163

FARLEY, THOMAS T.
B.CHICAGO,ILL.

YR	CL	LEA	POS	GP	G	REC
1884	WAS	AA	O		13	.213

FARMER, ALEXANDER JOHNSON
B.MAY 9,1880 NEW YORK,N.Y.
D.MAR.5,1920 NEW YORK,N.Y.

YR	CL	LEA	POS	GP	G	REC
1908	BRO	N	C		12	.167
			BRTR			

FARMER, EDWARD JOSEPH (ED)
B.OCT.18,1949 EVERGREEN PARK,ILL

YR	CL	LEA	POS	GP	G	REC
1971	CLE	A	P		43	5- 4
1972	CLE	A	P		46	2- 5
1973	CLE	A	P		16	0- 2
	DET	A	P		24	3- 0
1974	PHI	N	P		14	2- 1
1977	BAL	A	/P		1	0- 0
1978	MIL	A	/P		3	1- 0
			BRTR		147	13-12

FARMER, FLOYD HASKELL (JACK)
B.JULY 14,1892 GRANVILLE,TENN.
D.MAY 21,1970 COLUMBIA,LA.

YR	CL	LEA	POS	GP	G	REC
1916	PIT	N	2-O		55	.271
1918	CLE	A	O		7	.222
			BRTR		62	.269

FARMER, WILLIAM
B.DEC.27,1870

YR	CL	LEA	POS	GP	G	REC
1888	PIT	N	C		2	.000
	ATH	AA	C		3	.167
			BRTR		5	.125

FARRAR, SIDNEY DOUGLAS
B.AUG.10,1859 PARIS HILL,ME.
D.MAY 7,1935 NEW YORK,N.Y.

YR	CL	LEA	POS	GP	G	REC
1883	PHI	N	1		98	.230
1884	PHI	N	1		110	.246
1885	PHI	N	1		111	.245
1886	PHI	N	1		118	.248
1887	PHI	N	1		115	.344
1888	PHI	N	1		130	.246
1889	PHI	N	1		130	.268
1890	PHI	P	1		127	.251
			TR		939	.262

FARRELL, CHARLES ANDREW (DUKE)
B.AUG.31,1866 OAKDALE,MASS.
D.FEB.15,1925 BOSTON,MASS.

YR	CL	LEA	POS	GP	G	REC
1888	CHI	N	C-O		63	.232
1889	CHI	N	C-O		100	.263
1890	CHI	P	C-1		117	.296
1891	BOS	AA	C-3-O		122	.304
1892	PIT	N	3-O		152	.230
1893	WAS	N	C-3		122	.296
1894	NY	N	C		112	.282
1895	NY	N	C-3		89	.283
1896	NY	N	C		45	.279
	WAS	N	C-3		37	.326
1897	WAS	N	C		65	.327
1898	WAS	N	C-1		88	.316
1899	WAS	N	C		5	.333
	BRO	N	C		78	.294
1900	BRO	N	C		73	.277
1901	BRO	N	C-1		76	.293
1902	BRO	N	C-1		72	.237
1903	BOS	A	C		17	.404
1904	BOS	A	C		67	.219
1905	BOS	A	C		7	.238
			BBTR		1507	.280

FARRELL, EDWARD STEPHEN (DOC)
D.DEC.26,1901 JOHNSON CITY,N.Y.
D.DEC.20,1966 LIVINGSTON,N.J.

YR	CL	LEA	POS	GP	G	REC
1925	NY	N	2-S-3		27	.214
1926	NY	N	S		67	.287
1927	NY	N	S-3		42	.387
	BOS	N	2-S-3		110	.292
1928	BOS	N	S		134	.215
1929	BOS	N	2		5	.125
	NY	N	2-3		63	.213
1930	STL	N	S		23	.213
	CHI	N	S		46	.292
1932	NY	A	2		26	.175
1933	NY	A	2-S		44	.269
1935	BOS	A	2		4	.286
			BRTR		591	.260

FARRELL, JOHN (HARTFORD JACK)
D.FEB.10,1914

YR	CL	LEA	POS	GP	G	REC
1874	HAR	NA	O		3	-

FARRELL, JOHN A. (JACK) OR (MOOSE)
B.JULY 5,1857 NEWARK,N.J.
D.FEB.10,1914 OVERBROOK,N.J.

YR	CL	LEA	POS	GP	G	REC
1879	SYR	N	2		54	.304
	PRO	N	2		12	.260
1880	PRO	N	2		77	.270
1881	PRO	N	2-O		83	.237
1882	PRO	N	2		84	.254
1883	PRO	N	2		93	.304
1884	PRO	N	2-3		109	.220
1885	PRO	N	2		67	.206
1886	PHI	N	2		23	.171
	WAS	N	2		42	.252
1887	WAS	N	2-S		86	.264
1888	BAL	AA	2-S		103	.197
1889	BAL	AA	S		42	.204
			BRTR		875	.241

FARRELL, JOHN J. (JACK)
B.JUNE 16,1892 CHICAGO,ILL.
D.MAR.24,1918 CHICAGO,ILL.

YR	CL	LEA	POS	GP	G	REC
1914	CHI	F	2		157	.240
1915	CHI	F	2		69	.213
			BBTR		226	.232

FARRELL, JOHN STEPHEN
B.DEC.4,1876 COVINGTON,KY.
D.MAY 14,1921 KANSAS CITY,MO.

YR	CL	LEA	POS	GP	G	REC
1901	WAS	A	2-O		135	.277
1902	STL	N	2-S		139	.255
1903	STL	N	2		130	.272
1904	STL	N	2		130	.255
1905	STL	N	2		6	.182
			TR		540	.264

FARRELL, JOSEPH F.
B.1857 BROOKLYN,N.Y.
D.APR.18,1893 BROOKLYN,N.Y.

YR	CL	LEA	POS	GP	G	REC
1882	DET	N	2-S-3		66	.246
1883	DET	N	3		98	.246
1884	DET	N	3		108	.225
1886	BAL	AA	2-3		72	.212
					344	.233

FARRELL, MAJOR KERBY (KERBY)
B.SEPT.3,1913 LEAPWOOD,TENN.
D.DEC.17,1975 NASHVILLE,TENN.

YR	CL	LEA	POS	GP	G	REC
1943	BOS	N	P-1	5	85	0- 1
						.268
1945	CHI	A	1		103	.258
			BLTL	5	188	0- 1
						.262

NON-PLAYING MANAGER CLE[A] 1957

FARRELL, RICHARD JOSEPH (TURK)
B.APR.8,1934 BOSTON,MASS.
D.JUNE 10,1977 GREAT YARMOUTH,
ENGLAND

YR	CL	LEA	POS	GP	G	REC
1956	PHI	N	P		1	0- 1
1957	PHI	N	P		52	10- 2
1958	PHI	N	P		54	8- 9
1959	PHI	N	P		38	1- 6
1960	PHI	N	P		59	10- 6
1961	PHI	N	P		5	2- 1
	LA	N	P		50	6- 6
1962	HOU	N	P		43	10-20
1963	HOU	N	P		34	14-13
1964	HOU	N	P		32	11-10
1965	HOU	N	P		33	11-11
1966	HOU	N	P		32	6-10
1967	HOU	N	/P		7	1- 0
	PHI	N	P		50	9- 6
1968	PHI	N	P		54	4- 6
1969	PHI	N	P		46	3- 4
			BRTR		590	106-111

FARRELL, WILLIAM

YR	CL	LEA	POS	GP	G	REC
1883	BAL	AA	S		2	.000

FARROW, JOHN JACOB
B.1852 VERPLANCK S POINT,N.Y.
D.DEC.31,1914 PERTH AMBOY,N.J.

YR	CL	LEA	POS	GP	G	REC
1873	RES	NA	C-1-3-O		10	-
1874	ATL	NA	C-2		27	-
1884	BRO	AA	C		16	.190
			TR		53	-

FAST
B.MILWAUKEE,WIS.

YR	CL	LEA	POS	GP	G	REC
1887	IND	N	P		4	0- 1

FAST, DARCY RAE
B.MAR.10,1947 DALLAS,ORE.

YR	CL	LEA	POS	GP	G	REC
1968	CHI	N	/P		8	0- 1
			BLTL			

FASZHOLZ, JOHN EDWARD
(JACK) OR (PREACHER)
B.APR.11,1927 ST.LOUIS,MO.

YR	CL	LEA	POS	GP	G	REC
1953	STL	N	P		4	0- 0
			BRTR			

FAUL, WILLIAM ALVAN (BILL)
B.APR.21,1940 CINCINNATI,OHIO

YR	CL	LEA	POS	GP	G	REC
1962	DET	A	P		1	0- 0
1963	DET	A	P		28	5- 6
1964	DET	A	P		1	0- 0
1965	CHI	N	P		17	6- 6
1966	CHI	N	P		17	1- 4
1970	SF	N	/P		7	0- 0
			BRTR		71	12-16

FAULKNER, JAMES LEROY (LEFTY)
B.JULY 27,1899 BEATRICE,NEB.
D.JUNE 1,1962 W.PALM BEACH,FLA.

YR	CL	LEA	POS	GP	G	REC
1927	NY	N	P		3	1- 0
1928	NY	N	P		38	9- 8
1930	BRO	N	P		2	0- 0
			BBTL		43	10- 8
			BL 1927			

FAUSETT, ROBERT SHAW
(BUCK) OR (LEAKY)
B.APR.8,1908 SHERIDAN,ARK.

YR	CL	LEA	POS	GP	G	REC
1944	CIN	N	P-3	2	13	0- 0
						.097
			BLTR			

YR	CL LEA POS	GP	G	REC

FAUST, CHARLES VICTORY (VICTORY)
B.OCT.9,1880 MARION,KAN.
D.JUNE 18,1915 FORT STEILACOOM,WASH.
1911 NY   N P   2   0- 0
          TR

FAUTSCH, JOSEPH ROAMON
B.FEB.28,1887 MINNEAPOLIS,MINN.
D.MAR.16,1971 NEW HOPE,MINN.
1916 CHI A P   1   0- 0
          BRTR

FAUVER, CLAYTON KING (CAYT)
B.AUG.1,1872 N.EATON,OHIO
D.MAR.3,1942 CHATSWORTH,GA.
1899 LOU N P   1   1- 0
          BBTR

FAZIO, ERNEST JOSEPH (ERNIE)
B.JAN.25,1942 OAKLAND,CAL.
1962 HOU N S   12   .083
1963 HOU N 2-S-3   102   .184
1966 KC   A 2/S   27   .26o
          BRTR   141   .182

FEAR, LUVERN CARL (VERN)
B.AUG.21,1924 EVERLY,IOWA
D.SEPT.6,1976 SPENCER,IOWA
1952 CHI N P   4   0- 0
          BBTR

FEDEROFF, ALFRED (AL) OR (WHITEY)
B.JULY 11,1924 BAIRDFORD,PA.
1951 DET A 2   2   .000
1952 DET A 2-S   74   .242
          BRTR   76   .238

FEE, JOHN (JACK)
b.1870 CARBONDALE,PA.
D.MAR.3,1913 CARBONDALE,PA.
1889 IND N P   7   2- 2

FEHRING, WILLIAM PAUL (DUTCH)
B.MAY 31,1912 COLUMBUS,IND.
1934 CHI A C   1   .000
          BBTR

FEINBERG, EDWARD (ITZY)
B.SEPT.20,1918 PHILADELPHIA,PA.
1938 PHI N S-O   10   .150
1939 PHI N 2-S   6   .222
          BBTR   16   .184

FELDERMAN, MARVIN WILFRED
B.DEC.17,1917 BELLEVUE,IOWA
1942 CHI N C   3   .167
          BRTR

FELDMAN, HARRY
B.NOV.10,1919 NEW YORK,N.Y.
D.MAR.16,1962 FORT SMITH,ARK.
1941 NY   N P   3   1- 1
1942 NY   N P   31   7- 1
1943 NY   N P   31   44   4- 5
1944 NY   N P   40   54 11-13
1945 NY   N P   35   38 12-13
1946 NY   N P   3   0- 2
          BRTR   143 173 35-35

FELIX, AUGUST GUENTHER (GUS)
B.MAY 24,1895 CINCINNATI,OHIO
D.MAY 12,1960 MONTGOMERY,ALA.
1923 BOS N 2-3-O   139   .273
1924 BOS N O   59   .211
1925 BOS N O   121   .307
1926 BRO N O   134   .280
1927 BRO N O   130   .265
          BRTR   583   .274

FELIX, HARRY
B.1870 BROOKLYN,N.Y.
D.OCT.17,1961 MIAMI,FLA.
1901 NY   N P   1   0- 0
1902 PHI N P-3   9   16   1- 3
                                 .111
          TR   10   17   1- 3
                                 .105

FELLER, JACK LELAND
B.DEC.10,1936 ADRIAN,MICH.
1958 DET A C   1   .000
          BRTR

FELLER, ROBERT WILLIAM ANDREW
(BOB) OR (RAPID ROBERT)
B.NOV.3,1918 VAN METER,IOWA
1936 CLE A P   14   5- 3
1937 CLE A P   26   9- 7
1938 CLE A P   39 17-11
1939 CLE A P   39 24- 9
1940 CLE A P   43 27-11
1941 CLE A P   44 25-13
1945 CLE A P   9   5- 3
1946 CLE A P   48 26-15
1947 CLE A P   42 20-11
1948 CLE A P   44 19-15
1949 CLE A P   36 15-14
1950 CLE A P   35 16-11
1951 CLE A P   33 22- 8
1952 CLE A P   30   9-13
1953 CLE A P   25 10- 7
1954 CLE A P   19 13- 3
1955 CLE A P   25   4- 4
1956 CLE A P   19   0- 4
          BRTR   570 266-162

FELSCH, OSCAR EMIL (HAPPY)
B.AUG.22,1891 MILWAUKEE,WIS.
D.AUG.17,1964 MILWAUKEE,WIS.
1915 CHI A O   121   .248
1916 CHI A O   146   .301
1917 CHI A O   152   .308
1918 CHI A O   53   .252
1919 CHI A O   135   .275
1920 CHI A O   142   .338
          BRTR   749   .290

FELSKE, JOHN FREDERICK
B.MAY 30,1942 CHICAGO,ILL.
1968 CHI N /C   4   .000
1972 MIL A C/1   37   .138
1973 MIL A /C-1   13   .136
          BRTR   54   .135

FENNELLY, FRANCIS JOHN
B.FEB.18,1860 FALL RIVER,MASS.
D.AUG.4,1920 FALL RIVER,MASS.
1884 WAS AA 2-S-O   62   .288
     CIN AA S   28   .369
1885 CIN AA S   112   .259
1886 CIN AA S   132   .258
1887 CIN AA S   134   .368
1888 CIN AA 2-S-O   112   .191
     ATH AA S   15   .239
1889 ATH AA S   137   .259
1890 BRO AA S   47   .251
          BRTR   779   .278

FENNER, HORACE ALFRED (HOD)
B.JULY 12,1897 MARTIN,MICH.
D.NOV.20,1954 DETROIT,MICH.
1921 CHI A P   2   0- 0

FENWICK, ROBERT RICHARD (BOBBY)
B.DEC.10,1946 OKINAWA
1972 HOU N 2/S-3   36   .180
1973 STL N /2   5   .167
          BRTR   41   .179

FERENS, STANLEY (LEFTY)
B.MAR.5,1915 WENDELL,PA.
1942 STL A P   19   3- 4
1946 STL A P   34   2- 9
          BBTL   53   5-13

FERGUSON, CHARLES AUGUSTUS
B.MAY 10,1875 OKEMOS,MICH.
D.MAY 17,1931 SAULT STE.MARIE,MICH.
1901 CHI N P   1   0- 0

FERGUSON, CHARLES J.
B.APR.17,1863 CHARLOTTESVILLE,VA.
D.APR.29,1888 PHILADELPHIA,PA.
1884 PHI N P-O   46   51 20-22
                                 .251
1885 PHI N P-O   46   59 26-19
                                 .306
1886 PHI N P-O   43   71 32- 9
                                 .252
1887 PHI N P-2   33   69 21-10
                                 .412
          BBTR   168 250 99-60
                                 .313

FERGUSON, GEORGE CECIL (CECIL)
B.AUG.19,1886 ELLSWORTH,KAN.
D.SEPT.5,1943 ORLANDO,FLA.
1906 NY   N P   22   2- 1
1907 NY   N P   15   3- 2
1908 BOS N P   37 11-11
1909 BOS N P   36   5-23
1910 BOS N P   26   7- 7
1911 BOS N P   6   1- 3
          BRTR   142 29-47

FERGUSON, JAMES ALEXANDER (ALEX)
B.FEB.16,1897 MONTCLAIR,N.J.
D.APR.26,1976 SEPULVEDA,CAL.
1918 NY   A P   1   0- 0
1921 NY   A P   17   3- 1
1922 BOS A P   39   9-16
1923 BOS A P   34   9-13
1924 BOS A P   41 14-17
1925 BOS A P   5   0- 2
     NY   A P   21   4- 2
     WAS A P   7   5- 1
1926 WAS A P   19   3- 4
1927 PHI N P   31   8-16
1928 PHI N P   34   5-10
1929 PHI N P   5   1- 2
     BRO N P   3   0- 1
          BRTR   257 61-85

FERGUSON, JOSEPH VANCE (JOE)
B.SEP.19,1946 SAN FRANCISCO,CAL.
1970 LA   N /C   5   .250
1971 LA   N C   36   .216
1972 LA   N /C-O   8   .292
1973 LA   N *C-O   136   .263
1974 LA   N C-O   111   .252
1975 LA   N C-O   66   .208
1976 LA   N O-C   54   .222
     STL N O-C   71   .201
1977 HOU N *C/1   132   .257
1978 HOU N C   51   .207
     LA   N C/O   67   .237
          BRTR   737   .239

FERGUSON, ROBERT LESTER
B.APR.18,1919 BIRMINGHAM,ALA.
1944 CIN N P   9   0- 3
          BRTR

FERGUSON, ROBERT V. (BOB)
OR (DEATH TO FLYING THINGS)
B.1845 BROOKLYN,N.Y.
D.MAY 3,1894 BROOKLYN,N.Y.
1871 MUT NA M-C-2-3   34   -
1872 ATL NA M-3   35   .262
1873 ATL NA M-P-   1   53   0- 1
                      3
1874 ATL NA M-P-   1   56   0- 1
                     C-3
1875 HAR NA M-3   84   -
1876 HAR N M-3   69   .264
1877 HAR N M-P-   3   58   1- 1
                      3   .256
1878 CHI N M-S   60   .351
1879 TRO N M-3   29   .252
1880 TRO N M-2   82   .262
1881 TRO N M-2   84   .287
1882 TRO N M-2-S   79   .254
1883 PHI N M-P-   1   85   0- 0
                      2   .256
1884 PIT AA M-1-3-0   10   .154
          BBTR   6 818   1- 3

NON-PLAYING MANAGER MET[AA] 1886-87

FERNANDES, EDWARD PAUL
B.MAR.11,19.8 OAKLAND,CAL.
D.NOV.27,1968 HAYWARD,CAL.
1940 PIT N C   28   .121
1946 CHI A C   14   .250
          BBTR   42   .185

FERNANDEZ, FRANK
B.APR.16,1943 STATEN ISLAND,N.Y.
1967 NY   A /C-O   9   .214
1968 NY   A C/O   51   .170
1969 NY   A C-O   89   .223
1970 OAK A C/O   44   .214
1971 OAK A /C   4   .111
     WAS A /O-C   18   .100
     CHI N C   17   .171
1972 HOU N /C   3   .000
          BRTR   285   .199

FERNANDEZ, FROILAN (NANNY)
B.OCT.25,1918 WILMINGTON,CAL.
1942 BOS N 3-O   145   .255
1946 BOS N S-3-O   115   .255
1947 BOS N S-3-O   83   .206
1950 PIT N 3   65   .258
          BRTR   408   .248

FERNANDEZ, HUMBERTO [PEREZ] (CHICO)
B.MAR.2,1932 HAVANA,CUBA
1956 BRO N S   34   .227
1957 PHI N S   149   .262
1958 PHI N S   148   .230
1959 PHI N 2-S   45   .211
1960 DET A S   133   .241
1961 DET A S-3   133   .248
1962 DET A 1-S-3   141   .249
1963 DET A S   15   .143
     NY   N 2-S-3   58   .200
          BRTR   856   .240

FERNANDEZ, LORENZO MARTO
(MOSQUERA) (CHICO)
B.APR.23,1939 HAVANA,CUBA
1968 BAL A /S-2   24   .111
          BRTR

FERRARA, ALFRED JOHN
(AL) OR (THE BULL)
B.DEC.22,1939 BROOKLYN,N.Y.

YR	CL	LEA	POS	GP	G	REC
1963	LA	N	O		21	.199
1965	LA	N	O		41	.210
1966	LA	N	O		63	.270
1967	LA	N	O		122	.277
1968	LA	N	/O		2	.143
1969	SD	N	O		138	.260
1970	SD	N	O		138	.277
1971	SD	N	/O		17	.118
	CIN	N	/O		32	.182
		BRTR			574	.259

FERRARESE, DONALD HUGH (DON)
B.JUNE 19,1929 OAKLAND,CAL.

YR	CL	LEA	POS	GP	G	REC
1955	BAL	A	P		6	0- 0
1956	BAL	A	P		36	4-10
1957	BAL	A	P		8	1- 1
1958	CLE	A	P		28	3- 4
1959	CLE	A	P		15	5- 3
1960	CHI	A	P		5	0- 1
1961	PHI	N	P-O	42	43	5-12
						.171
1962	PHI	N	P		5	0- 1
	STL	N	P		38	1- 4
		BRTL		183	184	19-36
						.156

FERRARO, MICHAEL DENNIS (MIKE)
B.AUG.18,1944 KINGSTON,N.Y.

YR	CL	LEA	POS	GP	G	REC
1966	NY	A	3		10	.179
1968	NY	A	3		23	.161
1969	SEA	A	/H		5	.000
.972	MIL	A	*3/S		124	.255
		BRTR			162	.232

FERRAZZI, WILLIAM JOSEPH
B.APR.19,1907 W.QUINCY,MASS.

YR	CL	LEA	POS	GP	G	REC
1935	PHI	A	P		3	1- 2
		BRTR				

FERRELL, RICHARD BENJAMIN (RICK)
B.OCT.12,1905 DURHAM,N.C.

YR	CL	LEA	POS	GP	G	REC
1929	STL	A	C		64	.229
1930	STL	A	C		101	.268
1931	STL	A	C		117	.306
1932	STL	A	C		126	.315
1933	STL	A	C		22	.250
	BOS	A	C		118	.297
1934	BOS	A	C		132	.297
1935	BOS	A	C		133	.301
1936	BOS	A	C		121	.312
1937	BOS	A	C		18	.348
	WAS	A	C		86	.229
1938	WAS	A	C		135	.292
1939	WAS	A	C		87	.281
1940	WAS	A	C		103	.273
1941	WAS	A	C		21	.273
	STL	A	C		100	.252
1942	STL	A	C		99	.223
1943	STL	A	C		74	.239
1944	WAS	A	C		99	.277
1945	WAS	A	C		91	.266
1947	WAS	A	C		37	.303
		BRTR			1884	.281

FERRELL, WESLEY CHEEK (WES)
B.FEB.2,1908 GREENSBORO,N.C.
D.DEC.9,1976 SARASOTA,FLA.

YR	CL	LEA	POS	GP	G	REC
1927	CLE	A	P		1	0- 0
1928	CLE	A	P		2	0- 2
1929	CLE	A	P	43	47	21-10
1930	CLE	A	P	43	53	25-13
1931	CLE	A	P	40	48	22-12
1932	CLE	A	P	38	55	23-13
1933	CLE	A	P-O	28	61	11-12
						.271
1934	BOS	A	P	26	34	14- 5
1935	BOS	A	P	41	75	25- 4
1936	BOS	A	P	39	61	20-15
1937	BOS	A	P	12	18	3- 6
	WAS	A	P	25	53	11-13
1938	WAS	A	P	23	26	13- 8
	NY	A	P		5	2- 2
1939	NY	A	P		3	1- 2
1940	BRO	N	P	1	2	0- 0
1941	BOS	N	P		4	2- 1
		BRTR		374	548	193-128
						.280

FERRER, SERGIO [MARRERO]
B.JAN.29,1951 SANTURCE,P.R.

YR	CL	LEA	POS	GP	G	REC
1974	MIN	A	S/2		24	.281
1975	MIN	A	S-2		32	.247
1978	NY	N	S/2-3		37	.212
		BBTR			93	.251

FERRICK, THOMAS JEROME (TOM)
B.JAN.6,1915 NEW YORK,N.Y.

YR	CL	LEA	POS	GP	G	REC
1941	PHI	A	P		36	8-10
1942	CLE	A	P		31	3- 2
1946	CLE	A	P		9	0- 0
	STL	A	P		25	4- 1
1947	WAS	A	P		31	1- 7
1948	WAS	A	P		37	2- 5
1949	STL	A	P	50	51	6- 4
1950	STL	A	P		16	1- 3
	NY	A	P		30	6- 4
1951	NY	A	P		9	1- 1
1951	WAS	A	P		22	2- 0
1952	WAS	A	P		27	4- 3
		BRTR		323	324	40-40

FERRIS, ALBERT SAYLES (HOBE)
B.DEC.7,1877 PROVIDENCE,R.I.
D.MAR.18,1938 DETROIT,MICH.

YR	CL	LEA	POS	GP	G	REC
1901	BOS	A	2		138	.251
1902	BOS	A	2		133	.251
1903	BOS	A	2		141	.250
1904	BOS	A	2		156	.221
1905	BOS	A	2		141	.220
1906	BOS	A	2		130	.244
1907	BOS	A	2		143	.241
1908	STL	A	3		148	.270
1909	STL	A	2-3		148	.216
		BRTR			1278	.240

FERRISS, DAVID MEADOW
(DAVE) OR (BOO)
B.DEC.5,1921 SHAW,MISS.

YR	CL	LEA	POS	GP	G	REC
1945	BOS	A	P	35	61	21-10
1946	BOS	A	P	40	45	25- 6
1947	BOS	A	P	33	52	12-11
1948	BOS	A	P		31	7- 3
1949	BOS	A	P		4	0- 0
1950	BOS	A	P		1	0- 0
		BLTR		144	194	65-30

FERRY, ALFRED JOSEPH (CY)
B.SEPT.27,1878 HUDSON,N.Y.
D.SEPT.27,1938 PITTSFIELD,MASS.

YR	CL	LEA	POS	GP	G	REC
1904	DET	A	P		3	0- 1
1905	CLE	A	P		1	0- 0
		BRTR			4	0- 1

FERRY, JOHN FRANCIS (JACK)
B.APR.7,1887 PITTSFIELD,MASS.
D.AUG.29,1954 PITTSFIELD,MASS.

YR	CL	LEA	POS	GP	G	REC
1910	PIT	N	P		6	1- 2
1911	PIT	N	P		26	6- 4
1912	PIT	N	P		11	2- 0
1913	PIT	N	P		4	1- 0
		BRTR			47	10- 6

FERSON, ALEXANDER (COLONEL)
B.JULY 14,1866 PHILADELPHIA,PA.
D.SEPT.5,1957 BOSTON,MASS.

YR	CL	LEA	POS	GP	G	REC
1889	WAS	N	P		35	17-17
1890	BUF	P	P		10	1- 5
1892	BAL	N	P		2	0- 1
		TR			47	18-23

FESSENDEN, WALLACE CLIFTON
B.WATERTOWN,MASS.
NON-PLAYING MANAGER SYRACA(AA)1890

FETTE, LOUIS HENRY WILLIAM (LOU)
B.MAR.15,1907 ALMA,MO.

YR	CL	LEA	POS	GP	G	REC
1937	BOS	N	P	35	36	20-10
1938	BOS	N	P		33	11-13
1939	BOS	N	P		27	10-10
1940	BOS	N	P		7	0- 5
	BRO	N	P		2	0- 0
1945	BOS	N	P		5	0- 2
		BRTR		109	110	41-40

FETZER, WILLIAM MC KINNON (WILLY)
B.JUNE 24,1884 CONCORD,N.C.
D.MAY 3,1959 BUTNER,N.C.

YR	CL	LEA	POS	GP	G	REC
1906	PHI	A	O		1	.000

FEWSTER, WILSON LLOYD (CHICK)
B.NOV.10,1895 BALTIMORE,MD.
D.APR.16,1945 BALTIMORE,MD.

YR	CL	LEA	POS	GP	G	REC
1917	NY	A	2		11	.222
1918	NY	A	2		5	.500
1919	NY	A	S-O		81	.283
1920	NY	A	S		21	.286
1921	NY	A	2-O		66	.280
1922	NY	A	2-O		44	.228
	BOS	A	O		23	.316
1923	BOS	A	2-S		90	.236
1924	CLE	A	2		101	.267
1925	CLE	A	2-3		93	.248
1926	BRO	N	2		105	.244
1927	BRO	N	H		4	.000
		BRTR			644	.258

FICK, JOHN RALPH
B.MAY 18,1921 BALTIMORE,MD.
D.JUNE 9,1958 SOMERS POINT,N.J.

YR	CL	LEA	POS	GP	G	REC
1944	PHI	N	P		4	0- 0
		BLTL				

FIDRYCH, MARK STEVEN (BIRD)
B.AUG.14,1954 WORCESTER,MASS.

YR	CL	LEA	POS	GP	G	REC
1976	DET	A	P		31	19- 9
1977	DET	A	P		11	6- 4
1978	DET	A	/P		3	2- 0
		BRTR			45	27-13

FIEBER, CLARENCE THOMAS (LEFTY)
B.SEPT.4,1913 SAN FRANCISCO,CAL.

YR	CL	LEA	POS	GP	G	REC
1932	CHI	A	P		3	1- 0
		BLTL				

FIELD, JAMES C.
B.APR.2,1863 PHILADELPHIA,PA.
D.MAY 13,1953 ATLANTIC CITY,N.J

YR	CL	LEA	POS	GP	G	REC
1883	COL	AA	1		75	.239
1884	COL	AA	1		105	.229
1885	PIT	AA	1		56	.245
	BAL	AA	1		58	.213
1890	ROC	AA	1		51	.190
1898	WAS	N	1		5	.095
					330	.228

FIELD, SAMUEL JAY
B.OCT.12,1848 PHILADELPHIA,PA.
D.OCT.28,1904 SINKING SPRING,PA.

YR	CL	LEA	POS	GP	G	REC
1875	CEN	NA	C-O		3	-
	NAT	NA	C-O		5	-
1876	CIN	N	C-2		4	.000
		BRTR			12	-

FIELDS, GEORGE W.

YR	CL	LEA	POS	GP	G	REC
1872	MAN	NA	S-3-O		17	.282

FIELDS, JOHN JOSEPH (JOCKO)
B.OCT.20,1864 CORK,IRELAND
D.OCT.14,1950 JERSEY CITY,N.J.

YR	CL	LEA	POS	GP	G	REC
1887	PIT	N	O		39	.298
1888	PIT	N	O		44	.195
1889	PIT	N	C-O		74	.311
1890	PIT	N	P C-2-O		127	.277
1891	PIT	N	C		19	.239
	PHI	N	C		8	.233
1892	NY	N	C		17	.268
		BRTR			328	.274

FIENE, LOUIS HENRY (BIG FINN)
B.DEC.29,1884 FT.DODGE,IOWA
D.DEC.22,1964 CHICAGO,ILL.

YR	CL	LEA	POS	GP	G	REC
1906	CHI	A	P		6	1- 1
1907	CHI	A	P		4	0- 1
1908	CHI	A	P		1	0- 1
1909	CHI	A	P	13	15	2- 2
		BRTR		24	26	3- 5

FIFE, DANNY WAYNE
B.OCT.5,1949 HARRISBURG,ILL.

YR	CL	LEA	POS	GP	G	REC
1973	MIN	A	P		10	3- 2
1974	MIN	A	/P		4	0- 0
		BRTR			14	3- 2

FIFIELD, JOHN PROCTOR (JACK)
B.OCT.5,1871 ENFIELD,N.H.
D.NOV.27,1939 SYRACUSE,N.Y.

YR	CL	LEA	POS	GP	G	REC
1897	PHI	N	P		24	4-20
1898	PHI	N	P		20	11- 9
1899	PHI	N	P		13	3- 8
	WAS	N	P-3	6	7	2- 4
						.200
				63	64	20-41
						.200

FIGGEMEIER, FRANK Y.
B.APR.25,1873 ST.LOUIS,MO.

YR	CL	LEA	POS	GP	G	REC
1894	PHI	N	P		1	0- 1

FIGUEROA, EDUARDO [PADILLA] (ED)
B.OCT.14,1948 CIALES,P.R.

YR	CL	LEA	POS	GP	G	REC
1974	CAL	A	P		25	2- 8
1975	CAL	A	P		33	16-13
1976	NY	A	P		34	19-10
1977	NY	A	P		32	16-11
1978	NY	A	P		35	20- 9
		BRTR			159	73-51

FILE, LAWRENCE SAMUEL (SAM)
B.MAY 18,1922 CHESTER,PA.

YR	CL	LEA	POS	GP	G	REC
1940	PHI	N	S-3		7	.077
		BRTR				

FILES, CHARLES EDWARD (EDDIE)
B.MAY 19,1883 PORTLAND,ME.
D.MAY 10,1954 CORNISH,MAINE

YR	CL	LEA	POS	GP	G	REC
1908	PHI	A	P		2	0- 0
		BRTR				

FILIPOWICZ, STEPHEN CHARLES (FLIP)
B.JUNE 28,1921 DONORA,PA.
D.FEB.21,1975 WILKES-BARRE,PA.

YR	CL	LEA	POS	GP	G	REC
1944	NY	N	C-O		15	.195
1945	NY	N	O		35	.205
1948	CIN	N	O		7	.346
		BRTR			57	.223

FILLEY, MARCUS LUCIUS
B.FEB.28,1912 TROY,N.Y.

YR	CL	LEA	POS	GP	G	REC
1934	WAS	A	P		1	0- 0
		BRTR				

YR CL LEA POS   GP   G   REC

FILLINGIM, DANA
B.NOV.6,1893 COLUMBUS,GA.
D.FEB.3,1961 TUSKEGEE,ALA.
1915	PHI	A	P		8	0-4
1918	BOS	N	P		14	7-6
1919	BOS	N	P		32	6-13
1920	BOS	N	P	37	38	12-21
1921	BOS	N	P	44	45	15-10
1922	BOS	N	P		25	5-9
1923	BOS	N	P	35	36	1-9
1925	PHI	N	P		5	1-0
	BLTR			200	203	47-72

FINCHER, WILLIAM ALLEN
B.OCT.1,1894 ATLANTA,GA.
D.MAY 8,1946 SHREVEPORT,LA.
| 1916 | STL | A | P | | 12 | 0-1 |
| | BRTR | | | | | |

FINE, BENJAMIN J.
NON-PLAYING MANAGER STL[N] 1885

FINE, THOMAS MORGAN (TOMMY)
B.OCT.10,1914 CLEBURNE,TEX.
1947	BOS	A	P		9	1-2
1950	STL	A	P	14	16	0-1
	BBTR			23	25	1-3

FINGERS, ROLAND GLEN (ROLLIE)
B.AUG.25,1946 STEUBENVILLE,OHIO
1968	OAK	A	/P		1	0-0
1969	OAK	A	P		60	6-7
1970	OAK	A	P		45	7-9
1971	OAK	A	P		48	4-6
1972	OAK	A	P		65	11-9
1973	OAK	A	P		62	7-8
1974	OAK	A	P		76	9-5
1975	OAK	A	P	75	76	10-6
1976	OAK	A	P		70	13-11
1977	SD	N	P		78	8-9
1978	SD	N	P		67	6-13
	BRTR			647	648	81-83

FINIGAN, JAMES LeROY (JIM)
B.AUG.19,1928 QUINCY,ILL.
1954	PHI	A	3		136	.302
1955	KC	A	2-3		150	.255
1956	KC	A	2-3		91	.216
1957	DET	A	2-s		64	.270
1958	SF	N	2-3		23	.200
1959	BAL	A	2-S-3		48	.252
	BRTR				512	.264

FINK, HERMAN ADAM
B.AUG.22,1911 CONCORD,N.C.
1935	PHI	A	P		5	0-3
1936	PHI	A	P		34	8-16
1937	PHI	A	P		28	2-1
	BRTR				67	10-20

FINLAYSON, PEMBROKE
B.JULY 31,1888 CHERAW,S.C.
D.MAR.6,1912 BROOKLYN,N.Y.
1908	BRO	N	P		1	0-0
1909	BRO	N	P		1	0-0
	BRTR				2	0-0

FINLEY, ROBERT EDWARD
B.NOV.25,1915 ENNIS,TEX.
1943	PHI	N	C		28	.259
1944	PHI	N	C		94	.249
	BRTR				122	.252

FINLEY, WILLIAM JAMES
B.OCT.4,1863 NEW YORK,N.Y.
D.OCT.6,1912 ASBURY PARK,N.J.
| 1886 | NY | N | C-O | | 13 | .188 |

FINN, CORNELIUS FRANCIS
(NEAL) OR (MICKEY)
B.JAN.24,1904 BROOKLYN,N.Y.
D.JULY 7,1933 ALLENTOWN,PA.
1930	BRO	N	2		87	.278
1931	BRO	N	2		118	.274
1932	BRO	N	3		65	.238
1933	BRO	N	2		51	.237
	BRTR				321	.262

FINNERAN, JOSEPH IGNATIUS
(HAPPY) OR (SMOKEY JOE)
B.OCT.29,1891 E.ORANGE,N.J.
D.JULY 8,1942 ORANGE,N.J.
1912	PHI	N	P		14	0-2
1913	PHI	N	P		3	0-0
1914	BRO	F	P		27	12-11
1915	BRO	F	P		37	10-12
1918	DET	A	P		6	1-2
	NY	A	P		23	3-6
	BRTR				110	26-33

FINNEY, HAROLD WILSON
B.JULY 7,1905 LAFAYETTE,ALA.
1931	PIT	N	C		10	.308
1932	PIT	N	C		31	.212
1933	PIT	N	C		56	.233
1934	PIT	N	C		5	.000
1936	PIT	N	C		21	.000
	BRTR				123	.203

FINNEY, LOUIS KLOPSCHE (LOU)
B.AUG.13,1910 BUFFALO,ALA.
D.APR.22,1966 LAFAYETTE,ALA.
1931	PHI	A	O		9	.376
1933	PHI	A	O		74	.267
1934	PHI	A	1-O		92	.279
1935	PHI	A	1-O		109	.273
1936	PHI	A	1-O		151	.302
1937	PHI	A	1-O		92	.251
1938	PHI	A	1-O		122	.275
1939	PHI	A	O		9	.136
	BOS	A	1-O		95	.325
1940	BOS	A	1-O		130	.320
1941	BOS	A	1-O		127	.288
1942	BOS	A	1-O		113	.285
1944	BOS	A	1-O		68	.287
1945	BOS	A	H		2	.000
	STL	A	1-3-O		57	.277
1946	STL	A	O		16	.300
1947	PHI	N	H		4	.000
	BLTR				1270	.287

FIORE, MICHAEL GARY JOSEPH (MIKE)
B.OCT.11,1944 BROOKLYN,N.Y.
1968	BAL	A	/1-O		6	.059
1969	KC	A	1-O		107	.274
1970	KC	A	1		25	.181
	BOS	A	1/O		41	.140
1971	BOS	A	1		51	.177
1972	STL	N	/1-O		17	.100
	SD	N	/H		7	.000
	BLTL				254	.227

FIRTH, THEODORE JOHN
B.PHILADELPHIA,PA.
D.APR.18,1885 MARSHALLTOWN,IOWA
| 1884 | RIC | AA | P | | 1 | 0-1 |

FISCHER, CHARLES WILLIAM (CARL)
B.NOV.5,1905 MEDINA,N.Y.
D.DEC.10,1963 MEDINA,N.Y.
1930	WAS	A	P		8	1-1
1931	WAS	A	P		46	13-9
1932	WAS	A	P		12	3-2
	STL	A	P		24	3-7
1933	DET	A	P		35	11-15
1934	DET	A	P		20	6-4
1935	DET	A	P		3	0-1
	CHI	A	P		24	3-5
1937	CLE	A	P		2	0-1
	WAS	A	P		17	4-5
	BRTL				191	46-50

FISCHER, HENRY WILLIAM
(HANK) OR (BULLDOG)
B.JAN.11,1940 YONKERS,N.Y.
1962	MIL	N	P		29	2-3
1963	MIL	N	P		31	4-3
1964	MIL	N	P	37	38	11-10
1965	MIL	N	P	31	32	8-9
1966	ATL	N	P		14	2-3
	CIN	N	P		11	0-6
	BOS	A	/P		6	2-3
1967	BOS	A	/P		9	1-2
	BRTR			168	170	30-39

FISCHER, REUBEN WALTER (RUBE)
B.SEPT.19,1916 CARLOCK,S.D.
1941	NY	N	P		2	1-0
1943	NY	N	P		22	5-10
1944	NY	N	P		38	6-14
1945	NY	N	P		31	3-8
1946	NY	N	P		15	1-2
	BRTR				108	16-34

FISCHER, WILLIAM CHARLES
B.MAR.2,1891 NEW YORK,N.Y.
D.SEPT.4,1945 RICHMOND,VA.
1913	BRO	N	C		62	.267
1914	BRO	N	C		43	.257
1915	CHI	F	C		105	.326
1916	CHI	N	C		65	.197
	PIT	N	C		42	.254
1917	PIT	N	C		95	.286
	BLTR				412	.273

FISCHER, WILLIAM CHARLES (BILL)
B.OCT.11,1930 WAUSAU,WIS.
1956	CHI	A	P		3	0-0
1957	CHI	A	P		13	7-8
1958	CHI	A	P		17	2-3
	DET	A	P		22	2-4
	WAS	A	P		3	0-3
1959	WAS	A	P		34	9-11
1960	WAS	A	P		20	3-5
	DET	A	P		20	5-3
1961	DET	A	P		26	3-2
	KC	A	P		15	1-0
1962	KC	A	P		34	4-12
1963	KC	A	P		45	9-6
1964	MIN	A	P		9	0-1
	BRTR				281	45-58

FISCHLIN MICHAEL THOMAS (MIKE)
B.SEPT.13,1955 SACRAMENTO,CAL.
1977	HOU	N	S		13	.200
1978	HOU	N	S		44	.116
	BRTR				57	.129

FISHBURN, SAMUEL E.
B.MAY 15,1893 HAVERHILL,MASS.
D.APR.11,1965 BETHLEHEM,PA.
| 1919 | STL | N | 1-2 | | 9 | .333 |
| | BRTR | | | | | |

FISHEL, LEO
B.DEC.13,1877 BABYLON,N.Y.
D.MAY 19,1960 HEMPSTEAD,N.Y.
| 1899 | NY | N | P | | 1 | 0-1 |

FISHER
B.JOHNSTOWN,PA.
1884	KEY	U	P-1	8	10	1-7
						.222
	WIL	U	S-O		8	.069
1885	BUF	N	P	9	19	1-8
						.143

FISHER, AUGUST HARRIS (GUS)
B.OCT.2,1885 POTTSBOROUGH,TEX.
D.APR.8,1972 PORTLAND,ORE.
1911	CLE	A	C		70	.261
1912	NY	A	C		4	.200
	BLTR				74	.258

FISHER, CHAUNCEY BURR (PEACH)
(WHOA BILL)
B.JAN.8,1872 ANDERSON,IND.
D.APR.27,1939 LOS ANGELES,CAL.
1893	CLE	N	P		3	0-2
1894	CLE	N	P		3	0-2
	CIN	N	P		12	2-10
1896	CIN	N	P		20	9-7
1897	BRO	N	P		18	8-7
1901	NY	N	P		1	0-1
	STL	N	P		1	0-0
	BRTR				58	19-29

FISHER, CLARENCE HENRY
B.AUG.27,1898 LETART,W.VA.
D.NOV.2,1965 POINT PLEASANT,W.VA.
1919	WAS	A	P		2	0-0
1920	WAS	A	P		2	0-1
	BRTR				4	0-1

FISHER, DONALD RAYMOND
B.FEB.6,1916 CLEVELAND,OHIO
D.JULY 29,1973 MAYFIELD HEIGHTS OHIO
| 1945 | NY | N | P | | 2 | 1-0 |
| | BRTR | | | | | |

FISHER, EDDIE GENE
B.JULY 16,1936 SHREVEPORT,LA.
1959	SF	N	P		17	2-6
1960	SF	N	P		3	1-0
1961	SF	N	P		15	0-2
1962	CHI	A	P		57	9-5
1963	CHI	A	P		39	9-8
1964	CHI	A	P		59	6-3
1965	CHI	A	P		82	15-7
1966	CHI	A	P		23	1-3
	BAL	A	P		44	5-3
1967	BAL	A	P		46	4-3
1968	CLE	A	P		54	4-2
1969	CAL	A	P		52	3-2
1970	CAL	A	P		67	4-4
1971	CAL	A	P		57	10-8
1972	CAL	A	P		43	4-5
	CHI	A	P		6	0-1
1973	CHI	A	P		26	6-7
	STL	N	/P		6	2-1
	BRTR				690	85-70

FISHER, FREDERICK BROWN (FRITZ)
B.NOV.28,1941 ADRIAN,MICH.
| 1964 | DET | A | P | | 1 | 0-0 |
| | BLTL | | | | | |

FISHER, GEORGE ALOYS (SHOWBOAT)
B.JAN.16,1899 JENNINGS,IOWA
1923	WAS	A	O		13	.240
1924	WAS	A	O		15	.219
1930	STL	N	O		92	.374
1932	STL	A	O		18	.182
	BLTR				138	.335

FISHER, HARRY C.
B.PHILADELPHIA,PA.
1884	KC	U	S-3		10	.195
	CHI	U	3		1	.667
	CLE	N	C-2		6	.130
1889	LOU	AA	O		1	.000
					18	.147

FISHER, HARRY DEVEREUX
B.JAN.3,1926 NEWBURY,ONT.,CAN.
1951	PIT	N	H		3	.000
1952	PIT	N	P	8	15	1-2
	BLTR			8	18	1-2
						.278

FISHER, JOHN GUS (RED)
B.JUNE 22,1887 PITTSBURGH,PA.
D.JAN.31,1940 LOUISVILLE,KY.
| 1910 | STL | A | O | | 23 | .125 |
| | TR | | | | | |

FISHER, JOHN HOWARD (JACK) OR (FAT JACK)
B.MAR.4,1939 FROSTBURG,MD.

YR	CL	LEA	POS	GP	G	REC
1959	BAL	A	P		27	1- 6
1960	BAL	A	P		40	12-11
1961	BAL	A	P		36	10-13
1962	BAL	A	P	32	33	7- 9
1963	SF	N	P		36	6-10
1964	NY	N	P		40	10-17
1965	NY	N	P		43	8-24
1966	NY	N	P		38	11-14
1967	NY	N	P		39	9-18
1968	CHI	A	P		35	8-13
1969	CIN	N	P		34	4- 4
			BRTR	400	401	86-139

FISHER, MAURICE WAYNE
B.FEB.16,1931 UNIONDALE,IND.

YR	CL	LEA	POS	GP	G	REC
1955	CIN	N	P		1	0- 0
			BRTR			

FISHER, NEWTON
B.JUNE 16,1871 NASHVILLE,TENN.
D.FEB.28,1947 CHICAGO,ILL.

YR	CL	LEA	POS	GP	G	REC
1898	PHI	N	C		9	.154

FISHER, RAYMOND LYLE (CHIC)
B.OCT.4,1887 MIDDLEBURY,VT.

YR	CL	LEA	POS	GP	G	REC
1910	NY	A	P		15	5- 3
1911	NY	A	P		29	10-11
1912	NY	A	P		17	2- 8
1913	NY	A	P		43	11-17
1914	NY	A	P		29	10-12
1915	NY	A	P		30	18-11
1916	NY	A	P		31	11- 8
1917	NY	A	P		23	8- 9
1919	CIN	N	P		26	14- 5
1920	CIN	N	P		33	10-11
			BRTR		276	99-95

FISHER, ROBERT TAYLOR
B.NOV.3,1886 NASHVILLE,TENN.
D.AUG.4,1963 JACKSONVILLE,FLA.

YR	CL	LEA	POS	GP	G	REC
1912	BRO	N	S		82	.233
1913	BRO	N	S		132	.262
1914	CHI	N	S		15	.300
1915	CHI	N	S		147	.287
1916	CIN	N	2-S-O		61	.272
1918	STL	N	2		63	.317
1919	STL	N	2		3	.273
			BRTR		503	.276

FISHER, THOMAS CHALMERS (RED)
B.NOV.1,1880 ANDERSON,IND.
D.SEPT.3,1972 ANDERSON,IND.

YR	CL	LEA	POS	GP	G	REC
1902	DET	A	P		1	0- 0
1904	BOS	N	P	31	36	6-16
			BRTR	32	37	6-16

FISHER, THOMAS GENE (TOM)
B.APR.4,1942 CLEVELAND,OHIO

YR	CL	LEA	POS	GP	G	REC
1967	BAL	A	P		2	0- 0
			BRTR			

FISHER, WILBUR MC CULLOUGH
B.JULY 18,1894 GREENBOTTOM,W.VA
D.OCT.24,1960 WELCH,W.VA.

YR	CL	LEA	POS	GP	G	REC
1916	PIT	N	H		1	.000
			BBTR			

FISHER, WILLIAM CHARLES (CHEROKEE)
B.DEC.1845 PHILADELPHIA,PA.
D.SEPT.26,1912 NEW YORK,N.Y.

YR	CL	LEA	POS	GP	G	REC
1871	ROK	NA	P-1-O	22	25	5-17 / -
1872	BAL	NA	P-3-O	12	44	9- 3 / .205
1873	ATH	NA	P-1-O	4	49	2- 2 / -
1874	HAR	NA	P-S-3-O	35	52	13-22 / -
1875	PH1	NA	P-O	39	40	22-17 / .231
1876	CIN	N	P-1-S-O	25	35	4-20 / .248
1877	CHI	N	3		1	.000
1878	PRO	N	P		1	0- 1
			BRTR	138	248	55-62 / -

FISK, CARLTON ERNEST (PUDGE)
B.DEC.26,1947 BELLOWS FALLS,VT.

YR	CL	LEA	POS	GP	G	REC
1969	BOS	A	/C		2	.000
1971	BOS	A	C		14	.313
1972	BOS	A	*C		131	.293
1973	BOS	A	*C		135	.246
1974	BOS	A	C		52	.299
1975	BOS	A	C		79	.331
1976	BOS	A	*C		134	.255
1977	BOS	A	*C		152	.315
1978	BOS	A	*C/O		157	.284
			BRTR		856	.285

FISKE, MAXIMILIAN PATRICK (MAX) OR (SKI)
B.OCT.12,1888 CHICAGO,ILL.
D.MAY 15,1928 CHICAGO,ILL.

YR	CL	LEA	POS	GP	G	REC
1914	CHI	F	P		39	12-12
			BRTR			

FISLER, WESTON DICKSON
B.JULY 5,1841 CAMDEN,N.J.
D.DEC.25,1922 PHILADELPHIA,PA.

YR	CL	LEA	POS	GP	G	REC
1871	ATH	NA	1-2		28	.333
1872	ATH	NA	2		46	.327
1873	ATH	NA	1-2		43	-
1874	ATH	NA	1-2		37	.343
1875	ATH	NA	1-2-O		57	.276
1876	ATH	N	1-2-O		59	.286
					270	-

FITTERY, PAUL CLARENCE
B.OCT.10,1887 LEBANON,PA.
D.JAN.28,1974 CARTERSVILLE,GA.

YR	CL	LEA	POS	GP	G	REC
1914	CIN	N	P		11	0- 2
1917	PHI	N	P	17	19	1- 1
			BBTL	28	30	1- 3

FITZBERGER, CHARLES CASPER
B.FEB.13,1904 BALTIMORE,MD.
D.JAN.25,1965 BALTIMORE,MD.

YR	CL	LEA	POS	GP	G	REC
1928	BOS	N	H		7	.286
			BLTL			

FITZGERALD, D.G.

YR	CL	LEA	POS	GP	G	REC
1890	ROC	AA	P		12	3- 8

FITZGERALD, DENNIS S.
B.BOSTON,MASS.

YR	CL	LEA	POS	GP	G	REC
1890	ATH	AA	S		2	.429

FITZGERALD, EDWARD RAYMOND
B.MAY 21,1924 SANTA YNEZ,CAL.

YR	CL	LEA	POS	GP	G	REC
1948	PIT	N	C		102	.267
1949	PIT	N	C		75	.263
1950	PIT	N	C		6	.067
1951	PIT	N	C		55	.227
1952	PIT	N	C-3		51	.233
1953	PIT	N	C		6	.118
	WAS	A	C		88	.250
1954	WAS	A	C		115	.289
1955	WAS	A	C		74	.237
1956	WAS	A	C		64	.304
1957	WAS	A	C		45	.272
1958	WAS	A	C-1		58	.263
1959	WAS	A	C		19	.194
	CLE	A	C		49	.271
			BRTR		807	.260

FITZGERALD, HOWARD CHUMNEY (LEFTY)
B.MAY 16,1902 EAGLE LAKE,TEX.
D.FEB.27,1959 EAGLE FALLS,TEX.

YR	CL	LEA	POS	GP	G	REC
1922	CHI	N	O		16	.330
1924	CHI	N	O		7	.158
1926	BOS	A	O		31	.258
			BLTL		48	.259

FITZGERALD, JOHN FRANCIS
B.SEPT.15,1933 BROOKLYN,N.Y.

YR	CL	LEA	POS	GP	G	REC
1958	SF	N	P		1	0- 0
			BLTL			

FITZGERALD, JOHN H.
B.MAY 30,1870 NATICK,MASS.

YR	CL	LEA	POS	GP	G	REC
1891	BOS	AA	P		6	2- 1

FITZGERALD, JOHN T.
B.LEADVILLE,COL.

YR	CL	LEA	POS	GP	G	REC
1891	LOU	AA	P	31	32	12-17
1892	LOU	N	P		4	1- 3
				35	36	13-20

FITZGERALD, JUSTIN HOWARD
B.JUNE 22,1890 SAN MATEO,CAL.
D.JAN.17,1945 SAN MATEO,CAL.

YR	CL	LEA	POS	GP	G	REC
1911	NY	A	O		16	.270
1918	PHI	N	O		66	.293
			BLTR		82	.288

FITZGERALD, MATTHEW WILLIAM
B.AUG.31,1880 ALBANY,N.Y.
D.SEPT.22,1949 ALBANY,N.Y.

YR	CL	LEA	POS	GP	G	REC
1906	NY	N	C		4	.500
1907	NY	N	C		6	.133
			TR		10	.200

FITZGERALD, RAYMOND FRANCIS
B.DEC.5,1904 CHICOPEE,MASS.
D.SEPT.6,1977 WESTFIELD,MASS.

YR	CL	LEA	POS	GP	G	REC
1931	CIN	N	H		1	.000
			BRTR			

FITZKE, PAUL FREDERICK HERMAN (BOB)
B.JULY 30,1900 LACROSSE,WIS.
D.JUNE 30,1950 SACRAMENTO,CAL.

YR	CL	LEA	POS	GP	G	REC
1924	CLE	A	P		1	0- 0
			BLTL			

FITZMAURICE, SHAUN EARLE
B.AUG.25,1942 WORCESTER,MASS.

YR	CL	LEA	POS	GP	G	REC
1966	NY	N	/O		9	.154
			BRTR			

FITZMORRIS, ALAN JAMES (AL)
B.MAR.21,1946 BUFFALO,N.Y.

YR	CL	LEA	POS	GP	G	REC
1969	KC	A	/P		7	1- 1
1970	KC	A	P	43	45	8- 5
1971	KC	A	P		36	7- 5
1972	KC	A	P	38	39	2- 5
1973	KC	A	P		15	8- 3
1974	KC	A	P		34	13- 6
1975	KC	A	P		35	16-12
1976	KC	A	P	35	37	15-11
1977	CLE	A	P		29	6-10
1978	CLE	A	/P		7	0- 1
	CAL	A	/P		9	1- 0
			BBTR	288	293	77-59

FITZPATRICK, EDWARD HENRY
B.DEC.9,1889 PHILLIPSBURG,PA.
D.OCT.23,1965 BETHLEHEM,PA.

YR	CL	LEA	POS	GP	G	REC
1915	BOS	N	2-O		105	.221
1916	BOS	N	2-O		83	.213
1917	BOS	N	2-3-O		63	.253
			BRTR		251	.227

FITZSIMMONS, FREDERICK LANDIS (FAT FREDDIE)
B.JULY 28,1901 MISHAWAKA,IND.

YR	CL	LEA	POS	GP	G	REC
1925	NY	N	P		10	6- 3
1926	NY	N	P		37	14-10
1927	NY	N	P		42	17-10
1928	NY	N	P		40	20- 9
1929	NY	N	P		37	15-11
1930	NY	N	P		41	19- 7
1931	NY	N	P		35	18-11
1932	NY	N	P		35	11-11
1933	NY	N	P		36	16-11
1934	NY	N	P		38	18-14
1935	NY	N	P		18	4- 8
1936	NY	N	P		28	10- 7
1937	NY	N	P		6	2- 2
	BRO	N	P		13	4- 6
1938	BRO	N	P		27	11- 8
1939	BRO	N	P		27	7- 9
1940	BRO	N	P		20	16- 2
1941	BRO	N	P		13	6- 1
1942	BRO	N	P		1	0- 0
1943	BRO	N	P		9	3- 4
			BRTR		513	217-146

NON-PLAYING MANAGER PHI[N] 1943-45

FITZSIMMONS, THOMAS WILLIAM
B.APR.6,1890 OAKLAND,CAL.
D.DEC.20,1971 OAKLAND,CAL.

YR	CL	LEA	POS	GP	G	REC
1919	BRO	N	3		4	.000
			BRTR			

FLACK, MAX JOHN
B.FEB.5,1890 BELLEVILLE,ILL.
D.JULY 31,1975 BELLEVILLE,ILL.

YR	CL	LEA	POS	GP	G	REC
1914	CHI	F	O		135	.253
1915	CHI	F	O		141	.315
1916	CHI	N	O		141	.258
1917	CHI	N	O		131	.248
1918	CHI	N	O		123	.257
1919	CHI	N	O		116	.294
1920	CHI	N	O		135	.302
1921	CHI	N	O		133	.301
1922	CHI	N	O		17	.222
	STL	N	O		66	.292
1923	STL	N	O		128	.291
1924	STL	N	O		67	.263
1925	STL	N	O		79	.249
			BLTL		1412	.279

FLAGER, WALTER LEONARD
B.NOV.3,1921 CHICAGO HEIGHTS,ILL.

YR	CL	LEA	POS	GP	G	REC
1945	CHI	N	S		21	.212
	PHI	N	2-S		49	.250
			BLTR		70	.241

FLAGSTEAD, IRA JAMES (PETE)
B.SEPT.22,1893 MONTAGUE,MICH.
D.MAR.13,1940 OLYMPIA,WASH.

YR	CL	LEA	POS	GP	G	REC
1917	DET	A	O		4	.000
1919	DET	A	O		97	.331
1920	DET	A	O		110	.235
1921	DET	A	S-O		85	.305
1922	DET	A	O		4	.000
1923	DET	A	O		1	.000
	BOS	A	O		109	.312
1924	BOS	A	C		149	.304
1925	BOS	A	C		148	.280
1926	BOS	A	O		98	.299
1927	BOS	A	O		131	.285
1928	BOS	A	O		140	.290
1929	BOS	A	O		16	.325
	WAS	A	O		16	.143
	PIT	N	O		26	.280
1930	PIT	N	O		44	.250
			BRTR		1218	.290

FLAHERTY, P. J.
B.WORCESTER,MASS.

YR	CL	LEA	POS	GP	G	REC
1881	WOR	N	O		1	.000
			BLTL			

FLAHERTY, PATRICK HENRY
B.JUNE 24,1862 ST.LOUIS,MO.
D.JAN.30,1946 CHICAGO,ILL.

YR	CL	LEA	POS	GP	G	REC
1894	LOU	N	3		38	.295

YR	CL LEA POS	GP	G	REC

FLAHERTY, PATRICK JOSEPH
B.JUNE 29,1876 CARNEGIE,PA.
D.JAN.23,1968 ALEXANDRIA,LA.

1899 LOU N P		7	2- 3
1900 PIT N P		4	0- 1
1903 CHI A P		39	11-25
1904 CHI A P		5	3- 2
PIT N P	29	31	19- 9
1905 PIT N P	27	29	10-10
1907 BOS N P	27	35	12-15
1908 BOS N P		31	12-18
1910 PHI N P-O	1	2	0- 0
			.500
1911 BOS N P-O	2	23	0- 2
			.287
BLTL	172	206	69-85
			.196

FLAIR, ALBERT DELL (BROADWAY)
B.JULY 24,1916 NEW ORLEANS,LA.
| 1941 BOS A 1 | | 10 | .200 |
| BLTL |

FLANAGAN, CHARLES JAMES
B.DEC.31,1891 OAKLAND,CAL.
D.JAN.8,1930 SAN FRANCISCO,CAL.
| 1913 STL A 3 | | 4 | .000 |
| BRTR |

FLANAGAN, EDWARD J. (SLEEPY)
B.SEPT.15,1861 LOWELL,MASS.
D.NOV.10,1926 LOWELL,MASS.
1887 ATH AA 1		19	.277
1889 LOU AA 1		23	.247
		42	.255

FLANAGAN, JAMES PAUL (STEAMER)
B.APR.20,1881 KINGSTON,PA.
D.APR.21,1947 WILKES-BARRE,PA.
| 1905 PIT N O | | 7 | .280 |

FLANAGAN, MICHAEL KENDALL (MIKE)
B.DEC.16,1951 MANCHESTER,N.H.
1975 BAL A /P		2	0- 1
1976 BAL A P		20	3- 5
1977 BAL A P		36	15-10
1978 BAL A P		40	19-15
BLTL		98	37-31

FLANIGAN, RAYMOND ARTHUR
B.JAN.8,1923 MORGANTOWN,W.VA.
| 1946 CLE A P | | 3 | 0- 1 |
| BRTR |

FLANIGAN, THOMAS ANTHONY (TOM)
B.SEPT.6,1934 CINCINNATI,OHIO
1954 CHI A P		2	0- 0
1958 STL N P		1	0- 0
BRTL		3	0- 0

FLANNERY, JOHN MICHAEL
B.JAN.25,1957 LONG BEACH,CAL.
| 1977 CHI A /S-3 | | 7 | .000 |
| BRTR |

FLASKAMPER, RAYMOND HAROLD (FLASH)
B.OCT.31,1901 ST.LOUIS,MO.
D.FEB.3,1978 SAN ANTONIO,TEX.
| 1927 CHI A S | | 26 | .221 |
| BBTR |

FLATER, JOHN WILLIAM (JACK)
B.SEPT.22,1880 SANDYMOUNT,MD.
D.MAR.20,1970 WESTMINSTER,MD.
| 1908 PHI A P | | 5 | 1- 3 |
| TR |

FLAVIN, JOHN THOMAS
B.MAY 7,1942 ALBANY,CAL.
| 1964 CHI N P | | 5 | 0- 1 |
| BLTL |

FLEET, FRANK M.
B.1848 NEW YORK,N.Y.
D.JUNE 13,1900
1871 MUT NA P		1	0- 1
1872 ECK NA 2-3-O		13	.190
1873 RES NA P-1-	3	21	0- 3
			-
			2-3-S
1874 ATL NA C-2-O		19	-
1875 STL NA P		3	2- 1
ATL NA P-C-	1	25	0- 1
			2-S
		8	82	2- 6
			-

FLEITAS, ANGEL FELIX HUSTA
B.NOV.10,1914 CIENFUEGOS,CUBA
| 1948 WAS A S | | 15 | .077 |
| BRTR |

FLEMING, LESLIE FLETCHARD (BILL)
B.JULY 31,1913 ROWLAND,CAL.
1940 BOS A P		10	1- 2
1941 BOS A P		16	1- 1
1942 CHI N P		33	5- 6
1943 CHI N P		11	0- 1
1944 CHI N P	39	40	9-10
1946 CHI N P		14	0- 1
BRTR	123	124	16-21

FLEMING, LESLIE HARVEY (MOE)
B.AUG.7,1915 SINGLETON,TEX.
1939 DET A O		8	.000
1941 CLE A 1		2	.250
1942 CLE A 1-O		156	.292
1945 CLE A 1-O		42	.329
1946 CLE A 1-O		99	.278
1947 CLE A 1		103	.242
1949 PIT N 1		24	.258
BLTL		434	.277

FLEMING, THOMAS VINCENT (SLEUTH)
B.NOV.20,1873 PHILADELPHIA,PA.
D.DEC.26,1957 BOSTON,MASS.
1899 NY N O		20	.257
1902 PHI N O		5	.375
1904 PHI N O		2	.000
		27	.261

FLETCHER
| 1872 ECK NA O | | 2 | .250 |

FLETCHER, ALFRED VANDIDE (VAN)
B.AUG.6,1924 EAST BEND,N.C.
| 1955 DET A P | | 9 | 0- 0 |
| BRTR |

FLETCHER, ARTHUR
B.JAN.5,1885 COLLINSVILLE,ILL.
D.FEB.6,1950 LOS ANGELES,CAL.
1909 NY N S		29	.214
1910 NY N S		44	.224
1911 NY N S-3		108	.319
1912 NY N S		129	.282
1913 NY N S		136	.297
1914 NY N S		135	.286
1915 NY N S		149	.254
1916 NY N S		133	.286
1917 NY N S		151	.260
1918 PHI N S		124	.263
1919 NY N S		127	.277
1920 NY N S		41	.254
PHI N S		102	.297
1922 PHI N S		110	.280
BRTR	1518	.277
NON-PLAYING MANAGER
PHI[N] 1923-26, NY[A] 1929

FLETCHER, ELBURT PRESTON
B.MAR.18,1916 MILTON,MASS.
1934 BOS N 1		8	.500
1935 BOS N 1		39	.236
1937 BOS N 1		148	.247
1938 BOS N 1		147	.272
1939 BOS N 1		35	.245
PIT N 1		102	.303
1940 PIT N 1		147	.273
1941 PIT N 1		151	.288
1942 PIT N 1		145	.289
1943 PIT N 1		154	.283
1946 PIT N 1		148	.256
1947 PIT N 1		69	.242
1949 BOS N 1		122	.261
BLTL		1415	.271

FLETCHER, O. FRANK
B.MAR.6,1891 HILDRETH,ILL.
D.OCT.7,1974 ST.PETERSBURG,FLA.
| 1914 PHI N H | | 1 | .000 |
| BRTR |

FLETCHER, SAMUEL S.
B.ALTOONA,PA.
1909 BRO N P		1	0- 1
1912 CIN N P		2	0- 0
TR		3	0- 1

FLETCHER, THOMAS WAYNE
B.JUNE 28,1942 ELMIRA,N.Y.
| 1962 DET A P | | 1 | 0- 0 |
| BBTL |

FLICK, ELMER HARRISON
B.JAN.11,1876 BEDFORD,OHIO
D.JAN.9,1971 BEDFORD,OHIO
1898 PHI N O		133	.319
1899 PHI N O		125	.343
1900 PHI N O		138	.378
1901 PHI N O		138	.336
1902 PHI A O		11	.324
CLE A O		110	.293
1903 CLE A O		142	.299
1904 CLE A O		149	.303
1905 CLE A O		131	.306
1906 CLE A O		157	.311
1907 CLE A O		147	.302
1908 CLE A O		9	.212
1909 CLE A O		66	.255
1910 CLE A O		24	.265
BLTR		1480	.315

FLICK, LEWIS MILLER (NOISY)
B.FEB.18,1915 BRISTOL,TENN.
1943 PHI A O		1	.600
1944 PHI A O		19	.114
BLTL		20	.175

FLINN, DON RAPHAEL
B.NOV.17,1892 BLUFFDALE,TEX.
D.MAR.9,1959 WACO,TEX.
| 1917 PIT N O | | 14 | .298 |
| BRTR |

FLINN, JOHN RICHARD
B.SEPT.2,1954 MERCED,CAL.
| 1978 BAL A P | | 13 | 1- 1 |
| BRTR |

FLINT, FRANK SYLVESTER (SILVER)
B.AUG.3,1855 PHILADELPHIA,PA.
D.JAN.14,1892 CHICAGO,ILL.
1875 RS NA C-3		17	-
1878 IND N C		60	.228
1879 CHI N C		75	.290
1880 CHI N C-O		71	.167
1881 CHI N C-1-O		80	.310
1882 CHI N C-O		81	.250
1883 CHI N C-O		84	.265
1884 CHI N C-O		71	.207
1885 CHI N C-O		67	.208
1886 CHI N C		49	.202
1887 CHI N C		48	.282
1888 CHI N C		22	.181
1889 CHI N C		15	.232
BRTR		740	-

FLITCRAFT, HILDRETH MILTON (HILLY)
B.AUG.21,1923 WOODSTOWN,N.J.
| 1942 PHI N P | | 3 | 0- 0 |
| BLTL |

FLOHR, MORITZ HERMAN (DUTCH)
B.AUG.15,1911 CANISTEO,N.Y.
| 1934 PHI A P | | 15 | 0- 2 |
| BLTL |

FLOOD, CURTIS CHARLES (CURT)
B.JAN.18,1938 HOUSTON,TEX.
1956 CIN N H		5	.000
1957 CIN N 2-3		3	.333
1958 STL N 3-O		121	.261
1959 STL N 3-O		121	.255
1960 STL N 3-O		140	.237
1961 STL N O		132	.322
1962 STL N O		151	.296
1963 STL N O		158	.302
1964 STL N O		162	.311
1965 STL N *O		156	.310
1966 STL N *O		160	.267
1967 STL N *O		134	.335
1968 STL N *O		150	.301
1969 STL N *O		153	.285
1971 WAS A O		13	.200
BRTR		1759	.293

FLOOD, TIMOTHY A.
B.MAR.13,1877 MONTGOMERY CITY,MO.
D.JUNE 15,1929 ST.LOUIS,MO.
1899 STL N 2		9	.333
1902 BRO N 2-O		131	.228
1903 BRO N 2		87	.249
BRTR		227	.239

FLORENCE, PAUL ROBERT (PEP)
B.APR.22,1900 CHICAGO,ILL.
| 1926 NY N C | | 76 | .229 |
| BBTR |

FLORES, GILBERTO [GARCIA] (GIL)
B.OCT.27,1952 PONCE,P.R.
1977 CAL A O		104	.278
1978 NY N /O		11	.276
BRTR		115	.278

YR	CL	LEA	POS	GP	G	REC

FLORES, JESSE SANDOVAL
B.NOV.2,1914 GUADALAJARA,MEXICO

1942 CHI	N	P		4	0- 1
1943 PHI	A	P		31	12-14
1944 PHI	A	P		27	9-11
1945 PHI	A	P		29	7-10
1946 PHI	A	P		29	9- 7
1947 PHI	A	P		28	4-13
1950 CLE	AA	P		28	3- 3
BRTR				176	44-59

FLOWERS, BENNETT (BEN)
B.JUNE 15,1927 WILSON,N.C.

1951 BOS	A	P		1	0- 0
1953 BOS	A	P		32	1- 4
1955 DET	A	P		4	0- 0
STL	N	P		4	1- 0
1956 STL	N	P		3	1- 1
PHI	N	P		32	0- 2
BRTR				76	3- 7

FLOWERS, CHARLES RICHARD
B.185G PHILADELPHIA,PA.
D.OCT.9,1892

1871 TRO	NA	2-S		21	.303
1872 ATH	NA	S		3	.235
				24	.294

FLOWERS, CHARLES WESLEY (WES)
B.AUG.13,1913 VANNDALE,ARK.

1940 BRO	N	P		5	1- 1
1944 BRO	N	P		9	1- 1
BLTL				14	2- 2

FLOWERS, D'ARCY RAYMOND (JAKE)
B.MAR.16,1902 CAMBRIDGE,MD.
D.DEC.27,1962 CLEARWATER,FLA.

1923 STL	N	2-S-3		13	.094
1926 STL	N	2		40	.270
1927 BRO	N	S		67	.234
1928 BRO	N	2		103	.274
1929 BRO	N	2		46	.200
1930 BRO	N	2		89	.320
1931 BRO	N	2-S		22	.226
STL	N	2-S		45	.248
1932 STL	N	3		67	.255
1933 BRO	N	2-S-3-O		78	.233
1934 CIN	N	H		13	.333
BRTR				583	.255

FLOYD, LESLIE ROE (BUBBA)
B.JUNE 23,1917 DALLAS,TEX.

| 1944 DET | A | S | | 3 | .444 |
| BRTR | | | | | |

FLOYD, ROBERT NATHAN (BOBBY)
B.OCT.20,1943 HAWTHORNE,CAL.

1968 BAL	A	/S		5	.111
1969 BAL	A	2-S/3		39	.202
1970 BAL	A	/3		3	.000
KC	A	/S-3		14	.326
1971 KC	A	S/2-3		31	.152
1972 KC	A	3-S/2		61	.179
1973 KC	A	2-S		51	.333
1974 KC	A	/2-3-S		10	.111
BRTR				214	.219

FLUHRER, JOHN L.
[ALSO PLAYED UNDER NAME OF
WM. G. MORRIS 1 GAME IN 1915]
B.JAN.3,1894 ADRIAN,MICH.
D.JULY 7,1946 COLUMBUS,OHIO

| 1915 CHI | N | O | | 7 | .400 |
| BRTR | | | | | |

**FLYNN, CORNELIUS FRANCIS XAVIER
(CARNEY)**
B.JAN.23,1875 CINCINNATI,OHIO
D.FEB.10,1947 CINCINNATI,OHIO

1894 CIN	N	P		2	0- 0
1896 NY	N	P		3	0- 0
WAS	N	P		4	0- 1
BLTL				9	0- 2

FLYNN, EDWARD J.
B.CHICAGO,ILL.
1887 CLE | AA | 3 | | 7 | .215 |

FLYNN, GEORGE A. (DIBBY)
B.MAY 24,1870 CHICAGO,ILL.
D.DEC.28,1901 CHICAGO,ILL.

| 1896 CHI | N | O | | 29 | .267 |

FLYNN, JOHN A. (JOCKO)
B.JUNE 30,1864 LAWRENCE,MASS.
D.DEC.30,1907 LAWRENCE,MASS.

1886 CHI	N	P-O	32	56	24- 6
					.200
1887 CHI	N	O		1	.000
			32	57	24- 6
					.200

FLYNN, JOHN ANTHONY
B.SEPT.7,1883 PROVIDENCE,R.I.
D.MAR.23,1935 PROVIDENCE,R.I.

1910 PIT	N	1		93	.274
1911 PIT	N	1-3		32	.214
1912 WAS	A	1		20	.169
BRTR				145	.251

FLYNN, JOSEPH
B.PHILADELPHIA,PA.

1884 KEY	U	C-1-S-O		50	.244
BOS	U	C-1-O		9	.233
				59	.242

FLYNN, MICHAEL E.
B.LOWELL,MASS.

| 1891 BOS | AA | C | | 1 | .000 |

FLYNN, ROBERT DOUGLAS (DOUG)
B.APR.18,1951 LEXINGTON,KY.

1975 CIN	N	3-2-S		89	.268
1976 CIN	N	2-S		93	.283
1977 CIN	N	3/2-S		36	.250
NY	N	S-2/3		90	.191
1978 NY	N	*2-S		156	.237
BRTR				464	.238

FLYNN, WILLIAM (CLIPPER)
B.1850 NEW YORK
D.NOV.11,1881 LANSINGBURGH,N.Y.

1871 TRO	NA	1-3-O		29	.311
1872 OLY	NA	1		9	.220
				38	.291

FLYTHE, STUART MCGUIRE
B.DEC.9,1911 CONWAY,N.C.
D.OCT.18,1963 DURHAM,N.C.

| 1936 PHI | A | P | | 17 | 0- 0 |
| BRTR | | | | | |

FODGE, EUGENE ARLAN (GENE) OR (SUDS)
B.JULY 9,1931 SOUTH BEND,IND.

| 1958 CHI | N | P | | 16 | 1- 1 |
| BRTR | | | | | |

FOGARTY, JAMES G.
B.FEB.12,1864 SAN FRANCISCO,CAL
D.MAY 20,1891 PHILADELPHIA,PA.

1884 PHI	N	P-2-	1	95	0- 0
		S-3-O			.211
1885 PHI	N	2-S-3-O		111	.251
1886 PHI	N	O		76	.292
1887 PHI	N	O		126	.365
1888 PHI	N	O		120	.235
1889 PHI	N	O		128	.258
1890 PHI	P	M-O		91	.251
BR			1	747	0- 0
					.268

FOGARTY, JOSEPH J.
B.SAN FRANCISCO,CAL.
1885 STL | N | O | | 2 | .125 |

FOGEL, HORACE S.
B.MAR.2,1861 MACUNGIE,PA.
D.NOV.15,1928 PHILADELPHIA,PA.
NON-PLAYING MANAGER
IND[N] 1887; NY[N] 1902

FOHL, LEO ALEXANDER (LEE)
B.NOV.28,1870 PITTSBURGH,PA.
D.OCT.30,1965 CLEVELAND,OHIO

1902 PIT	N			1	.000
1903 CIN	N	C		4	.357
BLTR				5	.294

NON-PLAYING MANAGER
CLE[A] 1915-19, STL[A] 1921-23,
BOS[A] 1924-26

FOILES, HENRY LEE (HANK)
B.JUNE 10,1929 RICHMOND,VA.

1953 CIN	N	C		5	.154
CLE	A	C		7	.143
1955 CLE	A	C		62	.261
1956 CLE	A	C		1	.000
PIT	N	C		79	.262
1957 PIT	N	C		109	.270
1958 PIT	N	C		104	.205
1959 PIT	N	C		93	.225
1960 KC	A	C		6	.571
CLE	A	C		24	.279
DET	A	C		26	.250
1961 BAL	A	C		43	.274
1962 CIN	N	C		43	.275
1963 CIN	N	C		1	.000
LA	A	C		41	.214
1964 LA	A	H		4	.250
BRTR				608	.243

FOLEY, CHARLES JOSEPH (CURRY)
B.JAN.14,1856 MILLTOWN,IRELAND
D.OCT.20,1898 NEW YORK,N.Y.

1879 BOS	N	P-O	18	35	5- 8
					.313
1880 BOS	N	P-1-	28	78	14-14
		O			.285
1881 BUF	N	P-1-	6	83	2- 4
		O			.256
1882 BUF	N	P-O	1	84	0- 0
					.305
1883 BUF	N	P-O		23	1- 0
					.270
TL			54	303	22-26
					.283

FOLEY, JOHN J
B.HANNIBAL,MO.
1885 PRO | N | P | | 1 | 0- 1 |

FOLEY, MARVIS EDWIN (MARV)
B.AUG.29,1953 STANFORD,KY.

| 1978 CHI | A | C | | 11 | .353 |
| BLTR | | | | | |

FOLEY, RAYMOND KIRWIN
B.JUNE 23,1906 NAUGATUCK,CONN.

| 1928 NY | N | H | | 2 | .000 |
| BLTR | | | | | |

FOLEY, THOMAS J.
B.AUG.16,1842 CASHEL,IRELAND
D.NOV.3,1926
1871 CHI | NA | M-C-3-O | | 18 | - |

FOLEY, WILLIAM BROWN (WILL)
B.NOV.15,1855 CHICAGO,ILL.
D.NOV.15,1916 CHICAGO,ILL.

1875 CHI	NA	3		3	-
1876 CIN	N	C-3		58	.226
1877 CIN	N	3		56	.188
1878 MIL	N	C-3		55	.271
1879 CIN	N	2-3-O		55	.213
1884 CHI	U	3		5	.116
1884 CHI	U	3		18	.294
BRTR				250	-

FOLI, TIMOTHY JOHN (TIM)
B.DEC.6,1950 CULVER CITY,CAL.

1970 NY	N	/S-3		5	.364
1971 NY	N	2-3-S/O		97	.226
1972 MON	N	*S/2		149	.241
1973 MON	N	*S/2-O		122	.240
1974 MON	N	*S/3		121	.254
1975 MON	N	*S/2		152	.238
1976 MON	N	*S		149	.264
1977 MON	N	S		13	.175
SF	N	*S/2-3-O		164	.228
1978 NY	N	*S		113	.257
BRTR				1029	.244

FOLKERS, RICHARD NEVIN (RICH)
B.OCT.17,1946 WATERLOO,IOWA

1970 NY	N	P		16	0- 2
1972 STL	N	P		9	1- 0
1973 STL	N	P		34	4- 4
1974 STL	N	P		55	6- 2
1975 SD	N	P		45	6-11
.976 SD	N	P		33	2- 3
1977 MIL	A	/P		3	0- 1
BLTL				195	19-23

FONDY, DEE VIRGIL
B.OCT.31,1924 SLATON,TEX.

1951 CHI	N	1		49	.271
1952 CHI	N	1		145	.300
1953 CHI	N	1		150	.309
1954 CHI	N	1		141	.285
1955 CHI	N	1		150	.265
1956 CHI	N	1		137	.269
1957 CHI	N	1		11	.314
PIT	N	1		95	.313
1958 CIN	N	1-O		89	.218
BLTL				967	.283

FONSECA, LEWIS ALBERT (LEW)
B.JAN.21,1899 OAKLAND,CAL.

1921 CIN	N	1-2-O		82	.276
1922 CIN	N	2		81	.361
1923 CIN	N	1-2		65	.278
1924 CIN	N	1-2		20	.228
1925 PHI	N	1-2		126	.319
1927 CLE	A	1-2		112	.311
1928 CLE	A	1-3		75	.327
1929 CLE	A	1		148	.369
1930 CLE	A	1		40	.279
1931 CLE	A	1		26	.370
CHI	A	1-2-O		121	.299
1932 CHI	A	M-P-	1	18	0- 0
		O			.135
1933 CHI	A	M-1		23	.203
BRTR			1	937	0- 0
					.316

NON-PLAYING MANAGER CHI[A] 1934

FOOR, JAMES EMERSON (JIM)
B.JAN.19,1949 ST.LOUIS,MO.

1971 DET	A	/P		3	0- 0
1972 DET	A	/P		7	1- 0
1973 PIT	N	/P		3	0- 0
BLTL				13	1- 0

FOOTE, BARRY CLIFTON
B.FEB.16,1952 SMITHFIELD,N.C.

1973 MON	N	/H		6	.667
1974 MON	N	*C		125	.262
1975 MON	N	*C		118	.194
1976 MON	N	C/1		105	.234
1977 MON	N	C		15	.245
PHI	N	C		18	.219
1978 MON	N	C		39	.158
BRTR				426	.230

YR   CL LEA POS   GP   G   REC

FORAN, JAMES H.
B.1848 NEW YORK
1871 KEK NA 1-O   19   -

FORCE, DAVID W. (WEE DAVEY)
B.JULY 27,1849 NEW YORK,N.Y.
D.JUNE 21,1918 ENGLEWOOD,N.J.
1871 OLY NA S-3   32   -
1872 TRO NA S-3   25   .414
     BAL NA 3   18   .409
1873 BAL NA P-S-   2   48   1- 1
            3   -
1874 CHI NA S-3-O   59   -
1875 ATH NA S   77   .312
1876 ATH N S   60   .228
1877 STL N S-3   58   .258
1879 BUF N S   78   .209
1880 BUF N 2-S   78   .162
1881 BUF N 2-S-3-O   75   .179
1882 BUF N 2-S-3   73   .241
1883 BUF N 2-S-3   93   .213
1884 BUF N 2-S   102   .208
1885 BUF N 2-S-3   71   .225
1886 WAS N S   68   .181
     BRTR   2   1017   1- 1
                                 -

FORD, DARNELL GLENN (DAN)
B.MAY 19,1952 LOS ANGELES,CAL.
1975 MIN A *O   130   .280
1976 MIN A *O   145   .267
1977 MIN A *O   144   .267
1978 MIN A *O   151   .274
     BRTR   570   .272

FORD, DAVID ALAN (DAVE)
B.DEC.29,1956 CLEVELAND,OHIO
1978 BAL A /P   2   1- 0
     BRTR

FORD, E. L.
B.RICHMOND,VA.
1884 RIC AA 1-S   2   .000

FORD, EDWARD CHARLES (WHITEY)
OR (CHAIRMAN OF THE BOARD)
B.OCT.21,1928 NEW YORK,N.Y.
1950 NY A P   20   9- 1
1953 NY A P   32   33 18- 6
1954 NY A P   34 16- 8
1955 NY A P   39 18- 7
1956 NY A P   31 19- 6
1957 NY A P   24 11- 5
1958 NY A P   30 14- 7
1959 NY A P   35 16-10
1960 NY A P   33 12- 9
1961 NY A P   39 25- 4
1962 NY A P   38 17- 8
1963 NY A P   38 24- 7
1964 NY A P   39 17- 6
1965 NY A P   37   38 16-13
1966 NY A P   22   2- 5
1967 NY A /P   7   2- 4
     BLTL   498 500 236-106

FORD, EUGENE MATTHEW
B.JUNE 23,1912 FT.DODGE,IOWA
D.SEPT.7,1970 EMMETSBURG,IOWA
1936 BOS N P   2   0- 0
1938 CHI A P   4   0- 0
     BRTR   6   0- 0

FORD, EUGENE WYMAN
B.APR.16,1881 MILTON,N.S.,CAN.
D.AUG.21,1973 DUNEDIN,FLA.
1905 DET A P   7   0- 2
     BRTR

FORD, HORACE HILLS (HOD)
B.JULY 23,1897 NEW HAVEN,CONN.
D.JAN.29,1977 WINCHESTER,MASS.
1919 BOS N 2   10   .214
1920 BOS N 2-S   88   .241
1921 BOS N 2-S   152   .279
1922 BOS N 2-S   143   .271
1923 BOS N 2-S   111   .271
1924 PHI N 2   145   .272
1925 BRO N S   66   .273
1926 CIN N S   57   .279
1927 CIN N 2-S   115   .274
1928 CIN N S   149   .241
1929 CIN N 2-S   148   .276
1930 CIN N 2-S   132   .231
1931 CIN N 2-S-3   84   .229
1932 STL N S   1   .000
     BOS N 2-S   40   .274
1933 BOS N S   5   .067
     BRTR   1446   .263

FORD, PERCIVAL EDMUND WENTWORTH
(WENTY)
B.NOV.25,1946 NASSAU,BAHAMAS
1973 ATL N /P   4   1- 2
     BRTR

FORD, RUSSELL WILLIAM
B.APR.25,1883 BRANDON,MAN.,CAN.
D.JAN.24,1960 ROCKINGHAM,N.C.
1909 NY A P   1   0- 0
1910 NY A P   36   26- 6
1911 NY A P   37   22-11
1912 NY A P   36   39   13-21
1913 NY A P   33   11-18
1914 BUF F P   35   21- 6
1915 BUF F P   21   5- 9
     BRTR   199 202   98-71

FORD, THEODORE HENRY (TED)
B.FEB.7,1947 VINELAND,N.J.
1970 CLE A O   26   .174
1971 CLE A O   74   .194
1972 TEX A *O   129   .235
1973 CLE A *O   11   .225
     BRTR   240   .219

FORD, THOMAS WALTER
B.1866 CHATTANOOGA,TENN.
1890 COL AA P   1   0- 1
     BRO AA P-S   7   10   0- 6
                                .034
                   8   11   0- 7
                                .032

FOREMAN, AUGUST (HAPPY)
B.JULY 20,1897 MEMPHIS,TENN.
D.FEB.13,1953 NEW YORK,N.Y.
1924 CHI A P   5   0- 0
1926 BOS A P   3   0- 0
     BLTL   8   0- 0

FOREMAN, FRANCIS ISAIAH (MONKEY)
B.MAY 1,1863 BALTIMORE,MD.
D.NOV.19,1957 BALTIMORE,MD.
1884 CHI U P-O   3   1- 0
                                .091
     KC U P   1   0- 1
1885 BAL AA P-O   3   2- 1
                                .286
1889 BAL AA P   51   54   25-21
1890 CIN N P   24   13-11
1891 CIN N P   1   0- 0
     WAS AA P   44   49   22-22
1892 WAS N P   11   2- 5
     BAL N P   5   0- 2
1893 NY N P   2   0- 1
1895 CIN N P   25   11-14
1896 CIN N P   22   12- 6
1901 BOS A P   1   0- 1
     BAL A P   23   13- 7
1902 BAL A P   2   0- 2
     BLTL   218 226 101-94
                                .227

FOREMAN, JOHN DAVIS (BROWNIE)
B.AUG.6,1875 BALTIMORE,MD.
D.OCT.10,1926 BALTIMORE,MD.
1895 PIT N P   19   8- 7
1896 PIT N P   9   3- 4
     CIN N P   5   2- 3
     BLTL   33   13-14

FORMAN, WILLIAM ORANGE (BILL)
B.OCT.10,1886 VENANGO,PA.
D.OCT.3,1958 UNIONTOWN,PA.
1909 WAS A P   2   0- 2
1910 WAS A P   1   0- 0
     BBTR   3   0- 2

FORNIELES, JOSE MIGUEL (TORRES)
(MIKE)
B.JAN.18,1932 HAVANA,CUBA
1952 WAS A P   4   2- 2
1954 CHI A P   39   8- 7
1955 CHI A P   15   16   1- 2
1956 CHI A P   6   0- 1
1957 BAL A P   15   16   2- 6
     BOS A P   25   26   8- 7
1958 BOS A P   37   4- 6
1959 BOS A P   46   5- 3
1960 BOS A P   70   10- 5
1961 BOS A P   57   9- 8
1962 BOS A P   42   3- 6
1963 BOS A P   9   0- 0
     MIN A P   11   1- 1
     BRTR   432 440   63-64

FORSCH, KENNETH ROTH (KEN)
B.SEP.8,1946 SACRAMENTO,CAL.
1970 HOU N /P   4   1- 2
1971 HOU N P   33   8- 8
1972 HOU N P   30   6- 8
1973 HOU N P   46   9-12
1974 HOU N P   70   8- 7
1975 HOU N P   34   4- 8
1976 HOU N P   52   4- 3
1977 HOU N P   42   3- 8
1978 HOU N P   52   10- 6
     BRTR   363   55-62

FORSCH, ROBERT HERBERT (BOB)
B.JAN.13,1950 SACRAMENTO,CAL.
1974 STL N P   19   20   7- 4
1975 STL N P   34   35   15-10
1976 STL N P   33   35   8-10
1977 STL N P   35   20- 7
1978 STL N P   34   11-17
     BRTR   155 159   61-48

FORSTER, TERRY JAY
B.JAN.14,1952 SIOUX FALLS,S.D.
1971 CHI A P   45   2- 3
1972 CHI A P   62   63   6- 5
1973 CHI A P   51   53   6-11
1974 CHI A P   59   7- 8
1975 CHI A P   17   3- 3
1976 CHI A P   29   2-12
1977 PIT N P/O   33   36   6- 4
                                .346
1978 LA   N P   47   5- 4
     BLTL   343 349   37-50
                                .424

FORSTER, THOMAS W.
B.MAY 1,1859 NEW YORK,N.Y.
D.JULY 17,1946 NEW YORK,N.Y.
1882 DET N 2-3   20   .098
1884 PIT AA S-3   35   .212
1885 MET AA 2   57   .220
1886 MET AA 2   84   .205
                       196   .200

FORSYTHE, CLARENCE D.
B.1888 ST.LOUIS,MO.
1915 BAL F 3   1   .000
     TR

FORTUNE, GARRETT REESE (GARY)
B.OCT.11,1894 HIGH POINT,N.C.
D.SEPT.23,1955 WASHINGTON,D.C.
1916 PHI N P   1   0- 1
1918 PHI N P   8   0- 2
1920 BOS A P   14   0- 2
     BBTR   23   0- 5

FOSNOW, GERALD EUGENE (JERRY)
B.SEP.21,1940 DESHLER,OHIO
1964 MIN A P   7   0- 1
1965 MIN A P   29   3- 3
     BRTL   36   3- 4

FOSS, GEORGE DUEWARD (DEEBY)
B.JUNE 13,1897 REGISTER,VA.
D.NOV.10,1969 BRANDON,FLA.
1921 WAS A 3   4   .000
     BRTR

FOSS, LARRY CURTIS
B.APR.18,1936 CASTLETON,KAN.
1961 PIT N P   3   1- 1
1962 NY N P   5   0- 1
     BRTR   8   1- 2

FOSSE, RAYMOND EARL (RAY)
B.APR.4,1947 MARION,ILL.
1967 CLE A /C   7   .063
1968 CLE A /C   1   .000
1969 CLE A C   37   .172
1970 CLE A *C   120   .307
1971 CLE A *C/1   133   .276
1972 CLE A *C/1   134   .241
1973 OAK A *C   143   .256
1974 OAK A C   69   .196
1975 OAK A C/1-2   82   .140
1976 OAK A C/1   90   .301
1977 CLE A C/1   78   .265
     SEA A /C   11   .353
     BRTR   905   .257

FOSTER, ALAN BENTON
B.DEC.8,1946 PASADENA,CAL.
1967 LA   N /P   4   0- 1
1968 LA   N /P   3   0- 2
1969 LA   N P   24   3- 9
1970 LA   N P   33   10-13
1971 CLE A P   36   37   8-12
1972 CAL A /P   8   0- 1
1973 STL N P   35   13- 9
1974 STL N P   31   33   7-10
1975 SD   N P   17   19   3- 1
1976 SD   N P   26   29   3- 6
     BRTR   217 225   48-63

FOSTER, CLARENCE FRANCIS (POP)
B.APR.8,1878 NEW HAVEN,CONN.
D.APR.16,1944 PRINCETON,N.J.
1898 NY N O   31   .281
1899 NY N O   88   .305
1900 NY N O   20   .286
1901 WAS A O   104   .271
     CHI A O   11   .281
     TR   254   .285

```
YR  CL LEA POS    GP    G   REC        YR  CL LEA POS    GP    G   REC        YR  CL LEA POS    GP    G   REC

FOSTER, EDWARD CUNNINGHAM (KID)        FOUCAULT, STEVEN RAYMOND (STEVE)       FOWLER, RICHARD JOHN (DICK)
B.FEB.13,1887 CHICAGO,ILL.             B.OCT.3,1949 DULUTH,MINN.              B.MAR.30,1921 TORONTO,ONT.,CAN.
D.JAN.15,1937 WASHINGTON,D.C.          1973 TEX A  P      32   2- 4           D.MAY 22,1972 ONEONTA,N.Y.
1910 NY  A  S           30   .132      1974 TEX A  P      69   8- 9           1941 PHI A  P            4   1- 2
1912 WAS A  3          154   .285      1975 TEX A  P      59   8- 4           1942 PHI A  P      31   32   6-11
1913 WAS A  3          106   .247      1976 TEX A  P      46   8- 8           1945 PHI A  P       7   11   1- 2
1914 WAS A  3          156   .282      1977 DET A  P      44   7- 7           1946 PHI A  P           32   9-16
1915 WAS A  2-3        154   .275      1978 DET A  P      24   2- 4           1947 PHI A  P           36  12-11
1916 WAS A  2-3        158   .253        KC A  /P     3   0- 0                1948 PHI A  P           29  15- 8
1917 WAS A  2-3        143   .235        BLTR       277  35-36                1949 PHI A  P           31  15-11
1918 WAS A  3          129   .283                                            1950 PHI A  P           11   1- 5
1919 WAS A  3          120   .263      FOURNIER, F. HENRY (FRENCHY)           1951 PHI A  P           22   5-11
1920 BOS A  2-3        117   .259      B.SYRACUSE,N.Y.                        1952 PHI A  P           18   1- 2
1921 BOS A  2-3        120   .284      1894 CIN N  P       6   1- 3             BRTR      221  226  66-79
1922 BOS A  3           48   .211        TL
     STL A  3           37   .306                                            FOX, CHARLES FRANCIS (IRISH)
1923 STL A  2           27   .180      FOURNIER, JACQUES FRANK (JACK)         B.OCT.7,1921 NEW YORK,N.Y.
     BRTR            1499   .264        B.SEPT.29,1892 AU SABLE,MICH.         1942 NY  N  C            3   .429
                                        D.SEPT.5,1973 TACOMA,WASH.              BRTR
FOSTER, EDDY LEE (SLIM)                 1912 CHI A  1          35   .192      NON-PLAYING MANAGER
B.BIRMINGHAM,ALA.                       1913 CHI A  1-O        68   .234      SF[N] 1970-74, MON[N] 1976
D.MAR.1,1929 MONTGOMERY,ALA.            1914 CHI A  1         109   .311
1908 CLE A  P       6   1- 0           1915 CHI A  1-O       126   .322       FOX, ERVIN (PETE)
     TR                                 1916 CHI A  1         105   .240      B.MAR.8,1909 EVANSVILLE,IND.
                                        1917 CHI A  H           1   .000      D.JULY 5,1966 DETROIT,MICH.
FOSTER, ELMER ELLSWORTH                 1918 NY  A  1          27   .350      1933 DET A  O          128   .288
B.AUG.15,1861 MINNEAPOLIS,MINN.         1920 STL N  1         141   .306      1934 DET A  O          128   .285
D.JULY 22,1946 DEEPHAVEN,MINN.          1921 STL N  1         149   .343      1935 DET A  O          131   .321
1884 ATH AA C-O         3   .167        1922 STL N  P-1    1  128   0- 0      1936 DET A  O           73   .305
     KEY U  C           1   .333                                    .294      1937 DET A  O          148   .331
1886 MET AA O          18   .206        1923 BRO N  1         133   .351      1938 DET A  O          155   .293
1888 NY  N  O          37   .147        1924 BRO N  1         154   .334      1939 DET A  O          141   .295
1889 NY  N  O           2   .000        1925 BRO N  1         145   .350      1940 DET A  O           93   .289
1890 CHI N  O          27   .247        1926 BRO N  1          87   .284      1941 BOS A  O           73   .302
1891 CHI N  O           4   .187        1927 BOS N  1         122   .283      1942 BOS A  O           77   .262
     TR                92   .191          BLTR        1 1530   0- 0           1943 BOS A  O          127   .288
                                                                    .313      1945 BOS A  O           66   .245
FOSTER, GEORGE (RUBE)                                                           BRTR            1461   .298
B.JAN.5,1888 LEHIGH,OKLA                FOUSER, WILLIAM C.
D.MAR.1,1976 BOKOS4E,OKLA.              B.1855 PHILADELPHIA,PA.               FOX, GEORGE B. (PADDY)
1913 BOS A  P      19   20   3- 4      D.MAR.1,1919 PHILADELPHIA,PA.          B.DEC.1,1866 POTTSTOWN,PA.
1914 BOS A  P           32  14- 8      1876 ATH N  2-O        21   .135       D.MAY 8,1914 PHILADELPHIA,PA.
1915 BOS A  P      38   40  20- 9                                            1891 LOU AA 3            6   .105
1916 BOS A  P      34   38  14- 7      FOUTZ, DAVID LUTHER (SCISSORS)         1899 PIT N  C           13   .243
1917 BOS A  P           17   8- 7      B.SEPT.7,1856 CARROLL CO.,MD.                                19   .200
     BRTR          140  147  59-35      D.MAR.5,1897 WAVERLY,IND.
                                        1884 STL AA P-O   23   32  15- 6      FOX, HENRY H.
FOSTER, GEORGE ARTHUR                                               .233      1902 PHI N  P            1   0- 0
B.DEC.1,1948 TUSCALOOSA,ALA.            1885 STL AA P-1   47   65  33-14
1969 SF  N  /O          9   .400                                    .250      FOX, HOWARD FRANCIS (HOWIE)
1970 SF  N  /O          9   .316        1886 STL AA P-O   57   89  41-16      B.MAR.1,1921 COBURG,ORE.
1971 SF  N  O          36   .267                                    .282      D.OCT.9,1955 SAN ANTONIO,TEX.
     CIN N  *O        104   .234        1887 STL AA P-O   36  103  24-12      1944 CIN N  P            2   0- 0
1972 CIN N  O          59   .200                                    .393      1945 CIN N  P           45   8-13
1973 CIN N  O          17   .282        1888 BRO AA P-1   19  140  12- 7      1946 CIN N  P            4   0- C
1974 CIN N  O         106   .264                  O                 .283      1948 CIN N  P      34   35   6- 4
1975 CIN N  *O/1      134   .300        1889 BRO AA P-1    4  138   4- 0      1949 CIN N  P      38   41   6-19
1976 CIN N  *O/1      144   .306                                    .286      1950 CIN N  P      34   35  11- 8
1977 CIN N  O         158   .320        1890 BRO N  P-1    4  129   3- 1      1951 CIN N  P           40   9-14
1978 CIN N  *O        158   .281                                    .302      1952 PHI N  P           13   2- 7
     BRTR            934   .285         1891 BRO N  P-1    6  130   3- 3      1954 BAL A  P           38   1- 2
                                                                    .262        BRTR      248  253  43-72
FOSTER, LARRY LYNN                      1892 BRO N  P-O   22   53  12- 9
B.DEC.24,1937 LANSING,MICH.                                         .199      FOX, JACOB NELSON (NELLIE)
1963 DET A  P       1   0- 0           1893 BRO N  M-1-O      130   .272      B.DEC.25,1927 ST.THOMAS,PA.
     BLTR                               1894 BRO N  M-1        73   .310      D.DEC.1,1975 BALTIMORE,MD.
                                        1895 BRO N  M-O        28   .304      1947 PHI A  2            7   .000
FOSTER, LEONARD NORRIS (LEO)            1896 BRO N  M-1-O       2   .250      1948 PHI A  2            3   .154
B.FEB.2,1951 COVINGTON,KY.                BRTR       218 1112 147-68          1949 PHI A  2           88   .255
1971 ATL N  /S          9   .000                                    .286      1950 CHI A  2          130   .247
1973 ATL N  /S          3   .167                                            1951 CHI A  2          147   .313
1974 ATL N  S-2/3-O    72   .196                                            1952 CHI A  2          152   .296
1976 NY     /S-2       24   .203       FOUTZ, FRANK HAYES                     1953 CHI A  2          154   .285
1977 NY  N  2/S-3      36   .227       B.APR.8,1877 BALTIMORE,MD.             1954 CHI A  2          155   .319
     BRTR            144   .198         D.DEC.25,1961 LIMA,OHIO               1955 CHI A  2          154   .311
                                        1901 BAL A  1          20   .236      1956 CHI A  2          154   .296
                                          BRTR                                1957 CHI A  2          155   .317
FOSTER, OSCAR E. (REDDY)                                                      1958 CHI A  2          155   .300
B.1867 RICHMOND,VA.                     FOWLER, JESSE PETER (PETE)            1959 CHI A  2          156   .306
D.DEC.19,1908 RICHMOND,VA.             B.OCT.30,1898 SPARTANBURG,S.C.         1960 CHI A  2          150   .289
1896 NY  N  O           1   .000        D.SEPT.23,1973 COLUMBIA,S.C.          1961 CHI A  2          159   .251
                                        1924 STL N  P      13   1- 1          1962 CHI A  2          157   .267
                                          BRTL                                1963 CHI A  2          137   .260
FOSTER, ROY                                                                  1964 HOU N  2          133   .265
B.JULY 29,1945 BIXBY,MISS.              FOWLER, JOHN ARTHUR (ART)             1965 HOU N  /3-1-2      21   .268
1970 CLE A  *O        139   .268        B.JULY 3,1922 CONVERSE,S.C.             BLTR            2367   .288
1971 CLE A  *O        125   .245        1954 CIN N  P      40  12-10
1972 CLE A  O          73   .224        1955 CIN N  P      46  11-10          FOX, JOHN JOSEPH
     BRTR            337   .253         1956 CIN N  P      45  11-11          B.FEB.7,1859 ROXBURY,MASS.
                                        1957 CIN N  P      33   3- 0          D.APR.18,1893 BOSTON,MASS.
FOTHERGILL, ROBERT ROY                  1959 LA  N  P      36   3- 4          1881 BOS N  P-1-   17   30   6- 8
(BOB) OR (FATS)                         1961 LA  A  P      53   5- 8                   O                 .178
B.AUG.16,1897 MASSILLON,OHIO            1962 LA  A  P      48   4- 3          1883 BAL AA P-1-O      23   6-14
D.MAR.20,1938 DETROIT,MICH.             1963 LA  A  P      57   5- 3                                      1- 6
1922 DET A  O          42   .322        1964 LA  A  P       4   0- 2          1884 PIT AA P-S    7    8   1- 6
1923 DET A  O         101   .315          BRTR       362  54-51                                           0- 1
1924 DET A  O          54   .301                                            1886 WAS N  P            1   0- 1
1925 DET A  O          71   .353        FOWLER, JOSEPH CHESTER                                 48   62  13-29
1926 DET A  O         110   .367        (BOOB) OR (GINK)                                                 .179
1927 DET A  O         143   .359        B.NOV.11,1900 WACO,TEX.
1928 DET A  O         111   .317        1923 CIN N  S      11        .333     FOX, JOHN PAUL (JACK)
1929 DET A  O         115   .350        1924 CIN N  2-S-3  59        .333     B.MAY 21,1865 READING,PA.
1930 DET A  O          54   .254        1925 CIN N  S       6        .400     D.JUNE 28,1963 READING,PA.
     CHI A  O          52   .311        1926 BOS N  3       2        .125     1908 PHI A  O            8   .209
1931 CHI A  O         108   .282          BLTR        78        .326           BRTR
1932 CHI A  O         116   .295
1933 BOS A  O          28   .344
     BRTR            1105   .326
```

FOX, TERRENCE EDWARD (TERRY)
B.JULY 31,1935 CHICAGO,ILL.

YR	CL	LEA	POS	GP	G	REC
1960	MIL	N	P		5	0- 0
1961	DET	A	P		39	5- 2
1962	DET	A	P	44	47	3- 1
1963	DET	A	P		46	8- 6
1964	DET	A	P		32	4- 3
1965	DET	A	P		42	6- 4
1966	DET	A	/P		4	0- 1
	PHI	N	P	36	38	3- 2
			BRTR	248	253	29-19

FOX, WILLIAM HENRY
B.JAN.15,1872 FISKDALE,MASS.
D.MAY 7,1946 MINNEAPOLIS,MINN.

YR	CL	LEA	POS	GP	G	REC
1897	WAS	N	2-S		4	.250
1901	CIN	N	2		44	.163
			BBTR		48	.191

FOXEN, WILLIAM ALOYSIUS
B.MAY 31,1884 TENAFLY,N.J.
D.APR.17,1937 BROOKLYN,N.Y.

YR	CL	LEA	POS	GP	G	REC
1908	PHI	N	P		22	7- 7
1909	PHI	N	P		18	3- 7
1910	PHI	N	P		16	5- 5
	CHI	N	P		2	0- 0
1911	CHI	N	P		3	1- 1
			BLTL		61	16-20

FOXX, JAMES EMORY (JIMMIE)
(BEAST) OR (DOUBLE X)
B.OCT.22,1907 SUDLERSVILLE,MD.
D.JULY 21,1967 MIAMI,FLA.

YR	CL	LEA	POS	GP	G	REC
1925	PHI	A	C		10	.667
1926	PHI	A	C		26	.313
1927	PHI	A	1		61	.323
1928	PHI	A	C-1-3		118	.328
1929	PHI	A	1		149	.354
1930	PHI	A	1		153	.335
1931	PHI	A	1-3		139	.291
1932	PHI	A	1-3		154	.364
1933	PHI	A	1		149	.356
1934	PHI	A	1		150	.334
1935	PHI	A	C-1-3		147	.346
1936	BOS	A	1-O		155	.338
1937	BOS	A	1		150	.285
1938	BOS	A	1		149	.349
1939	BOS	A	P-1	1	124	0- 0
						.360
1940	BOS	A	C-1-3		144	.297
1941	BOS	A	1-3-O		135	.300
1942	BOS	A	1		30	.270
	CHI	N	C-1		70	.205
1944	CHI	N	C-3		15	.050
1945	PHI	N	P-1-	9	89	1- 0
			3			.268
			BRTR	10	2317	1- 0
						.325

FOY, JOSEPH ANTHONY (JOE)
B.FEB.21,1943 NEW YORK,N.Y.

YR	CL	LEA	POS	GP	G	REC
1966	BOS	A	*3-S		151	.262
1967	BOS	A	*3/O		130	.251
1968	BOS	A	*3/O		150	.225
1969	KC	A	*3-1-O/S-2		145	.262
1970	NY	N	3		99	.236
1971	WAS	A	3/2-S		41	.234
			BRTR		716	.248

FOYTACK, PAUL EUGENE
B.NOV.16,1930 SCRANTON,PA.

YR	CL	LEA	POS	GP	G	REC
1953	DET	A	P		6	0- 0
1955	DET	A	P		22	0- 1
1956	DET	A	P		43	15-13
1957	DET	A	P		38	14-11
1958	DET	A	P		39	15-13
1959	DET	A	P		39	14-14
1960	DET	A	P	28	29	2-11
1961	DET	A	P		32	11-10
1962	DET	A	P		29	10- 7
1963	DET	A	P		9	0- 1
	LA	A	P	25	26	5- 5
1964	LA	A	P		2	0- 1
			BRTR	312	314	86-87

FRAILING, KENNETH DOUGLAS (KEN)
B.JAN.19,1948 MARION,WIS.

YR	CL	LEA	POS	GP	G	REC
1972	CHI	A	/P		4	1- 0
1973	CHI	A	P		10	0- 0
1974	CHI	N	P	55	58	6- 9
1975	CHI	N	P		41	2- 5
1976	CHI	N	/P		6	1- 2
			BLTL	116	119	10-16

FRANCE, OSMAN BEVERLY (O.B.)
B.OCT.4,1858 GREENSBURG,OHIO
D.MAY 2,1947 AKRON,OHIO

YR	CL	LEA	POS	GP	G	REC
1890	CHI	N	P		1	0- 0
			BLTL			

FRANCIS, EARL COLEMAN
B.JULY 14,1935 SLAB FORK,W.VA.

YR	CL	LEA	POS	GP	G	REC
1960	PIT	N	P		7	1- 0
1961	PIT	N	P		23	2- 8
1962	PIT	N	P		36	9- 8
1963	PIT	N	P	33	34	4- 6
1964	PIT	N	P		2	0- 1
1965	STL	N	/P		2	0- 0
			BRTR	103	104	16-23

FRANCIS, RAY JAMES
B.MAR.8,1893 SHERMAN,TEX.
D.JULY 6,1934 ATLANTA,GA.

YR	CL	LEA	POS	GP	G	REC
1922	WAS	A	P		39	7-18
1923	DET	A	P	33	37	4- 8
1925	NY	A	P		4	0- 0
	BOS	A	P		6	0- 2
			BLTL	82	86	11-28

FRANCONA, JOHN PATSY (TITO)
B.NOV.4,1933 ALIQUIPPA,PA.

YR	CL	LEA	POS	GP	G	REC
1956	BAL	A	1-O		139	.258
1957	BAL	A	1-O		97	.233
1958	CHI	A	O		41	.258
	DET	A	1-O		45	.246
1959	CLE	A	1-O		122	.363
1960	CLE	A	1-O		147	.292
1961	CLE	A	1-O		155	.301
1962	CLE	A	1		158	.272
1963	CLE	A	1-O		142	.228
1964	CLE	A	1-O		111	.248
1965	STL	N	O-1		81	.259
1966	STL	N	1/O		83	.212
1967	PHI	N	1/O		27	.205
	ATL	N	1/O		82	.248
1968	ATL	N	O-1		122	.286
1969	ATL	N	O/1		51	.295
	OAK	A	1/O		32	.341
1970	OAK	A	/1-O		32	.242
	MIL	A	1		52	.231
			BLTL		1719	.272

FRANK, CHARLES
B.MAY 30,1870 MOBILE,ALA.
D.MAY 24,1922 MEMPHIS,TENN.

YR	CL	LEA	POS	GP	G	REC
1893	STL	N	O		40	.331
1894	STL	N	O		80	.246
					120	.272

FRANK, FREDERICK
B.MAR.11,1874 LOUISA,KY.
D.MAR.27,1950 ASHLAND,KY.

YR	CL	LEA	POS	GP	G	REC
1898	CLE	N	O		17	.208

FRANKHOUSE, FREDERICK MELOY
B.APR.9,1904 PORT ROYAL,PA.

YR	CL	LEA	POS	GP	G	REC
1927	STL	N	P		8	5- 1
1928	STL	N	P	21	22	3- 2
1929	STL	N	P	30	34	7- 2
1930	STL	N	P	8	9	2- 3
	BOS	N	P		27	7- 6
1931	BOS	N	P		26	8- 8
1932	BOS	N	P	37	40	4- 6
1933	BOS	N	P		43	16-15
1934	BOS	N	P		37	17- 9
1935	BOS	N	P		40	11-15
1936	BRO	N	P	41	42	13-10
1937	BRO	N	P	33	39	10-13
1938	BRO	N	P	30	31	3- 5
1939	BOS	N	P		23	0- 2
			BRTR	402	421	106-97

FRANKLIN

YR	CL	LEA	POS	GP	G	REC
1884	WAS	U	O		1	.000

FRANKLIN, JAMES WILFORD (JACK)
B.OCT.20,1919 PARIS,ILL.

YR	CL	LEA	POS	GP	G	REC
1944	BRO	N	P		1	0- 0
			BRTR			

FRANKLIN, JOHN WILLIAM (JAY)
B.MAR.16,1953 ARLINGTON,VA.

YR	CL	LEA	POS	GP	G	REC
1971	SD	N	/P		3	0- 1
			BRTR			

FRANKLIN, MURRAY ASHER (MOE)
B.APR.1,1914 CHICAGO,ILL.
D.MAR.16,1978 HARBOR CITY,CAL.

YR	CL	LEA	POS	GP	G	REC
1941	DET	A	S-3		13	.300
1942	DET	A	2-S		48	.260
			BRTR		61	.262

FRANKS, HERMAN LOUIS
B.JAN.4,1914 PRICE,UTAH

YR	CL	LEA	POS	GP	G	REC
1939	STL	N	C		17	.059
1940	BRO	N	C		65	.183
1941	BRO	N	C-O		57	.201
1947	PHI	A	C		8	.200
1948	PHI	A	C		40	.224
1949	NY	N	C		1	.667
			BLTR		188	.195

NON-PLAYING MANAGER
SF[N] 1965-68, CHI[N] 1977-78

FRASER, CHARLES CARROLTON (CHICK)
B.MAR.17,1871 CHICAGO,ILL.
D.MAY 8,1940 WENDELL,IOWA

YR	CL	LEA	POS	GP	G	REC
1896	LOU	N	P	41	43	13-25
1897	LOU	N	P		36	15-17
1898	LOU	N	P		26	7-19
	CLE	N	P		6	2- 3
1899	PHI	N	P	35	37	21-13
1900	PHI	N	P		26	16-10
1901	PHI	A	P	40	43	20-15
1902	PHI	N	P		27	12-13
1903	PHI	N	P	31	32	12-17
1904	PHI	N	P	42	44	13-24
1905	BOS	N	P	39	45	15-21
1906	CIN	N	P		31	10-20
1907	CHI	N	P		22	8- 5
1908	CHI	N	P		26	11- 9
1909	CHI	N	P		1	0- 0
			BRTR	429	445	175-211

FRASIER, VICTOR PATRICK
B.AUG.5,1904 RUSTON,LA.
D.JAN.10,1977 JACKSONVILLE,TEX.

YR	CL	LEA	POS	GP	G	REC
1931	CHI	A	P		46	13-15
1932	CHI	A	P		29	3-13
1933	CHI	A	P		10	1- 1
	DET	A	P		20	5- 5
1934	DET	A	P		8	1- 3
1937	BOS	N	P		3	0- 0
1939	CHI	A	P		10	0- 1
			BRTR		126	23-38

FRAZER, GEORGE KASSON
B.JAN.7,1861 SYRACUSE,N.Y.
D.FEB.5,1913 PHILADELPHIA,PA.
NON-PLAYING MANAGER SYR[AA]1890

FRAZIER, JOSEPH FILMORE (JOE)
B.OCT.6,1922 LIBERTY,N.C.

YR	CL	LEA	POS	GP	G	REC
1947	CLE	A	O		9	.071
1954	STL	N	1-O		81	.295
1955	STL	N	O		58	.200
1956	STL	N	O		14	.211
	CIN	N	O		10	.235
	BAL	A	O		45	.257
			BLTR		217	.241

NON-PLAYING MANAGER NY[N] 1976-77

FRAZIER, GEORGE ALLEN
B.OCT.13,1954 OKLAHOMA CITY,OKLA

YR	CL	LEA	POS	GP	G	REC
1978	STL	N	P		14	0- 3
			BRTR			

FREDERICK, JOHN HENRY
B.JAN.26,1902 DENVER,COLO.
D.JUNE 18,1977 TIGARD,ORE.

YR	CL	LEA	POS	GP	G	REC
1929	BRO	N	O		148	.328
1930	BRO	N	O		142	.334
1931	BRO	N	O		146	.270
1932	BRO	N	O		118	.299
1933	BRO	N	O		147	.308
1934	BRO	N	O		104	.296
			BLTL		805	.307

FREED, EDWIN CHARLES
B.AUG.22,1919 CENTRE VALLEY,PA.

YR	CL	LEA	POS	GP	G	REC
1942	PHI	N	O		13	.303
			BRTR			

FREED, ROGER VERNON
B.JUNE 2,1946 LOS ANGELES,CAL.

YR	CL	LEA	POS	GP	G	REC
1970	BAL	A	/1-O		4	.154
1971	PHI	N	*O/C		118	.221
1972	PHI	N	O		73	.225
1974	CIN	N	/1		6	.333
1976	MON	N	/1-O		8	.200
1977	STL	N	1/O		49	.398
1978	STL	N	1/O		52	.239
			BRTR		310	.245

FREEHAN, WILLIAM ASHLEY (BILL)
B.NOV.29,1941 DETROIT,MICH.

YR	CL	LEA	POS	GP	G	REC
1961	DET	A	C		4	.400
1963	DET	A	C-1		100	.243
1964	DET	A	C-1		144	.300
1965	DET	A	*C		130	.234
1966	DET	A	*C/1		136	.234
1967	DET	A	*C-1		155	.282
1968	DET	A	*C-1/O		155	.263
1969	DET	A	*C-1		143	.262
1970	DET	A	*C		117	.241
1971	DET	A	*C/O		148	.277
1972	DET	A	*C/1		111	.262
1973	DET	A	C/1		110	.234
1974	DET	A	1-C		130	.297
1975	DET	A	*C/1		120	.246
1976	DET	A	C/1		71	.270
			BRTR		1774	.262

FREEMAN, ALEXANDER VERNON (BUCK)
B.JULY 5,1896 MART,TEX.

YR	CL	LEA	POS	GP	G	REC
1921	CHI	N	P		38	9-10
1922	CHI	N	P		11	0- 1
			BBTR		49	9-11

FREEMAN, FRANK ELLSWORTH
(JERRY) OR (BUCK)
B.DEC.26,1879 PLACERVILLE,CAL.
D.SEPT.30,1952 LOS ANGELES,CAL.

YR	CL	LEA	POS	GP	G	REC
1908	WAS	A	1		154	.252
1909	WAS	A	1		19	.167
	BLTR				173	.245

FREEMAN, HARVEY BAYARD (BUCK)
B.DEC.22,1897 NOTTVILLE,MICH.
D.JAN.10,1970 KALAMAZOO,MICH.

YR	CL	LEA	POS	GP	G	REC
1921	PHI	A	P		18	1- 4
	BRTR					

FREEMAN, HERSHELL BASKIN
(HERSH) OR (BUSTER)
B.JULY 1,1928 GADSDEN,ALA.

YR	CL	LEA	POS	GP	G	REC
1952	BOS	A	P		4	1- 0
1953	BOS	A	P		18	1- 4
1955	BOS	A	P		2	0- 0
	CIN	N	P-3	52	53	7- 4
						.167
1956	CIN	N	P		64	14- 5
1957	CIN	N	P		52	7- 2
1958	CIN	N	P		5	0- 0
	CHI	N	P		9	0- 1
	BRTR			204	205	30-16
						.143

FREEMAN, JIMMY LEE
B.JUNE 29,1951 CARLSBAD,N.MEX.

YR	CL	LEA	POS	GP	G	REC
1972	ATL	N	/P	6	8	2- 2
1973	ATL	N	P	13	14	0- 2
	BLTL			19	22	2- 4

FREEMAN, JOHN EDWARD
B.JAN.24,1901 BOSTON,MASS.
D.APR.14,1958 WASHINGTON,D.C.

YR	CL	LEA	POS	GP	G	REC
1927	BOS	A	O		4	.000
	BRTR					

FREEMAN, JOHN FRANK (BUCK)
B.OCT.30,1871 CATASAUQUA,PA.
D.JUNE 25,1949 WILKES-BARRE,PA.

YR	CL	LEA	POS	GP	G	REC
1891	WAS	AA	P		6	0- 0
1898	WAS	N	O		29	.368
1899	WAS	N	O		155	.318
1900	BOS	N	1-O		109	.300
1901	BOS	A	1		129	.346
1902	BOS	A	O		138	.311
1903	BOS	A	O		141	.285
1904	BOS	A	O		157	.278
1905	BOS	A	1-O		130	.240
1906	BOS	A	1-O		121	.250
1907	BOS	A	O		4	.167
	BLTL			6	1119	0- 0
						.294

FREEMAN, JULIUS B.
B.NOV.7,1868 MISSOURI
D.JUNE 10,1921 ST.LOUIS,MO.

YR	CL	LEA	POS	GP	G	REC
1888	STL	AA	P		1	0- 1

FREEMAN, MARK PRICE
B.DEC.7,1930 MEMPHIS,TENN.

YR	CL	LEA	POS	GP	G	REC
1959	KC	A	P		3	0- 0
	NY	A	P		1	0- 0
1960	CHI	N	P		30	3- 3
	BRTR				34	3- 3

FREESE, EUGENE LEWIS
(GENE) OR (AUGIE)
B.JAN.8,1934 WHEELING,W.VA.

YR	CL	LEA	POS	GP	G	REC
1955	PIT	N	2-3		134	.253
1956	PIT	N	2-3		65	.208
1957	PIT	N	2-3-0		114	.283
1958	PIT	N	3		17	.167
	STL	N	2-S-3		62	.257
1959	PHI	N	2-3		132	.268
1960	CHI	A	3		127	.273
1961	CIN	N	2-3		152	.277
1962	CIN	N	3		18	.143
1963	CIN	N	3-0		66	.244
1964	PIT	N	3		99	.225
1965	PIT	N	3		43	.263
	CHI	A	/3		17	.281
1966	CHI	A	3		48	.208
	HOU	N	/3-2-0		21	.091
	BRTR				1115	.254

FREESE, GEORGE WALTER (BUD)
B.SEPT.12,1926 WHEELING,W.VA.

YR	CL	LEA	POS	GP	G	REC
1953	DET	A	H		1	.000
1955	PIT	N	3		51	.257
1961	CHI	N	H		9	.286
	BRTR				61	.257

FREEZE, CARL ALEXANDER (JAKE)
B.APR.25,1900 HUNTINGTON,ARK.

YR	CL	LEA	POS	GP	G	REC
1925	CHI	A	P		2	0- 0
	BRTR					

FREGOSI, JAMES LOUIS (JIM)
B.APR.4,1942 SAN FRANCISCO,CAL.

YR	CL	LEA	POS	GP	G	REC
1961	LA	A	S		11	.222
1962	LA	A	S		58	.291
1963	LA	A	S		154	.287
1964	LA	A	S		147	.277
1965	CAL	A	*S		161	.277
1966	CAL	A	*S/1		162	.252
1967	CAL	A	*S		151	.290
1968	CAL	A	*S		159	.244
1969	CAL	A	*S		101	.260
1970	CAL	A	*S/1		158	.278
1971	CAL	A	S-1/O		107	.233
1972	NY	N	3/S-1		101	.232
1973	NY	N	S-3/1-O		45	.234
	TEX	A	3-1/S		45	.268
1974	TEX	A	1-3		78	.261
1975	TEX	A	1-0/3		77	.262
1976	TEX	A	1-0/3		98	.233
1977	TEX	A	/1		13	.250
	PIT	N	1/3		36	.200
1978	PIT	N	/3-1		20	.200
	BRTR				1902	.265

NON-PLAYING MANAGER CAL[A] 1978

FREIBERGER, VERN DONALD
B.DEC.19,1923 DETROIT,MICH.

YR	CL	LEA	POS	GP	G	REC
1941	CLE	A	1		2	.125
	BRTL					

FREIGAU, HOWARD EARL (TY)
B.AUG.1,1902 DAYTON,OHIO
D.JULY 18,1932 CHATTANOOGA,TENN

YR	CL	LEA	POS	GP	G	REC
1922	STL	N	S-3		3	.000
1923	STL	N	1-2-S-3-O		113	.263
1924	STL	N	3		98	.269
1925	STL	N	S		9	.154
	CHI	N	1-S-3		117	.307
1926	CHI	N	3		140	.270
.927	CHI	N	3		30	.233
1928	BRO	N	S-3		17	.206
	BOS	N	2-S		52	.257
	BRTR				579	.272

FREISLEBEN, DAVID JAMES (DAVE)
B.OCT.31,1951 CORAOPOLIS,PA.

YR	CL	LEA	POS	GP	G	REC
1974	SD	N	P		33	9-14
1975	SD	N	P		36	5-14
1976	SD	N	P		34	10-13
1977	SD	N	P		33	7- 9
1978	SD	N	P		12	0- 3
	CLE	A	P		12	1- 4
	BRTR				160	32-57

FREITAS, ANTONIO (TONY)
B.MAY 5,1908 MILL VALLEY,CAL.

YR	CL	LEA	POS	GP	G	REC
1932	PHI	A	P		23	12- 5
1933	PHI	A	P		19	2- 4
1934	CIN	N	P	30	31	6-12
1935	CIN	N	P		31	5-10
1936	CIN	N	P		4	0- 2
	BRTL			107	108	25-33

FRENCH, CHARLES CALVIN
B.OCT.12,1883 INDIANAPOLIS,IND.
D.MAR.30,1962 INDIANAPOLIS,IND.

YR	CL	LEA	POS	GP	G	REC
1909	BOS	A	2-S		51	.251
1910	BOS	A	2		9	.200
	CHI	A	2		45	.165
	BLTR				105	.207

FRENCH, FRANK ALEXANDER (PAT)
B.SEPT.22,1893 DOVER,N.H.
D.JULY 13,1969 BATH,MAINE

YR	CL	LEA	POS	GP	G	REC
1917	PHI	A	O		4	.000
	BRTR					

FRENCH, LAWRENCE HERBERT
B.NOV.1,1907 VISALIA,CAL.

YR	CL	LEA	POS	GP	G	REC
1929	PIT	N	P		30	7- 5
1930	PIT	N	P		42	17-18
1931	PIT	N	P		39	15-13
1932	PIT	N	P		47	18-16
1933	PIT	N	P		47	18-13
1934	PIT	N	P		49	12-18
1935	PIT	N	P		42	17-10
1936	CHI	N	P		43	18- 9
1937	CHI	N	P		42	16-10
1938	CHI	N	P		43	10-19
1939	CHI	N	P		36	15- 8
1940	CHI	N	P		40	14-14
1941	CHI	N	P		26	5-14
	BRO	N	P		6	0- 0
1942	BRO	N	P		38	15+ 4
	BBTL				570	197-171
	BR 1929-33, 35-39					

FRENCH, RAYMOND EDWARD
B.JAN.9,1895 ALAMEDA,CAL.
D.APR.3,1978 ALAMEDA,CAL.

YR	CL	LEA	POS	GP	G	REC
1920	NY	A	S		2	.000
1923	BRO	N	S		43	.219
1924	BRO	N	S		37	.179
	BRTR				82	.193

FRENCH, RICHARD JAMES (JIM)
B.AUG.13,1941 WARREN,OHIO

YR	CL	LEA	POS	GP	G	REC
1965	WAS	A	C		13	.297
1966	WAS	A	C		10	.208
1967	WAS	A	/C		6	.063
1968	WAS	A	C		59	.194
1969	WAS	A	C		63	.184
1970	WAS	A	C/O		69	.211
1971	WAS	A	C		14	.146
	BLTR				234	.196

FRENCH, WALTER EDWARD
(PIGGY) OR (FITZ)
B.JULY 12,1899 MOORESTOWN,N.J.

YR	CL	LEA	POS	GP	G	REC
1923	PHI	A	O		16	.231
1925	PHI	A	O		67	.370
1926	PHI	A	O		112	.305
1927	PHI	A	O		109	.304
1928	PHI	A	O		49	.257
1929	PHI	A	O		45	.267
	BLTR				398	.303

FRENCH, WILLIAM
B.BALTIMORE,MD.

YR	CL	LEA	POS	GP	G	REC
1873	MAR	NA	P-1- O	1	5	0- 1

FREY, BENJAMIN RUDOLPH
B.APR.6,1906 DEXTER,MICH.
D.NOV.1,1937 JACKSON,MICH.

YR	CL	LEA	POS	GP	G	REC
1929	CIN	N	P		3	1- 2
1930	CIN	N	P		44	11-18
1931	CIN	N	P		34	8-12
1932	STL	N	P		2	0- 2
	CIN	N	P		28	4-10
1933	CIN	N	P	37	38	0- 4
1934	CIN	N	P	39	41	11-16
1935	CIN	N	P		38	6-10
1936	CIN	N	P	31	32	10- 8
	BRTR			256	260	57-82

FREY, LINUS REINHARD
(LONNY) OR (JUNIOR)
B.AUG.23,1910 ST.LOUIS,MO.

YR	CL	LEA	POS	GP	G	REC
1933	BRO	N	S		85	.319
1934	BRO	N	S-3		125	.284
1935	BRO	N	2-S		131	.262
1936	BRO	N	2-S		148	.279
1937	CHI	N	2-S		78	.278
1938	CIN	N	2-S		124	.265
1939	CIN	N	2		125	.291
1940	CIN	N	2		150	.266
1941	CIN	N	2		148	.254
1942	CIN	N	2		141	.266
1943	CIN	N	2		144	.203
1946	CIN	N	2-0		111	.246
1947	CIN	N	2		24	.209
	NY	A	2		24	.179
1948	NY	A	H		1	.000
	NY	N	2		29	.255
	BLTR				1535	.269
	BL 1939-43, 46-48					

FRIAS, JESUS MARIA (ANDUJAR) (PEPE)
B.JULY 14,1948 SAN DE PEDRO DE
MACORIS,D.R.

YR	CL	LEA	POS	GP	G	REC
1973	MON	N	S-2/3-O		100	.231
1974	MON	N	S-3-2/O		75	.214
1975	MON	N	S-3/2		51	.125
1976	MON	N	2-S/O		76	.248
1977	MON	N	2-S/3		53	.257
1978	MON	N	2/S		73	.267
	BRTR				428	.224
	BB 1976-78					

FRIBERG, AUGUSTAF BERNHARDT
[PLAYED UNDER NAME OF
BERNARD ALBERT FRIBERG]

FRIBERG, BERNARD ALBERT (BERNIE)
[REAL NAME
AUGUSTAF BERNHARDT FRIBERG]
B.AUG.18,1899 MANCHESTER,N.H.
D.DEC.8,1958 SWAMPSCOTT,MASS.

YR	CL	LEA	POS	GP	G	REC
1919	CHI	N	O		6	.200
1920	CHI	N	O		50	.211
1922	CHI	N	1-2-3-O		97	.311
1923	CHI	N	3		146	.318
1924	CHI	N	3		142	.279
1925	CHI	N	1-3		44	.257
	PHI	N	P-2- S-3-O	1	91	0- 0
						.270
1926	PHI	N	2		144	.268
1927	PHI	N	3		111	.233
1928	PHI	N	3		52	.202
1929	PHI	N	5-O		128	.301
1930	PHI	N	2-S-O		105	.341
1931	PHI	N	2-3		103	.261
1932	PHI	N	2		61	.240
1933	BOS	N	2-S-3		17	.317
	BRTR			1	1299	0- 0
						.280

YR	CL LEA POS	GP	G	REC

FRICANO, MARION JOHN
B.JULY 15,1923 BRANT,N.Y.
D.MAY 18,1976 TIJUANA,MEX.

1952 PHI A P		2	1- 0
1953 PHI A P	39	46	9-12
1954 PHI A P	37	42	5-11
1955 KC A P		10	0- 0
BRTR	88	100	15-23

FRIDAY, GRIER WILLIAM (SKIPPER)
B.OCT.26,1897 GASTONIA,N.C.
D.AUG.25,1962 GASTONIA,N.C.

1923 WAS A P		7	0- 1
BRTR			

FRIDLEY, JAMES RILEY (JIM)
OR (BIG JIM)
B.SEPT.6,1924 PHILIPPI,W.VA.

1952 CLE A O		62	.251
1954 BAL A O		85	.246
1958 CIN N O		5	.222
BRTR		152	.248

FRIED, ARTHUR EDWIN (CY)
B.JULY 23,1897 SAN ANTONIO,TEX.
D.OCT.10,1970 SAN ANTONIO,TEX.

1920 DET A P		2	0- 0
BLTL			

FRIEDRICH, ROBERT GEORGE
B.AUG.30,1906 CINCINNATI,OHIO
D.JAN.15,1924 PROVIDENCE,R.I.

1932 WAS A P		2	0- 0
BRTR			

FRIEL, PATRICK HENRY
B.JUNE 11,1860 LEWISBURG,W.VA.
D.JAN.15,1924 PROVIDENCE,R.I.

1890 SYR AA O		62	.238
1891 ATH AA O		2	.286
		64	.243

FRIEL, WILLIAM EDWARD
B.APR.1,1876 RENOVA,PA.
D.DEC.24,1959 ST.LOUIS,MO.

1901 MIL A 3-O		106	.271
1902 STL A ALL	1	79	0- 0
			.239
1903 STL A 2-3		98	.223
BLTR	1	283	0- 0
			.245

FRIEND, DANIEL SEBASTIAN
B.APR.8,1873 CINCINNATI,OHIO
D.JUNE 1,1942 CHILLICOTHE,OHIO

1895 CHI N P		5	2- 2
1896 CHI N P		33	19-14
1897 CHI N P	23	24	12-11
1898 CHI N P		2	0- 2
TL	63	64	33-29

FRIEND, FRANK B.
B.WASHINGTON,D.C.
D.SEPT.8,1897 ATLANTIC CITY,N.J

1896 LOU N C		2	.200

FRIEND, OWEN LACEY (RED)
B.MAR.21,1927 GRANITE CITY,ILL.

1949 STL A 2		2	.375
1950 STL A 2-S-3		119	.237
1953 DET A 2		31	.177
CLE A 2-S-3		34	.235
1955 BOS A 2-S		14	.262
CHI N S-3		6	.100
1956 CHI N H		2	.000
BRTR		208	.227

FRIEND, ROBERT BARTMESS
(BOB) OR (WARRIOR)
B.NOV.24,1930 LAFAYETTE,IND.

1951 PIT N P		34	6-10
1952 PIT N P		35	7-17
1953 PIT N P		32	8-11
1954 PIT N P		35	7-12
1955 PIT N P		44	14- 9
1956 PIT N P		49	17-17
1957 PIT N P		40	14-18
1958 PIT N P		38	22-14
1959 PIT N P		35	8-19
1960 PIT N P		38	18-12
1961 PIT N P		41	14-19
1962 PIT N P		39	18-14
1963 PIT N P		39	17-16
1964 PIT N P		35	13-18
1965 PIT N P		34	8-12
1966 NY N P		12	1- 4
NY A P		22	5- 8
BRTR		602	197-230

FRIERSON, ROBERT LAWRENCE (BUCK)
B.JULY 29,1917 CHICOTA,TEX.

1941 CLE A O		5	.273
BRTR			

FRIES, PETER MARTIN
B.OCT.30,1857 SCRANTON,PA.
D.JULY 30,1937 CHICAGO,ILL.

1883 COL AA P		3	0- 3
1884 IND AA O		1	.250
BLTL	3	4	0- 3
			.267

FRILL, JOHN EDMOND
B.APR.3,1879 READING,PA.
D.SEPT.29,1918 WESTERLY,R.I.

1910 NY A P		10	2- 2
1912 STL A P		3	1- 0
CIN N P		3	1- 0
BRTL		16	4- 2

FRINK, FRED FERDINAND
B.AUG.25,1911 MACON,GA.

1934 PHI N O		2	.000
BRTR			

FRISBEE, CHARLES AUGUSTUS (BUNT)
B.FEB.2,1874 DOWS,IOWA
D.NOV.7,1954 ALDEN,IOWA

1899 BOS N O		39	.331
1900 NY N O		4	.153
BBTR		43	.316

FRISCH, FRANK FRANCIS (FRANKIE)
OR (THE FORDHAM FLASH)
B.SEPT.9,1898 BRONX,N.Y.
D.MAR.12,1973 WILMINGTON,DEL.

1919 NY N 2-S-3		54	.226
1920 NY N 3		110	.280
1921 NY N 2-3		153	.341
1922 NY N 2-S-3		132	.326
1923 NY N 2-3		151	.348
1924 NY N 2-S-3		145	.328
1925 NY N 2-S-3		120	.331
1926 NY N 2		135	.314
1927 STL N 2		153	.337
1928 STL N 2		141	.300
1929 STL N 2-3		138	.334
1930 STL N 2-3		133	.346
1931 STL N 2		131	.311
1932 STL N 2-3		115	.292
1933 STL N M-2-S		147	.303
1934 STL N M-2-3		140	.305
1935 STL N M-2-3		103	.294
1936 STL N M-2-3		93	.274
1937 STL N M-2		17	.219
BBTR		2311	.316

NON-PLAYING MANAGER STL(N)1938,
PIT(N) 1940-46, CHI(N) 1949-51

FRISELLA, DANIEL VINCENT
(DANNY) OR (BEAR)
B.MAR.4,1946 SAN FRANCISCO,CAL.
D.JAN.1,1977 PHOENIX,ARIZ.

1967 NY N P		14	1- 6
1968 NY N P		19	2- 4
1969 NY N /P		3	0- 0
1970 NY N P		30	8- 3
1971 NY N P		53	8- 5
1972 NY N P		39	5- 8
1973 ATL N P		42	1- 2
1974 ATL N P		36	3- 4
1975 SD N P		65	1- 6
1976 STL N P		18	0- 0
MIL A P		32	5- 2
BLTR		351	34-40

FRISK, JOHN EMIL
B.OCT.19,1874 KALKASKA,MICH.
D.JAN.27,1922 SEATTLE,WASH.

1899 CIN N P		9	3- 6
1901 DET A P	12	19	5- 3
1905 STL A O		127	.261
1907 STL A H		5	.250
BLTR	21	160	8- 9
			.266

FRITZ, CHARLES CORNELIUS
B.JUNE 16,1882 MOBILE,ALA.
D.JULY 31,1944 MOBILE,ALA.

1907 PHI A P		1	1- 0
TL			

FRITZ, HARRY KOCH (DUTCHMAN)
B.SEPT.30,1890 PHILADELPHIA,PA.
D.NOV.4,1974 COLUMBUS,OHIO

1913 PHI A 3		5	.000
1914 CHI F 3		63	.229
1915 CHI F 3		72	.240
BRTR		140	.228

FRITZ, LAWRENCE JOSEPH (LARRY)
B.FEB.14,1949 E.CHICAGO,IND.

1975 PHI N /H		1	.000
BLTL			

FROATS, WILLIAM JOHN (BILL)
B.OCT.20,1930 NEW YORK,N.Y.

1955 DET A P		1	0- 0
BLTL			

FROCK, SAMUEL WILLIAM
B.DEC.23,1882 BALTIMORE,MD.
D.NOV.3,1925 BALTIMORE,MD.

1907 BOS N P		5	1- 3
1909 PIT N P		8	2- 1
1910 PIT N P		1	0- 0
BOS N P		45	12-19
1911 BOS N P		4	0- 1
BRTR		63	15-24

FROELICH, WILLIAM PALMER (BEN)
B.NOV.12,1887 PITTSBURGH,PA.
D.SEPT.1,1916 PITTSBURGH,PA.

1909 PHI N C		1	.000
TR			

FROMME, ARTHUR HENRY
B.SEPT.3,1883 QUINCY,ILL.
D.AUG.24,1956 LOS ANGELES,CAL.

1906 STL N P		5	1- 4
1907 STL N P		23	5-13
1908 STL N P		20	5-13
1909 CIN N P		37	19-13
1910 CIN N P		11	3- 4
1911 CIN N P		38	10-11
1912 CIN N P		43	16-19
1913 CIN N P		9	1- 4
NY N P		26	11- 6
1914 NY N P		38	9- 5
1915 NY N P		4	0- 1
BRTR		254	80-93

FROST, CARL DAVID (DAVE)
B.NOV.17,1952 LONG BEACH,CAL.

1977 CHI A /P		4	1- 1
1978 CAL A P		11	5- 4
BRTR		15	6- 5

FRY, JERRY RAY
B.FEB.29,1956 SALINAS,CAL.

1978 MON N /C		4	.000
BRTR			

FRY, JOHNSON (JAY)
B.NOV.21,1901 HUNTINGTON,W.VA.
D.APR.7,1959 CARMI,ILL.

1923 CLE A P		1	0- 0
BRTR			

FRYE, CHARLES ANDREW
B.JULY 17,1914 HICKORY,N.C.
D.MAY 25,1945 HICKORY,N.C.

1940 PHI N P	15	18	0- 6
BRTR			

FRYMAN, WOODROW THOMPSON (WOODIE)
B.APR.15,1940 EWING,KY.

1966 PIT N P		36	12- 9
1967 PIT N P		28	3- 8
1968 PHI N P		34	12-14
1969 PHI N P		36	12-15
1970 PHI N P		27	8- 6
1971 PHI N P		37	10- 7
1972 PHI N P		23	4-10
DET A P		16	10- 3
1973 DET A P		34	6-13
1974 DET A P		27	6- 9
1975 MON N P		38	9-12
1976 MON N P		34	13-13
1977 CIN N P		17	5- 5
1978 CHI N P		13	2- 4
MON N P		19	5- 7
BRTL		419	117-135

FUCHS, CHARLES THOMAS
B.NOV.18,1913 UNION CITY,N.J.
D.JUNE 10,1969 WEEHAWKEN,N.J.

1942 DET A P		9	3- 3
1943 PHI N P		17	2- 7
STL A P		13	0- 0
1944 BRO N P		8	1- 0
BBTR		47	6-10

FUCHS, EMIL EDMUND (JUDGE)
B.APR.17,1878 HAMBURG,GERMANY
D.DEC.5,1961 BOSTON,MASS.
NON-PLAYING MANAGER BOS(N) 1929

FUENTES, MIGUEL (PINET)
B.MAY 10,1946 LOIZA,P.R.
D.JAN.29,1970 LOIZA,P.R.

1969 SEA A /P		8	1- 3
BRTR			

YR	CL	LEA	POS	GP	G	REC

FUENTES, RIGOBERTO [PEAT] (TITO)
B.JAN.4,1944 HAVANA,CUBA

1965	SF	N	S/2-3		26	.208
1966	SF	N	S-2		133	.261
1967	SF	N	*2/S		133	.209
1969	SF	N	3-S		67	.295
1970	SF	N	2-S-3		123	.267
1971	SF	N	*2		152	.273
1972	SF	N	*2		152	.264
1973	SF	N	*2/3		160	.277
1974	SF	N	*2		108	.249
1975	SD	N	*2		146	.280
1976	SD	N	*2		135	.263
1977	DET	A	*2		151	.309
1978	OAK	A	2		13	.140
			BBTR		1499	.268
			BR 1965-67, 70 (PART)			

FUHR, OSCAR LAWRENCE
B.AUG.22,1893 DEFIANCE,MO.
D.MAR.27,1975 DALLAS,TEX.

1921	CHI	N	P	1	0- 0
1924	BOS	A	P	23	3- 6
1925	BOS	A	P	38	0- 6
			BLTL	62	3-12

FUHRMAN, ALFRED GEORGE (OLLIE)
B.JULY 20,1896 JORDAN,MINN.
D.JAN.11,1969 PEORIA,ILL.

| 1922 | PHI | A | C | 7 | .333 |
| | | | BBTR | | |

FULGHUM, JAMES LAVOISIER (DOT)
B.JULY 4,1900 VALDOSTA,GA.
D.NOV.11,1967 MIAMI,FLA.

| 1921 | PHI | A | S | 2 | .000 |
| | | | BRTR | | |

FULLER, CHARLES F. (NIG)
B.FEB.17,1866 INDIANA
D.APR.2,1931 HARTFORD,MICH.

| 1902 | BRO | N | C | 3 | .000 |
| | | | BRTR | | |

FULLER, EDWARD A.
B.MAR.22,1869 WASHINGTON,D.C.

| 1886 | WAS | N | P | 1 | 0- 1 |

FULLER, FRANK EDWARD (RABBIT)
B.JAN.1,1893 DETROIT,MICH.
D.OCT.29,1965 WARREN,MICH.

1915	DET	A	2		14	.156
1916	DET	A	2		20	.100
1923	BOS	A	2		6	.238
			BBTR		40	.177

FULLER, HENRY W. (HARRY)
B.DEC.5,1862 CINCINNATI,OHIO
D.DEC.12,1895 CINCINNATI,OHIO

| 1891 | STL | AA | 3 | 1 | .000 |

FULLER, JAMES HARDY (JIM)
B.NOV.26,1950 BETHESDA,MD.

1973	BAL	A	/O-1		9	.115
1974	BAL	A	O/1		64	.222
1977	HOU	N	D/1		34	.160
			BRTR		107	.194

FULLER, JOHN EDWARD
B.JAN.29,1950 LYNWOOD,CAL.

| 1974 | ATL | N | /O | 3 | .333 |
| | | | BLTL | | |

FULLER, VERNON GORDON (VERN)
B.MAR.1,1944 MENOMONIE,WIS.

1964	CLE	A	2		2	.000
1966	CLE	A	2		16	.234
1967	CLE	A	2/S		73	.223
1968	CLE	A	2-3/S		97	.242
1969	CLE	A	*2/3		108	.236
1970	CLE	A	2/3-.		29	.182
			BRTR		325	.232

FULLER, WILLIAM BENJAMIN (SHORTY)
B.OCT.10,1867 CINCINNATI,OHIO
D.APR.11,1904 CINCINNATI,OHIO

1888	WAS	N	S		49	.182
1889	STL	AA	S		140	.228
1890	STL	AA	S		130	.271
1891	STL	AA	2-S		135	.219
1892	LA	N	S		138	.236
1893	NY	N	S		130	.247
1894	NY	N	S		95	.282
1895	NY	N	S		126	.227
1896	NY	N	S		17	.180
			BRTR		960	.239

FULLERTON, CURTIS HOOPER
B.SEPT.13,1898 ELLSWORTH,ME.
D.JAN.2,1975 WINTHROP,MASS.

1921	BOS	A	P	4	0- 1
1922	BOS	A	P	31	1- 4
1923	BOS	A	P	37	2-15
1924	BOS	A	P	33	7-12
1925	BOS	A	P	4	0- 3
1933	BOS	A	P	6	0- 2
			BLTR	115	10-37

FULLIS, CHARLES PHILIP (CHICK)
B.FEB.27,1904 GIRARDVILLE,PA.
D.MAR.28,1946 ASHLAND,PA.

1928	NY	N	O		11	.000
1929	NY	N	O		86	.288
1930	NY	N	O		13	.000
1931	NY	N	O		89	.328
1932	NY	N	O		98	.298
1933	PHI	N	3-O		151	.309
1934	PHI	N	O		28	.225
		STL	N	O		69	.261
1936	STL	N	O		47	.281
			BRTR		590	.295

FULMER, CHARLES JOHN (CHICK)
B.FEB.12,1851 PHILADELPHIA,PA.
D.FEB.15,1940 PHILADELPHIA,PA.

1871	ROK	NA	1-S		16	-
1872	MUT	NA	S-3		36	.302
1873	PHI	NA	C-S		49	-
1874	PHI	NA	S-3		57	-
1875	PHI	NA	S-3		68	.222
1876	LOU	N	M-S		66	.272
1879	BUF	N	2		75	.266
1880	BUF	N	2		11	.152
1882	CIN	AA	M-S		79	.277
1883	CIN	AA	S		82	.247
1884	CIN	AA	S-3-O		30	.177
		STL	AA	2		1	.000
			TR		570	-

FULMER, CHRISTOPHER
B.JULY 4,1858 TAMAQUA,PA.
D.NOV.9,1931 TAMAQUA,PA.

1884	WAS	U	C-1-O		47	.282
1885	BAL	AA	C		79	.251
1887	BAL	AA	C		56	.368
1888	BAL	AA	C		51	.179
1889	BAL	AA	C		16	.278
			BRTR		250	.275

FULTZ, DAVID LEWIS
B.MAY 29,1875 STAUNTON,VA.
D.OCT.29,1959 DE LAND,FLA.

1898	PHI	N	O		16	.196
1899	PHI	N	S-3		2	.400
		BAL	N	3-O		54	.304
1901	PHI	A	2-O		132	.295
1902	PHI	A	2-O		129	.300
1903	NY	A	O		78	.240
1904	NY	A	O		96	.278
1905	NY	A	O		122	.232
			BRTR		629	.275

FUNK, ELIAS CALVIN (LIZ)
B.OCT.28,1904 LA CYGNE,KAN.
D.JAN.16,1968 NORMAN,OKLA.

1929	NY	A	H		1	.000
1930	DET	A	O		140	.275
1932	CHI	A	O		122	.259
1933	CHI	A	O		10	.222
			BLTL		273	.267

FUNK, FRANKLIN RAY (FRANK)
B.AUG.30,1935 WASHINGTON,D.C.

1960	CLE	A	P	9	4- 2
1961	CLE	A	P	56	11-11
1962	CLE	A	P	47	2- 1
1963	MIL	N	P	25	26	3- 3
			BRTR	137	138	20-17

FUNKHOUSER, LEONIDAS PYRRHUS
(PLAYED UNDER NAME OF
LEONIDAS PYRRHUS LEE)
B.OCT.26,1904 LA CYGNE,KAN.
D.JAN.16,1968 NORMAN,OKLA.

FURILLO, CARL ANTHONY (CARL)
(SKOONJ) OR (THE READING RIFLE)
B.MAR.8,1922 STONY CREEK MILLS,PA.

1946	BRO	N	O		117	.284
1947	BRO	N	O		124	.295
1948	BRO	N	O		148	.297
1949	BRO	N	O		142	.324
1950	BRO	N	O		153	.305
1951	BRO	N	O		158	.295
1952	BRO	N	O		134	.247
1953	BRO	N	O		132	.344
1954	BRO	N	O		150	.294
1955	BRO	N	O		140	.314
1956	BRO	N	O		149	.289
1957	BRO	N	O		119	.306
1958	LA	N	O		122	.290
1959	LA	N	O		50	.290
1960	LA	N	O		8	.200
			BRTR		1806	.299

FURNISS, THOMAS
B.CONNECTICUT
NON-PLAYING MANAGER BOS[U] 1884

FUSSELBACH, EDWARD L.
B.JULY 4,1858 PHILADELPHIA,PA.

1882	STL	AA	P-C-	2	35	0- 2
						.219
1884	BAL	U	C		65	.286
1885	ATH	AA	O		5	.316
1888	LOU	AA	O		1	.250
				2	106	0- 2
						.267

FUSSELL, FREDERICK MORRIS
(MOONLIGHT ACE)
B.OCT.7,1895 SHERIDAN,MO.
D.OCT.23,1966 SYRACUSE,N.Y.

1922	CHI	N	P	3	1- 1
1923	CHI	N	P	28	3- 5
1928	PIT	N	P	28	8- 9
1929	PIT	N	P	21	2- 2
			BLTL	80	14-17

FUSSELMAN, LESTER LEROY
B.MAR.7,1921 PRYOR,OKLA.
D.MAY 21,1970 CLEVELAND,OHIO

1952	STL	N	C		32	.159
1953	STL	N	C		11	.250
			BRTR		43	.169

GABLER, FRANK HAROLD (FRANK)
OR (THE GREAT GABBO)
B.NOV.6,1911 E.HIGHLANDS,CAL.
D.NOV.1,1967 LONG BEACH,CAL.

1935	NY	N	P	26	2- 1
1936	NY	N	P	43	4- 6
1937	NY	N	P	5	0- 0
		BOS	N	P	19	4- 7
1938	BOS	N	P	1	0- 0
		CHI	A	P	18	1- 7
			BRTR	113	16-23

GABLER, JOHN RICHARD (GABE)
B.OCT.2,1930 KANSAS CITY,MO.

1959	NY	A	P	3	1- 1
1960	NY	A	P	21	1- 3
1961	WAS	A	P	29	34	3- 8
			BBTR	53	58	7-12

GABLER, WILLIAM LOUIS (GABE)
B.AUG.4,1930 ST.LOUIS,MO.

| 1958 | CHI | N | H | 3 | .000 |
| | | | BLTR | | |

GABLES, KENNETH HARLIN (CORAL)
B.JAN.31,1919 WALNUT GROVE,MO.
D.JAN.2,1960 WALNUT GROVE,MO.

1945	PIT	N	P	29	11- 7
1946	PIT	N	P	32	2- 4
1947	PIT	N	P	1	0- 0
			BRTR	62	13-11

GABRIELSON, LEONARD GARY (LEN)
B.FEB.14,1940 OAKLAND,CAL.

1960	MIL	N	O		4	.000
1963	MIL	N	1-3-O		46	.217
1964	MIL	N	1-O		24	.184
		CHI	N	1-O		89	.246
1965	CHI	N	O/1		28	.250
		SF	N	O/1		88	.301
1966	SF	N	O/1		94	.217
1967	CAL	A	/O		11	.083
		LA	N	O		90	.261
1968	LA	N	O		108	.270
1969	LA	N	O/1		83	.270
1970	LA	N	/O-1		43	.190
			BLTR		708	.253

GABRIELSON, LEONARD HILBOURNE
B.SEPT.8,1915 OAKLAND,CAL.

| 1939 | PHI | N | 1 | 5 | .222 |
| | | | BLTL | | |

GADDY, JOHN WILSON (SHERIFF)
B.FEB.5,1914 WADESBORO,N.C.
D.MAY 3,1966 ALBEMARLE,N.C.

| 1938 | BRO | N | P | 2 | 2- 0 |
| | | | BRTR | | |

GAEDEL, EDWARD CARL (EDDIE)
B.JUNE 8,1925 CHICAGO,ILL.
D.JUNE 18,1961 CHICAGO,ILL.

| 1951 | STL | A | H | 1 | .000 |
| | | | BR | | |

GAFFKE, FABIAN SEBASTIAN
B.AUG.5,1913 MILWAUKEE,WIS.

1936	BOS	A	O		15	.127
1937	BOS	A	O		54	.288
1938	BOS	A	C-O		19	.100
1939	BOS	A	O		1	.000
1941	CLE	A	O		4	.250
1942	CLE	A	O		40	.164
			BRTR		129	.227

GAFFNEY, JOHN H.
B.JUNE 29,1855 ROXBURY,MASS.
D.AUG.8,1913 NEW YORK,N.Y.
NON-PLAYING MANAGER WAS[N] 1886-87

YR CL LEA POS   GP   G   REC   YR CL LEA POS   GP   G   REC   YR CL LEA POS   GP   G   REC

GAGLIANO, PHILIP JOSEPH (PHIL)
B.DEC.27,1941 MEMPHIS,TENN.
1963 STL N 2-3   10   .400
1964 STL N 1-2-3-0   40   .259
1965 STL N 2-0-3   122   .240
1966 STL N 3/1-0-2   90   .254
1967 STL N 2-3/1-5   73   .221
1968 STL N 2-3/0   53   .229
1969 STL N 2/1-3-0   62   .227
1970 STL N /3-1-2   18   .188
     CHI N 2/1-3   26   .150
1971 BOS A 0/2-3   47   .324
1972 BOS A 0/3-2-1   52   .256
1973 CIN N /3-2-1-0   63   .240
1974 CIN N /2-1-5   46   .065
     BRTR   702   .238

GAGLIANO, RALPH MICHAEL
B.OCT.8,1946 MEMPHIS,TENN.
1965 CLE A R   1   .000
     BLTR

GAGNIER, EDWARD J.
B.APR.16,1883 PARIS,FRANCE
D.SEPT.13,1946 DETROIT,MICH.
1914 BRO F S   94   .182
1915 BRO F S   19   .260
     BUF F 2   2   .000
     BRTR   115   .191

GAGNON, HAROLD DENNIS (CHICK)
B.SEPT.27,1897 MILLBURY,MASS.
D.APR.30,1970 WILMINGTON,DEL.
1922 DET A S   9   .250
1924 WAS A S   4   .200
     BRTR   13   .222

GAGUS, CHARLES
B.SAN FRANCISCO,CAL.
1884 WAS U P-S-   21   42 11- 9
          0   .240

GAINER, DELLOS CLINTON
(DEL) OR (SHERIFF)
B.NOV.10,1886 MONTROSE,W.VA.
D.JAN.29,1947 ELKINS,W.VA.
1909 DET A 1   2   .200
1911 DET A 1   70   .302
1912 DET A 1   51   .240
1913 DET A 1   104   .270
1914 DET A 1   1   .000
     BOS A 1   38   .238
1915 BOS A 1   82   .295
1916 BOS A 1   56   .253
1917 BOS A 1   52   .308
1919 BOS A 1-0   47   .237
1922 STL N 1-0   43   .268
     BRTR   546   .273

GAINES, ARNESTA JOE (JOE)
B.NOV.22,1936 BRYAN,TEX.
1960 CIN N 0   11   .200
1961 CIN N 0   5   .000
1962 CIN N 0   66   .231
1963 BAL A 0   66   .286
1964 BAL A 0   16   .154
     HOU N 0   89   .254
1965 HOU N 0   100   .227
1966 HOU N /0   11   .077
     BRTR   362   .241

GAINES, WILLARD ROLAND (NEMO)
B.DEC.23,1897 ALEXANDRIA,VA.
1921 WAS A P   4   0- 0
     BLTL

GAISER, FREDERICK JACOB
B.AUG.31,1885 STUTTGART,GERMANY
D.OCT.9,1918 TRENTON,N.J.
1908 STL N P   1   0- 0

GALAN, AUGUST JOHN (AUGIE)
B.MAY 25,1912 BERKELEY,CAL.
1934 CHI N 2   66   .260
1935 CHI N 0   154   .314
1936 CHI N 0   145   .264
1937 CHI N 0   147   .252
1938 CHI N 0   110   .286
1939 CHI N 0   148   .304
1940 CHI N 2-0   68   .230
1941 CHI N 0   65   .208
     BRO N 0   17   .259
1942 BRO N 1-2-0   69   .263
1943 BRO N 1-0   139   .287
1944 BRO N 2-0   151   .318
1945 BRO N 1-3-0   152   .307
1946 BRO N 1-3-0   99   .310
1947 CIN N 0   124   .314
1948 CIN N 0   54   .286
1949 NY N 1-0   22   .059
     PHI A 0   12   .308
     BBTR   1742   .287
     BL 1944-49

GALASSO, ROBERT JOSEPH (BOB)
B.JAN.13,1952 CONNELLSVILLE,PA.
1977 SEA A P   11   0- 6
     BLTR

GALATZER, MILTON (MILT)
B.MAY 4,1907 CHICAGO,IL..
D.JAN.29,1976 SAN FRANCISCO,CAL
1933 CLE A 1-0   57   .238
1934 CLE A 0   49   .270
1935 CLE A 0   93   .301
1936 CLE A P-0   1   49   0- 0
                               .237
1939 CIN N 1   3   .000
     BLTL   1 251 0- 0
                               .268

GALAZEWSKI, STANLEY JOSEPH
[PLAYED UNDER NAME OF
STANLEY JOSEPH GALLE]

GALE, RICHARD BLACKWELL (RICH)
B.JAN.19,1954 LITTLETON,N.H.
1978 KC A P   31 14- 8
     BRTR

GALEHOUSE, DENNIS WARD (DENNY)
B.DEC.7,1911 MARSHALLVILLE,OHIO
1934 CLE A P   1   0- 0
1935 CLE A P   3   1- 0
1936 CLE A P   36   8- 7
1937 CLE A P   36   9-14
1938 CLE A P   36   7- 8
1939 BOS A P   30   9-10
1940 BOS A P   25   6- 6
1941 STL A P   30   9-10
1942 STL A P   32 12-12
1943 STL A P   31 11-11
1944 STL A P   24   9-10
1946 STL A P   30   8-12
1947 STL A P   9   1- 3
     BOS A P   21 11- 7
1948 BOS A P   27   8- 8
1949 BOS A P   2   0- 0
     BRTR   375 109-118

GALLAGHER, ALAN MITCHELL EDWARD
GEORGE PATRICK HENRY (AL)
B.OCT.19,1945 SAN FRANCISCO,CAL.
1970 SF N 3   109   .266
1971 SF N *3   136   .277
1972 SF N 3   82   .223
1973 SF N /0   5   .222
     CAL A 3/2-S   110   .273
     BRTR   442   .263

GALLAGHER, D. F.
.901 CLE A 0   2   .000

GALLAGHER, DOUGLAS EUGENE
B.FEB.21,1940 FREMONT,OHIO
1962 DET A P   9   0- 4
     BRTL

GALLAGHER, EDWARD MICHAEL (LEFTY)
B.NOV.28,1910 DORCHESTER,MASS.
1932 BOS A P   9   0- 3
     BBTL

GALLAGHER, JAMES E.
B.FINDLAY,OHIO
D.MAR.29,1894 SCRANTON,PA.
1886 WAS N S   1   .200

GALLAGHER, JOHN C.
B.1894 PITTSBURGH,PA.
1915 BAL F 2   40   .200
     BRTR

GALLAGHER, JOHN LAURENCE (JACKIE)
B.JAN.28,1902 PROVIDENCE,R.I.
1923 CLE A 0   1 1.000
     BLTR

GALLAGHER, JOSEPH EMMETT (MUSCLES)
B.MAR.7,1914 BUFFALO,N.Y.
1939 NY A 0   14   .244
     STL A 0   71   .282
1940 STL A 0   23   .271
     BRO N 0   57   .264
     BRTR   165   .273

GALLAGHER, LAWRENCE KIRBY (GIL)
B.SEPT.5,1896 WASHINGTON,D.C.
D.JAN.6,1957 WASHINGTON,D.C.
1922 BOS N S   7   .045
     BBTR

GALLAGHER, ROBERT COLLINS (BOB)
B.JULY 7,1948 NEWTON,MASS.
1972 BOS A /H   7   .000
1973 HOU N 0/1   71   .264
1974 HOU N 0/1   102   .172
1975 NY N 0   33   .133
     BLTL   213   .220

GALLAGHER, WILLIAM H.
B.1875 LOWELL,MASS.
1896 PHI N S   14   .327

GALLAGHER, WILLIAM JOHN
B.PHILADELPHIA,PA.
1883 BAL AA P-S-   6   16   0- 3
          0   .159
     PHI N 0   2   .000
1884 KEY U P   3   1- 2
          TL   9   21   1- 5
                               .133

GALLE, STANLEY JOSEPH
[REAL NAME
STANLEY JOSEPH GALAZEWSKI]
B.FEB.7,1919 MILWAUKEE,WIS.
1942 WAS A 3   13   .111
     BRTR

GALLIA, MELVIN ALLYS (BERT)
B.OCT.14,1891 BEEVILLE,TEX.
D.MAR.19,1976 DEVINE,TEX.
1912 WAS A P   2   0- 0
1913 WAS A P   30   1- 5
1914 WAS A P   2   0- 0
1915 WAS A P   43 16-10
1916 WAS A P   49 17-13
1917 WAS A P   42 44   9-13
1918 STL A P   19   7- 6
1919 STL A P   34 12-14
1920 STL A P   2   0- 1
     PHI N P   18 19   2- 6
     BRTR   241 244 64-68

GALLIGAN, JOHN T.
B.1868 EASTON,PA.
D.JULY 17,1906 NEW YORK,N.Y.
1889 LOU AA 0   31   .167

GALLIVAN, PHILIP JOSEPH
B.MAY 29,1907 SEATTLE,WASH.
D.NOV.24,1969 ST.PAUL,MINN.
1931 BRO N P   6   0- 1
1932 CHI A P   13   1- 3
1934 CHI A P   35   4- 7
     BRTR   54   5-11

GALLOWAY, CLARENCE EDWARD (CHICK)
B.AUG.4,1896 CLINTON,S.C.
D.NOV.7,1969 CLINTON,S.C.
1919 PHI A S   17   .143
1920 PHI A S   98   .202
1921 PHI A S-3   131   .265
1922 PHI A S   155   .324
1923 PHI A S   134   .276
1924 PHI A S   129   .276
1925 PHI A S   149   .241
1926 PHI A S   133   .240
1927 PHI A S   77   .265
1928 DET A S-3   53   .264
     BRTR   1076   .264

GALLOWAY, JAMES CATO (BAD NEWS)
B.SEPT.16,1887 IREDELL,TEX.
D.MAY 3,1950 FORT WORTH,TEX.
1912 STL N 2   21   .185
     BBTR

GALVIN, JAMES FRANCIS (JIM)
(PUD), (GENTLE JEEMS)
OR (THE LITTLE STEAM ENGINE)
B.DEC.25,1856 ST.LOUIS,MO.
D.MAR.7,1902 PITTSBURGH,PA.
1875 STL NA P-0   6   11   4- 2
                               .146
1879 BUF N P   65   66 37-27
                               .211
1880 BUF N P-0   55   64 20-34
                               .211
1881 BUF N P-0   53   62 29-24
                               .211
1882 BUF N P-0   50   54 28-22
                               .213
1883 BUF N P-0   73   79 44-29
                               .220
1884 BUF N P   68 46-21
1885 BUF N M-P   32 12-19
     PIT AA P   11   3- 8
                               .108
1886 PIT AA P   50 29-21
1887 PIT N P   49 28-20
1888 PIT N P   50 23-25
1889 PIT N P   40 23-17
1890 PIT P P   26 11-14
1891 PIT N P   28 15-13
1892 PIT N P   11   5- 6
     STL N P   15   5- 6
     BRTR   682 716 362-308
                               .203

GALVIN, JAMES JOSEPH
B.AUG.11,1907 SOMERVILLE,MASS.
D.SEPT.30,1969 MARIETTA,GA.
1930 BOS A H   2   .000
     BRTR

GALVIN, JOHN
B.BROOKLYN,N.Y.
D.MAY 1904
1872 ATL NA 2   1   .000
1874 ATL NA 2   1   .000
                             2   .000

GALVIN, LOUIS
B.HAVERILL,MASS.
D.JUNE 17,1895

YR	CL	LEA	POS	GP	G	REC
1884	STP	U	P		3	0- 2

GAMBLE, JOHN ROBERT
B.FEB.10,1948 RENO,NEV.

YR	CL	LEA	POS	GP	G	REC
1972	DET	A	/S		6	.000
1973	DET	A	R		7	.000
		BRTR			13	.000

GAMBLE, LEE JESSE
B.JUNE 28,1910 RENOVO,PA.

YR	CL	LEA	POS	GP	G	REC
1935	CIN	N	O		2	.500
1938	CIN	N	O		53	.320
1939	CIN	N	O		72	.267
1940	CIN	N	O		38	.143
		BLTR			165	.266

GAMBLE, OSCAR CHARLES
B.DEC.20,1949 RAMER,ALA.

YR	CL	LEA	POS	GP	G	REC
1969	CHI	N	O		24	.225
1970	PHI	N	O		88	.262
1971	PHI	N	O		92	.221
1972	PHI	N	O/1		74	.237
1973	CLE	A	O-O		113	.267
1974	CLE	A	*O-O		135	.291
1975	CLE	A	O-O		121	.261
1976	NY	A	*O		110	.232
1977	CHI	A	O-O		137	.297
1978	SD	N	*O-O		126	.275
		BLTR			1020	.264

GAMBLE, ROBERT
B.1867 HAZELTON,PA.

YR	CL	LEA	POS	GP	G	REC
1888	ATH	AA	P		1	0- 1

GAMMON, JOHN FRANCIS
(PLAYED UNDER NAME OF
JOHN FRANCIS SMITH)

GAMMONS, JOHN ASHLEY (DAFF)
B.MAR.17,1876 NEW BEDFORD,MASS.
D.SEPT.24,1963 E.GREENWICH,R.I.

YR	CL	LEA	POS	GP	G	REC
1901	BOS	N	O		26	.211

GANDIL, CHARLES ARNOLD (CHICK)
B.JAN.19,1887 ST.PAUL,MINN.
D.DEC.13,1970 CALISTOGA,CAL.

YR	CL	LEA	POS	GP	G	REC
1910	CHI	A	1		77	.193
1912	WAS	A	1		117	.305
1913	WAS	A	1		147	.318
1914	WAS	A	1		145	.259
1915	WAS	A	1		136	.291
1916	CLE	A	1		146	.259
1917	CHI	A	1		149	.273
1918	CHI	A	1		114	.271
1919	CHI	A	1		115	.290
		BLTR			1146	.276

GANDY, ROBERT BRINKLEY (STRING)
B.AUG.25,1893 JACKSONVILLE,FLA.
D.JUNE 19,1945 JACKSONVILLE,FLA

YR	CL	LEA	POS	GP	G	REC
1916	PHI	N	O		1	.000
		BLTR				

GANLEY, ROBERT STEPHEN
B.APR.23,1875 LOWELL,MASS.
D.OCT.10,1945 LOWELL,MASS.

YR	CL	LEA	POS	GP	G	REC
1905	PIT	N	O		32	.315
1906	PIT	N	O		134	.258
1907	WAS	A	O		154	.276
1908	WAS	A	O		150	.239
1909	WAS	A	O		16	.000
	PHI	A	O		83	.207
		BLTL			569	.254

GANNON, JAMES EDWARD (GUSSIE)
B.NOV.26,1873 ERIE,PA.
D.APR.12,1966 ERIE,PA.

YR	CL	LEA	POS	GP	G	REC
1895	PIT	N	P		1	0- 0

GANNON, WILLIAM G.
B.NEW HAVEN,CONN.
D.APR.26,1927 FT.WORTH,TEX.

YR	CL	LEA	POS	GP	G	REC
1898	STL	N	O		1	0- 1
1901	CHI	N	O		15	.159
				1	16	0- 1
						.167

GANTENBEIN, JOSEPH STEPHEN (SEP)
B.AUG.25,1916 SAN FRANCISCO,CAL

YR	CL	LEA	POS	GP	G	REC
1939	PHI	A	2-3		111	.290
1940	PHI	A	1-S-3-O		75	.239
		BLTR			186	.272

GANTNER, JAMES ELMER (JIM)
B.JAN.5,1954 FOND DU LAC,WIS.

YR	CL	LEA	POS	GP	G	REC
1976	MIL	A	3		26	.246
1977	MIL	A	3		14	.298
1978	MIL	A	2-3/1-S		43	.216
		BLTR			83	.244

GANZEL, CHARLES WILLIAM
B.JUNE 18,1862 WATERFORD,WIS.
D.APR.7,1914 QUINCY,MASS.

YR	CL	LEA	POS	GP	G	REC
1884	STP	U	C-O		7	.208
1885	PHI	N	C-O		33	.168
1886	PHI	N	C		1	.000
	DET	N	C		53	.276
1887	DET	N	C		55	.285
1888	DET	N	C-2		93	.248
1889	BOS	N	C-O		71	.255
1890	BOS	N	C		38	.269
1891	BOS	N	C		68	.259
1892	BOS	N	C		51	.270
1893	BOS	N	C-O		69	.282
1894	BOS	N	C		65	.278
1895	BOS	N	C		74	.265
1896	BOS	N	C		44	.262
1897	BOS	N	C		27	.274
		BRTR			749	.264

GANZEL, FOSTER PIRIE (BABE)
B.MAY 22,1901 MALDEN,MASS.
D.FEB.6,1978 JACKSONVILLE,FLA.

YR	CL	LEA	POS	GP	G	REC
1927	WAS	A	O		13	.437
1928	WAS	A	O		10	.077
		BRTR			23	.311

GANZEL, JOHN HENRY
B.APR.7,1874 KALAMAZOO,MICH.
D.JAN.14,1959 ORLANDO,FLA.

YR	CL	LEA	POS	GP	G	REC
1898	PIT	N	1		14	.111
1900	PIT	N	1		78	.272
1901	NY	N	1		139	.220
1903	NY	A	1		129	.285
1904	NY	A	1		129	.261
1907	CIN	N	1		143	.254
1908	CIN	N	M-1		108	.250
		BRTR			740	.253

NON-PLAYING MANAGER BR[CIN] 1915

GARAGIOLA, JOSEPH HENRY (JOE)
B.FEB.12,1926 ST.LOUIS,MO.

YR	CL	LEA	POS	GP	G	REC
1946	STL	N	C		74	.237
1947	STL	N	C		77	.257
1948	STL	N	C		24	.107
1949	STL	N	C		81	.261
1950	STL	N	C		34	.318
1951	STL	N	C		27	.194
	PIT	N	C		72	.255
1952	PIT	N	C		118	.273
1953	PIT	N	C		27	.233
	CHI	N	C		74	.272
1954	CHI	N	C		63	.281
	NY	N	C		5	.273
		BLTR			676	.257

GARBACH, NATHANIEL MICHAEL
(PLAYED UNDER NAME OF
NATHANIEL MICHAEL GARBARK)

GARBACH, ROBERT MICHAEL
(PLAYED UNDER NAME OF
ROBERT MICHAEL GARBARK)

GARBARK, NATHANIEL MICHAEL
(REAL NAME
NATHANIEL MICHAEL GARBACH)
B.FEB.2,1916 HOUSTON,TEX.

YR	CL	LEA	POS	GP	G	REC
1944	NY	A	C		89	.261
1945	NY	A	C		60	.216
		BRTR			149	.244

GARBARK, ROBERT MICHAEL
(REAL NAME ROBERT MICHAEL GARBACH)
B.NOV.12,1909 HOUSTON,TEX.

YR	CL	LEA	POS	GP	G	REC
1934	CLE	A	C		5	.000
1935	CLE	A	C		6	.333
1937	CHI	N	C		1	.000
1938	CHI	N	C		23	.259
1939	CHI	N	C		24	.143
1944	PHI	A	C		18	.261
1945	BOS	A	C		68	.261
		BRTR			145	.248

GARBER, HENRY EUGENE (GENE)
B.NOV.13,1947 LANCASTER,PA.

YR	CL	LEA	POS	GP	G	REC
1969	PIT	N	/P		2	0- 0
1970	PIT	N	/P		14	0- 3
1972	PIT	N	/P		4	0- 0
1973	KC	A	P	48	49	9- 9
1974	KC	A	P		17	1- 2
	PHI	N	P		34	4- 0
1975	PHI	N	P		71	10-12
1976	PHI	N	P		59	9- 3
1977	PHI	N	P		64	8- 6
1978	PHI	N	P		22	2- 1
	ATL	N	P	43	44	4- 4
		BRTR		378	380	47-40

GARBER, ROBERT MITCHELL
B.SEPT.10,1928 HUNKER,PA.

YR	CL	LEA	POS	GP	G	REC
1956	PIT	N	P		2	0- 0
		BRTR				

GARBOWSKI, ALEXANDER
B.JUNE 25,1925 YONKERS,N.Y

YR	CL	LEA	POS	GP	G	REC
1952	DET	A	H		2	.000
		BRTR				

GARCIA, ALFONSO RAFAEL (KIKO)
B.OCT.14,1953 MARTINEZ,CAL.

YR	CL	LEA	POS	GP	G	REC
1976	BAL	A	S		11	.219
1977	BAL	A	S/2		65	.221
1978	BAL	A	S/2		79	.263
		BRTR			155	.244

GARCIA, DAMASO DOMINGO (SANCHEZ)
B.FEB.7,1957 MOCA,D.R.

YR	CL	LEA	POS	GP	G	REC
1978	NY	A	2/S		18	.195
		BRTR				

GARCIA, DAVID (DAVE)
B.SEPT.15,1920 E.ST.LOUIS,MO.
NON-PLAYING MANAGER CAL[A] 1977-78

GARCIA, EDWARD MIGUEL (MIKE)
OR (THE BIG BEAR)
B.NOV.17,1923 SAN GABRIEL,CAL.

YR	CL	LEA	POS	GP	G	REC
1948	CLE	A	P		1	0- 0
1949	CLE	A	P		41	14- 5
1950	CLE	A	P		33	11-11
1951	CLE	A	P		47	20-13
1952	CLE	A	P		46	22-11
1953	CLE	A	P		38	18- 9
1954	CLE	A	P		45	19- 8
1955	CLE	A	P		38	11-13
1956	CLE	A	P		35	11-12
1957	CLE	A	P		38	12- 8
1958	CLE	A	P		6	1- 0
1959	CLE	A	P		29	3- 6
1960	CHI	A	P		15	0- 0
1961	WAS	A	P		16	0- 1
		BRTR			428	142-97

GARCIA, PEDRO MODESTO [DELFI]
B.APR.17,1950 GUAYAMA,P.R.

YR	CL	LEA	POS	GP	G	REC
1973	MIL	A	*2		160	.245
1974	MIL	A	*2		141	.199
1975	MIL	A	2		98	.225
1976	MIL	A	2		41	.217
	DET	A	2		77	.198
1977	TOR	A	2		41	.208
		BRTR			558	.220

GARCIA, RALPH
B.DEC.14,1948 LOS ANGELES,CAL.

YR	CL	LEA	POS	GP	G	REC
1972	SD	N	/P		3	0- 0
1974	SD	N	/P		8	0- 0
		BRTR			11	0- 0

GARCIA, RAMON [GARCIA]
B.MAR.5,1924 LA ESPERANZA,CUBA

YR	CL	LEA	POS	GP	G	REC
1948	WAS	A	P		4	0- 0
		BRTR				

GARCIA, VINICIO UZCANGA (CHICO)
B.DEC.24,1924 VERICRUZ,MEXICO

YR	CL	LEA	POS	GP	G	REC
1954	BAL	A	2		39	.113
		BRTR				

GARDELLA, ALFRED STEPHAN (AL)
B.JAN.11,1918 NEW YORK,N.Y.

YR	CL	LEA	POS	GP	G	REC
1945	NY	N	1-0		17	.077
		BLTL				

GARDELLA, DANIEL LEWIS (DANNY)
B.FEB.26,1920 NEW YORK,N.Y.

YR	CL	LEA	POS	GP	G	REC
1944	NY	N	O		47	.250
1945	NY	N	1-O		121	.272
1950	STL	N	H		1	.000
		BLTL			169	.268

GARDINER, ARTHUR CECIL
B.DEC.26,1899 BROOKLYN,N.Y.

YR	CL	LEA	POS	GP	G	REC
1923	PHI	N	P		1	0- 0
		BRTR				

GARDNER, ALEXANDER
B.APR.28,1861 TORONTO,ONT.,CAN.
D.JUNE 18,1926 DANVERS,MASS.

YR	CL	LEA	POS	GP	G	REC
1884	WAS	AA	C		1	.000

GARDNER, ARTHUR JUNIOR (ART)
B.SEPT.21,1952 MADDEN,MISS.

YR	CL	LEA	POS	GP	G	REC
1975	HOU	N	/O		13	.194
1977	HOU	N	O		66	.154
1978	SF	N	/H		7	.000
		BLTL			86	.162

GARDNER, EARLE MC CLURKIN
B.JAN.24,1884 SPARTA,ILL.
D.MAR.2,1943 SPARTA,ILL.

YR	CL	LEA	POS	GP	G	REC
1908	NY	A	2		20	.213
1909	NY	A	2		22	.389
1910	NY	A	2		86	.244
1911	NY	A	2		102	.263
1912	NY	A	2		43	.281
		BRTR			273	.263

YR CL LEA POS   GP   G   REC   YR CL LEA POS   GP   G   REC   YR CL LEA POS   GP   G   REC

GARDNER, FRANKLIN W. (GID)
B.1859 E.CAMBRIDGE,MASS.
D.AUG.1,1914 CAMBRIDGE,MASS.
1879 TRO N P   2   0- 2
1880 CLE N P-O   9   10   2- 7
                             .200
1883 BAL AA P-2-   1   42   1- 0
            3-0   .290
1884 BAL AA O   41   .203
     CHI U P-3-   1   20   0- 0
            O   .173
     PIT U 2-O   16   .254
     BAL U S   1   .250
1885 BAL AA P-2   1   44   0- 1
                             .219
1887 IND N 2-O   18   .306
1888 WAS N 2   2   .200
                   14   196   3-10
                             .238

GARDNER, FREDERICK
B.PALMER,MASS.
1887 BAL AA P   4   0- 1

GARDNER, HARRY
B.SEP.20,1888 PORTLAND,ORE.
D.AUG.2,1961 BARLOW,ORE.
1911 PIT N P   13   1- 1
1912 PIT N P   1   10   0- 0
     TR   14   1- 1

GARDNER, JAMES ANDERSON
B.OCT.4,1874 PITTSBURGH,PA.
D.APR.24,1905 PITTSBURGH,PA.
1895 PIT N P   10   8- 2
1897 PIT N P   14   28   5- 5
1898 PIT N P   23   32 10-13
1899 PIT N P   7   1- 1
1902 CHI N P   3   1- 2
     TR   57   80 25-23

GARDNER, MILES GLENN
B.JAN.25,1916 BURNSVILLE,N.C.
D.JULY 7,1964 ROCHESTER,N.Y.
1945 STL N P   17   3- 1
     BRTR

GARDNER, RAYMOND VINCENT
B.OCT.25,1901 FREDERICK,MD.
D.MAY 1,1968 FREDERICK,MD.
1929 CLE A S   82   .262
1930 CLE A S   33   .077
     BRTR   115   .253

GARDNER, RICHARD FRANK (ROB)
B.DEC.19,1944 BINGHAMTON,N.Y.
1965 NY N /P   5   0- 2
1966 NY N P   41   43   4- 8
1967 CHI N P   18   0- 2
1968 CLE A P   5   0- 0
1970 NY A /P   1   1- 0
1971 OAK A /P   4   0- 0
     NY A /P   2   0- 0
1972 NY A P   20   8- 5
1973 CHI A /P   3   0- 0
     MIL A P   10   1- 1
     BRTL   109 111 14-18

GARDNER, WILLIAM FREDERICK
(BILLY) OR (SHOTGUN)
B.JULY 19,1927 WATERFORD,CONN.
1954 NY N 2-S-3   62   .213
1955 NY N 2-S-3   59   .203
1956 BAL A 2-S-3   144   .213
1957 BAL A 2-S   154   .262
1958 BAL A 2-S   151   .225
1959 BAL A 2-S-3   140   .217
1960 WAS A 2-S   145   .257
1961 MIN A 2-3   45   .234
     NY A 2-3   41   .212
1962 NY A 2-3   4   .000
     BOS A 2-S-3   53   .271
1963 BOS A 2-3   36   .190
     BRTR   1034   .237

GARDNER, WILLIAM LAWRENCE (LARRY)
B.MAY 13,1886 ENOSBURG FALLS,VT
D.MAR.11,1976 ST.GEORGE,VT.
1908 BOS A 3   3   .300
1909 BOS A 3   19   .207
1910 BOS A 2   113   .283
1911 BOS A 2-3   138   .284
1912 BOS A 3   143   .315
1913 BOS A 3   131   .281
1914 BOS A 3   155   .259
1915 BOS A 3   127   .258
1916 BOS A 3   148   .308
1917 BOS A 3   146   .265
1918 PHI A 3   127   .285
1919 CLE A 3   139   .300
1920 CLE A 3   154   .310
1921 CLE A 3   153   .319
1922 CLE A 3   137   .285
1923 CLE A 3   52   .253
1924 CLE A 3   38   .2OO
     BLTR   1923   .289

GARFIELD, WILLIAM MILTON
B.OCT.26,1867 SHEFFIELD,OHIO
D.DEC.16,1941 DANVILLE,ILL.
1889 PIT N P   4   0- 2
1890 CLE N P   8   1- 7
     TR   12   1- 9

GARIBALDI, ARTHUR EDWARD
B.AUG.20,1907 SAN FRANCISCO,CAL
D.OCT.19,1967 SACRAMENTO,CAL.
1936 STL N 2-3   71   .276

GARIBALDI, ROBERT ROY (BOB)
B.MAR.3,1942 STOCKTON,CAL.
1962 SF N P   9   0- 0
1963 SF N P   4   0- 1
1966 SF N /P   1   0- 0
1969 SF N /P   1   0- 1
     BLTR   15   0- 2

GARLAND, LOUIS LYMAN
B.JULY 16,1905 ARCHIE,MO.
1931 CHI A P   7   0- 2
     BRTR

GARLAND, MARCUS WAYNE (WAYNE)
B.OCT.26,1950 NASHVILLE,TENN.
1973 BAL A /P   4   0- 1
1974 BAL A P   20   5- 5
1975 BAL A P   29   2- 5
1976 BAL A P   38 20- 7
1977 CLE A P   38 13-19
1978 CLE A /P   6   2- 3
     BRTR   135 42-40

GARMAN, MICHAEL DOUGLAS (MIKE)
B.SEP.16,1949 CALDWELL,IDAHO
1969 BOS A /P   2   1- 0
1971 BOS A /P   3   1- 1
1972 BOS A /P   3   0- 1
1973 BOS A P   12   0- 0
1974 STL N P   64   7- 2
1975 STL N P   66   3- 8
1976 CHI N P   47   2- 4
1977 LA N P   49   4- 4
1978 LA N P   10   0- 1
     MON N P   47   4- 6
     BRTR   303 22-27

GARMS, DEBS C. (TEX)
B.JUNE 26,1908 BANGS,TEX.
1932 STL A O   34   .284
1933 STL A O   78   .317
1934 STL A O   91   .293
1935 STL A O   10   .267
1937 BOS N 3-O   125   .259
1938 BOS N 3-O   117   .315
1939 BOS N 3-O   132   .298
1940 PIT N 3-O   103   .355
1941 PIT N 3-O   83   .264
1943 PIT N S-3-O   90   .257
1944 STL N 3-O   73   .301
1945 STL N 3-O   74   .336
     BLTR   1010   .293

GARNER, PHILIP MASON (PHIL)
B.APR.30,1949 JEFFERSON CITY,TENN.
1973 OAK A /3   9   .000
1974 OAK A 3/S-2   30   .179
1975 OAK A *2/S   160   .246
1976 OAK A *2   159   .261
1977 PIT N *3-2-S   153   .260
1978 PIT N 2-3/S   154   .261
     BRTR   665   .256

GARONI, WILLIAM (WILLIE)
B.JULY 28,1877 FT.LEE,N.J.
D.SEPT.9,1914 FT.LEE,N.J.
1899 NY N P   3   0- 1

GARR, RALPH ALLEN
(RALPH) OR (ROAD RUNNER)
B.DEC.12,1945 MONROE,LA.
1968 ATL N H   11   .286
1969 ATL N /O   22   .222
1970 ATL N O   37   .281
1971 ATL N *O   154   .343
1972 ATL N *O   134   .325
1973 ATL N *O   148   .299
1974 ATL N *O   143   .353
1975 ATL N *O   151   .278
1976 CHI A *O   136   .300
1977 CHI A *O   134   .300
1978 CHI A *O   118   .275
     BLTR   1188   .309

GARRETT, CLARENCE RAYMOND (LAZ)
B.MAR.6,1891 READER,W.VA.
D.FEB.11,1977 MOUNDSVILLE,W.VA.
1915 CLE A P   4   2- 2
     BRTR

GARRETT, GREGORY (GREG)
B.MAR.12,1948 ATASCADERO,CAL.
1970 CAL A P   32   5- 6
1971 CIN N /P   2   0- 1
     BBTL   34   5- 7

GARRETT, HENRY ADRIAN
(ADRIAN) OR (PAT)
B.JAN.3,1943 BROOKSVILLE,FLA.
1966 ATL N /O   4   .000
1970 CHI N /H   3   .000
1971 OAK A /O   14   .143
1972 OAK A /O   14   .000
1973 CHI N /O-C   36   .222
1974 CHI N /C-1-O   10   .000
1975 CHI N /1   16   .095
     CAL A D-1/O-C   37   .262
1976 CAL A C/1   29   .125
     BLTR   163   .185

GARRETT, RONALD WAYNE (WAYNE)
B.DEC.3,1947 BROOKSVILLE,FLA.
1969 NY N 3-2/S   124   .218
1970 NY N 3-2/S   114   .254
1971 NY N 3/2   56   .213
1972 NY N 3-2   111   .232
1973 NY N *3/S-2   140   .256
1974 NY N *3/S   151   .224
1975 NY N 3/S   107   .266
1976 NY N 3-2/S   80   .223
     MON N 2/3   59   .243
1977 MON N 3/2   68   .270
1978 MON N 3   49   .174
     STL N 3   33   .333
     BLTR   1092   .239

GARRIDO, GIL GONZALO
B.JUNE 26,1941 PANAMA CITY,PAN.
1964 SF N S   14   .080
1968 ATL N S   18   .208
1969 ATL N S   82   .220
1970 ATL N S-2   101   .264
1971 ATL N S-3-2   79   .216
1972 ATL N 2-S/3   40   .267
     BRTR   334   .237

GARRIOTT, VIRGIL CECIL (CECIL)
B.AUG.15,1916 HARRISTOWN,ILL.
1946 CHI N H   6   .000
     BLTR

GARRISON, CLIFFORD WILLIAM
B.AUG.13,1905 BELMONT,OKLA.
1928 BOS A P   6   0- 0
     BRTR

GARRISON, ROBERT FORD (FORD)
(ROCKY) OR (SNAPPER)
B.AUG.29,1915 GREENVILLE,S.C.
1943 BOS A O   36   .279
1944 BOS A O   13   .245
     PHI A O   121   .269
1945 PHI A O   6   .304
1946 PHI A O   9   .108
     BRTR   185   .262

GARRITY, FRANCIS JOSEPH (HANK)
B.FEB.4,1908 BOSTON,MASS.
D.SEPT.1,1962 BOSTON,MASS.
1931 CHI A C   8   .214
     BRTR

GARRY, JAMES THOMAS
B.SEP.21,1869 GREAT BARRINGTON,MASS
D.JAN.15,1917 PITTSFIELD,MASS.
1893 BOS N P   1   0- 1

GARVER, NED FRANKLIN
B.DEC.25,1925 NEY,OHIO
1948 STL A P   38   46   7-11
1949 STL A P   41   55 12-17
1950 STL A P-O   37   51 13-18
                             .286
1951 STL A P   33   49 20-12
1952 STL A P   21   24   7-10
     DET A P   1   1- 0
1953 DET A P   30 11-11
1954 DET A P   35   36 14-11
1955 DET A P   33 12-16
1956 DET A P   6   0- 2
1957 KC A P   24   6-13
1958 KC A P   31 12-11
1959 KC A P   32 10-13
1960 KC A P   28   4- 9
1961 LA A P   12   0- 3
     BRTR   402 458 129-157
                             .218

GARVEY, STEVEN PATRICK (STEVE)
B.DEC.22,1948 TAMPA,FLA.
1969 LA N /H   3   .333
1970 LA N 3/2   34   .269
1971 LA N 3   81   .227
1972 LA N 3/1   96   .269
1973 LA N 1-O   114   .304
1974 LA N *1   156   .312
1975 LA N *1   160   .319
1976 LA N *1   162   .317
1977 LA N *1   162   .297
1978 LA N *1   162   .316
     BRTR   1130   .303

YR	CL	LEA	POS	GP	G	REC

GARVIN, THEODORE JARED (JERRY)
B.OCT.21,1955 OAKLAND,CAL.

YR	CL	LEA	POS	G	REC
1977	TOR	A	P	34	10-18
1978	TOR	A	P	26	4-12
		BLTL		60	14-30

GARVIN, VIRGIL LEE (NED)
B.JAN.1,1874 NAVASOTA,TEX.
D.JUNE 16,1908 FRESNO,CAL.

YR	CL	LEA	POS	G	REC
1896	PHI	N	P	2	0- 1
1899	CHI	N	P	22	9-13
1900	CHI	N	P	28	11-17
1901	MIL	A	P	37	8-21
1902	CHI	A	P	23	9-10
	BRO	N	P	2	1- 1
1903	BRO	N	P	38	15-18
1904	BRO	N	P	23	6-15
	NY	A	P	2	0- 1
		TR		177	59-97

GASPAR, HARRY LAMBERT
B.APR.28,1883 KINGSLEY,IOWA
D.MAY.14,1940 ORANGE,CAL.

YR	CL	LEA	POS	G	REC
1909	CIN	N	P	44	19-11
1910	CIN	N	P	48	15-17
1911	CIN	N	P	44	10-17
1912	CIN	N	P	7	1- 3
		BRTR		143	45-48

GASPAR, RODNEY EARL (ROD)
B.APR.3,1946 LONG BEACH,CAL.

YR	CL	LEA	POS	G	REC
1969	NY	N	/O	118	.228
1970	NY	N	/O	11	.000
1971	SD	N	/O	16	.118
1974	SD	N	/O-1	33	.214
		BBTR		178	.208

GASSAWAY, CHARLES CASON (SHERIFF)
B.AUG.12,1918 GASSAWAY,TENN.

YR	CL	LEA	POS	G	REC
1944	CHI	N	P	2	0- 1
1945	PHI	A	P	24	4- 7
1946	CLE	A	P	13	1- 1
		BLTL		39	5- 9

GASTALL, THOMAS EVERETT (TOM)
B.JUNE 13,1932 FALL RIVER,MASS.
D.SEPT.20,1956 RIVERA BEACH,MD.

YR	CL	LEA	POS	G	REC
1955	BAL	A	C	20	.148
1956	BAL	A	C	32	.196
		BRTR		52	.181

GASTFIELD, EDWARD (ED)
B.AUG.1,1869 CHICAGO,ILL.
D.DEC.1,1899 CHICAGO,ILL.

YR	CL	LEA	POS	G	REC
1884	DET	N	C-1-O	22	.063
1885	DET	N	P	1	0- 0
	CHI	N	C	1	.000
				24	0- 0
					.059

GASTON, ALEXANDER NATHANIEL
B.MAR.12,1893 NEW YORK,N.Y.

YR	CL	LEA	POS	G	REC
1920	NY	N	C	4	.100
1921	NY	N	C	20	.227
1922	NY	N	C	16	.192
1923	NY	N	C	22	.205
1926	BOS	A	C	98	.223
1929	BOS	A	C	55	.224
		BRTR		215	.218

GASTON, CLARENCE EDWIN (CITO)
B.MAR.17,1944 SAN ANTONIO,TEX.

YR	CL	LEA	POS	G	REC
1967	ATL	N	/O	9	.120
1969	SD	N	*O	129	.230
1970	SD	N	*O	146	.318
1971	SD	N	*O	141	.228
1972	SD	N	O	111	.269
1973	SD	N	*O	133	.250
1974	SD	N	O	106	.213
1975	ATL	N	O/1	64	.241
1976	ATL	N	O/1	69	.291
1977	ATL	N	/O-1	56	.271
1978	ATL	N	O/1	60	.229
	PIT	N	/O	2	.500
		BRTR		1026	.256

GASTON, NATHANIEL MILTON (MILT)
B.JAN.27,1896 RIDGEFIELD PARK,N.J.

YR	CL	LEA	POS	G	REC
1924	NY	A	P	28	5- 3
1925	STL	A	P	42	15-14
1926	STL	A	P	32	10-18
1927	STL	A	P	37	13-17
1928	WAS	A	P	28	6-12
1929	BOS	A	P	39	12-19
1930	BOS	A	P	38	13-20
1931	BOS	A	P	23	2-13
1932	CHI	A	P	28	7-17
1933	CHI	A	P	30	8-12
1934	CHI	A	P	29	6-19
		BRTR		354	97-164
		BB 1933			

GASTON, WELCOME THORNBURG
B.DEC.19,1872 GUERNSEY CO.,OHIO
D.DEC.13,1944 COLUMBUS,OHIO

YR	CL	LEA	POS	G	REC
1898	BRO	N	P	2	1- 1
1899	BRO	N	P	1	0- 1
		TL		3	1- 2

GASTREICH, HENRY CARL
[PLAYED UNDER NAME OF
HENRY CARL GASTRIGHT]

GASTRIGHT, HENRY CARL
[REAL NAME HENRY CARL GASTREICH]
B.MAR.29,1865 COVINGTON,KY.
D.OCT.9,1937 COLD SPRINGS,KY.

YR	CL	LEA	POS	G	REC
1889	COL	AA	P	31	11-13
1890	COL	AA	P	50	26-14
1891	COL	AA	P	35	12-19
1892	WAS	N	P	12	2- 6
1893	PIT	N	P	9	3- 2
	BOS	N	P	20	12- 4
1894	BRO	N	P	16	3- 4
1896	CIN	N	P	2	0- 1
		BRTR		175	69-63

GATES, JOSEPH DANIEL (JOE)
B.OCT.3,1954 GARY,IND.

YR	CL	LEA	POS	G	REC
1978	CHI	A	/2	8	.250
		BLTR			

GATEWOOD, AUBREY LEE
B.NOV.17,1938 LITTLE ROCK,ARK.

YR	CL	LEA	POS	GP	G	REC
1963	LA	A	P		4	1- 1
1964	LA	A	P	15	23	3- 3
1965	CAL	A	P		46	4- 5
1970	ATL	N	P		3	0- 0
		BRTR		68	76	8- 9

GATINS, FRANK ANTHONY
[REAL NAME FRANK ANTHONY GESTINO]
B.MAR.6,1871 JOHNSTOWN,PA.
D.NOV.8,1911 JOHNSTOWN,PA.

YR	CL	LEA	POS	G	REC
1896	WAS	N	S	16	.250
1901	BRO	N	3	49	.229
				65	.234

GAUDET, JAMES JENNINGS (JIM)
B.JUNE 3,1955 NEW ORLEANS,LA.

YR	CL	LEA	POS	G	REC
1978	KC	A	/C	3	.000

GAULE, MICHAEL JOHN
B.AUG.4,1869 BALTIMORE,MD.
D.JAN.24,1918 BALTIMORE,MD.

YR	CL	LEA	POS	G	REC
1889	LOU	AA	S	1	.000
		BLTL			

**GAUTREAU, WALTER PAUL
(DOC) OR (PUNK)**
B.JULY 26,1901 CAMBRIDGE,MASS.
D.AUG.23,1970 SALT LAKE CITY,UT

YR	CL	LEA	POS	G	REC
1925	PHI	A	2	4	.000
	BOS	N	2	68	.262
1926	BOS	N	2	79	.267
1927	BOS	N	2	87	.246
1928	BOS	N	2	23	.278
		BRTR		261	.257

GAUTREAUX, SIDNEY ALLEN (PUDGE)
B.MAY 4,1912 SCHRIEVER,LA.

YR	CL	LEA	POS	G	REC
1936	BRO	N	C	75	.268
1937	BRO	N	C	11	.100
		BBTR		86	.247

GAW, GEORGE JOSEPH (CHIPPY)
B.MAR.13,1892 W.NEWTON,MASS.
D.MAY 26,1968 BOSTON,MASS.

YR	CL	LEA	POS	G	REC
1920	CHI	N	P	6	1- 1
		BRTR			

GAZELLA, MICHAEL
B.OCT.13,1896 OLYPHANT,PA.
D.SEPT.11,1978 ODESSA,TEX.

YR	CL	LEA	POS	G	REC
1923	NY	A	2-S-3	8	.077
1926	NY	A	S-3	66	.232
1927	NY	A	3	54	.278
1928	NY	A	3	32	.232
		BRTR		160	.241

GEAR, DALE DUDLEY
B.FEB.2,1872 LONE ELM,KAN.
D.SEPT.23,1951 TOPEKA,KAN.

YR	CL	LEA	POS	GP	G	REC
1896	CLE	N	P		2	0- 2
1897	CLE	N	O		7	.167
1901	WAS	A	P-O	23	58	3-11
						.236
				25	67	3-13
						.239

GEARHART, LLOYD WILLIAM (GARY)
B.AUG.10,1923 NEW LEBANON,OHIO

YR	CL	LEA	POS	G	REC
1947	NY	N	O	73	.246
		BRTL			

GEARIN, DENNIS JOHN (DINTY)
B.OCT.15,1897 PROVIDENCE,R.I.
D.MAR.11,1959 PROVIDENCE,R.I.

YR	CL	LEA	POS	GP	G	REC
1923	NY	N	P		6	1- 1
1924	NY	N	P	6	10	1- 2
	BOS	N	P		1	0- 1
		BLTL		13	17	2- 4

GEARY, EUGENE FRANCIS JOSEPH (HUCK)
B.JAN.22,1917 BUFFALO,N.Y.

YR	CL	LEA	POS	G	REC
1942	PIT	N	S	9	.227
1943	PIT	N	S	46	.151
		BLTR		55	.160

GEARY, ROBERT NORTON (SPEED)
B.MAY 10,1891 CINCINNATI,OHIO

YR	CL	LEA	POS	G	REC
1918	PHI	A	P	16	3- 5
1919	PHI	A	P	9	0- 3
1921	CIN	N	P	10	1- 1
		BRTR		35	4- 9

GEBHARD, ROBERT HENRY (BOB)
B.JAN.3,1943 LAMBERTON,MINN.

YR	CL	LEA	POS	G	REC
1971	MIN	A	P	17	1- 2
1972	MIN	A	P	13	0- 1
1974	MON	N	/P	1	0- 0
		BRTR		31	1- 3

GEBRIAN, PETER (GABE)
B.AUG.10,1923 BAYONNE,N.J.

YR	CL	LEA	POS	G	REC
1947	CHI	A	P	27	2- 3
		BRTR			

GEDDES, JAMES LEE (JIM)
B.MAR.23,1949 COLUMBUS,OHIO

YR	CL	LEA	POS	GP	G	REC
1972	CHI	A	/P	5	6	0- 0
1973	CHI	A	/P		6	0- 0
		BRTR		11	12	0- 0

GEDEON, ELMER JOHN
B.APR.15,1917 CLEVELAND,OHIO
D.APR.15,1944 FRANCE

YR	CL	LEA	POS	G	REC
1939	WAS	A	O	5	.200
		BRTR			

GEDEON, ELMER JOSEPH (JOE)
B.DEC.5,1893 SACRAMENTO,CAL.
D.MAY 19,1941 SAN FRANCISCO,CAL

YR	CL	LEA	POS	GP	G	REC
1913	WAS	A	P-O	1	26	0- 0
						.188
1914	WAS	A	O		4	.000
1916	NY	A	2		122	.211
1917	NY	A	2		33	.239
1918	STL	A	2		123	.213
1919	STL	A	2		120	.254
1920	STL	A	2		153	.292
		BRTR		1	581	0- 0
						.244

GEDNEY, ALFRED W., (COUNT)
B.MAY 10,1849 BROOKLYN,N.Y.
D.MAR.26,1922

YR	CL	LEA	POS	GP	G	REC
1872	TRO	NA	O		9	.413
	ECK	NA	O		18	.158
1873	MUT	NA	O		54	-
1874	ATH	NA	1-O		54	-
1875	MUT	NA	P-O	1	68	1- 0
						-
				1	203	1- 0
						-

GEE, JOHN ALEXANDER (WHIZ)
B.DEC.7,1915 SYRACUSE,N.Y.

YR	CL	LEA	POS	G	REC
1939	PIT	N	P	3	1- 2
1941	PIT	N	P	3	0- 2
1943	PIT	N	P	15	4- 4
1944	PIT	N	P	4	0- 0
	NY	N	P	4	0- 0
1945	NY	N	P	2	0- 0
1946	NY	N	P	13	2- 4
		BLTL		44	7-12

GEER, GEORGE HARRISON
[PLAYED UNDER NAME OF
WILLIAM HENRY HARRISON GEER]

GEER, WILLIAM HENRY HARRISON
[REAL NAME GEORGE HARRISON GEER]
B.AUG.13,1849 SYRACUSE,N.Y.
D.JAN.5,1922

YR	CL	LEA	POS	G	REC
1874	MUT	NA	O	2	-
1875	NN	NA	2-S-3-O	37	-
1878	CIN	N	2-S	62	.215
1880	WOR	N	S-O	2	.000
1884	KEY	U	S	8	.226
	BRO	AA	S	107	.226
1885	LOU	AA	S	14	.113
		TR		232	-

YR	CL	LEA	POS	GP	G	REC

GEHRIG, HENRY LOUIS (LOU)
OR (THE IRON HORSE)
B.JUNE 19,1903 NEW YORK,N.Y.
D.JUNE 2,1941 NEW YORK,N.Y.

YR	CL	LEA	POS	GP	G	REC
1923	NY	A	1		13	.423
1924	NY	A	1		10	.500
1925	NY	A	1-0		126	.295
1926	NY	A	1		155	.313
1927	NY	A	1		155	.373
1928	NY	A	1		154	.374
1929	NY	A	1		154	.300
1930	NY	A	1		154	.379
1931	NY	A	1		155	.341
1932	NY	A	1		156	.349
1933	NY	A	1		152	.334
1934	NY	A	1-S		154	.363
1935	NY	A	1		149	.329
1936	NY	A	1		155	.354
1937	NY	A	1		157	.351
1938	NY	A	1		157	.295
1939	NY	A	1		8	.143
	BLTL				2164	.340

GEHRING, HENRY
B.JAN.24,1881 ST.PAUL,MINN.
D.APR.18,1912 KANSAS CITY,MO.

1907	WAS	A	P	14	20	3- 7
1908	WAS	A	P		5	0- 1
	TR			19	25	3- 8

GEHRINGER, CHARLES LEONARD
(CHARLIE) OR
(THE MECHANICAL MAN)
B.MAY 11,1903 FOWLERVILLE,MICH.

1924	DET	A	2		5	.545
1925	DET	A	2		8	.167
1926	DET	A	2		123	.277
1927	DET	A	2		133	.317
1928	DET	A	2		154	.320
1929	DET	A	2		155	.339
1930	DET	A	2		154	.330
1931	DET	A	2		101	.311
1932	DET	A	2		152	.298
1933	DET	A	2		155	.325
1934	DET	A	2		154	.356
1935	DET	A	2		150	.330
1936	DET	A	2		154	.354
1937	DET	A	2		144	.371
1938	DET	A	2		152	.306
1939	DET	A	2		118	.325
1940	DET	A	2		139	.313
1941	DET	A	2		127	.220
1942	DET	A	2		45	.267
	BLTR				2323	.320

GEHRMAN, PAUL ARTHUR (DUTCH)
B.MAY 3,1912 MT.ANGEL,ORE.

| 1937 | CIN | N | P | | 2 | 0- 1 |
| | BRTR | | | | | |

GEIER, PHILIP LOUIS (LITTLE PHIL)
B.NOV.3,1876 WASHINGTON,D.C.
D.SEPT.25,1967 SPOKANE,WASH.

1896	PHI	N	O		17	.232
1897	PHI	N	2-O		88	.265
1900	CIN	N	O		29	.273
1901	PHI	A	O		50	.236
	MIL	A	O		10	.184
1904	BOS	N	O		148	.243
	BLTR				342	.252

GEIGER, GARY MERLE
B.APR.4,1937 SAND RIDGE,ILL.

1958	CLE	A	P-3-O	1	91	0- 0
						.231
1959	BOS	A	O		120	.245
1960	BOS	A	O		77	.302
1961	BOS	A	O		140	.232
1962	BOS	A	O		131	.249
1963	BOS	A	1-O		121	.263
1964	BOS	A	O		5	.385
1965	BOS	A	O		24	.200
1966	ATL	N	O		78	.262
1967	ATL	N	O		69	.162
1969	HOU	N	O		93	.224
1970	HOU	N	/O		5	.250
	BLTL			1	954	0- 0
						.246

GEISEL, JOHN DAVID (DAVE)
B.JAN.18,1955 WINDBER,PA.

| 1978 | CHI | N | P | | 18 | 1- 0 |
| | BLTL | | | | | |

GEISHERT, VERNON WILLIAM (VERN)
B.JAN.10,1946 MADISON,WIS.

| 1969 | CAL | A | P | | 11 | 1- 1 |
| | BRTR | | | | | |

GEISS, EMIL M.
B.CHICAGO,ILL.

1882	BAL	AA	P-O	13	4- 9
						.159
1887	CHI	N	P		3	0- 1
	BR			16	4-10
						.140

GEISS, WILLIAM
B.1860 CHICAGO,ILL.

1884	DET	N	P-1-	1	75	0- 0
			2-0			.177
1891	STL	AA	2		76	.323
				1	151	0- 0
						.253

GELBERT, CHARLES MAGNUS
B.JAN.26,1906 SCRANTON,PA.
D.JAN.13,1967 EASTON,PA.

1929	STL	N	S		146	.262
1930	STL	N	S		139	.304
1931	STL	N	S		131	.289
1932	STL	N	S		122	.268
1935	STL	N	2-S-3		62	.292
1936	STL	N	S-3		93	.229
1937	CIN	N	2-S-3		43	.193
	DET	A	S		20	.085
1939	WAS	A	S-3		68	.255
1940	WAS	A	P-2-	2	22	0- 0
			S-3			.370
	BOS	A	3		30	.198
	BRTR			2	876	0- 0
						.267

GELNAR, JOHN RICHARD
B.JUNE 25,1943 GRANITE,OKLA

1964	PIT	N	P		7	0- 0
1967	PIT	N	P		10	0- 1
1969	SEA	A	P	39	40	3-10
1970	MIL	A	P		53	4- 3
1971	MIL	A	/P		2	0- 0
	BRTR			111	112	7-14

GENEWICH, JOSEPH EDWARD
B.JAN.15,1897 ELMIRA,N.Y.

1922	BOS	N	P		6	0- 2
1923	BOS	N	P		43	13-14
1924	BOS	N	P		34	10-19
1925	BOS	N	P		34	12-10
1926	BOS	N	P		37	8-16
1927	BOS	N	P		40	11- 8
1928	BOS	N	P		13	3- 7
	NY	N	P		26	11- 4
1929	NY	N	P	21	25	3- 7
1930	NY	N	P	18	21	2- 5
	BRTR			272	279	73-92

GENINS, C. FRANK (FRENCHY)
B.NOV.2,1866 ST.LOUIS,MO.
D.SEPT.30,1922 ST.LOUIS,MO.

1892	CIN	N	S		31	.195
	STL	N	S		14	.167
1895	PIT	N	3-O		64	.253
1901	CLE	A	O		26	.232
	TR				135	.228

GENOVESE, GEORGE MICHAEL
B.FEB.22,1922 STATEN ISLAND,N.Y

| 1950 | WAS | A | H | | 3 | .000 |
| | BLTR | | | | | |

GENTILE, JAMES EDWARD (JIM)
OR (DIAMOND JIM)
B.JUNE 3,1934 SAN FRANCISCO,CAL.

1957	BRO	N	1		4	.167
1958	LA	N	1		12	.133
1960	BAL	A	1		138	.292
1961	BAL	A	1		148	.302
1962	BAL	A	1		152	.251
1963	BAL	A	1		145	.248
1964	KC	A	1		136	.251
1965	KC	A	1		38	.246
	HOU	N	1		81	.242
1966	HOU	N	1		49	.243
	CLE	A	/1		33	.128
	BLTL				936	.260

GENTILE, SAMUEL CHRISTOPHER
B.OCT.12,1916 CHARLESTOWN,MASS.

| 1943 | BOS | N | H | | 8 | .250 |
| | BLTR | | | | | |

GENTRY, GARY EDWARD
B.OCT.6,1946 PHOENIX,ARIZ.

1969	NY	N	P		35	13-12
1970	NY	N	P		32	9- 9
1971	NY	N	P		32	12-11
1972	NY	N	P		32	7-10
1973	ATL	N	P	16	17	4- 6
1974	ATL	N	/P		3	0- 0
1975	ATL	N	/P		7	1- 1
	BRTR			157	158	46-49

GENTRY, HARVEY WILLIAM
B.MAY 27,1926 WINSTON-SALEM,N.C

| 1954 | NY | N | H | | 5 | .250 |
| | BLTR | | | | | |

GENTRY, JAMES RUFFUS (RUFE)
B.MAY 18,1918 WINSTON-SALEM,N.C.

1943	DET	A	P		4	1- 3
1944	DET	A	P		37	12-14
1946	DET	A	P		2	0- 0
1947	DET	A	P		1	0- 0
1948	DET	A	P		4	0- 0
	BRTR				48	13-17

GEORGE, ALEX THOMAS M.
B.SEPT.27,1938 KANSAS CITY,MO.

| 1955 | KC | A | S | | 5 | .100 |
| | BLTR | | | | | |

GEORGE, CHARLES PETER (GREEK)
B.DEC.25,1912 WAYCROSS,GA.

1935	CLE	A	C		2	.000
1936	CLE	A	C		23	.195
1938	BRO	N	C		7	.200
1941	CHI	N	C		35	.156
1945	PHI	A	C		51	.174
	BRTR				118	.177

GEORGE, THOMAS EDWARD (LEFTY)
B.AUG.13,1886 PITTSBURGH,PA.
D.MAY 13,1955 YORK,PA.

1911	STL	A	P		27	3-10
1912	CLE	A	P		11	0- 5
1915	CIN	N	P		7	2- 2
1918	BOS	N	P		10	1- 5
	BLTL				55	6-22

GEORGE, WILLIAM M.
B.JAN.27,1865 BELLAIRE,OHIO
D.AUG.23,1916 WHEELING,W.VA.

1887	NY	N	P		13	3- 9
1888	NY	N	P-O	4	9	2- 1
						.267
1889	NY	N	O		3	.267
	COL	AA	P-O	3	5	0- 0
						.308
	BRTL			20	30	5-10
						.220

GEORGY, OSCAR JOHN
B.NOV.25,1916 NEW ORLEANS,LA.

| 1938 | NY | N | P | | 1 | 0- 0 |
| | BRTR | | | | | |

GERAGHTY, BENJAMIN RAYMOND
B.JULY 19,1912 JERSEY CITY,N.J.
D.JUNE 18,1963 JACKSONVILLE,FLA

1936	BRO	N	S		51	.194
1943	BOS	N	2-S-3		8	.000
1944	BOS	N	2-3		11	.250
	BRTR				70	.199

GERARD, DAVID FREDERICK
B.AUG.6,1936 NEW YORK,N.Y.

| 1962 | CHI | N | P | | 39 | 2- 3 |
| | BRTR | | | | | |

GERBER, WALTER (SPOOKS)
B.AUG.18,1891 COLUMBUS,OHIO
D.JUNE 19,1951 COLUMBUS,OHIO

1914	PIT	N	S		17	.241
1915	PIT	N	S-3		56	.194
1917	STL	A	S		14	.308
1918	STL	A	S		56	.240
1919	STL	A	S		140	.227
1920	STL	A	S		154	.279
1921	STL	A	S		114	.278
1922	STL	A	S		153	.267
1923	STL	A	S		154	.281
1924	STL	A	S		148	.272
1925	STL	A	S		72	.272
1926	STL	A	S		131	.270
1927	STL	A	S		142	.224
1928	STL	A	S		6	.222
	BOS	A	S		104	.217
1929	BOS	A	2-S		61	.165
	BRTR			1522	.257

GERBERMAN, GEORGE ALOIS
B.MAR.8,1942 EL CAMPO,TEX.

| 1962 | CHI | N | P | | 1 | 0- 0 |
| | BRTR | | | | | |

GERHARDT, ALLEN RUSSELL (RUSTY)
B.AUG.13,1950 BALTIMORE,MD.

| 1974 | SD | N | P | | 23 | 2- 1 |
| | BBTL | | | | 23 | 2- 1 |

GERHARDT, JOHN JOSEPH
(JOE) OR (MOVE UP JOE)
B.FEB.14,1855 WASHINGTON,D.C.
D.MAR.11,1922 MIDDLETOWN,N.Y.

1873	NAT	NA	S		13	-
1874	BAL	NA	S		14	-
1875	MUT	NA	2-S-3-O		59	-
1876	LOU	N	1-2		65	.258
1877	LOU	N	1-2-S-O		59	.304
1878	CIN	N	2		61	.303
1879	CIN	N	1-2-3		78	.199
1881	DET	N	2-3		80	.242
1883	LOU	AA	M-2		77	.270
1884	LOU	AA	M-2		108	.220
1885	NY	N	2		112	.155
1886	NY	N	2		123	.196
1887	NY	N	3		1	.000
	MET	AA	2		85	.277
1890	BRO	AA	2		97	.211
	STL	AA	2		37	.260
1891	LOU	AA	2		2	.000
	BRTR			1071	-

YR	CL LEA POS	GP	G	REC
GERHEAUSER, ALBERT (AL) OR (LEFTY)				
B.JUNE 24,1917 ST.LOUIS,MO.				
D.MAY 28,1972 SPRINGFIELD,MO.				
1943 PHI N P		38	10-19	
1944 PHI N P	30	32	8-16	
1945 PIT N P		32	5-10	
1946 PIT N P-0	35	36	2- 2	
			.333	
1948 STL A P		14	0- 3	
BLTL	149	152	25-50	
			.209	
GERKEN, GEORGE HERBERT (PICKLES)				
B.JULY 28,1903 CHICAGO,ILL.				
D.OCT.23,1977 ARCADIA,CAL.				
1927 CLE A 0		6	.214	
1928 CLE A 0		38	.226	
BRTR		44	.225	
GERKIN, STEPHEN PAUL (SPLINTER)				
B.NOV.19,1915 GRAFTON,W.VA.				
1945 PHI A P		21	0-12	
BRTR				
GERLACH, JOHN GLENN (JOHNNY)				
B.MAY 11,1917 SHULLSBURG,WIS.				
1938 CHI A S		9	.280	
1939 CHI A 3		3	1.000	
BRTR		12	.333	
GERMAN, LESTER STANLEY				
B.JUNE 1,1869 BALTIMORE,MD.				
D.JUNE 10,1934 GERMANTOWN,MD.				
1890 BAL AA P		16	4-10	
1893 NY N P	18	20	10- 8	
1894 NY N P	17	19	7- 8	
1895 NY N P	20	31	7-13	
1896 NY N P		3	1- 1	
WAS N P		23	2-18	
1897 WAS N P-2	7	19	4- 3	
			.311	
	104	131	35-61	
			.252	
GERNER, EDWIN FREDERICK (LEFTY)				
B.JULY 22,1897 PHILADELPHIA,PA.				
D.MAY 15,1970 PHILADELPHIA,PA.				
1919 CIN N P		5	1- 0	
BLTL				
GERNERT, RICHARD EDWARD (DICK)				
B.SEPT.28,1928 READING,PA.				
1952 BOS A 1		102	.243	
1953 BOS A 1		139	.253	
1954 BOS A 1		14	.261	
1955 BOS A 1		7	.200	
1956 BOS A 1-0		106	.291	
1957 BOS A 1-0		99	.237	
1958 BOS A 1		122	.237	
1959 BOS A 1-0		117	.262	
1960 CHI N 1-0		52	.206	
DET A 1-0		21	.300	
1961 DET A 1		6	.200	
CIN N 1		40	.302	
1962 HOU N 1		10	.206	
BRTR		835	.254	
GERONIMO, CESAR FRANCISCO				
(ZORRILLA)				
B.MAR.11,1948 EL SEIBO,D.R.				
1969 HOU N /0		28	.250	
1970 HOU N 0		47	.243	
1971 HOU N 0		94	.220	
1972 CIN N *0		120	.275	
1973 CIN N *0		139	.210	
1974 CIN N *0		150	.281	
1975 CIN N *0		148	.257	
1976 CIN N *0		149	.307	
1977 CIN N *0		149	.266	
1978 CIN N *0		122	.226	
BLTL		1146	.263	
GERTENRICH, LOUIS WILHELM				
B.MAY 4,1875 CHICAGO,ILL.				
D.OCT.23,1933 CHICAGO,ILL.				
1901 MIL A 0		2	.333	
1903 PIT N 0		1	.000	
		3	.143	
GERVAIS, LUCIEN EDWARD (LEFTY)				
B.JULY 6,1890 GROVER,WIS.				
D.OCT.19,1960 LOS ANGELES,CAL.				
1913 BOS N P		6	0- 1	
BLTL				

YR	CL LEA POS	GP	G	REC
GESSLER, HARRY HOMER (DOC)				
B.DEC.23,1880 INDIANA,PA.				
D.DEC.26,1924 INDIANA,PA.				
1903 DET A 0		29	.238	
BRO N 0		43	.247	
1904 BRO N 0		89	.290	
1905 BRO N 1		119	.290	
1906 BRO N 1		9	.242	
0		22	.253	
1908 BOS A 0		128	.308	
1909 BOS A 0		111	.299	
WAS A 0		17	.182	
1910 WAS A 0		145	.259	
1911 WAS A 0		128	.282	
BLTR		840	.280	
NON-PLAYING MANAGER PIT[F] 1914				
GESSNER, CHARLES J.				
B.PHILADELPHIA,PA.				
1886 ATH AA P	1		0- 1	
GESTINO, FRANK ANTHONY				
[PLAYED UNDER NAME OF				
FRANK ANTHONY GATINS]				
GETTEL, ALLEN JONES (AL)				
B.SEPT.17,1917 NORFOLK,VA.				
1945 NY N P		27	9- 8	
1946 NY N P		26	6- 7	
1947 CLE A P	31	34	11-10	
1948 CLE A P		5	0- 1	
CHI A P-2	22	24	8-10	
			.241	
1949 CHI A P		19	2- 5	
WAS A P		16	0- 2	
1951 NY N P		30	1- 2	
1955 STL N P		8	1- 0	
BRTR	184	189	38-45	
			.228	
GETTIG, CHARLES H.				
[REAL NAME CHARLES H. GETTINGER]				
B.1875 CUMBERLAND,MD.				
1896 NY N P		6	1- 0	
1897 NY N P-S	2	20	1- 1	
			.203	
1898 NY N P-0	18	55	5- 4	
			.248	
1899 NY N P	15	31	7- 8	
			.241	
	41	112	14-13	
			.239	
GETTINGER, CHARLES H.				
[PLAYED UNDER NAME OF				
CHARLES H. GETTIG]				
GETTINGER, THOMAS L.				
B.1870 MOBILE,ALA.				
1889 STL AA 0		3	.455	
1890 STL AA 0		59	.260	
1895 LOU N P-0	1	60	0- 1	
			.281	
BLTL	1	122	0- 1	
			.277	
GETTMAN, JACOB JOHN				
B.OCT.25,1876 FRANK,RUSSIA				
D.OCT.4,1956 DENVER,COLO.				
1897 WAS N 0		37	.315	
1898 WAS N 0		140	.279	
1899 WAS N 0		16	.226	
BBTL		193	.280	
GETZ, GUSTAVE (GEE-GEE)				
B.AUG.3,1889 PITTSBURGH,PA.				
D.MAY 26,1969 KEANSBURG,N.J.				
1909 BOS N 3		40	.223	
1910 BOS N 3		47	.144	
1914 BRO N 3		55	.248	
1915 BRO N 3		130	.258	
1916 BRO N 3		40	.219	
1917 CIN N 2-3		7	.286	
1918 CLE A 3		6	.066	
PIT N 3		7	.200	
BRTR		332	.219	
GETZEIN, CHARLES H. (PRETZELS)				
B.FEB.14,1864 CHICAGO,ILL.				
D.JUNE 19,1932 CHICAGO,ILL.				
1884 DET N P		17	5-12	
1885 DET N P-0	38	39	12-26	
			.211	
1886 DET N P		43	31-11	
1887 DET N P		43	29-13	
1888 DET N P		45	18-26	
1889 IND N P		41	19-22	
1890 BOS N P		42	23-17	
1891 BOS N P-0	11	13	4- 6	
			.189	
CLE N P		1	0- 1	
1892 STL N P		14	5- 9	
BRTR	295	298	146-143	
			.207	

YR	CL LEA POS	GP	G	REC
GEYER, JACOB BOWMAN (RUBE)				
B.MAR.26,1884 ALLEGHENY,PA.				
D.OCT.12,1962 FORD TOWNSHIP,MINN.				
1910 STL N P		4	0- 1	
1911 STL N P		29	9- 6	
1912 STL N P		41	7-14	
1913 STL N P		30	1- 5	
BRTR		104	17-26	
GEYGAN, JAMES EDWARD (CHAPPIE)				
B.JUNE 3,1903 IRONTON,OHIO				
D.MAR.15,1966 COLUMBUS,OHIO				
1924 BOS A S		33	.256	
1925 BOS A S		3	.182	
1926 BOS A 3		4	.300	
BRTR		40	.252	
GHARRITY, EDWARD PATRICK (PATSY)				
B.MAR.13,1892 PARNELL,WIS.				
D.OCT.10,1966 BELOIT,WIS.				
1916 WAS A C-1		39	.228	
1917 WAS A 1		76	.284	
1918 WAS A C		4	.250	
1919 WAS A C-0		111	.271	
1920 WAS A C-1		131	.245	
1921 WAS A C		121	.316	
1922 WAS A C		96	.296	
1923 WAS A C-1		93	.207	
1929 WAS A H		3	.000	
1930 WAS A 1		2	.000	
BRTR		676	.249	
GIALLOMBARDO, ROBERT PAUL (BOB)				
B.MAY 20,1937 BROOKLYN,N.Y.				
1958 LA N P	6	8	1- 1	
BLTL				
GIANNINI, JOSEPH FRANCIS				
B.SEPT.8,1888 SAN FRANCISCO,CAL				
D.SEPT.26,1942 SAN FRANCISCO,CAL.				
1911 BOS A S	1		.500	
BLTR				
GIARD, JOSEPH OSCAR (PECO)				
B.OCT.7,1898 WARE,MASS.				
D.JULY 10,1956 WORCESTER,MASS.				
1925 STL A P		30	10- 5	
1926 STL A P		22	3-10	
1927 NY A P		16	0- 0	
BLTL		68	13-15	
GIBBON, JOSEPH CHARLES (JOE)				
B.APR.10,1935 HICKORY,MISS.				
1960 PIT N P		27	4- 2	
1961 PIT N P	30	31	13-10	
1962 PIT N P		19	3- 4	
1963 PIT N P	37	40	5-12	
1964 PIT N P	28	29	10- 7	
1965 PIT N P		31	4- 9	
1966 SF N P		37	4- 6	
1967 SF N P		28	0- 1	
1968 SF N P		29	1- 2	
1969 SF N P		16	1- 3	
PIT N P		35	5- 1	
1970 PIT N P		41	0- 1	
1971 CIN N P		5	0- 0	
HOU N /P		2	0- 0	
1972 CIN N /P		9	0- 0	
BRTL	419	424	61-65	
	48	1967-68		
GIBBS, JERRY DEAN (JAKE)				
B.NOV.7,1938 GRENADA,MISS.				
1962 NY A 3		2	.000	
1963 NY A C		4	.250	
1964 NY A C		3	.167	
1965 NY A C		37	.221	
1966 NY A C		62	.258	
1967 NY A C		116	.233	
1968 NY A *C		124	.213	
1969 NY A C		71	.224	
1970 NY A C		49	.301	
1971 NY A C		70	.218	
BLTR		538	.233	
GIBSON, CHARLES E.				
B.1877 PHILADELPHIA,PA.				
1905 STL A C		1	.000	
TR				
GIBSON, CHARLES GRIFFIN				
B.NOV.24,1899 LAGRANGE,GA.				
1924 PHI A C		12	.133	
BRTR				
GIBSON, FRANK GILBERT				
B.SEPT.27,1890 OMAHA,NEB.				
D.APR.27,1961 AUSTIN,TEX.				
1913 DET A C		20	.140	
1921 BOS N C		63	.264	
1922 BOS N C-1		66	.299	
1923 BOS N C		41	.300	
1924 BOS N C-1-3		90	.310	
1925 BOS N C-1		104	.278	
1926 BOS N C		24	.340	
1927 BOS N C		60	.222	
BBTR		468	.274	
BL 1913				

YR CL LEA POS GP G REC

GIBSON, GEORGE C. (MOON)
B.JULY 22,1880 LONDON,ONT.,CAN.
D.JAN.25,1967 LONDON,ONT.,CAN.

YR	CL	LEA	POS	GP	G	REC
1905	PIT	N	C		44	.178
1906	PIT	N	C		81	.178
1907	PIT	N	C		110	.220
1908	PIT	N	C		140	.228
1909	PIT	N	C		150	.265
1910	PIT	N	C		143	.259
1911	PIT	N	C		98	.209
1912	PIT	N	C		95	.240
1913	PIT	N	C		48	.280
1914	PIT	N	C		102	.285
1915	PIT	N	C		120	.251
1916	PIT	N	C		33	.202
1917	NY	N	C		35	.171
1918	NY	N	C		4	.500
	BRTR				1203	.236

NON-PLAYING MANAGER
PIT[N] 1920-22, CHI[N] 1925,
PIT[N] 1932-34

GIBSON, JOHN RUSSELL (RUSS)
B.MAY 6,1939 FALL RIVER,MASS.

YR	CL	LEA	POS	GP	G	REC
1967	BOS	A	C		49	.203
1968	BOS	A	C/1		76	.225
1969	BOS	A	C		85	.251
1970	SF	N	C		24	.232
1971	SF	N	C		29	.193
1972	SF	N	/C		5	.167
	BRTR				264	.228

GIBSON, LEIGHTON B. (LEE)
B.1866 LANCASTER,PA.

YR	CL	LEA	POS	GP	G	REC
1888	ATH	AA	C		1	.000
	TR					

GIBSON, NORWOOD RINGOLD (GIBBY)
B.MAR.11,1877 PEORIA,ILL.
D.JULY 7,1959 PEORIA,ILL.

YR	CL	LEA	POS	GP	G	REC
1903	BOS	A	P		25	11- 9
1904	BOS	A	P		33	17-14
1905	BOS	A	P		24	5-10
1906	BOS	A	P		5	0- 2
	BRTR				87	33-35

GIBSON, ROBERT (BOB)
B.NOV.9,1935 OMAHA,NEB.

YR	CL	LEA	POS	GP	G	REC
1959	STL	N	P	13	21	3- 5
1960	STL	N	P	27	40	3- 6
1961	STL	N	P	35	40	13-12
1962	STL	N	P	32	42	15-13
1963	STL	N	P	36	41	18- 9
1964	STL	N	P		40	19-12
1965	STL	N	P	38	42	20-12
1966	STL	N	P	35	40	21-12
1967	STL	N	P	24	27	13- 7
1968	STL	N	P	34	35	22- 9
1969	STL	N	P	35	37	20-13
1970	STL	N	P	34	40	23- 7
1971	STL	N	P		31	16-13
1972	STL	N	P		34	19-11
1973	STL	N	P		25	12-10
1974	STL	N	P		33	11-13
1975	STL	N	P		22	3-10
	BkTR			528	596	251-174

GIBSON, ROBERT MURRAY
B.AUG.20,1869 DUNCANSVILLE,PA.
D.DEC.19,1949 PITTSBURGH,PA.

YR	CL	LEA	POS	GP	G	REC
1890	CHI	N	P		1	1- 0
	PIT	N	P-O		3	0- 2
						.231
	BRTR				4	1- 2
						.176

GIBSON, SAMUEL BRAXTON
B.AUG.5,1899 KING,N.C.

YR	CL	LEA	POS	GP	G	REC
1926	DET	A	P	35	36	12- 9
1927	DET	A	P		33	11-12
1928	DET	A	P		20	5- 8
1930	NY	A	P		2	0- 1
1932	NY	N	P		41	4- 8
	BLTR			131	132	32-38

GICK, GEORGE EDWARD
B.OCT.18,1915 DUNNINGTON,IND.

YR	CL	LEA	POS	GP	G	REC
1937	CHI	A	P		1	0- 0
1938	CHI	A	P		1	0- 0
	BBTR				2	0- 0

GIDEON, JAMES LESLIE (JIM)
B.SEPT.26,1953 TAYLOR,TEX.

YR	CL	LEA	POS	GP	G	REC
1975	TEX	A	/P		1	0- 0
	BRTR					

GIEBEL, JOSEPH HENRY
B.NOV.30,1891 WASHINGTON,D.C.

YR	CL	LEA	POS	GP	G	REC
1913	PHI	A	C		1	.333
	BRTR					

GIEBELL, FLOYD GEORGE
B.DEC.10,1909 PENNSBORO,W.VA.

YR	CL	LEA	POS	GP	G	REC
1939	DET	A	P		9	1- 1
1940	DET	A	P		2	2- 0
1941	DET	A	P		17	0- 0
	BLTR				28	3- 1

GIEL, PAUL ROBERT
B.FEB.29,1932 WINONA,MINN.

YR	CL	LEA	POS	GP	G	REC
1954	NY	N	P		6	0- 0
1955	NY	N	P		34	4- 4
1958	SF	N	P		29	4- 5
1959	PIT	N	P		4	0- 0
1960	PIT	N	P		16	2- 0
1961	MIN	A	P	12	15	1- 0
	KC	A	P		1	0- 0
	BRTR			102	105	11- 9

GIFFORD, JAMES H.
B.OCT.18,1845 WARREN,N.Y.
D.DEC.19,1901 COLUMBUS,OHIO
NON-PLAYING MANAGER
IND[AA] 1884; MET[AA] 1885-86

GIGGIE, ROBERT THOMAS (BOB)
B.AUG.13,1933 DORCHESTER,MASS.

YR	CL	LEA	POS	GP	G	REC
1959	MIL	N	P		13	1- 0
1960	MIL	N	P		3	0- 0
	KC	A	P		10	1- 0
1962	KC	A	P		4	1- 1
	BRTR				30	3- 1

GIGON, NORMAN PHILLIP (NORM)
B.MAY 12,1938 TEANECK,N.J.

YR	CL	LEA	POS	GP	G	REC
1967	CHI	N	2/O-3		34	.171
	BRTR					

GIL, TOMAS GUSTAVO [GUILLEN] (GUS)
B.APR.19,1939 CARACAS,VENEZ.

YR	CL	LEA	POS	GP	G	REC
1967	CLE	A	2/1		51	.115
1969	SEA	A	3-2-S		92	.222
1970	MIL	A	2-3		64	.185
1971	MIL	A	2-3		14	.156
	BRTR				221	.186

GILBERT, ANDREW
B.JULY 18,1914 LATROBE,PA.

YR	CL	LEA	POS	GP	G	REC
1942	BOS	A	O		6	.091
1946	BOS	A	O		2	.000
	BRTR				8	.083

GILBERT, BENNETT HAROLD ROCHEFORT
[PLAYED UNDER NAME OF
BENNETT HAROLD ROCHEFORT]

GILBERT, CHARLES MADER
B.JULY 8,1919 NEW ORLEANS,LA.

YR	CL	LEA	POS	GP	G	REC
1940	BRO	N	O		57	.246
1941	CHI	N	O		39	.279
1942	CHI	N	O		74	.184
1943	CHI	N	O		8	.150
1946	CHI	N	O		15	.077
	PHI	N	O		88	.242
1947	PHI	N	O		83	.237
	BLTL				364	.229

GILBERT, DREW EDWARD (BUDDY)
B.JULY 26,1935 KNOXVILLE,TENN.

YR	CL	LEA	POS	GP	G	REC
1959	CIN	N	O		7	.150
	BLTR					

GILBERT, HAROLD JOSEPH (TOOKIE)
B.APR.4,1929 NEW ORLEANS,LA.
D.JUNE 23,1967 NEW ORLEANS,LA.

YR	CL	LEA	POS	GP	G	REC
1950	NY	N	1		113	.220
1953	NY	N	1		70	.169
	BLTR				183	.203

GILBERT, HARRY
B.POTTSTOWN,PA.

YR	CL	LEA	POS	GP	G	REC
1890	PIT	N	P		2	.250

GILBERT, JOE DENNIS
B.APR.20,1952 JASPER,TEX.

YR	CL	LEA	POS	GP	G	REC
1972	MON	N	P		22	0- 1
1973	MON	N	P		21	1- 2
	BRTL				43	1- 3

GILBERT, JOHN G.
B.JAN.6,1864 POTTSTOWN,PA.
D.NOV.12,1903 POTTSTOWN,PA.

YR	CL	LEA	POS	GP	G	REC
1890	PIT	N	S		2	.000

GILBERT, JOHN ROBERT (JACKRABBIT)
B.SEPT.14,1875 RHINEBECK,N.Y.
D.JULY 7,1941 ALBANY,N.Y.

YR	CL	LEA	POS	GP	G	REC
1898	WAS	N	O		2	.167
	NY	N	O		1	.250
1904	PIT	N	O		25	.241
					28	.237

GILBERT, LAWRENCE WILLIAM
B.DEC.3,1891 NEW ORLEANS,LA.
D.FEB.17,1965 NEW ORLEANS,LA.

YR	CL	LEA	POS	GP	G	REC
1914	BOS	N	O		72	.268
1915	BOS	N	O		45	.151
	BLTL				117	.230

GILBERT, PETER
B.SEPT.6,1867 BALTIC,CONN.
D.JAN.1,1912 SPRINGFIELD,MASS.

YR	CL	LEA	POS	GP	G	REC
1890	BAL	AA	3		29	.262
1891	BAL	AA	3		137	.229
1892	BAL	N	3		4	.200
1894	BRO	N	3		6	.000
	LOU	N	3		28	.287
	TR				204	.234

GILBERT, WALTER JOHN
B.DEC.19,1900 OSCODA,MICH.
D.SEPT.7,1958 DULUTH,MINN.

YR	CL	LEA	POS	GP	G	REC
1928	BRO	N	3		3	.203
1929	BRO	N	3		143	.304
1930	BRO	N	3		150	.294
1931	BRO	N	3		145	.266
1932	CIN	N	3		114	.214
	BRTR				591	.269

GILBERT, WILLIAM
B.HAVRE DE GRACE,MD.

YR	CL	LEA	POS	GP	G	REC
1892	BAL	N	P		2	0- 1

GILBERT, WILLIAM OLIVER
B.JUNE 21,1876 TULLYTOWN,PA.
D.AUG.8,1927 NEW YORK,N.Y.

YR	CL	LEA	POS	GP	G	REC
1901	NY	N	2		127	.269
1902	BAL	A	S		130	.243
1903	NY	N	2		128	.252
1904	NY	N	2		146	.253
1905	NY	N	2		115	.247
1906	NY	N	2		98	.231
1908	STL	N	2		89	.214
1909	STL	N	2		12	.172
	BRTR				845	.246

GILBREATH, RODNEY JOE (ROD)
B.SEP.24,1952 LAUREL,MISS.

YR	CL	LEA	POS	GP	G	REC
1972	ATL	N	/2-3		18	.237
1973	ATL	N	3		29	.284
1974	ATL	N	/2		3	.333
1975	ATL	N	2-3/S		90	.243
1976	ATL	N	*2/3-S		116	.251
1977	ATL	N	*2/3		128	.243
1978	ATL	N	3-2		116	.245
	BRTR				500	.248
	BB 1975 (PART)					

GILBRETH, WILLIAM FREEMAN (BILL)
B.SEP.3,1947 ABILENE,TEX.

YR	CL	LEA	POS	GP	G	REC
1971	DET	A	/P		9	2- 1
1972	DET	A	/P		2	0- 0
1974	CAL	A	/P		3	0- 0
	BLTL				14	2- 1

GILE, DONALD LOREN (DON) OR (BEAR)
B.APR.19,1935 MODESTO,CAL.

YR	CL	LEA	POS	GP	G	REC
1959	BOS	A	C		3	.200
1960	BOS	A	C-1		29	.176
1961	BOS	A	C-1		8	.278
1962	BOS	A	1		18	.049
	BRTR				58	.150

GILHAM, GEORGE LEWIS
B.SEPT.8,1899 SHAMOKIN,PA.
D.APR.25,1937 LANSDOWNE,PA.

YR	CL	LEA	POS	GP	G	REC
1920	STL	N	C		1	.000
1921	STL	N	C		1	.000
	BRTR				2	.000

GILHOOLEY, FRANK PATRICK (FLASH)
B.JUNE 10,1892 TOLEDO,OHIO
D.JULY 11,1959 TOLEDO,OHIO

YR	CL	LEA	POS	GP	G	REC
1911	STL	N	O		1	.000
1912	STL	N	O		13	.224
1913	NY	A	O		24	.341
1914	NY	A	O		1	.667
1915	NY	A	O		1	.000
1916	NY	A	O		98	.278
1917	NY	A	O		54	.242
1918	NY	A	O		112	.276
1919	BOS	A	O		48	.271
	BLTR				312	.271

GILKS, ROBERT JAMES
B.JULY 2,1867 CINCINNATI,OHIO
D.AUG.20,1944 BRUNSWICK,GA.

YR	CL	LEA	POS	GP	G	REC
1887	CLE	AA	P-O	11	22	6- 5
						.333
1888	CLE	AA	3-O		118	.232
1889	CLE	N	O		52	.238
1890	CLE	N	P-O	4	130	2- 2
						.213
1893	BAL	N	O		15	.000
	BRTR			15	337	8- 7
						.234

GILL, EDWARD JAMES
B.AUG.7,1896 SOMERVILLE,MASS.

YR	CL	LEA	POS	GP	G	REC
1919	WAS	N	P		16	1- 1
	BLTR					

```
YR   CL LEA POS     GP   G   REC
```

GILL, GEORGE LLOYD
B.FEB.13,1909 CATCHINGS,MISS.
```
1937 DET A  P        31  11- 4
1938 DET A  P        24  12- 9
1939 DET A  P         3   0- 1
     STL A  P        27   1-12
     BRTH            85  24-26
```

GILL, HAROLD EDMUND (HADDIE)
B.JAN.23,1899 BROCKTON,MASS.
D.AUG.1,1932 BROCKTON,MASS.
```
1923 CIN N  P         1   0- 0
     BLTL
```

GILL, JAMES C.
B.ST.LOUIS,MO.
```
1889 STL AA 2-O       2   .250
```

GILL, JOHN WESLEY (PATCHEYE)
B.MAR.27,1905 NASHVILLE,TENN.
```
1927 CLE A  O        21   .216
1928 CLE A  H         2   .000
1931 WAS A  O         8   .267
1934 WAS A  O        13   .245
1935 CHI N  H         3   .333
1936 CHI N  O        71   .253
     BLTR           118   .245
```

GILL, WARREN DARST (DOC)
B.DEC.21,1878 LADOGA,IND.
D.NOV.26,1952 LAGUNA BEACH,CAL.
```
1908 PIT N  1        25   .224
     BRTR
```

GILLELAND, SAMUEL
[PLAYED UNDER NAME OF SAMUEL GILLEN]

GILLEN, SAMUEL
[REAL NAME SAMUEL GILLELAND]
B.1870 PITTSBURGH,PA.
D.MAY 13,1905 PITTSBURGH,PA.
```
1893 PIT N  S         3   .000
1897 PHI N  S        74   .258
                     77   .253
```

GILLEN, THOMAS J.
B.MAY 18,1862 PHILADELPHIA,PA.
D.JAN.26,1889 PHILADELPHIA,PA.
```
1884 KEY U  C-O      28   .149
     PHI N  C         1   .333
1886 DET N  C         2   .400
                     31   .154
```

GILLENWATER, CARDEN EDISON
B.MAY 13,1918 RICEVILLE,TENN.
```
1940 STL N  O         7   .160
1943 BRO N  O         8   .176
1945 BOS N  O       144   .288
1946 BOS N  O        99   .228
1948 WAS A  O        77   .244
     BRTR           335   .260
```

GILLENWATER, CLARAL LEWIS
B.MAY 20,1900 SIMS,IND.
D.FEB.26,1978 BRADENTON,FLA.
```
1923 CHI A  P         5   1- 3
     BRTR
```

GILLESPIE, JAMES
B.BUFFALO,N.Y.
```
1890 BUF P  O         1   .000
```

GILLESPIE, JOHN PATRICK
(SILENT JOHN)
B.FEB.25,1900 OAKLAND,CAL.
D.FEB.15,1954 VALLEJO,CAL.
```
1922 CIN N  P        51   3- 3
     BRTR
```

GILLESPIE, PAUL ALLEN
B.SEPT.18,1920 CARTERSVILLE,GA.
```
1942 CHI N  C         5   .250
1944 CHI N  C         9   .269
1945 CHI N  C-O      75   .288
     BLTR            89   .283
```

GILLESPIE, PETER PATRICK (PETE)
B.NOV.30,1851 CARBONDALE,PA.
D.MAY 5,1910 CARBONDALE,PA.
```
1880 TRO N  O        82   .242
1881 TRO N  O        83   .277
1882 TRO N  O        72   .265
1883 NY  N  O        95   .314
1884 NY  N  O        97   .264
1885 NY  N  O       102   .292
1886 NY  N  O        98   .272
1887 NY  N  O        74   .293
     BL             703   .279
```

GILLESPIE, ROBERT WILLIAM (BUNCH)
B.OCT.8,1918 COLUMBUS,OHIO
```
1944 DET A  P         7   0- 1
1947 CHI A  P        25   5- 8
1948 CHI A  P        25   0- 4
1950 BOS A  P         1   0- 0
     BRTR            58   5-13
```

GILLIAM, JAMES WILLIAM
(JIM) OR (JUNIOR)
B.OCT.17,1928 NASHVILLE,TENN.
D.OCT.8,1978 INGLEWOOD,CAL.
```
1953 BRO N  2       151   .278
1954 BRO N  2-O     146   .282
1955 BRO N  2-O     147   .249
1956 BRO N  2-O     153   .300
1957 BRO N  2-O     149   .250
1958 LA  N  2-O     147   .261
1959 LA  N  2-3-O   145   .282
1960 LA  N  2-3     151   .248
1961 LA  N  2-3-O   144   .244
1962 LA  N  2-3-O   160   .270
1963 LA  N  2-3     148   .282
1964 LA  N  2-3-O   116   .228
1965 LA  N  3-O/2   111   .280
1966 LA  N  3/1-2    88   .217
     BBTR          1956   .265
```

GILLIFORD, PAUL GANT
(PAUL) OR (GORILLA)
B.JAN.12,1949 BRYN MAWR,PA.
```
1967 BAL A  /P        2   0- 0
     BRTL
```

GILLIGAN, ANDREW BERNARD (BARNEY)
B.JAN.3,1856 CAMBRIDGE,MASS.
D.APR.1,1934 LYNN,MASS.
```
1875 ATL NA C-O       2    -
1879 CLE N  C-O      52   .170
1880 CLE N  C-S-O    28   .179
1881 PRO N  C-2-S-O  45   .218
1882 PRO N  C-S      55   .223
1883 PRO N  C        72   .198
1884 PRO N  C-1-3    80   .244
1885 PRO N  C-S-O    69   .214
1886 WAS N  C        82   .190
1887 WAS N  C        27   .242
1888 DET N  C         1   .200
     BRTR           513    -
```

GILLIGAN, JOHN PATRICK (JACK)
B.OCT.18,1885 CHICAGO,ILL.
```
1909 STL A  P         3   1- 2
1910 STL A  P         9   0- 3
     BBTR            12   1- 5
```

GILLIS, GRANT
B.JAN.24,1901 GROVE HILL,ALA.
```
1927 WAS A  S        10   .222
1928 WAS A  S        24   .253
1929 BOS A  2        28   .247
     BRTR            62   .245
```

GILMAN, PITKIN CLARK
B.MAR.14,1864 LAPORTE,OHIO
D.AUG.17,1950 ELYRIA,OHIO
```
1884 CLE N  O         2   .100
1893 CLE N  3         2   .285
     BLTL             4   .176
```

GILMORE, ERNEST GROVER
B.NOV.1,1888 CHICAGO,ILL.
D.NOV.25,1919 SIOUX CITY,IOWA
```
1914 KC  F  O       138   .282
1915 KC  F  O       119   .282
     BLTL           257   .282
```

GILMORE, FRANK T.
B.APR.2,1864 WEBSTER,MASS.
D.JULY 26,1929 HARTFORD,CONN.
```
1886 WAS N  P         9   4- 4
1887 WAS N  P        27   7-20
1888 WAS N  P        13   1-10
     BR              49  12-34
```

GILMORE, JAMES
B.BALTIMORE,MD.
```
1875 NAT NA C-2-3     5    -
```

GILMORE, LEONARD PRESTON (MEOW)
B.NOV.3,1927 CLINTON,IND.
```
1944 PIT N  P         1   0- 1
     BRTR
```

GILPATRICK, GEORGE F.
B.FEB.28,1875 HOLDEN,MO.
D.DEC.15,1941 KANSAS CITY,MO.
```
1898 STL N  P         7   0- 1
```

GILROY
```
1874 CHI NA O         8    -
1875 ATH NA O         1   .000
                      9    -
```

GILROY, JOHN M.
B.OCT.26,1869 WASHINGTON,D.C.
D.AUG.4,1897 NORFOLK,VA.
```
1895 WAS N  P        11   1- 4
1896 WAS N  P         1   0- 0
                     12   1- 4
```

GILSON, HAROLD (HAL) OR (LEFTY)
B.FEB.9,1942 LOS ANGELES,CAL.
```
1968 STL N  P        13   0- 2
     HOU N  /P        2   0- 0
     BRTL        15  16   0- 2
```

GING, WILLIAM JOSEPH (BILLY)
B.NOV.7,1872 ELMIRA,N.Y.
D.SEPT.14,1950 ELMIRA,N.Y.
```
1899 BOS N  P         1   1- 0
```

GINGRAS, JOSEPH JOHN
B.JAN.10,1693 NEW YORK,N.Y.
D.SEPT.6,1947 JERSEY CITY,N.J.
```
1915 KC  F  P         2   0- 0
     BRTR
```

GINN, TINSLEY RUCKER
B.SEPT.26,1891 ROYSTON,GA.
D.AUG.30,1931 ATLANTA,GA.
```
1914 CLE A  O         2   .000
     BLTR
```

GINSBERG, MYRON NATHAN (JOE)
B.OCT.11,1926 NEW YORK,N.Y.
```
1948 DET A  C        11   .361
1950 DET A  C        36   .232
1951 DET A  C       102   .260
1952 DET A  C       113   .221
1953 DET A  C        18   .302
     CLE A  C        46   .284
1954 CLE A  C         3   .500
1956 KC  A  C        71   .246
     BAL A  C        15   .071
1957 BAL A  C        85   .274
1958 BAL A  C        61   .211
1959 BAL A  C        65   .181
1960 BAL A  C        14   .267
     CHI A  C        28   .253
1961 CHI A  C         6   .000
     BOS A  C        19   .256
1962 NY  N  C         2   .000
     BLTR           695   .241
```

GIONFRIDDO, ALBERT FRANCIS (AL)
B.MAR.8,1922 DYSART,PA.
```
1944 PIT N  O         4   .167
1945 PIT N  O       122   .284
1946 PIT N  O        64   .255
1947 PIT N  H         1   .000
     BRO N  H        37   .177
     BLTL           228   .256
```

GIORDANO, THOMAS ARTHUR
(TOMMY) OR (T-BONE)
B.OCT.9,1925 NEWARK,N.J.
```
1953 PHI A  2        11   .175
     BRTR
```

GIRARD, CHARLES A.
B.1686 BROOKLYN,N.Y.
```
1910 PHI N  P         7   1- 2
```

GIULIANI, ANGELO JOHN (TONY)
B.NOV.24,1912 ST.PAUL,MINN.
```
1936 STL A  C        71   .217
1937 STL A  C        19   .302
1938 WAS A  C        46   .217
1939 WAS A  C        54   .255
1940 BRO N  C         1   .000
1941 BRO N  C         3   .000
1943 WAS A  C        49   .226
     BRTR           243   .233
```

GIUSTI, DAVID JOHN (DAVE)
B.NOV.27,1939 SENECA FALLS,N.Y.
```
1962 HOU N  P    22  26   2- 3
1964 HOU N  P         8   6- C
1965 HOU N  P        38   8- 7
1966 HOU N  P    34  41  15-14
1967 HOU N  P    37  43  11- 5
1968 HOU N  P    37  38  11-14
1969 STL N  P        22   5- 7
1970 PIT N  P        66   9- 3
1971 PIT N  P        58   5- 6
1972 PIT N  P        54   7- 4
1973 PIT N  P        67   9- 2
1974 PIT N  P        64   7- 5
1975 PIT N  P        61   5- 4
1976 PIT N  P        40   5- 4
1977 OAK A  P        40   3- 3
     CHI N  P        20   0- 2
     BRTR       668 686 100-93
```

GLADD, JAMES WALTER
B.OCT.2,1922 FT.GIBSON,OKLA.
```
1946 NY  N  C         4   .691
     BRTR
```

GLADDING, FRED EARL
B.JUNE 28,1936 FLAT ROCK,MICH.
```
1961 DET A  P         8   1- 0
1962 DET A  P         6   0- C
1963 DET A  P        22   1- 1
1964 DET A  P        42   7- 4
1965 DET A  P        46   6- 2
1966 DET A  P        51   5- 0
1967 DET A  P        42   6- 4
1968 HOU N  /P        7   0- 0
1969 HOU N  P        57   4- 8
1970 HOU N  P        63   7- 4
1971 HOU N  P        48   4- 5
1972 HOU N  P        42   5- 6
1973 HOU N  P        16   2- 0
     BLTR           450  48-34
```

YR	CL LEA POS	GP	G	REC

GLADE, FREDERICK MONROE (LUCKY)
B.JAN.25,1876 DUBUQUE,IOWA
D.NOV.21,1934 GRAND ISLAND,NEB.

1902 CHI N	P	1		0- 1
1904 STL A	P	36	19-15
1905 STL A	P	32	6-24
1906 STL A	P	35	15-15
1907 STL A	P	32	13- 9
1908 NY A	P	5	0- 4
BRTR		141	53-68

GLADMAN, JOHN H. (BUCK)
B.1864 WASHINGTON,D.C.

1883 PHI N	3	1	.000
1884 WAS AA	3	56	.158
1886 WAS N	3	44	.138
		101	.149

GLADU, ROLAND EDOUARD
B.MAY 10,1913 MONTREAL,QUE.,CAN

| 1944 BOS N | 3-0 | 21 | .242 |
| BLTR | | | |

GLAISEK, JOHN BURKE (BERT)
B.JULY 28,1894 YOAKUM,TEX.
D.MAR.7,1959 HOUSTON,TEX.

| 1920 DET A | P | 9 | 0- 0 |
| BLTR | | | |

GLASS, THOMAS JOSEPH
B.APR.29,1898 GREENSBORO,N.C.

| 1925 PHI A | | 2 | 1- 0 |
| BRTR | | | |

GLASSCOCK, JOHN WESLEY (PEBBLY JACK)
B.JULY 22,1859 WHEELING,W.VA.
D.FEB.24,1947 WHEELING,W.VA.

1879 CLE N	2-3	80	.209
1880 CLE N	S	76	.247
1881 CLE N	2-S	84	.260
1882 CLE N	S	82	.285
1883 CLE N	2-S	93	.290
1884 CLE N	P-2-	2	72	0- 0
	S			.249
	CIN U	2-S	39	.388
1885 STL N	2-S	111	.280
1886 STL N	S	121	.325
1887 IND N	S	121	.349
1888 IND N	S	112	.269
1889 IND N	M-S	134	.359
1890 NY N	S	124	.336
1891 NY N	S	95	.243
1892 STL N	S	139	.273
1893 STL N	S	48	.301
	PIT N	S	66	.380
1894 PIT N	S	86	.262
1895 LOU N	S	18	.373
	WAS N	S	25	.233
BRTR		2 1726	0- 0
			.297

GLAVENICH, LUKE FRANK
B.JAN.17,1893 JACKSON,CAL.
D.MAY 22,1935 STOCKTON,CAL.

| 1913 CLE A | P | 1 | 0- 0 |

GLAVIANO, THOMAS GIATANO (TOMMY) OR (RABBIT)
B.OCT.26,1923 SACRAMENTO,CAL.

1949 STL N	2-3	87	.267
1950 STL N	2-S-0	115	.285
1951 STL N	2-0	54	.183
1952 STL N	2-3	80	.241
1953 STL N	2-S-3	53	.203
BRTR		389	.257

GLAZE, DANIEL RALPH
B.MAR.13,1882 DENVER,COL.
D.OCT.31,1908 ATASCADERO,CAL.

1906 BOS A	P	19	22	4- 6
1907 BOS A	P	32	9-13
1908 BOS A	P	10	2- 2
BRTR		61	64	15-21

GLAZNER, CHARLES FRANKLIN (WHITEY)
B.SEPT.17,1892 SYCAMORE,ALA.

1920 PIT N	P	2	0- 0
1921 PIT N	P	36	14- 5
1922 PIT N	P	33	11-12
1923 PIT N	P	7	2- 1
PHI N	P	28	7-14
1924 PHI N	P	35	7-16
BRTR		141	41-48

GLEASON, HARRY GILBERT
B.MAR.28,1875 CAMDEN,N.J.
D.OCT.21,1961 CAMDEN,N.J.

1901 BOS A	3	1	1.000
1902 BOS A	2-3-0	66	.224
1904 STL A	S-3	45	.214
1905 STL A	3	150	.217
TR		262	.217

GLEASON, JOHN DAY (JACK)
B.JULY 14,1854 ST.LOUIS,MO.
D.SEPT.4,1944 ST.LOUIS,MO.

1877 STL N	0	1	.250
1882 STL AA	3-0	78	.262
1883 STL AA	3-0	9	.205
LOU AA	S-3	84	.276
1884 STL U	3	77	.312
1885 STL N	3	2	.143
1886 STL AA	3	76	.195
BRTR		327	.262

GLEASON, JOSEPH PAUL
B.JULY 9,1895 PHELPS,N.Y.

1920 WAS A	P	2	0- 0
1922 WAS A	P	8	2- 2
BRTR		10	2- 2

GLEASON, ROY WILLIAM
B.APR.9,1943 MELROSE PARK,ILL.

| 1963 LA N | H | 8 | 1.000 |
| BBTR | | | |

GLEASON, WILLIAM
B.1866 CLEVELAND,OHIO
D.DEC.2,1893 CLEVELAND,OHIO

| 1890 CLE P | P | 1 | 0- 1 |

GLEASON, WILLIAM G. (WILL)
B.NOV.12,1858 ST.LOUIS,MO.
D.JULY 21,1932 ST.LOUIS,MO.

1882 STL AA	2-S	79	.286
1883 STL AA	S	95	.274
1884 STL AA	S	110	.269
1885 STL AA	S	112	.253
1886 STL AA	S	126	.267
1887 STL AA	S	135	.336
1888 ATH AA	S	123	.224
1889 LOU AA	S	15	.216
BRTR		795	.275

GLEASON, WILLIAM J. (KID)
B.OCT.26,1866 CAMDEN,N.J.
D.JAN.2,1933 PHILADELPHIA,PA.

1888 PHI N	P	24	7-17
1889 PHI N	P	25	28	9-14
1890 PHI N	P	56	58	39-17
1891 PHI N	P	50	60	24-22
1892 STL N	P	44	63	16-24
1893 STL N	P	46	55	21-25
1894 STL N	P	10	2- 6
BAL N	P	23	15- 6
1895 BAL N	P-2	4	107	3- 1
1896 NY N	2	133	.292
1897 NY N	2	134	.311
1898 NY N	2	149	.222
1899 NY N	2	148	.267
1900 NY N	2	111	.257
1901 DET A	2	136	.278
1902 DET A	2	118	.247
1903 PHI N	2	106	.284
1904 PHI N	2	153	.274
1905 PHI N	2	155	.247
1906 PHI N	2	135	.227
1907 PHI N	2	35	.143
1908 PHI N	2-0	2	.000
1912 CHI A	2	1	.500
BBTR		282 1944	136-136
			.262

NON-PLAYING MANAGER CHI[A] 1919-23

GLEASON, WILLIAM PATRICK (BILLY)
B.SEPT.6,1894 CHICAGO,ILL.
D.JAN.9,1957 HOLYOKE,MASS.

1916 PIT N	P	1	.000
1917 PIT N	2	14	.167
1921 STL A	2	26	.257
BRTR		41	.220

GLEESON, JAMES JOSEPH (GEE GEE)
B.MAR.5,1912 KANSAS CITY,MO.

1936 CLE A	0	41	.259
1939 CHI N	0	111	.223
1940 CHI N	0	129	.313
1941 CIN N	0	102	.233
1942 CIN N	0	9	.200
BBTR		392	.263

GLEICH, FRANK ELMER (INCH)
B.MAR.7,1894 COLUMBUS,OHIO
D.MAR.27,1949 COLUMBUS,OHIO

1919 NY A	0	4	.333
1920 NY A	0	24	.122
BLTR		28	.156

GLENALVIN, ROBERT J.
[REAL NAME ROBERT J. DOWLING]
B.JAN.17,1867 INDIANAPOLIS,IND.
D.MAR.24,1944 DETROIT,MICH.

1889 CHI N	2	66	.268
1893 CHI N	2	16	.400
TR		82	.294

GLENDON, MARTIN H.
B.1870 CHICAGO,ILL.

1902 CIN N	P	1	0- 1
1903 CLE A	P	3	1- 2
		4	1- 3

GLENN, BURDETTE (BOB)
B.JUNE 16,1894 W.SUNBURY,PA.

| 1920 STL N | P | 2 | 0- 0 |

GLENN, EDWARD C. (MOUSE)
B.SEPT.19,1860 RICHMOND,VA.
D.FEB.10,1892 RICHMOND,VA.

1884 RIC AA	0	42	.250
1886 PIT AA	0	71	.182
1888 KC AA	0	3	.000
BOS N	0	19	.154
BRTR		135	.196

GLENN, EDWARD D.
B.1874 LUDLOW,KY.
D.DEC.6,1911 LUDLOW,KY.

1898 NY N	S	2	.167
1902 CHI N	S	2	.000
		4	.158

GLENN, HARRY MELVILLE (HUSKY)
B.JUNE 9,1890 SHELBURN,IND.
D.OCT.12,1918 ST.PAUL,MINN.

| 1915 STL N | C | 6 | .312 |
| BRTR | | | |

GLENN, JOHN
B.JULY 10,1928 MOULTRIE,GA.

| 1960 STL N | 0 | 32 | .258 |
| BRTR | | | |

GLENN, JOHN W.
B.1849 ROCHESTER,N.Y.
D.NOV.10,1888 GLENS FALLS,N.Y.

1871 OLY NA	0	25	-
1872 OLY NA	0	9	.150
NAT NA	0	1	.500
1873 NAT NA	1	39	-
1874 CHI NA	1-3-0	54	-
1875 CHI NA	1-0	70	-
1876 CHI N	1-0	66	.292
1877 CHI N	1-0	50	.228
BRTR		314	-

GLENN, JOSEPH CHARLES (GABBY)
[REAL NAME JOSEPH CHARLES GURZENSKY]
B.NOV.19,1908 DICKSON CITY,PA.

1932 NY A	C	6	.125
1933 NY A	C	5	.143
1935 NY A	C	17	.233
1936 NY A	C	44	.271
1937 NY A	C	25	.283
1938 NY A	C	41	.260
1939 STL A	C	88	.273
1940 BOS A	C	22	.128
BRTR		248	.252

GLIATTO, SALVADOR MICHAEL
B.MAY 7,1902 CHICAGO,ILL.

| 1930 CLE A | P | 8 | 10 | 0- 0 |
| BBTR | | | |

GLOCKSON, NORMAN STANLEY
B.JUNE 15,1894 BLUE ISLAND,ILL.
D.AUG.5,1955 MAYWOOD,ILL.

| 1914 CIN N | C | 7 | .000 |
| BRTR | | | |

GLOSSOP, ALBAN (AL)
B.JULY 23,1915 CHRISTOPHER,ILL.

1939 NY N	0	10	.186
1940 NY N	2	27	.209
BOS N	2-S-0	60	.236
1942 PHI N	2-3	121	.225
1943 BRO N	2-S-3	87	.171
1946 CHI N	2-S	4	.000
BBTR		309	.209

GLYNN, EDWARD PAUL (ED)
B.JUNE 3,1953 FLUSHING,N.Y.

1975 DET A	/P	3	0- 2
1976 DET A	/P	5	1- 3
1977 DET A	/P	8	2- 1
1978 DET A	P	10	0- 0
BRTL		26	3- 6

GLYNN, WILLIAM VINCENT (BILL)
B.JULY 30,1925 SUSSEX,N.J.

1949 PHI N	1	8	.200
1952 CLE A	1	44	.272
1953 CLE A	1-0	147	.243
1954 CLE A	1-0	111	.251
BLTL		310	.249

GOAR, JOSHUA MERCER (JOT)
B.JAN.31,1870 NEW LISBON,IND.
D.APR.4,1947 NEW CASTLE,IND.

1896 PIT N	P	3	0- 0
1898 CIN N	P	1	0- 0
BRTR		4	0- 0

GOCHNAUER, JOHN PETER
B.SEPT.12,1875 ALTOONA,PA.
D.SEPT.27,1929 ALTOONA,PA.

1901 BRO N	S	3	.363
1902 CLE A	S	126	.183
1903 CLE A	S	136	.181
BRTR		265	.184

YR CL LEA POS GP G REC

GODAR, JOHN MICHAEL
B.OCT.25,1864 CINCINNATI,OHIO
D.JUNE 23,1949 PARK RIDGE,ILL.
1892 BAL N O 5 .333

GODBY, DANNY RAY
B.NOV.4,1946 LOGAN,W.VA.
1974 STL N /O 13 .154
BRTR

GODDARD, JOSEPH HAROLD (JOE)
B.JULY 23,1950 BECKLEY,W.VA.
1972 SD N C 12 .200
BRTR

GODWIN, JOHN HENRY (BUNNY)
B.MAR.10,1877 E.LIVERPOOL,OHIO
D.MAY 5,1956 E.LIVERPOOL,OHIO
1905 BOS A 2 16 .304
1906 BOS A 3 66 .187
BRTR 82 .209

GOEBEL, EDWIN
B.SEPT.1,1899 BROOKLYN,N.Y.
1922 WAS A O 37 .271
BRTR

GOECKEL, WILLIAM JOHN (BILLY)
B.SEPT.3,1871 WILKES-BARRE,PA.
D.NOV.1,1922 PHILADELPHIA,PA.
1899 PHI N 1 35 .283
BLTL

GOETZ, GEORGE BURT
B.GREENCASTLE,IND.
1889 BAL AA P 1 1- 0

GOETZ, JOHN HARDY
B.OCT.24,1937 GOETZVILLE,MICH.
1960 CHI N P 4 0- 0
BRTR

GOGGIN, CHARLES FRANCIS (CHUCK)
B.JULY 7,1945 POMPANO BEACH,FLA.
1972 PIT N /2 5 .286
1973 PIT N /C 1 1.000
ATL N 2/O-S-C 64 .289
1974 BOS A /2 2 .000
BBTR 72 .293

GOGOLEWSKI, WILLIAM JOSEPH (BILL)
B.OCT.26,1947 OSHKOSH,WIS.
1970 WAS A /P 8 2- 2
1971 WAS A P 27 6- 5
1972 TEX A P 36 4-11
1973 TEX A P 49 3- 6
1974 CLE A /P 5 0- 0
1975 CHI A P 19 0- 0
BLTR 144 15-24

GOLDEN, JAMES EDWARD (JIM)
B.MAR.20,1936 ELDON,MO.
1960 LA N P 1 1- 0
1961 LA N P 28 1- 1
1962 HOU N P 37 43 7-11
1963 HOU N P 3 0- 1
BLTR 69 75 9-13

GOLDEN, MICHAEL HENRY
B.SEPT.11,1851 SHIRLEY,MASS.
D.JAN.11,1929 ROCKLAND,ILL.
1875 WES NA P 13 1-12
CHI NA P-O 14 38 6- 8
-
1878 MIL N P-O 18 54 3-15
.209
BRTR 45 105 10-35
-

GOLDEN, ROY KRAMER
B.JULY 12,1888 MADISONVILLE,ILL
D.OCT.4,1961 NORWOOD,OHIO
1910 STL N P 7 2- 3
1911 STL N P 30 4- 9
TR 37 6-12

GOLDMAN, JONAH JOHN
B.AUG.29,1906 NEW YORK,N.Y.
1928 CLE A S 7 .238
1930 CLE A S-3 111 .242
1931 CLE A S 30 .129
BRTR 148 .224

GOLDSBERRY, GORDON FREDERICK
B.AUG.30,1927 SACRAMENTO,CAL.
1949 CHI A 1 39 .248
1950 CHI A 1-O 82 .268
1951 CHI A 1 10 .091
1952 STL A 1-O 86 .229
BLTL 217 .241

YR CL LEA POS GP G REC

GOLDSBY, WALTON HUGH
B.DEC.31,1861 LOUISIANA
D.JAN.11,1914 DALLAS,TEX.
1884 STL AA O 5 .211
WAS AA O 6 .375
RIC AA O 10 .222
1886 WAS N O 6 .111
1888 BAL AA O 44 .227
71 .233

GOLDSMITH, FRED ERNEST
B.MAY 15,1852 NEW HAVEN,CONN.
D.MAR.28,1939 BERKLEY,MICH.
1879 TRO N P-1-O 8 9 2- 4 .231
1880 CHI N P-1-O 25 35 22- 3 .260
1881 CHI N P-O 38 40 25-13 .240
1882 CHI N P-1 44 28-16 .229
1883 CHI N P-1-O 46 60 26-18 .221
1884 CHI N P-O 21 22 8-12 .135
BAL AA P-1 4 3- 1 .167
BRTR 186 214 116-67 .225

GOLDSMITH, HAROLD EUGENE
B.AUG.18,1898 PECONIC,N.Y.
1926 BOS N P 19 5- 7
1927 BOS N P 22 1- 3
1928 BOS N P 4 0- 0
1929 STL N P 2 0- 0
BRTR 47 6-10

GOLDSMITH, WALLACE
B.1849 BALTIMORE,MD.
1871 KEK NA C-S-3 19 -
1872 OLY NA 2-S 9 .225
1873 MAR NA 2 1 .000
1875 WES NA 3 13 -
NH NA 2 1 -
43 -

GOLDSTEIN, ISADORE (IZZY)
B.JUNE 6,1908 NEW YORK,N.Y.
1932 DET A P 16 3- 2
BBTR

GOLDSTEIN, LESLIE ELMER (LONNIE)
B.MAY 13,1918 AUSTIN,TEX.
1943 CIN N 1 5 .200
1946 CIN N H 6 .000
BLTL 11 .100

GOLDY, PURNAL WILLIAM
B.NOV.28,1937 CAMDEN,N.J.
1962 DET A O 20 .229
1963 DET A H 9 .250
BRTR 29 .231

GOLETZ, STANLEY (STASH)
B.MAY 21,1918 CRESCENT,OHIO
1941 CHI A H 5 .600
BLTL

GOLIAT, MIKE MITCHEL
B.NOV.5,1925 YATESBORO,PA.
1949 PHI N 1-2 55 .212
1950 PHI N 2 145 .234
1951 PHI N 2-3 41 .225
STL A 2 5 .182
1952 STL A 2 3 .000
BRTR 249 .225

GOLTZ, DAVID ALLAN (DAVE)
B.JUNE 23,1949 PELICAN RAPIDS,MINN.
1972 MIN A P 15 3- 3
1973 MIN A P 32 6- 4
1974 MIN A P 28 10-10
1975 MIN A P 32 14-14
1976 MIN A P 36 37 14-14
1977 MIN A P 39 41 20-11
1978 MIN A P 29 15-10
BRTR 211 214 82-66

GOLVIN, WALTER GEORGE
B.FEB.1,1894 HERSHEY,NEB.
D.JUNE 11,1973 GARDENA,CAL.
1922 CHI N 1 2 .000
BLTL

GOMEZ, JOSE LUIS [RODRIGUEZ] (CHILE)
B.MAY 23,1909 VILLAUNION,MEX.
1935 PHI N 2-S 67 .230
1936 PHI N 2-S 108 .232
1942 WAS A 2 25 .192
BRTR 200 .226

YR CL LEA POS GP G REC

GOMEZ, LUIS
B.AUG.19,1951 GUADALAJARA,MEX.
1974 MIN A S/2 82 .206
1975 MIN A S/2 89 .139
1976 MIN A S/2-3-O 38 .193
1977 MIN A 2/S-3-O 32 .246
1978 TOR A *S 153 .223
BRTR 394 .212

GOMEZ, PEDRO [MARTINEZ]
PLAYED UNDER NAME OF
PRESTON GOMEZ [MARTINEZ]]

GOMEZ, PRESTON [MARTINEZ]
[REAL NAME PEDRO GOMEZ [MARTINEZ]]
B.APR.20,1923 PRESTON,CUBA
1944 WAS A 2-S 8 .286
BRTR
NON-PLAYING MANAGER
SD[N] 1969-72, HOU[N] 1974-75

GOMEZ, RUBEN [COLON]
B.JULY 13,1927 ARROYO,P.R.
1953 NY N P 29 61 13-11
1954 NY N P 37 49 17- 9
1955 NY N P 33 42 9-10
1956 NY N P-O 40 52 7-17 .183
1957 NY N P-O 38 54 15-13 .184
1958 SF N P 42 48 10-12
1959 PHI N P 20 24 3- 8
1960 PHI N P 22 0- 3
1962 CLE A P 15 16 1- 2
MIN A P 6 1- 1
1967 PHI N /P 7 0- 0
BRTR 289 381 76-86 .199

GOMEZ, VERNON LOUIS
(LEFTY) OR (GOOFY)
B.NOV.26,1908 RODEO,CAL.
1930 NY A P 15 2- 5
1931 NY A P 40 21- 9
1932 NY A P 37 24- 7
1933 NY A P 35 16-10
1934 NY A P 38 26- 5
1935 NY A P 34 12-15
1936 NY A P 31 13- 7
1937 NY A P 34 21-11
1938 NY A P 32 18-12
1939 NY A P 26 12- 8
1940 NY A P 9 3- 3
1941 NY A P 23 15- 5
1942 NY A P 13 6- 4
1943 WAS A P 1 0- 1
BLTL 368 189-102

GONDER, JESSE LEMAR
B.JAN.20,1936 MONTICELLO,ARK.
1960 NY A C 7 .286
1961 NY A H 15 .333
1962 CIN N H 4 .000
1963 CIN N C 31 .313
NY N C 42 .302
1964 NY N C 131 .270
1965 NY N C 53 .238
MIL N C 31 .151
1966 PIT N C 59 .225
1967 PIT N C 22 .139
BLTR 395 .251

GONZALES, JOE MADRID (SMOKEY)
B.MAR.19,1915 SAN FRANCISCO,CAL
1937 BOS A P 8 1- 2
BRTR

GONZALES, JULIO ENRIQUE
B.DEC.20,1920 HAVANA,CUBA
1949 WAS A P 13 0- 0
BRTR

GONZALES, WENCESLAO O REILLY (VINCE)
B.SEPT.28,1925 QUIVICAN,CUBA
1955 WAS A P 1 0- 0
BLTL

GONZALEZ, ANDRES ANTONIO
[GONZALEZ] (TONY)
B.AUG.28,1936 CENTRAL CUNAGUA,CUBA
1960 CIN N O 39 .212
PHI N O 78 .299
1961 PHI N O 126 .277
1962 PHI N O 118 .302
1963 PHI N O 155 .306
1964 PHI N O 131 .278
1965 PHI N *O 108 .295
1966 PHI N *O 132 .286
1967 PHI N *O 149 .339
1968 PHI N *O 121 .264
1969 SD N O 53 .225
ATL N O 89 .294
1970 ATL N *O 123 .265
CAL A O 26 .304
1971 CAL A O 111 .245
BLTR 1559 .286

YR CL LEA POS   GP   G   REC

GONZALEZ, EUSEBIO MIGUEL
[LOPEZ] (PAPO)
B.JULY 13,1892 HAVANA,CUBA
D.FEB.14,1976 HAVANA,CUBA
1918 BOS A S-3   3   .400
       BRTR

GONZALEZ, JOSE FERNANDO
[QUINONES] (FERNANDO)
B.JUNE 19,1950 ARECIBO,P.R.
1972 PIT N /3   3   .000
1973 PIT N /3   37   .224
1974 KC A /3   9   .143
     NY A 2/3-S   51   .215
1977 PIT N 3-O/2-S 60   .276
1978 PIT N /2-3   9   .190
     SD N 2   101   .250
       BRTR   290   .243

GONZALEZ, JULIO CESAR
[HERNANDEZ]
B.DEC.25,1952 CAGUAS,P.R.
1977 HOU N S-2   110   .245
1978 HOU N 2-S/3   78   .233
       BRTR   188   .241

GONZALEZ, MIGUEL ANGEL
[CORDERO] (MIKE)
B.SEPT.24,1890 HAVANA,CUBA
D.FEB.19,1977 HAVANA,CUBA
1912 BOS N C   1   .000
1914 CIN N C   95   .233
1915 STL N C-1   51   .227
1916 STL N C-1   118   .239
1917 STL N C-1   106   .262
1918 STL N C-1-O 117   .252
1919 NY N C-1   58   .190
1920 NY N C   11   .251
1921 NY N C-1   13   .375
1924 STL N C   120   .296
1925 STL N C-1   22   .310
     CHI N C   70   .264
1926 CHI N C   60   .249
1927 CHI N C   39   .241
1928 CHI N C   49   .272
1929 CHI N C   60   .246
1931 STL N C   15   .105
1932 STL N C   17   .143
       BRTR   1042   .254
NON-PLAYING MANAGER
STL[N] 1938 AND 1940

GONZALEZ, ORLANDO EUGENE
B.NOV.15,1951 HAVANA,CUBA
1976 CLE A 1/O   28   .250
1978 PHI N O/1   26   .192
       BLTL   54   .234

GONZALEZ, PEDRO
B.DEC.12,1937 SAN PEDRO DE
MACORIS,D.R.
1963 NY A 2   14   .192
1964 NY A 1-2-3-O 80   .277
1965 NY A /H   7   .400
     CLE A *2/O-3   116   .253
1966 CLE A *2/O-3   110   .233
1967 CLE A 2/1-3-S   60   .228
       BRTR   407   .244

GOOCH, CHARLES FURMAN
B.JUNE 5,1902 SMYRNA,TENN.
1929 WAS A 1-S-3   39   .261
       BRTR

GOOCH, JOHN BEVERLEY
B.NOV.9,1897 SMYRNA,TENN.
D.MAR.15,1975 NASHVILLE,TENN.
1921 PIT N C   13   .237
1922 PIT N C   105   .328
1923 PIT N C   66   .277
1924 PIT N C   70   .290
1925 PIT N C   79   .298
1926 PIT N C   86   .271
1927 PIT N C   101   .258
1928 PIT N C   31   .238
     BRO N C   42   .317
1929 BRO N H   1   .000
     CIN N H   92   .300
1930 CIN N H   62   .243
1933 BOS A H   37   .162
       BBTR   805   .276

GOOCH, LEE CURRIN
d.FEB.23,1890 OXFORD,N.C.
D.MAY 18,1966 RALEIGH,N.C.
1915 CLE A H   2   .667
1917 PHI A O   17   .268
       BRTR   19   .295

GOOD, EUGENE J.
B.DEC.13,1882 ROXBURY,MASS.
D.AUG.6,1947 BOSTON,MASS.
1906 BOS N O   34   .151

GOOD, RALPH NELSON (HOLY)
B.APR.25,1886 MONTICELLO,ME.
D.NOV.24,1965 WATERVILLE,MAINE
1910 BOS N P   2   0- 0
       BRTR

GOOD, WILBUR DAVID (LEFTY)
B.SEPT.28,1885 PUNXSUTAWNEY,PA.
D.DEC.30,1963 BROOKSVILLE,FLA.
1905 NY A P   5   0- 1
1908 CLE A O   46   .279
1909 CLE A O   94   .214
1910 BOS N O   23   .337
1911 BOS N O   43   .267
     CHI N O   58   .269
1912 CHI N O   39   .143
1913 CHI N O   49   .253
1914 CHI N O   154   .272
1915 CHI N O   128   .259
1916 PHI N O   75   .250
1918 CHI A O   35   .250
       BLTL   5 749   0- 1
                            .258

GOODALL, HERBERT FRANK
B.MAR.10,1870 MANSFIELD,PA.
D.JAN.20,1938 MANSFIELD,PA.
1890 LOU AA P   18   10- 6
       BRTR

GOODELL, JOHN HENRY WILLIAM (LEFTY)
B.APR.5,1907 MUSKOGEE,OKLA.
1928 CHI A P   2   0- 0
       BRTL

GOODENOUGH, WILLIAM B.
B.1863 ST.LOUIS,MO.
D.MAY 24,1905 ST.LOUIS,MO.
1893 STL N O   10   .178

GOODFELLOW, MICHAEL J.
B.OCT.3,1866 PORT JERVIS,N.Y.
D.FEB.12,1920 NEWARK,N.J.
1887 STL AA C   1   .000
1888 STL AA O   69   .250
                    70   .246

GOODMAN, IVAL RICHARD
(IVAL) OR (GOODIE)
B.JULY 23,1908 NORTHVIEW,MO.
1935 CIN N O   148   .269
1936 CIN N O   136   .284
1937 CIN N O   147   .273
1938 CIN N O   145   .292
1939 CIN N O   124   .323
1940 CIN N O   136   .258
1941 CIN N O   42   .268
1942 CIN N O   87   .243
1943 CHI N O   80   .320
1944 CHI N O   62   .262
       BLTR   1107   .281

GOODMAN, JACOB
B.SEPT.14,1853 LANCASTER,PA.
D.MAR.9,1890 READING,PA.
1878 MIL N 1   59   .246
1882 PIT AA 1   10   .316
                    69   .256

GOODMAN, WILLIAM DALE (BILLY)
B.MAR.22,1926 CONCORD,N.C.
1947 BOS A O   12   .182
1948 BOS A 1-2-3   127   .310
1949 BOS A 1   122   .298
1950 BOS A 1-2-S-3-O 110   .354
1951 BOS A 1-2-3-O 141   .297
1952 BOS A 1-2-3-O 138   .306
1953 BOS A 1-2   128   .313
1954 BOS A 1-2-3-O 127   .303
1955 BOS A 1-2-3-O 149   .294
1956 BOS A 2   105   .293
1957 BOS A H   18   .063
     BAL A 1-2-S   73   .308
1958 CHI A 1-2-S-3 116   .299
1959 CHI A 2-3   104   .250
1960 CHI A 2-3   30   .234
1961 CHI A 1-2-3   41   .255
1962 HOU N 2-3   82   .255
       BLTR   1623   .300

GOODSON, JAMES EDWARD (ED)
B.JAN.25,1948 PULASKI,VA.
1970 SF N /1   7   .273
1971 SF N 1   20   .190
1972 SF N 1   58   .280
1973 SF N 3   102   .302
1974 SF N 1/3   98   .272
1975 SF N 1-3   39   .207
     ATL N 1/3   47   .211
1976 LA N 3/1-O-2 83   .229
1977 LA N 1/3   61   .167
       BLTR   515   .260

GOODWIN, ARTHUR INGRAM
B.FEB.27,1876 WHITLEY TWNSP.,PA
D.JUNE 19,1943 UNIONTOWN,PA.
1905 NY A P   1   0- 0

GOODWIN, CLAIRE VERNON (PEP)
D.DEC.19,1891 POCATELLO,IDAHO
D.FEB.15,1972 OAKLAND,CAL.
1914 KC F S-3   111   .243
1915 KC F 2-S   81   .235
       BLTR   192   .240

GOODWIN, CLYDE SAMUEL
B.NOV.12,1886 SHADE,OHIO
D.OCT.12,1963 DAYTON,OHIO
1906 WAS A P   3   0- 2
       BRTR

GOODWIN, DANNY KAY
B.SEPT.2,1953 ST.LOUIS,MO.
1975 CAL A /H   4   .100
1977 CAL A D   35   .209
1978 CAL A D   24   .276
       BLTR   63   .226

GOODWIN, JAMES PATRICK
B.AUG.15,1926 ST.LOUIS,MO.
1948 CHI A P   8   0- 0
       BLTL

GOODWIN, MARVIN MARDO
B.JAN.16,1891 GORDONSVILLE,VA.
D.OCT.21,1925 HOUSTON,TEX.
1916 WAS A P   3   0- 0
1917 STL N P   14   6- 4
1919 STL N P   33 34   11- 9
1920 STL N P   32   3- 8
1921 STL N P   14   1- 2
1922 STL N P   2   0- 0
1925 CIN N P   4   0- 2
       BRTR   102 103   21-25

GOOLSBY, RAYMOND DANIEL (OX)
B.SEPT.5,1919 FLORALA,ALA.
1946 WAS A O   3   .000
       BRTR

GOOSSEN, GREGORY BRYANT (GREG)
B.DEC.14,1945 LOS ANGELES,CAL.
1965 NY N /C   11   .290
1966 NY N C   13   .188
1967 NY N C   37   .159
1968 NY N 1/C   38   .208
1969 SEA A 1/O   52   .309
1970 MIL A 1   21   .255
     WAS A /O-1   21   .222
       BRTR   193   .241

GORBOUS, GLEN EDWARD
B.JULY 8,1930 DRUMHELLER,ALT.,CAN.
1955 CIN N O   8   .333
     PHI N O   91   .237
1956 PHI N O   15   .182
1957 PHI N H   3   .500
       BLTR   117   .238

GORCZYCA, JOHN JOSEPH PERRY
[PLAYED UNDER NAME OF
JOHN JOSEPH PERRY GORSICA]

GORDINIER, RAYMOND CORNELIUS (GORDY)
B.APR.11,1892 ROCHESTER,N.Y.
D.NOV.15,1960 ROCHESTER,N.Y.
1921 BRO N P   3   1- 0
1922 BRO N P   5   0- 0
       BRTR   8   1- 0

GORDON, JOSEPH LOWELL
(JOE) OR (FLASH)
B.FEB.18,1915 LOS ANGELES,CAL.
D.APR.14,1978 SACRAMENTO,CAL.
1938 NY A 2   127   .255
1939 NY A 2   151   .284
1940 NY A 2   155   .281
1941 NY A 2   156   .276
1942 NY A 2   147   .322
1943 NY A 2   152   .249
1946 NY A 2   112   .210
1947 CLE A 2   155   .272
1948 CLE A 2-S   144   .280
1949 CLE A 2   148   .251
1950 CLE A 2   119   .236
       BRTR   1566   .268
NON-PLAYING MANAGER
CLE[A] 1958-60, DET[A] 1960,
KC[A] 1961,1969

GORDON, MICHAEL WILLIAM (MIKE)
B.SEPT.11,1953 LEOMINSTER,MASS.
1977 CHI N /C   8   .043
1978 CHI N /C   4   .200
       BBTR   12   .71

GORDON, SIDNEY (SID)
B.AUG.13,1917 BROOKLYN,N.Y.
D.JUNE 17,1975 NEW YORK,N.Y.
1941 NY N O   9   .258
1942 NY N 3   6   .316
1943 NY N 1-2-3-O 131   .251
1946 NY N O   135   .293
1947 NY N O   130   .273
1948 NY N O   142   .299
1949 NY N 1-3-O 141   .284
1950 BOS N 3-O   134   .304
1951 BOS N 3-O   150   .287
1952 BOS N 3-O   144   .289
1953 MIL N 3-O   140   .274
1954 PIT N 3-O   131   .306
1955 PIT N 3-O   16   .170
     NY N 3-O   66   .243
       BRTR   1475   .283

YR	CL	LEA	POS	GP	G	REC

GORE, GEORGE F. (PIANO LEGS)
B.MAY 3,1852 SACCARAPPA,ME.
D.SEPT.16,1933 UTICA,N.Y.

1879	CHI	N	O		60	.268
1880	CHI	N	1-O		79	.365
1881	CHI	N	1-S-O		73	.297
1882	CHI	N	O		84	.318
1883	CHI	N	O		91	.334
1884	CHI	N	O		101	.316
1885	CHI	N	O		109	.312
1886	CHI	N	O		118	.304
1887	NY	N	O		111	.348
1888	NY	N	O		64	.220
1889	NY	N	O		119	.305
1890	NY	P	O		93	.335
1891	NY	N	O		130	.285
1892	NY	N	O		53	.254
	STL	N	O		20	.200
		BLTR			1301	.308

GORIN, CHARLES PERRY (CHARLIE)
B.FEB.6,1928 WACO,TEX.

1954	MIL	N	P		5	0- 1
1955	MIL	N	P		2	0- 0
		BLTL			7	0- 1

GORINSKI, ROBERT JOHN (BOB)
B.JAN.7,1952 LATROBE,PA.

1977	MIN	A	O		54	.195
		BRTR				

GORMAN, HERBERT ALLEN
B.DEC.18,1924 SAN FRANCISCO,CAL
D.APR.5,1953 SAN DIEGO,CAL.

1952	STL	N	H		1	.000
		BLTL				

GORMAN, HOWARD PAUL (LEFTY)
B.MAY 14,1913 PITTSBURGH,PA.

1937	PHI	N	O		13	.211
1938	PHI	N	H		1	.000
		BLTL			14	.200

GORMAN, JOHN F. (STOOPING JACK)
B.1859 ST.LOUIS,MO.
D.SEPT.9,1889 ST.LOUIS,MO.

1883	STL	AA	C-O		1	.000
1884	KC	U	1-3-O		33	.275
	PIT	AA	P-3-	3	8	1- 2
		O				.133
				3	42	1- 2
						.256

GORMAN, THOMAS ALOYSIUS (TOM)
B.JAN.4,1925 NEW YORK,N.Y.

1952	NY	A	P		12	6- 2
1953	NY	A	P		40	4- 5
1954	NY	A	P		23	0- 0
1955	KC	A	P		57	7- 6
1956	KC	A	P		52	9-10
1957	KC	A	P		38	5- 9
1958	KC	A	P		50	4- 4
1959	KC	A	P		17	1- 0
		BRTR			289	36-36

GORMAN, THOMAS DAVID (TOM)
OR (BIG TOM)
B.MAR.16,1916 NEW YORK,N.Y.

1939	NY	N	P		4	0- 0
		BRTL				

GORMLEY, JOSEPH
B.DEC.20,1866 SUMMIT HILL,PA.
D.JULY 2,1950 SUMMIT HILL,PA.

1891	PHI	N	P		1	0- 1
		BLTL				

GORNICKI, FRANK TED
B.JAN.14,1911 NIAGARA FALLS,N.Y.

1941	STL	N	P		4	1- 0
	CHI	N	P		1	0- 0
1942	PIT	N	P		25	5- 6
1943	PIT	N	P		42	9-13
1946	PIT	N	P		7	0- 0
		BRTR			79	15-19

GORSICA, JOHN JOSEPH PERRY
[REAL NAME
JOHN JOSEPH PERRY GORCZYCA]
B.MAR.29,1915 BAYONNE,N.J.

1940	DET	A	P		29	7- 7
1941	DET	A	P		33	9-11
1942	DET	A	P	28	31	3- 2
1943	DET	A	P	35	36	4- 5
1944	DET	A	P	34	40	6-14
1946	DET	A	P		14	0- 0
1947	DET	A	P		31	2- 0
		BRTR		204	214	31-39

GORYL, JOHN ALBERT (JOHNNY)
B.OCT.21,1933 CUMBERLAND,R.I.

1957	CHI	N	3		9	.211
1958	CHI	N	2-3		83	.242
1959	CHI	N	2-3		25	.168
1962	MIN	A	2-S		37	.192
1963	MIN	A	2-S-3		64	.287
1964	MIN	A	2-3		58	.140
		BRTR			276	.225

GOSGER, JAMES CHARLES (JIM)
B.NOV.6,1942 PORT HURON,MICH.

1963	BOS	A	O		19	.063
1965	BOS	A	O		81	.256
1966	BOS	A	O		40	.254
	KC	A	O		88	.224
1967	KC	A	*O		134	.242
1968	OAK	A	O		88	.180
1969	SEA	A	O		39	.109
	NY	N	/O		10	.133
1970	MON	N	O-1		91	.263
1971	MON	N	O/1		51	.157
1973	NY	N	O		38	.239
1974	NY	N	O		26	.091
		BLTL			705	.226

GOSLIN, LEON ALLEN (GOOSE)
B.OCT.16,1900 SALEM,N.J.
D.MAY 15,1971 BRIDGETON,N.J.

1921	WAS	A	O		14	.260
1922	WAS	A	O		101	.324
1923	WAS	A	O		150	.300
1924	WAS	A	O		154	.344
1925	WAS	A	O		150	.335
1926	WAS	A	O		147	.354
1927	WAS	A	O		148	.334
1928	WAS	A	O		135	.379
1929	WAS	A	O		145	.288
1930	WAS	A	O		47	.270
	STL	A	O		101	.327
1931	STL	A	O		151	.328
1932	STL	A	O		150	.299
1933	WAS	A	O		132	.297
1934	DET	A	O		151	.305
1935	DET	A	O		147	.292
1936	DET	A	O		147	.315
1937	DET	A	O		79	.238
1938	WAS	A	O		38	.158
		BLTR			2287	.316

GOSS, HOWARD WAYNE (HOWIE)
B.NOV.1,1934 WEWOKA,OKLA.

1962	PIT	N	O		89	.243
1963	HOU	N	O		133	.200
		BRTR			222	.216

GOSSAGE, RICHARD MICHAEL (RICH)
B.JULY 5,1951 COLORADO SPRINGS,COLO.

1972	CHI	A	P		36	7- 1
1973	CHI	A	P	20	21	0- 4
1974	CHI	A	P		39	4- 6
1975	CHI	A	P		62	9- 8
1976	CHI	A	P		31	9-17
1977	PIT	N	P		72	11- 9
1978	NY	A	P		63	10-11
		BRTR		323	324	50-56

GOSSETT, JOHN STAR (DICK)
B.AUG.21,1891 DENNISON,OHIO
D.OCT.6,1962 MASSILLON,OHIO

1913	NY	A	C		39	.162
1914	NY	A	C		10	.090
		BRTR			49	.151

GOTAY, JULIO ENRIQUE [SANCHEZ]
B.JUNE 9,1939 FAJARDO,P.R.

1960	STL	N	S-3		3	.375
1961	STL	N	S		10	.244
1962	STL	N	2-S-3-O		127	.255
1963	PIT	N	2		4	.500
1964	PIT	N	3		3	.400
1965	CAL	A	2/3-S		40	.247
1966	HOU	N	/3		4	.000
1967	HOU	N	2-S/3		77	.282
1968	HOU	N	2/3		73	.248
1969	HOU	N	2/3		46	.259
		BRTR			389	.260

GOULAIT, THEODORE LEE
B.AUG.11,1889 ST.CLAIR,MICH.
D.JULY 15,1936 ST.CLAIR,MICH.

1912	NY	N	P		1	0- 0
		BRTR				

GOULD, ALBERT FRANK (PUDGY)
B.JAN.20,1893 MUSCATINE,IOWA

1916	CLE	A	P		30	5- 7
1917	CLE	A	P		27	4- 4
		BRTR			57	9-11

GOULD, CHARLES HARVEY
B.AUG.21,1847 CINCINNATI,OHIO
D.APR.10,1917 FLUSHING,N.Y.

1871	BOS	NA	1-O		33	-
1872	BOS	NA	1-O		45	.256
1874	BAL	NA	C-1		33	-
1875	NH	NA	M-1-O		27	-
1876	CIN	N	M-P-	1	61	0- 0
			1			.240
1877	CIN	N	1-O		24	.275
		BRTR		1	223	0- 0
						-

GOULISH, NICHOLAS EDWARD
B.NOV.13,1917 PUNXSUTAWNEY,PA.

1944	PHI	N	H		1	.000
1945	PHI	N	O		13	.273
		BLTL			14	.250

GOUZZIE, CLAUDE
B.1881 PENNSYLVANIA
D.SEPT.21,1907 DENVER,COLO.

1903	STL	A	2		1	.000
		BRTR				

GOWDY, HENRY MORGAN (HANK)
B.AUG.24,1889 COLUMBUS,OHIO
D.AUG.1,1966 COLUMBUS,OHIO

1910	NY	N	1		5	.214
1911	NY	N	1		4	.250
	BOS	N	1		29	.289
1912	BOS	N	C		44	.271
1913	BOS	N	C		3	.000
1914	BOS	N	C		128	.243
1915	BOS	N	C		118	.247
1916	BOS	N	C		118	.252
1917	BOS	N	C		49	.214
1919	BOS	N	C-1		78	.279
1920	BOS	N	C		80	.243
1921	BOS	N	C		64	.299
1922	BOS	N	C-1		92	.316
1923	BOS	N	C		23	.125
	NY	N	C		53	.328
1924	NY	N	C		87	.325
1925	NY	N	C		47	.325
1929	BOS	N	C		10	.438
1930	BOS	N	C		16	.200
		BRTR			1043	.270

NON-PLAYING MANAGER CIN[N] 1946

GOWELL, LAWRENCE CLYDE (LARRY)
B.MAY 2,1948 LEWISTON,ME.

1972	NY	A	/P		2	0- 1
		BRTR				

GRABARKEWITZ, BILLY CORDELL
B.JAN.18,1946 LOCKHART,TEX.

1969	LA	N	S/3-2		34	.092
1970	LA	N	3-S-2		156	.289
1971	LA	N	2-3/S		44	.225
1972	LA	N	3-2/S		53	.167
1973	CAL	A	2-3/S-O		61	.163
	PHI	N	2/3-O		25	.286
1974	PHI	N	/O-3		34	.133
	CHI	N	2/S-3		53	.248
1975	OAK	A	/2		6	.000
		BRTR			466	.236

GRABER, RODNEY BLAINE
B.JUNE 20,1931 MARSHALLVILLE,O.

1958	CLE	A	O		4	.125
		BLTL				

GRABOWSKI, ALFONS FRANCIS
B.SEPT.6,1901 ST.LOUIS,MO.
D.OCT.29,1966 MEMPHIS,N.Y.

1929	STL	N	P		6	3- 2
1930	STL	N	P	33	35	6- 4
		BLTR		39	41	9- 6

GRABOWSKI, JOHN PATRICK (NIG)
B.JAN.7,1900 WARE,MASS.
D.MAY 23,1946 ALBANY,N.Y.

1924	CHI	A	C		20	.250
1925	CHI	A	C		21	.304
1926	CHI	A	C		48	.262
1927	NY	A	C		70	.277
1928	NY	A	C		75	.238
1929	NY	A	C		22	.203
1931	DET	A	C		40	.235
		BRTR			296	.292

GRABOWSKI, REGINALD JOHN
B.JULY 16,1907 SYRACUSE,N.Y.
D.APR.2,1955 SYRACUSE,N.Y.

1932	PHI	N	P		14	2- 2
1933	PHI	N	P		10	1- 3
1934	PHI	N	P		27	1- 3
		BRTR			51	4- 8

GRACE, JOSEPH LAVERNE (JOE)
B.JAN.3,1914 GORHAM,ILL.
D.SEPT.18,1969 MURPHYSBORO,ILL.

1938	STL	A	O		12	.340
1939	STL	A	O		74	.304
1940	STL	A	C-O		80	.258
1941	STL	A	C-O		115	.309
1946	STL	A	O		48	.230
	WAS	A	O		77	.302
1947	WAS	A	O		78	.248
		BLTR			484	.283

GRACE, MICHAEL LEE (MIKE)
B.JUNE 14,1956 PONTIAC,MICH.

1978	CIN	N	/3		5	.000
		BRTR				

YR	CL	LEA	POS	GP	G	REC

GRACE, ROBERT EARL (EARL)
B.FEB.24,1907 BARLOW,KY.
YR	CL	LEA	POS	GP	G	REC
1929	CHI	N	C		27	.250
1931	CHI	N	C		7	.111
	PIT	N	C		47	.280
1932	PIT	N	C		115	.274
1933	PIT	N	C		93	.289
1934	PIT	N	C		95	.270
1935	PHI	N	C		77	.263
1936	PHI	N	C		86	.249
1937	PHI	N	C		80	.211
	BLTR				627	.263

GRADY, JOHN J.
B.1860 LOWELL,MASS.
D.JULY 15,1893 LOWELL,MASS.
YR	CL	LEA	POS	GP	G	REC
1884	ALT	U	1-O		9	.289

GRADY, MICHAEL WILLIAM
B.DEC.23,1869 KENNETT SQUARE,PA
D.APR.3,1943 KENNETT SQUARE,PA.
YR	CL	LEA	POS	GP	G	REC
1894	PHI	N	C		50	.305
1895	PHI	N	C		33	.336
1896	PHI	N	C		62	.333
1897	PHI	N	1		4	.154
	STL	N	1		83	.281
1898	NY	N	C-O		83	.293
1899	NY	N	C-3		83	.336
1900	NY	N	C		75	.222
1901	WAS	A	C-1		94	.286
1904	STL	N	C		92	.313
1905	STL	N	C-1		91	.286
1906	STL	N	C-1		92	.250
	BRTR				842	.296

GRAFF, FREDERICK GOTTLEIB
B.AUG.25,1889 CANTON,OHIO
YR	CL	LEA	POS	GP	G	REC
1913	STL	A	3		4	.400
	BRTR					

GRAFF, JOHN F.
B.PHILADELPHIA,PA.
YR	CL	LEA	POS	GP	G	REC
1893	WAS	N	P		2	0- 1

GRAFF, LOUIS GEORGE
B.1866 PHILADELPHIA,PA.
YR	CL	LEA	POS	GP	G	REC
1890	SYR	AA	C		1	.400

GRAFF, MILTON EDWARD (MILT)
B.DEC.30,1930 JEFFERSON CENTER,PA.
YR	CL	LEA	POS	GP	G	REC
1957	KC	A	2		56	.181
1958	KC	A	2		5	.000
	BLTR				61	.179

GRAFFEN, S. MASON
B.1845 PHILADELPHIA,PA.
D.NOV.16,1883
NON-PLAYING MANAGER
STL(NA) 1875, STL(N) 1876

GRAHAM, ARCHIBALD WRIGHT (MOONLIGHT)
B.NOV.9,1876 FAYETTEVILLE,N.C.
D.AUG.25,1965 CHISOLM,MINN.
YR	CL	LEA	POS	GP	G	REC
1905	NY	N	O		1	.000

GRAHAM, ARTHUR WILLIAM (SKINNY)
B.AUG.12,1909 SOMERVILLE,MASS.
D.JULY 10,1967 CAMBRIDGE,MASS.
YR	CL	LEA	POS	GP	G	REC
1934	BOS	A	O		13	.234
1935	BOS	A	O		8	.300
	BLTR				21	.246

GRAHAM, BARNEY
B.PHILADELPHIA,PA.
D.DEC.31,1896 MOBILE,ALA.
YR	CL	LEA	POS	GP	G	REC
1889	ATH	AA	3		4	.167

GRAHAM, BERNARD
B.1860 BELOIT,WIS.
D.OCT.30,1886 MOBILE,ALA.
YR	CL	LEA	POS	GP	G	REC
1884	CHI	U	O		2	.500
	BAL	U	1-O		42	.271
					44	.303

GRAHAM, BERT (B.G.)
B.APR.3,1886 TILTON,ILL.
D.JUNE 19,1971 COTTONWOOD,ARIZ.
YR	CL	LEA	POS	GP	G	REC
1910	STL	A	1-2		8	.115
	BBTR					

GRAHAM, CHARLES HENRY
B.APR.25,1878 SANTA CLARA,CAL.
D.AUG.29,1948 SAN FRANCISCO,CAL
YR	CL	LEA	POS	GP	G	REC
1906	BOS	A	C		30	.233
	BRTR					

GRAHAM, DAWSON FRANCIS (TINY)
B.SEPT.9,1892 NASHVILLE,TENN.
D.DEC.29,1962 NASHVILLE,TENN.
YR	CL	LEA	POS	GP	G	REC
1914	CIN	N	1		25	.230
	BRTR					

GRAHAM, GEORGE FREDERICK (PEACHES)
B.MAR.23,1877 ALEDO,ILL.
D.JULY 25,1939 LONG BEACH,CAL.
YR	CL	LEA	POS	GP	G	REC
1902	CLE	A	2		2	.333
1903	CHI	N	P		1	0- 1
1908	BOS	N	C		67	.274
1909	BOS	N	C		81	.239
1910	BOS	N	C		91	.262
1911	BOS	N	C		33	.273
	CHI	N	C		36	.239
1912	PHI	N	C		24	.288
	BRTR	1	355			0- 1
						.265

GRAHAM, JOHN BERNARD (JACK)
B.DEC.4,1916 MINNEAPOLIS,MINN.
YR	CL	LEA	POS	GP	G	REC
1946	BRO	N	1		2	.200
	NY	N	1-O		100	.219
1949	STL	A	1		137	.238
	BLTL				239	.231

GRAHAM, KYLE (SKINNY)
B.AUG.14,1899 OAK GROVE,ALA.
D.DEC.1,1973 OAK GROVE,ALA.
YR	CL	LEA	POS	GP	G	REC
1924	BOS	N	P		5	0- 4
1925	BOS	N	P		34	7-12
1926	BOS	N	P		15	3- 3
1929	DET	A	P		13	1- 3
	BRTR				67	11-22

GRAHAM, OSCAR M.
B.1877 MANILLA,IOWA
D.SEPT.16,1931 MOLINE,ILL.
YR	CL	LEA	POS	GP	G	REC
1907	WAS	A	P	20	26	4-10
	TL					

GRAHAM, ROY VINCENT
B.FEB.22,1895 SAN FRANCISCO,CAL
D.APR.26,1933 MANILA,PHILLIPINES
YR	CL	LEA	POS	GP	G	REC
1922	CHI	A	C		5	.000
1923	CHI	A	C		36	.195
	BRTR				41	.188

GRAHAM, WAYNE LEON
B.APR.6,1937 YOAKUM,TEX.
YR	CL	LEA	POS	GP	G	REC
1963	PHI	N	O		10	.182
1964	NY	N	3		20	.091
	BRTR				30	.127

GRAHAM, WILLIAM J.
YR	CL	LEA	POS	GP	G	REC
1908	STL	A	P		21	6- 7
1909	STL	A	P		34	8-14
1910	STL	A	P		9	0- 8
	TL				64	14-29

GRAHAM, WILLIAM ALBERT (BILL)
B.JAN.22,1944 FLEMINGSBURG,KY.
YR	CL	LEA	POS	GP	G	REC
1966	DET	A	/P		1	0- 0
1967	NY	N	/P		5	1- 2
	BRTR				6	1- 2

GRAMLY, BERT THOMAS (TOMMY)
B.APR.19,1945 DALLAS,TEX.
YR	CL	LEA	POS	GP	G	REC
1968	CLE	A	/P	3	4	0- 1
	BRTR					

GRAMMAS, ALEXANDER PETER (ALEX)
B.APR.3,1926 BIRMINGHAM,ALA.
YR	CL	LEA	POS	GP	G	REC
1954	STL	N	S-3		142	.264
1955	STL	N	S		128	.240
1956	STL	N	S		6	.250
	CIN	N	2-S-3		77	.243
1957	CIN	N	2-S-3		73	.303
1958	CIN	N	2-S-3		105	.218
1959	STL	N	S		131	.269
1960	STL	N	2-S-3		102	.245
1961	STL	N	2-S-3		89	.212
1962	STL	N	S		21	.111
	CHI	N	2-S-3		23	.233
1963	CHI	N	S		16	.185
	BRTR				913	.247
NON-PLAYING MANAGER
PIT(N) 1969 (INTERIM),
MIL(A) 1976-77

GRAMPP, HENRY ERCHARDT (HANK)
B.SEPT.28,1903 NEW YORK,N.Y.
YR	CL	LEA	POS	GP	G	REC
1927	CHI	N	P		2	0- 0
1929	CHI	N	P		1	0- 1
	BRTR				3	0- 1

GRANEY, JOHN GLADSTONE (JACK)
B.JUNE 10,1886 ST.THOMAS,ONT.,CAN.
D.APR.20,1978 LOUISIANA,MO.
YR	CL	LEA	POS	GP	G	REC
1908	CLE	A	P		2	0- 0
1910	CLE	A	O		116	.236
1911	CLE	A	O		146	.269
1912	CLE	A	O		78	.242
1913	CLE	A	O		148	.267
1914	CLE	A	O		130	.265
1915	CLE	A	O		116	.260
1916	CLE	A	O		155	.241
1917	CLE	A	O		145	.228
1918	CLE	A	O		70	.237
1919	CLE	A	O		128	.234
1920	CLE	A	O		62	.296
1921	CLE	A	O		68	.299
1922	CLE	A	O		37	.155
	BLTL	2	1402			0- 0
						.250

GRANGER, WAYNE ALLAN
B.MAR.15,1944 SPRINGFIELD,MASS.
YR	CL	LEA	POS	GP	G	REC
1968	STL	N	P		34	4- 2
1969	CIN	N	P		90	9- 6
1970	CIN	N	P/O		67	6- 5
						.100
1971	CIN	N	P		70	7- 6
1972	MIN	A	P		63	4- 6
1973	STL	N	P		33	2- 4
	NY	A	/P		7	0- 1
1974	CHI	A	/P		5	0- 0
1975	HOU	N	P		55	2- 5
1976	MON	N	P		27	1- 0
	BRTR				451	35-35
						.103

GRANT, EDWARD LESLIE (HARVARD EDDIE)
B.MAY 21,1883 FRANKLIN,MASS.
D.OCT.5,1918 ARGONNE FOREST,FRANCE
YR	CL	LEA	POS	GP	G	REC
1905	CLE	A	2		2	.375
1907	PHI	N	3		74	.243
1908	PHI	N	3		147	.244
1909	PHI	N	3		154	.269
1910	PHI	N	3		152	.268
1911	CIN	N	3		133	.223
1912	CIN	N	S-3		96	.239
1913	CIN	N	3		27	.213
	NY	N	3		27	.200
1914	NY	N	2-S-3		88	.277
1915	NY	N	3		87	.208
	BLTR				987	.249

GRANT, GEORGE ADDISON
B.JAN.6,1903 E.TALLASSEE,ALA.
YR	CL	LEA	POS	GP	G	REC
1923	STL	A	P		4	0- 0
1924	STL	A	P		22	1- 2
1925	STL	A	P		12	0- 2
1927	CLE	A	P		25	4- 5
1928	CLE	A	P	28	29	10- 8
1929	CLE	A	P		12	0- 2
1931	PIT	N	P		11	0- 0
	BRTR			114	115	15-20

GRANT, JAMES CHARLES
B.OCT.6,1918 RACINE,WIS.
D.JULY 8,1970 ROCHESTER,MINN.
YR	CL	LEA	POS	GP	G	REC
1942	CHI	A	3		12	.167
1943	CHI	A	3		58	.259
	CLE	A	3		15	.136
1944	CLE	A	2-3		61	.273
	BLTR				146	.246

GRANT, JAMES RONALD
B.AUG.4,1894 COALVILLE,IOWA
YR	CL	LEA	POS	GP	G	REC
1923	PHI	N	P		2	0- 0
	BRTL					

GRANT, JAMES TIMOTHY
(JIM) OR (MUDCAT)
B.AUG.13,1935 LACOOCHEE,FLA.
YR	CL	LEA	POS	GP	G	REC
1958	CLE	A	P	44	54	10-11
1959	CLE	A	P	38	42	10- 7
1960	CLE	A	P	33	47	9- 8
1961	CLE	A	P	35	48	15- 9
1962	CLE	A	P	26	30	7-10
1963	CLE	A	P	38	53	13-14
1964	CLE	A	P	13	20	3- 4
	MIN	A	P	26	39	11- 9
1965	MIN	A	P	41	50	21- 7
1966	MIN	A	P		35	13-13
1967	MIN	A	P		27	5- 6
1968	LA	N	P	37	43	6- 4
1969	MON	N	P		11	1- 6
	STL	N	P	30	31	7- 5
1970	OAK	A	P		72	6- 2
	PIT	N	/P		8	2- 1
1971	PIT	N	P		42	5- 3
	OAK	A	P		15	1- 0
	BRTR			571	667	145-119

YR CL LEA POS   GP   G   REC

GRANTHAM, GEORGE FARLEY (BOOTS)
B.MAY 20,1900 GALENA,KAN.
D.MAR.16,1954 KINGMAN,ARIZ.
1922 CHI N 3   7   .174
1923 CHI N 2   152   .281
1924 CHI N 2-3   127   .316
1925 PIT N 1   114   .326
1926 PIT N 1   141   .319
1927 PIT N 1-2   151   .305
1928 PIT N 1   124   .323
1929 PIT N 1-2-0   110   .307
1930 PIT N 2   146   .324
1931 PIT N 1-2   127   .305
1932 CIN N 1-2   126   .292
1933 CIN N 1-2   87   .204
1934 NY N 1-3   32   .241
         BLTR   1444   .302

GRASMICK, LOUIS JUNIOR
B.SEPT.11,1924 BALTIMORE,MD.
1948 PHI N P   2   0- 0
         BRTR

GRASSO, NEWTON MICHAEL (MICKEY)
B.MAY 10,1920 NEWARK,N.J.
D.OCT.15,1975 MIAMI,FLA.
1946 NY N C   7   .136
1950 WAS A C   75   .287
1951 WAS A C   52   .206
1952 WAS A C   115   .216
1953 WAS A C   61   .209
1954 CLE A C   4   .333
1955 NY N C   8   .000
         BRTR   322   .226

GRATE, DONALD (DON) OR (BUCKEYE)
B.AUG.27,1923 GREENFIELD,OHIO
1945 PHI N P   4   5   0- 1
1946 PHI N P   3   1- 0
         BRTR   7   8   1- 1

GRAULICH, LEWIS
B.CAMDEN,N.J.
1891 PHI N C-1   7   .309

GRAVES, FRANK M.
B.NOV.2,1860 CINCINNATI,OHIO
1886 STL N C   41   .152

GRAVES, JOSEPH EBENEZER
B.FEB.27,1906 MARBLEHEAD,MASS.
1926 CHI N 3   2   .000
         BRTR

GRAVES, SAMUEL SIDNEY
(SID) OR (WHITEY)
B.NOV.30,1901 MARBLEHEAD,MASS.
1927 BOS N O   7   .250
         BRTR

GRAY, CHARLES
B.1867 INDIANAPOLIS,IND.
1890 PIT N P   5   0- 3

GRAY, DAVID ALEXANDER (DAVE)
B.JAN.7,1943 OGDEN,UTAH
1964 BOS A P   9   0- 0
         BRTR

GRAY, GARY GEORGE
B.SEPT.21,1952 NEW ORLEANS,LA.
1977 TEX A /O   1   .000
1978 TEX A D   17   .240
         BRTR   18   .231

GRAY, GEORGE EDWARD (CHUMMY)
B.JULY 17,1873 ROCKLAND,ME.
D.AUG.14,1913 ROCKLAND,MAINE
1899 PIT N P   9   4- 3
         TR

GRAY, JAMES D. (REDDY)
1890 PIT P 3   2   .222
     PIT N S   1   .000
1893 PIT N S   2   .500
                        5   .300

GRAY, JAMES W.
B.AUG.7,1862 PITTSBURGH,PA.
D.JAN.31,1938 ALLEGHENY,PA.
1884 PIT AA 3   1   1.000

GRAY, JOHN LEONARD (JOHNNY)
B.DEC.11,1927 W.PALM BEACH,FLA.
1954 PHI A P   18   19   3-12
1955 KC A P   8   0- 3
1957 CLE A P   7   1- 3
1958 PHI N P   15   0- 0
         BRTR   48   49   4-18

GRAY, MILTON MARSHALL
B.FEB.21,1914 LOUISVILLE,KY.
D.JUNE 30,1969 QUINCY,FLA.
1937 WAS A C   2   .000
         BRTR

GRAY, PETER J.
[REAL NAME PETER WYSHNER]
B.MAR.6,1915 NANTICOKE,PA.
1945 STL A O   77   .218
         BLTL

GRAY, RICHARD BENJAMIN (DICK)
B.JULY 11,1931 JEFFERSON,PA.
1958 LA N 3   58   .249
1959 LA N 3   21   .154
         STL N 2-S-3-0 36   .314
1960 STL N 2-3   9   .240
         BRTR   124   .240

GRAY, ROMER CARL
[PLAYED UNDER NAME OF
ROMER CARL GREY]

GRAY, SAMUEL DAVID
(SAM) OR (SAD SAM)
B.OCT.15,1897 VAN ALSTYNE,TEX.
D.APR.16,1953 MC KINNEY,TEX.
1924 PHI A P   34   8- 7
1925 PHI A P   32   16- 8
1926 PHI A P   38   11-12
1927 PHI A P   37   9- 6
1928 STL A P   35   20-12
1929 STL A P   43   18-15
1930 STL A P   27   4-15
1931 STL A P   43   11-24
1932 STL A P   32   7-12
1933 STL A P   38   7- 4
         BRTR   379   111-115

GRAY, STANLEY OSCAR (DOLLY)
B.DEC.10,1888 LADONIA,TEX.
D.OCT.11,1964 SNYDER,TEX.
1912 PHI N 1   7   .250

GRAY, TED GLENN
B.DEC.31,1924 DETROIT,MICH.
1946 DET A P   3   0- 2
1948 DET A P   26   6- 2
1949 DET A P   34   36   10-10
1950 DET A P   27   1C- 7
1951 DET A P   34   35   7-14
1952 DET A P   35   36   12-17
1953 DET A P   30   32   10-15
1954 DET A P   19   3- 5
1955 CHI A P   2   0- 0
     CLE A P   2   0- 0
     NY A P   1   0- 0
     BAL A P   9   1- 2
         BBTL   222 228   59-74
         BR 1946

GRAY, WILLIAM
B.NOV.4,1872 SAW MILL RUN,PA.
D.SEPT.7,1931 HOMESTEAD,PA.
1903 PIT N P   1   .333

GRAY, WILLIAM DENTON (DOLLY)
B.DEC.4,1878 ISHPEMING,MICH.
D.APR.4,1956 YUBA CITY,CAL.
1909 WAS A P   36   47   5-19
1910 WAS A P   34   35   8-19
1911 WAS A P   29   2-13
         BLTL   99 111   15-51

GROBA, ELI
B.AUG.9,1934 CHICAGO,ILL.
1959 NY A P   19   2- 5
1960 NY A P   24   27   6- 4
1961 LA A P   40   42   11-13
1962 LA A P   40   42   8- 9
1963 LA A P   12   13   1- 2
         BRTR   135 143   26-33

GREASON, WILLIAM HENRY
(BILL) OR (BOOSTER)
B.SEPT.3,1924 ATLANTA,GA.
1954 STL N P   3   0- 1
         BRTR

GREEN, EDWARD (DANNY)
B.NOV.6,1876 BURLINGTON,N.J.
D.NOV.9,1914 CAMDEN,N.J.
1898 CHI N O   47   .328
1899 CHI N O   114   .296
1900 CHI N O   100   .299
1901 CHI N O   132   .317
1902 CHI A O   129   .318
1903 CHI A O   136   .313
1904 CHI A O   148   .266
1905 CHI A O   112   .243
         BL   918   .296

GREEN, EDWARD M.
B.1850 PHILADELPHIA,PA.
D.MAR.22,1917 OGDEN,UTAH
1890 ATH AA P-2-   25   39   7-14
         S-3   .123

GREEN, ELIJAH JERRY (PUMPSIE)
B.OCT.27,1933 OAKLAND,CAL.
1959 BOS A 2-S   50   .233
1960 BOS A 2-S   133   .242
1961 BOS A 2-S   88   .260
1962 BOS A 2-S   56   .231
1963 NY N 3   17   .278
         BBTR   344   .246

GREEN, FRED ALLEN
B.SEP.14,1933 TITUSVILLE,N.J.
1959 PIT N P   17   1- 2
1960 PIT N P   45   8- 4
1961 PIT N P   13   0- 0
1962 WAS A P   5   0- 1
1964 PIT N P   8   0- 0
         BRTL   88   9- 7

GREEN, GENE LEROY
B.JUNE 26,1933 LOS ANGELES,CAL.
1957 STL N O   6   .200
1958 STL N C-O   137   .281
1959 STL N C-O   30   .189
1960 BAL A O   1   .250
1961 WAS A C-O   110   .286
1962 CLE A 1-O   66   .286
1963 CLE A O   43   .205
         CIN N C   15   .226
         BRTR   408   .267

GREEN, GEORGE DALLAS (DALLAS)
B.AUG.4,1934 NEWPORT,DEL.
1960 PHI N P   23   24   3- 6
1961 PHI N P   42   2- 4
1962 PHI N P   57   47   0- 6
1963 PHI N P   40   42   7- 5
1964 PHI N P   25   26   2- 1
1965 WAS A /P   6   0- 1
1966 NY N /P   4   0- 0
1967 PHI N /P   4   0- 0
         BLTR   165 199   20-22

GREEN, HARVEY GEORGE (BUCK)
B.FEB.9,1915 KENOSHA,WIS.
D.JULY 24,1970 FRANKLIN,LA.
1935 BRO N P   2   0- 0
         BBTR

GREEN, JAMES R.
B.CLEVELAND,OHIO
1884 WAS U 3-O   10   .139

GREEN, JOSEPH HENRY
[ALSO PLAYED UNDER NAME OF
JOSEPH HENRY GREENE]
B.SEPT.17,1897 PHILADELPHIA,PA.
D.FEB.4,1972 BRYN MAWR,PA.
1924 PHI A H   1   .000
         TR

GREEN, LEONARD CHARLES (LENNY)
B.JAN.6,1933 DETROIT,MICH.
1957 BAL A O   19   .182
1958 BAL A O   69   .231
1959 BAL A O   27   .292
         WAS A O   88   .242
1960 BAL A O   127   .294
1961 MIN A O   156   .285
1962 MIN A O   158   .271
1963 MIN A O   145   .239
1964 MIN A O   26   .000
         LA A O   39   .250
         BAL A O   19   .196
1965 BOS A C   119   .276
1966 BOS A L   65   .241
1967 DET A O   58   .278
1968 DET A /O   6   .250
         BLTL   1136   .267

GREEN, RICHARD LARRY (DICK)
B.APR.21,1941 SIOUX CITY,IOWA
1963 KC A 2-S   13   .270
1964 KC A 2   130   .264
1965 KC A *2   133   .232
1966 KC A *2/3   140   .256
1967 KC A 3-2/1-S   122   .198
1968 OAK A 2/C-3   76   .233
1969 OAK A *2   136   .275
1970 OAK A *2/3-C   133   .190
1971 OAK A *2/S   144   .244
1972 OAK A 2   26   .286
1973 OAK A *2/S-3   133   .262
1974 OAK A *2   100   .213
         BRTR   1288   .240

YR CL LEA POS	GP	G	REC

GREENBERG, HENRY BENJAMIN (HAMMERIN' HANK)
B.JAN.1,1911 NEW YORK,N.Y.

1930 DET A H	1		.000
1933 DET A 1	117		.301
1934 DET A 1	.53		.339
1935 DET A 1	152		.328
1936 DET A 1	12		.348
1937 DET A 1	154		.337
1938 DET A 1	155		.315
1939 DET A 1	138		.312
1940 DET A O	148		.340
1941 DET A O	19		.269
1945 DET A O	78		.311
1946 DET A 1	142		.277
1947 PIT N 1	125		.249
BRTR	1394		.313

GREENE, JOSEPH HENRY
[SEE JOSEPH HENRY GREEN]

GREENE, JULIUS FOUST (JUNE)
B.JUNE 25,1899 RAMSEUR,N.C.
D.MAR.19,1974 GLENDORA,CAL.

1928 PHI N P	1	11	0- 0
1929 PHI N P	5	21	0- 0
BLTR	6	32	0- 0

GREENE, NELSON GEORGE (LEFTY)
B.SEPT.20,1900 PHILADELPHIA,PA.

1924 BRO N P	4		0- 1
1925 BRO N P	11		2- 0
BLTL	15		2- 1

GREENE, PATRICK JOSEPH (PADDY) OR (PATSY)
[PLAYED UNDER NAME OF
PATRICK FOLEY IN 1902]
B.MAR.20,1875 PROVIDENCE,R.I.
D.OCT.20,1934 PROVIDENCE,R.I.

1902 PHI N 3	19		.188
1903 NY A 3	4		.308
DET A 3	1		.000
BRTR	24		.200

GREENFIELD, KENT
B.JULY 1,1902 GUTHRIE,KY.

1924 NY N P	1		0- 1
1925 NY N P	29		12- 8
1926 NY N P	39		13-12
1927 NY N P	12		2- 2
BOS N P	27		11-14
1928 BOS N P	32		3-11
1929 BOS N P	6		0- 0
BRO N P	6	7	0- 0
BRTR	152	153	41-48

GREENGRASS, JAMES RAYMOND (JIM)
B.OCT.24,1927 ADDISON,N.Y.

1952 CIN N O	18		.309
1953 CIN N O	154		.285
1954 CIN N O	139		.280
1955 CIN N O	13		.103
PHI N 3-O	94		.272
1956 PHI N 3-O	86		.205
BRTR	504		.269

GREENIG, JOHN A.
[PLAYED UNDER NAME OF
JOHN A. GREENING]

GREENING, JOHN A.
[REAL NAME JOHN A. GREENIG]
B.PHILADELPHIA,PA.

1888 WAS N P	1		0- 1

GREENWOOD, ROBERT CHANDLER (BOB) OR (GREENIE)
B.MAR.13,1928 CANANEA,MEXICO

1954 PHI N P	11	12	1- 2
1955 PHI N P	1		0- 0
BRTR	12	13	1- 2

GREENWOOD, WILLIAM F.
B.1857 PHILADELPHIA,PA.
D.MAY 2,1902 PHILADELPHIA,PA.

1882 ATH AA 2-O	7		.290
1884 BRO AA 2	92		.220
1887 BAL AA 2	119		.326
1888 BAL AA 2-S	113		.202
1889 COL AA 2	118		.219
1890 ROC AA 2	121		.226
BRTL	570		.246

GREER, BRIAN KEITH
B.MAY 14,1959 LYNWOOD,CAL.

1977 SD N /H	1		.000
BRTR			

GREER, EDWARD C.
B.PHILADELPHIA,PA.
D.FEB.4,1890 PHILADELPHIA,PA.

1885 BAL AA C-O	55		.199
1886 BAL AA C-O	10		.139
ATH AA O	72		.197
1887 BAL AA O	3		.182
BRO AA O	88		.302
BR	228		.237

GREGG, DAVID CHARLES (HIGHPOCKETS)
B.MAR.14,1891 CHEHALIS,WASH.
D.NOV.12,1965 CLARKSTON,WASH.

1913 CLE A P	1		0- 0
BRTR			

GREGG, HAROLD DANA (HAL) OR (SKEETS)
B.JULY 11,1921 ANAHEIM,CAL.

1943 BRO N P	5		0- 3
1944 BRO N P	39	42	9-16
1945 BRO N P		42	18-13
1946 BRO N P	26		6- 4
1947 BRO N P	37		4- 5
1948 PIT N P	22		2- 4
1949 PIT N P	8		1- 1
1950 PIT N P	5		0- 1
1952 NY N P	16		0- 1
BRTR	200	203	40-48

GREGG, SYLVEANUS AUGUSTUS (VEAN)
B.APR.13,1885 CHEHALIS,WASH.
D.JULY 29,1964 ABERDEEN,WASH.

1911 CLE A P	34		23- 7
1912 CLE A P	37		20-13
1913 CLE A P	44		20-13
1914 CLE A P	17		9- 3
BOS A P	12		3- 4
1915 BOS A P	18		5- 3
1916 BOS A P	21		2- 5
1918 PHI A P	30		8-14
1925 WAS A P	26		2- 2
BRTL	239		92-64

GREGORY, FRANK ERNST
B.JULY 25,1888 SPRING VALLEY TOWNSHIP,WIS.
D.NOV.5,1955 BELOIT,WIS.

1912 CIN N P	4		2- 0
BRTR			

GREGORY, GROVER LEROY (LEE)
B.JUNE 2,1938 BAKERSFIELD,CAL.

1964 CHI N P	11	19	0- 0
BLTL			

GREGORY, HOWARD WATTERSON
B.NOV.18,1886 HANNIBAL,MO.
D.MAY 30,1970 TULSA,OKLA.

1911 STL A P	3		0- 1
BLTR			

GREGORY, PAUL EDWIN (POP)
B.JUNE 9,1908 TOMNOLEN,MISS.

1932 CHI A P	33		5- 3
1933 CHI A P	23		4-11
BRTR	56		9-14

GREIF, WILLIAM BRILEY (BILL)
B.APR.25,1950 FT.STOCKTON,TEX.

1971 HOU N /P	7		1- 1
1972 SD N P	34		5-16
1973 SD N P	36		10-17
1974 SD N P	43	46	9-19
1975 SD N P	59		4- 6
1976 SD N /P	5		1- 3
STL N P	47		1- 5
BRTR	231	234	31-67

GREMMINGER, LORENZO EDWARD (BATTLESHIP)
B.MAR.30,1874 CANTON,OHIO
D.MAY 26,1942 CANTON,OHIO

1895 CLE N 3	19		.275
1902 BOS N 3	140		.250
1903 BOS N 3	140		.264
1904 DET A 3	82		.215
TR	381		.249

GREMP, LEWIS EDWARD (BUDDY)
B.AUG.5,1919 DENVER,COL.

1940 BOS N 1	4		.222
1941 BOS N C-1-2	37		.240
1942 BOS N 1-3	72		.217
BRTR	113		.224

GREVELL, WILLIAM J.
B.MAR.5,1898 WILLIAMSTOWN,N.J.
D.JUNE.22,1923 SPRINGFIELD TOWNSHIP,PA.

1919 PHI A P	5		0- 0
BRTR			

GREY, ROMER CARL (REDDY)
[REAL NAME ROMER CARL GRAY]
B.1875 ZANESVILLE,OHIO
D.NOV.9,1934 ALTADENA,CAL.

1903 PIT N O	1		.333

GREY, WILLIAM TOBIN
B.APR.5,1871 PHILADELPHIA,PA.
D.DEC.6,1932 PHILADELPHIA,PA.

1890 PHI N C	32		.242
1891 PHI N C	18		.264
1895 CIN N 3	47		.301
1896 CIN N C	35		.216
1898 PIT N 3	137		.232
	269		.246

GREYSON

1873 NAT NA P	8		1- 7

GRICH, ROBERT ANTHONY (BOBBY)
B.JAN.15,1949 MUSKEGON,MICH.

1970 BAL A S/2-3	30		.211
1971 BAL A /S-2	7		.300
1972 BAL A S-2-1/3	133		.278
1973 BAL A *2	162		.251
1974 BAL A *2	160		.263
1975 BAL A *2	150		.260
1976 BAL A *2/3	144		.266
1977 CAL A S	52		.243
1978 CAL A *2	144		.251
BRTR	982		.259

GRIESENBECK, CARLOS PHILLIPE TIMOTHY (TIM)
B.SAN ANTONIO,TEX.
D.MAR.25,1953 SAN ANTONIO,TEX.

1920 STL N *	5		.331
BRTR			

GRIEVE, THOMAS ALAN (TOM)
B.MAR.4,1948 PITTSFIELD,MASS.

1970 WAS A O	47		.198
1972 TEX A O	64		.204
1973 TEX A O	66		.309
1974 TEX A D-O/1	74		.255
1975 TEX A D-O	118		.276
1976 TEX A D-O	149		.255
1977 TEX A D-O	79		.225
1978 NY N D/1	54		.208
BRTR	651		.249

GRIFFIN, ALFREDO CLAUDINO (AL)
[REAL NAME ALFREDO CLAUDINO BAPTIST (GRIFFIN)]
B.OCT.6,1957 SANTO DOMINGO,D.R.

1976 CLE A /S	12		.250
1977 CLE A S	14		.146
1978 CLE A /S	5		.500
BBTR	31		.184

GRIFFIN, DOUGLAS LEE (DOUG)
B.JUNE 4,1947 SOUTH GATE,CAL.

1970 CAL A 2/3	18		.127
1971 BOS A *2	125		.244
1972 BOS A *2	129		.260
1973 BOS A *2	113		.255
1974 BOS A 2/S	93		.266
1975 BOS A 2/S	100		.240
1976 BOS A 2	49		.189
1977 BOS A /2	5		.000
BRTR	632		.245

GRIFFIN, FRANCIS ARTHUR (PUG)
B.APR.24,1896 LINCOLN,NEB.
D.OCT.12,1951 COLORADO SPRINGS,COLO.

1917 PHI A 1	18		.200
1920 NY N O	5		.250
BRTR	23		.207

GRIFFIN, IVY MOORE
B.DEC.25,1896 TOMASHVILLE,ALA.
D.AUG.25,1957 GAINESVILLE,FLA.

1919 PHI A 1	17		.294
1920 PHI A 1	129		.238
1921 PHI A 1	39		.321
BLTR	185		.257

GRIFFIN, JAMES LINTON (HANK) OR (PEPPER)
B.JULY 11,1886 WHITEHOUSE,TEX.
D.FEB.11,1950 TERRELL,TEX.

1911 CHI N P	1		0- 0
BOS N P	15		0- 6
1912 BOS N P	3		0- 0
BRTR	19		0- 6

GRIFFIN, MARTIN JOHN
B.SEPT.2,1901 SAN FRANCISCO,CAL
D.NOV.19,1951 LOS ANGELES,CAL.

1928 BRO N P	11	12	0- 3
BRTR			

YR	CL	LEA	POS	GP	G	REC

GRIFFIN, MICHAEL JOSEPH
B.MAR.20,1865 UTICA,N.Y.
D.APR.10,1908 UTICA,N.Y.

YR	CL	LEA	POS	GP	G	REC
1887	BAL	AA	O		136	.368
1888	BAL	AA	O		137	.261
1889	BAL	AA	S-O		137	.280
1890	PHI	P	O		115	.296
1891	BRO	N	O		133	.272
1892	BRO	N	O		129	.276
1893	BRO	N	O		93	.304
1894	BRO	N	O		106	.365
1895	BRO	N	O		132	.333
1896	BRO	N	O		122	.315
1897	BRO	N	O		134	.320
1698	BRO	N	M-O		134	.296
	BLTR				1508	.308

GRIFFIN, PATRICK RICHARD
B.MAY 6,1893 NILES,OHIO
D.JUNE 7,1927 YOUNGSTOWN,OHIO

YR	CL	LEA	POS	GP	G	REC
1914	CIN	N	P		1	0- 0
	BRTR					

GRIFFIN, THOMAS W.
B.ROCKFORD,ILL.

YR	CL	LEA	POS	GP	G	REC
1884	MIL	U	1		11	.295

GRIFFIN, TOBIAS CHARLES (SANDY)
B.JULY 19,1858 FAYETTEVILLE,N.Y
D.JUNE 5,1926 FAYETTEVILLE,N.Y.

YR	CL	LEA	POS	GP	G	REC
1884	NY	N	O		15	.64
1890	ROC	AA	O		107	.305
1891	WAS	AA	M-O		19	.273
1893	STL	N	O		23	.204
					164	.269

GRIFFIN, THOMAS JAMES (TOM)
B.FEB.22,1948 LOS ANGELES,CAL.

YR	CL	LEA	POS	GP	G	REC
1969	HOU	N	P		31	11-10
1970	HOU	N	P		23	3-13
1971	HOU	N	P		10	0- 6
1972	HOU	N	P		39	5- 4
1973	HOU	N	P		25	4- 6
1974	HOU	N	P	34	37	14-10
1975	HOU	N	P		17	3- 8
1976	HOU	N	P		20	3- 3
	SD	N	P	11	12	4- 3
1977	SD	N	P	38	39	6- 9
1978	CAL	A	P		24	3- 4
	BRTK			272	277	58-76

GRIFFITH, BARTHOLOMEW JOSEPH (BERT) OR (BUCK)
B.MAR.30,1896 ST.LOUIS,MO.
D.MAY 5,1973 BISHOP,CAL.

YR	CL	LEA	POS	GP	G	REC
1922	BRO	N	1-O		106	.308
1923	BRO	N	O		79	.294
1924	WAS	A	O		6	.111
	BRTR				191	.299

GRIFFITH, CLARK CALVIN (OLD FOX)
B.NOV.20,1869 CLEAR CREEK,MO.
D.OCT.27,1955 WASHINGTON,D.C.

YR	CL	LEA	POS	GP	G	REC
1891	STL	AA	P		27	11- 8
	BOS	AA	P		9	3- 1
1893	CHI	N	P		3	1- 1
1894	CHI	N	P	35	41	20-11
1895	CHI	N	P		39	25-14
1896	CHI	N	P		36	23-11
1897	CHI	N	P	40	46	18-18
1898	C-IN		P		38	25-12
1899	CHI	N	P	36	39	21-13
1900	CHI	N	P		30	14-13
1901	CHI	A	P		35	24- 8
1902	CHI	A	M-P	28	34	15- 9
			O			.220
1903	NY	A	M-P		24	14-10
1904	NY	A	M-P		16	6- 5
1905	NY	A	M-P		25	6- 5
1906	NY	A	M-P		17	2- 2
1907	NY	A	M-P		3	0- 0
1909	CIN	N	M-P		1	0- 1
1910	CIN	N	M-H		1	.000
1912	WAS	A	M-P		1	0- 0
1913	WAS	A	M-P		1	0- 0
1914	WAS	A	M-P		1	0- 0
	BRTR			447	469	228-142
						.233

NON-PLAYING MANAGER
NY(A) 1908, CIN(N) 1911,
WAS(A) 1915-20

GRIFFITH, EDWARD

YR	CL	LEA	POS	GP	G	REC
1892	CHI	N	P		1	0- 0

GRIFFITH, FRANK WESLEY
B.NOV.18,1872 GILMAN,ILL.
D.DEC.13,1908

YR	CL	LEA	POS	GP	G	REC
1894	CLE	N	P		7	3- 3

GRIFFITH, ROBERT DERRELL (DERRELL)
B.DEC.12,1943 ANADARKO,OKLA.

YR	CL	LEA	POS	GP	G	REC
1963	LA	N	2		1	.000
1964	LA	N	3-O		78	.290
1965	LA	N	O		22	.171
1966	LA	N	/O		23	.067
	BLTR				124	.260

GRIFFITH, THOMAS HERMAN
B.OCT.26,1889 PROSPECT,OHIO
D.APR.13,1967 CINCINNATI,OHIO

YR	CL	LEA	POS	GP	G	REC
1913	BOS	N	O		37	.252
1914	BOS	N	O		16	.104
1915	CIN	N	O		160	.307
1916	CIN	N	O		155	.266
1917	CIN	N	O		115	.270
1918	CIN	N	O		118	.265
1919	BRO	N	O		125	.261
1920	BRO	N	O		93	.260
1921	BRO	N	O		129	.312
1922	BRO	N	O		99	.316
1923	BRO	N	O		131	.293
1924	BRO	N	O		140	.251
1925	BRO	N	O		7	.000
	CHI	N	O		76	.285
	BLTR				1401	.279

GRIGGS, ART CARLE
B.DEC.10,1883 TOPEKA,KAN.
D.DEC.19,1938 LOS ANGELES,CAL.

YR	CL	LEA	POS	GP	G	REC
1909	STL	A	1-O		108	.280
1910	STL	A	1-2-O		123	.236
1911	CLE	A	1		27	.250
1912	CLE	A	1		89	.304
1914	BRO	F	1		38	.282
1915	BRO	F	1		27	.275
1918	DET	A	1		28	.364
	BRTR				440	.276

GRIGGS, HAROLD LLOYD (HAL)
B.AUG.24,1828 SHANNON,GA.

YR	CL	LEA	POS	GP	G	REC
1956	WAS	A	P	34	36	1- 6
1957	WAS	A	P		2	0- 1
1958	WAS	A	P		32	3-11
1959	WAS	A	P		37	2- 8
	BRTR			105	107	6-26

GRIGSBY, DENVER CLARENCE
B.MAR.25,1901 JACKSON,KY.
D.NOV.10,1973 SAPULPA,OKLA.

YR	CL	LEA	POS	GP	G	REC
1923	CHI	N	O		24	.292
1924	CHI	N	O		124	.299
1925	CHI	N	O		51	.255
	BLTR				199	.289

GRILLI, GUIDO JOHN
B.JAN.9,1939 MEMPHIS,TENN.

YR	CL	LEA	POS	GP	G	REC
1966	BOS	A	/P		6	0- 1
	KC	A	P		16	0- 1
	BLTL				22	0- 2

GRILLI, STEPHEN JOSEPH (STEVE)
B.MAY 2,1949 BROOKLYN,N.Y.

YR	CL	LEA	POS	GP	G	REC
1975	DET	A	/P		3	0- 0
1976	DET	A	P		36	3- 1
1977	DET	A	P		30	1- 2
	BRTR				69	4- 3

GRIM, JOHN HELM
B.AUG.9,1867 LEBANON,KY.
D.JULY 28,1961 INDIANAPOLIS,IND

YR	CL	LEA	POS	GP	G	REC
1888	PHI	N	2		2	.143
1890	ROC	AA	P-C-	2	50	2- 0
			S			.254
1891	MIL	AA	C		28	.233
1892	LOU	N	C		95	.254
1893	LOU	N	C		92	.287
1894	LOU	N	C-2		107	.290
1895	BRO	N	C		90	.288
1896	BRO	N	C		80	.269
1897	BRO	N	C		76	.261
1898	BRO	N	C		50	.275
1899	BRO	N	C		14	.271
			TR	2	684	2- 0
						.272

GRIM, ROBERT ANTON (BOB)
B.MAR.8,1930 NEW YORK,N.Y.

YR	CL	LEA	POS	GP	G	REC
1954	NY	A	P		37	20- 6
1955	NY	A	P		26	7- 5
1956	NY	A	P		26	6- 1
1957	NY	A	P		46	12- 8
1958	NY	A	P		41	0- 1
	KC	A	P		26	7- 6
1959	KC	A	P		40	6-10
1960	CLE	A	P		3	0- 1
	CIN	N	P		26	2- 2
	STL	N	P		13	1- 0
1962	KC	A	P		12	0- 1
	BRTR				268	61-41

GRIMES, BURLEIGH ARLAND (BURLEIGH) OR (OL STUBBLEBEARD)
B.AUG.18,1893 CLEAR LAKE,WIS.

YR	CL	LEA	POS	GP	G	REC
1916	PIT	N	P		6	2- 3
1917	PIT	N	P	37	42	3-16
1918	BRO	N	P		41	19- 9
1919	BRO	N	P	25	26	10-11
1920	BRO	N	P	40	43	23-11
1921	BRO	N	P		37	22-13
1922	BRO	N	P		36	17-14
1923	BRO	N	P	39	40	21-18
1924	BRO	N	P	38	40	22-13
1925	BRO	N	P	33	34	12-19
1926	BRO	N	P	36	31	12-13
1927	NY	N	P		39	19- 8
1928	PIT	N	P		48	25-14
1929	PIT	N	P		33	17- 7
1930	BOS	N	P		11	3- 5
	STL	N	P	22	23	13- 6
1931	STL	N	P		29	17- 9
1932	CHI	N	P		30	6-11
1933	CHI	N	P		17	3- 6
	STL	N	P		4	0- 1
1934	STL	N	P		4	2- 1
	PIT	N	P		8	1- 2
	NY	A	P		10	1- 2
	BRTR			617	632	270-212

NON-PLAYING MANAGER BRO(N) 1937-38

GRIMES, EDWARD ADELBERT
B.SEPT.8,1905 CHICAGO,ILL.
D.OCT.5,1974 CHICAGO,ILL.

YR	CL	LEA	POS	GP	G	REC
1931	STL	A	3		43	.263
1932	STL	A	3		31	.235
	BRTR				74	.248

GRIMES, JOHN THOMAS
B.APR.17,1869 WOODSTOCK,MD.
D.JAN.17,1964 SAN FRANCISCO,CAL

YR	CL	LEA	POS	GP	G	REC
1897	STL	N	P		3	0- 2
	BRTR					

GRIMES, AUSTIN ROY (SUMMER)
B.SEPT.11,1893 BERGHOLZ,OHIO
D.SEPT.,3,1974 GILFORD LAKE,O.

YR	CL	LEA	POS	GP	G	REC
1920	WAS	N	2		26	.156
	BRTR					

GRIMES, OSCAR RAY JR.
B.APR.13,1915 MINERVA,OHIO

YR	CL	LEA	POS	GP	G	REC
1938	CLE	A	1-2		4	.200
1939	CLE	A	1-2-S		114	.269
1940	CLE	A	1-3		11	.000
1941	CLE	A	1-2-3		77	.236
1942	CLE	A	1-2-3-3		54	.179
1943	NY	A	1-S		9	.256
1944	NY	A	S-3		116	.279
1945	NY	A	1-3		142	.265
1946	NY	A	2-S		14	.205
	PHI	A	2-S-3		59	.262
	BRTR				602	.256

GRIMES, OSCAR RAY SR.
B.SEPT.11,1893 BERGHOLZ,OHIO
D.MAY 23,1953 MINERVA,OHIO

YR	CL	LEA	POS	GP	G	REC
1920	BOS	A	1		1	.650
1921	CHI	N	1		147	.321
1922	CHI	N	1		138	.354
1923	CHI	N	1		64	.324
1924	CHI	N	1		51	.299
1926	PHI	N	1		32	.297
	BRTR				433	.324

GRIMM, CHARLES JOHN (JOLLY CHOLLY)
B.AUG.29,1896 ST.LOUIS,MO.

YR	CL	LEA	POS	GP	G	REC
1916	PHI	A	O		12	.091
1918	STL	N	1-3-O		50	.220
1919	PIT	N	1		14	.318
1920	PIT	N	1		148	.227
1921	PIT	N	1		151	.274
1922	PIT	N	1		154	.292
1923	PIT	N	1		152	.345
1924	PIT	N	1		151	.288
1925	CHI	N	1		141	.306
1926	CHI	N	1		147	.277
1927	CHI	N	1		147	.311
1928	CHI	N	1		147	.294
1929	CHI	N	1		120	.298
1930	CHI	N	1		114	.289
1931	CHI	N	1		146	.331
1932	CHI	N	M-1		149	.307
1933	CHI	N	M-1		107	.247
1934	CHI	N	M-1		75	.296
1935	CHI	N	M-1		2	.000
1936	CHI	N	M-1		39	.250
	BLTL				2166	.290

NON-PLAYING MANAGER
CHI(N) 1937-38, 1944-49,
BOS(N) 1952, MIL(N) 1953-56
CHI(N) 1960

GRIMSHAW, MYRON FREDERICK (MOOSE)
B.NOV.30,1875 ST.JOHNSVILLE,N.Y
D.DEC.11,1936 CANAJOHARIE,N.Y.

YR	CL	LEA	POS	GP	G	REC
1905	BOS	A	1		85	.239
1906	BOS	A	1		110	.290
1907	BOS	A	1-O		64	.204
	BBTR				259	.256

GRIMSLEY, ROSS ALBERT, I
B.JUNE 4,1922 AMERICUS,KAN.

YR	CL	LEA	POS	GP	G	REC
1951	CHI	A	P		7	0- 6
	BLTL					

GRIMSLEY, ROSS ALBERT, II
B.JAN.7,1950 TOPEKA,KAN.

YR	CL	LEA	POS	GP	G	REC
1971	CIN	N	P		26	10- 7
1972	CIN	N	P		30	14- 8
1973	CIN	N	P	38	39	13-10
1974	BAL	A	P		40	18-13
1975	BAL	A	P		35	10-13
1976	BAL	A	P		28	8- 7
1977	BAL	A	P		34	14-10
1978	MON	N	P		36	20-11
	BLTL			267	268	107-79

GRINER, DONALD DEXTER (RUSTY)
B.MAR.7,1888 CENTERVILLE,TENN.
D.JUNE 3,1950 BISHOPVILLE,S.C.

YR	CL	LEA	POS	GP	G	REC
1912	STL	N	P		12	3- 4
1913	STL	N	P		34	10-22
1914	STL	N	P		37	9-13
1915	STL	N	P	37	39	5-11
1916	STL	N	P		4	0- 0
1918	BRO	N	P		12	1- 5
	BLTR			136	138	28-55

GRISSOM, LEE THEO
B.OCT.23,1907 SHERMAN,TEX.

YR	CL	LEA	POS	GP	G	REC
1934	CIN	N	P		4	0- 1
1935	CIN	N	P		3	1- 1
1936	CIN	N	P		6	1- 1
1937	CIN	N	P	50	51	12-17
1938	CIN	N	P		14	2- 3
1939	CIN	N	P		33	9- 7
1940	NY	A	P		5	0- 0
	BRO	N	P		14	2- 5
1941	BRO	N	P		4	0- 0
	PHI	N	P		29	2-13
	BBTL			162	163	29-48
	BR 1934, 37					

GRISSOM, MARVIN EDWARD (MARV)
B.MAR.3,1918 LOS MOLINOS,CAL.

YR	CL	LEA	POS	GP	G	REC
1946	NY	N	P		4	0- 2
1949	DET	A	P		27	2- 4
1952	CHI	A	P		28	12-10
1953	BOS	A	P		13	2- 6
	NY	N	P		21	4- 2
1954	NY	N	P		56	10- 7
1955	NY	N	P		55	5- 4
1956	NY	N	P		43	1- 1
1957	NY	N	P		59	4- 4
1958	SF	N	P		51	7- 5
1959	STL	N	P		3	0- 0
	BRTR				356	47-45

GROAT, RICHARD MORROW (DICK)
B.NOV.4,1930 WILKINSBURG,PA.

YR	CL	LEA	POS	GP	G	REC
1952	PIT	N	S		95	.284
1955	PIT	N	S		151	.267
1956	PIT	N	S-3		142	.273
1957	PIT	N	S-3		125	.315
1958	PIT	N	S		151	.300
1959	PIT	N	S		147	.275
1960	PIT	N	S		138	.325
1961	PIT	N	S-3		148	.275
1962	PIT	N	S		161	.294
1963	STL	N	S		158	.319
1964	STL	N	S		161	.292
1965	STL	N	*S/3		153	.254
1966	PHI	N	*S-3/1		155	.260
1967	PHI	N	/S		10	.115
	SF	N	S/2		34	.171
	BRTR				1929	.286

GROB, CONRAD GEORGE (CONNIE)
B.NOV.9,1932 CROSS PLAINS,WIS.

YR	CL	LEA	POS	GP	G	REC
1956	WAS	A	P		37	4- 5
	BLTR					

GRODZICKI, JOHN (GROD)
B.FEB.26,1917 NANTICOKE,PA.

YR	CL	LEA	POS	GP	G	REC
1941	STL	N	P		5	2- 1
1946	STL	N	P		3	0- 0
1947	STL	N	P		16	0- 1
	BRTR				24	2- 2

GROH, HENRY KNIGHT (HEINIE)
B.SEPT.18,1889 ROCHESTER,N.Y.
D.AUG.22,1968 CINCINNATI,OHIO

YR	CL	LEA	POS	GP	G	REC
1912	NY	N	2		27	.271
1913	NY	N	2		4	.000
	CIN	N	2		117	.282
1914	CIN	N	2		139	.288
1915	CIN	N	2-3		160	.290
1916	CIN	N	2-S-3		149	.269
1917	CIN	N	2-3		156	.304
1918	CIN	N	M-3		126	.320
1919	CIN	N	3		122	.310
1920	CIN	N	3		145	.298
1921	CIN	N	3		97	.331
1922	NY	N	3		115	.265
1923	NY	N	3		123	.290
1924	NY	N	3		145	.281
1925	NY	N	2-3		25	.231
1926	NY	N	3		12	.229
1927	PIT	N	3		14	.286
	BRTR				1676	.292

GROH, LEWIS CARL (SILVER)
B.OCT.16,1883 ROCHESTER,N.Y.
D.OCT.20,1960 ROCHESTER,N.Y.

YR	CL	LEA	POS	GP	G	REC
1919	PHI	A	3		4	.000
	BRTR					

GROMEK, STEPHEN JOSEPH (STEVE)
B.JAN.15,1920 HAMTRAMCK,MICH.

YR	CL	LEA	POS	GP	G	REC
1941	CLE	A	P		9	1- 1
1942	CLE	A	P		14	2- 0
1943	CLE	A	P		3	0- 0
1944	CLE	A	P	35	44	10- 9
1945	CLE	A	P	33	37	19- 9
1946	CLE	A	P	29	37	5-15
1947	CLE	A	P	29	30	3- 5
1948	CLE	A	P		38	9- 3
1949	CLE	A	P		27	4- 6
1950	CLE	A	P		31	10- 7
1951	CLE	A	P		27	7- 4
1952	CLE	A	P	29	30	7- 2
1953	CLE	A	P		5	1- 1
	DET	A	P		19	6- 8
1954	DET	A	P		36	18-16
1955	DET	A	P		28	13-10
1956	DET	A	P		40	8- 6
1957	DET	A	P		15	0- 1
	BBTR			447	470	123-108

GROOM, ROBERT
B.SEPT.12,1884 BELLEVILLE,ILL.
D.FEB.19,1948 BELLEVILLE,ILL.

YR	CL	LEA	POS	GP	G	REC
1909	WAS	A	P	44	46	6-26
1910	WAS	A	P		34	12-17
1911	WAS	A	P		38	13-17
1912	WAS	A	P		43	24-13
1913	WAS	A	P		37	15-16
1914	STL	F	P		38	13-20
1915	STL	F	P		37	11-11
1916	STL	A	P		41	13- 9
1917	STL	A	P		38	8-19
1918	CLE	A	P		14	2- 2
	BRTR			368	370	117-150

GROSART, GEORGE ALBERT
B.1879 MEADVILLE,PA.
D.APR.18,1902 HOMESTEAD,PA.

YR	CL	LEA	POS	GP	G	REC
1901	BOS	N	O		7	.125

GROSKLOSS, HOWARD HOFFMAN (HOWDIE)
B.APR.10,1906 PITTSBURGH,PA.
B.APR.9,1907 PITTSBURGH,PA.

YR	CL	LEA	POS	GP	G	REC
1930	PIT	N	2		2	.333
1931	PIT	N	2		53	.280
1932	PIT	N	2		17	.100
	BRTR				72	.261

GROSS, DONALD JOHN (DON)
B.JUNE 30,1931 WEIDMAN,MICH.

YR	CL	LEA	POS	GP	G	REC
1955	CIN	N	P		17	4- 5
1956	CIN	N	P		19	3- 0
1957	CIN	N	P		43	7- 9
1958	PIT	N	P		40	5- 7
1959	PIT	N	P		21	1- 1
1960	PIT	N	P		5	0- 0
	BLTL				145	20-22

GROSS, EMIL MICHAEL
B.1859 CHICAGO,ILL.
D.AUG.24,1921 EAGLE RIVER,WIS.

YR	CL	LEA	POS	GP	G	REC
1879	PRO	N	C		30	.379
1880	PRO	N	C		84	.255
1881	PRO	N	C		51	.274
1883	PHI	N	C-O		56	.312
1884	STL	U	C-O		23	.326
1886	STL	N	C		1	.000
					245	.291

GROSS, EWELL (TURKEY)
B.FEB.21,1896 MESQUITE,TEX.
D.JAN.11,1936 DALLAS,TEX.

YR	CL	LEA	POS	GP	G	REC
1925	BOS	A	S		9	.094
	BRTR					

GROSS, GREGORY EUGENE (GREG)
B.AUG.1,1952 YORK,PA.

YR	CL	LEA	POS	GP	G	REC
1973	HOU	N	/O		14	.231
1974	HOU	N	*O		156	.314
1975	HOU	N	*O		132	.294
1976	HOU	N	*O		128	.286
1977	CIN	N	O		115	.322
1978	CHI	N	*O		124	.265
	BLTL				669	.295

GROSS, WAYNE DALE
B.JAN.14,1952 RIVERSIDE,CAL.

YR	CL	LEA	POS	GP	G	REC
1976	OAK	A	/1-O		10	.222
1977	OAK	A	*3/1		146	.233
1978	OAK	A	*3-1		118	.200
	BLTR				274	.221

GROSSMAN, HARLEY JOSEPH
B.MAY.5,1930 EVANSVILLE,IND.

YR	CL	LEA	POS	GP	G	REC
1952	WAS	A	P		1	0- 0
	BRTR					

GROTE, GERALD WAYNE (JERRY)
B.OCT.6,1942 SAN ANTONIO,TEX.

YR	CL	LEA	POS	GP	G	REC
1963	HOU	N	C		3	.200
1964	HOU	N	C		100	.181
1966	NY	N	*C/3		120	.237
1967	NY	N	*C		120	.195
1968	NY	N	*C		124	.282
1969	NY	N	*C		113	.252
1970	NY	N	*C		126	.255
1971	NY	N	*C		125	.270
1972	NY	N	C/3-O		64	.210
1973	NY	N	C/3		84	.256
1974	NY	N	C		97	.257
1975	NY	N	*C		119	.295
1976	NY	N	C/O		101	.272
1977	NY	N	C-3		42	.270
	LA	N	C/3		18	.259
1978	LA	N	C/3		41	.271
	BRTR				1397	.251

GROTH, ERNEST JOHN (DANGO)
B.DEC.24,1884 CEDARSBURG,WIS.
D.MAY 23,1950 MILWAUKEE,WIS.

YR	CL	LEA	POS	GP	G	REC
1904	CHI	N	P		3	0- 2
	BRTR					

GROTH, ERNEST WILLIAM
B.MAY 3,1922 BEAVER FALLS,PA.

YR	CL	LEA	POS	GP	G	REC
1947	CLE	A	P		2	0- 0
1948	CLE	A	P	1	2	0- 0
1949	CHI	A	P		3	0- 1
	BRTR			6	7	0- 1

GROTH, JOHN THOMAS (JOHNNY)
B.JULY 23,1926 CHICAGO,ILL.

YR	CL	LEA	POS	GP	G	REC
1946	DET	A	O		4	.000
1947	DET	A	O		2	.250
1948	DET	A	O		6	.471
1949	DET	A	O		103	.293
1950	DET	A	O		157	.306
1951	DET	A	O		118	.299
1952	DET	A	O		141	.284
1953	STL	A	O		141	.253
1954	CHI	A	O		125	.275
1955	CHI	A	O		32	.338
	WAS	A	O		63	.219
1956	KC	A	O		95	.258
1957	KC	A	O		55	.254
	DET	A	O		38	.291
1958	DET	A	O		88	.281
1959	DET	A	O		55	.235
1960	DET	A	O		25	.368
	BRTR				1248	.279

GROVE, ORVAL LEROY
B.AUG.29,1919 MINERAL,KAN.

YR	CL	LEA	POS	GP	G	REC
1940	CHI	A	P		3	0- 0
1941	CHI	A	P		2	0- 0
1942	CHI	A	P		12	4- 6
1943	CHI	A	P		32	15- 9
1944	CHI	A	P		34	14-15
1945	CHI	A	P		33	14-12
1946	CHI	A	P		33	8-13
1947	CHI	A	P		25	6- 8
1948	CHI	A	P		32	2-10
1949	CHI	A	P		1	0- 0
	BRTR				207	63-73

GROVE, ROBERT MOSES (LEFTY)
B.MAR.6,1900 LONACONING,MD.
D.MAY 22,1975 NORWALK,OHIO

YR	CL	LEA	POS	GP	G	REC
1925	PHI	A	P		45	10-12
1926	PHI	A	P		45	13-13
1927	PHI	A	P		51	20-13
1928	PHI	A	P		39	24- 8
1929	PHI	A	P		42	20- 6
1930	PHI	A	P		50	28- 5
1931	PHI	A	P		41	31- 4
1932	PHI	A	P		44	25-10
1933	PHI	A	P		45	24- 8
1934	BOS	A	P		22	8- 8
1935	BOS	A	P		35	20-12
1936	BOS	A	P		35	17-12
1937	BOS	A	P		32	17- 9
1938	BOS	A	P		24	14- 4
1939	BOS	A	P	23	25	15- 4
1940	BOS	A	P	22	23	7- 6
1941	BOS	A	P		21	7- 7
			BLTL	616	619	300-141

GROVER, CHARLES BURT (BUGS)
[BORN CHARLES BYRD GROVER]
B.JUNE 20,1890 HUNTINGTON
TOWNSHIP,OHIO
D.MAY 24,1971 EMMETT,MICH.

YR	CL	LEA	POS	GP	G	REC
1913	DET	A	P		2	0- 0
			BLTR			

GROVER, ROY ARTHUR
B.JAN.17,1892 SNOHOMISH,WASH.
D.FEB.7,1978 MILWAUKIE,ORE.

YR	CL	LEA	POS	GP	G	REC
1916	PHI	A	2		20	.272
1917	PHI	A	2		141	.224
1919	PHI	A	2		22	.232
	WAS	A	2		24	.187
			BRTR		207	.226

GRUBB, HARVEY HARRISON
B.SEPT.18,1890 LEXINGTON,N.C.
D.JAN.25,1970 CORPUS CHRISTI,TEX.

YR	CL	LEA	POS	GP	G	REC
1912	CLE	A	3		1	.000
			BRTR			

GRUBB, JOHN MAYWOOD
B.AUG.4,1948 RICHMOND,VA.

YR	CL	LEA	POS	GP	G	REC
1972	SD	N	/O		7	.333
1973	SD	N	*O/3		113	.311
1974	SD	N	*O/3		140	.286
1975	SD	N	*O		144	.269
1976	SD	N	O/1-3		109	.284
1977	CLE	A	O		34	.301
1978	CLE	A	*O		113	.265
	TEX	A	O		21	.394
			BLTR		681	.285

GRUBBS, THOMAS DILLARD (JUDGE)
B.FEB.22,1894 MT.STERLING,KY.

YR	CL	LEA	POS	GP	G	REC
1920	NY	N	P		1	0- 1
			BRTR			

GRUBE, FRANKLIN THOMAS (HANS)
B.JAN.7,1905 EASTON,PA.
D.JULY 2,1945 NEW YORK,N.Y.

YR	CL	LEA	POS	GP	G	REC
1931	CHI	A	C		88	.219
1932	CHI	A	C		93	.282
1933	CHI	A	C		85	.230
1934	STL	A	C		65	.288
1935	STL	A	C		3	.333
	CHI	A	C		9	.368
1936	CHI	A	C		33	.161
1941	STL	A	C		18	.154
			BRTR		394	.244

GRUBER, HENRY JOHN
B.DEC.14,1864 HAMDEN,CONN.
D.SEPT.26,1932 NEW HAVEN,CONN.

YR	CL	LEA	POS	GP	G	REC
1887	DET	N	P		9	5- 3
1888	DET	N	P		27	11-13
1889	CLE	N	P		23	7-16
1890	CLE	P	P		50	21-20
1891	CLE	N	P		38	16-21
			BRTL		147	60-73

GRUNWALD, ALFRED HENRY
(AL) OR (STRETCH)
B.FEB.13,1930 LOS ANGELES,CAL.

YR	CL	LEA	POS	GP	G	REC
1955	PIT	N	P		3	0- 0
1959	KC	A	P	6	7	0- 1
			BLTL	9	10	0- 1

GRYSKA, SIGMUND STANLEY
B.NOV.4,1915 CHICAGO,ILL.

YR	CL	LEA	POS	GP	G	REC
1938	STL	A	S		7	.476
1939	STL	A	S		18	.265
			BRTR		25	.329

GRZENDA, JOSEPH CHARLES (JOE)
B.JUNE 8,1937 SCRANTON,PA.

YR	CL	LEA	POS	GP	G	REC
1961	DET	A	P		4	1- 0
1964	KC	A	P		20	0- 2
1966	KC	A	P		21	0- 2
1967	NY	N	P		11	0- 0
1969	MIN	A	P		38	4- 1
1970	WAS	A	P		49	3- 6
1971	WAS	A	P		46	5- 2
1972	STL	N	P		30	1- 0
			BRTL		219	14-13

GUDAT, MARVIN JOHN (MARV)
B.AUG.27,1905 GOLIAD,TEX.
D.MAR.1,1954 LOS ANGELES,CAL.

YR	CL	LEA	POS	GP	G	REC
1929	CIN	N	P	7	9	1- 1
1932	CHI	N	P-O	1	60	0- 0
						.255
			BLTL	8	69	1- 1
						.250

GUERRA, FERMIN [ROMERO] (MIKE)
B.OCT.11,1912 HAVANA,CUBA

YR	CL	LEA	POS	GP	G	REC
1937	WAS	A	C		1	.000
1944	WAS	A	C-O		75	.281
1945	WAS	A	C		56	.210
1946	WAS	A	C		41	.253
1947	PHI	A	C		72	.215
1948	PHI	A	C		53	.211
1949	PHI	A	C		98	.265
1950	PHI	A	C		87	.282
1951	BOS	A	C		10	.156
	WAS	A	C		72	.200
			BRTR		565	.242

GUERRERO, MARIO MIGUEL [ABUD]
B.SEP.28,1949 SANTO DOMINGO,D.R.

YR	CL	LEA	POS	GP	G	REC
1973	BOS	A	S-2		66	.233
1974	BOS	A	S		93	.246
1975	STL	N	S		64	.239
1976	CAL	A	2-S		83	.284
1977	CAL	A	S-O-2		86	.283
1978	OAK	A	*S		143	.275
			BRTR		535	.263

GUERRERO, PEDRO
B.JUNE 29,1956 SAN PEDRO DE
MACORIS,D.R.

YR	CL	LEA	POS	GP	G	REC
1978	LA	N	/1		5	.625
			BBTR			

GUESE, THEODORE (WHITEY)
B.JAN.23,1873 NEW BREMEN,OHIO
D.APR.8,1951 WAPAKONETA,OHIO

YR	CL	LEA	POS	GP	G	REC
1901	CIN	N	P		6	1- 4
			BRTR			

GUIDRY, RONALD AMES (RON)
B.AUG.28,1950 LAFAYETTE,LA.

YR	CL	LEA	POS	GP	G	REC
1975	NY	A	P		10	0- 1
1976	NY	A	/P		7	0- 0
1977	NY	A	P	31	36	16- 7
1978	NY	A	P	35	37	25- 3
			BLTL	83	90	41-11

GUINDON, ROBERT JOSEPH (BOBBY)
B.SEP.4,1943 BROOKLINE,MASS.

YR	CL	LEA	POS	GP	G	REC
1964	BOS	A	1-O		5	.125
			BLTL			

GUINEY, BENJAMIN FRANKLIN
B.NOV.16,1858 DETROIT,MICH.
D.DEC.5,1930 DETROIT,MICH.

YR	CL	LEA	POS	GP	G	REC
1883	DET	N	2-O		1	.200
1884	DET	N	C		2	.000
			BBTR		3	.083

GUINN, DRANNON EUGENE (SKIP)
B.OCT.25,1944 ST.CHARLES,MO.

YR	CL	LEA	POS	GP	G	REC
1968	ATL	N	/P	3	7	0- 0
1969	HOU	N	P		28	1- 2
1971	HOU	N	/P		4	0- 0
			BRTL	35	39	1- 2

GUINTINI, BENJAMIN JOHN (BEN)
B.JAN.13,1920 LOS BANOS,CAL.

YR	CL	LEA	POS	GP	G	REC
1946	PIT	N	O		2	.000
1950	PHI	A	O		3	.000
			BRTR		5	.000

GUISE, WITT ORISON (LEFTY)
B.SEPT.18,1909 DRIGGS,ARK.
D.AUG.13,1966 LITTLE ROCK,ARK.

YR	CL	LEA	POS	GP	G	REC
1940	CIN	N	P		2	0- 0
			BLTL			

GUISTO, LOUIS JOSEPH
B.JAN.16,1894 NAPA,CAL.

YR	CL	LEA	POS	GP	G	REC
1916	CLE	A	1		6	.158
1917	CLE	A	1		73	.185
1921	CLE	A	1		2	.500
1922	CLE	A	1		35	.250
1923	CLE	A	1		40	.181
			BRTR		156	.196

GULDEN, BRADLEY LEE (BRAD)
B.JUNE 10,1956 NEW ULM,N.MEX.

YR	CL	LEA	POS	GP	G	REC
1978	LA	N	/C		3	.000
			BLTR			

GULLETT, DONALD EDWARD (DON)
B.JAN.6,1951 LYNN,KY.

YR	CL	LEA	POS	GP	G	REC
1970	CIN	N	P		44	5- 2
1971	CIN	N	P	35	40	16- 6
1972	CIN	N	P		31	9-10
1973	CIN	N	P	45	53	18- 8
1974	CIN	N	P	36	39	17-11
1975	CIN	N	P		22	15- 4
1976	CIN	N	P	23	25	11- 3
1977	NY	A	P		22	14- 4
1978	NY	A	/P		8	4- 2
			BRTL	266	284	109-50

GULLEY, THOMAS JEFFERSON
B.DEC.25,1899 GARNER,N.C.
D.NOV.24,1966 ST.CHARLES,ARK.

YR	CL	LEA	POS	GP	G	REC
1923	CLE	A	O		3	.500
1924	CLE	A	O		8	.150
1926	CHI	A	O		16	.229
			BLTR		27	.224

GULLIC, THEODORE JASPER (TED)
B.JAN.2,1907 KOSHKONONG,MO.

YR	CL	LEA	POS	GP	G	REC
1930	STL	A	O		92	.250
1933	STL	A	1-3-O		104	.243
			BRTR		196	.247

GUMBERT, ADDISON COURTNEY (AD)
B.OCT.10,1868 PITTSBURGH,PA.
D.APR.23,1925 PITTSBURGH,PA.

YR	CL	LEA	POS	GP	G	REC
1888	CHI	N	P		7	3- 3
1889	CHI	N	P	29	49	14-13
1890	BOS	P	P	39	45	22- 9
1891	CHI	N	P		29	17-10
1892	CHI	N	P	44	48	23-16
1893	PIT	N	P	19	24	13- 6
1894	PIT	N	P	32	33	18-14
1895	BRO	N	P		26	11-15
1896	BRO	N	P		5	0- 4
	PHI	N	P		11	6- 4
			BRTR	241	277	127-96

GUMPERT, HARRY EDWARD (GUNBOAT)
B.NOV.5,1909 ELIZABETH,PA.

YR	CL	LEA	POS	GP	G	REC
1935	NY	N	P		6	1- 2
1936	NY	N	P		39	11- 3
1937	NY	N	P		34	10-11
1938	NY	N	P	38	40	15-13
1939	NY	N	P	36	37	18-11
1940	NY	N	P		35	12-14
1941	NY	N	P		5	1- 1
	STL	N	P	33	34	11- 5
1942	STL	N	P		38	9- 5
1943	STL	N	P		21	10- 5
1944	STL	N	P		10	4- 2
	CIN	N	P		24	10- 8
1946	CIN	N	P		36	6- 8
1947	CIN	N	P		46	10-10
1948	CIN	N	P		61	10- 8
1949	CIN	N	P		29	4- 3
	PIT	N	P		16	1- 4
1950	PIT	N	P		1	0- 0
			BRTR	508	512	143-113

GUMBERT, WILLIAM SKEEN
B.AUG.8,1865 PITTSBURGH,PA.
D.APR.13,1946 PITTSBURGH,PA.

YR	CL	LEA	POS	GP	G	REC
1890	PIT	N	P		10	4- 4
1892	PIT	N	P		7	3- 2
1893	LOU	N	P		1	0- 0
			BRTR		18	7- 6

GUMPERT, RANDALL PENNINGTON (RANDY)
B.JAN.23,1918 MONOCACY,PA.

YR	CL	LEA	POS	GP	G	REC
1936	PHI	A	P		22	1- 2
1937	PHI	A	P		10	0- 0
1938	PHI	A	P		4	0- 2
1946	NY	A	P		33	11- 3
1947	NY	A	P	24	25	4- 1
1948	NY	A	P		15	1- 0
	CHI	A	P		16	2- 6
1949	CHI	A	P		34	13-16
1950	CHI	A	P	40	41	5-12
1951	CHI	A	P	33	37	9- 8
1952	BOS	A	P		10	1- 0
	WAS	A	P		20	4- 9
			BRTR	261	267	51-59

GUNKEL, WOODWARD WILLIAM (RED)
B.APR.15,1894 SHEFFIELD,ILL.
D.APR.19,1954 CHICAGO,ILL.

YR	CL	LEA	POS	GP	G	REC
1916	CLE	A	P		1	0- 0
			BBTR			

GUNKLE, FREDERICK W.
B.DUBUQUE,IOWA

YR	CL	LEA	POS	GP	G	REC
1879	CLE	N	C-O		1	.000

GUNNING, HYLAND
B.AUG.6,1888 MAPLEWOOD,N.J.
D.MAR.28,1975 TOGUS,ME.

YR	CL	LEA	POS	GP	G	REC
1911	BOS	A	1		4	.111
			BLTR			

YR	CL	LEA	POS	GP	G	REC

GUNNING, THOMAS FRANCIS
B.MAR.4,1862 NEWMARKET,N.H.
D.MAR.17,1931 FALL RIVER,MASS.

YR	CL	LEA	POS	GP	G	REC
1884	BOS	N	C		12	.095
1885	BOS	N	C		48	.224
1886	BOS	N	C		27	.224
1887	PHI	N	C		27	.293
1888	ATH	AA	C		23	.217
1889	ATH	AA	C		5	.375
					142	.216

GUNSON, JOSEPH BROOK
B.MAR.23,1863 PHILADELPHIA,PA.
D.NOV.15,1942 PHILADELPHIA,PA.

YR	CL	LEA	POS	G	REC
1884	WAS	U	C-0	44	.158
1889	KC	AA	C	34	.198
1892	BAL	N	C-0	85	.223
1893	STL	N	C	37	.280
	CLE	N	C	21	.296
	BRTR			221	.223

GURA, LAWRENCE CYRIL (LARRY)
B.NOV.26,1947 JOLIET,ILL.

YR	CL	LEA	POS	GP	G	REC
1970	CHI	N	P		20	1- 3
1971	CHI	N	/P		6	0- 0
1972	CHI	N	/P		7	0- 0
1973	CHI	N	P	21	22	2- 4
1974	NY	A	/P		8	5- 1
1975	NY	A	P		26	7- 8
1976	KC	A	P		20	4- 0
1977	KC	A	P		52	8- 5
1978	KC	A	P		35	16- 4
	BBTL			495	196	43-25
	8R 1970					

GURZENSKY, JOSEPH CHARLES
[PLAYED UNDER NAME OF
JOSEPH CHARLES GLENN]

GUST, ERNEST HERMAN FRANK (RED)
B.JAN.24,1888 BAY CITY,MICH.
D.OCT.26,1945 MAUPIN,ORE.

YR	CL	LEA	POS	G	REC
1911	STL	A	1	3	.000
	BRTR				

GUSTINE, FRANK WILLIAM (FRANKIE)
B.FEB.20,1920 HOOPESTON,ILL.

YR	CL	LEA	POS	G	REC
1939	PIT	N	3	22	.186
1940	PIT	N	2	133	.281
1941	PIT	N	2-3	121	.270
1942	PIT	N	C-2-S-3	115	.229
1943	PIT	N	1-2-S	112	.290
1944	PIT	N	2-S-3	127	.230
1945	PIT	N	C-2-S	128	.280
1946	PIT	N	2-S-3	131	.259
1947	PIT	N	3	156	.297
1948	PIT	N	3	131	.267
1949	CHI	N	2-3	76	.226
1950	STL	A	3	9	.158
	BRTR			1261	.265

GUTH, CHARLES HENRY (BUCKY)
B.AUG.18,1947 BALTIMORE,MD.

YR	CL	LEA	POS	G	REC
1972	MIN	A	/S	3	.000

GUTH, CHARLES J.
B.1856 CHICAGO,ILL.
D.JULY 1863 CHICAGO,ILL.

YR	CL	LEA	POS	G	REC
1880	CHI	N	P	1	1- 0

GUTIERREZ, CESAR DARIO
(CESAR) OR (COCA)
B.JAN.26,1943 CORO,VENEZ.

YR	CL	LEA	POS	G	REC
1967	SF	N	S/2	18	.143
1969	SF	N	/3-S	15	.217
	DET	A	S	17	.254
1970	DET	A	/S	135	.243
1971	DET	A	S/3-2	36	.189
	BRTR			223	.235

GUTTERIDGE, DONALD JOSEPH (DON)
B.JUNE 19,1912 PITTSBURG,KAN.

YR	CL	LEA	POS	G	REC
1936	STL	N	3	23	.319
1937	STL	N	3	119	.291
1938	STL	N	S-3	142	.255
1939	STL	N	3	148	.269
1940	STL	N	3	69	.269
1942	STL	A	2-3	147	.255
1943	STL	A	2	132	.273
1944	STL	A	2	148	.245
1945	STL	A	2-0	143	.238
1946	BOS	A	2-3	22	.234
1947	BOS	A	2-3	54	.168
1948	PIT	N	H	4	.000
	BRTR			1151	.256
NON-PLAYING MANAGER CHI[A] 1969-70

GUZMAN, SANTIAGO DONOVAN
B.JULY 25,1949 SAN PEDRO DE
MACORIS,D.R.

YR	CL	LEA	POS	G	REC
1969	STL	N	/P	1	0- 1
1970	STL	N	/P	8	1- 1
1971	STL	N	/P	2	0- 0
1972	STL	N	/P	1	0- 0
	BRTR			12	1- 2

YR	CL	LEA	POS	GP	G	REC

GYSELMAN, RICHARD RENALD
B.APR.6,1908 SAN FRANCISCO,CAL.

YR	CL	LEA	POS	G	REC
1933	BOS	N	2-S-3	58	.239
1934	BOS	N	3	24	.167
	BRTR			82	.225

HAAS, BERTHOLD JOHN (BERT)
B.FEB.6,1914 NAPERVILLE,ILL.

YR	CL	LEA	POS	G	REC
1937	BRO	N	1	16	.400
1938	BRO	N	H	1	.000
1942	CIN	N	1-3-0	154	.239
1943	CIN	N	1-3-0	101	.262
1946	CIN	N	1-3	140	.264
1947	CIN	N	1-0	135	.286
1948	PHI	N	1-3	95	.282
1949	PHI	N	H	2	.000
	NY	N	1-3	54	.260
1951	CHI	A	1-3-0	23	.163
	BRTR			721	.264

HAAS, BRUNO PHILIP (BOON)
B.MAY 5,1891 WORCESTER,MASS.
D.JUNE 5,1952 SARASOTA,FLA.

YR	CL	LEA	POS	G	REC
1915	PHI	A	P	12	0- 2
	BBTL				

HAAS, BRYAN EDMUND (MOOSE)
B.APR.22,1956 BALTIMORE,MD.

YR	CL	LEA	POS	GP	G	REC
1976	MIL	A	/P		5	0- 1
1977	MIL	A	/P	32	34	10-12
1978	MIL	A	/P		7	2- 3
	BRTR			44	46	12-16

HAAS, GEORGE EDWIN (EDDIE)
B.MAY 26,1935 PADUCAH,KY.

YR	CL	LEA	POS	G	REC
1957	CHI	N	0	14	.208
1958	CHI	N	0	9	.357
1960	MIL	N	0	32	.219
	BLTR			55	.243

HAAS, GEORGE WILLIAM (MULE)
B.OCT.15,1903 MONTCLAIR,N.J.
D.JUNE 30,1974 NEW ORLEANS,LA.

YR	CL	LEA	POS	G	REC
1925	PIT	N	0	4	.000
1928	PHI	A	0	9	.280
1929	PHI	A	0	139	.313
1930	PHI	A	0	132	.299
1931	PHI	A	0	102	.323
1932	PHI	A	0	143	.305
1933	PHI	A	0	106	.287
1934	PHI	A	0	106	.268
1935	CHI	A	0	92	.291
1936	CHI	A	0	119	.284
1937	CHI	A	1	54	.207
1938	PHI	A	0	40	.205
	BLTR			1168	.292

HABENICHT, ROBERT JULIUS
(BOB) OR (HOBBY)
B.FEB.13,1926 ST.LOUIS,MO.

YR	CL	LEA	POS	G	REC
1951	STL	N	P	3	0- 0
1953	STL	A	P	1	0- 0
	BRTR			4	0- 0

HABERER, EMIL KARL
B.FEB.2,1878 CINCINNATI,OHIO
D.OCT.19,1951 LOUISVILLE,KY.

YR	CL	LEA	POS	G	REC
1901	CIN	N	1	6	.167
1903	CIN	N	C	5	.154
1909	CIN	N	C	5	.187
	BRTR			16	.178

HACH, IRVIN (MAJOR)
B.JUNE 6,1873 LOUISVILLE,KY.
D.AUG.13,1936 LOUISVILLE,KY.

YR	CL	LEA	POS	G	REC
1897	LOU	N	2-3	15	.163

HACK, STANLEY CAMFIELD (STAN)
OR (SMILING STAN)
B.DEC.6,1909 SACRAMENTO,CAL

YR	CL	LEA	POS	G	REC
1932	CHI	N	3	72	.236
1933	CHI	N	3	20	.350
1934	CHI	N	3	111	.289
1935	CHI	N	1-3	124	.311
1936	CHI	N	1-3	149	.298
1937	CHI	N	3	154	.297
1938	CHI	N	3	152	.320
1939	CHI	N	3	156	.298
1940	CHI	N	3	149	.317
1941	CHI	N	1-3	151	.317
1942	CHI	N	3	144	.300
1943	CHI	N	3	144	.289
1944	CHI	N	1-3	98	.282
1945	CHI	N	1-3	150	.323
1946	CHI	N	3	92	.285
1947	CHI	N	3	76	.271
	BLTR			1938	.301
NON-PLAYING MANAGER
CHI[N] 1954-56, STL[N] 1958

HACKER, RICHARD WARREN (RICH)
B.OCT.6,1947 BELLEVILLE,ILL.

YR	CL	LEA	POS	G	REC
1971	MON	N	S	16	.121
	BBTR				

YR	CL	LEA	POS	GP	G	REC

HACKER, WARREN LOUIS
B.NOV.21,1924 MARISSA,ILL.

YR	CL	LEA	POS	GP	G	REC
1948	CHI	N	P		3	0- 1
1949	CHI	N	P	30	32	5- 8
1950	CHI	N	P		5	0- 1
1951	CHI	N	P		2	0- 0
1952	CHI	N	P	33	34	15- 9
1953	CHI	N	P	39	42	12-19
1954	CHI	N	P	39	43	6-13
1955	CHI	N	P		35	11-15
1956	CHI	N	P		34	3-13
1957	CIN	N	P		15	3- 2
	PHI	N	P		20	4- 4
1958	PHI	N	P		9	0- 1
1961	CHI	A	P		42	3- 3
	BRTR			306	316	62-89

HACKETT, CHARLES M.
B.HOLYOKE,MASS.
NON-PLAYING MANAGER
CLE[N] 1884, BRO[AA] 1885

HACKETT, JAMES JOSEPH (SUNNY JIM)
B.OCT.1,1877 JACKSONVILLE,ILL.
D.MAR.28,1961 DOUGLAS,MICH.

YR	CL	LEA	POS	GP	G	REC
1902	STL	N	P-0	4	6	0- 4
						.284
1903	STL	N	P-1	5	96	1- 3
						.228
	BRTR			9	102	1- 7
						.233

HACKETT, MORTIMER MARTIN (MERT)
B.NOV.1,1859 CAMBRIDGE,MASS.
D.FEB.22,1938 CAMBRIDGE,MASS.

YR	CL	LEA	POS	G	REC
1883	BOS	N	C-0	46	.234
1884	BOS	N	C-3	68	.203
1885	BOS	N	C	33	.182
1886	KC	N	C	62	.217
1887	IND	N	C	41	.272
	TR			250	.222

HACKETT, WALTER HENRY
B.AUG.15,1857 CAMBRIDGE,MASS.
D.OCT.2,1920 CAMBRIDGE,MASS.

YR	CL	LEA	POS	G	REC
1884	BOS	U	S	102	.248
1885	BOS	N	2-S	35	.184
				137	.233

HADDIX, HARVEY
(HARVEY) OR (THE KITTEN)
B.SEP.18,1925 MEDWAY,OHIO

YR	CL	LEA	POS	GP	G	REC
1952	STL	N	P-0	7	9	2- 2
						.214
1953	STL	N	P	36	46	20- 9
1954	STL	N	P	43	61	18-13
1955	STL	N	P		37	12-16
1956	STL	N	P	4	5	1- 0
	PHI	N	P	31	46	12- 8
1957	PHI	N	P	27	41	10-13
1958	CIN	N	P	29	42	8- 7
1959	PIT	N	P		31	12-12
1960	PIT	N	P		29	11-10
1961	PIT	N	P	29	31	10- 6
1962	PIT	N	P		28	9- 6
1963	PIT	N	P	49	50	3- 4
1964	BAL	A	P		49	5- 3
1965	BAL	A	P		24	3- 2
	BLTL			453	531	136-113
						.212

HADDOCK, GEORGE SILAS
(GENTLEMAN GEORGE)
B.DEC.25,1866 PORTSMOUTH,N.H.
D.APR.18,1926 BOSTON,MASS.

YR	CL	LEA	POS	GP	G	REC
1888	WAS	N	P		2	0- 2
1889	WAS	N	P		33	10-19
1890	BUF	P	P-0	35	42	9-26
						.240
1891	BOS	AA	P	52	58	33-11
1892	BRO	N	P		44	31-13
1893	BRO	N	P	18	26	8-10
1894	BRO	N	P		10	4- 3
	WAS	N	P-0	4	5	0- 4
						.250
	TR			198	220	95-88
						.219

HADDOW, JOHN FALCNOR
[PLAYED UNDER NAME OF JOHN B. BLACK]

THE OFFICIAL ENCYCLOPEDIA OF BASEBALL

YR	CL	LEA	POS	GP	G	REC

HADLEY, IRVING DARIUS (BUMP)
B.JULY 5,1904 LYNN,MASS.
D.FEB.15,1963 LYNN,MASS.

1926	WAS	A	P		1	0- 0
1927	WAS	A	P		30	14- 6
1928	WAS	A	P		33	12-13
1929	WAS	A	P		37	6-16
1930	WAS	A	P		42	15-11
1931	WAS	A	P		55	11-10
1932	CHI	A	P		3	1- 1
	STL	A	P		40	13-20
1933	STL	A	P		45	15-20
1934	STL	A	P		39	10-16
1935	WAS	A	P		35	10-15
1936	NY	A	P		31	14- 4
1937	NY	A	P		29	11- 8
1938	NY	A	P		29	9- 8
1939	NY	A	P		26	12- 6
1940	NY	A	P		25	3- 5
1941	NY	N	P		3	1- 0
	PHI	A	P		25	4- 6
	BRTR				528	161-165

HADLEY, KENT WILLIAM
B.DEC.17,1934 POCATELLO,IDAHO

1958	KC	A	1		3	.182
1959	KC	A	1		113	.253
1960	NY	A	1		55	.203
	BLTL				171	.242

HAEFNER, WILLIAM BERNHARD
B.JULY 8,1894 PHILADELPHIA,PA.

1915	PHI	A	C		3	.250
1920	PIT	N	C		54	.194
1928	NY	N	C		2	.000
	BPTR				59	.194

HAEFNER, MILTON ARNOLD (MICKEY)
B.OCT.9,1912 LENZBURG,ILL.

1943	WAS	A	P		36	11- 5
1944	WAS	A	P		31	12-15
1945	WAS	A	P		37	16-14
1946	WAS	A	P		33	14-11
1947	WAS	A	P		31	10-14
1948	WAS	A	P		28	5-13
1949	WAS	A	P	19	20	5- 5
	CHI	A	P		14	4- 6
1950	CHI	A	P		24	1- 0
	BOS	N	P		8	0- 2
	BLTL			261	262	76-93

HAFEY, CHARLES JAMES (CHICK)
B.FEB.12,1903 BERKELEY,CAL.
D.JULY 2,1973 CALISTOGA,CAL.

1924	STL	N	O		24	.253
1925	STL	N	O		93	.302
1926	STL	N	O		78	.271
1927	STL	N	O		103	.330
1928	STL	N	O		138	.337
1929	STL	N	O		134	.339
1930	STL	N	O		120	.336
1931	STL	N	O		122	.349
1932	CIN	N	O		83	.344
1933	CIN	N	O		144	.303
1934	CIN	N	O		140	.293
1935	CIN	N	O		15	.339
1937	CIN	N	O		89	.261
	BRTR				1283	.317

HAFEY, DANIEL ALBERT (BUD)
B.AUG.6,1912 BERKELEY,CAL.

1935	CHI	A	H		2	.000
	PIT	N	O		58	.228
1936	PIT	N	O		39	.212
1939	PIT	N	O		6	.154
	PHI	N	P-O	2	18	0- 0
						.176
	BRTR			2	123	0- 0
						.213

HAFEY, THOMAS FRANCIS (TOM)
(HEAVE-O) OR (THE ARM)
B.JULY 12,1913 BERKELEY,CAL.

1939	NY	N	3		70	.242
1944	STL	A	1-0		8	.357
	BRTR				78	.248

HAFFORD, LEO EDGAR
B.SEPT.17,1883 SOMERVILLE,MASS.
D.OCT.2,1911 WILLIMANTIC,CONN.

| 1906 | CIN | N | P | | 3 | 0- 0 |

HAGAN, ARTHUR CHARLES
B.MAR.17,1863 PROVIDENCE,R.I.
D.MAR.25,1936 PROVIDENCE,R.I.

1883	PHI	N	P		17	1-16
	BUF	N	P		2	0- 2
						.000
1884	BUF	N	P		3	1- 2
					22	2-20
						.115

HAGEMAN, KURT MORITZ (CASEY)
B.MAY 12,1887 MT.OLIVER,PA.
D.APR.21,1964 NEW BEDFORD,PA.

1911	BOS	A	P		2	0- 2
1912	BOS	A	P		2	0- 0
1914	STL	N	P		12	2- 4
	CHI	N	P		16	1- 1
	BRTR				32	3- 7

HAGENBUSH, JOHN ALBERT
[PLAYED UNDER NAME OF
JOHN ALBERT PFIESTER]

HAGERMAN, ZERIAH ZEQUIEL (RIP)
B.JUNE 20,1889 LINDEN,KAN.
D.JAN.29,1930 ALBUQUERQUE,N.M.

1909	CHI	N	P		13	4- 4
1914	CLE	A	P		37	9-15
1915	CLE	A	P		28	7-13
1916	CLE	A	P		2	0- 0
	BRTR				80	20-32

HAGUE, JOE CLARENCE
B.APR.25,1944 HUNTINGTON,W.VA.

1968	STL	N	/O-1		7	.235
1969	STL	N	O/1		40	.170
1970	STL	N	1-O		139	.271
1971	STL	N	1-O		129	.226
1972	STL	N	,/O		27	.237
	CIN	N	/O		69	.246
1973	CIN	N	/O-1		19	.152
	BLTL				430	.239

HAGUE, WILLIAM L.
[REAL NAME WILLIAM L. HAUG]
B.1852 PHILADELPHIA,PA.

1875	STL	NA	1-3		59	.206
1876	LOU	N	3		67	.264
1877	LOU	N	3		59	.267
1878	PRO	N	3		60	.207
1879	PRO	N	3		50	.227
	BRTR				295	.231

HAHN, DONALD ANTONE (DON)
B.NOV.16,1948 SAN FRANCISCO,CAL.

1969	MON	N	/O		4	.111
1970	MON	N	O		92	.255
1971	NY	N	O		98	.236
1972	NY	N	O		17	.162
1973	NY	N	O		93	.229
1974	N	*O		110	.251	
1975	PHI	N	/O		9	.000
	STL	N	/O		7	.125
	SD	N	O		34	.231
	BRTR				454	.236

HAHN, FRANK GEORGE (NOODLES)
B.APR.29,1879 NASHVILLE,TENN.
D.FEB.6,1960 CANDLER,N.C.

1899	CIN	N	P		38	23- 8
1900	CIN	N	P		40	16-21
1901	CIN	N	P		41	22-19
1902	CIN	N	P-1	36	37	23-12
			O			.183
1903	CIN	N	P		34	22-12
1904	CIN	N	P		35	15- 8
1905	CIN	N	P		12	5- 3
1906	NY	A	P		6	3- 2
	BLTL			242	243	129-95
						.178

HAHN, FREDERICK ALOYS
B.FEB.16,1929 NYACK,N.Y.

| 1952 | STL | N | P | | 1 | 0- 0 |
| | BRTL | | | | | |

HAHN, RICHARD FREDERICK
B.JULY 24,1916 CANTON,OHIO

| 1940 | WAS | A | C | | 1 | .000 |
| | BRTR | | | | | |

HAHN, WILLIAM EDGAR (ED)
B.AUG.27,1875 NEVADA,OHIO
D.NOV.29,1941 DES MOINES,IOWA

1905	NY	A	O		43	.319
1906	NY	A	O		11	.091
	CHI	A	O		130	.227
1907	CHI	A	O		156	.255
1908	CHI	A	O		122	.251
1909	CHI	A	O		76	.182
1910	CHI	A	O		15	.113
	BLTR				553	.237

HAID, HAROLD AUGUSTINE (HAL)
B.DEC.21,1897 BARBERTON,OHIO
D.AUG.13,1952 LOS ANGELES,CAL.

1919	STL	A	P		1	0- 0
1928	STL	N	P		27	2- 2
1929	STL	N	P		38	9- 9
1930	STL	N	P	20	21	3- 2
1931	BOS	N	P		27	0- 2
1933	CHI	A	P		6	0- 0
	BRTR			119	120	14-15

HAIGH, EDWARD E.
B.FEB.7,1867 PHILADELPHIA,PA.
D.FEB.15,1953 ATLANTIC CITY,N.J

| 1892 | STL | N | O | | 1 | .250 |

HAINES, HENRY LUTHER (HINKEY)
B.DEC.23,1898 RED LION,PA.

| 1923 | NY | A | O | | 28 | .160 |
| | BRTR | | | | | |

HAINES, JESSE JOSEPH (POP)
B.JULY 22,1893 CLAYTON,OHIO
D.AUG.5,1978 DAYTON,OHIO

1918	CIN	N	P		1	0- 0
1920	STL	N	P		47	48	13-20
1921	STL	N	P		37	39	18-12
1922	STL	N	P-1	29	30	11- 9
						.167
1923	STL	N	P		37	20-13
1924	STL	N	P		35	8-19
1925	STL	N	P		29	13-14
1926	STL	N	P		33	13- 4
1927	STL	N	P		38	24-10
1928	STL	N	P		33	20- 8
1929	STL	N	P		28	13-10
1930	STL	N	P		29	13- 8
1931	STL	N	P		19	12- 3
1932	STL	N	P		20	3- 5
1933	STL	N	P	32	33	9- 6
1934	STL	N	P		37	4- 4
1935	STL	N	P		36	6- 5
1936	STL	N	P		25	7- 5
1937	STL	N	P		16	3- 3
	BRTR			555	560	210-158
						.186

HAIRSTON, JERRY WAYNE
B.FEB.16,1952 BIRMINGHAM,ALA.

1973	CHI	A	O-1		60	.271
1974	CHI	A	U-O		45	.229
1975	CHI	A	O		69	.283
1976	CHI	A	C		44	.227
1977	CHI	A	O		13	.308
	PIT	N	C/2		51	.192
	BBTR				282	.257

HAIRSTON, JOHN LOUIS (JOHNNY)
B.AUG.29,1945 BIRMINGHAM,ALA.

| 1969 | CHI | N | /C-O | | 3 | .250 |
| | BRTR | | | | | |

HAIRSTON, SAMUEL (SAMMY)
B.JAN.28,1920 CRAWFORD,MISS.

| 1951 | CHI | A | C | | 4 | .400 |
| | BRTR | | | | | |

HAISLIP, JAMES CLIFTON (SLIM)
B.AUG.4,1891 FARMERSVILLE,TEX.
D.JAN.22,1970 DALLAS,TEX.

| 1913 | PHI | N | P | | 1 | 0- 0 |
| | BRTR | | | | | |

HAJDUK, CHESTER
B.JULY 21,1918 CHICAGO,ILL.

| 1941 | CHI | A | H | | 1 | .000 |
| | BRTR | | | | | |

HALAS, GEORGE STANLEY
B.FEB.2,1895 CHICAGO,ILL.

| 1919 | NY | A | O | | 12 | .091 |
| | BBTR | | | | | |

HALBRITER, EDWARD C.
B.AUBURN,N.Y.

| 1882 | ATH | AA | P | | . | 0- 1 |

HALDEMAN, JOHN AVERY
B.JAN.21,1855 PEE WEE VALLEY,KY.
D.SEPT.17,1899 LOUISVILLE,KY.

| 1877 | LOU | N | 2 | | 1 | .000 |
| | BLTR | | | | | |

HALE, ARVEL ODELL
(ODELL) OR (BAD NEWS)
B.AUG.10,1908 HOSSTON,LA.

1931	CLE	A	2-3		25	.283
1933	CLE	A	2-3		98	.276
1934	CLE	A	2-3		143	.302
1935	CLE	A	2-3		150	.304
1936	CLE	A	3		153	.316
1937	CLE	A	2-3		154	.267
1938	CLE	A	2		130	.278
1939	CLE	A	2		108	.312
1940	CLE	A	3		48	.220
1941	BOS	A	2-3		12	.206
	NY	N	2		41	.196
	BRTR				1062	.289

HALE, GEORGE WAGNER (DUCKY)
B.AUG.3,1894 DEXTER,KAN.
D.NOV.14,1945 WICHITA,KAN.

1914	STL	A	C		5	.271
1916	STL	A	O		4	.000
1917	STL	A	C		38	.197
1918	STL	A	C		12	.133
	BRTR				59	.184

```
YR  CL LEA POS    GP   G   REC        YR  CL LEA POS    GP   G   REC        YR  CL LEA POS    GP   G   REC

HALE, JOHN STEVEN                     HALL, HERBERT SILAS (IRON DUKE)       HALL, TOM EDWARD
B.AUG.5,1953 FRESNO,CAL.              B.JUNE 5,1893 STEELVILLE,ILL.         B.NOV.23,1947 THOMASVILLE,N.C.
1974 LA  N /O         4  1.000        D.JULY 1,1970 FRESNO,CAL.             1968 MIN A /P     8   11  2- 1
1975 LA  N  O        71   .211        1918 DET A  O     3   .000            1969 MIN A  P    31   32  8- 7
1976 LA  N  O        44   .154              BBTR                            1970 MIN A  P    52   53 11- 6
1977 LA  N  O        79   .241                                             1971 MIN A  P    48   49  4- 7
1978 SEA A  O       107   .171                                             1972 CIN N  P         47 10- 1
      BLTR          305   .199        HALL, IRVIN GLADSTONE                 1973 CIN N  P    54   55  8- 5
                                      B.OCT.7,1918 ALBERTON,MD.             1974 CIN N  P         40  3- 1
                                      1943 PHI A  2-S-3  151  .256          1975 CIN N /P          2  0- 0
HALE, RAY LUTHER (DAD)                1944 PHI A  1-2-S  143  .268                NY  N  P    34   35  4- 3
B.FEB.18,1879 ALLEGAN,MICH.           1945 PHI A  2      151  .261          1976 NY  N  P          5  1- 1
D.FEB.1,1946 ALLEGAN,MICH.            1946 PHI A  2-S     63  .249          1976 KC  A  P    31   33  1- 1
1902 BOS N  P     8  0- 3                   BRTR         508  .261          1977 KC  A /P          6  0- 0
      BAL A  P    3  0- 1                                                         BLTL      358  368 52-35
      BRTR       11  0- 4
                                      HALL, JAMES
                                      D.JAN.30,1886 BROOKLYN,N.Y.           HALL, WILLIAM BERNARD
HALE, ROBERT HOUSTON (BOB)            1872 ATL NA 2-O   13  .246            B.FEB.22,1892 CHARLESTON,W.VA.
B.NOV.7,1933 SARASOTA,FLA.            1874 ATL NA 2      2   -              1913 BRO N  P     3  0- 0
1955 BAL A  1    67  .357             1875 WES NA O      1   -                    BRTR
1956 BAL A  1    85  .237                               16   -
1957 BAL A  1    42  .250
1958 BAL A  1    19  .350                                                   HALL, WILLIAM LEMUEL (BILL)
1959 BAL A  1    40  .185             HALL, JIMMIE RANDOLPH                 B.JULY 30,1928 MOULTRIE,GA.
1960 CLE A  1    70  .360             B.MAR.4,7,1938 MT.HOLLY,N.C.          1954 PIT N  C     5  .000
1961 CLE A  H    42  .167             1963 MIN A  O    156  .260            1956 PIT N  C     1  .000
      NY  A  1   11  .154             1964 MIN A  O    149  .282            1958 PIT N  C    51  .284
      BLTL      376  .273             1965 MIN A  *O   148  .285                  BLTR       57  .262
                                      1966 MIN A  *O   120  .239
                                      1967 CAL A  *O   129  .249
HALE, SAMUEL DOUGLAS                  1968 CAL A  O     46  .214            HALLA, JOHN ARTHUR
B.SEPT.10,1896 GLEN ROSE,TEX.               CLE A  O     53  .198           B.MAY 13,1884 ST.LOUIS,MO.
D.SEPT.6,1974 WHEELER,TEX.            1969 CLE A  /O      4  .000           D.SEPT.30,1947 EL SEGUNDO,CAL.
1920 DET A  3-O   76  .293                  NY  A  O/1   80  .236           1905 CLE A  P     3  0- 1
1921 DET A  O      9  .000                  CHI N  /O    11  .208                 BLTL
1923 PHI A  3    115  .288            1970 CHI N  /O    28  .094
1924 PHI A  3     80  .318                  ATL N  O     39  .213
1925 PHI A  2-3  110  .345                  BLTR        963  .254           HALLAHAN, WILLIAM ANTHONY
1926 PHI A  3    111  .281                                                  (WILD BILL)
1927 PHI A  3    131  .313                                                  B.AUG.4,1902 BINGHAMTON,N.Y.
1928 PHI A  3     88  .309            HALL, JOHN SYLVESTER                  1925 STL N  P     6   1- 0
1929 PHI A  3    101  .277            B.JAN.9,1924 MUSKOGEE,OKLA.           1926 STL N  P    19   1- 4
1930 STL A  3     62  .274            1948 BRO N  P     3  0- 0             1929 STL N  P    20   4- 4
      BRTR       883  .302                  BRTR                            1930 STL N  P    35  15- 9
                                                                           1931 STL N  P    37  .9- 9
                                                                           1932 STL N  P    25   28 12- 7
HALEY, FRED                           HALL, MARCUS                          1933 STL N  P    36   37 16-13
B.WHEELING,W.VA.                      B.AUG.12,1887 JOPLIN,MO.              1934 STL N  P    32   8-12
1880 TRO N  C     2  .000             D.FEB.24,1915 JOPLIN,MO.              1935 STL N  P    40  15- 8
                                      1910 STL A  P     8  1- 7             1936 STL N  P     9   2- 2
                                      1913 DET A  P    30  9-12                   CIN N  P    23   5- 9
HALEY, RAYMOND TIMOTHY (PAT)          1914 DET A  P    25  4- 6             1937 CIN N  P    21   3- 0
B.JAN.23,1891 DANBURY,IOWA                            63  14-25            1938 PHI N  P    21   1- 6
D.OCT.8,1973 BRADENTON,FLA.                                                      BRTL      324  328 102-94
1915 BOS A  C     5  .143
1916 BOS A  C     1  .000             HALL, RICHARD WALLACE (DICK)
      PHI A  C    34  .220            B.SEP.27,1930 ST.LOUIS,MO.            HALLER, THOMAS FRANK (TOM)
1917 PHI A  C    41  .276             1952 PIT N  3-O   26  .138            B.JUNE 23,1937 LOCKPORT,ILL.
      BRTR       81  .250             1953 PIT N  2      7  .167            1961 SF  N  C     30  .145
                                      1954 PIT N  O    112  .239            1962 SF  N  C     99  .261
                                      1955 PIT N  P-O  15   21  6- 6        1963 SF  N  C-O   98  .255
HALICKI, EDWARD LOUIS (ED)            1956 PIT N  P-1  19   33  0- 7        1964 SF  N  C-O  117  .253
B.OCT.4,1950 KEARNY,N.J.                                      .345         1965 SF  N  *C   134  .251
1974 SF  N  P    16  1- 8             1957 PIT N  P     8   10  0- 0        1966 SF  N  *C/1 142  .240
1975 SF  N  P    24  9-13             1959 PIT N  P          2  0- 0        1967 SF  N  *C/O 141  .251
1976 SF  N  P    32  12-14            1960 KC  A  P    29   32  8-13        1968 LA  N  *C   144  .285
1977 SF  N  P    37  16-12            1961 BAL A  P    29   30  7- 5        1969 LA  N  *C   134  .263
1978 SF  N  P    29  9-10             1962 BAL A  P    43   44  6- 6        1970 LA  N  *C   112  .286
      BRTR      138  47-57            1963 BAL A  P    47   48  5- 5        1971 LA  N  C     84  .267
                                      1964 BAL A  P         45  9- 1        1972 DET A  C     59  .207
                                      1965 BAL A  P    48   44 11- 8              BLTR      1294  .257
HALL, ARCHIBALD W. (AL)               1966 BAL A  P         32  6- 2
B.WORCESTER,MASS.                     1967 PHI N  P    48  10- 8
D.FEB.10,1885 WARREN,PA.              1968 PHI N  P    32   4- 1            HALLETT, JACK PRICE
1879 TRO N  O    66  .255             1969 BAL A  P    39   5- 2            B.NOV.13,1913 TOLEDO,OHIO
1880 CLE N  O     2  .25              1970 BAL A  P    32  10- 5            1940 CHI A  P     2  1- 1
                 68  .252             1971 BAL A  P    27   6- 6            1941 CHI A  ?    22  5- 5
                                            BRTR      495  669 93-75        1942 PIT N  P     3  0- 1
                                                              .210         1943 PIT N  P     9  1- 2
HALL, CHARLES LOUIS (SEA LION)                                             1946 PIT N  P    35  5- 7
(REAL NAME CARLOS CLOLO)                                                   1948 NY  N  P     2  0- 0
B.JULY 27,1885 VENTURA,CAL.           HALL, ROBERT LEWIS (BOB)                   BRTR       73  12-16
D.DEC.6,1943 VENTURA,CAL.             B.DEC.22,1923 SWISSVALE,PA.
1906 CIN N  P    16  3- 6             1949 BOS N  P    31  6- 4
1907 CIN N  P    12  4- 3             1950 BOS N  P    21  0- 2             HALLIDAY, NEWTON
1909 BOS A  P    11  6- 4             1953 PIT N  P    37  3-12             B.1897 CHICAGO,ILL.
1910 BOS A  P    35   47  12- 9             BRTR       89  9-18             1916 PIT N  1     1  .000
1911 BOS A  P    32   39   8- 7                                                  BRTR
1912 BOS A  P         34  15- 8
1913 BOS A  P         35   4- 4       HALL, ROBERT PRILL
1916 STL N  P         10   0- 4       B.DEC.20,1878 BALTIMORE,MD.           HALLIGAN, WILLIAM E. (JOCKO)
1918 DET A  P          6   0- 1       D.DEC.1,1950 WELLESLEY,MASS.          B.DEC.8,1868 AVON,N.Y.
      BLTR      191  210  52-46       1904 PHI N  S-3  46  .160             D.FEB.13,1945 BUFFALO,N.Y.
                                      1905 NY  N  O     1  .333             1890 BUF P  C-O   53  .268
                                            BRO N  O    52  .236            1891 CIN N  O     61  .311
HALL, CHARLES W. (DOC)                      TR          99  .203            1892 CIN N  1-O   26  .287
1887 MET AA O     3  .214                                                        BAL N  1-O   44  .269
                                                                                            184  .287
                                      HALL, ROBERT RUSSELL (RUSS)
HALL, GEORGE W.                       B.SEPT.29,1871 SHELBYVILLE,KY.
B.1849 BROOKLYN,N.Y.                  D.JULY 1,1937 LOS ANGELES,CAL.        HALLINAN, EDWARD S.
1871 OLY NA O    32   -               1898 STL N  S    39  .252             B.AUG.23,1888 SAN FRANCISCO,CAL
1872 BAL NA 1-O  54  .300             1901 CLE A  S     1  .500             D.AUG.24,1940 SAN FRANCISCO,CAL
1873 BAL NA O    35   -                     TR          40  .259            1911 STL A  2-S   52  .207
1874 BOS NA O    47  .321                                                  1912 STL A  S     27  .221
1875 ATH N  O    77  .298                                                        BRTR        79  .212
1876 ATH N  O    60  .355
1877 LOU N  O    61  .322
      BL        366   -


HALL, HERBERT ERNEST (BERT)
B.OCT.15,1888 PORTLAND,ORE.
D.JUNE 18,1948 SEATTLE,WASH.
1911 PHI N  P     7  0- 1
      BRTR
```

HALLINAN, JAMES H.
B.MAY 27,1849 IRELAND
D.OCT.28,1879 CHICAGO,ILL.

YR	CL	LEA	POS	GP	G	REC
1871	KEK	NA	S	5		-
1875	WES	NA	S	13		-
	MUT	NA	2-S-3	44		-
1876	MUT	N	S	54		.277
1877	CIN	N	2	16		.370
	CHI	N	O	19		.281
1878	CHI	N	2-O	15		.231
	IND	N	O	3		.250
	BLTL			169		-

HALLMAN, WILLIAM HARRY
B.MAR.15,1876 PHILADELPHIA,PA.
D.APR.23,1950 PHILADELPHIA,PA.

YR	CL	LEA	POS	GP	G	REC
1901	MIL	A	O	139		.256
1903	CHI	A	O	64		.213
1906	PIT	N	O	23		.270
1907	PIT	N	O	84		.222
				310		.240

HALLMAN, WILLIAM WILSON (BILL)
B.MAR.31,1867 PITTSBURGH,PA.
D.SEPT.11,1920 PHILADELPHIA,PA.

YR	CL	LEA	POS	GP	G	REC
1888	PHI	N	2	16		.206
1889	PHI	N	S	119		.253
1890	PHI	P	C-2-3-O	85		.278
1891	ATH	AA	2	140		.288
1892	PHI	N	2	136		.292
1893	PHI	N	2	132		.328
1894	PHI	N	2	119		.327
1895	PHI	N	2	124		.315
1896	PHI	N	2	120		.318
1897	PHI	N	2	31		.248
	STL	N	M-2	81		.252
1898	BRO	N	2	133		.245
1901	CLE	A	S	5		.211
	PHI	N	2-3	122		.194
1902	PHI	N	3	73		.245
1903	PHI	N	2-3	57		.212
	BRTR			1493		.276

HALLSTROM, CHARLES E.
B.CHICAGO,ILL.

YR	CL	LEA	POS	GP	G	REC
1885	PRO	N	P	1		0- 1

HALPIN, JAMES NATHANIEL
B.OCT.4,1863 ENGLAND
D.JAN.4,1893 BOSTON,MASS.

YR	CL	LEA	POS	GP	G	REC
1882	WOR	N	3	2		.000
1884	WAS	U	S	44		.182
1885	DET	N	S	15		.129
				61		.163

HALT, ALVA WILLIAM
B.NOV.23,1890 SANDUSKY,OHIO
D.JAN.22,1973 SANDUSKY,OHIO

YR	CL	LEA	POS	GP	G	REC
1914	BRO	F	S	80		.235
1915	BRO	F	S-3	151		.245
1918	CLE	A	3	26		.174
	BRTR			257		.237

HAM, RALPH A.
B.1850 TROY,N.Y.
D.FEB.13,1905

YR	CL	LEA	POS	GP	G	REC
1871	ROK	NA	S-3-O	25		-
1872	MAN	NA	S	1		.333
				26		-

HAMANN, ELMER JOSEPH (DOC)
B.DEC.21,1900 NEW ULM,MINN.
D.JAN.11,1973 MILWAUKEE,WIS.

YR	CL	LEA	POS	GP	G	REC
1922	CLE	A	P	1		0- 0
	BRTR					

HAMBRICK, CHARLES H.
[PLAYED UNDER NAME OF
CHARLES H. HAMBURG]

HAMBRIGHT, ROGER DEE
B.MAR.26,1949 SUNNYSIDE,WASH.

YR	CL	LEA	POS	GP	G	REC
1971	NY	A	P	18		3- 1
	BRTR					

HAMBURG, CHARLES M.
[REAL NAME CHARLES H. HAMBRICK]
B.NOV.22,1863 LOUISVILLE,KY.

YR	CL	LEA	POS	GP	G	REC
1890	LOU	AA	O	134		.265

HAMBY, JAMES SANFORD (CRACKER)
B.JULY 29,1897 WILKESBORO,N.C.

YR	CL	LEA	POS	GP	G	REC
1926	NY	N	C	1		.000
1927	NY	N	2	21		.192
	BRTR			22		.182

HAMILL, JOHN ALEXANDER CHARLES
B.DEC.18,1860 NEW YORK,N.Y.
D.DEC.6,1911 BRISTOL,R.I.

YR	CL	LEA	POS	GP	G	REC
1884	WAS	AA	P	18	21	2-16
	BRTR					

HAMILTON, DAVID EDWARD (DAVE)
B.DEC.13,1947 SEATTLE,WASH.

YR	CL	LEA	POS	GP	G	REC
1972	OAK	A	P	25		6- 6
1973	OAK	A	P	16		6- 4
1974	OAK	A	P	29		7- 4
1975	OAK	A	P	11		1- 2
	CHI	A	P	30		6- 5
1976	CHI	A	P	45		6- 6
1977	CHI	A	P	55		4- 5
1978	STL	N	P	13		0- 0
	PIT	N	P	16		0- 2
	BLTL			240		36-34

HAMILTON, EARL ANDREW
B.JULY 19,1891 GIBSON,ILL.
D.NOV.17,1968 ANAHEIM,CAL.

YR	CL	LEA	POS	GP	G	REC
1911	STL	A	P	32		5-12
1912	STL	A	P	41		11-14
1913	STL	A	P	31		13-12
1914	STL	A	P	44		16-18
1915	STL	A	P	35		9-17
1916	STL	A	P	1		0- 0
	DET	A	P	5		2- 3
	STL	A	P	19		4- 6
1917	STL	A	P	27		0- 9
1918	PIT	N	P	6		0- 0
1919	PIT	N	P	28		8-11
1920	PIT	N	P	39		10-13
1921	PIT	N	P	35		13-15
1922	PIT	N	P	33		11- 7
1923	PIT	N	P	28		7- 9
1924	PHI	N	P	3		0- 1
	BLTL			407		115-147

HAMILTON, JACK EDWIN
B.DEC.25,1938 BURLINGTON,IOWA

YR	CL	LEA	POS	GP	G	REC
1962	PHI	N	P	41		9-12
1963	PHI	N	P	19		2- 1
1964	DET	A	P	5		0- 1
1965	DET	A	/P	4		1- 1
1966	NY	N	P	57		6-13
1967	NY	N	P	17		2- 0
	CAL	A	P	26		9- 6
1968	CAL	A	P	21		3- 1
1969	CAL	A	P	20		0- 2
	CHI	A	/P	8		0- 3
	BRTR			218		32-40

HAMILTON, STEVEN ABSHER (STEVE)
B.NOV.30,1935 COLUMBIA,KY.

YR	CL	LEA	POS	GP	G	REC
1961	CLE	A	P	2		0- 0
1962	WAS	A	P	41	43	3- 8
1963	WAS	A	P	3		0- 1
	NY	A	P	34		5- 1
1964	NY	A	P	30	32	7- 2
1965	NY	A	P	46		3- 1
1966	NY	A	P	44		8- 3
1967	NY	A	P	44		2- 4
1968	NY	A	P	40		2- 2
1969	NY	A	P	38		3- 4
1970	NY	A	P	35		4- 3
	CHI	A	/P	3		0- 0
1971	SF	N	P	39		2- 2
1972	CHI	N	P	22		1- 0
	BLTL			421	425	40-31

HAMILTON, THOMAS BALL (TOM) OR (HAM)
B.SEPT.29,1925 ALTOONA,KAN.
D.NOV.29,1973 TYLER,TEX.

YR	CL	LEA	POS	GP	G	REC
1952	PHI	A	1	9		.200
1953	PHI	A	1-O	58		.196
	BLTR			67		.197

HAMILTON, WILLIAM ROBERT
(SLIDING BILLY)
B.FEB.16,1866 NEWARK,N.J.
D.DEC.16,1940 WORCESTER,MASS.

YR	CL	LEA	POS	GP	G	REC
1888	KC	AA	O	35		.250
1889	KC	AA	O	137		.301
1890	PHI	N	O	123		.324
1891	PHI	N	O	133		.388
1892	PHI	N	O	136		.330
1893	PHI	N	O	82		.395
1894	PHI	N	O	131		.399
1895	PHI	N	O	121		.393
1896	BOS	N	O	131		.363
1897	BOS	N	O	125		.344
1898	BOS	N	O	109		.367
1899	BOS	N	O	81		.306
1900	BOS	N	O	135		.332
1901	BOS	N	O	99		.292
	BLTR			1578		.344

HAMLIN, KENNETH LEE (KEN)
B.MAY 18,1935 DETROIT,MICH.

YR	CL	LEA	POS	GP	G	REC
1957	PIT	N	S	2		.000
1959	PIT	N	S	3		.125
1960	KC	A	S	140		.224
1961	LA	A	S	42		.209
1962	WAS	A	2-S	98		.253
1965	WAS	A	2-S/3	117		.273
1966	WAS	A	2/3	66		.215
	BRTR			468		.241

HAMLIN, LUKE DANIEL
(LUKE) OR (HOT POTATO)
B.JULY 3,1904 FERRIS CENTER,MICH.
D.FEB.18,1978 CLARE,MICH.

YR	CL	LEA	POS	GP	G	REC
1933	DET	A	P	3		1- 0
1934	DET	A	P	20		2- 3
1937	BRO	N	P	39	41	11-13
1938	BRO	N	P	44		12-15
1939	BRO	N	P	40		20-13
1940	BRO	N	P	33	35	9- 8
1941	BRO	N	P	30		8- 8
1942	PIT	N	P	23		4- 4
1944	PHI	A	P	29		6-12
	BLTR			261	265	73-76

HAMM, PETER WHITFIELD (PETE)
B.SEP.20,1947 BUFFALO,N.Y.

YR	CL	LEA	POS	GP	G	REC
1970	MIN	A	P	10		0- 2
1971	MIN	A	P	13		2- 4
	BRTR			23		2- 6

HAMMOND, WALTER CHARLES
B.FEB.26,1891 AMSTERDAM,N.Y.
D.MAR.4,1942 KENOSHA,WIS.

YR	CL	LEA	POS	GP	G	REC
1915	CLE	A	2	35		.214
1922	CLE	A	2	1		.250
	PIT	N	2	9		.276
	BRTR			45		.232

HAMNER, GRANVILLE WILBUR (GRANNY)
B.APR.26,1927 RICHMOND,VA.

YR	CL	LEA	POS	GP	G	REC
1944	PHI	N	S	21		.247
1945	PHI	N	S	14		.171
1946	PHI	N	S	2		.143
1947	PHI	N	S	3		.286
1948	PHI	N	2-S-3	129		.260
1949	PHI	N	S	154		.263
1950	PHI	N	S	157		.270
1951	PHI	N	S	150		.255
1952	PHI	N	S	151		.275
1953	PHI	N	2-S	154		.276
1954	PHI	N	2-S	152		.299
1955	PHI	N	2-S	104		.257
1956	PHI	N	P-2-S	3	122	0- 1 / .224
1957	PHI	N	P-2-S	1	133	0- 0 / .227
1958	PHI	N	2-S-3	35		.301
1959	PHI	N	S-3	21		.297
	CLE	A	2-S-3	27		.164
1962	KC	A	P	3		0- 1
	BRTR			7	1531	0- 2 / .262

HAMNER, RALPH CONANT (BRUZ)
B.SEPT.12,1916 GIBSLAND,LA.

YR	CL	LEA	POS	GP	G	REC
1946	CHI	A	P	25		2- 7
1947	CHI	N	P	3		1- 2
1948	CHI	N	P.	27		5- 9
1949	CHI	N	P	6		0- 2
	BRTR			61		8-20

HAMNER, WESLEY GARVIN
B.MAR.18,1924 RICHMOND,VA.

YR	CL	LEA	POS	GP	G	REC
1945	PHI	N	2-S-3	32		.198
	BRTR					

HAMPTON, ISAAC BERNARD (IKE)
B.AUG.22,1951 CAMDEN,S.C.

YR	CL	LEA	POS	GP	G	REC
1974	NY	N	/C	4		.000
1975	CAL	A	C/S-3	31		.152
1976	CAL	A	/C-S	3		.000
1977	CAL	A	C	52		.295
1978	CAL	A	C/1	19		.214
	BBTR			109		.200

HAMRIC, ODBERT HERMAN (BERT)
B.MAR.1,1928 CLARKSBURG,W.VA.

YR	CL	LEA	POS	GP	G	REC
1955	BRO	N	H	2		.000
1958	BAL	A	H	8		.125
	BLTR			10		.111

HAMRICK, RAYMOND BERNARD
B.AUG.1,1921 NASHVILLE,TENN.

YR	CL	LEA	POS	GP	G	REC
1943	PHI	N	2-S	44		.200
1944	PHI	N	S	74		.205
	BRTR			118		.204

HANCKEN, MORRIS MEDLOCK (BUDDY)
B.AUG.30,1914 BIRMINGHAM,ALA.

YR	CL	LEA	POS	GP	G	REC
1940	PHI	A	C	1		.000
	BRTR					

HANCOCK, FRED JAMES
B.MAR.28,1920 ALLENPORT,PA.

YR	CL	LEA	POS	GP	G	REC
1949	CHI	A	S-3-O	39		.135
	BRTR					

HANCOCK, RONALD GARRY (GARRY)
B.JAN.23,1954 TAMPA,FLA.

YR	CL	LEA	POS	GP	G	REC
1978	BOS	A	O-D	38		.225
	BLTL					

YR	CL LEA POS	GP	G	REC

HAND, RICHARD ALLEN (RICH)
B.JULY 10,1948 BELLEVUE,WASH.

YR	CL LEA POS	GP	G	REC
1970	CLE A P		35	6-13
1971	CLE A P	19	16	2- 6
1972	TEX A P		30	10-14
1973	TEX A /P		8	2- 3
1973	CAL A P		16	4- 3
	BRTR	104	105	24-39

HANDIBOE, ALOYSIUS JAMES
(COALYARD MIKE)
B.JULY 21,1887 WASHINGTON,D.C.
D.JAN.31,1953 SAVANNAH,GA.

1911	NY A O		5	.067
	BLTL			

HANDIBOE, JAMES EDWARD (NICK)
B.JULY 17,1866 COLUMBUS,OHIO
D.NOV.8,1942 COLUMBUS,OHIO

1886	PIT AA P-O		14	7- 7
				.114
	BRTR			

HANDLEY, EUGENE LOUIS (GENE)
B.NOV.25,1914 KENNETT,MO.

1946	PHI A 2-S-3		89	.251
1947	PHI A 2-S-3		36	.256
	BRTR	125		.252

HANDLEY, LEE ELMER (JEEP)
B.JULY 31,1913 CLARION,IOWA
D.APR.8,1970 PITTSBURGH,PA.

1936	CIN N 2		24	.308
1937	PIT N 2		127	.250
1938	PIT N 3		139	.268
1939	PIT N 3		101	.265
1940	PIT N 2-3		98	.281
1941	PIT N 3		124	.288
1944	PIT N 2-S-3		40	.221
1945	PIT N 3		98	.298
1946	PIT N 2-3		116	.238
1947	PHI N 2-S-3		101	.253
	BRTR		968	.269

HANDRAHAN, JAMES VERNON (VERN)
B.NOV.27,1938 CHARLOTTETOWN,
P.E.I.,CANADA

1964	KC A P		18	0- 1
1966	KC A P		16	0- 1
	BLTR		34	0- 2

HANDS, WILLIAM ALFRED (BILL)
B.MAY.6,1940 HACKENSACK,N.J.

1965	SF N /P		4	0- 2
1966	CHI N P		41	8-13
1967	CHI N P		49	7- 8
1968	CHI N P		38	16-10
1969	CHI N P		41	20-14
1970	CHI N P		39	18-15
1971	CHI N P		36	12-18
1972	CHI N P		32	11- 8
1973	MIN A P		39	7-10
1974	MIN A P		35	4- 5
	TEX A /P		2	0- 0
1975	TEX A P		18	6- 7
	BRTR		374	111-110

HANEBRINK, HARRY ALOYSIUS
B.NOV.12,1927 ST.LOUIS,MO.

1953	MIL N 2-3		51	.238
1957	MIL N 3		6	.286
1958	MIL N 3-O		63	.188
1959	PHI N 2-3-O		57	.258
	BLTR		177	.224

HANEY, FRED GIRARD (PUDGE)
B.APR.25,1896 ALBUQUERQUE,N.MEX
D.NOV.9,1977 BEVERLY HILLS,CAL.

1922	DET A 1-3		81	.352
1923	DET A 2-S-3		142	.282
1924	DET A 3		86	.309
1925	DET A 3		114	.279
1926	BOS A 3		138	.221
1927	BOS A 3		47	.276
	CHI N H		4	.000
1929	STL N 3		10	.115
	BRTR		622	.275

NON-PLAYING MANAGER
STL(A) 1939-41, PIT(N) 1953-55,
MIL(N) 1956-59

HANEY, WALLACE LARRY (LARRY)
B.NOV.19,1942 CHARLOTTESVILLE,VA

1966	BAL A C		20	.161
1967	BAL A C		58	.268
1968	BAL A C		38	.236
1969	SEA A C		22	.254
	OAK A C		53	.151
1970	OAK A /C		2	.000
1972	OAK A /C-2		5	.000
1973	OAK A C		2	.500
	STL N /C		2	.000
1974	OAK A C/3-1		76	.165
1975	OAK A C/3		47	.192
1976	OAK A C		88	.226
1977	MIL A C		63	.228
1978	MIL A /C		4	.200
	BRTR		480	.215

HANFORD, CHARLES JOSEPH
B.JUNE 3,1881 TUNSTALL,ENGLAND
D.JULY 19,1963 TRENTON,N.J.

1914	BUF F O		156	.287
1915	CHI F O		74	.239
	BRTR		230	.276

HANIFIN, PATRICK JAMES
B.1868 NOVA SCOTIA,CANADA
D.NOV.5,1908 SPRINGFIELD,MASS.

1897	BRO N O		9	.200

HANKINS, DONALD WAYNE
B.FEB.9,1902 PENDLETON,IND.
D.MAY 16,1963 WINSTON-SALEM,N.C

1927	DET A P		20	2- 1
	BRTR			

HANKINS, JAY NELSON
B.NOV.7,1935 ST.LOUIS CO.,MO.

1961	KC A O		76	.185
1963	KC A O		10	.176
	BLTR		86	.184

HANKINSON, FRANK EDWARD
B.APR.29,1856 NEW YORK,N.Y.
D.APR.5,1911 PALISADES PARK,N.J

1878	CHI N P-3	1	57	0- 1
				.268
1879	CHI N P-O	24	41	14- 9
				.183
1880	CLE N P-3-	2	68	1- 1
	O			.209
1881	TRO N S-3		84	.196
1883	NY N 3		91	.221
1884	NY N 3		101	.255
1885	MET AA 3		96	.241
1886	MET AA 3		136	.240
1887	MET AA 3		127	.315
1888	KC AA 2		37	.175
	BRTR	27	838	15-11
				.239

HANLEY, JAMES PATRICK
B.OCT.13,1889 PROVIDENCE,R.I.
D.MAY 1,1961 ELMHURST,N.J.

1913	NY A P	1	0- 0
	TL		

HANLON, EDWARD HUGH (NED)
B.AUG.22,1857 MONTVILLE,CONN.
D.APR.14,1937 BALTIMORE,MD.

1880	CLE N S-3-O		72	.247
1881	DET N 3-O		75	.278
1882	DET N 3-O		79	.236
1883	DET N 2-O		97	.245
1884	DET N O		112	.268
1885	DET N 3-O		106	.301
1886	DET N O		126	.234
1887	DET N O		118	.316
1888	DET N O		108	.265
1889	PIT N M-O		115	.238
1890	PIT P M-O		119	.284
1891	PIT N M-O		115	.274
1892	BAL N M-O		8	.233
	BL		1250	.266

NON-PLAYING MANAGER
BAL(N)1893-98, BRO(N)1899-1905,
CIN(N) 1906-07

HANLON, WILLIAM (BIG BILL)
B.CALIFORNIA
D.MAR.18,1951 SACRAMENTO,CAL.

1903	CHI N 1		8	.045

HANNA, JOHN
B.PHILADELPHIA,PA.

1884	WAS AA C-O		24	.113
	RIC AA C-S		22	.206
			46	.162

HANNA, PRESTON LEE
B.SEPT.10,1954 PENSACOLA,FLA.

1975	ATL N /P		9	0- 0
1976	ATL N /P		5	0- 0
1977	ATL N P		17	2- 6
1978	ATL N P		29	7- 9
	BRTR		55	9-19

HANNAH, JAMES HARRISON (TRUCK)
B.JUNE 5,1891 LARIMORE,N.DAK.

1918	NY A C		90	.220
1919	NY A C		75	.238
1920	NY A C		79	.247
	BRTR		244	.235

HANNAHS, GERALD ELLIS (GERRY)
B.MAR.6,1953 BINGHAMTON,N.Y.

1976	MON N /P		3	2- 0
1977	MON N /P		8	1- 5
1978	LA N /P		1	0- 0
	BLTL		12	3- 5

HANNAN, JAMES JOHN (JIM)
B.JAN.7,1940 JERSEY CITY,N.J.

1962	WAS A P		42	2- 4
1963	WAS A P		13	2- 2
1964	WAS A P		49	4- 7
1965	WAS A /P		4	1- 1
1966	WAS A P		30	3- 9
1967	WAS A /P		8	1- 1
1968	WAS A P		25	10- 6
1969	WAS A P		35	7- 6
1970	WAS A P		42	9-11
1971	DET A P		7	1- 0
	MIL A P		21	1- 1
	BRTR		276	41-48

HANNIFIN, JOHN JOSEPH (JACK)
B.FEB.25,1883 HOLYOKE,MASS.
D.OCT.27,1945 NORTHAMPTON,MASS.

1906	PHI A H		1	.000
	NY N S-3		10	.200
1907	NY N 1-3		49	.228
1908	NY N 2		1	.000
	BOS N 3		79	.206
	BRTR		140	.214

HANNING, LOY VERNON
B.OCT.18,1917 BUNKER,MO.

1939	STL A P		4	0- 1
1942	STL A P		11	1- 1
	BRTR		15	1- 2

HANSEN, ANDREW VIGGO
(ANDY) OR (SWEDE)
B.NOV.12,1924 LAKE WORTH,FLA.

1944	NY N P	23	24	3- 3
1945	NY N P		23	4- 3
1947	NY N P		27	1- 5
1948	NY N P		36	5- 3
1949	NY N P		33	2- 6
1950	NY N P		31	0- 1
1951	PHI N P		24	3- 1
1952	PHI N P		43	5- 6
1953	PHI N P		30	0- 2
	BRTR	270	271	23-30

HANSEN, DOUGLAS WILLIAM
B.DEC.16,1926 LOS ANGELES,CAL.

1951	CLE A H		3	.000
	BRTR			

HANSEN, ROBERT JOSEPH (BOB)
B.MAY 26,1948 BOSTON,MASS.

1974	MIL A D/1		58	.295
1976	MIL A D/1		24	.164
	BLTL		82	.242

HANSEN, RONALD LAVERN (RON)
B.APR.5,1938 OXFORD,NEB.

1958	BAL A S		12	.000
1959	BAL A S		2	.000
1960	BAL A S		153	.255
1961	BAL A 2-S		155	.248
1962	BAL A S		71	.173
1963	CHI A S		144	.226
1964	CHI A S		158	.261
1965	CHI A *S/2		162	.235
1966	CHI A S		23	.176
1967	CHI A *S		157	.233
1968	WAS A S/3		86	.185
	CHI A 3/S-2		40	.230
1969	CHI A 2-1/S-3		85	.259
1970	NY A S-3/2		59	.297
1971	NY A 3/2-S		61	.207
1972	KC A /S-3-2		16	.133
	BRTR		1384	.234

HANSEN, ROY EMIL (SNIPE)
B.FEB.23,1907 CHICAGO,ILL.

1930	PHI N P		22	0- 7
1932	PHI N P		39	10-10
1933	PHI N P	32	33	6-14
1934	PHI N P		50	6-12
1935	PHI N P		2	0- 1
	STL A P		10	0- 1
	BBTL	155	156	22-45
	BL 1930			

HANSEN, ROY INGLOF (ING)
B.MAR.6,1898 BELOIT,WIS.
D.FEB.9,1977 BELOIT,WIS.

1918	WAS A P		5	1- 0
	BRTR			

HANSFORD, F. C.

1898	BRO N P		1	0- 1
	TL			

HANSKI, DONALD THOMAS
[REAL NAME DONALD THOMAS HANYZEWSKI]
B.FEB.27,1916 LAPORTE,IND.
D.SEPT.2,1957 WORTH,ILL.

1943	CHI A P-1	1	9	0- 0
				.238
1944	CHI A P		2	0- 0
	BLTL	3	11	0- 0
				.227

HANSON, EARL SYLVESTER (OLLIE)
B.JAN.19,1896 HOLBROOK,MASS.
D.AUG.19,1951 CLIFTON,N.J.

YR	CL	LEA	POS	GP	G	REC
1921	CHI	N	P		2	0- 2
		BRTR				

HANSON, JOSEPH
B.ST.LOUIS,MO.

YR	CL	LEA	POS	GP	G	REC
1913	NY	A	C		1	.000
		TR				

HANYZEWSKI, DONALD THOMAS
[PLAYED UNDER NAME OF
DONALD THOMAS HANSKI]

HANYZEWSKI, EDWARD MICHAEL
B.SEPT.18,1920 UNION MILLS,IND.

YR	CL	LEA	POS	GP	G	REC
1942	CHI	N	P		6	1- 1
1943	CHI	N	P		33	8- 7
1944	CHI	N	P		14	2- 5
1945	CHI	N	P		2	0- 0
1946	CHI	N	P		3	1- 0
		BRTR			58	12-13

HAPPENNY, JOHN CLIFFORD (CLIFF)
B.MAY 18,1901 WALT4AM,MASS.

YR	CL	LEA	POS	GP	G	REC
1923	CHI	A	2		32	.221
		BRTR				

**HARBIDGE, WILLIAM ARTHUR
(YALLER BILL)**
B.MAR.29,1855 PHILADELPHIA,PA.
D.MAR.17,1924 PHILADELPHIA,PA.

YR	CL	LEA	POS	GP	G	REC
1875	HAR	NA	C-1-2-0		50	-
1876	HAR	N	C-0		30	.211
1877	HAR	N	C-2-0		41	.222
1878	CHI	N	C-0		53	.298
1879	CHI	N	C-0		1	.000
1880	TRO	N	C-0		8	.370
1882	TRO	N	C-1-0		32	.187
1883	PHI	N	C-2-S-3-0		73	.221
1884	CIN	U	0		65	.271
		BLTL			353	-

**HARDER, MELVIN LEROY
(MEL) OR (CHIEF)**
B.OCT.15,1909 BEEMER,NEB.

YR	CL	LEA	POS	GP	G	REC
1928	CLE	A	P		23	0- 2
1929	CLE	A	P		11	1- 0
1930	CLE	A	P		36	11-10
1931	CLE	A	P		40	13-14
1932	CLE	A	P		39	15-13
1933	CLE	A	P	43	44	15-17
1934	CLE	A	P		44	20-12
1935	CLE	A	P		42	22-11
1936	CLE	A	P		36	15-15
1937	CLE	A	P		38	15-12
1938	CLE	A	P	38	39	17-10
1939	CLE	A	P		29	15- 9
1940	CLE	A	P		31	12-11
1941	CLE	A	P		15	5- 4
1942	CLE	A	P		29	13-14
1943	CLE	A	P		19	8- 7
1944	CLE	A	P		30	12-10
1945	CLE	A	P		11	3- 7
1946	CLE	A	P		13	5- 4
1947	CLE	A	P		15	6- 4
		BRTR		582	584	223-186

NON-PLAYING MANAGER CLE[A] 1961

HARDESTY, SCOTT D.
B.DAYTON,OHIO

YR	CL	LEA	POS	GP	G	REC
1899	NY	N	S		21	.228

HARDIE, LEWIS W.
B.AUG.24,1864 NEW YORK,N.Y.

YR	CL	LEA	POS	GP	G	REC
1884	PHI	N	C		2	.143
1886	CHI	N	C		16	.176
1890	BOS	N	C-0		47	.227
1891	BAL	AA	0		15	.232
					80	.223

HARDIN, JAMES WARREN (JIM)
B.AUG.6,1943 MORRIS CHAPEL,TENN.

YR	CL	LEA	POS	GP	G	REC
1967	BAL	A	P		19	8- 3
1968	BAL	A	P		35	18-13
1969	BAL	A	P		30	6- 7
1970	BAL	A	P		36	6- 5
1971	BAL	A	/P		6	0- 0
	NY	A	P		12	0- 2
1972	ATL	N	P		26	5- 2
		BRTR			164	43-32

HARDIN, WILLIAM EDGAR (BUD)
B.JUNE 14,1922 SHELBY,N.C.

YR	CL	LEA	POS	GP	G	REC
1952	CHI	N	2-S		3	.143
		BRTR				

HARDING, CHARLES HAROLD (SLIM)
B.JAN.3,1891 NASHVILLE,TENN.
D.OCT.30,1971 BOLD SRPINGS,TENN

YR	CL	LEA	POS	GP	G	REC
1913	DET	A	P		1	0- 0
		BRTR				

HARDING, LOUIS EDWARD (JUMBO)
B.SAN FRANCISCO,CAL.

YR	CL	LEA	POS	GP	G	REC
1886	STL	AA	C		1	.000

HARDY, CARROLL WILLIAM
B.MAY 18,1933 STURGIS,S.DAK.

YR	CL	LEA	POS	GP	G	REC
1958	CLE	A	0		27	.204
1959	CLE	A	0		32	.208
1960	CLE	A	0		29	.111
	BOS	A	0		73	.234
1961	BOS	A	0		85	.263
1962	BOS	A	0		115	.215
1963	HOU	N	0		15	.227
1964	HOU	N	0		46	.185
1967	MIN	A	/0		11	.375
		BRTR			433	.225

HARDY, DAVID ALEXANDER (DOONEY)
B.1877 TORONTO,ONT.,CANADA
D.APR.22,1940 TORONTO,ONT.,CAN.

YR	CL	LEA	POS	GP	G	REC
1902	CHI	N	P		4	2- 2
1903	CHI	N	P		3	1- 1
		TL			7	3- 3

HARDY, FRANCIS JOSEPH (RED)
B.JAN.16,1923 MARMARTH,N.DAK.

YR	CL	LEA	POS	GP	G	REC
1951	NY	N	P		2	0- 0
		BRTR				

HARDY, HARRY
B.NOV.5,1875 STEUBENVILLE,OHIO
D.SEPT.4,1944 STEUBENVILLE,OHIO

YR	CL	LEA	POS	GP	G	REC
1905	WAS	AA	P		8	3- 1
1906	WAS	A	P		5	0- 3
		BLTL			13	3- 4

HARDY, HOWARD LAWRENCE (LARRY)
B.JAN.10,1948 GOOSE CREEK,TEX.

YR	CL	LEA	POS	GP	G	REC
1974	SD	N	P		76	9- 4
1975	SD	N	/P		3	0- 0
1976	HOU	N	P		15	0- 0
		BRTR			94	9- 4

HARDY, JOHN DOOLITTLE
B.JUNE 23,1879 CLEVELAND,OHIO
D.OCT.20,1921 CLEVELAND,OHIO

YR	CL	LEA	POS	GP	G	REC
1903	CLE	A	0		5	.150
1907	CHI	N	C		1	.250
1909	WAS	A	C		10	.167
1910	WAS	A	C		7	.375
		TR			23	.196

HARGAN, STEVEN LOWELL (STEVE)
B.SEP.8,1942 FT.WAYNE,IND.

YR	CL	LEA	POS	GP	G	REC
1965	CLE	A	P		17	4- 3
1966	CLE	A	P		38	13-10
1967	CLE	A	P		30	14-13
1968	CLE	A	P		32	8-15
1969	CLE	A	P	32	34	5-14
1970	CLE	A	P	23	28	11- 3
1971	CLE	A	P		37	1-13
1972	CLE	A	P		12	0- 3
1974	TEX	A	P		37	12- 9
1975	TEX	A	P		33	9-10
1976	TEX	A	P		35	8- 8
1977	TOR	A	P		6	1- 3
	TEX	A	/P		6	1- 0
	ATL	N	P		16	0- 3
		BRTR		354	361	87-107

HARGRAVE, EUGENE FRANKLIN (BUBBLES)
B.JULY 15,1892 NEW HAVEN,IND.
D.FEB.23,1969 CINCINNATI,OHIO

YR	CL	LEA	POS	GP	G	REC
1913	CHI	N	C		3	.333
1914	CHI	N	C		23	.222
1915	CHI	N	C		15	.158
1921	CIN	N	C		93	.289
1922	CIN	N	C		98	.315
1923	CIN	N	C		118	.333
1924	CIN	N	C		98	.301
1925	CIN	N	C		87	.300
1926	CIN	N	C		105	.353
1927	CIN	N	C		102	.308
1928	CIN	N	C		65	.295
1930	NY	A	C		45	.278
		BRTR			652	.310

HARGRAVE, WILLIAM KC KINLEY (PINKY)
B.JAN.31,1896 NEW HAVEN,IND.
D.OCT.3,1942 FT.WAYNE,IND.

YR	CL	LEA	POS	GP	G	REC
1923	WAS	A	C		33	.288
1924	WAS	A	C		24	.152
1925	WAS	A	C		5	.333
	STL	A	C		67	.284
1926	STL	A	C		92	.281
1928	DET	A	C		121	.275
1929	DET	A	C		76	.330
1930	DET	A	C		55	.286
	WAS	A	C		10	.179
1931	WAS	N	C		40	.325
1932	BOS	N	C		82	.263
1933	BOS	N	C		45	.178
		BBTR			650	.278

BR 1923-26

HARGREAVES, CHARLES RUSSELL
B.DEC.14,1896 TRENTON,N.J.

YR	CL	LEA	POS	GP	G	REC
1923	BRO	N	C		20	.281
1924	BRO	N	C		15	.407
1925	BRO	N	C-1		45	.277
1926	BRO	N	C		85	.250
1927	BRO	N	C		46	.286
1928	BRO	N	C		20	.197
	PIT	N	C		79	.285
1929	PIT	N	C		102	.268
1930	PIT	N	C		11	.226
		BRTR			423	.270

HARGROVE, DUDLEY MICHAEL (MIKE)
B.OCT.26,1949 PERRYTON,TEX.

YR	CL	LEA	POS	GP	G	REC
1974	TEX	A	1-D/0		131	.323
1975	TEX	A	0-1-0		145	.303
1976	TEX	A	*1		7	.287
1977	TEX	A	*1		151	.305
1978	TEX	A	*1		146	.251
		BLTL			726	.293

HARGROVE, WILLIAM PATRICK (PAT)
B.MAY 10,1896 PALMYRA COURT
HOUSE,VA.

YR	CL	LEA	POS	GP	G	REC
1918	CHI	A	H		2	.000
		BRTR				

HARKINS, JOHN JOSEPH (PA)
B.APR.12,1859 NEW BRUNSWICK,N.J.
D.NOV.20,1940 NEW BRUNSWICK,N.J

YR	CL	LEA	POS	GP	G	REC
1884	CLE	N	P-S-	45	60	12-32
			3-0			.205
1885	BRO	AA	P		43	14-21
1886	BRO	AA	P-0	34	41	14-16
						.217
1887	BRO	AA	P		27	10-14
1888	BAL	AA	P		12	0- 1
		BRTR		150	172	50-84
						.235

HARKNESS, FREDERICK HARVEY (SPEC)
B.DEC.13,1887 LOS ANGELES,CAL.
D.MAY 16,1952 COMPTON,CAL.

YR	CL	LEA	POS	GP	G	REC
1910	CLE	A	P		26	10- 7
1911	CLE	A	P		12	2- 2
		BRTR			38	12- 9

HARKNESS, THOMAS WILLIAM (TIM)
B.DEC.23,1937 LACHINE,QUE.,CAN.

YR	CL	LEA	POS	GP	G	REC
1961	LA	N	1		5	.500
1962	LA	N	1		92	.258
1963	NY	N	1		123	.211
1964	NY	N	1		39	.282
		BLTL			259	.235

HARLEY, HENRY RISK (DICK)
B.AUG.18,1874 SPRINGFIELD,OHIO
D.MAY 16,1961 SPRINGFIELD,OHIO

YR	CL	LEA	POS	GP	G	REC
1905	BOS	N	P		7	2- 4
		BRTR				

HARLEY, RICHARD JOSEPH
B.SEPT.25,1872 PHILADELPHIA,PA.
D.APR.3,1952 PHILADELPHIA,PA.

YR	CL	LEA	POS	GP	G	REC
1897	STL	N	0		89	.288
1898	STL	N	0		142	.248
1899	CLE	N	0		145	.250
1900	CIN	N	0		5	.450
1901	CIN	N	0		133	.268
1902	DET	A	0		124	.276
1903	CHI	N	0		103	.231
		BLTR			741	.261

HARLOW, LARRY DUANE
B.NOV.13,1951 COLORADO SPRINGS,COLO.

YR	CL	LEA	POS	GP	G	REC
1975	BAL	A	/0		4	.333
1977	BAL	A	0		46	.208
1978	BAL	A	*0/P	1	147	0- 0
						.243
		BLTL		1	197	0- 0
						.241

HARMAN, WILLIAM BELL
B.JAN.2,1919 BRIDGEWATER,VA.

YR	CL	LEA	POS	GP	G	REC
1941	PHI	N	P-C		15	0- 0
						.071
		BRTR				

HARMON, CHARLES BYRON (CHUCK)
B.APR.23,1926 WASHINGTON,IND.

YR	CL	LEA	POS	GP	G	REC
1954	CIN	N	1-3		94	.238
1955	CIN	N	1-3-0		96	.253
1956	CIN	N	1-3-0		13	.000
	STL	N	1-3-0		20	.000
1957	STL	N	0		9	.333
	PHI	N	1-3-0		57	.256
		BRTR			289	.238

```
YR   CL LEA POS      GP    G    REC
```

HARMON, ROBERT GREEN (HICKORY BOB)
B.OCT.15,1887 LIBERAL,MO.
D.NOV.27,1961 MONROE,LA.
```
1909 STL N P              21   6-11
1910 STL N P              43  13-15
1911 STL N P              51  23-16
1912 STL N P       43  46 18-18
1913 STL N P       42  46  8-21
1914 PIT N P       37  44 13-17
1915 PIT N P       37  42 16-17
1916 PIT N P       31  35  8-11
1918 PIT N P       17  18  2- 7
     BBTR         322 346 107-133
```

HARMON, TERRY WALTER
B.APR.12,1944 TOLEDO,OHIO
```
1967 PHI N P               2  .000
1969 PHI N S-2/3          87  .239
1970 PHI N S-2/3          71  .248
1971 PHI N 2/S-3-1        79  .204
1972 PHI N 2-S/3          73  .284
1973 PHI N 2-S/3          72  .209
1974 PHI N /S-2           27  .133
1975 PHI N S/2-3          48  .181
1976 PHI N S-2/3          42  .295
1977 PHI N 2-S/3          46  .183
     BRTR               547  .233
```

HARPER, CHARLES WILLIAM (JACK)
B.APR.2,1878 GALLOWAY,PA.
D.SEPT.30,1950 JAMESTOWN,N.Y.
```
1899 CLE N P      5  1- 4
1900 STL N P      1  0- 1
1901 STL N P     36 23-13
1902 STL A P     29 17-10
1903 CIN N P     17  7- 7
1904 CIN N P     35 24- 8
1905 CIN N P     26  9-14
1906 CIN N P      5  0- 3
     CHI N P      1  0- 0
     BRTR       155 81-60
```

HARPER, GEORGE B.
B.AUG.17,1866 MILWAUKEE,WIS.
D.DEC.11,1931 STOCKTON,CAL.
```
1894 PHI N P     12  5- 3
1896 BRO N P     16  4- 8
                 28  9-11
```

HARPER, GEORGE WASHINGTON
B.JUNE 24,1892 ARLINGTON,KY.
D.AUG.18,1978 MAGNOLIA,ARK.
```
1916 DET A O          44  .161
1917 DET A O          47  .205
1918 DET A O          69  .243
1922 CIN N O         128  .339
1923 CIN N O          61  .256
1924 CIN N O          28  .270
     PHI N O         109  .295
1925 PHI N O         132  .349
1926 PHI N O          56  .314
1927 NY  N O         145  .331
1928 NY  N O          19  .228
     STL N O          99  .305
1929 BOS N O         136  .291
     BLTR           1073  .303
```

HARPER, HARRY CLAYTON
B.APR.24,1895 HACKENSACK,N.J.
D.APR.23,1963 NEW YORK,N.Y.
```
1913 WAS A P      4  1- 0
1914 WAS A P     23  2- 1
1915 WAS A P     19  5- 4
1916 WAS A P     36 15-10
1917 WAS A P     31 11-12
1918 WAS A P  35 36 11-10
1919 WAS A P     35  6-21
1920 BOS A P     27  5-14
1921 NY  A P      8  4- 3
1923 BRO N P
     BLTR      219 220 60-76
```

HARPER, JOHN WESLEY (JACK)
B.AUG.5,1893 HENDRICKS,W.VA.
D.JUNE 18,1927 HALSTEAD,KAN.
```
1915 PHI N P      3  0- 1
     BRTR
```

HARPER, TOMMY
B.OCT.14,1940 OAK GROVE,LA.
```
1962 CIN N 3           6  .174
1963 CIN N 3-0       129  .260
1964 CIN N 3-0       102  .243
1965 CIN N *O/3-2    159  .257
1966 CIN N *O        149  .278
1967 CIN N *O        103  .225
1968 CLE A *O/2      130  .217
1969 SEA A 2-3-0     148  .235
1970 MIL A *3-2-0    154  .296
1971 MIL A  O-3/2    152  .258
1972 BOS A *O        144  .254
1973 BOS A *O        147  .281
1974 BOS A O-D       118  .237
1975 CAL A  D-1/O     89  .239
     OAK A  1/O-3     34  .319
1976 BAL A  D/1-O     46  .234
     BRTR           1810  .257
```

HARPER, WILLIAM HOMER (BLUE SLEEVE)
B.JUNE 14,1889 BERTAND,MO.
D.JUNE 17,1951 SOMERVILLE,TENN.
```
1911 STL A P      2  0- 0
     BBTR
```

HARRAH, COLBERT DALE (TOBY)
B.OCT.26,1948 SISSONVILLE,W.VA.
```
1969 WAS A /S          8  .000
1971 WAS A *S/3      127  .230
1972 TEX A *S        116  .259
1973 TEX A  S-3      118  .260
1974 TEX A *S/3      161  .260
1975 TEX A *S-3-2    151  .293
1976 TEX A *S/3      155  .260
1977 TEX A *1/S      159  .263
1978 TEX A  3-S      139  .229
     BRTR           1134  .258
```

HARRELL, JOHN ROBERT
B.NOV.27,1947 LONG BEACH,CAL.
```
1969 SF  N /C          2  .500
     BRTR
```

HARRELL, OSCAR MARTIN (SLIM)
B.JULY 31,1890 GRANDVIEW,TEX.
D.APR.30,1971 HILLSBORO,TEX.
```
1912 PHI A P      1  0- 0
     BRTR
```

HARRELL, RAYMOND JAMES (COWBOY)
B.FEB.16,1912 PETROLIA,TEX.
```
1935 STL N P     11  1- 1
1937 STL N P     35  3- 7
1938 STL N P     32  2- 3
1939 CHI N P      4  0- 2
     PHI N P     22  3- 7
1940 PIT N P      3  0- 0
1945 NY  N P     12  0- 0
     BRTR       119  9-20
```

HARRELL, WILLIAM (BILLY)
B.JULY 18,1928 NORRISTOWN,PA.
```
1955 CLE A  S        13  .421
1957 CLE A  2-S-3    22  .263
1958 CLE A  2-S-3-0 101  .218
1961 BOS A  1-S-3    37  .162
     BRTR          173  .231
```

HARRELSON, DERREL MC KINLEY (BUD)
B.JUNE 6,1944 NILES,CAL.
```
1965 NY  N  S         19  .108
1966 NY  N  S         33  .222
1967 NY  N *S        151  .254
1968 NY  N *S        111  .219
1969 NY  N *S        123  .248
1970 NY  N *S        157  .243
1971 NY  N *S        142  .252
1972 NY  N *S        115  .215
1973 NY  N *S        106  .258
1974 NY  N  S        106  .227
1975 NY  N  S         34  .219
1976 NY  N *S        118  .234
1977 NY  N  S        107  .178
1978 PHI N  2-S       71  .214
     BBTR           1393  .234
     BR 1965, 1975 (PART)
```

HARRELSON, KENNETH SMITH
(KEN) OR (HAWK)
B.SEP.4,1941 WOODRUFF,S.C.
```
1963 KC  A  1-D       79  .230
1964 KC  A  1-D       49  .194
1965 KC  A *1/O      150  .238
1966 KC  A  1/O       63  .224
     WAS A  1         71  .248
1967 KC  A  1         26  .203
     KC  A  1         61  .305
     BOS A  O/1       23  .200
1968 BOS A *O-1      150  .275
1969 BOS A  1         10  .217
     CLE A *O-1      149  .222
1970 CLE A  1         17  .282
1971 CLE A  1/O       52  .199
     BRTR           900  .239
```

HARRELSON, WILLIAM CHARLES (BILL)
B.NOV.17,1945 TAHLEQUAH,OKLA.
```
1968 CAL A P     10  1- 6
     BBTR
```

HARRINGTON, ANDREW FRANCIS
B.NOV.13,1888 WAKEFIELD,MASS.
D.NOV.12,1936 MALDEN,MASS.
```
1913 CIN N P      1  0- 0
     BRTR
```

HARRINGTON, ANDREW MATTHEW
B.FEB.12,1903 MOUNTAIN VIEW,CAL
```
1925 DET A 2      1  .000
     BRTR
```

HARRINGTON, CHARLES MICHAEL (MICKEY)
B.OCT.8,1934 HATTIESBURG,MISS.
```
1963 PHI N R      1  .000
     BRTR
```

HARRINGTON, JEREMIAH PETER
B.AUG.12,1869 KEOKUK,IOWA
D.APR.16,1913 KEOKUK,IOWA
```
1890 CIN N C          65  .246
1891 CIN N C          90  .229
1892 CIN N C          18  .213
1893 LOU N C          10  .121
     TR              183  .228
```

HARRINGTON, JOSEPH C.
B.DEC.21,1869 FALL RIVER,MASS.
D.SEPT.13,1933 FALL RIVER,MASS.
```
1895 BOS N 2          18  .299
1896 BOS N 3          53  .203
                      71  .229
```

HARRINGTON, WILLIAM WOMBLE (BILL)
B.OCT.3,1927 SANFORD,N.C.
```
1953 PHI A P      1  0- 0
1955 KC  A P     34  3- 3
1956 KC  A P     23  2- 2
     BRTR        58  5- 5
```

HARRIS, ALONZO (CANDY)
B.SEP.17,1947 SELMA,ALA.
```
1967 HOU N /H      6  .000
     BBTR
```

HARRIS, BENJAMIN F.
B.1889 NASHVILLE,TENN.
```
1914 KC  F P     31  7- 7
1915 KC  F P      1  0- 0
     BRTR        32  7- 7
```

HARRIS, BOYD GAIL (GAIL)
B.OCT.15,1931 ABINGDON,VA.
```
1955 NY  N 1          79  .232
1956 NY  N 1          12  .132
1957 NY  N 1          90  .240
1958 DET A 1         134  .273
1959 DET A 1         114  .221
1960 DET A 1           8  .000
     BLTL           437  .240
```

HARRIS, CHALMER LUMAN (LUM)
B.JAN.17,1915 NEW CASTLE,ALA.
```
1941 PHI A P          33  4- 4
1942 PHI A P          26 11-15
1943 PHI A P          32  7-21
1944 PHI A P          23 10- 9
1946 PHI A P          34  3-14
1947 WAS A P           3  0- 0
     BRTR            151 35-63
```
NON-PLAYING MANAGER
BAL[A] 1961, HOU[N] 1964-65,
ATL[N] 1968-72

HARRIS, CHARLES (BUBBA)
B.FEB.19,1926 SULLIGENT,ALA.
```
1948 PHI A P     45  5- 2
1949 PHI A P     37  1- 1
1951 PHI A P      3  0- 0
     CLE A P      2  0- 0
     BRTR        87  6- 3
```

HARRIS, CHARLES JENKINS
B.OCT.21,1877 MACON,GA.
D.MAR.14,1963 GAINESVILLE,FLA.
```
1899 BAL N 3          21  .283
```

HARRIS, DAVID STANLEY (SHERIFF)
B.JULY 14,1900 SUMMERFIELD,N.C.
D.SEPT.18,1973 ATLANTA,GA.
```
1925 BOS N O          92  .265
1928 BOS N O           7  .118
1930 CHI A O          33  .235
     WAS A O          73  .320
1931 WAS A O          77  .312
1932 WAS A O          81  .327
1933 WAS A 1-3-0      82  .260
1934 WAS A O          97  .251
     BRTR            542  .281
```

HARRIS, FRANK W.
B.NOV.2,1858 PITTSBURGH,PA.
D.NOV.26,1939 E.MOLINE,ILL.
```
1884 ALT U 1-0        24  .242
```

HARRIS, HERBERT (HUB)
B.APR.24,1913 WHITING,IND.
```
1936 PHI N P      4  0- 0
     BLTL
```

HARRIS, JAMES WILLIAM (BILLY)
B.NOV.24,1943 HAMLET,N.C.
```
1968 CLE A  2-3/S     38  .213
1969 KC  A  /2         5  .286
     BLTR            43  .218
```

YR	CL	LEA	POS	GP	G	REC

HARRIS, JOSEPH (MOON)
B.MAY 30,1891 COULTERS,PA.
D.DEC.10,1959 RENTON,PA.

1914	NY	A	O		2	.000
1917	CLE	A	1		112	.304
1919	CLE	A	1		62	.375
1922	BOS	A	1-O		119	.316
1923	BOS	A	O		142	.335
1924	BOS	A	1		133	.301
1925	BOS	A	1		9	.150
	WAS	A	1-O		99	.324
1926	WAS	A	1-O		92	.307
1927	PIT	N	1		129	.326
1928	PIT	N	1		16	.391
	BRO	N	O		55	.236
	BRTR				.970	.317

HARRIS, JOSEPH WHITE
B.FEB.1,1882 MELROSE,MASS.
D.APR.12,1966 MELROSE,MASS.

1905	BOS	A	P		3	1- 2
1906	BOS	A	P		30	2-21
1907	BOS	A	P		12	0- 7
	TR				45	3-30

HARRIS, MAURICE CHARLES (MICKEY)
B.JAN.30,1917 NEW YORK,N.Y.
D.APR.15,1971 FARMINGTON,MICH.

1940	BOS	A	P		11	4- 2
1941	BOS	A	P		35	8-14
1946	BOS	A	P		34	17- 9
1947	BOS	A	P		15	5- 4
1948	BOS	A	P		20	7-10
1949	BOS	A	P		7	2- 3
	WAS	A	P		23	2-12
1950	WAS	A	P		53	5- 9
1951	WAS	A	P		41	6- 8
1952	WAS	A	P		1	0- 0
	CLE	A	P		29	3- 0
	BLTL				271	59-71

HARRIS, ROBERT ARTHUR
B.MAY 1,1916 GILLETTE,WYO.

1938	DET	A	P		3	1- 0
1939	DET	A	P		5	1- 1
	STL	A	P	28	29	9-12
1940	STL	A	P		35	11-15
1941	STL	A	P		34	12-14
1942	STL	A	P		6	1- 5
	PHI	A	P		16	1- 5
	BRTR			127	128	30-52

HARRIS, ROBERT NED (NED)
B.JULY 9,1916 AMES,IOWA
D.DEC.18,1976 W.PALM BEACH,FLA.

1941	DET	A	O		26	.213
1942	DET	A	O		121	.271
1943	DET	A	O		114	.254
1946	DET	A	H		1	.000
	BLTL				262	.259

HARRIS, SPENCER ANTHONY
B.AUG.12,1900 DULUTH,MINN.

1925	CHI	A	O		56	.283
1926	CHI	A	O		80	.252
1929	WAS	A	O		6	.214
1930	PHI	A	O		22	.184
	BLTL				164	.250

HARRIS, STANLEY RAYMOND (BUCKY)
B.NOV.8,1896 PORT JERVIS,N.Y.
D.NOV.8,1977 BETHESDA,MD.

1919	WAS	A	2		8	.214
1920	WAS	A	2		137	.300
1921	WAS	A	2		154	.289
1922	WAS	A	2		154	.269
1923	WAS	A	2		145	.282
1924	WAS	A	M-2		143	.268
1925	WAS	A	M-2		144	.287
1926	WAS	A	M-2		141	.283
1927	WAS	A	M-2		128	.267
1928	WAS	A	M-2		99	.204
1929	DET	A	M-2		7	.091
1931	DET	A	M-2		4	.125
	BRTR				1264	.274

NON-PLAYING MANAGER
DET(A) 1930, 32-33, BOS(A) 1934
WAS(A) 1935-42, PHI(N) 1943,
NY(A) 1947-48, WAS(A) 1950-54,
DET(A) 1955-56

HARRIS, VICTOR LANIER (VIC)
B.MAR.27,1950 LOS ANGELES,CAL.

1972	TEX	A	2/S		61	.140
1973	TEX	A	*0-3-2		152	.249
1974	CHI	N	2		62	.195
1975	CHI	N	O/3-2		51	.179
1976	STL	N	2-O-3/S		97	.228
1977	SF	N	2-S/3-O		69	.261
1978	SF	N	S-2/O		53	.150
	BBTR				545	.217

HARRIS, WALTER FRANCIS (BUDDY)
B.DEC.5,1948 PHILADELPHIA,PA.

1970	HOU	N	/P		2	0- 0
1971	HOU	N	P		20	1- 1
	BRTR				22	1- 1

HARRIS, WILLIAM MILTON
B.JUNE 23,1900 WYLIE,TEX.
D.AUG.21,1965 INDIAN TRAIL,N.C.

1923	CIN	N	P	22	3- 2
1924	CIN	N	P	3	0- 0
1931	PIT	N	P	4	2- 2
1932	PIT	N	P	37	10- 9
1933	PIT	N	P	31	4- 4
1934	PIT	N	P	11	0- 0
1938	BOS	A	P	13	5- 5
	BRTR			121	24-22

HARRIS, WILLIAM THOMAS
B.DEC.3,1931 DUGUAYVILLE,N.B.,CANADA

1957	BRO	N	P	1	0- 1
1959	LA	N	P	1	0- 1
	BRTR			2	0- 1

HARRISON

| 1875 | NH | NA | C | | 1 | - |

HARRISON, CHARLES WILLIAM (CHUCK)
B.APR.25,1941 ABILENE,TEX.

1965	HOU	N	1		15	.200
1966	HOU	N	*1		119	.256
1967	HOU	N	1		70	.221
1969	KC	A	1		75	.221
1971	KC	A	1		49	.217
	BRTR				328	.238

HARRISON, LEO J. (BEN)
B.1901 WAS A O

| 1901 | WAS | A | O | | 1 | .000 |

HARRISON, ROBERT LEE
B.SEPT.22,1930 ST.LOUIS,MO.

1955	BAL	A	P		1	0- 0
1956	BAL	A	P		1	0- 0
	BLTR				2	0- 0

HARRISON, RORIC EDWARD
B.SEP.20,1946 LOS ANGELES,CAL.

1972	BAL	A	P		39	3- 4
1973	ATL	N	P	38	39	11- 8
1974	ATL	N	P		20	6-11
1975	ATL	N	P		15	3- 4
	CLE	A	P		19	7- 7
1978	MIN	A	/P		9	0- 1
	BRTR			140	141	30-35

HARRISON, THOMAS JAMES (TOM)
B.JAN.18,1945 TRAIL,B.C.,CANADA

| 1965 | KC | A | P | 1 | 2 | 0- 0 |
| | BRTR | | | | | |

HARRISS, WILLIAM JENNINGS BRYAN (SLIM)
B.DEC.11,1896 BROWNWOOD,TEX.
D.SEPT.19,1963 TEMPLE,TEX.

1920	PHI	A	P		31	9-14
1921	PHI	A	P		39	11-16
1922	PHI	A	P		47	9-20
1923	PHI	A	P		46	10-16
1924	PHI	A	P		36	6-10
1925	PHI	A	P		46	19-12
1926	PHI	A	P		12	3- 5
	BOS	A	P		21	6-10
1927	BOS	A	P		44	14-21
1928	BOS	A	P		27	8-11
	BRTR				349	95-135

HARRIST, EARL (IRISH)
B.AUG.20,1919 DUBACH,LA.

1945	CIN	N	P		14	2- 4
1947	CHI	A	P		33	3- 8
1948	CHI	A	P		11	1- 3
	WAS	A	P		23	3- 3
1952	STL	A	P		36	2- 8
1953	CHI	A	P		7	1- 0
	DET	A	P		8	0- 2
	BRTR				132	12-28

HARSHANY, SAMUEL
B.MAY 1,1910 MADISON,ILL.

1937	STL	A	C		5	.091
1938	STL	A	C		11	.292
1939	STL	A	C		42	.241
1940	STL	A	C		3	.000
	BRTR				61	.210

HARSHMAN, JOHN ELVIN (JACK)
B.JULY 12,1927 SAN DIEGO,CAL.

1948	NY	N	1		5	.250
1950	NY	N	1		9	.125
1952	NY	N	P	2	3	0- 2
1954	CHI	A	P-1	35	36	14- 8
						.143
1955	CHI	A	P		32	11- 7
1956	CHI	A	P	34	36	15-11
1957	CHI	A	P		30	8- 8
1958	BAL	A	P-O	34	47	12-15
						.195
1959	BAL	A	P	14	15	0- 6
	BOS	A	P	8	9	2- 3
	CLE	A	P	13	21	5- 1
1960	CLE	A	P		15	2- 4
	BLTL			217	258	69-65
						.179

HARSTAD, OSCAR THEANDER
B.MAY 24,1892 PARKLAND,WASH.

| 1915 | CLE | A | P | | 32 | 3- 6 |

HART, JAMES (JIM)
B.MINNESOTA

| 1901 | BAL | A | 1 | | 58 | .312 |

HART, JAMES A.
B.JULY 10,1855 GIRARD,PA.
D.JULY 18,1919 CHICAGO,ILL.
NON-PLAYING MANAGER
LOU(AA) 1885-86, BOS(N) 1889

HART, JAMES HENRY (HUB)
B.FEB.2,1878 EVERETT,MASS.
D.OCT.10,1960 FORT WAYNE,IND.

1905	CHI	A	C		11	.125
1906	CHI	A	C		17	.162
1907	CHI	A	C		29	.271
	BLTR				57	.217

HART, JAMES RAY (JIM RAY)
B.OCT.30,1941 HOOKERTON,N.C.

1963	SF	N	3		7	.200
1964	SF	N	3-O		153	.286
1965	SF	N	*3-O		160	.299
1966	SF	N	*3-O		156	.285
1967	SF	N	3-O		158	.289
1968	SF	N	3-O		136	.258
1969	SF	N	O/3		95	.254
1970	SF	N	3-O		76	.282
1971	SF	N	/3-O		31	.256
1972	SF	N	3		24	.304
1973	SF	N	/3		5	.000
	NY	A	*O		114	.254
1974	NY	A	/H		10	.053
	BRTR				1125	.278

HART, JOSEPH L.
1890 STL AA P

| 1890 | STL | AA | P | | 28 | 12- 9 |

HART, THOMAS HENRY (BUSHY)
B.JUNE 15,1869 CANAAN,N.Y.
D.SEPT.17,1939 GARDNER,MASS.

| 1891 | WAS | AA | C-O | | 8 | .130 |

HART, WILLIAM FRANKLIN
B.JULY 19,1865 LOUISVILLE,KY.
D.SEPT.19,1936 CINCINNATI,OHIO

1886	ATH	AA	P		23	9-13
1887	ATH	AA	P		3	1- 2
1892	BRO	N	P	25	29	7-10
1895	PIT	N	P		31	14-15
1896	STL	N	P		40	46	13-26
1897	STL	N	P		37	43	9-23
1898	PIT	N	P		15	6- 9
1901	CLE	A	P		20	6-12
				194	210	65-110

HART, WILLIAM WOODROW
B.MAR.4,1913 WICONISCO,PA.
D.JULY 29,1968 LYKINS,PA.

1943	BRO	N	S		8	.158
1944	BRO	N	S-3		29	.178
1945	BRO	N	S-3		58	.230
	BRTR				95	.207

HARTENSTEIN, CHARLES OSCAR (CHUCK) OR (TWIGGY)
B.MAY.26,1942 SEGUIN,TEX.

1965	CHI	N	R		1	.000
1966	CHI	N	/P		5	0- 0
1967	CHI	N	P		45	9- 5
1968	CHI	N	P		28	2- 4
1969	PIT	N	P		56	5- 4
1970	PIT	N	P		17	1- 1
	STL	N	/P		6	0- 0
	BOS	A	P		17	0- 3
1977	TOR	A	P		13	0- 2
	BRTR			187	188	17-19
						.054

HARTER, FRANKLIN PIERCE (CHIEF)
B.SEPT.19,1886 KEYESPORT,ILL.
D.APR.14,1959 BREESE,ILL.

1912	CIN	N	P		6	1- 2
1913	CIN	N	P		17	1- 1
1914	IND	F	P		6	1- 2
	BRTR				29	3- 5

HARTFORD, BRUCE DANIEL
B.MAY 14,1892 CHICAGO,ILL.
D.MAY 25,1975 LOS ANGELES,CAL.

| 1914 | CLE | A | S | | 8 | .181 |

HARTJE, CHRISTIAN HENRY
B.MAR.25,1915 SAN FRANCISCO,CAL
D.JUNE 26,1946 SEATTLE,WASH.

| 1939 | BOS | N | C | | 9 | .313 |
| | BRTR | | | | | |

YR	CL LEA POS	GP	G	REC

HARTLEY, GROVER ALLEN (SLICK)
B.JULY 2,1888 OSGOOD,IND.
D.OCT.19,1964 DAYTONA BEACH,FLA

YR	CL LEA POS	GP	G	REC
1911	NY N C		10	.222
1912	NY N C		25	.235
1913	NY N C		23	.316
1914	STL F C		86	.286
1915	STL F C		117	.271
1916	STL A C		89	.225
1917	STL A C		19	.231
1924	NY N C		4	.286
1925	NY N C-1		46	.316
1926	NY N C		13	.048
1927	BOS A C		103	.275
1929	CLE A C		24	.273
1930	CLE A C		1	.750
1934	STL A C		5	.333
	BRTR		565	.267

HARTLEY, WALTER SCOTT (CHICK)
B.AUG.22,1880 PHILADELPHIA,PA.
D.JULY 18,1948 PHILADELPHIA,PA.

YR	CL LEA POS	GP	G	REC
1902	NY N O		1	.000
	BRTR			

HARTMAN, CHARLES OTTO
B.AUG.10,1888 LOS ANGELES,CAL.
D.OCT.22,1960 LOS ANGELES,CAL.

YR	CL LEA POS	GP	G	REC
1908	BOS A P		1	0- 0

HARTMAN, FREDERICK ORRIN (DUTCH)
B.APR.25,1868 ALLEGHENY,PA.
D.NOV.11,1938 MC KEESPORT,PA.

YR	CL LEA POS	GP	G	REC
1894	PIT N 3		49	.311
1897	STL N 3		126	.301
1898	STL N 3		122	.267
1899	NY N 3		52	.241
1901	CHI A 3		120	.313
1902	STL N 1-S-3		112	.221
	TR		581	.278

HARTMAN, J C (J C)
B.APR.15,1934 COTTONTON,ALA.

YR	CL LEA POS	GP	G	REC
1962	HOU N S		51	.223
1963	HOU N S		39	.122
	BRTR		90	.185

HARTMAN, ROBERT LOUIS
B.AUG.28,1937 KENOSHA,WIS.

YR	CL LEA POS	GP	G	REC
1959	MIL N P		3	0- 0
1962	CLE A P		8	0- 1
	BRTL		11	0- 1

HARTNETT, CHARLES LEO (GABBY)
B.DEC.20,1900 WOONSOCKET,R.I.
D.DEC.20,1972 PARK RIDGE,ILL.

YR	CL LEA POS	GP	G	REC
1922	CHI N C		31	.194
1923	CHI N C-1		85	.268
1924	CHI N C		111	.299
1925	CHI N C		117	.289
1926	CHI N C		93	.275
1927	CHI N C		127	.294
1928	CHI N C		120	.302
1929	CHI N C		25	.273
1930	CHI N C		141	.339
1931	CHI N C		116	.282
1932	CHI N C		121	.271
1933	CHI N C		140	.276
1934	CHI N C		130	.299
1935	CHI N C		116	.344
1936	CHI N C		121	.307
1937	CHI N C		110	.354
1938	CHI N M-C		88	.274
1939	CHI N M-C		97	.278
1940	CHI N M-C-1		37	.266
1941	NY N C		64	.300
	BRTR		1990	.298

HARTNETT, PATRICK J. (HAPPY)
B.OCT.20,1863 BOSTON,MASS.
D.APR.10,1935 BOSTON,MASS.

YR	CL LEA POS	GP	G	REC
1890	STL AA 1		13	.200

HARTRANFT, RAYMOND JOSEPH
B.SEPT.19,1890 QUAKERTOWN,PA.
D.FEB.10,1955 SPRING CITY,PA.

YR	CL LEA POS	GP	G	REC
1913	PHI N P		1	0- 0
	BLTL			

HARTS, GREGORY RUDOLPH (GREG)
B.APR.21,1950 ATLANTA,GA.

YR	CL LEA POS	GP	G	REC
1973	NY N /H		3	.500
	BLTL			

HARTSEL, TULLY FREDERICK (TOPSY)
B.JUNE 26,1874 POLK,OHIO
D.OCT.14,1944 TOLEDO,OHIO

YR	CL LEA POS	GP	G	REC
1898	LOU N O		21	.319
1899	LOU N O		20	.261
1900	CIN N O		18	.328
1901	CHI N O		140	.339
1902	PHI A O		137	.286
1903	PHI A O		98	.311
1904	PHI A O		147	.249
1905	PHI A O		148	.276
1906	PHI A O		144	.255
1907	PHI A O		143	.280
1908	PHI A O		129	.243
1909	PHI A O		83	.270
1910	PHI A O		90	.221
1911	PHI A O		25	.237
	BLTL		1343	.276

HARTSFIELD, ROY THOMAS (SPEC)
B.OCT.25,1925 CHATTAHOOCHEE,GA.

YR	CL LEA POS	GP	G	REC
1950	BOS N 2		107	.277
1951	BOS N 2		120	.271
1952	BOS N 2		38	.262
	BRTR		265	.273
NON-PLAYING MANAGER TOR[A] 1977-78

HARTUNG, CLINTON CLARENCE
(CLINT), (FLOPPY) OR
(THE HONDO HURRICANE)
B.AUG.10,1922 HONDO,TEX.

YR	CL LEA POS	GP	G	REC
1947	NY N P-O	23	34	9- 7
				.309
1948	NY N P	36	43	8- 8
1949	NY N P	33	38	9-11
1950	NY N P-1-	20	32	3- 3
	O			.302
1951	NY N O		21	.205
1952	NY N O		28	.218
	BRTR	112	196	29-29
				.212

HARTZELL, PAUL FRANKLIN
B.NOV.2,1953 BLOOMSBURG,PA.

YR	CL LEA POS	GP	G	REC
1976	CAL A P		37	7- 4
1977	CAL A P		41	8-12
1978	CAL A P		54	6-10
	BRTR		132	21-26

HARTZELL, ROY ALLEN
B.JULY 6,1881 GOLDEN,COLO.
D.NOV.6,1961 GOLDEN,UTAH

YR	CL LEA POS	GP	G	REC
1906	STL A 3		113	.213
1907	STL A 2-3		60	.236
1908	STL A S-O		115	.265
1909	STL A S-O		152	.271
1910	STL A S-3-O		151	.218
1911	NY A 3		144	.296
1912	NY A 3-O		123	.272
1913	NY A 2-3-O		141	.259
1914	NY A O		137	.233
1915	NY A O		119	.251
1916	NY A O		33	.187
	BLTR		1288	.252

HARVEL, LUTHER RAYMOND (RED)
B.SEPT.30,1905 CAMBRIA,ILL.

YR	CL LEA POS	GP	G	REC
1928	CLE A O		40	.220
	BRTR			

HARVEY, ERVIN KING
B.JAN.5,1879 SARATOGA,CAL.
D.JUNE 3,1954 SANTA MONICA,CAL.

YR	CL LEA POS	GP	G	REC
1900	CHI N P		2	0- 0
1901	CHI A P-O	3	17	2- 1
				.256
	CLE A P-O	7	44	0- 7
				.351
1902	CLE A O		12	.369
		12	75	2- 8
				.336

HASBROOK, ROBERT LYNDON (ZIGGY)
(ZIGGY)
B.NOV.21,1893 GRUNDY CENTER,IA.
D.FEB.9,1976 GARLAND,TEX.

YR	CL LEA POS	GP	G	REC
1916	CHI A 1		8	.125
1917	CHI A 2		2	.000
	BRTR		10	.111

HASENMAYER, DONALD IRVIN
B.APR.4,1927 ROSLYN,PA.

YR	CL LEA POS	GP	G	REC
1945	PHI N 2-3		5	.111
1946	PHI N 3		6	.083
	BRTR		11	.100

HASH, HERBERT HOWARD
B.FEB.13,1911 WOOLWINE,VA.

YR	CL LEA POS	GP	G	REC
1940	BOS A P	34	35	7- 7
1941	BOS A P		4	1- 0
	BRTR	38	39	8- 7

HASLIN, MICHAEL JOSEPH (MICKEY)
B.OCT.31,1910 WILKES-BARRE,PA.

YR	CL LEA POS	GP	G	REC
1933	PHI N 2		26	.236
1934	PHI N 2-3		72	.265
1935	PHI N 2-S-3		110	.265
1936	PHI N 2-3		16	.344
	BOS N 2-3		36	.279
1937	NY N 2-S-3		27	.190
1938	NY N 2-3		31	.324
	BRTR		318	.272

HASNEY, PETER JAMES
B.MAY 26,1865 ENGLAND
D.MAY 24,1908 PHILADELPHIA,PA.

YR	CL LEA POS	GP	G	REC
1890	ATH AA O		2	.125

HASSAMAER, WILLIAM LOUIS
(ROARING BILL)
B.JULY 26,1864 ST.LOUIS,MO.
D.MAY 29,1910 ST.LOUIS,MO.

YR	CL LEA POS	GP	G	REC
1894	WAS N 3-O		116	.326
1895	WAS N O		89	.278
	LOU N 1-O		20	.198
1896	LOU N 1		26	.248
	BRTR		251	.291

HASSETT, JOHN ALOYSIUS (BUDDY)
B.SEPT.5,1911 NEW YORK,N.Y.

YR	CL LEA POS	GP	G	REC
1936	BRO N 1		156	.310
1937	BRO N 1		137	.304
1938	BRO N O		115	.293
1939	BOS N 1-O		147	.309
1940	BOS N 1-O		124	.234
1941	BOS N 1		118	.296
1942	NY A 1		132	.284
	BLTL		929	.292

HASSEY, RONALD WILLIAM (RON)
B.FEB.27,1953 TUCSON,ARIZ.

YR	CL LEA POS	GP	G	REC
1978	CLE A C		25	.203
	BLTR			

HASSLER, ANDREW EARL (ANDY)
B.OCT.18,1951 TEXAS CITY,TEX.

YR	CL LEA POS	GP	G	REC
1971	CAL A /P		6	0- 3
1973	CAL A P		7	0- 4
1974	CAL A P		23	7-11
1975	CAL A P		30	3-12
1976	CAL A P		14	0- 6
	KC A P		19	5- 6
1977	KC A P	29	30	9- 6
1978	KC A P		11	1- 4
	BOS A P		13	2- 1
	BLTL	152	153	27-53

HASSLER, JOSEPH FREDERICK
B.APR.7,1905 FT.SMITH,ARK.
D.SEPT.4,1971 DUNCAN,OKLA.

YR	CL LEA POS	GP	G	REC
1928	PHI A S		28	.265
1929	PHI A S		4	.000
1930	STL A S		5	.250
	BRTR		37	.239

HASSON, CHARLES EUGENE (GENE)
B.JULY 20,1915 CONNELLSVILLE,PA

YR	CL LEA POS	GP	G	REC
1937	PHI A 1		28	.306
1938	PHI A 1		19	.275
	BLTL		47	.293

HASTINGS, CHARLES MORTON
B.NOV.11,1870 IRONTON,OHIO
D.AUG.3,1934 PARKERSBURG,W.VA.

YR	CL LEA POS	GP	G	REC
1893	CLE N P		16	4- 6
1896	PIT N P		17	5- 9
1897	PIT N P		15	7- 3
1898	PIT N P		18	4- 9
			66	20-27

HASTINGS, WINFIELD SCOTT (SCOTT)
B.AUG.10,1846 HILLSBORO,OHIO
D.AUG.14,1907 SAWTELLE,CAL.

YR	CL LEA POS	GP	G	REC
1871	ROK NA P-C-2	1	24	0- 1
1872	CLE NA M-C-2-O		21	.422
	BAL NA C-2		11	.196
1873	BAL NA C-1-2-O		32	-
1874	HAR NA C-2-O		52	-
1875	CHI NA C-2-O		66	-
1876	LOU N O		67	.254
1877	CIN N C-O		20	.141
	BRTR	1	292	0- 1

HASTY, ROBERT KELLER
B.MAY 3,1896 CANTON,GA.
D.MAY 28,1972 DALLAS,GA.

YR	CL LEA POS	GP	G	REC
1919	PHI A P		2	0- 2
1920	PHI A P		19	1- 3
1921	PHI A P		35	5-16
1922	PHI A P		28	9-14
1923	PHI A P		44	13-15
1924	PHI A P		18	1- 3
	BRTR		146	29-53

YR	CL LEA POS	GP	G	REC

HATFIELD, FRED JAMES
B.MAR.18,1925 LANETT,ALA.

YR	CL LEA POS	GP	G	REC
1950	BOS A 3		10	.250
1951	BOS A 3		80	.172
1952	BOS A 3		20	.286
	DET A S-3		111	.237
1953	DET A 2-S-3		109	.254
1954	DET A 2-3		81	.294
1955	DET A 2-S-3		122	.232
1956	DET A 2		8	.250
	CHI A 2-S-3		106	.262
1957	CHI A 3		69	.202
1958	CLE A 3		3	.125
	CIN N 2-3		3	.000
	BLTR		722	.241

HATFIELD, GILBERT (COLONEL)
B.JAN.27,1855 HOBOKEN,N.J.
D.MAY 27,1921 HOBOKEN,N.J.

YR	CL LEA POS	GP	G	REC
1885	BUF N 2-3		11	.125
1887	NY N 3		2	.429
1888	NY N 3		27	.181
1889	NY N P-S	6	32	0- 0
				.184
1890	NY P S-3		48	.301
	BOS P S		3	.143
	NY P P-S-3	2	20	0- 0
				.244
1891	WAS AA P-S-3	2	132	0- 2
				.258
1893	BRO N 3		33	.315
1895	LOU N S		5	.196
	TR	10	313	0- 2
				.246

HATFIELD, JOHN VAN BUREN
B.1847 NEW YORK,N.Y.
D.FEB.20,1909 LONG ISLAND CITY,N.Y.

YR	CL LEA POS	GP	G	REC
1871	MUT NA 2-3-0		34	-
1872	MUT NA 2		56	.303
1873	MUT NA 2-3		53	-
1874	MUT NA 3-0		64	-
1875	MUT NA 0		1	-
1876	MUT N 2		1	.250
			209	-

HATHAWAY, RAY WILSON
B.OCT.13,1916 GREENVILLE,OHIO

YR	CL LEA POS	GP	G	REC
1945	BRO N P		4	0- 1
	BRTR			

HATTEN, JOSEPH HILARIAN (JOE)
B.NOV.17,1916 BANCROFT,IOWA

YR	CL LEA POS	GP	G	REC
1946	BRO N P		42	14-11
1947	BRO N P		42	17- 8
1948	BRO N P	42	43	13-10
1949	BRO N P	37	39	12- 8
1950	BRO N P	23	27	2- 2
1951	BRO N P		11	1- 0
	CHI N		23	2- 6
1952	CHI N P	13	17	4- 4
	BRTL	233	244	65-49

HATTER, CLYDE MELNO
B.AUG.7,1908 POPLAR HILL,KY.
D.OCT.16,1937 YOSEMITE,KY.

YR	CL LEA POS	GP	G	REC
1935	DET A P		8	0- 0
1937	DET A P		3	1- 0
	BRTL		11	1- 0

HATTON, GRADY EDGEBERT
B.OCT.7,1922 BEAUMONT,TEX.

YR	CL LEA POS	GP	G	REC
1946	CIN N 3-0		116	.271
1947	CIN N 3		146	.281
1948	CIN N 2-S-3-0		133	.240
1949	CIN N 3		137	.263
1950	CIN N 2-S-3		130	.260
1951	CIN N 3-0		96	.254
1952	CIN N 2		128	.213
1953	CIN N 1-2-3		83	.233
1954	CIN N H		1	.000
	CHI A 1-3		13	.167
	BOS A 1-S-3		99	.281
1955	BOS A 2-3		126	.249
1956	BOS A H		5	.400
	STL N 2-3		44	.247
	BAL A 2-3		27	.148
1960	CHI N 2		28	.342
	BLTR		1312	.253

NON-PLAYING MANAGER HOU[N] 1966-68

HAUG, WILLIAM L.
[PLAYED UNDER NAME OF
WILLIAM L. HAGUE]

HAUGER, JOHN ARTHUR (ARTHUR)
B.NOV.18,1893 DELHI,OHIO
D.AUG.2,1944 REDWOOD CITY,CAL

YR	CL LEA POS	GP	G	REC
1912	CLE A O		15	.056
	BLTR			

HAUGHEY, CHRISTOPHER FRANCIS (BUD)
B.OCT.3,1925 ASTORIA,N.Y.

YR	CL LEA POS	GP	G	REC
1943	BRO N P		1	0- 1
	BRTR			

HAUGSTAD, PHILIP DONALD (PHIL)
B.FEB.23,1924 BLACK RIVER FALLS WIS.

YR	CL LEA POS	GP	G	REC
1947	BRO N P		6	1- 0
1948	BRO N P		1	0- 0
1951	BRO N P		21	0- 1
1952	CIN N P		9	0- 0
	BRTR		37	1- 1

HAUSER, ARNOLD GEORGE (PEEWEE) OR (STUB)
B.SEPT.25,1888 CHICAGO,ILL.
D.MAY 22,1966 AURORA,ILL.

YR	CL LEA POS	GP	G	REC
1910	STL N S		118	.205
1911	STL N S		136	.241
1912	STL N S		133	.259
1913	STL N S		22	.289
1915	CHI F S		20	.222
	BRTR		429	.238

HAUSER, JOSEPH JOHN (JOE) OR (UNSER CHOE)
B.JAN.12,1899 MILWAUKEE,WIS.

YR	CL LEA POS	GP	G	REC
1922	PHI A 1		111	.323
1923	PHI A 1		146	.307
1924	PHI A 1		149	.288
1926	PHI A 1		91	.192
1928	PHI A 1		95	.260
1929	CLE A 1		37	.250
	BLTL		629	.284

HAUSMAN, THOMAS MATTHEW (TOM)
B.MAR.31,1953 MOBRIDGE,S.D.

YR	CL LEA POS	GP	G	REC
1975	MIL A P		29	3- 6
1976	MIL A /P		3	0- 0
1978	NY N P		10	3- 3
	BRTR		42	6- 9

HAUSMANN, CLEMENS RAYMOND
B.AUG.17,1919 HOUSTON,TEX.
D.AUG.29,1972 BAYTOWN,TEX.

YR	CL LEA POS	GP	G	REC
1944	BOS A P		32	4- 7
1945	BOS A P		31	5- 7
1949	PHI N P		1	0- 0
	BRTR		64	9-14

HAUSMANN, GEORGE JOHN
B.FEB.11,1916 ST.LOUIS,MO.

YR	CL LEA POS	GP	G	REC
1944	NY N 2		131	.268
1945	NY N 2		154	.279
1949	NY N 2		16	.128
	BRTR		301	.268

HAWES, ROY LEE
B.JULY 5,1926 SHILOH,ILL.

YR	CL LEA POS	GP	G	REC
1951	WAS A 1		3	.167
	BLTL			

HAWES, WILLIAM HILDRETH
B.NOV.17,1853 NASHUA,N.H.
D.JUNE 16,1940 LOWELL,MASS.

YR	CL LEA POS	GP	G	REC
1879	BOS N O		37	.200
1884	CIN U 1-O		68	.260
	BRTR		105	.240

HAWK, EDWARD
B.MAY 11,1890 NEOSHO,MO.
D.MAR.26,1936 NEOSHO,MO.

YR	CL LEA POS	GP	G	REC
1911	STL A P		5	1- 4
	BLTR			

HAWKE, WILLIAM VICTOR (DICK)
B.APR.28,1870 ELSMERE,DEL.
D.DEC.11,1902 WILMINGTON,DEL.

YR	CL LEA POS	GP	G	REC
1892	STL N P		15	4- 5
1893	STL N P		3	0- 1
	BAL N P		28	11-17
1894	BAL N P		25	16- 9
	BRTR		71	31-32

HAWKES, THORNDIKE PROCTOR
B.OCT.15,1852 DANVERS,MASS.
D.FEB.3,1929 DANVERS,MASS.

YR	CL LEA POS	GP	G	REC
1879	TRO N 2		63	.206
1884	WAS AA 2		38	.226
			101	.256

HAWKINS, WYNN FIRTH (WYNN) OR (HAWK)
B.FEB.20,1936 E.PALESTINE,OHIO

YR	CL LEA POS	GP	G	REC
1960	CLE A P		15	4- 4
1961	CLE A P		30	7- 9
1962	CLE A P		3	1- 0
	BRTR		48	12-13

HAWKS, NELSON LOUIS (CHICKEN)
B.FEB.3,1896 SAN FRANCISCO,CAL.
D.MAY 26,1973 SAN RAFAEL,CAL.

YR	CL LEA POS	GP	G	REC
1921	NY A O		41	.288
1925	PHI N 1		105	.322
	BLTL		146	.316

HAWLEY, EMERSON P. (PINK)
B.DEC.5,1872 BEAVER DAM,WIS.
D.SEPT.19,1938 BEAVER DAM,WIS.

YR	CL LEA POS	GP	G	REC
1892	STL N P		19	6-13
1893	STL N P		33	5-17
1894	STL N P		48	18-25
1895	PIT N P		53	29-21
1896	PIT N P		48	21-21
1897	PIT N P		37	18-19
1898	CIN N P		42	26-12
1899	CIN N P		33	14-17
1900	NY N P		39	18-20
1901	MIL A P	24	28	7-13
	BLTR	376	380	162-178

HAWLEY, SCOTT

YR	CL LEA POS	GP	G	REC
1894	BOS N P		1	0- 0

HAWORTH, HOMER HOWARD (CULLY)
B.AUG.27,1893 NEWBERG,ORE.
D.AUG.13,1943 TROUTDALE,ORE.

YR	CL LEA POS	GP	G	REC
1915	CLE A C		7	.142
	BLTR			

HAYDEL, JOHN HAROLD (HAL)
B.JULY 9,1944 HOUMA,LA.

YR	CL LEA POS	GP	G	REC
1970	MIN A /P		4	2- 0
1971	MIN A P		31	4- 2
	BRTR		35	6- 2

HAYDEN, EUGENE FRANKLIN (LEFTY)
B.APR.14,1935 SAN FRANCISCO,CAL

YR	CL LEA POS	GP	G	REC
1958	CIN N P		3	0- 0
	BLTL			

HAYDEN, JOHN FRANCIS (JACK)
B.OCT.21,1880 BRYN MAWR,PA.
D.AUG.3,1942 HAVERFORD,PA.

YR	CL LEA POS	GP	G	REC
1901	PHI A O		51	.266
1906	BOS A O		85	.248
1908	CHI N O		11	.200
			147	.251

HAYES, FRANK WITMAN (BLIMP)
B.OCT.13,1914 JAMESBURG,N.J.
D.JUNE 22,1955 POINT PLEASANT,N.J.

YR	CL LEA POS	GP	G	REC
1933	PHI A C		3	.000
1934	PHI A C		92	.226
1936	PHI A C		144	.271
1937	PHI A C		60	.261
1938	PHI A C		99	.291
1939	PHI A C		124	.283
1940	PHI A C-1		136	.308
1941	PHI A C		126	.280
1942	PHI A C		21	.238
	STL A C		56	.252
1943	STL A C-1		88	.188
1944	PHI A C-1		155	.248
1945	PHI A C		32	.227
	CLE A C		119	.236
1946	CLE A C		51	.256
	CHI A C		53	.212
1947	BOS A C		5	.154
	BRTR		1364	.259

HAYES, JAMES MILLARD
B.FEB.11,1913 MONTEVALLO,ALA.

YR	CL LEA POS	GP	G	REC
1935	WAS A P		7	2- 4
	BLTR			

HAYES, JOHN J. (JACKIE)
B.JUNE 27,1861 BROOKLYN,N.Y.

YR	CL LEA POS	GP	G	REC
1882	WOR N C-S-3-0		78	.269
1883	PIT AA C-2-S-0		83	.263
1884	PIT AA C-1-2-0		34	.220
	BRO AA C-0		15	.220
1885	BRO AA C		42	.132
1886	WAS N C		26	.184
1887	BAL AA C		8	.143
1890	BRO P C		12	.191
	TR		298	.232

HAYES, MICHAEL
B.1853 CLEVELAND,OHIO

YR	CL LEA POS	GP	G	REC
1876	MUT N O		5	.182

HAYES, MINTER CARNEY (JACKIE)
B.JULY 19,1906 CLANTON,ALA.

YR	CL LEA POS	GP	G	REC
1927	WAS A S-3		10	.241
1928	WAS A 2-S		60	.257
1929	WAS A 2-3		123	.276
1930	WAS A 2		51	.283
1931	WAS A 2		38	.222
1932	CHI A 2-S-3		117	.257
1933	CHI A 2		138	.258
1934	CHI A 2		62	.257
1935	CHI A 2		89	.267
1936	CHI A 2-S		108	.312
1937	CHI A 2		143	.229
1938	CHI A 2		62	.328
1939	CHI A 2		72	.249
1940	CHI A 2		18	.195
	BRTR		1091	.265

HAYHURST, ELIAS HICKS
B.1826 PHILADELPHIA,PA.
D.DEC.18,1882 PHILADELPHIA,PA.
NON-PLAYING MANAGER ATH[AA] 1871-75

```
YR  CL LEA POS   GP    G    REC
```

HAYNES, JOSEPH WALTON (JOE)
B.SEPT.21,1917 LINCOLNTON,GA.
D.JAN.6,1967 HOPKINS,MINN.
```
1939 WAS A  P              27   8-12
1940 WAS A  P              22   3- 6
1941 CHI A  P               8   0- 0
1942 CHI A  P              40   8- 5
1943 CHI A  P              35   7- 2
1944 CHI A  P              33   5- 6
1945 CHI A  P         14   15   5- 5
1946 CHI A  P              32   7- 9
1947 CHI A  P              29  14- 6
1948 CHI A  P              27   9-10
1949 WAS A  P              37   2- 9
1950 WAS A  P              27   7- 5
1951 WAS A  P              26   1- 4
1952 WAS A  P              22   0- 3
         BRTR       379  380  76-82
```

HAYWOOD, WILLIAM KIERNAN (BILL)
B.APR.21,1937 COLON,PANAMA
```
1968 WAS A  P              14   0- 0
         BRTR
```

HAYWORTH, MYRON CLAUDE (RED)
B.MAY 14,1915 HIGH POINT,N.C.
```
1944 STL A  C              89   .223
1945 STL A  C              56   .194
         BRTR            145   .212
```

HAYWORTH, RAYMOND HALL
B.JAN.29,1904 HIGH POINT,N.C.
```
1926 DET A  C              12   .273
1929 DET A  C              14   .255
1930 DET A  C              77   .278
1931 DET A  C              88   .256
1932 DET A  C             109   .293
1933 DET A  C             134   .245
1934 DET A  C              54   .293
1935 DET A  C              51   .309
1936 DET A  C              81   .240
1937 DET A  C              30   .269
1938 DET A  C               8   .211
     BRO N  C               5   .000
1939 BRO N  C              21   .154
     NY  N  C               5   .231
1942 STL A  H               1  1.000
1944 BRO N  C               7   .000
1945 BRO N  C               2   .000
         BRTR            699   .265
```

HAZINSKI, STANLEY FRANK
[PLAYED UNDER NAME OF
STANLEY FRANK ROGERS]

HAZLE, ROBERT SIDNEY
(BOB) OR (HURRICANE)
B.DEC.9,1930 LAURENS,S.C.
```
1955 CIN N  O               6   .231
1957 MIL N  O              41   .403
1958 MIL N  O              20   .179
     DET A  O              43   .241
         BLTR            110   .310
```

HAZLETON, WILLARD CARPENTER (DOC)
B.AUG.28,1876 STRAFFORD,VT.
D.MAR.17,1941 BURLINGTON,VT.
```
1901 STL N  1               7   .125
1902 STL N  1               7   .130
                          14   .128
```

HEAD, EDWARD MARVIN (ED)
B.JAN.25,1918 SELMA,LA.
```
1940 BRO N  P         13   14   1- 2
1942 BRO N  P              36  10- 6
1943 BRO N  P              47   9-10
1944 BRO N  P               9   4- 3
1946 BRO N  P              13   3- 2
         BRTR       118  119  27-23
```

HEAD, RALPH
B.AUG.30,1893 TALLAPOOSA,GA.
D.OCT.8,1962 MUSCADINE,ALA.
```
1923 PHI N  P              35   2- 9
         BRTR
```

HEALEY, THOMAS
B.1853 CRANSTON,R.I.
D.FEB.6,1891 LEWISTON,MAINE
```
1878 PRO N  P               2   0- 2
     IND N  P-O      12   13   7- 5
                              .204
                     14   15   7- 7
                              .185
```

HEALY, FRANCIS XAVIER (FRAN)
B.SEP.6,1946 HOLYOKE,MASS.
```
1969 KC  A  /C               6   .400
1971 SF  N  C               47   .280
1972 SF  N  C               45   .152
1973 KC  A  C               95   .276
1974 KC  A  *C             139   .252
1975 KC  A  C               56   .255
1976 KC  A  /C               8   .125
     NY  A  C               46   .267
1977 NY  A  /C              27   .224
1978 NY  A  /C               1   .000
         BRTR            470   .250
```

HEALY, FRANCIS XAVIER PAUL
B.JUNE 29,1910 HOLYOKE,MASS.
```
1930 NY  N  O               7   .000
1931 NY  N  C               6   .143
1932 NY  N  C              14   .250
1934 STL N  C              15   .308
         BRTR             42   .241
```

HEALY, JOHN J.
(LONG JOHN) OR (EGYPTIAN)
B.OCT.27,1866 CAIRO,ILL.
D.MAR.16,1899 ST.LOUIS,MO.
```
1885 STL N  P               8   1- 7
1886 STL N  P         41   42  17-24
1887 IND N  P              40  12-28
1888 IND N  P              37  12-24
1889 WAS N  P              15   1-14
     CHI N  P               7   3- 4
1890 TOL AA P              47  22-19
1891 BAL AA P              23   8-12
1892 BAL N  P               9   2- 5
     LOU N  P               8   1- 1
         BRTR       235  236  79-138
```

HEALY, THOMAS FITZGERALD
B.OCT.30,1895 ALTOONA,PA.
```
1915 PHI A  3              23   .221
1916 PHI A  3               6   .261
         BRTR             29   .230
```

HEARD, CHARLES
B.JAN.30,1872 PHILADELPHIA,PA.
D.FEB.22,1945 PHILADELPHIA,PA.
```
1890 PIT N  P              12   0- 6
         BRTR
```

HEARD, JEHOSIE (JAY)
B.JAN.17,1925 ATLANTA,GA.
```
1954 BAL A  P               2   0- 0
         BLTL
```

HEARN
```
1872 OLY NA S-O            1   .333
```

HEARN, BUNN
B.MAY 21,1891 CHAPEL HILL,N.C.
D.OCT.19,1959 WILSON,N.C.
```
1910 STL N  P               5   1- 3
1911 STL N  P               2   0- 0
1913 NY  N  P               2   1- 1
1915 PIT F  P              29   6-11
1918 BOS N  P              17   5- 6
1920 BOS N  P              11   0- 3
         BLTL             66  13-24
```

HEARN, EDMUND
B.SEPT.17,1888 VENTURA,CAL.
D.SEPT.8,1952 SAWTELLE,CAL.
```
1910 BOS A  3               2   .000
     TR
```

HEARN, ELMER LAFAYETTE (BUNNY)
B.JAN.13,1904 BROOKLYN,N.Y.
D.MAR.31,1974 VENICE,FLA.
```
1926 BOS N  P              34   4- 9
1927 BOS N  P               8   0- 2
1928 BOS N  P               7   1- 0
1929 BOS N  P              10   2- 0
         BLTL             59   7-11
```

HEARN, JAMES TOLBERT (JIM)
B.APR.11,1921 ATLANTA,GA.
```
1947 STL N  P              37  12- 7
1948 STL N  P         34   36   8- 6
1949 STL N  P              17   1- 3
1950 STL N  P               6   0- 1
     NY  N  P              16  11- 3
1951 NY  N  P              34  17- 9
1952 NY  N  P              37  14- 7
1953 NY  N  P         36   37   9-12
1954 NY  N  P              29   8- 8
1955 NY  N  P         39   41  14-16
1956 NY  N  P         30   32   5-11
1957 PHI N  P              36   5- 1
1958 PHI N  P              39   5- 3
1959 PHI N  P               6   0- 2
         BRTR       396  403 109-89
```

HEARNE, HUGH JOSEPH (HUGHIE)
B.APR.18,1873 TROY,N.Y.
D.SEPT.22,1932 TROY,N.Y.
```
1901 BRO N  C               2   .500
1902 BRO N  C              62   .281
1903 BRO N  C              19   .281
         BRTR             83   .284
```

HEATH, JOHN GEOFFREY (JEFF)
B.APR.1,1915 FT.WILLIAM,ONT.,CANADA
D.DEC.9,1975 SEATTLE,WASH.
```
1936 CLE A  O              12   .341
1937 CLE A  O              20   .230
1938 CLE A  O             126   .343
1939 CLE A  O             121   .292
1940 CLE A  O             100   .219
1941 CLE A  O             151   .340
1942 CLE A  O             147   .278
1943 CLE A  O             118   .274
1944 CLE A  O              60   .331
1945 CLE A  O             102   .305
1946 WAS A  O              48   .283
1946 STL A  O              86   .275
1947 STL A  O             141   .251
1948 BOS N  O             115   .319
1949 BOS N  O              36   .306
         BLTR           1383   .293
```

HEATH, MICHAEL THOMAS (MIKE)
B.FEB.5,1955 TAMPA,FLA.
```
1978 NY  A  C              33   .228
         BRTR
```

HEATH, MINOR WILSON (MICKEY)
B.OCT.30,1903 TOLEDO,OHIO
```
1931 CIN N  1               7   .269
1932 CIN N  1              39   .201
         BLTL             46   .213
```

HEATH, SPENCER PAUL
B.NOV.5,1894 CHICAGO,ILL.
D.JAN.25,1930 CHICAGO,ILL.
```
1920 CHI A  P               4   0- 0
         BBTR
```

HEATH, THOMAS GEORGE
B.AUG.18,1913 AKRON,COL.
D.FEB.26,1967 LOS GATOS,CAL.
```
1935 STL A  C              47   .237
1937 STL A  C              17   .233
1938 STL A  C              70   .227
         BRTR            134   .230
```

HEATH, WILLIAM CHRIS (BILL)
B.MAR.10,1939 YUBA CITY,CAL.
```
1965 CHI A  /H              1   .000
1966 HOU N  C              55   .301
1967 HOU N  /C              9   .091
     DET A  /C             20   .125
1969 CHI N  /C             27   .156
         BLTR            112   .236
```

HEATHCOTE, CLIFTON EARL
B.JAN.24,1898 GLEN ROCK,PA.
D.JAN.19,1939 YORK,PA.
```
1918 STL N  1-O            88   .259
1919 STL N  1-O           114   .279
1920 STL N  O             133   .284
1921 STL N  O              62   .244
1922 STL N  O              34   .245
     CHI N  O              76   .276
1923 CHI N  O             117   .249
1924 CHI N  O             113   .309
1925 CHI N  O             109   .263
1926 CHI N  O             139   .276
1927 CHI N  O              83   .294
1928 CHI N  O              67   .285
1929 CHI N  O              82   .313
1930 CHI N  O              70   .260
1931 CIN N  O              90   .258
1932 CIN N  O               8   .000
     PHI N  O              30   .282
         BLTL           1415   .275
```

HEAVERLO, DAVID WALLACE (DAVE)
B.AUG.25,1950 ELLENSBURG,WASH.
```
1975 SF  N  P              42   3- 1
1976 SF  N  P              61   4- 4
1977 SF  N  P              56   5- 1
1978 OAK A  P              69   3- 6
         BRTR            228  15-12
```

HEBERT, WALLACE ANDREW (PREACHER)
B.AUG.21,1907 LAKE CHARLES,LA.
```
1931 STL A  P              23   6- 7
1932 STL A  P              35   1-12
1933 STL A  P              33   4- 6
1943 PIT N  P         34   35  10-11
         BLTL       125  126  21-36
```

HEBNER, RICHARD JOSEPH (RICHIE)
B.NOV.26,1947 BOSTON,MASS.
```
1968 PIT N  /H              2   .182
1969 PIT N  *3/1           129   .301
1970 PIT N  *3            120   .290
1971 PIT N  *3            112   .271
1972 PIT N  *3            124   .300
1973 PIT N  *3            144   .271
1974 PIT N  *3            144   .291
1975 PIT N  *3            128   .246
1976 PIT N  *3            132   .249
1977 PHI N  *1-3/2        118   .285
1978 PHI N  *1-3/2        137   .283
         BLTR           1292   .278
```

YR	CL	LEA	POS	GP	G	REC

HECHINGER, MICHAEL VINCENT
B.FEB.14,1890 CHICAGO,ILL.
D.AUG.13,1967 CHICAGO,ILL.

YR	CL	LEA	POS	GP	G	REC
1912	CHI	N	C		2	.000
1913	CHI	N	C		2	.000
	BRO	N	C		9	.222
	BRTR				13	.143

HECKER, GUY JACKSON
B.APR.3,1856 YOUNGVILLE,PA.
D.DEC.3,1938 WOOSTER,OHIO

YR	CL	LEA	POS	GP	G	REC
1882	LOU	AA	P-1-O	12	78	7- 5 .285
1883	LOU	AA	P-1-O	55	79	28-25 .264
1884	LOU	AA	P-1	76	79	52-20
1885	LOU	AA	P-1	54	72	30-24 .274
1886	LOU	AA	P-1	50	84	27-23 .342
1887	LOU	AA	P-1	33	91	19-12 .374
1888	LOU	AA	P-1	28	55	8-17 .255
1889	LOU	AA	P-1	17	82	5-11 .277
1890	PIT	N	M-P-1	14	86	2-12 .226
	BRTR			339	706	178-149 .292

HEDGPETH, HARRY MALCOLM
B.SEPT.4,1888 FAYETTEVILLE,N.C.
D.JULY 30,1966 RICHMOND,VA.

YR	CL	LEA	POS	GP	G	REC
1913	WAS	A	P		1	0- 0
	BLTL					

HEDLUND, MICHAEL DAVID
(MIKE) OR (RED)
B.AUG.11,1946 DALLAS,TEX.

YR	CL	LEA	POS	GP	G	REC
1965	CLE	A	/P		6	0- 0
1968	CLE	A	P		3	0- 0
1969	KC	A	/P		34	3- 6
1970	KC	A	/P		9	2- 3
1971	KC	A	P		32	15- 8
1972	KC	A	P		29	5- 7
	BBTR				113	25-24
	BR 1965, 72					

HEFFNER, DONALD HENRY (JEEP)
B.FEB.8,1911 ROUZERVILLE,PA.

YR	CL	LEA	POS	GP	G	REC
1934	NY	A	2		72	.261
1935	NY	A	2		10	.306
1936	NY	A	2-S-3		19	.229
1937	NY	A	2-S		60	.249
1938	STL	A	2		141	.245
1939	STL	A	2-S		110	.267
1940	STL	A	2		126	.236
1941	STL	A	2		110	.233
1942	STL	A	1-2		19	.167
1943	STL	A	1-2		18	.121
	PHI	A	1-2		52	.208
1944	DET	A	2		6	.211
	BRTR				743	.241

NON-PLAYING MANAGER CIN[N] 1966

HEFFNER, ROBERT FREDERIC (BOB)
B.SEP.13,1938 ALLENTOWN,PA.

YR	CL	LEA	POS	GP	G	REC
1963	BOS	A	P	20	21	4- 9
1964	BOS	A	P		55	7- 9
1965	BOS	A	P		27	0- 2
1966	CLE	A	/P		5	0- 1
1968	CAL	A	/P		7	0- 0
	BRTR			114	115	11-21

HEFLIN, RANDOLPH RUTHERFORD
B.SEPT.11,1918 FREDERICKSBURG,VA.

YR	CL	LEA	POS	GP	G	REC
1945	BOS	A	P		20	4-10
1946	BOS	A	P		25	4-11

HEGAN, JAMES EDWARD (JIM)
B.AUG.3,1920 LYNN,MASS.

YR	CL	LEA	POS	GP	G	REC
1941	CLE	A	C		16	.319
1942	CLE	A	C		68	.194
1946	CLE	A	C		88	.236
1947	CLE	A	C		135	.249
1948	CLE	A	C		144	.248
1949	CLE	A	C		152	.224
1950	CLE	A	C		131	.219
1951	CLE	A	C		133	.238
1952	CLE	A	C		112	.225
1953	CLE	A	C		112	.217
1954	CLE	A	C		139	.234
1955	CLE	A	C		116	.220
1956	CLE	A	C		122	.222
1957	CLE	A	C		58	.216
1958	DET	A	C		45	.192
	PHI	N	C		25	.220
1959	PHI	N	C		25	.196
	SF	N	C		21	.133
1960	CHI	N	C		24	.209
	BRTR				1666	.228

HEGAN, JAMES MICHAEL (MIKE)
B.JULY 21,1942 CLEVELAND,OHIO

YR	CL	LEA	POS	GP	G	REC
1964	NY	A	1		5	.000
1966	NY	A	1		13	.205
1967	NY	A	1-0		68	.136
1969	SEA	A	0-1		95	.292
1970	MIL	A	*1/0		148	.244
1971	MIL	A	1		46	.221
	OAK	A	1/0		65	.236
1972	OAK	A	1/0		98	.329
1973	OAK	A	1/0		75	.183
	NY	A	1		17	.275
1974	NY	A	1		18	.226
	MIL	A	0-1-0		89	.237
1975	MIL	A	0-1		93	.251
1976	MIL	A	0-0-1		80	.248
1977	MIL	A	/0-1		35	.170
	BLTL				965	.242

HEHL, HERMAN JACOB (JAKE)
B.OCT.8,1899 BROOKLYN,N.Y.
D.JULY 4,1961 BROOKLYN,N.Y.

YR	CL	LEA	POS	GP	G	REC
1918	BKO	N	P		1	0- 0
	BRTR					

HEIDEMANN, JACK SEALE
B.JULY 11,1949 BRENHAM,TEX.

YR	CL	LEA	POS	GP	G	REC
1969	CLE	A	/S		3	.000
1970	CLE	A	*S		133	.211
1971	CLE	A	S		81	.208
1972	CLE	A	S		10	.150
1974	CLE	A	/S-1-2		12	.091
	STL	N	S/3		47	.271
1975	NY	N	S/3-2		61	.214
1976	NY	N	/S-2		5	.083
	MIL	A	S-2		69	.219
1977	MIL	A	/2		5	.000
	BRTR				426	.211

HEIDRICK, R. EMMETT
(EMMETT) OR (SNAGS)
B.JULY 29,1876 QUEENSTOWN,PA.
D.JAN.20,1916 CLARION,PA.

YR	CL	LEA	POS	GP	G	REC
1898	CLE	N	O		19	.293
1899	STL	N	O		147	.329
1900	STL	N	O		83	.301
1901	STL	N	O		115	.339
1902	STL	A	P-S-3-O	1	110	0- 0 .288
1903	STL	A	O		121	.281
1904	STL	A	O		133	.269
1908	STL	A	O		26	.215
	TR			1	754	0- 0 .299

HEIFER, FRANKLIN (HECK)
B.JAN.18,1854 READING,PA.
D.AUG.29,1893

YR	CL	LEA	POS	GP	G	REC
1875	BOS	NA	1-0		11	.333

HEILBRONER, LOUIS WILBUR
B.JULY 4,1861 FT.WAYNE,IND.
D.DEC.21,1933 FT.WAYNE,IND.
NON-PLAYING MANAGER STL[N] 1900

HEILEMAN, JOHN GEORGE (CHINK)
B.AUG.10,1872 CINCINNATI,OHIO
D.JULY 19,1940 CINCINNATI,OHIO

YR	CL	LEA	POS	GP	G	REC
1901	CIN	N	3		5	.133
	TR					

HEILMANN, HARRY EDWIN (SLUG)
B.DEC.3,1894 SAN FRANCISCO,CAL.
D.JULY 9,1951 DETROIT,MICH.

YR	CL	LEA	POS	GP	G	REC
1914	DET	A	1-O		67	.225
1916	DET	A	1-O		136	.282
1917	DET	A	1-O		150	.281
1918	DET	A	1		79	.276
1919	DET	A	1		140	.320
1920	DET	A	1-O		145	.309
1921	DET	A	1		149	.394
1922	DET	A	O		118	.356
1923	DET	A	O		144	.403
1924	DET	A	O		153	.346
1925	DET	A	O		150	.393
1926	DET	A	O		141	.367
1927	DET	A	O		141	.398
1928	DET	A	1-O		151	.328
1929	DET	A	O		125	.344
1930	CIN	N	1-O		142	.333
1932	CIN	N	1		15	.258
	BRTR				2146	.342

HEIM, VAL RAYMOND
B.NOV.4,1920 PLYMOUTH,WIS.

YR	CL	LEA	POS	GP	G	REC
1942	CHI	A	O		13	.200
	BLTR					

HEIMACH, FREDERICK AMOS
(FRED) OR (LEFTY)
B.JAN.27,1901 CAMDEN,N.J.
D.JUNE 1,1973 FT.MYERS,FLA.

YR	CL	LEA	POS	GP	G	REC
1920	PHI	A	P		1	0- 1
1921	PHI	A	P		1	0- 0
1922	PHI	A	P		37	7-11
1923	PHI	A	P	40	63	6-12
1924	PHI	A	P	40	58	14-12
1925	PHI	A	P	10	15	0- 1
1926	PHI	A	P	13	14	1- 0
	BOS	A	P	20	26	2- 9
1928	NY	A	P	13	18	2- 3
1929	NY	A	P	35	36	11- 6
1930	BRO	N	P	9	13	0- 2
1931	BRO	N	P	31	39	9- 7
1932	BRO	N	P	36	37	9- 4
1933	BRO	N	P		10	0- 1
	BLTL			296	368	62-69

HEINE, WILLIAM HENRY (BUD)
B.SEPT.22,1900 ELMIRA,N.Y.
D.SEPT.2,1976 FT.LAUDERDALE,FLA

YR	CL	LEA	POS	GP	G	REC
1921	NY	N	2		1	.000
	BLTR					

HEINTZELMAN, KENNETH ALPHONSE (KEN)
B.OCT.14,1915 PERUQUE,MO.

YR	CL	LEA	POS	GP	G	REC
1937	PIT	N	P		1	1- 0
1938	PIT	N	P		1	0- 0
1939	PIT	N	P		17	1- 1
1940	PIT	N	P	39	41	8- 8
1941	PIT	N	P		35	11-11
1942	PIT	N	P		27	8-11
1946	PIT	N	P		32	8-12
1947	PIT	N	P		2	0- 0
	PHI	N	P		24	7-10
1948	PHI	N	P		27	6-11
1949	PHI	N	P		33	17-10
1950	PHI	N	P		23	3- 9
1951	PHI	N	P		35	6-12
1952	PHI	N	P		23	1- 3
	BRTL			319	321	77-98

HEINTZELMAN, THOMAS KENNETH (TOM)
B.NOV.3,1946 ST.CHARLES,MO.

YR	CL	LEA	POS	GP	G	REC
1973	STL	N	/2		23	.310
1974	STL	N	2-S/3		38	.230
1977	SF	N	/H		2	.000
1978	SF	N	/2-3-1		27	.229
	BRTR				90	.243

HEINZMAN, JOHN PETER (JACK)
B.SEPT.27,1863 NEW ALBANY,IND.
D.NOV.10,1914 LOUISVILLE,KY.

YR	CL	LEA	POS	GP	G	REC
1886	LOU	AA	1		1	.000
	BRTR					

HEISE, CLARENCE EDWARD (LEFTY)
B.AUG.7,1907 TOPEKA,KAN.

YR	CL	LEA	POS	GP	G	REC
1934	STL	N	P		1	0- 0
	BLTL					

HEISE, JAMES EDWARD
B.OCT.2,1932 SCOTTDALE,PA.

YR	CL	LEA	POS	GP	G	REC
1957	WAS	A	P		8	0- 3

HEISE, ROBERT LOWELL (BOBBY)
B.MAY 12,1947 SAN ANTONIO,TEX.

YR	CL	LEA	POS	GP	G	REC
1967	NY	N	2/S-3		16	.323
1968	NY	N	/S-2		16	.217
1969	NY	N	/S		4	.300
1970	SF	N	S-2/3		67	.234
1971	SF	N	/S-3-2		13	.000
	MIL	A	S-3/2-O		68	.254
1972	MIL	A	3/S		95	.266
1973	MIL	A	S/3-1-2		49	.204
1974	STL	N	/2		3	.143
	CAL	A	2/3-S		29	.267
1975	BOS	A	3-2/S-1		63	.214
1976	BOS	A	3/S-2		32	.268
1977	KC	A	2-S-3/1		54	.288
	BRTR				499	.247

HEISER, LE ROY BARTON (ROY)
B.JUNE 22,1942 BALTIMORE,MD.

YR	CL	LEA	POS	GP	G	REC
1961	WAS	A	P		3	0- 0
	BRTR					

HEISMANN, CHRISTIAN ERNEST (CRESE)
B.APR.16,1880 CINCINNATI,OHIO
D.NOV.19,1951 CINCINNATI,OHIO

YR	CL	LEA	POS	GP	G	REC
1901	CIN	N	P		3	0- 1
1902	CIN	N	P		5	2- 1
	BAL	A	P		3	0- 3
	BRTL					

HEIST, ALFRED MICHAEL (AL)
B.OCT.5,1927 BROOKLYN,N.Y.

YR	CL	LEA	POS	GP	G	REC
1960	CHI	N	O		41	.275
1961	CHI	N	O		109	.255
1962	HOU	N	O		27	.222
	BRTR				177	.255

YR	CL LEA POS	GP	G	REC

HEITMANN, HENRY ANTON
B.OCT.6,1896 ALBANY,N.Y.
D.DEC.15,1958 BROOKLYN,N.Y.
1918 BRO N P   1   0- 1

HEITMULLER, WILLIAM FREDERICK (HEINIE)
B.1883 SAN FRANCISCO,CAL.
D.OCT.8,1912 LOS ANGELES,CAL.
1909 PHI A O   64   .286
1910 PHI A O   31   .243
                               95   .271

HELD, MELVIN NICHOLAS (MEL) OR (COUNTRY)
B.APR.12,1929 EDON,OHIO
1956 BAL A P   4   0- 0
      BRTR

HELD, WOODSON GEORGE (WOODIE)
B.MAR.25,1932 SACRAMENTO,CAL.
1954 NY A S-3   4   .000
1957 NY A H   1   .000
      KC A O   92   .239
1958 KC A S-3-O   47   .214
      CLE A S-3-O   67   .194
1959 CLE A 2-S-3-O   143   .251
1960 CLE A S   109   .258
1961 CLE A S   146   .267
1962 CLE A S-3-O   139   .249
1963 CLE A 2-S-3-O   133   .248
1964 CLE A 2-3-O   118   .236
1965 WAS A *O/3-2-S 122   .247
1966 BAL A O/2-S-3   56   .207
1967 BAL A /2-3-O   26   .146
      CAL A 3-O-S/2   58   .220
1968 CHI A /2-S-3-O   33   .111
1969 CHI A O/3-2   40   .167
      CHI A S-3-2   56   .143
      BRTR   1390   .240

HELENIUS, ARTHUR DEWEY
[PLAYED UNDER NAME OF ARTHUR DEWEY DELANEY]

HELF, HENRY HARTZ (HANK)
B.AUG.26,1913 AUSTIN,TEX.
1938 CLE A C   6   .077
1940 CLE A C   1   .000
1946 CLE A C   71   .192
      BRTR   78   .184

HELFRICH, EMORY WILBUR (TY)
B.OCT.9,1890 PLEASANTVILLE,N.J.
D.MAR.18,1955 PLEASANTVILLE,N.J.
1915 BRO F 2   40   .245

HELLINGS
1875 ATL NA 2   1   .250

HELLMAN, ANTHONY J.
B.1861 CINCINNATI,OHIO
D.MAR.29,1898 CINCINNATI,OHIO
1886 BAL AA C   1   .000

HELMBOLD, HORACE
B.PHILADELPHIA,PA.
1890 ATH AA P   1   1- 0

HELMS, TOMMY VANN
B.MAY 5,1941 CHARLOTTE,N.C.
1964 CIN N H   2   .000
1965 CIN N /S-3-2   21   .381
1966 CIN N *3-2   138   .284
1967 CIN N 2-S   137   .274
1968 CIN N *2/S-3   127   .288
1969 CIN N *2/S   126   .269
1970 CIN N *2-S   150   .237
1971 CIN N *2   150   .258
1972 HOU N *2   139   .259
1973 HOU N *2   146   .287
1974 HOU N *2   137   .279
1975 HOU N 2/3-S   64   .207
1976 PIT N 3-2/S   62   .276
1977 PIT N H   15   .000
      BOS A O/3-2   21   .271
      BRTR   1435   .269

HELTZEL, WILLIAM WADE (HEINIE)
B.DEC.21,1913 YORK,PA.
1943 BOS N 3   29   .151
1944 BOS N S   11   .162
      BLTR   40   .157

HEMAN, RUSSELL FREDRICK (RUSS)
B.FEB.10,1933 OLIVE,CAL.
1961 CLE A P   6   0- 0
      LA N P   6   0- 0
      BRTR   12   0- 0

HEMINGWAY, EDSON MARSHALL
B.MAY 8,1893 SHERIDAN,MICH.
D.JULY 5,1969 GRAND RAPIDS,MICH
1914 STL A 3   4   .000
1917 NY N 1   7   .320
1918 PHI N 1-2-3   33   .213
      BBTR   44   .225

HEMMING, GEORGE EARL (GEORGE) OR (OLD WAX FIGGER)
B.DEC.15,1868 CARROLLTON,OHIO
D.JUNE 3,1930 SPRINGFIELD,MASS.
1890 CLE P P   3   0- 3
      BRO P P   16   7- 5
1891 BRO N P   22   8-14
1892 CIN N P   1   0- 0
      LOU N P   4   2- 1
1893 LOU N P   39   43 18-18
1894 LOU N P   32 11-20
      BAL N P   15   5- 0
1895 BAL N P   34 18-12
1896 BAL N P   25 15- 7
      .897 LOU N P   8   3- 5
      BRTR   199 203 87-85

HEMP, WILLIAM H. (DUCKY)
B.DEC.27,1867 ST.LOUIS,MO.
D.MAR.6,1923 ST.LOUIS,MO.
1887 LOU AA O   1   .250
1890 PIT N O   21   .213
      SYR AA O   9   .156
                      31   .200

HEMPHILL, CHARLES JUDSON (EAGLE EYE)
B.APR.20,1876 GREENVILLE,OHIO
D.JUNE 22,1953 DETROIT,MICH.
1899 STL N O   11   .243
      CLE N O   51   .280
1901 BOS A O   137   .269
1902 CLE A O   25   .272
      STL A O   103   .317
1903 STL A O   106   .238
1904 STL A O   114   .253
1906 STL A O   154   .289
1907 STL A O   153   .259
1908 NY A O   142   .297
1909 NY A O   73   .243
1910 NY A O   102   .239
1911 NY A O   69   .284
      BLTL   1240   .271

HEMPHILL, FRANK VERNON
B.MAY 13,1878 GREENVILLE,MICH.
D.NOV.16,1950 CHICAGO,ILL.
1906 CHI A O   13   .075
1909 WAS A O   1   .000
      BRTR   14   .070

HEMSLEY, RALSTON BURDETT (ROLLIE)
B.JUNE 24,1907 SYRACUSE,OHIO
D.JULY 31,1972 WASHINGTON,D.C.
1928 PIT N C   50   .271
1929 PIT N C   88   .289
1930 PIT N C   104   .253
1931 PIT N C   10   .171
      CHI N C   66   .309
1932 CHI N C   60   .238
1933 CIN N C   49   .190
      STL A C   32   .242
1934 STL A C-O   123   .309
1935 STL A C   144   .290
1936 STL A C   116   .263
1937 STL A C   100   .222
1938 CLE A C   66   .296
1939 CLE A C   107   .263
1940 CLE A C   119   .267
1941 CLE A C   98   .240
1942 CIN N C   36   .113
      NY A C   31   .294
1943 NY A C   62   .239
1944 NY A C   81   .268
1946 PHI N C   49   .223
1947 PHI N C   2   .333
      BRTR   1593   .262

HEMUS, SOLOMON JOSEPH (SOLLY)
B.APR.17,1923 PHOENIX,ARIZ.
1949 STL N 2   20   .333
1950 STL N 3   11   .133
1951 STL N 2-S   120   .281
1952 STL N S-3   151   .268
1953 STL N 2-S   154   .279
1954 STL N 2-S-3   124   .304
1955 STL N 2-S-3   96   .243
1956 STL N H   8   .200
      PHI N 2-3   78   .289
1957 PHI N 2   70   .185
1958 PHI N 3   105   .284
1959 STL N M-2-3   24   .235
      BLTR   961   .273
NON-PLAYING MANAGER STL[N] 1960-61

HENDERSON, ALBERT H.
B.BALTIMORE,MD.
NON-PLAYING MANAGER BAL[NA] 1872-74

HENDERSON, BERNARD (BERNIE) OR (BARNYARD)
B.APR.12,1899 DOUGLASSVILLE,TEX
D.JUNE 6,1966 LINDEN,TEX.
1921 CLE A P   2   3   0- 1
      BRTR

HENDERSON, EDWARD J.
[REAL NAME EUGENE J. BALL]
B.DEC.25,1884 NEWARK,N.J.
D.JAN.15,1964 NEW YORK,N.Y.
1914 PIT F P   6   0- 3
1914 IND F P   1   1- 0
      BLTL   7   1- 3

HENDERSON, JAMES HARDING (HARDIE)
B.OCT.31,1862 PHILADELPHIA,PA.
D.FEB.6,1903 PHILADELPHIA,PA.
1883 PHI N P-O   1   2   0- 0
                  3-O   .250
      BAL AA P-S-   45   50 10-30
                  3-O   .151
1884 BAL AA P   51   54 27-22
1885 BAL AA P   61 26-35
1886 BAL AA P   19   3-16
      BRO AA P   14 10- 4
1887 BRO AA P   14   4- 9
1888 PIT N P   5   1- 3
      BRTR   210 219 81-119
                                 .208

HENDERSON, JOSEPH LEE (JOE)
B.JULY 4,1946 LAKE CORMORANT,MISS.
1974 CHI A /P   5   1- 0
1976 CIN N /P   4   2- 0
1977 CIN N /P   7   0- 2
      BLTL   16   3- 2

HENDERSON, KENNETH JOSEPH (KEN)
B.JUNE 15,1946 CARROLL,IOWA
1965 SF N O   63   .192
1966 SF N O   11   .310
1967 SF N O   65   .190
1968 SF N /O   3   .333
1969 SF N *O/3   113   .225
1970 SF N *O   148   .294
1971 SF N *O/1   144   .264
1972 SF N *O   130   .257
1973 CHI A D-O   73   .260
1974 CHI A *O   162   .292
1975 CHI A *O   140   .251
1976 ATL N *O   133   .262
1977 TEX A O   75   .298
1978 NY N /O   7   .227
      CIN N O   64   .167
      BBTR   1328   .258

HENDERSON, STEVEN CURTIS (STEVE)
B.NOV.18,1952 HOUSTON,TEX.
1977 NY N O   99   .297
1978 NY N O   157   .266
      BRTR   256   .277

HENDERSON, WILLIAM C.
NON-PLAYING MANAGER BAL[U] 1884

HENDERSON, WILLIAM MAXWELL
B.NOV.4,1901 PENSACOLA,FLA.
D.OCT.6,1966 PENSACOLA,FLA.
1930 NY A P   3   0- 0
      BRTR

HENDLEY, CHARLES ROBERT (BOB)
B.APR.30,1939 MACON,GA.
1961 MIL N P   19   5- 7
1962 MIL N P   35   36 11-13
1963 MIL N P   41   46   9- 9
1964 SF N P   30 10-11
1965 SF N /P   8   0- 1
      CHI N P   18   4- 4
1966 CHI N P   43   4- 5
1967 CHI N /P   7   0- 0
      NY N P   15   3- 3
      BRTL   216 222 48-52

HENDRICK, GEORGE ANDREW
B.OCT.18,1949 LOS ANGELES,CAL.
1971 OAK A O   42   .237
1972 OAK A O   58   .182
1973 CLE A *O   113   .268
1974 CLE A *O   139   .279
1975 CLE A *O   145   .258
1976 CLE A *O   149   .265
1977 SD N *O   152   .311
1978 SD N O   36   .243
      STL N *O   102   .288
      BRTR   936   .272

HENDRICK, HARVEY LEE (GINK)
B.NOV.9,1897 MASON,TENN.
D.OCT.29,1941 COVINGTON,TENN.
1923 NY A O   37   .273
1924 NY A O   40   .263
1925 CLE A O   25   .286
1927 BRO N 1-O   128   .310
1928 BRO N 3-O   126   .318
1929 BRO N 1-O   110   .354
1930 BRO N O   68   .257
1931 BRO N H   1   .000
      CIN N 1   137   .315
1932 STL N 3   28   .250
      CIN N 1   94   .327
1933 CIN N 1-3-O   69   .291
1934 PHI N O   59   .293
      BLTR   922   .308

YR	CL LEA POS	GP	G	REC

HENDRICKS, EDWARD (BIG ED)
B.JUNE 20,1886 ZEELAND,MICH.
D.NOV.28,1930 JACKSON,MICH.
1910 NY N P   4   0- 1

HENDRICKS, ELROD JEROME
B.DEC.22,1940 CHARLOTTE AMALIE,V.I.
1968 BAL A C   79   .202
1969 BAL A C/1   105   .244
1970 BAL A C   106   .242
1971 BAL A C/1   101   .250
1972 BAL A C   33   .155
     CHI N C   17   .116
1973 BAL A C   41   .178
1974 BAL A C/1   66   .208
1975 BAL A C   85   .215
1976 BAL A C   28   .139
     NY A C   26   .226
1977 NY A /C   10   .273
1978 BAL A /C-P   1   13   0- 0
                            .333
     BLTR   1 710   0- 0
                            .220

HENDRICKS, JOHN CHARLES
B.APR.9,1875 JOLIET,ILL.
D.MAY 13,1943 CHICAGO,ILL.
1902 NY N O   7   .240
                       2   .500
1903 WAS A O   32   .183
     BLTL   41   .211
NON-PLAYING MANAGER
STL[N] 1918, CIN[N] 1924-29

HENDRICKSON, DONALD WILLIAMSON
B.JULY 14,1913 ROCHESTER,IND.
D.JAN.19,1977 NORFOLK,VA.
1945 BOS N P   37   4- 8
1946 BOS N P   2   0- 1
     BRTR   39   4- 9

HENDRIX, CLAUDE RAYMOND
B.APR.13,1889 OLATHE,KAN.
D.MAR.22,1944 ALLENTOWN,PA.
1911 PIT N P   22   4- 6
1912 PIT N P   46 24- 9
1913 PIT N P   42 53 14-15
1914 CHI F P   49 29-10
1915 CHI F P   40 46 16-15
1916 CHI N P   36 45   8-16
1917 CHI N P   40 48 10-12
1918 CHI N P   32 35 20- 7
1919 CHI N P   33 36 10-14
1920 CHI N P   27 34   9-12
     BRTR   367 414 144-116

HENDRYX, TIMOTHY GREEN
B.JAN.31,1891 LEROY,TEX.
D.AUG.14,1957 CORPUS CHRISTI,TEX.
1911 CLE A O   3   .265
1912 CLE A O   23   .243
1915 NY A O   13   .200
1916 NY A O   15   .290
1917 NY A O   125   .249
1918 STL A O   88   .279
1920 BOS A O   99   .328
1921 BOS A O   49   .241
     BRTR   415   .276

HENGLE, EDWARD S.
B.CHICAGO,ILL.
NON-PLAYING MANAGER CHI[U] 1884

HENGLE, EMORY J. (MOXIE)
B.1858
1884 CHI U 2   18   .222
     STP U 2   9   .132
1885 BUF N 2-O   7   .154
                      34   .172

HENION, LAFAYETTE M.
B.1901 SAN DIEGO,CAL.
D.JULY 22,1955 SAN LUIS OBISPO,CAL.
1919 BRO N P   1   0- 0
     BRTR

HENLEY, GAIL CURTICE
B.OCT.15,1928 WICHITA,KAN.
1954 PIT N O   14   .300
     BLTR

HENLEY, WELDON
B.OCT.25,1880 JASPER,GA.
D.NOV.16,1960 PALATKA,FLA.
1903 PHI A P   29 30 12- 9
1904 PHI A P   36 14-16
1905 PHI A P   25   4-12
1907 BRO N P   7   1- 5
     BRTR   97 98 31-42

HENLINE, WALTER JOHN (BUTCH)
B.DEC.20,1894 FT.WAYNE,IND.
D.OCT.9,1957 SARASOTA,FLA.
1921 NY N C   1   .000
     PHI N C   33   .306
1922 PHI N C   125   .316
1923 PHI N C-O   111   .324
1924 PHI N C-O   115   .284
1925 PHI N C-O   93   .304
1926 PHI N C   99   .283
1927 BRO N C   67   .266
1928 BRO N C   55   .212
1929 BRO N C   27   .242
1930 CHI A C   3   .125
1931 CHI A C   11   .067
     BRTR   740   .291

HENNESSEY, GEORGE (THREE STAR)
B.OCT.28,1907 SLATINGTON,PA.
1937 STL A P   5   0- 1
1942 PHI N P   5   1- 1
1945 CHI N P   2   0- 0
     BRTR   12   1- 2

HENNESSY, LESTER BAKER
B.DEC.12,1893 LYNN,MASS.
1913 DET A 2   14   .133
     BRTR

HENNIGAN, PHILLIP WINSTON (PHIL)
B.APR.10,1946 JASPER,TEX.
1969 CLE A /P   9   2- 1
1970 CLE A P   42   6- 3
1971 CLE A P   57   4- 3
1972 CLE A P   38   5- 3
1973 NY N P   30   0- 4
     BRTR   176 17-14

HENNING, ERNEST HERMAN (PETE)
B.DEC.28,1887 CROWN POINT,IND.
D.NOV.4,1939 DYER,IND.
1914 KC F P   28   5- 9
1915 KC F P   40   9-15
     BRTR   68 14-24

HENNINGER, RICHARD LEE (RICK)
B.JAN.11,1948 HASTINGS,NEB.
1973 TEX A /P   6   1- 0
     BRTR

HENRICH, FRANK WILDE (FRITZ)
B.MAY 8,1899 CINCINNATI,OHIO
D.MAY 1,1959 PHILADELPHIA,PA.
1924 PHI N O   36   .211
     BLTL

HENRICH, ROBERT EDWARD (BOBBY)
B.DEC.24,1938 LAWRENCE,KAN.
1957 CIN N 2-S-3-O   22   .200
1958 CIN N S   5   .000
1959 CIN N S   14   .000
     BRTR   48   .125

HENRICH, THOMAS DAVID (TOMMY)
(THE CLUTCH) OR (OLD RELIABLE)
B.FEB.20,1913 MASSILLON,OHIO
1937 NY A O   67   .320
1938 NY A O   131   .270
1939 NY A O   99   .277
1940 NY A 1-O   90   .307
1941 NY A O   144   .277
1942 NY A 1-O   127   .267
1946 NY A 1-O   150   .251
1947 NY A 1-O   142   .287
1948 NY A 1-O   146   .308
1949 NY A 1-O   115   .287
1950 NY A 1   73   .272
     BLTL   1284   .282

HENRIKSEN, OLAF (SWEDE)
B.APR.26,1888 KIRKERUP,DENMARK
D.OCT.17,1962 CANTON,MASS.
1911 BOS A O   27   .366
1912 BOS A O   37   .321
1913 BOS A O   30   .375
1914 BOS A O   61   .253
1915 BOS A O   73   .196
1916 BOS A O   68   .202
1917 BOS A O   15   .083
     BLTL   311   .267

HENRY, EARL CLIFFORD (HOOK)
B.JUNE 10,1917 ROSEVILLE,OHIO
1944 CLE A P   2   4   1- 1
1945 CLE A P   15 16   0- 3
     BLTL   17 20   1- 4

HENRY, FRANK JOHN (DUTCH)
B.MAY 12,1902 CLEVELAND,OHIO
D.AUG.23,1968 CLEVELAND,OHIO
1921 STL A P   1   0- 0
1922 STL A P   4   0- 0
1923 BRO N P   17   4- 6
1924 BRO N P   16   1- 2
1927 NY N P   15 11- 6
1928 NY N P   17   3- 6
1929 NY N P   27   5- 6
     CHI A P   2   1- 0
1930 CHI A P   35   2-17
     BLTL   164 27-43

HENRY, FREDERICK MARSHALL (SNAKE)
B.JULY 19,1895 WAYNESVILLE,N.C.
1922 BOS N 1   18   .197
1923 BOS N 1   11   .111
     BLTL   29   .187

HENRY, GEORGE WASHINGTON
B.AUG.10,1863 PHILADELPHIA,PA.
D.DEC.30,1934 LYNN,MASS.
1893 CIN N C   21   .273
     BRTR

HENRY, JAMES FRANCIS
B.JUNE 26,1910 DANVILLE,PA.
D.AUG.15,1976 MEMPHIS,TENN.
1936 BOS A P   21 22   5- 1
1937 BOS A P   3   1- 0
1939 PHI N P   9   0- 1
     BRTR   33 34   6- 2

HENRY, JOHN MICHAEL
B.SEPT.2,1863 SPRINGFIELD,MASS.
D.JUNE 11,1939 HARTFORD,CONN.
1884 CLE N P-O   5   9   1- 4
                            .154
1885 BAL AA P-O   9 10   2- 6
                            .273
1886 WAS N P   4   1- 3
1890 NY N O   37   .243
                  18 60   4-13
                            .241

HENRY, JOHN T.
B.DEC.26,1889 AMHERST,MASS.
D.NOV.24,1941 FORT HUACHUCA,ARIZ.
1910 WAS A C   29   .149
1911 WAS A C-1   85   .203
1912 WAS A C   68   .194
1913 WAS A C   96   .226
1914 WAS A C   91   .169
1915 WAS A C   95   .220
1916 WAS A C   117   .249
1917 WAS A C   65   .190
1918 BOS N C   43   .206
     BRTR   684   .207

HENRY, RONALD BAXTER (RON)
B.AUG.7,1936 CHESTER,PA.
1961 MIN A C-1   20   .143
1964 MIN A C   22   .122
     BRTR   42   .130

HENRY, WILLIAM FRANCIS (BILL)
B.FEB.15,1942 LONG BEACH,CAL.
1966 NY A /P   2   0- 0
     BLTL

HENRY, WILLIAM RODMAN (BILL)
B.OCT.15,1927 ALICE,TEX.
1952 BOS A P   13 14   5- 4
1953 BOS A P   21   5- 5
1954 BOS A P   24 25   3- 7
1955 BOS A P   17   2- 4
1958 CHI N P   44   5- 4
1959 CHI N P   65   9- 8
1960 CIN N P   51   1- 5
1961 CIN N P   47 48   2- 1
1962 CIN N P   40   4- 2
1963 CIN N P   47   1- 3
1964 CIN N P   37 38   2- 2
1965 CIN N /P   3   2- 0
     SF N P   35   2- 2
1966 SF N P   35   1- 1
1967 SF N P   28   2- 0
1968 SF N P   7   0- 2
     PIT N P   10   0- 0
1969 HOU N /P   3   0- 0
     BLTL   527 531 46-50

HENSHAW, ROY K.
B.JULY 29,1911 CHICAGO,ILL.
1933 CHI N P   21   2- 1
1935 CHI N P   31 13- 5
1936 CHI N P   39   9- 5
1937 BRO N P   42 43   5-12
1938 STL N P   27   5-11
1942 DET A P   23   2- 4
1943 DET A P   26   0- 2
1944 DET A P   7   0- 0
     BRTL   216 217 33-40

YR	CL	LEA	POS	GP	G	REC

HENSIEK, PHILIP FRANK (SID)
B.OCT.13,1901 ST.LOUIS,MO.
D.FEB.21,1972 ST.LOUIS,MO.
1935 WAS A P   6   0- 3
      BRTR

HEPLER, WILLIAM LEWIS (BILL)
B.SEP.25,1945 COVINGTON,VA.
1966 NY N P   37   3- 3
      BLTL

HERBEL, RONALD SAMUEL (RON)
B.JAN.16,1938 DENVER,COLO.
1963 SF N P   2   0- 0
1964 SF N P   40 41   9- 9
1965 SF N P   47 12- 9
1966 SF N P   32   4- 5
1967 SF N P   42   4- 5
1968 SF N P   28   0- 0
1969 SF N P   39   4- 1
1970 SD N P   64   7- 5
     NY N P   12   2- 2
1971 ATL N P   25   0- 1
      BRTR   331 332 42-37

HERBERT, ERNIE ALBERT (TEX)
B.JAN.30,1887 HALE,MO.
D.JAN.13,1968 DALLAS,TEX.
1913 CIN N P   6   0- 0
1914 STL F P   19 25   1- 0
1915 STL F P   11 12   1- 0
      BRTR   36 43   2- 0

HERBERT, FREDERICK
[REAL NAME HERBERT FREDERICK KEMMAN]
B.MAR.4,1887 LAGRANGE,ILL.
D.MAY 29,1963 TICE,FLA.
1915 NY N P   2   1- 1
      BRTR

HERBERT, RAYMOND ERNEST (RAY)
B.DEC.15,1929 DETROIT,MICH.
1950 DET A P   8   1- 2
1951 DET A P   5   4- 0
1953 DET A P   43   4- 6
1954 DET A P   42   3- 6
1955 KC A P   23 24   1- 8
1958 KC A P   42   8- 8
1959 KC A P   37 11-11
1960 KC A P   37 14-15
1961 KC A P   13   3- 6
     CHI A P   21   9- 6
1962 CHI A P   35 20- 9
1963 CHI A P   33 13-10
1964 CHI A P   20   6- 7
1965 PHI N P   25   5- 8
1966 PHI N P   23   2- 5
      BRTR   407 408 104-107

HERCHENROEDER, NICHOLAS
[PLAYED UNDER NAME OF
NICHOLAS REEDER]

HERMAN, ARTHUR
B.MAY 11,1871 OHIO
D.SEP.20,1955 LOS ANGELES,CAL.
1896 LOU N P   13   3- 5
1897 LOU N P   3   0- 0
                         16   3- 5

HERMAN, FLOYD CAVES (BABE)
B.JUNE 26,1903 BUFFALO,N.Y.
1926 BRO N 1-0   137 .319
1927 BRO N 1   130 .272
1928 BRO N O   134 .340
1929 BRO N O   146 .381
1930 BRO N O   153 .393
1931 BRO N O   151 .313
1932 CIN N O   148 .326
1933 CHI N O   137 .289
1934 CHI N O   125 .304
1935 PIT N 1-0   26 .235
     CIN N 1-0   92 .335
1936 CIN N 1-0   119 .279
1937 DET A O   17 .300
1945 BRO N O   37 .265
      BLTL   1552 .323

HERMAN, WILLIAM JENNINGS BRYAN (BILLY)
B.JULY 7,1909 NEW ALBANY,IND.
1931 CHI N 2   25 .327
1932 CHI N 2   154 .314
1933 CHI N 2   153 .279
1934 CHI N 2   113 .303
1935 CHI N 2   154 .341
1936 CHI N 2   153 .334
1937 CHI N 2   138 .335
1938 CHI N 2   152 .277
1939 CHI N 2   156 .307
1940 CHI N 2   135 .292
1941 CHI N 2   11 .291
     BRO N 2   133 .291
1942 BRO N 1-2   155 .256
1943 BRO N 2-3   153 .330
1946 BRO N 2-3   47 .288
     BOS N 1-2-3   75 .306
1947 PIT N M-1-2   15 .213
      BRTR   1922 .304
NON-PLAYING MANAGER BOS(A) 1964-66

HERMANN, ALBERT BARTEL
B.MAR.28,1901 MILLTOWN,N.J.
1923 BOS N 1-2-3   31 .237
1924 BOS N H   1 .000
      BRTR   32 .235

HERMANSKI, EUGENE VICTOR (GENE)
B.MAY 11,1920 PITTSFIELD,MASS.
1943 BRO N O   18 .300
1946 BRO N O   64 .200
1947 BRO N O   79 .275
1948 BRO N O   133 .290
1949 BRO N O   87 .299
1950 BRO N O   94 .298
1951 BRO N O   31 .250
     CHI N O   75 .282
1952 CHI N O   99 .255
1953 CHI N O   18 .150
     PIT N O   41 .177
      BLTR   739 .272

HERMOSO, ANGEL REMIGIO (REMY)
B.OCT.1,1947 CARABOBO,VENEZUELA
1967 ATL N /S-2   11 .308
1969 MON N 2/S   28 .162
1970 MON N /2-3   4 .000
1974 CLE A 2   48 .221
      BRTR   91 .211

HERNAIZ, JESUS RAFAEL [RODRIGUEZ]
B.JAN.8,1948 SANTURCE,P.R.
1974 PHI N P   27   2- 3
      BRTR

HERNANDEZ, ENZO OCTAVIO
B.FEB.12,1949 VALLE DE GUANAPE, VENEZ.
1971 SD N *S   143 .222
1972 SD N *S/O   114 .195
1973 SD N S   70 .223
1974 SD N *S   147 .232
1975 SD N *S   146 .218
1976 SD N *S   113 .256
1977 SD N /S   7 .000
1978 LA N /S   4 .000
      BRTR   714 .224

HERNANDEZ, GREGORIO EVELIO [LOPEZ]
B.DEC.24,1930 GUANABACOA,HAVANA,CUBA
1956 WAS A P   4   1- 1
1957 WAS A P   14   0- 0
      BRTR   18   1- 1

HERNANDEZ, GUILLERMO [VILLANUEVA] (WILLIE)
B.NOV.14,1955 AGUADA,P.R.
1977 CHI N P   67   8- 7
1978 CHI N P   54 55   8- 2
      BLTL   121 122 16- 9

HERNANDEZ, JACINTO [ZULUETA]
B.SEPT.11,1940 CENTRAL TINGUARO,CUBA
B.SEP.11,1940 MATANZAS,CUBA
1965 CAL A /S-3   6 .333
1966 CAL A 3/2-S-O   58 .043
1967 MIN A S-3   29 .143
1968 MIN A S/1   83 .176
1969 KC A *S   145 .222
1970 KC A S   83 .231
1971 PIT N S/3   88 .206
1972 PIT N S/3   72 .188
1973 PIT N S   54 .247
      BRTR   618 .208

HERNANDEZ, KEITH
B.OCT.20,1953 SAN FRANCISCO,CAL.
1974 STL N /1   14 .294
1975 STL N 1   64 .250
1976 STL N *1   129 .289
1977 STL N *1   161 .291
1978 STL N *1   159 .255
      BLTL   527 .274

HERNANDEZ, RAMON [GONZALEZ]
B.AUG.31,1940 CAROLINA,P.R.
1967 ATL N P   46   0- 2
1968 CHI N /P   8   0- 0
1971 PIT N P   10   0- 1
1972 PIT N P   53   5- 0
1973 PIT N P   59   4- 5
1974 PIT N P   58   5- 2
1975 PIT N P   46   7- 2
1976 PIT N P   37   2- 2
     CHI N /P   2   0- 0
1977 CHI N /P   6   0- 0
     BOS A P   12   0- 1
      BBTL   337 23-15

HERNANDEZ, RODOLFO [ACOSTA] (RUDY)
B.OCT.18,1951 ENPALME,MEXICO
1972 CHI A /S   8 .190
      BRTR

HERNANDEZ, RUDOLPH ALBERT
B.DEC.10,1931 SANTIAGO,D.R.
1960 WAS A P   24   4- 1
1961 WAS A P   7   0- 1
      BRTR   31   4- 2

HERNANDEZ, SALVADOR JOSE [RAMOS] (CHICO)
B.JAN.3,1916 HAVANA,CUBA
1942 CHI N C   47 .229
1943 CHI N C   43 .270
      BRTR   90 .250

HERNDON, LARRY DARNELL
B.NOV.3,1953 SUNFLOWER,TEX.
1974 STL N /O   12 1.000
1976 SF N *O   115 .288
1977 SF N   49 .239
1978 SF N *O   151 .259
      BRTR   327 .268

HERNON, THOMAS H.
B.NOV.4,1866 E.BRIDGEWATER,MASS
D.FEB.4,1902 NEW BEDFORD,MASS.
1897 CHI N O   4 .111

HEROUX, GEORGE L.
[PLAYED UNDER NAME OF
GEORGE L. WHEELER]

HERR, EDWARD JOSEPH
B.MAY 18,1862 ST.LOUIS,MO.
D.JULY 18,1943 ST.LOUIS,MO.
1887 CLE AA 3   11 .360
1888 STL AA S   43 .266
1890 STL AA 2-0   12 .233
                        66 .249

HERRELL, WALTER W.
B.FEB.1869 MARYLAND
1911 WAS A P   1   0- 0

HERRERA, JOSE CONCEPCION [CONTUEROS] (JOSE) OR (LOCO)
B.APR.8,1942 SAN LORENZO,VENEZ.
1967 HOU N /H   5 .250
1968 HOU N O/2   27 .240
1969 HOU N O/2-3   47 .286
1970 MON N /H   1 .000
      BRTR   80 .264

HERRERA, JUAN FRANCISCO [WILLAVICENCIO] (PANCHO)
B.JUNE 16,1934 SANTIAGO,CUBA
1958 PHI N 1-3   29 .270
1960 PHI N 1-2   145 .281
1961 PHI N 1   126 .258
      BRTR   300 .271

HERRERA, PROCOPIO RODRIGUEZ (BOBBY) OR (OTTO)
B.JULY 26,1926 NUEVO LAREDO,MEX
1951 STL A P   3   0- 0
      BRTR

HERRERA, RAMON (MIKE)
B.DEC.19,1897 HAVANA,CUBA
D.FEB.3,1978 HAVANA,CUBA
1925 BOS A 2   10 .385
1926 BOS A 2-3   74 .257
      BRTR   84 .275

HERRIAGE, WILLIAM TROY (TROY) OR (DUTCH)
B.DEC.20,1930 TIPTON,OKLA.
1956 KC A P   31 34   1-13
      BRTR

HERRIN, THOMAS EDWARD (TOM)
B.SEPT.12,1929 SHREVEPORT,LA.
1954 BOS A P   14   1- 2
      BRTR

YR CL LEA POS GP G REC

HERRING, ARTHUR L (RED) OR (SANDY)
B.MAR.10,1907 ALTUS,OKLA.
1929 DET A P 4 2- 1
1930 DET A P 23 3- 3
1931 DET A P 35 7-13
1932 DET A P 12 1- 2
1933 DET A P 24 1- 2
1934 BRO N P 14 2- 4
1939 CHI A P 7 0- 0
1944 BRO N P 12 3- 4
1945 BRO N P 23 7- 4
1946 BRO N P 35 7- 2
1947 PIT N P 11 1- 3
BRTR 200 34-38

HERRING, HERBERT LEE
B.JULY 22,1891 DANVILLE,ARK.
D.APR.22,1964 TUCSON,ARIZ.
1912 WAS A P 1 0- 0
BRTR

HERRING, SILAS CLARKE (LEFTY)
B.MAR.4,1880 PHILADELPHIA,PA.
1899 WAS N P 2 0- 0
1904 WAS A O 15 .174
BLTL 2 17 0- 0
.191

HERRING, WILLIAM FRANCIS
(BILL) OR (SMOKE)
B.OCT.31,1893 NEW YORK,N.Y.
D.SEPT.10,1962 HONESDALE,PA.
1915 BRO F P 3 0- 1

HERRMANN, EDWARD MARTIN (ED)
B.AUG.27,1946 SAN DIEGO,CAL.
1967 CHI A /C 2 .667
1969 CHI A C 102 .231
1970 CHI A C 96 .283
1971 CHI A C 101 .214
1972 CHI A *C 116 .249
1973 CHI A *C 119 .224
1974 CHI A *C 107 .259
1975 NY A D-C 80 .255
1976 CAL A C 29 .174
HOU N C 79 .204
1977 HOU N C 56 .291
1978 HOU N C 16 .111
MON N C 19 .175
BLTR 922 .240

HERRMANN, LEROY GEORGE
B.FEB.27,1906 STEWARD,ILL.
D.JULY 3,1972 LIVERMORE,CAL.
1932 CHI N P 7 2- 1
1933 CHI N P 9 0- 1
1935 CIN N P 29 3- 5
BRTR 45 5- 7

HERRMANN, MARTIN JOHN (LEFTY)
B.JAN.10,1893 OLDENBURG,IND.
D.SEPT.11,1956 CINCINNATI,OHIO
1918 BRO N P 1 0- 0
BLTL

HERRSCHER, RICHARD FRANKLIN (RICK)
B.NOV.3,1936 ST.LOUIS,MO.
1962 NY N 1-S-3-O 35 .220
BRTR

HERRNSTEIN, JOHN ELLETT
B.MAY 31,1938 HAMPTON,VA.
1962 PHI N O 6 .200
1963 PHI N 1-O 15 .167
1964 PHI N 1-O 125 .234
1965 PHI N 1-O 63 .200
1966 PHI N /O 4 .100
CHI N /1-O 9 .176
ATL N /O 17 .222
BLTL 239 .220

HERSH, EARL WALTER
B.MAY 21,1932 EBBVALE,MD.
1956 MIL N O 7 .231
BLTL

HERSHBERGER, NORMAN MICHAEL (MIKE)
B.OCT.9,1939 MASSILLON,OHIO
1961 CHI A O 15 .309
1962 CHI A O 148 .262
1963 CHI A O 135 .279
1964 CHI A O 141 .230
1965 KC A *O 150 .231
1966 KC A *O 146 .253
1967 KC A *O 142 .254
1968 OAK A O 99 .272
1969 OAK A O 51 .202
1970 MIL A O 49 .235
1971 CHI A O 74 .260
BRTR 1150 .252

HERSHBERGER, WILLARD MC KEE (BILL)
B.MAY 28,1910 LEMON COVE,CAL.
D.AUG.3,1940 BOSTON,MASS.
1938 CIN N C-2 49 .275
1939 CIN N C 63 .345
1940 CIN N C 48 .309
BRTR 160 .316

YR CL LEA POS GP G REC

HERSHEY, FRANK
B.DEC.13,1877 GORHAM,N.Y.
D.DEC.15,1949 CANADAIGUA,N.Y.
1905 BOS N P 2 0- 1

HERTWECK, NEAL CHARLES
B.NOV.22,1931 ST.LOUIS,MO.
1952 STL N 1 2 .000
BLTL

HERTZ, STEPHEN ALLAN (STEVE)
B.FEB.26,1945 DA,OHIO
1964 HOU N 3 5 .000
BRTR

HERZOG, CHARLES LINCOLN (BUCK)
B.JULY 9,1885 BALTIMORE,MD.
D.SEPT.4,1953 BALTIMORE,MD.
1908 NY N 2 59 .300
1909 NY N O 38 .185
1910 BOS N 3 105 .250
1911 BOS N 3 79 .310
NY N 3 69 .267
1912 NY N 3 140 .263
1913 NY N 3 96 .286
1914 CIN N M-S 138 .281
1915 CIN N M-1-S 155 .264
1916 CIN N M-S-3-O 79 .267
NY N 2-S-3 77 .261
1917 NY N 2 114 .235
1918 BOS N 1-2-S 118 .228
1919 BOS N 2 73 .276
CHI N 2 52 .280
1920 CHI N 2-3 91 .193
BRTR 1483 .259

HERZOG, DORREL NORMAN ELVERT
(WHITEY)
B.NOV.9,1931 NEW ATHENS,ILL.
1956 WAS A 1-O 117 .245
1957 WAS A O 36 .167
1958 WAS A O 8 .000
KC A 1-O 88 .240
1959 KC A 1-O 38 .293
1960 KC A 1-O 83 .266
1961 BAL A O 113 .291
1962 BAL A O 99 .266
1963 DET A 1-O 52 .151
BLTL 634 .257
NON-PLAYING MANAGER
TEX[A] 1973, CAL[A] 1974
(INTERIM), KC(A) 1975-78

HESLIN, THOMAS
[PLAYED UNDER NAME OF THOMAS HESS]

HESS, OTTO C.
B.OCT.10,1878 BERNE,SWITZERLAND
D.FEB.25,1926 TUCSON,ARIZ.
1902 CLE A P 7 2- 3
1904 CLE A P 21 34 9- 7
1905 CLE A P-O 27 54 10-12
.251
1906 CLE A P 42 53 20-17
1907 CLE A P 17 19 6- 6
1908 CLE A P-O 4 9 1- 0
.000
1912 BOS N P 33 12-17
1913 BOS N P 29 35 7-17
1914 BOS N P 14 31 5- 6
1915 BOS N P 4 5 0- 1
BLTL 198 280 72-86
.214

HESS, THOMAS
[REAL NAME THOMAS HESLIN]
B.AUG.15,1875 BROOKLYN,N.Y.
D.DEC.15,1945 ALBANY,N.Y.
1892 BAL N C 1 .000

HESSELBACHER, GEORGE EDWARD
B.JAN.18,1895 PHILADELPHIA,PA.
1916 PHI A P 6 0- 4
BRTR

HESTERFER, LAWRENCE
B.JUNE 9,1878 NEWARK,N.J.
D.SEPT.22,1943 CEDAR GROVE,N.J.
1901 NY N P 1 0- 1

HETKI, JOHN EDWARD (JOHNNY)
B.MAY 12,1922 LEAVENWORTH,KAN.
1945 CIN N P 5 1- 2
1946 CIN N P 32 6- 6
1947 CIN N P 37 3- 4
1948 CIN N P 3 0- 1
1950 CIN N P 22 1- 2
1952 STL A P 3 0- 1
1953 PIT N P 54 3- 6
1954 PIT N P 58 4- 4
BRTR 214 18-26

HETLING, AUGUST JULIUS (GUS)
B.NOV.21,1885 ST.LOUIS,MO.
D.OCT.13,1962 WICHITA,KAN.
1906 DET A 3 2 .143
BRTR

YR CL LEA POS GP G REC

HEUBEL, GEORGE A.
B.1849 PATERSON,N.J.
D.JAN.22,1896 PHILADELPHIA,PA.
1871 ATH NA 1-O 17 .321
1872 OLY NA O 5 .125
1876 MUT N 1 1 .000
23 .264

HEUSSER, EDWARD BURLTON (ED)
(THE WILD ELK OF THE WASATCH)
B.MAY 7,1909 MILL CREEK,UTAH
D.MAR.1,1956 AURORA,CAL.
1935 STL N P 33 5- 5
1936 STL N P 42 7- 3
1938 PHI N P 1 0- 0
1940 PHI A P 41 6-13
1943 CIN N P 26 4- 3
1944 CIN N P 30 13-11
1945 CIN N P 31 11-16
1946 CIN N P 29 7-14
1948 PHI N P 33 3- 2
BBTR 266 56-67
BR 1935-38

HEVING, JOHN ALOYSIUS (JOHNNY)
B.APR.29,1896 COVINGTON,KY.
D.DEC.24,1968 SALISBURY,N.C.
1920 STL A C 1 .000
1924 BOS A C 45 .284
1925 BOS A C 45 .168
1928 BOS A C 82 .259
1929 BOS A C 76 .319
1930 BOS A C 75 .277
1931 PHI A C 42 .239
1932 PHI A C 33 .273
BRTR 399 .265

HEVING, JOSEPH WILLIAM (JOE)
B.SEPT.2,1900 COVINGTON,KY.
D.APR.11,1970 COVINGTON,KY.
1930 NY N P 41 7- 5
1931 NY N P 22 1- 6
1933 CHI A P 40 7- 5
1934 CHI A P 33 1- 7
1937 CLE A P 40 8- 4
1938 CLE A P 3 1- 1
BOS A P 16 8- 1
1939 BOS A P 46 11- 3
1940 BOS A P 39 12- 7
1941 CLE A P 27 5- 2
1942 CLE A P 27 5- 3
1943 CLE A P 30 1- 1
1944 CLE A P 63 8- 3
1945 BOS N P 3 1- 0
BRTR 430 76-48

HEWETT, WALTER F.
B.1861 WASHINGTON,D.C.
D.OCT.7,1944 WASHINGTON,D.C.
NON-PLAYING MANAGER WAS[N] 1888

HEWITT, CHARLES JACOB (JAKE)
B.JUNE 6,1870 MAIDSVILLE,W.VA.
D.MAY 18,1959 MORGANTOWN,W.VA.
1895 PIT N P 3 1- 0
BLTL

HEYDEMAN, GREGORY GEORGE (GREG)
B.JAN.2,1952 CARMEL,CAL.
1973 LA N /P 1 0- 0
BRTR

HEYDON, MICHAEL EDWARD (ED)
B.JULY 15,1874 MISSOURI
D.OCT.13,1913 INDIANAPOLIS,IND.
1898 BAL N C 3 .111
1899 WAS N C 3 .000
1901 STL N C 14 .244
1904 CHI A C 5 .100
1905 WAS A C 77 .192
1906 WAS A C 49 .159
1907 WAS A C 62 .183
TR 213 .182

HEYNER, JOHN
B.HYDE PARK,ILL.
1890 PIT N P 1 0- 0

HIATT, JACK E
B.JULY 27,1942 BAKERSFIELD,CAL.
1964 LA A C-1 9 .375
1965 SF N C/1 40 .284
1966 SF N /1 18 .304
1967 SF N 1/C-O 73 .275
1968 SF N C-1 90 .232
1969 SF N C/1 69 .196
1970 MON N C/1 17 .326
CHI N C/1 66 .242
1971 HOU N C/1 69 .276
1972 HOU N C 10 .200
CAL A C 22 .289
BRTR 483 .251

HIBBARD, JOHN DENISON
B.DEC.2,1864 CHICAGO,ILL.
D.NOV.17,1937 HOLLYWOOD,CAL.
1884 CHI N P 2 1- 1
TL

YR CL LEA POS   GP   G   REC

HIBBS, JAMES KERR (JIM)
B.SEP.10,1944 KLAMATH FALLS,ORE.
1967 CAL A /H   3   .000
        BRTR

HICKEY, JAMES ROBERT (SID)
B.OCT.22,1920 N.ABINGTON,MASS.
1942 BOS N P   1   0- 1
1944 BOS N P   8   0- 0
        BRTR   9   0- 1

HICKEY, JOHN W.
B.NOV.3,1881 MINNEAPOLIS,MINN.
D.DEC.28,1941 SEATTLE,WASH.
1904 CLE A P   3   0- 3
        BRTL

HICKEY, MICHAEL F.
B.DEC.25,1871 CHICOPEE,MASS.
D.JUNE 11,1918 SPRINGFIELD,MASS
1899 BOS N 2   1   .333
1901 CHI N 3   10   .176
        BRTR   11   .212

HICKMAN, CHARLES TAYLOR
(CHEERFUL CHARLIE)
OR (PIANO LEGS)
B.MAY 4,1876 TAYLORTOWN,
DUNKARD TOWNSHIP,PA.
D.APR.19,1934 MORGANTOWN,W.VA.
1897 BOS N P   2   0- 0
1898 BOS N P   6   17   2- 2
1899 BOS N P   11   18   7- 0
1900 NY N 3   125   .313
1901 NY N P-S- 8   101   3- 5
                        3-0   .287
1902 BOS A O   28   .308
        CLE A P-1   1 102   0- 1
                             .376
1903 CLE A 1   130   .330
1904 CLE A 1   85   .415
        DET A 1   41   .254
1905 DET A 1-0   59   .221
        WAS A 2   88   .311
1906 WAS A 1-0   120   .284
1907 WAS A P-1-   1   60   0- 0
                   2   .300
        CHI A   21   .226
1908 CLE A 1-0   65   .234
        BRTR   47 1062   12- 8
                            .302

HICKMAN, DAVID JAMES
B.MAY 9,1894 UNION CITY,TENN.
1915 BAL F O   20   .210
1916 BRO N O   9   .200
1917 BRO N O   114   .219
1918 BRO N O   53   .234
1919 BRO N O   57   .192
        BRTR   253   .218

HICKMAN, ERNEST P.
B.1856 E.ST.LOUIS,ILL.
D.NOV.19,1891 E.ST.LOUIS,ILL.
1884 KC U P   18   3-13

HICKMAN, JAMES LUCIUS (JIM)
B.MAY 10,1937 HENNING,TENN.
1962 NY N O   140   .245
1963 NY N 3-O   146   .229
1964 NY N 3-O   139   .257
1965 NY N O-1-3 141   .236
1966 NY N O-1   58   .238
1967 LA N /P-   1 65   0- 0
             0/1-3   .163
1968 CHI N O   75   .223
1969 CHI N *O   134   .237
1970 CHI N O-1   149   .315
1971 CHI N O-1   117   .256
1972 CHI N 1-O   115   .272
1973 CHI N 1-O   92   .244
1974 STL N 1/3   58   .267
        BRTR   1 1421   0- 0
                         .252

HICKMAN, JESSE OWENS
B.FEB.18,1939 LECOMPTE,LA.
1965 KC A /P   12 14   0- 1
1966 KC A /P   1   0- 0
        BRTR   13 15   0- 1

HICKS, CLARENCE WALTER (BUDDY)
B.FEB.15,1927 BELVEDERE,CAL.
1956 DET A 2-S-3   26   .213
        BBTR

HICKS, JAMES EDWARD (JIM)
B.MAY 18,1940 EAST CHICAGO,IND.
1964 CHI A R   2   .000
1965 CHI A /O   13   .263
1966 CHI A O/1   18   .192
1969 STL N O   19   .182
        CAL A /P   37   .083
1970 CAL A /H   4   .250
        BRTR   .93 .163

YR CL LEA POS   GP   G   REC

HICKS, NATHANIEL WOODHULL
B.APR.19,1845 HEMPSTEAD,N.Y.
D.APR.21,1907 HOBOKEN,N.J.
1872 MUT NA C-O   56   .308
1873 MUT NA C   28   -
1874 PHI NA C-O   58   -
1875 MUT NA M-C-O   63   -
1876 MUT N C   45   .230
1877 CIN N C   8   .187
        BRTR   258   -

HICKS, WILLIAM JOSEPH (JOE)
B.APR.7,1933 IVY,VA.
1959 CHI A O   6   .429
1960 CHI A O   36   .191
1961 WAS A O   12   .172
1962 WAS A O   102   .224
1963 NY N O   56   .226
        BLTR   212   .221

HIGBE, WALTER KIRBY (KIRBY)
B.APR.8,1915 COLUMBIA,S.C.
1937 CHI N P   1   1- 0
1938 CHI N P   2   0- 0
1939 CHI N P   9   2- 1
        PHI N P   34   10-14
1940 PHI N P   41   14-19
1941 BRO N P   48   22- 9
1942 BRO N P   38   16-11
1943 BRO N P   35   13-10
1946 BRO N P   42   17- 8
1947 BRO N P   4   2- 0
        PIT N P   46   11-17
1948 PIT N P   56   8- 7
1949 PIT N P   7   0- 2
        NY N P   37   2- 0
1950 NY N P   18   0- 3
        BRTR   418 118-101

HIGBEE, MAHLON JESSE
B.AUG.16,1901 LOUISVILLE,KY.
D.APR.7,1968 DE PAUW,IND.
1922 NY N O   3   .400

HIGBY
1872 ATL NA O   1   .000

HIGDON, WILLIAM TRAVIS (BILL)
B.APR.27,1924 CAMP HILL,ALA.
1949 PHI N O   11   .304
        BLTR

HIGGINBOTHAM, IRVING CLINTON
B.APR.26,1882 HOMER,NEB.
D.JUNE 12,1959 SEATTLE,WASH.
1907 STL N P   7   1- 6
1908 STL N P   19   3- 8
1909 STL N P   3   1- 0
        CHI N P   19   5- 2
        TR   48   10-16

HIGGINS, DENNIS DEAN
B.AUG.4,1939 JEFFERSON CITY,MO.
1966 CHI A P   42   1- 0
1967 CHI A /P   9   1- 2
1968 WAS A P   59   4- 4
1969 WAS A P   55   10- 9
1970 CLE A P   58   4- 6
1971 STL N /P   3   1- 0
1972 STL N P   15   1- 2
        BRTR   241   22-23

HIGGINS, MICHAEL FRANKLIN
(MIKE) OR (PINKY)
B.MAY 27,1909 RED OAK,TEX.
D.MAR.21,1969 DALLAS,TEX.
1930 PHI A 2-S-3   14   .250
1933 PHI A 3   152   .314
1934 PHI A 3   144   .330
1935 PHI A 3   133   .296
1936 PHI A 3   146   .289
1937 BOS A 3   153   .302
1938 BOS A 3   139   .303
1939 DET A 3   132   .276
1940 DET A 3   131   .271
1941 DET A 3   147   .298
1942 DET A 3   143   .267
1943 DET A 3   138   .277
1944 DET A 3   148   .297
1946 DET A 3   18   .217
        BOS A 3   64   .275
        BRTR   1802   .292
NON-PLAYING MANAGER
BOS(A) 1955-59, 60-62

HIGGINS, ROBERT STONE
B.SEPT.23,1886 FAYETTEVILLE,TENN.
D.MAY 25,1941 CHATTANOOGA,TENN.
1909 BRO N C   8   .087
1911 BRO N C   4   .000
1912 BRO N C   1   .000
        BRTR   13   .143

YR CL LEA POS   GP   G   REC

HIGGINS, THOMAS EDWARD (EDDIE)
(DOC) OR (IRISH)
B.MAR.18,1888 NEVADA,ILL.
D.FEB.14,1959 ELGIN,ILL.
1909 STL N P   16   3- 3
1910 STL N P-O   2   0- 1
                         .400
        BRTR   18   3- 4
                         .231

HIGGINS, WILLIAM H.
B.OCT.3,1862 WILMINGTON,DEL.
D.SEPT.23,1926
1888 BOS N 2   14   .167
1890 STL AA 2   64   .251
        SYR AA 2   1   .250
        TR   79   .236

HIGH, ANDREW AIRD (HANDY ANDY)
B.NOV.21,1897 AVA,ILL.
1922 BRO N 2-S-3 153   .263
1923 BRO N 2-S-3 123   .270
1924 BRO N 2-S-3 144   .328
1925 BRO N 2-S-3   44   .200
        BOS N 2-3   60   .288
1926 BOS N 2-3   130   .296
1927 BOS N 3   113   .302
1928 STL N 2-3   111   .285
1929 STL N 2-3   146   .295
1930 STL N 3   72   .279
1931 STL N 2-3   63   .267
1932 CIN N 2-3   84   .188
1933 CIN N 2-3   24   .209
1934 PHI N 3   47   .206
        BLTR   1314   .284

HIGH, CHARLES EDWIN
B.DEC.1,1898 AVA,ILL.
D.SEPT.11,1960 OAK GROVE,ORE.
1919 PHI A O   11   .077
1920 PHI A O   17   .308
        BRTR   28   .242

HIGH, EDWARD T. (LEFTY)
B.DEC.26,1876 BALTIMORE,MD.
D.FEB.10,1926 BALTIMORE,MD.
1901 DET A P   5   3- 2
        TL

HIGH, HUGH JENKEN (BUNNY)
B.OCT.24,1887 POTTSTOWN,PA.
D.NOV.16,1962 ST.LOUIS,MO.
1913 DET A O   80   .230
1914 DET A O   80   .266
1915 NY A O   119   .258
1916 NY A O   115   .263
1917 NY A O   103   .236
1918 NY A O   6   .000
        BLTL   503   .250

HIGHAM, RICHARD
B.1852 ENGLAND
D.MAR.18,1905 CHICAGO,ILL.
1871 MUT NA C-2-O   22   -
1872 BAL NA C-1-2-3-O 46   .339
1873 MUT NA 2-O   23   -
        ATL NA 2   1   -
        MUT NA C-3-O   26   -
1874 MUT NA M-C-2-O   65   -
1875 CHI NA C-2-O   44   -
        MUT NA C-1-2-O 14   -
1876 HAR N C-O   67   .325
1878 PRO N O   60   .315
1880 TRO N C-O   1   .200
        BLTR   369   -

HILAND, JOHN W.
B.PHILADELPHIA,PA.
1885 PHI N 2   3   .000

HILCHER, WALTER FRANK (WHITEY)
B.FEB.28,1909 CHICAGO,ILL.
D.NOV.21,1962 MINNEAPOLIS,MINN.
1931 CIN N P   2   0- 1
1932 CIN N P   11   0- 3
1935 CIN N P   4   2- 0
1936 CIN N P   14   1- 2
        BRTR   31   3- 6

HILDEBRAND, GEORGE ALBERT
B.SEPT.6,1878 SAN FRANCISCO,CAL.
D.MAY 30,1960 WOODLAND HILLS,CAL.
1902 BRO N O   11   .227

HILDEBRAND, ORAL CLYDE
B.APR.7,1907 INDIANAPOLIS,IND.
D.SEPT.8,1977 SOUTHPORT,IND.
1931 CLE A P   5   2- 1
1932 CLE A P   27   8- 6
1933 CLE A P   36   16-11
1934 CLE A P   33   11- 9
1935 CLE A P   34   9- 8
1936 CLE A P   36   10-11
1937 STL A P   30   8-10
1938 STL A P   23 24   8-10
1939 NY A P   21   10- 4
1940 NY A P   13   1- 1
        BRTR   258 259 83-78

YR CL LEA POS   GP   G   REC   YR CL LEA POS   GP   G   REC   YR CL LEA POS   GP   G   REC

HILDEBRAND, PALMER MARION (PETE)
B.DEC.23,1884 SHAUCK,OHIO
D.JAN.25,1960 N.CANTON,OHIO
1913 STL N C   26   .164
BRTR

HILDEBRAND, R. E.
1902 CHI N O   1   .000

HILGENDORF, THOMAS EUGENE (TOM)
B.MAR.10,1942 CLINTON,IOWA
1969 STL N /P   6   0- 0
1970 STL N P   23   0- 4
1972 CLE A P   19   3- 1
1973 CLE A P   48   5- 3
1974 CLE A P   35   4- 3
1975 PHI N P   53   7- 3
BBTL   184 19-14

HILGERINK, WILLIAM EDWARD
[PLAYED UNDER NAME OF
WILLIAM EDWARD HILLY]

HILL, BELDEN L.
B.AUG.24,1864 KEWANEE,ILL.
D.OCT.22,1934 CEDAR RAPIDS,IOWA
1890 BAL AA 3   9   .133
BRTR

**HILL, CARMEN PROCTOR (CARMEN)
(SPECS) OR (BUNKER)**
B.OCT.1,1895 ROYALTON,MINN.
1915 PIT N P   8   2- 1
1916 PIT N P   2   0- 0
1918 PIT N P   6   2- 3
1919 PIT N P   4   0- 0
1922 NY N P   8   2- 1
1926 PIT N P   6   3- 3
1927 PIT N P   43 44 22-11
1928 PIT N P   36 16-10
1929 PIT N P   27   2- 3
STL N P   3   0- 0
1930 STL N P   4   0- 1
BRTR   147 148 49-33

HILL, CLIFFORD JOSEPH (RED)
B.JAN.20,1893 MARSHALL,TEX.
D.AUG.11,1938 EL PASO,TEX.
1917 PHI A P   1   0- 0
BBTL

HILL, DAVID BURNHAM
B.NOV.11,1937 NEW ORLEANS,LA.
1957 KC A P   2   0- 0
BRTL

HILL, GARRY ALTON
B.NOV.3,1946 RUTHERFORDTON,N.C.
1969 ATL N /P   1   0- 1
BRTR

HILL, HERBERT
B.AUG.19,1892 DALLAS,TEX.
1915 CLE A P   1   0- 0

HILL, HERMAN ALEXANDER
B.OCT.12,1945 TUSKEGEE,ALA.
D.DEC.14,1970 VALENCIA,VENEZ.
1969 MIN A /O   16   .000
1970 MIN A O   27   .091
BLTR   43   .083

HILL, HUGH ELLIS
B.JULY 21,1879 RINGGOLD,GA.
D.SEPT.6,1958 CINCINNATI,OHIO
1903 CLE A H   1   .000
1904 STL N O   23   .226
24   .233

HILL, HUNTER BENJAMIN
B.JUNE 21,1879 AUSTIN,TEX.
D.FEB.22,1959 AUSTIN,TEX.
1903 STL A 3   86   .249
1904 STL A 3   58   .220
WAS A 3   77   .229
1905 WAS A 3   103   .209
TR   324   .219

HILL, JESSE TERRILL
B.JAN.20,1907 YATES,MO.
1935 NY A O   107   .293
1936 WAS A O   85   .305
1937 WAS A O   33   .217
PHI A O   70   .293
BRTR   295   .289

HILL, MARC KEVIN
B.FEB.18,1952 ELSBERRY,MO.
1973 STL N /C   1   .000
1974 STL N /C   10   .238
1975 SF N C/3   72   .214
1976 SF N C/1   54   .183
1977 SF N *C/1   108   .250
1978 SF N *C/1   117   .243
BRTR   362   .232

HILL, OLIVER CLINTON
B.OCT.1,1912 POWDER SPRINGS,GA
D.SEPT.20,1970 DECATUR,GA.
1939 BOS N H   2   .500
BLTR

HILL, WILLIAM CICERO (STILL BILL)
B.AUG.2,1874 CHATTANOOGA,TENN.
D.JAN.28,1938 CINCINNATI,OHIO
1896 LOU N P   39 10-29
1897 LOU N P   26   6-18
1898 CIN N P   28 13-15
1899 CLE N P=O   11   3- 6
.121
BAL N P   8   3- 4
BRO N P   1   1- 0
BLTL   113 36-72
.166

HILLEBRAND, HOMER HILLER HENRY (DOC)
B.OCT.10,1879 FREEPORT,ILL.
D.JAN.23,1974 ELSINORE,CAL.
1905 PIT N P=1   10 36   4- 2
.236
1906 PIT N P   7   3- 2
1908 PIT N P   1   0- 0
.238
18 44   7- 4
.238

HILLER, CHARLES JOSEPH (CHUCK)
B.OCT.1,1934 JOHNSBURG,ILL.
1961 SF N 2   70   .238
1962 SF N 2   161   .276
1963 SF N 2   111   .223
1964 SF N 2-3   80   .160
1965 SF N /2   7   .143
NY N 2/0-3   100   .238
1966 NY N 2-3/0   108   .280
1967 NY N 2   25   .093
PHI N /2   31   .302
1968 PIT N /2   11   .385
BLTR   704   .243

HILLER, FRANK WALTER (DUTCH)
B.JULY 13,1920 NEWARK,N.J.
1946 NY A P   3   0- 2
1948 NY A P   22   5- 2
1949 NY A P   4   0- 2
1950 CHI N P   38 12- 5
1951 CHI N P   24   6-12
1952 CIN N P   28 29   5- 8
1953 NY N P   19   2- 1
BRTR   138 139 30-32

HILLER, HARVEY MAX (HOB)
B.MAY 12,1893 E.MAUCH CHUNK,PA.
D.DEC.27,1956 LEIGHTON,PA.
1920 BOS A 3   17   .172
1921 BOS A O   1   .000
BR   18   .167

HILLER, JOHN FREDERICK
B.APR.8,1943 TORONTO,ONT.,CANADA
1965 DET A /P   5   0- 0
1966 DET A /P   1   0- 0
1967 DET A P   23   4- 3
1968 DET A P   39   9- 6
1969 DET A P   40 41   4- 4
1970 DET A P   47   6- 6
1972 DET A P   24   2- 2
1973 DET A P   65 10- 5
1974 DET A P   59 17-14
1975 DET A P   36   2- 3
1976 DET A P   56 12- 8
1977 DET A P   45   8-14
1978 DET A P   51   9- 4
BRTL   491 492 82-69

HILLEY, EDWARD GARFIELD (WHITEY)
B.JUNE 17,1879 CLEVELAND,OHIO
D.NOV.14,1956 CLEVELAND,OHIO
1903 PHI A 3   1   .333
BRTR

HILLIS, MALCOLM DAVID (MACK)
B.JULY 23,1901 CAMBRIDGE,MASS.
D.JUNE 16,1961 CAMBRIDGE,MASS.
1924 NY A 2   1   .000
1928 PIT N 2   11   .250
BRTR   12   .243

HILLMAN, DARIUS DUTTON (DAVE)
B.SEPT.14,1927 DUNGANNON,VA.
1955 CHI N P   25 26   0- 0
1956 CHI N P   2   0- 2
1957 CHI N P   32 36   6-11
1958 CHI N P   31 32   4- 8
1959 CHI N P   39 42   8-11
1960 BOS A P   16   0- 3
1961 BOS A P   28   3- 2
1962 CIN N P   2   0- 0
NY N P   13   0- 0
BRTR   188 197 21-37

HILLY, WILLIAM EDWARD (PAT)
[REAL NAME WILLIAM EDWARD HILGERINK]
B.FEB.24,1887 FOSTORIA,OHIO
D.JULY 25,1953 EUREKA,MO.
1914 PHI N O   8   .300
BRTR

HILSEY, CHARLES
B.1864 PHILADELPHIA,PA.
1883 PHI N P   3   0- 3
1884 ATH AA P=O   3   6   2- 1
.261
6   9   2- 4
.235

HILT, BENJAMIN FRANKLIN
B.PHILADELPHIA,PA.
NON-PLAYING MANAGER PHI[P] 1890

HILTON, JOHN DAVID (DAVE)
B.SEP.15,1950 UVALDE,TEX.
1972 SD N 3   13   .213
1973 SD N 3-2   70   .197
1974 SD N 3-2   74   .240
1975 SD N /3   4   .000
BRTR   161   .213

HIMES, JOHN HERB (JACK)
B.SEPT.22,1978 BRYAN,OHIO
D.DEC.16,1949 JOLIET,ILL.
1905 STL N O   12   .156
1906 STL N O   40   .271
BLTR   52   .250

HIMSL, AVITUS BERNARD (VEDIE)
B.APR.2,1917 PLEVNA,MONT.
NON-PLAYING MANAGER CHI[N] 1961-62

HINCHMAN, HARRY SIBLEY
B.AUG.4,1878 PHILADELPHIA,PA.
D.JAN.19,1933 TOLEDO,OHIO
1907 CLE A 2   15   .216
BRTR

HINCHMAN, WILLIAM WHITE
B.APR.4,1883 PHILADELPHIA,PA.
D.FEB.21,1963 COLUMBUS,OHIO
1905 CIN N O   17   .255
1906 CIN N O   16   .204
1907 CLE A O   152   .228
1908 CLE A S=O   137   .231
1909 CLE A O   139   .258
1915 PIT N O   156   .307
1916 PIT N 1=O   152   .315
1917 PIT N 1=O   69   .189
1918 PIT N 1=O   50   .234
1920 PIT N O   18   .188
BRTR   906   .261

HINDS, SAMUEL RUSSELL (SAM)
B.JULY 11,1953 FREDERICK,MD.
1977 MIL A P   29   0- 3
BRTR

HINES, HENRY FRED (HUNKEY)
B.SEPT.29,1867 ELGIN,ILL.
D.JAN.2,1928 ROCKFORD,ILL.
1895 BRO N P   2   .250

HINES, MICHAEL P.
B.1864 IRELAND
D.MAR.14,1910 NEW BEDFORD,MASS.
1883 BOS N C=O   61   .228
1884 BOS N C   34   .181
1885 BOS N O   14   .250
BRO AA C   2   .167
PRO N C   1   .000
1888 BOS N C   3   .167
TL   115   .213

HINES, PAUL A.
B.MAR.1,1852 WASHINGTON,D.C.
D.JULY 10,1935 HYATTSVILLE,MD.
1872 NAT NA 1   11   .286
1873 NAT NA C-2=O   39   .328
1874 CHI NA 2-S=O   59   .276
1875 CHI NA 2=O   69   .314
1876 CHI N O   64   .330
1877 CHI N 2=O   60   .280
1878 PRO N O   60   .351
1879 PRO N O   84   .357
1880 PRO N 1-2=O   82   .306
1881 PRO N 2=O   79   .283
1882 PRO N O   84   .308
1883 PRO N 1=O   97   .298
PRO N P-1-   1 112   0- 0
O   .304
1885 PRO N 1-2-S-3=O   98   .273
1886 WAS N 3=O   121   .312
1887 WAS N O   123   .370
1888 IND N O   132   .280
1889 IND N 1   121   .264
1890 PIT N 1=O   31   .172
BOS N O   69   .266
1891 WAS AA O   54   .266
BRTR   1 1649   0- 0
.304

YR	CL LEA POS	GP	G	REC

HINKLE, DANIEL GORDON (GORDIE)
B.APR.3,1905 TORONTO,OHIO
D.MAR.19,1972 HOUSTON,TEX.
1934 BOS A C   27   .173
         BRTR

HINRICHS, PAUL EDWIN
(PAUL) OR (HERKY)
B.AUG.31,1925 MARENGO,IOWA
1951 BOS A P   4   0- 0
         BRTR

HINRICHS, WILLIAM LOUIS (DUTCH)
B.APR.27,1889 ORANGE,CAL.
D.AUG.18,1972 KINGSBURG,CAL.
1910 WAS A P   3   0- 1
         BRTR

HINSLEY, JERRY DEAN
B.APR.9,1944 HUGO,OKLA.
1964 NY N P   9   0- 2
1967 NY N /P   2   0- 0
         BRTR   11   0- 2

HINSON, JAMES PAUL
B.MAY 9,1934 VAN LEER,TENN.
D.SEPT.23,1960 MUSKOGEE,OKLA.
1928 BOS A H   3   .000
         BRTR

HINTON, CHARLES EDWARD (CHUCK)
B.MAY 3,1934 ROCKY MOUNT,N.C.
1961 WAS A O   106   .260
1962 WAS A 2-S-O   151   .310
1963 WAS A 1-S-3-O   150   .269
1964 WAS A 3-O   138   .274
1965 CLE A O-1-2/3   133   .255
1966 CLE A *O/1-2   123   .256
1967 CLE A *O/2   147   .245
1968 CAL A 1-O-3/2   116   .195
1969 CLE A O-3   94   .256
1970 CLE A 1-O/C-2-3   107   .318
1971 CLE A 1-O/C   88   .224
         BRTR   1353   .264

HINTON, JOHN R.
B.ALTOONA,PA.
1901 BOS N 3   4   .071
         TR

HINTON, RICHARD MICHAEL (RICH)
B.MAY 22,1947 TUCSON,ARIZ.
1971 CHI A P   18   3- 4
1972 NY A /P   7   1- 0
         TEX A /P   5   0- 1
1975 CHI A P   15   1- 0
1976 CIN N P   12   1- 2
1978 CHI A P   29   2- 6
         BLTL   86   8-13

HIPPAUF, HERBERT AUGUST (HERB)
B.MAY 9,1940 NEW YORK,N.Y.
1966 ATL N /P   3   0- 1
         BRTL

HISER, GENE TAYLOR
B.DEC.11,1948 BALTIMORE,MD.
1971 CHI N /O   5   .207
1972 CHI N O   32   .196
1973 CHI N O   100   .174
1974 CHI N /O   12   .235
1975 CHI N O/1   45   .242
         BLTL   206   .202

HISLE, LARRY EUGENE
B.MAY 5,1947 PORTSMOUTH,OHIO
1968 PHI N /O   7   .364
1969 PHI N *O   145   .266
1970 PHI N *O   126   .205
1971 PHI N O   36   .197
1973 MIN A O   143   .272
1974 MIN A *O   143   .286
1975 MIN A O-D   80   .314
1976 MIN A *O   155   .272
1977 MIN A *O   141   .302
1978 MIL A O-D   142   .290
         BRTR   1118   .274

HISNER, HARLEY PARNELL
B.NOV.6,1926 NAPLES,IND.
1951 BOS A P   1   0- 1
         BRTR

HITCHCOCK, JAMES FRANKLIN
B.JUNE 28,1911 INVERNESS,ALA.
D.JUNE 23,1959 MONTGOMERY,ALA.
1938 BOS N S   28   .171
         BRTR

HITCHCOCK, WILLIAM CLYDE (BILLY)
B.JULY 31,1916 INVERNESS,ALA.
1942 DET A S-3   85   .211
1946 DET A 2   3   .000
         WAS A S-3   98   .212
1947 STL A 1-2-5-3   80   .222
1948 BOS A 2-3   49   .298
1949 BOS A 1-2   55   .204
1950 PHI A 2-S   115   .273
1951 PHI A 1-2-3   77   .306
1952 PHI A 1-3   119   .246
1953 DET A 2-S-3   22   .211
         BRTR   703   .243
NON-PLAYING MANAGER DET[A] 1960
BAL[A] 1961-63; ATL[N] 1966-67

HITT, BRUCE SMITH
B.JAN.4,1897 COMANCHE,TEX.
D.NOV.10,1973 PORTLAND,ORE.
1917 STL N P   2   0- 0
         BRTR

HITT, ROY WESLEY (RHINO)
B.JUNE 22,1887 CARLETON,NEB.
D.FEB.8,1956 POMONA,CAL.
1907 CIN N P   21   6-10
         TL

HITTLE, LLOYD ELDON (RED)
B.FEB.21,1924 LODI,CAL.
1949 WAS A P   36   5- 7
1950 WAS A P   11   2- 4
         BRTL   47   7-11

HOAG, MYRIL OLIVER
B.MAR.9,1908 DAVIS,CAL.
D.JULY 28,1971 HIGH SPRINGS,FLA
1931 NY A O   44   .143
1932 NY A O   46   .370
1934 NY A O   97   .267
1935 NY A 3-O   48   .255
1936 NY A O   45   .301
1937 NY A O   106   .301
1938 NY A O   85   .277
1939 STL A P-O   1 129   0- 0
                                      .295
1940 STL A O   76   .262
1941 STL A O   1   .000
         CHI A O   106   .255
1942 CHI A O   113   .240
1944 CHI A O   17   .229
         CLE A O   67   .285
1945 CLE A P-O   2 40   0- 0
                                      .211
         BRTR   3 1020   0- 0
                                      .271

HOAK, DONALD ALBERT (DON) OR (TIGER)
B.FEB.5,1928 ROULETTE,PA.
D.OCT.9,1969 PITTSBURGH,PA.
1954 BRO N 3   88   .245
1955 BRO N 3   94   .240
1956 CHI N 3   121   .215
1957 CIN N 2-3   149   .293
1958 CIN N S-3   114   .261
1959 PIT N 3   155   .282
1960 PIT N 3   155   .282
1961 PIT N 3   145   .298
1962 PIT N 3   121   .241
1963 PHI N 3   115   .231
1964 PHI N H   6   .000
         BRTR   1263   .265

HOBBIE, GLEN FREDERICK
B.APR.24,1936 WITT,ILL.
1957 CHI N P   2   0- 0
1958 CHI N P   55   10- 6
1959 CHI N P   46   16-13
1960 CHI N P   46   16-20
1961 CHI N P   36   7-13
1962 CHI N P   42   5-14
1963 CHI N P   36   7-10
1964 CHI N P   8   0- 3
         STL N P   5   1- 2
         BRTR   284   62-81

HOBBS, WILLIAM LEE (SMOKEY)
B.MAY 7,1893 GRANT S LICK,KY.
D.JAN.5,1945 HAMILTON,OHIO
1913 CIN N 2   2   .000
1916 CIN N S   6   .182
         BRTR   8   .133

HOBLITZEL, RICHARD CARLETON (DOC)
[REAL NAME
RICHARD CARLETON HOBLITZELL]
B.OCT.26,1888 WAVERLY,W.VA.
D.NOV.14,1962 PARKERSBURG,W.VA.
1908 CIN N 1   32   .254
1909 CIN N 1   142   .308
1910 CIN N 1   155   .278
1911 CIN N 1   158   .289
1912 CIN N 1   148   .294
1913 CIN N 1   137   .285
1914 CIN N 1   78   .210
         BOS A 1   68   .319
1915 BOS A 1   124   .283
1916 BOS A 1   130   .259
1917 BOS A 1   120   .257
1918 BOS A 1   25   .159
         BRTR   1317   .278

HOBLITZELL, RICHARD CARLETON
[PLAYED UNDER NAME OF
RICHARD CARLETON HOBLITZEL]

HOBSON, CLELL LAVERN (BUTCH)
B.AUG.17,1951 TUSCALOOSA,ALA.
1975 BOS A /3   2   .250
1976 BOS A 3   76   .234
1977 BOS A *3   159   .265
1978 BOS A *3-D   147   .250
         BRTR   384   .253

HOCH, HARRY KELLER
B.JAN.9,1887 WOODSIDE,DEL.
1908 PHI N P   3   2- 1
1914 STL A P   15   0- 2
1915 STL A P   12   0- 3
         BRTR   30   2- 6

HOCK, EDWARD FRANCIS
B.MAR.27,1899 FRANKLIN FURNACE,OHIO
D.NOV.21,1963 PORTSMOUTH,OHIO
1920 STL N O   1   .000
1923 CIN N O   2   .000
1924 CIN N O   16   .100
         BLTL   19   .100

HOCKENBERY, CHARLES MARION (CHUCK)
B.DEC.15,1950 LACROSSE,WIS.
1975 CAL A /P   16   0- 5
         BBTR

HOCKETT, ORIS LEON (BROWN)
B.SEPT.29,1909 AMBOY,IND.
D.MAR.23,1969 TORRANCE,CAL.
1938 BRO N O   21   .329
1939 BRO N O   9   .231
1941 CLE A O   2   .333
1942 CLE A O   148   .250
1943 CLE A O   141   .276
1944 CLE A O   124   .289
1945 CHI A O   106   .293
         BLTR   551   .276

HOCKETTE, GEORGE EDWARD (LEFTY)
B.APR.7,1908 PERTH,MISS.
1934 BOS A P   3   2- 1
1935 BOS A P   23   2- 3
         BLTL   26   4- 4

HODAPP, URBAN JOHN (JOHNNY)
B.SEPT.26,1905 CINCINNATI,OHIO
1925 CLE A 3   37   .238
1926 CLE A 3   3   .200
1927 CLE A 3   79   .304
1928 CLE A 1-3   116   .323
1929 CLE A 2   90   .327
1930 CLE A 2   154   .354
1931 CLE A 2   122   .295
1932 CLE A H   7   .188
         CHI A O   68   .222
1933 BOS A 1-2   115   .312
         BRTR   791   .311

HODERLEIN, MELVIN ANTHONY (MEL)
B.JUNE 24,1923 MT.CARMEL,OHIO
1951 BOS A 2   9   .357
1952 WAS A 2   72   .269
1953 WAS A 2-S   23   .191
1954 WAS A 2-S   14   .160
         BBTR   118   .252

HODES, CHARLES
B.1848 NEW YORK,N.Y.
D.FEB.14,1875
1871 TRO NA C-S-3-O   28   -
1872 TRO NA C-S-3-O   13   .231
1874 ATL NA 2-O   21   -
                                 62   -

HODGE, CLARENCE CLEMET (SHOVEL)
B.JULY 6,1893 MOUNT ANDREW,ALA.
D.DEC.31,1967 FT.WALTON BEACH,FLA.
1920 CHI A P   4   1- 1
1921 CHI A P   36   6- 8
1922 CHI A P   35   7- 6
         BLTR   75   14-15

YR	CL	LEA	POS	GP	G	REC

HODGE, EDWARD BURTON (BERT)
B.MAY 25,1917 KNOXVILLE,TENN.
| 1942 | PHI | N | 3 | | 8 | .182 |
| | BLTR | | | | | |

HODGE, HAROLD MORRIS (GOMER)
B.APR.3,1944 RUTHERFORDTON,N.C.
| 1971 | CLE | A | /1-3-2 | | 80 | .205 |
| | BBTR | | | | | |

HODGES, GILBERT RAYMOND (GIL)
B.APR.4,1924 PRINCETON,IND.
D.APR.2,1972 WEST PALM BEACH,FLA
1943	BRO	N	3		1	.000
1947	BRO	N	C		28	.156
1948	BRO	N	C-1		134	.249
1949	BRO	N	1		156	.285
1950	BRO	N	1		153	.283
1951	BRO	N	1		158	.268
1952	BRO	N	1		153	.254
1953	BRO	N	1-0		141	.302
1954	BRO	N	1		154	.304
1955	BRO	N	1-0		150	.289
1956	BRO	N	C-1-0		153	.265
1957	BRO	N	1-2-3		150	.299
1958	LA	N	C-1-3-0		141	.259
1959	LA	N	1-3		124	.276
1960	LA	N	1-3		101	.198
1961	LA	N	1		109	.242
1962	NY	N	1		54	.252
1963	NY	N	1		11	.227
	BRTR				2071	.273
NON-PLAYING MANAGER
WAS[A] 1963-67, NY[N] 1968-71

HODGES, RONALD WRAY (RON)
B.JUNE 22,1949 ROCKY MOUNT,VA.
1973	NY	N	C		45	.260
1974	NY	N	C		59	.221
1975	NY	N	/C		9	.206
1976	NY	N	C		56	.226
1977	NY	N	C		66	.265
1978	NY	N	C		47	.255
	BLTR				282	.241

HODGIN, ELMER RALPH (RALPH)
B.FEB.10,1916 GREENSBORO,N.C.
1939	BOS	N	O		32	.208
1943	CHI	A	3-0		117	.314
1944	CHI	A	3-0		121	.295
1946	CHI	A	O		87	.252
1947	CHI	A	O		59	.294
1948	CHI	A	O		114	.266
	BLTR				530	.285

HODKEY, ALOYSIUS JOSEPH (ELI)
B.NOV.3,1917 LORAIN,OHIO
| 1946 | PHI | N | P | | 2 | 0- 1 |
| | BLTL | | | | | |

HODNETT, CHARLES
B.ST.LOUIS,MO.
1883	STL	AA	P-O		4	1- 1
						.154
1884	STL	U	P		15	12- 1
					19	13- 2
						.121

HODSON, GEORGE S.
B.1876 HARTFORD,CONN.
1894	BOS	N	P		11	4- 3
1895	PHI	N	P		4	0- 2
					15	4- 5

HOEFT, WILLIAM FREDERICK (BILLY)
B.MAY 17,1932 OSHKOSH,WIS.
1952	DET	A	P		34	2- 7
1953	DET	A	P	29	30	9-14
1954	DET	A	P	34	35	7-15
1955	DET	A	P	32	36	16- 7
1956	DET	A	P	38	42	20-14
1957	DET	A	P	34	42	9-11
1958	DET	A	P	36	43	10- 9
1959	DET	A	P	2	3	1- 1
	BOS	A	P	5	7	0- 3
	BAL	A	P		16	1- 1
1960	BAL	A	P		19	2- 1
1961	BAL	A	P		35	7- 4
1962	BAL	A	P		57	4- 8
1963	SF	N	P		23	2- 0
1964	MIL	N	P		42	4- 0
1965	CHI	N	P		29	2- 2
1966	CHI	N	P		36	1- 2
	SF	N	/P		4	0- 2
	BLTL			505	533	97-101

HOELSKOETTER, ARTHUR
(HOLLEY) OR (HOSS)
[ALSO PLAYED UNDER NAME OF
ARTHUR H. HOSTETTER]
B.SEPT.30,1882 ST.LOUIS,MO.
D.AUG.3,1954 ST.LOUIS,MO.
1905	STL	N	P-3	1	24	0- 1
						.241
1906	STL	N	P-S-	1	94	1- 0
			3			.224
1907	STL	N	1-2		118	.247
1908	STL	N	C		45	.232
	BRTR			2	281	1- 1
						.236

HOERNER, JOSEPH WALTER (JOE)
B.NOV.12,1936 DUBUQUE,IOWA
1963	HOU	N	P		1	0- 0
1964	HOU	N	P		7	0- 0
1966	STL	N	P		57	5- 1
1967	STL	N	P		57	4- 4
1968	STL	N	P		47	8- 2
1969	STL	N	P		45	2- 3
1970	PHI	N	P		44	6- 5
1971	PHI	N	P		49	4- 5
1972	PHI	N	P		15	0- 2
	ATL	N	P		25	1- 3
1973	ATL	N	P		20	2- 2
	KC	A	P		22	2- 0
1974	KC	A	P		30	2- 3
1975	PHI	N	P		25	0- 0
1976	TEX	A	P		41	0- 4
1977	CIN	N	/P		8	0- 0
	BRTL				493	39-34

HOERNSCHEMEYER, LEOPOLD CHRISTOPHER
[PLAYED UNDER NAME OF LEE MAGEE]

HOERST, FRANK JOSEPH (LEFTY)
B.AUG.11,1917 PHILADELPHIA,PA.
1940	PHI	N	P		6	1- 0
1941	PHI	N	P		37	3-10
1942	PHI	N	P		33	4-16
1946	PHI	N	P		18	1- 6
1947	PHI	N	P		4	1- 1
	BLTL				98	10-33

HOEY, FREDERICK C.
B.NEW YORK,N.Y.
D.DEC.7,1933
NON-PLAYING MANAGER NY[N] 1899

HOEY, JOHN B.
B.NOV.10,1881 WATERTOWN,MASS.
D.NOV.11,1947 NAUGATUCK,CONN.
1906	BOS	A	O		94	.244
1907	BOS	A	O		39	.219
1908	BOS	A	O		13	.139
					146	.230

HOFF, CHESTER CORNELIUS (RED)
B.MAY 8,1891 OSSINING,N.Y.
1911	NY	A	P		5	0- 2
1912	NY	A	P		5	0- 1
1913	NY	A	P		2	0- 0
1915	STL	A	P		11	2- 2
	BLTL				23	2- 5

HOFFER, WILLIAM LEOPOLD (BILL)
(CHICK) OR (WIZARD)
B.NOV.8,1870 CEDAR RAPIDS,IOWA
D.JULY 21,1959 CEDAR RAPIDS,IA.
1895	BAL	N	P		38	29- 8
1896	BAL	N	P		35	26- 7
1897	BAL	N	P	34	41	22-10
1898	BAL	N	P-O		5	0- 5
						.235
	PIT	N	P		4	3- 0
1899	PIT	N	P	19	30	8- 9
1901	CLE	A	P		17	6- 7
	BRTR			152	170	94-46
						.230

HOFFERTH, STEWART EDWARD (STEW)
B.JAN.27,1913 LOGANSPORT,IND.
1944	BOS	N	C		66	.200
1945	BOS	N	C		50	.235
1946	BOS	N	C		20	.207
	BRTR				136	.216

HOFFMAN, CLARENCE CASPER
(RED) OR (DUTCH)
B.JAN.28,1904 FREEBURG,ILL.
D.DEC.6,1962 BELLEVILLE,ILL.
| 1929 | CHI | A | O | | 107 | .258 |
| | BRTR | | | | | |

HOFFMAN, DANIEL JOHN
B.MAR.10,1880 CANTON,CONN.
D.MAR.14,1922 MANCHESTER,CONN.
1903	PHI	A	O		73	.235
1904	PHI	A	O		53	.305
1905	PHI	A	O		119	.262
1906	PHI	A	O		7	.217
	NY	A	O		100	.257
1907	NY	A	O		136	.253
1908	STL	A	O		99	.251
1909	STL	A	O		110	.269
1910	STL	A	O		106	.237
1911	STL	A	O		24	.210
	BLTR				827	.255

HOFFMAN, EDWARD ADOLPH (TEX)
B.NOV.30,1893 SAN ANTONIO,TEX.
D.MAY 19,1947 NEW ORLEANS,LA.
| 1915 | CLE | A | 3 | | 9 | .153 |
| | BLTR | | | | | |

HOFFMAN, FRANK J. (THE TEXAS WONDER)
B.HOUSTON,TEX.
| 1888 | KC | AA | P | | 12 | 3- 9 |

HOFFMAN, HARRY C. (IZZY)
B.JAN.5,1875 BRIDGEPORT,N.J.
D.NOV.13,1942 PHILADELPHIA,PA.
1904	WAS	A	O		10	.067
1907	BOS	N	O		19	.279
	BLTL				29	.224

HOFFMAN, JOHN EDWARD (JOHN)
(PORK CHOP)
B.OCT.31,1943 ABERDEEN,S.D.
1964	HOU	N	C		6	.067
1965	HOU	N	/C		2	.333
	BLTR				8	.143

HOFFMAN, LAWRENCE CHARLES
B.JULY 18,1882 CHICAGO,ILL.
D.DEC.29,1948 CHICAGO,ILL.
| 1901 | CHI | N | 3 | | 5 | .315 |
| | TR | | | | | |

HOFFMAN, OTTO CHARLES (HICKEY)
B.OCT.27,1856 CLEVELAND,OHIO
D.OCT.27,1915 PEORIA,ILL.
| 1879 | CLE | N | C | | 1 | .000 |

HOFFMAN, RAYMOND LAMONT
B.JUNE 14,1917 DETROIT,MICH.
| 1942 | WAS | A | 3 | | 7 | .053 |
| | BLTR | | | | | |

HOFFMAN, WILLIAM JOSEPH
B.MAR.3,1918 PHILADELPHIA,PA.
| 1939 | PHI | N | P | | 3 | 0- 0 |
| | BLTL | | | | | |

HOFFMEISTER, JESSE H.
B.TOLEDO,OHIO
| 1897 | PIT | N | 3 | | 47 | .312 |

HOFFNER, WILLIAM
B.DANVILLE,PA.
| 1888 | KC | AA | P | | 2 | 0- 2 |

HOFFORD, JOHN WILLIAM
B.PHILADELPHIA,PA.
1885	PIT	AA	P		3	0- 2
1886	PIT	AA	P		9	3- 6
					12	3- 8

HOFMAN, ARTHUR FREDERICK
(CIRCUS SOLLY)
B.OCT.29,1882 ST.LOUIS,MO.
D.MAR.10,1956 ST.LOUIS,MO.
1903	PIT	N	O		3	.000
1904	CHI	N	O		7	.269
1905	CHI	N	2		83	.237
1906	CHI	N	1-0		60	.256
1907	CHI	N	1-S-O		134	.268
1908	CHI	N	1-2-O		116	.243
1909	CHI	N	O		153	.285
1910	CHI	N	1-0		135	.325
1911	CHI	N	1-0		143	.252
1912	CHI	N	O		36	.272
	PIT	N	O		17	.283
1913	PIT	N	O		28	.229
1914	BRO	F	1-2-O		147	.291
1915	BUF	F	O		108	.233
1916	NY	A	O		6	.296
	CHI	N	O		5	.313
	BRTR				1181	.269

HOFMAN, ROBERT GEORGE (BOBBY)
B.OCT.5,1925 ST.LOUIS,MO.
1949	NY	N	2		19	.208
1952	NY	N	1-2-3		32	.286
1953	NY	N	2-3		74	.266
1954	NY	N	1-2-3		71	.224
1955	NY	N	C-1-2-3		96	.266
1956	NY	N	C-1-2-3		47	.179
1957	NY	N	H		2	.000
	BRTR				341	.248

```
YR  CL LEA POS      GP    G    REC        YR  CL LEA POS      GP    G    REC        YR  CL LEA POS      GP    G    REC

HOFMANN, FRED (BOOTNOSE)                  HOGSETT, ELON CHESTER (CHIEF)            HOLDSWORTH, FREDRICK WILLIAM (FRED)
B.JUNE 10,1894 ST.LOUIS,MO.              B.NOV.2,1903 BROWNELL,KAN.               B.MAY 29,1952 DETROIT,MICH.
D.NOV.19,1964 ST.HELENA,CAL.             1929 DET A  P              4   1- 2       1972 DET A /P              2   0- 1
1919 NY  A  C             1    .000      1930 DET A  P             33   9- 8       1973 DET A /P              5   0- 1
1920 NY  A  C            15    .292      1931 DET A  P             22   3- 9       1974 DET A /P              8   0- 3
1921 NY  A  C            23    .177      1932 DET A  P       47   48   11- 9       1976 BAL A  P             16   4- 1
1922 NY  A  C            37    .297      1933 DET A  P             45   6-10       1977 BAL A  P             12   0- 1
1923 NY  A  C            72    .290      1934 DET A  P             26   3- 2            MON N  P             14   3- 3
1924 NY  A  C            62    .175      1935 DET A  P             40   6- 6       1978 MON N /P              6   0- 0
1925 NY  A  C             3    .000      1936 DET A  P              3   0- 1            BRTR                63   7-10
1927 BOS A  C            87    .272           STL A  P       39   43   13-15
1928 BOS A  C            78    .226      1937 STL A  P       37   40   6-19       HOLDSWORTH, JAMES (LONG JIM)
     BRTR              378    .237       1938 WAS A  P       31   32   5- 6       B.NEW YORK
                                         1944 DET A  P              3   0- 0       1872 CLE NA S            21    .321
HOGAN, GEORGE EMMET                           BLTL          330  339   63-87           ECK NA S             2    .250
B.SEPT.25,1885 MARION,OHIO                                                         1873 MUT NA S            54    -
D.FEB.28,1922 BARTLESVILLE,OKLA          HOGUE, CALVIN GREY (CAL)                 1874 PHI NA S-3-O         56    -
1914 KC  F  P             4    3- 1      B.OCT.24,1927 DAYTON,OHIO                 1875 MUT NA S-O          69    -
                                         1952 PIT N  P             19   1- 8       1876 MUT N  O            52    .264
HOGAN, HARRY S.                          1953 PIT N  P              3   1- 1       1877 HAR N  O            55    .254
B.NOV.1,1875 SYRACUSE,N.Y.               1954 PIT N  P              3   0- 1       1882 TRO N  O             1    .000
D.JAN.24,1934 SYRACUSE,N.Y.                   BRTR                25   2-10       1884 IND AA O             5    .106
1901 CLE A  O             1    .000                                                    BRTR               315    -
                                         HOGUE, ROBERT CLINTON (BOBBY)
HOGAN, JAMES FRANCIS (SHANTY)            B.APR.5,1921 MIAMI,FLA.                  HOLKE, WALTER HENRY (UNION MAN)
B.MAR.21,1906 SOMERVILLE,MASS.           1948 BOS N  P             40   8- 2       B.DEC.25,1892 ST.LOUIS,MO.
D.APR.7,1967 BOSTON,MASS.                1949 BOS N  P             33   2- 2       D.OCT.12,1954 ST.LOUIS,MO.
1925 BOS N  O             9    .286      1950 BOS N  P             36   3- 5       1914 NY  N  1             2    .333
1926 BOS N  C             4    .286      1951 BOS N  P              3   0- 0       1916 NY  N  1            34    .351
1927 BOS N  C            71    .288           STL A  P            18   1- 1       1917 NY  N  1           153    .277
1928 NY  N  C           131    .333           NY  A  P             7   1- 0       1918 NY  N  1            88    .252
1929 NY  N  C           102    .300      1952 NY  A  P             27   3- 5       1919 BOS N  1           137    .292
1930 NY  N  C           122    .339           STL A  P             8   0- 1       1920 BOS N  1           144    .294
1931 NY  N  C           123    .301           BRTR               172   18-16      1921 BOS N  1           150    .261
1932 NY  N  C           140    .287                                               1922 BOS N  1           105    .241
1933 BOS N  C            96    .253      HOHMAN, WILLIAM HENRY                    1923 PHI N  P-1     1  147   0- 0
1934 BOS N  C            92    .262      B.NOV.27,1903 BROOKLYN,MD.                                              .311
1935 BOS N  C            59    .301      D.OCT.29,1968 BALTIMORE,MD.              1924 PHI N  1           148    .300
1936 WAS A  C            19    .323      1927 PHI N  O              7   .278      1925 PHI N  1            39    .244
1937 WAS A  C            21    .152           BRTR                                     CIN N  1            65    .280
     BRTR              989    .295                                                     BBTL          1 1212   0- 0
                                         HOHNHORST, EDWARD HENRY                                               .287
HOGAN, KENNETH TIMOTHY                   B.JAN.31,1885 KENTUCKY
B.OCT.9,1902 CLEVELAND,OHIO              D.MAR.28,1916 COVINGTON,KY.              HOLLAHAN, WILLIAM JAMES (HAPPY)
1921 CIN N  O             1    .000      1910 CLE A  1            17   .323       B.NOV.22,1896 NEW YORK,N.Y.
1923 CLE A  O             1    .000      1912 CLE A  1            15   .209       1920 WAS A  3             3    .167
1924 CLE A  O             1    .000           BLTL                32   .267
     BLTR                3    .000                                               HOLLAND, ALFRED WILLIS (AL)
                                         HOLBERT, WILLIAM H.                      B.AUG.16,1952 ROANOKE,VA.
HOGAN, MARTIN F.                         B.MAR.14,1855 BALTIMORE,MD.              1977 PIT N /P             2    0- 0
B.OCT.27,1871 WENSBURY,ENGLAND           D.MAR.11,1941 LAUREL,MD.                     BRTL
D.AUG.16,1923 YOUNGSTOWN,OHIO            1876 LOU N  C            12   .256
1894 CIN N  O             6    .174      1878 MIL N  C-O          44   .184       HOLLAND, HOWARD ARTHUR (MUL)
     STL N  O            23    .288      1879 SYR N  C-O          57   .199       B.JAN.6,1903 FRANKLIN,VA.
1895 STL N  O             5    .150           TRO N  C             4   .267       D.FEB.16,1969 WINCHESTER,VA.
                        34    .244       1880 TRO N  C-O          60   .188       1926 CIN N  P             3    0- 0
                                         1881 TRO N  C-O          44   .274       1927 NY  N  P             2    1- 0
HOGAN, ROBERT EDWARD (EDDIE)             1882 TRO N  C-1-3-O      68   .186       1929 STL N  P             8    0- 1
B.ST.LOUIS,MO.                           1883 MET AA C-2-O        71   .238           BRTR               13    1- 1
1882 STL AA P             1    0- 1      1884 MET AA C            65   .208
1884 MIL U  O            11    .077      1885 MET AA C            55   .190       HOLLAND, ROBERT CLYDE (DUTCH)
1887 MET AA O            32    .377      1886 MET AA C            48   .216       B.OCT.12,1903 MIDDLESEX,N.J.
1888 CLE AA O            77    .236      1887 MET AA C            70   .252       D.JUNE 16,1967 LUMBERTON,N.C.
     BR           1    121    0- 1       1888 BRO AA C            15   .115       1932 BOS N  O            39    .295
                               .277          BRTR               613   .213       1933 BOS N  O            13    .258
                                                                                 1934 CLE A  O            50    .250
HOGAN, WILLIAM HENRY (WILLIE)            HOLBOROW, WALTER ALBERT                       BRTR              102    .273
B.SEPT.14,1884 N.SAN JUAN,CAL.           B.NOV.30,1913 NEW YORK,N.Y.
D.SEPT.28,1974 SAN JOSE,CAL.             1944 WAS A  P             1   0- 0       HOLLAND, WILLARD A.
1911 PHI A  O             7    .105      1945 WAS A  P            15   1- 1       B.FT.WAYNE,IND.
     STL A  O           123    .260      1948 PHI A  P             5   1- 2       1889 BAL AA S            40    .182
1912 STL A  O           107    .214           BRTR                21   2- 3
     BRTR              237    .236                                               HOLLAND, WILLIAM DAVID (DUTCH)
                                         HOLBROOK, JAMES MARBURY (SAMMY)         B.JUNE 4,1915 VARINA,N.C.
HOGG, CARTER BRADLEY (BRAD)              B.JULY 17,1910 MERIDIAN,MISS.            1939 WAS A  P             3    0- 1
B.MAR.26,1888 BUENA VISTA,GA.            1935 WAS A  C            52   .259           BLTL
D.APR.2,1935 BUENA VISTA,GA.                  BRTR
1911 BOS N  P             8    0- 3                                              HOLLAWAY, KENNETH EUGENE (KEN)
1912 BOS N  P            10    1- 1      HOLCOMBE, KENNETH EDWARD (KEN)          (PLAYED UNDER NAME OF
1915 CHI N  P             2    1- 0      B.AUG.23,1918 BURNSVILLE,N.C.           KENNETH EUGENE HOLLOWAY)
1918 PHI N  P      30    39   13-13      1945 NY  A  P            23   3- 3
1919 PHI N  P      22    29    5-12      1948 CIN N  P             2   0- 0       HOLLEY, EDWARD EDGAR
     BRTR          72    84   20-29      1950 CHI A  P            24   3-10       B.JULY 23,1901 BENTON,KY.
                                         1951 CHI A  P            28   11-12      1928 CHI N  P            13    0- 0
HOGG, WILBERT GEORGE (BERT)              1952 CHI A  P             7   0- 5       1932 PHI N  P            34   11-14
B.APR.21,1913 DETROIT,MICH.                   STL A  P            12   0- 2       1933 PHI N  P            30   13-15
1934 BRO N  3             2    .000      1953 BOS A  P             3   1- 0       1934 PHI N  P      15    16   1- 8
     BRTR                                     BRTR                99   18-32           PIT N  P             5   0- 3
                                                                                      BRTR          97    98   25-40
HOGG, WILLIAM (BUFFALO BILL)             HOLDEN, JOSEPH FRANCIS (SOCKS)
B.1880 PORT HURON,MICH.                  B.JUNE 4,1913 ST.CLAIR,PA.              HOLLIDAY, JAMES WEAR (BUG)
D.DEC.8,1909 NEW ORLEANS,LA.             1934 PHI N  C            10   .071       B.FEB.8,1867 ST.LOUIS,MO.
1905 NY  A  P            39    9-16      1935 PHI N  C             6   .111       D.FEB.15,1910 CINCINNATI,OHIO
1906 NY  A  P            28   14-13      1936 PHI N  H             1   .000       1889 CIN AA O           135    .343
1907 NY  A  P      26    27   11- 8           BLTR                17   .083       1890 CIN N  O           131    .270
1908 NY  A  P            24    4-16                                              1891 CIN N  O           110    .318
     TR          117   118   38-53       HOLDEN, WILLIAM PAUL                    1892 CIN N  P-O     1  149   0- 1
                                         B.SEPT.7,1889 BIRMINGHAM,ALA.                                          .286
HOGRIEVER, GEORGE C.                     D.SEPT.14,1971 PENSACOLA,FLA.           1893 CIN N  O           122    .332
B.MAR.17,1869 CINCINNATI,OHIO            1913 NY  A  O            18   .302       1894 CIN N  O           122    .383
D.JAN.26,1961 APPLETON,WIS.              1914 NY  A  O            50   .182       1895 CIN N  O            31    .301
1895 CIN N  O            67    .278           CIN N  O            11   .214       1896 CIN N  O            22    .346
1901 MIL A  O            54    .243           BRTR                79   .211       1897 CIN N  O            53    .328
     BRTR              121    .261                                               1898 CIN N  O            26    .240
                                                                                      BRTR          1  901   0- 1
                                                                                                              .319
```

YR	CL LEA POS	GP	G	REC

HOLLING, CARL
B.JULY 9,1896 DANA,CAL.
D.JULY 18,1962 SONOMA,CAL.

1921 DET A P		35	3- 7
1922 DET A P		7	1- 1
BRTR		40	42	4- 8

HOLLINGSHEAD, JOHN SAMUEL
[ALSO PLAYED UNDER NAME OF
SAMUEL JOHN HOLLY]
B.JAN.17,1853 WASHINGTON,D.C.
D.OCT.6,1926

1872 NAT NA 2		9	.311
1873 NAT NA 2-0		30	-
1875 NAT NA 0		17	-
		56	-
NON-PLAYING MANAGER WAS[AA]1884

HOLLINGSWORTH, ALBERT WAYNE (BOOTS)
B.FEB.25,1908 ST.LOUIS,MO.

1935 CIN N P	38	39	6-13
1936 CIN N P	29	34	9-10
1937 CIN N P	43	46	9-15
1938 CIN N P	8	9	2- 2
PHI N P		24	5-16
1939 PHI N P		15	1- 9
BRO N P		9	1- 2
1940 WAS A P		3	1- 0
1942 STL A P	33	36	10- 6
1943 STL A P	35	36	6-13
1944 STL A P		26	5- 7
1945 STL A P	26	28	12- 9
1946 STL A P		5	0- 0
CHI A P		21	3- 2
BLTL	315	331	70-104

HOLLINGSWORTH, JOHN BURNETT (BONNIE)
B.DEC.26,1895 JACKSBORO,TENN.

1922 PIT N P		9	0- 0
1923 WAS A P		17	3- 7
1924 BRO N P		2	1- 0
1928 BOS N P		7	0- 2
BRTR		35	4- 9

HOLLISON, JOHN HENRY (SWEDE)
B.MAY 3,1870 CHICAGO,ILL.
D.AUG.19,1969 CHICAGO,ILL.

| 1892 CHI N P | | 1 | 0- 1 |
| BRTL |

**HOLLMIG, STANLEY ERNEST
(STAN) OR (HONDO)**
B.JAN.2,1926 FREDERICKSBURG,TEX

1949 PHI N 0		81	.255
1950 PHI N 0		11	.250
1951 PHI N H		2	.000
BRTR		94	.253

HOLLOCHER, CHARLES JACOB
B.JUNE 11,1896 ST.LOUIS,MO.
D.AUG.14,1940 FRONTENAC,MO.

1918 CHI N S		131	.316
1919 CHI N S		115	.270
1920 CHI N S		80	.319
1921 CHI N S		140	.289
1922 CHI N S		152	.339
1923 CHI N S		66	.342
1924 CHI N S		76	.245
BLTR		760	.304

HOLLOMAN, ALVA LEE (BOBO)
B.MAR.7,1925 THOMASTON,GA.

| 1953 STL A P | | 22 | 3- 7 |
| BRTR |

HOLLOWAY, JAMES MADISON
B.SEPT.22,1908 PLAQUEMINE,LA.

| 1929 PHI N P | | 3 | 0- 0 |
| BRTR |

**HOLLOWAY, KENNETH EUGENE
[REAL NAME KENNETH EUGENE HOLLAWAY]**
B.AUG.8,1897 THOMAS COUNTY,GA.
D.SEPT.25,1968 THOMASVILLE,GA.

1922 DET A P		1	0- 0
1923 DET A P		42	11-10
1924 DET A P		49	14- 6
1925 DET A P		38	13- 4
1926 DET A P		36	4- 5
1927 DET A P		36	11-12
1928 DET A P		30	4- 8
1929 CLE A P		25	6- 5
1930 CLE A P		12	1- 1
NY A P		16	0- 0
BRTR		285	64-51

HOLLY, EDWARD WILLIAM
B.JULY 6,1879 CHICAGO,ILL.
D.NOV.27,1973 WILLIAMSPORT,PA.

1906 STL N S		9	.067
1907 STL N S		150	.229
1914 PIT F S		100	.246
1915 PIT F S		16	.262
BRTR		275	.232

HOLLY, JEFFREY OWEN (JEFF)
B.MAR.1,1953 SAN PEDRO,CAL.

1977 MIN A P		18	2- 3
1978 MIN A P		15	1- 1
BLTL		33	3- 4

**HOLLY, SAMUEL JOHN
[ALSO PLAYED UNDER REAL NAME OF
JOHN SAMUEL HOLLINGSHEAD]**

HOLM, ROSCOE ALBERT (WATTIE)
B.DEC.28,1901 PETERSON,IOWA
D.MAY 19,1950 EVERLY,IOWA

1924 STL N C-3-0		81	.294
1925 STL N 0		13	.207
1926 STL N 0		55	.285
1927 STL N 0		110	.286
1928 STL N 3		102	.277
1929 STL N 0		64	.233
1932 STL N 0		11	.176
BRTR		436	.275

HOLM, WILLIAM FREDERICK
B.JAN.21,1912 CHICAGO,ILL.

1943 CHI N C		7	.067
1944 CHI N C		54	.148
1945 BOS A C		58	.185
BRTR		119	.156

HOLMAN, GARY RICHARD
B.JAN.25,1944 LONG BEACH,CAL.

1968 WAS A 1-0		75	.294
1969 WAS A 1/0		41	.161
BRTR		116	.259

HOLMES, EDWARD M.

| 1918 PHI A P | | 2 | 0- 0 |
| TR |

HOLMES, FREDERICK
B.CHICAGO,ILL.

1903 NY A 1		1	.000
1904 CHI N C		1	.333
TR		2	.333

HOLMES, HOWARD ELBERT (DUCKY)
B.JULY 8,1883 DAYTON,OHIO
D.SEPT.18,1945 DAYTON,OHIO

| 1906 STL N C | | 9 | .185 |
| TR |

HOLMES, JAMES SCOTT
B.AUG.2,1882 LAWRENCEBURG,KY.
D.MAR.10,1960 JACKSONVILLE,FLA.

1906 PHI A P		3	0- 1
1908 BRO N P		13	1- 4
		16	1- 5

HOLMES, JAMES WILLIAM (DUCKY)
B.JAN.28,1869 DES MOINES,IOWA
D.AUG.6,1932 TRURO,IOWA

1895 LOU N P-0	1	39	1- 0
			.382
1896 LOU N P-0	4	37	0- 2
			.276
1897 LOU N S		2	.000
NY N 0		78	.288
1898 STL N 0		23	.276
BAL N 0		112	.280
1899 BAL N 0		138	.319
1901 DET A 0		130	.294
1902 DET A 0		92	.253
1903 WAS A 2-3-0		21	.229
CHI A 0		86	.279
1904 CHI A 0		67	.308
1905 CHI A 0		92	.267
BLTL	5	917	1- 2
			.283

**HOLMES, THOMAS FRANCIS
(TOMMY) OR (KELLY)**
B.MAR.29,1917 BROOKLYN,N.Y.

1942 BOS N 0		141	.278
1943 BOS N 0		152	.270
1944 BOS N 0		155	.309
1945 BOS N 0		154	.352
1946 BOS N 0		149	.310
1947 BOS N 0		150	.309
1948 BOS N 0		139	.325
1949 BOS N 0		117	.266
1950 BOS N 0		105	.298
1951 BOS N M-0		27	.172
1952 BRO N 0		31	.111
BLTL		1320	.302
NON-PLAYING MANAGER BOS[N] 1952

HOLSHOUSER, HERMAN ALEXANDER
B.JAN.20,1907 ROCKWELL,N.C.

| 1930 STL A P | | 25 | 0- 1 |
| BRTR |

HOLT, JAMES EMMETT MADISON (RED)
B.JULY 25,1894 DAYTON,TENN.
D.FEB.2,1961 BIRMINGHAM,ALA.

| 1925 PHI A 1 | | 27 | .273 |
| BLTL |

HOLT, JAMES WILLIAM (JIM)
B.MAY 27,1944 GRAHAM,N.C.

1968 MIN A O/1		70	.208
1969 MIN A /O-1		12	.357
1970 MIN A *0/1		142	.266
1971 MIN A *0/1		126	.259
1972 MIN A /0-1		10	.444
1973 MIN A *0-1		132	.297
1974 MIN A 1/0		79	.254
OAK A 1		30	.143
1975 OAK A 1/0-C		102	.220
1976 OAK A /H		4	.286
BLTR		707	.265

**HOLTGRAVE, LAVERN GEORGE
(VERN) OR (WOODY)**
B.OCT.18,1942 AVISTON,ILL.

| 1965 DET A /P | | 1 | 0- 0 |
| BRTR |

HOLTZMAN, KENNETH DALE (KEN)
B.NOV.3,1945 ST.LOUIS,MO.

1965 CHI N /P		3	0- 0
1966 CHI N P		34	11-16
1967 CHI N P		12	9- 0
1968 CHI N P	34	35	11-14
1969 CHI N P		39	17-13
1970 CHI N P	39	40	17-11
1971 CHI N P		30	9-15
1972 OAK A P	39	40	19-11
1973 OAK A P	40	41	21-13
1974 OAK A P		39	19-17
1975 OAK A P		39	18-14
1976 BAL A P		13	5- 4
NY A P		21	9- 7
1977 NY A P		18	2- 3
1978 NY A /P		5	1- 0
CHI N P		23	0- 3
BRTL		428	432	168-141

HONAN, MARTIN W.
B.CHICAGO,ILL.
D.AUG.20,1908 CHICAGO,ILL.

1890 CHI N C		1	.000
1891 CHI N C		5	.167
		6	.133

HONEYCUTT, FREDERICK WAYNE (RICK)
B.JUNE 29,1952 CHATTANOOGA,TENN.

1977 SEA A P		10	0- 1
1978 SEA A P		26	5-11
BLTL		36	5-12

HOOD, ALBIE LARRISON (ABIE)
B.JAN.31,1903 SANFORD,N.C.

| 1925 BOS N 2 | | 5 | .286 |
| BLTR |

HOOD, DONALD HARRIS (DON)
B.OCT.16,1949 FLORENCE,S.C.

1973 BAL A /P		8	3- 2
1974 BAL A P	20	25	1- 1
1975 CLE A P	29	35	6-10
1976 CLE A P	33	34	3- 5
1977 CLE A P		41	42	2- 1
1978 CLE A P		36	5- 6
BLTL		167	180	20-25

HOOD, WALLACE JAMES JR.
B.SEPT.24,1925 LOS ANGELES,CAL.

| 1949 NY A P | | 2 | 0- 0 |
| BRTR |

HOOD, WALLACE JAMES SR.
B.FEB.9,1895 WHITTIER,CAL.
D.MAY 2,1965 HOLLYWOOD,CAL.

1920 BRO N 0		7	.154
PIT N 0		2	.000
1921 BRO N 0		56	.262
1922 BRO N 0		2	.000
BRTR		67	.238

HOOK, JAMES WESLEY (JAY)
B.NOV.18,1936 WAUKEGAN,ILL.

1957 CIN N P		3	0- 1
1958 CIN N P		1	0- 1
1959 CIN N P	17	19	5- 5
1960 CIN N P		36	11-18
1961 CIN N P		22	1- 3
1962 NY N P	37	41	8-19
1963 NY N P		41	4-14
1964 NY N P		3	0- 1
BLTR		160	166	29-62

HOOKER, WILLIAM EDWARD (BUCK)
B.AUG.28,1880 RICHMOND,VA.
D.JULY 2,1929 RICHMOND,VA.

1902 CIN N P		1	0- 1
1903 CIN N P		1	0- 0
TR		2	0- 1

HOOKS, ALEXANDER MARCUS
B.AUG.29,1906 EDGEWOOD,TEX.

| 1935 PHI A 1 | | 15 | .227 |
| BLTL |

```
YR   CL LEA POS      GP    G    REC          YR   CL LEA POS      GP   G    REC          YR   CL LEA POS      GP    G   REC

HOOPER, HARRY BARTHOLOMEW                    HOPKINS, JOHN WINTON (BUCK) OR (SIS)         HORNER, WILLIAM FRANK (JACK)
B.AUG.24,1887 BELL STATION,CAL.              B.JAN.3,1883 GRAFTON,VA.                     B.SEPT.21,1863 BALTIMORE,MD.
D.DEC.18,1974 SANTA CRUZ,CAL.                D.OCT.2,1929 PHOEBUS,VA.                     D.JULY 14,1910 NEW ORLEANS,LA.
1909 BOS A  O           81  .282             1907 STL N  O          15  .136              1894 BAL N  P          2   0- 1
1910 BOS A  O          155  .267                    BRTR
1911 BOS A  O          130  .311                                                          HORNSBY, ROGERS (RAJAH)
1912 BOS A  O          147  .242             HOPKINS, MEREDITH HILLIARD (MARTY)           B.APR.27,1896 WINTERS,TEX.
1913 BOS A  P-O    1   148   0- 0            B.FEB.22,1907 WOLFE CITY,TEX.                D.JAN.5,1963 CHICAGO,ILL.
                             .289            D.NOV.20,1963 DALLAS,TEX.                    1915 STL N  S          18  .246
1914 BOS A  O          141  .258             1934 PHI N  3          10  .120              1916 STL N  1-S-3     139  .313
1915 BOS A  O          149  .235             1935 CHI A  3          67  .214              1917 STL N  S         145  .327
1916 BOS A  O          151  .271                    CHI A  2-3      59  .222              1918 STL N  S-O       115  .281
1917 BOS A  O          151  .256                    BRTR         136  .211                1919 STL N  1-2-S-3   138  .318
1918 BOS A  O          126  .289                                                          1920 STL N  2         149  .370
1919 BOS A  O          128  .267             HOPKINS, MICHAEL JOSEPH (SKINNER)            1921 STL N  2         154  .397
1920 BOS A  O          139  .312             B.NOV.1,1872 GLASGOW,SCOTLAND                1922 STL N  2         154  .401
1921 CHI A  O          108  .327             D.FEB.5,1952 PITTSBURGH,PA.                  1923 STL N  1-2       107  .384
1922 CHI A  O          152  .304             1902 PIT N  C           1  1.000             1924 STL N  2         143  .424
1923 CHI A  O          145  .288                    BRTR                                  1925 STL N  M-2       138  .403
1924 CHI A  O          130  .328                                                          1926 STL N  M-2       134  .317
1925 CHI A  O          127  .265             HOPKINS, PAUL HENRY                          1927 NY  N  2         155  .361
        BLTR     1  2308   0- 0              B.SEPT.25,1904 CHESTER,CONN.                 1928 BOS N  M-2       140  .387
                             .281            1927 WAS A  P          2   1- 0              1929 CHI N  2         156  .380
                                             1929 WAS A  P          7   0- 1              1930 CHI N  M-2        42  .308
HOOPER, MICHAEL H.                                  STL A  P          2   0- 0            1931 CHI N  M-2-3     100  .331
B.FEB.7,1850 BALTIMORE,MD.                          BRTR          11   1- 1              1932 CHI N  M-O        19  .224
D.DEC.1,1917 BALTIMORE,MD.                                                                1933 STL N  2          46  .325
1873 MAR NA C-O        3    -                HOPP, JOHN LEONARD                                  STL A  M-H      11  .333
                                             (JOHNNY) OR (HIPPITY)                        1934 STL A  M-3-0      24  .304
HOOPER, ROBERT NELSON (BOB)                  B.JULY 18,1916 HASTINGS,NEB.                 1935 STL A  M-1-2-3    10  .208
B.MAY 30,1922 LEAMINGTON,ONT.,CANADA         1939 STL N  1           6  .500              1936 STL A  M-1         2  .400
1950 PHI A  P           45  15-10            1940 STL N  1-0        80  .270              1937 STL A  M-2        20  .321
1951 PHI A  P           38  12-10            1941 STL N  1-0       134  .303                      BRTR        2259  .358
1952 PHI A  P           43   8-15            1942 STL N  1          95  .258              NON-PLAYING MANAGER
1953 CLE A  P           43   5- 4            1943 STL N  1-0        91  .224              STL[A] 1952, CIN[N] 1952-53
1954 CLE A  P           17   0- 0            1944 STL N  1-0       139  .336
1955 CIN N  P            8   0- 2            1945 STL N  1-0       124  .289              HORNUNG, MICHAEL JOSEPH (MIKE)
        BRTR          194  40-41             1946 BOS N  1-0       129  .333              OR (UBBO UBBO)
                                             1947 BOS N  O         134  .288              B.JUNE 12,1857 CARTHAGE,N.Y.
HOOTEN, MICHAEL LEON (LEON)                  1948 PIT N  1-0       120  .278              D.OCT.30,1931 NEW YORK,N.Y.
B.APR.4,1948 DOWNEY,CAL.                     1949 PIT N  1-0       105  .318              1879 BUF N  O          78  .266
1974 OAK A  /P           6   0- 0                   BRO N  1-0       8  .000              1880 BUF N  P-1-   1   82   0- 0
        BRTR                                 1950 PIT N  1-0       106  .240                            2-O           .262
                                                    NY  A  1-0      19  .333              1881 BOS N  O          83  .240
HOOTON, BURT CARLTON                         1951 NY  A  1          46  .206              1882 BOS N  1-0        84  .301
B.FEB.17,1950 GREENVILLE,TEX.                1952 NY  A  1          15  .160              1883 BOS N  O          98  .278
1971 CHI N  /P           3   2- 0                   DET A  1-0      42  .217              1884 BOS N  1-0       110  .266
1972 CHI N  P           33  11-14                   BLTL        1393  .296               1885 BOS N  O          25  .201
1973 CHI N  P           42  14-17                                                         1886 BOS N  O          94  .257
1974 CHI N  P           48   7-11            HOPPER, C. F. (LEFTY)                        1887 BOS N  O          97  .299
1975 CHI N  P            3   0- 2            B.RIDGEWOOD,N.J.                             1888 BOS N  O         107  .239
        LA  N  P           31  18- 7         1898 BRO N  P          2   0- 2              1889 BAL AA O         135  .227
1976 LA  N  P           33  11-15                   TL                                    1890 NY  N  1-0       120  .238
1977 LA  N  P           32  12- 7                                                                BRTR     1  1113   0- 0
1978 LA  N  P           32  19-10            HOPPER, JAMES MC DANIEL                                              .259
        BRTR          257  94-83             B.SEPT.2,1919 CHARLOTTE,N.C.
                                             1946 PIT N  P          2   0- 1              HORSEY, HANSON
HOOVER, CHARLES E.                                  BRTR                                  B.NOV.26,1889 GALENA,MD.
B.SEPT.21,1865 MOUND CITY,ILL.                                                            D.DEC.1,1949 MILLINGTON,MD.
1888 KC  AA C           3  .200              HOPPER, WILLIAM BOOTH (BIRD DOG)             1912 CIN N  P          1   0- 0
1889 KC  AA C          71  .247              B.OCT.26,1890 JACKSON,TENN.                          BRTR
        TR            74  .245               D.JAN.14,1965 ALLEN PARK,MICH.
                                             1913 STL N  P          3   0- 3              HORTSMANN, OSCAR THEODORE
HOOVER, RICHARD LLOYD                        1914 STL N  P          3   0- 0              B.JUNE 2,1891 ALMA,MO.
B.DEC.11,1925 COLUMBUS,OHIO                  1915 WAS A  P         13   0- 1              D.MAY 11,1977 SALINA,KAN.
1952 BOS N  P          2   0- 0                     BRTR          19   0- 4              1917 STL N  P         35   9- 4
        BLTL                                                                              1918 STL N  P          9   0- 2
                                             HORAN, JOHN J.                               1919 STL N  P          6   0- 1
HOOVER, ROBERT JOSEPH (JOE)                  B.CHICAGO,ILL.                                      BRTR          50   9- 7
B.APR.15,1915 BRAWLEY,TEX.                   1884 CHI U  P-O    11  20   3- 3
D.SEPT.2,1965 LOS ANGELES,CAL.                                      .080                  HORTON, ANTHONY DARRIN (TONY)
1943 DET A  S         144  .243                                                           B.DEC.6,1944 SANTA MONICA,CAL.
1944 DET A  2-S       120  .236              HORAN, JOSEPH PATRICK (SHAGS)                1964 BOS A  1-0        36  .222
1945 DET A  S          74  .257              B.SEPT.6,1895 ST.LOUIS,MO.                   1965 BOS A  1          60  .294
        BRTR         338  .243               D.FEB.13,1969 TORRANCE,CAL.                  1966 BOS A  /1          6  .136
                                             1924 NY  A  O         22  .290               1967 BOS A  /1         21  .308
HOOVER, WILLIAM J. (BUSTER)                         BRTR                                         CLE A  1       106  .281
B.1863 PHILADELPHIA,PA.                                                                   1968 CLE A  *1        133  .249
1884 KEY U  P-1-   1   61   0- 0             HORAZDOVSKY, ALBERT W.                        1969 CLE A  *1        159  .278
              2-S-0          .355            (PLAYED UNDER NAME OF                        1970 CLE A  *1        115  .269
        PHI N  O           9  .211           ALBERT FRANCIS NELSON)                              BRTR         636  .268
1886 BAL AA O          40  .213
1892 CIN N  O          14  .176              HORLEN, JOEL EDWARD (JOE)                     HORTON, ELMER E. (HERKY JERKY)
        BRTR     1  124   0- 0               B.AUG.14,1937 SAN ANTONIO,TEX.               B.SEPT.4,1869 HAMILTON,OHIO
                             .285            1961 CHI A  P           5   1- 3             1896 PIT N  P          3   0- 2
                                             1962 CHI A  P          20   7- 6             1898 BRO N  P          1   0- 3
HOPE, SAMUEL                                 1963 CHI A  P          33  11- 7                                    4   0- 3
B.DEC.4,1878 BROOKLYN,N.Y.                   1964 CHI A  P          32  13- 9
D.JUNE 30,1946 GREENPORT,N.Y.                1965 CHI A  P      37  64  13-13
1907 PHI A  P          1   0- 0              1966 CHI A  P      35  51  10-13
                                             1967 CHI A  P      35  41  19- 7
HOPKINS, DONALD (DON)                        1968 CHI A  P          37  12-14
B.JAN.9,1952 WEST POINT,MISS.                1969 CHI A  P          35  13-16
1975 OAK A  D/O-R      82  .167              1970 CHI A  P      34  32   6-16
1976 OAK A  R           3  .000              1971 CHI A  P          32   8- 9
        BLTR          85  .167               1972 OAK A  P          32   3- 4
                                                    BRTR      361 412 116-117
HOPKINS, GAIL EASON
B.FEB.19,1943 TULSA,OKLA.                    HORNE, BERLYN DALE
1968 CHI A  /1         29  .216              (SONNY) OR (TRADER)
1969 CHI A  *1/1      124  .265              B.APR.12,1899 BACHMAN,OHIO
1970 CHI A  1/C       116  .286              1929 CHI N  P         11   1- 1
1971 KC  A  1         103  .278                     BBTR
1972 KC  A  1/3        53  .211
1973 KC  A  D-1        74  .246              HORNER, JAMES ROBERT (BOB)
1974 LA  N  /C-1       15  .222              B.AUG.6,1957 JUNCTION CITY,KAN.
        BLTR         514  .266               1978 ATL N  3         89  .266
                                                    BRTR
```

YR	CL LEA POS	GP	G	REC

HORTON, WILLIAM WATTERSON (WILLIE)
B.OCT.18,1942 ARNO,VA.

YR	CL LEA POS	GP	G	REC
1963	DET A O		15	.326
1964	DET A O		25	.163
1965	DET A *O/3		143	.273
1966	DET A *O		146	.262
1967	DET A *O		122	.274
1968	DET A *O		143	.285
1969	DET A *O		141	.262
1970	DET A O		96	.305
1971	DET A *O		119	.289
1972	DET A O		108	.231
1973	DET A *O		111	.316
1974	DET A O		72	.298
1975	DET A *O		159	.275
1976	DET A *O		114	.262
1977	DET A /O		1	.250
	TEX A *O-D		139	.289
1978	CLE A D		50	.249
	OAK A D/O		32	.314
	TOR A D		33	.205
	BRTR		1769	.275

HOSKINS, DAVID TAYLOR (DAVE)
B.AUG.3,1925 GREENWOOD,MISS.
D.APR.2,1970 FLINT,MICH.

1953	CLE A P	26	38	9- 3
1954	CLE A P	14	15	0- 1
	BLTR	40	53	9- 4

HOSLEY, TIMOTHY KENNETH (TIM)
B.MAY 10,1947 SPARTANBURG,S.C.

1970	OAK A /C		7	.167
1971	DET A /C-1		7	.188
1973	OAK A C		13	.214
1974	OAK A /C-1		11	.286
1975	CHI N C		62	.255
1976	OAK A C		37	.164
	CHI N /H		1	.000
1977	OAK A C-D/1		39	.192
1978	OAK A /C		13	.304
	BRTR		190	.222

HOST, EUGENE EARL (GENE)
(TWINKLES) OR (SLICK)
B.JAN.1,1933 LEEPER,PA.

1956	DET A P		1	0- 0
1957	KC A P		11	0- 2
	BBTL		12	0- 2

HOSTETLER, CHARLES CLOYD (CHUCK)
B.SEPT.22,1903 MC CLELLANDTOWN,PA.
D.FEB.19,1971 FORT COLLINS,COLO

1944	DET A O		90	.298
1945	DET A O		42	.159
	BLTR		132	.278

HOSTETTER, ARTHUR
(ALSO PLAYED UNDER NAME OF
ARTHUR HOELSKOETTER)

HOTALING, PETER JAMES (MONKEY)
B.DEC.16,1856 MOHAWK,N.Y.
D.JULY 3,1928 CLEVELAND,OHIO

1879	CIN N C-2-3-O		80	.278
1880	CLE N O		77	.240
1881	WOR N O		76	.306
1882	BOS N O		83	.253
1883	CLE N O		97	.255
1884	CLE N 2-O		101	.242
1885	BRO AA O		95	.277
1887	CLE AA O		127	.367
1888	CLE AA O		97	.290
	BRTR		833	.279

HOTTMAN, KENNETH ROGER (KEN)
B.MAY 7,1948 STOCKTON,CAL.

1971	CHI A /O		6	.125
	BRTR			

HOUCK, BYRON SIMON (DUKE)
B.AUG.28,1891 PROSPER,MINN.
D.JUNE 17,1969 SANTA CRUZ,CAL.

1912	PHI A P		30	8- 8
1913	PHI A P		40	15- 6
1914	PHI A P		3	0- 0
	BRO F P		17	2- 6
1918	STL A P		26	2- 4
	BRTR		116	27-24

HOUCK, SARGENT P. (SADIE)
B.1856 WASHINGTON,D.C.

1879	BOS N S-O		80	.264
1880	BOS N O		12	.170
	PRO N O		48	.197
1881	DET N S		75	.279
1883	DET N S		98	.291
1884	ATH AA S		110	.302
1885	ATH AA S		92	.259
1886	BAL AA S		61	.203
	WAS N S		51	.215
1887	MET AA S		10	.222
	BRTR		637	.254

HOUGH, CHARLES OLIVER (CHARLIE)
B.JAN.5,1948 HONOLULU,HAWAII

1970	LA N /P		8	0- 0
1971	LA N /P		4	0- 0
1972	LA N /P		2	0- 0
1973	LA N P		37	4- 2
1974	LA N P		49	9- 4
1975	LA N P		38	3- 7
1976	LA N P		77	12- 8
1977	LA N P		70	6-12
1978	LA N P		55	5- 5
	BRTR		340	39-38

HOUK, RALPH GEORGE (MAJOR)
B.AUG.9,1919 LAWRENCE,KAN.

1947	NY A C		41	.272
1948	NY A C		14	.276
1949	NY A C		5	.571
1950	NY A C		10	.111
1951	NY A C		3	.200
1952	NY A C		9	.333
1953	NY A C		8	.222
1954	NY A H		1	.000
	BRTR		91	.272

NON-PLAYING MANAGER
NY(A) 1961-63, 66-73,
DET(A) 1974-78

HOUSE, HENRY FRANKLIN
(FRANK) OR (PIG)
B.FEB.18,1930 BESSEMER,ALA.

1950	DET A C		5	.400
1951	DET A C		18	.220
1954	DET A C		114	.250
1955	DET A C		102	.259
1956	DET A C		94	.240
1957	DET A C		106	.259
1958	KC A C		76	.252
1959	KC A C		98	.236
1960	CIN N C		23	.179
1961	DET A C		17	.227
	BLTR		653	.248

HOUSE, PATRICK LORY (PAT)
B.SEP.1,1940 BOISE,IDAHO

1967	HOU N /P		6	1- 0
1968	HOU N P		18	1- 1
	BLTR		24	2- 1

HOUSE, THOMAS ROSS (TOM)
B.APR.29,1947 SEATTLE,WASH.

1971	ATL N P		11	1- 0
1972	ATL N /P		8	0- 0
1973	ATL N P		52	4- 2
1974	ATL N P		56	6- 2
1975	ATL N P		58	7- 7
1976	BOS A P		36	1- 3
1977	BOS A /P		8	1- 0
	SEA A P		26	4- 5
1978	SEA A P		34	5- 4
	BLTL		289	29-23

HOUSE, WILLARD EDWIN
B.OCT.3,1890 CABOOL,MO.
D.NOV.26,1923 KANSAS CITY,MO.

1913	DET A P		19	1- 2
	BRTR			

HOUSEHOLDER, CHARLES F.
B.1850 HARRISBURG,PA.

1884	CHI U P-S-	1	64	0- 0
	3-O			.232
	PIT U O	16		.270
	3-O			.240
		1	80	.240

HOUSEHOLDER, CHARLES W.
B.1856 HARRISBURG,PA.
D.DEC.26,1908 HARRISBURG,PA.

1882	BAL AA C-1		73	.244
1884	BRO AA C-1		76	.242
	BLTL		149	.243

HOUSEHOLDER, EDWARD H.
B.OCT.12,1869 PITTSBURGH,PA.
D.JULY 3,1924 LOS ANGELES,CAL.

1903	BRO N O		12	.209

HOUSEMAN, FRANK
B.BALTIMORE,MD.

1886	BAL AA P		1	0- 1

HOUSEMAN, JOHN FRANKLIN
B.JAN.10,1870 HOLLAND,MICH.
D.NOV.4,1922 CHICAGO,ILL.

1894	CHI N S		4	.353
1897	STL N N 2-O		76	.232
			80	.239

HOUSER, BENJAMIN FRANKLIN
B.NOV.30,1883 SHENANDOAH,PA.
D.JAN.19,1952 AUGUSTA,MAINE

1910	PHI A 1		34	.189
1911	BOS N 1		20	.254
1912	BOS N 1		108	.286
	BLTL		162	.267

HOUSER, JOSEPH WILLIAM
B.JULY 3,1891 STEUBENVILLE,OHIO
D.JAN.3,1953 ORLANDO,FLA.

1914	BUF F P		8	0- 1
	BLTL			

HOUTTEMAN, ARTHUR JOSEPH (ART)
B.AUG.7,1927 DETROIT,MICH.

1945	DET A P		13	0- 2
1946	DET A P		1	0- 1
1947	DET A P		23	7- 2
1948	DET A P		43	2-16
1949	DET A P	34	36	15-10
1950	DET A P		41	19-12
1952	DET A P	35	36	8-20
1953	DET A P		16	2- 6
	CLE A P	22	23	7- 7
1954	CLE A P		32	15- 7
1955	CLE A P		35	10- 6
1956	CLE A P	22	23	2- 2
1957	CLE A P		3	0- 0
	BAL A P		5	0- 0
	BRTR	325	330	87-91

HOUTZ, CHARLES
B.ST.LOUIS,MO.

1875	RS NA 1		19	-
1884	PIT AA 1-O		9	.226
			28	-

HOUTZ, FRED FRITZ (LEFTY)
B.SEPT.4,1875 CONNERSVILLE,IND.
D.FEB.15,1959 WAPAKONETA,OHIO

1899	CIN N O		5	.176
	BLTL			

HOVLEY, STEPHEN EUGENE (STEVE)
B.DEC.18,1944 VENTURA,CAL.

1969	SEA A O		91	.277
1970	MIL A O		40	.281
	OAK A O		72	.190
1971	OAK A O		24	.111
1972	KC A O		105	.270
1973	KC A O-D		104	.254
	BLTL		436	.258

HOVLIK, EDWARD CHARLES
B.AUG.20,1891 CLEVELAND,OHIO
D.MAR.19,1955 PAINESVILLE,OHIO

1918	WAS A P		8	2- 1
1919	WAS A P		3	0- 0
	BRTR		11	2- 1

HOVLIK, JOSEPH
B.AUG.16,1884 CZECHOSLOVAKIA
D.NOV.3,1951 OXFORD JUNCTION,IA

1909	WAS A P		3	0- 0
1910	WAS A P		1	0- 0
1911	CHI A P		12	2- 0
	BRTR		16	2- 0

HOWARD, BRUCE ERNEST
B.MAR.23,1943 SALISBURY,MD.

1963	CHI A P		7	2- 1
1964	CHI A P		3	2- 1
1965	CHI A P		30	9- 8
1966	CHI A P		27	9- 5
1967	CHI A P		30	3-10
1968	BAL A P		10	0- 2
	WAS A P		13	1- 4
	BBTR		120	26-31

HOWARD, DAVID AUSTIN (DEL)
B.MAY 1,1889 WASHINGTON,D.C.
D.JAN.26,1956 DALLAS,TEX.

1912	WAS A H		1	.000
1915	BRO F 2		20	.222
	BRTR		21	.222

HOWARD, DOUGLAS LYNN (DOUG)
B.FEB.6,1948 SALT LAKE CITY,UTAH

1972	CAL A /O-1-3		11	.263
1973	CAL A /O-1-3		8	.095
1974	CAL A /O-1		22	.231
1975	STL N /1		17	.207
1976	CLE A 1/O		39	.211
	BRTR		97	.212

HOWARD, EARL NYCUM
B.JUNE 25,1896 EVERETT,PA.
D.APR.5,1937 BEDFORD,PA.

1918	STL N P		1	0- 0
	TR			

HOWARD, ELSTON GENE
B.FEB.23,1929 ST.LOUIS,MO.

YR	CL	LEA	POS	G	REC
1955	NY	A	C-O	97	.290
1956	NY	A	C-O	98	.262
1957	NY	A	C-1-O	110	.253
1958	NY	A	C-1-O	103	.314
1959	NY	A	C-1-O	125	.273
1960	NY	A	C-O	107	.245
1961	NY	A	C-1	129	.348
1962	NY	A	C	136	.279
1963	NY	A	C	135	.287
1964	NY	A	C	150	.313
1965	NY	A	C/1-O	110	.233
1966	NY	A	*C-1	126	.256
1967	NY	A	C/1	66	.196
	BOS	A	C	42	.147
1968	BOS	A	C	71	.241
		BRTR		1605	.274

HOWARD, FRANK OLIVER
(FRANK), (HONDO)
OR (THE CAPITAL PUNISHER)
B.AUG.8,1936 COLUMBUS,OHIO

YR	CL	LEA	POS	G	REC
1958	LA	N	O	8	.241
1959	LA	N	O	9	.143
1960	LA	N	1-O	117	.268
1961	LA	N	1-O	92	.296
1962	LA	N	O	141	.296
1963	LA	N	O	123	.273
1964	LA	N	O	134	.226
1965	WAS	A	*O	149	.269
1966	WAS	A	*O	146	.278
1967	WAS	A	*O/1	149	.256
1968	WAS	A	*O-1	158	.274
1969	WAS	A	*O-1	161	.296
1970	WAS	A	*O-1	161	.283
1971	WAS	A	*O-1	153	.279
1972	TEX	A	1-O	95	.244
	DET	A	1/O	14	.242
1973	DET	A	D/1	85	.256
		BRTR		1895	.273

HOWARD, GEORGE ELMER (DEL)
B.DEC.24,1877 KENNEY,ILL.
D.DEC.24,1956 SEATTLE,WASH.

YR	CL	LEA	POS	G	REC
1905	PIT	N	1-O	119	.292
1906	BOS	N	2-O	147	.261
1907	BOS	N	O	48	.273
	CHI	N	1-O	41	.230
1908	CHI	N	1-O	89	.279
1909	CHI	N	1	57	.197
		BLTR		501	.262

HOWARD, IVON CHESTER
B.OCT.12,1882 KENNEY,ILL.
D.MAR.30,1967 MEDFORD,ORE.

YR	CL	LEA	POS	G	REC
1914	STL	A	1-3	81	.244
1915	STL	A	1-3-O	113	.278
1916	CLE	A	2	81	.187
1917	CLE	A	3	27	.102
		BBTR		302	.233

HOWARD, LAWRENCE RAYFORD (LARRY)
B.JUNE 6,1945 COLUMBUS,OHIO

YR	CL	LEA	POS	G	REC
1970	HOU	N	C/1-O	31	.307
1971	HOU	N	C	24	.234
1972	HOU	N	C	54	.223
1973	HOU	N	C	20	.167
	ATL	N	/C	4	.125
		BRTR		133	.236

HOWARD, LEE VINCENT
B.NOV.11,1923 STATEN ISLAND,N.Y

YR	CL	LEA	POS	G	REC
1946	PIT	N	P	3	0- 1
1947	PIT	N	P	2	0- 0
		BLTL		5	0- 1

HOWARD, PAUL JOSEPH (DEL)
B.MAY 20,1884 BOSTON,MASS.
D.AUG.29,1968 MIAMI,FLA.

YR	CL	LEA	POS	G	REC
1909	BOS	N	O	6	.230
		BRTR			

HOWARD, WILBUR LEON
B.JAN.8,1949 LOWELL,N.C.

YR	CL	LEA	POS	G	REC
1973	MIL	A	O	16	.205
1974	HOU	N	O	64	.216
1975	HOU	N	O	121	.283
1976	HOU	N	O/2	94	.220
1977	HOU	N	O/2	87	.257
1978	HOU	N	O/C-2	84	.230
		BBTR		466	.250

HOWARTH, JAMES EUGENE (JIMMY)
B.MAR.7,1947 BILOXI,MISS.

YR	CL	LEA	POS	G	REC
1971	SF	N	/O	7	.231
1972	SF	N	O/1	74	.235
1973	SF	N	O/1	65	.200
1974	SF	N	/O	6	.000
		BLTL		152	.217

HOWE, ARTHUR HENRY (ART)
B.DEC.15,1946 PITTSBURGH,PA.

YR	CL	LEA	POS	G	REC
1974	PIT	N	3/S	29	.243
1975	PIT	N	3/S	63	.171
1976	HOU	N	/3-2	21	.138
1977	HOU	N	2-3-S	125	.264
1978	HOU	N	*2-3/1	119	.293
		BRTR		357	.258

HOWE, CALVIN EARL
B.NOV.27,1924 ROCK FALLS,ILL.

YR	CL	LEA	POS	G	REC
1952	CHI	N	P	1	0- 0
		BLTL			

HOWE, JOHN (SHORTY)
B.NEW YORK,N.Y.

YR	CL	LEA	POS	G	REC
1890	NY	N	2	17	.172
1893	NY	N	3	1	.500
				18	.203

HOWE, LESTER CURTIS (LUCKY)
B.AUG.24,1895 BROOKLYN,N.Y.
D.JULY 16,1976 WOODMERE,N.Y.

YR	CL	LEA	POS	G	REC
1923	BOS	A	P	13	1- 0
1924	BOS	A	P	4	1- 0
		BRTR		17	2- 0

HOWELL, HENRY HARRY (HARRY)
B.NOV.14,1876 NEW JERSEY
D.MAY 22,1956 SPOKANE,WASH.

YR	CL	LEA	POS	GP	G	REC
1898	BRO	N	P		2	2- 0
1899	BAL	N	P		28	14- 7
1900	BRO	N	P		21	6- 3
1901	BAL	A	P	38	54	14-21
1902	BAL	A	P-1-	25	96	9-14
			2-S-3-O			.266
1903	NY	A	P	26	41	10- 7
1904	STL	A	P	34	35	13-21
1905	STL	A	P	38	41	14-21
1906	STL	A	P		36	15-13
1907	STL	A	P	42	44	16-15
1908	STL	A	P	40	41	18-18
1909	STL	A	P	10	18	1- 1
1910	STL	A	P		1	0- 0
		BRTR		341	458	132-141
						.217

HOWELL, HOMER ELLIOTT (DIXIE)
B.APR.24,1919 LOUISVILLE,KY.

YR	CL	LEA	POS	G	REC
1947	PIT	N	C	76	.276
1949	CIN	N	C	64	.244
1950	CIN	N	C	82	.223
1951	CIN	N	C	77	.251
1952	CIN	N	C	17	.189
1953	BRO	N	H	1	.000
1955	BRO	N	C	16	.262
1956	BRO	N	C	7	.231
		BRTR		340	.246

HOWELL, MILLARD (DIXIE)
B.JAN.7,1920 BOWMAN,KY.
D.MAR.18,1960 HOLLYWOOD,FLA.

YR	CL	LEA	POS	GP	G	REC
1940	CLE	A	P		3	0- 0
1949	CIN	N	P	5	9	0- 1
1955	CHI	A	P		35	8- 3
1956	CHI	A	P		34	5- 6
1957	CHI	A	P	37	42	6- 5
1958	CHI	A	P		1	0- 0
		BLTR		115	124	19-15

HOWELL, MURRAY DONALD
(RED) OR (PORKY)
B.JAN.29,1909 ATLANTA,GA.
D.OCT.1,1950 TRAVELERS REST,S.C

YR	CL	LEA	POS	G	REC
1941	CLE	A	N	11	.286
		BRTR			

HOWELL, ROLAND BOATNER (BILLIKEN)
B.JAN.3,1892 NAPOLEONVILLE,LA.
D.MAR.31,1973 BATON ROUGE,LA.

YR	CL	LEA	POS	G	REC
1912	STL	N	P	3	0- 0

HOWELL, ROY LEE
B.DEC.18,1953 LOMPOC,CAL.

YR	CL	LEA	POS	G	REC
1974	TEX	A	3	13	.250
1975	TEX	A	*3	125	.251
1976	TEX	A	*3	140	.253
1977	TEX	A	/O-1-3	7	.000
	TOR	A	3	96	.316
1978	TOR	A	*3/O	140	.270
		BLTR		521	.268

HOWERTON, WILLIAM RAY
(BILL) OR (HOPALONG)
B.DEC.12,1921 LOMPOC,CAL.

YR	CL	LEA	POS	G	REC
1949	STL	N	O	9	.308
1950	STL	N	O	110	.281
1951	STL	N	O	24	.262
	PIT	N	3-O	80	.274
1952	PIT	N	3	13	.320
	NY	N	O	11	.067
		BLTR		247	.274

HOWLEY, DANIEL PHILIP (DAN)
(HOWLING DAN) OR (DAPPER DAN)
B.OCT.16,1885 E.WEYMOUTH,MASS.
D.MAR.10,1944 E.WEYMOUTH,MASS.

YR	CL	LEA	POS	G	REC
1913	PHI	N	C	26	.125
		TR			

NON-PLAYING MANAGER
STL[A] 1927-29, CIN[N] 1930-32

HOWSER, RICHARD DALTON (DICK)
B.MAY 14,1937 MIAMI,FLA.

YR	CL	LEA	POS	G	REC
1961	KC	A	S	158	.280
1962	KC	A	S	83	.238
1963	KC	A	S	15	.195
	CLE	A	S	49	.247
1964	CLE	A	S	162	.256
1965	CLE	A	S-2	107	.235
1966	CLE	A	2-S	67	.229
1967	NY	A	2-3/S	63	.268
1968	NY	A	2/3-S	85	.153
		BRTR		789	.248

NON-PLAYING MANAGER
NY[A] 1978 [INTERIM]

HOY, WILLIAM ELLSWORTH (DUMMY)
B.MAY 23,1862 HOUCKSTOWN,OHIO
D.DEC.15,1961 CINCINNATI,OHIO

YR	CL	LEA	POS	G	REC
1888	WAS	N	O	136	.274
1889	WAS	N	O	127	.282
1890	BUF	P	O	122	.299
1891	STL	AA	O	139	.288
1892	WAS	N	O	149	.279
1893	WAS	N	O	130	.259
1894	CIN	N	O	128	.312
1895	CIN	N	O	107	.274
1896	CIN	N	O	121	.296
1897	CIN	N	O	128	.290
1898	LOU	N	O	148	.318
1899	LOU	N	O	155	.306
1901	CHI	A	O	130	.293
1902	CIN	N	O	72	.294
		BLTR		1792	.291

HOYLE, ROLAND EDISON (TEX)
B.JULY 17,1921 CARBONDALE,PA.

YR	CL	LEA	POS	G	REC
1952	PHI	A	P	3	0- 0
		BRTR			

HOYOT, FREDERICK
[PLAYED UNDER NAME OF
FREDERICK IOTT]

HOYT, WAITE CHARLES (SCHOOLBOY)
B.SEPT.9,1899 BROOKLYN,N.Y.

YR	CL	LEA	POS	G	REC
1918	NY	N	P	1	0- 0
1919	BOS	A	P	13	4- 6
1920	BOS	A	P	22	6- 6
1921	NY	A	P	43	19-13
1922	NY	A	P	37	19-12
1923	NY	A	P	37	17- 9
1924	NY	A	P	46	18-13
1925	NY	A	P	46	11-14
1926	NY	A	P	39	16-12
1927	NY	A	P	36	22- 7
1928	NY	A	P	42	23- 7
1929	NY	A	P	30	10- 9
1930	NY	A	P	8	2- 2
	DET	A	P	26	9- 8
1931	DET	A	P	16	3- 8
	PHI	A	P	16	10- 5
1932	BRO	N	P	8	1- 3
	NY	N	P	18	5- 7
1933	PIT	N	P	36	5- 7
1934	PIT	N	P	48	15- 6
1935	PIT	N	P	39	7-11
1936	PIT	N	P	22	7- 5
1937	PIT	N	P	11	1- 2
	BRO	N	P	27	7- 7
1938	BRO	N	P	6	0- 3
		BRTR		673	237-182

HRABOSKY, ALAN THOMAS (AL)
B.JULY 21,1949 OAKLAND,CAL.

YR	CL	LEA	POS	GP	G	REC
1970	STL	N	P		16	2- 1
1971	STL	N	/P		1	0- 0
1972	STL	N	P		5	1- 0
1973	STL	N	P		44	2- 4
1974	STL	N	P	65	65	8- 1
1975	STL	N	P		65	13- 3
1976	STL	N	P		68	8- 6
1977	STL	N	P		65	6- 5
1978	KC	A	P		58	8- 7
		BRTL		387	388	48-27

HRINIAK, WALTER JOHN (WALT)
B.MAY 22,1943 NATICK,MASS.

YR	CL	LEA	POS	G	REC
1968	ATL	N	/C	9	.346
1969	ATL	N	/C	7	.143
	SD	N	C	31	.227
		BLTR		47	.253

HUBBARD, ALLEN
[PLAYED UNDER NAME OF
AL WEST FOR PART OF 1883]
B.DEC.9,1860 WESTFIELD,MASS.
D.DEC.14,1930 NEWTON,MASS.

YR	CL	LEA	POS	G	REC
1883	ATH	AA	C-S	2	.286

HUBBARD, GLENN DEE
B.SEPT.25,1957 HAHN AFB,GERMANY

YR	CL	LEA	POS	G	REC
1978	ATL	N	2	44	.258
		BRTR			

YR	CL LEA POS	GP	G	REC

HUBBELL, CARL OWEN (KING CARL)
OR (THE MEAL TICKET)
B.JUNE 22,1903 CARTHAGE,MO.

1928 NY	N	P		20	10- 6
1929 NY	N	P		39	18-11
1930 NY	N	P		37	17-12
1931 NY	N	P		36	14-12
1932 NY	N	P		40	18-11
1933 NY	N	P		45	23-12
1934 NY	N	P		49	21-12
1935 NY	N	P		42	23-12
1936 NY	N	P		42	26- 6
1937 NY	N	P		39	22- 8
1938 NY	N	P		24	13-10
1939 NY	N	P		29	11- 9
1940 NY	N	P		31	11-12
1941 NY	N	P		26	11- 9
1942 NY	N	P		24	11- 8
1943 NY	N	P		12	4- 4
	BRTL			535	253-154
	BB 1928-29, 31-32				

HUBBELL, WILBERT WILLIAM
B.JUNE 17,1897 HENDERSON,COLO.

1919 NY	N	P		2	1- 1
1920 NY	N	P		14	0- 1
PHI	N	P		24	9- 9
1921 PHI	N	P		36	9-16
1922 PHI	N	P		35	7-15
1923 PHI	N	P	22	23	1- 6
1924 PHI	N	P		36	10- 9
1925 PHI	N	P		2	0- 0
BRO	N	P		33	3- 6
	BRTR		204	205	40-63

HUBBS, KENNETH DOUGLAS (KEN)
B.DEC.23,1941 RIVERSIDE,CAL.
D.FEB.13,1964 PROVO,UTAH

1961 CHI	N	2		10	.179
1962 CHI	N	2		160	.260
1963 CHI	N	2		154	.235
	BRTR			324	.247

HUBER, CLARENCE BILL (GILLY)
B.OCT.27,1896 TYLER,TEX.
D.FEB.22,1965 LAREDO,TEX.

1920 DET	A	3		10	.205
1921 DET	A	3		1	.000
1925 PHI	N	3		124	.284
1926 PHI	N	3		118	.245
	BRTR			253	.266

HUBER, OTTO
B.MAR.12,1914 GARFIELD,N.J.

1939 BOS	N	2-3		11	.273
	BRTR				

HUCKLEBERRY, EARL EUGENE
B.MAY 23,1910 KONAWA,OKLA.

1935 PHI	A	P		1	1- 0
	BRTR				

HUDGENS, JAMES PRICE
B.AUG.24,1902 NEWBURG,MO.
D.AUG.26,1955 ST.LOUIS,MO.

1923 STL	N	1-2		6	.250
1925 CIN	N	1		3	.429
1926 CIN	N	1		17	.250
	BLTR			26	.282

HUDLIN, GEORGE WILLIS
(WILLIS) OR (ACE)
B.MAY 23,1906 WAGONER,OKLA.

1926 CLE	A	P		8	1- 3
1927 CLE	A	P		43	18-12
1928 CLE	A	P		42	14-14
1929 CLE	A	P		40	17-15
1930 CLE	A	P		37	13-16
1931 CLE	A	P		44	15-14
1932 CLE	A	P		33	12- 8
1933 CLE	A	P		34	5-13
1934 CLE	A	P		36	15-10
1935 CLE	A	P	36	37	15-11
1936 CLE	A	P		27	1- 5
1937 CLE	A	P		35	12-11
1938 CLE	A	P		29	8- 8
1939 CLE	A	P		27	9-10
1940 CLE	A	P		4	2- 1
WAS	A	P		8	1- 2
STL	A	P		6	0- 1
NY	N	P		1	0- 1
1944 STL	A	P		1	0- 0
	BRTR		491	492	158-156

HUDSON, CHARLES (CHARLIE)
B.AUG.18,1949 ADA,OKLA.

1972 STL	N	P		12	1- 0
1973 TEX	A	P		25	4- 2
1975 CAL	N	/P		3	0- 1
	BLTL			40	5- 3

HUDSON, HAL CAMPBELL
(BUD) OR (LEFTY)
B.MAY 4,1927 GROSSE POINT,MICH.

1952 STL	A	P		3	0- 0
CHI	A	P		2	0- 0
1953 CHI	A	P		1	0- 0
	BLTL			6	0- 0

HUDSON, JESSE JAMES
B.JULY 22,1948 MASEFIELD,LA.

1969 NY	N	/P		1	0- 0
	BLTL				

HUDSON, JOHN WILSON (MR. CHIPS)
B.JUNE 30,1912 BRYAN,TEX.
D.NOV.7,1970 BRYAN,TEX.

1936 BRO	N	S		6	.167
1937 BRO	N	S		13	.185
1938 BRO	N	2		135	.261
1939 BRO	N	2-S		109	.254
1940 BRO	N	2-S-3		85	.218
1941 CHI	N	2-S-3		50	.202
1945 NY	N	2-3		28	.000
	BRTR			426	.242

HUDSON, NATHANIEL P.
B.JAN.12,1859 CHICAGO,ILL.
D.MAR.14,1928 CHICAGO,ILL.

1886 STL	AA	P	29	40	16-13
1887 STL	AA	P	8	13	3- 5
1888 STL	AA	P	37	55	26-10
1889 STL	AA	P-O	4	13	2- 2
					.245
	TR		78	121	47-30
					.255

HUDSON, REX HAUGHTON
B.AUG.11,1953 TULSA,OKLA.

1974 LA	N	/P		1	0- 0
	BBTR				

HUDSON, SIDNEY CHARLES (SID)
B.JAN.3,1917 COALFIELD,TENN.

1940 WAS	A	P		38	17-16
1941 WAS	A	P		33	13-14
1942 WAS	A	P	35	36	10-17
1946 WAS	A	P		31	8-11
1947 WAS	A	P		20	6- 9
1948 WAS	A	P		39	4-16
1949 WAS	A	P		40	8-17
1950 WAS	A	P	30	31	14-14
1951 WAS	A	P	23	24	5-12
1952 WAS	A	P		7	3- 4
BOS	A	P		21	7- 9
1953 BOS	A	P		30	6- 9
1954 BOS	A	P		33	3- 4
	BRTR		380	383	104-152

HUELSMAN, FRANK ELMER
B.JUNE 5,1874 ST.LOUIS,MO.
D.JUNE 9,1959 AFFTON,MO.

1897 STL	N	S		2	.286
1904 CHI	A	O		3	.167
DET	A	O		4	.333
CHI	A	H		1	.000
STL	A	O		20	.221
WAS	A	O		84	.241
1905 WAS	A	O		121	.271
	BRTR			235	.256

HUENKE, ALBERT A.
B.JUNE 26,1891 NEW BREMEN,OHIO
D.SEPT.20,1974 ST.MARYS,OHIO

1914 NY	N	P		1	0- 0
	BRTR				

HUFF, GEORGE A. (GEE)
B.JUNE 11,1872 CHAMPAIGN,ILL.
D.OCT.1,1936 CHAMPAIGN,ILL.
NON-PLAYING MANAGER BOS(A) 1907

HUFFMAN, BENJAMIN FRANKLIN
B.JUNE 26,1914 RILEYVILLE,VA.

1937 STL	A	C		76	.273
	BLTR				

HUG, EDWARD AMBROSE
B.JULY 14,1880 FAYETTEVILLE,O.
D.MAY 11,1953 CINCINNATI,OHIO

1903 BRO	N	C		1	.000
	BRTR				

HUGGINS, MILLER JAMES (MILLER)
(HUG) OR (MIGHTY MITE)
B.MAR.27,1879 CINCINNATI,OHIO
D.SEPT.25,1929 NEW YORK,N.Y.

1904 CIN	N	2		140	.263
1905 CIN	N	2		149	.273
1906 CIN	N	2		146	.292
1907 CIN	N	2		156	.248
1908 CIN	N	2		135	.239
1909 CIN	N	2-3		46	.213
1910 STL	N	2		151	.265
1911 STL	N	2		136	.261
1912 STL	N	2		120	.304
1913 STL	N	M-2		121	.285
1914 STL	N	M-2		148	.263
1915 STL	N	M-2		107	.241
1916 STL	N	M-2		18	.333
	BBTR			1573	.265

NON-PLAYING MANAGER
STL(N) 1917; NY(A) 1918-29

HUGHES, EDWARD
1902 CHI	N	O		1	.000

HUGHES, EDWARD
B.CHICAGO,ILL.

1902 CHI	A	C		1	.250
	TR				

HUGHES, EDWARD H.
B.1880 CHICAGO,ILL.

1905 BOS	A	P		6	3- 0
1906 BOS	A	P		2	0- 0
				8	3- 0

HUGHES, JAMES JAY (JAY)
B.JAN.22,1874 SACRAMENTO,CAL.
D.JUNE 2,1924 SACRAMENTO,CAL.

1898 BAL	N	P	35	49	21-11
1899 BRO	N	P		35	25- 5
1901 BRO	N	P		30	17-12
1902 BRO	N	P-O		29	15-11
					.202
	BRTR		129	143	78-39
					.223

HUGHES, JAMES MICHAEL (JIM)
B.AUG.11,1951 LOS ANGELES,CAL.

1974 MIN	A	/P		2	0- 2
1975 MIN	A	P		37	16-14
1976 MIN	A	P		37	9-14
1977 MIN	A	P		2	0- 0
	BRTR			78	25-30

HUGHES, JAMES ROBERT (JIM)
B.MAR.21,1923 CHICAGO,ILL.

1952 BRO	N	P		6	2- 1
1953 BRO	N	P		48	4- 3
1954 BRO	N	P		60	6- 4
1955 BRO	N	P		24	0- 2
1956 BRO	N	P		5	0- 0
CHI	N	P		25	1- 3
1957 CHI	A	P		4	0- 0
	BRTR			172	15-13

HUGHES, MICHAEL F. (MICKEY)
B.OCT.25,1866 NEW YORK,N.Y.
D.APR.10,1931 JERSEY CITY,N.J.

1888 BRO	AA	P		39	25-13
1889 BRO	AA	P		19	10- 6
1890 BRO	N	P		8	3- 5
ATH	AA	P		6	1- 5
	TR			72	39-29

HUGHES, RICHARD HENRY (DICK)
B.FEB.13,1938 STEPHENS,ARK.

1966 STL	N	/P		6	2- 1
1967 STL	N	P	37	40	16- 6
1968 STL	N	P		25	2- 2
	BRTR		68	71	20- 9

HUGHES, ROY JOHN (ROY)
(JEEP) OR (SAGE)
B.JAN.11,1911 CINCINNATI,OHIO

1935 CLE	A	2-S-3		82	.293
1936 CLE	A	2		152	.295
1937 CLE	A	2-3		104	.277
1938 STL	A	2		58	.281
1939 STL	A	2-S		17	.087
PHI	N	2		65	.228
1940 PHI	N	2		1	.000
1944 CHI	N	S-3		126	.287
1945 CHI	N	1-2-S-3		69	.261
1946 PHI	N	1-2-S-3		89	.236
	BRTR			763	.273

HUGHES, TERRY WAYNE
B.MAY 13,1949 SPARTANBURG,S.C.

1970 CHI	N	/3-0		2	.333
1973 STL	N	/3-1		11	.214
1974 BOS	A	3		41	.203
	BRTR			54	.209

HUGHES, THOMAS EDWARD
B.SEPT.13,1934 ANCON,C.Z.,PAN.

1959 STL	N	P		2	0- 2
	BLTR				

HUGHES, THOMAS FRANKLIN
B.AUG.6,1907 EMMET,ARK.

1930 DET	A	O		17	.373
	BLTR				

HUGHES, THOMAS JAMES (LONG TOM)
B.NOV.26,1878 CHICAGO,ILL.
D.FEB.8,1956 CHICAGO,ILL.

1900 CHI	N	P		3	1- 1
1901 CHI	N	P		33	10-23
1902 BAL	A	P		15	7- 8
BOS	A	P		8	
1903 BOS	A	P		32	21- 7
1904 NY	A	P		23	7-11
WAS	A	P		16	2-14
1905 WAS	A	P		39	16-16
1906 WAS	A	P		30	7-17
1907 WAS	A	P	34	36	7-13
1908 WAS	A	P		43	18-15
1909 WAS	A	P		22	4- 8
1911 WAS	A	P		34	10-17
1912 WAS	A	P		31	13-10
1913 WAS	A	P		36	4-12
	TR		399	401	129-176

```
YR  CL LEA POS    GP   G   REC          YR  CL LEA POS    GP   G   REC          YR  CL LEA POS    GP   G   REC

HUGHES, THOMAS L. (SALIDA TOM)          HULVEY, JAMES HENSEL (HANK)             HUNDLEY, CECIL RANDOLPH (RANDY)
B.JAN.28,1884 COAL CREEK,COLO.          B.JULY 18,1897 MT.SIDNEY,VA.            B.JUNE 1,1942 MARTINSVILLE,VA.
D.NOV.1,1961 LOS ANGELES,CAL.           1923 PHI A  P         1   0- 1          1964 SF  N  C         2    .000
1906 NY  A  P         3   0- 0               BBTR                               1965 SF  N /C         6    .067
1907 NY  A  P         3   2- 1                                                  1966 CHI N *C       149    .236
1909 NY  A  P        25   7- 8          HUME, THOMAS HUBERT (TOM)               1967 CHI N *C       152    .267
1910 NY  A  P        23   7- 9          B.MAR.29,1953 CINCINNATI,OHIO           1968 CHI N *C       160    .226
1914 BOS N  P         2   1- 0          1977 CIN N  P        14   3- 3          1969 CHI N *C       151    .255
1915 BOS N  P        50  16-14          1978 CIN N  P    42  43   8-11          1970 CHI N  C        73    .244
1916 BOS N  P        40  16- 3               BRTR        56  57  11-14          1971 CHI N /C         9    .333
1917 BOS N  P     11 13   5- 3                                                  1972 CHI N *C       114    .218
1918 BOS N  P         3   0- 2          HUMMEL, JOHN EDWIN (SILENT JOHN)        1973 CHI N *C       124    .226
     BRTR       160 162  54-40          B.APR.4,1883 BLOOMSBURG,PA.             1974 MIN A  C        32    .193
                                        D.MAY 18,1959 SPRINGFIELD,MASS.         1975 SD  N  C        74    .206
HUGHES, THOMAS OWEN (TOMMY)             1905 BRO N  2           30   .266        1976 CHI N /C        13    .167
B.OCT.7,1919 WILKES-BARRE,PA.           1906 BRO N  1-2-0       86   .199        1977 CHI N  C         2    .000
1941 PHI N  P        34 37   9-14       1907 BRO N  2-0         97   .234             BRTR           1061    .236
1942 PHI N  P        40 42  12-18       1908 BRO N  2-0        154   .241
1946 PHI N  P        29      6- 9       1909 BRO N  1-2-S-0    145   .280        HUNGLING, BERNARD HERMAN (BUD)
1947 PHI N  P        29 32   4-11       1910 BRO N  2          153   .244        B.MAR.5,1896 DAYTON,OHIO
1948 CIN N  P        12      0- 4       1911 BRO N  2          133   .270        D.MAR.30,1968 DAYTON,OHIO
     BRTR          144 152  31-56       1912 BRO N  2-0        122   .282        1922 BRO N  C        39    .255
                                        1913 BRO N  S-0        67   .242         1923 BRO N  C         2    .000
HUGHES, VERNON ALEXANDER (LEFTY)        1914 BRO N  1-0        73   .264         1930 STL A  C        10    .323
B.APR.15,1893 ETNA,PA.                  1915 BRO N  O          53   .230              BRTR             51    .241
D.SEPT.26,1961 SEWICKLEY,PA.            1918 NY  A  O          22   .295
1914 BAL F  P         3   0- 0               BRTR            1135   .254         HUNNEFIELD, WILLIAM FENTON
     BLTL                                                                        (WILD BILL)
                                        HUMPHREY, ALBERT                        B.JAN.5,1899 DEDHAM,MASS.
HUGHES, WILLIAM NESBERT                 B.FEB.26,1886 ASHTABULA,OHIO            D.AUG.28,1976 NANTUCKET,MASS.
B.NOV.18,1896 PHILADELPHIA,PA.          D.MAY 13,1961 ASHTABULA,OHIO            1926 CHI A  2-S-3   131    .274
D.FEB.25,1963 BIRMINGHAM,ALA.           1911 BRO N  O           8   .143         1927 CHI A  2-S     112    .285
1921 PIT N  P         1   0- 0               BLTR                               1928 CHI A  2        94    .294
     BRTR                                                                        1929 CHI A  2        47    .181
                                        HUMPHREY, TERRYAL GENE (TERRY)          1930 CHI A  S        31    .272
HUGHES, WILLIAM R.                      B.AUG.4,1949 CHICKASHA,OKLA.            1931 CLE A  S        21    .239
B.NOV.25,1866 BLADENSVILLE,ILL.         1971 MON N /C           9   .192             BOS N  2        11    .286
D.AUG.25,1943 SANTA ANA,CAL.            1972 MON N  C          69   .186             NY  N  2        64    .270
1884 WAS U  1-0           14   .122     1973 MON N  C          43   .147             BBTR            511    .272
1885 ATH AA P-0       2   4   0- 2      1974 MON N  C          20   .192
                              .188      1975 DET A  C          18   .244         HUNT, BENJAMIN FRANKLIN
                      2  18   0- 2      1976 CAL A  C          71   .245         (HIGH POCKETS)
                              .138      1977 CAL A *C         123   .227         B.1888 EUFAULA,OKLA.
                                        1978 CAL A  C/2-3      53   .219         1910 BOS A  P         7   2- 4
HUGHEY, JAMES ULYSSES                        BRTR             406   .214         1913 STL N  P         2   0- 1
(COLDWATER JIM)                                                                      BLTL             9   2- 5
B.MAR.8,1869 WAKASHMA,MICH.             HUMPHREYS, BRYON WILLIAM (BILL)
D.MAR.29,1945 COLDWATER,MICH.           B.JUNE 17,1911 VIENNA,MO.               HUNT, KENNETH LAWRENCE (KEN)
1891 MIL AA P         2   1- 1          1938 BOS A  P         2   0- 0          B.JULY 13,1934 GRAND FORKS,N.DAK
1893 CHI N  P         1   0- 1               BRTR                               1959 NY  A  O         6    .333
1896 PIT N  P        21   6- 8                                                  1960 NY  A  O        25    .273
1897 PIT N  P        20   6-13          HUMPHREYS, ROBERT WILLIAM (BOB)         1961 LA  A  2-O     149    .255
1898 STL N  P        34   7-24          B.AUG.18,1935 COVINGTON,VA.             1962 LA  A  1        13    .182
1899 CLE N  P        35   4-29          1962 DET A  P         4   0- 1          1963 LA  A  O        59    .183
1900 STL N  P        20   5- 8          1963 STL N  P         9   0- 1               WAS A  O         7    .200
     TR             133  29-84          1964 STL N  P        28   2- 0          1964 WAS A  O        51    .135
                                        1965 CHI N  P        41   2- 0               BRTR            310    .226
HUGHSON, CECIL CARLTON (TEX)            1966 WAS A  P        58   7- 3
B.FEB.9,1916 KYLE,TEX.                  1967 WAS A  P        48   6- 2          HUNT, KENNETH RAYMOND
1941 BOS A  P        12   5- 3          1968 WAS A  P        56   5- 7          D.DEC.14,1938 OGDEN,UTAH
1942 BOS A  P        38  22- 6          1969 WAS A  P        47   3- 3          1961 CIN N  P        29   9-10
1943 BOS A  P        35  12-15          1970 WAS A /P         5   0- 0               BRTR
1944 BOS A  P        28  18- 5               MIL A  P        23   2- 4
1946 BOS A  P        39  20-11               BRTR            319  27-21         HUNT, OLIVER JOEL (JOEL) OR (JODIE)
1947 BOS A  P        29  12-11                                                  B.OCT.11,1905 TEXICO,N.MEX.
1948 BOS A  P        15   3- 1          HUMPHRIES, ALBERT (BERT)                1931 STL N  O         4    .000
1949 BOS A  P        29   4- 2          B.SEPT.21,1945 ORLANDO,FLA.             1932 STL N  O        12    .190
     BRTR          225  96-54          B.SEPT.26,1880 CALIFORNIA,PA.                             16    .182
                                        1910 PHI N  P         5   0- 0
HUGHSON, GEORGE H.                      1911 PHI N  P        11   3- 3          HUNT, RICHARD M.
B.AUG.1,1834 ERIE CO.,N.Y.                   CIN N  P        14   4- 1          B.1847 NEW YORK
D.APR.22,1912                           1912 CIN N  P        30   9-11          1872 ECK NA 2-0      11    .288
NON-PLAYING MANAGER BUF[N] 1885         1913 CHI N  P        28  16- 4
                                        1914 CHI N  P    34  35  10-11          HUNT, RONALD KENNETH (RON)
                                        1915 CHI N  P        31   8-13          B.FEB.23,1941 ST.LOUIS,MO.
HUHN, EMIL HUGO (HAP)                                   153 154  50-43          1963 NY  N  2-3     143    .272
B.MAR.10,1892 NORT4 VERNON,IND.                                                 1964 NY  N  2-3     127    .303
D.SEPT.5,1925 CAMDEN,S.C.                                                       1965 NY  N  2/3      57    .240
1915 NEW F  C-1     124   .227          HUMPHRIES, JOHN HENRY                   1966 NY  N *2/S-3   132    .288
1916 CIN N  C-1-0    37   .255          B.NOV.12,1861 N.GOWER,ONT.,CAN.         1967 LA  N  2/3     110    .263
1917 CIN N  C-1      23   .196          D.NOV.29,1933 SALINAS,CAL.              1968 SF  N *2       148    .250
     BRTR          184   .229           1883 NY  N  C-0        26   .117         1969 SF  N *2/3     128    .262
                                        1884 WAS AA C-0        48   .178         1970 SF  N  2-3     117    .281
HULEN, WILLIAM FRANKLIN                      NY  N  C          19   .093         1971 MON N *2-3     152    .279
B.MAR.12,1869 DIXON,CAL.                     TL               93   .146         1972 MON N *2/3     129    .253
D.OCT.2,1947 PETALUMA,CAL.                                                      1973 MON N *2-3     113    .309
1896 PHI N  S        85   .268          HUMPHRIES, JOHN WILLIAM (JOHNNY)        1974 MON N  3-2/S   115    .268
1899 WAS N  S        19   .147          B.JUNE 23,1915 CLIFTON FORGE,VA              STL N /2        12    .174
     TL             104   .248          D.JUNE 24,1965 NEW ORLEANS,LA.               BRTR           1483    .273
                                        1938 CLE A  P        45   9- 8
HULIHAN, HARRY JOSEPH                   1939 CLE A  P        15   2- 4          HUNTER, EDISON FRANKLIN (EDDIE)
B.APR.18,1899 RUTLAND,VT.               1940 CLE A  P        19   0- 2          B.FEB.6,1905 BELLEVUE,KY.
1922 BOS N  P         7   2- 3          1941 CHI A  P        14   4- 2          D.MAR.14,1967 COLLRAIN TURNPIKE OHIO
     BRTL                               1942 CHI A  P        28  12-12          1933 CIN N  3         1    .000
                                        1943 CHI A  P        28  11-11               BRTR
HULSWITT, RUDOLPH EDWARD                1944 CHI A  P        30   8-10
B.FEB.23,1877 NEWPORT,KY.               1945 CHI A  P        22   6-14          HUNTER, FREDERICK CREIGHTON (NEWT)
D.JAN.16,1950 LOUISVILLE,KY.            1946 PHI N  P        10   0- 0          B.JAN.5,1880 CHILLICOTHE,OHIO
1899 LOU N  S         1   .000               BRTR           211  52-63         D.OCT.26,1963 COLUMBUS,OHIO
1902 PHI N  S-3     128   .272                                                  1911 PIT N  1        61    .254
1903 PHI N  S       138   .247                                                       BRTR
1904 PHI N  S       113   .244
1908 CIN N  S       119   .228
1909 STL N  S        77   .280
1910 STL N  S        32   .248
     BRTR          608   .253
```

YR CL LEA POS GP G REC

HUNTER, GEORGE HENRY
B.JULY 8,1887 BUFFALO,N.Y.
D.JAN.11,1968 HARRISBURG,PA.
1909 BRO N P-O 16 39 4-10
.228
1910 BRO N O 1 .000
BB 16 40 4-10
.228

HUNTER, GORDON WILLIAM (BILLY)
B.JUNE 4,1928 PUNXSUTAWNEY,PA.
1953 STL A S 154 .219
1954 BAL A S 125 .243
1955 NY A S 98 .227
1956 NY A S-3 39 .280
1957 KC A 2-S-3 116 .191
1958 KC A 2-S 22 .155
CLE A S-3 76 .195
BRTR 630 .219
NON-PLAYING MANAGER TEX[A] 1977-78

HUNTER, HAROLD JAMES (BUDDY)
B.AUG.9,1947 OMAHA,NEB.
1971 BOS A /2 8 .222
1973 BOS A /3-2 13 .429
1975 BOS A /2 1 .000
BRTR 22 .294

HUNTER, HERBERT HARRISON
B.DEC.25,1896 BOSTON,MASS.
D.JULY 25,1970 ORLANDO,FLA.
1916 NY N 3 21 .250
CHI N H 2 .000
1917 CHI N 2-3 3 .000
1920 BOS A O 4 .083
1921 STL N 1 9 .000
BLTR 39 .163

HUNTER, JAMES AUGUSTUS
(JIM) OR (CATFISH)
B.APR.8,1946 HERTFORD,N.C.
1965 KC A P 32 8- 8
1966 KC A P 30 9-11
1967 KC A P/1 35 37 13-17
.196
1968 OAK A P 36 39 13-13
1969 OAK A P 38 42 12-15
1970 OAK A P 40 43 18-14
1971 OAK A P 37 38 21-11
1972 OAK A P 38 39 21- 7
1973 OAK A P 36 37 21- 5
1974 OAK A P 41 25-12
1975 NY A P 39 23-14
1976 NY A P 36 17-15
1977 NY A P 22 9- 9
1978 NY A P 21 12- 6
BRTR 481 496 222-157
.226

HUNTER, ROBERT LEMJEL (LEM)
B.JAN.16,1863 WARREN,OHIO
D.NOV.9,1956 W.LAFAYETTE,OHIO
1883 CLE N P-O 1 0- 0
.250

HUNTER, WILLARD MITCHELL
B.MAR.8,1934 NEWARK,N.J.
1962 LA N P 1 10 0- 0
NY N P 27 1- 6
1964 NY N P 41 3- 3
BRTL 69 78 4- 9

HUNTER, WILLIAM ELLSWORTH
B.JULY 8,1887 BUFFALO,N.Y.
D.APR.10,1934 BUFFALO,N.Y.
1912 CLE A O 21 .165
BLTL

HUNTER, WILLIAM ROBERT
B.ST.THOMAS,ONT.,CAN.
1884 LOU AA C 2 .429

HUNTZ, STEPHEN MICHAEL (STEVE)
B.DEC.3,1945 CLEVELAND,OHIO
1967 STL N /2 3 .167
1969 STL N S-2/3 71 .194
1970 SD N S-3 106 .219
1971 CHI A 2/S-3 35 .209
1975 SD N 3/2 22 .151
BBTR 237 .206

HUNTZINGER, WALTER HENRY
(WALT) OR (SHAKES)
B.FEB.6,1899 POTTSVILLE,PA.
1923 NY N P 2 0- 1
1924 NY N P 12 1- 1
1925 NY N P 26 5- 1
1926 STL N P 9 0- 4
CHI N P 11 1- 1
BRTR 60 7- 8

HURD, THOMAS CARR (TOM) OR (WHITEY)
B.MAY 27,1924 DANVILLE,VA.
1954 BOS A P 16 2- 0
1955 BOS A P 43 8- 6
1956 BOS A P 40 3- 4
BRTR 99 13-10

YR CL LEA POS GP G REC

HURDLE, CLINTON MERRICK (CLINT)
B.JULY 30,1957 BIG RAPIDS,MICH.
1977 KC A /O 9 .308
1978 KC A O-1/3 133 .264
BLTR 142 .266

HURLEY, JEREMIAH JOSEPH
B.JUNE 15,1863 BOSTON,MASS.
D.SEPT.17,1950 BOSTON,MASS.
1889 BOS N C 1 .000
1890 PIT P C 8 .273
1891 CIN AA C-1-O 26 .220
TR 35 .227

HURLEY, JERRY J.
1901 CIN N C 7 .062
1907 BRO N C 1 .000
TR 8 .056

HURLEY, WILLIAM F. (DICK)
B.1847
1872 OLY NA O 2 .000

HURST, FRANK O DONNELL (DON)
B.AUG.12,1905 MAYSVILLE,KY.
D.DEC.6,1952 LOS ANGELES,CAL.
1928 PHI N 1 107 .285
1929 PHI N 1 154 .304
1930 PHI N 1 119 .327
1931 PHI N 1 137 .305
1932 PHI N 1 150 .339
1933 PHI N 1 147 .267
1934 PHI N 1 40 .262
CHI N 1 51 .199
BLTL 905 .292

HURST, TIMOTHY CARROLL
B.JUNE 30,1865 ASHLAND,PA.
D.JUNE 4,1915 POTTSVILLE,PA.
NON-PLAYING MANAGER STL[N] 1898

HUSTA, CARL LAWRENCE (SOX)
B.APR.8,1902 EGG HARBOR,N.J.
D.NOV.6,1951 KINGSTON,N.Y.
1925 PHI A S 6 .136
BRTR

HUSTED, WILLIAM J.
B.OCT.9,1867 GLOUCESTER,N.J.
1890 PHI P P 19 5-10

HUSTING, BERTHOLD JUNEAU (PETE)
B.MAR.6,1878 FOND DU LAC,WIS.
D.SEPT.3,1948 MILWAUKEE,WIS.
1900 PIT N P 2 0- 0
1901 MIL A P 35 9-15
1902 BOS A P 1 0- 1
PHI A P 32 14- 5
BRTR 70 23-21

HUSTON, HARRY EMANUEL KRESS
B.OCT.14,1883 BELLEFONTAINE,O.
D.OCT.13,1969 BLACKWELL,OKLA.
1906 PHI N C 2 .000
TR

HUSTON, WARREN LLEWELLYN
B.OCT.31,1913 NEWTONVILLE,MASS.
1937 PHI A 2-S 38 .130
1944 BOS N 2-S-3 33 .200
BRTR 71 .165

HUTCHENSON, JAMES F.
B.1863 NEW YORK,N.Y.
D.DEC.24,1941 NEW YORK,N.Y.
1884 KC U P 2 1- 1

HUTCHESON, JOSEPH JOHNSON
(SLUG) OR (POODLES)
B.FEB.5,1905 SPRINGTOWN,TEX.
1933 BRO N O 55 .234
BLTR

HUTCHINGS, JOHN RICHARD JOSEPH
B.APR.14,1916 CHICAGO,ILL.
D.APR.27,1963 INDIANAPOLIS,IND.
1940 CIN N P 19 2- 1
1941 CIN N P 8 0- 0
BOS N P 36 1- 6
1942 BOS N P 20 1- 0
1944 BOS N P 14 1- 4
1945 BOS N P 57 7- 6
1946 BOS N P 1 0- 1
BBTR 155 12-18

HUTCHINSON, EDWARD F.
B.1870 PITTSBURGH,PA.
1890 CHI N 2 7 .107

YR CL LEA POS GP G REC

HUTCHINSON, FREDERICK CHARLES (FRED)
B.AUG.12,1919 SEATTLE,WASH.
D.NOV.12,1964 BRADENTON,FLA.
1939 DET A P 13 3- 6
1940 DET A P 17 3- 7
1941 DET A H 2 .000
1946 DET A P 28 40 14-11
1947 DET A P 33 56 18-10
1948 DET A P 33 76 13-11
1949 DET A P 33 38 15- 7
1950 DET A P 39 44 17- 8
1951 DET A P 31 47 10-10
1952 DET A M-P 17 2- 1
1953 DET A M-P- 3 4 0- 0
1 .167
BLTR 242 354 95-71
.263
NON-PLAYING MANAGER DET[A] 1954
STL[N] 1956-58 CIN[N] 1959-64

HUTCHINSON, IRA KENDALL
B.AUG.31,1910 CHICAGO,ILL.
D.AUG.21,1973 CHICAGO,ILL.
1933 CHI A P 1 0- 0
1937 BOS N P 31 4- 6
1938 BOS N P 36 9- 8
1939 BRO N P 41 5- 2
1940 STL N P 20 4- 2
1941 STL N P 29 1- 5
1944 BOS N P 40 9- 7
1945 BOS N P 11 2- 3
BRTR 209 34-33

HUTCHINSON, WILLIAM FORREST
(WILD BILL)
B.DEC.17,1859 NEW HAVEN,CONN.
D.MAR.19,1926 KANSAS CITY,MO.
1889 CHI N P 37 16-17
1890 CHI N P 68 42-26
1891 CHI N P 63 64 43-19
1892 CHI N P 71 37-33
1893 CHI N P 40 41 16-24
1894 CHI N P 34 16-18
1895 CHI N P 34 13-18
1897 STL N P 6 1- 4
TR 353 355 184-159

HUTSON, GEORGE HERBERT (HERB)
B.JULY 17,1949 SAVANNAH,GA.
1974 CHI N P 20 0- 2
BRTR

HUTSON, ROY LEE
B.FEB.27,1902 LURAY,MO.
D.MAY 20,1957 LA MESA,CAL.
1925 BRO N O 7 .500
BLTR

HUTTO, JAMES NEAMON (JIM)
B.OCT.17,1947 NORFOLK,VA.
1970 PHI N O-1/C-3 57 .185
1975 BAL A /C 4 .000
BRTR 61 .175

HUTTON, THOMAS GEORGE (TOM)
B.APR.20,1946 LOS ANGELES,CAL.
1966 LA N /1 3 .000
1969 LA N 1 16 .271
1972 PHI N 1-O 134 .260
1973 PHI N 1 106 .263
1974 PHI N 1-O 96 .240
1975 PHI N 1-O 113 .248
1976 PHI N 1/O 95 .202
1977 PHI N 1/O 107 .309
1978 TOR A O/1 64 .254
MON N 1/O 39 .203
BLTL 773 .251

HYATT, ROBERT HAMILTON (HAM)
B.NOV.1,1884 BUNCOMBE CO.,N.C.
D.SEPT.11,1963 LIBERTY LAKE,WASH.
1909 PIT N O 49 .299
1910 PIT N 1 41 .263
1912 PIT N O 46 .289
1913 PIT N O 63 .333
1914 PIT N O 74 .215
1915 STL N 1-O 106 .268
1918 NY A O 53 .229
BLTR 432 .267

HYDE, RICHARD ELDE (DICK)
B.AUG.3,1928 HINDSBORO,ILL.
1955 WAS A P 3 0- 0
1957 WAS A P 52 4- 3
1958 WAS A P 53 10- 3
1959 WAS A P 37 2- 5
1960 WAS A P 9 0- 1
1961 BAL A P 15 1- 2
BRTR 169 17-14

HYNDMAN, JAMES WILLIAM
B.1864 KINGSTON,PA.
1886 ATH AA P 1 0- 1

```
YR  CL LEA POS    GP    G   REC        YR   CL LEA POS     GP    G   REC        YR   CL LEA POS    GP    G   REC

HYNES, PATRICK J.                      IRVIN, WILLIAM EDWARD (ED)              IZQUIERDO, ENRIQUE ROBERTO
B.MAR.12,1884 ST.LOUIS,MO.             B.1882 PHILADELPHIA,PA.                 (VALDES) (HANK)
D.MAR.12,1907 ST.LOUIS,MO.             D.FEB.18,1916 PHILADELPHIA,PA.          B.MAR.20,1931 MATANZAS,CUBA
1903 STL N  P          1    0- 1       1912 DET A  C          1   .667         1967 MIN A  C         16   .269
1904 STL A  P-O        3   66  1- 0         TR                                      BRTR
                              .240
     TL                4   67  1- 1    IRWIN, ARTHUR ALBERT                    JABLONOWSKI, PETER WILLIAM
                              .237     (DOC) OR (SANDY)                        [SEE PETER WILLIAM APPLETON]
                                       B.FEB.14,1858 TORONTO,ONT.,CAN.
IBURG, HERMAN EDWARD (HAM)             D.JULY 16,1921 ATLANTIC OCEAN           JABLONSKI, RAYMOND LEO
B.OCT.29,1877 SAN FRANCISCO,CAL        1880 WOR N  C-S-3     83   .260         (RAY) OR (JABBO)
D.FEB.11,1945 SAN FRANCISCO,CAL        1881 WOR N  S         49   .266         B.DEC.17,1926 CHICAGO,ILL.
1902 PHI N  P             30  11-19     1882 WOR N  1-S-3     84   .220         1953 STL N  3        157   .268
     BRTR                              1883 PRO N  2-S       98   .285         1954 STL N  1-3      152   .296
                                       1884 PRO N  P-S    1  99   0- 0         1955 CIN N  3-O       74   .240
IGNASIAK, GARY RAYMOND                                           .245         1956 CIN N  2-3      130   .256
B.SEP.1,1949 MT.CLEMENS,MICH.          1885 PRO N  2-S       59   .179         1957 NY  N  1-3-O    107   .289
1973 DET A  /P         3    0- 0       1886 PHI N  S        101   .233         1958 SF  N  3-O       86   .230
     BRTL                              1887 PHI N  S         99   .339         1959 STL N  S-3       60   .253
                                       1888 PHI N  S        124   .220              KC  A  3         25   .262
IMLAY, HARRY MILLER (DOC)              1889 PHI N  S         18   .219         1960 KC  A  3         21   .219
B.JAN.12,1889 ALLENTOWN,N.J.                WAS N  M-S       85   .233              BRTR           812   .268
D.OCT.7,1948 BORDENTOWN,N.J.           1890 BOS P  S         96   .264
1913 PHI N  P          9    0- 1       1891 BOS AA M-S        5   .154         JACKLITSCH, FREDERICK LAWRENCE
     BRTR                              1894 PHI N  M-S        1   .000         B.MAY 24,1876 BROOKLYN,N.Y.
                                            BLTR        1 1001   0- 0         D.JULY 18,1937
INGERSOLL, ROBERT RANDOLPH                                      .252         1900 PHI N  C          5   .181
B.JAN.8,1883 RAPID CITY,S.D.                                                  1901 PHI N  C         31   .292
D.JAN.13,1927 MINNEAPOLIS,MINN.        NON-PLAYING MANAGER                     1902 PHI N  C-O       27   .200
1914 CIN N  P          4    0- 0       WAS(N) 1892, PHI(N) 1895,               1903 BRO N  C         55   .267
     BRTR                              NY(N) 1896, WAS(N) 1898-99              1904 BRO N  C         23   .234
                                                                              1905 NY  A  C          1   .000
INGERTON, WILLIAM JOHN (SCOTTY)        IRWIN, CHARLES E.                       1907 PHI N  C         65   .213
B.APR.19,1886 PENINSULA,OHIO           B.FEB.15,1869 SHEFFIELD,ILL.            1908 PHI N  C         30   .221
D.JUNE 15,1956 CLEVELAND,OHIO          D.SEPT.21,1925 CHICAGO,ILL.             1909 PHI N  C         19   .310
1911 BOS N  3-O      133   .250        1893 CHI N  3         21   .324         1910 PHI N  C         17   .196
     BRTR                              1894 CIN N  S-3      130   .302         1914 BAL F  C        122   .275
                                       1895 CHI N  3          3   .240         1915 BAL F  C         48   .237
INGRAHAM, CHARLES                      1896 CIN N  3        127   .295         1917 BOS N  C          1   .000
B.1860 YOUNGSTOWN,OHIO                 1897 CIN N  3        134   .293              BRTR           444   .243
1883 BAL AA C          1   .250        1898 CIN N  3        135   .240
                                       1899 CIN N  3         87   .231         JACKSON, ALVIN NEIL (AL)
INGRAM, MELVIN DAVID                   1900 CIN N  S-3       85   .271         B.DEC.25,1935 WACO,TEX.
B.JULY 4,1904 ASHEVILLE,N.C.           1901 CIN N  3         67   .226         1959 PIT N  P          8   0- 0
1929 PIT N  H          3   .000             BRO N  3         64   .223         1961 PIT N  P       3  5   1- 0
                                       1902 BRO N  S-3      131   .273         1962 NY  N  P      36 44   8-20
INKS, ALBERT PRESTON (BERT)                 BLTR           984   .269         1963 NY  N  P      37 49  13-17
[REAL NAME ALBERT PRESTON INKSTEIN]                                           1964 NY  N  P      40 50  11-16
B.JAN.27,1871 LIGONIER,IND.            IRWIN, JOHN                             1965 NY  N  P      37 56   8-20
D.OCT.3,1941 LIGONIER,IND.             B.JULY 21,1861 TORONTO,ONT.,CAN         1966 STL N  P      36 51  13-15
1891 BRO N  P         13   3- 9        D.FEB.28,1934 BOSTON,MASS.              1967 STL N  P      38 41   9- 4
1892 BRO N  P          9   5- 1        1882 WOR N  1          1   .000         1968 NY  N  P      25 27   3- 7
     WAS N  P          8   2- 4        1884 BOS U  3        104   .235         1969 NY  N  /P         9   0- 0
1894 BAL N  P         16   8- 5        1886 ATH AA S          2   .333              CIN N  P         33   1- 0
     LOU N  P         11   2- 6        1887 WAS N  S          8   .382              BLTL     302 373  67-99
1895 LOU N  P         27   7-19        1888 WAS N  S         37   .222
1896 PHI N  P          5   0- 1        1889 WAS N  3         58   .289         JACKSON, CHARLES HERBERT (LEFTY)
     CIN N  P          3   1- 1        1890 BUF P  1-3       77   .220         B.FEB.7,1894 GRANITE CITY,ILL.
     BLTL             92  28-46        1891 BOS AA 3-O       20   .192         D.MAY 27,1968 RADFORD,VA.
                                            LOU AA 3         14   .038         1915 CHI A  H          1   .000
INKSTEIN, ALBERT PRESTON               1896 BAL N  2          1   .500         1917 PIT N  O         41   .240
[PLAYED UNDER NAME OF                       BLTR           322   .242              BLTL            42   .238
ALBERT PRESTON INKS]
                                       IRWIN, THOMAS ANDREW (TOMMY)             JACKSON, CHARLES BERNARD
IORG, DANE CHARLES                     B.DEC.20,1912 ALTOONA,PA.               B.AUG.4,1876 VERSAILLES,OHIO
B.MAY 11,1950 EUREKA,CAL.              1938 CLE A  S          3   .111         D.NOV.23,1957 SCOTTSBLUFF,NEB.
1977 PHI N  /1        12   .167             BRTR                              1905 DET A  P          2   0- 2
     STL N  /O        30   .313
1978 STL N   O        35   .271        IRWIN, WALTER KINGSLEY                   JACKSON, DARRELL PRESTON
     BLTR             77   .259        B.SEPT.23,1897 HENRIETTA,PA.            B.APR.3,1956 LOS ANGELES,CAL.
                                       D.AUG.18,1976 SPRING LAKE,MICH.         1978 MIN A  P         19   4- 6
IORG, GARTH RAY                        1921 STL N  H          4   .000              BBTL
B.OCT.12,1954 ARCATA,CAL.
1978 TOR A  2         19   .163        IRWIN, WILLIAM FRANKLIN (PHIL)           JACKSON, GEORGE CHRISTOPHER
     BRTR                              B.SEPT.16,1859 NEVILLE,OHIO             (HICKORY)
                                       D.AUG.7,1933 FT.THOMAS,KY.              B.OCT.14,1882 SPRINGFIELD,MO.
IOTT, CLARENCE EUGENE (HOOKS)          1886 CIN AA P          2   0- 2         D.NOV.25,1972 CLEBURNE,TEX.
B.DEC,3,1919 MOUNTAIN GROVE,MO.             BRTR                              1911 BOS N  O         39   .347
1941 STL A  P          2   0- 0                                               1912 BOS N  O        110   .262
1947 STL A  P          4   0- 1        ISBELL, WILLIAM FRANK                    1913 BOS N  O          3   .300
     NY  N  P         20   3- 8        (FRANK) OR (BALD EAGLE)                      BRTR           152   .285
     BBTL             26   3- 9        B.AUG.21,1875 DELEVAN,N.Y.
                                       D.JULY 15,1941 WICHITA,KAN.             JACKSON, GRANT DWIGHT
IOTT, FREDERICK                        1898 CHI N  P-O       10  41   4- 6     (GRANT) OR (BUCK)
(HAPPY JACK) OR (BIDDO)                                          .235         B.SEP.28,1942 FOSTORIA,OHIO
[REAL NAME FREDERICK HOYOT]            1901 CHI A  1        137   .261         1965 PHI N  /P         6   1- 1
B.JULY 7,1876 HOULTON,ME.              1902 CHI A  P-C-   1 137   1- 0         1966 PHI N  /P         2   0- 0
D.FEB.17,1941 ISLAND FALLS,ME.                     1-S          .266         1967 PHI N   P         4   2- 3
1903 CLE A   O         3   .200        1903 CHI A  1-3      138   .259         1968 PHI N   P     33 37   1- 6
     BRTR                              1904 CHI A  1-2       94   .208         1969 PHI N   P     38 40  14-18
                                       1905 CHI A  2-O       94   .296         1970 PHI N   P     32 52   5-15
IRELAN, HAROLD (GRUMP)                 1906 CHI A  2        143   .279         1971 BAL A   P        29   4- 3
B.AUG.5,1890 BURNETTSVILLE,IND.        1907 CHI A  P-2    1 125   0- 0         1972 BAL A   P        32   1- 1
D.JULY 16,1944 CARMEL,IND.                                      .243         1973 BAL A   P        45   8- 0
1914 PHI N  2         67   .236        1908 CHI A  P-1-   1  84   0- 0         1974 BAL A   P        49   6- 4
     BBTR                                          2            .247         1975 BAL A   P        41   4- 3
                                       1909 CHI A   1       120   .224         1976 BAL A   P        13   1- 1
IRVIN, MONTFORD (MONTE)                     BLTR        13 1113   5- 6             NY  A   P        21   6- 0
B.FEB.25,1919 COLUMBIA,ALA.                                     .254         1977 PIT N   P        49   5- 3
1949 NY  N  1-3-O     36   .224                                               1978 PIT N   P        60   7- 5
1950 NY  N  1-3-O    110   .300        IVIE, MICHAEL WILSON (MIKE)                  BLTL    493 519  65-63
1951 NY  N  1-O      151   .312        B.AUG.8,1952 ATLANTA,GA.                     BB 1965-70
1952 NY  N   O        46   .310        1971 SD  N  /C         6   .471
1953 NY  N   O       124   .329        1974 SD  N  1         12   .048         JACKSON, HENRY EVERETT
1954 NY  N  1-3-O    135   .262        1975 SD  N  1-3/C    111   .249         B.JUNE 23,1861 UNION CITY,IND.
1955 NY  N   O        51   .253        1976 SD  N  *1/C-3   140   .291         D.SEPT.14,1932 CHICAGO,ILL.
1956 CHI N   O       111   .271        1977 SD  N  *1-3     134   .272         1887 IND N  1         10   .263
     BRTR            764   .293        1978 SF  N   1-O     117   .308              BRTR
                                            BRTR           520   .277
```

YR	CL	LEA	POS	GP	G	REC

JACKSON, JAMES BENNER
B.NOV.28,1877 PHILADELPHIA,PA.
D.OCT.9,1955 PHILADELPHIA,PA.

YR	CL	LEA	POS	GP	G	REC
1901	BAL	A	O		97	.254
1902	NY	N	O		35	.193
1905	CLE	A	O		108	.257
1906	CLE	A	O		105	.214
		BRTR			345	.236

JACKSON, JOHN LEWIS
B.JULY 15,1909 WYNNEFIELD,PA.
D.OCT.24,1956 SOMERS POINT,N.J.

1933	PHI	N	P		10	2- 2
		BRTR				

JACKSON, JOSEPH JEFFERSON
(SHOELESS JOE)
B.JULY 16,1889 BRANDON MILLS,S.C.
D.DEC.5,1951 GREENVILLE,S.C.

1908	PHI	A	O		5	.131
1909	PHI	A	O		5	.177
1910	CLE	A	O		20	.387
1911	CLE	A	O		147	.408
1912	CLE	A	O		152	.395
1913	CLE	A	O		148	.373
1914	CLE	A	O		122	.338
1915	CLE	A	1-O		82	.326
	CHI	A	O		46	.269
1916	CHI	A	O		155	.341
1917	CHI	A	O		146	.301
1918	CHI	A	O		17	.354
1919	CHI	A	O		139	.351
1920	CHI	A	O		146	.362
		BLTR			1330	.356

JACKSON, LAWRENCE CURTIS (LARRY)
B.JUNE 2,1931 NAMPA,IDAHO

1955	STL	N	P	37	9-14
1956	STL	N	P	51	2- 2
1957	STL	N	P	41	15- 9
1958	STL	N	P	49	50	13-13
1959	STL	N	P	40	54	14-13
1960	STL	N	P	43	52	18-13
1961	STL	N	P	33	34	14-11
1962	STL	N	P	36	16-11
1963	CHI	N	P	37	14-18
1964	CHI	N	P	40	24-11
1965	CHI	N	P	39	49	14-21
1966	CHI	N	/P	3	0- 2
	PHI	N	P	35	36	15-13
1967	PHI	N	P	40	42	13-15
1968	PHI	N	P	34	37	13-17
		BRTR		558	599	194-183

JACKSON, LOUIS CLARENCE (LOU)
B.JULY 26,1935 RIVERTON,LA.
D.MAY 27,1969 TOKYO,JAPAN

1958	CHI	N	O		24	.171
1959	CHI	N	H		6	.250
1964	BAL	A	O		4	.375
		BLTR			34	.213

JACKSON, MICHAEL WARREN (MIKE)
B.MAR.27,1946 PATERSON,N.J.

1970	PHI	N	/P		5	1- 1
1971	STL	N	/P		1	0- 0
1972	KC	A	/P		7	1- 2
1973	KC	A	/P		9	0- 0
	CLE	A	/P		1	0- 0
		BLTR			23	2- 3

JACKSON, RANSOM JOSEPH (RANDY)
OR (HANDSOME RANSOM)
B.FEB.10,1926 LITTLE ROCK,ARK.

1950	CHI	N	3		34	.225
1951	CHI	N	3		145	.275
1952	CHI	N	3-O		116	.232
1953	CHI	N	3		139	.285
1954	CHI	N	3		126	.273
1955	CHI	N	3		138	.265
1956	BRO	N	3		101	.274
1957	BRO	N	3		48	.198
1958	LA	N	3		35	.185
	CLE	A	3		29	.242
1959	CLE	A	3		3	.143
	CHI	N	3-O		41	.243
		BRTR			955	.261

JACKSON, REGINALD MARTINEZ (REGGIE)
B.MAY 18,1946 WYNCOTE,PA.

1967	KC	A	O		35	.178
1968	OAK	A	*O		154	.250
1969	OAK	A	*O		152	.275
1970	OAK	A	*O		149	.237
1971	OAK	A	*O		150	.277
1972	OAK	A	*O		135	.265
1973	OAK	A	*O		151	.293
1974	OAK	A	*O-D		148	.289
1975	OAK	A	*O		157	.253
1976	BAL	A	*O-D		134	.277
1977	NY	A	*O-D		146	.286
1978	NY	A	*O-D		139	.274
		BLTR			1650	.269

JACKSON, ROLAND THOMAS (SONNY)
B.JULY 9,1944 WASHINGTON,D.C.

1963	HOU	N	S		1	.000
1964	HOU	N	S		9	.348
1965	HOU	N	/S-3		10	.130
1966	HOU	N	*S		150	.292
1967	HOU	N	*S		129	.237
1968	ATL	N	S		105	.226
1969	ATL	N	S		98	.239
1970	ATL	N	O		103	.259
1971	ATL	N	*O		149	.258
1972	ATL	N	S-O/3		60	.238
1973	ATL	N	O-S		117	.209
1974	ATL	N	/O		5	.429
		BLTR			936	.251

JACKSON, RONALD HARRIS (RON)
B.OCT.22,1933 KALAMAZOO,MICH.

1954	CHI	A	1		40	.280
1955	CHI	A	1		40	.203
1956	CHI	A	1		22	.214
1957	CHI	A	1		13	.317
1958	CHI	A	1		61	.233
1959	CHI	A	1		10	.214
1960	BOS	A	1		10	.226
		BRTR			196	.245

JACKSON, RONNIE D (RON)
B.MAY 9,1953 BIRMINGHAM,ALA.

1975	CAL	A	/O-3		13	.231
1976	CAL	A	*3/2-O		127	.227
1977	CAL	A	1-3-D/O-S		106	.243
1978	CAL	A	1-3/O		105	.297
		BRTR			351	.255

JACKSON, ROY LEE (ROY LEE)
B.MAY 1,1954 OPELIKA,ALA.

1977	NY	N	/P		4	0- 2
1978	NY	N	/P		4	0- 0
		BRTR			8	0- 2

JACKSON, SAMUEL
B.MAR.24,1849 RIPON,ENGLAND
D.AUG.4,1930

1871	BOS	NA	2-O		16	-
1872	ATL	N	O		3	.154
		BRTR			19	-

JACKSON, TRAVIS CALVIN (STONEWALL)
B.NOV.2,1903 WALDO,ARK.

1922	NY	N	S		3	.000
1923	NY	N	2-S-3		96	.275
1924	NY	N	S		151	.302
1925	NY	N	S		112	.285
1926	NY	N	S		111	.327
1927	NY	N	S		127	.318
1928	NY	N	S		150	.270
1929	NY	N	S		149	.294
1930	NY	N	S		116	.339
1931	NY	N	S		145	.310
1932	NY	N	S-3		52	.256
1933	NY	N	S-3		53	.246
1934	NY	N	S		137	.268
1935	NY	N	3		128	.301
1936	NY	N	3		126	.230
		BRTR			1656	.290

JACKSON, WILLIAM RILEY
B.APR.4,1881 PITTSBURGH,PA.
D.SEPT.24,1958 PEORIA,ILL.

1914	CHI	F	1		17	.040
1915	CHI	F	1		48	.165
		BLTL			65	.139

JACOBO, RICARDO ADOLFO [CARTY]
[PLAYED UNDER NAME OF
RICARDO ADOLFO JACOBO CARTY]

JACOBS, ANTHONY ROBERT (TONY)
B.AUG.5,1925 DIXMOOR,ILL.

1948	CHI	N	P		1	0- 0
1955	STL	N	P		1	0- 0
		BBTR			2	0- 0

JACOBS, ARTHUR EDWARD
B.AUG.28,1902 LUCKEY,OHIO
D.JUNE 8,1967 INGLEWOOD,CAL.

1939	CIN	N	P		1	0- 0
		BLTL				

JACOBS, FORREST VANDERGRIFT (SPOOK)
B.NOV.4,1925 CHESWOLD,DEL.

1954	PHI	A	2		132	.258
1955	KC	A	2		13	.261
1956	KC	A	2		32	.216
	PIT	N	2		11	.162
		BRTR			188	.247

JACOBS, LAMAR GARY (JAKE)
B.JUNE 9,1937 YOUNGSTOWN,OHIO

1960	WAS	A	H		6	.000
1961	MIN	A	O		4	.250
		BRTR			10	.200

JACOBS, MORRIS ELMORE (MIKE)
B.1877
D.MAR.21,1949 LOUISVILLE,KY.

1902	CHI	N	S		5	.210

JACOBS, NEWTON SMITH (BUCKY)
B.MAR.21,1913 ALTAVISTA,VA.

1937	WAS	A	P		11	1- 1
1939	WAS	A	P		2	0- 0
1940	WAS	A	P		9	0- 1
		BRTR			22	1- 2

JACOBS, OTTO ALBERT
B.APR.19,1889 CHICAGO,ILL.
D.NOV.19,1955 CHICAGO,ILL.

1918	CHI	A	C		29	.205
		BRTR				

JACOBS, RAYMOND F.
B.JAN.2,1902 SALT LAKE CITY,UTAH
D.APR.4,1952 LOS ANGELES,CAL.

1928	CHI	N	H		2	.000
		BRTR				

JACOBS, WILLIAM ELMER (ELMER)
B.AUG.10,1892 SALEM,MO.
D.FEB.10,1958 SALEM,MO.

1914	PHI	N	P		14	1- 3
1916	PIT	N	P		34	6-10
1917	PIT	N	P		38	6-19
1918	PIT	N	P		8	0- 1
	PHI	N	P		18	9- 5
1919	PHI	N	P		17	6-10
	STL	N	P		17	3- 6
1920	STL	N	P		23	4- 8
1924	CHI	N	P		38	11-12
1925	CHI	N	P		18	2- 3
1927	CHI	A	P		25	2- 4
		BRTR			250	50-81

JACOBSON, ALBERT L. (BEANY)
B.JUNE 5,1881 PORT WASHINGTON,WIS.
D.JAN.31,1933 DECATUR,ILL.

1904	WAS	A	P		33	5-23
1905	WAS	A	P		22	8- 9
1906	STL	A	P		25	9- 9
1907	STL	A	P		7	1- 5
	BOS	A	P		2	0- 0
		TL			89	23-46

JACOBSON, MERWIN JOHN WILLIAM (JAKE)
B.MAR.7,1894 NEW BRITAIN,CONN.
D.JAN.13,1978 BALTIMORE,MD.

1915	NY	N	O		8	.083
1916	CHI	N	O		4	.231
1926	BRO	N	O		110	.247
1927	BRO	N	O		11	.000
		BLTL			133	.230

JACOBSON, WILLIAM CHESTER
(BABY DOLL)
B.AUG.16,1890 CABLE,ILL.
D.JAN.16,1977 ORION,ILL.

1915	DET	A	O		38	.215
	STL	A	O		33	.249
1917	STL	A	O		148	.248
1919	STL	A	O		120	.323
1920	STL	A	O		154	.355
1921	STL	A	1-O		151	.352
1922	STL	A	O		145	.317
1923	STL	A	O		147	.309
1924	STL	A	O		152	.318
1925	STL	A	O		142	.341
1926	STL	A	O		50	.290
	BOS	A	O		98	.302
1927	BOS	A	O		45	.245
	CLE	A	O		32	.252
	PHI	A	O		17	.229
		BRTR			1472	.311

JACOBUS, STUART LOUIS (LARRY)
B.DEC.18,1893 CINCINNATI,OHIO
D.AUG.19,1965 N.COLLEGE HILL,O.

1918	CIN	N	P		5	0- 1
		BBTR				

JACOBY, HARRY
B.PHILADELPHIA,PA.

1882	BAL	AA	3-O		31	.213
1885	BAL	AA	2		11	.143
					42	.195

JACQUEZ, PATRICK THOMAS (PAT)
B.APR.23,1947 STOCKTON,CAL.

1971	CHI	A	/P		2	0- 0
		BRTR				

JAECKEL, PAUL HENRY (JAKE)
B.APR.1,1942 E.LOS ANGELES,CAL.

1964	CHI	N	P		4	1- 0
		BRTR				

JAEGER, CHARLES THOMAS
B.APR.17,1875 OTTAWA,ILL.
D.SEPT.27,1942 OTTAWA,ILL.

1904	DET	A	P		8	2- 3

JAEGER, JOSEPH PETER (ZIP)
B.MAR.3,1895 ST.CLOUD,MINN.
D.DEC.13,1963 HAMPTON,IOWA

1920	CHI	N	P		2	0- 0
		BRTR				

```
YR   CL LEA POS      GP    G    REC
```

JAHN, ARTHUR CHARLES
B.DEC.22,1895 STRUBLE,IOWA.
D.JAN.9,1948 LITTLE ROCK,ARK.
```
1925 CHI N  O              58   .301
1928 NY  N  O              10   .276
     PHI N  O              36   .223
          BRTR            104   .278
```

JAKUCKI, SIGMUND (SIG) OR (JACK)
B.AUG.20,1909 CAMDEN,N.J.
```
1936 STL A  P         7    0- 3
1944 STL A  P     35  36   13- 9
1945 STL A  P         30   12-10
          BRTR    72  73   25-22
```

JAMERSON, CHARLES DEWEY (LEFTY)
B.JAN.26,1900 ENFIELD,ILL.
```
1924 BOS A  P          1    0- 0
          BLTL
```

JAMES, ARTHUR (ART)
B.AUG.2,1952 DETROIT,MICH.
```
1975 DET A  O              11   .225
          BLTL
```

JAMES, BERTON HULON (JESSE)
B.JULY 7,1886 COOPERTOWN,TENN.
D.JAN.2,1959 ADAIRVILLE,KY.
```
1909 STL N  O               6   .285
          BLTR
```

JAMES, CHARLES WESLEY (CHARLIE)
B.DEC.22,1937 ST.LOUIS,MO.
```
1960 STL N  O              43   .180
1961 STL N  O             108   .255
1962 STL N  O             129   .276
1963 STL N  O             116   .268
1964 STL N  O              88   .223
1965 CIN N /O              26   .205
          BRTR            510   .255
```

JAMES, CLEO JOEL
B.AUG.31,1940 CLARKSDALE,MISS.
```
1968 LA  N /O              10   .200
1970 CHI N  O             100   .210
1971 CHI N  O/3            54   .287
1973 CHI N  O              44   .111
          BRTR            208   .228
```

JAMES, JAMES MC CUTCHEN
[PLAYED UNDER NAME OF
JAMES MC CUTCHEN MC JAMES]

JAMES, JEFFREY LYNN
(JEFF) OR (JESSE)
B.SEP.29,1941 INDIANAPOLIS,IND.
```
1968 PHI N  P              29    4- 4
1969 PHI N /P               6    2- 2
          BRTR             35    6- 6
```

JAMES, JOHN PHILLIP (JOHNNY)
B.JULY 23,1933 BONNER S FERRY,IDAHO
```
1958 NY  A  P               1    0- 0
1960 NY  A  P              28    5- 1
1961 NY  A  P               1    0- 0
     LA  N  P      36  43    0- 2
          BLTR    66  73    5- 3
```

JAMES, PHILIP ROBERT (SKIP)
B.OCT.21,1949 ELMHURST,ILL.
```
1977 SF  N /1              10   .267
1978 SF  N  1              41   .095
          BLTL             51   .167
```

JAMES, RICHARD LEE (RICK)
B.OCT.11,1947 SHEFFIELD,ALA.
```
1967 CHI N /P               3    0- 1
          BRTR
```

JAMES, ROBERT BYRNE (BERNIE)
B.SEPT.2,1905 ANGLETON,TEX.
```
1929 BOS N  2              46   .307
1930 BOS N  2               8   .182
1933 NY  N  2-S-3          60   .224
          BBTR            114   .257
```

JAMES, ROBERT HARVEY (BOB)
B.AUG.18,1958 GLENDALE,CAL.
```
1978 MON N /P               4    0- 1
          BRTR
```

JAMES, WILLIAM A. (LEFTY)
B.JULY 1,1889 GLENROY,OHIO
D.MAY 3,1933 PORTSMOUTH,OHIO
```
1912 CLE A  P               6    0- 1
1913 CLE A  P              11    2- 2
1914 CLE A  P              11    0- 3
          BLTL             28    2- 6
```

JAMES, WILLIAM HENRY (BIG BILL)
B.JAN.20,1887 DETROIT,MICH.
D.MAY 24,1942 VENICE,CAL.
```
1911 CLE A  P               8    3- 4
1912 CLE A  P               3    0- 0
1914 STL A  P              43   15-14
1915 STL A  P              34    6-10
     DET A  P              11    7- 3
1916 DET A  P              30    7-12
1917 DET A  P              34   13-10
1918 DET A  P              19    6-11
1919 DET A  P               3    3- 0
     BOS A  P              14    2- 5
     CHI A  P               5    3- 1
          BBTR            204   65-70
```

JAMES, WILLIAM LAWRENCE
(SEATTLE BILL)
B.MAR.12,1892 IOWA HILL,CAL.
D.MAR.10,1971 OROVILLE,CAL.
```
1913 BOS N  P              24    6-10
1914 BOS N  P     46  49   26- 7
1915 BOS N  P     13  14    5- 4
1919 BOS N  P               1    0- 0
          BRTR             88   37-21
```

JAMIESON, CHARLES DEVINE
(CHARLIE) OR (CUCKOO)
B.FEB.7,1893 PATERSON,N.J.
D.OCT.27,1969 PATERSON,N.J.
```
1915 WAS A  O              17   .279
1916 WAS A  P-O    1  64    0- 0
                                .248
1917 WAS A  P-O    1  20    0- 0
                                .171
     PHI A  O              85   .267
1918 PHI A  P-O    5 110    1- 1
                                .202
1919 CLE A  P-O    4  26    0- 0
                                .353
1920 CLE A  O             108   .319
1921 CLE A  O             140   .310
1922 CLE A  P-O    2 145    0- 0
                                .323
1923 CLE A  O             152   .345
1924 CLE A  O             143   .358
1925 CLE A  O             138   .296
1926 CLE A  O             143   .299
1927 CLE A  O             127   .309
1928 CLE A  O             112   .307
1929 CLE A  O             102   .291
1930 CLE A  O             103   .301
1931 CLE A  O              28   .302
1932 CLE A  O              16   .063
          BLTL    13 1779    1- 1
                                .303
```

JANESKI, GERARD JOSEPH (JERRY)
B.APR.18,1946 PASADENA,CAL.
```
1970 CHI A  P              35   10-17
1971 WAS A  P              23    1- 5
1972 TEX A /P               4    0- 1
          BRTR             62   11-23
```

JANOWICZ, VICTOR FELIX (VIC)
B.FEB.26,1930 ELYRIA,OHIO
```
1953 PIT N  C              42   .252
1954 PIT N  3-O            49   .151
          BRTR             83   .214
```

JANSEN, LAWRENCE JOSEPH (LARRY)
B.JULY 16,1920 VERBOORT,ORE.
```
1947 NY  N  P              42   21- 5
1948 NY  N  P              42   18-12
1949 NY  N  P              37   15-16
1950 NY  N  P              40   19-13
1951 NY  N  P              39   23-11
1952 NY  N  P              34   11-11
1953 NY  N  P              36   11-16
1954 NY  N  P              13    2- 2
1956 CIN N  P               8    2- 3
          BRTR            291  122-89
```

JANSEN, RAYMOND WILLIAM
B.JAN.16,1889 ST.LOUIS,MO.
D.MAR.19,1934 ST.LOUIS,MO.
```
1910 STL A  3               1   .800
          BRTR
```

JANTZEN, WALTER C. (HEINIE)
B.APR.9,1890 CHICAGO,ILL.
D.APR.1,1948 HINES,ILL.
```
1912 STL A  O              31   .185
          BRTR
```

JANVRIN, HAROLD CHANDLER
(HAL) OR (CHILDE HAROLD)
B.AUG.27,1892 HAVERHILL,MASS.
D.MAR.2,1962 BOSTON,MASS.
```
1911 BOS A  3              10   .153
1913 BOS A  S-3            86   .206
1914 BOS A  1-2-S         143   .238
1915 BOS A  S-3            99   .269
1916 BOS A  2-S           117   .223
1917 BOS A  2              55   .197
1919 WAS A  2              61   .178
     STL N  2               7   .214
1920 STL N  1-S-O          87   .274
1921 STL N  1              18   .281
     BRO N  1-S            44   .196
1922 BRO N  1-2-S-3-O      30   .298
          BRTR            757   .232
```

JARVIS, LEROY GILBERT (ROY)
B.JUNE 27,1926 SHAWNEE,OKLA.
```
1944 BRO N  C               1   .000
1946 PIT N  C               2   .250
1947 PIT N  C              18   .156
          BRTR             21   .160
```

JARVIS, RAYMOND ARNOLD (RAY)
B.MAY 10,1946 PROVIDENCE,R.I.
```
1969 BOS A  P              29    5- 6
1970 BOS A  P              15    0- 1
          BRTR             44    5- 7
```

JARVIS, ROBERT PATRICK (PAT)
B.MAR.18,1941 CARLYLE,ILL.
```
1966 ATL N  P              10    6- 2
1967 ATL N  P              32   15-10
1968 ATL N  P              34   16-12
1969 ATL N  P              37   13-11
1970 ATL N  P              36   16-16
1971 ATL N  P              35    6-14
1972 ATL N  P              37   11- 7
1973 MON N  P              28    2- 1
          BRTR            249   85-73
```

JASPER, HENRY W. (HI)
B.NOV.19,1880 ST.LOUIS,MO.
D.MAY 22,1937 ST.LOUIS,MO.
```
1914 CHI A  P              16    1- 0
1915 CHI A  P               3    1- 1
1916 STL N  P              21    5- 6
1919 CLE A  P              12    4- 5
          BRTR             52   11-12
```

JASTER, LARRY EDWARD
B.JAN.13,1944 MIDLAND,MICH.
```
1965 STL N /P               4    3- 0
1966 STL N  P              26   11- 5
1967 STL N  P     34  35    9- 7
1968 STL N  P              31    9-13
1969 MON N  P              24    1- 6
1970 ATL N  P              14    1- 1
1972 ATL N /P               5    1- 1
          BLTL   138 139   35-33
```

JATA, PAUL
B.SEP.4,1949 ASTORIA,N.Y.
```
1972 DET A  1-O/C          32   .230
          BRTR
```

JAVERY, ALVA WILLIAM (BEARTRACKS)
B.JUNE 5,1918 WORCESTER,MASS.
D.SEPT.13,1977 WOODSTOCK,CONN.
```
1940 BOS N  P              29    2- 4
1941 BOS N  P              34   10-11
1942 BOS N  P              42   12-16
1943 BOS N  P              41   17-16
1944 BOS N  P              40   10-19
1945 BOS N  P              17    2- 7
1946 BOS N  P               2    0- 1
          BRTR            205   53-74
```

JAVIER, IGNACIO ALFRED (AL)
[REAL NAME IGNACIO ALFREDO
WILKES (JAVIER)]
B.FEB.4,1954 SAN PEDRO DE
MACORIS,D.R.
```
1976 HOU N /O               8   .208
          BRTR
```

JAVIER, MANUEL JULIAN [LIRANZO]
(JULIAN)
B.AUG.9,1936 SAN FRANCISCO DE
MACORIS,D.R.
```
1960 STL N  2             119   .237
1961 STL N  2             113   .279
1962 STL N  2-S           155   .263
1963 STL N  2             161   .263
1964 STL N  2             155   .241
1965 STL N  2              77   .227
1966 STL N *2             147   .228
1967 STL N *2             140   .281
1968 STL N *2             139   .260
1969 STL N *2             143   .282
1970 STL N *2             139   .251
1971 STL N  2/3            90   .259
1972 CIN N  3/2-1          44   .209
          BRTR           1622   .257
```

```
YR  CL LEA POS    GP   G   REC

JAY, JOSEPH RICHARD (JOEY)
B.AUG.15,1935 MIDDLETOWN,CONN.
1953 MIL N  P          3   1- 0
1954 MIL N  P         15   1- 0
1955 MIL N  P         12   0- 0
1957 MIL N  P          1   0- 0
1958 MIL N  P         18   7- 5
1959 MIL N  P         34   6-11
1960 MIL N  P         32   9- 8
1961 CIN N  P         34  21-10
1962 CIN N  P         39  21-14
1963 CIN N  P         30   7-18
1964 CIN N  P         34  11-11
1965 CIN N  P         37   9- 8
1966 CIN N  P         12   0- 2
     ATL N /P          9   0- 4
     BBTR            310  99-91
     BR 1953

JEANES, ERNEST LEE (TEX)
B.DEC.19,1900 MAYPEARL,TEX.
D.APR.5,1973 LONGVIEW,TEX.
1921 CLE A  O          4   .500
1922 CLE A  O          1   0- 0
1925 WAS A  O         15   .263
1926 WAS A  O         21   .233
1927 NY  N  P      1  11   0- 0
     BRTR          2  52   0- 0
                           .278

JEFFCOAT, GEORGE EDWARD
B.DEC.24,1913 NEW BROOKLAND,S.C
D.OCT.13,1978 LEESVILLE,S.C.
1936 BRO N  P         40   5- 6
1937 BRO N  P         21   1- 3
1939 BRO N  P          1   0- 0
1943 BOS N  P          8   1- 2
     BRTR             70   7-11

JEFFCOAT, HAROLD BENTLEY (HAL)
B.SEPT.6,1924 W.COLUMBIA,S.C.
1948 CHI N  O        134   .279
1949 CHI N  O        108   .245
1950 CHI N  O         66   .235
1951 CHI N  O        113   .273
1952 CHI N  O        102   .219
1953 CHI N  O        106   .235
1954 CHI N  P-O   43  56   5- 6
                           .258
1955 CHI N  P     50  52   8- 6
1956 CIN N  P     38  49   8- 2
1957 CIN N  P     37  53  12-13
1958 CIN N  P-O   49  50   6- 8
                           .556
1959 CIN N  P         17   0- 1
     STL N  P     11  12   0- 1
     BRTR        245 918  39-37
                           .253

JEFFERSON, JESSE HARRISON
B.MAR.3,1949 MIDLOTHIAN,VA.
1973 BAL A  P         18   6- 5
1974 BAL A  P         20   1- 0
1975 BAL A /P          4   0- 2
     CHI A  P         22   5- 9
1976 CHI A  P         19   2- 5
1977 TOR A  P         33   9-17
1978 TOR A  P         31   7-16
     BRTR            147  30-54

JEFFRIES, IRVINE FRANKLIN
B.SEPT.10,1905 LOUISVILLE,KY.
1930 CHI A  S-3       40   .237
1931 CHI A  3         79   .224
1934 PHI N  2         56   .246
     BRTR            175   .234

JELINICH, FRANK ANTHONY (JELLY)
B.SEPT.3,1919 SAN JOSE,CAL.
1941 CHI N  O          4   .125
     BRTR

JENDRUS, GEORGE ANDREW
[PLAYED UNDER NAME OF
GEORGE JENDRUS ANDERSON]

JENKINS, FERGUSON ARTHUR
B.DEC.13,1943 CHATHAM,ONT.,CAN.
1965 PHI N /P          7   2- 1
1966 PHI N /P          1   0- 0
     CHI N  P         60   6- 8
1967 CHI N  P     38  39  20-13
1968 CHI N  P         40  20-15
1969 CHI N  P         43  21-15
1970 CHI N  P         40  22-16
1971 CHI N  P         39  24-13
1972 CHI N  P         36  20-12
1973 CHI N  P         38  14-16
1974 TEX A  P         41  25-12
1975 TEX A  P         37  17-18
1976 BOS A  P         30  12-11
1977 BOS A  P         28  10-10
1978 TEX A  P         34  18- 8
     BRTR        512 513 231-168
```

```
JENKINS, JOHN ROBERT
B.JULY 7,1896 BOSWORTH,MO.
D.AUG.3,1968 COLUMBIA,MO.
1922 CHI A  2-S        5   .000
     BRTR

JENKINS, JOSEPH DANIEL
B.OCT.12,1890 SHELBYVILLE,TENN.
D.JUNE 21,1974 FRESNO,CAL.
1914 STL A  C         19   .125
1917 CHI A  C         10   .111
1919 CHI A  C         11   .167
     BRTR             40   .136

JENKINS, THOMAS GRIFFITH (TUT)
B.APR.10,1898 CAMDEN,ALA.
1925 BOS A  O         15   .297
1926 BOS A  O         21   .180
     PHI A  O          6   .174
1929 STL A  O         21   .182
1930 STL A  O          2   .250
1931 STL A  O         81   .265
1932 STL A  O         25   .323
     BLTR            171   .259

JENKINS, WARREN WASHINGTON (JACKIE)
B.DEC.22,1942 COVINGTON,VA.
1962 WAS A  P          3   0- 1
1963 WAS A  P          4   0- 2
1969 LA  N /P          1   0- 0
     BRTR              8   0- 3

JENNINGS, ALFRED (ALAMAZOO)
B.1851 NEWPORT,KY.
D.NOV.2,1894 CINCINNATI,OHIO
1878 MIL N  C          1   .000

JENNINGS, HUGH AMBROSE
(HUGHIE) OR (EE-YAH)
B.APR.2,1869 PITTSTON,PA.
D.FEB.1,1928 SCRANTON,PA.
1891 LOU AA 1-S       87   .285
1892 LOU N  S        152   .232
1893 LOU N  S         23   .148
     BAL N  S         15   .241
1894 BAL N  S        128   .332
1895 BAL N  S        131   .386
1896 BAL N  S        129   .397
1897 BAL N  S        115   .353
1898 BAL N  2-S      143   .325
1899 BRO N  1         10   .200
     BAL N  2          2   .375
     BRO N  1-S       51   .320
1900 BRO N  1        112   .270
1901 PHI N  1         81   .274
1902 PHI N  1-2-S     78   .277
1903 BRO N  O          6   .235
1907 DET A  M-S        2   .250
1908 DET A  M-H        1   .000
1909 DET A  M-1        2   .500
1912 DET A  M-H        1   .000
1918 DET A  M-1        1   .000
     BRTR           1270   .314
NON-PLAYING MANAGER
DET[A] 1910-11, 13-17, 19-20

JENNINGS, WILLIAM LEE
B.SEPT.28,1925 ST.LOUIS,MO.
1951 STL A  S         64   .179
     BRTR

JENNINGS, WILLIAM MORLEY
[PLAYED UNDER NAME OF
WILLIAM M. MORLEY]

JENSEN, FORREST DOCENUS (WOODY)
B.AUG.11,1907 BREMERTON,WASH.
1931 PIT N  O         73   .243
1932 PIT N  O          7   .000
1933 PIT N  O         70   .296
1934 PIT N  O         88   .290
1935 PIT N  O        143   .324
1936 PIT N  O        153   .283
1937 PIT N  O        124   .279
1938 PIT N  O         68   .200
1939 PIT N  O         12   .167
     BLTL            738   .285

JENSEN, JACK EUGENE (JACKIE)
B.MAR.9,1927 SAN FRANCISCO,CAL.
1950 NY  A  O         45   .171
1951 NY  A  O         56   .298
1952 NY  A  O          7   .105
     WAS A  O        144   .286
1953 WAS A  O        147   .266
1954 BOS A  O        152   .276
1955 BOS A  O        152   .275
1956 BOS A  O        151   .315
1957 BOS A  O        145   .281
1958 BOS A  O        154   .286
1959 BOS A  O        148   .277
1961 BOS A  O        137   .263
     BRTR           1438   .279

JENSEN, WILLIAM
B.NOV.23,1888 NEW HAVEN,CONN.
1912 DET A  P          4   1- 2
1914 PHI A  P          2   0- 1
     BLTR              6   1- 3
```

```
JESSEE, DANIEL EDWARD
B.FEB.22,1901 OLIVE HILL,KY.
D.APR.30,1970 VENICE,FLA.
1929 CLE A  H          1   .000
     BLTR

JESTADT, GARRY ARTHUR
B.MAR.19,1947 CHICAGO,ILL.
1969 MON N /3          6   .000
1971 CHI N /3          3   .000
     SD  N  3-2/S      75   .291
1972 SD  N  2-3/S      92   .246
     BRTR            176   .260

JESTER, VIRGIL MILTON
B.JULY 23,1927 DENVER,COLO.
1952 BOS N  P         19   3- 5
1953 MIL N  P          2   0- 0
     BRTR             21   3- 5

JETER, JOHN (JOHNNY)
B.OCT.24,1944 SHREVEPORT,LA.
1969 PIT N  O         28   .310
1970 PIT N  O         85   .238
1971 SD  N  O         18   .320
1972 SD  N  O        110   .221
1973 CHI A  O         89   .240
1974 CLE A /O          6   .353
     BRTR            336   .244

JETHROE, SAMUEL (SAM) OR (JET)
B.JAN.20,1922 E.ST.LOUIS,ILL.
1950 BOS N  O        141   .273
1951 BOS N  O        148   .280
1952 BOS N  O        151   .232
1954 PIT N  O          2   .000
     BBTR            442   .261

JEWETT, NATHAN W.
B.1842
1872 ECK NA C          2   .125

JIMENEZ, FELIX ELVIO (ELVIO)
B.JAN.6,1940 SAN PEDRO DE
MACORIS,D.R.
1964 NY  A  O          1   .333
     BRTR

JIMENEZ, JUAN ANTONIO [MARTES]
B.MAR.8,1949 LA TORRE,LA VEGA,
D.R.
1974 PIT N /P          4   0- 0
     BRTR

JIMENEZ, MANUEL EMILIO (MANNY)
B.NOV.19,1938 SAN PEDRO DE
MACORIS,D.R.
1962 KC  A  O        139   .301
1963 KC  A  O         60   .280
1964 KC  A  O         95   .225
1966 KC  A  O         13   .114
1967 PIT N /O         50   .250
1968 PIT N /O         66   .303
1969 CHI N /H          6   .167
     BLTR            429   .272

JOHN, THOMAS EDWARD (TOMMY)
B.MAY 22,1943 TERRE HAUTE,IND.
1963 CLE A  P          6   0- 2
1964 CLE A  P         25   2- 9
1965 CHI A  P         39  14- 7
1966 CHI A  P         34  14-11
1967 CHI A  P         31  10-13
1968 CHI A  P         25  10- 5
1969 CHI A  P         33   9-11
1970 CHI A  P     37  38  12-17
1971 CHI A  P         38  13-16
1972 LA  N  P         29  11- 5
1973 LA  N  P         36  16- 7
1974 LA  N  P         22  13- 3
1976 LA  N  P         31  10-10
1977 LA  N  P         31  20- 7
1978 LA  N  P         33  17-10
     BRTL       450 451 171-133

JOHNS, AUGUSTUS FRANCIS
(AUGIE) OR (LEFTY)
B.SEPT.10,1899 ST.LOUIS,MO.
D.SEPT.12,1975 SAN ANTONIO,TEX.
1926 DET A  P         35   6- 4
1927 DET A  P          1   0- 0
     BLTL             36   6- 4

JOHNS, OLIVER TRACY
B.AUG.21,1879 TRENTON,OHIO
D.JUNE 17,1961 HAMILTON,OHIO
1905 CIN N  P          4   1- 0
     BLTL

JOHNS, THOMAS P.
B.BALTIMORE,MD.
1873 MAR NA O          1   .000

JOHNS, WILLIAM R. (PETE)
B.JAN.17,1889 CLEVELAND,OHIO
D.AUG.9,1964 CLEVELAND,OHIO
1915 CHI A  3         28   .210
1918 STL A  1         46   .180
     BRTR             74   .196
```

YR	CL LEA POS	GP	G	REC

JOHNSON, ABRAHAM
B.LONDON,ONT.,CAN.

YR	CL LEA POS	GP	G	REC
1893	CHI N P		1	0- 0

JOHNSON, ADAM RANKIN JR. (RANKIN)
B.MAR.1,1917 HAYDEN,ARIZ.

YR	CL LEA POS	GP	G	REC
1941	PHI A P		7	1- 0
	BRTR			

JOHNSON, ADAM RANKIN SR.
(RANKIN) OR (TEX)
B.FEB.4,1888 BURNET,TEX.
D.JULY 2,1972 WILLIAMSPORT,PA.

YR	CL LEA POS	GP	G	REC
1914	BOS A P		16	4- 9
	CHI F P		16	9- 5
1915	CHI F P		11	2- 5
	BAL F P		23	7-10
1918	STL N P		6	1- 1
	BRTR		72	22-30

JOHNSON, ALBERT J. (ABBIE)
B.CHICAGO,ILL.

YR	CL LEA POS	GP	G	REC
1896	LOU N 2		24	.232
1897	LOU N 2		44	.251
			68	.245

JOHNSON, ALEXANDER (ALEX)
B.DEC.7,1942 HELENA,ARK.

YR	CL LEA POS	GP	G	REC
1964	PHI N O		43	.303
1965	PHI N O		97	.294
1966	STL N O		25	.186
1967	STL N O		81	.223
1968	CIN N *O		149	.312
1969	CIN N *O		139	.315
1970	CAL A *O		156	.329
1971	CAL A O		65	.260
1972	CLE A O		108	.239
1973	TEX A *O-O		158	.287
1974	TEX A O-O		114	.291
	NY A /O		10	.214
1975	NY A O/O		52	.261
1976	DET A O-O		125	.268
	BRTR		1322	.288

JOHNSON, ARTHUR GILBERT
B.FEB.15,1897 WARREN,PA.

YR	CL LEA POS	GP	G	REC
1927	NY N P		1	0- 0
	BBTL			

JOHNSON, ARTHUR HENRY (LEFTY)
B.JULY 16,1916 WINCHESTER,MASS.

YR	CL LEA POS	GP	G	REC
1940	BOS N P		2	0- 1
1941	BOS N P	43	44	7-15
1942	BOS N P		4	0- 0
	BLTL	49	50	7-16

JOHNSON, BENJAMIN FRANKLIN
B.MAY 16,1931 GREENWOOD,S.C.

YR	CL LEA POS	GP	G	REC
1959	CHI N P		4	0- 0
1960	CHI N P		17	2- 1
	BRTR		21	2- 1

JOHNSON, CALEB CLARK
B.MAY 23,1844 USTICK TOWNSHIP,ILL.
D.MAR.7,1925

YR	CL LEA POS	GP	G	REC
1871	CLE NA 2-S-O		16	-

JOHNSON, CHARLES CLEVELAND
(HOME RUN)
B.MAR.12,1885 SLATINGTON,PA.
D.AUG.28,1940 MARCUS HOOK,PA.

YR	CL LEA POS	GP	G	REC
1908	PHI N O		9	.214

JOHNSON, CHESTER LILLIS
(CHET) OR (CHESTY CHET)
B.AUG.1,1917 REDMOND,WASH.

YR	CL LEA POS	GP	G	REC
1946	STL A P		5	0- 0
	BLTL			

JOHNSON, CLAIR BARTH (BART)
B.JAN.3,1950 TORRANCE,CAL.

YR	CL LEA POS	GP	G	REC
1969	CHI A /P		4	1- 3
1970	CHI A P		18	4- 7
1971	CHI A P		53	12-10
1972	CHI A /P		9	0- 3
1973	CHI A P		22	3- 3
1974	CHI A P		18	10- 4
1976	CHI A P		32	9-16
1977	CHI A P		29	4- 5
	BRTR		185	43-51

JOHNSON, CLIFFORD (CONNIE)
B.DEC.27,1922 STONE MOUNTAIN,GA

YR	CL LEA POS	GP	G	REC
1953	CHI A P	14	15	4- 4
1955	CHI A P	17	19	7- 4
1956	CHI A P		5	0- 1
	BAL A P		26	9-10
1957	BAL A P		35	14-11
1958	BAL A P		26	6- 9
	BRTR	123	126	40-39

JOHNSON, CLIFFORD (CLIFF)
B.JULY 22,1947 SAN ANTONIO,TEX.

YR	CL LEA POS	GP	G	REC
1972	HOU N /C		5	.250
1973	HOU N /1		7	.300
1974	HOU N C		83	.228
1975	HOU N 1-C/O		122	.276
1976	HOU N C-O-1		108	.226
1977	NY A O-1		51	.299
	NY A D-C-1		56	.296
1978	NY A D-C/1		76	.184
	BRTR		508	.251

JOHNSON, DARRELL DEAN
B.AUG.25,1928 HORACE,NEB.

YR	CL LEA POS	GP	G	REC
1952	STL A C		29	.282
	CHI A C		22	.108
1957	NY A C		21	.217
1958	NY A C		5	.250
1960	STL N C		8	.000
1961	PHI N C		21	.230
	CIN N C		20	.315
1962	CIN N C		2	.000
	BAL A C		6	.182
			134	.234

NON-PLAYING MANAGER
BOS[A] 1974-76, SEA[A] 1977-78

JOHNSON, DAVID ALLEN (DAVE)
B.JAN.30,1943 ORLANDO,FLA.

YR	CL LEA POS	GP	G	REC
1965	BAL A /3-2-S		20	.170
1966	BAL A *2/3		131	.257
1967	BAL A *2/3		148	.247
1968	BAL A *2-S		145	.242
1969	BAL A *2/S		142	.280
1970	BAL A *2/S		149	.281
1971	BAL A *2		142	.282
1972	BAL A *2		118	.221
1973	ATL N *2		157	.270
1974	ATL N 1-2		136	.251
1975	ATL N /H		11	1.000
1977	PHI N 1/2-3		78	.321
1978	PHI N 2/3-1		44	.191
	CHI N 3		24	.306
	BRTR		1435	.261

JOHNSON, DERON ROGER
B.JULY 17,1938 SAN DIEGO,CAL.

YR	CL LEA POS	GP	G	REC
1960	NY A 3		6	.500
1961	NY A 3		13	.105
	KC A 1-3-O		83	.216
1962	KC A 1-3-O		17	.105
1964	CIN N 1-3-O		140	.273
1965	CIN N *3		159	.287
1966	CIN N *O-1-3		142	.257
1967	CIN N 1-3		108	.224
1968	ATL N 1-3		127	.209
1969	PHI N O-3-1		138	.255
1970	PHI N *1/3		159	.256
1971	PHI N *1-3		158	.265
1972	PHI N 1		96	.213
1973	PHI N 1		12	.167
1974	OAK A *O-1		131	.246
	OAK A 1-D		50	.195
	MIL A D/1		49	.151
	BOS A /H		11	.120
1975	CHI A D-1		148	.233
	BOS A /1		3	.600
1976	BOS A /1		15	.132
	BRTR		1765	.244

JOHNSON, DONALD ROY (DON)
B.NOV.12,1926 PORTLAND,ORE.

YR	CL LEA POS	GP	G	REC
1947	NY A P		15	4- 3
1950	NY A P		8	1- 0
	STL A P		25	5- 6
1951	STL A P		6	0- 1
	WAS A P		21	7-11
1952	WAS A P		29	0- 5
1954	CHI A P		46	8- 7
1955	BAL A P		31	2- 4
1958	SF N P		17	0- 1
	BRTR		198	27-38

JOHNSON, DONALD SPORE (PEP)
B.DEC.7,1911 CHICAGO,ILL.

YR	CL LEA POS	GP	G	REC
1943	CHI N 2		10	.190
1944	CHI N 2		154	.278
1945	CHI N 2		138	.302
1946	CHI N 2		83	.242
1947	CHI N 2-3		120	.259
1948	CHI N 2-3		6	.250
	BRTR		911	.268

JOHNSON, EARL DOUGLAS
(EARL) OR (LEFTY)
B.APR.2,1919 REDMOND,WAS.

YR	CL LEA POS	GP	G	REC
1940	BOS A P	17	18	6- 2
1941	BOS A P		17	4- 5
1946	BOS A P		29	5- 4
1947	BOS A P	45	46	12-11
1948	BOS A P		35	10- 4
1949	BOS A P		19	3- 6
1950	BOS A P		11	0- 0
1951	DET A P		6	0- 0
	BLTL	179	181	40-32

JOHNSON, EDWIN CYRIL
B.MAR.31,1899 MORGANFIELD,KY.
D.JULY 3,1975 MORGANFIELD,KY.

YR	CL LEA POS	GP	G	REC
1920	WAS A 1-O		4	.230
	BLTR			

JOHNSON, ELLIS WALTER (WALT)
B.DEC.8,1892 MINNEAPOLIS,MINN.
D.JAN.4,1965 MINNEAPOLIS,MINN.

YR	CL LEA POS	GP	G	REC
1912	CHI A P		5	0- 0
1915	CHI A P		1	0- 0
1917	PHI A P		4	0- 2
	BRTR		10	0- 2

JOHNSON, ELMER ELLSWORTH (HICKORY)
B.JUNE 12,1884 BEARD,IND.
D.OCT.31,1966 HOLLYWOOD,FLA.

YR	CL LEA POS	GP	G	REC
1914	NY N C		11	.166
	BRTR			

JOHNSON, ERNEST RUDOLPH
B.APR.29,1888 CHICAGO,ILL.
D.MAY 1,1952 MONROVIA,CAL.

YR	CL LEA POS	GP	G	REC
1912	CHI A S		18	.262
1915	STL F S		152	.244
1916	STL A S		74	.229
1917	STL A 2-S		80	.248
1918	STL A S		29	.205
1921	CHI A S		142	.295
1922	CHI A S		145	.234
1923	CHI A S		12	.189
	NY A S		19	.447
1924	NY A S		64	.353
1925	NY A 2-S-3		76	.282
	BLTR		811	.267

JOHNSON, ERNEST THORWALD (ERNIE)
B.JUNE 16,1924 BRATTLEBORO,VT.

YR	CL LEA POS	GP	G	REC
1950	BOS N P		16	2- 0
1952	BOS N P		29	6- 3
1953	MIL N P		36	4- 3
1954	MIL N P		40	5- 2
1955	MIL N P		40	5- 7
1956	MIL N P		36	4- 3
1957	MIL N P		30	7- 3
1958	MIL N P		13	3- 1
1959	BAL A P		31	4- 1
	BRTR		273	40-23

JOHNSON, FRANK HERBERT
B.JULY 22,1942 EL PASO,TEX.

YR	CL LEA POS	GP	G	REC
1966	SF N O		15	.219
1967	SF N /O		8	.300
1968	SF N 3/O-S-2		67	.190
1969	SF N /O		7	.100
1970	SF N O-1		67	.273
1971	SF N /1-O		32	.082
	BRTR		196	.211

JOHNSON, FREDERICK EDWARD
(DEACON) OR (CACTUS)
B.MAR.10,1894 TOLAR,TEX.
D.JUNE 14,1973 KERRVILLE,TEX.

YR	CL LEA POS	GP	G	REC
1922	NY N P		2	0- 2
1923	NY N P		3	2- 0
1938	STL A P		17	3- 7
1939	STL A P		5	0- 1
	BRTR		27	5-10

JOHNSON, GEORGE HOWARD (MURPHY)
(BIG MURPH) OR (CHIEF)
B.MAR.30,1886 WINNEBAGO,NEB.
D.JUNE 11,1922 DES MOINES,IOWA

YR	CL LEA POS	GP	G	REC
1913	CIN N P		44	14-16
1914	CIN N P		1	0- 0
	KC F P		20	9-10
1915	KC F P		45	17-17
	BRTR		110	40-43

JOHNSON, HENRY WARD (HANK)
B.MAY 21,1906 BRADENTON,FLA.

YR	CL LEA POS	GP	G	REC
1925	NY A P		24	1- 3
1926	NY A P		1	0- 0
1928	NY A P		31	14- 9
1929	NY A P	12	13	3- 3
1930	NY A P	44	51	14-11
1931	NY A P		40	13- 8
1932	NY A P	5	6	2- 2
1933	BOS A P	25	26	8- 6
1934	BOS A P		31	6- 8
1935	BOS A P		13	2- 1
1936	PHI A P		3	2- 0
1939	CIN N P		20	0- 3
	BRTR	249	259	63-56
	BB 1933			

JOHNSON, JAMES BRIAN (JIM)
B.NOV.3,1945 MUSKEGON,MICH.

YR	CL	LEA	POS	GP	G	REC
1970	SF	N	/P		3	1- 0
	BLTL					

JOHNSON, JERRY MICHAEL
B.DEC.3,1943 MIAMI,FLA.

YR	CL	LEA	POS	GP	G	REC
1968	PHI	N	P		16	4- 4
1969	PHI	N	P		33	6-13
1970	STL	N	/P		7	2- 0
	SF	N	P		53	3- 4
1971	SF	N	P		67	12- 9
1972	SF	N	P		48	8- 6
1973	CLE	A	P		39	5- 6
1974	HOU	N	P		34	2- 1
1975	SD	N	P		21	3- 1
1976	SD	N	P		24	1- 3
1977	TOR	A	P		43	2- 4
	BRTR				365	48-51

JOHNSON, JOHN CLIFFORD (SWEDE)
B.SEPT.29,1914 BELMORE,OHIO

YR	CL	LEA	POS	GP	G	REC
1944	NY	A	P		22	0- 2
1945	CHI	A	P		29	3- 0
	BLTL				51	3- 2

JOHNSON, JOHN HENRY
B.AUG.21,1956 HOUSTON,TEX.

YR	CL	LEA	POS	GP	G	REC
1978	OAK	A	P	33	34	11-10
	BLTL					

JOHNSON, JOHN LOUIS (YOUNGY)
[REAL NAME JOHN LOUIS MERCER]
B.NOV.18,1869 PEKIN,ILL.
D.JAN.28,1941 KANSAS CITY,MO.

YR	CL	LEA	POS	GP	G	REC
1894	PHI	N	P		4	1- 3

JOHNSON, JOHN RALPH (SPUD)
B.1860 CHICAGO,ILL.

YR	CL	LEA	POS	GP	G	REC
1889	COL	AA	3-O		117	.285
1890	COL	AA	O		137	.354
1891	CLE	N	O		80	.263
	BL				334	.307

JOHNSON, KENNETH TRAVIS (KEN)
B.JUNE 16,1933 W.PALM BEACH,FLA.

YR	CL	LEA	POS	GP	G	REC
1958	KC	A	P		2	0- 0
1959	KC	A	P		2	1- 1
1960	KC	A	P		42	5-10
1961	KC	A	P		6	0- 4
	CIN	N	P		15	6- 2
1962	HOU	N	P		33	7-16
1963	HOU	N	P	37	38	11-17
1964	HOU	N	P		35	11-16
1965	HOU	N	/P		8	3- 2
	MIL	N	P		29	13- 8
1966	ATL	N	P		32	14- 8
1967	ATL	N	P		29	13- 9
1968	ATL	N	P		31	5- 8
1969	ATL	N	/P		9	0- 1
	NY	A	P		12	1- 2
	CHI	N	/P		9	1- 2
1970	MON	N	/P		3	0- 0
	BRTR			334	335	91-106

JOHNSON, KENNETH WANDERSEE (KEN) OR (HOOK)
B.JAN.14,1923 TOPEKA,KAN.

YR	CL	LEA	POS	GP	G	REC
1947	STL	N	P		2	1- 0
1948	STL	N	P	13	20	2- 4
1949	STL	N	P	14	21	0- 1
1950	STL	N	P		2	0- 0
	PHI	N	P	14	21	4- 1
1951	PHI	N	P	20	36	5- 8
1952	DET	A	P		9	0- 0
	BLTL			74	111	12-14

JOHNSON, LAMAR
B.SEPT.2,1950 BESSEMER,ALA.

YR	CL	LEA	POS	GP	G	REC
1974	CHI	A	/1		10	.345
1975	CHI	A	/1		8	.200
1976	CHI	A	O-1/3		82	.320
1977	CHI	A	D-1		118	.302
1978	CHI	A	*1-O		148	.273
	BRTR				366	.291

JOHNSON, LARRY DOBY
B.AUG.17,1950 CLEVELAND,OHIO

YR	CL	LEA	POS	GP	G	REC
1972	CLE	A	/C		1	.500
1974	CLE	A	R		1	.000
1975	MON	N	/C		1	.333
1976	MON	N	/C		6	.154
1978	MON	N	/C		3	.125
	BRTR				12	.192

JOHNSON, LLOYD WILLIAM (EPPA)
B.DEC.24,1910 SANTA ROSA,CAL.

YR	CL	LEA	POS	GP	G	REC
1934	PIT	N	P		1	0- 0
	BLTL					

JOHNSON, LOUIS BROWN (LOU) OR (SLICK)
B.SEP.22,1934 LEXINGTON,KY.

YR	CL	LEA	POS	GP	G	REC
1960	CHI	N	O		34	.206
1961	LA	A	O		1	.000
1962	MIL	N	O		61	.282
1965	LA	N	*O		131	.259
1966	LA	N	*O		152	.272
1967	LA	N	O		104	.270
1968	CHI	N	O		62	.244
1968	CLE	A	O		65	.257
1969	CAL	A	O		67	.203
	BRTR				677	.258

JOHNSON, MICHAEL NORTON (MIKE)
B.MAR.2,1951 SLAYTON,MINN.

YR	CL	LEA	POS	GP	G	REC
1974	SD	N	P		18	0- 2
	BRTR					

JOHNSON, OTIS L.
B.NOV.5,1883 MUNCIE,IND.
D.NOV.9,1915 BINGHAMTON,N.Y.

YR	CL	LEA	POS	GP	G	REC
1911	NY	A	2-S		71	.234
	BBTR					

JOHNSON, PAUL OSCAR
B.SEPT.2,1896 N.GROSVENORDALE,CONN.
D.FEB.14,1973 MC ALLEN,TEX.

YR	CL	LEA	POS	GP	G	REC
1918	BOS	N	H		1	.000
1920	PHI	A	O		18	.208
1921	PHI	A	O		48	.315
	BRTR				67	.276

JOHNSON, RICHARD ALLAN (FOOTER) OR (TREADS)
B.FEB.15,1932 DAYTON,OHIO

YR	CL	LEA	POS	GP	G	REC
1958	CHI	N	H		8	.000
	BLTL					

JOHNSON, ROBERT DALE (BOB)
B.APR.25,1943 AURORA,IND.

YR	CL	LEA	POS	GP	G	REC
1969	NY	N	/P		2	0- 0
1970	KC	A	P		40	8-13
1971	PIT	N	P		31	9-10
1972	PIT	N	P		31	4- 4
1973	PIT	N	P		50	4- 2
1974	CLE	A	P		14	3- 4
1977	ATL	N	P		15	0- 1
	BLTR				183	28-34

JOHNSON, ROBERT LEE (INDIAN BOB)
B.NOV.26,1906 PRYOR,OKLA.

YR	CL	LEA	POS	GP	G	REC
1933	PHI	A	O		142	.290
1934	PHI	A	O		141	.307
1935	PHI	A	O		147	.299
1936	PHI	A	2-O		153	.292
1937	PHI	A	O		138	.306
1938	PHI	A	O		152	.313
1939	PHI	A	O		150	.338
1940	PHI	A	O		138	.268
1941	PHI	A	1-O		149	.275
1942	PHI	A	O		149	.291
1943	WAS	A	1-3-O		144	.265
1944	BOS	A	O		144	.324
1945	BOS	A	O		143	.280
	BRTR				1863	.296

JOHNSON, ROBERT WALLACE (BOB)
B.MAR.4,1936 OMAHA,NEB.

YR	CL	LEA	POS	GP	G	REC
1960	KC	A	2-S-3		76	.205
1961	WAS	A	2-S-3		61	.295
1962	WAS	A	2-S-3-O		135	.288
1963	BAL	A	1-2-S-3		82	.295
1964	BAL	A	1-2-S-3-O		93	.248
1965	BAL	A	1-S-3/2		87	.242
1966	BAL	A	2-1/3		71	.217
1967	BAL	A	/H		4	.333
	NY	N	2-1-S/3		90	.348
1968	CIN	N	/S-1		16	.267
	ATL	N	3/2		52	.262
1969	STL	N	/3-1		19	.207
	OAK	A	/1-2		51	.343
1970	OAK	A	/3-1		30	.174
	BRTR				874	.272

JOHNSON, ROY (HARDROCK)
B.OCT.1,1895 MADILL,OKLA.

YR	CL	LEA	POS	GP	G	REC
1918	PHI	A	P		10	1- 5
	BRTR					

NON-PLAYING MANAGER CHI(N) 1944

JOHNSON, ROY CLEVELAND
B.FEB.23,1903 PRYOR,OKLA.
D.SEPT.10,1973 TACOMA,WASH.

YR	CL	LEA	POS	GP	G	REC
1929	DET	A	O		148	.314
1930	DET	A	O		125	.275
1931	DET	A	O		151	.279
1932	DET	A	O		49	.254
	BOS	A	O		94	.296
1933	BOS	A	O		133	.313
1934	BOS	A	O		143	.320
1935	BOS	A	O		145	.315
1936	NY	A	O		63	.265
1937	NY	A	O		12	.294
	BOS	N	O		85	.277
1938	BOS	N	O		7	.172
	BLTR				1155	.296

JOHNSON, RUSSELL CONWELL (JING)
B.OCT.9,1894 PARKER FORD,PA.
D.DEC.6,1950 POTTSTOWN,PA.

YR	CL	LEA	POS	GP	G	REC
1916	PHI	A	P		12	2- 9
1917	PHI	A	P	34	35	9-12
1919	PHI	A	P	34	35	9-14
1927	PHI	A	P		17	4- 2
1928	PHI	A	P		3	0- 0
	BRTR			100	102	24-37

JOHNSON, SILAS KENNETH (SI)
B.OCT.5,1906 MARSEILLES,ILL.

YR	CL	LEA	POS	GP	G	REC
1928	CIN	N	P		3	0- 0
1929	CIN	N	P		1	0- 0
1930	CIN	N	P		35	3- 1
1931	CIN	N	P		42	11-19
1932	CIN	N	P		42	13-15
1933	CIN	N	P		34	7-18
1934	CIN	N	P		46	7-22
1935	CIN	N	P		30	5-11
1936	CIN	N	P		2	0- 0
	STL	N	P		12	5- 3
1937	STL	N	P		38	12-12
1938	STL	N	P		6	0- 3
1940	PHI	N	P		37	5-14
1941	PHI	N	P		39	5-12
1942	PHI	N	P		39	8-19
1943	PHI	N	P		21	8- 3
1946	PHI	N	P		1	0- 0
	BOS	N	P		28	6- 5
1947	BOS	N	P		36	6- 8
	BRTR				492	101-165

JOHNSON, STANLEY LUCIUS
B.FEB.12,1937 DALLAS,TEX.

YR	CL	LEA	POS	GP	G	REC
1960	CHI	A	O		5	.167
1961	KC	A	O		3	.000
	BLTL				8	.111

JOHNSON, SYLVESTER W. (SYL)
B.DEC.31,1900 PORTLAND,ORE.

YR	CL	LEA	POS	GP	G	REC
1922	DET	A	P		29	7- 3
1923	DET	A	P		37	12- 7
1924	DET	A	P		29	5- 4
1925	DET	A	P		6	0- 2
1926	STL	N	P		19	0- 3
1927	STL	N	P		2	0- 0
1928	STL	N	P		34	8- 4
1929	STL	N	P		42	13- 7
1930	STL	N	P		32	12-10
1931	STL	N	P		19	1- 1
1932	STL	N	P		32	5-14
1933	STL	N	P		35	3- 3
1934	CIN	N	P		2	0- 0
	PHI	N	P		42	5- 9
1935	PHI	N	P		37	10- 8
1936	PHI	N	P		39	5- 7
1937	PHI	N	P		22	2-10
1938	PHI	N	P		22	2- 7
1939	PHI	N	P		22	8- 8
1940	PHI	N	P		17	2- 2
	BRTR				542	112-117

JOHNSON, THOMAS G.
B.SCRANTON,PA.

YR	CL	LEA	POS	GP	G	REC
1897	PHI	N	P		5	0- 2
1899	NY	N	P		1	0- 0
	BRTR				6	0- 2

JOHNSON, THOMAS RAYMOND (TOM)
B.APR.2,1951 ST.PAUL,MINN.

YR	CL	LEA	POS	GP	G	REC
1974	MIN	A	/P		4	2- 0
1975	MIN	A	P		18	1- 2
1976	MIN	A	P		18	3- 1
1977	MIN	A	P		71	16- 7
1978	MIN	A	P		18	1- 4
	BRTR				129	23-14

JOHNSON, TIMOTHY EVALD (TIM)
B.JULY 22,1949 GRAND FORKS,N.D.

YR	CL	LEA	POS	GP	G	REC
1973	MIL	A	*S		136	.213
1974	MIL	A	S-2/3-O		93	.245
1975	MIL	A	2-3-S/1		38	.141
1976	MIL	A	*2-3/1-S		105	.275
1977	MIL	A	2/S-3-O		30	.061
1978	MIL	A	/S		3	.000
	TOR	A	S-2		68	.241
	BLTR				473	.226

JOHNSON, VICTOR OSCAR (VIC)
B.AUG.3,1920 EAU CLAIRE,WIS.

YR	CL	LEA	POS	GP	G	REC
1944	BOS	A	P		2	0- 3
1945	BOS	A	P		26	6- 4
1946	CLE	A	P		9	0- 1
	BRTL				42	6- 8

YR CL LEA POS   GP   G   REC

JOHNSON, WALTER PERRY (BARNEY)
OR (THE BIG TRAIN)
B.NOV.6,1887 HUMBOLDT,KAN.
D.DEC.10,1946 WASHINGTON,D.C.

YR	CL	LEA	POS	GP	G	REC
1907	WAS	A	P		14	5- 9
1908	WAS	A	P		36	14-14
1909	WAS	A	P		40	13-25
1910	WAS	A	P		45	25-17
1911	WAS	A	P	40	42	25-13
1912	WAS	A	P	50	53	32-12
1913	WAS	A	P	48	51	36- 7
1914	WAS	A	P	51	54	28-18
1915	WAS	A	P	47	64	27-13
1916	WAS	A	P	48	59	25-20
1917	WAS	A	P	47	57	23-16
1918	WAS	A	P	39	65	23-13
1919	WAS	A	P	39	56	20-14
1920	WAS	A	P	21	35	8-10
1921	WAS	A	P	35	38	17-14
1922	WAS	A	P	41	43	15-16
1923	WAS	A	P		42	17-12
1924	WAS	A	P	38	39	23- 7
1925	WAS	A	P	30	36	20- 7
1926	WAS	A	P	33	35	15-16
1927	WAS	A	P	18	26	5- 6
		BRTR		802	930	416-279

NON-PLAYING MANAGER
WAS[A] 1929-32; CLE[A] 1933-35

JOHNSON, WILLIAM LAWRENCE
B.OCT.18,1892 CHICAGO,ILL.
D.NOV.3,1950 LOS ANGELES,CAL.

YR	CL	LEA	POS	GP	G	REC
1916	PHI	A	O		4	.267
1917	PHI	A	O		48	.174
		BLTR			52	.185

JOHNSON, WILLIAM RUSSELL (BULL)
B.AUG.30,1918 MONTCLAIR,N.J.

YR	CL	LEA	POS	GP	G	REC
1943	NY	A	3		155	.280
1946	NY	A	3		85	.260
1947	NY	A	3		132	.285
1948	NY	A	3		127	.294
1949	NY	A	1-2-3		113	.249
1950	NY	A	1-3		108	.260
1951	NY	A	3		15	.300
	STL	N	3		124	.262
1952	STL	N	3		94	.252
1953	STL	N	3		11	.200
		BRTR			964	.271

JOHNSON, WILLIAM T. (SLEEPY BILL)
B.CHESTER,PA.
D.1921

YR	CL	LEA	POS	GP	G	REC
1884	KEY	U	O		1	.000
1887	IND	N	O		11	.190
1890	BAL	AA	O		24	.354
1891	BAL	AA	O		127	.269
1892	BAL	N	O		4	.133
		BLTL			167	.264

JOHNSTON, JAMES HARLE
B.DEC.10,1889 CLEVELAND,TENN.
D.FEB.14,1967 CHATTANOOGA,TENN.

YR	CL	LEA	POS	GP	G	REC
1911	CHI	A	O		1	.000
1914	CHI	N	O		50	.228
1916	BRO	N	O		118	.252
1917	BRO	N	O		103	.270
1918	BRO	N	1-2-3-O		123	.281
1919	BRO	N	1-2-5-O		117	.261
1920	BRO	N	3		155	.291
1921	BRO	N	3		152	.325
1922	BRO	N	2-S-3		138	.319
1923	BRO	N	2-S-3		151	.325
1924	BRO	N	1-2-S-3-O		86	.298
1925	BRO	N	1-S-3-O		123	.297
1926	BOS	N	3-O		23	.246
	NY	N	O		37	.232
		BRTR			1377	.294

JOHNSTON, JOHN THOMAS
B.MAR.28,1890 LONGVIEW,TEX.
D.MAR.7,1940 SAN DIEGO,CAL.

YR	CL	LEA	POS	GP	G	REC
1913	STL	A	O		09	.226
		BLTR				

JOHNSTON, REX DAVID
B.NOV.6,1937 COLTON,CAL.

YR	CL	LEA	POS	GP	G	REC
1964	PIT	N	O		14	.000
		BBTR				

JOHNSTON, RICHARD FREDERICK
B.APR.6,1863 KINGSTON,N.Y.
D.APR.4,1934 DETROIT,MICH.

YR	CL	LEA	POS	GP	G	REC
1884	RIC	AA	S-O		39	.286
1885	BOS	N	O		26	.238
1886	BOS	N	O		109	.239
1887	BOS	N	O		124	.283
1888	BOS	N	O		135	.295
1889	BOS	N	O		131	.228
1890	BOS	P	O		2	.111
	NY	N	O		75	.257
1891	CIN	AA	O		99	.219
		BRTR			740	.256

JOHNSTON, WHEELER ROGER (DOC)
B.SEPT.9,1887 CLEVELAND,TENN.
D.FEB.17,1961 CHATTANOOGA,TENN.

YR	CL	LEA	POS	GP	G	REC
1909	CIN	N	1		3	.000
1912	CLE	A	1		43	.280
1913	CLE	A	1		133	.255
1914	CLE	A	1		103	.244
1915	PIT	N	1		147	.265
1916	PIT	N	1		114	.213
1918	CLE	A	1		74	.227
1919	CLE	A	1		102	.305
1920	CLE	A	1		147	.292
1921	CLE	A	1		118	.297
1922	PHI	A	1		71	.260
		BLTL			1055	.274

JOHNSTON, WILFRED IVY (FRED)
B.JULY 9,1900 PINEVILLE,N.C.
D.JULY 14,1959 TYLER,TEX.

YR	CL	LEA	POS	GP	G	REC
1924	BRO	N	2		4	.250
		BRTR				

JOHNSTONE, JOHN WILLIAM (JAY)
B.NOV.20,1945 MANCHESTER,ENN.

YR	CL	LEA	POS	GP	G	REC
1966	CAL	A	O		61	.264
1967	CAL	A	O		79	.209
1968	CAL	A	O		41	.261
1969	CAL	A	*O		148	.270
1970	CAL	A	*O		119	.238
1971	CHI	A	*O		124	.260
1972	CHI	A	O		113	.188
1973	OAK	A	/O-2		23	.107
1974	PHI	N	O		64	.295
1975	PHI	N	*O		122	.329
1976	PHI	N	*O/1		129	.318
1977	PHI	N	O-1		112	.284
1978	PHI	N	/1-O		35	.179
	NY	A	O		36	.262
		BLTR			1206	.267

JOINER, ROY MERRILL (POP)
B.OCT.30,1906 RED BLUFF,CAL.

YR	CL	LEA	POS	GP	G	REC
1934	CHI	N	P		20	0- 1
1935	CHI	N	P		2	0- 0
1940	NY	N	P		30	3- 2
		BLTL			52	3- 3

JOK, STANLEY EDWARD
(STAN) OR (TUCKER)
B.MAY 3,1926 BUFFALO,N.Y.
D.MAR.6,1972 BUFFALO,N.Y.

YR	CL	LEA	POS	GP	G	REC
1954	PHI	N	H		3	.000
	CHI	A	3		3	.167
1955	CHI	A	3-O		6	.250
		BRTR			12	.158

JOLLEY, SMEAD POWELL (SMEAD)
(GUINEA) OR (SMUDGE)
B.JAN.14,1902 WESSON,ARK.

YR	CL	LEA	POS	GP	G	REC
1930	CHI	A	O		152	.313
1931	CHI	A	O		54	.300
1932	CHI	A	O		12	.357
	BOS	A	O		137	.309
1933	BOS	A	O		118	.282
		BLTR			473	.305

JOLLY, DAVID (DAVE) OR (GABBY)
B.OCT.14,1924 STONY POINT,N.C.
D.MAY 27,1963 DURHAM,N.C.

YR	CL	LEA	POS	GP	G	REC
1953	MIL	N	P		24	0- 1
1954	MIL	N	P	47	48	11- 6
1955	MIL	N	P		36	2- 3
1956	MIL	N	P		29	2- 3
1957	MIL	N	P		23	1- 1
		BRTR		159	160	16-14

JONES
B.SYRACUSE,N.Y.

YR	CL	LEA	POS	GP	G	REC
1882	BAL	AA	C-O		4	.067
1884	KEY	U	C-O		4	.154
					8	.107

JONES, ALBERT EDWARD
(COWBOY) OR (BRONCO)
B.AUG.23,1874 GOLDEN,COLO.
D.FEB.9,1958 INGLEWOOD,CAL.

YR	CL	LEA	POS	GP	G	REC
1898	CLE	N	P		8	4- 4
1899	STL	N	P		14	6- 5
1900	STL	N	P		38	13-20
1901	STL	N	P		10	2- 6
		BLTL			70	25-35

JONES, ALEXANDER H.
B.1867 BRADFORD,PA.

YR	CL	LEA	POS	GP	G	REC
1889	PIT	N	P		1	1- 0
1892	LOU	N	P		18	6-12
	WAS	N	P		7	1- 2
1894	PHI	N	P		1	1- 0
1903	DET	A	P		2	0- 2
		TL			29	9-16

JONES, ARTHUR LENOX
B.FEB.7,1907 KERSHAW,S.C.

YR	CL	LEA	POS	GP	G	REC
1932	BRO	N	P		1	0- 0
		BRTR				

JONES, CARROLL ELMER (DEACON)
B.DEC.20,1892 ARCADIA,KAN.
D.DEC.28,1952 PITTSBURG,KAN.

YR	CL	LEA	POS	GP	G	REC
1916	DET	A	P		1	0- 0
1917	DET	A	P		24	4- 4
1918	DET	A	P	19	22	2- 2
		BRTR		44	47	6- 6

JONES, CHARLES C. (CASEY)
B.JUNE 2,1876 BUTLER,PA.
D.APR.2,1947 LUTSEN,MINN.

YR	CL	LEA	POS	GP	G	REC
1901	BOS	A	O		10	.119
1904	CHI	A	O		5	.235
1905	WAS	A	O		142	.208
1906	WAS	A	O		131	.241
1907	WAS	A	O		121	.265
1908	STL	A	O		74	.232
		TR			483	.233

JONES, CHARLES F.
B.NEW YORK,N.Y.

YR	CL	LEA	POS	GP	G	REC
1884	BRO	AA	2-3		24	.188
1885	MET	AA	1		1	.250
					25	.191

JONES, CHARLES LEANDER (BUMPUS)
B.JAN.1,1870 CEDARVILLE,OHIO
D.JUNE 25,1938 XENIA,OHIO

YR	CL	LEA	POS	GP	G	REC
1892	CIN	N	P		1	1- 0
1893	CIN	N	P		6	1- 3
	NY	N	P		4	0- 1
		BRTR			11	2- 4

JONES, CHARLES WESLEY (BABY)
[REAL NAME BENJAMIN WESLEY RIPPAY]
B.APR.30,1850 ALAMANCE CO.,N.C.

YR	CL	LEA	POS	GP	G	REC
1873	MAR	NA	O		1	-
1874	BAL	NA	C-O		5	-
1875	WES	NA	O		12	-
	HAR	NA	O		1	.000
1876	CIN	N	O		64	.279
1877	CIN	N	1-O		20	.329
	CHI	N	O		2	.375
1878	CIN	N	O		35	.336
1879	BOS	N	O		62	.297
1880	BOS	N	O		64	.297
1883	CIN	AA	O		85	.285
1884	CIN	AA	O		113	.322
1885	CIN	AA	O		112	.327
1886	CIN	AA	O		127	.274
1887	CIN	AA	O		41	.374
	MET	AA	O		63	.302
1888	KC	AA	O		6	.250
		BRTR			896	-

JONES, CLARENCE WOODROW
B.NOV.7,1941 ZANESVILLE,OHIO

YR	CL	LEA	POS	GP	G	REC
1967	CHI	N	O-1		53	.252
1968	CHI	N	/1		5	.000
		BLTL			58	.248

JONES, CLEON JOSEPH
B.AUG.4,1942 PLATEAU,ALA.

YR	CL	LEA	POS	GP	G	REC
1963	NY	N	O		6	.133
1965	NY	N	O		30	.149
1966	NY	N	*O	139	141	.275
1967	NY	N	*O		129	.246
1968	NY	N	*O		147	.297
1969	NY	N	*O-1		137	.340
1970	NY	N	*O		134	.277
1971	NY	N	*O		136	.319
1972	NY	N	O-1		106	.245
1973	NY	N	O		92	.260
1974	NY	N	O		124	.282
1975	NY	N	O		21	.240
1976	CHI	A	/O		12	.200
		BRTL			1213	.281

JONES, COBURN DYAS (COBE)
B.AUG.21,1907 DENVER,COLO.
D.JUNE 3,1969 DENVER,COLO.

YR	CL	LEA	POS	GP	G	REC
1928	PIT	N	S		1	.500
1929	PIT	N	S		25	.254
		BBTR			26	.262

JONES, DALE ELDON (NUBS)
B.DEC.17,1918 MARQUETTE,NEB.

YR	CL	LEA	POS	GP	G	REC
1941	PHI	N	P		2	0- 1
		BRTR				

JONES, DANIEL ALBION (JUMPING JACK)
B.OCT.23,1860 LITCHFIELD,CONN.
D.OCT.19,1936 WALLINGFORD,CONN.

YR	CL	LEA	POS	GP	G	REC
1883	DET	N	P-O		11	6- 4
						.243
	ATH	AA	P		7	5- 2
		TR			18	11- 6
						.197

YR CL LEA POS GP G REC

JONES, DAVID JEFFERSON
(DAVY) OR (KANGAROO)
B.JUNE 30,1880 CAMBRIA,WIS.
D.MAR.31,1972 MANKATO,MINN.
1901 MIL A O 14 .169
1902 STL A O 14 .224
CHI N O 63 .310
1903 CHI N O 130 .282
1904 CHI N O 97 .244
1906 DET A O 84 .260
1907 DET A O 126 .273
1908 DET A O 56 .207
1909 DET A O 69 .279
1910 DET A O 113 .265
1911 DET A O 98 .273
1912 DET A O 97 .294
1913 CHI A O 12 .288
1914 PIT F O 97 .272
1915 PIT F O 14 .327
1918 DET A O 2 .000
BLTR 1086 .270

JONES, DECATUR POINDEXTER (DICK)
B.MAY 22,1902 MEADVILLE,MISS.
1926 WAS A P 5 2- 1
1927 WAS A P 2 0- 0
BLTR 7 2- 1

JONES, EARL LESLIE (LEFTY)
B.JUNE 11,1919 FRESNO,CAL.
1945 STL A P 10 0- 0
BLTL

JONES, ELIJAH ALBERT
B.JAN.27,1882 OXFORD,MICH.
D.APR.28,1943 PONTIAC,MICH.
1907 DET A P 4 0- 2
1909 DET A P 2 1- 1
BRTR 6 1- 3

JONES, FIELDER ALLISON
B.AUG.13,1874 SHINGLEHOUSE,PA.
D.MAR.13,1934 PORTLAND,ORE.
1896 BRO N O 102 .353
1897 BRO N O 135 .322
1898 BRO N O 147 .304
1899 BRO N O 95 .286
1900 BRO N O 136 .309
1901 CHI A O 133 .325
1902 CHI A O 135 .318
1903 CHI A O 137 .304
1904 CHI A M-O 150 .245
1905 CHI A M-O 153 .245
1906 CHI A M-O 144 .230
1907 CHI A M-O 154 .261
1908 CHI A M-O 149 .253
1914 STL F M-H 5 .333
1915 STL F M-O 5 .000
BLTR 1780 .287
NON-PLAYING MANAGER STL[A] 1916-18

JONES, FRANK M.
B.DULUTH,MINN.
1884 DET N 2-S-O 34 .209

JONES, GARETH HOWELL (GARY)
B.JUNE 12,1945 HUNTINGTON PARK,CAL.
1970 NY A /P 2 0- 0
1971 NY A P 12 0- 0
BLTL 14 0- 0

JONES, GORDON BASSETT
B.APR.2,1930 PORTLAND,ORE.
1954 STL N P 11 4- 4
1955 STL N P 15 1- 4
1956 STL N P 5 0- 2
1957 NY N P 10 0- 1
1958 SF N P 11 3- 1
1959 SF N P 31 3- 2
1960 BAL A P 29 1- 1
1961 BAL A P 3 0- 0
1962 KC A P 21 3- 2
1964 HOU N P 34 0- 1
1965 HOU N /P 1 0- 0
BRTR 171 15-18

JONES, GROVER WILLIAM (DEACON)
B.APR.18,1934 WHITE PLAINS,N.Y.
1962 CHI A 1 18 .321
1963 CHI A 1 17 .188
1966 CHI A /H 5 .400
BLTR 40 .286

JONES, HAROLD MARION (HAL)
B.APR.9,1936 LOUISIANA,MO.
1961 CLE A 1 12 .171
1962 CLE A 1 5 .313
BRTR 17 .216

JONES, HENRY M. (BALDY)
B.CADILLAC,MICH.
1890 PIT N P 4 2- 2

JONES, HOWARD (COTTON)
B.MAR.1,1897 IRWIN,PA.
D.JULY 15,1972 JEANETTE,PA.
1921 STL N O 3 .000
BLTL

JONES, JAMES DALTON (DALTON)
B.DEC.10,1943 MC COMB,MISS.
1964 BOS A 2-S-3 118 .230
1965 BOS A 3/2 112 .270
1966 BOS A 2/3 115 .234
1967 BOS A 3-2/1 89 .289
1968 BOS A 1-2/3 111 .234
1969 BOS A 1/3-2 111 .220
1970 DET A 2-3-1 89 .220
1971 DET A O-3/1-2 83 .254
1972 DET A /H 7 .000
TEX A 3-2/1-O 72 .159
BLTR 907 .235

JONES, JAMES MURRELL (JAKE)
B.NOV.23,1920 EPPS,LA.
1941 CHI A 1 3 .000
1942 CHI A 1 7 .150
1946 CHI A 1 24 .266
1947 CHI A 1 45 .240
BOS A 1 109 .235
1948 BOS A 1 36 .200
BRTR 224 .229

JONES, JAMES TILFORD (SHERIFF)
B.DEC.25,1876 LONDON,KY.
D.MAY 6,1953 LONDON,KY.
1897 LOU N P 2 0- 0
1901 NY N P-O 1 21 0- 1
.209
1902 NY N O 65 .236
3 88 0- 1
.229

JONES, JESSE FRANK (BROADWAY)
B.NOV.15,1898 MILLSBORO,DEL.
D.SEPT.7,1977 LEWES,DEL.
1923 PHI N P 3 0- 0
BRTR

JONES, JOHN PAUL (ADMIRAL)
B.AUG.25,1892 ARCADIA,LA.
1919 NY N P 2 0- 0
1920 BOS N P 3 1- 0
BRTR 5 1- 0

JONES, JOHN JOSEPH (BINKY)
B.JULY 11,1899 ST.LOUIS,MO.
D.MAY 13,1961 ST.LOUIS,MO.
1924 BRO N S 10 .108
BRTR

JONES, JOHN WILLIAM (SKINS)
B.MAY 13,1901 COATESVILLE,PA.
D.NOV.3,1956 BALTIMORE,MD.
1923 PHI A O 1 .250
1932 PHI A O 4 .167
BLTL 5 .200

JONES, KENNETH FREDERICK (BROADWAY)
B.APR.13,1904 DOVER,N.J.
1924 DET A P 1 0- 0
1930 BOS N P 8 0- 1
BRTR 9 0- 1

JONES, MACK (MACK THE KNIFE)
B.NOV.6,1938 ALANTA,GA.
1961 MIL N O 28 .231
1962 MIL N O 91 .255
1963 MIL N O 93 .219
1965 MIL N *O 143 .262
1966 ATL N *O/1 118 .264
1967 ATL N *O 140 .253
1968 CIN N O 103 .252
1969 MON N *O 135 .270
1970 MON N O 108 .240
1971 MON N O 43 .165
BLTR 1002 .252

JONES, MAURICE MORRIS (RED)
B.NOV.2,1914 TIMPSON,TEX.
1940 STL N O 12 .091
BLTR

JONES, MICHAEL
B.HAMILTON,ONT.,CANADA
D.MAR.24,1894 HAMILTON,ONT.,CAN
1890 LOU AA P 4 4- 0

JONES, ODELL
B.JAN.13,1953 TULARE,CAL.
1975 PIT N /P 2 0- 0
1977 PIT N P 34 3- 7
1978 PIT N /P 3 2- 0
BRTR 39 5- 7

JONES, OSCAR WINFIELD (FLIP FLAP)
B.JAN.21,1879 LONDON GROVE,PA.
D.OCT.8,1946 PERKASIE,PA.
1903 BRO N P 38 19-14
1904 BRO N P 46 18-26
1905 BRO N P 29 30 7-14
BRTR 113 114 44-54

JONES, PERCY LEE
B.OCT.28,1899 HARWOOD,TEX.
1920 CHI N P 4 0- 0
1921 CHI N P 32 3- 5
1922 CHI N P 44 8- 9
1925 CHI N P 28 6- 6
1926 CHI N P 30 12- 7
1927 CHI N P 30 7- 8
1928 CHI N P 39 10- 6
1929 BOS N P 35 36 7-15
1930 PIT N P 9 0- 1
BRTL 251 252 53-57

JONES, RANDALL LEO (RANDY)
B.JAN.12,1950 FULLERTON,CAL.
1973 SD N P 20 7- 6
1974 SD N P 40 46 8-22
1975 SD N P 37 40 20-12
1976 SD N P 40 22-14
1977 SD N P 27 28 6-12
1978 SD N P 37 38 13-14
BRTL 201 212 76-80

JONES, ROBERT OLIVER (BOB)
B.OCT.11,1949 ELKTON,MD.
1974 TEX A /O 2 .000
1975 TEX A /O 9 .091
1976 CAL A O 78 .211
1977 CAL A /H 14 .176
BLTL 103 .196

JONES, ROBERT WALTER (DUCKY)
B.DEC.2,1889 CLAYTON,CAL.
D.AUG.30,1964 SAN DIEGO,CAL.
1917 DET A 2 46 .156
1918 DET A 3 75 .275
1919 DET A 3 127 .260
1920 DET A 3 81 .249
1921 DET A 3 141 .303
1922 DET A 3 124 .257
1923 DET A 3 100 .250
1924 DET A 3 110 .272
1925 DET A 3 50 .236
BLTR 854 .265

JONES, RUPPERT SANDERSON
B.MAR.12,1955 DALLAS,TEX.
1976 KC A O 28 .216
1977 SEA A *O 160 .263
1978 SEA A *O 129 .235
BLTL 317 .249

JONES, RYERSON L. (JACK)
(RI) OR (ANGEL SLEEVES)
B.CINCINNATI,OHIO
1883 LOU AA S-O 2 .000
1884 CIN U S 55 .265
TR 57 .258

JONES, SAMUEL (SAM)
OR (TOOTHPICK SAM)
B.DEC.14,1925 STEWARTSVILLE,OHIO
D.NOV.5,1971 MORGANTOWN,W.VA.
1951 CLE A P 2 0- 1
1952 CLE A P 14 2- 3
1955 CHI N P 36 14-20
1956 CHI N P 33 9-14
1957 STL N P 28 12- 9
1958 STL N P 35 14-13
1959 SF N P 50 21-15
1960 SF N P 39 18-14
1961 SF N P 37 8- 8
1962 DET A P 30 2- 4
1963 STL N P 11 2- 0
1964 BAL A P 7 0- 0
BRTR 322 102-101

JONES, SAMUEL POND (SAD SAM)
B.JULY 26,1892 WOODSFIELD,OHIO
D.JULY 6,1966 BARNESVILLE,OHIO
1914 CLE A P 1 0- 0
1915 CLE A P 48 3- 8
1916 BOS A P 12 13 0- 1
1917 BOS A P 9 0- 1
1918 BOS A P 24 16- 5
1919 BOS A P 35 13-20
1920 BOS A P 37 44 13-16
1921 BOS A P 40 43 23-16
1922 NY A P 45 13-13
1923 NY A P 39 21- 8
1924 NY A P 36 9- 6
1925 NY A P-O 43 46 15-21
.162
1926 NY A P 39 44 9- 8
1927 STL A P 30 32 8-14
1928 WAS A P 30 37 17- 7
1929 WAS A P 24 28 9- 9
1930 WAS A P 25 30 15- 7
1931 WAS A P 25 30 9-10
1932 CHI A P 30 39 10-15
1933 CHI A P 27 37 10-12
1934 CHI A P 27 31 8-12
1935 CHI A P 21 22 8- 7
BRTR 647 713 229-216
.197

YR	CL LEA POS	GP	G	REC

JONES, SHELDON LESLIE (AVAILABLE)
B.FEB.23,1922 TECUMSEH,NEB.

YR	CL LEA POS	GP	G	REC
1946	NY N P	6	1- 2	
1947	NY N P	15	2- 2	
1948	NY N P	55	16- 8	
1949	NY N P	42	15-12	
1950	NY N P	40	13-16	
1951	NY N P	41	6-11	
1952	BOS N P	39	1- 4	
1953	CHI N P	22	0- 2	
	BRTR	260	54-57	

JONES, SHERMAN JARVIS (ROADBLOCK)
B.FEB.10,1935 WINTON,N.C.

1960	SF N P	16	1- 1	
1961	CIN N P	24	1- 1	
1962	NY N P	8	0- 4	
	BLTR	48	2- 6	

JONES, STEVEN HOWELL (STEVE)
B.APR.22,1941 HUNTINGTON PARK,CAL.

1967	CHI A P	11	2- 2	
1968	WAS A /P	7	1- 2	
1969	KC A P	20	2- 3	
	BLTL	38	5- 7	

JONES, THOMAS
B.JAN.22,1877 HONESDALE,PA.
D.JUNE 21,1923

1902	BAL A 1-2	37	.283	
1904	STL A 1-2	156	.241	
1905	STL A 1	135	.242	
1906	STL A 1	144	.252	
1907	STL A 1	155	.250	
1908	STL A 1	155	.248	
1909	STL A 1	97	.254	
	DET A 1	44	.271	
1910	DET A 1	135	.255	
	BRTR	1058	.240	

JONES, THOMAS FREDRICK (RICK)
B.APR.16,1955 JACKSONVILLE,FLA<

1976	BOS A P	24	5- 3	
1977	SEA A P	10	1- 4	
1978	SEA A /P	3	0- 2	
	BLTL	37	6- 9	

JONES, TIMMOTHY BYRON (TIM)
B.JAN.24,1954 SACRAMENTO,CAL.

1977	PIT N /P	3	1- 0	
	BBTR			

JONES, VERNAL LEROY (NIPPY)
B.JUNE 29,1925 LOS ANGELES,CAL.

1946	STL N 2	16	.333	
1947	STL N 2-0	23	.247	
1948	STL N 1	132	.254	
1949	STL N 1	110	.300	
1950	STL N 1	13	.231	
1951	STL N 1	80	.263	
1952	PHI N 1	8	.167	
1957	MIL N 1-0	30	.266	
	BRTR	412	.267	

JONES, WILLIAM DENNIS (MIDGET)
B.APR.8,1887 HARTLAND,N.B.,CAN.
D.OCT.10,1946 BOSTON,MASS.

1911	BOS N 0	18	.216	
1912	BOS N 0	2	.500	
	BLTR	20	.226	

JONES, WILLIAM RODERICK (TEX)
B.AUG.4,1885 MARION,KAN.
D.FEB.26,1938 WICHITA,KAN.

1911	CHI A 1	9	.193	
	BRTR			

JONES, WILLIE EDWARD (PUDDIN HEAD)
B.AUG.16,1925 DILLON,S.C.

1947	PHI N 3	18	.226	
1948	PHI N 3	17	.333	
1949	PHI N 3	149	.245	
1950	PHI N 3	157	.267	
1951	PHI N 3	148	.285	
1952	PHI N 3	147	.250	
1953	PHI N 3	149	.225	
1954	PHI N 3	142	.271	
1955	PHI N 3	146	.258	
1956	PHI N 3	149	.277	
1957	PHI N 3	133	.218	
1958	PHI N 1-3	118	.271	
1959	PHI N 3	47	.269	
	CLE A 3	11	.222	
	CIN N 3	72	.249	
1960	CIN N 2-3	79	.268	
1961	CIN N 3	9	.000	
	BRTR	1691	.258	

JONNARD, CLARENCE JAMES (BUBBER)
B.NOV.23,1897 NASHVILLE,TENN.
D.AUG.23,1977 NEW YORK,N.Y.

1920	CHI A C	2	.000	
1922	PIT N C	10	.238	
1926	PHI N C	19	.118	
1927	PHI N C	53	.294	
1929	STL N C	18	.097	
1935	PHI N C	1	.000	
	BRTR	103	.230	

JONNARD, CLAUDE ALFRED
B.NOV.23,1897 NASHVILLE,TENN.
D.AUG.27,1959 NASHVILLE,TENN.

1921	NY N P	1	0- 0	
1922	NY N P	33	6- 1	
1923	NY N P	45	4- 3	
1924	NY N P	34	4- 5	
1926	STL A P	12	0- 2	
1929	CIN N P	12	0- 1	
	BRTR	137	14-12	

JOOST, EDWIN DAVID (EDDIE)
B.JUNE 5,1916 SAN FRANCISCO,CAL

1936	CIN N 2-S	13	.154	
1937	CIN N 2	6	.083	
1939	CIN N 2-S	42	.252	
1940	CIN N 2-S-3	88	.216	
1941	CIN N 1-2-S-3	152	.293	
1942	CIN N 2-S	142	.224	
1943	BOS N 2-S-3	124	.185	
1945	BOS N 2-3	35	.248	
1947	PHI A S	151	.206	
1948	PHI A S	135	.250	
1949	PHI A S	144	.263	
1950	PHI A S	131	.233	
1951	PHI A S	140	.289	
1952	PHI A S	146	.244	
1953	PHI A S	51	.249	
1954	PHI A M-2-S-3	19	.362	
1955	BOS A 2-S-3	55	.193	
	BRTR	1574	.239	

JORDAN, ADOLF OTTO (DUTCH)
B.JAN.5,1880 PITTSBURGH,PA.
D.DEC.23,1972 W.ALLEGHENY,PA.

1903	BRO N 2-3	77	.236	
1904	BRO N 2	89	.179	
	BRTR	162	.208	

JORDAN, BAXTER BYERLY (BUCK)
B.JAN.16,1907 COOLEEMEE,N.C.

1927	NY N H	5	.200	
1928	NY N N	2	.500	
1931	WAS A 1	9	.222	
1932	BOS N 1	49	.321	
1933	BOS N 1	152	.286	
1934	BOS N 1	124	.311	
1935	BOS N 1-3-0	130	.279	
1936	BOS N 1	138	.323	
1937	BOS N 1	8	.250	
	CIN N H	98	.282	
1938	CIN N H	9	.286	
	PH 1-3	87	.300	
	BLTL	811	.299	

JORDAN, CHARLES T. (KID)
B.OCT.4,1871 BALTIMORE,MD.
D.JUNE 1,1928 HAZLETON,PA.

1896	PHI N P	1	0- 0	

JORDAN, HARRY J.
B.TITUSVILLE,PA.

1894	PIT N P	1	1- 0	
1895	PIT N P	2	0- 2	
		3	1- 2	

JORDAN, JAMES WILLIAM (LORD)
B.JAN.13,1908 TUCAPAU,S.C.
D.DEC.4,1957 CHARLOTTE,N.C.

1933	BRO N 2-S	70	.256	
1934	BRO N 2-S	97	.266	
1935	BRO N 2-S-3	94	.278	
1936	BRO N 2	115	.234	
	BRTR	376	.257	

JORDAN, MICHAEL HENRY (MITTY)
B.FEB.7,1863 LAWRENCE,MASS.
D.SEPT.25,1940 LAWRENCE,MASS.

1890	PIT N 0	37	.096	

JORDAN, MILTON MIGNOT
B.MAY 24,1927 MINERAL SPRINGS,PA.

1953	DET A P	8	0- 1	
	BRTR			

JORDAN, NILES CHAPMAN
B.DEC.1,1925 LYMAN,WASH.

1951	PHI N P	5	2- 3	
1952	CIN N P	3	0- 1	
	BLTR	8	2- 4	

JORDAN, RAYMOND WILLIS (RIP) OR (LANKY)
B.SEPT.28,1889 PORTLAND,ME.
D.JUNE 5,1960 MERIDEN,CONN.

1912	CHI A P	1	0- 0	
1919	WAS A P	4	0- 0	
	BLTR	5	0- 0	

JORDAN, THOMAS JEFFERSON
B.SEPT.5,1919 LAWTON,OKLA.

1944	CHI A C	14	.267	
1946	CHI A C	10	.267	
	CLE A C	14	.200	
1948	STL A H	1	.000	
	BRTR	39	.240	

JORDAN, TIMOTHY JOSEPH
B.FEB.14,1879 NEW YORK,N.Y.
D.SEPT.13,1949 BRONX,N.Y.

1901	WAS A 1	5	.250	
	BAL A 1	1	.000	
1902	BAL A 0	1	.000	
1903	NY A 1	2	.125	
1906	BRO N 1	126	.262	
1907	BRO N 1	143	.274	
1908	BRO N 1	146	.247	
1909	BRO N 1	95	.273	
1910	BRO N H	5	.200	
	BLTL	524	.261	

JORGENS, ARNDT LUDWIG (ART)
B.MAY 18,1905 MODUM,NORWAY

1929	NY A C	18	.324	
1930	NY A C	16	.367	
1931	NY A C	46	.270	
1932	NY A C	56	.219	
1933	NY A C	21	.220	
1934	NY A C	58	.208	
1935	NY A C	36	.238	
1936	NY A C	31	.273	
1937	NY A C	13	.130	
1938	NY A C	9	.235	
1939	NY A C	3	.000	
	BRTR	307	.238	

JORGENS, ORVILLE EDWARD
B.JUNE 4,1908 ROCKFORD,ILL.

1935	PHI N P	53	10-15	
1936	PHI N P	39	8- 8	
1937	PHI N P	52	3- 4	
	BRTR	144	21-27	

JORGENSEN, CARL (PINKY)
B.NOV.21,1914 LATON,CAL.

1937	CIN N 0	6	.286	
	BRTR			

JORGENSEN, JOHN DONALD (SPIDER)
B.NOV.3,1919 FOLSOM,CAL.

1947	BRO N 3	129	.274	
1948	BRO N 3	31	.300	
1949	BRO N 3	53	.269	
1950	BRO N 3	2	.000	
	NY N 3	24	.135	
1951	NY N 3-0	28	.235	
	BLTR	267	.266	

JORGENSEN, MICHAEL (MIKE)
B.AUG.16,1948 PASSAIC,N.J.

1968	NY N /1	8	.143	
1970	NY N 1-0	76	.195	
1971	NY N 0/1	45	.220	
1972	MON N 1-0	113	.231	
1973	MON N *1-0	138	.230	
1974	MON N 1-0	131	.310	
1975	MON N *1/0	144	.261	
1976	MON N 1-0	125	.254	
1977	MON N /1	19	.200	
	OAK A 1-0	66	.246	
1978	TEX A 1/0	96	.196	
	BLTL	961	.246	

JOSEPH, RICARDO EMELINDO (RICK)
B.AUG.24,1939 SAN PEDRO DE
MACORIS,D.R.

1964	KC A 1-3	17	.222	
1967	PHI N 1	17	.220	
1968	PHI N 3-1/0	66	.219	
1969	PHI N 3-1/2	99	.273	
1970	PHI N 0-1/3	71	.227	
	BRTR	270	.243	

JOSEPHS, JOSEPH EMLEY
[SEE JOSEPH EMLEY BORDEN]

JOSEPHSON, DUANE CHARLES
B.JUNE 3,1942 NEW HAMPTON,IOWA

1965	CHI A /C	4	.111	
1966	CHI A C	11	.237	
1967	CHI A C	62	.238	
1968	CHI A *C	128	.247	
1969	CHI A C	52	.241	
1970	CHI A C	96	.316	
1971	BOS A C	91	.245	
1972	BOS A 1/C	26	.268	
	BRTR	470	.258	

JOSHUA, VON EVERETT
B.MAY 1,1948 OAKLAND,CAL.

1969	LA N /0	14	.250	
1970	LA N 0	72	.266	
1971	LA N /0	11	.000	
1973	LA N 0	75	.252	
1974	LA N 0	81	.234	
1975	SF N *0	129	.318	
1976	SF N 0	42	.263	
	MIL A *0	107	.267	
1977	MIL A *0	144	.261	
	BLTL	675	.274	

```
YR   CL LEA POS    GP    G    REC
```

JOSS, ADRIAN (ADDIE)
B.APR.12,1880 JUNEAU,WIS.
D.APR.14,1911 TOLEDO,OHIO
```
1902 CLE A P-1   32   33  17-13
                              .116
1903 CLE A P     32   34  18-13
1904 CLE A P     25   28  14- 8
1905 CLE A P     32   34  19-12
1906 CLE A P     34   36  21- 9
1907 CLE A P          42  27-11
1908 CLE A P          42  24-11
1909 CLE A P          33  14-13
1910 CLE A P     13        5- 5
     BRTR       285  295 159-95
                              .145
```

JOURDAN, THEODORE CHARLES
B.SEPT.5,1895 NEW ORLEANS,LA.
D.SEPT.23,1961 NEW ORLEANS,LA.
```
1916 CHI A H      3        .000
1917 CHI A 1     17        .148
1918 CHI A 1      7        .100
1920 CHI A 1     48        .240
     BLTL        75        .214
```

JOY, ALOYSIUS C. (POP)
B.JUNE 11,1860 WASHINGTON,D.C.
D.JUNE 28,1937 WASHINGTON,D.C.
```
1884 WAS U 1     35        .190
```

JOYCE, MICHAEL
[SEE MICHAEL JOYCE O NEILL]

JOYCE, MICHAEL LEWIS (MIKE)
B.FEB.12,1941 DETROIT,MICH.
```
1962 CHI A P     25        2- 1
1963 CHI A P      6        0- 0
     BRTR        31        2- 1
```

JOYCE, RICHARD EDWARD (DICK)
B.NOV.18,1943 PORTLAND,ME.
```
1965 KC  A /P     5        0- 1
     BLTL
```

JOYCE, ROBERT EMMETT
B.JAN.14,1915 STOCKTON,CAL.
```
1939 PHI A P     30        3- 5
1946 NY  N P     14        3- 4
     BRTR        44        6- 9
```

JOYCE, WILLIAM MICHAEL
(SCRAPPY BILL)
B.SEPT.21,1865 ST.LOUIS,MO.
D.MAY 8,1941 ST.LOUIS,MO.
```
1890 BRO P 3    133        .269
1891 BOS AA 3    65        .317
1892 BRO N 3     97        .249
1894 WAS N 3     98        .344
1895 WAS N 3    128        .308
1896 WAS N 3     80        .309
     NY  N M-3   49        .350
1897 NY  N M-3  110        .305
1898 NY  N M-1  143        .253
     BLTR       903        .293
```

JUDD, RALPH WESLEY
B.DEC.7,1901 PERRYSBURG,OHIO
D.MAY 6,1957 LAPEER,MICH.
```
1927 WAS A P      1        0- 0
1929 NY  N P     18        3- 0
1930 NY  N P      2        0- 0
     BLTR        21        3- 0
```

JUDD, THOMAS WILLIAM OSCAR
(OSCAR) OR (OSSIE)
B.FEB.14,1908 LONDON,ONT.,CAN.
```
1941 BOS A P      7   10   0- 0
1942 BOS A P     31   36   8-10
1943 BOS A P     23   27  11- 6
1944 BOS A P      9   10   1- 1
1945 BOS A P      2        0- 1
     PHI N P     23   27   5- 4
1946 PHI N P     30   46  11-12
1947 PHI N P     32   44   4-15
1948 PHI N P      4        0- 2
     BLTL       161  206  40-51
```

JUDE, FRANK
B.1885 MAHNOHMEN CO.,MINN.
D.MAY 4,1961
```
1906 CIN N O     80        .208
     BRTR
```

JUDGE, JOSEPH IGNATIUS (JOE)
B.MAY 25,1894 BROOKLYN,N.Y.
D.MAR.11,1963 WASHINGTON,D.C.
```
1915 WAS A 1     12        .353
1916 WAS A 1    103        .220
1917 WAS A 1    102        .285
1918 WAS A 1    130        .261
1919 WAS A 1    135        .288
1920 WAS A 1    126        .333
1921 WAS A 1    153        .301
1922 WAS A 1    148        .295
1923 WAS A 1    113        .314
1924 WAS A 1    140        .324
1925 WAS A 1    112        .314
1926 WAS A 1    134        .291
1927 WAS A 1    137        .308
1928 WAS A 1    153        .306
1929 WAS A 1    143        .315
1930 WAS A 1    126        .326
1931 WAS A 1     35        .284
1932 WAS A 1     82        .258
1933 BRO N 1     42        .214
     BOS A 1     34        .208
1934 BOS A 1     10        .333
     BLTL      2170        .298
```

JUDNICH, WALTER FRANKLIN (WALLY)
B.JAN.24,1917 SAN FRANCISCO,CAL
D.JULY 12,1971 GLENDALE,CAL.
```
1940 STL A O    137        .303
1941 STL A O    146        .284
1942 STL A O    132        .313
1946 STL A O    142        .262
1947 STL A 1-O  144        .258
1948 CLE A 1-O   79        .257
1949 PIT N O     10        .229
     BLTL       790        .281
```

JUDSON, HOWARD KOLLS (HOWIE)
B.FEB.16,1926 HEBRON,ILL.
```
1948 CHI A P     40   41   4- 5
1949 CHI A P          26   1-14
1950 CHI A P          46   2- 3
1951 CHI A P          27   5- 6
1952 CHI A P          21   0- 1
1953 CIN N P          10   0- 1
1954 CIN N P          37   5- 7
     BRTR       207  208  17-37
```

JUDY, LYLE LEROY (PUNCH)
B.NOV.15,1913 LAWRENCEVILLE,ILL
```
1935 STL N 2      8        .000
     BRTR
```

JUELICH, JOHN SAMUEL (RED)
B.SEPT.20,1916 ST.LOUIS,MO.
D.DEC.25,1970 ST.LOUIS,MO.
```
1939 PIT N 2     17        .239
     BRTR
```

JUMONVILLE, GEORGE BENEDICT
B.MAY 16,1917 MOBILE,ALA.
```
1940 PHI N S-3   11        .088
1941 PHI N 2-S    6        .429
     BRTR        17        .146
```

JUNGELS, KENNETH PETER (CURLY)
B.JUNE 23,1916 AURORA,ILL.
D.SEPT.4,1975 WEST BEND,WIS.
```
1937 CLE A P      2        0- 0
1938 CLE A P      9        1- 0
1940 CLE A P      2        0- 0
1941 CLE A P      6        0- 0
1942 PIT N P      6    9   0- 0
     BRTR        25   28   1- 0
```

JUREWICZ, MICHAEL ALLEN (MIKE)
B.SEP.20,1945 BUFFALO,N.Y.
```
1965 NY  A /P     2        0- 0
     BBTL
```

JURGES, WILLIAM FREDERICK (BILLY)
B.MAY 9,1908 BRONX,N.Y.
```
1931 CHI N 2-3   88        .201
1932 CHI N S    115        .253
1933 CHI N S    143        .269
1934 CHI N S    100        .246
1935 CHI N S    118        .241
1936 CHI N S    118        .280
1937 CHI N S    129        .298
1938 CHI N S    137        .245
1939 NY  N S    138        .285
1940 NY  N S     63        .252
1941 NY  N S    134        .293
1942 NY  N S    127        .256
1943 NY  N S-3  136        .229
1944 NY  N 2-S-3 85        .211
1945 NY  N S-3   61        .324
1946 NY  N 2-S-3 82        .222
1947 CHI N S     14        .200
     BRTR      1816        .258
NON-PLAYING MANAGER BOS[A] 1959-60
```

JURISICH, ALVIN JOSEPH
B.AUG.25,1921 NEW ORLEANS,LA.
```
1944 STL N P     30        7- 9
1945 STL N P     27        3- 3
1946 PHI N P     13        4- 3
1947 PHI N P     34        1- 7
     BRTR       104       15-22
```

JUST, JOSEPH ERWIN
[REAL NAME JOSEPH ERWIN JUSZCZAK]
B.JAN.8,1916 MILWAUKEE,WIS.
```
1944 CIN N C     11        .182
1945 CIN N C     14        .147
     BRTR        25        .156
```

JUSTIS, WALTER NEWTON (SMOKE)
B.AUG.17,1883 MOORES HILL,IND.
D.OCT.4,1941 LAWRENCEBURG,IND.
```
1905 DET A P      2        0- 0
```

JUSZCZAK, JOSEPH ERWIN
[PLAYED UNDER NAME OF
JOSEPH ERWIN JUST]

JUTZE, ALFRED HENRY (SKIP)
B.MAY 28,1946 QUEENS,N.Y.
```
1972 STL N C     21        .239
1973 HOU N C     90        .223
1974 HOU N /C     8        .231
1975 HOU N C     51        .226
1976 HOU N C     42        .152
1977 SEA A C     42        .220
     BRTR       254        .215
```

JUUL, EARL HEROLD (HEROLD)
B.MAY 21,1893 CHICAGO,ILL.
D.JAN.4,1942 CHICAGO,ILL.
```
1914 BRO F P      9        0- 3
     BRTR
```

JUUL, HERBERT VICTOR
B.FEB.2,1886 CHICAGO,ILL.
D.NOV.14,1928 CHICAGO,ILL.
```
1911 CIN N P      2        0- 0
     BLTL
```

KAAT, JAMES LEE (JIM)
B.NOV.7,1938 ZEELAND,MICH.
```
1959 WAS A P      3        0- 2
1960 WAS A P     13        1- 5
1961 MIN A P     36   47   9-17
1962 MIN A P     39   48  18-14
1963 MIN A P     31   36  10-10
1964 MIN A P     36   46  17-11
1965 MIN A P     45   56  18-11
1966 MIN A P     41   47  25-13
1967 MIN A P     42   45  16-13
1968 MIN A P     30   36  14-12
1969 MIN A P     40   43  14-13
1970 MIN A P     45   56  14-10
1971 MIN A P     39   54  13-14
1972 MIN A P     15   24  10- 2
1973 MIN A P     29   31  11-12
     CHI A /P     7        4- 1
1974 CHI A P     42       21-13
1975 CHI A P     43       20-14
1976 PHI N P     38   42  12-14
1977 PHI N P     35   36   6-11
1978 PHI N P     26        8- 5
     BLTL       675  781 261-217
```

KADING, JOHN FREDERICK (JACK)
B.NOV.17,1884 WAUKESHA,WIS.
D.JUNE 2,1964 CHICAGO,ILL.
```
1910 PIT N 1      3        .304
1914 CHI F H      3        .000
                 11        .292
```

KAFORA, FRANK JACOB
(JAKE) OR (TOMATOES)
B.OCT.16,1888 DETROIT,MICH.
D.MAR.23,1928 CHICAGO,ILL.
```
1913 PIT N C      1        .000
1914 PIT N C     21        .130
     BRTR        22        .125
```

KAHDOT, ISAAC LEONARD (CHIEF)
B.OCT.22,1901 GEORGETOWN,OKLA.
```
1922 CLE A P      4        0- 0
     BRTR
```

KAHL, NICHOLAS ALEXANDER
B.APR.10,1879 COULTERVILLE,ILL.
D.JULY 13,1959 SPARTA,ILL.
```
1905 CLE A 3     30        .221
     BRTR
```

KAHLE, ROBERT WAYNE
B.NOV.23,1915 NEWCASTLE,IND.
```
1938 BOS N H      8        .333
     BRTR
```

YR CL LEA POS   GP   G   REC   YR CL LEA POS   GP   G   REC   YR CL LEA POS   GP   G   REC

KAHLER, GEORGE RUNNELLS (KRUM)
B.SEPT.6,1889 ATHENS,OHIO
D.FEB.7,1924 BATTLE CREEK,VA.
1910 CLE A P   12   6- 4
1911 CLE A P   30   9- 8
1912 CLE A P   41   12-19
1913 CLE A P   24   5-11
1914 CLE A P   2   0- 1
         BRTR   109   32-43

KAHN, OWEN EARLE (JACK)
B.JUNE 5,190 RICHMOND,VA.
1930 BOS N H   1   .000
         BRTR

KAHOE, MICHAEL JOSEPH
B.SEPT.3,1873 YELLOW SPRINGS,O
D.MAY 14,1949 AKRON,OHIO
1895 CIN N C   3   .000
1899 CIN N C   14   .167
1900 CIN N C   49   .186
1901 CIN N C   4   .267
     CHI N C   65   .215
1902 CHI N C-S-3   7   .222
     STL A C   54   .251
1903 STL A C   74   .188
1904 STL A C   71   .215
1905 PHI N C   15   .255
1907 CHI N C   4   .286
     WAS A C   17   .191
1908 WAS A C   17   .185
1909 WAS A C   4   .125
         BRTR   398   .211

KAISER, ALFRED EDWARD (DEERFOOT)
B.AUG.3,1886 CINCINNATI,OHIO
D.APR.11,1969 CINCINNATI,OHIO
1911 CHI N O   26   .250
     BOS N O   66   .203
1912 BOS N O   4   .000
1914 IND F O   59   .226
         BRTR   155   .215

KAISER, CLYDE DONALD
(DON) OR (TIGER)
B.FEB.3,1935 BYNG,OKLA.
1955 CHI N P   11   0- 0
1956 CHI N P   27   4- 9
1957 CHI N P   20   2- 6
         BRTR   58   6-15

KAISER, ROBERT THOMAS (BOB)
B.APR.29,1950 CINCINNATI,OHIO
1971 CLE A /P   5   0- 0
         BBTL

KAISERLING, GEORGE
B.MAY 12,1893 STEUBENVILLE,OHIO
D.MAR.2,1918 STEUBENVILLE,OHIO
1914 IND F P   37   17-10
1915 NEW F P   41   15-16
         BRTR   78   32-26

KALAHAN, JOHN JOSEPH
B.SEPT.30,1878 PHILADELPHIA,PA.
D.JUNE 20,1952 PHILADELPHIA,PA.
1903 PHI A C   1   .000
         TR

KALBFUS, CHARLES HENRY (SKINNY)
B.DEC.28,1864 WASHINGTON,D.C.
D.NOV.18,1941 WASHINGTON,D.C.
1884 WAS U O   1   .200
         BR

KALFASS, WILLIAM PHILIP (LEFTY)
B.MAR.3,1916 NEW YORK,N.Y.
D.SEPT.8,1968 BROOKLYN,N.Y.
1937 PHI A P   3   1- 0
         BRTL

KALIN, FRANK BRUNO (FATS)
[REAL NAME FRANK BRUNO KALINKIEWICZ]
B.OCT.3,1917 STEUBENVILLIE,OHIO
D.JAN.12,1975 WEIRTON,W.VA.
1940 PIT N O   3   .000
1943 CHI A H   4   .000
         BRTR   7   .000

KALINE, ALBERT WILLIAM (AL)
B.DEC.19,1934 BALTIMORE,MD.
1953 DET A O   30   .250
1954 DET A O   138   .276
1955 DET A O   152   .340
1956 DET A O   153   .314
1957 DET A O   149   .295
1958 DET A O   146   .313
1959 DET A O   136   .327
1960 DET A O   147   .278
1961 DET A 3-O   153   .324
1962 DET A O   100   .304
1963 DET A O   145   .312
1964 DET A O   146   .293
1965 DET A *O/3   125   .281
1966 DET A *O   142   .288
1967 DET A *O   131   .308
1968 DET A O-1   102   .287
1969 DET A *O/1   131   .272
1970 DET A O-1   131   .278
1971 DET A *O/1   133   .294
1972 DET A O-1   106   .313
1973 DET A O-1   91   .255
1974 DET A *O   147   .262
         BRTR   2834   .297

KALINKIEWICZ, FRANK BRUNO
[PLAYED UNDER NAME OF
FRANK BRUNO KALIN]

KALLIO, RUDOLPH
B.DEC.14,1892 PORTLAND,ORE.
1918 DET A P   30   31   8-13
1919 DET A P   12   0- 0
1925 BOS A P   7   1- 4
         BRTR   49   50   9-17

KAMM, WILLIAM EDWARD (WILLIE)
B.FEB.2,1900 SAN FRANCISCO,CAL.
1923 CHI A 3   149   .292
1924 CHI A 3   147   .254
1925 CHI A 3   152   .279
1926 CHI A 3   143   .294
1927 CHI A 3   148   .270
1928 CHI A 3   155   .308
1929 CHI A 3   147   .268
1930 CHI A 3   111   .269
1931 CHI A 3   18   .254
     CLE A 3   114   .295
1932 CLE A 3   148   .286
1933 CLE A 3   133   .282
1934 CLE A 3   121   .269
1935 CLE A 3   6   .333
         BRTR   1692   .281

KAMMEYER, ROBERT LYNN (BOB)
B.DEC.2,1950 KANSAS CITY,KAN.
1978 NY A /P   7   0- 0
         BRTR

KAMP, ALPHONSE FRANCIS (IKE)
B.SEPT.5,1900 ROXBURY,MASS.
D.FEB.26,1955 BOSTON,MASS.
1924 BOS N P   1   0- 1
1925 BOS N P   24   2- 4
         BBTL   25   2- 5

KAMPOURIS, ALEXIS WILLIAM
B.NOV.13,1912 SACRAMENTO,CAL.
1934 CIN N 2   19   .197
1935 CIN N 2-S   148   .246
1936 CIN N 2   122   .239
1937 CIN N 2   146   .249
1938 CIN N 2   21   .257
     NY N 2   82   .246
1939 NY N 2-3   74   .249
1941 BRO N 2   16   .314
1942 BRO N 2   10   .238
1943 BRO N 2   19   .227
     WAS A 2-3-O   51   .207
         BRTR   708   .243

KANE, FRANCIS THOMAS (SUGAR)
[REAL NAME FRANCIS THOMAS KILEY]
B.MAR.9,1895 SCRANTON,PA.
D.DEC.2,1962 BROCKTON,MASS.
1915 BRO F O   3   .200
1919 NY A O   1   .000
         BLTR   4   .182

KANE, HARRY (KLONDIKE)
[REAL NAME HARRY COHEN]
B.JULY 27,1883 HAMBURG,ARK.
D.SEPT.15,1932 PORTLAND,ORE.
1902 STL A P   4   0- 1
1903 DET A P   3   0- 2
1905 PHI N P   2   1- 1
1906 PHI N P   6   1- 2
         BLTL   15   2- 6

KANE, JAMES JOSEPH (SHAMUS)
B.NOV.27,1881 SCRANTON,PA.
D.OCT.2,1947 OMAHA,NEB.
1908 PIT N 1   40   .241
         BLTL

KANE, JOHN FRANCIS
B.OCT.24,1883 PITTSBURG,KAN.
D.JAN.28,1934 ST.ANTHONY,IDAHO
1907 CIN N 3-O   75   .248
1908 CIN N O   127   .213
1909 CHI N 1   15   .089
1910 CHI N O   30   .242
         BRTR   247   .220

KANE, JOHN FRANCIS
B.FEB.19,1900 CHICAGO,ILL.
1925 CHI A 2-S   14   .179
         BBTR

KANE, THOMAS JOSEPH (SUGAR)
B.DEC.15,1906 CHICAGO,ILL.
1938 BOS N 2   2   .000
         BRTR

KANE, WILLIAM
B.1867 COLLINSVILLE,ILL.
1890 STL AA C-1   8   .160
         BRTR

KANEHL, RODERICK EDWIN
(ROD) OR (HOT ROD)
B.APR.1,1934 WICHITA,KAN.
1962 NY N 1-2-S-3-O   133   .248
1963 NY N 1-2-3-O   109   .241
1964 NY N 1-2-3-O   98   .232
         BRTR   340   .241

KANTLEHNER, ERVING LESLIE (PEANUTS)
B.JULY 31,1892 SAN JOSE,CAL.
1914 PIT N P   21   3- 2
1915 PIT N P   29   5-12
1916 PIT N P   34   5-15
     PHI N P   3   0- 0
         BLTL   87   13-29

KAPPEL, HENRY
B.1862 PHILADELPHIA,PA.
D.AUG.27,1905 PHILADELPHIA,PA.
1887 CIN AA 2-S-3-O   24   .294
1888 CIN AA 2-S-3-O   35   .254
1889 COL AA S-3   49   .269
         BRTR   108   .272

KAPPEL, JOSEPH
B.APR.27,1857 PHILADELPHIA,PA.
D.JULY 8,1929 PHILADELPHIA,PA.
1884 PHI N C   4   .067
1890 ATH AA S   57   .240
         BR   61   .227

KARDOW, PAUL OTTO (TEX)
B.SEPT.19,1915 HUMBLE,TEX.
D.APR.27,1968 SAN ANTONIO,TEX.
1936 CLE A P   2   0- 0
         BRTR

KARGER, EDWIN (ED) OR (LOOSE)
B.MAY 6,1883 SAN ANGELO,TEX.
D.SEPT.9,1957 DELTA,COLO.
1906 PIT N P   5   2- 3
     STL N P   29   5-16
1907 STL N P   39   15-19
1908 STL N P   22   4- 9
1909 STL N P   9   1- 3
     BOS A P   12   5- 2
1910 BOS A P   27   11- 7
1911 BOS A P   25   5- 8
         BRTL   164   48-67

KARL, ANTON ANDREW (ANDY)
B.APR.8,1914 MT.VERNON,N.Y.
1943 BOS A P   11   1- 1
     PHI N P   9   11   1- 2
1944 PHI N P   38   42   3- 2
1945 PHI N P   67   8- 8
1946 PHI N P   39   3- 7
1947 BOS N P   27   2- 3
         BRTR   191   197   18-23

KARLON, WILLIAM JOHN (HANK)
B.JAN.21,1909 PALMER,MASS.
D.DEC.7,1964 MONSON,MASS.
1930 NY A O   2   .000
         BRTR

KAROW, MARTIN GREGORY
B.JULY 18,1904 BRADDOCK,PA.
1927 BOS A S-3   6   .200
         BRTR

KARPEL, HERBERT (LEFTY)
B.DEC.27,1917 BROOKLYN,N.Y.
1946 NY A P   2   0- 0
         BLTL

```
YR   CL LEA POS     GP    G    REC
```

KARR, BENJAMIN JOYCE (BALDY)
B.NOV.28,1893 MT.PLEASANT,MISS.
D.DEC.8,1968 MEMPHIS,TENN.
```
1920 BOS A P      26   57   3- 8
1921 BOS A P      26   43   8- 7
1922 BOS A P      41   66   5-12
1925 CLE A P      32   46  11-12
1926 CLE A P      30   31   5- 6
1927 CLE A P           22   3- 3
       BLTR      177  265  35-48
```

KARST, JOHN GOTTLIEB (KING)
B.OCT.15,1893 PHILADELPHIA,PA.
D.MAY 21,1976 CAPE MAY COURT
HOUSE,N.J.
```
1915 BRO N 3            1   .000
       TR
```

KASKO, EDWARD MICHAEL (EDDIE)
B.JUNE 27,1932 LINDEN,N.J.
```
1957 STL N 2-S-3      134   .273
1958 STL N 2-S-3      104   .220
1959 CIN N 2-S-3      118   .283
1960 CIN N 2-S-3      126   .292
1961 CIN N 2-S-3      126   .271
1962 CIN N S-3        134   .278
1963 CIN N 2-S-3       76   .241
1964 HOU N S-3        133   .243
1965 HOU N S/3         68   .247
1966 BOS A S-3/2       58   .213
       BLTR          1077   .264
```
NON-PLAYING MANAGER BOS[A] 1970-73

KATOLL, JOHN (BIG JACK)
B.JUNE 24,1872 GERMANY
D.JUNE 18,1955 HARTLAND,ILL.
```
1898 CHI N P           2   0- 1
1899 CHI N P           3   1- 1
1901 CHI A P          27  13-12
1902 CHI A P           1   0- 0
     BAL A P-O   13   15   3-10
                           .152
       BLTR      46   48  17-24
                           .135
```

KATT, RAYMOND FREDERICK (RAY)
B.MAY 9,1927 NEW BRAUNFELS,TEX.
```
1952 NY N C            9   .222
1953 NY N C            8   .172
1954 NY N C           86   .255
1955 NY N C          124   .215
1956 NY N C           37   .228
     STL N C           47   .259
1957 NY N C           72   .230
1958 STL N C          19   .171
1959 STL N C          15   .292
       BLTR          417   .232
```

KATZ, ROBERT CLYDE
B.JAN.30,1911 LANCASTER,PA.
D.DEC.15,1962 ST.JOSEPH,MICH.
```
1944 CIN N P           6   0- 1
       BRTR
```

KAUFF, BENJAMIN MICHAEL
B.JAN.5,1890 POMEROY,OHIO
D.NOV.17,1961 COLUMBUS,OHIO
```
1912 NY  A O           5   .272
1914 IND F O         154   .366
1915 BRO F O         136   .344
1916 NY  N O         154   .264
1917 NY  N O         153   .308
1918 NY  N O          67   .315
1919 NY  N O         135   .277
1920 NY  N O          55   .274
       BLTR          859   .310
```

KAUFFMAN, HOWARD RICHARD (DICK)
B.JUNE 22,1888 E.LEWISBURG,PA.
D.APR.16,1948 MIFFLINBURG,PA.
```
1914 STL A 1           6   .333
1915 STL A 1          37   .258
       BBTR           43   .266
```

KAUFMANN, ANTHONY CHARLES
B.DEC.16,1900 CHICAGO,ILL.
```
1921 CHI N P           2   1- 0
1922 CHI N P     37   38   7-13
1923 CHI N P          33  14-10
1924 CHI N P     34   35  16-11
1925 CHI N P          31  13-13
1926 CHI N P     26   30   9- 7
1927 CHI N P           9   3- 3
     PHI N P      5    8   0- 3
     STL N P           1   0- 0
1928 STL N P      4    5   0- 0
1929 NY  N O          39   .031
1930 STL N P           2   0- 1
1931 STL N P     15   20   1- 1
1935 STL N P      3    7   0- 0
       BBTR     202  260  64-62
                           .220
```

KAVANAGH, CHARLES HUGH (SILK)
B.JUNE 9,1893 CHICAGO,ILL.
```
1914 CHI A O           5   .250
       BLTR
```

KAVANAGH, LEO DANIEL
B.AUG.9,1894 CHICAGO,ILL.
D.AUG.10,1950 CHICAGO,ILL.
```
1914 CHI F S           5   .273
       BRTR
```

KAVANAGH, MARTIN JOSEPH
B.JUNE 13,1891 HARRISON,N.J.
D.JULY 28,1960 ELOISE,MICH.
```
1914 DET A 2         127   .248
1915 DET A 1-2       113   .295
1916 DET A 2          58   .141
     CLE A 2          19   .250
1917 CLE A 2          14   .000
1918 CLE A 1          13   .211
     STL N 2          12   .181
     DET A 1          13   .273
       BRTR          369   .249
```

KAVANAUGH
```
1872 ECK NA 1-O        5   .185
```

KAY, WALTER BROCTON (KING BILL)
B.FEB.14,1878 NEW CASTLE,VA.
D.DEC.3,1945 ROANOKE,VA.
```
1907 WAS A O          25   .333
       BRTR
```

KAZAK, EDWARD TERRANCE (EDDIE)
[REAL NAME EDWARD TERRANCE TKACZUK]
B.JULY 18,1920 STEUBENVILLE,O.
```
1948 STL N 3           6   .273
1949 STL N 2-3        92   .304
1950 STL N 3          93   .256
1951 STL N 3          11   .182
1952 STL N 3           3   .000
     CIN N 1          13   .067
       BRTR          218   .273
```

KAZANSKI, THEODORE STANLEY
B.JUNE 25,1934 HAMTRAMCK,MICH.
```
1953 PHI N S          95   .217
1954 PHI N S          39   .135
1955 PHI N S-3         9   .083
1956 PHI N 2-S       117   .211
1957 PHI N 2-S-3      62   .265
1958 PHI N 2-S-3      95   .228
       BRTR          417   .217
```

KEALEY, STEVEN WILLIAM (STEVE)
B.MAY 13,1947 TORRANCE,CAL.
```
1968 CAL A /P          6   0- 1
1969 CAL A P          15   2- 0
1970 CAL A P          17   1- 0
1971 CHI A P          54   2- 2
1972 CHI A P          40   3- 2
1973 CHI A /P          7   0- 0
       BRTR          139   8- 5
```

KEANE, JOHN JOSEPH (JOHNNY)
B.NOV.3,1911 ST.LOUIS,MO.
D.JAN.6,1967 HOUSTON,TEX.
NON-PLAYING MANAGER
STL[N] 1961-64, NY[A] 1965-66

KEARNS, EDWARD JOSEPH (TEDDY)
B.JAN.21,1900 TRENTON,N.J.
D.DEC.21,1949 TRENTON,N.J.
```
1924 CHI N 1           4   .250
1925 CHI N 1           3   .500
       BRTR            7   .278
```

KEARNS, THOMAS J. (DASHER)
B.NOV.9,1869 ROCHESTER,N.Y.
D.DEC.7,1938
```
1880 BUF N C-O         9   .091
1882 DET N 2           4   .308
1884 DET N 2          18   .211
                      31   .188
```

KEARNS, W. A.
B.CHICAGO,ILL.
```
1901 BAL A P           4   1- 0
       TL
```

KEARSE, EDWARD PAUL (TRUCK)
B.FEB.23,1916 SAN FRANCISCO,CAL
D.JULY 15,1968 EUREKA,CAL.
```
1942 NY  A C          11   .192
       BRTR
```

KEAS, EDWARD JAMES
B.FEB.2,1863 DUBUQUE,IOWA
D.JAN.12,1940 DUBUQUE,IOWA
```
1888 CLE AA P          6   3- 3
```

KEATING, RAYMOND HERBERT
B.JULY 21,1891 BRIDGEPORT,CONN.
D.DEC.28,1963 SACRAMENTO,CAL.
```
1912 NY  A P           5   0- 3
1913 NY  A P          28   6-12
1914 NY  A P          34   7-11
1915 NY  A P          11   3- 6
1916 NY  A P          14   5- 6
1918 NY  A P          15   2- 2
1919 BOS N P     22   24   7-11
       BRTR     129  131  30-51
```

KEATING, ROBERT M.
B.SEPT.22,1862 SPRINGFIELD,MASS
D.JAN.19,1922 SPRINGFIELD,MASS.
```
1887 BAL AA P          1   0- 1
       BLTL
```

KEATING, WALTER FRANCIS (CHICK)
B.AUG.8,1891 PHILADELPHIA,PA.
D.JULY 13,1959 PHILADELPHIA,PA.
```
1913 CHI N S           2   .200
1914 CHI N S          20   .100
1915 CHI N S           4   .000
1926 PHI N S           4   .000
       BRTR           30   .087
```

KECK, FRANK JOSEPH (CACTUS)
B.JAN.13,1899 ST.LOUIS,MO.
```
1922 CIN N P          27   7- 6
1923 CIN N P          35   3- 6
       BRTR           62  10-12
```

KEEFE, DAVID EDWIN
B.JAN.9,1897 WILLISTON,VT.
D.FEB.4,1978 KANSAS CITY,MO.
```
1917 PHI A P           3   1- 0
1918 PHI A P           1   0- 1
1919 PHI A P           2   0- 1
1920 PHI A P     31   32   6- 7
1921 PHI A P          44   2- 9
1922 CLE A P          18   0- 0
       BLTR      99  100   9-18
```

KEEFE, GEORGE W.
B.JAN.7,1867 WASHINGTON,D.C.
D.AUG.24,1935 WASHINGTON,D.C.
```
1886 WAS N P           4   0- 3
1887 WAS N P           1   0- 1
1888 WAS N P          13   6- 7
1889 WAS N P          27   8-18
1890 BUF P            25   5-17
1891 WAS AA P          5   0- 5
       BLTL           75  19-51
```

KEEFE, JOHN THOMAS
B.JULY 16,1867 FITCHBURG,MASS.
D.AUG.10,1937 FITCHBURG,MASS.
```
1890 SYR AA P         44  14-23
```

KEEFE, ROBERT FRANCIS (BOBBY)
B.JUNE 16,1882 FOLSOM,CAL.
D.DEC.7,1964 SACRAMENTO,CAL.
```
1907 NY  A P          19   4- 4
1911 CIN N P          39  12-13
1912 CIN N P          17   1- 3
       BRTR           75  17-20
```

KEEFE, TIMOTHY JOHN (TIM)
(SMILING TIM) OR (SIR TIMOTHY)
B.JAN.1,1857 CAMBRIDGE,MASS.
D.APR.23,1933 CAMBRIDGE,MASS.
```
1880 TRO N P          12   6- 6
1881 TRO N P          46  19-27
1882 TRO N P-3-  43   51  17-26
          O                .225
1883 MET AA P-O       70  41-26
                           .220
1884 MET AA P    57   62  35-18
1885 NY  N P-O   45   46  32-13
                           .162
1886 NY  N P     63   64  42-20
1887 NY  N P          56  35-20
1888 NY  N P     50   51  35-12
1889 NY  N P          43  30-13
1890 NY  P P          30  17- 8
1891 NY  N P           8   2- 5
     PHI N P           9   3- 6
1892 PHI N P          36  21-14
1893 PHI N P          20  10-10
       BRTR     588  604 343-224
                           .199
```

KEEGAN, EDWARD CHARLES (ED)
B.JULY 8,1939 CAMDEN,N.J.
```
1959 PHI N P           3   0- 3
1961 KC  A P           6   0- 0
1962 PHI N P           5   0- 0
       BRTR           14   0- 3
```

KEEGAN, ROBERT CHARLES
(BOB) OR (SMILEY)
B.AUG.4,1920 ROCHESTER,N.Y.
```
1953 CHI A P          22   7- 5
1954 CHI A P     31   32  16- 9
1955 CHI A P          18   2- 5
1956 CHI A P          20   5- 7
1957 CHI A P          30  10- 8
1958 CHI A P          14   0- 2
       BRTR     135  136  40-36
```

YR	CL	LEA	POS	GP	G	REC

KEELER, WILLIAM HENRY (WEE WILLIE)
B.MAR.3,1872 BROOKLYN,N.Y.
D.JAN.1,1923 BROOKLYN,N.Y.

1892	NY	N	3		13	.306
1893	NY	N	2-S-0		7	.364
	BRO	N	3		19	.340
1894	BAL	N	O		128	.367
1895	BAL	N	O		131	.394
1896	BAL	N	O		127	.392
1897	BAL	N	O		128	.432
1898	BAL	N	O		128	.379
1899	BRO	N	O		143	.376
1900	BRO	N	O		137	.366
1901	BRO	N	O		136	.355
1902	BRO	N	O		132	.342
1903	NY	A	O		132	.318
1904	NY	A	O		143	.343
1905	NY	A	O		149	.302
1906	NY	A	O		152	.304
1907	NY	A	O		107	.234
1908	NY	A	O		91	.263
1909	NY	A	O		99	.264
1910	NY	A	O		17	.300
	BLTL				2119	.345

KEELEY, BURTON ELWOOD (SPEED)
B.NOV.2,1879 WILMINGTON,ILL.
D.MAY 3,1952 ELY,MINN.

1908	WAS	A	P	28	31	6-11
1909	WAS	A	P	2	0- 0	
	BRTR			30	33	6-11

KEELY, ROBERT WILLIAM (BOB)
B.AUG.22,1909 ST.LOUIS,MO.

1944	STL	N	C		1	.000
1945	STL	N	C		1	.000
	BRTR				2	.000

KEEN, HOWARD VICTOR (VIC)
B.MAR.16,1899 BELAIR,MD.
D.DEC.10,1976 SALISBURY,MD.

1918	PHI	A	P	1	1- 0	
1921	CHI	N	P	5	0- 3	
1922	CHI	N	P	7	1- 2	
1923	CHI	N	P	35	12- 8	
1924	CHI	N	P	40	15-14	
1925	CHI	N	P	30	2- 6	
1926	STL	N	P	26	10- 9	
1927	STL	N	P	21	2- 1	
	BRTR			165	43-43	

KEENAN, HARRY LEON (KID)
B.1875 LOUISVILLE,KY.
D.JUNE 11,1903 COVINGTON,KY.

| 1891 | CIN | AA | P | 1 | 0- 1 | |
| | TR | | | | | |

KEENAN, JAMES W.
B.FEB.10,1858 NEW HAVEN,CONN.
D.SEPT.21,1926 CINCINNATI,OHIO

1875	NH	NA	C-3	3	-	
1880	BUF	N	C	2	.125	
1882	PIT	AA	C-S-0	24	.206	
1884	IND	AA	C-1	68	.305	
1885	CIN	AA	P-C-	1	32	0- 0
			1-0			.282
1886	CIN	AA	P-C-	1	43	0- 0
			1-0			.278
1887	CIN	AA	C-1		47	.297
1888	CIN	AA	C-1		84	.229
1889	CIN	AA	C-1-3		87	.287
1890	CIN	N	C		54	.138
1891	CIN	N	C-1		75	.203
	BRTR			2	519	0- 0
						-

KEENAN, JAMES WILLIAM (SPARKPLUG)
B.MAY 25,1899 AVON,N.Y.

1920	PHI	N	P	1	0- 0	
1921	PHI	N	P	15	1- 2	
	BLTL			16	1- 2	

KEEN, WILLIAM BROWN (BUSTER)
B.AUG.16,1892 OGLETHORPE,GA.
D.JULY 16,1947 SOUTH POINT,OHIO

| 1911 | PIT | N | 1 | | 5 | .000 |
| | BRTR | | | | | |

KEENER, JOSEPH DONALD (JOE)
B.APR.21,1953 SAN PEDRO,CAL.

| 1976 | MON | N | /P | | 2 | 0- 1 |
| | BRTR | | | | | |

KEENER, JOSHUA HARRY (BEANS)
B.1869 EASTON,PA.
D.MAR.5,1912 EASTON,PA.

| 1896 | PHI | N | P | | 15 | 2-10 |

KEERL, GEORGE HENRY
B.APR.10,1847 BALTIMORE,MD.
D.SEPT.9,1923

| 1875 | CHI | NA | 2 | | 6 | - |

KEESEY, JAMES WARD
B.OCT.27,1902 PERRYVILLE,MO.
D.SEPT.15,1951 BOISE,IDAHO

1925	PHI	A	1		5	.400
1930	PHI	A	1		11	.250
	BRTR				16	.294

KEFFER, C. FRANK
B.PHILADELPHIA,PA.

| 1890 | SYR | AA | P | 1 | 0- 1 | |

KEHN, CHESTER LAWRENCE (CHET)
B.OCT.30,1921 SAN DIEGO,CAL.

| 1942 | BRO | N | P | 3 | 0- 0 | |
| | BRTR | | | | | |

KEIFER, SHERMAN C. (KATIE)
B.1892

| 1914 | IND | F | P | 1 | 1- 0 | |
| | BBTR | | | | | |

KEINZIL, WILLIAM
B.PHILADELPHIA,PA.

1882	ATH	AA	O	9	.297	
1884	KEY	U	O	61	.260	
	BLTL			70	.265	

KEISTER, WILLIAM HOFFMAN (WAGON TONGUE)
B.AUG.17,1874 BALTIMORE,MD.
D.AUG.19,1924 BALTIMORE,MD.

1896	BAL	N	2		13	.224
1898	BOS	N	2-S		9	.200
1899	BAL	N	2-S		134	.331
1900	STL	N	2		128	.298
1901	BAL	A	S		114	.328
1902	WAS	A	2-S-3-0		119	.303
1903	PHI	N	O		100	.320
	BLTR				617	.312

KEKICH, MICHAEL DENNIS (MIKE)
B.APR.2,1945 SAN DIEGO,CAL.

1965	LA	N	/P		9	0- 1
1968	LA	N	P	25	2-10	
1969	NY	A	P	28	4- 6	
1970	NY	A	P	26	6- 3	
1971	NY	A	P	37	10- 9	
1972	NY	A	P	29	10-13	
1973	NY	A	/P		5	1- 1
	CLE	A	P	16	19	1- 4
1975	TEX	A	P	23	0- 0	
1977	SEA	A	P	41	5- 4	
	BRTL			235	238	39-51

KELB, GEORGE FRANCIS (PUGGER) OR (LEFTY)
B.JULY 17,1870 TOLEDO,OHIO
D.OCT.20,1936 TOLEDO,OHIO

| 1898 | CLE | N | P | 3 | 0- 1 | |
| | TL | | | | | |

KELIHER, MAURICE MICHAEL (MICKEY)
B.JAN.11,1890 WASHINGTON,D.C.
D.SEPT.7,1930 WASHINGTON,D.C.

1911	PIT	N	1		3	.000
1912	PIT	N	H		2	.000
	BLTL				5	.000

KELL, EVERETT LEE (SKEETER)
B.OCT.11,1929 SWIFTON,ARK.

| 1952 | PHI | A | 2 | | 75 | .221 |

KELL, GEORGE CLYDE
B.AUG.23,1922 SWIFTON,ARK.

1943	PHI	A	3		1	.200
1944	PHI	A	3		139	.268
1945	PHI	A	3		147	.272
1946	PHI	A	3		26	.299
	DET	A	1-3		105	.327
1947	DET	A	3		152	.320
1948	DET	A	3		92	.304
1949	DET	A	3		134	.343
1950	DET	A	3		157	.340
1951	DET	A	3		147	.319
1952	DET	A	3		39	.296
	BOS	A	3		75	.319
1953	BOS	A	3-0		134	.307
1954	BOS	A	3		26	.258
	CHI	A	1-3-0		71	.283
1955	CHI	A	1-3-0		128	.312
1956	CHI	A	1-3		21	.313
	BAL	A	1-2-3		102	.261
1957	BAL	A	1-3		99	.297
	BRTR				1795	.306

KELLEHER, ALBERT ALOYSIUS (DUKE)
B.SEPT.30,1893 NEW YORK,N.Y.
D.SEPT.28,1947 STATEN ISLAND,N.Y.

| 1916 | NY | N | C | | 1 | .000 |
| | TR | | | | | |

KELLEHER, FRANCIS EUGENE
B.AUG.2,1916 SAN FRANCISCO,CAL

1942	CIN	N	O		38	.182
1943	CIN	N	O		9	.000
	BRTR				47	.167

KELLEHER, HAROLD JOSEPH
B.JUNE 24,1914 PHILADELPHIA,PA.

1935	PHI	N	P	3	2- 0	
1936	PHI	N	P	14	0- 5	
1937	PHI	N	P	27	30	2- 4
1938	PHI	N	P	6	0- 0	
	BRTR			50	53	4- 9

KELLEHER, JOHN PATRICK
B.SEPT.13,1893 BROOKLINE,MASS.
D.AUG.21,1960 BOSTON,MASS.

1912	STL	N	3		6	.363
1916	BRO	N	S-3		2	.000
1921	CHI	N	2-3		95	.309
1922	CHI	N	1-S-3		63	.259
1923	CHI	N	1-2-S-3		66	.306
1924	BOS	N	3		1	.000
	BRTR				233	.293

KELLEHER, MICHAEL DENNIS (MICK)
B.JULY 25,1947 SEATTLE,WASH.

1972	STL	N	S		23	.159
1973	STL	N	S		43	.184
1974	HOU	N	SS		19	.156
1975	STL	N	/S		7	.000
1976	CHI	N	*S-3/2		124	.228
1977	CHI	N	2-S/3		63	.230
1978	CHI	N	S-2-S		68	.253
	BRTR				347	.216

KELLER, CHARLES ERNEST (CHARLIE) OR (KING KONG)
B.SEPT.12,1916 MIDDLETOWN,MD.

1939	NY	A	O		111	.334
1940	NY	A	O		138	.286
1941	NY	A	O		140	.298
1942	NY	A	O		152	.292
1943	NY	A	O		141	.271
1945	NY	A	O		44	.301
1946	NY	A	O		150	.275
1947	NY	A	O		45	.238
1948	NY	A	O		83	.267
1949	NY	A	O		60	.250
1950	DET	A	O		50	.314
1951	DET	A	O		54	.258
1952	NY	A	O		2	.000
	BLTR				1170	.286

KELLER, HAROLD KEFAUVER (HAL)
B.JULY 7,1927 MIDDLETOWN,MD.

1949	WAS	A	H		3	.333
1950	WAS	A	C		11	.214
1952	WAS	A	C		11	.174
	BLTR				25	.204

KELLER, RONALD LEE (RON)
B.JUNE 3,1943 INDIANAPOLIS,IND.

1966	MIN	A	P	2	3	0- 0
1968	MIN	A	/P	7	8	0- 1
	BRTR			9	11	0- 1

KELLERT, FRANK WILLIAM
B.JULY 6,1924 OKLAHOMA CITY,OKLA.
D.NOV.19,1976 OKLAHOMA CITY,OKLA.

1953	STL	A	1		2	.000
1954	BAL	A	1		10	.096
1955	BRO	N	1		39	.325
1956	CHI	N	1		71	.186
	BRTR				122	.231

KELLETT, ALFRED HENRY
B.OCT.30,1901 RED BANK,N.J.
D.JULY 14,1960 NEW YORK,N.Y.

1923	PHI	A	P	5	0- 1	
1924	BOS	A	P	1	0- 0	
				6	0- 1	

KELLETT, DONALD STAFFORD (RED)
B.JULY 19,1909 BROOKLYN,N.Y.
D.NOV.5,1970 FT.LAUDERDALE,FLA.

| 1934 | BOS | A | 2-S-3 | | 9 | .040 |
| | BRTR | | | | | |

KELLEY, HARRY LEROY
B.FEB.13,1906 PARKIN,ARK.
D.MAR.23,1958 PARKIN,ARK.

1925	WAS	A	P		6	1- 1
1926	WAS	A	P		7	0- 0
1936	PHI	A	P	35	36	15-12
1937	PHI	A	P		41	13-21
1938	PHI	A	P		4	0- 2
	WAS	A	P		38	9- 8
1939	WAS	A	P		15	4- 3
	BRTR			146	147	42-47

YR CL LEA POS GP G REC

KELLEY, JOSEPH JAMES (JOE)
B.DEC.9,1871 CAMBRIDGE,MASS.
D.AUG.14,1943 BALTIMORE,MD.
1891 BOS N O 12 .244
PIT N O 2 .143
1892 PIT N O 56 .245
BAL N O 10 .250
1893 BAL N O 124 .312
1894 BAL N O 129 .391
1895 BAL N O 131 .370
1896 BAL N O 130 .370
1897 BAL N O 129 .389
1898 BAL N O 124 .328
1899 BRO N O 144 .329
1900 BRO N 1-O 118 .318
1901 BRO N 1 120 .309
1902 BAL A 1-3-O 60 .311
CIN N M-2-S-3-O 37 .327
1903 CIN N M-O 104 .316
1904 CIN N M-1 123 .281
1905 CIN N M-O 87 .277
1906 CIN N O 127 .228
1908 BOS N M-O 62 .259
BRTR 1829 .321

KELLEY, MICHAEL JOSEPH
B.DEC.2,1875 OTTER RIVER,MASS.
D.JUNE 6,1955 MINNEAPOLIS,MINN.
1899 LOU N 1 76 .247

KELLEY, RICHARD ANTHONY (DICK)
B.JAN.8,1940 BRIGHTON,MASS.
1964 MIL N P 2 0- 0
1965 MIL N P 21 22 1- 1
1966 ATL N P 20 7- 5
1967 ATL N P 39 2- 9
1968 ATL N P 31 2- 4
1969 SD N P 27 4- 8
1971 SD N P 48 2- 3
BRTL 188 189 18-30

KELLEY, THOMAS HENRY (TOM)
B.JAN.5,1944 MANCHESTER,CONN.
1964 CLE A P 6 0- 0
1965 CLE A /P 4 2- 1
1966 CLE A P 31 4- 8
1967 CLE A /P 1 0- 0
1971 ATL N P 28 9- 5
1972 ATL N P 27 5- 7
1973 ATL N /P 7 0- 1
BRTR 104 20-22

KELLIHER, FRANCIS MORTIMER (YUCKA)
B.MAY 23,1899 SOMERVILLE,MASS.
D.MAR.4,1956 SOMERVILLE,MASS.
1919 WAS A H 1 .000
BLTL

KELLNER, ALEXANDER RAYMOND (ALEX)
B.AUG.26,1924 TUCSON,ARIZ.
1948 PHI A P 13 0- 0
1949 PHI A P 38 20-12
1950 PHI A P 36 8-20
1951 PHI A P 33 11-14
1952 PHI A P 34 12-14
1953 PHI A P 25 11-12
1954 PHI A P 27 6-17
1955 KC A P 30 11- 8
1956 KC A P 20 21 7- 4
1957 KC A P 28 6- 5
1958 KC A P 7 8 0- 2
CIN N P 18 7- 3
1959 STL N P 12 2- 1
BRTL 321 323 101-112

KELLNER, WALTER JOSEPH (WALT)
B.APR.26,1929 TUCSON,ARIZ.
1952 PHI A P 1 0- 0
1953 PHI A P 2 0- 0
BRTR 3 0- 0

KELLOGG, ALBERT C.
1908 PHI A P 3 0- 2

KELLOGG, NATHANIEL M.
B.MANCHESTER,N.H.
1885 DET N S 5 .118

KELLOGG, RAYMOND NELSON
[PLAYED UNDER NAME OF
RAYMOND N. NELSON]

KELLOGG, WILLIAM DEARSTYNE
B.MAY 25,1884 ALBANY,N.Y.
D.DEC.12,1971 BALTIMORE,MD.
1914 CIN N 1 71 .175
BRTR

KELLUM, WINFORD ANSLEY
B.APR.11,1876 WATERFORD,ONT.,CANADA
D.AUG.10,1951 BIG RAPIDS,MICH.
1901 BOS A P 6 2- 3
1904 CIN N P 31 36 16- 8
1905 STL N P 11 3- 3
BBTL 48 53 21-14

YR CL LEA POS GP G REC

KELLY, ALBERT MICHAEL (RED)
B.NOV.15,1884 UNION,ILL.
D.FEB.4,1961 ZEPHYR HILLS,FLA.
1910 CHI A O 14 .155
TR

KELLY, CHARLES H.
1883 PHI N 3 2 .143
1886 ATH AA S 1 .000
3 .100

KELLY, EDWARD L.
B.1890 SPOKANE,WASH.
1914 BOS A P 3 0- 0
BRTR

KELLY, GEORGE LANGE (HIGH POCKETS)
B.SEPT.10,1895 SAN FRANCISCO,CAL.
1915 NY N 1 17 .158
1916 NY N 1 49 .158
1917 NY N P-1- 1 11 1- 0
O .000
PIT N 1 8 .087
1919 NY N 1 32 .290
1920 NY N 1 155 .266
1921 NY N 1 149 .308
1922 NY N 1 151 .327
1923 NY N 1 145 .307
1924 NY N 1-2-3-O 144 .324
1925 NY N 1-2-3 147 .309
1926 NY N 1-2 136 .303
1927 CIN N 1-2-O 61 .270
1928 CIN N 1-O 116 .296
1929 CIN N 1 147 .293
1930 CIN N 1 51 .288
CHI N 1 39 .331
1932 BRO N 1 64 .243
BRTR 1 1622 1- 0
.297

KELLY, HAROLD PATRICK (PAT)
B.JULY 30,1944 PHILADELPHIA,PA.
1967 MIN A /H 8 .000
1968 MIN A O 12 .114
1969 KC A *O 112 .264
1970 KC A *O 136 .235
1971 CHI A O 67 .291
1972 CHI A *O 119 .261
1973 CHI A *O 144 .280
1974 CHI A O-D 122 .281
1975 CHI A *O-D 133 .274
1976 CHI A O-D 107 .254
1977 BAL A *O 120 .256
1978 BAL A O 100 .274
BLTL 1180 .265

KELLY, HERBERT BARRETT (MOKE)
B.JUNE 4,1892 MOBILE,ALA.
D.MAY 18,1973 TORRANCE,CAL.
1914 PIT N P 5 0- 2
1915 PIT N P 5 1- 1
BLTL 10 1- 3

KELLY, JAMES ROBERT
[ALSO PLAYED UNDER REAL NAME OF
ROBERT JOHN TAGGERT IN 1918]
B.FEB.1,1884 BLOOMFIELD,N.J.
D.APR.10,1961 KINGSPORT,TENN.
1914 PIT N O 32 .227
1915 PIT F O 148 .290
1918 BOS N O 35 .329
BLTR 215 .294

KELLY, JAY THOMAS (TOM)
B.AUG.15,1950 GRACEVILLE,MINN.
1975 MIN A 1/O 49 .181
BLTL

KELLY, JOHN
1871 KEK NA O 18 -

KELLY, JOHN B.
B.MAR.13,1879 CLIFTON HEIGHTS,PA.
D.MAR.19,1944 BALTIMORE,MD.
1907 STL N O 52 .188

KELLY, JOHN FRANCIS
(KICK) OR (FATHER)
B.1859 PATERSON,N.J.
D.APR.13,1908 PATERSON,N.J.
1882 CLE N C 29 .134
1883 BAL AA C-O 46 .224
PHI N O 1 .000
1884 CIN U C 39 .253
WAS U C-O 4 .357
BRTR 119 .217

KELLY, JOHN O. (HONEST JOHN)
B.1856 NEW YORK,N.Y.
D.MAR.27,1926 MALBA,N.Y.
1879 SYR N C-1 9 .125
NON-PLAYING MANAGER LOU[AA]1887

YR CL LEA POS GP G REC

KELLY, JOSEPH HENRY
B.SEPT.23,1886 WEIR CITY,KAN.
D.AUG.16,1977 ST.JOSEPH,MO.
1914 PIT N O 141 .222
1916 CHI N O 54 .254
1917 BOS N O 116 .222
1918 BOS N O 47 .232
1919 BOS N O 18 .141
BRTR 376 .224

KELLY, JOSEPH JAMES
B.APR.23,1900 NEW YORK,N.Y.
D.NOV.24,1967 LYNBROOK,N.Y.
1926 CHI N O 65 .335
1928 CHI N 1 32 .212
BLTL 97 .307

KELLY, MICHAEL J.
B.NOV.9,1902 ST.LOUIS,MO.
1926 PHI N P 4 0- 0
BRTR

KELLY, MICHAEL JOSEPH (KING)
B.DEC.31,1857 TROY,N.Y.
D.NOV.8,1894 BOSTON,MASS.
1878 CIN N C-3-O 61 .281
1879 CIN N C-3-O 77 .348
1880 CHI N P-C- 1 82 0- 0
S-3-O .292
1881 CHI N C-3-O 80 .323
1882 CHI N C-1-S-3-O 84 .305
1883 CHI N P-C- 1 98 0- 0
2-3-O .253
1884 CHI N P-C- 2 107 0- 0
1-2-S-3-O .341
1885 CHI N C-1-2-3-O 107 .287
1886 CHI N C-O 118 .388
1887 BOS N C-2-O 114 .394
1888 BOS N C-O 105 .318
1889 BOS N C-O 125 .293
1890 BOS P M-C-S 90 .324
1891 CIN AA M-P- 3 74 0- 1
C-1-2-S-3-O .280
BOS AA C 3 .200
BOS N O 24 .239
1892 BOS N C 72 .201
1893 NY N C 16 .314
BRTR 7 1437 0- 1
.313

KELLY, R B (SPEEED)
B.AUG.12,1884 BRIAN,OHIO
D.MAY 6,1949 GOSHEN,IND.
1909 WAS A 3 17 .143
BRTR

KELLY, REYNOLDS JOSEPH (REN)
B.NOV.18,1899 SAN FRANCISCO,CAL
D.AUG.24,1963 MILLBRAE,CAL.
1923 PHI A P 1 0- 0
BRTR

KELLY, ROBERT EDWARD (BOB)
B.OCT.4,1927 CLEVELAND,OHIO
1951 CHI N P 35 7- 4
1952 CHI N P 31 4- 9
1953 CHI N P 14 0- 1
CIN N P 28 1- 2
1958 CIN N P 2 0- 0
CLE A P 13 0- 2
BRTR 123 12-18

KELLY, VAN HOWARD
B.MAR.18,1946 CHARLOTTE,N.C.
1969 SD N 3-2 73 .244
1970 SD N 3/2 38 .169
BLTR 111 .221

KELLY, WILLIAM HENRY (BIG BILL)
B.DEC.28,1899 SYRACUSE,N.Y.
1920 PHI A 1 8 .181
1928 PHI N 1 23 .169
BRTR 31 .171

KELLY, WILLIAM JOSEPH (BILLY)
B.MAY 1,1886 BALTIMORE,MD.
D.JUNE 3,1940 DETROIT,MICH.
1910 STL N C 2 .000
1911 PIT N C 6 .125
1912 PIT N C 48 .318
1913 PIT N C 48 .268
BRTR 104 .290

KELSEY, GEORGE W.
B.OHIO
1907 PIT N C 2 .400
TR

KELSO, WILLIAM EUGENE (BILL)
B.FEB.19,1940 KANSAS CITY,MO.
1964 LA A P 10 2- 0
1966 CAL A /P 5 1- 1
1967 CAL A P 69 5- 3
1968 CIN N P 35 4- 1
BRTR 119 12- 5

YR	CL	LEA	POS	GP	G	REC

KELTNER, KENNETH FREDERICK (KEN) OR (BUTCH)
B.OCT.31,1916 MILWAUKEE,WIS.

YR	CL	LEA	POS	GP	G	REC
1937	CLE	A	3		1	.000
1938	CLE	A	3		149	.276
1939	CLE	A	3		154	.325
1940	CLE	A	3		149	.254
1941	CLE	A	3		149	.269
1942	CLE	A	3		152	.287
1943	CLE	A	3		110	.260
1944	CLE	A	3		149	.295
1946	CLE	A	3		116	.241
1947	CLE	A	3		151	.257
1948	CLE	A	3		153	.297
1949	CLE	A	3		80	.232
1950	BOS	A	1-3		13	.321
		BRTR			1526	.276

KELTY, JOHN E.JOSEPH (CHIEF)
B.1867 JERSEY CITY,N.J.

1890	PIT	N	O		59	.236

KEMMAN, HERBERT FREDERICK
[PLAYED UNDER NAME OF FREDERICK HERBERT]

KEMMER, WILLIAM E.

1895	LOU	N	3		10	.139

KEMMERER, RUSSELL PAUL (RUSS) (RUSTY) OR (DUTCH)
B.NOV.1,1931 PITTSBURGH,PA.

YR	CL	LEA	POS	GP	G	REC
1954	BOS	A	P		19	5- 3
1955	BOS	A	P		7	1- 1
1957	BOS	A	P		1	0- 0
	WAS	A	P		39	7-11
1958	WAS	A	P		40	6-15
1959	WAS	A	P		37	8-17
1960	WAS	A	P		3	0- 2
	CHI	A	P		36	6- 3
1961	CHI	A	P		47	3- 3
1962	CHI	A	P		20	2- 1
	HOU	N	P		36	5- 8
1963	HOU	N	P		17	0- 0
		BRTR			302	43-59

KEMMLER, RUDOLPH
B.CHICAGO,ILL.
D.JUNE 20,1909 CHICAGO,ILL.

1879	PRO	N	C		2	.143
1881	CLE	N	C		1	.000
1882	CIN	AA	C-O		3	.091
	PIT	AA	C-O		25	.218
1883	COL	AA	C-O		85	.202
1884	PIT	AA	C		61	.202
1885	PIT	AA	C		18	.191
1886	STL	AA	C		35	.150
1889	COL	AA	C		8	.134
		BRTR			238	.195

KEMNER, HERMAN JOHN (DUTCH)
B.MAR.4,1899 QUINCY,ILL.

1929	CIN	N	P		9	0- 0
		BRTR				

KEMP, STEVEN F (STEVE)
B.AUG.7,1954 SAN ANGELO,TEX.

1977	DET	A	*O		151	.257
1978	DET	A	*O		159	.277
		BLTL			310	.267

KENDALL, FRED LYN
B.JAN.31,1949 TORRANCE,CAL.

1969	SD	N	/C		10	.154
1970	SD	N	/C-1-O		4	.000
1971	SD	N	C/1-3		49	.171
1972	SD	N	C/1		91	.216
1973	SD	N	*C		145	.282
1974	SD	N	*C		141	.231
1975	SD	N	C		103	.199
1976	SD	N	*C		146	.246
1977	CLE	A	*C		103	.249
1978	BOS	A	1/C		20	.195
		BRTR			812	.236

KENDERS, ALBERT DANIEL GEORGE
B.APR.4,1937 BARRINGTON,N.J.

1961	PHI	N	C		10	.174
		BRTR				

KENNA, EDWARD ALOYSIUS (EDDIE) OR (SCRAP IRON)
B.SEPT.30,1897 SAN FRANCISCO,CAL.
D.AUG.21,1972 SAN FRANCISCO,CAL

1928	WAS	A	C		41	.297
		BRTR				

KENNA, EDWARD BENNINGHAUS (THE PITCHING POET)
B.OCT.17,1877 CHARLESTON,W.VA.
D.MAR.22,1912 GRANT,FLA.

1902	PHI	A	P		3	1- 1
		TR				

KENNEDY, EDWARD
B.APR.1,1856 CARBONDALE,PA.
D.MAY 22,1905 NEW YORK,N.Y.

1883	MET	AA	O		97	.215
1884	MET	AA	O		103	.184
1885	MET	AA	O		96	.222
1886	BRO	AA	O		6	.181
					302	.209

KENNEDY, JAMES C.
B.1867 NEW YORK,N.Y.
D.APR.20,1904 BRIGHTON BEACH,N.Y.
NON-PLAYING MANAGER BRO[AA]1890

KENNEDY, JAMES EARL (JIM)
B.NOV.1,1946 TULSA,OKLA.

1970	STL	N	/S-2		12	.125
		BLTR				

KENNEDY, JOHN EDWARD
B.MAY 29,1941 CHICAGO,ILL.

1962	WAS	A	S-3		14	.262
1963	WAS	A	S-3		36	.177
1964	WAS	A	2-S-3		148	.230
1965	LA	N	3/S		104	.171
1966	LA	N	3-S-2		125	.201
1967	NY	A	S-3/2		78	.196
1969	SEA	A	S-3		61	.234
1970	MIL	A	2/3-S-1		25	.255
	BOS	A	3/2		43	.256
1971	BOS	A	2-S/3		74	.276
1972	BOS	A	2-S-3		71	.245
1973	BOS	A	2-3		67	.181
1974	BOS	A	/2-3		10	.133
		BRTR			856	.225

KENNEDY, JOHN IRVIN
B.NOV.23,1934 SUMTER,S.C.

1957	PHI	N	3		5	.000
		BRTR				

KENNEDY, JUNIOR RAYMOND
B.AUG.9,1950 FORT GIBSON,OKLA.

1974	CIN	N	2/3		22	.158
1978	CIN	N	2/3		89	.255
		BRTR			111	.244

KENNEDY, LLOYD VERNON (VERN)
B.MAR.20,1907 KANSAS CITY,MO.

YR	CL	LEA	POS	GP	G	REC
1934	CHI	A	P		3	0- 2
1935	CHI	A	P		31	11-11
1936	CHI	A	P		35	21- 9
1937	CHI	A	P		32	14-13
1938	DET	A	P		37	12- 9
1939	DET	A	P		4	0- 3
	STL	A	P		33	9-17
1940	STL	A	P		34	12-17
1941	STL	A	P		6	2- 4
	WAS	A	P	17	18	1- 7
1942	CLE	A	P	28	33	4- 8
1943	CLE	A	P	28	38	10- 7
1944	CLE	A	P	12	15	2- 5
	PHI	N	P	12	14	1- 3
1945	PHI	N	P	12	13	0- 3
	CIN	N	P		24	5-12
		BLTR		344	373	104-132

KENNEDY, MICHAEL JOSEPH (DOC)
B.AUG.11,1853 BROOKLYN,N.Y.
D.MAY 23,1920 GROVE,N.Y.

1879	CLE	N	C		47	.285
1880	CLE	N	C		66	.200
1881	CLE	N	C-3-O		38	.313
1882	CLE	N	C		1	.250
1883	BUF	N	C-1-O		5	.286
		BRTR			157	.257

KENNEDY, MONTIA CALVIN (MONTE)
B.MAY 11,1922 AMELIA,VA.

YR	CL	LEA	POS	GP	G	REC
1946	NY	N	P		38	9-10
1947	NY	N	P		34	9-12
1948	NY	N	P	25	26	3- 9
1949	NY	N	P	38	39	12-14
1950	NY	N	P		36	5- 4
1951	NY	N	P		29	1- 2
1952	NY	N	P	31	34	3- 4
1953	NY	N	P	18	19	0- 0
		BRTL		249	255	42-55

KENNEDY, RAYMOND LINCOLN
B.MAY 19,1895 PITTSBURGH,PA.
D.JAN.16,1969 CASSELBERRY,FLA.

1916	STL	A	C		1	.000
		BRTR				

KENNEDY, ROBERT DANIEL (BOB)
B.AUG.18,1920 CHICAGO,ILL.

YR	CL	LEA	POS	GP	G	REC
1939	CHI	A	3		3	.250
1940	CHI	A	3		154	.252
1941	CHI	A	3		76	.206
1942	CHI	A	3-O		113	.231
1946	CHI	A	3-O		113	.258
1947	CHI	A	3-O		115	.262
1948	CHI	A	O		30	.248
	CLE	A	1-2-O		66	.301
1949	CLE	A	3-O		121	.276
1950	CLE	A	O		146	.291
1951	CLE	A	O		108	.246
1952	CLE	A	3-O		22	.300
1953	CLE	A	O		100	.236
1954	CLE	A	O		1	.000
	BAL	A	3-O		106	.251
1955	BAL	A	1-3-O		26	.143
	CHI	A	1-3-O		83	.304
1956	CHI	A	3		8	.077
	DET	A	3-O		69	.232
1957	CHI	A	H		4	.000
	BRO	N	3-O		19	.129
		BRTR			1483	.254

NON-PLAYING MANAGER
CHI[N] 1963-65; OAK[A] 1968

KENNEDY, SHERMAN MONTGOMERY (SNAPPER)
B.NOV.1,1878 CONNEAUT,OHIO
D.AUG.15,1945 PASADENA,TEX.

1902	CHI	N	O		1	.000
		BBTR				

KENNEDY, TERRENCE EDWARD (TERRY)
B.JUNE 4,1956 EUCLID,OHIO

1978	STL	N	C		10	.172
		BLTR				

KENNEDY, THEODORE A.
B.FEB.1865 HENRY,ILL.
D.OCT.31,1907 ST.LOUIS,MO.

1885	CHI	N	P-3		9	7- 2
						.065
1886	ATH	AA	P		22	5-15
	LOU	AA	P		4	0- 4
	BL				35	12-21
						.043

KENNEDY, WILLIAM AULTON (LEFTY)
B.MAR.14,1921 CARNESVILLE,GA.

1948	CLE	A	P		6	1- 0
	STL	A	P		26	7- 8
1949	STL	A	P		48	4-11
1950	STL	A	P		1	0- 0
1951	STL	A	P		19	1- 5
1952	CHI	A	P		47	2- 2
1953	BOS	A	P		16	0- 0
1956	CIN	N	P		1	0- 0
1957	CIN	N	P		8	0- 2
		BLTL			172	15-28

KENNEDY, WILLIAM EDWARD (ED)
B.APR.5,1861 BELLEVUE,KY.
D.DEC.22,1912 CHEYENNE,WYOMING

1884	CIN	U	3-S-3-O		13	.213
		BRTR				

KENNEDY, WILLIAM GORMAN
B.DEC.22,1918 ALEXANDRIA,VA.

1942	WAS	A	P		8	0- 1
1946	WAS	A	P		21	1- 2
1947	WAS	A	P		2	0- 0
		BLTL			31	1- 3

KENNEDY, WILLIAM P. (BRICKYARD)
B.OCT.7,1867 BELLAIRE,OHIO
D.SEPT.23,1915 BELLAIRE,OHIO

YR	CL	LEA	POS	GP	G	REC
1892	BRO	N	P		22	13- 8
1893	BRO	N	P		45	25-18
1894	BRO	N	P		44	24-20
1895	BRO	N	P		36	19-13
1896	BRO	N	P		37	15-22
1897	BRO	N	P	40	42	19-21
1898	BRO	N	P		38	16-22
1899	BRO	N	P		37	18- 8
1900	BRO	N	P		37	22-15
1901	BRO	N	P		14	3- 5
1902	NY	N	P		6	1- 4
1903	PIT	N	P		18	9- 6
		BRTR		374	376	184-162

KENNEY, GERALD T (JERRY)
B.JUNE 30,1945 ST.LOUIS,MO.

1967	NY	A	S		20	.310
1969	NY	A	3-O-S		130	.257
1970	NY	A	*3/2		140	.193
1971	NY	A	*3/S-1		120	.262
1972	NY	A	S/3		50	.210
1973	CLE	A	/2		5	.250
		BLTR			465	.237

KENNEY, JOHN

1872	ATL	NA	2-O		5	.000

KENNEY, ARTHUR JOSEPH
B.APR.29,1916 MILFORD,MASS.

1938	BOS	N	P		2	0- 0
		BLTL				

YR	CL	LEA	POS	GP	G	REC

KENT, EDWARD C.
B.1859 NEW YORK
1884 TOL AA P   1   0- 1
TL

KENT, MAURICE ALLEN
B.SEPT.17,1885 MARSHALLTOWN,IA.
D.APR.19,1966 IOWA CITY,IOWA
1912 BRO N P   20   5- 5
1913 BRO N P   5   0- 0
BRTR   25   5- 5

KENWORTHY, RICHARD LEE (DICK)
B.APR.1,1941 RED OAK,IOWA
1962 CHI A 2   3   .000
1964 CHI A H   2   .000
1965 CHI A /H   9   .G00
1966 CHI A /3   9   .200
1967 CHI A 3   50   .227
1968 CHI A 3   58   .221
BRTR   125   .215

KENWORTHY, WILLIAM JENNINGS (DUKE)
B.JAN.1,1886 CAMBRIDGE,OHIO
D.SEPT.21,1950 EUREKA,CAL.
1912 WAS A 0   12   .289
1914 KC F 2   146   .316
1915 KC F 2   121   .299
1917 STL A 2   5   .100
BBTR   284   .305

KENZIE, WALTER H.
B.1859 CHICAGO,ILL.
1882 DET N S   13   .094
1884 CHI N S-3   19   .158
STL AA 2   2   .125
34   .133

KEOUGH, JOSEPH WILLIAM (JOE)
B.JAN.7,1946 POMONA,CAL.
1968 OAK A 0/1   34   .214
1969 KC A 0/1   70   .187
1970 KC A 0-1   57   .322
1971 KC A *0   110   .248
1972 KC A 0   56   .219
1973 CHI A /H   5   .000
BLTL   332   .246

KEOUGH, MATTHEW LON (MATT)
B.JULY 3,1955 POMONA,CAL.
1977 OAK A /P   7   8   1- 3
1978 OAK A P   32   33   8-15
BRTR   39   41   9-18

KEOUGH, RICHARD MARTIN (MARTY)
B.APR.14,1935 OAKLAND,CAL.
1956 BOS A H   3   .000
1957 BOS A 0   9   .059
1958 BOS A 1-0   68   .220
1959 BOS A 1-0   96   .243
1960 BOS A 0   38   .248
CLE A 0   65   .248
1961 WAS A 1-0   135   .249
1962 CIN N 1-0   111   .278
1963 CIN N 1-0   95   .227
1964 CIN N 1-0   109   .257
1965 CIN N 1/0   62   .116
1966 ATL N /1-0   17   .059
CHI N /0   33   .231
BLTL   841   .242

KERIAZAKOS, CONSTANTINE NICHOLAS (GUS)
B.JULY 28,1931 W.ORANGE,N.J.
1950 CHI A P   1   0- 1
1954 WAS A P   22   2- 3
1955 KC A P   5   0- 1
BRTR   28   2- 5

KERINS, JOHN NELSON
B.JULY 15,1858 INDIANAPOLIS,IND
D.SEPT.8,1919 LOUISVILLE,KY.
1884 IND AA 1   93   .210
1885 LOU AA C-1   113   .243
1886 LOU AA C-1   119   .268
1887 LOU AA C-1   112   .360
1888 LOU AA M-C-0   81   .139
1889 LOU AA C-0   2   .333
BAL AA C-1-S-0 16   .283
1890 STL AA C   19   .136
BRTR   555   .267

KERKSIECK, WAYMAN WILLIAM (BILL)
B.DEC.6,1913 ULM,ARK.
D.MAR.11,1970 STUTTGART,ARK.
1939 PHI N P   23   25   0- 2
BRTR

KERLIN, ORIE MILTON (CY)
B.JAN.23,1891 SUMMERFIELD,LA.
D.OCT.29,1974 SHREVEPORT,LA.
1915 PIT F C   3   .000
BLTR

KERN, JAMES LESTER (JIM)
B.MAR.15,1949 GLADWIN,MICH.
1974 CLE A /P   4   0- 1
1975 CLE A P   13   1- 2
1976 CLE A P   50 10- 7
1977 CLE A P   60   8-10
1978 CLE A P   58 10-10
BRTR   185 29-30

KERN, WILLIAM GEORGE
B.FEB.28,1933 COPLAY,PA.
1962 KC A 0   8   .250
BRTR

KERNAN, JOSEPH
B.BALTIMORE,MD.
1873 MAR NA 2-0   2   -

KERNEK, GEORGE BOYD
B.JAN.12,1940 HOLDENVILLE,OKLA.
1965 STL N /1   10   .290
1966 STL N 1   20   .240
BLTL   30   .259

KERNS, DANIEL P.
B.PHILADELPHIA,PA.
1920 PHI A H   1   .000

KERNS, RUSSELL ELDON
B.NOV.10,1920 FREMONT,OHIO
1945 DET A H   1   .000
BLTR

KERR, JOHN FRANCIS
B.NOV.26,1898 SAN FRANCISCO,CAL
1923 DET A S   19   .214
1924 DET A 3-0   17   .273
1929 CHI A 2   127   .258
1930 CHI A 2-S   70   .289
1931 CHI A 2   128   .268
1932 WAS A 2-S   51   .273
1933 WAS A 2-3   28   .200
1934 WAS A 3   31   .272
BRTR   471   .266
BB 1923-24

KERR, JOHN JONAS (DOC)
B.JAN.17,1882 DEL ROY,OHIO
D.JUNE 9,1937 BALTIMORE,MD.
1914 PIT F C   41   .254
BAL F C   14   .265
1915 BAL F C   3   .333
BBTR   58   .260

KERR, JOHN JOSEPH (BUDDY)
B.NOV.6,1922 ASTORIA,N.Y.
1943 NY N S   27   .286
1944 NY N S   150   .267
1945 NY N S   149   .249
1946 NY N S-3   145   .250
1947 NY N S   138   .287
1948 NY N S   144   .240
1949 NY N S   90   .209
1950 BOS N S   155   .227
1951 BOS N 2-S   69   .186
1067   .249

KERR, JOHN MELVILLE (MEL)
B.MAY 22,1903 SOURIS,MAN.,CAN.
1925 CHI N H   1   .000
BLTL

KERR, RICHARD HENRY (DICKIE)
B.JULY 3,1893 ST.LOUIS,MO.
D.MAY 4,1963 HOUSTON,TEX.
1919 CHI A P   39 13- 8
1920 CHI A P   46 21- 9
1921 CHI A P   44   45 19-17
1925 CHI A P   12   13   0- 1
BLTL   141 143 53-35

KERRIGAN, JOSEPH THOMAS (JOE)
B.NOV.30,1954 PHILADELPHIA,PA.
1976 MON N P   38   2- 6
1977 MON N P   66   3- 5
1978 BAL A P   26   3- 1
BRTR   130   8-12

KERSCHER, WOLFGANG ANDREW
[PLAYED UNDER NAME OF
MICHAEL ANDREW KIRCHER]

KERWIN, DANIEL P.
B.JULY 9,1879 PHILADELPHIA,PA.
1903 CIN N 0   1   .790
BLTL

KESSINGER, DONALD EULON (DON)
B.JULY 17,1942 FORREST CITY,ARK.
1964 CHI N S   4   .167
1965 CHI N *S   106   .201
1966 CHI N *S   150   .274
1967 CHI N *S   145   .231
1968 CHI N *S   160   .240
1969 CHI N *S   158   .273
1970 CHI N *S   154   .266
1971 CHI N *S   155   .258
1972 CHI N *S   149   .274
1973 CHI N *S   160   .262
1974 CHI N *S   153   .259
1975 CHI N *S-3   154   .243
1976 STL N *S-2/3 145   .239
1977 STL N S-2/3   59   .239
CHI A S-2/3   39   .235
1978 CHI A *S/2   131   .255
BBTR   2022   .253
BR 1964-65

KESSLER, HENRY (LUCKY)
B.JAN.9,1900 FRANKLIN,PA.
1873 ATL NA 1   1   -
1874 ATL NA C-2-3-0 14   -
1875 ATL NA 2-S-0   25   -
1876 CIN N S-3-0   59   .251
1877 CIN N C-1   6   .100
BRTR   105   -

KESTER, RICHARD LEE (RICK)
B.JULY 7,1946 IOLA,KAN.
1968 ATL N /P   5   0- 0
1969 ATL N /P   1   0- 0
1970 ATL N P   15   0- 0
BRTR   21   0- 0

KETCHUM, AUGUSTUS FRANKLIN
B.MAR.21,1897 ROYCE CITY,TEX.
1922 PHI A P   6   0- 1
BRTR

KETCHUM, FREDERICK L.
B.JULY 27,1875 ELMIRA,N.Y.
D.MAR.12,1908 CORTLAND,N.Y.
1899 LOU N 0   15   .311
1901 PHI A 0   5   .227
BLTR   20   .289

KETTER, PHILIP
B.HUTCHINSON,KAN.
1912 STL A C   2   .333
TR

KEUPPER, HENRY J.
B.JUNE 24,1887 STAUNTON,ILL.
D.AUG.14,1960 MARION,ILL.
1914 STL F P   42   7-20
BLTL

KIBBIE, HORACE KENT (HOD)
B.JULY 18,1903 FT.WORTH,TEX.
D.OCT.19,1975 FT.WORTH,TEX.
1925 BOS N 2-S   11   .268
BRTR

KIBBLE, JOHN WESTLY (JACK) OR (HAPPY)
B.JAN.2,1892 SEATONVILLE,ILL.
D.DEC.13,1969 ROUNDUP,MONT.
1912 CLE A 2-3   5   .000
BBTR

KIEFER, JOSEPH WILLIAM (HARLEM JOE) OR (SMOKE)
B.JULY 19,1899 W.LEYDEN,N.Y.
1920 CHI A P   2   0- 1
1925 BOS A P   2   0- 2
1926 BOS A P   11   0- 3
BRTR   15   0- 6

KIELY, LEO PATRICK (LEO) OR (KIKI)
B.NOV.30,1929 HOBOKEN,N.J.
1951 BOS A P   17   18   7- 7
1954 BOS A P   28   5- 8
1955 BOS A P   23   3- 3
1956 BOS A P   23   2- 2
1958 BOS A P   47   5- 2
1959 BOS A P   41   3- 3
1960 KC A P   20   1- 2
BLTL   209 210 26-27

KILDUFF, PETER JOHN
B.APR.4,1893 WEIR CITY,KAN.
D.FEB.14,1930 PITTSBURG,KAN.
1917 NY N 2-S   31   .205
CHI N 2-S   56   .277
1918 CHI N 2   30   .204
1919 CHI N 2-S-3   31   .273
BRO N 2-3   32   .301
1920 BRO N 2   141   .272
1921 BRO N 2   107   .288
BRTR   428   .270

KILEY, FRANCIS THOMAS
[PLAYED UNDER NAME OF
FRANCIS THOMAS KANE]

YR CL LEA POS   GP   G   REC

KILEY, JOHN FREDERICK
B.CAMBRIDGE,MASS.

YR	CL	LEA	POS	GP	G	REC
1884	WAS	AA	O		14	.203
1891	BOS	N	P		1	0- 1
			BLTL	1	15	0- 1
						.197

KILHULLEN, JOSEPH ISADORE (PAT)
B.AUG.10,1890 CARBONDALE,PA.
D.NOV.2,1922 OAKLAND,CAL.

YR	CL	LEA	POS	GP	G	REC
1914	PIT	N	C		1	.000
			BRTR			

KILKENNY, MICHAEL DAVID (MIKE)
B.APR.11,1945 BRADFORD,ONT.,CAN.

YR	CL	LEA	POS	GP	G	REC
1969	DET	A	P		39	8- 6
1970	DET	A	P	36	37	7- 6
1971	DET	A	P		30	4- 5
1972	DET	A	/P		1	0- 0
	OAK	A	/P		1	0- 0
	SD	N	/P		5	0- 0
	CLE	A	P		22	4- 1
1973	CLE	A	/P		5	0- 0
			BRTL	139	140	23-18

KILLEBREW, HARMON CLAYTON
(HARMON) OR (KILLER)
B.JUNE 29,1936 PAYETTE,IDAHO

YR	CL	LEA	POS	GP	G	REC
1954	WAS	A	2		9	.308
1955	WAS	A	2-3		38	.200
1956	WAS	A	2-3		44	.222
1957	WAS	A	2-3		9	.290
1958	WAS	A	3		13	.194
1959	WAS	A	3-O		153	.242
1960	WAS	A	1-3		124	.276
1961	MIN	A	1-3-O		150	.288
1962	MIN	A	1-O		155	.243
1963	MIN	A	O		142	.258
1964	MIN	A	O		158	.270
1965	MIN	A	1-3/O		113	.269
1966	MIN	A	*3-1-O		162	.281
1967	MIN	A	*1/3		163	.269
1968	MIN	A	1-3		100	.210
1969	MIN	A	*3-1		162	.276
1970	MIN	A	*3-1		157	.271
1971	MIN	A	1-3		147	.254
1972	MIN	A	*1		139	.231
1973	MIN	A	1		69	.242
1974	MIN	A	O-1		122	.222
1975	KC	A	O/1		106	.199
			BRTR		2435	.256

KILLEEN, EVANS HENRY
B.FEB.27,1936 BROOKLYN,N.Y.

YR	CL	LEA	POS	GP	G	REC
1959	KC	A	P		4	0- 0
			BRTR			

KILLEEN, HENRY
B.1871 TROY,N.Y.

YR	CL	LEA	POS	GP	G	REC
1891	CLE	N	P		1	0- 1

KILLEFER, WADE HAMPTON (RED)
B.APR.13,1884 BLOOMINGDALE,MICH
D.SEPT.4,1958 LOS ANGELES,CAL.

YR	CL	LEA	POS	GP	G	REC
1907	DET	A	O		1	.000
1908	DET	A	2		28	.213
1909	DET	A	2		23	.302
	WAS	A	O		40	.160
1910	WAS	A	2		106	.229
1914	CIN	N	O		42	.277
1915	CIN	N	1-O		155	.272
1916	CIN	N	O		70	.244
	NY	N	H		2	.500
			BRTR		467	.248

KILLEFER, WILLIAM LAVIER
(REINDEER BILL)
B.OCT.10,1887 BLOOMINGDALE,MICH
D.JULY 3,1960 ELSMERE,DEL.

YR	CL	LEA	POS	GP	G	REC
1909	STL	A	C		11	.172
1910	STL	A	C		74	.124
1911	PHI	N	C		6	.188
1912	PHI	N	C		85	.224
1913	PHI	N	C		120	.244
1914	PHI	N	C		98	.234
1915	PHI	N	C		105	.238
1916	PHI	N	C		97	.217
1917	PHI	N	C		125	.274
1918	CHI	N	C		104	.233
1919	CHI	N	C		103	.286
1920	CHI	N	C		62	.200
1921	CHI	N	M-C		45	.323
			BRTR		1035	.239

NON-PLAYING MANAGER
CHI[N] 1922-25, STL[A] 1930-33

KILLEN, FRANK BISSELL (LEFTY)
B.NOV.30,1870 PITTSBURGH,PA.
D.DEC.3,1939 PITTSBURGH,PA.

YR	CL	LEA	POS	GP	G	REC
1891	MIL	AA	P		11	8- 3
1892	WAS	N	P		54	29-25
1893	PIT	N	P		47	33-14
1894	PIT	N	P		24	14-10
1895	PIT	N	P		14	7- 6
1896	PIT	N	P		50	31-19
1897	PIT	N	P		41	16-23
1898	PIT	N	P		22	10-12
	WAS	N	P-O	17	20	7- 9
1899	WAS	N	P		5	0- 2
1899	BOS	N	P		12	7- 5
1900	CHI	N	P		6	3- 3
			TL	303	306	165-131
						.246

KILLIAN, EDWIN HENRY (ED)
OR (TWILIGHT ED)
B.NOV.12,1876 RACINE,WIS.
D.JULY 18,1928 DETROIT,MICH.

YR	CL	LEA	POS	GP	G	REC
1903	CLE	A	P		10	3- 5
1904	DET	A	P		40	15-20
1905	DET	A	P		39	22-14
1906	DET	A	P		20	9- 6
1907	DET	A	P	42	46	25-13
1908	DET	A	P	27	28	11-10
1909	DET	A	P		25	11- 9
1910	DET	A	P		11	4- 3
			BLTL	214	219	100-80

KILLILAY, JOHN WILLIAM (JACK)
B.MAY 24,1887 LEAVENWORTH,KAN.
D.OCT.21,1968 TULSA,OKLA.

YR	CL	LEA	POS	GP	G	REC
1911	BOS	A	P		14	4- 3
			BRTR			

KILROY, MATTHEW ALOYSIUS (MATCHES)
B.JUNE 21,1866 PHILADELPHIA,PA.
D.MAR.2,1940 PHILADELPHIA,PA.

YR	CL	LEA	POS	GP	G	REC
1886	BAL	AA	P		69	29-34
1887	BAL	AA	P		73	46-20
1888	BAL	AA	P	42	43	16-21
1889	BAL	AA	P	59	65	28-25
1890	BOS	P	P		31	10-13
1891	CIN	AA	P-O	7	8	1- 4
						.190
1892	WAS	N	P		4	1- 1
1893	LOU	N	P		5	3- 2
1894	LOU	N	P		6	0- 6
1898	CHI	N	P	12	25	6- 6
			TL	308	329	140-132
						.242

KILROY, MICHAEL JOSEPH
B.NOV.4,1872 PHILADELPHIA,PA.
D.OCT.2,1940 PHILADELPHIA,PA.

YR	CL	LEA	POS	GP	G	REC
1888	BAL	N	P		1	0- 1
1891	PHI	N	P		3	0- 1
			TR		4	0- 2

KIMBALL, EUGENE B.
B.AUG.31,1850 ROCHESTER,N.Y.
D.AUG.2,1882

YR	CL	LEA	POS	GP	G	REC
1871	CLE	NA	2-S-O		29	-

KIMBALL, NEWELL W. (NEWT)
B.MAR.27,1915 LOGAN,UTAH

YR	CL	LEA	POS	GP	G	REC
1937	CHI	N	P		2	0- 0
1938	CHI	N	P		1	0- 0
1940	BRO	N	P		21	3- 1
	STL	N	P		2	1- 0
1941	BRO	N	P		13	3- 1
1942	BRO	N	P		14	2- 0
1943	BRO	N	P		5	1- 1
	PHI	N	P		34	1- 6
			BRTR		94	11- 9

KIMBER, SAMUEL JACKSON
B.OCT.29,1852 PHILADELPHIA,PA.
D.NOV.7,1925 PHILADELPHIA,PA.

YR	CL	LEA	POS	GP	G	REC
1884	BRO	AA	P		41	18-20
1885	PRO	N	P		1	0- 1
			BRTR		42	18-21

KIMBERLIN, HARRY LYDLE
(MURPHY) OR (MULE TRADER)
B.MAR.13,1909 SULLIVAN,MO.

YR	CL	LEA	POS	GP	G	REC
1936	STL	A	P		13	0- 0
1937	STL	A	P		3	0- 2
1938	STL	A	P		1	0- 0
1939	STL	A	P		17	1- 2
			BRTR		34	1- 4

KIMBLE, RICHARD LEWIS
B.JULY 27,1915 BUCHTEL,OHIO

YR	CL	LEA	POS	GP	G	REC
1949	WAS	A	S		20	.245
			BLTR			

KIME, HAROLD LEE (LEFTY)
B.MAR.15,1899 W.SALEM,OHIO
D.MAY 16,1939 COLUMBUS,OHIO

YR	CL	LEA	POS	GP	G	REC
1920	STL	N	P		4	0- 0
			BLTL			

KIMM, BRUCE EDWARD
B.JUNE 29,1951 CEDAR RAPIDS,IOWA

YR	CL	LEA	POS	GP	G	REC
1976	DET	A	C		63	.263
1977	DET	A	C		14	.080
			BRTR		77	.237

KIMMICK, WALTER LYONS
B.MAY 30,1897 TURTLE CREEK,PA.

YR	CL	LEA	POS	GP	G	REC
1919	STL	N	S		2	.000
1921	CIN	N	3		3	.167
1922	CIN	N	2-S-3		39	.247
1923	CIN	N	2-S-3		29	.225
1925	PHI	N	2-S-3		70	.305
1926	PHI	N	1-S-3		20	.214
			BRTR		163	.261

KIMSEY, CLYDE ELIAS (CHAD)
B.AUG.6,1906 COPPERHILL,TENN.
D.DEC.3,1942 PRYOR,OKLA.

YR	CL	LEA	POS	GP	G	REC
1929	STL	A	P	24	29	3- 6
1930	STL	A	P	42	60	6-10
1931	STL	A	P	42	47	4- 6
1932	STL	A	P	33	34	4- 2
	CHI	A	P		7	1- 1
1933	CHI	A	P		28	4- 1
1936	DET	A	P		22	2- 3
			BLTR	198	227	24-29

KINDALL, GERALD DONALD
(JERRY) OR (SLIM)
B.MAY 27,1935 ST.PAUL,MINN.

YR	CL	LEA	POS	GP	G	REC
1956	CHI	N	S		32	.164
1957	CHI	N	2-S-3		72	.160
1958	CHI	N	2		3	.107
1960	CHI	N	2-S		89	.240
1961	CHI	N	2-S		96	.242
1962	CLE	A	2		154	.232
1963	CLE	A	1-2-S		86	.205
1964	CLE	A	1		23	.360
	MIN	A	1-2-S		62	.148
1965	MIN	A	*2-3/S		125	.196
			BRTR		742	.213
			BB 1960 (PART)			

KINDER, ELLIS RAYMOND
(ELLIS) OR (OLD FOLKS)
B.JULY 26,1914 ATKINS,ARK.
D.OCT.16,1968 JACKSON,TENN.

YR	CL	LEA	POS	GP	G	REC
1946	STL	A	P		33	3- 3
1947	STL	A	P		34	8-15
1948	BOS	A	P		28	10- 7
1949	BOS	A	P		43	23- 6
1950	BOS	A	P		48	14-12
1951	BOS	A	P		63	11- 2
1952	BOS	A	P		23	5- 6
1953	BOS	A	P		69	10- 6
1954	BOS	A	P		48	8- 8
1955	BOS	A	P		43	5- 5
1956	STL	N	P		22	2- 0
	CHI	A	P		29	3- 1
1957	CHI	A	P		1	0- 0
			BRTR		464	102-71

KINER, RALPH MC PHERRAN
B.OCT.27,1922 SANTA RITA,N.MEX.

YR	CL	LEA	POS	GP	G	REC
1946	PIT	N	O		144	.247
1947	PIT	N	O		152	.313
1948	PIT	N	O		156	.265
1949	PIT	N	O		152	.310
1950	PIT	N	O		150	.272
1951	PIT	N	1-O		151	.309
1952	PIT	N	O		149	.244
1953	PIT	N	O		41	.270
	CHI	N	O		117	.283
1954	CHI	N	O		147	.285
1955	CLE	A	O		113	.243
			BRTR		1472	.279

KING, CHARLES FREDERICK (SILVER)
[REAL NAME CHARLES FREDERICK KOENIG]
B.JAN.11,1868 ST.LOUIS,MO.
D.MAY 21,1938 ST.LOUIS,MO.

YR	CL	LEA	POS	GP	G	REC
1886	KC	N	P		7	1- 3
1887	STL	AA	P-O	46	62	34-11
1888	STL	AA	P		66	44-21
1889	STL	AA	P		54	33-17
1890	CHI	P	P		57	33-20
1891	PIT	N	P		48	17-31
1892	NY	N	P		52	24-24
1893	NY	N	P		15	5- 3
	CIN	N	P		13	7- 6
1896	WAS	N	P		16	10- 6
1897	WAS	N	P		18	9- 9
			BRTR	392	408	217-151
						.213

KING, CHARLES GILBERT (CHICK)
B.NOV.10,1930 PARIS,TENN.

YR	CL	LEA	POS	GP	G	REC
1954	DET	A	O		11	.214
1955	DET	A	O		7	.238
1956	DET	A	O		7	.222
1958	CHI	N	O		8	.250
1959	CHI	N	O		7	.000
	STL	N	O		5	.429
			BRTR		45	.237

KING, CLYDE EDWARD
B.MAY 23,1925 GOLDSBORO,N.C.

YR	CL	LEA	POS	GP	G	REC
1944	BRO	N	P		14	2-1
1945	BRO	N	P	42	43	5-5
1947	BRO	N	P		29	6-5
1948	BRO	N	P		9	0-1
1951	BRO	N	P		48	14-7
1952	BRO	N	P		23	2-0
1953	CIN	N	P		35	3-6
	BRTR			200	201	32-25

NON-PLAYING MANAGER
SF[N] 1969-70, ATL[N] 1974-75

KING, EDWARD LEE (LEE)
B.DEC.26,1892 HUNDRED,W.VA.
D.SEPT.16,1967 SHINNSTOWN,W.VA.

YR	CL	LEA	POS	G	REC
1916	PIT	N	O	8	.111
1917	PIT	N	O	111	.249
1918	PIT	N	O	36	.232
1919	NY	N	O	21	.100
1920	NY	N	O	93	.276
1921	NY	N	O	39	.223
	PHI	N	O	64	.269
1922	PHI	N	O	19	.226
	NY	N	1-O	20	.176
	BRTR			411	.247

KING, FREDERICK
[SEE JOHN ALBERT BUTLER]

KING, HAROLD (HAL)
B.FEB.1,1944 OVIEDO,FLA.

YR	CL	LEA	POS	G	REC
1967	HOU	N	C	15	.250
1968	HOU	N	C	27	.145
1970	ATL	N	C	89	.260
1971	ATL	N	C	86	.207
1972	TEX	A	C	50	.180
1973	CIN	N	/C	35	.186
1974	CIN	N	/C	20	.176
	BLTR			322	.214

KING, JAMES HUBERT (JIM)
B.AUG.27,1932 ELKINS,ARK.

YR	CL	LEA	POS	G	REC
1955	CHI	N	O	113	.256
1956	CHI	N	O	118	.249
1957	STL	N	O	22	.314
1958	SF	N	O	34	.214
1961	WAS	A	C-O	110	.270
1962	WAS	A	O	132	.243
1963	WAS	A	O	136	.231
1964	WAS	A	O	134	.241
1965	WAS	A	O	120	.213
1966	WAS	A	O	117	.248
1967	WAS	A	O/C	47	.210
	CHI	A	O	23	.120
	CLE	A	/O	19	.143
	BLTR			1125	.240

KING, LEE
B.MAR.28,1894 WALT4AM,MASS.
D.SEPT.7,1938 NEWTON CENTRE,MASS.

YR	CL	LEA	POS	G	REC
1916	PHI	A	O	42	.188
1919	BOS	N	O	2	.000
	BRTR			44	.186

KING, LYNN PAUL (DIG)
B.NOV.28,1907 VILLISCA,IOWA
D.MAY 11,1972 ATLANTIC,IOWA

YR	CL	LEA	POS	G	REC
1935	STL	N	O	8	.182
1936	STL	N	O	78	.190
1939	STL	N	O	89	.235
	BLTL			175	.208

KING, MARSHAL NEY (MART)
B.1849 TROY,N.Y.
D.OCT.19,1911

YR	CL	LEA	POS	G	REC
1871	CHI	NA	C-S-O	20	-
1872	TRO	NA	O	3	.000
				23	-

KING, NELSON JOSEPH (NELLIE)
B.MAR.15,1928 SHENANDOAH,PA.

YR	CL	LEA	POS	G	REC
1954	PIT	N	P	4	0-0
1955	PIT	N	P	17	1-3
1956	PIT	N	P	38	4-1
1957	PIT	N	P	36	2-1
	BRTR			95	7-5

KING, SAMUEL WARREN
B.MAY 17,1852 PEABODY,MASS.
D.AUG.11,1922 PEABODY,MASS.

YR	CL	LEA	POS	G	REC
1883	PHI	N	C	1	.000
1884	WAS	AA	C	12	.174
	TL			13	.174

KING, STEPHEN F.
B.1845 TROY,N.Y.
D.JULY 8,1895

YR	CL	LEA	POS	G	REC
1871	TRO	NA	O	29	.396
1872	TRO	NA	O	25	.297
1874	TRO	NA	O	12	-
				66	-

KINGDON, WESTCOTT WILLIAM
B.JULY 4,1900 LOS ANGELES,CAL.
D.APR.19,1975 CAPISTRANO,CAL.

YR	CL	LEA	POS	G	REC
1932	WAS	A	S-3	18	.324
	BRTR				

KINGMAN, DAVID ARTHUR (DAVE)
B.DEC.21,1948 PENDLETON,ORE.

YR	CL	LEA	POS	GP	G	REC
1971	SF	N	1-O		41	.278
1972	SF	N	3-1-O		135	.225
1973	SF	N	3-1/P	2	112	0-0 .203
1974	SF	N	1-3/O		121	.223
1975	NY	N	O-1-3		134	.231
1976	NY	N	*O-1		123	.238
1977	NY	N	O-1		58	.209
	SD	N	O-1/3		56	.238
	CAL	A	/1-O		10	.194
	NY	A	/H		8	.250
1978	CHI	N	*O/1		119	.266
	BRTR			2	917	0-0 .232

KINGMAN, HENRY LEES (HARRY)
B.APR.3,1892 TIENTSIN,CHINA

YR	CL	LEA	POS	G	REC
1914	NY	A	1	4	.000
	BLTL				

KINLOCK, WALTER
B.1878 ST.JOSEPH,MO.

YR	CL	LEA	POS	G	REC
1895	STL	N	3	1	.333

KINNEY, DENNIS PAUL
B.FEB.26,1952 TOLEDO,OHIO

YR	CL	LEA	POS	G	REC
1978	CLE	A	P	18	0-2
	SD	N	/P	7	0-1
	BLTL			25	0-3

KINNEY, WALTER WILLIAM
B.SEPT.9,1893 DENISON,TEX.
D.JULY 1,1971 ESCONDIDO,CAL.

YR	CL	LEA	POS	GP	G	REC
1918	BOS	A	P	5	6	0-0
1919	PHI	A	P	43	57	9-15
1920	PHI	A	P	10	13	2-4
1923	PHI	A	P		5	0-1
	BLTL			63	81	11-20

KINSELLA, EDWARD WILLIAM (RUBE)
B.JAN.15,1882 LEXINGTON,ILL.
D.JAN.17,1976 BLOOMINGTON,ILL.

YR	CL	LEA	POS	G	REC
1905	PIT	N	P	3	0-1
1910	STL	A	P	10	1-3
	BRTR			13	1-4

KINSELLA, ROBERT FRANCIS (RED)
B.JAN.5,1899 SPRINGFIELD,ILL.
D.DEC.30,1951 LOS ANGELES,CAL.

YR	CL	LEA	POS	G	REC
1919	NY	N	O	3	.222
1920	NY	N	O	1	.333
	BRTR			4	.250

KINSLER
B.STATEN ISLAND,N.Y.

YR	CL	LEA	POS	G	REC
1893	NY	N	P	1	.000

KINSLOW, THOMAS F.
B.JAN.12,1866 WASHINGTON,D.C.
D.FEB.22,1901 WASHINGTON,D.C.

YR	CL	LEA	POS	G	REC
1886	WAS	N	C	3	.333
1887	MET	AA	C	2	.000
1890	BRO	P	C	63	.277
1891	BRO	N	C	59	.238
1892	BRO	N	C	63	.309
1893	BRO	N	C	77	.299
1894	BRO	N	C	61	.298
1895	PIT	N	C	17	.230
1896	LOU	N	C	8	2.80
1898	WAS	N	C	3	.111
	STL	N	C	14	.278
	TR			370	.271

KINZY, HENRY HERSHEL (HARRY) OR (SLIM)
B.JULY 19,1910 HALLSVILLE,TEX.

YR	CL	LEA	POS	G	REC
1934	CHI	A	P	13	0-1

KIPP, FRED LEO
B.OCT.1,1931 PIQUA,KAN.

YR	CL	LEA	POS	GP	G	REC
1957	BRO	N	P		1	0-0
1958	LA	N	P	40	42	6-6
1959	LA	N	P		2	0-0
1960	NY	A	P		4	0-1
	BLTL			47	49	6-7

KIPPER, THORNTON JOHN
B.SEPT.27,1928 BAGLEY,WIS.

YR	CL	LEA	POS	G	REC
1953	PHI	N	P	20	3-3
1954	PHI	N	P	11	0-0
1955	PHI	N	P	24	0-1
	BRTR			55	3-4

KIPPERT, EDWARD AUGUST (KICKAPOO)
B.JAN.3,1880 DETROIT,MICH.
D.JUNE 3,1960 DETROIT,MICH.

YR	CL	LEA	POS	G	REC
1914	CIN	N	O	2	.000
	BRTR				

KIRBY, CLAYTON LAWS (CLAY)
B.JUNE 25,1948 WASHINGTON,D.C.

YR	CL	LEA	POS	GP	G	REC
1969	SD	N	P		35	7-20
1970	SD	N	P		36	10-16
1971	SD	N	P	38	40	15-13
1972	SD	N	P	34	35	12-14
1973	SD	N	P	34	35	8-18
1974	CIN	N	P		36	12-9
1975	CIN	N	P		26	10-6
1976	MON	N	P		22	1-8
	BRTR			261	265	75-104

KIRBY, JAMES HERSCHEL
B.MAY 5,1923 NASHVILLE,TENN.

YR	CL	LEA	POS	G	REC
1949	CHI	N	H	3	.500
	BRTR				

KIRBY, JOHN F.
B.JAN.13,1865 ST.LOUIS,MO.
D.OCT.6,1931 ST.LOUIS,MO.

YR	CL	LEA	POS	GP	G	REC
1884	KC	U	P-O		2	0-1 .167
1885	STL	N	P		14	5-8
1886	STL	N	P	38	41	12-25
1887	IND	N	P-O		8	1-7 .138
1888	KC	AA	P		6	1-5
	TR			73	76	19-51 .108

KIRBY, LARUE
B.DEC.30,1889 EUREKA,MICH.
D.JUNE 10,1961 LANSING,MICH.

YR	CL	LEA	POS	GP	G	REC
1912	NY	N	P		3	1-0
1914	STL	F	O		51	.253
1915	STL	F	O		59	.212
	BBTR			3	113	1-0 .233

KIRCHER, MICHAEL ANDREW
[REAL NAME WOLFGANG ANDREW KERSCHER]
B.SEPT.30,1897 ROCHESTER,N.Y.
D.JUNE 20,1972 ROCHESTER,N.Y.

YR	CL	LEA	POS	G	REC
1919	PHI	A	P	2	0-0
1920	STL	N	P	9	2-1
1921	STL	N	P	3	0-1
	BBTR			14	2-2

KIRK, THOMAS DANIEL
B.SEPT.27,1927 PHILADELPHIA,PA.
D.AUG.1,1974 PHILADELPHIA,PA.

YR	CL	LEA	POS	G	REC
1947	PHI	A	H	1	.000
	BLTL				

KIRK, WILLIAM PARTLEMORE
B.JULY 19,1935 COATESVILLE,PA.

YR	CL	LEA	POS	G	REC
1961	KC	A	P	1	0-0
	BLTL				

KIRKE, JUDSON FABIAN (JAY)
B.JUNE 16,1888 FLEISCHMANNS,N.Y N.Y.
D.AUG.31,1968 NEW ORLEANS,LA.

YR	CL	LEA	POS	G	REC
1910	DET	A	2	8	.192
1911	BOS	N	O	20	.360
1912	BOS	N	O	103	.320
1913	BOS	N	O	18	.237
1914	CLE	A	1-O	67	.273
1915	CLE	A	1	87	.310
1918	NY	N	1	17	.250
	BRTR			320	.301

KIRKLAND, WILLIE CHARLES
B.FEB.17,1934 SILURIA,ALA.

YR	CL	LEA	POS	G	REC
1958	SF	N	O	122	.258
1959	SF	N	O	126	.272
1960	SF	N	O	146	.252
1961	CLE	A	O	146	.259
1962	CLE	A	O	137	.200
1963	CLE	A	O	127	.230
1964	BAL	A	O	66	.200
	WAS	A	O	32	.216
1965	WAS	A	O	123	.231
1966	WAS	A	O	124	.190
	BLTR			1149	.240

KIRKPATRICK, EDGAR LEON (ED)
B.OCT.8,1944 SPOKANE,WASH.

YR	CL	LEA	POS	G	REC
1962	LA	A	C	3	.000
1963	LA	A	C-O	34	.195
1964	LA	A	O	75	.242
1965	CAL	A	O	19	.260
1966	CAL	A	*O/1	117	.192
1967	CAL	A	/C-O	3	.000
1968	CAL	A	O/C-1	89	.230
1969	KC	A	O/C-1-3-2	120	.257
1970	KC	A	C-O-1	134	.229
1971	KC	A	O/C	120	.219
1972	KC	A	*C/1	113	.275
1973	KC	A	*O-C	126	.263
1974	PIT	N	1-O/C	116	.247
1975	PIT	N	1-O	89	.236
1976	PIT	N	1-O-3	83	.233
1977	PIT	N	1/O-3	21	.143
	TEX	A	/O-1-C	20	.188
	MIL	A	O/3	29	.273
	BLTR			1311	.238

YR	CL LEA POS	GP	G	REC

KIRKPATRICK, ENOS CLAIRE
B.DEC.8,1885 PITTSBURGH,PA.
D.APR.14,1964 PITTSBURGH,PA.

YR	CL LEA POS	GP	G	REC
1912	BRO N 3		32	.191
1913	BRO N 2		48	.247
1914	BAL F 3		55	.259
1915	BAL F 2-3		60	.241
	BRTR		195	.239

KIRKWOOD, DONALD PAUL (DON)
B.SEPT.24,1949 PONTIAC,MICH.

YR	CL LEA POS	GP	G	REC
1974	CAL A /P		3	0- 0
1975	CAL A P	44	45	6- 5
1976	CAL A P		28	6-12
1977	CAL A P		13	1- 0
	CHI A P		16	1- 1
1978	TOR A P	16	17	4- 5
	BRTR	120	122	18-23

KIRRENE, JOSEPH JOHN (JOE)
B.OCT.4,1931 SAN FRANCISCO,CAL.

YR	CL LEA POS	GP	G	REC
1950	CHI A 3		1	.250
1954	CHI A 3		9	.304
	BRTR		10	.296

KIRSCH, HARRY LOUIS (CASEY)
B.OCT.17,1887 PITTSBURGH,PA.
D.DEC.25,1925 OVERBROOK,PA.

YR	CL LEA POS	GP	G	REC
1910	CLE A P		2	0- 0
	TR			

KISH, ERNEST ALEXANDER
B.FEB.6,1918 WASHINGTON,D.C.

YR	CL LEA POS	GP	G	REC
1945	PHI A O		43	.245
	BLTR			

KISINGER, CHARLES SAMUEL (RUBE)
B.DEC.13,1876 ADRIAN,MICH.
D.JULY 14,1941 HURON,OHIO

YR	CL LEA POS	GP	G	REC
1902	DET A P		5	1- 4
1903	DET A P		16	7- 9
	BRTR		21	8-13

KISLEAUSKAS, EDWARD WILLIAM
[PLAYED UNDER NAME OF
EDWARD WILLIAM COLE]

KISON, BRUCE EUGENE
B.FEB.18,1950 PASCO,WASH.

YR	CL LEA POS	GP	G	REC
1971	PIT N P		18	6- 5
1972	PIT N P		32	9- 7
1973	PIT N /P		7	3- 0
1974	PIT N P		40	9- 8
1975	PIT N P	33	35	12-11
1976	PIT N P		31	14- 9
1977	PIT N P	33	35	9-10
1978	PIT N P		28	6- 6
	BRTR	222	226	68-56

KISSINGER, WILLIAM FRANCIS (SHANG)
B.AUG.19,1871 DAYTON,KY.
D.APR.20,1929 CINCINNATI,OHIO

YR	CL LEA POS	GP	G	REC
1895	BAL N P		2	1- 1
	STL N P	24	27	5-10
1896	STL N P	19	22	2-13
1897	STL N P		11	0- 4
	BRTR	56	62	8-28

KITSON, FRANK L.
B.APR.11,1872 HOPKINS,MICH.
D.APR.14,1930 ALLEGAN,MICH.

YR	CL LEA POS	GP	G	REC
1898	BAL N P		23	8- 5
1899	BAL N P	38	40	20-16
1900	BRO N P	30	33	14-13
1901	BRO N P		32	19-11
1902	BRO N P		31	19-12
1903	DET A P	31	36	15-15
1904	DET A P	26	27	10-12
1905	DET A P		33	8-17
1906	WAS A P	32	33	6-14
1907	WAS A P		5	0- 1
	NY A P		11	3- 2
	BLTR	292	304	122-118

KITSOS, CHRISTOPHER ANESTOS
B.FEB.11,1928 NEW YORK,N.Y.

YR	CL LEA POS	GP	G	REC
1954	CHI N S		1	.000
	BBTR			

KITTRIDGE, MALACHI J. (JEDEDIAH)
B.OCT.12,1869 CLINTON,MASS.
D.JUNE 23,1928 GARY,IND.

YR	CL LEA POS	GP	G	REC
1890	CHI N C		96	.201
1891	CHI N C		70	.202
1892	CHI N C		66	.187
1893	CHI N C		67	.245
1894	CHI N C		50	.317
1895	CHI N C		58	.244
1896	CHI N C		61	.223
1897	CHI N C		77	.198
1898	LOU N C		88	.250
1899	LOU N C		46	.174
	WAS N C		41	.158
1901	BOS N C		113	.247
1902	BOS N C		72	.233
1903	BOS N C		30	.212
	WAS A C		59	.218
1904	WAS A M-C		80	.242
1905	WAS A C		77	.163
1906	WAS A C		22	.191
1906	CLE A C		5	.100
	BRTR		1178	.220

KLAERNER, HUGO EMIL (DUTCH)
B.OCT.15,1908 FREDERICKSBURG,TEX.

YR	CL LEA POS	GP	G	REC
1934	CHI A P		3	0- 2
	BRTR			

KLAGES, FREDERICK ALBERT ANTONY (FRED)
B.OCT.31,1943 AMBRIDGE,PA.

YR	CL LEA POS	GP	G	REC
1966	CHI A /P		3	1- 0
1967	CHI A P	11	12	4- 4
	BRTR	14	15	5- 4

KLAUS, ROBERT FRANCIS (BOBBY)
B.DEC.27,1937 SPRING GROVE,ILL.

YR	CL LEA POS	GP	G	REC
1964	CIN N 2-S-3		40	.183
	NY N 2-S-3		56	.244
1965	NY N 2-S-3		119	.191
	BRTR		215	.208

KLAUS, WILLIAM JOSEPH (BILLY)
B.DEC.9,1928 FOX LAKE,ILL.

YR	CL LEA POS	GP	G	REC
1952	BOS N S		7	.000
1953	MIL N H		2	.000
1955	BOS A S-3		135	.283
1956	BOS A S-3		.135	.271
1957	BOS A S		127	.252
1958	BOS A S		61	.159
1959	BAL A 2-S-3		104	.249
1960	BAL A 2-S-3		46	.209
1961	WAS A 2-S-3-O		91	.227
1962	PHI N 2-S		102	.206
1963	PHI N 2-S-3		11	.056
	BLTR		821	.249

KLAWITTER, ALBERT (DUTCH)
B.APR.12,1888 WILKES-BARRE,PA.
D.MAY 2,1950 MILWAUKEE,WIS.

YR	CL LEA POS	GP	G	REC
1909	NY N P		6	1- 1
1910	NY N P		1	0- 0
1913	DET A P		6	1- 2
	BRTR		13	2- 3

KLEE, OLLIE CHESTER (BABE)
B.MAY 20,1900 PIQUA,OHIO
D.FEB.9,1977 TOLEDO,OHIO

YR	CL LEA POS	GP	G	REC
1925	CIN N O		3	.000
	BLTL			

KLEIN, CHARLES HERBERT (CHUCK)
B.OCT.7,1904 INDIANAPOLIS,IND.
D.MAR.28,1958 INDIANAPOLIS,IND.

YR	CL LEA POS	GP	G	REC
1928	PHI N O		64	.360
1929	PHI N O		149	.356
1930	PHI N O		156	.386
1931	PHI N O		148	.337
1932	PHI N O		154	.348
1933	PHI N O		152	.368
1934	CHI N O		115	.301
1935	CHI N O		119	.293
1936	CHI N O		29	.294
	PHI N O		117	.309
1937	PHI N O		115	.325
1938	PHI N O		129	.247
1939	PHI N O		25	.191
	PIT N O		85	.300
1940	PHI N O		116	.218
1941	PHI N H		50	.123
1942	PHI N H		14	.071
1943	PHI N O		12	.100
1944	PHI N O		4	.143
	BLTR		1753	.320

KLEIN, LOUIS FRANK (LOU)
B.OCT.22,1918 NEW ORLEANS,LA.
D.JUNE 20,1976 METAIRIE,LA.

YR	CL LEA POS	GP	G	REC
1943	STL N 2-S		154	.287
1945	STL N 2-S-3-O		19	.228
1946	STL N 2		23	.194
1949	STL N 2-S-3		58	.219
1951	CLE A H		2	.000
	PHI A		49	.229
	BRTR		305	.259

NON-PLAYING MANAGER
CHI[N] 1961, 62, 65

KLEINE, HAROLD JOHN
B.JUNE 8,1923 ST.LOUIS,MO.
D.DEC.10,1957 ST.LOUIS,MO.

YR	CL LEA POS	GP	G	REC
1944	CLE A P	11	14	1- 2
1945	CLE A P		3	0- 0
	BLTL	14	17	1- 2

KLEINHANS, THEODORE OTTO
B.APR.8,1899 DEER PARK,WIS.

YR	CL LEA POS	GP	G	REC
1934	PHI N P		5	0- 0
	CIN N P	24	25	2- 6
1936	NY A P		19	1- 1
1937	CIN N P		7	1- 2
1938	CIN N P		1	0- 0
	BRTL	56	57	4- 9

KLEINKE, NORBERT GEORBE (NUB)
B.MAY 19,1911 FOND DU LAC,WIS.
D.MAR.16,1950 OFF MARIN COAST,CAL.

YR	CL LEA POS	GP	G	REC
1935	STL N P		4	0- 0
1937	STL N P		5	1- 1
	BRTR		9	1- 1

KLEINOW, JOHN PETER (RED)
B.JULY 20,1879 MILWAUKEE,WIS.
D.OCT.9,1929 NEW YORK,N.Y.

YR	CL LEA POS	GP	G	REC
1904	NY A C		67	.200
1905	NY A C		88	.221
1906	NY A C		96	.220
1907	NY A C		90	.264
1908	NY A C		96	.168
1909	NY A C		78	.228
1910	NY A C		5	.455
	BOS A C		51	.149
1911	BOS A C		8	.214
	PHI N C		4	.125
	BRTR		583	.212

KLEPFER, EDWARD LLOYD (BIG ED)
B.MAR.17,1888 SUMMERVILLE,PA.
D.AUG.9,1950 TULSA,OKLA.

YR	CL LEA POS	GP	G	REC
1911	NY A P		2	0- 0
1913	NY A P		8	0- 1
1915	CHI A P		2	0- 0
	CLE A P		2	2- 6
1916	CLE A P		31	6- 7
1917	CLE A P		41	14- 4
1919	CLE A P		5	0- 0
	BRTR		98	22-18

KLEVEN, JAY ALLEN
B.DEC.2,1949 OAKLAND,CAL.

YR	CL LEA POS	GP	G	REC
1976	NY N /C		2	.200
	BRTR			

KLIEMAN, EDWARD FREDERICK (ED) (SPECS) OR (BABE)
B.MAR.21,1918 NORWOOD,OHIO

YR	CL LEA POS	GP	G	REC
1943	CLE A P		1	0- 1
1944	CLE A P		47	11-18
1945	CLE A P		38	5- 8
1946	CLE A P		9	0- 0
1947	CLE A P		58	5- 4
1948	CLE A P		44	3- 2
1949	WAS A P		2	0- 0
	CHI A P		18	2- 0
1950	PHI A P		5	0- 0
	BRTR		222	26-28

KLIMCHOCK, LOUIS STEPHEN (LOU)
B.OCT.15,1939 HOSTETTER,PA.

YR	CL LEA POS	GP	G	REC
1958	KC A 2		2	.200
1959	KC A 2		17	.273
1960	KC A 2		10	.300
1961	KC A 1-2-3-0		57	.215
1962	MIL N H		8	.000
1963	WAS A 2		9	.143
	MIL N 1		24	.196
1964	MIL N 2-3		10	.333
1965	MIL N /1		34	.077
1966	NY N /H		5	.000
1968	CLE A /3-1-2		11	.133
1969	CLE A 3-2/C		90	.287
1970	CLE A /1-2		42	.161
	BLTR		318	.232

KLIMKOWSKI, RONALD BERNARD (RON)
B.MAR.1,1944 JERSEY CITY,N.J.

YR	CL LEA POS	GP	G	REC
1969	NY A /P		3	0- 0
1970	NY A P		45	6- 7
1971	OAK A P		26	2- 2
1972	NY A P		16	0- 3
	BRTR		90	8-12

KLINE, JOHN ROBERT (BOBBY)
B.JAN.27,1929 ST.PETERSBURG,FLA

YR	CL LEA POS	GP	G	REC
1955	WAS A P-2-S-3	1	77	0- 0
				.221
	BRTR			

KLINE, ROBERT GEORGE (JUNIOR)
B.DEC.9,1909 ENTERPRISE,OHIO

YR	CL LEA POS	GP	G	REC
1930	BOS A P		1	0- 0
1931	BOS A P		28	5- 5
1932	BOS A P		47	11-13
1933	BOS A P		46	7- 8
1934	PHI A P		20	6- 2
	WAS A P		6	1- 0
	BRTR		148	30-28

YR	CL	LEA	POS	GP	G	REC

KLINE, RONALD LEE (RON)
B.MAR.9,1932 CALLERY,PA.

YR	CL	LEA	POS	GP	G	REC
1952	PIT	N	P		27	0- 7
1955	PIT	N	P-3	36	37	6-13
						.132
1956	PIT	N	P		44	14-18
1957	PIT	N	P		40	9-16
1958	PIT	N	P	32	33	13-16
1959	PIT	N	P	33	38	11-13
1960	STL	N	P		34	4- 9
1961	LA	A	P		26	3- 6
	DET	A	P		10	5- 3
1962	DET	A	P		36	3- 6
1963	WAS	A	P		62	3- 8
1964	WAS	A	P		61	10- 7
1965	WAS	A	P		74	7- 6
1966	WAS	A	P		63	6- 4
1967	MIN	A	P		54	7- 1
1968	PIT	N	P		56	12- 5
1969	PIT	N	P		20	1- 3
	SF	N	/P		7	0- 2
	BOS	A	/P		16	0- 1
1970	ATL	N	/P		5	0- 0
	BRTR			736	743	114-144
						.092

KLINE, STEVEN JACK (STEVE)
B.OCT.6,1947 WENATCHEE,WASH.

YR	CL	LEA	POS	GP	G	REC
1970	NY	A	P		16	6- 6
1971	NY	A	P		31	12-13
1972	NY	A	P		32	16- 9
1973	NY	A	P		14	4- 7
1974	NY	A	/P		4	2- 2
	CLE	A	P		16	3- 8
1977	ATL	N	P		16	0- 0
	BRTR			129		43-45

KLING, JOHN GRADWOHL (NOISY)
B.FEB.25,1875 KANSAS CITY,MO.
D.JAN.31,1947 KANSAS CITY,MO.

YR	CL	LEA	POS	GP	G	REC
1900	CHI	N	C		15	.294
1901	CHI	N	C		70	.266
1902	CHI	N	C-S		113	.286
1903	CHI	N	C		132	.297
1904	CHI	N	C		120	.243
1905	CHI	N	C		110	.218
1906	CHI	N	C		99	.312
1907	CHI	N	C		100	.284
1908	CHI	N	C		125	.276
1910	CHI	N	C		86	.269
1911	CHI	N	C		27	.175
	BOS	N	C		75	.224
1912	BOS	N	M-C		81	.317
1913	CIN	N	M-C		80	.273
	BRTR				1233	.271

KLING, RUDOLPH A.
B.MAR.23,1870 ST.LOUIS,MO.
D.MAR.14,1937 ST.LOUIS,MO.

YR	CL	LEA	POS	GP	G	REC
1902	STL	N	S		4	.200
	TR					

KLING, WILLIAM
B.JAN.14,1867 KANSAS CITY,MO.
D.AUG.26,1934 KANSAS CITY,MO.

YR	CL	LEA	POS	GP	G	REC
1891	PHI	N	P		13	4- 3
1892	BAL	N	P		2	0- 1
1895	LOU	N	P		1	0- 0
	BLTR				16	4- 4

KLINGER, JOSEPH JOHN
B.AUG.2,1902 CANONSBURG,PA.
D.JULY 31,1960 LITTLE ROCK,ARK.

YR	CL	LEA	POS	GP	G	REC
1927	NY	N	0		3	.400
1930	CHI	A	C-1		4	.375
	BRTR				7	.389

KLINGER, ROBERT HAROLD (BOB)
B.JUNE 4,1908 ALLENTON,MO.
D.AUG.19,1977 VILLA RIDGE,MO.

YR	CL	LEA	POS	GP	G	REC
1938	PIT	N	P		28	12- 5
1939	PIT	N	P		37	14-17
1940	PIT	N	P		39	8-13
1941	PIT	N	P		35	9- 4
1942	PIT	N	P		37	8-11
1943	PIT	N	P		33	11- 8
1946	BOS	A	P		28	3- 2
1947	BOS	A	P		28	1- 1
	BRTR				265	66-61

KLIPPSTEIN, JOHN CALVIN (JOHNNY)
B.OCT.17,1927 WASHINGTON,D.C.

YR	CL	LEA	POS	GP	G	REC
1950	CHI	N	P	33	35	2- 9
1951	CHI	N	P		35	6- 6
1952	CHI	N	P		41	9-14
1953	CHI	N	P		48	10-11
1954	CHI	N	P		36	4-11
1955	CIN	N	P		39	9-10
1956	CIN	N	P		37	12-11
1957	CIN	N	P		46	8-11
1958	CIN	N	P		12	3- 2
	LA	N	P		45	3- 5
1959	LA	N	P		28	4- 0
1960	CLE	A	P		49	5- 5
1961	WAS	A	P		42	2- 2
1962	CIN	N	P		40	7- 6
1963	PHI	N	P		49	5- 6
1964	PHI	N	P		11	2- 1
	MIN	A	P		33	0- 4
1965	MIN	A	P		56	9- 3
1966	MIN	A	P		26	1- 1
1967	DET	A	/P		5	0- 0
	BRTR			711	713	101-118

KLOBEDANZ, FREDERICK AUGUSTUS (DUKE)
B.JUNE 13,1871 WATERBURY,CONN.
D.APR.12,1940 WATERBURY,CONN.

YR	CL	LEA	POS	GP	G	REC
1896	BOS	N	P		11	6- 4
1897	BOS	N	P		38	25- 8
1898	BOS	N	P		32	19-10
1899	BOS	N	P		5	1- 4
1902	BOS	N	P		1	1- 0
	BLTL				87	52-26

KLOPP, STANLEY HAROLD (BETZ)
B.DEC.22,1910 WOMELSDORF,PA.

YR	CL	LEA	POS	GP	G	REC
1944	BOS	N	P		24	1- 2
	BRTR					

KLOZA, JOHN CLARENCE (NAP)
B.SEPT.7,1903 POLAND
D.JUNE 11,1962 MILWAUKEE,WIS.

YR	CL	LEA	POS	GP	G	REC
1931	STL	A	O		3	.143
1932	STL	A	O		19	.154
	BRTR				22	.150

KLUGMANN, JOE
B.MAR.26,1895 ST.LOUIS,MO.
D.JULY 18,1951 MOBERLY,MO.

YR	CL	LEA	POS	GP	G	REC
1921	CHI	N	2		6	.286
1922	CHI	N	2		2	.250
1924	BRO	N	2-S		31	.165
1925	CLE	A	1-2-3		38	.333
	BRTR				77	.251

KLUMPP, ELMER EDWARD
B.AUG.26,1906 ST.LOUIS,MO.

YR	CL	LEA	POS	GP	G	REC
1934	WAS	A	C		12	.133
1937	BRO	N	C		5	.091
	BRTR				17	.115

KLUSMAN, WILLIAM F.
B.MAR.24,1865 CINCINNATI,OHIO
D.JUNE 24,1907 CINCINNATI,OHIO

YR	CL	LEA	POS	GP	G	REC
1888	BOS	N	2		28	.168
1890	STL	AA	1		15	.275
	BRTR				43	.206

KLUSZEWSKI, THEODORE BERNARD (TED) OR (BIG KLU)
B.SEPT.10,1924 ARGO,ILL.

YR	CL	LEA	POS	GP	G	REC
1947	CIN	N	1		9	.100
1948	CIN	N	1		113	.275
1949	CIN	N	1		136	.309
1950	CIN	N	1		134	.307
1951	CIN	N	1		154	.259
1952	CIN	N	1		135	.320
1953	CIN	N	1		149	.316
1954	CIN	N	1		149	.326
1955	CIN	N	1		153	.314
1956	CIN	N	1		138	.302
1957	CIN	N	1		69	.268
1958	PIT	N	1		100	.292
1959	PIT	N	1		60	.262
	CHI	A	1		31	.297
1960	CHI	A	1		81	.293
1961	LA	A	1		107	.243
	BLTL				1718	.298

KLUTTS, GENE ELLIS (MICKEY)
B.SEPT.20,1954 MONTEBELLO,CAL.

YR	CL	LEA	POS	GP	G	REC
1976	NY	A	/S		2	.000
1977	NY	A	/3-S		5	.267
1978	NY	A	/3		1	1.000
	BRTR				8	.300

KLUTTZ, CLYDE FRANKLIN
B.DEC.12,1917 ROCKWELL,N.C.

YR	CL	LEA	POS	GP	G	REC
1942	BOS	N	C		72	.267
1943	BOS	N	C		66	.246
1944	BOS	N	C		81	.279
1945	BOS	N	C		25	.296
	NY	N	C		73	.279
1946	NY	N	C		5	.375
	STL	N	C		52	.265
1947	PIT	N	C		73	.302
1948	PIT	N	C		94	.221
1951	STL	A	C		4	.500
	WAS	A	C		53	.308
1952	WAS	A	C		58	.229
	BRTR				656	.268

KNABE, FRANZ OTTO (DUTCH)
B.JUNE 2,1884 CARRICK,PA.
D.MAY 17,1961 PHILADELPHIA,PA.

YR	CL	LEA	POS	GP	G	REC
1905	PIT	N	3		3	.300
1907	PHI	N	2		126	.255
1908	PHI	N	2		151	.218
1909	PHI	N	2		111	.234
1910	PHI	N	2		136	.261
1911	PHI	N	2		142	.237
1912	PHI	N	2		126	.282
1913	PHI	N	2		148	.263
1914	BAL	F	M-2		146	.228
1915	BAL	F	M-2		100	.251
1916	PIT	N	2		28	.193
	CHI	N	2		51	.274
	BRTR				1268	.247

KNAPP, ROBERT CHRISTIAN (CHRIS)
B.SEPT.16,1953 CHERRY POINT,N.C.

YR	CL	LEA	POS	GP	G	REC
1975	CHI	A	/P		2	0- 0
1976	CHI	A	P		11	3- 1
1977	CHI	A	P		27	12- 7
1978	CAL	A	P		30	14- 8
	BRTR				70	29-16

KNAUPP, HENRY ANTONE (COTTON)
B.AUG.13,1889 SAN ANTONIO,TEX.
D.JULY 6,1967 NEW ORLEANS,LA.

YR	CL	LEA	POS	GP	G	REC
1910	CLE	A	S		18	.236
1911	CLE	A	S		13	.102
	BRTR				31	.184

KNAUSS, FRANK H.
B.1868 CLEVELAND,OHIO

YR	CL	LEA	POS	GP	G	REC
1890	COL	AA	P	33		21-11
1891	CLE	N	P		3	0- 3
1892	CIN	N	P		1	0- 1
1894	CLE	N	P		2	1- 1
1895	NY	N	P		1	0- 0
	BLTL				40	22-16

KNEISCH, RUDOLPH FRANK
B.APR.10,1899 BALTIMORE,MD.
D.APR.6,1965 BALTIMORE,MD.

YR	CL	LEA	POS	GP	G	REC
1926	DET	A	P		2	0- 1
	BRTL					

KNELL, PHILIP H.
B.1865 MILL VALLEY,CAL.

YR	CL	LEA	POS	GP	G	REC
1888	PIT	N	P		4	1- 2
1890	PHI	P	P		35	20-11
1891	COL	AA	P	58	66	27-27
1892	WAS	N	P		22	9-10
	PHI	N	P		11	4- 6
1894	PIT	N	P		4	0- 0
	LOU	N	P		40	7-22
1895	LOU	N	P		14	0- 6
	CLE	N	P		14	5- 4
	BRTL			192	200	73-88

KNELME, WILLIAM J.
(PLAYED UNDER NAME OF
WILLIAM J. KUEHNE]

KNEPPER, CHARLES
B.FEB.18,1871 ANDERSON,IND.
D.FEB.6,1946 MUNCIE,IND.

YR	CL	LEA	POS	GP	G	REC
1899	CLE	N	P		27	4-22
	BRTR					

KNEPPER, ROBERT WESLEY (BOB)
B.MAY 25,1954 AKRON,OHIO

YR	CL	LEA	POS	GP	G	REC
1976	SF	N	/P		4	1- 2
1977	SF	N	P		27	11- 9
1978	SF	N	P		36	17-11
	BLTL				67	29-22

KNERR, WALLACE LUTHER (LOU)
B.AUG.21,1921 DENVER,PA.

YR	CL	LEA	POS	GP	G	REC
1945	PHI	A	P	27	28	5-11
1946	PHI	A	P		30	3-16
1947	WAS	A	P		6	0- 0
	BRTR			63	64	8-27

YR	CL	LEA	POS	GP	G	REC

KNETZER, ELMER ELLSWORTH (BARON)
B.JULY 22,1885 CARRICK,PA.
D.OCT.3,1975 PITTSBURGH,PA.

YR	CL	LEA	POS	GP	G	REC
1909	BRO	N	P		5	1- 3
1910	BRO	N	P		20	7- 5
1911	BRO	N	P		35	11-12
1912	BRO	N	P		33	7- 9
1914	PIT	F	P		37	20-12
1915	PIT	F	P		41	18-14
1916	BOS	N	P		2	0- 2
1916	CIN	N	P	36	37	5-12
1917	CIN	N	P		11	0- 0
	BRTR			220	221	69-69

KNICKERBOCKER, AUSTIN JAY
B.OCT.15,1918 BANGALL,N.Y.

1947	PHI	A	O		21	.250
	BRTR					

KNICKERBOCKER, WILLIAM HART
B.DEC.29,1911 LOS ANGELES,CAL.
D.SEPT.8,1963 SEBASTOPOL,CAL.

1933	CLE	A	S		80	.226
1934	CLE	A	S		146	.317
1935	CLE	A	S		132	.298
1936	CLE	A	S		155	.294
1937	STL	A	S		121	.261
1938	NY	A	2		46	.250
1939	NY	A	2-S		6	.154
1940	NY	A	S-3		45	.242
1941	CHI	A	2		89	.245
1942	PHI	A	2-S		87	.253
	BRTR				907	.277

KNIGHT, ALONZO P. (LON)
B.JUNE 16,1853 PHILADELPHIA,PA.
D.APR.23,1932 PHILADELPHIA,PA.

1875	ATH	NA	P		13	6- 5
1876	ATH	N	P-1-	33	55	10-23
			O			.248
1880	WOR	N	O		48	.242
1881	DET	N	1-2-O		83	.270
1882	DET	N	1-O		83	.204
1883	ATH	AA	M-2-3-O		97	.237
1884	ATH	AA	P-O	1	110	0- 1
						.275
1885	ATH	AA	M-O		28	.186
	PRO	N	P-O	1	25	0- 0
						.160
	BRTR			48	542	16-29
						.246

KNIGHT, CHARLES RAY (RAY)
B.DEC.28,1952 ALBANY,GA.

1974	CIN	N	3		14	.182
1977	CIN	N	3-2/O-S		80	.261
1978	CIN	N	3/2-O-1-S		83	.200
	BRTR				177	.232

KNIGHT, ELMA RUSSELL (JACK)
B.JAN.12,1895 PITTSBORO,MISS.
D.JULY 30,1976 SAN ANTONIO,TEX.

1922	STL	N	P		1	0- 0
1925	PHI	N	P	33	40	7- 6
1926	PHI	N	P	35	40	3-12
1927	BOS	N	P		3	0- 0
	BLTR				84	10-18

KNIGHT, GEORGE HENRY
B.NOV.24,1855 LAKEVILLE,CONN.
D.OCT.4,1912

1875	NH	NA	P		1	1- 0

KNIGHT, JOHN WESLEY (SCHOOLBOY)
B.OCT.6,1885 PHILADELPHIA,PA.
D.DEC.19,1965 WALNUT CREEK,CAL.

1905	PHI	A	S		88	.234
1906	PHI	A	3		74	.194
1907	PHI	A	3		40	.212
	BOS	A	3		98	.215
1909	NY	A	1-2-S		116	.236
1910	NY	A	1-S		117	.312
1911	NY	A	1-2-S		132	.268
1912	WAS	A	2		32	.161
1913	NY	A	1-2		70	.236
	BRTR				767	.239

KNIGHT, JOSEPH WILLIAM (QUIET JOE)
B.SEPT.28,1859 POINT STANLEY,
ONT.,CANADA
D.OCT.11,1938 ST.THOMAS,ONT.,CAN.

1884	PHI	N	P		6	2- 4
1890	CIN	N	O		127	.312
	BLTL			6	133	2- 4
						.307

KNISELY, PETER COLE
B.AUG.11,1887 WAYNESBURG,PA.
D.JULY 1,1948 BROWNSVILLE,PA.

1912	CIN	N	O		21	.328
1913	CHI	N	O		2	.000
1914	CHI	N	O		37	.130
1915	CHI	N	O		64	.246
	BRTR				124	.235

KNODE, KENNETH THOMSON (MIKE)
B.NOV.6,1895 WESTMINSTER,MD.

1920	STL	N	O		42	.231
	BRTR					

KNODE, ROBERT TROXELL (BOB) OR (RAY)
B.JAN.28,1901 WESTMINSTER,MD.

1923	CLE	A	1		22	.289
1924	CLE	A	1		11	.243
1925	CLE	A	1		45	.250
1926	CLE	A	1		31	.333
	BLTL				109	.266

KNOLL, CHARLES ELMER (PUNCH)
B.OCT.7,1881 EVANSVILLE,IND.
D.FEB.7,1960 EVANSVILLE,IND.

1905	WAS	A	O		79	.213
	BRTR					

KNOLLS, OSCAR EDWARD (HUB)
B.DEC.18,1883 MEDARYVILLE,IND.
D.JULY 1,1946 CHICAGO,ILL.

1906	BRO	N	P		2	0- 0
	TR					

KNOOP, ROBERT FRANK (BOBBY)
B.OCT.18,1938 SIOUX CITY,IOWA

1964	LA	A	2		162	.216
1965	CAL	A	*2		142	.269
1966	CAL	A	*2		161	.232
1967	CAL	A	*2		159	.245
1968	CAL	A	2		152	.249
1969	CAL	A	2		27	.197
	CHI	A	*2		104	.229
1970	CHI	A	*2		130	.229
1971	KC	A	2/3		72	.205
1972	KC	A	2/3		44	.237
	BRTR				1153	.236

KNOTHE, GEORGE BERTRAM
B.JAN.12,1898 BAYONNE,N.J.

1932	PHI	N	2		6	.083
	BRTR					

KNOTHE, WILFRED EDGAR (FRITZ)
B.MAY 1,1903 PASSAIC,N.J.
D.MAR.27,1963 PASSAIC,N.J.

1932	BOS	N	3		89	.238
1933	BOS	N	S-3		44	.228
	PHI	N	2-3		41	.150
	BRTR				174	.220

KNOTT, JOHN HENRY (JACK)
B.MAR.2,1907 DALLAS,TEX.

1933	STL	A	P		20	1- 8
1934	STL	A	P		45	10- 3
1935	STL	A	P		48	11- 8
1936	STL	A	P		47	9-17
1937	STL	A	P		38	8-18
1938	STL	A	P		7	1- 2
	CHI	A	P		20	5-10
1939	CHI	A	P		25	11- 6
1940	CHI	A	P		25	11- 9
1941	PHI	A	P		27	13-11
1942	PHI	A	P		20	2-10
1946	PHI	A	P		3	0- 1
	BRTR				325	82-103

KNOTTS, JOSEPH STEVEN
B.MAR.3,1884 GREENSBORO,PA.
D.SEPT.15,1950 PHILADELPHIA,PA.

1907	BOS	N	C		3	.000
	BRTR					

KNOUFF, EDWARD (FRED)
B.1867 PHILADELPHIA,PA.
D.SEPT.14,1900 PHILADELPHIA,PA.

1885	ATH	AA	P-O		14	7- 6
						.204
1886	BAL	AA	P		1	0- 1
1887	BAL	AA	P		8	0- 6
	STL	AA	P-O	7	16	4- 3
						.190
1888	STL	AA	P		9	5- 4
	CLE	AA	P-2		10	6- 4
						.143
1889	ATH	AA	P		3	2- 0
	BRTR			52	61	24-24
						.194

KNOWDELL, JACOB AUGUSTUS (JAKE)
B.BROOKLYN,N.Y.

1874	ATL	NA	C-O		23	-
1875	ATL	NA	C-S-O		42	-
1878	MIL	N	C-O		4	.000
					69	-

KNOWLES, DAROLD DUANE
B.DEC.9,1941 BRUNSWICK,MO.

1965	BAL	A	/P		5	0- 1
1966	PHI	N	P		69	6- 5
1967	WAS	A	P		61	6- 8
1968	WAS	A	P		32	1- 1
1969	WAS	A	P		53	9- 2
1970	WAS	A	P		71	2-14
1971	WAS	A	P		12	2- 2
	OAK	A	P		43	5- 2
1972	OAK	A	P		54	5- 1
1973	OAK	A	P	52	53	6- 8
1974	OAK	A	P		45	3- 3
1975	CHI	N	P		58	6- 9
1976	CHI	N	P		58	5- 7
1977	TEX	A	P		42	5- 2
1978	MON	N	P		60	3- 3
	BLTL			715	716	64-68

KNOWLES, JAMES (DARBY)
B.1859 TORONTO,ONT.,CANADA
D.FEB.4,1912 NEW YORK,N.Y.

1884	PIT	AA	SS		46	.228
	BRO	AA	1-3		41	.237
1886	WAS	N	2-3		115	.212
1887	MET	AA	3		16	.262
1890	ROC	AA	3		124	.281
1892	NY	N	3		15	.169
					357	.240

KNOWLES, THOMAS H.
B.1895 RIDGWAY,PA.

1915	PHI	A	P		18	4- 7

KNOWLTON, WILLIAM YOUNG
B.AUG.18,1892 PHILADELPHIA,PA.
D.FEB.25,1944 PHILADELPHIA,PA.

1920	PHI	A	P		1	0- 1
	BRTR					

KNOX, ANDREW JACKSON (DASHER)
B.JAN.6,1864 PHILADELPHIA,PA.
D.SEPT.14,1940 PHILADELPHIA,PA.

1890	ATH	AA	1		21	.250
	BRTR					

KNOX, CLIFFORD HIRAM (BUD)
B.JAN.7,1902 COALVILLE,IOWA
D.SEPT.24,1965 OSKALOOSA,IOWA

1924	PIT	N	C		6	.222
	BBTR					

KNOX, JOHN CLINTON
B.JULY 26,1948 NEWARK,N.J.

1972	DET	A	/2		14	.077
1973	DET	A	/2		12	.281
1974	DET	A	2/3		55	.307
1975	DET	A	2/3		43	.267
	BLTR				124	.274

KOBACK, NICHOLAS NICHOLIE (NICK)
B.JULY 19,1935 HARTFORD,CONN.

1953	PIT	N	C		7	.125
1954	PIT	N	C		4	.000
1955	PIT	N	C		5	.286
	BRTR				16	.121

KOBEL, KEVIN RICHARD
B.OCT.2,1953 BUFFALO,N.Y.

1973	MIL	A	/P		2	0- 1
1974	MIL	A	P		34	6-14
1976	MIL	A	/P		3	0- 1
1978	NY	N	P		32	5- 6
	BRTL				71	11-22

KOCH, ALAN GOODMAN
B.MAR.25,1938 DECATUR,ALA.

1963	DET	A	P	7	8	1- 1
1964	DET	A	P		3	0- 0
	WAS	A	P		32	3-10
	BRTR			42	43	4-11

KOCH, BARNETT (BARNEY)
B.MAR.23,1923 CAMPBELL,NEB.

1944	BRO	N	2-S		33	.219
	BRTR					

KOCHER, BRADLEY WILSON
B.JAN.16,1888 WHITE HAVEN,PA.
D.JAN.13,1965 WHITE HAVEN,PA.

1912	DET	A	C		24	.206
1915	NY	N	C		4	.455
1916	NY	N	C		34	.108
	BRTR				62	.179

KOECHER, RICHARD FINLAY (HIGHPOCKETS)
B.MAR.30,1926 PHILADELPHIA,PA.

1946	PHI	N	P		1	0- 1
1947	PHI	N	P		3	0- 2
1948	PHI	N	P		3	0- 1
	BLTL				7	0- 4

YR	CL	LEA	POS	GP	G	REC

KOEGEL, PETER JOHN (PETE)
B.JULY 31,1947 MINEOLA,N.Y.

YR	CL	LEA	POS	GP	G	REC
1970	MIL	A	/O		7	.25C
1971	MIL	A	/1		2	.000
	PHI	N	/C-O		12	.231
1972	PHI	N	/1-C-3-O		41	.143
	BRTR				62	.174

KOEHLER, BENARD JAMES (BEN)
B.JAN.26,1877 SCHOERNDORN,GERMANY
D.MAY 21,1961 SOUTH BEND,IND.

1905	STL	A	O		142	.237
1906	STL	A	O		66	.220
	BRTR				208	.233

KOEHLER, HORACE LEVERING (PIP)
B.JAN.16,1902 GILBERT,PA.

| 1925 | NY | N | O | | 12 | .000 |
| | BRTR | | | | | |

KOENECKE, LEONARD GEORGE
B.JAN.18,1904 BARABOO,WIS.
D.SEPT.17,1935 TORONTO,ONT.,CAN

1932	NY	N	O		42	.255
1934	BRO	N	O		123	.320
1935	BRO	N	O		100	.283
	BLTR				265	.297

KOENIG, CHARLES FREDERICK
[PLAYED UNDER NAME OF
CHARLES FREDERICK KING]

KOENIG, MARK ANTHONY
B.JUL.19,1902 SAN FRANCISCO,CAL

1925	NY	A	S		28	.205
1926	NY	A	S		147	.271
1927	NY	A	S		123	.285
1928	NY	A	S		132	.319
1929	NY	A	S-3		116	.292
1930	NY	A	S		21	.243
	DET	A	P-S	2	76	0- 1
						.236
1931	DET	A	P-2-	3	106	0- 0
	S					.253
1932	CHI	N			33	.353
1933	CHI	N	2-S-3		80	.284
1934	CIN	N	1-2-S-3		151	.272
1935	NY	N	2-S-3		107	.283
1936	NY	N	S		42	.276
	BBTR			5	1162	0- 1
						.279

KOENIGSMARK, WILLIAM THOMAS
B.FEB.27,1896 WATERLOO,ILL.
D.JULY 1,1972 WATERLOO,ILL.

| 1919 | STL | N | P | 1 | 0- 0 |
| | BRTR | | | | |

KOESTNER, ELMER JOSEPH (BOB)
B.NOV.30,1885 PIPER CITY,ILL.
D.OCT.27,1959 FAIRBURY,ILL.

1910	CLE	A	P		27	5-10
1914	CHI	N	P		4	0- 0
	CIN	N	P		5	0- 0
	BRTR				36	5-10

KOHLER, HENRY
B.BALTIMORE,MD.

1871	KEK	NA	1-3		3	.167
1873	MAR	NA	3		6	-
1874	BAL	NA	C-1		5	-
					14	-

KOHLMAN, JOSEPH JAMES (BLACKIE)
B.JAN.28,1913 PHILADELPHIA,PA.

1937	WAS	A	P		2	1- 0
1938	WAS	A	P		7	0- 0
	BRTR				9	1- 0

KOKOS, RICHARD JEROME (DICK)
[REAL NAME RICHARD JEROME KOKOSZKA]
B.FEB.28,1928 CHICAGO,ILL.

1948	STL	A	O		71	.298
1949	STL	A	O		143	.261
1950	STL	A	O		143	.261
1953	STL	A	O		107	.241
1954	BAL	A	O		11	.200
	BLTR				475	.263

KOKOSZKA, RICHARD JEROME
[PLAYED UNDER NAME OF
RICHARD JEROME KOKOS]

KOLB, EDWARD WILLIAM
B.JULY 20,1880 CINCINNATI,OHIO

| 1899 | CLE | N | P | 1 | 0- 1 |
| | BRTR | | | | |

KOLB, GARY ALAN
B.MAR.13,1940 ROCK FALLS,ILL.

1960	STL	N	O		9	.000
1962	STL	N	O		6	.357
1963	STL	N	C-3-O		75	.271
1964	MIL	N	C-2-3-O		36	.188
1965	MIL	N	O		24	.259
	NY	N	O/1-3		40	.167
1968	PIT	N	O-C/3-2		74	.218
1969	PIT	N	/C		29	.081
	BLTR				293	.209

KOLLONIGE, JOSEPH EDWARD
[PLAYED UNDER NAME OF
JOSEPH EDWARD COLLINS]

KOLLOWAY, DONALD MARTIN (DON)
(BUTCH) OR (CAB)
B.AUG.4,1918 POSEN,ILL.

1940	CHI	A	2		10	.225
1941	CHI	A	1-2		71	.271
1942	CHI	A	1-2		147	.273
1943	CHI	A	2		85	.216
1946	CHI	A	2-3		123	.280
1947	CHI	A	1-2-3		124	.278
1948	CHI	A	2-3		119	.273
1949	CHI	A	3		4	.000
	DET	A	1-2-3		126	.294
1950	DET	A	1-2		125	.289
1951	DET	A	1		78	.255
1952	DET	A	1-2		65	.243
1953	PHI	A	3		2	.000
	BRTR				1079	.271

KOLP, RAYMOND CARL (JOCKEY)
B.OCT.1,1894 NEW BERLIN,OHIO
D.JULY 29,1967 NEW ORLEANS,LA.

1921	STL	A	P	37	39	8- 7
1922	STL	A	P		32	14- 4
1923	STL	A	P		34	5-12
1924	STL	A	P		25	5- 7
1927	CIN	N	P		24	3- 3
1928	CIN	N	P		44	13-10
1929	CIN	N	P		30	8-10
1930	CIN	N	P		37	7-12
1931	CIN	N	P		30	4- 9
1932	CIN	N	P		32	6-10
1933	CIN	N	P		30	6- 9
1934	CIN	N	P		28	0- 2
	BRTR			383	385	79-95

KOLSETH, KARL DICKEY (KOLEY)
B.DEC.25,1892 CAMBRIDGE,MASS.
D.MAY 3,1956 CUMBERLAND,MD.

| 1915 | BAL | F | 1 | | 6 | .217 |
| | BLTR | | | | | |

KOLSTAD, HAROLD EVERETTE (HAL)
B.JUNE 1,1935 RICE LAKE,WIS.

1962	BOS	A	P		27	0- 2
1963	BOS	A	P		7	0- 2
	BRTR				34	0- 4

KOMMERS, FREDERICK RAYMOND (BUGS)
B.MAR.31,1886 CHICAGO,ILL.
D.JUNE 14,1943 CHICAGO,ILL.

1913	PIT	N	O		40	.232
1914	STL	F	O		75	.308
	BAL	F	O		17	.220
	BLTR				132	.271

KONETCHY, EDWARD JOSEPH (BIG ED)
B.SEPT.3,1885 LACROSSE,WIS.
D.MAY 27,1947 FT.WORTH,TEX.

1907	STL	N	1		91	.251
1908	STL	N	1		154	.248
1909	STL	N	1		152	.286
1910	STL	N	P-1	1	144	0- 0
						.302
1911	STL	N	1		158	.289
1912	STL	N	1		143	.314
1913	STL	N	P-1	1	140	1- 0
						.276
1914	PIT	N	1		154	.249
1915	PIT	F	1		152	.310
1916	BOS	N	1		158	.260
1917	BOS	N	1		130	.272
1918	BOS	N	O-1	1	119	0- 1
						.236
1919	BRO	N	1		132	.298
1920	BRO	N	1		131	.308
1921	BRO	N	1		55	.269
	PHI	N	1		72	.321
	BRTR			3	2085	1- 1
						.281

KONIECZNY, DOUGLAS JAMES (DOUG)
B.SEP.27,1951 DETROIT,MICH.

1973	HOU	N	/P		2	0- 1
1974	HOU	N	/P		6	0- 3
1975	HOU	N	P		32	6-13
1977	HOU	N	/P		4	1- 1
	BRTR				44	7-18

KONIKOWSKI, ALEXANDER JAMES
(ALEX) OR (WHITEY)
B.JUNE 8,1928 THROOP,PA.

1948	NY	N	P		22	2- 3
1951	NY	N	P		3	0- 0
1954	NY	N	P		10	0- 0
	BRTR				35	2- 3

KONNICK, MICHAEL ALOYSIUS
B.JAN.19,1889 GLEN LYON,PA.
D.JULY 9,1971 WILKES-BARRE,PA.

1909	CIN	N	C		2	.400
1910	CIN	N	S		1	.000
	BRTR				3	.250

KONOPKA, BRUNO BRUCE (BRUCE)
B.SEPT.16,1919 HAMMOND,IND.

1942	PHI	A	1		5	.300
1943	PHI	A	H		2	.000
1946	PHI	A	1-0		38	.237
	BLTL				45	.238

KONSTANTY, CASIMIR JAMES (JIM)
B.MAR.2,1917 STRYKERSVILLE,N.Y.
D.JUNE 11,1976 ONEONTA,N.Y.

1944	CIN	N	P		20	6- 4
1946	BOS	N	P		10	0- 1
1948	PHI	N	P		6	1- 0
1949	PHI	N	P		53	9- 5
1950	PHI	N	P		74	16- 7
1951	PHI	N	P		58	4-11
1952	PHI	N	P		42	5- 3
1953	PHI	N	P		48	14-10
1954	PHI	N	P		33	2- 3
	NY	A	P		9	1- 1
1955	NY	A	P		45	7- 2
1956	NY	A	P		8	0- 0
	STL	N	P		27	1- 1
	BRTR				433	66-48

KOOB, ERNEST GERALD
B.SEPT.11,1893 KEELER,MICH.
D.NOV.12,1941 LEMAY,MO.

1915	STL	A	P		28	5- 6
1916	STL	A	P		33	11- 8
1917	STL	A	P		39	6-14
1919	STL	A	P		24	2- 4
	BLTL				124	24-32

KOONCE, CALVIN LEE (CAL)
B.NOV.18,1940 FAYETTEVILLE,N.C.

1962	CHI	N	P		35	10-10
1963	CHI	N	P		21	2- 6
1964	CHI	N	P		6	3- 0
1965	CHI	N	P		38	7- 9
1966	CHI	N	P		45	5- 5
1967	CHI	N	P		34	2- 2
	NY	N	P	11	13	3- 3
1968	NY	N	P		55	6- 4
1969	NY	N	P		40	6- 3
1970	NY	N	P		13	0- 2
	BOS	A	P		23	3- 4
1971	BOS	A	P		13	0- 1
	BRTR			334	336	47-49

KOONS, HARRY M.
B.1863 PHILADELPHIA,PA.

1884	ALT	U	C-3		21	.213
	CHI	U	3		1	.000
					22	.205

KOOSMAN, JEROME MARTIN (JERRY)
B.DEC.23,1942 APPLETON,MINN.

1967	NY	N	/P		9	0- 2
1968	NY	N	P		35	19-12
1969	NY	N	P		32	17- 9
1970	NY	N	P		30	12- 7
1971	NY	N	P		26	6-11
1972	NY	N	P		34	11-12
1973	NY	N	P		35	14-15
1974	NY	N	P		35	15-11
1975	NY	N	P		36	14-13
1976	NY	N	P		34	21-10
1977	NY	N	P		32	8-20
1978	NY	N	P		38	3-15
	BRTL			376	140-137

KOPACZ, GEORGE FELIX
(GEORGE) OR (SONNY)
B.FEB.26,1941 CHICAGO,ILL.

1966	ATL	N	/1		6	.000
1970	PIT	N	/1		10	.188
	BLTL				16	.120

KOPCHIA, JOSEPH
[PLAYED UNDER NAME OF
JOSEPH KOPPE]

KOPF, WALTER HENRY
B.JULY 10,1899 STONINGTON,CONN.

| 1921 | NY | N | 3 | | 2 | .333 |
| | BRTR | | | | | |

KOPF, WILLIAM LORENZ (LARRY)
[PLAYED UNDER NAME OF
FRED BRADY IN 1913]
B.NOV.3,1890 BRISTOL,CONN.

1913	CLE	A	2-3		6	.300
1914	PHI	A	2		35	.189
1915	PHI	A	S-3		118	.225
1916	CIN	N	S		11	.275
1917	CIN	N	S		148	.255
1919	CIN	N	S		135	.270
1920	CIN	N	2-S-3-O		126	.245
1921	CIN	N	S		107	.218
1922	BOS	N	2-S-3		126	.266
1923	BOS	N	2-S		39	.275
	BBTR				851	.249

YR	CL	LEA	POS	GP	G	REC

KOPLITZ, HOWARD DEAN (HOWIE)
B.MAY 4,1938 OSHKOSH,WIS.
```
1961 DET A  P          4    2- 0
1962 DET A  P     10  12    3- 0
196x WAS A  P          6    0- 0
1965 WAS A  P         33    4- 7
1966 WAS A  /P         1    0- 0
     BRTR        54  56    9- 7
```

KOPP, MERLIN HENRY (MANNY)
B.JAN.2,1892 TOLEDO,OHIO
D.MAY 6,1960 SACRAMENTO,CAL.
```
1915 WAS A  O         16     .250
1918 PHI A  O         96     .234
1919 PHI A  O         75     .226
     BBTR           187     .230
     BR 1915
```

KOPPE, GEORGE
[PLAYED UNDER NAME OF
GEORGE JOSEPH CUPPY]

KOPPE, JOSEPH (JOE)
[REAL NAME JOSEPH KOPCHIA]
B.OCT.19,1930 DETROIT,MICH.
```
1958 MIL N  S         16     .444
1959 PHI N  2-S      126     .261
1960 PHI N  S-3       58     .171
1961 PHI N  S          6     .000
     LA  A  2-S-3     91     .251
1962 LA  A  2-S-3    128     .227
1963 LA  A  2-S-3-O   76     .210
1964 LA  A  2-S-3     54     .257
1965 CAL A  2/S-3     23     .212
     BRTR           578     .236
```

KOPSHAW, GEORGE KARL
B.JULY 5,1895 PASSAIC,N.J.
D.DEC.26,1934 LYNCHBURG,VA.
```
1923 STL N  C          2     .200
     BRTR
```

**KORCHECK, STEPHEN JOSEPH
(STEVE) OR (HOSS)**
B.AUG.13,1932 MC CLELLANDTOWN,PA.
```
1954 WAS A  C          2     .143
1955 WAS A  C         13     .278
1958 WAS A  C         21     .078
1959 WAS A  C         22     .157
     BRTR            58     .159
```

KORES, ARTHUR EMIL (DUTCH)
B.JULY 22,1886 MILWAUKEE,WIS.
D.MAR.26,1974 MILWAUKEE,WIS.
```
1915 STL F  3         60     .229
     BRTR
```

**KORINCE, GEORGE EUGENE
(GEORGE) OR (MOOSE)**
B.JAN.10,1946 OTTAWA,ONT.,CANADA
```
1966 DET A  /P         2    0- 0
1967 DET A  /P         9    1- 0
     BRTR            11    1- 0
```

KORWAN, JAMES (LONG JIM)
B.MAR.4,1874 BROOKLYN,N.Y.
D.AUG.1899 BROOKLYN,N.Y.
```
1894 BRO N  P          1    0- 0
1897 CHI N  P          5    1- 2
                      6    1- 2
```

KOSCO, ANDREW JOHN (ANDY)
B.OCT.5,1941 YOUNGSTOWN,OHIO
```
1965 MIN A  O/1       23     .236
1966 MIN A  O/1       57     .222
1967 MIN A  /O         9     .143
1968 NY  A  O-1      131     .240
1969 LA  N  *O/1     120     .248
1970 LA  N  O/1       74     .228
1971 MIL A  O-1-3     98     .227
1972 CAL A  O         49     .239
     BOS A  O         17     .213
1973 CIN N  O/1       47     .280
1974 CIN N  /3-O      33     .189
     BRTR           658     .236
```

**KOSHOREK, CLEMENT JOHN
(CLEM) OR (SCOOTER)**
B.JUNE 20,1926 ROYAL OAK,MICH.
```
1952 PIT N  2-S-3     98     .261
1953 PIT N  H          1     .000
     BRTR            99     .260
```

**KOSKI, WILLIAM JOHN
(BILL) OR (T-BONE)**
B.FEB.6,1932 MADERA,CAL.
```
1951 PIT N  P         13    0- 1
     BRTR
```

KOSLO, GEORGE BERNARD (DAVE)
[REAL NAME GEORGE BERNARD KOSLOWSKI]
B.MAR.31,1920 MENASHA,WIS.
D.DEC.1,1975 MENASHA,WIS.
```
1941 NY  N  P          4    1- 2
1942 NY  N  P         19    3- 6
1946 NY  N  P     40  41   14-19
1947 NY  N  P         39   15-10
1948 NY  N  P         35    8-10
1949 NY  N  P     38  39   11-14
1950 NY  N  P         40   13-15
1951 NY  N  P         39   10- 9
1952 NY  N  P         41   10- 7
1953 NY  N  P         37    6-12
1954 BAL A  P          3    0- 1
     MIL N  P         12    1- 1
1955 MIL N  P          1    0- 1
     BLTL       348 350   92-107
```

KOSLOWSKI, GEORGE BERNARD
[PLAYED UNDER NAME OF
GEORGE BERNARD KOSLO]

KOSMAN, MICHAEL THOMAS
B.DEC.10,1917 HAMTRAMCK,MICH.
```
1944 CIN N  P          1     .000
     BRTR
```

KOSTAL, JOSEPH
```
1896 LOU N  C          2     .000
```

KOSTER, FREDERICK CHARLES (FRITZ)
B.DEC.21,1905 LOUISVILLE,KY.
```
1931 PHI N  O         76     .225
     BLTL
```

KOSTRO, FRANK JERRY
B.AUG.4,1937 WINDBER,PA.
```
1962 DET A  3         16     .268
1963 DET A  1-3-O     31     .231
     LA  A  1-3-O     43     .222
1964 MIN A  1-2-3-O   59     .272
1965 MIN A  /2-3-O    20     .161
1967 MIN A  /O-3      32     .323
1968 MIN A  O/1       63     .241
1969 MIN A  /H         2     .000
     BRTR           266     .244
```

KOUFAX, SANFORD (SANDY)
B.DEC.30,1935 BROOKLYN,N.Y.
```
1955 BRO N  P         12    2- 2
1956 BRO N  P         16    2- 4
1957 BRO N  P         34    5- 4
1958 LA  N  P         40   11-11
1959 LA  N  P         35    8- 6
1960 LA  N  P         37    8-13
1961 LA  N  P         42   18-13
1962 LA  N  P         28   14- 7
1963 LA  N  P         40   25- 5
1964 LA  N  P         29   19- 5
1965 LA  N  P         43   26- 8
1966 LA  N  P         41   27- 9
     BRTL           397  165-87
```

KOUKALIK, JOSEPH
B.MAR.3,1880 CHICAGO,ILL.
D.DEC.27,1945 CHICAGO,ILL.
```
1904 BRO N  P          1    0- 1
```

KOUPAL, LOUIS LADDIE
B.DEC.19,1898 TABOR,S.D.
D.DEC.8,1961 SAN GABRIEL,CAL.
```
1925 PIT N  P          7    0- 0
1926 PIT N  P          6    0- 0
1928 BRO N  P         17    1- 0
1929 BRO N  P         18    0- 1
     PHI N  P         15    3- 5
1930 PHI N  P         13    0- 4
1937 STL A  P         26    4- 9
     BRTR       101 102   10-21
```

KOWALEWSKI, HARRY FRANK
[PLAYED UNDER NAME OF
HARRY FRANK COVELESKI]

KOWALEWSKI, STANISLAUS
[PLAYED UNDER NAME OF
STANLEY ANTHONY COVELESKI]

KOWALIK, FABIAN LORENZ
B.APR.22,1908 FALLS CITY,TEX.
D.AUG.14,1954 KARNES CITY,TEX.
```
1932 CHI A  P          2    0- 1
1935 CHI N  P         20    2- 2
1936 CHI N  P          6    0- 2
     PHI N  P     22  42    1- 5
     BOS N  P      1   2    0- 1
     BBTR        51  76    3-11
     BR 1936
```

KOY, ERNEST ANYZ (CHIEF)
B.SEPT.17,1909 SEALY,TEX.
```
1938 BRO N  O        142     .299
1939 BRO N  O        125     .276
1940 BRO N  O         24     .229
     STL N  O         93     .310
1941 STL N  O         13     .200
     CIN N  O         67     .250
1942 CIN N  H          3     .000
     PHI N  O         91     .244
     BRTR           558     .279
```

KOZAR, ALBERT KENNETH (AL)
B.JULY 5,1922 MC KEES ROCKS,PA.
```
1948 WAS A  2        150     .250
1949 WAS A  2        105     .269
1950 WAS A  2         20     .200
     CHI A  2-3       10     .300
     BRTR           285     .254
```

KRACHER, JOSEPH PETER (JUG)
B.NOV.4,1915 PHILADELPHIA,PA.
```
1939 PHI N  C          5     .200
     BRTR
```

KRAFT, CLARENCE OTTO (BIG BOY)
B.JUNE 9,1887 EVANSVILLE,IND.
D.MAR.26,1958 FORT WORTH,TEX.
```
1914 BOS N  1-3        3     .333
     BRTR
```

KRAKAUSKAS, JOSEPH VICTOR LAWRENCE
B.MAR.28,1915 MONTREAL,QUE.,CAN
D.JULY 8,1960 HAMILTON,ONT.,CAN
```
1937 WAS A  P          5    4- 1
1938 WAS A  P         29    7- 5
1939 WAS A  P         39   11-17
1940 WAS A  P         32    1- 6
1941 CLE A  P         12    1- 2
1942 CLE A  P          3    0- 0
1946 CLE A  P         29    2- 5
     BLTL           149   26-36
```

KRALICK, JOHN FRANCIS (JACK)
B.JUNE 1,1935 YOUNGSTOWN,OHIO
```
1959 WAS A  P          6    0- 0
1960 WAS A  P         35    8- 6
1961 MIN A  P         33   13-11
1962 MIN A  P         39   12-11
1963 MIN A  P      5   6    1- 4
     CLE A  P         28   13- 5
1964 CLE A  P         30   12- 7
1965 CLE A  P         30    5-11
1966 CLE A  P         27    3- 4
1967 CLE A  /P         2    0- 2
     BLTL       235 236   67-65
```

**KRALY, STEVE CHARLES
(STEVE) OR (LEFTY)**
B.APR.18,1929 WHITING,IND.
```
1953 NY  A  P          5    0- 2
     BLTL
```

KRAMER, JOHN HENRY (JACK)
B.JAN.5,1918 NEW ORLEANS,LA.
```
1939 STL A  P         40    9-16
1940 STL A  P         16    3- 7
1941 STL A  P         29    4- 3
1943 STL A  P          3    0- 0
1944 STL A  P         33   17-13
1945 STL A  P         29   10-15
1946 STL A  P         31   13-11
1947 STL A  P         33   11-16
1948 BOS A  P         29   18- 5
1949 BOS A  P         21    6- 8
1950 NY  A  P         35    3- 6
1951 NY  N  P          4    0- 0
     NY  A  P          4    1- 0
     BRTR           322   95-103
```

KRANEPOOL, EDWARD EMIL (ED)
B.NOV.8,1944 NEW YORK,N.Y.
```
1962 NY  N  1          3     .167
1963 NY  N  1-O       86     .209
1964 NY  N  1-O      119     .257
1965 NY  N  *1       153     .253
1966 NY  N  *1-O     146     .254
1967 NY  N  *1       141     .269
1968 NY  N  *1/O     127     .231
1969 NY  N  *1/O     112     .238
1970 NY  N  /1        43     .170
1971 NY  N  *1-O     122     .280
1972 NY  N  *1/O     122     .269
1973 NY  N  1        100     .239
1974 NY  N  O-1       94     .300
1975 NY  N  1/O      106     .323
1976 NY  N  1-O      123     .292
1977 NY  N  O-1      108     .281
1978 NY  N  O/1       66     .210
     BLTL          1771     .262
```

KRAPP, EUGENE H. (RUBBER ARM)
B.MAY 12,1887 ROCHESTER,N.Y.
D.APR.13,1923 DETROIT,MICH.
```
1911 CLE A  P     35  36   12- 8
1912 CLE A  P          9    2- 5
1914 BUF F  P         37   16-14
1915 BUF F  P         38    9-19
     BRTR           120   39-46
```

YR	CL	LEA	POS	GP	G	REC

KRAUS, JOHN WILLIAM (JACK)
(TEX) OR (TEXAS JACK)
B.APR.26,1918 SAN ANTONIO,TEX.
D.JAN.2,1976 SAN ANTONIO,TEX.

YR	CL	LEA	POS	GP	G	REC
1943	PHI	N	P	34	35	9-15
1945	PHI	N	P		19	4- 9
1946	NY	N	P		17	2- 1
		BRTL		70	71	15-25

KRAUSE, HARRY WILLIAM (HAL)
B.JULY 12,1887 SAN FRANCISCO,CAL.
D.OCT.23,1940 SAN FRANCISCO,CAL

1908	PHI	A	P		4	1- 1
1909	PHI	A	P		32	18- 8
1910	PHI	A	P		16	6- 6
1911	PHI	A	P		28	11- 7
1912	PHI	A	P		3	0- 1
	CLE	A	P		3	0- 1
		BBTL			86	36-24

KRAUSSE, LEWIS BERNARD, JR. (LEW)
B.APR.25,1943 MEDIA,PA.

1961	KC	A	P	12	13	2- 5
1964	KC	A	P	5	8	0- 2
1965	KC	A	/P	7	10	2- 4
1966	KC	A	P	36	40	14- 9
1967	KC	A	P	48	49	7-17
1968	OAK	A	P		36	10-11
1969	OAK	A	P		43	7- 7
1970	MIL	A	P	37	38	13-18
1971	MIL	A	P		43	8-12
1972	BOS	A	P		24	1- 3
1973	STL	N	/P		1	0- 0
1974	ATL	N	P		29	4- 3
		BRTR		321	334	68-91

KRAUSSE, LEWIS BERNARD, SR.
B.JUNE 8,1912 MEDIA,PA.

1931	PHI	A	P		3	1- 0
1932	PHI	A	P		20	4- 1
		BRTR			23	5- 1

KRAVEC, KENNETH PETER (KEN)
B.JULY 29,1951 CLEVELAND,OHIO

1975	CHI	A	P	2	0- 1
1976	CHI	A	/P	9	1- 5
1977	CHI	A	P	26	11- 8
1978	CHI	A	P	30	11-16
		BBTL		67	23-30

KRAVITZ, DANIEL (DANNY)
(DUSTY) OR (BEAK)
B.DEC.21,1930 LOPEZ,PA.

1956	PIT	N	C-3		32	.265
1957	PIT	N	C		19	.146
1958	PIT	N	C		45	.240
1959	PIT	N	C		52	.253
1960			C		8	.000
	KC	A	C		59	.234
		BLTR			215	.236

KREEVICH, MICHAEL ANDREAS (MIKE)
B.JUNE 10,1908 MT.OLIVE,ILL.

1931	CHI	N	O		5	.167
1935	CHI	A	3		6	.435
1936	CHI	A	O		137	.307
1937	CHI	A	O		144	.302
1938	CHI	A	O		129	.297
1939	CHI	A	O		145	.323
1940	CHI	A	O		144	.255
1941	CHI	A	O		121	.232
1942	PHI	A	O		116	.255
1943	STL	A	O		60	.255
1944	STL	A	O		105	.301
1945	STL	A	O		84	.237
	WAS	A	O		45	.272
		BRTR			1241	.283

KREHMEYER, CHARLES L.
B.JULY 5,1863 ST.LOUIS,MO.
D.FEB.10,1926 ST.LOUIS,MO.

1884	STL	AA	C-O		20	.257
1885	LOU	AA	C-1-O		7	.212
	STL	N	C-O		1	.000
					28	.250

KREITNER, ALBERT JOSEPH (MICKEY)
B.OCT.10,1922 NASHVILLE,TENN.

1943	CHI	N	C		3	.375
1944	CHI	N	C		39	.152
		BRTR			42	.172

KREITZ, RALPH WESLEY (RED)
B.NOV.13,1885 PLUM CREEK,NEB.
D.JULY 20,1941 PORTLAND,ORE.

1911	CHI	A	P		7	.176
		BRTR				

KREMER, REMY PETER (RAY) OR (WIZ)
B.MAR.23,1893 OAKLAND,CAL.
D.FEB.8,1965 PINOLE,CAL.

1924	PIT	N	P	41	42	18-10
1925	PIT	N	P		40	17- 8
1926	PIT	N	P		37	20- 6
1927	PIT	N	P		35	19- 8
1928	PIT	N	P		34	15-13
1929	PIT	N	P		34	18-10
1930	PIT	N	P		39	20-12
1931	PIT	N	P		30	11-15
1932	PIT	N	P		11	4- 3
1933	PIT	N	P		7	1- 0
		BRTR		308	309	143-85

KREMMEL, JAMES LOUIS (JIM)
B.FEB.28,1948 BELLEVILLE,ILL.

1973	TEX	A	/P		4	0- 2
1974	CHI	N	P		23	0- 2
		BLTL			27	0- 4

KRESS, CHARLES STEVEN (CHUCK)
B.DEC.9,1921 PHILADELPHIA,PA.

1947	CIN	N	1		11	.148
1949	CIN	N	1		27	.207
	CHI	A	1		97	.278
1950	CHI	A	1		3	.000
1954	DET	A	1-O		24	.189
	BRO	N	1		13	.083
		BLTL			175	.249

KRESS, RALPH (RED)
B.JAN.2,1907 COLUMBIA,CAL.
D.NOV.29,1962 LOS ANGELES,CAL.

1927	STL	A	S		7	.304
1928	STL	A	S		150	.273
1929	STL	A	S		147	.305
1930	STL	A	S-3		154	.313
1931	STL	A	1-S-3-O		150	.311
1932	STL	A	3		14	.191
	CHI	A	S-3-O		135	.283
1933	CHI	A	1-O		129	.248
1934	CHI	A	O		8	.286
	WAS	A	O		56	.228
1935	WAS	A	P-1-	3	84	0- 0
			2-S-O			.298
1936	WAS	A	2-S		109	.284
1938	STL	A	S		150	.302
1939	STL	A	S		13	.279
	DET	A	S		51	.242
1940	DET	A	S-3		33	.222
1946	NY	N	P		1	0- 0
		BRTR		4	1391	0- 0
						.286

KRETLOW, LOUIS HENRY (LOU) OR (LENA)
B.JUNE 27,1923 APACHE,OKLA.

1946	DET	A	P		1	1- 0
1948	DET	A	P		5	2- 1
1949	DET	A	P		23	3- 2
1950	STL	A	P	9	10	2- 9
	CHI	A	P		11	0- 0
1951	CHI	A	P		26	6- 9
1952	CHI	A	P		19	4- 4
1953	CHI	A	P		9	0- 0
	STL	A	P		22	1- 5
1954	BAL	A	P		32	6-11
1955	BAL	A	P		24	4- 9
1956	KC	A	P		25	4- 9
		BRTR		199	200	27-47

KREUGER, RICHARD ALLEN (RICK)
B.NOV.3,1948 GRAND RAPIDS,MICH.

1975	BOS	A	/P		2	0- 0
1976	BOS	A	/P		8	2- 1
1977	BOS	A	/P		1	0- 1
1978	CLE	A	P		6	0- 0
		BRTL			17	2- 2

KREUTZER, FRANKLIN JAMES (FRANK)
B.FEB.7,1939 BUFFALO,N.Y.

1962	CHI	A	P		1	0- 0
1963	CHI	A	P		1	1- 0
1964	CHI	A	P		17	3- 1
	WAS	A	P		13	2- 6
1965	WAS	A	P		33	2- 6
1966	WAS	A	/P		9	0- 5
1969	WAS	A	/P		4	0- 0
		BRTL			78	8-18

KRICHELL, PAUL BERNARD
B.DEC.19,1882 NEW YORK,N.Y.
D.JUNE 4,1957 NEW YORK,N.Y.

1911	STL	A	C		28	.232
1912	STL	A	C		57	.217
		BRTR			85	.222

KRIEG, WILLIAM FREDERICK
B.JAN.29,1859 PETERSBURG,ILL.
D.MAR.25,1930 CHILLICOTHE,ILL.

1884	CHI	U	C-1-O		59	.231
	PIT	U	C-O		10	.350
1885	CHI	N	C-O		1	.000
	BRO	AA	C		17	.150
1886	WAS	N	1		27	.255
1887	WAS	N	1		24	.304
		BRTR			138	.248

KRIEGER

1884	KC	U	P		1	0- 1

KRIEGER, KURT FERDINAND (DUTCH)
B.SEPT.16,1926 TRAISEN,AUSTRIA
D.AUG.16,1970 ST.LOUIS,MO.

1949	STL	N	P		1	0- 0
1951	STL	N	P		2	0- 0
		BRTR			3	0- 0

KRIST, HOWARD WILBUR (SPUD)
B.FEB.28,1916 W.HENRIETTA,N.Y.

1937	STL	N	P		6	3- 1
1938	STL	N	P		2	0- 0
1941	STL	N	P		37	10- 0
1942	STL	N	P	34	35	13- 3
1943	STL	N	P		34	11- 5
1946	STL	N	P		15	0- 0
		BLTR		128	129	37-11

KROCK, AUGUST H. (GUS)
B.MAY 9,1866 MILWAUKEE,WIS.
D.MAR.22,1905 PASADENA,CAL.

1888	CHI	N	P		39	25-14
1889	CHI	N	P		8	4- 4
	IND	N	P		7	5- 2
	WAS	N	P		7	1- 6
1890	BUF	P	P		4	0- 3
		TL			65	35-29

KROH, FLOYD MYRON (RUBE)
B.AUG.25,1886 FRIENDSHIP,N.Y.
D.MAR.17,1944 NEW ORLEANS,LA.

1906	BOS	A	P		1	1- 0
1907	BOS	A	P		7	0- 4
1908	CHI	N	P		2	0- 0
1909	CHI	N	P		17	9- 4
1910	CHI	N	P		6	3- 1
1912	BOS	N	P		3	0- 0
		BLTL			36	13- 9

KROL, JOHN THOMAS (JACK)
B.JULY 9,1936 CHICAGO,ILL.
NON-PLAYING MANAGER
STL[N] 1978 [INTERIM]

KROLL, GARY MELVIN
B.JULY 8,1941 CULVER CITY,CAL.

1964	PHI	N	P		2	0- 0
	NY	N	P		8	0- 1
1965	NY	N	P		32	6- 6
1966	HOU	N	P		10	0- 0
1969	CLE	A	P		19	0- 0
		BRTR			71	6- 7

KRONER, JOHN HAROLD
B.NOV.13,1908 ST.LOUIS,MO.
D.AUG.26,1968 ST.LOUIS,MO.

1935	BOS	A	3		2	.250
1936	BOS	A	2-S-3		84	.239
1937	CLE	A	2-3		86	.237
1938	CLE	A	2		51	.248
		BRTR			223	.262

KROUSE, WILLIAM
B.AURORA,ILL.

1901	CIN	N	2		1	.250
		TR				

KRSNICH, MICHAEL (MIKE)
B.AUG.5,1927 W.ALLIS,WIS.

1960	MIL	N	O		4	.333
1962	MIL	N	1-3-O		11	.083
		BRTR			15	.190

KRSNICH, ROCCO PETER (ROCKY)
B.DEC.4,1927 W.ALLIS,WIS.

1949	CHI	A	3		16	.218
1952	CHI	A	3		40	.231
1953	CHI	A	3		64	.202
		BRTR			120	.215

KRUEGER, ERNEST GEORGE
B.DEC.27,1890 CHICAGO,ILL.
D.APR.22,1976 WAUKEGAN,ILL.

1913	CLE	A	C		5	.000
1915	NY	A	C		10	.172
1917	NY	N	C		8	.000
	BRO	N	C		31	.272
1918	BRO	N	C		30	.267
1919	BRO	N	C		80	.248
1920	BRO	N	C		52	.288
1921	BRO	N	C		65	.264
1925	CIN	N	C		37	.307
		BRTR			318	.264

KRUEGER, ARTHUR WILLIAM (OOM PAUL)
B.SEPT.17,1876 CHICAGO,ILL.
D.FEB.20,1961 ST.LOUIS,MO.

1899	CLE	N	3		13	.227
1900	STL	N	2		12	.400
1901	STL	N	3		142	.274
1902	STL	N	S-3		125	.264
1903	PIT	N	S-O		71	.246
1904	PIT	N	S-O		75	.194
1905	PHI	N	P-S	1	30	0- 1
						.184
		BRTR		1	468	0- 1
						.250

YR	CL	LEA	POS	GP	G	REC

KRUG, EVERETT BEN (CHRIS)
B.DEC.25,1939 LOS ANGELES,CAL.
1965 CHI N C 60 .201
1966 CHI N C 11 .214
1969 SD N /C 8 .059
BRTK 79 .192

KRUG, HENRY CHARLES
B.DEC.4,1876 SAN FRANCISCO,CAL.
D.JAN.14,1908 SAN FRANCISCO,CAL
1902 PHI N 2-S-3-O 53 .225
TR

KRUG, MARTIN JOHN
B.SEPT.10,1888 COBLENZ,GERMANY
D.JUNE 27,1966 GLENDALE,CAL.
1912 BOS A S 15 .308
1922 CHI N 2-S-3 127 .275
BRTR 142 .278

KRUGER, ABRAHAM
B.FEB.14,1885 MORRIS RUN,PA.
D.JULY 4,1962 ELMIRA,N.Y.
1908 BRO N P 1 0-1
BRTR

KRUGER, ARTHUR T.
B.MAR.16,1881 SAN ANTONIO,TEX.
D.NOV.28,1949 HONOJ,CAL.
1907 CIN N O 96 .233
1910 CLE A O 62 .170
BOS N O 1 .000
1914 KC F O 122 .290
1915 KC F O 80 .234
BRTR 361 .228

KRUKOW, MICHAEL EDWARD (MIKE)
B.JAN.21,1952 LONG BEACH,CAL.
1976 CHI N /P 2 0-0
1977 CHI N P 34 8-14
1978 CHI N P 27 9-3
BRTR 63 17-17

KRUMM, ALBERT
B.COLUMBUS,OHIO
1889 PIT N P 1 0-1
TR

KRYHOSKI, RICHARD DAVID (DICK)
B.MAR.24,1925 LEONIA,N.J.
1949 NY A 1 54 .294
1950 DET A 1 53 .219
1951 DET A 1 119 .287
1952 STL A 1 111 .243
1953 STL A 1 104 .278
1954 BAL A 1 100 .260
1955 KC A 1 28 .213
BLTL 569 .264

KUBEK, ANTHONY CHRISTOPHER (TONY)
B.OCT.12,1936 MILWAUKEE,WIS.
1957 NY A 2-S-3-O 127 .297
1958 NY A 1-2-S-O 138 .265
1959 NY A 2-S-3-O 132 .279
1960 NY A S-O 147 .273
1961 NY A S 153 .276
1962 NY A S-O 45 .314
1963 NY A S-O 135 .257
1964 NY A S 106 .229
1965 NY A S/O-1 109 .218
BLTR 1092 .266

KUBIAK, THEODORE RODGER (TED)
B.MAY 12,1942 NEW BRUNSWICK,N.J.
1967 KC A S-2/3 53 .157
1968 OAK A 2-S 48 .250
1969 OAK A S-2 92 .249
1970 MIL A 2-S 158 .252
1971 MIL A 2-S 89 .227
STL N S-2 32 .250
1972 TEX A 2-S/3 46 .224
OAK A 2/3 51 .181
1973 OAK A 2-S/3 106 .220
1974 OAK A 2-S-3 99 .209
1975 OAK A /S-3-2 20 .250
SD N 3-2/1 87 .224
1976 SD N 3-2/S-1 96 .163
BBTR 977 .231

KUBISZYN, JOHN HENRY (JACK)
B.DEC.17,1936 BUFFALO,N.Y.
1961 CLE A 2-S-3 25 .214
1962 CLE A S-3 25 .169
BRTR 50 .188

KUCAB, JOHN ALBERT (JOHNNY)
B.DEC.4,1919 OLYPHANT,PA.
D.MAY 26,1977 YOUNGSTOWN,OHIO
1950 PHI A P 1 1-1
1951 PHI A P 30 4-3
1952 PHI A P 28 28 0-1
BRTR 59 62 5-5

KUCEK, JOHN ANDREW CHARLES (JACK)
B.JUNE 8,1953 WARREN,OHIO
1974 CHI A /P 9 1-4
1975 CHI A /P 2 0-0
1976 CHI A /P 2 0-0
1977 CHI A /P 8 0-1
1978 CHI A P 10 2-3
BRTR 31 3-8

KUCKS, JOHN CHARLES (JOHNNY)
B.JULY 27,1933 HOBOKEN,N.J.
1955 NY A P 29 8-7
1956 NY A P 34 18-9
1957 NY A P 37 8-10
1958 NY A P 34 8-8
1959 NY A P 9 0-1
KC A P 33 8-11
1960 KC A P 31 4-10
BRTR 207 54-56

KUCZEK, STANISLAW LEO (STEVE)
B.DEC.28,1924 AMSTERDAM,N.Y.
1949 BOS N H 1 1.000
BRTR

KUCZYNSKI, BERNARD CARL (BERT)
B.JAN.8,1920 PHILADELPHIA,PA.
1943 PHI A P 6 0-1
BRTR

KUEHL, KARL OTTO
B.SEPT.9,1937 MONTEREY PARK,CAL.
NON-PLAYING MANAGER MON[N] 1976

KUEHNE, WILLIAM J.
[REAL NAME WILLIAM J. KNELME]
B.OCT.24,1858 LEIPZIG,GERMANY
D.OCT.27,1921 SULPHUR SPRINGS,O
1883 COL AA 2-S-3-O 96 .222
1884 COL AA 3 110 .238
1885 PIT AA 3 105 .216
1886 PIT AA 3-O 117 .211
1887 PIT N S 101 .322
1888 PIT N S-3 137 .234
1889 PIT N 3 97 .246
1890 PIT N 3 126 .243
1891 COL AA 3 56 .214
LOU AA 3 40 .275
1892 LOU N 3 76 .164
STL N S-3 6 .167
CIN N 3 6 .217
STL N 3 1 .000
TR 1074 .236

KUENN, HARVEY EDWARD
B.DEC.4,1930 W.ALLIS,WIS.
1952 DET A S 19 .325
1953 DET A S 155 .308
1954 DET A S 155 .306
1955 DET A S 145 .306
1956 DET A S-O 146 .332
1957 DET A 1-S-3 151 .277
1958 DET A O 139 .319
1959 DET A O 139 .353
1960 CLE A 3-O 126 .308
1961 SF N S-3-O 131 .265
1962 SF N 3-O 130 .304
1963 SF N 3-O 120 .290
1964 SF N 1-3-O 111 .262
1965 SF N O/1 23 .237
CHI N O/1 54 .217
1966 CHI N /O 3 .333
PHI N O-1/3 86 .296
BRTR 1833 .303
NON-PLAYING MANAGER
MIL[A] 1975 [INTERIM]

KUHAULUA, FRED MAHELE
B.FEB.23,1953 HONOLULU,HAWAII
1977 CAL A /P 3 0-0
BLTL

KUHEL, JOSEPH ANTHONY (JOE)
B.JUNE 25,1906 CLEVELAND,OHIO
1930 WAS A 1 18 .286
1931 WAS A 1 139 .269
1932 WAS A 1 101 .291
1933 WAS A 1 153 .322
1934 WAS A 1 63 .289
1935 WAS A 1 151 .261
1936 WAS A 1 149 .321
1937 WAS A 1 136 .283
1938 CHI A 1 117 .267
1939 CHI A 1 139 .300
1940 CHI A 1 155 .280
1941 CHI A 1 153 .250
1942 CHI A 1 115 .249
1943 WAS A 1 153 .213
1944 WAS A 1 139 .278
1945 WAS A 1 142 .285
1946 WAS A 1 14 .150
CHI A 1 64 .273
1947 CHI A H 4 .000
BLTL 2105 .277
NON-PLAYING MANAGER WAS[A] 1948-49

KUHN, BERNARD DANIEL (BUB)
B.OCT.12,1899 VICKSBURG,MICH.
D.NOV.20,1956 DETROIT,MICH.
1924 CLE A P 1 0-1
BLTR

KUHN, KENNETH HAROLD (KENNY)
B.MAR.20,1937 LOUISVILLE,KY.
1955 CLE A S 4 .333
1956 CLE A 2-S 27 .273
1957 CLE A 2-S-3 40 .170
BLTR 71 .210

KUHN, WALTER CHARLES (RED)
B.FEB.2,1884 FRESNO,CAL.
D.JUNE 14,1935 FRESNO,CAL.
1912 CHI A C 75 .202
1913 CHI A C 26 .160
1914 CHI A C 17 .275
BRTR 118 .205

KUHNS, CHARLES B.
B.FREEPORT,PA.
D.JULY 15,1922 PITTSBUGH,PA.
1897 PIT N 3 2 .000
1899 BOS N S-3 6 .267
8 .217

KUIPER, DUANE EUGENE
B.JUNE 19,1950 RACINE,WIS.
1974 CLE A /2 10 .500
1975 CLE A 2 90 .292
1976 CLE A *2/1 135 .263
1977 CLE A *2 148 .277
1978 CLE A *2 149 .283
BLTR 532 .280

KULL, JOHN A.
B.JUNE 24,1882 SHENANDOAH,PA.
D.MAR.30,1936 SCHUYLKILL,PA.
1909 PHI A P 1 1-0
BLTL

KUME, JOHN MICHAEL (MIKE)
B.MAY 19,1926 PREMIER,W.VA.
1955 KC A P 6 0-2
BRTR

KUNKEL, WILLIAM GUSTAVE JAMES (BILL)
B.JULY 7,1936 HOBOKEN,N.J.
1961 KC A P 58 3-4
1962 KC A P 9 0-0
1963 NY A P 22 3-2
BRTR 89 6-6

KUNZ, EARL DEWEY (PINCHES)
B.DEC.25,1899 SACRAMENTO,CAL.
D.APR.14,1963 SACRAMENTO,CAL.
1923 PIT N P 21 1-2

KUROSAKI, RYAN YOSHITOMO
B.JULY 3,1952 HONOLULU,HAWAII
1975 STL N /P 7 0-0

KUROWSKI, GEORGE JOHN (WHITEY)
B.APR.19,1918 READING,PA.
1941 STL N 3 5 .333
1942 STL N S-3-O 115 .254
1943 STL N S-3 139 .287
1944 STL N 2-S-3 149 .270
1945 STL N S-3 133 .323
1946 STL N 3 142 .301
1947 STL N 3 146 .310
1948 STL N 3 77 .214
1949 STL N 3 10 .143
BRTR 916 .286

KURTZ, HAROLD JAMES (HAL) OR (BUD)
B.AUG.20,1943 WASHINGTON,D.C.
1968 CLE A P 28 30 1-2
BRTR

KUSEL, EDWARD
B.FEB.15,1886 CLEVELAND,OHIO
D.OCT.20,1948 CLEVELAND,OHIO
1909 STL A P 3 0-3

KUSH, EMIL BENEDICT
B.NOV.4,1916 CHICAGO,ILL.
D.NOV.26,1969 RIVER GROVE,ILL.
1941 CHI N P 2 0-0
1942 CHI N P 1 0-0
1946 CHI N P 40 9-2
1947 CHI N P 47 8-3
1948 CHI N P 34 1-4
1949 CHI N P 26 3-3
BRTR 150 21-12

KUSICK, CRAIG ROBERT
B.SEP.30,1948 MILWAUKEE,WIS.
1973 MIN A 1/O 15 .250
1974 MIN A 1 76 .239
1975 MIN A 1 57 .237
1976 MIN A O-1 109 .259
1977 MIN A O-1 115 .254
1978 MIN A O-1/O 77 .173
BRTR 449 .236

YR	CL	LEA	POS	GP	G	REC

KUSNYER, ARTHUR WILLIAM (ART)
B.DEC.19,1945 AKRON,OHIO
1970	CHI	A	/C		4	.100
1971	CAL	A	/C		6	.154
1972	CAL	A	C	64		.207
1973	CAL	A	C	41		.125
1976	MIL	A	C	15		.118
1978	KC	A	/C		9	.231
			BRTR	139		.176

KUSTUS, JOSEPH J. (JUL)
B.SEPT.5,1882 DETROIT,MICH.
D.APR.27,1916 ELOISE,MICH.
| 1909 | BRO | N | O | | 50 | .145 |
| | | | BRTR | | | |

KUTINA, JOSEPH PETER
B.JAN.16,1885 CHICAGO,ILL.
D.APR.13,1945 CHICAGO,ILL.
1911	STL	A	1	26		.259
1912	STL	A	1	67		.205
			BRTR	93		.222

KUTYNA, MARION JOHN (MARTY)
B.NOV.14,1932 PHILADELPHIA,PA.
1959	KC	A	P		4	0- 0
1960	KC	A	P	51		3- 2
1961	WAS	A	P	50		6- 8
1962	WAS	A	P	54		5- 6
			BRTR	159		14-16

KUZAVA, ROBERT LEROY (BOB) OR (SARGE)
B.MAY 28,1923 WYANDOTTE,MICH.
1946	CLE	A	P		2	1- 0
1947	CLE	A	P		4	1- 1
1949	CHI	A	P		29	10- 6
1950	CHI	A	P		10	1- 3
	WAS	A	P		22	8- 7
1951	CHI	A	P		8	3- 3
	NY	A	P	23	24	8- 4
1952	NY	A	P		28	8- 8
1953	NY	A	P		33	6- 5
1954	NY	A	P		20	1- 3
	BAL	A	P		4	1- 3
1955	BAL	A	P		6	0- 1
	PHI	N	P		17	1- 0
1957	PIT	N	P		4	0- 0
	STL	N	P		3	0- 0
			BBTL	213	214	49-44

KVASNAK, ALEXANDER
B.JAN.11,1921 SAGAMORE,PA.
| 1942 | WAS | A | O | | 5 | .182 |
| | | | BRTR | | | |

KWIETNIEWSKI, CASIMIR EUGENE
[PLAYED UNDER NAME OF
CASIMIR EUGENE MICHAELS]

KYLE, ANDREW EWING
B.OCT.29,1889 TORONTO,ONT.,CAN.
D.SEPT.6,1971 TORONTO,ONT.,CAN.
| 1912 | CIN | N | O | | 8 | .350 |
| | | | BLTL | | | |

LAABS, CHESTER PETER (CHET)
B.APR.30,1912 MILWAUKEE,WIS.
1937	DET	A	O		72	.240
1938	DET	A	O		64	.237
1939	DET	A	O		5	.313
	STL	A	O		95	.300
1940	STL	A	O		105	.271
1941	STL	A	O		118	.278
1942	STL	A	O		144	.275
1943	STL	A	O		151	.250
1944	STL	A	O		66	.234
1945	STL	A	O		35	.239
1946	STL	A	O		80	.261
1947	PHI	A	O		15	.219
			BRTR	950		.262

LABINE, CLEMENT WALTER (CLEM)
B.AUG.6,1926 LINCOLN,R.I.
1950	BRO	N	P		1	0- 0
1951	BRO	N	P		14	5- 1
1952	BRO	N	P	25	26	8- 4
1953	BRO	N	P		37	11- 6
1954	BRO	N	P		47	7- 6
1955	BRO	N	P		60	13- 5
1956	BRO	N	P		62	10- 6
1957	BRO	N	P		58	5- 7
1958	LA	N	P		52	6- 6
1959	LA	N	P		56	5-10
1960	LA	N	P		13	0- 1
	DET	A	P		14	0- 3
	PIT	N	P		15	3- 0
1961	PIT	N	P		56	4- 1
1962	NY	N	P		3	0- 0
			BRTR	513	514	77-56

LABOY, JOSE ALBERTO (COCO)
B.JULY 3,1940 PONCE,P.R.
1969	MON	N	*3	157		.258
1970	MON	N	*3/2	137		.199
1971	MON	N	3/2	76		.252
1972	MON	N	3/2-S	28		.261
1973	MON	N	3/2-O	22		.121
			BRTR	420		.233

LACEY, ROBERT JOSEPH (BOB)
B.AUG.25,1953 FREDERICKSBURG,VA.
1977	OAK	A	P		64	6- 8
1978	OAK	A	P		74	8- 9
			BRTL	138		14-17

LA CHANCE, GEORGE JOSEPH (CANDY)
B.FEB.15,1870 WATERBURY,CONN.
D.AUG.18,1932 WATERTOWN,VT.
1893	BRO	N	C		11	.176
1894	BRO	N	1		65	.329
1895	BRO	N	1		128	.320
1896	BRO	N	1		89	.280
1897	BRO	N	1		125	.308
1898	BRO	N	1-S		135	.243
1899	BAL	N	1		126	.307
1901	CLE	A	1		133	.306
1902	BOS	A	1		138	.275
1903	BOS	A	1		141	.258
1904	BOS	A	1		157	.231
1905	BOS	A	1		12	.128
			BB	1260		.281

LACHEMANN, MARCEL ERNEST
B.JUNE 13,1941 LOS ANGELES,CAL.
1969	OAK	A	P		28	4- 1
1970	OAK	A	P		41	3- 3
1971	OAK	A	/P		1	0- 0
			BRTR		70	7- 4

LACHEMANN, RENE GEORGE
B.MAY 4,1945 LOS ANGELES,CAL.
1965	KC	A	C	92		.227
1966	KC	A	/C	7		.200
1968	OAK	A	C	19		.150
			BRTR	118		.210

LA CLAIRE, GEORGE LEWIS (FRENCHY)
B.OCT.18,1886 MILTON,VT.
D.OCT.10,1918 FARNHAM,QUE.,CAN.
1914	PIT	F	P		22	5- 2
1915	PIT	F	P		14	3- 2
	BUF	F	P		1	0- 0
	BAL	F	P		18	0- 6
			TR		55	8-10

LA COCK, RALPH PIERRE (PETER)
B.JAN.17,1952 BURBANK,CAL.
1972	CHI	N	/O		9	.500
1973	CHI	N	/O		11	.250
1974	CHI	N	O-1		35	.182
1975	CHI	N	1-O		106	.229
1976	CHI	N	1-O		106	.221
1977	KC	A	1-O-D		88	.303
1978	KC	A	*1		118	.295
			BLTL	469		.257

LA CORTE, FRANK JOSEPH
B.OCT.13,1951 SAN JOSE,CAL.
1975	ATL	N	/P		3	0- 3
1976	ATL	N	P	19	21	3-12
1977	ATL	N	P		14	1- 8
1978	ATL	N	/P		2	0- 1
			BRTR	38	40	4-24

LA COSS, MICHAEL JAMES (MIKE)
B.MAY 30,1956 GLENDALE,CAL.
| 1978 | CIN | N | P | 16 | 17 | 4- 8 |
| | | | BRTR | | | |

LACY, LEONDAUS (LEON)
B.APR.10,1948 LONGVIEW,TEX.
1972	LA	N	2		60	.259
1973	LA	N	2		57	.207
1974	LA	N	2/3		48	.282
1975	LA	N	2-O/S		101	.314
1976	ATL	N	2/O-3		50	.272
	LA	N	O/3-2		93	.266
1977	LA	N	O-2-3		75	.266
1978	LA	N	O-2/3-S		103	.261
			BRTR	547		.270

LACY, OSCEOLA GUY (GUY)
B.JUNE 12,1897 CLEVELAND,TENN.
D.NOV.19,1935 CLEVELAND,TENN.
| 1926 | CLE | A | 2 | | 13 | .167 |

LADD, ARTHUR CLIFFORD HIRAM (HI)
B.FEB.9,1870 WILLIMANTIC,CONN.
D.MAY 7,1948 CRANSTON,R.I.
| 1898 | PIT | N | O | | 1 | .000 |
| | BOS | N | O | | 2 | .000 |

LADE, DOYLE MARION (PORKY)
B.FEB.17,1921 FAIRBURY,NEB.
1946	CHI	N	P		3	0- 2
1947	CHI	N	P	34	35	11-10
1948	CHI	N	P		19	5- 6
1949	CHI	N	P		36	4- 5
1950	CHI	N	P		34	5- 6
			BRTR	126	127	25-29
			BB	1946-47		

LADEW, STEPHEN
B.ST.LOUIS,MO.
| 1889 | KC | AA | P | | 2 | 0- 0 |

LAFATA, JOSEPH JOSEPH (JOE)
B.AUG.3,1921 DETROIT,MICH.
1947	NY	N	O		62	.221
1948	NY	N	H		1	.000
1949	NY	N	1		64	.256
			BLTL	127		.229

LAFFERTY, FRANK BERNARD (FLIP)
B.MAY 4,1854 SCRANTON,PA.
D.FEB.8,1910 WILMINGTON,DEL.
1876	ATH	N	P		1	0- 1
1877	LOU	N	O		4	.059
			TR	1	5	0- 1
						.050

LAFITTE, EDWARD FRANCIS (DOC)
B.APR.7,1886 NEW ORLEANS,LA.
D.APR.12,1971 JENKINTOWN,PA.
1909	DET	A	P		3	0- 1
1911	DET	A	P	29	31	11- 8
1912	DET	A	P		1	0- 0
1914	BRO	F	P		42	18-15
1915	BRO	F	P		17	7- 9
	BUF	F	P		14	2- 2
			BRTR	106	108	38-35

LA FOREST, BYRON JOSEPH (TY)
B.APR.18,1919 EDMUNDSTON,N.B.,CANADA
D.MAY 5,1947 ARLINGTON,MASS.
| 1945 | BOS | A | 3-O | | 52 | .280 |
| | | | BRTR | | | |

LAGGER, EDWIN JOSEPH
B.JULY 14,1912 JOLIET,ILL.
| 1934 | PHI | A | P | | 8 | 0- 0 |
| | | | BRTR | | | |

LA GROW, LERRIN HARRIS
B.JULY 8,1948 PHOENIX,ARIZ.
1970	DET	A	P		10	0- 1
1972	DET	A	P		16	0- 1
1973	DET	A	P		21	1- 5
1974	DET	A	P		37	8-19
1975	DET	A	P		32	7-14
1976	STL	N	/P		8	0- 1
1977	CHI	A	P		66	7- 3
1978	CHI	A	P		52	6- 5
			BRTR	242		29-49

LAHOUD, JOSEPH MICHAEL (JOE)
B.APR.14,1947 DANBURY,CONN.
1968	BOS	A	O		29	.192
1969	BOS	A	O/1	101		.188
1970	BOS	A	O		17	.245
1971	BOS	A	O		107	.215
1972	MIL	A	O		111	.237
1973	MIL	A	O-D		96	.204
1974	CAL	A	*O-D	127		.271
1975	CAL	A	O-D		76	.214
1976	CAL	A	O		42	.177
	TEX	A	D/O		38	.225
1977	KC	A	O		34	.262
1978	KC	A	/O		13	.125
			BLTL	791		.223

LAJESKIE, RICHARD EDWARD
B.JAN.8,1926 PASSAIC,N.J.
D.AUG.15,1976 RAMSEY,N.J.
| 1946 | NY | N | 2 | | 6 | .200 |
| | | | BRTR | | | |

LAJOIE, NAPOLEON (NAP) OR (LARRY)
B.SEPT.5,1875 WOONSOCKET,R.I.
D.FEB.7,1959 DAYTONA BEACH,FLA.
1896	PHI	N	1		39	.328
1897	PHI	N	1-O		126	.363
1898	PHI	N	2		147	.328
1899	PHI	N	2		72	.379
1900	PHI	N	2		102	.346
1901	PHI	A	2		131	.422
1902	PHI	A	2		1	.200
	CLE	A	2		86	.369
1903	CLE	A	2		126	.355
1904	CLE	A	2-S		140	.381
1905	CLE	A	M-2		65	.329
1906	CLE	A	M-2-3		152	.355
1907	CLE	A	M-2		137	.299
1908	CLE	A	M-2		157	.289
1909	CLE	A	M-2		128	.324
1910	CLE	A	2		159	.384
1911	CLE	A	1-2		90	.365
1912	CLE	A	1-2		117	.368
1913	CLE	A	2		137	.335
1914	CLE	A	1-2		121	.258
1915	PHI	A	2		129	.280
1916	PHI	A	2		113	.246
			BRTR	2475		.339

YR	CL	LEA	POS	GP	G	REC

LAKE, EDWARD ERVING
(EDDIE) OR (SPARKY)
B.MAR.18,1916 ANTIOCH,CAL.
```
1939 STL N  S              2    .250
1940 STL N  2-S           32    .212
1941 STL N  2-S-3         45    .105
1943 BOS A  S             75    .199
1944 BOS A  P-2-     6    57    0- 0
            S-3                 .206
1945 BOS A  S            133    .279
1946 DET A  S            155    .254
1947 DET A  S            158    .211
1948 DET A  2-3          64     .263
1949 DET A  2-S-3        94     .196
1950 DET A  S-3          20     .000
           BRTR     6   835    0- 0
                                .231
```

LAKE, FREDERICK LOVETT
B.OCT.16,1866 NOVA SCOTIA,CAN.
D.NOV.24,1931 BOSTON,MASS.
```
1891 BOS N  C              5    .142
1894 LOU N  C-2           16    .292
1897 BOS N  C             17    .272
1898 PIT N  1              5    .083
1910 BOS N  M-H            3    .000
           BRTR           46    .238
NON-PLAYING MANAGER BOS[A] 1908-09
```

LAKE, JOSEPH HENRY
B.JAN.6,1881 BROOKLYN,N.Y.
D.JUNE 30,1950 BROOKLYN,N.Y.
```
1908 NY  A  /P     37    44    9-21
1909 NY  A  P            32   14-11
1910 STL A  P      35    37   11-18
1911 STL A  P            30   10-15
1912 STL A  P            15    3-10
1913 DET A  P            22    9- 9
     DET A  P            28    8- 7
           BRTR   199   208   64-91
```

LAKEMAN, ALBERT WESLEY
(AL) OR (MOOSE)
B.DEC.31,1918 CINCINNATI,OHIO
D.MAY 25,1976 SPARTANBURG,S.C.
```
1942 CIN N  C             20    .158
1943 CIN N  C             22    .255
1944 CIN N  -H             1    .000
1945 CIN N  -H            76    .256
1946 CIN N  C             23    .133
1947 CIN N  H              2    .000
     PHI N  C-1           55    .159
1948 PHI N  P-C           32    0- 0
                                .162
1949 BOS N  1              3    .167
1954 DET A  C              5    .000
           BRTR          239    0- 0
                                .203
```

LALLY, DANIEL J. (DAN)
B.AUG.12,1867 JERSEY CITY,N.J.
D.APR.14,1936 MILWAUKEE,WIS.
```
1891 PIT N  O             41    .225
1897 STL N  O             87    .278
           BRTR          128    .263
```

LAMABE, JOHN ALEXANDER (JACK)
B.OCT.3,1936 FARMINGDALE,N.Y.
```
1962 PIT N  P             46    3- 1
1963 BOS A  P             65    7- 4
1964 BOS A  P             39    9-13
1965 BOS A  P             14    0- 3
     HOU N  /P             3    0- 2
1966 CHI A  /P            34    7- 9
1967 CHI A  /P             3    1- 0
     NY  N  P             16    0- 3
     STL N  P             23    3- 4
1968 CHI N  P             42    3- 2
           BRTR          285   33-41
```

LA MACCHIA, ALFRED ANTHONY
B.JULY 22,1921 ST.LOUIS,MO.
```
1943 STL A  P              1    0- 1
1945 STL A  P              5    2- 0
1946 STL A  P              8    0- 0
     WAS A  P              2    0- 1
           BRTR           16    2- 2
```

LA MANNA, FRANK (HANK)
B.AUG.22,1919 WATERTOWN,PA.
```
1940 BOS N  P              5    1- 0
1941 BOS N  P-O    35     47    5- 4
                                .281
1942 BOS N  P       5     10    0- 1
           BRTR    45     62    6- 5
                                .256
```

LAMANNO, RAYMOND SIMONO (RAY)
B.NOV.17,1919 OAKLAND,CAL.
```
1941 CIN N  C              1    .000
1942 CIN N  C            111    .264
1946 CIN N  C             85    .243
1947 CIN N  C            118    .257
1948 CIN N  C            127    .242
           BRTR          442    .252
```

LAMANSKE, FRANK JAMES (LEFTY)
B.SEPT.30,1906 OGLESBY,ILL.
D.AUG.4,1971 OLNEY,ILL.
```
1935 BRO N  P              2    0- 0
           BLTL
```

LAMAR, WILLIAM HARMONG
(GOOD TIME BILL)
B.MAR.21,1897 ROCKVILLE,MD.
D.MAY 24,1970 ROCKPORT,MASS.
```
1917 NY  A  O             11    .244
1918 NY  A  O             26    .227
1919 NY  A  O             11    .188
     BOS A  O             48    .291
1920 BRO N  O             24    .273
1921 BRO N  O              3    .333
1924 PHI A  O             87    .330
1925 PHI A  O            138    .356
1926 PHI A  O            116    .284
1927 PHI A  O             84    .299
           BLTR          550    .310
```

LA MASTER, WAYNE LEE
B.FEB.13,1907 SPEED,IND.
```
1937 PHI N  P      50     51   15-19
1938 PHI N  P            18     4- 7
     BRO N  P             3     0- 1
           BLTL    71     74   19-27
```

LAMB, JOHN ANDREW
B.JULY 20,1946 SHARON,CONN.
```
1970 PIT N  P             23    0- 1
1971 PIT N  /P             2    0- 0
1973 PIT N  P             22    0- 1
           BRTR           47    0- 2
```

LAMB, LAYMON RAYMOND
B.MAR.17,1895 LINCOLN,NEB.
D.OCT.15,1955 FAYETTEVILLE,ARK.
```
1920 STL A  O              9    .375
1921 STL A  O             45    .253
           BRTR           54    .272
```

LAMB, RAYMOND RICHARD (RAY)
B.DEC.23,1944 GLENDALE,CAL.
```
1969 LA  N  P             10    0- 1
1970 LA  N  P             35    6- 1
1971 CLE A  P             43    6-12
1972 CLE A  P             34    5- 6
1973 CLE A  P             32    3- 3
           BRTR          154   20-23
```

LAMBERT, CLAYTON PATRICK
B.MAR.26,1917 SUMMITT,ILL.
```
1946 CIN N  P             23    2- 2
1947 CIN N  P              3    0- 0
           BRTR           26    2- 2
```

LAMBERT, EUGENE MARION
B.APR.26,1921 CRENSHAW,MISS.
```
1941 PHI N  P              2    0- 1
1942 PHI N  P              1    0- 0
           BRTR            3    0- 1
```

LAMBETH, OTIS SAMUEL
B.MAY 13,1890 BERLIN,KAN.
D.JUNE 5,1976 MORAN,KAN.
```
1916 CLE A  P      15     16    4- 3
1917 CLE A  P            26     7- 6
1918 CLE A  P             2     0- 0
           BRTR    43     44   11- 9
```

LAMER, PIERRE (PETE)
B.1874 HOBOKEN,N.J.
D.OCT.24,1931 BROOKLYN,N.Y.
```
1902 CHI N  C              2    .222
1907 CIN N  C              1    .000
           TR              3    .182
```

LAMLEIN, FREDERICK ARTHUR (DUTCH)
[PLAYED UNDER NAME OF
FREDERICK ARTHUR LAMLINE]

LAMLINE, FREDERICK ARTHUR
[REAL NAME FREDERICK ARTHUR LAMLEIN]
B.AUG.14,1867 PORT HURON,MICH.
D.SEPT.20,1970 PORT HURON,MICH.
```
1912 CHI A  P              1    0- 0
1915 STL N  P              4    0- 0
           BRTR            5    0- 0
```

LAMONT, GENE WILLIAM
B.DEC.25,1946 ROCKFORD,ILL.
```
1970 DET A  C             15    .295
1971 DET A  /C             7    .067
1972 DET A  /C             1    .000
1974 DET A  /C            60    .217
1975 DET A  /C             4    .375
           BLTR           87    .233
```

LA MOTTE, ROBERT EUGENE (BOBBY)
B.FEB.15,1898 SAVANNAH,GA.
D.NOV.24,1970 CHATHAM,GA.
```
1920 WAS A  S              4    .000
1921 WAS A  S             16    .195
1922 WAS A  3             68    .252
1925 STL A  S-3           97    .273
1926 STL A  S             36    .202
           BRTR          221    .253
```

LAMP, DENNIS PATRICK
B.SEPT.23,1952 LOS ANGELES,CAL.
```
1977 CHI N  P             11    0- 2
1978 CHI N  P             37    7-15
           BRTR           48    7-17
```

LAMPARD, CHRISTOPHER KEITH (KEITH)
B.DEC.20,1945 WARRINGTON,ENGLAND
```
1969 HOU N  /O             9    .250
1970 HOU N  O/1           53    .236
           BLTR           62    .238
```

LAMPE, HENRY JOSEPH
B.SEPT.19,1872 BOSTON,MASS.
D.SEPT.16,1936 DORCHESTER,MASS.
```
1894 BOS N  P              2    0- 1
1895 PHI N  P              7    0- 2
           BRTL            9    0- 3
```

LANAHAN, RICHARD ANTHONY
B.SEPT.27,1911 WASHINGTON,D.C.
D.MAR.12,1975 ROCHESTER,MINN.
```
1935 WAS A  P              3    0- 3
1937 WAS A  P              6    0- 1
1940 PIT N  P             40    6- 8
1941 PIT N  P              7    0- 1
           BLTL           56    6-13
```

LANCE, GARY DEAN
B.SEPT.21,1948 GREENVILLE,S.C.
```
1977 KC  A  /P             1    0- 1
           BBTR
```

LAND, DOC BURRELL
[PLAYED UNDER NAME OF
WILLIAM GILBERT LAND]

LAND, GROVER CLEVELAND
B.SEPT.22,1884 FRANKFORT,KY.
D.JULY 22,1958 PHOENIX,ARIZ.
```
1908 CLE A  C              7    .230
1909 CLE A  C              1    .500
1910 CLE A  C             34    .207
1911 CLE A  C             35    .140
1913 CLE A  C             17    .235
1914 BRO F  C            103    .282
1915 BRO F  C             96    .261
           BRTR          293    .247
```

LAND, WILLIAM GILBERT (DOC)
[REAL NAME DOC BURRELL LAND]
B.MAY 14,1903 BINNSVILLE,MASS.
```
1929 WAS A  O              1    .000
           BLTL
```

LANDENBERGER, KENNETH HENRY
(KEN) OR (RED)
B.JULY 29,1928 LYNDHURST,OHIO
D.JULY 28,1960 CLEVELAND,OHIO
```
1952 CHI A  1              2    .200
           BLTL
```

LANDESTOY, RAFAEL SILVIALDO
[SANTANA]
B.MAY 28,1953 BANI,D.R.
```
1977 LA  N  /2-S          15    .278
1978 HOU N  S/O-2         59    .266
           BBTR           74    .267
           BR 1977
```

LANDIS, JAMES HENRY (JIM)
B.MAR.9,1934 FRESNO,CAL.
```
1957 CHI A  O             96    .212
1958 CHI A  O            142    .277
1959 CHI A  O            149    .272
1960 CHI A  O            148    .253
1961 CHI A  O            140    .283
1962 CHI A  O            149    .228
1963 CHI A  O            133    .225
1964 CHI A  O            106    .208
1965 KC  A  *O           118    .239
1966 CLE A  O             85    .222
1967 DET A  O             25    .208
     BOS A  /O             5    .143
     HOU N  O             50    .252
           BRTR         1346    .247
```

LANDIS, SAMUEL H. (DOC)
B.AUG.16,1854 PHILADELPHIA,PA.
```
1882 ATH AA P-O     2      3    1- 1
                                .167
     BAL AA P-O    43     51   11-28
                                .160
                   45     54   12-29
                                .161
```

LANDIS, WILLIAM HENRY (BILL)
B.OCT.8,1942 HANFORD,CAL.
```
1963 KC  A  P              1    0- 0
1967 BOS A  P      18     21    1- 0
1968 BOS A  P            38     3- 3
1969 BOS A  P      45     46    5- 5
           BLTL   102    106    9- 8
```

LANDREAUX, KENNETH FRANCIS (KEN)
B.DEC.22,1954 LOS ANGELES,CAL.
```
1977 CAL A  O             23    .250
1978 CAL A  O             93    .223
           BLTR          116    .229
```

LANDRETH, LARRY ROBERT
B.MAR.11,1955 STRATFORD,ONT.,CAN

YR	CL	LEA	POS	GP	G	REC
1976	MON	N	/P		3	1- 2
1977	MON	N	/P		4	0- 2
		BRTR			7	1- 4

LANDRITH, HOBERT NEAL (HOBIE)
B.MAR.16,1930 DECATUR,ILL.

YR	CL	LEA	POS	GP	G	REC
1950	CIN	N	C		4	.214
1951	CIN	N	C		4	.385
1952	CIN	N	C		15	.260
1953	CIN	N	C		52	.240
1954	CIN	N	C		48	.198
1955	CIN	N	C		43	.253
1956	CHI	N	C		111	.221
1957	STL	N	C		75	.243
1958	STL	N	C		70	.215
1959	SF	N	C		109	.251
1960	SF	N	C		71	.242
1961	SF	N	C		43	.239
1962	NY	N	C		23	.289
	BAL	A	C		60	.222
1963	BAL	A	C		2	.000
	WAS	A	C		42	.175
		BLTR			772	.233

LANDRUM, DONALD LEROY (DON)
B.FEB.16,1936 SANTA ROSA,CAL.

YR	CL	LEA	POS	GP	G	REC
1957	PHI	N	O		2	.143
1960	STL	N	O		13	.245
1961	STL	N	2-O		28	.167
1962	STL	N	O		32	.314
	CHI	N	O		83	.282
1963	CHI	N	O		84	.242
1964	CHI	N	O		11	.000
1965	CHI	N	*O		131	.226
1966	SF	N	O		72	.186
		BLTR			456	.234

LANDRUM, JESSE GLENN
B.JULY 31,1912 CROCKETT,TEX.

YR	CL	LEA	POS	GP	G	REC
1938	CHI	A	2		4	.000
		BRTR				

LANDRUM, JOSEPH BUTLER
B.DEC.13,1928 COLUMBIA,S.C.

YR	CL	LEA	POS	GP	G	REC
1950	BRO	N	P		7	0- 0
1952	BRO	N	P		9	1- 3
		BRTR			16	1- 3

LANE, GEORGE M. (CHAPPY)
B.PITTSBURGH,PA.

YR	CL	LEA	POS	GP	G	REC
1882	PIT	AA	C-1-O		54	.167
1884	TOL	AA	1-O		56	.231
					110	.200

LANE, JAMES HUNTER
(HUNTER) OR (DODO)
B.JULY 20,1900 PULASKI,TENN.

YR	CL	LEA	POS	GP	G	REC
1924	BOS	N	2-3		7	.067
		BRTR				

LANE, JERALD HAL (JERRY)
B.FEB.7,1926 ASHLAND,N.Y.

YR	CL	LEA	POS	GP	G	REC
1953	WAS	A	P		20	1- 4
1954	CIN	N	P		3	1- 0
1955	CIN	N	P		8	0- 2
		BRTR			31	2- 6

LANE, MARVIN
B.JAN.18,1950 SANDERSVILLE,GA.

YR	CL	LEA	POS	GP	G	REC
1971	DET	A	/O		8	.143
1972	DET	A	/O		8	.000
1973	DET	A	/O		6	.250
1974	DET	A	O		50	.233
1976	DET	A	O		18	.188
		BRTR			90	.207

LANE, RICHARD HARRISON (DICK)
B.JUNE 28,1927 HIGHLAND PARK,MICH.

YR	CL	LEA	POS	GP	G	REC
1949	CHI	A	O		12	.119
		BRTR				

LANFORD, LEWIS GROVER (SAM)
B.JAN.8,1886 WOODRUFF,S.C.
D.SEPT.14,1970 WOODRUFF,S.C.

YR	CL	LEA	POS	GP	G	REC
1907	WAS	A	P		2	0- 0
		BRTR				

LANFRANCONI, WALTER OSWALD
B.NOV.9,1916 BARRE,VT.

YR	CL	LEA	POS	GP	G	REC
1941	CHI	N	P		2	0- 1
1947	BOS	N	P	36	37	4- 4
		BRTR		38	39	4- 5

LANG, DONALD CHARLES (DON)
B.MAR.15,1915 SELMA,CAL.

YR	CL	LEA	POS	GP	G	REC
1938	CIN	N	2-3		21	.260
1948	STL	N	2-3		117	.269
		BRTR			138	.268

LANG, MARTIN JOHN
B.SEPT.27,1905 HOOPER,NEB.
D.JAN.13,1968 LAKEWOOD,COLO.

YR	CL	LEA	POS	GP	G	REC
1930	PIT	N	P		2	0- 0
		BRTL				

LANG, ROBERT DAVID (CHIP)
B.AUG.21,1952 PITTSBURGH,PA.

YR	CL	LEA	POS	GP	G	REC
1975	MON	N	/P		1	0- 0
1976	MON	N	P		29	1- 3
		BRTR			30	1- 3

LANGE, FRANK HERMAN (SEAGAN)
B.OCT.28,1883 COLUMBIA,WIS.
D.DEC.26,1945 MADISON,WIS.

YR	CL	LEA	POS	GP	G	REC
1910	CHI	A	P		23	9- 4
1911	CHI	A	P	29	54	8- 8
1912	CHI	A	P	31	36	10-10
1913	CHI	A	P	12	16	1- 4
		BRTR		95	129	28-26

LANGE, ERWIN HENRY (ERV)
B.AUG.12,1887 FOREST PARK,ILL.
D.APR.24,1971 MAYWOOD,ILL.

YR	CL	LEA	POS	GP	G	REC
1914	CHI	F	P		37	12-11
		BRTR				

LANGE, RICHARD OTTO (DICK)
B.SEP.1,1948 HARBOR BEACH,MICH.

YR	CL	LEA	POS	GP	G	REC
1972	CAL	A	/P		2	0- 0
1973	CAL	A	P		17	2- 1
1974	CAL	A	P	21	29	3- 8
1975	CAL	A	P		30	4- 6
		BRTR		70	78	9-15

LANGE, WILLIAM ALEXANDER
(BILL) OR (LITTLE EVA)
B.JUNE 6,1871 SAN FRANCISCO,CAL
D.JULY 23,1950 SAN FRANCISCO,CAL.

YR	CL	LEA	POS	GP	G	REC
1893	CHI	N	2-O		116	.288
1894	CHI	N	O		112	.324
1895	CHI	N	O		122	.388
1896	CHI	N	O		123	.333
1897	CHI	N	O		117	.352
1898	CHI	N	O		111	.332
1899	CHI	N	O		107	.324
		BRTR			808	.336

LANGFORD, ELTON J. (SAM)
B.MAY 21,1900 BRIGGS,TEX.

YR	CL	LEA	POS	GP	G	REC
1926	BOS	A	O		1	.000
1927	CLE	A	O		20	.269
1928	CLE	A	O		110	.276
		BLTR			131	.275

LANGFORD, JAMES RICK (RICK)
B.MAR.20,1952 FARMVILLE,VA.

YR	CL	LEA	POS	GP	G	REC
1976	PIT	N	P		12	0- 1
1977	OAK	A	P		37	8-19
1978	OAK	A	P	37	40	7-13
		BRTR		86	89	15-33

LANGSFORD, ROBERT WILLIAM
[REAL NAME ROBERT HUGO LANKSWERT]
B.AUG.5,1865 LOUISVILLE,KY.
D.JAN.10,1907 LOUISVILLE,KY.

YR	CL	LEA	POS	GP	G	REC
1899	LOU	N	S		1	.000
		BRTR				

LANIER, HAROLD CLIFTON (HAL)
B.JULY 4,1942 DENTON,N.C.

YR	CL	LEA	POS	GP	G	REC
1964	SF	N	2-S		98	.274
1965	SF	N	*2/S		159	.226
1966	SF	N	*2-S		149	.231
1967	SF	N	*S-2		151	.213
1968	SF	N	*S		151	.206
1969	SF	N	*S		150	.228
1970	SF	N	*S/2-1		134	.231
1971	SF	N	3-2/S-1		109	.233
1972	NY	A	3/S-2		60	.214
1973	NY	A	S/2-3		35	.209
		BRTR			1196	.228
		BB 1966-70				

LANIER, HUBERT MAX (MAX)
B.AUG.18,1915 DENTON,N.C.

YR	CL	LEA	POS	GP	G	REC
1938	STL	N	P		18	0- 3
1939	STL	N	P		7	2- 1
1940	STL	N	P		35	9- 6
1941	STL	N	P		35	10- 8
1942	STL	N	P		34	13- 8
1943	STL	N	P		32	15- 7
1944	STL	N	P		33	17-12
1945	STL	N	P		4	2- 2
1946	STL	N	P		6	6- 0
1949	STL	N	P		15	5- 4
1950	STL	N	P		27	11- 9
1951	STL	N	P		31	11- 9
1952	NY	N	P	37	38	7-12
1953	NY	N	P		3	0- 0
	STL	A	P		10	0- 1
		BRTL		327	328	108-82

LANIER, LORENZO
B.OCT.19,1948 TUSKEGEE,ALA.

YR	CL	LEA	POS	GP	G	REC
1971	PIT	N	/H		6	.000
		BLTR				

LANKSWERT, ROBERT HUGO
[PLAYED UNDER NAME OF
ROBERT WILLIAM LANGSFORD]

LANNING, JOHN YOUNG
(TOBACCO CHEWIN JOHNNY)
B.SEPT.6,1910 ASHEVILLE,N.C.

YR	CL	LEA	POS	GP	G	REC
1936	BOS	N	P		28	7-11
1937	BOS	N	P		32	5- 7
1938	BOS	N	P		32	8- 7
1939	BOS	N	P		37	5- 6
1940	PIT	N	P		38	8- 4
1941	PIT	N	P		34	11-11
1942	PIT	N	P		34	6- 8
1943	PIT	N	P		12	4- 1
1945	PIT	N	P		1	0- 0
1946	PIT	N	P		27	4- 5
1947	BOS	N	P		3	0- 0
		BRTR			278	58-60

LANNING, LESTER ALFRED (RED)
B.MAY 13,1895 HARVARD,ILL.
D.JUNE 13,1962 BRISTOL,CONN.

YR	CL	LEA	POS	GP	G	REC
1916	PHI	A	P-O	5	19	0- 3
						.182
		BLTL				

LANNING, THOMAS NEWTON (TOM)
B.APR.22,1909 BILTMORE,N.C.
D.NOV.4,1967 MARIETTA,GA.

YR	CL	LEA	POS	GP	G	REC
1938	PHI	N	P		3	0- 1
		BLTL				

LANSFORD, CARNEY RAY
B.FEB.7,1957 SAN JOSE,CAL.

YR	CL	LEA	POS	GP	G	REC
1978	CAL	A	*3/S		121	.294
		BRTR				

LANSING, EUGENE HEWITT
B.JAN.11,1898 ALBANY,N.Y.
D.JAN.18,1945 RENSSELAER,N.Y.
D.JAN.18,1945

YR	CL	LEA	POS	GP	G	REC
1922	BOS	N	P		15	0- 1
		BRTR				

LA PALME, PAUL EDMORE
(PAUL) OR (LEFTY)
B.DEC.14,1923 SPRINGFIELD,MASS.

YR	CL	LEA	POS	GP	G	REC
1951	PIT	N	P		22	1- 5
1952	PIT	N	P		31	1- 2
1953	PIT	N	P		35	8-16
1954	PIT	N	P		33	4-10
1955	STL	N	P		56	4- 3
1956	STL	N	P		1	0- 0
	CIN	N	P		11	2- 4
	CHI	A	P		29	3- 1
1957	CHI	A	P	35	36	1- 4
		BLTL		253	254	24-45

LAPAN, PETER NELSON
B.JUNE 25,1891 EASTHAMPTON,MASS
D.JAN.5,1953 NORWALK,CAL.

YR	CL	LEA	POS	GP	G	REC
1922	WAS	A	C		11	.324
1923	WAS	A	C		2	.000
		BRTR			13	.306

LAPIHUSKA, ANDREW (APPLES)
B.NOV.1,1922 DELMONT,N.J.

YR	CL	LEA	POS	GP	G	REC
1942	PHI	N	P		3	0- 2
1943	PHI	N	P		1	0- 0
		BLTR			4	0- 2

LA POINTE, RALPH ROBERT
B.JAN.8,1922 WINOOSKI,VT.
D.SEPT.13,1967 BURLINGTON,VT.

YR	CL	LEA	POS	GP	G	REC
1947	PHI	N	S		56	.308
1948	STL	N	2-S-3		87	.225
		BRTR			143	.266

LA PORTE, FRANK BREYFOGLE (POT)
B.FEB.6,1880 UHRICHSVILLE,OHIO
D.SEPT.25,1939 NEWCOMERSTOWN,O.

YR	CL	LEA	POS	GP	G	REC
1905	NY	A	2		11	.375
1906	NY	A	3		123	.264
1907	NY	A	3-O		130	.270
1908	BOS	A	2-3		60	.245
	NY	A	2		41	.253
1909	NY	A	2		89	.298
1910	NY	A	2-O		124	.264
1911	STL	A	2		136	.314
1912	STL	A	3-O		80	.308
	WAS	A	2		39	.316
1913	WAS	A	2-3-O		80	.250
1914	IND	F	2		133	.311
1915	NEW	F	2		148	.251
		BRTR			1194	.281

LAPP, JOHN WALKER (JACK)
B.SEPT.10,1884 FRAZER,PA.
D.FEB.6,1920 PHILADELPHIA,PA.

YR	CL	LEA	POS	GP	G	REC
1908	PHI	A	C		13	.143
1909	PHI	A	C		21	.336
1910	PHI	A	C		71	.234
1911	PHI	A	C		68	.353
1912	PHI	A	C		90	.292
1913	PHI	A	C		84	.228
1914	PHI	A	C		69	.231
1915	PHI	A	C		112	.272
1916	CHI	A	C		40	.208
		BLTR			568	.263

YR	CL	LEA	POS	GP	G	REC

LA RIVIERE, EDMOND ARMAND
[PLAYED UNDER NAME OF
EDMOND ARMAND WINGO]

LARKER, NORMAN HOWARD JOHN (NORM)
B.DEC.27,1930 BEAVER MEADOWS,PA.
1958	LA	N	1-O		99	.277
1959	LA	N	1-O		108	.289
1960	LA	N	1-O		133	.323
1961	LA	N	1-O		97	.270
1962	HOU	N	1-O		147	.263
1963	MIL	N	1		64	.177
	SF	N	1		19	.071
	BLTL				667	.275

LARKIN, EDWARD FRANCIS
B.JULY 1,1885 WYALUSING,PA.
D.MAR.26,1934 WYALUSING,PA.
| 1909 | PHI | A | C | | 2 | .167 |
| | BRTR | | | | | |

LARKIN, FRANK (TERRY)
B.NEW YORK,N.Y.
1876	MUT	N	P		1	0- 1
1877	HAR	N	P-2-	56	58	29-25
			3			.228
1878	CHI	N	P	55	57	29-26
1879	CHI	N	P	55	58	30-23
1880	TRO	N	P-S-O		5	0- 5
						.118
1884	WAS	U	3		17	.257
	RIC	AA	2		39	.179
	BRTR			172	235	88-80
						.242

LARKIN, HENRY E. (TED)
B.JAN.12,1860 READING,PA.
D.JAN.31,1942 READING,PA.
1884	ATH	AA	O		87	.296
1885	ATH	AA	O		108	.338
1886	ATH	AA	O		139	.327
1887	ATH	AA	1-O		125	.374
1888	ATH	AA	1		135	.283
1889	ATH	AA	1		133	.324
1890	CLE	P	M-1		125	.327
1891	ATH	AA	1-O		133	.277
1892	WAS	N	1		116	.282
1893	WAS	N	1		81	.322
	BRTR				1182	.313

LARKIN, STEPHEN PATRICK
B.OCT.9,1910 CINCINNATI,OHIO
D.MAY 2,1969 NORRISTOWN,PA.
| 1934 | DET | A | P | | 2 | 0- 0 |
| | BRTR | | | | | |

LARMORE, ROBERT MC KAHAN (RED)
B.DEC.6,1896 ANDERSON,IND.
D.JAN.15,1964 ST.LOUIS,MO.
| 1918 | STL | N | S | | 4 | .285 |
| | BRTR | | | | | |

LA ROCHE, DAVID EUGENE (DAVE)
B.MAY 14,1948 COLORADO SPRINGS,COLO.
1970	CAL	N	P		38	4- 1
1971	CAL	N	P		56	5- 1
1972	MIN	A	P		62	5- 7
1973	CHI	N	P		45	4- 1
1974	CHI	N	P	49	50	5- 6
1975	CLE	A	P		61	5- 3
1976	CLE	A	P		61	1- 4
1977	CLE	A	P		13	2- 2
	CAL	A	P		46	6- 5
1978	CAL	A	P		59	10- 9
	BLTL			490	491	47-39

LA ROQUE, SAMUEL H. J.
B.FEB.26,1864 ST.MATHIAS,QUE.,CANADA
1888	DET	N	2		2	.444
1890	PIT	N	2-S		111	.242
1891	PIT	N	P		1	.000
	LOU	AA	2		9	.333
					123	.249

LA ROSE, HENRY JOHN (JOHN)
B.OCT.25,1951 PAWTUCKET,R.I.
| 1978 | BOS | A | P | | 1 | 0- 0 |
| | BLTL | | | | | |

LA ROSE, VICTOR RAYMOND (VIC)
B.DEC.23,1944 LOS ANGELES,CAL.
| 1968 | CHI | N | /2-S | | 4 | .000 |
| | BRTR | | | | | |

LA ROSS, HARRY RAYMOND (SPIKE)
D.MAR.22,1954 CHICAGO,ILL.
B.JAN.2,1888 EASTON,PA.
| 1914 | CIN | N | O | | 22 | .229 |

LARSEN, DONALD JAMES (DON)
B.AUG.7,1929 MICHIGAN CITY,IND.
1953	STL	A	P	38	50	7-12
						.284
1954	BAL	A	P	29	44	3-21
1955	NY	A	P	19	21	9- 2
1956	NY	A	P	38	45	11- 5
1957	NY	A	P	27	31	10- 4
1958	NY	A	P	19	28	9- 6
1959	NY	A	P	25	29	6- 7
1960	KC	A	P	22	23	1-10
1961	KC	A	P-O	8	18	1- 0
						.300
	CHI	A	P		25	7- 2
1962	SF	N	P	49	52	5- 4
1963	SF	N	P		46	7- 7
1964	SF	N	P		6	0- 1
	HOU	N	P	30	31	4- 8
1965	HOU	N	/P		1	0- 0
	BAL	A	P		27	1- 2
1967	CHI	N	/P		3	0- 0
	BRTR			412	480	81-91
						.242

LARSEN, ERLING ADELI (SWEDE)
B.NOV.15,1913 JERSEY CITY,N.J.
| 1936 | BOS | N | 2 | | 3 | .000 |
| | BRTR | | | | | |

LARSON, DANIEL JAMES (DAN)
B.JULY 4,1954 LOS ANGELES,CAL.
1976	HOU	N	P	13	14	5- 8
1977	HOU	N	P	32	33	1- 7
1978	PHI	N	/P		1	0- 0
	BRTR			46	48	6-15

LA RUSSA, ANTHONY (TONY)
B.OCT.4,1944 TAMPA,FLA.
1963	KC	A	2-S		34	.250
1968	OAK	A	/H		5	.333
1969	OAK	A	/H		8	.000
1970	OAK	A	2		52	.198
1971	OAK	A	/2-S-3		23	.000
	ATL	N	/2		9	.286
1973	CHI	N	P		1	.000
	BRTR				132	.199

LARY, ALFRED ALLEN (AL)
B.SEPT.26,1929 NORTHPORT,ALA.
1954	CHI	N	P	1	2	0- 0
1955	CHI	N	H		4	.000
1962	CHI	N	P	15	23	0- 1
	BRTR			16	29	0- 1
						.250

LARY, FRANK STRONG (FRANK)
(MULE) OR (THE YANKEE KILLER)
B.APR.10,1930 NORTHPORT,ALA.
1954	DET	A	P		3	0- 0
1955	DET	A	P		36	14-15
1956	DET	A	P		41	21-13
1957	DET	A	P		40	11-16
1958	DET	A	P		39	16-15
1959	DET	A	P		32	17-10
1960	DET	A	P	38	39	15-15
1961	DET	A	P	36	42	23- 9
1962	DET	A	P	17	22	2- 6
1963	DET	A	P		16	4- 9
1964	DET	A	P		6	0- 2
	NY	N	P		13	2- 3
	MIL	N	P		5	1- 0
1965	NY	N	P		14	1- 3
	CHI	A	P		14	1- 0
	BRTR			350	362	128-116

LARY, LYNFORD HOBART
(LYN) OR (BROADWAY)
B.JAN.28,1906 ARMONA,CAL.
D.JAN.9,1973 DOWNEY,CAL.
1929	NY	A	S-3		80	.309
1930	NY	A	S		117	.289
1931	NY	A	S		155	.280
1932	NY	A	S		91	.232
1933	NY	A	1-S-3-O		52	.220
1934	NY	A	S		1	.000
	BOS	A	1-S		129	.241
1935	WAS	A	S		39	.194
	STL	A	S		93	.288
1936	STL	A	S		155	.289
1937	CLE	A	S		156	.290
1938	CLE	A	S		141	.268
1939	CLE	A	S		3	.000
	BRO	N	S-3		29	.161
	STL	N	S-3		34	.167
1940	STL	A	2-S		27	.056
	BRTR				1302	.269

LASHER, FREDERICK WALTER (FRED)
B.AUG.19,1941 POUGHKEEPSIE,N.Y.
1963	MIN	A	P		11	0- 0
1967	DET	A	P		17	2- 1
1968	DET	A	P		34	5- 1
1969	DET	A	P		32	2- 1
1970	DET	A	P		12	1- 3
	CLE	A	P		43	1- 7
1971	CAL	A	/P		2	0- 0
	BRTR				151	11-13

LASLEY, WILLARD ALMOND
B.JULY 13,1902 MARIETTA,OHIO
| 1924 | STL | A | P | | 2 | 0- 0 |
| | BBTR | | | | | |

LA SORDA, THOMAS CHARLES (TOM)
B.SEPT.22,1927 NORRISTOWN,PA.
1954	BRO	N	P		4	0- 0
1955	BRO	N	P		4	0- 0
1956	KC	A	P	18	19	0- 4
	BLTL			26	27	0- 4
NON-PLAYING MANAGER LA[N] 1976-78

LASSETTER, DONALD O NEAL (DON)
B.MAR.27,1933 NEWNAN,GA.
| 1957 | STL | N | O | | 4 | .154 |
| | BRTR | | | | | |

LATHAM, GEORGE WARREN (JUICE)
B.SEPT.6,1852 UTICA,N.Y.
D.MAY 26,1914 UTICA,N.Y.
1875	BOS	NA	1		16	.320
	NH	NA	1-S-3		20	-
1877	LOU	N	1		59	.290
1882	ATH	AA	1		75	.300
1883	LOU	AA	1-2-S		90	.248
1884	LOU	AA	1		78	.161
	BRTR				338	-

LATHAM, WALTER ARLINGTON (ARLIE) OR
(THE FRESHEST MAN ON EARTH)
B.MAR.15,1860 W.LEBANON,N.H.
D.NOV.29,1952 GARDEN CITY,N.Y.
1880	BUF	N	C-S-O		22	.125
1883	STL	AA	3		97	.228
1884	STL	AA	3		110	.276
1885	STL	AA	3		110	.213
1886	STL	AA	3		134	.303
1887	STL	AA	3		136	.307
1888	STL	AA	3		133	.264
1889	STL	AA	3		118	.254
1890	CHI	P	3		52	.241
	CIN	N	3		63	.250
1891	CIN	N	3		133	.271
1892	CIN	N	3		150	.239
1893	CIN	N	3		125	.296
1894	CIN	N	3		130	.313
1895	CIN	N	3		110	.310
1896	STL	N	M-3		8	.229
1899	WAS	N	2		6	.143
1909	NY	N	2		4	.000
	BRTR				1621	.266

LATHERS, CHARLES TEN EYCK (CHICK)
B.OCT.22,1888 DETROIT,MICH.
D.JULY 26,1971 PETOSKEY,MICH.
1910	DET	A	3		41	.232
1911	DET	A	3		29	.222
	BLTR				70	.228

LATHROP, WILLIAM GEORGE
B.AUG.12,1891 HANOVER,WIS.
D.NOV.20,1958 JANESVILLE,WIS.
1913	CHI	A	P		6	0- 0
1914	CHI	A	P		19	1- 2
	BRTR				25	1- 2

LATIMER, CLIFFORD WESLEY (TACKS)
B.NOV.30,1877 LOVELAND,OHIO
D.APR.24,1936 LOVELAND,OHIO
1898	NY	N	C		3	.400
1899	LOU	N	C		8	.280
1900	PIT	N	C		4	.333
1901	BAL	A	C		1	.250
1902	BRO	N	C		8	.041
	TR				24	.209

LATMAN, ARNOLD BARRY (BARRY)
B.MAY 21,1936 LOS ANGELES,CAL.
1957	CHI	A	P		7	1- 2
1958	CHI	A	P		13	3- 0
1959	CHI	A	P		37	8- 5
1960	CLE	A	P		44	7-12
1961	CLE	A	P		45	13- 5
1962	CLE	A	P		45	8-13
1963	CLE	A	P		38	7-12
1964	LA	A	P		40	6-10
1965	CAL	A	P		18	1- 1
1966	HOU	N	P		31	2- 7
1967	HOU	N	P		39	3- 6
	BRTR				344	59-68

LATTEMORE, WILLIAM HERSHEL
(BILL) OR (SLOATHFUL BILL)
B.MAY 25,1884 ROXTON,TEX.
D.OCT.30,1919 COLORADO SPRINGS,COLO.
| 1908 | CLE | A | P | | 4 | 1- 2 |
| | BLTL | | | | | |

LAU, CHARLES RICHARD (CHARLIE)
B.APR.12,1933 ROMULUS,MICH.

YR	CL	LEA	POS	GP	G	REC
1956	DET	A	C		3	.222
1958	DET	A	C		30	.147
1959	DET	A	C		2	.167
1960	MIL	N	C		21	.189
1961	MIL	N	C		28	.207
	BAL	A	C		17	.170
1962	BAL	A	C		81	.294
1963	BAL	A	C		29	.188
	KC	A	C		62	.294
1964	KC	A	C		43	.271
	BAL	A	C		62	.259
1965	BAL	A	C		68	.295
1966	BAL	A	H		18	.500
1967	BAL	A	H		11	.125
	ATL	N	H		52	.200
	BLTR				527	.255

LAUDEL, ARTHUR
[PLAYED UNDER NAME OF
ARTHUR LOUDELL]

LAUDER, WILLIAM (BILLY)
B.FEB.23,1874 NEW YORK,N.Y.
D.MAY 20,1933 NORWALK,CONN.

YR	CL	LEA	POS	GP	G	REC
1898	PHI	N	3		97	.272
1899	PHI	N	3		149	.263
1901	PHI	A	3		2	.125
1902	NY	N	3-0		126	.239
1903	NY	N	3		108	.281
	BRTR				482	.262

LAUGHLIN, BENJAMIN

YR	CL	LEA	POS	GP	G	REC
1873	RES	NA	2-3		11	-

LAUTERBORN, WILLIAM BERNARD
B.JUNE 9,1879 HORNELL,N.Y.
D.APR.19,1965 ANDOVER,N.Y.

YR	CL	LEA	POS	GP	G	REC
1904	BOS	N	2		20	.275
1905	BOS	N	2-3		57	.185
	BRTR				77	.208

LAUZERIQUE, GEORGE ALBERT
B.JULY 22,1947 HAVANA,CUBA

YR	CL	LEA	POS	GP	G	REC
1967	KC	A	/P		3	0- 2
1968	OAK	A	/P		1	0- 0
1969	OAK	A	P		19	3- 4
1970	MIL	A	P		11	1- 2
	BRTR				34	4- 8

LAVAGETTO, HARRY ARTHUR (COOKIE)
B.DEC.1,1912 OAKLAND,CAL.

YR	CL	LEA	POS	GP	G	REC
1934	PIT	N	2		87	.220
1935	PIT	N	2-3		78	.290
1936	PIT	N	2-3		40	.244
1937	BRO	N	2-3		149	.282
1938	BRO	N	3		137	.273
1939	BRO	N	3		153	.300
1940	BRO	N	3		118	.257
1941	BRO	N	3		132	.277
1946	BRO	N	3		88	.236
1947	BRO	N	1-3		41	.261
	BRTR				1043	.269

NON-PLAYING MANAGER
WAS[A] 1957-60, MIN[A] 1961

LAVAN, JOHN LEONARD (DOC)
B.OCT.28,1890 GRAND RAPIDS,MICH
D.MAY 29,1952 DETROIT,MICH.

YR	CL	LEA	POS	GP	G	REC
1913	STL	A	S		46	.147
	PHI	A	S		6	.067
1914	STL	A	S		74	.263
1915	STL	A	S		157	.218
1916	STL	A	S		110	.236
1917	STL	A	S		118	.239
1918	WAS	A	S		117	.278
1919	STL	N	S		100	.242
1920	STL	N	S		142	.289
1921	STL	N	S		150	.259
1922	STL	N	S-3		89	.227
1923	STL	N	1-2-S-3		50	.198
1924	STL	N	2-S		4	.000
	BRTR				1163	.246

LAVELLE, GARY ROBERT
B.JAN.3,1949 SCRANTON,PA.

YR	CL	LEA	POS	GP	G	REC
1974	SF	N	P		10	0- 3
1975	SF	N	P		65	6- 3
1976	SF	N	P		65	10- 6
1977	SF	N	P		73	7- 7
1978	SF	N	P		67	13-10
	BBTL				280	36-29

LAVENDER, JAMES SANFORD (JIMMY)
B.MAR.25,1884 BARNESVILLE,GA.
D.JAN.12,1960 CARTERSVILLE,GA.

YR	CL	LEA	POS	GP	G	REC
1912	CHI	N	P		42	16-13
1913	CHI	N	P		40	10-14
1914	CHI	N	P		37	11-11
1915	CHI	N	P		41	10-16
1916	CHI	N	P		36	10-14
1917	PHI	N	P		28	6- 8
	BRTR				224	63-76

LAVER, JOHN CHARLES (CHUCK)
B.1865 PITTSBURGH,PA.

YR	CL	LEA	POS	GP	G	REC
1884	PIT	AA	P-1-	3	13	0- 2
			0			.109
1889	PIT	N	C		4	.231
1890	CHI	N	C		2	.375
	TR			3	19	0- 2
						.179

LAVIGNE, ARTHUR DAVID
B.JAN.26,1885 WORCESTER,MASS.
D.JULY 18,1950 WORCESTER,MASS.

YR	CL	LEA	POS	GP	G	REC
1914	BUF	F	C		45	.200
	BRTR					

LAVIN, JOHN
B.BAY CITY,MICH.

YR	CL	LEA	POS	GP	G	REC
1884	STL	N	O		16	.204

LAW, RONALD DAVID (RON)
B.MAR.14,1946 HAMILTON,ONT.,CAN.

YR	CL	LEA	POS	GP	G	REC
1969	CLE	A	P		35	3- 4
	BRTR					

LAW, RUDY KARL
B.OCT.7,1956 WACO,TEX.

YR	CL	LEA	POS	GP	G	REC
1978	LA	N	/O		11	.250
	BLTL					

LAW, VERNON SANDERS
(VERN) OR (DEACON)
B.MAR.12,1930 MERIDIAN,IDAHO

YR	CL	LEA	POS	GP	G	REC
1950	PIT	N	P		27	7- 9
1951	PIT	N	P		28	6- 9
1954	PIT	N	P-0	39	50	9-13
						.231
1955	PIT	N	P	43	44	10-10
1956	PIT	N	P		39	8-16
1957	PIT	N	P	31	34	10- 8
1958	PIT	N	P	35	36	14-12
1959	PIT	N	P	34	38	18- 9
1960	PIT	N	P		35	20- 9
1961	PIT	N	P		11	3- 4
1962	PIT	N	P		23	10- 7
1963	PIT	N	P	18	21	4- 5
1964	PIT	N	P	35	36	12-13
1965	PIT	N	P	29	34	17- 9
1966	PIT	N	P	31	34	12- 8
1967	PIT	N	P	25	26	2- 6
	BRTR			483	516	162-147
						.216

LAWING, GARLAND FREDERICK (KNOBBY)
B.AUG.29,1919 GASTONIA,N.C.

YR	CL	LEA	POS	GP	G	REC
1946	CIN	N	0		2	.000
	NY	N	0		8	.167
	BRTR				10	.133

LAWLOR, MICHAEL H.
B.MAR.11,1854 TROY,N.Y.
D.AUG.3,1918 TROY,N.Y.

YR	CL	LEA	POS	GP	G	REC
1880	TRO	N	C		4	.100
1884	WAS	U	C		2	.000
					6	.059

LAWRENCE, BROOKS ULYSSES
(BROOKS) OR (BULL)
B.JAN.30,1925 SPRINGFIELD,OHIO

YR	CL	LEA	POS	GP	G	REC
1954	STL	N	P		35	15- 6
1955	STL	N	P		46	3- 8
1956	CIN	N	P		49	19-10
1957	CIN	N	P		49	16-13
1958	CIN	N	P		46	8-13
1959	CIN	N	P		43	7-12
1960	CIN	N	P		7	1- 0
	BRTR				275	69-62

LAWRENCE, JAMES ROSS (JIM)
B.FEB.12,1939 HAMILTON,ONT.,CAN.

YR	CL	LEA	POS	GP	G	REC
1963	CLE	A	C		2	.000
	BLTR					

LAWRENCE, ROBERT ANDREW (LARRY)
B.DEC.14,1899 BROOKLYN,N.Y.

YR	CL	LEA	POS	GP	G	REC
1924	CHI	A	P		1	0- 0
	BRTR					

LAWRENCE, WILLIAM HENRY
B.MAR.11,1906 SAN MATEO,CAL.

YR	CL	LEA	POS	GP	G	REC
1932	DET	A	0		25	.217
	BRTR					

LAWRY, OTIS CARROLL (RABBIT)
B.NOV.1,1893 FAIRFIELD,ME.
D.OCT.23,1965 CHINA,MAINE

YR	CL	LEA	POS	GP	G	REC
1916	PHI	A	2		41	.203
1917	PHI	A	2		30	.164
	BLTR				71	.191

LAWSON, ALBERT W.
B.BLOOMINGTON,ILL.

YR	CL	LEA	POS	GP	G	REC
1890	BOS	N	P		1	0- 1
	PIT	N	P		2	0- 1
	BRTR				3	0- 2

LAWSON, ALFRED VOYLE (ROXIE)
B.APR.13,1906 DONNELLSON,IOWA
D.APR.9,1977 STOCKPORT,IOWA

YR	CL	LEA	POS	GP	G	REC
1930	CLE	A	P		7	1- 2
1931	CLE	A	P		17	0- 2
1933	DET	A	P		4	0- 1
1935	DET	A	P		7	3- 1
1936	DET	A	P		41	8- 6
1937	DET	A	P		37	18- 7
1938	DET	A	P		27	8- 9
1939	DET	A	P		2	1- 1
	STL	A	P	36	37	3- 7
1940	DET	A	P		30	5- 3
	BRTR			208	209	47-39

LAWSON, ROBERT BAKER
B.AUG.23,1876 BROOKNEAL,VA.
D.OCT.28,1952 CHAPEL HILL,N.C.

YR	CL	LEA	POS	GP	G	REC
1901	BOS	N	P		10	2- 2
1902	BAL	A	P		3	0- 2
	BRTR				13	2- 4

LAWSON, STEVEN GEORGE (STEVE)
B.DEC.28,1950 OAKLAND,CAL.

YR	CL	LEA	POS	GP	G	REC
1972	TEX	A	P		13	0- 0
	BRTL					

LAXTON, WILLIAM HARRY (BILL)
B.JAN.5,1948 CAMDEN,N.J.

YR	CL	LEA	POS	GP	G	REC
1970	PHI	N	/P		2	0- 0
1971	SD	N	P		18	0- 2
1974	SD	N	P		30	0- 1
1976	DET	A	P		26	0- 5
1977	SEA	A	P		43	3- 2
	CLE	A	/P		2	0- 0
	BLTL				121	3-10

LAYDEN, EUGENE FRANCIS
B.MAR.14,1894 PITTSBURGH,PA.

YR	CL	LEA	POS	GP	G	REC
1915	NY	A	0		3	.286
	BLTL					

LAYDON, PETER JOHN (PETE)
B.DEC.30,1919 DALLAS,TEX.

YR	CL	LEA	POS	GP	G	REC
1948	STL	A	0		41	.250
	BRTR					

LAYNE, HERMAN
B.FEB.13,1901 NEW HAVEN,W.VA.
D.AUG.27,1973 GALLIPOLIS,OHIO

YR	CL	LEA	POS	GP	G	REC
1927	PIT	N	0		11	.000
	BRTR					

LAYNE, IVORIA HILLIS
(HILLIS) OR (TONY)
B.FEB.23,1918 WHITWELL,TENN.

YR	CL	LEA	POS	GP	G	REC
1941	WAS	A	3		13	.280
1944	WAS	A	2-3		33	.195
1945	WAS	A	3		61	.299
	BLTR				107	.264

LAYTON, LESTER LEE (LES)
B.NOV.18,1921 NARDIN,OKLA.

YR	CL	LEA	POS	GP	G	REC
1948	NY	N	0		63	.231
	BRTR					

LAZAR, JOHN DANIEL (DANNY)
B.NOV.14,1943 EAST CHICAGO,IND.

YR	CL	LEA	POS	GP	G	REC
1968	CHI	A	/P		8	0- 1
1969	CHI	A	/P		9	0- 0
	BLTL				17	0- 1

LAZOR, JOHN PAUL (JOHNNY)
B.SEPT.9,1912 TAYLOR,WASH.

YR	CL	LEA	POS	GP	G	REC
1943	BOS	A	0		83	.226
1944	BOS	A	C-0		16	.083
1945	BOS	A	0		101	.310
1946	BOS	A	0		23	.138
	BLTR				223	.263

LAZZERI, ANTHONY MICHAEL
(TONY) OR (POOSH EM UP TONY)
B.DEC.6,1903 SAN FRANCISCO,CAL.
D.AUG.6,1946 SAN FRANCISCO,CAL.

YR	CL	LEA	POS	GP	G	REC
1926	NY	A	2		155	.275
1927	NY	A	2-S		153	.309
1928	NY	A	2		116	.332
1929	NY	A	2		147	.354
1930	NY	A	2-3		143	.303
1931	NY	A	2-3		135	.267
1932	NY	A	2		142	.300
1933	NY	A	2		139	.294
1934	NY	A	2-3		123	.267
1935	NY	A	2-S		130	.273
1936	NY	A	2		150	.287
1937	NY	A	2		126	.244
1938	CHI	N	S		54	.267
1939	BRO	N	2-3		14	.282
	NY	N	3		13	.295
	BRTR				1740	.292

YR	CL LEA POS	GP	G	REC

LEACH, FREDERICK M. (FREDDY)
B.NOV.23,1897 SPRINGFIELD,MO.
1923	PHI N O		52	.260
1924	PHI N O		8	.464
1925	PHI N O		65	.312
1926	PHI N O		129	.329
1927	PHI N O		140	.306
1928	PHI N 1-O		145	.304
1929	NY N O		113	.290
1930	NY N O		126	.327
1931	NY N O		129	.309
1932	BOS N O		84	.247
	BLTR		991	.307

LEACH, THOMAS WILLIAM (TOMMY)
B.NOV.4,1877 FRENCH CREEK,N.Y.
D.SEPT.29,1969 HAINES CITY,FLA.
1898	LOU N 3		3	.300
1899	LOU N S-3		106	.289
1900	PIT N 3		45	.215
1901	PIT N 3		93	.298
1902	PIT N 3		135	.280
1903	PIT N 3		127	.298
1904	PIT N 3		146	.257
1905	PIT N 3-O		131	.257
1906	PIT N 3-O		126	.286
1907	PIT N 3-O		149	.303
1908	PIT N 3		152	.259
1909	PIT N O		151	.261
1910	PIT N O		133	.270
1911	PIT N O		102	.238
1912	PIT N O		28	.299
	CHI N O		82	.240
1913	CHI N O		131	.287
1914	CHI N 3-O		153	.263
1915	CIN N O		107	.224
1918	PIT N S-O		30	.194
	BRTR		2130	.270

LEADLEY, ROBERT H.
B.1851 DETROIT,MICH.
NON-PLAYING MANAGER
DET[N] 1886, CLE[N] 1890-91

LEAHY, DANIEL C.
B.AUG.8,1870 NASHVILLE,TENN.
D.DEC.25,1915
| 1896 | PHI N S | | 2 | .333 |

LEAHY, THOMAS JOSEPH
B.JUNE 2,1869 NEW HAVEN,CONN.
D.JUNE 12,1951 NEW HAVEN,CONN.
1897	PIT N O		23	.242
	WAS N C-2-3-O		20	.426
1898	WAS N C		15	.182
1901	MIL N C		33	.240
	PHI A C		3	.294
1905	STL N C		29	.227
	TR		123	.256

LEAR, CHARLES BERNARD (KING)
B.JAN.23,1891 GREENCASTLE,PA.
D.OCT.31,1976 GREENCASTLE,PA.
1914	CIN N P		17	1- 2
1915	CIN N P		40	6-10
	BRTR		57	7-12

LEAR, FREDERICK FRANCIS (KING)
B.APR.7,1894 NEW YORK,N.Y.
D.OCT.13,1955 E.ORANGE,N.J.
1915	PHI A 3		2	.000
1918	CHI N 2		2	.000
1919	CHI N 2		40	.224
1920	NY N 3		31	.253
	BRTR		75	.235

LEARD, WILLIAM WALLACE (WILD BILL)
B.OCT.14,1885 ONEIDA,N.Y.
D.JAN.19,1970 SAN FRANCISCO,CAL
| 1917 | BRO N 2 | | 3 | .000 |
| | TR | | | |

LEARY, FRANCIS PATRICK
B.FEB.26,1881 WAYLAND,MASS.
D.OCT.4,1907 BOSTON,MASS.
| 1907 | CIN N P | | 2 | 1- 1 |

LEARY, JOHN J. (JACK)
B.1858 NEW HAVEN,CONN.
1880	BOS N P-O		1	0- 1
				.000
1881	DET N P-O	2	3	0- 2
				.273
1882	PIT AA P-1-	3	61	1- 0
	2-3-O			.293
	BAL AA P-O	3	4	2- 1
				.167
1883	LOU AA S		40	.183
	BAL AA 2		3	.182
1884	ALT U P-3-	3	8	0- 3
	O			.088
	CHI U P-2-	2	10	0- 0
	3-O			.184
	TL	14	130	3- 7
				.230

LEARY, JOHN LOUIS (JACK)
B.MAY 2,1898 WALTHAM,MASS.
D.AUG.18,1961 WALTHAM,MASS.
1914	STL A 1		144	.265
1915	STL A 1		75	.243
	BRTR		219	.258

LEATHERS, HAROLD LANGFORD
B.DEC.2,1898 SELMA,CAL.
D.APR.12,1977 MODESTO,CAL.
| 1920 | CHI N S | | 7 | .319 |

LEBER, EMIL BOHMIEL
B.MAY 15,1881 CLEVELAND,OHIO
D.NOV.6,1924 CLEVELAND,OHIO
| 1905 | CLE A 3 | | 2 | .000 |

LE BOURVEAU, DE WITT WILEY (BEVO)
B.AUG.24,1894 DANA,CAL.
D.DEC.9,1947 NEVADA CITY,CAL.
1919	PHI N O		17	.270
1920	PHI N O		84	.257
1921	PHI N O		93	.295
1922	PHI N O		74	.269
1929	PHI A O		12	.312
	BLTR		280	.275

LEDBETTER, RALPH OVERTON (RAZOR)
B.DEC.8,1894 RUTHERFORD COLLEGE N.C.
D.FEB.1,1969 W.PALM BEACH,FLA.
| 1915 | DET A P | | 1 | 0- 0 |
| | BRTR | | | |

LEDWITH, MICHAEL
B.BROOKLYN,N.Y.
| 1874 | ATL NA C | | 1 | - |

LEE, CLIFFORD WALKER
B.AUG.4,1896 LEXINGTON,NEB.
1919	PIT N C-O		42	.196
1920	PIT N O		37	.237
1921	PHI N 1-O		88	.308
1922	PHI N 1-3-O		122	.322
1923	PHI N O		107	.321
1924	PHI N 1-O		21	.250
	CIN N O		6	.333
1925	CLE A O		77	.322
1926	CLE A O		21	.175
	BRTR		521	.300

LEE, DONALD EDWARD (DON)
B.FEB.26,1934 GLOBE,ARIZ.
1957	DET A P		11	1- 3
1958	DET A P		1	0- 0
1960	WAS A P		44	8- 7
1961	MIN A P		37	3- 6
1962	MIN A P		9	3- 3
	LA A P		27	8- 8
1963	LA A P		40	8-11
1964	LA A P		33	5- 4
1965	CAL A P		10	0- 1
	HOU N /P		7	0- 0
1966	HOU N /P		9	2- 0
	CHI N P		16	2- 1
	BRTR		244	40-44

LEE, ERNEST DUDLEY (DUD)
[PLAYED UNDER NAME OF
ERNEST DUDLEY IN 1920-21]
B.AUG.22,1899 DENVER,COLO.
D.JAN.7,1971 DENVER,COLO.
1920	STL A S		1	1.000
1921	STL A 2-S		72	.167
1924	BOS A S		94	.253
1926	BOS A S		84	.224
	BLTR		253	.223

LEE, HAROLD BURNHAM (SHERIFF)
B.FEB.15,1905 LUDLOW,MISS.
1930	BRO N O		22	.162
1931	PHI N O		44	.221
1932	PHI N O		149	.303
1933	PHI N O		46	.287
	BOS N O		88	.221
1934	BOS N O		139	.292
1935	BOS N O		112	.303
1936	BOS N O		152	.293
	BRTR		752	.275

LEE, LEONIDAS PYRRHUS
[REAL NAME
LEONIDAS PYRRHUS FUNKHOUSER]
B.DEC.13,1860 ST.LOUIS,MO.
D.JUNE 11,1912 HENDERSONVILLE,N.C.
| 1877 | STL N S-O | | 4 | .278 |

LEE, LE RON
B.MAR.4,1948 BAKERSFIELD,CAL.
1969	STL N /O		7	.217
1970	STL N O		121	.227
1971	STL N /O		25	.179
	SD N O		79	.273
1972	SD N O		101	.300
1973	SD N O		118	.237
1974	CLE A O		79	.233
1975	CLE A /O		13	.130
	LA N O		48	.256
1976	LA N O		23	.133
	BLTR		614	.250

LEE, MARK LINDEN
B.JUNE 14,1953 INGLEWOOD,CAL.
| 1978 | SD N P | | 56 | 5- 1 |
| | BBTR | | | |

LEE, MICHAEL RANDALL (MIKE)
B.MAY 19,1941 BELL,CAL.
1960	CLE A P		7	0- 0
1963	LA A P		6	1- 1
	BLTL		13	1- 1

LEE, ROBERT DEAN (BOB)
(MOOSE) OR (HORSE)
B.NOV.26,1937 OTTUMWA,IOWA
1964	LA A P		64	6- 5
1965	CAL A P		69	9- 7
1966	CAL A P		61	5- 4
1967	LA N /P		4	0- 0
	CIN N P		27	3- 3
1968	CIN N P		44	2- 4
	BRTR		269	25-23

LEE, ROY EDWIN
B.SEPT.28,1917 ELMIRA,N.Y.
| 1945 | NY N P | | 3 | 0- 2 |
| | BLTL | | | |

LEE, THOMAS F.
B.JUNE 9,1862 MILWAUKEE,WIS.
D.MAR.4,1886 MILWAUKEE,WIS.
1884	CHI N P-S	5	6	1- 4
				.125
	BAL U P-1-	15	21	5- 8
	S-3-O			.300
		20	27	6-12
				.260

LEE, THORNTON STARR (LEFTY)
B.SEPT.13,1906 SONOMA,CAL.
1933	CLE A P		3	1- 1
1934	CLE A P		1	1- 1
1935	CLE A P		32	7-10
1936	CLE A P		43	3- 5
1937	CHI A P		30	12-10
1938	CHI A P	33	34	13-12
1939	CHI A P		33	15-11
1940	CHI A P		28	12-13
1941	CHI A P		35	22-11
1942	CHI A P		11	2- 6
1943	CHI A P		19	5- 9
1944	CHI A P		15	3- 9
1945	CHI A P		29	15-12
1946	CHI A P		7	2- 4
1947	CHI A P		21	3- 7
1948	NY N P		11	1- 3
	BLTL	374	375	117-124

LEE, WILLIAM CRUTCHER (BIG BILL)
B.OCT.21,1909 PLAQUEMINE,LA.
D.JUNE 15,1977 PLAQUEMINE,LA.
1934	CHI N P	35	40	13-14
1935	CHI N P		39	20- 6
1936	CHI N P		43	18-11
1937	CHI N P		42	14-15
1938	CHI N P		44	22- 9
1939	CHI N P		37	19-15
1940	CHI N P		37	9-17
1941	CHI N P		28	8-14
1942	CHI N P		32	13-13
1943	CHI N P		13	3- 7
	PHI N P		13	1- 5
1944	PHI N P		31	10-11
1945	PHI N P		13	3- 6
	BOS N P		16	6- 3
1946	BOS N P		25	10- 9
1947	CHI N P		14	0- 2
	BRTR	462	467	169-157

LEE, WILLIAM FRANCIS (BILL)
B.DEC.28,1946 BURBANK,CAL.
1969	BOS A P		20	1- 3
1970	BOS A P		11	2- 2
1971	BOS A P		47	9- 2
1972	BOS A P		47	7- 4
1973	BOS A P		38	17-11
1974	BOS A P		38	17-15
1975	BOS A P		41	17- 9
1976	BOS A P	24	26	5- 7
1977	BOS A P		27	9- 5
1978	BOS A P		28	10-10
	BLTL	321	323	94-68

YR	CL	LEA	POS	GP	G	REC

LEE, WILLIAM JOSEPH
B.JAN.9,1895 BAYONNE,N.J.
```
1915 STL A 3-0        18   .186
1916 STL A O           7   .182
     BRTR             25   .186
```

LEE, WYATT ARNOLD (WATTY)
B.AUG.12,1879 LYNCH S STATION,VA.
D.MAR.6,1936 WASHINGTON,D.C.
```
1901 WAS A P      36  42  16-16
1902 WAS A P-O    12 108   4- 6
                          .261
1903 WAS A P-O    23  76   8-13
                          .207
1904 PIT N P       5   8   1- 2
     TL           76 234  29-37
                          .247
```

LEEK, EUGENE HAROLD (GENE)
B.JULY 15,1936 SAN DIEGO,CAL.
```
1959 CLE A S-3    13   .222
1961 LA A S-3-0   57   .226
1962 LA A 3        7   .143
     BRTR         77   .221
```

LEES, GEORGE EDWARD
B.FEB.2,1895 BETHLEHEM,PA.
```
1921 CHI A C      20   .214
     BRTR
```

LEEVER, SAMUEL (SAM), (DEACON)
OR (THE GOSHEN SCHOOLMASTER)
B.DEC.23,1871 GOSHEN,OHIO
D.MAY 19,1953 GOSHEN,OHIO
```
1898 PIT N P          4   1- 0
1899 PIT N P         50  20-23
1900 PIT N P         28  15-13
1901 PIT N P         19  14- 5
1902 PIT N P-O       26  16- 7
                         .178
1903 PIT N P         36  25- 7
1904 PIT N P         34  18-12
1905 PIT N P         33  19- 6
1906 PIT N P         36  22- 7
1907 PIT N P         31  14- 9
1908 PIT N P         38  15- 7
1909 PIT N P         19   8- 1
1910 PIT N P         26   6- 5
     BRTR           380 193-102
                         .186
```

LEFEBVRE, JAMES KENNETH (JIM)
B.JAN.7,1943 HAWTHORNE,CAL.
```
1965 LA  N *2      157   .250
1966 LA  N *2-3    152   .274
1967 LA  N 3-2/1   136   .261
1968 LA  N 2-3/O-1  84   .241
1969 LA  N 3-2/1    95   .236
1970 LA  N 2-3/1   109   .252
1971 LA  N *2/3    119   .245
1972 LA  N 2-3      70   .201
     BBTR          922   .251
```

LE FEBVRE, WILFRID HENRY
(BILL) OR (LEFTY)
B.NOV.11,1915 NATICK,R.I.
```
1938 BOS A P       1   0- 0
1939 BOS A P    5  7   1- 1
1943 WAS A P    6  7   2- 0
1944 WAS A P-1 24 60   2- 4
                      .258
     BLTL       36 75   5- 5
                      .276
```

LE FEVRE, ALFREDO MODESTO
B.SEPT.16,1898 NEW YORK,N.Y.
```
1920 NY N 2-S     17   .148
     BRTR
```

LEFLER, WADE HAMPTON
B.JUNE 5,1896 COOLEEMEE,N.C.
```
1924 BOS N H       1   .000
     WAS A O       5   .625
     BL            6   .556
```

LE FLORE, RONALD (RON)
B.JUNE 16,1948 DETROIT,MICH.
```
1974 DET A O      59   .260
1975 DET A *O    136   .258
1976 DET A *O    135   .316
1977 DET A *O    154   .325
1978 DET A *O    155   .297
     BRTR        639   .296
```

LEGETT, LOUIS ALFRED (DOC)
B.JUNE 1,1901 NEW ORLEANS,LA.
```
1929 BOS N C      39   .160
1933 BOS A C       8   .200
1934 BOS A C      19   .289
1935 BOS A H       2   .000
     BRTR         68   .208
```

LEHANE, MICHAEL PATRICK
B.RHODE ISLAND
```
1884 WAS U S-3     3   .333
1890 COL AA 1    140   .185
1891 COL AA 1    137   .217
                 280   .204
```

LEHENY, REGIS FRANCIS
B.JAN.9,1908 PITTSBURGH,PA.
D.NOV.2,1976 PITTSBURGH,PA.
```
1932 BOS A P      2   0- 0
     BLTL
```

LEHEW, JAMES ANTHONY (JIM)
B.AUG.19,1937 BALTIMORE,MD.
```
1961 BAL A P      2   0- 0
1962 BAL A P      6   0- 0
     BRTR         8   0- 0
```

LEHMAN, KENNETH KARL (KEN)
B.JUNE 10,1928 SEATTLE,WASH.
```
1952 BRO N P          4   1- 2
1956 BRO N P         25   2- 3
1957 BRO N P          3   0- 0
1958 BAL A P     30  33   8- 3
1961 PHI N P     41  42   1- 1
     BLTL       134 138  14-10
```

LEHNER, PAUL EUGENE (PAUL)
(PEANUTS) OR (GULLIVER)
B.JULY 1,1920 DOLOMITE,ALA.
D.DEC.27,1967 BIRMINGHAM,ALA.
```
1946 STL A O      16   .222
1947 STL A O     135   .248
1948 STL A 1-O   103   .276
1949 STL A 1-O   104   .229
1950 PHI A O     114   .309
1951 PHI A O       9   .143
     CHI A O      23   .208
     STL A O      21   .134
     CLE A O      12   .231
1952 BOS A O       3   .667
     BLTL         540  .257
```

LEHR, CLARENCE EMANUEL (KING)
B.MAY 16,1886 ESCANABA,MICH.
D.JAN.31,1948 DETROIT,MICH.
```
1911 PHI N 2-S-O  22   .148
     TR
```

LEHR, NORMAN CARL MICHAEL (KING)
B.MAY 28,1901 ROCHESTER,N.Y.
D.JULY 17,1968 LIVONIA,N.Y.
```
1926 CLE A P      4   0- 0
     TR
```

LEIBER, HENRY EDWARD (HANK)
B.JAN.17,1911 PHOENIX,ARIZ.
```
1933 NY  N O        6   .200
1934 NY  N O       63   .241
1935 NY  N O      154   .331
1936 NY  N O      101   .279
1937 NY  N O       51   .293
1938 NY  N O       98   .269
1939 CHI N O      112   .310
1940 CHI N 1-O    117   .302
1941 NY  N 1-O     53   .216
1942 NY  N P-O  1  58   0- 1
                       .218
     BRTR       1 813   0- 1
                       .288
```

LEIBOLD, HARRY LORAN (NEMO)
B.FEB.17,1892 BUTLER,IND.
D.FEB.4,1977 DETROIT,MICH.
```
1913 CLE A O      84   .260
1914 CLE A O     114   .244
1915 CLE A O      56   .246
     CHI A O      37   .284
1916 CHI A O      45   .244
1917 CHI A O     125   .236
1918 CHI A O     116   .250
1919 CHI A O     122   .302
1920 CHI A O     108   .220
1921 BOS A O     123   .306
1922 BOS A O      81   .258
1923 BOS A O      11   .111
     WAS A O      96   .305
1924 WAS A O      84   .293
1925 WAS A 3-O    56   .273
     BLTR       1258   .266
```

LEIFER, ELMER EDWIN
B.MAY 23,1893 CLARINGTON,OHIO
D.SEPT.26,1948 EVERETT,WASH.
```
1921 CHI A O      9   .300
     BLTR
```

LEIFIELD, ALBERT PETER (LEFTY)
B.SEPT.5,1883 TRENTON,ILL.
D.OCT.10,1970 ALEXANDRIA,VA.
```
1905 PIT N P       8    5- 2
1906 PIT N P      37   18-13
1907 PIT N P      40   20-16
1908 PIT N P      34   15-14
1909 PIT N P      32   19- 8
1910 PIT N P      40   15-13
1911 PIT N P   42 43   16-16
1912 PIT N P       6    1- 2
     CHI N P      13    7- 2
1913 CHI N P       6    0- 1
1918 STL A P      15    2- 6
1919 STL A P      19    6- 4
1920 STL A P       4    0- 0
     BLTL     296 297 124-97
```

LEIGHTON, JOHN ATKINSON
B.OCT.4,1861 PEABODY,MASS.
D.OCT.31,1956 LYNN,MASS.
```
1890 SYR AA O      7   .266
```

LEINHAUSER, WILLIAM CHARLES
B.NOV.4,1893 PHILADELPHIA,PA.
D.APR.14,1976 ELKINS PARK,PA.
```
1912 DET A O       1   .000
```

LEIP, EDGAR ELLSWORTH
B.NOV.29,1910 TRENTON,N.J.
```
1939 WAS A 2       9   .344
1940 PIT N 2       3   .200
1941 PIT N 2-3    15   .200
1942 PIT N H       3   .000
     BRTR         30   .274
```

LEIPER, JOHN HENRY THOMAS
B.DEC.23,1867 CHESTER,PA.
D.AUG.23,1960 WEST GOSHEN,PA.
```
1891 COL AA P      6   2- 3
     TL
```

LEITH, WILLIAM (SHADY BILL)
B.MAY 31,1873 BEACON,N.Y.
D.JULY 16,1940 BEACON,N.Y.
```
1899 WAS N P       1   0- 0
```

LEITNER, GEORGE ALOYSIUS (DOC)
B.SEPT.14,1865 PIERMONT,N.Y.
D.MAY 18,1937 NEW YORK,N.Y.
```
1887 IND N P       9   2- 7
     BRTR
```

LEITNER, GEORGE MICHAEL (DUMMY)
B.JUNE 19,1871 PARKTON,MD.
D.FEB.20,1960 BALTIMORE,MD.
```
1901 PHI A P       1   0- 0
     NY  N P       2   0- 2
1902 CLE A P       1   0- 1
     CHI A P       1   0- 0
                   5   0- 3
```

LEJA, FRANK JOHN
B.FEB.7,1936 HOLYOKE,MASS.
```
1954 NY A 1       12   .200
1955 NY A 1        7   .000
1962 LA A 1        7   .000
     BLTL         26   .043
```

LE JEUNE, SHELDON ALDENBERT (LARRY)
B.JULY 22,1885 CHICAGO,ILL.
D.APR.21,1952 ELOISE,MICH.
```
1911 BRO N O       6   .157
1915 PIT N O      18   .169
                  24   .167
```

LE JOHN, DONALD EVERETT (DON)
B.MAY 13,1934 DAISYTOWN,PA.
```
1965 LA N 3       34   .256
     BRTR
```

LELIVELT, JOHN FRANK (JACK)
B.NOV.14,1885 CHICAGO,ILL.
D.JAN.20,1941 SEATTLE,WASH.
```
1909 WAS A O      91   .292
1910 WAS A O     110   .265
1911 WAS A O      72   .320
1912 NY  A O      36   .362
1913 NY  A O      18   .214
     CLE A O      16   .409
1914 CLE A O      32   .328
     BLTL        375   .301
```

LELIVELT, WILLIAM JOHN
B.OCT.21,1884 CHICAGO,ILL.
D.FEB.14,1968 CHICAGO,ILL.
```
1909 DET A P       4   0- 2
1910 DET A P       1   0- 1
     BRTR          5   0- 3
```

LEMANCZYK, DAVID LAWRENCE (DAVE)
B.AUG.17,1950 SYRACUSE,N.Y.
```
1973 DET A P       1   0- 0
1974 DET A /P     22   2- 1
1975 DET A P      26   2- 7
1976 DET A P      20   4- 6
1977 TOR A P      34  13-16
1978 TOR A P      29   4-14
     BRTR        132  25-44
```

LEMASTER, DENVER CLAYTON (DENNY)
B.FEB.25,1939 CORONA,CAL.
```
1962 MIL N P      17   3- 4
1963 MIL N P      46  11-14
1964 MIL N P      39  17-11
1965 MIL N P      32   7-13
1966 ATL N P      27  11- 8
1967 ATL N P      31   9- 9
1968 HOU N P      33  10-15
1969 HOU N P      38  13-17
1970 HOU N P      39   7-12
1971 HOU N P      42   0- 2
1972 MON N P      13   2- 0
     BRTL        357  90-105
```

YR CL LEA POS   GP   G   REC

LE MASTER, JOHNNIE LEE
B.JUNE 19,1954 PORTSMOUTH,OHIO
1975 SF N S   22   .189
1976 SF N S   33   .210
1977 SF N S/3   68   .149
1978 SF N S/2   101   .235
     BRTR   224   .205

LE MAY, RICHARD PAUL (DICK)
B.AUG.28,1938 CINCINNATI,OHIO
1961 SF N P   27   3- 6
1962 SF N P   9   0- 1
1963 SF N P   9   0- 1
     BLTL   45   3- 8

LEMBO, STEPHEN NEAL (STEVE)
B.NOV.13,1926 BROOKLYN,N.Y.
1950 BRO N C   5   .167
1952 BRO N C   2   .200
     BRTR   7   .182

LEMON, CHESTER EARL (CHET)
B.FEB.12,1955 JACKSON,MISS.
1975 CHI A /3-O   9   .257
1976 CHI A *O   132   .246
1977 CHI A *O   150   .273
1978 CHI A O-D   105   .300
     BRTR   396   .271

LEMON, JAMES ROBERT (JIM)
B.MAR.23,1928 COVINGTON,VA.
1950 CLE A O   12   .176
1953 CLE A 1-O   16   .174
1954 WAS A O   37   .234
1955 WAS A O   10   .200
1956 WAS A O   146   .271
1957 WAS A 1-O   137   .284
1958 WAS A O   142   .246
1959 WAS A O   147   .279
1960 WAS A O   148   .269
1961 MIN A O   129   .258
1962 MIN A O   12   .176
1963 MIN A O   7   .118
     PHI N O   31   .271
     CHI A 1   36   .200
     BRTR   1010   .262
NON-PLAYING MANAGER WAS(A) 1968

LEMON, ROBERT GRANVILLE (BOB)
B.SEPT.22,1920 SAN BERNARDINO,CAL.
1941 CLE A 3   5   .250
1942 CLE A 3   5   .000
1946 CLE A P-O   32   55   4- 5
                             .180
1947 CLE A P-O   37   47 11- 5
                             .321
1948 CLE A P   43   52 20-14
1949 CLE A P   37   44 22-10
1950 CLE A P   44   72 23-11
1951 CLE A P   42   56 17-14
1952 CLE A P   42   54 22-11
1953 CLE A P   41   51 21-15
1954 CLE A P   36   40 23- 7
1955 CLE A P   35   49 18-10
1956 CLE A P   39   43 20-14
1957 CLE A P   21   25   6-11
1958 CLE A P   11   15   0- 1
     BLTR   460 615 207-128
                             .222
NON-PLAYING MANAGER
KC(A) 1970-72, CHI(A) 1977-78,
NY(A) 1978

LEMONDS, DAVID LEE (DAVE)
B.JULY 5,1948 CHARLOTTE,N.C.
1969 CHI N /P   2   0- 1
1972 CHI A P   31   34   4- 7
     BLTL   33   36   4- 8

LEMONGELLO, MARK
B.JULY 21,1955 JERSEY CITY,N.J.
1976 HOU N /P   4   3- 1
1977 HOU N P   34   35   9-14
1978 HOU N P   33   9-14
     BRTR   71   72 21-29

LENHARDT, DONALD EUGENE
(DON) OR (FOOTSIE)
B.OCT.4,1922 ALTON,ILL.
1950 STL A 1-3-O   139   .273
1951 STL A 1-O   31   .262
     CHI A 1-O   64   .266
1952 BOS A O   30   .295
     DET A O   45   .188
     STL A O   18   .271
1953 STL A 3-O   97   .317
1954 BAL A 1-O   13   .152
     BOS A 3-O   44   .273
     BRTR   481   .271

LENNON, EDWARD FRANCIS
B.AUG.17,1897 PHILADELPHIA,PA.
D.SEPT.13,1947 PHILADELPHIA,PA.
1928 PHI N P   5   0- 0
     BRTR

LENNON, ROBERT ALBERT
(BOB) OR (ARCH)
B.SEPT.15,1928 BROOKLYN,N.Y.
1954 NY N H   3   .000
1956 NY N O   26   .182
1957 CHI N O   9   .143
     BLTL   38   .165

LENNON, WILLIAM F.
B.1848 BROOKLYN,N.Y.
1871 KEK NA M-C   11   -
1872 NAT NA C   11   .231
1873 MAR NA C-1   5   -
                        27   -

LENNOX, JAMES EDGAR (EGGIE)
B.NOV.3,1885 CAMDEN,N.J.
D.OCT.26,1939 CAMDEN,N.J.
1906 PHI A 3   6   .059
1909 BRO N 3   121   .262
1910 BRO N 3   100   .259
1912 CHI N 3   27   .235
1914 PIT F 3   124   .317
1915 PIT F 3   55   .321
     BRTR   433   .276

LENTINE, JAMES MATTHEW (JIM)
B.JULY 16,1954 LOS ANGELES,CAL.
1978 STL N /O   8   .182
     BRTR

LENTZ
1872 ECK NA C   4   .133

LEON, EDUARDO ANTONIO (EDDIE)
B.AUG.11,1946 TUCSON,ARIZ.
1968 CLE A /S   6   .000
1969 CLE A S   64   .239
1970 CLE A *2-S/3   152   .248
1971 CLE A *2-S   131   .261
1972 CLE A 2-S   89   .200
1973 CHI A *S/2   127   .228
1974 CHI A S/2-3   31   .109
1975 NY A /S   1   .000
     BRTR   601   .236

LEON, ISIDORO [BECERRA] (IZZY)
B.JAN.4,1911 CRUCES,LAS VILLAS,CUBA
1945 PHI N P   14   0- 4
     BRTR

LEON, MAXIMINO [MOLINA] (MAX)
B.FEB.4,1950 POZO HONDO, ACULO,
MEXICO
1973 ATL N P   12   16   2- 2
1974 ATL N P   34   4- 7
1975 ATL N P   50   2- 1
1976 ATL N P   30   2- 4
1977 ATL N P   31   33   4- 4
1978 ATL N /P   5   6   0- 0
     BRTR   162 169 14-18

LEONARD
1892 STL N O   1   .000

LEONARD, ANDREW JACKSON (ANDY)
B.JUNE 1,1846 COUNTY CAVAN,IRELAND
D.AUG.22,1903 ROXBURY,MASS.
1871 OLY NA 2-S-O   31   -
1872 BOS NA 2-S-O   46   .341
1873 BOS NA 2-S-O   58   .327
1874 BOS NA 2-S-O   71   .342
1875 BOS NA 2-S-3-O   80   .323
1876 BOS N 2-O   64   .277
1877 BOS N S-O   58   .286
1878 BOS N O   60   .259
1880 CIN N 2-S-O   33   .210
1882 STL AA O   1   .250
     BRTR   502   -

LEONARD, DENNIS PATRICK
B.MAY 18,1951 BROOKLYN,N.Y.
1974 KC N /P   5   0- 4
1975 KC A P   35 15- 7
1976 KC A P   35 17-10
1977 KC A P   38   39 20-12
1978 KC A P   40 21-17
     BRTR   150 151 73-50

LEONARD, ELMER ELLSWORTH (TINY)
B.NOV.12,1888 NAPA,CAL.
1911 PHI A P   5   2- 2
     BRTR

LEONARD, EMIL JOHN (DUTCH)
B.MAR.25,1909 AUBURN,ILL.
1933 BRO N P   10   2- 3
1934 BRO N P   44 14-11
1935 BRO N P   43   2- 9
1936 BRO N P   16   0- 0
1938 WAS A P   33 12-15
1939 WAS A P   34 20- 8
1940 WAS A P   35 14-19
1941 WAS A P   34 18-13
1942 WAS A P   6   2- 2
1943 WAS A P   31 11-13
1944 WAS A P   32 14-14
1945 WAS A P   31 17- 7
1946 WAS A P   26 10-10
1947 PHI N P   32 17-12
1948 PHI N P   34 12-17
1949 CHI N P   33   7-16
1950 CHI N P   35   5- 1
1951 CHI N P   41 10- 6
1952 CHI N P   45   2- 2
1953 CHI N P   45   2- 3
     BRTR   640 191-181

LEONARD, HUBERT BENJAMIN (DUTCH)
B.APR.16,1892 BIRMINGHAM,OHIO
D.JULY 11,1952 FRESNO,CAL.
1913 BOS A P   42 14-16
1914 BOS A P   35 19- 5
1915 BOS A P   32 15- 7
1916 BOS A P   48 18-12
1917 BOS A P   37 16-17
1918 BOS A P   16   8- 6
1919 DET A P   29 14-13
1920 DET A P   28 10-17
1921 DET A P   30 11-13
1924 DET A P   9   3- 2
1925 DET A P   18 11- 4
     BLTL   330 139-112

LEONARD, JEFFREY N (JEFF)
B.SEPT.22,1955 PHILADELPHIA,PA.
1977 LA N O   11   .300
1978 HOU N /O   8   .385
     BRTR   19   .361

LEONARD, JOSEPH HOWARD
B.NOV.15,1894 W.CHICAGO,ILL.
D.MAY 1,1920 WASHINGTON,D.C.
1914 PIT N 3   53   .198
1916 CLE A 3   2   .000
     WAS A 3   42   .274
1917 WAS A 1-3   99   .192
1919 WAS A 2-3   71   .258
1920 WAS A H   1   .000
     BLTR   269   .226

LEONHARD, DAVID PAUL (DAVE)
B.JAN.22,1942 ARLINGTON,VA.
1967 BAL A /P   3   0- 0
1968 BAL A P   28   30   7- 7
1969 BAL A P   37   38   7- 4
1970 BAL A P   23   25   0- 0
1971 BAL A P   12   13   2- 3
1972 BAL A P   14   16   0- 0
     BRTR   117 125 16-14

LEOPOLD, RUDOLPH MATAS
B.JULY 27,1905 GRAND CANE,LA.
D.SEPT.3,1965 BATON ROUGE,LA.
1928 CHI A H   2   0- 0
     BLTL

LEOVICH, JOHN JOSEPH
B.MAY 5,1918 PORTLAND,ORE.
1941 PHI A C   1   .500
     BRTR

LEPCIO, THADDEUS STANLEY (TED)
B.JULY 28,1930 UTICA,N.Y.
1952 BOS A 2-S-3   84   .263
1953 BOS A 2-S-3   66   .236
1954 BOS A 2-S-3   116   .256
1955 BOS A 3   51   .231
1956 BOS A 2-3   83   .261
1957 BOS A 2   79   .241
1958 BOS A 2   50   .199
1959 BOS A 2   3   .333
     DET A 2-S-3   76   .279
1960 PHI N 2-S-3   69   .227
1961 CHI A 3   5   .000
     MIN A 2-S-3   47   .170
     BRTR   729   .245

LEPINE, LOUIS JOSEPH (PETE)
B.SEPT.5,1876 MONTREAL,QUE.,CAN
D.DEC.3,1949 WOONSOCKET,R.I.
1902 DET A 1-O   29   .202
     BLTL

LEPPERT, DON EUGENE (DON) OR (TIGER)
B.NOV.20,1930 MEMPHIS,TENN.
1955 BAL A 2   40   .114
     BLTR

LEPPERT, DONALD GEORGE (DON)
B.OCT.19,1931 INDIANAPOLIS,IND.

YR	CL	LEA	POS	GP	G	REC
1961	PIT	N	C		22	.267
1962	PIT	N	C		45	.266
1963	WAS	A	C		73	.237
1964	WAS	A	C		50	.156
	BRTR				190	.229

LERCH, RANDY LOUIS
B.OCT.9,1954 SACRAMENTO,CAL.

YR	CL	LEA	POS	GP	G	REC
1975	PHI	N	/P		3	0- 0
1976	PHI	N	/P		1	0- 0
1977	PHI	N	P	32	33	10- 6
1978	PHI	N	P	33	36	11- 8
	BLTL			69	73	21-14

LERCHEN, BERTRAM ROE (DUTCH)
B.APR.4,1889 DETROIT,MICH.
D.JAN.7,1962 DETROIT,MICH.

YR	CL	LEA	POS	GP	G	REC
1910	BOS	A	S		6	.067
	TR					

LERCHEN, GEORGE EDWARD
B.DEC.1,1922 DETROIT,MICH.

YR	CL	LEA	POS	GP	G	REC
1952	DET	A	O		14	.156
1953	CIN	N	O		22	.294
	BBTR				36	.204
	BL 1953					

LERIAN, WALTER IRVIN (PECK)
B.FEB.10,1903 BALTIMORE,MD.
D.OCT.22,1929 BALTIMORE,MD.

YR	CL	LEA	POS	GP	G	REC
1928	PHI	N	C		96	.272
1929	PHI	N	C		105	.223
	BRTR				201	.246

LE ROY, LOUIS PAUL (CHIEF)
B.FEB.18,1879 OMRO VILLAGE,WIS.
D.OCT.10,1944 SHAWANO,WIS.

YR	CL	LEA	POS	GP	G	REC
1905	NY	A	P		3	2- 1
1906	NY	A	P		11	2- 0
1910	BOS	A	P		1	0- 0
	BRTR				15	4- 1

LERSCH, BARRY LEE
B.SEP.7,1944 DENVER,COLO.

YR	CL	LEA	POS	GP	G	REC
1969	PHI	N	P		10	0- 3
1970	PHI	N	P		42	6- 3
1971	PHI	N	P	38	44	5-14
1972	PHI	N	P	36	37	4- 6
1973	PHI	N	P		42	3- 6
1974	STL	N	/P		1	0- 0
	BLTR			169	177	18-32
	BB 1969-72					

LESHNOCK, DONALD LEE (DON)
B.NOV.25,1946 YOUNGSTOWN,OHIO

YR	CL	LEA	POS	GP	G	REC
1972	DET	A	/P		1	0- 0
	BRTL					

LESLIE, ROY REID
B.AUG.23,1894 BAILEY,TEX.
D.APR.9,1972 SHERMAN,TEX.

YR	CL	LEA	POS	GP	G	REC
1917	CHI	N	1		7	.211
1919	STL	N	1		12	.208
1922	PHI	N	1		141	.270
	BRTR				160	.266

LESLIE, SAMUEL ANDREW (SAMBO)
B.JULY 26,1905 MOSS POINT,MISS.

YR	CL	LEA	POS	GP	G	REC
1929	NY	N	O		1	.000
1930	NY	N	H		2	.500
1931	NY	N	1		53	.302
1932	NY	N	1		77	.293
1933	NY	N	1		40	.321
	BRO	N	1		96	.283
1934	BRO	N	1		146	.332
1935	BRO	N	1		142	.308
1936	NY	N	1		117	.295
1937	NY	N	1		72	.309
1938	NY	N	1		76	.293
	BLTL				822	.304

LETCHAS, CHARLIE
B.OCT.3,1915 THOMASVILLE,GA.

YR	CL	LEA	POS	GP	G	REC
1939	PHI	N	2		12	.227
1941	WAS	A	2		2	.125
1944	PHI	N	2-S-3		116	.238
1946	PHI	N	2		6	.231
	BRTR				136	.234

LETCHER, THOMAS F.
B.1868 GRAND RAPIDS,MICH.

YR	CL	LEA	POS	GP	G	REC
1891	MIL	AA	O		6	.130

LEVAN, JESSE ROY
B.JULY 15,1926 READING,PA.

YR	CL	LEA	POS	GP	G	REC
1947	PHI	N	O		2	.444
1954	WAS	A	1-3		7	.300
1955	WAS	A	H		16	.188
	BLTR				25	.286

LEVERENZ, WALTER FRED (TINY)
B.JULY 21,1887 CHICAGO,ILL.
D.MAR.19,1973 ATASCADERO,CAL.

YR	CL	LEA	POS	GP	G	REC
1913	STL	A	P		30	6-17
1914	STL	A	P	27	28	1-12
1915	STL	A	P		5	1- 2
	BLTL			62	63	8-31

LEVERETT, GORHAM VANCE (DIXIE)
B.MAR.29,1894 GEORGETOWN,TEX.
D.FEB.20,1957 BEAVERTON,ORE.

YR	CL	LEA	POS	GP	G	REC
1922	CHI	A	P		33	13-10
1923	CHI	A	P		38	10-13
1924	CHI	A	P		21	2- 3
1926	CHI	A	P		6	1- 1
1929	BOS	N	P		24	3- 7
	BRTR				122	29-34

LEVERETTE, HORACE WILBUR (HOD)
B.FEB.4,1889 SHREVEPORT,LA.
D.APR.10,1958 ST.PETERSBURG,FLA

YR	CL	LEA	POS	GP	G	REC
1920	STL	A	P		3	0- 2
	BRTR					

LEVEY, JAMES JULIUS (JIM)
B.SEPT.13,1906 PITTSBURGH,PA.
D.MAR.14,1970 DALLAS,TEX.

YR	CL	LEA	POS	GP	G	REC
1930	STL	A	S		8	.243
1931	STL	A	S		139	.209
1932	STL	A	S		152	.280
1933	STL	A	S		141	.195
	BBTR				440	.230
	BR 1930-31					

LEVIS, CHARLES H.
B.ST.LOUIS,MO.

YR	CL	LEA	POS	GP	G	REC
1884	BAL	U	M-1-3		88	.228
	WAS	U	1		1	.000
	IND	AA	1		3	.200
1885	BAL	AA	1		1	.333
					93	.226

LEVSEN, EMIL HENRY (DUTCH)
B.APR.29,1898 WYOMING,IOWA
D.MAR.12,1972 ST.LOUIS PARK,MINN.

YR	CL	LEA	POS	GP	G	REC
1923	CLE	A	P		3	0- 0
1924	CLE	A	P		4	1- 1
1925	CLE	A	P		4	1- 2
1926	CLE	A	P		33	16-13
1927	CLE	A	P		25	3- 7
1928	CLE	A	P		11	0- 3
	BRTR				80	21-26

LEVY, EDWARD CLARENCE
[REAL NAME EDWARD CLARENCE WHITNER]
B.OCT.28,1916 BIRMINGHAM,ALA.

YR	CL	LEA	POS	GP	G	REC
1940	PHI	N	H		1	.000
1942	NY	A	i		13	.122
1944	NY	A	O		40	.242
	BRTR				54	.215

LEWALLYN, DENNIS DALE
B.AUG.11,1953 PENSACOLA,FLA.

YR	CL	LEA	POS	GP	G	REC
1975	LA	N	/P		2	0- 0
1976	LA	N	/P		4	1- 1
1977	LA	N	/P		5	3- 1
1978	LA	N	/P		1	0- 0
	BRTR				12	4- 2

LEWIS
B.BROOKLYN,N.Y.

YR	CL	LEA	POS	GP	G	REC
1890	BUF	P	P		1	0- 0

LEWIS, ALLAN SYDNEY (ALLAN)
OR (THE PANAMANIAN EXPRESS)
B.DEC.12,1941 COLON,PANAMA

YR	CL	LEA	POS	GP	G	REC
1967	KC	A	R/H		34	.167
1968	OAK	A	R/O		26	.250
1969	OAK	A	R/O		12	.000
1970	OAK	A	R/O		25	.250
1972	OAK	A	R/O		24	.200
1973	OAK	A	R/O		35	.000
	BBTR				156	.207

LEWIS, EDWARD MORGAN
(TED) OR (PARSON)
B.DEC.25,1872 MACHYNLLETH,WALES
D.MAY 24,1936 DURHAM,N.H.

YR	CL	LEA	POS	GP	G	REC
1896	BOS	N	P		6	1- 4
1897	BOS	N	P		35	20-12
1898	BOS	N	P		34	25- 8
1899	BOS	N	P		28	17-11
1900	BOS	A	P		26	13-12
1901	BOS	A	P		38	17-16
					167	93-63

LEWIS, FREDERICK MILLER
B.OCT.13,1858 BUFFALO,N.Y.
D.JUNE 5,1945 UTICA,N.Y.

YR	CL	LEA	POS	GP	G	REC
1881	BOS	N	O		27	.195
1883	PHI	N	O		38	.242
	STL	AA	O		50	.295
1884	STL	AA	O		72	.322
	STL	U	O		8	.281
1885	STL	N	O		45	.292
1886	CIN	AA	O		67	.325
	BBTR				307	.296

LEWIS, GEORGE EDWARD (DUFFY)
B.APR.18,1888 SAN FRANCISCO,CAL

YR	CL	LEA	POS	GP	G	REC
1910	BOS	A	O		151	.283
1911	BOS	A	O		130	.307
1912	BOS	A	O		154	.284
1913	BOS	A	P-O	1	149	0- 0
						.298
1914	BOS	A	O		146	.278
1915	BOS	A	O		152	.291
1916	BOS	A	O		152	.268
1917	BOS	A	O		150	.302
1919	NY	A	O		141	.272
1920	NY	A	O		107	.271
1921	WAS	A	O		27	.186
	BLTL			1	459	0- 0
						.284

LEWIS, JOHN DAVID (JACK)
B.FEB.25,1956 STEUBENVILLE,OHIO

YR	CL	LEA	POS	GP	G	REC
1911	BOS	A	2		18	.271
1914	PIT	F	2		117	.234
1915	PIT	F	2		77	.268
	BRTR				212	.249

LEWIS, JOHN KELLY (BUDDY)
B.AUG.10,1916 GASTONIA,N.C.

YR	CL	LEA	POS	GP	G	REC
1935	WAS	A	3		8	.107
1936	WAS	A	3		143	.291
1937	WAS	A	3		156	.314
1938	WAS	A	3		151	.296
1939	WAS	A	3		140	.319
1940	WAS	A	3-O		148	.317
1941	WAS	A	3-O		149	.297
1945	WAS	A	O		69	.333
1946	WAS	A	O		150	.292
1947	WAS	A	O		140	.261
1949	WAS	A	O		95	.245
	BLTR				1349	.297

LEWIS, JOHNNY JOE
B.AUG.10,1939 GREENVILLE,ALA.

YR	CL	LEA	POS	GP	G	REC
1964	STL	N	O		40	.234
1965	NY	N	*O		148	.245
1966	NY	N	O		65	.193
1967	NY	N	O		13	.118
	BRTR				266	.227

LEWIS, PHILIP
B.OCT.7,1883 PITTSBURGH,PA.
D.AUG.8,1959 PORT WENTWORTH,GA.

YR	CL	LEA	POS	GP	G	REC
1905	BRO	N	S		118	.254
1906	BRO	N	S		135	.243
1907	BRO	N	S		136	.248
1908	BRO	N	S		116	.219
	BRTR				505	.242

LEWIS, WILLIAM BURTON (BERT)
B.OCT.3,1895 TONAWANDA,N.Y.
D.MAR.24,1950 TONAWANDA,N.Y.

YR	CL	LEA	POS	GP	G	REC
1924	PHI	N	P		12	0- 0
	BRTR					

LEWIS, WILLIAM HENRY (BUDDY)
B.OCT.15,1904 RIPLEY,TENN.
D.OCT.24,1977 MEMPHIS,TENN.

YR	CL	LEA	POS	GP	G	REC
1933	STL	N	C		15	.400
1935	BOS	N	C		6	.000
1936	BOS	N	C		29	.306
	BRTR				50	.327

LEY, TERRENCE RICHARD (TERRY)
B.FEB.21,1947 PORTLAND,ORE.

YR	CL	LEA	POS	GP	G	REC
1971	NY	A	/P		6	0- 0
	BLTL					

LEZCANO, SIXTO JOAQUIN
(CURRAS)
B.NOV.28,1953 ARECIBO,P.R.

YR	CL	LEA	POS	GP	G	REC
1974	MIL	A	O		15	.241
1975	MIL	A	*O		134	.247
1976	MIL	A	*O		145	.285
1977	MIL	A	*O		109	.273
1978	MIL	A	*O		132	.292
	BRTR				535	.274

LIBBY, STEPHEN AUGUSTUS
B.DEC.8,1853 SCARBOROUGH,ME.

YR	CL	LEA	POS	GP	G	REC
1879	BUF	N	1		1	.000

LIBKE, ALBERT WALTER
B.SEPT.12,1918 TACOMA,WASH.

YR	CL	LEA	POS	GP	G	REC
1945	CIN	N	P-1-	4	130	0- 0
						.283
1946	CIN	N	P-O	1	124	0- 0
						.253
	BLTR			5	254	0- 0
						.268

LIBRAN, FRANCISCO (ROSAS) (FRANKIE)
B.MAY 6,1948 MAYAGUEZ,P.R.

YR	CL	LEA	POS	GP	G	REC
1969	SD	N	/S		10	.100
	BRTR					

YR	CL LEA POS	GP	G	REC

LIDDLE, DONALD EUGENE (DON)
B.MAY 25,1925 MT.CARMEL,ILL.

YR	CL LEA POS	GP	G	REC
1953	MIL N P		31	7- 6
1954	NY N P	28	29	9- 4
1955	NY N P		33	10- 4
1956	NY N P		11	1- 2
1956	STL N P	14	15	1- 2
	BLTL	117	119	28-18

LIEBER, CHARLES EDWIN (DUTCH)
B.FEB.1,1910 ALAMEDA,CAL.
D.DEC.31,1961 SAWTELLE,CAL.

1935	PHI A P		19	1- 1
1936	PHI A P		3	0- 1
	BRTR		22	1- 2

LIEBHARDT, GLENN IGNATIUS
(GLENN) OR (SANDY)
B.JULY 31,1910 CLEVELAND,OHIO

1930	PHI A P		5	0- 1
1936	STL A P		24	0- 0
1938	STL A P		2	0- 0
	BRTR		31	0- 1

LIEBHARDT, GLENN JOHN
B.MAR.10,1883 MILTON,IND.
D.JULY 13,1956 CLEVELAND,OHIO

1906	CLE A P		2	2- 0
1907	CLE A P		38	18-14
1908	CLE A P		38	15-16
1909	CLE A P		12	1- 5
			90	36-35

LIESE, FREDERICK RICHARD
B.OCT.7,1885 WISCONSIN
D.JUNE 30,1967 LOS ANGELES,CAL.

1910	BOS N P		4	0- 0

LIFSIT, HENRY LANDERS
[PLAYED UNDER NAME OF
HENRY LANDERS BOSTICK]

LILLARD, ROBERT EUGENE (GENE)
B.NOV.12,1913 SANTA BARBARA,CAL

1936	CHI N S-3		19	.206
1939	CHI N P	20	23	3- 5
1940	STL N P		2	0- 1
	BRTR	22	44	3- 6
				.182

LILLARD, WILLIAM BEVERLY
B.JAN.10,1918 GOLETA,CAL.

1939	PHI A S		7	.316
1940	PHI A 2-S		73	.238
	BRTR		80	.244

LILLIE, JAMES J. (GRASSHOPPER)
B.1862 NEW HAVEN,CONN.
D.NOV.9,1890 KANSAS CITY,MO.

1883	BUF N P-2- 3-0	1	50	0- 0 .231
1884	BUF N P-C- O	1	110	0- 1 .219
1885	BUF N 1-S-0		112	.248
1886	KC N O		114	.175
		2	386	0- 1 .217

LILLIS, ROBERT PERRY (BOB)
B.JUNE 2,1930 ALTADENA,CAL.

1958	LA N S		20	.391
1959	LA N S		30	.229
1960	LA N 2-S-3		48	.267
1961	LA N 2-S-3		19	.111
	STL N 2-S		86	.217
1962	HOU N 2-S-3		129	.249
1963	HOU N 2-S-3		147	.198
1964	HOU N 2-S-3		109	.266
1965	HOU N *S/3-2		124	.221
1966	HOU N 2-S/3		68	.232
1967	HOU N S/2-3		37	.244
	BRTR		817	.236

LIMMER, LOUIS (LOU)
B.MAR.10,1925 NEW YORK,N.Y.

1951	PHI A 1		94	.159
1954	PHI A 1		115	.231
	BRTR		209	.202

LINCOLN, EZRA PERRY
B.NOV.17,1868 RAYNHAM,MASS.
D.MAY 7,1951 TAUNTON,MASS.

1890	CLE N P		15	3-10
	SYR AA P		3	0- 3
	TL		18	3-13

LIND, HENRY CARL (CARL) OR (HOOKS)
B.SEPT.19,1903 NEW ORLEANS,LA.
D.AUG.2,1946 NEW YORK,N.Y.

1927	CLE A 2		12	.135
1928	CLE A 2		154	.294
1929	CLE A 2		66	.240
1930	CLE A 2-S		24	.247
	BRTR		256	.272

LIND, JACKSON HUGH (JACK)
B.JUNE 8,1946 DENVER,COL.

1974	MIL A /S-2		9	.235
1975	MIL A /S-3-1		17	.050
	BBTR		26	.135

LINDAMAN, VIVAN ALEXANDER (VIVE)
B.OCT.26,1877 CHARLES CITY,IOWA
D.FEB.13,1927 CHARLES CITY,IOWA

1906	BOS N P		39	12-23
1907	BOS N P		34	11-15
1908	BOS N P		43	12-16
1909	BOS N P		15	1- 6
	BRTR		131	36-60

LINDBECK, EMERIT DESMOND (EM)
B.AUG.27,1935 KEWANEE,ILL.

1960	DET A P		2	.000
	BLTR			

LINDBLAD, PAUL AARON
B.AUG.9,1941 CHANUTE,KAN.

1965	KC A /P		4	0- 1
1966	KC A P		38	5-10
1967	KC A P	46	48	5- 8
1968	OAK A P		47	4- 3
1969	OAK A P		60	9- 6
1970	OAK A P		62	8- 2
1971	OAK A /P		8	1- 0
	WAS A P		43	6- 4
1972	TEX A P		66	5- 8
1973	OAK A P		36	1- 5
1974	OAK A P		45	4- 4
1975	OAK A P		68	9- 1
1976	OAK A P		65	6- 5
1977	TEX A P		42	4- 5
1978	TEX A P		18	1- 1
	NY A /P		7	0- 0
	BLTL	655	657	68-63

LINDE, LYMAN GILBERT
B.SEPT.20,1920 BEAVER DAM,WIS.

1947	CLE A P		1	0- 0
1948	CLE A P		3	0- 0
	BRTR		4	0- 0

LINDELL, JOHN HARLAN (JOHNNY)
B.AUG.30,1916 GREELEY,COLO.

1941	NY A P		1	.000
1942	NY A O	23	27	2- 1
1943	NY A O		122	.245
1944	NY A O		149	.300
1945	NY A O		41	.283
1946	NY A 1-O		102	.259
1947	NY A O		127	.275
1948	NY A O		88	.317
1949	NY A O		78	.242
1950	NY A O		7	.190
	STL N O		36	.186
1953	PIT N P-1	27	58	5-16 .286
	PHI N P-O	5	11	1- 1 .389
1954	PHI N H		7	.200
	BRTR	55	854	8-18 .273

LINDEMAN, ERNEST
B.JUNE 10,1883 NEW YORK,N.Y.
D.DEC.27,1951 BROOKLYN,N.Y.

1907	BOS N P		1	0- 0
	BRTR			

LINDEN, WALTER CHARLES
B.MAR.27,1924 CHICAGO,ILL.

1950	BOS N C		3	.400
	BRTR			

LINDERMANN, ROBERT J.
B.CHESTER,PA.

1901	PHI A O		3	.100

LINDQUIST, CARL EMIL
B.MAY 9,1919 MORRIS RUN,PA.

1943	BOS N P		2	0- 2
1944	BOS N P		5	0- 0

LINDSAY, CHRISTIAN HALLER
(CHRIS), (PINKY) OR (THE CRAB)
B.JULY 24,1878 BAKER S YARD,
MOON TOWNSHIP, BEAVER COUNTY,PA
D.JAN.25,1941 CLEVELAND,OHIO

1905	DET A 1		88	.267
1906	DET A 1-2		141	.224
	BRTR		229	.240

LINDSAY, WILLIAM GIBBONS
B.FEB.24,1881 MADISON,N.C.
D.JULY 14,1963 GREENSBORO,N.C.

1911	CLE A 3		19	.242

LINDSEY, JAMES KENDRICK (JIM)
B.JAN.24,1898 GREENSBURG,LA.
D.OCT.25,1963 JACKSON,LA.

1922	CLE A P		29	4- 5
1924	CLE A P		3	0- 0
1929	STL N P		2	1- 1
1930	STL N P		39	7- 5
1931	STL N P		35	6- 4
1932	STL N P		33	3- 3
1933	STL N P		1	0- 0
1934	CIN N P		4	0- 0
	STL N P		11	0- 1
1937	BRO N P		20	0- 1
	BRTR		177	21-20

LINDSTROM, AXEL OLAF
B.AUG.26,1895 GUSTAVSBERG,SWEDEN
D.JUNE 24,1940 ASHEVILLE,N.C.

1916	PHI A P		1	0- 0
	BRTR			

LINDSTROM, CHARLES WILLIAM (CHUCK)
B.SEPT.7,1936 CHICAGO,ILL.

1958	CHI A C		1	1.000
	BRTR			

LINDSTROM, FREDERICK CHARLES
(FREDDY)
B.NOV.21,1905 CHICAGO,ILL.

1924	NY N 2-3		52	.253
1925	NY N 2-S-3		104	.287
1926	NY N 3		140	.302
1927	NY N 3-O		138	.306
1928	NY N 3		153	.358
1929	NY N 3		150	.319
1930	NY N 3		148	.379
1931	NY N O		78	.300
1932	NY N 3-O		144	.271
1933	PIT N O		138	.310
1934	PIT N O		90	.290
1935	CHI N 3-O		90	.275
1936	BRO N O		26	.264
	BRTR		1438	.311

LINES, RICHARD GEORGE (DICK)
B.AUG.17,1938 MONTREAL,QUE.,CAN.

1966	WAS A P		53	5- 2
1967	WAS A P		54	2- 5
	BRTL		107	7- 7

LINHART, CARL JAMES
B.DEC.14,1929 ZBOROV,CZECH.

1952	DET A H		3	.000
	BLTR			

LINKE, EDWARD KARL (BABE)
B.NOV.9,1911 CHICAGO,ILL.

1933	WAS A P		3	1- 0
1934	WAS A P	7	8	2- 2
1935	WAS A P		40	11- 7
1936	WAS A P		13	1- 5
1937	WAS A P	36	37	0- 1
1938	STL A P		21	1- 7
	BRTR	120	122	22-22

LINKE, FREDERICK L. (LADOIE)

1910	CLE A P		22	5- 6
	STL A P		3	0- 0
			25	5- 6

LINT, ROYCE JAMES
B.JAN.1,1921 BIRMINGHAM,ALA.

1954	STL N P	30	31	2- 3
	BLTL			

LINTON, CLAUDE C. (BOB)
B.APR.18,1903 EMERSON,ARK.

1929	PIT N C		17	.111
	BLTR			

LINTZ, LARRY
B.OCT.10,1949 MARTINEZ,CAL.

1973	MON N 2-S		52	.250
1974	MON N 2-S/3		113	.238
1975	MON N 2/S		46	.197
	STL N /2-S		27	.278
1976	OAK A /2-O-R		68	.000
1977	OAK A 2/S-3		41	.133
1978	CLE A R		3	.000
	BBTR		350	.227

LINZ, PHILIP FRANCIS (PHIL)
B.JUNE 4,1939 BALTIMORE,MD.

1962	NY A 2-S-3-O		71	.287
1963	NY A 2-S-3-O		72	.269
1964	NY A 2-S-3-O		112	.250
1965	NY A S/3-O-2		99	.207
1966	PHI N 3/S-2		40	.200
1967	PHI N /S-3		23	.222
	NY N 2/S-3-O		24	.207
1968	NY N 2		78	.209
	BRTR		519	.235

YR	CL	LEA	POS	GP	G	REC

LINZY, FRANK ALFRED
B.SEP.15,1940 FT.GIBSON,OKLA.

YR	CL	LEA	POS	G	REC
1963	SF	N	P	8	0- 0
1965	SF	N	P	57	9- 3
1966	SF	N	P	51	7-11
1967	SF	N	P	57	7- 7
1968	SF	N	P	57	9- 8
1969	SF	N	P	58	14- 9
1970	SF	N	P	20	2- 1
	STL	N	P	47	3- 5
1971	STL	N	P	50	4- 3
1972	MIL	A	P	47	2- 2
1973	MIL	A	P	42	2- 6
1974	PHI	N	P	22	3- 2
	BRTR			516	62-57

LI PETRI, MICHAEL ANGELO (ANGELO)
B.JULY 6,1930 BROOKLYN,N.Y.

1956	PHI	N	P	6	0- 0
1958	PHI	N	P	4	0- 0
	BRTR			10	0- 0

LIPON, JOHN JOSEPH
(JOHNNY) OR (SKIDS)
B.NOV.10,1922 MARTIN S FERRY,O.

1942	DET	A	S	34	.191
1946	DET	A	S-3	14	.300
1948	DET	A	2-S-3	121	.290
1949	DET	A	S	127	.251
1950	DET	A	S	147	.293
1951	DET	A	S	129	.265
1952	DET	A	S	39	.221
	BOS	A	S-3	79	.205
1953	BOS	A	S	60	.214
	STL	A	2-3	7	.222
1954	CIN	N	H	1	.000
	BRTR			758	.259

NON-PLAYING MANAGER CLE(A) 1971

LIPP, THOMAS C.
B.1871 BALTIMORE,MD.

1897	PHI	N	P	1	0- 1

LIPSCOMB, GERARD (NIG)
B.FEB.24,1911 RUTHERFORDTON,N.C
D.FEB.27,1978 HUNTERSVILLE,N.C.

YR	CL	LEA	POS	GP	G	REC
1937	STL	A	P-2	3	36	0- 0
						.323

LIPSKI, ROBERT PETER (BOB)
B.JULY 7,1938 SCRANTON,PA.

1963	CLE	A	C	2	.000
	BLTR				

LIS, JOSEPH ANTHONY (JOE)
B.AUG.15,1946 SOMERVILLE,N.J.

1970	PHI	N	/O	13	.189
1971	PHI	N	O	59	.211
1972	PHI	N	1-O	62	.243
1973	MIN	A	1	103	.245
1974	MIN	A	1	24	.195
	CLE	A	1/3-O	57	.202
1975	CLE	A	/1	9	.308
1976	CLE	A	1	20	.314
1977	SEA	A	/1-C	9	.231
	BRTR			356	.233

LISENBEE, HORACE MILTON (HOD)
B.SEPT.23,1898 CLARKSVILLE,TENN

1927	WAS	A	P	39	18- 9
1928	WAS	A	P	16	2- 6
1929	BOS	A	P	5	0- 0
1930	BOS	A	P	37	10-17
1931	BOS	A	P	41	5-12
1932	BOS	A	P	19	0- 4
1936	PHI	A	P	19	1- 7
1945	CIN	N	P	31	1- 3
	BRTR			207	37-58

LISKA, ADOLPH JAMES (AD)
B.JULY 10,1906 DWIGHT,NEB.

YR	CL	LEA	POS	GP	G	REC
1929	WAS	A	P		24	3- 9
1930	WAS	A	P		32	9- 7
1931	WAS	A	P		2	0- 1
1932	PHI	N	P		8	2- 0
1933	PHI	N	P-O	45	47	3- 1
						.071
	BRTR			111	113	17-18
						.108

LISTER, MORRIS ELMER (PETE)
B.JULY 21,1881 SAVANNA,ILL.
D.MAY 12,1948 ST.PETERSBURG,FLA

1907	CLE	A	1	22	.277
	BRTR				

LITTELL, MARK ALAN
B.JAN.17,1953 CAPE GIRARDEAU,MO.

1973	KC	A	/P	8	1- 3
1975	KC	A	/P	7	1- 2
1976	KC	A	P	60	8- 4
1977	KC	A	P	48	8- 4
1978	STL	N	P	72	4- 8
	BLTR			195	22-21

LITTLE, GEORGE HARRY
B.ST.LOUIS,MO.
D.JAN.25,1892

1877	STL	N	O	1	.200
	LOU	N	2	1	.000
	STL	N	O	2	.143
	TR			4	.133

LITTLE, WILLIAM ARTHUR (JACK)
B.MAR.12,1891 MART,TEX.
D.JULY 27,1961 DALLAS,TEX.

1912	NY	A	O	3	.250
	BRTR				

LITTLEFIELD, RICHARD BERNARD (DICK)
B.MAR.18,1926 DETROIT,MICH.

YR	CL	LEA	POS	GP	G	REC
1950	BOS	A	P		15	2- 2
1951	CHI	A	P		4	1- 1
1952	DET	A	P		28	0- 3
	STL	A	P		7	2- 3
1953	STL	A	P	36	38	7-12
1954	BAL	A	P		3	0- 0
	PIT	N	P		23	10-11
1955	PIT	N	P		35	5-12
1956	PIT	N	P		6	0- 0
	STL	N	P		3	0- 2
	NY	N	P		31	4- 4
1957	CHI	N	P		48	2- 3
1958	MIL	N	P		4	0- 1
	BLTL			243	245	33-54

LITTLEJOHN, CHARLES CARLISLE
(CARLISLE)
B.OCT.6,1901 IRENE,TEX.

1927	STL	N	P	14	15	3- 1
1928	STL	N	P		12	2- 1
	BRTR			26	27	5- 2

LITTLEJOHN, DENNIS GERALD
B.OCT.4,1954 SANTA MONICA,CAL.

1978	SF	N	/C	2	.000
	BRTR				

LITTRELL, JACK NAPIER
B.JAN.22,1929 LOUISVILLE,KY.

1952	PHI	A	S-3	4	.000
1954	PHI	A	S	9	.300
1955	KC	A	1-2-S	37	.200
1957	KC	A	2-S-3	61	.190
	BRTR			111	.204

LITWHILER, DANIEL WEBSTER (DANNY)
B.AUG.31,1916 RINGTOWN,PA.

1940	PHI	N	O	36	.345
1941	PHI	N	O	151	.305
1942	PHI	N	O	151	.271
1943	PHI	N	O	36	.258
	STL	N	O	80	.279
1944	STL	N	O	140	.264
1946	STL	N	H	6	.292
	BOS	N	3-O	79	.292
1947	BOS	N	O	91	.261
1948	BOS	N	O	13	.273
	CIN	N	3-O	106	.275
1949	CIN	N	3-O	102	.291
1950	CIN	N	O	54	.259
1951	CIN	N	O	12	.276
	BRTR			1057	.281

LIVELY, EVERETT ADRIAN
(BUDDY) OR (RED)
B.FEB.14,1925 BIRMINGHAM,ALA.

1947	CIN	N	P	38	4- 7
1948	CIN	N	P	10	0- 0
1949	CIN	N	P	31	4- 6
	BRTR			79	8-13

LIVELY, HENRY EVERETT (JACK)
B.MAY 29,1885 JOPPA,ALA.
D.DEC.5,1967 ARAB,ALA.

YR	CL	LEA	POS	GP	G	REC
1911	DET	A	P	18	20	7- 5
	BR					

LIVENGOOD, WESLEY AMOS
B.JULY 18,1910 SALISBURY,N.C.

1939	CIN	N	P	5	0- 0
	BRTR				

LIVINGSTON, PATRICK JOSEPH (PADDY)
B.JAN.14,1880 CLEVELAND,OHIO
D.SEPT.19,1977 CLEVELAND,OHIO

1901	CLE	A	1	1	.000
1906	CIN	N	C	47	.158
1909	PHI	A	C	64	.234
1910	PHI	A	C	37	.208
1911	PHI	A	C	27	.239
1912	CLE	A	C	19	.234
1917	STL	N	C	7	.200
	BRTR			202	.208

LIVINGSTON, THOMPSON ORVILLE
(MICKEY)
B.NOV.15,1914 NEWBERRY,S.C.

1938	WAS	A	C	2	.750
1941	PHI	N	C-1	95	.203
1942	PHI	N	C-1	84	.205
1943	PHI	N	C-1	84	.249
	CHI	N	C-1	36	.261
1945	CHI	N	C-1	71	.254
1946	CHI	N	C	66	.256
1947	CHI	N	C	19	.212
	NY	N	C	5	.167
1948	NY	N	C	45	.212
1949	NY	N	C	19	.298
	BOS	N	C	28	.234
1951	BRO	N	C	2	.400
	BRTR			561	.238

LIVINGSTONE, ALBANY
B.NEW YORK

1901	NY	N	P	2	0- 2

LIZOTTE, ABEL
B.APR.13,1870 LEWISTON,ME.
D.DEC.4,1926 WILKES-BARRE,PA.

1896	PIT	N	1	7	.104

LLENAS, WINSTON ENRIQUILLO
(DAVILA)
B.SEP.23,1943 SANTIAGO,D.R.

1968	CAL	A	/3	16	.128
1969	CAL	A	/3	34	.170
1972	CAL	A	3/2-O	44	.266
1973	CAL	A	3-D/O	78	.269
1974	CAL	A	O-2-D/3	72	.261
1975	CAL	A	2-O/1-3	56	.186
	BRTR			300	.230

LLEWELLYN, CLEMENT MANLEY (LEW)
B.AUG.1,1895 DOBSON,N.C.
D.NOV.26,1969 CONCORD,N.C.

1922	NY	A	P	1	1- 0
	BLTR				

LOAN, WILLIAM JOSEPH (MIKE)
B.SEPT.27,1894 PHILADELPHIA,PA.
D.NOV.21,1966 SPRINGFIELD,PA.

1912	PHI	N	C	1	.500
	TR				

LOANE, ROBERT KENNETH
B.AUG.6,1914 BERKELEY,CAL.

1939	WAS	A	O	3	.000
1940	PHI	N	O	13	.227
	BRTR			16	.161

LOBERT, FRANK JOHN
B.NOV.26,1883 WILLIAMSPORT,PA.
D.MAY 29,1932 PITTSBURGH,PA.

1914	BAL	F	3	10	.167
	TR				

LOBERT, JOHN BERNARD
(HANS) OR (HONUS)
B.OCT.18,1881 WILMINGTON,DEL.
D.SEPT.14,1968 PHILADELPHIA,PA.

1903	PIT	N	3	3	.077
1905	CHI	N	3	14	.196
1906	CIN	N	S-3	76	.310
1907	CIN	N	S	147	.246
1908	PHI	N	S-3-O	155	.293
1909	CIN	N	3	122	.212
1910	CIN	N	3	90	.309
1911	PHI	N	3	147	.285
1912	PHI	N	3	65	.327
1913	PHI	N	3	150	.300
1914	PHI	N	3	135	.275
1915	NY	N	3	106	.251
1916	NY	N	3	48	.224
1917	NY	N	3	50	.192
	BRTR			1310	.275

NON-PLAYING MANAGER PHI(N) 1938, 42

LOCK, DON WILSON
B.JULY 27,1936 WICHITA,KAN.

1962	WAS	A	O	71	.253
1963	WAS	A	O	149	.252
1964	WAS	A	O	152	.248
1965	WAS	A	*O	143	.215
1966	WAS	A	*O	138	.233
1967	PHI	N	O	112	.252
1968	PHI	N	O	99	.210
1969	PHI	N	/O	4	.000
	BOS	A	O/1	53	.224
	BRTR			921	.238

LOCKE, CHARLES EDWARD (CHUCK)
B.MAY 5,1932 MALDEN,MO.

1955	BAL	A	P	2	0- 0
	BRTR				

```
YR  CL LEA POS      GP   G    REC

LOCKE, LAWRENCE DONALD (BOBBY)
B.MAR.3,1934 ROWES RUN,PA.
1959 CLE A P             24   3- 2
1960 CLE A P         32  35   3- 5
1961 CLE A P             37   4- 4
1962 STL N P             1    0- 0
     PHI N P             5    1- 0
1963 PHI N P             9    0- 0
1964 PHI N P             8    0- 0
1965 CIN N P             11   0- 1
1967 CAL A /P            9    3- 0
1968 CAL A P             29   2- 3
     BRTR       165  168  16-15

LOCKE, MARSHALL
B.INDIANAPOLIS,IND.
1874 BAL NA S            1    .000
1884 IND AA O            7    .241
                         8    .233

LOCKE, RONALD THOMAS (RON)
B.APR.4,1942 WAKEFIELD,R.I.
1964 NY  N P             25   1- 2
     BRTL

LOCKER, ROBERT AWTRY (BOB)
B.MAR.15,1938 GEORGE,IOWA
1965 CHI A P             51   5- 2
1966 CHI A P             56   9- 8
1967 CHI A P             77   7- 5
1968 CHI A P             70   5- 4
1969 CHI A P             17   2- 3
     SEA A P             51   3- 3
1970 MIL A P             28   0- 1
     OAK A P             38   3- 3
1971 OAK A P             47   7- 2
1972 OAK A P             56   6- 1
1973 CHI N P             63  10- 6
1975 CHI N P             22   0- 1
     BBTR            576  57-39
     BR 1965-67

LOCKHEAD, HARRY P.
B.CALIFORNIA
1899 CLE N S            146   .223
1901 DET A S            1     .500
     PHI A S            9     .088
     TR               156     .217

LOCKLEAR, GENE
B.JULY 19,1949 LUMBERTON,N.C.
1973 CIN N /O           29    .192
     SD   N O           67    .240
1974 SD  N O            39    .270
1975 SD  N O           100    .321
1976 SD  N O            43    .224
     NY  A /O           13    .219
1977 NY  A /O           1     .600
     BLTR              292    .274

LOCKLIN, STUART CARLTON (STU)
B.JULY 22,1928 APPLETON,WIS.
1955 CLE A O            16    .167
1956 CLE A O            9     .167
     BLTL               25    .167

LOCKMAN, CARROLL WALTER (WHITEY)
B.JULY 25,1926 LOWELL,N.C.
1945 NY  N O            32    .341
1947 NY  N H            2     .500
1948 NY  N O           146    .286
1949 NY  N O           151    .301
1950 NY  N O           129    .295
1951 NY  N 1-O         153    .282
1952 NY  N 1           154    .290
1953 NY  N 1-O         150    .295
1954 NY  N 1-O         148    .251
1955 NY  N 1-O         147    .273
1956 NY  N 1-O          48    .272
     STL N 1-O          70    .249
1957 NY  N 1-O         133    .248
1958 SF  N 1-2-O        92    .238
1959 BAL A 1-2-0        38    .217
     CIN N 1-2-3-0      52    .262
1960 CIN N 1            21    .200
     BLTR             1666    .279
NON-PLAYING MANAGER CIN(N) 1972-74

LOCKWOOD, CLAUDE EDWARD (SKIP)
B.AUG.17,1946 ROSLINDALE,MASS.
1965 KC  A /3           42    .121
1969 SEA A /P           6     0- 1
1970 MIL A P            27    5-12
1971 MIL A P        33  36   10-15
1972 MIL A P        29  31    8-15
1973 MIL A P            37    5-12
1974 CAL A P            37    2- 5
1975 NY  N P            24    1- 3
1976 NY  N P            56   10- 7
1977 NY  N P            63    4- 8
1978 NY  N P            57    7-13
     BRTR       369  416  52-91
                              .151

LOCKWOOD, MILO HATHAWAY
B.APR.7,1858 SOLON,OHIO
D.OCT.9,1897 ECONOMY,PA.
1884 WAS U  P-3-    10  20   1- 9
            O                 .209
```

```
YR  CL LEA POS       GP   G    REC

LODIGIANI, DARIO ANTONIO
B.JUNE 6,1916 SAN FRANCISCO,CAL.
1938 PHI A 2-3          93    .280
1939 PHI A 2-3         121    .260
1940 PHI A H            1     .000
1941 CHI A 3           87     .239
1942 CHI A 2-3         59     .280
1946 CHI A 3           44     .245
     BRTR             405     .260

LOEPP, GEORGE HERBERT
B.SEPT.11,1901 DETROIT,MICH.
D.SEPT.4,1967 LOS ANGELES,CAL.
1928 BOS A O            15    .176
1930 WAS A O            50    .276
     BRTR               65    .249

LOES, WILLIAM (BILLY)
B.DEC.13,1929 LONG ISLAND CITY,N.Y.
1950 BRO N P            10    0- 0
1952 BRO N P        38  39   13- 8
1953 BRO N P            32   14- 8
1954 BRO N P            28   13- 5
1955 BRO N P            22   10- 4
1956 BRO N P            1     0- 1
     BAL A P            21    2- 7
1957 BAL A P            31   12- 7
1958 BAL A P            32    9- 9
1959 BAL A P            37    4- 7
1960 SF  N P            37    3- 2
1961 SF  N P            26    6- 5
     BRTR       315  316  80-63

LOFTUS, FRANCIS PATRICK
B.MAR.10,1898 SCRANTON,PA.
1926 WAS A P            1     0- 0
     BRTR

LOFTUS, RICHARD JOSEPH
B.MAR.7,1901 CONCORD,MASS.
JAN.21,1972 CONCORD,MASS.
1924 BRO N 1-O          46    .272
1925 BRO N O            51    .237
     BLTR               97    .250

LOFTUS, THOMAS JOSEPH
B.NOV.15,1856 ST.LOUIS,MO.
D.APR.16,1910 DUBUQUE,IOWA
1877 STL N O            3     .182
1883 STL AA O           9     .167
NON-PLAYING MANAGER CLE(AA)1888
  CLE(N) 1889, CIN(N) 1890-91,
  CHI(N) 1900-01, WAS(A) 1902-03

LOGAN, JOHN (JOHNNY) OR (YATCHA)
B.MAR.23,1927 ENDICOTT,N.Y.
1951 BOS N S            62    .219
1952 BOS N S           117    .283
1953 MIL N S           150    .273
1954 MIL N S           154    .275
1955 MIL N S           154    .297
1956 MIL N S           148    .281
1957 MIL N S           129    .273
1958 MIL N S           145    .226
1959 MIL N S           138    .291
1960 MIL N S           136    .245
1961 MIL N S            18    .105
     PIT N S-3          27    .231
1962 PIT N S            3     .300
1963 PIT N S-3          81    .232
     BRTR             1503    .268

LOGAN, ROBERT DEAN (LEFTY)
B.FEB.10,1910 THOMPSON,NEB.
D.MAY 20,1978 INDIANAPOLIS,IND.
1935 BRO N P            2     0- 1
1937 DET A P            1     0- 0
     CHI N P            4     0- 0
1938 CHI N P            14    0- 2
1941 CIN N P            2     0- 1
1945 BOS N P            34    7-11
     BRTL               57    7-15

LOHMAN, GEORGE F. (PETE)
B.OCT.21,1864 LAKE ELMO,MINN.
D.NOV.21,1928 LOS ANGELES,CAL.
1891 WAS AA C           32    .200

LOHR, HOWARD SYLVESTER
B.JUNE 3,1892 PHILADELPHIA,PA.
D.JAN.9,1977 PHILADELPHIA,PA.
1914 CIN N O            8     .213
1916 CLE A O            3     .143
     BRTR               21    .204

LOHRKE, JACK WAYNE (LUCKY)
B.FEB.25,1924 LOS ANGELES,CAL.
1947 NY  N 3           112    .240
1948 NY  N 2-3         97     .250
1949 NY  N 2-S-3       55     .267
1950 NY  N 3           30     .186
1951 NY  N S-3         23     .200
1952 PHI N S-3         25     .207
1953 PHI N 2-S-3       12     .154
     BRTR             354     .242
```

```
YR  CL LEA POS       GP   G    REC

LOHRMAN, WILLIAM LE ROY (BILL)
B.MAY 22,1913 BROOKLYN,N.Y.
1934 PHI N P            4     0- 1
1937 NY  N P            2     1- 0
1938 NY  N P            31    9- 6
1939 NY  N P            38   12-13
1940 NY  N P            31   10-15
1941 NY  N P            33    9-10
1942 STL N P            5     1- 1
     NY  N P            26   13- 4
1943 NY  N P        17  21    5- 6
     BRO N P            6     0- 2
1944 BRO N P            3     0- 0
     CIN N P            2     0- 1
     BRTR       198  202  60-59

LOIS, ALBERTO
[REAL NAME ALBERTO LOUIS]
B.MAY 6,1956 HATO MAYOR,D.R.
1978 PIT N /O           3     .250
     BRTR

LOLICH, MICHAEL STEPHEN (MICKEY)
B.SEP.12,1940 PORTLAND,ORE.
1963 DET A P            33    5- 9
1964 DET A P            44   18- 9
1965 DET A P            43   15- 9
1966 DET A P            40   14-14
1967 DET A P        31  32   14-13
1968 DET A P        39  41   17- 9
1969 DET A P        37  38   19-11
1970 DET A P        40  42   14-19
1971 DET A P            45   25-14
1972 DET A P            41   22-14
1973 DET A P            42   16-15
1974 DET A P            41   16-21
1975 DET A P            32   12-18
1976 NY  N P            31    8-13
1978 SD  N P            20    2- 1
     BBTL       559  565 217-189

LOLICH, RONALD JOHN (RON)
B.SEP.19,1946 PORTLAND,ORE.
1971 CHI A /O           2     .125
1972 CLE A O            24    .188
1973 CLE A O-D          61    .229
     BRTR               87    .211

LOLLAR, JOHN SHERMAN (SHERM)
B.AUG.23,1924 DURHAM,ARK.
D.SEPT.24,1977 SPRINGFIELD,MO.
1946 CLE A C            28    .242
1947 NY  A C            11    .219
1948 NY  A C            22    .211
1949 STL A C           109    .261
1950 STL A C           126    .280
1951 STL A C-3         98     .252
1952 CHI A C           132    .240
1953 CHI A C-1         113    .287
1954 CHI A C           107    .244
1955 CHI A C           138    .261
1956 CHI A C           136    .293
1957 CHI A C           101    .256
1958 CHI A C           127    .273
1959 CHI A C-1         140    .265
1960 CHI A C           129    .252
1961 CHI A C           116    .282
1962 CHI A C            84    .268
1963 CHI A C-1         35     .233
     BRTR             1752    .264

LOMBARDI, ERNESTO NATALI
(ERNIE), (SCHNOZZ) OR (BOCCI)
B.APR.6,1908 OAKLAND,CAL.
D.SEPT.26,1977 SANTA CRUZ,CAL.
1931 BRO N C            73    .297
1932 CIN N C           118    .303
1933 CIN N C           107    .283
1934 CIN N C           132    .305
1935 CIN N C           120    .343
1936 CIN N C           121    .333
1937 CIN N C           120    .334
1938 CIN N C           129    .342
1939 CIN N C           130    .287
1940 CIN N C           109    .319
1941 CIN N C           117    .264
1942 BOS N C           105    .330
1943 NY  N C           104    .305
1944 NY  N C           117    .255
1945 NY  N C           115    .307
1946 NY  N C            88    .290
1947 NY  N C            48    .282
     BRTR             1853    .306

LOMBARDI, VICTOR ALVIN (VIC)
B.SEPT.20,1922 REEDLEY,CAL.
1945 BRO N P        38  45   10-11
1946 BRO N P        41  43   13-10
1947 BRO N P        33  36   12-11
1948 PIT N P        38  39   10- 9
1949 PIT N P        34  43    5- 5
1950 PIT N P        39  42    0- 5
     BLTL       223  248  50-51

LOMBARDO, LOUIS
B.NOV.18,1929 CARLSTADT,N.J.
1948 NY  N P            2     0- 0
     BLTL
```

```
YR  CL LEA POS    GP   G   REC        YR  CL LEA POS    GP   G   REC        YR  CL LEA POS    GP   G   REC

LONBORG, JAMES REYNOLD (JIM)          LONG, THOMAS AUGUSTUS                 LOPEZ, ALFONSO RAMON (AL)
B.APR.16,1942 SANTA MARIA,CAL.        B.JUNE 1,1890 MITCHUM,ALA.            B.AUG.20,1908 TAMPA,FLA.
1965 BOS A P      32   9-17           D.JUNE 15,1972 MOBILE,ALA.            1928 BRO N C       3  .000
1966 BOS A P   45 46  10-10           1911 WAS A O      14  .208            1930 BRO N C     128  .309
1967 BOS A P      39  22- 9           1912 WAS A O       1  .000            1931 BRO N C     111  .269
1968 BOS A P      23   6-10           1915 STL N O     140  .294            1932 BRO N C     126  .275
1969 BOS A P      29   7-11           1916 STL N O     119  .293            1933 BRO N C-2   126  .301
1970 BOS A /P      9   4- 1           1917 STL N O     144  .232            1934 BRO N C     140  .275
1971 BOS A P      27  10- 7              BRTR          418  .269            1935 BRO N C     128  .251
1972 MIL A P      33  14-12                                                 1936 BOS N C     128  .242
1973 PHI N P      38  13-16           LONG, THOMAS FRANCIS (LITTLE HAWK)    1937 BOS N C     105  .204
1974 PHI N P      39  17-13           B.APR.22,1898 MEMPHIS,TENN.           1938 BOS N C      71  .267
1975 PHI N P      27   8- 6           D.SEPT.16,1973 LOUISVILLE,KY.         1939 BOS N C     131  .252
1976 PHI N P      33  18-10           1924 BRO N P       1   0- 0           1940 BOS N C      36  .294
1977 PHI N P      25  11- 4              BLTL                               1940 PIT N C      59  .259
1978 PHI N P      22   8-1C                                                 1941 PIT N C     114  .205
   BRTR      421 422 157-136          LONNETT, JOSEPH PAUL (JOE)            1942 PIT N C     103  .256
                                      B.FEB.7,1927 BEAVER FALLS,PA.         1943 PIT N C-3   118  .263
LONERGAN, WALTER E.                   1956 PHI N C      16  .182            1944 PIT N C-3   115  .230
B.SEPT.22,1885 BOSTON,MASS.           1957 PHI N C      67  .169            1945 PIT N C-3    91  .218
D.JAN.23,1958 LEXINGTON,MASS.         1958 PHI N C      17  .140            1946 PIT N C-3    56  .307
1911 BOS A 2-S-3   9  .269            1959 PHI N C      43  .172            1947 CLE A C-3    61  .262
   BRTR                                  BRTR          143  .166               BRTR         1950  .261
                                                                            NON-PLAYING MANAGER CLE[A] 1951-56,
LONG, DANIEL W.                       LOOK, BRUCE MICHAEL                   CHI[A] 1957-65, 68-69
B.AUG.27,1867 BOSTON,MASS.            B.JUNE 9,1943 LANSING,MICH.
D.APR.30,1929 SAUSALITO,CAL.          1968 MIN A C      59  .246            LOPEZ, ARTURO (ART)
1888 LOU AA O      1  .000               BLTR                               B.JUNE 8,1937 MAYAGUEZ,P.R.
1890 BAL AA O     21  .177                                                  1965 NY  A O      38  .143
                  22  .173            LOOK, DEAN ZACHARY                       BLTL
                                      B.JULY 23,1937 LANSING,MICH.
LONG, HERMAN C. (GERMANY) OR          1961 CHI A O       3  .000            LOPEZ, AURELIO ALEJANDRO [RIOS]
(FLYING DUTCHMAN)                        BRTR                               B.SEPT.21,1948 TECAMACHALCO
B.APR.13,1866 CHICAGO,ILL.                                                  PUEBLA,MEXICO
D.SEPT.17,1909 DENVER,COLO.           LOOS, PETER                          1974 KC  A /P      8   0- 0
1889 KC  AA S    136  .280            B.PHILADELPHIA,PA.                    1978 STL N P      25   4- 2
1890 BOS N  S    101  .250            1901 PHI A P       1   0- 1              BRTR           33   4- 2
1891 BOS N  S    139  .287
1892 BOS N  S    151  .286            LOPAT, EDMUND WALTER (EDDIE)          LOPEZ, CARLOS ANTONIO [MORALES]
1893 BOS N  S    128  .294            (REAL NAME EDMUND WALTER LOPATYNSKI)  B.SEPT.27,1950 MAZATLAN,MEXICO
1894 BOS N  S    103  .324            B.JUNE 21,1918 NEW YORK,N.Y.          1976 CAL A /O      9  .000
1895 BOS N  S    124  .319            1944 CHI A P   27 30  11-10           1977 SEA A O      99  .283
1896 BOS N  S    119  .334            1945 CHI A P   26 32  10-13           1978 BAL A *O    129  .238
1897 BOS N  S    106  .327            1946 CHI A P   29 30  13-13              BRTR          237  .260
1898 BOS N  S    142  .275            1947 CHI A P   31 35  16-13
1899 BOS N  S    145  .257            1948 NY  A P   33 34  17-11           LOPEZ, HECTOR HEADLEY
1900 BOS N  S    124  .256            1949 NY  A P      31  15-10           B.JULY 8,1932 COLON,PANAMA
1901 BOS N  S    138  .238            1950 NY  A P   35 36  18- 8           1955 KC  A 2-3     128  .290
1902 BOS N  2-S  120  .227            1951 NY  A P      31  21- 9           1956 KC  A 2-S-3-O 151  .273
1903 NY  A  S     22  .225            1952 NY  A P      20  10- 5           1957 KC  A 2-3-O   121  .294
    DET A  2-S    69  .218            1953 NY  A P   25 26  16- 4           1958 KC  A 2-S-3-O 151  .261
1904 PHI N  2      1  .250            1954 NY  A P      26  12- 4           1959 KC  A 2        36  .281
   BLTR          1868  .280           1955 NY  A P      16   4- 8               NY  A 3       112  .283
                                          BAL A P      10   3- 4           1960 NY  A 2-3-O   131  .284
LONG, JAMES ALBERT (JIMMIE)              BLTL     340 357 166-112           1961 NY  A O        93  .222
B.JUNE 29,1898 FT.DODGE,IOWA          NON-PLAYING MANAGER KC[A] 1963-64     1962 NY  A 2-3-O   106  .275
D.SEPT.14,1970 FT.DODGE,IOWA                                                1963 NY  A 2-O     130  .249
1922 CHI A C       3  .000            LOPATA, STANLEY EDWARD               1964 NY  A 3-O     127  .260
   BRTR                               (STAN) OR (STASH)                     1965 NY  A O/1     111  .261
                                      B.SEPT.12,1925 DELRAY,MICH.          1966 NY  A O        54  .214
LONG, JAMES M.                        1948 PHI N C       6  .133              BRTR           1451  .269
B.NOV.15,1862 LOUISVILLE,KY.          1949 PHI N C      83  .271
D.DEC.12,1932 LOUISVILLE,KY.          1950 PHI N C      58  .209            LOPEZ, JOSE RAMON [HEVIA] (RAMON)
1891 LOU AA O      6  .243            1951 PHI N C       3  .000            B.MAY 26,1937 LAS VILLAS,CUBA
1893 BAL N  O     55  .225            1952 PHI N C      57  .274            1966 CAL A /P      4   5   0- 1
                  61  .227            1953 PHI N C      81  .239              BRTR
                                      1954 PHI N C-1    86  .290
LONG, JEOFFREY KEITH (JEOFF)          1955 PHI N C-1    99  .271            LOPEZ, MARCELINO PONS
B.OCT.9,1941 COVINGTON,KY.            1956 PHI N C-1   146  .267            B.SEP.23,1943 HAVANA,CUBA
1963 STL N H       5  .200            1957 PHI N C     116  .237            1963 PHI N P       4   5   1- 0
1964 STL N 1-O    28  .233            1958 PHI N C      86  .248            1965 CAL A P    35 52  14-13
    CHI A 1-O     23  .143            1959 MIL N C-1    25  .104            1966 CAL A P    37 55   7-14
   BRTR           56  .193            1960 MIL N C       7  .125            1967 CAL A /P      4   7   0- 2
                                         BRTR          853  .254               BAL A /P       4   6   1- 0
LONG, LESTER (LEP)                                                          1969 BAL A P      27   5- 3
B.JULY 12,1888 SUMMIT,N.J.            LOPATKA, ARTHUR JOSEPH               1970 BAL A P      25   1- 1
D.OCT.21,1958 BIRMINGHAM,ALA.         B.MAY 28,1920 CHICAGO,ILL.           1971 MIL A P    31 34   2- 7
1911 PHI A P       4   0- 0           1945 STL N P       4   1- 0           1972 CLE A /P      4   0- 0
   BRTR                               1946 PHI N P       4   0- 1              BRTL     171 215  31-40
                                         BBTL            8   1- 1
LONG, NELSON (RED)                                                         LORD, BRISTOL ROBOTHAM (BRIS)
B.SEPT.28,1876 BURLINGTON,ONT.,       LOPATYNSKI, EDMUND WALTER            OR (THE HUMAN EYEBALL)
CANADA                                (PLAYED UNDER NAME OF                 B.SEPT.21,1883 UPLAND,PA.
D.AUG.11,1929 HAMILTON,ONT.,CAN       EDMUND WALTER LOPAT)                  D.NOV.13,1964 ANNAPOLIS,MO.
1902 BOS N P       1   0- 0                                                 1905 PHI A O      66  .239
   BRTR                                                                     1906 PHI A P-O  1 118   0- 0
                                                                                                  .233
LONG, RICHARD DALE (DALE)             LOPES, DAVID EARL (DAVEY)            1907 PHI A O      57  .182
B.FEB.6,1926 SPRINGFIELD,MO.          B.MAY 3,1946 E.PROVIDENCE,R.I.        1909 CLE A O      69  .269
1951 PIT N 1      10  .167            1972 LA  N 2       11  .214           1910 CLE A O      57  .226
    STL A 1-O     34  .238            1973 LA  N *2/O-S-3 142  .275            PHI A O       69  .274
1955 PIT N 1     131  .291            1974 LA  N *2     145  .266           1911 PHI A O     134  .310
1956 PIT N 1     148  .263            1975 LA  N *2-O-S 155  .262           1912 PHI A O      96  .238
1957 PIT N 1       7  .182            1976 LA  N *2-O   117  .241           1913 BOS N O      73  .251
    CHI N 1      123  .305            1977 LA  N *2     134  .283              BRTR        1 739   0- 0
1958 CHI N C-1   142  .271            1978 LA  N *2/O   151  .278                                 .256
1959 CHI N 1     110  .236               BRTR          855  .268
1960 SF  N 1      37  .167
    NY  A 1       26  .366
1961 WAS A 1     123  .249
1962 WAS A 1      67  .241
    NY  A 1       41  .298
1963 NY  A 1      14  .200
   BLTL         1013  .267
```

YR	CL LEA POS	GP	G	REC

LORD, HARRY DONALD
B.MAR.8,1882 PORTER,ME.
D.AUG.9,1948 WESTBROOK,MAINE

YR	CL LEA POS	GP	G	REC
1907	BOS A 3		10	.184
1908	BOS A 3		145	.259
1909	BOS A 3		136	.311
1910	BOS A 3		77	.243
	CHI A 3		44	.310
1911	CHI A 3		141	.321
1912	CHI A 3-0		151	.267
1913	CHI A 3		150	.263
1914	CHI A 3		21	.189
1915	BUF F M-3		97	.273
	BLTR		972	.278

LORD, WILLIAM CARLTON (CARLTON)
B.JAN.7,1900 PHILADELPHIA,PA.
D.AUG.15,1947 CHESTER,PA.

| 1923 | PHI N 3 | | 17 | .234 |
| | BRTR | | | |

LORENZEN, ADOLPH ANDREAS (LEFTY)
B.JAN.12,1893 DAVENPORT,IOWA
D.MAR.5,1963 DAVENPORT,IOWA

| 1913 | DET A P | 1 | | 0- 0 |
| | BLTR | | | |

LOTZ, JOSEPH PETER (SMOKEY)
B.JAN.2,1891 REMSEN,IOWA
D.JAN.1,1971 CASTRO VALLEY,CAL.

| 1916 | STL N P | 12 | | 0- 3 |
| | BRTR | | | |

LOUDELL, ARTHUR
[REAL NAME ARTHUR LAUDEL]
B.APR.10,1882 LATHAM,MO.
D.FEB.19,1961 KANSAS CITY,MO.

| 1910 | DET A P | 5 | | 0- 1 |
| | BR | | | |

LOUDEN, WILLIAM (BALDY)
B.AUG.27,1885 PIEDMONT,W.VA.
D.DEC.8,1935 PIEDMONT,W.VA.

1907	NY A 3		2	.167
1912	DET A 2		121	.241
1913	DET A 2		72	.241
1914	BUF F S		127	.313
1915	BUF F 2-S-3		137	.280
1916	CIN N 2-S		134	.219
	BRTR		593	.261

LOUDENSLAGER, CHARLES EDWARD
B.MAY 21,1881 BALTIMORE,MD.
D.OCT.31,1933 BALTIMORE,MD.

| 1904 | BRO N 2 | | 1 | .000 |
| | TR | | | |

LOUGHLIN, LARRY JOHN
B.AUG.16,1941 TACOMA,WASH.

| 1967 | PHI N /P | 3 | | 0- 0 |
| | BLTL | | | |

LOUGHLIN, WILLIAM H.
B.BALTIMORE,MD.

| 1883 | BAL AA 0 | 1 | | .400 |

LOUGHRAN
B.NEW YORK,N.Y.

| 1884 | NY N C-0 | 8 | | .120 |

LOUIS, ALBERTO
[PLAYED UNDER NAME OF ALBERTO LOIS]

LOUN, DONALD NELSON (DON)
B.NOV.9,1940 FREDERICK,MD.

| 1964 | WAS A P | 2 | | 1- 1 |
| | BRTL | | | |

LOVE, EDWARD HAUGHTON (SLIM)
B.AUG.1,1890 LOVE,MISS.
D.NOV.30,1942 MEMPHIS,TENN.

1913	WAS A P	5		2- 0
1916	NY A P	20		2- 0
1917	NY A P	33		6- 5
1918	NY A P	38		13-12
1919	DET A P	22		5- 4
1920	DET A P	1		0- 0
	BLTL	119		28-21

LOVELACE, GROVER THOMAS
B.SEPT.8,1896 WOLFE CITY,TENN.

| 1922 | PIT N 0 | 1 | | .000 |
| | BRTR | | | |

LOVENGUTH, LYNN RICHARD
B.NOV.29,1922 CAMDEN,N.Y.

1955	PHI N P	14		0- 1
1957	STL N P	2	3	0- 1
	BLTR	16	17	0- 2

LOVETT, JOHN
B.MAY 6,1877 MONDAY,OHIO
D.DEC.5,1937 MURRAY CITY,OHIO

| 1903 | STL N P | 3 | | 0- 0 |

LOVETT, LEONARD WALKER
B.JULY 17,1852 LANCASTER CO.,PA
D.NOV.18,1922

1873	RES NA P		1	0- 1
1875	CEN NA P		5	-
	BRTR	1	6	0- 1

LOVETT, MERRITT MARWOOD (MEM)
B.JUNE 15,1912 CHICAGO,ILL.

| 1933 | CHI A N | 1 | | .000 |

LOVETT, THOMAS JOSEPH
B.DEC.7,1863 PROVIDENCE,R.I.
D.MAR.20,1928 PROVIDENCE,R.I.

1885	ATH AA P	16		7- 8
1889	BRO AA P		30	18-10
1890	BRO N P		44	31-11
1891	BRO N P		42	24-18
1893	BRO N P	14	18	3- 6
1894	BOS N P		15	7- 4
	BR	161	165	90-57

LOVITTO, JOSEPH (JOE)
B.JAN.6,1951 SAN PEDRO,CAL.

1972	TEX A *0		117	.224
1973	TEX A 3/0		26	.136
1974	TEX A *0/1		113	.223
1975	TEX A 0/1-C		50	.208
	BBTR		306	.216

LOVRICH, PETER (PETE)
B.OCT.16,1942 BLUE ISLAND,ILL.

| 1963 | KC A P | 20 | | 1- 1 |
| | BRTR | | | |

LOW, FLETCHER
B.APR.7,1893 ESSEX,MASS.
D.JUNE 6,1973 HANOVER,N.H.

| 1915 | BOS N 3 | 1 | | .250 |
| | BRTR | | | |

LOWDERMILK, GROVER CLEVELAND (SLIM)
B.JAN.15,1885 SANBORN,IND.
D.MAR.31,1968 ODIN,ILL.

1909	STL N P		7	0- 2
1911	STL N P		11	0- 1
1912	CHI N P		2	0- 1
1915	STL A P		38	9-18
	DET A P		7	4- 1
1916	DET A P		2	0- 0
	CLE A P		10	1- 5
1917	STL A P		3	2- 1
1918	STL A P		13	2- 6
1919	STL A P		7	0- 0
	CHI A P		20	5- 5
1920	CHI A P		3	0- 0
	BRTR	123		23-40

LOWDERMILK, LOUIS BAILEY
B.FEB.23,1887 SANBORN,IND.
D.DEC.27,1975 CENTRALIA,ILL.

1911	STL N P	16		3- 4
1912	STL N P	4		1- 1
	BRTL	20		4- 5

LOWE
B.1884 DET N C

| | | 1 | | .250 |

LOWE, CHARLES
B.BALTIMORE,MD.

| 1872 | ATL NA 2 | | 6 | .148 |

LOWE, GEORGE WESLEY
B.APR.25,1895 RIDGEFIELD PARK,N.J.

| 1920 | CIN N P | 1 | | 0- 0 |

LOWE, ROBERT LINCOLN
(BOBBY) OR (LINK)
B.JULY 10,1868 PITTSBURGH,PA.
D.DEC.8,1951 DETROIT,MICH.

1890	BOS N S-0		52	.280
1891	BOS N 2-0		124	.281
1892	BOS N 2		124	.244
1893	BOS N 2		120	.316
1894	BOS N 2		133	.341
1895	BOS N 2		99	.301
1896	BOS N 2		79	.320
1897	BOS N 2		121	.314
1898	BOS N 2		147	.272
1899	BOS N 2		152	.267
1900	BOS N 2		127	.279
1901	BOS N 2-3		129	.259
1902	CHI N 2-3		121	.260
1903	CHI N 2		28	.267
1904	PIT N H		1	.000
	DET A M-2		140	.205
1905	DET A 3-0		58	.193
1906	DET A 2-S		41	.207
1907	DET A 3		17	.243
	BRTR		1807	.275

LOWENSTEIN, JOHN LEE
B.JAN.27,1947 WOLF POINT,MONT.

1970	CLE A 2/3-0-S		17	.256
1971	CLE A 2-0/S		58	.186
1972	CLE A 0/1		68	.212
1973	CLE A 0*2/3-1		98	.292
1974	CLE A *0/3-1/2		140	.242
1975	CLE A 0-0/3-2		91	.242
1976	CLE A 0-0/1		93	.205
1977	CLE A 0-0/1		81	.242
1978	TEX A 3-0-0		77	.222
	BLTR		723	.238

LOWN, OMAR JOSEPH (TURK)
B.MAY 30,1924 BROOKLYN,N.Y.

1951	CHI N P		31	4- 9
1952	CHI N P		33	4-11
1953	CHI N P		49	8- 7
1954	CHI N P	15	16	0- 2
1956	CHI N P		61	9- 8
1957	CHI N P		67	5- 7
1958	CHI N P		4	0- 0
	CIN N P		11	0- 2
	CHI A P		27	3- 3
1959	CHI A P		60	9- 2
1960	CHI A P		45	2- 3
1961	CHI A P	59	60	7- 5
1962	CHI A P		42	4- 2
	BRTR		504	55-61

LOWREY, HARRY LEE (PEANUTS)
B.AUG.27,1918 CULVER CITY,CAL.

1942	CHI N 0		27	.190
1943	CHI N 2-S-0		130	.292
1945	CHI N S-0		143	.283
1946	CHI N 3-0		144	.257
1947	CHI N 2-3-0		115	.281
1948	CHI N 2-S-3-0		129	.294
1949	CHI N 3-0		38	.270
	CIN N 0		89	.224
1950	CIN N 2-0		91	.227
	STL N 2-3-0		17	.268
1951	STL N 2-3-0		114	.303
1952	STL N 3-0		132	.286
1953	STL N 2-3-0		104	.269
1954	STL N 0		74	.115
1955	PHI N 1-2-0		54	.189
	BRTR		1401	.273

LOWRY, JOHN D.
B.BALTIMORE,MD.

| 1875 | NAT NA 0 | | 6 | - |

LOWRY, SAMUEL JOSEPH
B.MAR.25,1920 PHILADELPHIA,PA.

1942	PHI A P		1	0- 0
1943	PHI A P		5	0- 0
	BRTR		6	0- 0

LUBY, HUGH MAX (HAL)
B.JUNE 13,1913 BLACKFOOT,IDAHO

1936	PHI A 2		9	.184
1944	NY N 1-2-3		111	.254
	BRTR		120	.247

LUBY, JOHN PERKINS (PAT)
B.1868 CHARLESTON,S.C.
D.APR.24,1899 CHARLESTON,S.C.

1890	CHI N P-1-0		30	20- 8
				.342
1891	CHI N P	22	24	10-12
1892	CHI N P	30	40	9-21
1895	LOU N P		15	1- 5
	TR	97	109	40-46
				.250

LUCADELLO, JOHN (JOHNNY)
B.FEB.22,1919 THURBER,TEX.

1938	STL A 3		7	.150
1939	STL A 2		9	.233
1940	STL A 2		17	.317
1941	STL A 2-S-3-0		107	.279
1946	STL A 2-3		87	.248
1947	NY A 2		12	.083
	BBTR		239	.264

YR	CL	LEA	POS	GP	G	REC

LUCAS, CHARLES FREDERICK (RED)
OR (THE NASHVILLE NARCISSUS)
B.APR.28,1902 COLUMBIA,TENN.

YR	CL	LEA	POS	GP	G	REC
1923	NY	N	P		3	0- 0
1924	BOS	N	P-3	27	33	1- 4
						.333
1925	BOS	N	2		6	.150
1926	CIN	N	P-2	39	66	8- 5
						.303
1927	CIN	N	P-2-	37	80	18-11
			S-O			.313
1928	CIN	N	P	27	39	13- 9
1929	CIN	N	P	32	76	19-12
1930	CIN	N	P	33	80	14-16
1931	CIN	N	P	29	97	14-13
1932	CIN	N	P	31	76	13-17
1933	CIN	N	P	29	75	10-16
1934	PIT	N	P	29	68	10- 9
1935	PIT	N	P	20	47	8- 6
1936	PIT	N	P	27	69	15- 4
1937	PIT	N	P	20	59	8-10
1938	PIT	N	P	13	33	6- 3
	BLTR			396	907	157-135
						.281

LUCAS, FREDERICK WARRINGTON
B.JAN.19,1903 VINELAND,N.J.

YR	CL	LEA	POS	GP	G	REC
1935	PHI	N	O		20	.265
	BRTR					

LUCAS, HENRY V.
B.SEPT.5,1857 ST.LOUIS,MO.
D.NOV.15,1910 ST.LOUIS,MO.
NON-PLAYING MANAGER STL[N] 1885

LUCAS, JOHN CHARLES (BUSTER)
B.FEB.10,1903 GLEN CARBON,ILL.
D.OCT.31,1970 MARYVILLE,ILL.

YR	CL	LEA	POS	GP	G	REC
1931	BOS	A	O		3	.000
1932	BOS	A	O		1	.000
	BRTL				4	.000

LUCAS, J. R. C.
NON-PLAYING MANAGER STL[N] 1877

LUCAS, RAY WESLEY (LUKE)
B.OCT.2,1908 SPRINGFIELD,OHIO
D.OCT.9,1969 HARRISON,MICH.

YR	CL	LEA	POS	GP	G	REC
1929	NY	N	P		3	0- 0
1930	NY	N	P		6	0- 0
1931	NY	N	P		1	0- 0
1933	BRO	N	P		2	0- 0
1934	BRO	N	P		10	1- 1
	BRTR				22	1- 1

LUCE, FRANK EDWARD
B.DEC.6,1896 SPENCER,OHIO
D.FEB.3,1942 MILWAUKEE,WIS.

YR	CL	LEA	POS	GP	G	REC
1923	PIT	N	O		9	.500
	BLTR					

LUCEY, JOSEPH EARL (SCOTCH)
B.MAR.27,1897 HOLYOKE,MASS.

YR	CL	LEA	POS	GP	G	REC
1920	NY	A	2		3	.000
1925	BOS	A	P-S	7	10	0- 1
						.133
	BRTR			7	13	0- 1
						.118

LUCCHESI, FRANK JOSEPH
B.APR.24,1927 SAN FRANCISCO,CAL.
NON-PLAYING MANAGER
PHI[N] 1970-72, TEX[A] 1975-77

LUCID, CORNELIUS CONRAD (CON)
B.FEB.24,1869 DUBLIN,IRELAND

YR	CL	LEA	POS	GP	G	REC
1893	LOU	N	P		2	0- 1
1894	BRO	N	P		10	4- 3
1895	BRO	N	P		21	11- 6
	PHI	N	P		10	6- 3
1896	PHI	N	P		5	1- 4
1897	STL	N	P		6	1- 5
					54	23-22

LUCIER, LOUIS JOSEPH
B.MAR.23,1918 NORTHBRIDGE,MASS.

YR	CL	LEA	POS	GP	G	REC
1943	BOS	A	P		16	3- 4
1944	BOS	A	P		3	0- 0
	PHI	N	P		1	0- 0
1945	PHI	N	P		13	0- 1
	BRTR				33	3- 5

LUCKEY, HOWARD J.
B.PHILADELPHIA,PA.

YR	CL	LEA	POS	GP	G	REC
1890	ATH	AA	P		1	0- 0

LUDERUS, FREDERICK WILLIAM (FRED)
B.SEPT.12,1885 MILWAUKEE,WIS.
D.JAN.4,1961 MILWAUKEE,WIS.

YR	CL	LEA	POS	GP	G	REC
1909	CHI	N	1		11	.305
1910	CHI	N	1		17	.204
	PHI	N	1		19	.294
1911	PHI	N	1		146	.301
1912	PHI	N	1		148	.257
1913	PHI	N	1		155	.262
1914	PHI	N	1		121	.248
1915	PHI	N	1		141	.315
1916	PHI	N	1		146	.281
1917	PHI	N	1		154	.261
1918	PHI	N	1		125	.288
1919	PHI	N	1		138	.293
1920	PHI	N	1		16	.156
	BLTR				1337	.277

LUDOLPH, WILLIAM FRANCIS
(WEE WILLIE)
B.JAN.21,1900 SAN FRANCISCO,CAL
D.APR.8,1952 OAKLAND,CAL.

YR	CL	LEA	POS	GP	G	REC
1924	DET	A	P		3	0- 0
	BRTR					

LUDWIG, WILLIAM LAWRENCE
B.MAY 27,1882 LOUISVILLE,KY.
D.SEPT.5,1947 LOUISVILLE,KY.

YR	CL	LEA	POS	GP	G	REC
1908	STL	N	C		52	.182
	TR					

LUEBBE, ROY JOHN
B.SEPT.17,1900 PARKERSBURG,IOWA

YR	CL	LEA	POS	GP	G	REC
1925	NY	A	C		8	.000
	BBTR					

LUEBBER, STEPHEN LEE (STEVE)
B.JULY 9,1949 CLINTON,MO.

YR	CL	LEA	POS	GP	G	REC
1971	MIN	A	P	18	19	2- 5
1972	MIN	A	/P		2	0- 0
1976	MIN	A	P		38	4- 5
	BRTR				58	6-10

LUEBKE, RICHARD RAYMOND (DICK)
B.APR.8,1935 CHICAGO,ILL.
D.DEC.4,1974 SAN DIEGO,CAL.

YR	CL	LEA	POS	GP	G	REC
1962	BAL	A	P		10	0- 1
	BRTL					

LUFF, HENRY T.
B.SEPT.14,1856 PHILADELPHIA,PA.
D.OCT.11,1916 PHILADELPHIA,PA.

YR	CL	LEA	POS	GP	G	REC
1875	NH	NA	P-3-	8	38	1- 7
			O			-
1882	DET	N	2-O		3	.273
	CIN	AA	1-O		28	.223
1883	LOU	AA	1-O		6	.174
1884	KEY	U	1-O		24	.266
	KC	U	3-O		5	.053
				8	104	1- 7
						-

LUHRSEN, WILLIAM FERDINAND
(WILD BILL)
B.APR.14,1884 BUCKLEY,ILL.
D.AUG.15,1973 LITTLE ROCK,ARK.

YR	CL	LEA	POS	GP	G	REC
1913	PIT	N	P		5	3- 1
	BRTR					

LUKENS, ALBERT P.
B.1872 VINELAND,N.J.

YR	CL	LEA	POS	GP	G	REC
1894	PHI	N	P		3	0- 1

LUKON, EDWARD PAUL (MONGOOSE)
B.AUG.5,1920 BURGETTSTOWN,PA.

YR	CL	LEA	POS	GP	G	REC
1941	CIN	N	O		23	.267
1945	CIN	N	O		2	.125
1946	CIN	N	O		102	.250
1947	CIN	N	O		86	.205
	BLTL				213	.236

LUM, MICHAEL KEN-WAI (MIKE)
B.OCT.27,1945 HONOLULU,HAWAII

YR	CL	LEA	POS	GP	G	REC
1967	ATL	N	/O		9	.231
1968	ATL	N	O		122	.224
1969	ATL	N	O		121	.268
1970	ATL	N	O		123	.254
1971	ATL	N	*O/1		145	.269
1972	ATL	N	*O/1		123	.228
1973	ATL	N	1-O		138	.294
1974	ATL	N	1-O		106	.233
1975	ATL	N	1-O		124	.228
1976	CIN	N	O		84	.228
1977	CIN	N	O/1		81	.160
1978	CIN	N	O/1		86	.267
	BLTL				1262	.248

LUMENTI, RAPHAEL ANTHONY (RALPH)
B.DEC.21,1936 MILFORD,MASS.

YR	CL	LEA	POS	GP	G	REC
1957	WAS	A	P		3	0- 1
1958	WAS	A	P		8	1- 2
1959	WAS	A	P		2	0- 0
	BLTL				13	1- 3

LUMLEY, HARRY G. (JUDGE)
B.SEPT.29,1880 FOREST CITY,PA.
D.MAY 22,1938 BINGHAMTON,N.Y.

YR	CL	LEA	POS	GP	G	REC
1904	BRO	N	O		150	.279
1905	BRO	N	O		129	.293
1906	BRO	N	O		131	.324
1907	BRO	N	O		118	.267
1908	BRO	N	O		116	.216
1909	BRO	N	M-O		52	.250
1910	BRO	N	O		8	.100
	BLTR				704	.275

LUMPE, JERRY DEAN
B.JUNE 2,1933 LINCOLN,MO.

YR	CL	LEA	POS	GP	G	REC
1956	NY	A	S-3		20	.258
1957	NY	A	S-3		40	.340
1958	NY	A	S-3		81	.254
1959	NY	A	2-S-3		18	.222
	KC	A	2-S-3		108	.243
1960	KC	A	2-S		146	.272
1961	KC	A	2		148	.293
1962	KC	A	2*S		156	.301
1963	KC	A	2		157	.271
1964	DET	A	2		158	.256
1965	DET	A	*2		145	.257
1966	DET	A	2		113	.231
1967	DET	A	2/3		81	.232
	BLTR				1371	.268

LUNA, GUILLERMO ROMERO (MEMO)
B.JUNE 25,1930 TACUBAYA,MEXICO

YR	CL	LEA	POS	GP	G	REC
1954	STL	N	P		1	0- 1
	BLTL					

LUND, DONALD ANDREW (DON)
B.MAY 18,1923 DETROIT,MICH.

YR	CL	LEA	POS	GP	G	REC
1945	BRO	N	H		4	.000
1947	BRO	N	O		11	.300
1948	BRO	N	O		27	.188
	STL	A	O		63	.248
1949	DET	A	H		2	.000
1952	DET	A	O		8	.304
1953	DET	A	O		131	.257
1954	DET	A	O		35	.130
	BRTR				281	.240

LUND, GORDON THOMAS (GORDY)
B.FEB.23,1941 IRON MOUNTAIN,MICH.

YR	CL	LEA	POS	GP	G	REC
1967	CLE	A	/S		3	.250
1969	SEA	A	S/2-3		20	.263
	BRTR				23	.261

LUNDBOM, JOHN FREDERICK (JACK)
B.MAR.10,1877 MANISTEE,MICH.
D.OCT.31,1949 MANISTEE,MICH.

YR	CL	LEA	POS	GP	G	REC
1902	CLE	N	P		8	2- 1
	BRTR					

LUNDGREN, CARL LEONARD
B.FEB.16,1880 MARENGO,ILL.
D.AUG.21,1934 MARENGO,ILL.

YR	CL	LEA	POS	GP	G	REC
1902	CHI	N	P-S	18	19	9- 9
						.106
1903	CHI	N	P		27	11- 9
1904	CHI	N	P		31	17-10
1905	CHI	N	P		23	13- 4
1906	CHI	N	P	27	28	17- 6
1907	CHI	N	P		28	18- 7
1908	CHI	N	P		23	6- 9
1909	CHI	N	P		2	0- 1
	BRTR			179	181	91-55
						.157

LUNDGREN, EBIN DELMAR (DEL)
B.SEPT.21,1900 LINDSBORG,KAN.

YR	CL	LEA	POS	GP	G	REC
1924	PIT	N	P		8	0- 1
1926	BOS	A	P		18	0- 2
1927	BOS	A	P		30	5-12
	BRTR				56	5-15

LUNDSTEDT, THOMAS ROBERT (TOM)
B.APR.10,1949 DAVENPORT,IOWA

YR	CL	LEA	POS	GP	G	REC
1973	CHI	N	/C		4	.000
1974	CHI	N	C		22	.094
1975	MIN	A	C		18	.107
	BBTR				44	.092

LUNTE, HARRY AUGUST
B.SEPT.15,1892 ST.LOUIS,MO.
D.JULY 27,1965 ST.LOUIS,MO.

YR	CL	LEA	POS	GP	G	REC
1919	CLE	A	S		2	.195
1920	CLE	A	S		23	.197

LUPIEN, ULYSSES JOHN (TONY)
B.APR.23,1917 CHELMSFORD,MASS.

YR	CL	LEA	POS	GP	G	REC
1940	BOS	A	1		10	.474
1942	BOS	A	1		128	.281
1943	BOS	A	1		154	.255
1944	PHI	N	1		153	.283
1945	PHI	N	1		15	.315
1948	CHI	A	1		154	.246
	BLTL				614	.268

YR CL LEA POS   GP   G   REC

LUPLOW, ALVIN DAVID (AL)
B.MAR.13,1939 SAGINAW,MICH.
YR	CL	LEA	POS	GP	G	REC
1961	CLE	A	O		5	.056
1962	CLE	A	3		97	.277
1963	CLE	A	O		100	.234
1964	CLE	A	O		19	.111
1965	CLE	A	/O		53	.133
1966		NY	*O		111	.251
1967	NY	N	O		41	.205
	PIT	N	O		55	.184
	BLTR				481	.235

LUQUE, ADOLFO (DOLF)
OR (THE PRIDE OF HAVANA)
B.AUG.4,1890 HAVANA,CUBA
D.JULY 3,1957 HAVANA,CUBA
YR	CL	LEA	POS	GP	G	REC
1914	BOS	N	P		2	0- 1
1915	BOS	N	P		2	0- 0
1918	CIN	N	P-O	12	13	6- 3
						.321
1919	CIN	N	P-3	30	31	10- 3
						.125
1920	CIN	N	P		37	13- 9
1921	CIN	N	P	41	42	17-19
1922	CIN	N	P		39	13-23
1923	CIN	N	P	41	43	27- 8
1924	CIN	N	P-O	31	33	10-15
						.178
1925	CIN	N	P	36	37	16-18
1926	CIN	N	P		34	13-16
1927	CIN	N	P		29	13-12
1928	CIN	N	P		33	11-10
1929	CIN	N	P		32	5-16
1930	BRO	N	P		31	14- 8
1931	BRO	N	P		19	7- 6
1932	NY	N	P		38	6- 7
1933	NY	N	P		35	8- 2
1934	NY	N	P		26	4- 3
1935	NY	N	P		2	1- 0
	BRTR			550	558	194-179
						.227

LUSH, ERNEST BENJAMIN
B.OCT.31,1884 BRIDGEPORT,CONN.
D.FEB.26,1937 DETROIT,MICH.
YR	CL	LEA	POS	GP	G	REC
1910	STL	N	O		1	.000
	TL					

LUSH, JOHN CHARLES
B.OCT.8,1885 WILLIAMSPORT,PA.
D.NOV.18,1946 BEVERLY HILLS,CAL
YR	CL	LEA	POS	GP	G	REC
1904	PHI	N	P-1	7	102	0- 5
			O			.276
1905	PHI	N	P		6	2- 0
1906	PHI	N	P-O	37	61	18-15
						.264
1907	PHI	N	P		12	5- 6
	STL	N	P		16	5- 9
1908	STL	N	P		38	11-18
1909	STL	N	P	34	45	11-18
1910	STL	N	P		36	14-13
	BLTL			186	316	66-84
						.253

LUSH, WILLIAM LUCAS
B.NOV.10,1873 BRIDGEPORT,CONN.
D.AUG.28,1951 HAWTHORNE,N.Y.
YR	CL	LEA	POS	GP	G	REC
1895	WAS	N	O		5	.210
1896	WAS	N	O		91	.245
1897	WAS	N	O		2	.000
1901	BOS	N	O		7	.185
1902	BOS	N	3-O		118	.231
1903	DET	A	O		117	.278
1904	CLE	A	O		138	.272
	BBTR				478	.254

LUSKEY, CHARLES MELTON
B.APR.6,1876 WASHINGTON,D.C.
D.DEC.20,1962 BETHESDA,MD.
YR	CL	LEA	POS	GP	G	REC
1901	WAS	A	C-O		11	.195

LUTENBERG, CHARLES WILLIAM
B.OCT.4,1864 QUINCY,ILL.
D.DEC.24,1938 QUINCY,ILL.
YR	CL	LEA	POS	GP	G	REC
1894	LOU	N	1		70	.192

LUTTRELL, LYLE KENNETH
B.FEB.22,1930 BLOOMINGTON,ILL.
YR	CL	LEA	POS	GP	G	REC
1956	WAS	A	S		38	.189
1957	WAS	A	S		19	.200
	BRTR				57	.192

LUTZ, LOUIS WILLIAM (RED)
B.DEC.17,1898 CINCINNATI,OHIO
YR	CL	LEA	POS	GP	G	REC
1922	CIN	N	C		1	1.000

LUTZ, ROLLIN JOSEPH (JOE)
B.FEB.18,1925 KEOKUK,IOWA
YR	CL	LEA	POS	GP	G	REC
1951	STL	A	1		14	.167
	BLTL					

LUTZKE, WALTER JOHN (RUBE)
B.APR.17,1897 MILWAUKEE,WIS.
D.MAR.6,1938 GRANVILLE,WIS.
YR	CL	LEA	POS	GP	G	REC
1923	CLE	A	3		143	.256
1924	CLE	A	3		106	.243
1925	CLE	A	2-3		81	.219
1926	CLE	A	3		142	.261
1927	CLE	A	3		100	.251
	BRTR				572	.249

LUZINSKI, GREGORY MICHAEL (GREG)
B.NOV.22,1950 CHICAGO,ILL.
YR	CL	LEA	POS	GP	G	REC
1970	PHI	N	/1		8	.167
1971	PHI	N	1		28	.300
1972	PHI	N	*O/1		150	.281
1973	PHI	N	*O		161	.285
1974	PHI	N	O		85	.272
1975	PHI	N	*O		161	.300
1976	PHI	N	*O		149	.304
1977	PHI	N	*O		149	.309
1978	PHI	N	*O		155	.265
	BRTR				1046	.289

LYLE, ALBERT WALTER (SPARKY)
B.JULY 22,1944 DUBOIS,PA.
YR	CL	LEA	POS	GP	G	REC
1967	BOS	A	P		27	1- 2
1968	BOS	A	P		49	6- 1
1969	BOS	A	P		71	8- 3
1970	BOS	A	P		63	1- 7
1971	BOS	A	P		50	6- 4
1972	NY	A	P		59	9- 5
1973	NY	A	P		51	5- 9
1974	NY	A	P		66	9- 3
1975	NY	A	P		49	5- 7
1976	NY	A	P		64	7- 8
1977	NY	A	P		72	13- 5
1978	NY	A	P		59	9- 3
	BLTL				680	79-57

LYLE, JAMES CHARLES
B.JULY 24,1900 LAKE,MISS.
D.OCT.10,1977 WILLIAMSPORT,PA.
YR	CL	LEA	POS	GP	G	REC
1925	WAS	A	P		1	0- 0
	BRTR					

LYNCH, ADRIAN RYAN
B.FEB.9,1897 LAURENS,IOWA
D.MAR.16,1934 DAVENPORT,IOWA
YR	CL	LEA	POS	GP	G	REC
1920	STL	A	P		5	2- 0
	BRTR					

LYNCH, GERALD THOMAS (JERRY)
B.JULY 17,1930 BAY CITY,MICH.
YR	CL	LEA	POS	GP	G	REC
1954	PIT	N	O		98	.239
1955	PIT	N	C-O		88	.284
1956	PIT	N	O		19	.158
1957	CIN	N	C-O		67	.258
1958	CIN	N	O		122	.312
1959	CIN	N	O		117	.260
1960	CIN	N	O		102	.289
1961	CIN	N	O		96	.315
1962	CIN	N	O		114	.281
1963	CIN	N	O		22	.250
	PIT	N	O		88	.266
1964	PIT	N	O		114	.273
1965	PIT	N	O		73	.281
1966	PIT	N	O		64	.214
	BLTR				1184	.277

LYNCH, HENRY W.
B.1866 WORCESTER,MASS.
D.NOV.23,1925 WORCESTER,MASS.
YR	CL	LEA	POS	GP	G	REC
1893	CHI	N	O		4	.214

LYNCH, JOHN H. (JACK)
B.FEB.5,1857 NEW YORK,N.Y
D.APR.20,1923
YR	CL	LEA	POS	GP	G	REC
1881	BUF	N	P-O	19	23	10- 9
						.166
1883	MET	AA	P		29	13-16
1884	MET	AA	P		54	34-14
1885	MET	AA	P		45	23-21
1886	MET	AA	P		51	20-30
1887	MET	AA	P		23	7-15
1890	BRO	AA	P		2	0- 2
	BRTR			223	227	112-107
						.151

LYNCH, MATTHEW DANIEL (DUMMY)
B.FEB.7,1927 DALLAS,TEX.
YR	CL	LEA	POS	GP	G	REC
1948	CHI	N	2		7	.286
	BRTR					

LYNCH, MICHAEL JOSEPH
B.SEPT.10,1875 ST.PAUL,MINN.
D.APR.1,1947 JENNINGS LODGE,ORE
YR	CL	LEA	POS	GP	G	REC
1902	CHI	N	O		7	.166

LYNCH, MICHAEL JOSEPH
B.JUNE 28,1880 HOLYOKE,MASS.
D.APR.2,1927 GARRISON,N.Y.
YR	CL	LEA	POS	GP	G	REC
1904	PIT	N	P		27	14-11
1905	PIT	N	P		33	17- 7
1906	PIT	N	P		18	6- 5
1907	PIT	N	P		7	2- 2
	NY	N	P		12	3- 6
	BRTR				97	42-21

LYNCH, THOMAS (DUMMY)
B.1863 PERU,ILL.
D.MAY 13,1903 PERU,ILL.
YR	CL	LEA	POS	GP	G	REC
1884	CHI	N	P-1		5	3- 2
						.000

LYNCH, THOMAS JAMES
B.APR.3,1860 BENNINGTON,VT.
D.MAR.28,1955 COHOES,N.Y.
YR	CL	LEA	POS	GP	G	REC
1884	WIL	U	C-1-O		16	.281
	PHI	N	P-C-	1	12	0- 1
			O			.318
1885	PHI	N	2-O		13	.189
	BLTR			1	41	0- 1
						.261

LYNCH, WALTER EDWARD (JABBER)
B.APR.15,1897 BUFFALO,N.Y.
D.DEC.21,1976 DAYTONA BEACH,FLA
YR	CL	LEA	POS	GP	G	REC
1922	BOS	A	C		3	.667
	TR					

LYNN, BYRD (BIRDIE)
B.MAR.13,1889 UNIONVILLE,ILL.
D.FEB.5,1940 NAPA,CAL.
YR	CL	LEA	POS	GP	G	REC
1916	CHI	A	C		31	.225
1917	CHI	A	C		35	.222
1918	CHI	A	C		4	.142
1919	CHI	A	C		29	.227
1920	CHI	A	C		16	.320
	BRTR				115	.237

LYNN, FREDRIC MICHAEL (FRED)
B.FEB.3,1952 CHICAGO,ILL.
YR	CL	LEA	POS	GP	G	REC
1974	BOS	A	O		15	.419
1975	BOS	A	*O		145	.331
1976	BOS	A	*O		132	.314
1977	BOS	A	*O		129	.260
1978	BOS	A	*O		150	.298
	BLTL				571	.303

LYNN, JAPHET MONROE (RED)
B.DEC.27,1913 KENNEY,TEX.
D.OCT.27,1977 BELLVILLE,TEX.
YR	CL	LEA	POS	GP	G	REC
1939	DET	A	P		4	0- 1
	NY	N	P		26	1- 0
1940	NY	N	P		33	4- 3
1944	CHI	N	P		22	5- 4
	BRTR				85	10- 8

LYNN, JEROME EDWARD
B.APR.14,1916 SCRANTON,PA.
D.SEPT.25,1972 SCRANTON,PA.
YR	CL	LEA	POS	GP	G	REC
1937	WAS	A	2		1	.667
	BRTR					

LYON, RUSSELL MAYO
B.JUNE 26,1913 BALL GROUND,GA.
YR	CL	LEA	POS	GP	G	REC
1944	CLE	A	C		7	.182
	BRTR					

LYONS, ALBERT HAROLD (AL)
B.JULY 18,1918 ST.JOSEPH,MO.
D.DEC.20,1965 INGLEWOOD,CAL.
YR	CL	LEA	POS	GP	G	REC
1944	NY	A	P	11	19	0- 0
1946	NY	A	P		2	0- 1
1947	NY	A	P	6	8	1- 0
	PIT	N	P	13	15	1- 2
1948	BOS	N	P-O	7	16	1- 0
						.167
	BRTR			39	60	3- 3
						.293

LYONS, DENNIS PATRICK ALOYSIUS (DENNY)
B.MAR.12,1866 CINCINNATI,OHIO
D.JAN.3,1929 W.COVINGTON,KY.
YR	CL	LEA	POS	GP	G	REC
1885	PRO	N	3		4	.125
1886	ATH	AA	3		32	.226
1887	ATH	AA	3		137	.469
1888	ATH	AA	3		111	.325
1889	ATH	AA	3		131	.327
1890	ATH	AA	3		88	.351
1891	STL	AA	3		120	.312
1892	NY	N	3		108	.260
1893	PIT	N	3		131	.318
1894	PIT	N	3		72	.311
1895	STL	N	3		33	.290
1896	PIT	N	3		116	.306
1897	PIT	N	1		36	.206
	BRTR				1119	.325

LYONS, EDWARD HOYTE (MOUSE)
B.MAY 12,1923 WINSTON-SALEM,N.C
YR	CL	LEA	POS	GP	G	REC
1947	WAS	A	2		7	.154
	BRTR					

LYONS, GEORGE TONY (SMOOTH)
B.JAN.25,1891 BIBLE GROVE,ILL.
YR	CL	LEA	POS	GP	G	REC
1920	STL	N	P		7	2- 1
1924	STL	A	P		26	3- 2
	BRTR				33	5- 3

YR	CL	LEA	POS	GP	G	REC

LYONS, HARRY P.
B.MAR.25,1866 CHESTER,PA.
D.JUNE 30,1912 MAURICETOWN,N.J.
1887	PHI	N	O		1	.200
	STL	AA	O		2	.125
1888	STL	AA	O		123	.190
1889	NY	N	O		5	.100
1890	ROC	AA	O		132	.264
1892	NY	N	O		96	.245
1893	NY	N	O		46	.272
					405	.236

LYONS, HERSCHEL ENGLEBERT
B.JULY 23,1919 FRESNO,CAL.
| 1941 | STL | N | P | | 1 | 0- 0 |
BRTR

LYONS, PATRICK JERRY
B.CANADA
D.JAN.20,1914 SPRINGFIELD,OHIO
| 1890 | CLE | N | 2 | | 11 | .052 |

LYONS, TERENCE HILBERT
B.DEC.14,1908 NEW HOLLAND,OHIO
D.SEPT.9,1959 DAYTON,OHIO
| 1929 | PHI | N | 1 | | 1 | .000 |
BRTR

LYONS, THEODORE AMAR (TED)
B.DEC.28,1900 LAKE CHARLES,LA.
1923	CHI	A	P		9	2- 1
1924	CHI	A	P		41	12-11
1925	CHI	A	P		43	21-11
1926	CHI	A	P	39	41	18-16
1927	CHI	A	P	39	41	22-14
1928	CHI	A	P	39	49	15-14
1929	CHI	A	P	37	40	14-20
1930	CHI	A	P	42	57	22-15
1931	CHI	A	P	22	42	4- 6
1932	CHI	A	P	33	49	10-15
1933	CHI	A	P	36	51	10-21
1934	CHI	A	P	30	50	11-13
1935	CHI	A	P	23	29	15- 8
1936	CHI	A	P		26	10-13
1937	CHI	A	P	22	23	12- 7
1938	CHI	A	P	23	24	9-11
1939	CHI	A	P		21	14- 6
1940	CHI	A	P		22	12- 8
1941	CHI	A	P		22	12-10
1942	CHI	A	P		20	14- 6
1946	CHI	A	M-P		5	1- 4
		BBTR		594	705	260-230
NON-PLAYING MANAGER CHI[A] 1947-48

LYONS, THOMAS A. (TOBY)
B.MAR.27,1869 CAMBRIDGE,MASS.
D.AUG.29,1920 BOSTON,MASS.
| 1890 | SYR | AA | P | | 3 | 1- 2 |

LYSTON, WILLIAM EDWARD
B.1863 NEAR BALTIMORE,MD.
D.AUG 4,1944 BALTIMORE,MD.
1891	COL	AA	P		1	0- 0
1894	CLE	N	P		1	0- 1
	TR				2	0- 1

LYTLE, EDWARD BENSON (DAD) OR (POP)
B.MAR.10,1862 RACINE,WIS.
D.DEC.21,1950 LONG BEACH,CAL.
1890	CHI	N	O		1	.000
	PIT	N	2-O		15	.123
					16	.115

LYTTLE, JAMES LAWRENCE (JIM)
B.MAY 20,1946 HAMILTON,OHIO
1969	NY	A	O		28	.181
1970	NY	A	O		87	.310
1971	NY	A	O		49	.198
1972	CHI	A	O		44	.232
1973	MON	N	O		49	.259
1974	MON	N	O		25	.333
1975	MON	N	O		44	.273
1976	MON	N	O		42	.271
	LA	N	O		23	.221
	BLTR				391	.248

MAAS, DUANE FREDRICK (DUKE)
B.JAN.31,1929 UTICA,MICH.
D.DEC.7,1976 MT.CLEMENS,MICH.
1955	DET	A	P		18	5- 6
1956	DET	A	P		26	0- 7
1957	DET	A	P		45	10-14
1958	KC	A	P		10	4- 5
	NY	A	P		22	7- 3
1959	NY	A	P		38	14- 8
1960	NY	A	P		35	5- 1
1961	NY	A	P		1	0- 0
	BRTR				195	45-44

MABE, ROBERT LEE (BOB)
B.OCT.8,1929 DANVILLE,VA.
1958	STL	N	P	31	32	3- 9
1959	CIN	N	P		18	4- 2
1960	BAL	A	P		2	0- 0
	BRTR	KU			52	7-11

MAC CORMACK, FRANK LOUIS
B.SEPT.21,1954 JERSEY CITY,N.J.
1976	DET	A	/P		9	0- 5
1977	SEA	A	/P		3	0- 0
	BRTR				12	0- 5

MAC DONALD, HARVEY FORSYTH
B.MAY 18,1898 NEW YORK,N.Y.
D.OCT.4,1965 MANOA,PA.
| 1928 | PHI | N | O | | 13 | .250 |
BLTL

MACDONALD, WILLIAM PAUL (BILL)
B.MAR.28,1929 ALAMEDA,CAL.
1950	PIT	N	P		32	8-10
1953	PIT	N	P		4	0- 1
	BRTR				36	8-11

MACE, HARRY L. (JIMMY)
B.WASHINGTON,D.C.
| 1891 | WAS | AA | P | | 5 | 0- 4 |

MACEY
B.COLUMBUS,OHIO
| 1890 | ATH | AA | C | | 1 | .000 |

MAC FAYDEN, DANIEL KNOWLES (DANNY) OR (DEACON DANNY)
B.JUNE 10,1905 N.TRURO,MASS.
D.AUG.26,1972 BRUNSWICK,ME.
1926	BOS	A	P		3	0- 1
1927	BOS	A	P	35	37	5- 8
1928	BOS	A	P	33	35	9-15
1929	BOS	A	P		32	10-18
1930	BOS	A	P		36	11-14
1931	BOS	A	P		35	16-12
1932	BOS	A	P		12	1-10
	NY	A	P		16	7- 9
1933	NY	A	P		25	3- 2
1934	NY	A	P		22	4- 3
1935	CIN	N	P		7	1- 2
	BOS	N	P		28	5-13
1936	BOS	N	P		37	17-13
1937	BOS	N	P		32	14-14
1938	BOS	N	P		29	14- 9
1939	BOS	N	P		33	8-14
1940	PIT	N	P		35	5- 4
1941	WAS	A	P		5	0- 1
1943	BOS	N	P		10	2- 1
	BRTR			465	469	132-159

MAC GAMWELL, EDWARD M.
B.JAN.6,1879 BUFFALO,N.Y.
D.MAY 26,1924 ALBANY,N.Y.
| 1905 | BRO | N | 1 | | 4 | .267 |
BLTL

MACHA, KENNETH EDWARD (KEN)
B.SEPT.29,1950 MONROEVILLE,PA.
1974	PIT	N	/C		5	.600
1977	PIT	N	3-1/0		35	.274
1978	PIT	N	3		29	.212
	BRTR				69	.263

MACHEMEHL, CHARLES WALTER (CHUCK)
B.APR.20,1947 BRENHAM,TEX.
| 1971 | CLE | A | P | | 14 | 0- 2 |
BRTR

MACHEMER, DAVID RITCHIE (DAVE)
B.MAY 24,1951 ST.JOSEPH,MO.
| 1978 | CAL | A | /2-3-S | | 10 | .273 |
BRTR

MACIARZ, JOSEPH JOHN
[PLAYED UNDER NAME OF JOE JOHN MACK]

MACK, CORNELIUS ALEXANDER (CONNIE) OR (THE TALL TACTICIAN)
[REAL NAME CORNELIUS ALEXANDER MC GILLICUDDY]
B.DEC.22,1862 E.BROOKFIELD,MASS
D.FEB.8,1956 GERMANTOWN,PA.
1886	WAS	N	C		10	.361
1887	WAS	N	C		80	.220
1888	WAS	N	C		85	.186
1889	WAS	N	C-1-O		97	.292
1890	BUF	P	C		123	.268
1891	PIT	N	C		71	.210
1892	PIT	N	C		86	.257
1893	PIT	N	C		36	.325
1894	PIT	N	M-C		63	.257
1895	PIT	N	M-C		14	.362
1896	PIT	N	M-C-1		30	.207
	BRTR				695	.252
NON-PLAYING MANAGER PHI[A] 1901-50

MACK, DENNIS JOSEPH
[REAL NAME DENNIS JOSEPH MC GEE]
B.1851 EASTON,PA.
D.APR.10,1888 WILKES-BARRE,PA.
1871	ROK	NA	P-1-S	1	25	0- 1
1872	ATH	NA	1-S		46	.247
1873	PHI	NA	1-2-O		45	-
1874	PHI	NA	1		56	-
1876	STL	N	S		48	.204
1880	BUF	N	2-S		17	.203
1882	LOU	AA	2-5-O		72	.193
1883	PIT	AA	1-S		60	.200
	BRTR			1	369	0- 1
						-

MACK, EARLE THADDEUS
[REAL NAME EARLE THADDEUS MC GILLICUDDY]
B.FEB.1,1890 E.BROOKFIELD,MASS.
D.FEB.4,1967 UPPER DARBY TOWNSHIP,PA.
1910	PHI	A	C		1	.500
1911	PHI	A	3		2	.000
1914	PHI	A	1		2	.000
	BLTR				5	.133

MACK, FRANK GEORGE (STUBBY)
B.FEB.2,1900 OKAHOMA CITY,OKLA.
1922	CHI	A	P		8	2- 2
1923	CHI	A	P		12	0- 1
1925	CHI	A	P		8	0- 0
	BRTR				28	2- 3

MACK, JOSEPH (REDDY)
[REAL NAME JOSEPH MC NAMARA]
B.MAY 22,1866 IRELAND
D.DEC.30,1916 NEWPORT,KY.
1885	LOU	AA	2		11	.244
1886	LOU	AA	2		137	.244
1887	LOU	AA	2		128	.410
1888	LOU	AA	2		110	.228
1889	BAL	AA	2		136	.236
1890	BAL	AA	2		26	.272
					548	.285

MACK, JOE JOHN
[REAL NAME JOSEPH JOHN MACIARZ]
B.JAN.4,1912 CHICAGO,ILL.
| 1945 | BOS | N | 1 | | 66 | .231 |
BBTL

MACK, RAYMOND JAMES (RAY)
[REAL NAME RAYMOND JAMES MLCKOVSKY]
B.AUG.31,1916 CLEVELAND,OHIO
D.MAY 7,1969 BUCYRUS,OHIO
1938	CLE	A	2		2	.333
1939	CLE	A	2		36	.152
1940	CLE	A	2		146	.283
1941	CLE	A	2		145	.228
1942	CLE	A	2		143	.225
1943	CLE	A	2		153	.220
1944	CLE	A	2		83	.232
1946	CLE	A	2		61	.205
1947	NY	A	H		1	.000
	CHI	N	2		21	.218
	BRTR				791	.232

MACK, WILLIAM FRANCIS
B.FEB.12,1885 ELMIRA,N.Y.
D.SEPT.30,1971 ELMIRA,N.Y.
| 1908 | CHI | N | P | | 2 | 0- 0 |

MACKANIN, PETER (PETE)
B.AUG.1,1951 CHICAGO,ILL.
1973	TEX	A	S-3		44	.100
1974	TEX	A	/S		2	.167
1975	MON	N	*2/S-3		130	.225
1977	MON	N	*2/3-S-O		114	.224
1977	MON	N	/2-S-3-O		55	.224
1978	PHI	N	/1-3		5	.250
	BRTR				350	.213

MAC KENZIE, ERIC HUGH
B.AUG.29,1932 GLENDON,ALT.,CAN.
| 1955 | KC | A | C | | 1 | .000 |
BLTR

MAC KENZIE, HENRY GORDON (GORDON)
B.JULY 9,1937 ST.PETERSBURG,FLA
| 1961 | KC | A | C | | 11 | .125 |
BRTR

MAC KENZIE, KENNETH PURVIS (KEN)
B.MAR.10,1934 GORE BAY,ONT.,CAN.
1960	MIL	N	P		9	0- 1
1961	MIL	N	P		5	0- 1
1962	NY	N	P		42	5- 4
1963	NY	N	P		34	3- 1
	STL	N	P		8	0- 0
1964	SF	N	P		10	0- 0
1965	HOU	N	P		21	0- 3
	BRTL				129	8-10

YR	CL	LEA	POS	GP	G	REC

MACKIEWICZ, FELIX THADDEUS
B.NOV.20,1917 CHICAGO,ILL.

YR	CL	LEA	POS	G	REC
1941	PHI	A	O	5	.285
1942	PHI	A	O	6	.214
1943	PHI	A	O	9	.063
1945	CLE	A	O	120	.273
1946	CLE	A	O	78	.260
1947	CLE	A	O	2	.000
	WAS	A	O	3	.167
	BRTR			223	.259

MACKINSON, JOHN JOSEPH
B.OCT.29,1923 ORANGE,N.J.

YR	CL	LEA	POS	GP	G	REC
1953	PHI	A	P		1	0-0
1955	STL	N	P	8	9	0-1
	BRTR			9	10	0-1

MAC LEOD, WILLIAM DANIEL (BILLY)
B.MAY 13,1942 GLOUCESTER,MASS.

YR	CL	LEA	POS	G	REC
1962	BOS	A	P	2	0-1
	BLTL				

MACON, MAX CULLEN
B.OCT.14,1915 PENSACOLA,FLA.

YR	CL	LEA	POS	GP	G	REC
1938	STL	N	P	38	46	4-11
1940	BRO	N	P		2	1-0
1942	BRO	N	P	14	26	5-3
1943	BRO	N	P	25	43	7-5
						.164
1944	BOS	N	P-1-	1	106	0-0
			O			.273
1947	BOS	N	P		1	0-0
	BLTL			81	226	17-19
						.265

MAC PHEE, WALTER SCOTT (WADDY)
B.DEC.23,1899 BROOKLYN,N.Y.

YR	CL	LEA	POS	G	REC
1922	NY	N	3	2	.286
	BRTR				

MAC PHERSON, HARRY WILLIAM
B.JULY 10,1926 N.ANDOVER,MASS.

YR	CL	LEA	POS	G	REC
1944	BOS	N	P	1	0-0

MACULLAR, JAMES F. (LITTLE MAC)
B.JAN.6,1855 BOSTON,MASS.
D.APR.8,1924 BALTIMORE,MD.

YR	CL	LEA	POS	G	REC
1879	SYR	N	S-O	63	.231
1882	CIN	AA	O	79	.282
1883	CIN	AA	S-O	14	.151
1884	BAL	AA	S	108	.193
1885	BAL	AA	S	100	.202
1886	BAL	AA	S	76	.227
	BRTL			440	.210

MADDEN
B.PITTSBURGH,PA.

YR	CL	LEA	POS	G	REC
1914	PIT	F	C	2	.500

MADDEN, EUGENE
B.JUNE 5,1890 ELM GROVE,W.VA.
D.APR.6,1949 UTICA,N.Y.

YR	CL	LEA	POS	G	REC
1916	PIT	N	O	1	.000
	BLTR				

MADDEN, LEONARD JOSEPH (LEFTY)
B.JULY 2,1890 TOLEDO,OHIO
D.SEPT.9,1949 TOLEDO,OHIO

YR	CL	LEA	POS	G	REC
1912	CHI	N	P	6	0-1
	BLTL				

MADDEN, MICHAEL JOSEPH (KID)
B.OCT.29,1866 PORTLAND,ME.
D.MAR.16,1896 PORTLAND,MAINE

YR	CL	LEA	POS	GP	G	REC
1887	BOS	N	P		37	22-14
1888	BOS	N	P		19	7-12
1889	BOS	N	P	20	21	10-10
1890	BOS	P	P		14	3-2
1891	BOS	AA	P		4	0-2
	BAL	AA	P-O	31	36	14-10
						.257
	TL			125	131	56-50
						.281

MADDEN, THOMAS FRANCIS (BUNNY)
B.SEPT.14,1882 BOSTON,MASS.
D.JAN.24,1954 CAMBRIDGE,MASS.

YR	CL	LEA	POS	G	REC
1909	BOS	A	C	12	.168
1910	BOS	A	C	14	.400
1911	BOS	A	C	4	.200
	PHI	N	C	22	.276
	BRTR			52	.285

MADDEN, THOMAS JOSEPH
B.JULY 31,1883 PHILADELPHIA,PA.
D.JULY 26,1930 PHILADELPHIA,PA.

YR	CL	LEA	POS	G	REC
1906	BOS	N	O	4	.267
1910	NY	A	O	1	.000
	BLTL			5	.250

MADDERN, CLARENCE JAMES
B.SEPT.26,1921 BISBEE,ARIZ.

YR	CL	LEA	POS	G	REC
1946	CHI	N	O	3	.000
1948	CHI	N	O	80	.252
1949	CHI	N	1	10	.333
1951	CLE	A	O	11	.167
	BRTR			104	.248

MADDOX, ELLIOTT
B.DEC.21,1947 EAST ORANGE,N.J.

YR	CL	LEA	POS	G	REC
1970	DET	A	3-O-S/2	109	.248
1971	WAS	A	*O-3	128	.217
1972	TEX	A	O	98	.252
1973	TEX	A	O/3	100	.238
1974	NY	A	*O/2-3	137	.303
1975	NY	A	O/2	55	.307
1976	NY	A	O	18	.217
1977	BAL	A	O/3	49	.262
1978	NY	N	O-3/1	119	.257
	BRTR			813	.263

MADDOX, GARRY LEE
B.SEP.1,1949 CINCINNATI,OHIO

YR	CL	LEA	POS	G	REC
1972	SF	N	*O	125	.266
1973	SF	N	*O	144	.319
1974	SF	N	*O	135	.284
1975	SF	N	O	17	.135
1976	PHI	N	*O	99	.291
1976	PHI	N	*O	146	.330
1977	PHI	N	*O	139	.292
1978	PHI	N	*O	155	.288
	BRTR			960	.294

MADDOX, JERRY GLENN
B.JULY 26,1953 WHITTIER,CAL.

YR	CL	LEA	POS	G	REC
1978	ATL	N	/3	7	.214
	BRTR				

MADDOX, NICHOLAS
B.NOV.9,1886 GAVANSTOWN,MD.
D.NOV.27,1954 PITTSBURGH,PA.

YR	CL	LEA	POS	G	REC
1907	PIT	N	P	6	5-1
1908	PIT	N	P	36	23-8
1909	PIT	N	P	31	13-8
1910	PIT	N	P	20	2-3
	TR			93	43-20

MADIGAN, WILLIAM (TICE)
B.1868 WASHINGTON,D.C.
D.DEC.4,1954 WASHINGTON,D.C.

YR	CL	LEA	POS	G	REC
1886	WAS	N	P	14	1-13
	TR				

MADISON, ARTHUR
B.JAN.14,1872 CLARKSBURG,MASS.
D.JAN.27,1933 N.ADAMS,MASS.

YR	CL	LEA	POS	G	REC
1895	PHI	N	2-S	10	.400
1899	PIT	N	2-S	33	.269
	BRTR			43	.288

MADISON, DAVID PLEDGER (DAVE)
B.FEB.1,1921 BOROKSVILLE,MISS.

YR	CL	LEA	POS	G	REC
1950	NY	A	P	1	0-0
1952	STL	A	P	31	4-2
	DET	A	P	10	1-1
1953	DET	A	P	32	3-4
	BRTR			74	8-7

MADJESKI, EDWARD WILLIAM
(REAL NAME EDWARD WILLIAM MAJEWSKI)
B.JULY 24,1909 FAR ROCKAWAY,N.Y

YR	CL	LEA	POS	G	REC
1932	PHI	A	C	17	.229
1933	PHI	A	C	51	.282
1934	PHI	A	C	8	.375
	CHI	A	C	85	.221
1937	NY	N	C	5	.200
	BRTR			166	.241

MADLOCK, WILLIAM (BILL)
B.JAN.2,1951 MEMPHIS,TENN.

YR	CL	LEA	POS	G	REC
1973	TEX	A	3	21	.351
1974	CHI	N	*3	128	.313
1975	CHI	N	*3	130	.354
1976	CHI	N	*3	142	.339
1977	SF	N	*3/2	140	.302
1978	SF	N	*2/1	122	.309
	BRTR			683	.325

MADRID, SALVADOR (SAL)
B.JUNE 9,1920 EL PASO,TEX.
D.FEB.24,1977 FT.WAYNE,IND.

YR	CL	LEA	POS	G	REC
1947	CHI	N	S	8	.125
	BRTR				

MAESTRI, HECTOR ANIBAL
B.APR.19,1935 HAVANA,CUBA

YR	CL	LEA	POS	G	REC
1960	WAS	A	P	1	0-0
1961	WAS	A	P	1	0-1
	BRTR			2	0-1

MAGEE, LEO CHRISTOPHER (LEE)
(REAL NAME LEOPOLD CHRISTOPHER HOERNSCHEMEYER)
B.JUNE 4,1889 CINCINNATI,OHIO
D.MAR.14,1966 COLUMBUS,OHIO

YR	CL	LEA	POS	G	REC
1911	STL	N	2	21	.261
1912	STL	N	2-O	128	.290
1913	STL	N	2-O	137	.267
1914	STL	N	1-O	142	.284
1915	BRO	F	M-2	121	.330
1916	NY	A	O	131	.257
1917	NY	A	O	51	.220
	STL	A	O	36	.185
1918	CIN	N	2-3	119	.290
1919	BRO	N	2	45	.238
	CHI	N	2-S-3-O	79	.292
	BBTR			1010	.276

MAGEE, SHERWOOD ROBERT (SHERRY)
B.AUG.6,1884 CLARENDON,PA.
D.MAR.13,1929 PHILADELPHIA,PA.

YR	CL	LEA	POS	G	REC
1904	PHI	N	O	95	.277
1905	PHI	N	O	155	.299
1906	PHI	N	O	154	.282
1907	PHI	N	O	139	.328
1908	PHI	N	O	142	.283
1909	PHI	N	O	143	.270
1910	PHI	N	O	154	.331
1911	PHI	N	O	120	.288
1912	PHI	N	O	132	.306
1913	PHI	N	O	138	.306
1914	PHI	N	1-S-O	146	.314
1915	BOS	N	1-O	156	.280
1916	BOS	N	O	122	.241
1917	BOS	N	O	72	.255
	CIN	N	1-O	45	.324
1918	CIN	N	1-2-O	115	.297
1919	CIN	N	2-3-O	56	.215
	BRTR			2084	.291

MAGEE, WILLIAM M.
B.JAN.11,1868 BOSTON,MASS.

YR	CL	LEA	POS	G	REC
1897	LOU	N	P	20	4-13
1898	LOU	N	P	35	16-14
1899	LOU	N	P	11	4-6
	PHI	N	P	10	3-5
	WAS	N	P	5	1-4
1901	STL	N	P	1	0-1
	NY	N	P	6	0-3
1902	NY	N	P	3	0-0
	PHI	N	P	8	2-4
				99	30-50

MAGGERT, HARL VESS
B.FEB.13,1883 CROMWELL,IND.
D.JAN.7,1963 FRESNO,CAL.

YR	CL	LEA	POS	G	REC
1907	PIT	N	O	3	.000
1912	PHI	A	O	72	.256
	BLTR			75	.250

MAGGERT, HARL WARREN
B.MAY 4,1914 LOS ANGELES,CAL.

YR	CL	LEA	POS	G	REC
1938	BOS	N	O	66	.281
	BRTR				

MAGLIE, SALVATORE ANTHONY
(SAL) OR (THE BARBER)
B.APR.26,1917 NIAGARA FALLS,N.Y

YR	CL	LEA	POS	GP	G	REC
1945	NY	N	P	13	14	5-4
1950	NY	N	P		47	18-4
1951	NY	N	P		42	23-6
1952	NY	N	P		35	18-8
1953	NY	N	P		27	8-9
1954	NY	N	P		34	14-6
1955	NY	N	P		23	9-5
	CLE	A	P		10	0-2
1956	CLE	A	P		2	0-0
	BRO	N	P		28	13-5
1957	BRO	N	P		19	6-6
	NY	A	P		6	2-0
1958	NY	A	P		7	1-1
	STL	N	P		10	2-6
	BRTR			303	304	119-62

MAGNER, EDMUND BURKE (STUBBY)
B.FEB.20,1888 KALAMAZOO,MICH.
D.SEPT.6,1956 CHILLICOTHER,OHIO

YR	CL	LEA	POS	G	REC
1911	NY	A	2	12	.194
	BRTR				

MAGNER, WILLIAM JOHN
B.1855

YR	CL	LEA	POS	G	REC
1879	CIN	N	O	1	.000

MAGNUSON, JAMES ROBERT (JIM)
B.AUG.18,1946 MARINETTE,WIS.

YR	CL	LEA	POS	G	REC
1970	CHI	A	P	13	1-5
1971	CHI	A	P	15	1-1
1973	NY	A	/P	8	0-1
	BRTL			36	2-7

MAGOON, GEORGE HENRY
(MAGGIE) OR (TOPSY)
B.MAR.27,1875 ST.ALBANS,MAINE
D.DEC.6,1943 ROCHESTER,N.H.

YR	CL	LEA	POS	G	REC
1898	BRO	N	S	93	.227
1899	BAL	N	S	61	.252
	CHI	N	S	59	.235
1901	CIN	N	S	128	.251
1902	CIN	N	2-S	44	.275
1903	CIN	N	2	41	.216
	CHI	A	2	94	.227
	BRTR			520	.240

MAGRINI, PETER ALEXANDER (PETE)
B.JUNE 8,1942 SAN FRANCISCO,CAL.

YR	CL	LEA	POS	G	REC
1966	BOS	A	A/P	3	0-1
	BRTR				

YR	CL LEA POS	GP	G	REC

MAGUIRE, FREDERICK EDWARD
B.MAY 10,1899 ROCBURY,MASS.
D.NOV.3,1961 BRIGHTON,MASS.

1922	NY N 2		5	.333
1923	NY N 2-3		41	.200
1928	CHI N 2		140	.279
1929	BOS N 2		138	.252
1930	BOS N 2		146	.267
1931	BOS N 2		148	.228
	BRTR		618	.252

MAGUIRE, JACK
B.FEB.5,1925 ST.LOUIS,MO.

1950	NY N 1-0		29	.175
1951	NY N 0		16	.400
	PIT N 2-3		8	.000
	STL A 2-3-0		41	.244
	BRTR		94	.240

MAHADY, JAMES BERNARD
B.APR.22,1901 CORTLAND,N.Y.
D.AUG.9,1936 CORTLAND,N.Y.

| 1921 | NY N 2 | | 1 | .000 |
| | BRTR | | | |

MAHAFFEY, ARTHUR (ART)
B.JUNE 4,1938 CINCINNATI,OHIO

1960	PHI N P		14	7- 3
1961	PHI N P		36	11-19
1962	PHI N P	41	42	19-14
1963	PHI N P		26	7-10
1964	PHI N P		34	12- 9
1965	PHI N P		22	2- 5
1966	STL N P		12	1- 4
	BRTR	185	186	59-64

MAHAFFEY, LEE ROY (POPEYE)
B.FEB.9,1903 BELTON,S.C.
D.JULY 23,1969 ANDERSON,S.C.

1926	PIT N P		4	0- 0
1927	PIT N P		2	1- 0
1930	PHI A P		33	9- 5
1931	PHI A P		30	15- 4
1932	PHI A P		37	13-13
1933	PHI A P		33	13-10
1934	PHI A P		37	6- 7
1935	PHI A P		27	8- 4
1936	STL A P		21	2- 6
	BRTR		224	67-49

MAHAFFY, LOUIS W.
B.1874 MADISON,WIS.
D.1898 LOU N P

| 1898 | LOU N P | | 2 | 0- 1 |

MAHAN, ARTHUR LEO
B.JUNE 8,1913 SOMERVILLE,MASS.

1940	PHI N P-1	1	146	0- 0
				.244
	BLTL			

MAHARG, WILLIAM
B.MAR.19,1887 PHILADELPHIA,PA.

1912	DET A 3		1	.000
1916	PHI N P		1	.000
	TR		2	.000

MAHER, FRANK
B.PHILADELPHIA,PA.

| 1902 | PHI N S | | 2 | .000 |
| | TR | | | |

MAHER, THOMAS
B.PHILADELPHIA,PA.

| 1902 | PHI N 0 | | 1 | .000 |

MAHLBERG, GREGORY JOHN (GREG)
B.AUG.8,1952 MILWAUKEE,WIS.

| 1978 | TEX A /C | | 1 | .000 |
| | BRTR | | | |

MAHLER, MICHAEL JAMES (MICKEY)
B.JULY 30,1952 MONTGOMERY,ALA.

1977	ATL N /P		5	1- 2
1978	ATL N P		34	4-11
	BBTL		39	5-13

MAHON, ALFRED GWIN (LEFTY)
B.SEPT.23,1910 ALBION,NEB.

| 1930 | PHI A P | | 3 | 0- 0 |
| | BLTL | | | |

MAHONEY, CHRISTOPHER JOHN
B.JUNE 11,1885 MILTON,MASS.
D.JULY 15,1954 VISALIA,CAL.

| 1910 | BOS A P | | 3 | 0- 1 |
| | BRTR | | | |

MAHONEY, DANIEL J.
B.MAR.20,1864 SPRINGFIELD,MASS.
D.FEB.1,1904 SPRINGFIELD,MASS.

1892	CIN N C		5	.190
1895	WAS N C		6	.167
	BRTR		11	.182

MAHONEY, DANIEL JOSEPH
B.SEPT.6,1888 HAVERHILL,MASS.
D.SEPT.28,1960 UTICA,N.Y.

| 1911 | CIN N H | | 1 | .000 |

MAHONEY, GEORGE W. (BIG MIKE)
B.DEC.5,1873 BOSTON,MASS.
D.JAN.3,1940 BOSTON,MASS.

1897	BOS N C		2	.500
1898	STL N 1		2	.000
			4	.111

MAHONEY, JAMES THOMAS (JIM) OR (MOE)
B.MAY 26,1934 ENGLEWOOD,N.J.

1959	BOS A S		31	.130
1961	WAS A 2-S		43	.241
1962	CLE A 2-S-3		41	.243
1965	HOU N /S		5	.200
	BRTR		120	.229

MAHONEY, ROBERT PAUL (BOB)
B.JUNE 20,1928 LE ROY,MINN.

1951	CHI A P		3	0- 0
	STL A P		30	2- 5
1952	STL A P		3	0- 0
	BRTR		36	2- 5

MAIER, ROBERT PHILLIP
B.SEPT.5,1915 DUNELLEN,N.J.

| 1945 | DET A 3-0 | | 132 | .263 |
| | BRTR | | | |

MAILHO, EMIL PIERRE (LEFTY)
B.DEC.16,1909 BERKELEY,CAL.

| 1936 | PHI A 0 | | 21 | .056 |
| | BLTL | | | |

MAILS, JOHN WALTER (WALTER)
(DUSTER) OR (THE GREAT)
B.OCT.1,1895 SAN QUENTIN,CAL.
D.JULY 5,1974 SAN FRANCISCO,CAL

1915	BRO N P		2	0- 1
1916	BRO N P		11	0- 1
1920	CLE A P		9	7- 0
1921	CLE A P		34	14- 8
1922	CLE A P		26	4- 7
1925	STL N P		21	7- 7
1926	STL N P		1	0- 1
	BLTL		104	32-25

MAIN, FORREST HARRY (WOODY)
B.FEB.12,1922 DELANO,CAL.

1948	PIT N P		17	1- 1
1950	PIT N P		12	1- 0
1952	PIT N P		48	2-12
1953	PIT N P		2	0- 0
	BRTR		79	4-13

MAIN, MILES GRANT (ALEX)
B.MAY 13,1884 MONTROSE,MICH.
D.DEC.29,1965 ROYAL OAK,MICH.

1914	DET A P		32	6- 6
1915	KC F P		35	13-14
1918	PHI N P	8	9	2- 2
	BLTR	75	76	21-22

MAINS, JAMES ROYAL
B.JULY 7,1868 N.WINDHAM,MAINE
D.MAY 23,1923 BRIDGTON,MAINE

| 1943 | PHI A P | | 1 | 0- 1 |
| | BRTR | | | |

MAINS, WILLARD EBEN (GRASSHOPPER)
B.JULY 7,1868 N.WINDHAM,ME.
D.MAY 23,1923

1888	CHI N P		2	1- 1
1891	CIN AA P-0	26	27	12-10
				.280
	MIL AA P		2	0- 2
1896	BOS N P		10	3- 2
	TR	40	41	16-15
				.306

MAISEL, CHARLES LOUIS
B.APR.21,1894 CATONSVILLE,MD.
D.AUG.25,1953 BALTIMORE,MD.

| 1915 | BAL A F C | | 1 | .000 |
| | BRTR | | | |

MAISEL, FREDERICK CHARLES
(FRITZ) OR (FLASH)
B.DEC.23,1889 CATONSVILLE,MD.
D.APR.22,1967 BALTIMORE,MD.

1913	NY A 3		51	.257
1914	NY A 3		149	.239
1915	NY A 3		135	.281
1916	NY A 0		53	.228
1917	NY A 3		113	.198
1918	STL A 3		90	.232
	BRTR		591	.242

MAISEL, GEORGE JOHN
B.MAR.12,1892 CATONSVILLE,MD.
D.NOV.20,1968 BALTIMORE,MD.

1913	STL A 0		11	.157
1916	DET A 3		8	.000
1921	CHI N 3		111	.310
1922	CHI N 3		58	.190
	BRTR		168	.281

MAJESKI, HENRY (HANK) OR (HEENEY)
B.DEC.13,1916 STATEN ISLAND,N.Y

1939	BOS N 3		106	.272
1940	BOS N H		3	.000
1941	BOS N 3		19	.145
1946	NY A 3		8	.083
	PHI A 3		78	.250
1947	PHI A 2-S-3		141	.280
1948	PHI A 5-3		148	.310
1949	PHI A 3		114	.277
1950	CHI A 3		122	.309
1951	CHI A 3		12	.257
	PHI A 3		89	.285
1952	PHI A 3		34	.256
	CLE A 2-3		36	.296
1953	CLE A 2-3-0		50	.300
1954	CLE A 2-3		57	.281
1955	CLE A 2-3		36	.188
	BAL A 2-3		16	.171
	BRTR		1069	.279

MAJEWSKI, EDWARD WILLIAM
(PLAYED UNDER NAME OF
EDWARD WILLIAM MADJESKI)

MAKOSKY, FRANK
B.JAN.20,1912 BOONTON,N.J.

| 1937 | NY A P | | 26 | 5- 2 |
| | BRTR | | | |

MAKOWSKI, THOMAS ANTHONY (TOM)
B.DEC.22,195C BUFFALO,N.Y.

| 1975 | DET A /P | | 3 | 0- 0 |
| | BRTL | | | |

MAKOWSKY, HARRY DUQUESNE
(PLAYED UNDER NAME OF
HARRY DUQUESNE MARKELL)

MALARKEY, JOHN S. (LIZ)
B.MAY 4,,872 SPRINGFIELD,OHIO
D.OCT.29,1949 CINCINNATI,OHIO

1894	WAS N P		4	2- 1
1895	WAS N P		22	0- 8
1896	WAS N P		1	0- 1
1899	CHI N P		1	0- 1
1902	BOS N P-2		20	9-11
				.210
1903	BOS N P		32	11-15
			80	22-37
				.172

MALARKEY, WILLIAM JOHN
B.NOV.26,1878 PORT BYRON,ILL.
D.DEC.12,1956 PHOENIX,ARIZ.

| 1908 | NY N P | | 15 | 0- 2 |
| | BRTR | | | |

MALAY, CHARLES FRANCIS
B.JUNE 13,1879 BROOKLYN,N.Y.
D.SEPT.18,1949 BROOKLYN,N.Y.

| 1905 | BRO N 2-0 | | 101 | .252 |
| | B8TR | | | |

MALAY, JOSEPH CHARLES
B.OCT.25,1935 BROOKLYN,N.Y.

1933	NY N 1		8	.125
1935	NY N H		1	1.000
	BLTL		9	.100

MALINOSKY, ANTHONY FRANCIS
B.OCT.5,1909 COLLINSVILLE,ILL.

| 1937 | BRO N S-3 | | 35 | .228 |
| | BRTR | | | |

MALIS, CYRUS SOL
B.FEB.26,1907 PHILADELPHIA,PA.
D.JAN.12,1971 N.HOLLYWOOD,CAL.

| 1934 | PHI N P | | 1 | 0- 0 |
| | BRTR | | | |

MALKMUS, ROBERT EDWARD (BOBBY)
B.JULY 4,1931 NEWARK,N.J.

1957	MIL N 2		13	.091
1958	WAS A 2-S-3		41	.186
1959	WAS A H		6	.000
1960	PHI N 2-S-3		79	.211
1961	PHI N 2-S-3		121	.231
1962	PHI N S		8	.200
	BRTR		268	.215

MALLETT, GERALD GORDON (JERRY)
B.SEPT.18,1935 BONNE TERRE,MO.

| 1959 | BOS A 0 | | 4 | .267 |
| | BRTR | | | |

MALLETTE, MALCOLM FRANCIS (MAL)
B.JAN.30,1922 SYRACUSE,N.Y.

| 1950 | BRO N P | | 2 | 0- 0 |
| | BLTL | | | |

MALLON, LESLIE CLYDE
B.NOV.21,1905 SWEETWATER,TEX.
DECEASED

1931	PHI N 2		122	.309
1932	PHI N 2		103	.259
1934	BOS N 2		42	.295
1935	BOS N 2-3-0		116	.274
	BRTR		383	.283

YR	CL LEA POS	GP	G	REC

MALONEE, HOWARD BENNETT
(BEN) OR (LEFTY)
B.MAR.31,1894 BALTIMORE,MD.
D.FEB.19,1978 BALTIMORE,MD.

YR	CL	LEA	POS	GP	G	REC
1921	PHI	A	O		7	.261
	BLTL					

MALLONEE, JULIUS NORRIS
B.APR.4,1900 CHARLOTTE,N.C.
D.DEC.26,1934 CHARLOTTE,N.C.

YR	CL	LEA	POS	GP	G	REC
1925	CHI	A	O		2	.000
	BLTR					

MALLORY, JAMES BAUGH (SUNNY JIM)
B.SEPT.1,1918 LAWRENCEVILLE,VA.

YR	CL	LEA	POS	GP	G	REC
1940	WAS	A	O		4	.167
1945	STL	N	O		13	.233
	NY	N	O		37	.298
	BRTR				54	.268

MALLORY, SHELDON
B.JULY 16,1953 ARGO,ILL.

YR	CL	LEA	POS	GP	G	REC
1977	OAK	A	O/1		64	.214
	BLTL					

MALLOY, ARCHIBALD ALEXANDER
(ALEX) OR (LICK)
B.OCT.31,1886 LAURINBURG,N.C.
D.MAR.1,1961 FERRIS,TEX.

YR	CL	LEA	POS	GP	G	REC
1910	STL	A	P		7	0- 6
	BRTR					

MALLOY, HERMAN (TUG)
B.JUNE 1,1885 MASSILLON,OHIO
D.MAY 9,1942 NIMISHILLEN,OHIO

YR	CL	LEA	POS	GP	G	REC
1907	DET	A	P		1	0- 1
1908	DET	A	P		3	0- 2
	BRTR				4	0- 3

MALLOY, ROBERT PAUL
B.MAY 28,1918 CANONSBURG,PA.

YR	CL	LEA	POS	GP	G	REC
1943	CIN	N	P		6	0- 0
1944	CIN	N	P		9	1- 1
1946	CIN	N	P		27	2- 5
1947	CIN	N	P		1	0- 0
1949	STL	A	P		5	1- 1
	BRTR				48	4- 7

MALMBERG, HARRY WILLIAM
(HARRY) OR (SWEDE)
B.JULY 31,1926 FAIRFIELD,ALA.
D.OCT.29,1976 SAN FRANCISCO,CAL.

YR	CL	LEA	POS	GP	G	REC
1955	DET	A	2		67	.216
	BRTR					

MALONE

YR	CL	LEA	POS	GP	G	REC
1872	ECK	NA	P-O	3	4	0- 3
						.250

MALONE, EDWARD RUSSELL
B.JUNE 16,1920 CHICAGO,ILL.

YR	CL	LEA	POS	GP	G	REC
1949	CHI	A	C		55	.271
1950	CHI	A	C		31	.225
	BRTR				86	.257

MALONE, FERGUSON G.
B.1842 IRELAND
D.JAN.18,1905 SEATTLE,WASH.

YR	CL	LEA	POS	GP	G	REC
1871	ATH	NA	C		27	.366
1872	ATH	NA	C-1		39	.269
1873	PHI	NA	C-S		52	-
1874	CHI	NA	C		47	-
1875	PHI	NA	C-1-O		27	.228
1876	ATH	N	C		22	.229
1884	KEY	U	M-C		1	.250
	BRTL				215	-

MALONE, LEWIS ALOYSIUS
B.MAR.13,1897 BALTIMORE,MD.
D.FEB.17,1972 BROOKLYN,N.Y.

YR	CL	LEA	POS	GP	G	REC
1915	PHI	A	2		76	.204
1916	PHI	A	S		5	.000
1917	BRO	N	H		1	.000
1919	BRO	N	2-S-3		51	.204
	BRTR				133	.202

MALONE, PERCE LEIGH (PAT)
B.SEPT.25,1902 ALTOONA,PA.
D.MAY 13,1943 ALTOONA,PA.

YR	CL	LEA	POS	GP	G	REC
1928	CHI	N	P		42	18-13
1929	CHI	N	P		40	22-10
1930	CHI	N	P		45	20- 9
1931	CHI	N	P		36	16- 9
1932	CHI	N	P		37	15-17
1933	CHI	N	P		31	10-14
1934	CHI	N	P		34	14- 7
1935	NY	A	P		29	3- 5
1936	NY	A	P		35	12- 4
1937	NY	A	P		28	4- 4
	BLTR				357	134-92

MALONEY, CHARLES MICHAEL
B.MAY 22,1886 CAMBRIDGE,MASS.
D.JAN.17,1967 ARLINGTON,MASS.

YR	CL	LEA	POS	GP	G	REC
1908	BOS	N	P		1	0- 0
	BRTR					

MALONEY, JAMES WILLIAM (JIM)
B.JUNE 2,1940 FRESNO,CAL.

YR	CL	LEA	POS	GP	G	REC
1960	CIN	N	P		11	2- 6
1961	CIN	N	P-O	27	30	6- 7
						.379
1962	CIN	N	P	22	24	9- 7
1963	CIN	N	P	33	34	23- 7
1964	CIN	N	P		31	15-10
1965	CIN	N	P	33	35	20- 9
1966	CIN	N	P	32	35	16- 8
1967	CIN	N	P	30	33	15-11
1968	CIN	N	P	33	38	16-10
1969	CIN	N	P		30	12- 5
1970	CIN	N	/P		7	0- 1
1971	CAL	A	P		13	0- 3
	BLTR			302	321	134-84
						.201

MALONEY, JOHN
D.JULY 21,1890

YR	CL	LEA	POS	GP	G	REC
1876	MUT	N	O		2	.286
1877	HAR	N	O		1	.250
					3	.273

MALONEY, PATRICK WILLIAM
B.JAN.19,1888 GROSVENORDALE,CONN.

YR	CL	LEA	POS	GP	G	REC
1912	NY	A	O		22	.215

MALONEY, WILLIAM ALPHONSE (BILLY)
B.JUNE 5,1878 LEWISTON,ME.
D.SEPT.2,1960 BRECKENRIDGE,TEX.

YR	CL	LEA	POS	GP	G	REC
1901	MIL	A	C-O		84	.297
1902	STL	A	C-O		30	.203
	CIN	N	C-O		24	.228
1905	CHI	N	O		143	.260
1906	BRO	N	O		151	.221
1907	BRO	N	O		144	.229
1908	BRO	N	O		107	.195
	BLTR				685	.236

MALOY, PAUL AUGUSTUS (BIFF)
B.JUNE 4,1892 BASCOM,OHIO
D.MAR.18,1976 SANDUSKY,OHIO

YR	CL	LEA	POS	GP	G	REC
1913	BOS	A	P		2	0- 0
	BRTR					

MALTZBERGER, GORDON RALPH
(GORDON) OR (MALTZY)
B.SEPT.4,1912 UTOPIA,TEX.
D.DEC.11,1974 RIALTO,TEX.

YR	CL	LEA	POS	GP	G	REC
1943	CHI	A	P		37	7- 4
1944	CHI	A	P		46	10- 5
1946	CHI	A	P		19	2- 0
1947	CHI	A	P		33	1- 4
	BRTR				135	20-13

MALZONE, FRANK JAMES
B.FEB.28,1930 BRONX,N.Y.

YR	CL	LEA	POS	GP	G	REC
1955	BOS	A	3		6	.350
1956	BOS	A	3		27	.165
1957	BOS	A	3		153	.292
1958	BOS	A	3		155	.295
1959	BOS	A	3		154	.280
1960	BOS	A	3		152	.271
1961	BOS	A	3		151	.266
1962	BOS	A	3		156	.283
1963	BOS	A	3		151	.291
1964	BOS	A	3		148	.264
1965	BOS	A	3		106	.239
1966	CAL	A	3		82	.206
	BRTR				1441	.274

MAMAUX, ALBERT LEON
B.MAY 30,1894 PITTSBURGH,PA.
D.JAN.2,1963 SANTA MONICA,CAL.

YR	CL	LEA	POS	GP	G	REC
1913	PIT	N	P		1	0- 0
1914	PIT	N	P		13	5- 2
1915	PIT	N	P		38	21- 8
1916	PIT	N	P		45	21-15
1917	PIT	N	P		16	2-11
1918	BRO	N	P		2	0- 1
1919	BRO	N	P		30	10-12
1920	BRO	N	P		41	12- 8
1921	BRO	N	P		12	3- 3
1922	BRO	N	P		37	1- 4
1923	BRO	N	P		5	0- 2
1924	NY	A	P		14	1- 1
	BRTR				254	76-67

MANCUSO, AUGUST RODNEY
(GUS) OR (BLACKIE)
B.DEC.5,1905 GALVESTON,TEX.

YR	CL	LEA	POS	GP	G	REC
1928	STL	N	C		11	.184
1930	STL	N	C		76	.366
1931	STL	N	C		67	.262
1932	STL	N	C		103	.284
1933	NY	N	C		144	.264
1934	NY	N	C		122	.245
1935	NY	N	C		128	.298
1936	NY	N	C		139	.301
1937	NY	N	C		86	.279
1938	NY	N	C		52	.348
1939	CHI	N	C		80	.231
1940	BRO	N	C		60	.229
1941	STL	N	C		106	.229
1942	STL	N	C		5	.077
	NY	N	C		39	.193
1943	NY	N	C		94	.198
1944	NY	N	C		78	.251
1945	PHI	N	C		70	.199
	BRTR				1460	.265

MANCUSO, FRANK OCTAVIUS
B.MAY 23,1918 HOUSTON,TEX.

YR	CL	LEA	POS	GP	G	REC
1944	STL	A	C		88	.205
1945	STL	A	C		119	.268
1946	STL	A	C		87	.240
1947	WAS	A	C		43	.229
	BRTR				337	.241

MANDA, CARL ALAN
B.NOV.16,1886 LITTLE RIVER,KAN.

YR	CL	LEA	POS	GP	G	REC
1914	CHI	A	2		9	.333
	BRTR					

MANDERS, HAROLD CARL
B.JUNE 14,1917 WAUKEE,IOWA

YR	CL	LEA	POS	GP	G	REC
1941	DET	A	P		8	1- 0
1942	DET	A	P		18	2- 0
1946	DET	A	P		2	0- 0
	CHI	N	P		2	0- 0
	BRTR				30	3- 1

MANGAN, JAMES DANIEL (JIM)
B.SEPT.24,1929 SAN FRANCISCO,CAL

YR	CL	LEA	POS	GP	G	REC
1952	PIT	N	C		11	.154
1954	PIT	N	C		14	.192
1956	NY	N	C		20	.100
	BRTR				45	.153

MANGUAL, ANGEL LUIS (GUILBE)
B.MAR.19,1947 JUANA DIAZ,P.R.

YR	CL	LEA	POS	GP	G	REC
1969	PIT	N	/O		6	.250
1971	OAK	A	O		94	.286
1972	OAK	A	O		91	.246
1973	OAK	A	O-D/1-2		74	.224
1974	OAK	A	O-D/3		115	.233
1975	OAK	A	O-D		62	.220
1976	OAK	A	/O		8	.167
	BRTR				450	.245

MANGUAL, JOSE MANUEL [GUILBE] (PEPE)
B.MAY 23,1952 PONCE,P.R.

YR	CL	LEA	POS	GP	G	REC
1972	MON	N	O		8	.273
1973	MON	N	O		33	.177
1974	MON	N	O		23	.311
1975	MON	N	*O		140	.245
1976	MON	N	O		66	.260
	NY	N	O		41	.186
1977	NY	N	/O		8	.143
	BRTR				319	.242

MANGUM, LEO ALLAN (BLACKIE)
B.MAY 24,1896 DURHAM,N.C.
D.JULY 9,1974 LIMA,OHIO

YR	CL	LEA	POS	GP	G	REC
1924	CHI	A	P		13	1- 4
1925	CHI	A	P		7	1- 0
1928	NY	N	P		1	0- 0
1932	BOS	N	P		7	0- 0
1933	BOS	N	P		25	4- 3
1934	BOS	N	P		29	5- 3
1935	BOS	N	P		3	0- 0
	BRTR				85	11-10

MANGUS, GEORGE GRAHAM
B.MAY 22,1890 RED CREEK,N.Y.
D.AUG.10,1933 RUTLAND,MASS.

YR	CL	LEA	POS	GP	G	REC
1912	PHI	N	O		10	.200
	BLTR					

MANION, CLYDE JENNINGS (PETE)
B.OCT.30,1896 JEFFERSON CITY,MO
D.SEPT.4,1967 DETROIT,MICH.

YR	CL	LEA	POS	GP	G	REC
1920	DET	A	C		32	.275
1921	DET	A	C		11	.111
1922	DET	A	C		42	.275
1923	DET	A	C		23	.136
1924	DET	A	C		14	.231
1926	DET	A	C		75	.198
1927	DET	A	H		1	.000
1928	STL	A	C		76	.226
1929	STL	A	C		35	.243
1930	STL	A	C		57	.216
1932	CIN	N	C		49	.207
1933	CIN	N	C		36	.167
1934	CIN	N	C		25	.185
	BRTR				476	.218

MANKOWSKI, PHILIP ANTHONY (PHIL)
B.JAN.9,1953 BUFFALO,N.Y.

YR	CL	LEA	POS	GP	G	REC
1976	DET	A	3		24	.271
1977	DET	A	3/2		94	.276
1978	DET	A	3		88	.275
	BLTR				206	.275

MANLOVE, CHARLES HENRY (CHICK)
B.OCT.8,1862 PHILADELPHIA,PA.
D.FEB.12,1952 ALTOONA,PA.

YR	CL	LEA	POS	GP	G	REC
1884	ALT	U	C		1	.750
	NY	N	C		2	.000
	BRTR				3	.231

MANN, BEN GARTH (GARTH) OR (RED)
B.NOV.16,1915 BRANDON,TEX.

YR	CL	LEA	POS	GP	G	REC
1944	CHI	N	H		1	.000
	BRTR					

MANN, FRED I.
B.APR.1,1858 SUTTON,VT.
D.APR.6,1916 SPRINGFIELD,MASS.

YR	CL	LEA	POS	GP	G	REC
1882	WOR	N	1-3		19	.241
	ATH	AA	3		29	.224
1883	COL	AA	1-S-3-O		96	.230
1884	COL	AA	O		99	.276
1885	PIT	AA	O		100	.253
1886	PIT	AA	O		117	.259
1887	CLE	AA	O		64	.375
	ATH	AA	O		55	.310
	BL				579	.277

MANN, JOHN LEO
B.FEB.4,1898 FONTANET,IND.
D.MAR.31,1977 TERRE HAUTE,IND.

YR	CL	LEA	POS	GP	G	REC
1928	CHI	A	3		6	.286

MANN, LESLIE (LES) OR (MAJOR)
B.NOV.18,1893 LINCOLN,NEB.
D.JAN.14,1962 PASADENA,CAL.

YR	CL	LEA	POS	GP	G	REC
1913	BOS	N	O		120	.253
1914	BOS	N	O		126	.247
1915	CHI	F	O		135	.306
1916	CHI	N	O		127	.272
1917	CHI	N	O		117	.273
1918	CHI	N	O		129	.288
1919	CHI	N	O		80	.227
	BOS	N	O		40	.285
1920	BOS	N	O		115	.276
1921	STL	N	O		97	.328
1922	STL	N	O		84	.347
1923	STL	N	O		38	.371
	CIN	N	O		8	.000
1924	BOS	N	O		32	.275
1925	BOS	N	O		60	.342
1926	BOS	N	O		50	.302
1927	BOS	N	O		29	.258
	NY	N	O		29	.328
1928	NY	N	O		82	.264
	BRTR				1498	.282

MANNING, ERNEST DEVON (ED)
B.OCT.9,1890 FLORALA,ALA.
D.APR.28,1973 PENSACOLA,FLA.

YR	CL	LEA	POS	GP	G	REC
1914	STL	A	P		7	0- 0
	BLTR					

MANNING, JAMES BENJAMIN
B.JULY 21,1943 L ANSE,MICH.

YR	CL	LEA	POS	GP	G	REC
1962	MIN	N	P		5	0- 0
	BRTR					

MANNING, JAMES H.
B.JAN.31,1862 FALL RIVER,MASS.
D.OCT.22,1929 EDINBURG,TEX.

YR	CL	LEA	POS	GP	G	REC
1884	BOS	N	2-S-3-O		84	.241
1885	BOS	N	S-O		84	.206
	DET	N	S		20	.269
1886	POR	N	O		26	.185
1887	DET	N	O		13	.250
1889	KC	AA	M-2-O		132	.204
	TR				359	.217

NON-PLAYING MANAGER WAS[A] 1901

MANNING, JOHN E. (JACK)
B.DEC.20,1853 BRAINTREE,MASS.
D.AUG.19,1929 BOSTON,MASS.

YR	CL	LEA	POS	GP	G	REC
1873	BOS	NA	1-O		33	.311
1874	BAL	NA	P-2-	19	42	4-15
			S			-
	HAR	NA	S		1	-
1875	BOS	NA	P-1-	16	77	14- 2
			3-O			.285
1876	BOS	N	P-O	21	70	15- 6
						.258
1877	CIN	N	P-1-	9	58	0- 4
			2-S-O			.315
1878	BOS	N	P-O	1	60	1- 0
						.254
1880	CIN	N	1-O		48	.216
1881	BUF	N	O		1	.000
1883	PHI	N	O		97	.265
1884	PHI	N	O		103	.272
1885	PHI	N	O		107	.256
1886	BAL	AA	O		137	.227
	BRTR			66	834	34-27
						-

MANNING, RICHARD EUGENE (RICK)
B.SEPT.2,1954 NIAGARA FALLS,N.Y.

YR	CL	LEA	POS	GP	G	REC
1975	CLE	A	*O		120	.285
1976	CLE	A	*O		138	.292
1977	CLE	A	O		68	.226
1978	CLE	A	*O		148	.263
	BLTR				474	.272

MANNING, TIMOTHY E.
B.CHICAGO,ILL.

YR	CL	LEA	POS	GP	G	REC
1882	PRO	N	C-S		19	.105
1883	BAL	AA	2		35	.233
1884	BAL	AA	2		91	.207
1885	BAL	AA	2		43	.201
	PRO	N	S		10	.086
					198	.193

MANNING, WALTER S. (RUBE)
B.APR.29,1883 CHAMBERSBURG,PA.
D.APR.23,1930 WILLIAMSPORT,PA.

YR	CL	LEA	POS	GP	G	REC
1907	NY	A	P		1	0- 1
1908	NY	A	P	42	44	13-16
1909	NY	A	P		26	7-11
1910	NY	A	P		16	2- 4
	BRTR			85	87	22-32

MANNO, DONALD D.
B.MAY 15,1915 WILLIAMSPORT,PA.

YR	CL	LEA	POS	GP	G	REC
1940	BOS	N	O		3	.286
1941	BOS	N	1-3-O		22	.167
	BRTR				25	.189

MANSELL, JOHN
B.1861 AUBURN,N.Y.
D.FEB.20,1925 WILLARD,N.Y.

YR	CL	LEA	POS	GP	G	REC
1882	ATH	AA	O		32	.237
	BL					

MANSELL, MICHAEL R.
B.JAN.15,1858 AUBURN,N.Y.
D.DEC.4,1902 AUBURN,N.Y.

YR	CL	LEA	POS	GP	G	REC
1879	SYR	N	O		66	.211
1880	CIN	N	O		53	.192
1882	PIT	AA	O		73	.283
1883	PIT	AA	O		90	.240
1884	PIT	AA	O		27	.131
	ATH	AA	O		20	.194
	RIC	AA	O		29	.301
	BL				358	.235

MANSELL, THOMAS E. (BRICK)
B.JAN.1,1855 AUBURN,N.Y.
D.OCT.6,1934 AUBURN,N.Y.

YR	CL	LEA	POS	GP	G	REC
1879	TRO	N	O		39	.242
	SYR	N	O		1	.255
1883	DET	N	P-O	1	34	0- 0
						.213
	STL	AA	O		28	.370
1884	CIN	AA	O		65	.244
	COL	AA	O		23	.211
	BL			1	190	0- 0
						.254

MANSKE, LOUIS HUGO
B.JULY 4,1884 MILWAUKEE,WIS.
D.APR.27,1963 MILWAUKEE,WIS.

YR	CL	LEA	POS	GP	G	REC
1906	PIT	N	P		2	0- 0
	BLTL					

MANTILLA, FELIX (LAMELA)
B.JULY 29,1934 ISABELA,P.R.

YR	CL	LEA	POS	GP	G	REC
1956	MIL	N	S-3		35	.283
1957	MIL	N	2-S-3-O		71	.236
1958	MIL	N	2-S-3-O		85	.221
1959	MIL	N	2-S-3-O		103	.215
1960	MIL	N	S-O		63	.257
1961	MIL	N	2-S-3-O		45	.215
1962	NY	N	2-S-3		141	.275
1963	BOS	A	2-S-O		66	.315
1964	BOS	A	2-S-3-O		133	.289
1965	BOS	A	*2-O/1		150	.275
1966	HOU	N	1-3/2-O		77	.219
	BRTR				969	.261

MANTLE, MICKEY CHARLES
(MICKEY) OR (THE COMMERCE COMET)
B.OCT.20,1931 SPAVINAW,OKLA.

YR	CL	LEA	POS	GP	G	REC
1951	NY	A	O		96	.267
1952	NY	A	3-O		142	.311
1953	NY	A	O		127	.295
1954	NY	A	2-S-O		146	.300
1955	NY	A	S-O		147	.306
1956	NY	A	O		150	.353
1957	NY	A	O		144	.365
1958	NY	A	O		150	.304
1959	NY	A	O		144	.285
1960	NY	A	O		153	.275
1961	NY	A	O		153	.317
1962	NY	A	O		123	.321
1963	NY	A	O		65	.314
1964	NY	A	O		143	.303
1965	NY	A	*O		122	.255
1966	NY	A	O		108	.288
1967	NY	A	*1		144	.245
1968	NY	A	*1		144	.237
	BBTR				2401	.298

MANUEL, CHARLES FUQUA (CHARLIE)
B.JAN.4,1944 NORTH FORK,W.VA.

YR	CL	LEA	POS	GP	G	REC
1969	MIN	A	O		83	.207
1970	MIN	A	O		59	.188
1971	MIN	A	/O		18	.125
1972	MIN	A	O		63	.205
1974	LA	N	/H		4	.333
1975	LA	N	H		15	.133
	BLTR				242	.198

MANUEL, JERRY
B.DEC.23,1953 HAHIRA,GA.

YR	CL	LEA	POS	GP	G	REC
1975	DET	A	/2		6	.056
1976	DET	A	2/S		54	.140
	BBTR				60	.115

MANUEL, MARK GARFIELD (MOXIE)
B.OCT.16,1881 METROPOLIS,ILL.
D.APR.26,1924 MEMPHIS,TENN.

YR	CL	LEA	POS	GP	G	REC
1905	WAS	A	P		3	0- 0
1908	CHI	A	P	17		2- 4
	BRTB			20		2- 4

MANUSH, FRANK BENJAMIN
B.SEPT.18,1883 TUSCUMBIA,ALA.
D.JAN.5,1965 LAGUNA BEACH,CAL.

YR	CL	LEA	POS	GP	G	REC
1908	PHI	A	3		23	.156
	BRTR					

MANUSH, HENRY EMMETT (HEINIE)
B.JULY 20,1901 TUSCUMBIA,ALA.
D.MAY 12,1971 SARASOTA,FLA.

YR	CL	LEA	POS	GP	G	REC
1923	DET	A	O		109	.334
1924	DET	A	O		120	.289
1925	DET	A	O		99	.303
1926	DET	A	O		136	.378
1927	DET	A	O		152	.299
1928	STL	A	O		154	.378
1929	STL	A	O		142	.355
1930	STL	A	O		49	.328
	WAS	A	O		88	.362
1931	WAS	A	O		146	.307
1932	WAS	A	O		149	.342
1933	WAS	A	O		153	.336
1934	WAS	A	O		137	.349
1935	WAS	A	O		119	.273
1936	BOS	A	O		82	.291
1937	BRO	N	O		132	.333
1938	BRO	N	O		17	.235
	PIT	N	O		15	.308
1939	PIT	N	O		10	.000
	BLTL				2009	.331

MANVILLE, RICHARD WESLEY (DICK)
B.DEC.25,1926 DES MOINES,IOWA

YR	CL	LEA	POS	GP	G	REC
1950	BOS	N	P		1	0- 0
1952	CHI	N	P		11	0- 0
	BRTR				12	0- 0

MAPEL, ROLLA HAMILTON (LEFTY)
B.MAR.9,1890 LEE S SUMMITT,MO.
D.APR.6,1966 SAN DIEGO,CAL.

YR	CL	LEA	POS	GP	G	REC
1919	STL	A	P		4	0- 3
	BLTL					

MAPES, CLIFFORD FRANKLIN (CLIFF)
B.MAR.13,1922 SUTHERLAND,NEB.

YR	CL	LEA	POS	GP	G	REC
1948	NY	A	O		53	.250
1949	NY	A	O		111	.247
1950	NY	A	O		108	.247
1951	NY	A	O		45	.216
	STL	A	O		56	.274
1952	DET	A	O		86	.197
	BLTR				459	.242

MAPLE, HOWARD ALBERT (MAPE)
B.JULY 20,1903 ADRIAN,MO.
D.NOV.9,1970 PORTLAND,ORE.

YR	CL	LEA	POS	GP	G	REC
1932	WAS	A	C		44	.244
	BLTR					

MAPPES, GEORGE RICHARD (DICK)
B.DEC.25,1865 ST.LOUIS,MO.
D.FEB.20,1934 ST.LOUIS,MO.

YR	CL	LEA	POS	GP	G	REC
1885	BAL	AA	2		6	.211
1886	STL	N	C		6	.143
					12	.182

MARANDA, GEORGES HENRI
B.JAN.15,1932 LEVIS,QUE.,CAN.

YR	CL	LEA	POS	GP	G	REC
1960	SF	N	P		17	1- 4
1962	MIN	A	P		32	1- 3
	BRTR				49	2- 7

```
YR   CL LEA POS      GP    G    REC        YR   CL LEA POS      GP    G    REC        YR   CL LEA POS      GP    G    REC
```

MARANVILLE, WALTER JAMES
VINCENT (RABBIT)
B.NOV.11,1891 SPRINGFIELD,MASS.
D.JAN.5,1954 NEW YORK,N.Y.
```
1912 BOS N S             26   .209
1913 BOS N S            143   .247
1914 BOS N S            156   .246
1915 BOS N S            149   .244
1916 BOS N S            155   .235
1917 BOS N S            142   .260
1918 BOS N S             11   .316
1919 BOS N S            131   .267
1920 BOS N S            134   .266
1921 PIT N S            153   .294
1922 PIT N 2-S          155   .294
1923 PIT N S            141   .277
1924 PIT N 2            152   .266
1925 CHI N M-2-S         75   .233
1926 BRO N 2-S           78   .235
1927 STL N S              9   .241
1928 STL N S            112   .240
1929 BOS N S            146   .284
1930 BOS N S            142   .281
1931 BOS N 2-S          145   .260
1932 BOS N 2            149   .235
1933 BOS N 2            143   .218
1935 BOS N 2             23   .149
          BRTR        2670   .258
```

MARBERRY, FREDRICK (FIRPO)
B.NOV.30,1898 STREETMAN,TEX.
D.AUG.1976 MEXIA,TEX.
```
1923 WAS A P             11   4- 0
1924 WAS A P             50  11-12
1925 WAS A P             55   8- 6
1926 WAS A P             64  11- 7
1927 WAS A P             56  10- 7
1928 WAS A P             48  13-13
1929 WAS A P             49  19-12
1930 WAS A P             33  15- 5
1931 WAS A P             45  16- 4
1932 WAS A P             54   8- 4
1933 DET A P             38  13- 5
1934 DET A P              5   0- 1
1935 DET A P             13   5- 5
1936 NY  N P              1   0- 0
     WAS A P              5   0- 2
          BRTR          551 146-89
```

MARBET, WALTER WILLIAM
B.SEPT.13,1890 PLYMOUTH CO.,IA.
D.SEPT.24,1956 HOHENWALD,TENN.
```
1913 STL N P              3   0- 1
```

MARCANO, JESUS MANUEL [TRILLO]
[SEE JESUS MANUEL MARCANO TRILLO]

MARCHILDON, PHILIP JOSEPH
(PHIL) OR (BABE)
B.OCT.25,1913 PENETANGUISHENE,
ONT.,CANADA
```
1940 PHI A P              2   0- 2
1941 PHI A P             30  10-15
1942 PHI A P             38  17-14
1945 PHI A P              3   0- 1
1946 PHI A P             36  13-16
1947 PHI A P             35  19- 9
1948 PHI A P             33   9-15
1949 PHI A P              7   0- 3
1950 BOS A P              1   0- 0
          BRTR          185  68-75
```

MARCUM, JOHN ALFRED (FOOTSIE)
B.SEPT.9,1909 CAMPBELLSBURG,KY.
```
1933 PHI A P          5      3- 2
1934 PHI A P         37  58  14-11
1935 PHI A P         39  64  17-12
1936 BOS A P         31  48   8-13
1937 BOS A P         37  51  13-11
1938 BOS A P         15  19   5- 6
1939 STL A P         12  16   2- 5
     CHI A P         19  38   3- 3
          BLTR      195 299  65-63
```

MARCZLEWICZ, CHARLES ANTHONY
[PLAYED UNDER NAME OF
CHARLES ANTHONY MARSHALL]

MARENTETTE, LEO JOHN
B.FEB.16,1941 DETROIT,MICH.
```
1965 DET A /P             2   0- 0
1969 MON N /P             3   0- 0
          BRTR            5   0- 0
```

MARES
```
1894 LOU N O              1   .000
```

†ARGONERI, JOSEPH EMANUEL (JOE)
i.JAN.13,1930 SOMERSET,PA.
```
1956 NY  N P             23   6- 6
1957 NY  N P             13   1- 1
          BLTL           36   7- 7
```

MARICHAL, JUAN ANTONIO [SANCHEZ]
(JUAN) OR (MANITO)
B.OCT.20,1937 LAGUNA VERDE,D.R.
```
1960 SF N P              11   6- 2
1961 SF N P          29  30  13-10
1962 SF N P          37  38  18-11
1963 SF N P          41  42  25- 8
1964 SF N P              33  21- 8
1965 SF N P              39  22-13
1966 SF N P              37  25- 6
1967 SF N P              26  14-10
1968 SF N P              38  26- 9
1969 SF N P          37  38  21-11
1970 SF N P              34  12-10
1971 SF N P              37  18-11
1972 SF N P              25   6-16
1973 SF N P              34  11-15
1974 BOS A P             11   5- 1
1975 LA  N /P             2   0- 1
          BRTR      471 475 243-142
```

MARION, DONALD G. (RUBE)
B.1890
D.JAN.18,1933 MILWAUKEE,WIS.
```
1914 BRO F P             17   3- 3
1915 BRO F P             35  12- 9
          BRTR           52  15-12
```

MARION, JOHN WYETH (RED)
B.MAR.14,1914 RICHBURG,S.C.
D.MAR.13,1975 SAN JOSE,CAL.
```
1935 WAS A O              4   .182
1943 WAS A O             14   .176
          BRTR           18   .179
```

MARION, MARTIN WHITFORD (MARTY)
(SLATS) (THE OCTOPUS)
B.DEC.1,1917 RICHBURG,S.C.
```
1940 STL N S            125   .278
1941 STL N S            155   .252
1942 STL N S            147   .276
1943 STL N S            129   .280
1944 STL N S            144   .267
1945 STL N S            123   .277
1946 STL N S            146   .233
1947 STL N S            149   .272
1948 STL N S            144   .252
1949 STL N S            134   .272
1950 STL N S            106   .247
1952 STL A M-S           67   .247
1953 STL A M-3            3   .000
          BRTR        1572   .263
```
NON-PLAYING MANAGER
STL[N] 1951, CHI[A] 1954-56

MARIS, ROGER EUGENE
B.SEPT.10,1934 FARGO,N.D.
```
1957 CLE A O            116   .235
1958 CLE A O             51   .225
     KC  A O             99   .247
1959 KC  A O            122   .273
1960 NY  A O            136   .283
1961 NY  A O            161   .269
1962 NY  A O            157   .256
1963 NY  A O             90   .269
1964 NY  A O            141   .281
1965 NY  A O             46   .239
1966 NY  A O            119   .233
1967 STL N *O           125   .261
1968 STL N O            100   .255
          BLTR        1463   .260
```

MARKELL, HARRY DUQUESNE (DUKE)
[REAL NAME HARRY DUQUESNE MAKOWSKY]
B.AUG.17,1923 PARIS,FRANCE
```
1951 STL A P              5   1- 1
          BRTR
```

MARKLAND, CLENETH EUGENE (MOUSEY)
B.DEC.26,1919 DETROIT,MICH.
```
1950 PHI A 2              5   .125
          BRTR
```

MARKLE, CLIFFORD MONROE
B.MAY 3,1894 DRAVOSBURG,PA.
D.MAY 24,1974 TEMPLE CITY,CAL.
```
1915 NY  A P              3   2- 0
1916 NY  A P             11   4- 3
1921 CIN N P             10   2- 6
1922 CIN N P             25   4- 5
1924 NY  A P              7   0- 3
          BRTR           56  12-17
```

MARLOWE, RICHARD BURTON (DICK)
B.JUNE 27,1929 HICKORY,N.C.
D.DEC.30,1968 TOLEDO,OHIO
```
1951 DET A P              2   0- 1
1952 DET A P              4   0- 2
1953 DET A P             42   6- 7
1954 DET A P             38   5- 4
1955 DET A P              4   1- 0
1956 DET A P              7   1- 1
     CHI A P              1   0- 0
          BRTR           98  13-15
```

MARNIE, HARRY SYLVESTER (HAL)
B.JULY 6,1918 PHILADELPHIA,PA.
```
1940 PHI N 2             11   .176
1941 PHI N 2-S-3         61   .241
1942 PHI N 2-S-3         24   .167
          BRTR           96   .221
```

MAROLEWSKI, FRED DANIEL (FRITZ)
B.OCT.6,1928 CHICAGO,ILL.
```
1953 STL N 1              1   .000
```

MARONE, LOUIS STEPHEN (LOU)
B.DEC.3,1945 SAN DIEGO,CAL.
```
1969 PIT N P             29   1- 1
1970 PIT N /P             1   0- 0
          BRTL           30   1- 1
```

MARQUARD, RICHARD WILLIAM (RUBE)
B.OCT.9,1889 CLEVELAND,OHIO
```
1908 NY  N P              1   0- 1
1909 NY  N P             29   5-13
1910 NY  N P             13   4- 4
1911 NY  N P             45  24- 7
1912 NY  N P             43  26-11
1913 NY  N P             42  23-10
1914 NY  N P             39  12-22
1915 NY  N P             27   9- 8
     BRO N P              6   2- 2
1916 BRO N P             36  13- 6
1917 BRO N P             37  19-12
1918 BRO N P             34   9-16
1919 BRO N P              8   3- 3
1920 BRO N P             28  10- 7
1921 CIN N P             39  17-14
1922 BOS N P             39  11-15
1923 BOS N P             38  11-14
1924 BOS N P              6   1- 2
1925 BOS N P             26   2- 8
          BBTL          536 201-177
```

MARQUARDT, ALBERT LUDWIG (OLLIE)
B.SEPT.22,1902 TOLEDO,OHIO
D.FEB.7,1968 FORT CLINTON,OHIO
```
1931 BOS A 2             17   .179
          BRTR
```

MARQUEZ, GONZALO ENRIQUE [MOYA]
B.MAR.31,1946 CAUPANO,VENEZ.
```
1972 OAK A /1            23   .381
1973 OAK A /2-1-0        23   .240
     CHI N 1             19   .224
1974 CHI N /1            11   .000
          BLTL           76   .235
```

MARQUEZ, LUIS ANGEL
(LUIS) OR (CANENA)
B.OCT.28,1925 AGUADILLA,P.R.
```
1951 BOS N O             68   .197
1954 PIT N O             17   .083
     PIT N O             14   .111
          BRTR           99   .182
```

MARQUIS, JAMES MILBURN
B.NOV.18,1900 YOAKUM,TEX.
```
1925 NY  A P              2   0- 0
```

MARQUIS, ROBERT RUDOLPH (BOB)
B.DEC.23,1924 OKLAHOMA CITY,OKLA.
```
1953 CIN N O             40   .273
          BLTL
```

MARQUIS, ROGER JULIAN
(ROGER) OR (NOONIE)
B.APR.5,1937 HOLYOKE,MASS.
```
1955 BAL A O              1   .000
          BLTL
```

MARR, CHARLES W. (LEFTY)
B.SEPT.19,1862 CINCINNATI,OHIO
D.JAN.11,1912 NEW BRITAIN,CONN.
```
1886 CIN AA O             7   .269
1889 COL AA S-3-O       139   .303
1890 CIN N  3-O         130   .299
1891 CIN N  O            72   .244
     CIN AA O            14   .204
          BLTL          362   .289
```

MARRERO, CONRADO EUGENIO
[RAMOS] (CONNIE)
B.APR.25,1911 LAS VILLAS,CUBA
```
1950 WAS A P             27   6-10
1951 WAS A P             25  11- 9
1952 WAS A P             22  11- 8
1953 WAS A P             22   8- 7
1954 WAS A P             22   3- 6
          BRTR          118  39-40
```

MARRIOTT, WILLIAM EARL
B.APR.18,1893 PRATT,KAN.
D.AUG.11,1969 BERKELEY,CAL.
```
1917 CHI N H              3   .000
1920 CHI N 2             14   .279
1921 CHI N 2             10   .316
1925 BOS N 3-O          103   .268
1926 BRO N 3            109   .267
1927 BRO N 3              6   .111
          BLTR          265   .268
```

MARROW, CHARLES KENNON (BUCK)
B.AUG.29,1909 TARBORO,N.C.

YR	CL	LEA	POS	GP	G	REC
1932	DET	A	P		18	2- 5
1937	BRO	N	P		6	1- 2
1938	BRO	N	P		15	0- 1
		BRTR			39	3- 8

MARS, EDWARD M.
B.1863 CHICAGO,ILL.

YR	CL	LEA	POS	GP	G	REC
1890	SYR	AA	P		17	9- 6

MARSANS, ARMANDO
B.OCT.3,1887 MATANZAS,CUBA
D.SEPT.3,1960 HAVANA,CUBA

YR	CL	LEA	POS	GP	G	REC
1911	CIN	N	O		36	.261
1912	CIN	N	O		110	.317
1913	CIN	N	1-O		118	.297
1914	CIN	N	O		36	.298
	STL	F	2-S		9	.350
1915	STL	F	O		36	.177
1916	STL	A	O		151	.254
1917	STL	A	O		75	.230
	NY	A	O		25	.227
1918	NY	A	O		37	.236
		BRTR			633	.269

MARSH, FRED FRANCIS
B.JAN.5,1924 VALLEY FALLS,KAN.

YR	CL	LEA	POS	GP	G	REC
1949	CLE	A	H		1	.000
1951	STL	A	2-S-3		130	.243
1952	STL	A	2-S		11	.217
	WAS	A	2-O		9	.042
	STL	A	S-3		76	.286
1953	CHI	A	1-2-S-3		67	.200
1954	CHI	A	1-S-3-O		62	.306
1955	BAL	A	2-S-3		89	.218
1956	BAL	A	2-S-3		20	.125
		BRTR			465	.239

MARSHALL, CHARLES ANTHONY
[REAL NAME
CHARLES ANTHONY MARCZLEWICZ]
B.AUG.28,1919 WILMINGTON,DEL.

YR	CL	LEA	POS	GP	G	REC
1941	STL	N	C		1	.000
		BRTR				

MARSHALL, CLARENCE WESTLY (CUDDLES)
B.APR.28,1925 BELLINGHAM,WASH.

YR	CL	LEA	POS	GP	G	REC
1946	NY	A	P		23	3- 4
1948	NY	A	P		1	0- 0
1949	NY	A	P		21	3- 0
1950	STL	A	P		28	1- 3
		BRTR			73	7- 7

MARSHALL, DAVID LEWIS (DAVE)
B.JAN.14,1943 ARTESIA,CAL.

YR	CL	LEA	POS	GP	G	REC
1967	SF	N	R		1	.000
1968	SF	N	O		76	.264
1969	SF	N	O		110	.232
1970	NY	N	O		92	.243
1971	NY	N	O		100	.238
1972	NY	N	O		72	.250
1973	SD	N	/O		39	.286
		BLTR			490	.246

MARSHALL, EDWARD HERBERT (DOC)
B.JUNE 4,1906 NEW ALBANY,MISS.

YR	CL	LEA	POS	GP	G	REC
1929	NY	N	2		5	.400
1930	NY	N	2-S		78	.309
1931	NY	N	2-S		68	.201
1932	NY	N	S		68	.248
		BRTR			219	.259

MARSHALL, JOSEPH ELMER
B.AUG.22,1875 SAN FRANCISCO,CAL
D.MAY 4,1934 WALLA WALLA,WASH.

YR	CL	LEA	POS	GP	G	REC
1903	PIT	N	2-O		9	.261
1906	STL	N	O		27	.158
		BRTR			36	.178

MARSHALL, KEITH ALAN
B.JULY 2,1951 SAN FRANCISCO,CAL.

YR	CL	LEA	POS	GP	G	REC
1973	KC	A	/O		8	.222

MARSHALL, MICHAEL GRANT (MIKE)
B.JAN.15,1943 ADRIAN,MICH.

YR	CL	LEA	POS	GP	G	REC
1967	DET	A	P		37	1- 3
1969	SEA	A	P	20	21	3-10
1970	HOU	N	/P		4	0- 1
	MON	N	P		24	3- 7
1971	MON	N	P		66	5- 8
1972	MON	N	P		65	14- 8
1973	MON	N	P		92	14-11
1974	LA	N	*P		106	15-12
1975	LA	N	P	57	58	9-14
1976	LA	N	P		30	4- 3
	ATL	N	P		24	2- 1
1977	ATL	N	/P		4	1- 0
	TEX	A	P		12	2- 2
1978	MIN	A	P		54	10-12
		BRTR		595	597	83-92

MARSHALL, MILO MAX (MAX)
B.SEPT.18,1913 SHENANDOAH,IOWA

YR	CL	LEA	POS	GP	G	REC
1942	CIN	N	O		131	.255
1943	CIN	N	O		132	.236
1944	CIN	N	O		66	.245
		BLTR			329	.245

MARSHALL, ROY DE VERNE (RUBE) OR (CY)
B.JAN.19,1890 SALINEVILLE,OHIO

YR	CL	LEA	POS	GP	G	REC
1912	PHI	N	P		2	0- 1
1913	PHI	N	P		13	1- 3
1914	PHI	N	P		27	6- 7
1915	BUF	F	P		21	2- 1
		BRTR			63	9-12

MARSHALL, RUFUS JAMES (JIM)
B.MAY 25,1931 DANVILLE,ILL.

YR	CL	LEA	POS	GP	G	REC
1958	BAL	A	1-O		85	.215
	CHI	N	1-O		26	.272
1959	CHI	N	1-O		108	.252
1960	SF	N	1-O		75	.237
1961	SF	N	1-O		44	.222
1962	NY	N	1-O		17	.344
	PIT	N	1		55	.220
		BLTL			410	.242

NON-PLAYING MANAGER CHI[N] 1974-76

MARSHALL, WILLARD WARREN
B.FEB.8,1921 RICHMOND,VA.

YR	CL	LEA	POS	GP	G	REC
1942	NY	N	O		116	.257
1946	NY	N	O		131	.282
1947	NY	N	O		155	.291
1948	NY	N	O		143	.272
1949	NY	N	O		141	.307
1950	BOS	N	O		105	.235
1951	BOS	N	O		136	.281
1952	BOS	N	O		21	.227
	CIN	N	O		107	.267
1953	CIN	N	O		122	.266
1954	CHI	A	O		47	.254
1955	CHI	A	O		22	.171
		BLTR			1246	.274

MARSHALL, WILLIAM HENRY
B.FEB.14,1911 DORCHESTER,MASS.
D.MAY 5,1977 SACRAMENTO,CAL.

YR	CL	LEA	POS	GP	G	REC
1931	BOS	A	H		1	.000
1934	CIN	N	2		6	.125
		BRTR			7	.125

MARSHALL, WILLIAM RIDDLE (DOC)
B.SEPT.22,1875 BUTLER,PA.
D.DEC.11,1959 CLINTON,ILL.

YR	CL	LEA	POS	GP	G	REC
1904	PHI	N	C		8	.100
	NY	N	C		1	.000
	BOS	N	C		13	.209
	NY	N	H		10	.393
1906	NY	N	C-O		29	.167
	STL	N	C		38	.276
1907	STL	N	C		83	.202
1908	STL	N	C		6	.071
	CHI	N	C		9	.300
1909	BRO	N	C		47	.202
		BRTR			244	.210

MARTEL, LEON ALPHONSE (DOC) OR (MARTY)
B.JAN.29,1883 WEYMOUTH,MASS.
D.OCT.11,1947 WASHINGTON,D.C.

YR	CL	LEA	POS	GP	G	REC
1909	PHI	N	C		24	.268
1910	BOS	N	1		10	.000
	TR				34	.211

MARTIN, ALBERT
[PLAYED UNDER NAME OF ALBERT MAY]

MARTIN, ALFRED MANUEL (BILLY)
B.MAY 16,1928 BERKELEY,CAL.

YR	CL	LEA	POS	GP	G	REC
1950	NY	A	2-3		34	.250
1951	NY	A	2-S-3-O		51	.259
1952	NY	A	2		109	.267
1953	NY	A	2-S		149	.257
1955	NY	A	2-S		20	.300
1956	NY	A	2-3		121	.264
1957	NY	A	2-3		43	.241
	KC	A	2-S-3		73	.257
1958	DET	A	S-3		131	.255
1959	CLE	A	2-3		73	.260
1960	CIN	N	2		103	.246
1961	MIL	N	H		6	.000
	MIN	A	2-S		108	.246
		BRTR			1021	.257

NON-PLAYING MANAGER
MIN[A] 1969, DET[A] 1971-73
TEX[A] 1973-75, NY[A] 1975-78

MARTIN, ALPHONSE CASE
B.AUG.4,1845 NEW YORK,N.Y.
D.MAY 24,1933

YR	CL	LEA	POS	GP	G	REC
1872	TRO	NA	P-O	3	25	1- 2
						.287
	ECK	NA	P-O	10	18	2- 8
						.183
1873	MUT	NA	P-C-O	2	30	0- 2
						-
1874	ATL	NA	2-O		7	-
1875	ATL	NA	O		5	-
				15	89	3-12
						-

MARTIN, BARNES ROBERTSON (BARNEY)
B.MAR.3,1923 COLUMBIA,S.C.

YR	CL	LEA	POS	GP	G	REC
1953	CIN	N	P		1	0- 0
		BRTR				

MARTIN, BORIS MICHAEL (BABE)
[REAL NAME
BORIS MICHAEL MARTINOVICH]
B.MAR.28,1920 SEATTLE,WASH.

YR	CL	LEA	POS	GP	G	REC
1944	STL	A	O		2	.750
1945	STL	A	1-O		54	.200
1946	STL	A	C		3	.222
1948	BOS	A	C		4	.500
1949	BOS	A	C		2	.000
1953	STL	A	C		4	.000
		BRTR			69	.214

MARTIN, ELWOOD GOOD (SPEED)
B.SEPT.15,1893 WAWAWAI,WASH.

YR	CL	LEA	POS	GP	G	REC
1917	STL	A	P	9	10	0- 3
1918	CHI	N	P		9	5- 2
1919	CHI	N	P		35	8- 8
1920	CHI	N	P		35	4-15
1921	CHI	N	P		37	11-15
1922	CHI	N	P		1	1- 0
		BRTR		126	127	29-43

MARTIN, FRANK
B.1877 CHICAGO,ILL.

YR	CL	LEA	POS	GP	G	REC
1897	LOU	N	2		2	.222
1898	CHI	N	2		1	.000
1899	NY	N	2		17	.254
					20	.235

MARTIN, FRED TURNER
B.JUNE 27,1915 WILLIAMS,OKLA.

YR	CL	LEA	POS	GP	G	REC
1946	STL	N	P		6	2- 1
1949	STL	N	P		21	6- 0
1950	STL	N	P	30	31	4- 2
		BRTR		57	58	12- 3

MARTIN, HAROLD WINTHROP (DOC)
B.SEPT.23,1887 ROXBURY,MASS.
D.APR.15,1935 MILTON,MASS.

YR	CL	LEA	POS	GP	G	REC
1908	PHI	A	P		1	0- 1
1911	PHI	A	P		11	1- 3
1912	PHI	A	P		2	0- 0
		BRTR			14	1- 4

MARTIN, HERSHEL RAY
B.SEPT.19,1909 BIRMINGHAM,ALA.

YR	CL	LEA	POS	GP	G	REC
1937	PHI	N	O		141	.283
1938	PHI	N	O		120	.298
1939	PHI	N	O		111	.282
1940	PHI	N	O		33	.253
1944	NY	A	O		85	.302
1945	NY	A	O		117	.267
		BBTR			607	.285

MARTIN, JERRY LINDSEY
B.MAY 11,1949 COLUMBIA,S.C.

YR	CL	LEA	POS	GP	G	REC
1974	PHI	N	O		13	.214
1975	PHI	N	O		57	.212
1976	PHI	N	*O/1		130	.248
1977	PHI	N	*O/1		116	.260
1978	PHI	N	*O		128	.271
		BRTR			444	.254

MARTIN, JOHN CHRISTOPHER (JACK)
B.APR.19,1887 PLAINFIELD,N.J.

YR	CL	LEA	POS	GP	G	REC
1912	NY	A	S		69	.225
1914	BOS	N	3		33	.212
	PHI	N	S		83	.253
		BRTR			185	.237

MARTIN, JOHN LEONARD ROOSEVELT (PEPPER) OR
(THE WILD HORSE OF THE OSAGE)
B.FEB.29,1904 TEMPLE,OKLA.
D.MAR.5,1965 MC ALESTER,OKLA.

YR	CL	LEA	POS	GP	G	REC
1928	STL	N	O		39	.308
1930	STL	N	O		6	.000
1931	STL	N	O		123	.300
1932	STL	N	3-O		85	.238
1933	STL	N	3		145	.316
1934	STL	N	P-3	1	110	0- 0
						.289
1935	STL	N	3-O		135	.299
1936	STL	N	P-3-O	1	143	0- 0
						.309
1937	STL	N	O		98	.304
1938	STL	N	O		91	.294
1939	STL	N	3-O		88	.306
1940	STL	N	3-O		86	.316
1944	STL	N	O		40	.279
		BRTR		2	1189	0- 0
						.298

MARTIN, JOSEPH CLIFTON (J.C.)
B.DEC.13,1936 AXTON,VA.

YR	CL	LEA	POS	GP	G	REC
1959	CHI	A	3		3	.250
1960	CHI	A	1-3		7	.100
1961	CHI	A	1-3		110	.230
1962	CHI	A	C-1-3		18	.077
1963	CHI	A	C-1-3		105	.205
1964	CHI	A	C		122	.197
1965	CHI	A	*C/1-3		119	.261
1966	CHI	A	C		67	.255
1967	CHI	A	C/1		101	.234
1968	NY	N	C-1		78	.225
1969	NY	N	C/1		66	.209
1970	NY	N	C/1		40	.156
1971	CHI	N	C/0		47	.264
1972	CHI	N	C		25	.240
		BLTR			908	.222

MARTIN, JOSEPH SAMUEL (SILENT JOE)
B.JAN.1,1876 HOLLIDAYSBURG,PA.
D.MAY 25,1964 ALTOONA,PA.

YR	CL	LEA	POS	G	REC
1903	WAS	A	2-3-0	36	.208
	STL	A	3-0	44	.231
		BLTR		80	.221

MARTIN, MORRIS WEBSTER
(MORRIE) (LEFTY)
B.SEPT.3,1922 DIXON,MO.

YR	CL	LEA	POS	G	REC
1949	BRO	N	P	10	1- 3
1951	PHI	A	P	35	11- 4
1952	PHI	A	P	5	0- 2
1953	PHI	A	P	58	10-12
1954	PHI	A	P	13	2- 4
	CHI	A	P	35	5- 4
1955	CHI	A	P	37	2- 3
1956	CHI	A	P	10	1- 0
	BAL	A	P	9	1- 1
1957	STL	N	P	4	0- 0
1958	STL	N	P	17	3- 1
	CLE	A	P	14	2- 0
1959	CHI	N	P	3	0- 0
		BLTL		250	38-34

MARTIN, PATRICK FRANCIS
B.APR.13,1894 BROOKLYN,N.Y.

YR	CL	LEA	POS	G	REC
1919	PHI	A	P	2	0- 2
1920	PHI	A	P	8	1- 4
		BLTL		10	1- 6

MARTIN, PAUL CHARLES
B.MAR.10,1932 BROWNSTONE,PA.

YR	CL	LEA	POS	G	REC
1955	PIT	N	P	7	0- 1

MARTIN, RAYMOND JOSEPH
B.MAR.13,1925 NORWOOD,MASS.

YR	CL	LEA	POS	G	REC
1943	BOS	N	P	2	0- 0
1947	BOS	N	P	1	1- 0
1948	BOS	N	P	2	0- 0
		BRTR		5	1- 0

MARTIN, STUART MC GUIRE
B.NOV.17,1913 RICH SQUARE,N.C.

YR	CL	LEA	POS	G	REC
1936	STL	N	2	92	.298
1937	STL	N	2	90	.260
1938	STL	N	2	114	.278
1939	STL	N	2	120	.268
1940	STL	N	2-3	112	.238
1941	PIT	N	1-2-3	88	.304
1942	PIT	N	1-2-S	42	.225
1943	CHI	N	1-2-3	64	.220
		BLTR		722	.268

MARTIN, THOMAS EUGENE (GENE)
B.JAN.12,1947 AMERICUS,GA.

YR	CL	LEA	POS	G	REC
1968	WAS	A	/0	9	.364
		BLTR			

MARTIN, WILLIAM LLOYD (BILLY)
B.FEB.13,1894 WASHINGTON,D.C.
D.SEPT.14,1949 ARLINGTON,VA.

YR	CL	LEA	POS	G	REC
1914	BOS	N	S	1	.000
		BRTR			

MARTIN, WILLIAM JOSEPH (SMOKEY JOE)
B.AUG.28,1911 SEYMOUR,MO.
D.SEPT.28,1960 BUFFALO,N.Y.

YR	CL	LEA	POS	G	REC
1936	NY	N	3	7	.267
1938	CHI	A	H	1	.000
		BRTR		8	.267

MARTINA, JOSEPH JOHN (OYSTER JOE)
B.JULY 8,1889 NEW ORLEANS,LA.
D.MAR.22,1962 NEW ORLEANS,LA.

YR	CL	LEA	POS	GP	G	REC
1924	WAS	A	P	24	25	6- 8
		BRTR				

MARTINEZ, FELIX ANTHONY (TIPPY)
B.MAY 31,1950 LAJUNTA,COL.

YR	CL	LEA	POS	GP	G	REC
1974	NY	A	P		10	0- 0
1975	NY	A	P		23	1- 2
1976	NY	A	P		11	2- 0
	BAL	A	P		28	3- 1
1977	BAL	A	P		41	5- 1
1978	BAL	A	P	42	43	3- 3
		BLTL		155	156	14- 7

MARTINEZ, GABRIEL ANTONIO (DIAZ)
(TONY)
B.MAR.18,1941 PERICO,CUBA

YR	CL	LEA	POS	G	REC
1963	CLE	A	S	43	.156
1964	CLE	A	2-S	9	.214
1965	CLE	A	/H	4	.000
1966	CLE	A	/S-2	17	.294
		BRTR		73	.171

MARTINEZ, JOHN ALBERT (BUCK)
B.NOV.7,1948 REDDING,CAL.

YR	CL	LEA	POS	G	REC
1969	KC	A	C/0	72	.229
1970	KC	A	/C	6	.111
1971	KC	A	C	22	.152
1973	KC	A	C	14	.250
1974	KC	A	C	43	.215
1975	KC	A	C	80	.226
1976	KC	A	C	95	.228
1977	KC	A	C	29	.225
1978	MIL	A	C	89	.219
		BRTR		450	.221

MARTINEZ, JOSE (AIZCUIZ)
B.JULY 26,1942 CARDENAS,CUBA

YR	CL	LEA	POS	G	REC
1969	PIT	N	2-S/3-0	77	.268
1970	PIT	N	/3-2-S	19	.050
		BRTR		96	.245

MARTINEZ, JOSE DENNIS (EMILIA)
(DENNIS)
B.MAY 14,1955 GRANADA,NICARAGUA

YR	CL	LEA	POS	G	REC
1976	BAL	A	/P	4	1- 2
1977	BAL	A	P	42	14- 7
1978	BAL	A	P	40	16-11
		BRTR		86	31-20

MARTINEZ, ORLANDO (OLIVA) (MARTY)
B.AUG.23,1941 HAVANA,CUBA

YR	CL	LEA	POS	GP	G	REC
1962	MIN	A	S-3		37	.167
1967	ATL	N	S/2-C-3-1		44	.288
1968	ATL	N	S-3-2-C		113	.230
1969	HOU	N	P	21	78	0- 0
			O-S-3/C-2			.308
1970	HOU	N	S-3/C-2		75	.220
1971	HOU	N	/2-S-1-3		32	.258
1972	STL	N	/S-2-3		9	.429
	OAK	A	2/S-3		22	.125
	TEX	A	/S-3-2		26	.146
		BBTR		1	436	0- 0
						.243

BR 1962

MARTINEZ, ROGELIO (ULLOA) (LIMONAR)
B.NOV.5,1918 MATANZAS,CUBA

YR	CL	LEA	POS	G	REC
1950	WAS	A	P	2	0- 1
		BRTR			

MARTINEZ, RODOLFO HECTOR
(SANTOS) (HECTOR)
B.MAY 11,1939 LAS VILLAS,CUBA

YR	CL	LEA	POS	G	REC
1962	KC	A	H	1	.000
1963	KC	A	0	6	.286
		BRTR		7	.267

MARTINEZ, SILVIO RAMON (CABRERA)
B.AUG.19,1955 SANTIAGO,D.R.

YR	CL	LEA	POS	G	REC
1977	CHI	A	P	10	0- 1
1978	STL	N	P	22	9- 8
		BRTR		32	9- 9

MARTINEZ, TEODORO NOEL
(ENCARNACION) (TED)
B.DEC.10,1947 CENTRAL BARAHONA,
D.R.

YR	CL	LEA	POS	G	REC
1970	NY	N	/2-S	4	.063
1971	NY	N	S-2/3-0	38	.288
1972	NY	N	2-S-0/3	103	.224
1973	NY	N	S-0-3/2	92	.255
1974	NY	N	S-3-2-0	116	.219
1975	STL	N	/0-2-S-3	16	.190
	OAK	A	S-2-3	86	.172
1977	LA	N	2-S-3	67	.299
1978	LA	N	S-3-2	54	.255
		BRTR		576	.238

BB 1973 (PART)

MARTINI, GUIDO JOE
(SOUTHERN) OR (WEDO)
B.JULY 1,1913 BIRMINGHAM,ALA.
D.OCT.28,1970 PHILADELPHIA,PA.

YR	CL	LEA	POS	G	REC
1935	PHI	A	P	3	0- 2
		BRTR			

MARTINOVICH, BORIS MICHAEL
[PLAYED UNDER NAME OF
BORIS MICHAEL MARTIN]

MARTY, JOSEPH ANTON (JOE)
B.SEPT.1,1913 SACRAMENTO,CAL.

YR	CL	LEA	POS	GP	G	REC
1937	CHI	N	0		88	.290
1938	CHI	N	0		76	.243
1939	CHI	N	0		23	.132
	PHI	N	P-0	1	91	0- 0
						.254
1940	PHI	N	0		123	.270
1941	PHI	N	0		137	.268
		BRTR		1	538	0- 0
						.261

MARTYN, ROBERT GORDON (BOB)
B.AUG.15,1930 WEISER,IDAHO

YR	CL	LEA	POS	G	REC
1957	KC	A	0	58	.267
1958	KC	A	0	95	.261
1959	KC	A	H	1	.000
		BLTR		154	.263

MARTZ, GARY ARTHUR
B.JAN.10,1951 SPOKANE,WASH.

YR	CL	LEA	POS	G	REC
1975	KC	A	/0	1	.000
		BRTR			

MASHORE, CLYDE WAYNE
B.MAY 29,1945 CONCORD,CAL.

YR	CL	LEA	POS	G	REC
1969	CIN	N	/H	2	.000
1970	MON	N	0	13	.160
1971	MON	N	0/3	66	.193
1972	MON	N	0	93	.227
1973	MON	N	0/2	67	.204
		BRTR		241	.208

MASI, PHILIP SAMUEL (PHIL)
B.JAN.6,1917 CHICAGO,ILL.

YR	CL	LEA	POS	G	REC
1939	BOS	N	C	46	.254
1940	BOS	N	C	63	.196
1941	BOS	N	C	87	.222
1942	BOS	N	C-0	57	.218
1943	BOS	N	C	80	.273
1944	BOS	N	C-1-3	89	.275
1945	BOS	N	C-1	114	.272
1946	BOS	N	C	133	.267
1947	BOS	N	C	126	.304
1948	BOS	N	C	113	.253
1949	BOS	N	C	37	.210
	PIT	N	C-1	48	.274
1950	CHI	A	C	122	.279
1951	CHI	A	C	84	.271
1952	CHI	A	C	30	.254
		BRTR		1229	.264

MASKREY, HARRY H.
B.DEC.21,1861 MERCER,PA.
D.AUG.17,1930 MERCER,PA.

YR	CL	LEA	POS	G	REC
1882	LOU	AA	0	1	.000

MASKREY, SAMUEL LEECH (LEECH)
B.FEB.11,1854 MERCER,PA.
D.APR.11,1922 MERCER,PA.

YR	CL	LEA	POS	G	REC
1882	LOU	AA	M-2-0	76	.225
1883	LOU	AA	M-S-0	96	.190
1884	LOU	AA	0	107	.247
1885	LOU	AA	0	110	.230
1886	LOU	AA	0	5	.158
	CIN	AA	0	27	.204
				421	.227

MASON, ADELBERT WILLIAM (DEL)
B.OCT.29,1883 NEWFANE,N.Y.
D.DEC.31,1962 WINTER PARK,FLA.

YR	CL	LEA	POS	G	REC
1904	WAS	A	P	5	0- 3
1906	CIN	N	P	2	0- 1
1907	CIN	N	P	25	5-12
		BRTR		32	5-16

MASON, CHARLES E.
B.JUNE 25,1853 ARKANSAS
D.OCT.21,1936 PHILADELPHIA,PA.

YR	CL	LEA	POS	G	REC
1875	CEN	NA	1-0	12	-
	NAT	NA	0	8	-
1883	ATH	AA	M-0	1	.500
		TR		21	-

NON-PLAYING MANAGER
ATH[AA] 1882, 84-87

MASON, DONALD STETSON (DON)
B.DEC.20,1944 BOSTON,MASS.

YR	CL	LEA	POS	G	REC
1966	SF	N	/2	42	.120
1967	SF	N	/2	4	.000
1968	SF	N	/2-S-3	10	.158
1969	SF	N	2-3/S	104	.228
1970	SF	N	2	46	.139
1971	SD	N	2/3	113	.212
1972	SD	N	/2	9	.182
1973	SD	N	/2	8	.000
		BLTR		336	.205

MASON, ERNEST
B.NEW ORLEANS,LA.
D.JULY 30,1904 COVINGTON,LA.

YR	CL	LEA	POS	G	REC
1894	STL	N	P	4	0- 2

MASON, HENRY (HANK)
B.JUNE 19,1931 MARSHALL,MO.

YR	CL	LEA	POS	G	REC
1958	PHI	N	P	1	0- 0
1960	PHI	N	P	3	0- 0
		BRTR		4	0- 0

MASON, JAMES PERCY (JIM)
B.AUG.14,1950 MOBILE,ALA.

YR	CL	LEA	POS	G	REC
1971	WAS	A	/S	3	.333
1972	TEX	A	S-3	46	.197
1973	TEX	A	S-2/3	92	.206
1974	NY	A	*S	152	.250
1975	NY	A	S/2	94	.152
1976	NY	A	S	93	.180
1977	TOR	A	S	22	.165
	TEX	A	S/3	36	.218
1978	TEX	A	S-3/2	55	.190
		BLTR		593	.204

YR CL LEA POS   GP   G   REC

MASSA, GORDON RICHARD (GORDON)
(MOOSE) OR (DUKE)
B.SEPT.2,1935 CINCINNATI,OHIO
1957 CHI N C   6   .467
1958 CHI N H   2   .000
        BLTR   8   .412

MASSEY, ROY HARDEE (RED)
B.OCT.9,1890 SEVIERVILLE,TENN.
D.JUNE 23,1954 ATLANTA,GA.
1918 BOS N 1-S-3-O   66   .291
        BLTR

MASSEY, WILLIAM HARRY (BIG BILL)
B.JAN.1871 PHILADELPHIA,PA.
D.OCT.9,1940 MANILA,PHILIPPINES
1894 CIN N 1   13   .294

MASSEY, WILLIAM HERBERT (MIKE)
B.SEPT.28,1893 GALVESTON,TEX.
D.OCT.17,1971 SHREVEPORT,LA.
1917 BOS N 2   31   .198
        BBTR

MASTERS, WALTER THOMAS
B.MAR.28,1907 PEN ARGYL,PA.
1931 WAS A P   3   0- 0
1937 PHI N P   1   0- 0
1939 PHI A P   4   0- 0
        BRTR   8   0- 0

MASTERSON, PAUL NICKALIS
(PAUL) OR (LEFTY)
B.OCT.16,1915 CHICAGO,ILL.
1940 PHI N P   2   0- 0
1941 PHI N P   2   1- 0
1942 PHI N P   4   0- 0
        BLTL   8   1- 0

MASTERSON, WALTER EDWARD (WALT)
B.JUNE 22,1920 PHILADELPHIA,PA.
1939 WAS A P   24   2- 2
1940 WAS A P   31   3-13
1941 WAS A P   34   4- 3
1942 WAS A P   25 26   5- 9
1945 WAS A P   4   1- 2
1946 WAS A P   29   3- 6
1947 WAS A P   35 36   12-16
1948 WAS A P   33   8-15
1949 WAS A P   10 11   3- 2
     BOS A P   18   3- 4
1950 BOS A P   33   8- 6
1951 BOS A P   30   3- 0
1952 BOS A P   5   1- 1
     WAS A P   24   9- 8
1953 WAS A P   29   10-12
1956 DET A P   35   1- 1
        BRTR   399 402   78-100

MATARAZZO, LEONARD
B.SEPT.12,1928 NEW CASTLE,PA.
1952 PHI A P   1   0- 0
        BRTR

MATCHICK, JOHN THOMAS (TOMMY)
B.SEP.7,1943 HAZLETON,PA.
1967 DET A /S   8   .167
1968 DET A S-2/1   80   .203
1969 DET A 2-3/S-1   94   .242
1970 BOS A /3-2-S   10   .071
     KC A S-2/3   55   .196
1971 MIL A 3/2   42   .219
1972 BAL A /3   3   .222
        BLTR   292   .215

MATHES, JOSEPH JOHN
B.JULY 28,1891 MILWAUKEE,WIS.
1912 PHI A 3   4   .154
1914 STL F 2   24   .298
1916 BOS N 2   2   .000
        BBTR   30   .276

MATHEWS, EDWIN LEE (EDDIE)
B.OCT.13,1931 TEXARKANA,TEX.
1952 BOS N 3   145   .242
1953 MIL N 3   157   .302
1954 MIL N 3-O   138   .290
1955 MIL N 3   141   .289
1956 MIL N 3   151   .272
1957 MIL N 3   148   .292
1958 MIL N 3   149   .251
1959 MIL N 3   148   .306
1960 MIL N 3   153   .277
1961 MIL N 3   152   .306
1962 MIL N 1-3   152   .265
1963 MIL N 3-O   158   .263
1964 MIL N 1-3   141   .233
1965 MIL N *3   156   .251
1966 ATL N 3   134   .250
1967 HOU N 1-3   101   .238
     DET A 3-1   36   .231
1968 DET A /1-3   31   .212
        BLTR   2391   .271
NON-PLAYING MANAGER ATL(N) 1972-74

MATHEWS, NELSON ELMER
B.JULY 21,1941 COLUMBIA,ILL.
1960 CHI N O   3   .250
1961 CHI N O   3   .111
1962 CHI N O   15   .306
1963 CHI N O   61   .155
1964 KC A O   157   .239
1965 KC A O   67   .212
        BRTR   306   .223

MATHEWS, ROBERT T. (BOBBY)
B.NOV.21,1851 BALTIMORE,MD.
D.APR.17,1898 BALTIMORE,MD.
1871 KEK NA P   19   6-13
1872 BAL NA P-2-   42 47 26-16
              O   .229
1873 MUT NA P-O   25 26 10-15
                                .229

ATL NA P   1   1- 0
MUT NA P   26 19- 7
1874 MUT NA P   65 42-23
1875 MUT NA P   70 29-38
1876 MUT N P   56 21-34
1877 CIN N P-S-O   15   3-12
                                .169
1879 PRO N P-O   19 42 11- 5
                                .200
1881 PRO N P-O   13 15   4- 7
                                .155
     BOS N P   5   19   1- 0
                                .169
1882 BOS N P-S-   34 45 19-14
              O   .224
1883 ATH AA P-O   44 30-14
                                .173
1884 ATH AA P   49 30-18
1885 ATH AA P   48 30-17
1886 ATH AA P   23 13- 9
1887 ATH AA P   8   3- 5
        BRTR   572 618 298-247

MATHEWSON, CHRISTOPHER
(CHRISTY), (MATTY) OR (BIG SIX)
B.AUG.12,1878 FACTORYVILLE,PA.
D.OCT.7,1925 SARANAC LAKE,N.Y.
1900 NY N P   6   0- 2
1901 NY N P   37 20-16
1902 NY N P-1-   34 41 13-18
              O   .200
1903 NY N P   45 30-13
1904 NY N P   48 33-12
1905 NY N P   43 32- 8
1906 NY N P   38 22-12
1907 NY N P   41 24-12
1908 NY N P   56 37-11
1909 NY N P   37 25- 6
1910 NY N P   38 27- 9
1911 NY N P   45 26-13
1912 NY N P   43 23-12
1913 NY N P   40 25-11
1914 NY N P   41 24-13
1915 NY N P   27   8-14
1916 NY N P   12   3- 4
     CIN N M-P   1   1- 0
        BRTR   632 636 373-186
                                .214
NON-PLAYING MANAGER CIN(N) 1917-18

MATHEWSON, HENRY
B.DEC.24,1886 FACTORYVILLE,PA.
D.JULY 1,1917 FACTORYVILLE,PA.
1906 NY N P   2   0- 1
1907 NY N P   1   0- 0
                      3   0- 1

MATHIAS, CARL LYNWOOD
(CARL) OR (STUBBY)
B.JUNE 13,1936 BECHTELSVILLE,PA
1960 CLE A P   7   0- 1
1961 WAS A P   4   0- 1
        BBTL   11   0- 2

MATHISON, I. I.
B.BALTIMORE,MD.
1902 BAL A S-3   28   .275
        TR

MATIAS, JOHN ROY
B.AUG.15,1944 HONOLULU,HAWAII
1970 CHI A O-1   58   .188
        BLTL

MATLACK, JONATHAN TRUMPBOUR (JON)
B.JAN.19,1950 WEST CHESTER,PA.
1971 NY N /P   7   0- 3
1972 NY N P   34   15-10
1973 NY N P   34 35   14-16
1974 NY N P   34   13-15
1975 NY N P   33   16-12
1976 NY N P   35   17-10
1977 NY N P   26   7-15
1978 TEX A P   35   15-13
        BLTL   238 239 97-94

MATTERN, ALONZO ALBERT
B.JUNE 16,1883 W.RUSH,N.Y.
D.NOV.6,1958 WEST RUSH,N.Y.
1908 BOS N P   5   1- 2
1909 BOS N P   47   15-21
1910 BOS N P   51   16-19
1911 BOS N P   33   4-15
1912 BOS N P   2   0- 1
        BLTR   138   36-56

MATTERSON, C. V.
B.OHIO
1884 STL U P-O   1   1- 0
                            .000

MATTESON, HENRY EDSON
(EDDIE) OR (MATTY)
B.SEPT.7,1884 GUYS MILLS,PA.
D.SEPT.1,1943 WESTFIELD,N.Y.
1914 PHI N P   13   3- 2
1918 WAS A P   14   5- 3
        BRTR   29   8- 5

MATTHEWS, JAMES VINCENT
B.SEPT.29,1899 BALTIMORE,MD.
1922 BOS N P   3   0- 1
        BRTL

MATTHEWS, GARY NATHANIEL
B.JULY 5,1950 SAN FERNANDO,CAL.
1972 SF N O   20   .290
1973 SF N *O   148   .300
1974 SF N *O   154   .287
1975 SF N *O   116   .280
1976 SF N *O   156   .279
1977 ATL N *O   148   .283
1978 ATL N *O   129   .285
        BRTR   871   .286

MATTHEWS, ROBERT
B.CAMDEN,N.J.
1891 ATH AA O   1   .333

MATTHEWS, WID CURRY (WID) OR (MATTY)
B.OCT.20,1896 RALEIGH,ILL.
D.OCT.5,1965 HOLLYWOOD,CAL.
1923 PHI A O   129   .274
1924 WAS A O   53   .302
1925 WAS A O   10   .444
        BLTL   192   .284

MATTHEWS, WILLIAM CALCIN
B.JAN.12,1878 MAHANOY CITY,PA.
D.JAN.23,1946 MAHANOY CITY,PA.
1909 BOS A P   5   0- 0
        TR

MATTHEWSON, DALE WESLEY
B.MAY 15,1923 CATASAUQUA,PA.
1943 PHI N P   11 12   0- 3
1944 PHI N P   17   0- 0
        BRTR   28 29   0- 3

MATTHIAS, STEPHEN J.
B.MITCHELLVILLE,MD.
1884 CHI U S   35   .274

MATTICK, ROBERT JAMES (BOBBY)
B.DEC.5,1915 SIOUX CITY,IOWA
1938 CHI N S   1   1.000
1939 CHI N S   51   .287
1940 CHI N S-3   128   .218
1941 CIN N 2-S-3   20   .183
1942 CIN N S   6   .200
        BRTR   206   .233

MATTICK, WALTER JOSEPH (CHINK)
B.MAR.12,1887 ST.LOUIS,MO.
D.NOV.5,1968 LOS ALTOS,CAL.
1912 CHI A O   88   .260
1913 CHI A O   68   .188
1918 STL N O   8   .142
        BRTR   164   .227

MATTIMORE, MICHAEL JOSEPH
B.1859 RENOVO,PA.
D.APR.29,1931 BUTTE,MONT.
1887 NY N P   8   3- 4
1888 ATH AA P   26 41 15-10
1889 ATH AA P-O   4 23   2- 2
                                .257
     KC AA P-O   2 19   1- 1
                                .147
1890 BRO AA P-O   20 33   6-14
                                .126
        BLTR   60 124 27-31
                                .206

MATTINGLY, LAURENCE EARL (EARL)
B.NOV.4,1904 NEWPORT,MD.
1931 BRO N P   8   0- 1
        BRTR

MATTIS, RALPH (MATTY)
B.AUG.24,1890 ROXBOROUGH,PA.
D.SEPT.13,1960 WILLIAMSPORT,PA.
1914 PIT F O   35   .247
        BRTR

YR	CL	LEA	POS	GP	G	REC

MATTOX, CLOY MITCHELL (MONK)
B.NOV.21,1902 LEESVILLE,VA.
1929 PHI A C   3 .167
     BLTR

MATTOX, JAMES POWELL
B.DEC.17,1896 LEESVILLE,VA.
D.OCT.12,1973 MYRTLE BEACH,S.C.
1922 PIT N C   29 .294
1923 PIT N C   22 .188
     BLTR   51 .253

MATUZAK, HARRY GEORGE (MATTY)
B.JAN.27,1910 OMER,MICH.
D.NOV.16,1978 FAIR HOPE,ALA.
1934 PHI A P   11 0- 3
1936 PHI A P   6 0- 1
     BRTR   17 0- 4

MAUCH, GENE WILLIAM (GENE) OR (SKIP)
B.NOV.18,1925 SALINA,KAN.
1944 BRO N S   5 .133
1947 PIT N 2-S   16 .300
1948 BRO N 2-S   12 .154
     CHI N 2-S   53 .203
1949 CHI N 2-S-3   72 .247
1950 BOS N 2-S-3   48 .231
1951 BOS N 2-S-3   19 .100
1952 STL N S   7 .000
1956 BOS A 2   7 .320
1957 BOS A 2   65 .270
     BRTR   304 .239
NON-PLAYING MANAGER
PHI[N] 1960-68, MON[N] 1969-75,
MIN[A] 1976-78

MAUCK, ALFRED MARIS (HAL)
B.MAR.6,1869 PRINCETON,IND.
D.APR.27,1921 GIBSON COUNTY,IND
1893 CHI N P   18 8- 9

MAUL, ALBERT JOSEPH (SMILING AL)
B.OCT.9,1865 PHILADELPHIA,PA.
D.MAY 3,1958 PHILADELPHIA,PA.
1884 KEY U P   1 0- 1
1887 PHI N P   7 16 5- 2
1888 PIT N P-1-   2 73 0- 1
          O   .211
1889 PIT N P-O   6 67 1- 3
                         .276
1890 PIT P P-O   32 44 17-11
                         .265
1891 PIT N P-O   6 40 1- 2
                         .194
1893 WAS N P   34 39 10-23
1894 WAS N P   28 35 11-15
1895 WAS N P   17 20 11- 6
1896 WAS N P   9 5- 2
1897 WAS N P   1 0- 0
     BAL N P   1 0- 0
1898 BAL N P   28 29 20- 7
1899 BRO N P   4 2- 0
1900 PHI N P   5 2- 3
1901 NY N P   3 0- 2
     BRTR   184 387 85-78
                         .251

MAULDIN, MARSHALL REESE
B.NOV.5,1914 ATLANTA,GA.
1934 CHI A 3   10 .263
     BRTR

MAUN, ERNEST GERALD
B.FEB.3,1901 CLEARWATER,KAN.
1924 NY N P   22 1- 1
1926 PHI N P   14 1- 4
     BLTR   36 2- 5

MAUNEY, RICHARD
B.JAN.26,1920 CONCORD,N.C.
D.FEB.6,1970 ALBEMARLE,N.C.
1945 PHI N P   20 22 6-10
1946 PHI N P   24 25 6- 4
1947 PHI N P   9 15 0- 0
     BRTR   53 62 12-14

MAUPIN, HENRY CARR (HARRY)
B.JULY 11,1872 WELLESVILLE,MO.
D.AUG.22,1952
1898 STL N P   2 0- 2
1899 CLE N P   5 0- 3
                      7 0- 5

MAURIELLO, RALPH (RALPH) OR (TAMI)
B.AUG.25,1934 BROOKLYN,N.Y.
1958 LA N P   3 1- 1
     BRTR

MAURO, CARMEN LOUIS
B.NOV.10,1926 ST.PAUL,MINN.
1948 CHI N O   3 .200
1950 CHI N O   62 .227
1951 CHI N O   13 .172
1953 BRO N C   8 .000
     WAS A O   17 .174
     PHI A 3-O   64 .267
     BLTR   167 .231

MAVIS, ROBERT HENRY (BOB)
B.APR.8,1918 MILWAUKEE,WIS.
1949 DET A H   1 .000
     BLTR

MAXIE, LARRY HANS
B.OCT.10,1940 UPLAND,CAL.
1969 ATL N /P   2 0- 0

MAXVILL, CHARLES DALLAN (DAL)
B.FEB.18,1939 GRANITE CITY,ILL.
1962 STL N S-3   79 .222
1963 STL N 2-S-3   53 .235
1964 STL N 2-S-3-O   37 .231
1965 STL N 2-S   68 .135
1966 STL N *S/2-O   134 .244
1967 STL N *S/2   152 .227
1968 STL N *S   151 .253
1969 STL N *S   132 .175
1970 STL N *S-2   152 .201
1971 STL N *S   142 .225
1972 STL N S-2   105 .250
     OAK A 2/S   27 .250
1973 OAK A S-2/3   29 .211
     PIT N S   74 .189
1974 PIT N /S   8 .182
     OAK A 2-S/3   60 .192
1975 OAK A S/2   20 .200
     BRTR   1423 .217

**MAXWELL, CHARLES RICHARD
(CHARLIE) OR (SMOKEY)**
B.APR.28,1927 LAWTON,MICH.
1950 BOS A O   2 .000
1951 BOS A O   49 .188
1952 BOS A 1-O   8 .067
1954 BOS A O   74 .250
1955 BAL A H   4 .000
     DET A 1-O   55 .266
1956 DET A O   141 .326
1957 DET A O   138 .276
1958 DET A 1-O   131 .272
1959 DET A O   145 .251
1960 DET A O   134 .237
1961 DET A O   79 .229
1962 DET A 1-O   30 .194
     CHI A 1-O   69 .296
1963 CHI A 1-O   71 .231
1964 CHI A H   2 .000
     BLTL   1132 .264

MAXWELL, JAMES ALBERT (BERT)
B.OCT.17,1886 TEXARKANA,ARK.
D.DEC.10,1961 BRADY,TEX.
1906 PIT N P   1 0- 1
1908 PHI A P   4 0- 0
1911 NY N P   4 1- 2
1914 BRO F P   12 3- 4
     BBTR   21 4- 7

**MAY, ALBERT
(REAL NAME ALBERT MARTIN)**
1872 ECK NA 2   4 .263

MAY, CARLOS
B.MAY 17,1948 BIRMINGHAM,ALA.
1968 CHI A D   17 .179
1969 CHI A *O   100 .281
1970 CHI A *O/1   150 .285
1971 CHI A *1/O   141 .294
1972 CHI A *O/1   148 .308
1973 CHI A D-O/1   149 .268
1974 CHI A *O-D   149 .249
1975 CHI A 1-D-O   128 .271
1976 CHI A D/O   20 .175
     NY A D/O-1   87 .278
1977 NY A D/O   65 .227
     CAL A /1   11 .333
     BLTR   1165 .274

MAY, DAVID LA FRANCE (DAVE)
B.DEC.23,1943 NEW CASTLE,DEL.
1967 BAL A O   36 .235
1968 BAL A O   84 .191
1969 BAL A O   78 .242
1970 BAL A /O   25 .194
     MIL A O   101 .240
1971 MIL A *O   144 .277
1972 MIL A *O   143 .238
1973 MIL A *O   156 .303
1974 MIL A *O   135 .226
1975 ATL N O   82 .276
1976 ATL N O   105 .215
1977 TEX A *O   120 .241
1978 TEX A *O   39 .195
     PIT N /H   5 .000
     BLTR   1253 .251

MAY, FRANK SPRUIELL (JAKIE)
B.NOV.25,1895 YOUNGSVILLE,N.C.
D.JUNE 3,1970 WENDELL,N.C.
1917 STL N P   15 0- 0
1918 STL N P   29 5- 6
1919 STL N P   28 3-12
1920 STL N P   16 1- 4
1921 STL N P   5 1- 3
1924 CIN N P   38 3- 3
1925 CIN N P   36 8- 9
1926 CIN N P   45 13- 9
1927 CIN N P   44 15-12
1928 CIN N P   21 3- 5
1929 CIN N P   41 10-14
1930 CIN N P   26 3-11
1931 CHI N P   31 9- 5
1932 CHI N P   35 2- 2
     BRTL   410 72-95

MAY, JERRY LEE
B.DEC.14,1943 STAUNTON,VA.
1964 PIT N C   11 .298
1965 PIT N /C   4 .500
1966 PIT N C   42 .250
1967 PIT N *C   110 .271
1968 PIT N *C   137 .219
1969 PIT N C   62 .232
1970 PIT N C   51 .209
1971 KC A C   71 .252
1972 KC A C   53 .100
1973 KC A C   11 .133
     NY N /C   4 .250
     BRTR   556 .234

MAY, LEE ANDREW
B.MAR.23,1943 BIRMINGHAM,ALA.
1965 CIN N /H   5 .000
1966 CIN N 1   25 .333
1967 CIN N 1-O   127 .265
1968 CIN N *1-O   146 .290
1969 CIN N *1/O   158 .278
1970 CIN N *1   153 .253
1971 CIN N *1   147 .278
1972 HOU N *1   148 .284
1973 HOU N *1   148 .270
1974 HOU N *1   152 .268
1975 BAL A *1   146 .262
1976 BAL A *1   148 .258
1977 BAL A *1-D   150 .253
1978 BAL A *D/1   148 .246
     BRTR   1801 .268

MAY, MERRILL GLEND (PINKY)
B.JAN.18,1911 LACONIA,IND.
1939 PHI N 3   135 .287
1940 PHI N 5-3   136 .293
1941 PHI N 3   142 .267
1942 PHI N 3   115 .238
1943 PHI N 3   137 .282
     BRTR   665 .275

MAY, MILTON SCOTT (MILT)
B.AUG.1,1950 GARY,IND.
1970 PIT N /H   5 .500
1971 PIT N C   49 .278
1972 PIT N C   57 .281
1973 PIT N C   101 .269
1974 HOU N *C   127 .289
1975 HOU N *C   111 .241
1976 DET A /C   6 .280
1977 DET A *C   115 .249
1978 DET A C   105 .250
     BLTR   676 .263

MAY, RUDOLPH (RUDY)
B.JULY 18,1944 COFFEYVILLE,KAN.
1965 CAL A P   30 4- 9
1969 CAL A P   43 44 10-13
1970 CAL A P   38 7-13
1971 CAL A P   32 11-12
1972 CAL A P   35 12-11
1973 CAL A P   34 7-17
1974 CAL A P   18 0- 1
     NY A P   17 8- 4
1975 NY A P   32 14-12
1976 NY A P   11 4- 3
     BAL A P   24 11- 7
1977 BAL A P   37 18-14
1978 MON N P   27 8-10
     BLTL   378 379 114-126

MAY, WILLIAM HERBERT (BUCKSHOT)
B.DEC.13,1899 BAKERSFIELD,CAL.
1924 PIT N P   1 0- 0
     BRTR

YR	CL	LEA	POS	GP	G	REC

MAYBERRY, JOHN CLAIBORN
B.FEB.18,1949 DETROIT,MICH.

YR	CL	LEA	POS	GP	G	REC
1968	HOU	N	/1		4	.000
1969	HOU	N	/H		5	.000
1970	HOU	N	1		50	.216
1971	HOU	N	1		46	.182
1972	KC	A	*1		149	.298
1973	KC	A	*1		152	.278
1974	KC	A	*1-0		126	.234
1975	KC	A	*1-0		156	.291
1976	KC	A	*1		161	.232
1977	KC	A	*1		153	.230
1978	TOR	A	*1		152	.250
	BLTL				1154	.254

MAYE, ARTHUR LEE (LEE)
B.DEC.11,1934 TUSCALOOSA,ALA.

YR	CL	LEA	POS	GP	G	REC
1959	MIL	N	O		51	.300
1960	MIL	N	O		41	.301
1961	MIL	N	O		110	.271
1962	MIL	N	O		99	.244
1963	MIL	N	O		124	.271
1964	MIL	N	3-0		153	.304
1965	MIL	N	O		15	.302
	HOU	N	*O		108	.251
1966	HOU	N	O		115	.288
1967	CLE	A	O/2		115	.259
1968	CLE	A	O/1		109	.281
1969	CLE	A	O		43	.250
	WAS	A	O		71	.290
1970	WAS	A	O/3		96	.263
	CHI	A	/H		6	.167
1971	CHI	A	O		32	.205
	BLTR				1288	.274

MAYER, EDWARD H.
B.AUG.16,1866 MARSHALL,ILL.

YR	CL	LEA	POS	GP	G	REC
1890	PHI	N	3		117	.241
1891	PHI	N	3-0		65	.201
					182	.217

MAYER, EDWIN DAVID
B.NOV.30,1931 SAN FRANCISCO,CAL

YR	CL	LEA	POS	GP	G	REC
1957	CHI	N	P		3	0-0
1958	CHI	N	P		19	2-2
	BLTL				22	2-2

MAYER, ERSKINE JOHN
[REAL NAME JAMES ERSKINE]
B.JAN.16,1889 ATLANTA,GA.
D.MAR.10,1957 LOS ANGELES,CAL.

YR	CL	LEA	POS	GP	G	REC
1912	PHI	N	P		7	0-1
1913	PHI	N	P		39	9-9
1914	PHI	N	P		48	21-19
1915	PHI	N	P		43	21-15
1916	PHI	N	P		28	7-7
1917	PHI	N	P		28	11-6
1918	PHI	N	P		13	7-4
	PIT	N	P		15	9-3
1919	PIT	N	P		18	5-3
	CHI	A	P		6	1-3
	BRTR				245	91-70

MAYER, SAMUEL FRANKEL
[REAL NAME SAMUEL FRANKEL ERSKINE]
B.FEB.28,1893 ATLANTA,GA.
D.JULY 1,1962 ATLANTA,GA.

YR	CL	LEA	POS	GP	G	REC
1915	WAS	A	P-1-	1	11	0-0
			O			.231
	BRTL					

MAYER, WALTER A.
B.AUG.3,1889 CINCINNATI,OHIO
D.NOV.18,1951 MINNEAPOLIS,MINN.

YR	CL	LEA	POS	GP	G	REC
1911	CHI	A	C		1	.000
1912	CHI	A	C		9	.000
1914	CHI	A	C		39	.165
1915	CHI	A	C		22	.222
1917	BOS	A	C		4	.167
1918	BOS	A	C		26	.224
1919	STL	A	C		30	.226
	BRTR				131	.183

MAYES, ADAIR BUSHYHEAD (PADDY)
B.MAR.17,1885 LOCUST GROVE,OKLA
D.MAY 28,1962 FAYETTEVILLE,ARK.

YR	CL	LEA	POS	GP	G	REC
1911	PHI	N	O		5	.000
	BLTR					

MAYNARD, JAMES WALTER (BUSTER)
B.MAR.25,1913 HENDERSON,S.C.

YR	CL	LEA	POS	GP	G	REC
1940	NY	N	O		7	.276
1942	NY	N	2-3-O		89	.247
1943	NY	N	3-O		121	.206
1946	NY	N	O		7	.000
	BRTR				224	.221

MAYNARD, LE ROY EVANS (CHICK)
B.NOV.2,1896 TURNERS FALLS,MASS
D.JAN.31,1957 BANGOR,MAINE

YR	CL	LEA	POS	GP	G	REC
1922	BOS	A	S		12	.125
	TR					

MAYNARD, RICHARD WHEELER
[PLAYED UNDER NAME OF
RICHARD WHEELER]

**MAYO, EDWARD JOSEPH
(EDDIE) OR (HOTSHOT)
[REAL NAME EDWARD JOSEPH MAYOSKI]**
B.APR.15,1910 HOLYOKE,MASS.

YR	CL	LEA	POS	GP	G	REC
1936	NY	N	3		46	.199
1937	BOS	N	3		65	.227
1938	BOS	N	S-3		8	.214
1943	PHI	A	3		128	.219
1944	DET	A	2-S		154	.249
1945	DET	A	2		134	.285
1946	DET	A	2		51	.252
1947	DET	A	2		142	.279
1948	DET	A	2-3		106	.249
	BLTR				834	.253

MAYO, JOHN LEWIS (JACKIE)
B.JULY 26,1925 LITCHFIELD,ILL.

YR	CL	LEA	POS	GP	G	REC
1948	PHI	N	O		12	.229
1949	PHI	N	O		45	.128
1950	PHI	N	O		18	.222
1951	PHI	N	O		9	.143
1952	PHI	N	1-O		50	.244
1953	PHI	N	O		5	.000
	BLTR				139	.213

MAYOSKI, EDWARD JOSEPH
[PLAYED UNDER NAME OF
EDWARD JOSEPH MAYO]

MAYS, ALBERT C.
B.MAY 17,1865 CANAL DOVER,OHIO
D.MAY 7,1905 PARKERSBURG,W.VA.

YR	CL	LEA	POS	GP	G	REC
1885	LOU	AA	P		17	6-11
1886	MET	AA	P		41	11-27
1887	MET	AA	P		62'	17-34
1888	BRO	AA	P		18	9-9
1889	COL	AA	P		22	9-9
1890	COL	AA	P		1	0-1
	BR				161	52-91

MAYS, CARL WILLIAM (CARL) OR (SUB)
B.NOV.12,1891 LIBERTY,KY.
D.APR.4,1971 EL CAJON,CAL.

YR	CL	LEA	POS	GP	G	REC
1915	BOS	A	P		38	4-6
1916	BOS	A	P	44	48	18-13
1917	BOS	A	P		35	22-9
1918	BOS	A	P	35	38	21-13
1919	BOS	A	P	21	22	8-12
	NY	A	P		13	5-2
1920	NY	A	P		45	26-11
1921	NY	A	P	49	51	27-9
1922	NY	A	P	34	35	12-14
1923	NY	A	P		23	5-2
1924	CIN	N	P	37	38	20-9
1925	CIN	N	P		12	3-5
1926	CIN	N	P		39	19-12
1927	CIN	N	P		14	3-7
1928	CIN	N	P		14	4-1
1929	NY	N	P		37	7-2
	BLTR			490	502	204-127

**MAYS, WILLIE HOWARD
(WILLIE) OR (SAY HEY)**
B.MAY 6,1931 WESTFIELD,ALA.

YR	CL	LEA	POS	GP	G	REC
1951	NY	N	O		121	.274
1952	NY	N	O		34	.236
1954	NY	N	O		151	.345
1955	NY	N	O		152	.319
1956	NY	N	O		152	.296
1957	NY	N	O		152	.333
1958	SF	N	O		152	.347
1959	SF	N	O		151	.313
1960	SF	N	O		153	.319
1961	SF	N	O		154	.308
1962	SF	N	O		162	.304
1963	SF	N	S-O		157	.314
1964	SF	N	1-S-3-O		157	.296
1965	SF	N	*O		157	.317
1966	SF	N	*O		152	.288
1967	SF	N	*O		141	.263
1968	SF	N	*O/1		148	.289
1969	SF	N	*O/1		117	.283
1970	SF	N	*O/1		139	.291
1971	SF	N	O-1		136	.271
1972	SF	N	O		19	.184
	NY	N	O-1		69	.267
1973	NY	N	O-1		66	.211
	BRTR				2992	.302

**MAZEROSKI, WILLIAM STANLEY
(BILL) OR (MAZ)**
B.SEP.5,1936 WHEELING,W.VA.

YR	CL	LEA	POS	GP	G	REC
1956	PIT	N	2		81	.243
1957	PIT	N	2		148	.283
1958	PIT	N	2		152	.275
1959	PIT	N	2		135	.241
1960	PIT	N	2		151	.273
1961	PIT	N	2		152	.265
1962	PIT	N	2		159	.271
1963	PIT	N	2		142	.245
1964	PIT	N	2		162	.268
1965	PIT	N	*2		130	.271
1966	PIT	N	*2		162	.262
1967	PIT	N	*2		163	.261
1968	PIT	N	*2		143	.251
1969	PIT	N	*2		67	.229
1970	PIT	N	*2		112	.229
1971	PIT	N	2/3		70	.254
1972	PIT	N	2/3		34	.188
	BRTR				2163	.260

MAZZERA, MELVIN LEONARD (MIKE)
B.JAN.31,1914 STOCKTON,CAL.

YR	CL	LEA	POS	GP	G	REC
1935	STL	A	O		12	.233
1937	STL	A	H		7	.286
1938	STL	A	O		86	.279
1939	STL	A	O		34	.297
1940	PHI	N	1-O		69	.237
	BLTL				208	.268

MAZZILLI, LEE LOUIS
B.MAR.25,1955 NEW YORK,N.Y.

YR	CL	LEA	POS	GP	G	REC
1976	NY	N	O		24	.195
1977	NY	N	*O		159	.250
1978	NY	N	*O		148	.273
	BBTR				331	.257

MC ADAMS, GEORGE D. (JACK)
B.DEC.17,1886 BENTON,ARK.
D.MAY 21,1937 SAN FRANCISCO,CAL

YR	CL	LEA	POS	GP	G	REC
1911	STL	N	P		6	0-0
	BRTR					

MC AFEE, WILLIAM FORT
B.SEPT.7,1907 SMITHVILLE,GA.
D.JULY 8,1958 CULPEPPER,VA.

YR	CL	LEA	POS	GP	G	REC
1930	CHI	N	P		2	0-0
1931	BOS	N	P		18	0-1
1932	WAS	A	P		8	6-1
1933	WAS	A	P-2		27	3-2
						.267
1934	STL	A	P		28	1-0
	BRTR				83	10-4
						.173

MC ALEER, JAMES ROBERT (LOAFER)
B.JULY 10,1864 YOUNGSTOWN,OHIO
D.APR.29,1931 YOUNGSTOWN,OHIO

YR	CL	LEA	POS	GP	G	REC
1889	CLE	N	O		109	.235
1890	CLE	P	O		86	.272
1891	CLE	N	O		135	.246
1892	CLE	N	O		150	.241
1893	CLE	N	O		91	.253
1894	CLE	N	O		64	.298
1895	CLE	N	O		132	.291
1896	CLE	N	O		116	.288
1897	CLE	N	O		23	.224
1898	CLE	N	O		104	.235
1901	CLE	A	M-O		3	.125
1902	STL	A	M-O		2	.167
1907	STL	A	M-H		1	.000
	BRTR				1017	.259

NON-PLAYING MANAGER
STL[A] 1903-09, WAS[A] 1910-11

MC ALEESE, JOHN JAMES (JACK)
B.AUG.22,1878 SHARON,PA.
D.NOV.14,1950 NEW YORK,N.Y.

YR	CL	LEA	POS	GP	G	REC
1901	CHI	A	P		1	0-0
1909	STL	A	O		85	.213
	TR			1	86	0-0
						.213

MC ALLESTER, WILLIAM LUSK
B.DEC.29,1889 CHATTANOOGA,TENN.
D.MAR.3,1970 CHATTANOOGA,TENN.

YR	CL	LEA	POS	GP	G	REC
1913	STL	A	C		46	.153
	BRTR					

MC ALLISTER, JACK
[SEE ANDREW JAMES COAKLEY]

YR	CL LEA POS	GP	G	REC

MC ALLISTER, LEWIS WILLIAM (SPORT)
B.JULY 23,1874 AUSTIN,MISS.
D.JULY 17,1962 WYANDOTTE,MICH.

YR	CL LEA POS	GP	G	REC
1896	CLE N P-C-	3	7	0- 0
	O			.185
1897	CLE N P	7	40	2- 3
				.211
1898	CLE N P	9	16	3- 3
1899	CLE N P-0	1	110	0- 1
				.238
1901	DET A C-1		91	.287
1902	DET A C-1-2-S-3-0		20	.200
	BAL A 1-2-3		3	.091
	DET A C-1-2-S-3-0		44	.209
1903	DET A C-S		78	.264
	BBTR	20	409	5- 7
				.245

MC ANALLY, ERNEST LEE (ERNIE)
B.AUG.15,1946 PITTSBURG,TEX.

1971	MON N P		31	11-12
1972	MON N P		29	6-15
1973	MON N P		27	7- 9
1974	MON N P		25	6-13
	BBTR		112	30-49

MC ANANY, JAMES (JIM)
B.SEPT.4,1936 LOS ANGELES,CAL.

1958	CHI A 0		5	.000
1959	CHI A 0		67	.276
1960	CHI A H		3	.000
1961	CHI N P		11	.300
1962	CHI N H		7	.000
	BBTR		93	.253

MC ANDREW, JAMES CLEMENT (JIM)
B.JAN.11,1944 LOST NATION,IOWA

1968	NY N P		12	4- 7
1969	NY N P		27	6- 7
1970	NY N P		32	10-14
1971	NY N P		24	2- 5
1972	NY N P		28	11- 8
1973	NY N P	23	24	3- 8
1974	SD N P		15	1- 4
	BBTR	161	162	37-53

MC ARTHUR, MALCOLM (MAC)
B.1862 DETROIT,MICH.

1884	IND AA P		6	1- 5
	TR			

MC ARTHUR, OLAND ALEXANDER (DIXIE)
B.FEB.1,1892 VERNON,ALA.

1914	PIT N P		1	0- 0
	BRTR			

MC ATEE, MICHAEL JAMES (BUTCH)
B.1846 LANSINGBURG,N.Y.
D.OCT.18,1876

1871	CHI NA 1		26	-
1872	TRO NA 1		25	.209
			51	-

MC AULEY, JAMES EARL (IKE)
B.AUG.19,1891 WICHITA,KAN.
D.APR.6,1928 DES MOINES,IOWA

1914	PIT N 2-S-3		15	.125
1915	PIT N S		5	.133
1916	PIT N S		4	.250
1917	STL N S		3	.286
1925	CHI N S		37	.280
	BRTR		64	.246

MC AULIFFE, EUGENE LEO
B.JAN.8,1872 RANDOLPH,MASS.
D.APR.29,1953 RANDOLPH,MASS.

1904	BOS N C		1	.500
	TR			

MC AULIFFE, RICHARD JOHN (DICK)
B.NOV.29,1939 HARTFORD,CONN.

1960	DET A S		8	.259
1961	DET A S-3		80	.256
1962	DET A 2-S-3		139	.263
1963	DET A 2-S		150	.262
1964	DET A S		162	.241
1965	DET A *S		113	.260
1966	DET A *S-3		124	.274
1967	DET A *2/S		153	.239
1968	DET A *2/S		151	.249
1969	DET A 2		74	.262
1970	DET A *S-S-3		146	.234
1971	DET A *2/S		128	.208
1972	DET A *2/S-3		122	.240
1973	DET A *2/S		106	.274
1974	BOS A 2-3/S		100	.210
1975	BOS A /3		7	.133
	BLTR		1763	.247

MC AVOY, GEORGE H.

1914	PHI N H		1	.000

MC AVOY, JAMES EUGENE (WICKEY)
B.OCT.22,1894 ROCHESTER,N.Y.
D.JULY 5,1973 ROCHESTER,N.Y.

1913	PHI A C		4	.111
1914	PHI A C		8	.111
1915	PHI A C		68	.190
1917	PHI A C		10	.250
1918	PHI A C		83	.244
1919	PHI A C		62	.141
	BRTR		235	.199

MC AVOY, THOMAS JOHN (TOM)
B.AUG.12,1936 BROOKLYN,N.Y.

1959	WAS A P		1	0- 0
	BLTL			

MC BEAN, ALVIN O NEAL (AL)
B.MAY 15,1938 CHARLOTTE AMALIE,V.I.

1961	PIT N P	27	28	3- 2
1962	PIT N P	33	34	15-10
1963	PIT N P	55	59	13- 3
1964	PIT N P		58	8- 3
1965	PIT N P/0		62	6- 6
				.222
1966	PIT N P	47	50	4- 3
1967	PIT N P		51	7- 4
1968	PIT N P	36	43	9-12
1969	SD N /P		1	0- 1
	LA N /P		31	2- 6
1970	LA N /P		1	0- 0
	PIT N /P		7	0- 0
	BRTR	409	425	67-50
				.197

MC BEE, PRYOR EDWARD (LEFTY)
B.JUNE 20,1901 BLANCO,OKLA.
D.APR.19,1963 ROSEVILLE,CAL.

1926	CHI A P		1	0- 0
	BRTL			

MC BRIDE, ALGERNON BRIGGS
B.MAY.23,1869 MARTINSVILLE,IND.
D.JAN.10,1956 GEORGETOWN,OHIO

1896	CIN N 0		9	.233
1898	CIN N 0		120	.300
1899	CIN N 0		62	.352
1900	CIN N 0		109	.277
1901	CIN N 0		30	.254
	NY N 0		62	.277
	BLTL		392	.294

MC BRIDE, ARNOLD RAY (BAKE)
B.FEB.3,1949 FULTON,MO.

1973	STL N 0		40	.302
1974	STL N *0		150	.309
1975	STL N *0		116	.300
1976	STL N 0		72	.335
1977	STL N 0		43	.262
	PHI N 0		85	.339
1978	PHI N *0		122	.269
	BLTR		628	.303

MC BRIDE, GEORGE FLORIAN
B.NOV.20,1880 MILWAUKEE,WIS.
D.JULY 2,1973 MILWAUKEE,WIS.

1901	MIL A S			.250
1905	PIT N S-3		25	.218
	STL N S		81	.253
1906	STL N S		90	.169
1908	WAS A S		155	.232
1909	WAS A S		155	.234
1910	WAS A S		154	.230
1911	WAS A S		154	.236
1912	WAS A S		192	.226
1913	WAS A S		150	.214
1914	WAS A S		156	.203
1915	WAS A S		146	.204
1916	WAS A S		139	.227
1917	WAS A S		50	.192
1918	WAS A S		18	.132
1919	WAS A S		15	.200
1920	WAS A S		14	.219
	BRTR		1655	.218

NON-PLAYING MANAGER WAS[A] 1921

MC BRIDE, JAMES DICKSON (DICK)
B.1845 PHILADELPHIA,PA.
D.OCT.10,1916 PHILADELPHIA,PA.

1871	ATH NA P		25	20- 5
1872	ATH NA P		46	31-15
1873	ATH NA P-0	46	48	24-21
1874	ATH NA P		55	33-22
1875	ATH NA P		59	43-14
1876	BOS N P		4	0- 4
	TR	235	237	151-81

MC BRIDE, JOHN F.

1890	ATH AA 0		1	.000

MC BRIDE, KENNETH FAYE (KEN)
B.AUG.12,1935 HUNTSVILLE,ALA.

1959	CHI A P		11	0- 1
1960	CHI A P		5	0- 1
1961	LA A P	38	45	12-15
1962	LA A P		24	11- 5
1963	LA A P	36	38	13-12
1964	LA A P		29	4-13
1965	CAL A /P		8	0- 3
	BRTR	151	160	40-50

MC BRIDE, PETER WILLIAM
B.JULY 9,1875 ADAMS,MASS.
D.JULY 3,1944 N.ADAMS,MASS.

1898	CLE N P		1	0- 1
1899	STL N P		11	2- 5
			12	2- 6

MC BRIDE, THOMAS RAYMOND (TOM)
B.NOV.2,1914 BONHAM,TEX.

1943	BOS A 0		26	.240
1944	BOS A 1-0		71	.245
1945	BOS A 1-0		100	.305
1946	BOS A 0		61	.301
1947	BOS A 0		2	.200
	WAS A 3-0		56	.271
1948	WAS A 0		92	.257
	BRTR		408	.275

MC CABE, JAMES ARTHUR (SWAT)
B.NOV.20,1881 TOWANDA,PA.
D.DEC.9,1944 BRISTOL,CONN.

1909	CIN N 0		4	.461
1910	CIN N 0		13	.257
	BLTR		17	.313

MC CABE, JOSEPH ROBERT (JOE)
B.AUG.27,1938 INDIANAPOLIS,IND.

1964	MIN A C		14	.158
1965	WAS A C		14	.185
	BRTR		28	.174

MC CABE, RALPH HERBERT (MACK)
B.OCT.21,1918 NAPANEE,ONT.,CAN.
D.MAY 3,1974 WINDSOR,ONT.,CAN.

1946	CLE A P		1	0- 1
	BRTR			

MC CABE, RICHARD JAMES
B.FEB.21,1896 MAMARONECK,N.Y.
D.APR.11,1950 BUFFALO,N.Y.

1918	BOS A P		3	0- 1
1922	CHI A P		3	1- 0
			6	1- 1

MC CABE, TIMOTHY J. (TIM)
B.OCT.19,1894 IRONTON,MO.
D.APR.12,1977 IRONTON,MO.

1915	STL A P		7	3- 1
1916	STL A P		13	3- 0
1917	STL A P		1	0- 0
1918	STL A P		2	0- 0
	BRTR		23	6- 1

MC CABE, WILLIAM FRANCIS
B.OCT.28,1892 CHICAGO,ILL.
D.SEPT.2,1966 CHICAGO,ILL.

1918	CHI N 2-0		29	.178
1919	CHI N S-3-0		33	.155
1920	CHI N 0		3	.500
	BRO N 0		41	.147
	BBTR		106	.161
	BL 1918			

MC CAFFERY, HARRY CHARLES
B.NOV.25,1858 ST.LOUIS,MO.
D.APR.19,1928 ST.LOUIS,MO.

1882	STL AA 1-2-3-0		37	.268
1883	STL AA 0		5	.053
1885	CIN AA P		1	1- 0
	BRTR	1	43	1- 0
				.237

MC CAFFREY, CHARLES P. (SPARROW)
B.PHILADELPHIA,PA.
D.MAY 1894 PHILADELPHIA,PA.

1889	COL AA C		2	.167
1890	ATH AA C		1	.250
			3	.200

MC CAHAN, WILLIAM GLENN (BILL)
B.JUNE 7,1921 PHILADELPHIA,PA.

1946	PHI A P		4	1- 1
1947	PHI A P		29	10- 5
1948	PHI A P		17	4- 7
1949	PHI A P		7	1- 1
	BRTR		57	16-14

MC CALL, BRIAN ALLEN
(BRIAN) OR (BAM)
B.JAN.25,1943 KENTFIELD,CAL.

1962	CHI A 0		4	.375
1963	CHI A 0		3	.000
	BLTL		7	.200

MC CALL, JOHN WILLIAM (WINDY)
B.JUL.18,1925 SAN FRANCISCO,CAL

YR	CL	LEA	POS	GP	G	REC
1948	BOS	A	P		1	0- 1
1949	BOS	A	P		5	0- 0
1950	PIT	N	P		2	0- 0
1954	NY	N	P		33	2- 5
1955	NY	N	P		42	6- 5
1956	NY	N	P		46	3- 4
1957	NY	N	P		5	0- 0
	BLTL				134	11-15

MC CALL, LARRY STEPHEN
B.SEPT.8,1952 ASHEVILLE,N.C.

YR	CL	LEA	POS	GP	G	REC
1977	NY	A	/P	2	3	0- 1
1978	NY	A	/P		5	1- 1
	BLTR			7	8	1- 2

MC CALL, ROBERT LEONARD (DUTCH)
B.DEC.27,1920 COLUMBIA,TENN.

YR	CL	LEA	POS	GP	G	REC
1948	CHI	N	P		30	4-13
	BLTL					

MC CALLISTER, JOHN (JACK)
B.JAN.19,1879 MARIETTA,OHIO
D.OCT.18,1946 COLUMBUS,OHIO
NON-PLAYING MANAGER CLE[A] 1927

MC CANDLESS, JOHN C.
B.1895 PITTSBURGH,PA.

YR	CL	LEA	POS	GP	G	REC
1914	BAL	F	O		11	.258
1915	BAL	F	O		116	.218
	BLTR				127	.221

MC CANN, HENRY EUGENE (GENE) OR (MIKE)
B.JUNE 13,1876 BALTIMORE,MD.
D.APR.26,1943 NEW YORK,N.Y.

YR	CL	LEA	POS	GP	G	REC
1901	BRO	N	P		6	2- 3
1902	BRO	N	P		3	1- 2
	TR				9	3- 5

MC CANN, ROBERT EMMETT (EMMETT)
B.MAR.4,1902 PHILADELPHIA,PA.
D.APR.15,1937 PHILADELPHIA,PA.

YR	CL	LEA	POS	GP	G	REC
1920	PHI	A	S		10	.286
1921	PHI	A	S		52	.223
1926	BOS	A	S		6	.000
	BRTR				68	.222

MC CARDELL, ROGER MORTON
B.AUG.29,1932 GORSJCH MILLS,MD.

YR	CL	LEA	POS	GP	G	REC
1959	SF	N	C		4	.000
	BRTR					

MC CARREN, WILLIAM JOSEPH
B.NOV.4,1895 FORTENIA,PA.

YR	CL	LEA	POS	GP	G	REC
1923	BRO	N	3-O		69	.245
	BRTR					

MC CARTHY, ALEXANDER GEORGE
B.MAY 12,1888 CHICAGO,ILL.
D.MAR.12,1978 SALISBURY,MD.

YR	CL	LEA	POS	GP	G	REC
1910	PIT	N	S		3	.046
1911	PIT	N	S		46	.240
1912	PIT	N	2		111	.277
1913	PIT	N	S		31	.203
1914	PIT	N	3		57	.150
1915	PIT	N	2		21	.204
	CHI	N	2		23	.264
1916	CHI	N	2-S		37	.245
	PIT	N	2-S		50	.197
1917	PIT	N	3		49	.219
	BRTR				428	.229

MC CARTHY, ARCHIBALD J.
B.YPSILANTI,MICH.

YR	CL	LEA	POS	GP	G	REC
1902	DET	A	P		10	1- 7

MC CARTHY, JEROME FRANCIS
B.MAY 23,1923 BROOKLYN,N.Y.
D.OCT.3,1965 OCEANSIDE,N.Y.

YR	CL	LEA	POS	GP	G	REC
1948	STL	A	1		2	.333
	BLTL					

MC CARTHY, JOHN ARTHUR (JACK)
B.MAR.26,1869 GILBERTVILLE,MASS
D.SEPT.11,1931 CHICAGO,ILL.

YR	CL	LEA	POS	GP	G	REC
1893	CIN	N	O		48	.285
1894	CIN	N	1-O		40	.267
1898	PIT	N	O		137	.289
1899	PIT	N	O		139	.307
1900	CHI	N	O		123	.296
1901	CLE	A	O		86	.314
1902	CLE	A	O		95	.276
1903	CLE	A	O		109	.265
	CHI	N	O		24	.277
1904	CHI	N	O		115	.264
1905	CHI	N	O		43	.276
1906	BRO	N	O		86	.304
1907	BRO	N	O		25	.220
	BLTL				1070	.289

MC CARTHY, JOHN JOSEPH (JOHNNY)
B.JAN.7,1910 CHICAGO,ILL.
D.SEPT.13,1973 MUNDELEIN,ILL.

YR	CL	LEA	POS	GP	G	REC
1934	BRO	N	1		17	.179
1935	BRO	N	1		22	.250
1936	NY	N	1		4	.438
1937	NY	N	1		114	.279
1938	NY	N	1		134	.272
1939	NY	N	P-1	1	50	0- 0
						.262
1940	NY	N	1		51	.239
1941	NY	N	1-O		14	.325
1943	BOS	N	1		78	.304
1946	BOS	N	1		2	.143
1948	BOS	N	1		56	.263
	BLTL			1	542	0- 0
						.277

MC CARTHY, JOSEPH N.
B.DEC.25,1881 SYRACUSE,N.Y.
D.JAN.12,1937 SYRACUSE,N.Y.

YR	CL	LEA	POS	GP	G	REC
1905	NY	A	C		1	.000
1906	STL	N	C		14	.237
	TR				15	.225

MC CARTHY, JOSEPH VINCENT (MARSE JOE)
B.APR.21,1887 PHILADELPHIA,PA.
D.JAN.13,1978 BUFFALO,N.Y.
NON-PLAYING MANAGER
CHI[N] 1926-30, NY[A] 1931-46,
BOS(A) 1948-50

MC CARTHY, THOMAS FRANCIS MICHAEL (TOMMY)
B.JULY 24,1864 BOSTON,MASS.
D.AUG.5,1922 BOSTON,MASS.

YR	CL	LEA	POS	GP	G	REC
1884	BOS	U	P-O	7	53	0- 7
						.218
1885	BOS	N	O		40	.182
1886	PHI	N	O		8	.185
1887	PHI	N	O		18	.208
1888	STL	AA	P-O	1	131	0- 0
						.276
1889	STL	AA	O		139	.297
1890	STL	AA	M-O		133	.332
1891	STL	AA	O		135	.302
1892	BOS	N	O		152	.244
1893	BOS	N	O		116	.360
1894	BOS	N	O		126	.349
1895	BOS	N	O		116	.291
1896	BRO	N	O		101	.253
	BRTR			8	1268	0- 7
						.294

MC CARTHY, THOMAS PATRICK
B.MAY 22,1884 FT.WAYNE,IND.
D.MAR.28,1933 MISHAWAKA,IND.

YR	CL	LEA	POS	GP	G	REC
1908	CIN	N	P		1	0- 1
	PIT	N	P		2	0- 0
	BOS	N	P		14	7- 3
1909	BOS	N	P		8	0- 5
	TR				25	7- 9

MC CARTHY, WILLIAM JOHN
B.BOSTON,MASS.
D.FEB.4,1928 WASHINGTON,D.C.

YR	CL	LEA	POS	GP	G	REC
1905	BOS	N	C		1	.000
1907	CIN	N	C		3	.125
	TR				4	.091

MC CARTHY, WILLIAM THOMAS
B.APR.11,1882 ASHLAND,MASS.
D.MAY 29,1939 BOSTON,MASS.

YR	CL	LEA	POS	GP	G	REC
1906	BOS	N	P		1	0- 0
	BRTR					

MC CARTON, FRANK
B.MIDDLETOWN,CONN.

YR	CL	LEA	POS	GP	G	REC
1872	MAN	NA	O		19	.271

MC CARTY, GEORGE LEWIS (LEW)
B.NOV.17,1888 MILTON,PA.
D.JUNE 9,1930 READING,PA.

YR	CL	LEA	POS	GP	G	REC
1913	BRO	N	C		9	.192
1914	BRO	N	C		90	.254
1915	BRO	N	C		84	.239
1916	BRO	N	C-1		55	.311
	NY	N	C		25	.400
1917	NY	N	C		56	.247
1918	NY	N	C		85	.269
1919	NY	N	C		85	.281
1920	NY	N	C		36	.192
	STL	N	C		5	.286
1921	STL	N	C		1	.000
	BRTR				532	.277

MC CARTY, JOHN A.
B.ST.LOUIS,MO.

YR	CL	LEA	POS	GP	G	REC
1889	KC	AA	P		20	8- 6
	TR					

MC CARVER, JAMES TIMOTHY (TIM)
B.OCT.16,1941 MEMPHIS,TENN.

YR	CL	LEA	POS	GP	G	REC
1959	STL	N	C		8	.167
1960	STL	N	C		10	.200
1961	STL	N	C		22	.239
1963	STL	N	C		127	.289
1964	STL	N	C		143	.288
1965	STL	N	*C		113	.276
1966	STL	N	*C		150	.274
1967	STL	N	*C		138	.295
1968	STL	N	*C		128	.253
1969	STL	N	*C		138	.260
1970	PHI	N	C		44	.287
1971	PHI	N	*C		134	.278
1972	PHI	N	C		45	.237
	MON	N	C-O/3		77	.251
1973	STL	N	1-C		130	.266
1974	STL	N	C/1		74	.250
	BOS	A	/C		11	.250
1975	BOS	A	/C-1		12	.381
	PHI	N	C/1		47	.254
1976	PHI	N	C/1		90	.277
1977	PHI	N	C/1		93	.320
1978	PHI	N	C-1		90	.247
	BLTR				1824	.272

MC CATTY, STEVEN EARL (STEVE)
B.MAR.20,1954 DETROIT,MICH.

YR	CL	LEA	POS	GP	G	REC
1977	OAK	A	/P		4	0- 0
1978	OAK	A	/P		9	0- 0
	BRTR				13	0- 0

MC CAULEY, ALLEN A.
B.MAR.4,1863 INDIANAPOLIS,IND.

YR	CL	LEA	POS	GP	G	REC
1884	IND	AA	P-1	9	17	2- 7
						.189
1890	PHI	N	1		112	.244
1891	WAS	AA	1		57	.283
	BLTL			9	186	2- 7
						.262

MC CAULEY, JAMES A.
B.1861 STANLEY,N.Y.

YR	CL	LEA	POS	GP	G	REC
1884	STL	AA	C		1	.000
1885	BUF	N	C-O		24	.205
	CHI	N	C-O		3	.100
1886	BRO	AA	C		10	.233
	BRTR				38	.200

MC CAULEY, PATRICK M.
B.JUNE 10,1870 WARE,MASS.
D.JAN.23,1917 NEWARK,N.J.

YR	CL	LEA	POS	GP	G	REC
1893	STL	N	C		5	.067
1896	WAS	N	C		21	.247
1903	NY	A	C		6	.096
	TR				32	.200

MC CAULEY, WILLIAM H.
B.1870 WASHINGTON,D.C.

YR	CL	LEA	POS	GP	G	REC
1895	WAS	N	S		1	.000

MC CHESNEY, HARRY VINCENT (PUD)
B.JUNE 1,1880 PITTSBURGH,PA.
D.AUG.11,1960 PITTSBURGH,PA.

YR	CL	LEA	POS	GP	G	REC
1904	CHI	N	O		22	.261
	BRTR					

MC CLAIN, JOSEPH FRED (JOE)
B.MAY 5,1933 JOHNSON CITY,TENN.

YR	CL	LEA	POS	GP	G	REC
1961	WAS	A	P		33	8-18
1962	WAS	A	P		10	0- 3
	BRTR				43	8-22

MC CLANAHAN, PETER
B.OCT.24,1906 COLDSPRING,TEX.

YR	CL	LEA	POS	GP	G	REC
1931	PIT	N	H		7	.500

MC CLELLAN, HERVEY MC DOWELL (LITTLE MAC)
B.DEC.22,1894 CYNTHIANA,KY.
D.NOV.6,1925 CYNTHIANA,KY.

YR	CL	LEA	POS	GP	G	REC
1919	CHI	A	S-3		7	.333
1920	CHI	A	3		10	.300
1921	CHI	A	2-S-O		63	.179
1922	CHI	A	3		91	.226
1923	CHI	A	S		141	.235
1924	CHI	A	S		32	.176
	BRTR				344	.221

MC CLELLAN, WILLIAM HENRY
B.MAR.22,1856 CHICAGO,ILL.
D.JULY 3,1929 CHICAGO,ILL.

YR	CL	LEA	POS	GP	G	REC
1878	CHI	N	2		46	.241
1881	PRO	N	2-S-O		65	.164
1883	PHI	N	S-O		78	.230
1884	PHI	N	S		110	.256
1885	BRO	AA	2-3		113	.251
1886	BRO	AA	2		142	.262
1887	BRO	AA	2		136	.350
1888	BRO	AA	2-O		75	.214
	CLE	AA	2-S-O		22	.222
	BLTL				787	.258

MC CLESKEY, JEFFERSON LAMAR
B.NOV.6,1891 AMERICUS,GA.
D.MAY 11,1971 AMERICUS,GA.

YR	CL	LEA	POS	GP	G	REC
1913	BOS	N	3		2	.000
	BLTR					

```
YR  CL LEA POS    GP    G   REC

MC CLOSKEY
1875 NAT NA C         10     -

MC CLOSKEY, JAMES ELLWOOD (IRISH)
B.MAY 26,1910 DANVILLE,PA.
D.AUG.18,1971 JERSEY CITY,N.J.
1936 BOS N  P          4    0- 0
        BLTL

MC CLOSKEY, JAMES JOHN
B.AUG.20,1882 WYOMING,PA.
D.MAR.1,1919 LEWISBURG,PA.
1906 PHI N  P          9    3- 3
1907 PHI N  P          2    0- 0
                      11    3- 3

MC CLOSKEY, JOHN JOSEPH
(HONEST JOHN)
B.APR.4,1862 LOUISVILLE,KY.
D.NOV.17,1940 LOUISVILLE,KY.
NON-PLAYING MANAGER
LOUEN] 1895-96, STLEN] 1906-08

MC CLOSKEY, WILLIAM GEORGE
B.PHILADELPHIA,PA.
1884 WIL U  C-O        9   .133

MC CLURE, HAROLD MURRAY (MAC)
B.AUG.8,1859 LEWISBURG,PA.
D.JUNE 5,1919 WILKES-BARRE,PA.
1882 BOS N  O          2   .333
        TR

MC CLURE, LAWRENCE LEDWITH
B.OCT.3,1885 WAYNE,W.VA.
D.AUG.31,1949 HUNTINGTON,W.VA.
1910 NY A   O          1   .000
        BR

MC CLURE, ROBERT CRAIG (BOB)
B.APR.29,1952 OAKLAND,CAL.
1975 KC A   P         12    1- 0
1976 KC A  /P          8    0- 0
1977 MIL A  P         68    2- 1
1978 MIL A  P         44    2- 6
        BRTL    132  133    5- 7

MC CLUSKEY, HARRY ROBERT
B.MAR.29,1892 CLAY CENTER,OHIO
D.JUNE 7,1962 TOLEDO,OHIO
1915 CIN N  P          3    0- 0
        BLTL

MC COLL, ALEXANDER BOYD (RED)
B.MAR.29,1894 EAGLEVILLE,OHIO
1933 WAS A  P          4    1- 0
1934 WAS A  P         42    3- 4
        BBTR          46    4- 4

MC CONNAUGHEY, RALPH JAMES
B.AUG.5,1889 PENNSYLVANIA
D.JUNE 4,1966 DETROIT,MICH.
1914 IND F  P          7    0- 2
        BRTR

MC CONNELL, AMBROSE MOSES (AMBY)
B.APR.29,1883 N.POWNAL,VT.
D.MAY 20,1942 UTICA,N.Y.
1908 BOS A  2        140   .279
1909 BOS A  2        121   .238
1910 BOS A  2         12   .125
     CHI A  2         32   .296
1911 CHI A  2        104   .280
        BLTR        409   .264

MC CONNELL, GEORGE NEELY (SLATS)
B.SEPT.16,1877 SHELBYVILLE,TENN.
D.MAY 10,1964 CHATTANOOGA,TENN.
1909 NY A   P-1        1   13   0- 1
                                .209
1912 NY A   P         23   42   8-12
1913 NY A   P              35   5-15
1914 CHI N  P               1   0- 1
1915 CHI F  P         44   50  25-10
1916 CHI N  P              28   4-12
        BRTR    132  169  42-51
                                .182

MC CONNELL, SAMUEL FAULKNER
B.JUNE 8,1895 PHILADELPHIA,PA.
1915 PHI A  3          6   .191
        BLTR

MC COOL, WILLIAM JOHN (BILLY)
B.JULY 14,1944 BATESVILLE,IND.
1964 CIN N  P         40    6- 5
1965 CIN N  P         62    9-10
1966 CIN N  P         57    8- 8
1967 CIN N  P         31    3- 7
1968 CIN N  P         30    3- 4
1969 SD N   P         54    3- 5
1970 STL N  P         18    0- 3
        BRTL         292   32-42


MC CORMICK, FRANK ANDREW (BUCK)
B.JUNE 9,1911 NEW YORK,N.Y.
1934 CIN N  1          12   .313
1937 CIN N  1-2-O      24   .325
1938 CIN N  1         151   .326
1939 CIN N  1         156   .332
1940 CIN N  1         155   .309
1941 CIN N  1         154   .269
1942 CIN N  1         145   .277
1943 CIN N  1         126   .303
1944 CIN N  1         153   .305
1945 CIN N  1         152   .276
1946 PHI N  1         135   .284
1947 PHI N  1          15   .225
     BOS N  1          81   .354
1948 BOS N  1          75   .250
        BRTR         1534   .299

MC CORMICK, HARRY ELWOOD (MOOSE)
B.FEB.28,1881 PHILADELPHIA,PA.
D.JULY 9,1962 LEWISBURG,PA.
1904 NY N   O          54   .266
     PIT N  O          66   .290
1908 PHI N  O           5   .091
     NY N   O          65   .302
1909 NY N   O         110   .290
1912 NY N   O          42   .333
1913 NY N   O          57   .275
        TL            399   .285

MC CORMICK, JAMES (JIM)
B.1856 SCOTLAND
D.MAR.10,1918 PATERSON,N.J.
1878 IND N  P          14   15   4- 9
1879 CLE N  M-P        60   75  20-40
     O                           .219
1880 CLE N  M-P        73   77  44-29
                                 .250
1881 CLE N  M-P        57   69  26-31
     2-O                         .257
1882 CLE N  P          65   67  35-29
                                 .216
1883 CLE N  M-P        40   41  27-13
     O                           .235
1884 CLE N  P-O        41   48  19-22
                                 .263
     CIN U  P-O        26   28  22- 4
                                 .237
1885 PRO N  P           4        1- 3
     CHI N  P-O        25       20- 4
                                 .231
1886 CHI N  P          42       31-11
1887 PIT N  P          36       13-23
        BRTR    483  527 262-218
                                 .237

MC CORMICK, JAMES AMBROSE
B.NOV.2,1868 SPENCER,MASS.
D.FEB.1,1948 SACO,MAINE
1892 STL N  2          2   .000
        BRTR

MC CORMICK, JOHN (JERRY)
B.PHILADELPHIA,PA.
D.SEPT.19,1905 PHILADELPHIA,PA.
1883 BAL AA 3         98   .261
1884 KEY U  2-S-3-O   66   .206
     WAS U  S-3       42   .237
                     206   .268

MC CORMICK, MICHAEL FRANCIS (MIKE)
B.SEP.29,1938 PASADENA,CAL.
1956 NY N   P           3   0- 1
1957 NY N   P          24   3- 1
1958 SF N   P          42  11- 8
1959 SF N   P          47  12-16
1960 SF N   P          49  15-12
1961 SF N   P          40  13-16
1962 SF N   P      28  29   5- 5
1963 BAL A  P          25   6- 8
1964 BAL A  P           4   0- 2
1965 WAS A  P      44  45   8- 8
1966 WAS A  P          41  11-14
1967 SF N   P      40  41  22-10
1968 SF N   P          38  12-14
1969 SF N   P          32  11- 9
1970 SF N   P          23   3- 4
     NY A  /P           9   2- 0
1971 KC A  /P           4   0- 0
        BLTL    484 487 134-128

MC CORMICK, MICHAEL J.
(KID) OR (DUDE)
B.1883 JERSEY CITY,N.J.
D.NOV.18,1953 JERSEY CITY,N.J.
1904 BRO N  3        105   .184
        BRTR


MC CORMICK, MYRON WINTHROP (MIKE)
B.MAY 6,1917 ANGELS CAMP,CAL.
D.APR.14,1976 VENTURA,CAL.
1940 CIN N  O         110   .300
1941 CIN N  O         110   .287
1942 CIN N  O          40   .237
1943 CIN N  O           4   .133
1946 CIN N  O          23   .216
     BOS N  O          59   .262
1947 BOS N  O          92   .285
1948 BOS N  O         115   .303
1949 BRO N  O          55   .209
1950 NY N   H           4   .000
     CHI A  O          55   .232
1951 WAS A  O          81   .288
        BRTR          748   .275

MC CORMICK, PATRICK HENRY (HARRY)
B.OCT.25,1895 SYRACUSE,N.Y.
D.AUG.8,1889 SYRACUSE,N.Y.
1879 SYR N  P      49   55  11-13
1881 WOR N  P-O         12   1- 8
                             .122
1882 CIN AA P-O    25   26  13-12
                             .126
1883 CIN AA P           14   9- 5
        TR     100  107  34-38
                             .207

MC CORMICK, WILLIAM J. (BARRY)
B.DEC.25,1874 CINCINNATI,OHIO
D.JAN.28,1956 CINCINNATI,OHIO
1895 LOU N  S          3   .273
1896 CHI N  3         45   .219
1897 CHI N  S-3      100   .273
1898 CHI N  3        136   .248
1899 CHI N  2        102   .234
1900 CHI N  S-3      110   .215
1901 CHI N  S        115   .234
1902 STL A  S-3-O    139   .246
1903 STL A  2         59   .192
     WAS A  2-3       62   .225
1904 WAS A  2        112   .219
        TR           983   .237

MC CORRY, WILLIAM CHARLES
B.JULY 9,1887 SARANAC LAKE,N.Y.
D.MAR.22,1973 AUGUSTA,GA.
1909 STL A  P          2   0- 2
        BLTR

MC COSKY, WILLIAM BARNEY (BARNEY)
B.APR.11,1918 COAL RUN,PA.
1939 DET A  O        147   .311
1940 DET A  O        143   .340
1941 DET A  O        127   .324
1942 DET A  O        154   .293
1946 DET A  O         25   .198
     PHI A  O         92   .354
1947 PHI A  O        137   .328
1948 PHI A  O        135   .326
1950 PHI A  O         66   .240
1951 PHI A  O         12   .296
     CIN N  O         25   .320
     CLE A  O         31   .213
1952 CLE A  O         54   .213
1953 CLE A  H         22   .190
        BLTR         1170   .312

MC COVEY, WILLIE LEE
(WILLIE) OR (STRETCH)
B.JAN.10,1938 MOBILE,ALA.
1959 SF N   1          52   .354
1960 SF N   1         101   .238
1961 SF N   1         106   .271
1962 SF N   1-O        91   .293
1963 SF N   1-O       152   .280
1964 SF N   1-O       130   .220
1965 SF N   *1        160   .276
1966 SF N   *1        150   .295
1967 SF N   *1        135   .276
1968 SF N   *1        148   .293
1969 SF N   *1        149   .320
1970 SF N   *1        152   .289
1971 SF N   1         105   .277
1972 SF N   1          81   .213
1973 SF N   *1        130   .266
1974 SD N   *1        128   .253
1975 SD N   *1        122   .252
1976 SD N   1          71   .203
     OAK A  /H         11   .208
1977 SF N   *1        141   .280
1978 SF N   1         108   .228
        BLTL         2423   .272

MC COY, A. G.
B.DANVILLE,PA.
1889 WAS N  O          2   .000

MC COY, BENJAMIN JENISON (BENNY)
B.NOV.9,1915 JENISON,MICH.
1938 DET A  2-3        7   .200
1939 DET A  2-S       55   .302
1940 PHI A  2-3      134   .257
1941 PHI A  2        141   .271
        BLTR         337   .269
```

YR	CL LEA POS	GP	G	REC

MC CRABB, LESTER WILLIAM (BUSTER)
B.NOV.4,1914 WAKEFIELD,PA.

YR	CL LEA POS	GP	G	REC
1939	PHI A P	5		1- 2
1940	PHI A P	4		0- 0
1941	PHI A P	26		9-13
1942	PHI A P	1		0- 0
1950	PHI A P	2		0- 0
	BRTR	38		10-15

MC CRAW, TOMMY LEE
B.NOV.21,1940 MALVERN,ARK.

1963	CHI A 1	102		.254
1964	CHI A 1-O	125		.261
1965	CHI A 1-O	133		.238
1966	CHI A *1-O	151		.229
1967	CHI A *1/O	125		.236
1968	CHI A *1	136		.235
1969	CHI A 1-O	93		.258
1970	CHI A 1-O	129		.220
1971	WAS A O-1	122		.213
1972	CLE A O-1	129		.258
1973	CAL A O-1	99		.265
1974	CAL A 1-O	56		.286
	CLE A 1/O	45		.304
1975	CAL A 1/O	23		.275
	BLTL	1468		.246

MC CREA, FRANCIS WILLIAM
B.SEPT.6,1896 JERSEY CITY,N.J.

1925	CLE A C	1		.200
	BRTR			

MC CREDIE, WALTER HENRY (JUDGE)
B.NOV.29,1876 MANCHESTER,IOWA
D.JULY 29,1934 PORTLAND,ORE.

1903	BRO N O	56		.324
	BLTR			

MC CREERY, EDWARD P.
B.1891 DECEASED

1914	DET A P	3		1- 0
	BRTR			

MC CREERY, THOMAS LIVINGSTON
B.OCT.19,1874 BEAVER,PA.
D.JULY 3,1941 BEAVER,PA.

1895	LOU N P-1-	5	29	3- 2
				.336
1896	LOU N P-O	1	110	0- 1
				.351
1897	LOU N O		89	.283
	NY N Z-O		49	.290
1898	NY N O		34	.198
	PIT N O		51	.304
1899	PIT N O		113	.325
1900	PIT N O		33	.223
1901	BRO N O		84	.302
1902	BRO N 1-O		111	.246
1903	BRO N O		38	.217
	BOS N O		23	.217
	BB	6	764	3- 3
				.292

MC CUE, FRANK ALOYSIUS
B.OCT.4,1898 CHICAGO,ILL.
D.JULY 5,1953 CHICAGO,ILL.

1922	PHI A 3	2		.000
	BBTR			

MC CULLOUGH, CHARLES
B.1867 DUBLIN,IRELAND

1890	BRO AA P	24		4-20
	SYR AA P	5		2- 2
		29		6-22

MC CULLOUGH, CLYDE EDWARD
B.MAR.4,1917 NASHVILLE,TENN.

1940	CHI N C	9		.154
1941	CHI N C	125		.227
1942	CHI N C	109		.282
1943	CHI N C	87		.237
1946	CHI N C	95		.287
1947	CHI N C	86		.252
1948	CHI N C	69		.209
1949	PIT N C	91		.237
1950	PIT N C	103		.254
1951	PIT N C	92		.297
1952	CHI N C-1	66		.233
1953	CHI N C	77		.258
1954	CHI N C-3	31		.259
1955	CHI N C	44		.198
1956	CHI N C	14		.211
	BRTR	1098		.252

MC CULLOUGH, PAUL WILLARD
B.JULY 28,1898 NEW CASTLE,PA.
D.NOV.7,1970 NEW CASTLE,PA.

1929	WAS A P	3		0- 0
	BRTR			

MC CULLOUGH, PINSON LAMAR (PHIL)
B.JULY 22,1917 STOCKBRIDGE,GA.

1942	WAS A P	1		0- 0

MC CURDY, HARRY HENRY (HANK)
B.SEPT.15,1699 STEVENS POINT,WIS.
D.JULY 21,1972 HOUSTON,TEX.

1922	STL N C-1	13		.196
1923	STL N C	67		.265
1926	CHI A C	44		.326
1927	CHI A C	86		.286
1928	CHI A C	49		.262
1930	PHI N C	80		.331
1931	PHI N C	66		.287
1932	PHI N C	62		.235
1933	PHI N C	73		.278
1934	CIN N C	3		.000
	BLTR	543		.282

MC DANIEL, LYNDALL DALE (LINDY)
B.DEC.13,1935 HOLLIS,OKLA.

1955	STL N P	4		0- 0
1956	STL N P	39		7- 6
1957	STL N P	30	31	15- 9
1958	STL N P	26		5- 7
1959	STL N P	62		14-12
1960	STL N P	65		12- 4
1961	STL N P	55		10- 6
1962	STL N P	55		3-10
1963	CHI N P	57		13- 7
1964	CHI N P	63		1- 7
1965	CHI N P	71		5- 6
1966	SF N P	64		10- 5
1967	SF N P	41		2- 6
1968	SF N P	12		0- 0
	NY A P	24		4- 1
1969	NY A P	51		5- 6
1970	NY A P	62		9- 5
1971	NY A P	44		5-10
1972	NY A P	37		3- 1
1973	NY A P	47		12- 6
1974	KC A P	38		1- 4
1975	KC A P	40		5- 1
	BRTR	987	988	141-119

MC DANIEL, MAX VON (VON)
B.APR.18,1939 HOLLIS,OKLA.

1957	STL N P	17		7- 5
1958	STL N P	2		0- 0
	BRTR	19		7- 5

MC DERMOTT, FRANK A. (RED)
B.NOV.12,1889 PHILADELPHIA,PA.
D.SEPT.11,1964 PHILADELPHIA,PA.

1912	DET A O	5		.250
	BRTR			

MC DERMOTT, JOSEPH

1871	KEK NA O	2		-
1872	ECK NA P	7		0- 7
1873	RES NA S	1		-
		7	10	0- 7
				-

MC DERMOTT, MAURICE JOSEPH (MICKEY)
B.AUG.29,1928 POUGHKEEPSIE,N.Y.

1948	BOS A P	7		0- 0
1949	BOS A P	12		5- 4
1950	BOS A P	38	39	7- 3
1951	BOS A P	34	43	8- 8
1952	BOS A P	30	36	10- 9
1953	BOS A P	32	43	18-10
1954	WAS A P	30	54	7-15
1955	WAS A P	31	70	10-10
1956	NY A P	23	46	2- 6
1957	KC A P-1	29	58	1- 4
				.245
1958	DET A P	2	4	0- 0
1961	STL N P	19	22	1- 0
	KC A P	4	7	0- 0
	BLTL	291	443	69-69
				.252

MC DERMOTT, MICHAEL JOSEPH
B.SEPT.7,1862 ST.LOUIS,MO.
D.JUNE 30,1943 ST.LOUIS,MO.

1889	LOU AA P	9		1- 7
1895	LOU N P	26		4-19
1896	LOU N P	12		2- 7
1897	CLE N P	9		3- 4
	STL N P	7		3- 4
	TR	63		13-41

MC DERMOTT, TERRENCE MICHAEL (TERRY)
B.MAR.20,1951 ROCKVILLE CEN.,N.Y.

1972	LA N /1	9		.130
	BRTR			

MC DEVITT, DANIEL EUGENE (DANNY)
B.NOV.18,1932 NEW YORK,N.Y.

1957	BRO N P	22		7- 4
1958	LA N P	13		2- 6
1959	LA N P	39		10- 8
1960	LA N P	24		0- 4
1961	NY A P	8		1- 2
	MIN A P	16		1- 0
1962	KC A P	33		0- 3
	BLTL	155		21-27

MC DONALD, CHARLES E. (TEX)
[REAL NAME CHARLES C. CRABTREE]
B.JAN.31,1891 FARMERSVILLE,TEX.
D.MAR.31,1943 HOUSTON,TEX.

1912	CIN N S	61		.257
1913	CIN N S	11		.364
	BOS N 3	62		.353
1914	PIT F 2-3	67		.318
	BUF F O	69		.295
1915	BUF F O	87		.271
	BLTR	357		.296

MC DONALD, DANIEL
B.1847 BROOKLYN,N.Y.
D.NOV.23,1880

1872	ATL NA O	14		.214
	ECK NA S	1		.000
		15		.197

MC DONALD, DAVID BRUCE (DAVE)
B.MAY 20,1943 NEW ALBANY,IND.

1969	NY A /1	9		.217
1971	MON N /1-O	24		.103
	BLTR	33		.145

MC DONALD, EDWARD C.
B.OCT.28,1886 ALBANY,N.Y.
D.MAR.11,1946 ALBANY,N.Y.

1911	BOS N 3	54		.206
1912	BOS N 3	121		.259
1913	CHI N H	1		.000
	BRTR	176		.244

MC DONALD, HENRY MONROE (HANK)
B.JAN.16,1911 SANTA MONICA,CAL.

1931	PHI A P	19		2- 4
1933	PHI A P	4		1- 1
	STL A P	25		0- 4
	BRTR	48		3- 9

MC DONALD, JAMES
B.PHILADELPHIA,PA.

1902	NY N O	2		.333

MC DONALD, JAMES A.
B.AUG.6,1860 SAN FRANCISCO,CAL.
D.SEPT.14,1914 SAN FRANCISCO,CAL.

1884	WAS U C-O	2		.167
	PIT AA 3-O	38		.151
1885	BUF N S-O	5		.000
		45		.139

MC DONALD, JIMMIE LE ROY (HOT ROD)
B.MAY 17,1927 GRANTS PASS,ORE.

1950	BOS A P	9		1- 0
1951	STL A P	16	17	4- 7
1952	NY A P	26		3- 4
1953	NY A P	27	29	9- 7
1954	NY A P	16		4- 1
1955	BAL A P	21		3- 5
1956	CHI A P	8		0- 2
1957	CHI A P	10		0- 1
1958	CHI A P	3		0- 0
	BRTR	136	139	24-27

MC DONALD, JOHN JOSEPH
B.DEC.11,1881 NESQUEHONING,PA.
D.NOV.6,1972 ALLENTOWN,PA.

	BRTR			
1907	WAS A P	1		0- 0
	TR			

MC DONALD, MALCOLM JOSEPH
B.APR.9,1888 TEXAS
D.MAY 30,1963 BAYTOWN,TEX.

1910	STL A 3	10		.156
	BRTR			

MC DONNELL, JAMES WILLIAM (MACK)
B.AUG.15,1922 GAGETOWN,MICH.

1943	CLE A C	2		.000
1944	CLE A C	20		.233
1945	CLE A C	28		.196
	BLTR	50		.211

MC DONOUGH, EDWARD SEBASTIAN
B.SEPT.11,1886 ELGIN,ILL.
D.SEPT.2,1926 ELGIN,ILL.

1909	PHI N C	1		.000
1910	PHI N C	4		.111
	BRTR	5		.095

MC DOOLAN

1873	MAR NA P	1		0- 1
1875	RS NA P	1		0- 1
		2		0- 2

MC DOUGAL, JAMES A. (SANDY)
B.FEB.18,1878 BUFFALO,N.Y.
D.OCT.4,1910 BUFFALO,N.Y.

1905	STL N P	5		1- 4

MC DOUGAL, JOHN A.

1895	BRO N P	5		0- 0

YR CL LEA POS   GP   G   REC

MC DOUGAL, JOHN H. (DEWEY)
B.SEPT.19,1871 ALEDO,ILL.
D.APR.28,1936 GALESBURG,ILL.
```
1895 STL N  P              15   4-11
1896 STL N  P               3   0- 1
                           18   4-12
```

MC DOUGALD, GILBERT JAMES (GIL)
B.MAY 19,1928 SAN FRANCISCO,CAL
```
1951 NY  A  2-3       131       .306
1952 NY  A  2-3       152       .263
1953 NY  A  2-3       141       .285
1954 NY  A  2-3       126       .259
1955 NY  A  2-3       141       .285
1956 NY  A  2-S-3     120       .311
1957 NY  A  2-S-3     141       .289
1958 NY  A  2-S       138       .250
1959 NY  A  2-S-3     127       .251
1960 NY  A  2-3       119       .258
        BRTR        1336       .276
```

MC DOWELL, SAMUEL EDWARD THOMAS
(SAM) OR (SUDDEN SAM)
B.SEP.21,1942 PITTSBURGH,PA.
```
1961 CLE A  P               1   0- 0
1962 CLE A  P          25   3- 7
1963 CLE A  P     14   15   3- 5
1964 CLE A  P          31  11- 6
1965 CLE A  P     42   43  17-11
1966 CLE A  P     35   36   9- 8
1967 CLE A  P          37  13-15
1968 CLE A  P          38  15-14
1969 CLE A  P          39  18-14
1970 CLE A  P-    39   40  20-12
        /1-2                 .124
1971 CLE A  P          35  13-17
1972 SF  N  P          28  10- 8
1973 SF  N  P          18   1- 2
        NY  A  P          16   5- 8
1974 NY  A  P          13   1- 6
1975 PIT N  P          14   2- 1
        BLTL      425  429 141-134
                            .154
```

MC ELROY, JAMES D.
B.SAN FRANCISCO,CAL.
D.FEB,24,1889 ALBUQUERQUE,N.M.
```
1884 PHI N  P-O        13   1-12
                            .136
        WIL U  P-O         1   0- 1
                            .000
                       14   1-13
                            .131
```

MC ELVEEN, PRYOR MYNATT (HUMPY)
B.NOV.5,1883 ATLANTA,GA.
D.OCT.27,1951 PLEASANT HILL,TENN.
```
1909 BRO N  3          67  .198
1910 BRO N  3          64  .225
1911 BRO N  3          16  .193
        TR            147  .209
```

MC ELWEE, LELAND STANFORD
B.MAY 23,1894 LA MESA,CAL.
D.FEB.8,1957 UNION,MAINE
```
1916 PHI A  3          54  .265
        BRTR
```

MC ELYEA, FRANK
B.AUG.4,1918 CARMI,ILL.
```
1942 BOS N  O           7  .000
        BRTR
```

MC ENANEY, WILLIAM HENRY (WILL)
B.FEB.14,1952 SPRINGFIELD,OHIO
```
1974 CIN N  P          24   2- 1
1975 CIN N  P          70   5- 2
1976 CIN N  P          55   2- 6
1977 MON N  P          69   3- 5
1978 PIT N /P           6   0- 0
        BLTL          224  12-14
```

MC EVOY, LOUIS ANTHONY
B.MAY 30,1902 WILLIAMSBURG,KAN.
D.DEC.17,1953 WEBSTER GROVES,MO
```
1930 NY  A  P          28   1- 3
1931 NY  A  P           6   0- 0
        BRTR           34   1- 3
```

MC FADDEN, BERNARD JOSEPH (BARNEY)
B.FEB.22,1874 ECKLEY,PA.
D.APR.28,1924 MAUCH CHUNK,PA.
```
1901 CIN N  P           8   3- 4
1902 PHI N  P           1   0- 1
        BRTR            9   3- 5
```

MC FADDEN, GUY
```
1895 STL N  1           4  .200
```

MC FADDEN, LEON
B.APR.26,1944 LITTLE ROCK,ARK.
```
1968 HOU N  S          16  .277
1969 HOU N  O/S        44  .176
1970 HOU N  R           2  .000
        BRTR           62  .215
```

MC FARLAN, ALEXANDER SHEPHERD
B.OCT.11,1869 ST.LOUIS,MO.
D.MAR.2,1939 PEEWEE VALLEY,KY.
```
1892 LOU N  O          14  .162
```

MC FARLAN, ANDERSON DANIEL (DAN)
B.NOV.26,1874 GAINESVILLE,TEX.
D.SEPT.24,1924 LOUISVILLE,KY.
```
1895 LOU N  P           7   0- 6
1899 BRO N  P           1   0- 0
        WAS N  P          29   8-18
                       37   8-24
```

MC FARLAND, CHARLES A. (CHAPPIE)
B.ST.LOUIS,MO.
D.DEC.15,1924 HOUSTON,TEX.
```
1902 STL N  P           2   0- 1
1903 STL N  P          28   9-19
1904 STL N  P          32  13-18
1905 STL N  P          31   9-18
1906 STL N  P           7   3- 4
        PIT N  P           6   1- 3
        BRO N  P           1   0- 1
        TR            107  35-64
```

MC FARLAND, CLAUDE
```
1884 BAL U  P-O         1   3   0- 1
                            .286
```

MC FARLAND, EDWARD WILLIAM
B.AUG.3,1874 CLEVELAND,OHIO
D.NOV.28,1959 CLEVELAND,OHIO
```
1893 CLE N  O           9  .370
1896 STL N  C          80  .239
1897 STL N  C-1-2-O    31  .324
        PHI N  C          36  .221
1898 PHI N  C         118  .274
1899 PHI N  C          90  .333
1900 PHI N  C          90  .307
1901 PHI N  C          72  .278
1902 CHI A  C-1-O      71  .231
1903 CHI A  C          61  .210
1904 CHI A  C          50  .263
1905 CHI A  C          80  .280
1906 CHI A  C          12  .181
1907 CHI A  C          52  .283
1908 BOS A  C          19  .208
        BRTR          871  .272
```

MC FARLAND, HERMAS WALTER
B.MAR.11,1870 DES MOINES,IOWA
D.SEPT.21,1935 RICHMOND,VA.
```
1896 LOU N  O          25  .198
1898 CIN N  O          15  .286
1901 CHI A  O         132  .265
1902 CHI A  O           7  .185
        BAL A  O          63  .321
1903 NY  A  O         103  .223
        BLTR          345  .257
```

MC FARLAND, HOWARD ALEXANDER
B.MAR.7,1911 EL RENO,OKLA.
```
1945 WAS A  P           6  .091
        BRTR
```

MC FARLAND, LA MONT A. (MONTE)
B.1871 ILLINOIS
D.NOV.15,1913 PEORIA,ILL.
```
1895 CHI N  P           2   2- 0
1896 CHI N  P           3   0- 3
                        5   2- 3
```

MC FARLANE, ORLANDO DEJESUS
(QUESADA)
B.JUNE 28,1938 ORIENTE,CUBA
```
1962 PIT N  C           8  .087
1964 PIT N  C-O        37  .244
1966 DET A  C          49  .254
1967 CAL A /C          12  .227
1968 CAL A /C          18  .290
        BRTR          124  .240
```

MC FETRIDGE, JOHN R. (JACK)
B.AUG.25,1869 PHILADELPHIA,PA.
D.JAN.10,1917 PHILADELPHIA,PA.
```
1890 PHI N  P           1   1- 0
1903 PHI N  P          14   1-11
                       15   2-11
```

MC GAFFIGAN, MARK ANDREW (PATSY)
B.SEPT.12,1888 CARLYLE,ILL.
D.DEC.22,1940 CARLYLE,ILL.
```
1917 PHI N  S          19  .167
1918 PHI N  2-S        54  .203
        BRTR           73  .194
```

MC GAH, EDWARD JOSEPH (EDDIE)
B.SEPT.30,1921 OAKLAND,CAL.
```
1946 BOS A  C          15  .216
1947 BOS A  C           9  .000
        BRTR           24  .157
```

MC GAHA, FRED MELVIN (MEL)
B.SEPT.26,1926 BASTROP,LA.
NON-PLAYING MANAGER
CLE[A] 1962, KC[A] 1964-65

MC GANN, DENNIS LAWRENCE
(DAN) OR (CAP)
B.JULY 15,1871 SHELBYVILLE,KY.
D.DEC.13,1910 LOUISVILLE,KY.
```
1895 LOU N  S-3        17  .313
1896 BOS N  2          42  .315
1898 BAL N  1         145  .298
1899 BRO N  1          63  .245
        WAS N  1          75  .338
1900 STL N  1         124  .301
1901 STL N  1         113  .265
1902 BAL A  1          68  .304
        NY  N  1          61  .301
1903 NY  N  1         129  .270
1904 NY  N  1         141  .286
1905 NY  N  1         136  .299
1906 NY  N  1         133  .237
1907 NY  N  1          81  .298
1908 BOS N  1         130  .240
        BBTR         1458  .283
```

MC GARR, JAMES B. (CHIPPY)
B.MAY 10,1863 WORCESTER,MASS.
D.JUNE 6,1904 WORCESTER,MASS.
```
1884 CHI U  2          18  .160
1886 ATH AA S          72  .271
1887 ATH AA S         127  .331
1888 STL AA S          35  .187
1889 KC  AA 2-S-3-O    25  .287
        BAL AA S           3  .143
1890 BOS N  3         121  .236
1893 CLE N  3          63  .309
1894 CLE N  3         127  .272
1895 CLE N  3         112  .270
1896 CLE N  3         111  .266
        BRTR          814  .273
```

MC GARR, JAMES VINCENT (REDS)
B.NOV.9,1888 PHILADELPHIA,PA.
```
1912 DET A  O           1  .000
```

MC GARVEY, DANIEL
```
1912 DET A  O           1  .000
```

MC GEACHY, JOHN CHARLES (JACK)
B.MAY 23,1864 CLINTON,MASS.
D.APR.5,1930
```
1886 DET N  O           7  .333
        STL N  O          58  .216
1887 IND N  O          99  .278
1888 IND N  O         118  .219
1889 IND N  O         131  .267
1890 BRO P  O         104  .253
1891 ATH AA O          46  .217
        BOS AA O          41  .250
        BR            604  .248
```

MC GEARY, MICHAEL HENRY
B.1851 PHILADELPHIA,PA.
```
1871 TRO NA C-S        29  .244
1872 ATH NA C-S-O      46  .344
1873 ATH NA C-S        51   -
1874 ATH NA C-S-O      54   -
1875 PHI NA 2-S-3-O    68  .294
1876 STL N  2          60  .259
1877 STL N  2-3        57  .253
1879 PRO N  2-3        84  .276
1880 PRO N  2-S-3      17  .129
        CLE N  3-O        31  .233
1881 CLE N  3          10  .211
1882 DET N  2-S        33  .149
        BRTR          540   -
```

MC GEE, DANIEL ALOYSIUS
B.SEPT.29,1913 NEW YORK,N.Y.
```
1934 BOS N  S           7  .136
```

MC GEE, DENNIS JOSEPH
[PLAYED UNDER NAME OF
DENNIS JOSEPH MACK]

MC GEE, F.
```
1874 ATL NA 2-S-O      16   -
1875 MUT NA O          22   -
        ATL NA 2-3-O      21   -
1884 WAS U  C-3-O       4  .188
                       63   -
```

MC GEE, FRANCIS D. (TUBBY)
B.APR.28,1899 COLUMBUS,OHIO
D.JAN.30,1934 COLUMBUS,OHIO
```
1925 WAS A  1           2  .000
        BRTR
```

MC GEE, WILLIAM HENRY (FIDDLER BILL)
B.NOV.16,1909 BATCHTOWN,ILL.
```
1935 STL N  P           1   1- 0
1936 STL N  P           7   1- 1
1937 STL N  P           4   1- 0
1938 STL N  P          47   7-12
1939 STL N  P          43  12- 5
1940 STL N  P          38  16-10
1941 STL N  P           4   0- 1
        NY  N  P          22   2- 9
1942 NY  N  P          31   6- 3
        BRTR          197  46-41
```

YR	CL LEA POS	GP	G	REC

MC GEEHAN, CORNELIUS BERNARD (CONNY)
B.AUG.25,1882 DRIFTON,PA.
D.JULY 4,1907 HAZLETON,PA.
1903 PHI A P   6   1- 0

MC GEEHAN, DANIEL DE SALES
B.JUNE 7,1885 JEDDO,PA.
D.JULY 12,1955 HAZLETON,PA.
1911 STL N 2   3   .222
             BRTR

MC GEHEE, PATRICK HENRY
B.JULY 2,1888 MEADVILLE,MISS.
D.DEC.30,1946 PADUCAH,KY.
1912 DET A P   1   0- 1
             BLTR

MC GHEE, WARREN EDWARD (ED)
B.SEPT.29,1924 PERRY,ARK.
1950 CHI A 0   3   .167
1953 PHI A 0   104   .263
1954 PHI A 0   21   .208
     CHI A 0   42   .227
1955 PHI A 0   26   .077
             BRTR   196   .246

MC GHEE, WILLIAM MAC (FIBBER)
B.SEPT.5,1908 SHAWMUT,ALA.
1944 PHI A 1   77   .289
1945 PHI A 1-0   93   .252
             BLTL   170   .272

MC GILBERRY, RANDALL KENT (RANDY)
B.OCT.29,1953 MOBILE,ALA.
1977 KC A /P   3   0- 1
1978 KC A P   18   0- 1
             BBTR   21   0- 2

MC GILL, WILLIAM JOHN (PARSON)
B.JUNE 29,1880 GALVA,KAN.
D.AUG.7,1959 ALVA,OKLA.
1907 STL A P   2   1- 0
             BRTR

MC GILL, WILLIAM VANESS
(KID) OR (WILLIE)
B.NOV.10,1873 ATLANTA,GA.
D.AUG.29,1944 INDIANAPOLIS,IND.
1890 CLE P P   24 11- 9
1891 CIN AA P   8   2- 4
     STL AA P   36 19- 9
1892 CIN N P   3   1- 1
1893 CIN N P   35 17-17
1894 CIN N P   26   6-19
1895 PHI N P   19 10- 8
1896 PHI N P   12   4- 4
     TL   163 70-71

MC GILLEN, JOHN JOSEPH
B.AUG.6,1917 EDDYSTONE,PA.
1944 PHI A P   2   0- 0
             BLTL

MC GILLICUDDY, CORNELIUS ALEXANDER
[PLAYED UNDER NAME OF
CORNELIUS ALEXANDER MACK]

MC GILLICUDDY, EARLE THADDEUS
[PLAYED UNDER NAME OF
EARLE THADDEUS MACK]

MC GILVRAY, WILLIAM ALEXANDER
(BIG BILLY)
B.APR.29,1883 PORTLAND,ORE.
D.MAY 23,1952 DENVER,COLO.
1908 CIN N H   2   .000

MC GINLEY, JAMES WILLIAM
B.OCT.2,1878 GROVELAND,MASS.
D.SEPT.20,1961 HAVERHILL,MASS.
1904 STL N P   3   2- 1
1905 STL N P   1   0- 1
                       4   2- 2

MC GINLEY, TIMOTHY S.
B.PHILADELPHIA,PA.
D.NOV.2,1899 OAKLAND,CAL.
1875 CEN NA C-0   13   -
     NH NA C   32   -
1876 BOS N C   9   .150
                      54   -

MC GINN, DANIEL MICHAEL (DAN)
B.NOV.29,1943 OMAHA,NEB.
1968 CIN N P   14   0- 1
1969 MON N P   74   7-10
1970 MON N P   52   7-10
1971 MON N P   28   1- 4
1972 CHI N P   42   43   0- 5
             BLTL   210 211 15-30

MC GINN, FRANK J.
B.CINCINNATI,OHIO
D.NOV.19,1897 CINCINNATI,OHIO
1890 PIT N 0   1   .000

MC GINNIS, AUGUST (GUS)
B.1870 PAINESVILLE,OHIO
1893 CHI N P   13   2- 6
     PHI N P   5   1- 3
                      18   3- 9

MC GINNIS, GEORGE W. (JUMBO)
B.FEB.22,1864 ST.LOUIS,MO.
D.MAY 18,1934 ST.LOUIS,MO.
1882 STL AA P-2-   46   51 25-21
             0   .227
1883 STL AA P-0   44 29-15
                           .211
1884 STL AA P   40 24-16
1885 STL AA P   13   6- 6
1886 STL AA P   10   5- 2
             BAL AA P 26 11-12
1887 CIN AA P   9   3- 6
                     188 193 103-78
                           .215

MC GINNITY, JOSEPH JEROME
(JOE) OR (IRON MAN)
B.MAR.19,1871 ROCK ISLAND,ILL.
D.NOV.14,1929 BROOKLYN,N.Y.
1899 BAL N P   43 28-17
1900 BRO N P   41 29- 9
1901 BAL A P   48 26-19
1902 BAL A P-0 26   27 13-10
                           .295
     NY N P-2-   16   19   8- 8
             0   .123
1903 NY N P   55 31-20
1904 NY N P   51 35- 8
1905 NY N P   46 22-16
1906 NY N P   45 27-12
1907 NY N P   47 18-17
             BRTR   455 463 247-139
                           .193

MC GLONE, JOHN T.
B.1864 BROOKLYN,N.Y.
1886 WAS N 3   3   .091
1887 CLE AA 3   21   .329
1888 CLE AA 3   55   .183
                      79   .221

MC GLOTHEN, LYNN EVERETT
B.MAR.27,1950 MONROE,LA.
1972 BOS A P   22   8- 7
1973 BOS A /P   6   1- 2
1974 STL N P   31 16-12
1975 STL N P   39 15-13
1976 STL N P   33 13-15
1977 SF N P   21   2- 9
1978 SF N /P   5   0- 0
     CHI N P   49   5- 3
             BLTR   202 60-61

MC GLOTHIN, EZRA MAC (PAT)
B.OCT.20,1920 COALFIELD,TENN.
1949 BRO N P   7   1- 1
1950 BRO N P   1   0- 0
             BLTR   8   1- 1

MC GLOTHLIN, JAMES MILTON
(JIM) OR (RED)
B.OCT.6,1943 LOS ANGELES,CAL.
D.DEC.23,1975 UNION,KY.
1965 CAL A /P   3   0- 3
1966 CAL A P   19   3- 1
1967 CAL A P   32 12- 8
1968 CAL A P   40 10-15
1969 CAL A P   37   8-16
1970 CIN N P   35 14-10
1971 CIN N P   30   8-12
1972 CIN N P   31   9- 8
1973 CIN N P   24   3- 3
     CHI A /P   5   0- 1
             BRTR   256 67-77

MC GLYNN, ULYSSES SIMPSON GRANT
(STONEY)
B.MAY 26,1872 LANCASTER,PA.
D.AUG.26,1941 MANITOWOC,WIS.
1906 STL N P   9   4- 2
1907 STL N P   45 14-25
1908 STL N P   16 11- 6
             BRTR   67 19-33

MC GOVERN, ARTHUR JOHN
B.FEB.27,1882 ST.JOHN,N.B.,CAN.
D.NOV.14,1912 THORNTON,R.I.
1905 BOS A C   15   .114

MC GOWAN, FRANK BERNARD (BEAUTY)
B.NOV.8,1901 BRANFORD,CONN.
1922 PHI A 0   99   .230
1923 PHI A 0   95   .254
1928 STL A 0   47   .363
1929 STL A 0   125   .254
1937 BOS N 0   9   .083
             BLTR   375   .262

MC GOWAN, TULLIS EARL (MICKEY)
B.NOV.26,1921 DOTHAN,ALA.
1948 NY N P   3   0- 0
             BLTL

MC GRANER, HOWARD (MUCK)
B.SEPT.11,1869 HANLEY RUN,OHIO
D.OCT.22,1952 ZALESKI,OHIO
1912 CIN N P   2   1- 0
             BLTL

MC GRAW, JAMES LEO
B.1890
D.NOV.14,1918 CLEVELAND,OHIO
1914 BRO F P   1   0- 0

MC GRAW, FRANK EDWIN (TUG)
B.AUG.30,1944 MARTINEZ,CAL.
1965 NY N P   37   38   2- 7
1966 NY N P   15   2- 9
1967 NY N /P   4   0- 3
1969 NY N P   42   43   9- 3
1970 NY N P   57   4- 6
1971 NY N P   51 11- 4
1972 NY N P   54   8- 6
1973 NY N P   60   5- 6
1974 NY N P   41   6-11
1975 PHI N P   56   9- 6
1976 PHI N P   58   7- 6
1977 PHI N P   45   7- 3
1978 PHI N P   55   8- 7
             BRTL   575 977 78-77

MC GRAW, JOHN JOSEPH
(JOHN) OR (LITTLE NAPOLEON)
B.APR.7,1873 TRUXTON,N.Y.
D.FEB.25,1934 NEW ROCHELLE,N.Y.
1891 BAL AA S   31   .245
1892 BAL N 2-0   76   .267
1893 BAL N S   127   .328
1894 BAL N 3   123   .340
1895 BAL N 3   93   .374
1896 BAL N 3   19   .356
1897 BAL N 3   105   .326
1898 BAL N 3   141   .334
1899 BAL N M-3   118   .390
1900 STL N 3   98   .337
1901 BAL A M-3   73   .352
1902 BAL A M-3   20   .286
     NY N M-3   34   .226
1903 NY N M-2   12   .273
1904 NY N M-2   3   .300
1905 NY N M-0   3   .000
1906 NY N M-3   4   .000
             BLTR   1080   .334
NON-PLAYING MANAGER NY[N] 1907-32

MC GRAW, ROBERT EMMETT
B.APR.10,1895 LA VETA,COLO.
1917 NY A P   2   0- 1
1918 NY A P   1   0- 1
1919 NY A P   6   0- 2
     BOS A P   10   1- 0
1920 NY A P   15   0- 0
1925 BRO N P   2   0- 2
1926 BRO N P   33   9-13
1927 BRO N P   1   0- 1
     STL N P   18   4- 5
1928 PHI N P   39   7- 8
1929 PHI N P   41   5- 5
             BRTR   168 26-38

MC GREGOR, SCOTT HOUSTON
B.JAN.18,1954 INGLEWOOD,CAL.
1976 BAL A /P   3   0- 1
1977 BAL A P   29   3- 5
1978 BAL A P   35 15-13
             BBTL   67 18-19

MC GREW, WALTER HOWARD (SLIM)
B.AUG.5,1899 YOAKUM,TEX.
D.AUG.21,1967 HOUSTON,TEX.
1922 WAS A P   1   0- 0
1923 WAS A P   3   0- 1
1924 WAS A P   6   0- 1
             BRTR   10   0- 2

MC GRILLIS, MARK
1892 STL N 3   1   .000

MC GUCKIN, JOSEPH W.
B.1862 PATERSON,N.J.
D.DEC.31,1903 YONKERS,N.Y.
1890 BAL AA 0   10   .056

MC GUINNESS, JOHN J.
1876 LOU N 2   1   .000
1879 SYR N 1   12   .294
1884 KEY U 1   52   .243
                      65   .249

MC GUIRE, JAMES A.
B.FEB.4,1875 DUNKIRK,N.Y.
D.JAN.26,1917 BUFFALO,N.Y.
1901 CLE A S   18   .232
             TR

MC GUIRE, JAMES THOMAS (DEACON)
B.NOV.2,1865 YOUNGSTOWN,OHIO
D.OCT.31,1936 ALBION,MICH.

YR	CL	LEA	POS	GP	G	REC
1884	TOL	AA	C		45	.184
1885	DET	N	C-O		34	.190
1886	PHI	N	C		48	.197
1887	PHI	N	C		40	.354
1888	PHI	N	C		12	.333
1888	DET	N	C		3	.000
	CLE	AA	C		25	.207
1890	ROC	AA	C		87	.301
1891	WAS	AA	C		111	.296
1892	WAS	N	C		87	.241
1893	WAS	N	C		59	.262
1894	WAS	N	C		102	.304
1895	WAS	N	C		133	.330
1896	WAS	N	C		95	.325
1897	WAS	N	C		82	.338
1898	WAS	N	M-C-1		128	.273
1899	WAS	N	C		56	.277
	BRO	N	C		43	.338
1900	BRO	N	C		68	.280
1901	BRO	N	C		84	.293
1902	DET	A	C		72	.229
1903	DET	A	C		71	.241
1904	NY	A	C		100	.211
1905	NY	A	C		71	.219
1906	NY	A	C		51	.299
1907	NY	A	H		1	.000
	BOS	A	M-C		6	.500
1908	BOS	A	M-1		1	.000
	CLE	A	C		1	.250
1910	CLE	A	M-C		1	.000
1912	DET	A	C		1	.500
			BRTR		1718	.279

NON-PLAYING MANAGER CLE[A] 1909, 11

MC GUIRE, MICKEY C.
B.JAN.18,1941 DAYTON,OHIO

YR	CL	LEA	POS	GP	G	REC
1962	BAL	A	S		6	.000
1967	BAL	A	/2		10	.235
			BRTR		16	.190

MC GUIRE, MURRAY MASON
B.JAN.19,1872 RICHMOND,VA.
D.SEPT.10,1945 RICHMOND,VA.

YR	CL	LEA	POS	GP	G	REC
1894	CIN	N	P		1	0- 0

MC GUIRE, THOMAS PATRICK (ELMER)
B.FEB.1,1892 CHICAGO,ILL.
D.DEC.7,1959 PHOENIX,ARIZ.

YR	CL	LEA	POS	GP	G	REC
1914	CHI	F	P	24	37	5- 6
1919	CHI	A	P		1	0- 0
			BRTR	25	38	5- 6

MC GUNNIGLE, WILLIAM HENRY (GUNNER)
B.JAN.1,1855 STOUGHTON,MASS.
D.MAR.9,1899 BROCKTON,MASS.

YR	CL	LEA	POS	GP	G	REC
1879	BUF	N	M-P-O	13	46	7- 5 .180
1880	BUF	N	M-P-O	5	7	2- 3 .174
	WOR	N	P		1	0- 0
1882	CLE	N	O		1	.200
			BRTR	19	55	9- 8 .177

NON-PLAYING MANAGER
BRO[AA] 1888-89, BRO[N] 1890,
PIT(N) 1891, LOU(N) 1896

MC HALE, JAMES BERNARD
B.DEC.17,1875 MINERS MILLS,PA.
D.JUNE 18,1959 LOS ANGELES,CAL.

YR	CL	LEA	POS	GP	G	REC
1908	BOS	A	O		21	.224
			BRTR			

MC HALE, JOHN JOSEPH
B.SEPT.21,1921 DETROIT,MICH.

YR	CL	LEA	POS	GP	G	REC
1943	DET	A	H		4	.000
1944	DET	A	H		1	.000
1945	DET	A	1		19	.143
1947	DET	A	1		39	.211
1948	DET	A	H		1	.000
			BLTR		64	.193

MC HALE, MARTIN JOSEPH
B.OCT.30,1888 STONEHAM,MASS.

YR	CL	LEA	POS	GP	G	REC
1910	BOS	A	P		2	0- 2
1911	BOS	A	P		4	0- 0
1913	NY	A	P		7	2- 4
1914	NY	A	P	31	32	7-16
1915	NY	A	P		13	3- 7
1916	BOS	A	P		2	0- 1
	CLE	A	P		5	0- 0
			BRTR	64	65	12-30

MC HALE, ROBERT E. (RABBIT)
B.FEB.7,1870 SACRAMENTO,CAL.

YR	CL	LEA	POS	GP	G	REC
1898	WAS	N	O		10	.171

MC HENRY, AUSTIN BUSH (MAC)
B.SEPT.22,1895 WRIGHTSVILLE,O.
D.NOV.27,1922 JEFFERSON,OHIO

YR	CL	LEA	POS	GP	G	REC
1918	STL	N	O		80	.261
1919	STL	N	2-3-O		110	.286
1920	STL	N	O		137	.282
1921	STL	N	O		152	.350
1922	STL	N	O		64	.303
			BRTR		543	.302

MC ILREE, VANCE ELMER
B.OCT.14,1897 RIVERSIDE,IOWA
D.MAY 6,1959 KANSAS CITY,MO.

YR	CL	LEA	POS	GP	G	REC
1921	WAS	A	P		1	0- 0
			BRTR			

MC ILVEEN, HENRY COOKE (IRISH)
B.JULY 27,1880 BELFAST,IRELAND
D.OCT.18,1960 LORAIN,OHIO

YR	CL	LEA	POS	GP	G	REC
1906	PIT	N	P		5	0- 1
1908	NY	A	O		44	.213
1909	NY	A	H		4	.000
			TL	5	53	0- 1 .212

MC ILWAIN, STOVER WILLIAM
(STOVER) OR (SMOKEY)
B.SEPT.22,1939 SAVANNAH,GA.
D.JAN.15,1966 BUFFALO,N.Y.

YR	CL	LEA	POS	GP	G	REC
1957	CHI	A	P		1	0- 0
1958	CHI	A	P		1	0- 0
			BRTR		2	0- 0

MC INNIS, JOHN PHALEN
(STUFFY) OR (JACK)
B.SEPT.19,1890 GLOUCESTER,MASS.
D.FEB.16,1960 IPSWICH,MASS.

YR	CL	LEA	POS	GP	G	REC
1909	PHI	A	S		19	.239
1910	PHI	A	S		38	.301
1911	PHI	A	1-S		126	.321
1912	PHI	A	1		153	.327
1913	PHI	A	1		148	.326
1914	PHI	A	1		149	.314
1915	PHI	A	1		119	.314
1916	PHI	A	1		140	.295
1917	PHI	A	1		150	.303
1918	BOS	A	1-3		117	.272
1919	BOS	A	1		120	.305
1920	BOS	A	1		148	.297
1921	BOS	A	1		152	.307
1922	CLE	A	1		142	.305
1923	BOS	N	1		154	.315
1924	BOS	N	1		146	.291
1925	PIT	N	1		59	.368
1926	PIT	N	1		47	.299
1927	PHI	N	M-1		1	.000
			BRTR		2128	.308

MC INTIRE, JOHN REID (HARRY)
B.JAN.11,1879 DAYTON,OHIO
D.JAN.9,1949 DAYTONA BEACH,FLA.

YR	CL	LEA	POS	GP	G	REC
1905	BRO	N	P	40	45	9-27
1906	BRO	N	P	39	42	13-21
1907	BRO	N	P		28	7-15
1908	BRO	N	P		40	11-20
1909	BRO	N	P		32	7-17
1910	CHI	N	P		28	13- 9
1911	CHI	N	P		25	11- 7
1912	CHI	N	P		7	1- 2
1913	CIN	N	P		1	0- 1
			BRTR	240	248	72-119

MC INTOSH, JOSEPH ANTHONY (JOE)
B.AUG.4,1951 BILLINGS,MONT.

YR	CL	LEA	POS	GP	G	REC
1974	SD	N	P		10	0- 4
1975	SD	N	P	37	38	8-15
			BBTR	47	48	8-19

MC INTYRE, FRANK W.
D.DETROIT,MICH.

YR	CL	LEA	POS	GP	G	REC
1883	DET	N	P		1	1- 0
	COL	AA	P		2	1- 1
					3	2- 1

MC INTYRE, MATTHEW W.
B.JUNE 12,1880 STONINGTON,CONN.
D.APR.2,1920 DETROIT,MICH.

YR	CL	LEA	POS	GP	G	REC
1901	PHI	A	O		82	.283
1904	DET	A	O		152	.254
1905	DET	A	O		131	.265
1906	DET	A	O		133	.260
1907	DET	A	O		20	.284
1908	DET	A	O		151	.295
1909	DET	A	O		125	.244
1910	DET	A	O		83	.236
1911	CHI	A	O		146	.323
1912	CHI	A	O		45	.167
			BLTL		1068	.270

MC IVOR, EDWARD OTTO
B.JULY 26,1884 GREENVILLE,TEX.
D.MAY 4,1954 DALLAS,TEX.

YR	CL	LEA	POS	GP	G	REC
1911	STL	N	O		17	.226
			BBTL			

MC JAMES, JAMES MC CUTCHEN (DOC)
[REAL NAME JAMES MC CUTCHEN JAMES]
B.AUG.27,1873 WILLIAMSBURG,S.C.
D.SEPT.23,1901 CHARLESTON,S.C.

YR	CL	LEA	POS	GP	G	REC
1895	WAS	N	P		3	1- 1
1896	WAS	N	P		34	12-21
1897	WAS	N	P		41	14-24
1898	BAL	N	P		42	27-14
1899	BRO	N	P		33	17-11
1901	BRO	N	P		13	4- 6
			TR		166	75-77

MC KAIN, ARCHIE RICHARD (HAPPY)
B.MAY 12,1911 DELPHOS,KAN.

YR	CL	LEA	POS	GP	G	REC
1937	BOS	A	P	36	38	8- 8
1938	BOS	A	P		37	5- 4
1939	DET	A	P		32	5- 6
1940	DET	A	P		27	5- 0
1941	DET	A	P		15	2- 1
	STL	A	P		8	0- 1
1943	STL	A	P		10	1- 1
			BBTL	165	167	26-21
			BL 1941-43			

MC KAIN, HAROLD LE ROY
B.JULY 10,1906 LOGAN,IOWA
D.JAN.24,1970 SACRAMENTO,CAL.

YR	CL	LEA	POS	GP	G	REC
1927	CLE	A	P		2	0- 1
1929	CHI	A	P		34	6- 9
1930	CHI	A	P	32	33	6- 4
1931	CHI	A	P	27	32	6- 9
1932	CHI	A	P		8	0- 0
			BLTR	103	109	18-23

MC KAY, DAVID LAWRENCE (DAVE)
B.MAR.14,1950 VANCOUVER,B.C.,CAN

YR	CL	LEA	POS	GP	G	REC
1975	MIN	A	3		33	.256
1976	MIN	A	3/S		45	.203
1977	TOR	A	2-3-S		95	.197
1978	TOR	A	*2/S-3		145	.238
			BBTR		318	.225
			BR 1975-76			

MC KAY, REEVE STEWART (RIP)
B.NOV.16,1881 MORGAN,TEX.
D.JAN.18,1946 DALLAS,TEX.

YR	CL	LEA	POS	GP	G	REC
1915	STL	A	P		1	0- 0
			TR			

MC KEAN, EDWIN JOHN (ED) OR (MACK)
B.JUNE 6,1864 GRAFTON,OHIO
D.AUG.16,1919 CLEVELAND,OHIO

YR	CL	LEA	POS	GP	G	REC
1887	CLE	AA	S		132	.364
1888	CLE	AA	S-O		130	.297
1889	CLE	N	S		123	.302
1890	CLE	N	S		136	.296
1891	CLE	N	S		141	.280
1892	CLE	N	S		128	.269
1893	CLE	N	S		125	.325
1894	CLE	N	S		130	.354
1895	CLE	N	S		132	.344
1896	CLE	N	S		133	.335
1897	CLE	N	S		127	.273
1898	CLE	N	S		151	.285
1899	STL	N	S		67	.281
			BRTR		1655	.311

MC KECHNIE, WILLIAM BOYD
(BILL) OR (DEACON)
B.AUG.7,1886 WILKINSBURG,PA.
D.OCT.29,1965 BRADENTON,FLA.

YR	CL	LEA	POS	GP	G	REC
1907	PIT	N	2		3	.125
1910	PIT	N	2		60	.217
1911	PIT	N	1-2		92	.227
1912	PIT	N	2-S		24	.247
1913	BOS	N	O		1	.000
	NY	A	2		44	.134
1914	IND	F	3		149	.305
1915	NEW	F	M-3		126	.257
1916	NY	N	M-3		71	.238
	CIN	N	M-3		37	.292
1917	CIN	N	2-S-3		48	.254
1918	PIT	N	3		126	.255
1920	PIT	N	3		40	.218
			BBTR		821	.252

NON-PLAYING MANAGER
PIT[N] 1922-26, STL[N] 1928-29,
BOS(N) 1930-37, CIN(N) 1938-46

MC KEE

YR	CL	LEA	POS	GP	G	REC
1884	WAS	U	C-3-O		4	.188

MC KEE, JAMES F.
B.ROCKFORD,ILL.
D.JUNE 26,1912
NON-PLAYING MANAGER MIL[U] 1884

MC KEE, JAMES MARION (JIM)
B.FEB.1,1947 COLUMBUS,OHIO

YR	CL	LEA	POS	GP	G	REC
1972	PIT	N	/P		2	1- 0
1973	PIT	N	P		15	0- 1
			BRTR		17	1- 1

MC KEE, RAYMOND ELLIS (RED)
B.JULY 20,1890 SHAWNEE,OHIO
D.AUG.5,1972 SAGINAW,MICH.

YR	CL	LEA	POS	GP	G	REC
1913	DET	A	C		67	.283
1914	DET	A	C		32	.187
1915	DET	A	C		55	.274
1916	DET	A	C		32	.211
			BLTR		186	.254

MC KEE, ROGERS HORNSBY
B.SEPT.16,1926 SHELBY,N.C.

YR	CL	LEA	POS	GP	G	REC
1943	PHI	N	P		4	1- 0
1944	PHI	N	P		1	0- 0
			BLTL		5	1- 0

YR CL LEA POS   GP   G   REC

MC KEEVER, JAMES
B.APR.19,1861 NEWFOUNDLAND,CAN.
D.AUG.19,1897 BOSTON,MASS.
1884 BOS U C-0   16   .141

MC KEITHAN, EMMETT JAMES (TIM)
B.NOV.2,1906 LAWNDALE,N.C.
D.AUG.20,1969 FOREST CITY,N.C.
1932 PHI A P   4   0- 1
1933 PHI A P   3   1- 0
1934 PHI A P   3   0- 0
     BRTR   10   1- 1

MC KELVEY, JOHN WELLINGTON
B.AUG.27,1847 ROCHESTER,N.Y.
D.MAY.31,1944
1875 NH NA 3-0   43   -

MC KELVY, RUSSELL ERRETT
B.SEPT.8,1856 MEADVILLE,PA.
D.OCT.19,1915 OMAHA,NEB.
1878 IND N P-0   3   60   0- 0
                              .222
1882 PIT AA O   1   0- 0
                             1.000
     TR   3   61   0- 0
                              .219

MC KENNA, EDWARD J.
B.ST.LOUIS,MO.
1874 PHI NA 1   1   .000
1877 STL N O   1   .200
1884 WAS U C-0   32   .188
                       34   .184

MC KENNA, JAMES WILLIAM (KIT)
B.FEB.10,1873 LYNCHBURG,VA.
D.MAR.31,1941 LYNCHBURG,VA.
1898 BRO N P   14   1- 7
1899 BAL N P   9   2- 4
                       23   3-11

MC KENRY, FRANK GORDON (BIG PETE)
B.AUG.13,1888 PINEY FLATS,TENN.
D.NOV.1,1956 FRESNO,CAL.
1915 CIN N P   21   5- 5
1916 CIN N P   6   1- 1
     BRTR   27   6- 6

MC KEON, JOHN ALOYSIUS (JACK)
B.NOV.23,1930 SOUTH AMBOY,N.J.
NON-PLAYING MANAGER
KC[A] 1973-75, OAK[A] 1977-78

MC KEON, LAWRENCE G.
B.MAR.25,1866 NEW YORK
D.JULY 18,1915 INDIANAPOLIS,IND
1884 IND AA P-1   61   70   18-41
                              .215
1885 CIN AA P-0   33   20-13
                              .157
1886 CIN AA P-1- 17   18   8- 9
                              .250
     KC N P   2   0- 2
                 113 123   46-65
                              .203

MC KEOUGH, DAVID J.
B.1865 UTICA,N.Y.
D.JULY 10,1901 UTICA,N.Y.
1890 ROC AA C   63   .218
1891 ATH AA C   15   .278
                       78   .231

MC KINNEY, BUCK
B.LOUISVILLE,KY.
NON-PLAYING MANAGER LOU[AA]1889

MC KINNEY, CHARLES RICHARD (RICH)
B.NOV.22,1946 PIQUA,OHIO
1970 CHI A 3-S   43   .168
1971 CHI A 2-0/3   114   .271
1972 NY A 3   37   .215
1973 OAK A 3/2-0   48   .246
1974 OAK A /2   5   .243
1975 OAK A /1   8   .143
1977 OAK A 1-0/3-0-2   86   .177
     BRTR   341   .225

MC KINNEY, ROBERT FRANCIS
B.OCT.4,1875 MC SHERRYSTOWN,PA.
D.AUG.19,1946 CHICAGO,ILL.
1901 PHI A 2   2   .000

MC KINNON, ALEXANDER J.
B.AUG.14,1856 BOSTON,MASS.
D.JULY 24,1887 CHARLESTOWN,MASS
1884 NY N 1   112   .275
1885 STL N 1   100   .270
1886 STL N 1   122   .301
1887 PIT N 1   48   .365
                      382   .301

MC KNIGHT, DENNIS HAMAR
B.1847 PITTSBURGH,PA.
D.MAY 5,1900 PITTSBURGH,PA.
NON-PLAYING MANAGER PIT[AA]1884

MC KNIGHT, JAMES ARTHUR (JIM)
B.JUNE 1,1936 BEE BRANCH,ARK.
1960 CHI N 2-0   3   .333
1962 CHI N 2-0   60   .224
     BRTR   63   .231

MC LAIN, DENNIS DALE (DENNY)
B.MAR.29,1944 CHICAGO,ILL.
1963 DET A P   3   2- 1
1964 DET A P   19   20   4- 5
1965 DET A P   33   16- 6
1966 DET A P   38   20-14
1967 DET A P   37   38   17-16
1968 DET A P   41   44   31- 6
1969 DET A P   42   24- 9
1970 DET A P   14   3- 5
1971 WAS A P   33   10-22
1972 OAK A /P   5   1- 2
     ATL N P   15   3- 5
     BRTR   280 285 131-91

MC LANE, EDWARD CAMERON
B.AUG.20,1881 WESTON,MASS.
1907 BRO N O   1   .000

MC LARNEY, ARTHUR JAMES
B.DEC.20,1908 FT.WORDEN,WASH.
1932 NY N S   9   .130
     BBTR

MC LARRY, HOWARD ZELL (POLLY)
B.MAR.25,1891 LEONARD,TEX.
D.NOV.4,1971 BONHAM,TEX.
1912 CHI A H   2   .000
1915 CHI N 1-2   68   .197
                       70   .194

MC LAUGHLIN, BERNARD
B.1857 IRELAND
D.FEB.13,1921 LOWELL,MASS.
1882 WOR N S-0   15   .207
1884 WAS U S   10   .189
     KC U P-2-   6   40   0- 4
                              .218
1887 PHI N 2   50   .259
1890 SYR AA S   81   .260
                  6   196   0- 4
                              .245

MC LAUGHLIN, BYRON SCOTT
B.SEPT.29,1955 VAN NUYS,CAL.
1977 SEA A /P   1   0- 0
1978 SEA A P   20   4- 8
     BRTR   21   4- 8

MC LAUGHLIN, FRANCIS EDWARD
B.JUNE 19,1856 LOWELL,MASS.
D.APR.5,1917 LOWELL,MASS.
1883 PIT AA P-2-   1   27   0- 0
           S-0   .200
1884 CIN U S   15   .246
     CHI U 2-S   .284
     KC U P-2-   4   33   1- 1
           S-3-0   .219
     BRTR   5   90   1- 1
                              .235

MC LAUGHLIN, JAMES ANSON
(KID) OR (SUNSHINE)
B.APR.12,1888 RANDOLPH,N.Y.
D.NOV.13,1934 ALLEGHENY,N.Y.
1914 CIN N O   3   .000
     BLTR

MC LAUGHLIN, JAMES C.
B.1860 CLEVELAND,OHIO
D.NOV.16,1895 CLEVELAND,OHIO
1884 WAS U S-3   10   .194
     BAL AA P-0   3   5   1- 7
                              .227
       TL   3   15   1- 2
                              .207

MC LAUGHLIN, JAMES ROBERT
B.JAN.3,1902 ST.LOUIS,MO.
D.DEC.18,1968 MOUNT VERNON,ILL.
1932 STL A 3   1   .000
     BRTR

MC LAUGHLIN, JOEY RICHARD
B.JULY 11,1956 TULSA,OKLA.
1977 ATL N /P   3   0- 0
     BRTR

MC LAUGHLIN, JUSTIN THEODORE (JUD)
B.MAR.24,1912 BRIGHTON,MASS.
D.SEPT.27,1964 CAMBRIDGE,MASS.
1931 BOS A P   9   0- 0
1932 BOS A P   1   0- 0
1933 BOS A P   6   0- 0
     BLTL   16   0- 0

MC LAUGHLIN, MICHAEL DUANE
B.OCT.23,1953 OAKLAND,CAL.
1976 HOU N P   17   4- 5
1977 HOU N P   46   4- 7
1978 HOU N P   12   0- 1
     BRTR   75   8-13

MC LAUGHLIN, PATRICK ELMER
B.AUG.17,1910 TAYLOR,TEX.
1937 DET A P   10   11   0- 2
1940 PHI A P   1   0- 0
1945 DET A P   1   0- 0
     BRTR   12   13   0- 2

MC LAUGHLIN, THOMAS
B.LOUISVILLE,KY.
1883 LOU AA 1-2-S-3-0 42   .206
1884 LOU AA S   100   .191
1885 LOU AA 2   113   .215
1886 MET AA 2   74   .137
1891 WAS AA 2   14   .250
                      343   .198

MC LAUGHLIN, WARREN A.
B.JAN.22,1876 N.PLAINFIELD,N.J.
D.OCT.22,1923 PLAINFIELD,N.J.
1900 PHI N P   1   0- 0
1902 PIT N P   3   3- 0
1903 PIT N P   3   0- 2
                        7   3- 2

MC LAURIN, RALPH EDGAR
B.MAY 23,1885 KISSIMMEE,FLA.
D.FEB.11,1943 MC COLL,S.C.
1908 STL N O   8   .227

MC LEAN, ALBERT ELDON (ELROD)
B.SEPT.20,1912 CHICAGO,ILL.
1935 WAS A P   4   0- 0
     BRTR

MC LEAN, JOHN BANNERMAN (LARRY)
B.JULY 18,1881 CAMBRIDGE,MASS.
D.MAR.24,1921 BOSTON,MASS.
1901 BOS A 1   9   .210
1903 CHI N C   1   .000
1904 STL N C   24   .167
1906 CIN N C   12   .191
1907 CIN N C   101   .289
1908 CIN N C-1   88   .217
1909 CIN N C   95   .256
1910 CIN N C   119   .298
1911 CIN N C   98   .287
1912 CIN N C   102   .243
1913 STL N C   48   .270
     NY N C   30   .320
1914 NY N C   79   .260
1915 NY N C   13   .152
     BRTR   819   .263

MC LELAND, WAYNE GAFFNEY
(WAYNE) OR (NUBBIN)
B.AUG.29,1924 MILTON,IOWA
1951 DET A P   6   0- 1
1952 DET A P   4   0- 0
     BRTR   10   0- 1

MC LEOD, RALPH ALTON
B.OCT.19,1916 N.QUINCY,MASS.
1938 BOS N O   6   .286
     BLTL

MC LEOD, SOULE JAMES (JIM)
B.SEPT.12,1908 JONES,LA.
1930 WAS A 3   18   .265
1932 WAS A S   7   .000
1933 PHI N 3   67   .194
     BRTR   92   .203

MC LISH, CALVIN COOLIDGE JULIUS
CAESAR TUSKAHOMA
(CAL) OR (BUSTER)
B.DEC.1,1925 ANADARKO,OKLA.
1944 BRO N P   23   31   3-10
1946 BRO N P   1   0- 0
1947 PIT N P   1   0- 0
1948 PIT N P   2   3   0- 0
1949 CHI N P   8   9   1- 1
1951 CHI N P   30   31   4-10
1956 CLE A P   37   39   2- 4
1957 CLE A P   42   44   9- 7
1958 CLE A P   39   16- 8
1959 CLE A P   35   19- 8
1960 CIN N P   37   4-14
1961 CHI A P   31   10-13
1962 PHI N P   32   11- 5
1963 PHI N P   32   33   13-11
1964 PHI N P   2   0- 1
     BBTR   352 368   92-92

MC MACKIN, SAMUEL
B.1872 CLEVELAND,OHIO
D.FEB.2,1903 COLUMBUS,OHIO
1902 CHI A P   1   0- 0
     DET A P   1   0- 0
                        2   0- 0

MC MAHAN, JACK WALLY
B.JULY 25,1932 HOT SPRINGS,ARK.
1956 PIT N P   11   0- 0
     KC A P   23   0- 5
     BRTL   34   0- 5

YR	CL LEA POS	GP	G	REC

MC MAHON, DONALD JOHN (DON)
B.JAN.4,1930 BROOKLYN,N.Y.

YR	CL LEA POS	GP	G	REC
1957 MIL N P		32	2- 3	
1958 MIL N P		38	7- 2	
1959 MIL N P		60	5- 3	
1960 MIL N P		48	3- 6	
1961 MIL N P		53	6- 4	
1962 MIL N P		2	0- 1	
	HOU N P		51	5- 5
1963 HOU N P		49	1- 5	
1964 CLE A P		70	6- 4	
1965 CLE A P		58	3- 3	
1966 CLE A P		12	1- 1	
	BOS A P		49	8- 7
1967 BOS A P		11	1- 2	
	CHI A P		52	5- 0
1968 CHI A P		25	2- 1	
	DET A P		20	3- 1	
1969 DET A P		34	3- 5	
	SF N P		13	3- 1
1970 SF N P		61	9- 5	
1971 SF N P		61	10- 6	
1972 SF N P		44	3- 3	
1973 SF N P		22	4- 0	
1974 SF N /P		9	0- 0	
	BRTR		874	90-68

MC MAHON, HENRY JOHN (DOC)
B.DEC.19,1886 WOBURN,MASS.
D.DEC.11,1929 WOBURN,MASS.

1908 BOS A P		1	1- 0	

MC MAHON, JOHN HENRY (JACK)
B.OCT.15,1869 WATERBURY,CONN.
D.DEC.30,1894 BRIDGEPORT,CONN.

1892 NY N 1		36	.239
1893 NY N C		11	.333
	TL		47	.256

MC MAHON, JOHN JOSEPH (SADIE)
B.SEPT.19,1867 WILMINGTON,DEL.
D.FEB.20,1954 DELAWARE CITY,DEL.

1889 ATH AA P	29	30	15-11
1890 ATH AA P		51	29-17
	BAL AA P		12	7- 3
1891 BAL AA P		60	34-25
1892 BAL N P		47	19-28
1893 BAL N P		40	23-16
1894 BAL N P		34	25- 8
1895 BAL N P		15	10- 4
1896 BAL N P		21	12- 8
1897 BRO N P		9	0- 0
	BRTR	318	319	174-120

MC MAKIN, JOHN WEAVER
(SPARTANBURG JOHN)
B.MAR.6,1878 SPARTANBURG,S.C.
D.SEPT.25,1956 LYMAN,S.C.

1902 BRO N P		4	2- 2	
	BRTL			

MC MANUS, FRANCIS E.
B.SEPT.21,1875 LAWRENCE,MASS.
D.SEPT.1,1923 SYRACUSE,N.Y.

1899 WAS N C		7	.400
1903 BRO N C		2	.000
1904 DET A C		1	.000
	NY A C		4	.000
	TR		14	.235

MC MANUS, GEORGE
B.1846
D.OCT.2,1918 NEW YORK,N.Y.
NON-PLAYING MANAGER STL[N] 1877

MC MANUS, JAMES MICHAEL
B.JULY 20,1936 BROOKLINE,MASS.

1960 KC A 1		5	.308
	BLTL			

MC MANUS, JOAB LOGAN (JOE)
B.SEPT.7,1887 PALMYRA,ILL.
D.DEC.23,1955 BECKLEY,W.VA.

1913 CIN N P		1	0- 0	
	BRTR			

MC MANUS, MARTIN JOSEPH (MARTY)
B.MAR.14,1900 CHICAGO,ILL.
D.FEB.18,1966 ST.LOUIS,MO.

1920 STL A 3		1	.200
1921 STL A 1-2-3		121	.260
1922 STL A 2		154	.312
1923 STL A 1-2		154	.309
1924 STL A 2		123	.333
1925 STL A 2		154	.288
1926 STL A 3		149	.284
1927 DET A 2-S-3		108	.268
1928 DET A 1-3		139	.288
1929 DET A 3		154	.280
1930 DET A 3		142	.320
1931 DET A 2-3		107	.273
	BOS A 2-3		17	.276
1932 BOS A M-2-3		93	.235
1933 BOS A M-1-2-3		106	.284
1934 BOS N 2-3		119	.276
	BRTR		1831	.289

MC MANUS, PATRICK
B.1879 TRO N P

1879 TRO N P		2	0- 2	

MC MATH, JIMMY LEE
B.AUG.10,1949 TUSCALOOSA,ALA.

1968 CHI N /O		6	.143	
	BLTL			

MC MILLAN, GEORGE A. (REDDY)
B.EVANSVILLE,IND.

1890 NY N O		10	.138	

MC MILLAN, NORMAN ALEXIS (BUB)
B.OCT.5,1895 LATTA,S.C.
D.SEPT.28,1969 MARION,S.C.

1922 NY A O		33	.256
1923 BOS A 2-S-3		131	.253
1924 STL A 2-3		76	.279
1928 CHI N 2-3		49	.220
1929 CHI N 3		124	.271
	BRTR		413	.260

MC MILLAN, ROY DAVID
B.JULY 17,1930 BONHAM,TEX.

1951 CIN N 2-S-3		85	.211
1952 CIN N S		154	.244
1953 CIN N S		155	.233
1954 CIN N S		154	.250
1955 CIN N S		151	.268
1956 CIN N S		150	.263
1957 CIN N S		151	.272
1958 CIN N S		145	.229
1959 CIN N S		79	.264
1960 CIN N 2-S		124	.236
1961 MIL N S		154	.220
1962 MIL N S		137	.246
1963 MIL N S		100	.250
1964 MIL N S		8	.308
	NY N *S		113	.211
1965 NY N *S		157	.242
1966 NY N S		76	.213
	BRTR		2093	.243
NON-PLAYING MANAGER
MIL[A] 1972 [INTERIM]
NY[N] 1975

MC MILLAN, THOMAS ERWIN (TOM)
B.SEPT.13,1951 RICHMOND,VA.

1977 SEA A /S		2	.000	
	BRTR			

MC MILLIAN, THOMAS LAW (RABBIT)
B.APR.17,1888 PITTSTON,PA.
D.JULY 15,1966 ORLANDO,FLA.

1908 BRO N S		43	.238
1909 BRO N S		108	.212
1910 BRO N S		23	.176
1912 NY A S		82	.185
	NY A S		41	.228
	BRTR		297	.209

MC MULLEN, GEORGE
B.CALIFORNIA

1887 MET AA P		3	1- 2	

MC MULLEN, HUGH RAPHAEL
B.DEC.16,1901 LA CYGNE,KAN.

1925 NY N C		5	.133
1926 NY N C		57	.187
1928 WAS A H		1	.000
1929 CIN N C		1	.000
	BBTR		64	.176

MC MULLEN, KENNETH LEE (KEN)
B.JUNE 1,1942 OXNARD,CAL.

1962 LA N O		6	.273
1963 LA N 2-3-O		79	.236
1964 LA N 1-3-O		24	.209
1965 WAS A *3/O-1		150	.263
1966 WAS A *3/1-O		147	.233
1967 WAS A 3		146	.245
1968 WAS A *3-S		151	.248
1969 WAS A 3		158	.272
1970 WAS A 3		15	.203
	CAL A *3		124	.232
1971 CAL A *3		160	.250
1972 CAL A 3		137	.269
1973 LA N 3		42	.247
1974 LA N /3-2		44	.250
1975 LA N 3/1		39	.239
1976 OAK A 3-1-O/O-2		98	.220
1977 MIL A D-1/3		63	.228
	BRTR		1583	.248

MC MULLIN, FREDERICK WILLIAM
B.OCT.13,1891 SCAMMON,KAN.
D.NOV.21,1952 LOS ANGELES,CAL.

1914 DET A S		1	.000
1916 CHI A 3		68	.257
1917 CHI A 3		59	.237
1918 CHI A 3		70	.276
1919 CHI A 3		60	.294
1920 CHI A 3		46	.197
	BRTR		304	.256

MC MULLIN, JOHN F. (LEFTY)
B.1848 PHILADELPHIA,PA.
D.APR.11,1881

1871 TRO NA P		29	13-15
1872 MUT NA P-O	2	54	2- 0
				.231
1873 ATH NA P-O	1	51	1- 0
				.231
1874 ATH NA C-O		55	.387
1875 PHI NA P-O	1	53	0- 1
				.249
	BLTL	33	242	16-16
				-

MC NABB, CARL MAC (SKINNY)
B.JAN.25,1917 STEVENSON,ALA.

1945 DET A H		1	.000	
	BRTR			

MC NABB, EDGAR J. (TEXAS)
B.OCT.24,1865 MT.VERNON,OHIO
D.FEB.28,1894 PITTSBURGH,PA.

1893 BAL N P		17	8- 8	

**MC NAIR, DONALD ERIC
(ERIC) OR (BOOB)**
B.APR.12,1909 MERIDIAN,MISS.
D.MAR.11,1949 MERIDIAN,MISS.

1929 PHI A S		4	.500
1930 PHI A S-3		78	.266
1931 PHI A 2-S-3		79	.271
1932 PHI A S		135	.285
1933 PHI A 2-S		89	.261
1934 PHI A S		151	.280
1935 PHI A 1-S-3		137	.270
1936 BOS A 2-S-3		128	.268
1937 BOS A 2		126	.292
1938 BOS A 2-S		46	.156
1939 CHI A 2-3		129	.324
1940 CHI A 2-3		66	.227
1941 DET A S-3		23	.186
1942 DET A S		26	.162
	PHI A 2-S		34	.243
	BRTR		1251	.274

MC NALLY, DAVID ARTHUR (DAVE)
B.OCT.31,1942 BILLINGS,MONT.

1962 BAL A P		1	1- 0
1963 BAL A P		29	7- 8
1964 BAL A P		30	9-11
1965 BAL A P		35	11- 6
1966 BAL A P		34	13- 6
1967 BAL A P		24	7- 7
1968 BAL A P		35	22-10
1969 BAL A P		41	20- 7
1970 BAL A P	40	41	24- 9
1971 BAL A P		30	21- 5
1972 BAL A P		36	13-17
1973 BAL A P		38	17-17
1974 BAL A P		39	16-10
1975 MON N P		12	3- 6
	BRTL	424	425	184-119

**MC NALLY, MICHAEL JOSEPH (MIKE)
OR (MINOOKA MIKE)**
B.SEPT.9,1892 MINOOKA,PA.
D.MAY 29,1965 BETHLEHEM,PA.

1915 BOS A 3		23	.151
1916 BOS A 2		87	.171
1917 BOS A 3		42	.300
1919 BOS A 3		33	.262
1920 BOS A 2		93	.256
1921 NY A 2-3		71	.260
1922 NY A 3		52	.252
1923 NY A 2-3		30	.211
1924 NY A 2-3		49	.247
1925 WAS A 2-S-3		12	.143
	BRTR		492	.238

MC NAMARA, GEORGE FRANCIS
B.JAN.11,1903 CHICAGO,ILL.

1922 WAS A O		3	.272	
	BLTR			

MC NAMARA, JOHN FRANCIS
B.JUNE 4,1932 SACRAMENTO,CAL.
NON-PLAYING MANAGER
OAK[A] 1969-70, SD[N] 1974-77

MC NAMARA, JOHN RAYMOND (DINNY)
B.SEPT.16,1905 LEXINGTON,MASS.
D.DEC.20,1963 LEXINGTON,MASS.

1927 BOS N O		11	.000
1928 BOS N O		9	.250
	BLTR		20	.077

MC NAMARA, JOSEPH
[PLAYED UNDER NAME OF JOSEPH MACK]

MC NAMARA, ROBERT MAXEY
B.SEPT.19,1916 DENVER,COLO.

1939 PHI A 3		9	.222	
	BRTR			

MC NAMARA, THOMAS HENRY
B.NOV.5,1895 ROXBURY,MASS.
D.MAY 5,1974 DANVERS,MASS.

1922 PIT N H		1	.000	
	BR			

MC NAMARA, TIMOTHY ALOYSIUS
B.NOV.20,1898 MILLVILLE,MASS.

YR	CL	LEA	POS	GP	G	REC
1922	BOS	N	P		24	3- 4
1923	BOS	N	P		32	3-13
1924	BOS	N	P		35	8-12
1925	BOS	N	P		1	0- 0
1926	NY	N	P		6	0- 0
		BRTR			98	14-29

MC NAUGHTON, GORDON JOSEPH
B.JULY 31,1910 CHICAGO,ILL.
D.AUG.6,1942 CHICAGO,ILL.

YR	CL	LEA	POS	GP	G	REC
1932	BOS	A	P		6	0- 1
		BRTR				

MC NEAL, JOHN HARLEY (HARRY)
B.AUG.11,1877 IBERIA,OHIO
D.JAN.11,1945 CLEVELAND,OHIO

YR	CL	LEA	POS	GP	G	REC
1901	CLE	A	P		11	5- 6
		BRTR				

MC NEELY, GEORGE EARL (EARL)
B.MAY 12,1898 SACRAMENTO,CAL.
D.JULY 16,1971 SACRAMENTO,CAL.

YR	CL	LEA	POS	GP	G	REC
1924	WAS	A	O		43	.330
1925	WAS	A	O		122	.285
1926	WAS	A	O		124	.303
1927	WAS	A	O		73	.276
1928	STL	A	O		127	.236
1929	STL	A	O		69	.243
1930	STL	A	1-O		76	.272
1931	STL	A	O		49	.225
		BRTR			683.	.272

MC NEIL, NORMAN FRANCIS
B.OCT.22,1892 CHICAGO,ILL.
D.APR.11,1942 BUFFALO,N.Y.

YR	CL	LEA	POS	GP	G	REC
1919	BOS	A	C		5	.273
		BRTR				

MC NERTNEY, GERALD EDWARD (JERRY)
B.AUG.7,1936 BOONE,IOWA

YR	CL	LEA	POS	GP	G	REC
1964	CHI	A	C		73	.215
1966	CHI	A	C		44	.220
1967	CHI	A	C		56	.228
1968	CHI	A	C/1		74	.219
1969	SEA	A	*C		128	.241
1970	MIL	A	C-1		111	.243
1971	STL	N	C		56	.289
1972	STL	N	C		39	.208
1973	PIT	N	/C		9	.250
		BRTR			590	.237

MC NICHOL, EDWARD
B.1880 WHEELING,W.VA.

YR	CL	LEA	POS	GP	G	REC
1904	BOS	N	P		17	2-13
		TR				

MC NULTY, PATRICK HOWARD
B.FEB.27,1899 CLEVELAND,OHIO
D.MAY 4,1963 HOLLYWOOD,CAL.

YR	CL	LEA	POS	GP	G	REC
1922	CLE	A	O		22	.271
1924	CLE	A	O		101	.268
1925	CLE	A	O		118	.314
1926	CLE	A	O		48	.250
1927	CLE	A	O		19	.317
		BLTR			308	.290

MC NULTY, WILLIAM FRANCIS (BILL)
B.AUG.29,1946 SACRAMENTO,CAL.

YR	CL	LEA	POS	GP	G	REC
1969	OAK	A	/O		5	.000
1972	OAK	A	/3		4	.100
		BRTR			9	.037

MC PARTLIN, FRANK
B.FEB.16,1872 HOOSICK FALLS,N.Y
D.1940

YR	CL	LEA	POS	GP	G	REC
1899	NY	N	P		1	0- 0
		TR				

MC PHEE, JOHN ALEXANDER (BID)
B.NOV.1,1859 MASSENA,N.Y.
D.JAN.3,1942 SAN DIEGO,CAL.

YR	CL	LEA	POS	GP	G	REC
1882	CIN	AA	2		78	.218
1883	CIN	AA	C-2		94	.235
1884	CIN	AA	2		113	.292
1885	CIN	AA	2		110	.275
1886	CIN	AA	2		140	.272
1887	CIN	AA	2		129	.354
1888	CIN	AA	2		110	.230
1889	CIN	AA	2-3		135	.269
1890	CIN	N	2		132	.255
1891	CIN	N	2		138	.257
1892	CIN	N	2		144	.294
1893	CIN	N	2		127	.307
1894	CIN	N	2		128	.320
1895	CIN	N	2		114	.295
1896	CIN	N	2		116	.299
1897	CIN	N	2		80	.307
1898	CIN	N	2		131	.246
1899	CIN	N	2		106	.283
		BRTR			2125	.281

NON-PLAYING MANAGER CIN[N] 1901-02

MC PHERSON, JOHN JACOB
B.MAR.9,1869 EASTON,PA.
D.SEPT.30,1941 EASTON,PA.

YR	CL	LEA	POS	GP	G	REC
1901	PHI	A	P		1	0- 1
1904	PHI	N	P		15	1- 9
					16	1-10

MC QUAID, HERBERT GEORGE
B.MAR.29,1899 SAN FRANCISCO,CAL
D.APR.4,1966 RICHMOND,CAL.

YR	CL	LEA	POS	GP	G	REC
1923	CIN	N	P		12	1- 0
1926	NY	A	P		17	1- 0
		BRTR			29	2- 0

MC QUAID, JAMES H.
B.CHICAGO,ILL.

YR	CL	LEA	POS	GP	G	REC
1891	STL	AA	2		4	.333
1898	WAS	N	O		1	.000
					5	.333

MC QUAIG, GERALD JOSEPH
B.JAN.31,1912 DOUGLAS,GA.

YR	CL	LEA	POS	GP	G	REC
1934	PHI	A	O		7	.063
		BRTR				

MC QUEEN, MICHAEL ROBERT (MIKE)
B.AUG.30,1950 OKLAHOMA CITY,OKLA

YR	CL	LEA	POS	GP	G	REC
1969	ATL	N	P		1	0- 0
1970	ATL	N	P		22	1- 5
1971	ATL	N	P		17	4- 1
1972	ATL	N	P		23	0- 5
1974	CIN	N	P		10	0- 0
		BLTL			73	5-11

MC QUERY, WILLIAM THOMAS (MOX)
B.JUNE 28,1861 GARRARD CO.,KY.
D.JUNE 12,1900 COVINGTON,KY.

YR	CL	LEA	POS	GP	G	REC
1884	CIN	U	1		32	.248
1885	DET	N	1		70	.273
1886	KC	N	1		122	.247
1890	SYR	AA	1		120	.295
1891	WAS	AA	1		68	.236
					412	.266

MC QUILLAN, GEORGE WATT
B.MAY 1,1885 BROOKLYN,N.Y.
D.MAR.30,1940 COLUMBUS,OHIO

YR	CL	LEA	POS	GP	G	REC
1907	PHI	N	P		6	2- 0
1908	PHI	N	P		48	23-17
1909	PHI	N	P		41	13-16
1910	PHI	N	P		24	9- 6
1911	CIN	N	P		19	2- 6
1913	PIT	N	P		25	8- 6
1914	PIT	N	P		45	13-17
1915	PIT	N	P		31	8-10
	PHI	N	P		9	4- 3
1916	PHI	N	P		21	1- 7
1918	CLE	A	P		5	0- 1
		BRTR			274	83-89

MC QUILLAN, HUGH A. (HANDSOME HUGH)
B.SEPT.15,1897 NEW YORK,N.Y.
D.AUG.26,1947 NEW YORK,N.Y.

YR	CL	LEA	POS	GP	G	REC
1918	BOS	N	P		1	1- 0
1919	BOS	N	P-O	16	20	2- 3
						.222
1920	BOS	N	P		38	11-15
1921	BOS	N	P		45	13-17
1922	BOS	N	P	28	32	5-10
	NY	N	P		15	6- 9
1923	NY	N	P	38	41	15-14
1924	NY	N	P	27	35	14- 8
1925	NY	N	P	14	16	2- 3
1926	NY	N	P	33	34	11-10
1927	NY	N	P		11	5- 4
	BOS	N	P		13	3- 5
		BRTR		279	301	88-94
						.195

MC QUILLEN, GLENN RICHARD (RED)
B.APR.19,1915 STRASBURG,VA.

YR	CL	LEA	POS	GP	G	REC
1938	STL	A	O		43	.284
1941	STL	A	O		7	.333
1942	STL	A	O		100	.283
1946	STL	A	O		59	.241
1947	STL	A	H		1	.000
		BRTR			210	.274

MC QUINN, GEORGE HARTLEY
B.MAY 29,1910 ARLINGTON,VA.

YR	CL	LEA	POS	GP	G	REC
1936	CIN	N	1		38	.201
1938	STL	A	1		148	.324
1939	STL	A	1		154	.316
1940	STL	A	1		151	.279
1941	STL	A	1		130	.297
1942	STL	A	1		145	.262
1943	STL	A	1		125	.243
1944	STL	A	1		146	.250
1945	STL	A	1		139	.277
1946	PHI	A	1		136	.225
1947	NY	A	1		144	.304
1948	NY	A	1		94	.248
		BLTL			1550	.276

MC RAE, HAROLD ABRAHAM (HAL)
B.JULY 10,1946 AVON PARK,FLA.

YR	CL	LEA	POS	GP	G	REC
1968	CIN	N	2		17	.196
1970	CIN	N	O/3-2		70	.248
1971	CIN	N	O		99	.264
1972	CIN	N	O-3		61	.278
1973	KC	A	O-D/3		106	.234
1974	KC	A	D-O/3		148	.310
1975	KC	A	*D-O/3		126	.306
1976	KC	A	*D-O		149	.332
1977	KC	A	*D/O		162	.298
1978	KC	A	*D/O		156	.273
		BRTR			1094	.289

MC RAE, NORMAN (NORM)
B.SEP.26,1947 ELIZABETH,N.J.

YR	CL	LEA	POS	GP	G	REC
1969	DET	A	/P		3	0- 0
1970	DET	A	P		19	0- 0
		BRTR			22	0- 0

MC REMER

YR	CL	LEA	POS	GP	G	REC
1884	WAS	U	P		1	0- 0

MC SHANNIC, PETER ROBERT
B.MAR.20,1864 PITTSBURGH,PA.
D.NOV.30,1940 TOLEDO,OHIO

YR	CL	LEA	POS	GP	G	REC
1888	PIT	N	3		26	.194
		BB				

MC SORLEY, JOHN BERNARD (TRICK)
B.DEC.6,1858 ST.LOUIS,MO.
D.FEB.9,1936 ST.LOUIS,MO.

YR	CL	LEA	POS	GP	G	REC
1875	RS	NA	3-O		13	-
1884	TOL	AA	1		21	.249
1885	STL	N	3		2	.500
1886	STL	AA	5		5	.150
		TR			41	-

MC SWEENEY, PAUL
B.ST.LOUIS,MO.

YR	CL	LEA	POS	GP	G	REC
1891	STL	AA	2		3	.250

MC TAMANY, JAMES EDWARD (JIM)
B.JULY 1,1863 PHILADELPHIA,PA.
D.APR.16,1916 LENNI,PA.

YR	CL	LEA	POS	GP	G	REC
1885	BRO	AA	O		35	.238
1886	BRO	AA	O		113	.248
1887	BRO	AA	O		134	.354
1888	KC	AA	O		116	.251
1889	COL	AA	O		139	.279
1890	COL	AA	O		125	.256
1891	COL	AA	O		77	.266
	ATH	AA	O		53	.209
		BRTR			792	.275

MC TIGUE, WILLIAM PATRICK (REBEL)
B.JAN.3,1891 NASHVILLE,TENN.
D.MAY 8,1920 NASHVILLE,TENN.

YR	CL	LEA	POS	GP	G	REC
1911	BOS	N	P		14	0- 5
1912	BOS	N	P		10	2- 0
1913	BOS	N	P		1	0- 0
1916	DET	A	P		3	0- 1
		BLTL			28	2- 6

MC VEY, CALVIN ALEXANDER (CAL)
B.AUG.30,1850 MONTROSE LEE CO.,IOWA
D.AUG.20,1926 SAN FRANCISCO,CAL.

YR	CL	LEA	POS	GP	G	REC
1871	BOS	NA	C-O		32	.366
1872	BOS	NA	C-O		46	.306
1873	BAL	NA	C-1-2-S-3-O		36	-
1874	BOS	NA	C-O		70	.385
1875	BOS	NA	P-C-1-O	2	82	1- 1 / .352
1876	CHI	N	P-1	6	63	6- 0 / .345
1877	CHI	N	P-C-1-2-3	17	60	4- 8 / .368
1878	CIN	N	M-P-C-3	2	62	1- 0 / .293
1879	CIN	N	M-P-C-1-3-O	3	80	0- 2 / .299
		BRTR		30	531	12-11 / -

MC VEY, GEORGE W.
B.1864 PORT JERVIS,N.Y.
D.MAY 3,1896 QUINCY,ILL.

YR	CL	LEA	POS	GP	G	REC
1885	BRO	AA	C-1		6	.143

MC WEENY, DOUGLAS LAWRENCE (BUZZ)
B.AUG.17,1896 CHICAGO,ILL.
D.JAN.1,1953 MELROSE PARK,ILL.

YR	CL	LEA	POS	GP	G	REC
1921	CHI	A	P		27	3- 6
1922	CHI	A	P		4	0- 1
1924	CHI	A	P		13	1- 3
1926	BRO	N	P		42	11-13
1927	BRO	N	P		34	4- 8
1928	BRO	N	P		42	14-14
1929	BRO	N	P		36	4-10
1930	BRO	N	P		8	0- 2
		BRTR			206	37-57

MC WILLIAMS, LARRY DEAN
B.FEB.10,1954 WICHITA,KAN.

YR	CL	LEA	POS	GP	G	REC
1978	ATL	N	P		15	9- 3
		BLTL				

YR CL LEA POS   GP   G   REC   YR CL LEA POS   GP   G   REC   YR CL LEA POS   GP   G   REC

MC WILLIAMS, WILLIAM HENRY
B.NOV.28,1910 DUBUQUE,IOWA
1931 BOS A H   2   .000
      BRTR

MEAD, CHARLES RICHARD
B.APR.9,1921 VERMILION,ALT.,CANADA
1943 NY N O   37   .274
1944 NY N O   39   .179
1945 NY N O   11   .270
      BLTR   87   .245

MEADOR, JOHN DAVIS (JOHNNY)
B.DEC.4,1892 MADISON,N.C.
D.APR.11,1970 WINSTON-SALEM,N.C
1920 PIT N P   12   0- 2
      BRTR

MEADOWS, HENRY LEE (LEE) OR (SPECS)
B.JULY 12,1894 OXFORD,N.C.
D.JAN.29,1963 DAYTONA BEACH,FLA
1915 STL N P   39 13-11
1916 STL N P   51 12-23
1917 STL N P   43 15- 9
1918 STL N P   30 31   8-10
1919 STL N P   22   4-10
     PHI N P   18 21   8-10
1920 PHI N P   35 39 16-14
1921 PHI N P   28 11-16
1922 PHI N P   33 12-18
1923 PHI N P   8   1- 3
     PIT N P   31 16-10
1924 PIT N P   36 13-12
1925 PIT N P   35 19-10
1926 PIT N P   36 20- 9
1927 PIT N P   40 19-10
1928 PIT N P   4   1- 1
1929 PIT N P   1   0- 0
      BLTR   490 498 188-180
      BB 1920-21, 26, 28

MEADOWS, RUFUS RIVERS
B.AUG.25,1907 CHASE CITY,VA.
D.MAY 10,1970 WICHITA,KAN.
1926 CIN N P   1   0- 0
      BLTL

MEAKIM, GEORGE CLINTON
B.JULY 11,1865 BROOKLYN,N.Y.
D.FEB.17,1923 QUEENS,N.Y.
1890 LOU AA P   30 10- 8
1891 ATH AA P   6   2- 3
1892 CHI N P   2   0- 1
     CIN N P   3   1- 1
1895 LOU N P   1   0- 0
                           42 13-13

MEANS, HARRY L.
B.JUNE 15,1869 HOPKINSVILLE,KY.
D.FEB.1,1945
NON-PLAYING MANAGER LOU[AA]1889

MEANEY, PATRICK J.
B.1892 PHILADELPHIA,PA.
D.OCT.20,1922 PHILADELPHIA,PA.
1912 DET A S   1   .000
      TR

MEARA, CHARLES EDWARD (GOGGY)
B.APR.13,1891 NEW YORK,N.Y.
D.FEB.8,1962 BRONX,N.Y.
1914 NY N O   4   .286
      BLTR

MEDEIROS, RAY ANTONE (PEP)
B.MAY 9,1926 OAKLAND,CAL.
1945 CIN N H   1   .000
      BRTR

MEDICH, GEORGE FRANCIS (DOC)
B.DEC.9,1948 ALIQUIPPA,PA.
1972 NY A /P   1   0- 0
1973 NY A P   34 14- 9
1974 NY A P   38 39 19-15
1975 NY A P   38 16-16
1976 PIT N P   29   8-11
1977 OAK A P   26 10- 6
     SEA A /P   3   2- 0
     NY A /P   1   0- 1
1978 TEX A P   28   9- 8
      BRTR   198 199 78-66

MEDLINGER, IRVING JOHN (IRV)
B.JUNE 18,1927 CHICAGO,ILL.
D.SEPT.3,1975 WHEELING,ILL.
1949 STL A P   3   0- 0
1951 STL A P   6   0- 0
      BLTL   9   0- 0

MEDWICK, JOSEPH MICHAEL
(JOE), (DUCKY) OR (MUSCLES)
B.NOV.24,1911 CARTERET,N.J.
D.MAR.21,1975 ST.PETERSBURG,FLA
1932 STL N O   26   .349
1933 STL N O   148   .306
1934 STL N O   149   .319
1935 STL N O   154   .353
1936 STL N O   155   .351
1937 STL N O   156   .374
1938 STL N O   146   .322
1939 STL N O   150   .332
1940 STL N O   37   .304
     BRO N O   106   .300
1941 BRO N O   133   .318
1942 BRO N O   142   .300
1943 BRO N O   48   .272
     NY N 1-3   78   .281
1944 NY N O   128   .337
1945 NY N O   26   .304
     BOS N 1-O   66   .284
1946 BRO N 1-O   41   .312
1947 STL N O   75   .307
1948 STL N O   20   .324
      BRTR   1984   .324

MEE, THOMAS WILLIAM (JUDGE)
B.MAR.18,1890 CHICAGO,ILL.
1910 STL A S   7   .167

MEEGAN, PETER J. (STEADY PETE)
B.NOV.13,1863 SAN FRANCISCO,CAL
D.MAR.15,1905 SAN FRANCISCO,CAL
1884 RIC AA P-O   22 23   7-12
                                .156
1885 PIT AA P   19   7- 8
                     41 42 14-20
                                .156

MEEHAN, WILLIAM THOMAS
B.SEPT.3,1891 OSCEOLA,PA.
1915 PHI A P   1   0- 1

MEEK, FRANK J. (DAD)
B.ST.LOUIS,MO.
D.DEC.26,1922 ST.LOUIS,MO.
1889 STL AA C   2   .500
1890 STL AA C   4   .333
                            6   .353

MEEKER, CHARLES ROY (ROY)
B.SEPT.15,1900 LEAD MINES,MO.
D.MAR.25,1929 ORLANDO,FLA.
1923 PHI A P   5   3- 0
1924 PHI A P   30   5-12
1926 CIN N P   7   0- 2
      BLTL   42   8-14

MEEKIN, JOUETT
B.FEB.21,1867 NEW ALBANY,IND.
D.DEC.14,1944 NEW ALBANY,IND.
1891 LOU AA P   29 33 10-17
1892 LOU N P   25   7-10
     WAS N P   13   2-11
1893 WAS N P   28 29 10-17
1894 NY N P   47 48 36-10
1895 NY N P   30 16-11
1896 NY N P   40 26-13
1897 NY N P   35 38 20-11
1898 NY N P   36 16-20
1899 NY N P   16   5-11
     BOS N P   17   7- 6
1900 PIT N P   2   0- 2
                    318 327 155-139

MEEKS, SAMUEL MACK (SAMMY)
B.APR.23,1923 ANDERSON,S.C.
1948 WAS A 2-S   24   .121
1949 CIN N 2-S   16   .306
1950 CIN N S-3   39   .284
1951 CIN N S-3   23   .229
      BRTR   102   .251

MEELER, CHARLES PHILLIP (PHIL)
B.JULY 3,1948 SOUTH BOSTON,VA.
1972 DET A /P   7   0- 1
      BRTR

MEERS, RUSSELL HARLAN (BABE)
B.AUG.28,1918 TILTON,ILL.
1941 CHI N P   5   0- 1
1946 CHI N P   7   1- 2
1947 CHI N P   35   2- 0
      BLTL   43   3- 3

MEIER, ARTHUR ERNST (DUTCH)
B.MAR.30,1879 ST.LOUIS,MO.
D.MAR.23,1948 CHICAGO,ILL.
1906 PIT N S-O   68   .256
      BRTR

MEIKLE, ARTHUR FRANCIS
[PLAYED UNDER NAME OF
ARTHUR FRANCIS NICHOLDS]

MEINE, HENRY WILLIAM (HEINIE)
OR (THE COUNT OF LUXEMBURG)
B.MAY 1,1896 ST.LOUIS,MO.
D.MAR.18,1968 ST.LOUIS,MO.
1922 STL A P   1   0- 0
1929 PIT N P   22   7- 6
1930 PIT N P   20   6- 8
1931 PIT N P   36 19-13
1932 PIT N P   28 12- 9
1933 PIT N P   32 15- 8
1934 PIT N P   26   7- 6
      BRTR   165 66-50

MEINERT, WALTER HENRY
B.DEC.11,1890 NEW YORK,N.Y.
D.NOV.9,1958 DECATUR,ILL.
1913 STL A O   4   .375
      BLTL

MEINKE, FRANK LOUIS
B.OCT.18,1863 CHICAGO,ILL.
D.NOV.8,1931 CHICAGO,ILL.
1884 DET N P-2-   33 90   8-21
            S-3   .167
1885 DET N P-O   1   0- 1
                                .000
                     34 91   8-21
                                .166

MEINKE, ROBERT BERNARD
B.JUNE 25,1887 CHICAGO,ILL.
D.DEC.29,1952 CHICAGO,ILL.
1910 CIN N S   2   .000
      BRTR

MEISTER, JOHN F.
B.ALTOONA,PA.
D.JAN.28,1923
1884 TOL AA 3   34   .199
1886 MET AA 2   45   .240
1887 MET AA O   39   .282
                          118   .245

MEISTER, KARL DANIEL (DUTCH)
B.MAY 15,1891 MARIETTA,OHIO
D.AUG.15,1967 MARIETTA,OHIO
1913 CIN N O   4   .285
      BRTR

MEIXELL, MERTEN MERRILL (MOXIE)
B.OCT.18,1887 LAKE CRYSTAL,MINN
1912 CLE A O   3   .500
      BLTR

MEJIAS, ROMAN [GOMEZ]
B.AUG.9,1930 RIO DAMUJI,CUBA
1955 PIT N O   71   .216
1957 PIT N O   58   .275
1958 PIT N O   76   .268
1959 PIT N O   96   .236
1960 PIT N H   3   .000
1961 PIT N O   4   .000
1962 HOU N O   146   .286
1963 BOS A O   111   .227
1964 BOS A O   62   .238
      BRTR   627   .254

MEJIAS, SAMUEL ELIAS (SAM)
B.MAY 9,1952 SANTIAGO,D.R.
1976 STL N O   18   .143
1977 MON N O   74   .228
1978 MON N O/P   1 67   0- 0
                                .232
      BRTR   1 159   0- 0
                                .219

MELE, ALBERT ERNEST (DUTCH)
B.JAN.11,1915 NEW YORK,N.Y.
D.FEB.12,1975 HOLLYWOOD,FLA.
1937 CIN N O   6   .143
      BLTL

MELE, SABATH ANTHONY (SAM)
B.JAN.21,1923 ASTORIA,N.Y.
1947 BOS A 1-O   123   .302
1948 BOS A O   66   .233
1949 BOS A O   18   .196
     WAS A 1-O   78   .242
1950 WAS A 1-O   126   .274
1951 WAS A 1-O   143   .274
1952 WAS A O   9   .429
     CHI A 1-O   123   .248
1953 CHI A 1-O   140   .274
1954 BAL A O   72   .239
     BOS A 1-O   42   .318
1955 BOS A O   14   .129
     CIN N 1-O   35   .210
1956 CLE A 1-O   57   .254
      BRTR   1046   .260
NON-PLAYING MANAGER MIN[A] 1961-67

MELENDEZ, LUIS ANTONIO [SANTANA]
B.AUG.11,1949 AIBONITO,P.R.

YR	CL	LEA	POS	GP	G	REC
1970	STL	N	O		21	.300
1971	STL	N	O		88	.225
1972	STL	N	*O		118	.238
1973	STL	N	O		121	.267
1974	STL	N	O/S		83	.218
1975	STL	N	O		110	.265
1976	STL	N	/C		20	.125
1976	SD	N	O		72	.244
1977	SD	N	/O		8	.000
	BRTR				641	.248

MELILLO, OSCAR DONALD
(SKI) OR (SPINACH)
B.AUG.4,1899 CHICAGO,ILL.
D.NOV.14,1963 CHICAGO,ILL.

YR	CL	LEA	POS	GP	G	REC
1926	STL	A	2-3		99	.255
1927	STL	A	2		107	.225
1928	STL	A	2-3		51	.189
1929	STL	A	2		141	.296
1930	STL	A	2		149	.256
1931	STL	A	2		151	.306
1932	STL	A	2		154	.242
1933	STL	A	2		132	.292
1934	STL	A	2		144	.241
1935	STL	A	2		19	.206
	BOS	A	2		106	.261
1936	BOS	A	2		98	.226
1937	BOS	A	2		26	.250
	BRTR				1377	.260

NON-PLAYING MANAGER STL[A] 1938

MELLANA, JOSEPH PETER
B.MAR.2,1905 OAKLAND,CAL.
D.NOV.1,1969 LARKSPUR,CAL.

YR	CL	LEA	POS	GP	G	REC
1927	PHI	A	3		4	.286
	BRTR					

MELLOR, WILLIAM HARPIN
B.JUNE 6,1874 CAMDEN,N.J.
D.NOV.5,1940 BRIDGETON,R.I.

YR	CL	LEA	POS	GP	G	REC
1902	BAL	A	1		10	.361
	BRTR					

MELOAN, PAUL B. (MOLLY)
B.AUG.23,1888 PAYNESVILLE,MO.
D.FEB.11,1950 TAFT,CAL.

YR	CL	LEA	POS	GP	G	REC
1910	CHI	A	O		65	.243
1911	CHI	A	O		1	.333
	STL	A	O		64	.262
	BRTL				130	.253

MELTER, STEPHEN BLAZIUS
B.JAN.2,1886 CHEROKEE,IOWA
D.JAN.28,1962 MISHAWAKA,IND.

YR	CL	LEA	POS	GP	G	REC
1909	STL	N	P		23	0-1
	BRTR					

MELTON, CLIFFORD GEORGE
(CLIFF) OR (MICKEY MOUSE)
OR (MOUNTAIN MUSIC)
B.JAN.3,1912 BREVARD,N.C.

YR	CL	LEA	POS	GP	G	REC
1937	NY	N	P		46	20-9
1938	NY	N	P		36	14-14
1939	NY	N	P		41	12-15
1940	NY	N	P		37	10-11
1941	NY	N	P		42	8-11
1942	NY	N	P		23	11-5
1943	NY	N	P		34	9-13
1944	NY	N	P		13	2-2
	BLTL				272	86-80

MELTON, DAVID OLIN (DAVE)
B.OCT.3,1928 PAMPA,TEX.

YR	CL	LEA	POS	GP	G	REC
1956	KC	A	O		3	.333
1958	KC	A	O		9	.000
	BRTR				12	.111

MELTON, REUBEN FRANKLIN (RUBE)
B.FEB.27,1917 CRAMERTON,N.C.
D.SEPT.11,1971 GREER,S.C.

YR	CL	LEA	POS	GP	G	REC
1941	PHI	N	P		25	1-5
1942	PHI	N	P		42	9-20
1943	BRO	N	P		30	5-8
1944	BRO	N	P		37	9-13
1946	BRO	N	P		24	6-3
1947	BRO	N	P		4	0-1
	BRTR				162	30-50

MELTON, WILLIAM EDWIN (BILL)
B.JULY 7,1945 GULFPORT,MISS.

YR	CL	LEA	POS	GP	G	REC
1968	CHI	A	3		34	.266
1969	CHI	A	*3-O		157	.255
1970	CHI	A	O-3		141	.263
1971	CHI	A	*3		150	.269
1972	CHI	A	3		57	.245
1973	CHI	A	*3		152	.277
1974	CHI	A	*3-O		136	.242
1975	CHI	A	*3-O		149	.240
1976	CAL	A	O-1-3		118	.208
1977	CLE	A	1-O-3		50	.241
	BRTR				1144	.253

MENDOZA, CRISTOBAL RIGOBERTO
[CARRERAS] (MINNIE)
B.NOV.16,1933 CEIBA DEL AGUA,CUBA

YR	CL	LEA	POS	GP	G	REC
1970	MIN	A	/3-2		16	.188
	BRTR					

MENDOZA, MARIO [AIZPURU]
B.DEC.26,1950 CHIHUAHUA,MEX.

YR	CL	LEA	POS	GP	G	REC
1974	PIT	N	S		91	.221
1975	PIT	N	S/3		56	.180
1976	PIT	N	S/3-2		50	.185
1977	PIT	N	S-3/P	1	70	0-0
						.198
1978	PIT	N	2-3-S		57	.218
	BRTR			1	324	0-0
						.204

MENEFEE, JOHN (JOCK)
B.JAN.15,1868 WEST VIRGINIA
D.MAR.11,1953 BELLE VERNON,PA.

YR	CL	LEA	POS	GP	G	REC
1892	PIT	N	P		2	0-0
1893	LOU	N	P	17	21	8-8
1894	LOU	N	P		34	8-15
	PIT	N	P		13	3-8
1895	PIT	N	P		2	0-1
1898	NY	N	P		1	0-1
1900	CHI	N	P		17	9-5
1901	CHI	N	P-O	20	46	8-12
						.251
1902	CHI	N	P-1-	22	64	12-10
			2-3-O			.231
1903	CHI	N	P		22	8-10
	BRTR			148	222	56-69
						.223

MENKE, DENIS JOHN
B.JULY 21,1940 ALGONA,IOWA

YR	CL	LEA	POS	GP	G	REC
1962	MIL	N	1-2-S-3-O		50	.192
1963	MIL	N	1-2-S-3-O		146	.234
1964	MIL	N	2-S-3		151	.283
1965	MIL	N	S/1-3		71	.243
1966	ATL	N	*S-3/1		138	.251
1967	ATL	N	*S/3		129	.227
1968	HOU	N	*2-S/1-3		150	.249
1969	HOU	N	*S-2/1-3		154	.269
1970	HOU	N	*S-2/1-3-O		154	.304
1971	HOU	N	*1-3-S/2		146	.246
1972	CIN	N	*3-1		140	.233
1973	CIN	N	*3/S-2-1		139	.191
1974	HOU	N	1/3-2-S		30	.103
	BRTR				1598	.250

MENOSKY, MICHAEL WILLIAM
(LEAPING MIKE)
B.OCT.16,1894 GLEN CAMPBELL,PA.

YR	CL	LEA	POS	GP	G	REC
1914	PIT	F	O		60	.260
1915	PIT	F	O		16	.100
1916	WAS	A	O		11	.162
1917	WAS	A	O		114	.258
1919	WAS	A	O		116	.287
1920	BOS	A	O		141	.297
1921	BOS	A	O		133	.300
1922	BOS	A	O		126	.283
1923	BOS	A	O		84	.229
	BLTR				801	.278

MENSOR, EDWARD (THE MIDGET)
B.NOV.7,1886 WOODVILLE,ORE.
D.APR.20,1970 SALEM,ORE.

YR	CL	LEA	POS	GP	G	REC
1912	PIT	N	O		39	.263
1913	PIT	N	O		44	.179
1914	PIT	N	O		44	.202
	BB				127	.221

MENZE, THEODORE CHARLES
B.NOV.4,1897 ST.LOUIS,MO.
D.DEC.23,1969 ST.LOUIS,MO.

YR	CL	LEA	POS	GP	G	REC
1918	STL	N	O		2	.000
	BRTR					

MEOLA, EMILE MICHAEL (MIKE)
B.OCT.19,1905 NEW YORK,N.Y.
D.SEPT.1,1976 FAIR LAWN,N.J.

YR	CL	LEA	POS	GP	G	REC
1933	BOS	A	P		3	0-0
1936	STL	A	P		9	0-1
	BOS	A	P		6	0-2
	BRTR				18	0-3

MEOLI, RUDOLPH BARTHOLOMEW (RUDY)
B.MAY 1,1951 TROY,N.Y.

YR	CL	LEA	POS	GP	G	REC
1971	CAL	A	/H		7	.000
1973	CAL	A	S-3/2		120	.223
1974	CAL	A	3/S-1-2		36	.244
1975	CAL	A	S-3-2		70	.214
1978	CHI	N	/2-3		47	.103
	BLTR				280	.217

MERCANTELLI, EUGENE RUDOLPH
[PLAYED UNDER NAME OF
EUGENE RUDOLPH RYE]

MERCER, GEORGE BARCLAY (WIN)
B.JUNE 20,1874 CHESTER,W.VA.
D.JAN.12,1903 SAN FRANCISCO,CAL

YR	CL	LEA	POS	GP	G	REC
1894	WAS	N	P	40	43	16-23
1895	WAS	N	P	38	54	14-24
1896	WAS	N	P		44	25-19
1897	WAS	N	P		45	24-21
1898	WAS	N	P-S-	29	73	12-16
			O			.334
1899	WAS	N	P-3	21	98	7-14
						.303
1900	NY	N	P-3	29	72	13-16
						.308
1901	WAS	A	P	24	50	9-13
1902	DET	A	P		35	15-18
	TR			305	514	135-164
						.293

MERCER, JOHN (JACK)

YR	CL	LEA	POS	GP	G	REC
1910	PIT	N	P		1	0-0

MERCER, JOHN LOCKE
B.JAN.22,1892 TAYLORTOWN,LA.

YR	CL	LEA	POS	GP	G	REC
1912	STL	N	1		1	.000

MERCER, JOHN LOUIS
[PLAYED UNDER NAME OF
JOHN LOUIS JOHNSON]

MERCHANT, JAMES ANDERSON (ANDY)
B.AUG.30,1950 MOBILE,ALA.

YR	CL	LEA	POS	GP	G	REC
1975	BOS	A	/C		1	.500
1976	BOS	A	/C		2	.000
	BLTR				3	.333

MERENA, JOHN JOSEPH (SPIKE)
B.NOV.18,1909 PATERSON,N.J.
D.MAR.8,1977 BRIDGEPORT,CONN.

YR	CL	LEA	POS	GP	G	REC
1934	BOS	A	P		4	1-2
	BLTL					

MEREWETHER, ARTHUR FRANCIS (MERRY)
B.JULY 1,1902 E.PROVIDENCE,R.I.

YR	CL	LEA	POS	GP	G	REC
1922	PIT	N	2		1	.000
	BRTR					

MERKLE, FREDERICK CHARLES (FRED)
B.DEC.20,1888 WATERTOWN,WIS.
D.MAR.2,1956 DAYTONA BEACH,FLA.

YR	CL	LEA	POS	GP	G	REC
1907	NY	N	1		15	.255
1908	NY	N	1		18	.268
1909	NY	N	1		71	.191
1910	NY	N	1		144	.292
1911	NY	N	1		148	.283
1912	NY	N	1		129	.309
1913	NY	N	1		153	.261
1914	NY	N	1		146	.258
1915	NY	N	1-O		140	.299
1916	NY	N	1		112	.241
	BRO	N	1		23	.208
1917	BRO	N	1		2	.125
	CHI	N	1		146	.266
1918	CHI	N	1		129	.297
1919	CHI	N	1-2		133	.267
1920	CHI	N	1		92	.285
1925	NY	A	1		7	.385
1926	NY	A	1		1	1.000
	BRTR				1609	.273

MERRILL, EDWARD S.
B.1860 CHICAGO,ILL.

YR	CL	LEA	POS	GP	G	REC
1882	WOR	N	3		2	.125
1884	IND	AA	2		54	.183
					56	.181

MERRIMAN, LLOYD ARCHER
(LLOYD) OR (CITATION)
B.AUG.2,1924 CLOVIS,CAL.

YR	CL	LEA	POS	GP	G	REC
1949	CIN	N	O		103	.230
1950	CIN	N	O		92	.258
1951	CIN	N	O		114	.262
1954	CIN	N	O		73	.268
1955	CHI	A	H		1	.000
	CHI	N	O		72	.214
	BLTL				455	.242

MERRITT, GEORGE WASHINGTON
B.APR.14,1880 PATERSON,N.J.
D.FEB.21,1938 MEMPHIS,TENN.

YR	CL	LEA	POS	GP	G	REC
1901	PIT	N	P		4	3-0
1902	PIT	N	P-O	1	2	0-0
						.333
1903	PIT	N	P		8	0-0
	TR			13	14	3-0
						.214

MERRITT, HERMAN G.
B.NOV.12,1900 INDEPENDENCE,MO.
D.MAY 26,1927 KANSAS CITY,MO.

YR	CL	LEA	POS	GP	G	REC
1921	DET	A	S		20	.370
	BRTR					

YR	CL LEA POS	GP	G	REC

MERRITT, JAMES JOSEPH (JIM)
B.DEC.6,1943 ALTADENA,CAL.
1965 MIN A P		16	5- 4
1966 MIN A P		31	7-14
1967 MIN A P		37	13- 7
1968 MIN A P		38	12-16
1969 CIN N P		42	17- 9
1970 CIN N P		35	20-12
1971 CIN N P	28	29	1-11
1972 CIN N /P		4	1- 0
1973 TEX A P		35	5-13
1974 TEX A P		26	0- 0
1975 TEX A /P		5	0- 0
BLTL	297	298	81-86

MERRITT, JOHN HOWARD
B.OCT.12,1894 TUPELO,MISS.
D.NOV.3,1955 TUPELO,MISS.
| 1913 NY N O | | 1 | .000 |

MERRITT, LLOYD WESLEY
B.APR.8,1933 ST.LOUIS,MO.
| 1957 STL N P | | 44 | 1- 2 |
| BRTR | | | |

MERRITT, WILLIAM HENRY
B.JULY 30,1870 LOWELL,MASS.
D.NOV.17,1937 LOWELL,MASS.
1891 CHI N C		11	.218
1892 LOU N C		45	.195
1893 BOS N C		35	.363
1894 BOS N C-O		10	.231
PIT N C		26	.300
CIN N C-1-3-O		30	.316
1895 CIN N C		21	.213
PIT N C		66	.273
1896 PIT N C		70	.296
1897 PIT N C		56	.270
1899 BOS N C		1	.000
		371	.274

MERSON
| 1914 BRO F H | | 1 | .000 |

MERSON, JOHN WARREN (JACK)
B.JAN.17,1922 ELK RIDGE,MD.
1951 PIT N 2		13	.360
1952 PIT N 2-3		111	.246
1953 BOS A 2		1	.000
BRTR		125	.257

MERTES, SAMUEL BLAIR (SANDOW)
B.AUG.6,1872 SAN FRANCISCO,CAL.
D.MAR.11,1945 SAN FRANCISCO,CAL
1896 PHI N O		35	.248
1898 CHI N O		70	.304
1899 CHI N O		109	.305
1900 CHI N 1-O		125	.294
1901 CHI A 2		137	.280
1902 CHI A P-C-	1	129	0- 0
1-2-S-3			.263
1903 NY N O		138	.280
1904 NY N O		148	.276
1905 NY N O		150	.279
1906 NY N O		71	.237
STL N O		53	.246
BRTR	1	1165	0- 0
			.280

MERTZ, JAMES VERLIN
B.AUG.10,1916 LIMA,OHIO
| 1943 WAS A P | | 33 | 5- 7 |
| BRTR | | | |

MERULLO, LEONARD RICHARD (LENNIE)
B.MAY 5,1917 BOSTON,MASS.
1941 CHI N S		7	.353
1942 CHI N S		143	.256
1943 CHI N S		129	.254
1944 CHI N 1-S		66	.212
1945 CHI N 1-S		121	.239
1946 CHI N S		65	.151
1947 CHI N 1-S		108	.241
BRTR		639	.240

MESNER, STEPHAN MATHIAS (STEVE)
B.JAN.13,1918 LOS ANGELES,CAL.
1938 CHI N S		2	.250
1939 CHI N S		17	.279
1941 STL N 3		24	.145
1943 CIN N 3		137	.272
1944 CIN N 3		121	.242
1945 CIN N 2-3		150	.254
BRTR		451	.252

MESSENGER, ANDREW WARREN (BUD)
B.FEB.1,1898 GRAND BLANC,MICH.
D.NOV.4,1971 LANSING,MICH.
| 1924 CLE A P | | 5 | 2- 0 |
| BRTR | | | |

MESSENGER, CHARLES WALTER (BOBBY)
B.MAR.19,1884 BANGOR,ME.
D.JULY 10,1951 BATH,MAINE
1909 CHI A O		31	.170
1910 CHI A O		9	.185
1911 CHI A O		13	.133
1914 STL N O		1	.000
BBTR		54	.165

MESSERSMITH, JOHN ALEXANDER (ANDY)
B.AUG.6,1945 TOMS RIVER,N.J.
1968 CAL A P	28	29	4- 2
1969 CAL A P	40	42	16-11
1970 CAL A P	37	38	11-10
1971 CAL A P	38	39	20-13
1972 CAL A P	25	26	8-11
1973 LA A P	33	34	14-10
1974 LA A P		39	20- 6
1975 LA N P	42	44	19-14
1976 ATL N P		29	11-11
1977 ATL N P		16	5- 4
1978 NY A /P		6	0- 3
BRTR	333	342	128-95

MESSITT, THOMAS JOHN
B.JULY 27,1874 FRANKFORT,PA.
D.SEPT.22,1934 CHICAGO,ILL.
| 1899 LOU N C | | 2 | .125 |

METCALF, ROBERT
B.BROOKLYN,N.Y.
| 1875 MUT NA S-3-O | | 7 | - |

METCALF, THOMAS JOHN (TOM)
B.JULY 16,1940 AMHERST,WIS.
| 1963 NY A P | | 8 | 1- 0 |
| BRTR | | | |

METHA, FRANK JOSEPH (SCAT)
B.DEC.13,1913 LOS ANGELES,CAL.
| 1940 DET A 2-3 | | 26 | .243 |
| BRTR | | | |

METHENY, ARTHUR BEAUREGARD (BUD)
B.JUNE 1,1915 ST.LOUIS,MO.
1943 NY A O		103	.261
1944 NY A O		137	.239
1945 NY A O		133	.248
1946 NY A H		3	.000
BLTL		376	.247

METIVIER, GEORGE DEWEY (DEWEY)
B.MAY 6,1898 CAMBRIDGE,MASS.
D.MAR.2,1947 CAMBRIDGE,MASS.
1922 CLE A P		2	2- 0
1923 CLE A P		26	4- 2
1924 CLE A P		26	1- 5
BLTR		54	7- 7

METKOVICH, GEORGE MICHAEL (CATFISH)
B.OCT.8,1921 ANGEL S CAMP,CAL.
1943 BOS A 1-O		78	.246
1944 BOS A 1-O		134	.277
1945 BOS A 1-O		138	.260
1946 BOS A O		86	.246
1947 CLE A 1-O		126	.254
1949 CHI A O		93	.237
1951 PIT N 1-O		120	.293
1952 PIT N 1-O		125	.271
1953 PIT N 1-O		26	.146
CHI N 1-O		61	.234
1954 PIT N 1-O		68	.276
BLTL		1055	.261

METRO, CHARLES
(REAL NAME CHARLES MORESKONICH)
B.APR.28,1919 NANTY-GLO,PA.
1943 DET A O		44	.200
1944 DET A O		38	.192
PHI A 2-3-O		24	.100
1945 PHI A O		65	.210
BRTR		171	.193
NON-PLAYING MANAGER
CHI(N) 1962, KC(A) 1970

METZ, LEONARD RAYMOND
B.JULY 6,1899 LOUISVILLE,COLO.
D.FEB.24,1953 DENVER,COLO.
1923 PHI N 2-S		12	.297
1924 PHI N S		7	.286
1925 PHI N 2-S		11	.000
BRTR		30	.169

METZGER, CLARENCE EDWARD (BUTCH)
B.MAY 23,1952 LAFAYETTE,IND.
1974 SF N P		10	1- 0
1975 SD N /P		4	1- 0
1976 SD N P		77	11- 4
1977 SD N P		17	0- 0
STL N P		58	4- 2
1978 NY N P		25	1- 3
BRTR		191	18- 9

METZGER, ROGER HENRY
B.OCT.10,1947 FREDERICKSBURG,TEX
1970 CHI N /S		1	.000
1971 HOU N *S		150	.235
1972 HOU N *S		153	.222
1973 HOU N *S		154	.250
1974 HOU N *S		143	.253
1975 HOU N *S		127	.227
1976 HOU N *S/2		152	.210
1977 HOU N S/2		97	.186
1978 HOU N S/2		45	.220
SF N S		75	.260
BBTR		1097	.231
BL 1970			

METZIG, WILLIAM ANDREW
B.DEC.4,1918 FT.DODGE,IOWA
| 1944 CHI A 2 | | 5 | .125 |
| BRTR | | | |

METZLER, ALEXANDER
B.JAN.4,1903 FRESNO,CAL.
D.NOV.30,1973 FRESNO,CAL.
1925 CHI N O		9	.184
1926 PHI A O		20	.242
1927 CHI A O		134	.319
1928 CHI A O		139	.304
1929 CHI A O		52	.275
1930 CHI A O		56	.176
STL A O		56	.261
BLTR		560	.285

MEUSEL, EMIL FREDERICK (IRISH)
B.JUNE 9,1893 OAKLAND,CAL.
D.MAR.1,1963 LONG BEACH,CAL.
1914 WAS A O		1	.000
1918 PHI N 2-O		124	.279
1919 PHI N O		135	.305
1920 PHI N O		138	.309
1921 PHI N O		84	.353
NY N O		62	.329
1922 NY N O		154	.330
1923 NY N O		146	.297
1924 NY N O		139	.310
1925 NY N O		135	.328
1926 NY N O		129	.292
1927 BRO N O		42	.243
		1289	.310

MEUSEL, ROBERT WILLIAM (LONG BOB)
B.JULY 19,1896 SAN JOSE,CAL.
D.NOV.28,1977 DOWNEY,CAL.
1920 NY A 3-O		119	.328
1921 NY A O		149	.318
1922 NY A O		121	.319
1923 NY A O		132	.313
1924 NY A O		143	.325
1925 NY A 3-O		156	.292
1926 NY A O		108	.315
1927 NY A O		135	.337
1928 NY A O		131	.297
1929 NY A O		100	.261
1930 CIN N O		113	.289
BRTR		1407	.309

MEYER, BERNHARD (EARACHE)
B.JAN.1,1888 HEMATITE,MO.
D.FEB.6,1974 FESTUS,MO.
1913 BRO N O		38	.195
1914 BAL F O		141	.302
1915 BAL F O		35	.233
BUF F O		93	.237
1925 PHI N 2		1	1.000
BRTR		308	.265

MEYER, DANIEL THOMAS (DAN)
B.AUG.3,1952 HAMILTON,OHIO
1974 DET A O		13	.200
1975 DET A O-1		122	.236
1976 DET A O-1		105	.252
1977 SEA A *1		159	.273
1978 SEA A *1/O		123	.227
BLTR		522	.247

MEYER, GEORGE FRANCIS
B.AUG.22,1912 CHICAGO,ILL.
| 1938 CHI A 2 | | 24 | .296 |
| BRTR | | | |

MEYER, JOHN ROBERT (JACK)
B.MAR.23,1932 PHILADELPHIA,PA.
D.MAR.6,1967 PHILADELPHIA,PA.
1955 PHI N P		50	6-11
1956 PHI N P		41	7-11
1957 PHI N P		19	0- 2
1958 PHI N P		37	3- 6
1959 PHI N P		47	5- 3
1960 PHI N P		7	3- 1
1961 PHI N P		1	0- 0
BRTR		202	24-34

MEYER, LAMBERT DALTON (DUTCH)
B.OCT.6,1915 WACO,TEX.
1937 CHI N H		1	.000
1940 DET A 2		23	.259
1941 DET A 2		46	.190
1942 DET A 2		14	.327
1945 CLE A 2		130	.292
1946 CLE A 2		72	.232
BRTR		286	.264

MEYER, LEE
| 1909 BRO N S | | 7 | .130 |
| TR | | | |

MEYER, ROBERT BERNARD (BOB)
B.AUG.4,1939 TOLEDO,OHIO
1964 NY A P		7	0- 3
LA A P		6	1- 0
KC A P	9	12	1- 4
1969 SEA A /P		6	0- 3
1970 MIL A P		10	0- 1
BRTL	38	41	2-12

YR	CL	LEA	POS	GP	G	REC

METER, RUSSELL CHARLES (RUSS)
(ROWDY) OR (THE MAD MONK)
B.OCT.25,1923 PERU,ILL.

YR	CL	LEA	POS	GP	G	REC
1946	CHI	N	P		4	0- 0
1947	CHI	N	P		23	3- 2
1948	CHI	N	P		29	10-10
1949	PHI	N	P		37	17- 8
1950	PHI	N	P		32	9-11
1951	PHI	N	P		28	8- 9
1952	PHI	N	P		37	13-14
1953	BRO	N	P		34	15- 5
1954	BRO	N	P		36	11- 6
1955	BRO	N	P		18	6- 2
1956	PHI	N	P		20	1- 6
	CIN	N	P		1	0- 0
1957	BOS	A	P		2	0- 0
1959	KC	A	P		18	1- 0
	BBTR				319	94-73

MEYER, SCOTT WILLIAM
B.AUG.19,1957 EVERGREEN PARK,ILL

YR	CL	LEA	POS	GP	G	REC
1978	OAK	A	/C		8	.111
	BRTR					

MEYER, WILLIAM ADAM (BILLY)
B.JAN.14,1892 KNOXVILLE,TENN.
D.MAR.31,1957 KNOXVILLE,TENN.

YR	CL	LEA	POS	GP	G	REC
1913	CHI	A	C		1	1.000
1916	PHI	A	C		50	.232
1917	PHI	A	C		62	.236
	BRTR				113	.236

NON-PLAYING MANAGER PIT[N] 1948-52

MEYERLE, LEVI SAMUEL (LONG LEVI)
B.1849 PHILADELPHIA,PA.
D.NOV.4,1921 PHILADELPHIA,PA.

YR	CL	LEA	POS	GP	G	REC
1871	ATH	NA	3		26	.448
1872	ATH	NA	S-3-O		27	.318
1873	PHI	NA	3		47	-
1874	CHI	NA	2-S-3-O		52	-
1875	PHI	NA	1-2-3		67	.314
1876	ATH	N	P-3	2	55	0- 2
						.336
1877	CIN	N	2-S-O		27	.327
1884	KEY	U	1-O		3	.091
	BRTR			2	304	0- 2
						-

MEYERS, HENRY L.
B.1860 PHILADELPHIA,PA.
D.JUNE 28,1898 HARRISBURG,PA.

YR	CL	LEA	POS	GP	G	REC
1890	ATH	AA	1-3		5	.167

MEYERS, JOHN TORTES (CHIEF)
B.JULY 29,1880 RIVERSIDE,CAL.
D.JULY 25,1971 SAN BERNARDINO,CAL.

YR	CL	LEA	POS	GP	G	REC
1909	NY	N	C		64	.277
1910	NY	N	C		117	.285
1911	NY	N	C		128	.332
1912	NY	N	C		126	.358
1913	NY	N	C		120	.312
1914	NY	N	C		134	.286
1915	NY	N	C		110	.232
1916	BRO	N	C		80	.247
1917	BRO	N	C		47	.214
	BOS	N	C		25	.246
	BRTR				951	.291

MEYERS, LEWIS HENRY (CRAZY HORSE)
B.DEC.9,1859 CINCINNATI,OHIO
D.NOV.30,1920 CINCINNATI,OHIO

YR	CL	LEA	POS	GP	G	REC
1884	CIN	U	C-O		1	.000
	BRTR					

MICELOTTA, ROBERT PETER (MICKEY)
B.OCT.20,1928 CORONA,N.Y.

YR	CL	LEA	POS	GP	G	REC
1954	PHI	N	S		13	.000
1955	PHI	N	S		4	.000
	BRTR				17	.000

MICHAEL, EUGENE RICHARD
(GENE) OR (STICK)
B.JUNE 2,1938 KENT,OHIO

YR	CL	LEA	POS	GP	G	REC
1966	PIT	N	/S-2-3		30	.152
1967	LA	N	S		98	.202
1968	NY	A	S/P	1	61	0- 0
						.198
1969	NY	A	*S		119	.272
1970	NY	A	*S/3-2		134	.214
1971	NY	A	*S		139	.224
1972	NY	A	*S		126	.233
1973	NY	A	*S		129	.225
1974	NY	A	2-S/3		81	.260
1975	DET	A	S/2-3		56	.214
	BBTR			1	973	0- 0
						.229

MICHAELS, CASIMIR EUGENE (CASS)
(PLAYED IN 1943 UNDER REAL NAME
OF CASIMIR EUGENE KWIETNIEWSKI)
B.MAR.4,1926 DETROIT,MICH.

YR	CL	LEA	POS	GP	G	REC
1943	CHI	A	3		2	.000
1944	CHI	A	S-3		27	.176
1945	CHI	A	2-S		129	.245
1946	CHI	A	2-S-3		91	.258
1947	CHI	A	2-3		110	.273
1948	CHI	A	2-S-O		145	.248
1949	CHI	A	2		154	.308
1950	CHI	A	2		36	.312
	WAS	A	2		106	.250
1951	WAS	A	2		138	.258
1952	WAS	A	2		22	.233
	STL	A	2-3		55	.265
	PHI	A	2		55	.250
1953	PHI	A	2		117	.251
1954	CHI	A	2-3		101	.262
	BRTR				1288	.262

MICHAELS, JOHN JOSEPH
B.JULY 10,1907 BRIDGEPORT,CONN.

YR	CL	LEA	POS	GP	G	REC
1932	BOS	A	P		29	1- 6
	BLTL					

MICHAELS, RALPH JOSEPH
B.MAY 3,1902 ETNA,PA.

YR	CL	LEA	POS	GP	G	REC
1924	CHI	N	S		8	.364
1925	CHI	N	1-2-S-3		22	.280
1926	CHI	N	H		2	.000
	BRTR				32	.295

MICHAELSON, JOHN AUGUST (MIKE)
B.AUG.12,1893 TIVALKOSKI,FINLAND
D.APR.16,1968 WOODRUFF,WIS.

YR	CL	LEA	POS	GP	G	REC
1921	CHI	A	P		2	0- 0
	BRTR					

MICKELSON, EDWARD ALLEN (ED)
B.SEPT.9,1926 OTTAWA,ILL.

YR	CL	LEA	POS	GP	G	REC
1950	STL	N	1		5	.100
1953	STL	A	1		7	.133
1957	CHI	N	1		6	.000
	BRTR				18	.081

MICKENS, GLENN ROGER
B.JULY 26,1930 WILMAR,CAL.

YR	CL	LEA	POS	GP	G	REC
1953	BRO	N	P		4	0- 1
	BRTR					

MIDDLETON, JAMES BLAINE (RIFLE JIM)
B.MAY 28,1889 ARGOS,IND.
D.JAN.12,1974 ARGOS,IND.

YR	CL	LEA	POS	GP	G	REC
1917	NY	N	P		13	1- 1
1921	DET	A	P		38	6-11
	BRTR				51	7-12

MIDDLETON, JOHN WAYNE (LEFTY)
B.APR.11,1900 MT.CALM,TEX.

YR	CL	LEA	POS	GP	G	REC
1922	CLE	A	P		2	0- 0
	BLTL					

MIDKIFF, EZRA MILLINGTON (SALT ROCK)
B.NOV.13,1882 SALT ROCK,W.VA.
D.MAR.20,1957 HUNTINGTON,W.VA.

YR	CL	LEA	POS	GP	G	REC
1909	CIN	N	3		1	.000
1912	NY	A	3		21	.244
1913	NY	A	3		68	.215
	BLTR				90	.222

MIDKIFF, RICHARD
B.SEPT.28,1914 GONZALES,TEX.
D.OCT.30,1956 TEMPLE,TEX.

YR	CL	LEA	POS	GP	G	REC
1938	BOS	A	P		13	1- 1
	BBTL					

MIERKOWICZ, EDWARD FRANK (ED)
(BUTCH) OR (MOUSE)
B.MAR.6,1924 WYANDOTTE,MICH.

YR	CL	LEA	POS	GP	G	REC
1945	DET	A	O		10	.133
1947	DET	A	O		21	.190
1948	DET	A	O		3	.200
1950	STL	N	H		1	.000
	BRTR				35	.175

MIGGINS, LAWRENCE EDWARD
(LARRY) OR (IRISH)
B.AUG.20,1925 BRONX,N.Y.

YR	CL	LEA	POS	GP	G	REC
1948	STL	N	H		1	.000
1952	STL	N	1-O		42	.229
	BRTR				43	.227

MIHALIC, JOHN MICHAEL
B.NOV.13,1911 CLEVELAND,OHIO

YR	CL	LEA	POS	GP	G	REC
1935	WAS	A	S		6	.227
1936	WAS	A	2		25	.239
1937	WAS	A	2		38	.252
	BRTR				69	.244

MIKKELSEN, PETER JAMES (PETE)
B.OCT.25,1939 STATEN ISLAND,N.Y.

YR	CL	LEA	POS	GP	G	REC
1964	NY	A	P		50	7- 4
1965	NY	A	P		41	4- 9
1966	PIT	N	P		71	9- 8
1967	PIT	N	P		32	1- 2
	CHI	N	/P		7	0- 0
1968	CHI	N	/P		3	0- 0
	STL	N	/P		5	0- 0
1969	LA	N	P		48	7- 5
1970	LA	N	P		33	4- 2
1971	LA	N	P		41	8- 5
1972	LA	N	P		33	5- 5
	BRTR				364	45-40

MIKLOS, JOHN JOSEPH (HANK)
B.NOV.27,1910 CHICAGO,ILL.

YR	CL	LEA	POS	GP	G	REC
1944	CHI	N	P		2	0- 0
	BLTL					

MIKSIS, EDWARD THOMAS (EDDIE)
B.SEPT.11,1926 BURLINGTON,N.J.

YR	CL	LEA	POS	GP	G	REC
1944	BRO	N	S-3		26	.220
1946	BRO	N	2-3		23	.146
1947	BRO	N	2-S-3-O		45	.267
1948	BRO	N	2-S-3		86	.213
1949	BRO	N	1-2-S-3		50	.221
1950	BRO	N	2-S-3		51	.250
1951	BRO	N	2-3		19	.200
	CHI	N	2		102	.266
1952	CHI	N	2-S		93	.232
1953	CHI	N	2-S		142	.251
1954	CHI	N	2-3-O		38	.202
1955	CHI	N	3-O		131	.235
1956	CHI	N	2-S-3		114	.239
1957	STL	N	2		49	.211
	BAL	A	H		1	.000
1958	BAL	A	S		3	.000
	CIN	N	1-2-S-3-O		69	.140
	BRTR				1042	.236

MILAN, HORACE ROBERT
B.APR.7,1894 LINDEN,TENN.
D.JUNE 29,1955 TEXARKANA,ARK.

YR	CL	LEA	POS	GP	G	REC
1915	WAS	A	O		10	.375
1917	WAS	A	O		31	.288
	BRTR				41	.320

MILAN, JESSE CLYDE
(CLYDE) OR (DEERFOOT)
B.MAR.25,1887 LINDEN,TENN.
D.MAR.3,1953 ORLANDO,FLA.

YR	CL	LEA	POS	GP	G	REC
1907	WAS	A	O		48	.279
1908	WAS	A	O		130	.239
1909	WAS	A	O		130	.200
1910	WAS	A	O		142	.279
1911	WAS	A	O		154	.315
1912	WAS	A	O		154	.306
1913	WAS	A	O		154	.299
1914	WAS	A	O		115	.295
1915	WAS	A	O		153	.288
1916	WAS	A	O		150	.273
1917	WAS	A	O		155	.294
1918	WAS	A	O		128	.290
1919	WAS	A	O		88	.287
1920	WAS	A	O		126	.322
1921	WAS	A	O		112	.288
1922	WAS	A	M-O		42	.230
	BLTR				1981	.285

MILBOURNE, LAWRENCE WILLIAM (LARRY)
B.FEB.14,1951 PORT NORRIS,N.J.

YR	CL	LEA	POS	GP	G	REC
1974	HOU	N	2/S-O		112	.279
1975	HOU	N	2-S		73	.212
1976	HOU	N	2		59	.248
1977	SEA	A	2-S/3		86	.219
1978	SEA	A	3-S-2-O		93	.226
	BBTR				423	.233

MILES, CARL THOMAS
B.MAR.22,1918 TRENTON,MO.

YR	CL	LEA	POS	GP	G	REC
1940	PHI	A	P		2	0- 0
	BBTL					

MILES, DONALD RAY
B.MAR.13,1936 INDIANAPOLIS,IND.

YR	CL	LEA	POS	GP	G	REC
1958	LA	N	O		8	.182
	BLTR					

MILES, JAMES CHARLIE (JIM)
B.AUG.8,1943 GRENADA,MISS.

YR	CL	LEA	POS	GP	G	REC
1968	WAS	A	/P		3	0- 0
1969	WAS	A	P	10	12	0- 1
	BRTR			13	15	0- 1

MILES, WILSON DANIEL (DEE)
B.FEB.19,1909 KELLERMAN,ALA.
D.NOV.2,1976 BIRMINGHAM,ALA.

YR	CL	LEA	POS	GP	G	REC
1935	WAS	A	O		60	.264
1936	WAS	A	O		25	.237
1939	PHI	A	O		106	.300
1940	PHI	A	O		88	.301
1941	PHI	A	O		80	.312
1942	PHI	A	O		99	.272
1943	BOS	A	O		45	.215
	BLTR				503	.280

YR CL LEA POS   GP   G   REC

MILEY, MICHAEL WILFRED (MIKE)
B.MAR.30,1953 YAZOO CITY,MISS.
D.JAN.6,1977 BATON ROUGE,LA.
1975 CAL A S   70   .174
1976 CAL A S   14   .184
     BBTR   84   .176

MILJUS, JOHN KENNETH (JOHN)
(JOVO) OR (BIG SERB)
B.JUNE 30,1895 PITTSBURGH,PA.
D.FEB.11,1976 POULSON,MONTANA
1915 PIT F P   1   0- 0
1917 BRO N P   4   0- 1
1920 BRO N P   9   10   1- 0
1921 BRO N P   28   6- 3
1927 PIT N P   19   8- 3
1928 PIT N P   21   5- 7
     CLE A P   11   1- 4
1929 CLE A P   34   8- 8
     BRTR   127   128   29-26

MILLAN, FELIX BERNARDO
[MARTINEZ]
B.AUG.21,1943 YABUCOA,P.R.
1966 ATL N 2/S-3   37   .275
1967 ATL N 2   41   .235
1968 ATL N *2   149   .289
1969 ATL N *2   162   .267
1970 ATL N *2   142   .310
1971 ATL N *2   143   .289
1972 ATL N *2   125   .257
1973 NY N *2   153   .290
1974 NY N *2   136   .268
1975 NY N *2   162   .283
1976 NY N *2   139   .282
1977 NY N 2   91   .248
     BRTR   1480   .279

MILLARD, FRANK E.
B.JULY 4,1865 E.ST.LOUIS,ILL.
D.JULY 4,1892 GALVESTON,TEX.
1890 STL AA 2   1   .000

MILLER, BERT
1897 PHI N 2   3   .200

MILLER, BURT
B.KALAMAZOO,MICH.
1897 LOU N P   4   0- 0

MILLER, CHARLES BRADLEY (DUSTY)
B.SEPT.10,1868 OIL CITY,PA.
D.JAN.14,1943 ST.MARTINSVILLE,LA.
1889 BAL AA O   11   .125
1890 STL AA O   27   .203
1895 CIN N O   132   .329
1896 CIN N O   125   .318
1897 CIN N O   119   .317
1898 CIN N O   152   .299
1899 CIN N O   60   .260
     STL N O   10   .231
     BLTR   656   .299

MILLER, CHARLES BRUCE (BRUCE)
B.MAR.4,1947 FORT WAYNE,IND.
1973 SF N /3-2-S   12   .143
1974 SF N 3-S/2   73   .278
1975 SF N 3-2/S   99   .239
1976 SF N /2-3   12   .160
     BRTR   196   .246

MILLER, CHARLES ELMER
B.JAN.4,1892 WARRENSBURG,MO.
D.APR.23,1972 WARRENSBURG,MO.
1912 STL A S   1   .000
     TR

MILLER, CHARLES HESS
B.DEC.30,1877 CONTESTOGA CENTER PA.
D.JAN.13,1951 MILLERSVILLE,PA.
1915 BAL F H   1   .000

MILLER, CHARLES MARION (CHUCK)
B.SEPT.18,1889 WOODVILLE,OHIO
D.JUNE 16,1961 HOUSTON,TEX.
1913 STL N O   4   .091
1914 STL N O   36   .194
     BLTL   40   .170

MILLER, DAKIN EVANS
B.SEPT.2,1877 MALVERN,IOWA
D.APR.20,1950 STOCKTON,CAL.
1902 CHI N O   50   .225

MILLER, DYAR K
B.MAY 29,1946 BATESVILLE,IND.
1975 BAL A P   30   6- 3
1976 BAL A P   49   2- 4
1977 BAL A P   12   2- 2
     CAL A P   41   4- 4
1978 CAL A P   41   6- 2
     BRTR   173   20-15

MILLER, EDMUND JOHN (BING)
B.AUG.30,1894 VINTON,IOWA
D.MAY 7,1966 PHILADELPHIA,PA.
1921 WAS A O   114   .288
1922 PHI A O   143   .336
1923 PHI A O   123   .299
1924 PHI A O   113   .342
1925 PHI A 1-O   124   .318
1926 PHI A O   38   .291
     STL A O   94   .331
1927 STL A O   144   .325
1928 PHI A O   139   .329
1929 PHI A O   147   .335
1930 PHI A O   154   .303
1931 PHI A O   137   .281
1932 PHI A O   95   .295
1933 PHI A 1-O   67   .275
1934 PHI A O   81   .243
1935 BOS A O   78   .304
1936 BOS A O   30   .298
     BRTR   1821   .312

MILLER, EDWARD LEE (EDDIE)
B.JUNE 29,1957 SAN PABLO,CAL.
1977 TEX A /O   17   .333
1978 ATL N /O   6   .143
     BBTR   23   .185

MILLER, EDWARD ROBERT (EPPIE)
B.NOV.26,1916 PITTSBURGH,PA.
1936 CIN N S   5   .100
1937 CIN N S-3   36   .190
1939 BOS N S   77   .267
1940 BOS N S   151   .276
1941 BOS N S   154   .239
1942 BOS N S   142   .244
1943 CIN N S   154   .224
1944 CIN N S   155   .209
1945 CIN N S   115   .238
1946 CIN N S   91   .194
1947 CIN N S   151   .268
1948 PHI N S   130   .246
1949 PHI N 2-S   85   .207
1950 STL N 2-S   64   .22/
     BRTR   1510   .238

MILLER, EDWIN J. (BIG ED)
B.NOV.24,1888 ANNVILLE,PA.
1912 STL A 1-S   12   .155
1914 STL A 1   34   .138
1918 CLE A 1   32   .229
     BRTR   78   .195

MILLER, ELMER
B.JULY 28,1890 SANDUSKY,OHIO
D.NOV.26,1944 BELOIT,WIS.
1912 STL N O   12   .189
1915 NY A O   26   .145
1916 NY A O   43   .224
1917 NY A O   114   .251
1918 NY A O   67   .243
1921 NY A O   56   .298
1922 NY A O   51   .286
     BOS A O   44   .172
     BRTR   413   .243

MILLER, ELMER LE ROY
B.APR.17,1904 DETROIT,MICH.
1929 PHI N P   31   0- 1
     BLTL

MILLER, FRANK LEE (BULLET)
B.MAY 13,1886 ALLEGAN,MICH.
D.FEB.19,1974 ALLEGAN,MICH.
1913 CHI A P   1   0- 1
1916 PIT N P   30   7-10
1917 PIT N P   38 39   10-19
1918 PIT N P   23   11- 8
1919 PIT N P   32   13-12
1922 BOS N P   31   11-13
1923 BOS N P   8   0- 3
     BRTR   163   164   52-66

MILLER, FREDERICK
B.PHILADELPHIA,PA.
1892 WAS N S   1   .000

MILLER, FREDERICK HOLMAN (SPEEDY)
B.JUNE 28,1886 FAIRFIELD,IND.
D.MAY 2,1953 BROOKVILLE,IND.
1910 BRO N P   3   1- 1
     BLTL

MILLER, GEORGE C.
B.FEB.19,1853 NEWPORT,KY.
D.JULY 24,1929 NORWOOD,OHIO
1877 CIN N C   11   .162
1884 CIN AA C   6   .250
     BRTR   17   .190

MILLER, GEORGE FREDERICK (FOGHORN)
(CALLIOPE) OR (DOGGIE)
B.AUG.15,1864 BROOKLYN,N.Y.
D.APR.6,1909 BROOKLYN,N.Y.
1884 PIT AA C-O   88   .222
1885 PIT AA C   42   .161
1886 PIT AA C   83   .258
1887 PIT N C-O   87   .313
1888 PIT N C-O   103   .277
1889 PIT N C-O   102   .267
1890 PIT N 3-O   138   .273
1891 PIT N C-S-3-O   131   .285
1892 PIT N C-S-O   147   .268
1893 PIT N C   40   .194
1894 STL N M-C-2-3   125   .341
1895 STL N C-3-O   123   .290
1896 LOU N C-2   84   .273
     BRTR   1293   .274

MILLER, HENRY D.
1892 CHI N P   4   1- 2
     TL

MILLER, HUGH STANLEY (COTTON)
B.DEC.28,1887 ST.LOUIS,MO.
D.DEC.24,1945 ST.LOUIS,MO.
1911 PHI N H   1   .000
1914 STL F 1   132   .225
1915 STL F 1   6   .500
     BRTR   139   .228

MILLER, JACOB GEORGE
B.FEB.5,1897 BALTIMORE,MD.
1922 PIT N O   3   .091

MILLER, JAMES MC CURDY (RABBIT)
B.OCT.2,1880 PITTSBURGH,PA.
D.FEB.7,1937 PITTSBURGH,PA.
1901 NY N 2   18   .136
     BRTR

MILLER, JAMES ELDRIDGE (HACK)
B.FEB.13,1913 CELESTE,TEX.
D.NOV.22,1966 DALLAS,TEX.
1944 DET A C   5   .200
1945 DET A C   2   .750
     BRTR   7   .444

MILLER, JOHN ALLEN
B.MAR.14,1944 ALHAMBRA,CAL.
1966 NY A /1-O   6   .087
1969 LA N /O-1-3-2   26   .211
     BRTR   32   .164

MILLER, JOHN ANTHONY (OX)
B.MAY 4,1915 GAUSE,TEX.
1943 WAS A P   3   0- 0
     STL A P   2   0- 0
1945 STL A P   4   6   2- 1
1946 STL A P   11   1- 3
1947 CHI N P   4   1- 2
     BRTR   24   26   4- 6

MILLER, JOHN BARNEY (DOTS)
B.SEPT.9,1886 KEARNY,N.J.
D.SEPT.5,1923 SARANAC LAKE,N.Y.
1909 PIT N 2   150   .279
1910 PIT N 2   119   .227
1911 PIT N 2   129   .268
1912 PIT N 1   148   .275
1913 PIT N 1   154   .272
1914 STL N 1-S   155   .290
1915 STL N 1-2   150   .264
1916 STL N 1-2-S   143   .238
1917 STL N 1-2   148   .248
1919 STL N 1-2   101   .231
1920 PHI N 2-3   98   .254
1921 PHI N 1-3   84   .297
     BRTR   1579   .263

MILLER, JOHN ERNEST
B.MAY 30,1941 BALTIMORE,MD.
1962 BAL A P   2   1- 1
1963 BAL A P   3   1- 1
1965 BAL A P   16   6- 4
1966 BAL A P   23   4- 8
1967 BAL A /P   2   0- 0
     BRTR   46   12-14

MILLER, JOSEPH A.
B.FEB.17,1861 BALTIMORE,MD.
D.APR.23,1928 WHEELING,W.V.A
1884 TOL AA S   105   .236
1885 LOU AA 2-S-3   97   .192
                      202   .217

MILLER, JOSEPH H. (CYCLONE)
B.SEPT.24,1859 SPRINGFIELD,MASS
D.OCT.13,1916 NEW LONDON,CONN.
1884 CHI U P   1   0- 0
     PRO N P-O   6   2- 4
                            .045
1886 ATH AA P   21   10- 9
     TL   29   12-14
                            .259

YR	CL	LEA	POS	GP	G	REC

MILLER, JOSEPH WICK
B.JULY 24,1850 GERMANY
D.AUG.30,1891

YR	CL	LEA	POS	GP	G	REC
1872	NAT	NA	M-1	1		.250
1875	WES	NA	2	13		-
	CHI	NA	2-0	16		-
				30		-

MILLER, KENNETH ALBERT (WHITEY)
B.MAY 2,1915 ST.LOUIS,MO.

| 1944 | NY | N | P | 5 | 0- 1 |
| | | BRTR | | | |

MILLER, L. EDWARD
B.TECUMSEH,MICH.

| 1884 | TOL | AA | O | 8 | .208 |

MILLER, LARRY DON
B.JUNE 19,1937 TOPEKA,KAN.

1964	LA	N	P	16	4- 8
1965	NY	N	P	28	1- 4
1966	NY	N	/P	4	0- 2
		BLTL		48	5-14

MILLER, LAWRENCE H. (HACK)
B.JAN.1,1894 NEW YORK,N.Y.
D.SEPT.17,1971 OAKLAND,CAL.

1916	BRO	N	O	3	.333
1918	BOS	A	O	12	.276
1922	CHI	N	O	122	.351
1923	CHI	N	O	135	.301
1924	CHI	N	O	53	.336
1925	CHI	N	O	24	.279
		BRTR		349	.323

MILLER, LEO ALPHONSO (RED)
B.FEB.11,1897 PHILADELPHIA,PA.
D.OCT.20,1973 ORLANDO,FLA.

| 1923 | PHI | N | P | 1 | 0- 0 |
| | | BRTR | | | |

MILLER, LOWELL OTTO (MOONIE)
B.JUNE 1,1889 MINDEN,NEB.
D.MAR.29,1962 BROOKLYN,N.Y.

1910	BRO	N	C	28	.197
1911	BRO	N	C	22	.210
1912	BRO	N	C	98	.278
1913	BRO	N	C	104	.212
1914	BRO	N	C	54	.231
1915	BRO	N	C	84	.224
1916	BRO	N	C	73	.255
1917	BRO	N	C	92	.230
1918	BRO	N	C-1	75	.193
1919	BRO	N	C	51	.226
1920	BRO	N	C	90	.289
1921	BRO	N	C	91	.234
1922	BRO	N	C	59	.261
		BRTR		921	.245

MILLER, NORMAN CALVIN (NORM)
B.FEB.5,1946 LOS ANGELES,CAL.

1965	HOU	N	/O	11	.200
1966	HOU	N	/O-3	11	.147
1967	HOU	N	O	64	.205
1968	HOU	N	O	79	.237
1969	HOU	N	*O	119	.264
1970	HOU	N	O/C	90	.239
1971	HOU	N	O/C	45	.257
1972	HOU	N	O	67	.243
1973	HOU	N	/O	3	.000
	ATL	N	/O	9	.375
1974	ATL	N	/O	42	.171
		BLTR		540	.238

MILLER, OTIS LOUIS (OTTO)
B.FEB.2,1901 BELLEVILLE,ILL.
D.JULY 26,1959 BELLEVILLE,ILL.

1927	STL	A	S-3	51	.224
1930	BOS	A	2-3	112	.286
1931	BOS	A	2-3	107	.272
1932	BOS	A	O	2	.000
		BRTR		272	.273

MILLER, RALPH DARWIN
B.MAR.15,1873 CINCINNATI,OHIO
D.MAY 8,1973 CINCINNATI,OHIO

1898	BRO	N	P	19	21	5-14
1899	BAL	N	P	6		1- 2
		BRTR		25	27	6-16

MILLER, RALPH HENRY
(MOOSE) OR (LEFTY)
B.JAN.14,1899 VINTON,IOWA
D.FEB.18,1967 WHITE BEAR LAKE,MINN.

| 1921 | WAS | A | P | 1 | 0- 0 |
| | | BRTL | | | |

MILLER, RALPH JOSEPH
B.FEB.29,1896 FT.WAYNE,IND.
D.MAR.18,1939 FT.WAYNE,IND.

1920	PHI	N	3	97	.219
1921	PHI	N	S	57	.304
1924	WAS	A	2	9	.133
		BRTR		163	.248

MILLER, RANDALL SCOTT (RANDY)
B.MAR.18,1953 OXNARD,CAL.

1977	BAL	A	/P	1	0- 0
1978	MON	N	/P	5	0- 1
		BRTR		6	0- 1

MILLER, RAYMOND PETER
B.FEB.12,1888 PITTSBURGH,PA.
D.APR.7,1927 PITTSBURGH,PA.

1917	CLE	A	1	19	.190
	PIT	N	1	6	.148
				25	.188

MILLER, RICHARD ALAN (RICK)
B.APR.19,1948 GRAND RAPIDS,MICH.

1971	BOS	A	O	15	.333
1972	BOS	A	O	89	.214
1973	BOS	A	*O	143	.261
1974	BOS	A	*O	114	.261
1975	BOS	A	O	77	.194
1976	BOS	A	O	105	.283
1977	BOS	A	O	86	.254
1978	CAL	A	*O	132	.263
		BLTL		761	.259

MILLER, ROBERT GERALD (BOB)
B.JULY 15,1935 BERWYN,ILL.

1953	DET	A	P	13		1- 2
1954	DET	A	P	32	34	1- 1
1955	DET	A	P	7	9	2- 1
1956	DET	A	P		11	0- 2
1962	CIN	N	P		6	0- 0
	NY	N	P		17	2- 2
		BRTL		86	90	6- 8

MILLER, ROBERT JOHN (BOB)
B.JUNE 16,1926 DETROIT,MICH.

1949	PHI	N	P	3	0- 0
1950	PHI	N	P	35	11- 6
1951	PHI	N	P	17	2- 1
1952	PHI	N	P	3	0- 1
1953	PHI	N	P	35	8- 9
1954	PHI	N	P	30	7- 9
1955	PHI	N	P	40	8- 4
1956	PHI	N	P	49	3- 6
1957	PHI	N	P	32	2- 5
1958	PHI	N	P	17	1- 1
		BRTR		261	42-42

MILLER, ROBERT LANE (BOB)
B.FEB.18,1939 ST.LOUIS,MO.

1957	STL	N	P	5	7	0- 0
1959	STL	N	P		1	0- 0
1960	STL	N	P	15	17	4- 3
1961	STL	N	P	34	35	1- 3
1962	NY	N	P	33	40	1-12
1963	LA	N	P		42	10- 8
1964	LA	N	P		74	7- 7
1965	LA	N	P		61	6- 7
1966	LA	N	P		46	4- 2
1967	LA	N	P		52	2- 9
1968	MIN	A	P		45	0- 3
1969	MIN	A	P		48	5- 5
1970	CLE	A	P		19	2- 2
	CHI	A	P	15	16	4- 6
	CHI	N	/P		7	0- 0
1971	CHI	N	/P		2	0- 0
	SD	N	P		38	7- 3
	PIT	N	P		16	1- 2
1972	PIT	N	P		36	5- 2
1973	SD	N	P		18	0- 0
	NY	N	/P		1	0- 0
	DET	A	P		22	4- 2
1974	NY	N	P		58	2- 2
		BRTR		694	707	69-81

MILLER, ROBERT W.
B.1862

1890	ROC	AA	P	13	3- 8
1891	WAS	AA	P	7	2- 3
				20	5-11

MILLER, RODNEY CARTER
B.JAN.16,1940 PORTLAND,ORE.

| 1957 | BRO | N | H | 1 | .000 |
| | | BLTR | | | |

MILLER, ROGER WESLEY
B.AUG.1,1954 CONNELLSVILLE,PA.

| 1974 | MIL | A | /P | 2 | 0- 0 |
| | | BRTR | | | |

MILLER, ROLAND ARTHUR (RONNIE)
B.AUG.28,1918 MASON CITY,IOWA

| 1941 | WAS | A | P | 1 | 0- 0 |
| | | BBTR | | | |

MILLER, ROSCOE CLYDE
(ROXY) OR (RUBBERLEGS)
B.DEC.2,1876 GREENVILLE,IND.
D.APR.18,1913 CORYDON,IND.

1901	DET	A	P	39	23-13
1902	DET	A	P	20	6-11
	NY	N	P	10	1- 8
1903	NY	N	P	15	2- 5
1904	PIT	N	P	19	7- 9
				103	39-46

MILLER, ROY OSCAR (DOC)
B.1883 CHATHAM,ONT.,CANADA
D.JULY 31,1938 JERSEY CITY,N.J.

1910	CHI	N	O	1	.000
	BOS	N	O	130	.286
1911	BOS	N	O	146	.333
1912	BOS	N	O	51	.234
	PHI	N	O	67	.288
1913	PHI	N	O	69	.345
1914	CIN	N	O	93	.255
		BLTL		557	.295

MILLER, RUDEL CHARLES (RUDY)
B.JULY 12,1900 KALAMAZOO,MICH.

| 1929 | PHI | A | 3 | 2 | .250 |
| | | BRTR | | | |

MILLER, RUSSELL LEWIS
B.MAR.25,1900 ETNA,OHIO
D.APR.30,1962 BUCYRUS,OHIO

1927	PHI	N	P	2	1- 1
1928	PHI	N	P	33	36	0-12
		BRTR		35	38	1-13

MILLER, STUART LEONARD (STU)
B.DEC.26,1927 NORTHAMPTON,MASS.

1952	STL	N	P		12	6- 3
1953	STL	N	P	40	42	7- 8
1954	STL	N	P	19	20	2- 3
1956	STL	N	P		3	0- 1
	PHI	N	P	24	29	5- 6
1957	NY	N	P		38	7- 9
1958	SF	N	P	41	42	6- 9
1959	SF	N	P		59	8- 7
1960	SF	N	P		47	7- 6
1961	SF	N	P	63	64	14- 5
1962	SF	N	P	59	60	5- 8
1963	BAL	A	P		71	5- 8
1964	BAL	A	P		66	7- 7
1965	BAL	A	P		67	14- 7
1966	BAL	A	P		51	9- 4
1967	BAL	A	P		42	3-10
1968	ATL	N	P		2	0- 0
		BRTR		704	716	105-103

MILLER, THOMAS P. (REDDY)
B.PHILADELPHI,APA.
D.MAY 29,1876

| 1875 | STL | NA | C-3 | 52 | .166 |

MILLER, THOMAS ROYALL
B.JULY 5,1897 POWHATAN COURT
HOUSE,VA.

1918	BOS	N	H	2	.000
1919	BOS	N	O	7	.333
		BLTR		9	.250

MILLER, WALTER JACOB (JAKE)
B.FEB.28,1897 WAGRAM,OHIO
D.AUG.20,1975 VENICE,FLA.

1924	CLE	A	P	2	0- 1
1925	CLE	A	P	32	10-13
1926	CLE	A	P	18	7- 4
1927	CLE	A	P	34	10- 8
1928	CLE	A	P	25	8- 9
1929	CLE	A	P	29	14-12
1930	CLE	A	P	24	4- 4
1931	CLE	A	P	10	2- 1
1933	CHI	A	P	26	30	5- 6
		BLTL		200	204	60-58

MILLER, WALTER W.
B.OCT.19,1884 GAS CITY,IND.
D.MAR.1,1956 MARION,IND.

| 1911 | BRO | N | P | 3 | 0- 1 |
| | | BRTR | | | |

MILLER, WARD TAYLOR
(WINDY) OR (GRUMP)
B.JULY 5,1884 MT.CARROLL,ILL.
D.SEPT.4,1958 DIXON,ILL.

1909	PIT	N	O	14	.143
	CIN	N	O	43	.310
1910	CIN	N	O	26	.238
1912	CHI	N	O	86	.307
1913	CHI	N	O	80	.236
1914	STL	F	O	119	.295
1915	STL	F	O	155	.307
1916	STL	A	O	146	.266
1917	STL	A	O	43	.207
		BLTR		712	.278

MILLER, WARREN W.

1909	WAS	A	O	26	.216
1911	WAS	A	O	21	.148
				47	.188

MILLER, WILLIAM
B.CLEVELAND,OHIO

| 1902 | PIT | N | O | 1 | .200 |

MILLER, WILLIAM FRANCIS (WILD BILL)
B.APR.12,1910 HANNIBAL,MO.

| 1937 | STL | A | P | 1 | 0- 1 |
| | | BRTR | | | |

YR CL LEA POS   GP   G   REC   YR CL LEA POS   GP   G   REC   YR CL LEA POS   GP   G   REC

MILLER, WILLIAM PAUL (BILL)
(LEFTY) OR (HOOKS)
B.JULY 26,1927 MINERSVILLE,PA.
1952 NY A P   21   4- 6
1953 NY A P   13   2- 1
1954 NY A P   2   0- 1
1955 BAL A P   5   0- 1
       BLTL   41   6- 9

MILLIES, WALTER LOUIS
B.OCT.18,1906 CHICAGO,ILL.
1934 BRO N C   2 .000
1936 WAS A C   74 .312
1937 WAS A C   59 .223
1939 PHI N C   84 .234
1940 PHI N C   26 .070
1941 PHI N C   1 .000
       BRTR   246 .243

MILLIGAN, JOHN (JOCKO)
B.AUG.8,1861 PHILADELPHIA,PA.
D.AUG.29,1923 PHILADELPHIA,PA.
1884 ATH AA C   66 .295
1885 ATH AA C   7 .286
1886 ATH AA C-1   76 .249
1887 ATH AA C-1   96 .344
1888 STL AA C   63 .202
1889 STL AA C   72 .370
1890 PHI P C   62 .315
1891 ATH AA C-1   117 .300
1892 WAS N C-1   76 .277
1893 BAL N C-1   23 .240
     NY N   40 .243
       BRTR   698 .293

MILLIGAN, JOHN ALEXANDER
B.JAN.22,1904 SCHUYLERVILLE,N.Y.
D.MAY 15,1972 FORT PIERCE,FLA.
1928 PHI N P   13   2- 5
1929 PHI N P   8   0- 1
1930 PHI N P   9   1- 2
1931 PHI N P   3   0- 0
1934 WAS A P   2   0- 0
       BRTL   35   3- 8

MILLIGAN, WILLIAM J. (BILLY)
B.AUG.19,1878 BUFFALO,N.Y.
D.OCT.14,1928 BUFFALO,N.Y.
1901 PHI A P   7   0- 3
1904 NY N P   5   0- 1
       TL   12   0- 4

MILLIKEN, ROBERT FOGLE (BOBO)
B.AUG.25,1926 MAJORSVILLE,W.VA.
1953 BRO N P   37   8- 4
1954 BRO N P   24   5- 2
       BRTR   61 13- 6

MILLS, ABBOTT PAIGE (JACK)
B.OCT.23,1889 S.WILLIAMSTOWN,MASS.
D.JUNE 3,1973 WASHINGTON,D.C.
1911 CLE A S   13 .294
       BLTR

MILLS, ARTHUR GRANT
B.MAR.2,1903 UTICA,N.Y.
D.JULY 23,1975 UTICA,N.Y.
1927 BOS N P   15   0- 0
1928 BOS N P   4   0- 0
       BRTR   19   0- 1

MILLS, CHARLES
B.BROOKLYN,N.Y.
D.APR.10,1874
1871 MUT NA C-O   33   -
1872 MUT NA C-3-O   6 .133
                      39   -

MILLS, COLONEL BUSTER (BUS)
B.SEPT.16,1908 RANGER,TEX.
1934 STL N O   29 .236
1935 BRO N O   17 .214
1937 BOS A O   123 .295
1938 STL A O   123 .285
1940 NY A O   34 .397
1942 CLE A O   80 .277
1946 CLE A O   9 .273
       BRTR   415 .287
NON-PLAYING MANAGER CIN[N] 1953

MILLS, EVERETT
B.1845 NEWARK,N.J.
D.JUNE 22,1908 NEWARK,N.J.
1871 OLY NA 1   31   -
1872 BAL NA 1   53 .274
1873 BAL NA 1-O   54   -
1874 HAR NA 1   53   -
1875 HAR NA 1   78   -
1876 HAR N 1   63 .259
                     332   -

MILLS, FRANK LE MOYNE
B.MAY 13,1895 KNOXVILLE,OHIO
1914 CLE A C   4 .142
       BLTR

MILLS, HOWARD ROBINSON (LEFTY)
B.MAY 12,1910 DEDHAM,MASS.
1934 STL A P   4   0- 0
1937 STL A P   2   1- 1
1938 STL A P   30 10-12
1939 STL A P   34   4-11
1940 STL A P   26   0- 6
       BLTL   96 15-30

MILLS, RICHARD ALAN (DICK)
B.JAN.29,1945 BOSTON,MASS.
1970 BOS A /P   2   0- 0
       BRTR

MILLS, RUPERT FRANK
B.OCT.12,1892 NEWARK,N.J.
D.JULY 20,1929 LAKE HOPATCONG,N.J.
1915 NEW F 1   41 .205
       BRTR

MILLS, WILLIAM GRANT (WEE WILLIE)
B.AUG.15,1877 SCHENEVUS,N.Y.
D.JULY 5,1914 NORWOOD,N.Y.
1901 NY N P   2   0- 2
       BR

MILLS, WILLIAM HENRY
B.NOV.2,1920 BOSTON,MASS.
1944 PHI A C   5 .250
       BRTR

MILNAR, ALBERT JOSEPH (HAPPY)
B.DEC.26,1913 CLEVELAND,OHIO
1936 CLE A P   4   1- 2
1938 CLE A P   23 24   3- 1
1939 CLE A P   37 41 14-12
1940 CLE A P   37 18-10
1941 CLE A P   35 12-19
1942 CLE A P   28 40   6- 8
1943 CLE A P   16 19   1- 3
     STL A P   3- 2
1946 STL A P   4- 1
     PHI N P   1   0- 0
       BLTL   188 208 57-58

MILNE, WILLIAM JAMES (PETE)
B.APR.10,1925 MOBILE,ALA.
1948 NY N O   12 .222
1949 NY N O   31 .241
1950 NY N H   4 .250
       BLTR   47 .233

MILNER, BRIAN TATE
B.NOV.17,1959 FORT WORTH,TEX.
1978 TOR A /C   2 .444
       BRTR

MILNER, JOHN DAVID
(JOHN) OR (THE HAMMER)
B.DEC.28,1949 ATLANTA,GA.
1971 NY N /O   9 .167
1972 NY N O-1   117 .238
1973 NY N 1-O   129 .239
1974 NY N *1   137 .252
1975 NY N O-1   91 .191
1976 NY N *O-1   127 .271
1977 NY N 1-O   131 .255
1978 PIT N O-1   108 .271
       BLTL   849 .248

MILOSEVICH, MICHAEL (MOLLIE)
B.JAN.13,1915 ZEIGLER,ILL.
D.FEB.3,1966 E.CHICAGO,IND.
1944 NY A S   94 .247
1945 NY A 2-S   30 .217
       BRTR   124 .242

MILSTEAD, GEORGE EARL (COWBOY)
B.JUNE 26,1903 CLEBURNE,TEX.
D.AUG.9,1977 CLEBURNE,TEX.
1924 CHI N P   13   1- 1
1925 CHI N P   5   1- 1
1926 CHI N P   18   1- 5
       BLTL   36   3- 7

MILTON, S. LAWRENCE (TUG)
B.PITTSBURG,KAN.
1903 STL N P   1   0- 0
       TR

MINAHAN, DANIEL JOSEPH
B.NOV.28,1865 TROY,N.Y.
D.AUG.8,1929 TROY,N.Y.
1895 LOU N 3   8 .361
       BRTR

MINAHAN, EDMUND JOSEPH (COTTON)
B.DEC.10,1882 SPRINGFIELD,OHIO
D.MAY 20,1958 E.ORANGE,N.J.
1907 CIN N P   2   0- 2
       BRTR

MINARCIN, RUDY ANTHONY
(RUDY) OR (BUSTER)
B.MAR.25,1930 N.VANDERGRIFT,PA.
1955 CIN N P   41   5- 9
1956 BOS A P   3   1- 0
1957 BOS A P   26   0- 0
       BRTR   70   6- 9

MINCHER, DONALD RAY (DON)
B.JUNE 24,1938 HUNTSVILLE,ALA.
1960 WAS A 1   27 .241
1961 MIN A 1   35 .188
1962 MIN A 1   86 .240
1963 MIN A 1   82 .258
1964 MIN A 1   120 .237
1965 MIN A 1/O   128 .251
1966 MIN A *1   139 .251
1967 CAL A *1/O   147 .273
1968 CAL A *1   120 .236
1969 SEA A *1   140 .246
1970 OAK A *1   140 .246
1971 OAK A 1   28 .239
     WAS A 1   100 .291
1972 TEX A 1   61 .236
     OAK A 1   47 .148
       BLTR   1400 .249

MINCHER, EDWARD JOHN
B.BALTIMORE,MD.
1871 KEK NA O   9   -
1872 NAT NA O   11 .118
                      20   -

MINER, RAYMOND THEADORE (LEFTY)
B.APR.4,1897 GLENS FALLS,N.Y.
D.SEPT.15,1963 GLENRIDGE,N.Y.
1921 PHI A P   1   0- 0
       BRTL

MINETTO, CRAIG STEPHEN
B.APR.25,1954 STOCKTON,CAL.
1978 OAK A /P   4   0- 0
       BLTL

MINGORI, STEPHEN BERNARD (STEVE)
B.FEB.29,1944 KANSAS CITY,MO.
1970 CLE A P   21   1- 0
1971 CLE A P   54   1- 2
1972 CLE A P/O   41 42   0- 6
                               .125
1973 CLE A /P   5   0- 0
     KC A P   19   3- 3
1974 KC A P   36   2- 3
1975 KC A P   36   0- 3
1976 KC A P   55   5- 5
1977 KC A P   43   2- 4
1978 KC A P   45   1- 4
       BLTL   355 356 15-30
                               .167

MINNER, PAUL EDISON (LEFTY)
B.JULY 30,1923 NEW WILMINGTON,PA.
1946 BRO N P   3   0- 1
1948 BRO N P   28 31   4- 3
1949 BRO N P   27   3- 1
1950 CHI N P   29 43   8-13
1951 CHI N P   33 36   6-17
1952 CHI N P   28 29 14- 9
1953 CHI N P   31 12-15
1954 CHI N P   32 33 11-11
1955 CHI N P   22   9- 9
1956 CHI N P   10   2- 5
       BLTL   253 265 69-84

MINNICK, DONALD ATHEY
B.APR.14,1931 LYNCHBURG,VA.
1957 WAS A P   2   0- 1
       BRTR

MINOSO, SATURNINO ORESTES ARMAS
(ARRIETA) (MINNIE)
B.NOV.29,1922 HAVANA,CUBA
1949 CLE A O   9 .188
1951 CLE A 1   8 .429
     CHI A S-3-O   138 .324
1952 CHI A S-3-O   147 .281
1953 CHI A 3-O   151 .313
1954 CHI A 3-O   153 .320
1955 CHI A 3-O   139 .288
1956 CHI A 1-3-O   151 .316
1957 CHI A O   153 .310
1958 CLE A 3-O   149 .302
1959 CLE A O   148 .302
1960 CHI A O   154 .311
1961 CHI A O   152 .280
1962 STL N O   39 .196
1963 WAS A 3-O   109 .229
1964 CHI A O   30 .226
1976 CHI A /H   3 .125
       BRTR   1833 .298

MINSHALL, JAMES EDWARD (JIM)
B.JULY 4,1947 COVINGTON,KY.
1974 PIT N /P   5   0- 1
1975 PIT N /P   1   0- 0
       BRTR   6   0- 1

MINTON, GREGORY BRIAN (GREG)
B.JULY 29,1951 LUBBOCK,TEX.
1975 SF N /P   4   1- 1
1976 SF N /P   10 11   0- 3
1977 SF N /P   2   3   1- 1
1978 SF N P   11   0- 1
       BBTR   27 29   2- 6

YR	CL LEA POS	GP	G	REC

MIRABELLA, PAUL THOMAS
B.MAR.20,1954 BELLEVILLE,N.J.
| 1978 TEX A | P | | 10 | 3- 2 |
| | BLTL | | | |

MIRANDA, GUILLERMO [PEREZ] (WILLIE)
B.MAY 24,1926 VELASCO,CUBA
1951 WAS A	1-S		7	.444
1952 CHI A	2-S-3		12	.250
	STL A	S		7	.091
	CHI A	2-S-3	58	.218
1953 STL A	S-3		17	.167
	NY A	S		48	.224
1954 NY A	2-S-3		92	.250
1955 BAL A	2-S		153	.255
1956 BAL A	S		148	.217
1957 BAL A	S		115	.194
1958 BAL A	S		102	.201
1959 BAL A	2-S-3		65	.159
	BBTR		824	.221

MISSE, JOHN BEVERLY
B.MAY 30,1885 HIGHLAND,KAN.
D.MAR.18,1970 ST.JOSEPH,MO.
| 1914 STL F | 2-S | | 97 | .189 |
| | BRTR | | | |

MITCHELL, ALBERT ROY (ROY)
B.APR.19,1885 BELTON,TEX.
D.SEPT.8,1959 TEMPLE,TEX.
1910 STL A	P		6	4- 2
1911 STL A	P	28	29	4- 8
1912 STL A	P		13	3- 4
1913 STL A	P		33	13-16
1914 STL A	P		28	4- 5
1918 CHI A	P		2	0- 1
	CIN N	P		9	0- 1
1919 CIN N	P		7	0- 1
	BRTR		122	123	32-37

MITCHELL, CLARENCE ELMER
B.FEB.22,1891 FRANKLIN,NEB.
D.NOV.6,1963 GRAND ISLAND,NEB.
1911 DET A	P		5	1- 0
1916 CIN N	P-1-	29	56	11-10
	O			.239
1917 CIN N	P-1-	32	47	9-15
	O			.278
1918 BRO N	P	1	10	0- 1
1919 BRO N	P	23	34	7- 5
1920 BRO N	P	19	55	5- 2
1921 BRO N	P	37	46	11- 9
1922 BRO N	P-1	5	56	0- 3
				.290
1923 PHI N	P	29	53	9-10
1924 PHI N	P	29	69	6-13
1925 PHI N	P-1	32	52	10-17
				.196
1926 PHI N	P	28	39	9-14
1927 PHI N	P	13	18	6- 3
1928 PHI N	P	3	5	0- 0
	STL N	P		19	8- 9
1929 STL N	P	25	26	8-11
1930 STL N	P		1	1- 0
	NY N	P		24	10- 3
1931 NY N	P		27	13-11
1932 NY N	P		8	1- 3
	BLTL		390	650	125-139
				.252

MITCHELL, CRAIG SETON
B.APR.14,1954 SANTA ROSA,CAL.
1975 OAK A	/P		1	0- 1
1976 OAK A	/P		1	0- 0
1977 OAK A	/P		3	0- 1
1978 SEA A	P		29	8-14
	BRTR		34	8-16

MITCHELL, FREDERICK FRANCIS
[REAL NAME FREDERICK FRANCIS YAPP]
B.JUNE 5,1878 CAMBRIDGE,MASS.
D.OCT.13,1970 NEWTON,MASS.
1901 BOS A	P		20	6- 9
1902 BOS A	P		1	0- 1
	PHI A	P-O	19	20	5- 8
				.184
1903 PHI N	P		28	11-14
1904 PHI N	P		25	4- 8
	BRO N	P		8	2- 4
1905 BRO N	P		25	3- 7
1910 NY N	P		68	.230
1913 BOS N	C		4	.333
	BRTR		126	199	31-51
				.209

NON-PLAYING MANAGER
CHI[N] 1917-20, BOS[N] 1921-23

MITCHELL, JOHN FRANKLIN
B.AUG.9,1894 DETROIT,MICH.
D.NOV.4,1965 BIRMINGHAM,MICH.
1921 NY A	S		13	.262
1922 NY A	S		4	.000
	BOS A	S		59	.251
1923 BOS A	S		92	.225
1924 BRO N	S		64	.263
1925 BRO N	S		97	.250
	BBTR		329	.245

MITCHELL, LOREN DALE (DALE)
B.AUG.23,1921 COLONY,OKLA.
1946 CLE A	O		11	.432
1947 CLE A	O		123	.316
1948 CLE A	O		141	.336
1949 CLE A	O		149	.317
1950 CLE A	O		130	.308
1951 CLE A	O		134	.290
1952 CLE A	O		134	.323
1953 CLE A	O		134	.300
1954 CLE A	1-O		53	.283
1955 CLE A	1-O		61	.259
1956 CLE A	O		38	.133
	BRO N	O		19	.292
	BLTL		1127	.312

MITCHELL, MICHAEL FRANCIS
B.DEC.12,1879 SPRINGFIELD,OHIO
D.JULY 16,1961 PHOENIX,ARIZ.
1907 CIN N	O		148	.292
1908 CIN N	O		119	.222
1909 CIN N	O		145	.310
1910 CIN N	O		156	.286
1911 CIN N	O		140	.291
1912 CIN N	O		147	.283
1913 CHI N	O		82	.262
	PIT N	O		54	.271
1914 PIT N	O		76	.234
	WAS A	O		55	.285
	BRTR		1122	.278

MITCHELL, MONROE BARR
B.SEPT.11,1901 STARKVILLE,MISS.
D.SEPT.4,1976 VALDOSTA,GA.
| 1923 WAS A | P | | 10 | 2- 4 |
| | BRTL | | | |

MITCHELL, PAUL MICHAEL
B.AUG.19,1949 WORCESTER,MASS.
1975 BAL A	P		11	3- 0
1976 OAK A	P		26	9- 7
1977 OAK A	/P		9	0- 3
	SEA A	/P		9	3- 3
	BRTR		51	15-13

MITCHELL, ROBERT MC KASHA
B.FEB.6,1856 CINCINNATI,OHIO
D.MAY 1,1933 SPRINGFIELD,OHIO
1877 CIN N	P-O	12	13	6- 5
				.204
1878 CIN N	P-S-	9	14	7- 2
	O			.250
1879 CLE N	P-O	22	30	4-13
				.146
1882 STL AA	P-O		1	0- 0
				.000
	BLTL		44	58	17-20
				.182

MITCHELL, ROBERT VANCE (BOBBY)
B.OCT.22,1943 NORRISTOWN,PA.
1970 NY A	/O		10	.227
1971 MIL A	O		35	.182
1973 MIL A	O-O		47	.223
1974 MIL A	O-O		88	.243
1975 MIL A	O-O		93	.249
	BRTR		273	.235

MITCHELL, WILLIAM (WILLIE)
B.DEC.1,1889 PLEASANT GROVE,MISS.
D.NOV.23,1973 SARDIS,MISS.
1909 CLE A	P		3	1- 2
1910 CLE A	P		35	12- 8
1911 CLE A	P	31	32	7-14
1912 CLE A	P		29	5- 8
1913 CLE A	P		35	14- 8
1914 CLE A	P		39	12-17
1915 CLE A	P		36	11-14
1916 CLE A	P		11	2- 5
	DET A	P		24	8- 4
1917 DET A	P	30	31	12- 8
1918 DET A	P		1	0- 1
1919 DET A	P		3	1- 2
	BRTL		277	279	85-91

MITTERLING, RALPH (SARGE)
B.APR.19,1890 FREEBURG,PA.
D.JAN.22,1956 PITTSBURGH,PA.
| 1916 PHI A | O | | 13 | .154 |

MITTERWALD, GEORGE EUGENE
B.JUNE 7,1945 BERKELEY,CAL.
1966 MIN A	/C		3	.200
1968 MIN A	C		11	.206
1969 MIN A	C/O	69		.257
1970 MIN A	*C		117	.222
1971 MIN A	*C		125	.250
1972 MIN A	C		66	.184
1973 MIN A	*C		125	.259
1974 CHI N	C		78	.251
1975 CHI N	C-1		84	.220
1976 CHI N	C-1		101	.215
1977 CHI N	*C/1		110	.238
	BRTR		887	.236

MIZE, JOHN ROBERT (JOHNNY)
OR (THE BIG CAT)
B.JAN.7,1913 DEMOREST,GA.
1936 STL N	1		126	.329
1937 STL N	1		145	.364
1938 STL N	1		149	.337
1939 STL N	1		153	.349
1940 STL N	1		155	.314
1941 STL N	1		126	.317
1942 NY N	1		142	.305
1946 NY N	1		101	.337
1947 NY N	1		154	.302
1948 NY N	1		152	.289
1949 NY N	1		106	.263
	NY A	1		13	.261
1950 NY A	1		90	.277
1951 NY A	1		113	.259
1952 NY A	1		78	.263
1953 NY A	1		81	.250
	BLTR		1884	.313

MIZELL, WILMER DAVID (VINEGAR BEND)
B.AUG.13,1930 LEAKESVILLE,MISS.
1952 STL N	P		30	10- 8
1953 STL N	P		33	13-11
1956 STL N	P		33	14-14
1957 STL N	P		33	8-10
1958 STL N	P		30	10-14
1959 STL N	P		31	13-10
1960 STL N	P		9	1- 3
	PIT N	P		23	13- 5
1961 PIT N	P		25	7-10
1962 PIT N	P		4	1- 1
	NY N	P		17	0- 2
	BRTL		268	90-88

MIZEUR, WILLIAM FRANCIS (BAD BILL)
B.JUNE 22,1897 NOKOMIS,ILL.
D.AUG.27,1976 DECATUR,ILL.
1923 STL A	O		1	.000
1924 STL A	O		1	.000
	BLTR		2	.000

MLCKOVSKY, RAYMOND JAMES
[PLAYED UNDER NAME OF
RAYMOND JAMES MACK]

MOATES, DAVID ALLAN (DAVE)
B.JAN.30,1948 GREAT LAKES,ILL.
1974 TEX A	R		1	.000
1975 TEX A	O		54	.274
1976 TEX A	O		85	.241
	BLTL		140	.260

MODAK, MICHAEL JOSEPH ALOYSIUS
B.MAY 18,1922 CAMPBELL,OHIO
| 1945 CIN N | P | | 20 | 1- 2 |
| | BRTR | | | |

MOELLER, DANIEL EDWARD
B.MAR.23,1885 DE WITT,IOWA
D.APR.14,1951 FLORENCE,ALA.
1907 PIT N	O		11	.285
1908 PIT N	O		27	.193
1912 WAS A	O		132	.276
1913 WAS A	O		153	.236
1914 WAS A	O		151	.250
1915 WAS A	O		118	.226
1916 WAS A	O		78	.245
	CLE A	O		25	.069
	BBTR		695	.243

MOELLER, JOSEPH DOUGLAS (JOE)
B.FEB.15,1943 BLUE ISLAND,ILL.
1962 LA N	P		19	6- 5
1964 LA N	P		27	7-13
1966 LA N	P		29	2- 4
1967 LA N	/P		6	0- 0
1968 LA N	/P		3	1- 1
1969 LA N	P		23	1- 0
1970 LA N	P		31	7- 9
1971 LA N	P		28	2- 4
	BRTR		166	26-36

MOELLER, RONALD RALPH
(RON) OR (THE KID)
B.OCT.13,1938 CINCINNATI,OHIO
1956 BAL A	P		4	0- 1
1958 BAL A	P		4	0- 0
1961 LA A	P	33	35	4- 8
1963 LA A	P		3	0- 0
	WAS A	P		8	2- 0
	BLTL		52	54	6- 9

MOFFETT, JOSEPH W.
B.WHEELING,W.VA.
| 1884 TOL AA | 1-3 | | 56 | .207 |

MOFFET, SAMUEL R.
B.1857 WHEELING,W.VA.
D.1907 BUTTE,MONTANA
1884 CLE N	P-1-	22	66	3-19
	2-3-O			.179
1887 IND N	P		11	1- 5
1888 IND N	P-O	7	10	2- 5
				.114
	TR		40	87	6-29
				.167

MOFFITT, RANDALL JAMES (RANDY)
B.OCT.13,1948 LONG BEACH,CAL.

YR	CL	LEA	POS	GP	G	REC
1972	SF	N	P		40	1- 5
1973	SF	N	P		60	4- 4
1974	SF	N	P		61	5- 7
1975	SF	N	P		55	4- 5
1976	SF	N	P		58	6- 6
1977	SF	N	P		64	4- 9
1978	SF	N	P		70	8- 4
			BRTR		408	32-40

MOFORD, HERBERT (HERB)
B.AUG.6,1928 BROOKSVILLE,KY.

YR	CL	LEA	POS	GP	G	REC
1955	STL	N	P		14	1- 1
1958	DET	A	P		25	4- 9
1959	BOS	A	P		4	0- 2
1962	NY	N	P		7	0- 1
			BRTR		50	5-13

MOGRIDGE, GEORGE ANTHONY
B.FEB.18,1889 ROCHESTER,N.Y.
D.MAR.4,1962 ROCHESTER,N.Y.

YR	CL	LEA	POS	GP	G	REC
1911	CHI	A	P		4	0- 2
1912	CHI	A	P		17	3- 4
1915	NY	A	P		6	2- 3
1916	NY	A	P	30	31	6-12
1917	NY	A	P		29	9-11
1918	NY	A	P	45	48	15-13
1919	NY	A	P		36	10- 8
1920	NY	A	P		26	5- 9
1921	WAS	A	P		38	18-14
1922	WAS	A	P		34	18-13
1923	WAS	A	P		33	13-13
1924	WAS	A	P		30	16-11
1925	WAS	A	P		10	4- 3
	STL	A	P		2	1- 1
1926	BOS	N	P	39	40	6-10
1927	BOS	N	P		20	6- 4
			BLTL	399	404	132-131

MOHARDT, JOHN HENRY
B.JAN.21,1898 PITTSBURGH,PA.
D.NOV.24,1961 LA JOLLA,CAL.

YR	CL	LEA	POS	GP	G	REC
1922	DET	A	O		5	1.000

MOHART, GEORGE BENJAMIN
B.MAR.6,1892 BUFFALO,N.Y.
D.OCT.2,1970 SILVER CREEK,N.Y.

YR	CL	LEA	POS	GP	G	REC
1920	BRO	N	P		13	0- 1
1921	BRO	N	P		2	0- 0
			BRTR		15	0- 1

MOHLER, ERNEST FOLLETTE (KID)
B.DEC.13,1874 ONEIDA,ILL.
D.NOV.4,1961 SAN FRANCISCO,CAL.

YR	CL	LEA	POS	GP	G	REC
1894	WAS	N	S		3	.125
			BLTL			

MOISAN, WILLIAM JOSEPH
B.JULY 30,1925 BRADFORD,MASS.

YR	CL	LEA	POS	GP	G	REC
1953	CHI	N	P		3	0- 0
			BLTR			

MOKAN, JOHN LEO
B.SEPT.23,1895 BUFFALO,N.Y.

YR	CL	LEA	POS	GP	G	REC
1921	PIT	N	O		19	.269
1922	PIT	N	O		31	.258
	PHI	N	3-O		47	.252
1923	PHI	N	3-O		113	.313
1924	PHI	N	O		96	.260
1925	PHI	N	O		75	.330
1926	PHI	N	O		127	.303
1927	PHI	N	O		74	.286
			BRTR		582	.291

MOLE, FENTON LE ROY (MUSCLES)
B.JUNE 14,1925 SAN LEANDRO,CAL.

YR	CL	LEA	POS	GP	G	REC
1949	NY	A	1		10	.185
			BLTL			

MOLESWORTH, CARLTON
B.FEB.15,1876 FREDERICK,MD.
D.JULY 25,1961 FREDERICK,MD.

YR	CL	LEA	POS	GP	G	REC
1895	WAS	N	P		4	0- 2
			TL			

MOLINARO, ROBERT JOSEPH (BOB)
B.MAY 21,1950 NEWARK,N.J.

YR	CL	LEA	POS	GP	G	REC
1975	DET	A	/O		6	.263
1977	DET	A	/H		4	.250
	CHI	A	/O		1	.500
1978	CHI	A	O-D		105	.262
			BLTR		116	.264

MOLITOR, PAUL LEO
B.AUG.22,1956 ST.PAUL,MINN.

YR	CL	LEA	POS	GP	G	REC
1978	MIL	A	2-S/3		125	.273
			BRTR			

MOLLENKAMP, FREDERICK HENRY
B.MAR.15,1890 CINCINNATI,OHIO
D.NOV.1,1948 CINCINNATI,OHIO

YR	CL	LEA	POS	GP	G	REC
1914	PHI	N	1		3	.125

MOLLWITZ, FREDERICK AUGUST (FRITZ)
B.JUNE 16,1890 COBURG,GERMANY
D.OCT.3,1967 BRADENTON,FLA.

YR	CL	LEA	POS	GP	G	REC
1913	CHI	N	1		3	.428
1914	CHI	N	1		12	.143
	CIN	N	1		33	.164
1915	CIN	N	1		153	.259
1916	CIN	N	1		65	.224
	CHI	N	1		33	.268
1917	PIT	N	1		36	.257
1918	PIT	N	1		119	.269
1919	PIT	N	1-O		56	.167
	STL	N	1		25	.241
			BRTR		535	.241

MOLONEY, RICHARD HENRY (RICHIE)
B.JUNE 7,1950 BROOKLINE,MASS.

YR	CL	LEA	POS	GP	G	REC
1970	CHI	A	/P		1	0- 0
			BRTR			

MOLYNEAUX, VINCENT LEO
B.AUG.17,1888 LEWISTON,N.Y.
D.MAY 4,1950 STAMFORD,CONN.

YR	CL	LEA	POS	GP	G	REC
1917	STL	A	P		7	0- 0
1918	BOS	A	P		6	1- 0
			BRTR		13	1- 0

MONACO, BLAS
B.NOV.16,1915 SAN ANTONIO,TEX.

YR	CL	LEA	POS	GP	G	REC
1937	CLE	A	2		5	.286
1946	CLE	A	H		12	.000
			BBTR		17	.154

MONAHAN, EDWARD FRANCIS (RINTY)
B.APR.28,1928 BROOKLYN,N.Y.

YR	CL	LEA	POS	GP	G	REC
1953	PHI	A	P		4	0- 0
			BRTR			

MONBOUQUETTE, WILLIAM CHARLES (BILL)
B.AUG.11,1936 MEDFORD,MASS.

YR	CL	LEA	POS	GP	G	REC
1958	BOS	A	P		10	3- 4
1959	BOS	A	P	34	35	7- 7
1960	BOS	A	P	35	38	14-11
1961	BOS	A	P	32	33	14-14
1962	BOS	A	P		35	15-13
1963	BOS	A	P		37	20-10
1964	BOS	A	P	36	39	13-14
1965	BOS	A	P	35	36	10-18
1966	DET	A	P		30	7- 8
1967	DET	A	/P		2	0- 0
	NY	A	P		33	6- 5
1968	NY	A	P		17	5- 7
	SF	N	/P		7	0- 1
			BRTR	343	352	114-112

MONCEWICZ, FREDERICK ALFRED
B.SEPT.1,1903 BROCKTON,MASS.
D.APR.23,1969 BROCKTON,MASS.

YR	CL	LEA	POS	GP	G	REC
1928	BOS	A	S		3	.000
			BRTR			

MONCHAK, ALEX
B.DEC.22,1919 BAYONNE,N.J.

YR	CL	LEA	POS	GP	G	REC
1940	PHI	N	2-S		19	.143
			BRTR			

MONDAY, ROBERT JAMES (RICK)
B.NOV.20,1945 BATESVILLE,ARK.

YR	CL	LEA	POS	GP	G	REC
1966	KC	A	O		17	.098
1967	KC	A	*O		124	.251
1968	OAK	A	*O		148	.274
1969	OAK	A	*O		122	.271
1970	OAK	A	*O		112	.290
1971	OAK	A	*O		116	.245
1972	CHI	N	*O		138	.249
1973	CHI	N	*O		149	.267
1974	CHI	N	*O		142	.294
1975	CHI	N	*O		136	.267
1976	CHI	N	*O-1		137	.272
1977	LA	N	*O/1		118	.230
1978	LA	N	*O/1		119	.254
			BLTL		1578	.264

MONEY, DONALD WAYNE
(DON) OR (BROOKS)
B.JUNE 7,1947 WASHINGTON,D.C.

YR	CL	LEA	POS	GP	G	REC
1968	PHI	N	/S		4	.231
1969	PHI	N	*S		127	.229
1970	PHI	N	*3/S		120	.295
1971	PHI	N	3-O-2		121	.223
1972	PHI	N	*3/S		152	.222
1973	MIL	A	*3-S		145	.284
1974	MIL	A	*3/2		159	.283
1975	MIL	A	3/S		109	.277
1976	MIL	A	*3-D/S		117	.267
1977	MIL	A	*2-O-3		152	.279
1978	MIL	A	1-2-3-D/S		137	.293
			BRTR		1343	.266

MONGE, ISIDRO PEDROZA (SID)
B.APR.11,1951 AGUA PREITA,MEXICO

YR	CL	LEA	POS	GP	G	REC
1975	CAL	A	/P		4	0- 2
1976	CAL	A	P		32	6- 7
1977	CAL	A	/P		4	0- 1
	CLE	A	P		33	1- 2
1978	CLE	A	P		48	4- 3
			BBTL		121	11-15

MONROE, EDWARD OLIVER (PECK)
B.FEB.22,1895 LOUISVILLE,KY.
D.APR.29,1969 LOUISVILLE,KY.

YR	CL	LEA	POS	GP	G	REC
1917	NY	A	P		9	1- 0
1918	NY	A	P		1	0- 0
			BRTR		10	1- 0

MONROE, FRANK W.
B.HAMILTON,OHIO

YR	CL	LEA	POS	GP	G	REC
1884	IND	AA	C		1	.000

MONROE, JOHN ALLEN
B.AUG.24,1898 FARMERSVILLE,TEX.
D.JUNE 19,1956 CONROE,TEX.

YR	CL	LEA	POS	GP	G	REC
1921	NY	N	2		19	.143
	PHI	N	2		41	.286
			BLTR		60	.266

MONROE, LAWRENCE JAMES (LARRY)
B.JUNE 20,1956 DETROIT,MICH.

YR	CL	LEA	POS	GP	G	REC
1976	CHI	A	/P		8	0- 1
			BRTR			

MONROE, ZACHARY CHARLES (ZACH)
B.JULY 8,1931 PEORIA,ILL.

YR	CL	LEA	POS	GP	G	REC
1958	NY	A	P		21	4- 2
1959	NY	A	P		3	0- 0
			BRTR		24	4- 2

MONTAGUE, EDWARD FRANCIS
B.JULY 24,1905 SAN FRANCISCO,CAL.

YR	CL	LEA	POS	GP	G	REC
1928	CLE	A	S		32	.235
1930	CLE	A	S-3		58	.263
1931	CLE	A	S		64	.285
1932	CLE	A	S-3		66	.245
			BRTR		220	.262

MONTAGUE, JOHN EVANS
B.SEP.12,1947 NEWPORT NEWS,VA.

YR	CL	LEA	POS	GP	G	REC
1973	MON	N	/P		4	0- 0
1974	MON	N	P		46	3- 4
1975	MON	N	P	12	13	0- 1
	PHI	N	/P		3	0- 0
1977	SEA	A	P		47	8-12
1978	SEA	A	P		19	1- 3
			BRTR	131	132	12-20

MONTANEZ, GUILLERMO [NARANJO]
(WILLIE)
B.APR.1,1948 CATANO,P.R.

YR	CL	LEA	POS	GP	G	REC
1966	CAL	A	/1		8	.000
1970	PHI	N	O/1		18	.240
1971	PHI	N	*O/1		158	.255
1972	PHI	N	*O-1		147	.247
1973	PHI	N	1-O		146	.263
1974	PHI	N	*1/O		143	.304
1975	PHI	N	1		21	.286
	SF	N	*1		135	.305
1976	SF	N	1		60	.309
	ATL	N	*1		103	.321
1977	ATL	N	*1		136	.287
1978	NY	N	*1		159	.256
			BLTL		1234	.279

MONTEAGUDO, AURELIO FAUSTINO
[CINTRA]
B.NOV.19,1943 CAIBARIEN,CUBA

YR	CL	LEA	POS	GP	G	REC
1963	KC	A	P		4	0- 0
1964	KC	A	P		11	0- 4
1965	KC	A	/P	4	5	0- 0
1966	KC	A	/P		6	0- 0
	HOU	N	P		10	0- 0
1967	CHI	A	/P		1	0- 1
1970	KC	A	P		21	1- 1
1973	CAL	A	P		15	2- 1
			BRTR	72	73	3- 7

MONTEAGUDO, RENE [MIRANDA]
B.MAR.12,1916 HAVANA,CUBA
D.SEPT.14,1973 HIALEAH,FLA.

YR	CL	LEA	POS	GP	G	REC
1938	WAS	A	P		5	1 -1
1940	WAS	A	P		27	2- 6
1944	WAS	A	O		10	.289
1945	PHI	N	P-O	14	114	0- 0
						.301
			BLTL	46	156	3- 7
						.289

MONTEFUSCO, JOHN JOSEPH
(JOHN) OR (COUNT)
B.MAY 25,1950 LONG BRANCH,N.J.

YR	CL	LEA	POS	GP	G	REC
1974	SF	N	/P		7	3- 2
1975	SF	N	P		35	15- 9
1976	SF	N	P	37	38	16-14
1977	SF	N	P		26	7-12
1978	SF	N	P	36	37	11- 9
			BRTR	141	143	52-46

MONTEJO, MANUEL (PETE)
B.OCT.16,1936 HAVANA,CUBA

YR	CL	LEA	POS	GP	G	REC
1961	DET	A	P		12	0- 0
			BRTR			

MONTEMAYOR, FELIPE ANGEL
(FELIPE) OR (MONTY)
B.FEB.7,1930 MONTERREY,MEXICO

YR	CL	LEA	POS	GP	G	REC
1953	PIT	N	O		28	.109
1955	PIT	N	O		36	.211
			BLTL		64	.173

THE OFFICIAL ENCYCLOPEDIA OF BASEBALL

YR CL LEA POS   GP   G   REC

MONTGOMERY, ALVIN ATLAS
B.JULY 3,1920 LOVI4G,VA,MEX.
D.APR.26,1942 WAVERLY,VA.
1941 BOS N C   42   .192
     BRTR

MONTGOMERY, MONTY BRYSON
B.SEP.1,1946 ALBEMARLE,N.C.
1971 KC A /P   3   3- 0
1972 KC A /P   9   3- 3
     BRTR   12   6- 3

MONTGOMERY, ROBERT EDWARD (BOB)
B.APR.16,1944 NASHVILLE,TENN.
1970 BOS A C   22   .179
1971 BOS A C   67   .239
1972 BOS A C   24   .286
1973 BOS A C   34   .320
1974 BOS A C   88   .252
1975 BOS A C/1   62   .226
1976 BOS A C   31   .247
1977 BOS A C   17   .300
1978 BOS A C   10   .241
     BRTR   355   .251

MONTREUIL, ALLAN ARTHUR (AL)
B.AUG.23,1943 NEW ORLEANS,LA.
1972 CHI N /2   5   .091
     BRTR

MONZANT, RAMON (SEGUNDO)
B.JAN.4,1933 MARACAIBO,VENEZ.
1954 NY N P   6   0- 0
1955 NY N P   28   29   4- 8
1956 NY N P   4   6   1- 0
1957 NY N P   24   3- 2
1958 SF N P   43   44   8-11
1960 SF N P   1   0- 0
     BRTR   106 110 16-21

MONZON, DANIEL FRANCISCO (DAN)
B.MAY 17,1946 BRONX,N.Y.
1972 MIN A 2/3-S-O   55   .273
1973 MIN A 2-3/O   39   .224
     BRTR   94   .244

MOOCK, JOSEPH GEOFFREY (JOE)
B.MAR.12,1944 PLAQUEMINE,LA.
1967 NY N 3   13   .225
     BLTR

MOOLIC, GEORGE HENRY (PRUNES)
B.MAR.12,1867 LAWRENCE,MASS.
D.FEB.19,1915 LAWRENCE,MASS.
1886 CHI N C   15   .145

MOON, LEO (LEFTY)
B.JUNE 22,1899 BELMONT,N.C.
D.AUG.25,1970 NEW ORLEANS,LA.
1932 CLE A P   1   0- 0
     BRTL

MOON, WALLACE WADE (WALLY)
B.APR.3,1930 BAY,ARK.
1954 STL N O   151   .304
1955 STL N 1-O   152   .295
1956 STL N 1-O   149   .298
1957 STL N O   142   .295
1958 STL N O   108   .238
1959 LA N 1-O   145   .302
1960 LA N O   138   .299
1961 LA N O   134   .328
1962 LA N 1-O   95   .242
1963 LA N O   122   .262
1964 LA N O   68   .220
1965 LA N O   53   .202
     BLTR   1457   .289

MOONEY, JIM IRVING
B.SEPT.4,1906 MOORESBURG,TENN.
1931 NY N P   10   7- 1
1932 NY N P   29   6-10
1933 STL N P   21   2- 5
1934 STL N P   32   2- 4
     BRTL   92 17-20

MOORE, ALBERT JAMES
B.AUG.4,1902 BROOKLYN,N.Y.
D.NOV.29,1974 AT SEA N.Y.TO P.R
1925 NY N O   2   .125
1926 NY N O   28   .222
     BRTR   30   .213

MOORE, ALVIN EARL (JUNIOR)
B.JAN.25,1953 WASKOM,TEX.
1976 ATL N /3-2-O   20   .269
1977 ATL N *3/2   112   .260
1978 CHI A O/3-O   24   .292
     BRTR   156   .265

MOORE, ANSELM WINN
B.SEPT.22,1917 DEL4I,LA.
1946 DET A C   51   .209
     BLTR

MOORE, ARCHIE FRANCIS
B.AUG.30,1941 UPPER DARBY,PA.
1964 NY A 1-O   31   .174
1965 NY A /O   9   .412
     BLTL   40   .275

MOORE, BALOR LILBON
B.JAN.25,1951 SMITHVILLE,TEX.
1970 MON N /P   6   0- 2
1972 MON N P   22   9- 9
1973 MON N P   35   7-16
1974 MON N /P   8   0- 2
1977 CAL A /P   7   0- 2
1978 TOR A P   37   6- 9
     BLTL   115 22-40

MOORE, CARLOS WHITMAN
B.AUG.13,1906 CLINTON,TENN.
D.JULY 2,1958 NEW ORLEANS,LA.
1930 WAS A P   4   0- 0
     BRTR

MOORE, CHARLES WESLEY
B.DEC.1,1884 JACKSON CO.,IND.
D.JULY 29,1970 PORTLAND,ORE.
1912 CHI N 2-3   5   .222

MOORE, CHARLES WILLIAM (CHARLIE)
B.JUNE 21,1953 BIRMINGHAM,ALA.
1973 MIL A /C   8   .185
1974 MIL A C   72   .245
1975 MIL A C-O   73   .290
1976 MIL A C-O/3   87   .191
1977 MIL A *C   138   .248
1978 MIL A C   96   .269
     BRTR   474   .248

MOORE, D C (DEE)
B.APR.6,1914 HEDLEY,TEX.
1936 CIN N P-C   2   6   0- 0
                              .400
1937 CIN N C   7   .077
1943 BRO N C-3   37   .253
     PHI N C-1-3   37   .239
1946 PHI N C-1   11   .077
     BRTR   2   98   0- 0
                              .232

MOORE, DONNIE RAY
B.FEB.13,1954 LUBBOCK,TEX.
1975 CHI N /P   4   0- 0
1977 CHI N P   27   4- 2
1978 CHI N P   71   9- 7
     BLTR   102 13- 9

MOORE, EARL ALONZO (EARL)
(BIG EBBIE) OR (CROSSFIRE)
B.JULY 29,1879 PICKERINGTON,O.
D.NOV.28,1961 COLUMBUS,OHIO
1901 CLE A P   31 16-14
1902 CLE A P   36 17-18
1903 CLE A P   29 22- 7
1904 CLE A P   26 13-11
1905 CLE A P   30 16-14
1906 CLE A P   5   1- 1
1907 CLE A P   3   0- 3
     NY A P   12   3- 4
1908 PHI N P   3   2- 1
1909 PHI N P   38 18-12
1910 PHI N P   46 22-15
1911 PHI N P   42 15-19
1912 PHI N P   31   9-14
1913 PHI N P   12   0- 0
     CHI N P   7   1- 1
1914 BUF F P   36 11-15
     BRTR   387 166-149

MOORE, EUEL WALTON (CHIEF)
B.MAY 27,1908 REAGAN,OKLA.
1934 PHI N P   20   5- 7
1935 PHI N P   15   1- 6
     NY N P   6   2- 0
1936 PHI N P   20   2- 3
     BRTR   61   9-16

MOORE, EUGENE JR. (GENE) OR (ROWDY)
B.AUG.26,1909 LANCASTER,TEX.
D.MAR.12,1978 JACKSON,MISS.
1931 CIN N O   4   .143
1933 STL N O   11   .395
1934 STL N H   9   .278
1935 STL N H   3   .000
1936 BOS N O   151   .290
1937 BOS N O   148   .283
1938 BOS N O   54   .272
1939 BRO N O   107   .225
1940 BRO N O   10   .300
     BOS N O   103   .292
1941 BOS N O   129   .272
1942 WAS A O   1   .000
1943 WAS A 1-O   92   .268
1944 STL A 1-O   110   .238
1945 STL A 1-O   110   .260
     BLTL   1042   .270

MOORE, EUGENE SR.
(GENE) OR (BLUE GOOSE)
B.NOV.9,1885 LANCASTER,TEX.
D.AUG.31,1938 DALLAS,TEX.
1909 PIT N P   1   0- 0
1910 PIT N P   4   2- 1
1912 CIN N P   5   0- 1
     BRTR   10   2- 2

MOORE, FERDINAND DEPAGE
B.FEB.21,1896 CAMDEN,N.J.
D.MAY 6,1947 ATLANTIC CITY,N.J.
1914 PHI A /P   2   .250

MOORE, GARY DOUGLAS
B.FEB.24,1945 TULSA,OKLA.
1970 LA N /O-1   7   .188
     BRTL

MOORE, GEORGE RAYMOND
B.NOV.25,1872 CAMBRIDGE,MASS.
D.NOV.17,1948 HYANNIS,MASS.
1905 PIT N P   1   0- 0
     BBTR

MOORE, GRAHAM EDWARD (EDDIE)
B.JAN.18,1899 BARLOW,KY.
D.FEB.10,1976 FT.MYERS,FLA.
1923 PIT N S   6   .269
1924 PIT N 2-3-O   72   .359
1925 PIT N 2-3-O   142   .298
1926 PIT N 2-S-3   43   .227
     BOS N 2-S-3   54   .266
1927 BOS N 2-3-O   112   .302
1928 BOS N O   68   .237
1929 BRO N 2-S   111   .296
1930 BRO N 2-S-O   76   .281
1932 NY N S   37   .264
1934 CLE A 2   27   .154
     BRTR   748   .285

MOORE, HENRY S. (HARRY)
1884 WAS U O   107   .337

MOORE, JACKIE SPENCER
B.FEB.19,1939 JAY,FLA.
1965 DET A C   21   .094
     BRTR

MOORE, JAMES STANFORD
B.DEC.14,1903 PRESCOTT,ARK.
D.MAY 19,1973 SEATTLE,WASH.
1928 CLE A P   1   0- 1
1929 CLE A P   2   0- 0
1930 CHI A P   9   2- 1
1931 CHI A P   33   0- 2
1932 CHI A P   1   0- 0
     BRTR   46   2- 4

MOORE, JAMES WILLIAM
B.APR.24,1903 PARIS,TENN.
1930 CHI A O   16   .205
     PHI A O   15   .380
1931 PHI A O   49   .223
     BRTR   80   .254

MOORE, JEREMIAH S. (JERRIE)
B.DETROIT,MICH.
1884 ALT U C-O   20   .298
     CLE N C   10   .235
1885 DET N C   5   .200
                        35   .266

MOORE, JOHN FRANCIS
B.MAR.23,1902 WATERVILLE,CONN.
1928 CHI N H   4   .000
1929 CHI N O   37   .286
1931 CHI N O   39   .240
1932 CHI N O   119   .305
1933 CIN N O   135   .263
1934 CIN N O   16   .190
     PHI N O   116   .365
1935 PHI N O   153   .323
1936 PHI N O   124   .328
1937 PHI N O   96   .319
1945 CHI N H   7   .167
     BLTR   846   .308

MOORE, JOSEPH GREGG
(JO-JO) OR (THE GAUSE GHOST)
B.DEC.25,1908 GAUSE,TEX.
1930 NY N O   3   .200
1931 NY N O   4   .250
1932 NY N O   86   .305
1933 NY N O   132   .292
1934 NY N O   139   .331
1935 NY N O   155   .295
1936 NY N O   152   .316
1937 NY N O   142   .310
1938 NY N O   125   .302
1939 NY N O   138   .269
1940 NY N O   138   .276
1941 NY N O   121   .273
     BLTR   1335   .298

```
YR  CL LEA POS      GP   G    REC
```

MOORE, LLOYD ALBERT (WHITEY)
B.JUNE 10,1912 TUSCARAWAS,OHIO
```
1936 CIN N  P           1    1- 0
1937 CIN N  P          13    0- 3
1938 CIN N  P          19    6- 4
1939 CIN N  P          42   13-12
1940 CIN N  P          25    8- 8
1941 CIN N  P          23    2- 1
1942 CIN N  P           1    0- 0
     STL N  P           9    0- 1
     BRTR             133   30-29
```

MOORE, MAURICE
D.FEB.22,1881
```
1875 ATL NA 1-S-3      21     -
```

MOORE, RANDOLPH EDWARD (RANDY)
B.JUNE 21,1905 NAPLES,TEX.
```
1927 CHI A  O           6    .000
1928 CHI A  O          24    .213
1930 BOS N  3-O        83    .288
1931 BOS N  3-O        83    .260
1932 BOS N  1-3-O     107    .293
1933 BOS N  1-O       135    .302
1934 BOS N  1-O       123    .284
1935 BOS N  1-O       125    .275
1936 BRO N  O          42    .239
1937 BRO N  C          13    .186
     STL N  O           8    .000
     BLTR             749    .279
```

MOORE, RAYMOND LEROY
(RAY) OR (FARMER)
B.JUNE 1,1926 MEADOWS,MD.
```
1952 BRO N  P          14    1- 2
1953 BRO N  P           1    0- 1
1955 BAL A  P          46   10-10
1956 BAL A  P          32   12- 7
1957 BAL A  P          34   11-13
1958 CHI A  P          32    9- 7
1959 CHI A  P          29    3- 6
1960 CHI A  P          14    1- 1
     WAS A  P          37    3- 2
1961 MIN A  P          46    4- 4
1962 MIN A  P          49    8- 3
1963 MIN A  P          31    1- 3
     BRTR             365   63-59
```

MOORE, ROBERT BARRY (BARRY)
B.APR.3,1943 STATESVILLE,N.C.
```
1965 WAS A  /P          1    0- 0
1966 WAS A  P          12    3- 3
1967 WAS A  P          27    7-11
1968 WAS A  P    32    34    4- 6
1969 WAS A  P    31    32    9- 8
1970 CLE A  P          13    3- 5
     CHI A  P          24    0- 4
     BLTL        140  143   26-37
```

MOORE, ROY DANIEL
B.OCT.26,1898 AUSTIN,TEX.
D.APR.5,1951 SEATTLE,WASH.
```
1920 PHI A  P    24    27    1-13
1921 PHI A  P    29    31   10-10
1922 PHI A  P          15    0- 3
     DET A  P           9    0- 0
1923 DET A  P     3     4    0- 0
     BBTL         80    86   11-26
```

MOORE, TERRY BLUFORD
B.MAY 27,1912 VERNON,ALA.
```
1935 STL N  O         119    .287
1936 STL N  O         143    .264
1937 STL N  O         115    .267
1938 STL N  O          94    .272
1939 STL N  P-O   1   130    0- 0
                            .295
1940 STL N  O         136    .304
1941 STL N  O         122    .294
1942 STL N  3-O       130    .288
1946 STL N  O          91    .263
1947 STL N  O         127    .283
1948 STL N  O          91    .232
     BRTR          1  1298    0- 0
                            .281
```
NON-PLAYING MANAGER PHI[N] 1954

MOORE, TOMMY JOE
B.JULY 7,1948 LYNWOOD,CAL.
```
1972 NY  N  /P          3    0- 0
1973 NY  N  /P    3     4    0- 1
1975 STL N  P          10    0- 0
     TEX A  P    12    14    0- 2
1977 SEA A  P          14    2- 1
     BRTR          42   45    2- 4
```

MOORE, WILLIAM ALLEN (SCRAPPY)
B.DEC.16,1892 ST.LOUIS,MO.
D.OCT.13,1964 LITTLE ROCK,ARK.
```
1917 STL A  3                .125
     BRTR
```

MOORE, WILLIAM AUSTIN (CY)
B.FEB.7,1905 ELBERTON,GA.
D.MAR.28,1972 AUGUSTA,GA.
```
1929 BRO N  P          32    3- 3
1930 BRO N  P           1    0- 0
1931 BRO N  P          23    1- 2
1932 BRO N  P    20    21    0- 3
1933 PHI N  P          36    8- 9
1934 PHI N  P          35    4- 9
     BRTR         147  148   16-26
```

MOORE, WILLIAM CHRISTOPHER
B.SEPT.3,1902 CORNING,N.Y.
```
1925 DET A  P           1    0- 0
     BRTR
```

MOORE, WILLIAM HENRY (WILLIE)
B.DEC.12,1901 KANSAS CITY,MO.
D.MAR.24,1972 KANSAS CITY,MO.
```
1926 BOS A  C           5    .167
1927 BOS A  C          44    .217
     BLTR              49    .207
```

MOORE, WILLIAM WILCY (CY)
B.MAY 20,1897 BONITA,TEX.
D.MAR.29,1963 HOLLIS,OKLA.
```
1927 NY  A  P          50   19- 7
1928 NY  A  P          35    4- 4
1929 NY  A  P          41    6- 4
1931 BOS A  P          53   11-13
1932 BOS A  P          37    4-10
     NY  A  P          10    2- 0
1933 NY  A  P          35    5- 6
     BRTR             261   51-44
```

MOORHEAD, CHARLES ROBERT (BOB)
B.JAN.23,1938 CHAMBERSBURG,PA.
```
1962 NY  N  P          38    0- 2
1965 NY  N  /P          9    0- 1
     BRTR              47    0- 3
```

MOOSE, ROBERT RALPH (BOB)
B.OCT.9,1947 EXPORT,PA.
D.OCT.9,1976 MARTINS FERRY,OHIO
```
1967 PIT N  /P          2    1- 0
1968 PIT N  P          38    8-12
1969 PIT N  P          44   14- 3
1970 PIT N  P    28    29   11-10
1971 PIT N  P          30   11- 7
1972 PIT N  P    31    32   13-10
1973 PIT N  /P   33    37   12-13
1974 PIT N  /P          7    1- 5
1975 PIT N  P          23    2- 2
1976 PIT N  P          53    3- 9
     BRTR         289  295   76-71
```

MOOTY, J T (JAKE)
B.APR.13,1913 BENNETT,TEX.
D.APR.20,1970 FORT WORTH,TEX.
```
1936 CIN N  P           8    0- 0
1937 CIN N  P    14    15    0- 3
1940 CIN N  P    20    24    6- 6
1941 CHI N  P          33    8- 9
1942 CHI N  P          19    2- 5
1943 CHI N  P           2    0- 0
1944 DET A  P          15    0- 0
     BRTR         111  116   16-23
```

MORA, ANDRES [IBARRA]
B.MAY 25,1955 RIO BRAVO,MEX.
```
1976 BAL A  O-O        73    .218
1977 BAL A  O/3        77    .245
1978 BAL A  O          76    .214
     BRTR             226    .226
```

MORALES, JOSE MANUEL [HERNANDEZ]
B.DEC.30,1944 FREDERIKSTED,V.I.
```
1973 OAK A  /H          6    .286
     MON N  /H          5    .400
1974 MON N  /C         25    .269
1975 MON N  1/O-C      93    .301
1976 MON N  1-C       104    .316
1977 MON N  /C-1       65    .203
1978 MIN A  D/C-1-O   101    .314
     BRTR             399    .298
```

MORALES, JULIO RUBEN [TORRES]
(JERRY)
B.FEB.18,1949 YABUCAO,P.R.
```
1969 SD  N  O          19    .195
1970 SD  N  O          28    .155
1971 SD  N  /O         12    .118
1972 SD  N  O/3       115    .239
1973 SD  N  *O        122    .281
1974 SD  N  *O        151    .273
1975 CHI N  *O        153    .270
1976 CHI N  *O        140    .274
1977 CHI N  *O        136    .290
1978 STL N  *O        130    .239
     BRTR            1006    .264
```

MORALES, RICHARD ANGELO (RICH)
B.SEP.20,1943 SAN FRANCISCO,CAL.
```
1967 CHI A  /S          8    .000
1968 CHI A  /S-2       10    .172
1969 CHI A  2-S/3      55    .215
1970 CHI A  S-3-2      62    .161
1971 CHI A  S-3/2-O    84    .243
1972 CHI A  S-2-3     110    .206
1973 CHI A  /3-2        7    .000
1973 SD  N  2-S        90    .164
1974 SD  N  S-2/3-1    54    .197
     BRTR             480    .195
```

MORAN, ALBERT THOMAS (HIKER)
B.JAN.1,1912 ROCHESTER,N.Y.
```
1938 BOS N  P           1    0- 0
1939 BOS N  P           6    1- 1
     BRTR               7    1- 1
```

MORAN, CARL WILLIAM
#BILL# OR #BUGS#
B.SEPT.26,1950 PORTSMOUTH,VA.
```
1974 CHI A  P          15    1- 3
     BRTR
```

MORAN, CHARLES BARTHELL
(UNCLE CHARLIE)
B.FEB.22,1878 NASHVILLE,TENN.
D.JUNE 14,1949 HORSE CAVE,KY.
```
1903 STL N  P-S   3     4    0- 1
                            .429
1908 STL N  C          16    .175
     BRTR          3    20    0- 1
                            .221
```

MORAN, CHARLES VINCENT
B.MAR.26,1879 WASHINGTON,D.C.
D.APR.11,1934 WASHINGTON,D.C.
```
1903 WAS A  S          98    .232
1904 WAS A  S          61    .209
     STL A  3          81    .241
1905 STL A  2          28    .195
     TR               268    .210
```

MORAN, HARRY EDWIN
B.APR.2,1889 SLATER,W.VA.
D.NOV.28,1962 BECKLEY,W.VA.
```
1912 DET A  P           4    0- 2
1914 BUF F  P          34   10- 7
1915 NEW F  P          34   13- 9
     BLTL              72   23-18
```

MORAN, JOHN HERBERT (HERBIE)
B.FEB.16,1884 COSTELLO,PA.
D.SEPT.21,1954 CLARKSON,N.Y.
```
1908 PHI A  O          19    .153
     BOS N  O           8    .266
1909 BOS N  O           8    .233
1910 BOS N  O          20    .119
1912 BRO N  O         130    .276
1913 BRO N  O         132    .266
1914 CIN N  O         107    .235
     BOS N  O          41    .266
1915 BOS N  O         130    .200
     BLTR             595    .243
```

MORAN, PATRICK JOSEPH (PAT)
B.FEB.7,1876 FITCHBURG,MASS.
D.MAR.7,1924 ORLANDO,FLA.
```
1901 BOS N  C          53    .216
1902 BOS N  C-1-O      72    .250
1903 BOS N  C         108    .250
1904 BOS N  C-3       111    .226
1905 BOS N  C          78    .240
1906 CHI N  C          61    .250
1907 CHI N  C          59    .227
1908 CHI N  C          45    .260
1909 CHI N  C          74    .219
1910 PHI N  C          56    .236
1911 PHI N  C          32    .184
1912 PHI N  C          13    .115
1913 PHI N  C           1    .000
1914 PHI N  C           1    .000
     TR               764    .236
```
NON-PLAYING MANAGER
PHI[N] 1915-18, CIN[N] 1919-23

MORAN, RICHARD ALAN (AL)
B.DEC.5,1938 DETROIT,MICH.
```
1963 NY  N  S-3       119    .193
1964 NY  N  S-3        16    .227
     BRTR             135    .195
```

MORAN, ROY ELLIS (DEEDLE)
B.SEPT.17,1884 VINCENNES,IND.
D.JULY 18,1966 ATLANTA,GA.
```
1912 WAS A  O           7    .077
     BRTR
```

MORAN, SAMUEL
B.SEPT.16,1870 ROCHESTER,N.Y.
D.AUG.29,1897 ROCHESTER,N.Y.
```
1895 PIT N  P          10    2- 5
     TL
```

YR CL LEA POS   GP   G   REC

MORAN, WILLIAM L.
B.OCT.10,1869 JOLIET,ILL.
D.APR.8,1916 JOLIET,ILL.
1892 STL N C   22   .153
1895 CHI N C   15   .163
                        37   .157

MORAN, WILLIAM NELSON (BILLY)
B.NOV.27,1933 MONTGOMERY,ALA.
1958 CLE A 2-S   115   .226
1959 CLE A 2-S   11   .294
1961 LA A 2-S   54   .260
1962 LA A 2   160   .282
1963 LA A 2   153   .275
1964 LA A 2-S-3   50   .268
     CLE A 1-2-3   69   .205
1965 CLE A /2-S   22   .125
     BRTR   634   .263

MORE, FORREST
B.SEPT.30,1883 HAYDEN,IND.
D.AUG.17,1968 COLUMBUS,IND.
1909 STL N P   15   1- 5
     BOS N P   10   1- 5
                        25   2-10

MOREHART, RAYMOND ANDERSON
B.DEC.2,1899 NEAR ABNER,TEX.
1924 CHI A S   31   .200
1926 CHI A 2   73   .318
1927 NY A 2   73   .256
     BLTR   177   .269

MOREHEAD, DAVID MICHAEL
(DAVE) OR (MOE)
B.SEP.5,1942 SAN DIEGO,CAL.
1963 BOS A P   29 10-13
1964 BOS A P   32   8-15
1965 BOS A P   34 10-18
1966 BOS A P   12   1- 2
1967 BOS A P   10   5- 4
1968 BOS A P   11   1- 4
1969 KC A P   21   2- 3
1970 KC A P   28   3- 5
     BRTR   177 40-64

MOREHEAD, SETH MARVIN
(SETH) OR (MOE)
B.AUG.15,1934 HOUSTON,TEX.
1957 PHI N P   34   1- 1
1958 PHI N P   27   1- 6
1959 PHI N P   3   0- 2
     CHI N P   11   0- 1
1960 CHI N P   45   2- 9
1961 MIL N P   12   1- 0
     BLTL   132   5-19

MOREJON, DANIEL [TORRES] (DANNY)
B.JULY 21,1930 HAVANA,CUBA
1958 CIN N O   12   .192
     BRTR

MORELAND, BOBBY KEITH (KEITH)
B.MAY 2,1954 DALLAS,TEX.
1978 PHI N /C   1   .000
     BRTR

MORELOCK, A. HARRY
B.PHILADELPHIA,PA.
1891 PHI N 3   4   .071
1892 PHI N 3   1   .000
                         5   .059

MOREN, LEWIS HOWARD (LEW) OR (HICKS)
B.AUG.4,1883 PITTSBURGH,PA.
D.NOV.2,1966 PITTSBURGH,PA.
1903 PIT N P   1   0- 1
1904 PIT N P   1   0- 0
1907 PHI N P   37 11-18
1908 PHI N P   28   8- 9
1909 PHI N P   40 16-15
1910 PHI N P   34 13-14
     TR   141 48-57

MORENO, JULIO [GONZALEZ]
B.JAN.28,1921 GUINES,CUBA
1950 WAS A P   4   1- 1
1951 WAS A P   31   5-11
1952 WAS A P   26   9- 9
1953 WAS A P   12   3- 1
     BRTR   73 18-22

MORENO, OMAR RENAN [QUINTERO]
B.OCT.24,1952 PUERTO ARMUELLES,
PANAMA
1975 PIT N /O   6   .167
1976 PIT N O   48   .270
1977 PIT N *O   150   .240
1978 PIT N *O   155   .235
     BLTL   359   .241

MORESKONICH, CHARLES
[PLAYED UNDER NAME OF CHARLES METRO]

MORET, ROGELIO [TORRES]
B.SEP.16,1949 GUAYAMA,P.R.
1970 BOS A /P   3   1- 0
1971 BOS A P   13   4- 3
1972 BOS A /P   3   0- 0
1973 BOS A P   30 13- 2
1974 BOS A P   31   9-10
1975 BOS A P   36   37 14- 3
1976 ATL N P   27   3- 5
1977 TEX A P   18   3- 3
1978 TEX A /P   7   0- 1
     BBTL   168   169 47-27

MOREY, DAVID BEALE
B.FEB.25,1889 MALDEN,MASS.
1913 PHI A P   2   0- 0
     BLTR

MORGAN, CHESTER COLLINS (CHICK)
B.JUNE 6,1910 CLEVELAND,MISS.
1935 DET A O   14   .174
1938 DET A O   74   .284
     BLTR   88   .277

MORGAN, CYRIL ARLON (CY)
B.SEPT.11,1896 LAKEVILLE,MASS.
D.SEPT.11,1946 LAKEVILLE,MASS.
1921 BOS N P   17   1- 1
1922 BOS N P   2   0- 0
     BRTR   19   1- 1

MORGAN, EDWARD CARRE (ED)
B.MAY 22,1904 CAIRO,ILL.
1928 CLE A 1-3-0   76   .313
1929 CLE A O   93   .318
1930 CLE A 1-O   150   .350
1931 CLE A 1   131   .351
1932 CLE A 1   144   .293
1933 CLE A 1-O   39   .264
1934 BOS A 1   138   .267
     BRTR   771   .313

MORGAN, EDWIN WILLIS (PEPPER)
B.NOV.19,1914 BRADY LAKE,OHIO
1936 STL N O   8   .278
1937 BRO N O   31   .188
     BLTL   39   .212

MORGAN, HARRY RICHARD (CY)
B.NOV.10,1878 POMEROY,OHIO
D.JUNE 28,1962 WHEELING,W.VA.
1903 STL A P   2   0- 2
1904 STL A P   8   0- 2
1905 STL A P   13   2- 6
1907 STL A P   13   2- 5
     BOS A P   13   6- 6
1908 BOS A P   30 13-14
1909 BOS A P   12   3- 9
     PHI A P   27 15- 8
1910 PHI A P   36 18-12
1911 PHI A P   38 15- 7
1912 PHI A P   16   3- 8
1913 CIN N P   1   0- 1
     BRTR   209 77-80

MORGAN, HENRY WILLIAM (BILL)
B.BROOKLYN,N.Y.
1875 RS NA P-3- 5   19   1- 4
            O   -
1878 MIL N 2-3-0   14   .175
1882 PIT AA C-0   16   .279
1883 PIT AA C-2-S-0   30   .167
1884 WAS AA C-2-S-0   44   .181
     RIC AA C-2-0   6   .100
     BAL U C-2-0   2   .250
            5   131   1- 4
                              -

MORGAN, JAMES EDWARD (RED)
B.OCT.6,1883 NEOLA,IOWA DECEASED
1906 BOS A 3   88   .215
     TR

MORGAN, JOHN P.
1916 PHI A 3   1   .250
     TR

MORGAN, JOE LEONARD
B.SEP.19,1943 BONHAM,TEX.
1963 HOU N 2   8   .240
1964 HOU N 2   10   .189
1965 HOU N *2   157   .271
1966 HOU N 2   122   .285
1967 HOU N *2/O   133   .275
1968 HOU N /2-0   10   .250
1969 HOU N *2-0   147   .236
1970 HOU N *2   144   .268
1971 HOU N *2   160   .256
1972 CIN N *2   149   .292
1973 CIN N *2   157   .290
1974 CIN N *2   149   .293
1975 CIN N *2   146   .327
1976 CIN N *2   141   .320
1977 CIN N *2   153   .288
1978 CIN N *2   132   .236
     BLTR   1918   .279

MORGAN, JOSEPH MICHAEL (JOE)
B.NOV.19,1930 WALPOLE,MASS.
1959 MIL N 2   13   .217
     KC A 3   20   .190
1960 PHI N 3   26   .133
     CLE A 3-0   22   .298
1961 CLE A O   4   .200
1964 STL N H   3   .000
     BLTR   88   .193

MORGAN, MICHAEL THOMAS (MIKE)
B.OCT.8,1959 TULARE,CAL.
1978 OAK A /P   3   0- 3
     BRTR

MORGAN, RAYMOND CARYLL (RAY)
B.JUNE 14,1889 BALTIMORE,MD.
D.FEB.15,1940 BALTIMORE,MD.
1911 WAS A 3   25   .213
1912 WAS A 2   80   .238
1913 WAS A 2   137   .272
1914 WAS A 2   147   .257
1915 WAS A 2   62   .233
1916 WAS A 2   99   .267
1917 WAS A 2   101   .266
1918 WAS A 2   68   .233
     BRTR   739   .254

MORGAN, ROBERT MORRIS (BOBBY)
B.JUNE 29,1926 OKLAHOMA CITY,OKLA.
1950 BRO N S-3   67   .226
1952 BRO N 2-S-3   67   .236
1953 BRO N S-3   69   .260
1954 PHI N 2-S-3   135   .262
1955 PHI N 1-2-S-3   136   .232
1956 PHI N 2-3   8   .200
     STL N 2-S-3   61   .195
1957 PHI N 2   2   .000
     CHI N 2-3   125   .207
1958 CHI N H   1   .000
     BRTR   671   .233

MORGAN, TOM STEPHEN
(TOM) OR (PLOWBOY)
B.MAY 20,1930 EL MONTE,CAL.
1951 NY A P   27   9- 3
1952 NY A P   16   5- 4
1954 NY A P   32 11- 5
1955 NY A P   40   7- 3
1956 NY A P   41   6- 7
1957 KC A P   46   9- 7
1958 DET A P   39   2- 5
1959 DET A P   46   1- 4
1960 DET A P   22   3- 2
     WAS A P   14   1- 3
1961 LA A P   59   8- 2
1962 LA A P   48   5- 2
1963 LA A P   13   0- 0
     BRTR   443 67-47

MORGAN, VERNON THOMAS (VERN)
B.AUG.8,1928 EMPORIA,VA.
D.NOV.8,1975 MINNEAPOLIS,MINN.
1954 CHI N 3   24   .234
1955 CHI N 3   7   .143
     BLTR   31   .225

MORHARDT, MEREDITH GOODWIN (MOE)
B.JAN.16,1937 MANCHESTER,CONN.
1961 CHI N 1   7   .278
1962 CHI N H   18   .125
     BLTR   25   .206

MORIARTY, EDWARD JEROME
B.OCT.12,1912 HOLYOKE,MASS.
1935 BOS N 2   8   .324
1936 BOS N H   6   .167
     BRTR   14   .300

MORIARTY, EUGENE JOHN·
B.HOLYOKE,MASS.
1884 BOS N O   4   .063
     IND AA P-3- 2   10   0- 2
         O   +.216
1885 DET N P-S- 1   11   0- 0
         3-0   .026
1892 STL N O   46   .175
     BL   3   71   0- 2
                            .160

MORIARTY, GEORGE JOSEPH
B.JULY 7,1884 CHICAGO,ILL.
D.APR.8,1964 MIAMI,FLA.
1903 CHI N 3   1   .000
1904 CHI N 3-0   5   .000
1906 NY A 3   65   .234
1907 NY A 1-3   126   .277
1908 NY A 1-3   101   .236
1909 DET A 3   133   .273
1910 DET A 3   136   .251
1911 DET A 3   130   .243
1912 DET A 1-3   105   .248
1913 DET A 3   102   .239
1914 DET A 3   130   .254
1915 DET A 3   31   .211
1916 CHI A 3   7   .200
     TR   1072   .251
NON-PLAYING MANAGER DET[A] 1927-28

YR CL LEA POS   GP   G   REC

MORIARTY, WILLIAM JOSEPH
B.1863 CHICAGO,ILL.
D.DEC.25,1916 ELGIN,ILL.
1909 CIN N S   6   .250
        BRTR

MORLAN, JOHN GLEN
B.NOV.22,1947 COLUMBUS,OHIO
1973 PIT N P   10   2- 2
1974 PIT N P   39   0- 3
                        49   2- 5

MORLEY, WILLIAM M.
[REAL NAME WILLIAM MORLEY JENNINGS]
B.JAN.23,1890 HOLLAND,MICH.
1913 WAS A 2   2   .000
        BRTR

MORONEY, JAMES FRANCIS
B.DEC.4,1885 BOSTON,MASS.
D.FEB.26,1929 PHILADELPHIA,PA.
1906 BOS N P   3   0- 3
1910 PHI N P   12   1- 2
1912 CHI N P   10   1- 1
        BLTL   25   2- 6

MORRELL, WILLARD BLACKMER
B.APR.9,1900 BOSTON,MASS.
D.AUG.5,1975 BRIMINGHAM,ALA.
1926 WAS A P   26   3- 3
1930 NY N P   2   0- 0
1931 NY N P   20   5- 3
        BRTR   48   8- 6

MORRILL, JOHN FRANCIS (HONEST JOHN)
B.FEB.19,1855 BOSTON,MASS.
D.APR.2,1932 BOSTON,MASS.
1876 BOS N C-2   66 .260
1877 BOS N 1-2-3-0   61 .302
1878 BOS N 1   60 .240
1879 BOS N 1-3   84 .281
1880 BOS N P-1-   2   84 0- 0
            3   .240
1881 BOS N P-1-   1   80 0- 1
            2-3   .289
1882 BOS N M-P-   1   82 0- 0
            1-2-S-3-0   .289
1883 BOS N M-P-   1   97 1- 0
            1-2-S-3-0   .319
1884 BOS N M-P-   1   106 0- 0
            1-2-3   .265
1885 BOS N M-1-2-3   111 .225
1886 BOS N M-1-2-S   117 .246
1887 BOS N M-1   124 .331
1888 BOS N M-1   134 .197
1889 WAS N M-1   44 .185
1890 BOS P 1-S   2 .143
        BRTR   6 1252 1- 1
                             .264

MORRIS, DANNY WALKER
B.JUNE 11,1946 GREENVILLE,KY.
1968 MIN A /P   3   0- 1
1969 MIN A /P   3   0- 1
        BRTR   6   0- 2

MORRIS, DOYT THEODORE
B.JULY 15,1916 STANLEY,N.C.
1937 PHI A H   6   .154
        BR

MORRIS, E.
B.TRENTON,N.J.
1884 BAL U P-O   1   0- 0
                             .000

MORRIS, EDWARD (CANNONBALL)
B.SEPT.29,1862 BROOKLYN,N.Y.
D.APR.12,1937 PITTSBURGH,PA.
1884 COL AA P   49   57 35-13
1885 PIT AA P   64 39-24
1886 PIT AA P   63 41-20
1887 PIT N P   37 14-22
1888 PIT N P   54 29-24
1889 PIT N P   21   7-14
1890 PIT N P   18   8- 6
        BRTL   306 314 173-123

MORRIS, JOHN SCOTT (JACK)
B.MAY 16,1955 ST.PAUL,MINN.
1977 DET A /P   7   1- 1
1978 DET A P   28   3- 5
        BRTR   35   4- 6

MORRIS, JOHN WALLACE
B.AUG.23,1941 LEWES,DEL.
1966 PHI N P   13   1- 1
1968 BAL A P   19   2- 0
1969 SEA A /P   6   0- 0
1970 MIL A P   20   4- 3
1971 MIL A P   43   2- 2
1972 SF N /P   7   0- 0
1973 SF N /P   7   1- 0
1974 SF N /P   17   1- 1
        BRTL   132 11- 7

MORRIS, JOHN WALTER (WALTER)
B.JAN.31,1880 ROCKWALL,TEX.
D.AUG.24,1961 DALLAS,TEX.
1908 STL N S   23   .178
        BRTR

MORRIS, JOSEPH HARLEY (BUGS)
[PLAYED UNDER NAME OF
JOSEPH HARLEY BENNETT IN 1918]
B.APR.19,1892 KANSAS CITY,MO.
D.NOV.21,1957 NOEL,MO.
1918 STL A P   4   0- 2
1921 CHI A P   4   0- 4
        STL A P   1   0- 0
        BRTR   9   0- 6

MORRIS, P.
B.ROCKFORD,ILL.
1884 WAS U S   1   .000

MORRIS, WALTER EDWARD (BIG ED)
B.DEC.7,1899 FOSHEE,ALA.
D.MAR.3,1932 CENTURY,FLA.
1922 CHI N P   5   0- 0
1928 BOS A P   47 19-15
1929 BOS A P   33 14-14
1930 BOS A P   18   4- 9
1931 BOS A P   37   5- 7
        BRTR   140 42-45

MORRIS, WILLIAM G.
[SEE JOHN L. FLUHRER]

MORRISETTE, WILLIAM LEE
B.JAN.17,1893 BALTIMORE,MD.
D.MAR.25,1966 VIRGINIA BEACH,VA
1915 PHI A P   1   2- 0
1916 PHI A P   1   0- 0
1920 DET A P   8   1- 1
        BRTR   13   3- 1

MORRISON, JAMES FORREST (JIM)
B.SEPT.23,1952 PENSACOLA,FLA.
1977 PHI N /3   5   .429
1978 PHI N 2/3-0   53   .157
        BRTR   58   .174

MORRISON, JOHN DEWEY
(JUGHANDLE JOHNNY)
B.OCT.22,1895 PELLVILLE,KY.
D.MAR.20,1966 LOUISVILLE,KY.
1920 PIT N P   2   1- 0
1921 PIT N P   21   9- 7
1922 PIT N P   45 17-11
1923 PIT N P   42 25-13
1924 PIT N P   41 11-16
1925 PIT N P   44 17-14
1926 PIT N P   26   6- 8
1927 PIT N P   21   3- 2
1929 BRO N P   39 13- 7
1930 BRO N P   16   1- 2
        BRTR   297 103-80

MORRISON, JONATHAN W.
B.1859 PORT HURON,MICH.
1884 IND AA O   43 .256
1887 MET AA O   9 .231
                        52 .252

MORRISON, MICHAEL
B.FEB.6,1867 ERIE,PA.
D.JUNE 16,1955 ERIE,PA.
1887 CLE AA P   41 15-26
1888 CLE AA P   4   1- 3
1890 SYR AA P-O   15   32   7- 8
                             .238
        BAL AA P   4   1- 3
        BRTR   64   81 24-40
                             .234

MORRISON, PHILIP MELVIN
B.OCT.18,1894 ROCKPORT,IND.
D.JAN.18,1955 LEXINGTON,KY.
1921 PIT N P   1   0- 0
        BBTR

MORRISON, STEPHEN HENRY (HANK)
B.MAY 22,1866 OLNEYVILLE,R.I.
D.SEPT.30,1927 ATTLEBORO,MASS.
1887 IND N P   8   3- 5
        BRTR

MORRISON, THOMAS J.
B.1861
1895 LOU N S-3   5   .272
1896 LOU N 3   8   .107
                        13   .208

MORRISON, WALTER GUY
B.AUG.29,1895 HINTON,W.VA.
D.AUG.14,1934 GRAND RAPIDS,MICH
1927 BOS N P   11   1- 2
1928 BOS N P   1   0- 0
        BRTR   12   1- 2

MORRISSEY, FRANK FREDERICK (DEACON)
B.BALTIMORE,MD.
1901 BOS A P   1   0- 0
1902 CHI N P-3   5   7   1- 3
                             .090
                     6   8   1- 3
                             .080

MORRISSEY, JOHN ALBERT
(JACK) OR (KING)
B.MAY 2,1876 LANSING,MICH.
D.OCT.30,1936 LANSING,MICH.
1902 CIN N 2-O   12 .289
1903 CIN N 2-S   27 .247
        BBTR   39 .254

MORRISSEY, JOHN H.
D.APR.29,1884 JANESVILLE,WIS.
B.APR.29,1884
1881 BUF N 3   12 .191
1882 DET N 3   14 .286
                            .204

MORRISSEY, JOSEPH ANSELM (JO-JO)
B.JAN.16,1904 WARREN,R.I.
D.MAY 2,1950 WORCESTER,MASS.
1932 CIN N 2-S-3   89 .242
1933 CIN N 2-S-3   148 .230
1936 CHI A 2-S-3   17 .184
        BRTR   254 .232

MORRISSEY, THOMAS J.
B.1861 JANESVILLE,WIS.
D.SEPT.23,1941 JANESVILLE,WIS.
1884 MIL U 3   12 .174

MORROW, ROBERT
B.SEPT.27,1838 ENGLAND
D.FEB.6,1898
NON-PLAYING MANAGER PRO[N] 1881

MORSE, JACOB CHARLES
B.JUNE 7,1860 CONCORD,MASS.
D.APR.12,1937 BROOKLINE,MASS.
NON-PLAYING MANAGER BOS[U] 1884

MORSE, NEWELL OBEDIAH (BUD)
B.SEPT.4,1904 BERKELEY,CAL.
1929 PHI A 2   8   .074
        BLTR

MORSE, PETER RAYMOND (PETE) OR (HAP)
B.DEC.6,1886 ST.PAUL,MINN.
D.JUNE 19,1974 ST.PAUL,MINN.
1911 STL N S-O   4   .000
        BRTR

MORTON, CARL WENDLE
B.JAN.18,1944 KANSAS CITY,MO.
1969 MON N /P   8   0- 3
1970 MON N P   43 18-11
1971 MON N P   36 10-18
1972 MON N P   27   35   7-13
1973 ATL N P   38   40 15-10
1974 ATL N P   38 16-12
1975 ATL N P   39 17-16
1976 ATL N P   26   27   4- 9
        BRTR   255 266 87-92

MORTON, CHARLES HAZEN
B.OCT.12,1854 KINGSVILLE,OHIO
D.DEC.9,1921 MASSILLON,OHIO
1882 PIT AA 2-S-3-0   23 .278
        STL AA 2-O   9 .059
1884 TOL AA M-P-   1   31   0- 1
             3-O   .188
1885 DET N M-S-3   22 .177
        TR   1   85   0- 1
                             .199

MORTON, GUY JR. (MOOSE)
B.NOV.4,1930 TUSCALOOSA,ALA.
1954 BOS A H   1   .000
        BRTR

MORTON, GUY SR. (GUY)
OR (THE ALABAMA BLOSSOM)
B.JUNE 1,1893 VERNON,ALA.
D.OCT.18,1934 SHEFFIELD,ALA.
1914 CLE A P   25   1-13
1915 CLE A P   34 15-15
1916 CLE A P   27 12- 8
1917 CLE A P   35 10-10
1918 CLE A P   30 14- 8
1919 CLE A P   26   9- 9
1920 CLE A P   29   8- 6
1921 CLE A P   30   8- 3
1922 CLE A P   38 14- 9
1923 CLE A P   33   6- 6
1924 CLE A P   10   0- 1
        BRTR   317 97-88

MORTON, WILLIAM H. (SPARROW)
1884 PHI N P   2   0- 2
        TL

MORTON, WYCLIFFE NATHANIEL (BUBBA)
B.DEC.13,1931 WASHINGTON,D.C.

YR	CL	LEA	POS	GP	G	REC
1961	DET	A	O		77	.287
1962	DET	A	1-O		90	.262
1963	DET	A	1-O		6	.091
	MIL	N	1-O		15	.179
1966	CAL	A	O		15	.220
1967	CAL	A	O		80	.313
1968	CAL	A	O/3		81	.270
1969	CAL	A	O/1		87	.244
	BRTR				451	.267

MORYN, WALTER JOSEPH (WALT) OR (MOOSE)
B.APR.12,1926 ST.PAUL,MINN.

YR	CL	LEA	POS	GP	G	REC
1954	BRO	N	O		48	.275
1955	BRO	N	O		11	.263
1956	CHI	N	O		147	.285
1957	CHI	N	O		149	.289
1958	CHI	N	O		143	.264
1959	CHI	N	O		117	.234
1960	CHI	N	O		38	.294
	STL	N	O		75	.245
1961	STL	N	O		17	.125
	PIT	N	O		40	.200
	BLTR				785	.266

MOSCHITTO, ROSAIRE ALLEN (ROSS)
B.FEB.15,1945 FRESNO,CAL.

YR	CL	LEA	POS	GP	G	REC
1965	NY	A	O		96	.185
1967	NY	A	/O		14	.111
	BRTR				110	.167

MOSELEY, EARL VICTOR (VIC)
B.SEPT.7,1884 MIDDLEBURG,OHIO
D.JULY 1,1963 ALLIANCE,OHIO

YR	CL	LEA	POS	GP	G	REC
1913	BOS	A	P		24	9- 5
1914	IND	F	P		43	19-18
1915	NEW	F	P		38	15-15
1916	CIN	N	P		31	7-10
	BRTR				136	50-48

MOSER, ARNOLD ROBERT
B.AUG.9,1915 HOUSTON,TEX.

YR	CL	LEA	POS	GP	G	REC
1937	CIN	N	H		5	.000
	BRTR					

MOSER, WALTER FREDRICK
B.FEB.27,1881 CONCORD,N.C.
D.DEC.10,1946 PHILADELPHIA,PA.

YR	CL	LEA	POS	GP	G	REC
1906	PHI	N	P		6	0- 3
1911	BOS	A	P		6	0- 1
	STL	A	P		2	0- 1
	BRTR				14	0- 5

MOSES, FELIX I.
B.RICHMOND,VA.
NON-PLAYING MANAGER RIC[AA]1884

MOSES, GERALD BRAHEEN (JERRY)
B.AUG.9,1946 YAZOO CITY,MISS.

YR	CL	LEA	POS	GP	G	REC
1965	BOS	A	/H		4	.250
1968	BOS	A	/C		6	.333
1969	BOS	A	C		53	.304
1970	BOS	A	C/O		92	.263
1971	CAL	A	C/O		69	.227
1972	CLE	A	C/1		52	.220
1973	NY	A	C		21	.254
1974	DET	A	C		74	.237
1975	SD	N	/C		13	.158
	CHI	A	/1		2	.500
	BRTR				386	.251

MOSES, WALLACE (WALLY)
B.OCT.8,1910 UVALDA,GA.

YR	CL	LEA	POS	GP	G	REC
1935	PHI	A	O		85	.325
1936	PHI	A	O		146	.345
1937	PHI	A	O		154	.320
1938	PHI	A	O		142	.307
1939	PHI	A	O		115	.307
1940	PHI	A	O		142	.309
1941	PHI	A	O		116	.301
1942	CHI	A	O		146	.270
1943	CHI	A	O		150	.245
1944	CHI	A	O		136	.280
1945	CHI	A	O		140	.295
1946	CHI	A	O		56	.274
	BOS	A	O		48	.206
1947	BOS	A	O		90	.275
1948	BOS	A	O		78	.259
1949	PHI	A	O		110	.276
1950	PHI	A	O		88	.264
1951	PHI	A	O		70	.191
	BLTL				2012	.291

MOSKAU, PAUL RICHARD
B.DEC.20,1953 ST.JOSEPH,MO.

YR	CL	LEA	POS	GP	G	REC
1977	CIN	N	P	20	22	6- 6
1978	CIN	N	P	26	29	6- 4
	BRTR			46	51	12-10

MOSKIMAN, WILLIAM BANKHEAD (DOC)
B.DEC.20,1879 OAKLAND,CAL.
D.JAN.11,1953 SAN LEANDRO,CAL.

YR	CL	LEA	POS	GP	G	REC
1910	BOS	A	P-1	1	5	0- 0
			O			.111
	BRTR					

MOSOLF, JAMES FREDERICK
B.AUG.21,1905 PUYALLUP,WASH.

YR	CL	LEA	POS	GP	G	REC
1929	PIT	N	O		8	.462
1930	PIT	N	P-O	1	40	0- 0
						.333
1931	PIT	N	O		39	.250
1933	CHI	N	O		31	.268
	BLTR			1	118	0- 0
						.295

MOSS, CHARLES CROSBY
B.MAR.20,1911 MERIDIAN,MISS.

YR	CL	LEA	POS	GP	G	REC
1934	PHI	A	C		10	.200
1935	PHI	A	C		4	.333
1936	PHI	A	C		33	.250
	BRTR				47	.246

MOSS, CHARLES MALCOLM (MAL)
B.APR.18,1905 SULLIVAN,IND.

YR	CL	LEA	POS	GP	G	REC
1930	CHI	N	P		12	0- 0
	BRTL					

MOSS, HOWARD GLENN
B.OCT.17,1919 GASTONIA,N.C.

YR	CL	LEA	POS	GP	G	REC
1942	NY	N	O		7	.000
1946	CIN	N	O		7	.192
	CLE	A	3		8	.063
	BRTR				22	.097

MOSS, JOHN LESTER (LES)
B.MAY 14,1925 TULSA,OKLA.

YR	CL	LEA	POS	GP	G	REC
1946	STL	A	C		12	.371
1947	STL	A	C		96	.157
1948	STL	A	C		107	.257
1949	STL	A	C		97	.291
1950	STL	A	C		84	.266
1951	STL	A	C		16	.170
	BOS	A	C		71	.198
1952	STL	A	C		52	.246
1953	STL	A	C		78	.276
1954	BAL	A	C		50	.246
1955	BAL	A	C		29	.339
	CHI	A	C		32	.254
1956	CHI	A	C		56	.244
1957	CHI	A	C		42	.270
1958	CHI	A	H		2	.000
	BRTR				824	.247

NON-PLAYING MANAGER
CHI[A] 1968 [INTERIM]

MOSS, RAYMOND EARL
B.DEC.5,1901 CHATTANOOGA,TENN.

YR	CL	LEA	POS	GP	G	REC
1926	BRO	N	P		1	0- 0
1927	BRO	N	P		1	1- 0
1928	BRO	N	P	22	24	0- 3
1929	BRO	N	P	39	42	11- 6
1930	BRO	N	P		36	9- 6
1931	BRO	N	P		1	0- 0
	BOS	N	P		12	1- 3
	BRTR			112	117	22-18

MOSSI, DONALD LOUIS (DON) OR (THE SPHINX)
B.JAN.11,1929 ST.HELENA,CAL.

YR	CL	LEA	POS	GP	G	REC
1954	CLE	A	P		40	6- 1
1955	CLE	A	P		57	4- 3
1956	CLE	A	P		48	6- 5
1957	CLE	A	P		36	11-10
1958	CLE	A	P		43	7- 8
1959	DET	A	P	34	36	17- 9
1960	DET	A	P		23	9- 8
1961	DET	A	P		35	15- 7
1962	DET	A	P	35	36	11-13
1963	DET	A	P		24	7- 7
1964	CHI	A	P		34	3- 1
1965	KC	A	P		51	5- 8
	BLTL			460	463	101-80

MOSSOR, EARL DALTON
B.JULY 21,1925 FORBES,TENN.

YR	CL	LEA	POS	GP	G	REC
1951	BRO	N	P		3	0- 0
	BLTR					

MOSTIL, JOHN ANTHONY (JOHNNY) OR (BANANAS)
B.JUNE 1,1896 CHICAGO,ILL.
D.DEC.10,1970 MIDLOTHIAN,ILL.

YR	CL	LEA	POS	GP	G	REC
1918	CHI	A	2		10	.273
1921	CHI	A	O		100	.304
1922	CHI	A	O		132	.304
1923	CHI	A	O		153	.291
1924	CHI	A	O		118	.325
1925	CHI	A	O		153	.299
1926	CHI	A	O		148	.328
1927	CHI	A	O		13	.125
1928	CHI	A	O		133	.270
1929	CHI	A	O		12	.229
	BRTR				972	.301

**MOTA, JOSE ANTONIO [BAEZ]
[PLAYED UNDER NAME OF
JOSE ANTONIO BAEZ]**

MOTA, MANUEL RAFAEL [GERONIMO] (MANNY)
B.FEB.18,1938 SANTO DOMINGO,D.R.

YR	CL	LEA	POS	GP	G	REC
1962	SF	N	2-3-O		47	.176
1963	PIT	N	2-O		59	.270
1964	PIT	N	C-2-O		115	.277
1965	PIT	N	O		121	.279
1966	PIT	N	O/3		116	.332
1967	PIT	N	O/3		120	.321
1968	PIT	N	O/2-3		111	.281
1969	MON	N	O		31	.315
	LA	N	O		85	.323
1970	LA	N	*O/3		124	.305
1971	LA	N	O		91	.312
1972	LA	N	O		118	.323
1973	LA	N	O		89	.314
1974	LA	N	/O		66	.281
1975	LA	N	/O		52	.265
1976	LA	N	/O		50	.288
1977	LA	N	/O		49	.395
1978	LA	N	H		37	.303
	BRTR				1481	.303

MOTT, ELISHA MATTHEW (BITSY)
B.JUNE 12,1918 ARCADIA,FLA.

YR	CL	LEA	POS	GP	G	REC
1945	PHI	N	2-S-3		90	.222
	BRTR					

MOTTON, CURTELL HOWARD (CURT)
B.SEP.24,1940 DARNELL,LA.

YR	CL	LEA	POS	GP	G	REC
1967	BAL	A	O		27	.200
1968	BAL	A	O		83	.198
1969	BAL	A	O		56	.303
1970	BAL	A	O		52	.226
1971	BAL	A	O		38	.189
1972	MIL	A	/O		6	.167
	CAL	A	/O		42	.154
1973	BAL	A	/O		5	.333
1974	BAL	A	/O		7	.000
	BRTR				316	.213

MOTZ, FRANK H.
B.OCT.1,1869 FREEBURG,PA.

YR	CL	LEA	POS	GP	G	REC
1890	PHI	N	1		1	.000
1893	CIN	N	1		42	.267
1894	CIN	N	1		18	.204
					61	.244

MOULDER, GLEN HUBERT
B.SEPT.28,1917 CLEVELAND,OKLA.

YR	CL	LEA	POS	GP	G	REC
1946	BRO	N	P		1	0- 0
1947	STL	A	P		32	4- 2
1948	CHI	A	P		33	3- 6
	BRTR				66	7- 8

MOULTON, ALBERT THEODORE (ALLIE)
B.JAN.16,1886 MEDWAY,MASS.
D.SEPT.10,1968 PEABODY,MASS.

YR	CL	LEA	POS	GP	G	REC
1911	STL	A	2		4	.067
	BRTR					

MOUNTAIN, FRANK HENRY
B.MAY 17,1860 FT.EDWARD,N.Y.
D.NOV.19,1939 SCHENECTADY,N.Y.

YR	CL	LEA	POS	GP	G	REC
1880	TRO	N	P		2	1- 1
1881	DET	N	P		7	3- 4
1882	WOR	N	P		5	0- 5
	ATH	AA	P-O	8	9	2- 6
						.308
	WOR	N	P-1-	18	20	2-11
			O			.264
1883	COL	AA	P-O	60	71	26-33
						2.16
1884	COL	AA	P-O	43	58	24-17
						.237
1885	PIT	AA	P		5	1- 4
1886	PIT	AA	P-1	2	18	0- 2
						.148
	TR			150	195	59-83
						.221

MOUNTJOY, WILLIAM R. (MEDICINE BILL)
B.1857 PORT HURON,MICH.
D.MAY 19,1934 LONDON,ONT.,CAN.

YR	CL	LEA	POS	GP	G	REC
1883	CIN	AA	P		1	0- 1
1884	CIN	AA	P-O	32	34	20-12
						.171
1885	CIN	AA	P		17	10- 7
	BAL	AA	P-O	6	7	2- 4
						.063
				56	59	32-24
						.157

MOWE, RAYMOND BENJAMIN
B.JULY 12,1889 ROCHESTER,IND.
D.AUG.14,1968 SARASOTA,FLA.

YR	CL	LEA	POS	GP	G	REC
1913	BRO	N	S		5	.111
	BLTR					

MOWREY, HARRY HARLAN (MIKE)
B.APR.20,1884 BROWNS MILL,PA.
D.MAR.20,1947 CHAMBERSBURG,PA.

YR	CL	LEA	POS	GP	G	REC
1905	CIN	N	3		7	.266
1906	CIN	N	3		17	.321
1907	CIN	N	3		138	.252
1908	CIN	N	3		63	.220
1909	CIN	N	3		35	.191
	STL	N	3		8	.241
1910	STL	N	3		141	.282
1911	STL	N	3		135	.267
1912	STL	N	3		114	.255
1913	STL	N	3		132	.260
1914	PIT	N	3		79	.254
1915	PIT	F	3		151	.282
1916	BRO	N	3		144	.244
1917	BRO	N	3		83	.214
	BRTR				1247	.251

MOWRY, JOSEPH ALOYSIUS
B.APR.6,1908 ST.LOUIS,MO.

YR	CL	LEA	POS	GP	G	REC
1933	BOS	N	O		86	.221
1934	BOS	N	O		25	.215
1935	BOS	N	O		81	.265
	BBTR				192	.233

MOYER, CHARLES EDWARD
B.AUG.15,1885 ANDOVER,OHIO

YR	CL	LEA	POS	GP	G	REC
1910	WAS	A	P		6	0-3

MOYNAHAN, MICHAEL
B.1860 CHICAGO,ILL.

YR	CL	LEA	POS	GP	G	REC
1880	BUF	N	S		27	.296
1881	CLE	N	3-O		33	.225
	DET	N	3		2	.333
1883	ATH	AA	S		93	.283
1884	ATH	AA	S		1	.000
	CLE	N	2-S-O		12	.304
	BL				168	.285

MROZINSKI, RONALD FRANK (RON)
B.SEPT.16,1930 WHITE HAVEN,PA.

YR	CL	LEA	POS	GP	G	REC
1954	PHI	N	P		15	1-1
1955	PHI	N	P		22	0-2
	BRTL				37	1-3

MUDROCK, PHILIP RAY (PHIL)
B.JUNE 12,1937 LOUISVILLE,COLO.

YR	CL	LEA	POS	GP	G	REC
1963	CHI	N	P		1	0-0
	BRTR					

MUELLER, CLARENCE FRANCIS (HEINIE)
B.SEPT.16,1899 CREVE COEUR,MO.
D.JAN.23,1975 DE SOTO,MO.

YR	CL	LEA	POS	GP	G	REC
1920	STL	N	O		4	.318
1921	STL	N	O		55	.352
1922	STL	N	O		61	.270
1923	STL	N	O		78	.343
1924	STL	N	1-O		92	.264
1925	STL	N	O		78	.313
1926	STL	N	O		52	.267
	NY	N	O		85	.249
1927	NY	N	O		84	.289
1928	BOS	N	O		42	.225
1929	BOS	N	O		46	.204
1935	STL	A	1-O		16	.185
	BLTL				693	.282

MUELLER, DONALD FREDERICK (DON)
OR (MANDRAKE THE MAGICIAN)
B.APR.14,1927 ST.LOUIS,MO.

YR	CL	LEA	POS	GP	G	REC
1948	NY	N	O		36	.358
1949	NY	N	O		51	.232
1950	NY	N	O		132	.291
1951	NY	N	O		122	.277
1952	NY	N	O		126	.281
1953	NY	N	O		131	.333
1954	NY	N	O		153	.342
1955	NY	N	O		147	.306
1956	NY	N	O		138	.269
1957	NY	N	O		135	.258
1958	CHI	A	O		70	.253
1959	CHI	A	H		4	.500
	BLTR				1245	.296

MUELLER, EMMETT JEROME (HEINIE)
B.JULY 20,1912 ST.LOUIS,MO.

YR	CL	LEA	POS	GP	G	REC
1938	PHI	N	2-3		136	.250
1939	PHI	N	2-3-O		115	.279
1940	PHI	N	1-2-3-O		97	.247
1941	PHI	N	2-3-O		93	.227
	BBTR				441	.253

MUELLER, JOSEPH GORDON (GORDIE)
B.DEC.10,1922 BALTIMORE,MD.

YR	CL	LEA	POS	GP	G	REC
1950	BOS	A	P		8	0-0
	BRTR					

MUELLER, LESLIE CLYDE
B.MAR.4,1919 BELLEVILLE,ILL.

YR	CL	LEA	POS	GP	G	REC
1941	DET	A	P		4	0-0
1945	DET	A	P		26	6-8
	BRTR				30	6-8

MUELLER, RAY COLEMAN
(RAY) OR (IRON MAN)
B.MAR.20,1912 PITTSBURG,KAN.

YR	CL	LEA	POS	GP	G	REC
1935	BOS	N	C		42	.227
1936	BOS	N	C		24	.197
1937	BOS	N	C		64	.251
1938	BOS	N	C		83	.237
1939	PIT	N	C		86	.233
1940	PIT	N	C		4	.333
1943	CIN	N	C		141	.260
1944	CIN	N	C		155	.286
1946	CIN	N	C		114	.254
1947	CIN	N	C		71	.250
1948	CIN	N	C		14	.206
1949	CIN	N	C		32	.274
	NY	N	C		56	.224
1950	NY	N	C		4	.091
	PIT	N	C		67	.269
1951	BOS	N	C		28	.157
	BRTR				985	.252

MUELLER, WALTER JOHN
B.DEC.6,1894 CENTRAL,MO.
D.AUG.16,1971 ST.LOUIS,MO.

YR	CL	LEA	POS	GP	G	REC
1922	PIT	N	O		32	.270
1923	PIT	N	O		40	.306
1924	PIT	N	O		30	.260
1926	PIT	N	O		19	.242
	BRTR				121	.275

MUELLER, WILLARD LAWRENCE (WILLIE)
B.AUG.30,1956 WEST BEND,WIS.

YR	CL	LEA	POS	GP	G	REC
1978	MIL	A	/P		5	1-0
	BRTR					

MUELLER, WILLIAM LAWRENCE (HAWK)
B.NOV.9,1920 BAY CITY,MICH.

YR	CL	LEA	POS	GP	G	REC
1942	CHI	A	O		26	.165
1945	CHI	A	O		13	.000
	BRTR				39	.149

MUFFETT, BILLY ARNOLD
(BILLY) OR (MUFF)
B.SEPT.21,1930 HAMMOND,IND.

YR	CL	LEA	POS	GP	G	REC
1957	STL	N	P		23	3-2
1958	STL	N	P		35	4-6
1959	SF	N	P		5	0-0
1960	BOS	A	P		23	6-4
1961	BOS	A	P		38	3-11
1962	BOS	A	P		1	0-0
	BRTR				125	16-23

MUICH, IGNATIUS ANDREW (JOE)
B.NOV.23,1903 ST.LOUIS,MO.

YR	CL	LEA	POS	GP	G	REC
1924	BOS	N	P		3	0-0
	BRTR					

MUIR, JOSEPH ALLEN
B.NOV.26,1922 ORIOLE,MO.

YR	CL	LEA	POS	GP	G	REC
1951	PIT	N	P		9	0-2
1952	PIT	N	P		12	2-3
	BLTL				21	2-5

MULCAHY, HUGH NOYES (HUGH)
OR (LOSING PITCHER)
B.SEPT.9,1913 BRIGHTON,MASS.

YR	CL	LEA	POS	GP	G	REC
1935	PHI	N	P-O	18	19	1-5
						.000
1936	PHI	N	P		3	1-1
1937	PHI	N	P		56	8-18
1938	PHI	N	P	46	47	10-20
1939	PHI	N	P		38	9-16
1940	PHI	N	P	36	37	13-22
1945	PHI	N	P		5	1-3
1946	PHI	N	P		16	2-4
1947	PIT	N	P		2	0-0
	BRTR			220	223	45-89
						.165

MULDOON, MICHAEL
B.HARTFORD,CONN.

YR	CL	LEA	POS	GP	G	REC
1882	CLE	N	3-O		82	.252
1883	CLE	N	3		95	.224
1884	CLE	N	2-3-O		109	.239
1885	BAL	AA	3		103	.250
1886	BAL	AA	2-3		101	.205
	BL				490	.235

MULLANE, ANTHONY JOHN
(TONY) OR (COUNT)
OR (THE APOLLO OF THE BOX)
B.JAN.20,1859 CORK,IRELAND
D.APR.26,1944 CHICAGO,ILL.

YR	CL	LEA	POS	GP	G	REC
1881	DET	N	P		5	1-4
1882	LOU	AA	P-1-2-O	55	77	31-23
						.255
1883	STL	AA	P-1-2-O	52	77	35-17
						.201
1884	TOL	AA	P-1-O	66	95	36-26
						.276
1886	CIN	AA	P-1-2-S-O	71	103	31-27
						.228
1887	CIN	AA	P-O	51	61	31-17
						.284
1888	CIN	AA	P-1-2-O	44	51	27-16
						.251
1889	CIN	AA	P-1-3-O	29	62	11-8
						.307
1890	CIN	N	P-3-O	22	81	12-10
						.276
1891	CIN	N	P	49	61	24-23
1892	CIN	N	P		34	20-14
1893	CIN	N	P		16	7-7
	BAL	N	P		38	12-15
1894	BAL	N	P		14	7-6
	CLE	N	P		8	2-1
	BBTB			554	783	287-214
						.250

BL 1882

MULLEAVY, GREGORY THOMAS (MOE)
B.SEPT.25,1905 DETROIT,MICH.

YR	CL	LEA	POS	GP	G	REC
1930	CHI	A	S		77	.263
1932	CHI	A	2		1	.000
1933	BOS	A	H		1	.000
	BRTR				79	.260

MULLEN

YR	CL	LEA	POS	GP	G	REC
1872	CLE	NA	O		1	.667

MULLEN, CHARLES GEORGE
B.MAR.15,1889 SEATTLE,WASH.
D.JUNE 6,1963 SEATTLE,WASH.

YR	CL	LEA	POS	GP	G	REC
1910	CHI	A	1		41	.195
1911	CHI	A	1		20	.203
1914	NY	A	1		93	.260
1915	NY	A	1		40	.267
1916	NY	A	1-2		59	.267
	BRTR				253	.247

MULLEN, FORD PARKER (MOON)
B.FEB.9,1917 OLYMPIA,WASH.

YR	CL	LEA	POS	GP	G	REC
1944	PHI	N	2-3		118	.267
	BLTR					

MULLEN, WILLIAM JOHN (BILLY)
B.JAN.23,1896 ST.LOUIS,MO.
D.MAY 4,1971 ST.LOUIS,MO.

YR	CL	LEA	POS	GP	G	REC
1920	STL	A	2		2	.000
1921	STL	A	3		4	.000
1923	BRO	N	3		11	.273
1926	DET	A	3		11	.077
1928	STL	A	3		15	.389
	BRTR				36	.220

MULLER, FREDERICK WILLIAM
B.DEC.21,1907 NEWARK,CAL.
D.OCT.20,1976 DAVIS,CAL.

YR	CL	LEA	POS	GP	G	REC
1933	BOS	A	2		15	.188
1934	BOS	A	2-3		2	.000
	BRTR				17	.184

MULLER, JOHN

YR	CL	LEA	POS	GP	G	REC
1874	ATH	NA	C		4	-
1876	ATH	N	C		1	.000
	BLTL				5	-

MULLIGAN

YR	CL	LEA	POS	GP	G	REC
1884	WAS	U	3		1	.000

MULLIGAN, EDWARD JOSEPH (BIG JOE)
B.AUG.27,1894 ST.LOUIS,MO.

YR	CL	LEA	POS	GP	G	REC
1915	CHI	N	S-3		11	.363
1916	CHI	N	S		58	.153
1921	CHI	A	3		152	.251
1922	CHI	A	3		103	.234
1928	PIT	N	2-3		27	.233
	BRTR				351	.232

MULLIGAN, JOSEPH IGNATIUS
B.JULY 31,1913 E.WEYMOUTH,MASS.

YR	CL	LEA	POS	GP	G	REC
1934	BOS	A	P		14	1-0
	BRTR					

MULLIGAN, RICHARD CHARLES
B.MAR.18,1918 WILKES-BARRE,PA.

YR	CL	LEA	POS	GP	G	REC
1941	WAS	A	P		1	0-1
1946	PHI	N	P		19	2-2
	BOS	N	P		4	1-0
1947	BOS	N	P		1	0-0
	BLTL				25	3-3

YR CL LEA POS   GP   G   REC

MULLIN, GEORGE JOSEPH (GEORGE)
OR (WABASH GEORGE)
B.JULY 4,1880 TOLEDO,OHIO
D.JAN.7,1944 WABASH,IND.
```
1902 DET A  P-O   33   37  14-15
                             .328
1903 DET A  P     40   46  19-14
1904 DET A  P     45   52  16-24
1905 DET A  P     44   47  22-18
1906 DET A  P-2   40   50  21-18
     O                       .225
1907 DET A  P-1   47   70  20-20
                             .217
1908 DET A  P     38   55  17-12
1909 DET A  P     40   52  29- 8
1910 DET A  P     38   50  21-12
1911 DET A  P     30   40  18-10
1912 DET A  P     30   37  12-17
1913 DET A  P          12   2- 7
     WAS A  P      6   12   2- 4
1914 IND F  P     36   40  14-10
1915 NEW F  P           6   2- 2
       BLTR      485  606 229-191
                             .262
```

MULLIN, HENRY
B.BOSTON,MASS.
```
1884 WAS AA O     34  .139
     BOS U  O      2  .000
                  36  .131
```

MULLIN, JAMES HENRY
B.OCT.16,1883 NEW YORK,N.Y.
D.JAN.24,1925 PHILADELPHIA,PA.
```
1904 PHI A  1     26  .415
     WAS A  2     26  .168
     PHI A  2     17  .157
1905 WAS A  2     49  .190
       TR        118  .197
```

MULLIN, PATRICK JOSEPH (PAT)
B.NOV.1,1917 TROTTER,PA.
```
1940 DET A  O      4  .000
1941 DET A  O     54  .345
1946 DET A  O     93  .246
1947 DET A  O    116  .256
1948 DET A  O    138  .288
1949 DET A  O    104  .268
1950 DET A  O     69  .218
1951 DET A  O    110  .281
1952 DET A  O     97  .251
1953 DET A  O     79  .268
       BLTR      864  .271
```

MULLINIKS, STEVEN RANCE (RANCE)
B.JAN.15,1956 TULARE,CAL.
```
1977 CAL A  S     78  .269
1978 CAL A  S     50  .185
       BLTR      128  .244
```

MULRENAN, DOMINIC JOSEPH
B.DEC.18,1893 WOBURN,MASS.
D.JULY 27,1964 MELROSE,MASS.
```
1921 CHI A  P     12   2- 8
        TR
```

MULRONEY, FRANCIS JOSEPH
B.APR.8,1903 MALLARD,IOWA
```
1930 BOS A  P      2   0- 1
        BRTR
```

MULVEY, JOSEPH H.
B.OCT.27,1858 PROVIDENCE,R.I.
D.AUG.21,1928 PHILADELPHIA,PA.
```
1883 PRO N  2-S    4  .053
     PHI N  3      3  .500
1884 PHI N  3     99  .229
1885 PHI N  3    106  .268
1886 PHI N  3    105  .267
1887 PHI N  3    109  .317
1888 PHI N  3     99  .215
1889 PHI N  3    129  .288
1890 PHI P  3    120  .291
1891 ATH AA 3    112  .247
1892 PHI N  3     25  .142
1893 WAS N  3     55  .242
1895 BRO N  3     13  .327
       BRTR      979  .266
```

MUMPHREY, JERRY WAYNE
B.SEPT.9,1952 TYLER,TEX.
```
1974 STL N  /O     5  .000
1975 STL N  /O    11  .375
1976 STL N  /O   112  .258
1977 STL N  *O   145  .287
1978 STL N  *O   125  .262
       BBTR      398  .271
```

MUNCE, JOHN L. (BIG JOHN)
B.PHILADELPHIA,PA.
```
1884 WIL U  O      7  .190
```

MUNCH, JACOB FERDINAND
B.NOV.16,1890 MORTON,PA.
D.JUNE 8,1966 LANSDOWNE,PA.
```
1918 PHI A  1     22  .267
        BLTL
```

MUNCRIEF, ROBERT CLEVELAND (BOB)
B.JAN.28,1916 MADILL,OKLA.
```
1937 STL A  P          1   0- 0
1939 STL A  P          2   0- 0
1941 STL A  P     36  13- 9
1942 STL A  P     24   6- 8
1943 STL A  P     35  13-12
1944 STL A  P     33  13- 8
1945 STL A  P     27  28  13- 4
1946 STL A  P     29   3-12
1947 STL A  P     31   8-14
1948 CLE A  P     21   5- 4
1949 PIT N  P     13   1- 5
     CHI N  P     34   5- 6
1951 NY  A  P          2   0- 0
       BRTR      288 289  80-82
```

MUNDINGER, GEORGE
B.NEW ORLEANS,LA.
```
1884 IND AA C      3  .200
```

MUNDY, WILLIAM EDWARD
B.JUNE 28,1889 SALINEVILLE,OHIO
D.SEPT.23,1958 KALAMAZOO,MICH.
```
1913 BOS A  1     17  .255
        BLTL
```

MUNGER, GEORGE DAVID (RED)
B.OCT.4,1918 HOUSTON,TEX.
```
1943 STL N  P     32   9- 5
1944 STL N  P     21  11- 3
1946 STL N  P     10   2- 2
1947 STL N  P     40  16- 5
1948 STL N  P     39  10-11
1949 STL N  P     35  15- 8
1950 STL N  P     32   7- 8
1951 STL N  P     23   4- 6
1952 STL N  P      1   0- 1
     PIT N  P      5   0- 3
1956 PIT N  P     35   3- 4
       BRTR      273  77-56
```

MUNGO, VAN LINGLE
B.JUNE 8,1911 PAGELAND,S.C.
```
1931 BRO N  P          5   3- 1
1932 BRO N  P     39  13-11
1933 BRO N  P     41  16-15
1934 BRO N  P     45   46  18-16
1935 BRO N  P     37   44  16-10
1936 BRO N  P     45   50  18-19
1937 BRO N  P     25   28   9-11
1938 BRO N  P     24   32   4-11
1939 BRO N  P     14   29   4- 5
1940 BRO N  P      7    8   1- 0
1941 BRO N  P          2   0- 0
1942 NY  N  P          9   1- 2
1943 NY  N  P     45   49   3- 7
1945 NY  N  P     26   28  14- 7
       BRTR      364  410 120-115
```

MUNIZ, MANUEL [RODRIGUEZ] (MANNY)
B.DEC.31,1947 CAGUAS,P.R.
```
1971 PHI N  /P     5   0- 1
        BRTR
```

MUNN
```
1875 ATL NA 2      1    -
```

MUNNS, LESLIE ERNEST
(BIG ED) OR (NEMO)
B.DEC.1,1908 FORT BRAGG,CAL.
```
1934 BRO N  P     33   34   3- 7
1935 BRO N  P     21   22   1- 3
1936 STL N  P      7    8   0- 3
       BRTR       61   64   4-13
```

MUNSON, CLARENCE HANFORD (RED)
B.JULY 31,1883 CINCINNATI,OHIO
DECEASED
```
1905 PHI N  C      9  .222
        TR
```

MUNSON, JOSEPH MARTIN NAPOLEON
[REAL NAME
JOSEPH MARTIN NAPOLEON CARLSON]
B.NOV.6,1899 RENOVO,PA.
```
1925 CHI N  O      9  .371
1926 CHI N  O     33  .257
        BLTR      42  .287
```

MUNSON, THURMAN LEE
B.JUNE 7,1947 AKRON,OHIO
```
1969 NY  A  C          26  .256
1970 NY  A  *C        132  .302
1971 NY  A  *C/O      125  .251
1972 NY  A  *C        140  .280
1973 NY  A  *C        147  .301
1974 NY  A  *C        144  .261
1975 NY  A  *C-O/1-O-3 157  .318
1976 NY  A  *C-O      152  .302
1977 NY  A  *C-O      149  .308
1978 NY  A  *C-O-O    154  .297
       BRTR          1326  .292
```

MUNYAN, JOHN B.
B.NOV.14,1860 CHESTER,PA.
D.FEB.18,1945 ENDICOTT,N.Y.
```
1887 CLE AA O     16  .276
1890 COL AA O      2  .167
     STL AA C     94  .270
1891 STL AA C     59  .234
                 171  .261
```

MURA, STEPHEN ANDREW (STEVE)
B.FEB.12,1955 NEW ORLEANS,LA.
```
1978 SD  N  /P     5   0- 2
        BRTR
```

MURAKAMI, MASANORI
B.MAY 6,1944 OTSUKI,JAPAN
```
1964 SF  N  P      9   1- 0
1965 SF  N  P     45   4- 1
        BLTL      54   5- 1
```

MURCER, BOBBY RAY
B.MAY 20,1946 OKLAHOMA CITY,OKLA
```
1965 NY  A  S         11  .243
1966 NY  A  S         21  .174
1969 NY  A  *O-3     152  .259
1970 NY  A  *O       159  .251
1971 NY  A  *O       146  .331
1972 NY  A  *O       153  .292
1973 NY  A  *O       160  .304
1974 NY  A  *O       156  .274
1975 SF  N  *O       147  .298
1976 SF  N  *O       147  .259
1977 CHI N  *O/2-S   154  .265
1978 CHI N  *O       146  .281
        BLTR        1552  .280
```

MURCH, SIMEON AUGUSTUS (SIMMY)
B.NOV.21,1880 CASTINE,ME.
D.JUNE 6,1939 EXETER,N.H.
```
1904 STL N  2-3   13  .137
1905 STL N  2-S    4  .111
1908 BRO N  1      6  .181
        TR        23  .143
```

MURCHISON, THOMAS MALCOLM (TIM)
B.OCT.8,1896 LIBERTY,N.C.
D.OCT.20,1962 LIBERTY,N.C.
```
1917 STL N  P      1   0- 0
1920 CLE A  P      2   0- 0
        BRTL       3   0- 0
```

MURDOCK, WILBUR E.
```
1908 STL N  O     16  .258
```

MURFF, JOHN ROBERT (RED)
B.APR.1,1921 BURLINGTON,TEX.
```
1956 MIL N  P     14   0- 0
1957 MIL N  P     12   2- 2
        BRTR      26   2- 2
```

MURNANE, TIMOTHY HAYES (TIM)
B.JUNE 4,1852 NAUGATUCK,CONN.
D.FEB.13,1917 BOSTON,MASS.
```
1872 MAN NA 1       24  .296
1873 ATH NA 1-2-O   42   -
1874 ATH NA 1-2-O   19   -
1875 PHI NA 1-2-O   68  .285
1876 BOS N  1       69  .275
1877 BOS N  1-O     35  .279
1878 PRO N  1-O     48  .245
1884 BOS U  M-1-O   76  .235
        BLTR       381   -
```

MURPHY, CLARENCE
```
1886 LOU AA O      1  .000
```

MURPHY, CORNELIUS B. (MONK)
OR (RAZZLE DAZZLE)
B.OCT.15,1863 WORCESTER,MASS.
D.AUG.1,1914 WORCESTER,MASS.
```
1884 ALT U  P     14   4- 6
     PHI N  P      3   0- 3
1890 BRO P  P     20   5-10
     BRO AA P     15   3- 9
     BRO P  P      2   0- 0
        TR        54  12-28
```

MURPHY, CORNELIUS DAVID (STONE FACE)
B.NOV.1,1870 NORTHFIELD,MASS.
D.DEC.14,1949 NEW BEDFORD,MASS.
```
1893 CIN N  C      3  .000
1894 CIN N  C      1  .000
        BLTR       4  .000
```

MURPHY, DALE BRYAN
B.MAR.12,1956 PORTLAND,ORE.
```
1976 ATL N  C     19  .262
1977 ATL N  C     18  .316
1978 ATL N  *1-C 151  .226
        BRTR     168  .240
```

```
YR  CL LEA POS    GP    G    REC
```

MURPHY, DANIEL FRANCIS (DANNY)
B.AUG.11,1876 PHILADELPHIA,PA.
D.NOV.22,1955 JERSEY CITY,N.J.
```
1900 NY  N  2          21    .250
1901 NY  N  2           5    .200
1902 PHI A  2          76    .313
1903 PHI A  2         133    .275
1904 PHI A  2         149    .286
1905 PHI A  2         150    .278
1906 PHI A  2         119    .301
1907 PHI A  2         124    .271
1908 PHI A  2-0       142    .265
1909 PHI A  0         149    .281
1910 PHI A  0         151    .300
1911 PHI A  0         141    .329
1912 PHI A  0          36    .323
1913 PHI A  0          40    .322
1914 BRO F  0          50    .311
1915 BRO F  0           5    .166
     BRTR            1491    .290
```

MURPHY, DANIEL FRANCIS (DANNY)
B.AUG.23,1942 BEVERLY,MASS.
```
1960 CHI N  0          31    .120
1961 CHI N  0           4    .385
1962 CHI N  0          14    .200
1969 CHI A  P          17    2- 1
1970 CHI A  P          51    2- 3
     BLTR       68    117    4- 4
                             .177
```

MURPHY, DANIEL JOSEPH (HANDSOME DAN)
B.SEPT.10,1864 BROOKLYN,N.Y.
D.DEC.14,1915 BROOKLYN,N.Y.
```
1892 NY  N  C           8    .115
```

MURPHY, DAVID FRANCIS (DIRTY DAVE)
B.MAY 4,1876 ADAMS,MASS.
D.APR.8,1940 ADAMS,MASS.
```
1905 BOS N  S-3         3    .167
     TR
```

MURPHY, DWAYNE KEITH
B.MAR.18,1955 MERCED,CAL.
```
1978 OAK A  0          60    .192
     BLTR
```

MURPHY, EDWARD J.
B.JAN.22,1877 AUBURN,N.Y.
D.JAN.29,1935 WEEDSPORT,N.Y.
```
1898 PHI N  P           7    1- 3
1901 STL N  P          20   10- 9
1902 STL N  P          19   10- 6
1903 STL N  P    16    24    4- 8
     TR          62    70   25-26
```

MURPHY, EDWARD JOSEPH
B.AUG.23,1918 JOLIET,ILL.
```
1942 PHI N  1          13    .250
     BRTR
```

MURPHY, FRANK J. (TONY)
B.BROOKLYN,N.Y.
```
1884 MET AA C           1    .333
```

MURPHY, FRANK MORTON
B.1880 HACKENSACK,N.J.
D.NOV.2,1912 NEW YORK,N.Y.
```
1901 BOS N  0          45    .271
     NY  N  0          34    .143
                       79    .218
```

MURPHY, HERBERT COURTLAND (DUMMY)
B.DEC.18,1886 OLNEY,ILL.
D.AUG.10,1962 TALLAHASSEE,FLA.
```
1914 PHI N  S           9    .160
     BRTR
```

MURPHY, HOWARD
B.JAN.1,1882 BIRMINGHAM,ALA.
D.SEPT.5,1926 RIVERSIDE,TEX.
```
1909 STL N  0          19    .200
```

MURPHY, JOHN EDWARD (EDDIE)
B.OCT.2,1891 HANCOCK,N.Y.
D.FEB.21,1969 DUNMORE,PA.
```
1912 PHI A  0          33    .317
1913 PHI A  0         136    .295
1914 PHI A  0         148    .272
1915 PHI A  0          60    .231
     CHI A  0          78    .315
1916 CHI A  0          51    .210
1917 CHI A  0          53    .314
1918 CHI A  0          91    .297
1919 CHI A  0          30    .486
1920 CHI A  0          58    .339
1921 CHI A  0           6    .200
1926 PIT N  0          16    .118
     BLTR             760    .287
```

MURPHY, JOHN H.
B.MAR.8,1867 PHILADELPHIA,PA.
```
1884 ALT U  2-0        13    .158
     WIL U  P-2-  7    10    0- 6
           S-3-0             .065
                       23    0- 6
                             .133
```

MURPHY, JOHN JOSEPH (GRANDMA)
FIREMAN(OR)FORDHAM JOHNNY)
B.JULY 14,1908 NEW YORK,N.Y.
D.JAN.14,1970 NEW YORK,N.Y.
```
1932 NY  A  P           2    0- 0
1934 NY  A  P          40   14-10
1935 NY  A  P          40   10- 5
1936 NY  A  P          27    9- 3
1937 NY  A  P          39   13- 4
1938 NY  A  P          32    8- 2
1939 NY  A  P          38    3- 6
1940 NY  A  P          35    8- 4
1941 NY  A  P          35    8- 3
1942 NY  A  P          31    4-10
1943 NY  A  P          37   12- 4
1946 NY  A  P          27    4- 2
1947 BOS A  P          32    0- 0
     BRTR             415   93-53
```

MURPHY, JOHN P. (SOLDIER BOY)
B.1879 NEW HAVEN,CONN.
D.JUNE 1,1914 BAKER,ORE.
```
1902 STL N  3           1    .600
1903 DET A  S           5    .182
                        6    .240
```

MURPHY, JOSEPH AKIN
B.SEPT.7,1866 ST.LOUIS,MO.
D.MAR.28,1951 CORAL GABLES,FLA.
```
1886 CIN AA P           5    2- 3
     STL N  P           4    0- 4
     STL AA P           1    1- 0
1887 STL AA P           1    1- 0
                       11    4- 7
```

MURPHY, LAWRENCE PATRICK
```
1891 WAS AA 0         107    .255
     BL
```

MURPHY, LEO JOSEPH (RED)
B.JAN.7,1889 TERRE HAUTE,IND.
D.AUG.12,1960 RACINE,WIS.
```
1915 PIT N  C          31    .098
     BRTR
```

MURPHY, MICHAEL JEROME
B.AUG.19,1888 FORESTVILLE,PA.
D.OCT.26,1952 JOHNSON CITY,N.Y.
```
1912 STL N  C           1    .000
1916 PHI A  C          14    .107
     BRTR              15    .103
```

MURPHY, MORGAN EDWARD
B.FEB.14,1867 E.PROVIDENCE,R.I.
D.OCT.3,1938 PROVIDENCE,R.I.
```
1890 BOS P  C          60    .238
1891 BOS AA C         107    .218
1892 CIN N  C          69    .192
1893 CIN N  C          56    .234
1894 CIN N  C          76    .268
1895 CIN N  C          22    .272
1896 STL N  C          48    .251
1897 STL N  C          55    .177
1898 PIT N  C           5    .125
     PHI N  C          25    .202
1900 PHI N  C          11    .277
1901 PHI N  C-1         9    .179
     BRTR             543    .221
```

MURPHY, PATRICK J.
B.JAN.2,1857 AUBURN,MASS.
D.MAY 16,1927 WORCESTER,MASS.
```
1887 NY  N  C          16    .245
1888 NY  N  C          28    .169
1889 NY  N  C           8    .280
1890 NY  N  C          32    .235
                       84    .223
```

MURPHY, RICHARD LEE
B.OCT.25,1931 CINCINNATI,OHIO
```
1954 CIN N  H           6    .000
     BLTL
```

MURPHY, ROBERT J.
B.DEC.26,1866 DUTCHESS CO.,N.Y.
```
1890 NY  N  P           3    1- 1
```

MURPHY, ROBERT R. (BUZZ)
B.APR.26,1895 DENVER,COLO.
D.MAY 11,1938 DENVER,COLO.
```
1918 BOS N  0           9    .375
1919 WAS A  0          79    .262
     BLTL              88    .271
```

MURPHY, THOMAS ANDREW (TOM)
B.DEC.30,1945 CLEVELAND,OHIO
```
1968 CAL A  P          15    5- 6
1969 CAL A  P          36   10-16
1970 CAL A  P          39   16-13
1971 CAL A  P          37    6-17
1972 CAL A  /P          6    0- 0
     KC  A  P    18    21    4- 4
1973 STL N  P          19    3- 7
1974 MIL A  P          70   10-10
1975 MIL A  P    52    53    1- 9
1976 MIL A  P          15    0- 1
     BOS A  P          37    4- 5
1977 BOS A  P          16    0- 1
     TOR A  P          19    2- 1
1978 TOR A  P          50    6- 9
     BRTR      429    433   67-99
```

MURPHY, WALTER JOSEPH
B.SEPT.27,1907 NEW YORK,N.Y.
```
1931 BOS A  P           2    0- 0
     BRTR
```

MURPHY, WILLIAM EUGENE (BILLY)
B.MAY 7,1944 PINEVILLE,LA.
```
1966 NY  N  0          84    .230
     BRTR
```

MURPHY, WILLIAM HENRY (YALE)
B.NOV.11,1869 SOUTHVILLE,MASS.
D.FEB.14,1906 SOUTHVILLE,MASS.
```
1894 NY  N  S-0        73    .271
1895 NY  N  0          47    .209
1897 NY  N  S           4    .000
                      124    .242
```

MURPHY, WILLIAM N.
(WILLIE) OR (GENTLE WILLIE)
B.1865 BOSTON,MASS.
```
1884 CLE N  S-0        42    .226
     WAS AA 3-0         5    .454
     BOS U  C-0         1    .000
                       48    .249
```

MURRAY, ANTHONY JOSEPH
B.APR.30,1904 CHICAGO,ILL.
D.MAR.19,1974 CHICAGO,ILL.
```
1923 CHI N  0           2    .250
     BRTR
```

MURRAY, DALE ALBERT
B.FEB.2,1950 CUERO,TEX.
```
1974 MON N  P          32    1- 1
1975 MON N  P          63   15- 8
1976 MON N  P          81    4- 9
1977 CIN N  P          61    7- 2
1978 CIN N  P          15    1- 1
     NY  N  P          53    8- 5
     BRTR             305   36-26
```

MURRAY, EDDIE CLARENCE
B.FEB.24,1956 LOS ANGELES,CAL.
```
1977 BAL A  *0-1/0    160    .283
1978 BAL A  #1/3      161    .285
     BBTR             321    .284
```

MURRAY, EDWARD FRANCIS
B.MAY 8,1895 MYSTIC,CONN.
D.NOV.8,1970 CHEYENNE,WYOMING
```
1917 STL A  S           1    .000
     BRTR
```

MURRAY, GEORGE KING (SMILER)
B.SEPT.23,1898 CHARLOTTE,N.C.
D.OCT.18,1955 MEMPHIS,TENN.
```
1922 NY  A  P          22    3- 2
1923 BOS A  P          39    7-11
1924 BOS A  P          28    2- 9
1926 WAS A  P          12    6- 3
1927 WAS A  P           7    1- 1
1933 CHI A  P           2    0- 0
     BRTR             110   19-26
```

MURRAY, JAMES FRANCIS (BIG JIM)
B.DEC.31,1900 SCRANTON,PA.
D.JULY 15,1973 NEW YORK,N.Y.
```
1922 BRO N  P           4    0- 0
     BBTL
```

MURRAY, JAMES OSCAR
B.JAN.16,1878 GALVESTON,TEX.
D.APR.25,1945 GALVESTON,TEX.
```
1902 CHI N  0          11    .166
1911 STL A  0          31    .186
1914 BRO N  0          39    .232
     BRTL              81    .195
```

MURRAY, JEREMIAH J. (MIAH)
B.JAN.1,1865 BOSTON,MASS.
D.JAN.11,1922 BOSTON,MASS.
```
1884 PRO N  C-1-0       8    .185
1885 LOU AA C-1        11    .162
1888 WAS N  C          12    .098
1891 WAS AA C           2    .000
     BRTR              33    .138
```

MURRAY, JOHN JOSEPH (RED)
B.MAR.4,1884 ARNOT,PA.
D.DEC.4,1958 SAYRE,PA.

YR	CL	LEA	POS	GP	G	REC
1906	STL	N	O		41	.257
1907	STL	N	O		131	.262
1908	STL	N	O		154	.282
1909	NY	N	O		149	.263
1910	NY	N	O		148	.277
1911	NY	N	O		131	.291
1912	NY	N	O		143	.277
1913	NY	N	O		147	.267
1914	NY	N	O		86	.223
1915	NY	N	O		45	.220
	CHI	N	O		51	.299
1917	NY	N	O		22	.045
	BRTR				1248	.270

MURRAY, JOSEPH AMBROSE (AMBY)
B.JUNE 4,1913 FALL RIVER,MASS.

YR	CL	LEA	POS	GP	G	REC
1936	BOS	N	P		4	0-0
	BLTL					

MURRAY, JOSEPH AMBROSE
B.NOV.11,1920 WILKES-BARRE,PA.

YR	CL	LEA	POS	GP	G	REC
1950	PHI	A	P		8	0-3
	BLTL					

MURRAY, LARRY
B.APR.1,1953 CHICAGO,ILL.

YR	CL	LEA	POS	GP	G	REC
1974	NY	A	/O		6	.000
1975	NY	A	/O		6	.000
1976	NY	A	/O		8	.100
1977	OAK	A	O/S		90	.179
1978	OAK	A	/O		11	.083
	BBTR				121	.167

MURRAY, PATRICK JOSEPH
B.JULY 18,1897 SCOTTSVILLE,N.Y.

YR	CL	LEA	POS	GP	G	REC
1919	PHI	N	P		8	0-2
	BRTL					

MURRAY, RAYMOND LEE
(RAY) OR (DEACON)
B.OCT.1,1917 SPRING HOPE,N.C.

YR	CL	LEA	POS	GP	G	REC
1948	CLE	A	H		4	.000
1950	CLE	A	C		55	.273
1951	CLE	A	C		1	1.000
	PHI	A	C		40	.213
1952	PHI	A	C		44	.206
1953	PHI	A	C		84	.284
1954	BAL	A	C		22	.246
	BRTR				250	.252

MURRAY, ROBERT HAYES
B.JULY 4,1898 ST.ALBANS,VT.

YR	CL	LEA	POS	GP	G	REC
1923	WAS	A	3		10	.162
	TR					

MURRAY, THOMAS W.
B.1866 SAVANNAH,GA.

YR	CL	LEA	POS	GP	G	REC
1894	PHI	N	S		1	.000

MURRAY, WILLIAM ALLENWOOD (DASHER)
B.SEPT.6,1893 VINALHAVEN,ME.
D.SEPT.14,1943 BOSTON,MASS.

YR	CL	LEA	POS	GP	G	REC
1917	WAS	A	2		8	.143
	BBTR					

MURRAY, WILLIAM JEREMIAH
B.APR.13,1864 PEABODY,MASS.
D.MAR.25,1937 YOUNGSTOWN,OHIO
NON-PLAYING MANAGER PHI[N] 1907-09

MURRELL, IVAN AUGUSTUS
B.APR.24,1945 ALMIRANTE,PANAMA

YR	CL	LEA	POS	GP	G	REC
1963	HOU	N	O		2	.200
1964	HOU	N	O		10	.143
1967	HOU	N	/O		10	.310
1968	HOU	N	O		32	.102
1969	SD	N	O/1		111	.255
1970	SD	N	*O/1		125	.245
1971	SD	N	O		103	.235
1972	SD	N	/O		5	.143
1973	SD	N	O-1		93	.229
1974	ATL	N	O-1		73	.248
	BRTR				564	.236

MURTAUGH, DANIEL EDWARD (DANNY)
B.OCT.8,1917 CHESTER,PA.
D.DEC.2,1976 CHESTER,PA.

YR	CL	LEA	POS	GP	G	REC
1941	PHI	N	2-S		85	.219
1942	PHI	N	2-S-3		144	.241
1943	PHI	N	2		113	.273
1946	PHI	N	2		6	.211
1947	BOS	N	3		3	.125
1948	PIT	N	2		146	.290
1949	PIT	N	2		75	.203
1950	PIT	N	2		118	.294
1951	PIT	N	2-3		77	.199
	BRTR				767	.254

NON-PLAYING MANAGER
PIT[N]1957-64, 67, 70-71, 73-76

MUSER, ANTHONY JOSEPH (TONY)
B.AUG.1,1947 VAN NUYS,CAL.

YR	CL	LEA	POS	GP	G	REC
1969	BOS	A	/1		2	.111
1971	CHI	A	/1		11	.313
1972	CHI	A	1/O		44	.279
1973	CHI	A	1-D/O		109	.285
1974	CHI	A	1-D		103	.291
1975	CHI	A	1		43	.243
	BAL	A	1		80	.317
1976	BAL	A	*1-O-D		136	.227
1977	BAL	A	1-O		120	.229
1978	MIL	A	1		15	.133
	BLTL				663	.259

MUSGRAVES, DENNIS EUGENE
B.DEC.25,1943 INDIANAPOLIS,IND.

YR	CL	LEA	POS	GP	G	REC
1965	NY	N	/P		5	0-0
	BRTR					

MUSIAL, STANLEY FRANK
(STAN) OR (STAN THE MAN)
B.NOV.21,1920 DONORA,PA.

YR	CL	LEA	POS	GP	G	REC
1941	STL	N	O		12	.426
1942	STL	N	O		140	.315
1943	STL	N	O		157	.357
1944	STL	N	O		146	.347
1946	STL	N	1-O		156	.365
1947	STL	N	1		149	.312
1948	STL	N	1-O		155	.376
1949	STL	N	1-O		157	.338
1950	STL	N	1-O		146	.346
1951	STL	N	1-O		152	.355
1952	STL	N	P-1-O	1	154	0-0 .336
1953	STL	N	O		157	.337
1954	STL	N	1-O		153	.330
1955	STL	N	1-O		154	.319
1956	STL	N	1-O		156	.310
1957	STL	N	1		134	.351
1958	STL	N	1		135	.337
1959	STL	N	1-O		115	.255
1960	STL	N	1-O		116	.275
1961	STL	N	O		123	.288
1962	STL	N	O		135	.330
1963	STL	N	O		124	.255
	BLTL			1	3026	0-0 .331

MUSSER, PAUL
B.JUNE 24,1889 MILLHEIM,PA.

YR	CL	LEA	POS	GP	G	REC
1912	WAS	A	P		8	1-0
1919	BOS	A	P		5	0-2
	BRTR				13	1-2

MUSSER, WILLIAM DANIEL (DANNY)
B.SEPT.5,1905 ZION,PA.

YR	CL	LEA	POS	GP	G	REC
1932	WAS	A	3		1	.500
	BLTR					

MUSSILL, BERNARD JAMES
B.OCT.1,1919 WOODVILLE,PA.

YR	CL	LEA	POS	GP	G	REC
1944	PHI	N	P		16	0-1
	BRTL					

MUSTAIKIS, ALEXANDER DOMINICK
B.MAR.26,1909 CHELSEA,MASS.
D.JAN.17,1970 SCRANTON,PA.

YR	CL	LEA	POS	GP	G	REC
1940	BOS	A	P		6	0-1
	BRTR					

MUTRIE, JAMES J. (TRUTHFUL JIM)
B.JUNE 13,1851 CHELSEA,MASS.
D.JAN.24,1938 NEW YORK,N.Y.
NON-PLAYING MANAGER
MET[AA] 1883-84, NY[N] 1885-91

MYATT, GEORGE EDWARD (GEORGE)
(MERCURY),(STUD) OR (FOGHORN)
B.JUNE 14,1914 DENVER,COLO.

YR	CL	LEA	POS	GP	G	REC
1938	NY	N	S-3		43	.306
1939	NY	N	3		22	.189
1943	WAS	A	2-S-3		42	.245
1944	WAS	A	2-S-O		140	.284
1945	WAS	A	2-S-3-O		133	.296
1946	WAS	A	2-3		15	.235
1947	WAS	A	2		12	.000
	BLTR				407	.283

NON-PLAYING MANAGER
PHI[N] 1968-69 [INTERIM]

MYATT, GLENN CALVIN
B.JULY 9,1897 ARGENTA,ARK.
D.AUG.9,1969 HOUSTON,TEX.

YR	CL	LEA	POS	GP	G	REC
1920	PHI	A	C-O		70	.250
1921	PHI	A	C		44	.203
1923	CLE	A	C		92	.286
1924	CLE	A	C		105	.342
1925	CLE	A	C-O		106	.271
1926	CLE	A	C		56	.246
1927	CLE	A	C		55	.245
1928	CLE	A	C		58	.288
1929	CLE	A	C		59	.233
1930	CLE	A	C		86	.294
1931	CLE	A	C		65	.247
1932	CLE	A	C		82	.246
1933	CLE	A	C		40	.234
1934	CLE	A	C		36	.318
1935	CLE	A	C		10	.083
	NY	N	C		13	.222
1936	DET	A	C		27	.218
	BLTR				1004	.270

MYER, CHARLES SOLOMON (BUDDY)
B.MAR.16,1904 ELLISVILLE,MISS.
D.OCT.31,1974 BATON ROUGE,LA.

YR	CL	LEA	POS	GP	G	REC
1925	WAS	A	S		4	.250
1926	WAS	A	S		132	.304
1927	WAS	A	S		15	.216
	BOS	A	S		123	.288
1928	BOS	A	3		147	.313
1929	WAS	A	2-3		141	.300
1930	WAS	A	2		138	.303
1931	WAS	A	2		139	.293
1932	WAS	A	2		143	.279
1933	WAS	A	2		131	.302
1934	WAS	A	2		139	.305
1935	WAS	A	2		151	.349
1936	WAS	A	2		51	.269
1937	WAS	A	2		125	.293
1938	WAS	A	2		127	.336
1939	WAS	A	2		83	.302
1940	WAS	A	2		71	.290
1941	WAS	A	2		53	.252
	BLTR				1923	.303

MYERS, ELMER GLENN
B.MAR.2,1894 YORK SPRINGS,PA.
D.JULY 29,1976 COLLINGWOOD,N.J.

YR	CL	LEA	POS	GP	G	REC
1915	PHI	A	P		1	1-0
1916	PHI	A	P	44	53	14-23
1917	PHI	A	P		38	9-16
1918	PHI	A	P		18	4-8
1919	CLE	A	P		23	8-7
1920	CLE	A	P		16	2-4
	BOS	A	P		12	9-1
1921	BOS	A	P		30	8-12
1922	BOS	A	P		3	0-1
	BRTR			185	194	55-72

MYERS, GEORGE D.
B.NOV.13,1860 BUFFALO,N.Y.
D.DEC.14,1926 BUFFALO,N.Y.

YR	CL	LEA	POS	GP	G	REC
1884	BUF	N	C-O		76	.186
1885	BUF	N	C-O		89	.205
1886	STL	N	C		78	.189
1887	IND	N	C		66	.284
1888	IND	N	C		66	.238
1889	IND	N	C-O		39	.194
	BR				414	.219

MYERS, HENRY C.
B.MAY 1858 PHILADELPHIA,PA.
D.APR.18,1895 PHILADELPHIA,PA.

YR	CL	LEA	POS	GP	G	REC
1881	PRO	N	S		1	.000
1882	BAL	AA	M-P-	2	69	0-2
			S			.223
1884	WIL	U	2-S		4	.167
	BRTR			2	76	0-2 .216

MYERS, HENRY HARRISON (HI)
B.APR.27,1889 E.LIVERPOOL,OHIO
D.MAY 1,1965 MINERVA,OHIO

YR	CL	LEA	POS	GP	G	REC
1909	BRO	N	O		6	.227
1911	BRO	N	O		12	.179
1914	BRO	N	O		70	.286
1915	BRO	N	O		153	.248
1916	BRO	N	O		113	.262
1917	BRO	N	1-2-3-O		120	.268
1918	BRO	N	O		107	.256
1919	BRO	N	O		133	.307
1920	BRO	N	O		154	.304
1921	BRO	N	2-O		144	.288
1922	BRO	N	2-O		153	.317
1923	STL	N	O		96	.300
1924	STL	N	2-3-O		43	.210
1925	STL	N	O		1	.000
	CIN	N	O		3	.167
	STL	N	H		1	1.000
	BRTR				1309	.281

MYERS, JAMES ALBERT (BERT)
B.APR.8,1874 FREDERICK,MD.
D.OCT.12,1915 WASHINGTON,D.C.

YR	CL	LEA	POS	GP	G	REC
1896	STL	N	3		122	.258
1898	WAS	N	3		31	.261
1900	PHI	N	3		7	.185
	BRTR				160	.236

YR	CL LEA POS	GP	G	REC

MYERS, JAMES ALBERT (COD)
B.OCT.22,1863 DANVILLE,ILL.
D.DEC.24,1927 MARSHALL,ILL.

YR	CL LEA POS	G	REC
1884	MIL U 2	12	.326
1885	PHI N 2	93	.204
1886	KC N 2	118	.276
1887	WAS N 2-S	105	.308
1888	WAS N 2	132	.207
1889	WAS N 2	46	.262
	PHI N 2	75	.269
1890	PHI N 2	117	.277
1891	PHI N 2	134	.238
		832	.255

MYERS, JOSEPH WILLIAM
B.MAR.18,1882 WILMINGTON,DEL.
D.FEB.11,1956 DELAWARE CITY,DEL

| 1905 | PHI A P | 1 | 0- 0 |
| | BRTR | | |

MYERS, LYNNWOOD LINCOLN
B.FEB.23,1914 ENOLA,PA.

1938	STL N S	70	.242
1939	STL N S-3	74	.239
	BRTR	144	.241

MYERS, RALPH EDWARD (HAP)
B.APR.8,1888 SAN FRANCISCO,CAL.
D.JUN.30,1967 SAN FRANCISCO,CAL

1910	BOS A C	3	.333
1911	STL A 1	11	.297
	BOS A 1	13	.368
1913	BOS N 1	140	.273
1914	BRO F 1	89	.226
1915	BRO F 1	115	.282
		371	.268

MYERS, RICHARD
B.APR.7,1930 SACRAMENTO,CAL.

| 1956 | CHI N H | 4 | .000 |
| | BR | | |

MYERS, WILLIAM HARRISON (BILLY)
B.AUG.14,1910 ENOLA,PA.

1935	CIN N S	117	.267
1936	CIN N S	98	.269
1937	CIN N 2-S	124	.251
1938	CIN N 2-S	134	.253
1939	CIN N S	151	.281
1940	CIN N S	90	.202
1941	CHI N 2-S	24	.222
	BRTR	738	.297

MYRICK, ROBERT HOWARD (BOB)
B.OCT.1,1952 HATTIESBURG,MISS.

1976	NY N P	21	1- 1
1977	NY N P	44	2- 2
1978	NY N P	17	0- 3
	BRTL	82	3- 6

NABORS, HERMAN JOHN (JACK)
B.NOV.19,1887 MONTEVALLO,ALA.
D.NOV.20,1923 WILTON,ALA.

1915	PHI A P	10	0- 5
1916	PHI A P	40	1-21
1917	PHI A P	2	0- 0
	BRTR	52	1-26

NAGEL, WILLIAM TAYLOR
B.AUG.19,1915 MEMPHIS,TENN.

YR	CL LEA POS	GP	G	REC
1939	PHI A P-2-3	1	105	0- 0
				.252
1941	PHI N 2-3-0		17	.143
1945	CHI A 1-3		67	.209
	BRTR	1	189	0- 0
				.227

NAGELEISEN, LOUIS MARCELLUS
[PLAYED UNDER NAME OF
LOUIS MARCELLUS NAGELSEN]

NAGELSEN, LOUIS MARCELLUS
[REAL NAME
LOUIS MARCELLUS NAGELEISEN]
B.JUNE 29,1887 PIQUA,OHIO
D.OCT.22,1965 FORT WAYNE,IND.

| 1912 | CLE A C | 2 | .000 |
| | BRTR | | |

NAGELSON, RUSSELL CHARLES (RUSS)
B.SEP.19,1944 CINCINNATI,OHIO

1968	CLE A /H	5	.333
1969	CLE A /O-1	12	.353
1970	CLE A /O	17	.125
	DET A /O-1	28	.188
	BLTR	62	.211

NAGLE, THOMAS EDWARD
B.OCT.30,1865 MILWAUKEE,WIS.
D.MAR.9,1946 MILWAUKEE,WIS.

1890	CHI N C	38	.264
1891	CHI N C	8	.120
	BRTR	46	.243

NAGLE, WALTER HAROLD
(LUCKY) OR (JUDGE)
B.MAR.10,1880 SANTA ROSA,CAL.
D.MAY 27,1971 SANTA ROSA,CAL.

1911	PIT N P	8	4- 2
	BOS A P	5	1- 1
		13	5- 3

NAGY, STEPHEN (STEVE)
B.MAY 28,1919 FRANKLIN,N.J.

YR	CL LEA POS	GP	G	REC
1947	PIT N P		6	1- 3
1950	WAS A P	9	15	2- 5
	BLTL	15	21	3- 8

NAGY, MICHAEL TIMOTHY (MIKE)
B.MAR.25,1948 NEW YORK,N.Y.

1969	BOS A P	33	34	12- 2
1970	BOS A P		23	6- 5
1971	BOS A P		12	1- 3
1972	BOS A /P		1	0- 0
1973	CIN N /P		9	0- 2
1974	HOU N /P		9	1- 1
	BRTR	87	88	20-13

NAHEM, SAMUEL RALPH (SUBWAY)
B.OCT.19,1915 NEW YORK,N.Y.

1938	BRO N P	1	1- 0
1941	STL N P	26	5- 2
1942	PHI N P	35	1- 3
1948	PHI N P	28	3- 3
	BRTR	90	10- 8

NAHORODNY, WILLIAM GERARD (BILL)
B.AUG.31,1953 HAMTRAMCK,MICH.

1976	PHI N /C	3	.200
1977	CHI A /C	7	.261
1978	CHI A *C/1	107	.236
	BRTR	117	.237

NAKTENIS, PETER ERNEST
B.JUNE 12,1914 ABERDEEN,WASH.

1936	PHI A P	7	0- 1
1939	CIN N P	3	0- 0
	BLTL	10	0- 1

NALEWAY, FRANK (CHICK)
B.JULY 5,1902 CHICAGO,ILL.
D.JAN.28,1949 CHICAGO,ILL.

| 1924 | CHI A S | 1 | .000 |

NANCE, WILLIAM G. (KID)
[REAL NAME WILLIE G. COOPER]
B.AUG.2,1876 FT.WORTH,TEX.
D.MAY 28,1958 FORT WORTH,TEX.

1897	LOU N O	34	.241
1898	LOU N O	22	.329
1901	DET A O	133	.290
1904	STL A C	1	.333
	BRTR	190	.286

NAPIER, SKELTON LE ROY (BUDDY)
B.DEC.18,1889 BYRONVILLE,GA.
D.MAR.29,1968 HUTCHINS,TEX.

1912	STL A P	6	0- 2
1918	CIN N P	1	0- 0
1920	CIN N P	9	4- 2
1921	CIN N P	22	0- 2
	BRTR	38	4- 6

NAPLES, ALOYSIUS FRANCIS
B.AUG.29,1927 ST.GEORGE,S.I.,N.Y.

| 1949 | STL A S | 2 | .143 |

NAPOLEON, DANIEL (DANNY)
B.JAN.11,1942 CLAYSBURG,PA.

1965	NY N O/3	68	.144
1966	NY N O	12	.212
	BRTR	80	.162

NARAGON, HAROLD RICHARD (HAL)
B.OCT.1,1928 ZANESVILLE,OHIO

1951	CLE A C	3	.250
1954	CLE A C	46	.238
1955	CLE A C	57	.323
1956	CLE A C	53	.287
1957	CLE A C	57	.256
1958	CLE A H	9	.333
1959	CLE A C	14	.278
	WAS A C	71	.241
1960	WAS A C	33	.207
1961	MIN A C	57	.302
1962	MIN A C	24	.229
	BLTR	424	.266

NARANJO, LAZARO RAMON GONZALO
(GONZALO)
B.NOV.25,1934 HAVANA,CUBA

| 1956 | PIT N P | 17 | 1- 2 |
| | BLTR | | |

NARLESKI, RAYMOND EDMOND (RAY)
B.NOV.25,1928 CAMDEN,N.J.

1954	CLE A P	42	3- 3
1955	CLE A P	60	9- 1
1956	CLE A P	32	3- 2
1957	CLE A P	46	11- 5
1958	CLE A P	44	13-10
1959	DET A P	42	4-12
	BRTR	266	43-33

NARLESKI, WILLIAM EDWARD (CAP)
B.JUNE 14,1899 PERTH AMBOY,N.J.
D.JULY 22,1964 LAUREL SPRINGS,N.J.

1929	BOS A 2-S	96	.277
1930	BOS A S-3	39	.235
	BRTR	135	.262

NARRON, SAMUEL (SAM)
B.AUG.25,1913 MIDDLESEX,N.C.

1935	STL N C	4	.429
1942	STL N C	10	.400
1943	STL N C	10	.091
	BRTR	24	.286

NARUM, LESLIE FERDINAND (BUSTER)
B.NOV.16,1940 PHILADELPHIA,PA.

1963	BAL A P	7	0- 0
1964	WAS A P	38	9-15
1965	WAS A P	46	4-12
1966	WAS A /P	3	0- 0
1967	WAS A /P	2	1- 0
	BRTR	96	14-27

NASH, CHARLES FRANCIS (COTTON)
B.JULY 24,1942 JERSEY CITY,N.J.

1967	CHI A /1	3	.000
1969	MIN A /1-0	6	.222
1970	MIN A /1	4	.250
	BRTR	13	.188

NASH, JAMES EDWIN (JIM)
B.FEB.9,1945 HAWTHORNE,NEV.

YR	CL LEA POS	GP	G	REC
1966	KC A P		18	12- 1
1967	KC A P		37	12-17
1968	OAK A P		34	13-13
1969	OAK A P		26	8- 8
1970	ATL N P		34	13- 9
1971	ATL N P	32	33	9- 7
1972	ATL N P		11	1- 1
	PHI N /P		0	0- 8
	BRTR	201	202	68-64

NASH, KENNETH LELAND
[PLAYED ONE GAME IN 1912
UNDER NAME OF COSTELLO]
B.JULY 14,1888 S.WEYMOUTH,MASS.
D.FEB.16,1977 EPSOM,N.H.

1912	CLE A S	10	.182
1914	STL N 1-2-S-3	24	.275
	BBTR	34	.247

NASH, WILLIAM MITCHELL
B.JUNE 24,1865 RICHMOND,VA.
D.NOV.15,1929 E.ORANGE,N.J.

1884	RIC AA 3	44	.188
1885	BOS N 2-3	26	.255
1886	BOS N S-3	109	.280
1887	BOS N 3	118	.368
1888	BOS N 2-3	135	.283
1889	BOS N 3	127	.274
1890	BOS P 3	129	.284
1891	BOS N 3	139	.276
1892	BOS N 3	135	.265
1893	BOS N 3	128	.304
1894	BOS N 3	132	.294
1895	BOS N 3	133	.296
1896	PHI N M-3	64	.242
1897	PHI N S-3	102	.258
1898	PHI N 3	20	.232
	BRTR	1541	.286

NASTU, PHILIP
B.MAR.8,1955 BRIDGEPORT,CONN.

| 1978 | SF N /P | 3 | 0- 1 |
| | BLTL | | |

NATON, PETER ALPHONSUS
B.SEPT.9,1931 FLUSHING,N.Y.

| 1953 | PIT N C | 6 | .167 |
| | BRTR | | |

NAVA, VINCENT P. (SANDY)
[REAL NAME IRWIN SANDY]
B.APR.12,1850 SAN FRANCISCO,CAL
D.JUNE 15,1906 BALTIMORE,MD.

1882	PRO N C-O	27	.206
1883	PRO N C-O	27	.240
1884	PRO N C-2-S-O	32	.089
1885	BAL AA C	8	.148
1886	BAL AA C-S	2	.200
		96	.176

YR	CL LEA POS	GP	G	REC

NAVARRO, JULIO [VENTURA]
(JULIO) OR (WHIPLASH)
B.JAN.9,1936 VIEQUES,P.R.

1962	LA A P		9	1- 1
1963	LA A P		57	4- 5
1964	LA A P		5	0- 0
	DET A P		26	2- 1
1965	DET A P		15	0- 2
1966	DET A /P		1	0- 0
1970	ATL N P		17	0- 0
	BRTR		130	7- 9

NAYLOR, EARL EUGENE
B.MAY 19,1919 KANSAS CITY,MO.

1942	PHI N P-O	20	76	0- 5
				.196
1943	PHI N O		33	.175
1946	BRO N H		3	.000
	BRTR	20	112	0- 5
				.186

NAYLOR, ROLEINE CECIL (ROLLIE)
B.FEB.4,1892 CRUM,TEX.
D.JUNE 18,1966 FORT WORTH,TEX.

1917	PHI A P		5	2- 2
1919	PHI A P		31	5-18
1920	PHI A P		42	10-23
1921	PHI A P	32	33	3-13
1922	PHI A P	35	36	10-15
1923	PHI A P		26	12- 7
1924	PHI A P		10	0- 5
	BRTR	181	183	42-83

NAYMICK, MICHAEL JOHN (MIKE)
B.SEPT.6,1917 BERLIN,PA.

1939	CLE A P		2	0- 1
1940	CLE A P		13	1- 2
1943	CLE A P		29	4- 4
1944	CLE A P		7	0- 0
	STL N P		1	0- 0
	BRTR		52	5- 7

NEAGLE, JOHN HENRY (JACK)
B.JAN.2,1858 SYRACUSE,N.Y.
D.SEPT.20,1904 SYRACUSE,N.Y.

1879	CIN N P-O	2	3	0- 1
				.167
1883	PHI N P-O	8	18	1- 4
				.162
	BAL AA P-O	6	9	1- 4
				.270
	PIT AA P-O	17	29	3-13
				.168
1884	PIT AA P	37	41	11-26
				.169
	BRTR	70	100	16-48
				.169

NEAL, CHARLES LENARD (CHARLIE)
B.JAN.30,1931 LONGVIEW,TEX.

1956	BRO N 2-S		62	.287
1957	BRO N 2-S-3		128	.270
1958	LA N 2-3		140	.254
1959	LA N 2-S		151	.287
1960	LA N 2-S		139	.256
1961	LA N 2		108	.235
1962	NY N 2-S-3		136	.260
1963	NY N S-3		72	.225
	CIN N 2-S-3		34	.156
	BRTR		970	.259

NEAL, JOSEPH H.
B.1865 WADSWORTH,OHIO

1886	LOU AA P-O	1	2	0- 1
				.000
1887	LOU AA P		5	0- 4
1890	STL AA P		10	3- 3
1891	STL AA P		15	6- 4
	BRTR	31	32	9-11
				.119

NEAL, THEOPHILUS FOUNTAIN (OFFA)
B.JUNE 5,1876 LOGAN,ILL.
D.APR.12,1950 MT.VERNON,ILL.

| 1905 | NY N 2-3 | | 4 | .077 |
| | BLTR | | | |

NEALE, ALFRED EARLE (GREASY)
B.NOV.5,1891 PARKERSBURG,W.VA.
D.NOV.2,1973 LAKE WORTH,FLA.

1916	CIN N O		138	.262
1917	CIN N O		121	.294
1918	CIN N O		107	.270
1919	CIN N O		139	.242
1920	CIN N O		150	.255
1921	PHI N O		22	.211
	CIN N O		63	.241
1922	CIN N O		25	.233
1924	CIN N O		3	.000
	BLTR		768	.259

NEALON, JAMES JOSEPH
B.DEC.15,1884 SACRAMENTO,CAL.
D.APR.2,1910 SAN FRANCISCO,CAL.

1906	PIT N 1		154	.255
1907	PIT N 1		104	.257
			258	.256

NECCIAI, RONALD ANDREW (RON)
B.JUNE 16,1932 MANOWN,PA.

| 1952 | PIT N P | | 12 | 1- 6 |
| | BRTR | | | |

NEEDHAM, THOMAS J. (DEERFOOT)
B.APR.7,1879 IRELAND
D.DEC.13,1926 STEUBENVILLE,OHIO

1904	BOS N C		78	.260
1905	BOS N C		82	.218
1906	BOS N C		81	.190
1907	BOS N C		79	.196
1908	NY N C		47	.209
1909	CHI N C		10	.200
1910	CHI N C		28	.184
1911	CHI N C		23	.194
1912	CHI N C		33	.178
1913	CHI N C		20	.238
1914	CHI N C		9	.118
	BRTR		490	.209

NEEMAN, CALVIN AMANOUS (CAL)
B.FEB.18,1929 VALMEYER,ILL.

1957	CHI N C		122	.258
1958	CHI N C		76	.259
1959	CHI N C		44	.162
1960	CHI N C		9	.154
	PHI N C		59	.181
1961	PHI N C		19	.226
1962	PIT N C		24	.180
1963	CLE A C		9	.000
	WAS A C		14	.056
	BRTR		376	.224

NEGRAY, RONALD ALVIN (RON)
B.FEB.26,1930 AKRON,OHIO

1952	BRO N P		4	0- 0
1955	PHI N P		19	4- 3
1956	PHI N P		39	2- 3
1958	LA N P		4	0- 0
	BRTR		66	6- 6

NEHER, JAMES GILMORE
B.FEB.5,1889 ROCHESTER,N.Y.
D.NOV.11,1951 BUFFALO,N.Y.

| 1912 | CLE A P | | 1 | 0- 0 |
| | BRTR | | | |

NEHF, ARTHUR NEUKOM (ART)
B.JULY 31,1892 TERRE HAUTE,IND.
D.DEC.18,1960 PHOENIX,ARIZ.

1915	BOS N P		12	5- 4
1916	BOS N P	22	23	7- 5
1917	BOS N P		38	17- 8
1918	BOS N P-O	32	35	15-15
				.257
1919	BOS N P-O	21	22	8- 9
				.197
	NY N P		13	9- 2
1920	NY N P		40	21-12
1921	NY N P	41	42	20-10
1922	NY N P		37	19-13
1923	NY N P		34	13-10
1924	NY N P-O	30	33	14- 4
				.231
1925	NY N P	30	33	11- 9
				.228
1926	NY N P		2	0- 0
	CIN N P		7	0- 1
1927	CIN N P		21	3- 5
	CHI N P		8	1- 1
1928	CHI N P		31	13- 7
1929	CHI N P		32	8- 5
	BLTL	451	463	184-120
				.211

NEIBAUER, GARY WAYNE
B.OCT.29,1944 BILLINGS,MONT.

1969	ATL N P		29	1- 2
1970	ATL N /P		7	0- 3
1971	ATL N /P		6	1- 0
1972	ATL N /P		8	0- 0
	PHI N /P		9	0- 2
1973	ATL N /P		16	2- 1
	BRTR		75	4- 8

NEIGER, ALVIN EDWARD
B.MAR.26,1939 WILMINGTON,DEL.

| 1960 | PHI N P | | 6 | 0- 0 |
| | BLTL | | | |

NEIGHBORS, CECIL F. (CY)
B.SEPT.23,1880 MISSOURI
D.MAY 20,1964 TACOMA,WASH.

| 1908 | PIT N O | | 1 | .000 |

NEIGHBORS, ROBERT OTIS
B.NOV.9,1917 TALAHINA,OKLA.
D.AUG 8,1952 NORTH KOREA [MIA]

| 1939 | STL A S | | 7 | .182 |
| | BRTR | | | |

NEILL, THOMAS WHITE
B.NOV.7,1919 HARTSELLE,ALA.

1946	BOS N O		13	.267
1947	BOS N O		7	.200
	BLTR		20	.255

NEIS, BERNARD EDMUND
B.SEPT.26,1895 BLOOMINGTON,ILL.
D.NOV.29,1972 INVERNESS,FLA.

1920	BRO N O		95	.253
1921	BRO N O		102	.257
1922	BRO N O		61	.229
1923	BRO N O		126	.274
1924	BRO N O		80	.303
1925	BOS N O		106	.285
1926	BOS N O		30	.215
1927	CLE A O		32	.302
	CHI A O		45	.289
	BBTR		677	.272
	BR 1920-21			

NEITZKE, ERNEST FREDRICH
B.NOV.13,1894 TOLEDO,OHIO
D.APR.27,1977 SYLVANIA,OHIO

| 1921 | BOS A P | | 11 | 0- 0 |
| | BRTR | | | |

NEKOLA, FRANCIS JOSEPH (BOTS)
B.DEC.10,1906 NEW YORK,N.Y.

1929	NY A P		9	0- 0
1933	DET A P		2	0- 0
	BLTL		11	0- 0

NELSON, ALBERT FRANCIS (RED)
[REAL NAME ALBERT W. HORAZDOVSKY]
B.MAY 19,1886 CLEVELAND,OHIO
D.OCT.26,1956 ST.PETERSBURG,FLA

1910	STL A P		7	5- 1
1911	STL A P		15	3- 9
1912	STL A P		8	0- 3
	PHI N P		4	2- 0
1913	PHI N P		2	0- 0
	CIN N P		2	0- 0
	BRTR		38	10-13

NELSON, ANDREW (PEACHES)

| 1908 | CHI A P | | 3 | 1- 0 |

NELSON, DAVID EARL (DAVE)
B.JUNE 20,1944 FORT STILL,OKLA.

1968	CLE A 2-S		88	.233
1969	CLE A 2/O		52	.203
1970	WAS A 2		47	.159
1971	WAS A 3/2		85	.280
1972	TEX A *3-O		145	.226
1973	TEX A *2		142	.286
1974	TEX A *2		121	.236
1975	TEX A 2		28	.213
1976	KC A 2/1		78	.235
1977	KC A 2		27	.188
	BRTR		813	.244
	BB 1968 (PART)			

NELSON, GEORGE EMMETT
(EMMETT) OR (RAMROD)
B.FEB.26,1905 VIBORG,S.DAK.
D.AUG.25,1967 SIOUX FALLS,S.D.

1935	CIN N P		19	4- 4
1936	CIN N P		6	1- 0
	BRTR		25	5- 4

NELSON, GLENN RICHARD (ROCKY)
B.NOV.18,1924 PORTSMOUTH,OHIO

1949	STL N 1		82	.221
1950	STL N 1		76	.247
1951	STL N 1-O		9	.222
	PIT N 1-O		71	.267
	CHI A H		6	.000
1952	BRO N 1		37	.256
1954	CLE A 1		4	.000
1956	BRO N 1		30	.208
	STL N 1-O		38	.232
1959	PIT N 1-O		98	.291
1960	PIT N 1		93	.300
1961	PIT N 1		75	.197
	BLTL		620	.249

NELSON, JACKSON W. (CANDY)
B.MAR.14,1849 BROOKLYN,N.Y.
D.SEPT.4,1910 BROOKLYN,N.Y.

1872	TRO NA S-O		4	.368
	ECK NA 2-3-O		18	.235
1873	MUT NA 2-3-O		37	-
1874	MUT NA 2-S		65	-
1875	MUT NA 2-3-O		70	-
1878	IND N S		18	.136
1879	TRO N S-O		28	.246
1881	WOR N S		23	.275
1883	MET AA S		96	.291
1884	MET AA S		111	.259
1885	MET AA S		107	.251
1886	MET AA S-O		109	.230
1887	MET AA S-O		68	.361
	NY N 3		1	.000
1890	BRO AA S		60	.234
	BLTR		815	-

```
YR  CL LEA POS      GP    G    REC
```

NELSON, JAMES LORIN (JIM)
B.JULY 4,1947 BIRMINGHAM,ALA.
```
1970 PIT N  P            15    4- 2
1971 PIT N  P            17    2- 2
     BRTR                32    6- 4
```

NELSON, LUTHER MARTIN (LUKE)
B.DEC.4,1893 CABLE,ILL.
```
1919 NY  A  P             9    3- 0
     BRTR
```

NELSON, LYNN BERNARD
(LYNN) OR (LINE DRIVE)
B.FEB.24,1905 SHELDON,N.DAK.
D.FEB.15,1955 KANSAS CITY,MO.
```
1930 CHI N  P            37    3- 2
1933 CHI N  P       24   29    5- 5
1934 CHI N  P             2    0- 1
1937 PHI A  P       30   74    4- 9
1938 PHI A  P       32   67   10-11
1939 PHI A  P       35   40   10-13
1940 DET A  P        6   19    1- 1
     BRTL          166  268   33-42
```

NELSON, MELVIN FREDERICK (MEL)
B.MAY 30,1936 SAN DIEGO,CAL.
```
1960 STL N  P             2    0- 1
1963 LA  A  P       36   39    2- 3
1965 MIN A  P            28    0- 4
1967 MIN A /P             1    0- 0
1968 STL N  P            18    2- 1
1969 STL N /P             8    0- 1
     BRTL           93   96    4-10
```

NELSON, RAYMOND (KELL)
(REAL NAME RAYMOND NELSON KELLOGG)
B.AUG.4,1875 HOLYOKE,MASS.
D.JAN.8,1961 MT.VERNON,N.Y.
```
1901 NY  N  2            36    .205
     BRTR
```

NELSON, ROBERT SIDNEY
(TEX) OR (BABE)
B.AUG.7,1936 DALLAS,TEX.
```
1955 BAL A 1-0           25    .194
1956 BAL A  O            39    .206
1957 BAL A  P            15    .217
     BLTL                79    .205
```

NELSON, ROGER EUGENE
(ROGER) OR (SPIDER)
B.JUNE 7,1944 ALTADENA,CAL.
```
1967 CHI A /P             5    0- 1
1968 BAL A  P            19    4- 3
1969 KC  A  P            29    7-13
1970 KC  A /P             6    0- 2
1971 KC  A  P            13    0- 1
1972 KC  A  P            34   11- 6
1973 CIN N  P            14    3- 2
1974 CIN N  P            14    4- 4
1976 KC  A /P             3    0- 0
     BRTR               135   29-32
```

NELSON, TOM COUSINEAU (TOMMY)
B.MAY 1,1917 CHICAGO,ILL.
D.SEPT.24,1973 SAN DIEGO,CAL.
```
1945 BOS N  2-3          40    .165
     BRTR
```

NELSON, WILLIAM F.
B.SEPT.28,1863 TERRE HAUTE,IND.
D.JUNE 23,1941 TERRE HAUTE,IND.
```
1884 PIT AA P             3    1- 2
     TR
```

NEN, RICHARD LEROY (DICK)
B.SEP.24,1939 SOUTH GATE,CAL.
```
1963 LA  N 1              7    .125
1965 WAS A 1             69    .260
1966 WAS A 1             94    .213
1967 WAS A 1/0          110    .218
1968 CHI N 1             81    .181
1970 WAS A /1             6    .200
     BLTL               367    .224
```

NESS, JOHN CHARLES (JACK)
B.NOV.11,1885 CHICAGO,ILL.
D.DEC.3,1957 DE LAND,FLA.
```
1911 DET A 1            12    .161
1916 CHI A 1            75    .267
     BRTR               87    .248
```

NETTLES, GRAIG
B.AUG.20,1944 SAN DIEGO,CAL.
```
1967 MIN A /H             3    .333
1968 MIN A  0/3-1        22    .224
1969 MIN A  0-3          96    .222
1970 CLE A *3/0         157    .235
1971 CLE A *3           158    .261
1972 CLE A *3           150    .253
1973 NY  A *3           160    .234
1974 NY  A *3/S         155    .246
1975 NY  A *3           157    .267
1976 NY  A *3           158    .254
1977 NY  A *3           158    .255
1978 NY  A *3/S         159    .276
     BLTR              1533    .252
```

NETTLES, JAMES WILLIAM (JIM)
B.MAR.2,1947 SAN DIEGO,CAL.
```
1970 MIN A  0            13    .250
1971 MIN A  0            70    .250
1972 MIN A  0/1         102    .204
1974 DET A  0            43    .227
     BLTL               228    .225
```

NETTLES, MORRIS
B.JAN.26,1952 LOS ANGELES,CAL.
```
1974 CAL A  0            56    .274
1975 CAL A  0           112    .231
     BLTL               168    .247
```

NETZEL, MILES A. (MILO)
B.MAY 12,1886 ELDRED,PA.
D.MAR.18,1938 OXNARD,CAL.
```
1909 CLE A 3-0          10    .186
     TR
```

NEU, OTTO ADAM
B.SEPT.24,1894 SPRINGFIELD,OHIO
D.SEPT.19,1932 KENTON,OHIO
```
1917 STL A  H            1    .000
     BRTR
```

NEUBAUER, HAROLD CHARLES
B.MAY 13,1902 HOBOKEN,N.J.
D.SEPT.9,1949 BARRINGTON,R.I.
```
1925 BOS A P             7    1- 0
     BRTR
```

NEUER, JOHN S. (TEX)
B.JUNE 14,1877 FREMONT,OHIO
D.JAN.14,1966 NORTHUMBERLAND,PA
```
1907 NY  A P             7    4- 2
     BRTR
```

NEUMEIER, DANIEL GEORGE (DAN)
B.MAR.9,1948 SHAWANO,WIS.
```
1972 CHI A /P            3    0- 0
     BRTR
```

NEUN, JOHN HENRY (JOHNNY)
B.OCT.28,1900 BALTIMORE,MD.
```
1925 DET A 1            60    .266
1926 DET A 1            97    .298
1927 DET A 1            79    .323
1928 DET A 1            36    .213
1930 BOS N 1            81    .325
1931 BOS N 1            79    .221
     BBTL              432    .289
```
NON-PLAYING MANAGER
NY(A) 1946; CIN(N) 1947-48

NEVEL, ERNIE WYRE
B.AUG.17,1919 CHARLESTON,MO.
```
1950 NY  A P             3    0- 1
1951 NY  A P             1    0- 0
1953 CIN N P            10    0- 0
     BRTR               14    0- 1
```

NEVERS, ERNEST ALONZO (ERNIE)
B.JUNE 11,1903 WILLOW RIVER,MINN.
D.MAY 3,1976 SAN RAFAEL,CAL.
```
1926 STL A P        11   12    2- 4
1927 STL A P            27    3- 8
1928 STL A P             6    1- 0
     BRTR           44   45    6-12
```

NEVINS
```
1873 RES NA 2-3-0       13    —
```

NEWCOMBE, DONALD (DON) OR (NEWK)
B.JUNE 14,1926 MADISON,N.J.
```
1949 BRO N P        38   39   17- 8
1950 BRO N P            40   19-11
1951 BRO N P            40   20- 9
1954 BRO N P        29   31    9- 8
1955 BRO N P        34   57   20- 5
1956 BRO N P        38   52   27- 7
1957 BRO N P        28   34   11-12
1958 LA  N P            11    0- 6
     CIN N P        20   39    7- 7
1959 CIN N P        30   61   13- 8
1960 CIN N P        16   24    4- 6
     CLE A P        20   24    2- 3
     BLTR          344  452  149-90
```

NEWELL, JOHN A.
B.JAN.14,1868 WILMINGTON,DEL.
D.JAN.28,1919 WILMINGTON,DEL.
```
1891 PIT N 3             5    .111
     BRTL
```

NEWELL, T. E.
B.ST.LOUIS,MO.
```
1877 STL N S             1    .000
```

NEWHAUSER, DONALD LOUIS (DON)
B.NOV.7,1947 MIAMI,FLA.
```
1972 BOS A P            31    4- 2
1973 BOS A /P            9    0- 1
1974 BOS A /P            2    0- 0
     BRTR               42    4- 3
```

NEWHOUSER, HAROLD (HAL)
B.MAY 20,1921 DETROIT,MICH.
```
1939 DET A P             1    0- 1
1940 DET A P            28    9- 9
1941 DET A P            33    9-11
1942 DET A P        38   39    8-14
1943 DET A P            37    8-17
1944 DET A P            47   29- 9
1945 DET A P            40   25- 9
1946 DET A P            37   26- 9
1947 DET A P            40   17-17
1948 DET A P            39   21-12
1949 DET A P            38   18-11
1950 DET A P            35   15-13
1951 DET A P        15   17    6- 6
1952 DET A P        25   26    9- 9
1953 DET A P             7    0- 1
1954 CLE A P            26    7- 2
1955 CLE A P             2    0- 0
     BLTL          488  492  207-150
```

NEWKIRK, FLOYD ELMO
(FLOYD) OR (THREE-FINGER)
B.JULY 16,1908 NORRIS CITY,ILL.
D.APR.15,1976 CLAYTON,MO.
```
1934 NY  A P             1    0- 0
     BRTR
```

NEWKIRK, JOEL IVAN
B.MAY 1,1896 KYANA,IND.
```
1919 CHI N P             1    0- 0
1920 CHI N P             2    0- 1
     BRTR                3    0- 1
```

NEWLIN, MAURICE MILTON (MICKEY)
B.JUNE 22,1914 BLOOMINGDALE,IND
```
1940 STL A P             1    1- 0
1941 STL A P            14    0- 2
     BRTR               15    1- 2
```

NEWMAN, CHARLES C.
B.INDIANAPOLIS,IND.
```
1891 STL AA C            1    .000
1892 NY  N O             2    .375
     CHI N O            14    .148
                        17    .244
```

NEWMAN, FREDERICK WILLIAM (FRED)
B.FEB.21,1942 BOSTON,MASS.
```
1962 LA  A P             4    0- 1
1963 LA  A P            12    1- 5
1964 LA  A P        32   39   13-10
1965 CAL A P            36   14-16
1966 CAL A P            21    4- 7
1967 CAL A /P            3    1- 0
     BRTR          108  115   33-39
```

NEWMAN, JEFFREY LYNN (JEFF)
B.SEPT.11,1948 FORT WORTH,TEX.
```
1976 OAK A C            43    .195
1977 OAK A C/P       1  94    0- 0
                                .222
1978 OAK A C-1         105    .239
     BRTR            1 242    0- 0
                                .227
```

NEWMAN, RAYMOND FRANCIS (RAY)
B.JUNE 22,1945 EVANSVILLE,IND.
```
1971 CHI N P            30    1- 2
1972 MIL A /P            4    0- 0
1973 MIL A P            11    2- 1
     BLTL               45    3- 3
```

NEWNAM, PATRICK HENRY
B.DEC.10,1880 HEMPSTEAD,TEX.
D.JUNE 20,1938 SAN ANTONIO,TEX.
```
1910 STL A 1           103    .216
1911 STL A 1            20    .194
     BRTR              123    .213
```

YR	CL	LEA	POS	GP	G	REC
NEWSOM, LOUIS NORMAN						
(BUCK) OR (BOBO)						
B.AUG.11,1907 HARTSVILLE,S.C.						
D.DEC.7,1962 ORLANDO,FLA.						
1929	BRO	N	P		3	0- 3
1930	BRO	N	P		2	0- 0
1932	CHI	N	P		1	0- 0
1934	STL	A	P	47	50	16-20
1935	STL	A	P		7	0- 6
	WAS	A	P		28	11-12
1936	WAS	A	P	43	44	17-15
1937	WAS	A	P	11	13	3- 4
	BOS	A	P	30	31	13-10
1938	STL	A	P	44	46	20-16
1939	STL	A	P		6	3- 1
	DET	A	P		35	17-10
1940	DET	A	P		36	21- 5
1941	DET	A	P		43	12-20
1942	WAS	A	P		30	11-17
	BRO	N	P		6	2- 2
1943	BRO	N	P		22	9- 4
	STL	A	P		10	1- 6
	WAS	A	P		6	3- 3
1944	PHI	A	P		37	13-15
1945	PHI	A	P		36	8-20
1946	PHI	A	P		10	3- 5
	WAS	A	P		24	11- 8
1947	WAS	A	P		14	4- 6
	NY	A	P		17	7- 5
1948	NY	N	P		11	0- 4
1952	WAS	A	P		10	1- 1
	PHI	A	P		14	3- 3
1953	PHI	A	P		17	2- 1
		BRTR		600	609	211-222
NEWSOME, HEBER HAMPTON (DICK)						
B.DEC.13,1909 AHOSKIE,N.C.						
D.DEC.15,1965 AHOSKIE,N.C.						
1941	BOS	A	P		36	19-10
1942	BOS	A	P		24	8-10
1943	BOS	A	P		27	8-13
		BRTR			87	35-33
NEWSOME, LAMAR ASHBY (SKEETER)						
B.OCT.18,1910 PHENIX CITY,ALA.						
1935	PHI	A	2-S-3-O		59	.207
1936	PHI	A	S		127	.225
1937	PHI	A	S		122	.253
1938	PHI	A	S		17	.271
1939	PHI	A	S		99	.222
1941	BOS	A	2-S		93	.225
1942	BOS	A	2-S-3		29	.274
1943	BOS	A	S-3		114	.265
1944	BOS	A	2-S-3		136	.242
1945	BOS	A	2-S-3		125	.290
1946	PHI	N	2-S-3		112	.232
1947	PHI	N	2-S-3		95	.229
		BRTR			1128	.245
NEWTON, EUSTACE JAMES (DOC)						
B.OCT.26,1877 INDIANAPOLIS,IND.						
D.MAY 14,1931 MEMPHIS,TENN.						
1900	CIN	N	P		30	9-14
1901	CIN	N	P		20	4-13
	BRO	N	P		13	7- 5
1902	BRO	N	P-1	30	32	15-14
						.174
1905	NY	A	P		12	2- 4
1906	NY	A	P		21	7- 5
1907	NY	A	P		19	7-10
1908	NY	A	P		23	4- 5
1909	NY	A	P		4	0- 3
		BLTL		172	174	55-73
						.172
NIARHOS, CONSTANTINE GREGORY (GUS)						
B.DEC.6,1920 BIRMINGHAM,ALA.						
1946	NY	A	C		37	.225
1948	NY	A	C		83	.268
1949	NY	A	C		32	.279
1950	NY	A	H		1	.000
	CHI	A	C		41	.324
1951	CHI	A	C		66	.256
1952	BOS	A	C		29	.103
1953	BOS	A	C		16	.200
1954	PHI	N	C		3	.200
1955	PHI	N	C		7	.111
		BRTR			315	.252
NICE, CHARLES REIFF						
[PLAYED UNDER NAME OF						
CHARLES REIFF NYCE]						
NICHOL, SAMUEL ANDERSON						
B.APR.20,1869 IRELAND						
D.APR.19,1937 STEUBENVILLE,OHIO						
1888	PIT	N	O		8	.045
1890	COL	AA	O		14	.188
					22	.147
NICHOLAS, DONALD LEIGH (DON)						
B.OCT.30,1930 PHOENIX,ARIZ.						
1952	CHI	A	H		3	.000
1954	CHI	A	H		7	.000
		BLTR			10	.000

YR	CL	LEA	POS	GP	G	REC
NICHOLLS, SIMON BURDETTE						
B.JULY 18,1882 GERMANTOWN,MD.						
D.MAR.12,1911 BALTIMORE,MD.						
1903	DET	A	S		2	.375
1906	PHI	A	S		12	.219
1907	PHI	A	2-S		124	.302
1908	PHI	A	2-S		150	.216
1909	PHI	A	3		21	.211
1910	CLE	A	S		3	.000
		BLTR			312	.252
NICHOLS, ALFRED H.						
B.BROOKLYN,N.Y.						
1875	ATL	NA	3		32	-
1876	MUT	N	3		57	.177
1877	LOU	N	1-2-S-3		6	.211
					95	-
NICHOLS, ARTHUR FRANCIS						
[REAL NAME ARTHUR FRANCIS MEIKLE]						
B.JULY 14,1871 MANCHESTER,N.H.						
D.AUG.9,1945 WILLIMANTIC,CONN.						
1898	CHI	N	C		13	.264
1899	CHI	N	C		17	.277
1900	CHI	N	C		8	.208
1901	STL	N	C-O		82	.247
1902	STL	N	C-1-O		69	.272
1903	STL	N	1		33	.192
					222	.248
NICHOLS, CHARLES AUGUSTUS (KID)						
B.SEPT.14,1869 MADISON,WIS.						
D.APR.11,1953 KANSAS CITY,MO.						
1890	BOS	N	P		47	27-19
1891	BOS	N	P		50	30-17
1892	BOS	N	P	53	54	35-16
1893	BOS	N	P	46	47	32-14
1894	BOS	N	P		46	33-13
1895	BOS	N	P		43	27-16
1896	BOS	N	P		45	30-14
1897	BOS	N	P		43	32-11
1898	BOS	N	P		45	33-12
1899	BOS	N	P	38	41	20-18
1900	BOS	N	P		29	13-14
1901	BOS	N	P		46	18-15
1904	STL	N	M-P		36	20-12
1905	STL	N	M-P		8	1- 5
	PHI	N	P		18	10- 6
1906	PHI	N	P		4	0- 2
		BBTR		597	602	361-204
NICHOLS, CHESTER RAYMOND JR. (CHET)						
B.FEB.22,1931 PAWTUCKET,R.I.						
1951	BOS	N	P		33	11- 8
1954	MIL	N	P		35	9-11
1955	MIL	N	P		34	9- 8
1956	MIL	N	P		2	0- 1
1960	BOS	A	P		6	0- 2
1961	BOS	A	P		26	3- 2
1962	BOS	A	P		29	1- 1
1963	BOS	A	P		21	1- 3
1964	CIN	N	P		3	0- 0
		BBTL			189	34-36
NICHOLS, CHESTER RAYMOND SR. (NICK)						
B.JULY 3,1897 WOONSOCKET,R.I.						
1926	PIT	N	P		3	0- 0
1927	PIT	N	P		8	0- 3
1928	NY	N	P		3	0- 0
1930	PHI	N	P	16	26	1- 2
1931	PHI	N	P		3	0- 1
1932	PHI	N	P		11	0- 2
		BRTR		44	54	1- 8
NICHOLS, DOLAN LEVON						
(DOLAN) OR (NICK)						
B.FEB.28,1930 TISHOMINGO,MISS.						
1958	CHI	N	P		24	0- 4
		BRTR				
NICHOLS, FREDERICK C. (TRICKY)						
B.1856 BRIDGEPORT,CONN.						
1875	NH	NA	P-O	32	33	4-28
						-
1876	BOS	N	P		1	1- 0
1877	STL	N	P-O	42	51	18-23
						.168
1878	PRO	N	P		11	4- 7
1880	WOR	N	P		2	0- 2
1882	BAL	AA	P-O	14	27	1-13
						.154
		BRTR		112	125	28-73
						-
NICHOLS, ROY						
B.MAR.3,1921 LITTLE ROCK,ARK.						
1944	NY	N	2-3		11	.222
		BRTR				
NICHOLSON, DAVID LAWRENCE (DAVE)						
B.AUG.29,1939 ST.LOUIS,MO.						
1960	BAL	A	O		54	.186
1962	BAL	A	O		97	.173
1963	CHI	A	O		126	.229
1964	CHI	A	O		97	.204
1965	CHI	A	O		54	.153
1966	HOU	N	O		100	.246
1967	ATL	N	/O		10	.200
		BRTR			538	.212

YR	CL	LEA	POS	GP	G	REC
NICHOLSON, FRANK COLLINS						
B.AUG.29,1889 BERLIN,PA.						
D.NOV.10,1972 JERSEY SHORE,PA.						
1912	PHI	N	P		2	0- 0
		BRTR				
NICHOLSON, FREDERICK (SHOEMAKER)						
B.SEPT.1,1894 HONEY GROVE,TEX.						
1917	DET	A	O		13	.286
1919	PIT	N	1-O		30	.273
1920	PIT	N	O		99	.360
1921	BOS	N	O		83	.327
1922	BOS	N	O		78	.252
		BRTR			303	.311
NICHOLSON, OVID EDWARD						
B.DEC.30,1888 SALEM,IND.						
D.MAR.24,1968 SALEM,IND.						
1912	PIT	N	O		6	.454
		BLTR				
NICHOLSON, THOMAS C.						
(PARSON) OR (BEACON)						
B.APR.14,1863 BLAINE,OHIO						
D.FEB.28,1917 BELLAIRE,OHIO						
1888	DET	N	2		24	.259
1890	TOL	AA	2		133	.261
1895	WAS	N	S		10	.184
					167	.256
NICHOLSON, WILLIAM BECK (SWISH)						
B.DEC.11,1914 CHESTERTOWN,MD.						
1936	PHI	A	O		11	.000
1939	CHI	N	O		58	.295
1940	CHI	N	O		135	.297
1941	CHI	N	O		147	.254
1942	CHI	N	O		152	.294
1943	CHI	N	O		154	.309
1944	CHI	N	O		156	.287
1945	CHI	N	O		151	.243
1946	CHI	N	O		105	.220
1947	CHI	N	O		148	.244
1948	CHI	N	O		143	.261
1949	PHI	N	O		98	.234
1950	PHI	N	O		41	.224
1951	PHI	N	O		85	.241
1952	PHI	N	O		55	.273
1953	PHI	N	O		38	.210
		BLTR			1677	.268
NICKLIN, SAMUEL STRANG						
[PLAYED UNDER NAME OF						
SAMUEL NICKLIN STRANG]						
NICOL, GEORGE EDWARD						
B.OCT.17,1870 BARRY,ILL.						
D.AUG.10,1924 MILWAUKEE,WIS.						
1890	STL	AA	P		4	2- 2
1891	CHI	N	P		3	0- 1
1894	PIT	N	P		9	4- 2
	LOU	N	P-O	6	28	3- 3
						.345
		TL		22	44	9- 8
						.344
NICOL, HUGH						
B.JAN.1,1858 CAMPSIE,SCOTLAND						
D.JUNE 27,1921 LAFAYETTE,IND.						
1881	CHI	N	S-O		26	.203
1882	CHI	N	S-O		47	.198
1883	STL	AA	2-O		85	.263
1884	STL	AA	2-O		110	.270
1885	STL	AA	O		112	.211
1886	STL	AA	O		67	.204
1887	CIN	AA	O		126	.334
1888	CIN	AA	2-S-O		134	.236
1889	CIN	AA	2-3-O		122	.246
1890	CIN	N	O		50	.209
		BRTR			879	.254
NON-PLAYING MANAGER STL[N] 1897						
NICOSIA, STEVEN RICHARD (STEVE)						
B.AUG.6,1955 PATERSON,N.J.						
1978	PIT	N	/C		3	.000
		BRTR				
NIEBERGALL, CHARLES ARTHUR (NIG)						
B.MAY 23,1899 NEW YORK,N.Y.						
1921	STL	N	C		5	.167
1923	STL	N	C		9	.107
1924	STL	N	C		40	.293
		BRTR			54	.231
NIEHAUS, ALBERT BERNARD						
B.JUNE 1,1899 CINCINNATI,OHIO						
D.OCT.14,1931 CINCINNATI,OHIO						
1925	PIT	N	1		17	.219
	CIN	N	1		51	.299
		BRTR			68	.275
NIEHAUS, RICHARD J.						
B.OCT.24,1892 COVINGTON,KY.						
D.MAR.12,1957 ATLANTA,GA.						
1913	STL	N	P		3	0- 2
1914	STL	N	P		8	1- 0
1915	STL	N	P		15	2- 1
1920	CLE	A	P		19	1- 2
		BLTL			45	4- 5

```
YR  CL LEA POS    GP   G   REC          YR  CL LEA POS    GP   G   REC          YR  CL LEA POS    GP   G   REC

NIEHOFF, JOHN ALBERT (BERT)             NIGGELING, JOHN ARNOLD (JOHNNY)         NIXON, WILLARD LEE
B.MAY 13,1884 LOUISVILLE,COLO.          B.JULY 10,1903 REMSEN,IOWA              B.JUNE 17,1928 TAYLORSVILLE,GA.
D.DEC.8,1974 INGLEWOOD,CAL.             D.SEPT.16,1963 LE MARS,IOWA             1950 BOS A  P        22   8- 6
1913 CIN N  3          2    .000        1938 BOS N  P         2   1- 0          1951 BOS A  P    33  34   7- 4
1914 CIN N  3        142    .242        1939 CIN N  P        10   2- 1          1952 BOS A  P    23  33   5- 4
1915 PHI N  3        148    .238        1940 STL A  P        28   7-11          1953 BOS A  P        23   4- 8
1916 PHI N  3        146    .243        1941 STL A  P        24   7- 9          1954 BOS A  P        31  11-12
1917 PHI N  3        114    .255        1942 STL A  P        28  15-11          1955 BOS A  P        31  12-10
1918 STL N  3         22    .176        1943 STL A  P        20   6- 8          1956 BOS A  P        23   9- 8
     NY  N  3          7    .261             WAS A  P         6   4- 2          1957 BOS A  P    29  32  12-13
     BRTR           581    .240         1944 WAS A  P        24  10- 8          1958 BOS A  P        10   1- 7
                                        1945 WAS A  P        26   7-12               BLTR      225 239  69-72
                                        1946 BOS N  P         8   2- 5
NIEKRO, JOSEPH FRANKLIN (JOE)                BRTR          184  64-69          NOBLE, RAFAEL MIGUEL (RAY)
B.NOV.7,1944 MARTINS FERRY,OHIO                                                 B.MAR.15,1922 CENTRAL HATILLO,CUBA
1967 CHI N  P        36  10- 7                                                  1951 NY  N  C        55   .234
1968 CHI N  P        34  14-10          NILAND, THOMAS JAMES (HONEST TOM)       1952 NY  N  C         6   .000
1969 CHI N /P         4   0- 1          B.APR.14,1870 BROOKFIELD,MASS.          1953 NY  N  C        46   .206
     SD  N  P    37  38   8-17          D.APR.30,1950 LYNN,MASS.                     BRTR          107   .218
1970 DET A  P    38  39  12-13          1896 STL N  S-O      18   .162
1971 DET A  P    31  32   6- 7               BRTR                              NOFTSKER, GEORGE W.
1972 DET A  P        18   3- 2                                                  B.AUG.24,1859 SHIPPENSBURG,PA.
1973 ATL N  P        20   2- 4                                                  D.MAY 8,1931 SHIPPENSBURG,PA.
1974 ATL N  P        27   3- 2          NILES, HERBERT CLYDE (HARRY)            1884 ALT U  C-O      7   .042
1975 HOU N  P        40   6- 4          B.SEPT.10,1880 BUCHANAN,MICH.
1976 HOU N  P        36   4- 8          D.APR.18,1953 STURGIS,MICH.
1977 HOU N  P        44  13- 8          1906 STL A  3-O     142   .229         NOLAN, EDWARD SYLVESTER (THE ONLY)
1978 HOU N  P    35  36  14-14          1907 STL A  2       120   .289         B.NOV.7,1857 PATERSON,N.J.
     BRTR      400 404  95-97                BOS A  2        95   .250         D.MAY 18,1913 PATERSON,N.J.
                                             BOS A  2        18   .235         1878 IND N  P        35  13-22
                                        1909 BOS A  O       145   .245         1881 CLE N  P-3- 21  40   7-13
NIEKRO, PHILIP HENRY (PHIL)             1910 BOS A  O        18   .214                       O         .251
B.APR.1,1939 BLAINE,OHIO                     CLE A  O        70   .212         1883 PIT AA P-O      7   0- 6
1964 MIL N  P        10   0- 0               BRTR          608   .246                                  .296
1965 MIL N  P    41  42   2- 3                                                 1884 WIL U  P-O   5   9   1- 4
1966 ATL N  P        28   4- 3                                                                         .242
1967 ATL N  P        46  11- 9          NILES, WILLIAM A.                       1885 PHI N  P-O      8   1- 7
1968 ATL N  P        37  14-12          B.1869 COVINGTON,KY.                                           .133
1969 ATL N  P        40  23-13          1895 PIT N  3        11   .205               BLTR       76  99  22-52
1970 ATL N  P        34  12-18                                                                         .247
1971 ATL N  P        42  15-14
1972 ATL N  P        38  16-12          NILL, GEORGE CHARLES (RABBIT)          NOLAN, GARY LYNN
1973 ATL N  P        42  13-10          B.JULY 14,1881 FT.WAYNE,IND.           B.MAY 27,1948 HERLONG,CAL.
1974 ATL N  P        41  20-13          D.MAY 24,1962 FORT WAYNE,IND.          1967 CIN N  P        33  14- 8
1975 ATL N  P        39  15-15          1904 WAS A  2        15   .167         1968 CIN N  P        23   9- 4
1976 ATL N  P        38  17-11          1905 WAS A  2-3     103   .182         1969 CIN N  P    16  17   8- 8
1977 ATL N  P        44  16-20          1906 WAS A  2-S-O    89   .235         1970 CIN N  P        37  18- 7
1978 ATL N  P    44  45  19-18          1907 WAS A  2-S-3    66   .218         1971 CIN N  P        35  12-15
     BRTR      564 566 197-171               CLE A  2        12   .286         1972 CIN N  P        25  15- 5
                                        1908 CLE A  S        11   .215         1973 CIN N /P         2   0- 1
                                             BRTR          296   .212         1975 CIN N  P        32  15- 9
NIELSEN, MILTON ROBERT                                                         1976 CIN N  P        34  15- 9
B.FEB.8,1925 TYLER,MINN.                                                       1977 CIN N /P         8   4- 1
1949 CLE A  O         3   .111          NIPPERT, MERLIN LEE                         CAL A /P     5   6   0- 3
1951 CLE A  H        16   .000          B.SEPT.1,1938 MANGUM,OKLA.                  BRTR      250 252 110-70
     BLTL            19   .067          1962 BOS A  P         4   0- 0
                                             BRTR                              NOLAN, JOSEPH WILLIAM (JOE)
                                                                               B.MAY 12,1951 ST.LOUIS,MO.
NIEMAN, ELMER LE ROY (BUTCH)                                                   1972 NY  N /C         4   .000
B.FEB.8,1918 HERKIMER,KAN.              NISCHWITZ, RONALD LEE (RON)            1975 ATL N /C         4   .250
1943 BOS N  O       101   .251          B.JULY 1,1937 DAYTON,OHIO              1977 ATL N  C        62   .280
1944 BOS N  O       134   .265          1961 DET A  P         6   0- 1         1978 ATL N  C        95   .230
1945 BOS N  O        97   .247          1962 DET A  P        48   4- 5              BLTR          165   .236
     BLTL           332   .256          1963 DET A  P        14   0- 2
                                        1965 DET A  P        20   1- 0         NOLD, RICHARD LOUIS (DICK)
                                             BBTL            88   5- 8         B.MAY 4,1943 SAN FRANCISCO,CAL.
NIEMAN, ROBERT CHARLES (BOB)                                                   1967 WAS A /P         7   0- 2
B.JAN.26,1927 CINCINNATI,OHIO                                                       BRTR
1951 STL A  O        12   .372          NITCHOLAS, OTHO JAMES
1952 STL A  O       131   .289          B.SEPT.13,1908 MC KINNEY,TEX.          NONNENKAMP, LEO WILLIAM (RED)
1953 DET A  O       142   .281          1945 BRO N  P         7   1- 0         B.JULY 7,1911 ST.LOUIS,MO.
1954 DET A  O        91   .263               BRTR                             1933 PIT N  H         1   .000
1955 CHI A  O        99   .283                                                 1938 BOS A  O        87   .283
1956 CHI A  O        14   .300                                                 1939 BOS A  O        58   .240
     BAL A  O       114   .322          NIXON, ALBERT RICHARD                  1940 BOS A  H         9   .000
1957 BAL A  O       129   .276          (HUMPTY DUMPTY)                             BLTL          155   .262
1958 BAL A  O       105   .325          B.APR.11,1886 ATLANTIC CITY,N.J
1959 BAL A  O       118   .292          D.NOV.9,1960 OPELOUSAS,LA.             NOONAN, PETER JOHN
1960 STL N  O        81   .287          1915 BRO N  O        14   .231         B.NOV.24,1881 W.STOCKBRIDGE,MASS.
1961 STL N  O         6   .471          1916 BRO N  O         1  1.000         D.JAN.11,1965 PITTSFIELD,MASS.
     CLE A  O        39   .354          1918 BRO N  O         6   .454         1904 PHI A  C        38   .202
1962 CLE A  H         2   .000          1921 BOS N  O        55   .239         1906 CHI N  C         1   .333
     SF  N  O        30   .300          1922 BOS N  O        86   .264              STL N  C-1      39   .168
     BRTR          1113   .295          1923 BOS N  O        88   .274         1907 STL N  C        70   .224
                                        1926 PHI N  O        93   .293              BRTR          148   .205
                                        1927 PHI N  O        54   .312
NIEMES, JACOB LELAND                    1928 PHI N  O        25   .234         NOPS, JEREMIAH H.
B.OCT.19,1919 CINCINNATI,OHIO                BRTL          422   .276          B.JUNE 23,1875 TOLEDO,OHIO
D.MAR.4,1966 HAMILTON,OHIO                                                     D.MAR.26,1937 CAMDEN,N.J.
1943 CIN N  P         3   0- 0                                                 1896 PHI N  P         1   1- 0
     BRTL                               NIXON, RUSSELL EUGENE (RUSS)                BAL N  P         3   2- 1
                                        B.FEB.19,1935 CLEVELAND,OHIO           1897 BAL N  P        28  20- 7
                                        1957 CLE A  C        62   .281         1898 BAL N  P        29  19-10
NIEMIEC, ALFRED JOSEPH (AL)             1958 CLE A  C       113   .301         1899 BAL N  P    31  32  16-12
B.MAY 18,1911 MERIDEN,CONN.             1959 CLE A  C        82   .240         1900 BAL N  P         9   3- 4
1934 BOS A  2         9   .219          1960 CLE A  C        25   .244         1901 BAL A  P        27  11-12
1936 PHI A  2        69   .197               BOS A  C        80   .298              BRTR      128 129  72-46
     BRTR            78   .200          1961 BOS A  C        87   .289
                                        1962 BOS A  C        65   .278         NORDBROOK, TIMOTHY CHARLES (TIM)
                                        1963 BOS A  C        98   .268         B.JULY 7,1949 BALTIMORE,MD.
NIESON, CHARLES BASSETT (CHUCK)         1964 BOS A  C        81   .233         1974 BAL A /S-2      6   .267
B.SEP.24,1942 HANFORD,CAL.              1965 BOS A  C        59   .270         1975 BAL A  S/2     40   .118
1964 MIN N  P         2   0- 0          1966 MIN A  C        51   .260         1976 BAL A  2-S     27   .227
     BRTR                               1967 MIN A  C        74   .239              CAL A /S-2      5   .000
                                        1968 BOS A  C        29   .153         1977 CHI A  S/3     15   .250
                                             BLTR          906   .268              TOR A  S        24   .175
                                                                               1978 TOR A /S        7   .000
                                                                                    MIL A /S         2   .000
                                                                                    TL            126   .174
```

YR CL LEA POS   GP   G   REC

NORDHAGEN, WAYNE OREN
B.JULY 4,1948 THIEF RIVER FALLS, MINN.
1976 CHI A O/C   22   .189
1977 CHI A O/C   52   .315
1978 CHI A O-D-C   68   .301
     BRTR   142   .290

NORDSTROM, ANDREW ARTHUR
[PLAYED UNDER NAME OF
ANDREW ARTHUR CAREY]

NORDYKE, LOUIS ELLIS
B.AUG.7,1876 BRIGHTON,IOWA
D.SEPT.27,1945 LOS ANGELES,CAL.
1906 STL A 1   25   .245
     TR

NOREN, IRVING ARNOLD (IRV)
B.NOV.29,1924 JAMESTOWN,N.Y.
1950 WAS A 1-O   138   .295
1951 WAS A O   129   .279
1952 WAS A O   12   .245
     NY A 1-O   93   .235
1953 NY A O   109   .267
1954 NY A 1-O   125   .319
1955 NY A O   132   .253
1956 NY A 1-O   29   .216
1957 KC A 1-O   81   .213
     STL N O   17   .367
1958 STL N O   117   .264
1959 STL N 1-O   8   .125
     CHI N 1-O   65   .321
1960 CHI N 1-O   12   .091
     LA N H   26   .200
     BLTL   1093   .275

NORIEGA, JOHN ALAN
B.DEC.20,1943 OGDEN,UTAH
1969 CIN N /P   5   0- 0
1970 CIN N /P   8   0- 0
     BRTR   13   0- 0

NORMAN, DANIEL EDMUND (DAN)
B.JAN.11,1955 LOS ANGELES,CAL.
1977 NY N /O   7   .250
1978 NY N O   19   .266
     BRTR   26   .262

NORMAN, FREDIE HUBERT (FRED)
B.AUG.20,1942 SAN ANTONIO,TEX.
1962 KC A P   2   0- 0
1963 KC A P   2   0- 1
1964 CHI N P   8   0- 4
1966 CHI N /P   2   0- 0
1967 CHI N /P   1   0- 0
1970 LA N P   30   2- 0
     STL N /P   1   0- 0
1971 STL N /P   4   0- 0
     SD N P   20   25   3-12
1972 SD N P   42   43   9-11
1973 SD N P   12   1- 7
     CIN N P   24   12- 6
1974 CIN N P   35   13-12
1975 CIN N P   34   12- 6
1976 CIN N P   33   12- 7
1977 CIN N P   35   14-13
1978 CIN N P   36   11- 9
     BBTL   321 327   89-86
     BL 1962-70

NORMAN, HENRY WILLIS PATRICK (BILL)
B.JULY 16,1910 ST.LOUIS,MO.
D.APR.21,1962 MILWAUKEE,WIS.
1931 CHI A O   24   .182
1932 CHI A O   13   .229
     BRTR   37   .204
NON-PLAYING MANAGER DET[A] 1958-59

NORMAN, NELSON AUGUSTO
B.MAY 23,1958 SAN PEDRO DE MACORIS,D.R.
1978 TEX A S/3   23   .265
     BRTR

NORRIS, JAMES FRANCIS (JIM)
B.DEC.20,1948 BROOKLYN,N.Y.
1977 CLE A *O/1   133   .270
1978 CLE A O-D/1   113   .283
     BLTL   246   .275

NORRIS, LEO JOHN
B.MAY 17,1908 BAY ST.LOUIS,MISS
1936 PHI N 2-S   154   .265
1937 PHI N 2-S-3   116   .257
     BRTR   270   .262

NORRIS, MICHAEL KELVIN (MIKE)
B.MAR.19,1955 SAN FRANCISCO,CAL.
1975 OAK A /P   4   1- 0
1976 OAK A P   24   4- 5
1977 OAK A P   16   17   2- 7
1978 OAK A P   14   15   0- 5
     BRTR   58   60   7-17

NORTH, LOUIS ALEXANDER
B.JUNE 15,1891 ELGIN,ILL.
D.MAY 16,1974 SHELTON,CONN.
1913 DET A 1   1   0- 1
1917 STL N 1   5   0- 0
1920 STL N 1   26   3- 2
1921 STL N 1   4   4- 4
1922 STL N 1   93   10- 3
1923 STL N 1   34   3- 4
1924 STL N 1   9   0- 0
     BOS N 1   6   1- 2
     BRTR   172 174   21-16

NORTH, WILLIAM ALEX (BILL)
B.MAY 15,1948 SEATTLE,WASH.
1971 CHI N /O   1   .375
1972 CHI N O   66   .181
1973 OAK A *O   146   .285
1974 OAK A *O   149   .260
1975 OAK A *O   140   .273
1976 OAK A *O   154   .276
1977 OAK A O   56   .261
1978 OAK A O   24   .212
     LA N *O   110   .234
     BRTR   853   .264
     BR 1971

NORTHEN, HUBBARD ELWIN
B.AUG.16,1885 ATLANTA,TEX.
D.OCT.16,1947 SHREVEPORT,LA.
1910 STL A O   26   .198
1911 CIN N O   1   .000
     BRO N O   19   .316
1912 BRO N O   118   .282
     BLTL   164   .272

NORTHEY, RONALD JAMES (RON)
B.APR.26,1920 MAHANOY CITY,PA.
D.APR.16,1971 PITTSBURGH,PA.
1942 PHI N O   127   .251
1943 PHI N O   147   .278
1944 PHI N O   152   .288
1946 PHI N O   128   .249
1947 PHI N O   13   .255
     STL N 3-O   110   .293
1948 STL N O   96   .321
1949 STL N O   90   .260
1950 STL N O   27   .260
     CHI N O   53   .281
1952 CHI N H   1   .000
1955 CHI A O   14   .357
1956 CHI A O   53   .354
1957 CHI A H   40   .185
     PHI N H   33   .269
     BLTR   1084   .275

NORTHEY, SCOTT RICHARD
B.OCT.15,1946 PHILADELPHIA,PA.
1969 KC A O   20   .262
     BRTR

NORTHROP, GEORGE HOWARD
(JAKE) OR (JERKY)
B.MAR.5,1888 MONROETON,PA.
D.NOV.16,1945 MONROETON,PA.
1918 BOS N P   7   5- 1
1919 BOS N P   12   1- 5
     BLTR   19   6- 6

NORTHRUP, JAMES THOMAS (JIM)
B.NOV.24,1939 BRECKENRIDGE,MICH.
1964 DET A O   5   .083
1965 DET A O   80   .205
1966 DET A *O   123   .265
1967 DET A *O   144   .271
1968 DET A *O   154   .264
1969 DET A *O   148   .295
1970 DET A *O   139   .262
1971 DET A *O-1   136   .270
1972 DET A *O/1   134   .261
1973 DET A *O   119   .307
1974 DET A O   97   .237
     MON N O   21   .241
     BAL A /O   8   .571
1975 BAL A O   84   .273
     BLTR   1392   .267

NORTON, ELISHA STRONG
(EFFIE) OR (LEITER)
B.AUG.17,1873 CONNEAUT,OHIO
D.MAR.5,1950 ASPINWALL,PA.
1896 WAS N P   8   3- 2
1897 WAS N P   8   1- 1
     BRTR   16   4- 3

NORTON, J. J.
[PLAYED UNDER NAME OF
THOMAS JOHN CAREY]

NORTON, PETER J.
B.JUNE 19,1850 WISCONSIN
D.FEB.8,1923
1871 OLY NA O   1   .000

NORTON, THOMAS JOHN (TOM)
B.APR.26,1950 ELYRIA,OHIO
1972 MIN A P   21   0- 1
     BRTR

NORWOOD, WILLIE
B.NOV.7,1950 GREEN COUNTY,ALA.
1977 MIN A O   39   .229
1978 MIN A *O   125   .255
     BRTR   164   .250

NOSSEK, JOSEPH RUDOLPH (JOE)
B.NOV.8,1940 CLEVELAND,OHIO
1964 MIN A O   7   .000
1965 MIN A O/3   87   .218
1966 MIN A /O   4   .000
     KC A O/3   87   .261
1967 KC A O   87   .205
1969 OAK A O   13   .000
     STL N /O   9   .200
1970 STL N /H   1   .000
     BRTR   295   .228

NOTTEBART, DONALD EDWARD (DON)
B.JAN.23,1936 WEST NEWTON,MASS.
1960 MIL N P   5   1- 0
1961 MIL N P   38   6- 7
1962 MIL N P   39   2- 2
1963 HOU N P   31   11- 8
1964 HOU N P   28   6-11
1965 HOU N P   29   4-15
1966 CIN N P   59   5- 4
1967 CIN N P   47   0- 3
1969 NY A /P   4   0- 0
     CHI N P   16   1- 1
     BRTR   296   36-51

NOURSE, CHESTER LINWOOD (CHET)
B.AUG.7,1887 IPSWICH,MASS.
D.APR.20,1958 CLEARWATER,FLA.
1909 BOS A P   3   0- 0

NOVIKOFF, LOUIS ALEXANDER
(LOU) OR (THE MAD RUSSIAN)
B.OCT.12,1915 GLENDALE,ARIZ.
D.SEPT.30,1970 SOUTH GATE,CAL.
1941 CHI N O   62   .241
1942 CHI N O   128   .300
1943 CHI N O   78   .279
1944 CHI N O   71   .281
1946 PHI N O   17   .364
     BRTR   356   .282

NOVOTNEY, RALPH JOSEPH (RUBE)
B.AUG.5,1924 STREATOR,ILL.
1949 CHI N C   22   .269
     BRTR

NOYES, WINFIELD CHARLES (WIN)
B.JUNE 16,1889 PLEASANTON,NEB.
D.APR.8,1969 CASHMERE,WASH.
1913 BOS N P   11   0- 0
1917 PHI A P   27   10-10
1919 PHI A P   10   1- 5
     CHI A P   1   0- 0
     BRTR   49   11-15

NUNAMAKER, LESLIE GRANT (LES)
B.JAN.25,1889 MALCOLM,NEB.
D.NOV.14,1938 HASTINGS,NEB.
1911 BOS A C   62   .257
1912 BOS A C   35   .259
1913 BOS A C   30   .227
1914 BOS A C   5   .200
     NY A C   86   .265
1915 NY A C   87   .225
1916 NY A C   91   .296
1917 NY A C   104   .261
1918 STL A C   85   .259
1919 CLE A C   26   .256
1920 CLE A C   34   .333
1921 CLE A C   46   .359
1922 CLE A C   25   .302
     BRTR   716   .268

NUNN, HOWARD RALPH (HOWIE)
B.OCT.19,1935 WESTFIELD,N.C.
1959 STL N P   16   2- 2
1961 CIN N P   24   2- 1
1962 CIN N P   6   0- 0
     BRTR   46   4- 3

NUSZ
1884 WAS U O   1   .000

NUTTER, EVERETT CLARENCE (DIZZY)
B.AUG.27,1893 ROSEVILLE,OHIO
D.JULY 25,1958 BATTLE CREEK,MICH.
1919 BOS N O   18   .212
     BLTR

```
YR   CL LEA POS    GP    G   REC        YR   CL LEA POS    GP    G   REC        YR   CL LEA POS    GP    G   REC

NUXHALL, JOSEPH HENRY (JOE)             OBRADOVICH, JAMES THOMAS (JIM)          O BRIEN, PETER J.
B.JULY 30,1928 HAMILTON,OHIO            B.SEPT.13,1949 FORT CAMPBELL,KY.        B.JUNE 17,1877 BINGHAMTON,N.Y.
1944 CIN N  P            1   0- 0       1978 HOU N /1          10   .176         D.JAN.31,1917 JERSEY CITY,N.J.
1952 CIN N  P           37   1- 4           BLTL                                1901 CIN N  2          15   .208
1953 CIN N  P           30   9-11                                               1906 STL A  2-3       151   .233
1954 CIN N  P    35  36 12- 5           O BRIEN, DANIEL JOQUES (DAN)            1907 CLE A  3          43   .244
1955 CIN N  P    50  53 17-12           B.APR.22,1954 ST.PETERSBURG,FLA.            WAS A  2          39   .185
1956 CIN N  P        44 13-11           1978 STL N /P           7   0- 2            BLTR      248   .231
1957 CIN N  P    39  42 10-10               BRTR
1958 CIN N  P        36 12-11                                                   O BRIEN, RAYMOND JOSEPH
1959 CIN N  P        28  9- 9           O BRIEN, EDWARD JOSEPH (EDDIE)          B.OCT.31,1892 ST.LOUIS,MO.
1960 CIN N  P    38  39  1- 8           B.DEC.11,1930 S.AMBOY,N.J.              D.MAR.31,1942 ST.LOUIS,MO.
1961 KC  A  P    37  56  5- 8           1953 PIT N  S          89   .238        1916 PIT N  O          16   .211
1962 LA  A  P         9  0- 0           1955 PIT N  S-3-0      75   .233            BLTL
1962 CIN N  P        12  5- 0           1956 PIT N  P-2-   1   63  0- 0
1963 CIN N  P        35 15- 8                 S-3-0                .264         O BRIEN, ROBERT ALLEN (BOB)
1964 CIN N  P    32  34  9- 8           1957 PIT N  P           3   1- 0        B.APR.23,1939 PITTSBURGH,PA.
1965 CIN N  P        32 11- 4           1958 PIT N  P           1   0- 0        1971 LA  N  P          14   2- 2
1966 CIN N  P        35  6- 8               BRTR       5 231   1- 0                 BRTR
    BLTL      526 555 135-117                                    .236
                                                                                O BRIEN, SYDNEY LLOYD (SID)
NYCE, CHARLES REIFF                     O BRIEN, FRANK ALOYSIUS (MICKEY)        B.DEC.18,1944 COMPTON,CAL.
[REAL NAME CHARLES REIFF NICE]          B.SEPT.13,1894 SAN FRANCISCO,CAL.       1969 BOS A  3-S-2     100   .243
B.JULY 1,1870 PHILADELPHIA,PA.          D.NOV.4,1971 MONTEREY PARK,CAL.         1970 CHI A  3-2/S     121   .247
D.MAY 9,1908 PHILADELPHIA,PA.           1923 PHI N  C          15   .333        1971 CAL A  S/2-3-1-0  90   .199
1895 BOS N  S         9   .229              BRTR                                1972 CAL A /3-S-2-1    36   .179
                                                                                    MIL A /3-2        31   .207
NYE, RICHARD RAYMOND (RICH)             O BRIEN, GEORGE JOSEPH                      BRTR      378   .230
B.AUG.4,1944 OAKLAND,CAL.               B.NOV.4,1889 CLEVELAND,OHIO
1966 CHI N /P         3   0- 2          D.MAR.24,1966 COLUMBUS,OHIO             O BRIEN, THOMAS EDWARD
1967 CHI N  P        35 13-10           1915 STL A  C           2   .222        (TOMMY) OR (OBIE)
1968 CHI N  P        27  7-12               BRTR                                B.DEC.19,1918 ANNISTON,LA.
1969 CHI N  P    34  36  3- 5                                                   1943 PIT N  3-0       89   .310
1970 STL N /P         6   0- 0          O BRIEN, JEREMIAH                       1944 PIT N  3-0       85   .250
    MON N /P      8  10   3- 2          B.WORCESTER,MASS.                       1945 PIT N  O         58   .335
    BLTL      113 117 26-31             D.JULY 5,1911                           1949 BOS A  O         49   .224
                                        1887 WAS N  2           1   .000        1950 BOS A  O          9   .129
NYMAN, GERALD SMITH (JERRY)                                                         WAS A  O          3   .111
B.NOV.23,1942 LOGAN,UTAH                O BRIEN, JOHN E.                            BRTR      293   .275
1968 CHI A /P         8   2- 1          1884 BAL U  O          18   .256
1969 CHI A  P    20  21  4- 4                                                   O BRIEN, THOMAS H.
1970 SD  N /P     2   3   0- 2          O BRIEN, JOHN F. (DARBY)                B.SALEM,MASS.
    BLTL       30  32   6- 7            B.APR.19,1867 TROY,N.Y.                 D.APR.21,1921 WORCESTER,MASS.
                                        D.MAR.12,1892 W.TROY,N.Y.               1882 WOR N  2-3-0     22   .202
NYMAN, NYLS WALLACE REX                 1888 CLE AA P    30  31 11-19           1883 BAL AA 2-0       33   .294
B.MAR.7,1954 DETROIT,MICH.              1889 CLE N  P        41 22-17           1884 BOS U  2        102   .265
1974 CHI A /O         5   .643          1890 CLE P  P        26  8-16           1885 BAL AA 1-2        8   .182
1975 CHI A /O       106   .226          1891 BOS AA P        41 19-13           1887 MET AA 1         29   .248
1976 CHI A /O         8   .133              BRTR      138 139 60-65            1890 ROC AA 1         73   .181
1977 CHI A /H         1   .000                                                                267   .239
    BLTR      120 238                   O BRIEN, JOHN J. (CHEWING GUM)
                                        B.JULY 14,1870 ST.JOHN,N.B.,CAN         O BRIEN, THOMAS J.
DANA, HENRY KAUHANE (PRINCE)            D.MAY 13,1913 LEWISTON,MAINE            B.FEB.20,1873 VERONA,PA.
B.JAN.22,1908 WAIPAHU,HAWAII            1891 BRO N  2          43   .251        D.FEB.4,1901 PHOENIX,ARIZONA
D.JUNE 19,1974 AUSTIN,TEX.              1893 CHI N  2           4   .416        1897 BAL N  1         38   .268
1934 PHI N  O         6   .238          1895 LOU N  2         128   .262        1898 BAL N  O         19   .217
1943 DET A  P    10  20  3- 2           1896 LOU N  2          49   .333            PIT N  1-0       104   .259
1945 DET A  P         4  0- 0               WAS N  2          69   .270        1899 NY  N  3-0       152   .305
    BRTR       14  30  3- 2             1897 WAS N  2          84   .242        1900 PIT N  1-0       94   .294
                         .308           1899 BAL N  2          39   .190                       407   .294
                                            PIT N  2          76   .223
OATES, JOHNNY LANE                          BLTR      492   .256               O BRIEN, THOMAS JOSEPH (BUCK)
B.JAN.21,1946 SYLVA,N.C.                                                       B.MAY 9,1882 BROCKTON,MASS.
1970 BAL A /C         5   .278          O BRIEN, JOHN JOSEPH (JACK)             D.JULY 25,1959 DORCHESTER,MASS.
1972 BAL A  C    85   .261              B.FEB.5,1873 WATERVLIET,N.Y.            1911 BOS A  P           6   5- 1
1973 ATL N  C    93   .248              D.JUNE 13,1933 WATERVLIET,N.Y.          1912 BOS A  P    37  18-13
1974 ATL N  C   100   .223              1899 WAS N  O         121   .279        1913 BOS A  P    15   4- 9
1975 ATL N /C     8   .222              1901 WAS A  O          12   .184            CHI A  P     7   0- 3
    PHI N  C    90   .286                   CLE A  O          91   .206            BRTR       65  27-26
1976 PHI N  C    37   .293              1903 BOS A  O          96   .212
1977 LA  N  C    60   .269                             320   .259              O BRIEN, WILLIAM D. (DARBY)
1978 LA  N  C    40   .307                                                     B.SEPT.1,1863 PEORIA,ILL.
    BLTR      518   .258                O BRIEN, JOHN K. (JACK)                 D.JUNE 15,1893 PEORIA,ILL.
                                        [REAL NAME JOHN K. BYRNE]               1887 MET AA O        129   .353
OBERKFELL, KENNETH RAY (KEN)            B.JUNE 12,1860 PHILADELPHIA,PA.         1888 BRO AA O        136   .275
B.MAY 4,1956 HIGHLAND,ILL.              D.NOV.2,1910 PHILADELPHIA,PA.           1889 BRO AA O        136   .312
1977 STL N /2     9   .111              1882 ATH AA C-1-0      62   .304        1890 BRO N  O         85   .314
1978 STL N 2/3   24   .120              1883 ATH AA C-1-S-3-0  93   .281        1891 BRO N  O        102   .260
    BLTR       33   .119                1884 ATH AA C-0        38   .300        1892 BRO N  O        121   .245
                                        1885 ATH AA C          61   .261            BRTR      709   .292
OBERLANDER, HARTMAN LOUIS (DOC)         1886 ATH AA C-1-3     105   .257
B.MAY 12,1864 WAUKEGAN,ILL.             1887 BRO AA C          30   .269        O BRIEN, WILLIAM SMITH
D.NOV.14,1922 PRYOR,MONTANA             1888 BAL AA C          57   .224        B.MAR.14,1860 ALBANY,N.Y.
1888 CLE AA P     3   1- 2              1890 ATH AA 1         110   .270        D.MAY 26,1911 KANSAS CITY,MO.
                                            BRTR      556   .276               1884 STP U  P-3    3   8   1- 1
OBERLIN, FRANK RUFUS (FLOSSIE)                                                                           .241
B.MAR.29,1876 ELSIE,MICH.               O BRIEN, JOHN THOMAS (JOHNNY)               KC  U  1-3        4   .293
D.JAN.6,1952 ASHLEY,IND.                B.DEC.11,1930 S.AMBOY,N.J.              1887 WAS N  1        113   .310
1906 BOS A  P     4   1- 3              1953 PIT N  2-S        89   .247        1888 WAS N  1        133   .225
1907 BOS A  P    12   1- 5              1955 PIT N  2          84   .299        1889 WAS N  1          2   .000
    WAS A  P    11  12   2- 6           1956 PIT N  P-2-   8   73  1- 0         1890 BRO AA 1         95   .277
1909 WAS A  P    10   1- 3                    S                   .173             BR         3 355   1- 1
1910 WAS A  P     8   1- 6              1957 PIT N  P-2-  16   34  0- 3                              .266
    BRTR       45  46  6-23                   S                   .314
                                        1958 PIT N  H           3   .000        OCK, HAROLD DAVID (WHITEY)
                                            STL N  P-2-   1   12  0- 0          B.MAR.17,1912 BROOKLYN,N.Y.
                                              S                   .000          D.MAR.18,1975 MT.KISCO,N.Y.
                                        1959 MIL N  2          44   .198        1935 BRO N  C           1   .000
                                            BRTR       25 339   1- 3                BRTR
                                                                 .250
                                                                                OCKEY, WALTER ANDREW (FOOTIE)
                                        O BRIEN, PETER F.                       [REAL NAME WALTER ANDREW OKPYCH]
                                        B.JUNE 16,1868 CHICAGO,ILL.             B.JAN.4,1920 NEW YORK,N.Y.
                                        1890 CHI N  2          27   .275        D.DEC.4,1971 STATEN ISLAND,N.Y.
                                                                                1944 NY  N  P           2   0- 0
                                                                                    BRTR
```

YR	CL	LEA	POS	GP	G	REC

O CONNELL, DANIEL FRANCIS (DANNY)
B.JAN.21,1927 PATERSON,N.J.
D.OCT.2,1969 CLIFTON,N.J.

YR	CL	LEA	POS	GP	G	REC
1950	PIT	N	S-3		79	.292
1953	PIT	N	2-3		149	.294
1954	MIL	N	1-2-S		146	.279
1955	MIL	N	2-S-3		124	.225
1956	MIL	N	2-S-3		139	.239
1957	MIL	N	2		48	.235
	NY	N	2-3		95	.266
1958	SF	N	2-3		107	.232
1959	SF	N	2-3		34	.190
1961	WAS	A	2-3		138	.260
1962	WAS	A	2-3		84	.263
		BRTR			1143	.260

O CONNELL, JAMES JOSEPH
B.FEB.11,1901 SACRAMENTO,CAL.
D.NOV.11,1976 BAKERSFIELD,CAL.

1923	NY	N	1-O		87	.250
1924	NY	N	2-O		52	.317
		BLTR			139	.270

O CONNELL, JOHN CHARLES
B.JUNE 13,1904 PITTSBURGH,PA.

1928	PIT	N	C		1	1.000
1929	PIT	N	C		2	.143
		BRTR			3	.125

O CONNELL, JOHN JOSEPH
B.MAY 16,1872 LAWRENCE,MASS.

1891	BAL	AA	2-S		7	.172
1902	DET	A	1-2		8	.136
					15	.157

O CONNELL, PATRICK
B.1862
D.MAY 5,1892

1890	BRO	AA	3		11	.237

O CONNELL, PATRICK H.
B.JUNE 10,1861 BANGOR,ME.
D.JAN.24,1943 LEWISTON,MAINE

1886	BAL	AA	O		42	.186

O CONNOR, ANDREW JAMES
B.SEPT.14,1884 ROXBURY,MASS.

1908	NY	A	P		1	0- 1

O CONNOR, DANIEL CORNELIUS
B.AUG.1868 GUELPH,ONT.,CANADA
D.MAR.3,1942 GUELPH,ONT.,CANADA

1890	LOU	AA	1		6	.480

O CONNOR, FRANK HENRY
B.SEPT.15,1870 KEESEVILLE,N.Y.
D.DEC.26,1913 BRATTLEBORO,VT.

1893	PHI	N	P		3	0- 0
		TL				

O CONNOR, JAMES MATTHEW
[PLAYED UNDER NAME OF
JAMES MATTHEW CONNOR]

O CONNOR, JOHN J.

1916	CHI	N			1	.000
		TR				

O CONNOR, JOHN JOSEPH (JACK)
(ROWDY JACK) OR (PEACH PIE)
B.JUNE 2,1869 ST.LOUIS,MO.
D.NOV.14,1937 ST.LOUIS,MO.

1887	CIN	AA	C-O		12	.133
1888	CIN	AA	C-O		36	.201
1889	COL	AA	C		107	.269
1890	COL	AA	C-O		118	.341
1891	COL	AA	C-O		56	.260
1892	CLE	N	C-O		139	.253
1893	CLE	N	C-O		93	.309
1894	CLE	N	C-O		80	.324
1895	CLE	N	C-1		88	.293
1896	CLE	N	C		60	.300
1897	CLE	N	1-O		100	.290
1898	CLE	N	C-1		129	.262
1899	STL	N	C-1		79	.261
1900	STL	N	C		10	.219
	PIT	N	C		38	.242
1901	PIT	N	C		56	.200
1902	PIT	N	C-1		45	.292
1903	NY	A	C		64	.197
1904	STL	A	C		13	.193
1906	STL	A	C		58	.190
1907	STL	A	C		25	.157
1910	STL	A	M-C		1	1.000
		BRTR			1407	.268

NON-PLAYING MANAGER STL(N) 1909

O CONNOR, PATRICK FRANCIS (PADDY)
B.AUG.4,1879 WINDSOR LOCKS,CONN
D.AUG.17,1950 SPRINGFIELD,MASS.

1908	PIT	N	C		12	.187
1909	PIT	N	C		9	.312
1910	PIT	N	C		1	.250
1914	STL	N	C		10	.000
1915	PIT	F	C		70	.224
1918	NY	A	C		1	.333
		BRTR			103	.222

O DAY, HENRY FRANCIS (HANK)
B.JULY 8,1862 CHICAGO,ILL.
D.JULY 2,1935 CHICAGO,ILL.

1884	TOL	AA	P-O	40	65	10-29
						.209
1885	PIT	AA	P		14	5- 7
1886	WAS	N	P		6	2- 2
1887	WAS	N	P	30	34	8-19
1888	WAS	N	P		47	16-31
1889	WAS	N	P		13	4- 5
1890	NY	P	P		43	22-15
		TR		208	237	76-114
						.198

NON-PLAYING MANAGER
CIN(N) 1912, CHI(N) 1914

O DEA, JAMES KENNETH (KEN)
B.MAR.16,1913 LIMA,N.Y.

1935	CHI	N	C		76	.257
1936	CHI	N	C		80	.307
1937	CHI	N	C		83	.301
1938	CHI	N	C		86	.263
1939	NY	N	C		52	.175
1940	NY	N	C		48	.240
1941	NY	N	C		59	.213
1942	STL	N	C		58	.234
1943	STL	N	C		71	.281
1944	STL	N	C		85	.249
1945	STL	N	C		100	.254
1946	STL	N	C		22	.123
	BOS	N	C		12	.219
		BLTR			832	.255

O DEA, PAUL (LEFTY)
B.JULY 3,1920 CLEVELAND,OHIO

1944	CLE	A	P-1-	3	76	0- 0
			O			.318
1945	CLE	A	P-O	1	87	0- 0
						.235
		BLTL		4	163	0- 0
						.272

O DELL, WILLIAM OLIVER (BILLY)
B.FEB.10,1933 WHITMIRE,S.C.

1954	BAL	A	P		7	1- 1
1956	BAL	A	P		4	0- 0
1957	BAL	A	P	35	37	4-10
1958	BAL	A	P	41	42	14-11
1959	BAL	A	P	38	43	10-12
1960	SF	N	P	43	49	8-13
1961	SF	N	P	46	49	7- 5
1962	SF	N	P	43	49	19-14
1963	SF	N	P	36	47	14-10
1964	SF	N	P	36	50	8- 7
1965	MIL	N	P/1		62	10- 6
						.174
1966	ATL	N	P	24	26	2- 3
	PIT	N	P		37	3- 2
1967	PIT	N	P	27	28	5- 6
		BBTL		479	530	105-100
						.125

ODENWALD, THEODORE JOSEPH (LEFTY)
B.JAN.4,1902 HUDSON,WIS.
D.OCT.23,1965 SHAKOPEE,MINN.

1921	CLE	A	P		10	1- 0
1922	CLE	A	P		1	0- 0
		BRTL			11	1- 0

ODOM, DAVID EVERETT
(BLIMP) OR (PORKY)
B.JUNE 5,1918 DINUBA,CAL.

1943	BOS	N	P		22	0- 3
		BRTR				

ODOM, HERMAN BOYD (HEINIE)
B.OCT.13,1900 RUSK,TEX.
D.AUG.31,1970 RUSK,TEX.

1925	NY	A	3		1	1.000
		BBTR				

ODOM, JOHNNY LEE (BLUE MOON)
B.MAY 29,1945 MACON,GA.

1964	KC	A	P		5	1- 2
1965	KC	A	/P		1	0- 0
1966	KC	A	P	14	17	5- 5
1967	KC	A	P	29	33	3- 8
1968	OAK	A	P	32	42	16-10
1969	OAK	A	P	32	43	15- 6
1970	OAK	A	P	29	37	9- 8
1971	OAK	A	P	25	37	10-12
1972	OAK	A	P	31	59	15- 6
1973	OAK	A	P	30	51	5-12
1974	OAK	A	P	34	43	1- 5
1975	OAK	A	/P	7	8	0- 2
	CLE	A	/P		3	1- 0
	ATL	N	P		15	1- 7
1976	CHI	A	/P		8	2- 2
		BRTR		295	402	84-85

O DONNELL

1884	KEY	U	C		1	.250

O DONNELL, EDWARD
[PLAYED UNDER NAME OF
EDWARD DONNELLY]

O DONNELL, GEORGE DANA
B.MAY 27,1929 WINCHESTER,ILL.

1954	PIT	N	P		21	3- 9
		BRTR				

O DONNELL, HARRY HERMAN (BUTCH)
B.APR.2,1894 PHILADELPHIA,PA.
D.JAN.31,1958 PHILADELPHIA,PA.

1927	PHI	N	C		16	.063
		BRTR				

O DONOGHUE, JOHN EUGENE
B.OCT.7,1939 KANSAS CITY,MO.

1963	KC	A	P		1	0- 1
1964	KC	A	P	39	40	10-14
1965	KC	A	P	34	39	9-18
1966	CLE	A	P		32	6- 8
1967	CLE	A	P		33	8- 9
1968	BAL	A	P		16	0- 0
1969	SEA	A	P		55	2- 2
1970	MIL	A	P		25	2- 0
	MON	N	/P		9	2- 3
1971	MON	N	P		2	0- 0
		BRTL		257	263	39-55

O DOUL, FRANCIS JOSEPH (LEFTY)
B.MAR.4,1897 SAN FRANCISCO,CAL.
D.DEC.7,1969 SAN FRANCISCO,CAL.

1919	NY	A	P	3	19	0- 0
1920	NY	A	P	2	13	0- 0
1922	NY	A	P	6	8	0- 0
1923	BOS	A	P	23	36	1- 1
1928	NY	N	O		114	.319
1929	PHI	N	O		154	.398
1930	PHI	N	O		140	.383
1931	BRO	N	O		134	.336
1932	BRO	N	O		148	.368
1933	BRO	N	O		43	.252
	NY	N	O		78	.306
1934	NY	N	O		83	.316
		BLTL		34	970	1- 1
						.349

ODWELL, FREDERICK WILLIAM (FRITZ)
B.SEPT.25,1872 DOWNSVILLE,N.Y.
D.AUG.19,1948 DOWNSVILLE,N.Y.

1904	CIN	N	O		126	.284
1905	CIN	N	O		126	.241
1906	CIN	N	O		57	.223
1907	CIN	N	O		84	.270
		BLTR			393	.258

OERTEL, CHARLES FRANK (CHUCK)
(DUCKY) OR (SNUFFY)
B.MAR.12,1931 COFFEYVILLE,KAN.

1958	BAL	A	O		14	.167
		BLTR				

OESCHGER, JOSEPH CARL (JOE)
B.MAY 24,1891 CHICAGO,ILL.

1914	PHI	N	P		32	4- 8
1915	PHI	N	P		6	1- 0
1916	PHI	N	P		14	1- 0
1917	PHI	N	P	42	43	15-14
1918	PHI	N	P		30	6-18
1919	PHI	N	P		5	0- 1
	NY	N	P		5	0- 1
	BOS	N	P		7	4- 2
1920	BOS	N	P		38	15-13
1921	BOS	N	P		46	20-14
1922	BOS	N	P		46	6-21
1923	BOS	N	P		44	5-15
1924	NY	N	P		10	2- 0
	PHI	N	P		19	2- 7
1925	BRO	N	P		21	1- 2
		BRTR		365	366	82-116

OESTER, RONALD JOHN (RON)
B.MAY 5,1956 CINCINNATI,OHIO

1978	CIN	N	/S		6	.375
		BBTR				

O FARRELL, ROBERT ARTHUR (BOB)
B.OCT.19,1896 WAUKEGAN,ILL.

1915	CHI	N	C		2	.667
1916	CHI	N	C		1	.000
1917	CHI	N	C		3	.375
1918	CHI	N	C		52	.283
1919	CHI	N	C		49	.216
1920	CHI	N	C		44	.248
1921	CHI	N	C		96	.250
1922	CHI	N	C		128	.323
1923	CHI	N	C		131	.319
1924	CHI	N	C		71	.241
1925	CHI	N	C		17	.182
	STL	N	C		94	.278
1926	STL	N	C		147	.293
1927	STL	N	M-C		61	.264
1928	STL	N	C		16	.212
	NY	N	C		75	.195
1929	NY	N	C		91	.306
1930	NY	N	C		94	.301
1931	NY	N	C		85	.224
1932	NY	N	C		50	.239
1933	STL	N	C		55	.239
1934	CIN	N	M-C		44	.244
	CHI	N	C		22	.224
1935	STL	N	C		14	.000
		BRTR			1492	.273

```
YR  CL LEA POS      GP   G    REC

OFFICE, ROWLAND JOHNIE
B.OCT.25,1952 SACRAMENTO,CAL.
1972 ATL N /D            2   .400
1974 ATL N *D          131   .246
1975 ATL N *D          126   .290
1976 ATL N  D           99   .281
1977 ATL N *D/1        124   .241
1978 ATL N *D          146   .250
     BLTL              628   .262

OGDEN, JOHN MAHLON (JACK)
B.NOV.5,1897 OGDEN,PA.
D.NOV.9,1977 PHILADELPHIA,PA.
1918 NY  N  P            5   0- 0
1928 STL A  P           38  15-16
1929 STL A  P           34   4- 8
1931 CIN N  P    22     23   4- 8
1932 CIN N  P    24     27   2- 2
     BRTR       123    127  25-34

OGDEN, WARREN HARVEY (CURLY)
B.JAN.24,1901 OGDEN,PA.
D.AUG.6,1964 CHESTER,PA.
1922 PHI A  P    15     17   1- 4
1923 PHI A  P    18     19   1- 2
1924 PHI A  P            5   0- 3
     WAS A  P    16     17   9- 5
1925 WAS A  P           17   3- 1
1926 WAS A  P           22   4- 4
     BRTR        94     97  18-19

OGLESBY, JAMES DORN
B.AUG.10,1905 SCHOFIELD,MO.
D.SEPT.1,1955 TULSA,OKLA.
1936 PHI A  1            3   .182
     BLTL

OGLIVIE, BENJAMIN AMBROSIO (BEN)
B.FEB.11,1949 COLON,PANAMA
1971 BOS A  O           14   .263
1972 BOS A  O           94   .241
1973 BOS A  O-D         58   .218
1974 DET A  O-1         92   .270
1975 DET A  O/1        100   .286
1976 DET A  O/1        115   .285
1977 DET A *D          132   .262
1978 MIL A  O-D-1      128   .303
     BLTL              733   .273

OGRODOWSKI, AMBROSE FRANCIS
(BRUCE) OR (BRUSIE)
B.FEB.17,1912 HOYTVILLE,PA.
D.MAR.5,1956 SAN FRANCISCO,CAL.
1936 STL N  C           94   .228
1937 STL N  C           90   .233
     BRTR              184   .231

OGRODOWSKI, JOSEPH ANTHONY
B.NOV.20,1906 HOYTVILLE,PA.
D.JUNE 24,1959 ELMIRA,N.Y.
1925 BOS N  P            1   0- 0
     BRTR

O HAGEN, HARRY P.
B.SEPT.30,1873 WASHINGTON,D.C.
D.JAN.14,1913 NEWARK,N.J.
1892 WAS N  C            1   .250
1902 CHI N  1           53   .188
     NY  N              24   .138
     CLE A  1            3   .384
                        61   .177

O HARA, JAMES FRANCIS (KID)
B.DEC.19,1875 WILKES-BARRE,PA.
D.DEC.1,1954 CANTON,OHIO
1904 BOS N  O            8   .207
     BBTR

O HARA, THOMAS F.
B.JULY 13,1885 WAVERLY,N.Y.
D.JUNE 8,1954 DENVER,COLO.
1906 STL N  O           14   .321
1907 STL N  O           47   .237
                        61   .257

O HARA, WILLIAM ALEXANDER
B.AUG.14,1883 TORONTO,ONT.,CAN.
D.JUNE 15,1931 JERSEY CITY,N.J.
1909 NY  N  O          111   .236
1910 STL N  P-1-    1    9   0- 0
            O                .150
     BLTR           1  120   0- 0
                             .231

OHL, JOSEPH EARL
B.JAN.10,1888 JOBSTOWN,N.J.
D.DEC.18,1951 CAMDEN,N.J.
1909 WAS A  P            4   0- 0
     BLTL

OKPYCH, WALTER ANDREW
[PLAYED UNDER NAME OF
WALTER ANDREW OCKEY]

OKRIE, FRANK ANTHONY (LEFTY)
B.OCT.28,1896 DETROIT,MICH.
D.OCT.16,1959 DETROIT,MICH.
1920 DET A  P           21   1- 2
     BLTL


OKRIE, LEONARD JOSEPH (LEN)
B.JULY 16,1923 DETROIT,MICH.
1948 WAS A  C           19   .238
1950 WAS A  C           17   .222
1951 WAS A  C            5   .125
1952 BOS A  C            1   .000
     BRTR               42   .218

OLDFIELD, DAVID
B.PHILADELPHIA,PA.
1883 BAL AA C            1   .000
1885 BRO AA C-O         10   .308
1886 BRO AA C           14   .240
     WAS N  C           19   .158
     TR                 44   .211

OLDHAM, JOHN CYRUS (RED)
B.JULY 15,1893 ZION,MD.
D.JAN.28,1961 COSTA MESA,CAL.
1914 DET A  P            9   2- 4
1915 DET A  P           17   2- 0
1920 DET A  P           39   8-13
1921 DET A  P    43     42  11-14
1922 DET A  P           43  10-13
1925 PIT N  P           11   3- 2
1926 PIT N  P           17   2- 2
     BBTL              176  178  38-48
     BL 1922-26

OLDHAM, JOHN HARDIN
B.NOV.6,1932 SALINAS,CAL.
1956 CIN N  H            1   .000
     BL

OLDIS, ROBERT CARL (BOB)
B.JAN.5,1928 PRESTON,IOWA
1953 WAS A  C            7   .250
1954 WAS A  C-3         11   .333
1955 WAS A  C            6   .000
1960 PIT N  C           22   .200
1961 PIT N  C            4   .000
1962 PHI N  C           38   .263
1963 PHI N  C           47   .224
     BRTR              135   .237

OLDRING, REUBEN HENRY (RUBE)
B.MAY 30,1884 NEW YORK,N.Y.
D.SEPT.9,1961 BRIDGETON,N.J.
1905 NY  A  S            8   .300
1906 PHI A  3           39   .241
1907 PHI A  O          117   .286
1908 PHI A  O          116   .221
1909 PHI A  O           90   .230
1910 PHI A  O          134   .308
1911 PHI A  O          121   .297
1912 PHI A  O           98   .301
1913 PHI A  O          136   .283
1914 PHI A  O          119   .277
1915 PHI A  O          107   .248
1916 PHI A  O           40   .247
     NY  A  O           43   .234
1918 PHI A  O           49   .233
     BRTR             1237   .270

O LEARY, CHARLES TIMOTHY
B.OCT.15,1882 CHICAGO,ILL.
D.JAN.6,1941 CHICAGO,ILL.
1904 DET A  S          135   .215
1905 DET A  S          148   .213
1906 DET A  S          128   .219
1907 DET A  S          139   .241
1908 DET A  S           65   .251
1909 DET A  3           76   .203
1910 DET A  2-S         65   .242
1911 DET A  2           74   .266
1912 DET A  2            3   .200
1913 STL N  2-S        121   .217
1934 STL A  H            1  1.000
     BRTR              955   .234

O LEARY, DANIEL (HUSTLING DAN)
B.OCT.24,1856 DETROIT,MICH.
D.JUNE 22,1922 CHICAGO,ILL.
1879 PRO N  O            2   .429
1880 BOS N  O            3   .250
1881 DET N  O            2   .000
1882 WOR N  O            6   .167
1884 CIN U  M-O         27   .252
     BL                 40   .235

OLIN, FRANKLIN WALTER
B.JAN.9,1860 WOODFORD,VT.
D.MAY 20,1951 ST.LOUIS,MO.
1884 WAS AA 2-O         21   .386
     WAS U  O            1   .000
     TOL AA O           26   .271
1885 DET N  3            1   .500
                        49   .306


OLIVA, PEDRO (LOPEZ) (TONY)
B.JULY 20,1940 PINAR DEL RIO,CUBA
1962 MIN A  D            9   .444
1963 MIN A  H            7   .429
1964 MIN A  O          161   .323
1965 MIN A *D          149   .321
1966 MIN A *D          159   .307
1967 MIN A *O          126   .289
1968 MIN A *O          128   .289
1969 MIN A *O          153   .309
1970 MIN A *O          157   .325
1971 MIN A *O          126   .337
1972 MIN A /O           10   .321
1973 MIN A *D          146   .291
1974 MIN A  D          127   .285
1975 MIN A *D          131   .270
1976 MIN A  D           67   .211
     BLTR             1676   .304

OLIVARES, EDWARD (BALZAC)
B.NOV.5,1938 MAYAGUEZ,P.R.
1960 STL N  3            3   .000
1961 STL N  O           21   .167
     BRTR               24   .143

OLIVER, ALBERT (AL)
B.OCT.14,1946 PORTSMOUTH,OHIO
1968 PIT N /O            4   .125
1969 PIT N *1-O        129   .285
1970 PIT N  O-1        151   .270
1971 PIT N *O-1        143   .282
1972 PIT N *O/1        140   .312
1973 PIT N *O-1        158   .292
1974 PIT N  O-1        147   .321
1975 PIT N *O/1        155   .280
1976 PIT N *O/1        121   .323
1977 PIT N *O          154   .308
1978 TEX A *O-D        133   .324
     BLTR             1435   .299

OLIVER, DAVID JACOB (DAVE)
B.APR.7,1951 STOCKTON,CAL.
1977 CLE A /2            7   .318
     BLTR

OLIVER, EUGENE GEORGE (GENE)
B.MAR.22,1935 MOLINE,ILL.
1959 STL N  C-1-O       68   .244
1961 STL N  C-O         22   .269
1962 STL N  C-1-O      122   .258
1963 STL N  C           39   .225
     MIL N  C-1-O        95   .250
1964 MIL N  C-1         93   .276
1965 MIL N  C-1/O      122   .270
1966 ATL N  C/1-O       76   .194
1967 ATL N  C           17   .196
     PHI N  C/1         85   .224
1968 BOS A  C/O         16   .143
     CHI N /1-C-O        8   .364
1969 CHI N /C           23   .222
     BRTR              786   .246

OLIVER, NATHANIEL (NATE) OR (PEEWEE)
B.DEC.13,1940 ST.PETERSBURG,FLA.
1963 LA  N  2-S         65   .239
1964 LA  N  2-S         99   .243
1965 LA  N /2            8  1.000
1966 LA  N  2/S-3       80   .193
1967 LA  N  2-S/O       77   .237
1968 SF  N  2-S/3       36   .178
1969 NY  A  /H           1   .000
     CHI N  2           44   .159
     BRTR              410   .226

OLIVER, RICHARD
[SEE TRACY SOUTER BARRETT]

OLIVER, ROBERT LEE (BOB)
B.FEB.8,1943 SHREVEPORT,LA.
1965 PIT N /O            3   .000
1969 KC  A  O-1/3      118   .254
1970 KC  A *1-3        160   .260
1971 KC  A  1-O/3      128   .244
1972 KC  A  O           16   .270
     CAL A *1/O        134   .269
1973 CAL A  3-O-1-O    151   .265
1974 CAL A  1-3/O      110   .248
     BAL A /1            9   .150
1975 NY  A /1-3         18   .132
     BRTR              847   .256

OLIVER, THOMAS NOBLE (REBEL)
B.JAN.15,1903 MONTGOMERY,ALA.
1930 BOS A  O          154   .293
1931 BOS A  O          148   .276
1932 BOS A  O          122   .264
1933 BOS A  O           90   .258
     BRTR              514   .277

OLIVO, DIOMEDES ANTONIO
[MALDONADO]
B.JAN.22,1919 GUAYUBIN,D.R.
D.FEB.15,1977 SANTO DOMINGO,D.R.
1960 PIT N  P            3   0- 0
1962 PIT N  P           62   5- 1
1963 STL N  P           19   0- 5
     BLTL               85   5- 6
```

YR	CL LEA POS	GP	G	REC

OLIVO, FEDERICO EMILIO
[MOLDONADO] (CHI-CHI)
B.MAR.18,1928 GUAYBIN,D.R.
D.FEB.3,1977 GUAYBIN,D.R.

1961 MIL N	P		3	0- 0
1964 MIL N	P		38	2- 1
1965 MIL N	/P		8	0- 1
1966 ATL N	P		47	5- 4
BRTR			96	7- 6

OLLOM, JAMES DONALD (JIM)
B.JULY 8,1945 SNOHOMISH,WASH.

1966 MIN A	/P		3	0- 0
1967 MIN A	P		21	0- 1
BRTL			24	0- 1

OLMO, LUIS FRANCISCO
[RODRIGUEZ]
B.AUG.11,1919 ARECIBO,P.R.

1943 BRO N	O		57	.303
1944 BRO N	2-3-O		136	.258
1945 BRO N	2-3-O		141	.313
1949 BRO N	O		38	.305
1950 BOS N	3-O		69	.227
1951 BOS N	O		21	.196
BRTR			462	.281

OLMSTEAD, FREDERIC WILLIAM
B.JULY 3,1881 GRAND RAPIDS,MICH
D.OCT.22,1936 MUSKOGEE,OKLA.

1908 CHI A	P		1	1- 0
1909 CHI A	P		8	3- 2
1910 CHI A	P		32	10-12
1911 CHI A	P		25	6- 6
BRTR			66	20-20

OLMSTED, HENRY THEODORE
B.JAN.12,1879 SAGINAW BAY,MICH.
D.JAN.6,1969 BRADENTON,FLA.

1905 BOS A	P		3	1- 2

OLSEN, ALBERT WILLIAM (OLE)
B.MAR.30,1921 SAN DIEGO,CAL.

1943 BOS A	H		1	.000
BLTL				

OLSEN, ARTHUR (OLE)
B.SEPT.12,1894 S.NORWALK,CONN.

1922 DET A	P	37	39	7- 6
1923 DET A	P		17	1- 1
BRTR		54	56	8- 7

OLSEN, BERNARD CHARLES (BARNEY)
B.SEPT.11,1919 EVERETT,MASS.

1941 CHI N	O		24	.288
BRTR				

OLSEN, VERN JARL
B.MAR.16,1918 HILLSBORO,ORE.

1939 CHI N	P		4	1- 0
1940 CHI N	P	34	35	13- 9
1941 CHI N	P		37	10- 8
1942 CHI N	P		32	6- 9
1946 CHI N	P		5	0- 0
BRTL		112	113	30-26

OLSON, IVAN MASSIE (IVY)
B.OCT.14,1885 KANSAS CITY,MO.
D.SEPT.1,1965 INGLEWOOD,CAL.

1911 CLE A	S		140	.261
1912 CLE A	S-3		123	.253
1913 CLE A	1-3		104	.248
1914 CLE A	2-S-3		89	.242
1915 CIN N	1-2-3		63	.232
BRO N	3		18	.077
1916 BRO N	3		108	.254
1917 BRO N	S		139	.269
1918 BRO N	S		126	.239
1919 BRO N	S		140	.278
1920 BRO N	2-S		143	.254
1921 BRO N	2-S		151	.267
1922 BRO N	2-S		136	.272
1923 BRO N	1-2-S-3		82	.260
1924 BRO N	2-S		10	.222
BRTR			1572	.267

OLSON, KARL ARTHUR (KARL) OR (OLE)
B.JULY 6,1930 ROSS,CAL.

1951 BOS A	O		5	.100
1953 BOS A	O		25	.123
1954 BOS A	O		101	.260
1955 BOS A	O		26	.250
1956 WAS A	O		106	.246
1957 WAS A	O		8	.167
DET A	O		8	.143
BRTR			279	.235

OLSON, MARVIN CLEMENT
(MARV) OR (SPARKY)
B.MAY 28,1907 GAYVILLE,S.DAK.

1931 BOS A	2		15	.189
1932 BOS A	2		115	.248
1933 BOS A	2		3	.000
BRTR			133	.241

OLSON, THEODORE OTTO
B.AUG.27,1912 QUINCY,MASS.

1936 BOS A	P		5	1- 1
1937 BOS A	P		11	0- 0
1938 BOS A	P		2	0- 0
BRTR			18	1- 1

O MARA, OLIVER EDWARD
B.MAR.8,1891 ST.LOUIS,MO.

1912 DET A	S		1	.000
1914 BRO N	S		67	.263
1915 BRO N	S		149	.244
1916 BRO N	S		72	.202
1918 BRO N	3		121	.213
1919 BRO N	3		2	.000
TR			412	.231

O MEARA, THOMAS EDWARD
B.DEC.12,1872 CHICAGO,ILL.
D.FEB.16,1902 FORT WAYNE,IND.

1895 CLE N	C		1	.000
1896 CLE N	C		9	.148
			10	.135

O NEAL

1874 HAR NA	O		1	.000

O NEAL, ORAN HERBERT (SKINNY)
B.MAY 2,1899 GATEWOOD,MO.

1925 PHI N	P		11	0- 0
1927 PHI N	P		2	0- 0
BRTR			13	0- 0

O NEIL, DENNIS
B.1861 IRELAND

1893 STL N	1		7	.120

O NEIL, EDWARD J.
B.MAR.11,1859 FALL RIVER,MASS.
D.SEPT.30,1892 FALL RIVER,MASS.

1890 TOL AA	P		3	2- 1
ATH AA	P-3-	8	11	0- 8
	O			.176
TR		11	14	2- 9
				.136

O NEIL, GEORGE MICHAEL (MICKEY)
B.APR.12,1900 ST.LOUIS,MO.
D.APR.8,1964 ST.LOUIS,MO.

1919 BOS N	C		11	.214
1920 BOS N	C		112	.283
1921 BOS N	C		98	.249
1922 BOS N	C		83	.223
1923 BOS N	C		96	.212
1924 BOS N	C		106	.246
1925 BOS N	C		70	.258
1926 BRO N	C		75	.209
1927 WAS A	C		5	.000
NY N	C		16	.132
BRTR			672	.239

O NEIL, JOHN FRANCIS
B.APR.19,1920 SHELBIANA,KY.

1946 PHI N	S		46	.266
BRTR				

O NEIL
B.BEDFORD,PA.

1875 ATL NA	P-S-	4	6	0- 4
	O			-

O NEILL, FREDERICK JAMES (TIP)
B.1865 LONDON,ONTARIO,CANADA
D.MAR.7,1892 LONDON,ONT.,CAN.

1887 MET AA	O		5	.391

O NEILL, HARRY MINK
B.MAY 8,1917 PHILADELPHIA,PA.
D.MAR.6,1945 IWO JIMA,MARIANAS
ISLANDS

1939 PHI A	C		1	.000
BRTR				

O NEILL, JAMES EDWARD (TIP)
B.MAY 25,1858 WOODSTOCK,ONT.,CANADA
D.DEC.31,1915 WOODSTOCK,ONT.,CANADA.

1883 NY N	P-O	20	23	7-13
				.178
1884 STL AA	P-O	17	77	10- 4
				.272
1885 STL AA	O		51	.342
1886 STL AA	O		138	.329
1887 STL AA	O		123	.492
1888 STL AA	O		130	.332
1889 STL AA	O		133	.337
1890 CHI P	O		137	.302
1891 STL AA	O		127	.321
1892 CIN N	O		107	.250
BRTR		37	1046	17-17
				.332

O NEILL, JAMES LEO
B.FEB.23,1893 MINOOKA,PA.
D.SEPT.5,1976 CHAMBERSBURG,PA.

1920 WAS A	S		86	.289
1923 WAS A	2-S		23	.273
BRTR			109	.287

O NEILL, JOHN J.
B.NEW YORK,N.Y.

1899 NY N	C		2	.000
1902 NY N	C		2	.000
TR			4	.000

O NEILL, JOHN JOSEPH (JACK)
B.JAN.10,1873 GALWAY,IRELAND
D.JUNE 29,1935 SCRANTON,PA.

1902 STL N	C		56	.154
1903 STL N	C		74	.236
1904 CHI N	C		49	.214
1905 CHI N	C		50	.198
1906 BOS N	C		51	.180
TR			280	.199

O NEILL, JOSEPH HENRY (HARRY)
B.FEB.20,1897 RIDGETOWN,ONT.,CANADA
D.SEPT.5,1969 RIDGETOWN,ONT.,CAN.

1922 PHI A	P		1	0- 0
1923 PHI A	P		3	0- 0
BRTR			4	0- 0

O NEILL, MICHAEL JOYCE
[PLAYED UNDER NAME OF
MICHAEL JOYCE IN 1901]
B.SEPT.7,1877 GALWAY,IRELAND
D.AUG.12,1959 SCRANTON,PA.

1901 STL N	P		6	2- 2
1902 STL N	P-O	33	36	16-15
				.318
1903 STL N	P	19	32	4-13
1904 STL N	P	25	28	10-14
1907 CIN N	O		9	.069
BRTR		83	111	32-44
				.255

O NEILL, PHILIP BERNARD (PEACHES)
B.AUG.30,1879 ANDERSON,IND.
D.AUG.2,1955 ANDERSON,IND.

1904 CIN N	C		8	.267
TR				

O NEILL, ROBERT EMMETT
(EMMETT) OR (PINKY)
B.JAN.13,1918 SAN MATEO,CAL.

1943 BOS A	P		11	1- 4
1944 BOS A	P		28	6-11
1945 BOS A	P		24	8-11
1946 CHI N	P		1	0- 0
CHI A	P		2	0- 0
BRTR			66	15-26

O NEILL, STEPHEN FRANCIS (STEVE)
B.JULY 6,1891 MINOOKA,PA.
D.JAN.26,1962 CLEVELAND,OHIO

1911 CLE A	C		9	.111
1912 CLE A	C		68	.228
1913 CLE A	C		78	.295
1914 CLE A	C		86	.253
1915 CLE A	C		121	.236
1916 CLE A	C		130	.235
1917 CLE A	C		129	.184
1918 CLE A	C		114	.242
1919 CLE A	C		125	.289
1920 CLE A	C		149	.321
1921 CLE A	C		106	.322
1922 CLE A	C		133	.311
1923 CLE A	C		113	.248
1924 BOS A	C		106	.238
1925 NY A	C		35	.286
1927 STL A	C		74	.230
1928 STL A	C		10	.292
BRTR			1586	.263

NON-PLAYING MANAGER
CLE[A] 1935-37, DET[A] 1943-48,
BOS[A] 1950-51, PHI[N] 1952-54

O NEILL, WILLIAM JOHN
B.JAN.22,1880 ST.JOHN,N.B.,CAN.
D.JULY 27,1920 ST.JOHN,N.B.,CAN

1904 BOS A	O		18	.192
WAS A	O		94	.277
1906 WAS A	O		94	.248
BB			206	.242

ONIS, MANUEL DOMINGUEZ
(RALPH) OR (CURLY)
B.OCT.24,1908 TAMPA,FLA.

1935 BRO N	C		1	1.000
BRTR				

ONSLOW, EDWARD JOSEPH (EDDIE)
B.FEB.17,1893 MEADVILLE,PA.

1912 DET A	1		35	.227
1913 DET A	1		17	.255
1918 CLE A	O		2	.200
1927 WAS A	1		9	.222
BLTL			63	.232

ONSLOW, JOHN JAMES (JACK)
B.OCT.13,1888 SCOTTDALE,PA.
D.DEC.22,1960 CONCORD,MASS.

1912 DET A	C		31	.159
1917 NY N	C		9	.250
BRTR			40	.169

NON-PLAYING MANAGER CHI[A] 1949-50

YR	CL	LEA	POS	GP	G	REC

ONTIVEROS, STEVEN ROBERT (STEVE)
B.OCT.26,1951 BAKERSFIELD,CAL.

1973	SF	N	/1-0		24	.242
1974	SF	N	3-1/0	120		.265
1975	SF	N	3/0-1	108		.289
1976	SF	N	/3-0-1	59		.176
1977	CHI	N	*3	156		.299
1978	CHI	N	3/1	82		.243
			BBTR	549		.273

ORAN, THOMAS
D.SEPT.21,1886

| 1875 | RS | NA | O | | 19 | - |

ORAVETZ, ERNEST EUGENE (ERNIE)
B.JAN.24,1932 JOHNSTOWN,PA.

1955	WAS	A	O		100	.270
1956	WAS	A	O		88	.248
			BBTL		188	.263

ORDENNA, ANTONIO [RODRIGUEZ] (MOSQUITO)
B.OCT.30,1918 GUANABACOA,HAVANA,CUBA

| 1943 | PIT | N | S | | 1 | .500 |
| | | | BRTR | | | |

ORENGO, JOSEPH CHARLES (JOE)
B.NOV.29,1914 SAN FRANCISCO,CAL

1939	STL	N	S		7	.000
1940	STL	N	2-S-3	129		.287
1941	NY	N	2-S-3	77		.214
1943	NY	N	1		83	.218
	BRO	N	3		7	.200
1944	DET	A	1-2-S-3	46		.201
1945	CHI	A	2-3	17		.067
			BRTR		366	.238

O RILEY, DONALD LEE (DON)
B.MAR.12,1945 TOPEKA,KAN.

1969	KC	A	P	18	19	1- 1
1970	KC	A	/P		9	0- 0
			BRTR	27	28	1- 1

ORME, GEORGE WILLIAM
B.SEPT.16,1891 LEBANON,IND.
D.MAR.16,1962 INDIANAPOLIS,IND.

| 1920 | BOS | A | O | | 4 | .323 |
| | | | BRTR | | | |

ORNDOORFF, JESSE WALWORTH THAYER
B.JAN.15,1881 CHICAGO,ILL.
D.SEPT.28,1960 CARDIFF-BY-THE-SEA,CAL.

| 1907 | BOS | N | C | | 5 | .100 |
| | | | BBTR | | | |

O ROURKE

| 1872 | ECK | NA | P | | 1 | 0- 1 |

O ROURKE, FRANCIS JAMES (BLACKIE)
B.NOV.28,1894 HAMILTON,ONT.,CAN

1912	BOS	N	S		61	.122
1917	BRO	N	3		64	.237
1918	BRO	N	2		4	.167
1920	WAS	A	S		14	.277
1921	WAS	A	S	123		.234
1922	BOS	A	S-3	67		.264
1924	DET	A	2		47	.276
1925	DET	A	2-S-3	124		.293
1926	DET	A	2-S-3	111		.242
1927	STL	A	2-3	140		.268
1928	STL	A	3		99	.263
1929	STL	A	3	154		.251
1930	STL	A	S-3	115		.268
1931	STL	A	1-S		8	.222
			BRTR	1131		.254

O ROURKE, JAMES HENRY (ORATOR JIM)
B.AUG.24,1852 BRIDGEPORT,CONN.
D.JAN.8,1919 BRIDGEPORT,CONN.

1872	MAN	NA	S		23	.287
1873	BOS	NA	C-1-0	57		.347
1874	BOS	NA	1		69	.349
1875	BOS	NA	1-3-0	74		.289
1876	BOS	N	O		70	.312
1877	BOS	N	O		61	.362
1878	BOS	N	O		60	.274
1879	PRO	N	1-0		80	.351
1880	BOS	N	C-1-S-3-0	84		.281
1881	BUF	N	M-C-1-S-3-0	83		.301
1882	BUF	N	M-C-S-3-0	84		.281
1883	BUF	N	M-P-	1	93	0- 0
			C-S-3-0			.327
1884	BUF	N	M-P-	4	104	0- 1
			C-1-3-3			.350
1885	NY	N	C-O		112	.299
1886	NY	N	C-O		104	.309
1887	NY	N	C-3-O	103		.344
1888	NY	N	O		107	.273
1889	NY	N	O		128	.320
1890	NY	P	O		111	.366
1891	NY	N	O		136	.301
1892	NY	N	O		112	.297
1893	WAS	N	M-1-O	129		.305
1904	NY	N	C		1	.250
			BRTR	5	1985	0- 1
						.317

O ROURKE, JAMES PATRICK (CHARLIE)
B.JUNE 22,1937 WALLA WALLA,WASH

| 1959 | STL | N | H | | 2 | .000 |
| | | | BRTR | | | |

O ROURKE, JAMES STEPHEN (QUEENIE)
B.DEC.26,1883 BRIDGEPORT,CONN.
D.DEC.22,1955 SPARROWS POINT,MD

| 1908 | NY | A | 2-S-3-0 | | 34 | .231 |
| | | | BRTR | | | |

O ROURKE, JOHN
B.1853 BRIDGEPORT,CONN.
D.JUNE 23,1911 BOSTON,MASS.

1879	BOS	N	O		70	.341
1880	BOS	N	O		78	.282
1883	MET	AA	1-0		79	.256
			BL		227	.299

O ROURKE, JOSEPH LEO JR.
B.OCT.28,1904 PHILADELPHIA,PA.

| 1929 | PHI | N | H | | 3 | .000 |
| | | | BLTR | | | |

O ROURKE, JOSEPH LEO SR. (PATSY)
B.APR.13,1881 PHILADELPHIA,PA.
D.APR.18,1956 PHILADELPHIA,PA.

| 1908 | STL | N | S | | 53 | .195 |
| | | | TR | | | |

O ROURKE, MICHAEL J.

| 1890 | BAL | AA | P | | 9 | 2- 2 |

O ROURKE, THOMAS JOSEPH
B.1863 NEW YORK,N.Y.
D.JULY 19,1929 NEW YORK,N.Y.

1887	BOS	N	C		21	.223
1888	BOS	N	C		20	.175
1890	NY	N	C		2	.000
	SYR	AA	C		43	.227
			TR		86	.211

O ROURKE, TIMOTHY PATRICK (VOICELESS TIM)
B.MAY 18,1864 CHICAGO,ILL.
D.APR.20,1938 SEATTLE,WASH.

1890	SYR	AA	3		82	.288
1891	COL	AA	3		34	.261
1892	BAL	N	S		62	.317
1893	BAL	N	S		31	.379
	LOU	N	S		90	.290
1894	LOU	N	1-3-0		55	.284
	STL	N	1-3-0		18	.274
	WAS	N	1		7	.179
			TR		379	.295

ORR, DAVID L.
B.SEPT.29,1859 NEW YORK,N.Y.
D.JUNE 3,1915 BROOKLYN,N.Y.

1883	MET	AA	1		1	.250
	NY	N	O		12	.000
	MET	AA	1		12	.326
1884	MET	AA	1	110		.352
1885	MET	AA	1	107		.366
1886	MET	AA	1	136		.346
1887	MET	AA	M-1	85		.403
1888	BRO	AA	1		95	.303
1889	COL	AA	1	134		.325
1890	BRO	P	1	107		.387
			BLTR		788	.353

ORR, WILLIAM JOHN (BILLY)
B.APR.22,1891 SAN FRANCISCO,CAL

1913	PHI	A	S		27	.200
1914	PHI	A	S		10	.167
			BRTR		37	.191

ORRELL, FORREST GORDON (JOE)
B.OCT.6,1917 NATIONAL CITY,CAL.

1943	DET	A	P	10	0- 0
1944	DET	A	P		10	2- 1
1945	DET	A	P		12	2- 3
			BRTR		32	4- 4

ORSATTI, ERNEST RALPH (ERNIE)
B.SEPT.8,1902 LOS ANGELES,CAL.
D.SEPT.4,1968 CANOGA PARK,CAL.

1927	STL	N	O		27	.315
1928	STL	N	O		27	.304
1929	STL	N	1-0	113		.332
1930	STL	N	1-0		48	.321
1931	STL	N	O		70	.291
1932	STL	N	O		101	.336
1933	STL	N	1-0	120		.298
1934	STL	N	O		105	.300
1935	STL	N	O		90	.240
			BLTL		701	.306

ORSINO, JOHN JOSEPH (JOHN) OR (HORSE)
B.APR.22,1938 TEANECK,N.J.

1961	SF	N	C		25	.277
1962	SF	N	C		18	.271
1963	BAL	A	C-1	116		.272
1964	BAL	A	C-1	81		.222
1965	BAL	A	C/1	77		.233
1966	WAS	A	/1-C	14		.174
1967	WAS	A	/H		1	.000
			BRTR		332	.249

ORTA, JORGE [NUNEZ]
B.NOV.26,1950 MAZATLAN,MEXICO

1972	CHI	A	S-2/3		51	.202
1973	CHI	A	*2/S	128		.266
1974	CHI	A	*2-D/S	139		.316
1975	CHI	A	*2	140		.304
1976	CHI	A	O-3-D	158		.274
1977	CHI	A	*2	144		.282
1978	CHI	A	*2	117		.274
			BLTR	877		.283

ORTEGA, FILOMENO CORONADA (PHIL) OR (KEMO)
B.OCT.7,1939 GILBERT,ARIZ.

1960	LA	N	P		3	0- 0
1961	LA	N	P		4	0- 2
1962	LA	N	P		24	0- 2
1963	LA	N	P		1	0- 0
1964	LA	N	P	34	35	7- 9
1965	WAS	A	P		35	12-15
1966	WAS	A	P		33	12-12
1967	WAS	A	P		34	10-10
1968	WAS	A	P		31	5-12
1969	CAL	A	/P		5	0- 0
			BRTR	204	205	46-62

ORTENZIO, FRANK JOSEPH
B.FEB.24,1951 FRESNO,CAL.

| 1973 | KC | A | /1 | | 9 | .280 |

ORTH, ALBERT LEWIS (SMILING AL) OR (THE CURVELESS WONDER)
B.SEPT.5,1872 TIPTON,IND.
D.OCT.8,1948 LYNCHBURG,VA.

1895	PHI	N	P		11	8- 1
1896	PHI	N	P		24	15- 9
1897	PHI	N	P	33	42	14-19
1898	PHI	N	P	27	32	15-12
1899	PHI	N	P		17	13- 3
1900	PHI	N	P	30	35	14-14
1901	PHI	N	P		35	21-12
1902	WAS	A	P-1-	38	54	19-18
			S-O			.218
1903	WAS	A	P	37	54	10-21
1904	WAS	A	P-O	10	32	3- 4
						.236
	NY	A	P-O	18	24	11- 5
						.365
1905	NY	A	P		40	18-18
1906	NY	A	P	45	47	27-17
1907	NY	A	P	37	43	14-21
1908	NY	A	P	21	38	2-13
1909	NY	A	P	1	22	1- 0
			BLTR	424	550	205-187
						.276

ORTIZ, JOSE LUIS [IRIZARRY]
B.JUNE 25,1947 PONCE,P.R.

1969	CHI	A	/O		16	.273
1970	CHI	A	/O		15	.333
1971	CHI	N	O		36	.295
			BRTR		67	.301

ORTIZ, OLIVERIO [NUNEZ] (BABY)
B.DEC.5,1919 CAMAGUEY,CUBA

| 1944 | WAS | A | P | | 2 | 0- 2 |
| | | | BRTR | | | |

ORTIZ, ROBERTO GONZALO [NUNEZ]
B.JUNE 30,1915 CAMAGUEY,CUBA
D.SEPT.15,1971 MIAMI,FLA.

1941	WAS	A	O		22	.329
1942	WAS	A	O		20	.167
1943	WAS	A	O		1	.250
1944	WAS	A	O		85	.253
1949	WAS	A	O		40	.279
1950	WAS	A	O		39	.227
	PHI	A	O		6	.071
			BRTR		213	.255

ORWOLL, OSWALD CHRISTIAN (OSSIE)
B.NOV.17,1900 PORTLAND,ORE.
D.MAY 8,1967 DECORAH,IOWA

1928	PHI	A	P-1	27	64	6- 5
						.306
1929	PHI	A	P	12	30	0- 2
			BLTL	39	94	6- 7
						.294

OSBORN, DANNY LEON (OZZIE)
B.JUNE 19,1946 SPRINGFIELD,MO.

| 1975 | CHI | A | P | | 24 | 3- 0 |
| | | | BRTR | | | |

YR	CL LEA POS	GP	G	REC

OSBORN, JOHN BODE (BOB)
B.APR.17,1903 SAN DIEGO,TEX.
D.APR.19,1960 PARIS,ARK.

YR	CL LEA POS	GP	G	REC
1925	CHI N P		1	0- 0
1926	CHI N P		31	6- 5
1927	CHI N P		24	5- 5
1929	CHI N P		3	0- 0
1930	CHI N P		35	10- 6
1931	PIT N P		27	6- 1
	BRTR		121	27-17

OSBURN, LARRY PATRICK (PAT)
B.MAY 4,1949 MURRAY,KY.

1974	CIN N /P		6	0- 0
1975	MIL A /P		6	0- 1
	BLTL		12	0- 1

OSBORN, WILFRED PEARL (OSSIE)
B.NOV.28,1883 NEVADA,OHIO
D.SEPT.2,1954 UPPER SANDUSKY,O.

1907	PHI N O		37	.276
1908	PHI N O		152	.267
1909	PHI N O		54	.183
	BLTR		243	.252

OSBORNE, EARNEST PRESTON (TINY)
B.APR.9,1893 PORTERDALE,GA.
D.JAN.5,1969 ATLANTA,GA.

1922	CHI N P		41	9- 5
1923	CHI N P		37	8-15
1924	CHI N P		2	0- 0
	BRO N /P		21	6- 5
1925	BRO N P		41	8-15
	BLTR		142	31-40

OSBORNE, FREDERICK W.
B.HAMPTON,IOWA

| 1890 | PIT N P-O | 6 | 41 | 0- 6 |
| | | | | .238 |

OSBORNE, LAWRENCE SIDNEY (BOBO)
B.OCT.12,1935 CHATTAHOOCHEE,GA.

1957	DET A 1-O		11	.148
1958	DET A H		2	.000
1959	DET A 1-O		86	.191
1961	DET A 1-3		71	.215
1962	DET A C-1-3		64	.230
1963	WAS A 1-3		125	.212
	BLTR		359	.206

OSBORNE, WAYNE HAROLD
(OSSIE) OR (FISH HOOK)
B.OCT.11,1912 WATSONVILLE,CAL.

1935	PIT N P	2	3	0- 0
1936	BOS N P		5	1- 1
	BLTR	7	8	1- 1

OSGOOD, CHARLES BENJAMIN
B.NOV.23,1926 SOMERVILLE,MASS.

| 1944 | BRO N P | | 1 | 0- 0 |
| | BRTR | | | |

O SHEA, FRANCIS JOSEPH
[PLAYED UNDER NAME OF
FRANCIS JOSEPH SHEA]

OSINSKI, DANIEL (DAN)
B.NOV.17,1933 CHICAGO,ILL.

1962	KC A P		4	0- 0
	LA A P		33	6- 4
1963	LA A P		47	8- 8
1964	LA A P		47	3- 3
1965	MIL N P		61	0- 3
1966	BOS A P		44	4- 3
1967	BOS A P		34	3- 1
1969	CHI A P		51	5- 5
1970	HOU N /P		3	0- 1
	BRTR		324	29-28

OSTDIEK, HENRY GIRARD (HARRY)
B.APR.12,1881 OTTUMWA,IOWA
D.MAY 6,1956 MINNEAPOLIS,MINN.

1904	CLE A C		7	.157
1908	BOS A C		1	.000
	BRTR		8	.143

OSTEEN, CLAUDE WILSON
B.AUG.9,1939 CANEY SPRINGS,TENN.

1957	CIN N P		3	0- 0
1959	CIN N P		2	0- 0
1960	CIN N P	20	26	0- 1
1961	CIN N P-O	1	6	0- 0
				.000
	WAS A P		3	1- 1
1962	WAS A P		28	37	8-13
1963	WAS A P		40	49	9-14
1964	WAS A P		37	40	15-13
1965	LA N P		40	42	15-15
1966	LA N P		39	17-14
1967	LA N P		39	42	17-17
1968	LA N P		39	40	12-18
1969	LA N P		41	44	20-15
1970	LA N P		37	39	16-14
1971	LA N P		38	39	14-11
1972	LA N P		33	36	20-11
1973	LA N P		33	16-11
1974	HOU N P		23	9- 9
	STL N /P		8	0- 2
1975	CHI A P		37	7-16
	BLTL	541	588	196-195
				.188

OSTEEN, JAMES CHAMPLIN (CHAMP)
B.FEB.24,1877 HENDERSONVILLE,N.C.
D.DEC.14,1962 GREENVILLE,S.C.

1903	WAS A S		10	.195
1904	NY A 3		27	.202
1908	STL N S		29	.196
1909	STL N S		16	.199
	BLTR		82	.199

OSTEEN, MILTON DARRELL (DARRELL)
B.FEB.14,1943 OKLAHOMA CITY,OKLA

1965	CIN N /P		3	0- 0
1966	CIN N P	13	16	0- 2
1967	CIN N P	10	14	0- 2
1970	OAK A /P		3	1- 0
	BRTR	29	36	1- 4

OSTENDORF, FREDERICK K.
B.AUG.5,1890 BALTIMORE,MD.
D.MAR.2,1965 KEOUGHTAN,VA.

| 1914 | IND F P | | 1 | 0- 0 |
| | BLTL | | | |

OSTER, WILLIAM CHARLES
B.JAN.2,1933 NEW YORK,N.Y.

| 1954 | PHI A P | | 8 | 0- 1 |
| | BLTL | | | |

OSTERGARD, ROBERT LUND (RED)
B.MAY 11,1898 GALVESTON,TEX.

| 1921 | CHI A S | | 12 | .364 |
| | BLTR | | | |

OSTERHOUT, CHARLES H.
B.1857 SYRACUSE,N.Y.
D.MAY 21,1933 SYRACUSE,N.Y.

| 1879 | SYR N C-2 | | 2 | .000 |
| | TR | | | |

OSTERMUELLER, FREDERICK RAYMOND
(FRITZ)
B.SEPT.15,1907 QUINCY,ILL.
D.DEC.17,1957 QUINCY,ILL.

1934	BOS A P		23	10-13
1935	BOS A P		22	7- 8
1936	BOS A P		43	10-16
1937	BOS A P		25	3- 7
1938	BOS A P	31	33	13- 5
1939	BOS A P		34	11- 7
1940	BOS A P	31	33	5- 9
1941	STL A P	15	16	0- 3
1942	STL A P		10	3- 1
1943	STL N P		11	0- 2
	BRO N P	7	8	1- 1
1944	BRO N P	10	11	2- 1
	PIT N P	28	29	11- 7
1945	PIT N P		14	5- 4
1946	PIT N P	27	28	13-10
1947	PIT N P		26	12-10
1948	PIT N P		23	8-11
	BLTL	390	399	114-115

OSTROSSER, BRIAN LEONARD
B.JUNE 17,1949 HAMILTON,ONT.,CAN

| 1973 | NY N /S | | 4 | .000 |
| | BLTR | | | |

OSTROWSKI, JOHN THADDEUS (JOHNNY)
B.OCT.17,1917 CHICAGO,ILL.

1943	CHI N 3-O		10	.207
1944	CHI N O		8	.154
1945	CHI N 3		7	.300
1946	CHI N 2-3		64	.213
1948	BOS A H		1	.000
1949	CHI A 3-O		49	.266
1950	CHI A O		21	.222
	WAS A O		55	.227
	CHI A O		1	.500
	BRTR		216	.234

OSTROWSKI, JOSEPH PAUL (JOE)
(PROFESSOR) OR (SPECS)
B.NOV.15,1916 W.WYOMING,PA.

1948	STL A P		26	4- 6
1949	STL A P		40	8- 8
1950	STL A P		9	2- 4
	NY A P		21	1- 1
1951	NY A P		34	6- 4
1952	NY A P		20	2- 2
	BLTL		150	23-25

OTERO, REGINO JOSEPH [GOMEZ]
(REGGIE)
B.SEPT.7,1915 HAVANA,CUBA

| 1945 | CHI N 1 | | 14 | .391 |
| | BLTR | | | |

OTEY, WILLIAM TILFORD
(STEAMBOAT BILL)
B.DEC.16,1886 DAYTON,OHIO
D.APR.23,1931 DAYTON,OHIO

1907	PIT N P		3	0- 1
1910	WAS A P		9	0- 1
1911	WAS A P		12	1- 4
	BLTL		24	1- 6

OTIS, AMOS JOSEPH
B.APR.26,1947 MOBILE,ALA.

1967	NY N O/3		19	.220
1969	NY N O/3		48	.151
1970	KC A *O		159	.284
1971	KC A *O		147	.301
1972	KC A *O		143	.293
1973	KC A *O-D		148	.300
1974	KC A *O		146	.284
1975	KC A *O		132	.247
1976	KC A *O		153	.279
1977	KC A *O		142	.251
1978	KC A *O		141	.298
	BRTR		1378	.286

OTIS, HARRY GEORGE (CANNONBALL)
B.OCT.5,1886 W.NEW YORK,N.J.
D.JAN.29,1976 TEANECK,N.J.

| 1909 | CLE A P | | 5 | 2- 2 |
| | TL | | | |

OTIS, PAUL FRANKLIN (BILL)
B.DEC.24,1889 SCITUATE,MASS.

| 1912 | NY A O | | 4 | .000 |

O TOOLE, DENNIS JOSEPH
B.MAR.13,1949 CHICAGO,ILL.

1969	CHI A /P		2	0- 0
1970	CHI A /P		3	0- 0
1971	CHI A /P		1	0- 0
1972	CHI A /P		3	0- C
1973	CHI A /P		6	0- 0
	BRTR		15	0- 0

O TOOLE, JAMES JEROME (JIM)
B.JAN.10,1937 CHICAGO,ILL.

1958	CIN N P		1	0- 1
1959	CIN N P	28	29	5- 8
1960	CIN N P		34	12-12
1961	CIN N P		39	19- 9
1962	CIN N P		36	16-13
1963	CIN N P		33	17-14
1964	CIN N P		30	17- 7
1965	CIN N P		29	3-10
1966	CIN N P		25	5- 7
1967	CHI A P		15	4- 3
	BBTL	270	271	98-84

O TOOLE, MARTIN JAMES
B.NOV.27,1888 WM.PENN,PA.
D.FEB.18,1949 ABERDEEN,WASH.

1908	CIN N P		3	1- 0
1911	PIT N P		5	3- 2
1912	PIT N P		37	15-17
1913	PIT N P		26	6- 8
1914	PIT N P		19	1- 8
	NY N P		10	1- 1
	BRTR		100	27-36

YR	CL	LEA	POS	GP	G	REC

OTT, MELVIN THOMAS (MEL)
OR (MASTER MELVIN)
B.MAR.2,1909 GRETNA,LA.
D.NOV.21,1958 NEW ORLEANS,LA.

YR	CL	LEA	POS	GP	G	REC
1926	NY	N	O		35	.383
1927	NY	N	O		82	.282
1928	NY	N	O		124	.322
1929	NY	N	O		150	.328
1930	NY	N	O		148	.349
1931	NY	N	O		138	.292
1932	NY	N	O		154	.318
1933	NY	N	O		152	.283
1934	NY	N	O		153	.326
1935	NY	N	3-O		152	.322
1936	NY	N	O		150	.328
1937	NY	N	3-O		151	.294
1938	NY	N	3-O		150	.311
1939	NY	N	3-O		125	.308
1940	NY	N	3-O		151	.289
1941	NY	N	O		148	.286
1942	NY	N	M-O		152	.295
1943	NY	N	M-3-O		125	.234
1944	NY	N	M-3-O		120	.288
1945	NY	N	M-O		135	.308
1946	NY	N	M-O		31	.074
1947	NY	N	M-H		4	.000
			BLTR		2730	.304

NON-PLAYING MANAGER NY[N] 1948

OTT, NATHAN EDWARD (ED)
B.JULY 11,1951 MUNCY,PA.

YR	CL	LEA	POS	GP	G	REC
1974	PIT	N	/O		7	.000
1975	PIT	N	/C		5	.200
1976	PIT	N	/C		27	.308
1977	PIT	N	C		104	.264
1978	PIT	N	C/O		112	.269
			BLTR		255	.267

OTT, WILLIAM JOSEPH (BILLY)
B.NOV.23,1940 NEW YORK,N.Y.

YR	CL	LEA	POS	GP	G	REC
1962	CHI	N	O		12	.143
1964	CHI	N	O		20	.179
			BBTR		32	.164

OTTEN JAMES EDWARD (JIM)
B.JULY 1,1951 LEWISTON,MONT.

YR	CL	LEA	POS	GP	G	REC
1974	CHI	A	/P		5	0- 1
1975	CHI	A	/P		2	0- 0
1976	CHI	A	/P		2	0- 0
			BRTR		9	0- 1

OTTEN, JOSEPH G.
B.MURPHYSBORO,ILL.

YR	CL	LEA	POS	GP	G	REC
1895	STL	N	C		24	.233
			TR			

OTTERSON, WILLIAM JOHN (BILLY)
B.MAY 4,1862 PITTSBURGH,PA.
D.SEPT.21,1940 PITTSBURGH,PA.

YR	CL	LEA	POS	GP	G	REC
1887	BRO	AA	S		30	.269
			BRTR			

OULLIBER, JOHN ANDREW
B.FEB.24,1911 NEW ORLEANS,LA.

YR	CL	LEA	POS	GP	G	REC
1933	CLE	A	O		22	.267
			BRTR			

OUTEN, WILLIAM AUSTIN (CHICK)
B.JUNE 17,1905 MT.HOLLY,N.C.
D.SEPT.11,1961 DURHAM,N.C.

YR	CL	LEA	POS	GP	G	REC
1933	BRO	N	C		93	.248
			BLTR			

OUTLAW, JAMES PAULUS (JIMMY)
B.JAN.20,1913 ORME,TENN.

YR	CL	LEA	POS	GP	G	REC
1937	CIN	N	3		49	.273
1938	CIN	N	H		4	.000
1939	BOS	N	O		65	.263
1943	DET	A	O		20	.269
1944	DET	A	O		139	.273
1945	DET	A	3-O		132	.271
1946	DET	A	3-O		92	.261
1947	DET	A	3-O		70	.228
1948	DET	A	3-O		74	.283
1949	DET	A	H		5	.250
			BRTR		650	.268

OVERALL, ORVAL
B.FEB.2,1881 VISALIA,CAL.
D.JULY 14,1947 FRESNO,CAL.

YR	CL	LEA	POS	GP	G	REC
1905	CIN	N	P		42	17-23
1906	CIN	N	P		13	4- 5
	CHI	N	P		18	12- 3
1907	CHI	N	P		36	23- 7
1908	CHI	N	P		37	15-11
1909	CHI	N	P		38	20-11
1910	CHI	N	P	23	24	12- 6
1913	CHI	N	P		10	4- 5
			BBTR	217	218	107-71

OVERBECK, HENRY A.
B.ST.LOUIS,MO.

YR	CL	LEA	POS	GP	G	REC
1883	PIT	AA	1		2	.222
	STL	AA	O		4	.000
1884	BAL	U	P-3-	1	33	0- 0
			O			.159
	KC	U	P-1-	4	26	0- 3
			3-O			.174
				5	65	0- 3
						.157

OVERMIRE, FRANK (STUBBY)
B.MAY 16,1919 MOLINE,MICH.
D.MAR.3,1977 LAKELAND,FLA.

YR	CL	LEA	POS	GP	G	REC
1943	DET	A	P		29	7- 6
1944	DET	A	P		32	11-11
1945	DET	A	P		31	9- 9
1946	DET	A	P		24	5- 7
1947	DET	A	P		28	11- 5
1948	DET	A	P		37	3- 4
1949	DET	A	P		14	1- 3
1950	STL	A	P		31	9-12
1951	STL	A	P		8	1- 6
	NY	A	P		15	1- 1
1952	STL	A	P		17	0- 3
			BRTL		266	58-67

OVERY, HARRY MICHAEL (MIKE)
B.JAN.27,1951 CLINTON,ILL.

YR	CL	LEA	POS	GP	G	REC
1976	CAL	A	/P		5	0- 2
			BRTR			

OVITZ, ERNEST GAYHEART
B.OCT.7,1885 MINERAL POINT,WIS.

YR	CL	LEA	POS	GP	G	REC
1911	CHI	N	P		1	0- 0

OWCHINKO, ROBERT DENNIS (BOB)
B.JAN.1,1955 DETROIT,MICH.

YR	CL	LEA	POS	GP	G	REC
1976	SD	N	/P		2	0- 2
1977	SD	N	P		30	9-12
1978	SD	N	P		36	10-13
			BLTL		68	19-27

OWEN, ARNOLD MALCOLM (MICKEY)
B.APR.4,1916 NIXA,MO.

YR	CL	LEA	POS	GP	G	REC
1937	STL	N	C		80	.231
1938	STL	N	C		122	.267
1939	STL	N	C		131	.259
1940	STL	N	C		117	.264
1941	BRO	N	C		128	.231
1942	BRO	N	C		133	.259
1943	BRO	N	C-S		106	.260
1944	BRO	N	C-2		130	.273
1945	BRO	N	C		24	.286
1949	CHI	N	C		62	.273
1950	CHI	N	C		86	.243
1951	CHI	N	C		58	.184
1954	BOS	A	C		32	.235
			BRTR		1209	.255

OWEN, FRANK MALCOLM (YIP)
B.DEC.23,1879 YPSILANTI,MICH.
D.NOV.27,1942 DETROIT,MICH.

YR	CL	LEA	POS	GP	G	REC
1901	DET	A	P		9	1- 4
1903	CHI	A	P		26	8-11
1904	CHI	A	P		37	21-15
1905	CHI	A	P		42	22-14
1906	CHI	A	P		42	22-13
1907	CHI	A	P		11	2- 3
1908	CHI	A	P		25	6- 7
1909	CHI	A	P		3	1- 1
			TR		195	83-68

OWEN, MARVIN JAMES (MARV) OR (FRECK)
B.MAR.22,1906 AGNEW,CAL.

YR	CL	LEA	POS	GP	G	REC
1931	DET	A	1-S-3		105	.223
1933	DET	A	3		138	.262
1934	DET	A	3		154	.317
1935	DET	A	3		134	.263
1936	DET	A	3		154	.295
1937	DET	A	3		107	.288
1938	CHI	A	3		141	.281
1939	CHI	A	3		58	.237
1940	BOS	A	1-3		20	.211
			BRTR		1011	.275

OWENS, FRANK WALTER (YIP)
B.JAN.26,1886 TORONTO,ONT.,CAN.
D.JULY 2,1958 MINNEAPOLIS,MINN.

YR	CL	LEA	POS	GP	G	REC
1905	BOS	A	C		1	.000
1909	CHI	A	C		64	.201
1914	BRO	F	C		55	.274
1915	BAL	F	C		98	.245
			BRTR		218	.241

OWENS, FURMAN LEE
B.MAY 6,1908 CONVERSE,S.C.
D.NOV.14,1958 GREENVILLE,S.C.

YR	CL	LEA	POS	GP	G	REC
1935	PHI	A	C		2	.250
			BRTR			

OWENS, JAMES PHILIP (JIM) OR (BEAR)
B.JAN.16,1934 GIFFORD,PA.

YR	CL	LEA	POS	GP	G	REC
1955	PHI	N	P		3	0- 2
1956	PHI	N	P		10	0- 4
1958	PHI	N	P		1	1- 0
1959	PHI	N	P		31	12-12
1960	PHI	N	P		31	4-14
1961	PHI	N	P-O	20	21	5-10
						.074
1962	PHI	N	P		23	2- 4
1963	CIN	N	P		19	0- 2
1964	HOU	N	P		48	8- 7
1965	HOU	N	P		50	6- 5
1966	HOU	N	P		40	4- 7
1967	HOU	N	P		10	0- 1
			BRTR	286	287	42-68
						.101

OWENS, PAUL FRANCIS
B.FEB.7,1924 SALAMANCA,N.Y.
NON-PLAYING MANAGER PHI[N] 1972

OWENS, THOMAS LLEWELLYN (RED)
B.NOV.1,1874 POTTSVILLE,PA.
D.AUG.20,1952 HARRISBURG,PA.

YR	CL	LEA	POS	GP	G	REC
1899	PHI	N	2		8	.045
1905	BRO	N	2		43	.215
			BRTR		51	.196

OXLEY, HENRY HAVELOCK
B.JAN.4,1858 COVEHEAD,P.E.I.,CANADA.
D.OCT.12,1945 SOMERVILLE,MASS.

YR	CL	LEA	POS	GP	G	REC
1884	NY	N	C		2	.000
	MET	AA	C		1	.000
					3	.000

OYLER, ANDREW PAUL (PEPPER)
B.MAY 5,1880 NEWVILLE,PA.
D.OCT.24,1970 E.PENNSBORO TWP.,
CUMBERLAND COUNTY,PA.

YR	CL	LEA	POS	GP	G	REC
1902	BAL	A	2-S-3-O		26	.227
			BRTR			

OYLER, RAYMOND FRANCIS (RAY)
B.AUG.4,1938 INDIANAPOLIS,IND.

YR	CL	LEA	POS	GP	G	REC
1965	DET	A	S-2/1-3		82	.186
1966	DET	A	S		71	.171
1967	DET	A	*S		148	.207
1968	DET	A	*S		111	.135
1969	SEA	A	*S		106	.165
1970	CAL	A	S/3		24	.083
			BRTR		542	.175

OZARK, DANIEL LEONARD (DANNY)
B.NOV.26,1923 BUFFALO,N.Y.
NON-PLAYING MANAGER PHI[N] 1973-78

OZMER, HORACE ROBERT (DOC)
B.MAY 25,1901 ATLANTA,GA.
D.DEC.28,1970 ATLANTA,GA.

YR	CL	LEA	POS	GP	G	REC
1923	PHI	A	P		1	0- 0
			BRTR			

PABOR, CHARLES HENRY
B.SEPT.24,1849 NEW YORK,N.Y.
D.APR.22,1913 NEW HAVEN,CONN.

YR	CL	LEA	POS	GP	G	REC
1871	CLE	NA	M-P-	1	29	0- 1
			O			—
1872	PHI	NA	P-O	2	20	1- 1
						.269
1873	ATL	NA	O		55	—
1874	PHI	NA	O		5	—
1875	ATL	NA	M-O		41	—
	NH	NA	O		6	—
			TL	3	156	1- 2

PABST, EDWARD D. A.
B.1868 ST.LOUIS,MO.

YR	CL	LEA	POS	GP	G	REC
1890	ATH	AA	O		8	.345
	STL	AA	O		4	.143
					12	.279

PACELLA, JOHN LEWIS
B.SEPT.15,1956 BROOKLYN,N.Y.

YR	CL	LEA	POS	GP	G	REC
1977	NY	N	/P		3	0- 0
			BRTR			

PACIOREK, JOHN FRANCIS
B.FEB.11,1945 DETROIT,MICH.

YR	CL	LEA	POS	GP	G	REC
1963	HOU	N	O		1	1.000
			BRTR			

PACIOREK, THOMAS MARIAN (TOM)
B.NOV.2,1946 DETROIT,MICH.

YR	CL	LEA	POS	GP	G	REC
1970	LA	N	/O		8	.222
1971	LA	N	/O		2	.500
1972	LA	N	/1-O		11	.255
1973	LA	N	O/1		96	.262
1974	LA	N	O/1		85	.240
1975	LA	N	O		62	.193
1976	ATL	N	O-1/3		111	.290
1977	ATL	N	1/O-3		72	.239
1978	ATL	N	/1		5	.333
	SEA	A	O-D/1		70	.299
			BRTR		522	.263

YR	CL	LEA	POS	GP	G	REC

PACK, FRANK (FRANKIE)
B.APR.10,1928 MORRISTOWN,TENN.
| 1949 STL | A | H | | | 1 | .000 |
| | BLTR | | | | | |

PACKARD, EUGENE MILO
B.JULY 13,1887 COLORADO SPRINGS
COLORADO
D.MAY 19,1959 RIVERSIDE,CAL.
1912 CIN	N	P			1	1- 0
1913 CIN	N	P	39	43	7-11
1914 KC	F	P		42	20-14
1915 KC	F	P		42	20-12
1916 CHI	N	P	37	44	10- 6
1917 CHI	N	P		2	0- 0
STL	N	P	34	36	9- 6
1918 STL	N	P	30	36	12-12
1919 PHI	N	P	21	27	6- 8
	BLTL		248	273	85-69

PACTWA, JOSEPH MARTIN (JOE)
B.JUNE 2,1948 HAMMOND,IND.
| 1975 CAL | A | P | | | 4 | 1- 0 |
| | BLTL | | | | | |

PADDEN, RICHARD JOSEPH (BRAINS)
B.SEPT.17,1870 MARTINS FERRY,O.
D.OCT.31,1922 MARTINS FERRY,O.
1896 PIT	N	2			60	.239
1897 PIT	N	2			135	.281
1898 PIT	N	2			128	.256
1899 WAS	N	2-S			131	.272
1901 STL	A	2			123	.253
1902 STL	A	2			117	.265
1903 STL	A	2			29	.202
1904 STL	A	2			132	.238
1905 STL	A	2			16	.172
	BRTR				871	.256

PADDEN, THOMAS FRANCIS (TOM)
B.OCT.6,1908 MANCHESTER,N.H.
D.JUNE 10,1973 MANCHESTER,N.H.
1932 PIT	N	C			47	.263
1933 PIT	N	C			30	.211
1934 PIT	N	C			82	.321
1935 PIT	N	C			97	.272
1936 PIT	N	C			88	.249
1937 PIT	N	C			35	.286
1943 PHI	N	C			17	.293
WAS	A	C			3	.000
	BRTR				399	.272

PADDOCK, DELMAR HAROLD
B.JUNE 8,1887 VOLGA,S.DAK.
D.FEB.6,1952 REMER,MINN
1912 CHI	A	H			1	.000
NY	A	3			45	.287
	BLTR				46	.287

PADGETT, DON WILSON
B.DEC.5,1911 CAROLEEN,N.C.
1937 STL	N	O			123	.314
1938 STL	N	1-O			110	.271
1939 STL	N	C			92	.399
1940 STL	N	C-1			93	.242
1941 STL	N	C-1-O			107	.247
1946 BRO	N	C			19	.167
BOS	N	C			44	.255
1947 PHI	N	C			75	.316
1948 PHI	N	C			36	.230
	BLTR				699	.288

PADGETT, ERNEST KITCHEN (RED)
B.MAR.1,1899 PHILADELPHIA,PA.
D.APR.15,1957 E.ORANGE,N.J.
1923 BOS	N	2-S			4	.182
1924 BOS	N	2			138	.255
1925 BOS	N	2-S-3			86	.305
1926 CLE	A	3			36	.210
1927 CLE	A	2			7	.286
	BRTR				271	.266

PAEPKE, DENNIS RAY
B.APR.17,1949 LONG BEACH,CAL.
1969 KC	A	/C			12	.111
1971 KC	A	C-O			60	.204
1972 KC	A	/C			2	.000
1974 KC	A	/C-O			.6	.167
	BRTR				80	.183

PAFKO, ANDREW (ANDY)
(HANDY ANDY) OR (PRUSCHKA)
B.FEB.25,1921 BOYCEVILLE,WIS.
1943 CHI	N	O			13	.379
1944 CHI	N	O			128	.269
1945 CHI	N	O			144	.298
1946 CHI	N	O			65	.282
1947 CHI	N	O			129	.302
1948 CHI	N	3			142	.312
1949 CHI	N	3-O			144	.281
1950 CHI	N	O			146	.304
1951 CHI	N	O			49	.264
BRO	N	O			84	.249
1952 BRO	N	3-O			150	.287
1953 MIL	N	O			140	.297
1954 MIL	N	O			138	.286
1955 MIL	N	3-O			86	.266
1956 MIL	N	O			45	.258
1957 MIL	N	O			83	.277
1958 MIL	N	O			95	.238
1959 MIL	N	O			71	.218
	BRTR				1852	.285

PAGAN, DAVID PERCY (DAVE)
B.SEP.15,1949 NIPAWIN,SASK.,CAN.
1973 NY	A	/P			4	0- 0
1974 NY	A	P			16	1- 3
1975 NY	A	P			13	0- 0
1976 NY	A	/P			7	1- 1
BAL	A	P			20	1- 4
1977 SEA	A	P			24	1- 1
PIT	N	/P			1	0- 0
	BRTR				85	4- 9

PAGAN, JOSE ANTONIO [RODRIGUEZ]
B.MAY 5,1935 BARCELONETA,P.R.
1959 SF	N	2-S-3			31	.174
1960 SF	N	S-3			18	.286
1961 SF	N	S-O			134	.253
1962 SF	N	S			164	.259
1963 SF	N	2-S-O			148	.234
1964 SF	N	S-O			134	.223
1965 SF	N	S			26	.205
PIT	N	3/S			42	.237
1966 PIT	N	3-S/2-O			109	.264
1967 PIT	N	3-O-S/2-C			81	.289
1968 PIT	N	3-O/S-2-1			80	.221
1969 PIT	N	3-O/2			108	.285
1970 PIT	N	3/O-1-2			95	.265
1971 PIT	N	3/O-1			57	.241
1972 PIT	N	3/O			53	.252
1973 PHI	N	3/1-O-2			46	.205
	BRTR				1326	.250

PAGE, JOSEPH FRANCIS
(JOE) OR (FIREMAN)
B.OCT.28,1917 CHERRY VALLEY,PA.
1944 NY	A	P			19	5- 7
1945 NY	A	P			20	6- 3
1946 NY	A	P	31	32	9- 8
1947 NY	A	P		56	14- 8
1948 NY	A	P		55	7- 8
1949 NY	A	P		60	13- 8
1950 NY	A	P		37	3- 7
1954 PIT	N	P			7	0- 0
	BLTL		285	286	57-49

PAGE, MICHAEL RANDY (MIKE)
B.JULY 12,1940 WOODRUFF,S.C.
| 1968 ATL | N | /O | | | 20 | .179 |
| | BLTR | | | | | |

PAGE, MITCHELL OTIS
B.OCT.15,1951 LOS ANGELES,CAL.
1977 OAK	A	*O			145	.307
1978 OAK	A	*O-O			147	.285
	BLTR				292	.296

PAGE, PHILIP RAUSAC
B.AUG.23,1905 SPRINGFIELD,MASS.
D.JUNE 26,1958 SPRINGFIELD,MASS
1928 DET	A	P			3	2- 0
1929 DET	A	P			10	0- 2
1930 DET	A	P			12	0- 1
1934 BRO	N	P			6	1- 0
	BRTL				31	3- 3

PAGE, SAMUEL WALTER
B.FEB.11,1916 WOODRUFF,S.C.
| 1939 PHI | A | P | | | 4 | 0- 3 |
| | BLTR | | | | | |

PAGE, VANCE LINWOOD
B.SEPT.19,1905 ELM CITY,N.C.
D.JULY 14,1951 WILSON,N.C.
1938 CHI	N	P			13	5- 4
1939 CHI	N	P			27	7- 7
1940 CHI	N	P	30	31	1- 3
1941 CHI	N	P			25	2- 2
	BRTR		95	96	15-16

PAGEL, KARL DOUGLAS
B.MAR.29,1955 MADISON,WIS.
| 1978 CHI | N | /H | | | 2 | .000 |
| | BLTL | | | | | |

PAGLIARONI, JAMES VINCENT
(JIM) OR (PAG)
B.DEC.8,1937 DEARBORN,MICH.
1955 BOS	A	C			1	.000
1960 BOS	A	C			28	.306
1961 BOS	A	C			120	.242
1962 BOS	A	C			90	.258
1963 PIT	N	C			92	.230
1964 PIT	N	C			97	.295
1965 PIT	N	*C			134	.268
1966 PIT	N	*C			123	.235
1967 PIT	N	C			44	.200
1968 OAK	A	C			66	.246
1969 OAK	A	/C			14	.148
SEA	A	C/1-O			40	.264
	BRTR				849	.252

PAIGE, GEORGE LYNN (PIGGY)
B.MAY 5,1883 PAW PAW,MICH.
D.JUNE 8,1939 BERLIN,WIS.
| 1911 CLE | A | P | | | 2 | 1- 0 |
| | BLTR | | | | | |

PAIGE, LEROY ROBERT (SATCHEL)
B.JULY 7,1906 MOBILE,ALA.
1948 CLE	A	P			21	6- 1
1949 CLE	A	P			31	4- 7
1951 STL	A	P			23	3- 4
1952 STL	A	P			46	12-10
1953 STL	A	P			57	3- 9
1965 KC	A	/P			1	0- 0
	BRTR				179	28-31

PAINE, PHILLIPS STEERE (FLIP)
B.JUNE 8,1930 CHEPACHET,R.I.
D.FEB.19,1978 LEBANON,PA.
1951 BOS	N	P			21	2- 0
1954 MIL	N	P			11	1- 0
1955 MIL	N	P			15	2- 0
1956 MIL	N	P			1	0- 0
1957 MIL	N	P			1	0- 0
1958 STL	N	P			46	5- 1
	BRTR				95	10- 1

PALAGYI, MICHAEL RAYMOND
B.JULY 4,1917 CONNEAUT,OHIO
| 1939 WAS | A | P | | | 1 | 0- 0 |
| | BRTR | | | | | |

PALICA, ERVIN MARTIN (ERV)
[REAL NAME
ERVIN MARTIN PAVLIECIVICH]
B.FEB.9,1928 LOMITA,CAL.
1945 BRO	N	H			2	.000
1947 BRO	N	P			3	0- 1
1948 BRO	N	P	41	45	6- 6
1949 BRO	N	P			49	8- 9
1950 BRO	N	P	43	48	13- 8
1951 BRO	N	P	19	20	2- 6
1953 BRO	N	P			4	0- 0
1954 BRO	N	P	25	28	3- 3
1955 BAL	A	P			33	5-11
1956 BAL	A	P	29	30	4-11
	BRTR		246	262	41-55
						.198

PALM, RICHARD PAUL (MIKE)
B.FEB.13,1925 BOSTON,MASS.
| 1948 BOS | A | P | | | 3 | 0- 0 |
| | BRTR | | | | | |

PALMER
B.ST.LOUIS,MO.
| 1885 STL | N | P | | | 4 | 0- 4 |

PALMER, DAVID WILLIAM
B.AUG.19,1957 GLENS FALLS,N.Y.
| 1978 MON | N | /P | | | 5 | 0- 1 |
| | BRTR | | | | | |

PALMER, EDWIN HENRY (BALDY)
B.JUNE 1,1893 PETTY,TEX.
| 1917 PHI | A | 3 | | | 16 | .212 |
| | BRTR | | | | | |

PALMER, JAMES ALVIN (JIM)
B.OCT.15,1945 NEW YORK,N.Y.
1965 BAL	A	P	27	29	5- 4
1966 BAL	A	P	30	36	15-10
1967 BAL	A	/P			9	3- 1
1969 BAL	A	P	26	27	16- 4
1970 BAL	A	P	39	44	20-10
1971 BAL	A	P	37	38	20- 9
1972 BAL	A	P		36	21-10
1973 BAL	A	P		38	22- 9
1974 BAL	A	P		26	7-12
1975 BAL	A	P		39	23-11
1976 BAL	A	P		40	22-13
1977 BAL	A	P		39	20-11
1978 BAL	A	P		38	21-12
	BRTR		424	439	215-116

YR	CL LEA POS	GP	G	REC
PALMER, LOWELL RAYMOND				
B.AUG.18,1947 SACRAMENTO,CAL.				
1969 PHI N P		26	2- 8
1970 PHI N P		38	1- 2
1971 PHI N /P		3	0- 0
1972 STL N P	16	17	0- 3
CLE A /P		1	0- 0
1974 SD N P	22	23	2- 5
BRTR	106	108	5-18
PALMERO, EMILIO ANTONIO (PAL)				
B.JUNE 13,1895 GUANABACOA,CUBA				
D.JULY 15,1970 TOLEDO,OHIO				
1915 NY N P		3	0- 2
1916 NY N P		5	0- 3
1921 STL A P	24	29	4- 7
1926 WAS A P		7	2- 2
1928 BOS N P		3	0- 1
BLTL	42	47	6-15
BB 1915-16			
PALMISANO, JOSEPH				
B.NOV.19,1902 WEST POINT,GA.				
D.NOV.5,1971 ALBUQUERQUE,N.MEX.				
1931 PHI A C		19	.227
BRTR			
PALMQUIST, EDWIN LEE (ED)				
B.JUNE 10,1933 LOS ANGELES,CAL.				
1960 LA N P		22	0- 1
1961 LA N P		5	0- 1
MIN A P		9	1- 1
BRTR		36	1- 3
PALYS, STANLEY FRANCIS (STAN)				
B.MAY 1,1930 BLAKELY,PA.				
1953 PHI N O		2	.000
1954 PHI N O		2	.250
1955 PHI N O		15	.288
CIN N 1-O		79	.230
1956 CIN N O		40	.226
BRTR		138	.237
PANER, GEORGE WASHINGTON				
[PLAYED UNDER NAME OF				
GEORGE WASHINGTON PAYNTER]				
PANTHER, JAMES EDWARD (JIM)				
B.MAR.1,1945 BURLINGTON,IOWA				
1971 OAK A /P		4	0- 1
1972 TEX A P		58	5- 9
1973 ATL N P		23	2- 3
BRTR		85	7-13
PAOLINELLI, RINALDO ANGELO				
[PLAYED UNDER NAME OF				
RALPH ARTHUR PINELLI]				
PAPA, JOHN PAUL				
B.DEC.5,1940 BRIDGEPORT,CONN.				
1961 BAL A P		2	0- 0
1962 BAL A P		1	0- 0
BRTR		3	0- 0
PAPAI, ALFRED THOMAS				
B.MAY 7,1919 DIVERNON,ILL.				
1948 STL N P	10	11	0- 1
1949 STL A P		42	4-11
1950 BOS A P		16	4- 2
STL N P		13	1- 0
1955 CHI A P		7	0- 0
BRTR	88	89	9-14
PAPASTEGIOS, MILTIADES STERGIOS				
[PLAYED UNDER NAME OF				
MILTON STEPHEN PAPPAS]				
PAPE, KENNETH WAYNE (KEN)				
B.OCT.1,1951 SAN ANTONIO,REX.				
1976 TEX A /S-3-2		21	.217
BRTR			
PAPE, LAWRENCE ALBERT				
B.JULY 21,1883 NORWOOD,OHIO				
D.AUG.3,1918 PITTSBURGH,PA.				
1909 BOS A P		11	2- 0
1911 BOS A P		27	10- 8
1912 BOS A P		13	1- 1
BRTR		51	13- 9
PAPI, STANLEY GERARD (STAN)				
B.FEB.4,1951 FRESNO,CAL.				
1974 STL N /S-2		8	.250
1977 MON N 3/S-2		13	.233
1978 MON N S-3/2		67	.230
BRTR		88	.231
PAPISH, FRANK RICHARD				
(FRANK) OR (PAP)				
B.OCT.21,1917 PUEBLO,COLO.				
D.AUG.30,1965 PUEBLO,COLO.				
1945 CHI A P		19	4- 4
1946 CHI A P		31	7- 5
1947 CHI A P		38	12-12
1948 CHI A P		32	2- 8
1949 CLE A P		25	1- 0
1950 PIT N P		4	0- 0
BRTL		149	26-29

YR	CL LEA POS	GP	G	REC
PAPPALAU, JOHN JOSEPH				
B.APR.3,1875 ALBANY,N.Y.				
D.MAY 12,1944 ALBANY,N.Y.				
1897 CLE N P		2	0- 0
PAPPAS, MILTON STEPHEN				
(MILT) OR (GIMPY)				
[REAL NAME				
MILTIADES STERGIOS PAPASTEGIOS]				
B.MAY 11,1939 DETROIT,MICH.				
1957 BAL A P		4	0- 0
1958 BAL A P-2	31	32	10-10
			.143
1959 BAL A P		33	15- 9
1960 BAL A P		30	15-11
1961 BAL A P		26	13- 9
1962 BAL A P		35	12-10
1963 BAL A P	34	36	16- 9
1964 BAL A P		37	16- 7
1965 BAL A P		34	13- 9
1966 CIN N P	33	36	12-11
1967 CIN N P		34	16-13
1968 CIN N P	15	16	2- 5
ATL N P		22	10- 8
1969 ATL N P		26	6-10
1970 ATL N P		11	2- 2
CHI N P		21	10- 8
1971 CHI N P		35	17-14
1972 CHI N P		29	17- 7
1973 CHI N P		30	7-12
BRTR	520	527	209-164
			.123
PARENT, FREDERICK ALFRED (FRED)				
B.NOV.25,1875 BIDDEFORD,ME.				
D.NOV.2,1972 SANFORD,MAINE				
1899 STL N 2		2	.125
1901 BOS A S		138	.318
1902 BOS A S		139	.288
1903 BOS A S		139	.304
1904 BOS A S		155	.296
1905 BOS A S		153	.234
1906 BOS A S		149	.235
1907 BOS A S-O		114	.276
1908 CHI A S-O		119	.207
1909 CHI A S-O		136	.261
1910 CHI A S		81	.178
1911 CHI A 2		3	.444
BRTR		1328	.265
PARISSE, LOUIS PETER (TONY)				
B.JUNE 25,1911 PHILADELPHIA,PA.				
D.JUNE 2,1956 PHILADELPHIA,PA.				
1943 PHI A C		6	.176
1944 PHI A C		30	.000
BRTR		10	.143
PARK, JAMES				
B.NOV.10,1892 RICHMOND,KY.				
D.DEC.17,1970 LEXINGTON,KY.				
1915 STL A P		3	2- 0
1916 STL A P		26	1- 4
1917 STL A P		13	1- 1
BRTR		42	4- 5
PARKER, CLARENCE MC KAY (ACE)				
B.MAY 17,1912 PORTSMOUTH,VA.				
1937 PHI A S		38	.117
1938 PHI A S		56	.230
BRTR		94	.179
PARKER, CLARENCE PERKINS (PAT)				
B.MAY 22,1893 SOMERVILLE,MASS.				
D.MAR.21,1967 CLAREMONT,N.H.				
1915 STL A O		3	.167
PARKER, DAVID GENE (DAVE)				
B.JUNE 9,1951 CALHOUN,MISS.				
1973 PIT N O		54	.288
1974 PIT N O/1		73	.282
1975 PIT N *O		148	.308
1976 PIT N *O		138	.313
1977 PIT N *O/2		159	.338
1978 PIT N *O		148	.334
BLTR		720	.318
PARKER, DOUGLAS WOOLLEY (DIXIE)				
B.APR.24,1895 FOREST HOME,ALA.				
D.MAY 19,1972 TUSCALOOSA,ALA.				
1923 PHI N C		4	.200
BLTR			
PARKER, FRANCIS JAMES (SALTY)				
B.JULY 6,1913 E.ST.LOUIS,ILL.				
1936 DET A 1-S		11	.260
NON-PLAYING MANAGER				
NY[N] 1967 [INTERIM],				
HOU[N] 1972 [INTERIM]				
PARKER, HARLEY PARK (DOC)				
B.JUNE 14,1874 THERESA,N.Y.				
D.MAR.3,1941 CHICAGO,ILL.				
1893 CHI N P		1	0- 0
1895 CHI N P		7	4- 3
1896 CHI N P		10	1- 5
1901 CIN N P		1	0- 1
BRTR		19	5- 9

YR	CL LEA POS	GP	G	REC
PARKER, HARRY WILLIAM				
B.SEP.14,1947 HIGHLAND,ILL.				
1970 STL N /P		7	1- 1
1971 STL N /P		4	0- 0
1973 NY N P		38	8- 4
1974 NY N P		40	4-12
1975 NY N P		18	2- 3
STL N P		14	0- 1
1976 CLE A /P		3	0- 0
BRTR		124	15-21
PARKER, JAY				
1899 PIT N P		1	0- 0
PARKER, MAURICE WESLEY (WES)				
B.NOV.13,1939 EVANSTON,ILL.				
1964 LA N 1-O		124	.257
1965 LA N *1/O		154	.238
1966 LA N *1-O		156	.253
1967 LA N *1-O		139	.247
1968 LA N *1-O		135	.239
1969 LA N *1/O		132	.278
1970 LA N *1		161	.319
1971 LA N *1-O		157	.274
1972 LA N *1/O		130	.279
BBTL		1288	.267
PARKER, ROY W.				
B.1897				
1919 STL N P		2	0- 0
BRTR			
PARKER, WILLIAM DAVID (BILLY)				
B.JAN.14,1947 HAYNEVILLE,ALA.				
1971 CAL A 2		20	.229
1972 CAL A 3/2-O-S		36	.213
1973 CAL A 2/S		38	.225
BRTR		94	.222
PARKINSON, FRANK JOSEPH				
(FRANK) OR (PARKY)				
B.MAR.23,1895 DICKSON CITY,PA.				
D.JULY 4,1960 TRENTON,N.J.				
1921 PHI N S		108	.253
1922 PHI N 2		141	.275
1923 PHI N 2-5-3		67	.242
1924 PHI N 2-5-3		62	.212
BRTR		378	.256
PARKS, ARTIE WILLIAM				
B.NOV.1,1911 PARIS,ARK.				
1937 BRO N O		7	.313
1939 BRO N O		71	.272
BLTR		78	.275
PARKS, VERNON HENRY (SLICKER)				
B.NOV.10,1895 FOWLER,MICH.				
1921 DET A P		10	3- 2
BRTR			
PARKS, WILLIAM ROBERT				
B.JUNE 4,1849 EASTON,PA.				
D.OCT.10,1911 EASTON,PA.				
1875 NAT NA P-O	12	25	3- 9
PHI NA O		2	-
1876 BOS N O		1	.000
		28	3- 9
			-
PARMELEE, LE ROY EARL				
(ROY) OR (TARZAN)				
B.APR.25,1907 LAMBERTVILLE,MICH				
1929 NY N P		2	1- 0
1930 NY N P		11	0- 1
1931 NY N P		13	2- 2
1932 NY N P		8	0- 3
1933 NY N P	32	33	13- 8
1934 NY N P		22	10- 6
1935 NY N P		34	14-10
1936 STL N P		37	11-11
1937 CHI N P	33	37	7- 8
1939 PHI A P	14	16	1- 6
BRTR	206	213	59-55
PARNELL, MELVIN LLOYD				
(MEL) OR (DUSTY)				
B.JUNE 13,1922 NEW ORLEANS,LA.				
1947 BOS A P		15	2- 3
1948 BOS A P		35	15- 8
1949 BOS A P		39	25- 7
1950 BOS A P		40	18-10
1951 BOS A P	36	37	18-11
1952 BOS A P	33	35	12-12
1953 BOS A P		38	21- 8
1954 BOS A P		19	3- 7
1955 BOS A P	13	14	2- 3
1956 BOS A P		21	7- 6
BLTL	289	293	123-75
PARNHAM, JAMES ARTHUR (RUBE)				
B.FEB.1,1894 HEIDELBERG,PA.				
D.NOV.25,1963 MC KEESPORT,PA.				
1916 PHI A P		4	2- 1
1917 PHI A P		2	0- 1
BRTR		6	2- 2

YR	CL	LEA	POS	GP	G	REC

PARRILLA, SAMUEL (SAM)
B.JUNE 12,1943 SANTURCE,P.R.
| 1970 | PHI | N | /O | | 11 | .125 |
| | BRTR | | | | | |

PARRISH, LANCE MICHAEL
B.JUNE 15,1956 MC KEESPORT,PA.
1977	DET	A	C		12	.196
1978	DET	A	C		85	.219
	BRTR				97	.216

PARRISH, LARRY ALTON
B.NOV.10,1953 WINTER HAVEN,FLA.
1974	MON	N	3		25	.203
1975	MON	N	#3/2-S		145	.274
1976	MON	N	#3		154	.232
1977	MON	N	#3		123	.246
1978	MON	N	#3		144	.277
	BRTR				591	.256

PARROTT, MICHAEL EVERETT ARCH (MIKE)
B.DEC.6,1954 OXNARD,CAL.
1977	BAL	A	/P	3	0- 0	
1978	SEA	A	P	27	1- 5	
	BRTR			30	1- 5	

PARROTT, THOMAS WILLIAM (TACKY TOM)
B.APR.10,1868 PORTLAND,ORE.
D.JAN.1,1932 DUNDEE,ORE.
1893	CHI	N	P	5	0- 4	
	CIN	N		24	9- 8	
1894	CIN	N	P	38	59	19-19
1895	CIN	N	P	31	47	11-20
1896	STL	N	P-O	6	118	1- 1
						.288
	BRTR			104	253	40-52
						.304

PARROTT, WALTER EDWARD (JIGGS)
B.JULY 14,1871 PORTLAND,ORE.
D.APR.16,1898 PHOENIX,ARIZ.
1892	CHI	N	3		79	.215
1893	CHI	N	3		113	.292
1894	CHI	N	2		128	.244
1895	CHI	N	S		3	.200
					321	.240

PARSON, WILLIAM EDWIN (JIGGS)
B.DEC.28,1885 PARKER,S.DAK.
D.MAY 18,1967 LOS ANGELES,CAL.
1910	BOS	N	P	10	0- 2	
1911	BOS	N	P	7	0- 1	
	BRTR			17	0- 3	

PARSONS, CHARLES JAMES
B.JULY 18,1863 CHERRY FLATS,PA.
D.MAR.24,1936 MANSFIELD,PA.
1886	BOS	N	P	2	0- 2	
1887	MET	AA	P	4	1- 1	
1890	CLE	N	P	2	0- 1	
	TL			8	1- 4	

PARSONS, EDWARD DIXON (DIXIE)
B.MAY 12,1916 TALLADEGA,ALA.
1939	DET	A	C	5	.000	
1942	DET	A	C	63	.197	
1943	DET	A	C	40	.142	
	BRTR			108	.176	

PARSONS, JOHN S.
B.NAPOLEON,OHIO
| 1884 | CIN | AA | O | 1 | .000 | |

PARSONS, THOMAS ANTHONY (TOM)
B.SEP.13,1939 LAKEVILLE,CONN.
1963	PIT	N	P	1	0- 1	
1964	NY	N	P	4	1- 2	
1965	NY	N	P	35	1-10	
	BRTR			40	2-13	

PARSONS, WILLIAM RAYMOND (BILL)
B.AUG.17,1948 RIVERSIDE,CAL.
1971	MIL	A	P	36	13-17	
1972	MIL	A	P	33	13-13	
1973	MIL	A	P	20	3- 6	
1974	OAK	A	/P	4	0- 0	
	BRTR			93	29-36	

PARTEE, ROY ROBERT
B.SEPT.7,1917 LOS ANGELES,CAL.
1943	BOS	A	C	96	.281	
1944	BOS	A	C	89	.243	
1946	BOS	A	C	40	.315	
1947	BOS	A	C	60	.231	
1948	STL	A	C	82	.203	
	BRTR			367	.246	

PARTENHEIMER, HAROLD PHILIP (STEVE)
B.AUG.30,1891 GREENFIELD,MASS.
D.JUNE 16,1971 MANSFIELD,OHIO
| 1913 | DET | A | 3 | 1 | .000 | |
| | TR | | | | | |

PARTENHEIMER, STANWOOD WENDELL (STAN) OR (PARTY)
B.OCT.21,1922 CHICOPEE FALLS,MASS.
1944	BOS	A	P	1	0- 0	
1945	STL	N	P	8	0- 0	
	BRTL			9	0- 0	
	BL 1944					

PARTRIDGE, JAMES BUGG (JAY)
B.NOV.15,1902 MOUNTVILLE,GA.
D.JAN.14,1974 NASHVILLE,TENN.
1927	BRO	N	2	146	.260	
1928	BRO	N	2	37	.247	
	BLTR			183	.259	

PASCHAL, BENJAMIN EDWIN (BEN)
B.OCT.13,1895 ENTERPRISE,ALA.
D.NOV.10,1974 CHARLOTTE,N.C.
1915	CLE	A	O	9	.111	
1920	BOS	A	O	9	.250	
1924	NY	A	O	4	.272	
1925	NY	A	O	89	.360	
1926	NY	A	O	96	.287	
1927	NY	A	O	50	.317	
1928	NY	A	O	65	.316	
1929	NY	A	O	42	.208	
	BRTR			364	.309	

PASCHALL, WILLIAM HERBERT (BILL)
B.APR.22,1954 NORFOLK,VA.
| 1978 | KC | A | /P | 2 | 0- 1 | |

PASCUAL, CAMILO ALBERTO [LUS] (CAMILO) OR (LITTLE POTATO)
B.JAN.20,1934 HAVANA,CUBA
1954	WAS	A	P	48	4- 7	
1955	WAS	A	P	43	2-12	
1956	WAS	A	P	39	43	6-18
1957	WAS	A	P	29	32	8-17
1958	WAS	A	P	31	8-12	
1959	WAS	A	P	32	17-10	
1960	WAS	A	P	26	27	12- 8
1961	MIN	A	P	35	15-16	
1962	MIN	A	P	34	20-11	
1963	MIN	A	P	31	33	21- 9
1964	MIN	A	P	36	15-12	
1965	MIN	A	P	27	9- 3	
1966	MIN	A	P	21	8- 6	
1967	WAS	A	P	28	12-10	
1968	WAS	A	P	31	13-12	
1969	WAS	A	P	14	17	2- 5
	CIN	N	/P	5	0- 0	
1970	LA	N	P	10	0- 0	
1971	CLE	A	/P	9	2- 2	
	BRTR			529	542	174-170

PASCUAL, CARLOS A. [LUS]
B.MAR.13,1930 HAVANA,CUBA
| 1950 | WAS | A | P | 2 | 1- 1 | |
| | BRTR | | | | | |

PASEK, JOHN PAUL
B.JUNE 25,1905 NIAGARA FALLS,N.Y.
D.MAR.13,1976 NIAGARA FALLS,N.Y
1933	DET	A	C	28	.246	
1934	CHI	A	C	4	.333	
	BRTR			32	.257	

PASKERT, GEORGE HENRY (DODE)
B.AUG.28,1881 CLEVELAND,OHIO
D.FEB.12,1959 CLEVELAND,OHIO
1907	CIN	N	O	16	.280	
1908	CIN	N	O	116	.243	
1909	CIN	N	O	88	.251	
1910	CIN	N	O	141	.300	
1911	PHI	N	O	153	.273	
1912	PHI	N	O	145	.315	
1913	PHI	N	O	124	.262	
1914	PHI	N	O	132	.264	
1915	PHI	N	O	109	.244	
1916	PHI	N	O	149	.279	
1917	PHI	N	O	141	.251	
1918	CHI	N	3-O	127	.286	
1919	CHI	N	O	88	.196	
1920	CHI	N	O	139	.279	
1921	CIN	N	O	27	.174	
	BRTR			1695	.268	

PASLEY, KEVIN PATRICK
B.JULY 22,1953 BROOKLYN,N.Y.
1974	LA	N	C	1	.000	
1976	LA	N	C	23	.231	
1977	LA	N	/C	2	.333	
	SEA	A	/C	4	.385	
1978	SEA	A	C	25	.241	
	BRTR			55	.254	

PASQUARIELLO, MICHAEL JOHN (TONEY)
B.NOV.7,1898 PHILADELPHIA,PA.
D.APR.3,1965 BRIDGEPORT,CONN.
1919	PHI	N	1	1	1.000	
	STL	N	H	1	.000	
	BRTR			2	.500	

PASSEAU, CLAUDE WILLIAM
B.APR.9,1909 WAYNESBORO,MISS.
1935	PIT	N	P	1	0- 1	
1936	PHI	N	P	49	50	11-15
1937	PHI	N	P	14-18		
1938	PHI	N	P	44	45	11-18
1939	PHI	N	P	8	2- 4	
	CHI	N	P	34	35	13- 9
1940	CHI	N	P	46	20-13	
1941	CHI	N	P	34	14-14	
1942	CHI	N	P	35	19-14	
1943	CHI	N	P	35	15-12	
1944	CHI	N	P	34	15- 9	
1945	CHI	N	P	34	17- 9	
1946	CHI	N	P	21	9- 8	
1947	CHI	N	P	19	2- 6	
	BRTR			444	447	162-150

PASTORIUS, JAMES W. (SUNNY JIM)
B.JULY 12,1881 PITTSBURGH,PA.
D.MAY 10,1941 PITTSBURGH,PA.
1906	BRO	N	P	29	10-14	
1907	BRO	N	P	28	16-12	
1908	BRO	N	P	28	4-20	
1909	BRO	N	P	12	1- 9	
	BLTL			97	31-55	

PATE, JOSEPH WILLIAM
B.JUNE 6,1892 ALICE,TEX.
D.DEC.26,1948 FORT WORTH,TEX.
1926	PHI	A	P	47	9- 0	
1927	PHI	A	P	32	0- 3	
	BLTL			79	9- 3	

PATEK, FREDERICK JOSEPH (FREDDIE) OR (THE FLEA)
B.OCT.9,1944 SEGUIN,TEX.
1968	PIT	N	S/O-3	61	.255	
1969	PIT	N	*S	147	.239	
1970	PIT	N	S	84	.245	
1971	KC	A	*S	147	.267	
1972	KC	A	*S	136	.212	
1973	KC	A	*S	135	.234	
1974	KC	A	*S	149	.225	
1975	KC	A	*S	136	.228	
1976	KC	A	*S	144	.241	
1977	KC	A	*S	154	.262	
1978	KC	A	*S	138	.248	
	BRTR			1431	.241	

PATRICK, ROBERT LEE
B.OCT.27,1917 FT.SMITH,ARK.
1941	DET	A	O	5	.286	
1942	DET	A	O	4	.250	
	BRTR			9	.267	

PATTEE, HARRY ERNEST
B.JAN.17,1882 CHARLESTOWN,MASS.
D.JULY 17,1971 LYNCHBURG,VA.
| 1908 | BRO | N | 2 | 74 | .216 | |
| | BLTR | | | | | |

PATTEN, CASE LYMAN (CASEY)
B.MAY 7,1876 WESTPORT,N.Y.
D.MAY 31,1935 ROCHESTER,N.Y.
1901	WAS	A	P	31	18-10	
1902	WAS	A	P-O	36	39	17-17
						.095
1903	WAS	A	P	35	10-23	
1904	WAS	A	P	44	15-21	
1905	WAS	A	P	43	16-20	
1906	WAS	A	P	38	19-16	
1907	WAS	A	P	36	12-17	
1908	WAS	A	P	5	1- 3	
	BOS	A	P	1	0- 0	
1909	BOS	A	P	1	0- 0	
	BBTL			270	273	108-127
						.132

PATTERSON, DANIEL THOMAS
B.1846
1871	MUT	NA	O	32	-	
1872	ECK	NA	1-O	12	.160	
1874	MUT	NA	1	1	-	
1875	ATL	NA	2-O	10	-	
				55	-	

PATTERSON, DARYL ALAN
B.NOV.21,1943 COALINGA,CAL.
1968	DET	A	P	38	2- 3	
1969	DET	A	P	18	0- 2	
1970	DET	A	P	43	7- 1	
1971	DET	A	P	12	0- 1	
	OAK	A	/P	4	0- 0	
	STL	N	P	13	0- 1	
1974	PIT	N	P	14	2- 1	
	BLTR			142	11- 9	

PATTERSON, GILBERT THOMAS (GIL)
B.SEPT.5,1955 PHILADELPHIA,PA.
| 1977 | NY | A | P | 10 | 1- 2 | |
| | BRTR | | | | | |

PATTERSON, HAMILTON
B.OCT.13,1877 BELLEVILLE,ILL.
D.NOV.25,1945 E.ST.LOUIS,ILL.
1909	STL	A	1-O	17	.204	
	CHI	A	O	1	.000	
	TR			18	.192	

```
YR  CL LEA POS    GP   G    REC        YR  CL LEA POS    GP   G    REC        YR  CL LEA POS    GP   G    REC
```

PATTERSON, HENRY JOSEPH COLQUIT (HANK)
B.JULY 17,1907 SAN FRANCISCO,CAL.
D.SEPT.30,1970 PANORAMA CITY,CAL.
```
1932 BOS A C              1   .000
          TR
```

PATTERSON, LORENZO CLAIRE (CLAIRE)
B.OCT.5,1887 ARKANSAS CITY,KAN.
D.MAR.28,1913 MOJAVE,CAL.
```
1909 CIN N O              4   .125
          BLTR
```

PATTERSON, ROY LEWIS (BOY WONDER)
B.DEC.17,1876 STODDARD,WIS.
D.APR.14,1953 ST.CROIX FALLS,WIS.
```
1901 CHI A P             40   20-16
1902 CHI A P             34   20-13
1903 CHI A P             34   14-16
1904 CHI A P             22   7- 9
1905 CHI A P             13   4- 5
1906 CHI A P             22   10- 7
1907 CHI A P             19   4- 6
          BRTR          184   79-72
```

PATTERSON, WILLIAM JENNINGS BRYAN (PAT)
B.JAN.29,1901 BELLEVILLE,ILL.
D.OCT.1,1977 ST.LOUIS,MO.
```
1921 NY N 3              23   .400
          BRTR
```

PATTIN, MARTIN WILLIAM (MARTY)
B.APR.6,1943 CHARLESTON,ILL.
```
1968 CAL A P             52   4- 4
1969 SEA A P      34     39   7-12
1970 MIL A P      37     43   14-12
1971 MIL A P             36   14-14
1972 BOS A P             38   17-13
1973 BOS A P             34   15-15
1974 KC  A P             25   3- 7
1975 KC  A P      44     45   10-10
1976 KC  A P             44   8-14
1977 KC  A P             31   10- 3
1978 KC  A P             32   3- 3
          BRTR  407     419   105-107
```

PATTISON, GEORGE
```
1884 KEY U O              2   .146
```

PATTISON, JAMES WELLS
B.DEC.18,1908 NEW YORK,N.Y.
```
1929 BRO N P              6   0- 1
          BLTL
```

PATTON, GENE TUNNEY
B.JULY 8,1926 COATESVILLE,PA.
```
1944 BOS N H              1   .000
          BLTR
```

PATTON, GEORGE WILLIAM (BILL)
B.OCT.7,1912 CORNWALL,PA.
```
1935 PHI A C              9   .300
          BRTR
```

PATTON, HARRY C.
B.DAVENPORT,IOWA
```
1910 STL N P              1   0- 0
```

PATTON, THOMAS ALLEN
B.SEPT.5,1935 HONEY BROOK,PA.
```
1957 BAL A C              1   .000
          BRTR
```

PAUL, LOUIS
```
1876 ATH N C              3   .167
```

PAUL, MICHAEL GEORGE (MIKE)
B.APR.18,1945 DETROIT,MICH.
```
1968 CLE A P/1           36   5- 8
                              .167
1969 CLE A P             47   5-10
1970 CLE A P             30   2- 8
1971 CLE A P             17   2- 7
1972 TEX A P             49   8- 9
1973 TEX A P      36     37   5- 4
     CHI N P             11   0- 1
1974 CHI N /P             2   0- 1
          BLTL  228     229   27-48
                              .115
```

PAULA, CARLOS CONILL
B.NOV.4,1928 HAVANA,CUBA
```
1954 WAS A O              9   .167
1955 WAS A O            115   .299
1956 WAS A O             33   .183
          BRTR          157   .271
```

PAULETTE, EUGENE EDWARD (GENE)
B.MAY 26,1892 CENTRALIA,ILL.
D.FEB.8,1966 LITTLE ROCK,ARK.
```
1911 NY  N 1             10   .167
1916 STL A H              5   .500
1917 STL A 1             12   .182
     STL N 1             95   .265
1918 STL N ALL    1     125   0- 0
                              .273
1919 STL N 1-2-S         43   .215
     PHI N 1-2-O         67   .259
1920 PHI N 1            143   .288
          BRTR    1     500   0- 0
                              .268
```

PAULSEN, GUILFORD PAUL HANS (GIL)
B.NOV.14,1902 GRAETTINGER,IOWA
```
1925 STL N P              1   0- 0
          BRTR
```

PAUXTIS, SIMON FRANCIS
B.JULY 20,1885 PITTSTON,PA.
D.MAR.13,1961 PHILADELPHIA,PA.
```
1909 CIN N C              4   .125
          BRTR
```

PAVESKOVICH, JOHN MICHAEL
[PLAYED UNDER NAME OF
JOHN MICHAEL PESKY]

PAVLETICH, DONALD STEPHEN (DON)
B.JULY 13,1938 MILWAUKEE,WIS.
```
1957 CIN N H              1   .000
1959 CIN N H              1   .000
1962 CIN N C-1           34   .222
1963 CIN N C-1           71   .208
1964 CIN N C-1           34   .242
1965 CIN N C/1           68   .319
1966 CIN N C-1           83   .294
1967 CIN N C/1-3         74   .238
1968 CIN N 1/C           46   .286
1969 CHI A C-1           78   .245
1970 BOS A 1-C           32   .138
1971 BOS A /C            14   .259
          BRTR          536   .254
```

PAVLIECICVICH, ERVIN MARTIN
[PLAYED UNDER NAME OF
ERVIN MARTIN PALICA]

PAWELEK, THEODORE JOHN
(TED) OR (PORKY)
B.AUG.15,1919 CHICAGO HEIGHTS,ILL.
D.FEB.12,1964 CHICAGO HEIGHTS,ILL.
```
1946 CHI N C              4   .250
          BLTR
```

PAWLOSKI, STANLEY WALTER
B.SEPT.6,1931 WANAMIE,PA.
```
1955 CLE A 2              2   .125
          BRTR
```

PAXTON, MICHAEL DE WAYNE (MIKE)
B.SEPT.3,1953 MEMPHIS,TENN.
```
1977 BOS A P             29   10- 5
1978 CLE A P             33   12-11
          BRTR           62   22-16
```

PAYNE, FREDERICK THOMAS
B.SEPT.2,1880 CAMDEN,N.Y.
D.JAN.16,1954 CAMDEN,N.Y.
```
1906 DET A C-O           72   .270
1907 DET A C             53   .167
1908 DET A C             20   .067
1909 CHI A C             32   .244
1910 CHI A C             91   .222
1911 CHI A C             66   .203
          BRTR          334   .215
```

PAYNE, GEORGE WASHINGTON
B.MAY 23,1894 MT.VERNON,KY.
D.JAN.24,1959 LONG BEACH,CAL.
```
1920 CHI A P             12   1- 1
          BRTR
```

PAYNE, HARLEY FENWICK (LADY)
B.JAN.9,1868 WINDSOR,ONT.,CAN.
D.DEC.29,1935 ORWELL,OHIO
```
1896 BRO N P      31     32   14-13
1897 BRO N P      34     39   13-21
1898 BRO N P              1   1- 0
1899 PIT N P              4   1- 3
          TL      70     76   29-37
```

PAYNTER, GEORGE WASHINGTON
[REAL NAME GEORGE WASHINGTON PANER]
B.JULY 6,1871 CINCINNATI,OHIO
D.OCT.1,1950 CINCINNATI,OHIO
```
1894 STL N O              1   .000
```

PAZIK, MICHAEL JOSEPH (MIKE)
B.JAN.26,1950 LYNN,MASS.
```
1975 MIN A /P             5   0- 4
1976 MIN A /P             5   0- 0
1977 MIN A /P             3   1- 0
          BLTL           13   1- 4
```

PEACOCK, JOHN GASTON (JOHNNY)
B.JAN.10,1910 FREMONT,N.C.
```
1937 BOS A C              9   .313
1938 BOS A C             72   .303
1939 BOS A C             92   .277
1940 BOS A C             63   .282
1941 BOS A C             79   .284
1942 BOS A C             88   .266
1943 BOS A C              4   .202
1944 BOS A C              4   .000
     PHI N C-2           83   .225
1945 PHI N C             33   .203
     BRO N C             48   .255
          BLTR          619   .262
```

PEAK, ELIAS
B.PHILADELPHIA,PA.
```
1884 BOS U O              1   .000
     KEY U 2-S-O         54   .199
                         55   .196
```

PEARCE, FRANKLIN THOMAS
B.AUG.31,1905 MIDDLETOWN,KY.
D.SEPT.3,1950 VAN BUREN,N.Y.
```
1933 PHI N P             20   5- 4
1934 PHI N P              7   0- 0
1935 PHI N P              5   0- 0
          BRTR           32   5- 6
```

PEARCE, GEORGE THOMAS (FILBERT)
B.JAN.10,1888 AURORA,ILL.
D.OCT.11,1935 JOLIET,ILL.
```
1912 CHI N P              3   0- 0
1913 CHI N P             25   13- 5
1914 CHI N P             30   9-12
1915 CHI N P             36   13- 9
1916 CHI N P              4   0- 0
1917 STL N P              5   1- 1
          BLTL          103   36-27
```

PEARCE, GRAYSON S. (GRACE)
B.NEW YORK,N.Y.
D.AUG.29,1894 NEW YORK,N.Y.
```
1876 LOU N P              1   0- 0
1882 LOU AA 2-O           9   .294
     BAL AA 2-S-O        42   .210
1883 COL AA 2-O          11   .220
     NY  N 2-O           18   .095
1884 MET AA 2-O           5   .250
          BRTR    1      86   0- 0
                              .200
```

PEARCE, HARRY JAMES
B.JULY 12,1889 PHILADELPHIA,PA.
D.JAN.8,1942 PHILADELPHIA,PA.
```
1917 PHI N S              4   .250
1918 PHI N 1-2-S         60   .244
1919 PHI N 2-S-3         68   .180
          BRTR          132   .208
```

PEARCE, JAMES MADISON (JIM)
B.JUNE 9,1925 ZEBULON,N.C.
```
1949 WAS A P              2   0- 1
1950 WAS A P             20   2- 1
1953 WAS A P              4   0- 1
1954 CIN N P              2   1- 0
1955 CIN N P              2   0- 1
          BRTR           30   3- 4
```

PEARCE, RICHARD J. (DICKEY)
B.JAN.2,1836 BROOKLYN,N.Y.
D.OCT.12,1908 ONSET,MASS.
```
1871 MUT NA S            34   -
1872 MUT NA M-S-O        43   .188
1873 ATL NA S            55   -
1874 ATL NA S            36   -
     PHI NA S             1   -
     ATL NA S-3          20   -
1875 STL NA S            67   .256
1876 STL NA S            25   .200
1877 STL NA S             8   .172
          BRTR          289   -
```

PEARCE, WILLIAM C. (DUCKY)
B.MAR.17,1885 CORNING,OHIO
D.MAY 22,1933 BROWNSTOWN,IND.
```
1908 CIN N C              2   .000
1909 CIN N C              2   .000
          BRTR            4   .000
```

PEARS, FRANK T.
B.ST.LOUIS,MO.
```
1889 KC  AA P             3   0- 2
1893 STL N P              1   0- 0
          TR              4   0- 2
```

PEARSON, ALBERT GREGORY (ALBIE)
B.SEP.12,1934 ALHAMBRA,CAL.
```
1958 WAS A O            146   .275
1959 WAS A O             25   .188
     BAL A O             80   .232
1960 BAL A O             48   .244
1961 LA  A O            144   .288
1962 LA  A O            160   .261
1963 LA  A O            154   .304
1964 LA  A O            107   .223
1965 CAL A *O           122   .278
1966 CAL A /O             2   .000
          BLTL          988   .270
```

Column 1

PEARSON, ALEXANDER FRANKLIN
B.MAR.7,1877 GREENSBORO,PA.
D.OCT.30,1966 ROCHESTER,PA.

YR	CL	LEA	POS	GP	G	REC
1902	STL	N	P		11	2- 6
1903	CLE	A	P		4	1- 2
		BRTR			15	3- 8

PEARSON, DAVID P.
[REAL NAME DAVID P. PIERSON]
B.AUG.20,1855 WILKES-BARRE,PA.
D.NOV.11,1922 TRENTON,N.J.

1876	CIN	N	P-C-	1	56	0- 1
			O			.235
		BRTR				

PEARSON, ISAAC OVERTON (IKE)
B.MAR.1,1917 GRENADA,MISS.

1939	PHI	N	P	26	27	2-13
1940	PHI	N	P		29	3-14
1941	PHI	N	P		46	4-14
1942	PHI	N	P		35	1- 6
1946	PHI	N	P		5	1- 0
1948	CHI	A	P		23	2- 3
		BRTR		164	165	13-50

PEARSON, MONTGOMERY MARCELLUS (MONTE) OR (HOOT)
B.SEPT.2,1909 OAKLAND,CAL.
D.JAN.27,1978 FRESNO,CAL.

1932	CLE	A	P		8	0- 0
1933	CLE	A	P		19	10- 5
1934	CLE	A	P		39	18-13
1935	CLE	A	P		30	8-13
1936	NY	A	P		33	19- 7
1937	NY	A	P		22	9- 3
1938	NY	A	P		28	16- 7
1939	NY	A	P		22	12- 5
1940	NY	A	P		16	7- 5
1941	CIN	N	P	7	8	1- 3
		BRTR		224	225	101-61

PEASLEY, MARVIN WARREN
B.JULY 16,1888 JONESPORT,ME.
D.DEC.27,1948 SAN FRANCISCO,CAL

1910	DET	A	P		2	0- 1
		BLTL				

PECHINEY, GEORGE ADOLPHE (PISCH)
B.SEPT.20,1861 CINCINNATI,OHIO
D.JULY 14,1943 CINCINNATI,OHIO

1885	CIN	AA	P		11	7- 4
1886	CIN	AA	P-O	38	43	17-21
						.221
1887	CLE	AA	P		10	1- 9
		BRTR		59	64	25-34
						.220

PECHOUS, CHARLES EDWARD
B.OCT.5,1896 CHICAGO,ILL.

1915	CHI	F	3		18	.220
1916	CHI	N	3		22	.145
1917	CHI	N	S		13	.244
		BRTR			53	.193

PECK, HAROLD ARTHUR (HAL)
B.APR.20,1917 BIG BEND,WIS.

1943	BRO	N	H		1	.000
1944	PHI	A	O		2	.250
1945	PHI	A	O		112	.276
1946	PHI	A	O		48	.247
1947	CLE	A	O		114	.293
1948	CLE	A	O		45	.286
1949	CLE	A	O		33	.310
		BLTL			355	.279

PECKINPAUGH, ROGER THORPE
B.FEB.5,1891 WOOSTER,OHIO
D.NOV.17,1977 CLEVELAND,OHIO

1910	CLE	A	S		15	.200
1912	CLE	A	S		69	.212
1913	CLE	A	S		1	.000
	NY	A	S		95	.268
1914	NY	A	M-S		157	.223
1915	NY	A	S		142	.220
1916	NY	A	S		142	.255
1917	NY	A	S		148	.260
1918	NY	A	S		122	.231
1919	NY	A	S		122	.305
1920	NY	A	S		139	.270
1921	NY	A	S		149	.288
1922	WAS	A	S		147	.254
1923	WAS	A	S		154	.264
1924	WAS	A	S		155	.272
1925	WAS	A	1-S		126	.294
1926	WAS	A	S		57	.238
1927	CHI	A	S		68	.295
		BRTR			2008	.259

NON-PLAYING MANAGER
CLE[A] 1928-33, 41

PEDEN, LESLIE EARL (GOOCH)
B.SEPT.17,1923 AZLE,TEX.

1953	WAS	A	C		9	.250
		BRTR				

PEDROES, CHARLES P.
B.OCT.27,1869 CHICAGO,ILL.
D.AUG.6,1927 CHICAGO,ILL.

1902	CHI	N	O		2	.000

Column 2

PEEK, STEPHEN GEORGE
B.JULY 30,1914 SPRINGFIELD,MASS

YR	CL	LEA	POS	GP	G	REC
1941	NY	A	P		17	4- 2
		BBTR				

PEEL, HOMER HEFNER
B.OCT.10,1902 PORT SULLIVAN,TEX

1927	STL	N	O		2	.000
1929	PHI	N	O		53	.269
1930	STL	N	O		26	.164
1933	NY	N	O		84	.257
1934	NY	N	O		21	.195
		BRTR			186	.238

PEERSON, JACK CHILES
B.AUG.28,1910 BRUNSWICK,GA.
D.OCT.23,1966 FT.WALTON BEACH,FLA.

1935	PHI	A	S		10	.316
1936	PHI	A	2-S		8	.324
		BRTR			18	.321

PEERY, GEORGE A. (RED)
B.AUG.15,1906 PAYSON,UTAH

1927	PIT	N	P		1	0- 0
1929	BOS	N	P	9	10	0- 1
		BLTL		10	11	0- 1

PEETE, CHARLES (CHARLIE) OR (MULE)
B.FEB.22,1929 FRANKLIN,VA.
D.NOV.27,1956 CARACAS,VENEZ.

1956	STL	N	O		23	.192
		BLTR				

PEFFER, MONTE
B.1891 NEW YORK,N.Y.

1913	PHI	A	S		1	.000
		BRTR				

PEITZ, HENRY CLEMENT (HEINIE)
B.NOV.28,1870 ST.LOUIS,MO.
D.OCT.23,1943 CINCINNATI,OHIO

1893	STL	N	C		94	.266
1894	STL	N	C-1-3		100	.274
1895	STL	N	C		90	.288
1896	CIN	N	C		67	.298
1897	CIN	N	C		73	.297
1898	CIN	N	C		100	.281
1899	CIN	N	C		91	.271
1900	CIN	N	C		84	.251
1901	CIN	N	C-2		73	.311
1902	CIN	N	C-1-2-3		104	.313
1903	CIN	N	C		102	.260
1904	CIN	N	C-1		82	.243
1905	PIT	N	C		88	.223
1906	PIT	N	C		38	.240
1913	STL	N	C-O		3	.333
		BRTR			1189	.274

PEITZ, JOSEPH

1892	STL	N	O		1	.000
1894	STL	N	O		5	.421
		BRTR			6	.364

PELLAGRINI, EDWARD CHARLES (EDDIE)
B.MAR.13,1918 BOSTON,MASS.

1946	BOS	A	S-3		22	.211
1947	BOS	A	S-3		74	.203
1948	STL	A	S		105	.238
1949	STL	A	S		79	.238
1951	PHI	N	2-S-3		86	.234
1952	CIN	N	2-S-3		46	.170
1953	PIT	N	2-S-3		78	.253
1954	PIT	N	2-S-3		73	.226
		BRTR			563	.226

PELOUZE

1886	STL	N	O		1	.000

PELTY, BARNEY
B.SEPT.10,1880 FARMINGTON,MO.
D.MAY 24,1939 FARMINGTON,MO.

1903	STL	A	P		8	4- 4
1904	STL	A	P		40	14-18
1905	STL	A	P		31	13-14
1906	STL	A	P		35	17-12
1907	STL	A	P		36	12-21
1908	STL	A	P	20	21	7- 4
1909	STL	A	P	27	37	11-11
1910	STL	A	P		27	5-10
1911	STL	A	P	28	29	7-15
1912	STL	A	P		6	0- 3
	WAS	A	P		11	2- 6
		BRTR		269	281	92-118

PELTZ, JOHN
B.APR.23,1861 NEW ORLEANS,LA.
D.FEB.27,1906 NEW ORLEANS,LA.

1884	IND	AA	O		106	.213
1888	BAL	AA	O		1	.250
1890	BRO	AA	O		99	.234
	SYR	AA	O		5	.176
	TOL	AA	O		18	.227
		BRTR			229	.223

PEMBERTON, BROCK
B.NOV.6,1953 TULSA,OKLA.

1974	NY	N	/1		11	.182
1975	NY	N	/H		2	.000
		BBTL			13	.167

Column 3

PENA, JOSE [GUTIERREZ]
B.DEC.3,1942 JUAREZ,MEXICO

YR	CL	LEA	POS	GP	G	REC
1969	CIN	N	/P		6	1- 1
1970	LA	N	P		29	4- 3
1971	LA	N	P		21	2- 0
1972	LA	N	P		5	0- 0
		BRTR			61	7- 4

PENA, ORLANDO GREGORIO [QUEVARA]
B.NOV.17,1933 VICTORIA DE LAS TUNAS,CUBA

1958	CIN	N	P		9	1- 0
1959	CIN	N	P		46	5- 9
1960	CIN	N	P		4	0- 1
1962	KC	A	P		13	6- 4
1963	KC	A	P		35	12-20
1964	KC	A	P	40	42	12-14
1965	KC	A	P		12	0- 6
	DET	A	P		30	4- 6
1966	DET	A	P		54	4- 2
1967	DET	A	P		2	0- 1
	CLE	A	P		48	0- 3
1970	PIT	N	P		23	2- 1
1971	BAL	A	/P		5	0- 1
1973	BAL	A	P		11	1- 1
	STL	N	P		42	4- 4
1974	STL	N	P		42	5- 2
	CAL	A	/P		4	0- 0
1975	CAL	A	/P		7	0- 2
		BRTR		420	429	56-77

PENA, ROBERTO CESAR [RAMIREZ]
B.APR.17,1940 SANTO DOMINGO,D.R.

1965	CHI	N	S		51	.218
1966	CHI	N	/S		6	.176
1968	PHI	N	*S		138	.260
1969	SD	N	S-2-3-1		139	.250
1970	OAK	A	S/3		19	.259
	MIL	A	S-2/1		121	.238
1971	MIL	A	1-3-S/2		113	.237
		BRTR			587	.245

PENCE, ELMER CLAIR
B.AUG.17,1900 VALLEY SPRINGS,CAL.
D.SEPT.17,1968 SAN FRANCISCO,CAL.

1922	CHI	A	O		1	.000
		BRTR				

PENCE, RUSSELL WILLIAM (RUSTY)
B.MAR.11,1900 MARINE,ILL.
D.AUG.11,1971 HOT SRPINGS,ARK.

1921	CHI	A	P		4	0- 0
		BRTR				

PENDLETON, JAMES EDWARD (JIM)
B.JAN.7,1924 ST.CHARLES,MO.

1953	MIL	N	S-O		120	.299
1954	MIL	N	O		71	.220
1955	MIL	N	S-3-O		8	.000
1956	MIL	N	1-2-S-3		14	.000
1957	PIT	N	S-3-O		46	.305
1958	PIT	N	H		3	.333
1959	CIN	N	S-3-O		65	.257
1962	HOU	N	1-S-3-O		117	.246
		BRTR			444	.255

PENNER, KENNETH WILLIAM (KEN)
B.APR.24,1896 BOONEVILLE,IND.
D.MAY 28,1959 SACRAMENTO,CAL.

1916	CLE	A	P		4	1- 0
1929	CHI	N	P		5	0- 1
		BLTR			9	1- 1

PENNINGTON, GEORGE LOUIS (KEWPIE)
B.SEPT.24,1896 NEW YORK,N.Y.
D.MAY 3,1953 NEWARK,N.J.

1917	STL	A	P		1	0- 0
		BRTR				

PENNOCK, HERBERT JEFFERIS (HERB) OR (THE KNIGHT OF KENNETT SQUARE)
B.FEB.19,1894 KENNETT SQUARE,PA
D.JAN.30,1948 NEW YORK,N.Y.

1912	PHI	A	P		17	1- 2
1913	PHI	A	P		14	4- 1
1914	PHI	A	P		28	11- 4
1915	PHI	A	P		11	3- 5
	BOS	A	P		5	0- 0
1916	BOS	A	P	9	11	0- 2
1917	BOS	A	P		24	5- 5
1919	BOS	A	P		32	17- 8
1920	BOS	A	P	37	38	16-13
1921	BOS	A	P		32	12-14
1922	BOS	A	P		32	10-17
1923	NY	A	P		35	19- 6
1924	NY	A	P		40	21- 9
1925	NY	A	P		47	16-17
1926	NY	A	P		40	23-11
1927	NY	A	P		34	19- 8
1928	NY	A	P		28	17- 6
1929	NY	A	P		27	9-11
1930	NY	A	P		25	11- 7
1931	NY	A	P		25	11- 6
1932	NY	A	P		22	9- 5
1933	NY	A	P		23	7- 4
1934	BOS	A	P		30	2- 0
		BBTL		617	620	243-161

YR   CL LEA POS   GP   G   REC

PENSON, PAUL EUGENE
B.JULY 12,1931 KANSAS CITY,KAN.
```
1954 PHI N  P              5   1- 1
        BRTR
```

PENTZ, EUGENE DAVID (GENE)
B.JUNE 21,1953 JOHNSTOWN,PA.
```
1975 DET A  P             13   0- 4
1976 HOU N  P             40   3- 3
1977 HOU N  P             41   5- 2
1978 HOU N  P             10   0- 0
        BRTR            104   8- 9
```

PEOPLES, JAMES ELSWORTH
B.OCT.8,1863 BIG BEAVER,MICH.
D.AUG.29,1920 DETROIT,MICH.
```
1884 CIN AA C-1-S-3-0     70  .180
1885 CIN AA P-C-    2   7   0- 2
           O                .136
           BRO AA C        40  .205
1886 BRO AA C             94  .221
1887 BRO AA C             73  .283
1888 BRO AA C             33  .198
1889 COL AA C             28  .223
           TR        2 345   0- 2
                            .224
```

PEPITONE, JOSEPH ANTHONY (JOE) OR (PEPI)
B.OCT.9,1940 BROOKLYN,N.Y.
```
1962 NY  A  1-0           63  .239
1963 NY  A  1-0          157  .271
1964 NY  A  1-0          160  .251
1965 NY  A  *1-0         143  .247
1966 NY  A  *1-0         152  .255
1967 NY  A  *0/1         133  .251
1968 NY  A  0-1          108  .245
1969 NY  A  *1           135  .242
1970 HOU N  1-0           75  .251
         CHI N  0-1       56  .268
1971 CHI N  1-0          115  .307
1972 CHI N  1            66  .262
1973 CHI N  1            31  .268
         ATL N /1         3  .364
         BLTL          1397  .258
```

PEPLOSKI, HENRY STEPHEN (PEP)
B.SEPT.15,1905 GARLIN,POLAND
```
1929 BOS N  3             6  .200
        BLTR
```

PEPLOSKI, JOSEPH ALOYSIUS (PEPPER)
B.SEPT.12,1891 BROOKLYN,N.Y.
DECEASED
```
1913 DET A  3             2  .500
        BRTR
```

PEPPER, DONALD HOYTE (DON)
B.OCT.8,1943 SARATOGA SPRGS.,N.Y
```
1966 DET A /1             4  .000
        BLTR
```

PEPPER, HUGH MC LAURIN (LAURIN)
B.JAN.18,1931 VAUGHAN,MISS.
```
1954 PIT N  P            14   1- 5
1955 PIT N  P            14   0- 1
1956 PIT N  P            11   1- 1
1957 PIT N  P      5      0- 1
        BRTR      44  46   2- 8
```

PEPPER, RAYMOND WATSON
B.AUG.5,1905 DECATUR,ALA.
```
1932 STL N  O            21  .246
1933 STL N  O             3  .222
1934 STL A  O           148  .298
1935 STL A  O            92  .253
1936 STL A  O            75  .282
        BRTR           339  .281
```

PEPPER, ROBERT ERNEST
B.MAY 3,1895 ROSSTON,PA.
D.APR.8,1968 FORT CLIFF,PA.
```
1915 PHI A  P             1   0- 0
        BRTR
```

PEPPER, WILLIAM HARRISON
B.WEBB CITY,MO.
```
1894 LOU N  P             2   0- 1
```

PERAZA, LUIS [RIOS]
B.JUNE 17,1942 RIO PIEDRAS,P.R.
```
1969 PHI N /P             8   0- 0
        BRTR
```

PERDUE, HERBERT RODNEY (HUB) OR (THE GALLATIN SQUASH)
B.JUNE 7,1882 BETHPAGE,TENN.
D.OCT.31,1968 GALLATIN,TEX.
```
1911 BOS N  P            24   6-10
1912 BOS N  P            37  13-16
1913 BOS N  P            38  16-13
1914 BOS N  P             9   2- 5
         STL N  P        22   8- 8
1915 STL N  P            31   6-12
        BRTR           161  51-64
```

PEREZ, ATANACIO [RIGAL] (TONY)
B.MAY 14,1942 CAMAGUEY,CUBA
```
1964 CIN N  1            12  .080
1965 CIN N  1           104  .260
1966 CIN N  1            99  .265
1967 CIN N *3-1/2       156  .290
1968 CIN N *3           160  .282
1969 CIN N *3           160  .294
1970 CIN N *3/1         158  .317
1971 CIN N *3-1         158  .269
1972 CIN N *1           136  .283
1973 CIN N *1           151  .314
1974 CIN N *1           158  .265
1975 CIN N *1           137  .282
1976 CIN N *1           139  .260
1977 MON N *1           154  .283
1978 MON N *1           148  .290
        BRTR          2030  .283
```

PEREZ, CESAR LEONARDO [TOVAR]
[PLAYED UNDER NAME OF
CESAR LEONARDO TOVAR]

PEREZ, GEORGE THOMAS
B.DEC.29,1937 SAN FERNANDO,CAL.
```
1958 PIT N  P             4   0- 1
```

PEREZ, MARTIN ROMAN (MARTY)
B.FEB.28,1947 VISALIA,CAL.
```
1969 CAL A /3-2-3        13  .231
1970 CAL A /S             3  .000
1971 ATL N *S/2         130  .227
1972 ATL N *S           141  .228
1973 ATL N *S           141  .250
1974 ATL N *2-3/S       127  .260
1975 ATL N *2/S         120  .275
1976 ATL N  2-5/3        31  .250
         SF  N  2/S      93  .259
1977 NY  A /3            1  .500
         OAK A *2-3/S   105  .231
1978 OAK A  3/S-2        16  .200
        BRTR           931  .246
```

PERKINS, BRODERICK PHILLIP
B.NOV.23,1954 PITTSBURG,CAL.
```
1978 SD  N  1            62  .240
        BLTL
```

PERKINS, CECIL BOYCE
B.DEC.1,1940 BALTIMORE,MD.
```
1967 NY  A /P             2   0- 1
        BRTR
```

PERKINS, CHARLES SULLIVAN (LEFTY)
B.SEPT.9,1905 BIRMINGHAM,ALA.
```
1930 PHI A  P             8   0- 0
1934 BRO N  P            11   0- 3
        BLTL             19   0- 3
```

PERKINS, RALPH FOSTER (CY)
B.FEB.27,1896 GLOUCESTER,MASS.
D.OCT.2,1963 PHILADELPHIA,PA.
```
1915 PHI A  C             7  .190
1917 PHI A  C             6  .167
1918 PHI A  C            68  .188
1919 PHI A  C           101  .252
1920 PHI A  C           148  .260
1921 PHI A  C           141  .288
1922 PHI A  C           148  .267
1923 PHI A  C           143  .270
1924 PHI A  C           128  .242
1925 PHI A  C-3          65  .307
1926 PHI A  C            63  .291
1927 PHI A  C            59  .256
1928 PHI A  C            19  .172
1929 PHI A  C            38  .211
1930 PHI A  C            20  .158
1931 NY  A  C            16  .255
1934 DET A  H             1  .000
        BRTR          1171  .259
```

PERKOVICH, JOHN JOSEPH
B.MAR.10,1924 CHICAGO,ILL.
```
1950 CHI A  P             1   0- 0
        BRTR
```

PERKOWSKI, HARRY WALTER
B.SEPT.6,1922 DANTE,VA.
```
1947 CIN N  P             3   0- 0
1949 CIN N  P             5   1- 1
1950 CIN N  P      22  32   0- 0
1951 CIN N  P      35  37   3- 6
1952 CIN N  P            33  12-10
1953 CIN N  P            33  12-11
1954 CIN N  P            28   2- 8
1955 CHI N  P      25  26   3- 4
        BLTL      184  197  33-40
```

PERLOZZO, SAMUEL BENEDICT (SAM)
B.MAR.4,1951 CUMBERLAND,MD.
```
1977 MIN A  2/3          10  .292
        BRTR
```

PERME, LEONARD JOHN
B.NOV.25,1917 CLEVELAND,OHIO
```
1942 CHI A  P             4   0- 1
1946 CHI A  P             4   0- 0
        BLTL              8   0- 1
```

PERNOLL, HENRY HUBBARD (HUB)
B.MAR.14,1888 GRANT S PASS,ORE.
D.FEB.18,1944 GRANT S PASS,ORE.
```
1910 DET A  P            11   4- 3
1912 DET A  P             3   0- 0
        BRTL             14   4- 3
```

PERRANOSKI, RONALD PETER (RON)
B.APR.1,1936 PATERSON,N.J.
```
1961 LA  N  P            53   7- 5
1962 LA  N  P            70   6- 6
1963 LA  N  P            69  16- 3
1964 LA  N  P            72   5- 7
1965 LA  N  P            59   6- 6
1966 LA  N  P            55   6- 7
1967 LA  N  P            70   6- 7
1968 MIN A  P            66   8- 7
1969 MIN A  P            75   9-10
1970 MIN A  P            67   7- 8
1971 MIN A  P            36   1- 4
         DET A  P        11   0- 1
1972 DET A  P            17   0- 1
         LA  N /P         9   2- 0
1973 CAL A /P             8   0- 2
        BLTL           737  79-74
```

PERRIN, JOHN STEPHENSON
B.FEB.4,1898 ESCANABA,MICH.
D.JUNE 24,1969 DETROIT,MICH.
```
1921 BOS N  O             4  .231
        BLTR
```

PERRIN, WILLIAM JOSEPH (LEFTY)
B.JUNE 23,1910 NEW ORLEANS,LA.
D.JUNE 30,1974 NEW ORLEANS,LA.
```
1934 CLE A  P             1   0- 1
        BRTL
```

PERRINE, JOHN GROVER (NIG)
B.JAN.14,1885 CLINTON,WIS.
D.AUG.13,1948 KANSAS CITY,MO.
```
1907 WAS A  2-S          44  .171
        TR
```

PERRING, GEORGE WILSON
B.AUG.13,1884 SHARON,WIS.
D.AUG.20,1960 BELOIT,WIS.
```
1908 CLE A  S-3          89  .216
1909 CLE A  3            88  .223
1910 CLE A  3            39  .221
1914 KC  F  1-3         144  .282
1915 KC  F  1-2-3       153  .257
        BRTR           513  .249
```

PERRITT, WILLIAM DAYTON (POL)
B.AUG.30,1892 ARCADIA,LA.
D.OCT.15,1947 SHREVEPORT,LA.
```
1912 STL N  P             6   1- 1
1913 STL N  P            36   6-14
1914 STL N  P            41  16-13
1915 NY  N  P            35  12-18
1916 NY  N  P            40  18-11
1917 NY  N  P            35  17- 7
1918 NY  N  P      35  36  18-13
1919 NY  N  P            11   1- 1
1920 NY  N  P             8   0- 0
1921 NY  N  P             5   2- 0
         DET A  P         4   1- 0
        BRTR      256  257  92-78
```

PERRY, BOYD GLENN
B.MAR.21,1914 SNOW CAMP,N.C.
```
1941 DET A  2-S          36  .181
```

PERRY, CLAYTON SHIELDS
B.DEC.18,1881 RICE LAKE,WIS.
D.JAN.16,1954 RICE LAKE,WIS.
```
1908 DET A  3             7  .118
        TR
```

PERRY, GAYLORD JACKSON
B.SEP.15,1938 WILLIAMSTON,N.C.
```
1962 SF  N  P            13   3- 1
1963 SF  N  P      31  32   1- 6
1964 SF  N  P      44  46  12-11
1965 SF  N  P      47  49   8-12
1966 SF  N  P            36  21- 8
1967 SF  N  P      39  42  15-17
1968 SF  N  P            39  16-15
1969 SF  N  P            40  19-14
1970 SF  N  P            41  23-13
1971 SF  N  P      37  38  16-12
1972 CLE A  P            41  24-16
1973 CLE A  P            41  19-19
1974 CLE A  P            37  21-13
1975 CLE A  P            15   6- 9
         TEX A  P        22  12- 8
1976 TEX A  P            32  15-14
1977 TEX A  P            34  15-12
1978 SD  N  P            37  21- 6
        BRTR      626  635 267-206
```

YR	CL LEA POS	GP	G	REC

PERRY, HERBERT SCOTT (SCOTT)
B.APR.17,1891 DENNISON,TEX.
D.OCT.27,1959 KANSAS CITY,MO.

YR	CL LEA POS	GP	G	REC
1915 STL A P		1	0- 0
1916 CHI N P		4	2- 1
1917 CIN N P		4	0- 0
1918 PHI A P		44	21-19
1919 PHI A P		25	4-17
1920 PHI A P		42	11-25
1921 PHI A P		12	3- 6
BRTR		132	41-68

PERRY, JAMES EVAN (JIM)
B.OCT.30,1936 WILLIAMSTON,N.C.

1959 CLE A P			44	12-10
1960 CLE A P	41	42	18-10
1961 CLE A P		35	10-17
1962 CLE A P		35	12-12
1963 CLE A P		5	0- 0
MIN A P		35	9- 9
1964 MIN A P		42	6- 3
1965 MIN A P		36	12- 7
1966 MIN A P		33	11- 7
1967 MIN A P	37	39	8- 7
1968 MIN A P		32	8- 6
1969 MIN A P	46	47	20- 6
1970 MIN A P/O	40	41	24-12
			.247
1971 MIN A P		40	17-17
1972 MIN A P		35	13-16
1973 DET A P		35	14-13
1974 CLE A P		36	17-12
1975 CLE A /P		8	1- 6
OAK A P		15	3- 4
BBTR	630	635	215-174
			.199

PERRY, MELVIN GRAY (BOB)
B.SEP.14,1934 NEW BERN,N.C.

1963 LA A O		61	.253
1964 LA A O		70	.276
BRTR		131	.266

PERRY, WILLIAM HENRY
(HANK) OR (SOCKS)
B.JULY 28,1886 HOWELL,MICH.
D.JULY 16,1956 PONTIAC,MICH.

| 1912 DET A P | | 13 | .162 |
| BLTR | | | |

PERRYMAN, EMMETT KEY (PARSON)
B.OCT.24,1888 EVERETT SPRINGS,GA.
D.SEPT.12,1966 STARKE,FLA.

| 1915 STL A P | | 24 | 2- 3 |
| BRTR | | | |

PERSICO, SALVATORE GIUSEPPE
[PLAYED UNDER NAME OF JOSEPH SMITH]

PERTICA, WILLIAM ANDREW
B.MAR.5,1897 SANTA BARBARA,CAL.
D.DEC.28,1967 LOS ANGELES,CAL.

1918 BOS A P		1	0- 0
1921 STL N P		38	14-10
1922 STL N P-S	34	35	8- 8
			.181
1923 STL N P		1	0- 0
BRTR	74	75	22-18
			.152

PERZANOWSKI, STANLEY (STAN)
B.AUG.25,1950 EAST CHICAGO,ILL.

1971 CHI A /P		5	0- 1
1974 CHI A /P		2	0- 0
1975 TEX A P		12	3- 3
1976 TEX A /P		5	0- 0
1978 MIN A /P		13	2- 7
BBTR		37	5-11

PESKY, JOHN MICHAEL (JOHNNY)
[REAL NAME JOHN MICHAEL PAVESKOVICH]
B.SEPT.27,1919 PORTLAND,ORE.

1942 BOS A S		147	.331
1946 BOS A S		153	.335
1947 BOS A S-3		155	.324
1948 BOS A 3		143	.281
1949 BOS A 3		148	.306
1950 BOS A S-3		127	.312
1951 BOS A 2-S-3		131	.313
1952 BOS A S-3		25	.149
DET A 2-S-3		69	.254
1953 DET A 2		103	.292
1954 DET A H		20	.176
WAS A 2-S		49	.253
BLTR		1270	.307
NON-PLAYING MANAGER BOS(A) 1963-64			

PETERMAN, WILLIAM DAVID
B.MAR.20,1921 PHILADELPHIA,PA.

| 1942 PHI N C | | 1 | 1.000 |
| BRTR | | | |

PETERS, GARY CHARLES
B.APR.21,1937 GROVE CITY,PA.

1959 CHI A P		2	0- 0
1960 CHI A P		2	0- 0
1961 CHI A P		3	0- 0
1962 CHI A P		5	0- 1
1963 CHI A P	41	50	19- 8
1964 CHI A P	37	54	20- 8
1965 CHI A P	33	42	10-12
1966 CHI A P	30	38	12-10
1967 CHI A P	38	48	16-11
1968 CHI A P	31	46	4-13
1969 CHI A P	36	37	10-15
1970 BOS A P	34	37	16-11
1971 BOS A P	34	53	14-11
1972 BOS A P		33	3- 3
BLTL	359	450	124-103

PETERS, JOHN PAUL
B.APR.8,1850 LOUISIANA,MO.
D.JAN.3,1924 ST.LOUIS,MO.

1874 CHI NA 2-S-3		54	-
1875 CHI NA 2-S		70	-
1876 CHI N S		66	.348
1877 CHI N S		60	.317
1878 MIL N 2-S		54	.311
1879 CHI N S		79	.254
1880 PRO N S		83	.230
1881 BUF N 5-O		54	.214
1882 PIT AA 2-S		72	.278
1883 PIT AA S		8	.107
1884 PIT AA S		1	.000
BRTR		601	-

PETERS, OSCAR C. (RUBE)
B.MAR.15,1886 GRAND FORK,ILL.

1912 CHI A P		28	5- 6
1914 BRO F P		11	1- 1
BR		39	6- 7

PETERS, RAYMOND JAMES (RAY)
B.AUG.27,1946 BUFFALO,N.Y.

| 1970 MIL A /P | | 2 | 0- 2 |
| BRTR | | | |

PETERS, RUSSELL DIXON (RUSTY)
B.DEC.14,1914 ROANOKE,VA.

1936 PHI A S-3		45	.218
1937 PHI A 2-S-3		116	.260
1938 PHI A S		2	.000
1940 CLE A 1-2-S-3		30	.239
1941 CLE A 2-S-3		29	.206
1942 CLE A 2-S-3		34	.224
1943 CLE A 2-S-3-O		79	.219
1944 CLE A 2-S-3		88	.223
1946 CLE A S		9	.286
1947 STL A 2-S		39	.340
BRTR		471	.236

PETERSON, CARL FRANCIS (BUDDY)
B.APR.23,1925 PORTLAND,ORE.

1955 CHI A S		6	.286
1957 BAL A S		7	.176
BRTR		13	.237

PETERSON, CHARLES ANDREW (CAP)
B.AUG.15,1942 TACOMA,WASH.

1962 SF N S		4	.167
1963 SF N 2-S-3-O		22	.259
1964 SF N 1-2-3-O		66	.203
1965 SF N O		63	.248
1966 SF N O/1		89	.237
1967 WAS A *O		122	.240
1968 WAS A O		94	.204
1969 CLE A O/3		76	.227
BRTR		536	.230

PETERSON, FRED INGELS
[PLAYED UNDER NAME OF
FRITZ FRED PETERSON]

PETERSON, FRITZ FRED
[REAL NAME FRED INGELS PETERSON]
B.FEB.8,1942 CHICAGO,ILL.

1966 NY A P		34	12-11
1967 NY A P		36	8-14
1968 NY A P		36	12-11
1969 NY A P		37	17-16
1970 NY A P		39	20-11
1971 NY A P		37	15-13
1972 NY A P		35	17-15
1973 NY A /P		31	8-15
1974 NY A /P		3	0- 0
CLE A P		29	9-14
1975 CLE A /P		25	14- 8
1976 CLE A /P		9	0- 3
TEX A /P		4	1- 0
BBTL		355	133-131

PETERSON, HARDING WILLIAM (HARDY)
B.OCT.17,1929 PERTH AMBOY,N.J.

1955 PIT N C		32	.247
1957 PIT N C		30	.301
1958 PIT N C		2	.333
1959 PIT N C		2	.000
BRTR		66	.273

PETERSON, JAMES NIELS
B.AUG.18,1908 PHILADELPHIA,PA.
D.APR.8,1975 PALM BEACH,FLA.

1931 PHI A P		6	0- 1
1937 BRO N P		32	2- 5
BRTR		41	2- 6

PETERSON, KENT FRANKLIN (PETE)
B.DEC.21,1925 GOSHEN,UTAH

1944 CIN N P		1	0- 0
1947 CIN N P		37	6-13
1948 CIN N P		43	2-15
1949 CIN N P		30	4- 5
1950 CIN N P		9	0- 3
1951 CIN N P		9	1- 1
1952 PHI N P		3	0- 0
1953 PHI N P		15	0- 1
BRTL		147	13-38

PETERSON, ROBERT A.
B.PHILADELPHIA,PA.

1906 BOS A C		39	.203
1907 BOS A C		4	.000
TR		43	.183

PETERSON, SIDNEY HERBERT
B.JAN.31,1918 HAVELOCK,N.DAK.

| 1943 STL A P | | 3 | 2- 0 |
| BRTR | | | |

PETOSKEY, FREDERICK LEE (TED)
B.JAN.5,1911 ST.CHARLES,MICH.

1934 CIN N O		6	.000
1935 CIN N O		4	.400
BRTR		10	.167

PETROCELLI, AMERICO PETER (RICO)
B.JUNE 27,1943 BROOKLYN,N.Y.

1963 BOS A S		1	.250
1965 BOS A S		103	.232
1966 BOS A *S/3		139	.238
1967 BOS A *S		142	.259
1968 BOS A *S/1		123	.234
1969 BOS A *S/3		154	.297
1970 BOS A *S-3		157	.261
1971 BOS A *3		158	.251
1972 BOS A *3		147	.240
1973 BOS A 3		100	.244
1974 BOS A *3		129	.267
1975 BOS A *3		115	.239
1976 BOS A 3/2-1-S		85	.213
BRTR		1553	.251

PETROSKEY, JAMES
[PLAYED UNDER NAME OF JAMES CLARK]

PETTEE, PATRICK E.
B.JAN.10,1863 NATICK,MASS.
D.OCT.9,1934 NATICK,MASS.

| 1891 LOU AA 2 | | 2 | .167 |
| TR | | | |

PETTIGREW, JIM NED (NED)
B.AUG.25,1881 HONEY GROVE,TEX.
D.AUG.20,1952 DUNCAN,OKLA.

| 1914 BUF F H | | 2 | .000 |

PETTIT, GEORGE WILLIAM PAUL
(PAUL) OR (LEFTY)
B.NOV.29,1931 LOS ANGELES,CAL.

1951 PIT N P		2	0- 0
1953 PIT N P	10	11	1- 2
BLTL	12	13	1- 2

PETTIT, LEON ARTHUR (LEFTY)
B.JUNE 23,1902 WAYNESBURG,PA.
D.NOV.21,1974 COLUMBIA,TENN.

1935 WAS A P		41	8- 5
1937 PHI N P		3	0- 1
BLTL		44	8- 6

PETTIT, ROBERT HENRY
B.JULY 19,1861 WILLIAMSTOWN,MASS.
D.NOV.1,1910 DERBY,CONN.

1887 CHI N O		32	.301
1888 CHI N O		43	.254
1891 MIL AA 3		21	.174
		96	.254

PETTY, CHARLES E.
B.JUNE 28,1866 NASHVILLE,TENN.

1889 CIN AA P		5	2- 3
1893 NY N P		9	5- 2
1894 WAS N P		15	3- 8
CLE N P		3	0- 2
TR		32	10-15

PETTY, JESSE LEE (JESSE)
OR (THE SILVER FOX)
B.NOV.23,1894 ORR,OKLA.
D.OCT.23,1971 ST.PAUL,MINN.

YR	CL	LEA	POS	GP	G	REC
1921	CLE	A	P		4	0- 0
1925	BRO	N	P		28	9- 9
1926	BRO	N	P		38	17-17
1927	BRO	N	P		42	13-18
1928	BRO	N	P		40	15-15
1929	PIT	N	P		36	11-10
1930	PIT	N	P		10	1- 6
	CHI	N	P		9	1- 3
		BRTL			207	67-78

PEZOLD, LORENZ JOHANNES (LARRY)
B.JUNE 22,1893 NEW ORLEANS,LA.
D.OCT.22,1957 BATON ROUGE,LA.

YR	CL	LEA	POS	GP	G	REC
1914	CLE	A	3		23	.226
		BRTR				

PEZZOLO, FRANCESCO STEPHANO
[PLAYED UNDER NAME OF
FRANK L. BODIE]

PEZZULLO, JOHN (PRETZEL)
B.DEC.10,1910 BRIDGEPORT,CONN.

YR	CL	LEA	POS	GP	G	REC
1935	PHI	N	P		41	3- 5
1936	PHI	N	P		1	0- 0
		BLTL			42	3- 5

PFEFFER, EDWARD JOSEPH (JEFF)
B.MAR.4,1888 SEYMOUR,ILL.
D.AUG.15,1972 CHICAGO,ILL.

YR	CL	LEA	POS	GP	G	REC
1911	STL	A	P		2	0- 0
1913	BRO	N	P		5	0- 1
1914	BRO	N	P	43	44	23-12
1915	BRO	N	P		40	19-14
1916	BRO	N	P	41	43	25-11
1917	BRO	N	P	30	31	11-15
1918	BRO	N	P		1	1- 0
1919	BRO	N	P		30	17-13
1920	BRO	N	P		30	16- 9
1921	BRO	N	P		6	1- 5
	STL	N	P		18	9- 3
1922	STL	N	P	44	45	19-12
1923	STL	N	P		26	8- 9
1924	STL	N	P		16	4- 5
	PIT	N	P		15	5- 3
		BRTR		347	352	158-112

PFEFFER, FRANCIS XAVIER (BIG JEFF)
B.MAR.31,1882 CHAMPAIGN,ILL.
D.DEC.19,1954 KANKAKEE,ILL.

YR	CL	LEA	POS	GP	G	REC
1905	CHI	N	P		15	5- 5
1906	BOS	N	P	35	50	13-22
1907	BOS	N	P		19	6- 8
1908	BOS	N	P		4	0- 0
1910	CHI	N	P-O	13	14	1- 0
						.158
1911	BOS	N	P	26	30	7- 5
		BRTR		112	132	32-40
						.203

PFEFFER, NATHANIEL FREDERICK
(FRED), (FRITZ) OR (DANDELION)
B.MAR.17,1860 LOUISVILLE,KY.
D.APR.10,1932 CHICAGO,ILL.

YR	CL	LEA	POS	GP	G	REC
1882	TRO	N	S-3		83	.221
1883	CHI	N	1-2-S-O		96	.234
1884	CHI	N	P-2	1	111	0- 0
						.289
1885	CHI	N	P-2-	4	112	3- 1
			O			.240
1886	CHI	N	2		119	.263
1887	CHI	N	2		123	.325
1888	CHI	N	2		135	.249
1889	CHI	N	2		134	.241
1890	CHI	P	2		123	.268
1891	CHI	N	2		137	.246
1892	LOU	N	M-2		124	.261
1893	LOU	N	2		124	.269
1894	LOU	N	2-S		104	.297
1895	LOU	N	1-2-S		11	.288
1896	NY	N	2		4	.143
	CHI	N	2		95	.244
1897	CHI	N	2		32	.230
		BRTR		5	1667	3- 1
						.262

PFEIL, ROBERT RAYMOND (BOB)
B.NOV.13,1943 PASSAIC,N.J.

YR	CL	LEA	POS	GP	G	REC
1969	NY	N	3-2/O		62	.232
1971	PHI	N	3/C-O-1-2-S		44	.271
		BRTR			106	.242

PFIESTER, JOHN ALBERT (JACK)
OR (JACK THE GIANT KILLER)
[REAL NAME JOHN ALBERT HAGENBUSH]
B.MAY 24,1878 CINCINNATI,OHIO
D.SEPT.3,1953 LOVELAND,OHIO

YR	CL	LEA	POS	GP	G	REC
1903	PIT	N	P		3	0- 3
1904	PIT	N	P		3	1- 1
1906	CHI	N	P		31	20- 8
1907	CHI	N	P		30	14- 9
1908	CHI	N	P		33	12-10
1909	CHI	N	P		29	17- 6
1910	CHI	N	P		14	6- 3
1911	CHI	N	P		6	2- 4
		BRTL			149	72-44

PFISTER, DANIEL ALBIN (DAN)
B.DEC.20,1936 PLAINFIELD,N.J.

YR	CL	LEA	POS	GP	G	REC
1961	KC	A	P		2	0- 0
1962	KC	A	P	41	52	4-14
1963	KC	A	P	3	4	1- 0
1964	KC	A	P	19	20	1- 5
		BRTR		65	78	6-19

PFISTER, GEORGE EDWARD
B.SEPT.4,1918 BOUND BROOK,N.J.

YR	CL	LEA	POS	GP	G	REC
1941	BRO	N	C		1	.000
		BRTR				

PFLANN, WILLIAM F.
B.BROOKLYN,N.Y.

YR	CL	LEA	POS	GP	G	REC
1894	CIN	N	P		1	0- 1

PFUND, LE ROY HERBERT (LEE)
B.OCT.10,1918 OAK PARK,ILL.

YR	CL	LEA	POS	GP	G	REC
1945	BRO	N	P		15	3- 2
		BRTR				

PFYL, MEINHARD CHARLES (MONTE)
B.MAY 11,1884 ST.LOUIS,MO.
D.OCT.18,1945 SAN FRANCISCO,CAL

YR	CL	LEA	POS	GP	G	REC
1907	NY	N	1		1	.000
		BLTL				

PHEBUS, RAYMOND WILLIAM (BILL)
B.AUG.9,1909 CHERRYVALE,KAN.

YR	CL	LEA	POS	GP	G	REC
1936	WAS	A	P		2	0- 0
1937	WAS	A	P		6	3- 2
1938	WAS	A	P		5	0- 0
		BRTR			13	3- 2

PHELAN, ARTHUR THOMAS (DUGAN)
B.AUG.14,1887 NIANTIC,ILL.
D.DEC.27,1964 FT.WORTH,TEX.

YR	CL	LEA	POS	GP	G	REC
1910	CIN	N	3		17	.214
1912	CIN	N	3		130	.243
1913	CHI	N	2-3		91	.249
1914	CHI	N	S		25	.283
1915	CHI	N	2-3		133	.219
		BRTR			396	.236

PHELAN, DANIEL B.
B.WATERBURY,CONN.

YR	CL	LEA	POS	GP	G	REC
1890	LOU	AA	1		8	.250

PHELAN, JAMES D. (DICK)
B.DEC.10,1854 TOWANDA,PA.
D.FEB.13,1931 SAN ANTONIO,TEX.

YR	CL	LEA	POS	GP	G	REC
1884	BAL	U	2		97	.254
1885	BUF	N	2		4	.133
	STL	N	3		2	.250
					103	.249

PHELAN, LEWIS G.
NON-PLAYING MANAGER STL[N] 1895

PHELPS, CORNELIUS CARMAN (NEAL)
B.NOV.19,1840 NEW YORK,N.Y.
D.FEB.12,1885 NEW YORK,N.Y.

YR	CL	LEA	POS	GP	G	REC
1871	KEK	NA	1		1	.000
1873	MUT	NA	O		1	.000
1874	MUT	NA	O		4	-
1875	MUT	NA	O		2	-
1876	MUT	N	O		1	.000
	ATH	N	C		1	.000
					10	-

PHELPS, EDWARD JAYKILL (YALLER)
B.MAR.3,1879 ALBANY,N.Y.
D.JAN.31,1942 E.GREENBUSH,N.Y.

YR	CL	LEA	POS	GP	G	REC
1902	PIT	N	C-1		18	.197
1903	PIT	N	C		79	.282
1904	PIT	N	C		92	.242
1905	CIN	N	C		44	.231
1906	CIN	N	C		12	.275
	PIT	N	C		40	.237
1907	PIT	N	C		36	.212
1908	PIT	N	C		20	.234
1909	STL	N	C		83	.248
1910	STL	N	C		80	.263
1912	BRO	N	C		52	.288
1913	BRO	N	C		15	.222
		BRTR			571	.251

PHELPS, ERNEST GORDON
(BABE) OR (BLIMP)
B.APR.19,1908 ODENTON,MD.

YR	CL	LEA	POS	GP	G	REC
1931	WAS	A	H		3	.333
1933	CHI	N	C		3	.286
1934	CHI	N	C		44	.286
1935	BRO	N	C		47	.364
1936	BRO	N	C		115	.367
1937	BRO	N	C		121	.313
1938	BRO	N	C		66	.308
1939	BRO	N	C		98	.285
1940	BRO	N	C-1		118	.295
1941	BRO	N	C		16	.233
1942	PIT	N	C		95	.284
		BLTR			726	.310

PHELPS, RAYMOND CLIFFORD
B.DEC.11,1903 DUNLAP,TENN.
D.JULY 7,1971 FORT PIERCE,FLA.

YR	CL	LEA	POS	GP	G	REC
1930	BRO	N	P		36	14- 7
1931	BRO	N	P		28	7- 9
1932	BRO	N	P		20	4- 5
1935	CHI	A	P		27	4- 8
1936	CHI	A	P		15	4- 6
		BRTR			126	33-35

PHILLEY, DAVID EARL (DAVE)
B.MAY 16,1920 PARIS,TEX.

YR	CL	LEA	POS	GP	G	REC
1941	CHI	A	O		7	.222
1946	CHI	A	O		17	.353
1947	CHI	A	3-O		143	.258
1948	CHI	A	O		137	.287
1949	CHI	A	O		146	.286
1950	CHI	A	O		156	.242
1951	CHI	A	O		7	.240
	PHI	A	3-O		125	.263
1952	PHI	A	3-O		151	.263
1953	PHI	A	3-O		157	.303
1954	CLE	A	O		133	.226
1955	CLE	A	O		44	.306
	BAL	A	3-O		82	.296
1956	BAL	A	3-O		32	.205
	CHI	A	1-O		86	.265
1957	CHI	A	1-O		22	.324
	DET	A	1-3-O		65	.283
1958	PHI	N	1-O		91	.309
1959	PHI	N	1-O		99	.291
1960	PHI	N	1-O		14	.333
	SF	N	3-O		39	.164
	BAL	A	3-O		14	.265
1961	BAL	A	3-O		99	.250
1962	BOS	A	O		38	.143
		BBTR			1904	.270

PHILLIPPE, CHARLES LOUIS (DEACON)
B.MAY 23,1872 RURAL RETREAT,VA.
D.MAR.30,1952 AVALON,PA.

YR	CL	LEA	POS	GP	G	REC
1899	LOU	N	P	39	42	20-17
1900	PIT	N	P		32	18-14
1901	PIT	N	P		34	22-12
1902	PIT	N	P		30	20- 9
1903	PIT	N	P	36	37	25- 9
1904	PIT	N	P		21	10-10
1905	PIT	N	P		38	22-13
1906	PIT	N	P		33	15-10
1907	PIT	N	P		35	14-11
1908	PIT	N	P		5	0- 0
1909	PIT	N	P		22	8- 3
1910	PIT	N	P		31	14- 2
1911	PIT	N	P		3	0- 0
		BRTR		359	363	188-110

PHILLIPS, ADOLFO EMILIO [LOPEZ]
B.DEC.16,1941 BETHANIA,PANAMA

YR	CL	LEA	POS	GP	G	REC
1964	PHI	N	O		13	.231
1965	PHI	N	O		41	.230
1966	PHI	N	/O		2	.000
	CHI	N	*O		116	.262
1967	CHI	N	*O		144	.268
1968	CHI	N	*O		143	.241
1969	CHI	N	O		28	.224
	MON	N	O		58	.216
1970	MON	N	O		92	.238
1972	CLE	A	O		12	.000
		BRTR			649	.247

PHILLIPS, ALBERT ABERNATHY (BUZ)
B.MAY 25,1904 NEWTON,N.C.
D.NOV.6,1964 BALTIMORE,MD.

YR	CL	LEA	POS	GP	G	REC
1930	PHI	N	P		14	0- 0
		BRTR				

PHILLIPS, CLARENCE LEMUEL (RED)
B.NOV.3,1908 PAULS VALLEY,OKLA.

YR	CL	LEA	POS	GP	G	REC
1934	DET	A	P		7	2- 0
1936	DET	A	P		22	2- 4
		BRTR			29	4- 4

PHILLIPS, DAMON ROSWELL (DEE)
B.JUNE 8,1919 CORSICANA,TEX.

YR	CL	LEA	POS	GP	G	REC
1942	CIN	N	S		28	.202
1944	BOS	N	S-3		140	.258
1946	BOS	N	H		2	.500
		BRTR			170	.250

PHILLIPS, EDWARD DAVID
B.FEB.17,1901 WORCESTER,MASS.
D.JAN.26,1968 BUFFALO,N.Y.

YR	CL	LEA	POS	GP	G	REC
1924	BOS	N	C		3	.000
1929	DET	A	C		68	.235
1931	PIT	N	C		106	.232
1932	NY	A	C		9	.290
1934	WAS	A	C		56	.195
1935	CLE	A	C		70	.273
		BRTR			312	.237

PHILLIPS, HAROLD ROSS (LEFTY)
B.JUNE 16,1919 LOS ANGELES,CAL.
D.JUNE 12,1972 FULLERTON,CAL.
NON-PLAYING MANAGER CAL[A] 1969-71

PHILLIPS, HORACE B.
B.MAY 14,1853 SALEM,OHIO
NON-PLAYING MANAGER COL[AA]1883
PIT[AA] 1884-86, PIT[N] 1887-89

YR	CL LEA POS	GP	G	REC

PHILLIPS, HOWARD EDWARD (EDDIE)
B.JULY 8,1931 ST.LOUIS,MO.
| 1953 STL N H | | 9 | .000 |
| BBTR | | | |

PHILLIPS, JACK DORN (STRETCH)
B.SEPT.6,1921 CLARENCE,N.Y.
1947 NY A 1		16	.278
1948 NY A 1		1	.000
1949 NY A 1		45	.308
PIT N 1-3		18	.232
1950 PIT N P-1-	1	69	0- 0
3			.293
1951 PIT N 1-3		70	.237
1952 PIT N 1		1	.000
1955 DET A 1-3		55	.316
1956 DET A 1-2-0		67	.295
1957 DET A H		1	.000
BRTR	1	343	0- 0
			.283

PHILLIPS, JOHN MELVIN (BUBBA)
B.JUNE 16,1930 WEST POINT,MISS.
1955 DET A 3-0		95	.234
1956 CHI A 3-0		67	.273
1957 CHI A 3-0		121	.270
1958 CHI A 3-0		84	.273
1959 CHI A 3-0		117	.264
1960 CLE A S-3-0		113	.207
1961 CLE A 3		143	.264
1962 CLE A 2-3-0		148	.258
1963 DET A 3-0		128	.246
1964 DET A 3-0		46	.253
BRTR		1062	.255

PHILLIPS, JOHN STEPHEN (JACK)
B.MAY 24,1919 ST.LOUIS,MO.
D.JUNE 16,1958 ST.LOUIS,MO.
| 1945 NY N P | | 2 | 0- 0 |
| BRTR | | | |

PHILLIPS, MARR B.
B.JUNE 16,1857 PITTSBURGH,PA.
D.APR.13,1928 PITTSBURGH,PA.
1884 IND AA S		97	.266
1885 DET N S		33	.208
PIT AA S		2	.375
1890 ROC AA S		65	.196
		197	.235

PHILLIPS, MICHAEL DWAINE (MIKE)
B.AUG.19,1950 BEAUMONT,TEX.
1973 SF N 3-S/2		63	.240
1974 SF N 3-2-S		100	.219
1975 SF N /2-3		10	.194
NY N *S/2		116	.256
1976 NY N S-2-3		87	.256
1977 NY N S/3-2		38	.209
STL N 2/S-3		48	.241
1978 STL N 2-S/3		76	.268
BLTR		538	.244

PHILLIPS, NORMAN EDWIN (ED)
B.SEP.20,1944 ARDMORE,OKLA.
| 1970 BOS N P | | 18 | 0- 2 |
| BRTR | | | |

PHILLIPS, RICHARD EUGENE (DICK)
B.NOV.24,1931 RACINE,WIS.
1962 SF N 1		5	.000
1963 WAS A 1-2-3		124	.237
1964 WAS A 1-3		109	.231
1966 WAS A /1		25	.162
BLTR		263	.229

PHILLIPS, THOMAS GERALD
B.APR.5,1889 PHILLIPSBURG,PA.
D.APR.12,1929 PHILLIPSBURG,PA.
1915 STL A P		5	1- 3
1919 CLE A P		22	3- 2
1921 WAS A P		1	1- 0
1922 WAS A P		17	3- 7
BRTR		45	8-12

PHILLIPS, WILLIAM B.
B.1857 ST.JOHN,N.B.,CANADA
D.OCT.7,1900 CHICAGO,ILL.
1879 CLE N 1		81	.271
1880 CLE N 1		84	.255
1881 CLE N 1		84	.270
1882 CLE N C-1		76	.266
1883 CLE N 1		94	.244
1884 CLE N 1		110	.272
1885 BRO AA 1		100	.293
1886 BRO AA 1		142	.281
1887 BRO AA 1		132	.322
1888 KC AA 1		129	.235
BRTR		1032	.273

**PHILLIPS, WILLIAM CORCORAN
(WHOA BILL) OR (SILVER BILL)**
B.NOV.9,1868 ALLENPORT,PA.
D.OCT.25,1941 CHARLEROI,PA.
1890 PIT N P		15	1- 9
1895 CIN N P		17	5- 5
1899 CIN N P	28	31	17- 8
1900 CIN N P	23	27	9-11
1901 CIN N P		33	14-18
1902 CIN N P		33	16-17
1903 CIN N P		16	7- 6
TR	165	172	69-74
NON-PLAYING MANAGER
IND[F] 1914; NEW[F] 1915

**PHILLIPS, WILLIAM TAYLOR
(TAYLOR) OR (TAY)**
B.JUNE 18,1933 ATLANTA,GA.
1956 MIL N P		23	5- 3
1957 MIL N P		27	3- 2
1958 CHI N P		39	7-10
1959 CHI N P		7	0- 2
PHI N P		32	1- 4
1960 PHI N P		10	0- 1
1963 CHI A P		9	0- 0
BLTL		147	16-22

PHOEBUS, THOMAS HAROLD (TOM)
B.APR.7,1942 BALTIMORE,MD.
1966 BAL A /P		3	2- 1
1967 BAL A P		33	14- 9
1968 BAL A P		36	15-15
1969 BAL A P		35	14- 7
1970 BAL A P		27	5- 5
1971 SD N P		29	3-11
1972 SD N /P		1	0- 1
CHI N P	37	38	3- 3
BRTR	201	202	56-52

PHYLE, WILLIAM JOSEPH
B.JUNE 25,1875 DULUTH,MINN.
D.AUG.6,1953 LOS ANGELES,CAL.
1898 CHI N P		2	2- 1
1899 CHI N P		10	2- 8
1901 NY N P		20	7-10
1906 STL N 3		21	.178
TR	33	54	11-19
			.176

**PIATT, WILEY HAROLD
(WILEY) OR (IRON MAN)**
B.JULY 13,1874 BLUE CREEK,OHIO
D.SEPT.20,1946 CINCINNATI,OHIO
1898 PHI N P		38	24-14
1899 PHI N P		39	23-15
1900 PHI N P		19	9- 9
1901 PHI A P		18	7-11
CHI A P		8	3- 5
1902 CHI A P		31	12-13
1903 BOS N P		25	9-15
BLTL		178	87-82

PICCIOLO, ROBERT MICHAEL (ROB)
B.FEB.4,1953 SANTA MONICA,CAL.
1977 OAK A *S		148	.200
1978 OAK A S-2-3		78	.226
BRTR		226	.205

PICCIUTO, NICHOLAS THOMAS
B.AUG.27,1921 NEWARK,N.J.
| 1945 PHI N 2-3 | | 36 | .135 |
| BRTR | | | |

PICHE, RONALD JACQUES (RON)
B.MAY 22,1935 VERDUN,QUE.,CANADA
1960 MIL N P		37	3- 5
1961 MIL N P		12	2- 2
1962 MIL N P	14	16	3- 2
1963 MIL N P		37	1- 1
1965 CAL A P		14	0- 3
1966 STL N P		20	1- 3
BRTR	134	136	10-16

PICINICH, VALENTINE JOHN (VAL)
B.SEPT.8,1896 NEW YORK,N.Y.
D.DEC.5,1942 NOBLEBORO,MAINE
1916 PHI A C		40	.195
1917 PHI A C		2	.333
1918 WAS A C		47	.230
1919 WAS A C		60	.274
1920 WAS A C		48	.203
1921 WAS A C		45	.277
1922 WAS A C		76	.229
1923 BOS A C		87	.276
1924 BOS A C		69	.273
1925 BOS A C-1		90	.255
1926 CIN N C		89	.263
1927 CIN N C		65	.254
1928 CIN N C		96	.302
1929 BRO N C		93	.260
1930 BRO N C		23	.217
1931 BRO N C		24	.267
1932 BRO N C		41	.257
1933 BRO N C		6	.167
PIT N C		16	.250
BRTR		1037	.258

PICK, CHARLES THOMAS
B.APR.10,1888 BROOKNEAL,VA.
D.JUNE 26,1954 LYNCHBURG,VA.
1914 WAS A O		10	.347
1915 WAS A H		3	.000
1916 PHI A 3		121	.241
1918 CHI N 2-3		29	.326
1919 CHI N 2-3		75	.231
BOS N 1-2-3-0		34	.273
1920 BOS N 2		95	.274
BLTR		367	.260

PICK, EDGAR EVERETT
B.MAY 7,1899 ATTLEBORO,MASS.
D.MAY 13,1967 SANTA MONICA,CAL.
1923 CIN N O		9	.375
1924 CIN N O		3	.000
1927 CHI N 3		54	.171
BBTR		66	.178

PICKERING, OLIVER DANIEL (OLLIE)
B.APR.9,1870 OLNEY,ILL.
D.JAN.20,1952 VINCENNES,IND.
1896 LOU N O		45	.303
1897 LOU N O		62	.258
CLE N 2-0		47	.346
1901 CLE A O		138	.308
1902 CLE A 1-O		60	.259
1903 PHI A O		137	.281
1904 PHI A O		122	.224
1907 STL A O		151	.276
1908 WAS A O		113	.225
BLTR		875	.272

PICKERING, URBANE HENRY (PICK)
B.JUNE 3,1899 HOXIE,KAN.
D.MAY 13,1970 MODESTO,CAL.
1931 BOS A 2-3		103	.252
1932 BOS A 3		132	.260
BRTR		235	.257

PICKETT, CHARLES A.
B.COLUMBUS,OHIO
| 1910 STL N P | | 2 | 0- 0 |

PICKETT, DAVID T.
B.MAY 26,1874 BROOKLINE,MASS.
| 1898 BOS N O | | 14 | .272 |

PICKETT, JOHN THOMAS
B.FEB.10,1866 CHICAGO,ILL.
D.JULY 4,1922 CHICAGO,ILL.
1889 KC AA O		41	.223
1890 PHI P 2		100	.281
1892 BAL N 2		36	.208
BRTR		177	.250

PICKREL, CLARENCE DOUGLAS
B.MAR.28,1911 GRENTA,VA.
1933 PHI N P		9	1- 0
1934 BOS N P		10	0- 0
BRTR		19	1- 0

PICKUP, CLARENCE WILLIAM (TY)
B.OCT.29,1897 PHILADELPHIA,PA.
D.AUG.2,1974 PHILADELPHIA,PA.
| 1918 PHI N O | | 1 | 1.000 |

PICONE, MARIO PETER (BABE)
B.JULY 5,1926 BROOKLYN,N.Y.
1947 NY N P		2	0- 0
1952 NY N P		2	0- 1
1954 NY N P		5	0- 0
CIN N P		4	0- 1
BRTR		13	0- 2

PICUS, JOHN QUINN
[PLAYED UNDER NAME OF
JOHN PICUS QUINN]

PIECHOTA, ALOYSIUS EDWARD (PIE)
B.JAN.19,1914 CHICAGO,ILL.
1940 BOS N P		21	2- 5
1941 BOS N P		1	0- 0
BRTR		22	2- 5

PIEH, EDWIN JOHN (CY)
B.SEPT.29,1886 WAUNAKEE,WIS.
D.SEPT.12,1945 JACKSONVILLE,FLA
1913 NY A P		4	1- 0
1914 NY A P		18	4- 4
1915 NY A P		21	4- 5
BRTR		43	9- 9

PIERCE, LAVERN JACK (JACK)
B.JUNE 2,1948 LAUREL,MISS.
1973 ATL N /1		11	.050
1974 ATL N /1		6	.111
1975 DET A 1		53	.235
BLTR		70	.211

PIERCE, MAURICE
B.WASHINGTON,D.C.
| 1884 WAS U 3 | | 2 | .143 |

```
YR   CL LEA POS      GP   G   REC
```

PIERCE, RAYMOND LESTER (LEFTY)
B.JUNE 6,1897 EMPORIA,KAN.
D.MAY 4,1963 DENVER,COLO.
```
1924 CHI N P              6   0- 0
1925 PHI N P             23   5- 4
1926 PHI N P     37  39   2- 7
     BLTL        66  68   7-11
```

PIERCE, TONY MICHAEL
B.JAN.29,1946 BRUNSWICK,GA.
```
1967 KC  A P             49   3- 4
1968 OAK A P             17   1- 2
     BRTL            66   4- 6
```

PIERCE, WALTER WILLIAM (BILLY)
B.APR.2,1927 DETROIT,MICH.
```
1945 DET A P              5   0- 0
1948 DET A P             22   3- 0
1949 CHI A P     32  39   7-15
1950 CHI A P     33  40  12-16
1951 CHI A P     37  39  15-14
1952 CHI A P     33  35  15-12
1953 CHI A P-1   40  42  18-12
                         .126
1954 CHI A P     36  38   9-10
1955 CHI A P     33  34  15-10
1956 CHI A P     35  39  20- 9
1957 CHI A P     37  41  20-12
1958 CHI A P         35  17-11
1959 CHI A P         34  14-15
1960 CHI A P         32  14- 7
1961 CHI A P         39  10- 9
1962 SF  N P         30  16- 6
1963 SF  N P         38   3-11
1964 SF  N P         34   3- 0
     BLTL   585 616 211-169
                         .184
```

PIERCY, ANDREW J.
B.AUG.1856 SAN JOSE,CAL.
D.DEC.27,1932 SAN JOSE,CAL.
```
1881 CHI N 2-3       2   .250
     TR
```

PIERCY, WILLIAM BENTON (WILD BILL)
B.MAY 2,1896 EL MONTE,CAL.
D.AUG.28,1951 LONG BEACH,CAL.
```
1917 NY  A P             1   0- 1
1921 NY  A P            14   5- 4
1922 BOS A P            29   3- 9
1923 BOS A P            30   8-17
1924 BOS A P            23   5- 7
1926 CHI N P            19   6- 5
     BRTR   116  27-43
```

PIEROTTI, MARINO PAUL (CHICK)
B.SEPT.23,1920 LUCCA,ITALY
```
1945 WAS A P            44  14-13
1946 WAS A P            30   2- 2
1947 WAS A P            23   2- 4
1948 WAS A P      8  13   0- 2
     CHI A P     21  32   8-10
1949 CHI A P     39  48   4- 6
1950 CLE A P     29  30   0- 1
     BRTR   194 220  30-38
```

PIEROTTI, ALBERT FELIX
B.OCT.24,1895 BOSTON,MASS.
D.FEB.12,1964 REVERE,MASS.
```
1920 BOS N P             6   1- 1
1921 BOS N P             2   0- 1
     BRTR        8   1- 2
```

PIERRE, RICHARD J.
B.GRAND HAVEN,MICH.
```
1883 PHI N S         5   .158
```

PIERRO, WILLIAM LEONARD (BILL)
OR (WILD BILL)
B.APR.19,1926 BROOKLYN,N.Y.
```
1950 PIT N P            13   0- 2
     BRTR
```

PIERSALL, JAMES ANTHONY (JIM)
B.NOV.14,1929 WATERBURY,CONN.
```
1950 BOS A O             6   .286
1952 BOS A S-3-O        56   .267
1953 BOS A O           151   .272
1954 BOS A O           133   .285
1955 BOS A O           149   .283
1956 BOS A O           159   .293
1957 BOS A O           151   .261
1958 BOS A O           130   .237
1959 CLE A 3-O         100   .246
1960 CLE A O           138   .282
1961 CLE A O           121   .322
1962 WAS A O           135   .244
1963 WAS A O            29   .245
     NY  A O            40   .194
     LA  A O            20   .308
1964 LA  A O            87   .314
1965 CAL A O            53   .268
1966 CAL A O            75   .211
1967 CAL A /O            5   .000
     BRTR  1734   .272
```

PIERSON, DAVID P.
[PLAYED UNDER NAME OF
DAVID. P. PEARSON]

PIERSON, EDMUND DANA
B.1858 NEWARK,N.J.
D.JULY 20,1922 NEWARK,N.J.
```
1885 MET AA 2       3   .091
     TR
```

PIERSON, WILLIAM MORRIS
B.JUNE 14,1899 ATLANTIC CITY,N.J.
D.FEB.20,1959 ATLANTIC CITY,N.J
```
1919 PHI A P             8   0- 1
1919 PHI A P             2   0- 0
1924 PHI A P             1   0- 0
     BLTL       11   0- 1
```

PIET, ANTHONY FRANCIS
[REAL NAME
ANTHONY FRANCIS PIETRUSZKA]
B.DEC.7,1906 BERWICK,PA.
```
1931 PIT N 2            44   .299
1932 PIT N 2           154   .282
1933 PIT N 2           107   .323
1934 CIN N 2-3         106   .259
1935 CIN N O             6   .200
     CHI A 2-3          77   .298
1936 CHI A 2-3         109   .273
1937 CHI A 2-3         100   .235
1938 DET A 3            41   .213
     BRTR   744   .277
```

PIETRUSZKA, ANTHONY FRANCIS
[PLAYED UNDER NAME OF
ANTHONY FRANCIS PIET]

PIEZ, CHARLES WILLIAM (SANDY)
B.OCT.13,1888 NEW YORK,N.Y.
D.DEC.29,1930 ATLANTIC CITY,N.J
```
1914 NY  N O        35   .375
     BRTR
```

PIGNATANO, JOSEPH BENJAMIN (JOE)
B.AUG.4,1929 BROOKLYN,N.Y.
```
1957 BRO N C             8   .214
1958 LA  N C            63   .218
1959 LA  N C            52   .237
1960 LA  N C            58   .233
1961 KC  A C-3          92   .243
1962 SF  N C             7   .200
     NY  N C            27   .232
     BRTR   307   .234
```

PIKE, JAY
B.BROOKLYN,N.Y.
```
1877 HAR N O         1   .250
```

PIKE, JESS WILLARD
B.JULY 31,1916 DUSTIN,OKLA.
```
1946 NY  N O        16   .171
     BLTR
```

PIKE, LIPMAN EMANUEL
B.MAY 25,1845 NEW YORK,N.Y.
D.OCT.10,1893 BROOKLYN,N.Y.
```
1871 TRO NA M-1-2-O     28   .351
1872 BAL NA 2-S-O       54   .296
1873 BAL NA 2-O         56   -
1874 HAR NA M-2-S-O     52   -
1875 STL NA 2-O         67   .342
1876 STL N  O           63   .314
1877 CIN N  M-2-S-O     58   .297
1878 CIN N  O           28   .326
     PRO N  2            5   .227
1881 WOR N  O           5   .091
1887 MET AA O           1   .000
     BLTL   417   -
```

PIKTUZIS, GEORGE RICHARD
B.JAN.3,1932 CHICAGO,ILL.
```
1956 CHI N P         2   0- 0
     BRTL
```

PILARCIK, ALFRED JAMES (AL)
B.JULY 3,1930 WHITING,IND.
```
1956 KC  A O            69   .251
1957 BAL A O           142   .278
1958 BAL A O           141   .243
1959 BAL A O           130   .282
1960 BAL A O           104   .247
1961 KC  A O            35   .200
     CHI A O            47   .177
     BLTL   668   .256
```

PILLETTE, DUANE XAVIER (DEE)
B.JULY 24,1922 DETROIT,MICH.
```
1949 NY  A P            12   2- 4
1950 NY  A P             4   0- 0
     STL A P     24  27   3- 5
1951 STL A P     35  41   6-14
1952 STL A P     30  35  10-13
1953 STL A P         31   7-13
1954 BAL A P         23  10-14
1955 BAL A P          7   0- 3
1956 PHI N P         20   0- 0
     BRTR   188 202  38-66
```

PILLETTE, HERMAN POLYCARP
(OLD FOLKS)
B.DEC.26,1895 ST.PAUL,ORE.
D.APR.30,1960 SACRAMENTO,CAL.
```
1917 CIN N P             1   0- 0
1922 DET A P            40  19-12
1923 DET A P            47  14-19
1924 DET A P            19   1- 1
     BRTR   107  34-32
```

PILLION, CECIL RANDOLPH (SQUIZ)
B.APR.13,1894 HARTFORD,CONN.
D.SEPT.30,1962 PITTSBURGH,PA.
```
1915 PHI A P         2   0- 0
     TL
```

PILNEY, ANTONE JAMES (ANDY)
B.JAN.19,1913 FRONTENAC,LA.
```
1936 BOS N H         3   .000
```

PINA, HORACIO [GARCIA]
B.MAR.12,1945 COAHUILA,MEXICO
```
1968 CLE A P            12   1- 1
1969 CLE A P            31   4- 2
1970 WAS A P            61   5- 3
1971 WAS A P            56   1- 1
1972 TEX A P            60   2- 7
1973 OAK A P            47   6- 3
1974 CHI N P            34   3- 4
     CAL A P            11   1- 2
1978 PHI N /P            2   0- 0
     BRTR   314  23-23
```

PINELLI, RALPH ARTHUR (BABE)
[REAL NAME
RINALDO ANGELO PAOLINELLI]
B.OCT.18,1895 SAN FRANCISCO,CAL
```
1918 CHI A 3            24   .231
1920 DET A S-3         102   .229
1922 CIN N 3           156   .305
1923 CIN N 3           117   .277
1924 CIN N 3           144   .306
1925 CIN N S-3         130   .283
1926 CIN N 2-S-3        71   .222
1927 CIN N 2-S-3        30   .197
     BRTR   774   .276
```

PINIELLA, LOUIS VICTOR (LOU)
B.AUG.28,1943 TAMPA,FLA.
```
1964 BAL A H             4   .000
1968 CLE A /O            6   .000
1969 KC  A *O/1        135   .282
1970 KC  A *O/1        144   .301
1971 KC  A *O          126   .279
1972 KC  A *O          151   .312
1973 KC  A *O          144   .250
1974 NY  A *O/1        140   .305
1975 NY  A O            74   .196
1976 NY  A O-D         100   .281
1977 NY  A O-D/1       103   .330
1978 NY  A *O-D        130   .314
     BRTR  1257   .290
```

PINKHAM, EDWARD
B.1849 BROOKLYN,N.Y.
```
1871 CHI NA P-3-    1  24   1- 0
         O                -
     TL
```

PINKNEY, GEORGE BURTON
B.JAN.11,1862 ORANGE PRAIRIE,ILL.
D.NOV.10,1926 PEORIA,ILL.
```
1884 CLE N  2-S         35   .309
1885 BRO AA 2-3        111   .288
1886 BRO AA 3          142   .260
1887 BRO AA 3          138   .326
1888 BRO AA 3          143   .260
1889 BRO AA 3          138   .253
1890 BRO N  3          126   .309
1891 BRO N  3          135   .278
1892 STL N  3           78   .172
1893 LOU N  3          118   .226
     BRTR  1164   .272
```

PINNANCE, EDWARD D. (PEANUTS)
B.OCT.22,1879 WALPOLE ISLAND,
ONT.,CANADA
D.DEC.12,1944 WALPOLE ISLAND,
ONTARIO,CANADA
```
1903 PHI A P         2   0- 1
     BLTR
```

```
YR  CL LEA POS    GP    G    REC        YR  CL LEA POS    GP    G    REC        YR  CL LEA POS    GP    G    REC

PINSON, VADA EDWARD                     PITLOCK, LEE PATRICK THOMAS (SKIP)      PLANK, EDWARD STEWART (EDDIE)
B.AUG.11,1938 MEMPHIS,TENN.             B.NOV.6,1947 HILLSIDE,ILL.              OR (GETTYSBURG EDDIE)
1958 CIN N   O          27   .271       1970 SF  N   P          18   5- 5        B.AUG.31,1875 GETTYSBURG,PA.
1959 CIN N   O         154   .316       1974 CHI A   P          40   3- 3        D.FEB.24,1926 GETTYSBURG,PA.
1960 CIN N   O         154   .287       1975 CHI A  /P           1   0- 0        1901 PHI A   P          33  16-14
1961 CIN N   O         154   .343            BLTL               59   8- 8        1902 PHI A   P          36  20-15
1962 CIN N   O         155   .292                                                1903 PHI A   P      41  43  23-16
1963 CIN N   O         162   .313                                                1904 PHI A   P      44  45  26-15
1964 CIN N   O         156   .266                                                1905 PHI A   P          41  26-12
1965 CIN N  *O         159   .305       PITTINGER, CHARLES RENO (TOGIE)         1906 PHI A   P          26  19- 6
1966 CIN N  *O         156   .288       B.1871 GREENCASTLE,PA.                   1907 PHI A   P          43  24-16
1967 CIN N   O         158   .288       D.JAN.14,1909 GREENCASTLE,PA.            1908 PHI A   P          36  14-16
1968 CIN N  *O         130   .271       1900 BOS N   P          18   2- 9        1909 PHI A   P      34  35  19-10
1969 STL N  *O         132   .255       1901 BOS N   P          32  15-16        1910 PHI A   P          38  16-10
1970 CLE A  *O/1       148   .286       1902 BOS N   P          44  27-15        1911 PHI A   P          40  22- 8
1971 CLE A  *O/1       146   .263       1903 BOS N   P          44  18-22        1912 PHI A   P          37  26- 6
1972 CAL A  *O/1       136   .275       1904 BOS N   P          38  14-21        1913 PHI A   P          41  17-10
1973 CAL A  *O         124   .260       1905 PHI N   P          46  23-16        1914 PHI A   P          34  16- 6
1974 KC  A  *O/1       115   .276       1906 PHI N   P          20  8-10         1915 STL F   P          42  21-11
1975 KC  A   O/1       103   .223       1907 PHI N   P          16   9- 5        1916 STL A   P          37  16-15
     BLTL            2469   .286             BLTR             258 116-114        1917 STL A   P          20   5- 6
                                                                                      BLTL          623 627 326-192

PINTO, WILLIAM LERTON (LERTON)
B.APR.8,1898 CHILLICOTHE,OHIO
1922 PHI N   P           9   0- 1       PITTINGER, CLARKE ALONZO (PINKY)        PLARSKI, DONALD JOSEPH (DON)
1924 PHI N   P           3   0- 0       B.FEB.24,1899 HUDSON,MICH.              B.NOV.9,1929 CHICAGO,ILL.
     BLTL               12   0- 1       D.NOV.4,1977 FT.LAUDERDALE,FLA.         1955 KC  A   O           8   .091
                                        1921 BOS A   O          40   .198            BRTR
                                        1922 BOS A   S-3        66   .259
PIPGRAS, EDWARD JOHN                    1923 BOS A   2          60   .215
B.JUNE 15,1904 SCHLESWIG,IOWA           1925 CHI N   S-3        59   .312       PLASKETT, ELMO ALEXANDER
D.APR.13,1964 CURRIE,MINN.              1927 CIN N   2-S-3      31   .274       B.JUNE 27,1938 FREDERIKSTED,V.I.
1932 BRO N   P           5   0- 1       1928 CIN N   2-S-3      40   .237       1962 PIT N   C           7   .286
     BRTR                               1929 CIN N   2-S-3      77   .295       1963 PIT N   C-3        10   .143
                                             BRTR              373   .252            BRTR               17   .200

PIPGRAS, GEORGE WILLIAM
B.DEC.20,1899 IDA GROVE,IOWA
1923 NY  A   P           8   1- 3                                               PLATT, MIZELL GEORGE (WHITEY)
1924 NY  A   P           9   0- 1       PITTS, GAYLEN RICHARD                    B.AUG.21,1920 W.PALM BEACH,FLA.
1927 NY  A   P          29  10- 3       B.JUNE 6,1946 WICHITA,KAN.              D.JULY 27,1970 W.PALM BEACH,FLA.
1928 NY  A   P          46  24-13       1974 OAK A   3/2-1      18   .244       1942 CHI N   O           4   .063
1929 NY  A   P          39  18-12       1975 OAK A   /3-S-2     10   .333       1943 CHI N   O          20   .171
1930 NY  A   P          44  15-15            BRTR               28   .250       1946 CHI A   O          84   .251
1931 NY  A   P          36   7- 6                                               1948 STL A   O         123   .271
1932 NY  A   P          32  16- 9                                               1949 STL A   1-O       102   .258
1933 NY  A   P           4   2- 2                                                    BRTR             333   .255
     BOS A   P          22   9- 8       PITULA, STANLEY (STAN)
1934 BOS A   P           2   0- 0       B.MAR.23,1931 HACKENSACK,N.J.
1935 BOS A   P           5   0- 1       D.AUG.15,1965 HACKENSACK,N.J.           PLATTE, ALFRED FREDERICK JOSEPH
     BRTR             276 102-73        1957 CLE A   P      23  24   2- 2       B.APR.13,1890 GRAND RAPIDS,MICH
                                             BRTR                               D.AUG.29,1976 GRAND RAPIDS,MICH
                                                                                1913 DET A   O           9   .111
PIPP, WALTER CLEMENT (WALLY)                                                         BLTL
B.FEB.17,1893 CHICAGO,ILL.
D.JAN.11,1965 GRAND RAPIDS,MICH         PITZ, HERMAN
1913 DET A   1          11   .178       B.JULY 18,1865 BROOKLYN,N.Y.            PLEIS, WILLIAM (BILL)
1915 NY  A   1         136   .246       D.SEPT.3,1924 FAR ROCKAWAY,N.Y.         B.AUG.5,1937 ST.LOUIS,MO.
1916 NY  A   1         151   .262       1890 BRO AA C          61   .129        1961 MIN A   P          37   4- 2
1917 NY  A   1         155   .244            SYR AA C-S-O      29   .216        1962 MIN A   P          21   2- 5
1918 NY  A   1          91   .304                              90   .155        1963 MIN A   P          36   6- 2
1919 NY  A   1         138   .275                                               1964 MIN A   P          47   4- 1
1920 NY  A   1         153   .280                                               1965 MIN A   P          41   4- 4
1921 NY  A   1         153   .296                                               1966 MIN A  /P           8   1- 2
1922 NY  A   1         152   .329       PIZARRO, JUAN RAMON [CORDOVA]                BLTL             190  21-16
1923 NY  A   1         144   .304       B.FEB.7,1937 SANTURCE,P.R.
1924 NY  A   1         153   .295       1957 MIL N   P      24  25   5- 6
1925 NY  A   1          62   .230       1958 MIL N   P          16   6- 4       PLESS, RANCE
1926 CIN N   1         155   .291       1959 MIL N   P          29   6- 2       B.DEC.6,1925 GREENEVILLE,TENN.
1927 CIN N   1         122   .260       1960 MIL N   P      21  23   6- 7       1956 KC  A   1-3        48   .271
1928 CIN N   1          95   .283       1961 CHI A   P      39  40  14- 7            BRTR
     BLTL            1871   .281        1962 CHI A   P      36  37  12-14
                                        1963 CHI A   P          32  16- 8
                                        1964 CHI A   P          33  19- 9       PLEWS, HERBERT EUGENE (HERB)
PIPPEN, HENRY HAROLD (COTTON)           1965 CHI A   P      18  19   6- 3       B.JUNE 14,1928 HELENA,MONT.
B.APR.2,1910 CISCO,TEX.                 1966 CHI A   P          34   8- 6       1956 WAS A   2-S-3      91   .270
1936 STL N   P           6   0- 2       1967 PIT N   P          50   8-10       1957 WAS A   2-S-3     104   .271
1939 PHI A   P          25   4-11       1968 PIT N   P      12  13   1- 1       1958 WAS A   2-3        111   .256
     DET A   P           3   0- 1            BOS A   P      19  20   6- 8       1959 WAS A   2          27   .225
1940 DET A   P           4   1- 2       1969 BOS A  /P           6   0- 1            BOS A   H          13   .083
     BRTR               38   5-16            CLE A   P          48   3- 3            BLTR             346   .262
                                             OAK A  /P           3   1- 1
                                        1970 CHI N   P          12   0- 0
PIRTLE, GERALD EUGENE (GERRY)           1971 CHI N   P          16   7- 6       PLITT, NORMAN WILLIAM
B.DEC.3,1947 TULSA,OKLA.                1972 CHI N   P          16   4- 5       B.FEB.21,1893 YORK,PA.
1978 MON N   P          19   0- 2       1973 CHI N  /P           2   0- 1       D.FEB.1,1954 NEW YORK,N.Y.
     BRTR                               HOU N   P          15   2- 2            1918 BRO N   P           1   0- 0
                                        1974 PIT N  /P           7   1- 1       1927 BRO N   P          19   2- 6
                                             BLTL             488 496 131-105        NY  N   P           3   1- 0
PISONI, JAMES PETE (JIM)                                                             BRTR               23   3- 6
B.AUG.14,1929 ST.LOUIS,MO.
1953 STL A   O           3   .083
1956 KC  A   O          10   .267       PLANETA, EMIL JOSEPH                    PLOCK, WALTER S.
1957 KC  A   O          44   .237       B.JAN.31,1909 HIGGANUM,CONN.            B.JULY 2,1869 PHILADELPHIA,PA.
1959 MIL N   O           9   .167       D.FEB.2,1963 ROCKY HILL,CONN.           D.APR.28,1900 RICHMOND,VA.
     NY  A   O          17   .176       1931 NY  N   P           2   0- 0       1891 PHI N   O           2   .400
1960 NY  A   O          20   .111            BRTR
     BRTR             103   .212
                                                                                PLODINEC, TIMOTHY ALFRED (TIM)
                                                                                B.JAN.27,1947 ALIQUIPPA,PA.
PITKO, ALEXANDER (SPUNK)                PLANK, EDWARD ARTHUR (ED)               1972 STL N  /P           1   0- 0
B.NOV.22,1914 BURLINGTON,N.J.           B.APR.9,1952 CHICAGO,ILL.                    BRTR
1938 PHI N   O           7   .316       1978 SF  N  /P           5   0- 0
1939 WAS A   O           4   .125            BRTR
     BRTR               11   .259                                               PLUMMER, WILLIAM FRANCIS (BILL)
                                                                                B.MAR.21,1947 OAKLAND,CAL.
                                                                                1968 CHI N /C           2   .000
PITLER, JACOB ALBERT (JAKE)                                                     1970 CIN N /C           4   .125
B.APR.22,1894 NEW YORK,N.Y.                                                     1971 CIN N /C-3        10   .000
D.FEB.3,1968 BINGHAMTON,N.Y.                                                    1972 CIN N  C/1-3      38   .186
1917 PIT N   2         109   .233                                               1973 CIN N  C/3        50   .125
1918 PIT N   2           3   .000                                               1974 CIN N  C/3        50   .151
     BRTR             112   .232                                                1975 CIN N  C          65   .182
                                                                                1976 CIN N  C          56   .248
                                                                                1977 CIN N  C          51   .137
                                                                                1978 SEA A  C          41   .215
                                                                                     BRTR             367   .188
```

YR	CL	LEA	POS	GP	G	REC

POAT, RAYMOND WILLIS (RAY)
B.DEC.19,1917 CHICAGO,ILL.

1942	CLE	A	P		4	1- 3
1943	CLE	A	P		17	2- 5
1944	CLE	A	P		36	4- 8
1947	NY	N	P		7	4- 3
1948	NY	N	P		39	11-10
1949	NY	N	P		2	0- 0
	PIT	N	P		11	0- 1
	BRTR				116	22-30

POCOROBA, BIFF
B.JULY 25,1953 BURBANK,CAL.

1975	ATL	N	C		67	.255
1976	ATL	N	C		54	.241
1977	ATL	N	*C		113	.290
1978	ATL	N	C		92	.242
	BBTR				326	.260

BL 1975 (PART),
1977 (PART)

PODBIELAN, CLARENCE ANTHONY (BUD)
B.MAR.6,1924 CURLEW,WASH.

1949	BRO	N	P		7	0- 1
1950	BRO	N	P		20	5- 4
1951	BRO	N	P		27	2- 2
1952	BRO	N	P	3	4	0- 0
	CIN	N	P		24	4- 5
1953	CIN	N	P		36	6-16
1954	CIN	N	P		27	7-10
1955	CIN	N	P		17	1- 2
1957	CIN	N	P		5	0- 1
1959	CLE	A	P		6	0- 1
	BRTR			172	173	25-42

PODGAJNY, JOHN SIGMUND (SPECS)
B.JUNE 10,1920 CHESTER,PA.
D.MAR.2,1971 CHESTER,PA.

1940	PHI	N	P		4	1- 3
1941	PHI	N	P	34	35	9-12
1942	PHI	N	P	43	44	6-14
1943	PHI	N	P		13	4- 4
	PIT	N	P	15	21	0- 4
1946	CLE	A	P		6	0- 0
	BRTR			115	123	20-37

PODRES, JOHN JOSEPH (JOHNNY)
B.SEP.30,1932 WITHERBEE,N.Y.

1953	BRO	N	P	33	34	9- 4
1954	BRO	N	P	29	38	11- 7
1955	BRO	N	P	27	32	9-10
1957	BRO	N	P	31	35	12- 9
1958	LA	N	P	39	42	13-15
1959	LA	N	P		34	14- 9
1960	LA	N	P		34	14-12
1961	LA	N	P		32	18- 5
1962	LA	N	P		40	15-13
1963	LA	N	P		37	14-12
1964	LA	N	P		2	0- 2
1965	LA	N	P		27	7- 6
1966	LA	N /P		1	0- 0
	DET	A	P		36	4- 5
1967	DET	A	P		21	3- 1
1969	SD	N	P		17	5- 6
	BLTL			440	462	148-116

POEPPING, MICHAEL HAROLD (MIKE)
B.AUG.7,1950 LITTLE FALLS,MINN.

| 1975 | MIN | A | O | | 14 | .135 |
| | BRTR | | | | | |

POETZ, JOSEPH FRANK (BULL MONTANA)
B.JUNE 22,1900 ST.LOUIS,MO.
D.FEB.7,1942 ST.LOUIS,MO.

| 1926 | NY | N | P | | 2 | 0- 1 |
| | BRTR | | | | | |

POFAHL, JAMES WILLARD
B.JUNE 18,1917 FARIBAULT,MINN.

1940	WAS	A	2-S		119	.234
1941	WAS	A	S		22	.187
1942	WAS	A	2-S-3		84	.208
	BRTR				225	.220

POFFENBERGER, CLETUS ELWOOD (BOOTS)
B.JULY 1,1915 WILLIAMSPORT,MD.

1937	DET	A	P		29	10- 5
1938	DET	A	P		25	6- 7
1939	BRO	N	P		3	0- 0
	BRTR				57	16-12

POHOLSKY, THOMAS GEORGE (TOM)
B.AUG.26,1929 DETROIT,MICH.

1950	STL	N	P		5	0- 0
1951	STL	N	P		38	7-13
1954	STL	N	P		23	5- 7
1955	STL	N	P-O		30	9-11
						.182
1956	STL	N	P		33	9-14
1957	CHI	N	P		28	1- 7
	BRTR				159	31-52
						.171

POINDEXTER, CHESTER JENNINGS
(JENNINGS) OR (JINX)
B.SEPT.30,1910 PAULS VALLEY,OKLA.

1936	BOS	A	P		3	0- 2
1939	PHI	N	P		11	0- 0
	BLTL				14	0- 2

POINTER, AARON ELTON
(AARON) OR (HAWK)
B.APR.19,1942 LITTLE ROCK,ARK.

1963	HOU	N	O		2	.200
1966	HOU	N	O		11	.346
1967	HOU	N	O		27	.157
	BRTR				40	.208

POLACHANIN, NICHOLAS JOSEPH
[PLAYED UNDER NAME OF
NICHOLAS JOSEPH POLLY]

POLAND, HUGH REID
B.JAN.19,1913 TOMPKINSVILLE,KY.

1943	NY	N	C		4	.083
	BOS	N	C		44	.191
1944	BOS	N	C		8	.130
1946	BOS	N	C		4	.167
1947	PHI	N	C		4	.000
	CIN	N	C		16	.333
1948	CIN	N	H		3	.333
	BLTR				83	.185

POLCHOW, LOUIS WILLIAM
B.MAR.14,1881 MANKATO,MINN.
D.AUG.15,1912 GOOD THUNDER,MINN

| 1902 | CLE | A | P | | 1 | 0- 1 |

POLE, RICHARD HENRY (DICK)
B.OCT.13,1950 TROUT CREEK,MICH.

1973	BOS	A	P		12	3- 2
1974	BOS	A	P		15	1- 1
1975	BOS	A	P		18	4- 6
1976	BOS	A	P		31	6- 5
1977	SEA	A	P		25	7-12
1978	SEA	A	P		21	4-11
	BRTR			122	25-37

POLHEMUS, MARK L. (MARK)
OR (HUMPTY DUMPTY)
B.OCT.4,1864 BROOKLYN,N.Y.

| 1887 | IND | N | O | | 19 | .259 |

POLIVKA, KENNETH LYLE (SOUP)
B.JAN.21,1921 CHICAGO,ILL.

| 1947 | CIN | N | P | | 2 | 0- 0 |
| | BLTL | | | | | |

POLLET, HOWARD JOSEPH (HOWIE)
B.JUNE 26,1921 NEW ORLEANS,LA.
D.AUG.8,1974 HOUSTON,TEX.

1941	STL	N	P		9	5- 2
1942	STL	N	P		27	7- 5
1943	STL	N	P		16	8- 4
1946	STL	N	P		40	21-10
1947	STL	N	P		37	9-11
1948	STL	N	P	36	38	13- 8
1949	STL	N	P		39	20- 9
1950	STL	N	P	37	38	14-13
1951	STL	N	P		6	0- 3
	PIT	N	P		21	6-10
1952	PIT	N	P		31	7-16
1953	PIT	N	P		5	1- 1
	CHI	N	P		25	5- 6
1954	CHI	N	P		20	8-10
1955	CHI	N	P		24	4- 3
1956	CHI	N	P		11	12	3- 1
	PIT	N	P		19	0- 4
	BLTL			403	407	131-116

POLLI, LOUIS AMERICO (CRIP)
B.JULY 9,1901 BARRE,VT.

1932	STL	A	P		5	0- 0
1944	NY	N	P		19	0- 2
	BRTR				24	0- 2

POLLY, NICHOLAS JOSEPH
[REAL NAME
NICHOLAS JOSEPH POLACHANIN]
B.APR.18,1917 CHICAGO,ILL.

1937	BRO	N	3		10	.222
1945	BOS	A	3		4	.143
	BRTR				14	.200

POLONI, JOHN PAUL
B.FEB.28,1954 DEARBORN,MICH.

| 1977 | TEX | A /P | | 2 | 1- 0 |
| | BLTL | | | | | |

POMORSKI, JOHN LEON
B.DEC.30,1905 BROOKLYN,N.Y.
D.DEC.6,1977 BRAMPTON,ONT.,CAN.

| 1934 | CHI | A | P | | 3 | 0- 0 |
| | BRTR | | | | | |

POND, ERASMUS ARLINGTON (ARLIE)
B.JAN.19,1872 RUTLAND,VT.
D.SEPT.19,1930 CEBU,PHILIPPINES

1895	BAL	N	P		7	0- 1
1896	BAL	N	P		24	15- 8
1897	BAL	N	P	27	31	18- 9
1898	BAL	N	P		2	1- 1
	TR			60	64	34-19

POND, RALPH BENJAMIN
B.MAY 4,1888 EAU CLAIRE,WIS.
D.SEPT.18,1947 CLEVELAND,OHIO

| 1910 | BOS | A | O | | 1 | .333 |

PONDER, CHARLES ELMER (ELMER)
B.JUNE 26,1893 REED,OKLA.
D.APR.20,1974 ALBUQUERQUE,N.MEX

1917	PIT	N	P		3	1- 1
1919	PIT	N	P		9	0- 5
1920	PIT	N	P		33	11-13
1921	PIT	N	P		8	2- 0
	CHI	N	P		16	3- 6
	BRTR				69	17-27

POOL, HARLIN WELTY (SAMSON)
B.MAR.12,1908 LAKEPORT,CAL.
D.FEB.15,1963 RODEO,CAL.

1934	CIN	N	O		99	.327
1935	CIN	N	O		28	.176
	BLTR				127	.303

POOLE, EDWARD I.
B.SEPT.7,1874 CANTON,OHIO
D.MAR.11,1919 MALVERN,OHIO

1900	PIT	N	P		2	1- 0
1901	PIT	N	P		23	5- 4
1902	PIT	N	P		1	0- 0
	CIN	N	P		16	12- 4
1903	CIN	N	P		25	8-13
1904	BRO	N	P		24	7-14
	TR				91	33-35

POOLE, JAMES ROBERT (EASY)
B.MAY 12,1895 TAYLORSVILLE,N.C.
D.JAN.2,1975 HICKORY,N.C.

1925	PHI	A	1		133	.298
1926	PHI	A	1		112	.294
1927	PHI	A	1		38	.222
	BLTR				283	.288

POOLE, RAYMOND HERMAN
B.JAN.16,1920 SALISBURY,N.C.

1941	PHI	A	H		2	.000
1947	PHI	A	H		13	.231
	BLTR				15	.200

POORMAN, THOMAS IVERSON
B.OCT.14,1857 LOCK HAVEN,PA.
D.FEB.18,1905 LOCK HAVEN,PA.

1880	BUF	N	P-O		11	19	1- 8
							.159
	CHI	N	P-O		2	7	1- 0
							.200
1884	TOL	AA	P-O		1	93	0- 1
							.224
1885	BOS	N	O			55	.241
1886	BOS	N	O			88	.261
1887	ATH	AA	O			135	.316
1888	ATH	AA	O			85	.227
	BLTR			14	482	2- 9
						.260

POPE, DAVID (DAVE)
B.JUNE 17,1925 TALLADEGA,ALA.

1952	CLE	A	O		12	.294
1954	CLE	A	O		60	.294
1955	CLE	A	O		35	.298
	BAL	A	O		86	.248
1956	BAL	A	O		12	.158
	CLE	A	O		25	.243
	BLTR				230	.265

POPOVICH, PAUL EDWARD
B.AUG.18,1940 FLEMINGTON,W.VA.

1964	CHI	N	H		1	1.000
1966	CHI	N /2		2	.000
1967	CHI	N	S-2/3		49	.214
1968	LA	N	2-S/3		134	.232
1969	LA	N	2/S		28	.200
	CHI	N	2/S-3-O		60	.312
1970	CHI	N	2-S/3		78	.253
1971	CHI	N	2-3/S		89	.217
1972	CHI	N	2/S-3		58	.194
1973	CHI	N	2/S-3		99	.236
1974	PIT	N	2-S		59	.217
1975	PIT	N /2-S		25	.200
	BBTR			682	.233

BR 1964-67

POPOWSKI, EDWARD JOSEPH (EDDIE)
B.AUG.20,1913 SAYERVILLE,N.J.
NON-PLAYING MANAGER BOS[A]
1969 [INTERIM], 1973 [INTERIM]

POPP, WILLIAM PETER
B.JUNE 7,1877 ST.LOUIS,MO.
D.SEPT.5,1909 ST.LOUIS,MO.

| 1902 | STL | N | P | | 9 | 2- 6 |
| | TR | | | | | |

POPPLEIN, GEORGE J.
B.BALTIMORE,MD.

| 1873 | MAR | NA | O | | 1 | .000 |

POQUETTE, THOMAS ARTHUR (TOM)
B.OCT.30,1951 EAU CLAIRE,WIS.

1973	KC	A	O		21	.214
1976	KC	A	O		104	.302
1977	KC	A	O		106	.292
1978	KC	A	O		80	.216
	BLTR				311	.277

PORRAY, EDMUND JOSEPH
B.DEC.5,1888 AT SEA ON ATLANTIC OCEAN
D.JULY 13,1954 LACKAWAXEN,PA.

YR	CL	LEA	POS	GP	G	REC
1914	BUF	F	P		3	0- 1
			BRTR			

PORTER, DANIEL EDWARD
B.OCT.17,1931 DECATUR,ILL.

YR	CL	LEA	POS	GP	G	REC
1951	WAS	A	O		13	.211
			BLTL			

PORTER, DARRELL RAY
B.JAN.17,1952 JOPLIN,MO.

YR	CL	LEA	POS	GP	G	REC
1971	MIL	A	C		22	.214
1972	MIL	A	C		18	.125
1973	MIL	A	C-O		117	.254
1974	MIL	A	*C		131	.241
1975	MIL	A	*C		130	.232
1976	MIL	A	*C		119	.208
1977	KC	A	*C		130	.275
1978	KC	A	*C		150	.265
			BLTR		817	.244

PORTER, HENRY
B.1861 VERGENNES,VT.
D.DEC.30,1906 BROCKTON,MASS.

YR	CL	LEA	POS	GP	G	REC
1884	MIL	U	P-1-O	6	10	3- 2
						.278
1885	BRO	AA	P		55	33-21
1886	BRO	AA	P		48	28-20
1887	BRO	AA	P		40	16-23
1888	KC	AA	P		55	17-37
1889	KC	AA	P		4	0- 3
			BRTR	208	212	97-106
						.190

PORTER, IRVING MARBLE
B.MAY 17,1888 LYNN,MASS.
D.FEB.20,1971 LYNN,MASS.

YR	CL	LEA	POS	GP	G	REC
1914	CHI	A	O		1	.000
			BBTR			

PORTER, J W (JAY) OR (J W)
B.JAN.17,1933 SHAWNEE,OKLA.

YR	CL	LEA	POS	GP	G	REC
1952	STL	A	3-O		33	.250
1955	DET	A	C-1-O		24	.236
1956	DET	A	C-O		14	.095
1957	DET	A	C-1-O		58	.250
1958	CLE	A	C-1-3		40	.200
1959	WAS	A	C-1		37	.226
	STL	N	C-1		23	.212
			BRTR		229	.228

PORTER, MATTHEW S.
D.KANSAS CITY,MO.
B.KANSAS CITY,MO.

YR	CL	LEA	POS	GP	G	REC
1884	KC	U	O		3	.083

PORTER, NED SWINDELL
B.JULY 6,1905 APALACHICOLA,FLA.
D.JUNE 30,1968 GAINESVILLE,FLA.

YR	CL	LEA	POS	GP	G	REC
1926	NY	N	P		2	0- 0
1927	NY	N	P		1	0- 0
			BRTR		3	0- 0

PORTER, ODIE OSCAR
B.MAY 24,1877 BORDEN,IND.
D.MAY 2,1903 BORDEN,IND.

YR	CL	LEA	POS	GP	G	REC
1902	PHI	A	P		1	0- 1

PORTER, RICHARD TWILLEY (DICK)
(WIGGLES) OR (TWITCHES)
B.DEC.30,1901 PRINCESS ANNE,MD.
D.SEPT.24,1974 PHILADELPHIA,PA.

YR	CL	LEA	POS	GP	G	REC
1929	CLE	A	2-O		71	.328
1930	CLE	A	O		119	.350
1931	CLE	A	O		114	.312
1932	CLE	A	O		146	.308
1933	CLE	A	O		132	.267
1934	CLE	A	O		13	.227
	BOS	N			80	.302
			BLTR		675	.308

PORTERFIELD, ERWIN COOLIDGE (BOB)
B.AUG.10,1923 NEWPORT,VA.

YR	CL	LEA	POS	GP	G	REC
1948	NY	A	P		16	5- 3
1949	NY	A	P		12	2- 5
1950	NY	A	P	10	11	1- 1
1951	NY	A	P		2	0- 0
	WAS	A	P		19	9- 8
1952	WAS	A	P		31	13-14
1953	WAS	A	P	34	37	22-10
1954	WAS	A	P		32	13-15
1955	WAS	A	P		30	10-17
1956	BOS	A	P		25	3-12
1957	BOS	A	P		28	4- 4
1958	BOS	A	P		2	0- 0
	PIT	N	P		37	4- 6
1959	PIT	N	P		36	1- 2
	CHI	N	P		4	0- 0
			BRTR	318	322	87-97

PORTO, ALFRED (AL) OR (LEFTY)
B.JUNE 27,1926 HEILWOOD,PA.

YR	CL	LEA	POS	GP	G	REC
1948	PHI	N	P		3	0- 0
			BLTL			

PORTOCARRERO, ARNOLD MARIO (ARNIE)
B.JULY 5,1931 NEW YORK,N.Y.

YR	CL	LEA	POS	GP	G	REC
1954	PHI	A	P		34	9-18
1955	KC	A	P		24	5- 9
1956	KC	A	P		3	0- 1
1957	KC	A	P		33	4- 9
1958	BAL	A	P		32	15-11
1959	BAL	A	P		27	2- 7
1960	BAL	A	P		13	3- 2
			BRTR		166	38-57

POSADA, LEOPOLDO JESUS (HERNANDEZ) (LEO)
B.APR.15,1936 HAVANA,CUBA

YR	CL	LEA	POS	GP	G	REC
1960	KC	A	O		10	.361
1961	KC	A	O		116	.253
1962	KC	A	O		29	.196
			BRTR		155	.256

POSEDEL, WILLIAM JOHN
(SAILOR BILL) OR
(BARNACLE BILL)
B.AUG.2,1906 SAN FRANCISCO,CAL.

YR	CL	LEA	POS	GP	G	REC
1938	BRO	N	P		33	8- 9
1939	BOS	N	P		33	15-13
1940	BOS	N	P		35	12-17
1941	BOS	N	P		18	4- 4
1946	BOS	N	P		19	2- 0
			BRTR		138	41-43

POSER, JOHN FALK (BOB)
B.MAR.16,1910 COLUMBUS,WIS.

YR	CL	LEA	POS	GP	G	REC
1932	CHI	A	P	1	5	0- 0
1935	STL	A	P		4	1- 1
			BLTR	5	9	1- 1

POSSEHL, LOUIS THOMAS
B.APR.12,1926 CHICAGO,ILL.

YR	CL	LEA	POS	GP	G	REC
1946	PHI	N	P		1	1- 2
1947	PHI	N	P		2	0- 0
1948	PHI	N	P	3	4	1- 1
1951	PHI	N	P		2	0- 1
1952	PHI	N	P		4	0- 1
			BRTR	15	16	2- 5

POST, SAMUEL GILBERT
B.NOV.17,1896 RICHMOND,VA.
D.MAR.31,1971 PORTSMOUTH,VA.

YR	CL	LEA	POS	GP	G	REC
1922	BRO	N	1		9	.280
			BLTL			

POST, WALTER CHARLES (WALLY)
B.JULY 9,1929 ST.WENDELIN,OHIO

YR	CL	LEA	POS	GP	G	REC
1949	CIN	N	O		6	.250
1951	CIN	N	O		15	.220
1952	CIN	N	O		19	.155
1953	CIN	N	O		11	.242
1954	CIN	N	O		130	.255
1955	CIN	N	O		154	.309
1956	CIN	N	O		143	.249
1957	CIN	N	O		134	.244
1958	PHI	N	O		110	.282
1959	PHI	N	O		132	.254
1960	PHI	N	O		34	.286
	CIN	N			77	.281
1961	CIN	N	O		99	.294
1962	CIN	N	O		109	.263
1963	CIN	N	O		5	.000
	MIN	A	O		21	.191
1964	CLE	A	O		5	.000
			BRTR		1204	.266

POSTE, E.

YR	CL	LEA	POS	GP	G	REC
1902	DET	A	O		3	.083

POTT, NELSON ADOLPH (LEFTY)
B.JULY 16,1899 CINCINNATI,OHIO
D.DEC.3,1963 CINCINNATI,OHIO

YR	CL	LEA	POS	GP	G	REC
1922	CLE	A	P		2	0- 0
			BLTL			

POTTER, MARYLAND DYKES (DYKES)
B.SEPT.7,1910 ASHLAND,KY.

YR	CL	LEA	POS	GP	G	REC
1938	BRO	N	P		2	0- 0
			BRTR			

POTTER, MICHAEL GARY (MIKE)
B.MAY 16,1951 MONTEBELLO,CAL.

YR	CL	LEA	POS	GP	G	REC
1976	STL	N	/O		9	.000
1977	STL	N	/O		5	.000
			BRTR		14	.000

POTTER, NELSON THOMAS (NELLIE)
B.AUG.23,1911 MT.MORRIS,ILL.

YR	CL	LEA	POS	GP	G	REC
1936	STL	N	P		1	0- 0
1938	PHI	A	P	35	38	2-12
1939	PHI	A	P		41	8-12
1940	PHI	A	P		31	9-14
1941	PHI	A	P		10	1- 1
	BOS	A	P		10	2- 0
1943	STL	A	P		33	10- 5
1944	STL	A	P		32	19- 7
1945	STL	A	P		32	15-11
1946	STL	A	P		23	8- 9
1947	STL	A	P		32	4-10
1948	STL	A	P		2	1- 1
	PHI	A	P		8	2- 2
	BOS	N	P		18	5- 2
1949	BOS	N	P		41	6-11
			BLTR	349	352	92-97

POTTER, SQUIRE
B.MAR.18,1902 FLATWOODS,KY.

YR	CL	LEA	POS	GP	G	REC
1923	WAS	A	P		1	0- 0
			BRTR			

POTTS, DANIEL
B.KENT,OHIO

YR	CL	LEA	POS	GP	G	REC
1892	WAS	N	C		1	.333

POTTS, JOHN FREDERICK (FRED)
B.FEB.6,1887 TIPP CITY,OHIO
D.SEPT.5,1962 CLEVELAND,OHIO

YR	CL	LEA	POS	GP	G	REC
1914	KC	F	O		40	.287
			BLTR			

POULSEN, KEN STERLING
B.AUG.4,1947 VAN NUYS,CAL.

YR	CL	LEA	POS	GP	G	REC
1967	BOS	A	/3-S		5	.200
			BLTR			

POUNDS, JEARED WELLS (BILL)
B.MAR.11,1878 PATERSON,N.J.
D.JULY 7,1936 PATERSON,N.J.

YR	CL	LEA	POS	GP	G	REC
1903	CLE	A	P		1	0- 0
	BRO	N	P		1	0- 0
			BRTR		2	0- 0

POWELL, ALVIN JACOB (JAKE)
B.JULY 15,1908 SILVER SPRING,MD
D.NOV.4,1948 WASHINGTON,D.C.

YR	CL	LEA	POS	GP	G	REC
1930	WAS	A	O		3	.000
1934	WAS	A	O		9	.286
1935	WAS	A	2-O		139	.312
1936	WAS	A	O		53	.290
	NY	A	O		87	.306
1937	NY	A	O		97	.263
1938	NY	A	O		45	.256
1939	NY	A	O		31	.244
1940	NY	A	O		12	.185
1943	WAS	A	O		37	.265
1944	WAS	A	3-O		96	.240
1945	WAS	A	O		31	.194
	PHI	N	O		48	.231
			BRTR		688	.271

POWELL, CHARLES ABNER
(ABNER) OR (AB)
B.DEC.15,1860 SHENANDOAH,PA.
D.AUG.7,1953 NEW ORLEANS,LA.

YR	CL	LEA	POS	GP	G	REC
1884	WAS	U	P-2-3-O	19	47	4-12
						.270
1886	BAL	AA	P-O	7	10	2- 5
						.147
	CIN	AA	P-C-S-O	4	19	0- 1
						.230
			BRTR	30	76	6-18
						.246

POWELL, GROVER DAVID
B.OCT.10,1940 SAYRE,PA.

YR	CL	LEA	POS	GP	G	REC
1963	NY	N	P		20	1- 1
			BLTL			

POWELL, HOSKEN
B.MAY 14,1955 SELMA,ALA.

YR	CL	LEA	POS	GP	G	REC
1978	MIN	A	*O		121	.247
			BLTL			

POWELL, JAMES E.
B.1859 RICHMOND,VA.

YR	CL	LEA	POS	GP	G	REC
1884	RIC	AA	1		40	.243

```
YR  CL LEA POS      GP   G    REC

POWELL, JOHN JOSEPH (JACK) OR (RED)
B.JULY 9,1874 BLOOMINGTON,ILL.
D.OCT.17,1944 CHICAGO,ILL.
1897 CLE N  P       26   28  15- 9
1898 CLE N  P            40  24-15
1899 STL N  P       44   46  23-21
1900 STL N  P            37  17-18
1901 STL N  P            37  19-18
1902 STL A  P-C-    43   44  22-17
                             1-0      .217
1903 STL A  P       38   39  15-19
1904 NY  A  P            47  23-19
1905 NY  A  P            37   9-11
     STL A  P             3   2- 1
1906 STL A  P            29  13-14
1907 STL A  P            35  13-16
1908 STL A  P            33  16-13
1909 STL A  P            34  12-16
1910 STL A  P            21   7-11
1911 STL A  P            32   8-19
1912 STL A  P            32   9-16
     BRTR          568  574 247-253
                                    .191

POWELL, JOHN WESLEY (BOOG)
B.AUG.17,1941 LAKELAND,FLA.
1961 BAL A  0             4  .077
1962 BAL A  1-0         124  .243
1963 BAL A  1-0         140  .265
1964 BAL A  1-0         134  .290
1965 BAL A  1-0         144  .248
1966 BAL A  *1          140  .287
1967 BAL A  *1          125  .234
1968 BAL A  *1          156  .249
1969 BAL A  *1          152  .304
1970 BAL A  *1          154  .297
1971 BAL A  *1          128  .256
1972 BAL A  *1          140  .252
1973 BAL A  *1          114  .265
1974 BAL A  *1          110  .265
1975 CLE A  *1          134  .297
1976 CLE A  1           95  .215
1977 LA  N  /1          50  .244
     BLTR            2042  .266

POWELL, MARTIN J.
B.MAR.25,1856 FITCHBURG,MASS.
D.FEB.5,1888 FITCHBURG,MASS.
1881 DET N  C-1         59  .310
1882 DET N  1           77  .247
1883 DET N  1           97  .267
1884 CIN U  1           45  .314
1885 ATH AA 1           18  .164
     BL              292  .276

POWELL, PAUL RAY
B.MAR.19,1948 SAN ANGELO,TEX.
1971 MIN A  0           20  .161
1973 LA  N  /0           2  .000
1975 LA  N  /C-0         8  .200
     BRTR             30  .167

POWELL, RAYMOND REATH (RABBIT)
B.NOV.20,1888 SILOAM SPRINGS,ARK.
D.OCT.16,1962 CHILLICOTHE,MO.
1913 DET A  0            2  .000
1917 BOS N  0           88  .272
1918 BOS N  0           53  .213
1919 BOS N  0          123  .236
1920 BOS N  0          147  .225
1921 BOS N  0          149  .306
1922 BOS N  0          142  .296
1923 BOS N  0           97  .302
1924 BOS N  0           74  .261
     BRTR            875  .271

POWELL, ROBERT LEROY (LEROY)
B.OCT.17,1933 FLINT,MICH.
1955 CHI A  H            1  .000
1957 CHI A  H            1  .000
     BRTR              2  .000

POWELL, SAMUEL
1913 STL A  P            2  0- 0

POWELL, WILLIAM BURRIS (BIG BILL)
B.MAY 8,1885 RICHMOND,VA.
D.SEPT.28,1967 E.LIVERPOOL,OHIO
1909 PIT N  P            3  0- 1
1910 PIT N  P           12  4- 6
1912 CHI N  P            1  0- 0
1913 CIN N  P            1  0- 1
     BRTR             17  4- 8

POWER, THOMAS E.
B.SAN FRANCISCO,CAL.
D.FEB.25,1898 SAN FRANCISCO,CAL
1890 BAL AA 1           38  .211


POWER, VICTOR PELLOT (VIC)
B.NOV.1,1931 ARECIBO,P.R.
1954 PHI A  1-S-3-0    127  .255
1955 KC  A  1          147  .319
1956 KC  A  1-2-0      127  .309
1957 KC  A  1-2-0      129  .259
1958 KC  A  1-2         52  .302
     CLE A  1-2-S-3-0   93  .317
1959 CLE A  1-2-3      147  .289
1960 CLE A  1-S-3      147  .288
1961 CLE A  1-2        147  .268
1962 MIN A  1-2        144  .290
1963 MIN A  1-2-3      138  .270
1964 MIN A  1-2         19  .222
     LA  A  1-2-3       68  .249
     PHI N  1           18  .208
1965 CAL A  *1/2-3     124  .259
     BRTR           1627  .284

POWERS, ELLIS FOREE (MIKE)
B.MAR.2,1906 CRESTWOOD,KY.
1932 CLE A  0           14  .182
1933 CLE A  0           24  .277
     BLTL             38  .238

POWERS, JAMES T.
B.1868 NEW YORK,N.Y.
1890 BRO AA P            4  1- 2

POWERS, JOHN CALVIN
B.JULY 8,1929 BIRMINGHAM,ALA.
1955 PIT N  0            2  .250
1956 PIT N  0           11  .048
1957 PIT N  0           20  .286
1958 PIT N  0           57  .183
1959 CIN N  0           43  .236
1960 BAL A  0           10  .111
     CLE A  0            8  .167
     BLTR            151  .195

POWERS, JOHN LLOYD (IKE)
B.MAR.13,1906 HANCOCK,MD.
D.DEC.22,1968 HANCOCK,MD.
1927 PHI A  P           11  1- 1
1928 PHI A  P            9  1- 0
     BRTR             20  2- 1

POWERS, LESLIE EDWIN
B.NOV.5,1912 SEATTLE,WASH.
1938 NY  N  H            2  .000
1939 PHI N  1           19  .346
     BLTL             21  .327

POWERS, MICHAEL RILEY
B.SEPT.22,1870 PITTSFIELD,MASS.
D.APR.26,1909 PHILADELPHIA,PA.
1898 LOU N  C           27  .298
1899 LOU N  C           41  .211
     WAS N  C-1         14  .333
1901 PHI A  C          116  .248
1902 PHI A  C-1         71  .271
1903 PHI A  C           74  .227
1904 PHI A  C           57  .187
1905 PHI A  C           22  .183
     NY  A  C           11  .083
     PHI A  C           19  .161
1906 PHI A  C           58  .157
1907 PHI A  C           59  .182
1908 PHI A  C           62  .180
1909 PHI A  C            1  .250
     BRTR            632  .218

POWERS, PATRICK THOMAS
B.JUNE 27,1860 TRENTON,N.J.
D.AUG.29,1925 BELMAR,N.J.
NON-PLAYING MANAGER
ROC[AA] 1890; NY[N] 1892

POWERS, PHILLIP B. (GRANDMOTHER)
B.JULY 26,1854 NEW YORK,N.Y.
D.DEC.22,1914 NEW YORK,N.Y.
1878 CIN N  C-0          9  .140
1880 BOS N  C-0         35  .148
1881 CLE N  C-3          6  .143
1882 CIN AA C-1-0       15  .212
1883 CIN AA C-0         29  .234
1884 CIN AA C-1-0       35  .158
1885 CIN AA C           15  .267
     BAL AA C-0          9  .121
     BRTR            153  .184

POWIS, CARL EDGAR (CARL) OR (JUG)
B.JAN.11,1928 PHILADELPHIA,PA.
1957 BAL A  0           15  .195
     BRTR

PRALL, WILFRED ANTHONY (WILLIE)
B.APR.20,1950 HACKENSACK,N.J.
1975 CHI N  /P           3  0- 2
     BLTL

PRAMESA, JOHN STEVEN (JOHNNY)
B.AUG.28,1925 BARTON,OHIO
1949 CIN N  C           17  .240
1950 CIN N  C           74  .307
1951 CIN N  C           72  .229
1952 CHI N  C           22  .283
     BRTR            185  .268


PRATT, ALBERT GEORGE (UNCLE AL)
B.NOV.19,1848 ALLEGHENY,PA.
D.NOV.21,1937
1871 CLE NA P-O     28   29  10-18
                                 -
1872 CLE NA P-O     11   15   3- 8
                                .261
                    39   44  13-26

NON-PLAYING MANAGER PIT[AA] 1882-83

PRATT, DERRILL BURNHAM (DEL)
B.JAN.10,1888 WALHALLA,S.C.
D.SEPT.30,1977 TEXAS CITY,TEX.
1912 STL A  2-S        151  .302
1913 STL A  2          154  .296
1914 STL A  2          158  .282
1915 STL A  2          159  .291
1916 STL A  2          158  .267
1917 STL A  2          123  .247
1918 NY  A  2          126  .275
1919 NY  A  2          140  .292
1920 NY  A  2          154  .314
1921 BOS A  2          135  .324
1922 BOS A  2          154  .302
1923 DET A  1-2        101  .310
1924 DET A  1-2        121  .303
     BRTR           1834  .292

PRATT, FRANCIS BRUCE (TRUCKHORSE)
B.AUG.24,1897 BLOCTON,ALA.
D.MAR.8,1974 CENTREVILLE,ALA.
1921 CHI A  H            1  .000
     TR

PRATT, LESTER JOHN (LARRY)
B.OCT.8,1886 GIBSON CITY,ILL.
D.JAN.8,1969 PEORIA,ILL.
1914 BOS A  C            5  .000
1915 BRO F  C           20  .191
     NEW F  C            5  .500
     BRTR             30  .196

PRATT, THOMAS J.
B.1844 WORCESTER,MASS.
D.SEPT.29,1908
1871 ATH NA 1            1    -
1884 BAL AA 0            2  .250
NON-PLAYING MANAGER KEY[U] 1884

PREGENZER, JOHN ARTHUR
B.AUG.2,1935 BURLINGTON,WIS.
1963 SF  N  P            6  0- 0
1964 SF  N  P           13  2- 0
     BRTR             19  2- 0

PREIBISCH, MELVIN ADOLPHUS (PRIMO)
B.NOV.23,1914 SEALY,TEX.
1940 BOS N  0           11  .225
1941 BOS N  0            5  .000
     BRTR             16  .205

PRENDERGAST, JAMES BARTHOLOMEW (JIM)
B.AUG.23,1917 BROOKLYN,N.Y.
1948 BOS N  P           10  1- 1
     BLTL

PRENDERGAST, MICHAEL THOMAS
B.DEC.15,1888 ARLINGTON,ILL.
D.NOV.18,1967 OMAHA,NEB.
1914 CHI F  P           30  5- 9
1915 CHI F  P           42  14-12
1916 CHI N  P           35  6-11
1917 CHI N  P           35  3- 6
1918 PHI N  P           33  13-14
1919 PHI N  P            5  0- 1
     BRTR            180  41-53

PRENTISS, GEORGE PEPPER
(PLAYED UNDER NAME OF
GEORGE PEPPER WILSON IN 1901)
B.JUNE 10,1876 WILMINGTON,DEL.
D.SEPT.8,1902 WILMINGTON,DEL.
1901 BOS A  P            2  1- 0
1902 BOS A  P            6  2- 2
     BAL A  P            6  3- 3
     BB               14  6- 5

PRESCOTT, GEORGE BERTRAND (BOBBY)
B.MAR.27,1931 COLON,PANAMA
1961 KC  A  0           10  .083
     BRTR

PRESKO, JOSEPH EDWARD (JOE)
OR (LITTLE JOE)
B.OCT.7,1928 KANSAS CITY,MO.
1951 STL N  P           15  7- 4
1952 STL N  P           28  7-10
1953 STL N  P      34   35  6-13
1954 STL N  P      37   38  4- 9
1957 DET A  P            7  1- 1
1958 DET A  P            7  0- 0
     BRTR          128  130 25-37
```

YR	CL	LEA	POS	GP	G	REC

PRESSNELL, FOREST CHARLES (TOT)
B.AUG.8,1906 FINDLAY,OHIO

YR	CL	LEA	POS	GP	G	REC
1938	BRO	N	P		43	11-14
1939	BRO	N	P		31	9- 7
1940	BRO	N	P		24	6- 5
1941	CHI	N	P		29	5- 3
1942	CHI	N	P		27	1- 1
		BRTR			154	32-30

PRESTON, WALTER B.
B.1871 GALVESTON,TEX.

1895	LOU	N	3-0		49	.292

PRICE, GILBERT EUGENE
[PLAYED UNDER NAME OF
(LEFTY) SCHEGG]

PRICE, JAMES L.
NON-PLAYING MANAGER NY[N] 1884

PRICE, JIMMIE WILLIAM
B.OCT.13,1941 HARRISBURG,PA.

1967	DET	A	C		44	.261
1968	DET	A	C		64	.174
1969	DET	A	C		72	.234
1970	DET	A	C		52	.182
1971	DET	A	C		29	.241
		BRTR			261	.214

PRICE, JOHN THOMAS REID
(JACKIE) OR (JOHNNY)
B.NOV.13,1912 WINDBORN,MISS.
D.OCT.2,1967 SAN FRANCISCO,CAL.

1946	CLE	A	S		7	.231
		BLTR				

PRICE, JOSEPH PRESTON (LUMBER)
B.APR.10,1897 MILLIGAN COLLEGE,TENN.
D.JAN.19,1961 WASHINGTON,D.C.

1928	NY	N	0		1	.000
		BRTR				

PRICE, WILLIAM
B.PHILADELPHIA,PA.

1890	ATH	AA	P		1	1- 0

PRICHARD, ROBERT ALEXANDER
B.OCT.21,1917 PARIS,TEX.

1939	WAS	A	3		26	.235
		BLTL				

PRIDDY, GERALD EDWARD (JERRY)
B.NOV.9,1919 LOS ANGELES,CAL.

1941	NY	A	1-2-3		56	.213
1942	NY	A	1-2-S-3		59	.280
1943	WAS	A	2-S-3		149	.271
1946	WAS	A	2		138	.254
1947	WAS	A	2		147	.214
1948	STL	A	2		151	.296
1949	STL	A	2		145	.290
1950	DET	A	2		157	.277
1951	DET	A	2-S		154	.260
1952	DET	A	2		75	.283
1953	DET	A	1-2-3		65	.235
		BRTR			1296	.265

PRIDDY, ROBERT SIMPSON (BOB)
B.DEC.10,1939 PITTSBURGH,PA.

1962	PIT	N	P		2	1- 0
1964	PIT	N	P		19	1- 2
1965	SF	N	/P		9	1- 0
1966	SF	N	P		38	6- 3
1967	WAS	A	P		46	3- 7
1968	CHI	A	P		35	42	3-11
1969	CHI	A	/P		4	0- 0
	CAL	A	P		15	0- 1
	ATL	N	/P		1	0- 0
1970	ATL	N	P		41	5- 5
1971	ATL	N	P		40	4- 9
		BRTR		249	261	24-38

PRIEST, JOHN GOODING
B.JUNE 23,1886 ST.JOSEPH,MO.

1911	NY	A	2		8	.142
1912	NY	A	H		2	.500
		BRTR			10	.174

PRIM, RAYMOND LEE (POP)
B.OCT.3,1906 SALITPA,ALA.

1933	WAS	A	P		2	0- 1
1934	WAS	A	P		8	0- 2
1935	PHI	N	P		29	3- 4
1943	CHI	N	P		29	4- 3
1945	CHI	N	P		34	13- 8
1946	CHI	N	P		14	2- 3
		BRTL			116	22-21

PRINCE, DONALD MARK
B.APR.5,1938 CLARKTON,N.C.

1962	CHI	N	P		1	0- 0
		BRTR				

PRINCE, WALTER F.
B.1860 N.ANDOVER,MASS.
D.MAR.2,1938

1883	LOU	AA	1-S-0		4	.182
1884	DET	N	0		7	.130
	WAS	AA	1		43	.211
	WAS	U	1		1	.250
		BRTR			55	.200

PRITCHARD, HAROLD WILLIAM (BUDDY)
B.JAN.25,1936 SOUTH GATE,CAL.

1957	PIT	N	S-0		23	.091
		BRTR				

PROCTOR, JAMES ARTHUR
B.SEPT.9,1935 BRANDYWINE,MD.

1959	DET	A	P		2	0- 1
		BRTR				

PROCTOR, L. (LOU)

1912	STL	A	H		1	.000

PROCTOR, NOAH RICHARD (RED)
B.OCT.27,1900 WILLIAMSBURG,VA.
D.DEC.17,1954 RICHMOND,VA.

1923	CHI	A	P		2	0- 0
		BRTR				

PROESER, GEORGE (YATZ)
B.MAY 30,1864 CINCINNATI,OHIO
D.OCT.13,1941 NEW BURLINGTON,O.

1888	CLE	AA	P		7	3- 4
1890	SYR	AA	0		13	.264
		BLTL		7	20	3- 4
						.276

PROLY, MICHAEL JAMES (MIKE)
B.DEC.15,1950 JAMAICA,N.Y.

1976	STL	N	P		14	1- 0
1978	CHI	A	P		14	5- 2
		BRTR			28	6- 2

PROPST, WILLIAM JACOB (JAKE)
B.MAR.10,1895 KENNEDY,ALA.
D.FEB.24,1967 COLUMBUS,MISS.

1923	WAS	A	H		1	.000

PROTHRO, JAMES THOMPSON (DOC)
B.JULY 16,1893 MEMPHIS,TENN.
D.OCT.14,1971 MEMPHIS,TENN.

1920	WAS	A	3		6	.385
1923	WAS	A	3		6	.250
1924	WAS	A	3		46	.333
1925	BOS	A	S-3		119	.313
1926	CIN	N	3		3	.200
		BRTR			180	.319
NON-PLAYING MANAGER PHI[N] 1939-41

PROUGH, HERSCHEL CLINTON
(BILL) OR (CLINT)
B.NOV.28,1887 MARKLE,IND.
D.DEC.29,1936 RICHMOND,IND.

1912	CIN	N	P		1	0- 0
		BRTR				

PRUDHOMME, JOHN OLGUS (AUGIE)
B.NOV.20,1902 FRIERSON,LA.

1929	DET	A	P		34	1- 6
		BRTR				

PRUESS, EARL HENRY (GIBBY)
B.APR.2,1895 CHICAGO,ILL.

1920	STL	A	0		1	.000

PRUETT, HUBERT SHELBY (SHUCKS)
B.SEPT.1,1900 MALDEN,MO.

1922	STL	A	P		39	7- 7
1923	STL	A	P		32	4- 7
1924	STL	A	P		33	3- 4
1927	PHI	N	P		31	7-17
1928	PHI	N	P		13	2- 4
1930	NY	N	P		45	5- 4
1932	BOS	N	P		18	1- 5
		BLTL			211	29-48

PRUETT, JAMES CALVIN
B.DEC.16,1917 NASHVILLE,TENN.

1944	PHI	A	C		3	.250
1945	PHI	A	C		6	.222
		BRTR			9	.231

PRUIETT, CHARLES LE ROY (TEX)
B.APR.10,1883 OSGOOD,IND.
D.MAR.6,1953 VENTURA,CAL.

1907	BOS	A	P		35	3-11
1908	BOS	A	P		13	1- 7
		BLTR			48	4-18

PRUITT, RONALD RALPH (RON)
B.OCT.21,1951 FLINT,MICH.

1975	TEX	A	C/0		14	.176
1976	CLE	A	0/C-3-1		47	.267
1977	CLE	A	0/C-3		78	.288
1978	CLE	A	C-0/3		71	.235
		BRTR			210	.261

PRYOR, GREGORY RUSSELL (GREG)
B.OCT.2,1949 MARIETTA,OHIO

1976	TEX	A	/2-S-3		5	.375
1978	CHI	A	2-S-3		82	.261
		BRTR			87	.265

PUCCINELLI, GEORGE LAWRENCE
(POOCH) OR (COUNT)
B.JUNE 22,1907 SAN FRANCISCO,CAL.
D.APR.16,1956 SAN FRANCISCO,CAL.

1930	STL	N	0		11	.563
1932	STL	N	0		31	.278
1934	STL	A	0		10	.231
1936	PHI	A	0		135	.278
		BRTR			187	.283

PUCKETT, TROY LEVI
B.DEC.10,1889 WINCHESTER,IND.
D.APR.13,1971 WINCHESTER,IND.

1911	PHI	N	P		1	0- 0
		BLTR				

PUENTE, MIGUEL ANTONIO [AGUILAR]
B.MAY 8,1948 SAN LUIS POTOSI,MEX

1970	SF	N	/P		6	1- 3
		BRTR				

PUHL, JOHN G.
B.1875 BAYONNE,N.J.
D.AUG.24,1900 BAYONNE,N.J.

1898	NY	N	3		2	.250
1899	NY	N	3		1	.000
					3	.200

PUHL, TERRY STEPHEN
B.JULY 8,1956 MELVILLE,SASK.,CAN

1977	HOU	N	0		60	.301
1978	HOU	N	*0		149	.289
		BLTR			209	.292

PUIG, RICHARD GERALD (RICH)
B.MAR.16,1953 TAMPA,FLA.

1974	NY	N	/2-3		4	.000
		BLTR				

PUJOLS, LUIS BIENVENIDO
[TORIBIO]
B.NOV.18,1955 SANTIAGO,D.R.

1977	HOU	N	/C		6	.067
1978	HOU	N	C/1		56	.131
		BRTR			62	.125

PUMPELLY, SPENCER ARMSTRONG
B.APR.11,1893 OWEGO,N.Y.
D.DEC.5,1973 SAYRE,PA.

1925	WAS	A	P		1	0- 0

PURCELL, WILLIAM ALOYSIUS (BLONDIE)
B.MAR.16,1854 PATERSON,N.J.
D.FEB.20,1912 TRENTON,N.J.

1879	SYR	N	P-C-		22	62	4-14
			0				.269
	CIN	N	P-0		2	12	0- 2
							.231
1880	CIN	N	P-S-		26	76	3-16
			0				.283
1881	CLE	N	0			20	.165
	BUF	N	P-0		9	30	4- 1
							.267
1882	BUF	N	P-0		4	84	2- 2
							.276
1883	PHI	N	P-S-		10	96	2- 8
			3-0				.270
1884	PHI	N	P-0		7	102	2- 5
							.244
1885	ATH	AA	P-0		1	66	0- 1
							.298
	BOS	N	0			21	2.18
1886	BAL	AA	0			27	.224
1887	BAL	AA	0			140	.305
1888	BAL	AA	0			101	.233
	ATH	AA	3-0			18	.167
1889	ATH	AA	0			130	.306
1890	ATH	AA	0			106	.287
				81	1091	17-49
						.272

PURDIN, JOHN NOLAN
B.JULY 16,1942 LYNX,OHIO

1964	LA	N	P		3	2- 0
1965	LA	N	P		11	2- 1
1968	LA	N	P		35	36	2- 3
1969	LA	N	/P		9	0- 0
		BRTR			58	59	6- 4

PURDY, EVERETT VIRGIL (PID)
B.JUNE 15,1904 BEATRICE,NEB.
D.JAN.16,1951 BEATRICE,NEB.

1926	CHI	A	0		11	.182
1927	CIN	N	0		18	.355
1928	CIN	N	0		70	.309
1929	CIN	N	0		82	.271
		BLTR			181	.293

YR	CL LEA POS	GP	G	REC

PURKEY, ROBERT THOMAS (BOB)
B.JULY 14,1929 PITTSBURGH,PA.
1954	PIT N P	36		3- 8
1955	PIT N P	14		2- 7
1956	PIT N P	2		0- 0
1957	PIT N P	48		11-14
1958	CIN N P	37		17-11
1959	CIN N P	38		13-18
1960	CIN N P	41		17-11
1961	CIN N P	36		16-12
1962	CIN N P	37		23- 5
1963	CIN N P	21		6-10
1964	CIN N P	34		11- 9
1965	STL N P	32		10- 9
1966	PIT N P	10	11	0- 1
	BRTR	386	387	129-115

PURNELL, JESSE RHOADES
B.MAY 11,1881 GLENSIDE,PA.
D.JULY 4,1966 PHILADELPHIA,PA.
| 1904 | PHI N 3 | 7 | | .105 |

PURNER, OSCAR E.
B.1873 WASHINGTON,D.C.
| 1895 | WAS N P | 1 | | 0- 0 |

PURTELL, WILLIAM PATRICK
B.JAN.6,1886 COLUMBUS,OHIO
D.MAR.17,1962 BRADENTON,FLA.
1908	CHI A 3	26		.130
1909	CHI A 2-3	103		.258
1910	CHI A 3	102		.222
	BOS A 3	49		.211
1911	BOS A 3	27		.280
1914	DET A 3	26		.171
	BRTR	333		.227

PUTNAM, EDDY WILLIAM (ED)
B.SEPT.25,1953 LOS ANGELES,CAL.
1976	CIN N /C-1	5		.429
1978	CHI N /3-1-C	17		.200
	BRTR	22		.250

PUTNAM, AUGUSTUS
B.NOV.21,1617 HARTFORD,CONN.
D.JAN.13,1890
NON-PLAYING MANAGER MAN[NA]1872

PUTNAM, PATRICK EDWARD (PAT)
B.DEC.3,1953 BETHEL,VT.
1977	TEX A /1	11		.308
1978	TEX A D/1	20		.152
	BLTR	31		.208

**PUTTMANN, AMBROSE NICHOLAS
(PUTTY) OR (BROSE)**
B.SEPT.9,1880 CINCINNATI,OHIO
D.JUNE 21,1936 JAMAICA,N.Y.
1903	NY A P	3		2- 0
1904	NY A P	10		2- 0
1905	NY A P	17		3- 7
1906	STL N P	4		2- 2
	TL	34		9- 9

PYBURN, JAMES EDWARD (JIM)
B.NOV.1,1932 FAIRFIELD,ALA.
1955	BAL A 3-0	39		.204
1956	BAL A 0	84		.173
1957	BAL A C-0	35		.225
	BRTR	158		.190

PYECHA, JOHN NICHOLAS
B.NOV.25,1931 ALIQUIPPA,PA.
| 1954 | CHI N P | 1 | | 0- 1 |
| | BRTR | | | |

PYLE, HARLAN ALBERT (FIRPO)
B.NOV.29,1905 BURCHARD,NEB.
| 1928 | CIN N P | 2 | | 0- 0 |
| | BRTR | | | |

PYLE, HARRY THOMAS (SHADOW)
B.OCT.30,1861 READING,PA.
D.NOV.26,1908 READING,PA.
1884	PHI N P	1		0- 1
1887	CHI N P	4		1- 3
		5		1- 4

**PYLE, HERBERT EWALD
(EWALD) OR (LEFTY)**
B.AUG.27,1910 ST.LOUIS,MO.
1939	STL A P	6		0- 2
1942	STL A P	2		0- 0
1943	WAS A P	18		4- 8
1944	NY N P	31		7-10
1945	NY N P	6		0- 0
	BOS N P	4		0- 1
	BLTL	67		11-21

PYTLAK, FRANK ANTHONY
B.JULY 30,1908 BUFFALO,N.Y.
D.MAY 8,1977 BUFFALO,N.Y.
1932	CLE A C	12		.241
1933	CLE A C	80		.310
1934	CLE A C	91		.260
1935	CLE A C	55		.295
1936	CLE A C	75		.321
1937	CLE A C	125		.315
1938	CLE A C	113		.308
1939	CLE A C	63		.268
1940	CLE A C-0	62		.141
1941	BOS A C	106		.271
1945	BOS A C	9		.118
1946	BOS A C	4		.143
	BRTR	795		.282

QUALLS, JAMES ROBERT (JIM)
B.OCT.9,1946 EXETER,CAL.
1969	CHI N 0/2	43		.250
1970	MON N /2-0	9		.111
1972	CAL A /0	11		.000
	BBTR	63		.223

**QUALTERS, THOMAS FRANCIS
(TOM) OR (MONEY BAGS)**
B.APR.1,1935 MC KEESPORT,PA.
1953	PHI N P	1		0- 0
1957	PHI N P	6		0- 0
1958	PHI N P	1		0- 0
	CHI A P	26		0- 0
	BRTR	34		0- 0

QUARLES, WILLIAM H.
B.1869 PETERSBURG,VA.
D.MAR.25,1897 PETERSBURG,VA.
1891	WAS AA P	4		2- 2
1893	BOS N P	4		2- 2
		8		4- 4

QUEEN, MELVIN DOUGLAS (MEL)
B.MAR.26,1942 JOHNSON CITY,N.Y.
1964	CIN N P	48		.200
1965	CIN N /0	5		.000
1966	CIN N 0/P	7	56	0- 0
				+127
1967	CIN N P	31	49	14- 8
1968	CIN N /P	5	10	0- 1
1969	CIN N /P	2		1- 0
1970	CAL A P	34	37	3- 6
1971	CAL A P	44	45	2- 2
1972	CAL A P	17		0- 0
	BLTR	140	269	20-17
				.179

QUEEN, MELVIN JOSEPH (MEL)
B.MAR.4,1918 MAXWELL,PA.
1942	NY A P	4		1- 0
1944	NY A P	10		6- 3
1946	NY A P	14		1- 1
1947	NY A P	5		0- 0
	PIT N P	14		3- 7
1948	PIT N P	25		4- 4
1950	PIT N P	33		5-14
1951	PIT N P	39		7- 9
1952	PIT N P	2		0- 2
	BRTR	146		27-40

**QUEEN, WILLIAM EDDLEMAN
(BILLY) OR (DOC)**
B.NOV.28,1928 GASTONIA,N.C.
| 1954 | MIL N 0 | 3 | | .000 |
| | BRTR | | | |

QUELLICH, GEORGE WILLIAM
B.FEB.10,1903 JOHNSVILLE,CAL.
D.AUG.21,1958 PLUMAS COUNTY,CAL
| 1931 | DET A 0 | 13 | | .222 |
| | BRTR | | | |

QUEST, JOSEPH L.
B.1852 NEW CASTLE,PA.
1871	CLE NA 2-S	3		-
1878	IND N 2	59		.213
1879	CHI N 2	79		.220
1880	CHI N 2-S	80		.245
1881	CHI N 2-S	77		.249
1882	DET N 2	42		.201
1883	DET N 2	36		.204
	STL AA 2	20		.253
1884	STL AA 2	81		.200
	PIT AA 2-S	12		.209
1885	DET N 2-S	55		.195
1886	ATH AA S	41		.200
	BRTR	585		-

QUICK, EDWARD (EDDIE)
B.BALTIMORE,MD.
D.MAY 19,1913 ROCKY FORD,COLO.
| 1903 | NY A P | 1 | | 0- 1 |

QUICK, JAMES HAROLD
B.OCT.4,1919 ROME,GA.
| 1939 | WAS A S | 12 | | .244 |
| | BRTR | | | |

**QUILICI, FRANCIS RALPH
(FRANK) OR (GUIDO)**
B.MAY 11,1939 CHICAGO,ILL.
1965	MIN A 2/S	56		.208
1967	MIN A 2/3-S	23		.105
1968	MIN A 2-3/S-1	97		.245
1969	MIN A 3-2/S	118		.174
1970	MIN A 2-3/S	111		.227
	BRTR	405		.214
NON-PLAYING MANAGER MIN[A] 1972-75

QUILLEN, LEON ABNER (LEE)
B.MAY 5,1882 NORTH BRANCH,MINN.
D.MAY 14,1965 ST.PAUL,MINN.
1906	CHI A S	3		.111
1907	CHI A 3	49		.192
	TR	52		.186

QUINLAN
B.1874 PHI NA S
| 1874 | PHI NA S | 1 | | .000 |

QUINLAN, LAWRENCE A.
B.MARLBORO,MASS.
| 1891 | BOS AA C | 2 | | .000 |

QUINLAN, THOMAS FINNERS
B.OCT.21,1887 SCRANTON,PA.
D.FEB.17,1966 SCRANTON,PA.
1913	STL N 0	13		.160
1915	CHI A 0	42		.193
	BLTL	55		.183

QUINN, CLARENCE C. (TAD)
B.TORRINGTON,CONN.
D.AUG.7,1946 WATERBURY,CONN.
1902	PHI A P	1		0- 1
1903	PHI A P	2		0- 0
	TR	3		0- 1

QUINN, FRANK J.
B.GRAND RAPIDS,MICH.
D.FEB.17,1920 CAMDEN,IND.
| 1899 | CHI N 0 | 12 | | .181 |

QUINN, FRANK WILLIAM
B.NOV.27,1927 SPRINGFIELD,MASS.
1949	BOS A P	8		0- 0
1950	BOS A P	1		0- 0
	BRTR	9		0- 0

QUINN, JOHN EDWARD (PICK)
B.SEPT.12,1885 FRAMINGHAM,MASS.
D.APR.9,1956 MARLBORO,MASS.
| 1911 | PHI N 0 | 1 | | .000 |
| | BRTR | | | |

**QUINN, JOHN PICUS (JACK)
[REAL NAME JOHN QUINN PICUS]**
B.JULY 5,1883 JANESVILLE,PA.
D.APR.17,1946 POTTSVILLE,PA.
1909	NY A P	22		9- 5
1910	NY A P	35		18-12
1911	NY A P	39		8- 9
1912	NY A P	18		5- 7
1913	BOS N P	8		4- 3
1914	BAL F P	46	48	26-14
1915	BAL F P	44	54	9-22
1918	CHI A P	6		5- 1
1919	NY A P	38		15-14
1920	NY A P	41		18-10
1921	NY A P	33		8- 7
1922	BOS A P	40		13-15
1923	BOS A P	42		13-17
1924	BOS A P	44		12-13
1925	BOS A P	19		7- 8
	PHI A P	18		6- 3
1926	PHI A P	31		10-11
1927	PHI A P	34		15-10
1928	PHI A P	31		18- 7
1929	PHI A P	35		11- 9
1930	PHI A P	35		9- 7
1931	BRO N P	39		5- 4
1932	BRO N P	42		3- 7
1933	CIN N P	14		0- 1
	BRTR	754	766	247-216

QUINN, JOSEPH C.
B.1851 CHICAGO,ILL.
D.JAN.2,1909 CHICAGO,ILL.
1871	KEK NA C	4		-
1875	WES NA C-0	11		-
	HAR NA C-0	4		-
	CHI NA C-0	16		-
1881	BOS N 1	1		.000
	WOR N C	2		.125
		38		-

YR	CL	LEA	POS	GP	G	REC

QUINN, JOSEPH J.
B.DEC.25,1864 SYDNEY,AUSTRALIA
D.NOV.12,1940 ST.LOUIS,MO.

YR	CL	LEA	POS	GP	G	REC
1884	STL	U	1		82	.261
1885	STL	N	1-3-0		97	.212
1886	STL	N	2-0		75	.232
1888	BOS	N	2		38	.201
1889	BOS	N	2-S		111	.261
1890	BOS	P	2		129	.296
1891	BOS	N	2		123	.247
1892	BOS	N	2		142	.219
1893	STL	N	2		135	.241
1894	STL	N	2		106	.274
1895	STL	N	M-2		134	.309
1896	STL	N	2		48	.231
	BAL	N	2		20	.295
1897	BAL	N	S-3		71	.264
1898	BAL	N	2-3-0		11	.281
	STL	N	2		99	.250
1899	CLE	N	M-2		146	.292
1900	STL	N	2-S-3		22	.259
	CIN	N	2		72	.279
1901	WAS	A	2		66	.251
	BRTR				1727	.262

QUINN, PATRICK
B.BOSTON,MASS.
D.MAR,1893

YR	CL	LEA	POS	GP	G	REC
1873	RES	NA	C		1	-
1875	ATL	NA	3-0		2	-
1877	CHI	N	0		4	.071
					7	-

QUINN, THOMAS OSCAR
B.APR.25,1864 ANNAPOLIS,MD.
D.JULY 24,1932 PITTSBURGH,PA.

YR	CL	LEA	POS	GP	G	REC
1886	PIT	AA	C		3	.000
1889	BAL	AA	C		54	.174
1890	PIT	P	C		56	.207
					113	.181

QUINN, WELLINGTON HUNT (WIMPY)
B.MAY 12,1918 BIRMINGHAM,ALA.
D.SEPT.1,1954 SANTA MONICA,CAL.

YR	CL	LEA	POS	GP	G	REC
1941	CHI	N	P		3	0- 0
	BRTR					

QUINTANA, LUIS JOAQUIN [SANTOS]
B.DEC.25,1951 VEGA BAJA,P.R.

YR	CL	LEA	POS	GP	G	REC
1974	CAL	A	P	18	2- 1	
1975	CAL	A	/P	4	0- 2	
	BLTL			22	2- 3	

QUINTON, MARSHALL J.
B.PHILADELPHIA,PA.

YR	CL	LEA	POS	GP	G	REC
1884	RIC	AA	C-0		26	.231
1885	ATH	AA	C		7	.207
					33	.226

QUIRK, ARTHUR LINCOLN (ART)
B.APR.11,1938 PROVIDENCE,R.I.

YR	CL	LEA	POS	GP	G	REC
1962	BAL	A	P	7	2- 2	
1963	WAS	A	P	7	1- 0	
	BRTL			14	3- 2	

QUIRK, JAMES PATRICK (JAMIE)
B.OCT.22,1954 WHITTIER,CAL.

YR	CL	LEA	POS	GP	G	REC
1975	KC	A	0/3		14	.256
1976	KC	A	0-S-3/1		64	.246
1977	MIL	A	0-0/3		93	.217
1978	KC	A	3/S		17	.207
	BLTR				188	.228

RABBITT, JOSEPH PATRICK
B.JAN.16,1900 FRONTENAC,KAN.
D.DEC.5,1969 NORWALK,CONN.

YR	CL	LEA	POS	GP	G	REC
1922	CLE	A	0		2	.333
	BLTR					

RABE, CHARLES HENRY (CHARLIE)
B.MAY 6,1932 BOYCE,TEX.

YR	CL	LEA	POS	GP	G	REC
1957	CIN	N	P		2	0- 1
1958	CIN	N	P		9	0- 3
	BLTL				11	0- 4

RACHUNOK, STEPHEN STEPANOVICH
(STEVE) OR (THE MAD RUSSIAN)
B.DEC.5,1916 RITTMAN,OHIO

YR	CL	LEA	POS	GP	G	REC
1940	BRO	N	P		2	0- 1
	BRTR					

RACKLEY, MARVIN EUGENE (MARV)
B.JULY 25,1921 SENECA,S.C.

YR	CL	LEA	POS	GP	G	REC
1947	BRO	N	0		18	.222
1948	BRO	N	0		88	.327
1949	BRO	N	0		9	.444
	PIT	N	0		11	.314
	BRO	N	0		54	.291
1950	CIN	N	H		5	.500
	BLTL				185	.317

RADATZ, RICHARD RAYMOND (DICK)
B.APR.2,1937 DETROIT,MICH.

YR	CL	LEA	POS	GP	G	REC
1962	BOS	A	P		62	9- 6
1963	BOS	A	P		66	15- 6
1964	BOS	A	P		79	16- 9
1965	BOS	A	P		63	9-11
1966	BOS	A	P		16	0- 2
	CLE	A	/P		39	0- 3
1967	CLE	A	P		3	0- 0
1967	CHI	N	P		20	1- 0
1969	DET	A	P		11	2- 2
	MON	N	P		22	0- 4
	BRTR				381	52-43

RADBORN, CHARLES GARDNER
(CHARLEY) OR (OLD HOSS)
B.DEC.11,1854 ROCHESTER,N.Y.
D.FEB.5,1897 BLOOMINGTON,ILL.

YR	CL	LEA	POS	GP	G	REC
1880	BUF	N	2-0		6	.143
1881	PRO	N	P-2-	37	70	25-12
			S-0			.221
1882	PRO	N	P-S-	54	83	33-19
			0			.239
1883	PRO	N	P-1-	72	89	44-23
			0			.283
1884	PRO	N	P-1-	72	85	60-12
			2-S-3-0			.233
1885	PRO	N	P-2-	49	65	28-21
			0			.232
1886	BOS	N	P	58	66	27-31
1887	BOS	N	P		48	24-23
1888	BOS	N	P		24	7-16
1889	BOS	N	P	32	35	20-11
1890	BOS	P	P		43	26-12
1891	CIN	N	P	25	27	12-12
	BRTR			514	641	306-192
						.241

RADBOURN, GEORGE B. (DORDY)
B.APR.8,1856 BLOOMINGTON,ILL.
D.JAN.1,1904 BLOOMINGTON,ILL.

YR	CL	LEA	POS	GP	G	REC
1883	DET	N	P-0		3	1- 1
						.154

RADCLIFF, JOHN J.
B.1846 CAMDEN,N.J.
D.JULY 26,1911

YR	CL	LEA	POS	GP	G	REC
1871	ATH	NA	S		28	.333
1872	BAL	NA	2-S-3		54	.283
1873	BAL	NA	2-S-3-0		45	-
1874	PHI	NA	1-2-S-3-0		22	-
1875	CEN	NA	S		5	-
					154	-

RADCLIFF, RAYMOND ALLEN (RIP)
B.JAN.19,1906 KIOWA,OKLA.
D.MAY 23,1962 ENID,OKLA.

YR	CL	LEA	POS	GP	G	REC
1934	CHI	A	0		14	.268
1935	CHI	A	0		146	.286
1936	CHI	A	0		138	.335
1937	CHI	A	0		144	.325
1938	CHI	A	1-0		129	.330
1939	CHI	A	1-0		113	.264
1940	STL	A	1-0		150	.342
1941	STL	A	0		19	.282
	DET	A	0		96	.317
1942	DET	A	1-0		62	.250
1943	DET	A	1-0		70	.261
	BLTL				1081	.311

RADEBAUGH, ROY
B.FEB.22,1884 CHAMPAIGN,ILL.
D.JAN.17,1945 CEDAR RAPIDS,IOWA

YR	CL	LEA	POS	GP	G	REC
1911	STL	N	P		2	0- 0
	BRTR					

RADER, DAVID MARTIN (DAVE)
B.DEC.26,1948 CLAREMORE,OKLA.

YR	CL	LEA	POS	GP	G	REC
1971	SF	N	/C		3	.000
1972	SF	N	*C		133	.259
1973	SF	N	*C		148	.229
1974	SF	N	*C		113	.291
1975	SF	N	C		98	.291
1976	SF	N	C		88	.263
1977	STL	N	C		66	.263
1978	CHI	N	*C		116	.203
	BLTR				765	.254

RADER, DONALD RUSSELL
B.SEPT.5,1893 WOLCOTT,IND.

YR	CL	LEA	POS	GP	G	REC
1913	CHI	A	3-0		4	.333
1921	PHI	N	S		9	.281
	BLTR				13	.286

RADER, DOUGLAS LEE (DOUG)
(ROJO) OR (THE RED ROOSTER)
B.JULY 30,1944 CHICAGO,ILL.

YR	CL	LEA	POS	GP	G	REC
1967	HOU	N	1/3		47	.333
1968	HOU	N	3/1		98	.267
1969	HOU	N	*3/1		155	.246
1970	HOU	N	*3/1		156	.252
1971	HOU	N	*3		135	.244
1972	HOU	N	*3		152	.237
1973	HOU	N	*3		154	.254
1974	HOU	N	*3		152	.257
1975	HOU	N	*3/S		129	.223
1976	SD	N	*3		139	.257
1977	SD	N	3		52	.271
	TOR	A	3-0/1-0		96	.240
	BRTR				1465	.251

RADER, DREW LEON (LEFTY)
B.MAY 14,1901 ELMIRA,N.Y.
D.JUNE 5,1975 CATSKILL,N.Y.

YR	CL	LEA	POS	GP	G	REC
1921	PIT	N	P		1	0- 0
	BRTL					

RADFORD, PAUL REVERE (SHORTY)
B.OCT.14,1861 ROXBURY,MASS.
D.FEB.21,1945 BOSTON,MASS.

YR	CL	LEA	POS	GP	G	REC
1883	BOS	N	0		71	.205
1884	PRO	N	P-1-	2	96	0- 0
			S-0			.202
1885	PRO	N	P-S-	2	105	.242
			0			
1886	KC	N	S-0		122	.229
1887	MET	AA	S-0		128	.404
1888	BRO	AA	0		91	.224
1889	CLE	N	0		136	.236
1890	CLE	P	S-0		122	.292
1891	BOS	AA	S		133	.257
1892	WAS	N	S-3-0		124	.254
1893	WAS	N	0		124	.228
1894	WAS	N	2-S-0		93	.233
	BRTR			4	1355	0- 1
						.259

RADTKE, JACK WILLIAM
B.APR.14,1913 DENVER,COLO.

YR	CL	LEA	POS	GP	G	REC
1936	BRO	N	2		33	.097
	BBTR					

RAETHER, HAROLD HERMAN
(HAL) OR (BUD)
B.OCT.10,1932 LAKE MILLS,WIS.

YR	CL	LEA	POS	GP	G	REC
1954	PHI	A	P		1	0- 0
1957	KC	A	P		1	0- 0
	BRTR				4	0- 0

RAFFENSBERGER, KENNETH DAVID (KEN)
B.AUG.8,1917 YORK,PA.

YR	CL	LEA	POS	GP	G	REC
1939	STL	N	P		1	0- 0
1940	CHI	N	P		43	7- 9
1941	CHI	N	P		10	0- 1
1943	PHI	N	P		1	0- 1
1944	PHI	N	P	37	38	13-20
1945	PHI	N	P		5	0- 3
1946	PHI	N	P		39	8-15
1947	PHI	N	P		10	2- 6
	CIN	N	P		19	8- 5
1948	CIN	N	P		40	11-12
1949	CIN	N	P		41	18-17
1950	CIN	N	P		38	14-19
1951	CIN	N	P		42	16-17
1952	CIN	N	P		38	17-13
1953	CIN	N	P		39	7-14
1954	CIN	N	P		6	0- 2
	BRTL			396	397	119-154

RAFFO, ALBERT MARTIN (AL)
B.NOV.27,1941 SAN FRANCISCO,CAL.

YR	CL	LEA	POS	GP	G	REC
1969	PHI	N	P		45	1- 3
	BRTR					

RAFTER, JOHN CORNELIUS (JACK)
B.FEB.20,1875 TROY,N.Y.
D.JAN.5,1943 TROY,N.Y.

YR	CL	LEA	POS	GP	G	REC
1904	PIT	N	C		1	.000
	TR					

RAFTERY, THOMAS FRANCIS
B.OCT.5,1881 BOSTON,MASS.
D.DEC.31,1954 BOSTON,MASS.

YR	CL	LEA	POS	GP	G	REC
1909	CLE	A	0		8	.269

YR CL LEA POS GP G REC

RAGAN, DON CARLOS PATRICK (PAT)
B.NOV.15,1888 BLANCHARD,IOWA
D.SEPT.4,1956 LOS ANGELES,CAL.

YR	CL	LEA	POS	GP	G	REC
1909	CIN	N	P		2	0- 1
	CHI	N	P		2	0- 0
1911	BRO	N	P		22	4- 3
1912	BRO	N	P		36	7-18
1913	BRO	N	P		44	15-18
1914	BRO	N	P		38	10-15
1915	BRO	N	P		4	1- 0
	BOS	N	P		34	16-12
1916	BOS	N	P		31	9- 9
1917	BOS	N	P		30	6- 9
1918	BOS	N	P		30	8-17
1919	BOS	N	P		4	0- 2
	NY	N	P		7	1- 0
	CHI	A	P		1	0- 0
1923	PHI	N	P		1	0- 0
	BRTR				286	77-104

RAGLAND, FRANK ROLAND
B.MAY 26,1904 WATER VALLEY,MISS
D.JULY 28,1959 PARIS,MISS.

YR	CL	LEA	POS	GP	G	REC
1932	WAS	A	P		12	1- 0
1933	PHI	N	P		11	0- 4
	BRTR				23	1- 4

RAGLAND, THOMAS (TOM)
B.JUNE 16,1946 TALLADEGA,ALA.

YR	CL	LEA	POS	GP	G	REC
1971	WAS	A	2		10	.174
1972	TEX	A	2/3-S		25	.172
1973	CLE	A	2/S		67	.257
	BRTR				102	.231

RAICH, ERIC JAMES
B.NOV.1,1951 DETROIT,MICH.

YR	CL	LEA	POS	GP	G	REC
1975	CLE	A	P		18	7- 8
1976	CLE	A	/P		1	0- 0
	BRTR				19	7- 8

RAINES, LAWRENCE GLENN HOPE (LARRY)
B.MAR.9,1930 ST.ALBANS,W.VA.

YR	CL	LEA	POS	GP	G	REC
1957	CLE	A	2-S-3-O		96	.262
1958	CLE	A	2		7	.000
	BRTR				103	.253

RAINEY, JOHN PAUL
B.JULY 26,1864 BIRMINGHAM,MICH.
D.NOV.11,1912 DETROIT,MICH.

YR	CL	LEA	POS	GP	G	REC
1887	NY	N	3		17	.349
1890	BUF	P	O		42	.248
	BLTR				59	.276

RAJSICH, DAVID CHRISTOPHER (DAVE)
B.SEPT.28,1951 YOUNGSTOWN,OHIO

YR	CL	LEA	POS	GP	G	REC
1978	NY	A	/P		4	0- 0
	BLTL					

RAKOW, EDWARD CHARLES (ED) OR (ROCK)
B.MAY 30,1936 PITTSBURGH,PA.

YR	CL	LEA	POS	GP	G	REC
1960	LA	N	P		9	0- 1
1961	KC	A	P		45	2- 8
1962	KC	A	P		42	14-17
1963	KC	A	P		34	9-10
1964	DET	A	P		42	8- 9
1965	DET	A	/P		6	0- 0
1967	ATL	N	P		17	3- 2
	BBTR				195	36-47
	BR 1960-61					

RALEIGH, JOHN AUSTIN
B.APR.21,1890 ELKHORN,WIS.
D.AUG.24,1955 ESCONDIDO,CAL.

YR	CL	LEA	POS	GP	G	REC
1909	STL	N	P		15	1-10
1910	STL	N	P		3	0- 0
	BRTL				18	1-10

RALSTON, SAMUEL BERYL (DOC)
B.AUG.3,1885 PIERPONT,OHIO
D.AUG.29,1950 LANCASTER,PA.

YR	CL	LEA	POS	GP	G	REC
1910	WAS	A	O		22	.205
	BRTR					

RAMAZZOTTI, ROBERT LOUIS (BOB)
B.JAN.16,1917 ELANORA,PA.

YR	CL	LEA	POS	GP	G	REC
1946	BRO	N	2-3		62	.208
1948	BRO	N	2		4	.000
1949	BRO	N	3		5	.154
	CHI	N	2-S-3		65	.179
1950	CHI	N	2-S-3		61	.262
1951	CHI	N	2-S-3		73	.247
1952	CHI	N	2		50	.284
1953	CHI	N	2		26	.154
	BRTR				346	.230

RAMBERT, ELMER DONALD (PEP)
B.AUG.1,1916 CLEVELAND,OHIO

YR	CL	LEA	POS	GP	G	REC
1939	PIT	N	P		2	0- 0
1940	PIT	N	P		3	0- 1
	BRTR				5	0- 1

RAMBO, WARREN DAWSON (PETE)
B.NOV.1,1906 THOROJGHFARE,N.J.

YR	CL	LEA	POS	GP	G	REC
1926	PHI	N	P		1	0- 0
	BRTR					

YR CL LEA POS GP G REC

RAMIREZ, MILTON [BARBOZA] (MILT)
B.APR.2,1950 MAYAGUEZ,P.R.

YR	CL	LEA	POS	GP	G	REC
1970	STL	N	S/3		62	.190
1971	STL	N	/S		4	.273
	BRTR				66	.200

RAMIREZ, ORLANDO [LEAL]
B.DEC.18,1951 CARTAGENA,COLOMBIA

YR	CL	LEA	POS	GP	G	REC
1974	CAL	A	S		31	.163
1975	CAL	A	S		44	.240
1976	CAL	A	S		30	.200
1977	CAL	A	/2-S		25	.077
	BRTR				130	.197

RAMOS, DOMINGO ANTONIO
[DE RAMOS]
B.MAR.29,1958 SANTIAGO,D.R.

YR	CL	LEA	POS	GP	G	REC
1978	NY	A	/S		1	.000
	BRTR					

RAMOS, JESUS MANUEL [GARCIA]
(CHUCHO)
B.APR.12,1918 MATURIN,VENEZ.

YR	CL	LEA	POS	GP	G	REC
1944	CIN	N	O		4	.500
	BRTL					

RAMOS, PEDRO [GUERRA]
(PEDRO) OR (PETE)
B.APR.28,1935 PINAR DEL RIO,CUBA

YR	CL	LEA	POS	GP	G	REC
1955	WAS	A	P	45	59	5-11
1956	WAS	A	P	37	56	12-10
1957	WAS	A	P	43	56	12-16
1958	WAS	A	P	43	53	14-18
1959	WAS	A	P	37	45	13-19
1960	WAS	A	P	43	53	11-18
1961	MIN	A	P	42	53	11-20
1962	CLE	A	P	37	39	10-12
1963	CLE	A	P	36	54	9- 8
1964	CLE	A	P	36	44	7-10
	NY	A	P		13	1- 0
1965	NY	A	P		65	5- 5
1966	NY	A	P		52	3- 9
1967	PHI	N	/P		6	0- 0
1969	PIT	N	/P		5	0- 1
	CIN	N	P		38	4- 3
1970	WAS	A	/P	4	5	0- 0
	BBTR			582	696	117-160
	BR 1955-59					

RAMOS, ROBERTO
B.NOV.5,1955 HAVANA,CUBA

YR	CL	LEA	POS	GP	G	REC
1978	MON	N	/C		2	.000
	BRTR					

RAMSDELL, JAMES WILLARD
(WILLIE) OR (THE KNUCK)
B.APR.4,1916 WILLIAMSBURG,KAN.
D.OCT.8,1969 WICHITA,KAN.

YR	CL	LEA	POS	GP	G	REC
1947	BRO	N	P		2	1- 1
1948	BRO	N	P		27	4- 4
1950	BRO	N	P		5	1- 2
	CIN	N	P		27	7-12
1951	CIN	N	P		31	9-17
1952	CHI	N	P		19	2- 3
	BRTR				111	24-39

RAMSEY, MICHAEL JEFFREY (MIKE)
B.MAR.29,1954 ROANOKE,VA.

YR	CL	LEA	POS	GP	G	REC
1978	STL	N	/S		12	.200
	BBTR					

RAMSEY, THOMAS A. (TOAD)
B.AUG.8,1864 INDIANAPOLIS,IND.
D.MAR.27,1906 INDIANAPOLIS,IND.

YR	CL	LEA	POS	GP	G	REC
1885	LOU	AA	P		9	3- 4
1886	LOU	AA	P		66	37-27
1887	LOU	AA	P		66	39-27
1888	LOU	AA	P	38	41	8-30
1889	LOU	AA	P		20	2-18
	STL	AA	P		6	4- 2
1890	STL	AA	P		44	22-14
	BRTL			249	252	115-122

RAMSEY, WILLIAM THRACE
(BILL) OR (SQUARE JAW)
B.FEB.20,1921 OSCEOLA,ARK.

YR	CL	LEA	POS	GP	G	REC
1945	BOS	N	O		78	.292
	BRTR					

RAND, RICHARD HILTON (DICK)
B.MAR.7,1931 SOUTH GATE,CAL.

YR	CL	LEA	POS	GP	G	REC
1953	STL	N	C		9	.290
1955	STL	N	C		3	.300
1957	PIT	N	C		60	.219
	BRTR				72	.240

RANDALL, NEWTON J.
B.FEB.3,1881 NEW LOWELL,ONT.,CANADA
D.MAY 3,1955 DULUTH,MINN.

YR	CL	LEA	POS	GP	G	REC
1907	CHI	N	O		21	.205
	BOS	N	O		73	.213
					94	.211

RANDALL, ROBERT LEE (BOB)
B.JUNE 6,1948 NORTON,KAN.

YR	CL	LEA	POS	GP	G	REC
1976	MIN	A	*2		153	.267
1977	MIN	A	*2/1-3		103	.239
1978	MIN	A	*2/3		119	.270
	BRTR				375	.260

YR CL LEA POS GP G REC

RANDLE, LEONARD SHENOFF (LEN)
B.FEB.12,1949 LONG BEACH,CAL.

YR	CL	LEA	POS	GP	G	REC
1971	WAS	A	2		75	.219
1972	TEX	A	2/S-O		74	.193
1973	TEX	A	/2-O		10	.207
1974	TEX	A	3-2-O/S		151	.302
1975	TEX	A	2-O-3/C-S		156	.276
1976	TEX	A	*2-O/3		142	.224
1977	NY	N	*3-2/O-S		136	.304
1978	NY	N	*3/2		132	.233
	BBTR				876	.259
	BR 1971					

RANDOLPH, WILLIAM LARRY (WILLIE)
B.JULY 6,1954 HOLLY HILL,S.C.

YR	CL	LEA	POS	GP	G	REC
1975	PIT	N	2/3		30	.164
1976	NY	A	*2		125	.267
1977	NY	A	*2		147	.274
1978	NY	A	*2		134	.279
	BRTR				436	.269

RANEW, MERRITT THOMAS
B.MAY 10,1938 ALBANY,GA.

YR	CL	LEA	POS	GP	G	REC
1962	HOU	N	C		71	.234
1963	CHI	N	C-1		78	.338
1964	CHI	N	C		16	.091
	MIL	N	C		9	.118
1965	CAL	A	C		41	.209
1969	SEA	A	C/O-3		54	.247
	BLTR				269	.247

RANEY, FRANK ROBERT DONALD (RIBS)
[REAL NAME FRANK
ROBERT DONALD RANISZEWSKI]
B.FEB.16,1923 DETROIT,MICH.

YR	CL	LEA	POS	GP	G	REC
1949	STL	A	P		3	1- 2
1950	STL	A	P		1	0- 1
	BRTR				4	1- 3

RANISZEWSKI, FRANK ROBERT DONALD
[PLAYED UNDER NAME OF
FRANK ROBERT DONALD RANEY]

RAPP, EARL WELLINGTON
B.MAY 20,1921 CORUNNA,MICH.

YR	CL	LEA	POS	GP	G	REC
1949	DET	A	H		1	.000
	CHI	A	O		19	.259
1951	NY	N	H		13	.091
	STL	A	O		26	.327
1952	STL	A	O		30	.143
	WAS	A	O		46	.284
	BLTR				135	.262

RAPP, JOSEPH ALOYSIUS (GOLDIE)
B.FEB.6,1892 CINCINNATI,OHIO
D.JULY 1,1966 LA MESA,CAL.

YR	CL	LEA	POS	GP	G	REC
1921	NY	N	3		58	.215
	PHI	N	3		52	.277
1922	PHI	N	S-3		119	.253
1923	PHI	N	3		47	.263
	BBTR				276	.253

RAPP, VERNON FRED (VERN)
B.MAY 11,1928 ST.LOUIS,MO.
NON-PLAYING MANAGER STL[N] 1977-78

RARIDEN, WILLIAM ANGEL (BILL)
OR (BEDFORD BILL)
B.FEB.4,1888 BEDFORD,IND.
D.AUG.28,1942 BEDFORD,IND.

YR	CL	LEA	POS	GP	G	REC
1909	BOS	N	C		13	.167
1910	BOS	N	C		49	.226
1911	BOS	N	C		69	.228
1912	BOS	N	C		79	.223
1913	BOS	N	C		95	.236
1914	IND	F	C		132	.236
1915	NEW	F	C		142	.278
1916	NY	N	C		120	.222
1917	NY	N	C		101	.271
1918	NY	N	C		69	.224
1919	CIN	N	C		74	.216
1920	CIN	N	C		39	.248
	BRTR				982	.239

RASCHI, VICTOR JOHN ANGELO (VIC)
B.MAR.28,1919 W.SPRINGFIELD,MASS.

YR	CL	LEA	POS	GP	G	REC
1946	NY	A	P		2	2- 0
1947	NY	A	P		15	7- 2
1948	NY	A	P		36	19- 8
1949	NY	A	P		38	21-10
1950	NY	A	P		33	21- 8
1951	NY	A	P		35	21-10
1952	NY	A	P		31	16- 6
1953	NY	A	P		28	13- 6
1954	STL	N	P		30	8- 9
1955	STL	N	P		1	0- 1
	KC	A	P		20	4- 6
	BRTR				269	132-66

RASMUSSEN, ERIC RALPH
[BORN HAROLD RALPH RASMUSSEN]
B.MAR.22,1952 RACINE,WIS.

YR	CL	LEA	POS	GP	G	REC
1975	STL	N	P		14	5- 5
1976	STL	N	P		43	6-12
1977	STL	N	P		34	11-17
1978	STL	N	P		10	2- 5
	SD	N	P		27	12-10
	BRTR				128	36-49

```
YR  CL LEA POS      GP    G    REC
```

RASMUSSEN, HENRY
B.APR.18,1895 CHICAGO,ILL.
1915 CHI F P   2   0- 0

RATH, FREDERICK HELSHER (FRED)
B.SEP.1,1943 LITTLE ROCK,ARK.
1968 CHI A /P   5   0- 0
1969 CHI A /P   3   0- 2
       BRTR   8   0- 2

RATH, MORRIS CHARLES
B.DEC.25,1886 MOBEETIE,TEX.
D.NOV.18,1945 UPPER DARBY,PA.
1909 PHI A S-3   7   .269
1910 PHI A 3   15   .160
     CLE A 3   27   .191
1912 CHI A 2   157   .272
1913 CHI A 2   90   .197
1919 CIN N 2   138   .264
1920 CIN N 2-3-0   129   .267
       BLTR   563   .254

RATLIFF, KELLY EUGENE (GENE)
B.SEP.28,1945 MACON,GA.
1965 HOU N /H   4   .000
       BRTR

RATLIFF, PAUL HAWTHORNE
B.JAN.23,1944 SAN DIEGO,CAL.
1963 MIN A C   10   .190
1970 MIN A C   69   .268
1971 MIN A C   21   .159
     MIL A C   23   .171
1972 MIL A C   22   .071
       BLTR   145   .205

RAU, DOUGLAS JAMES (DOUG)
B.DEC.15,1948 COLUMBUS,TEX.
1972 LA N /P   7   2- 2
1973 LA N P   31   4- 2
1974 LA N P   36 13-11
1975 LA N P   38 15- 9
1976 LA N P   34 16-12
1977 LA N P   32 14- 8
1978 LA N P   30 15 -9
       BLTL   208 79-35

RAUB, THOMAS JEFFERSON
B.DEC.1,1870 RAUBSVILLE,PA.
D.FEB.16,1949 PHILLIPSBURG,N.J.
1903 CHI N C   27   .226
1906 STL N C   22   .282
       BRTR   49   .253

RAUCH, ROBERT JOHN (BOB)
B.JUNE 16,1949 BROOKINGS,S.D.
1972 NY N P   19   0- 1
       BRTR

RAUDMAN, ROBERT JOYCE
(BOB) OR (SHORTY)
B.MAR.14,1942 ERIE,PA.
1966 CHI N /O   8   .241
1967 CHI N /O   8   .154
       BLTL   16   .200

RAUTZHAN, CLARENCE GEORGE (LANCE)
B.AUG.20,1952 POTTSVILLE,PA.
1977 LA N P   25   4- 1
1978 LA N P   43   2- 1
       BRTL   68   6- 2

RAWLEY, SHANE WILLIAM
B.JULY 27,1955 RACINE,WIS.
1978 SEA A P   52   53 4- 9
       BRTL

RAWLINGS, JOHN WILLIAM (RED)
B.AUG.17,1892 BLOOMFIELD,IOWA
D.OCT.16,1972 INGLEWOOD,CAL.
1914 CIN N 3   33   .217
     KC F S   61   .209
1915 KC F S   120   .213
1917 BOS N 2-S   122   .256
1918 BOS N 2-S-0   111   .207
1919 BOS N 2-S-0   77   .255
1920 BOS N 2   5   .000
     PHI N 2   98   .234
1921 PHI N 2   60   .291
     NY N 2   86   .267
1922 NY N 2-3   88   .282
1923 PIT N 2   119   .284
     PIT N H   3   .333
1925 PIT N 2   36   .282
1926 PIT N 2   61   .232
       BRTR   1080   .249

RAY, CARL GRADY
B.JAN.31,1889 DANBURY,N.C.
D.APR.3,1970 WALNUT COVE,N.C.
1915 PHI A P   2   0- 1
1916 PHI A P   3   0- 1
       BLTL   5   0- 2

RAY, IRVING BURTON (STUBBY)
B.JAN.22,1864 HARRINGTON,ME.
D.FEB.23,1948 HARRINGTON,ME.
1888 BOS N S   50   .247
1889 BOS N S   9   .312
     BAL AA S   27   .330
1890 BAL AA S   38   .347
1891 BAL AA S-0   103   .277
       TL   227   .290

RAY, JAMES FRANCIS (JIM) OR (STING)
B.DEC.1,1944 ROCK HILL,S.C.
1965 HOU N /P   3   0- 2
1968 HOU N /P   1   0- 0
1969 HOU N P   41   42 2- 3
1969 HOU N P   40   8- 2
1970 HOU N P   52   6- 3
1971 HOU N P   47   10- 4
1972 HOU N P   54   10- 9
1973 HOU N P   42   6- 4
1974 DET A P   28   1- 3
       BRTR   308 309 43-30

RAY, ROBERT HENRY (FARMER)
B.SEP.7,1886 FT.LYON,COLO.
D.MAR.11,1963 ELECTRA,TEX.
1910 STL A P   21   4-10

RAYDON, CURTIS LOWELL (CURT)
B.NOV.18,1933 BLOOMINGTON,ILL.
1958 PIT N P   31   8- 4
       BRTR

RAYMER, FREDERICK CHARLES
B.NOV.12,1875 LEAVENWORTH,KAN.
D.JUNE 11,1957 LOS ANGELES,CAL.
1901 CHI N S-3   118   .235
1904 BOS N 2   114   .210
1905 BOS N 2   136   .211
       TR   368   .218

RAYMOND, ARTHUR LAWRENCE (BUGS)
B.FEB.24,1882 CHICAGO,ILL.
D.SEPT.7,1912 CHICAGO,ILL.
1904 DET A P   5   0- 1
1907 STL N P   10   3- 4
1908 STL N P   48 13-25
1909 NY N P   39 18-12
1910 NY N P   19   4-11
1911 NY N P   17   6- 4
       BRTR   138 46-57

RAYMOND, HARRY H. (JACK)
[REAL NAME HARRY H. TRUMAN]
B.FEB.20,1862 UTICA,N.Y.
D.MAR.21,1925 SAN DIEGO,CAL.
1888 LOU AA 3   32   .208
1889 LOU AA P-3   1 130   0- 0
                           .241
1890 LOU AA 3   122   .280
1891 LOU AA S   14   .207
1892 PIT N 3   11   .083
     WAS N 3   4   .067
                   1 313   0- 0
                           .247

RAYMOND, JOSEPH CLAUDE MARC
(CLAUDE) OR (FRENCHY)
B.MAY 7,1937 ST.JEAN,QUE.,CANADA
1959 CHI A P   3   0- 0
1961 MIL N P   13   1- 0
1962 MIL N P   26   5- 5
1963 MIL N P   45   4- 6
1964 HOU N P   38   41 5- 5
1965 HOU N P   33   34 7- 4
1966 HOU N P   62   7- 5
1967 HOU N P   21   0- 4
     ATL N P   28   4- 1
1968 ATL N P   36   3- 5
1969 ATL N P   33   2- 2
     MON N P   15   1- 2
1970 MON N P   59   6- 7
1971 MON N P   37   1- 7
       BRTR   449 453 46-53

RAYMOND, LOUIS ANTHONY
B.DEC.11,1894 BUFFALO,N.Y.
1919 PHI N 2   1   .500

RAZIANO, BARRY JOHN
B.FEB.5,1947 NEW ORLEANS,LA.
1973 KC A P   2   0- 0
1974 CAL A P   13   1- 2
       BBTR   15   1- 2

REACH, ALFRED JAMES
B.MAY 25,1840 LONDON,ENGLAND
D.JAN.14,1928
1871 ATH NA 2   26   .371
1872 ATH NA 1-0   23   .191
1873 ATH NA 2-0   12   -
1874 ATH NA 0   14   -
1875 ATH NA 2-0   5   -
       TL   80   -

REACH, ROBERT
B.AUG.28,1843 WILLIAMSBURG,N.Y.
D.MAY 9,1922
1872 OLY NA S   1   .200
1873 NAT NA S   1   -
                       2   -

REAGAN, ARTHUR (RIP)
B.1882 FT.SCOTT,KAN.
1903 CIN N P   3   0- 2
       BRTR

REAGAN, J.
1898 NY N O   2   .200

REAMS, LEROY
B.AUG.11,1943 PINE BLUFF,ARK.
1969 PHI N /H   1   .000
       BLTR

REARDON, JEREMIAH
B.1866 ST.LOUIS,MO. DECEASED
1886 STL N P   1   0- 1
     CIN AA P-0   1   0- 1
                           .000
                       2   0- 2
                           .143

REARDON, PHILIP MICHAEL
B.OCT.3,1883 BROOKLYN,N.Y.
D.SEPT.28,1920 BROOKLYN,N.Y.
1906 BRO N O   5   .071
       BRTR

REBEL, ARTHUR ANTHONY
B.MAR.4,1915 CINCINNATI,OHIO
1938 PHI N O   7   .222
1945 STL N O   26   .347
       BLTL   33   .333

REBERGER, FRANK BEALL
(FRANK) OR (CRANE)
B.JUNE 7,1944 CALDWELL,IDAHO
1968 CHI N /P   3   0- 1
1969 SO N P   67   1- 2
1970 SF N P   45   48 7- 8
1971 SF N P   13   16 3- 0
1972 SF N P   20   22 3- 4
       BRTR   148 196 14-15

RECCIUS, J. WILLIAM (BILL)
B.1847 FRANKFURT-ON-MAIN,GERMANY
D.JAN.25,1911 LOUISVILLE,KY.
NON-PLAYING MANAGER LOU[AA] 1882-83

RECCIUS, JOHN
B.JUNE 7,1862 LOUISVILLE,KY.
D.SEPT.1,1930 LOUISVILLE,KY.
1882 LOU AA S   14   73 4- 6
                           .216
1883 LOU AA P-0   1   17   0- 0
                           .154
                  19   90   4- 6
                           .205

RECCIUS, PHILLIP
B.JUNE 7,1862 LOUISVILLE,KY.
D.FEB.19,1903 LOUISVILLE,KY.
1882 LOU AA O   3   .091
1883 LOU AA O   1   .333
1884 LOU AA P-S-   13   75 0- 7
     3   .249
1885 LOU AA P-3   5 105 0- 5
                           .240
1886 LOU AA P-0   1   5 0- 1
                           .267
1887 LOU AA S-0   11   .341
     CLE AA 3   62   .295
1888 LOU AA 3   2   .223
1890 ROC AA 0   1   .000
                           5-13
                      19 265 .243

REDDING, PHILIP HAYDEN
B.JAN.25,1890 CRYSTAL SPRINGS,MISS.
D.MAR.31,1928 GREENWOOD,MISS.
1912 STL N P   3   2- 1
1913 STL N P   1   0- 0
       BLTR   4   2- 1

REDER, JOHN ANTHONY
B.SEPT.24,1909 LUBLIN,POLAND
1932 BOS A 1   17   .135
       BRTR

REDFERN, GEORGE HOWARD (BUCK)
B.APR.7,1902 ASHEVILLE,N.C.
D.SEPT.8,1964 ASHEVILLE,N.C.
1928 CHI A 2   86   .234
1929 CHI A 2   21   .130
       BRTR   107   .218

REDFERN, PETER IRVINE (PETE)
B.AUG.25,1954 GLENDALE,CAL.
1976 MIN A P   23   8- 8
1977 MIN A P   30   6- 9
1978 MIN A /P   3   0- 2
       BRTR   56 14-19

YR	CL LEA POS	GP	G	REC

REDMON, GLENN VINCENT
B.JAN.11,1948 DETROIT,MICH.
1974 SF N /2   7   .235
    BRTR

REDMOND, HARRY JOHN
B.SEPT.13,1887 CLEVELAND,OHIO
D.JULY 10,1960 CLEVELAND,OHIO
1909 BRO N 2   6   .100
    TR

REDMOND, HOWARD WAYNE (WAYNE)
B.NOV.25,1945 ATHENS,ALA.
1965 DET A /O   4   .000
1969 DET A /H   5   .000
    BRTR   9   .000

REDMOND, JOHN MC KITTRICK (RED)
B.SEPT.3,1910 FLORENCE,ARIZ.
D.JULY 27,1968 GARLAND,TEX.
1935 WAS A C   22   .176
    BLTR

REDMOND, WILLIAM T.
B.BROOKLYN,N.Y.
1875 RS NA S-3   19   -
1877 CIN N S   3   .250
1878 MIL N S-O   47   .229
    BLTL   69   -

REECE, ROBERT SCOTT (BOB)
B.JAN.5,1951 SACRAMENTO,CAL.
1978 MON N /C   9   .182
    BRTR

REED
1874 BAL NA O   1   .000

REED, HOWARD DEAN (HOWIE) OR (OIZ)
B.DEC.21,1936 DALLAS,TEX.
1958 KC A P   3   1- 0
1959 KC A P   6   0- 3
1960 KC A P   1   0- 0
1964 LA N P   26   3- 4
1965 LA N P   38   7- 5
1966 LA N /P   1   0- 0
    CAL A P   19   0- 1
1967 HOU N /P   4   1- 1
1969 MON N P   31   6- 7
1970 MON N P   57   6- 5
1971 MON N P   43   2- 3
    BRTR   229   26-29

REED, JOHN BURWELL (JACK)
B.FEB.2,1933 SILVER CITY,MISS.
1961 NY A O   28   .154
1962 NY A O   88   .302
1963 NY A O   106   .205
    BRTR   222   .233

REED, MILTON D.
B.JULY 4,1890 ATLANTA,GA.
D.JULY 27,1938 ATLANTA,GA.
1911 STL N H   1   .000
1913 PHI N 2-S   13   .240
1914 PHI N S   44   .206
1915 BRO F 2   10   .290
    BLTR   68   .224

REED, RALPH EDWIN (TED)
B.OCT.18,1890 BEAVER,PA.
D.FEB.16,1959 BEAVER,PA.
1915 NEW F 3   20   .247
    BRTR

REED, ROBERT EDWARD (BOB)
B.JAN.12,1945 BOSTON,MASS.
1969 DET A /P   8   0- 0
1970 DET A P   16   17   2- 4
    BRTR   24   25   2- 4

REED, RONALD LEE (RON)
B.NOV.2,1942 LAPORTE,IND.
1966 ATL N /P   2   1- 1
1967 ATL N /P   3   1- 1
1968 ATL N P   11   11-10
1969 ATL N P   36   37   18-10
1970 ATL N P   21   22   7-10
1971 ATL N P   32   13-14
1972 ATL N P   31   11-15
1973 ATL N P   20   21   4-11
1974 ATL N P   28   10-11
1975 ATL N P   10   4- 5
    STL N P   24   9- 8
1976 PHI N P   59   8- 7
1977 PHI N P   60   7- 5
1978 PHI N P   66   3- 4
    BRTR   427   430   107-112

REED, WILLIAM JOSEPH (BILLY)
B.NOV.12,1922 SHAWANO,WIS.
1952 BOS N 2   15   .250
    BLTR

REEDER, JAMES EDWARD (ICICLE)
B.1865 CINCINNATI,OHIO
1884 CIN AA O   3   .143
    WAS U O   3   .167
     6   .154

REEDER, NICHOLAS
(REAL NAME NICHOLAS HERCHENROEDER)
B.MAR.22,1867 LOUISVILLE,KY.
D.SEPT.26,1894 LOUISVILLE,KY.
1891 LOU AA 3   1   .000
    BRTR

REEDER, WILLIAM EDGAR
B.FEB.20,1922 DIKE,TEXAS
1949 STL N P   21   1- 1
    BRTR

REES, STANLEY MILTON (NELLIE)
B.FEB.25,1899 CYNTHIANA,KY.
D.AUG.30,1967 LEXINGTON,KY.
1918 WAS A P   2   1- 0
    BLTL

REESE, ANDREW JACKSON
B.FEB.7,1904 TUPELO,MISS.
D.JAN.10,1966 TUPELO,MISS.
1927 NY N 3-O   97   .265
1928 NY N 2-O   109   .308
1929 NY N 2   58   .263
1930 NY N 3-O   67   .278
    BRTR   331   .281

REESE, HAROLD HENRY (PEEWEE)
B.JULY 23,1918 EKRON,KY.
1940 BRO N S   84   .272
1941 BRO N S   152   .228
1942 BRO N S   151   .255
1946 BRO N S   152   .284
1947 BRO N S   142   .284
1948 BRO N S   151   .274
1949 BRO N S   155   .279
1950 BRO N S-3   141   .260
1951 BRO N S   154   .286
1952 BRO N S   149   .272
1953 BRO N S   140   .271
1954 BRO N S   141   .309
1955 BRO N S   145   .282
1956 BRO N S-3   147   .257
1957 BRO N S-3   103   .224
1958 LA N S-3   59   .224
    BRTR   2166   .269

REESE, JAMES HERMAN (JIMMIE)
(REAL NAME JAMES HERMAN SOLOMAN)
B.OCT.1,1905 LOS ANGELES,CAL.
1930 NY A 2   77   .346
1931 NY A 2   65   .241
1932 STL N 2   90   .265
    BLTR   232   .278

REESE, RICHARD BENJAMIN (RICH)
B.SEP.29,1941 LEIPSIC,OHIO
1964 MIN A 1   10   .000
1965 MIN A /1-O   14   .286
1966 MIN A /H   3   .000
1967 MIN A 1-O   95   .248
1968 MIN A 1-O   126   .259
1969 MIN A *1/O   132   .322
1970 MIN A *1   153   .261
1971 MIN A 1/O   120   .219
1972 MIN A 1-O   132   .218
1973 DET A 1-O   59   .137
    MIN A 1   22   .174
    BLTL   866   .253

REEVES, ROBERT EDWIN (GUNNER)
B.JUNE 24,1904 HILL CITY,TENN.
1926 WAS A 3   20   .224
1927 WAS A S-3   112   .255
1928 WAS A 2-S   102   .303
1929 BOS A 3   140   .248
1930 BOS A 2-S-3   92   .217
1931 BOS A P-2   1   36   0- 0
    .167
    BRTR   1   502   0- 0
    .252

REGALADO, RUDOLPH VALENTINO (RUDY)
B.MAY 21,1930 LOS ANGELES,CAL.
1954 CLE A 2-3   65   .250
1955 CLE A 2-3   10   .240
1956 CLE A 1-3   16   .234
    BRTR   91   .246

REGAN, MICHAEL JOSEPH
B.NOV.19,1887 PHOENIX,N.Y.
D.MAY 22,1961 ALBANY,N.Y.
1917 CIN N P   22   33   11-10
1918 CIN N P   22   23   5- 5
1919 CIN N P   1   0- 0
    BRTR   55   57   16-15

REGAN, PHILIP RAYMOND
(PHIL) OR (THE VULTURE)
B.APR.6,1937 OTSEGO,MICH.
1960 DET A P   17   0- 4
1961 DET A P   32   33   10- 7
1962 DET A P   35   11- 9
1963 DET A P   38   15- 9
1964 DET A P   32   33   5-10
1965 DET A P   16   1- 5
1966 LA N P   65   14- 1
1967 LA N P   55   6- 9
1968 LA N /P   5   2- 0
    CHI N P   68   10- 5
1969 CHI N P   71   12- 6
1970 CHI N P   54   5- 9
1971 CHI N P   48   5- 5
1972 CHI N /P   5   0- 1
    CHI A P   10   0- 1
    BRTR   551   553   96-81

REGAN, WILLIAM WRIGHT
B.JAN.23,1899 PITTSBURGH,PA.
D.JUNE 11,1968 PITTSBURGH,PA.
1926 BOS A 2   108   .263
1927 BOS A 2   129   .274
1928 BOS A 2   138   .264
1929 BOS A 2-3   104   .288
1930 BOS A 2   134   .266
1931 PIT N 2   28   .202
    BRTR   641   .267

REGO, ANTONE (TONY)
(REAL NAME ANTONE DO REGO)
B.OCT.31,1897 WAILUKU,HAWAII
D.JAN.6,1978 TULSA,OKLA.
1924 STL A C   24   .220
1925 STL A C   20   .406
    BRTR   44   .286

REHG, WALTER PHILLIP
B.AUG.31,1888 SUMMERFIELD,ILL.
D.APR.5,1946 BURBANK,CAL.
1912 PIT N O   7   .000
1913 BOS A O   30   .277
1914 BOS A O   84   .218
1915 BOS A O   5   .200
1917 BOS N O   87   .270
1918 BOS N O   40   .241
1919 CIN N O   5   .167
    BRTR   258   .251

REIBER, FRANK BERNARD
(FRANK) OR (TUBBY)
B.SEPT.19,1909 HUNTINGTON,W.VA.
1933 DET A C   13   .278
1934 DET A H   3   .000
1935 DET A C   8   .273
1936 DET A C   20   .273
    BRTR   44   .271

REICH, HERMAN CHARLES
B.NOV.23,1917 BELL,CAL.
1949 WAS A H   2   .000
    CLE A O   1   .500
    CHI N 1-O   108   .280
    BRTL   111   .279

REICHARDT, FREDERIC CARL (RICK)
B.MAR.16,1943 MADISON,WIS.
1964 LA A O   11   .162
1965 CAL A O   20   .267
1966 CAL A O   89   .288
1967 CAL A *O   146   .265
1968 CAL A *O   151   .255
1969 CAL A *O/1   137   .254
1970 CAL A /O   9   .167
    WAS A O/3   107   .253
1971 CHI A *O/1   138   .278
1972 CHI A O   101   .251
1973 CHI A O   46   .275
    KC A D/O   41   .220
1974 KC A /H   1   1.000
    BRTR   997   .261

REICHLE, RICHARD WENDELL
B.NOV.23,1896 LINCOLN,ILL.
D.JUNE 13,1967 ST.LOUIS,MO.
1922 BOS A O   6   .250
1923 BOS A O   122   .258
    BLTR   128   .257

REID, EARL PERCY
B.JUNE 8,1913 BANGOR,ALA.
1946 BOS N P   2   1- 0
    BLTR

REID, SCOTT DONALD
B.JAN.7,1947 CHICAGO,ILL.
1969 PHI N /O   13   .211
1970 PHI N O   25   .122
    BLTR   38   .147

REID, WILLIAM ALEXANDER (SANDY)
B.MAY 17,1857 LONDON,ONT.,CAN.
D.JUNE 26,1940 LONDON,ONT.,CAN.
1883 BAL AA 2-S   16   .285
1884 PIT AA O   19   .246
     35   .269

YR	CL	LEA	POS	GP	G	REC

REIDY, WILLIAM JOSEPH
B.OCT.9,1873 CLEVELAND,OHIO
D.OCT.14,1915 CLEVELAND,OHIO

YR	CL	LEA	POS	GP	G	REC
1896	NY	N	P		2	0- 1
1899	BRO	N	P		2	0- 0
1901	MIL	A	P		36	15-18
1902	STL	A	P-O	11	13	3- 5
						.195
1903	STL	A	P		6	1- 5
	BRO	N	P		15	6- 7
1904	BRO	N	P-2	6	11	0- 4
						.196
			BRTR	78	85	25-40
						.150

REILLEY, ALEXANDER ALOYSIUS
(DUKE) OR (MIDGET)
B.AUG.25,1884 CHICAGO,ILL.
D.MAR.4,1968 INDIANAPOLIS,IND.

1909	CLE	A	O		20	.210
			BBTR			

REILLEY, CHARLES E.
B.1856 HARTFORD,CONN.
D.1888

1879	TRO	N	C-1		61	.232
1880	CIN	N	C-3-O		29	.204
1881	DET	N	C-1-S-3-O		18	.179
	WOR	N	C		2	.375
1882	PRO	N	C		3	.182
			BRTR		113	.214

REILLY, ARCHER EDWIN
B.AUG.17,1891 ALTON,ILL.
D.NOV.29,1949 COLUMBUS,OHIO

1917	PIT	N	3		1	.000
			BRTR			

REILLY, BERNARD EUGENE (BARNEY)
B.FEB.7,1884 BROCKTON,MASS.
D.NOV.15,1934 ST.JOSEPH,MO.

1909	CHI	A	2		12	.120
			BRTR			

REILLY, CHARLES (JOSH)
B.1868 SAN FRANCISCO,CAL.
D.JUNE 13,1938 SAN FRANCISCO,CAL.

1896	CHI	N	2		9	.205

REILLY, CHARLES THOMAS
(PRINCETON CHARLIE)
B.JUNE 24,1855 PRINCETON,N.J.
D.DEC.16,1937 LOS ANGELES,CAL.

1889	COL	AA	3		6	.478
1890	COL	AA	3		137	.270
1891	PIT	N	3		110	.211
1892	PHI	N	3		81	.201
1893	PHI	N	3		104	.252
1894	PHI	N	3		36	.272
1895	PHI	N	S		44	.267
1897	WAS	N	3		101	.275
			BBTR		619	.250

REILLY, HAROLD J.

1919	CHI	N	O		1	.000

REILLY, JOHN GOOD (LONG JOHN)
B.OCT.5,1858 CINCINNATI,OHIO
D.MAY 31,1937 CINCINNATI,OHIO

1880	CIN	N	1-O		72	.195
1883	CIN	AA	1		97	.289
1884	CIN	AA	1-S-O		106	.339
1885	CIN	AA	1-O		106	.308
1886	CIN	AA	1-O		115	.270
1887	CIN	AA	1-O		134	.334
1888	CIN	AA	1-O		126	.324
1889	CIN	AA	1-O		111	.261
1890	CIN	N	1		133	.300
1891	CIN	N	1-O		133	.200
			BRTR		1133	.284

REILLY, JOSEPH J.
B.NEW YORK,N.Y.

1884	BOS	U	3-O		3	.000
1885	MET	AA	2-3		10	.122
					13	.096

REILLY, THOMAS HENRY
B.AUG.3,1884 ST.LOUIS,MO.
D.OCT.18,1918 NEW ORLEANS,LA.

1908	STL	N	S		29	.173
1909	STL	N	S		4	.167
1914	CLE	A	H		1	.000
			BRTR		34	.170

REINBACH, MICHAEL WAYNE (MIKE)
B.AUG.6,1949 SAN DIEGO,CAL.

1974	BAL	A	/O		12	.250
			BLTR			

REINHART, ARTHUR CONRAD
B.MAY 29,1899 ACKLEY,IOWA
D.NOV.11,1946 HOUSTON,TEX.

1919	STL	N	P		1	0- 0
1925	STL	N	P	20	28	11- 5
1926	STL	N	P	27	40	10- 5
1927	STL	N	P	21	27	5- 2
1928	STL	N	P	23	27	4- 6
			BLTL	92	123	30-18

REINHOLZ, ARTHUR AUGUST
B.JAN.27,1903 DETROIT,MICH.

1928	CLE	A	3		2	.333
			BRTR			

REINICKER, WALTER
[REAL NAME WALTER SMITH]

1915	BAL	F	3		3	.125
			TR			

REIPSCHLAGER, CHARLES W.
B.1855 NEW YORK,N.Y. DECEASED

1883	MET	AA	C-O		35	.189
1884	MET	AA	C		59	.236
.885	MET	AA	C		72	.234
1886	MET	AA	C		66	.221
1887	CLE	AA	C		63	.248
			BRTR		295	.229

REIS, HARRIE CRANE (JACK)
B.JUNE 14,1890 CINCINNATI,OHIO
D.JULY 20,1939 CINCINNATI,OHIO

1911	STL	N	P		3	0- 0
			BRTR			

REIS, LAWRENCE P. (LAURIE)

1877	CHI	N	P		4	3- 1
1878	CHI	N	P-O	4	5	1- 3
						.150
			BRTR	8	9	4- 4
						.140

REIS, ROBERT JOSEPH THOMAS
B.JAN.2,1909 WOODSIDE,N.Y.
D.MAY 1,1973 ST.PAUL,MINN.

1931	BRO	N	2-3		6	.294
1932	BRO	N	3		1	.250
1935	BRO	N	P-1-	14	52	3- 2
			2-3-O			.247
1936	BOS	N	P	35	37	6- 5
1937	BOS	N	P-O	4	45	0- 0
						.244
1938	BOS	N	P-O	16	34	1- 0
						.184
			BRTR	69	175	10-13
						.233

REIS, THOMAS EDWARD
B.AUG.6,1914 NEWPORT,KY.

1938	PHI	N	P		4	0- 1
	BOS	N	P		4	0- 0
			BRTR		8	0- 1

REISER, HAROLD PATRICK (PETE)
B.MAR.17,1919 ST.LOUIS,MO.

1940	BRO	N	S-3-O		58	.293
1941	BRO	N	O		137	.343
1942	BRO	N	O		125	.310
1946	BRO	N	3-O		122	.277
1947	BRO	N	O		110	.309
1948	BRO	N	O		64	.236
1949	BOS	N	3-O		84	.272
1950	BOS	N	3-O		53	.205
1951	PIT	N	3-O		74	.271
1952	CLE	A	O		34	.136
			BLTR		861	.295
			BB 1940 (PART),			
			1948-52 (PART)			

REISGEL, JACOB (BUGS)
B.DEC.12,1887 BROOKLYN,N.Y.
D.FEB.24,1957 AMSTERDAM,N.Y.

1911	CLE	A	P		2	0- 1
			BRTR			

REISING, CHARLES

1884	IND	AA	O		1	.000

REISLING, FRANK CARL (DOC)
B.JULY 25,1874 MARTINS FERRY,O.
D.MAR.4,1955 TULSA,OKLA.

1904	BRO	N	P		7	3- 3
1905	BRO	N	P		2	0- 0
1909	WAS	A	P	10	12	2- 4
1910	WAS	A	P	30	31	9-10
			BRTR	49	52	14-17

REISS, ALBERT ALLEN
B.JAN.8,1909 ELIZABETH,N.J.

1932	PHI	A	S		9	.200
			BBTR			

REITZ, HENRY P. (HEINIE)
B.JUNE 29,1867 CHICAGO,ILL.
D.NOV.10,1914 SAN FRANCISCO,CAL.

1893	BAL	N	2		130	.297
1894	BAL	N	2		109	.306
1895	BAL	N	2-3		63	.281
1896	BAL	N	2		119	.283
1897	BAL	N	2		127	.289
1898	WAS	N	2		132	.302
1899	PIT	N	2		35	.263
			BLTR		715	.293

REITZ, KENNETH JOHN (KEN)
B.JUNE 24,1951 SAN FRANCISCO,CAL

1972	STL	N	3		21	.359
1973	STL	N	*3/S		147	.235
1974	STL	N	*3/S-2		154	.271
1975	STL	N	*3		161	.269
1976	SF	N	*3/S		155	.267
1977	STL	N	*3		177	.261
1978	STL	N	*3		150	.246
			BRTR		945	.262

REMENTER, WILLIS J. (BUTCH)
B.MAR.14,1878 PHILADELPHIA,PA.
D.SEPT.23,1922 PHILADELPHIA,PA.

1904	PHI	N	C		1	.000
			TR			

REMNEAS, ALEXANDER NORMAN
B.FEB.21,1886 MINNEAPOLIS,MINN.
D.AUG.27,1975 PHOENIX,ARIZ.

1912	DET	A	P		1	0- 0
1915	STL	A	P		2	0- 0
			BRTR		3	0- 0

REMSEN, JOHN J. (JACK)
B.1851 BROOKLYN,N.Y.

1872	ATL	NA	O		35	.205
1873	ATL	NA	O		51	-
1874	MUT	NA	O		64	-
1875	HAR	NA	O		85	-
1876	HAR	N	O		69	.274
1877	STL	N	O		33	.260
1878	CHI	N	O		55	.233
1879	CHI	N	1-O		39	.248
1881	CLE	N	O		48	.174
1884	PHI	N	O		10	.222
	BRO	AA	O		81	.238
			BR		570	-

REMY, GERALD PETER (JERRY)
B.NOV.8,1952 FALL RIVER,MASS.

1975	CAL	A	*2		147	.258
1976	CAL	A	*2		143	.263
1977	CAL	A	*2/3		154	.252
1978	BOS	A	*2/S		148	.278
			BLTR		592	.263

RENFER, ERWIN ARTHUR
B.DEC.11,1895 ELGIN,ILL.
D.OCT.26,1958 SYCAMORE,ILL.

1913	DET	A	P		1	0- 1
			BRTR			

RENFROE, MARSHALL DANIEL
B.MAY 25,1936 CENTURY,FLA.
D.DEC.10,1970 PENSACOLA,FLA.

1959	SF	N	P		1	0- 0
			BLTL			

RENICK, WARREN RICHARD (RICK)
B.MAR.16,1944 LONDON,OHIO

1968	MIN	A	S		42	.216
1969	MIN	A	3-O/S		71	.245
1970	MIN	A	3-O/S		81	.229
1971	MIN	A	/3-O		27	.222
1972	MIN	A	O/1-3-S		55	.172
			BRTR		276	.221

RENIFF, HAROLD EUGENE
(HAL) OR (PORKY)
B.JULY 2,1938 WARREN,OHIO

1961	NY	A	P		25	2- 0
1962	NY	A	P		2	0- 0
1963	NY	A	P		48	4- 3
1964	NY	A	P	41	44	6- 4
1965	NY	A	P		51	3- 4
1966	NY	A	P		56	3- 7
1967	NY	A	P		24	0- 2
	NY	N	P		29	3- 3
			BRTR	276	279	21-23

RENINGER, JAMES DAVID
B.MAR.7,1913 AURORA,ILL.

1938	PHI	A	P		4	0- 2
1939	PHI	A	P		4	0- 2
			BRTR		8	0- 4

RENKO, STEVEN (STEVE)
B.DEC.10,1944 KANSAS CITY,KAN.

1969	MON	N	P		18	6- 7
1970	MON	N	P	41	41	13-11
1971	MON	N	P	40	41	15-14
1972	MON	N	P/1	30	32	1-10
						.292
1973	MON	N	P	36	41	15-11
1974	MON	N	P		37	12-16
1975	MON	N	P	31	33	6-12
1976	MON	N	/P		5	0- 1
	CHI	N	P	28	29	6-11
1977	CHI	N	P		13	2- 2
	CHI	A	/P		8	5- 0
1978	OAK	A	P		27	6-12
			BRTR	314	325	89-107
						.216

YR   CL LEA POS   GP   G   REC

RENNA, WILLIAM BENEDITTO (BILL)
OR (BIG BILL)
B.OCT.14,1924 HANFORD,CAL.
1953 NY A O   61 .314
1954 PHI A O   123 .232
1955 KC A O   100 .213
1956 KC A O   33 .271
1958 BOS A O   39 .268
1959 BOS A O   14 .091
        BRTR   370 .239

RENSA, TONY GEORGE (PUG)
B.SEPT.29,1901 PARSONS,PA.
1930 DET N C   20 .270
     PHI N C   54 .285
1931 PHI N C   19 .103
1933 NY A C   8 .310
1937 CHI A C   26 .298
1938 CHI A C   59 .248
1939 CHI A C   14 .200
        BRTR   200 .261

REPASS, ROBERT WILLIS
B.NOV.6,1917 W.PITTSTON,PA.
1939 STL N 2   3 .333
1942 WAS A 2-S-3   81 .239
        BRTR   84 .242

REPLOGLE, ANDREW DAVID (ANDY)
B.OCT.7,1953 SOUTH BEND,IND.
1978 MIL A P   32 9- 5
        BRTR

REPOZ, ROGER ALLEN
B.AUG.3,1940 BELLINGHAM,WASH.
1964 NY A O   11 .000
1965 NY A O   79 .220
1966 NY A O   37 .349
     KC A O-1   101 .216
1967 KC A O   40 .241
     CAL A O   74 .250
1968 CAL A *O   133 .240
1969 CAL A O-1   103 .164
1970 CAL A *O-1   137 .238
1971 CAL A O-1   113 .199
1972 CAL A /H   3 .333
        BLTL   831 .224

REPULSKI, ELDON JOHN (RIP)
B.OCT.4,1927 SAUK RAPIDS,MINN.
1953 STL N O   153 .275
1954 STL N O   152 .283
1955 STL N O   147 .270
1956 STL N O   112 .277
1957 PHI N O   134 .260
1958 PHI N O   85 .244
1959 LA N O   53 .255
1960 LA N O   4 .200
     BOS A O   73 .243
1961 BOS A O   15 .284
        BRTR   928 .269

RESCIGNO, XAVIER FREDERICK (MR. X.)
B.OCT.13,1913 NEW YORK,N.Y.
1943 PIT N P   37 6- 9
1944 PIT N P   48 10- 8
1945 PIT N P   44 3- 5
        BRTR   129 19-22

RESSLER, LAWRENCE P.
1875 NAT NA 2-O   25   -

RESTELLI, DINO PAUL (DINGO)
B.SEPT.23,1924 ST.LOUIS,MO.
1949 PIT N 1-O   72 .250
1951 PIT N O   21 .184
        BRTR   93 .241

RETTENMUND, MERVIN WELDON (MERV)
B.JUNE 6,1943 FLINT,MICH.
1968 BAL A O   31 .297
1969 BAL A O   95 .247
1970 BAL A O   106 .322
1971 BAL A *O   141 .318
1972 BAL A O   102 .233
1973 BAL A O   95 .262
1974 CIN N O   80 .216
1975 CIN N O/3   93 .239
1976 SD N O   86 .229
1977 SD N O/3   107 .286
1978 CAL A O-D   50 .269
        BRTR   986 .272

RETTGER, GEORGE EDWARD
B.JULY 29,1868 CLEVELAND,OHIO
D.JUNE 5,1921 LAKEWOOD,OHIO
1891 STL AA P   15 10- 3
1892 CLE N P   6 1- 4
     CIN N P-O   1   2 1- 0
                          .125
        TR   22 23 12- 7
                          .092

RETTIG, ADOLPH JOHN (OTTO)
B.JAN.29,1894 NEW YORK,N.Y.
D.JUNE 16,1977 STUART,FLA.
1922 PHI A P   4 1- 2
        BRTR

RETZER, KENNETH LEO (KEN)
B.APR.30,1934 WOOD RIVER,ILL.
1961 WAS A C   16 .340
1962 WAS A C   109 .285
1963 WAS A C   95 .242
1964 WAS A C   17 .094
        BLTR   237 .264

REULBACH, EDWARD MARVIN (BIG ED)
B.DEC.1,1882 DETROIT,MICH.
D.JULY 17,1961 GLENS FALLS,N.Y.
1905 CHI N P   34 17-13
1906 CHI N P   33 34 19- 4
1907 CHI N P   27 17- 4
1908 CHI N P   46 24- 7
1909 CHI N P   35 19-10
1910 CHI N P   24 12- 8
1911 CHI N P   33 16- 9
1912 CHI N P   39 10- 6
1913 CHI N P   9 1- 3
     BRO N P   16 7- 6
1914 BRO N P   44 11-18
1915 NEW F P   33 21-10
1916 BOS N P   21 7- 6
1917 BOS N P   5 0- 1
        BRTR   399 400 181-105

REUSCHEL, PAUL RICHARD
B.JAN.12,1947 QUINCY,ILL.
1975 CHI N P   28 1- 3
1976 CHI N P   50 4- 2
1977 CHI N P   69 5- 6
1978 CHI N P   16 2- 0
     CLE A P   18 2- 4
        BRTR   181 14-15

REUSCHEL, RICKEY EUGENE (RICK)
B.MAY 16,1949 QUINCY,ILL.
1972 CHI N P   21 10- 8
1973 CHI N P   36 14-15
1974 CHI N P   41 13-12
1975 CHI N P   38 11-17
1976 CHI N P   38 14-12
1977 CHI N P   39 41 20-10
1978 CHI N P   35 14-15
        BRTR   248 250 96-89

REUSS, JERRY
B.JUNE 19,1949 ST.LOUIS,MO.
1969 STL N /P   1 1- 0
1970 STL N P   20 7- 8
1971 STL N P   36 14-14
1972 HOU N P   33 9-13
1973 HOU N P   41 42 16-13
1974 PIT N P   35 16-11
1975 PIT N P   32 18-11
1976 PIT N P   31 14- 9
1977 PIT N P   33 35 10-13
1978 PIT N P   23 3- 2
        BLTL   285 288 108-94

REVELS
1874 BAL NA O   1 .000

REVERING, DAVID ALVIN (DAVE)
B.FEB.12,1953 ROSEVILLE,CAL.
1978 OAK A *1   152 .271
        BLTR

REXTER
1875 ATL NA O   1 .000

REYES, NAPOLEON AGUILERA
B.NOV.24,1919 SAN LUIS,CUBA
1943 NY N 1-3   40 .256
1944 NY N 1-3-O   116 .289
1945 NY N 1-3   122 .288
1950 NY N 1   1 .000
        BRTR   279 .284

REYNOLDS, ALLIE PIERCE
(ALLIE) OR (SUPERCHIEF)
B.FEB.10,1915 BETHANY,OKLA.
1942 CLE A P   2 0- 0
1943 CLE A P   34 39 11-12
1944 CLE A P   28 41 11- 8
1945 CLE A P   44 18-12
1946 CLE A P   31 35 11-15
1947 NY A P   34 38 19- 8
1948 NY A P   39 41 16- 7
1949 NY A P   35 37 17- 6
1950 NY A P   35 36 16-12
1951 NY A P   40 43 17- 8
1952 NY A P   35 41 20- 8
1953 NY A P   41 42 13- 7
1954 NY A P   36 13- 4
        BRTR   434 475 182-107

REYNOLDS, ARCHIE EDWARD
B.JAN.3,1946 GLENDALE,CAL.
1968 CHI N /P   7 0- 1
1969 CHI N /P   2 0- 1
1970 CHI N /P   7 0- 2
1971 CAL A /P   15 0- 3
1972 MIL N /P   5 0- 1
        BRTR   36 0- 8

REYNOLDS, CARL NETTLES
B.FEB.1,1903 LA RUE,TEX.
D.MAY 29,1978 HOUSTON,TEX.
1927 CHI A O   14 .214
1928 CHI A O   84 .323
1929 CHI A O   131 .317
1930 CHI A O   138 .359
1931 CHI A O   118 .290
1932 WAS A O   102 .305
1933 STL A O   135 .286
1934 BOS A O   113 .303
1935 BOS A O   78 .270
1936 WAS A O   89 .276
1937 CHI N O   7 .273
1938 CHI N O   125 .302
1939 CHI N O   88 .246
        BRTR   1222 .302

REYNOLDS, CHARLES E.
B.JULY 31,1857 ALLEGANY,N.Y.
D.MAY 1,1913 BUFFALO,N.Y.
1882 ATH AA P-O   2 1- 1
                          .125

REYNOLDS, CHARLES L.
B.MAY 1,1865 WILLIAMSBURGH,IND.
1889 KC AA C   1 .250
     BRO AA C   11 .222
                      12 .225

REYNOLDS, DANIEL VANCE (SQUIRREL)
B.NOV.27,1919 STONY POINT,N.C.
1945 CHI A 2-S   29 .167
        BRTR

REYNOLDS, DONALD EDWARD (DON)
B.APR.16,1953 ARKADELPHIA,ARK.
1978 SD N O   57 .253
        BRTR

REYNOLDS, GORDON CRAIG (CRAIG)
B.DEC.27,1952 HOUSTON,TEX.
1975 PIT N S   31 .224
1976 PIT N /S-2   7 .250
1977 SEA A *S   135 .248
1978 SEA A *S   148 .292
        BLTR   321 .269

REYNOLDS, KENNETH LEE (KEN)
B.JAN.4,1947 TREVOSE,PA.
1970 PHI N /P   4 0- 0
1971 PHI N P   35 36 5- 9
1972 PHI N P   33 48 2-15
1973 MIL A P   2 0- 1
1975 STL N P   10 0- 1
1976 SD N P   19 0- 3
        BLTL   103 119 7-29

REYNOLDS, ROBERT ALLEN (BOB)
B.JAN.21,1947 SEATTLE,WASH.
1969 MON N /P   1 0- 0
1971 STL N /P   4 0- 0
     MIL A /P   3 0- 1
1972 BAL A /P   3 0- 0
1973 BAL A P   42 7- 5
1974 BAL A P   54 7- 5
1975 BAL A /P   7 0- 1
     DET A P   21 0- 2
     CLE A /P   5 0- 2
        BRTR   140 14-16

REYNOLDS, ROSS ERNEST (DOC)
B.AUG.20,1887 BARKSDALE,TEX.
D.JUNE 23,1970 ADA,OKLA.
1914 DET A P   26 5- 3
1915 DET A P   4 0- 1
        BRTR   30 5- 4

REYNOLDS, TOMMIE D
B.AUG.15,1941 ARIZONA,LA.
1963 KC A O   8 .053
1964 KC A 3-O   31 .202
1965 KC A O/3   90 .237
1967 NY N O/3-C   101 .206
1969 OAK A O   107 .257
1970 CAL A O/3   59 .250
1971 CAL A O/3   45 .186
1972 MIL A O/1-3   72 .200
        BBTR   513 .226
        BB 1967 (PART)

REYNOLDS, WILLIAM DEE
B.AUG.14,1884 EASTLAND,TEX.
D.JUNE 5,1924 CARNEGIE,OKLA.
1913 NY A C   5 .000
1914 NY A C   4 .400
        BRTR   9 .200

RHAWN, ROBERT JOHN (ROCKY)
B.FEB.13,1919 CATAWISSA,PA.
1947 NY N 2-3   13 .311
1948 NY N S-3   36 .273
1949 NY N 2   14 .172
     PIT N 3   3 .143
     CHI A S-3   24 .205
        BRTR   90 .237

YR	CL LEA POS	GP	G	REC

RHEAM, KENNETH JOHNSTON (CY)
B.SEPT.28,1893 PITTSBURGH,PA.
D.OCT.23,1947 PITTSBURGH,PA.

YR	CL	LEA	POS	GP	G	REC
1914	PIT	F	1		72	.209
1915	PIT	F	O		27	.174
	BRTR				99	.201

RHEM, CHARLES FLINT
(FLINT) OR (SHAD)
B.JAN.24,1901 RHEMS,S.C.
D.JULY 30,1969 COLUMBIA,S.C.

YR	CL	LEA	POS	GP	G	REC
1924	STL	N	P		6	2- 2
1925	STL	N	P		30	8-13
1926	STL	N	P		34	20- 7
1927	STL	N	P		27	10-12
1928	STL	N	P		28	11- 8
1930	STL	N	P		26	12- 8
1931	STL	N	P		33	11-10
1932	STL	N	P		6	4- 2
	PHI	N	P		26	11- 7
1933	PHI	N	P		28	5-14
1934	STL	N	P		5	1- 0
		N	P		25	8- 8
1935	BOS	N	P		10	0- 5
1936	STL	N	P		10	2- 1
	BRTR				294	105-97

RHIEL, WILLIAM JOSEPH
B.AUG.16,1900 YOUNGSTOWN,OHIO
D.AUG.16,1946 YOUNGSTOWN,OHIO

YR	CL	LEA	POS	GP	G	REC
1929	BRO	N	2		76	.278
1930	BOS	N	3		20	.170
1932	DET	A	1-3		85	.260
1933	DET	A	O		19	.176
	BRTR				200	.266

RHINES, WILLIAM PEARL (BUNKER)
B.MAR.14,1869 RIDGWAY,PA.
D.JAN.30,1922 RIDGWAY,PA.

YR	CL	LEA	POS	GP	G	REC
1890	CIN	N	P		45	28-17
1891	CIN	N	P		43	16-27
1892	CIN	N	P		12	3- 4
1893	LOU	N	P		5	1- 3
1895	CIN	N	P		32	20-12
1896	CIN	N	P		17	10- 7
1897	CIN	N	P		36	19-15
1898	PIT	N	P		31	12-15
1899	PIT	N	P		10	4- 3
	BRTR				231	113-103

RHOADS, ROBERT BARTON (DUSTY)
B.OCT.4,1879 WOOSTER,OHIO
D.FEB.12,1967 SAN BERNARDINO,CAL.

YR	CL	LEA	POS	GP	G	REC
1902	CHI	N	P		16	4- 8
1903	STL	N	P	17	18	5- 8
	CLE	A	P		5	2- 3
1904	CLE	A	P	22	29	11- 9
1905	CLE	A	P	29	33	17-12
1906	CLE	A	P		38	22-10
1907	CLE	A	P		35	15-14
1908	CLE	A	P		37	18-12
1909	CLE	A	P		20	5- 9
	TR			219	231	99-84

RHODEN, RICHARD ALAN (RICK)
B.MAY 16,1953 BOYNTON BEACH,FLA.

YR	CL	LEA	POS	GP	G	REC
1974	LA	N	/P		4	1- 0
1975	LA	N	P		26	3- 3
1976	LA	N	P		27	12- 3
1977	LA	N	P	31	32	16-10
1978	LA	N	P		30	10- 8
	BRTR			118	119	42-24

RHODES, CHARLES ANDERSON (DUSTY)
B.APR.7,1885 CANEY,KAN.
D.OCT.26,1918 CANEY,KAN.

YR	CL	LEA	POS	GP	G	REC
1906	STL	N	P		9	4- 5
1908	CIN	N	P		1	0- 0
	STL	N	P		4	1- 2
1909	STL	N	P		12	3- 5
	BRTR				26	8-12

RHODES, JAMES LAMAR (DUSTY)
B.MAY 13,1927 MATHEWS,ALA.

YR	CL	LEA	POS	GP	G	REC
1952	NY	N	O		67	.250
1953	NY	N	O		76	.233
1954	NY	N	O		82	.341
1955	NY	N	O		94	.305
1956	NY	N	O		111	.217
1957	NY	N	O		92	.205
1959	SF	N	H		54	.188
	BLTR				576	.253

RHODES, JOHN GORDON (DUSTY)
B.AUG.11,1907 WINNEMUCCA,NEV.
D.MAR.24,1960 LONG BEACH,CAL.

YR	CL	LEA	POS	GP	G	REC
1929	NY	N	P		10	0- 4
1930	NY	N	P		3	0- 0
1931	NY	N	P		18	0- 3
1932	NY	N	P		10	1- 2
	BOS	A	P		12	1- 8
1933	BOS	A	P	34	35	12-15
1934	BOS	A	P		44	12-12
1935	BOS	A	P	34	36	2-10
1936	PHI	A	P		35	9-20
	BRTR			200	203	43-74

RHODES, WILLIAM CLARENCE
B.POTTSTOWN,PA.

YR	CL	LEA	POS	GP	G	REC
1893	LOU	N	P		17	5-12

RHYNE, HAROLD J.
B.MAR.30,1899 PASO ROBLES,CAL.
D.JAN.7,1971 ORANGEVILLE,CAL.

YR	CL	LEA	POS	GP	G	REC
1926	PIT	N	2-S		109	.251
1927	PIT	N	2-3		62	.274
1929	BOS	A	S		120	.252
1930	BOS	A	S		107	.203
1931	BOS	A	S		147	.273
1932	BOS	A	S		71	.227
1933	CHI	A	2-S-3		39	.265
	BRTR				655	.250

RIBANT, DENNIS JOSEPH
B.SEP.20,1941 DETROIT,MICH.

YR	CL	LEA	POS	GP	G	REC
1964	NY	N	P	14	17	1- 5
1965	NY	N	P		19	1- 3
1966	NY	N	P	39	40	11- 9
1967	PIT	N	P	38	47	9- 8
1968	DET	A	P	14	16	2- 2
	CHI	A	P		17	0- 2
1969	STL	N	/P	1	2	0- 0
	CIN	N	/P		7	0- 0
	BRTR			149	165	24-29

RICCELLI, FRANK JOSEPH
B.FEB.24,1953 SYRACUSE,N.Y.

YR	CL	LEA	POS	GP	G	REC
1976	SF	N	/P		4	1- 1
1978	HOU	N	/P		2	0- 0
	BLTL				6	1- 1

RICE, DELBERT W (DEL)
B.OCT.27,1922 PORTSMOUTH,OHIO

YR	CL	LEA	POS	GP	G	REC
1945	STL	N	C		83	.261
1946	STL	N	C		55	.273
1947	STL	N	C		97	.218
1948	STL	N	C		100	.197
1949	STL	N	C		92	.236
1950	STL	N	C		130	.244
1951	STL	N	C		122	.251
1952	STL	N	C		147	.259
1953	STL	N	C		135	.236
1954	STL	N	C		56	.252
1955	STL	N	C		20	.203
	MIL	N	C		27	.197
1956	MIL	N	C		71	.213
1957	MIL	N	C		54	.229
1958	MIL	N	C		43	.223
1959	MIL	N	C		13	.207
1960	CHI	N	C		18	.231
	STL	N	C		1	.000
	BAL	A	C		1	.000
1961	CAL	A	C		44	.241
	BRTR				1309	.237

NON-PLAYING MANAGER CAL(A) 1972

RICE, EDGAR CHARLES (SAM)
B.FEB.20,1890 MOROCCO,IND.
D.OCT.13,1974 ROSSMOR,MD.

YR	CL	LEA	POS	GP	G	REC
1915	WAS	A	P		4	1- 0
1916	WAS	A	P-O	5	58	0- 1
						.299
1917	WAS	A	O		155	.302
1918	WAS	A	O		7	.348
1919	WAS	A	O		141	.321
1920	WAS	A	O		153	.338
1921	WAS	A	O		143	.330
1922	WAS	A	O		154	.295
1923	WAS	A	O		148	.316
1924	WAS	A	O		154	.334
1925	WAS	A	O		152	.350
1926	WAS	A	O		152	.337
1927	WAS	A	O		142	.297
1928	WAS	A	O		148	.328
1929	WAS	A	O		150	.323
1930	WAS	A	O		147	.349
1931	WAS	A	O		120	.310
1932	WAS	A	O		106	.323
1933	WAS	A	O		73	.294
1934	CLE	A	O		97	.293
	BLTR			9	2404	1- 1
						.322

RICE, HAROLD HOUSTEN (HOOT)
B.FEB.11,1924 MORGANETTE,W.VA.

YR	CL	LEA	POS	GP	G	REC
1948	STL	N	O		8	.323
1949	STL	N	O		40	.196
1950	STL	N	O		14	.211
1951	STL	N	O		69	.254
1952	STL	N	O		98	.288
1953	STL	N	H		8	.250
	PIT	N	O		78	.311
1954	PIT	N	O		28	.173
	CHI	N	O		51	.193
	BLTR				424	.260

RICE, HARRY FRANCIS
B.NOV.22,1901 WARE STATION,ILL.
D.JAN.1,1971 PORTLAND,ORE.

YR	CL	LEA	POS	GP	G	REC
1923	STL	A	H		4	.006
1924	STL	A	3		44	.279
1925	STL	A	C-1-2-3-O		103	.359
1926	STL	A	O		148	.313
1927	STL	A	O		137	.287
1928	DET	A	O		131	.302
1929	DET	A	O		130	.304
1930	DET	A	O		37	.305
1930	NY	A	O		100	.298
1931	WAS	A	O		47	.265
1933	CIN	N	3-O		143	.261
	BLTR				1024	.299

RICE, JAMES EDWARD (JIM)
B.MAR.8,1953 ANDERSON,S.C.

YR	CL	LEA	POS	GP	G	REC
1974	BOS	A	D/O		24	.269
1975	BOS	A	D-O		144	.309
1976	BOS	A	D-O		153	.282
1977	BOS	A	*D-O		160	.320
1978	BOS	A	*D-O		163	.315
	BRTR				644	.306

RICE, LEONARD OLIVER
B.SEPT.2,1918 LEAD,S.DAK.

YR	CL	LEA	POS	GP	G	REC
1944	CIN	N	C		10	.000
1945	CHI	N	C		32	.232
	BRTR				42	.223

RICE, ROBERT TURNBULL
B.MAY 28,1899 PHILADELPHIA,PA.

YR	CL	LEA	POS	GP	G	REC
1926	PHI	N	3		19	.146

RICH, WOODROW EARL (WOODY)
B.MAR.9,1917 MORGANTON,N.C.

YR	CL	LEA	POS	GP	G	REC
1939	BOS	A	P		21	4- 3
1940	BOS	A	P		3	1- 0
1941	BOS	A	P		2	0- 0
1944	BOS	N	P		7	1- 1
	BLTR				33	6- 4

RICHARD, JAMES RODNEY (J.R.)
B.MAR.7,1950 VIENNA,LA.

YR	CL	LEA	POS	GP	G	REC
1971	HOU	N	/P		4	2- 1
1972	HOU	N	/P		4	1- 0
1973	HOU	N	P		16	6- 2
1974	HOU	N	P		2	2- 3
1975	HOU	N	P		33	12-10
1976	HOU	N	P		39	20-15
1977	HOU	N	P		36	18-12
1978	HOU	N	P	36	37	18-11
	BRTR			183	184	79-54

RICHARD, LEE EDWARD (BEEBEE)
B.SEP.18,1948 LAFAYETTE,LA.

YR	CL	LEA	POS	GP	G	REC
1971	CHI	A	S-O		87	.231
1972	CHI	A	/O-S		11	.241
1974	CHI	A	3/S-2-O		32	.164
1975	CHI	A	3/S-2		43	.200
1976	STL	N	2-S/3		66	.176
	BRTR				239	.209
	BB 1975					

RICHARDS, DUANE LEE
B.DEC.16,1936 SPARTANBURG,IND.

YR	CL	LEA	POS	GP	G	REC
1960	CIN	N	P		2	0- 0
	BRTR					

RICHARDS, EUGENE (GENE)
B.SEPT.29,1953 MONTICELLO,S.C.

YR	CL	LEA	POS	GP	G	REC
1977	SD	N	*O-1		146	.290
1978	SD	N	*O-1		154	.308
	BLTL				300	.299

RICHARDS, FRED CHARLES
(FRED) OR (FUZZY)
B.NOV.3,1927 WARREN,OHIO

YR	CL	LEA	POS	GP	G	REC
1951	CHI	N	1		10	.296
	BLTL					

RICHARDS, PAUL RAPIER
B.NOV.21,1908 WAXAHACHIE,TEX.

YR	CL	LEA	POS	GP	G	REC
1932	BRO	N	C		3	.000
1933	NY	N	C		51	.195
1934	NY	N	C		42	.160
1935	NY	N	C		7	.250
	PHI	A	C		85	.245
1943	DET	A	C		100	.220
1944	DET	A	C		95	.237
1945	DET	A	C		83	.256
1946	DET	A	C		57	.201
	BRTR				523	.227

NON-PLAYING MANAGER
CHI(A) 1951-54, BAL(A) 1955-61,
CHI(A) 1976

RICHARDSON
B.BOSTON,MASS.

YR	CL	LEA	POS	GP	G	REC
1884	CHI	U	2		1	.000

YR	CL LEA POS	GP	G	REC

RICHARDSON, ABRAM HARDING
(HARDY) OR (OLD TRUE BLUE)
B.APR.21,1855 CLARKSBORO,N.J.
D.JAN.14,1931 UTICA,N.Y.
1879 BUF N 3   78 .278
1880 BUF N C-3   80 .252
1881 BUF N 2-S-O   83 .290
1882 BUF N 2   83 .271
1883 BUF N 2   90 .310
1884 BUF N 1-2-3-O 98 .301
1885 BUF N P-2- 1 96 0- 0
          S-O   .319
1886 DET N 2-O   125 .351
1887 DET N 2-O   120 .363
1888 DET N 2   57 .289
1889 BOS N 2-O   132 .304
1890 BOS P O   130 .332
1891 BOS AA O   74 .264
1892 WAS N 2-O   9 .114
     NY N 2-O   61 .223
        BRTR   1 1316 0- 0
                       .302

RICHARDSON, CLIFFORD NOLEN (NOLEN)
B.JAN.18,1903 CHATTANOOGA,TENN.
D.SEPT.25,1951 ATHENS,GA.
1929 DET A S   13 .190
1931 DET A 3   38 .270
1932 DET A 3   69 .219
1935 NY A S   12 .217
1938 CIN N S   35 .290
1939 CIN N S   1 .000
        BRTR   168 .247

RICHARDSON, DANIEL (DANNY)
B.JAN.25,1863 ELMIRA,N.Y.
D.SEPT.12,1926 NEW YORK,N.Y.
1884 NY N S-O   70 .259
1885 NY N P-3- 9 48 5- 1
          O   .262
1886 NY N P-O   1 64 0- 1
                       .232
1887 NY N 2   122 .332
1888 NY N 2   135 .226
1889 NY N 2   124 .279
1890 NY P 2-S   123 .258
1891 NY N 2   123 .262
1892 WAS N M-2-S   142 .240
1893 BRO N 2   51 .246
1894 LOU N S   116 .255
        BRTR   10 1118 5- 2
                       .261

RICHARDSON, GORDON CLARK (GORDIE)
B.JULY 19,1938 COLQUITT,GA.
1964 STL N P   19 4- 2
1965 NY N P   35 2- 2
1966 NY N P   15 0- 2
        BRTL   69 6- 6

RICHARDSON, JOHN WILLIAM (JACK)
B.OCT.3,1891 CENTRAL CITY,ILL.
D.JAN.18,1970 MARION,ILL.
1915 PHI A P   3 0- 1
1916 PHI A P   1 0- 0
        BBTR   4 0- 1

RICHARDSON, KENNETH FRANKLIN
B.MAY 2,1915 ORLEANS,IND.
1942 PHI A 1-3-O   6 .067
1946 PHI N 2   6 .150
        BRTR   12 .114

RICHARDSON, ROBERT CLINTON (BOBBY)
B.AUG.19,1935 SUMTER,S.C.
1955 NY A 2-S   11 .154
1956 NY A 2   5 .143
1957 NY A 2   97 .256
1958 NY A 2-S-3   73 .247
1959 NY A 2-S-3   134 .301
1960 NY A 2-3   150 .252
1961 NY A 2   162 .261
1962 NY A 2   161 .302
1963 NY A 2   151 .265
1964 NY A 2-S   159 .267
1965 NY A *2   160 .247
1966 NY A *2/3   149 .251
        BRTR   1412 .266

RICHARDSON, THOMAS MITCHELL
B.AUG.7,1863 LOUISVILLE,ILL.
D.NOV.15,1939 ONAWA,IOWA
1917 STL A H   1 .000
        BRTR

RICHARDSON, WILLIAM HEZEKIAH
B.OCT.8,1877 DECATUR COUNTY,IND
D.APR.11,1954 BATESVILLE,IND.
1901 STL N 1   15 .211

RICHBOURG, LANCELOT CLAYTON (LANCE)
B.DEC.18,1897 DE FUNIAK SPRINGS FLA.
D.SEPT.10,1975 CRESTVIEW,FLA.
1921 PHI N 2   10 .200
1924 WAS A O   15 .281
1927 BOS N O   115 .309
1928 BOS N O   148 .337
1929 BOS N O   139 .305
1930 BOS N O   130 .304
1931 BOS N O   97 .287
1932 CIN N O   44 .257
        BLTR   698 .308

RICHERT, PETER GERARD (PETE)
B.OCT.29,1939 FLORAL PARK,N.Y.
1962 LA N P   19 5- 4
1963 LA N P   20 5- 3
1964 LA N P   8 2- 3
1965 WAS A P   34 42 15-12
1966 WAS A P   36 43 14-14
1967 WAS A P   11 12 2- 6
     BAL A P   26 27 7-10
1968 BAL A P   36 6- 3
1969 BAL A P   44 7- 4
1970 BAL A P   50 7- 2
1971 BAL A P   35 3- 5
1972 LA N P   37 2- 3
1973 LA N P   39 3- 3
1974 STL N P   13 0- 0
     PHI N P   21 2- 1
        BLTL   429 446 80-73

RICHIE, LEWIS A.
B.AUG.23,1883 AMBLER,PA.
D.AUG.15,1936 AMBLER,PA.
1906 PHI N P   33 9-11
1907 PHI N P   25 6- 6
1908 PHI N P   25 7-10
1909 PHI N P   11 1- 1
          BOS N P   25 7- 7
1910 BOS N P   4 0- 3
          CHI N P   28 11- 4
1911 CHI N P   36 15-11
1912 CHI N P   39 16- 8
1913 CHI N P   16 2- 4
        BRTR   242 74-65

RICHMOND, BERYL JUSTICE
B.AUG.24,1907 GLEN EASTON,W.VA.
1933 CIN N P   5 0- 0
1934 CIN N P   6 1- 2
        BBTL   11 1- 2
        BR 1933

RICHMOND, DONALD LESTER (DON)
B.OCT.27,1919 GILLETT,PA.
1941 PHI A 3   9 .200
1946 PHI A 3   16 .290
1947 PHI A 2-3   19 .190
1951 STL N 3   12 .088
        BLTR   56 .211

RICHMOND, JOHN H.
B.PHILADELPHIA,PA.
1875 ATH NA C-2-O   27 .213
1879 SYR N S-O   61 .211
1880 BOS N S-O   31 .248
1881 BOS N S-O   26 .275
1882 CLE N O   39 .154
          ATH AA O 19 .173
1883 COL AA S   91 .274
1884 COL AA S   105 .237
1885 PIT AA S   34 .206
          TR   433 .231

RICHMOND, JOHN LEE
B.MAY 5,1857 SHEFFIELD,OHIO
D.OCT.1,1929 TOLEDO,OHIO
1879 BOS N P   1 1- 0
1880 WOR N P-O   67 75 31-33
                       .224
1881 WOR N P-O   52 60 25-27
                       .251
1882 WOR N P-O   47 55 14-33
                       .280
1883 PRO N P-O   11 48 3- 8
                       .283
1886 CIN AA P-O   3 8 0- 1
                       .260
          TL   181 247 74-102
                       .258

RICHMOND, RAYMOND SINCLAIR
B.JUNE 15,1896 FILLMORE,ILL.
D.OCT.21,1969 DE SOTO,MO.
1920 STL A P   2 2- 0
1921 STL A P   6 0- 1
        BRTR   8 2- 1

RICHTER, ALLEN GORDON (AL)
B.FEB.7,1927 NORFOLK,VA.
1951 BOS A S   5 .091
1953 BOS A S   1 .000
        BRTR   6 .091

RICHTER, EMIL HENRY (REGGIE)
B.SEPT.14,1888 DUSSELDORF,GERMANY
D.AUG.2,1934 WINFIELD,ILL.
1911 CHI N P   22 1- 3
        BRTR

RICHTER, JOHN M.
B.LOUISVILLE,KY.
1898 LOU N 3   3 .154

RICKERT, JOSEPH FRANCIS
(JOE) OR (DIAMOND JOE)
B.DEC.12,1876 LONDON,OHIO
D.OCT.15,1943 SPRINGFIELD,OHIO
1898 PIT N O   2 .167
1901 BOS N O   13 .175
                    15 .174

RICKERT, MARVIN AUGUST
(MARV) OR (TWITCH)
B.JAN.8,1921 LONG BRANCH,WASH.
D.JUNE 3,1978 OAKVILLE,WASH.
1942 CHI N O   8 .269
1946 CHI N O   111 .263
1947 CHI N 1-O   71 .146
1948 CIN N H   8 .167
          BOS N O   3 .231
1949 BOS N 1-O   100 .292
1950 PIT N O   17 .150
          CHI A 1-O 84 .237
        BLTR   402 .247

RICKETTS, DAVID WILLIAM (DAVE)
B.JULY 12,1935 POTTSTOWN,PA.
1963 STL N C   3 .250
1965 STL N C   11 .241
1967 STL N C   52 .273
1968 STL N /C   20 .136
1969 STL N /C   30 .273
1970 PIT N /C   14 .182
        BBTR   130 .249

RICKETTS, RICHARD JAMES (DICK)
B.DEC.4,1933 POTTSTOWN,PA.
1959 STL N P   12 1- 6
        BLTR

RICKEY, WESLEY BRANCH
(BRANCH) OR (THE MAHATMA)
B.DEC.20,1881 LUCASVILLE,OHIO
D.DEC.9,1965 COLUMBIA,MO.
1905 STL A C   1 .000
1906 STL A C   64 .284
1907 NY A C-O   52 .182
1914 STL A M-H   2 .000
        BLTR   119 .239
NON-PLAYING MANAGER
STL(A) 1913-15, STL(N) 1919-25

RICKLEY, CHRISTIAN
B.PHILADELPHIA,PA.
1884 KEY U S   7 .207

RICKS, JOHN
1891 STL AA 3   5 .158
1894 STL N 3   1 .000
                     6 .150

RICO, ALFREDO [CRUZ] (FRED)
B.JULY 4,1944 JEROME,ARIZ.
1969 KC A /O-3   12 .231
        BRTR

RICO, ARTHUR RAYMOND
B.JULY 23,1896 ROXBURY,MASS.
D.JAN.3,1919 BOSTON,MASS.
1916 BOS N C   4 .000
1917 BOS N C   13 .286
        BRTR   17 .222

RICONDA, HENRY PAUL (HARRY)
B.MAR.17,1897 NEW YORK,N.Y.
D.NOV.13,1958 MAHOPAC,N.Y.
1923 PHI A 3   55 .263
1924 PHI A 3   83 .293
1926 BOS N 3   4 .167
1928 BRO N 2-S-3   92 .224
1929 PIT N S   8 .467
1930 CIN N H   1 .000
        BRTR   243 .243

RIDDLE, ELMER RAY
B.JULY 31,1914 COLUMBUS,GA.
1939 CIN N P   1 0- 0
1940 CIN N P   15 1- 2
1941 CIN N P   33 19- 4
1942 CIN N P   29 7-11
1943 CIN N P   36 21-11
1944 CIN N P   4 2- 2
1945 CIN N P   12 1- 4
1947 CIN N P   16 1- 0
1948 PIT N P   28 29 12-10
1949 PIT N P   16 1- 8
        BRTR   190 191 65-52

YR	CL	LEA	POS	GP	G	REC

RIDDLE, JOHN H.
B.PHILADELPHIA,PA.

YR	CL	LEA	POS	GP	G	REC
1889	WAS	N	C		11	.210
1890	ATH	AA	C-O		25	.115
					36	.147

RIDDLE, JOHN LUDY (MUTT)
B.OCT.3,1905 CLINTON,S.C.

1930	CHI	A	C		25	.241
1937	WAS	A	C		8	.269
	BOS	N	C		2	.000
1938	BOS	N	C		19	.281
1941	CIN	N	C		10	.300
1944	CIN	N	C		1	.000
1945	CIN	N	C		23	.178
1948	PIT	N	C		10	.200
	BRTR				98	.238

RIDDLEMOSER, DENNIS MICHAEL
B.NOV.22,1945 CLIFTON FORGE,VA.

1970	WAS	A	/P		8	0- 0
1971	WAS	A	P		57	3- 1
1972	CLE	A	P		38	1- 3
	BRTL				103	4- 4

RIDDLEMOSER, DORSEY LEE
B.MAR.25,1875 FREDERICK,MD.
D.MAY 11,1954 FREDERICK,MD.

| 1899 | WAS | N | P | | 1 | 0- 0 |
| | BRTR | | | | | |

RIDGEWAY, JOHN A. (JACK)
B.1891 PHILADELPHIA,PA.

| 1914 | BAL | F | P | | 4 | 0- 0 |
| | BLTR | | | | | |

RIDZIK, STEPHEN GEORGE (STEVE)
B.APR.29,1929 YONKERS,N.Y.

1950	PHI	N	P		1	0- 0
1952	PHI	N	P		24	4- 2
1953	PHI	N	P		42	9- 6
1954	PHI	N	P		35	4- 5
1955	PHI	N	P		3	0- 1
	CIN	N	P		13	0- 3
1956	NY	N	P	41	44	6- 2
1957	NY	N	P	15	16	0- 2
1958	CLE	A	P		6	0- 2
1963	WAS	A	P		20	5- 6
1964	WAS	A	P		49	5- 5
1965	WAS	A	P		63	6- 4
1966	PHI	N	/P		2	0- 0
	BRTR			314	318	39-38

RIEBE, HARVEY DONALD (HANK)
B.OCT.10,1921 CLEVELAND,OHIO

1942	DET	A	C		11	.314
1947	DET	A	C		8	.000
1948	DET	A	C		25	.194
1949	DET	A	C		17	.182
	BRTR				61	.212

RIEGER, ELMER JAY
B.FEB.25,1889 PERRIS,CAL.
D.OCT.21,1959 LOS ANGELES,CAL.

| 1910 | STL | N | P | | 13 | 0- 2 |
| | BBTR | | | | | |

RIGGERT, JOSEPH ALOYSIUS
B.DEC.11,1886 JANESVILLE,WIS.
D.DEC.10,1973 KANSAS CITY,MO.

1911	BOS	A	O		50	.212
1914	BRO	N	O		27	.190
	STL	N	O		34	.216
1919	BOS	N	O		63	.283
	BRTR				174	.240

RIGGS, LEWIS SIDNEY
B.APR.22,1910 MEBANE,N.C.
D.AUG.12,1975 DURHAM,N.C.

1934	STL	N	H		2	.000
1935	CIN	N	3		142	.278
1936	CIN	N	3		141	.257
1937	CIN	N	2-S-3		122	.242
1938	CIN	N	3		142	.252
1939	CIN	N	3		22	.158
1940	CIN	N	3		41	.292
1941	BRO	N	1-2-3		77	.305
1942	BRO	N	1-3		70	.278
1946	BRO	N	3		1	.000
	BLTR				760	.262

RIGNEY, EMORY ELMO (TOPPER)
B.JAN.7,1897 GROVETON,TEX.
D.JUNE 6,1972 SAN ANTONIO,TEX.

1922	DET	A	S		155	.300
1923	DET	A	S		129	.315
1924	DET	A	S		147	.289
1925	DET	A	S-3		62	.247
1926	BOS	A	S		148	.270
1927	BOS	A	3		7	.118
	WAS	A	S-3		46	.271
	BRTR				694	.288

RIGNEY, JOHN DUNCAN (JOHNNY)
B.OCT.28,1914 OAK PARK,ILL.

1937	CHI	A	P		22	2- 5
1938	CHI	A	P		38	9- 9
1939	CHI	A	P		35	15- 8
1940	CHI	A	P	39	40	14-18
1941	CHI	A	P		30	13-13
1942	CHI	A	P		7	3- 3
1946	CHI	A	P		15	5- 5
1947	CHI	A	P		11	2- 3
	BRTR			197	198	63-64

RIGNEY, WILLIAM JOSEPH (BILL)
(SPECS) OR (THE CRICKET)
B.JAN.29,1918 ALAMEDA,CAL.

1946	NY	N	S-3		110	.236
1947	NY	N	2-S-3		130	.267
1948	NY	N	2-S		113	.264
1949	NY	N	2-S-3		122	.278
1950	NY	N	2-3		56	.181
1951	NY	N	2-3		44	.232
1952	NY	N	1-2-S-3		60	.300
1953	NY	N	2-3		19	.250
	BRTR				654	.259

NON-PLAYING MANAGER
NY(N) 1956-57, SF(N) 1958-60,
LA(A) 1963-65, CAL(A) 1966-69,
MIN(A) 1970-72, SF(N) 1976

RIKARD, CULLEY
B.MAY 9,1914 OXFORD,MISS.

1941	PIT	N	O		6	.200
1942	PIT	N	O		38	.192
1947	PIT	N	O		109	.287
	BLTR				153	.270

RILEY, JAMES JOSEPH
B.NOV.10,1886 BUFFALO,N.Y.
D.MAR.25,1949 BUFFALO,N.Y.

| 1910 | BOS | N | O | | 1 | .000 |
| | BRTR | | | | | |

RILEY, JAMES NORMAN
B.MAY 25,1895 BAYFIELD,N.B.,CAN
D.MAY 25,1969 SEGUIN,TEX.

1921	STL	A	3		4	.000
1923	WAS	A	1		2	.000
	BLTR				6	.000

RILEY, LEON FRANCIS (LEE)
B.AUG.20,1906 PRINCETON,NEB.
D.SEPT.13,1970 SCHENECTADY,N.Y.

| 1944 | PHI | N | O | | 4 | .083 |
| | BLTR | | | | | |

RILEY, WILLIAM JAMES (PIGTAIL BILLY)
B.1857 CINCINNATI,OHIO
O.NOV.9,1887 CINCINNATI,OHIO

1875	WES	NA	O		8	-
1879	CLE	N	O		43	.142
					51	-

RING, JAMES JOSEPH (JIMMY)
B.FEB.15,1895 BROOKLYN,N.Y.
D.JULY 6,1965 NEW YORK,N.Y.

1917	CIN	N	P		24	3- 7
1918	CIN	N	P		21	9- 5
1919	CIN	N	P		32	10- 9
1920	CIN	N	P		42	17-16
1921	PHI	N	P		34	10-19
1922	PHI	N	P		40	12-18
1923	PHI	N	P	39	41	18-16
1924	PHI	N	P		32	10-12
1925	PHI	N	P		38	14-16
1926	NY	N	P		39	11-10
1927	STL	N	P		13	0- 4
1928	PHI	N	P		35	4-17
	BRTR			389	391	118-149

RINGO, FRANK C.
B.OCT.12,1861 LIBERTY,MO.
D.APR.12,1889 KANSAS CITY,MO.

1883	PHI	N	C-2-S-3-O		57	.183
1884	PHI	N	C		25	.132
	ATH	AA	C		2	.000
1885	DET	N	C-3-O		16	.246
	PIT	AA	C		3	.182
1886	PIT	AA	C-1		16	.241
	KC	N	C		16	.232
					135	.193

RINKER, ROBERT JOHN
B.APR.21,1921 AUDENRIED,PA.

| 1950 | PHI | A | C | | 3 | .333 |
| | BRTR | | | | | |

RIOS, JUAN O. [VELEZ]
B.JULY 14,1945 MAYAGUEZ,P.R.

| 1969 | KC | A | 2-S/3 | | 87 | .224 |
| | BRTR | | | | | |

RIPLEY, ALLEN STEVENS
B.OCT.18,1952 NORWOOD,MASS.

| 1978 | BOS | A | P | | 15 | 2- 5 |
| | BRTR | | | | | |

RIPLEY, WALTER FRANKLIN
B.NOV.26,1916 WORCESTER,MASS.

| 1935 | BOS | A | P | | 2 | 0- 0 |
| | BRTR | | | | | |

RIPPAY, BENJAMIN WESLEY
[PLAYED UNDER NAME OF
CHARLES WESLEY JONES]

RIPPELMEYER, RAYMOND ROY (RAY)
B.JULY 9,1933 VALMEYER,ILL.

| 1962 | WAS | A | P | | 18 | 1- 2 |
| | BRTR | | | | | |

RIPPLE, CHARLES DAWSON
B.DEC.1,1921 BOLTON,N.C.

1944	PHI	N	P		1	0- 0
1945	PHI	N	P		4	0- 1
1946	PHI	N	P		6	1- 0
	BLTL				11	1- 1

RIPPLE, JAMES ALBERT (JIMMY)
B.OCT.14,1909 EXPORT,PA.
D.JULY 16,1959 GREENSBURG,PA.

1936	NY	N	O		96	.305
1937	NY	N	O		121	.317
1938	NY	N	O		134	.261
1939	NY	N	O		66	.228
	BRO	N	O		28	.330
1940	BRO	N	O		7	.231
	CIN	N	O		32	.307
1941	CIN	N	O		38	.216
1943	PHI	A	O		32	.238
	BLTR				554	.282

RISBERG, CHARLES AUGUST (SWEDE)
B.OCT.13,1894 SAN FRANCISCO,CAL
D.OCT.13,1975 RED BLUFF,CAL.

1917	CHI	A	S		149	.203
1918	CHI	A	2-S-3		82	.256
1919	CHI	A	1-S		119	.256
1920	CHI	A	S		126	.266
	BRTR				476	.243

RISING, PERRY SUMNER (POP)
B.INDUSTRY,PA.

| 1905 | BOS | A | O | | 11 | .100 |

RITCHEY, CLAUDE CASSIUS
(CLAUDE) OR (LITTLE ALL RIGHT)
B.OCT.5,1873 EMLENTON,PA.
D.NOV.8,1951 EMLENTON,PA.

1897	CIN	N	S-O		100	.288
1898	LOU	N	2-S		152	.259
1899	LOU	N	2		147	.309
1900	PIT	N	2		123	.295
1901	PIT	N	2		140	.298
1902	PIT	N	2-O		114	.275
1903	PIT	N	2		137	.287
1904	PIT	N	2		156	.263
1905	PIT	N	2		153	.255
1906	PIT	N	2		151	.269
1907	BOS	N	2		144	.255
1908	BOS	N	2		120	.273
1909	BOS	N	2		25	.172
	BBTR				1662	.276

RITCHIE, JAY SEAY
B.NOV.20,1936 SALISBURY,N.C.

1964	BOS	A	P		21	1- 1
1965	BOS	A	P		44	1- 2
1966	ATL	N	P		22	0- 1
1967	ATL	N	P		52	4- 6
1968	CIN	N	P		28	2- 3
	BRTR				167	8-13

RITTER

| 1885 | BUF | N | 2 | | 2 | .167 |

RITTER, FLOYD ALEXANDER
B.JUNE 1,1870 DORSET,OHIO
D.FEB.7,1943 STEVENSON,WASH.

| 1890 | TOL | AA | C | | 1 | .000 |
| | BRTR | | | | | |

RITTER, LEWIS ELMER (OLD DOG)
B.SEPT.7,1875 LIVERPOOL,PA.
D.MAY 27,1952 HARRISBURG,PA.

1902	BRO	N	C		16	.250
1903	BRO	N	C		75	.236
1904	BRO	N	C		63	.248
1905	BRO	N	C		90	.219
1906	BRO	N	C		67	.208
1907	BRO	N	C		89	.203
1908	BRO	N	C		37	.192
	BRTR				437	.221

RITTER, WILLIAM HERBERT (HANK)
B.OCT.12,1893 MC COYSVILLE,PA.
D.SEPT.3,1964 AKRON,OHIO

1912	PHI	N	P		3	0- 0
1914	NY	N	P		1	1- 0
1915	NY	N	P		22	2- 1
1916	NY	N	P		3	1- 0
	BRTR				29	4- 1

```
YR  CL LEA POS      GP   G    REC
```

RITTERSON, E. W.
1876 ATH N C   15   .250

RITTWAGE, JAMES MICHAEL (JIM)
B.OCT.23,1944 CLEVELAND,OHIO
1970 CLE A /P-3   8   1- 1
                               .375
     BRTR

RITZ, JAMES L.
B.1874 PITTSBURGH,PA.
D.NOV.10,1896 PITTSBURGH,PA.
1894 PIT N 3   1   .000

RIVERA, JESUS MANUEL (TORRES)
(BOMBO)
B.AUG.2,1952 PONCE,PR.
1975 MON N /O   5   .111
1976 MON N O   68   .276
1978 MIN A O   101   .271
     BRTR   174   .270

RIVERA, MANUEL JOSEPH (JIM)
OR (JUNGLE JIM)
B.JULY 22,1922 NEW YORK,N.Y.
1952 STL A O   97   .256
     CHI A O   53   .249
1953 CHI A O   156   .259
1954 CHI A O   145   .286
1955 CHI A O   147   .264
1956 CHI A O   139   .255
1957 CHI A 1-O   125   .256
1958 CHI A O   116   .225
1959 CHI A O   80   .220
1960 CHI A O   48   .294
1961 CHI A H   1   .000
     KC A   64   .241
     BLTL   1171   .256

RIVIERE, ARTHUR BERNARD (TINK)
B.AUG.2,1899 LIBERTY,TEX.
D.SEPT.27,1965 LIBERTY,TEX.
1921 STL N P   18   1- 0
1925 CHI A P   3   0- 0
     BRTR   21   1- 0

RIVERS, JOHN MILTON (MICKEY)
B.OCT.31,1948 MIAMI,FLA.
1970 CAL A /O   17   .320
1971 CAL A O   78   .265
1972 CAL A O   56   .214
1973 CAL A O   30   .349
1974 CAL A *O   118   .285
1975 CAL A O   155   .284
1976 NY A *O   137   .312
1977 NY A *O   138   .326
1978 NY A *O   141   .265
     BLTL   872   .291

RIXEY, EPPA (JEPTHA)
B.MAY 3,1891 CULPEPER,VA.
D.FEB.28,1963 CINCINNATI,OHIO
1912 PHI N P   23   10-10
1913 PHI N P   35   9- 5
1914 PHI N P   24   2-11
1915 PHI N P   29   11-12
1916 PHI N P   38   22-10
1917 PHI N P   39   16-21
1919 PHI N P   23   6-12
1920 PHI N P   41 43   11-22
1921 CIN N P   40   19-18
1922 CIN N P   40   25-13
1923 CIN N P   42   20-15
1924 CIN N P   35   15-14
1925 CIN N P   39   21-11
1926 CIN N P   37   14- 8
1927 CIN N P   34   12-10
1928 CIN N P   43   19-18
1929 CIN N P   35   10-13
1930 CIN N P   32   9-13
1931 CIN N P   22   4- 7
1932 CIN N P   25   5- 5
1933 CIN N P   16   6- 3
     BRTL   692 694 266-251

RIZZO, JOHN COSTA (JOHNNY)
B.JULY 30,1912 HOUSTON,TEX.
D.DEC.4,1977 HOUSTON,TEX.
1938 PIT N O   143   .301
1939 PIT N O   94   .261
1940 PIT N O   9   .179
     CIN N O   31   .282
     PHI N 3-O   103   .292
1941 PHI N 3-O   99   .217
1942 BRO N O   78   .230
     BRTR   557   .270

RIZZUTO, PHILIP FRANCIS
(PHIL) OR (SCOOTER)
B.SEPT.25,1917 BROOKLYN,N.Y.
1941 NY A S   133   .307
1942 NY A S   144   .284
1946 NY A S   126   .257
1947 NY A S   153   .273
1948 NY A S   128   .252
1949 NY A S   153   .275
1950 NY A S   155   .324
1951 NY A S   144   .274
1952 NY A S   152   .254
1953 NY A S   134   .271
1954 NY A 2-S   127   .195
1955 NY A 2-S   81   .259
1956 NY A S   31   .231
     BRTR   1661   .273

ROACH, JAMES MICHAEL (MIKE)
B.1876 NEW YORK,N.Y.
D.NOV.12,1916 BINGHAMTON,N.Y.
1899 WAS N C   21   .237

ROACH, JOHN F.
B.ATHENS,PA.
D.MAR.1,1915 SANDUSKY,OHIO
1867 NY N P   1   0- 1
     TL

ROACH, MELVIN EARL (MEL)
B.JAN.25,1933 RICHMOND,VA.
1953 MIL N 2   5   .000
1954 MIL N 1   3   .000
1957 MIL N 2   7   .167
1958 MIL N 1-2-O   44   .309
1959 MIL N 2-3-O   19   .097
1960 MIL N 1-2-3-O   48   .300
1961 MIL N 1-O   13   .167
     CHI N 1-2   23   .128
1962 PHI N 1-2-3-O   65   .190
     BRTR   227   .239

ROACH, WILBUR CHARLES (ROXEY)
B.NOV.c.8,1882 ANITA,PA.
D.DEC.26,1947 BAY CITY,MICH.
1910 NY A S   70   .214
1911 NY A S   12   .250
1912 WAS A S   2   .500
1915 BUF F S   92   .270
     BRTR   176   .249

ROARKE, MICHAEL THOMAS (MIKE)
B.NOV.8,1930 WEST WARWICK,R.I.
1961 DET A C   86   .223
1962 DET A C   56   .213
1963 DET A C   23   .318
1964 DET A C   29   .232
     BRTR   194   .230

ROAT, FREDERICK
B.FEB.10,1868 OREGON,ILL.
1890 PIT N 3   57   .223
1892 CHI N 2   8   .200
                         65   .220

ROBELLO, THOMAS VARDASCO (TONY)
B.FEB.9,1913 SAN LEANDRO,CAL.
1933 CIN N 2-3   14   .233
1934 CIN N H   2   .000
     BRTR   16   .219

ROBERGE, JOSEPH ALBERT ARMAND
(SKIPPY)
B.MAY 19,1917 LOWELL,MASS.
1941 BOS N 2-S-3   55   .216
1942 BOS N 2-3   74   .215
1946 BOS N 3   48   .231
     BRTR   177   .220

ROBERSON, JOHN HENRY
[PLAYED UNDER NAME OF
JOHN HENRY ROBINSON]

ROBERTS, CHARLES EMORY (RED)
B.AUG.8,1918 CARROLLTON,GA.
1943 WAS A S-3   9   .261
     BRTR

ROBERTS, CLARENCE ASHLEY (SKIPPER)
B.JAN.11,1888 WARDNER,IDAHO
D.DEC.24,1963 LONG BEACH,CAL.
1913 STL N C   26   .146
1914 PIT F C   32   .226
     CHI F C   4   .333
     PIT F C   18   .228
     BLTR   80   .210

ROBERTS, CURTIS BENJAMIN (CURT)
B.AUG.16,1929 PINELAND,TEX.
D.NOV.14,1969 OAKLAND,CAL.
1954 PIT N 2   134   .232
1955 PIT N 2   6   .118
1956 PIT N 2   31   .177
     BRTR   171   .223

ROBERTS, DALE
(DALE) OR (MOUNTAIN MAN)
B.APR.12,1942 OWENTON,KY.
1967 NY A /P   2   0- 0
     BRTL

ROBERTS, DAVID ARTHUR (DAVE)
B.SEP.11,1944 GALLIPOLIS,OHIO
1969 SD N P   22 23   0- 3
1970 SD N P   43   8-14
1971 SD N P   37 38 14-17
1972 HOU N P   35 12- 7
1973 HOU N P   39 41 17-11
1974 HOU N P   34 35 10-12
1975 HOU N P   32   8-14
1976 DET A P   36 16-17
1977 DET A P   22   4-10
     CHI N P   17   1- 1
1978 CHI N P   35 37   6- 8
     BLTL   352 359 96-114

ROBERTS, DAVID LEONARD (DAVE)
B.JUNE 30,1933 PANAMA CITY,PAN.
1962 HOU N 1-O   16   .245
1964 HOU N 1-O   61   .184
1966 PIT N /1   14   .125
     BLTL   91   .196

ROBERTS, DAVID WAYNE (DAVE)
B.FEB.17,1951 LEBANON,ORE.
1972 SD N 3-2/S-C   100   .244
1973 SD N *3-2   127   .286
1974 SD N *3/S-O   113   .167
1975 SD N 3/2   32   .263
1977 SD N C/2-3-S   82   .220
1978 SD N C/1-O   54   .216
     BRTR   509   .240

ROBERTS, JAMES NEWSON (BIG JIM)
B.OCT.13,1895 ARTESIA,MISS.
1924 BRO N P   11   0- 3
1925 BRO N P   1   0- 0
     BRTR   12   0- 3

ROBERTS, LEON KAUFFMAN
B.JAN.22,1951 VICKSBURG,MICH.
1974 DET A O   17   .270
1975 DET A *O   129   .257
1976 HOU N O   8   .074
1977 HOU N /O   19   .074
1978 SEA A *O   134   .301
     BRTR   386   .277

ROBERTS, RAYMOND
B.AUG.25,1895 CRUGER,MISS.
D.JAN.30,1962 CRUGER,MISS.
1919 PHI A P   3   0- 2
     BLTR

ROBERTS, ROBIN EVAN
B.SEP.30,1926 SPRINGFIELD,ILL.
1948 PHI N P   20 21   7- 9
1949 PHI N P   43 15-15
1950 PHI N P   40 20-11
1951 PHI N P   44 21-15
1952 PHI N P   39 28- 7
1953 PHI N P   44 23-16
1954 PHI N P   45 23-15
1955 PHI N P   41 51 23-14
1956 PHI N P   43 19-18
1957 PHI N P   39 10-22
1958 PHI N P   35 36 17-14
1959 PHI N P   35 15-17
1960 PHI N P   35 12-16
1961 PHI N P   26   1-10
1962 BAL A P   27 10- 9
1963 BAL A P   35 14-13
1964 BAL A P   31 13- 7
1965 BAL A P   20   5- 7
1966 BAL A P   10   5- 2
     HOU N P   13   3- 5
     CHI N P   11   2- 3
     BBTR   676 688 286-245
     BR 1948-52

ROBERTS, THOMAS
B.BALTIMORE,MD.
1874 ATL NA O   1   .000

ROBERTSON, ALFRED JAMES (JIM)
B.JAN.29,1928 CHICAGO,ILL.
1954 PHI A C   63   .184
1955 KC A C   6   .250
     BRTR   69   .187

ROBERTSON, CHARLES CULBERTSON
B.JAN.31,1896 DEXTER,TEX.

YR	CL	LEA	POS	GP	G	REC
1919	CHI	A	P		1	0- 1
1922	CHI	A	P		37	14-15
1923	CHI	A	P		38	13-18
1924	CHI	A	P		17	4-10
1925	CHI	A	P		24	8-12
1926	STL	A	P		8	1- 2
1927	BOS	N	P		28	7-17
1928	BOS	N	P		13	2- 5
BLTR					166	49-80

ROBERTSON, DARYL BERDENE
B.JAN.5,1936 CRIPPLE CREEK,COLO

YR	CL	LEA	POS	G	REC
1962	CHI	N	S-3	9	.105
BRTR					

ROBERTSON, DAVIS AYDELOTTE (DAVE)
B.SEPT.25,1889 PORTSMOUTH,VA.
D.NOV.5,1970 VIRGINIA BEACH,VA.

YR	CL	LEA	POS	G	REC
1912	NY	N	1-O	3	.000
1914	NY	N	O	82	.266
1915	NY	N	O	141	.294
1916	NY	N	O	150	.307
1917	NY	N	O	142	.259
1919	NY	N	O	1	.000
	CHI	N	O	27	.208
1920	CHI	N	O	134	.300
1921	CHI	N	O	22	.222
	PIT	N	O	60	.322
1922	NY	N	O	42	.276
BLTL				804	.287

ROBERTSON, DONALD ALEXANDER
B.OCT.15,1930 HARVEY,ILL.

YR	CL	LEA	POS	G	REC
1954	CHI	N	O	14	.000
BLTL					

ROBERTSON, EUGENE EDWARD
B.DEC.29,1899 ST.LOUIS,MO.

YR	CL	LEA	POS	G	REC
1919	STL	A	S	5	.143
1922	STL	A	S-3	18	.296
1923	STL	A	3	78	.247
1924	STL	A	3	121	.319
1925	STL	A	S-3	134	.271
1926	STL	A	S-3	78	.251
1928	NY	A	3	83	.291
1929	NY	A	3	90	.298
	BOS	N	3	8	.286
1930	BOS	N	3	21	.186
BLTR				636	.280

ROBERTSON, JERRY LEE
B.OCT.13,1943 WINCHESTER,KAN.

YR	CL	LEA	POS	G	REC
1969	MON	N	P	38	5-16
1970	DET	A	P	11	0- 0
BBTR				49	5-16

ROBERTSON, PRESTON (DICK)
B.1891 WASHINGTON,D.C.
D.OCT.2,1944 NEW ORLEANS,LA.

YR	CL	LEA	POS	GP	G	REC
1913	CIN	N	P		2	0- 1
1918	BRO	N	P	13	14	3- 6
1919	WAS	A	P		7	0- 2
BRTR				22	23	3- 9

ROBERTSON, RICHARD PAUL (RICH)
B.OCT.14,1944 ALBANY,CAL.

YR	CL	LEA	POS	G	REC
1966	SF	N	/P	1	0- 0
1967	SF	N	/P	1	0- 0
1968	SF	N	/P	3	2- 0
1969	SF	N	P	17	1- 3
1970	SF	N	P	41	8- 9
1971	SF	N	P	23	2- 2
BRTR				86	13-14

ROBERTSON, ROBERT EUGENE (BOB)
B.OCT.2,1946 FROSTBURG,MD.

YR	CL	LEA	POS	G	REC
1967	PIT	N	/1	9	.171
1969	PIT	N	1	32	.208
1970	PIT	N	1/3-O	117	.287
1971	PIT	N	*1	131	.271
1972	PIT	N	1-O-3	115	.193
1973	PIT	N	*1	119	.239
1974	PIT	N	1	91	.229
1975	PIT	N	1	75	.274
1976	PIT	N	1	61	.217
1978	SEA	A	O-1	64	.230
BRTR				814	.244

ROBERTSON, SHERRARD ALEXANDER (SHERRY)
B.JAN.1,1919 MONTREAL,QUE.,CAN.
D.OCT.23,1970 HOUGHTON,S.DAK.

YR	CL	LEA	POS	G	REC
1940	WAS	A	S	10	.212
1941	WAS	A	S	1	.000
1943	WAS	A	S-3	59	.217
1946	WAS	A	2-S-3-O	74	.200
1947	WAS	A	2-3-O	95	.233
1948	WAS	A	O	71	.246
1949	WAS	A	2-3-O	110	.241
1950	WAS	A	2-3-O	71	.260
1951	WAS	A	O	62	.193
1952	WAS	A	H	1	.000
	PHI	N	2-3-O	43	.200
BLTR				597	.230

ROBINSON, AARON ANDREW
B.JUNE 23,1915 LANCASTER,S.C.
D.MAR.9,1966 LANCASTER,S.C.

YR	CL	LEA	POS	G	REC
1943	NY	A	H	1	.000
1945	NY	A	H	50	.281
1946	NY	A	H	100	.297
1947	NY	A	H	82	.270
1948	CHI	A	H	98	.252
1949	DET	A	H	110	.269
1950	DET	A	H	107	.226
1951	DET	A	H	36	.207
	BOS	A	H	26	.203
BLTR				610	.260

ROBINSON, ALFRED V.

YR	CL	LEA	POS	G	REC
1872	OLY	NA	O	7	.188

ROBINSON, BROOKS CALBERT
B.MAY 18,1937 LITTLE ROCK,ARK.

YR	CL	LEA	POS	G	REC
1955	BAL	A	3	6	.091
1956	BAL	A	2-3	15	.227
1957	BAL	A	3	50	.239
1958	BAL	A	2-3	145	.238
1959	BAL	A	2-3	88	.284
1960	BAL	A	2-3	152	.294
1961	BAL	A	2-S-3	163	.287
1962	BAL	A	2-S-3	162	.303
1963	BAL	A	S-3	161	.251
1964	BAL	A	3	163	.317
1965	BAL	A	*3	144	.297
1966	BAL	A	*3	157	.269
1967	BAL	A	*3	158	.269
1968	BAL	A	*3	162	.253
1969	BAL	A	*3	156	.234
1970	BAL	A	*3	158	.276
1971	BAL	A	*3	156	.272
1972	BAL	A	*3	153	.250
1973	BAL	A	*3	155	.257
1974	BAL	A	*3	153	.288
1975	BAL	A	*3	144	.201
1976	BAL	A	3	71	.211
1977	BAL	A	3	24	.149
BRTR				2896	.267

ROBINSON, BRUCE PHILIP
B.APR.16,1954 LA JOLLA,CAL.

YR	CL	LEA	POS	G	REC
1978	OAK	A	C	28	.250
BLTR					

ROBINSON, CHARLES HENRY
B.JULY 27,1856 WESTERLY,R.I.
D.MAY 10,1913

YR	CL	LEA	POS	G	REC
1884	IND	AA	C-S-O	19	.286
1885	BRO	AA	O	12	.143
				31	.241

ROBINSON, CLYDE (RABBIT)
B.MAR.5,1882 WELLSBURG,W.VA.
D.APR.9,1915 WATERBURY,CONN.

YR	CL	LEA	POS	G	REC
1903	WAS	A	2-S-O	103	.219
1904	DET	A	2-S-3-O	97	.204
1910	CIN	N	3	2	.000
BRTR				202	.210

ROBINSON, CRAIG GEORGE
B.AUG.21,1948 ABINGTON,PA.

YR	CL	LEA	POS	G	REC
1972	PHI	N	/S	5	.200
1973	PHI	N	S/2	46	.226
1974	ATL	N	*S	145	.230
1975	ATL	N	/S	10	.059
	SF	N	S/2	29	.069
1976	SF	N	/2-3-S	15	.308
	ATL	N	/2-S-3	15	.235
1977	ATL	N	S	27	.207
BRTR				292	.219

ROBINSON, DAVID TANNER (DAVE)
B.MAY 22,1946 MINNEAPOLIS,MINN.

YR	CL	LEA	POS	G	REC
1970	SD	N	O	15	.316
1971	SD	N	/H	7	.000
BBTR				22	.273

ROBINSON, DON ALLEN
B.JUNE 8,1957 ASHLAND,KY.

YR	CL	LEA	POS	G	REC
1978	PIT	N	P	35	14- 6
BRTR					

ROBINSON, EARL JOHN
B.NOV.3,1936 NEW ORLEANS,LA.

YR	CL	LEA	POS	G	REC
1958	LA	N	3	8	.200
1961	BAL	A	O	96	.266
1962	BAL	A	O	29	.286
1964	BAL	A	O	37	.273
BRTR				170	.268

ROBINSON, FLOYD ANDREW
B.MAY 9,1936 PRESCOTT,ARK.

YR	CL	LEA	POS	G	REC
1960	CHI	A	O	22	.283
1961	CHI	A	O	132	.310
1962	CHI	A	O	156	.312
1963	CHI	A	O	146	.283
1964	CHI	A	O	141	.301
1965	CHI	A	*O	156	.265
1966	CHI	A	*O	127	.237
1967	CIN	N	O	55	.238
1968	OAK	A	O	53	.247
	BOS	A	O	24	.125
BLTR				1012	.283

ROBINSON, FRANK
B.AUG.31,1935 BEAUMONT,TEX.

YR	CL	LEA	POS	G	REC
1956	CIN	N	O	152	.290
1957	CIN	N	1-O	150	.322
1958	CIN	N	3-O	148	.269
1959	CIN	N	1-O	146	.311
1960	CIN	N	1-3-O	139	.297
1961	CIN	N	3-O	153	.323
1962	CIN	N	O	162	.342
1963	CIN	N	1-O	140	.259
1964	CIN	N	O	156	.306
1965	CIN	N	*O	156	.296
1966	BAL	A	*O/1	155	.316
1967	BAL	A	*O/1	129	.311
1968	BAL	A	*O/1	130	.268
1969	BAL	A	*O-1	148	.308
1970	BAL	A	*O/1	132	.306
1971	BAL	A	O-1	133	.281
1972	LA	N	O	103	.251
1973	CAL	A	*O-O	147	.266
1974	CAL	A	*O/O	129	.251
	CLE	A	O/1	15	.200
1975	CLE	A	O-M	49	.237
1976	CLE	A	O-M/1-O	36	.224
BRTR				2808	.294

ROBINSON, FREDERIC HENRY
B.JULY 6,1856 SOUTH ACTON,MASS.
D.DEC.18,1933 HUDSON,MASS.

YR	CL	LEA	POS	G	REC
1884	CIN	U	2	3	.231
BRTR					

ROBINSON, HUMBERTO VALENTINO
B.JUNE 25,1930 COLON,PANAMA

YR	CL	LEA	POS	G	REC
1955	MIL	N	P	13	3- 1
1956	MIL	N	P	1	0- 0
1958	MIL	N	P	19	2- 4
1959	CLE	A	P	5	1- 0
	PHI	N	P	31	2- 4
1960	PHI	N	P	33	0- 4
BRTR				102	8-13

ROBINSON, JACK ROOSEVELT (JACKIE)
B.JAN.31,1919 CAIRO,GA.
D.OCT.24,1972 STAMFORD,CONN.

YR	CL	LEA	POS	G	REC
1947	BRO	N	1	151	.296
1948	BRO	N	1-2	147	.296
1949	BRO	N	2	156	.342
1950	BRO	N	2	144	.328
1951	BRO	N	2	153	.338
1952	BRO	N	2	149	.308
1953	BRO	N	1-2-S-3-O	136	.329
1954	BRO	N	2-3-O	124	.311
1955	BRO	N	1-2-3-O	105	.256
1956	BRO	N	1-2-3-O	117	.275
BRTR				1382	.311

ROBINSON, JOHN (JACK) OR (BRIDGEPORT)
B.E.GREENWICH,CONN.

YR	CL	LEA	POS	G	REC
1902	NY	N	C	4	.000
TR					

ROBINSON, JOHN EDWARD (JACK)
B.FEB.20,1921 ORANGE,N.J.

YR	CL	LEA	POS	G	REC
1949	BOS	A	P	3	0- 0
BRTR					

ROBINSON, JOHN HENRY (HANK) OR (RUBE)
[REAL NAME JOHN HENRY ROBERSON]
B.AUG.16,1889 FLOYD,ARK.
D.JULY 3,1965 N.LITTLE ROCK,ARK.

YR	CL	LEA	POS	G	REC
1911	PIT	N	P	5	0- 1
1912	PIT	N	P	33	12- 7
1913	PIT	N	P	43	14- 9
1914	STL	N	P	26	7- 8
1915	STL	N	P	32	7- 8
1918	NY	A	P	11	2- 4
BRTL				150	42-37

ROBINSON, WILBERT (UNCLE ROBBY)
B.JUNE 29,1863 BOLTON,MASS.
D.AUG.8,1934 ATLANTA,GA.

YR	CL	LEA	POS	G	REC
1886	ATH	AA	C-1	87	.205
1887	ATH	AA	C	68	.286
1888	ATH	AA	C	67	.268
1889	ATH	AA	C	69	.242
1890	ATH	AA	C	83	.236
	BAL	AA	C-1	14	.271
1891	BAL	N	C	93	.221
1892	BAL	N	C	83	.270
1893	BAL	N	C	91	.338
1894	BAL	N	C	106	.348
1895	BAL	N	C	74	.264
1896	BAL	N	C	66	.354
1897	BAL	N	C	47	.313
1898	BAL	N	C	77	.276
1899	BAL	N	C	105	.284
1900	STL	N	C	56	.255
1901	BAL	A	C	71	.298
1902	BAL	A	M-C	90	.292
BRTR				1347	.286

NON-PLAYING MANAGER BRO[N] 1914-31

YR	CL LEA POS	GP	G	REC

ROBINSON, WILLIAM EDWARD (EDDIE)
B.DEC.15,1920 PARIS,TEX.
```
1942 CLE A  1          8   .125
1946 CLE A  1          7   .467
1947 CLE A  1         95   .245
1948 CLE A  1        134   .254
1949 WAS A  1        143   .294
1950 WAS A  1         36   .240
     CHI A  1        119   .311
1951 CHI A  1        151   .282
1952 CHI A  1        155   .296
1953 PHI A  1        156   .247
1954 NY  A  1         85   .261
1955 NY  A  1         88   .208
1956 NY  A  1         26   .222
     KC  A  1         75   .198
1957 DET A  H         13   .000
     CLE A  1         19   .222
     BAL A  H          4   .000
     BLTR          1314   .268
```

ROBINSON, WILLIAM H. (YANK)
B.SEPT.19,1859 PHILADELPHIA,PA.
D.AUG.25,1894 ST.LOUIS,MO.
```
1882 DET N  P-S-    1  11   0- 0
              D                 
1884 BAL U  P-C-    6  98   2- 3
              S-3              .269
1885 STL AA C-2-0      78   .259
1886 STL AA P-2     1 133   0- 1
                               .279
1887 STL AA 2         124   .426
1888 STL AA 2-S       134   .231
1889 STL AA 2         132   .210
1890 PIT P  2          98   .239
1891 CIN AA 2-S        97   .178
1892 WAS N  3          64   .160
     BRTR          8 969   2- 4
                               .262
```

ROBINSON, WILLIAM HENRY (BILL)
B.JUNE 26,1943 MCKEESPORT,PA.
```
1966 ATL N  /O         6   .273
1967 NY  A  *O       116   .196
1968 NY  A  O        107   .240
1969 NY  A  O/1       87   .171
1972 PHI N  O         82   .239
1973 PHI N  *O-3     124   .288
1974 PHI N  O        100   .236
1975 PIT N  O         92   .280
1976 PIT N  O-3/1    122   .303
1977 PIT N  1-O-3    137   .304
1978 PIT N  *O-3/1   136   .246
     BRTR          1109   .257
```

ROBISON, MATTHEW STANLEY
B.MAR.30,1859 PITTSBURGH,PA.
D.MAR.24,1911
NON-PLAYING MANAGER STL[N] 1905

ROBITAILLE, JOSEPH ANTHONY (CHICK)
B.MAR.2,1879 WHITEHALL,N.Y.
D.JULY 30,1947 WATERFORD,N.Y.
```
1904 PIT N  P          9   5- 3
1905 PIT N  P         17   7- 6
     BRTR            26  12- 9
```

ROBLE, RAFAEL [BATISTA]
[SEE RAFAEL BATISTA]

ROBLES, RAFAEL ORLANDO [NATERA]
B.OCT.20,1947 SAN PEDRO DE
MACORIS,D.R.
```
1969 SD  N  /S         6   .100
1970 SD  N  S         23   .213
1972 SD  N  S/3       18   .167
     BRTR            47   .188
```

ROBLES, SERGIO [VALENZUELA]
B.APR.16,1946 MAGDALENA,MEXICO
```
1972 BAL A  /C         2   .200
1973 BAL A  /C         8   .077
1976 LA  N  /C         6   .000
     BRTR            16   .095
```

ROBSON, THOMAS JAMES (TOM)
B.JAN.15,1946 ROCHESTER,N.Y.
```
1974 TEX A  /1         6   .231
1975 TEX A  /1        17   .200
     BRTR            23   .208
```

ROCAP, ADAM
B.1854 PHILADELPHIA,PA.
D.MAR.29,1892
```
1875 ATH NA 2-O       13   .186
```

ROCCO, MICHAEL DOMINICK (MIKE)
B.MAR.2,1916 ST.PAUL,MINN.
```
1943 CLE A  1        108   .240
1944 CLE A  1        155   .266
1945 CLE A  1        143   .264
1946 CLE A  1         34   .245
     BLTL           440   .258
```

ROCHE, ARMANDO [BAEZ]
B.DEC.7,1926 HAVANA,CUBA
```
1945 WAS A  P          2   0- 0
```

ROCHE, JOHN JOSEPH (JACK) OR (RED)
B.NOV.22,1890 LOS ANGELES,CAL.
```
1914 STL N  C         12   .667
1915 STL N  C         46   .205
1917 STL N  C          1   .000
     BRTR            59   .286
```

ROCHEFORT, BENNETT HAROLD
[REAL NAME BENNETT
HAROLD ROCHEFORT GILBERT]
B.AUG.15,1896 CAMDEN,N.J.
```
1914 PHI A  1          1   .500
     BLTR
```

ROCHELLI, LOUIS JOSEPH
B.JAN.11,1919 WILLIAMSON,ILL.
```
1944 BRO N  2          5   .176
     BRTR
```

ROCK, LESTER HENRY
[REAL NAME LESTER HENRY SCHWARZROCK]
B.AUG.19,1912 SPRINGFIELD,MINN.
```
1936 CHI A  1          2   .000
     BLTR
```

ROCKENFIELD, ISAAC BROC
B.NOV.3,1876 OMAHA,NEB.
D.FEB.21,1927 SAN DIEGO,CAL.
```
1905 STL A  2         95   .217
1906 STL A  2         27   .239
     BRTR           122   .222
```

ROCKETT, PATRICK EDWARD (PAT)
B.JAN.9,1955 SAN ANTONIO,TEX.
```
1976 ATL N  /S         4   .200
1977 ATL N  S         93   .254
1978 ATL N  S         55   .141
     BRTR           152   .214
```

RODGERS, KENNETH ANDRE IAN
(ANDRE) OR (ANDY)
B.DEC.2,1934 NASSAU,BAHAMAS
```
1957 NY  N  S-3       32   .244
1958 SF  N  S         22   .206
1959 SF  N  S         71   .250
1960 SF  N  1-S-3-0   81   .244
1961 CHI N  1-2-S-O   73   .266
1962 CHI N  1-S      138   .278
1963 CHI N  S        150   .229
1964 CHI N  S        129   .239
1965 PIT N  S-3/1-2   75   .287
1966 PIT N  /S-3/1    36   .184
1967 PIT N  /1-3-S-2  47   .230
     BRTR           854   .249
```

RODGERS, ROBERT LEROY (BOB)
B.AUG.16,1938 DELAWARE,OHIO
```
1961 LA  A  C         16   .321
1962 LA  A  C        155   .258
1963 LA  A  C        100   .233
1964 LA  A  *C       148   .243
1965 CAL A  *C       132   .209
1966 CAL A  *C       133   .236
1967 CAL A  *C/O     139   .219
1968 CAL A  C         91   .190
1969 CAL A  C         18   .196
     BBTR           932   .232
```

RODGERS, WILBUR KINCAID
(RAWMEAT BILL)
B.APR.18,1887 PLEASANT RIDGE,O.
```
1915 CLE A  2         16   .298
     BOS A  2         11   .000
     CIN N  2-S-3-0   72   .239
1916 CIN N  2-S        3   .000
     BLTR           102   .243
```

RODGERS, WILLIAM SHERMAN
B.DEC.5,1922 HARRISBURG,PA.
```
1944 PIT N  O          2   .250
1945 PIT N  H          1  1.000
     BLTL             3   .400
```

RODIN, ERIC CHAPMAN
B.FEB.5,1930 ORANGE,N.J.
```
1954 NY  N  O          5   .000
     BRTR
```

RODRIGUEZ, ANTONIO ORDENANA
[PLAYED UNDER NAME OF
ANTONIO ORDENANA]

RODRIGUEZ, AURELIO [ITUARTE]
B.DEC.28,1947 CANANEA,SONORA,MEX
```
1967 CAL A  3         29   .238
1968 CAL A  3/2       76   .242
1969 CAL A  3        159   .225
1970 CAL A  3         17   .270
     WAS A  *3/S     142   .251
1971 DET A  *3/S     154   .253
1972 DET A  *3/S     153   .236
1973 DET A  *3/S     160   .222
1974 DET A  *3       159   .222
1975 DET A  *3       151   .245
1976 DET A  *3       128   .240
1977 DET A  3/S       96   .219
1978 DET A  *3       134   .265
     BRTR          1558   .239
```

RODRIGUEZ, EDUARDO (REYES)
B.MAR.6,1952 BARCELONETA,P.R.
```
1973 MIL A  P         30   9- 7
1974 MIL A  P         43   7- 4
1975 MIL A  P         43   7- 0
1976 MIL A  P         45   5-13
1977 MIL A  P         42   5- 6
1978 MIL A  P         32   5- 5
     BRTR           235  38-35
```

RODRIGUEZ, ELISEO [DELGADO] (ELLIE)
B.MAY 24,1946 FAJARDO,P.R.
```
1968 NY  A  /C         9   .208
1969 KC  A  C         95   .236
1970 KC  A  C         80   .225
1971 MIL A  *C       115   .210
1972 MIL A  *C       116   .285
1973 MIL A  *C        94   .269
1974 CAL A  *C       140   .253
1975 CAL A  C         90   .233
1976 LA  N  C         36   .212
     BRTR           775   .245
```

RODRIGUEZ, FERNANDO PEDRO
[BORREGO] (FREDDY)
B.APR.29,1924 HAVANA,CUBA
```
1958 CHI N  P          7   0- 0
1959 PHI N  P          1   0- 0
     BRTR             8   0- 0
```

RODRIGUEZ, HECTOR ANTONIO
[ORDENANA]
B.JUNE 13,1920 ALQUIZAR,CUBA
```
1952 CHI A  3        124   .265
     BRTR
```

RODRIGUEZ, JOSE (EL HOMBRE GOMA)
B.FEB.23,1894 HAVANA,CUBA
D.JAN.21,1953 HAVANA,CUBA
```
1916 NY  N  H          1   .000
1917 NY  N  1          7   .200
1918 NY  N  1-2-3     50   .160
     BRTR            58   .166
```

RODRIGUEZ, ROBERTO [MUNOZ]
B.NOV.29,1941 CARACAS,VENEZ.
```
1967 KC  A  P         15   1- 1
1970 OAK A  /P         6   0- 0
     SD  N  P         10   0- 0
     CHI N  P         27  11- 2
     BRTR            57   4- 3
```

ROE, ELWIN CHARLES (PREACHER)
B.FEB.26,1915 ASH FLAT,ARK.
```
1938 STL N  P          1   0- 0
1944 PIT N  P         39  13-11
1945 PIT N  P         33  14-13
1946 PIT N  P         21   3- 8
1947 PIT N  P         38   4-15
1948 BRO N  P         34  12- 8
1949 BRO N  P         30  15- 6
1950 BRO N  P         36  19-11
1951 BRO N  P         34  22- 3
1952 BRO N  P         27  11- 2
1953 BRO N  P         25  11- 3
1954 BRO N  P         15   3- 4
     BRTL           333 127-84
```

ROE, JAMES CLAY (CLAY) OR (SHAD)
B.JAN.7,1904 GREEN BRIAR,TENN.
D.APR.4,1956 CLEVELAND,MISS.
```
1923 WAS A  P          1   0- 1
     BLTL
```

ROEBUCK, EDWARD JACK (ED)
B.JULY 3,1931 EAST MILLSBORO,PA.
```
1955 BRO N  P         47   5- 6
1956 BRO N  P         43   5- 4
1957 BRO N  P         44   8- 2
1958 LA  N  P         32   0- 1
1960 LA  N  P         58   8- 3
1961 LA  N  P          5   2- 0
1962 LA  N  P         64  10- 2
1963 LA  N  P         29   2- 4
     WAS A  P         26   2- 1
1964 WAS A  P          2   0- 0
     PHI N  P         60   5- 3
1965 PHI N  P         44   5- 3
1966 PHI N  /P         6   0- 2
     BRTR           460  52-31
```

ROENICKE, GARY STEVEN
B.DEC.5,1954 COVINA,CAL.
```
1976 MON N  O         29   .222
1978 BAL A  O         27   .259
     BRTR            56   .236
```

ROETTGER, OSCAR FREDERICK LOUIS
(OKKIE)
B.FEB.19,1900 ST.LOUIS,MO.
```
1923 NY  A  P          5   0- 0
1924 NY  A  P          1   0- 0
1927 BRO N  O          5   .000
1932 PHI A  1         26   .233
     BRTR           6  37   0- 0
                               .212
```

YR	CL LEA POS	GP	G	REC

ROETTGER, WALTER HENRY
B.AUG.28,1902 ST.LOUIS,MO.
D.SEPT.14,1951 CHAMPAIGN,ILL.

1927	STL N O		5	.000
1928	STL N O		68	.341
1929	STL N O		79	.253
1930	NY N O		121	.283
1931	CIN N O		44	.351
	STL N O		45	.285
1932	CIN N O		106	.277
1933	CIN N O		84	.239
1934	PIT N O		47	.245
	BRTR		599	.285

ROETZ, EDWARD BERNARD
B.AUG.6,1905 PHILADELPHIA,PA.
D.MAR.16,1965 PHILADELPHIA,PA.

| 1929 | STL A 1-2-S | | 16 | .244 |
| | BRTR | | | |

ROGALSKI, JOSEPH ANTHONY
B.JULY 15,1912 ASHLAND,WIS.
D.NOV.20,1951 ASHLAND,WIS.

| 1938 | DET A P | 2 | | 0- 0 |
| | BRTR | | | |

ROGELL, WILLIAM GEORGE (BILLY)
B.NOV.24,1904 SPRINGFIELD,ILL.

1925	BOS A 2-S		58	.195
1927	BOS A 3		82	.266
1928	BOS A 2-S		102	.233
1930	DET A S-3		54	.166
1931	DET A S		48	.303
1932	DET A S		144	.271
1933	DET A S		155	.295
1934	DET A S		154	.296
1935	DET A S		150	.275
1936	DET A S		146	.274
1937	DET A S		146	.276
1938	DET A S		136	.259
1939	DET A S-3		74	.230
1940	CHI N 2-S-3		33	.136
	BBTR		1482	.267

ROGERS, EMMETT
B.1865 ROME,N.Y.

| 1890 | TOL AA C | | 35 | .184 |
| | BL | | | |

ROGERS, FRALEY W.
B.1850 BROOKLYN,N.Y.
D.MAY 10,1881

| 1872 | BOS NA 1-O | | 46 | .294 |

ROGERS, JAMES F.
B.APR.9,1872 HARTFORD,CONN.

1896	WAS N 2-3-O		38	.279
	LOU N 2		74	.256
1897	LOU N M-2		40	.148
			152	.235

ROGERS, JAY LEWIS
B.AUG.5,1888 SANDUSKY,N.Y.
D.JULY 1,1964 CARLISLE,N.Y.

| 1914 | NY A C | | 5 | .000 |
| | BRTR | | | |

ROGERS, LEE OTIS (LEE) OR (BUCK)
B.OCT.8,1913 TUSCALOOSA,ALA.

1938	BOS A P		14	1- 1
	BKO N P	12	14	0- 2
	BRTL	26	28	1- 3

**ROGERS, ORLIN WOODROW
(BUCK) OR (LEFTY)**
B.NOV.5,1912 SPRING GARDEN,VA.

| 1935 | WAS A P | 2 | | 0- 1 |
| | BRTL | | | |

ROGERS, STANLEY FRANK (PACKY)
[REAL NAME STANLEY FRANK HAZINSKI]
B.APR.26,1913 SWOYERSVILLE,PA.

| 1938 | BKO N 2-S-3 | | 23 | .189 |
| | BRTR | | | |

ROGERS, STEPHEN DOUGLAS (STEVE)
B.OCT.26,1949 JEFFERSON CITY,MO.

1973	MON N P		17	10- 5
1974	MON N P		38	15-22
1975	MON N P		35	11-12
1976	MON N P	33	35	7-17
1977	MON N P		40	17-16
1978	MON N P		30	13-10
	BRTR	193	195	73-82

ROGERS, THOMAS ANDREW (SHOTGUN)
B.FEB.12,1892 SPARTA,TENN.
D.MAR.7,1936 NASHVILLE,TENN.

1917	STL A P		24	3- 6
1918	STL A P		29	8-10
1919	STL A P		2	0- 1
	PHI A P		23	4-12
1921	NY A P	5	6	0- 1
	BRTR	83	84	15-30

ROGGE, FRANCIS CLINTON (CLINT)
B.JULY 19,1889 MEMPHIS,MICH.
D.JAN.6,1969 MT.CLEMENS,MICH.

1915	PIT F P		37	17-11
1921	CIN N P		6	1- 2
	BLTR		43	18-13

ROGGENBURK, GARRY EARL
B.APR.16,1940 CLEVELAND,OHIO

1963	MIN A P		36	2- 4
1965	MIN A P		12	1- 0
1966	MIN A P		12	1- 2
	BOS A /P		1	0- 0
1968	BOS A /P		4	0- 0
1969	BOS A /P		7	0- 1
	SEA A /P		7	2- 2
	BRTL		79	6- 9

ROGODZINSKI, MICHAEL GEORGE (MIKE)
B.FEB.22,1948 EVANSTON,ILL.

1973	PHI N O		66	.238
1974	PHI N /O		17	.067
1975	PHI N /O		16	.263
	BLTR		99	.219

ROGOVIN, SAUL WALTER
B.OCT.10,1922 BROOKLYN,N.Y.

1949	DET A P		5	0- 1
1950	DET A P		11	2- 1
1951	DET A P		5	1- 1
	CHI A P	22	24	11- 7
1952	CHI A P		33	14- 9
1953	CHI A P		22	7-12
1955	BAL A P	14	15	1- 8
	PHI N P	12	13	5- 3
1956	PHI N P		22	7- 6
1957	PHI N P		4	0- 0
	BRTR	150	154	48-48

**ROHE, GEORGE ANTHONY
(GEORGE) OR (WHITEY)**
B.SEPT.15,1875 CINCINNATI,OHIO
D.JUNE 10,1957 CINCINNATI,OHIO

1901	BAL A 3		14	.294
1905	CHI A 2-3		34	.212
1906	CHI A 3		74	.258
1907	CHI A 2-S-3		144	.213
	BRTR		266	.227

ROHR, LESLIE NORVIN (LES)
B.MAR.5,1946 LOWESTOFT,ENGLAND

1967	NY N /P		3	2- 1
1968	NY N /P		2	0- 2
1969	NY N /P		1	0- 0
	BLTL		6	2- 3

ROHR, WILLIAM JOSEPH (BILLY)
B.JULY 1,1945 SAN DIEGO,CAL.

1967	BOS A P		10	2- 3
1968	CLE A P		17	1- 0
	BLTL		27	3- 3

ROHWER, RAY
B.JUNE 5,1895 DIXON,CAL.

1921	PIT N O		30	.250
1922	PIT N O		53	.294
	BLTL		83	.284

ROIG, ANTON AMBROSE (TONY)
B.DEC.23,1927 NEW ORLEANS,LA.

1953	WAS A 2		3	.125
1955	WAS A 2-S-3		29	.228
1956	WAS A 2-S		44	.210
	BRTR		76	.212

ROJAS, FELIPE [ALOU]
[SEE FELIPE ROJAS ALOU]

ROJAS, JESUS MARIA [ALOU]
[SEE JESUS MARIA ROJAS ALOU]

ROJAS, MATEO [ALOU]
[SEE MATEO ROJAS ALOU]

**ROJAS, MINERVINO ALEJANDRO
(LANDIN) (MINNIE)**
B.NOV.29,1938 REMEDIOS,
LAS VILLAS,CUBA

1966	CAL A P		47	7- 4
1967	CAL A P		72	12- 9
1968	CAL A P		38	4- 3
	BRTR		157	23-16

**ROJAS, OCTAVIO VICTOR (RIVAS)
(COOKIE)**
B.MAR.6,1939 HAVANA,CUBA

1962	CIN N 2-3		39	.221
1963	PHI N 2-O		64	.221
1964	PHI N C-2-S-3-O		109	.291
1965	PHI N 2-O-S/C-1		142	.303
1966	PHI N *2-O/S		156	.268
1967	PHI N *P	137	147	0- 0
	*2/O-C-S-3			.259
1968	PHI N *2/C		152	.232
1969	PHI N 2/O		110	.228
1970	STL N 2/O-S		23	.106
	KC A 2		98	.260
1971	KC A *2/S-O		115	.300
1972	KC A *2/3-S		137	.261
1973	KC A *2		139	.276
1974	KC A *2		144	.271
1975	KC A *2		120	.254
1976	KC A 2/3-1		63	.242
1977	KC A 3-2		64	.256
	BRTR	1	1822	0- 0
				.263

ROJEK, STANLEY ANDREW (STAN)
B.APR.21,1919 N.TONAWANDA,N.Y.

1942	BRO N H		1	.000
1946	BRO N 2-S-3		45	.277
1947	BRO N 2-S-3		32	.263
1948	PIT N S		156	.290
1949	PIT N S		144	.244
1950	PIT N 2-S		76	.257
1951	PIT N S		58	.188
	STL N S		51	.274
1952	STL A 2-S		9	.143
	BRTR		522	.266

ROLAND, JAMES IVAN (JIM)
B.DEC.14,1942 FRANKLIN,N.C.

1962	MIN A P		1	0- 0
1963	MIN A P		10	4- 1
1964	MIN A P		30	2- 6
1966	MIN A /P		1	0- 0
1967	MIN A P		25	0- 1
1968	MIN A P	28	29	4- 1
1969	OAK A P		39	5- 1
1970	OAK A P		28	3- 3
1971	OAK A P		31	1- 3
1972	OAK A /P		2	0- 0
	NY A P		16	0- 1
	TEX A /P		5	0- 0
	BRTR	216	217	19-17

ROLFE, ROBERT ABIAL (RED)
B.OCT.17,1908 PENACOOK,N.H.
D.JULY 8,1969 GUILFORD,N.H.

1931	NY A S		1	.000
1934	NY A S-3		89	.287
1935	NY A S-3		149	.300
1936	NY A 3		135	.319
1937	NY A 3		154	.276
1938	NY A 3		151	.311
1939	NY A 3		152	.329
1940	NY A 3		139	.250
1941	NY A 3		136	.264
1942	NY A 3		69	.219
	BLTR		1175	.289
NON-PLAYING MANAGER DET[A] 1949-52				

ROLLING, RAYMOND COPELAND
B.SEPT.8,1886 MARTINSBURG,MO.
D.AUG.25,1966 ST.PAUL,MINN.

| 1912 | STL N 2 | | 5 | .200 |
| | BRTR | | | |

ROLLINGS, WILLIAM RUSSELL (RED)
B.MAR.21,1904 MOBILE,ALA.
D.DEC.31,1964 MOBILE,ALA.

1927	BOS A 1-3		82	.266
1928	BOS A 1-2-3		50	.229
1930	BOS N 2-3		52	.230
	BLTR		184	.251

**ROLLINS, RICHARD JOHN
(RICH) OR (RED)**
B.APR.16,1938 MOUNT PLEASANT,PA.

1961	MIN A 2-3		13	.294
1962	MIN A S-3		159	.298
1963	MIN A 3		136	.307
1964	MIN A 3		148	.270
1965	MIN A *3-2		140	.249
1966	MIN A 3/2-O		90	.245
1967	MIN A 3		109	.245
1968	MIN A 3		93	.241
1969	SEA A 3/S		58	.225
1970	MIL A /3		14	.200
	CLE A /3		42	.233
	BRTR		1002	.269

ROLLINSON

| 1884 | WAS U C | | 1 | .000 |

ROMAN, WILLIAM ANTHONY (BILL)
B.OCT.11,1938 DETROIT,MICH.

1964	DET A 1		3	.375
1965	DET A /1		21	.074
	BLTL		24	.143

```
YR  CL LEA POS     GP   G   REC
```

ROMANO, JAMES KING
B.APR.6,1927 BROOKLYN,N.Y.
1950 BRO N P   3   0- 0
     BRTR

ROMANO, JOHN ANTHONY
(JOHN) OR (HONEY)
B.AUG.23,1934 HOBOKEN,N.J.
1958 CHI A C   4   .286
1959 CHI A C   53   .294
1960 CLE A C   108   .272
1961 CLE A C   142   .299
1962 CLE A C   135   .261
1963 CLE A C-O   89   .216
1964 CLE A C-1   106   .241
1965 CHI A *C/O-1   122   .242
1966 CHI A *C   122   .231
1967 STL N C   24   .121
     BRTR   905   .255

ROMBERGER, ALLEN ISAIAH (DUTCH)
B.MAY 26,1927 KLINGERSTOWN,PA.
1954 PHI A P   10   1- 1
     BRTR

ROMMEL, EDWIN AMERICUS (EDDIE)
B.SEPT.13,1897 BALTIMORE,MD.
D.AUG.26,1970 BALTIMORE,MD.
1920 PHI A P   33 34   7- 7
1921 PHI A P   46 16-23
1922 PHI A P   51 27-13
1923 PHI A P   56 18-19
1924 PHI A P   43 45 18-15
1925 PHI A P   52 21-10
1926 PHI A P   37 11-11
1927 PHI A P   30 11- 3
1928 PHI A P   43 13- 5
1929 PHI A P   32 12- 2
1930 PHI A P   35   9- 4
1931 PHI A P   25 29   7- 5
1932 PHI A P   17   1- 2
     BRTR   500 507 171-119

ROMERO, EDGARDO RALPH [RIVERA] (ED)
B.DEC.9,1957 SANTURCE,P.R.
1977 MIL A S   10   .280
     BRTR

ROMO, ENRIQUE [NAVARRO] (HENRY)
B.JULY 15,1947 SANTA ROSALIA,MEX
1977 SEA A P   58   8-10
1978 SEA A P   56 11- 7
     BRTR   114 19-17

ROMO, VICENTE [NAVARRO]
(VICENTE) OR (HUEVO)
B.APR.12,1943 SANTA ROSALIA,MEX.
1968 LA N /P   1   0- 0
     CLE A P   40   5- 3
1969 CLE A /P   3   1- 1
     BOS A P   52   7- 9
1970 BOS A P   48   7- 3
1971 BOS A P   45   1- 7
1972 CHI A P   28   3- 0
1973 SD N P   49   2- 3
1974 SD N P   54   5- 5
     BRTR   320 31-31

ROMONOSKY, JOHN
B.JULY 7,1929 HARRISBURG,PA.
1953 STL N P   2   0- 0
1958 WAS A P   18 27   2- 4
1959 WAS A P   12 20   1- 0
     BRTR   32 49   3- 4

RONDEAU, HENRI JOSEPH
B.MAY 5,1887 DANIELSON,CONN.
D.MAY 28,1943 WOONSOCKET,R.I.
1913 DET A C-1   35   .186
1915 WAS A   O   14   .154
1916 WAS A   O   50   .222
     BRTR   99   .203

RONDON, GILBERT
B.NOV.18,1953 BRONX,N.Y.
1976 HOU N P   19   2- 2
     BRTR

ROOF, PHILLIP ANTHONY (PHIL)
B.MAR.5,1941 PADUCAH,KY.
1961 MIL N C   1   .000
1964 MIL N C   1   .000
1965 CAL A /C   9   .136
     CLE A C   43   .173
1966 KC A *C/1   127   .209
1967 KC A *C   114   .205
1968 OAK A C   34   .188
1969 OAK A *C   106   .235
1970 MIL A *C/1   110   .227
1971 MIL A C   41   .193
     MIN A C   31   .241
1972 MIN A C   61   .205
1973 MIN A C   47   .197
1974 MIN A C   44   .196
1975 MIN A C   63   .302
1976 MIN A C   18   .217
     CHI A /C   4   .111
1977 TOR A /C   3   .000
     BRTR   857   .215

ROOKER, JAMES PHILLIP (JIM)
B.SEP.23,1941 LAKEVIEW,ORE.
1968 DET A /P   2   0- 0
1969 KC A P   28 34   4-16
1970 KC A P/O 38 41 10-15
                              .200
1971 KC A P   20 21   2- 7
1972 KC A P   18   5- 6
1973 PIT N P   41 42 10- 6
1974 PIT N P   33 15-11
1975 PIT N P   28 13-11
1976 PIT N P   30 33 15- 8
1977 PIT N P   30 14- 9
1978 PIT N P   28 32   9-11
     BRTL   296 314 97-100
                              .216

ROOKS, GEORGE BRINTON MC CLELLAN
[REAL NAME GEORGE
BRINTON MC CLELLAN RUCKSER]
B.OCT.21,1863 CHICAGO,ILL.
D.MAR.11,1935 CHICAGO,ILL.
1891 BOS N O   5   .125

ROONEY, FRANK
[REAL NAME FRANK ROVNY]
B.OCT.12,1884 PODEBRADY,BOHEMIA
[AUSTRIA-HUNGARY]
D.APR.6,1977 BESSEMER,MICH.
1914 IND F 1   12   .212

ROOT, CHARLES HENRY
(CHARLIE) OR (CHINSKI)
B.MAR.17,1899 MIDDLETOWN,OHIO
D.NOV.5,1970 HOLLISTER,CAL.
1923 STL A P   27   0- 4
1926 CHI N P   42 18-17
1927 CHI N P   48 26-15
1928 CHI N P   40 14-18
1929 CHI N P   43 19- 6
1930 CHI N P   37 16-14
1931 CHI N P   39 17-14
1932 CHI N P   39 15-10
1933 CHI N P   35 15-10
1934 CHI N P   34   4- 7
1935 CHI N P   38 15- 8
1936 CHI N P   33   3- 6
1937 CHI N P   43 13- 5
1938 CHI N P   44   8- 7
1939 CHI N P   35   8- 8
1940 CHI N P   36   2- 4
1941 CHI N P   19   8- 7
     BRTR   632 201-160

ROQUE, JOSE [VARGAS]
B.APR.28,1950 PONCE,P.R.
1970 STL N /O   5   .000
1971 STL N /O   3   .300
1972 STL N O   32   .148
1973 MON N O   25   .148
     BRTR   65   .137

ROSADO, LUIS [ROBLES]
B.DEC.6,1955 SANTURCE,P.R.
1977 NY N /1-C   9   .208

ROSAR, WARREN VINCENT (BUDDY)
B.JULY 3,1914 BUFFALO,N.Y.
1939 NY A C   43   .276
1940 NY A C   73   .298
1941 NY A C   67   .287
1942 NY A C   69   .230
1943 CLE A C   115   .283
1944 CLE A C   99   .263
1945 PHI A C   92   .210
1946 PHI A C   121   .283
1947 PHI A C   102   .259
1948 PHI A C   90   .255
1949 PHI A C   32   .200
1950 BOS A C   27   .269
1951 BOS A C   58   .229
     BRTR   988   .261

ROSARIO, ANGEL RAMON (JIM)
B.MAY 5,1945 BAYAMON,P.R.
1971 SF N O   92   .234
1972 SF N /O   7   .000
1976 MIL A O   15   .189
     BBTR   114   .216

ROSARIO, SANTIAGO
B.JULY 25,1939 GUAYANILLA,P.R.
1965 KC A 1/O   81   .235
     BLTL

ROSE, CHARLES ALFRED
B.SEPT.1,1885 MACON,MO.
D.AUG.4,1961 SALINA,KAN.
1909 STL A P   3   1- 2
     BLTL

ROSE, DONALD GARY (DON)
B.MAR.19,1947 COVINA,CAL.
1971 NY N /P   1   0- 0
1972 CAL A P   16   1- 4
1974 SF N /P   2   0- 0
     BRTR   19   1- 4

ROSE, PETER EDWARD (PETE)
OR (CHARLIE HUSTLE)
B.APR.14,1941 CINCINNATI,OHIO
1963 CIN N O   157   .273
1964 CIN N 2   136   .269
1965 CIN N *2   162   .312
1966 CIN N *2-3   156   .313
1967 CIN N *O-2   148   .301
1968 CIN N *O/2-1   149   .335
1969 CIN N *O/2   156   .348
1970 CIN N *O   159   .316
1971 CIN N *O   160   .304
1972 CIN N *O   154   .307
1973 CIN N *O   160   .338
1974 CIN N *O   163   .284
1975 CIN N *3-O   162   .317
1976 CIN N *3/O   162   .323
1977 CIN N *3   162   .311
1978 CIN N *3/O-1   159   .302
     BBTR   2505   .310

ROSEBORO, JOHN
B.MAY 13,1933 ASHLAND,OHIO
1957 BRO N C-1   35   .145
1958 LA N C-O   114   .271
1959 LA N C   118   .232
1960 LA N C-1-3   103   .213
1961 LA N C   128   .251
1962 LA N C   128   .249
1963 LA N C   135   .236
1964 LA N C   134   .287
1965 LA N *C/3   136   .233
1966 LA N *C   142   .276
1967 LA N *C   116   .272
1968 MIN A *C   135   .216
1969 MIN A C   115   .263
1970 WAS A C   46   .233
     BLTR   1585   .249

ROSEBROUGH, ELI E. (ZEKE)
B.CHARLESTON,ILL.
1898 PIT N P   4   0- 2
1899 PIT N P   2   0- 1
     BRTR   6   0- 3

ROSELLI, ROBERT EDWARD (BOB)
B.DEC.10,1931 SAN FRANCISCO,CAL
1955 MIL N C   6   .222
1956 MIL N C   4   .500
1958 MIL N H   1   .000
1961 CHI A C   22   .263
1962 CHI A C   35   .188
     BRTR   68   .219

ROSELLO, DAVID [RODRIGUEZ] (DAVE)
B.JUNE 26,1950 MAYAGUEZ,P.R.
1972 CHI N /S   5   .250
1973 CHI N 2/S   16   .263
1974 CHI N 2-S   62   .203
1975 CHI N S   19   .239
1976 CHI N S/2   91   .242
1977 CHI N 3-S/2   56   .220
     BRTR   249   .232

ROSEMAN, JAMES J. (CHIEF)
B.1856 NEW YORK,N.Y.
1882 TRO N O   80   .236
1883 MET AA 1-O   93   .260
1884 MET AA O   107   .295
1885 MET AA P-O   1 101   0- 1
                              .284
1886 MET AA O   134   .228
1887 ATH AA O   21   .325
     MET AA O   59   .281
                            1 .250
1890 STL AA M-O   80   .322
     LOU AA O   2   .250
                   1 678   0- 1
                              .271

ROSEN, ALBERT LEONARD (FLIP)
B.FEB.29,1924 SPARTANBURG,S.C.
1947 CLE A 3-O   7   .111
1948 CLE A 3   5   .200
1949 CLE A 3   23   .159
1950 CLE A 3   155   .287
1951 CLE A 3   154   .265
1952 CLE A 1-S-3   148   .302
1953 CLE A 1-S-3   155   .336
1954 CLE A 1-2-S-3 137   .300
1955 CLE A 1-3   139   .244
1956 CLE A 3   121   .267
     BRTR   1044   .285

ROSEN, GOODWIN GEORGE (GOODY)
B.AUG.28,1912 TORONTO,ONT,CAN.
1937 BRO N O   22   .312
1938 BRO N O   138   .281
1939 BRO N O   54   .251
1944 BRO N O   89   .261
1945 BRO N O   145   .325
1946 BRO N O   3   .333
     NY N O   100   .281
     BLTL   551   .291

ROSENBERG, HARRY
B.JUNE 22,1909 SAN FRANCISCO,CAL.
1930 NY N O   9   .000
     BRTR

YR	CL	LEA	POS	GP	G	REC

ROSENBERG, LOUIS C.
B.MAR.5,1903 SAN FRANCISCO,CAL.

YR	CL	LEA	POS	GP	G	REC
1923	CHI	A	2-0		3	.250
		BRTR				

ROSENFELD, MAX
B.DEC.23,1902 NEW YORK,N.Y.
D.MAR.10,1969 MIAMI,FLA.

YR	CL	LEA	POS	GP	G	REC
1931	BRO	N	O		3	.222
1932	BRO	N	O		34	.359
1933	BRO	N	O		5	.111
		BRTR			42	.298

ROSENTHAL, LAWRENCE JOHN
B.MAY 21,1912 ST.PAUL,MINN.

YR	CL	LEA	POS	GP	G	REC
1936	CHI	A	O		85	.281
1937	CHI	A	O		58	.289
1938	CHI	A	O		61	.286
1939	CHI	A	O		107	.265
1940	CHI	A	O		107	.301
1941	CHI	A	O		20	.237
	CLE	A	1-0		45	.187
1944	NY	A	O		36	.198
	PHI	A	O		32	.264
1945	PHI	A	O		28	.200
		BLTL			579	.263

ROSENTHAL, SIMON (SI)
B.NOV.13,1903 BOSTON,MASS.
D.APR.7,1969 BOSTON,MASS.

YR	CL	LEA	POS	GP	G	REC
1925	BOS	A	O		19	.264
1926	BOS	A	O		104	.267
		BLTL			123	.266

ROSER, EMERSON COREY (STEVE)
B.JAN.25,1918 ROME,N.Y.

YR	CL	LEA	POS	GP	G	REC
1944	NY	A	P		16	4-3
1945	NY	A	P		11	0-0
1946	NY	A	P		4	1-1
	BOS	N	P		14	1-1
		BRTR			45	6-5

ROSER, JOHN WILLIAM JOSEPH
(BUNNY) OR (JACK)
B.NOV.15,1901 ST.LOUIS,MO.

YR	CL	LEA	POS	GP	G	REC
1922	BOS	N	O		32	.239
		BLTL				

ROSS, CHESTER FRANKLIN (BUSTER)
B.MAR.11,1903 KUTTAWA,KY.

YR	CL	LEA	POS	GP	G	REC
1924	BOS	A	P		30	4-3
1925	BOS	A	P		33	3-8
1926	BOS	A	P		1	0-1
		BLTL			64	7-12

ROSS, CHESTER JAMES (CHET)
B.APR.1,1917 BUFFALO,N.Y.

YR	CL	LEA	POS	GP	G	REC
1939	BOS	N	O		11	.323
1940	BOS	N	O		149	.281
1941	BOS	N	O		29	.120
1942	BOS	N	O		76	.195
1943	BOS	N	O		94	.218
1944	BOS	N	O		54	.227
		BRTR			413	.241

ROSS, CLIFFORD DAVIS
B.AUG.3,1928 PHILADELPHIA,PA.

YR	CL	LEA	POS	GP	G	REC
1954	CIN	N	P		4	0-0
		BLTL				

ROSS, DONALD RAYMOND (DON)
B.JULY 16,1914 PASADENA,CAL.

YR	CL	LEA	POS	GP	G	REC
1938	DET	A	3		77	.260
1940	BRO	N	3		10	.289
1942	DET	A	3-0		87	.274
1943	DET	A	2-S-3-0		89	.267
1944	DET	A	1-0		66	.210
1945	DET	A	3		8	.379
	CLE	A	3		106	.262
1946	CLE	N	3-0		55	.268
		BRTR			498	.262

ROSS, ERNEST BERTRAM (CURLY)
B.MAR.31,1880 TORONTO,ONT.,CAN.
D.MAR.28,1950 TORONTO,ONT.,CAN.

YR	CL	LEA	POS	GP	G	REC
1902	BAL	A	P		2	1-1

ROSS, FLOYD ROBERT (BOB)
B.NOV.2,1928 FULLERTON,CAL.

YR	CL	LEA	POS	GP	G	REC
1950	WAS	A	P		6	0-1
1951	WAS	A	P		11	0-1
1956	PHI	N	P		3	0-0
		BRTR			20	0-2

ROSS, GARY DOUGLAS
B.SEP.16,1947 MCKEESPORT,PA.

YR	CL	LEA	POS	GP	G	REC
1968	CHI	N	P		13	1-1
1969	CHI	N	/P		2	0-0
	SD	N	P		46	3-12
1970	SD	N	P		33	2-3
1971	SD	N	P		13	1-3
1972	SD	N	P		60	4-3
1973	SD	N	P		58	4-4
1974	SD	N	/P		9	0-0
1975	CAL	A	/P		1	0-1
1976	CAL	A	P		34	8-16
1977	CAL	A	P		14	2-4
		BRTR			283	25-47

ROSS, GEORGE SIDNEY
B.JUNE 27,1892 SAN RAFAEL,CAL.
D.APR.22,1935 AMITYVILLE,N.Y.

YR	CL	LEA	POS	GP	G	REC
1918	NY	N	P		1	0-0
		BLTL				

ROSS, LEE RAVON (BUCK)
B.FEB.3,1915 NORWOOD,N.C.

YR	CL	LEA	POS	GP	G	REC
1936	PHI	A	P		30	9-14
1937	PHI	A	P		28	5-10
1938	PHI	A	P		29	9-16
1939	PHI	A	P		29	6-14
1940	PHI	A	P		24	5-10
1941	PHI	A	P		1	0-1
	CHI	A	P		20	3-8
1942	CHI	A	P		22	5-7
1943	CHI	A	P		21	11-7
1944	CHI	A	P		20	2-7
1945	CHI	A	P		13	1-1
		BRTR			237	56-95

ROSSI, JOSEPH ANTHONY (JOE)
B.MAR.13,1923 OAKLAND,CAL.

YR	CL	LEA	POS	GP	G	REC
1952	CIN	N	C		55	.221
		BRTR				

ROSSMAN, CLAUDE R.
B.JUNE 17,1881 PHILMONT,N.Y.
D.JAN.16,1928 POUGHKEEPSIE,N.Y.

YR	CL	LEA	POS	GP	G	REC
1904	CLE	A	O		18	.190
1906	CLE	A	1		118	.308
1907	DET	A	1		153	.277
1908	DET	A	1		138	.294
1909	DET	A	1		80	.246
	STL	A	1		4	.467
		BLTL			511	.282

ROSSO, FRANCIS JAMES
B.MAR.1,1921 AGAWAM,MASS.

YR	CL	LEA	POS	GP	G	REC
1944	NY	N	P		3	0-0
		BRTR				

ROTBLATT, MARVIN JOSEPH (MARV)
B.OCT.18,1927 CHICAGO,ILL.

YR	CL	LEA	POS	GP	G	REC
1948	CHI	A	P		7	0-1
1950	CHI	A	P		2	0-0
1951	CHI	A	P		26	4-2
		BBTL			35	4-3

ROTH, FRANCIS CHARLES (FRANK)
B.OCT.11,1878 CHICAGO,ILL.
D.MAR.27,1955 BURLINGTON,WIS.

YR	CL	LEA	POS	GP	G	REC
1903	PHI	N	C		61	.273
1904	PHI	N	C		68	.258
1905	STL	A	C		35	.262
1906	CHI	A	C		16	.196
1909	CIN	N	C		52	.238
1910	CIN	N	C		27	.200
		BRTR			259	.248

ROTH, ROBERT FRANK (BRAGGO)
B.AUG.28,1892 BURLINGTON,WIS.
D.SEPT.11,1936 CHICAGO,ILL.

YR	CL	LEA	POS	GP	G	REC
1914	CHI	A	O		34	.294
1915	CHI	A	3-0		69	.257
	CLE	A	O		40	.287
1916	CLE	A	O		125	.286
1917	CLE	A	O		145	.285
1918	CLE	A	O		106	.283
1919	PHI	A	O		48	.323
	BOS	A	O		63	.256
1920	WAS	A	O		138	.290
1921	NY	A	O		43	.283
		BRTR			811	.284

ROTHEL, ROBERT BURTON
B.SEPT.17,1923 COLUMBIA STATION OHIO

YR	CL	LEA	POS	GP	G	REC
1945	CLE	A	3		4	.200
		BRTR				

ROTHERMEL, EDWARD HILL (BOBBY)
B.DEC.18,1870 FLEETWOOD,PA.
D.FEB.11,1927 DETROIT,MICH.

YR	CL	LEA	POS	GP	G	REC
1899	BAL	N	2		10	.095

ROTHFUSS, JOHN ALBERT (JACK)
B.APR.18,1872 NEWARK,N.J.
D.APR.20,1947 BASKING RIDGE,N.J

YR	CL	LEA	POS	GP	G	REC
1897	PIT	N	1		31	.348

ROTHGEB, CLAUDE JAMES
B.JAN.1,1880 MILFORD,ILL.
D.JULY 6,1944 MANITOWOC,WIS.

YR	CL	LEA	POS	GP	G	REC
1905	WAS	A	O		6	.133
		BB				

ROTHROCK, JOHN HOUSTON (JACK)
B.MAR.14,1905 LONG BEACH,CAL.

YR	CL	LEA	POS	GP	G	REC
1925	BOS	A	S		22	.345
1926	BOS	A	S		15	.294
1927	BOS	A	1-2-5-3		117	.260
1928	BOS	A	P-1-	1	117	0-0
			S-3-0			.267
1929	BOS	A	O		143	.300
1930	BOS	A	3-0		45	.277
1931	BOS	A	2-0		133	.278
1932	BOS	A	O		12	.208
	CHI	A	O		39	.188
1934	STL	N	O		154	.284
1935	STL	N	O		129	.273
1937	PHI	A	O		88	.267
		BBTR		1	1014	0-0
						.276

ROUNSAVILLE, VIRLE GENE (GENE)
B.SEP.27,1944 KONAWA,OKLA.

YR	CL	LEA	POS	GP	G	REC
1970	CHI	A	/P		8	0-1
		BRTR				

ROUSH, EDD J
B.MAY 8,1893 OAKLAND CITY,IND.

YR	CL	LEA	POS	GP	G	REC
1913	CHI	A	O		9	.100
1914	IND	F	O		74	.333
1915	NEW	F	O		145	.298
1916	NY	N	O		39	.188
	CIN	N	O		69	.287
1917	CIN	N	O		136	.341
1918	CIN	N	O		113	.333
1919	CIN	N	O		133	.321
1920	CIN	N	1-2-0		149	.339
1921	CIN	N	O		112	.352
1922	CIN	N	O		49	.351
1923	CIN	N	O		138	.351
1924	CIN	N	O		121	.348
1925	CIN	N	O		134	.339
1926	CIN	N	1-0		144	.323
1927	NY	N	O		140	.304
1928	NY	N	O		46	.252
1929	NY	N	O		115	.324
1931	CIN	N	O		101	.271
		BLTL			1967	.323

ROUTCLIFFE, PHILIP JOHN (CHICKEN)
B.OCT.24,1870 OSWEGO,N.Y.
D.OCT.4,1918 OSWEGO,N.Y.

YR	CL	LEA	POS	GP	G	REC
1890	PIT	N	O		1	.250

ROVNY, FRANK
[PLAYED UNDER NAME OF FRANK ROONEY]

ROWAN, DAVID
[REAL NAME DAVID DROHAN]
B.DEC.6,1882 ELORA,ONT.,CANADA
D.JULY 30,1955 TORONTO,ONT.,CAN

YR	CL	LEA	POS	GP	G	REC
1911	STL	A	1		18	.384
		BLTL				

ROWAN, JOHN ALBERT
B.JUNE 16,1887 NEW CASTLE,PA.
D.SEPT.29,1966 DAYTON,OHIO

YR	CL	LEA	POS	GP	G	REC
1906	DET	A	P		1	0-1
1908	CIN	N	P		8	3-3
1909	CIN	N	P		38	11-12
1910	CIN	N	P		42	14-13
1911	PHI	N	P		12	3-4
	CHI	N	P		1	0-0
1913	CIN	N	P		5	0-4
1914	CIN	N	P		12	1-3
		BRTR			119	32-40

ROWE, DAVID ELI
B.FEB.1856 JACKSONVILLE,ILL.

YR	CL	LEA	POS	GP	G	REC
1877	CHI	N	P-O	1	2	0-1
						.286
1882	CLE	N	P-O	1	23	0-1
						.247
1883	BAL	AA	P-1-S-0	1	59	0-0
						.297
1884	STL	U	P-S-O	1	87	1-0
						.292
1885	STL	N	O		16	.161
1886	KC	N	M-O		105	.240
1888	KC	AA	M-0		32	.195
		BR		4	324	1-2
						.257

ROWE, DONALD HOWARD (DON)
B.APR.3,1936 BRAWLEY,CAL.

YR	CL	LEA	POS	GP	G	REC
1963	NY	N	P		26	0-0
		BLTL				

ROWE, HARLAND STIMSON (HYPIE)
B.APR.20,1896 SPRINGVALE,ME.
D.MAY 26,1969 SPRINGVALE,MAINE

YR	CL	LEA	POS	GP	G	REC
1916	PHI	A	3		17	.139
		BLTR				

```
YR   CL LEA POS      GP    G    REC
```

ROWE, JOHN CHARLES (JACK)
B.DEC.8,1857 HARRISBURG,PA.
D.APR.26,1911 ST.LOUIS,MO.
```
1879 BUF N C-O              8   .382
1880 BUF N C-3-O           77   .256
1881 BUF N C-S-3-O         61   .333
1882 BUF N C-S-3-O         75   .266
1883 BUF N C-S-O           86   .275
1884 BUF N C-S-O           91   .310
1885 BUF N C-S-O           98   .289
1886 DET N S              111   .303
1887 DET N S              123   .363
1888 DET N S              105   .277
1889 PIT N S               74   .258
1890 BUF P M-S            125   .250
     BLTR               1034   .292
```

ROWE, KENNETH DARRELL (KEN)
B.DEC.31,1933 FERNDALE,MICH.
```
1963 LA  N P               14   1- 1
1964 BAL A P                6   1- 0
1965 BAL A /P               6   0- 0
     BRTR                  26   2- 1
```

ROWE, LYNWOOD THOMAS (SCHOOLBOY)
B.JAN.11,1910 WACO,TEX.
D.JAN.8,1961 EL DORADO,ARK.
```
1933 DET A P       19   21   7- 4
1934 DET A P       45   51  24- 8
1935 DET A P       42   45  19-13
1936 DET A P       41   45  19-10
1937 DET A P            10   1- 4
1938 DET A P             4   0- 2
1939 DET A P       28   31  10-12
1940 DET A P            27  16- 3
1941 DET A P       27   32   8- 6
1942 DET A P             2   1- 0
     BRO N P        9   14   1- 0
1943 PHI N P       27   82  14- 8
1946 PHI N P       17   30  11- 4
1947 PHI N P       31   43  14-10
1948 PHI N P       30   31  10-10
1949 PHI N P            23   3- 7
     BRTR         382  491 158-101
```

ROWELL, CARVEL WILLIAM (BAMA)
B.JAN.13,1916 CITRONELLE,ALA.
```
1939 BOS N O               21   .186
1940 BOS N 2-O            130   .305
1941 BOS N 2-3-O          138   .267
1946 BOS N O               95   .280
1947 BOS N 2-3-O          113   .276
1948 BOS N 2-3-O           77   .240
     BRTR                 574   .275
```

ROWEN, W. EDWARD (ED)
B.OCT.2,1857 BRIDGEPORT,CONN.
D.FEB.22,1892 BRIDGEPORT,CONN.
```
1882 BOS N C-S-3-O         82   .245
1883 ATH AA C-2-3-O        49   .227
1884 ATH AA C               4   .400
     BRTR                 135   .243
```

ROWLAND, CHARLES LELAND (CHUCK)
B.JULY 23,1899 WARRENTON,N.C.
```
1923 PHI N C                6   .000
     BRTR
```

ROWLAND, CLARENCE HENRY (PANTS)
B.FEB.12,1879 PLATTEVILLE,WIS.
D.MAY 17,1969 CHICAGO,ILL.
NON-PLAYING MANAGER CHI[A] 1915-18

ROXBURGH, JAMES A.
B.SAN FRANCISCO,CAL.
```
1884 BAL U A                2   .333
1887 ATH AA C               2   .125
     BRTR                   4   .214
```

ROY, CHARLES ROBERT
B.JUNE 22,1884 BEAULIEU,MINN.
D.FEB.10,1950 BLACKFOOT,IDAHO
```
1906 PHI N P                8   0- 1
```

ROY, EMILE ARTHUR
B.MAY 26,1907 BRIGHTON,MASS.
```
1933 PHI A P                1   0- 1
     BRTR
```

ROY, JEAN-PIERRE
B.JUNE 26,1920 MONTREAL,QUE.,CAN.
```
1946 BRO N P                3   0- 0
     BBTR
```

ROY, LUTHER FRANKLIN
B.JULY 21,1902 OOLTEWAH,TENN.
D.JULY 24,1963 GRAND RAPIDS,MICH.
```
1924 CLE A P       16   0- 0
1925 CLE A P        6   0- 0
1927 CHI N P       11   3- 1
1929 BRO N P       21   3- 6
     BRO N P        2   0- 0
     BRTR          56   6-12
```

ROY, NORMAN BROOKS
(NORMIE) OR (JUMBO)
B.NOV.15,1928 NEWTON,MASS.
```
1950 BOS N P               19   4- 3
     BRTR
```

ROYSTER, JERON KENNIS (JERRY)
B.OCT.18,1952 SACRAMENTO,CAL.
```
1973 LA  N /2-3-2          10   .211
1974 LA  N /2-3-O           6   .000
1975 LA  N /O-2-3-S        13   .250
1976 ATL N *3/S           149   .248
1977 ATL N  3-S-2/O       140   .216
1978 ATL N  2-S/3         140   .259
     BRTR                 458   .242
```

ROZEK, RICHARD LOUIS (DICK)
B.MAR.27,1927 CEDAR RAPIDS,IOWA
```
1950 CLE A P               12   0- 0
1951 CLE A P                7   0- 0
1952 CLE A P               10   1- 0
1953 PHI A P                2   0- 0
1954 PHI A P                2   0- 0
     BLTL                  33   1- 0
```

ROZEMA, DAVID SCOTT (DAVE)
B.AUG.5,1956 GRAND RAPIDS,MICH.
```
1977 DET A P               28  15- 7
1978 DET A P               28   9-12
     BRTR                  56  24-19
```

ROZNOVSKY, VICTOR JOSEPH (VIC)
B.OCT.19,1938 SHINER,TEX.
```
1964 CHI N C               35   .197
1965 CHI N C               71   .221
1966 BAL A C               41   .237
1967 BAL A C               45   .206
1969 PHI N /C              13   .231
     BLTR                 205   .218
```

RUBELING, ALBERT WILLIAM
B.MAY 10,1913 BALTIMORE,MD.
```
1940 PHI A 2-3            108   .245
1941 PHI A 3                6   .263
1943 PIT N 2-3            47   .262
1944 PIT N 2-3-O          92   .245
     BRTR                 253   .249
```

RUBERTO, JOHN EDWARD (SONNY)
B.JAN.2,1946 STATEN ISLAND,N.Y.
```
1969 SD  N C               19   .143
1972 CIN N /C               2   .000
     BRTR                  21   .125
```

RUBIO, JORGE JESUS [CHAVEZ]
B.APR.23,1945 MEXICALI,MEXICO
```
1966 CAL A /P               7   2- 1
1967 CAL A /P               3   0- 2
     BRTR                  10   2- 3
```

RUBLE, WILLIAM ARTHUR
(ART) OR (SPEEDY)
B.MAR.11,1903 KNOXVILLE,TENN.
```
1927 DET A O               56   .165
1934 PHI N O               19   .278
     BLTR                  75   .207
```

RUCKER, GEORGE NAPOLEON (NAP)
B.AUG.5,1970 CRABAPPLE,GA.
D.DEC.19,1970 ALPHARETTA,GA.
```
1907 BRO N P               37  15-13
1908 BRO N P               42  17-19
1909 BRO N P               38  13-19
1910 BRO N P               41  17-18
1911 BRO N P               48  22-18
1912 BRO N P               45  18-21
1913 BRO N P               41  14-15
1914 BRO N P               16   7- 6
1915 BRO N P               19   9- 4
1916 BRO N P                9   2- 1
     BRTL                 336 134-134
```

RUCKER, JOHN JOEL (JOHNNY)
B.JAN.15,1917 CRABAPPLE,GA.
```
1940 NY  N O               86   .298
1941 NY  N O              143   .284
1943 NY  N O              132   .223
1944 NY  N O              144   .244
1945 NY  N O              105   .273
1946 NY  N O               95   .264
     BLTR                 705   .272
```

RUCKSER, GEORGE BRINTON MC CLELLAN
[PLAYED UNDER NAME OF GEORGE
BRINTON MC CLELLAN ROOKS]

RUDDERHAM, JOHN EDMUND
B.AUG.30,1863 QUINCY,MASS.
D.APR.3,1942 RANDOLPH,MASS.
```
1884 BOS U O                1   .250
     BRTR
```

RUDI, JOSEPH ODEN (JOE)
B.SEP.7,1946 MODESTO,CAL.
```
1967 KC  A /1-O            19   .186
1968 OAK A O               68   .177
1969 OAK A O-1             35   .189
1970 OAK A O-1            106   .309
1971 OAK A *O/1           127   .267
1972 OAK A *O/3           147   .305
1973 OAK A *O/1           120   .270
1974 OAK A *O-1           158   .293
1975 OAK A  1-O           126   .278
1976 OAK A *O/1           130   .270
1977 CAL A  O              64   .264
1978 CAL A *O-O-D-1       133   .256
     BRTR                1233   .273
```

RUDOLPH, ERNEST WILLIAM
B.FEB.13,1910 BLACK RIVER FALLS WIS.
```
1945 BRO N P                7   1- 0
     BLTR
```

RUDOLPH, FREDERICK DONALD (DON)
B.AUG.16,1931 BALTIMORE,MD.
D.SEPT.12,1968 GRANADA HILLS,CAL
```
1957 CHI A P                5   1- 0
1958 CHI A P                7   1- 0
1959 CHI A P                4   0- 0
     CIN N P                5   0- 0
1962 CLE A P                1   0- 0
     WAS A P               37   8-10
1963 WAS A P               37   7-19
1964 WAS A P               28   1- 3
     BLTL                 124  18-32
```

RUDOLPH, JOHN HERMAN (DUTCH)
B.JULY 10,1882 NATRONA,PA.
D.APR.17,1907 NATRONA,PA.
```
1903 PHI N H                1   .000
1904 CHI N O                2   .250
                           3   .200
```

RUDOLPH, KENNETH VICTOR (KEN)
B.DEC.29,1946 ROCKFORD,ILL.
```
1969 CHI N C/O             27   .206
1970 CHI N C               20   .100
1971 CHI N C               25   .197
1972 CHI N C               42   .236
1973 CHI N C               64   .206
1974 SF  N C               57   .259
1975 STL N C               44   .200
1976 STL N C               27   .160
1977 SF  N C               11   .200
     BAL A C               11   .286
     BRTR                 328   .213
```

RUDOLPH, RICHARD (DICK) OR (BALDY)
B.AUG.25,1887 NEW YORK,N.Y.
D.OCT.20,1949 BRONX,N.Y.
```
1910 NY  N P                3   0- 1
1911 NY  N P                1   0- 0
1913 BOS N P      33   35  14-13
1914 BOS N P      42   43  27-10
1915 BOS N P      44   45  22-19
1916 BOS N P           41  19-12
1917 BOS N P      31   32  13-13
1918 BOS N P           21   9-10
1919 BOS N P           37  13-18
1920 BOS N P           14   4- 8
1922 BOS N P            3   0- 2
1923 BOS N P            4   1- 2
1927 BOS N P            1   0- 0
     BRTR         279  284 122-108
             88 1919-27
```

RUEL, HEROLD DOMINIC (MUDDY)
B.FEB.20,1896 ST.LOUIS,MO.
D.NOV.13,1963 PALO ALTO,CAL.
```
1915 STL A C               10   .000
1917 NY  A C                6   .118
1918 NY  A C                3   .333
1919 NY  A C               81   .240
1920 NY  A C               82   .268
1921 BOS A C              113   .277
1922 BOS A C              116   .255
1923 WAS A C              136   .316
1924 WAS A C              149   .283
1925 WAS A C-1            127   .310
1926 WAS A C              117   .299
1927 WAS A C              131   .308
1928 WAS A C              108   .257
1929 WAS A C               69   .245
1930 WAS A C               66   .253
1931 BOS A C               33   .301
     DET A C               14   .120
1932 DET A C               51   .235
1933 STL A C               36   .190
1934 CHI A C               22   .211
     BRTR                1470   .276
```
NON-PLAYING MANAGER STL[A] 1947

RUETHER, WALTER HENRY (DUTCH)
B.SEPT.13,1893 ALAMEDA,CAL.
D.MAY 16,1970 PHOENIX,ARIZ.

YR	CL	LEA	POS	GP	G	REC
1917	CHI	N	P	10	31	2- 0
	CIN	N	P	7	19	1- 2
1918	CIN	N	P		2	0- 1
1919	CIN	N	P	33	42	19- 6
1920	CIN	N	P	37	45	16-12
1921	BRO	N	P	36	49	10-13
1922	BRO	N	P	35	67	21-12
1923	BRO	N	P-1	34	49	13-14
						.274
1924	BRO	N	P	30	33	8-13
1925	WAS	A	P-1	30	55	18- 7
						.333
1926	WAS	A	P	23	47	13- 6
	NY	A	P	5	13	2- 3
1927	NY	A	P	27	35	13- 6
	BLTL			309	487	138-95
						.258

RUFER, RUDOLPH JOSEPH (RUDY)
B.OCT.28,1926 RIDGEWOOD,N.Y.

YR	CL	LEA	POS	GP	G	REC
1949	NY	N	S		7	.067
1950	NY	N	S		15	.091
	BRTR				22	.077

RUFFING, CHARLES HERBERT (RED)
B.MAY 3,1904 GRANVILLE,ILL.

YR	CL	LEA	POS	GP	G	REC
1924	BOS	A	P		8	0- 0
1925	BOS	A	P		37	9-18
1926	BOS	A	P		37	6-15
1927	BOS	A	P	26	29	5-13
1928	BOS	A	P	42	60	10-25
1929	BOS	A	P	35	60	9-22
1930	BOS	A	P	4	6	0- 3
	NY	A	P	34	52	15- 5
1931	NY	A	P	37	48	16-14
1932	NY	A	P	35	55	18- 7
1933	NY	A	P	35	55	9-14
1934	NY	A	P	36	45	19-11
1935	NY	A	P	30	50	16-11
1936	NY	A	P	33	53	20-12
1937	NY	A	P	31	54	20- 7
1938	NY	A	P	31	45	21- 7
1939	NY	A	P	28	44	21- 7
1940	NY	A	P	30	33	15-12
1941	NY	A	P	23	38	15- 6
1942	NY	A	P	24	30	14- 7
1945	NY	A	P	11	21	7- 3
1946	NY	A	P		8	5- 1
1947	CHI	A	P	9	14	3- 5
	BRTR			624	882	273-225
						.269

RUHLE, VERNON GERALD (VERN)
B.JAN.25,1951 COLEMAN,MICH.

YR	CL	LEA	POS	GP	G	REC
1974	DET	A	/P		5	2- 0
1975	DET	A	P		32	11-12
1976	DET	A	P		32	9-12
1977	DET	A	P		14	3- 5
1978	HOU	N	P		13	3- 3
	BRTR				96	28-32

RUIZ, HIRALDO SABLON (CHICO)
B.DEC.5,1938 SANTO DOMINGO,CUBA
D.FEB.9,1972 SAN DIEGO,CAL.

YR	CL	LEA	POS	GP	G	REC
1964	CIN	N	2-3		77	.244
1965	CIN	N	/3-S		29	.111
1966	CIN	N	3/0-S		82	.255
1967	CIN	N	2-3-S/0		105	.220
1968	CIN	N	2-1/3-S		85	.259
1969	CIN	N	2-S/3-1-0		88	.245
1970	CAL	A	3/2-S-1-C		68	.243
1971	CAL	A	/3-2		31	.263
	BBTR				565	.240

RUIZ, MANUEL (CRUZ) (CHICO)
B.NOV.1,1951 SANTURCE,P.R.

YR	CL	LEA	POS	GP	G	REC
1978	ATL	N	2/3		18	.283
	BRTR					

RULLO, JOSEPH VINCENT
B.JUNE 16,1916 NEW YORK,N.Y.
D.OCT.28,1969 PHILADELPHIA,PA.

YR	CL	LEA	POS	GP	G	REC
1943	PHI	A	2		16	.291
1944	PHI	A	1-2		35	.167
	BRTR				51	.212

RUMLER, WILLIAM GEORGE
B.MAR.27,1891 MILFORD,NEB.
D.MAY 26,1966 LINCOLN,NEB.

YR	CL	LEA	POS	GP	G	REC
1914	STL	A	C		33	.174
1916	STL	A	O		27	.324
1917	STL	A	O		78	.261
	BRTR				138	.251

RUNNELLS, JAMES EDWARD
[PLAYED UNDER NAME OF
JAMES EDWARD RUNNELS]

RUNNELS, JAMES EDWARD (PETE)
[REAL NAME JAMES EDWARD RUNNELLS]
B.JAN.28,1928 LUFKIN,TEX.

YR	CL	LEA	POS	GP	G	REC
1951	WAS	A	S		78	.278
1952	WAS	A	2-S		152	.285
1953	WAS	A	2-S		137	.257
1954	WAS	A	2-S-O		139	.268
1955	WAS	A	2-S		134	.284
1956	WAS	A	1-2-S		147	.310
1957	WAS	A	1-2-3		134	.230
1958	BOS	A	1-2		147	.322
1959	BOS	A	1-2-S		147	.314
1960	BOS	A	1-2-3		143	.320
1961	BOS	A	1-2-S-3		143	.317
1962	BOS	A	1		152	.326
1963	HOU	N	1-2-3		124	.253
1964	HOU	N	1		22	.196
	BLTR				1799	.291

NON-PLAYING MANAGER
BOS [A] 1966 [INTERIM]

RUSH, JESSE HOWARD (ANDY)
B.DEC.26,1889 LONGTON,KAN.
D.MAR.16,1969 FRESNO,CAL.

YR	CL	LEA	POS	GP	G	REC
1925	BRO	N	P		4	0- 1
	BRTR					

RUSH, ROBERT RANSOM (BOB)
B.DEC.21,1925 BATTLE CREEK,MICH

YR	CL	LEA	POS	GP	G	REC
1948	CHI	N	P	36	38	5-11
1949	CHI	N	P		35	10-18
1950	CHI	N	P	39	40	13-20
1951	CHI	N	P		37	11-12
1952	CHI	N	P		34	17-13
1953	CHI	N	P		29	9-14
1954	CHI	N	P		33	13-15
1955	CHI	N	P		33	13-11
1956	CHI	N	P		32	13-10
1957	CHI	N	P		31	6-16
1958	MIL	N	P		28	10- 6
1959	MIL	N	P		31	5- 6
1960	MIL	N	P		10	2- 0
	CHI	A	P		9	0- 0
	BRTR			417	420	127-152

RUSIE, AMOS WILSON (AMOS)
OR (THE HOOSIER THUNDERBOLT)
B.MAY 30,1871 MOORESVILLE,IND.
D.DEC.6,1942 SEATTLE,WASH.

YR	CL	LEA	POS	GP	G	REC
1889	IND	N	P		26	11-11
1890	NY	N	P	64	73	28-33
1891	NY	N	P		56	34-20
1892	NY	N	P	62	65	32-28
1893	NY	N	P	54	56	33-21
1894	NY	N	P		50	36-13
1895	NY	N	P		47	23-22
1897	NY	N	P		37	28- 8
1898	NY	N	P	35	36	20-11
1901	CIN	N	P		3	0- 1
	BRTR			434	448	245-168

RUSSELL, ALLAN E. (RUBBERARM)
B.JULY 31,1893 BALTIMORE,MD.
D.OCT.20,1972 BALTIMORE,MD.

YR	CL	LEA	POS	GP	G	REC
1915	NY	A	P		5	1- 2
1916	NY	A	P	34	35	6-10
1917	NY	A	P	25	30	7- 8
1918	NY	A	P	27	29	8-11
	BOS	A	P		23	9- 4
1919	NY	A	P		21	8- 5
	BOS	A	P	16	17	5- 6
1920	BOS	A	P		39	7-11
1921	BOS	A	P		34	6- 7
1922	WAS	A	P	52	54	10- 7
1923	WAS	A	P		37	5- 1
1924	WAS	A	P		41	2- 4
1925	WAS	A	P		32	2- 4
	BBTR			345	356	74-76

RUSSELL, BENJAMIN PAUL (PAUL)
B.1870 READING,PA.
D.POTTSTOWN,PA.

YR	CL	LEA	POS	GP	G	REC
1894	STL	N	O		3	.100

RUSSELL, CLARENCE DICKSON (LEFTY)
B.JULY 8,1890 BALTIMORE,MD.
D.JAN.22,1962 BALTIMORE,MD.

YR	CL	LEA	POS	GP	G	REC
1910	PHI	A	P		1	1- 0
1911	PHI	A	P		7	0- 2
1912	PHI	A	P		3	0- 2
	BLTL				11	1- 4

RUSSELL, EWELL ALBERT (REB)
B.APR.12,1889 JACKSON,MISS.
D.SEPT.30,1973 INDIANAPOLIS,IND

YR	CL	LEA	POS	GP	G	REC
1913	CHI	A	P	51	52	22-16
1914	CHI	A	P	38	39	8-12
1915	CHI	A	P	41	45	11-12
1916	CHI	A	P		56	18-11
1917	CHI	A	P	35	39	15- 5
1918	CHI	A	P	19	27	6- 5
1919	CHI	A	P		1	0- 0
1922	PIT	N	O		60	.368
1923	PIT	N	O		94	.289
	BLTL			241	413	80-61
						.269

RUSSELL, GLEN DAVID (RIP)
B.JAN.26,1915 LOS ANGELES,CAL.
D.SEPT.26,1976 LOS ALAMITOS,CAL

YR	CL	LEA	POS	GP	G	REC
1939	CHI	N	1		143	.273
1940	CHI	N	1-3		68	.247
1941	CHI	N	1		6	.294
1942	CHI	N	1-2-3-0		102	.242
1946	BOS	A	2-3		80	.208
1947	BOS	A	3		26	.154
	BRTR				425	.255

RUSSELL, HARVEY HOLMES
B.JAN.10,1887 MARSHALL,VA.

YR	CL	LEA	POS	GP	G	REC
1914	BAL	F	C		79	.247
1915	BAL	F	C		52	.243
	BLTR				131	.246

RUSSELL, JACK ERWIN
B.OCT.24,1905 PARIS,TEX.

YR	CL	LEA	POS	GP	G	REC
1926	BOS	A	P		37	0- 5
1927	BOS	A	P	34	35	4- 9
1928	BOS	A	P	32	35	11-14
1929	BOS	A	P	35	37	6-18
1930	BOS	A	P	35	41	9-20
1931	BOS	A	P	36	41	10-18
1932	BOS	A	P		11	1- 7
	CLE	A	P	18	20	5- 7
1933	WAS	A	P		50	12- 6
1934	WAS	A	P		54	5-10
1935	WAS	A	P		43	4- 9
1936	WAS	A	P		18	3- 2
	BOS	A	P		23	0- 3
1937	DET	A	P		25	2- 5
1938	CHI	N	P		42	6- 1
1939	CHI	N	P	39	43	4- 3
1940	STL	N	P		26	3- 4
	BRTR			558	581	85-141

RUSSELL, JAMES WILLIAM (JIM)
B.OCT.1,1918 FAYETTE CITY,PA.

YR	CL	LEA	POS	GP	G	REC
1942	PIT	N	O		5	.071
1943	PIT	N	1-O		146	.259
1944	PIT	N	O		152	.312
1945	PIT	N	O		146	.284
1946	PIT	N	1-O		146	.277
1947	PIT	N	O		128	.253
1948	BOS	N	O		89	.264
1949	BOS	N	O		130	.231
1950	BRO	N	O		79	.229
1951	BRO	N	O		16	.000
	BBTR				1035	.267

RUSSELL, JOHN ALBERT
B.OCT.20,1895 SAN MATEO,CAL.
D.NOV.20,1930 ELY,NEV.

YR	CL	LEA	POS	GP	G	REC
1917	BRO	N	P		5	0- 1
1918	BRO	N	P		1	0- 0
1921	CHI	A	P		11	2- 5
1922	CHI	A	P		5	0- 1
	BLTL				22	2- 7

RUSSELL, LLOYD OPAL
B.APR.10,1913 ATOKA,OKLA.
D.MAY 24,1968 WACO,TEX.

YR	CL	LEA	POS	GP	G	REC
1938	CLE	A	H		2	.000
	BRTR					

RUSSELL, WILLIAM ELLIS (BILL)
B.OCT.21,1948 PITTSBURG,KANS.

YR	CL	LEA	POS	GP	G	REC
1969	LA	N	O		98	.226
1970	LA	N	O/S		81	.259
1971	LA	N	2-O/S		91	.227
1972	LA	N	*S/O		129	.272
1973	LA	N	*S		162	.265
1974	LA	N	*S/O		160	.269
1975	LA	N	S		84	.206
1976	LA	N	*S		149	.274
1977	LA	N	*S		153	.278
1978	LA	N	*S		155	.286
	BRTR				1262	.265
	BB 1971					

RUSSO, MARIUS UGO (LEFTY)
B.JULY 19,1914 BROOKLYN,N.Y.

YR	CL	LEA	POS	GP	G	REC
1939	NY	A	P		21	8- 3
1940	NY	A	P		30	14- 8
1941	NY	A	P		28	14-10
1942	NY	A	P		9	4- 1
1943	NY	A	P		24	5-10
1946	NY	A	P	8	10	0- 2
	BRTL			120	122	45-34

RUST
B.LOUISVILLE,KY.

YR	CL	LEA	POS	GP	G	REC
1882	BAL	AA	P-O		1	0- 0
						.333

RUSTECK, RICHARD FRANK (DICK)
B.JULY 12,1941 CHICAGO,ILL.

YR	CL	LEA	POS	GP	G	REC
1966	NY	N	/P		8	1- 2
	BRTL					

RUSZKOWSKI, HENRY ALEXANDER (HANK)
B.NOV.6,1925 CLEVELAND,OHIO

YR	CL	LEA	POS	GP	G	REC
1944	CLE	A	C		3	.375
1945	CLE	A	C		14	.204
1947	CLE	A	C		23	.259
	BRTR				40	.238

YR   CL LEA POS   GP   G   REC

RUTH, GEORGE HERMAN (BABE)
(THE BAMBINO) OR
(THE SULTAN OF SWAT)
B.FEB.6,1895 BALTIMORE,MD.
D.AUG.16,1948 NEW YORK,N.Y.

YR	CL	LEA	POS	GP	G	REC
1914	BOS	A	P	4	5	2- 1
1915	BOS	A	P	32	42	18- 6
1916	BOS	A	P	44	67	23-12
1917	BOS	A	P	41	52	24-13
1918	BOS	A	P-1	20	95	13- 7
			O			.300
1919	BOS	A	P-O	17	130	8- 5
						.322
1920	NY	A	P-O	1	142	1- 0
						.376
1921	NY	A	P-O	2	152	2- 0
						.378
1922	NY	A	O		110	.315
1923	NY	A	O		152	.393
1924	NY	A	O		153	.378
1925	NY	A	O		98	.290
1926	NY	A	O		152	.372
1927	NY	A	O		151	.356
1928	NY	A	O		154	.323
1929	NY	A	O		135	.345
1930	NY	A	P-O	1	145	1- 0
						.359
1931	NY	A	O		145	.373
1932	NY	A	O		133	.341
1933	NY	A	P	1	137	1- 0
						.301
1934	NY	A	O		125	.288
1935	BOS	N	O		28	.181
	BLTL			163	2503	93-44
						.342

RUTHERFORD, JAMES HOLLIS
B.SEPT.26,1886 STILLWATER,MINN.
D.SEPT.18,1956 CLEVELAND,OHIO
| 1910 | CLE | A | O | | 1 | .500 |

RUTHERFORD, JOHN WILLIAM (DOC)
B.MAY 5,1925 BELLEVILLE,ONT.,CANADA
| 1952 | BRO | N | P | | 22 | 7- 7 |
| | BLTR | | | | | |

RUTHVEN, RICHARD DAVID (DICK)
B.MAR.27,1951 SACRAMENTO,CAL.
1973	PHI	N	P	25	27	6- 9
1974	PHI	N	P		35	9-13
1975	PHI	N	P	11	12	2- 2
1976	ATL	N	P	36	37	14-17
1977	ATL	N	P		25	7-13
1978	ATL	N	P		13	2- 6
	PHI	N	P	20	21	13- 5
	BRTR			165	170	53-65

RUTNER, MILTON (MICKEY)
B.MAR.18,1920 HEMPSTEAD,N.Y.
| 1947 | PHI | A | 3 | | 12 | .250 |
| | BRTR | | | | | |

RYAN, CORNELIUS JOSEPH (CONNIE)
B.FEB.27,1920 NEW ORLEANS,LA.
1942	NY	N	2		11	.185
1943	BOS	N	2-3		132	.212
1944	BOS	N	2-3		88	.295
1946	BOS	N	2-3		143	.241
1947	BOS	N	2-S		150	.265
1948	BOS	N	2-3		51	.213
1949	BOS	N	1-2-S-3		85	.250
1950	BOS	N	2		20	.194
	CIN	N	2		106	.259
1951	CIN	N	1-2-3-O		136	.237
1952	PHI	N	2		154	.241
1953	PHI	N	1-2		90	.296
	CHI	A	3		17	.222
1954	CIN	N	H		1	.000
	BRTR				1184	.248
NON-PLAYING MANAGER
ATL(N) 1975 (INTERIM)
TEX(A) 1977 (INTERIM)

RYAN, DANIEL R. (CYCLONE)
B.1866 CAPPERWHITE,IRELAND
D.JAN.30,1917 MEDFIELD,MASS.
1887	MET	AA	1		8	.285
1891	BOS	N	P	1	1	0- 0
				1	9	0- 0
						.278

RYAN, J. (MIKE)
B.ST.LOUIS,MO.
| 1895 | STL | N | 3 | | 2 | .000 |

RYAN, JACK (GULFPORT)
B.SEPT.19,1884 LAWRENCEVILLE,ILL.
D.OCT.16,1949 HONDSBORO,MISS.
1908	CLE	A	P		8	1- 0
1909	BOS	A	P	13	14	4- 3
1911	BRO	N	P		3	0- 1
	TR			24	25	5- 4

RYAN, JAMES E. (JIMMY)
B.FEB.11,1863 CLINTON,MASS.
D.OCT.26,1923 CHICAGO,ILL.
1885	CHI	N	S-O		3	.462
1886	CHI	N	O		84	.306
1887	CHI	N	P-O	1	126	0- 0
						.355
1888	CHI	N	P-O	4	130	3- 1
						.331
1889	CHI	N	S-O		135	.324
1890	CHI	P	O		118	.330
1891	CHI	N	O		118	.289
1892	CHI	N	O		127	.289
1893	CHI	N	O		82	.304
1894	CHI	N	O		108	.359
1895	CHI	N	O		108	.322
1896	CHI	N	O		127	.312
1897	CHI	N	O		135	.309
1898	CHI	N	O		143	.322
1899	CHI	N	O		124	.301
1900	CHI	N	O		106	.276
1902	WAS	A	O		120	.317
1903	WAS	A	O		114	.245
	BRTL			5	2008	3- 1
						.314

RYAN, JOHN A.
[PLAYED 1 GAME UNDER REAL
NAME OF DANIEL SHEEHAN]
B.BIRMINGHAM,MICH.
| 1884 | BAL | U | P-O | | 6 | 3- 2 |
| | | | | | | .095 |

RYAN, JOHN BENNETT
B.NOV.12,1868 HAVERHILL,MASS.
1889	LOU	AA	C		21	.163
1890	LOU	AA	C		94	.219
1891	LOU	AA	C		75	.212
1894	BOS	N	C		49	.271
1895	BOS	N	C		49	.295
1896	BOS	N	C		8	.094
1898	BRO	N	C		82	.189
1899	BAL	N	C		2	.500
1901	STL	N	C		80	.196
1902	STL	N	C-1-2-S-3		74	.177
1903	STL	N	C-1		66	.238
1912	WAS	A	3		1	.000
1913	WAS	A	C		1	.000
	BRTR				602	.216

RYAN, JOHN BUDD (BUDDY)
B.OCT.6,1885 KANSAS
D.JULY 9,1956 SACRAMENTO,CAL.
1912	CLE	A	O		93	.271
1913	CLE	A	O		73	.296
	BLTR				166	.282

RYAN, JOHN COLLINS (BLONDY)
B.JAN.4,1906 LYNN,MASS.
D.NOV.28,1959 SWAMPSCOTT,MASS.
1930	CHI	A	3		28	.207
1933	NY	N	S		146	.238
1934	NY	N	2-S-3		110	.242
1935	PHI	N	2-S-3		39	.264
	NY	A	S		30	.238
1937	NY	N	S		21	.240
1938	NY	N	2-S-3		12	.208
	BRTR				386	.239

RYAN, JOHN FRANCIS (JACK)
B.MAY 5,1905 MINERAL,MINN.
D.SEPT.24,1967 ROCHESTER,MINN.
| 1929 | BOS | A | S-O | | 2 | .000 |

RYAN, JOHN JOSEPH
B.PHILADELPHIA,PA.
D.MAR.22,1902 PHILADELPHIA,PA.
1873	PHI	NA	1		1	-
1874	BAL	NA	O		47	-
1875	NH	NA	P-C-	6	37	1- 5
			S-3-O			-
1876	LOU	N	O		65	.247
1877	CIN	N	O		6	.154

RYAN, JOHN M.
B.HAMILTON,OHIO
1884	WAS	U	3-O		7	.143
	WIL	U	O		2	.167
					9	.147

RYAN, LYNN NOLAN (NOLAN)
B.JAN.31,1947 REFUGIO,TEX.
1966	NY	N	/P		2	0- 1
1968	NY	N	P		21	6- 9
1969	NY	N	P		25	6- 3
1970	NY	N	P		27	7-11
1971	NY	N	P		30	10-14
1972	CAL	A	P		39	19-16
1973	CAL	A	P		41	21-16
1974	CAL	A	P		42	22-16
1975	CAL	A	P		28	14-12
1976	CAL	A	P		39	17-18
1977	CAL	A	P		37	19-16
1978	CAL	A	P		31	10-13
	BRTR				362	151-145

RYAN, MICHAEL JAMES (MIKE)
B.NOV.25,1941 HAVERHILL,MASS.
1964	BOS	A	C		1	.333
1965	BOS	A	C		33	.159
1966	BOS	A	*C		116	.214
1967	BOS	A	C		79	.199
1968	PHI	N	C		96	.179
1969	PHI	N	*C		133	.204
1970	PHI	N	C		46	.179
1971	PHI	N	C		43	.164
1972	PHI	N	C		46	.179
1973	PHI	N	C		28	.232
1974	PIT	N	C		15	.100
	BRTR				636	.193

RYAN, WILFRED PATRICK DOLAN (ROSY)
B.MAR.15,1898 WORCESTER,MASS.
1919	NY	N	P		4	1- 2
1920	NY	N	P		3	0- 1
1921	NY	N	P		36	7-10
1922	NY	N	P		46	17-12
1923	NY	N	P		45	16- 5
1924	NY	N	P		37	8- 6
1925	BOS	N	P	37	38	2- 8
1926	BOS	N	P		7	0- 2
1928	NY	A	P		3	0- 0
1933	BRO	N	P		30	1- 1
	BLTR			248	249	52-47

RYBA, DOMINIC JOSEPH (MIKE)
B.JUNE 9,1903 DE LANCEY,PA.
D.DEC.13,1971 BROOKLINE STATION MO.
1935	STL	N	P		2	1- 1
1936	STL	N	P	14	18	5- 1
1937	STL	N	P	38	41	9- 6
1938	STL	N	P		3	1- 1
1941	BOS	A	P		40	7- 3
1942	BOS	A	P-C	18	21	3- 3
						.294
1943	BOS	A	P		40	7- 5
1944	BOS	A	P		42	12- 7
1945	BOS	A	P		34	7- 6
1946	BOS	A	P		9	0- 1
	BRTR			240	250	52-34
						.214

RYDER, THOMAS
| 1884 | STL | U | O | | 8 | .214 |

RYE, EUGENE RUDOLPH (HALF-PINT)
[REAL NAME
EUGENE RUDOLPH MERCANTELLI]
B.NOV.15,1906 CHICAGO,ILL.
| 1931 | BOS | A | O | | 17 | .179 |
| | BLTR | | | | | |

RYERSON, GARY LAWRENCE
B.JUNE 7,1948 LOS ANGELES,CAL.
1972	MIL	A	P		20	3- 8
1973	MIL	A	/P		9	0- 1
	BRTL				29	3- 9

SABO, ALEXANDER (GIZ)
[REAL NAME ALEXANDER SZABO]
B.FEB.14,1910 NEW BRUNSWICK,N.J
1936	WAS	A	C		4	.375
1937	WAS	A	C		1	.000
	BRTR				5	.375

SACKA, FRANK
B.AUG.30,1924 ROMULUS,MICH.
1951	WAS	A	C		7	.250
1953	WAS	A	C		7	.278
	BRTR				14	.265

SADECKI, RAYMOND MICHAEL (RAY)
B.DEC.26,1940 KANSAS CITY,KAN.
1960	STL	N	P	26	29	9- 9
1961	STL	N	P	31	36	14-10
1962	STL	N	P	22	24	6- 8
1963	STL	N	P	36	39	10-10
1964	STL	N	P	37	39	20-11
1965	STL	N	P		36	6-15
1966	STL	N	/P	5	6	2- 1
	SF	N	P		26	3- 7
1967	SF	N	P	35	37	12- 6
1968	SF	N	P	38	43	12-18
1969	SF	N	P	29	30	5- 8
1970	NY	N	P		28	8- 4
1971	NY	N	P		34	7- 7
1972	NY	N	P		34	2- 1
1973	NY	N	P		31	5- 4
1974	NY	N	P		34	8- 8
1975	STL	N	/P		8	1- 0
	ATL	N	P		25	2- 3
	KC	A	/P		5	1- 0
1976	KC	A	/P		3	0- 0
	MIL	A	P		36	2- 0
1977	NY	N	/P		4	0- 1
	BLTL			563	587	135-131

SADEK, MICHAEL GEORGE (MIKE)
B.MAY 30,1946 MINNEAPOLIS,MINN.
1973	SF	N	C		39	.167
1975	SF	N	C		42	.236
1976	SF	N	C		55	.204
1977	SF	N	C		61	.230
1978	SF	N	C		40	.239
	BRTR				237	.220

```
YR  CL LEA POS    GP   G    REC
```

SADOWSKI, EDWARD ROMAN (ED)
B.JAN,19,1932 PITTSBURGH,PA.
```
1960 BOS A  C          38   .215
1961 LA  A  C          69   .232
1962 LA  A  C          27   .200
1963 LA  A  C          80   .172
1966 ATL N  /C          3   .111
     BRTR             217   .202
```

SADOWSKI, JAMES MICHAEL (JIM)
B.AUG.7,1951 PITTSBURGH,PA.
```
1974 PIT N  /P           4  0- 1
     BRTR
```

SADOWSKI, ROBERT (BOB)
B.FEB.19,1938 PITTSBURGH,PA.
```
1963 MIL N  P          19   5- 7
1964 MIL N  P          51   9-10
1965 MIL N  P          34   5- 9
1966 BOS A  P          11   1- 1
     BRTR             115  20-27
```

SADOWSKI, ROBERT FRANK
(BOB) OR (SID)
B.JAN,15,1937 ST.LOUIS,MO.
```
1960 STL N  2           1   .000
1961 PHI N  3          16   .130
1962 CHI A  2-3        79   .231
1963 LA  A  2-3-0      88   .250
     BLTR             184   .222
```

SADOWSKI, THEODORE (TED)
B.APR.1,1936 PITTSBURGH,PA.
```
1960 WAS A  P           9   1- 0
1961 MIN A  P          15   0- 2
1962 MIN A  P          19   1- 1
     BRTR              43   2- 3
```

SAFFELL, THOMAS JUDSON (TOM)
B.JULY 26,1921 ETOWAH,TENN.
```
1949 PIT N  O          73   .322
1950 PIT N  O          67   .205
1951 PIT N  O          49   .200
1955 PIT N  O          73   .168
     KC  A  O           9   .216
     BLTR             271   .238
```

SAGE, HARRY (DOC)
B.MAR.16,1864 ROCK ISLAND,ILL.
D.MAY 27,1947 ROCK ISLAND,ILL.
```
1890 TOL AA P-C    1   58   0- 1
                             .139
     BRTR
```

SAGER, SAMUEL B. (PONY)
B.1847 MARSHALLTOWN,IOWA
```
1871 ROK NA S-O        8   -
```

SAIER, VICTOR SYLVESTER (VIC)
B.MAY 4,1891 LANSING,MICH.
D.MAY 14,1967 E.LANSING,MICH.
```
1911 CHI N  1          73   .259
1912 CHI N  1         122   .288
1913 CHI N  1         149   .289
1914 CHI N  1         153   .240
1915 CHI N  1         144   .264
1916 CHI N  1         147   .253
1917 CHI N  1           6   .238
1919 PIT N  1          58   .223
     BLTR             852   .262
```

SAIN, JOHN FRANKLIN (JOHNNY)
B.SEPT.25,1917 HAVANA,ARK.
```
1942 BOS N  P          40   4- 7
1946 BOS N  P     37   40  20-14
1947 BOS N  P     38   40  21-12
1948 BOS N  P     42   43  24-15
1949 BOS N  P     37   39  10-17
1950 BOS N  P          37  20-13
1951 BOS N  P          26   5-13
     NY  A  P           7   2- 1
1952 NY  A  P     35   47  11- 6
1953 NY  A  P     40   41  14- 7
1954 NY  A  P          45   6- 6
1955 NY  A  P           3   0- 0
     KC  A  P          25   2- 5
     BRTR        412  433 139-116
```

ST.CLAIRE, EDWARD JOSEPH (EBBA)
B.AUG.5,1921 WHITEHALL,N.Y.
```
1951 BOS N  C          72   .282
1952 BOS N  C          39   .213
1953 MIL N  C          33   .200
1954 NY  N  C          20   .262
     BBTR             164   .249
```

ST.VRAIN, JAMES MARCELLIN
B.JUNE 6,1871 RALLS COUNTY,MO.
D.JUNE 12,1937 BUTTE,MONTANA
```
1902 CHI N  P          12   9- 6
     BRTL
```

SAKATA, LENN HARUKI
B.JUNE 8,1954 HONOLULU,HAWAII
```
1977 MIL A  2          53   .162
1978 MIL A  2          30   .192
                       83   .172
```

SALE, FREDERICK LINK (FREDDY)
B.MAY 2,1902 CHESTER,S.C.
D.MAY 27,1996 HERMOSA BEACH,CAL
```
1924 PIT N  P           1   0- 0
     BRTR
```

SALES, EDWARD A.
B.1861 HARRISBURG,PA.
D.AUG.10,1912 NEW HAVEN,CONN.
```
1890 PIT N  S          51   .228
     TR
```

SALISBURY, HENRY H. (HARRY)
B.MAY 15,1855 PROVIDENCE,R.I.
D.MAR.29,1933 CHICAGO,ILL.
```
1879 TRO N  P-O        10   4- 6
                             .056
1882 PIT AA P-O        39  20-19
                             .152
     BL                49  24-25
                             .143
```

SALISBURY, WILLIAM A.
B.1876 IOWA
```
1902 PHI N  P           2   0- 0
```

SALKELD, WILLIAM FRANKLIN (BILL)
B.MAR.8,1917 POCATELLO,IDAHO
D.APR.22,1967 LOS ANGELES,CAL.
```
1945 PIT N  C          99   .311
1946 PIT N  C          69   .294
1947 PIT N  C          47   .213
1948 BOS N  C          78   .242
1949 BOS N  C          66   .255
1950 CHI A  C           1   .000
     BLTR             356   .273
```

SALLEE, HARRY FRANKLIN
(SLIM) OR (SCATTER)
B.FEB.3,1885 HIGGINSPORT,OHIO
D.MAR.23,1950 HIGGINSPORT,OHIO
```
1908 STL N  P          23   3- 8
1909 STL N  P          32  10-11
1910 STL N  P          18   7- 8
1911 STL N  P          36  15- 9
1912 STL N  P          48  16-17
1913 STL N  P          50  19-15
1914 STL N  P          46  18-17
1915 STL N  P          46  13-17
1916 STL N  P          16   5- 5
     NY  N  P          15   9- 4
1917 NY  N  P          34  18- 7
1918 NY  N  P          18   8- 8
1919 CIN N  P          29  21- 7
1920 CIN N  P          21   5- 6
     NY  N  P           5   1- 0
1921 NY  N  P          37   6- 4
     BLTL             476 174-143
```

SALMON, ROGER ELLIOTT
B.MAY 11,1891 NEWARK,N.J.
D.JUNE 17,1974 BELFAST,ME.
```
1912 PHI A  P           1   1- 0
     BLTL
```

SALMON, RUTHFORD EDUARDO (CHICO)
B.DEC.3,1940 COLON,PANAMA
```
1964 CLE A  1-2-0      86   .307
1965 CLE A  1-0/2-3    79   .242
1966 CLE A  S-2-1-0/3 126   .256
1967 CLE A  0-1-2-S/3  90   .227
1968 CLE A  2-3-S-0-1 103   .214
1969 BAL A  1/2-S-3-0  52   .297
1970 BAL A  S-2-3/1    63   .250
1971 BAL A  /1-2-3-S   42   .179
1972 BAL A  /1-3       17   .063
     BRTR             658   .249
```

SALTZGAVER, OTTO HAMLIN (JACK)
B.JAN.23,1903 CROTON,IOWA
D.FEB.1,1978 KEOKUK,IOWA
```
1932 NY  A  2          20   .128
1934 NY  A  1-3        94   .271
1935 NY  A  1-2-3      61   .262
1936 NY  A  3          34   .211
1937 NY  A  1          17   .182
1945 PIT N  2-3        52   .325
     BLTR             278   .260
```

SALVE, AUGUSTUS WILLIAM (GUS)
B.DEC.29,1885 BOSTON,MASS.
D.MAR.29,1971 PROVIDENCE,R.I.
```
1908 PHI A  P           2   0- 1
     TL
```

SALVESON, JOHN THEODORE (JACK)
B.JAN.5,1914 FULLERTON,CAL.
D.DEC.28,1974 NORWALK,CAL.
```
1933 NY  N  P           8   0- 2
1934 NY  N  P     12   13   3- 1
1935 PIT N  P           5   0- 1
     CHI A  P          20   1- 2
1943 CLE A  P          23   5- 3
1945 CLE A  P          19   0- 0
     BRTR         87   88   9- 9
```

SALVO, MANUEL (GYP)
B.JUNE 30,1913 SACRAMENTO,CAL.
```
1939 NY  N  P          32   4-10
1940 BOS N  P          21  10- 9
1941 BOS N  P          35   7-16
1942 BOS N  P          25   7- 8
1943 BOS N  P           1   0- 0
     PHI N  P           1   0- 0
     BOS N  P          20   5- 7
     BRTR             135  33-50
```

SAMBITO, JOSEPH CHARLES (JOE)
B.JUNE 28,1952 BROOKLYN,N.Y.
```
1976 HOU N  P          20   3- 2
1977 HOU N  P          54   5- 5
1978 HOU N  P          62   4- 9
     BLTL             136  12-16
```

SAMCOFF, EDWARD WILLIAM (ED)
B.SEPT.1,1924 SACRAMENTO,CAL.
```
1951 PHI A  2           4   .000
     BRTR
```

SAMFORD, RONALD EDWARD (RON)
B.FEB.28,1930 DALLAS,TEX.
```
1954 NY  N  2          12   .000
1955 DET A  S           1   .000
1957 DET A  2-S-3      54   .220
1959 WAS A  2-S        91   .224
     BRTR             158   .219
```

SAMPLE, WILLIAM AMOS (BILL)
B.APR.2,1955 ROANOKE,VA.
```
1978 TEX A  /O          8   .467
     BRTR
```

SAMUEL, AMADO RUPERTO
B.DEC.6,1938 SAN PEDRO DE
MACORIS,D.R.
```
1962 MIL N  2-S-3      76   .206
1963 MIL N  2-S-3      15   .176
1964 NY  N  2-S-3      53   .232
     BRTR             144   .215
```

SAMUELS, JOSEPH JONAS (SKABOTCHI)
B.MAR.21,1905 SCRANTON,PA.
```
1930 DET A  3          22   .186
     BRTR
```

SAMUELS, SAMUEL EARL (IKE)
B.FEB.20,1876 CHICAGO,ILL.
```
1895 STL N  3          22   .186
     BRTR
```

SANBERG, GUSTAVE E.
B.FEB.23,1896 LONG ISLAND CITY,N.Y.
D.FEB.3,1930 LOS ANGELES,CAL.
```
1923 CIN N  C           7   .176
1924 CIN N  C          24   .173
     BRTR              31   .174
```

SANCHEZ, CELERINO (PEREZ)
B.FEB.3,1944 VERACRUZ,MEXICO
```
1972 NY  A  3          71   .248
1973 NY  A  3-0/S-0    34   .219
     BRTR             105   .242
```

SANCHEZ, RAUL GUADALUPE
(RODRIGUEZ)
B.DEC.12,1930 MARIANAO,CUBA
```
1952 WAS A  P           3   1- 1
1957 CIN N  P          38   3- 2
1960 CIN N  P           8   1- 0
     BRTR              49   5- 3
```

SAND, JOHN HENRY (HEINIE)
B.JULY 3,1897 SAN FRANCISCO,CAL
D.NOV.3,1958 SAN FRANCISCO,CAL.
```
1923 PHI N  S-3       132   .228
1924 PHI N  S         137   .245
1925 PHI N  S         148   .278
1926 PHI N  S         149   .272
1927 PHI N  S-3       141   .299
1928 PHI N  S         141   .211
     BRTR             848   .258
```

SANDERS, ALEXANDER BENNETT (BEN)
B.FEB.16,1865 CATHARPEN,VA.
D.AUG.29,1930 MEMPHIS,TENN.
```
1888 PHI N  P-O   31   57  19-10
1889 PHI N  P     40   41  19-17
1890 PHI P  P          44  21-19
1891 ATH AA P-O   21   41  12- 7
                             .253
1892 LOU N  P-1   31   53  12-17
                             .267
     BRTR        167  236  83-70
                             .267
```

SANDERS, DEE WILMA
B.APR.8,1921 QUITMAN,TEX.
```
1945 STL A  P           2   0- 0
     BRTR
```

SANDERS, JOHN FRANK
B.NOV.20,1945 GRAND ISLAND,NEB.
```
1965 KC  A  R           1   .000
     BRTR
```

YR CL LEA POS   GP   G   REC

SANDERS, KENNETH GEORGE (KEN) OR (DAFFY)
B.JULY 8,1941 ST.LOUIS,MO.
```
1964 KC  A  P              21   0- 2
1966 BOS A  P              24   3- 6
     KC  A  P              38   3- 4
1968 OAK A /P               7   0- 1
1970 MIL A  P              50   5- 2
1971 MIL A  P              83   7-12
1972 MIL A  P              62   2- 9
1973 MIN A  P              27   2- 4
     CLE A  P              15   5- 1
1974 CLE A /P               9   0- 1
     CAL A /P               9   0- 0
1975 NY  N  P         29   30   1- 1
1976 NY  N  P              31   1- 2
     KC  A /P               3   0- 0
     BRTR          408  409   29-45
```

SANDERS, RAYMOND FLOYD (RAY)
B.DEC.4,1916 BONNE TERRE,MO.
```
1942 STL N  1              95  .252
1943 STL N  1             144  .280
1944 STL N  1             154  .295
1945 STL N  1             143  .276
1946 BOS N  1              80  .243
1948 BOS N  H               5  .250
1949 BOS N  1               9  .143
     BLTR               630  .275
```

SANDERS, REGINALD JEROME (REGGIE)
B.SEPT.9,1949 BIRMINGHAM,ALA.
```
1974 DET A  1              26  .273
     BRTR
```

SANDERS, ROY GARVIN (BUTCH) OR (PEPE)
B.AUG.1,1892 STAFFORD,KAN.
D.JAN.17,1950 KANSAS CITY,MO.
```
1917 CIN N  P          2    3   0- 1
1918 PIT N  P              28   7- 9
     BRTR           30   31   7-10
```

SANDERS, ROY L. (SIMON)
B.1894
```
1918 NY  A  P               6   0- 2
1920 STL A  P               8   1- 1
     BRTR                14   1- 3
```

SANDERS, WARREN WILLIAMS
B.AUG.2,1877 MAYNARDVILLE,TENN.
D.AUG.3,1962 CHATTANOOGA,TENN.
```
1903 STL N  P               8   1- 6
1904 STL N  P               4   1- 2
     BRTL                12   2- 8
```

SANDERSON, SCOTT DOUGLAS
B.JULY 22,1956 DEARBORN,MICH.
```
1978 MON N  P              10   4- 2
     BRTR
```

SANDLOCK, MICHAEL JOSEPH (MIKE)
B.OCT.17,1915 OLD GREENWICH,CONN.
```
1942 BOS N  S               2 1.000
1944 BOS N  S-3            30  .100
1945 BRO N  C-2-S-3        80  .282
1946 BRO N  C-3            19  .147
1953 PIT N  C              64  .231
     BBTR               195  .240
     BL 1944
```

SANDS, CHARLES DUANE (CHARLIE)
B.DEC.17,1947 NEWPORT NEWS,VA.
```
1967 NY  A /H               1  .000
1971 PIT N /C              28  .200
1972 PIT N /H               1  .000
1973 CAL A  C              17  .273
1974 CAL A  D/C            43  .193
1975 OAK A /H               3  .500
     BLTR                93  .214
```

SANDT, THOMAS JAMES (TOMMY)
B.DEC.22,1950 BROOKLYN,N.Y.
```
1975 OAK A /2               1  .000
1976 OAK A  S/2-3          41  .209
     BRTR                42  .209
```

SANDY, IRWIN
[PLAYED UNDER NAME OF VINCENT NAVA]

SANFORD, JOHN DOWARD (JACK)
B.JUNE 23,1917 CHATHAM,VA.
```
1940 WAS A  1              34  .197
1941 WAS A  1               3  .400
1946 WAS A  1              10  .231
     BRTR                47  .209
```

SANFORD, JOHN FREDERICK (FRED)
B.AUG.9,1919 GARFIELD,UTAH
```
1943 STL A  P               3   0- 0
1946 STL A  P               3   2- 1
1947 STL A  P              34   7-16
1948 STL A  P         42   43  12-21
1949 NY  A  P              29   7- 3
1950 NY  A  P              26   5- 4
1951 NY  A  P              11   0- 3
     WAS A  P               7   2- 3
     STL A  P               9   2- 4
     BBTR          164  165  37-55
     BR 1948
```

SANFORD, JOHN STANLEY (JACK)
B.MAY 18,1929 WELLESLEY HILLS,MASS.
```
1956 PHI N  P               3   1- 0
1957 PHI N  P              33  19- 8
1958 PHI N  P              38  10-13
1959 SF  N  P              36  15-12
1960 SF  N  P              37  12-14
1961 SF  N  P         38   39  13- 9
1962 SF  N  P              39  24- 7
1963 SF  N  P         42   43  16-13
1964 SF  N  P         18   19   5- 7
1965 SF  N  P              23   4- 5
     CAL A /P               9   1- 2
1966 CAL A  P              50  13- 7
1967 CAL A  P              12   3- 2
     KC  A  P              10   1- 2
     BRTR          388  393  137-101
```

SANGUILLEN, MANUEL DE JESUS (MAGAN) (MANNY)
B.MAR.21,1944 COLON,PANAMA
```
1967 PIT N  C              30  .271
1969 PIT N *C             129  .303
1970 PIT N *C             128  .325
1971 PIT N *C             138  .319
1972 PIT N *C/O           136  .298
1973 PIT N  C-O           149  .282
1974 PIT N *C             151  .287
1975 PIT N *C             133  .328
1976 PIT N *C             114  .290
1977 OAK A  C-O/O-1       152  .275
1978 PIT N  1-C            85  .264
     BRTR              1345  .298
```

SANICKI, EDWARD ROBERT (BUTCH)
B.JULY 7,1924 WALLINGTON,N.J.
```
1949 PHI N  O               7  .231
1951 PHI N  O              13  .500
     BRTR                20  .294
```

SANKEY, BENJAMIN TURNER
B.SEPT.2,1907 NAUVOO,ALA.
```
1929 PIT N  S               2  .143
1930 PIT N  2-S            13  .167
1931 PIT N  2-S            57  .227
     BRTR                72  .213
```

SANTIAGO, JOSE GUILLERMO (JOSE) OR (PANTS)
B.SEPT.4,1928 COAMO,P.R.
```
1954 CLE A  P               1   0- 0
1955 CLE A  P              17   2- 0
1956 KC  A  P               9   1- 2
     BRTR                27   3- 2
```

SANTIAGO, JOSE RAFAEL (ALFONSO)
B.AUG.15,1940 JUANA DIAZ,P.R.
```
1963 KC  A  P               4   1- 0
1964 KC  A  P              34   0- 6
1965 KC  A /P               4   0- 0
1966 BOS A  P         35   38  12-13
1967 BOS A  P              50  12- 4
1968 BOS A  P         18   23   9- 4
1969 BOS A  P              10   0- 0
1970 BOS A /P          8    9   0- 2
     BRTR          163  172  34-29
```

SANTO, RONALD EDWARD (RON)
B.FEB.25,1940 SEATTLE,WASH.
```
1960 CHI N  3              95  .251
1961 CHI N  3             154  .284
1962 CHI N  S-3           162  .227
1963 CHI N  3             162  .297
1964 CHI N  3             161  .313
1965 CHI N *3             164  .285
1966 CHI N *3/S           155  .312
1967 CHI N *3             161  .300
1968 CHI N *3             162  .246
1969 CHI N *3             160  .289
1970 CHI N *3/O           154  .267
1971 CHI N *3/O           154  .267
1972 CHI N *3/2-S-O       133  .302
1973 CHI N *3             149  .267
1974 CHI A  D-2-3/1-S     117  .221
     BRTR              2243  .277
```

SANTORINI, ALAN JOEL (AL)
B.MAY 19,1948 IRVINGTON,N.J.
```
1968 ATL N /P               1   0- 1
1969 SD  N  P              32   8-14
1970 SD  N  P              21   1- 8
1971 SD  N  P              18   0- 2
     STL N  P              19   0- 2
1972 STL N  P              30   8-11
1973 STL N /P               6   0- 0
     BRTR               127  17-38
```

SANTRY, EDWARD
B.CHICAGO,ILL.
```
1884 DET N  2-S             6  .174
```

SARGENT, JOSEPH ALEXANDER (JOE) OR (HORSE BELLY)
B.SEPT.24,1893 ROCHESTER,N.Y.
D.JULY 5,1950 ROCHESTER,N.Y.
```
1921 DET A  2-S-3          66  .253
     BRTR
```

SARMIENTO, MANUEL EDUARDO (APONTE) (MANNY)
B.FEB.2,1956 CAGUA,VENEZ.
```
1976 CIN N  P              22   5- 1
1977 CIN N  P              24   0- 0
1978 CIN N  P         63   64   9- 7
     BRTR          109  110  14- 8
```

SARNI, WILLIAM F. (BILL)
B.SEPT.19,1927 LOS ANGELES,CAL.
```
1951 STL N  C              36  .174
1952 STL N  C               3  .200
1954 STL N  C             123  .300
1955 STL N  C             107  .256
1956 STL N  C              43  .291
     NY  N  C              78  .231
     BRTR               390  .263
```

SATRIANO, THOMAS VICTOR NICHOLAS (TOM)
B.AUG.28,1940 PITTSBURGH,PA.
```
1961 LA  A  2-S-3          35  .198
1962 LA  A  3              10  .421
1963 LA  A  C-1-3          23  .180
1964 LA  A  C-1-2-S-3     108  .200
1965 CAL A  3-C-2/1        47  .165
1966 CAL A  C-1-3/2       103  .239
1967 CAL A  3-C-2/1        90  .224
1968 CAL A  C-2-3/1       111  .253
1969 CAL A  C/1-2          41  .259
     BOS A  C              47  .189
1970 BOS A  C              59  .236
     BLTR               674  .225
```

SAUCIER, FRANCIS FIELD (FRANK)
B.MAY 28,1926 LESLIE,MO.
```
1951 STL A  O              18  .071
     BLTR
```

SAUCIER, KEVIN ANDREW
B.AUG.9,1956 PENSACOLA,FLA.
```
1978 PHI N /P               1   0- 1
     BLTL
```

SAUER, EDWARD (EDDIE) OR (HORN)
B.JAN.3,1920 PITTSBURGH,PA.
```
1943 CHI N  O              14  .273
1944 CHI N  O              23  .220
1945 CHI N  O              49  .258
1949 STL N  H              24  .222
     BOS N  O              79  .266
     BRTR               189  .256
```

SAUER, HENRY JOHN (HANK)
B.MAR.17,1919 PITTSBURGH,PA.
```
1941 CIN N  O               9  .303
1942 CIN N  1               7  .250
1945 CIN N  1-O            31  .293
1948 CIN N  1-O           145  .260
1949 CIN N  1-O            42  .237
     CHI N  O              96  .291
1950 CHI N  1-O           145  .274
1951 CHI N  O             141  .263
1952 CHI N  O             151  .270
1953 CHI N  O             108  .263
1954 CHI N  O             142  .288
1955 CHI N  O              79  .211
1956 STL N  O              75  .298
1957 NY  N  O             127  .259
1958 SF  N  O              88  .250
1959 SF  N  O              13  .067
     BRTR              1399  .266
```

SAUNDERS, DENNIS JAMES
B.JAN.4,1949 ALHAMBRA,CAL.
```
1970 DET A /P               8   1- 1
     BBTR
```

SAUNDERS, RUSSELL COLLIER (RUSTY)
B.MAR.12,1906 TRENTON,N.J.
D.NOV.24,1967 TRENTON,N.J.
```
1927 PHI A  O               5  .133
     BRTR
```

YR	CL LEA POS	GP	G	REC

SAUTERS, AL
B.PHILADELPHIA,PA.
1890 ATH AA 3   14   .098

SAVAGE, DONALD ANTHONY
B.MAR.5,1919 BLOOMFIELD,N.J.
D.DEC.25,1961 MONTCLAIR,N.J.
1944 NY A 3   71   .264
1945 NY A 3-O   34   .224
    BRTR   105   .256

SAVAGE, EPHESIAN
[PLAYED UNDER NAME OF
THEODORE EDMUND SAVAGE]

SAVAGE, JAMES HAROLD (JIMMIE)
B.AUG.29,1883 SOUTHINGTON,CONN.
D.JUNE 26,1940 NEW CASTLE,PA.
1912 PHI N 2   2   .000
1914 PIT F 3-O   132   .285
1915 PIT F O   14   .150
    BBTR   148   .280

SAVAGE, JOHN ROBERT (BOB)
B.DEC.1,1921 MANCHESTER,N.H.
1942 PHI A P   8   0- 1
1946 PHI A P   40   3-15
1947 PHI A P   44   8-10
1948 PHI A P   33   5- 1
1949 STL A P   4   0- 0
    BRTR   129   16-27

SAVAGE, THEODORE EDMUND (TED)
[REAL NAME EPHESIAN SAVAGE]
B.FEB.21,1937 VENICE,ILL.
1962 PHI N O   127   .266
1963 PIT N O   85   .195
1965 STL N O   30   .159
1966 STL N /O   16   .172
1967 STL N /H   9   .125
   CHI N O/3   96   .218
1968 CHI N /O   3   .250
   LA N O   61   .206
1969 CIN N O/2   68   .227
1970 MIL A O/1   114   .279
1971 MIL A /O   14   .176
   KC A /O   19   .172
    BRTR   642   .233

SAVERINE, ROBERT PAUL
(BOB) OR (RABBIT)
B.JUNE 2,1941 NORWALK,CONN.
1959 BAL A R   1   .000
1962 BAL A 2   8   .238
1963 BAL A 2-S-O   115   .234
1964 BAL A S-O   46   .147
1966 WAS A 2-3-S/O   120   .251
1967 WAS A 2-S/3-O   89   .236
    BBTR   379   .239

SAVIDGE, DONALD SNYDER
B.AUG.28,1908 BERWICK,PA.
1929 WAS A 3   3   0- 0
    BRTR

SAVIDGE, RALPH AUSTIN
(THE HUMAN WHIPCORD)
B.FEB.3,1879 JERSEYTOWN,PA.
D.JULY 22,1959 BERWICK,PA.
1908 CIN N P   4   0- 1
1909 CIN N P   1   0- 0
    BRTR   5   0- 1

SAVRANSKY, MORRIS (MOE)
B.JAN.13,1929 CLEVELAND,OHIO
1954 CIN N P   16   0- 2
    BLTL

SAWATSKI, CARL ERNEST
(CARL) OR (SWATS)
B.NOV.4,1927 SHICKSHINNY,PA.
1948 CHI N H   2   .000
1950 CHI N C   38   .175
1953 CHI N C   43   .220
1954 CHI A C   43   .183
1957 MIL N C   58   .234
1958 MIL N C   10   .100
   PHI N C   60   .230
1959 PHI N C   74   .293
1960 STL N C   78   .229
1961 STL N C-O   86   .299
1962 STL N C   89   .252
1963 STL N C   56   .238
    BLTR   633   .242

SAWYER, CARL EVERETT (HUCK)
B.OCT.19,1890 SEATTLE,WASH.
D.JAN.17,1957 LOS ANGELES,CAL.
1915 WAS A 2   10   .117
1916 WAS A 2   16   .194
    BRTR   26   .190

SAWYER, EDWIN MILBY (EDDIE)
B.SEPT.10,1910 WESTERLY,R.I.
NON-PLAYING MANAGER
PHI[N] 1948-52, 58-60

SAWYER, RICHARD CLYDE (RICK)
B.APR.7,1948 BAKERSFIELD,CAL.
1974 NY A /P   1   0- 0
1975 NY A /P   4   0- 0
1976 SD N P   13   5- 3
1977 SD N P   56   7- 6
    BRTR   74   12- 9

SAWYER, WILLARD NEWTON
B.JULY 29,1864 BRIMFIELD,OHIO
D.JAN.5,1936 KENT,OHIO
1883 CLE N P   17   4-10
    BLTL

SAX, ERIK OLIVER (OLLIE)
B.NOV.5,1904 BRANFORD,CONN.
1928 STL A 3   16   .176
    BRTR

SAY, JAMES I.
B.1862 BALTIMORE,MD.
D.JUNE 23,1894 BALTIMORE,MD.
1882 LOU AA 3   1   .500
   ATH AA S   1   .500
1884 WIL U 3   16   .220
   KC U 3   2   .250
1887 CLE AA 3   15   .367
     35   .304

SAY, LEWIS I.
B.FEB.4,1854 BALTIMORE,MD.
D.JUNE 5,1930 FALLSTON,MD.
1873 MAR NA S-O   3   -
1874 BAL NA S   18   -
1875 NAT NA 2-S-O   9   -
1880 CIN N S   47   .202
1882 ATH AA S   71   .221
1883 BAL AA S   84   .260
1884 BAL U S   79   .236
   KC U 2-S   17   .217
    BRTR   328   -

SAYLES, WILLIAM NISBETH
B.JULY 27,1917 PORTLAND,ORE.
1939 BOS A P   5   0- 0
1943 NY N P   18   19   1- 3
   BRO N P   5   6   0- 0
    BRTR   28   30   1- 3

SAYLOR, PHILIP ANDREW (LEFTY)
B.JAN.2,1871 VAN WERT CO.,OHIO
D.JULY 23,1937 W.ALEXANDRIA,O.
1891 PHI N P   1   0- 0
    TL

SCALA, GERARD DANIEL (JERRY)
B.SEPT.27,1926 BAYONNE,N.J.
1948 CHI A O   3   .000
1949 CHI A O   37   .250
1950 CHI A O   40   .194
    BLTR   80   .223

SCALZI, FRANK JOHN (SKEETER)
B.JUNE 16,1913 LAFFERTY,OHIO
1939 NY N S-3   11   .333
    BRTR

SCALZI, JOHN ANTHONY
B.MAR.22,1907 STAMFORD,CONN.
D.SEPT.27,1962 PORT CHESTER,N.Y
1931 BOS N H   2   .000
    BRTR

SCANLAN, FRANK ALOYSIUS
B.APR.28,1890 SYRACUSE,N.Y.
D.APR.9,1969 BROOKLYN,N.Y.
1909 PHI N P   6   0- 0

SCANLAN, WILLIAM DENNIS (DOC)
B.MAR.7,1881 SYRACUSE,N.Y.
D.MAY 29,1949 BROOKLYN,N.Y.
1903 PIT N P   1   0- 1
1904 PIT N P   4   1- 2
   BRO N P   14   7- 7
1905 BRO N P   33   15-11
1906 BRO N P   38   18-13
1907 BRO N P   17   6- 8
1909 BRO N P   19   8- 7
1910 BRO N P   34   9-11
1911 BRO N P   22   3-10
    BLTR   182   67-70

SCANLON, JAMES PATRICK (PAT)
B.SEPT.23,1952 MINNEAPOLIS,MINN.
1974 MON N /3   2   .250
1975 MON N 3/1   60   .183
1976 MON N /3-1   11   .185
1977 SD N 2-3/O   47   .190
    BLTR   120   .187

SCANLON, M. J.
B.CHICAGO,ILL.
1890 NY N 1   3   .000

SCANLON, MICHAEL B.
B.1847 CORK,IRELAND
D.JAN.18,1929
NON-PLAYING MANAGER
WAS[U] 1884, WAS[N] 1886

SCANNELL, JOHN J.
1884 BOS U O   6   .304

SCANTLEBURY, PATRICO ATHELSTAN (PAT)
B.NOV.11,1925 GATUN,CANAL ZONE
1956 CIN N P   8   0- 1
    BLTL

SCARBOROUGH, RAE WILSON
[PLAYED UNDER NAME OF
RAY WILSON SCARBOROUGH]

SCARBOROUGH, RAY WILSON
[REAL NAME RAE WILSON SCARBOROUGH]
B.JULY 23,1917 MT.GILEAD,N.C.
1942 WAS A P   17   2- 1
1943 WAS A P   24   4- 4
1946 WAS A P   32   7-11
1947 WAS A P   33   6-13
1948 WAS A P   31   15- 8
1949 WAS A P   34   13-11
1950 WAS A P   8   3- 5
   CHI A P   27   10-13
1951 BOS A P   37   12- 9
1952 BOS A P   28   1- 5
   NY A P   9   5- 1
1953 NY A P   25   2- 2
   DET A P   13   0- 2
    BRTR   318   80-85

SCARCE, GUERRANT MC CURDY (MAC)
B.APR.8,1949 DANVILLE,VA.
1972 PHI N P   31   1- 2
1973 PHI N P   52   1- 8
1974 PHI N P   58   3- 8
1975 NY N P   1   0- 0
1978 MIN A P   17   1- 1
    BLTL   159   6-19

SCARRITT, RUSSELL MALLORY
B.JAN.14,1903 PENSACOLA,FLA.
1929 BOS A O   151   .294
1930 BOS A O   113   .289
1931 BOS A O   10   .154
1932 PHI N O   11   .182
    BLTR   285   .285

SCARSELLA, LESLIE GEORGE (LES)
B.NOV.23,1913 SANTA CRUZ,CAL.
D.DEC.17,1958 SAN FRANCISCO,CAL
1935 CIN N 1   6   .200
1936 CIN N 1   115   .313
1937 CIN N 1-O   110   .246
1939 CIN N H   16   .143
1940 BOS N 1   18   .300
    BLTR   265   .285

SCHAAL, PAUL
B.MAR.3,1943 PITTSBURGH,PA.
1964 LA A 2-3   17   .125
1965 CAL A *3/2   155   .224
1966 CAL A *3   138   .244
1967 CAL A 3/S-2   99   .188
1968 CAL A 3   60   .210
1969 KC A 3/2-S   61   .263
1970 KC A 3-S/2   124   .268
1971 KC A *3   161   .274
1972 KC A *3/S   127   .228
1973 KC A *3   121   .288
1974 KC A 3   121   .276
   CAL A 3   53   .248
    BRTR   1128   .244

SCHACHT, ALEXANDER (AL)
B.NOV.11,1892 NEW YORK,N.Y.
1919 WAS A P   2   2- 0
1920 WAS A P   22   6- 4
1921 WAS A P   30   6- 6
    BRTR   54   14-10

SCHACHT, SIDNEY (SID)
B.FEB.31,1918 BOGOTA,N.J.
1950 STL A P   9   0- 0
1951 STL A P   5   0- 0
   BOS N P   5   0- 2
    BRTR   20   0- 2

SCHACKER, HAROLD
B.APR.6,1925 BROOKLYN,N.Y.
1945 BOS N P   6   0- 1
    BRTR

SCHAEFER, HERMAN A. (GERMANY)
B.FEB.4,1877 CHICAGO,ILL.
D.MAY 16,1919 SARANAC LAKE,N.Y.

YR	CL	LEA	POS	GP	G	REC
1901	CHI	N	2		2	.375
1902	CHI	N	1-3-0		60	.188
1905	DET	A	2		153	.244
1906	DET	A	2		124	.238
1907	DET	A	2-S		109	.258
1908	DET	A	2-S-3		153	.259
1909	DET	A	2		87	.250
	WAS	A	2		37	.155
1910	WAS	A	2-0		74	.275
1911	WAS	A	1		125	.334
1912	WAS	A	1-2-0		60	.247
1913	WAS	A	P-2	1	52	0- 0
						.320
1914	WAS	A	2		25	.241
1915	NEW	F	O		58	.214
1916	NY	A	O		1	.000
1918	CLE	A	2		1	.000
	BRTR			1	1141	0- 0
						.256

SCHAEFFER, HARRY EDWARD (LEFTY)
B.JUNE 23,1924 READING,PA.

YR	CL	LEA	POS	GP	G	REC
1952	NY	A	P		5	0- 1
	BLTL					

SCHAFER, HARRY C. (SILK STOCKING)
B.AUG.14,1846 PHILADELPHIA,PA.
D.FEB.28,1935 PHILADELPHIA,PA.

YR	CL	LEA	POS	GP	G	REC
1871	BOS	NA	3		33	-
1872	BOS	NA	3-0		48	.262
1873	BOS	NA	3-0		60	.284
1874	BOS	NA	3		71	.275
1875	BOS	NA	3		51	.295
1876	BOS	N	3		70	.248
1877	BOS	N	S-3-0		33	.277
1878	BOS	N	O		4	.235
1879	CIN	N	S		1	.000
	BRTR				371	-

SCHAFER, JOHN W.
B.LOCK HAVEN,PA.

YR	CL	LEA	POS	GP	G	REC
1886	MET	AA	P		8	5- 3
1887	MET	AA	P		13	2-11
					21	7-14

SCHAEFFER, MARK PHILIP
B.JUNE 5,1948 SANTA MONICA,CAL.

YR	CL	LEA	POS	GP	G	REC
1972	SD	N	P		41	2- 0
	BLTL					

SCHAFFER, JIMMIE RONALD
B.APR.5,1936 LIMEPORT,PA.

YR	CL	LEA	POS	GP	G	REC
1961	STL	N	C		68	.255
1962	STL	N	C		70	.242
1963	CHI	N	C		57	.239
1964	CHI	N	C		54	.205
1965	CHI	A	C		17	.194
	NY	N	C		24	.135
1966	PHI	N	/C		8	.133
1967	PHI	N	/C		2	.000
1968	CIN	N	/C		4	.167
	BRTR				304	.223

SCHAFFERNOTH, JOSEPH ARTHUR (JOE)
B.AUG.6,1937 TRENTON,N.J.

YR	CL	LEA	POS	GP	G	REC
1959	CHI	N	P		5	1- 0
1960	CHI	N	P		33	2- 3
1961	CHI	N	P		21	0- 4
	CLE	A	P		15	0- 1
	BRTR				74	3- 8

SCHAIVE, JOHN EDWARD (JOHNNY)
B.FEB.25,1934 SPRINGFIELD,ILL.

YR	CL	LEA	POS	GP	G	REC
1958	WAS	A	H		7	.250
1959	WAS	A	2		16	.153
1960	WAS	A	2		6	.250
1962	WAS	A	2-3		82	.253
1963	WAS	A	H		3	.000
	BRTR				114	.232

SCHALK, LE ROY JOHN (ROY)
B.NOV.9,1908 CHICAGO,ILL.

YR	CL	LEA	POS	GP	G	REC
1932	NY	A	2		3	.250
1944	CHI	A	2-S		146	.220
1945	CHI	A	2		133	.248
	BRTR				282	.233

SCHALK, RAYMOND WILLIAM (RAY) OR (CRACKER)
B.AUG.12,1892 HARVEY,ILL.
D.MAY 19,1970 CHICAGO,ILL.

YR	CL	LEA	POS	GP	G	REC
1912	CHI	A	C		23	.286
1913	CHI	A	C		128	.244
1914	CHI	A	C		135	.270
1915	CHI	A	C		135	.266
1916	CHI	A	C		129	.232
1917	CHI	A	C		140	.227
1918	CHI	A	C		108	.219
1919	CHI	A	C		131	.282
1920	CHI	A	C		151	.270
1921	CHI	A	C		128	.252
1922	CHI	A	C		142	.281
1923	CHI	A	C		123	.228
1924	CHI	A	C		57	.196
1925	CHI	A	C		125	.274
1926	CHI	A	C		82	.265
1927	CHI	A	M-C		16	.231
1928	CHI	A	M-C		2	1.000
1929	NY	N	C		5	.000
	BRTR				1760	.253

SCHALLER, WALTER (BIFF)
B.SEPT.23,1889 CHICAGO,ILL.
D.OCT.9,1939 EMERYVILLE,CAL.

YR	CL	LEA	POS	GP	G	REC
1911	DET	A	O		40	.133
1913	CHI	A	O		34	.219
					74	.186

SCHALLICK, AUGUST
[PLAYED UNDER NAME OF AUGUST SHALLIX]

SCHALLOCK, ARTHUR LAWRENCE (ART)
B.APR.25,1924 MILL VALLEY,CAL.

YR	CL	LEA	POS	GP	G	REC
1951	NY	A	P		11	3- 1
1952	NY	A	P		2	0- 0
1953	NY	A	P		7	0- 0
1954	NY	A	P		6	0- 1
1955	NY	A	P		2	0- 0
	BAL	A	P		30	3- 5
	BLTL				58	6- 7

SCHANG, ROBERT MARTIN
B.DEC.7,1886 WALES CENTER,N.Y.
D.AUG.24,1966 SACRAMENTO,CAL.

YR	CL	LEA	POS	GP	G	REC
1914	PIT	N	C		10	.250
1915	PIT	N	C		56	.184
	NY	N	C		12	.143
1927	STL	N	C		3	.200
	BRTR				81	.188

SCHANG, WALTER HENRY (WALLY)
B.AUG.22,1889 S.WALES,N.Y.
D.MAR.6,1965 ST.LOUIS,MO.

YR	CL	LEA	POS	GP	G	REC
1913	PHI	A	C		77	.266
1914	PHI	A	C		107	.287
1915	PHI	A	C-3-0		116	.248
1916	PHI	A	C-0		110	.266
1917	PHI	A	C		118	.285
1918	BOS	A	C-0		88	.245
1919	BOS	A	C-0		113	.306
1920	BOS	A	C-0		122	.305
1921	NY	A	C		134	.316
1922	NY	A	C		124	.319
1923	NY	A	C		84	.276
1924	NY	A	C		114	.292
1925	NY	A	C		73	.240
1926	STL	A	C		103	.330
1927	STL	A	C		97	.318
1928	STL	A	C		91	.285
1929	STL	A	C		94	.237
1930	PHI	A	C		45	.174
1931	DET	A	C		30	.184
	BBTR				1840	.284

SCHANZ, CHARLEY MURRELL
B.JUNE 8,1919 ANACORTES,WASH.

YR	CL	LEA	POS	GP	G	REC
1944	PHI	N	P		40	13-16
1945	PHI	N	P		35	4-15
1946	PHI	N	P		32	6- 6
1947	PHI	N	P		34	2- 4
1950	BOS	A	P		14	3- 2
	BRTR				155	28-43

SCHAPPERT, JOHN
B.BROOKLYN,N.Y.
D.JULY 29,1916 ROCKAWAY BEACH,N.Y.

YR	CL	LEA	POS	GP	G	REC
1882	STL	AA	P-0		15	8- 7
						.173
	BRTR					

SCHARDT, WILBURT (BIG BILL)
B.JAN.20,1886 CLEVELAND,OHIO
D.JULY 20,1964 VERMILION,OHIO

YR	CL	LEA	POS	GP	G	REC
1911	BRO	N	P		39	5-15
1912	BRO	N	P		7	0- 1
					46	5-16

SCHAREIN, ARTHUR OTTO (SCOOP)
B.JUNE 30,1905 DECATUR,ILL.
D.JULY 21,1969 SAN ANTONIO,TEX.

YR	CL	LEA	POS	GP	G	REC
1932	STL	A	3		81	.304
1933	STL	A	2-S-3		123	.204
1934	STL	A	H		1	.500
	BRTR				205	.244

SCHAREIN, GEORGE ALBERT (TOM)
B.NOV.21,1914 DECATUR,ILL.

YR	CL	LEA	POS	GP	G	REC
1937	PHI	N	S		146	.241
1938	PHI	N	2-S		117	.238
1939	PHI	N	S		118	.238
1940	PHI	N	S		7	.294
	BRTR				388	.240

SCHARF, EDWARD T.
B.1859 BALTIMORE,MD.
D.MAR.12,1937 BALTIMORE,MD.

YR	CL	LEA	POS	GP	G	REC
1882	BAL	AA	3-0		10	.243
1883	BAL	AA	S		13	.216

SCHATZEDER, DANIEL ERNEST (DAN)
B.DEC.1,1954 ELMHURST,ILL.

YR	CL	LEA	POS	GP	G	REC
1977	MON	N	/P		6	2- 1
1978	MON	N	P	29	32	7- 7
	BLTL			35	38	9- 8

SCHAUER, ALEXANDER JOHN (RUBE)
[REAL NAME DIMITRI IVANOVICH DIMITRIHOFF]
B.MAR.19,1891 ODESSA,RUSSIA
D.APR.15,1957 MINNEAPOLIS,MINN.

YR	CL	LEA	POS	GP	G	REC
1913	NY	N	P		3	0- 1
1914	NY	N	P		6	0- 0
1915	NY	N	P		32	2- 8
1916	NY	N	P		19	1- 4
1917	PHI	A	P		33	7-16
	BRTR				93	10-29

SCHEER, ALLAN G.
B.OCT.21,1888 DAYTON,OHIO
D.MAY 6,1959 LOGANSPORT,IND.

YR	CL	LEA	POS	GP	G	REC
1913	BRO	N	O		6	.272
1914	IND	F	O		117	.309
1915	NEW	F	O		155	.269
	BLTR				278	.283

SCHEER, HENRY (HEINIE)
B.JULY 31,1900 NEW YORK,N.Y.
D.MAR.21,1976 NEW HAVEN,CONN.

YR	CL	LEA	POS	GP	G	REC
1922	PHI	A	2-3		51	.171
1923	PHI	A	2		69	.238
	BRTR				120	.212

SCHEEREN, FREDERICK (FRITZ) OR (DUTCH)
B.SEPT.8,1891 KOKOMO,IND.
D.JUNE 17,1973 OIL CITY,PA.

YR	CL	LEA	POS	GP	G	REC
1914	PIT	N	O		11	.267
1915	PIT	N	O		4	.000
	BRTR				15	.243

SCHEETZ, OWEN FRANKLIN
B.DEC.24,1913 NEW BEDFORD,OHIO

YR	CL	LEA	POS	GP	G	REC
1943	WAS	A	P		6	0- 0
	BRTR					

SCHEFFING, ROBERT BODEN (BOB)
B.AUG.11,1915 OVERLAND,MO.

YR	CL	LEA	POS	GP	G	REC
1941	CHI	N	C		51	.242
1942	CHI	N	C		44	.196
1946	CHI	N	C		63	.278
1947	CHI	N	C		110	.264
1948	CHI	N	C		102	.300
1949	CHI	N	C		55	.268
1950	CHI	N	C		12	.188
	CIN	N	C		21	.277
1951	CIN	N	C		47	.254
	STL	N	C		12	.111
	BRTR				517	.263

NON-PLAYING MANAGER
CHI[N] 1957-59, DET[A] 1961-63

SCHEFFLER, THEODORE J.
B.NEW YORK,N.Y.

YR	CL	LEA	POS	GP	G	REC
1888	DET	N	O		27	.202
1890	ROC	AA	O		117	.239
					144	.233

SCHEGG, (LEFTY)
[REAL NAME GILBERT EUGENE PRICE]
B.AUG.26,1889 LEESVILLE,OHIO
D.FEB.27,1963 NILES,OHIO

YR	CL	LEA	POS	GP	G	REC
1912	WAS	A	P		2	0- 0
	TL					

SCHEIB, CARL ALVIN
B.JAN.1,1927 GRATZ,PA.

YR	CL	LEA	POS	GP	G	REC
1943	PHI	A	P		6	0- 1
1944	PHI	A	P		15	0- 0
1945	PHI	A	P		4	0- 0
1947	PHI	A	P	21	22	4- 6
1948	PHI	A	P-0	32	52	14- 8
						.298
1949	PHI	A	P	38	47	9-12
1950	PHI	A	P	43	50	3-10
1951	PHI	A	P	46	48	1-12
1952	PHI	A	P	30	44	11- 7
1953	PHI	A	P	28	35	3- 7
1954	PHI	A	P	3	1	0- 1
	STL	N	P		3	0- 1
	BRTR			267	327	45-65
						.250

```
YR  CL LEA POS   GP   G   REC
```

SCHEIBECK, FRANK S.
B.JUNE 28,1865 DETROIT,MICH.
D.OCT.22,1956 DETROIT,MICH.
```
1887 CLE AA P-3    1    3   0- 0
                            .364
1888 DET N  S      1       .000
1890 TOL AA S    134       .234
1894 PIT N  2-S-3-0  26    .347
     WAS N  S     49       .238
1895 WAS N  S     48       .182
1899 WAS N  S     27       .287
1901 CLE A  S     93       .217
1906 DET A  2      3       .125
          BRTR   1 384     0- 0
                           .243
```

SCHEIBLE, JOHN G. (JACK)
B.FEB.16,1866 YOUNGSTOWN,OHIO
D.AUG.9,1897 YOUNGSTOWN,OHIO
```
1893 CLE N  P      3       1- 1
1894 PHI N  P              0- 1
          TL       4       1- 2
```

SCHEINBLUM, RICHARD ALAN (RICHIE)
B.NOV.5,1942 NEW YORK,N.Y.
```
1965 CLE A  /H     4       .000
1967 CLE A  O     18       .318
1968 CLE A  O     19       .218
1969 CLE A  O    102       .166
1971 WAS A  O     27       .143
1972 KC  A  *O   134       .300
1973 CIN N  O     29       .222
     CAL A  O     77       .328
1974 CAL A  /O    10       .154
     KC  A  D/O   36       .181
     STL N  /H     6       .333
          BBTR   462       .263
```

SCHELL, CLYDE DANIEL (DANNY)
B.DEC.26,1927 FOSTORIA,OHIO
D.MAY 11,1972 MAYVILLE,MICH.
```
1954 PHI N  O     92       .283
1955 PHI N  H      2       .000
          BRTR    94       .281
```

SCHELLE, GERARD ANTHONY (JIM)
B.APR.13,1917 BALTIMORE,MD.
```
1939 PHI A  P      1       0- 0
          BRTR
```

SCHELLHASSE, ALBERT HERMAN
B.MAR.22,1864 EVANSVILLE,IND.
D.JAN.4,1919 EVANSVILLE,IND.
```
1890 BOS N  C-0    9       .096
1891 LOU AA C      6       .156
          TR      15       .120
```

SCHEMANSKE, FREDERICK GEORGE (BUCK)
B.APR.28,1903 DETROIT,MICH.
D.FEB.18,1960 DETROIT,MICH.
```
1923 WAS A  P      2       0- 0
          BRTR
```

SCHEMER, MICHAEL
B.NOV.20,1917 BALTIMORE,MD.
```
1945 NY  N  1     31       .333
1946 NY  N  H      1       .000
          BLTL    32       .330
```

SCHENCK, WILLIAM G.
B.BROOKLYN,N.Y.
```
1882 LOU AA P-S-   3   59   1- 0
            3-0             .265
1884 RIC AA 2-S   41       .287
1885 BRO AA 3      1       .000
                 1 101     1- 0
                           .237
```

SCHENEBERG, JOHN BLUFORD
B.NOV.20,1887 GUYANDOTTE,W.VA.
D.SEPT.26,1950 HUNTINGTON,W.VA.
```
1913 PIT N  P      1       0- 1
1920 STL N  P      1       0- 0
          BBTR     2       0- 1
```

SCHENZ, HENRY LEONARD (HANK)
B.APR.11,1919 NEW RICHMOND,OHIO
```
1946 CHI N  3      6       .182
1947 CHI N  3      7       .071
1948 CHI N  2-3   96       .261
1949 CHI N  3      7       .429
1950 PIT N  2-S-3 58       .228
1951 PIT N  2-3   25       .213
     NY  N  H      8       .000
          BRTR   207       .247
```

SCHEPNER, JOSEPH MAURICE
(GENTLEMAN JOE)
B.AUG.10,1899 ALIQUIPPA,PA.
D.JULY 25,1959 MOBILE,ALA.
```
1919 STL A  3     14       .212
          BRTR
```

SCHERBARTH, ROBERT ELMER (BOB)
B.JAN.18,1926 MILWAUKEE,WIS.
```
1950 BOS A  C      1       .000
          BRTR
```

SCHERER, HARRY
```
1889 LOU AA O      1       .333
```

SCHERMAN, FREDERICK JOHN (FRED)
B.JULY 25,1944 DAYTON,OHIO
```
1969 DET A  /P             4    1- 0
1970 DET A  P             48    4- 4
1971 DET A  P             69   11- 6
1972 DET A  P             57    7- 3
1973 DET A  P     34      35    2- 2
1974 HOU N  P             53    2- 5
.975 HOU N  P             16    0- 1
     MON N  P             34    4- 3
1976 MON N  P             31    2- 2
          BLTL   346 347  33-26
```

SCHESLER, CHARLES (DUTCH)
B.JUNE 1,1900 FRANKFURT,GERMANY
D.NOV.19,1953 HARRISBURG,PA.
```
1931 PHI N  P     17       0- 0
          BRTR
```

SCHETTLER, LOUIS MARTIN
B.JUNE 12,1886 PITTSBURGH,PA.
D.MAY 1,1960 YOUNGSTOWN,OHIO
```
1910 PHI N  P     27       2- 6
          BRTR
```

SCHIAPPACASSE, LOUIS JOSEPH
B.MAR.29,881 ANN ARBOR,MICH.
D.SEPT.20,1910 ANN ARBOR,MICH.
```
1902 DET A  O      2       .000
          BR
```

SCHICK, MAURICE FRANCIS
B.APR.17,1892 CHICAGO,ILL.
```
1917 CHI N  O     14       .147
          BRTR
```

SCHILLING, CHARLES THOMAS (CHUCK)
B.OCT.25,1937 BROOKLYN,N.Y.
```
1961 BOS A  2    158       .259
1962 BOS A  2    119       .230
1963 BOS A  2    146       .234
1964 BOS A  2     47       .196
1965 BOS A  2     71       .240
          BRTR   541       .239
```

SCHILLINGS, ELBERT ISAIAH (RED)
B.MAR.29,1900 DEPORT,TEX.
D.JAN.7,1954 OKLAHOMA CITY,OKLA
```
1922 PHI A  P      4       0- 0
          BRTR
```

SCHINDLER, WILLIAM GIBBONS
B.JULY 10,1896 PERRYVILLE,MO.
```
1920 STL N  C      1       .000
          BRTR
```

SCHIRICK, HARRY ERNEST (DUTCH)
B.JUNE 15,1890 RUBY,N.Y.
D.NOV.12,1968 KINGSTON,N.Y.
```
1914 STL A  H      1       .000
          BRTR
```

SCHLAFLY, HARRY LINTON (LARRY)
B.SEPT.20,1878 PORT WASHINGTON,OHIO
D.JUNE 27,1919 CANTON,OHIO
```
1902 CHI N  2-S-3-0  10     .333
1906 WAS A  2    123       .246
1907 WAS A  2     24       .135
1914 BUF F  M-2   52       .254
          BRTR   209       .239
```
NON-PLAYING MANAGER BUF[F] 1915

SCHLEI, GEORGE HENRY (ADMIRAL)
B.JAN.12,1878 CINCINNATI,OHIO
D.JAN.24,1958 HUNTINGTON,W.VA.
```
1904 CIN N  C     88       .237
1905 CIN N  C     95       .226
1906 CIN N  C-1  112       .245
1907 CIN N  C     72       .272
1908 CIN N  C     88       .220
1909 NY  N  C     89       .244
1910 NY  N  C     49       .192
1911 NY  N  C      1       .000
          BRTR   594       .237
```

SCHLESINGER, WILLIAM CORDES (RUDY)
B.NOV.5,1941 CINCINNATI,OHIO
```
1965 BOS A  /H     1       .000
          BRTR
```

SCHLIEBNER, FREDERICK PAUL (DUTCH)
B.MAY 19,1891 CHARLOTTENBURG,GERMANY
D.APR.15,1975 TOLEDO,OHIO
```
1923 BRO N  1     19       .250
     STL A  1    127       .275
          BRTR   146       .271
```

SCHLITZER, VICTOR JOSEPH (BIFF)
B.DEC.4,1884 ROCHESTER,N.Y.
D.JAN.4,1948 WELLESLEY HILLS,MASS.
```
1908 PHI A  P     23       6- 8
1909 PHI A  P      9       2- 6
     BOS A  P      9       2- 2
1914 BUF F  P      3       0- 0
          BRTR    44      10-16
```

SCHLUETER, JAY D
B.JULY 31,1949 PHOENIX,ARIZ.
```
1971 HOU N  /O     7       .333
          BRTR
```

SCHLUETER, NORMAN JOHN (DUKE)
B.SEPT.25,1916 BELLEVILLE,ILL.
```
1938 CHI A  C     35       .229
1939 CHI A  C     34       .232
1944 CLE A  C     49       .123
          BRTR   118       .186
```

SCHMANDT, RAYMOND HENRY
B.JAN.25,1896 ST.LOUIS,MO.
D.FEB.1,1969 ST.LOUIS,MO.
```
1915 STL A  1      2       .000
1918 BRO N  2     34       .307
1919 BRO N  1-2-3 47       .165
1920 BRO N  1     28       .238
1921 BRO N  1     95       .306
1922 BRO N  1    110       .267
          BRTR   316       .269
```

SCHMEES, GEORGE EDWARD
(GEORGE) OR (ROCKY)
B.SEPT.6,1924 CINCINNATI,OHIO
```
1952 STL A  1-0   34       .131
     BOS A  P-1-   2   42   0- 0
           O               .203
          BLTL    2   76   0- 0
                           .168
```

SCHMELZ, ALAN GEORGE (AL)
B.NOV.12,1943 WHITTIER,CAL.
```
1967 NY  N  /P     2       0- 0
          BRTR
```

SCHMELZ, GUSTAVIUS HEINRICH
B.SEPT.26,1850 COLUMBUS,OHIO
D.OCT.13,1925 COLUMBUS,OHIO
NON-PLAYING MANAGER
COL(AA) 1884, STL(N) 1886,
CIN(AA) 1887-89, CLE(N) 1890
COL(AA) 1890-91, WAS(N) 1894-97

SCHMIDT, CHARLES (BOSS)
B.SEPT.12,1880 COAL HILL,ARK.
D.NOV.14,1932 CLARKSVILLE,ARK.
```
1906 DET A  C     68       .218
1907 DET A  C    104       .244
1908 DET A  C    122       .265
1909 DET A  C     84       .209
1910 DET A  C     71       .259
1911 DET A  C     28       .283
          BBTR   477       .243
```

SCHMIDT, CHARLES JOHN (BUTCH)
OR (BUTCHER BOY)
B.JULY 19,1886 BALTIMORE,MD.
D.SEPT.4,1952 BALTIMORE,MD.
```
1909 NY  A  P      1       0- 0
1913 BOS N  1     22       .308
1914 BOS N  1    147       .285
1915 BOS N  1    127       .251
          BLTL   1 297     0- 0
                           .272
```

SCHMIDT, FRANK ELMER
[PLAYED UNDER NAME OF
FRANK ELMER SMITH]

SCHMIDT, FREDERICK ALBERT
B.FEB.9,1916 HARTFORD,CONN.
```
1944 STL N  P     37       7- 3
1946 STL N  P     16       1- 0
1947 STL N  P      2       0- 0
     PHI N  P     29       5- 8
     CHI N  P      1       0- 0
          BRTR    85      13-11
```

SCHMIDT, HENRY M.
B.JUNE 26,1873 BROWNSVILLE,TEX.
D.APR.23,1926 NASHVILLE,TENN.
```
1903 BRO N  P     40   41  22-13
```

SCHMIDT, HERMAN (PETE)
B.ST.LOUIS,MO.
```
1913 STL A  P      1       0- 0
          TL
```

SCHMIDT, MICHAEL JACK (MIKE)
B.SEP,27,1949 DAYTON,OHIO
```
1972 PHI N  3/2      13     .206
1973 PHI N  #3/2-1-S 132    .196
1974 PHI N  *3      162     .282
1975 PHI N  #3-S    158     .249
1976 PHI N  #3      160     .262
1977 PHI N  #3/S-2  154     .274
1978 PHI N  #3/S    145     .251
          BRTR     924      .255
```

SCHMIDT, ROBERT BENJAMIN (BOB)
B.APR.22,1933 ST.LOUIS,MO.

YR	CL	LEA	POS	GP	G	REC
1958	SF	N	C		127	.244
1959	SF	N	C		71	.243
1960	SF	N	C		110	.267
1961	SF	N	C		2	.167
	CIN	N	C		27	.129
1962	WAS	A	C		88	.242
1963	WAS	A	C		9	.200
1965	NY	A	C		20	.250
		BRTR			454	.243

SCHMIDT, WALTER JOSEPH
B.MAR.20,1887 COAL HILL,ARK.
D.JULY 4,1973 MODESTO,CAL.

YR	CL	LEA	POS	GP	G	REC
1916	PIT	N	C		64	.190
1917	PIT	N	C		72	.246
1918	PIT	N	C		105	.238
1919	PIT	N	C		85	.251
1920	PIT	N	C		94	.277
1921	PIT	N	C		114	.282
1922	PIT	N	C		40	.328
1923	PIT	N	C		97	.248
1924	PIT	N	C		58	.243
1925	STL	N	C		37	.253
		BRTR			766	.257

SCHMIDT, WILLARD RAYMOND
B.MAY 29,1928 HAYS,KAN.

YR	CL	LEA	POS	GP	G	REC
1952	STL	N	P		18	2- 3
1953	STL	N	P		6	0- 2
1955	STL	N	P		20	7- 6
1956	STL	N	P		33	6- 8
1957	STL	N	P		40	10- 3
1958	CIN	N	P		41	3- 5
1959	CIN	N	P		36	3- 2
		BRTR			194	31-29

SCHMIT, FREDERICK M.
(CRAZY) OR (GERMANY)
B.FEB.13,1866 CHICAGO,ILL.
D.OCT.5,1940 CHICAGO,ILL.

YR	CL	LEA	POS	GP	G	REC
1890	PIT	N	P		11	1- 9
1892	BAL	N	P		7	1- 4
1893	BAL	N	P		9	3- 2
	NY	N	P		4	0- 2
1899	CLE	N	P	19	21	2-17
1901	BAL	A	P		4	0- 2
		BLTL		54	56	7-36

SCHMITZ, JOHN ALBERT
(JOHNNY) OR (BEAR TRACKS)
B.NOV.27,1920 WAUSAU,WIS.

YR	CL	LEA	POS	GP	G	REC
1941	CHI	N	P		6	2- 0
1942	CHI	N	P		23	3- 7
1946	CHI	N	P		42	11-11
1947	CHI	N	P		38	13-18
1948	CHI	N	P		34	18-13
1949	CHI	N	P		36	11-13
1950	CHI	N	P		39	10-16
1951	CHI	N	P		8	1- 2
	BRO	N	P		16	1- 4
1952	BRO	N	P		10	1- 1
	NY	A	P		5	1- 1
	CIN	N	P		3	1- 0
1953	NY	A	P		3	0- 0
	WAS	A	P		24	2- 7
1954	WAS	A	P		29	11- 8
1955	WAS	A	P		32	7-10
1956	BOS	A	P		2	0- 0
	BAL	A	P		18	0- 3
		BRTL			368	93-114

SCHMULBACH, HENRY ALRIVES
B.JAN.17,1925 E.ST.LOUIS,ILL.

YR	CL	LEA	POS	GP	G	REC
1943	STL	A	H		1	.000
		BLTR				

SCHMUTZ, CHARLES OTTO (KING)
B.JAN.1,1890 SAN DIEGO,CAL.
D.JUNE 27,1962 SEATTLE,WASH.

YR	CL	LEA	POS	GP	G	REC
1914	BRO	N	P		18	1- 3
1915	BRO	N	P		1	0- 0
		BRTR			19	1- 3

SCHNECK, DAVID LEE (DAVE)
B.JUNE 18,1949 ALLENTOWN,PA.

YR	CL	LEA	POS	GP	G	REC
1972	NY	N	O		37	.187
1973	NY	N	O		13	.194
1974	NY	N	O		93	.205
		BLTL			143	.199

SCHNEIBERG, FRANK FREDERICK
B.MAR.12,1882 MILWAUKEE,WIS.
D.MAY 18,1948 MILWAUKEE,WIS.

YR	CL	LEA	POS	GP	G	REC
1910	BRO	N	P		1	0- 0

SCHNEIDER, DANIEL LOUIS (DAN)
B.AUG.29,1942 EVANSVILLE,IND.

YR	CL	LEA	POS	GP	G	REC
1963	MIL	N	P		30	1- 0
1964	MIL	N	P	13	14	1- 2
1966	ATL	N	P		14	0- 0
1967	HOU	N	P	54	55	0- 2
1969	HOU	N	/P		6	0- 1
		BLTL		117	119	2- 5

SCHNEIDER, EMANUEL SEBASTIAN
[PLAYED UNDER NAME OF
EMANUEL SEBASTIAN SNYDER]

SCHNEIDER, PETER JOSEPH (PETE)
B.AUG.20,1895 LOS ANGELES,CAL.
D.JUNE 1,1957 LOS ANGELES,CAL.

YR	CL	LEA	POS	GP	G	REC
1914	CIN	N	P	29	31	5-13
1915	CIN	N	P		48	14-19
1916	CIN	N	P	44	49	10-19
1917	CIN	N	P	46	49	20-19
1918	CIN	N	P	33	36	10-15
1919	NY	A	P		7	0- 1
		BRTR		207	220	59-86

SCHNELL, KARL OTTO
B.SEPT.20,1899 LOS ANGELES,CAL.

YR	CL	LEA	POS	GP	G	REC
1922	CIN	N	P		10	0- 0
1923	CIN	N	P		1	0- 0
		BRTR			11	0- 0

SCHOEN, GERALD THOMAS (GERRY)
B.JAN.15,1947 NEW ORLEANS,LA.

YR	CL	LEA	POS	GP	G	REC
1968	WAS	A	/P		1	0- 1
		BRTR				

SCHOENDIENST, ALBERT FRED (RED)
B.FEB.2,1923 GERMANTOWN,ILL.

YR	CL	LEA	POS	GP	G	REC
1945	STL	N	2-S-O		137	.278
1946	STL	N	2-S-3		142	.281
1947	STL	N	2-3-O		151	.253
1948	STL	N	2		119	.272
1949	STL	N	2-S-3-O		151	.297
1950	STL	N	2-S-3		153	.276
1951	STL	N	2-S		135	.289
1952	STL	N	2-S-3		152	.303
1953	STL	N	2		146	.342
1954	STL	N	2		148	.315
1955	STL	N	2		145	.268
1956	STL	N	2		40	.314
	NY	N	2		92	.296
1957	NY	N	2		57	.307
	MIL	N	2-O		93	.310
1958	MIL	N	2		106	.262
1959	MIL	N	2		5	.000
1960	MIL	N	2		68	.257
1961	STL	N	2		72	.300
1962	STL	N	2-3		98	.301
1963	STL	N	H		6	.000
		BBTR			2216	.289

NON-PLAYING MANAGER STL[N] 1965-76

SCHOENECK, LEWIS W. (JUMBO)
B.1862 CHICAGO,ILL.

YR	CL	LEA	POS	GP	G	REC
1884	CHI	U	1-O		70	.315
	PIT	U	1		18	.276
	BAL	U	1		16	.283
1888	IND	N	1		48	.237
1889	IND	N	1		16	.242
		TR			168	.280

SCHOFIELD, JOHN RICHARD
(DICK) OR (DUCKY)
B.JAN.7,1935 SPRINGFIELD,ILL.

YR	CL	LEA	POS	GP	G	REC
1953	STL	N	S		33	.179
1954	STL	N	S		43	.143
1955	STL	N	S		12	.000
1956	STL	N	S		16	.100
1957	STL	N	S		65	.161
1958	STL	N	S		39	.213
	PIT	N	S-3		26	.148
1959	PIT	N	2-S-O		81	.234
1960	PIT	N	2-S-3		65	.333
1961	PIT	N	2-S-3-O		60	.192
1962	PIT	N	2-S-3		54	.288
1963	PIT	N	2-S-3		138	.246
1964	PIT	N	S		121	.246
1965	PIT	N	S		31	.229
	SF	N	S		101	.203
1966	SF	N	/S		11	.063
	NY	A	S		25	.155
	LA	N	3/S		20	.257
1967	LA	N	S/2-3		84	.216
1968	STL	N	S-2		69	.220
1969	BOS	A	2-S/3-O		94	.257
1970	BOS	A	2-3/S		76	.187
1971	MIL	A	3/S-2		23	.107
	STL	N	S-2/3		34	.217
		BBTR			1321	.227

SCHOMBERG, OTTO H.
[REAL NAME OTTO H. SHAMBRICK]
B.NOV.14,1864 MILWAUKEE,WIS.
D.MAY 3,1927

YR	CL	LEA	POS	GP	G	REC
1886	PIT	AA	1		72	.295
1887	IND	N	1		112	.389
1888	IND	N	1		29	.214
		TL			213	.329

SCHOONMAKER, JERALD LEE (JERRY)
B.DEC.14,1933 SEYMOUR,MO.

YR	CL	LEA	POS	GP	G	REC
1955	WAS	A	O		20	.152
1957	WAS	A	O		30	.087
		BRTR			50	.130

SCHORR, EDWARD WALTER
B.FEB.14,1891 BREMEN,OHIO
D.SEPT.12,1969 ATLANTIC CITY,N.J.

YR	CL	LEA	POS	GP	G	REC
1915	CHI	N	P		2	0- 0
		BRTR				

SCHOTT, EUGENE ARTHUR (GENE)
B.JULY 14,1913 BATAVIA,OHIO

YR	CL	LEA	POS	GP	G	REC
1935	CIN	N	P	33	36	8-11
1936	CIN	N	P	31	39	11-11
1937	CIN	N	P	37	50	4-13
1938	CIN	N	P		31	5- 5
1939	PHI	N	P	4	8	0- 1
	BRO	N	R		1	.000
		BRTR		136	165	28-41
						.211

SCHRAMKA, PAUL EDWARD
B.MAR.22,1928 MILWAUKEE,WIS.

YR	CL	LEA	POS	GP	G	REC
1953	CHI	N	O		2	.000
		BLTL				

SCHRECKENGOST, OSSEE FREEMAN
[ALSO PLAYED UNDER NAME
OF OSSEE SCHRECK]
B.APR.11,1875 NEW BETHLEHEM,PA.
D.JULY 9,1914 PHILADELPHIA,PA.

YR	CL	LEA	POS	GP	G	REC
1897	LOU	N	C		1	.000
1898	CLE	N	C		5	.367
1899	STL	N	1-O		6	.000
	CLE	N	C-1-S-O		43	.315
	STL	N	C		60	.306
1901	BOS	A	C		83	.320
1902	CLE	A	1		18	.338
	PHI	A	C-1-O		78	.312
1903	PHI	A	C		91	.222
1904	PHI	A	C		94	.189
1905	PHI	A	C		114	.274
1906	PHI	A	C		98	.284
1907	PHI	A	C		101	.272
1908	PHI	A	C		71	.222
	CHI	A	C		6	.188
		BRTR			869	.272

SCHREIBER, DAVID HENRY (BARNEY)
B.MAY 8,1882 WAVERLY,OHIO
D.OCT.6,1964 CHILLICOTHE,OHIO

YR	CL	LEA	POS	GP	G	REC
1911	CIN	N	P		3	0- 1
		BLTL				

SCHREIBER, HENRY WALTER (HANK)
B.JULY 12,1891 CLEVELAND,OHIO
D.FEB.23,1968 INDIANAPOLIS,IND.

YR	CL	LEA	POS	GP	G	REC
1914	CHI	A	O		1	.000
1917	BOS	N	S-3		2	.286
1919	CIN	N	S-3		19	.224
1921	NY	N	2-S		4	.167
1926	CHI	N	2-S-3		10	.056
		BRTR			36	.187

SCHREIBER, PAUL FREDERICK
(PAUL) OR (VON)
B.OCT.8,1902 JACKSONVILLE,FLA.

YR	CL	LEA	POS	GP	G	REC
1922	BRO	N	P		1	0- 0
1923	BRO	N	P		9	0- 0
1945	NY	A	P		2	0- 0
		BRTR			12	0- 0

SCHREIBER, THEODORE HENRY (TED)
B.JULY 11,1938 BROOKLYN,N.Y.

YR	CL	LEA	POS	GP	G	REC
1963	NY	N	2-S-3		39	.160
		BRTR				

SCHRIVER, WILLIAM FREDERICK (POP)
B.JULY 11,1865 BROOKLYN,N.Y.
D.DEC.27,1932 BROOKLYN,N.Y.

YR	CL	LEA	POS	GP	G	REC
1886	BRO	AA	C-O		9	.040
1888	PHI	N	C		39	.194
1889	PHI	N	C		55	.265
1890	PHI	N	C		57	.273
1891	CHI	N	C		25	.311
1892	CHI	N	C		89	.222
1893	CHI	N	C		59	.295
1894	CHI	N	C		94	.269
1895	NY	N	C		24	.290
1897	CIN	N	C		52	.310
1898	PIT	N	C		93	.227
1899	PIT	N	C		84	.297
1900	PIT	N	C		23	.317
1901	STL	N	C-1		44	.286
		BRTR			747	.263

SCHRODER, ROBERT JAMES (BOB)
B.DEC.30,1944 RIDGEFIELD,N.J.

YR	CL	LEA	POS	GP	G	REC
1965	SF	N	/2-3		31	.222
1966	SF	N	/S		10	.242
1967	SF	N	2/3		62	.230
1968	SF	N	2/S-3		35	.159
		BLTR			138	.217

SCHROLL, ALBERT BRINGHURST
(AL) OR (BULL)
B.MAR.22,1932 NEW ORLEANS,LA.

YR	CL	LEA	POS	GP	G	REC
1958	BOS	A	P		5	0- 0
1959	PHI	N	P		3	1- 1
	BOS	A	P		14	1- 4
1960	CHI	N	P		2	0- 0
1961	MIN	A	P		11	4- 4
		BRTR			35	6- 9

```
YR  CL LEA POS    GP    G   REC

SCHUBLE, HENRY GEORGE (HEINIE)
B.NOV.1,1906 HOUSTON,TEX.
1927 STL N  S         65   .257
1929 DET A  S         92   .233
1932 DET A  S-3      102   .271
1933 DET A  2-S-3     49   .219
1934 DET A  2-S-3     11   .267
1935 DET A  2-3       11   .250
1936 STL N  3          2   .000
        BRTR         332   .251

SCHUELER, RONALD RICHARD (RON)
B.APR.14,1948 CATHERINE,KAN.
1972 ATL N  P         37   5- 8
1973 ATL N  P         39   8- 7
1974 PHI N  P         44  11-16
1975 PHI N  P         46   4- 4
1976 PHI N  P         35   1- 0
1977 MIN A  P         52   8- 7
1978 CHI A  P    30   31   3- 5
        BRTR    283  284  40-47

SCHUERHOLZ, FRED PETER
[PLAYED UNDER NAME OF
FRED PETER SHERRY]

SCHULMERICH, EDWARD WESLEY (WES)
B.APR.21,1901 HILLSBORO,ORE.
1931 BOS N  O         95   .309
1932 BOS N  O        119   .260
1933 BOS N  O         29   .247
     PHI N  O         97   .334
1934 PHI N  O         15   .250
     CIN N  O         74   .263
        BRTR         429   .289

SCHULT, ARTHUR WILLIAM (DUTCH)
B.JUNE 20,1928 BROOKLYN,N.Y.
1953 NY  A  H          7   .000
1956 CIN N  O          5   .429
1957 CIN N  O         21   .265
     WAS A  1-O       77   .263
1959 CHI N  1-O       42   .271
1960 CHI N  1-O       12   .133
        BRTR         164   .264

SCHULT, FRED WILLIAM
[PLAYED UNDER NAME OF
FRED WILLIAM SCHULTE]

SCHULTE, FRANK M. (WILDFIRE)
B.SEPT.17,1882 COHOCTON,N.Y.
D.OCT.2,1949 OAKLAND,CAL.
1904 CHI N  O         20   .286
1905 CHI N  O        123   .274
1906 CHI N  O        146   .281
1907 CHI N  O         92   .287
1908 CHI N  O        102   .236
1909 CHI N  O        140   .264
1910 CHI N  O        150   .301
1911 CHI N  O        154   .300
1912 CHI N  O        139   .264
1913 CHI N  O        132   .278
1914 CHI N  O        137   .241
1915 CHI N  O        151   .249
1916 CHI N  O         72   .305
     PIT N  O         55   .241
1917 PIT N  O         30   .216
     PHI N  O         64   .213
1918 WAS A  O         93   .288
        BLTR        1800   .270

SCHULTE, FRED WILLIAM
(FRED) OR (FRITZ)
[REAL NAME FRED WILLIAM SCHULT]
B.JAN.13,1901 BELVIDERE,ILL.
1927 STL A  O         60   .317
1928 STL A  O        146   .286
1929 STL A  O        121   .307
1930 STL A  O        113   .278
1931 STL A  O        134   .304
1932 STL A  O        146   .294
1933 WAS A  O        144   .295
1934 WAS A  O        136   .298
1935 WAS A  O         75   .268
1936 PIT N  O         74   .261
1937 PIT N  O         29   .100
        BRTR        1178   .292

SCHULTE, HERMAN JOSEPH (HAM)
[REAL NAME
HERMAN JOSEPH SCHULTEHENRICH]
B.SEPT.1,1912 ST.CHARLES,MO.
1940 PHI N  2-S      120   .236
        BRTR

SCHULTE, JOHN CLEMENT
B.SEPT.8,1896 FREDERICKTOWN,MO.
D.JUNE 28,1978 ST.LOUIS,MO.
1923 STL A  C          7   .000
1927 STL N  C         64   .288
1928 PHI N  C         65   .248
1929 CHI N  C         31   .261
1932 STL N  C         15   .208
     BOS N  C         10   .222
        BLTR         192   .261


SCHULTE, JOHN HERMAN FRANK (JACK)
B.NOV.15,1881 CINCINNATI,OHIO
D.AUG.17,1975 ROSEVILLE,MICH.
1906 BOS N  S          2   .000
        BRTR

SCHULTE, LEONARD WILLIAM
[REAL NAME
LEONARD WILLIAM SCHULTEHENRICH]
B.DEC.5,1916 ST.CHARLES,MO.
1944 STL A  H          1   .000
1945 STL A  2-S-3    119   .247
1946 STL A  2-3        4   .400
        BRTR         124   .248

SCHULTEHENRICH, HERMAN JOSEPH
[PLAYED UNDER NAME OF
HERMAN JOSEPH SCHULTE]

SCHULTEHENRICH, LEONARD WILLIAM
[PLAYED UNDER NAME OF
LEONARD WILLIAM SCHULTE]

SCHULTZ, CHARLES BUDD (BUDDY)
B.SEPT.19,1950 CLEVELAND,OHIO
1975 CHI N  /P         6   2- 0
1976 CHI N  P         29   1- 1
1977 STL N  P    40   41   6- 1
1978 STL N  P         62   2- 4
        BRTL    137  138  11- 6

SCHULTZ, GEORGE WARREN (BARNEY)
B.AUG.15,1926 BEVERLY,N.J.
1955 STL N  P         19   1- 2
1959 DET A  P         13   1- 2
1961 CHI N  P         41   7- 6
1962 CHI N  P         51   5- 5
1963 CHI N  P         15   1- 0
     STL N  P         24   2- 0
1964 STL N  P         30   1- 3
1965 STL N  P         34   2- 2
        BRTR         227  20-20

SCHULTZ, HOWARD HENRY (HOWIE)
(STRETCH) OR (STEEPLE)
B.JULY 3,1922 ST.PAUL,MINN.
1943 BRO N  1         45   .269
1944 BRO N  1        138   .255
1945 BRO N  1         39   .239
1946 BRO N  1         90   .253
1947 BRO N  1          2   .000
     PHI N  1        114   .223
1948 PHI N  1          6   .077
     CIN N  1         36   .167
        BRTR         470   .241

SCHULTZ, JOHN
B.ST.LOUIS,MO.
1891 STL AA C          1   .000

SCHULTZ, JOSEPH CHARLES JR. (DODE)
B.AUG.29,1918 CHICAGO,ILL.
1939 PIT N  C          4   .286
1940 PIT N  C         16   .194
1941 PIT N  C          9   .500
1943 STL A  C         46   .239
1944 STL A  C          3   .250
1945 STL A  C         41   .295
1946 STL A  C         42   .386
1947 STL A  H         43   .184
1948 STL A  H         43   .189
        BLTR         240   .259
NON-PLAYING MANAGER
SEA[A] 1969, DET[A] 1973

SCHULTZ, JOSEPH CHARLES SR.
(GERMANY)
B.JULY 24,1893 PITTSBURGH,PA.
D.APR.13,1941 COLUMBIA,S.C.
1912 BOS N  2          4   .250
1913 BOS N  O          8   .222
1915 BRO N  3         56   .292
     CHI N  3          7   .250
1916 PIT N  2-3       77   .260
1919 STL N  O         88   .253
1920 STL N  O         99   .263
1921 STL N  O         92   .309
1922 STL N  O        112   .313
1923 STL N  O          2   .286
1924 STL N  O         12   .167
     PHI N  O         88   .285
1925 PHI N  O         24   .344
     CIN N  2-O       33   .323
        BRTR         702   .285

SCHULTZ, ROBERT DUFFY (BILL)
B.NOV.27,1923 LOUISVILLE,KY.
1951 CHI N  P         17   3- 6
1952 CHI N  P         29   6- 3
1953 CHI N  P          7   0- 2
     PIT N  P         11   0- 2
1955 DET A  P          1   0- 0
        BRTL          65   9-13

SCHULTZ, WEBB CARL
B.JAN.31,1898 WAUTOMA,WIS.
1924 CHI A  P          1   0- 0
        BRTR


SCHULTZ, WILLIAM MICHAEL (MIKE)
B.DEC.17,1926 SYRACUSE,N.Y.
1947 CIN N  P          1   0- 0
        BLTL

SCHULTZE, JOHN F.
B.BURLINGTON,N.J.
1891 PHI N  P          6   0- 3

SCHULZ, ALBERT CHRISTOPHER
B.MAY 12,1889 TOLEDO,OHIO
D.DEC.13,1931 GALLIPOLIS,OHIO
1912 NY  A  P          3   1- 0
1913 NY  A  P         38   8-14
1914 NY  A  P          4   1- 3
     BUF F  P         27   9-12
1915 BUF F  P         42  21-14
1916 CIN N  P         44   8-19
        BRTL         158  48-62

SCHULZ, WALTER FREDERICK
B.APR.16,1900 ST.LOUIS,MO.
D.FEB.27,1928 PRESCOTT,ARK.
1920 STL N  P          2   0- 0
        BRTR

SCHUMACHER, HAROLD HENRY
(PRINCE HAL)
B.NOV.23,1910 HINCKLEY,N.Y.
1931 NY  N  P          8   1- 1
1932 NY  N  P    27   30   5- 6
1933 NY  N  P    35   39  19-12
1934 NY  N  P    41   44  23-10
1935 NY  N  P    33   38  19- 9
1936 NY  N  P    35   46  11-13
1937 NY  N  P    38   45  13-12
1938 NY  N  P    28   36  13- 8
1939 NY  N  P    29   30  13-10
1940 NY  N  P    34   35  13-13
1941 NY  N  P-O  30   38  12-10
                            .152
1942 NY  N  P    29   37  12-13
1946 NY  N  P         24   4- 4
        BRTR    391  450 158-121
                            .202

SCHUMANN, CARL J. (HACK)
B.AUG.13,1884 BUFFALO,N.Y.
D.MAR.25,1946 BUFFALO,N.Y.
1906 PHI A  P          4   0- 2
        TR

SCHUPP, FERDINAND MAURICE
B.JAN.16,1891 LOUISVILLE,KY.
D.DEC.16,1971 LOS ANGELES,CAL.
1913 NY  N  P          5   0- 0
1914 NY  N  P          8   0- 0
1915 NY  N  P         23   1- 0
1916 NY  N  P         30   9- 3
1917 NY  N  P         36  21- 7
1918 NY  N  P         10   0- 1
1919 NY  N  P          9   1- 3
     STL N  P         10   4- 4
1920 STL N  P    38   39  16-13
1921 STL N  P          9   2- 0
     BRO N  P         20   3- 4
1922 CHI A  P         18   4- 4
        BRTR    216  217  61-39

SCHURR, WAYNE ALLEN
B.AUG.6,1937 GARRETT,IND.
1964 CHI N  P         26   0- 0
        BRTR

SCHUSTER, WILLIAM CHARLES
(BROADWAY BILL)
B.AUG.4,1912 BUFFALO,N.Y.
1937 PIT N  S          3   .500
1939 BOS N  S-3        2   .000
1943 CHI N  S         13   .294
1944 CHI N  2-S       60   .221
1945 CHI N  2-S-3     45   .191
        BRTR         123   .234

SCHWALL, DONALD BERNARD (DON)
B.MAR.2,1936 WILKES-BARRE,PA.
1961 BOS A  P    25   27  15- 7
1962 BOS A  P    33   34   9-15
1963 PIT N  P         33   6-12
1964 PIT N  P    15   16   4- 3
1965 PIT N  P         43   9- 6
1966 PIT N  P         11   3- 2
     ATL N  P         11   3- 3
1967 ATL N  /P         1   0- 0
        BRTR    172  176  49-48

SCHWAMB, RALPH RICHARD (BLACKIE)
B.AUG.6,1926 LOS ANGELES,CAL.
1948 STL A  P         12   1- 1
        BRTR

SCHWARTZ, DOUGLAS RANDALL (RANDY)
B.FEB.9,1944 LOS ANGELES,CAL.
1965 KC  A  /1         6   .286
1966 KC  A  /1        10   .091
        BLTL          16   .167
```

YR	CL LEA POS	GP	G	REC

SCHWARTZ, WILLIAM AUGUST
(SCOOPER BILL)
B.APR.3,1864 JAMESTOWN,KY.
D.DEC.22,1940 NEWPORT,KY.

YR	CL LEA POS	GP	G	REC
1883	COL AA C-1	2		.250
1884	CIN U C	24		.263
	BRTR	26		.262

SCHWARTZ, WILLIAM CHARLES (BLAB)
B.APR.22,1884 CLEVELAND,OHIO
D.AUG.29,1961 NASHVILLE,TENN.

YR	CL LEA POS	GP	G	REC
1904	CLE A 1	24		.151
	TR			

SCHWARZ, WILLIAM DE WITT
B.JAN.30,1891 BIRMINGHAM,ALA.
D.JUNE 24,1949 JACKSONVILLE,FLA

YR	CL LEA POS	GP	G	REC
1914	NY A C	1		.000
	TR			

SCHWARZROCK, LESTER HENRY
[PLAYED UNDER NAME OF
LESTER HENRY ROCK]

SCHWEITZER, ALBERT CASPAR
(AL) OR (CHEESE)
B.DEC.23,1882 CLEVELAND,OHIO
D.JAN.27,1969 NEWARK,OHIO

YR	CL LEA POS	GP	G	REC
1908	STL A O	64		.291
1909	STL A O	27		.224
1910	STL A O	113		.230
1911	STL A O	76		.215
	BRTR	280		.238

SCHWENCK, RUDOLPH CHRISTIAN (RUDY)
B.APR.6,1884 LOUISVILLE,KY.
D.NOV.27,1941 ANCHORAGE,KY.

YR	CL LEA POS	GP	G	REC
1909	CHI N P	3		1- 1

SCHWENK, HAROLD EDWARD (HAL)
B.AUG.23,1890 SCHUYLKILL HAVEN,PA.
D.SEPT.3,1955 KANSAS CITY,MO.

YR	CL LEA POS	GP	G	REC
1913	STL A P	1		1- 0
	BLTL			

SCHWERT, PIUS LOUIS (PI)
B.NOV.22,1892 ANGOLA,N.Y.
D.MAR.11,1941 WASHINGTON,D.C.

YR	CL LEA POS	GP	G	REC
1914	NY A C	2		.000
1915	NY A C	9		.278
	BRTR	11		.208

SCHWIND, ARTHUR EDWIN
B.NOV.4,1889 FT.WAYNE,IND.
D.JAN.13,1968 SULLIVAN,ILL.

YR	CL LEA POS	GP	G	REC
1912	BOS N 3	1		.000
	BBTR			

SCHYPINSKI, GERALD ALBERT (JERRY)
B.SEPT.16,1931 DETROIT,MICH.

YR	CL LEA POS	GP	G	REC
1955	KC A 2-S	22		.217
	BLTR			

SCOFFIC, LOUIS (WEASER)
B.MAY 20,1913 HERRIN,ILL.

YR	CL LEA POS	GP	G	REC
1936	STL N O	4		.429

SCOGGINS, LYNN J. (JIM) OR (LEFTY)
B.JULY 19,1891 KILLEEN,TEX.
D.AUG.16,1923 COLUMBIA,S.C.

YR	CL LEA POS	GP	G	REC
1913	CHI A P	1		0- 0
	BLTL			

SCORE, HERBERT JUDE (HERB)
B.JUNE 7,1933 ROSEDALE,N.Y.

YR	CL LEA POS	GP	G	REC
1955	CLE A P	33		16-10
1956	CLE A P	35		20- 9
1957	CLE A P	5		2- 1
1958	CLE A P	12		2- 3
1959	CLE A P	30		9-11
1960	CHI A P	23		5-10
1961	CHI A P	8		1- 2
1962	CHI A P	4		0- 0
	BLTL	150		55-46

SCOTT
YR	CL LEA POS	GP	G	REC
1884	BAL U 3-O	13		.226

SCOTT, AMOS RICHARD (DICK)
B.FEB.5,1882 BETHEL,OHIO
D.APR.11,1911 CHICAGO,ILL.

YR	CL LEA POS	GP	G	REC
1901	CIN N P	3		0- 2
	BRTR			

SCOTT, ANTHONY (TONY)
B.SEP.18,1951 CINCINNATI,OHIO

YR	CL LEA POS	GP	G	REC
1973	MON N /O	11		.000
1974	MON N O	19		.286
1975	MON N O	92		.182
1977	STL N O	95		.291
1978	STL N O	96		.228
	BBTR	313		.246

SCOTT, EDWARD
B.AUG.12,1870 WALBRIDGE,OHIO
D.NOV.1,1933 TOLEDO,OHIO

YR	CL LEA POS	GP	G	REC
1900	CIN N P	39		17-20
1901	CLE A P	16		7- 6
	BRTR	55		24-26

SCOTT, FLOYD JOHN (PETE)
B.DEC.21,1898 WOODLAND,CAL.
D.MAY 3,1953 DALY CITY,CAL.

YR	CL LEA POS	GP	G	REC
1926	CHI N O	77		.286
1927	CHI N O	71		.314
1928	PIT N O	60		.311
	BRTR	208		.303

SCOTT, GEORGE CHARLES
(GEORGE) OR (BOOMER)
B.MAR.23,1944 GREENVILLE,MISS.

YR	CL LEA POS	GP	G	REC
1966	BOS A *1/3	162		.245
1967	BOS A *1/3	159		.303
1968	BOS A *1/3	124		.171
1969	BOS A *3-1	152		.253
1970	BOS A 3-1	127		.296
1971	BOS A *1	146		.263
1972	MIL A *1-3	152		.266
1973	MIL A *1	158		.306
1974	MIL A *1	158		.281
1975	MIL A *1-D/3	158		.285
1976	MIL A *1	156		.274
1977	BOS A *1	157		.269
1978	BOS A *1	120		.233
	BRTR	1929		.269

SCOTT, GEORGE WILLIAM
B.NOV.17,1896 TRENTON,MO.

YR	CL LEA POS	GP	G	REC
1920	STL N P	2		0- 0
	BRTR			

SCOTT, JAMES (JIM)
OR (DEATH VALLEY JIM)
B.APR.23,1888 DEADWOOD,S.DAK.
D.APR.7,1957 PALM SPRINGS,CAL.

YR	CL LEA POS	GP	G	REC
1909	CHI A P	36		12-12
1910	CHI A P	40		8-18
1911	CHI A P	39		14-11
1912	CHI A P	5		2- 2
1913	CHI A P	48		20-20
1914	CHI A P	43		14-18
1915	CHI A P	48		24-11
1916	CHI A P	32		7-14
1917	CHI A P	24		6- 7
	BRTR	315		107-113

SCOTT, JAMES WALTER
B.SEPT.22,1888 SHENANDOAH,PA.
D.MAY 12,1972 S.PASADENA,FLA.

YR	CL LEA POS	GP	G	REC
1914	PIT F S	8		.250
	BRTR			

SCOTT, JOHN HENRY
B.JAN.24,1952 JACKSON,MISS.

YR	CL LEA POS	GP	G	REC
1974	SD N /O	14		.067
1975	SD N /O	25		.000
1977	TOR A O	79		.240
	BRTR	118		.222

SCOTT, JOHN WILLIAM (JACK)
B.APR.18,1892 RIDGEWAY,N.C.
D.NOV.30,1959 DURHAM,N.C.

YR	CL LEA POS	GP	G	REC
1916	PIT N P	3		0- 0
1917	BOS N P	7		1- 2
1919	BOS N P-O	19	24	6- 6
				.185
1920	BOS N P		44	10-21
1921	BOS N P	47	51	15-13
1922	CIN N P		1	0- 0
	NY N P		17	8- 2
1923	NY N P		40	16- 7
1925	NY N P	36	41	14-15
1926	NY N P	50	51	13-15
1927	PHI N P	48	83	9-21
1928	NY N P		16	4- 1
1929	NY N P		30	7- 6
	BLTR	358	408	103-109
				.275

SCOTT, LE GRANT EDWARD
B.JULY 25,1910 CLEVELAND,OHIO

YR	CL LEA POS	GP	G	REC
1939	PHI N O	78		.280
	BLTL			

SCOTT, LEWIS EVERETT (DEACON)
B.NOV.19,1892 BLUFFTON,IND.
D.NOV.2,1960 FORT WAYNE,IND.

YR	CL LEA POS	GP	G	REC
1914	BOS A S	144		.239
1915	BOS A S	100		.201
1916	BOS A S	123		.323
1917	BOS A S	157		.241
1918	BOS A S	126		.221
1919	BOS A S	138		.278
1920	BOS A S	154		.269
1921	BOS A S	154		.262
1922	NY A S	154		.269
1923	NY A S	152		.246
1924	NY A S	153		.250
1925	NY A S	22		.217
	WAS A S	33		.272
1926	CHI A S	40		.252
	CIN N S	4		.667
	BRTR	1654		.249

SCOTT, MARSHALL (LEFTY)
B.JULY 15,1915 ROSWELL,N.MEX.
D.MAR.3,1964 HOUSTON,TEX.

YR	CL LEA POS	GP	G	REC
1945	PHI N P	8		0- 2
	BRTL			

SCOTT, MILTON PARKER (MIKADO MILT)
B.JAN.17,1866 CHICAGO,ILL.
D.NOV.3,1938 BALTIMORE,MD.

YR	CL LEA POS	GP	G	REC
1882	CHI N 1	1		.400
1884	DET N 1	108		.249
1885	DET N 1	38		.263
	PIT AA 1	55		.241
1886	BAL AA 1	137		.192
		339		.232

SCOTT, RALPH ROBERT (MICKEY)
B.JULY 25,1947 WEIMAR,GERMANY

YR	CL LEA POS	GP	G	REC
1972	BAL A P	15		0- 1
1973	BAL A /P	1		0- 0
	MON N P	22		1- 2
1975	CAL A P	50		4- 2
1976	CAL A P	33	35	3- 0
1977	CAL A P		12	0- 2
	BLTL	133	135	8- 7

SCOTT, RICHARD LEWIS (DICK)
B.MAR.13,1933 PORTSMOUTH,N.H.

YR	CL LEA POS	GP	G	REC
1963	LA N P	9		0- 0
1964	CHI N P	3		0- 0
	BRTL	12		0- 0

SCOTT, RODNEY DARRELL (ROD)
B.OCT.16,1953 INDIANAPOLIS,CAL.

YR	CL LEA POS	GP	G	REC
1975	KC A D-R/2-S	48		.067
1976	MON N /2-S	7		.400
1977	OAK A 2-S/3-O	133		.261
1978	DET N 3-O/2-S	78		.282
	BBTR	266		.266
	BR 1975			

SCRIVENER, WAYNE ALLISON (CHUCK)
B.OCT.3,1947 ALEXANDRIA,VA.

YR	CL LEA POS	GP	G	REC
1975	DET A /3-S	4		.250
1976	DET A 2-S/3	80		.221
1977	DET A S/2-3	61		.083
	BRTR	145		.190

SCZEPKOWSKI, THEODORE WALTER
[PLAYED UNDER NAME OF
THEODORE WALTER SEPKOWSKI]

SEALE, JOHNNY RAY
(JOHNNIE) OR (DURANGO KID)
B.NOV.14,1938 EDGEWATER,COLO.

YR	CL LEA POS	GP	G	REC
1964	DET A P	4		1- 0
1965	DET A /P	4		0- 0
	BLTL	8		1- 0

SEARS, KENNETH EUGENE (ZIGGY)
B.JULY 6,1917 STREATOR,ILL.
D.JULY 17,1968 BRIDGEPORT,TEX.

YR	CL LEA POS	GP	G	REC
1943	NY A C	60		.278
1946	STL A C	7		.333
	BLTR	67		.282

SEATON, THOMAS GORDON
B.AUG.30,1887 BLAIR,NEB.
D.APR.10,1940 EL PASO,TEX.

YR	CL LEA POS	GP	G	REC
1912	PHI N P	44		16-12
1913	PHI N P	92		27-12
1914	BRO F P	44		25-14
1915	BRO F P	26		7- 7
	NEW F P	18		7-10
1916	CHI N P	31		6- 6
1917	CHI N P	16		5- 4
	BBTR	231		93-65

SEATS, THOMAS EDWARD
B.SEPT.24,1911 FARMINGTON,N.C.

YR	CL LEA POS	GP	G	REC
1940	DET A P	26		2- 2
1945	BRO N P	31		10- 7
	BBTL	57		12- 9
	BR 1945			

YR	CL LEA POS	GP	G	REC

SEAVER, GEORGE THOMAS (TOM)
B.NOV.17,1944 FRESNO,CAL.

YR	CL LEA POS	GP	G	REC
1967	NY N P	35	36	16-13
1968	NY N P	36	38	16-12
1969	NY N P	36	39	25- 7
1970	NY N P	37	42	18-12
1971	NY N P	36	39	20-10
1972	NY N P	35	36	21-12
1973	NY N P	36	39	19-10
1974	NY N P		32	11-11
1975	NY N P	36	37	22- 9
1976	NY N P		35	14-11
1977	NY N P		13	7- 3
	CIN N P		20	14- 3
1978	CIN N P		36	16-14
	BRTR	423	442	219-127

SEBRING, JAMES DENNISON
B.MAR.22,1882 LIBERTY,PA.
D.DEC.22,1909 WILLIAMSPORT,PA.

1902	PIT N O		19	.338
1903	PIT N O		124	.277
1904	PIT N O		80	.269
	CIN N O		56	.225
1905	CIN N O		56	.286
1909	BRO N O		25	.099
	WAS A O		1	.000
	BLTL		361	.262

SECHRIST, THEODORE O HARA (DOC)
B.FEB.10,1876 WILLIAMSTOWN,KY.
D.APR.2,1950 LOUISVILLE,KY.

1899	NY N P	1		0- 0
	BRTR			

SECORY, FRANK EDWARD
B.AUG.24,1912 MASON CITY,IOWA

1940	DET A H		1	.000
1942	CIN N O		2	.000
1944	CIN N O		22	.321
1945	CHI N O		35	.158
1946	CHI N O		33	.233
	BRTR		93	.228

SECRIST, DONALD LAVERNE (DON)
B.FEB.26,1944 SEATTLE,WASH.

1969	CHI A P		19	0- 1
1970	CHI A /P		9	0- 0
	BLTL		28	0- 1

SEDGWICK, HENRY KENNETH (DUKE)
B.JUNE 1,1899 MARTINS FERRY,O.

1921	PHI N P		16	1- 3
1923	WAS A P		5	0- 1
	BRTR		21	1- 4

SEE, CHARLES HENRY (CHAD)
B.OCT.13,1896 PLEASANTVILLE,N.Y
D.JULY 19,1948 BRIDGEPORT,CONN.

1919	CIN N O		8	.286
1920	CIN N P-O	1	47	0- 0
				.305
1921	CIN N O		37	.245
	BLTR	1	92	0- 0
				.267

SEEDS, ROBERT IRA (SUITCASE BOB)
B.FEB.24,1907 RINGGOLD,TEX.

1930	CLE A O		85	.285
1931	CLE A O		48	.306
1932	CLE A O		2	.000
	CHI A O		116	.291
1933	BOS A 1-O		82	.243
1934	BOS A O		8	.167
	CLE A O		61	.247
1936	NY A O		13	.262
1938	NY N O		81	.291
1939	NY N O		63	.266
1940	NY N O		56	.290
	BRTR		615	.277

SEELBACH, CHARLES FREDERICK (CHUCK)
B.MAR.20,1948 LAKEWOOD,OHIO

1971	DET A /P		5	0- 0
1972	DET A P		61	9- 8
1973	DET A /P		5	1- 0
1974	DET A /P		4	0- 0
	BRTR		75	10- 8

SEEREY, JAMES PATRICK (PAT)
B.MAR.17,1923 WILBURTON,OKLA.

1943	CLE A O		26	.222
1944	CLE A O		101	.234
1945	CLE A O		126	.237
1946	CLE A O		117	.225
1947	CLE A O		82	.171
1948	CLE A O		10	.261
	CHI A O		95	.229
1949	CHI A O		4	.000
	BRTR		561	.224

SEERY, JOHN EMMETT (EMMETT)
B.FEB.13,1861 PRINCEVILLE,ILL.

1884	BAL U C-3-O		107	.309
	KC U O		1	.400
1885	STL N 3-O		58	.162
1886	STL N 3-O		126	.238
1887	IND N 3-O		122	.326
1888	IND N 3-O		133	.220
1889	IND N 3-O		127	.313
1890	BRO P 3-O		104	.222
1891	CIN AA 3-O		97	.282
1892	LOU N 3-O		42	.194
	BLTR		917	.266

SEGRIST, KAL HILL
B.APR.14,1931 GREENVILLE,TEX.

1952	NY A 2-3		13	.043
1955	BAL A 1-2-3		7	.333
	BRTR		20	.125

SEGUI, DIEGO PABLO [GONZALEZ]
B.AUG.17,1937 HOLGUIN,CUBA

1962	KC A P		39	8- 5
1963	KC A P		38	9- 6
1964	KC A P		40	8-17
1965	KC A P	40	41	5-15
1966	WAS A P		21	3- 7
1967	KC A P		36	3- 4
1968	OAK A P		52	6- 5
1969	SEA A P		66	12- 6
1970	OAK A P		47	10-10
1971	OAK A P		26	10- 8
1972	OAK A /P		7	0- 1
	STL N P		33	3- 1
1973	STL N P		65	7- 6
1974	BOS A P		58	6- 8
1975	BOS A P		33	2- 5
1977	SEA A P		40	0- 7
	BRTR	639	640	92-111

SEIBOLD, HARRY (SOCKS)
B.APR.3,1896 PHILADELPHIA,PA.
D.SEPT.21,1965 PHILADELPHIA,PA.

1915	PHI A P		10	.115
1916	PHI A P		5	1- 2
1917	PHI A P	32	36	4-16
1919	PHI A P	14	15	2- 3
1929	BOS N P		33	12-17
1930	BOS N P		36	15-16
1931	BOS N P		33	10-18
1932	BOS N P		28	3-10
1933	BOS N P		11	1- 4
	BRTR	192	207	48-86
				.196

SELBACH, ALBERT KARL (KIP)
B.MAR.24,1872 COLUMBUS,OHIO
D.FEB.17,1956 COLUMBUS,OHIO

1894	WAS N S-O		96	.300
1895	WAS N O		129	.324
1896	WAS N O		121	.316
1897	WAS N O		126	.317
1898	WAS N O		131	.302
1899	CIN N O		139	.302
1900	NY N O		141	.345
1901	NY N O		125	.292
1902	BAL A O		128	.321
1903	WAS A O		141	.252
1904	WAS A O		48	.264
	BOS A O		98	.258
1905	BOS A O		115	.246
1906	BOS A O		60	.211
	BRTR		1598	.296

SELEE, FRANK GIBSON
B.OCT.26,1859 AMHERST,N.Y.
D.JULY 5,1909 DENVER,COLO.
NON-PLAYING MANAGER
BOS(N)1890-1901, CHI(N)1902-05

SELKIRK, GEORGE ALEXANDER (TWINKLETOES)
B.JAN.4,1899 HUNTSVILLE,ONT.,CANADA

1934	NY A O		46	.313
1935	NY A O		128	.312
1936	NY A O		137	.308
1937	NY A O		78	.328
1938	NY A O		99	.254
1939	NY A O		128	.306
1940	NY A O		118	.269
1941	NY A O		70	.220
1942	NY A O		42	.192
	BLTR		846	.290

SELL, LESTER ELWOOD (EPP)
B.APR.26,1897 LLEWELLYN,PA.
D.FEB.19,1961 READING,PA.

1922	STL N P		7	4- 2
1923	STL N P		5	0- 1
	BRTR		12	4- 3

SELLERS, OLIVER (RUBE)
B.MAR.7,1881 DUQUESNE,PA.
D.JAN.14,1952 PITTSBURGH,PA.

1910	BOS N O		12	.156

SELLS, DAVID WAYNE (DAVE)
B.SEP.18,1946 VACAVILLE,CAL.

1972	CAL A P		10	2- 0
1973	CAL A P		51	7- 2
1974	CAL A P		20	2- 3
1975	CAL A /P		4	0- 0
	LA N /P		5	0- 2
	BRTR		90	11- 7

SELMA, RICHARD JAY (DICK)
B.NOV.4,1943 SANTA ANA,CAL.

1965	NY N /P	4	7	2- 1
1966	NY N P	30	31	4- 6
1967	NY N P	38	43	2- 4
1968	NY N P	33	39	9-10
1969	SD N /P		4	2- 2
	CHI N P		36	10- 8
1970	PHI N P/3-1		73	8- 9
				.150
1971	PHI N P	17	18	0- 2
1972	PHI N P	46	47	2- 9
1973	PHI N /P		6	1- 1
1974	CAL A P		18	2- 2
	MIL A /P		2	0- 0
	BRTR	307	324	42-54
				.172

BB 1966 (PART)

SELMAN, FRANK C.
[ALSO PLAYED UNDER NAME OF FRANK C. WILLIAMS]
B.BALTIMORE,MD.
D.OCT.14,1890

1871	KEK NA C-3	14		-
1872	OLY NA C-3	8		.275
1873	MAR NA P	1		0- 1
1874	BAL NA C-S-O	12		-
1875	NAT NA 1	1		-
		1	36	0- 1

SELPH, CAREY ISOM
B.DEC.5,1901 DONALDSON,ARK.
D.FEB.24,1976 HOUSTON,TEX.

1929	STL N 2		25	.235
1932	CHI A 3		116	.283
	BRTR		141	.277

SEMBER, MICHAEL DAVID (MIKE)
B.FEB.24,1953 HAMMOND,IND.

1977	CHI N /2		3	.250
1978	CHI N /3-S		9	.333
	BRTR		12	.286

SEMBERA, CARROLL WILLIAM
B.JULY 26,1941 SHINER,TEX.

1965	HOU N /P		2	0- 1
1966	HOU N P		24	1- 2
1967	HOU N P		43	2- 6
1969	MON N P		23	0- 2
1970	MON N /P		5	0- 0
	BRTR		99	3-11

SEMINICK, ANDREW WASIL (ANDY)
B.SEPT.12,1920 PIERCE,W.VA.

1943	PHI N C		22	.181
1944	PHI N C-O		22	.222
1945	PHI N C-3-O		80	.239
1946	PHI N C		124	.264
1947	PHI N C		111	.252
1948	PHI N C		125	.225
1949	PHI N C		109	.243
1950	PHI N C		130	.288
1951	PHI N C		101	.227
1952	CIN N C		108	.256
1953	CIN N C		119	.235
1954	CIN N C		86	.235
1955	CIN N C		6	.133
	PHI N C		93	.246
1956	PHI N C		60	.199
1957	PHI N C		8	.091
	BRTR		1304	.243

SEMPROCH, ROMAN ANTHONY (ROMAN) OR (BABY)
B.JAN.7,1931 CLEVELAND,OHIO

1958	PHI N P		36	13-11
1959	PHI N P		30	3-10
1960	DET A P		17	3- 0
1961	LA A P		2	0- 0
	BRTR		85	19-21

SENERCHIA, EMANUEL ROBERT (SONNY)
B.APR.6,1931 NEWARK,N.J.

1952	PIT N 3		29	.220
	BRTR			

SENSENDERFER, JOHN PHILLIPS JENKINS
B.DEC.28,1847 PHILADELPHIA,PA.
D.MAY 3,1903

1871	ATH NA O		25	.371
1872	ATH NA O		1	.400
1873	ATH NA O		19	-
1874	ATH NA O		4	-
			49	-

YR CL LEA POS — GP — G — REC

SENTELL, LEOPOLD THEODORE (PAUL)
B.AUG.27,1879 NEW ORLEANS,LA.
D.APR.27,1923 CINCINNATI,OHIO

YR	CL	LEA	POS	GP	G	REC
1906	PHI	N	2-3	55		.229
1907	PHI	N	S	3		.000
	TR			58		.226

SEOANE, MANUEL MODESTO (MANNY)
B.JUNE 26,1955 TAMPA,FLA.

YR	CL	LEA	POS	GP	G	REC
1977	PHI	N	/P	2		0- 0
1978	CHI	N	/P	7		1- 0
	BRTR			9		1- 0

SEPKOWSKI, THEODORE WALTER
[REAL NAME
THEODORE WALTER SCZEPKOWSKI]
B.NOV.9,1923 BALTIMORE,MD.

YR	CL	LEA	POS	GP	G	REC
1942	CLE	A	2	5		.100
1946	CLE	A	3	2		.500
1947	CLE	A	P	10		.125
	NY	A	H	2		.000
	BLTR			19		.231

SERAD, WILLIAM I.
B.1863 PHILADELPHIA,PA.
D.NOV.1,1925 CHESTER,PA.

YR	CL	LEA	POS	GP	G	REC
1884	BUF	N	P-0	38		17-21
						.175
1885	BUF	N	P	29		8-21
1887	CIN	AA	P-0	22		11-11
						.278
1888	CIN	AA	P	6		1- 3
	BRTR			95		37-56
						.183

SERAFIN, JOSEPH STANLEY
[PLAYED UNDER NAME OF
JOSEPH STANLEY COBB]

SERENA, WILLIAM ROBERT (BILL)
B.OCT.2,1924 ALAMEDA,CAL.

YR	CL	LEA	POS	GP	G	REC
1949	CHI	N	3	12		.216
1950	CHI	N	3	127		.239
1951	CHI	N	3	13		.333
1952	CHI	N	2-3	122		.274
1953	CHI	N	2-3	93		.251
1954	CHI	N	2-3	41		.159
	BRTR			408		.251

SERUM, GARY WAYNE
B.OCT.24,1956 FARGO,N.D.

YR	CL	LEA	POS	GP	G	REC
1977	MIN	A	/P	8		0- 0
1978	MIN	A	P	34		9- 9
	BRTR			42		9- 9

SESSI, WALTER ANTHONY (WATSIE)
B.JULY 23,1918 FINLEYVILLE,PA.

YR	CL	LEA	POS	GP	G	REC
1941	STL	N	0	5		.000
1946	STL	N	H	15		.143
	BLTL			20		.074

SETTLEMIRE, EDGAR MERLE (LEFTY)
B.JAN.19,1903 SANTA FE,OHIO

YR	CL	LEA	POS	GP	G	REC
1928	BOS	A	P	33		0- 6
	BLTL					

SEVCIK, JOHN JOSEPH
B.JULY 11,1942 OAK PARK,ILL.

YR	CL	LEA	POS	GP	G	REC
1965	MIN	A	C	12		.063
	BRTR					

SEVEREID, HENRY LEVAI (HANK)
B.JUNE 1,1891 STORY CITY,IOWA
D.DEC.17,1968 SAN ANTONIO,TEX.

YR	CL	LEA	POS	GP	G	REC
1911	CIN	N	C	22		.304
1912	CIN	N	C	50		.237
1913	CIN	N	C	8		.200
1915	STL	A	C	80		.222
1916	STL	A	C	100		.273
1917	STL	A	C	143		.265
1918	STL	A	C	91		.256
1919	STL	A	C	112		.248
1920	STL	A	C	123		.277
1921	STL	A	C	143		.324
1922	STL	A	C	137		.321
1923	STL	A	C	122		.308
1924	STL	A	C	137		.308
1925	STL	A	C	34		.358
	WAS	A	C	50		.364
1926	WAS	A	C	22		.212
	NY	A	C	41		.266
	BRTR			1375		.289

SEVERINSEN, ALBERT HENRY (AL)
B.NOV.9,1944 BROOKLYN,N.Y.

YR	CL	LEA	POS	GP	G	REC
1969	BAL	A	P	12		1- 1
1971	SD	N	P	59		2- 5
1972	SD	N	P	17		0- 1
	BRTR			88		3- 7

SEVERSON, RICHARD ALLEN (RICH)
B.DEC.16,1945 ARTESIA,CAL.

YR	CL	LEA	POS	GP	G	REC
1970	KC	A	S-2	77		.250
1971	KC	A	/2-S-3	16		.300
	BBTR			93		.256

SEWARD, EDWARD WILLIAM
[REAL NAME EDWARD WILLIAM SOURHARDT]
B.JUNE 29,1867 CLEVELAND,OHIO
D.JULY 30,1947 CLEVELAND,OHIO

YR	CL	LEA	POS	GP	G	REC
1885	PRO	N	P	1		0- 1
1887	ATH	AA	P	55	75	25-24
1888	ATH	AA	P	57	64	34-19
1889	ATH	AA	P	38	45	21-16
1890	ATH	AA	P	21	27	1-13
1891	CLE	N	P	7		1- 0
	TR			179	219	87-73

SEWARD, FRANK MARTIN
B.APR.7,1921 PENNSAUKEN,N.J.

YR	CL	LEA	POS	GP	G	REC
1943	NY	N	P	1		0- 1
1944	NY	N	P	25		3- 2
	BRTR			26		3- 3

SEWARD, GEORGE E.
B.ST.LOUIS,MO.

YR	CL	LEA	POS	GP	G	REC
1875	STL	NA	C-2-0	23		.210
1876	MUT	N	2	1		.000
1882	STL	AA	C-0	38		.195
				62		.198

SEWELL, JAMES LUTHER (LUKE)
B.JAN.5,1901 TITUS,ALA.

YR	CL	LEA	POS	GP	G	REC
1921	CLE	A	C	3		.000
1922	CLE	A	C	41		.264
1923	CLE	A	C	10		.200
1924	CLE	A	C	63		.291
1925	CLE	A	C-0	74		.232
1926	CLE	A	C	126		.238
1927	CLE	A	C	128		.293
1928	CLE	A	C	122		.270
1929	CLE	A	C	124		.236
1930	CLE	A	C	76		.257
1931	CLE	A	C	108		.275
1932	CLE	A	C	87		.253
1933	WAS	A	C	141		.264
1934	WAS	A	C-1-2-3-0	72		.237
1935	CHI	A	C	118		.285
1936	CHI	A	C	128		.251
1937	CHI	A	C	122		.269
1938	CHI	A	C	65		.213
1939	CLE	A	C	16		.150
1942	STL	A	M-C	6		.143
	BRTR			1630		.259

NON-PLAYING MANAGER STL[A]
1941, 43-46; CIN[N] 1949-52

SEWELL, JOSEPH WHEELER (JOE)
B.OCT.9,1898 TITUS,ALA.

YR	CL	LEA	POS	GP	G	REC
1920	CLE	A	S	22		.329
1921	CLE	A	S	154		.318
1922	CLE	A	2-S	153		.299
1923	CLE	A	S	153		.353
1924	CLE	A	S	153		.316
1925	CLE	A	2-S	155		.335
1926	CLE	A	S	154		.324
1927	CLE	A	S	153		.316
1928	CLE	A	S-3	155		.323
1929	CLE	A	3	152		.315
1930	CLE	A	3	109		.289
1931	NY	A	3	130		.302
1932	NY	A	3	125		.272
1933	NY	A	3	135		.273
	BLTR			1903		.312

SEWELL, THOMAS WESLEY
B.APR.16,1906 TITUS,ALA.
D.JULY 30,1956 MONTGOMERY,ALA.

YR	CL	LEA	POS	GP	G	REC
1927	CHI	N	P	1		.000
	BLTR					

SEWELL, TRUETT BANKS (RIP)
B.MAY 11,1907 DECATUR,ALA.

YR	CL	LEA	POS	GP	G	REC
1932	DET	A	P	5		0- 0
1938	PIT	N	P	17		0- 1
1939	PIT	N	P	52		10- 9
1940	PIT	N	P	33	47	16- 5
1941	PIT	N	P	39	42	14-17
1942	PIT	N	P	40	41	17-15
1943	PIT	N	P	35	41	21- 9
1944	PIT	N	P	38	44	21-12
1945	PIT	N	P	33	35	11- 9
1946	PIT	N	P	25	26	8-12
1947	PIT	N	P		24	6- 4
1948	PIT	N	P		21	13- 3
1949	PIT	N	P		28	6- 1
	BLTR			390	423	143-97

SEXAUER, ELMER GEORGE
B.MAY 21,1926 ST.LOUIS CO.,MO.

YR	CL	LEA	POS	GP	G	REC
1948	BRO	N	P	2		0- 0
	BRTR					

SEXTON, FRANK JOSEPH
B.JULY 8,1872 BROCKTON,MASS.
D.JAN.4,1938 BRIGHTON,MASS.

YR	CL	LEA	POS	GP	G	REC
1895	BOS	N	P	10		1- 4

SEXTON, JIMMY DALE
B.DEC.15,1951 MOBILE,ALA.

YR	CL	LEA	POS	GP	G	REC
1977	SEA	A	S	14		.216
1978	HOU	N	S/3-2	88		.206
	BRTR			102		.208

SEXTON, THOMAS W.
B.MAR.14,1865 ROCK ISLAND,ILL.
D.FEB.8,1934 ROCK ISLAND,ILL.

YR	CL	LEA	POS	GP	G	REC
1884	MIL	U	S	12		.229

SEYBOLD, RALPH ORLANDO (SOCKS)
B.NOV.23,1870 WASHINGTONVILLE,O
D.DEC.22,1921 GREENSBURG,PA.

YR	CL	LEA	POS	GP	G	REC
1899	CIN	N	0	22		.221
1901	PHI	A	1-0	114		.332
1902	PHI	A	0	137		.317
1903	PHI	A	1-0	137		.299
1904	PHI	A	0	143		.282
1905	PHI	A	0	132		.271
1906	PHI	A	0	116		.316
1907	PHI	A	0	147		.271
1908	PHI	A	0	48		.215
	BRTR			996		.293

SEYFRIED, GORDON CLAY
B.JULY 4,1937 LONG BEACH,CAL.

YR	CL	LEA	POS	GP	G	REC
1963	CLE	A	P	3		0- 1
1964	CLE	A	P	2		0- 0
	BRTR			5		0- 1

SEYMOUR, JAMES BENTLEY (CY)
B.DEC.9,1872 ALBANY,N.Y.
D.SEPT.20,1919 NEW YORK,N.Y.

YR	CL	LEA	POS	GP	G	REC
1896	NY	N	P	12		2- 4
1897	NY	N	P	34	41	20-14
1898	NY	N	P-0	44	78	25-17
						.273
1899	NY	N	P	33	45	13-18
1900	NY	N	P	11	21	2- 2
1901	BAL	A	0	137		.302
1902	BAL	A	0	72		.278
	CIN	N	P+3-	1	60	0- 0
						.349
1903	CIN	N	0	135		.342
1904	CIN	N	0	130		.312
1905	CIN	N	0	149		.377
1906	CIN	N	0	79		.357
	NY	N	0	72		.320
1907	NY	N	0	126		.294
1908	NY	N	0	155		.267
1909	NY	N	0	73		.310
1910	NY	N	0	78		.265
1913	BOS	N	0	39		.178
	BLTL			135	1500	62-55
						.307

SEYMOUR, THOMAS
B.1858 PITTSBURGH,PA.
D.FEB.17,1916 BOISE,IDAHO

YR	CL	LEA	POS	GP	G	REC
1882	PIT	AA	P	1		0- 1

SHAFER, ARTHUR JOSEPH (TILLIE)
B.MAR.22,1889 LOS ANGELES,CAL.
D.JAN.10,1962 LOS ANGELES,CAL.

YR	CL	LEA	POS	GP	G	REC
1909	NY	N	3	31		.179
1910	NY	N	3	27		.182
1912	NY	N	S	76		.288
1913	NY	N	2-S-3-0	138		.287
	BBTR			274		.273

SHAFER, RALPH NEWTON
B.MAR.17,1894 CINCINNATI,OHIO
D.FEB.5,1950 AKRON,OHIO

YR	CL	LEA	POS	GP	G	REC
1914	PIT	N	H	1		.000

SHAFFER

YR	CL	LEA	POS	GP	G	REC
1875	ATL	NA	0	1		.000

SHAFFER, FRANK

YR	CL	LEA	POS	GP	G	REC
1884	ALT	U	C-3-0	19		.284
	KC	U	C-2-S-3-0	43		.172
	BAL	U	0	3		.077
				65		.200

SHAFFER, GEORGE (ORATOR)
B.1852 PHILADELPHIA,PA.

YR	CL	LEA	POS	GP	G	REC
1874	HAR	NA	0	9		-
	MUT	NA	0	1		-
1875	PHI	NA	1-3-0	16		.262
1877	LOU	N	1-0	61		.285
1878	IND	N	0	60		.344
1879	CHI	N	0	70		.319
1880	CLE	N	0	82		.265
1881	CLE	N	0	84		.257
1882	CLE	N	0	82		.218
1883	BUF	N	0	94		.292
1884	STL	U	0	89		.354
1885	STL	N	0	69		.194
	ATH	AA	0	2		.222
1886	ATH	AA	0	21		.344
1890	ATH	AA	0	106		.286
	BLTR			846		-

SHAFFER, TAYLOR
B.PHILADELPHIA,PA.

YR	CL	LEA	POS	GP	G	REC
1890	ATH	AA	2	70		.178

YR	CL	LEA	POS	GP	G	REC

SHALLIX, AUGUST
[REAL NAME AUGUST SCHALLICK]
B.MAR.29,1858 PADERBORN,
WESTPHALIA,GERMANY
D.OCT.28,1937 CINCINNATI,OHIO

YR	CL	LEA	POS	GP	G	REC
1884	CIN	AA	P		23	11-10
1885	CIN	AA	P-O		13	7- 4
						.128
	BRTR				36	18-14
						.085

SHAMBRICK, OTTO H.
[PLAYED UNDER NAME OF
OTTO H. SCHOMBERG]

SHAMSKY, ARTHUR LOUIS (ART)
B.OCT.14,1941 ST.LOUIS,MO.

YR	CL	LEA	POS	GP	G	REC
1965	CIN	N	O/1		64	.260
1966	CIN	N	O		96	.231
1967	CIN	N	O		76	.197
1968	NY	N	O-1		116	.238
1969	NY	N	O/1		100	.300
1970	NY	N	O-1		122	.293
1971	NY	N	O/1		68	.185
1972	CHI	N	/1		15	.125
	OAK	A	/H		8	.000
	BLTL				665	.253

SHANABROOK, WARREN H.
B.NOV.30,1880 MASSILLON,OHIO
D.MAR.10,1964 N.CANTON,OHIO

YR	CL	LEA	POS	GP	G	REC
1906	WAS	A	1		1	.000
	BRTR					

SHANAHAN, PAUL GREGORY (GREG)
B.DEC.11,1947 EUREKA,CAL.

YR	CL	LEA	POS	GP	G	REC
1973	LA	N	/P		7	0- 0
1974	LA	N	/P		4	0- 0
	BRTR				11	0- 0

SHANDLEY, JAMES J.
B.NEW YORK
D.NOV.7,1904 BROOKLYN,N.Y.

YR	CL	LEA	POS	GP	G	REC
1870	MUT	N	0		2	.125

SHANER, WALTER DEDAKER (SKINNY)
B.MAY 24,1900 LYNCHBURG,VA.

YR	CL	LEA	POS	GP	G	REC
1923	CLE	A	3		3	.250
1926	BOS	A	0		69	.283
1927	BOS	A	0		122	.273
1929	CIN	N	1-0		13	.321
	BBTR				207	.278

SHANK, HARVEY TILLMAN
B.JULY 29,1946 TORONTO,ONT.,CAN.

YR	CL	LEA	POS	GP	G	REC
1970	CAL	A	/P		1	0- 0
	BRTR					

SHANKS, HOWARD SAMUEL (HANK)
B.JULY 21,1890 CHICAGO,ILL.
D.JULY 30,1941 MONACA,PA.

YR	CL	LEA	POS	GP	G	REC
1912	WAS	A	0		115	.236
1913	WAS	A	0		109	.254
1914	WAS	A	0		143	.224
1915	WAS	A	3-0		141	.250
1916	WAS	A	3-0		140	.259
1917	WAS	A	S-0		126	.202
1918	WAS	A	2-0		120	.257
1919	WAS	A	2-S		135	.248
1920	WAS	A	1-3-0		128	.268
1921	WAS	A	3		154	.302
1922	WAS	A	3-0		84	.283
1923	BOS	A	2-3		131	.254
1924	BOS	A	S-3		72	.259
1925	NY	A	2-3-0		66	.258
	BRTR				1664	.253

SHANLEY, HARRY ROOT (DOC)
B.1890 GRANBURY,TEX.
D.DEC.13,1934 ST.PETERSBURG,FLA

YR	CL	LEA	POS	GP	G	REC
1912	STL	A	S		5	.000
	BRTR					

SHANNER, WILFRED WILLIAM (BILL)
B.NOV.4,1894 OAKLAND CITY,IND.

YR	CL	LEA	POS	GP	G	REC
1920	PHI	N	P		1	0- 0
	BLTR					

SHANNON, DANIEL W.
B.MAR.23,1865 BRIDGEPORT,CONN.
D.OCT.25,1913 BRIDGEPORT,CONN.

YR	CL	LEA	POS	GP	G	REC
1889	LOU	AA	M-2		120	.262
1890	PHI	P	2		18	.260
	NY	P	2-S-3		83	.238
1891	WAS	AA	M-S		19	.118
					240	.238

SHANNON, FRANK E. (TOD)
B.DEC.3,1873 SAN FRANCISCO,CAL.

YR	CL	LEA	POS	GP	G	REC
1892	WAS	N	S		1	.200
1895	WAS	N	S		1	.200
1896	LOU	N	S		31	.161
					33	.163

SHANNON, JOSEPH ALOYSIUS
B.FEB.11,1897 JERSEY CITY,N.J.
D.JULY 28,1955 JERSEY CITY,N.J.

YR	CL	LEA	POS	GP	G	REC
1915	BOS	N	0		5	.200
	BRTR					

SHANNON, MAURICE JOSEPH (RED)
B.FEB.11,1897 JERSEY CITY,N.J.
D.MAY 27,1970 JERSEY CITY,N.J.

YR	CL	LEA	POS	GP	G	REC
1915	BOS	N	S		1	.000
1917	PHI	A	S		11	.257
1918	PHI	A	2-S		72	.240
1919	PHI	A	2		39	.271
	BOS	A	2		80	.259
1920	WAS	A	S		48	.288
	PHI	A	S		24	.167
1921	PHI	A	N		1	.000
1926	CHI	N	S		19	.333
	BBTR				310	.257

**SHANNON, THOMAS MICHAEL
(MIKE) OR (MOONMAN)**
B.JULY 5,1939 ST.LOUIS,MO.

YR	CL	LEA	POS	GP	G	REC
1962	STL	N	0		10	.133
1963	STL	N	0		32	.308
1964	STL	N	0		88	.261
1965	STL	N	*O/C		124	.221
1966	STL	N	*O/C		137	.288
1967	STL	N	*#3/O		130	.245
1968	STL	N	*3		156	.266
1969	STL	N	*3		150	.254
1970	STL	N	3		55	.213
					882	.255

SHANNON, OWEN DENNIS IGNATIUS
B.DEC.22,1885 OMAHA,NEB.
D.APR.10,1918 OMAHA,NEB.

YR	CL	LEA	POS	GP	G	REC
1903	STL	A	C		8	.200
1907	WAS	A	C		4	.143
	BRTR				12	.188

SHANNON, WALTER CHARLES (WALLY)
B.JAN.23,1934 CLEVELAND,OHIO

YR	CL	LEA	POS	GP	G	REC
1959	STL	N	2-S		47	.284
1960	STL	N	2-S		18	.174
	BLTR				65	.263

SHANNON, WILLIAM PORTER (SPIKE)
B.FEB.7,1878 PITTSBURGH,PA.
D.MAY 16,1940 MINNEAPOLIS,MINN.

YR	CL	LEA	POS	GP	G	REC
1904	STL	N	0		133	.280
1905	STL	N	0		140	.268
1906	STL	N	0		80	.258
	NY	N	0		69	.268
1907	NY	N	0		155	.265
1908	NY	N	0		74	.224
	PIT	N	0		32	.197
					690	.259

SHANTZ, ROBERT CLAYTON (BOBBY)
B.SEP.26,1925 POTTSTOWN,PA.

YR	CL	LEA	POS	GP	G	REC
1949	PHI	A	P		33	6- 8
1950	PHI	A	P	36	37	8-14
1951	PHI	A	P	32	36	18-10
1952	PHI	A	P	33	34	24- 7
1953	PHI	A	P	16	21	5- 9
1954	PHI	A	P	2	7	1- 0
1955	KC	A	P	23	26	5-10
1956	KC	A	P	45	51	2- 7
1957	NY	A	P	30	33	11- 5
1958	NY	A	P-O		33	7- 6
						.229
1959	NY	A	P	33	40	7- 3
1960	NY	A	P	42	43	5- 4
1961	PIT	N	P	43	44	6- 3
1962	HOU	N	P	3	7	1- 1
	STL	N	P		28	5- 3
1963	STL	N	P		55	6- 4
1964	STL	N	P		16	1- 3
	CHI	N	P		20	0- 1
	PHI	N	P		14	1- 1
	BRTL			537	578	119-99
						.195

SHANTZ, WILMER EBERT (BILLY)
B.JULY 31,1927 POTTSTOWN,PA.

YR	CL	LEA	POS	GP	G	REC
1954	PHI	A	C		51	.256
1955	KC	A	C		79	.258
1960	NY	A	C		1	.000
	BRTR				131	.257

SHARMAN, RALPH EDWARD (BALLY)
B.APR.11,1895 CLEVELAND,OHIO
D.MAY 24,1918 CAMP SHERIDAN,ALA

YR	CL	LEA	POS	GP	G	REC
1917	PHI	A	O		13	.297
	BRTR					

SHARON, RICHARD LOUIS (DICK)
B.APR.15,1950 SAN MATEO,CAL.

YR	CL	LEA	POS	GP	G	REC
1973	DET	A	0		91	.242
1974	DET	A	0		60	.217
1975	SD	N	0		91	.194
	BRTR				242	.218

SHARP, WILLIAM HOWARD (BILL)
B.JAN.18,1950 LIMA,OHIO

YR	CL	LEA	POS	GP	G	REC
1973	CHI	A	0		77	.276
1974	CHI	A	0		100	.253
1975	CHI	A	0		18	.200
	MIL	A	*0		125	.255
1976	MIL	A	0		78	.244
	BLTL				398	.255

SHARPE, BAYARD HESTON (BUD)
B.AUG.6,1881 WEST CHESTER,PA.
D.MAY 31,1916 HADDOCK,GA.

YR	CL	LEA	POS	GP	G	REC
1905	BOS	N	0		45	.182
1910	BOS	N	1		113	.239
	PIT	N	1		4	.188
	BLTR				162	.222

SHARROTT, GEORGE OSCAR
B.NOV.2,1869 W.NEW BRIGHTON,
S.I.,N.Y.
D.JAN.6,1932 JAMAICA,N.Y.

YR	CL	LEA	POS	GP	G	REC
1893	BRO	N	P		11	4- 7
1894	BRO	N	P		3	1- 1
	BLTR				14	5- 8

SHARROTT, JOHN HENRY (JACK)
B.AUG.13,1869 BANGOR,ME.
D.DEC.31,1927 LOS ANGELES,CAL.

YR	CL	LEA	POS	GP	G	REC
1890	NY	N	P	23	29	11- 9
1891	NY	N	P		10	4- 3
1892	NY	N	P-O	1	5	0- 1
						.000
1893	PHI	N	P-O	8	30	2- 3
						.254
	BRTR			42	74	17-16
						.236

SHARSIG, WILLIAM A.
B.1855 PHILADELPHIA,PA.
D.FEB.1,1902 PHILADELPHIA,PA.
NON-PLAYING MANAGER ATH[AA] 1882-91

SHAUGHNESSY, FRANCIS JOSEPH (SHAG)
B.APR.8,1883 AMBOY,ILL.
D.MAY 15,1969 MONTREAL,QUE.,CAN

YR	CL	LEA	POS	GP	G	REC
1905	WAS	A	0		1	.000
1908	PHI	A	0		8	.321
	BRTR				9	.290

SHAUTE, JOSEPH BENJAMIN (LEFTY)
B.AUG.1,1899 PECKVILLE,PA.
D.FEB.21,1970 SCRANTON,PA.

YR	CL	LEA	POS	GP	G	REC
1922	CLE	A	P		2	5- 0
1923	CLE	A	P	33	34	10- 8
1924	CLE	A	P		46	20-17
1925	CLE	A	P	26	29	4-12
1926	CLE	A	P		34	14-10
1927	CLE	A	P		45	9-16
1928	CLE	A	P		36	13-17
1929	CLE	A	P		26	8- 8
1930	CLE	A	P		4	0- 0
1931	BRO	N	P		25	11- 6
1932	BRO	N	P	34	35	7- 7
1933	BRO	N	P		41	3- 4
1934	CIN	N	P		8	0- 2
	BLTL			360	368	99-109

SHAW, ALBERT SIMPSON
B.MAR.1,1881 TOLEDO,ILL.
D.DEC.30,1974 DANVILLE,ILL.

YR	CL	LEA	POS	GP	G	REC
1907	STL	N	0		8	.303
1908	STL	N	0		96	.264
1909	STL	N	0		92	.248
1914	BRO	F	0		110	.321
1915	KC	F	0		132	.279
	BLTR				438	.279

SHAW, ALFRED (SHODDY)
B.OCT.3,1874 BURSLEM,ENGLAND
D.MAR.25,1958 UHRICHSVILLE,OHIO

YR	CL	LEA	POS	GP	G	REC
1901	DET	A	C		57	.215
1907	BOS	A	C		76	.192
1908	CHI	A	C		32	.082
1909	BOS	N	C		18	.100
	BRTR				183	.207

SHAW, BENJAMIN NATHANIEL
B.JUNE 18,1893 LA CENTER,KY.
D.MAR.16,1959 AURORA,OHIO

YR	CL	LEA	POS	GP	G	REC
1917	PIT	N	O		2	.000
1918	PIT	N	O		21	.194
	BRTR				23	.184

SHAW, DONALD WELLINGTON (DON)
B.FEB.23,1944 PITTSBURGH,PA.

YR	CL	LEA	POS	GP	G	REC
1967	NY	N	P		40	4- 5
1968	NY	N	/P		7	0- 0
1969	MON	N	P		35	2- 5
1971	STL	N	P		45	7- 2
1972	STL	N	/P		8	0- 1
	OAK	A	/P		3	0- 1
	BLTL				138	13-14

YR	CL	LEA	POS	GP	G	REC

SHAW, FREDERICK LANDER (DUPEE)
B.MAY 31,1859 CHARLESTOWN,MASS.
D.JUNE 11,1938 EVERETT,MASS.

YR	CL	LEA	POS	GP	G	REC
1883	DET	N	P-O	29	38	11-18
						.189
1884	DET	A	P-O	26	36	8-18
						.191
	BOS	U	P-O	39	44	22-15
						.235
1885	PRO	N	P-O		49	23-26
						.133
1886	WAS	N	P		45	14-31
1887	WAS	N	P		21	7-14
1888	WAS	N	P		3	0-3
	TL			212	236	85-125
						.174

SHAW, JAMES ALOYSIUS (GRUNTING JIM)
B.AUG.19,1893 PITTSBURGH,PA.
D.JAN.27,1962 WASHINGTON,D.C.

YR	CL	LEA	POS	GP	G	REC
1913	WAS	A	P		2	0-1
1914	WAS	A	P		48	15-17
1915	WAS	A	P		25	5-12
1916	WAS	A	P		26	3-8
1917	WAS	A	P		47	19-14
1918	WAS	A	P		41	16-12
1919	WAS	A	P		45	16-17
1920	WAS	A	P		38	11-18
1921	WAS	A	P		15	1-0
	BRTR			287		82-99

SHAW, ROBERT JOHN (BOB)
B.JUNE 29,1933 BRONX,N.Y.

YR	CL	LEA	POS	GP	G	REC
1957	DET	A	P		7	0-1
1958	DET	A	P	11	12	1-2
	CHI	A	P		29	4-2
1959	CHI	A	P		47	18-6
1960	CHI	A	P		36	13-13
1961	CHI	A	P		14	3-4
	KC	A	P	26	28	9-10
1962	MIL	N	P		38	15-9
1963	MIL	N	P		48	7-11
1964	SF	N	P		61	7-6
1965	SF	N	P		42	16-9
1966	SF	N	P		13	1-4
	NY	N	P		26	11-10
1967	NY	N	P		23	3-9
	CHI	N	/P		9	0-2
	BRTR			430	433	108-98

SHAW, ROYAL N
B.SEPT.29,1884 YAKIMA,WASH.
D.JULY 3,1969 YAKIMA,WASH.

YR	CL	LEA	POS	GP	G	REC
1908	PIT	N	O		1	.000
	BBTR					

SHAW, SAMUEL E.
B.1863 BALTIMORE,MD.

YR	CL	LEA	POS	GP	G	REC
1888	BAL	AA	P		6	2-4
1893	CHI	N	P		2	1-0
	BRTR				8	3-4

SHAWKEY, JAMES ROBERT (BOB)
B.DEC.4,1890 SIGEL,PA.

YR	CL	LEA	POS	GP	G	REC
1913	PHI	A	P		18	7-5
1914	PHI	A	P		38	16-8
1915	PHI	A	P		17	6-5
	NY	A	P		16	4-8
1916	NY	A	P		53	24-14
1917	NY	A	P		32	13-15
1918	NY	A	P		3	1-1
1919	NY	A	P		41	20-11
1920	NY	A	P		38	20-13
1921	NY	A	P		38	18-12
1922	NY	A	P		39	20-12
1923	NY	A	P		36	16-11
1924	NY	A	P		38	16-11
1925	NY	A	P		32	6-14
1926	NY	A	P		29	8-7
1927	NY	A	P		19	2-3
	BRTR			487		197-150
NON-PLAYING MANAGER NY[A] 1930

SHAY, ARTHUR JOSEPH (MARTY)
B.APR.25,1896 BOSTON,MASS.
D.FEB.20,1951 WORCESTER,MASS.

YR	CL	LEA	POS	GP	G	REC
1916	CHI	N	2		2	.286
1924	BOS	N	2-S		19	.235
	BRTR				21	.240

SHAY, DANIEL C.
B.NOV.8,1876 SPRINGFIELD,OHIO
D.DEC.1,1927 KANSAS CITY,MO.

YR	CL	LEA	POS	GP	G	REC
1901	CLE	A	S		19	.226
1904	STL	N	S		98	.256
1905	STL	N	2-S		78	.238
1907	NY	N	S		24	.190
	TR				219	.240

SHEA, FRANCIS JOSEPH (SPEC)
OR (THE NAUGATUCK NUGGET)
[REAL NAME FRANCIS JOSEPH O SHEA]
B.OCT.2,1920 NAUGATUCK,CONN.

YR	CL	LEA	POS	GP	G	REC
1947	NY	A	P		27	14-5
1948	NY	A	P		28	9-10
1949	NY	A	P		20	1-1
1951	NY	A	P		25	5-5
1952	WAS	A	P		22	11-7
1953	WAS	A	P		23	12-7
1954	WAS	A	P		23	2-9
1955	WAS	A	P		27	2-2
	BRTR			195		56-46

SHEA, GERALD J.
B.JULY 26,1881 ST.LOUIS,MO.
D.MAY 3,1964 BERKELEY,MO.

YR	CL	LEA	POS	GP	G	REC
1905	STL	N	C		2	.333
	TR					

SHEA, JOHN EDWARD
(NAP) OR (NAPOLEON)
B.MAY 23,1874 WARE,MASS.
D.JULY 8,1968 BLOOMFIELD HILLS,MICH.

YR	CL	LEA	POS	GP	G	REC
1902	PHI	N	C		3	.111
	BRTR					

SHEA, JOHN MICHAEL JOSEPH (LEFTY)
B.DEC.27,1904 EVERETT,MASS.
D.NOV.30,1956 MALDEN,MASS.

YR	CL	LEA	POS	GP	G	REC
1928	BOS	A	P		1	0-0
	BLTL					

SHEA, MERVYN DAVID JOHN (MERV)
B.SEPT.5,1900 SAN FRANCISCO,CAL
D.JAN.27,1953 SACRAMENTO,CAL.

YR	CL	LEA	POS	GP	G	REC
1927	DET	A	C		34	.176
1928	DET	A	C		39	.236
1929	DET	A	C		50	.290
1933	BOS	A	C		16	.143
	STL	A	C		94	.262
1934	CHI	A	C		62	.199
1935	CHI	A	C		46	.230
1936	CHI	A	C		14	.125
1937	CHI	A	C		25	.211
1938	BRO	N	C		48	.183
1939	DET	A	C		4	.000
1944	PHI	N	C		7	.267
	BRTR				439	.220

SHEA, MICHAEL J.
B.MAR.10,1867 NEW ORLEANS,LA.

YR	CL	LEA	POS	GP	G	REC
1887	CIN	AA	P		2	1-1

SHEA, PATRICK HENRY (RED)
B.NOV.29,1898 WARE,MASS.

YR	CL	LEA	POS	GP	G	REC
1918	PHI	A	P		3	0-0
1921	NY	N	P		9	5-2
1922	NY	N	P		11	0-3
	BRTR				23	5-5

SHEA, STEVEN FRANCIS (STEVE)
B.DEC.5,1942 WORCESTER,MASS.

YR	CL	LEA	POS	GP	G	REC
1968	HOU	N	P		30	4-4
1969	MON	N	P		10	0-0
	BRTR				40	4-4

SHEALY, ALBERT BERLEY
B.MAR.20,1900 CHAPIN,S.C.
D.MAR.7,1967 HAGERSTOWN,MD.

YR	CL	LEA	POS	GP	G	REC
1928	NY	A	P		23	8-6
1930	CHI	N	P		24	0-0
	BRTR				47	8-6

SHEAN, DAVID WILLIAM
B.JULY 9,1883 ARLINGTON,MASS.
D.MAY 22,1963 BOSTON,MASS.

YR	CL	LEA	POS	GP	G	REC
1906	PHI	A	2		22	.213
1908	PHI	N	S		14	.106
1909	PHI	N	2		29	.232
	BOS	N	2		72	.044
1910	BOS	N	2		148	.239
1911	CHI	N	2-S		43	.193
1912	BOS	N	S		2	.400
1917	CIN	N	2		131	.210
1918	BOS	A	2		115	.264
1919	BOS	A	2		29	.140
	BRTR				605	.228

SHEARER, RAY SOLOMON
B.SEPT.19,1929 JACOBUS,PA.

YR	CL	LEA	POS	GP	G	REC
1957	MIL	N	O		2	.500
	BRTR					

SHEARON, JOHN M.
B.1870 PITTSBURGH,PA.

YR	CL	LEA	POS	GP	G	REC
1891	CLE	N	P-O	6	30	1-4
						.234
1896	CLE	N	O		15	.174
				6	45	1-4
						.214

SHEARS, GEORGE PENFIELD
B.APR.13,1890 MARSHALL,MO.

YR	CL	LEA	POS	GP	G	REC
1912	NY	A	P		4	0-0
	BRTL					

SHECKARD, SAMUEL JAMES TILDEN
(JIMMY)
B.NOV.23,1878 UPPER CHANCEFORD,PA.
D.JAN.15,1947 LANCASTER,PA.

YR	CL	LEA	POS	GP	G	REC
1897	BRO	N	S-O		13	.326
1898	BRO	N	O		105	.290
1899	BAL	N	O		147	.298
1900	BRO	N	O		75	.305
1901	BRO	N	O		133	.353
1902	BAL	A	O		4	.266
	BRO	N	O		122	.273
1903	BRO	N	O		139	.332
1904	BRO	N	O		143	.239
1905	BRO	N	O		129	.292
1906	CHI	N	O		149	.262
1907	CHI	N	O		142	.267
1908	CHI	N	O		115	.231
1909	CHI	N	O		148	.255
1910	CHI	N	O		143	.256
1911	CHI	N	O		156	.276
1912	CHI	N	O		146	.245
1913	STL	N	O		52	.199
	CIN	N	O		47	.190
	BLTR				2108	.276

SHEEHAN, DANIEL
[SEE JOHN J. RYAN]

SHEEHAN, DANIEL
B.DEC.18,1872 CLEVELAND,OHIO

YR	CL	LEA	POS	GP	G	REC
1900	NY	N	S		1	.000

SHEEHAN, JAMES THOMAS (BIG JIM)
B.JUNE 3,1913 NEW HAVEN,CONN.

YR	CL	LEA	POS	GP	G	REC
1936	NY	N	C		1	.000
	BRTR					

SHEEHAN, JOHN THOMAS (JACK)
B.APR.15,1893 CHICAGO,ILL.

YR	CL	LEA	POS	GP	G	REC
1920	BRO	N	3		1	.400
1921	BRO	N	3		5	.000
	BRTR				9	.176

SHEEHAN, THOMAS CLANCY
B.MAR.31,1894 GRAND RIDGE,ILL.

YR	CL	LEA	POS	GP	G	REC
1915	PHI	A	P		15	4-8
1916	PHI	A	P		38	1-15
1921	NY	A	P		12	1-0
1924	CIN	N	P	39	41	9-11
1925	CIN	N	P		10	1-0
	PIT	N	P	23	24	1-1
1926	PIT	N	P		9	0-2
	BRTR			146	149	17-37
NON-PLAYING MANAGER SF[N] 1960

SHEEHAN, THOMAS H.
B.NOV.6,1877 SACRAMENTO,CAL.
D.MAY 22,1959 PANAMA CITY,PAN.

YR	CL	LEA	POS	GP	G	REC
1906	PIT	N	3		90	.241
1907	PIT	N	3		67	.274
1908	BRO	N	3		145	.214
	TR				302	.236

SHEEHAN, TIMOTHY JAMES (BIFF)
B.FEB.13,1868 HARTFORD,CONN.
D.OCT.21,1923 HARTFORD,CONN.

YR	CL	LEA	POS	GP	G	REC
1895	STL	N	O		49	.324
1896	STL	N	O		5	.133
					54	.309

SHEELY, EARL HOMER
(EARL) OR (WHITEY)
B.FEB.12,1893 BUSHNELL,ILL.
D.SEPT.16,1952 SEATTLE,WASH.

YR	CL	LEA	POS	GP	G	REC
1921	CHI	A	1		154	.304
1922	CHI	A	1		149	.317
1923	CHI	A	1		156	.296
1924	CHI	A	1		146	.320
1925	CHI	A	1		153	.315
1926	CHI	A	1		145	.299
1927	CHI	A	1		45	.209
1929	PIT	N	1		139	.293
1931	BOS	N	1		147	.273
	BRTR				1234	.300

SHEELY, HOLLIS KIMBALL (BUD)
B.NOV.26,1920 SPOKANE,WASH.

YR	CL	LEA	POS	GP	G	REC
1951	CHI	A	C		34	.180
1952	CHI	A	C		36	.240
1953	CHI	A	C		31	.217
	BLTR				101	.210

SHEERIN, CHARLES JOSEPH (CHUCK)
B.APR.17,1909 BROOKLYN,N.Y.

YR	CL	LEA	POS	GP	G	REC
1936	PHI	N	2-3		39	.264
	BRTR					

SHELDON, BOB MITCHELL
B.NOV.27,1950 MONTEBELLO,CAL.

YR	CL	LEA	POS	GP	G	REC
1974	MIL	A	/2		10	.118
1975	MIL	A	2		53	.287
1977	MIL	A	D/2		31	.203
	BLTR				94	.256

YR	CL	LEA	POS	GP	G	REC

SHELDON, ROLAND FRANK (ROLLIE)
B.DEC.17,1936 PUTNAM,CONN.

YR	CL	LEA	POS	GP	G	REC
1961	NY	A	P	35	36	11- 5
1962	NY	A	P		34	7- 8
1964	NY	A	P		19	5- 2
1965	NY	A	P		3	0- 0
1965	KC	A	P		32	10- 8
1966	KC	A	P		14	4- 7
	BOS	A	P		23	1- 6
	BRTR			160	161	38-36

SHELLENBACK, FRANK VICTOR
B.DEC.16,1898 JOPLIN,MO.
D.AUG.17,1969 NEWTON,MASS.

1918	CHI	A	P	28	29	10-12
1919	CHI	A	P		8	1- 3
	BRTR			36	37	11-15

SHELLENBACK, JAMES PHILIP (JIM)
B.NOV.18,1943 RIVERSIDE,CAL.

1966	PIT	N	/P		2	0- 0
1967	PIT	N	/P		6	1- 1
1969	PIT	N	/P		8	0- 0
	WAS	A	P		30	4- 7
1970	WAS	A	P	39	40	6- 7
1971	WAS	A	P		40	3-11
1972	TEX	A	P		22	2- 4
1973	TEX	A	/P		2	0- 0
1974	TEX	A	P		11	0- 0
1977	MIN	A	/P		5	0- 0
	BLTL			165	166	16-30

SHELLEY, HUBERT LENEIRRE (HUGH)
B.OCT.26,1910 ROGERS,TEX.

1935	DET	A	O		7	.250
	BRTR					

SHELTON, ANDREW KEMPER (SKEETER)
B.JUNE 29,1888 HUNTINGTON,W.VA.
D.JAN.9,1954 HUNTINGTON,W.VA.

1915	NY	A	O		10	.025
	BRTR					

SHEMO, STEPHEN MICHAEL
B.APR.9,1915 SWOYERSVILLE,PA.

1944	BOS	N	2-3		18	.290
1945	BOS	N	2-S-3		17	.239
	BRTR				35	.260

SHEPARD, JACK LEROY
B.MAY 13,1932 CLOVIS,CAL.

1953	PIT	N	C		2	.250
1954	PIT	N	C		82	.304
1955	PIT	N	C		94	.239
1956	PIT	N	C-1		100	.242
	BRTR			278		.260

SHEPARDSON, RAYMOND FRANCIS
B.MAY 3,1897 LITTLE FALLS,N.Y.
D.NOV.8,1975 LITTLE FALLS,N.Y.

1924	STL	N	P		3	.000
	BRTR					

SHEPPARD, JOHN
B.BALTIMORE,MD.

1873	MAR	NA	C-O		3	.000

SHERDEL, WILLIAM HENRY (WEE WILLIE)
B.AUG.15,1896 MC SHERRYSTOWN,PA
D.NOV.14,1968 MC SHERRYSTOWN,PA.

1918	STL	N	P		35	6-12
1919	STL	N	P	36	40	5- 9
1920	STL	N	P	43	49	11-10
1921	STL	N	P	38	39	9- 8
1922	STL	N	P	47	48	17-13
1923	STL	N	P	39	45	15-13
1924	STL	N	P-O	35	49	8- 9
						.200
1925	STL	N	P	32	33	15- 6
1926	STL	N	P	34	36	16-12
1927	STL	N	P		39	17-12
1928	STL	N	P		38	21-10
1929	STL	N	P		33	10-15
1930	STL	N	P		13	3- 2
	BOS	N	P		21	8- 5
1931	BOS	N	P		27	6-10
1932	BOS	N	P		1	0- 0
	STL	N	P		3	0- 0
	BLTL			514	549	165-146
						.223

SHERID, ROYDAN RICHARD (ROY)
B.JAN.25,1908 MORRISTOWN,PA.

1929	NY	A	P	33	6- 6
1930	NY	A	P		37	12-13
1931	NY	A	P		17	5- 5
	BRTR			87	23-24

SHERIDAN

1875	ATL	NA	O		1	.000

SHERIDAN, EUGENE ANTHONY (RED)
B.NOV.14,1896 BROOKLYN,N.Y.
D.NOV.25,1975 QUEENS VILLAGE,N.Y.

1918	BRO	N	2		2	.250
1920	BRO	N	S		2	.000
	BRTR				4	.167

SHERIDAN, NEILL RAWLINS
(NEILL) OR (WILD HORSE)
B.NOV.20,1921 SACRAMENTO,CAL.

1948	BOS	A	H		2	.000
	BRTR					

SHERLING EDWARD CREECH (SHINE)
B.JULY 17,1897 COALSBURG,PA.
D.NOV.16,1965 ENTERPRISE,CAL.

1924	PHI	A	H		4	.500
	BRTR					

SHERLOCK, JOHN CLINTON (MONK)
B.OCT.26,1904 BUFFALO,N.Y.

1930	PHI	N	1		92	.324
	BRTR					

SHERLOCK, VINCENT THOMAS (BALDY)
B.MAR.27,1909 BUFFALO,N.Y.

1935	BRO	N	2		9	.462
	BRTR					

SHERMAN, DANIEL L. (BABE)
B.1892 CONNECTICUT

1914	CHI	F	P		1	0- 1
	BRTR					

SHERMAN, JOEL POWERS (JOE)
B.NOV.4,1890 YARMOUTH,MASS.

1915	PHI	A	P		2	1- 0
	BRTR					

SHERRILL, DENNIS LEE
B.MAR.3,1956 MIAMI,FLA.

1978	NY	A	/3		2	.000
	BRTR					

SHERRY, FRED PETER
[REAL NAME FRED PETER SCHUERHOLZ]
B.JAN.13,1880 HONESDALE,PA.
D.JULY 27,1975 HONESDALE,PA.

1911	WAS	A	P		10	0- 4
	BRTR					

SHERRY, LAWRENCE (LARRY)
B.JULY 25,1935 LOS ANGELES,CAL.

1958	LA	N	P		5	0- 0
1959	LA	N	P		23	7- 2
1960	LA	N	P		57	14-10
1961	LA	N	P		53	4- 4
1962	LA	N	P		58	7- 3
1963	LA	N	P		36	2- 6
1964	DET	A	P		38	7- 5
1965	DET	A	P		39	3- 6
1966	DET	A	P		55	8- 5
1967	DET	A	P		20	0- 1
	HOU	N	P		29	1- 2
1968	CAL	A	/P		3	0- 0
	BRTR			416	53-44

SHERRY, NORMAN BURT (NORM)
B.JULY 16,1931 NEW YORK,N.Y.

1959	LA	N	C		2	.333
1960	LA	N	C		47	.283
1961	LA	N	C		47	.256
1962	LA	N	C		35	.182
1963	NY	N	C		63	.136
	BRTR			194	.215

NON-PLAYING MANAGER CAL[A] 1976-77

SHETRONE, BARRY STEVAN
B.JULY 6,1938 BALTIMORE,MD.

1959	BAL	A	O		33	.203
1960	BAL	A	R		1	.000
1961	BAL	A	O		3	.143
1962	BAL	A	O		21	.250
1963	WAS	A	H		2	.000
	BLTR			60	.205

SHETTSLINE, WILLIAM JOSEPH
B.OCT.25,1863 PHILADELPHIA,PA.
D.FEB.22,1933 PHILADELPHIA,PA.
NON-PLAYING MANAGER PHI[N] 1898-1902

SHETZLINE, JOHN HENRY
B.1850 PHILADELPHIA,PA.
D.DEC.15,1892 PHILADELPHIA,PA.

1882	BAL	AA	2-S-3-O	76	.226

SHEVLIN, JAMES CORNELIUS
B.JULY 9,1909 CINCINNATI,OHIO
D.OCT.30,1978 FT.LAUDERDALE,FLA

1930	DET	A	1		28	.143
1932	CIN	N	1		7	.208
1934	CIN	N	1		18	.308
	BLTL			53	.247

SHIELDS, BENJAMIN COWAN
(BIG BEN) OR (LEFTY)
B.JUNE 17,1903 HUNTERSVILLE,N.C

1924	NY	A	P		2	0- 0
1925	NY	A	P		4	3- 0
1930	BOS	A	P		3	0- 0
1931	PHI	N	P		4	1- 0
	BBTL			13	4- 0

SHIELDS, CHARLES S.
B.DEC.10,1879 JACKSON,TENN.
D.AUG.27,1953 MEMPHIS,TENN.

1902	BAL	A	P-O		23	3- 9
						.163
	STL	A	P		4	3- 0
1907	STL	N	P		3	0- 3
	BLTL			30	6-12
						.219

SHIELDS, FRANCIS LEROY (PETE)
B.SEPT.21,1891 SWIFTWATER,MISS.
D.FEB.11,1961 JACKSON,MISS.

1915	CLE	A	1		23	.208
	BRTR					

SHIELDS, VINCENT WILLIAM
B.NOV.18,1900 FREDERICTON,N.B.,
CANADA
D.OCT.17,1952 PLASTER ROCK,N.B.
CANADA

1924	STL	N	P		3	1- 1
	BLTR					

SHIFFLETT, GARLAND JESSIE
(GARLAND) OR (DUCK)
B.MAR.28,1935 ELKTON,VA.

1957	WAS	A	P		6	0- 0
1964	MIN	A	P		10	0- 2
	BRTR			16	0- 2

SHILLING, JAMES ROBERT
B.MAY 14,1915 TULSA,OKLA.

1939	CLE	A	2		31	.276
	PHI	N	2-S-3		11	.303
	BRTR			42	.282

SHINAULT, ENOCH ERSKINE (GINGER)
B.SEPT.7,1892 BENTON,ARK.
D.DEC.29,1930 DENVER,COLO.

1921	CLE	A	C		22	.378
1922	CLE	A	C		13	.133
	BRTR			35	.295

SHINDLE, WILLIAM
B.DEC.5,1863 GLOUCESTER,N.J.
D.1920 GLOUCESTER CITY,N.J.

1886	DET	N	S		5	.333
1887	DET	N	3		20	.340
1888	BAL	AA	3		135	.216
1889	BAL	AA	3		138	.315
1890	PHI	P	S		132	.236
1891	PHI	N	3		103	.210
1892	BAL	N	3		143	.253
1893	BAL	N	3		125	.259
1894	BRO	N	3		117	.300
1895	BRO	N	3		118	.278
1896	BRO	N	3		131	.281
1897	BRO	N	3		134	.289
1898	BRO	N	3		120	.228
	TR			1421	.271

SHINNERS, RALPH PETER
B.OCT.4,1895 MONCHES,WIS.
D.JULY 23,1962 MILWAUKEE,WIS.

1922	NY	N	O		56	.251
1923	NY	N	O		33	.154
1925	STL	N	O		74	.295
	BRTR			163	.276

SHINNICK, TIMOTHY JAMES (TIM)
(DANDY) OR (GOOD EYE)
B.NOV.6,1867 EXETER,N.H.
D.MAY 18,1944 EXETER,N.H.

1890	LOU	AA	2		133	.267
1891	LOU	AA	2		135	.225
	BBTR			268	.244

SHIPKE, WILLIAM MARTIN (TONY)
(SKIPPER BILL) OR
(MUSKRAT BILL)
[REAL NAME
WILLIAM MARTIN SHIPKRETHAVER]
B.NOV.18,1882 ST.LOUIS,MO.
D.SEPT.10,1940 OMAHA,NEB.

1906	CLE	A	3		2	.000
1907	WAS	A	3		64	.196
1908	WAS	A	3		111	.208
1909	WAS	A	3		8	.154
	TR			185	.200

SHIPKRETHAVER, WILLIAM MARTIN
[PLAYED UNDER NAME OF
WILLIAM MARTIN SHIPKE]

YR	CL LEA POS	GP	G	REC

SHIPLEY, JOSEPH CLARK
(JOE) OR (MOSES)
B.MAY 9,1935 MORRISTOWN,TENN.
1958 SF N P — 1 0- 0
1959 SF N P — 10 0- 0
1960 SF N P — 15 0- 0
1963 CHI A P — 3 0- 1
BRTR — 29 0- 1

SHIRES, CHARLES ARTHUR
(ART) OR (ART THE GREAT)
B.AUG.13,1907 ITALY,TEX.
D.JULY 13,1967 ITALY,TEX.
1928 CHI A 1 — 33 .341
1929 CHI A 1 — 100 .312
1930 CHI A 1 — 37 .260
WAS A 1 — 38 .365
1932 BOS N 1 — 82 .238
BLTR — 290 .291

SHIREY, CLAIR LEE (DUKE)
B.JUNE 20,1898 JERSEY SHORE,PA.
D.SEPT.1,1962 HAGERSTOWN,PA.
1920 WAS A P — 2 0- 1
BR

SHIRLEY, ALVIS NEWMAN (TEX)
B.APR.25,1918 BIRTHRIGHT,TEX.
1941 PHI A P — 5 0- 1
1942 PHI A P — 15 0- 1
1944 STL A P 23 30 5- 4
1945 STL A P 32 43 8-12
1946 STL A P 27 35 6-12
BBTR 102 128 19-30
BR 1941-42

SHIRLEY, BARTON ARVIN (BART)
B.JAN.4,1940 CORPUS CHRISTI,TEX.
1964 LA N S-3 — 18 .274
1966 LA N /S — 12 .200
1967 NY N /2 — 6 .000
1968 LA N S-2 — 39 .181
BRTR — 75 .204

SHIRLEY, ERNEST RAEFORD (MULE)
B.MAY 24,1901 SNOW HILL,N.C.
D.AUG.4,1955 GOLDSBORO,N.C.
1924 WAS A 1 — 30 .234
1925 WAS A 1 — 14 .130
BLTL — 44 .210

SHIRLEY, ROBERT CHARLES (BOB)
B.JUNE 25,1954 CUSHING,OKLA.
1977 SD N P — 39 12-18
1978 SD N P — 50 8-11
BRTL — 89 20-29

SHIVER, IVEY MERWIN (CHICK)
B.JAN.22,1907 SYLVESTER,GA.
D.AUG.31,1972 SAVANNAH,GA.
1931 DET A O — 2 .111
1934 CIN N O — 19 .203
BRTR — 21 .191

SHOCH, GEORGE QUINTUS
B.JAN.6,1859 PHILADELPHIA,PA.
D.SEPT.30,1937 PHILADELPHIA,PA.
1886 WAS N O — 26 .294
1887 WAS N O — 69 .294
1888 WAS N S-O — 90 .183
1889 WAS N O — 30 .238
1891 MIL AA 2-S — 34 .299
1892 BAL N S — 75 .279
1893 BRO N 3-O — 93 .276
1894 BRO N O — 63 .320
1895 BRO N O — 58 .263
1896 BRO N 2 — 75 .278
1897 BRO N 2 — 79 .290
BRTR — 692 .271

SHOCKCOR, URBAIN JACQUES
[PLAYED UNDER NAME OF
URBAN JAMES SHOCKER]

SHOCKER, URBAN JAMES
[REAL NAME URBAIN JACQUES SHOCKCOR]
B.AUG.22,1890 CLEVELAND,OHIO
D.SEPT.9,1928 DENVER,COLO.
1916 NY A P — 12 4- 3
1917 NY A P — 26 8- 5
1918 STL A P — 14 6- 5
1919 STL A P — 30 13-11
1920 STL A P — 38 20-10
1921 STL A P — 47 27-12
1922 STL A P — 48 24-17
1923 STL A P — 43 20-12
1924 STL A P — 40 16-13
1925 NY A P — 41 12-12
1926 NY A P — 41 19-11
1927 NY A P — 31 18- 6
1928 NY A P — 1 0- 0
BRTR — 412 187-117

SHOCKLEY, JOHN COSTEN (COSTEN)
B.FEB.8,1942 GEORGETOWN,DEL.
1964 PHI N 1 — 11 .229
1965 CAL A 1/O — 40 .187
BLTL — 51 .197

SHOEMAKER, CHARLES LANDIS (CHARLIE)
B.AUG.10,1939 LOS ANGELES,CAL.
1961 KC A 2 — 7 .385
1962 KC A 2 — 5 .182
1964 KC A 2 — 16 .212
BLTR — 28 .258

SHOENECK, LEWIS N.
[SEE LEWIS N. SCHOENECK]

SHOFFNER, MILBURN JAMES (MILT)
B.NOV.13,1905 SHERMAN,TEX.
D.JAN.19,1978 MADISON,OHIO
1929 CLE A P — 11 2- 3
1930 CLE A P — 24 3- 4
1931 CLE A P — 12 2- 3
1937 BOS N P — 6 3- 1
1938 BOS N P 26 27 8- 7
CIN N P — 10 2- 2
1939 BOS N P — 25 4- 6
CIN N P — 10 2- 2
1940 CIN N P — 20 1- 0
BLTL 134 135 25-26

SHOFNER, FRANK STRICKLAND (STRICK)
B.JULY 23,1919 CRAWFORD,TEX.
1947 BOS A 3 — 5 .154
BLTR

SHOKES, EDWARD CHRISTOPHER
B.JAN.27,1920 CHARLESTON,S.C.
1941 CIN N H — 1 .000
1946 CIN N 1 — 31 .120
BLTL — 32 .119

SHOMBERG, OTTO H.
[SEE OTTO H. SCHOMBERG]

SHOOK, RAYMOND CURTIS
B.NOV.18,1889 PERRY,OHIO
D.SEPT.16,1970 SOUTH BEND,IND.
1916 CHI A H — 1 .000

SHOOP, RONALD LEE (RON)
B.SPET.19,1931 RURAL VALLEY,PA.
1959 DET A C — 3 .143
BRTR

SHOPAY, THOMAS MICHAEL (TOM)
B.FEB.21,1945 BRISTOL,CONN.
1967 NY A /O — 8 .296
1969 NY A /O — 28 .083
1971 BAL A O — 47 .257
1972 BAL A /O — 49 .225
1975 BAL A O/C — 14 .200
1976 BAL A O/C — 14 .200
1977 BAL A O — 67 .188
BLTR — 253 .201

SHORE, ERNEST GRADY (ERNIE)
B.MAR.24,1891 EAST BEND,N.C.
1912 NY N P — 1 0- 0
1914 BOS A P — 19 10- 4
1915 BOS A P — 38 19- 7
1916 BOS A P — 38 16-10
1917 BOS A P — 29 13-10
1919 NY A P — 20 5- 8
1920 NY A P — 14 2- 2
BRTR — 159 65-41

SHORE, RAYMOND EVERETT (RAY)
B.JUNE 9,1921 CINCINNATI,OHIO
1946 STL A P — 1 0- 0
1948 STL A P — 17 1- 2
1949 STL A P — 13 0- 1
BRTR — 31 1- 3

SHORES, WILLIAM DAVID
B.MAY 26,1904 ABILENE,TEX.
1928 PHI A P — 3 1- 1
1929 PHI A P — 39 11- 6
1930 PHI A P — 31 12- 4
1931 PHI A P — 6 0- 3
1933 NY N P — 8 2- 1
1936 CHI A P — 9 0- 0
BRTR — 96 26-15

SHORT, CHRISTOPHER JOSEPH (CHRIS)
B.SEP.19,1937 MILFORD,DEL.
1959 PHI N P — 3 0- 0
1960 PHI N P — 42 6- 9
1961 PHI N P-C 39 40 6-12
.162
1962 PHI N P 47 48 11- 9
1963 PHI N P — 38 9-12
1964 PHI N P 42 44 17- 9
1965 PHI N P — 47 18-11
1966 PHI N P — 42 20-10
1967 PHI N P — 29 9-11
1968 PHI N P 42 43 19-13
1969 PHI N P — 2 0- 0
1970 PHI N P — 36 9-16
1971 PHI N P — 31 7-14
1972 PHI N P — 19 1- 1
1973 MIL A P — 42 3- 5
BRTL 501 506 135-132
.126
88 1970-71

SHORT, DAVID ORVIS
B.MAY 11,1917 MAGNOLIA,ARK.
1940 CHI A H — 4 .333
1941 CHI A O — 3 .000
BLTR — 7 .091

SHORT, WILLIAM ROSS (BILL)
B.NOV.27,1937 KINGSTON,N.Y.
1960 NY A P — 10 3- 5
1962 BAL A P — 5 0- 0
1966 BAL A /P — 6 2- 3
BOS A /P — 8 0- 0
1967 PIT N /P — 6 0- 0
1968 NY N P — 34 0- 3
1969 CIN N /P — 4 0- 0
BLTL — 73 5-11

SHORTEN, CHARLES HENRY (CHICK)
B.APR.19,1892 SCRANTON,PA.
D.OCT.23,1965 SCRANTON,PA.
1915 BOS A O — 6 .214
1916 BOS A O — 53 .295
1917 BOS A O — 69 .179
1919 DET A O — 95 .315
1920 DET A O — 116 .288
1921 DET A O — 92 .272
1922 STL A O — 55 .275
1924 CIN N O — 41 .275
BLTL — 527 .275

SHOTTON, BURTON EDWIN (BARNEY)
B.OCT.18,1884 BROWNHELM,OHIO
D.JULY 29,1962 LAKE WALES,FLA.
1909 STL A O — 17 .262
1911 STL A O — 139 .255
1912 STL A O — 154 .290
1913 STL A O — 149 .293
1914 STL A O — 154 .269
1915 STL A O — 156 .283
1916 STL A O — 157 .282
1917 STL A O — 118 .224
1918 WAS A O — 126 .261
1919 STL N O — 85 .285
1920 STL N O — 62 .228
1921 STL N O — 38 .250
1922 STL N O — 34 .200
1923 STL N O — 1 .000
BLTR — 1390 .270
NON-PLAYING MANAGER
PHI(N) 1928-33, CIN(N) 1934,
BRO(N) 1947, 48-50

SHOUN, CLYDE MITCHELL (HARDROCK)
B.MAR.20,1912 MOUNTAIN CITY,TENN.
D.MAR.20,1968 MOUNTAIN HOME,TENN.
1935 CHI N P — 5 1- 0
1936 CHI N P — 4 0- 0
1937 CHI N P — 37 7- 7
1938 STL N P — 40 6- 6
1939 STL N P — 53 3- 1
1940 STL N P — 54 13-11
1941 STL N P — 26 3- 5
1942 STL N P — 2 0- 0
CIN N P — 34 1- 3
1943 CIN N P — 45 14- 5
1944 CIN N P — 38 13-10
1946 CIN N P — 27 1- 6
1947 CIN N P — 10 0- 0
BOS N P — 26 5- 3
1948 BOS N P — 36 5- 1
1949 BOS N P — 1 0- 0
CHI A P — 16 1- 1
BLTL — 454 73-59

SHOUPE, JOHN F.
B.SEPT.30,1851 CINCINNATI,OHIO
D.FEB.13,1920 CINCINNATI,OHIO
1879 TRO N S — 10 .097
1882 STL AA 2 — 2 .000
1884 WAS U O — 1 .750
BLTR — 13 .135

SHOVLIN, JOHN JOSEPH (BRODE)
B.JAN.14,1891 DRIFTON,PA.
D.FEB.16,1976 BETHESDA,MD.
1911 PIT N H — 2 .000
1919 STL A 2 — 9 .212
1920 STL A 2 — 7 .286
BRTR — 18 .220

SHREVE, LEVEN LAWRENCE (LEV)
B.JAN.14,1869 LOUISVILLE,KY.
D.OCT.18,1942 DETROIT,MICH.
1887 BAL AA P — 6 2- 1
IND N P — 15 5-10
1888 IND N P 35 36 11-24
1889 IND N P — — 0- 3
TR 59 60 18-38

SHRIVER, HARRY GRAYDON (POP)
B.SEPT.2,1896 WADESTOWN,W.VA.
D.JAN.7,1970 MORGANTOWN,W.VA.
1922 BRO N P — 25 4- 6
1923 BRO N P — 1 0- 0
BRTR — 26 4- 6

```
YR  CL LEA POS      GP    G    REC
```

SHUBA, GEORGE THOMAS (SHOTGUN)
B.DEC.13,1924 YOUNGSTOWN,OHIO
```
1948 BRO N O        63        .267
1949 BRO N H         1       1.000
1950 BRO N O        34        .207
1952 BRO N O        94        .305
1953 BRO N O        74        .254
1954 BRO N O        45        .154
1955 BRO N O        44        .275
     BLTR          355        .259
```

SHUGART, WILLIAM FRANK (FRANK)
B.1867 CHICAGO,ILL.
```
1890 CHI P S        29        .177
1891 PIT N S        75        .285
1892 PIT N S       137        .276
1893 PIT N S-O      52        .274
     STL N S-O      57        .297
1894 STL N O       133        .285
1895 LOU N S-O     112        .256
1897 PHI N S        40        .251
1901 CHI A S       107        .251
     BLTR          742        .268
```

SHULTZ, WALLACE LUTHER (TOOTS)
B.OCT.10,1888 HOMESTEAD,PA.
D.JAN.30,1959 MC KEESPORT,PA.
```
1911 PHI N P         5        0- 3
1912 PHI N P        22   23   1- 4
     BRTR           27   28   1- 7
```

SHUMAN, HARRY
B.MAR.5,1916 PHILADELPHIA,PA.
```
1942 PIT N P         1        0- 0
1943 PIT N P        11        0- 0
1944 PIT N P        18        0- 0
     BRTR           30        0- 0
```

SHUPE, VINCENT WILLIAM
B.SEPT.5,1921 E.CANTON,OHIO
D.APR.5,1962 CANTON,OHIO
```
1945 BOS N 1        78        .269
     BLTL
```

SICKING, EDWARD JOSEPH
B.MAR.30,1897 ST.BERNARD,OHIO
D.AUG.30,1978 CINCINNATI,OHIO
```
1916 CHI N 3         1       1.000
1918 NY  N 2-S-3    46        .250
1919 NY  N 2-S       6        .333
     PHI N 2-S-3    61        .216
1920 NY  N 3        46        .172
     CIN N 2-S-3    37        .266
1927 PIT N 2         6        .143
     BRTR          203        .226
```

SIEBERN, NORMAN LEROY (NORM)
B.JULY 26,1933 ST.LOUIS,MO.
```
1956 NY  A O        54        .204
1958 NY  A O       136        .300
1959 NY  A 1-O     120        .271
1960 KC  A 1-O     144        .279
1961 KC  A 1-O     153        .296
1962 KC  A 1       162        .308
1963 KC  A 1-O     152        .272
1964 BAL A 1       150        .245
1965 BAL A 1       106        .256
1966 CAL A 1       125        .247
1967 SF  N 1-O      46        .155
     BOS A 1/O      33        .205
1968 BOS A /1-O     27        .067
     BLTR         1408        .272
```

SIEBERT, PAUL EDWARD
B.JUNE 5,1953 MINNEAPOLIS,MINN.
```
1974 HOU N /P        5        1- 1
1975 HOU N /P        7        0- 2
1976 HOU N P        19        0- 2
1977 SD  N /P        4        0- 0
     NY  N P        25        2- 1
1978 NY  N P        27        0- 2
     BLTL           87        3- 8
```

SIEBERT, RICHARD WALTHER (DICK)
B.FEB.19,1912 FALL RIVER,MASS.
D.DEC.9,1978 MINNEAPOLIS,MINN.
```
1932 BRO N 1         6        .286
1936 BRO N O         2        .000
1937 STL N 1        22        .184
1938 STL N H         1       1.000
     PHI A 1        48        .284
1939 PHI A 1       101        .294
1940 PHI A 1       154        .286
1941 PHI A 1       123        .334
1942 PHI A 1       153        .260
1943 PHI A 1       146        .251
1944 PHI A 1-O     132        .306
1945 PHI A 1       147        .267
     BLTL         1035        .282
```

SIEBERT, WILFRED CHARLES (SONNY)
B.JAN.14,1937 ST.MARY S,MO.
```
1964 CLE A P        41   42   7- 9
1965 CLE A P        39   40  16- 8
1966 CLE A P             34  16- 8
1967 CLE A P             34  10-12
1968 CLE A P        31   33  12-10
1969 CLE A /P             2   0- 1
     BOS A P             43  14-10
1970 BOS A P             33  15- 8
1971 BOS A P             32  16-10
1972 BOS A P        32   33  12-12
1973 BOS A /P             2   0- 1
     TEX A P             25   7-11
1974 STL N P             28   8- 8
1975 SD  N /P        6    7   3- 2
     OAK A P             17   4- 4
     BRTR          399  405 140-114
```

SIEBLER, DWIGHT LEROY
B.AUG.5,1937 COLUMBUS,NEB.
```
1963 MIN A P         7        2- 1
1964 MIN A P         9        0- 0
1965 MIN A /P        7        0- 0
1966 MIN A /P       23        2- 2
1967 MIN A /P        2        0- 0
     BRTR           48        4- 3
```

SIEFKE, FREDERICK EDWIN
B.MAR.27,1870 NEW YORK,N.Y.
D.APR.18,1893 NEW YORK,N.Y.
```
1890 BRO AA 3       16        .137
```

SIEGEL, JOHN
B.YORK,PA.
```
1884 KEY U 3         8        .226
```

SIEGLE, JOHN HERBERT
B.JULY 8,1874 URBANA,OHIO
D.FEB.12,1968 URBANA,OHIO
```
1905 CIN N O        16        .304
1906 CIN N O        21        .118
     BRTR           37        .202
```

SIEMER, OSCAR SYLVESTER (COTTON)
B.AUG.14,1901 ST.LOUIS,MO.
D.DEC.5,1959 ST.LOUIS,MO.
```
1925 BOS N C        16        .304
1926 BOS N C        31        .205
     BRTR           47        .244
```

SIEVER, EDWARD T.
B.APR.2,1878 LEWISTOWN,ILL.
D.FEB.5,1920 DETROIT,MICH.
```
1901 DET A P        37       18-11
1902 DET A P        25        8-13
1903 STL A P        32       14-15
1904 STL A P        30       11-16
1906 DET A P        29       14-10
1907 DET A P        38       19-10
1908 DET A P        11        2- 6
     BLTL          202       86-81
```

SIEVERS, ROY EDWARD
(ROY) OR (SQUIRREL)
B.NOV.18,1926 ST.LOUIS,MO.
```
1949 STL A 3-O     140        .306
1950 STL A 3-O     113        .238
1951 STL A O        31        .225
1952 STL A 1        11        .200
1953 STL A 1        92        .270
1954 WAS A 1-O     145        .232
1955 WAS A 1-3-O   144        .271
1956 WAS A 1-O     152        .253
1957 WAS A 1-O     152        .301
1958 WAS A 1-O     148        .295
1959 WAS A 1-O     115        .242
1960 CHI A 1-O     127        .295
1961 CHI A 1       141        .295
1962 PHI N 1-O     144        .262
1963 PHI N 1       138        .240
1964 PHI N 1        49        .183
     WAS A 1        33        .172
1965 WAS A /1       12        .190
     BRTR         1887        .267
```

SIFFEL, FRANK
B.PHILADELPHIA,PA.
```
1884 ATH AA C        7        .143
1885 ATH AA C-O      3        .100
                    10        .129
```

SIGAFOOS, FRANCIS LEONARD
B.MAR.21,1904 EASTON,PA.
D.APR.12,1968 INDIANAPOLIS,IND.
```
1926 PHI A S        13        .255
1929 DET A 2-S-3    14        .174
     CHI A H         7        .333
1931 CIN N S-3      21        .169
     BRTR           55        .201
```

SIGLIN, WESLEY PETER (PADDY)
B.SEPT.24,1891 AURELIA,IOWA
D.AUG.5,1956 OAKLAND,CAL.
```
1914 PIT N 2        14        .154
1915 PIT N 2         6        .285
1916 PIT N 2         3        .250
     BRTR           23        .180
```

SIGMAN, WESLEY TRIPLETT (TRIPP)
B.JAN.17,1899 MOORESVILLE,N.C.
D.MAR.8,1971 AUGUSTA,GA.
```
1929 PHI N O        10        .517
1930 PHI N O        52        .270
     BLTR           62        .325
```

SIGNER, WALTER DONALD ALOYSIUS
B.OCT.12,1910 NEW YORK,N.Y.
D.JULY 23,1974 GREENWICH,CONN.
```
1943 CHI N P         4        2- 1
1945 CHI N P         6        0- 0
     BRTR           10        2- 1
```

SIGSBY, SETH DEWITT
B.TROY,N.Y.
```
1893 NY N P          1        0- 0
```

SILBER, EDWARD JAMES
B.JUNE 6,1914 PHILADELPHIA,PA.
```
1937 STL A O        22        .313
1939 STL A H         1        .000
     BRTR           23        .310
```

SILCH, EDWARD (BALDY)
B.FEB.22,1865 ST.LOUIS,MO.
D.JAN.15,1895 ST.LOUIS,MO.
```
1888 BRO AA O       13        .260
     TR
```

SILVA, DANIEL JAMES
B.OCT.5,1896 EVERETT,MASS.
D.APR.4,1974 HYANNIS,MASS.
```
1919 WAS A 3         1        .250
     BRTR
```

SILVERA, AARON ALBERT (AL)
B.AUG.26,1935 SAN DIEGO,CAL.
```
1955 CIN N O        13        .143
1956 CIN N O         1        .000
     BRTR           14        .143
```

SILVERA, CHARLES ANTHONY RYAN
(CHARLIE) OR (SWEDE)
B.OCT.13,1924 SAN FRANCISCO,CAL
```
1948 NY  A C         4        .571
1949 NY  A C        58        .315
1950 NY  A C        18        .160
1951 NY  A C        18        .275
1952 NY  A C        20        .327
1953 NY  A C-3      42        .280
1954 NY  A C        20        .270
1955 NY  A C        14        .192
1956 NY  A C         7        .222
1957 CHI N C        26        .208
     BRTR          227        .282
```

SILVERIO, LUIS PASCUAL
(DELMONTE)
B.OCT.23,1956 VILLA GONZALEZ,D.R
```
1978 KC A /O         8        .545
     BRTR
```

SILVERIO, TOMAS ROBERTO (TOM)
B.OCT.14,1945 SANTIAGO,D.R.
```
1970 CAL A /O-1     15        .000
1971 CAL A /O        3        .333
1972 CAL A /O       13        .167
     BLTL           31        .100
```

SILVERMAN, MICHAEL
[PLAYED UNDER NAME OF JESSE BAKER]

SILVESTRI, KENNETH JOSEPH
(KEN) OR (HAWK)
B.MAY 3,1916 CHICAGO,ILL.
```
1939 CHI A C        22        .173
1940 CHI A C        28        .250
1941 NY  A C        17        .250
1946 NY  A C        13        .286
1947 NY  A C         3        .200
1949 PHI N C-2-S     4        .000
1950 PHI N C        11        .250
1951 PHI N C-2       4        .222
     BBTR          102        .217
```
NON-PLAYING MANAGER
ATL[N] 1967 [INTERIM]

SIMA, ALBERT (AL)
B.OCT.7,1921 MAHWAH,N.J.
```
1950 WAS A P        17        4- 5
1951 WAS A P        18        3- 7
1953 WAS A P        31        2- 3
1954 CHI A P         5        0- 1
     PHI A P        29        2- 5
     BRTL          100       11-21
```

SIMMONS, ALOYSIUS HARRY
(AL) OR (BUCKETFOOT AL)
[REAL NAME ALOYS SZYMANSKI]
B.MAY 22,1902 MILWAUKEE,WIS.
D.MAY 26,1956 MILWAUKEE,WIS.

YR	CL	LEA	POS	GP	G	REC
1924	PHI	A	O		152	.308
1925	PHI	A	O		153	.386
1926	PHI	A	O		147	.343
1927	PHI	A	O		106	.392
1928	PHI	A	O		119	.351
1929	PHI	A	O		143	.365
1930	PHI	A	O		138	.381
1931	PHI	A	O		128	.390
1932	PHI	A	O		154	.322
1933	CHI	A	O		146	.331
1934	CHI	A	O		138	.344
1935	CHI	A	O		128	.267
1936	DET	A	O		143	.327
1937	WAS	A	O		103	.279
1938	WAS	A	O		125	.302
1939	BOS	N	O		93	.282
	CIN	N	O		9	.143
1940	PHI	A	O		37	.309
1941	PHI	A	O		9	.125
1943	BOS	A	O		40	.203
1944	PHI	A	O		4	.500
		BRTR			2215	.334

SIMMONS, CURTIS THOMAS (CURT)
B.MAY.19,1929 EGYPT,PA.

YR	CL	LEA	POS	GP	G	REC
1947	PHI	N	P		1	1- 0
1948	PHI	N	P		31	7-13
1949	PHI	N	P	38	39	4-10
1950	PHI	N	P	31	34	17- 8
1952	PHI	N	P		28	14- 8
1953	PHI	N	P		32	16-13
1954	PHI	N	P	34	38	14-15
1955	PHI	N	P	25	27	8- 8
1956	PHI	N	P	33	39	15-10
1957	PHI	N	P	32	38	12-11
1958	PHI	N	P	29	38	7-14
1959	PHI	N	P	7	8	0- 0
1960	PHI	N	P		4	0- 0
	STL	N	P	23	29	7- 4
1961	STL	N	P	30	32	9-10
1962	STL	N	P		31	10-10
1963	STL	N	P		32	15- 9
1964	STL	N	P		34	18- 9
1965	STL	N	P		34	9-15
1966	STL	N	P		10	1- 1
	CHI	N	P		19	4- 7
1967	CHI	N	P		17	3- 7
	CAL	A	P		14	2- 1
		BLTL		569	609	193-183

SIMMONS, GEORGE WASHINGTON (HACK)
B.JAN.29,1885 BROOKLYN,N.Y.
D.APR.26,1942 ARVERNE,N.Y.

YR	CL	LEA	POS	GP	G	REC
1910	DET	A	1		42	.191
1912	NY	A	2		110	.239
1914	BAL	F	2-O		113	.269
1915	BAL	F	O		39	.205
		BRTR			304	.242

SIMMONS, JOHN EARL
B.JULY 7,1924 BIRMINGHAM,ALA.

YR	CL	LEA	POS	GP	G	REC
1949	WAS	A	O		62	.215
		BRTR				

SIMMONS, JOSEPH S.
B.JUNE 13,1845 NEW YORK,N.Y.

YR	CL	LEA	POS	GP	G	REC
1871	CHI	NA	1-O		27	-
1872	CLE	NA	1-O		17	.230
1875	WES	NA	1-O		13	-
					57	-

NON-PLAYING MANAGER WIL[U] 1884

SIMMONS, LEWIS
B.AUG.27,1838 NEW CASTLE,PA.
D.SEPT.2,1911 ALLENTOWN,PA.
NON-PLAYING MANAGER ATH[AA]1886

SIMMONS, PATRICK CLEMENT
[REAL NAME PATRICK CLEMENT SIMONI]
B.NOV.29,1908 WATERVLIET,N.Y.
D.JULY 3,1968 ALBANY,N.Y.

YR	CL	LEA	POS	GP	G	REC
1928	BOS	A	P		31	0- 2
1929	BOS	A	P		2	0- 0
		BRTR			33	0- 2

SIMMONS, TED LYLE
B.AUG.9,1949 HIGHLAND PARK,MICH.

YR	CL	LEA	POS	GP	G	REC
1968	STL	N	/C		2	.333
1969	STL	N	/C		5	.214
1970	STL	N	C		82	.243
1971	STL	N	*C		133	.304
1972	STL	N	*C-1		152	.303
1973	STL	N	*C/1-O		161	.310
1974	STL	N	*C-1		152	.272
1975	STL	N	*C/1-O		157	.332
1976	STL	N	*C-1/O-3		150	.291
1977	STL	N	*C/O		150	.318
1978	STL	N	*C-O		152	.287
		BBTR			1296	.298

SIMON, HENRY JOSEPH (HANK)
B.AUG.25,1862 HAWKINSVILLE,N.Y.
D.JAN.1,1925 ALBANY,N.Y.

YR	CL	LEA	POS	GP	G	REC
1887	CLE	AA	O		3	.100
1890	BRO	AA	O		90	.248
1890	SYR	AA	O		37	.294
		BRTR			130	.257

SIMON, MICHAEL EDWARD
B.APR.13,1883 HAYDEN,IND.
D.JUNE 10,1963 LOS ANGELES,CAL.

YR	CL	LEA	POS	GP	G	REC
1909	PIT	N	C		12	.167
1910	PIT	N	C		20	.213
1911	PIT	N	C		68	.228
1912	PIT	N	C		42	.301
1913	PIT	N	C		92	.247
1914	STL	F	C		93	.219
1915	BRO	F	C		47	.175
		BRTR			374	.229

SIMON, SYLVESTER ADAM (SAMMY)
B.DEC.14,1897 EVANSVILLE,IND.
D.FEB.28,1973 CHANDLER,IND.

YR	CL	LEA	POS	GP	G	REC
1923	STL	A	H		1	.000
1924	STL	A	S-3		23	.250
		BRTR			24	.242

SIMONI, PATRICK CLEMENT
[PLAYED UNDER NAME OF
PATRICK CLEMENT SIMMONS]

SIMONS, MELBERN ELLIS (BUTCH)
B.JULY 1,1900 CARLYLE,ILL.
D.NOV.10,1974 PADUCAH,KY.

YR	CL	LEA	POS	GP	G	REC
1931	CHI	A	O		68	.275
1932	CHI	A	O		7	.000
		BLTR			75	.268

SIMPSON, HARRY LEON (HARRY)
(SUITCASE) OR (GOODY)
B.DEC.3,1925 ATLANTA,GA.

YR	CL	LEA	POS	GP	G	REC
1951	CLE	A	1-O		122	.229
1952	CLE	A	1-O		146	.266
1953	CLE	A	1-O		82	.227
1955	CLE	A	H		3	.000
	KC	A	1-O		112	.301
1956	KC	A	1-O		141	.293
1957	KC	A	1-O		50	.296
	NY	A	1-O		75	.250
1958	NY	A	O		24	.216
	KC	A	1-O		78	.264
1959	KC	A	1		8	.286
	CHI	A	1-O		38	.187
	PIT	N	O		9	.267
		BLTR			888	.266

SIMPSON, JOE ALLEN
B.DEC.31,1951 PURCELL,OKLA.

YR	CL	LEA	POS	GP	G	REC
1975	LA	N	/O		9	.333
1976	LA	N	O		23	.133
1977	LA	N	O/1		29	.174
1978	LA	N	O		10	.400
		BLTL			71	.188

SIMPSON, MARTIN
B.BALTIMORE,MD.

YR	CL	LEA	POS	GP	G	REC
1873	MAR	NA	C-2		4	-

SIMPSON, RICHARD CHARLES (DICK)
B.JULY 28,1943 WASHINGTON,D.C.

YR	CL	LEA	POS	GP	G	REC
1962	LA	A	O		6	.250
1964	LA	A	O		21	.140
1965	CAL	A	/O		8	.222
1966	CIN	N	O		92	.238
1967	CIN	N	O		44	.259
1968	STL	N	O		26	.232
	HOU	N	O		59	.186
1969	NY	A	/O		6	.273
	SEA	A	O		26	.176
		BRTR			288	.207

SIMPSON, STEVEN EDWARD (STEVE)
B.AUG.30,1948 ST.JOSEPH,MO.

YR	CL	LEA	POS	GP	G	REC
1972	SD	N	/P		9	0- 2
		BRTR				

SIMPSON, THOMAS LEO (DUKE)
B.SEPT.15,1927 COLUMBUS,OHIO

YR	CL	LEA	POS	GP	G	REC
1953	CHI	N	P		30	1- 2
		BRTR				

SIMPSON, WAYNE KIRBY
B.DEC.2,1948 LOS ANGELES,CAL.

YR	CL	LEA	POS	GP	G	REC
1970	CIN	N	P	26	27	14- 3
1971	CIN	N	P		22	4- 7
1972	CIN	N	P		24	8- 5
1973	KC	A	P		16	3- 4
1975	PHI	N	/P		7	1- 0
1977	CAL	A	P		27	6-12
		BRTR		122	123	36-31

SIMS, CLARENCE (PETE)
B.MAY 24,1891 CROWN CITY,OHIO
D.DEC.2,1968 DALLAS,TEX.

YR	CL	LEA	POS	GP	G	REC
1915	STL	A	P		3	1- 0
		BRTR				

SIMS, DUANE B (DUKE)
B.JUNE 5,1941 SALT LAKE CITY,UT.

YR	CL	LEA	POS	GP	G	REC
1964	CLE	A	C		2	.000
1965	CLE	A	C		48	.178
1966	CLE	A	C		52	.263
1967	CLE	A	C		88	.202
1968	CLE	A	C-1/O		122	.249
1969	CLE	A	*C/O-1		114	.236
1970	CLE	A	C-O-1		110	.264
1971	LA	N	C		90	.274
1972	LA	N	C		51	.192
	DET	A	C/O		38	.316
1973	DET	A	C/O		80	.242
	NY	A	/C		4	.333
1974	NY	A	/C		5	.133
	TEX	A	C/O		39	.208
		BLTR			843	.239

SIMS, GREGORY EMMETT (GREG)
B.JUNE 28,1946 SAN FRANCISCO,CAL

YR	CL	LEA	POS	GP	G	REC
1966	HOU	N	/O		7	.167
		BBTR				

SINCOCK, HERBERT SYLVESTER (BERT)
B.SEPT.8,1887 BARKERVILLE,B.C.
CANADA
D.AUG.1,1946 HOUGHTON,MICH.

YR	CL	LEA	POS	GP	G	REC
1908	CIN	N	P		1	0- 0

SINER, HOSEA JOHN
B.MAR.20,1885 SHELBURN,IND.
D.JUNE 11,1948 NEW LEBANON,IND.

YR	CL	LEA	POS	GP	G	REC
1909	BOS	N	3		10	.130
		BRTR				

SINGER, WILLIAM ROBERT (BILL)
OR (THE SINGER THROWING MACHINE)
B.APR.24,1944 LOS ANGELES,CAL.

YR	CL	LEA	POS	GP	G	REC
1964	LA	N	P		2	0- 1
1965	LA	N	/P		2	0- 0
1966	LA	N	/P		3	0- 0
1967	LA	N	P	32	34	12- 8
1968	LA	N	P		37	13-17
1969	LA	N	P		41	20-12
1970	LA	N	P		16	8- 5
1971	LA	N	P		31	10-17
1972	LA	N	P		26	6-16
1973	CAL	A	P		40	20-14
1974	CAL	A	P		14	7- 4
1975	CAL	A	P		29	7-15
1976	TEX	A	P		10	4- 1
	MIN	A	P		26	9- 9
1977	TOR	A	P		13	2- 8
		BRTR		322	324	118-127

SINGLETON, BERT ELMER
(ELMER) OR (SMOKY)
B.JUNE 26,1918 OGDEN,UTAH

YR	CL	LEA	POS	GP	G	REC
1945	BOS	N	P		7	1- 4
1946	BOS	N	P	15	16	0- 1
1947	PIT	N	P	36	41	2- 2
1948	PIT	N	P		38	4- 6
1950	WAS	A	P		21	1- 2
1957	CHI	N	P	5	6	0- 1
1958	CHI	N	P		2	1- 0
1959	CHI	N	P		21	2- 1
		BRTR		145	152	11-17
		BB 1957-58				

SINGLETON, JOHN EDWARD (SHERIFF)
B.NOV.27,1896 GALLIPOLIS,OHIO
D.OCT.23,1937 DAYTON,OHIO

YR	CL	LEA	POS	GP	G	REC
1922	PHI	N	P		22	1-10
		BRTR				

SINGLETON, KENNETH WAYNE (KEN)
B.JUNE 10,1947 NEW YORK,N.Y.

YR	CL	LEA	POS	GP	G	REC
1970	NY	N	O		69	.263
1971	NY	N	O		115	.245
1972	MON	N	*O		142	.274
1973	MON	N	*O		162	.302
1974	MON	N	*O		148	.276
1975	BAL	A	*O		155	.300
1976	BAL	A	*O-D		154	.278
1977	BAL	A	*O		152	.328
1978	BAL	A	*O		149	.293
		BBTR			1246	.289

SINGTON, FREDERICK WILLIAM
B.FEB.24,1910 BRIMINGHAM,ALA.

YR	CL	LEA	POS	GP	G	REC
1934	WAS	A	O		9	.286
1935	WAS	A	O		20	.182
1936	WAS	A	O		25	.319
1937	WAS	A	O		78	.237
1938	BRO	N	O		17	.358
1939	BRO	N	O		32	.274
		BRTR			181	.273

SIPEK, RICHARD FRANCIS
B.JAN.16,1923 CHICAGO,ILL.

YR	CL	LEA	POS	GP	G	REC
1945	CIN	N	O		82	.244
		BLTR				

SIPIN, JOHN WHITE
B.AUG.29,1946 WATSONVILLE,CAL.

YR	CL	LEA	POS	GP	G	REC
1969	SD	N	2		68	.223
		BRTR				

```
YR  CL LEA POS      GP   G    REC
```

SISK, TOMMIE WAYNE
B.APR.12,1942 ARDMORE,OKLA.
```
1962 PIT N  P            5    0- 2
1963 PIT N  P           57    1- 3
1964 PIT N  P           42    1- 4
1965 PIT N  P       38  39    7- 3
1966 PIT N  P           34   10- 5
1967 PIT N  P           37   13-13
1968 PIT N  P           33    5- 5
1969 SD  N  P           53    2-13
1970 CHI A  P           17    1- 1
        BRTR       316 317   40-49
```

SISLER, DAVID MICHAEL (DAVE)
B.OCT.16,1931 ST.LOUIS,MO.
```
1956 BOS A  P           39    9- 8
1957 BOS A  P           22    7- 8
1958 BOS A  P           30    8- 9
1959 BOS A  P            3    0- 0
     DET A  P           32    1- 3
1960 DET A  P           41    7- 5
1961 WAS A  P           45    2- 8
1962 CIN N  P           35    4- 3
        BRTR           247   38-44
```

SISLER, GEORGE HAROLD
(GEORGEOUS GEORGE)
B.MAR.24,1893 MANCHESTER,OHIO
D.MAR.26,1973 RICHMOND HEIGHTS,MO.
```
1915 STL A  P-1-   15  81    4- 4
            O                .285
1916 STL A  P-1-    3 151    1- 2
            3                .305
1917 STL A  1-2       135    .353
1918 STL A  P-1     2 114    0- 0
                             .341
1919 STL A  1         132    .352
1920 STL A  P-1     1 154    0- 0
                             .407
1921 STL A  1         138    .371
1922 STL A  1         142    .420
1924 STL A  M-1       151    .305
1925 STL A  M-P-    1 150    0- 0
            1                .345
1926 STL A  M-P-    1 150    0- 0
            1                .289
1927 STL A  1         149    .327
1928 WAS A  1-0        20    .245
     BOS N  P-1     1 118    0- 0
                             .340
1929 BOS N  1         154    .326
1930 BOS N  1         116    .309
        BRTL       24 2055   5- 6
                             .340
```

SISLER, RICHARD ALLAN (DICK)
B.NOV.2,1920 ST.LOUIS,MO.
```
1946 STL N  1-0        83    .260
1947 STL N  1-0        46    .203
1948 PHI N  1         121    .274
1949 PHI N  1         121    .289
1950 PHI N  O         141    .296
1951 PHI N  O         125    .287
1952 CIN N  O          11    .185
     STL N  1         119    .261
1953 STL N  1          32    .296
        BRTR          799    .276
```
NON-PLAYING MANAGER CIN[N] 1964-65

SISTI, SEBASTIAN DANIEL (SIBBY)
B.JULY 26,1920 BUFFALO,N.Y.
```
1939 BOS N  2-S-3      63    .226
1940 BOS N  2-3       123    .251
1941 BOS N  2-S-3     140    .259
1942 BOS N  2-0       129    .211
1946 BOS N  3           1    .000
1947 BOS N  2-S        56    .281
1948 BOS N  2-S        83    .244
1949 BOS N  2-S-3     101    .257
1950 BOS N  1-2-S-3-0  69    .171
1951 BOS N  1-2-S-3-0 114    .279
1952 BOS N  2-S-3-0    90    .212
1953 MIL N  2-S-3      38    .217
1954 MIL N  H           9    .000
        BRTR         1016    .244
```

SITTON, CARL VETTER
B.SEPT.22,1882 PENDLETON,S.C.
D.SEPT.11,1931 VALDOSTA,GA.
```
1909 CLE A  P          14    3- 2
        TR
```

SIVESS, PETER
B.SEPT.23,1913 SOUTH RIVER,N.J.
```
1936 PHI N  P          17    3- 4
1937 PHI N  P           6    1- 1
1938 PHI N  P          39    3- 6
        BRTR           62    7-11
```

SIXSMITH, EDWARD
B.FEB.26,1863 PHILADELPHIA,PA.
D.DEC.12,1926 PHILADELPHIA,PA.
```
1884 PHI N  C           1    .000
        BRTR
```

SIZEMORE, THEODORE CRAWFORD (TED
B.APR.15,1945 GADSDEN,ALA.
```
1969 LA  N  *2-S/O    159    .271
1970 LA  N  2/O-S      96    .306
1971 STL N  2-S-O/3   135    .264
1972 STL N  *2        120    .264
1973 STL N  *2/3      142    .282
1974 STL N  *2/S-O    129    .250
1975 STL N  *2        153    .240
1976 LA  N  2/3-C      84    .241
1977 PHI N  *2        152    .281
1978 PHI N  *2        108    .219
        BRTR         1278    .263
```

SKAFF, FRANCIS MICHAEL (FRANK)
B.SEPT.30,1913 LA CROSSE,WIS.
```
1935 BRO N  3           6    .545
1943 PHI A  1-S-3      32    .281
        BRTR           38    .320
```

SKAGGS, DAVID LINDSEY (DAVE)
B.JUNE 12,1951 SANTA MONICA,CAL.
```
1977 BAL A  C          80    .287
1978 BAL A  C          36    .151
        BRTR          116    .248
```
NON-PLAYING MANAGER DET[A] 1966

SKAUGSTAD, DAVID WENDELL
B.JAN.10,1940 ALGONA,IOWA
```
1957 CIN N  P           2    0- 0
        BLTL
```

SKEELS, DAVID
B.DEC.29,1892 WASHINGTON STATE
D.DEC.2,1926 SPOKANE,WASH.
```
1910 DET A  P           1    0- 0
        BLTR
```

SKETCHLEY, HARRY CLEMENT (BUD)
B.MAR.30,1919 VIRDEN,MAN.,CAN.
```
1942 CHI A  O          13    .194
        BLTL
```

SKIDMORE, ROBERT ROE (ROE)
B.OCT.30,1945 DECATUR,ILL.
```
1970 CHI N  /H          1   1.000
        BRTR
```

SKIFF, WILLIAM FRANKLIN
B.OCT.16,1895 NEW ROCHELLE,N.Y.
D.DEC.25,1976 BRONXVILLE,N.Y.
```
1921 PIT N  C          16    .289
1926 NY  A  C           6    .099
        BRTR           22    .250
```

SKINNER
```
1884 BAL U  O           1    .333
     CHI U  O           1    .333
                        2    .333
```

SKINNER, ELISHA HARRISON (CAMP)
B.JUNE 25,1897 DOUGLASVILLE,GA.
D.AUG.4,1944 DOUGLASVILLE,GA.
```
1922 NY  A  O          27    .182
1923 BOS A  O           7    .230
        BLTR           34    .196
```

SKINNER, ROBERT RALPH (BOB)
B.OCT.3,1931 LAJOLLA,CAL.
```
1954 PIT N  1-0       132    .249
1956 PIT N  1-3-0     113    .202
1957 PIT N  1-3-0     126    .305
1958 PIT N  O         144    .321
1959 PIT N  1-0       143    .280
1960 PIT N  O         145    .273
1961 PIT N  O         119    .268
1962 PIT N  O         144    .302
1963 PIT N  O          34    .270
     CIN N  O          72    .253
1964 CIN N  O          25    .220
     STL N  O          55    .271
1965 STL N  O          80    .309
1966 STL N  H          49    .156
        BLTR         1381    .277
```
NON-PLAYING MANAGER PHI[N] 1968-69
SD[N] 1977 (INTERIM)

SKIZAS, LOUIS PETER (LOU)
OR (THE NERVOUS GREEK)
B.JUNE 2,1932 CHICAGO,ILL.
```
1956 NY  A  H           6    .167
     KC  A  O          83    .316
1957 KC  A  3-0       119    .245
1958 DET A  3-0        23    .242
1959 CHI A  O           8    .077
        BRTR          239    .270
```

SKOK, CRAIG RICHARD
B.SEP.1,1947 DOBBS FERRY,N.Y.
```
1973 BOS A  P          11    0- 1
1976 TEX A  /P          9    0- 1
1978 ATL N  P          43    3- 2
        BRTL           63    3- 4
```

SKOPEC, JOHN S. (BUCKSHOT)
B.MAY 8,1880 CHICAGO,ILL.
D.OCT.12,1912 CHICAGO,ILL.
```
1901 CHI A  P          10    6- 4
1903 DET A  P           6    2- 2
        BLTL           16    8- 6
```

SKOWRON, WILLIAM JOSEPH
(BILL) OR (MOOSE)
B.DEC.18,1930 CHICAGO,ILL.
```
1954 NY  A  1-2-3      87    .340
1955 NY  A  1-3       108    .319
1956 NY  A  1-3       134    .308
1957 NY  A  1         122    .304
1958 NY  A  1-3       126    .273
1959 NY  A  1          74    .298
1960 NY  A  1         146    .309
1961 NY  A  1         150    .267
1962 NY  A  1         140    .270
1963 LA  N  1-3        89    .203
1964 NY  A  1          73    .271
     CHI A  1          73    .293
1965 CHI A  *1        146    .274
1966 CHI A  1         120    .249
1967 CHI A  /H          8    .000
     CAL A  1          62    .220
        BRTR         1658    .282
```

SLADE, GORDON LEIGH (OSKIE)
B.OCT.9,1904 SALT LAKE CITY,UTAH
D.JAN.2,1974 LONG BEACH,CAL.
```
1930 BRO N  S          25    .216
1931 BRO N  S          85    .239
1932 BRO N  S-3        79    .240
1933 STL N  2-S        39    .113
1934 CIN N  2-S       138    .285
1935 CIN N  2-S-3-0    71    .281
        BRTR          437    .257
```

SLADEN, ARTHUR
B.LOWELL,MASS.
```
1884 BOS U  O           2    .000
```

SLAGLE, JAMES FRANKLIN (JIMMY)
(RABBIT) OR (SHORTY)
B.JULY 11,1873 WORTHVILLE,PA.
D.MAY 10,1956 CHICAGO,ILL.
```
1899 WAS N  O         146    .273
1900 PHI N  O         141    .299
1901 PHI N  O          48    .189
     BOS N  O          65    .278
1902 CHI N  O         114    .313
1903 CHI N  O         139    .298
1904 CHI N  O         120    .260
1905 CHI N  O         159    .269
1906 CHI N  O         127    .239
1907 CHI N  O         136    .258
1908 CHI N  O         101    .222
        BLTR         1292    .269
```

SLAGLE, JOHN A.
B.LAWRENCE,IND.
```
1891 CIN AA P           1    0- 0
```

SLAGLE, WALTER JENNINGS
B.DEC.15,1878 KENTON,OHIO
D.JUNE 17,1974 SAN GABRIEL,CAL.
```
1910 CIN N  P           1    0- 0
        BBTR
```

SLAPNICKA, CYRIL CHARLES (CY)
B.MAR.23,1886 CEDAR RAPIDS,IOWA
```
1911 CHI N  P           3    0- 2
1918 PIT N  P           7    1- 4
        BBTR           10    1- 6
```

SLAPPEY, JOHN HENRY
B.AUG.8,1898 ALBANY,GA.
D.JUNE 10,1957 MARIETTA,GA.
```
1920 PHI A  P           3    0- 1
        BLTL
```

SLATON, JAMES MICHAEL (JIM)
B.JUNE 19,1950 LONG BEACH,CAL.
```
1971 MIL A  P          26   10- 8
1972 MIL A  P           9    1- 6
1973 MIL A  P          38   13-15
1974 MIL A  P          40   13-16
1975 MIL A  P          37   11-18
1976 MIL A  P          38   14-15
1977 MIL A  P          32   10-14
1978 DET A  P          35   17-11
        BRTR          255   89-103
```

SLATTERY, JOHN TERRENCE (JACK)
B.JAN.6,1878 S.BOSTON,MASS.
D.JULY 17,1949
```
1901 BOS A  C           1    .500
1903 CLE A  1           4    .000
     CHI A  C-1        61    .231
1906 STL N  C           2    .000
1909 WAS A  C          32    .214
        TR            100    .221
```
NON-PLAYING MANAGER BOS[N] 1928

YR CL LEA POS   GP   G   REC

SLATTERY, MICHAEL J.
B.OCT.28,1865 BOSTON,MASS.
D.OCT.16,1904 BOSTON,MASS.
1884 BOS U O   105   .208
1888 NY N O   103   .245
1889 NY N O   12   .286
1890 NY N P   97   .290
1891 CIN N O   41   .221
     WAS AA O   15   .283
          BLTL   373   .249

SLATTERY, PHILIP RYAN
B.FEB.25,1893 HARPER,IOWA
D.MAR.2,1968 LONG BEACH,CAL.
1915 PIT N P   3   0- 0
          BRTL

SLAUGHTER, BYRON ATKINS (BARNEY)
B.OCT.6,1884 SMYRNA,DEL.
D.MAY 17,1961 PHILADELPHIA,PA.
1910 PHI N P   8   0- 1
          BRTR

SLAUGHTER, ENOS BRADSHER (COUNTRY)
B.APR.27,1916 ROXBORO,N.C.
1938 STL N O   112   .276
1939 STL N O   149   .320
1940 STL N O   140   .306
1941 STL N O   113   .311
1942 STL N O   152   .318
1946 STL N O   156   .300
1947 STL N O   147   .294
1948 STL N O   146   .321
1949 STL N O   151   .336
1950 STL N O   148   .290
1951 STL N O   123   .281
1952 STL N O   140   .300
1953 STL N O   143   .291
1954 NY A O   69   .248
1955 NY A H   10   .111
     KC A O   108   .322
1956 KC A O   91   .278
     NY A O   24   .289
1957 NY A O   96   .254
1958 NY A O   77   .304
1959 NY A O   74   .172
     MIL N O   11   .167
          BLTR   2380   .300

SLAUGHTER, STERLING F.
B.NOV.18,1941 DANVILLE,ILL.
1964 CHI N P   20   2- 4
          BRTR

SLAYBACK, ELBERT (SCOTTIE)
B.OCT.5,1901 PADUCAH,KY.
1926 NY N 2   2   .000
          BRTR

SLAYBACK, WILLIAM GROVER (BILL)
B.FEB.21,1948 HOLLYWOOD,CAL.
1972 DET A P   23   5- 6
1973 DET A /P   3   0- 0
1974 DET A P   16   1- 3
          BRTR   42   6- 9

SLAYTON, FOSTER HERBERT (STEVE)
B.APR.26,1902 BARRE,VT.
1928 BOS A P   3   0- 0
          BRTR

SLEATER, LOUIS MORTIMER (LOU)
B.SEPT.8,1926 ST.LOUIS,MO.
1950 STL A P   1   0- 0
1951 STL A P   20   25   1- 9
1952 STL A P   4   0- 1
     WAS A P   14   15   4- 2
1955 KC A P   16   21   1- 1
1956 MIL N P   25   2- 2
1957 DET A P   41   3- 3
1958 DET A P   4   0- 0
     BAL A P   6   9   1- 0
          BLTL   131   145 12-18

SLOAN, BRUCE ADAMS
(BRUCE) OR (FATSO)
B.OCT.4,1914 MC ALESTER,OKLA.
D.OCT.23,1973 OKLAHOMA CITY,OKLA.
1944 NY N O   59   .269
          BLTL

SLOAN, YALE YEASTMAN (TOD)
B.DEC.24,1890 MADISONVILLE,TENN
D.SEPT.12,1956 AKRON,OHIO
1913 STL A O   7   .269
1917 STL A O   109   .230
1919 STL A O   27   .238
          BLTR   143   .234

SLOAT, DWAIN CLIFFORD (LEFTY)
B.DEC.1,1918 NOKOMIS,ILL.
1948 BRO N P   4   0- 1
1949 CHI N P   5   0- 0
          BRTL   9' 0- 1

SLOCUM, RONALD REECE (RON)
B.JULY 2,1945 MODESTO,CAL.
1969 SD N /2-3-S   13   .292
1970 SD N C-S-3/2   60   .141
1971 SD N /3   7   .000
          BRTR   80   .150

SMADT, JAN
[PLAYED UNDER NAME OF
JOHN WILLIAM SMITH]

SMALL, CHARLES ALBERT
B.OCT.24,1905 AUBURN,ME.
D.JAN.14,1953 AUBURN,ME.
1930 BOS A O   25   .167
          BLTR

SMALL, GEORGE HENRY (HANK)
B.JULY 31,1953 ATLANTA,GA.
1978 ATL N /1   1   .000
          BRTR

SMALL, JAMES ARTHUR (JIM)
B.MAR.8,1937 PORTLAND,ORE.
1955 DET A O   12   .000
1956 DET A O   58   .319
1957 DET A O   36   .214
1958 KC A O   2   .000
          BLTL   108   .270

SMALLEY, ROY FREDERICK JR.
B.OCT.25,1952 LOS ANGELES,CAL.
1975 TEX A S-2/C   78   .228
1976 TEX A 2/S   41   .225
     MIN A *S   103   .271
1977 MIN A *S   150   .231
1978 MIN A *S   158   .273
          BBTR   530   .251

SMALLEY, ROY FREDERICK SR.
B.JUNE 9,1926 SPRINGFIELD,MO.
1948 CHI N S   124   .216
1949 CHI N S   135   .245
1950 CHI N S   154   .230
1951 CHI N S   79   .231
1952 CHI N S   87   .222
1953 CHI N S   82   .249
1954 MIL N 1-2-S   25   .222
1955 PHI N 2-S-3   92   .196
1956 PHI N S   65   .226
1957 PHI N S   28   .161
1958 PHI N S   1   .000
          BRTR   872   .227

SMALLEY, WILLIAM DARWIN (DEACON)
B.JUNE 27,1871 OAKLAND,CAL.
D.OCT.11,1891 BAY CITY,MICH.
1890 CLE N 3   136   .213
1891 WAS AA 3   9   .171
          BRTR   145   .208

SMALLWOOD, WALTER CLAYTON
B.APR.24,1893 DAYTON,MO.
D.APR.29,1967 BALTIMORE,MD.
1917 NY A P   2   0- 0
1919 NY A P   6   0- 0
          BRTR   8   0- 0

SMAZA, JOSEPH PAUL
B.JULY 7,1923 DETROIT,MICH.
1946 CHI A O   2   .200
          BLTL

SMEJKAL, FRANK JOHN
[PLAYED UNDER NAME OF
FRANK JOHN SMYKAL]

SMILEY, WILLIAM B.
B.1856 BALTIMORE,MD.
D.JULY 11,1884 BALTIMORE,MD.
1874 BAL NA 3   2   -
1882 STL AA 2-S-0   58   .208
     BAL AA 2-S   16   .113
                            76   -

SMITH, ALBERT EDGAR
B.OCT.15,1860 NORTH HAVEN,CONN.
1883 BOS N O   29   .217

SMITH, ALEXANDER BENJAMIN
(BROADWAY ALECK)
B.1871 NEW YORK,N.Y.
D.JULY 9,1919 NEW YORK,N.Y.
1897 BRO N C-O   61   .309
1898 BRO N C-O   48   .260
1899 BRO N C   16   .164
     BAL N C-1-O   41   .383
1900 BRO N C-3   7   .240
1901 NY N P-C   1   29   0- 1
                                 .168
1902 BAL N C-1-2-3-O   40   .234
1903 BOS A C   12   .333
1904 CHI N C   10   .173
1906 NY N C-1   14   .185
          TR   1   278   0- 1
                                 .263

SMITH, ALEXANDER CHARLES
B.SEPT.12,1855 TROY,N.Y.
D.MAR.29,1932
1882 TRO N 1   34   .236
     WOR N 1   19   .216
                            53   .230

SMITH, ALFRED JOHN (AL)
B.OCT.12,1907 BELLEVILLE,ILL.
D.APR.28,1977 BROWNSVILLE,TEX.
1934 NY N P   30   3- 5
1935 NY N P   40 10- 8
1936 NY N P   43 14-13
1937 NY N P   33   5- 4
1938 PHI N P   37   1- 4
1939 PHI N P   5   0- 0
1940 CLE A P   31 15- 7
1941 CLE A P   29   30 12-13
1942 CLE A P   30 10-15
1943 CLE A P   29   30 17- 7
1944 CLE A P   28   7-13
1945 CLE A P   21   22   5-12
          BLTL   356   359 99-101

SMITH, ALFRED KENDRICKS
B.DEC.13,1903 NORRISTOWN,PA.
1926 NY N P   1   0- 0
          BRTR

SMITH, ALPHONSE EUGENE
(AL) OR (FUZZY)
B.FEB.7,1928 KIRKWOOD,MO.
1953 CLE A 3-O   47   .240
1954 CLE A S-3-O   131   .281
1955 CLE A 2-S-3-O   154   .306
1956 CLE A 2-3-O   141   .274
1957 CLE A 3-O   135   .247
1958 CLE A 3-O   139   .252
1959 CHI A 3-O   129   .237
1960 CHI A O   142   .315
1961 CHI A 3-O   147   .278
1962 CHI A 3-O   142   .292
1963 BAL A O   120   .272
1964 CLE A 3-O   61   .162
     BOS A 3-O   29   .216
          BRTR   1517   .272

SMITH, ANTHONY (TONY)
B.MAY 14,1884 CHICAGO,ILL.
D.FEB.27,1964 GALVESTON,TEX.
1907 WAS A S   51   .187
1910 BRO N S   106   .181
1911 BRO N S   12   .138
          BRTR   169   .180

SMITH, ARMSTRONG FREDERICK
(KLONDIKE)
B.JAN.4,1887 LONDON,ENGLAND
D.NOV.15,1959 SPRINGFIELD,MASS.
1912 NY N P   7   .185
          BLTL

SMITH, ARTHUR LAIRD
B.JUNE 21,1906 BOSTON,MASS.
1932 CHI A P   3   0- 1
          BRTR

SMITH, BILLY EDWARD
B.JULY 14,1953 HODGE,LA.
1975 CAL A S/1-3   59   .203
1976 CAL A S   13   .375
1977 BAL A *2/S-1-3   109   .215
1978 BAL A 2/S   85   .260
          BBTR   266   .229

SMITH, BOBBY GENE (BOBBY GENE)
B.MAY 28,1934 HOOD RIVER,ORE.
1957 STL N O   93   .211
1958 STL N O   28   .284
1959 STL N O   43   .217
1960 PHI N 3-O   98   .286
1961 PHI N O   79   .253
1962 NY N O   8   .136
     CHI N O   13   .172
     STL N O   91   .231
1965 CAL A O   23   .228
          BRTR   476   .243

SMITH, CALVIN BERNARD (BERNIE)
B.SEP.4,1941 PONCHATOULA,LA.
1970 MIL A O   44   .276
1971 MIL A O   15   .139
          BRTR   59   .232

YR	CL	LEA	POS	GP	G	REC

SMITH, CARL REGINALD (REGGIE)
B.APR.2,1945 SHREVEPORT,LA.

YR	CL	LEA	POS	GP	G	REC
1966	BOS	A	/O		6	.154
1967	BOS	A	*O/2		158	.246
1968	BOS	A	*O		155	.265
1969	BOS	A	*O		143	.309
1970	BOS	A	*O		147	.303
1971	BOS	A	*O		159	.283
1972	BOS	A	*O		131	.270
1973	BOS	A	*O/1		115	.303
1974	STL	N	*O/1		143	.309
1975	STL	N	O-1/3		135	.302
1976	STL	N	1-0-3		47	.216
	LA	N	O/3		65	.280
1977	LA	N	*O		148	.307
1978	LA	N	*O		128	.295
	BBTR				1680	.287

SMITH, CARR E.
B.APR.8,1901 KERNERSVILLE,N.C.

YR	CL	LEA	POS	GP	G	REC
1923	WAS	A	O		5	.111
1924	WAS	A	O		6	.191
	BRTR				11	.150

SMITH, CHARLES E.
B.APR.20,1880 CLEVELAND,OHIO
D.JAN.3,1929 CLEVELAND,OHIO

YR	CL	LEA	POS	GP	G	REC
1902	CLE	A	P		3	0- 1
1906	WAS	A	P		33	9-16
1907	WAS	A	P	36	37	11-21
1908	WAS	A	P	26	30	9-13
1909	WAS	A	P		21	2-12
	BOS	A	P		5	4- 0
1910	BOS	A	P		23	11- 6
1911	BOS	A	P		1	0- 0
	CHI	N	P		7	3- 2
1912	CHI	N	P		21	7- 4
1913	CHI	N	P		20	7- 9
1914	CHI	N	P		16	2- 4
	BRTR			212	217	65-88

SMITH, CHARLES J.
B.DEC.11,1840 BROOKLYN,N.Y.
D.NOV.15,1897

YR	CL	LEA	POS	GP	G	REC
1871	MUT	NA	2-3		15	-

SMITH, CHARLES MARVIN (POP)
B.OCT.12,1856 DIGBY,N.S.,CANADA
D.APR.18,1927 BOSTON,MASS.

YR	CL	LEA	POS	GP	G	REC
1880	CIN	N	2		82	.199
1881	CLE	N	3		10	.118
	WOR	N	2-O		11	.068
	BUF	N	2		3	.000
1882	ATH	AA	2-S-3-O		20	.090
	BAL	AA	O		1	.000
	LOU	AA	S		3	.182
1883	COL	AA	P-2-	2	96	0- 0
			3			.258
1884	COL	AA	2		108	.240
1885	PIT	AA	2		106	.258
1886	PIT	AA	2-S		126	.223
1887	PIT	N	2-S		122	.263
1888	PIT	N	2-S		130	.207
1889	PIT	N	S		72	.210
	BOS	N	S		59	.257
1890	BOS	N	2		134	.229
1891	WAS	AA	2		27	.161
	BRTR			2	1110	0- 0
						.228

SMITH, CHARLES WILLIAM (CHARLEY)
B.SEP.15,1937 CHARLESTON,S.C.

YR	CL	LEA	POS	GP	G	REC
1960	LA	N	3		18	.167
1961	LA	N	S-3		9	.250
	PHI	N	S-3		112	.248
1962	CHI	N	3		65	.207
1963	CHI	N	S		4	.286
1964	CHI	N	3		2	.143
	NY	N	S-3-O		127	.239
1965	NY	N	*3/S-2		135	.244
1966	STL	N	*3/S		116	.266
1967	NY	A	*3		135	.224
1968	NY	A	3		46	.229
1969	CHI	N	/H		2	.000
	BRTR				771	.239

SMITH, CLARENCE OSSIE (POP-BOY)
B.MAY 23,1892 NEWPORT,TENN.
D.FEB.16,1924 SWEETWATER,TEX.

YR	CL	LEA	POS	GP	G	REC
1913	CHI	A	P		15	0- 1
1916	CLE	A	P		5	1- 3
1917	CLE	A	P		6	0- 1
	BRTR				26	1- 5

SMITH, CLAY JAMIESON
B.SEPT.11,1914 CAMBRIDGE,KAN.

YR	CL	LEA	POS	GP	G	REC
1938	CLE	A	P		4	0- 0
1940	DET	A	P		14	1- 1
	BRTR				18	1- 1

SMITH, DAVID MERWIN
B.DEC.17,1914 SELLERS,S.C.

YR	CL	LEA	POS	GP	G	REC
1938	PHI	A	P		21	2- 1
1939	PHI	A	P		1	0- 0
	BRTR				22	2- 1

SMITH, DOUGLASS WELDON
B.MAY 25,1892 MILLERS FALLS,MASS.
D.SEPT.18,1973 GREENFIELD,MASS.

YR	CL	LEA	POS	GP	G	REC
1912	BOS	A	P		1	0- 0
	BLTL					

SMITH, E. J.

YR	CL	LEA	POS	GP	G	REC
1890	BUF	P	1		1	.000

SMITH, EARL CALVIN
B.MAR.14,1928 SUNNYSIDE,WASH.

YR	CL	LEA	POS	GP	G	REC
1955	PIT	N	O		9	.063
	BRTR					

SMITH, EARL LEONARD (SHERIFF)
B.JAN.20,1891 OAK HILL,OHIO
D.MAR.14,1943 PORTSMOUTH,OHIO

YR	CL	LEA	POS	GP	G	REC
1916	CHI	N	O		14	.259
1917	STL	A	O		52	.281
1918	STL	A	O		89	.269
1919	STL	A	O		88	.250
1920	STL	A	3-O		103	.306
1921	STL	A	3-O		25	.333
	WAS	A	O		59	.217
1922	WAS	A	O		65	.259
	BBTR				495	.271

SMITH, EARL SUTTON (OIL)
B.FEB.14,1897 HOT SPRINGS,ARK.
D.JUNE 9,1963 LITTLE ROCK,ARK.

YR	CL	LEA	POS	GP	G	REC
1919	NY	N	C		21	.250
1920	NY	N	C		91	.294
1921	NY	N	C		89	.336
1922	NY	N	C		90	.277
1923	NY	N	C		24	.206
	BOS	N	C		72	.288
1924	BOS	N	C		33	.271
	PIT	N	C		39	.369
1925	PIT	N	C		109	.313
1926	PIT	N	C		105	.346
1927	PIT	N	C		66	.270
1928	PIT	N	C		32	.247
	STL	N	C		24	.224
1929	STL	N	C		57	.345
1930	STL	N	C		8	.000
	BLTR				860	.303

SMITH, EDGAR
B.DEC.14,1913 COLUMBUS,N.J.

YR	CL	LEA	POS	GP	G	REC
1936	PHI	A	P		2	1- 1
1937	PHI	A	P	38	40	4-17
1938	PHI	A	P		43	3-10
1939	PHI	A	P		3	1- 0
	CHI	A	P		29	9-11
1940	CHI	A	P		32	14- 9
1941	CHI	A	P		34	13-17
1942	CHI	A	P		29	7-20
1943	CHI	A	P		25	11-11
1946	CHI	A	P		24	8-11
1947	CHI	A	P		15	1- 3
	BOS	A	P		8	1- 3
	BBTL			282	284	73-113

SMITH, EDGAR EUGENE
B.JUNE 12,1862 PROVIDENCE,R.I.
D.NOV.3,1892 PROVIDENCE,R.I.

YR	CL	LEA	POS	GP	G	REC
1883	PRO	N	1-O		2	.222
	PHI	N	P-O		1	0- 1
						.750
1884	WAS	AA	P-O	3	14	0- 2
						.089
1885	PRO	N	P		1	1- 0
1890	CLE	N	P		7	1- 4
	BRTR			14	25	2- 7
						.173

SMITH, EDWARD MAYO (MAYO)
B.JAN.17,1915 NEW LONDON,MO.
D.NOV.24,1977 BOYNTON BEACH,FLA

YR	CL	LEA	POS	GP	G	REC
1945	PHI	A	O		73	.212
	BLTR					

NON-PLAYING MANAGER
PHI(N) 1955-58; CIN(N) 1959,
DET(A) 1967-70

SMITH, ELMER ELLSWORTH (MIKE)
B.MAR.23,1868 PITTSBURGH,PA.
D.NOV.5,1945 PITTSBURGH,PA.

YR	CL	LEA	POS	GP	G	REC
1886	CIN	AA	P-O		9	4- 5
						.308
1887	CIN	AA	P-O	51	52	33-18
						.288
1888	CIN	AA	P-O	39	40	22-17
						.220
1889	CIN	AA	P		29	10-12
1892	PIT	N	P-O	13	136	7- 6
						.282
1893	PIT	N	O		128	.306
1894	PIT	N	O		125	.352
1895	PIT	N	O		124	.296
1896	PIT	N	O		120	.358
1897	PIT	N	O		122	.311
1898	CIN	N	O		122	.344
1899	CIN	N	O		87	.295
1900	CIN	N	O		29	.207
	NY	N	O		87	.274
1901	PIT	N	O		4	.000
	BOS	N	O		18	.240
	BLTL			141	1232	76-58
						.314

SMITH, ELMER JOHN
B.SEPT.21,1892 SANDUSKY,OHIO

YR	CL	LEA	POS	GP	G	REC
1914	CLE	A	O		13	.333
1915	CLE	A	O		144	.248
1916	CLE	A	O		79	.277
	WAS	A	O		45	.214
1917	WAS	A	O		35	.222
	CLE	A	O		64	.261
1919	CLE	A	O		114	.278
1920	CLE	A	O		129	.316
1921	CLE	A	O		129	.290
1922	BOS	A	O		73	.282
	NY	A	O		21	.208
1923	NY	A	O		70	.306
1925	CIN	N	O		96	.271
	BLTR				1012	.277

SMITH, ELWOOD HOPE (MIKE)
B.NOV.16,1904 NORFOLK,VA.

YR	CL	LEA	POS	GP	G	REC
1926	NY	N	O		4	.143
	BLTR					

SMITH, ERNEST HENRY
(KANSAS CITY KID)
B.OCT.11,1899 TOTOWA,N.J.
D.APR.6,1973 BROOKLYN,N.Y.

YR	CL	LEA	POS	GP	G	REC
1930	CHI	A	S		24	.241
	BRTR					

SMITH, FRANK ELMER (NIG)
OR (PIANO MOVER)
(REAL NAME FRANK ELMER SCHMIDT)
B.OCT.28,1879 PITTSBURGH,PA.
D.NOV.3,1952 PITTSBURGH,PA.

YR	CL	LEA	POS	GP	G	REC
1904	CHI	A	P		26	16-10
1905	CHI	A	P		39	19-12
1906	CHI	A	P		20	5- 5
1907	CHI	A	P	41	42	22-11
1908	CHI	A	P	41	43	16-17
1909	CHI	A	P	51	53	25-17
1910	CHI	A	P	19	24	4-10
	BOS	A	P		4	1- 1
1911	BOS	A	P		1	0- 0
	CIN	N	P		34	10-14
1912	CIN	N	P		8	1- 1
1914	BAL	F	P		39	10- 8
1915	BAL	F	P		17	4- 6
	BRO	F	P		15	5- 0
	BRTR			355	365	138-112

SMITH, FRANK L.
B.1857 CANANDAIGUA,N.Y.

YR	CL	LEA	POS	GP	G	REC
1884	PIT	AA	C-O		10	.263

SMITH, FRANK THOMAS
B.APR.4,1928 PIERREPONT MANOR,N.Y.

YR	CL	LEA	POS	GP	G	REC
1950	CIN	N	P		38	2- 7
1951	CIN	N	P		50	5- 5
1952	CIN	N	P		53	12-11
1953	CIN	N	P		50	8- 1
1954	CIN	N	P		50	5- 8
1955	STL	N	P		28	3- 1
1956	CIN	N	P		2	0- 0
	BRTR				271	35-33

SMITH, FREDERICK
B.NOV.24,1878 NEW DIGGINS,WIS.
D.FEB.4,1964 LOS ANGELES,CAL.

YR	CL	LEA	POS	GP	G	REC
1907	CIN	N	P		18	2- 7
	BLTR					

SMITH, FREDERICK C.
B.1863

YR	CL	LEA	POS	GP	G	REC
1890	TOL	AA	P		37	19-14
	BLTR					

YR   CL LEA POS   GP   G   REC

SMITH, FREDERICK VINCENT
B.JULY 29,1891 CLEVELAND,OHIO
D.MAY 28,1961 CLEVELAND,OHIO

YR	CL	LEA	POS	GP	G	REC
1913	BOS	N	3		92	.228
1914	BUF	F	S-3		146	.222
1915	BUF	F	S		35	.220
	BRO	F	S		109	.245
1917	STL	N	3		56	.182
	BRTR				438	.225

SMITH, GEORGE ALLEN
(COLUMBIA GEORGE)
B.MAY 31,1892 BYRAM,CONN.
D.JAN.7,1965 GREENWICH,CONN.

YR	CL	LEA	POS	GP	G	REC
1916	NY	N	P		9	3- 0
1917	NY	N	P		14	0- 3
1918	CIN	N	P		10	2- 3
	NY	N	P		5	2- 3
1919	NY	N	P		8	4- 1
	PHI	N	P		31	5-11
1920	PHI	N	P		43	13-18
1921	PHI	N	P		39	4-20
1922	PHI	N	P		42	5-14
1923	BRO	N	P		25	3- 6
	BRTR				229	41-81

SMITH, GEORGE CORNELIUS
B.JULY 7,1938 ST.PETERSBURG,FLA.

YR	CL	LEA	POS	GP	G	REC
1963	DET	A	2		52	.216
1964	DET	A	2		5	.286
1965	DET	A	2/S-3		32	.094
1966	BOS	A	*2-S		128	.213
	BRTR				217	.205

SMITH, GEORGE HENRY (HEINIE)
B.OCT.24,1871 PITTSBURGH,PA.
D.JUNE 25,1939 BUFFALO,N.Y.

YR	CL	LEA	POS	GP	G	REC
1897	LOU	N	2		21	.280
1898	LOU	N	2		31	.207
1899	PIT	N	2		15	.264
1902	NY	N	M-2		140	.248
1903	DET	A	2		93	.222
	BRTR				300	.239

SMITH, GEORGE J. (GERMANY)
B.APR.21,1863 PITTSBURGH,PA.
D.DEC.1,1927 ALTOONA,PA.

YR	CL	LEA	POS	GP	G	REC
1884	ALT	U	P-S	1	25	0- 0
						.307
	CLE	N	2-S		71	.258
1885	BRO	AA	S		109	.256
1886	BRO	AA	S		117	.249
1887	BRO	AA	S		104	.307
1888	BRO	AA	S		103	.214
1889	BRO	AA	S		121	.233
1890	BRO	N	S		129	.191
1891	CIN	N	S		138	.205
1892	CIN	N	S		138	.248
1893	CIN	N	S		130	.244
1894	CIN	N	S		128	.266
1895	CIN	N	S		127	.297
1896	CIN	N	S		119	.282
1897	BRO	N	S		113	.207
1898	STL	N	S		51	.156
	BRTR			1	1723	0- 0
						.245

SMITH, GEORGE L.
NON-PLAYING MANAGER SYR[N] 1879

SMITH, GEORGE SHELBY
B.OCT.27,1901 LOUISVILLE,KY.

YR	CL	LEA	POS	GP	G	REC
1926	DET	A	P		23	1- 2
1927	DET	A	P		30	4- 1
1928	DET	A	P		39	1- 1
1929	DET	A	P		14	3- 2
1930	BOS	A	P	27	29	1- 2
	BRTR			133	135	10- 8

SMITH, HAROLD LAVERNE
B.JUNE 30,1902 CRESTON,IOWA

YR	CL	LEA	POS	GP	G	REC
1932	PIT	N	P		2	1- 0
1933	PIT	N	P		28	8- 7
1934	PIT	N	P		20	3- 4
1935	PIT	N	P		1	0- 0
	BRTR				51	12-11

SMITH, HAROLD RAYMOND
(HAL) OR (CURA)
B.JUNE 1,1931 BARLING,ARK.

YR	CL	LEA	POS	GP	G	REC
1956	STL	N	C		75	.282
1957	STL	N	C		100	.279
1958	STL	N	C		77	.227
1959	STL	N	C		142	.270
1960	STL	N	C		127	.228
1961	STL	N	C		45	.248
1965	PIT	N	/C		4	.000
	BRTR				570	.258

SMITH, HAROLD WAYNE (HAL)
B.DEC.7,1930 W.FRANKFORT,ILL.

YR	CL	LEA	POS	GP	G	REC
1955	BAL	A	C		135	.271
1956	BAL	A	C		78	.262
	KC	A	C		36	.275
1957	KC	A	C		107	.303
1958	KC	A	C-1-3		99	.273
1959	KC	A	C-3		108	.288
1960	PIT	N	C		77	.295
1961	PIT	N	C		67	.223
1962	HOU	N	C-1-3		109	.235
1963	HOU	N	C		31	.241
1964	CIN	N	C		32	.121
	BRTR				879	.267

SMITH, HARRISON MORTON
B.AUG.15,1889 UNION,NEB.
D.JULY 26,1964 DUNBAR,NEB.

YR	CL	LEA	POS	GP	G	REC
1912	CHI	A	P		1	1- 0
	BRTR					

SMITH, HARRY THOMAS
B.OCT.31,1874 YORKSHIRE,ENGLAND
D.FEB.17,1933 SALEM,N.J.

YR	CL	LEA	POS	GP	G	REC
1901	PHI	A	C		11	.308
1902	PIT	N	C		49	.187
1903	PIT	N	C		61	.175
1904	PIT	N	C		47	.248
1905	PIT	N	C		1	.000
1906	PIT	N	C		1	.000
1907	PIT	N	C		18	.263
1908	BOS	N	C		38	.246
1909	BOS	N	M-C		31	.168
1910	BOS	N	C		38	.238
	BRTR				295	.212

SMITH, HARRY W.
B.FEB.5,1856 N.VERNON,IND.
D.JUNE 4,1898 N.VERNON,IND.

YR	CL	LEA	POS	GP	G	REC
1877	CIN	N	2-0		24	.202
	CIN	N	C-2-0		9	.281
1889	LOU	AA	C		1	1.000
	BRTR				34	.228

SMITH, HARVEY FETTERHOFF
B.JULY 24,1871 UNION DEPOSIT,PA
D.NOV.12,1962 HARRISBURG,PA.

YR	CL	LEA	POS	GP	G	REC
1896	WAS	N	3		34	.288
	BLTR					

SMITH, HENRY JOSEPH (HAPPY)
B.JULY 14,1883 COQUILLE,ORE.
D.FEB.26,1961 SAN JOSE,CAL.

YR	CL	LEA	POS	GP	G	REC
1910	BRO	N	C		16	.237
	BLTR					

SMITH, JACK
B.JUNE 23,1895 CHICAGO,ILL.
D.MAY 2,1972 WESTCHESTER,ILL.

YR	CL	LEA	POS	GP	G	REC
1915	STL	N	O		4	.187
1916	STL	N	O		130	.244
1917	STL	N	O		137	.297
1918	STL	N	O		42	.211
1919	STL	N	O		119	.223
1920	STL	N	O		91	.332
1921	STL	N	O		116	.328
1922	STL	N	O		143	.309
1923	STL	N	O		124	.310
1924	STL	N	O		124	.283
1925	STL	N	O		80	.251
1926	STL	N	O		1	.000
	BOS	N	O		96	.311
1927	BOS	N	O		84	.317
1928	BOS	N	O		96	.280
1929	BOS	N	O		19	.250
	BLTL				1406	.287

SMITH, JACK HATFIELD
B.NOV.15,1935 PIKEVILLE,KY.

YR	CL	LEA	POS	GP	G	REC
1962	LA	N	P		8	0- 0
1963	LA	N	P		4	0- 0
1964	MIL	N	P		22	2- 2
	BRTR				34	2- 2

SMITH, JACOB G.
B.DUBOIS,PA.

YR	CL	LEA	POS	GP	G	REC
1911	PHI	N	P		2	0- 0

SMITH, JAMES
[PLAYED UNDER NAME OF
JAMES BLUEJACKET]

SMITH, JAMES A. (STUB)
B.NOV.26,1876 ELMWOOD,ILL.

YR	CL	LEA	POS	GP	G	REC
1898	BOS	N	S		3	.100

SMITH, JAMES CARLISLE (RED)
B.APR.6,1890 GREENVILLE,S.C.
D.OCT.11,1966 ATLANTA,GA.

YR	CL	LEA	POS	GP	G	REC
1911	BRO	N	3		28	.261
1912	BRO	N	3		128	.286
1913	BRO	N	3		151	.296
1914	BRO	N	3		90	.245
	BOS	N	3		60	.314
1915	BOS	N	3		3	.158
1916	BOS	N	3		150	.259
1917	BOS	N	3		147	.295
1918	BOS	N	3		119	.298
1919	BOS	N	3-0		87	.245
	BRTR				1117	.278

SMITH, JAMES HARRY (HARRY)
B.MAY 15,1890 BALTIMORE,MD.
D.APR.1,1922 CHARLOTTE,N.C.

YR	CL	LEA	POS	GP	G	REC
1914	NY	N	C		5	.428
1915	NY	N	C		21	.125
	BRO	F	C		25	.215
1917	CIN	N	C		8	.118
1918	CIN	N	C		13	.185
	BRTR				72	.189

SMITH, JAMES LAWRENCE
(GREENFIELD JIMMY)
B.MAY 15,1895 PITTSBURGH,PA.
D.JAN.1,1974 PITTSBURGH,PA.

YR	CL	LEA	POS	GP	G	REC
1914	CHI	F	S		3	.500
1915	CHI	F	S		94	.217
	BAL	F	S		33	.191
1916	PIT	N	S		36	.188
1917	NY	N	2		36	.229
1918	BOS	N	2-S-3-0		34	.225
1919	CIN	N	2-S-3-0		28	.275
1921	PHI	N	2		67	.231
1922	PHI	N	2-S-3		38	.219
	BBTR				369	.221
	BR 1914					

SMITH, JOHN
B.BALTIMORE,MD.

YR	CL	LEA	POS	GP	G	REC
1873	MAR	NA	S-0		5	-
1874	BAL	NA	S		5	-
1875	NH	NA	S		1	-
					11	-

SMITH, JOHN FRANCIS (PHENOMENAL)
[REAL NAME JOHN FRANCIS GAMMON]
B.DEC.12,1864 PHILADELPHIA,PA.
D.APR.3,1952 MANCHESTER,N.H.

YR	CL	LEA	POS	GP	G	REC
1884	BAL	U	P-0	8	10	3- 5
						.158
	ATH	AA	P	1		0- 1
	PIT	AA	P	1		0- 1
1885	BRO	AA	P	1		0- 1
	ATH	AA	P	1		0- 1
1886	DET	N	P	3		1- 1
1887	BAL	AA	P		62	29-29
1888	BAL	AA	P		35	19-20
	ATH	AA	P	3		2- 0
1889	ATH	AA	P	4		1- 3
1890	PHI	N	P		22	7-15
	PIT	N	P	5		2- 3
1891	PHI	N	P	3		1- 2
	BLTL			149	151	61-82
						.279

SMITH, JOHN JOSEPH
[PLAYED UNDER NAME OF
JOHN FRANCIS COFFEY]

SMITH, JOHN MARSHALL
B.SEPT.27,1906 WASHINGTON,D.C.

YR	CL	LEA	POS	GP	G	REC
1931	BOS	A	1		4	.133
	BBTR					

SMITH, JOHN WILLIAM (CHICK)
[REAL NAME JAN SMADT]
B.DEC.2,1892 DAYTON,KY.
D.OCT.11,1935 DAYTON,OHIO

YR	CL	LEA	POS	GP	G	REC
1913	CIN	N	P		5	0- 1
	BLTL					

SMITH, JOSEPH
[REAL NAME
SALVATORE GIUSEPPE PERSICO]
B.DEC.29,1893 NEW YORK,N.Y.

YR	CL	LEA	POS	GP	G	REC
1913	NY	N	C		14	.161
	BRTR					

SMITH, JUDSON GRANT
B.JAN.13,1869 GREEN OAK,MICH.
D.DEC.7,1947 LOS ANGELES,CAL.

YR	CL	LEA	POS	GP	G	REC
1893	CIN	N	S-3-0		16	.233
	STL	N	3		4	.067
1896	PIT	N	3		4	.333
1898	WAS	N	3		65	.302
1901	PIT	N	3		6	.130
	BRTR				95	.275

SMITH, KEITH LAVARNE
B.MAY 3,1953 PALMETTO,FLA.

YR	CL	LEA	POS	GP	G	REC
1977	TEX	A	O		23	.239
	BRTR					

YR	CL	LEA	POS	GP	G	REC

SMITH, LAWRENCE PATRICK (PADDY)
B.MAY 16,1894 PELHAM,N.Y.
1920 BOS A C   2   .000
BLTR

SMITH, LEO H.
B.MAY 13,1863 BROOKLYN,N.Y.
1890 ROC AA S   35   .190

SMITH, LONNIE
B.DEC.22,1955 CHICAGO,ILL.
1978 PHI N O   17   .000
BRTR

SMITH, LOUIS O. (BULL)
B.MAY 16,1894 PELHAM,N.Y.
1904 PIT N O   13   .142
1906 CHI N H   1   .000
1911 WAS A H   1   .000
TR   15   .140

SMITH, MARVIN HAROLD (RED)
B.JULY 17,1900 ASHLEY,ILL.
D.FEB.19,1961 LOS ANGELES,CAL.
1925 PHI A S-3   20   .286
BLTR

SMITH, MILTON (MILT)
B.MAR.27,1929 COLUMBUS,GA.
1955 CIN N 2-3   36   .196
BRTR

SMITH, NATHANIEL BEVERLY
B.APR.26,1935 CHICAGO,ILL.
1962 BAL A C   5   .222

SMITH, OLIVER H.
B.1868 MT.VERNON,OHIO
1894 LOU N O   89   .288

SMITH, OSBORNE EARL (OZZIE)
B.DEC.26,1954 MOBILE,ALA.
1978 SD N *S   159   .258
BBTR

SMITH, PAUL LESLIE
B.MAR.19,1931 NEW CASTLE,PA.
1953 PIT N 1-O   118   .283
1957 PIT N 1-O   81   .293
1958 PIT N H   6   .333
     CHI N 1   18   .150
BLTL   223   .270

SMITH, PAUL STONER
B.MAY 7,1888 MT.ZION,ILL.
D.JULY 3,1958 DECATUR,ILL.
1916 CIN N O   10   .227
BLTR

SMITH, PETER LUKE (PETE)
B.MAR.19,1940 NATICK,MASS.
1962 BOS A P   1   0- 1
1963 BOS A P   6   0- 0
BRTR   7   0- 1

SMITH, REGINALD
B.LOUISVILLE,KY.
1886 ATH AA P   1   0- 1

SMITH, RHESA EDWARD (ED)
B.FEB.21,1879 MENTONE,IND.
D.MAR.20,1955 TARPON SPRINGS,FLA.
1906 STL N P   19   7-10
BRTR

SMITH, RICHARD ARTHUR (DICK)
B.MAY 17,1939 LEBANON,ORE.
1963 NY N 1-O   20   .238
1964 NY N 1-O   46   .223
1965 LA N /O   10   .000
BRTR   76   .218

SMITH, RICHARD HARRISON (DICK)
B.JULY 21,1927 BLANDBURG,PA.
1951 PIT N 3   12   .174
1952 PIT N 2-S-3   29   .106
1953 PIT N S   13   .163
1954 PIT N 3   12   .097
1955 PIT N S   4   .000
BRTR   70   .134

SMITH, RICHARD KELLY (DICK)
B.AUG.25,1944 LINCOLNTON,N.C.
1969 WAS A /O   21   .107
BRTR

SMITH, RICHARD PAUL (RED)
B.MAY 18,1904 BROKAW,WIS.
1927 NY N C   1   .000
BRTR

SMITH, ROBERT ASHLEY
B.JULY 19,1891 HARDWICK,VT.
1913 CHI A P   1   0- 0
1915 BUF F P   1   0- 0
BRTR   2   0- 0

SMITH, ROBERT ELDRIDGE
B.APR.22,1898 ROGERSVILLE,TENN.
1923 BOS N 2-S   115   .251
1924 BOS N S-3   106   .228
1925 BOS N P-2-
     S-O   13   58   5- 3
     S-O   .282
1926 BOS N P   33   40   10-13
1927 BOS N P   41   54   10-18
1928 BOS N P   38   39   13-17
1929 BOS N P   34   39   11-17
1930 BOS N P   38   39   10-14
1931 CHI N P   36   15-12
1932 CHI N P   34   36   4- 3
1933 CIN N P-S   16   23   4- 4
               .200
     BOS N P   14   4- 3
1934 BOS N P   39   42   6- 9
1935 BOS N P   46   47   8-18
1936 BOS N P   35   6- 7
1937 BOS N P   18   19   0- 1
BRTR   435   742   106-139
               .242

SMITH, ROBERT GILCHRIST (BOB)
B.FEB.1,1931 WOODSVILLE,N.H.
1955 BOS A P   1   0- 0
1957 STL N P   6   0- 0
     PIT N P   20   2- 4
1958 PIT N P   35   2- 2
1959 PIT N P   20   0- 0
     DET A P   9   0- 3
BRTL   91   4- 9

**SMITH, ROBERT WALKAY
(BOB) OR (RIVERBOAT)**
B.MAY 13,1928 CLARENCE,MD.
1958 BOS A P   17   4- 3
1959 CHI N P   1   0- 0
     CLE A P   12   0- 1
BBTL   30   4- 4
BL 1958

SMITH, RUFUS FRAZIER (SHIRT)
B.JAN.24,1905 GUILFORD COLLEGE,N.C.
1927 DET A P   1   0- 0
BRTL

SMITH, SAMUEL (SKYROCKET)
B.1857 BALTIMORE,MD.
1888 LOU AA 1   56   .246
BR

SMITH, SHERROD MALONE (SHERRY)
B.FEB.18,1891 MONTICELLO,GA.
D.SEPT.12,1949 REIDSVILLE,GA.
1911 PIT N P   1   0- 0
1912 PIT N P   3   0- 0
1915 BRO N P   29   14- 8
1916 BRO N P   36   38   14-10
1917 BRO N P   38   43   12-12
1919 BRO N P   30   7-12
1920 BRO N P   33   11- 9
1921 BRO N P   35   7-11
1922 BRO N P   28   4- 8
     CLE A P   2   1- 0
1923 CLE A P   30   9- 6
1924 CLE A P   39   40   12-14
1925 CLE A P   31   11-14
1926 CLE A P   27   11-10
1927 CLE A P   11   1- 4
BRTL   373   381   114-118

SMITH, SYDNEY E.
B.AUG.31,1883 SMITHVILLE,S.C.
D.JUNE 5,1961 ORANGEBURG,S.C.
1908 PHI A C   43   .205
     STL A C   28   .182
1910 CLE A C   9   .346
1911 CLE A C   58   .299
1914 PIT N C   4   .300
1915 PIT N H   1   .000
BRTR   145   .247

SMITH, THOMAS E.
B.DEC.5,1871 BOSTON,MASS.
D.MAR.2,1929 DORCHESTER,MASS.
1894 BOS N P   2   0- 0
1895 PHI N P   11   3- 3
1896 LOU N P   14   1- 5
1898 STL N P   1   0- 1
            28   4- 9

SMITH, THOMAS N.
B.BALTIMORE,MD.
1875 ATL NA 2   3   -

SMITH, TOMMY ALEXANDER
B.AUG.1,1948 ALBERMARLE,N.C.
1973 CLE A O   14   .244
1974 CLE A O   23   .097
1975 CLE A /O   8   .125
1976 CLE A O   55   .256
1977 SEA A O   21   .259
BLTR   121   .232

SMITH, VINCENT AMBROSE
B.DEC.7,1915 RICHMOND,VA.
1941 PIT N C   9   .303
1946 PIT N C   7   .190
BRTR   16   .259

SMITH, WALLACE H.
B.MAR.13,1889 PHILADELPHIA,PA.
D.JUNE 10,1930 FLORENCE,ARIZ.
1911 STL N S-3   60   .216
1912 STL N S-3   79   .256
1914 WAS A 2   45   .196
BRTR   180   .229

SMITH, WALTER
[PLAYED UNDER NAME OF
WALTER REINICKER]

SMITH, WILBUR FLOYD (WIB)
B.AUG.30,1886 EVART,MICH.
D.NOV.18,1959 FARGO,N.D.
1909 STL A C   17   .190
BLTR

SMITH, WILLARD JEHU (RED)
B.APR.11,1892 LOGANSPORT,IND.
D.JULY 17,1972 NOBLESVILLE,IND.
1917 PIT N C   11   .143
1918 PIT N C   15   .167
BRTR   26   .156

SMITH, WILLIAM
D.OCT.28,1897 GUELPH,ONT.,CAN.
1886 DET N P   10   5- 4

SMITH, WILLIAM E.
B.E.LIVERPOOL,OHIO
1884 CLE N O   1   .000

SMITH, WILLIAM GARLAND
B.JUNE 8,1934 WASHINGTON,D.C.
1958 STL N P   2   0- 1
1959 STL N P   6   0- 0
1962 PHI N P   24   1- 5
BLTL   32   1- 6

SMITH, WILLIAM J.
B.BALTIMORE,MD.
D.AUG.9,1886
1873 MAR NA M-C-2-O   6   -

SMITH, WILLIE
B.FEB.11,1939 ANNISTON,ALA.
1963 DET A P   11   17   1- 0
1964 LA A P-O   15   118   1- 4
               .301
1965 CAL A *O/1   136   .261
1966 CAL A O   90   .185
1967 CLE A /O-1   21   .219
1968 CLE A /1-P-O   2   33   0- 0
               .143
     CHI N O/1-P   1   55   0- 0
               .275
1969 CHI N O-1   103   .246
1970 CHI N 1/O   87   .216
1971 CIN N 1   31   .164
BLTL   29   691   2- 4
               .248

SMOLL, CLYDE HETRICK (LEFTY)
B.APR.17,1914 QUAKERTOWN,PA.
1940 PHI N P   33   2- 8
BBTL

SMOOT, HOMER VERNON (DOC)
B.MAR.26,1878 GALESTOWN,MD.
D.MAR.25,1928 SALISBURY,MD.
1902 STL N O   129   .310
1903 STL N O   129   .296
1904 STL N O   137   .281
1905 STL N O   138   .311
1906 STL N O   86   .248
     CIN N O   59   .259
BLTR   678   .290

SMOWERY, HENRY NEITZ
[PLAYED UNDER NAME OF
HENRY NEITZ SMOYER]

SMOYER, HENRY NEITZ (HARRY)
[REAL NAME HENRY NEITZ SMOWERY]
B.APR.25,1890 FREDERICKSBURG,PA
D.FEB.28,1956 DUBOIS,PA.
1912 STL A S-3   6   .214
TR

SMYKAL, FRANK JOHN
[REAL NAME FRANK JOHN SMEJKAL]
B.OCT.13,1889 CHICAGO,ILL.
D.AUG.11,1950 CHICAGO,ILL.
1916 PIT N S   6   .300
BRTR

SMYRES, CLARENCE MELVIN (CLANCY)
B.MAY 24,1922 CULVER CITY,CAL.
1944 BRO N H   5   .000
BBTR

SMYTH, JAMES DANIEL (RED)
B.JAN.30,1893 HOLLY SPRINGS,MISS.
D.APR.14,1958 INGLEWOOD,CAL.

YR	CL	LEA	POS	GP	G	REC
1915	BRO	N	O		19	.136
1916	BRO	N	O		2	.000
1917	BRO	N	O		29	.120
	STL	N	O		38	.211
1918	STL	N	2-O		40	.212
		BLTR			128	.193

SMYTHE, WILLIAM HENRY (HARRY)
B.OCT.24,1904 AUGUSTA,GA.

YR	CL	LEA	POS	GP	G	REC
1929	PHI	N	P	19	20	4- 6
1930	PHI	N	P		25	0- 3
1934	NY	A	P		8	0- 2
	BRO	N	P	8	10	1- 1
		BLTL			63	5-12

SNEED, JONATHON L. (JOHN)
B.COLUMBUS,OHIO
D.JAN.4,1899 MEMPHIS,TENN.

YR	CL	LEA	POS	GP	G	REC
1884	IND	AA	O		27	.105
1890	TOL	AA	O		9	.167
	COL	AA	O		128	.309
1891	COL	AA	O		99	.261
					263	.267

SNELL, CHARLES ANTHONY
B.NOV.29,1892 READING,PA.

YR	CL	LEA	POS	GP	G	REC
1912	STL	A	C		8	.222
		BRTR				

SNELL, WALTER HENRY (DOC)
B.MAY 19,1889 BRIDGEWATER,MASS.

YR	CL	LEA	POS	GP	G	REC
1913	BOS	A	C		6	.250
		BRTR				

SNIDER, EDWIN DONALD (DUKE)
OR (THE SILVER FOX)
B.SEP.19,1926 LOS ANGELES,CAL.

YR	CL	LEA	POS	GP	G	REC
1947	BRO	N	O		40	.241
1948	BRO	N	O		53	.244
1949	BRO	N	O		146	.292
1950	BRO	N	O		152	.321
1951	BRO	N	O		150	.277
1952	BRO	N	O		144	.303
1953	BRO	N	O		153	.336
1954	BRO	N	O		149	.341
1955	BRO	N	O		148	.309
1956	BRO	N	O		151	.292
1957	BRO	N	O		139	.274
1958	LA	N	O		106	.312
1959	LA	N	O		126	.308
1960	LA	N	O		101	.243
1961	LA	N	O		85	.296
1962	LA	N	O		80	.278
1963	NY	N	O		129	.243
1964	SF	N	O		91	.210
		BLTR			2143	.295

SNIPES, WYATT EURE (ROXY) OR (ROCK)
B.OCT.28,1896 MARION,S.C.
D.MAY 1,1941 FAYETTEVILLE,N.C.

YR	CL	LEA	POS	GP	G	REC
1923	CHI	A	H		1	.000
		BLTR				

SNODGRASS, AMZIE BEAL
B.MAR.18,1870 SPRINGFIELD,OHIO
D.SEPT.9,1951 NEW YORK,N.Y.

YR	CL	LEA	POS	GP	G	REC
1901	BAL	A	O		2	.100
		BRTR				

SNODGRASS, FREDERICK CARLISLE
(FRED) OR (SNOW)
B.OCT.19,1887 VENTURA,CAL.
D.APR.5,1974 VENTURA,CAL.

YR	CL	LEA	POS	GP	G	REC
1908	NY	N	C		5	.250
1909	NY	N	O		22	.300
1910	NY	N	O		112	.321
1911	NY	N	O		151	.294
1912	NY	N	1-O		146	.269
1913	NY	N	O		141	.291
1914	NY	N	O		113	.263
1915	NY	N	O		80	.151
	BOS	N	O		23	.278
1916	BOS	N	O		112	.249
		BRTR			905	.275

SNOOK, FRANK WALTER
B.MAR.28,1949 SOMERVILLE,N.J.

YR	CL	LEA	POS	GP	G	REC
1973	SD	N	P		18	0- 2
		BRTR				

SNOVER, COLONEL LESTER (BOSCO)
B.MAY 16,1895 HALLSTEAD,PA.
D.APR.30,1969 ROCHESTER,N.Y.

YR	CL	LEA	POS	GP	G	REC
1919	NY	N	P		2	0- 1
		BLTL				

SNOW
B.BOSTON,MASS.

YR	CL	LEA	POS	GP	G	REC
1874	ATL	NA	O		1	.000

SNYDER, BERNARD AUSTIN
B.AUG.25,1913 PHILADELPHIA,PA.

YR	CL	LEA	POS	GP	G	REC
1935	PHI	A	2-S		10	.344
		BRTR				

SNYDER, CHARLES
B.CAMDEN,N.J.
D.MAR.10,1901 PHILADELPHIA,PA.

YR	CL	LEA	POS	GP	G	REC
1890	ATH	AA	C-O		9	.419

SNYDER, CHARLES N. (POP)
B.OCT.6,1854 WASHINGTON,D.C.
D.OCT.29,1924 WASHINGTON,D.C.

YR	CL	LEA	POS	GP	G	REC
1873	NAT	NA	C-O		28	-
1874	BAL	NA	C		34	-
1875	PHI	NA	C		65	.233
1876	LOU	N	C		56	.195
1877	LOU	N	C-S-O		61	.258
1878	BOS	N	C		60	.212
1879	BOS	N	C		81	.234
1881	BOS	N	C-2-S-O		60	.228
1882	CIN	AA	C-1-O		72	.289
1883	CIN	AA	M-C-S		58	.245
1884	CIN	AA	M-C-1-O		68	.284
1885	CIN	AA	C-1		38	.250
1886	CIN	AA	C-1-O		52	.195
1887	CLE	AA	C		73	.276
1888	CLE	AA	C		63	.216
1889	CLE	N	C		21	.192
1890	CLE	P	C		12	.183
1891	WAS	AA	M-C		8	.179
		BRTR			910	-

SNYDER, EMANUEL SEBASTIAN (REDLEG)
[REAL NAME
EMANUEL SEBASTIAN SCHNEIDER]
B.DEC.12,1853 CAMDEN,N.J.
D.NOV.11,1933 CAMDEN,N.J.

YR	CL	LEA	POS	GP	G	REC
1876	CIN	N	O		55	.150
1884	WIL	U	1-O		17	.192
		BRTR				

SNYDER, FRANK C. (COONEY)
B.TORONTO,ONTARIO,CANADA
D.MAR.9,1917 TORONTO,ONT.,CAN.

YR	CL	LEA	POS	GP	G	REC
1898	LOU	N	C		15	.169

SNYDER, FRANK ELTON (PANCHO)
B.MAY 27,1893 SAN ANTONIO,TEX.
D.JAN.5,1962 SAN ANTONIO,TEX.

YR	CL	LEA	POS	GP	G	REC
1912	STL	N	C		11	.111
1913	STL	N	C		7	.190
1914	STL	N	C		100	.230
1915	STL	N	C		144	.298
1916	STL	N	C-1		132	.259
1917	STL	N	C		115	.237
1918	STL	N	C-1		39	.250
1919	STL	N	C-1		50	.182
	NY	N	C		32	.228
1920	NY	N	C		87	.250
1921	NY	N	C		108	.320
1922	NY	N	C		104	.343
1923	NY	N	C		120	.256
1924	NY	N	C		118	.302
1925	NY	N	C		107	.240
1926	NY	N	C		55	.216
1927	STL	N	C		63	.258
		BRTR			1392	.265

SNYDER, GENE WALTER
B.MAR.31,1931 YORK,PA.

YR	CL	LEA	POS	GP	G	REC
1959	LA	N	P		11	1- 1
		BRTL				

SNYDER, GEORGE T.
B.1849 PHILADELPHIA,PA.
D.AUG.2,1905 PHILADELPHIA,PA.

YR	CL	LEA	POS	GP	G	REC
1882	ATH	AA	P		1	1- 0

SNYDER, GERALD GEORGE (JERRY)
B.JULY 21,1929 JENKS,OKLA.

YR	CL	LEA	POS	GP	G	REC
1952	WAS	A	2-S		36	.158
1953	WAS	A	2-S		29	.339
1954	WAS	A	2-S		64	.234
1955	WAS	A	2-S		46	.224
1956	WAS	A	2-S		43	.270
1957	WAS	A	2-S-3		42	.151
1958	WAS	A	2-S		6	.111
		BRTR			266	.230

SNYDER, JAMES
B.1851 NEW YORK
D.1881

YR	CL	LEA	POS	GP	G	REC
1872	ECK	NA	C-S-O		26	.275

SNYDER, JAMES ROBERT (JIM)
B.AUG.15,1932 DEARBON,MICH.

YR	CL	LEA	POS	GP	G	REC
1961	MIN	A	2		3	.000
1962	MIN	A	1-2		12	.100
1964	MIN	A	2		26	.155
		BRTR			41	.140

SNYDER, JOHN WILLIAM (JACK)
B.1892 ALLEGHENY CO.,PA.

YR	CL	LEA	POS	GP	G	REC
1914	BUF	F	C		1	.000
1917	BRO	N	C		7	.273
		BRTR			8	.273

SNYDER, JOSHUA
B.1844
D.APR.21,1881 BROOKLYN,N.Y.

YR	CL	LEA	POS	GP	G	REC
1872	ECK	NA	O		9	.171

SNYDER, RUSSELL HENRY (RUSS)
B.JUNE 22,1934 OAK,NEB.

YR	CL	LEA	POS	GP	G	REC
1959	KC	A	O		73	.313
1960	KC	A	O		125	.260
1961	BAL	A	O		115	.292
1962	BAL	A	O		139	.305
1963	BAL	A	O		148	.256
1964	BAL	A	O		56	.290
1965	BAL	A	*O		132	.270
1966	BAL	A	*O		117	.306
1967	BAL	A	O		108	.236
1968	CHI	A	O		38	.134
	CLE	A	O/1		68	.281
1969	CLE	A	O		122	.248
1970	MIL	A	*O		124	.232
		BLTR			1365	.271

SNYDER, WILLIAM NICHOLS
B.JAN.28,1898 MANSFIELD,OHIO
D.OCT.8,1934 KALAMAZOO,MICH.

YR	CL	LEA	POS	GP	G	REC
1919	WAS	A	P		2	0- 1
1920	WAS	A	P		16	2- 1
		BRTR			18	2- 2

SOCKALEXIS, LEWIS M. (CHIEF)
B.OCT.24,1871 OLD TOWN,MAINE
D.DEC.24,1913 BURLINGTON,MAINE

YR	CL	LEA	POS	GP	G	REC
1897	CLE	N	O		66	.331
1898	CLE	N	O		20	.222
1899	CLE	N	O		7	.252
		BLTR			93	.307

SODD, WILLIAM
B.SEPT.18,1914 FT.WORTH,TEX.

YR	CL	LEA	POS	GP	G	REC
1937	CLE	A	H		1	.000
		BRTR				

SODERHOLM, ERIC THANE
B.SEP.24,1948 CORTLAND,N.Y.

YR	CL	LEA	POS	GP	G	REC
1971	MIN	A	3		21	.156
1972	MIN	A	3		93	.188
1973	MIN	A	3/S		35	.297
1974	MIN	A	*3/S		141	.276
1975	MIN	A	*3		117	.286
1977	CHI	A	*3		130	.280
1978	CHI	A	*3-D/2		143	.258
		BRTR			680	.262

SOLAITA, TOLIA (TONY)
B.JAN.15,1947 NUUYLI,AMER.SOMOA

YR	CL	LEA	POS	GP	G	REC
1968	NY	A	/1		1	.000
1974	KC	A	1-D/O		96	.268
1975	KC	A	D-1		93	.260
1976	KC	A	D/1		31	.235
	CAL	A	1		63	.270
1977	CAL	A	1		116	.241
1978	CAL	A	D-1		60	.223
		BLTL			460	.253

SOLIS, MARCELINO
B.JULY 19,1930 SAN LUIS POTOSI,
MEXICO

YR	CL	LEA	POS	GP	G	REC
1958	CHI	N	P		15	3- 3
		BLTL				

SOLOMAN, JAMES HERMAN
[PLAYED UNDER NAME OF
JAMES HERMAN REESE]

SOLOMON, EDDIE
B.FEB.9,1951 PERRY,GA.

YR	CL	LEA	POS	GP	G	REC
1973	LA	N	/P		4	0- 0
1974	LA	N	/P		4	0- 0
1975	CHI	N	/P		6	0- 0
1976	STL	N	P		26	1- 1
1977	ATL	N	P		18	6- 6
1978	ATL	N	P	37	38	4- 6
		BRTR		95	96	11-13

SOLOMON, MOSES H. (MOE)
OR (THE RABBI OF SWAT)
B.DEC.8,1900 NEW YORK,N.Y.
D.JUNE 25,1966 MIAMI,FLA.

YR	CL	LEA	POS	GP	G	REC
1923	NY	N	O		2	.375
		BLTL				

SOLTERS, JULIUS JOSEPH (MOOSE)
[REAL NAME JULIUS JOSEPH SOLTESZ]
B.MAR.22,1906 PITTSBURGH,PA.
D.SEPT.28,1975 PITTSBURGH,PA.

YR	CL	LEA	POS	GP	G	REC
1934	BOS	A	O		101	.299
1935	BOS	A	O		24	.241
	STL	A	O		127	.330
1936	STL	A	O		152	.291
1937	CLE	A	O		152	.323
1938	CLE	A	O		67	.201
1939	CLE	A	O		41	.275
	STL	A	O		40	.206
1940	CHI	A	O		116	.308
1941	CHI	A	O		76	.259
1943	CHI	A	O		42	.155
		BRTR			938	.289

SOLTESZ, JULIUS JOSEPH
[PLAYED UNDER NAME OF
JULIUS JOSEPH SOLTERS]

YR	CL LEA POS	GP	G	REC

SOMERLOTT, JOHN WESLEY (JOCK)
B.OCT.26,1882 FLINT,IND.
D.APR.21,1965 BUTLER,IND.
```
1910 WAS A  1          16    .222
1911 WAS A  1          13    .175
        TR             29    .204
```

SOMERVILLE, EDWARD
B.PHILADELPHIA,PA.
D.SEPT.30,1877 HAMILTON,ONT.,CANADA
```
1875 CEN NA 2-3        14    -
     NH  NA 1-2-S-3    33    -
1876 LOU N  2          64    .187
        BRTR          111    -
```

SOMMER, JOSEPH JOHN
B.NOV.20,1858 COVINGTON,KY.
D.JAN.16,1938 CINCINNATI,OHIO
```
1880 CIN N  S-3-O      20    .182
1882 CIN AA O          80    .280
1883 CIN AA P-3-   1   97    0- 9
            O                .281
1884 BAL AA 3-O       107    .272
1885 BAL AA O         110    .250
1886 BAL AA 2-O       139    .215
1887 BAL AA O         131    .355
1888 BAL AA S-O        79    .215
1889 BAL AA O         106    .224
1890 CLE N  P-O    1    9    0- 1
                             .294
     BAL AA O          38    .239
        BRTR       2  916    0- 1
                             .262
```

SOMMERS, JOSEPH ANDREWS (PETE)
B.OCT.26,1866 CLEVELAND,OHIO
D.JULY 22,1908 CLEVELAND,OHIO
```
1887 MET AA C          32    .219
1888 BOS N  C           4    .231
1889 CHI N  C          12    .239
     IND N  C          19    .241
1890 NY  N  C-1-O      17    .070
     CLE N  C-O         8    .192
        BR             92    .209
```

SOMMERS, RUDOLPH
B.OCT.30,1888 CINCINNATI,OHIO
D.MAR.18,1949 LOUISVILLE,KY.
```
1912 CHI N  P           1    0- 1
1914 BRO F  P          23    2- 7
1926 BOS A  P           2    0- 0
1927 BOS A  P           7    0- 0
        BBTL           33    2- 8
```

SOMMERS, WILLIAM (KID)
B.TORONTO,ONT.,CANADA
D.OCT.16,1895 TORONTO,ONT.,CAN.
```
1889 CLE N  C           2    .000
1893 STL N  C           2    .000
        TR              4    .000
```

SOMMERS, WILLIAM DJNN (BILL)
B.FEB.17,1923 BROOKLYN,N.Y.
```
1950 STL A  2-3        65    .255
        BRTR
```

SOMMERVILLE, ANDREW HENRY
CREAL NAME
HENRY TRAVERS SUMMERSGILL]
B.FEB.6,1876 BROOKLYN,N.Y.
D.JUNE 16,1931 RICHMOND HILL,N.Y.
```
1894 BRO N  P           1    0- 1
```

SONGER, DONALD C.
B.JAN.3,1900 WALNJT,KAN.
D.OCT.3,1962 KANSAS CITY,MO.
```
1924 PIT N  P           4    0- 0
1925 PIT N  P           8    0- 1
1926 PIT N  P          35    7- 8
1927 PIT N  P           2    0- 0
     NY  N  P          22    3- 5
        BLTL           71   10-14
```

SORENSEN, LARY ALAN
B.OCT.4,1955 DETROIT,MICH.
```
1977 MIL A  P          23    7-10
1978 MIL A  P          37   18-12
        BRTR           60   25-22
```

SORRELL, VICTOR GARLAND (VIC)
B.APR.9,1901 MORRISVILLE,N.C.
D.MAY 4,1972 RALEIGH,N.C.
```
1928 DET A  P          29    8-11
1929 DET A  P          36   14-15
1930 DET A  P          35   16-11
1931 DET A  P          35   13-14
1932 DET A  P     32   34   14-14
1933 DET A  P          36   11-15
1934 DET A  P          28    6- 9
1935 DET A  P          12    6- 3
1936 DET A  P          30    6- 7
1937 DET A  P           7    0- 2
        BRTR     280  281   92-101
```

SORRELL, WILLIAM (BILL)
B.OCT.14,1940 MOREHEAD,KY.
```
1965 PHI N /3          10    .385
1967 SF  N /O          18    .176
1970 KC  A  3/0-1      57    .267
        BLTR           85    .267
```

SORRELLS, RAYMOND EDWIN (CHICK)
B.JULY 31,1896 STRINGTOWN,OKLA.
```
1922 CLE A  S           2    .000
        BRTR
```

SOSA, ELIAS [MARTINEZ]
B.JUNE 10,1950 LA VEGA,D.R.
```
1972 SF  N /P           8    0- 1
1973 SF  N  P          71   10- 4
1974 SF  N  P          68    9- 7
1975 STL N  P          14    0- 3
     ATL N  P          43    2- 2
1976 ATL N  P          21    4- 4
     LA  N  P          24    2- 4
1977 LA  N  P     44   45    2- 2
1978 OAK A  P          68    8- 2
        BRTR     361  362   37-29
```

SOSA, JOSE YNOCENCIO
[REAL NAME JOSE YNOCENCIO [SOSA]]
B.DEC.28,1952 SANTO DOMINGO,D.R.
```
1975 HOU N  P     25   26    1- 3
1976 HOU N  P           9    0- 0
        BRTR     34   35    1- 3
```

SOTHERN, DENNIS ELWOOD
B.JAN.20,1904 WASHINGTON,D.C.
```
1926 PHI N  O          14    .245
1928 PHI N  O         141    .285
1929 PHI N  O          76    .306
1930 PHI N  O          90    .280
     PIT N  O          17    .176
1931 BRO N  O          19    .161
        BRTR          357    .280
```

SOTHORON, ALLEN SUTTON
B.APR.27,1893 BRADFORD,OHIO
D.JUNE 17,1939 ST.LOUIS,MO.
```
1914 STL A  P           1    0- 0
1915 STL A  P           3    0- 1
1917 STL A  P          49   14-19
1918 STL A  P          29   13-12
1919 STL A  P          39   20-12
1920 STL A  P          36    8-15
1921 STL N  P           5    1- 2
     BOS A  P           2    0- 2
     CLE A  P          22   12- 4
1922 CLE A  P           6    1- 3
1924 STL N  P          29   10-16
1925 STL N  P          28   10-10
1926 STL N  P          15    3- 3
        BBTR          264   92-99
     BR 1924-26
NON-PLAYING MANAGER STL[A] 1933
```

SOTO, MARIO MELVIN
B.JULY 12,1956 BANI,D.R.
```
1977 CIN N  P          12    2- 6
1978 CIN N /P           5    1- 0
        BRTR           17    3- 6
```

SOUCHOCK, STEPHEN (BUD)
B.MAR.3,1919 YATESBORO,PA.
```
1946 NY  A  1          47    .302
1948 NY  A  1          44    .203
1949 CHI A  1-O        84    .234
1951 DET A  1-2-3-O    91    .245
1952 DET A  1-3-O      92    .249
1953 DET A  1-O        89    .302
1954 DET A  3-O        25    .179
1955 DET A  H           1   1.000
        BRTR          473    .255
```

SOURHARDT, EDWARD WILLIAM
[PLAYED UNDER NAME OF
EDWARD WILLIAM SEWARD]

SOUTHWICK, CLYDE AUBRA
B.NOV.3,1886 MAXWELL,IOWA
D.OCT.14,1961 FREEPORT,ILL.
```
1911 STL A  C           4    .250
```

SOUTHWORTH, WILLIAM FREDERICK (BILL)
B.NOV.10,1945 MADISON,WIS.
```
1964 MIL N  3           3    .286
        BRTR
```

SOUTHWORTH, WILLIAM HARRISON (BILLY)
B.MAR.9,1893 HARVARD,NEB.
D.NOV.15,1969 COLUMBUS,OHIO
```
1913 CLE A  O           1    .000
1915 CLE A  O          60    .220
1918 PIT N  O          64    .341
1919 PIT N  O         121    .280
1920 PIT N  O         146    .284
1921 BOS N  O         141    .308
1922 BOS N  O          43    .322
1923 BOS N  2-O       153    .319
1924 NY  N  O          94    .256
1925 NY  N  O         123    .292
1926 NY  N  O          36    .328
     STL N  O          99    .317
1927 STL N  O          92    .301
1929 STL N  M-O        19    .188
        BLTR         1192    .298
NON-PLAYING MANAGER
STL[N] 1940-45, BOS[N] 1946-51
```

SOWDERS, JOHN
B.DEC.10,1866 LOUISVILLE,KY.
D.JULY 29,1908 INDIANAPOLIS,IND
```
1887 IND N  P           1    0- 0
1889 KC  AA P     26   28    6-16
                       40   18-16
        BRTL     67   69   24-32
```

SOWDERS, LEONARD
B.JUNE 29,1861 LOUISVILLE,KY.
D.NOV.19,1888 INDIANAPOLIS,IND.
```
1886 BAL AA O          23    .267
```

SOWDERS, WILLIAM JEFFERSON
(LITTLE BILL)
B.NOV.29,1864 LOUISVILLE,KY.
D.FEB.22,1931 INDIANAPOLIS,IND.
```
1888 BOS N  P          35   19-15
1889 BOS N  P           4    2- 2
     PIT N  P-O   12   14    5- 4
                             .256
1890 PIT N  P          17    3- 7
        BRTR     68   70   29-28
                             .189
```

SPADE, ROBERT
B.JAN.4,1877 AKRON,OHIO
D.SEPT.7,1924 CINCINNATI,OHIO
```
1907 CIN N  P           3    1- 1
1908 CIN N  P          35   17-12
1909 CIN N  P          14    5- 5
1910 CIN N  P           3    1- 2
     STL A  P           7    1- 3
        BRTR           62   25-23
```

SPAHN, WARREN EDWARD
B.APR.23,1921 BUFFALO,N.Y.
```
1942 BOS N  P           4    0- 0
1946 BOS N  P          24    8- 5
1947 BOS N  P     40   41   21-10
1948 BOS N  P          36   15-12
1949 BOS N  P     38   40   21-14
1950 BOS N  P          41   21-17
1951 BOS N  P     39   42   22-14
1952 BOS N  P     40   52   14-19
1953 MIL N  P     35   38   23- 7
1954 MIL N  P     39   41   21-12
1955 MIL N  P     39   40   17-14
1956 MIL N  P          39   20-11
1957 MIL N  P          39   21-11
1958 MIL N  P     38   41   22-11
1959 MIL N  P          40   21-15
1960 MIL N  P          40   21-10
1961 MIL N  P     38   39   21-13
1962 MIL N  P     34   36   18-14
1963 MIL N  P          33   23- 7
1964 MIL N  P     38   39    6-13
1965 NY  N  P     20   21    4-12
     SF  N  P          16    3- 4
        BLTL     750  782  363-245
```

SPALDING, ALBERT GOODWILL
B.SEPT.2,1850 BYRON,ILL.
D.SEPT.9,1915 POINT LOMA,CAL.
```
1871 BOS NA P          33   21-10
1872 BOS NA P          48   36- 8
                             .338
1873 BOS NA P-O   57   60   41-15
                             .359
1874 BOS NA P          71   52-18
1875 BOS NA P-1-  66   74   56- 5
                O            .318
1876 CHI N  M-P-  60   66   46-14
                O            .306
1877 CHI N  M-P-   4   60    0- 0
                1-2-3        .256
1878 CHI N  2           1    .500
        BRTR     339  413  252-70
                             .318
```

SPALDING, CHARLES HARRY (DICK)
B.OCT.13,1893 PHILADELPHIA,PA.
D.FEB.3,1950 PHILADELPHIA,PA.
```
1927 PHI N  O         115    .296
1928 WAS A  O          16    .348
        BLTL          131    .299
```

YR	CL	LEA	POS	GP	G	REC

SPANGLER, ALBERT DONALD (AL)
B.JULY 8,1933 PHILADELPHIA,PA.
```
1959 MIL N  O            6    .417
1960 MIL N  O          101    .267
1961 MIL N  O           68    .268
1962 HOU N  O          129    .285
1963 HOU N  O          120    .281
1964 HOU N  O          135    .245
1965 HOU N  O           38    .214
     CAL A  O           51    .260
1966 CAL A  /O           6    .667
1967 CHI N  O           62    .254
1968 CHI N  O           88    .271
1969 CHI N  O           82    .211
1970 CHI N  /O          21    .143
1971 CHI N  /H           5    .400
     BLTL              912    .262
```

SPANSWICK, WILLIAM HENRY (BILL)
B.JULY 8,1938 SPRINGFIELD,MASS.
```
1964 BOS A  P           29   2- 3
     BLTL
```

SPARKS, THOMAS FRANK (TULLY)
B.DEC.12,1874 AETNA,GA.
D.JULY 15,1937 ANNISTON,ALA.
```
1897 PHI N  P            1   0- 1
1899 PIT N  P           25   9- 7
1901 MIL A  P           30   6-17
1902 NY  N  P           15   4-11
     BOS A  P           17   7- 8
1903 PHI N  P           28  11-15
1904 PHI N  P           26   9-16
1905 PHI N  P           34  13-11
1906 PHI N  P           42  19-16
1907 PHI N  P           33  22- 8
1908 PHI N  P           33  16-15
1909 PHI N  P           24   6-11
1910 PHI N  P            3   0- 2
     BRTR              311 122-138
```

SPARMA, JOSEPH BLASE (JOE)
B.FEB.4,1942 MASSILLON,OHIO
```
1964 DET A  P           21    5- 6
1965 DET A  P           30   13- 8
1966 DET A  P           29    2- 7
1967 DET A  P           37   16- 9
1968 DET A  P           34   10-10
1969 DET A  P           23    2- 8
1970 MON N  /P           9    0- 4
     BRTR          183 185  52-52
```

SPEAKE, ROBERT CHARLES
(BOB) OR (SPOOK)
B.AUG.22,1930 SPRINGFIELD,MO.
```
1955 CHI N  1-O         95    .218
1957 CHI N  1-O        129    .232
1958 SF  N  O           66    .211
1959 SF  N  H           15    .091
     BLTR              305    .223
```

SPEAKER, TRISTRAM E
(TRIS) OR (THE GREY EAGLE)
B.APR.4,1888 HUBBARD,TEX.
D.DEC.8,1958 LAKE WHITNEY,TEX.
```
1907 BOS A  O            7    .158
1908 BOS A  O           31    .220
1909 BOS A  O          143    .309
1910 BOS A  O          141    .340
1911 BOS A  O          141    .327
1912 BOS A  O          153    .383
1913 BOS A  O          141    .366
1914 BOS A  P-O      1 158   0- 0
                             .338
1915 BOS A  O          150    .322
1916 CLE A  O          151    .386
1917 CLE A  O          142    .352
1918 CLE A  O          127    .319
1919 CLE A  M-O        134    .296
1920 CLE A  M-O        150    .388
1921 CLE A  M-O        132    .362
1922 CLE A  M-O        131    .378
1923 CLE A  M-O        150    .380
1924 CLE A  M-O        135    .344
1925 CLE A  M-O        117    .389
1926 CLE A  M-O        150    .304
1927 WAS A  1-O        141    .327
1928 PHI A  O           64    .267
     BLTL         1 2789   0- 0
                             .344
```

SPEECE, BYRON FRANKLIN
B.JAN.6,1897 WEST BADEN,IND.
D.SEPT.29,1974 ELGIN,ORE.
```
1924 WAS A  P           21   2- 1
1925 CLE A  P           28   3- 5
1926 CLE A  P            2   0- 0
1930 PHI N  P           11   0- 0
     BRTR               62   5- 6
```

SPEED, HORACE ARTHUR
B.OCT.4,1951 LOS ANGELES,CAL.
```
1975 SF  N  /O          17    .133
1978 CLE A  O           70    .226
     BRTR               87    .215
```

SPEER, FLOYD VERNIE
B.JAN.27,1913 BOONEVILLE,ARK.
D.MAR.22,1969 LITTLE ROCK,ARK.
```
1943 CHI A  P            1   0- 0
1944 CHI A  P            2   0- 0
     BRTR                3   0- 0
```

SPEER, GEORGE NATHAN (KID)
B.JUNE 16,1886 CORNING,MO.
D.JAN.13,1940 EDMONTON,ALBERTA,
CANADA
```
1909 DET A  P           13   4- 4
     BLTL
```

SPEIER, CHRIS EDWARD
B.JUNE 28,1950 ALAMEDA,CAL.
```
1971 SF  N  *S         157    .235
1972 SF  N  *S         150    .269
1973 SF  N  *S/2       153    .249
1974 SF  N  *S/3       141    .250
1975 SF  N  *S/3       141    .271
1976 SF  N  *S/2-3-1   145    .226
1977 SF  N  /S           6    .176
     MON N  *S         139    .235
1978 MON N  *S         150    .251
     BRTR             1182    .248
```

SPENCE, HARRISON L.
B.FEB.22,1856 NEW YORK,N.Y.
D.MAY 19,1908 CHICAGO,ILL.
NON-PLAYING MANAGER INDEN] 1888

SPENCE, JOHN ROBERT (BOB)
B.FEB.10,1946 SAN DIEGO,CAL.
```
1969 CHI A  /1          12    .154
1970 CHI A  1           46    .223
1971 CHI A  /1          14    .148
     BLTR               72    .202
```

SPENCE, STANLEY ORVILLE (STAN)
B.MAR.20,1915 S.PORTSMOUTH,KY.
```
1940 BOS A  O           51    .279
1941 BOS A  1-O         86    .232
1942 WAS A  O          149    .323
1943 WAS A  O          149    .267
1944 WAS A  1-O        153    .313
1946 WAS A  O          152    .292
1947 WAS A  O          147    .279
1948 BOS A  1-O        114    .235
1949 BOS A  O            7    .150
     STL A  1-O        104    .245
     BLTL             1112    .282
```

SPENCER
```
1872 NAT NA S            2    .200
```

SPENCER, CHESTER ARTHUR
B.MAR.4,1883 S.WEBSTER,OHIO
D.NOV.20,1938 PORTSMOUTH,OHIO
```
1906 BOS N  O            7    .148
```

SPENCER, DARYL DEAN
(DARYL) OR (BIG DEE)
B.JULY 13,1929 WICHITA,KAN.
```
1952 NY  N  S-3          7    .294
1953 NY  N  2-S-3      118    .208
1956 NY  N  2-S-3      146    .221
1957 NY  N  2-S-3      148    .249
1958 SF  N  2-S        148    .256
1959 SF  N  2-S        152    .265
1960 STL N  2-S        148    .258
1961 STL N  S           37    .254
     LA  N  S-3         60    .243
1963 LA  N  S-3         77    .236
     LA  N  3            7    .111
     CIN N  3           50    .239
     BRTR             1098    .244
```

SPENCER, EDWARD RUSSELL (TUBBY)
B.JAN.26,1884 OIL CITY,PA.
D.FEB.1,1945 SAN FRANCISCO,CAL.
```
1905 STL A  C           35    .235
1906 STL A  C           58    .176
1907 STL A  C           71    .265
1908 STL A  C           91    .210
1909 BOS A  C           28    .162
1911 PHI N  C           11    .156
1916 DET A  C           19    .370
1917 DET A  C           70    .239
1918 DET A  C           66    .219
     BRTR              449    .225
```

SPENCER, FRANK G.
B.1886 MINNEAPOLIS,MINN.
```
1912 STL A  P            1   0- 0
     BRTR
```

SPENCER, GEORGE ELWELL
B.JULY 7,1926 COLUMBUS,OHIO
```
1950 NY  N  P           10   1- 0
1951 NY  N  P           57  10- 4
1952 NY  N  P           35   3- 5
1953 NY  N  P            1   0- 0
1954 NY  N  P            6   1- 0
1955 NY  N  P            1   0- 0
1958 DET A  P            7   1- 0
1960 DET A  P            5   0- 1
     BRTR              122  16-10
```

SPENCER, GLENN EDWARD
B.SEPT.11,1905 CORNING,N.Y.
D.DEC.30,1958 BINGHAMTON,N.Y.
```
1928 PIT N  P            4   0- 0
1930 PIT N  P           41   8- 9
1931 PIT N  P           38  11-12
1932 PIT N  P           39   4- 8
1933 NY  N  P           17   0- 2
     BRTR              139  23-31
```

SPENCER, HUBERT THOMAS (TOMMY)
B.FEB.28,1951 GALLIPOLIS,OHIO
```
1978 CHI A  O           29    .185
     BRTR
```

SPENCER, JAMES LLOYD (JIM)
B.JULY 30,1947 HANOVER,PA.
```
1968 CAL A  1           19    .191
1969 CAL A  *1         113    .254
1970 CAL A  *1         146    .274
1971 CAL A  *1         148    .237
1972 CAL A  1-O         82    .222
1973 CAL A  1           29    .241
     TEX A  1          102    .267
1974 TEX A  1-O        118    .278
1975 TEX A  1-O        132    .266
1976 CHI A  *1         150    .253
1977 CHI A  *1         128    .247
1978 NY  A  O-1         71    .227
     BLTL             1238    .254
```

SPENCER, LLOYD BENJAMIN (BEN)
B.MAY 15,1890 PATAPSCO,MD.
D.SEPT.1,1970 FINKSBURG,MD.
```
1913 WAS A  O            8    .300
     BLTL
```

SPENCER, ROY HAMPTON
B.FEB.22,1900 SCRANTON,N.C.
D.FEB.8,1973 PORT CHARLOTTE,FLA
```
1925 PIT N  C           14    .214
1926 PIT N  C           28    .395
1927 PIT N  C           38    .283
1929 WAS A  C           50    .155
1930 WAS A  C           93    .255
1931 WAS A  C          145    .275
1932 WAS A  C          102    .246
1933 CLE A  C           75    .203
1934 CLE A  C            5    .143
1936 NY  N  C           19    .278
1937 BRO N  C           51    .205
1938 BRO N  C           16    .267
     BRTR              636    .247
```

SPENCER, VERNON MURRAY
B.FEB.23,1896 WIXOM,MICH.
```
1920 NY  N  O           45    .200
```

SPERAW, PAUL BACHMAN
(POLLY) OR (BIRDIE)
B.OCT.5,1893 ANNVILLE,PA.
D.FEB.22,1962 CEDAR RAPIDS,IOWA
```
1920 STL A  3            1    .000
     BRTR
```

SPERBER, EDWIN GEORGE
B.JAN.21,1895 CINCINNATI,OHIO
D.JAN.5,1976 CINCINNATI,OHIO
```
1924 BOS N  O           24    .288
1925 BOS N  O            2    .000
     BLTL               26    .279
```

SPERRING, ROBERT WALTER (ROB)
B.OCT.10,1949 SAN FRANCISCO,CAL.
```
1974 CHI N  2/S         42    .206
1975 CHI N  3-2-S/O     65    .208
1976 CHI N  3-S/2-O     43    .258
1977 HOU N  S-2-3       58    .186
     BRTR              208    .211
```

SPERRY, STANLEY KENNETH
B.FEB.19,1914 EVANSVILLE,WIS.
D.SEPT.27,1962 EVANSVILLE,WIS.
```
1936 PHI N  2           20    .135
1938 PHI A  2           60    .273
     BLTR               80    .255
```

SPICER, ROBERT OBERTON (BOB)
B.APR.11,1925 RICHMOND,VA.
```
1955 KC  A  P            2   0- 0
1956 KC  A  P            2   0- 0
     BLTR                4   0- 0
```

SPIES, HENRY (HARRY)
B.JUNE 12,1866 NEW ORLEANS,LA.
D.JULY 8,1942 LOS ANGELES,CAL.
```
1895 CIN N  C           14    .200
     LOU N  C           69    .268
                        83    .257
```

SPIEZIO, EDWARD WAYNE (ED)
B.OCT.31,1941 JOLIET,ILL.

YR	CL	LEA	POS	GP	G	REC
1964	STL	N	H		12	.333
1965	STL	N	/3		10	.167
1966	STL	N	3		26	.219
1967	STL	N	3/O		55	.210
1968	STL	N	O/3		29	.157
1969	SD	N	3/O		121	.234
1970	SD	N	3		110	.285
1971	SD	N	3/O		97	.231
1972	SD	N	/3		20	.138
	CHI	A	3		74	.238
	BRTR				554	.238

SPIKES, LESLIE CHARLES (CHARLIE)
B.JAN.23,1951 BOGALUSA,LA.

YR	CL	LEA	POS	GP	G	REC
1972	NY	A	/O		14	.147
1973	CLE	A	*O-O		140	.237
1974	CLE	A	*O		155	.271
1975	CLE	A	O		111	.229
1976	CLE	A	O		101	.237
1977	CLE	A	O		32	.232
1978	DET	A	/O		10	.250
	BRTR				563	.244

SPILLNER, DANIEL RAY (DAN)
B.NOV.27,1951 CASPER,WYO.

YR	CL	LEA	POS	GP	G	REC
1974	SD	N	P		30	9-11
1975	SD	N	P		37	5-13
1976	SD	N	P	32	33	2-11
1977	SD	N	P		76	7- 6
1978	SD	N	P		17	1- 0
	CLE	A	P		36	3- 1
	BRTR			228	229	27-42

SPILMAN, WILLIAM HARRY (HARRY)
B.JULY 18,1954 ALBANY,GA.

YR	CL	LEA	POS	GP	G	REC
1978	CIN	N	/H		4	.250
	BLTR					

SPINDEL, HAROLD STEWART
B.MAY 27,1913 CHANDLER,OKLA.

YR	CL	LEA	POS	GP	G	REC
1939	STL	A	C		48	.269
1945	PHI	N	C		36	.230
1946	PHI	N	C		1	.333
	BRTR				85	.254

SPINKS, SCIPIO RONALD
B.JULY 12,1947 CHICAGO,ILL.

YR	CL	LEA	POS	GP	G	REC
1969	HOU	N	/P		1	0- 0
1970	HOU	N	/P	5	6	0- 1
1971	HOU	N	/P		5	1- 0
1972	STL	N	P	16	21	5- 5
1973	STL	N	/P		8	1- 5
	BRTR			35	41	7-11

SPLITTORFF, PAUL WILLIAM
B.OCT.8,1946 EVANSVILLE,IND.

YR	CL	LEA	POS	GP	G	REC
1970	KC	A	/P		2	0- 1
1971	KC	A	P		22	8- 9
1972	KC	A	P		35	12-12
1973	KC	A	P		38	20-11
1974	KC	A	P	36	37	13-19
1975	KC	A	P		35	9-10
1976	KC	A	P		26	11- 8
1977	KC	A	P		37	16- 6
1978	KC	A	P		39	19-13
	BLTL			270	271	108-89

SPOGNARDI, ANDREA ETTORE (ANDY)
B.OCT.18,1908 BOSTON,MASS.

YR	CL	LEA	POS	GP	G	REC
1932	BOS	A	2-S-3		17	.294

SPOHRER, ALFRED RAY (AL)
B.DEC.3,1902 PHILADELPHIA,PA.
D.JULY 17,1972 PLYMOUTH,N.H.

YR	CL	LEA	POS	GP	G	REC
1928	NY	N	C		2	.000
	BOS	N	C		51	.218
1929	BOS	N	C		114	.272
1930	BOS	N	C		112	.317
1931	BOS	N	C		114	.240
1932	BOS	N	C		104	.269
1933	BOS	N	C		67	.250
1934	BOS	N	C		100	.223
1935	BOS	N	C		92	.242
	BRTR				756	.259

SPONGBERG, CARL GUSTAV
B.MAY 21,1884 IDAHO FALLS,IDAHO
D.JULY 21,1938 LOS ANGELES,CAL.

YR	CL	LEA	POS	GP	G	REC
1908	CHI	N	P		1	0- 0
	BRTR					

SPOONER, KARL BENAJMIN
B.JUNE 23,1931 ORISKANY FALLS,N.Y.

YR	CL	LEA	POS	GP	G	REC
1954	BRO	N	P		2	2- 0
1955	BRO	N	P		29	8- 6
	BRTL				31	10- 6

SPOTTS, JAMES RUSSELL
B.APR.10,1909 HONEY BROOK,PA.
D.JUNE 15,1964 MEDFORD,N.J.

YR	CL	LEA	POS	GP	G	REC
1930	PHI	N	C		3	.000
	BRTR					

SPRAGINS, HOMER FRANKLIN
B.NOV.9,1920 GRENADA,MISS.

YR	CL	LEA	POS	GP	G	REC
1947	PHI	N	P		4	0- 0
	BRTR					

SPRAGUE, CHARLES WELLINGTON
B.OCT.10,1864 CLEVELAND,OHIO
D.DEC.31,1912 DES MOINES,IOWA

YR	CL	LEA	POS	GP	G	REC
1887	CHI	N	P		3	1- 1
1889	CLE	N	P		3	0- 3
1890	TOL	AA	P-O	14	51	6- 7
						.245
				20	57	7-11
						.236

SPRAGUE, EDWARD NELSON (ED)
B.SEP.16,1945 BOSTON,MASS.

YR	CL	LEA	POS	GP	G	REC
1968	OAK	A	P		47	3- 4
1969	OAK	A	P		27	1- 1
1971	CIN	N	/P		7	1- 0
1972	CIN	N	P		33	3- 3
1973	CIN	N	P		28	1- 3
	STL	N	/P		8	0- 0
	MIL	A	/P		7	0- 1
1974	MIL	A	P		20	7- 2
1975	MIL	A	P		18	1- 7
1976	MIL	A	/P		3	0- 2
	BRTR				198	17-23

SPRATT, HENRY LEE (JACK)
B.JULY 10,1868 BROADFORD,VA.
D.JULY 3,1969 WASHINGTON,D.C.

YR	CL	LEA	POS	GP	G	REC
1911	BOS	N	S		41	.240
1912	BOS	N	S		27	.258
	BLTR				68	.247

SPRIGGS, GEORGE HERMAN
B.MAY 22,1941 NEWELL,MD.

YR	CL	LEA	POS	GP	G	REC
1965	PIT	N	/O		9	.500
1966	PIT	N	/H		9	.143
1967	PIT	N	O		38	.175
1969	KC	A	/O		23	.138
1970	KC	A	O		51	.208
	BLTR				130	.191

SPRING, JACK RUSSELL
B.MAR.11,1933 SPOKANE,WASH.

YR	CL	LEA	POS	GP	G	REC
1955	MIN	N	P		2	0- 1
1957	BOS	A	P		1	0- 0
1958	WAS	A	P		3	0- 0
1961	LA	A	P		18	3- 0
1962	LA	A	P		57	4- 2
1963	LA	A	P		45	3- 0
1964	LA	A	P		6	1- 0
	CHI	N	P		7	0- 0
	STL	N	P		2	0- 0
1965	CLE	A	P		14	1- 2
	BRTL				155	12- 5

SPRINGER, BRADFORD LOUIS
B.MAY 9,1904 DETROIT,MICH.
D.JAN.4,1970 BIRMINGHAM,MICH.

YR	CL	LEA	POS	GP	G	REC
1925	STL	A	P		2	0- 0
1926	CIN	N	P		1	0- 0
	BLTL				3	0- 0

SPRINGER, EDWARD E.
B.DETROIT,MICH.

YR	CL	LEA	POS	GP	G	REC
1889	LOU	AA	P		1	0- 1

SPRINZ, JOSEPH CONRAD
(JOE) OR (MULE)
B.AUG.3,1902 ST.LOUIS,MO.

YR	CL	LEA	POS	GP	G	REC
1930	CLE	A	C		17	.178
1931	CLE	A	C		1	.000
1933	STL	N	C		3	.200
	BRTR				21	.170

SPROULL, CHARLES WILLIAM
B.JAN.9,1919 TAYLORSVILLE,GA.

YR	CL	LEA	POS	GP	G	REC
1945	PHI	N	P		34	4-10
	BRTR					

SPROUT, ROBERT SAMUEL
B.DEC.5,1941 FLORIN,PA.

YR	CL	LEA	POS	GP	G	REC
1961	LA	A	P		1	0- 0
	BLTL					

SPROWL, ROBERT JOHN (BOBBY)
B.APR.14,1956 SANDUSKY,OHIO

YR	CL	LEA	POS	GP	G	REC
1978	BOS	A	/P		3	0- 2
	BLTL					

SPURGEON, FRED (FREDDY)
B.OCT.9,1900 WABASH,IND.
D.NOV.5,1970 KALAMAZOO,MICH.

YR	CL	LEA	POS	GP	G	REC
1924	CLE	A	2		2	.167
1925	CLE	A	2-S-3		107	.287
1926	CLE	A	2		149	.294
1927	CLE	A	2		57	.252
	BRTR				315	.285

SPURNEY, EDWARD FREDERICK
B.JAN.9,1872 CLEVELAND,OHIO
D.OCT.12,1932 CLEVELAND,OHIO

YR	CL	LEA	POS	GP	G	REC
1891	PIT	N	S		3	.285

SQUIRES, MICHAEL LYNN (MIKE)
B.MAR.5,1952 KALAMAZOO,MICH.

YR	CL	LEA	POS	GP	G	REC
1975	CHI	A	1		20	.231
1977	CHI	A	/1		3	.000
1978	CHI	A	1		46	.280
	BLTL				69	.261

STACEK, ALBERT JOHN
[PLAYED UNDER NAME OF
ALBERT JOHN STOKES]

STACK, WILLIAM EDWARD (EDDIE)
B.OCT.2,1887 CHICAGO,ILL.
D.AUG.28,1958 CHICAGO,ILL.

YR	CL	LEA	POS	GP	G	REC
1910	PHI	N	P		20	6- 7
1911	PHI	N	P		12	5- 5
1912	BRO	N	P		28	7- 5
1913	BRO	N	P		23	4- 4
	CHI	N	P		11	4- 2
1914	CHI	N	P		6	0- 1
	BRTR				100	26-24

STAEHLE, MARVIN GUSTAVE (MARV)
B.MAR.13,1942 OAK PARK,ILL.

YR	CL	LEA	POS	GP	G	REC
1964	CHI	A	H		6	.400
1965	CHI	A	/H		7	.429
1966	CHI	A	/2		8	.133
1967	CHI	A	2/S		32	.111
1969	MON	N	/2		6	.412
1970	MON	N	2/S		104	.218
1971	ATL	N	/2-3		22	.111
	BLTR				185	.207

STAFFORD, HENRY ALEXANDER (HEINIE)
B.NOV.1,1891 ORLEANS,VT.
D.JAN.29,1972 LAKE WORTH,FLA.

YR	CL	LEA	POS	GP	G	REC
1916	NY	N	H		1	.000
	TR					

STAFFORD, JAMES JOSEPH
(GENERAL) OR (JAMSEY)
B.JULY 9,1868 WEBSTER,MASS.
D.SEPT.11,1923 WORCESTER,MASS.

YR	CL	LEA	POS	GP	G	REC
1890	BUF	P	P		15	3- 9
1893	NY	N	O		67	.301
1894	NY	N	3		11	.229
1895	NY	N	2		123	.293
1896	NY	N	O		59	.282
1897	NY	N	S-O		7	.091
	LOU	N	S		112	.280
1898	LOU	N	O		42	.312
	BOS	N	1-O		37	.270
1899	BOS	N	O		50	.313
	WAS	N	2-S-3		30	.243
	BRTR			15	553	3- 9
						.284

STAFFORD, JOHN HENRY (DOC)
B.APR.8,1870 DUDLEY,MASS.
D.JULY 3,1940 WORCESTER,MASS.

YR	CL	LEA	POS	GP	G	REC
1893	CLE	N	P		2	0- 0
	BRTR					

STAFFORD, ROBERT LEE

YR	CL	LEA	POS	GP	G	REC
1890	ATH	AA	O		1	.000

STAFFORD, WILLIAM CHARLES (BILL)
B.AUG.13,1939 CATSKILL,N.Y.

YR	CL	LEA	POS	GP	G	REC
1960	NY	A	P	11	12	3- 1
1961	NY	A	P		36	14- 9
1962	NY	A	P		35	14- 9
1963	NY	A	P		28	4- 8
1964	NY	A	P		31	5- 0
1965	NY	A	P		22	3- 8
1966	KC	A	P		9	0- 4
1967	KC	A	P		14	0- 1
	BRTR			186	187	43-40

STAGGS, STEPHEN ROBERT (STEVE)
B.MAY 6,1951 ANCHORAGE,ALASKA

YR	CL	LEA	POS	GP	G	REC
1977	TOR	A	2		72	.258
1978	OAK	A	2/S-3		47	.244
	BRTR				119	.255

STAHL, CHARLES SYLVESTER (CHICK)
B.JAN.10,1873 FT.WAYNE,IND.
D.MAR.28,1907 W.BADEN,IND.

YR	CL	LEA	POS	GP	G	REC
1897	BOS	N	O		111	.359
1898	BOS	N	O		125	.311
1899	BOS	N	O		148	.348
1900	BOS	N	O		134	.293
1901	BOS	A	O		130	.310
1902	BOS	A	O		127	.318
1903	BOS	A	O		78	.279
1904	BOS	A	O		157	.300
1905	BOS	A	O		134	.258
1906	BOS	A	M-O		155	.286
	BLTL				1299	.306

YR	CL	LEA	POS	GP	G	REC

STAHL, GARLAND (JAKE)
B.APR.13,1879 ELKHART,IND.
D.SEPT.18,1922 LOS ANGELES,CAL.

YR	CL	LEA	POS	GP	G	REC
1903	BOS	A	C		38	.239
1904	WAS	A	1-O		141	.261
1905	WAS	A	M-1		140	.250
1906	WAS	A	M-1		137	.222
1908	NY	A	1-O		74	.239
	BOS	A	1		79	.240
1909	BOS	A	1		127	.294
1910	BOS	A	1		144	.271
1912	BOS	A	M-1		95	.301
1913	BOS	A	M-1		1	.000
	BRTR				976	.260

STAHL, LARRY FLOYD
B.JUNE 29,1941 BELLEVILLE,ILL.

YR	CL	LEA	POS	GP	G	REC
1964	NY	N	O		15	.261
1965	KC	A	O		28	.198
1966	KC	A	O		119	.250
1967	NY	N	O		71	.239
1968	NY	N	O/1		53	.235
1969	SD	N	O-1		95	.198
1970	SD	N	O		52	.182
1971	SD	N	O/1		114	.253
1972	SD	N	O/1		107	.226
1973	CIN	N	O/1		76	.225
	BLTL				730	.232

STAIGER, ROY JOSEPH
B.JAN.6,1950 TULSA,OKLA.

YR	CL	LEA	POS	GP	G	REC
1975	NY	N	3		13	.158
1976	NY	N	3/S		95	.220
1977	NY	N	3/S		40	.252
	BRTR				148	.226

STAINBACK, GEORGE TUCKER (TUCK)
B.AUG.4,1910 LOS ANGELES,CAL.

YR	CL	LEA	POS	GP	G	REC
1934	CHI	N	O		104	.306
1935	CHI	N	O		47	.255
1936	CHI	N	O		44	.173
1937	CHI	N	O		72	.231
1938	STL	N	O		6	.000
	PHI	N	O		30	.259
	BRO	N	O		35	.327
1939	BRO	N	O		68	.269
1940	DET	A	O		15	.225
1941	DET	A	O		94	.245
1942	NY	A	O		15	.200
1943	NY	A	O		71	.260
1944	NY	A	O		30	.218
1945	NY	A	O		95	.257
1946	PHI	A	O		91	.244
	BRTR				817	.258

STALBERGER, WILLIAM
B.DETROIT,MICH.

YR	CL	LEA	POS	GP	G	REC
1885	PRO	N	P		1	0- 1

STALEY, GEORGE GAYLORD (GALE)
B.MAY 2,1899 DE PERE,WIS.

YR	CL	LEA	POS	GP	G	REC
1925	CHI	N	2		7	.423
	BLTR					

STALEY, GERALD LEE (GERRY)
B.AUG.21,1920 BRUSH PRAIRIE,WASH.

YR	CL	LEA	POS	GP	G	REC
1947	STL	N	P		18	1- 0
1948	STL	N	P		31	4- 4
1949	STL	N	P		45	10-10
1950	STL	N	P		42	13-13
1951	STL	N	P		42	19-13
1952	STL	N	P		35	17-14
1953	STL	N	P		40	18- 9
1954	STL	N	P		48	7-13
1955	CIN	N	P		30	5- 8
	NY	A	P		2	0- 0
1956	NY	A	P		1	0- 0
	CHI	A	P		26	8- 3
1957	CHI	A	P		47	5- 1
1958	CHI	A	P		50	4- 5
1959	CHI	A	P		67	8- 5
1960	CHI	A	P		64	13- 8
1961	CHI	A	P		16	0- 3
	KC	A	P		23	1- 1
	DET	A	P		13	1- 1
	BRTR				640	134-111

STALEY, HENRY E. (HARRY)
B.NOV.3,1866 JACKSONVILLE,ILL.
D.JAN.12,1910 BATTLE CREEK,MICH

YR	CL	LEA	POS	GP	G	REC
1888	PIT	N	P		24	12-12
1889	PIT	N	P	48	49	21-26
1890	PIT	P	P		47	21-23
1891	PIT	N	P		9	2- 4
	BOS	N	P		27	19- 8
1892	BOS	N	P		35	24-11
1893	BOS	N	P		32	19-10
1894	BOS	N	P		27	13-14
1895	STL	N	P		18	5-13
	BRTR			267	268	136-121

STALLARD, EVAN TRACY (TRACY)
B.AUG.31,1937 COEBURN,VA.

YR	CL	LEA	POS	GP	G	REC
1960	BOS	A	P		4	0- 0
1961	BOS	A	P		43	2- 7
1962	BOS	A	P		1	0- 0
1963	NY	N	P		39	6-17
1964	NY	N	P		36	10-20
1965	STL	N	P		40	11- 8
1966	STL	N	P		20	1- 5
	BRTR				183	30-57

STALLCUP, THOMAS VIRGIL (RED)
B.JAN.3,1922 RAVENSFORD,N.&C.

YR	CL	LEA	POS	GP	G	REC
1947	CIN	N	S		8	.000
1948	CIN	N	S		149	.228
1949	CIN	N	S		141	.254
1950	CIN	N	S		136	.251
1951	CIN	N	S		121	.241
1952	CIN	N	S		2	.000
	STL	N	S		29	.129
1953	CIN	N	H		1	.000
	BRTR				587	.241

STALLER, GEORGE WALBORN
(GEORGE) OR (STOPPER)
B.APR.1,1916 RUTHERFORD HEIGHTS,PA.

YR	CL	LEA	POS	GP	G	REC
1943	PHI	A	O		21	.271
	BLTL					

STALLINGS, GEORGE TWEEDY
(GEORGE) OR (GENTLEMAN GEORGE)
B.NOV.17,1867 AUGUSTA,GA.
D.MAY 13,1929 HADDOCK,GA.

YR	CL	LEA	POS	GP	G	REC
1890	BRO	N	C		4	.000
1897	PHI	N	M-1		1	.400
	BRTR				5	.100

NON-PLAYING MANAGER
PHI(N) 1898; DET(A) 1901,
NY(A) 1909-10, BOS(N) 1913-20

STANAGE, OSCAR HARLAND
B.MAR.17,1883 TULARE,CAL.
D.NOV.11,1964 DETROIT,MICH.

YR	CL	LEA	POS	GP	G	REC
1906	CIN	N	C		1	1.000
1909	DET	A	C		77	.262
1910	DET	A	C		88	.207
1911	DET	A	C		141	.264
1912	DET	A	C		119	.261
1913	DET	A	C		80	.224
1914	DET	A	C		122	.193
1915	DET	A	C		100	.223
1916	DET	A	C		94	.237
1917	DET	A	C		99	.205
1918	DET	A	C		54	.253
1919	DET	A	C		38	.242
1920	DET	A	C		78	.231
1925	DET	A	C		3	.200
	BRTR				1094	.234

STALBERGER... [STANCEAU, CHARLES]
B.JAN.9,1916 CANTON,OHIO
D.APR.3,1969 CANTON,OHIO

YR	CL	LEA	POS	GP	G	REC
1941	NY	A	P		22	3- 3
1946	NY	A	P		3	0- 0
	PHI	N	P		14	2- 4
	BRTR				39	5- 7

STANDAERT, JEROME JOHN
B.NOV.2,1901 CHICAGO,ILL.
D.AUG.4,1964 CHICAGO,ILL.

YR	CL	LEA	POS	GP	G	REC
1925	BRO	N	H		1	.000
1926	BRO	N	2-3		66	.345
1929	BOS	A	1		19	.167
	BRTR				86	.318

STANDRIDGE, ALFRED PETER (PETE)
B.APR.25,1891 BLACK DIAMOND,WASH.
D.AUG.2,1963 SAN FRANCISCO,CAL.

YR	CL	LEA	POS	GP	G	REC
1911	STL	N	P		2	0- 0
1915	CHI	N	P	29	30	4- 1
	BRTR			31	32	4- 1

STANEK, ALBERT WILFRED
(AL) OR (LEFTY)
B.DEC.24,1943 SPRINGFIELD,MASS.

YR	CL	LEA	POS	GP	G	REC
1963	SF	N	P		11	0- 0
	BLTL					

STANGE, ALBERT LEE (LEE)
B.OCT.27,1936 CHICAGO,ILL.

YR	CL	LEA	POS	GP	G	REC
1961	MIN	A	P		7	1- 0
1962	MIN	A	P		44	4- 3
1963	MIN	A	P		32	12- 5
1964	MIN	A	P		3	3- 6
	CLE	A	P	23	24	4- 8
1965	CLE	A	P		41	8- 4
1966	CLE	A	/P		8	1- 0
	BOS	A	P		28	7- 9
1967	BOS	A	P		35	8-10
1968	BOS	A	P		30	5- 5
1969	BOS	A	P		41	6- 9
1970	BOS	A	P		20	2- 2
	CHI	A	P		16	1- 0
	BRTR			359	360	62-61

STANHOUSE, DONALD JOSEPH (DON)
B.FEB.12,1951 DU QUOIN,ILL.

YR	CL	LEA	POS	GP	G	REC
1972	TEX	A	P	24	26	2- 9
1973	TEX	A	P	21	23	1- 7
1974	TEX	A	P		18	1- 1
1975	MON	N	/P		4	0- 0
1976	MON	N	P		34	9-12
1977	MON	N	P		47	10-10
1978	BAL	A	P		56	6- 9
	BRTR			204	208	29-48

STANKA, JOE DONALD
B.JULY 23,1931 HAMMON,OKLA.

YR	CL	LEA	POS	GP	G	REC
1959	CHI	A	P		2	1- 0
	BRTR					

STANKARD, THOMAS FRANCIS
B.MAR.20,1882 WALTHAM,MASS.
D.JUNE 13,1958 WALTHAM,MASS.

YR	CL	LEA	POS	GP	G	REC
1904	PIT	N	3		2	.000
	BRTR					

STANKY, EDWARD RAYMOND (EDDIE)
(THE BRAT) OR (MUGGSY)
B.SEPT.3,1916 PHILADELPHIA,PA.

YR	CL	LEA	POS	GP	G	REC
1943	CHI	N	2-S-3		142	.245
1944	CHI	N	2-S-3		13	.240
	BRO	N	2-S-3		89	.276
1945	BRO	N	2-S		153	.258
1946	BRO	N	2		144	.273
1947	BRO	N	2		146	.252
1948	BOS	N	2		67	.320
1949	BOS	N	2		138	.285
1950	NY	N	2		152	.300
1951	NY	N	2		145	.247
1952	STL	N	M-2		53	.229
1953	STL	N	M-2		17	.267
	BRTR				1259	.268

NON-PLAYING MANAGER
STL(N) 1954-55, CHI(A) 1966-68
TEX(A) 1977 (ONE GAME)

STANLEY, FREDERICK BLAIR (FRED)
B.AUG.13,1947 FARNHAMVILLE,IOWA

YR	CL	LEA	POS	GP	G	REC
1969	SEA	A	S/2		17	.279
1970	MIL	A	/2		6	.000
1971	CLE	A	S/2		60	.225
1972	CLE	A	/S-2		6	.167
	SD	N	2-S/3		39	.200
1973	NY	A	S/2		26	.212
1974	NY	A	S-2		33	.184
1975	NY	A	S-2/3		117	.222
1976	NY	A	*S/2		110	.238
1977	NY	A	S/3-2		48	.261
1978	NY	A	S-2/3		81	.219
	BRTR				543	.225
	BB 1969-71					

STANLEY, JAMES F.
B.1889

YR	CL	LEA	POS	GP	G	REC
1914	CHI	F	S		46	.206

STANLEY, JOHN LEONARD (BUCK)
B.NOV.13,1889 WASHINGTON,D.C.
D.AUG.13,1940 NORFOLK,VA.

YR	CL	LEA	POS	GP	G	REC
1911	PHI	N	P		4	0- 1
	BLTL					

STANLEY, JOSEPH
B.NEW JERSEY

YR	CL	LEA	POS	GP	G	REC
1884	BAL	U	O		5	.217

STANLEY, JOSEPH BERNARD
B.APR.2,1881 WASHINGTON,D.C.
D.SEPT.13,1967 DETROIT,MICH.

YR	CL	LEA	POS	GP	G	REC
1897	WAS	N	P		1	0- 0
1902	WAS	A	P		3	.333
1903	BOS	N	P-O	1	79	0- 0
						.250
1904	BOS	N	O		3	.000
1905	WAS	A	O		28	.261
1906	WAS	A	O		73	.163
1909	CHI	N	O		16	.135
	BBTR			2	203	0- 0
						.213

STANLEY, MITCHELL JACK (MICKEY)
B.JULY 20,1942 GRAND RAPIDS,MICH

YR	CL	LEA	POS	GP	G	REC
1964	DET	A	O		4	.273
1965	DET	A	O		30	.239
1966	DET	A	O		92	.289
1967	DET	A	*O/1		145	.210
1968	DET	A	*O-1/S-2		153	.259
1969	DET	A	*O-S/1		149	.235
1970	DET	A	*O/1		142	.252
1971	DET	A	*O		139	.292
1972	DET	A	*O		142	.234
1973	DET	A	*O		157	.244
1974	DET	A	O-1/2		99	.221
1975	DET	A	O-1/3		52	.256
1976	DET	A	O-1-3/S-2		84	.257
1977	DET	A	O/1-S		75	.230
1978	DET	A	O-1		53	.265
	BRTR				1516	.248

YR	CL	LEA	POS	GP	G	REC

STANLEY, ROBERT WILLIAM (BOB)
B.NOV.10,1954 PORTLAND,MAINE

YR	CL	LEA	POS	GP	G	REC
1977	BOS	A	P		41	8- 7
1978	BOS	A	P		52	15- 2
	BRTR				93	23- 9

STANSBURY, JOHN JAMES (JACK)
B.DEC.6,1885 PHILLIPSBURG,N.J.
D.DEC.26,1970 EASTON,PA.

1918	BOS	A	3		20	.128
	BRTR					

STANTON, GEORGE WASHINGTON (BUCK)
B.JUNE 19,1906 STANTONSBURG,N.C

1931	STL	N	O		13	.200
	BLTL					

STANTON, HARRY ANDREW
B.ST.LOUIS,MO.

1900	STL	N	C		1	.000
1904	CHI	N	C		1	.000
	TR				2	.000

STANTON, LEROY BOBBY
B.APR.10,1946 LATTA,S.C.

1970	NY	N	/O		4	.250
1971	NY	N	/O		5	.190
1972	CAL	A	*O		127	.251
1973	CAL	A	*O		119	.235
1974	CAL	A	*O		118	.267
1975	CAL	A	*O		137	.261
1976	CAL	A	O		93	.190
1977	SEA	A	O-D		133	.275
1978	SEA	A	O-D		93	.182
	BRTR				829	.244

STANTON, MICHAEL THOMAS (MIKE)
B.SEPT.25,1952 PHENIX CITY,ALA.

1975	HOU	N	/P		7	0- 2
	BRTR					

STAPLES, JOSEPH F.
B.BUFFALO,N.Y.

1885	BUF	N	2-O		7	.045

STARGELL, WILVER DORNEL (WILLIE)
B.MAR.6,1940 EARLSBORO,OKLA.

1962	PIT	N	O		10	.290
1963	PIT	N	1-O		108	.243
1964	PIT	N	1-O		117	.273
1965	PIT	N	*O/1		144	.272
1966	PIT	N	*O-1		140	.315
1967	PIT	N	O-1		134	.271
1968	PIT	N	*O-1		128	.237
1969	PIT	N	*O-1		145	.307
1970	PIT	N	O/1		136	.264
1971	PIT	N	*O		141	.295
1972	PIT	N	/1-O		138	.293
1973	PIT	N	*O		148	.299
1974	PIT	N	*O/1		140	.301
1975	PIT	N	*1		124	.269
1976	PIT	N	*1		117	.257
1977	PIT	N	1		63	.274
1978	PIT	N	*1		122	.295
	BLTL				2055	.283

STARK, MONROE RANDOLPH (DOLLY)
B.JAN.19,1885 RIPLEY,MISS.
D.DEC.1,1924 MEMPHIS,TENN.

1909	CLE	A	S		19	.200
1910	BRO	N	S		30	.165
1911	BRO	N	2-S		55	.295
1912	BRO	N	S		8	.182
	BRTR				112	.238

STARKEL, CONRAD
B.NOV.16,1880 GERMANY
D.JAN.19,1933 TACOMA,WASH.

1906	WAS	A	P		1	0- 0
	BRTR					

STARNAGLE, GEORGE HENRY
[REAL NAME GEORGE HENRY STEUERNAGEL]
B.OCT.6,1873 BELLEVILLE,ILL.
D.FEB.19,1946 BELLEVILLE,ILL.

1902	CLE	A	C		1	.000
	BRTR					

STARR, CHARLES WATKIN
B.AUG.30,1878 PIKE CO.,OHIO
D.OCT.18,1937 PASADENA,CAL.

1905	STL	A	2		24	.206
1908	PIT	N	S		19	.186
1909	BOS	N	2		61	.222
	PHI	N	2		3	.000
	TR				107	.211

STARR, RAYMOND FRANCIS
(RAY) OR (IRON MAN)
B.APR.23,1906 NOWATA,OKLA.
D.FEB.9,1963 BAYLIS,ILL.

1932	STL	N	P		3	1- 1
1933	NY	N	P		6	0- 1
	BOS	N	P		9	0- 1
1941	CIN	N	P		7	3- 2
1942	CIN	N	P		37	15-13
1943	CIN	N	P		36	11-10
1944	PIT	N	P		27	6- 5
1945	PIT	N	P		4	0- 2
	CHI	N	P		9	1- 0
	BRTR				138	37-35

STARR, RICHARD EUGENE (DICK)
B.MAR.2,1921 KITTANNING,PA.

1947	NY	A	P		4	1- 0
1948	NY	A	P		1	0- 0
1949	STL	A	P		30	1- 7
1950	STL	A	P	32	33	7- 5
1951	STL	A	P		15	2- 5
	WAS	A	P		11	1- 7
	BRTR			.0	94	12-24

STARR, WILLIAM (CHICK)
B.FEB.26,1911 BROOKLYN,N.Y.

1935	WAS	A	C		12	.208
1936	WAS	A	C		1	.000
	BRTR				13	.208

STARRETTE, HERMAN PAUL
B.NOV.20,1938 STATESVILLE,N.C.

1963	BAL	A	P		18	0- 1
1964	BAL	A	P		5	1- 0
1965	BAL	A	/P		4	0- 0
	BRTR				27	1- 1

START, JOSEPH (JOE)
(OLD RELIABLE) OR (ROCKS)
B.OCT.14,1842 NEW YORK,N.Y.
D.MAR.27,1927 PROVIDENCE,R.I.

1871	MUT	NA	1		34	-
1872	MUT	NA	1		55	.274
1873	MUT	NA	1		54	-
1874	MUT	NA	1		54	-
1875	MUT	NA	1		69	.210
1876	MUT	N	1		56	.276
1877	HAR	N	1		60	.332
1878	CHI	N	1		60	.345
1879	PRO	N	1		65	.318
1880	PRO	N	1		79	.260
1881	PRO	N	1		79	.327
1882	PRO	N	1		82	.328
1883	PRO	N	1		87	.283
1884	PRO	N	1		90	.273
1885	PRO	N	1		99	.275
1886	WAS	N	1		29	.229
	BLTL				1062	-

STATON, JOSEPH (JOE)
B.MAR.8,1948 SEATTLE,WASH.

1972	DET	A	/1		6	.000
1973	DET	A	/1		9	.235
	BLTL				15	.211

STATZ, ARNOLD JOHN (JIGGER)
B.OCT.20,1897 WAUKEGAN,ILL.

1919	NY	N	2-O		21	.300
1920	NY	N	O		16	.133
	BOS	A	O		2	.000
1922	CHI	N	O		110	.297
1923	CHI	N	O		154	.319
1924	CHI	N	2-O		135	.277
1925	CHI	N	O		38	.257
1927	BRO	N	O		130	.274
1928	BRO	N	O		77	.234
	BRTR				683	.285
	BB 1922 (PART)					

STAUB, DANIEL JOSEPH (RUSTY)
B.APR.1,1944 NEW ORLEANS,LA.

1963	HOU	N	1-O		150	.224
1964	HOU	N	1-O		89	.216
1965	HOU	N	*O/1		131	.256
1966	HOU	N	*O/1		153	.280
1967	HOU	N	*O		149	.333
1968	HOU	N	*1-O		161	.291
1969	MON	N	*O		158	.302
1970	MON	N	*O		160	.274
1971	MON	N	*O		162	.311
1972	NY	N	O		66	.293
1973	NY	N	*O		152	.279
1974	NY	N	*O		151	.258
1975	NY	N	*O		155	.282
1976	DET	A	*O-D		161	.299
1977	DET	A	*D		158	.278
1978	DET	A	*D		162	.273
	BLTR				2318	.280

STAUFFER, CHARLES EDWARD (ED)
B.JAN.10,1898 EMSWORTH,PA.

1923	CHI	N	P		1	0- 0
1925	STL	A	P		20	0- 1
	BRTR				21	0- 1

STEARNS, DANIEL ECKFORD
B.OCT.17,1861 BUFFALO,N.Y.
D.JUNE 28,1944 GLENDALE,CAL.

1880	BUF	N	C-2-S-3-O		21	.232
1881	DET	N	S		3	.100
1882	CIN	AA	1-2-S-O		49	.302
1883	BAL	AA	1-O		94	.248
1884	BAL	AA	1		101	.241
1885	BAL	AA	1		67	.186
	BUF	N	C-1-S		30	.200
1889	KC	AA	1		139	.288
	BLTR				504	.252

STEARNS, JOHN HARDIN
B.AUG.21,1951 DENVER,COL.

1974	PHI	N	/C		1	.500
1975	NY	N	C		59	.189
1976	NY	N	C		32	.262
1977	NY	N	*C/1		139	.251
1978	NY	N	*C/3		143	.264
	BRTR				374	.249

STEARNS, WILLIAM

1871	OLY	NA	P		2	2- 0
1872	NAT	NA	P		11	0-11
1873	NAT	NA	P		31	7-24
1874	HAR	NA	P-O	18	32	2-16
1875	NAT	NA	P-O	14	19	2-12
				76	95	13-63

STECHER, CHARLES
B.BORDENTOWN,N.J.

1890	ATH	AA	P		10	0- 7

STEDRONSKE
B.TROY,N.Y.

1879	CHI	N	2-3		4	.083

STEELE, ELMER RAE
B.MAY 17,1886 MUITZESKILL,N.Y.
D.MAR.9,1966 RHINEBECK,N.Y.

1907	BOS	A	P		4	0- 1
1908	BOS	A	P		16	5- 7
1909	BOS	A	P		15	4- 2
1910	PIT	N	P		3	0- 3
1911	PIT	N	P		31	9- 9
	BRO	N	P		5	0- 0
	BBTR				74	18-22

STEELE, ROBERT WESLEY
B.JAN.5,1894 CASSBURN,ONT.,CAN.
D.JAN.27,1962 OCALA,FLA.

1916	STL	N	P		29	5-15
1917	STL	N	P		12	1- 3
	PIT	N	P	27	33	5-11
1918	PIT	N	P		10	2- 3
	NY	N	P		12	3- 5
1919	NY	N	P		1	0- 1
	BBTL				91	97	16-38

STEELE, WILLIAM MITCHELL (BIG BILL)
B.OCT.5,1885 MILFORD,PA.
D.OCT.19,1949 OVERLAND,PA.

1910	STL	N	P		9	4- 4
1911	STL	N	P		43	18-19
1912	STL	N	P	40	41	9-13
1913	STL	N	P		12	4- 4
1914	STL	N	P		17	1- 2
	BRO	N	P		8	1- 1
	BRTR			129	130	37-43

STEELMAN, MORRIS JAMES (FARMER)
B.JUNE 29,1875 MILLVILLE,N.J.
D.SEPT.16,1944 MERCHANTVILLE,N.J.

1899	LOU	N	C		5	.062
1900	BRO	N	C		1	.000
1901	BRO	N	C		1	.333
	PHI	A	C		27	.267
1902	PHI	A	C-O		10	.187
	TR				44	.220

STEEN, WILLIAM JOHN
B.NOV.11,1887 PITTSBURGH,PA.

1912	CLE	A	P		26	9- 8
1913	CLE	A	P		22	4- 5
1914	CLE	A	P		30	9-14
1915	CLE	A	P		10	0- 4
	DET	A	P		20	6- 1
	BRTR				108	28-32

STEENGRAFE, MILTON HENRY
B.MAY 26,1900 SAN FRANCISCO,CAL
D.JUNE 2,1977

1924	CHI	A	P		3	0- 0
1926	CHI	A	P		13	1- 2
	BRTR				16	1- 2

STEERE, FRED EUGENE
B.AUG.16,1872 S.SCITUATE,R.I.
D.MAR.13,1942

1894	PIT	N	S		10	.184

YR	CL LEA POS	GP	G	REC

STEEVENS, MORRIS DALE
B.OCT.7,1940 ADDIE,ILL.
1962 CHI N	P	12	0- 1
1964 PHI N	P	4	0- 0
1965 PHI N	/P	6	0- 1
	BLTL	22	0- 2

STEGMAN, DAVID WILLIAM (DAVE)
B.JAN.30,1954 INGLEWOOD,CAL.
| 1978 DET A | /O | 8 | .286 |
| | BRTR | | |

STEIN, EDWARD F.
B.SEPT.5,1869 DETROIT,MICH.
D.MAY 10,1928 DETROIT,MICH.
1890 CHI N	P	18	11- 6
1891 CHI N	P	13	6- 6
1892 BRO N	P	45	27-18
1893 BRO N	P	35	19-14
1894 BRO N	P	41	26-14
1895 BRO N	P	28	15-13
1896 BRO N	P	17	3- 7
1898 BRO N	P	3	0- 2
		200	107-80

STEIN, IRVIN MICHAEL
B.MAY 21,1911 MADISONVILLE,LA.
| 1932 PHI A | P | 1 | 0- 0 |
| | BRTR | | |

STEIN, JUSTIN MARION (OTT)
B.AUG.9,1911 ST.LOUIS,MO.
1938 PHI N	2-3	11	.256
	CIN N	2-5	11	.333
	BRTR	22	.281

STEIN, WILLIAM ALLEN (BILL)
B.JAN.21,1947 BATTLE CREEK,MICH.
1972 STL N	/3-O	14	.314
1973 STL N	O/1-3	32	.218
1974 CHI A	3	13	.279
1975 CHI A	2-3-O/O	76	.270
1976 CHI A	2-3/1-S-O	117	.268
1977 SEA A	*3/S	151	.259
1978 SEA A	*3	114	.261
	BRTR	517	.263

STEIN, WILLIAM RANDOLPH (RANDY)
B.MAR.7,1953 POMONA,CAL.
| 1978 MIL A | P | 31 | 3- 2 |
| | BRTR | | |

STEINBACHER, HENRY JOHN (HANK)
B.MAR.22,1913 SACRAMENTO,CAL.
D.APR.3,1977 SACRAMENTO,CAL.
1937 CHI A	O	26	.260
1938 CHI A	O	106	.331
1939 CHI A	O	71	.171
	BLTR	203	.292

STEINBRENNER, EUGENE GASS
B.NOV.17,1892 PITTSBURGH,PA.
D.APR.29,1970 PITTSBURGH,PA.
| 1912 PIT N | 2 | 3 | .100 |
| | TR | | |

STEINECKE, WILLIAM ROBERT
B.FEB.7,1907 CINCINNATI,OHIO
| 1931 PIT N | C | 4 | .000 |
| | BRTR | | |

STEINEDER, RAYMOND J.
B.NOV.13,1895 SALEM,N.J.
1923 PIT N	P	15	2- 0
1924 PIT N	P	5	0- 1
	PHI N	P	9	1- 1
	BRTR	29	3- 2

STEINER, BENAJMIN SAUNDERS (BEN)
B.JULY 28,1921 ALEXANDRIA,VA.
1945 BOS A	2	78	.257
1946 BOS A	3	3	.250
1947 DET A	H	1	.000
	BLTR	82	.256

STEINER, JAMES HARRY (RED)
B.JAN.9,1915 LOS ANGELES,CAL.
1945 CLE A	C	12	.143
	BOS A	C	26	.207
	BLTR	38	.190

STEINFELDT, HARRY M.
B.SEPT.29,1877 ST.LOUIS,MO.
D.AUG.17,1914 BELLEVUE,KY.
1898 CIN N	2-O	83	.289
1899 CIN N	2-3	107	.242
1900 CIN N	2-3	136	.247
1901 CIN N	2-3	105	.250
1902 CIN N	3-S-O	128	.276
1903 CIN N	3	118	.312
1904 CHI N	3	98	.244
1905 CHI N	3	106	.271
1906 CHI N	3	151	.327
1907 CHI N	3	151	.266
1908 CHI N	3	150	.241
1909 CHI N	3	151	.252
1910 CHI N	3	128	.252
1911 BOS N	3	19	.254
	BRTR	1631	.267

STELLBAUER, WILLIAM JENNINGS
B.MAR.20,1894 BREMOND,TEX.
D.FEB.16,1974 NEW BRAUNFELS,TEX
| 1916 PHI A | O | 25 | .270 |
| | BRTR | | |

STELZLE, JACOB CHARLES
[PLAYED UNDER NAME OF
JACOB CHARLES STENZEL]

STELMASZEK, RICHARD FRANCIS (RICK)
B.OCT.8,1948 CHICAGO,ILL.
1971 WAS A	/C	6	.000
1973 TEX A	/C	7	.111
	CAL A	C	22	.154
1974 CAL A	C	25	.227
	BLTR	60	.170

STEM, FREDERICK BOOTHE
B.SEPT.22,1885 OXFORD,N.C.
D.SEPT.5,1964 DARLINGTON,S.C.
1908 BOS N	1	19	.278
1909 BOS N	1	68	.208
	BLTR	87	.224

STEMMEYER, WILLIAM (CANNON BALL)
B.MAY 6,1865 CLEVELAND,OHIO
D.MAY 3,1945 CLEVELAND,OHIO
1885 BOS N	P	2	1- 1
1886 BOS N	P	41	22-18
1887 BOS N	P	14	6- 8
1888 CLE AA	P	3	0- 2
	BRTR	60	29-29

STENGEL, CHARLES DILLON (CASEY)
OR (THE OLD PROFESSOR)
B.JULY 30,1890 KANSAS CITY,MO.
D.SEPT.29,1975 GLENDALE,CAL.
1912 BRO N	O	17	.316
1913 BRO N	O	124	.272
1914 BRO N	O	126	.316
1915 BRO N	O	132	.237
1916 BRO N	O	127	.279
1917 BRO N	O	150	.257
1918 PIT N	O	39	.246
1919 PIT N	O	89	.293
1920 PHI N	O	129	.292
1921 PHI N	O	24	.305
	NY N	O	18	.227
1922 NY N	O	84	.368
1923 NY N	O	75	.339
1924 BOS N	O	131	.280
1925 BOS N	O	12	.077
	BLTL	1277	.284
NON-PLAYING MANAGER
BRO(N) 1934-36, BOS(N) 1938-43,
NY(A) 1949-60, NY(N) 1962-65

STENHOUSE, DAVID ROTCHFORD (DAVE)
B.SEP.12,1933 WESTERLY,R.I.
1962 WAS A	P	34	11-12
1963 WAS A	P	16	3- 9
1964 WAS A	P	26	2- 7
	BRTR	76	16-28

STENNETT, RENALDO ANTONIO
[PORTE] (RENNIE)
B.APR.5,1951 COLON,PANAMA
1971 PIT N	2	50	.353
1972 PIT N	2-O/S	109	.286
1973 PIT N	2-S/O	128	.242
1974 PIT N	*2/O	157	.291
1975 PIT N	*2	148	.286
1976 PIT N	*2/S	157	.257
1977 PIT N	*2	116	.336
1978 PIT N	2/3	106	.243
	BRTR	971	.281

STENZEL, JACOB CHARLES (JAKE)
[REAL NAME JACOB CHARLES STELZLE]
B.JUNE 24,1867 CINCINNATI,OHIO
D.JAN.6,1919 CINCINNATI,OHIO
1890 CHI N	C-O	11	.209
1892 PIT N	O	2	.000
1893 PIT N	O	51	.409
1894 PIT N	O	131	.351
1895 PIT N	O	131	.384
1896 PIT N	O	112	.366
1897 BAL N	O	131	.351
1898 BAL N	O	35	.254
	STL N	O	105	.287
1899 STL N	O	32	.270
	CIN N	O	9	.321
	BRTR	750	.344

STEPHEN, LOUIS ROBERTS (BUZZ)
B.JULY 13,1944 PORTERVILLE,CAL.
| 1968 MIN A | /P | 2 | 1- 1 |
| | BRTR | | |

STEPHENS, BRYAN MARIS
B.JULY 14,1920 FAYETTEVILLE,ARK
1947 CLE A	P	31	5-10
1948 STL A	P	43	3- 6
	BRTR	74	8-16

STEPHENS, CLARENCE WRIGHT
B.AUG.19,1863 CINCINNATI,OHIO
D.FEB.28,1945 CINCINNATI,OHIO
1886 CIN AA	P	1	1- 0
1891 CIN N	P	1	0- 1
1892 CIN N	P	2	0- 1
	TR	4	1- 2

STEPHENS, GEORGE BENJAMIN
B.SEPT.28,1867 ROMEO,MICH.
D.AUG.5,1896 ARMADA,MICH.
1892 BAL N	P	5	1- 0
1893 WAS N	P	9	1- 6
1894 WAS N	P	3	0- 3
		17	2- 9

STEPHENS, GLEN EUGENE (GENE)
B.JAN.20,1933 GRAVETTE,ARK.
1952 BOS A	O	21	.226
1953 BOS A	O	78	.204
1955 BOS A	O	109	.293
1956 BOS A	O	104	.270
1957 BOS A	O	120	.266
1958 BOS A	O	134	.219
1959 BOS A	O	92	.278
1960 BOS A	O	35	.229
	BAL A	O	84	.238
1961 BAL A	O	32	.190
	KC A	O	62	.208
1962 KC A	H	5	.000
1963 CHI A	O	6	.389
1964 CHI A	O	82	.234
	BLTR	964	.240

STEPHENS, JAMES WALTER
(JIM) OR (LITTLE NEMO)
B.DEC.10,1883 SALINEVILLE,OHIO
D.JAN.2,1965 OXFORD,ALA.
1907 STL A	C	58	.202
1908 STL A	C	47	.200
1909 STL A	C	79	.220
1910 STL A	C	99	.241
1911 STL A	C	70	.231
1912 STL A	C	74	.249
	BRTR	427	.227

STEPHENS, VERNON DECATUR (VERN)
(JUNIOR) OR (BUSTER)
B.OCT.23,1920 MC ALISTER,N.MEX.
D.NOV.3,1968 LONG BEACH,CAL.
1941 STL A	S	3	.500
1942 STL A	S	145	.294
1943 STL A	S-O	137	.289
1944 STL A	S	145	.293
1945 STL A	S-3	149	.289
1946 STL A	S	115	.307
1947 STL A	S	150	.279
1948 BOS A	S	155	.269
1949 BOS A	S	155	.290
1950 BOS A	S	149	.295
1951 BOS A	S-3	109	.300
1952 BOS A	S-3	92	.254
1953 CHI A	S-3	44	.186
	STL A	3	46	.321
1954 BAL A	3	101	.285
1955 BAL A	3	3	.167
	CHI A	3	22	.250
	BRTR	1720	.286

STEPHENSON, CHESTER EARL (EARL)
B.JULY 31,1947 BENSON,N.C.
1971 CHI N	P	16	1- 0
1972 MIL A	P	35	3- 5
1977 BAL A	/P	1	0- 0
1978 BAL A	/P	2	0- 0
	BLTL	54	4- 5

STEPHENSON, JACKSON RIGGS
(RIGGS) OR (OLD HOSS)
B.JAN.5,1898 AKRON,ALA.
1921 CLE A	2	65	.330
1922 CLE A	2-3	86	.339
1923 CLE A	2	91	.319
1924 CLE A	2	71	.371
1925 CLE A	O	19	.296
1926 CHI N	O	82	.338
1927 CHI N	O	152	.344
1928 CHI N	O	137	.324
1929 CHI N	O	136	.362
1930 CHI N	O	109	.367
1931 CHI N	O	80	.319
1932 CHI N	O	147	.324
1933 CHI N	O	97	.329
1934 CHI N	O	38	.216
	BRTR	1310	.336

STEPHENSON, JERRY JOSEPH
B.OCT.6,1943 DETROIT,MICH.
1963 BOS A	P	1	0- 0
1965 BOS A	P	15	1- 5
1966 BOS A	P	15	2- 5
1967 BOS A	/P	8	3- 1
1968 BOS A	P	23	2- 8
1969 SEA A	/P	2	0- 0
1970 LA N	/P	3	0- 0
	BLTR	67	8-19

YR	CL	LEA	POS	GP	G	REC

STEPHENSON, JOHN HERMAN
B.JUNE.13,1941 S.PORTSMOUTH,KY.

YR	CL	LEA	POS	GP	G	REC
1964	NY	N	3-O	37		.158
1965	NY	N	C/O	62		.215
1966	NY	N	C/O	63		.196
1967	CHI	N	C	18		.224
1968	CHI	N	/H	2		.000
1969	SF	N	/C-3	22		.222
1970	SF	N	/C-O	23		.070
1971	CAL	A	C	98		.219
1972	CAL	A	C	66		.274
1973	CAL	A	C	60		.246
	BLTR			451		.216

STEPHENSON, JOSEPH CHESTER
B.JUNE 30,1921 DETROIT,MICH.

YR	CL	LEA	POS	GP	G	REC
1943	NY	N	C	9		.250
1944	CHI	N	C	4		.125
1947	CHI	A	C	16		.143
	BRTR			29		.179

STEPHENSON, REUBEN CRANDOL (DUMMY)
B.SEPT.22,1869 PETERSBURG,N.J.
D.DEC.1,1924 TRENTON,N.J.

YR	CL	LEA	POS	GP	G	REC
1892	PHI	N	O	8		.277

STEPHENSON, ROBERT LLOYD (BOB)
B.AUG.11,1928 BLAIR,OKLA.

YR	CL	LEA	POS	GP	G	REC
1955	STL	N	2-S-3	67		.243
	BRTR					

STEPHENSON, WALTER MC QUEEN (TARZAN)
B.MAR.27,1911 SALUDA,N.C.

YR	CL	LEA	POS	GP	G	REC
1935	CHI	N	C	16		.385
1936	CHI	N	C	6		.083
1937	PHI	N	C	10		.261
	BRTR			32		.279

STERLING, JOHN A.
B.PHILADELPHIA,PA.

YR	CL	LEA	POS	GP	G	REC
1890	ATH	AA	P	1		0-1

STERLING, RANDALL WAYNE (RANDY)
B.APR.21,1951 KEY WEST,FLA.

YR	CL	LEA	POS	GP	G	REC
1974	NY	N	/P	3		1-1
	BBTR					

STERRETT, CHARLES HURLBUT (DUTCH)
B.OCT.1,1889 MILROY,PA.
D.DEC.8,1965 BALTIMORE,MD.

YR	CL	LEA	POS	GP	G	REC
1912	NY	A	1-O	66		.265
1913	NY	A	C	21		.171
	BRTR			87		.253

STEUERNAGEL, GEORGE HENRY
[PLAYED UNDER NAME OF
GEORGE HENRY STARNAGLE]

STEVENS, CHARLES AUGUSTUS (CHUCK)
B.JULY 10,1918 VAN HOUTEN,N.MEX

YR	CL	LEA	POS	GP	G	REC
1941	STL	A	1	4		.154
1946	STL	A	1	122		.248
1948	STL	A	1	85		.260
	BBTL			211		.251

STEVENS, EDWARD LEE (ED) OR (BIG ED)
B.JAN.12,1925 GALVESTON,TEX.

YR	CL	LEA	POS	GP	G	REC
1945	BRO	N	1	55		.274
1946	BRO	N	1	103		.242
1947	BRO	N	1	5		.154
1948	PIT	N	1	128		.254
1949	PIT	N	1	67		.262
1950	PIT	N	1	17		.196
	BLTL			375		.252

STEVENS, JAMES ARTHUR
(JIM) OR (STEVE)
B.AUG.25,1889 WILLIAMSBURG,MD.
D.SEPT.25,1966 BALTIMORE,MD.

YR	CL	LEA	POS	GP	G	REC
1914	WAS	A	P	2		0-0
	BRTR					

STEVENS, R C
B.JULY 22,1934 MOULTRIE,GA.

YR	CL	LEA	POS	GP	G	REC
1958	PIT	N	1	59		.267
1959	PIT	N	1	3		.269
1960	PIT	N	1	9		.000
1961	WAS	A	1	33		.129
	BLTR			104		.210

STEVENS, ROBERT JORDAN
B.APR.17,1907 CHEVY CHASE,MD.

YR	CL	LEA	POS	GP	G	REC
1931	MIN	N	S	12		.343
	BLTR					

STEWART, ASA (ACE)
B.FEB.14,1869 TERRE HAUTE,IND.
D.APR.17,1912 TERRE HAUTE,IND.

YR	CL	LEA	POS	GP	G	REC
1895	CHI	N	2	97		.244
	BRTR					

STEWART, CHARLES EUGENE (TUFFY)
B.JULY 31,1883 CHICAGO,ILL.
D.NOV.18,1934 CHICAGO,ILL.

YR	CL	LEA	POS	GP	G	REC
1913	CHI	N	O	9		.125
1914	CHI	N	H	1		.000
	BLTL			10		.111

STEWART, DAVID KEITH (DAVE)
B.FEB.19,1957 OAKLAND,CAL.

YR	CL	LEA	POS	GP	G	REC
1978	LA	N	/P	1		0-0
	BRTR					

STEWART, EDWARD PERRY (BUD)
B.JUNE 15,1916 SACRAMENTO,CAL.

YR	CL	LEA	POS	GP	G	REC
1941	PIT	N	O	73		.267
1942	PIT	N	2-3-0	82		.219
1948	NY	A	H	6		.200
	WAS	A	O	118		.279
1949	WAS	A	O	118		.284
1950	WAS	A	O	118		.267
1951	CHI	A	O	95		.276
1952	CHI	A	O	92		.267
1953	CHI	A	O	53		.271
1954	CHI	A	O	18		.077
	BLTR			773		.268

STEWART, FRANK
B.SEPT.8,1906 MINNEAPOLIS,MINN.

YR	CL	LEA	POS	GP	G	REC
1927	CHI	A	P	1		0-1

STEWART, GLEN WELDON (GABBY)
B.SEPT.29,1912 TULLAHOMA,TENN.

YR	CL	LEA	POS	GP	G	REC
1940	NY	N	S-3	15		.138
1943	PHI	N	C-1-2-S	110		.211
1944	PHI	N	2-S-3	118		.220
	BRTR			243		.213

STEWART, JAMES FRANKLIN (JIMMY)
B.JUNE 11,1939 OPELIKA,ALA.

YR	CL	LEA	POS	GP	G	REC
1963	CHI	N	2-S	13		.297
1964	CHI	N	2-S-3-O	132		.253
1965	CHI	N	O-S	116		.223
1966	CHI	N	O/2-S-3	57		.178
1967	CHI	N	/H	6		.167
	CHI	A	/O-2-S	24		.167
1969	CIN	N	O-2/3-S	119		.253
1970	CIN	N	S-O-2/C-1	101		.267
1971	CIN	N	O/3-2	80		.232
1972	HOU	N	O/1-2-3	68		.219
1973	HOU	N	/3-O-2	61		.191
	BRTR			777		.237

STEWART, JOHN FRANKLIN (STUFFY)
B.JAN.31,1894 JASPER,FLA.

YR	CL	LEA	POS	GP	G	REC
1916	STL	N	2	9		.176
1917	STL	N	2	13		.000
1921	STL	A	H	3		.333
1922	PIT	N	2	3		.154
1923	BRO	N	2	4		.364
1925	WAS	A	2-3	7		.353
1926	WAS	A	2	62		.270
1927	WAS	A	2	56		.240
1929	WAS	A	2	22		.000
	BRTR			179		.238

STEWART, JOSEPH LAWRENCE (ACE)
B.MAR.11,1879 MONROE,N.C.
D.FEB.9,1913 YOUNGSTOWN,OHIO

YR	CL	LEA	POS	GP	G	REC
1904	BOS	N	P	2		0-0

STEWART, MARK (BIG SLICK)
B.OCT.11,1889 WHITLOCK,TENN.
D.JAN.17,1932 MEMPHIS,TENN.

YR	CL	LEA	POS	GP	G	REC
1913	CIN	N	C	1		.000
	BLTR					

STEWART, SAMUEL LEE (SAMMY)
B.OCT.28,1954 ASHEVILLE,N.C.

YR	CL	LEA	POS	GP	G	REC
1978	BAL	A	/P	2		1-1
	BRTR					

STEWART, VESTON GOFF (BUNKY)
B.JAN.7,1931 JASPER,N.C.

YR	CL	LEA	POS	GP	G	REC
1952	WAS	A	P	1		0-0
1953	WAS	A	P	2		0-2
1954	WAS	A	P	29		0-2
1955	WAS	A	P	7		0-0
1956	WAS	A	P	33	34	5-7
	BLTL			72	73	5-11

STEWART, WALTER CLEVELAND (LEFTY)
B.SEPT.23,1900 SPARTA,TENN.
D.SEPT.26,1974 KNOXVILLE,TENN.

YR	CL	LEA	POS	GP	G	REC
1921	DET	A	P	5		0-0
1927	STL	A	P	27	28	8-11
1928	STL	A	P	29		7-9
1929	STL	A	P	23		9-6
1930	STL	A	P	35		20-12
1931	STL	A	P	36		14-17
1932	STL	A	P	41		15-19
1933	WAS	A	P-2	34	35	15-6
						.143
1934	WAS	A	P	24	25	7-11
1935	WAS	A	P	1		0-1
	CLE	A	P	24		6-6
	BRTL			279	282	101-98
						.204

STEWART, WALTER NESBITT (NEB)
B.MAY 21,1918 S.CHARLESTON,OHIO

YR	CL	LEA	POS	GP	G	REC
1940	PHI	N	O	10		.129
	BRTR					

STEWART, WILLIAM MACKLIN (MACK)
B.SEPT.23,1914 STEVENSON,ALA.
D.MAR.21,1960 MACON,GA.

YR	CL	LEA	POS	GP	G	REC
1944	CHI	N	P	8		0-0
1945	CHI	N	P	16		0-1
	BRTR			24		0-1

STEWART, WILLIAM WAYNE (BILL)
B.APR.15,1928 BAY CITY,MICH.

YR	CL	LEA	POS	GP	G	REC
1955	KC	A	O	11		.111
	BRTR					

STIELY, FREDERICK WARREN
B.JUNE 1,1901 VALLEY VIEW,PA.

YR	CL	LEA	POS	GP	G	REC
1929	STL	A	P	1		1-0
1930	STL	A	P	4	5	0-1
1931	STL	A	P	4		0-0
	BLTL			9	10	1-1

STIGMAN, RICHARD LEWIS (DICK)
B.JAN.24,1936 NIMROD,MINN.

YR	CL	LEA	POS	GP	G	REC
1960	CLE	A	P	41		5-11
1961	CLE	A	P	22		2-5
1962	MIN	A	P	40		12-5
1963	MIN	A	P	33		15-15
1964	MIN	A	P	32		6-15
1965	MIN	A	P	33		4-2
1966	BOS	A	P	34		2-1
	BRTL			235		46-54

STILES, ROLLAND MAYS (LENA)
B.NOV.17,1906 RATCLIFF,ARK.

YR	CL	LEA	POS	GP	G	REC
1930	STL	A	P	20		3-6
1931	STL	A	P	34		3-1
1933	STL	A	P	31		3-7
	BRTR			85		9-14

STILLMAN, ROYLE ELDON
B.JAN.2,1951 SANTA MONICA,CAL.

YR	CL	LEA	POS	GP	G	REC
1975	BAL	A	/O	13		.429
1976	BAL	A	/1	20		.091
1977	CHI	A	O-D/1	56		.210
	BLTL			89		.213

STILLWELL, RONALD ROY (RON)
B.DEC.3,1939 LOS ANGELES,CAL.

YR	CL	LEA	POS	GP	G	REC
1961	WAS	A	S	8		.125
1962	WAS	A	2-S	6		.273
	BRTR			14		.211

STIMMEL, ARCHIBALD MAY (LUMBAGO)
B.MAY 30,1873 WOODSBORO,MD.
D.AUG.18,1958 FREDERICK,MD.

YR	CL	LEA	POS	GP	G	REC
1900	CIN	N	P	2		1-1
1901	CIN	N	P	20		4-14
1902	CIN	N	P	4		0-4
	BRTR			26		5-19

STIMSON, CARL REMUS
B.JULY 18,1894 HAMBURG,IOWA
D.NOV.9,1936 OMAHA,NEB.

YR	CL	LEA	POS	GP	G	REC
1923	BOS	A	P	2		0-0
	BBTR					

STINE, HARRY C.
B.FEB.20,1864 SHENANDOAH,PA.
D.JUNE 5,1924 NIAGARA FALLS,N.Y

YR	CL	LEA	POS	GP	G	REC
1890	ATH	AA	P	1		0-1

STINE, LEE ELBERT
B.NOV.17,1913 STILLWATER,OKLA.

YR	CL	LEA	POS	GP	G	REC
1934	CHI	A	P	4		0-0
1935	CHI	A	P	1		0-0
1936	CIN	N	P	40		3-9
1938	NY	A	P	4		0-0
	BRTR			49		3-8

STINSON, GORRELL ROBERT (BOB)
B.OCT.11,1945 ELKIN,N.C.

YR	CL	LEA	POS	GP	G	REC
1969	LA	N	/C	4		.375
1970	LA	N	/C	4		.000
1971	STL	N	/C-O	17		.211
1972	HOU	N	C/O	27		.171
1973	MON	N	C/3	48		.261
1974	MON	N	C	38		.172
1975	KC	A	C/1-2-O	63		.265
1976	KC	A	C	79		.263
1977	SEA	A	C	105		.269
1978	SEA	A	*C	124		.258
	BBTR			509		.254
	BR 1969					

STIRES, GARRETT
B.OCT.13,1849 HUNTERDON CO.,N.J
D.JUNE 13,1933

YR	CL	LEA	POS	GP	G	REC
1871	ROK	NA	O	25		-

STIRNWEISS, GEORGE HENRY (SNUFFY)
B.OCT.26,1918 NEW YORK,N.Y.
D.SEPT.15,1958 NEWARK BAY,N.J.

YR	CL	LEA	POS	GP	G	REC
1943	NY	A	2-S		83	.219
1944	NY	A	2		154	.319
1945	NY	A	2		152	.309
1946	NY	A	2-S-3		129	.251
1947	NY	A	2		148	.256
1948	NY	A	2		141	.252
1949	NY	A	2-3		70	.261
1950	NY	A	2		7	.000
	STL	A	2-S-3		93	.218
1951	CLE	A	2-3		50	.216
1952	CLE	A	3		1	.000
	BRTR				1028	.268

STIVETTS, JOHN ELMER (HAPPY JACK)
B.MAR.31,1868 ASHLAND,PA.
D.APR.18,1930 ASHLAND,PA.

YR	CL	LEA	POS	GP	G	REC
1889	STL	AA	P	25	26	12- 7
1890	STL	AA	P	54	67	31-20
1891	STL	AA	P-O	66	85	31-21
						.305
1892	BOS	N	P-O	47	64	33-14
						.300
1893	BOS	N	P	33	41	21-12
1894	BOS	N	P	41	57	25-14
1895	BOS	N	P	34	38	16-16
1896	BOS	N	P	39	59	22-13
1897	BOS	N	P-O	16	49	12- 4
						.388
1898	BOS	N	P-O	1	27	0- 1
						.252
1899	CLE	N	P	6	18	0- 4
	BRTR			362	531	203-126
						.305

STOBBS, CHARLES KLEIN (CHUCK)
B.JULY 2,1929 WHEELING,W.VA.

YR	CL	LEA	POS	GP	G	REC
1947	BOS	A	P		4	0- 1
1948	BOS	A	P		6	0- 0
1949	BOS	A	P		26	11- 6
1950	BOS	A	P		32	12- 7
1951	BOS	A	P		34	10- 9
1952	CHI	A	P		38	7-12
1953	WAS	A	P		27	11- 8
1954	WAS	A	P		31	11-11
1955	WAS	A	P		41	4-14
1956	WAS	A	P	37	38	15-15
1957	WAS	A	P		42	8-20
1958	WAS	A	P		19	2- 6
	STL	N	P		17	1- 3
1959	WAS	A	P		41	1- 8
1960	WAS	A	P		40	12- 7
1961	MIN	A	P		24	2- 3
	BLTL			459	460	107-130

STOCK, MILTON JOSEPH (MILT)
B.JULY 11,1893 CHICAGO,ILL.
D.JULY 16,1977 MONTROSE,ALA.

YR	CL	LEA	POS	GP	G	REC
1913	NY	N	S		7	.176
1914	NY	N	3		115	.263
1915	PHI	N	3		69	.260
1916	PHI	N	S-3		132	.281
1917	PHI	N	S-3		150	.264
1918	PHI	N	3		123	.274
1919	STL	N	2-3		135	.307
1920	STL	N	3		155	.319
1921	STL	N	3		149	.307
1922	STL	N	S-3		151	.304
1923	STL	N	2-3		151	.289
1924	BRO	N	3		142	.242
1925	BRO	N	2-3		146	.328
1926	BRO	N	2		3	.000
	BRTR				1628	.289

STOCK, WESLEY GAY (WES)
B.APR.10,1934 LONGVIEW,WASH.

YR	CL	LEA	POS	GP	G	REC
1959	BAL	A	P		7	0- 0
1960	BAL	A	P		17	2- 2
1961	BAL	A	P		35	5- 0
1962	BAL	A	P		53	3- 2
1963	BAL	A	P		47	7- 0
1964	BAL	A	P		14	2- 0
	KC	A	P		50	6- 3
1965	KC	A	P		62	0- 4
1966	KC	A	P		35	2- 2
1967	KC	A	/P		1	0- 0
	BRTR				321	27-13

STOCKSDALE, OTIS HINKLEY (OTIS)
OR (OLD GRAY FOX)
B.AUG.7,1871 NEAR ARCADIA,MD.
D.MAR.15,1933 PENNSVILLE,N.J.

YR	CL	LEA	POS	GP	G	REC
1893	WAS	N	P		12	2- 8
1894	WAS	N	P	16	19	5- 8
1895	WAS	N	P		20	5-10
	BOS	N	P-1	7	8	2- 2
						.308
1896	BAL	N	P		2	0- 0
	BLTR			57	61	14-28
						.323

STOCKWELL, LEONARD C.
B.AUG.25,1859 CORDOVA,ILL.
D.SEPT.15,1904 CORDOVA,ILL.

YR	CL	LEA	POS	GP	G	REC
1879	CLE	N	O		2	.000
1884	LOU	AA	C-O		2	.111
1890	CLE	N	C		2	.286
	TR				6	.136

STODDARD

YR	CL	LEA	POS	GP	G	REC
1875	ATL	NA	O		2	-

STODDARD, TIMOTHY PAUL (TIM)
B.JAN.24,1953 E.CHICAGO,IND.

YR	CL	LEA	POS	GP	G	REC
1975	CHI	A	/P		1	0- 0
1978	BAL	A	/P		8	0- 1
	BRTR				9	0- 1

STOKES, ALBERT JOHN
[REAL NAME ALBERT JOHN STACEK]
B.JAN.1,1900 CHICAGO,ILL.

YR	CL	LEA	POS	GP	G	REC
1925	BOS	A	C		17	.212
1926	BOS	A	C		30	.163
	BRTR				47	.181

STOKES, ARTHUR MILTON
B.SEPT.13,1896 EMMITSBURG,MD.
D.JUNE 3,1962 TITUSVILLE,PA.

YR	CL	LEA	POS	GP	G	REC
1925	PHI	A	P		12	1- 1
	BRTR					

STONE, CHARLES RICHARD (DICK)
B.DEC.5,1911 OKLAHOMA CITY,OKLA

YR	CL	LEA	POS	GP	G	REC
1945	WAS	A	P		3	0- 0
	BLTL					

STONE, DARRAH DEAN (DEAN)
B.SEP.1,1930 MOLINE,ILL.

YR	CL	LEA	POS	GP	G	REC
1953	WAS	A	P		3	0- 1
1954	WAS	A	P		31	12-10
1955	WAS	A	P		43	6-13
1956	WAS	A	P	41	42	5- 7
1957	WAS	A	P		3	0- 0
	BOS	A	P		17	1- 3
1959	STL	N	P		18	0- 1
1962	HOU	N	P		15	3- 2
	CHI	A	P		27	1- 0
1963	BAL	A	P		17	1- 2
	BLTL			215	216	29-39

STONE, DWIGHT ELY
B.AUG.2,1886 HOLT CO.,NEB.
D.JUNE 3,1976 GLENDALE,CAL.

YR	CL	LEA	POS	GP	G	REC
1913	STL	A	P		18	2- 6
1914	KC	F	P		39	7-14
	BRTR				57	9-20

STONE, EDWIN ARNOLD (ARNIE)
B.OCT.9,1892 NORTH CREEK,N.Y.
D.JULY 29,1948

YR	CL	LEA	POS	GP	G	REC
1923	PIT	N	P		9	0- 1
1924	PIT	N	P		26	4- 2
	BRTL				35	4- 3

STONE, EUGENE DANIEL (GENE)
B.JAN.16,1944 BURBANK,CAL.

YR	CL	LEA	POS	GP	G	REC
1969	PHI	N	/1		18	.214
	BLTL					

STONE, GEORGE HEARD
B.JULY 9,1946 RUSTON,LA.

YR	CL	LEA	POS	GP	G	REC
1967	ATL	N	/P		2	0- 0
1968	ATL	N	P		17	7- 4
1969	ATL	N	P		36	13-10
1970	ATL	N	P		35	11-11
1971	ATL	N	P	27	30	6- 8
1972	ATL	N	P	31	33	6-11
1973	NY	N	P	27	28	12- 3
1974	NY	N	P		15	2- 7
1975	NY	N	P		13	3- 3
	BLTL			203	209	60-57

STONE, GEORGE ROBERT
B.SEPT.3,1877 LOST NATION,IOWA
D.JAN.3,1945 CLINTON,IOWA

YR	CL	LEA	POS	GP	G	REC
1903	BOS	A	H		2	.000
1905	STL	A	O		154	.296
1906	STL	A	O		154	.358
1907	STL	A	O		155	.320
1908	STL	A	O		148	.281
1909	STL	A	O		83	.287
1910	STL	A	O		152	.256
	BLTL				848	.301

STONE, HARRY RONALD (RON)
B.SEP.9,1942 CORNING,CAL.

YR	CL	LEA	POS	GP	G	REC
1966	KC	A	/O-1		26	.273
1969	PHI	N	O		103	.239
1970	PHI	N	O/1		123	.262
1971	PHI	N	O/1		95	.227
1972	PHI	N	O		41	.167
	BLTL				388	.241

STONE, JOHN VERNON (ROCKY)
B.AUG.23,1918 REDDING,CAL.

YR	CL	LEA	POS	GP	G	REC
1943	CIN	N	P		13	0- 1
	BRTR					

STONE, JOHN THOMAS (JONATHAN)
(JOHN) OR (ROCKY)
B.OCT.10,1905 LYNCHBURG,TENN.
D.NOV.30,1955 SHELBYVILLE,TENN.

YR	CL	LEA	POS	GP	G	REC
1928	DET	A	O		26	.354
1929	DET	A	O		51	.260
1930	DET	A	O		126	.313
1931	DET	A	O		147	.327
1932	DET	A	O		145	.297
1933	DET	A	O		148	.280
1934	WAS	A	O		113	.315
1935	WAS	A	O		125	.315
1936	WAS	A	O		123	.341
1937	WAS	A	O		139	.330
1938	WAS	A	O		56	.244
	BLTR				1199	.310

STONE, STEVEN MICHAEL (STEVE)
B.JULY 14,1947 EUCLID,OHIO

YR	CL	LEA	POS	GP	G	REC
1971	SF	N	P		24	5- 9
1972	SF	N	P		27	6- 8
1973	CHI	A	P	36	39	6-11
1974	CHI	N	P	38	42	8- 6
1975	CHI	N	P	33	34	12- 8
1976	CHI	N	P		17	3- 6
1977	CHI	A	P		31	15-12
1978	CHI	A	P		30	12-12
	BRTR			236	244	67-72

STONE, WILLIAM ARTHUR (TIGE)
B.SEPT.18,1901 MACON,GA.
D.JAN.1,1960 JACKSONVILLE,FLA.

YR	CL	LEA	POS	GP	G	REC
1923	STL	N	P-O	1	5	0- 0
						1.000

STONEHAM, JOHN ANDREW
B.NOV.8,1908 WOOD RIVER,ILL.

YR	CL	LEA	POS	GP	G	REC
1933	CHI	A	O		10	.120
	BLTR					

STONEMAN, WILLIAM HAMBLY (BILL)
B.APR.7,1944 OAK PARK,ILL.

YR	CL	LEA	POS	GP	G	REC
1967	CHI	N	P		28	2- 4
1968	CHI	N	P		18	0- 1
1969	MON	N	P		42	11-19
1970	MON	N	P	40	42	7-15
1971	MON	N	P	39	41	17-16
1972	MON	N	P	36	40	12-14
1973	MON	N	P		29	4- 8
1974	CAL	A	P		13	1- 8
	BRTR			245	253	54-85

STONER, ULYSSES SIMPSON GRANT (LIL)
B.FEB.28,1899 BOWIE,TEX.
D.JUNE 26,1966 ENID,OKLA.

YR	CL	LEA	POS	GP	G	REC
1922	DET	A	P		17	4- 4
1924	DET	A	P	36	37	11-11
1925	DET	A	P		34	10- 9
1926	DET	A	P		32	7-10
1927	DET	A	P		38	10-13
1928	DET	A	P		36	5- 8
1929	DET	A	P		24	3- 3
1930	PIT	N	P		5	0- 0
1931	PHI	N	P		7	0- 0
	BRTR			229	230	50-58

STORIE, HOWARD EDWARD (SPONGE)
B.MAY 15,1911 PITTSFIELD,MASS.
D.JULY 27,1968 PITTSFIELD,MASS.

YR	CL	LEA	POS	GP	G	REC
1931	BOS	A	C		6	.118
1932	BOS	A	C		6	.375
	BRTR				12	.200

STORKE, ALAN MARSHALL
B.SEPT.27,1884 AUBURN,N.Y.
D.MAR.18,1910 NEWTON,MASS.

YR	CL	LEA	POS	GP	G	REC
1906	PIT	N	S-3		5	.250
1907	PIT	N	1-3		102	.258
1908	PIT	N	1		56	.252
1909	PIT	N	1		32	.254
	STL	N	S		48	.282
	TR				243	.260

STORTI, LINDO IVAN
B.DEC.5,1906 SANTA MONICA,CAL.

YR	CL	LEA	POS	GP	G	REC
1930	STL	A	2		7	.321
1931	STL	A	3		86	.220
1932	STL	A	3		53	.259
1933	STL	A	2-3		70	.195
	BBTR				216	.227

STOTTLEMYRE, MELVIN LEON (MEL)
B.NOV.13,1941 HAZELTON,MO.

YR	CL	LEA	POS	GP	G	REC
1964	NY	A	P	13	14	9- 3
1965	NY	A	P		37	20- 9
1966	NY	A	P		37	12-20
1967	NY	A	P		36	15-15
1968	NY	A	P		36	21-12
1969	NY	A	P		39	20-14
1970	NY	A	P	37	38	15-13
1971	NY	A	P		35	16-12
1972	NY	A	P	36	37	14-18
1973	NY	A	P		38	16-16
1974	NY	A	P	16	19	6- 7
	BRTR			360	366	164-139

YR CL LEA POS GP G REC

STOUCH, THOMAS CARL
B.DEC.2,1870 PERRYVILLE,OHIO
D.OCT.7,1956 LANCASTER,PA.
1898 LOU N 2 4 .377
  BRTR

STOUT, ALLYN MC CLELLAND (FISH HOOK)
B.OCT.31,1904 PEORIA,ILL.
D.DEC.22,1974 SIKESTOWN,MO.
1931 STL N P 30 6- 0
1932 STL N P 36 4- 5
1933 STL N P 1 0- 0
 CIN N P 23 2- 3
1934 CIN N P 41 6- 8
1935 NY N P 40 1- 4
1943 BOS N P 9 1- 0
  BRTR 180 20-20

STOVALL, GEORGE THOMAS (FIREBRAND)
B.NOV.23,1878 INDEPENDENCE,MO.
D.NOV.5,1951 BURLINGTON,IOWA
1904 CLE A 1 51 .297
1905 CLE A 1-2 111 .272
1906 CLE A 1-2-3 116 .273
1907 CLE A 1 124 .236
1908 CLE A 1 138 .292
1909 CLE A 1 145 .246
1910 CLE A 1 142 .261
1911 CLE A M-1 126 .271
1912 STL A M-1 115 .254
1913 STL A M-1 89 .287
1914 KC F M-1 122 .270
1915 KC F M-1 130 .233
  BRTR 1409 .264

STOVALL, JESSE CRAMER (SCOUT)
B.JULY 24,1875 INDEPENDENCE,MO.
D.JULY 12,1955 SAN DIEGO,CAL.
1903 CLE A P 6 5- 1
1904 DET A P 21 23 2-13
  BLTR 27 29 7-14

STOVEY, HARRY DUFFIELD
[REAL NAME HARRY DUFFIELD STOWE]
B.DEC.20,1856 PHILADELPHIA,PA.
D.SEPT.20,1937 NEW BEDFORD,MASS
1880 WOR N P-1- 1 81 0- 0
 O .258
1881 WOR N 1-O 74 .270
1882 WOR N 1-O 84 .288
1883 ATH A P-C- 1 93 0- 0
 1-O .318
1884 ATH AA 1 106 .404
1885 ATH AA 1-O 112 .342
1886 ATH AA 1-O 123 .317
1887 ATH AA 1-O 124 .402
1888 ATH AA O 130 .318
1889 ATH AA O 138 .330
1890 BOS P O 118 .308
1891 BOS N O 133 .279
1892 BOS N O 38 .171
 BAL N O 74 .374
1893 BAL N O 8 .167
 BRO N O 45 .266
  BRTR 2 1481 0- 0
   .320

STOVIAK, RAYMOND THOMAS
B.JUNE 6,1915 SCOTTDALE,PA.
1938 PHI N O 10 .000
  BLTL

STOWE, HAROLD RUDOLPH (HAL)
B.AUG.29,1937 GASTONIA,N.C.
1960 NY A P 1 0- 0
  BLTL

STOWE, HARRY DUFFIELD
[PLAYED UNDER NAME OF
HARRY DUFFIELD STOVEY]

STRAHLER, MICHAEL WAYNE (MIKE)
B.MAR.14,1947 CHICAGO,ILL.
1970 LA N /P 6 1- 1
1971 LA N /P 6 0- 0
1972 LA N P 19 1- 2
1973 DET A P 22 4- 5
  BRTR 53 6- 8

STRAHS, RICHARD BERNARD (DICK)
B.DEC.4,1924 EVANSTON,ILL.
1954 CHI A P 9 0- 0
  BLTR

STRAMPE, ROBERT EDWIN (BOB)
B.JUNE 13,1950 JANESVILLE,WIS.
1972 DET A /P 7 0- 0
  BBTR

STRAND, PAUL EDWARD
B.DEC.19,1893 CARBONADO,WASH.
D.JULY 2,1974 SALT LAKE CITY,UTAH
1913 BOS N P 7 0- 0
1914 BOS N P 16 18 6- 2
1915 BOS N P 6 24 1- 1
1924 PHI A O 47 .228
  BRTL 29 96 7- 3
   .215

STRANDS, JOHN LAWRENCE (LARRY)
B.DEC.5,1885 CHICAGO,ILL.
D.JAN.19,1957 FOREST PARK,ILL.
1915 NEW F 2-3 34 .187
  BRTR

STRANDS, LEWIS
1915 CHI F 2 1 .000

STRANG, SAMUEL NICKLIN
(SAM) OR [THE DIXIE THRUSH]
[REAL NAME SAMUEL STRANG NICKLIN]
B.DEC.16,1876 CHATTANOOGA,TENN.
D.MAR.13,1932 CHATTANOOGA,TENN.
1896 LOU N S 14 .222
1900 CHI N 3 25 .276
1901 NY N 2-3 135 .291
1902 CHI A 3 137 .273
 CIN N 2-3 3 .363
1903 BRO N 3 135 .272
1904 BRO N 2 76 .192
1905 NY N 2-O 96 .259
1906 NY N 2-O 104 .319
1907 NY N O 95 .252
1908 NY N 3 22 .094
  BBTR 842 .266

STRANGE, ALAN COCHRANE (INKY)
B.NOV.7,1909 PHILADELPHIA,PA.
1934 STL A S 127 .233
1935 STL A S 49 .231
 WAS A S 20 .185
1940 STL A 2-S 5 .186
1941 STL A 1-S-3 45 .232
1942 STL A 2-S-3 19 .270
  BRTR 314 .223

STRATTON, ASA EVANS
B.FEB.10,1853 GRAFTON,MASS.
D.AUG.14,1925 FITCHBURG,MASS.
1881 WOR N S 1 .250

STRATTON, C. SCOTT (SCOTT)
B.OCT.2,1869 CAMPBELLSBURG,KY.
D.MAR.8,1939 LOUISVILLE,KY.
1888 LOU AA P-O 34 65 10-17
   .266
1889 LOU AA P-O 19 62 3-14
   .280
1890 LOU AA P 54 34-15
1891 PIT N P 3 0- 2
 LOU AA P 22 33 6-12
1892 LOU N P-O 41 60 21-20
1893 LOU N P-O 38 58 12-24
   .252
1894 LOU N P-O 7 13 1- 3
   .282
 CHI N P 15 20 9- 6
1895 CHI N P 3 2- 3
 TR 241 376 98-116
   .280

STRATTON, EDWARD
B.BALTIMORE,MD.
1873 MAR NA P-O 3 4 0- 3
   -

STRATTON, MONTY FRANKLIN PIERCE
(MONTY) OR (GANDER)
B.MAY 21,1912 CELESTE,TEX.
1934 CHI A P 1 0- 0
1935 CHI A P 5 1- 2
1936 CHI A P 16 5- 7
1937 CHI A P 22 15- 5
1938 CHI A P 26 27 15- 9
  BRTR 70 71 36-23

STRAUB, JOSEPH
B.JAN.19,1858 MILWAUKEE,WIS.
1880 TRO N C 3 .231
1882 ATH AA C-O 8 .188
1883 COL AA C-1-O 27 .135
  38 .152

STRAUSS, JOSEPH (DUTCH)
(JOE) OR (THE SOCKER)
B.1844 HUNGARY
D.JUNE 25,1906 CINCINNATI,OHIO
1884 KC U C-2-3-O 15 .208
1885 LOU AA C-O 2 .167
1886 LOU AA O 77 .210
 BRO AA C-O 9 .235
 TR 103 .213

STREAKER, JOHN A.
[PLAYED UNDER NAME OF
JOHN A. STRICKER]

STREET, CHARLES EVARD
(GABBY) OR (OLD SARGE)
B.SEPT.30,1882 HUNTSVILLE,ALA.
D.FEB.6,1951 JOPLIN,MO.
1904 CIN N C 11 .121
1905 CIN N C 2 .000
 BOS N C 3 .167
 CIN N C 27 .247
1908 WAS A C 131 .206
1909 WAS A C 137 .211
1910 WAS A C 89 .203
1911 WAS A C 72 .222
1912 NY A C 28 .182
1931 STL N M-C 1 .000
  BRTR 501 .208
NON-PLAYING MANAGER
STL[N] 1930, 32-33, STL[A] 1938

STREIT, OSCAR WILLIAM
B.JULY 7,1873 FLORENCE,ALA.
D.OCT.10,1935 BIRMINGHAM,ALA.
1899 BOS N P 2 1- 0
1902 CLE A P 8 0- 7
  BLTL 10 1- 7

STRELECKI, EDWARD HENRY
B.APR.10,1905 NEWARK,N.J.
D.JAN.9,1968 NEWARK,N.J.
1928 STL A P 22 0- 2
1929 STL A P 7 1- 1
1931 CIN N P 13 0- 0
  BRTR 42 1- 3

STREMMEL, PHILIP
B.APR.16,1880 ZANESVILLE,OHIO
D.DEC.26,1947 CHICAGO,ILL.
1909 STL A P 2 0- 2
1910 STL A P 5 0- 3
  BRTR 7 0- 5

STREULI, WALTER HERBERT (WALT)
B.SEPT.26,1935 MEMPHIS,TENN.
1954 DET A C 1 .000
1955 DET A C 2 .290
1956 DET A C 3 .250
  BRTR 6 .250

STRICKER, JOHN A. (CUB)
[REAL NAME JOHN A. STREAKER]
B.JUNE 8,1859 PHILADELPHIA,PA.
1882 ATH AA P-2- 1 74 1- 0
 O .203
1883 ATH AA C-2-3 89 .254
1884 ATH AA 2 109 .236
1885 ATH AA 2 106 .211
1887 CLE AA 2 131 .333
1888 CLE AA 2 126 .231
1889 CLE N 2 136 .251
1890 CLE P 2 127 .248
1891 BOS AA 2 139 .225
1892 STL N 2-S 28 .206
 BAL N 2 72 .275
1893 WAS N 2 59 .181
  BRTR 1 1196 1- 0
   .240

STRICKLAND, GEORGE BEVAN (BO)
B.JAN.10,1926 NEW ORLEANS,LA.
1950 PIT N S-3 23 .111
1951 PIT N 2-S 138 .216
1952 PIT N 1-2-S-3 76 .177
 CLE A 2-S 31 .216
1953 CLE A 1-S 123 .284
1954 CLE A S 112 .213
1955 CLE A S 130 .209
1956 CLE A 2-S-3 85 .211
1957 CLE A 2-S-3 89 .234
1959 CLE A 2-S-3 132 .238
1960 CLE A 2-S-3 32 .167
  BRTR 971 .224
NON-PLAYING MANAGER CLE[A] 1966

STRICKLAND, JAMES MICHAEL (JIM)
B.JUNE 12,1946 LOS ANGELES,CAL.
1971 MIN A P 24 1- 0
1972 MIN A P 25 3- 1
1973 MIN A /P 7 0- 1
1975 CLE A /P 4 0- 0
  BLTL 60 4- 2

STRICKLAND, WILLIAM GOSS
B.MAR.29,1908 NASHVILLE,GA.
1937 STL A P 9 0- 0
  BRTR

STRICKLETT, ELMER GRIFFIN (SPITBALL)
B.AUG.29,1876 GLASCO,KAN.
D.JUNE 7,1964 SANTA CRUZ,CAL.
1904 CHI A P 1 0- 1
1905 BRO N P 33 8-20
1906 BRO N P 41 14-18
1907 BRO N P 29 30 12-14
 TR 104 105 34-53

YR	CL LEA POS	GP	G	REC

STRIEF, GEORGE ANDREW
B.OCT.16,1856 CINCINNATI,OHIO
D.APR.1,1946 CLEVELAND,OHIO

1879	CLE N	2-O		71	.174
1882	PIT AA	2-S		73	.202
1883	STL AA	2-O		78	.211
1884	STL AA	O		47	.193
	KC U	2		14	.094
	PIT U	2		15	.182
	CLE N	3-O		8	.241
1885	ATH AA	2-S-3		44	.270
				350	.197

STRIKE, JOHN
B.PHILADELPHIA,PA.

1882	LOU AA	C-1-2-S-O		33	.142
1886	PHI N	P		2	1- 1
			2	35	1- 1
					.134

STRIKER, WILBUR SCOTT (JAKE)
B.OCT.23,1933 NEW WASHINGTON,O.

1959	CLE A	P		1	1- 0
1960	CHI A	P		2	0- 0
	BLTL			3	1- 0

**STRINCEVICH, NICHOLAS MIHAILOVICH
(NICK) OR (JUMBO)**
B.MAR.1,1915 GARY,IND.

1940	BOS N	P	32	33	4- 8
1941	BOS N	P		3	0- 0
	PIT N	P		12	1- 2
1942	PIT N	P		7	0- 0
1944	PIT N	P		40	14- 7
1945	PIT N	P		36	16-10
1946	PIT N	P		32	10-15
1947	PIT N	P		32	1- 6
1948	PIT N	P		3	0- 0
	PHI N	P		6	0- 1
	BRTR		203	204	46-49

STRINGER, LOUIS BERNARD (LOU)
B.MAY 13,1917 GRAND RAPIDS,MICH

1941	CHI N	2-S		145	.246
1942	CHI N	2-3		121	.236
1946	CHI N	2-S-3		80	.244
1948	BOS A	2		4	.091
1949	BOS A	2		35	.268
1950	BOS A	2-S-3		24	.294
	BRTR			409	.242

**STRIPP, JOSEPH VALENTINE
(JERSEY JOE)**
B.FEB.3,1903 HARRISON,N.J.

1928	CIN N	S-3-O		42	.288
1929	CIN N	2-3		64	.214
1930	CIN N	1-3		130	.306
1931	CIN N	1-3		105	.324
1932	BRO N	1-3		138	.303
1933	BRO N	3		141	.277
1934	BRO N	3		104	.315
1935	BRO N	1-3-O		109	.306
1936	BRO N	3		110	.317
1937	BRO N	1-3		90	.243
1938	STL N	3		54	.286
	BOS N	3		59	.275
	BRTR			1146	.294

STROBEL, ALBERT IRVING (ALLIE)
B.JUNE 11,1884 BOSTON,MASS.
D.FEB.10,1955 HOLLYWOOD,FLA.

1905	BOS N	3-O		5	.103
1906	BOS N	2		99	.202
	TR			104	.196

STROHMAYER, JOHN EMERY
B.OCT.13,1946 BELLE FOURCHE,S.D.

1970	MON N	P		42	3- 1
1971	MON N	P		27	7- 5
1972	MON N	P		48	1- 2
1973	MON N	P		17	0- 0
	NY N	/P		7	0- 0
1974	NY N	/P		1	0- 0
	BRTR			142	11- 9

STROM, BRENT TERRY
B.OCT.14,1948 SAN DIEGO,CAL.

1972	NY N	P		11	0- 3
1973	CLE N	P		27	2-10
1975	SD N	P		18	8- 8
1976	SD N	P	36	38	12-16
1977	SD N	N /P		8	0- 2
	BRTL		100	102	22-39

STROMME, FLOYD MARVIN (ROCK)
B.AUG.1,1916 COPPERSTOWN,N.DAK.

1939	CLE A	P		5	0- 1
	BRTR				

STRONER, JAMES M.
B.SEPT.26,1892 CHICAGO,ILL.
D.NOV.16,1971 CHICAGO,ILL.

1929	PIT N	3		6	.375
	BRTR				

STROUD, EDWIN MARVIN (ED)
B.OCT.31,1939 LAPINE,ALA.

1966	CHI A	O		12	.167
1967	CHI A	O		20	.296
	WAS A	O		87	.201
1968	WAS A	O		105	.239
1969	WAS A	O		123	.252
1970	WAS A	*O		129	.266
1971	CHI A	O		53	.177
	BLTR			529	.237

STROUD, RALPH VIVIAN (SAILOR)
B.MAY 15,1885 IRONIA,N.J.
D.APR.11,1970 STOCKTON,CAL.

1910	DET A	P		28	5- 9
1915	NY N	P		32	12- 9
1916	NY N	P		10	3- 2
	BRTR			70	20-20

STRUNK, AMOS AARON
B.JAN.22,1889 PHILADELPHIA,PA.

1908	PHI A	O		12	.222
1909	PHI A	O		11	.114
1910	PHI A	O		16	.333
1911	PHI A	O		74	.256
1912	PHI A	O		120	.289
1913	PHI A	O		93	.305
1914	PHI A	O		122	.275
1915	PHI A	1-O		132	.297
1916	PHI A	O		150	.316
1917	PHI A	O		148	.281
1918	BOS A	O		114	.256
1919	BOS A	O		48	.271
	PHI A	O		60	.211
1920	PHI A	O		57	.307
	CHI A	O		52	.220
1921	CHI A	O		121	.332
1922	CHI A	O		92	.289
1923	CHI A	O		94	.315
1924	CHI A	O		1	.000
	CHI A	O		30	.143
	BLTL			1507	.283

STRUSS, CLARENCE HERBERT (STEAMBOAT)
B.FEB.24,1909 RIVERDALE,ILL.

1934	PIT N	P		2	0- 1
	BRTR				

STRYKER, STERLING ALPA (DUTCH)
B.JULY 29,1895 ATLANTIC
HIGHLANDS,N.J.
D.NOV.5,1964 RED BANK,N.J.

1924	BOS N	P		20	3- 8
1926	BRO N	P		2	0- 0
	BRTR			22	3- 8

STUART, JOHN DAVIS (STUD)
B.APR.27,1901 CLINTON,TENN.
D.MAY 13,1970 CHARLESTON,W.VA.

1922	STL N	P		2	0- 0
1923	STL N	P		37	9- 5
1924	STL N	P-3	28	30	9-11
					.204
1925	STL N	P		15	2- 2
	BRTR		82	84	20-18
					.228

STUART, LUTHER LANE (LUKE)
B.MAY 23,1892 ALAMANCE CO.,N.C.
D.JUNE 15,1947 WINSTON-SALEM,N.C.

1921	STL A	2		3	.333
	BRTR				

STUART, MARLIN HENRY
B.AUG.8,1918 PARAGOULD,ARK.

1949	DET A	P		14	0- 2
1950	DET A	P		19	3- 1
1951	DET A	P		29	4- 6
1952	DET A	P		30	3- 2
	STL A	P		12	1- 2
1953	STL A	P		60	8- 2
1954	BAL A	P		22	1- 2
	NY A	P		10	3- 0
	BLTR		196	197	23-17

**STUART, RICHARD LEE (DICK)
OR (DR. STRANGEGLOVE)**
B.NOV.7,1932 SAN FRANCISCO,CAL.

1958	PIT N	1		67	.268
1959	PIT N	1-O		118	.297
1960	PIT N	1		122	.260
1961	PIT N	1-O		138	.301
1962	PIT N	1		114	.228
1963	BOS A	1		157	.261
1964	BOS A	1		156	.279
1965	PHI N	*1/3		149	.234
1966	NY N	1		31	.218
	LA N	1		38	.264
1969	CAL A	1		22	.157
	BRTR			1112	.264

STUART, WILLIAM ALEXANDER (CHAUNCEY)
B.DONORA,PA.

1895	PIT N	S		19	.259
1899	NY N	2		1	.000
				20	.250

STUBING, LAWRENCE GEORGE (LARRY)
B.MAR.31,1938 BRONX,N.Y.

1967	CAL A	/H		5	.000
	BLTL				

STUDLEY, SEYMOUR L. (WARHORSE)
B.WASHINGTON,D.C.
D.1874

1872	NAT NA	O		5	.136

STUELAND, GEORGE ANTON
B.MAR.2,1899 ALGONA,IOWA
D.SEPT.9,1964 ONAWA,IOWA

1921	CHI N	P		2	0- 1
1922	CHI N	P		35	9- 4
1923	CHI N	P		6	0- 1
1925	CHI N	P		2	0- 0
	BBTR			45	9- 6

STUFFEL, PAUL HARRINGTON
B.MAR.22,1927 CANTON,OHIO

1950	PHI N	P		3	0- 0
1952	PHI N	P		2	1- 0
1953	PHI N	P		2	0- 0
	BRTR			7	1- 0

STULTZ, GEORGE IRVIN
B.JUNE 30,1873 LOUISVILLE,KY.

1894	BOS N	P		1	1- 0

STUMP, JAMES GILBERT (JIM)
B.FEB.10,1932 LANSING,MICH.

1957	DET A	P		6	1- 0
1959	DET A	P		5	0- 0
	BRTR			11	1- 0

STUMPF, GEORGE FREDERICK
B.DEC.15,1910 NEW ORLEANS,LA.

1931	BOS A	O		7	.250
1932	BOS A	O		79	.201
1933	BOS A	O		22	.341
1936	CHI A	O		10	.273
	BLTL			118	.235

STUMPF, WILLIAM FREDERICK
B.MAR.21,1892 BALTIMORE,MD.
D.FEB.14,1966 CROWNSVILLE,MD.

1912	NY A	S		40	.240
1913	NY A	S		12	.207
	BRTR			52	.236

**STURDIVANT, THOMAS VIRGIL
(TOM) OR (SNAKE)**
B.APR.28,1930 GORDON,KAN.

1955	NY A	P		33	1- 3
1956	NY A	P		32	16- 8
1957	NY A	P		28	16- 6
1958	NY A	P		15	3- 6
1959	NY A	P		7	0- 2
	KC A	P	36	37	2- 6
1960	BOS A	P		40	3- 3
1961	WAS A	P		15	2- 6
	PIT N	P		13	5- 2
1962	PIT N	P		49	9- 5
1963	PIT N	P		3	0- 0
	DET A	P		28	1- 2
	KC A	P		17	1- 2
1964	KC A	P		3	0- 0
	NY N	P		16	0- 0
	BLTR		335	336	59-51

STURDY, GUY R.
B.AUG.7,1899 SHERMAN,TEX.
D.MAY 4,1965 MARSHALL,TEX.

1927	STL A	1		5	.429
1928	STL A	1		54	.222
	BLTL			59	.288

STURGEON, ROBERT HOWARD (BOBBY)
B.AUG.6,1919 CLINTON,IND.

1940	CHI N	S		7	.190
1941	CHI N	2-S-3		129	.245
1942	CHI N	2-S-3		63	.247
1946	CHI N	2-S		100	.296
1947	CHI N	2-S-3		87	.254
1948	BOS N	2-S-3		34	.218
	BRTR			420	.257

STURGIS, DEAN DONNELL
B.DEC.1,1892 BELOIT,KAN.
D.JUNE 4,1920 UNIONTOWN,PA.

1914	PHI A	C		4	.250

STURM JOHN PETER JOSEPH
B.JAN.23,1916 ST.LOUIS,MO.

1941	NY A	1		124	.239
	BLTL				

STUTZ, GEORGE (KID) OR (SATAN)
B.FEB.12,1893 PHILADELPHIA,PA.
D.DEC.29,1930 PHILADELPHIA,PA.

1926	PHI N	S		6	.000
	BLTR				

YR CL LEA POS   GP   G   REC   YR CL LEA POS   GP   G   REC   YR CL LEA POS   GP   G   REC

STYLES, WILLIAM GRAVES (LENA)
B.NOV.27,1899 GURLEY,ALA.
D.MAR.14,1956 GURLEY,ALA.
1919 PHI A C		8	.273
1920 PHI A C		24	.260
1921 PHI A C		4	.200
1930 CIN N C-1		7	.250
1931 CIN N C		34	.241
BRTR		77	.249

STYNES, CORNELIUS WILLIAM (NEIL)
B.DEC.10,1868 ARLINGTON,MASS.
D.MAR.26,1944 SOMERVILLE,MASS.
| 1890 CLE P C | | 2 | .000 |

SUAREZ, KENNETH RAYMOND (KEN)
B.APR.12,1943 TAMPA,FLA.
1966 KC A C		35	.145
1967 KC A C		39	.238
1968 CLE A C/2-3-0		17	.100
1969 CLE A C		36	.294
1971 CLE A C		50	.203
1972 TEX A C		25	.152
1973 TEX A C		93	.248
BRTR		295	.227

SUAREZ, LUIS ABELARDO
B.AUG.24,1916 ALTO SONGO,CUBA
| 1944 WAS A 3 | | 1 | .000 |
| BRTR | | | |

SUCH, RICHARD STANLEY (DICK)
B.OCT.15,1944 SANFORD,N.C.
| 1970 WAS A P | 21 | 22 | 1- 5 |
| BLTR | | | |

SUCHE, CHARLES MORRIS
B.AUG.15,1915 CRANES MILL,TEX.
| 1938 CLE A P | 1 | 0- 0 |
| BRTL | | | |

SUCHECKI, JAMES JOSEPH (JIM)
B.AUG.25,1927 CHICAGO,ILL.
1950 BOS A P		4	0- 0
1951 STL A P		29	0- 6
1952 PIT N P		5	0- 0
BRTR		38	0- 6

SUCK, ANTHONY
B.JUNE 11,1858 CHICAGO,ILL.
D.JAN.29,1895 CHICAGO,ILL.
1883 BUF N C-0		2	.000
1884 CHI U C-S-3-0		43	.149
PIT U C		10	.182
BAL U C		3	.300
		58	.156

SUDAKIS, WILLIAM PAUL
(BILL) OR (SUDS)
B.MAR.27,1946 JOLIET,ILL.
1968 LA N 3		24	.276
1969 LA N *3		132	.234
1970 LA N C-3/0-1		94	.264
1971 LA N C/3-1-0		41	.193
1972 NY N /1-C		18	.143
1973 TEX A 3-1/C-0		82	.255
1974 NY A D-1/3-C		89	.232
1975 CAL A D/C-1		30	.121
CLE A 1/C		20	.196
BRTR		530	.234

SUDER, PETER (PETE) OR (PECKY)
B.APR.16,1916 ALIQUIPPA,PA.
1941 PHI A S-3		139	.245
1942 PHI A 2-S-3		128	.256
1943 PHI A 2-S-3		131	.221
1946 PHI A 1-2-S-3-0		128	.281
1947 PHI A 2-S-3		145	.241
1948 PHI A 2		148	.241
1949 PHI A 2-S-3		118	.267
1950 PHI A 1-2-S-3		77	.246
1951 PHI A 2-S-3		123	.245
1952 PHI A 2-S-3		74	.241
1953 PHI A 2-S-3		115	.286
1954 PHI A 2-S-3		69	.200
1955 KC A 2		26	.210
BRTR		1421	.249

SUDHOFF, JOHN WILLIAM (WEE WILLIE)
B.SEPT.17,1874 ST.LOUIS,MO.
D.MAY 25,1917 ST.LOUIS,MO.
1897 STL N P		11	1- 8
1898 STL N P		38	11-26
1899 CLE N P		14	3- 8
STL N P		30	12-10
1900 STL N P	16	32	6- 8
1901 STL N P		33	17-11
1902 STL A P-0		31	11-13
			.171
1903 STL A P	38	41	21-16
1904 STL A P		29	7-14
1905 STL A P		32	10-20
1906 WAS A P		8	0- 2
TR	280	299	99-136
			.180

SUGDEN, JOSEPH
B.JULY 31,1870 PHILADELPHIA,PA.
D.JUNE 28,1959 PHILADELPHIA,PA.
1893 PIT N C		25	.273
1894 PIT N C		39	.333
1895 PIT N C		45	.310
1896 PIT N C		77	.298
1897 PIT N C		83	.219
1898 STL N C		80	.259
1899 CLE N C		78	.281
1901 CHI A C		48	.283
1902 STL A P-C	1	69	0- 0
	1-0		.231
1903 STL A C		79	.214
1904 STL A C-1		104	.262
1905 STL A P-C	1	91	0- 1
			.173
1912 DET A 1		1	.333
BBTR	2	819	0- 1
			.255

SUGGS, GEORGE FRANKLIN
B.JULY 7,1882 KINSTON,N.C.
D.APR.4,1949 KINSTON,N.C.
1908 DET A P		6	1- 0
1909 DET A P		9	1- 3
1910 CIN N P		35	20-12
1911 CIN N P		36	15-13
1912 CIN N P		42	19-16
1913 CIN N P		36	8-15
1914 BAL F P		46	24-14
1915 BAL F P		35	11-17
BRTR		245	99-90

SUHR, AUGUST RICHARD (GUS)
B.JAN.3,1906 SAN FRANCISCO,CAL.
1930 PIT N 1		151	.286
1931 PIT N 1		87	.211
1932 PIT N 1		154	.263
1933 PIT N 1		154	.267
1934 PIT N 1		151	.283
1935 PIT N 1-0		153	.272
1936 PIT N 1		156	.312
1937 PIT N 1		151	.278
1938 PIT N 1		145	.294
1939 PIT N 1		63	.289
PHI N 1		60	.318
1940 PHI N 1		10	.160
BLTR		1435	.281

SUKEFORTH, CLYDE LEROY
(CLYDE) OR (SUKEY)
B.NOV.30,1901 WASHINGTON,ME.
1926 CIN N H		1	.000
1927 CIN N C		38	.190
1928 CIN N C		33	.182
1929 CIN N C		84	.354
1930 CIN N C		94	.284
1931 CIN N C		112	.256
1932 BRO N C		59	.234
1933 BRO N C		20	.056
1934 BRO N C		27	.163
1945 BRO N C		18	.294
BRTR		486	.264
NON-PLAYING MANAGER BRO(N) 1947

SUKLA, EDWARD ANTHONY (ED)
B.MAR.3,1943 LONG BEACH,CAL.
1964 LA A P		2	0- 1
1965 CAL A P		25	2- 3
1966 CAL A P		12	1- 1
BRTR		39	3- 5

SULIK, ERNEST RICHARD (DAVE)
B.JULY 7,1910 SAN FRANCISCO,CAL.
D.MAY 31,1963 OAKLAND,CAL.
| 1936 PHI N 0 | | 122 | .287 |
| BLTL | | | |

SULLIVAN
| 1875 NH NA 0 | | 2 | - |

SULLIVAN, ANDREW R.
B.AUG.30,1884 SOUTHBOROUGH,MASS
D.FEB.14,1920 FRAMINGHAM,MASS.
| 1904 BOS N S | | 1 | .000 |
| TR | | | |

SULLIVAN, CARL MANCEL (JACKIE)
B.FEB.22,1918 PRINCETON,TEX.
| 1944 DET A 2 | | 1 | .000 |
| BRTR | | | |

SULLIVAN, CHARLES EDWARD
B.MAY 23,1903 YADKIN VALLEY,N.C
D.MAY 28,1935 MAIDEN,N.C.
1928 DET A P		3	0- 2
1930 DET A P		40	1- 5
1931 DET A P		31	3- 2
BLTR		74	4- 9

SULLIVAN, DANIEL C. (LINK)
B.MAY 9,1857 PROVIDENCE,R.I.
D.OCT.26,1893 PROVIDENCE,R.I.
1882 LOU AA C-S-3-0		67	.284
1883 LOU AA C-S-3-0		36	.225
1884 LOU AA C		64	.245
1885 LOU AA C		13	.156
STL AA C		17	.138
1886 PIT AA C		1	.000
TR		198	.242

SULLIVAN, DENNIS J.
B.1854 BOSTON,MASS.
1879 PRO N C		5	.250
1880 BOS N C		1	.250
		6	.250

SULLIVAN, DENNIS WILLIAM
B.SEPT.28,1882 HILLSBORO,WIS.
D.JUNE 2,1956 W.LOS ANGELES,CAL
1905 WAS A 0		3	.000
1907 BOS A 0		144	.245
1908 BOS A 0		100	.241
CLE A 0		4	.000
1909 CLE A 0		3	.667
BLTR		254	.239

SULLIVAN, EDWARD TROWBRIDGE
[SEE EDWARD TROWBRIDGE COLLINS SR]

SULLIVAN, FLORENCE P. (FLEURY)
B.1862 E.ST.LOUIS,ILL.
D.FEB.19,1897 E.ST.LOUIS,ILL.
| 1884 PIT AA P | | 51 | 54 | 16-35 |

SULLIVAN, FRANKLIN LEAL (FRANK)
B.JAN.23,1930 HOLLYWOOD,CAL.
1953 BOS A P		14	1- 1
1954 BOS A P		36	15-12
1955 BOS A P		35	18-13
1956 BOS A P		34	14- 7
1957 BOS A P		31	14-11
1958 BOS A P		32	13- 9
1959 BOS A P		30	9-11
1960 BOS A P		40	6-16
1961 PHI N P		49	3-16
1962 PHI N P		19	0- 2
MIN A P		21	4- 1
1963 MIN A P		10	0- 1
BRTR		351	97-100

SULLIVAN, HARRY ANDREW
B.APR.12,1888 ROCKFORD,ILL.
D.SEPT.22,1919 ROCKFORD,ILL.
| 1909 STL N P | | 2 | 0- 0 |
| BLTL | | | |

SULLIVAN, HAYWOOD COOPER
B.DEC.15,1930 DONALSONVILLE,GA.
1955 BOS A C		2	.000
1957 BOS A C		2	.000
1959 BOS A C		4	.000
1960 BOS A C		52	.161
1961 KC A C-1-0		117	.242
1962 KC A C-1		95	.248
1963 KC A C		40	.212
BRTR		312	.226
NON-PLAYING MANAGER KC(A) 1965

SULLIVAN, JAMES E.
B.APR.25,1869 CHARLESTOWN,MASS.
D.NOV.30,1901 ROXBURY,MASS.
1891 BOS N P		1	0- 0
COL AA P		1	0- 1
1895 BOS N P	25	26	11- 9
1896 BOS N P		24	11-13
1897 BOS N P		13	4- 4
	64	65	26-27

SULLIVAN, JAMES P.
D.MAY 22,1898
NON-PLAYING MANAGER COL(AA)1890

SULLIVAN, JAMES RICHARD
B.APR.5,1894 MINE RUN,VA.
D.FEB.12,1972 BURTONSVILLE,MD.
1921 PHI A P		2	0- 2
1922 PHI A P		20	0- 2
1923 CLE A P		3	0- 1
BRTR		25	0- 5

SULLIVAN, JOHN EUGENE
B.FEB.16,1873 ILLINOIS
D.JUNE 5,1924 ST.PAUL,MINN.
1905 DET A C		13	.176
1908 PIT N C		1	.000
TR		14	.171

SULLIVAN, JOHN FRANK (CHUB)
B.JAN.12,1856 BOSTON,MASS.
D.SEPT.12,1881 BOSTON,MASS.
1877 BOS N 1		8	.250
1878 CIN N 1		62	.255
1880 WOR N 1		42	.267
BRTR		112	.262

YR	CL LEA POS	GP	G	REC

SULLIVAN, JOHN JEREMIAH (LEFTY)
B.MAY 31,1894 CHICAGO,ILL.
D.JULY 7,1958 CHICAGO,ILL.
1919 CHI A P   4   0- 1
        BLTL

SULLIVAN, JOHN LAWRENCE
B.MAR.21,1890 WILLIAMSPORT,PA.
D.APR.1,1967 MILTON,PA.
1920 BOS N O   81 .296
1921 BOS N O   5 .000
     CHI N O   76 .329
        BRTR   162 .309

SULLIVAN, JOHN PAUL
B.NOV.2,1920 CHICAGO,ILL.
1942 WAS A S   94 .235
1943 WAS A S   134 .206
1944 WAS A S   138 .251
1947 WAS A 2-S   49 .256
1948 WAS A 2-S   85 .208
1949 STL A 2-S-3   105 .226
        BRTR   605 .230

SULLIVAN, JOHN PETER
B.JAN.3,1941 SOMERVILLE,N.J.
1963 DET A C   3 .000
1964 DET A C   2 .000
1965 DET A C   34 .267
1967 NY N C   65 .218
1968 PHI N /C   12 .222
        BLTR   116 .228

SULLIVAN, JOE
B.SEPT.26,1910 MASON CITY,ILL.
1935 DET A P   25 6- 6
1936 DET A P   26 2- 5
1939 BOS N P   31 33 6- 9
1940 BOS N P   36 10-14
1941 BOS N P   16 2- 2
     PIT N   16 4- 1
        BLTL   150 152 30-37

SULLIVAN, JOSEPH DANIEL
B.JAN.6,1870 CHARLESTOWN,MASS.
D.NOV.2,1897 CHARLESTOWN,MASS.
1893 WAS N S   127 .271
1894 WAS N 2-S-3   17 .239
     PHI N S   76 .358
1895 PHI N S   91 .340
1896 PHI N 3-O   38 .269
     STL N O   60 .287
                     409 .304

SULLIVAN, MARTIN J.
B.OCT.20,1862 LOWELL,MASS.
D.JAN.5,1894 LOWELL,MASS.
1887 CHI N O   115 .334
1888 CHI N O   75 .235
1889 IND N O   69 .285
1890 BOS N O   121 .285
1891 BOS N O   17 .224
     CLE N O   1 .250
        BRTR   398 .288

SULLIVAN, MICHAEL JOSEPH
B.JUNE 10,1860 WEBSTER,MASS.
D.MAR.21,1929 WEBSTER,MASS.
1888 ATH AA 3-O   28 .277
        BRTR

SULLIVAN, MICHAEL JOSEPH
(MIKE) OR (BIG MIKE)
B.OCT.23,1866 BOSTON,MASS.
D.JUNE 14,1906 BOSTON,MASS.
1889 WAS N P   9 0- 3
1890 CHI N P   12 5- 6
1891 ATH AA P   2 0- 2
     NY N P   3 1- 2
1892 CIN N P   18 12- 6
1893 CIN N P   22 7-13
1894 WAS N P   14 2-10
     CLE N P   12 6- 4
1895 CLE N P   5 1- 4
1896 NY N P   23 10-12
1897 NY N P   21 8- 7
1898 BOS N P   3 0- 2
1899 BOS N P   1 1- 0
        BL   145 53-71

SULLIVAN, PATRICK B.
B.DEC.2,1862 MILWAUKEE,WIS.
1884 KC U P-C   1 31 0- 1
                3-O   .193
        TR

SULLIVAN, PAUL THOMAS (LEFTY)
B.SEPT.7,1916 NASHVILLE,TENN.
1939 CLE A P   7 0- 1
        BLTL

SULLIVAN, RUSSELL GUY (RUSS)
B.FEB.19,1923 FREDERICKSBURG,VA
1951 DET A O   7 .192
1952 DET A O   15 .327
1953 DET A O   23 .250
        BLTR   45 .267

SULLIVAN, SUTER G.
B.1872 BALTIMORE,MD.
1898 STL N S   40 .225
1899 CLE N 3-O   126 .250
                     166 .245

SULLIVAN, THOMAS
B.MAR.1,1860 NEW YORK,N.Y.
D.APR.12,1947 CINCINNATI,OHIO
1884 COL AA P   4 2- 2
1886 LOU AA P   9 2- 7
1888 KC AA P-O   24 28 8-16
                          .109
1889 KC AA P   10 2- 8
                  47 51 14-33
                          .116

SULLIVAN, THOMAS AUGUSTIN
B.OCT.18,1895 BOSTON,MASS.
D.SEPT.23,1962 W.ROXBURY,MASS.
1922 PHI N P   3 0- 0
        BLTL

SULLIVAN, THOMAS BRANDON
B.DEC.19,1906 NOME,ALASKA
D.AUG.16,1994 SEATTLE,WASH.
1925 CIN N C   1 .000
        BRTR

SULLIVAN, THOMAS JEFFERSON
(SLEEPER) OR (OLD IRON HANDS)
B.ST.LOUIS,MO.
D.SEPT.25,1899 CAMDEN,N.J.
1881 BUF N C-O   31 .190
1882 STL AA C   51 .182
1883 STL AA C-O   8 .148
1884 STL U P-C   1   2 1- 0
                          .167
        TR   1 92 1- 0
                          .185

SULLIVAN, TIMOTHY PAUL (TED)
B.1851 COUNTY CLARE,IRELAND
D.JULY 5,1929 WASHINGTON,D.C.
1884 KC U M-S-O   3 .333
NON-PLAYING MANAGER
STL(A) 1882-83; STL(U) 1884,
WAS(N) 1888

SULLIVAN, WILLIAM
B.JULY 4,1853 HOLYOKE,MASS.
D.NOV.13,1884 HOLYOKE,MASS.
1878 CHI N O   2 .000

SULLIVAN, WILLIAM JOSEPH JR.
B.OCT.23,1910 CHICAGO,ILL.
1931 CHI A 3   92 .275
1932 CHI A 1-3   93 .316
1933 CHI A C-1   54 .192
1935 CIN N 1-2-3   85 .266
1936 CLE A C   93 .351
1937 CLE A C   72 .286
1938 STL A C   111 .277
1939 STL A C-O   118 .289
1940 DET A C-3   78 .309
1941 DET A C   85 .282
1942 BRO N C   43 .267
1947 PIT N C   38 .255
        BLTR   962 .289

SULLIVAN, WILLIAM JOSEPH SR.
B.FEB.1,1875 OAKLAND,WIS.
D.JAN.28,1965 NEWBERG,ORE.
1899 BOS N C   22 .284
1900 BOS N C   66 .267
1901 CHI A C   98 .245
1902 CHI A C-1-O   78 .151
1903 CHI A C   32 .188
1904 CHI A C   108 .235
1905 CHI A C   98 .201
1906 CHI A C   118 .214
1907 CHI A C   112 .179
1908 CHI A C   137 .191
1909 CHI A M-C   97 .162
1910 CHI A M-C   45 .183
1911 CHI A M-C   89 .215
1912 CHI A M-C   39 .209
1914 CHI A M-C   1 .000
1916 DET A M-C   1 .000
        BRTR   1141 .213

SULLIVAN, WILLIAM T.
1890 SYR AA P   6 2- 4

SUMMA, HOMER WAYNE
B.NOV.3,1898 GENTRY,MO.
D.JAN.29,1966 LOS ANGELES,CAL.
1920 PIT N O   10 .318
1922 CLE A O   12 .348
1923 CLE A O   137 .328
1924 CLE A O   111 .290
1925 CLE A 3-O   75 .390
1926 CLE A O   154 .308
1927 CLE A O   145 .286
1928 CLE A O   134 .284
1929 PHI A O   37 .272
1930 PHI A O   25 .278
        BLTR   840 .301

SUMMERS, JOHN JUNIOR (CHAMP)
B.JUNE 15,1946 BREMERTON,WASH.
1974 OAK A O   20 .125
1975 CHI N O   76 .231
1976 CHI N O-1/C   83 .206
1977 CIN N O/3   59 .171
1978 CIN N O   13 .257
        BLTR   251 .205

SUMMERS, ORON EDGAR
(KICKAPOO ED) OR (CHIEF)
B.DEC.5,1884 LADOGA,IND.
D.MAY 12,1953 INDIANAPOLIS,IND.
1908 DET A P   40 24-12
1909 DET A P   35 19- 9
1910 DET A P   30 13-12
1911 DET A P   30 11-11
1912 DET A P   3 2- 1
        BBTR   138 69-45

SUMMERSGILL, HENRY TRAVERS
[PLAYED UNDER NAME OF
ANDREW SOMMERVILLE]

SUMNER, CARL RINGDAHL (LEFTY)
B.SEPT.28,1908 CAMBRIDGE,MASS.
1928 BOS A O   16 .276
        BLTL

SUNDAY, ARTHUR
[REAL NAME AUGUST WACHER]
B.JAN.21,1862 SPRINGFIELD,OHIO
1890 BRO P O   24 .292

SUNDAY, WILLIAM ASHLEY (BILLY)
(PARSON) OR (THE EVANGELIST)
B.NOV.9,1862 AMES,IOWA
D.NOV.6,1935 CHICAGO,ILL.
1883 CHI N O   15 .259
1884 CHI N O   43 .221
1885 CHI N O   46 .255
1886 CHI N O   25 .242
1887 CHI N O   46 .359
1888 PIT N O   119 .233
1889 PIT N O   80 .239
1890 PIT N O   85 .268
     PHI N O   31 .256
        BL   488 .258

SUNDBERG, JAMES HOWARD (JIM)
B.MAY 18,1951 GALESBURG,ILL.
1974 TEX A *C   132 .247
1975 TEX A *C   155 .199
1976 TEX A *C   140 .228
1977 TEX A *C   149 .291
1978 TEX A *C   149 .278
        BRTR   725 .249

SUNDIN, GORDON VINCENT
B.OCT.10,1937 MINNEAPOLIS,MINN.
1956 BAL A P   1 0- 0
        BRTR

SUNDRA, STEPHEN RICHARD
(STEVE) OR (SMOKEY)
B.MAR.27,1910 LUXOR,PA.
D.MAR.23,1952 CLEVELAND,OHIO
1936 NY A P   1 0- 0
1938 NY A P   25 6- 4
1939 NY A P   24 11- 1
1940 NY A P   27 4- 6
1941 WAS A P   28 9-13
1942 WAS A P   6 1- 3
     STL A P   20 8- 3
1943 STL A P   32 15-11
1944 STL A P   3 2- 0
1946 STL A P   2 0- 0
        BBTR   168 56-41
        BR 1941-43

SUNKEL, THOMAS JACOB (LEFTY)
B.AUG.9,1912 PARIS,ILL.
1937 STL N P   9 0- 0
1939 STL N P   20 4- 4
1941 NY N P   2 1- 1
1942 NY N P   1 0- 1
1944 BRO N P   12 1- 3
        BLTL   63 9-15

SURKONT, MATTHEW CONSTANTINE (MAX)
B.JUNE 16,1922 CENTRAL FALLS,R.I.
1949 CHI A P   44 3- 5
1950 BOS N P   9 5- 2
1951 BOS N P   37 12-16
1952 BOS N P   31 12-13
1953 MIL N P   28 11- 5
1954 PIT N P   33 9-18
1955 PIT N P   35 7-14
1956 PIT N P   1 0- 0
     STL N P   5 0- 0
     NY N P   8 2- 2
1957 NY N P   5 0- 1
        BRTR   236 61-76

YR	CL LEA POS	GP	G	REC

SUSCE, GEORGE CYRIL METHODIUS
(GOOD KID)
B.AUG.13,1908 PITTSBURGH,PA.

YR	CL LEA POS	GP	G	REC
1929 PHI N C		17	.294
1932 DET A C		2	.000
1939 PIT N C		31	.227
1940 STL A C		61	.212
1941 CLE A C		1	.000
1942 CLE A C		2	1.000
1943 CLE A C		3	.000
1944 CLE A C		29	.230
BRTR		146	.228

SUSCE, GEORGE DANIEL
B.SEPT.13,1931 PITTSBURGH,PA.

1955 BOS A P		29	9- 7
1956 BOS A P		21	2- 4
1957 BOS A P		29	7- 3
1958 BOS A P		2	0- 0
DET A P		27	4- 3
1959 DET A P		9	0- 0
BRTR		117	22-17

SUSKO, PETER JONATHAN
B.JULY 2,1904 LAURA,OHIO
D.MAY 22,1978 JACKSONVILLE,FLA.

| 1934 WAS A 1 | | 58 | .286 |
| BLTL | | | |

SUTCLIFFE, CHARLES INIGO (BUTCH)
B.JULY 22,1915 FALL RIVER,MASS.

| 1938 BOS N C | | 4 | .250 |

SUTCLIFFE, EDWARD ELMER (SY)
B.APR.15,1863 WHEATON,ILL.
D.FEB.13,1893 WHEATON,ILL.

1884 CHI N C		4	.200
1885 CHI N C-O		11	.195
STL N C-O		15	.140
1888 DET N S		49	.257
1889 CLE N C		65	.248
1890 CLE P C-O		99	.329
1891 WAS AA C-O		51	.365
1892 BAL N 1		66	.275
BL		360	.273

SUTCLIFFE, RICHARD LEE (RICK)
B.JUNE 21,1956 INDEPENDENCE,MO.

1976 LA N /P		1	0- 0
1978 LA N /P		2	0- 0
BLTR		3	0- 0

SUTER, HARRY RICHARD
(HANDSOME HARRY) OR (RUBE)
B.SEPT.15,1887 INDEPENDENCE,MO.
D.JULY 24,1971 TOPEKA,KAN.

| 1909 CHI A P | | 18 | 2- 3 |
| BLTR | | | |

SUTHERLAND, DARRELL WAYNE
B.NOV.14,1941 GLENDALE,CAL.

1964 NY N P		10	0- 3
1965 NY N P		18	3- 1
1966 NY N P		31	2- 0
1968 CLE A /P		3	0- 0
BRTR		62	5- 4

SUTHERLAND, GARY LYNN
B.SEP.27,1944 GLENDALE,CAL.

1966 PHI N /S		3	.000
1967 PHI N S-O		103	.247
1968 PHI N 2-S-3/O		67	.275
1969 MON N *2-S/O		141	.239
1970 MON N 2-S/3		116	.206
1971 MON N 2-S/O-3		111	.257
1972 HOU N /2-3		5	.125
1973 HOU N 2/S		16	.259
1974 DET A *2-S/3		149	.254
1975 DET A *2		129	.258
1976 DET A 2		42	.205
MIL A 2/1		59	.217
1977 SD N 2-3/1		80	.243
1978 STL N /2		10	.167
BRTR		1031	.243

SUTHERLAND, HARVEY SCOTT (SUDS)
D.FEB.20,1894 BEAVERTON,ORE.
D.MAY 11,1972 PORTLAND,ORE.

| 1921 DET A P | 13 | 17 | 6- 2 |
| BRTR | | | |

SUTHERLAND, HOWARD ALVIN (DIZZY)
B.APR.9,1923 WASHINGTON,D.C.

| 1949 WAS A P | | 1 | 0- 1 |
| BLTL | | | |

SUTTER, HOWARD BRUCE (BRUCE)
B.JAN.8,1953 LANCASTER,PA.

1976 CHI N P		52	6- 3
1977 CHI N P		62	7- 3
1978 CHI N P		64	8-10
BRTR		178	21-16

SUTTHOFF, JOHN GERHARD
(JACK) OR (SUNNY JACK)
B.JUNE 29,1873 CINCINNATI,OHIO
D.AUG.3,1942 CINCINNATI,OHIO

1898 WAS N P		2	0- 2
1899 STL N P		2	1- 1
1901 CIN N P-O	10	11	1- 6
			.121
1903 CIN N P		30	16-11
1904 CIN N P		12	3- 3
PHI N P		19	4-13
1905 PHI N P		13	3- 3
BLTR	88	89	28-39
			.149

SUTTON, DONALD HOWARD (DON)
B.APR.2,1945 CLIO,ALA.

1966 LA N P	37	38	12-12
1967 LA N P	37	43	11-15
1968 LA N P	35	36	11-15
1969 LA N P		41	17-18
1970 LA N P	38	40	15-13
1971 LA N P	38	39	17-12
1972 LA N P		33	19- 9
1973 LA N P		33	18-10
1974 LA N P		40	19- 9
1975 LA N P		35	16-13
1976 LA N P		35	21-10
1977 LA N P		33	14- 8
1978 LA N P		34	15-11
BRTR	469	480	205-155

SUTTON, JOHNNY IKE (JOHN)
B.NOV.13,1952 DALLAS,TEX.

1977 STL N P		14	2- 1
1978 MIN A P		17	0- 0
BRTR		31	2- 1

SUTTON, EZRA BALLOU
B.SEPT.17,1850 SENECA,N.Y.
D.JUNE 20,1907 BRAINTREE,MASS.

1871 CLE NA 3		29	-
1872 CLE NA 3		21	.282
1873 ATH NA 2-S-3		50	-
1874 ATH NA S-3		55	-
1875 ATH NA 1-3-0		75	.328
1876 ATH N 1-2-3		54	.293
1877 BOS N S-3		58	.292
1878 BOS N 3		60	.226
1879 BOS N S-3		84	.248
1880 BOS N S-3		74	.250
1881 BOS N S-3		83	.291
1882 BOS N S-3		80	.255
1883 BOS N S-3-0		94	.323
1884 BOS N 3		106	.349
1885 BOS N S-3		108	.312
1886 BOS N 2-S-3-0		116	.276
1887 BOS N S-0		74	.327
1888 BOS N 3		28	.218
BLTR		1249	-

SWABACH, WILLIAM

| 1887 NY N P | | 2 | 0- 1 |

SWACINA, HARRY JOSEPH (SWATS)
B.AUG.22,1881 ST.LOUIS,MO.
D.JUNE 23,1944 BIRMINGHAM,ALA.

1907 PIT N 1		26	.200
1908 PIT N 1		50	.216
1914 BAL F 1		158	.276
1915 BAL F 1		85	.247
BRTR		319	.254

SWAIM, JOHN HILLARY (CY)
B.MAR.11,1874 CADWALLADER,OHIO
D.NOV.8,1918 OAKLAND,CAL.

1897 WAS N P		24	5-12
1898 WAS N P		15	3-11
		39	8-23

SWAN, ANDREW J.

1884 WAS AA 1-3		5	.143
RIC AA 1		3	.500
		8	.258

SWAN, CRAIG STEVEN
B.NOV.30,1950 VAN NUYS,CAL.

1973 NY N /P		3	0- 1
1974 NY N /P		7	1- 3
1975 NY N /P		6	1- 3
1976 NY N P		23	6- 9
1977 NY N P		26	9-10
1978 NY N P		29	9- 6
BRTR		94	26-32

SWANDELL, JOHN MARTIN (MARTY)
B.1845 NEW YORK

1872 ECK NA 1-2-3-0		14	.207
1873 RES NA 1		2	-
		16	-

SWANDER, EDWARD D. (PINKY)
B.JULY 4,1880 PORTSMOUTH,OHIO
D.OCT.24,1944 SPRINGFIELD,MASS.

1903 STL A O		14	.250
1904 STL A O		1	.000
BLTR		15	.245

SWANN, HENRY (DUCKY)
B.1892

| 1914 KC F P | | 1 | 0- 1 |
| BRTR | | | |

SWANSON, ARTHUR LEONARD (RED)
B.OCT.15,1936 BATON ROUGE,LA.

1955 PIT N P		1	0- 0
1956 PIT N P	9	10	0- 0
1957 PIT N P		32	3- 3
BRTR	42	43	3- 3

SWANSON, ERNEST EVAR (EVAR)
B.OCT.15,1902 DE KALB,ILL.
D.JULY 17,1973 GALESBURG,ILL.

1929 CIN N O		148	.300
1930 CIN N O		95	.309
1932 CHI A O		14	.308
1933 CHI A O		144	.306
1934 CHI A O		117	.298
BRTR		518	.303

SWANSON, KARL EDWARD
B.DEC.17,1903 N.HENDERSON,ILL.

1928 CHI A 2		22	.141
1929 CHI A H		2	.000
BLTR		24	.138

SWANSON, STANLEY LAWRENCE (STAN)
B.MAY 19,1944 YUBA CITY,CAL.

| 1971 MON N O | | 49 | .245 |
| BRTR | | | |

SWANSON, WILLIAM ANDREW
B.OCT.12,1888 NEW YORK,N.Y.
D.OCT.14,1954 NEW YORK,N.Y.

| 1914 BOS A 2 | | 11 | .211 |
| BBTR | | | |

SWARTWOOD, CYRUS EDWARD (ED)
B.JAN.12,1859 ROCKFORD,ILL.
D.MAY 15,1924 PITTSBURGH,PA.

1881 BUF N O		1	.250
1882 PIT AA 1-O		71	.319
1883 PIT AA C-1-O		95	.369
1884 PIT AA O		102	.330
1885 BRO AA O		100	.242
1886 BRO AA O		123	.262
1887 BRO AA O		91	.344
1890 TOL AA O		126	.309
1892 PIT N O		12	.263
TR		721	.309

SWARTZ, MONROE (MONTY) OR (DAZZY)
B.JAN.1,1897 FARMERSVILLE,OHIO

| 1920 CIN N P | | 1 | 0- 1 |

SWARTZ, SHERWIN MERLE (BUD)
B.JUNE 3,1929 TULSA,OKLA.

| 1947 STL A P | | 5 | 0- 0 |
| BLTL | | | |

SWARTZEL, PARK B.
B.NOV.21,1865 KNIGHTSTOWN,IND.
D.JAN.3,1940 LOS ANGELES,CAL.

| 1889 KC AA P | 48 | 52 | 19-26 |
| BRTR | | | |

SWASEY, CHARLES JAMES
[PLAYED UNDER NAME OF
CHARLES JAMES SWEAZY]

SWEAZY, CHARLES JAMES
[REAL NAME CHARLES JAMES SWASEY]
B.NOV.2,1847 NEWARK,N.J.
D.MAR.30,1908 NEWARK,N.J.

1871 OLY NA 2		4	-
1872 CLE NA 2-O		11	.222
1873 BOS NA 2		1	-
1874 BAL NA 2-O		8	-
ATL NA 2		10	-
1875 RS NA M-2		19	-
1876 CIN N 2-O		56	.203
1878 PRO N 2		54	.178
BRTR		163	-

SWEENEY, CHARLES A.

| 1914 PHI A O | | 1 | .000 |

SWEENEY, CHARLES J.
B.APR.13,1863 SAN FRANCISCO,CAL.
D.APR.4,1902 SAN FRANCISCO,CAL.

1882 ATH AA P-O	21	24	8-11
			.175
PRO N		1	.000
1883 PRO N P-1-O		21	11- 9
			.218
1884 PRO N P-1- O	25	40	17- 7
			.302
STL U P-1- O	34	46	24- 7
			.307
1885 STL N P-O		38	73 12-20
			.207
1886 STL N P		17	5- 6
1887 CLE AA P-1	3	36	0- 3
			.329
	142	258	77-64
			.259

YR CL LEA POS | GP | G | REC

SWEENEY, DANIEL J.
B.JAN.28,1868 PHILADELPHIA,PA.
D.JULY 13,1913 LOUISVILLE,KY.

YR	CL	LEA	POS	GP	G	REC
1895	LOU	N	O	21		.279

SWEENEY, EDWARD FRANCIS
(ED) OR (JEFF)
B.JULY 19,1888 CHICAGO,ILL.
D.JULY 4,1947 CHICAGO,ILL.

YR	CL	LEA	POS	GP	G	REC
1908	NY	A	C	32		.146
1909	NY	A	C	67		.267
1910	NY	A	C	78		.200
1911	NY	A	C	83		.231
1912	NY	A	C	110		.266
1913	NY	A	C	117		.265
1914	NY	A	C	87		.213
1915	NY	A	C	53		.190
1919	PIT	N	C	17		.095
		BRTR		644		.232

SWEENEY, HARRY LEON (HANK)
B.DEC.28,1915 FRANKLIN,TENN.

YR	CL	LEA	POS	GP	G	REC
1944	PIT	N	1	1		.000
		BLTL				

SWEENEY, JEREMIAH H.
B.1860 BOSTON,MASS.
D.AUG.25,1891 BOSTON,MASS.

YR	CL	LEA	POS	GP	G	REC
1884	KC	U	1	30		.260

SWEENEY, JOHN J. (ROONEY)
B.1860
D.AUG.10,1886

YR	CL	LEA	POS	GP	G	REC
1883	BAL	AA	C-2-O	25		.232
1884	BAL	U	C-O	43		.239
1885	STL	N	C-O	3		.091
				71		.231

SWEENEY, PETER JAY
B.DEC.31,1863 CALIFORNIA
D.AUG.22,1901 SAN FRANCISCO,CAL

YR	CL	LEA	POS	GP	G	REC
1888	WAS	N	3	11		.181
1889	WAS	N	3	49		.228
	STL	AA	3	9		.310
1890	STL	AA	3	49		.162
	LOU	AA	3	2		.143
	ATH	AA	3	14		.157
		BRTR		134		.202

SWEENEY, WILLIAM J.
B.PHILADELPHIA,PA.
D.APR.13,1908 PATERSON,N.J.

YR	CL	LEA	POS	GP	G	REC
1884	BAL	U	P	64	83	40-21

SWEENEY, WILLIAM JOHN
B.MAR.6,1886 COVINGTON,KY.
D.MAY 26,1948 CAMBRIDGE,MASS.

YR	CL	LEA	POS	GP	G	REC
1907	CHI	N	3	3		.100
	BOS	N	S-3	57		.262
1908	BOS	N	3	127		.244
1909	BOS	N	S-3	138		.243
1910	BOS	N	1-S-3	147		.267
1911	BOS	N	2	136		.314
1912	BOS	N	2	153		.344
1913	BOS	N	2	139		.257
1914	CHI	N	2	134		.218
		BRTR		1034		.272

SWEENEY, WILLIAM JOSEPH
B.DEC.29,1904 CLEVELAND,OHIO
D.APR.18,1957 SAN DIEGO,CAL.

YR	CL	LEA	POS	GP	G	REC
1928	DET	A	1	89		.252
1930	BOS	A	1	88		.309
1931	BOS	A	1	131		.295
		BRTR		308		.286

SWEET, RICKY JOE (RICK)
B.SEPT.7,1952 LONGVIEW,WASH.

YR	CL	LEA	POS	GP	G	REC
1978	SD	N	C	88		.221
		BLTR				

SWEETLAND, LESTER LEO
[BORN LEO SWEETLAND]
B.AUG.15,1901 ST.IGNACE,MICH.
D.MAR.4,1974 MELBOURNE,FLA.

YR	CL	LEA	POS	GP	G	REC
1927	PHI	N	P	21	25	2-10
1928	PHI	N	P	37	41	3-15
1929	PHI	N	P	43	53	13-11
1930	PHI	N	P	34	35	7-15
1931	CHI	N	P	26	29	8- 7
		BBTL		161	183	33-58
		BR 1927-29				

SWEIGERT

YR	CL	LEA	POS	GP	G	REC
1890	ATH	AA	O	1		.000

SWENTOR, AUGUST WILLIAM
B.NOV.21,1899 SEYMOUR,CONN.
D.NOV.10,1969 WATERBURY,CONN.

YR	CL	LEA	POS	GP	G	REC
1922	CHI	A	3	1		.000
		BRTR				

SWETONIC, STEPHEN ALBERT
B.AUG.13,1903 MT.PLEASANT,PA.
D.APR.22,1974 CANONSBURG,PA.

YR	CL	LEA	POS	GP	G	REC
1929	PIT	N	P	41	42	8-10
1930	PIT	N	P		23	6- 6
1931	PIT	N	P		14	0- 2
1932	PIT	N	P		24	11- 6
1933	PIT	N	P		31	12-12
1935	PIT	N	R		1	.000
		BRTR		133	135	37-36
						.170

SWETT, CHARLES A. (POP)
B.APR.15,1868 SAN FRANCISCO,CAL

YR	CL	LEA	POS	GP	G	REC
1890	BOS	P	C	37		.193

SWIFT, ROBERT VIRGIL (BOB)
B.MAR.6,1915 SALINA,KAN.
D.OCT.17,1966 DETROIT,MICH.

YR	CL	LEA	POS	GP	G	REC
1940	STL	A	C	130		.244
1941	STL	A	C	63		.259
1942	STL	A	C	29		.187
	PHI	A	C	60		.229
1943	PHI	A	C	77		.192
1944	DET	A	C	80		.255
1945	DET	A	C	95		.233
1946	DET	A	C	42		.234
1947	DET	A	C	97		.251
1948	DET	A	C	113		.223
1949	DET	A	C	74		.238
1950	DET	A	C	67		.227
1951	DET	A	C	44		.192
1952	DET	A	C	28		.138
1953	DET	A	C	2		.333
		BRTR		1001		.231

NON-PLAYING MANAGER DET[A] 1966

SWIFT, WILLIAM VINCENT (BILL)
B.JAN.10,1908 ELMIRA,N.Y.
D.FEB.23,1969 BARTOW,FLA.

YR	CL	LEA	POS	GP	G	REC
1932	PIT	N	P		39	14-10
1933	PIT	N	P		37	14-10
1934	PIT	N	P		37	11-13
1935	PIT	N	P		39	15- 8
1936	PIT	N	P		45	16-16
1937	PIT	N	P		36	9-10
1938	PIT	N	P		36	7- 5
1939	PIT	N	P		36	5- 7
1940	BOS	N	P		4	1- 1
1941	BRO	N	P		9	3- 0
1943	CHI	A	P		18	0- 2
		BRTR		336		95-82

SWIGART, OADIS VAUGHN
B.FEB.13,1915 ARCHIE,MO.

YR	CL	LEA	POS	GP	G	REC
1939	PIT	N	P		3	1- 1
1940	PIT	N	P		7	0- 2
		BLTR			10	1- 3

SWIGLER, ADAM WILLIAM (DOC)
B.SEPT.21,1895 PHILADELPHIA,PA.
D.FEB.5,1975 PHILADELPHIA,PA.

YR	CL	LEA	POS	GP	G	REC
1917	NY	N	P		1	0- 1

SWINDELL, JOSHUA ERNEST
B.JULY 5,1885 ROSE HILL,KAN.
B.OCT.26,1878 ROSE HILL,KAN.

YR	CL	LEA	POS	GP	G	REC
1911	CLE	A	P		4	0- 1
1913	CLE	A	P		1	.000
		TR		4	5	0- 1
						.200

SWINDELLS, CHARLES JAY (SWIN)
B.OCT.26,1878 ROCKFORD,ILL.
D.JULY 22,1940 PORTLAND,ORE.

YR	CL	LEA	POS	GP	G	REC
1904	STL	N	C	3		.125
		TR				

SWISHER, STEVEN EUGENE (STEVE)
B.AUG.9,1951 PARKERSBURG,W.VA.

YR	CL	LEA	POS	GP	G	REC
1974	CHI	N	C	90		.214
1975	CHI	N	C	93		.213
1976	CHI	N	*C	109		.236
1977	CHI	N	C	74		.190
1978	STL	N	C	45		.278
		BRTR		411		.223

SWOBODA, RONALD ALAN
(RON) OR (ROCKY)
B.JUNE 30,1944 BALTIMORE,MD.

YR	CL	LEA	POS	GP	G	REC
1965	NY	N	*O	135		.228
1966	NY	N	O	112		.222
1967	NY	N	*O-1	134		.281
1968	NY	N	*O	132		.242
1969	NY	N	O	109		.235
1970	NY	N	*O	115		.233
1971	MON	N	O	39		.259
	NY	A	O	54		.261
1972	NY	A	O/1	63		.248
1973	NY	A	O	35		.116
		BRTR		928		.242

SWORMSTEDT, LEONARD B.
B.OCT.6,1878 CINCINNATI,OHIO
D.JULY 19,1964 SALEM,MASS.

YR	CL	LEA	POS	GP	G	REC
1901	CIN	N	P		4	2- 1
1902	CIN	N	P		2	0- 1
1906	BOS	A	P		3	1- 1
		BRTR			9	3- 3

SYKES, ROBERT JOSEPH (BOB)
B.DEC.11,1954 NEPTUNE,N.J.

YR	CL	LEA	POS	GP	G	REC
1977	DET	A	P		32	5- 7
1978	DET	A	P		22	6- 6
		BBTL			54	11-13

SYLVESTER, LOUIS J.
B.FEB.14,1855 SPRINGFIELD,ILL.

YR	CL	LEA	POS	GP	G	REC
1884	CIN	U	P-O	2	70	0- 2
						.264
1886	LOU	AA	O	54		.227
	CIN	AA	O	14		.156
1887	STL	AA	O	28		.298
		BRTR		2	166	0- 2
						.253

SZABO, ALEXANDER
[PLAYED UNDER NAME OF
ALEXANDER SABO]

SZEKELY, JOSEPH
B.FEB.2,1925 CLEVELAND,OHIO

YR	CL	LEA	POS	GP	G	REC
1953	CIN	N	O	5		.077
		BRTR				

SZOTKIEWICZ, KENNETH JOHN (KEN)
B.FEB.25,1947 WILMINGTON,DEL.

YR	CL	LEA	POS	GP	G	REC
1970	DET	A	S	47		.107
		BLTR				

SZYMANSKI, ALOYS
[PLAYED UNDER NAME OF
ALOYSIUS HARRY SIMMONS]

TABB, JERRY LYNN
B.MAR.17,1952 ALTUS,OKLA.

YR	CL	LEA	POS	GP	G	REC
1976	CHI	N	/1	11		.292
1977	OAK	A	1	51		.222
1978	OAK	A	/1	12		.111
		BRTR		74		.226

TABER, EDWARD TIMOTHY (LEFTY)
B.JAN.11,1900 ROCK ISLAND,ILL.

YR	CL	LEA	POS	GP	G	REC
1926	PHI	N	P		6	0- 0
1927	PHI	N	P		3	0- 1
		BLTL			9	0- 1

TABER, JOHN PARDON
B.JUNE 28,1868 ACUSHNET,MASS.
D.FEB.21,1940 BOSTON,MASS.

YR	CL	LEA	POS	GP	G	REC
1890	BOS	N	P		2	0- 1

TABOR, JAMES REUBIN
(JIM) OR (RAWHIDE)
B.NOV.5,1913 OWENS CROSSROADS,ALA.
D.AUG.22,1953 SACRAMENTO,CAL.

YR	CL	LEA	POS	GP	G	REC
1938	BOS	A	3	19		.316
1939	BOS	A	3	149		.289
1940	BOS	A	3	120		.285
1941	BOS	A	3	126		.279
1942	BOS	A	3	139		.252
1943	BOS	A	3-O	137		.242
1944	BOS	A	3	116		.285
1946	PHI	N	3	124		.268
1947	PHI	N	3	75		.235
		BRTR		1005		.270

TAFF, JOHN GALLATIN
B.JUNE 3,1890 AUSTIN,TEX.
D.MAY 15,1961 HOUSTON,TEX.

YR	CL	LEA	POS	GP	G	REC
1913	PHI	A	P		5	0- 1
		BRTR				

TAGGERT, ROBERT JOHN
[SEE JAMES ROBERT KELLY]

TAITT, DOUGLAS JOHN (POCO)
B.AUG.3,1902 BAY CITY,MICH.
D.DEC.12,1970 PORTLAND,ORE.

YR	CL	LEA	POS	GP	G	REC
1928	BOS	A	P-O	1	143	0- 0
						.299
1929	BOS	A	O	26		.281
	CHI	A	O	47		.168
1931	PHI	N	O	38		.225
1932	PHI	N	H	4		.190
		BLTR		1	258	0- 0
						.263

TALBOT, FREDERICK LEALAND
(FRED) OR (BUBBY)
B.JUNE 28,1941 WASHINGTON,D.C.

YR	CL	LEA	POS	GP	G	REC
1963	CHI	A	P		1	0- 0
1964	CHI	A	P	17	18	4- 5
1965	KC	A	P	39	47	10-12
1966	KC	A	P		11	4- 4
	NY	A	P		23	7- 7
1967	NY	A	P	29	30	6- 8
1968	NY	A	P		29	1- 9
1969	NY	A	/P		8	0- 0
	SEA	A	P	25	27	5- 8
	OAK	A	P		12	1- 2
1970	OAK	A	/P		1	0- 1
		BRTR		195	207	38-56

TALBOT, ROBERT DALE (BOB)
B.JUNE 6,1927 VISALIA,CAL.

YR	CL	LEA	POS	GP	G	REC
1953	CHI	N	O	8		.333
1954	CHI	N	O	114		.241
		BRTR		122		.247

YR CL LEA POS GP G REC

TALCOTT, LE ROY EVERETT (ROY)
B.JAN.16,1920 BROOKLINE,MASS.
1943 BOS N P 1 0- 0
BRTR

TALTON, MARION LEE (TIM)
B.JAN.14,1939 PIKEVILLE,N.C.
1966 KC A C/1 37 .340
1967 KC A C/1 46 .254
BLTR 83 .295

TAMARGO, JOHN FELIX
B.NOV.7,1951 TAMPA,FLA.
1976 STL N /C 10 .300
1977 STL N /C 4 .000
1978 STL N /C 6 .000
SF N C 36 .239
BBTR 56 .223

TAMULIS, VITAUTIS CASIMIRUS (VITO)
B.JULY 11,1911 CAMBRIDGE,MASS.
D.MAY 5,1974 NASHVILLE,TENN.
1934 NY A P 1 1- 0
1935 NY A P 30 10- 5
1938 STL A P 3 0- 3
BRO N P 38 39 12- 6
1939 BRO N P 39 9- 8
1940 BRO N P-1 41 42 8- 5
.130
1941 PHI N P 6 0- 1
BRO N P 12 0- 0
BLTL 170 172 40-28
.175

TANANA, FRANK DARYL
B.JULY 3,1953 DETROIT,MICH.
1973 CAL A /P 4 2- 2
1974 CAL A P 39 14-19
1975 CAL A P 34 16- 9
1976 CAL A P 34 35 19-10
1977 CAL A P 31 15- 9
1978 CAL A P 33 18-12
BLTL 175 176 84-61

TANKERSLEY, LAWRENCE WILLIAM (LEO)
B.JUNE 8,1901 TERRELL,TEX.
1925 CHI A C 1 .000
BRTR

TANNEHILL, JESSE NILES (POWDER)
B.JULY 14,1874 DAYTON,KY.
D.SEPT.22,1956 DAYTON,KY.
1894 CIN N P 5 1- 1
1897 PIT N P-O 17 53 8- 8
.266
1898 PIT N P 38 45 24-14
1899 PIT N P 38 40 23-14
1900 PIT N P 28 32 20- 7
1901 PIT N P 32 40 18-10
1902 PIT N P-O 27 41 20- 6
.289
1903 NY A P 32 39 15-15
1904 BOS A P 33 45 20-10
1905 BOS A P 37 23-10
1906 BOS A P 26 31 13-11
1907 BOS A P 18 21 6- 7
1908 BOS A P 1 1- 0
WAS A P 10 26 1- 4
1909 WAS A P 5 16 1- 1
1911 CIN N P 1 0- 0
BBTL 346 473 194-118
.261
BL 1903

TANNEHILL, LEE FORD
B.OCT.26,1880 DAYTON,KY.
D.FEB.16,1938 LIVE OAK,FLA.
1903 CHI A S 136 .220
1904 CHI A 3 153 .226
1905 CHI A 3 142 .200
1906 CHI A S-3 112 .175
1907 CHI A 3 33 .241
1908 CHI A 3 141 .216
1909 CHI A S-3 155 .222
1910 CHI A 1-S 67 .222
1911 CHI A 2-S 141 .254
1912 CHI A 3 2 .000
BRTR 1082 .219

TANNER, CHARLES WILLIAM (CHUCK)
B.JULY 4,1929 NEW CASTLE,PA.
1955 MIL N O 97 .247
1956 MIL N O 60 .238
1957 MIL N O 22 .246
CHI N O 95 .286
1958 CHI N O 73 .262
1959 CLE A O 14 .250
1960 CLE A O 21 .280
1961 LA A O 7 .125
1962 LA A O 7 .125
BLTL 396 .261
NON-PLAYING MANAGER
CHI[A] 1970-75, OAK[A] 1976
PIT[N] 1977-78

YR CL LEA POS GP G REC

TAPPAN, WALTER VAN DORN (TAP)
B.OCT.8,1890 CARLINVILLE,ILL.
D.DEC.19,1967 LYNWOOD,CAL.
1914 KC F 3 18 .200
BRTR

TAPPE, ELVIN WALTER (EL)
B.MAY 21,1927 QUINCY,ILL.
1954 CHI N C 46 .185
1955 CHI N C 2 .000
1956 CHI N C 3 .000
1958 CHI N C 17 .214
1960 CHI N C 51 .233
1962 CHI N M-C 26 .208
BRTR 145 .207
NON-PLAYING MANAGER CHI[N] 1961

TAPPE, THEODORE NASH (TED)
B.FEB.2,1931 SEATTLE,WASH.
1950 CIN N H 7 .200
1951 CIN N H 4 .333
1955 CHI N O 23 .260
BLTR 34 .259

TARBERT, WILBUR ARLINGTON (ARLIE)
B.SEPT.10,1904 CLEVELAND,OHIO
D.NOV.27,1946 CLEVELAND,OHIO
1927 BOS A O 33 .189
1928 BOS A O 6 .176
BRTR 39 .186

TARTABULL, JOSE MILAGES [GUZMAN]
B.NOV.27,1938 CIENFUEGOS,CUBA
1962 KC A O 107 .277
1963 KC A O 79 .240
1964 KC A O 104 .200
1965 KC A O 68 .312
1966 KC A O 37 .236
BOS A O 68 .277
1967 BOS A O 115 .223
1968 BOS A O 72 .281
1969 OAK A O 75 .267
1970 OAK A /O 24 .231
BLTL 749 .261

TASBY, WILLIE
B.JAN.8,1933 SHREVEPORT,LA.
1958 BAL A O 18 .200
1959 BAL A O 142 .250
1960 BAL A O 39 .212
BOS A O 105 .281
1961 WAS A O 141 .251
1962 WAS A O 11 .206
CLE A 3-O 75 .241
1963 CLE A 2-O 52 .224
BRTR 583 .250

TATE, ALVIN WALTER
B.JULY 1,1918 COLEMAN,OKLA.
1946 PIT N P 2 0- 1
BRTR

TATE, EDWARD CHRISTOPHER
(POP) OR (DIMPLES)
B.DEC.22,1860 RICHMOND,VA.
D.JUNE 25,1932 RICHMOND,VA.
1885 BOS N C 4 .167
1886 BOS N C 31 .226
1887 BOS N C 55 .271
1888 BOS N C 40 .229
1889 BAL AA C 72 .178
1890 BAL AA C 20 .219
BRTL 222 .225

TATE, HENRY BENNETT (BENNIE)
B.DEC.3,1901 WHITWELL,TENN.
D.OCT.27,1973 W.FRANKFORT,ILL.
1924 WAS A C 21 .302
1925 WAS A C 16 .481
1926 WAS A C 59 .267
1927 WAS A C 61 .313
1928 WAS A C 57 .246
1929 WAS A C 81 .294
1930 WAS A C 14 .231
CHI A C 72 .326
1931 CHI A C 89 .267
1932 CHI A C 4 .100
BOS A C 81 .245
1934 CHI N C 11 .125
BLTR 566 .279

TATE, HUGH HENRY (HUGHIE)
B.MAY 19,1880 EVERETT,PA.
D.AUG.7,1956 GREENVILLE,PA.
1905 WAS A O 4 .230
BRTR

TATE, LEE WILLIE (SKEETER)
B.MAR.18,1932 BLACK ROCK,ARK.
1958 STL N S 10 .200
1959 STL N 2-S-3 41 .140
BRTR 51 .165

TATE, RANDALL LEE (RANDY)
B.OCT.23,1952 FLORENCE,ALA.
1975 NY N P 26 5-13
BRTR

YR CL LEA POS GP G REC

TATUM, JARVIS
B.OCT.11,1946 FRESNO,CAL.
1968 CAL A O 17 .176
1969 CAL A /O 10 .318
1970 CAL A O 75 .238
BRTR 102 .232

TATUM, KENNETH RAY (KEN)
B.APR.25,1944 ALEXANDRIA,LA.
1969 CAL A P 45 7- 2
1970 CAL A P 62 7- 4
1971 BOS A P 36 2- 4
1972 BOS A P 22 0- 2
1973 BOS A /P 1 0- 0
1974 CHI A P 10 0- 0
BRTR 176 16-12

TATUM, V T (TOMMY)
B.JULY 16,1919 BOYD,TEX.
1941 BRO N O 8 .167
1947 BRO N O 4 .000
CIN N 2-O 69 .273
BRTR 81 .258

TAUBENSEE, FRED JOSEPH
[PLAYED UNDER NAME OF
FRED JOSEPH TAUBY]

TAUBY, FRED JOSEPH
[REAL NAME FRED JOSEPH TAUBENSEE]
B.MAR.27,1906 CANTON,OHIO
D.NOV.23,1955 CONCORDIA,CAL.
1935 CHI A O 13 .125
1937 PHI N O 11 .000
BRTR 24 .077

TAUSCHER, WALTER EDWARD
B.NOV.22,1901 LA SALLE,ILL.
1928 PIT N P 17 0- 0
1931 WAS A P 6 1- 0
BRTR 23 1- 0

TAUSSIG, DONALD FRANKLIN (DON)
B.FEB.19,1932 NEW YORK,N.Y.
1958 SF N O 39 .200
1961 STL N O 98 .287
1962 HOU N O 16 .200
BRTR 153 .262

TAVENER, JOHN ADAM
(JACKIE) OR (RABBIT)
B.DEC.27,1897 CELINA,OHIO
D.SEPT.14,1969 FORT WORTH,TEX.
1921 DET A S 2 .000
1925 DET A S 134 .245
1926 DET A S 156 .265
1927 DET A S 116 .274
1928 DET A S 132 .260
1929 CLE A S 92 .212
BLTR 632 .255

TAVERAS, ALEJANDRO ANTONIO
[BETANCES] (ALEX)
B.OCT.9,1955 SANTIAGO,D.R.
1976 HOU N /2-S 14 .217
BRTR

TAVERAS, FRANKLIN CRISOSTOMO
[FABIAN] (FRANK)
B.DEC.24,1949 LAS MATAS DE
SANTA CRUZ,D.R.
1971 PIT N R 1 .000
1972 PIT N /S 4 .000
1974 PIT N *S 126 .246
1975 PIT N *S 134 .212
1976 PIT N *S 144 .258
1977 PIT N *S 147 .252
1978 PIT N *S 157 .278
BRTR 713 .253

TAYLOR
1874 BAL NA 1 12 -

TAYLOR, ANTONIO NEMESIO
[SANCHEZ] (TONY)
B.DEC.19,1935 CENTRAL ALARA,CUBA
1958 CHI N 2-3 140 .235
1959 CHI N 2-S 150 .280
1960 CHI N 2 19 .263
PHI N 2-3 127 .287
1961 PHI N 2-3 106 .250
1962 PHI N 2-S 152 .259
1963 PHI N 2-3 157 .281
1964 PHI N 2 154 .251
1965 PHI N 2/3 106 .229
1966 PHI N 2-3 125 .242
1967 PHI N 1-3-2/S 132 .238
1968 PHI N *3/2-1 145 .250
1969 PHI N 3-2-1 138 .262
1970 PHI N 2-3-O/S 124 .301
1971 PHI N 2-3/1 36 .234
DET A 2/3 55 .287
1972 DET A 2/3-1 78 .303
1973 DET A 2/1-3-O 84 .229
1974 PHI N /1-3-2 62 .328
1975 PHI N 3/1-2 79 .243
1976 PHI N /2-3 26 .261
BRTR 2195 .261

YR	CL	LEA	POS	GP	G	REC

TAYLOR, ARLISS W.
B.CLEARFIELD,PA.

YR	CL	LEA	POS	GP	G	REC
1921	PHI	A	P	1		0- 1

TAYLOR, BENJAMIN HARRISON
B.APR.2,1889 PAOLI,IND.
D.NOV.3,1946 MARTIN COUNTY,IND.

YR	CL	LEA	POS	GP	G	REC
1912	CIN	N	P	2		0- 0
			TR			

TAYLOR, BENJAMIN EJGENE (BEN)
B.SEPT.30,1927 METROPOLIS,ILL.

YR	CL	LEA	POS	GP	G	REC
1951	STL	A	1	33		.258
1952	DET	A	1	7		.167
1955	MIL	N	1	12		.100
			BLTL	52		.231

TAYLOR, BRUCE BELL
B.APR.16,1953 HOLDEN,MASS.

YR	CL	LEA	POS	GP	G	REC
1977	DET	A	P	19		1- 0
1978	DET	A	/P	1		0- 0
			BRTR	20		1- 0

TAYLOR, C L (CHINK)
B.FEB.9,1898 BURNET,TEX.

YR	CL	LEA	POS	GP	G	REC
1925	CHI	N	O	8		.000
			BRTR			

TAYLOR, CARL MEANS
B.JAN.20,1944 SARASOTA,FLA.

YR	CL	LEA	POS	GP	G	REC
1968	PIT	N	C/O	44		.211
1969	PIT	N	O-1	104		.348
1970	STL	N	O-1/3	104		.249
1971	PIT	N	/O	7		.167
	KC	A	0	20		.179
1972	KC	A	C/O-1-3	63		.265
1973	KC	A	C/1	69		.228
			BRTR	411		.266

TAYLOR, CHARLES GILBERT (CHUCK)
B.APR.18,1942 SHELBYVILLE,TENN.

YR	CL	LEA	POS	GP	G	REC
1969	STL	N	P	27		7- 5
1970	STL	N	P	56		6- 7
1971	STL	N	P	43		3- 1
1972	NY	N	P	20		0- 0
	MIL	A	/P	5		0- 0
1973	MON	N	/P	8		2- 0
1974	MON	N	P	61		6- 2
1975	MON	N	P	54		2- 2
1976	MON	N	P	31		2- 3
			BRTR	305		28-20

TAYLOR, DANIEL TURNEY
B.DEC.23,1900 LASH,PA.
D.OCT.11,1972 LATROBE,PA.

YR	CL	LEA	POS	GP	G	REC
1926	WAS	A	0	21		.300
1929	CHI	N	0	2		.000
1930	CHI	N	0	74		.283
1931	CHI	N	0	88		.300
1932	CHI	N	0	6		.227
	BRO	N	0	105		.324
1933	BRO	N	0	103		.285
1934	BRO	N	0	120		.299
1935	BRO	N	0	112		.290
1936	BRO	N	0	43		.293
			BRTR	674		.297

TAYLOR, EDWARD

YR	CL	LEA	POS	GP	G	REC
1903	STL	N	P	1		0- 0

TAYLOR, EDWARD JAMES
B.NOV.17,1901 CHICAGO,ILL.

YR	CL	LEA	POS	GP	G	REC
1926	BOS	N	S-3	92		.268
			BRTR			

TAYLOR, FREDERICK RANKIN
B.DEC.3,1924 ZANESVILLE,OHIO

YR	CL	LEA	POS	GP	G	REC
1950	WAS	A	1	6		.125
1951	WAS	A	1	6		.167
1952	WAS	A	1	10		.263
			BLTR	22		.191

TAYLOR, GARY WILLIAM
B.OCT.19,1945 DETROIT,MICH.

YR	CL	LEA	POS	GP	G	REC
1969	DET	A	/P	7		0- 1
			BRTR			

TAYLOR, GEORGE EDWARD
(GEORGE) OR (LIVE)
B.FEB.3,1855 BELFAST,ME.
D.FEB.19,1888 SAN FRANCISCO,CAL

YR	CL	LEA	POS	GP	G	REC
1884	PIT	AA	O	41		.202

TAYLOR, GEORGE J.
B.NOV.22,1853 NEW YORK
NON-PLAYING MANAGER BRO[AA]1884

TAYLOR, HARRY EVANS
B.DEC.2,1935 SAN ANGELO,TEX.

YR	CL	LEA	POS	GP	G	REC
1957	KC	A	P	2		0- 0
			BRTR			

TAYLOR, HARRY LEONARD
B.APR.14,1866 HALSEY VALLEY,N.Y
D.JULY 12,1955 BUFFALO,N.Y.

YR	CL	LEA	POS	GP	G	REC
1890	LOU	AA	1	134		.279
1891	LOU	AA	1	91		.289
1892	LOU	N	1-O	123		.274
1893	BAL	N	1	88		.294
			BL	436		.283

TAYLOR, HARRY WARREN
B.DEC.26,1907 MC KEESPORT,PA.
D.APR.27,1969 TOLEDO,OHIO

YR	CL	LEA	POS	GP	G	REC
1932	CHI	N	1	10		.125
			BLTL			

TAYLOR, JAMES B. (SANDY)

YR	CL	LEA	POS	GP	G	REC
1879	TRO	N	O	24		.214

TAYLOR, JAMES HARRY (HARRY)
B.MAY 20,1919 E.GLENN,IND.

YR	CL	LEA	POS	GP	G	REC
1946	BRO	N	P	4		0- 0
1947	BRO	N	P	33		10- 5
1948	BRO	N	P	17		2- 7
1950	BOS	A	P	3		2- 0
1951	BOS	A	P	31		4- 9
1952	BOS	A	P	2		1- 0
			BRTR	90		19-21

TAYLOR, JAMES WREN (ZACK)
B.JULY 27,1898 YULEE,FLA.
D.SEPT.19,1974 ORLANDO,FLA.

YR	CL	LEA	POS	GP	G	REC
1920	BRO	N	C	5		.167
1921	BRO	N	C	30		.196
1922	BRO	N	C	7		.214
1923	BRO	N	C	96		.288
1924	BRO	N	C	99		.290
1925	BRO	N	C	109		.310
1926	BOS	N	C	125		.255
1927	BOS	N	C	30		.240
	NY	N	C	83		.233
1928	BOS	N	C	125		.251
1929	BOS	N	C	34		.268
	CHI	N	C	64		.274
1930	CHI	N	C	32		.232
1931	CHI	N	C	8		.250
1932	CHI	N	C	21		.200
1933	CHI	N	C	16		.000
1934	NY	A	C	4		.143
1935	BRO	N	C	26		.130
			BRTR	914		.261

NON-PLAYING MANAGER
STL[A] 1946, 48-51

TAYLOR, JOE CEPHUS
B.MAR.2,1926 CHAPMAN,ALA.

YR	CL	LEA	POS	GP	G	REC
1954	PHI	A	O	18		.224
1957	CIN	N	O	33		.262
1958	STL	N	O	18		.304
	BAL	A	O	36		.273
1959	BAL	A	O	14		.156
			BRTR	119		.249

TAYLOR, JOHN BUDD (BREWERY JACK)
B.MAY 23,1873 W.NEW BRIGHTON,N.Y.
D.FEB.7,1900 STATEN ISLAND,N.Y.

YR	CL	LEA	POS	GP	G	REC
1891	NY	N	P	1		0- 1
1892	PHI	N	P	3		2- 0
1893	PHI	N	P	19		8- 8
1894	PHI	N	P	34		24-10
1895	PHI	N	P	40		26-13
1896	PHI	N	P	44		21-20
1897	PHI	N	P	36	37	18-18
1898	PHI	N	P	47	49	16-31
1899	CIN	N	P	24		8-10
				246	251	123-111

TAYLOR, JOHN W. (JACK)
B.JAN.14,1874 NEW
STRAIGHTSVILLE,OHIO
D.MAR.4,1938 COLUMBUS,OHIO

YR	CL	LEA	POS	GP	G	REC
1898	CHI	N	P	5		5- 0
1899	CHI	N	P	41	42	18-22
1900	CHI	N	P	27		9-17
1901	CHI	N	P	33		13-19
1902	CHI	N	P-1-	38	53	22-11
			2-3-O			.239
1903	CHI	N	P	37	39	21-14
1904	STL	N	P	41		22-19
1905	STL	N	P	37	39	15-20
1906	STL	N	P	17		8- 9
	CHI	N	P	17		12- 3
1907	CHI	N	P	18		7- 5
			BRTR	309	331	152-139
						.222

TAYLOR, LEO THOMAS (CHINK)
B.MAY 13,1901 WALLA WALLA,WASH.

YR	CL	LEA	POS	GP	G	REC
1923	CHI	A	H	1		.000
			BRTR			

TAYLOR, LUTHER HADEN (DUMMY)
B.FEB.21,1875 OSKALOOSA,KAN.
D.AUG.22,1958 JACKSONVILLE,ILL.

YR	CL	LEA	POS	GP	G	REC
1900	NY	N	P	11		4- 3
1901	NY	N	P	45		18-27
1902	CLE	A	P	4		1- 3
	NY	N	P	23		8-15
1903	NY	N	P	33		13-13
1904	NY	N	P	37		21-15
1905	NY	N	P	32		16- 9
1906	NY	N	P	31		17- 9
1907	NY	N	P	28	29	11- 7
1908	NY	N	P	27		8- 5
			BRTR	271	272	117-106

TAYLOR, OAK
B.CINCINNATI,OHIO

YR	CL	LEA	POS	GP	G	REC
1877	HAR	N	O	2		.375

TAYLOR, PHILIP WILEY (WILEY)
B.MAR.18,1888 WAMEGO,KAN.
D.JULY 8,1954 WESTMORELAND,KAN.

YR	CL	LEA	POS	GP	G	REC
1911	DET	A	P	3		0- 2
1912	CHI	A	P	3		0- 1
1913	STL	A	P	5		0- 2
1914	STL	A	P	16		2- 5
			BRTR	27		2-10

TAYLOR, ROBERT DALE (HAWK)
B.APR.3,1939 METROPOLIS,ILL.

YR	CL	LEA	POS	GP	G	REC
1957	MIL	N	P	7		.000
1958	MIL	N	0	4		.125
1961	MIL	N	C-0	20		.192
1962	MIL	N	0	20		.255
1963	MIL	N	0	16		.069
1964	NY	N	C-0	92		.240
1965	NY	N	C/1	25		.152
1966	NY	N	C-1	53		.174
1967	NY	N	C	13		.243
	CAL	A	C	23		.308
1969	KC	A	O/C	64		.270
1970	KC	A	/C-1	57		.164
			BRTR	394		.218

TAYLOR, ROBERT LEE (BOB)
B.MAR.20,1944 LELAND,MISS.

YR	CL	LEA	POS	GP	G	REC
1970	SF	N	O/C	63		.190
			BLTR			

TAYLOR, RONALD WESLEY (RON)
B.DEC.13,1937 TORONTO,ONT.,CAN.

YR	CL	LEA	POS	GP	G	REC
1962	CLE	A	P	8		2- 2
1963	STL	N	P	54		9- 7
1964	STL	N	P	63		8- 4
1965	STL	N	P	25		2- 1
	HOU	N	P	32		1- 5
1966	HOU	N	P	36		2- 3
1967	NY	N	P	50		4- 6
1968	NY	N	P	58		1- 5
1969	NY	N	P	59		9- 4
1970	NY	N	P	57		5- 4
1971	NY	N	P	45		2- 2
1972	SD	N	/P	4		0- 0
			BRTR	491		45-43

TAYLOR, SAMUEL DOUGLAS (SAMMY)
B.FEB.27,1933 WOODRUFF,S.C.

YR	CL	LEA	POS	GP	G	REC
1958	CHI	N	C	96		.259
1959	CHI	N	C	110		.269
1960	CHI	N	C	74		.207
1961	CHI	N	C	89		.238
1962	CHI	N	C	7		.133
	NY	N	C	68		.222
1963	NY	N	C	22		.257
	CIN	N	C	3		.000
	CLE	A	C	4		.300
			BLTR	473		.245

TAYLOR, THOMAS LIVINGSTONE CARLTON
B.SEPT.17,1892 MEXIA,TEX.
D.APR.5,1956 GREENVILLE,MISS.

YR	CL	LEA	POS	GP	G	REC
1924	WAS	A	3	26		.260
			BRTR			

TAYLOR, VERNON CHARLES (PETE)
B.NOV.26,1927 SEVERN,MD.

YR	CL	LEA	POS	GP	G	REC
1952	STL	A	P	1		0- 0
			BRTR			

TAYLOR, WALLACE NAPOLEON
B.1872 PITTSBURGH,PA.
D.SEPT.13,1905 CINCINNATI,OHIO

YR	CL	LEA	POS	GP	G	REC
1898	LOU	N	3	9		.200

```
YR   CL LEA POS      GP   G   REC        YR   CL LEA POS      GP   G   REC        YR   CL LEA POS      GP   G   REC

TAYLOR, WILLIAM HENRY                    TEKULVE, KENTON CHARLES (KENT)           TENNEY, FREDERICK CLAY
(BOLLICKY BILL)                          B.MAR.5,1947 CINCINNATI,OHIO             B.JUNE 9,1859 MARLBORO,N.H.
B.1855 WASHINGTON,D.C.                    1974 PIT N /P          8   1- 1           1884 WAS U 1-O        30  .236
D.MAY 14,1900 JACKSONVILLE,FLA.           1975 PIT N P          34   1- 2                BOS U P          5   0- 1
 1881 WOR N P-O    1    6   0- 1          1976 PIT N P          64   5- 3                WIL U P          1   0- 1
                           .111          1977 PIT N P          72  10- 1                            6  36   4- 2
      DET N 3          1    .500          1978 PIT N P          91   8- 7                                    .217
      CLE N P-3-   1   25   0- 0               BRTR          269  25-14
           O               .222                                                    TEPEDINO, FRANK RONALD
 1882 PIT AA P-C-  1   65   0- 0         TEMPLE, JOHN ELLIS (JOHNNY)              B.NOV.23,1947 BROOKLYN,N.Y.
           1-3-O           .286          B.AUG.8,1928 LEXINGTON,N.C.               1967 NY A /1           9  .400
 1883 PIT AA P-C- 11   83   3- 8          1952 CIN N 2          30  .196           1969 NY A O           13  .231
           1-O             .259           1953 CIN N 2          63  .264           1970 NY A /1-O        16  .316
 1884 STL U P-1-  31   42  24- 2          1954 CIN N 2         146  .307           1971 NY A /O           6  .000
           O               .371           1955 CIN N 2-S       150  .281                MIL A 1          53  .198
      ATH AA P            32 18-12        1956 CIN N 2-O       154  .285           1972 NY A /H           8  .000
 1885 ATH AA P         6    1- 5          1957 CIN N 2         145  .284           1973 ATL N 1          74  .304
                           .333           1958 CIN N 1-2       141  .306           1974 ATL N 1          78  .231
 1886 BAL AA P-O   7   10   1- 6          1959 CIN N 2         149  .311           1975 ATL N /H          8  .000
      TR          91  271  48-34          1960 CLE A 2-3        98  .268                BLTL           265  .241
                           .278           1961 CLE A 2         129  .276
                                          1962 BAL A 2          78  .263          TEPSIC, JOSEPH JOHN
TAYLOR, WILLIAM MICHAEL (BILL)                 HOU N 2-3        31  .263          B.SEPT.18,1923 SLOVAN,PA.
B.DEC.30,1929 ALHAMBRA,CAL.               1963 HOU N 2-3       100  .264           1946 BRO N O          15  .000
 1954 NY N O          55  .185            1964 CIN N H           6  .000                BRTR
 1955 NY N O          65  .266                 BRTR           1420  .284
 1956 NY N O           1  .250                                                    TERLECKI, ROBERT JOSEPH (BOB)
 1957 NY N H          11  .000           TEMPLETON, CHARLES SHERMAN (CHUCK)       B.FEB.14,1945 TRENTON,N.J.
      DET A O          9  .348           B.JUNE 1,1932 DETROIT,MICH.               1972 PHI N /P          9   0- 0
 1958 DET A O          8  .375            1955 BRO N P           4   0- 1                BRTR
      BLTR           149  .237            1956 BRO N P           6   0- 1
                                               BRTL             10   0- 2         TERLECKY, GREGORY JOHN (GREG)
TEACHOUT, ARTHUR JOHN (BUD)                                                       B.MAR.20,1952 CULVER CITY,CAL.
B.FEB.27,1904 LOS ANGELES,CAL.           TEMPLETON, GARRY LEWIS                    1975 STL N P          20   0- 1
 1930 CHI N P     40   42  11- 4         B.MAR.24,1956 LOCKEY,TEX.                      BRTR
 1931 CHI N P     27   37   1- 2          1976 STL N S          53  .291
 1932 STL N P      1    0- 0              1977 STL N *S        153  .322          TERPKO, JEFFREY MICHAEL (JEFF)
      BRTL        68   80  12- 6          1978 STL N *S        155  .280          B.OCT.16,1950 SAYRE,PA.
                                               BBTR           361  .305           1974 TEX A /P          3   0- 0
TEBBETTS, GEORGE ROBERT (BIRDIE)                                                  1976 TEX A P          32   3- 3
B.NOV.10,1912 BURLINGTON,VT.             TENER, JOHN KINLEY                        1977 MON N P          13   0- 1
 1936 DET A C         10  .303           B.JULY 25,1863 COUNTY TYRONE,IRELAND           BRTR             48   3- 4
 1937 DET A C         50  .191           D.MAY 19,1946 PITTSBURGH,PA.
 1938 DET A C         53  .294            1885 BAL AA O          1   .000         TERRELL, JERRY WAYNE
 1939 DET A C        106  .261            1888 CHI N P          14   7- 5         B.JULY 13,1946 WASECA,MINN.
 1940 DET A C        111  .296            1889 CHI N P      31   38  14-15         1973 MIN A S-3-2/O   124  .265
 1941 DET A C        110  .284            1890 PIT P P          19   3-13          1974 MIN A S-2-3-D/O-1 116 .245
 1942 DET A C         99  .247                 BRTR         65   72  24-33         1975 MIN A S-2-1-3/O 108  .286
 1946 DET A C         87  .243                                     .235           1976 MIN A 2-3-S/O    89  .246
 1947 DET A C         20  .094                                                    1977 MIN A 3-2/S-1-O  93  .224
      BOS A C         90  .299           TENACE, FURY GENE (GENE)                  1978 KC A 2-3-S/1     73  .203
 1948 BOS A C        128  .280           (REAL NAME FIORE GINO TENNACI)                 BRTR            603  .254
 1949 BOS A C        122  .270           B.OCT.10,1946 RUSSELLTON,PA.                   BB 1974 (PART)
 1950 BOS A C         79  .310            1969 OAK A C          16  .158
 1951 CLE A C         55  .263            1970 OAK A C          38  .305          TERRELL, THOMAS
 1952 CLE A C         42  .248            1971 OAK A C/O        65  .274          B.LOUISVILLE,KY.
      BRTR          1162  .270            1972 OAK A C/O-1-2-3  82  .225          D.JULY 9,1893 LOUISVILLE,KY.
NON-PLAYING MANAGER                       1973 OAK A *1-C/2    160  .259           1886 LOU AA C          1  .250
CIN(N) 1954-58, MIL(N) 1961-62,           1974 OAK A *1-C/2    158  .211
CLE(A) 1963-66                            1975 OAK A *C-1      158  .255          TERRY
                                          1976 OAK A 1-C       128  .233          1875 NAT NA 1-O        5   -
TEBEAU, CHARLES ALBERT (PUSSY)            1977 SD N C-1-3      147  .233
B.PITTSFIELD,MASS.                        1978 SD N 1-C/3      142  .224          TERRY, JOHN
 1895 CLE N P          2   .500                BRTR           1094  .241          B.ST.LOUIS,MO.
                                                                                   1902 DET A P           1   0- 1
TEBEAU, GEORGE E. (WHITE WINGS)          TENNACI, FIORE GINO                       1903 STL A P           3   1- 0
B.DEC.26,1861 ST.LOUIS,MO.               [PLAYED UNDER NAME OF                                           4   1- 1
D.FEB.4,1923 DENVER,COLO.                FURY GENE TENACE]
 1887 CIN AA P-O   1   88   0- 0                                                  TERRY, LANCELOT YANK (YANK)
                           .361                                                   B.FEB.11,1911 BEDFORD,IND.
 1888 CIN AA O       121  .228           TENNANT, JAMES MC DONNELL                 1940 BOS A P           4   1- 0
 1889 CIN AA 1-O     135  .255           B.MAR.3,1907 SHEPHERDSTOWN,W.VA           1942 BOS A P          20   6- 5
 1890 TOL AA O        96  .261           D.APR.16,1967 TRUMBULL,CONN.              1943 BOS A P          30   7- 9
 1894 WAS N O         60  .226            1929 NY N P            1   0- 0          1944 BOS A P          27   6-10
      CLE N O         45  .316                 BRTR                                1945 BOS A P          12   0- 4
 1895 CLE N 1-O       87  .323                                                         BRTR             93  20-28
      BRTR         1  632   0- 0         TENNANT, THOMAS FRANCIS
                           .284          B.JULY 3,1882 MONROE,WIS.                TERRY, RALPH WILLARD
                                         D.FEB.15,1955 SAN CARLOS,CAL.            B.JAN.9,1936 BIG CABIN,OKLA.
TEBEAU, OLIVER WENDELL (PATSY)            1912 STL A N           2   .000          1956 NY A P            3   1- 2
B.DEC.5,1864 ST.LOUIS,MO.                      BLTL                                1957 NY A P            7   1- 1
D.MAY 15,1918 ST.LOUIS,MO.                                                             KC A P       21   22   4-11
 1887 CHI N 3         20  .208                                                     1958 KC A P           40  11-13
 1889 CLE N 3        136  .282           TENNEY, FREDERICK (FRED)                  1959 KC A P            9   2- 4
 1890 CLE P M-3      108  .292           B.NOV.26,1871 GEORGETOWN,MASS.                 NY A P           24   3- 7
 1891 CLE N M-3       61  .261           D.JULY 3,1952 BOSTON,MASS.                1960 NY A P           35  10- 8
 1892 CLE N M-3       84  .246            1894 BOS N C          24  .387           1961 NY A P           31  16- 3
 1893 CLE N M-1-3    119  .359            1895 BOS N C-O        42  .276           1962 NY A P           43  23-12
 1894 CLE N M-1      110  .305            1896 BOS N C-O        86  .342           1963 NY A P           40  17-15
 1895 CLE N M-1       66  .329            1897 BOS N 1         131  .325           1964 NY A P           27   7-11
 1896 CLE N M-1      132  .271            1898 BOS N 1         117  .335           1965 CLE A P          30  11- 6
 1897 CLE N M-1-2    111  .267            1899 BOS N 1         150  .350           1966 KC A P           19   1- 5
 1898 CLE N M-1-2    130  .254            1900 BOS N 1         111  .284                NY N P           11   0- 1
 1899 STL N M-1       76  .263            1901 BOS N 1         113  .278           1967 NY N /P           2   0- 0
 1900 STL N M-1        1  .000            1902 BOS N 1         134  .314                BRTR        338 339 107-99
      BRTR          1150  .284            1903 BOS N 1         122  .313
                                          1904 BOS N 1         147  .270
TEDROW, ALLEN SEYMOUR                     1905 BOS N M-1       148  .288
B.DEC.14,1891 WESTERVILLE,OHIO            1906 BOS N M-1       143  .283
D.JAN.23,1958 WESTERVILLE,OHIO            1907 BOS N M-1       149  .273
 1914 CLE A P          4   1- 2           1908 NY N 1          156  .256
      BRTL                                1909 NY N 1           98  .235
                                          1911 BOS N M-1        98  .263
                                               BLTL           1969  .295
TEED, RICHARD LEROY (DICK)
B.MAR.8,1926 SPRINGFIELD,MASS.
 1953 BRO N H          1   .000
      BBTR
```

TERRY, WILLIAM HAROLD (MEMPHIS BILL)
B.OCT.30,1898 ATLANTA,GA.

YR	CL	LEA	POS	GP	G	REC
1923	NY	N	1		3	.143
1924	NY	N	1		77	.239
1925	NY	N	1		133	.319
1926	NY	N	1-O		98	.289
1927	NY	N	1		150	.326
1928	NY	N	1		149	.326
1929	NY	N	1		150	.372
1930	NY	N	1		154	.401
1931	NY	N	1		153	.349
1932	NY	N	M-1		154	.350
1933	NY	N	M-1		123	.322
1934	NY	N	M-1		153	.354
1935	NY	N	M-1		145	.341
1936	NY	N	M-1		79	.310
	BLTL				1721	.341

NON-PLAYING MANAGER NY[N] 1937-41

TERRY, WILLIAM H. (ADONIS)
B.AUG.7,1864 WESTFIELD,MASS.
D.FEB.24,1915 MILWAUKEE,WIS.

YR	CL	LEA	POS	GP	G	REC
1884	BRO	AA	P-O	55	67	19-35
						.235
1885	BRO	AA	P-O	25	70	6-16
						.162
1886	BRO	AA	P-O	33	75	18-15
						.250
1887	BRO	AA	P-O	40	86	17-16
						.335
1888	BRO	AA	P	24	30	13-8
1889	BRO	AA	P	40	48	21-16
1890	BRO	N	P-O	44	99	26-15
						.278
1891	BRO	N	P	23	25	6-15
1892	BAL	N	P		6	1-1
	PIT	N	P		27	20-7
1893	PIT	N	P		21	12-7
1894	PIT	N	P		6	0-1
	CHI	N	P		24	4-12
1895	CHI	N	P	37	39	21-14
1896	CHI	N	P		29	14-15
1897	CHI	N	P		1	0-0
	BRTR			435	653	198-193
						.271

TERRY, ZEBULON ALEXANDER (ZEB)
B.JUNE 17,1891 DENISON,TEX.

YR	CL	LEA	POS	GP	G	REC
1916	CHI	A	S		94	.190
1917	CHI	A	S		2	.100
1918	BOS	N	S		28	.305
1919	PIT	N	S		129	.227
1920	CHI	A	2-S		133	.280
1921	CHI	A	2		123	.275
1922	CHI	A	2-S-3		131	.286
	BRTR				640	.260

TERWILLIGER, RICHARD MARTIN
B.JUNE 27,1906 SAND LAKE,MICH.
D.JAN.21,1969 GREENVILLE,MICH.

YR	CL	LEA	POS	GP	G	REC
1932	STL	N	P		1	0-0

TERWILLIGER, WILLARD WAYNE (WAYNE) OR (TWIG)
B.JUNE 27,1925 CLARE,MICH.

YR	CL	LEA	POS	GP	G	REC
1949	CHI	N	2		36	.223
1950	CHI	N	1-2-3-O		133	.242
1951	CHI	N	2		50	.214
	BRO	N	2-3		37	.280
1953	WAS	A	2		134	.252
1954	WAS	A	2-S-3		106	.208
1955	NY	N	2-S-3		80	.257
1957	NY	N	2		14	.222
1959	KC	A	2-S-3		74	.267
1960	KC	A	2		2	.000
	BRTR				666	.240

TESCH, ALBERT JOHN (TINY)
B.JAN.27,1891 JERSEY CITY,N.J.
D.AUG.3,1947 JERSEY CITY,N.J.

YR	CL	LEA	POS	GP	G	REC
1915	BRO	F	2		7	.286
	BBTR					

TESREAU, CHARLES MONROE (JEFF)
B.MAR.5,1889 SILVER MINE,MO.
D.SEPT.24,1946 HANOVER,N.H.

YR	CL	LEA	POS	GP	G	REC
1912	NY	N	P		36	17-7
1913	NY	N	P		41	22-13
1914	NY	N	P		42	26-10
1915	NY	N	P		43	19-16
1916	NY	N	P	40	41	14-14
1917	NY	N	P		33	13-8
1918	NY	N	P		12	4-4
	BRTR			247	248	115-72

TESTA, NICHOLAS (NICK)
B.JUNE 29,1928 NEW YORK,N.Y.

YR	CL	LEA	POS	GP	G	REC
1958	SF	N	C		1	.000
	BRTR					

TETTELBACH, RICHARD MORLEY (DICK) OR (TUT)
B.JUNE 26,1929 NEW HAVEN,CONN.

YR	CL	LEA	POS	GP	G	REC
1955	NY	A	O		2	.000
1956	WAS	A	O		18	.156
1957	WAS	A	O		9	.182
	BRTR				29	.150

TEXTOR, GEORGE BERNHARDT
B.DEC.27,1888 NEWPORT,KY.
D.MAR.10,1954 MASSILLON,OHIO

YR	CL	LEA	POS	GP	G	REC
1914	IND	F	C		20	.179
1915	NEW	F	C		3	.333
	BBTR				23	.194

THACKER, MORRIS BENTON (MOE)
B.MAY 21,1934 LOUISVILLE,KY.

YR	CL	LEA	POS	GP	G	REC
1958	CHI	N	C		11	.250
1960	CHI	N	C		54	.156
1961	CHI	N	C		25	.171
1962	CHI	N	C		65	.187
1963	STL	N	C		3	.000
	BRTR				158	.177

THAKE, ALBERT
B.1847 NEW YORK,N.Y.
D.SEPT.11,1872

YR	CL	LEA	POS	GP	G	REC
1872	ATL	NA	2-O		17	.274

THATCHER, ULYSSES GRANT (GRANT)
B.FEB.23,1877 MAYTOWN,PA.
D.MAR.17,1936 LANCASTER,PA.

YR	CL	LEA	POS	GP	G	REC
1903	BRO	N	P		4	3-1
1904	BRO	N	P		1	1-0
	TR				5	4-1

THAYER, EDWARD L.
B.MECHANIC FALLS,ME.

YR	CL	LEA	POS	GP	G	REC
1876	MUT	N	2		1	.000

THAYER, GREGORY ALLEN (GREG)
B.OCT.23,1949 CEDAR RAPIDS,IOWA

YR	CL	LEA	POS	GP	G	REC
1978	MIN	A	P		20	1-1
	BRTR					

THEIS, JOHN LOUIS (JACK)
B.JULY 23,1891 GEORGETOWN,OHIO
D.JULY 6,1941 GEORGETOWN,OHIO

YR	CL	LEA	POS	GP	G	REC
1920	CIN	N	P		1	0-0
	BRTR					

THEISS, DUANE CHARLES
B.NOV.20,1953 ZANESVILLE,OHIO

YR	CL	LEA	POS	GP	G	REC
1977	ATL	N	P		17	1-1
1978	ATL	N	/P		3	0-0
	BRTR				20	1-1

THEOBALD, RONALD MERRILL (RON)
B.JULY 28,1943 OAKLAND,CAL.

YR	CL	LEA	POS	GP	G	REC
1971	MIL	A	*2/S-3		126	.276
1972	MIL	A	*2		125	.220
	BRTR				251	.248

THEODORE, GEORGE BASIL
B.NOV.13,1947 SALT LAKE CITY,UT.

YR	CL	LEA	POS	GP	G	REC
1973	NY	N	O/1		45	.259
1974	NY	N	1-O		60	.158
	BRTR				105	.219

THESENGA, ARNOLD JOSEPH (JUG)
B.APR.27,1914 JEFFERSON,S.DAK.

YR	CL	LEA	POS	GP	G	REC
1944	WAS	A	P		5	0-0
	BRTR					

THEVENOW, THOMAS JOSEPH (TOMMY)
B.SEPT.6,1903 MADISON,IND.
D.JULY 29,1957 MADISON,IND.

YR	CL	LEA	POS	GP	G	REC
1924	STL	N	S		23	.202
1925	STL	N	S		50	.269
1926	STL	N	S		156	.256
1927	STL	N	S		59	.194
1928	STL	N	S		69	.205
1929	PHI	N	S		90	.227
1930	PHI	N	S		156	.286
1931	PIT	N	S		120	.213
1932	PIT	N	S-3		59	.237
1933	PIT	N	2-S-3		73	.312
1934	PIT	N	2-3		122	.271
1935	PIT	N	2-S-3		110	.238
1936	CIN	N	2-S-3		106	.234
1937	BOS	N	S		21	.118
1938	PIT	N	2-S-3		15	.200
	BRTR				1229	.248

THIEL, MAYNARD BERT (BERT)
B.MAY 4,1926 MARION,WIS.

YR	CL	LEA	POS	GP	G	REC
1952	BOS	N	P		4	1-1

THIELMAN, HENRY JOSEPH
B.OCT.3,1880 ST.CLOUD,MINN.
D.SEPT.24,1942 NEW YORK,N.Y.

YR	CL	LEA	POS	GP	G	REC
1902	NY	N	P-O	5	6	0-1
						.111
	CIN	N	P		29	9-15
1903	BRO	N	P		8	0-3
	BRTR			42	43	9-19
						.121

THIELMAN, JOHN PETER (JAKE)
B.MAY 20,1879 ST.CLOUD,MINN.
D.JAN.28,1928 MINNEAPOLIS,MINN.

YR	CL	LEA	POS	GP	G	REC
1905	STL	N	P	32	33	15-16
1906	STL	N	P		3	0-3
1907	CLE	A	P	20	21	11-8
1908	CLE	A	P		11	3-3
	BOS	A	P		1	1-0
	BRTR			67	69	30-30

THIES, DAVID ROBERT (DAVE)
B.MAR.21,1937 MINNEAPOLIS,MINN.

YR	CL	LEA	POS	GP	G	REC
1963	KC	A	P		9	0-1
	BRTR					

THIES, VERNON ARTHUR (JAKE)
B.APR.1,1926 ST.LOUIS,MO.

YR	CL	LEA	POS	GP	G	REC
1954	PIT	N	P		33	3-9
1955	PIT	N	P		1	0-1
	BRTR				34	3-10

THOENEN, RICHARD CRISPIN (DICK)
B.JAN.9,1944 MEXICO,MO.

YR	CL	LEA	POS	GP	G	REC
1967	PHI	N	/P		1	0-0
	BRTR					

THOENY, JOHN
[PLAYED UNDER NAME OF JOHN THONEY]

THOMAS, ALPHONSE (TOMMY)
B.DEC.23,1899 BALTIMORE,MD.

YR	CL	LEA	POS	GP	G	REC
1926	CHI	A	P		44	15-12
1927	CHI	A	P		40	19-16
1928	CHI	A	P		36	17-16
1929	CHI	A	P	36	37	14-18
1930	CHI	A	P		34	5-13
1931	CHI	A	P		43	10-14
1932	CHI	A	P		12	3-3
	WAS	A	P		16	8-7
1933	WAS	A	P		35	7-7
1934	WAS	A	P		33	8-9
1935	WAS	A	P		1	0-0
	PHI	N	P		4	0-1
1936	STL	A	P		36	11-9
1937	STL	A	P		17	0-1
	BOS	A	P		9	0-2
	BRTR			398	399	117-128

THOMAS, BLAINE M.
B.1888 PAYSON,ARIZ.
D.AUG.21,1915 GLOBE,ARIZ.

YR	CL	LEA	POS	GP	G	REC
1911	BOS	A	P		2	0-0
	BRTR					

THOMAS, CARL LESLIE
B.MAY 28,1932 MINNEAPOLIS,MINN.

YR	CL	LEA	POS	GP	G	REC
1960	CLE	A	P		5	1-0
	BRTR					

THOMAS, CHESTER DAVID (PINCH)
B.JAN.24,1888 CAMP POINT,ILL.
D.DEC.24,1953 MODESTO,CAL.

YR	CL	LEA	POS	GP	G	REC
1912	BOS	A	C		13	.194
1913	BOS	A	C		37	.286
1914	BOS	A	C		63	.192
1915	BOS	A	C		86	.236
1916	BOS	A	C		99	.264
1917	BOS	A	C		83	.238
1918	CLE	A	C		32	.247
1919	CLE	A	C		34	.109
1920	CLE	A	C		7	.333
1921	CLE	A	C		21	.257
	BLTR				475	.237

THOMAS, CLARENCE FLETCHER (LEFTY)
B.OCT.4,1903 GLADE SPRINGS,VA.
D.MAR.21,1952 CHARLOTTESVILLE,VA.

YR	CL	LEA	POS	GP	G	REC
1925	WAS	A	P		2	0-2
1926	WAS	A	P		6	0-0
	BLTL				8	0-2

THOMAS, CLAUDE ALFRED (LEFTY)
B.MAY 15,1890 STANBERRY,MO.
D.MAR.6,1946 SULPHUR,OKLA.

YR	CL	LEA	POS	GP	G	REC
1916	WAS	A	P		7	0-3
	BLTL					

THOMAS, DANNY LEE (DAN)
B.MAY 9,1951 BIRMINGHAM,ALA.

YR	CL	LEA	POS	GP	G	REC
1976	MIL	A	O		32	.276
1977	MIL	A	/O		22	.271
	BRTR				54	.274

THOMAS, DERRELL OSBON
B.JAN.14,1951 LOS ANGELES,CAL.

YR	CL	LEA	POS	GP	G	REC
1971	HOU	N	/2		5	.000
1972	SD	N	2-S/O		130	.230
1973	SD	N	S-2		113	.238
1974	SD	N	*2-3-O/S		141	.247
1975	SF	N	*2/O		144	.276
1976	SF	N	2/O-S-3		81	.232
1977	SF	N	O-2-S/3-1		148	.267
1978	SD	N	O-2-3-1		128	.227
	BBTR				890	.247

YR CL LEA POS | GP | G | REC

THOMAS, FAY WESLEY (SCOW)
B.OCT.10,1904 HOLYROOD,KAN.
```
1927 NY  N  P            9   0- 0
1931 CLE A  P           16   2- 4
1932 BRO N  P            7   0- 1
1935 STL A  P           49   7-15
     BRTR               81   9-20
```

THOMAS, FORREST (FROSTY)
B.MAY 23,1881 FAUCETT,MO.
D.MAR.18,1970 ST.JOSEPH,MO.
```
1905 DET A  P            2   0- 2
     BRTR
```

THOMAS, FRANK JOSEPH
B.JUNE 11,1929 PITTSBURGH,PA.
```
1951 PIT N  O           39   .264
1952 PIT N  O            6   .095
1953 PIT N  O          128   .255
1954 PIT N  O          153   .298
1955 PIT N  O          142   .245
1956 PIT N  2-3-O      157   .282
1957 PIT N  1-3-O      151   .290
1958 PIT N  1-3-O      149   .281
1959 CIN N  1-3-O      108   .225
1960 CHI N  1-3-O      135   .238
1961 CHI N  1-O         15   .260
     MIL N  1-3-O      124   .284
1962 NY  N  1-3-O      156   .266
1963 NY  N  1-3-O      126   .260
1964 NY  N  1-3-O       60   .254
     PHI N  1           39   .294
1965 PHI N  O-1/3       35   .260
     HOU N  1/3-O       23   .172
     MIL N  /1-O        15   .212
1966 CHI N  /H           5   .000
     BRTR             1766   .266
```

**THOMAS, FREDERICK HARVEY
(FRED) OR (TOMMY)**
B.DEC.19,1892 MILWAUKEE,WIS.
```
1918 BOS A  3           44   .257
1919 PHI A  3          124   .212
1920 PHI A  3           77   .233
     WAS A  3            2   .000
     BRTR              247   .225
```

THOMAS, FREDERICK L.
B.INDIANA
NON-PLAYING MANAGER IND[N] 1887

THOMAS, GEORGE EDWARD
B.NOV.29,1937 MINNEAPOLIS,MINN.
```
1957 DET A  3            1   .000
1958 DET A  O            1   .000
1961 DET A  5-O         17   .000
     LA  A  3-O         79   .280
1962 LA  A  O           56   .238
1963 LA  A  1-3-O       53   .210
     DET A  2-O         49   .239
1964 DET A  3-O        105   .286
1965 DET A  O/2         79   .213
1966 BOS A  O/3-C-1     69   .237
1967 BOS A  O/1-C       65   .213
1968 BOS A  /O          12   .200
1969 BOS A  O-1/C-3     29   .353
1970 BOS A  O/3         38   .343
1971 BOS A  /O           9   .077
     MIN A  O/1-3       23   .267
     BRTR              685   .255
```

THOMAS, HERBERT MARK
B.MAY 26,1902 SAMPSON CITY,FLA.
```
1924 BOS N  O           32   .220
1925 BOS N  2            5   .235
1927 BOS N  2           24   .230
     NY  N  O           13   .176
     BRTR               74   .221
```

THOMAS, IRA FELIX
B.JAN.22,1881 BALLSTON SPA,N.Y.
D.OCT.11,1958 PHILADELPHIA,PA.
```
1906 NY  A  C           44   .200
1907 NY  A  C           80   .192
1908 DET A  C           40   .307
1909 PHI A  C           84   .223
1910 PHI A  C           60   .277
1911 PHI A  C          103   .273
1912 PHI A  C           46   .216
1913 PHI A  C           21   .283
1914 PHI A  C            2   .000
1915 PHI A  C            1   .000
     BRTR              481   .242
```

T-HOMAS, JAMES GORMAN (GORMAN)
B.DEC.12,1950 CHARLESTON,S.C.
```
1973 MIL A  O/3         59   .187
1974 MIL A  O           17   .261
1975 MIL A  *O         121   .179
1976 MIL A  O/3         99   .198
1978 MIL A  *O         137   .246
     BRTR              433   .214
```

THOMAS, JAMES LEROY (LEE)
B.FEB.5,1936 PEORIA,ILL.
```
1961 NY  A  H            2   .500
     LA  A  1-O        130   .284
1962 LA  A  1-O        160   .290
1963 LA  A  1-O        149   .220
1964 LA  A  1-O         47   .273
     BOS A  1-O        107   .257
1965 BOS A  *1-O       151   .271
1966 ATL N  1           39   .198
     CHI N  1-O         75   .242
1967 CHI N  O-1         77   .220
1968 HOU N  O/1         90   .194
     BLTR             1027   .255
```

THOMAS, JOHN TILLMAN (BUD)
B.MAR.10,1929 SEDALIA,MO.
```
1951 STL A  S           14   .350
     BRTR
```

THOMAS, KEITH MARSHALL (KITE)
B.APR.27,1924 KANSAS CITY,KAN.
```
1952 PHI A  O           75   .250
1953 PHI A  O           24   .122
     WAS A  C-O         38   .293
     BRTR              137   .233
```

THOMAS, LEO RAYMOND (LEO) OR (TOMMY)
B.JULY 26,1923 TURLOCK,CAL.
```
1950 STL A  3           35   .198
1952 STL A  2-S-3       41   .234
     CHI A  3           19   .167
     BRTR               95   .212
```

THOMAS, LUTHER BAXTER (BUD)
B.SEPT.9,1910 FABER,VA.
```
1932 WAS A  P            2   0- 0
1933 WAS A  P            2   0- 0
1937 PHI A  P           35   8-15
1938 PHI A  P           42   9-14
1939 PHI A  P            2   0- 1
     WAS A  P            4   0- 0
     DET A  P           27   7- 0
1940 DET A  P            3   0- 1
1941 DET A  P           26   1- 3
     BRTR              143  25-34
```

THOMAS, MYLES LEWIS
B.OCT.22,1897 STATE COLLEGE,PA.
D.DEC.12,1963 TOLEDO,OHIO
```
1926 NY  A  P           33   6- 6
1927 NY  A  P           21   7- 4
1928 NY  A  P     12    13   1- 0
1929 NY  A  P            5   0- 2
     WAS A  P           22   7- 8
1930 WAS A  P     12    14   2- 2
     BRTR        105   108  23-22
```

THOMAS, RAYMOND JOSEPH
B.JULY 9,1910 DOVER,N.H.
```
1938 BRO N  C            1   .333
```

THOMAS, ROBERT WILLIAM (RED)
B.APR.25,1898 HARGROVE,ALA.
D.MAR.29,1962 FREMONT,OHIO
```
1921 CHI N  O            8   .267
     BRTR
```

THOMAS, ROY ALLEN
B.MAR.24,1874 NORRISTOWN,PA.
D.NOV.20,1959 NORRISTOWN,PA.
```
1899 PHI N  O          148   .324
1900 PHI N  P-O    1   139   .324
                              .325
1901 PHI N  O          128   .305
1902 PHI N  O          138   .292
1903 PHI N  O          130   .327
1904 PHI N  O          139   .290
1905 PHI N  O          147   .317
1906 PHI N  O          142   .254
1907 PHI N  O          121   .243
1908 PHI N  O            6   .167
     PIT N  O          101   .256
1909 BOS N  O           77   .263
1910 PHI N  O           20   .183
1911 PHI N  O           21   .133
     BLTL        1    1457   .291
                              .291
```

THOMAS, ROY JUSTIN
B.JUNE 22,1953 QUANTICO,VA.
```
1977 HOU N  /P           4   0- 0
1978 STL N  P           16   1- 1
     BRTR               20   1- 1
```

THOMAS, STANLEY BROWN (STAN)
B.JULY 11,1949 RUMFORD,ME.
```
1974 TEX A  P           12   0- 0
1975 TEX A  P           46   4- 4
1976 CLE A  P           37   4- 4
1977 SEA A  P           13   2- 6
     NY  A  /P           3   1- 0
     BRTR              111  11-14
```

THOMAS, THOMAS WILLIAM (SAVAGE TOM)
B.DEC.27,1873 SHAWNEE,OHIO
D.SEPT.22,1942 SHAWNEE,OHIO
```
1899 STL N  P            4   1- 1
1900 STL N  P            5   1- 0
                         9   2- 1
```

THOMAS, VALMY
B.OCT.21,1928 SANTURCE,P.R.
```
1957 NY  N  C           88   .249
1958 SF  N  C           63   .259
1959 PHI N  C-3         66   .200
1960 BAL A  C            8   .063
1961 CLE A  C           27   .209
     BRTR              252   .230
```

THOMAS, WALTER W.
```
1908 BOS N  S            5   .154
     TR
```

THOMAS, WILLIAM MISKEY
B.DEC.8,1877 NORRISTOWN,PA.
D.JAN.14,1950 EVANSBURG,PA.
```
1902 PHI N  1-2-O        6   .176
     TR
```

THOMASON, ARTHUR WILSON
B.FEB.12,1889 LIBERTY,MO.
D.MAY 2,1944 KANSAS CITY,MO.
```
1910 CLE A  O           17   .158
     BLTL
```

THOMASON, MELVIN ERSKINE (ERSKINE)
B.AUG.13,1948 LAURENS,S.C.
```
1974 PHI N  /P           1   0- 0
     BRTR
```

THOMASSON, GARY LEAH
B.JULY 29,1951 SAN DIEGO,CAL.
```
1972 SF  N  /1-O         10   .333
1973 SF  N  1-O         112   .285
1974 SF  N  O-1         120   .244
1975 SF  N  O-1         114   .227
1976 SF  N  O-1         103   .259
1977 SF  N  *O-1        145   .256
1978 OAK A  O/1          47   .201
     NY  A  O            54   .276
     BLTL              705   .251
```

THOMPSON, A. M.
B.ST.PAUL,MINN.
```
1875 NAT NA C-O         10    -
     ATL NA O            1    -
                        11    -
NON-PLAYING MANAGER STP[U] 1884
```

THOMPSON, ARTHUR J.
```
1884 WAS U  P            1   0- 1
```

THOMPSON, BOBBY LA RUE
B.NOV.3,1953 CHARLOTTE,N.C.
```
1978 TEX A  O           64   .225
     BBTR
```

THOMPSON, CHARLES LEMOINE (TIM)
B.MAR.1,1924 COALPORT,PA.
```
1954 BRO N  C           10   .154
1956 KC  A  C           92   .272
1957 KC  A  C           81   .204
1958 DET A  C            4   .167
     BLTR              187   .238
```

THOMPSON, DANNY LEON
B.FEB.1,1947 WICHITA,KAN.
D.DEC.10,1976 ROCHESTER,MINN.
```
1970 MIN A  2-3/S       96   .219
1971 MIN A  3/2-S       48   .263
1972 MIN A  *S         144   .276
1973 MIN A  S/3         99   .225
1974 MIN A  S/3         97   .250
1975 MIN A  *S/3-2     112   .270
1976 MIN A  S           34   .234
     TEX A  3-2-S       64   .214
     BRTR              694   .248
```

THOMPSON, DAVID FORREST (FORREST)
B.MAR.3,1918 MOORESVILLE,N.C.
```
1948 WAS A  P           46   6-10
1949 WAS A  P      9    10   1- 3
     BLTL         55    56   7-13
```

THOMPSON, DONALD NEWLIN (DON)
B.DEC.28,1923 SWEPSONVILLE,N.C.
```
1949 BOS N  O            7   .182
1951 BRO N  O           80   .229
1953 BRO N  O           96   .242
1954 BRO N  O           34   .040
     BLTL              217   .218
```

THOMPSON, EUGENE EARL (JUNIOR)
B.JUNE 7,1917 LATHAM,ILL.
```
1939 CIN N  P           42  13- 5
1940 CIN N  P           33  16- 9
1941 CIN N  P           27   6- 6
1942 CIN N  P           29   4- 7
1946 NY  N  P           39   4- 6
1947 NY  N  P           15   4- 2
     BRTR              185  47-35
```

```
YR  CL LEA POS    GP    G   REC        YR  CL LEA POS    GP    G   REC        YR  CL LEA POS    GP    G   REC

THOMPSON, FRANK E                      THOMPSON, RUPERT LOCKHART (TOMMY)      THORNTON, ANDRE (ANDY)
B.JULY 4,1893 SPRINGFIELD,MO.          B.MAY 19,1910 ELKHART,ILL.             B.AUG.13,1949 TUSKEGEE,ALA.
D.JUNE 27,1940 MINERAL TWSP.,MO        D.MAY 24,1971 AUBURN,CAL.              1973 CHI N /1          17   .200
1920 STL A 3          22   .170        1933 BOS N O          24   .186        1974 CHI N 1/3        107   .261
          BRTR                         1934 BOS N O         105   .265        1975 CHI N *1/3       120   .293
                                       1935 BOS N O         112   .273        1976 CHI N 1           27   .200
THOMPSON, FULLER WEIDNER               1936 BOS N 1-O       106   .286             MON N 1-O          69   .191
B.MAY 1,1889 LOS ANGELES,CAL.          1938 CHI A 1          19   .111        1977 CLE A *1         131   .263
D.FEB.19,1972 LOS ANGELES,CAL.         1939 CHI A O           1   .000        1978 CLE A *1         145   .262
1911 BOS N P           3   0- 0             STL A O           30   .302                 BRTR        616   .257
          BRTR                                   BLTR        397   .266
                                                                              THORNTON, JOHN
THOMPSON, HAROLD (HARRY)               THOMPSON, SAMUEL LUTHER                B.1870 WASHINGTON,D.C.
B.MAR.25,1893 NANTICOKE,PA.            (SAM) OR (BIG SAM)                     D.AUG.31,1893 PENSACOLA,FLA.
D.FEB.14,1951 RENO,NEV.                B.MAR.5,1860 DANVILLE,IND.             1889 WAS N P           1       0- 1
1919 WAS A P      12  18   0- 3        D.NOV.7,1922 DETROIT,MICH.             1891 PHI N P          3G      15-11
     PHI A         3   5   0- 1        1885 DET N O          63   .303        1892 PHI N P-O     3   5       0- 1
          BLTL    15  23   0- 4        1886 DET N O         122   .310                                       .385
                                       1887 DET N O         127   .406             STL N O               1   .000
THOMPSON, HENRY CURTIS (HANK)          1888 DET N O          55   .281                          34  37      15-13
B.DEC.8,1925 OKLAHOMA CITY,OKLA        1889 PHI N O         128   .296                                       .157
D.SEPT.30,1969 FRESNO,CAL.             1890 PHI N O         132   .313
1947 STL A 2          27   .256        1891 PHI N O         133   .295        THORNTON, OTIS BENJAMIN
1949 NY  N 2-3        75   .280        1892 PHI N O         151   .303        B.JUNE 30,1945 DOCENA,ALA.
1950 NY  N 3-O       148   .289        1893 PHI N O         130   .377        1973 HOU N /C           2   .000
1951 NY  N 3          87   .235        1894 PHI N O         102   .403                 BRTR
1952 NY  N 2-3-O     128   .260        1895 PHI N O         118   .394
1953 NY  N 2-3-O     114   .302        1896 PHI N O         119   .305        THORNTON, WALTER MILLER
1954 NY  N 2-3-O     136   .263        1897 PHI N O           3   .250        B.FEB.18,1875 LEWISTON,MAINE
1955 NY  N 2-S-3     135   .245        1898 PHI N O          14   .365        D.JULY 14,1960 LOS ANGELES,CAL.
1956 NY  N 2-3-O      83   .235        1906 DET A O           8   .225        1895 CHI N P           9   3- 2
          BRTR      933   .267                   BLTR       1405   .336        1896 CHI N P       5   9   2- 1
                                                                              1897 CHI N P-O    16  71   6- 9
THOMPSON, JAMES ALFRED (SHAG)          THOMPSON, THOMAS CARL                                                .329
B.APR.29,1893 HAW RIVER,N.C.           B.NOV.7,1889 SPRING CITY,TENN.         1898 CHI N P-O    24  56  12- 9
1914 PHI A O          16   .172        D.JAN.16,1963 LA JOLLA,CAL.                                          .283
1915 PHI A O          17   .333        1912 NY  N P           8   0- 2             TL         54 145  23-21
1916 PHI A O          15   .000                 BRTR                                                        .313
          BLTR        48   .203
                                       THOMPSON, THOMAS HOMER (HOMER)         THORPE, BENJAMIN ROBERT (BOB)
THOMPSON, JASON DOLPH                  B.JUNE 19,1892 SPRING CITY,TENN.       B.NOV.19,1926 CARYVILLE,FLA.
B.JULY 6,1954 HOLLYWOOD,CAL.           D.SEPT.12,1957 ATLANTA,GA.             1951 BOS N P           2   .500
1976 DET A *1        123   .218        1912 NY  N C           1   .000        1952 BOS N O          81   .260
1977 DET A *1        158   .270                 BRTR                          1953 MIL N O          27   .162
1978 DET A *1        153   .287                                                         BRTR       110   .291
          BLTR      434   .263         THOMPSON, VERNON SCOT (SCOT)
                                       B.DEC.7,1955 GROVE CITY,PA.            THORPE, JAMES FRANCIS (JIM)
THOMPSON, JOHN DUDLEY                  1978 CHI N /O-1       19   .417         B.MAY 28,1888 PRAGUE,OKLA.
(LEE) OR (LEFTY)                                 BLTL                          D.MAR.28,1953 LONG BEACH,CAL.
B.FEB.26,1898 SMITHFIELD,UTAH                                                 1913 NY  N O          19   .143
D.FEB.17,1963 SANTA BARBARA,CAL.       THOMPSON, WILL MC LAIN                 1914 NY  N O          30   .194
1921 CHI A P           4   0- 3        B.AUG.30,1870 PITTSBURGH,PA.           1915 NY  N O          17   .231
          BLTL                         D.JUNE 9,1962 PITTSBURGH,PA.           1917 CIN N O          77   .247
                                       1892 PIT N P           1   0- 1             NY  N O          26   .200
THOMPSON, JOHN GUSTAV (GUS)                      BRTR                          1918 NY  N O          58   .248
B.JUNE 22,1877 HUMBOLDT,IOWA                                                  1919 NY  N O           2   .333
D.MAR.28,1958 KALISPELL,MONT.          THOMSON, ROBERT BROWN (BOBBY)              BOS N 1-O          60   .327
1903 PIT N P           5   2- 2        OR (THE STATEN ISLAND SCOT)                      BRTR       289   .252
1906 STL N P          17   2-11        B.OCT.25,1923 GLASGOW,SCOTLAND              BB 1915
                      22   4-13        1946 NY  N 3          18   .315
                                       1947 NY  N 2-O       138   .283        THORPE, ROBERT JOSEPH (BOB)
THOMPSON, JOHN P. (TUG)                1948 NY  N O         138   .248        B.JAN.12,1935 SAN DIEGO,CAL.
B.INDIANAPOLIS,IND.                    1949 NY  N O         156   .309        D.MAR.17,1960 SAN DIEGO,CAL.
D.JULY 1895 WILMINGTON,DEL.            1950 NY  N O         149   .252        1955 CHI N P           2   0- 0
1882 CIN AA O          1   .200        1951 NY  N 3-O       148   .294                 BRTR
1884 IND AA C-O       24   .204        1952 NY  N 3-O       153   .270
                      25   .204        1953 NY  N O         154   .288        THRASHER, FRANK EDWARD (BUCK)
                                       1954 MIL N O          43   .232        B.AUG.6,1889 WATKINSVILLE,GA.
THOMPSON, JOHN SAMUEL (JOCKO)          1955 MIL N O         101   .257        D.JUNE 12,1938 CLEVELAND,OHIO
B.JAN.17,1920 BEVERLY,MASS.            1956 MIL N 3-O       142   .235        1916 PHI A O           7   .310
1948 PHI N P           2   1- 0        1957 MIL N O          41   .236        1917 PHI A O          23   .234
1949 PHI N P       8   9   1- 3             NY  N 3-O         41   .242                 BRTR         30   .255
1950 PHI N P           2   0- 0        1958 CHI N 3-O       192   .283
1951 PHI N P      29  30   4- 8        1959 CHI N O         122   .259        THRONEBERRY, MARVIN EUGENE
          BLTL    41  43   6-11        1960 BOS A 1-O        40   .263        (MARV) OR (MARVELOUS MARV)
                                            BAL A O            3   .000        B.SEPT.2,1933 COLLIERVILLE,TENN.
THOMPSON, LAFAYETTE FRESCO                       BRTR       1779   .270        1955 NY  A O           1  1.000
(FRESCO) OR (TOMMY)                                                           1958 NY  A 1-O        60   .227
B.JUNE 6,1902 CENTERVILLE,ALA.         THONEY, JOHN (BULLET JACK)             1959 NY  A 1-O        80   .240
D.NOV.20,1968 FULLERTON,CAL.           (REAL NAME JOHN THOENY)                1960 KC  A 1         104   .250
1925 PIT N 2          14   .243        B.DEC.8,1879 FT.THOMAS,KY.             1961 KC  A 1-O        40   .238
1926 NY  N 2           2   .625        D.OCT.24,1948 COVINGTON,KY.                 BAL A 1-O         56   .208
1927 PHI N 2         153   .303        1902 CLE A 2-S-O      28   .291        1962 BAL A O           9   .000
1928 PHI N 2         152   .287             BAL A 3            3   .000             NY  N 1         116   .244
1929 PHI N 2         148   .324        1903 CLE A O          32   .213        1963 NY  N 1          14   .143
1930 PHI N 2         122   .282        1904 WAS A O          17   .300                 BLTL       480   .237
1931 BRO N 2-S        74   .265             3-O              35   .231
1932 BRO N H           3   .000        1908 BOS A O         109   .255        THRONEBERRY, MAYNARD FAYE (FAYE)
1934 NY  N H           1   .000        1909 BOS A O          14   .184        B.JUNE 22,1931 MEMPHIS,TENN.
          BRTR      669   .298         1911 BOS A O          26   .250        1952 BOS A O          98   .258
                                                 BRTR       264   .235        1955 BOS A O          60   .220
THOMPSON, MICHAEL WAYNE (MIKE)                                                1956 BOS A O          24   .222
B.SEP.6,1949 DENVER,COLO.              THORMAHLEN, HERBERT EHLER              1957 BOS A H           1   .000
1971 WAS A P          16   1- 6        (HANK) OR (LEFTY)                           WAS A O           68   .185
1973 STL N /P          2   0- 0        B.JULY 5,1896 JERSEY CITY,N.J.         1958 WAS A O          44   .184
1974 STL N P          19   0- 3        D.FEB.6,1955 HOLLYWOOD,CAL.            1959 WAS A O         117   .251
     ATL N /P          1   0- 0        1917 NY  A P           1   0- 1        1960 WAS A O          85   .248
1975 ATL N P          16   0- 6        1918 NY  A P          16   7- 3        1961 LA  A O          24   .194
          BRTR        54   1-15        1919 NY  A P          30  13- 9                 BLTR       521   .236
                                       1920 NY  A P          29   9- 6
                                       1921 BOS A P          23   1- 7        THROOP, GEORGE LYNFORD
                                       1925 BRO N P           5   0- 3        B.NOV.24,1950 PASADENA,CAL.
                                                 BLTL       104  30-29        1975 KC  A /P          7   0- 0
                                                                              1977 KC  A /P          4   0- 0
                                       THORMODSGARD, PAUL GAYTON              1978 KC  A /P          1   1- 0
                                       B.NOV.10,1953 SAN FRANCISCO,CAL.                 BRTR        12   1- 0
                                       1977 MIN A P          37  11-15
                                       1978 MIN A P          11   1- 6
                                                 BRTR        49  12-21
```

YR	CL	LEA	POS	GP	G	REC

THUMAN, LOUIS CHARLES FRANK
B.DEC.13,1916 BALTIMORE,MD.

YR	CL	LEA	POS	GP	G	REC
1939	WAS	A	P		3	0- 0
1940	WAS	A	P		2	0- 1
		BRTR			5	0- 1

THURMAN, ROBERT BURNS (BOB)
B.MAY 14,1921 WICHITA,KAN.

YR	CL	LEA	POS	G	REC
1955	CIN	N	O	82	.217
1956	CIN	N	O	80	.295
1957	CIN	N	O	74	.247
1958	CIN	N	O	94	.230
1959	CIN	N	H	4	.250
		BLTL		334	.246

THURSTON, HOLLIS JOHN (SLOPPY)
B.JUNE 2,1899 FREMONT,NEB.
D.SEPT.14,1973 LOS ANGELES,CAL.

YR	CL	LEA	POS	GP	G	REC
1923	STL	A	P		2	0- 0
	CHI	A	P	44	45	7- 8
1924	CHI	A	P	38	51	20-14
1925	CHI	A	P	36	44	10-14
1926	CHI	A	P	31	38	6- 8
1927	WAS	A	P	29	42	13-13
1930	BRO	N	P	24	36	6- 4
1931	BRO	N	P		24	9- 9
1932	BRO	N	P	28	29	12- 8
1933	BRO	N	P		32	6- 8
		BRTR		288	343	89-86

TIANT, LUIS CLEMENTE [VEGA]
B.NOV.23,1940 MARIANAO,CUBA

YR	CL	LEA	POS	G	REC
1964	CLE	A	P	19	10- 4
1965	CLE	A	P	41	11-11
1966	CLE	A	P	46	12-11
1967	CLE	A	P	33	12- 9
1968	CLE	A	P	34	21- 9
1969	CLE	A	P	38	9-20
1970	MIN	A	P	18	7- 3
1971	BOS	A	P	21	1- 7
1972	BOS	A	P	43	15- 6
1973	BOS	A	P	35	20-13
1974	BOS	A	P	38	22-13
1975	BOS	A	P	33	18-14
1976	BOS	A	P	38	21-12
1977	BOS	A	P	32	12- 8
1978	BOS	A	P	32	13- 8
		BRTR		503	204-148

TIDROW, RICHARD WILLIAM (DICK)
B.MAY 14,1947 SAN FRANCISCO,CAL.

YR	CL	LEA	POS	G	REC
1972	CLE	A	P	39	14-15
1973	CLE	A	P	42	14-16
1974	CLE	A	/P	4	1- 3
	NY	A	P	33	11- 9
1975	NY	A	P	37	6- 3
1976	NY	A	P	47	4- 5
1977	NY	A	P	49	11- 4
1978	NY	A	P	31	7-11
		BRTR		282	68-66

TIEFENAUER, BOBBY GENE
B.OCT.10,1929 DESLOGE,MO.

YR	CL	LEA	POS	G	REC
1952	STL	N	P	6	0- 0
1955	STL	N	P	18	1- 4
1960	CLE	A	P	6	0- 1
1961	STL	N	P	3	0- 0
1962	HOU	N	P	43	2- 4
1963	MIL	N	P	12	1- 1
1964	MIL	N	P	46	4- 6
1965	MIL	N	/P	6	0- 1
	NY	A	P	10	1- 1
	CLE	A	P	15	0- 5
1967	CLE	A	P	5	0- 1
1968	CHI	N	/P	9	0- 1
		BRTR		179	9-25

TIEFENTHALER, VERLE MATTHEW
B.JULY 11,1937 BREDA,IOWA

YR	CL	LEA	POS	G	REC
1962	CHI	A	P	3	0- 0
		BLTR			

TIEMEYER, EDWARD CARL
B.MAY 9,1885 CINCINNATI,OHIO
D.SEPT.27,1946 CINCINNATI,OHIO

YR	CL	LEA	POS	GP	G	REC
1906	CIN	N	P-3	1	5	0- 0
						.181
1907	CIN	N	H		1	.000
1909	MIL	A	1		4	.363
		BRTR		1	10	0- 0
						.273

TIERNAN, MICHAEL JOSEPH
(SILENT MIKE)
B.JAN.21,1867 TRENTON,N.J.
D.NOV.9,1918 NEW YORK,N.Y.

YR	CL	LEA	POS	G	REC
1887	NY	N	O	103	.340
1888	NY	N	O	113	.293
1889	NY	N	O	122	.334
1890	NY	N	O	133	.303
1891	NY	N	O	133	.303
1892	NY	N	O	114	.297
1893	NY	N	O	124	.327
1894	NY	N	O	112	.282
1895	NY	N	O	119	.354
1896	NY	N	O	133	.361
1897	NY	N	O	129	.331
1898	NY	N	O	103	.286
1899	NY	N	O	36	.250
		BLTL		1474	.318

TIERNEY, JAMES ARTHUR (COTTON)
B.FEB.10,1894 KANSAS CITY,KAN.
D.APR.18,1953 KANSAS CITY,MO.

YR	CL	LEA	POS	G	REC
1920	PIT	N	2	12	.260
1921	PIT	N	2-3	117	.299
1922	PIT	N	2-S-3-O	122	.345
1923	PIT	N	2	29	.292
	PHI	N	2-3-O	121	.317
1924	BOS	N	2-3	136	.259
1925	BRO	N	1-2+3	93	.257
		BRTR		630	.296

TIERNEY, WILLIAM J.
B.MAY 14,1858 BOSTON,MASS.
D.SEPT.21,1898 BOSTON,MASS.

YR	CL	LEA	POS	G	REC
1882	CIN	AA	1	1	.000
1884	BAL	U	O	1	.333
				2	.125

TIETJE, LESLIE WILLIAM (TOOTS)
B.SEPT.11,1911 SUMNER,IOWA

YR	CL	LEA	POS	GP	G	REC
1933	CHI	A	P		3	2- 0
1934	CHI	A	P		34	5-14
1935	CHI	A	P		30	9-15
1936	CHI	A	P		2	0- 0
	STL	A	P	14	16	3- 5
1937	STL	A	P		5	1- 2
1938	STL	A	P		18	2- 5
		BRTR		106	108	22-41

TIFT, RAYMOND FRANK
B.JUNE 21,1884 FITCHBURG,MASS.
D.MAR.29,1945 VERONA,N.J.

YR	CL	LEA	POS	G	REC
1907	NY	A	P	4	0- 0
		TR			

TIGHE, JOHN THOMAS (JACK)
B.AUG.9,1913 KEARNY,N.J.
NON-PLAYING MANAGER DET[A] 1957-58

TILLEY, JOHN C.
B.1856 NEW YORK,N.Y.

YR	CL	LEA	POS	G	REC
1882	CLE	N	O	15	.089
1884	TOL	AA	O	17	.182
	STP	U	O	9	.148
				41	.138

TILLMAN, JOHN LAWRENCE (DUCKY)
B.OCT.6,1893 BRIDGEPORT,CONN.
D.APR.7,1964 HARRISBURG,PA.

YR	CL	LEA	POS	G	REC
1915	STL	A	P	2	0- 0
		BBTR			

TILLMAN, JOHN ROBERT (BOB)
B.MAR.24,1937 NASHVILLE,TENN.

YR	CL	LEA	POS	G	REC
1962	BOS	A	C	81	.229
1963	BOS	A	C	96	.225
1964	BOS	A	C	131	.278
1965	BOS	A	*C	111	.215
1966	BOS	A	C	78	.230
1967	BOS	A	C	30	.188
	NY	A	C	22	.254
1968	ATL	N	C	86	.220
1969	ATL	N	C	69	.195
1970	ATL	N	C	71	.238
		BRTR		775	.232

TILLOTSON, THADDEUS ASA (THAD)
B.DEC.20,1940 MERCED,CAL.

YR	CL	LEA	POS	G	REC
1967	NY	A	P	43	3- 9
1968	NY	A	/P	7	1- 0
		BRTR		50	4- 9

TIMBERLAKE, GARY DALE
B.AUG.8,1948 LACONIA,IND.

YR	CL	LEA	POS	G	REC
1969	SEA	A	/P	2	0- 0
		BRTL			

TIMMERMANN, THOMAS HENRY (TOM)
B.MAY 12,1940 BREESE,ILL.

YR	CL	LEA	POS	GP	G	REC
1969	DET	A	P		31	4- 3
1970	DET	A	P		61	6- 7
1971	DET	A	P		52	7- 6
1972	DET	A	P	34	39	8-10
1973	DET	A	P		17	1- 1
	CLE	A	P		29	8- 7
1974	CLE	A	/P		4	1- 1
		TR		228	229	35-35

TINCUP, AUSTIN BEN (BEN)
B.DEC.14,1890 ADAIR,OKLA.

YR	CL	LEA	POS	GP	G	REC
1914	PHI	N	P	28	31	8-10
1915	PHI	N	P		11	0- 0
1916	PHI	N	P		1	0- 0
1918	PHI	N	P	8	11	0- 1
1928	CHI	N	P		2	0- 0
		BLTR		50	56	8-11

TINKER, JOSEPH BERT (JOE)
B.JULY 27,1880 MUSCOTAH,KAN.
D.JULY 27,1948 ORLANDO,FLA.

YR	CL	LEA	POS	G	REC
1902	CHI	N	S-3	133	.273
1903	CHI	N	S-3	124	.291
1904	CHI	N	S	141	.221
1905	CHI	N	S	149	.247
1906	CHI	N	S	148	.233
1907	CHI	N	S	113	.221
1908	CHI	N	S	157	.266
1909	CHI	N	S	143	.256
1910	CHI	N	S	132	.288
1911	CHI	N	S	143	.278
1912	CHI	N	S	142	.282
1913	CIN	N	M-S	110	.317
1914	CHI	F	M-S	127	.259
1915	CHI	F	M-S	30	.275
1916	CHI	N	M-2	7	.100
		BRTR		1799	.263

TINNING, LYLE FORREST (BUD)
B.MAR.12,1906 PILGER,NEB.
D.JAN.17,1961 EVANSVILLE,IND.

YR	CL	LEA	POS	G	REC
1932	CHI	N	P	24	5- 3
1933	CHI	N	P	32	13- 6
1934	CHI	N	P	39	4- 6
1935	STL	N	P	4	0- 0
		BBTR		99	22-15
		BR 1934-35			

TIPPER, JAMES
B.JUNE 18,1849 MIDDLETOWN,CONN.
D.APR.19,1895

YR	CL	LEA	POS	G	REC
1872	MAN	NA	3-O	24	.264
1874	HAR	NA	O	45	-
1875	NH	NA	O	41	-
				110	-

TIPPLE, DANIEL E.
(BIG DAN) OR (RUSTY)
B.FEB.13,1890 ROCKFORD,ILL.
D.MAR.26,1960 OMAHA,NEB.

YR	CL	LEA	POS	G	REC
1915	NY	A	P	3	1- 1
		BRTR			

TIPTON, ERIC GORDON (THE RED)
(DUKIE) OR (BLUE DEVIL)
B.APR.20,1915 PETERSBURG,VA.

YR	CL	LEA	POS	G	REC
1939	PHI	A	O	47	.231
1940	PHI	A	O	2	.125
1941	PHI	A	O	1	.500
1942	CIN	N	O	63	.222
1943	CIN	N	O	140	.288
1944	CIN	N	O	140	.301
1945	CIN	N	O	108	.242
		BRTR		501	.270

TIPTON, JOE HICKS
B.FEB.18,1923 MC CAYSVILLE,GA.

YR	CL	LEA	POS	G	REC
1948	CLE	A	C	47	.289
1949	CHI	A	C	67	.204
1950	PHI	A	C	64	.266
1951	PHI	A	C	72	.239
1952	PHI	A	C	23	.191
	CLE	A	C	43	.248
1953	CLE	A	C	47	.229
1954	WAS	A	C	54	.223
		BRTR		417	.236

TISCHINSKI, THOMAS ARTHUR (TOM)
B.JULY 12,1944 KANSAS CITY,MO.

YR	CL	LEA	POS	G	REC
1969	MIN	A	C	37	.191
1970	MIN	A	C	24	.196
1971	MIN	A	C	21	.130
		BRTR		82	.181

TISING, JOHNNIE JOSEPH (JACK)
B.OCT.9,1903 HIGH POINT,MO.
D.SEPT.5,1967 LEADVILLE,OHIO

YR	CL	LEA	POS	G	REC
1936	PIT	N	P	10	1- 3
		BLTR			

TITCOMB, LEDELL (CANNONBALL)
B.AUG.21,1866 W.BALDWIN,ME.
D.JUNE 8,1950 KINGSTON,N.H.

YR	CL	LEA	POS	G	REC
1886	PHI	N	P	5	0- 5
1887	ATH	AA	P	3	1- 2
	NY	N	P	9	4- 3
1888	NY	N	P	23	14- 8
1889	NY	N	P	4	2- 2
1890	ROC	AA	P	21	9- 8
		BLTL		65	30-28

YR	CL LEA POS	GP	G	REC

TITUS, JOHN FRANKLIN (SILENT JOHN)
B.FEB.21,1876 ST.CLAIR,PA.
D.JAN.8,1943 ST.CLAIR,PA.

YR	CL LEA POS	GP	G	REC
1903	PHI N O	72		.286
1904	PHI N O	140		.294
1905	PHI N O	147		.308
1906	PHI N O	142		.267
1907	PHI N O	142		.275
1908	PHI N O	149		.286
1909	PHI N O	149		.270
1910	PHI N O	142		.241
1911	PHI N O	60		.284
1912	PHI N O	45		.274
	BOS N O	96		.325
1913	BOS N O	87		.297
	BLTL	1371		.282

TKACZUK, EDWARD TERRANCE
[PLAYED UNDER NAME OF
EDWARD TERRANCE KAZAK]

TOBIK, DAVID VANCE (DAVE)
B.MAR.2,1953 EUCLID,OHIO

1978	DET A /P	5		0- 0
	BRTR			

TOBIN, JAMES ANTHONY
(JIM) OR (ABBA DABBA)
B.DEC.27,1912 OAKLAND,CAL.
D.MAY 19,1969 OAKLAND,CAL.

1937	PIT N P	20	21	6- 3
1938	PIT N P	40	56	14-12
1939	PIT N P	25	43	9- 9
1940	BOS N P	15	20	7- 3
1941	BOS N P	33	43	12-12
1942	BOS N P	37	47	12-21
1943	BOS N P-1	33	46	14-14
				.280
1944	BOS N P	43	62	18-19
1945	BOS N P	27	41	9-14
	DET A P	14	17	4- 5
	BRTR	287	396	105-112
				.230

TOBIN, JOHN MARTIN (TIP)
B.SEPT.15,1906 JAMAICA PLAIN,MASS.

1932	NY N H	1		.000
	BRTR			

TOBIN, JOHN PATRICK (JACKIE)
B.JAN.6,1921 OAKLAND,CAL.

1945	BOS A 2-3-0	84		.252
	BLTR			

TOBIN, JOHN THOMAS (JACK)
B.MAY 4,1892 ST.LOUIS,MO.
D.DEC.10,1969 ST.LOUIS,MO.

1914	STL F O	135		.270
1915	STL F O	158		.299
1916	STL A O	77		.213
1918	STL A O	122		.277
1919	STL A O	127		.327
1920	STL A O	147		.340
1921	STL A O	150		.352
1922	STL A O	146		.331
1923	STL A O	151		.317
1924	STL A 1	136		.299
1925	STL A 1-O	77		.301
1926	WAS A O	27		.212
	BOS A O	51		.273
1927	BOS A O	111		.310
	BLTL	1615		.309

TOBIN, MARION BROOKS (PAT)
B.JAN.28,1916 HERMITAGE,ARK.
D.JAN.21,1975 SHREVEPORT,LA.

1941	PHI A P	1		0- 0
	BRTR			

TOBIN, WILLIAM F.
B.OCT.10,1854 HARTFORD,CONN.
D.OCT.11,1912 HARTFORD,CONN.

1880	WOR N 1	5		.125
	TRO N 1	32		.152
	BL	37		.142

TODD, ALFRED CHESTER
B.JAN.7,1902 TROY,N.Y.

1932	PHI N C	33		.229
1933	PHI N C-O	73		.206
1934	PHI N C	91		.318
1935	PHI N C	107		.290
1936	PIT N C	76		.273
1937	PIT N C	133		.307
1938	PIT N C	133		.265
1939	BRO N C	86		.277
1940	CHI N C	104		.249
1941	CHI N H	6		.167
1943	CHI N C	21		.133
	BRTR	863		.276

TODD, FRANK
B.ABERDEEN,MD.

1898	LOU N P	3		0- 3
	TL			

TODD, JACKSON A
B.NOV.20,1951 TULSA,OKLA.

1977	NY N P	19		3- 6
	BRTR			

TODD, JAMES RICHARD (JIM)
B.SEPT.21,1947 LANCASTER,PA.

1974	CHI N P	43		4- 2
1975	OAK A P	58		8- 3
1976	OAK A P	49		7- 8
1977	CHI N P	20		1- 1
1978	SEA A P	49		3- 4
	BLTR	219		23-18

TODT, PHILIP JULIUS (HOOK)
B.AUG.9,1901 ST.LOUIS,MO.
D.NOV.15,1973 ST.LOUIS,MO.

1924	BOS A 1	52		.262
1925	BOS A 1	141		.278
1926	BOS A 1	154		.255
1927	BOS A 1	140		.236
1928	BOS A 1	144		.252
1929	BOS A 1	153		.262
1930	BOS A 1	111		.269
1931	PHI A 1	62		.244
	BLTL	957		.258

TOENES, WILLIAM HARREL (HAL)
B.OCT.8,1917 MOBILE,ALA.

1947	WAS A P	3		0- 1
	BRTR			

TOLAN, ROBERT (BOBBY)
B.NOV.19,1945 LOS ANGELES,CAL.

1965	STL N O	17		.188
1966	STL N O/1	43		.172
1967	STL N O-1	110		.253
1968	STL N O/1	92		.230
1969	CIN N *O	152		.305
1970	CIN N *O	152		.316
1972	CIN N *O	149		.283
1973	CIN N *O	129		.206
1974	SD N O	95		.266
1975	SD N *O-1	147		.255
1976	PHI N 1-O	110		.261
1977	PHI N /1	19		.125
	PIT N 1/O	49		.203
	BLTL	1260		.265

TOLSON, CHARLES JULIUS
(CHICK) OR (TOBY)
B.MAY 3,1895 MARYLAND

1925	CLE A 1	3		.250
1926	CHI N 1	57		.313
1927	CHI N 1	39		.296
1929	CHI N 1	32		.257
1930	CHI N 1	13		.300
	BRTR	144		.284

TOMANEK, RICHARD CARL
(DICK) OR (BONES)
B.JAN.6,1931 AVON LAKE,OHIO

1953	CLE A P	1		1- 0
1954	CLE A P	1		0- 0
1957	CLE A P	34		2- 1
1958	CLE A P	18	20	2- 3
	KC A P	36		5- 5
1959	KC A P	16		0- 1
	BLTL	108		10-10

TOMASIC, ANDREW JOHN
B.DEC.10,1919 HOKENDAUQUA,PA.

1949	NY N P	2		0- 1
	BRTR			

TOMER, GEORGE CLARENCE
B.NOV.26,1895 PERRY,IOWA

1913	STL A H	1		.000
	BLTR			

TOMLIN, DAVID ALLEN (DAVE)
B.JUNE 22,1949 MAYSVILLE,KY.

1972	CIN N /P	3		0- 0
1973	CIN N P	16		1- 2
1974	SD N P	47		2- 0
1975	SD N P	67		4- 2
1976	SD N P	49		0- 1
1977	SD N P	76		4- 4
1978	CIN N P	57		9- 1
	BLTL	315		20-10

TOMNEY, PHILIP HOWARD (BUSTER)
B.JULY 17,1863 READING,PA.
D.MAR.18,1892 READING,PA.

1888	LOU AA S	34		.149
1889	LOU AA S	112		.215
1890	LOU AA S	110		.264
	BRTR	256		.229

TOMPKINS, CHARLES HERBERT (CHUCK)
B.SEPT.1,1889 PRESCOTT,ARK.
D.SEPT.20,1979 PRESCOTT,ARK.

1912	CIN N P	1		0- 0
	BRTR			

TOMPKINS, RONALD EVERETT
(RON) OR (STRETCH)
B.NOV.27,1944 SAN DIEGO,CAL.

1965	KC A /P	5		0- 0
1971	CHI N P	35		0- 2
	BRTR	40		0- 2

TOMS, THOMAS HOWARD (TOMMY)
B.OCT.15,1951 CHARLOTTESVILLE,VA

1975	SF N /P	7		0- 1
1976	SF N /P	7		0- 1
1977	SF N /P	4		0- 1
	BRTR	18		0- 3

TONEY, FREDERICK ARTHUR (FRED)
B.DEC.11,1887 NASHVILLE,TENN.
D.MAR.11,1953 NASHVILLE,TENN.

1911	CHI N P	18		1- 1
1912	CHI N P	9		1- 2
1913	CHI N P	7		2- 2
1915	CIN N P	36		17- 6
1916	CIN N P	41		14-17
1917	CIN N P	43		24-16
1918	CIN N P	22		6-10
	NY N P	11		6- 2
1919	NY N P	24		13- 6
1920	NY N P	42		21-11
1921	NY N P	42		18-11
1922	NY N P	13		5- 6
1923	STL N P	29		11-12
	BRTR	337		139-102

TONKIN, HARRY GLENVILLE (DOC)
B.AUG.11,1881 CONCORD,N.H.
D.MAY 30,1959 MIAMI,FLA.

1907	WAS A P	1		0- 0
	BLTL			

TONNEMAN, CHARLES RICHARD (TONY)
B.SEPT.10,1881 CHICAGO,ILL.
D.AUG.7,1951 PRESCOTT,ARIZ.

1911	BOS A C	2		.200
	BRTR			

TOOLE, STEPHEN J.
B.1862 NEW ORLEANS,LA.

1886	BRO AA P	13		6- 6
1887	BRO AA P	26		13-10
1888	KC AA P	13		4- 6
1890	BRO AA P	6		2- 4
	BRTL	58		25-26

TOOLEY, ALBERT R. (BERT)
B.AUG.30,1886 HOWELL,MICH.
D.AUG.17,1976 MARSHALL,MICH.

1911	BRO N S	114		.206
1912	BRO N S	77		.234
	BRTR	191		.216

TORPORCER, GEORGE (SPECS)
B.FEB.9,1899 NEW YORK,N.Y.

1921	STL N 2	22		.264
1922	STL N 2-S-3-O	116		.323
1923	STL N 1-2-S-3	97		.254
1924	STL N 2-S-3	70		.313
1925	STL N 2-S	83		.284
1926	STL N 2	64		.250
1927	STL N S-3	86		.248
1928	STL N 1-2	8		.000
	BLTR	546		.279

TOPPIN, RUPERTO
B.DEC.7,1941 PANAMA CITY,PANAMA

1962	KC A P	2		0- 0
	BRTR			

TORBORG, JEFFREY ALLEN (JEFF)
B.NOV.26,1941 PLAINFIELD,N.J.

1964	LA N C	28		.233
1965	LA N C	56		.240
1966	LA N C	46		.225
1967	LA N C	76		.214
1968	LA N C	37		.161
1969	LA N C	51		.185
1970	LA N C	64		.231
1971	CAL A C	55		.203
1972	CAL A C	59		.209
1973	CAL A *C	102		.220
	BRTR	574		.214

NON-PLAYING MANAGER CLE[A] 1977-78

TORGESON, CLIFFORD EARL (EARL)
OR (THE EARL OF SNOHOMISH)
B.JAN.1,1924 SNOHOMISH,WASH.

YR	CL	LEA	POS	GP	G	REC
1947	BOS	N	1		128	.281
1948	BOS	N	1		134	.253
1949	BOS	N	1		25	.260
1950	BOS	N	1		156	.290
1951	BOS	N	1		155	.263
1952	BOS	N	1-0		122	.230
1953	PHI	N	1		111	.274
1954	PHI	N	1		135	.271
1955	PHI	N	1		47	.267
	DET	A	1		89	.283
1956	DET	A	1		117	.264
1957	DET	A	1		30	.240
	CHI	A	1-0		86	.295
1958	CHI	A	1		96	.266
1959	CHI	A	1		127	.220
1960	CHI	A	1		68	.263
1961	CHI	A	1		20	.067
	NY	A	1		22	.111
	BLTL				1668	.265

TORKELSON, CHESTER LEROY (RED)
B.MAR.19,1894 CHICAGO,ILL.
D.SEPT.22,1964 CHICAGO,ILL.

YR	CL	LEA	POS	GP	G	REC
1917	CLE	A	P		4	2-1
	BRTR					

TORPHY, WALTER ANTHONY (RED)
B.NOV.6,1891 FALL RIVER,MASS.

YR	CL	LEA	POS	GP	G	REC
1920	BOS	N	1		3	.200
	BRTR					

TORRE, FRANK JOSEPH
B.DEC.30,1931 BROOKLYN,N.Y.

YR	CL	LEA	POS	GP	G	REC
1956	MIL	N	1		111	.258
1957	MIL	N	1		129	.272
1958	MIL	N	1		138	.309
1959	MIL	N	1		115	.228
1960	MIL	N	1		21	.205
1962	PHI	N	1		108	.310
1963	PHI	N	1		92	.250
	BLTL				714	.273

TORRE, JOSEPH PAUL (JOE)
B.JULY 18,1940 BROOKLYN,N.Y.

YR	CL	LEA	POS	GP	G	REC
1960	MIL	N	H		2	.500
1961	MIL	N	C		113	.278
1962	MIL	N	C		80	.282
1963	MIL	N	C-1-0		142	.293
1964	MIL	N	C-1		154	.321
1965	MIL	N	*C-1		148	.291
1966	ATL	N	*C-1		148	.315
1967	ATL	N	*C-1		135	.277
1968	ATL	N	C-1		115	.271
1969	STL	N	*1-C		159	.289
1970	STL	N	C-3/1		161	.325
1971	STL	N	*3		161	.363
1972	STL	N	*3-1		149	.289
1973	STL	N	*1-3		141	.287
1974	STL	N	*1-3		147	.282
1975	NY	N	3-1		114	.247
1976	NY	N	1/3		114	.306
1977	NY	N	M-1/3		26	.176
	BRTR				2209	.297

NON-PLAYING MANAGER NY[N] 1978

TORREALBA, PABLO ARNOLDO
[TORREALBA]
B.APR.28,1948 BARQUISIMENTO,VEN.

YR	CL	LEA	POS	GP	G	REC
1975	ATL	N	/P		6	0-1
1976	ATL	N	P		36	0-2
1977	OAK	A	P		41	4-6
1978	CHI	A	P		25	2-4
	BLTL				108	6-13

TORRES, ANGEL RAFAEL [RUIZ]
B.OCT.24,1952 LAS CIENGAS,AZUA, D.R.

YR	CL	LEA	POS	GP	G	REC
1977	CIN	N	/P		5	0-0
	BLTL					

TORRES, DON GILBERTO [NUNEZ] (GIL)
B.AUG.23,1915 REGLA,CUBA

YR	CL	LEA	POS	GP	G	REC
1940	WAS	A	P		2	0- 0
1944	WAS	A	1-2-3		134	.267
1945	WAS	A	S-3		147	.237
1946	WAS	A	P-2-S-3	3	63	0- 0 / .254
	BRTR			5	346	0- 0 / .252

TORRES, FELIX [SANCHEZ]
B.MAY 1,1932 PONCE,P.R.

YR	CL	LEA	POS	GP	G	REC
1962	LA	A	3		127	.259
1963	LA	A	1-3		138	.261
1964	LA	A	1-3		100	.231
	BRTR				365	.254

TORRES, HECTOR EPITACIO
[MARROQUIN]
B.SEP.16,1945 MONTERREY,MEXICO

YR	CL	LEA	POS	GP	G	REC
1968	HOU	N	*S/2		128	.223
1969	HOU	N	S		34	.159
1970	HOU	N	S/2		31	.246
1971	CHI	N	S/2		31	.224
1972	HOU	N	/P-2-S/0-3	1	83	0- 0 / .155
1973	HOU	N	S-2		38	.091
1975	SD	N	S-3-2		112	.259
1976	SD	N	S/3-2		74	.195
1977	TOR	N	S-2/3		91	.241
	BRTR			1	622	0- 0 / .216

TORRES, RICARDO J.
B.1894 CUBA
D.HAVANA,CUBA

YR	CL	LEA	POS	GP	G	REC
1920	WAS	A	C-1		16	.333
1921	WAS	A	C		2	.333
1922	WAS	A	C		4	.000
	BRTR				22	.297

TORRES, ROSENDO [HERNANDEZ] (RUSTY)
B.SEP.30,1948 AQUADILLA,P.R.

YR	CL	LEA	POS	GP	G	REC
1971	NY	A	/O		9	.385
1972	NY	A	O		80	.211
1973	CLE	A	*O		122	.205
1974	CLE	A	O		108	.187
1976	CAL	A	*O/3		120	.205
1977	CAL	A	O		58	.156
1978	CHI	A	O		16	.318
	BBTR				513	.209

TORREZ, MICHAEL AUGUSTINE (MIKE)
B.AUG.28,1946 TOPEKA,KAN.

YR	CL	LEA	POS	GP	G	REC
1967	STL	N	/P		3	0- 1
1968	STL	N	/P		5	2- 1
1969	STL	N	P		24	10- 4
1970	STL	N	P		30	8-10
1971	STL	N	/P		9	1- 2
	MON	N	/P		1	0- 0
1972	MON	N	P		34	16-12
1973	MON	N	P	35	36	9-12
1974	MON	N	P	32	36	15- 8
1975	BAL	A	P		36	20- 9
1976	OAK	A	/P		39	16-12
1977	OAK	A	/P		4	3- 1
	NY	A	P		31	14-12
1978	BOS	A	P		36	16-13
	BRTR			319	524	130-97

TOST, LOUIS EUGENE
B.JUNE 1,1911 CUMBERLAND,WASH.
D.FEB.22,1967 SANTA CLARA,CAL.

YR	CL	LEA	POS	GP	G	REC
1942	BOS	N	P		35	10-10
1943	BOS	N	P		3	0- 1
1947	PIT	N	P		1	0- 0
	BLTL				39	10-11

TOTH, PAUL LOUIS
B.JUNE 30,1935 MCROBERTS,KY.

YR	CL	LEA	POS	GP	G	REC
1962	STL	N	P		6	1- 0
	CHI	N	P		6	3- 1
1963	CHI	N	P		27	5- 9
1964	CHI	N	P		4	0- 2
	BRTR				43	9-12

TOUCHSTONE, CLAYLAND MAFFITT
B.JAN.24,1903 MOORE,PA.
D.APR.28,1949 BEAUMONT,TEX.

YR	CL	LEA	POS	GP	G	REC
1928	BOS	N	P		5	0- 0
1929	BOS	N	P		1	0- 0
1945	CHI	A	P		6	0- 0
	BRTR				12	0- 0

TOVAR, CESAR LEONARDO
(CESAR) OR (PEPITO)
[REAL NAME CESAR LEONARD PEREZ [TOVAR]]
B.JULY 3,1940 CARACAS,VENEZ.

YR	CL	LEA	POS	GP	G	REC
1965	MIN	A	/2-3-0-S		18	.200
1966	MIN	A	2-S-0		134	.260
1967	MIN	A	O-3-2/S		164	.267
1968	MIN	A	/P-O-3-S-2/C-1	1	157	0- 0 / .272
1969	MIN	A	*O-2-3		158	.288
1970	MIN	A	*O/2-3		161	.300
1971	MIN	A	*O/3-2		157	.311
1972	MIN	A	*O		141	.265
1973	PHI	N	3-O-2		97	.268
1974	TEX	A	*O		138	.292
1975	TEX	A	O-0/2		102	.258
	OAK	A	3/2-S		19	.231
1976	OAK	A	O		29	.178
	NY	A	O/2		13	.154
	BRTR			1	1488	0- 0 / .278

TOWNE, JAY KING (BABE)
B.MAR.12,1880 COON RAPID,IOWA
D.OCT.29,1938 DES MOINES,IOWA

YR	CL	LEA	POS	GP	G	REC
1906	CHI	A	C		13	.290
	BLTR					

TOWNSEND, GEORGE HODGSON
(GEORGE) OR (SLEEPY)
B.JUNE 4,1867 HARTSDALE,N.Y.
D.MAR.15,1930 NEW HAVEN,CONN.

YR	CL	LEA	POS	GP	G	REC
1887	ATH	AA	C		14	.217
1888	ATH	AA	C		43	.150
1890	BAL	AA	C		19	.214
1891	BAL	AA	C		59	.178
	BRTR				155	.186

TOWNSEND, IRA DANCE (PAT)
B.JAN.9,1894 WEIMAR,TEX.
D.JULY 21,1965 SCHULENBERG,TEX.

YR	CL	LEA	POS	GP	G	REC
1920	BOS	N	P		4	0- 0
1921	BOS	N	P		4	0- 0
	BRTR				8	0- 0

TOWNSEND, JOHN (HAPPY)
B.APR.9,1879 TOWNSEND,DEL.
D.DEC.1,1963 WILMINGTON,DEL.

YR	CL	LEA	POS	GP	G	REC
1901	PHI	N	P		18	9- 6
1902	WAS	A	P		27	9-16
1903	WAS	A	P		20	2-11
1904	WAS	A	P	36	38	5-27
1905	WAS	A	P		34	6-17
1906	CLE	A	P		16	3- 7
	BRTR			151	153	34-84

TOWNSEND, LEO ALPHONSE (LEFTY)
B.JAN.15,1891 MOBILE,ALA.
D.DEC.3,1976 MOBILE,ALA.

YR	CL	LEA	POS	GP	G	REC
1920	BOS	N	P		7	2- 2
1921	BOS	N	P		1	0- 1
	BLTL				8	2- 3

TOY, JAMES MADISON
B.FEB.20,1858 BEAVER FALLS,PA.
D.MAR.13,1919 BEAVER FALLS,PA.

YR	CL	LEA	POS	GP	G	REC
1887	CLE	AA	1		109	.239
1890	BRO	AA	C		43	.172
					152	.218

TOZIER, WILLIAM LOUIS
B.JULY 3,1882 ST.LOUIS,MO.
D.FEB.23,1955 BELMONT,CAL.

YR	CL	LEA	POS	GP	G	REC
1908	CIN	N	P		4	0- 0
	BRTR					

TRACEWSKI, RICHARD JOSEPH (DICK)
B.FEB.3,1935 EYNON,PA.

YR	CL	LEA	POS	GP	G	REC
1962	LA	N	S		15	.000
1963	LA	N	2-S		104	.226
1964	LA	N	2-S-3		106	.247
1965	LA	N	3-2/S		78	.215
1966	DET	A	2/S		81	.194
1967	DET	A	S-2-3		74	.280
1968	DET	A	S-3-2		90	.156
1969	DET	A	S-2/3		66	.139
	BRTR				614	.213

TRAFFLEY, JOHN
B.1862 CHICAGO,ILL.
D.JULY 17,1900 BALTIMORE,MD.

YR	CL	LEA	POS	GP	G	REC
1889	LOU	AA	O		1	.500

TRAFFLEY, WILLIAM F.
B.DEC.21,1859 STATEN ISLAND,N.Y
D.JUNE 24,1908 DENVER,COLO.

YR	CL	LEA	POS	GP	G	REC
1878	CHI	N	C		2	.111
1883	CIN	AA	C-2-S		29	.200
1884	BAL	AA	C-O		54	.186
1885	BAL	AA	C		70	.156
1886	BAL	AA	C		25	.224
	BRTR				180	.181

TRAGESSER, WALTER JOSEPH
B.JUNE 14,1887 LAFAYETTE,IND.
D.DEC.14,1970 LAFAYETTE,IND.

YR	CL	LEA	POS	GP	G	REC
1913	BOS	N	C		1	.000
1915	BOS	N	C		7	.000
1916	BOS	N	C		41	.204
1917	BOS	N	C		98	.222
1918	BOS	N	C		7	.000
1919	BOS	N	C		20	.272
	PHI	N	C		35	.164
1920	PHI	N	C		62	.210
	BRTR				271	.215

TRAMBACK, STEPHEN JOSEPH (RED)
B.OCT.1,1915 ISELIN,PA.

YR	CL	LEA	POS	GP	G	REC
1940	NY	N	O		2	.250
	BLTL					

TRAMMELL, ALAN STUART
B.FEB.21,1958 GARDEN GROVE,CAL.

YR	CL	LEA	POS	GP	G	REC
1977	DET	A	S		19	.186
1978	DET	A	*S		139	.268
	BRTR				158	.261

TRAUTMAN, FREDERICK ORLANDO
B.MAR.24,1892 BUCYRUS,OHIO
D.FEB.15,1964 BUCYRUS,OHIO

YR	CL	LEA	POS	GP	G	REC
1915	NEW	F	P		1	0- 0
	BRTR					

TRAUX, FREDERICK W.

YR	CL	LEA	POS	GP	G	REC
1890	PIT	N	O		1	.333

```
YR   CL LEA POS    GP    G    REC        YR   CL LEA POS    GP    G    REC        YR   CL LEA POS    GP    G    REC
```

TRAVERS, ALOYSIUS JOSEPH
(ALLAN) OR (JOE)
B.MAY 7,1892 PHILADELPHIA,PA.
D.APR.19,1968 PHILADELPHIA,PA.
```
1912 DET A  P            1   0- 1
     BRTR
```

TRAVERS, WILLIAM EDWARD (BILL)
B.OCT.27,1952 NORWOOD,MASS.
```
1974 MIL A  P           23   2- 3
1975 MIL A  P           28   6-11
1976 MIL A  P           34  15-16
1977 MIL A  P           19   4-12
1978 MIL A  P           28  12-11
     BLTL              132  39-53
```

TRAVIS, CECIL HOWELL
B.AUG.8,1913 RIVERDALE,GA.
```
1933 WAS A  3           18   .302
1934 WAS A  3          109   .319
1935 WAS A  3-0        138   .318
1936 WAS A  S-0        138   .317
1937 WAS A  S          135   .344
1938 WAS A  S          146   .335
1939 WAS A  S          130   .292
1940 WAS A  S-3        136   .322
1941 WAS A  S-3        152   .359
1945 WAS A  3           15   .241
1946 WAS A  S-3        137   .252
1947 WAS A  S-3         74   .216
     BLTR             1328   .313
```

TRAY, JAMES
B.FEB.14,1860 JACKSON,MICH.
D.JULY 26,1905 JACKSON,MICH.
```
1884 IND AA C-1         6   .261
```

TRAYNOR, HAROLD JOSEPH (PIE)
B.NOV.11,1899 FRAMINGHAM,MASS.
D.MAR.16,1972 PITTSBURGH,PA.
```
1920 PIT N  S           17   .212
1921 PIT N  3            7   .203
1922 PIT N  S-3        142   .281
1923 PIT N  3          153   .338
1924 PIT N  3          142   .294
1925 PIT N  S-3        150   .320
1926 PIT N  3          152   .317
1927 PIT N  3          149   .342
1928 PIT N  3          144   .337
1929 PIT N  3          130   .356
1930 PIT N  3          130   .366
1931 PIT N  3          155   .298
1932 PIT N  3          135   .329
1933 PIT N  3          154   .304
1934 PIT N  M-3        119   .309
1935 PIT N  M-1-3       57   .279
1937 PIT N  M-3          5   .167
     BRTR             1941   .320
```
NON-PLAYING MANAGER
PIT[N] 1936, 38-39

TREACEY, FREDERICK S.
B.1847 BROOKLYN,N.Y.
```
1871 CHI NA O          25    -
1872 ATH NA O          46   .256
1873 PHI NA O          51    -
1874 CHI NA O          35    -
1875 CEN NA O          11    -
     PHI NA O          42    -
1876 MUT N  O          57   .210
                      267    -
```

TREACEY, PETER
B.1852 BROOKLYN,N.Y.
```
1876 MUT N  S           2   .167
```

TREADAWAY, EDGAR RAYMOND (RAY)
B.OCT.31,1907 RAGLAND,ALA.
D.OCT.12,1935 CHATTANOOGA,TENN.
```
1930 WAS A  3           6   .211
     BLTR
```

TREADWAY, GEORGE B.
B.NOV.11,1866 GREENUP CO.,KY.
D.NOV.17,1928 RIVERSIDE,CAL.
```
1893 BAL N  O         114   .268
1894 BRO N  O         122   .336
1895 BRO N  O          85   .262
1896 LOU N  O           2   .143
     BL               323   .292
```

TREADWAY, THADFORD LEON (RED)
B.APR.28,1920 ATHALONE,N.C.
```
1944 NY  N  O          50   .300
1945 NY  N  O          88   .241
     BLTR             138   .267
```

TRECHOCK, FRANK ADAM
B.DEC.24,1915 WINDBER,PA.
```
1937 WAS A  S           1   .500
     BRTR
```

TREKELL, HARRY ROY
B.NOV.18,1892 BREDA,ILL.
D.NOV.4,1965 SPOKANE,WASH.
```
1913 STL N  P           7   0- 1
     BRTR
```

TREMARK, NICHOLAS JOSEPH
B.OCT.15,1912 YONKERS,N.Y.
```
1934 BRO N  O          17   .250
1935 BRO N  O          10   .231
1936 BRO N  O           8   .250
     BLTL              35   .247
```

TREMBLY, EDWARD J.
[PLAYED UNDER NAME OF
EDWARD J. TRUMBULL]

TREMEL, WILLIAM LEONARD
(BILL) OR (MUMBLES)
B.JULY 4,1929 LILLY,PA.
```
1954 CHI N  P          33   1- 2
1955 CHI N  P          23   3- 0
1956 CHI N  P           1   0- 0
     BRTR              57   4- 2
```

TREMPER, CARLTON OVERTON (OVERTON)
B.MAR.22,1906 BROOKLYN,N.Y.
```
1927 BRO N  O          26   .233
1928 BRO N  O          10   .194
     BRTR              36   .220
```

TRENWITH, GEORGE
D.FEB.1,1890
```
1875 CEN NA 3          10    -
     NH  NA 3           6    -
                       16    -
```

TRESH, MICHAEL (MIKE)
B.FEB.23,1914 HAZLETON,PA.
D.OCT.4,1966 DETROIT,MICH.
```
1938 CHI A  C          10   .241
1939 CHI A  C         119   .259
1940 CHI A  C         135   .281
1941 CHI A  C         115   .251
1942 CHI A  C          72   .232
1943 CHI A  C          86   .215
1944 CHI A  C          93   .260
1945 CHI A  C         150   .249
1946 CHI A  C          80   .217
1947 CHI A  C          90   .241
1948 CHI A  C          39   .250
1949 CLE A  C          38   .216
     BRTR             1027   .249
```

TRESH, THOMAS MICHAEL (TOM)
B.SEP.20,1937 DETROIT,MICH.
```
1961 NY  A  S           9   .250
1962 NY  A  S-0       157   .286
1963 NY  A  O         145   .269
1964 NY  A  O         153   .246
1965 NY  A  *O        156   .279
1966 NY  A  O-3       151   .233
1967 NY  A  *O        130   .219
1968 NY  A  *S-O      152   .195
1969 NY  A  S          45   .182
     DET A  S-0/3      94   .224
     BBTR            1192   .245
```

TREVINO, ALEJANDRO [CASTRO] (ALEX)
B.AUG.26,1957 MONTERREY,MEX.
```
1978 NY  N  /C-3        6   .250
     BRTR
```

TREVINO, CARLOS [CASTRO] (BOBBY)
B.AUG.15,1943 MONTERREY,MEXICO
```
1968 CAL A  O          17   .225
     BRTR
```

TRIANDOS, GUS
B.JULY 30,1930 SAN FRANCISCO,CAL
```
1953 NY  A  C-1        18   .157
1954 NY  A  C           2   .000
1955 BAL A  C-1-3     140   .277
1956 BAL A  C-1-3     131   .279
1957 BAL A  C         129   .254
1958 BAL A  C         137   .245
1959 BAL A  C         126   .216
1960 BAL A  C         109   .269
1961 BAL A  C         115   .244
1962 BAL A  C          66   .159
1963 DET A  C         106   .239
1964 PHI N  C-1        73   .250
1965 PHI N  C          30   .171
     HOU N  C          24   .181
     BRTR             1206   .244
```

TRICE, ROBERT LEE (BOB)
B.AUG.28,1926 NEWTON,GA.
```
1953 PHI A  P            3   2- 1
1954 PHI A  P     19    20   7- 8
1955 KC  A  P            4   0- 0
     BRTR         26    27   9- 9
```

TRIEBEL, GEORGE W.
[PLAYED UNDER NAME OF
GEORGE W. CREAMER]

TRILLO, JESUS MANUEL MARCANO (MANNY)
[REAL NAME
JESUS MANUEL MARCANO [TRILLO]]
B.DEC.25,1950 CARIPITO,VEN.
```
1973 OAK A  2           2   .250
1974 OAK A  2          21   .152
1975 CHI N  *2/S      154   .248
1976 CHI N  *2/S      158   .239
1977 CHI N  *2        152   .280
1978 CHI N  *2        152   .261
     BRTR             654   .254
```

TRIMBLE, JOSEPH GERARD (JOE)
B.OCT.12,1930 PROVIDENCE,R.I.
```
1955 BOS A  P           2   0- 0
1957 PIT N  P           5   0- 2
     BRTR               7   0- 2
```

TRIMBLE, WILLIAM T.
D.JULY 29,1927 COLUMBUS,OHIO
NON-PLAYING MANAGER WAS[NA]1875

TRINKLE, KENNETH WAYNE (KEN)
B.DEC.15,1919 PAOLI,IND.
```
1943 NY  N  P          11   1- 5
1946 NY  N  P          48   7-14
1947 NY  N  P          62   8- 4
1948 NY  N  P          53   4- 5
1949 PHI N  P          42   1- 1
     BRTR             216  21-29
```

TRIPLETT, HERMAN COAKER (COAKER)
B.DEC.18,1911 BOONE,N.C.
```
1938 CHI N  O          12   .250
1941 STL N  O          76   .286
1942 STL N  O          64   .273
1943 STL N  O           9   .080
     PHI N  O         105   .272
1944 PHI N  O          84   .234
1945 PHI N  O         120   .240
     BRTR             470   .256
```

TROEDSON, RICHARD LA MONTE (RICH)
B.MAY 1,1950 PALO ALTO,CAL.
```
1973 SD  N  P          50   7- 9
1974 SD  N  P          15   1- 1
     BLTL              65   8-10
```

TROSKY, HAROLD ARTHUR JR.
(HAL) OR (HOOT)
[REAL NAME
HAROLD ARTHUR TROYAVESKY JR.]
B.SEPT.29,1936 CLEVELAND,OHIO
```
1958 CHI A  P           2   1- 0
```

TROSKY, HAROLD ARTHUR SR. (HAL)
[REAL NAME
HAROLD ARTHUR TROYAVESKY SR.]
B.NOV.11,1912 NORWAY,IOWA
```
1933 CLE A  1          11   .295
1934 CLE A  1         154   .330
1935 CLE A  1         154   .271
1936 CLE A  1         151   .343
1937 CLE A  1         153   .298
1938 CLE A  1         150   .334
1939 CLE A  1         122   .335
1940 CLE A  1         140   .295
1941 CLE A  1          89   .294
1944 CHI A  1         135   .241
1946 CHI A  1          88   .254
     BLTR             1347   .302
```

TROST, MICHAEL J.
B.1866 PHILADELPHIA,PA.
D.MAR.24,1901 PHILADELPHIA,PA.
```
1890 STL AA C          17   .250
1895 LOU N  1           2   .111
                       19   .217
```

TROTT, SAMUEL W.
B.1858 WASHINGTON,D.C.
D.JUNE 5,1925 CATONSVILLE,MD.
```
1880 BOS N  C-O        38   .197
1881 DET N  C           6   .192
1882 DET N  C-1-2-S-O  30   .246
1883 DET N  C-1-2-0    73   .233
1884 BAL AA C          72   .254
1885 BAL AA C          20   .289
1887 BAL AA C          85   .302
1888 BAL AA C          31   .275
     BLTR             355   .258
```
NON-PLAYING MANAGER WAS[AA]1891

TROTTER, WILLIAM FELIX (BILL)
B.AUG.10,1908 CISNE,ILL.
```
1937 STL A  P          34   2- 9
1938 STL A  P           1   0- 1
1939 STL A  P          41   6-13
1940 STL A  P          36   7- 6
1941 STL A  P          29   4- 2
1942 STL A  P           3   0- 1
     WAS A  P          17   3- 1
1944 STL N  P           2   0- 1
     BRTR             163  22-34
```

YR CL LEA POS	GP	G	REC

TROUPE, QUINCY THOMAS
B.DEC.25,1912 DUBLIN,GA.
| 1952 CLE A C | 6 | .100 | |
| BBTR | | | |

TROUT, PAUL HOWARD (DIZZY)
B.JUNE 29,1915 SANDCUT,IND.
D.FEB.28,1972 HARVEY,ILL.
1939 DET A P	33	35	9-10
1940 DET A P	33		3- 7
1941 DET A P	37	40	9- 9
1942 DET A P	35	36	12-18
1943 DET A P	44	45	20-12
1944 DET A P	49	51	27-14
1945 DET A P	41	42	18-15
1946 DET A P	38	40	17-13
1947 DET A P	32	34	10-11
1948 DET A P		32	10-14
1949 DET A P		33	3- 6
1950 DET A P		34	13- 5
1951 DET A P		42	9-14
1952 DET A P		10	1- 5
BOS A P		26	9- 8
1957 BAL A P		2	0- 0
BBTR	521	535	170-161

TROUT, STEVEN RUSSELL (STEVE)
B.JULY 30,1957 DETROIT,MICH.
| 1978 CHI A /P | 4 | 3- 0 | |
| BLTL | | | |

TROWBRIDGE, ROBERT (BOB)
B.JUNE 27,1930 HUDSON,N.Y.
1956 MIL N P	19	3- 2	
1957 MIL N P	32	7- 5	
1958 MIL N P	27	1- 3	
1959 MIL N P	16	1- 0	
1960 KC N P	22	1- 3	
BRTR	116	13-13	

TROY, JOHN JOSEPH (DASHER)
B.MAY 8,1856 NEW YORK,N.Y.
D.MAR.30,1938 OZONE PARK,N.Y.
1881 TRO N 2-3	11	.304	
1882 DET N 2-S	39	.232	
PRO N S	4	.235	
1883 NY N 2-S	82	.216	
1884 MET AA 2	107	.264	
1885 MET AA 2	46	.225	
BRTR	289	.242	

TROY, ROBERT (BUN)
B.AUG.22,1888 GERMANY
D.OCT.7,1918 MEUSE,FRANCE
| 1912 DET A P | 1 | 0- 1 | |
| BRTR | | | |

TROYAVESKY, HAROLD ARTHUR JR.
[PLAYED UNDER NAME OF
HAROLD ARTHUR TROSKY JR.]

TROYAVESKY, HAROLD ARTHUR SR.
[PLAYED UNDER NAME OF
HAROLD ARTHUR TROSKY SR.]

TRUBY, HARRY GARVIN (BIRD EYE)
B.MAY 12,1870 IRONTON,OHIO
D.MAR.21,1953 IRONTON,OHIO
1895 CHI N 2	33	.339	
1896 PHI N 2	27	.266	
PIT N 2	8	.156	
TR	68	.286	

TRUCKS, VIRGIL OLIVER (FIRE)
B.APR.26,1919 BIRMINGHAM,ALA.
1941 DET A P	1	0- 0	
1942 DET A P	28	14- 8	
1943 DET A P	33	16-10	
1945 DET A P	1	0- 0	
1946 DET A P	32	14- 9	
1947 DET A P	36	10-12	
1948 DET A P	43	14-13	
1949 DET A P	41	19-11	
1950 DET A P	7	3- 1	
1951 DET A P	37	13- 8	
1952 DET A P	35	5-19	
1953 STL A P	16	5- 4	
CHI A P	24	15- 6	
1954 CHI A P	40	19-12	
1955 CHI A P	32	13- 8	
1956 DET A P	22	6- 5	
1957 KC A P	48	9- 7	
1958 KC A P	16	0- 1	
NY A P	25	2- 1	
BRTR	517	177-135	

TRUESDALE, FRANK O.
B.DEC.12,1885 KIRKWOOD,MO.
1910 STL A 2	123	.219	
1911 STL A 2	1	.000	
1914 NY A 2	77	.212	
1918 BOS N 2	15	.278	
BBTR	216	.220	

TRUMAN, HARRY H.
[PLAYED UNDER NAME OF
HARRY H. RAYMOND]

YR CL LEA POS	GP	G	REC

TRUMBULL, EDWARD J.
[REAL NAME EDWARD J. TREMBLY]
B.NOV.3,1860 CHICOPEE FALLS,MASS.
| 1884 WAS AA P-O | 10 | 24 | 1- 9 |
| | | | .109 |

TSITOURIS, JOHN PHILIP
B.MAY 4,1936 MONROE,N.C.
1957 DET A P	2	1- 0	
1958 KC A P	1	0- 0	
1959 KC A P	24	4- 3	
1960 KC A P	14	0- 2	
1962 CIN N P	4	1- 0	
1963 CIN N P	30	12- 8	
1964 CIN N P	37	9-13	
1965 CIN N P	31	6- 9	
1966 CIN N /P	1	0- 0	
1967 CIN N /P	2	1- 0	
1968 CIN N /P	3	0- 3	
BRTR	149	34-38	

TUCKER, OLIVER DINWIDDIE (OLLIE)
B.JAN.27,1902 RADIANT,VA.
D.JULY 13,1940 RADIANT,VA.
1927 WAS A O	20	.208	
1928 CLE A O	14	.128	
BLTR	34	.155	

TUCKER, THOMAS JOSEPH (FOGHORN)
B.OCT.28,1863 HOLYOKE,MASS.
D.OCT.22,1935 MONTAGUE,MASS.
1887 BAL AA 1	136	.315	
1888 BAL AA 1	136	.291	
1889 BAL AA 1	134	.375	
1890 BOS N 1	132	.295	
1891 BOS N 1	140	.272	
1892 BOS N 1	148	.281	
1893 BOS N 1	121	.299	
1894 BOS N 1	122	.328	
1895 BOS N 1	126	.254	
1896 BOS N 1	122	.304	
1897 BOS N 1	2	.143	
WAS N 1	96	.333	
1898 BRO N 1	73	.278	
STL N 1	72	.238	
1899 CLE N 1	126	.237	
BBTR	1686	.295	

TUCKER, THURMAN LOWELL (JOE E.)
B.SEPT.26,1917 GORDON,TEX.
1942 CHI A O	7	.125	
1943 CHI A O	139	.235	
1944 CHI A O	124	.287	
1945 CHI A O	121	.288	
1947 CHI A O	89	.236	
1948 CHI A O	83	.260	
1949 CLE A O	80	.244	
1950 CLE A O	57	.178	
1951 CLE A H	1	.000	
BLTR	701	.255	

TUCKEY, THOMAS H. (TABASCO TOM)
B.OCT.7,1883 CONNECTICUT
D.OCT.17,1950 NEW YORK,N.Y.
1908 BOS N P	8	3- 3	
1909 BOS N P	17	0- 9	
TL	25	3-12	

TUERO, OSCAR [MONZON]
B.DEC.17,1892 HAVANA,CUBA
1918 STL N P	11	12	1- 2
1919 STL N P		45	5- 7
1920 STL N P		2	0- 0
BRTR	58	59	6- 9

TURBEVILLE, GEORGE ELKINS
B.AUG.24,1914 TURBEVILLE,S.C.
1935 PHI A P	19	0- 3	
1936 PHI A P	12	2- 5	
1937 PHI A P	31	0- 4	
BRTL	62	2-12	

TURBIDY, JEREMIAH
B.JULY 4,1852 DUDLEY,MASS.
D.SEPT.5,1920 WEBSTER,MASS.
| 1884 KC U S | 12 | .279 | |

TURCHIN, EDWARD LAWRENCE (SMILEY)
B.FEB.10,1917 NEW YORK,N.Y.
| 1943 CLE A S-3 | 11 | .231 | |
| BRTR | | | |

TURGEON, EUGENE JOSEPH (PETE)
B.JAN.31,1897 MINNEAPOLIS,MINN.
D.JAN.24,1977 WICHITA FALLS,TEX
D.JAN.24,1977 WICHITA FALLS,TEX
| 1923 CHI N S | 3 | .167 | |
| BRTR | | | |

TURK, LUCAS NEWTON
(HARLEM) OR (CHIEF)
B.MAY 2,1898 HOMER,GA.
| 1922 WAS A P | 5 | 0- 0 | |
| BRTR | | | |

YR CL LEA POS	GP	G	REC

TURLEY, ROBERT LEE (BOB)
OR (BULLET BOB)
B.SEP.19,1930 TROY,ILL.
1951 STL A P	1	0- 1	
1953 STL A P	10	2- 6	
1954 STL A P	35	14-15	
1955 NY A P	36	17-13	
1956 NY A P	27	8- 4	
1957 NY A P	32	13+ 6	
1958 NY A P	33	21- 7	
1959 NY A P	33	8-11	
1960 NY A P	34	9- 3	
1961 NY A P	15	3- 5	
1962 NY A P	24	3- 3	
1963 LA A P	19	2- 7	
BOS A P	11	1- 4	
BRTR	310	101-85	

TURNER, EARL EDWIN
B.MAY 6,1923 PITTSFIELD,MASS.
1948 PIT N C	2	.000	
1950 PIT N C	40	.243	
BRTR	42	.240	

TURNER, GEORGE A. (TUCK)
B.FEB.13,1873 W.NEW BRIGHTON,N.Y.
D.JULY 16,1945 STATEN ISLAND,N.Y.
1893 PHI N O	35	.324	
1894 PHI N O	77	.423	
1895 PHI N O	48	.388	
1896 PHI N O	11	.231	
STL N O	48	.255	
1897 STL N O	102	.289	
1898 STL N O	34	.210	
BL	355	.325	

TURNER, JAMES RILEY (MILKMAN)
B.AUG.6,1903 ANTIOCH,TENN.
1937 BOS N P	33	39	20-11
1938 BOS N P		35	14-18
1939 BOS N P		25	4-11
1940 CIN N P	24	25	14- 7
1941 CIN N P		23	6- 4
1942 CIN N P		3	0- 0
NY A P		5	1- 1
1943 NY A P		18	3- 0
1944 NY A P		35	4- 4
1945 NY A P		30	3- 4
BLTR	231	238	69-60

TURNER, JOHN WEBBER (JERRY)
B.JAN.17,1954 TEXARKANA,ARK.
1974 SD N O	17	.292	
1975 SD N /O	11	.273	
1976 SD N O	105	.267	
1977 SD N O	118	.246	
1978 SD N O	106	.280	
BLTL	357	.265	

TURNER, KENNETH CHARLES (KEN)
B.AUG.17,1943 FRAMINGHAM,MASS.
| 1967 CAL A P | 13 | 1- 2 | |
| BRTL | | | |

TURNER, ROBERT EDWARD (TED)
B.NOV.19,1938 CINCINNATI,OHIO
NON-PLAYING MANAGER
ATL[N] 1977 [ONE GAME]

TURNER, TERRENCE LAMONT
(TERRY) OR (COTTON TOP)
B.FEB.28,1881 SANDY LAKE,PA.
D.JULY 18,1960 CLEVELAND,OHIO
1901 PIT N 3	2	.428	
1904 CLE A S	111	.236	
1905 CLE A S	154	.263	
1906 CLE A S	147	.291	
1907 CLE A S	142	.242	
1908 CLE A S-O	60	.239	
1909 CLE A 2-S	53	.250	
1910 CLE A S-3	150	.230	
1911 CLE A 3	117	.252	
1912 CLE A 3	103	.308	
1913 CLE A 2-S-3	120	.248	
1914 CLE A 2-3	120	.243	
1915 CLE A 2-3	75	.252	
1916 CLE A 2-3	124	.262	
1917 CLE A 2-3	69	.205	
1918 CLE A 2-3	74	.249	
1919 PHI A S	38	.189	
BRTR	1659	.256	

TURNER, THEODORE HOLHOT
B.MAY 4,1892 LAWRENCEBURG,KY.
D.FEB.4,1958 LEXINGTON,KY.
| 1920 CHI N P | 1 | 0- 0 | |
| BRTR | | | |

TURNER, THOMAS LOVATT (TINK)
B.FEB.20,1890 SWARTHMORE,PA.
D.FEB.25,1962 PHILADELPHIA,PA.
| 1915 PHI A P | 1 | 0- 1 | |
| BRTR | | | |

TURNER, THOMAS RICHARD
B.SEPT.8,1916 CUSTER CO.,OKLA.

YR	CL	LEA	POS	GP	G	REC
1940	CHI	A	C		37	.208
1941	CHI	A	C		38	.238
1942	CHI	A	C		56	.242
1943	CHI	A	C		51	.240
1944	CHI	A	C		36	.230
	STL	A	C		15	.320
	BRTR				233	.237

TUTTLE, WILLIAM ROBERT (BILL)
B.JULY 4,1929 ELWOOD,ILL.

YR	CL	LEA	POS	GP	G	REC
1952	DET	A	O		7	.240
1954	DET	A	O		147	.266
1955	DET	A	O		154	.279
1956	DET	A	O		140	.253
1957	DET	A	O		133	.251
1958	KC	A	O		148	.231
1959	KC	A	O		126	.300
1960	KC	A	O		151	.256
1961	KC	A	O		25	.262
	MIN	A	2-3-O		113	.246
1962	MIN	A	O		110	.210
1963	MIN	A	O		16	.000
	BRTR				1270	.259

TUTWILER, ELMER STRANGE
B.NOV.19,1905 CARBON HILL,ALA.
D.MAY 3,1976 PENSACOLA,FLA.

YR	CL	LEA	POS	GP	G	REC
1928	PIT	N	P		2	0- 0

TUTWILER, GUY ISBELL
(GUY) OR (KING TUT)
B.JULY 17,1889 COALBURG,ALA.
D.AUG.19,1930 BIRMINGHAM,ALA.

YR	CL	LEA	POS	GP	G	REC
1911	DET	A	2-O		13	.186
1913	DET	A	1		14	.191
	BLTR				27	.190

TWINEHAM, ARTHUR W. (OLD HOSS)
B.NOV.26,1866 GALESBURG,ILL.

YR	CL	LEA	POS	GP	G	REC
1893	STL	N	C		14	.325
1894	STL	N	C		31	.314
	BLTR				45	.317

TWINING, HOWARD EARLE
(TWINK) OR (DOC)
B.MAY 30,1894 HORSHAM,PA.
D.JUNE 14,1973 LANSDALE,PA.

YR	CL	LEA	POS	GP	G	REC
1916	CIN	N	P		1	0- 0
	BRTR					

TWITCHELL, LAWRENCE GRANT
B.FEB.18,1864 CLEVELAND,OHIO
D.APR.23,1930 CLEVELAND,OHIO

YR	CL	LEA	POS	GP	G	REC
1886	DET	N	P		4	2- 2
1887	DET	N	P-O	11	63	10- 1
						.352
1888	DET	N	O		130	.244
1889	CLE	N	O		134	.275
1890	CLE	P	P-O	3	56	0- 0
						.224
	8UF	P	P-O	12	44	5- 7
						.216
1891	COL	AA	P-O	2	57	1- 1
						.275
1892	WAS	N	O		51	.221
1893	LOU	N	O		45	.331
1894	LOU	N	O		51	.265
	BRTR			32	635	18-11
						.266

TWITCHELL, WAYNE LEE
B.MAR.10,1948 PORTLAND,ORE.

YR	CL	LEA	POS	GP	G	REC
1970	MIL	A	/P		2	0- 0
1971	PHI	N	/P		6	1- 0
1972	PHI	N	P		49	5- 9
1973	PHI	N	P		34	13- 9
1974	PHI	N	P		25	6- 9
1975	PHI	N	P		36	5-10
1976	PHI	N	P		26	3- 1
1977	PHI	N	P		12	0- 5
	MON	N	P		22	6- 5
1978	MON	N	P		33	4-12
	BRTR				245	43-60

TWOMBLY, CLARENCE EDWARD (BABE)
B.JAN.18,1896 JAMAICA PLAIN,MASS.
D.NOV.23,1974 SAN CLEMENTE,CAL.

YR	CL	LEA	POS	GP	G	REC
1920	CHI	N	O		78	.235
1921	CHI	N	O		87	.377
	BLTR				165	.304

TWOMBLY, EDWIN PARKER (CY)
B.JUNE 15,1897 GROVELAND,MASS.
D.DEC.3,1974 SAVANNAH,GA.

YR	CL	LEA	POS	GP	G	REC
1921	CHI	A	P			1- 2
	BLTL					

TWOMBLY, GEORGE FREDERICK
(SILENT GEORGE)
B.JUNE 4,1692 BOSTON,MASS.
D.FEB.17,1975 LEXINGTON,MASS.

YR	CL	LEA	POS	GP	G	REC
1914	CIN	N	O		68	.233
1915	CIN	N	O		46	.197
1916	CIN	N	O		3	.000
1917	BOS	N	O		32	.186
1919	WAS	A	O		1	.000
	BRTR				150	.211

TYACK, JAMES FREDERICK
B.JAN.9,1911 FLORENCE,MONT.

YR	CL	LEA	POS	GP	G	REC
1943	PHI	A	O		54	.258
	BLTR					

TYLER, FREDERICK FRANKLIN (CLANCY)
B.DEC.16,1891 DERRY,N.H.
D.OCT.14,1945 E.DERRY,N.H.

YR	CL	LEA	POS	GP	G	REC
1914	BOS	N	C		6	.105
	TR					

TYLER, GEORGE ALBERT (LEFTY)
B.DEC.14,1889 DERRY,N.H.
D.SEPT.29,1953 LOWELL,MASS.

YR	CL	LEA	POS	GP	G	REC
1910	BOS	N	P		4	0- 0
1911	BOS	N	P		28	7-10
1912	BOS	N	P		42	12-22
1913	BOS	N	P	39	43	16-17
1914	BOS	N	P		38	16-14
1915	BOS	N	P	32	45	10- 9
1916	BOS	N	P	34	39	17-10
1917	BOS	N	P	32	61	14-12
1918	CHI	N	P	33	38	19- 8
1919	CHI	N	P		6	2- 2
1920	CHI	N	P	27	29	11-12
1921	CHI	N	P	10	19	3- 2
	BLTL			325	392	127-118

TYLER, JOHN ANTHONY (JOHNNIE)
(TY TY) OR (KATZ)
[REAL NAME JOHN TYLKA]
B.JULY 30,1906 MT.PLEASANT,PA.
D.JULY 11,1972 MT.PLEASANT,PA.

YR	CL	LEA	POS	GP	G	REC
1934	BOS	N	O		3	.167
1935	BOS	N	O		13	.340
	BBTR				16	.321

TYLKA, JOHN
[PLAYED UNDER NAME OF
JOHN ANTHONY TYLER]

TYNG, JAMES ALEXANDER
B.MAY 27,1856 PHILADELPHIA,PA.
D.OCT.30,1931 NEW YORK,N.Y.

YR	CL	LEA	POS	GP	G	REC
1879	BOS	N	P		3	1- 2
1888	PHI	N	P		1	0- 0
					4	1- 2

TYREE, EARL CARLTON (TY)
B.MAR.4,1890 HUNTSVILLE,ILL.
D.MAY 17,1954 RUSHVILLE,ILL.

YR	CL	LEA	POS	GP	G	REC
1914	CHI	N	C		1	.000
	BRTR					

TYRIVER, DAVID BURTON
B.OCT.31,1937 OSHKOSH,WIS.

YR	CL	LEA	POS	GP	G	REC
1962	CLE	A	P		4	0- 0
	BRTR					

TYRONE, JAMES VERNON (JIM)
B.JAN.29,1949 ALICE,TEX.

YR	CL	LEA	POS	GP	G	REC
1972	CHI	N	/O		13	.000
1974	CHI	N	O/3		57	.185
1975	CHI	N	/O		11	.227
1977	OAK	A	O/1-S		96	.245
	BRTR				177	.227

TYRONE, OSCAR WAYNE (WAYNE)
B.AUG.1,1950 ALICE,TEX.

YR	CL	LEA	POS	GP	G	REC
1976	CHI	N	/O-1-3		30	.228
	BRTR					

TYSON, ALBERT THOMAS (TY)
B.JUNE 1,1892 WILKES-BARRE,PA.
D.AUG.16,1953 BUFFALO,N.Y.

YR	CL	LEA	POS	GP	G	REC
1926	NY	N	O		97	.293
1927	NY	N	O		43	.264
1928	BRO	N	O		59	.271
	BRTR				199	.280

TYSON, CECIL WASHINGTON
(TURKEY) OR (SLIM)
B.DEC.6,1914 ELM CITY,N.C.

YR	CL	LEA	POS	GP	G	REC
1944	PHI	N	H		1	.000
	BLTR					

TYSON, MICHAEL RAY (MIKE)
B.JAN.13,1950 ROCKY MOUNT,N.C.

YR	CL	LEA	POS	GP	G	REC
1972	STL	N	2/S		13	.189
1973	STL	N	*S-2		144	.243
1974	STL	N	*S-2		151	.223
1975	STL	N	S-2/3		122	.246
1976	STL	N	2		76	.286
1977	STL	N	*2		138	.246
1978	STL	N	*2		125	.233
	BRTR				769	.246
	BB 1972					

UCHRINSCKO, JAMES EMERSON
B.OCT.20,1900 W.NEWTON,PA.

YR	CL	LEA	POS	GP	G	REC
1926	WAS	A	P		3	0- 0
	BLTR					

UECKER, ROBERT GEORGE (BOB)
B.JAN.26,1935 MILWAUKEE,WIS.

YR	CL	LEA	POS	GP	G	REC
1962	MIL	N	C		33	.250
1963	MIL	N	C		13	.250
1964	STL	N	C		40	.198
1965	STL	N	C		53	.228
1966	PHI	N	C		78	.208
1967	PHI	N	C		18	.171
	ATL	N	C		62	.146
	BRTR				297	.200

UHALT, BERNARD BARTHOLOMEW (FRENCHY)
B.APR.27,1910 BAKERSFIELD,CAL.

YR	CL	LEA	POS	GP	G	REC
1934	CHI	A	O		57	.242
	BLTR					

UHLAENDER, THEODORE OTTO (TED)
B.OCT.21,1940 CHICAGO, HEIGHTS,ILL.

YR	CL	LEA	POS	GP	G	REC
1965	MIN	A	/O		13	.182
1966	MIN	A	*O		105	.226
1967	MIN	A	*O		133	.258
1968	MIN	A	*O		140	.283
1969	MIN	A	*O		152	.273
1970	CLE	A	*O		141	.268
1971	CLE	A	*O		141	.288
1972	CIN	N	O		73	.159
	BLTR				898	.263

UHLE, GEORGE ERNEST (THE BULL)
B.SEPT.18,1898 CLEVELAND,OHIO

YR	CL	LEA	POS	GP	G	REC
1919	CLE	A	P		26	10- 5
1920	CLE	A	P		27	4- 5
1921	CLE	A	P	41	48	16-13
1922	CLE	A	P	50	56	22-16
1923	CLE	A	P	54	58	26-16
1924	CLE	A	P	28	59	9-15
1925	CLE	A	P	29	55	13-11
1926	CLE	A	P	39	50	27-11
1927	CLE	A	P	25	43	8- 9
1928	CLE	A	P	31	55	12-17
1929	DET	A	P	32	40	15-11
1930	DET	A	P	33	59	12-12
1931	DET	A	P	29	53	11-12
1932	DET	A	P	33	38	6- 6
1933	DET	A	P		1	0- 0
	NY	N	P	6	8	1- 1
	NY	A	P		12	6- 1
1934	NY	A	P		10	2- 4
1936	CLE	A	P	7	24	0- 1
	BRTR			513	722	200-166
						.288

UHLE, ROBERT ELLWOOD
(BOB) OR (LEFTY)
B.SEPT.17,1913 SAN FRANCISCO,CAL.

YR	CL	LEA	POS	GP	G	REC
1938	CHI	A	P		1	0- 0
1940	DET	A	P		1	0- 0
	BBTL				2	0- 0

UHLER, MAURICE W.
B.DEC.14,1886 PIKESVILLE,MD.
D.MAY 4,1918 BALTIMORE,MD.

YR	CL	LEA	POS	GP	G	REC
1914	CIN	N	O		46	.214
	BRTR					

UHLIR, CHARLES
B.JULY 30,1912 CHICAGO,ILL.

YR	CL	LEA	POS	GP	G	REC
1934	CHI	A	O		14	.148
	BLTL					

ULATOWSKI, CLEMENT LAMBERT
[PLAYED UNDER NAME OF
CLEMENT LAMBERT CLEMENS]

ULISNEY, MICHAEL EDWARD
(MIKE) OR (SLUGS)
B.SEPT.28,1917 GREENWALD,PA.

YR	CL	LEA	POS	GP	G	REC
1945	BOS	N	C		11	.389
	BRTR					

ULLRICH, CARLOS SANTIAGO
(CASTELLO) (SANDY)
B.JULY 25,1921 HAVANA,CUBA

YR	CL	LEA	POS	GP	G	REC
1944	WAS	A	P		3	0- 0
1945	WAS	A	P		28	3- 3
	BRTR				31	3- 3

ULRICH, FRANK W. (DUTCH)
B.NOV.18,1899 BALTIMORE,MD.
D.FEB.11,1929 BALTIMORE,MD.

YR	CL	LEA	POS	GP	G	REC
1925	PHI	N	P		21	3- 3
1926	PHI	N	P		45	16-13
1927	PHI	N	P		32	8-11
	BRTR				98	19-27

ULRICH, GEORGE F.
B.PHILADELPHIA,PA.

YR	CL	LEA	POS	GP	G	REC
1892	WAS	N	S		6	.291
1893	CIN	N	O		1	.000
1896	NY	N	O		14	.178
					21	.208

YR	CL	LEA	POS	GP	G	REC

UMBACH, ARNOLD WILLIAM
B.DEC.6,1942 WILLIAMSBURG,VA.
1964	MIL	N	P		1	1- 0
1966	ATL	N	P		22	0- 2
			BRTR		23	1- 2

UMBARGER, JAMES HAROLD (JIM)
B.FEB.17,1953 BURBANK,CAL.
1975	TEX	A	P		56	8- 7
1976	TEX	A	P		30	10-12
1977	OAK	A	P		12	1- 5
	TEX	A	/P		3	1- 1
1978	TEX	A	P		32	5- 8
			BLTL		133	25-33

UMBRICHT, JAMES (JIM)
B.SEP.17,1930 CHICAGO,ILL.
D.APR.8,1964 HOUSTON,TEX.
1959	PIT	N	P		1	0- 0
1960	PIT	N	P		17	1- 2
1961	PIT	N	P		1	0- 0
1962	HOU	N	P		34	4- 0
1963	HOU	N	P		35	4- 3
			BRTR		88	9- 5

UMPHLETT, THOMAS MULLEN (TOM)
B.MAY 12,1930 SCOTLAND NECK,N.C
1953	BOS	A	O		137	.283
1954	WAS	A	1-O		114	.219
1955	WAS	A	O		110	.217
			BRTR		361	.246

UNDERHILL, WILLIE VERN
B.SEPT.6,1904 YOWELL,TEX.
D.OCT.26,1970 BAY CITY,TEX.
1927	CLE	A	P		4	0- 2
1928	CLE	A	P		11	1- 2
			BRTR		15	1- 4

UNDERWOOD, FRED G.
B.1869 KANSAS
D.JAN.26,1906 KANSAS CITY,MO.
| 1894 | BRO | N | P | | 7 | 2- 3 |

UNDERWOOD, THOMAS GERALD (TOM)
B.DEC.22,1953 KOKOMO,IND.
1974	PHI	N	/P		7	1- 0
1975	PHI	N	P		35	14-13
1976	PHI	N	P	33	34	10- 5
1977	PHI	N	P		14	3- 2
	STL	N	P		19	6- 9
1978	TOR	A	P		31	6-14
			BRTL	139	140	40-43

UNGLAUB, ROBERT ALEXANDER
B.JULY 31,1881 BALTIMORE,MD.
D.NOV.29,1916 BALTIMORE,MD.
1904	NY	A	3		6	.211
	BOS	A	3		7	.182
1905	BOS	A	3		43	.223
1907	BOS	A	M-1		139	.255
1908	BOS	A	1		72	.262
	WAS	A	1		72	.307
1909	WAS	A	1-2-O		130	.264
1910	WAS	A	1		124	.234
			BRTR		593	.258

UNSER, ALBERT BERNARD (AL)
B.OCT.12,1912 MORRISONVILLE,ILL
1942	DET	A	C		4	.375
1943	DET	A	C		38	.248
1944	DET	A	C-2		11	.120
1945	CIN	N	C		67	.265
			BRTR		120	.252

UNSER, DELBERT BERNARD (DEL)
B.DEC.9,1944 DECATUR,ILL.
1968	WAS	A	*O/1		156	.230
1969	WAS	A	*O		153	.286
1970	WAS	A	*O		119	.258
1971	WAS	A	*O		153	.255
1972	CLE	A	*O		132	.238
1973	PHI	N	*O		136	.289
1974	PHI	N	*O		142	.264
1975	NY	N	*O		147	.294
1976	NY	N	O		77	.228
	MON	N	O		69	.227
1977	MON	N	O-1		113	.273
1978	MON	N	1-O		130	.196
			BLTL		1527	.258

UPCHURCH, JEFFERSON WOODROW (WOODY)
B.APR.13,1911 BUIES CREEK,N.C.
D.OCT.23,1971 BUIES CREEK,N.C.
1935	PHI	A	P		3	0- 2
1936	PHI	A	P		7	0- 2
			BRTL		10	0- 4

UPHAM, JOHN LESLIE
B.DEC.29,1941 WINDSOR,ONT.,CAN.
1967	CHI	N	/P		5	8	0- 1
1968	CHI	N	/P-O	2	13	0- 0
						.200
			BLTL	7	21	0- 1
						.308

UPHAM, WILLIAM LAWRENCE
B.APR.4,1888 AKRON,OHIO
D.SEPT.14,1959 NEWARK,N.J.
1915	BRO	F	P		33	6- 8
1918	BOS	N	P		3	1- 1
			BBTR		36	7- 9

UPP, GEORGE HENRY (JERRY)
B.DEC.10,1883 SANDUSKY,OHIO
D.JUNE 30,1937 SANDUSKY,OHIO
| 1909 | CLE | A | P | | 7 | 2- 1 |
| | | | TL | | | |

UPRIGHT, ROY T. (DIXIE)
B.MAY 30,1926 KANNAPOLIS,N.C.
| 1953 | STL | A | H | | 9 | .250 |
| | | | BLTL | | | |

UPSHAW, CECIL LEE
B.OCT.22,1942 SPEARSVILLE,LA.
1966	ATL	N	/P		1	0- 0
1967	ATL	N	P		30	2- 3
1968	ATL	N	P		52	8- 7
1969	ATL	N	P		62	6- 4
1971	ATL	N	P		49	11- 6
1972	ATL	N	P		42	3- 5
1973	ATL	N	/P		5	0- 1
	HOU	N	P		35	2- 3
1974	CLE	A	/P		7	0- 1
	NY	A	P		36	1- 5
1975	CHI	A	P		29	1- 1
			BRTR		348	34-36

UPSHAW, WILLIE CLAY
B.APR.27,1957 BLANCO,TEX.
| 1978 | TOR | A | O-0-1 | | 95 | .237 |
| | | | BLTL | | | |

UPTON, THOMAS HERBERT (TOM) OR (MUSCLES)
B.DEC.29,1926 ESTER,MO.
1950	STL	A	2-S-3		124	.237
1951	STL	A	S		52	.198
1952	WAS	A	S		5	.000
			BRTR		181	.225

UPTON, WILLIAM RAY
B.JULY 18,1929 ESTHER,MO.
| 1954 | PHI | A | P | | 2 | 0- 0 |
| | | | BRTR | | | |

URBAN, JACK ELMER
B.DEC.5,1928 OMAHA,NEB.
1957	KC	A	P	31	37	7- 4
1958	KC	A	P	30	31	8-11
1959	STL	N	P		8	0- 0
			BRTR	69	76	15-15

URBAN, LOUIS JOHN (LUKE)
B.MAR.22,1898 FALL RIVER,MASS.
1927	BOS	N	C		35	.288
1928	BOS	N	C		15	.176
			BRTR		50	.273

URBANSKI, WILLIAM MICHAEL (BILLY)
B.JUNE 5,1903 LINOLEUMVILLE,N.Y
D.JULY 12,1973 PERTH AMBOY,N.J.
1931	BOS	N	S-3		82	.238
1932	BOS	N	S		136	.272
1933	BOS	N	S		144	.251
1934	BOS	N	S		146	.293
1935	BOS	N	S		132	.229
1936	BOS	N	S-3		122	.261
1937	BOS	N	H		1	.000
			BRTR		763	.260

URREA, JOHN GODOY
B.FEB.9,1955 LOS ANGELES,CAL.
1977	STL	N	P		41	7- 6
1978	STL	N	P		27	4- 9
			BRTR		68	11-15

URY, LOUIS NETOWN (LON) OR (OLD SLEEP)
B.1877 FT.SCOTT,KAN.
D.MAR.4,1918 KANSAS CITY,MO.
| 1903 | STL | N | 1 | | 2 | .142 |
| | | | TR | | | |

USHER, ROBERT ROYCE (BOB)
B.MAR.1,1925 SAN DIEGO,CAL.
1946	CIN	N	3-O		92	.204
1947	CIN	N	O		9	.182
1950	CIN	N	O		106	.259
1951	CIN	N	O		114	.208
1952	CHI	N	H		1	.000
1957	CLE	A	3-O		10	.125
	WAS	A	O		96	.261
			BRTR		428	.235

USSAT, WILLIAM AUGUST (DUTCH)
B.APR.11,1904 DAYTON,OHIO
D.MAY 29,1959 DAYTON,OHIO
1925	CLE	A	2		1	.000
1927	CLE	A	3		4	.187
			BRTR		5	.187

VACHE, ERNEST LEWIS (TEX)
B.NOV.17,1895 SANTA MONICA,CAL.
D.JUNE 11,1953 LOS ANGELES,CAL.
| 1925 | BOS | A | O | | 110 | .313 |
| | | | BRTR | | | |

VADEBONCOEUR, EUGENE F.
B.SYRACUSE,N.Y.
D.OCT.16,1935 HAVERHILL,MASS.
| 1884 | PHI | N | C | | 4 | .214 |

VAHRENHORST, HARRY HENRY (VAN)
B.FEB.13,1885 ST.LOUIS,MO.
D.OCT.10,1943 ST.LOUIS,MO.
| 1904 | STL | A | H | | 1 | .000 |
| | | | BRTR | | | |

VAIL, MICHAEL LEWIS (MIKE)
B.NOV.19,1951 SAN FRANCISCO,CAL.
1975	NY	N	O		38	.302
1976	NY	N	O		53	.217
1977	NY	N	O		108	.262
1978	CLE	A	/O		14	.235
	CHI	N	O/3		74	.333
			BRTR		287	.277

VAIL, ROBERT GARFIELD (DOC)
B.SEPT.24,1881 LINNEUS,MAINE
D.MAY 26,1948 PITTSBURGH,PA.
| 1908 | PIT | N | P | | 4 | 1- 2 |

VALDES, ARMANDO VIERA
B.MAY 2,1922 CARDENAS,CUBA
| 1944 | WAS | A | H | | 1 | .000 |
| | | | BRTR | | | |

VALDES, RENE (GUTIERREZ)
B.JUNE 2,1929 GUANABACOA,CUBA
| 1957 | BRO | N | P | | 5 | 1- 1 |
| | | | BRTR | | | |

VALDESPINO, HILARIO [BORROTO] (SANDY)
B.JAN.14,1939 SAN JOSE DE LAS LAJAS, CUBA
1965	MIN	A	O		108	.261
1966	MIN	A	O		52	.176
1967	MIN	A	O		99	.165
1968	ATL	N	O		36	.233
1969	HOU	N	O		41	.244
	SEA	A	/O		20	.211
1970	MIL	A	/O		8	.000
1971	KC	A	O		18	.317
			BLTL		382	.230

VALDIVIELSO, JOSE [LOPEZ]
B.MAY 22,1934 MATANZAS,CUBA
1955	WAS	A	S		94	.221
1956	WAS	A	S		90	.236
1959	WAS	A	S		24	.286
1960	WAS	A	S-3		117	.213
1961	MIN	A	2-S-3		76	.195
			BRTR		401	.219

VALENTINE, ELLIS CLARENCE
B.JULY 30,1954 HELENA,ARK.
1975	MON	N	O		12	.364
1976	MON	N	O		94	.279
1977	MON	N	*O		127	.293
1978	MON	N	*O		151	.289
			BRTR		384	.290

VALENTINE, FRED LEE (FRED) OR (SQUEAKY)
B.JAN.19,1935 CLARKSDALE,MISS.
1959	BAL	A	O		12	.316
1963	BAL	A	O		26	.268
1964	WAS	A	O		102	.228
1965	WAS	A	O		12	.241
1966	WAS	A	*O/1		146	.276
1967	WAS	A	*O		151	.234
1968	WAS	A	O		37	.238
	BAL	A	O		47	.247
			BBTR		533	.247

VALENTINE, HAROLD LEWIS (CORKY)
B.JAN.4,1929 TROY,OHIO
1954	CIN	N	P		36	12-11
1955	CIN	N	P		10	2- 1
			BRTR		46	14-12

VALENTINE, JOHN G.
B.NOV.21,1855 BROOKLYN,N.Y.
| 1883 | COL | AA | P-O | | 15 | 2- 9 |
| | | | | | | .294 |

VALENTINE, ROBERT
| 1876 | MUT | N | C | | 1 | .000 |

```
YR   CL LEA POS      GP   G   REC

VALENTINE, ROBERT JOHN (BOBBY)
8.MAY 13,195G STAMFORD,CONN.
1969 LA  N  R            5   .000
1971 LA  N  S-3-2-O    101   .249
1972 LA  N  2-3-0-S    119   .274
1973 CAL A  S/O         32   .302
1974 CAL A  O-S-3/2    117   .261
1975 CAL A  3-O/1-O     26   .281
     SD  N  /O           7   .133
1976 SD  N  O/1         15   .367
1977 SD  N  S-3/1       44   .179
1977 NY  N  1-S/3       42   .133
1978 NY  N  2/3         69   .269
     BRTR             577   .259

VALENTINETTI, VITO JOHN
B.SEPT.16,1928 W.NEW YORK,N.J.
1954 CHI A  P           1   0-0
1956 CHI A  P          42   6-4
1957 CHI N  P           9   0-0
     CLE A  P          11   2-2
1958 DET A  P          15   1-0
     WAS A  P          23   4-6
1959 WAS A  P           7   0-2
     BRTR            108   13-14

VALENZUELA, BENJAMIN BELTRAN
(BENNY) OR (PAPELERO)
B.JUNE 2,1933 LOS MOCHIS,MEXICO
1958 STL N  3          10   .214
     BRTR

VALESTIN, EDWARD JOSEPH
[PLAYED UNDER NAME OF
EDWARD JOSEPH FALLENSTEIN]

VALLE, HECTOR JOSE
B.OCT.27,1940 VEGA BAJA,P.R.
1965 LA  N  /C          9   .308
     BRTR

VALO, ELMER WILLIAM
B.MAR.5,1921 RIBNIK,CZECH.
1940 PHI A  O           6   .348
1941 PHI A  O          15   .420
1942 PHI A  O         133   .251
1943 PHI A  O          77   .221
1946 PHI A  O         108   .307
1947 PHI A  O         112   .300
1948 PHI A  O         113   .305
1949 PHI A  O         150   .283
1950 PHI A  O         129   .280
1951 PHI A  O         123   .302
1952 PHI A  O         129   .281
1953 PHI A  O          50   .224
1954 PHI A  O          95   .214
1955 KC  A  O         112   .364
1956 KC  A  O           9   .222
     PHI N  O          98   .289
1957 BRO N  O          81   .273
1958 LA  N  O          65   .248
1959 CLE A  O          34   .292
1960 NY  A  O           8   .000
     WAS A  O          76   .281
1961 MIN A  O          33   .156
     PHI N  O          50   .186
     BRTR           1806   .282

VAN ALSTYNE, CLAYTON EMORY (SPIKE)
B.MAY 24,1900 STUYVESANT,N.Y.
D.JAN.5,1960 HUDSON,N.Y.
1927 WAS A  P           2   0-0
1928 WAS A  P           4   0-0
     BRTR              6   0-0

VAN ATTA, RUSSELL (SHERIFF)
B.JUNE 12,1906 AUGUSTA,N.J.
1933 NY  A  P          26   12-4
1934 NY  A  P          28   3-5
1935 NY  A  P           5   0-0
     STL A  P          53   9-16
1936 STL A  P     52   53   4-7
1937 STL A  P          16   1-2
1938 STL A  P          25   4-7
1939 STL A  P           2   0-0
     BLTL        207  208  33-41

VAN BRABANT, CAMILLE OSCAR (OZZIE)
B.SEPT.28,1926 KINGSVILLE,ONT.,
CANADA
1954 PHI A  P           9   0-2
1955 KC  A  P           2   0-0
     BRTR             11   0-2

VAN BUREN, EDWARD EUGENE (DEACON)
B.DEC.14,1870 LA SALLE CO.,ILL.
D.JUNE 29,1957 PORTLAND,ORE.
1904 BRO N  O           1  1.000
     PHI N  O          12   .233
     BLTR             13   .250

VAN CAMP, ALBERT JOSEPH
B.SEPT.7,1903 MOLINE,ILL.
1928 CLE A  1           5   .235
1931 BOS A  1-O       101   .275
1932 BOS A  1          34   .223
     BRTR            140   .261


VANCE, CLARENCE ARTHUR (DAZZY)
B.MAR.4,1891 ORIENT,IOWA
D.FEB.16,1961 HOMOSASSA SPRINGS FLA
1915 PIT N  P           1   0-1
     NY  A  P           8   0-3
1918 NY  A  P           2   0-0
1922 BRO N  P          36   18-12
1923 BRO N  P          37   18-15
1924 BRO N  P          35   28-6
1925 BRO N  P          31   22-9
1926 BRO N  P          22   9-10
1927 BRO N  P          34   16-15
1928 BRO N  P          38   22-10
1929 BRO N  P          31   14-13
1930 BRO N  P          35   17-15
1931 BRO N  P          30   11-13
1932 BRO N  P          27   12-11
1933 STL N  P          28   6-2
1934 CIN N  P           6   0-2
     STL N  P          19   1-1
1935 BRO N  P          20   3-2
     BRTR            440  197-140

VANCE, GENE COVINGTON (SANDY)
B.JAN.5,1947 LAMAR,COLO.
1970 LA  N  P          20   7-7
1971 LA  N  P          10   2-1
     BRTR             30   9-8

VANCE, JOSEPH ALBERT (SANDY)
B.SEPT.16,1905 DEVINE,TEX.
D.JULY 4,1978 DEVINE,TEX.
1935 CHI A  P          10   2-2
1937 NY  A  P           2   1-0
1938 NY  A  P      3    4   0-0
     BRTR         15   16   3-2

VAN CUYK, CHRISTIAN GERALD (CHRIS)
B.MAR.1,1927 KIMBERLY,WIS.
1950 BRO N  P          12   1-3
1951 BRO N  P           9   1-2
1952 BRO N  P          23   5-6
     BLTL             44   7-11

VAN CUYK, JOHN HENRY (JOHNNY)
B.JULY 7,1921 LITTLE CHUTE,WIS.
1947 BRO N  P           2   0-0
1948 BRO N  P           3   0-0
1949 BRO N  P           2   0-0
     BLTL              7   0-0

VANDAGRIFT, CARL WILLIAM
B.APR.22,1883 CANTRALL,ILL.
D.OCT.9,1920 FORT WAYNE,IND.
1914 IND F  2          42   .246
     BRTR

VANDEMANN, FREDERICK H.
[PLAYED UNDER NAME OF
FREDERICK H. ABBOTT]

VANDENBERG, HAROLD HARRIS (HY)
B.MAR.17,1907 ABILENE,KAN.
1935 BOS A  P           3   0-0
1937 NY  N  P           1   0-1
1938 NY  N  P           6   0-1
1939 NY  N  P           2   0-0
1940 NY  N  P          13   1-1
1944 CHI N  P          35   7-4
1945 CHI N  P          30   7-3
     BRTR             90   15-10

VANDER MEER, JOHN SAMUEL
(JOHNNY), (DOUBLE NO-HIT)
OR (THE DUTCH MASTER)
B.NOV.2,1914 PROSPECT PARK,N.J.
1937 CIN N  P     19   21   3-5
1938 CIN N  P     32   33   15-10
1939 CIN N  P          30   5-9
1940 CIN N  P     10   12   3-1
1941 CIN N  P     33   33   16-13
1942 CIN N  P     33   37   18-12
1943 CIN N  P     36   40   15-16
1946 CIN N  P     29   33   10-12
1947 CIN N  P          30   9-14
1948 CIN N  P     33   41   17-14
1949 CIN N  P     28   33   5-4
1950 CHI N  P     32   35   3-4
1951 CLE A  P           1   0-1
     8BTL        346  382  119-121

VAN DUSEN, FREDERICK WILLIAM (FRED)
B.JULY 31,1937 JACKSON HEIGHTS,N.Y.
1955 PHI N  H           1   .000
     BL

VAN DYKE, BENJAMIN HARRISON
B.AUG.15,1888 CLINTONVILLE,PA.
D.OCT.22,1973 SARASOTA,FLA.
1909 PHI N  P           2   0-0
1912 BOS A  P           3   1-0
     BRTL              5   1-0


VAN DYKE, WILLIAM JENNINGS
B.DEC.15,1863 PARIS,ILL.
D.MAY 9,1933 EL PASO,TEX.
1890 TOL AA O         128   .266
1892 STL N  O           3   .000
1893 BOS N  O           3   .250
     BRTR            134   .262

VANGILDER, ELAM RUSSELL
B.APR.23,1896 CAPE GIRARDEAU,MO
D.APR.30,1977 CAPE GIRARDEAU,MO
1919 STL A  P           3   1-0
1920 STL A  P          24   3-8
1921 STL A  P          31   11-12
1922 STL A  P     43   45   19-13
1923 STL A  P     41   45   16-17
1924 STL A  P          43   5-10
1925 STL A  P          52   14-8
1926 STL A  P          42   9-11
1927 STL A  P          44   10-12
1928 DET A  P          38   11-10
1929 DET A  P           6   0-1
     BRTR        367  373  99-102

VAN HALTREN, GEORGE EDWARD
MARTIN (GEORGE) OR (RIP)
B.MAR.30,1866 ST.LOUIS,MO.
D.SEPT.29,1945 OAKLAND,CAL.
1887 CHI N  P-O   19   44   12-7
                             .278
1888 CHI N  P-O   27   81   13-11
                             .283
1889 CHI N  O         134   .322
1890 BRO P  P-O   26   92   15-10
                             .346
1891 BAL AA M-P-   6  136   0-1
           S-O               .316
1892 BAL N  M-P-   4  135   0-0
           O                 .304
     PIT N  O          13   .212
1893 PIT N  O         123   .350
1894 NY  N  O         139   .333
1895 NY  N  P-O    1  131   0-0
                             .338
1896 NY  N  P-O    2  133   1-0
                             .353
1897 NY  N  O         131   .332
1898 NY  N  O         155   .315
1899 NY  N  O         153   .301
1900 NY  N  P-O    1  141   0-0
                             .319
1901 NY  N  O      1  133   0-1
                             .342
1902 NY  N  O          26   .250
1903 NY  N  O          75   .257
     BLTL         87 1975   41-30
                             .322

VANN, JOHN SILAS
B.JUNE 7,1893 FAIRLAND,OKLA.
D.JUNE 10,1958 SHREVEPORT,LA.
1913 STL N  H           1   .000
     BRTR

VAN NOY, JAY LOWELL
B.NOV.4,1928 GARLAND,UTAH
1951 STL N  O           6   .000
     BLTR

VAN ROBAYS, MAURICE RENE (BOMBER)
B.NOV.15,1914 DETROIT,MICH.
D.MAR.1,1965 DETROIT,MICH.
1939 PIT N  O          27   .314
1940 PIT N  1-O       145   .273
1941 PIT N  O         129   .282
1942 PIT N  O         100   .232
1943 PIT N  O          69   .288
1946 PIT N  1-O        59   .212
     BRTR            529   .267

VAN ZANDT, CHARLES ISAAC (IKE)
B.1877 BROOKLYN,N.Y.
D.SEPT.14,1908 NASHUA,N.H.
1901 NY  N  P           3   0-0
1904 CHI N  O           3   .000
1905 STL A  O          94   .233
                3  100   0-0
                             .224

VAN ZANT, RICHARD
(DICK) OR (FOGHORN DICK)
B.RICHMOND,IND.
1888 CLE AA 3          10   .187

VARGA, ANDREW WILLIAM (ANDY)
B.DEC.11,1930 CHICAGO,ILL.
1950 CHI N  P           1   0-0
1951 CHI N  P           2   0-0
     BRTL              3   0-0

VARGAS, ROBERTO ENRIQUE
B.MAY 29,1929 SANTURCE,P.R.
1955 MIL N  P          25   0-0
     BLTL
```

YR	CL	LEA	POS	GP	G	REC

VARGUS, WILLIAM FAY
B.NOV.11,1899 N.SCITUATE,MASS.
1925 BOS N P 11 1- 1
1926 BOS N P 4 0- 0
BLTL 15 1- 1

VARNER, GLEN GANN (BUCK)
B.AUG.17,1930 HIXSON,TENN.
1952 WAS A O 2 .000
BLTR

VARNEY, LAWRENCE DELANO (DIKE)
B.AUG.9,1880 DOVER,N.H.
D.APR.23,1950 LONG ISLAND CITY,N.Y.
1902 CLE A P 3 2- 1

VARNEY, RICHARD FRED (PETE)
B.APR.10,1949 ROXBURY,MASS.
1973 CHI A /C 5 .060
1974 CHI A /C 9 .250
1975 CHI A C 36 .271
1976 CHI A C 14 .244
ATL N /C 5 .100
BRTR 69 .247

VASBINDER, MOSES CALHOUN (CAL)
B.JULY 19,1880 SCIO,OHIO
D.DEC.22,1950 CADIZ,OHIO
1902 CLE A P 2 0- 0
BRTR

VAUGHAN, CECIL PORTER
(PORTER) OR (LEFTY)
B.MAY 11,1919 STEVENSVILLE,VA.
1940 PHI A P 18 2- 9
1941 PHI A P 5 0- 2
1946 PHI A P 1 0- 0
BRTL 24 2-11

VAUGHAN, CHARLES WAYNE (CHARLIE)
B.OCT.6,1947 MERCEDES,TEX.
1966 ATL N /P 1 1- 0
1969 ATL N /P 1 0- 0
BRTL 2 1- 0

VAUGHAN, GLENN EDWARD
(GLENN) OR (SPARKY)
B.FEB.19,1944 COMPTON,CAL.
1963 HOU N S-3 9 .167
BBTR

VAUGHAN, JOSEPH FLOYD (ARKY)
B.MAR.9,1912 CLIFTY,ARK.
D.AUG.30,1952 EAGLEVILLE,CAL.
1932 PIT N S 129 .318
1933 PIT N S 152 .314
1934 PIT N S 149 .333
1935 PIT N S 137 .385
1936 PIT N S 156 .335
1937 PIT N S-0 126 .322
1938 PIT N S 148 .322
1939 PIT N S 152 .306
1940 PIT N S 156 .300
1941 PIT N S-3 106 .316
1942 BRO N 2-S-3 128 .277
1943 BRO N S-3 149 .305
1947 BRO N 3-0 64 .325
1948 BRO N 3-0 65 .244
BLTR 1817 .318

VAUGHN, CLARENCE LEROY (ROY)
B.SEPT.4,1911 SEDALIA,MO.
D.MAR.1,1937 MARTINSVILLE,VA.
1934 PHI A P 2 0- 0
BBTR

VAUGHN, FREDERICK THOMAS
(FRED) OR (MUSCLES)
B.OCT.18,1918 COALINGA,CAL.
D.MAR.2,1964 NEAR LAKE WALES,FLA.
1944 WAS A 2-3 23 .257
1945 WAS A 2-S 80 .235
BRTR 110 .242

VAUGHN, HARRY FRANCIS (FARMER)
B.MAR.1,1864 RURAL DALE,OHIO
D.FEB.21,1914 CINCINNATI,OHIO
1886 CIN AA C 1 .000
1888 LOU AA C-0 49 .203
1889 LOU AA C 90 .233
1890 NY P C 45 .248
1891 CIN AA P-C- 1 45 0- 0
          1-3-0 .255
MIL AA C-1 24 .330
1892 CIN N C 85 .257
1893 CIN N C-1-0 119 .299
1894 CIN N C 67 .309
1895 CIN N C 88 .305
1896 CIN N C-1 113 .297
1897 CIN N 1 50 .305
1898 CIN N 1 73 .303
1899 CIN N 1 28 .178
BRTR 1 877 0- 0
              .276

VAUGHN, JAMES LESLIE (HIPPO)
B.APR.9,1888 WEATHERFORD,TEX.
D.MAY 29,1966 CHICAGO,ILL.
1908 NY A P 2 0- 0
1910 NY A P 29 13-11
1911 NY A P 26 8-10
1912 NY A P 15 2- 8
WAS A P 12 4- 3
1913 CHI N P 7 5- 1
1914 CHI N P 42 21-13
1915 CHI N P 41 43 20-12
1916 CHI N P 44 17-15
1917 CHI N P 41 23-13
1918 CHI N P 35 22-10
1919 CHI N P 38 21-14
1920 CHI N P 40 19-16
1921 CHI N P 17 3-11
BBTL 389 178-137

VAUGHN, ROBERT
B.JULY 4,1885 STAMFORD,N.Y.
D.APR.11,1965 SEATTLE,WASH.
1909 NY A 2 5 .143
1915 STL F 2 144 .274
BRTR 149 .271

VEACH, ALVIS LINDELL
B.AUG.6,1909 MAYLENE,ALA.
1935 PHI A P 2 0- 2
BRTR

VEACH, ROBERT HAYES (BOBBY)
B.JUNE 29,1888 ISLAND,KY.
D.AUG.7,1945 DETROIT,MICH.
1912 DET A O 23 .342
1913 DET A O 138 .269
1914 DET A O 149 .275
1915 DET A O 152 .313
1916 DET A O 150 .306
1917 DET A O 154 .319
1918 DET A P-O 1 127 0- 0
                    .279
1919 DET A O 139 .355
1920 DET A O 154 .307
1921 DET A O 150 .338
1922 DET A O 155 .327
1923 DET A O 114 .321
1924 BOS A O 142 .295
1925 BOS A O 1 .200
NY A O 56 .353
WAS A O 18 .243
BLTR 1 1822 0- 0
                .310

VEACH, WILLIAM WALTER (PEAK-A-BOO)
B.JUNE 15,1862 INDIANAPOLIS,IND
D.NOV.12,1937 INDIANAPOLIS,IND.
1884 KC U P-O 14 27 2- 9
                    .127
1887 LOU AA P 1 0- 1
1890 CLE N 1 62 .237
PIT N 1 8 .300
        15 98 2-10
                .216

VEAL, ORVILLE INMAN (COOT)
B.JULY 9,1932 SANDERSVILLE,GA.
1958 DET A S 58 .256
1959 DET A S 77 .202
1960 DET A 2-S-3 27 .297
1961 WAS A S 69 .202
1962 PIT N H 1 .000
1963 DET A S 15 .219
BRTR 247 .231

VEALE, ROBERT ANDREW (BOB)
B.OCT.28,1935 BIRMINGHAM,ALA.
1962 PIT N P 11 2- 2
1963 PIT N P 34 35 5- 2
1964 PIT N P 40 41 18-12
1965 PIT N P 39 17-12
1966 PIT N P 38 16-12
1967 PIT N P 33 16- 8
1968 PIT N P 36 13-14
1969 PIT N P 34 13-14
1970 PIT N P 34 10-15
1971 PIT N P 37 6- 0
1972 PIT N /P 5 0- 0
BOS A P 2 2- 0
1973 BOS A P 32 2- 3
1974 BOS A P 18 0- 1
BBTR 397 399 120-95

VEDDER, LOUIS EDWARD
B.AUG.20,1897 OAKVILLE,MICH.
1920 DET A P 1 0- 0
BRTR

VEIGEL, ALLEN FRANCIS
B.JAN.30,1917 DOVER,OHIO
1939 BOS N P 2 0- 1
BRTR

VEIL, FREDERICK WILLIAM (BUCKY)
B.AUG.24,1881 TYRONE,PA.
D.APR.16,1931 ALTOONA,PA.
1903 PIT N P 12 5- 3
1904 PIT N P 1 0- 0
BRTR 13 5- 3

VELAZQUEZ, CARLOS (QUINONES)
B.MAR.22,1948 LOIZA,P.R.
1973 MIL A P 18 2- 2
BRTR

VELAZQUEZ, FEDERICO ANTONIO
(FREDDIE)
B.DEC.6,1937 SANTO DOMINGO,D.R.
1969 SEA A /C 6 .125
1973 ATL N C 15 .348
BRTR 21 .256

VELEZ, OTONIEL (FRANCESCHI) (OTTO)
B.NOV.29,1950 PONCE,P.R.
1973 NY A O 23 .195
1974 NY A 1/0-3 27 .209
1975 NY A /1 6 .250
1976 NY A O/1-3 49 .266
1977 TOR A O-O 120 .256
1978 TOR A O/1 91 .266
BRTR 316 .251

VELTMAN, ARTHUR PATRICK (PAT)
B.MAR.24,1906 MOBILE,ALA.
1926 CHI A O 4 .000
1928 NY N O 1 .333
1929 NY N C 2 .000
1931 BOS N H 1 .000
1932 NY N H 2 .000
1934 PIT N C 12 .107
BRTR 22 .132

VENTURA, VINCENT
B.APR.18,1917 NEW YORK,N.Y.
1945 WAS A O 18 .207
BRTR

VERBAN, EMIL MATTHEW (EMIL)
(DUTCH) OR (ANTELOPE)
B.AUG.27,1915 LINCOLN,ILL.
1944 STL N 2 146 .257
1945 STL N 2 155 .278
1946 STL N 2 1 .000
PHI N 2 138 .275
1947 PHI N 2 155 .285
CHI N 2 55 .231
1948 CHI N 2 56 .295
1949 CHI N 2 98 .289
1950 CHI N 2-S-3-0 45 .108
BOS N 2 4 .000
BRTR 853 .272

VERBANIC, JOSEPH MICHAEL (JOE)
B.APR.24,1943 WASHINGTON,PA.
1966 PHI N P 17 1- 1
1967 NY A P 28 4- 3
1968 NY A P 40 6- 7
1970 NY A /P 7 1- 0
BRTR 92 12-11

VERBLE, GENE KERMIT
(GENE) OR (SATCHEL)
B.JUNE 29,1928 CONCORD,N.C.
1951 WAS A 2-S-3 68 .203
1953 WAS A S 13 .190
BRTR 81 .202

VERDEL, ALBERT ALFRED
(AL) OR (STUMPY)
B.JUNE 10,1921 PUNXSUTAWNEY,PA.
1944 PIT N P 1 0- 0
BRTR

VERDI, FRANK MICHAEL
B.JUNE 2,1926 BROOKLYN,N.Y.
1953 NY A S 1 .000
BRTR

VEREKER, JOHN JAMES (TOMMY)
B.DEC.2,1893 BALTIMORE,MD.
D.APR.2,1974 BALTIMORE,MD.
1915 BAL F P 2 0- 0
BRTR

VERGEZ, JOHN LOUIS
B.JULY 9,1906 OAKLAND,CAL.
1931 NY N 3 152 .278
1932 NY N 3 118 .261
1933 NY N 3 123 .271
1934 NY N 3 108 .200
1935 PHI N S-3 148 .249
1936 PHI N 3 15 .275
STL N 3 8 .167
BRTR 672 .255

VERHOEVEN, JOHN C
B.JULY 3,1953 LONG BEACH,CAL.
1976 CAL A P 21 0- 2
1977 CAL A /P 3 0- 0
CHI A /P 6 0- 0
BRTR 30 0- 4

YR	CL	LEA	POS	GP	G	REC

VERNON, JAMES BARTON (MICKEY)
B.APR.22,1918 MARCUS HOOK,PA.

YR	CL	LEA	POS	GP	G	REC
1939	WAS	A	1	76		.257
1940	WAS	A	1	5		.158
1941	WAS	A	1	138		.299
1942	WAS	A	1	151		.271
1943	WAS	A	1	145		.268
1946	WAS	A	1	148		.353
1947	WAS	A	1	154		.265
1948	WAS	A	1	150		.242
1949	CLE	A	1	153		.291
1950	CLE	A	1	28		.189
	WAS	A	1	90		.306
1951	WAS	A	1	141		.293
1952	WAS	A	1	154		.251
1953	WAS	A	1	152		.337
1954	WAS	A	1	151		.290
1955	WAS	A	1	150		.301
1956	BOS	A	1	119		.310
1957	BOS	A	1	102		.241
1958	CLE	A	1	119		.293
1959	MIL	N	1-0	74		.220
1960	PIT	N	H	9		.125
	BLTL			2409		.286

NON-PLAYING MANAGER WAS[A] 1961-63

VERNON, JOSEPH HENRY
B.NOV.25,1889 MANSFIELD,MASS.
D.MAR.13,1955 PHILADELPHIA,PA.

YR	CL	LEA	POS	GP	G	REC
1912	CHI	N	P	1		0- 0
1914	BRO	F	P	1		0- 0
	BRTR			2		0- 0

VERSALLES, ZOILO CASANOVA
[RODRIGUEZ] (ZOILO) OR (ZORRO)
B.DEC.18,1939 HAVANA,CUBA

YR	CL	LEA	POS	GP	G	REC
1959	WAS	A	S	29		.153
1960	WAS	A	S	15		.133
1961	MIN	A	S	129		.280
1962	MIN	A	S	160		.241
1963	MIN	A	S	159		.261
1964	MIN	A	S	166		.259
1965	MIN	A	S	160		.273
1966	MIN	A	*S	137		.249
1967	MIN	A	*S	160		.200
1968	LA	N	*S	122		.196
1969	CLE	A	2-3/S	72		.226
	WAS	A	S/2-3	31		.267
1971	ATL	N	3-S/2	66		.191
	BRTR			1400		.242

VERYZER, THOMAS MARTIN (TOM)
B.FEB.11,1953 PORT JEFFERSON,N.Y

YR	CL	LEA	POS	GP	G	REC
1973	DET	A	S	18		.300
1974	DET	A	S	22		.236
1975	DET	A	*S	128		.252
1976	DET	A	S	97		.234
1977	DET	A	*S	123		.197
1978	CLE	A	*S	130		.271
				520		.241

VIAU, LEON (LEE)
B.JULY 5,1866 CORINTH,VT.
D.DEC.3,1947 PATERSON,N.J.

YR	CL	LEA	POS	GP	G	REC
1888	CIN	AA	P-0	41		27-14
						.085
1889	CIN	AA	P	47		21-19
1890	CIN	N	P	12		7- 3
	CLE	N	P	14		4-10
1891	CLE	N	P	39		18-20
1892	CLE	N	P	1		1- 0
	LOU	N	P	15	20	4-11
	BOS	N	P	2		1- 0
	BRTR			171	176	83-77
						.141

VICK, HENRY ARTHUR (ERNIE)
B.JULY 2,1900 TOLEDO,OHIO

YR	CL	LEA	POS	GP	G	REC
1922	STL	N	C	3		.333
1924	STL	N	C	16		.348
1925	STL	N	C	14		.188
1926	STL	N	C	24		.196
	BRTR			57		.232

VICK, SAMUEL BRUCE
B.APR.12,1895 BATESVILLE,MISS.

YR	CL	LEA	POS	GP	G	REC
1917	NY	A	0	10		.278
1918	NY	A	0	2		.667
1919	NY	A	0	106		.248
1920	NY	A	0	51		.220
1921	BOS	A	0	44		.260
	BRTR			213		.248

VICKERS, HARRY PORTER (RUBE)
B.MAY 17,1878 PITTSFORD,MICH.
D.DEC.9,1958 BELLEVILLE,MICH.

YR	CL	LEA	POS	GP	G	REC
1902	CIN	N	P-C	3	4	0- 3
						.363
1903	BRO	N	P-0	2	3	0- 1
						.000
1907	PHI	A	P	10		2- 2
1908	PHI	A	P	53		18-19
1909	PHI	A	P	18		2- 2
	BLTR			86	88	22-27
						.167

VICKERY, THOMAS GILL (VINEGAR TOM)
B.MAY 5,1867 MILFORD,MASS.
D.MAR.21,1921 BURLINGTON,N.J.

YR	CL	LEA	POS	GP	G	REC
1890	PHI	N	P	45		24-18
1891	CHI	N	P	14		6- 5
1892	BAL	N	P	19		8-11
1893	PHI	N	P	14		5- 5
				92		43-39

VICO, GEORGE STEVE (SAM)
B.AUG.4,1923 SAN FERNANDO,CAL.

YR	CL	LEA	POS	GP	G	REC
1948	DET	A	1	144		.267
1949	DET	A	1	67		.190
	BLTR			211		.250

VIDAL, JOSE [NICOLAS]
(JOSE) OR (PAPITO)
B.APR.3,1940 BATEY LECHUGAS,D.R.

YR	CL	LEA	POS	GP	G	REC
1966	CLE	A	0	17		.188
1967	CLE	A	0	16		.118
1968	CLE	A	0/1	37		.167
1969	SEA	A	/0	18		.192
	BRTR			88		.164

VINES, ROBERT EARL
B.FEB.25,1897 WAXAHACHIE,TEX.

YR	CL	LEA	POS	GP	G	REC
1924	STL	N	P	2		0- 0
1925	PHI	N	P	3		0- 0
	BRTR			5		0- 0

VINEYARD, DAVID KENT (DAVE)
B.FEB.25,1941 CLAY,W.VA.

YR	CL	LEA	POS	GP	G	REC
1964	BAL	A	P	19		2- 5
	BRTR					

VINSON, CHARLES ANTHONY
(CHARLIE) OR (CHUCK)
B.JAN.5,1944 WASHINGTON,D.C.

YR	CL	LEA	POS	GP	G	REC
1966	CAL	A	1	13		.182
	BLTL					

VINSON, ERNEST AUGUSTUS (RUBE)
B.MAR.20,1879 DOVER,DEL.
D.OCT.12,1951 CHESTER,PA.

YR	CL	LEA	POS	GP	G	REC
1904	CLE	A	0	15		.269
1905	CLE	A	0	38		.195
1906	CHI	A	0	10		.250
				63		.220

VINTON, WILLIAM MILLER
B.APR.27,1865 WINTHROP,MASS.
D.SEPT.3,1893 PAWTUCKET,R.I.

YR	CL	LEA	POS	GP	G	REC
1884	PHI	N	P	21		9- 8
1885	PHI	N	P	9		3- 0
	ATH	AA	P-0	7		4- 3
						.192
	BRTR			37		16-17
						.119

VIOX, JAMES HARRY
B.DEC.30,1890 LOCKLAND,OHIO
D.JAN.6,1969 ERLANGER,KY.

YR	CL	LEA	POS	GP	G	REC
1912	PIT	N	3	33		.186
1913	PIT	N	2	137		.317
1914	PIT	N	2	143		.265
1915	PIT	N	2	150		.256
1916	PIT	N	2	43		.250
	BRTR			506		.272

VIRDON, WILLIAM CHARLES (BILL)
B.JUNE 9,1931 HAZEL PARK,MICH.

YR	CL	LEA	POS	GP	G	REC
1955	STL	N	0	144		.281
1956	STL	N	0	24		.211
	PIT	N	0	133		.334
1957	PIT	N	0	144		.251
1958	PIT	N	0	144		.267
1959	PIT	N	0	144		.254
1960	PIT	N	0	120		.264
1961	PIT	N	0	146		.260
1962	PIT	N	0	156		.247
1963	PIT	N	0	142		.269
1964	PIT	N	0	145		.243
1965	PIT	N	*0	135		.279
1968	PIT	N	/0	6		.333
	BLTR			1583		.267

NON-PLAYING MANAGER
PIT[N] 1972-73, NY[A] 1974-75,
HOU[N] 1975-78

VIRGIL, OSVALDO JOSE [PICHARDO]
(OZZIE)
B.MAY 17,1933 MONTECRISTI,D.R.

YR	CL	LEA	POS	GP	G	REC
1956	NY	N	3	3		.417
1957	NY	N	S-3-0	96		.235
1958	DET	A	3	49		.244
1960	DET	A	C-2-S-3	62		.227
1961	DET	A	C-2-S-3	20		.133
	KC	A	C-3	11		.143
1962	BAL	A	H	1		.000
1965	PIT	N	C/3-2	39		.265
1966	SF	N	C-3/1-2-0	42		.213
1969	SF	N	/H	1		.000
	BRTR			324		.231

VIRTUE, JACOB KITCHLINE
(JAKE) OR (GUESSES)
B.MAR.2,1865 PHILADELPHIA,PA.
D.FEB.3,1943 CAMDEN,N.J.

YR	CL	LEA	POS	GP	G	REC
1890	CLE	N	1	62		.305
1891	CLE	N	1	139		.262
1892	CLE	N	1	147		.282
1893	CLE	N	1	95		.287
1894	CLE	N	0	23		.276
	BBTR			466		.282

VISNER, JOSEPH P.
B.SEPT.27,1862 MINNEAPOLIS,MINN

YR	CL	LEA	POS	GP	G	REC
1885	BAL	AA	0	4		.214
1889	BRO	AA	C-0	80		.249
1890	PIT	P	0	127		.265
1891	WAS	AA	0	13		.229
	STL	AA	0	5		.136
	BLTR			229		.256

VITELLI, ANTONIO JOSEPH (JOE)
B.APR.12,1908 MCKEES ROCKS,PA.
D.FEB.7,1967 PITTSBURGH,PA.

YR	CL	LEA	POS	GP	G	REC
1944	PIT	N	P	4		0- 0
1945	PIT	N	P	1		.000
	BRTR			4	5	0- 0
						.000

VITT, OSCAR JOSEPH (OSSIE)
B.JAN.4,1890 SAN FRANCISCO,CAL.
D.JAN.31,1963 OAKLAND,CAL.

YR	CL	LEA	POS	GP	G	REC
1912	DET	A	2-3-0	73		.245
1913	DET	A	2-3	99		.240
1914	DET	A	2-3	66		.251
1915	DET	A	3	152		.250
1916	DET	A	3	153		.226
1917	DET	A	3	140		.254
1918	DET	A	3	81		.239
1919	BOS	A	3	133		.243
1920	BOS	A	2-3	87		.220
1921	BOS	A	3	78		.190
	BRTR			1062		.240

NON-PLAYING MANAGER CLE[A] 1938-40

VOGEL, OTTO HENRY
B.OCT.26,1899 MENDOTA,ILL.
D.JULY 19,1969 IOWA CITY,IOWA

YR	CL	LEA	POS	GP	G	REC
1923	CHI	N	3-0	41		.210
1924	CHI	N	0	70		.207
	BRTR			111		.249

VOIGT, OLEN EDWARD (ODE)
B.JAN.29,1900 WHEATON,ILL.
D.APR.7,1970 SCOTTSDALE,ARIZ.

YR	CL	LEA	POS	GP	G	REC
1924	STL	A	P	8		1- 0
	BLTR					

VOISELLE, WILLIAM SYMMES (BILL)
(BIG BILL) OR (NINETY-SIX)
B.JAN.29,1919 GREENWOOD,S.C.

YR	CL	LEA	POS	GP	G	REC
1942	NY	N	P	2		0- 1
1943	NY	N	P	4		1- 2
1944	NY	N	P	43	44	21-16
1945	NY	N	P	41		14-14
1946	NY	N	P	36		9-15
1947	NY	N	P	11		1- 4
	BOS	N	P	22		8- 7
1948	BOS	N	P	37		13-13
1949	BOS	N	P	30		7- 8
1950	CHI	N	P	19		0- 4
	BRTR			245	246	74-84

VOLLMER, CLYDE FREDERICK
B.SEPT.24,1921 CINCINNATI,OHIO

YR	CL	LEA	POS	GP	G	REC
1942	CIN	N	0	12		.093
1946	CIN	N	0	5		.182
1947	CIN	N	0	78		.219
1948	CIN	N	0	7		.111
	WAS	A	0	1		.400
1949	WAS	A	0	129		.253
1950	WAS	A	0	6		.286
	BOS	A	0	57		.284
1951	BOS	A	0	115		.251
1952	BOS	A	H	90		.264
1953	BOS	A	H	1		.000
	WAS	A	0	118		.260
1954	WAS	A	0	62		.256
	BRTR			685		.251

VOLZ, JACOB PHILLIP
(JAKE) OR (SILENT JAKE)
B.APR.4,1878 SAN ANTONIO,TEX.
D.AUG.11,1962 SAN ANTONIO,TEX.

YR	CL	LEA	POS	GP	G	REC
1901	BOS	A	P	1		1- 0
1905	BOS	N	P	3		0- 2
1908	CIN	N	P	7		1- 2
	BRTR			11		2- 4

VON DER AHE, CHRISTIAN
FREDERICK WILHELM (CHRIS)
B.NOV.7,1851 HILLE,GERMANY
D.JUNE 7,1913 ST.LOUIS,MO.
NON-PLAYING MANAGER
STL[AA] 1884, STL[N] 1892,95,97

YR CL LEA POS   GP   G   REC

VON FRICKEN, ANTHONY (TONY)
B.MAY 30,1870 BROOKLYN,N.Y.
D.MAR.22,1947 TROY,N.Y.

YR	CL LEA POS	GP	G	REC
1890	BOS N P		1	0- 1
	BBTR			

VON HOFF, BRUCE FREDERICK
B.NOV.17,1943 OAKLAND,CAL.

YR	CL LEA POS	GP	G	REC
1965	HOU N /P		3	0- 0
1967	HOU N P		10	0- 3
	BRTR		13	0- 3

VON KOLNITZ, ALFRED HOLMES (FRITZ)
B.MAY 20,1893 CHARLESTON,S.C.
D.MAR.18,1948 MOUNT PLEASANT,S.C.

YR	CL LEA POS	GP	G	REC
1914	CIN N 3		41	.221
1915	CIN N C-1-S-3-O		50	.192
1916	CHI A 3		24	.227
	BRTR		115	.212

VORHEES, HENRY BERT (CY)
B.SEPT.30,1874 LODI,OHIO
D.FEB.8,1910 PERRY,OHIO

YR	CL LEA POS	GP	G	REC
1902	PHI N P		10	3- 2
	WAS A P		1	0- 1
			11	3- 3

VOSMIK, JOSEPH FRANKLIN (JOE)
B.APR.4,1910 CLEVELAND,OHIO
D.JAN.27,1962 CLEVELAND,OHIO

YR	CL LEA POS	GP	G	REC
1930	CLE A O		9	.231
1931	CLE A O		149	.320
1932	CLE A O		153	.312
1933	CLE A O		119	.263
1934	CLE A O		104	.341
1935	CLE A O		152	.348
1936	CLE A O		138	.287
1937	STL A O		144	.325
1938	BOS A O		146	.324
1939	BOS A O		145	.276
1940	BRO N O		116	.282
1941	BRO N O		25	.196
1944	WAS A O		14	.194
	BRTR		1414	.307

VOSS, ALEXANDER
B.1859 ATLANTA,GA.
D.AUG.31,1906 CINCINNATI,OHIO

YR	CL LEA POS	GP	G	REC
1884	WAS U P-1-	26	63	7-14
	S-3-O			.190
	KC U P-O	8	14	1- 7
				.089
	BRTR	34	77	8-21
				.173

VOSS, WILLIAM EDWARD (BILL)
B.OCT.31,1943 GLENDALE,CAL.

YR	CL LEA POS	GP	G	REC
1965	CHI A O		9	.182
1966	CHI A /O		2	.000
1967	CHI A O		13	.091
1968	CHI A O		61	.156
1969	CAL A *O/1		133	.261
1970	CAL A O		80	.243
1971	MIL A O		97	.251
1972	MIL A O		27	.083
	OAK A O		40	.227
	STL N /O		11	.207
	BLTL		475	.227

VOWINKEL, JOHN HENRY (RIP)
B.NOV.18,1884 OSWEGO,N.Y.
D.JULY 13,1966 OSWEGO,N.Y.

YR	CL LEA POS	GP	G	REC
1905	CIN N P		6	3- 3
	BRTR			

VOYLES, PHILIP VANCE
B.MAY 12,1900 MURPHY,N.C.
D.NOV.3,1972 MARLBORO,MASS.

YR	CL LEA POS	GP	G	REC
1929	BOS N O		20	.235

VUCKOVICH, PETER DENNIS (PETE)
B.OCT.27,1952 JOHNSTOWN,PA.

YR	CL LEA POS	GP	G	REC
1975	CHI A /P		4	0- 1
1976	CHI A P		33	7- 4
1977	TOR A P		53	7- 7
1978	STL N P		45	12-12
	BRTR		135	26-24

VUKOVICH, JOHN CHRISTOPHER
B.JULY 31,1947 SACRAMENTO,CAL.

YR	CL LEA POS	GP	G	REC
1970	PHI N /S-3		3	.125
1971	PHI N 3		74	.166
1973	MIL A 3-1/S		55	.125
1974	MIL A 3-3-2/1		38	.188
1975	CIN N 3		31	.211
1976	PHI N /3-1		4	.125
1977	PHI N /H		2	.000
	BRTR		207	.160

WACHER, AUGUST
[PLAYED UNDER NAME OF ARTHUR SUNDAY]

WACHTEL, PAUL HORINE
B.APR.30,1888 MYERSVILLE,MD.
D.DEC.15,1964 SAN ANTONIO,TEX.

YR	CL LEA POS	GP	G	REC
1917	BRO N P		2	0- 0
	BRTR			

WACKER, CHARLES JAMES
B.DEC.8,1883 JEFFERSONVILLE,IND
D.AUG.7,1948 EVANSVILLE,IND.

YR	CL LEA POS	GP	G	REC
1909	PIT N P		1	0- 0
	BLTL			

WADDELL, GEORGE EDWARD (RUBE)
B.OCT.13,1876 BRADFORD,PA.
D.APR.1,1914 SAN ANTONIO,TEX.

YR	CL LEA POS	GP	G	REC
1897	LOU N P		2	0- 1
1899	LOU N P		10	7- 2
1900	PIT N P	29	30	10-10
1901	PIT N P		2	0- 2
	CHI N P		31	14-14
1902	PHI A P		33	24- 7
1903	PHI A P		38	22-16
1904	PHI A P		46	26-17
1905	PHI A P		46	26-11
1906	PHI A P		43	16-16
1907	PHI A P		43	19-13
1908	STL A P		43	19-14
1909	STL A P		31	11-14
1910	STL A P		10	3- 1
	BRTL	405	406	197-138

WADDEY, FRANK ORUM
B.AUG.21,1905 MEMPHIS,TENN.

YR	CL LEA POS	GP	G	REC
1931	STL A O		14	.273

WADE, ABRAHAM LINCOLN (HAM)
B.DEC.20,1880 SPRING CITY,PA.
D.JULY 21,1968 RIVERSIDE,N.J.

YR	CL LEA POS	GP	G	REC
1907	NY N O		1	.000
	BRTR			

WADE, BENJAMIN STYRON (BEN)
B.NOV.26,1922 MOREHEAD CITY,N.C

YR	CL LEA POS	GP	G	REC
1948	CHI N P		2	0- 1
1952	BRO N P		37	11- 9
1953	BRO N P		32	7- 5
1954	BRO N P		23	1- 1
	STL N P		13	0- 0
1955	PIT N P		11	0- 1
	BLTL		118	19-17

WADE, GALEARD LEE (GALE)
B.JAN.20,1929 HOLLISTER,MO.

YR	CL LEA POS	GP	G	REC
1955	CHI N O		9	.182
1956	CHI N O		10	.000
	BLTR		19	.133

WADE, JACOB FIELDS (WHISTLING JAKE)
B.APR.1,1912 MOREHEAD CITY,N.C.

YR	CL LEA POS	GP	G	REC
1936	DET A P		13	4- 5
1937	DET A P		33	7-10
1938	DET A P		27	3- 2
1939	BOS A P		20	1- 4
	STL A P		4	0- 2
1942	CHI A P		15	5- 5
1943	CHI A P		21	3- 7
1944	CHI A P		19	2- 4
1946	NY A P		13	2- 1
	WAS A P		6	0- 0
	BLTL		171	27-40

WADE, RICHARD FRANK (RIP)
B.JAN.12,1898 DULUTH,MINN.
D.JUNE 16,1957 SANDSTONE,MINN.

YR	CL LEA POS	GP	G	REC
1923	WAS A O		33	.232
	BLTR			

WADSWORTH, JOHN L. (JACK)
B.OCT.16,1868 WELLINGTON,OHIO
D.JULY 8,1941 ELYRIA,OHIO

YR	CL LEA POS	GP	G	REC
1890	CLE N P		20	2-15
1893	BAL N P		3	0- 2
1894	LOU N P		23	4-17
1895	LOU N P		2	0- 1
	BLTR		48	6-35

WAGENHURST, ELWOOD OTTO
B.JUNE 3,1863 KUTZTOWN,PA.
D.FEB.12,1946

YR	CL LEA POS	GP	G	REC
1888	PHI N 3		2	.125

WAGNER, ALBERT (BUTTS)
B.SEPT.17,1869 CARNEGIE,PA.
D.NOV.26,1928 PITTSBURGH,PA.

YR	CL LEA POS	GP	G	REC
1898	WAS N 3		57	.237
	BRO N 3		11	.237
			68	.233

WAGNER, CHARLES F. (HEINIE)
B.SEPT.23,1880 NEW YORK,N.Y.
D.MAR.20,1943 NEW ROCHELLE,N.Y.

YR	CL LEA POS	GP	G	REC
1902	NY N S		17	.214
1906	BOS A 2		9	.250
1907	BOS A S		111	.213
1908	BOS A S		153	.247
1909	BOS A S		124	.256
1910	BOS A S		142	.273
1911	BOS A 2-S		80	.257
1912	BOS A S		144	.274
1913	BOS A S		109	.226
1915	BOS A 2		84	.239
1916	BOS A S		4	.500
1918	BOS A 2		3	.125
	BRTR		980	.249
NON-PLAYING MANAGER BOS[A] 1930

WAGNER, CHARLES THOMAS
(CHARLIE) OR (BROADWAY)
B.DEC.3,1912 READING,PA.

YR	CL LEA POS	GP	G	REC
1938	BOS A P		13	1- 3
1939	BOS A P	9	11	3- 1
1940	BOS A P	12	13	1- 0
1941	BOS A P		29	12- 8
1942	BOS A P		29	14-11
1946	BOS A P		8	1- 0
	BRTR	100	103	32-23

WAGNER, GARY EDWARD
B.JUNE 26,1940 BRIDGEPORT,ILL.

YR	CL LEA POS	GP	G	REC
1965	PHI N P		59	7- 7
1966	PHI N /P		5	0- 1
1967	PHI N P		1	0- 0
1968	PHI N P		44	4- 4
1969	PHI N /P		9	0- 3
	BOS A /P		6	1- 3
1970	BOS A P		38	3- 1
	BRTR		162	15-19

WAGNER, HAROLD EDWARD (HAL)
B.JULY 2,1915 E.RIVERTON,N.J.

YR	CL LEA POS	GP	G	REC
1937	PHI A C		1	.000
1938	PHI A C		33	.227
1939	PHI A C		5	.125
1940	PHI A C		34	.253
1941	PHI A C		46	.221
1942	PHI A C		104	.236
1943	PHI A C		111	.239
1944	PHI A C		5	.250
	BOS A C		66	.332
1946	BOS A C		117	.230
1947	BOS A C		21	.231
	DET A C		71	.284
1948	DET A C		54	.202
	PHI N C		3	.000
1949	PHI N C		1	.000
	BLTR		672	.248

WAGNER, JACOB EARLE
B.NOV.6,1861 YORK,PA.
D.NOV.10,1943
NON-PLAYING MANAGER WAS[N] 1892-93

WAGNER, JOHN PETER (HONUS)
OR (THE FLYING DUTCHMAN)
B.FEB.24,1874 CARNEGIE,PA.
D.DEC.6,1955 CARNEGIE,PA.

YR	CL LEA POS	GP	G	REC
1897	LOU N O		61	.344
1898	LOU N 1-3		148	.305
1899	LOU N 3-O		144	.359
1900	PIT N O		134	.381
1901	PIT N S-3-O		141	.352
1902	PIT N P-1-	1	137	0- 0
	2-S-O			.329
1903	PIT N S		129	.355
1904	PIT N S		132	.349
1905	PIT N S		147	.363
1906	PIT N S		140	.339
1907	PIT N S		142	.350
1908	PIT N S		151	.354
1909	PIT N S		137	.339
1910	PIT N S		150	.320
1911	PIT N 1-S		130	.334
1912	PIT N S		145	.324
1913	PIT N S		114	.300
1914	PIT N S-3		150	.252
1915	PIT N S		156	.274
1916	PIT N 1-S		123	.287
1917	PIT N M-1-3		74	.265
	BRTR	1	2785	0- 0
				.329

WAGNER, JOSEPH BERNARD
B.APR.24,1889 NEW YORK,N.Y.
D.NOV.15,1948 BRONX,N.Y.

YR	CL LEA POS	GP	G	REC
1915	CIN N 2-S-3-O		75	.178

WAGNER, LEON LAMAR
B.MAY 13,1934 CHATTANOOGA,TENN.

YR	CL	LEA	POS	GP	G	REC
1958	SF	N	O		74	.317
1959	SF	N	O		87	.225
1960	STL	N	O		39	.214
1961	LA	A	O		133	.280
1962	LA	A	O		160	.268
1963	LA	A	O		149	.291
1964	CLE	A	O		163	.253
1965	CLE	A	*O		144	.294
1966	CLE	A	*O		150	.279
1967	CLE	A	*O		135	.242
1968	CLE	A	O		38	.184
	CHI	A	O		69	.284
1969	SF	N	/O		11	.333
	BLTR				1352	.272

WAGNER, MARK DUANE
B.MAR,4,1954 CONNEAUT,OHIO

YR	CL	LEA	POS	GP	G	REC
1976	DET	A	S		39	.261
1977	DET	A	S/2		22	.146
1978	DET	A	S/2		39	.239
	BRTR				100	.232

WAGNER, WILLIAM GEORGE (BULL)
B.JAN,1,1888 LILLEY,MICH.
D.OCT,2,1967 MUSKEGON,MICH.

YR	CL	LEA	POS	GP	G	REC
1913	BRO	N	P		18	4-2
1914	BRO	N	P		6	0-1
	BRTR				24	4-3

WAGNER, WILLIAM JOSEPH
B.JAN,2,1894 JESSUP,IOWA
D.JAN,11,1951 WATERLOO,IOWA

YR	CL	LEA	POS	GP	G	REC
1914	PIT	N	C		3	.000
1915	PIT	N	C		5	.000
1916	PIT	N	C		19	.237
1917	PIT	N	C		53	.205
1918	BOS	N	C		13	.213
	BRTR				93	.207

WAHL, KERMIT EMERSON
B.NOV,18,1922 COLUMBIA,S.DAK.

YR	CL	LEA	POS	GP	G	REC
1944	CIN	N	3		4	.000
1945	CIN	N	2-S-3		71	.201
1947	CIN	N	2-S-3		39	.173
1950	PHI	A	2-S-3		89	.257
1951	PHI	A	3		20	.186
	STL	A	3		8	.333
	BRTR				231	.226

WAITKUS, EDWARD STEPHEN (EDDIE)
B.SEPT,4,1919 CAMBRIDGE,MASS.
D.SEPT,15,1972 JAMAICA PLAIN,MASS.

YR	CL	LEA	POS	GP	G	REC
1941	CHI	N	1		12	.179
1946	CHI	N	1		113	.304
1947	CHI	N	1		130	.292
1948	CHI	N	1-O		139	.296
1949	PHI	N	1		54	.306
1950	PHI	N	1		154	.284
1951	PHI	N	1		145	.257
1952	PHI	N	1		146	.289
1953	PHI	N	1		81	.291
1954	BAL	A	1		95	.283
1955	BAL	A	1		38	.259
	PHI	N	1		33	.280
	BLTL				1140	.285

WAITS, MICHAEL RICHARD (RICK)
B.MAY 15,1952 ATLANTA,GA.

YR	CL	LEA	POS	GP	G	REC
1973	TEX	A	/P		1	0-0
1975	CLE	A	P		16	6-2
1976	CLE	A	P	26	36	7-9
1977	CLE	A	P	37	38	9-7
1978	CLE	A	P	34	35	13-15
	BLTL			114	126	35-33

WAITT, CHARLES C.
B.OCT,14,1853 HALLOWELL,ME.

YR	CL	LEA	POS	GP	G	REC
1875	STL	NA	O		30	.211
1877	CHI	N	O		10	.098
1882	BAL	AA	O		72	.154
1883	PHI	N	O		1	.333
					113	.167

WAKEFIELD, HOWARD JOHN
B.APR,2,1884 BUCYRUS,OHIO
D.APR,16,1941 CHICAGO,ILL.

YR	CL	LEA	POS	GP	G	REC
1905	CLE	A	C		10	.111
1906	WAS	A	C		77	.280
1907	CLE	A	C		26	.135
	BRTR				113	.248

WAKEFIELD, RICHARD CUMMINGS (DICK)
B.MAY 6,1921 CHICAGO,ILL.

YR	CL	LEA	POS	GP	G	REC
1941	DET	A	O		7	.143
1943	DET	A	O		155	.316
1944	DET	A	O		78	.355
1946	DET	A	O		111	.268
1947	DET	A	O		110	.276
1948	DET	A	O		59	.206
1950	NY	A	H		3	.500
1952	NY	N	H		3	.000
	BLTR				638	.293

WAKEFIELD, WILLIAM SUMNER (BILL)
B.MAY 24,1941 KANSAS CITY,MO.

YR	CL	LEA	POS	GP	G	REC
1964	NY	N	P		62	3-5
	BRTR					

WALBERG, GEORGE ELVIN (RUBE)
B.JULY 27,1896 PINE CITY,MINN.
D.OCT,27,1978 TEMPE,ARIZ.

YR	CL	LEA	POS	GP	G	REC
1923	NY	N	P		2	0-0
	PHI	A	P		26	4-8
1924	PHI	A	P		6	0-0
1925	PHI	A	P		53	8-14
1926	PHI	A	P		40	12-10
1927	PHI	A	P	46	47	16-12
1928	PHI	A	P		38	17-12
1929	PHI	A	P		40	18-11
1930	PHI	A	P		38	13-12
1931	PHI	A	P	44	45	20-12
1932	PHI	A	P		41	17-10
1933	PHI	A	P	40	41	9-13
1934	BOS	A	P		30	6-7
1935	BOS	A	P		44	5-9
1936	BOS	A	P		24	5-4
1937	BOS	A	P		32	5-7
	BLTL			544	547	155-141

WALCZAK, EDWIN JOSEPH
(ED) OR (HUSKY)
B.SEPT,21,1916 ARTIC,R.I.

YR	CL	LEA	POS	GP	G	REC
1945	PHI	N	2-S		20	.211
	BRTR					

WALDBAUER, ALBERT CHARLES (DOC)
B.FEB,22,1892 RICHMOND,VA.
D.JULY 16,1969 YAKIMA,WASH.

YR	CL	LEA	POS	GP	G	REC
1917	WAS	A	P		2	0-0

WALDEN, THOMAS FRED
B.JUNE 25,1890 FAYETTE,MO.
D.SEPT,27,1955 JEFFERSON BARRACKS,MO.

YR	CL	LEA	POS	GP	G	REC
1912	STL	A	C		1	.000

WALDO, HIRAM HUNGERFORD
B.NOV,23,1827 ELBA,N.Y.
D.APR,26,1912 ROCKFORD,ILL.
NON-PLAYING MANAGER ROK[NA]1871

WALDRON, IRVING
B.JAN,21,1876 HILLSIDE,N.Y.
D.JULY 22,1944 WORCESTER,MASS.

YR	CL	LEA	POS	GP	G	REC
1901	MIL	A	O		62	.288
	WAS	A	O		79	.321
	BRTR				141	.306

WALENTOSKI, NORMAN EDWARD
[PLAYED UNDER NAME OF
NORMAN EDWARD WALLEN]

WALKER, ALBERT BLUFORD (RUBE)
B.MAY 16,1926 LENOIR,N.C.

YR	CL	LEA	POS	GP	G	REC
1948	CHI	N	C		79	.275
1949	CHI	N	C		56	.244
1950	CHI	N	C		74	.230
1951	CHI	N	C		37	.234
	BRO	N	C		36	.243
1952	BRO	N	C		46	.259
1953	BRO	N	C		43	.242
1954	BRO	N	C		50	.181
1955	BRO	N	C		48	.252
1956	BRO	N	C		54	.212
1957	BRO	N	C		60	.181
1958	LA	N	C		25	.114
	BLTR				608	.227

WALKER, CHARLES FRANKLIN (FRANK)
B.SEPT,22,1894 ENOREE,S.C.
D.SEPT,16,1974 BRISTOL,TENN.

YR	CL	LEA	POS	GP	G	REC
1917	DET	A	O		2	.000
1918	DET	A	O		55	.198
1920	PHI	A	O		24	.231
1921	PHI	A	O		19	.227
1925	NY	N	O		39	.222
	BRTR				139	.214

WALKER, CLARENCE WILLIAM (TILLY)
B.SEPT,4,1887 TELFORD,TENN.
D.SEPT,21,1959 UNICOI,TENN.

YR	CL	LEA	POS	GP	G	REC
1911	WAS	A	O		98	.278
1912	WAS	A	O		36	.273
1913	STL	A	O		23	.294
1914	STL	A	O		151	.298
1915	STL	A	O		144	.269
1916	BOS	A	O		128	.263
1917	BOS	A	O		106	.246
1918	PHI	A	O		114	.294
1919	PHI	A	O		125	.292
1920	PHI	A	O		149	.268
1921	PHI	A	O		142	.304
1922	PHI	A	O		153	.283
1923	PHI	A	O		52	.275
	BRTR				1421	.281

WALKER, EDWARD HARRISON
B.AUG,11,1874 CAMBOIS,ENGLAND
D.SEPT,29,1947 AKRON,OHIO

YR	CL	LEA	POS	GP	G	REC
1902	CLE	A	P		1	0-1
1903	CLE	A	P		3	0-0
	BLTL				4	0-1

WALKER, ERNEST ROBERT
B.SEPT,17,1890 BLOSSBURG,ALA.
D.APR,1,1965 PELL CITY,ALA.

YR	CL	LEA	POS	GP	G	REC
1913	STL	A	O		7	.214
1914	STL	A	O		71	.298
1915	STL	A	O		50	.211
	BLTR				128	.256

WALKER, EWART GLADSTONE (DIXIE)
B.JUNE 1,1887 BROWNSVILLE,PA.
D.NOV,14,1965 LEEDS,ALA.

YR	CL	LEA	POS	GP	G	REC
1909	WAS	A	P		4	3-1
1910	WAS	A	P		29	11-11
1911	WAS	A	P	32	34	8-14
1912	WAS	A	P		9	3-6
	BRTR			74	76	25-32

WALKER, FRED (DIXIE)
OR (THE PEOPLE S CHERCE)
B.SEPT,24,1910 VILLA RICA,GA.

YR	CL	LEA	POS	GP	G	REC
1931	NY	A	O		2	.300
1933	NY	A	O		98	.274
1934	NY	A	O		17	.118
1935	NY	A	O		8	.154
1936	NY	A	O		6	.350
	CHI	A	O		26	.271
1937	CHI	A	O		154	.302
1938	DET	A	O		127	.308
1939	DET	A	O		43	.305
	BRO	N	O		61	.280
1940	BRO	N	O		143	.308
1941	BRO	N	O		148	.311
1942	BRO	N	O		118	.290
1943	BRO	N	O		138	.302
1944	BRO	N	O		147	.357
1945	BRO	N	O		154	.300
1946	BRO	N	O		150	.319
1947	BRO	N	O		148	.306
1948	PIT	N	O		129	.316
1949	PIT	N	1-O		88	.282
	BLTR				1905	.306

WALKER, FREDERICK MITCHELL (MYSTERIOUS)
B.MAR,21,1884 UTICA,NEB.
D.FEB,11,1958 OAK PARK,ILL.

YR	CL	LEA	POS	GP	G	REC
1910	CIN	N	P		1	0-0
1913	BRO	N	P		10	1-3
1914	PIT	N	P		35	4-16
1915	BRO	N	P		13	2-4
	BRTR				59	7-23

WALKER, GEORGE A.
B.HAMILTON,ONT.,CANADA

YR	CL	LEA	POS	GP	G	REC
1888	BAL	AA	P		4	1-3

WALKER, GERALD HOLMES (GEE)
B.MAR,19,1908 GULFPORT,MISS.

YR	CL	LEA	POS	GP	G	REC
1931	DET	A	O		59	.296
1932	DET	A	O		127	.323
1933	DET	A	O		127	.280
1934	DET	A	O		98	.300
1935	DET	A	O		98	.301
1936	DET	A	O		134	.353
1937	DET	A	O		151	.335
1938	CHI	A	O		120	.305
1939	CHI	A	O		149	.291
1940	WAS	A	O		140	.294
1941	CLE	A	O		121	.283
1942	CIN	N	O		119	.230
1943	CIN	N	O		114	.245
1944	CIN	N	O		121	.278
1945	CIN	N	3-O		106	.253
	BRTR				1784	.294

WALKER, HARRY WILLIAM (THE HAT)
B.OCT,22,1916 PASCAGOULA,MISS.

YR	CL	LEA	POS	GP	G	REC
1940	STL	N	O		7	.185
1941	STL	N	O		7	.267
1942	STL	N	2-O		74	.314
1943	STL	N	2-O		148	.294
1946	STL	N	1-O		112	.237
1947	STL	N	O		10	.200
	PHI	N	O		130	.371
1948	PHI	N	1-3-O		112	.292
1949	CHI	N	O		42	.264
	CIN	N	1-O		86	.318
1950	STL	N	1-O		60	.207
1951	STL	N	1-O		8	.308
1959	STL	N	M-O		11	.357
	BLTR				807	.296

NON-PLAYING MANAGER
PIT[N] 1965-67, HOU[N] 1968-72

WALKER, HARVEY WILLOS (HUB)
B.AUG,17,1906 GULFPORT,MISS.

YR	CL	LEA	POS	GP	G	REC
1931	DET	A	O		90	.286
1935	DET	A	O		9	.160
1936	CIN	N	C-1-O		92	.275
1937	DET	A	2-O		78	.249
1945	DET	A	O		28	.130
	BRTR				297	.263

YR	CL	LEA	POS	GP	G	REC

WALKER, JAMES LUKE (LUKE)
B.SEP.2,1943 DEKALB,TEX.

YR	CL	LEA	POS	GP	G	REC
1965	PIT	N	/P		2	0- 0
1966	PIT	N	P		10	0- 1
1968	PIT	N	P		39	0- 3
1969	PIT	N	P		31	4- 6
1970	PIT	N	P		42	15- 6
1971	PIT	N	P		28	10- 8
1972	PIT	N	P		26	4- 6
1973	PIT	N	P		37	7-12
1974	DET	A	P		28	5- 5
		BLTL			243	45-47

WALKER, JAMES ROY (DIXIE)
B.APR.15,1893 LAWRENCEBURG,TENN
D.FEB.10,1962 NEW ORLEANS,LA.

1912	CLE	A	P		2	0- 0
1915	CLE	A	P		25	5- 9
1917	CHI	N	P		2	0- 1
1918	CHI	N	P		13	1- 3
1921	STL	N	P		38	11-12
1922	STL	N	P		12	1- 2
		BBTR			92	18-27
		BR 1912-15, 21				

WALKER, JERRY ALLEN
B.FEB.12,1939 ADA,OKLA.

1957	BAL	A	P		13	1- 0
1958	BAL	A	P		6	0- 0
1959	BAL	A	P	30	31	11-10
1960	BAL	A	P	29	35	3- 4
1961	KC	A	P	36	45	8-14
1962	KC	A	P	31	36	8- 9
1963	CLE	A	P		39	6- 6
1964	CLE	A	P		6	0- 1
		BBTR		190	211	37-44
		BR 1963-64				

WALKER, JOHN MILES
B.DEC.11,1896 TOULON,ILL.
D.AUG.19,1976 HOLLYWOOD,FLA.

1919	PHI	A	C		3	.000
1920	PHI	A	C		6	.235
1921	PHI	A	1		113	.258
1922	PHI	A	C		2	.000
		BRTR			124	.252

WALKER, JOSEPH RICHARD (SPEED)
B.JAN.23,1898 MUNHALL,PA.
D.JUNE 20,1959 W.MIFFLIN,PA.

| 1923 | STL | N | 2 | | 2 | .286 |
| | | BRTR | | | | |

WALKER, MARTIN VAN BUREN (BUDDY)
B.MAR.27,1899 PHILADELPHIA,PA.
D.APR.24,1978 PHILADELPHIA,PA.

| 1928 | PHI | N | P | | 1 | 0- 1 |
| | | BLTL | | | | |

WALKER, MOSES FLEETWOOD (FLEET)
B.OCT.7,1857 MT.PLEASANT,OHIO
D.MAY 11,1924 STEUBENVILLE,OHIO

| 1884 | TOL | AA | C | | 41 | .251 |
| | | BRTR | | | | |

WALKER, OSCAR
B.MAR.18,1854 BROOKLYN,N.Y.
D.MAY 30,1889 BROOKLYN,N.Y.

1875	ATL	NA	O		1	.000
1879	BUF	N	1		70	.266
1880	BUF	N	P		33	.233
1882	STL	AA	1-2-O		76	.233
1884	BRO	AA	1-O		95	.268
		BLTL			275	.253

WALKER, ROBERT THOMAS (TOM)
B.NOV.7,1948 TAMPA,FLA.

1972	MON	N	P		46	2- 2
1973	MON	N	P		54	7- 5
1974	MON	N	P		33	4- 5
1975	DET	A	P		36	3- 8
1976	STL	N	P		10	1- 2
1977	MON	N	P		11	1- 1
	CAL	A	/P		1	0- 0
		BRTR			191	18-23

WALKER, THOMAS WILLIAM
B.AUG.1,1881 PHILADELPHIA,PA.
D.JULY 10,1944 WOODBURY HEIGHTS N.J.

1902	PHI	A	P		1	0- 1
1904	CIN	N	P		25	15-10
1905	CIN	N	P		23	10- 6
		BRTR			49	25-17

WALKER, WALTER S.
B.IONIA,MICH.

1884	DET	N	C		1	.250
1885	BAL	AA	O		3	.000
					4	.077

WALKER, WELDAY WILBERFORCE
B.JUNE 1859 STEUBENVILLE,OHIO
D.NOV.23,1937 STEUBENVILLE,OHIO

| 1884 | TOL | AA | O | | 5 | .222 |

WALKER, WILLIAM CURTIS (CURT)
B.JULY 3,1896 BEEVILLE,TEX.
D.DEC.9,1955 BEEVILLE,TEX.

YR	CL	LEA	POS	GP	G	REC
1919	NY	A	H		1	.000
1920	NY	N	O		8	.000
1921	NY	N	O		64	.286
	PHI	N	O		21	.338
1922	PHI	N	O		148	.337
1923	PHI	N	1-O		140	.281
1924	PHI	N	1-O		24	.296
	CIN	N	1-O		109	.300
1925	CIN	N	1-O		145	.318
1926	CIN	N	1-O		155	.306
1927	CIN	N	1-O		146	.292
1928	CIN	N	1-O		123	.279
1929	CIN	N	1-O		141	.313
1930	CIN	N	1-O		134	.307
		BLTR			1359	.304

WALKER, WILLIAM HENRY (BILL)
B.OCT.7,1903 E.ST.LOUIS,ILL.
D.JUNE 14,1966 E.ST.LOUIS,ILL.

1927	NY	N	P		3	0- 0
1928	NY	N	P		22	3- 6
1929	NY	N	P		29	14- 7
1930	NY	N	P	39	40	17-15
1931	NY	N	P		37	16- 9
1932	NY	N	P		31	8-12
1933	STL	N	P		29	9-10
1934	STL	N	P		24	12- 4
1935	STL	N	P	37	38	13- 8
1936	STL	N	P	21	22	5- 6
		BRTL		272	275	97-77

WALKUP, JAMES ELTON (JIM)
B.DEC.14,1909 HAVANA,ARK.

1934	STL	A	P		3	0- 0
1935	STL	A	P		55	6- 9
1936	STL	A	P		5	0- 3
1937	STL	A	P		27	9-12
1938	STL	A	P		18	1-12
1939	STL	A	P		1	0- 1
	DET	A	P		7	0- 0
		BRTR			116	16-38

WALKUP, JAMES HUEY (JIM)
B.NOV.3,1895 HAVANA,ARK.

| 1927 | DET | A | P | | 2 | 0- 0 |
| | | BRTL | | | | |

WALL
1873 NAT NA S | | | | | 1 | - |

WALL, JOSEPH FRANCIS (GUMMY)
B.JULY 24,1873 BROOKLYN,N.Y.
D.JULY 17,1936 BROOKLYN,N.Y.

1901	NY	N	C		3	.286
1902	NY	N	P		6	.357
	BRO	N	C		5	.176
		BLTL			14	.282

WALL, MURRAY WESLEY
B.SEPT.19,1926 DALLAS,TEX.
D.OCT.8,1971 LONE OAK,TEX.

1950	BOS	N	P		1	0- 0
1957	BOS	A	P		11	3- 0
1958	BOS	A	P		52	8- 9
1959	BOS	A	P		15	1- 4
	WAS	A	P		1	0- 0
	BOS	A	P		11	1- 1
		BRTR			91	13-14

WALL, STANLEY ARTHUR (STAN)
B.JUNE 16,1951 BUTLER,MO.

1975	LA	N	P		10	0- 1
1976	LA	N	P		31	2- 2
1977	LA	N	P		25	2- 3
		BLTL			66	4- 6

WALLACE, CLARENCE EUGENE (JACK)
B.AUG.6,1890 WINNFIELD,LA.
D.OCT.15,1960 WINNFIELD,LA.

| 1915 | CHI | N | C | | 2 | .285 |
| | | BRTR | | | | |

WALLACE, DAVID WILLIAM (DAVE)
B.SEP.7,1947 WATERBURY,CONN.

1973	PHI	N	/P		4	0- 0
1974	PHI	N	/P		3	0- 1
1978	TOR	A	/P		6	0- 0
		BRTR			13	0- 1

WALLACE, DONALD ALLEN (DON)
B.AUG.25,1940 SAPULPA,OKLA.

| 1967 | CAL | A | /2-1-3 | | 23 | .000 |
| | | BLTR | | | | |

WALLACE, FREDERICK RENSHAW
(DOC) OR (JESSE)
B.SEPT.30,1893 CHURCH HILL,MD.
D.DEC.31,1964 HAVERFORD,PA.

| 1919 | PHI | N | S | | 2 | .200 |
| | | TR | | | | |

WALLACE, HARRY CLINTON
(HUCK) OR (LEFTY)
B.JULY 27,1882 RICHMOND,IND.
D.JULY 6,1951 CLEVELAND,OHIO.

YR	CL	LEA	POS	GP	G	REC
1912	PHI	N	P		4	0- 0
		BLTL				

WALLACE, JAMES HAROLD (LEFTY)
B.AUG.12,1921 EVANSVILLE,IND.

1942	BOS	N	P		19	1- 3
1945	BOS	N	P	5	6	1- 0
1946	BOS	N	P		27	3- 3
		BLTL		51	52	5- 6

WALLACE, JAMES L.
B.NOV.14,1894 REVERE,MASS.
D.MAY 16,1953 REVERE,MASS.

| 1905 | PIT | N | O | | 7 | .214 |
| | | BLTL | | | | |

WALLACE, MICHAEL SHERMAN (MIKE)
B.FEB.3,1951 GASTONIA,N.C.

1973	PHI	N	P		20	1- 1
1974	PHI	N	/P		8	1- 0
	NY	A	P		23	6- 0
1975	NY	A	/P		3	0- 0
	STL	N	/P		9	0- 0
1977	TEX	A	/P		54	3- 2
		BLTL			117	11- 3

WALLACE, RHODERICK JOHN (BOBBY)
B.NOV.4,1873 PITTSBURGH,PA.
D.NOV.3,1960 TORRANCE,CAL.

1894	CLE	N	P		4	2- 2
1895	CLE	N	P		27	14-10
1896	CLE	N	P	15	33	9- 6
1897	CLE	N	3		131	.339
1898	CLE	N	3		153	.269
1899	STL	N	S-3		151	.302
1900	STL	N	S		129	.272
1901	STL	N	S		135	.322
1902	STL	A	P-S-	1	133	0- 0
			O			.287
1903	STL	A	S		136	.245
1904	STL	A	S		139	.273
1905	STL	A	S		156	.271
1906	STL	A	S		139	.258
1907	STL	A	S		147	.257
1908	STL	A	S		137	.253
1909	STL	A	S-3		116	.238
1910	STL	A	S-3		138	.258
1911	STL	A	M-S		125	.232
1912	STL	A	M-S		99	.241
1913	STL	A	S		52	.211
1914	STL	A	S		26	.219
1915	STL	A	S		9	.231
1916	STL	A	S-3		14	.278
1917	STL	N	S-3		8	.100
1918	STL	N	2-S-3		32	.133
		BRTR		47	2369	25-18
						.268

NON-PLAYING MANAGER CIN(N) 1937

WALLAESA, JOHN (JACK)
B.AUG.31,1919 EASTON,PA.

1940	PHI	A	S		6	.150
1942	PHI	A	S		36	.256
1946	PHI	A	S		83	.196
1947	CHI	A	S-3-O		81	.195
1948	CHI	A	S-O		33	.188
		BBTR			219	.205
		BR 1940				

WALLEN, NORMAN EDWARD
[REAL NAME NORMAN EDWARD WALENTOSKI]
B.FEB.13,1917 MILWAUKEE,WIS.

| 1945 | BOS | N | 3 | | 4 | .133 |
| | | BRTR | | | | |

WALLER, JOHN FRANCIS (RED)
B.JUNE 16,1883 WASHINGTON,D.C.
D.FEB.9,1915 SECAUCUS TOWNSHIP,N.J.

| 1909 | NY | N | P | | 1 | 0- 0 |

WALLING, DENNIS MARTIN
B.APR.17,1954 NEPTUNE,N.J.

1975	OAK	A	/O		6	.125
1976	OAK	A	/O		3	.273
1977	HOU	N	/O		6	.286
1978	HOU	N	O		120	.251
		BLTR			135	.251

WALLIS, HAROLD JOSEPH (JOE)
B.JAN.9,1952 E.ST.LOUIS,ILL.

1975	CHI	N	O		16	.286
1976	CHI	N	O		121	.254
1977	CHI	N	O		56	.250
1978	CHI	N	O		28	.309
	OAK	A	O		85	.237
		BBTR			306	.254

YR	CL	LEA	POS	GP	G	REC

WALLS, RAY LEE (LEE)
B.JAN.6,1933 SAN DIEGO,CAL.

YR	CL	LEA	POS	GP	G	REC
1952	PIT	N	O		32	.188
1956	PIT	N	O		143	.274
1957	PIT	N	O		8	.182
	CHI	N	3-O		117	.240
1958	CHI	N	O		136	.304
1959	CHI	N	O		120	.257
1960	CIN	N	1-O		29	.274
	PHI	N	1-3-O		65	.199
1961	PHI	N	1-3-O		91	.280
1962	LA	N	1-3-O		60	.266
1963	LA	N	1-3-O		64	.233
1964	LA	N	C-O		37	.179
			BRTR		902	.262

WALSH, AUGUST S.
B.AUG.9,1904 WILMINGTON,DEL.

YR	CL	LEA	POS	GP	G	REC
1927	PHI	N	P		1	0- 1
1928	PHI	N	P	38	39	4- 9
			BRTR	39	40	4-10

WALSH, AUSTIN
B.1892

YR	CL	LEA	POS	GP	G	REC
1914	CHI	F	O		52	.235
			BLTL			

WALSH, CORNELIUS R.
B.APR.23,1882 ST.LOUIS,MO.
D.APR.5,1953 ST.LOUIS,MO.

YR	CL	LEA	POS	GP	G	REC
1907	PIT	N	P		1	0- 0

WALSH, EDWARD ARTHUR
B.FEB.11,1905 MERIDEN,CONN.
D.OCT.31,1937 MERIDEN,CONN.

YR	CL	LEA	POS	GP	G	REC
1928	CHI	A	P		14	4- 7
1929	CHI	A	P	24	25	6-11
1930	CHI	A	P	37	39	1- 4
1932	CHI	A	P		4	0- 2
			BRTR	79	82	11-24

WALSH, EDWARD AUGUSTINE
(ED) OR (BIG ED)
B.MAY 14,1881 PLAINS,PA.
D.MAY 26,1959 POMPANO BEACH,FLA

YR	CL	LEA	POS	GP	G	REC
1904	CHI	A	P		18	5- 5
1905	CHI	A	P	22	29	8- 5
1906	CHI	A	P	41	42	17-13
1907	CHI	A	P	56	57	24-18
1908	CHI	A	P		66	40-15
1909	CHI	A	P	31	32	15-11
1910	CHI	A	P	45	52	18-20
1911	CHI	A	P	55	62	27-18
1912	CHI	A	P		62	27-17
1913	CHI	A	P		16	8- 3
1914	CHI	A	P	9	11	2- 3
1915	CHI	A	P	3	5	3- 0
1916	CHI	A	P		2	0- 1
1917	BOS	N	P		4	0- 1
			BRTR	430	458	194-130

WALSH, JAMES CHARLES
B.SEPT.22,1885 KALLILA,IRELAND
D.JULY 3,1962 SYRACUSE,N.Y.

YR	CL	LEA	POS	GP	G	REC
1912	PHI	A	O		31	.252
1913	PHI	A	O		94	.255
1914	NY	A	O		43	.207
	PHI	A	O		67	.226
1915	PHI	A	O		117	.206
1916	PHI	A	O		112	.222
	BOS	A	O		15	.348
1917	BOS	A	O		57	.265
			BLTR		536	.231

WALSH, JAMES GERALD (JUNIOR)
B.MAR.7,1919 NEWARK,N.J.

YR	CL	LEA	POS	GP	G	REC
1946	PIT	N	P		4	0- 1
1948	PIT	N	P		2	1- 0
1949	PIT	N	P		9	1- 4
1950	PIT	N	P		38	1- 1
1951	PIT	N	P		36	1- 4
			BRTR		89	4-10

WALSH, JAMES THOMAS
B.JULY 10,1894 ROXBURY,MASS.
D.MAY 13,1967 BOSTON,MASS.

YR	CL	LEA	POS	GP	G	REC
1921	DET	A	P		3	0- 0
			BLTL			

WALSH, JOHN
B.WILKES-BARRE,PA.

YR	CL	LEA	POS	GP	G	REC
1903	PHI	N	3		1	.000
			TR			

WALSH, JOSEPH A. (REDDY)
B.NOV.1865 CHICAGO,ILL.

YR	CL	LEA	POS	GP	G	REC
1891	BAL	AA	2-S		25	.189

WALSH, JOSEPH FRANCIS
B.OCT.14,1887 WATERBURY,CONN.
D.JAN.6,1967 BUFFALO,N.Y.

YR	CL	LEA	POS	GP	G	REC
1910	NY	A	C		2	.333
1911	NY	A	C		4	.222
			BRTR		6	.267

WALSH, JOSEPH PATRICK (TWEET)
B.MAR.13,1917 ROXBURY,MASS.

YR	CL	LEA	POS	GP	G	REC
1938	BOS	N	S		4	.000
			BRTR			

WALSH, LEO THOMAS (DEE)
B.MAR.28,1890 ST.LOUIS,MO.
D.JULY 14,1971 ST.LOUIS,MO.

YR	CL	LEA	POS	GP	G	REC
1913	STL	A	S		23	.170
1914	STL	A	S		7	.087
1915	STL	A	P-O	1	59	0- 0
						.220
			BBTR		89	0- 0
						.195

WALSH, MICHAEL JOHN
B.AUG.6,1852 BALTIMORE,MD.
D.MAR.17,1924 SPRINGFIELD,MO.
NON-PLAYING MANAGER LOU[AA]1884

WALSH, MICHAEL TIMOTHY (RUNT)
B.MAR.25,1886 LIMA,OHIO
D.JAN.21,1947 BALTIMORE,MD.

YR	CL	LEA	POS	GP	G	REC
1910	PHI	N	2-O		67	.248
1911	PHI	N	ALL	1	84	0- 0
						.270
1912	PHI	N	2		51	.267
1913	PHI	N	2		26	.333
1914	BAL	F	3		117	.310
1915	BAL	F	3		109	.304
	STL	F	3		14	.200
			BRTR	1	468	0- 0
						.269

WALSH, THOMAS JOSEPH
B.FEB.28,1885 DAVENPORT,IOWA
D.MAR.16,1963 NAPLES,FLA.

YR	CL	LEA	POS	GP	G	REC
1906	CHI	N	C		2	.000
			TR			

WALSH, WALTER WILLIAM
B.APR.30,1897 NEWARK,N.J.
D.JAN.15,1966 AVON BY THE SEA,N.J.

YR	CL	LEA	POS	GP	G	REC
1920	PHI	N	H		1	.000
			BRTR			

WALTER, JAMES BERNARD (BERNIE)
B.AUG.15,1908 DOVER,TENN.

YR	CL	LEA	POS	GP	G	REC
1930	PIT	N	P		1	0- 0
			BRTR			

WALTERS, ALFRED JOHN (ROXY)
B.NOV.5,1892 SAN FRANCISCO,CAL.
D.JUNE 3,1956 ALMEDA,CAL.

YR	CL	LEA	POS	GP	G	REC
1915	NY	A	C		2	.333
1916	NY	A	C		66	.266
1917	NY	A	C		61	.263
1918	NY	A	C		64	.199
1919	BOS	A	C		48	.193
1920	BOS	A	C		88	.198
1921	BOS	A	C		54	.201
1922	BOS	A	C		38	.194
1923	BOS	A	C		40	.250
1924	CLE	A	C		32	.257
1925	CLE	A	C		5	.200
			BRTR		498	.222

WALTERS, CHARLES LEONARD (CHARLIE)
B.FEB.21,1947 MINNEAPOLIS,MINN.

YR	CL	LEA	POS	GP	G	REC
1969	MIN	A	/P		6	0- 0
			BRTR			

WALTERS, FRED JAMES
(FRED) OR (WHALE)
B.SEPT.4,1912 LAUREL,MISS.

YR	CL	LEA	POS	GP	G	REC
1945	BOS	A	C		40	.172
			BRTR			

WALTERS, KENNETH ROGERS (KEN)
B.NOV.11,1933 FRESNO,CAL.

YR	CL	LEA	POS	GP	G	REC
1960	PHI	N	O		124	.239
1961	PHI	N	1-3-O		86	.228
1963	CIN	N	1-O		49	.187
			BRTR		259	.231

WALTERS, WILLIAM HENRY (BUCKY)
B.APR.19,1909 PHILADELPHIA,PA.

YR	CL	LEA	POS	GP	G	REC
1931	BOS	N	2-3		9	.211
1932	BOS	N	3		22	.187
1933	BOS	A	2-3		52	.256
1934	BOS	A	3		23	.216
	PHI	N	P-3	2	83	0- 0
						.260
1935	PHI	N	P-2-3-O	24	49	9- 9
						.250
1936	PHI	N	P	40	64	11-21
1937	PHI	N	P	37	56	14-15
1938	PHI	N	P	12	15	4- 8
	CIN	N	P	27	36	11- 6
1939	CIN	N	P	39	40	27-11
1940	CIN	N	P	36	37	22-10
1941	CIN	N	P	37	39	19-15
1942	CIN	N	P-O	34	40	15-14
						.242
1943	CIN	N	P	34	37	15-15
1944	CIN	N	P	34	37	23- 8
1945	CIN	N	P	22	24	10-10
1946	CIN	N	P	22	24	10- 7
1947	CIN	N	P		20	8- 8
1948	CIN	N	M-P		7	0- 3
1950	BOS	N	P		1	0- 0
			BRTR	428	715	198-160
						.242

NON-PLAYING MANAGER CIN[N] 1949

WALTON, DANIEL JAMES
(DANNY) OR (MICKEY)
B.JULY 14,1947 LOS ANGELES,CAL.

YR	CL	LEA	POS	GP	G	REC
1968	HOU	N	/H		2	.000
1969	SEA	A	O		23	.217
1970	MIL	A	*O		117	.257
1971	MIL	A	O/3		30	.203
	NY	A	/O		5	.143
1973	MIN	A	O-D/3		37	.177
1975	MIN	A	/1-C		42	.175
1976	LA	N	H		18	.133
1977	HOU	N	/1		13	.190
			BRTR		287	.224
			BB 1975-77			

WALTON, ZACH
[SEE JONATHAN
THOMPSON WALTON ZACHARY]

WALTZ, JOHN J.
NON-PLAYING MANAGER BAL[N] 1892

WAMBSGANSS, WILLIAM ADOLPH
B.MAR.19,1894 CLEVELAND,OHIO

YR	CL	LEA	POS	GP	G	REC
1914	CLE	A	S		43	.217
1915	CLE	A	2-3		121	.195
1916	CLE	A	2-S-3		136	.246
1917	CLE	A	2		141	.255
1918	CLE	A	2		87	.295
1919	CLE	A	2		139	.278
1920	CLE	A	2		153	.244
1921	CLE	A	2		107	.285
1922	CLE	A	2-S		143	.262
1923	CLE	A	2		101	.290
1924	BOS	A	2		155	.275
1925	BOS	A	1-2		111	.231
1926	PHI	A	S		54	.352
			BRTR		1491	.259

WANER, LLOYD JAMES (LITTLE POISON)
B.MAR.16,1906 HARRAH,OKLA.

YR	CL	LEA	POS	GP	G	REC
1927	PIT	N	O		150	.355
1928	PIT	N	O		152	.335
1929	PIT	N	O		151	.353
1930	PIT	N	O		68	.362
1931	PIT	N	O		154	.314
1932	PIT	N	O		134	.333
1933	PIT	N	O		121	.276
1934	PIT	N	O		140	.283
1935	PIT	N	O		122	.309
1936	PIT	N	O		106	.321
1937	PIT	N	O		129	.330
1938	PIT	N	O		147	.313
1939	PIT	N	O		112	.285
1940	PIT	N	O		72	.259
1941	PIT	N	O		3	.250
	BOS	N	O		19	.412
	CIN	N	O		55	.256
1942	PHI	N	O		101	.261
1944	BRO	N	O		15	.286
	PIT	N	O		19	.357
1945	PIT	N	O		23	.263
			BLTR		1993	.316

WANER, PAUL GLEE (BIG POISON)
B.APR.16 1903 HARRAH,OKLA.
D.AUG.29 1965 SARASOTA,FLA.

YR	CL	LEA	POS	GP	G	REC
1926	PIT	N	O		144	.336
1927	PIT	N	1-O		155	.380
1928	PIT	N	1-O		152	.370
1929	PIT	N	O		151	.336
1930	PIT	N	O		145	.368
1931	PIT	N	1-O		150	.322
1932	PIT	N	O		154	.341
1933	PIT	N	O		154	.309
1934	PIT	N	O		146	.362
1935	PIT	N	O		139	.321
1936	PIT	N	O		148	.373
1937	PIT	N	O		154	.354
1938	PIT	N	O		148	.280
1939	PIT	N	O		125	.328
1940	PIT	N	1-O		89	.290
1941	BRO	N	O		11	.171
	BOS	N	1-O		95	.279
1942	BOS	N	O		114	.258
1943	BRO	N	O		82	.311
1944	BRO	N	O		83	.287
	NY	A	O		9	.143
1945	NY	A	O		1	.000
			BLTL		2549	.333

WANNER, CLARENCE CURTIS (JOHNNY)
B.NOV.29,1885 GENESEO,ILL.
D.MAY 28,1919 GENESEO,ILL.

YR	CL	LEA	POS	GP	G	REC
1909	NY	A	S		3	.125
			BRTR			

WANNINGER, PAUL LOUIS (PEE-WEE)
B.DEC.12,1902 BIRMINGHAM,ALA.

YR	CL	LEA	POS	GP	G	REC
1925	NY	A	2-S-3		117	.236
1927	BOS	A	S		18	.200
	CIN	N	S		28	.247
			BLTR		163	.234

WANTZ, RICHARD CARTER (DICK)
B.APR.11,1940 SOUTH GATE,CAL.
D.MAY 13,1965 INGLEWOOD,CAL.

YR	CL	LEA	POS	GP	G	REC
1965	CAL	A	/P		1	0- 0
			BRTR			

YR	CL	LEA	POS	GP	G	REC

WARD, AARON LEE
B.AUG.28,1896 BOONEVILLE,ARK.
D.JAN.30,1961 NEW ORLEANS,LA.

1917	NY	A	S		8	.115
1918	NY	A	S		20	.125
1919	NY	A	1-S		27	.205
1920	NY	A	3		127	.256
1921	NY	A	2-3		153	.306
1922	NY	A	2		154	.267
1923	NY	A	2		192	.284
1924	NY	A	2		120	.253
1925	NY	A	2-3		125	.246
1926	NY	A	1		22	.323
1927	CHI	A	2		145	.270
1928	CLE	A	2-S-3		6	.111
		BRTR			1059	.268

WARD, CHARLES WILLIAM (CHUCK)
B.JULY 30,1894 ST.LOUIS,MO.
D.APR.4,1969 INDIAN ROCKS,FLA.

1917	PIT	N	S		125	.236
1918	BRO	N	S		2	.333
1919	BRO	N	3		45	.233
1920	BRO	N	S		19	.155
1921	BRO	N	S		12	.071
1922	BRO	N	S		33	.274
		BRTR			236	.228

WARD, CHRIS GILBERT
B.MAY 18,1949 OAKLAND,CAL.

1972	CHI	N	/H		1	.000
1974	CHI	N	O/1		92	.204
		BLTL			93	.203

WARD, E. (HAP)

| 1912 | DET | A | O | | 1 | .000 |

WARD, FRANK GRAY (PIGGY)
B.APR.16,1867 CHAMBERSBURG,PA.
D.OCT.24,1912 ALTOONA,PA.

1883	PHI	N	3		1	.000
1889	PHI	N	2		7	.160
1891	PIT	N	O		5	.333
1892	BAL	N	O		53	.282
1893	BAL	N	O		11	.250
		CIN	N	O	38	.261
1894	WAS	N	2		89	.303
					204	.286

WARD, JAMES H.
B.MAR.1855 BOSTON,MASS.
D.JUNE 4,1886 BOSTON,MASS.

| 1876 | ATH | N | C | | 1 | .500 |

WARD, JOHN ANDREW
B.FEB.6,1879 NEW LEXINGTON,OHIO
D.JAN.17,1945 AKRON,OHIO

| 1902 | BRO | N | O | | 13 | .290 |

WARD, JOHN E.
B.WASHINGTON,D.C.

1884	WAS	U	O		1	.250
1885	PRO	N	P		1	0- 1
				1	2	0- 1
						.143

WARD, JOHN FRANCIS (JAY)
B.SEP.9,1938 BROOKFIELD,MO.

1963	MIN	A	3-O		9	.067
1964	MIN	A	2-O		12	.226
1970	CIN	N	/3-1-2		6	.000
		BRTR			27	.163

WARD, JOHN MONTGOMERY (MONTE)
B.MAR.3,1860 BELLEFONTE,PA.
D.MAR.4,1925 AUGUSTA,GA.

1878	PRO	N	P		35	22-13
1879	PRO	N	P-3	65	82	44-18
						.287
1880	PRO	N	P-3-	63	82	40-23
				O		.226
1881	PRO	N	P-S-	36	83	18-18
				O		.241
1882	PRO	N	P-S-	32	83	19-13
				O		.245
1883	NY	N	P-2-	33	88	12-14
				S-3-O		.258
1884	NY	N	P-2-	9	109	3- 3
				O		.249
1885	NY	N	S		111	.226
1886	NY	N	S		122	.273
1887	NY	N	S		129	.371
1888	NY	N	S		122	.251
1889	NY	N	S		114	.298
1890	BRO	P	M-S		128	.371
1891	BRO	N	M-2-S		104	.287
1892	BRO	N	M-2		148	.273
1893	NY	N	M-2		134	.348
1894	NY	N	M-2		136	.262
		BLTR		273	1810	158-102
						.284
		BB 1888				

WARD, JOSEPH A.
B.SEPT.2,1884 PHILADELPHIA,PA.
D.AUG.11,1934

1906	PHI	N	3		30	.295
1909	NY	A	2		9	.179
		PHI	N	2	63	.266
1910	PHI	N	1		33	.145
		TR			135	.237

WARD, PETER THOMAS (PETE)
B.JULY 26,1939 MONTREAL,QUE.,CAN

1962	BAL	A	O		8	.143
1963	CHI	A	2-S-3		157	.295
1964	CHI	A	3		144	.282
1965	CHI	A	*3/2		138	.247
1966	CHI	A	O-3/1		84	.219
1967	CHI	A	O-1-3		146	.233
1968	CHI	A	3-1-O		125	.216
1969	CHI	A	1-3/O		105	.246
1970	NY	A	1		66	.260
		BLTR			973	.254

WARD, PRESTON MEYER
B.JULY 24,1927 COLUMBIA,MO.

1948	BRO	N	1		42	.260
1950	CHI	N	1		80	.253
1953	CHI	N	1-O		3	.230
		PIT	N	1	88	.210
1954	PIT	N	1-3-O		117	.269
1955	PIT	N	1-O		84	.212
1956	PIT	N	1-O		16	.333
		CLE	A	1-O	87	.253
1957	CLE	A	1		10	.182
1958	CLE	A	1-3-O		48	.338
		KC	A	1-3-O	81	.254
1959	KC	A	1-O		58	.248
		BLTR			744	.253

WARD, RICHARD O.
B.MAY 21,1909 HERRICK,S.DAK.
D.MAY 30,1966 FREELAND,WASH.

1934	CHI	N	P		3	0- 0
1935	STL	N	P		1	0- 0
		BRTR			4	0- 0

WARDEN, JONATHAN EDGAR
(JON) OR (WARBLER)
B.OCT.1,1946 COLUMBUS,OHIO

| 1968 | DET | A | P | | 28 | 4- 1 |
| | | BBTL | | | | |

WARE, GEORGE
NON-PLAYING MANAGER PRO[N] 1878

WARES, CLYDE ELLSWORTH (BUZZY)
B.MAY 23,1886 VANDALIA,MICH.
D.MAY 26,1964 SOUTH BEND,IND.

1913	STL	A	S		10	.286
1914	STL	A	S		81	.209
		BRTR			91	.220

WARHOP, JOHN MILTON (JACK)
(CHIEF) OR (CRAB)
[REAL NAME JOHN MILTON WAUHOP]
B.JULY 4,1884 HINTON,W.VA.
D.OCT.4,1960 FREEPORT,ILL.

1908	NY	A	P		5	1- 3
1909	NY	A	P		36	13-15
1910	NY	A	P		37	14-14
1911	NY	A	P	30	32	12-13
1912	NY	A	P		39	10-19
1913	NY	A	P		15	4- 4
1914	NY	A	P		37	8-15
1915	NY	A	P		21	7- 9
		BRTR		220	222	69-92

WARMOTH, WALLACE WALTER (CY)
B.FEB.2,1893 BONE GAP,ILL.
D.JUNE 20,1957 MT.CARMEL,ILL.

1916	STL	N	P		3	0- 0
1922	WAS	A	P		5	1- 0
1923	WAS	A	P		21	7- 4
		BLTL			29	8- 4

WARNEKE, LONNIE (LON)
OR (THE ARKANSAS HUMMINGBIRD)
B.MAR.28,1909 MT.IDA,ARK.
D.JUNE 23,1976 HOT SPRINGS,ARK.

1930	CHI	N	P		1	0- 0
1931	CHI	N	P		20	2- 4
1932	CHI	N	P		35	22- 6
1933	CHI	N	P	36	39	18-13
1934	CHI	N	P	43	52	22-10
1935	CHI	N	P	42	44	20-13
1936	CHI	N	P		40	16-13
1937	STL	N	P		36	18-11
1938	STL	N	P		31	13- 8
1939	STL	N	P		34	13- 7
1940	STL	N	P		33	16-10
1941	STL	N	P		37	17- 9
1942	STL	N	P		12	6- 4
		CHI	N	P	15	5- 7
1943	CHI	N	P		21	4- 5
1945	CHI	N	P		9	0- 1
		BRTR		445	459	192-121

WARNER, EDWARD EMORY
B.JUNE 20,1889 FITCHBURG,MASS.
D.FEB.5,1954 NEW YORK,N.Y.

| 1912 | PIT | N | P | | 11 | 1- 1 |
| | | BRTL | | | | |

WARNER, FREDERICK JOHN RODNEY
B.1855 PHILADELPHIA,PA.
D.FEB.13,1886 PHILADELPHIA,PA.

1875	CEN	NA	O		14	-
1876	ATH	N	O		1	.000
1878	IND	N	S		41	.243
1879	CLE	N	3-O		76	.243
1883	PHI	N	3		38	.233
1884	BRO	AA	3		85	.212
					255	-

WARNER, HOKE HAYDEN (HOOKS)
B.MAY 22,1894 DEL RIO,TEX.
D.FEB.19,1947 SAN FRANCISCO,CAL

1916	PIT	N	3		44	.238
1917	PIT	N	3		3	.200
1919	PIT	N	3		6	.125
1921	CHI	N	3		14	.211
		BLTR			67	.228

WARNER, JACK DYER
B.JULY 12,1940 BRANDYWINE,W.VA.

1962	CHI	N	P		7	0- 0
1963	CHI	N	P		8	0- 1
1964	CHI	N	P		7	0- 0
1965	CHI	N	P		11	0- 1
		BRTR			33	0- 2

WARNER, JOHN JOSEPH
B.AUG.15,1872 NEW YORK,N.Y.
D.DEC.21,1943 QUEENS,N.Y.

1895	BOS	N	C		3	.143
		LOU	N	C	60	.263
1896	LOU	N	C-1	33	.209
		NY	N	C	16	.264
1897	NY	N	C		110	.274
1898	NY	N	C		108	.289
1899	NY	N	C		83	.271
1900	NY	N	C		31	.269
1901	NY	N	C		77	.239
1902	BOS	A	C		64	.234
1903	NY	N	C		85	.284
1904	NY	N	C		86	.199
1905	STL	N	C		41	.235
		DET	A	C	36	.202
1906	DET	A	C		49	.242
		WAS	A	C	33	.204
1907	WAS	A	C		72	.256
1908	WAS	A	C		51	.241
		BLTR			1038	.250

WARNER, JOHN JOSEPH (JACKIE)
B.AUG.1,1943 MONROVIA,CAL.

| 1966 | CAL | A | O | | 45 | .277 |
| | | BRTR | | | | |

WARNER, JOHN RALPH
B.AUG.29,1903 EVANSVILLE,IND.

1925	DET	A	3		10	.333
1926	DET	A	3		100	.251
1927	DET	A	3		139	.267
1928	DET	A	3		75	.214
1929	BRO	N	S		17	.274
1930	BRO	N	3		21	.320
1931	BRO	N	S-3		9	.500
1933	PHI	N	2-S-3		107	.224
		BRTR			478	.250

WARNOCK, HAROLD CHARLES (HAL)
B.JAN.6,1912 NEW YORK,N.Y.

| 1935 | STL | A | O | | 6 | .286 |
| | | BLTR | | | | |

WARREN, BENNIE LOUIS
B.MAR.2,1912 ELK CITY,OKLA.

1939	PHI	N	C		18	.232
1940	PHI	N	C-1		106	.246
1941	PHI	N	C		121	.215
1942	PHI	N	C-1		90	.209
1946	NY	N	C		39	.159
1947	NY	N	C		3	.200
		BRTR			377	.219

WARREN, THOMAS GENTRY
B.JULY 5,1917 TULSA,OKLA.
D.JAN.2,1968 TULSA,OKLA.

| 1944 | BRO | N | P | 22 | 41 | 1- 4 |
| | | BBTL | | | | |

WARREN, WILLIAM
[SEE WILLIAM WARREN WHITE]

WARREN, WILLIAM H.
B.FEB.11,1887 CAIRO,ILL.

1914	IND	F	C		23	.239
1915	NEW	F	C		5	.333
		BLTR			28	.245

WARSTLER, HAROLD BURTON (RABBIT)
B.SEPT.13,1903 N.CANTON,OHIO
D.MAY 31,1964 N.CANTON,OHIO

YR	CL	LEA	POS	GP	G	REC
1930	BOS	A	S		54	.185
1931	BOS	A	2-S		66	.243
1932	BOS	A	S		115	.211
1933	BOS	A	S		92	.217
1934	PHI	A	2		117	.236
1935	PHI	A	2-3		138	.250
1936	PHI	A	2		66	.250
	BOS	N	S		74	.211
1937	BOS	N	S		149	.223
1938	BOS	N	S		142	.231
1939	BOS	N	2-S-3		114	.243
1940	BOS	N	2		33	.211
	CHI	N	2-S		45	.226
		BRTR			1205	.229

WARTHEN, DANIEL DEAN (DAN)
B.DEC.1,1952 OMAHA,NEB.

YR	CL	LEA	POS	GP	G	REC
1975	MON	N	P		40	8- 6
1976	MON	N	P		23	2-10
1977	MON	N	P		12	2- 3
	PHI	N	/P		3	0- 1
1978	HOU	N	/P		5	0- 1
		BBTL			83	12-21

WARWICK, CARL WAYNE
B.FEB.27,1937 DALLAS,TEX.

YR	CL	LEA	POS	GP	G	REC
1961	LA	N	O		19	.091
	STL	N	O		55	.250
1962	STL	N	O		13	.348
	HOU	N	O		130	.260
1963	HOU	N	1-O		150	.254
1964	STL	N	O		88	.259
1965	STL	N	O/1		50	.156
	BAL	A	/O		9	.000
1966	CHI	N	O		16	.227
		BRTL			530	.248

WARWICK, FIRMIN NEWTON (BILL)
B.NOV.26,1897 PHILADELPHIA,PA.

YR	CL	LEA	POS	GP	G	REC
1921	PIT	N	C		1	.000
1925	STL	N	C		13	.293
1926	STL	N	C		9	.357
		BRTR			23	.304

WASDELL, JAMES CHARLES (JIMMY)
B.MAY 15,1914 CLEVELAND,OHIO

YR	CL	LEA	POS	GP	G	REC
1937	WAS	A	1		32	.255
1938	WAS	A	1		53	.236
1939	WAS	A	1		29	.303
1940	WAS	A	1		10	.086
	BRO	N	1-O		77	.278
1941	BRO	N	O		94	.299
1942	PIT	N	1-O		122	.259
1943	PIT	N	H		4	.500
	PHI	N	1-O		141	.261
1944	PHI	N	1-O		133	.277
1945	PHI	N	1-O		134	.300
1946	PHI	N	1-O		26	.255
	CLE	A	1-O		32	.268
1947	CLE	A	H		1	.000
		BLTL			888	.273

WASEM, LINCOLN WILLIAM
B.JAN.30,1911 BIRMINGHAM,OHIO

YR	CL	LEA	POS	GP	G	REC
1937	BOS	N	C		2	.000
		BRTR				

WASHBURN, GEORGE EDWARD
B.OCT.6,1914 SOLON,ME.

YR	CL	LEA	POS	GP	G	REC
1941	NY	A	P		1	0- 1
		BLTR				

WASHBURN, GREGORY JAMES (GREG)
B.DEC.3,1946 COAL CITY,ILL.

YR	CL	LEA	POS	GP	G	REC
1969	CAL	A	/P		8	0- 2
		BRTR				

WASHBURN, LIBEUS (LIBE)
B.JUNE 16,1874 LYME,N.H.
D.MAR.22,1940 MALONE,N.Y.

YR	CL	LEA	POS	GP	G	REC
1902	NY	N	O		6	.444
1903	PHI	N	P	4	8	0- 4
		BBTL		4	14	0- 4
						.286

WASHBURN, RAY CLARK
B.MAY 31,1938 PASCO,WASH.

YR	CL	LEA	POS	GP	G	REC
1961	STL	N	P		3	1- 1
1962	STL	N	P		34	12- 9
1963	STL	N	P		11	5- 3
1964	STL	N	P		15	3- 4
1965	STL	N	P		28	9-11
1966	STL	N	P		27	11- 9
1967	STL	N	P		27	10- 7
1968	STL	N	P		31	14- 8
1969	STL	N	P		28	3- 8
1970	CIN	N	P		35	4- 4
		BRTR			239	72-64

WASHER, WILLIAM (BUCK)
B.OCT.11,1882 AKRON,OHIO
D.DEC.8,1955 AKRON,OHIO

YR	CL	LEA	POS	GP	G	REC
1905	PHI	N	P		1	0- 0
		TR				

WASHINGTON, CLAUDELL
B.AUG.31,1954 LOS ANGELES,CAL.

YR	CL	LEA	POS	GP	G	REC
1974	OAK	A	D-O		73	.285
1975	OAK	A	*O		148	.308
1976	OAK	A	*O		134	.257
1977	TEX	A	*O		129	.284
1978	TEX	A	/O		12	.167
	CHI	A	O		86	.264
		BLTL			582	.280

WASHINGTON, HERBERT LEE (HERB)
B.NOV.16,1951 BELZONIA,MISS.

YR	CL	LEA	POS	GP	G	REC
1974	OAK	A	R		92	.000
1975	OAK	A	R		13	.000
		BRTR			105	.000

WASHINGTON, LA RUE
B.SEPT.7,1953 LONG BEACH,CAL.

YR	CL	LEA	POS	GP	G	REC
1978	TEX	A	/2		3	.000
		BRTR				

WASHINGTON, RONALD (RON)
B.APR.29,1952 NEW ORLEANS,LA.

YR	CL	LEA	POS	GP	G	REC
1977	LA	N	S		10	.368
		BRTR				

WASHINGTON, SLOANE VERNON
(GEORGE) OR (VERN)
B.JUNE 7,1907 LINDEN,TEX.

YR	CL	LEA	POS	GP	G	REC
1935	CHI	A	O		108	.288
1936	CHI	A	O		20	.163
		BLTR			128	.268

WASHINGTON, U L (U L)
B.OCT.27,1953 STRINGTOWN,OKLA.

YR	CL	LEA	POS	GP	G	REC
1977	KC	A	/S		10	.200
1978	KC	A	S-2		69	.264
		BBTR			79	.255

WASLEWSKI, GARY LEE
B.JULY 21,1941 MERIDEN,CONN.

YR	CL	LEA	POS	GP	G	REC
1967	BOS	A	P		12	2- 2
1968	BOS	A	P	34	39	4- 7
1969	STL	N	P		12	0- 2
	MON	N	P		30	3- 7
1970	MON	N	/P		6	0- 2
	NY	A	P		26	2- 2
1971	NY	A	P		24	0- 1
1972	OAK	A	/P		8	0- 3
		BRTR		152	157	11-26

WATERBURY, STEVEN CRAIG (STEVE)
B.APR.6,1952 CARBONDALE,ILL.

YR	CL	LEA	POS	GP	G	REC
1976	STL	N	/P		5	0- 0
		BRTR				

WATERMAN, FREDERICK A.
B.1846 NEW YORK,N.Y.
D.DEC.16,1899

YR	CL	LEA	POS	GP	G	REC
1871	OLY	NA	C-3		32	-
1872	OLY	NA	C-3		9	.400
1873	NAT	NA	S-3-O		15	-
1875	CHI	NA	2-3		4	-
					60	-

WATERS, FRED WARREN
B.FEB.2,1927 BENTON,MISS.

YR	CL	LEA	POS	GP	G	REC
1955	PIT	N	P		2	0- 0
1956	PIT	N	P		23	2- 2
		BLTL			25	2- 2

WATHAN, JOHN DAVID
B.OCT.4,1949 CEDAR RAPIDS,IOWA

YR	CL	LEA	POS	GP	G	REC
1976	KC	A	C/1		27	.286
1977	KC	A	C/1		55	.328
1978	KC	A	1-C		67	.300
		BRTR			149	.308

WATKINS, DAVID ROGER (DAVE)
B.MAR.15,1944 OWENSBORO,KY.

YR	CL	LEA	POS	GP	G	REC
1969	PHI	N	C/O-3		69	.176
		BRTR				

WATKINS, EDWARD

YR	CL	LEA	POS	GP	G	REC
1902	PHI	N	O		1	.000

WATKINS, GEORGE ARCHIBALD
B.JUNE 4,1900 FREESRONE CO.,TEX
D.JUNE 1,1970 HOUSTON,TEX.

YR	CL	LEA	POS	GP	G	REC
1930	STL	N	1-O		119	.373
1931	STL	N	O		131	.288
1932	STL	N	O		127	.312
1933	STL	N	O		138	.278
1934	NY	N	O		105	.247
1935	PHI	N	O		150	.270
1936	PHI	N	O		19	.243
	BRO	N	O		105	.256
		BLTR			894	.288

WATKINS, HARVEY L.
NON-PLAYING MANAGER NY[N] 1895

WATKINS, ROBERT CECIL (BOB)
B.MAR.12,1948 SAN FRANCISCO,CAL.

YR	CL	LEA	POS	GP	G	REC
1969	HOU	N	/P		5	0- 0
		BRTR				

WATKINS, WILLIAM HENRY
B.MAY 5,1858 BRANTFORD,ONT.,CAN
D.JUNE 9,1937

YR	CL	LEA	POS	GP	G	REC
1884	IND	AA	M-2-3		34	.211

NON-PLAYING MANAGER
DET[N] 1885-88, KC[AA] 1888-89,
STL(N) 1893, PIT(N) 1898-99

WATLINGTON, JULIUS NEAL (NEAL)
B.DEC.25,1922 YANCEYVILLE,N.C.

YR	CL	LEA	POS	GP	G	REC
1953	PHI	A	C		21	.159
		BLTR				

WATSON, ARTHUR STANHOPE (WATTY)
B.JAN.11,1884 JEFFERSONVILLE,IND.
D.MAY 9,1950 BUFFALO,N.Y.

YR	CL	LEA	POS	GP	G	REC
1914	BRO	F	C		19	.289
1915	BRO	F	C		8	.294
	BUF	F	C		21	.452
		BLTR			48	.344

WATSON, CHARLES JOHN
B.JAN.30,1885 OHIO
D.DEC.30,1949 SAN DIEGO,CAL.

YR	CL	LEA	POS	GP	G	REC
1913	CHI	N	P		1	1- 0
1914	CHI	F	P		26	9- 8
	STL	F	P		9	3- 4
1915	STL	F	P		33	9- 9
		BRTL			69	22-21

WATSON, JOHN REEVES (MULE)
B.OCT.15,1896 HOMER,LA.
D.AUG.25,1949 SHREVEPORT,LA.

YR	CL	LEA	POS	GP	G	REC
1918	PHI	A	P		21	6-10
1919	PHI	A	P		4	0- 1
1920	BOS	N	P		1	0- 0
	PIT	N	P		5	0- 0
	BOS	N	P		12	5- 4
1921	BOS	N	P		44	14-13
1922	BOS	N	P		41	8-14
1923	BOS	N	P		11	1- 2
	NY	N	P		17	8- 5
1924	NY	N	P		22	7- 4
		BRTR			178	49-53

WATSON, JOHN THOMAS
B.JAN.16,1908 TAZEWELL,VA.
D.APR.29,1965 HUNTINGTON,W.VA.

YR	CL	LEA	POS	GP	G	REC
1930	DET	A	S		4	.250
		BLTR				

WATSON, MILTON W.
B.1893 PARIS,TEX.

YR	CL	LEA	POS	GP	G	REC
1916	STL	N	P		18	4- 6
1917	STL	N	P		41	10-13
1918	PHI	N	P		23	5- 7
1919	PHI	N	P		8	2- 4
		BRTR			90	21-30

WATSON, ROBERT JOSE (BOB) OR (BULL)
B.APR.10,1946 LOS ANGELES,CAL.

YR	CL	LEA	POS	GP	G	REC
1966	HOU	N	/H		1	.000
1967	HOU	N	/1		6	.214
1968	HOU	N	O		45	.229
1969	HOU	N	/O-1-C		20	.275
1970	HOU	N	1/C-O		97	.272
1971	HOU	N	O-1		129	.288
1972	HOU	N	*O/1		147	.312
1973	HOU	N	*O-1/C		158	.312
1974	HOU	N	*O-1		150	.296
1975	HOU	N	*1/O		132	.324
1976	HOU	N	*1		157	.313
1977	HOU	N	*1		151	.289
1978	HOU	N	*1		139	.289
		BRTR			1332	.299

WATSON, WALTER L. (MOTHER)
B.JAN.27,1865 MIDDLEPORT,OHIO
D.NOV.23,1898 MIDDLEPORT,OHIO

YR	CL	LEA	POS	GP	G	REC
1887	CIN	AA	P-O		2	1- 1
						.222

WATT, ALBERT BAILEY (ALLIE)
B.DEC.12,1899 PHILADELPHIA,PA.
D.MAR.15,1968 NORFOLK,VA.

YR	CL	LEA	POS	GP	G	REC
1920	WAS	A	2		1	1.000
		BRTR				

WATT, EDWARD DEAN (EDDIE)
B.APR.4,1942 LAMONI,IOWA

YR	CL	LEA	POS	GP	G	REC
1966	BAL	A	P		43	9- 7
1967	BAL	A	P		49	3- 5
1968	BAL	A	P		59	5- 5
1969	BAL	A	P		56	5- 2
1970	BAL	A	P		53	7- 7
1971	BAL	A	P		35	3- 1
1972	BAL	A	P		38	2- 3
1973	BAL	A	P		30	3- 4
1974	PHI	N	P		42	1- 1
1975	CHI	N	/P		6	0- 1
		BRTR			411	38-36

WATT, FRANK MARION (KILO)
B.DEC.15,1902 WASHINGTON,D.C.
D.AUG.31,1956 WASHINGTON,D.C.

YR	CL	LEA	POS	GP	G	REC
1931	PHI	N	P		38	5- 5
		BRTR				

YR	CL	LEA	POS	GP	G	REC

WATWOOD, JOHN CLIFFORD
B.AUG.17,1906 ALEXANDER CITY,ALA.

1929	CHI	A	O		85	.302
1930	CHI	A	1-O		133	.302
1931	CHI	A	O		128	.283
1932	CHI	A	O		13	.296
	BOS	A	1-O		95	.249
1933	BOS	A	O		13	.133
1939	PHI	N	1		2	.167
	BLTL				469	.283

WAUGH, JAMES ELDEN (JIM)
B.NOV.25,1933 LANCASTER,OHIO

1952	PIT	N	P		17	1- 6
1953	PIT	N	P		29	4- 5
	BRTR				46	5-11

WAUHOP, JOHN MILTON
[PLAYED UNDER NAME OF
JOHN MILTON WARHOP]

WAY, ROBERT CLINTON
B.APR.2,1906 EMLENTON,PA.
D.JUNE 20,1974 PITTSBURGH,PA.

| 1927 | CHI | A | 2 | | 5 | .333 |
| | BRTR | | | | | |

WAYENBERG, FRANK
B.AUG.27,1898 FRANKLIN,KAN.
D.APR.16,1975 ZANESVILLE,OHIO

| 1924 | CLE | A | P | | 2 | 0- 0 |
| | BRTR | | | | | |

WEAFER, KENNETH ALBERT (HAL) OR (AL)
B.FEB.6,1914 WOBURN,MASS.

| 1936 | BOS | N | P | | 1 | 0- 0 |
| | BRTR | | | | | |

WEATHERLY, CYRIL ROY
(ROY) OR (STORMY)
B.FEB.25,1915 WARREN,TEX.

1936	CLE	A	O		84	.335
1937	CLE	A	O		53	.201
1938	CLE	A	O		83	.262
1939	CLE	A	O		95	.310
1940	CLE	A	O		135	.303
1941	CLE	A	O		102	.289
1942	CLE	A	O		128	.258
1943	NY	A	O		77	.264
1946	NY	A	H		2	.500
1950	NY	N	O		52	.261
	BLTR				811	.286

WEAVER, ARTHUR COGGSHALL
(SIX O CLOCK)
B.APR.7,1879 WICHITA,KAN.
D.MAR.23,1917 DENVER,COLO.

1902	STL	N	C		11	.171
1903	PIT	N	C		16	.245
	PIT	N	C		15	.239
1905	STL	A	C		28	.120
1908	CHI	A	C		15	.200
	TR				85	.184

WEAVER, DAVID FLOYD (FLOYD)
B.MAY 12,1941 BEN FRANKLIN,TEX.

1962	CLE	A	P		1	1- 0
1965	CLE	A	P		32	2- 2
1970	CHI	A	P		31	1- 2
1971	MIL	A	P		21	0- 1
	BRTR				85	4- 5

WEAVER, EARL SIDNEY
B.AUG.14,1930 ST.LOUIS,MO.
NON-PLAYING MANAGER BAL[A] 1968-78

WEAVER, GEORGE DAVIS (BUCK)
B.AUG.18,1890 STOWE,PA.
D.JAN.31,1956 CHICAGO,ILL.

1912	CHI	A	S		147	.224
1913	CHI	A	S		151	.272
1914	CHI	A	S		136	.246
1915	CHI	A	S		148	.268
1916	CHI	A	S-3		151	.227
1917	CHI	A	S-3		118	.284
1918	CHI	A	S-3		112	.300
1919	CHI	A	S-3		140	.296
1920	CHI	A	S-3		151	.333
	BBTR				1254	.272
	BR 1912-16					

WEAVER, HARRY ABRAHAM
B.FEB.26,1892 CLARENDON,PA.

1915	PHI	A	P		2	0- 2
1916	PHI	A	P		3	0- 0
1917	CHI	N	P		4	1- 1
1918	CHI	N	P		8	2- 2
1919	CHI	N	P		2	0- 1
	BRTR				19	3- 6

WEAVER, JAMES BRIAN (JIM) OR (FLUFF)
B.FEB.19,1939 LANCASTER,PA.

1967	CAL	A	P		13	3- 0
1968	CAL	A	P		14	0- 1
	BLTL				27	3- 1

WEAVER, JAMES DEMENT (BIG JIM)
B.NOV.25,1903 FULTON,KY.

1928	WAS	A	P		3	0- 0
1931	NY	A	P		17	2- 1
1934	STL	A	P		5	2- 0
	CHI	N	P		27	11- 9
1935	PIT	N	P		33	14- 8
1936	PIT	N	P		38	14- 8
1937	PIT	N	P		32	8- 5
1938	STL	A	P		1	0- 1
	CIN	N	P		30	6- 4
1939	CIN	N	P		3	0- 0
	BRTR				189	57-36

WEAVER, MONTGOMERY MORTON
(MONTE) OR (PROF)
B.JUNE 15,1906 HILTON,N.C.

1931	WAS	A	P		3	1- 0
1932	WAS	A	P	43	44	22-10
1933	WAS	A	P		23	10- 5
1934	WAS	A	P		31	11-15
1935	WAS	A	P		5	1- 1
1936	WAS	A	P		26	6- 4
1937	WAS	A	P		30	12- 9
1938	WAS	A	P		31	7- 6
1939	BOS	A	P		9	1- 0
	BLTR			201	202	71-50

WEAVER, ORVILLE FOREST (ORLIE)
B.JUNE 4,1886 NEWPORT,KY.
D.NOV.28,1970 NEW ORLEANS,LA.

1910	CHI	N	P		7	1- 1
1911	CHI	N	P		6	2- 2
	BOS	N	P		27	3-12
	BRTR				40	6-15

WEAVER, SAMUEL H.
B.JULY 10,1855 PHILADELPHIA,PA.
D.FEB.1,1914 PHILADELPHIA,PA.

1875	PHI	NA	P		1	1- 0
1878	MIL	N	P	42	47	12-30
1882	ATH	AA	P-O	41	42	26-15
						.240
1883	LOU	AA	P-1-	46	50	24-20
			O			.195
1884	KEY	U	P		20	5-12
1886	ATH	AA	P		2	0- 2
	BRTR			152	162	68-79
						.211

WEAVER, WILLIAM B. (FARMER)
B.MAR.23,1865 PARKERSBURG,W.VA.
D.JAN.25,1943 AKRON,OHIO

1886	BRO	AA	C		1	.000
1888	LOU	AA	O		26	.274
1889	LOU	AA	O		124	.290
1890	LOU	AA	O		130	.292
1891	LOU	AA	O		133	.284
1892	LOU	N	O		136	.268
1893	LOU	N	C-O		104	.309
1894	LOU	N	C		60	.206
	PIT	N	C-S-3-O		30	.352
					744	.285

WEBB, CLEON EARL (LEFTY)
B.MAR.1,1885 MT.GILEAD,OHIO
D.JAN.12,1958 CIRCLEVILLE,OHIO

| 1910 | PIT | N | P | | 7 | 2- 1 |
| | BBTL | | | | | |

WEBB, HENRY GAYLON MATTHEW (HANK)
B.MAY 21,1950 COPIAGUE,N.Y.

1972	NY	N	/P		6	0- 0
1973	NY	N	/P		2	0- 0
1974	NY	N	/P		3	0- 2
1975	NY	N	/P	29	31	7- 6
1976	NY	N	/P		8	0- 1
1977	LA	N	/P		5	0- 0
	BRTR			53	55	7- 9

WEBB, JAMES LAVERNE (SKEETER)
B.NOV.4,1909 MERIDIAN,MISS.

1932	STL	N	S		1	.000
1938	CLE	A	S		20	.276
1939	CLE	A	S		81	.264
1940	CHI	A	2-S-3		84	.237
1941	CHI	A	2-S-3		29	.190
1942	CHI	A	2		32	.170
1943	CHI	A	2		58	.235
1944	CHI	A	2-S		139	.211
1945	DET	A	2-S		118	.199
1946	DET	A	2-S		64	.219
1947	DET	A	2-S		50	.203
1948	PHI	A	2-S		23	.148
					699	.219

WEBB, SAMUEL HENRY (RED)
B.SEPT.25,1924 WASHINGTON,D.C.

1948	NY	N	P		5	2- 1
1949	NY	N	P		20	1- 1
	BLTR				25	3- 2

WEBB, WILLIAM EARL (EARL)
B.SEPT.17,1898 BON AIR,TENN.
D.MAY 23,1965 JAMESTOWN,TENN.

1925	NY	N	O		4	.000
1927	CHI	N	O		102	.301
1928	CHI	N	O		62	.250
1930	BOS	A	O		127	.323
1931	BOS	A	O		151	.333
1932	BOS	A	O		52	.281
	DET	A	O		88	.287
1933	DET	A	O		6	.273
	CHI	A	O		58	.308
	BLTR				650	.306

WEBB, WILLIAM FREDERICK
B.DEC.12,1913 ATLANTA,GA.

| 1943 | PHI | N | P | | 1 | 0- 0 |
| | BRTR | | | | | |

WEBB, WILLIAM JOSEPH
B.JUNE 25,1895 CHICAGO,ILL.
D.JAN.12,1943 CHICAGO,ILL.

| 1917 | PIT | N | 2-S | | 5 | .200 |
| | BRTR | | | | | |

WEBBER, JOSEPH EDWARD
B.1861 HAMILTON,ONT.,CANADA
D.DEC.15,1921 HAMILTON,ONT.,CAN

| 1884 | IND | AA | C | | 3 | .000 |

WEBBER, LESTER ELMER
B.MAY 6,1915 LAKEPORT,CAL.

1942	BRO	N	P		19	3- 2
1943	BRO	N	P		54	2- 2
1944	BRO	N	P		48	7- 8
1945	BRO	N	P		17	7- 3
1946	BRO	N	P		11	3- 3
	CLE	A	P		4	1- 1
1948	CLE	A	P		1	0- 0
	BRTR				154	23-19

WEBER, CHARLES P. (COUNT)
B.OCT.22,1868 CINCINNATI,OHIO
D.JUNE 13,1914 BEAUMONT,TEX.

| 1898 | WAS | N | P | | 1 | 0- 1 |

WEBER, HARRY
B.INDIANAPOLIS,IND.

| 1884 | DET | N | O | | 2 | .000 |

WEBSTER, RAMON ALBERTO (RAY)
B.AUG.31,1942 COLON,PANAMA

1967	KC	A	1-O		122	.256
1968	OAK	A	1		66	.214
1969	OAK	A	1		64	.260
1970	SD	N	1/O		95	.259
1971	SD	N	H		10	.125
	OAK	A	/1		7	.000
	CHI	N	/1		16	.313
	BLTL				380	.244

WEBSTER, RAYMOND GEORGE (RAY)
B.NOV.15,1937 GRASS VALLEY,CAL.

1959	CLE	A	2-3		40	.203
1960	BOS	A	2		7	.000
	BRTR				47	.195

WECKBECKER, PETER
B.AUG.30,1864 BUTLER,PA.
D.MAY 16,1935 HAMPTON,VA.

1889	IND	N	C		1	.000
1890	LOU	AA	C		30	.234
					31	.232

WEEDEN, CHARLES ALBERT (BERT)
B.DEC.21,1882 NORTHWOOD,N.H.
D.JAN.7,1939 NORTHWOOD,N.H.

| 1911 | BOS | N | H | | 1 | .000 |
| | BLTL | | | | | |

WEEKLY, JOHNNY
B.JUNE 14,1937 WATERPROOF,LA.
D.NOV.24,1974 WALNUT CREEK,CAL.

1962	HOU	N	O		13	.192
1963	HOU	N	O		34	.225
1964	HOU	N	O		6	.133
	BRTR				53	.207

WEGENER, MICHAEL DENIS (MIKE)
B.OCT.5,1946 DENVER,COLO.

1969	MON	N	P		32	5-14
1970	MON	N	P		25	3- 6
	BRTR				57	8-20

WEHDE, WILBUR (BIGGS)
B.NOV.23,1906 HOLSTEIN,IOWA
D.SEPT.21,1970 SIOUX FALLS,S.DAK.

1930	CHI	A	P		4	0- 0
1931	CHI	A	P		8	1- 0
	BRTR				12	1- 0

```
YR  CL LEA POS      GP    G    REC

WEHMEIER, HERMAN RALPH (HERM)
B.FEB.18,1927 CINCINNATI,OHIO
D.MAY 21,1973 DALLAS,TEX.
1945 CIN N P        2    3   0- 1
1947 CIN N P             1   0- 0
1948 CIN N P       33   36  11- 8
1949 CIN N P       33   36  11-12
1950 CIN N P       41   54  10-18
1951 CIN N P       39   46   7-10
1952 CIN N P       33   41   9-11
1953 CIN N P       28   29   1- 6
1954 CIN N P       12   13   0- 3
     PHI N P            25  10- 8
1955 PHI N P       31   34  10-12
1956 PHI N P             3   0- 2
     STL N P            42  12- 9
1957 STL N P       36   40  10- 7
1958 STL N P             3   0- 1
     DET A P             7   1- 0
        BRTR      361  413  92-108

WEHRMEISTER, DAVID THOMAS (DAVE)
B.NOV.9,1952 BERWYN,ILL.
1976 SD  N /P            7   0- 4
1977 SD  N  P           30   1- 3
1978 SD  N /P            4   1- 0
        BRTR       41   2- 7

WEICHBRODT, RUDOLPH C.
[PLAYED UNDER NAME OF SKELL ROACH]

WEIDMAN, GEORGE E. (STUMP)
B.FEB.17,1861 ROCHESTER,N.Y.
D.MAR.3,1905 NEW YORK,N.Y.
1880 BUF N P-O     17   23   0-10
                              .400
1881 DET N P            13   8- 5
1882 DET N P-S-    46   50  26-20
        O                     .217
1883 DET N P-2-    45   76  19-23
                              .173
1884 DET N P-2-    27   79   5-22
        S-O                   .162
1885 DET N P-O     38   43  14-23
                              .156
1886 KC  N P       49   51  12-37
1887 DET N P            21  13- 6
     MET AA P-O    12   14   4- 8
                              .229
     NY  N P             2   0- 2
1888 NY  N P             2   1- 1
        BRTR      272  374 102-157
                              .177

WEIGEL, RALPH RICHARD
(RALPH) OR (WIG)
B.OCT.2,1921 COLDWATER,OHIO
1946 CLE A C             6   .167
1948 CHI A C-O     66   .233
1949 WAS A C       34   .233
        BRTR      106   .230

WEIHE, JOHN GARIBALDI (PODGE)
B.NOV.13,1862 CINCINNATI,OHIO
D.APR.15,1914 CINCINNATI,OHIO
1883 CIN AA O       1   .250
1884 IND AA O      64   .261
        BRTR       65   .260

WEIK, RICHARD HENRY (DICK) OR (LEGS)
B.NOV.17,1927 WATERLOO,IOWA
1948 WAS A P             3   1- 2
1949 WAS A P       27   28   3-12
1950 WAS A P            14   1- 3
     CLE A P            11   1- 3
1953 CLE A R             1   .000
     DET A P            12   0- 1
1954 DET A P             9   0- 1
        BRTR       76   78   6-22
                              .226

WEILAND, EDWIN NICHOLAS
B.NOV.26,1914 EVANSTON,ILL.
D.JULY 12,1971 CHICAGO,ILL.
1940 CHI A P             5   0- 0
1942 CHI A P             5   0- 0
        BLTR       10   0- 0

WEILAND, ROBERT GEORGE (LEFTY)
B.DEC.14,1905 CHICAGO,ILL.
1928 CHI A P             1   1- 0
1929 CHI A P            15   2- 4
1930 CHI A P            14   0- 4
1931 CHI A P            15   2- 7
1932 BOS A P            43   6-16
1933 BOS A P            39   8-14
1934 BOS A P            11   1- 5
     CLE A P            16   1- 5
1935 STL N P            14   0- 2
1937 STL N P            41  15-14
1938 STL N P            35  16-11
1939 STL N P            32  10-12
1940 STL N P             1   0- 0
        BLTL      277  62-94

WEILENMANN, CARL WOOLWORTH
[PLAYED UNDER NAME OF
CARL WOOLWORTH WEILMAN]


WEILMAN, CARL WOOLWORTH (ZEKE)
[REAL NAME
CARL WOOLWORTH WEILENMANN]
B.NOV.29,1889 HAMILTON,OHIO
D.MAY 25,1924 HAMILTON,OHIO
1912 STL A P             9   2- 4
1913 STL A P            39  10-20
1914 STL A P            45  19-13
1915 STL A P            47  18-18
1916 STL A P            46  17-18
1917 STL A P             5   1- 2
1919 STL A P            20  10- 6
1920 STL A P            30   9-13
        BLTL      241  86-94

WEIMER, JACOB (JAKE)
OR (TORNADO JAKE)
B.NOV.29,1873 OTTUMWA,IOWA
D.JUNE 17,1928 CHICAGO,ILL.
1903 CHI N P            35  20- 8
1904 CHI N P            37  20-13
1905 CHI N P            33  18-13
1906 CIN N P            41  20-14
1907 CIN N P            29  11-14
1908 CIN N P            15   8- 7
1909 NY  N P             1   0- 0
        BRTL      191  97-69

WEINERT, PHILLIP WALTER (LEFTY)
B.APR.21,1902 PHILADELPHIA,PA.
D.APR.17,1973 ROCKLEDGE,FLA.
1919 PHI N P             1   0- 0
1920 PHI N P            10   1- 1
1921 PHI N P             8   1- 0
1922 PHI N P            34   8-11
1923 PHI N P       38   39   4-17
1924 PHI N P             8   0- 1
1927 CHI N P             5   1- 1
1928 CHI N P            10   1- 0
1931 NY  A P            17   2- 2
        BLTL      131  132  18-33

WEINGARTNER, ELMER WILLIAM (DUTCH)
B.AUG.13,1918 CLEVELAND,OHIO
1945 CLE A S            20   .231
        BRTR

WEINTRAUB, PHILIP (MICKEY)
B.OCT.12,1907 CHICAGO,ILL.
1933 NY  N O             8   .200
1934 NY  N O            31   .351
1935 NY  N 1-O          64   .241
1937 CIN N O            49   .271
     NY  N O             6   .333
1938 PHI N 1           100   .311
1944 NY  N 1           104   .316
1945 NY  N 1            82   .272
        BLTL      444   .295

WEIR, WILLIAM FRANKLIN
(ROY) OR (BILL)
B.FEB.25,1911 PORTLAND,MAINE
1936 BOS N P       12   13   4- 3
1937 BOS N P            10   1- 1
1938 BOS N P             5   1- 0
1939 BOS N P             2   0- 0
        BLTL       29   30   6- 4

WEIS, ALBERT JOHN (AL)
B.APR.2,1938 FRANKLIN SQUARE,N.Y
1962 CHI A 2-S-3         7   .083
1963 CHI A 2-S-3        99   .271
1964 CHI A 2-S-O       133   .247
1965 CHI A 2/S-3-O     103   .296
1966 CHI A 2-S         125   .155
1967 CHI A 2-S          50   .245
1968 NY  N S-2/3        90   .172
1969 NY  N 2-S         103   .215
1970 NY  N 2-S          75   .207
1971 NY  N /2-3         11   .000
        BBTR      800   .219
        BR 1969-71

WEIS, ARTHUR JOHN (BUTCH)
B.MAR.2,1903 ST.LOUIS,MO.
1922 CHI N O             2   .500
1923 CHI N O            22   .231
1924 CHI N O            37   .278
1925 CHI N O            67   .267
        BLTL      128   .270

WEISER, HARRY BUDSON (BUD)
B.JAN.8,1891 SHAMOKIN,PA.
D.JULY 31,1961 SHAMOKIN,PA.
1915 PHI N O            37   .141
1916 PHI N O             4   .300
        BRTR       41   .162

WEISS, JOSEPH HAROLD
B.JAN.27,1894 CHICAGO,ILL.
1919 CHI F 1       29   .239


WELAJ, JOHN LUDWIG
B.MAY 27,1914 MOSS CREEK,PA.
1939 WAS A O            63   .274
1940 WAS A O            88   .256
1941 WAS A O            49   .208
1943 PHI A O            93   .242
        BRTR      293   .250

WELCH, CURTIS BENTON
B.FEB.11,1862 E.LIVERPOOL,OHIO
D.AUG.29,1896 E.LIVERPOOL,OHIO
1884 TOL AA O          109   .224
1885 STL AA O          112   .266
1886 STL AA O          138   .285
1887 STL AA O          131   .307
1888 ATH AA O          136   .291
1889 ATH AA O          125   .273
1890 ATH AA O          106   .283
     BAL AA 1-O         19   .122
1891 BAL AA O          130   .278
1892 BAL N  O           63   .233
     CIN N  O           24   .220
1893 LOU N  O           14   .181
        BR       1107   .269

WELCH, FRANK TIGUER
(FRANK) OR (BUGGER)
B.AUG.10,1897 BIRMINGHAM,ALA.
D.JULY 25,1957 BIRMINGHAM,ALA.
1919 PHI A O            13   .167
1920 PHI A O           100   .258
1921 PHI A O           115   .285
1922 PHI A O           114   .259
1923 PHI A O           125   .297
1924 PHI A O            94   .290
1925 PHI A O            85   .277
1926 PHI A O            75   .281
1927 BOS A O            15   .179
        BRTR      738   .284

WELCH, HERBERT M. (DUTCH)
B.OCT.19,1898 RO ELLEN,TENN.
D.APR.13,1967 MEMPHIS,TENN.
1925 BOS A S            13   .289
        BLTR

WELCH, JOHN VERNON
B.DEC.2,1906 WASHINGTON,D.C.
D.SEPT.2,1940 ST.LOUIS,MO.
1926 CHI N P             3   0- 0
1927 CHI N P             3   0- 0
1928 CHI N P             3   0- 0
1931 CHI N P             8   2- 1
1932 BOS A P       20   23   4- 6
1933 BOS A P            47   4- 9
1934 BOS A P            41  13-15
1935 BOS A P            31  10- 9
1936 BOS A P             9   2- 1
     PIT N P             9   0- 0
        BLTR      172  175  35-41

WELCH, MICHAEL FRANCIS
(SMILING MICKEY)
B.JULY 4,1859 BROOKLYN,N.Y.
D.JULY 30,1941 NASHUA,N.H.
1880 TRO N P-O     64   66  34-30
                              .286
1881 TRO N P            39  20-18
1882 TRO N P-O     30   37  14-16
                              .240
1883 NY  N P-O     48   81  27-21
                              .239
1884 NY  N P-O     60   67  39-21
                              .250
1885 NY  N P-O          58  47-11
                              .206
1886 NY  N P       58   59  33-23
1887 NY  N P            40  23-15
1888 NY  N P            47  26-19
1889 NY  N P            41  28-12
1890 NY  N P            35  18-13
1891 NY  N P       18   19   5-11
1892 NY  N P             2   1- 1
        BLTR      540  591 315-211
                              .229

WELCH, MILTON EDWARD
B.JULY 26,1924 FARMERSVILLE,ILL
1945 DET A C             1   .000
        BRTR

WELCH, ROBERT LYNN (BOB)
B.NOV.3,1956 DETROIT,MICH.
1978 LA  N P            23   7- 4
        BBTR

WELCH, THEODORE
B.1893
1914 STL F P             3   0- 0
        BLTR

WELCHONCE, HARRY MONROE
(HARRY) OR (WELCH)
B.NOV.20,1883 NORTH POINT,PA.
D.FEB.26,1977 ARCADIA,CAL.
1911 PHI N O            17   .212
        BLTR
```

YR	CL LEA POS	GP	G	REC

WELDAY, LYNDON EARL (MIKE)
B.DEC.19,1879 CONWAY,IOWA
D.MAY 28,1942 LEAVENWORTH,KAN.
1907 CHI A O   24   .229
1909 CHI A O   29   .189
    BLTL   53   .202

WELF, OLIVER HENRY
B.JAN.17,1889 CLEVELAND,OHIO
D.JUNE 15,1967 CLEVELAND,OHIO
1916 CLE A H   1   .000
    BRTL

WELLMAN, ROBERT JOSEPH
B.JULY 15,1925 NORWOOD,OHIO
1948 PHI A 1-O   4   .200
1950 PHI A O   11   .333
    BRTR   15   .280

WELLS, EDWIN LEE (SATCHELFOOT)
B.JUNE 7,1900 ASHLAND,OHIO
1923 DET A P   7   1- 0
1924 DET A P   29   6- 8
1925 DET A P   35   6- 9
1926 DET A P   30   12-10
1927 DET A P   8   0- 1
1929 NY A P   31   13- 9
1930 NY A P   27   29   2- 3
1931 NY A P   27   28   9- 5
1932 NY A P   22   24   3- 3
1933 STL A P   36   38   6-14
1934 STL A P   33   1- 7
    BLTL   291 298 69-69

WELLS, JACOB
B.AUG.9,1863 MEMPHIS,TENN.
D.MAR.16,1927 HENDERSONVILLE,N.C.
1888 DET N C   16   .157
1890 STL AA C   28   .238
    BRTR   44   .210

WELLS, JOHN FREDERICK
B.NOV.25,1922 JUNCTION CITY,KAN
1944 BRO N P   4   0- 2
    BRTR

WELLS, LEO DONALD
B.JULY 18,1917 KANSAS CITY,KAN.
1942 CHI A S   35   .194
1946 CHI A S-3   45   .189
    BRTR   80   .190

WELSH, JAMES DANIEL
B.OCT.9,1902 DENVER,COLO.
D.OCT.30,1970 OAKLAND,CAL.
1925 BOS N 2-O   122   .312
1926 BOS N O   134   .278
1927 BOS N O   131   .288
1928 NY N O   124   .307
1929 NY N O   38   .248
    BOS N O   53   .290
1930 BOS N O   113   .275
    BLTR   715   .290

WELSH, JAMES J. (TUB)
B.JULY 3,1866 ST.LOUIS,MO.
1890 TOL AA C   33   .263
1895 LOU N C-1   39   .224
             72   .241

WELTEROTH, RICHARD JOHN (DICK)
B.AUG.3,1927 WILLIAMSPORT,PA.
1948 WAS A P   33   2- 1
1949 WAS A P   52   2- 5
1950 WAS A P   5   0- 0
    BRTR   90   4- 6

WELZER, ANTON FRANK (TONY)
B.APR.5,1899 GERMANY
D.MAR.18,1971 MILWAUKEE,WIS.
1926 BOS A P   40   4- 2
1927 BOS A P   37   6-11
    BRTR   77   10-13

WENDELL, LEWIS CHARLES
B.MAR.22,1892 NEW YORK,N.Y.
D.JULY 11,1953 BROOKLYN,N.Y.
1915 NY N C   20   .222
1916 NY N C   2   .000
1924 PHI N C   21   .250
1925 PHI N C   18   .077
1926 PHI N C   1   .000
    BRTR   62   .180

WENSLOFF, CHARLES WILLIAM (BUTCH)
B.DEC.3,1915 SAUSALITO,CAL.
1943 NY A P   29   13-11
1947 NY N P   11   3- 1
1948 CLE A P   1   0- 1
    BRTR   41   16-13

WENTZ, JOHN GEORGE
[REAL NAME JOHN GEORGE WERNZ]
B.MAR.4,1863 LOUISVILLE,KY.
D.SEPT.14,1907 LOUISVILLE,KY.
1891 LOU AA 2   1   .250

WENTZEL, STANLEY AARON
B.JAN.13,1917 LORANE,PA.
1945 BOS N O   4   .211
    BRTR

WENZ, FREDERICK CHARLES
(FRED) OR (FIREBALL)
B.AUG.26,1941 BOUND BROOK,N.J.
1968 BOS A /P   1   0- 0
1969 BOS A /P   8   1- 0
1970 PHI N P   22   2- 0
    BRTR   31   3- 0

WERA, JULIAN VALENTINE (JULIE)
B.FEB.9,1902 WINONA,MINN.
D.DEC.12,1975 ROCHESTER,MINN.
1927 NY A 3   38   .239
1929 NY A 3   5   .417
    BRTR   43   .259

WERBER, WILLIAM MURRAY (BILLY)
B.JUNE 20,1908 BERWYN,MD.
1930 NY A S-3   4   .286
1933 NY A H   3   .000
    BOS A S-3   108   .258
1934 BOS A S-3   152   .321
1935 BOS A 3   124   .255
1936 BOS A 3-O   145   .275
1937 PHI A 3   128   .292
1938 PHI A 3   134   .259
1939 CIN N 3   147   .289
1940 CIN N 3   143   .277
1941 CIN N 3   109   .239
1942 NY N 3   98   .205
    BRTR   1295   .271

WERDEN, PERCIVAL WHERITT (PERRY)
B.JULY 21,1865 ST.LOUIS,MO.
D.JAN.9,1934 MINNEAPOLIS,MINN.
1884 STL U P-O   15   18   11- 1
                     .237
1888 WAS N O   3   .300
1890 TOL AA 1   129   .283
1891 BAL AA 1   137   .292
1892 STL N 1   148   .255
1893 STL N 1   124   .284
1897 LOU N 1   134   .301
    BRTR   15 693   11- 1
                     .283

WERHAS, JOHN CHARLES
(JOHNNY) OR (PEACHES)
B.FEB.7,1938 HIGHLAND PARK,MICH.
1964 LA N 3   29   .193
1965 LA N /1   4   .000
1967 LA N /H   7   .143
    CAL A 3/1-O   49   .160
    BRTR   89   .173

WERLE, WILLIAM GEORGE
(BILL) OR (BUGS)
B.DEC.21,1920 OAKLAND,CAL.
1949 PIT N P   35   12-13
1950 PIT N P   48   8-16
1951 PIT N P   59   8- 6
1952 PIT N P   5   0- 0
    STL N P   19   1- 2
1953 BOS A P   5   0- 1
1954 BOS A P   14   0- 1
    BLTL   185   29-39

WERLEY, GEORGE WILLIAM
B.SEPT.8,1938 ST.LOUIS,MO.
1956 BAL A /P   1   0- 0
    BRTR

WERNER, DONALD PAUL (DON)
B.MAR.8,1953 APPLETON,WIS.
1975 CIN N /C   7   .125
1976 CIN N /C   3   .500
1977 CIN N C   10   .174
1978 CIN N C   50   .150
    BRTR   70   .162

WERNZ, JOHN GEORGE
[PLAYED UNDER NAME OF
JOHN GEORGE WENTZ]

WERRICK, JOSEPH ABRAHAM
B.OCT.25,1861 ST.PAUL,MINN.
D.MAY 10,1943 ST.PETER,MINN.
1884 STP U S   9   .071
1886 LOU AA 3   136   .250
1887 LOU AA 3   136   .333
1888 LOU AA 3   109   .210
    TR   390   .266

WERT, DONALD RALPH (DON)
B.JULY 29,1938 STRASBURG,PA.
1963 DET A 2-S-3   78   .259
1964 DET A S-3   148   .257
1965 DET A *3/S-2   162   .261
1966 DET A *3   150   .268
1967 DET A *3/S   142   .257
1968 DET A *5/S   150   .200
1969 DET A *3   132   .225
1970 DET A *3/2   128   .218
1971 WAS A /S-3-2   20   .050
    BRTR   1110   .242

WERTZ, DWIGHT LEWIS (DEL)
B.1891
1914 BUF F S   3   .000
    BRTR

WERTZ, HENRY LEVI (JOHNNY)
B.APR.20,1898 POMARIA,S.C.
1926 BOS N P   32   11- 9
1927 BOS N P   42   4-10
1928 BOS N P   10   0- 2
1929 BOS N P   4   0- 0
    BRTR   88   15-21

WERTZ, VICTOR WOODROW (VIC)
B.FEB.9,1925 YORK,PA.
1947 DET A O   102   .288
1948 DET A O   119   .248
1949 DET A O   155   .304
1950 DET A O   149   .308
1951 DET A O   136   .285
1952 DET A O   85   .246
    STL A O   37   .346
1953 STL A O   128   .268
1954 BAL A O   29   .202
    CLE A 1-O   94   .275
1955 CLE A 1-O   74   .253
1956 CLE A 1   136   .264
1957 CLE A 1   144   .282
1958 CLE A 1   25   .279
1959 BOS A 1   94   .275
1960 BOS A 1   131   .282
1961 BOS A 1   99   .262
    DET A H   8   .167
1962 DET A 1   74   .324
1963 DET A H   6   .000
    MIN A 1   35   .136
    BLTR   1860   .277

WEST, AL
[SEE ALLEN HUBBARD]

WEST, FRANK
B.1873 WILMERDING,PA.
1894 BOS N P   1   0- 0

WEST, JAMES HIRAM (HI)
B.AUG.8,1884 ROSEVILLE,ILL.
D.MAY 25,1963 LOS ANGELES,CAL.
1905 CLE A P   6   2- 2
1911 CLE A P   13   2- 4
    BRTR   19   4- 6

WEST, MAX EDWARD
B.NOV.28,1916 DEXTER,MO.
1938 BOS N O   123   .234
1939 BOS N O   130   .285
1940 BOS N 1-O   139   .261
1941 BOS N O   138   .277
1942 BOS N 1-O   134   .255
1946 BOS N 1   1   .000
    CIN N O   72   .213
1948 PIT N 1-O   87   .178
    BLTR   824   .254

WEST, MILTON DOUGLAS (BUCK)
B.AUG.29,1860 SPRING MILL,OHIO
D.JAN.13,1929 MANSFIELD,OHIO
1884 CIN AA O   33   .292
1890 CLE N O   37   .245
    BRTR   70   .265

WEST, RICHARD THOMAS
B.NOV.24,1915 LOUISVILLE,KY.
1938 CIN N H   1   .000
1939 CIN N C-O   8   .211
1940 CIN N C   7   .393
1941 CIN N C   67   .215
1942 CIN N C-O   33   .177
1943 CIN N H   3   .000
    BRTR   119   .221

WEST, SAMUEL FILMORE (SAM)
B.OCT.5,1904 LONGVIEW,TEX.
1927 WAS A O   38   .239
1928 WAS A O   125   .301
1929 WAS A O   142   .267
1930 WAS A O   120   .328
1931 WAS A O   132   .333
1932 WAS A O   146   .287
1933 STL A O   133   .300
1934 STL A O   122   .326
1935 STL A O   138   .300
1936 STL A O   152   .278
1937 STL A O   122   .328
1938 STL A O   44   .309
    WAS A O   92   .302
1939 WAS A 1-O   115   .282
1940 WAS A 1-O   57   .253
1941 WAS A O   26   .270
1942 CHI A O   49   .232
    BLTL   1753   .283

WEST, WALTER MAXWELL (MAX)
B.JULY 14,1904 SUNSET,TEX.
D.APR.25,1971 HOUSTON,TEX.
1928 BRO N O   7   .286
1929 BRO N O   5   .250
    BRTR   12   .276

YR	CL LEA POS	GP	G	REC

WEST, WELDON EDISON (LEFTY)
B.SEPT.3,1915 GIBSONVILLE,N.C.
1944 STL A P   11   0- 0
1945 STL A P   24   3- 4
         BRTL   35   3- 4

WEST, WILLIAM NELSON
B.AUG.21,1840 PHILADELPHIA,PA.
D.AUG.18,1891 PHILADELPHIA,PA.
1874 ATL NA 2   10   -
1876 MUT N 2   1   .000
                       11   -

WESTERBERG, OSCAR W.
B.1882
D.APR.17,1909 W.ALAMEDA CO.,CAL
1907 BOS N S   3   .222
         TR

WESTERVELT, HUYLER
B.OCT.1,1870 PIERMONT,N.Y.
1894 NY N P   18   7- 9

WESTLAKE, JAMES PATRICK (JIM)
B.JULY 3,1930 SACRAMENTO,CAL.
1955 PHI N H   1   .000
         BLTL

WESTLAKE, WALDON THOMAS (WALLY)
B.NOV.8,1920 GRIDLEY,CAL.
1947 PIT N O   112   .273
1948 PIT N O   132   .285
1949 PIT N O   147   .282
1950 PIT N O   139   .285
1951 PIT N 3-O   50   .282
         STL N O   73   .235
1952 STL N O   21   .216
         CIN N O   59   .202
         CLE A O   29   .232
1953 CLE A O   82   .330
1954 CLE A O   85   .263
1955 CLE A O   16   .250
         BAL A O   8   .125
1956 PHI N H   5   .000
         BRTR   958   .272

WESTON, ALFRED JOHN
B.DEC.11,1905 LYNN,MASS.
1929 BOS N H   3   .000

WESTRUM, WESLEY NOREEN (WES)
B.NOV.28,1922 CLEARBROOK,MINN.
1947 NY N C   6   .417
1948 NY N C   66   .160
1949 NY N C   64   .243
1950 NY N C   140   .236
1951 NY N C   124   .219
1952 NY N C   114   .231
1953 NY N C-3   107   .224
1954 NY N C   98   .187
1955 NY N C   69   .212
1956 NY N C   68   .220
1957 NY N C   63   .165
         BRTR   919   .217
NON-PLAYING MANAGER
NY[N] 1965-67, SF[N] 1974-75

WETZEL, CHARLES EDWARD (BUZZ)
B.AUG.25,1894 JAY,OKLA.
D.MAR.7,1941 GLOBE,ARIZ.
1927 PHI A P   2   0- 0
         BRTR

WETZEL, FRANKLIN BURTON (DUTCH)
B.JULY 7,1893 COLUMBUS,IND.
D.MAR.5,1942 HOLLYWOOD,CAL.
1920 STL A P   7   .428
1921 STL A P   61   .210
         BRTR   68   .243

WETZEL, GEORGE WILLIAM (SHORTY)
B.1868 PHILADELPHIA,PA.
D.FEB.25,1899 DAYTON,OHIO
1885 BAL AA P   2   0- 2

WEYHING, AUGUST (CANNONBALL)
B.SEPT.29,1866 LOUISVILLE,KY.
D.SEPT.4,1955 LOUISVILLE,KY.
1887 ATH AA P   55 27-27
1888 ATH AA P   48   49 29-18
1889 ATH AA P   53 30-20
1890 BRO P P   49 31-15
1891 ATH AA P   53   54 31-20
1892 PHI N P   53   54 28-23
1893 PHI N P   40   41 24-16
1894 PHI N P   36 17-14
1895 PHI N P   24   8-19
         PIT N P   3   1- 0
         LOU N P   27   8-19
1896 LOU N P   6   2- 3
1898 WAS N P   43 15-26
1899 WAS N P   40 16-21
1900 STL N P   7   3- 4
         BRO N P   8   3- 2
1901 CLE A P   2   0- 0
         CIN N P   1   0- 1
         BRTR   526 530 265-231

WEYHING, JOHN
B.JUNE 24,1869 LOUISVILLE,KY.
D.JUNE 20,1890 LOUISVILLE,KY.
1888 CIN AA P   8   3- 4
1889 COL AA P   1   0- 0
         BLTL   9   3- 4

WHALEY, WILLIAM CARL
B.FEB.10,1899 INDIANAPOLIS,IND.
D.MAR.3,1943 INDIANAPOLIS,IND.
1923 STL A O   23   .240
         BRTR

WHALING, ALBERT JAMES (BERT)
B.JUNE 22,1888 LOS ANGELES,CAL.
D.JAN.21,1965 SAWTELLE,CAL.
1913 BOS N C   79   .242
1914 BOS N C   60   .209
1915 BOS N C   72   .221
         BRTR   211   .225

WHEAT, LEROY WILLIAM (LEE)
B.SEPT.15,1929 EDWARDSVILLE,ILL
1954 PHI A P   8   0- 2
1955 KC A P   3   0- 0
         BRTR   11   0- 2

WHEAT, MC KINLEY DAVIS (MACK)
B.JUNE 9,1893 POLO,MO.
1915 BRO N C   8   .071
1916 BRO N C   2   .000
1917 BRO N C   29   .133
1918 BRO N C-O   57   .217
1919 BRO N C   41   .205
1920 PHI N C   78   .226
1921 PHI N C   10   .185
         BRTR   225   .204

WHEAT, ZACHARY DAVIS
(ZACH) OR (BUCK)
B.MAY 23,1886 HAMILTON,MO.
D.MAR.11,1972 SEDALIA,MO.
1909 BRO N O   26   .304
1910 BRO N O   156   .284
1911 BRO N O   136   .287
1912 BRO N O   123   .305
1913 BRO N O   138   .301
1914 BRO N O   145   .319
1915 BRO N O   146   .258
1916 BRO N O   149   .312
1917 BRO N O   109   .312
1918 BRO N O   105   .335
1919 BRO N O   137   .297
1920 BRO N O   148   .328
1921 BRO N O   148   .320
1922 BRO N O   152   .335
1923 BRO N O   98   .375
1924 BRO N O   141   .375
1925 BRO N O   150   .359
1926 BRO N O   111   .290
1927 PHI A O   88   .324
         BLTR   2406   .317

WHEATLEY, CHARLES
B.JUNE 27,1893 ROSEDALE,KAN.
1912 DET A P   5   0- 4
         BRTR

WHEATON, ELWOOD PIERCE (WOODY)
B.OCT.3,1914 PHILADELPHIA,PA.
1943 PHI A O   7   .200
1944 PHI A P-O   11   30 0- 1
                            .186
         BLTL   11   37 0- 1
                            .191

WHEELER, DONALD WESLEY (SCOTT)
B.SEPT.29,1922 MINNEAPOLIS,MINN
1949 CHI A C   67   .240
         BRTR

WHEELER, EDWARD
B.JUNE 15,1878 SHERMAN,MICH.
D.AUG.19,1947 FT.WORTH,TEX.
1902 BRO N 2-S-3   24   .127
         BBTR

WHEELER, EDWARD RAYMOND
B.MAY 24,1917 LOS ANGELES,CAL.
1945 CLE A S-3   46   .194
         BRTR

WHEELER, FLOYD CLARK (RIP)
B.MAR.2,1898 MARION,KY.
D.SEPT.16,1968 MARION,KY.
1921 PHI N P   1   0- 0
1922 PIT N P   1   0- 0
1923 CHI N P   3   1- 2
1924 CHI N P   29   3- 6
         BRTR   34   4- 8

WHEELER, GEORGE HARRISON (HEAVY)
B.NOV.10,1881 SHELBURN,IND.
D.JUNE 14,1918 CLINTON,IND.
1910 CIN N O   3   .000
         BLTR

WHEELER, GEORGE L.
[REAL NAME GEORGE L. HEROUX]
B.AUG.3,1869 METHEUN,MASS.
D.MAY 23,1946 SANTA ANA,CAL.
1896 PHI N P   3   1- 1
1897 PHI N P   25 10-10
1898 PHI N P   15   6- 9
1899 PHI N P   5   3- 2
                       48 20-22

WHEELER, HARRY EUGENE
B.MAR.3,1858 VERSAILLES,IND.
D.OCT.9,1900 CINCINNATI,OHIO
1878 PRO N P   7   6- 1
1879 CIN N P-O   1   0- 1
                            .000
1880 CLE N O   1   .250
         CIN N 3-O   17   .108
1882 CIN AA P-1-   3   75   1- 2
                            .250
1883 COL AA P-O   1   83   0- 1
                            .225
1884 STL AA O   5   .200
         KC U P-O   1 14   0- 1
                            .246
         CHI U O   19   .241
         PIT U O   17   .236
         BAL U O   17   .254
         BRTR   13 256   7- 6
                            .225

WHEELER, RICHARD
[REAL NAME RICHARD WHEELER MAYNARD]
B.JAN.14,1898 KEENE,N.H.
D.FEB.12,1962 LEXINGTON,MASS.
1918 STL N O   5   .000

WHEELOCK, GARY RICHARD
B.NOV.29,1951 BAKERSFIELD,CAL.
1976 CAL A /P   2   0- 0
1977 SEA A P   17   6- 9
         BRTR   19   6- 9

WHEELOCK, WARREN H. (BOBBY)
B.AUG.6,1864 CHARLESTOWN,MASS.
D.MAR.13,1928 BOSTON,MASS.
1887 BOS N S-O   44   .314
1890 COL AA S   59   .267
1891 COL AA S   136   .230
         BRTR   239   .257

WHELAN, JAMES FRANK
B.1890
1913 STL N O   1   .000
         BRTR

WHELAN, THOMAS JOSEPH
B.JAN.3,1894 LYNN,MASS.
D.JUNE 26,1957 BOSTON,MASS.
1920 BOS N 1   1   .000
         BRTR

WHICKER, KEMP CASWELL
[PLAYED UNDER NAME OF
KEMP CASWELL WICKER]

WHILLOCK, JACK KENNETH
B.NOV.4,1942 CLINTON,ARK.
1971 DET A /P   7   0- 2
         BRTR

WHISENANT, THOMAS PETER (PETE)
B.DEC.14,1929 ASHEVILLE,N.C.
1952 BOS N O   24   .192
1955 STL N O   58   .191
1956 CHI N O   103   .239
1957 CIN N O   67   .211
1958 CIN N 2-O   85   .236
1959 CIN N O   36   .239
1960 CIN N H   1   .000
         CLE A O   7   .167
         WAS A O   58   .226
1961 MIN A O   10   .000
         CIN N C-3-O   26   .200
         BRTR   475   .224

WHISENTON, LARRY
B.JULY 3,1956 ST.LOUIS,MO.
1977 ATL N /H   4   .250
1978 ATL N /O   6   .188
         BLTL   10   .200

WHISTLER, LEWIS
[REAL NAME LEWIS WISSLER]
B.MAR.10,1868 ST.LOUIS,MO.
D.DEC.30,1959 ST.LOUIS,MO.
1890 NY N 1   45   .288
1891 NY N S-O   71   .245
1892 BAL N 1   52   .227
         LOU N 1   80   .252
1893 LOU N 1   13   .222
         STL N 1   10   .243
                      271   .250

YR	CL LEA POS	GP	G	REC

WHITAKER, LOUIS RODMAN (LOE)
B.MAY 12,1957 BROOKLYN,N.Y.
1977 DET A /2		11	.250
1978 DET A *2	139		.285
BLTR	150		.263

WHITAKER, STEPHEN EDWARD (STEVE)
B.MAY 7,1943 TACOMA,WASH.
1966 NY A O	31		.246
1967 NY A *O	122		.243
1968 NY A O	28		.117
1969 SEA A O	69		.250
1970 SF N /O	16		.111
BLTR	266		.230

WHITAKER, WILLIAM H. (PAT)
B.1865 ST.LOUIS,MO.
1888 BAL AA P	2	1- 1	
1889 BAL AA P	1	1- 0	
TR	3	2- 1	

WHITBY, WILLIAM EDWARD (BILL)
B.JULY 29,1943 CREWE,VA.
| 1964 MIN A P | 4 | 0- 0 | |
| BRTR | | | |

WHITCHER, ROBERT ARTHUR
B.APR.29,1917 BERLIN,N.H.
| 1945 BOS N P | 9 | 0- 2 | |
| BLTL | | | |

WHITE, ADELL (ABE)
B.MAY 16,1906 WINDER,GA.
| 1937 STL N P | 5 | 0- 1 | |
| BRTL | | | |

WHITE, ALBERT EUGENE (FUZZ)
B.JUNE 27,1918 SPRINGFIELD,MO.
1940 STL A H	2		.000
1947 NY N H	7		.231
BLTR	9		.200

WHITE, C B.
B.WAKEMAN,OHIO
| 1883 PHI N 3 | 1 | | .000 |

WHITE, CHARLES (CHARLIE)
B.AUG.14,1928 KINSTON,N.C.
1954 MIL N C	50		.237
1955 MIL N C	12		.233
BLTR	62		.236

WHITE, DONALD WILLIAM (DON)
B.JAN.8,1919 EVERETT,WASH.
1948 PHI A 3-O	86		.245
1949 PHI A 3-O	57		.213
BRTR	143		.232

WHITE, EDWARD PERRY (ED)
B.APR.6,1926 ANNISTON,ALA.
| 1955 CHI A O | 3 | | .500 |
| BRTR | | | |

WHITE, ELDER LAFAYETTE
B.DEC.23,1934 COLERAIN,N.C.
| 1962 CHI N 2-S | 23 | | .151 |
| BRTR | | | |

WHITE, ELMER
B.MAY 23,1850 CATON,N.Y.
D.JULY 19,1938
| 1871 CLE NA C-O | 16 | | - |

WHITE, ERNEST DANIEL (ERNIE)
B.SEPT.5,1916 PACOLET MILLS,S.C
D.MAY 22,1974 AUGUSTA,GA.
1940 STL N P	8	9	1- 1
1941 STL N P	32	33	17- 7
1942 STL N P	26	27	7- 5
1943 STL N P	14	21	5- 5
1946 BOS N P	12	14	0- 1
1947 BOS N P		1	0- 0
1948 BOS N P	15	16	0- 2
BRTL	108	121	30-21

WHITE, FRANK
B.SEP.4,1950 GREENVILLE,MISS.
1973 KC A S-2	51		.223
1974 KC A 2-S-3	99		.221
1975 KC A 2-S/3-C	111		.250
1976 KC A *2-S	152		.229
1977 KC A *2/S	152		.245
1978 KC A *2	143		.275
BRTR	708		.245

WHITE, GEORGE FREDERICK (DEKE)
B.SEPT.8,1872 ALBANY,N.Y.
D.NOV.27,1957 ALBANY,N.Y.
| 1895 PHI N P | 3 | 1- 0 | |
| BBTL | | | |

WHITE, GUY HARRIS (DOC)
B.APR.9,1879 WASHINGTON,D.C.
D.FEB.19,1969 SILVER SPRING,MD.
1901 PHI N P		28	14-13
1902 PHI N P-O	36	50	16-20
			.274
1903 CHI A P		38	17-16
1904 CHI A P		30	16-10
1905 CHI A P		34	18-14
1906 CHI A P		28	18- 6
1907 CHI A P	47	48	27-13
1908 CHI A P	41	51	19-13
1909 CHI A P-O	23	71	10- 9
			.238
1910 CHI A P	33	56	15-13
1911 CHI A P	34	39	10-14
1912 CHI A P		32	8-10
1913 CHI A P	19	20	2- 4
BLTL	423	525	190-155
			.217

WHITE, HAROLD GEORGE (HAL)
B.MAR.18,1919 UTICA,N.Y.
1941 DET A P		4	0- 0
1942 DET A P		34	12-12
1943 DET A P		32	7-12
1946 DET A P		11	1- 1
1947 DET A P		35	4- 5
1948 DET A P		27	2- 1
1949 DET A P		10	1- 0
1950 DET A P		42	9- 6
1951 DET A P		38	3- 4
1952 DET A P		41	1- 8
1953 STL N P	9	10	0- 0
STL N P		49	6- 5
1954 STL N P		4	0- 0
BRTR	336	337	46-54

WHITE, JAMES LAURIE (DEACON)
B.DEC.7,1847 CATON,N.Y.
D.JULY 7,1939 AURORA,ILL.
1871 CLE NA C-2-O	29		-
1872 CLE NA C-2-O	21		.336
1873 BOS NA C-O	60		.389
1874 BOS NA C-1-O	68		.326
1875 BOS NA C-1-O	80		.355
1876 CHI N C	66		.335
1877 BOS N C-1-O	59		.387
1878 CIN N C-3-O	60		.313
1879 CIN N M-C-1-O	77		.330
1880 CIN N 1-2-O	34		.302
1881 BUF N C-1-2-3-O	78		.310
1882 BUF N C-3	83		.281
1883 BUF N C-3	93		.289
1884 BUF N C-3	106		.325
1885 BUF N 3	98		.292
1886 DET N 3	124		.289
1887 DET N 3	111		.341
1888 DET N 3	125		.298
1889 PIT N 3		95	.253
1890 BUF P P-1-	1	122	0- 1
	3		.264
BLTR	1	1549	0- 1
			-

WHITE, JEROME CARDELL (JERRY)
B.AUG.23,1952 SHIRLEY,MASS.
1974 MON N /O	9		.400
1975 MON N O	39		.299
1976 MON N O	114		.249
1977 MON N /O	16		.190
1978 MON N /O	18		.200
CHI N O	59		.272
BBTR	255		.261

WHITE, JOHN WALLACE (DOC)
B.JAN.19,1878 INDIANAPOLIS,IND.
D.SEPT.30,1963 INDIANAPOLIS,IND
| 1904 BOS N O | 1 | | .000 |
| BRTR | | | |

WHITE, JOHN PETER (JACK)
B.AUG.31,1905 NEW YORK,N.Y.
D.JUNE 19,1971 FLUSHING,N.Y.
1927 CIN N 2-S	5		.000
1928 CIN N 2	1		.000
BBTR	6		.000

WHITE, JOYNER CLIFFORD (JO-JO)
B.JUNE 1,1909 RED OAK,GA.
1932 DET A O	80		.260
1933 DET A O	91		.252
1934 DET A O	115		.313
1935 DET A O	114		.240
1936 DET A O	58		.275
1937 DET A O	94		.246
1938 DET A O	78		.262
1943 PHI A O	139		.248
1944 PHI A S-O	85		.221
CIN N O	24		.235
BLTR	878		.256
NON-PLAYING MANAGER
CLE[A] 1960 [INTERIM]

WHITE, JOYNER MICHAEL (MIKE)
B.DEC.18,1938 DETROIT,MICH.
1963 HOU N 2	3		.286
1964 HOU N 2-3-O	89		.271
1965 HOU N /3	8		.000
BRTR	100		.264

WHITE, OLIVER KIRBY (KIRBY)
(RED) OR (BUCK)
B.JAN.3,1884 HILLSBORO,OHIO
D.APR.22,1943 HILLSBORO,OHIO
1909 BOS N P	23	6-13	
1910 BOS N P	3	1- 2	
PIT N P	30	10- 9	
1911 PIT N P	2	0- 1	
BLTR	58	17-25	

WHITE, MYRON ALAN
B.AUG.1,1957 LONG BEACH,CAL.
| 1978 LA N /O | 7 | | .500 |
| BLTL | | | |

WHITE, ROY HILTON
B.DEC.27,1943 LOS ANGELES,CAL.
1965 NY A O/2	14		.333
1966 NY A O/2	115		.225
1967 NY A O-3	70		.224
1968 NY A *O	159		.267
1969 NY A *O	130		.290
1970 NY A *O	162		.296
1971 NY A *O	147		.292
1972 NY A *O	155		.270
1973 NY A *O	162		.246
1974 NY A O-D	136		.275
1975 NY A *O/1	148		.290
1976 NY A *O	156		.286
1977 NY A *O	143		.268
1978 NY A O-D	103		.269
BBTR	1800		.273

WHITE, SAMUEL
B.1895
| 1919 BOS N C | 1 | | .000 |
| BRTR | | | |

WHITE, SAMUEL CHARLES (SAMMY)
B.JULY 7,1928 WENATCHEE,WASH.
1951 BOS A C	4		.182
1952 BOS A C	115		.281
1953 BOS A C	136		.273
1954 BOS A C	137		.282
1955 BOS A C	143		.261
1956 BOS A C	114		.245
1957 BOS A C	111		.215
1958 BOS A C	102		.259
1959 BOS A C	119		.284
1961 MIL N C	21		.222
1962 PHI N C	41		.216
BRTR	1043		.262

WHITE, STEPHEN VINCENT
B.DEC.21,1884 DORCHESTER,MASS.
D.JAN.29,1975 BRAINTREE,MASS.
1912 WAS A P	1	0- 0	
BOS N P	3	0- 0	
BRTR	4	0- 0	

WHITE, WILLIAM BARNEY
B.JUNE 25,1924 PARIS,TEX.
| 1945 BRO N S-3 | 4 | | .000 |
| BRTR | | | |

WHITE, WILLIAM DEKOVA (BILL)
B.JAN.28,1934 LAKEWOOD,FLA.
1956 NY N 1-O	138		.256
1958 SF N O	26		.241
1959 STL N 1-O	138		.302
1960 STL N 1-O	144		.283
1961 STL N 1	153		.286
1962 STL N 1-O	159		.324
1963 STL N 1	162		.304
1964 STL N 1	160		.303
1965 STL N *1	148		.289
1966 PHI N *1	159		.276
1967 PHI N 1	110		.250
1968 PHI N 1	127		.239
1969 STL N 1	49		.211
BLTL	1673		.286

WHITE, WILLIAM DIGHTON
B.MAY 1,1860 BRIDGEPORT,OHIO
D.DEC.29,1924 BELLAIRE,OHIO
1884 PIT AA S-3	74		.219
1886 LOU AA S	135		.262
1887 LOU AA S	132		.311
1888 LOU AA S-3	49		.283
STL AA S	60		.176
	450		.259

WHITE, WILLIAM EDWARD
B.MILNER,GA.
| 1879 PRO N 1 | 1 | | .250 |

YR	CL	LEA	POS	GP	G	REC

WHITE, WILLIAM HENRY
(WILL) OR (WHOOP-LA)
B.OCT.11,1854 CATON,N.Y.
D.AUG.31,1911 PORT CARLING,ONT.
CANADA

YR	CL	LEA	POS	GP	G	REC
1877	BOS	N	P		3	2- 1
1878	CIN	N	P-O		51	29-21
						.132
1879	CIN	N	P		75	38-30
1880	CIN	N	P-O		61	18-43
						.163
1881	DET	N	P		2	0- 2
1882	CIN	AA	P-1-O		54	40-12
						.264
1883	CIN	AA	P		65	43-22
1884	CIN	AA	M-P		54	34-18
1885	CIN	AA	P		35	17-15
1886	CIN	AA	P		3	1- 2
		BBTR			403	222-166
						.185

WHITE, WILLIAM WARREN
[ALSO PLAYED UNDER NAME OF
WILLIAM WARREN]
D.MAR.3,1898

YR	CL	LEA	POS	GP	G	REC
1871	OLY	NA	2		1	.000
1872	NAT	NA	S-3		10	.318
1873	NAT	NA	S-3		39	-
1874	BAL	NA	3		45	-
1875	CHI	NA	2-S-3-O		70	-
1884	WAS	U	2-3		2	.000
					167	-

WHITEHEAD, BURGESS URQUHART
(BURGESS) OR (WHITEY)
B.JUNE 29,1910 TARBORO,N.C.

YR	CL	LEA	POS	GP	G	REC
1933	STL	N	2-S		12	.286
1934	STL	N	2-S-3		100	.277
1935	STL	N	2-S-3		107	.263
1936	NY	N	2		154	.278
1937	NY	N	2		152	.286
1939	NY	N	2		95	.239
1940	NY	N	2-S-3		133	.282
1941	NY	N	2-3		116	.228
1946	PIT	N	2-S-3		55	.220
		BRTR			924	.263

WHITEHEAD, JOHN HENDERSON
(SILENT JOHN)
B.APR.27,1909 COLEMAN,TEX.
D.OCT.20,1964 BONHAM,TEX.

YR	CL	LEA	POS	GP	G	REC
1935	CHI	A	P		28	13-13
1936	CHI	A	P		34	13-13
1937	CHI	A	P		26	11- 8
1938	CHI	A	P		32	10-11
1939	CHI	A	P		7	0- 3
	STL	A	P		26	1- 3
1940	STL	A	P		15	1- 3
1942	STL	A	P		4	0- 0
		BRTR			172	49-54

WHITEHEAD, MILTON P.

YR	CL	LEA	POS	GP	G	REC
1884	STL	U	P-2-	1	100	0- 1
			S-3-O			.225
	KC	U	2-S-3		5	.150
				1	105	0- 1
						.222

WHITEHILL, EARL OLIVER
B.FEB.7,1900 CEDAR RAPIDS,IOWA
D.OCT.22,1954 OMAHA,NEB.

YR	CL	LEA	POS	GP	G	REC
1923	DET	A	P		8	2- 0
1924	DET	A	P	35	37	17- 9
1925	DET	A	P	35	36	11-11
1926	DET	A	P		36	16-13
1927	DET	A	P		41	16-14
1928	DET	A	P		31	11-16
1929	DET	A	P		38	14-15
1930	DET	A	P		34	17-13
1931	DET	A	P		34	13-16
1932	DET	A	P		33	16-12
1933	WAS	A	P-O	39	40	22- 8
						.222
1934	WAS	A	P	32	35	14-11
1935	WAS	A	P		34	14-13
1936	WAS	A	P		28	14-11
1937	CLE	A	P		33	8- 8
1938	CLE	A	P		26	9- 8
1939	CHI	N	P		24	4- 7
		BLTR		541	548	218-185

WHITEHORN, ARTHUR LEE
[SEE ARTHUR LEE DALEY]

WHITEHOUSE, CHARLES EVIS
(CHARLIE) OR (LEFTY)
B.JAN.25,1894 CHARLESTON,ILL.
D.JULY 19,1960 INDIANAPOLIS,IND

YR	CL	LEA	POS	GP	G	REC
1914	IND	F	P		8	2- 0
1915	NEW	F	P		11	2- 2
1919	WAS	A	P		6	0- 1
		BBTL			25	4- 3

WHITEHOUSE, GILBERT
[PLAYED UNDER NAME OF
GILBERT ARTHUR WHITEHOUSE]

WHITEHOUSE, GILBERT ARTHUR
[REAL NAME GILBERT WHITEHOUSE]
B.OCT.15,1893 SOMERVILLE,MASS.
D.FEB.14,1926 BREWER,ME.

YR	CL	LEA	POS	GP	G	REC
1912	BOS	N	C		1	.000
1915	NEW	F	O		35	.217
		BBTR			36	.211

WHITELEY, GURDON W.
B.OCT.5,1859 ASHAWAY,R.I.
D.NOV.24,1924 CRANSTON,R.I.

YR	CL	LEA	POS	GP	G	REC
1884	CLE	N	O		8	.147
1885	BOS	N	C-O		33	.185
					41	.178

WHITEMAN, GEORGE (LUCKY)
B.DEC.23,1882 PEORIA,ILL.
D.FEB.10,1947 HOUSTON,TEX.

YR	CL	LEA	POS	GP	G	REC
1907	BOS	A	O		4	.167
1913	NY	A	O		11	.343
1918	BOS	A	O		71	.267
		BRTR			86	.271

WHITFIELD, FRED DWIGHT
B.JAN.7,1938 VANDIVER,ALA.

YR	CL	LEA	POS	GP	G	REC
1962	STL	N	1		73	.266
1963	CLE	A	1		109	.251
1964	CLE	A	1		101	.270
1965	CLE	A	*1		132	.293
1966	CLE	A	1		137	.241
1967	CLE	A	1		100	.218
1968	CIN	N	1		87	.257
1969	CIN	N	1		74	.149
1970	MON	N	/1		4	.067
		BLTL			817	.253

WHITFIELD, TERRY BERTLAND
B.JAN.12,1953 BLYTHE,CAL.

YR	CL	LEA	POS	GP	G	REC
1974	NY	A	/O		2	.200
1975	NY	A	O		28	.272
1976	NY	A	/O		1	.000
1977	SF	N	O		114	.285
1978	SF	N	*O		149	.289
		BLTR			294	.286

WHITING, EDWARD C.
[ALSO PLAYED UNDER NAME OF
HARRY ZIEBER]
B.PHILADELPHIA,PA.

YR	CL	LEA	POS	GP	G	REC
1882	BAL	AA	C-1-O		73	.267
1883	LOU	AA	C-1-3-O		55	.295
1884	LOU	AA	C		42	.220
1886	WAS	N	C		6	.000
		BLTR			176	.254

WHITING, JESSE W.

YR	CL	LEA	POS	GP	G	REC
1902	PHI	N	P		1	0- 1
1906	BRO	N	P		3	1- 1
1907	BRO	N	P		2	0- 0
					6	1- 2

WHITMAN, DICK CORWIN
B.NOV.9,1920 WOODBURN,ORE.

YR	CL	LEA	POS	GP	G	REC
1946	BRO	N	O		104	.260
1947	BRO	N	O		4	.000
1948	BRO	N	O		60	.291
1949	BRO	N	O		23	.184
1950	PHI	N	O		75	.250
1951	PHI	N	O		19	.118
		BLTR			285	.259

WHITMAN, WALTER FRANKLIN
(FRANK) OR (HOOKER)
B.AUG.15,1924 MARENGO,IND.

YR	CL	LEA	POS	GP	G	REC
1946	CHI	A	1-2-S		17	.063
1948	CHI	A	S		3	.000
		BRTR			20	.045

WHITNER, EDWARD CLARENCE
[PLAYED UNDER NAME OF
EDWARD CLARENCE LEVY]

WHITNEY, ARTHUR CARTER (PINKY)
B.JAN.2,1905 SAN ANTONIO,TEX.

YR	CL	LEA	POS	GP	G	REC
1928	PHI	N	3		151	.301
1929	PHI	N	3		154	.327
1930	PHI	N	3		149	.342
1931	PHI	N	3		130	.287
1932	PHI	N	3		154	.298
1933	PHI	N	3		31	.264
	BOS	N	2-3		100	.246
1934	BOS	N	2-3		146	.259
1935	BOS	N	2-3		126	.273
1936	BOS	N	3		10	.175
	PHI	N	3		114	.294
1937	PHI	N	3		138	.341
1938	PHI	N	3		102	.277
1939	PHI	N	3		34	.187
		BRTR			1539	.295

WHITNEY, ARTHUR WILSON
B.JAN.16,1858 BROCKTON,MASS.
D.AUG.15,1943 LOWELL,MASS.

YR	CL	LEA	POS	GP	G	REC
1880	WOR	N	3		75	.222
1881	DET	N	3		58	.182
1882	PRO	N	S		11	.071
	DET	N	P-S-	3	30	0- 1
			3			.177
1884	PIT	AA	3		22	.299
1885	PIT	AA	S		90	.227
1886	PIT	AA	S-3		136	.225
1887	PIT	N	3		119	.343
1888	NY	N	3		90	.219
1889	NY	N	3		129	.217
1890	NY	P	S-3		119	.212
1891	CIN	AA	S-3		86	.200
	STL	AA	S-3		2	.000
		BRTR		3	967	0- 1
						.235

WHITNEY, FRANK THOMAS (JUMBO)
B.FEB.18,1856 BROCKTON,MASS.
D.OCT.30,1943 BALTIMORE,MD.

YR	CL	LEA	POS	GP	G	REC
1876	BOS	N	O		34	.236
		BRTR				

WHITNEY, JAMES EVANS (JIM)
OR (GRASSHOPPER JIM)
B.NOV.10,1857 CONKLIN,N.Y.
D.MAY 21,1891 BINGHAMTON,N.Y.

YR	CL	LEA	POS	GP	G	REC
1881	BOS	N	P-1-	64	74	31-33
			O			.255
1882	BOS	N	P-1-	46	60	24-22
			O			.325
1883	BOS	N	P-1-	62	96	38-22
			O			.282
1884	BOS	N	P-1-	48	62	24-17
			3-O			.260
1885	BOS	N	P-1-	50	72	17-32
			O			.234
1886	KC	N	P-O	46	67	12-32
						.239
1887	WAS	N	P	46	52	24-21
1888	WAS	N	M-P	40	42	19-21
1889	IND	N	P		10	2- 7
1890	ATH	AA	P		7	2- 3
		BLTR		419	542	193-210
						.266

WHITROCK, WILLIAM FRANKLIN
B.MAR.4,1870 CINCINNATI,OHIO
D.JULY 26,1935 DERBY,CONN.

YR	CL	LEA	POS	GP	G	REC
1890	STL	AA	P		13	6- 7
1893	LOU	N	P		8	2- 4
1894	LOU	N	P		2	0- 1
	CIN	N	P	10	17	2- 5
1896	PHI	N	P		2	0- 1
		TR		35	42	10-18

WHITSON, EDDIE LEE
B.MAY 19,1955 JOHNSON CITY,TENN.

YR	CL	LEA	POS	GP	G	REC
1977	PIT	N	/P		5	1- 0
1978	PIT	N	/P		43	5- 6
		BRTR			48	6- 6

WHITT, LEO ERNEST (ERNIE)
B.JUNE 13,1952 DETROIT,MICH.

YR	CL	LEA	POS	GP	G	REC
1977	TOR	A	C		23	.171
1978	TOR	A	/C		2	.000
1976	BOS	A	/C		8	.222
		BLTR			25	.156

WHITTAKER, WALTER ELTON (DOC)
B.JUNE 11,1894 CHELSEA,MASS.
D.AUG.9,1965 PEMBROKE,MASS.

YR	CL	LEA	POS	GP	G	REC
1916	PHI	A	P		1	0- 0
		BLTR				

WHITTED, GEORGE BOSTIC (POSSUM)
B.FEB.4,1890 DURHAM,N.C.
D.OCT.16,1962 WILMINGTON,N.C.

YR	CL	LEA	POS	GP	G	REC
1912	STL	N	3		12	.282
1913	STL	N	S-3-O		123	.220
1914	STL	N	O		20	.129
	BOS	N	O		66	.216
1915	PHI	N	O		128	.281
1916	PHI	N	1-O		147	.281
1917	PHI	N	O		149	.280
1918	PHI	N	O		24	.244
1919	PHI	N	2		78	.249
	PIT	N	3-O		35	.398
1920	PIT	N	O		134	.261
1921	PIT	N	O		108	.280
1922	BRO	N	O		1	.000
		BRTR			1025	.270

WICKER, FLOYD EULISS
B.SEP.12,1943 BURLINGTON,N.C.

YR	CL	LEA	POS	GP	G	REC
1968	STL	N	/H		5	.500
1969	MON	N	O		41	.103
1970	MIL	A	O		15	.195
1971	MIL	A	H		11	.125
	SF	N	/O		9	.143
		BLTR			81	.159

WICKER, KEMP CASWELL
[REAL NAME KEMP CASWELL WHICKER]
B.AUG.13,1906 KERNERSVILLE,N.C.
D.JUNE 11,1973 KERNERSVILLE,N.C

YR	CL	LEA	POS	GP	G	REC
1936	NY	A	P		7	1- 2
1937	NY	A	P		16	7- 3
1938	NY	A	P		1	1- 0
1941	BRO	N	P		16	1- 2
			BRTL		40	10- 7

WICKER, ROBERT KITRIDGE
B.MAY 24,1878 BEDFORD,IND.
D.JAN.22,1955 EVANSTON,ILL.

YR	CL	LEA	POS	GP	G	REC
1901	STL	N	P		3	0- 0
1902	STL	N	P-O	19	22	5-11
						.234
1903	STL	N	P		1	0- 0
	CHI	N	P		32	20- 9
1904	CHI	N	P-O	30	50	17-10
						.219
1905	CHI	N	P	22	25	13- 7
1906	CHI	N	P		10	3- 5
	CIN	N	P		20	6-11
			BRTR	137	163	64-53
						.206

WICKERSHAM, DAVID CLIFFORD (DAVE)
B.SEP.27,1935 ERIE,PA.

YR	CL	LEA	POS	GP	G	REC
1960	KC	A	P		5	0- 0
1961	KC	A	P		17	2- 1
1962	KC	A	P		30	11- 4
1963	KC	A	P		38	12-15
1964	DET	A	P		40	19-12
1965	DET	A	P		34	9-14
1966	DET	A	P		38	8- 3
1967	DET	A	P		36	4- 5
1968	PIT	N	P		11	1- 0
1969	KC	A	P		34	2- 3
			BRTR		283	68-57

WICKLAND, ALBERT
B.JAN.27,1888 CHICAGO,ILL.

YR	CL	LEA	POS	GP	G	REC
1913	CIN	N	O		26	.215
1914	CHI	F	O		158	.288
1915	CHI	F	O		30	.235
	PIT	F	O		110	.303
1918	BOS	N	O		95	.262
1919	NY	A	O		26	.152
			BLTL		445	.275

WIDMAR, ALBERT JOSEPH (AL)
B.MAR.20,1925 CLEVELAND,OHIO

YR	CL	LEA	POS	GP	G	REC
1947	BOS	A	P		2	0- 0
1948	STL	A	P		49	2- 6
1950	STL	A	P		36	7-15
1951	STL	A	P		26	4- 9
1952	CHI	A	P		1	0- 0
			BRTR		114	13-30

WIDNER, WILLIAM WATERFIELD
(WILD BILL)
B.JUNE 3,1867 CINCINNATI,OHIO
D.DEC.10,1908 CINCINNATI,OHIO

YR	CL	LEA	POS	GP	G	REC
1887	CIN	AA	P		1	1- 0
1888	WAS	N	P		15	4- 7
1889	COL	AA	P	39	40	13-22
1890	COL	AA	P		13	4- 8
1891	CIN	AA	P		1	0- 1
			BRTR	69	70	22-38

WIEAND, FRANKLIN DELANO
ROOSEVELT (TED)
B.APR.4,1933 WALNUTPORT,PA.

YR	CL	LEA	POS	GP	G	REC
1958	CIN	N	P		1	0- 0
1960	CIN	N	P		5	0- 1
			BRTR		6	0- 1

WIEDEMEYER, CHARLES JOHN
B.JAN.31,1915 CHICAGO,ILL.

YR	CL	LEA	POS	GP	G	REC
1934	CHI	N	P		4	0- 0
			BRTL			

WIENEKE, JOHN
B.MAR.10,1894 SALTZBURG,PA.
D.MAR.16,1933 PLEASANT RIDGE,MICH.

YR	CL	LEA	POS	GP	G	REC
1921	CHI	N	P		10	0- 1
			BRTL			

WIESLER, ROBERT GEORGE (BOB)
B.AUG.13,1930 ST.LOUIS,MO.

YR	CL	LEA	POS	GP	G	REC
1951	NY	A	P		4	0- 2
1954	NY	A	P		6	3- 2
1955	NY	A	P		16	0- 2
1956	WAS	A	P	37	38	3-12
1957	WAS	A	P		3	1- 1
1958	WAS	A	P		4	0- 0
			BBTL	70	71	7-19

WIETELMANN, WILLIAM FREDERICK
(WHITEY)
B.MAR.15,1919 ZANESVILLE,OHIO

YR	CL	LEA	POS	GP	G	REC
1939	BOS	N	S		23	.203
1940	BOS	N	2-S-3		35	.195
1941	BOS	N	2-S-3		16	.091
1942	BOS	N	2-S		13	.206
1943	BOS	N	S		193	.215
1944	BOS	N	2-S-3		125	.240
1945	BOS	N	P-2-	1	123	0- 0
			S-3			.271
1946	BOS	N	P-2-	3	44	0- 0
			S-3			.205
1947	PIT	N	1-2-S-3		48	.234
			BBTR	4	580	0- 0
						.232

BR 1939-41

WIGGS, JAMES ALVIN (BIG JIM)
B.SEPT.1,1876 TRONDHEIM,NORWAY
D.JAN.20,1963 XENIA,OHIO

YR	CL	LEA	POS	GP	G	REC
1903	CIN	N	P		2	0- 1
1905	DET	N	P		6	3- 3
1906	DET	A	P		4	1- 1
			BBTR		12	4- 5

WIGHT, WILLIAM ROBERT
(BILL) OR (LEFTY)
B.APR.12,1922 RIO VISTA,CAL.

YR	CL	LEA	POS	GP	G	REC
1946	NY	A	P		14	2- 2
1947	NY	A	P		1	1- 0
1948	CHI	A	P		34	9-20
1949	CHI	A	P		35	15-13
1950	CHI	A	P		30	10-16
1951	BOS	A	P		34	7- 7
1952	BOS	A	P		10	2- 1
	DET	A	P		23	5- 9
1953	DET	A	P		13	0- 3
	CLE	A	P		20	2- 1
1955	CLE	A	P		17	0- 0
	BAL	A	P-1	19	6- 8	
						.083
1956	BAL	A	P		35	9-12
1957	BAL	A	P		27	6- 6
1958	CIN	N	P		7	0- 1
	STL	N	P		28	3- 0
			BLTL		347	77-99
						.115

WIGINTON, FREDERICK THOMAS
B.DEC.16,1897 ROGERS,NEB.

YR	CL	LEA	POS	GP	G	REC
1923	STL	N	P		4	0- 0
			BRTR			

WILBER, DELBERT QUENTIN
(DEL) OR (BABE)
B.FEB.24,1919 LINCOLN PARK,MICH

YR	CL	LEA	POS	GP	G	REC
1946	STL	N	C		4	.000
1947	STL	N	C		51	.232
1948	STL	N	C		27	.190
1949	STL	N	C		2	.250
1951	PHI	N	C		84	.278
1952	PHI	N	H		2	.000
	BOS	A	H		47	.267
1953	BOS	A	C-1		58	.241
1954	BOS	A	C		24	.131
			BRTR		299	.242

NON-PLAYING MANAGER
TEX[A] 1973 [INTERIM]

WILBORN, CLAUDE EDWARD
B.SEPT.1,1912 WOODSDALE,N.C.

YR	CL	LEA	POS	GP	G	REC
1940	BOS	N	O		5	.000
			BLTR			

WILCOX, MILTON EDWARD (MILT)
B.APR.20,1950 HONOLULU,HAWAII

YR	CL	LEA	POS	GP	G	REC
1970	CIN	N	P		5	3- 1
1971	CIN	N	P		18	2- 2
1972	CLE	A	P		32	7-14
1973	CLE	A	P	26	27	8-10
1974	CLE	A	P		41	2- 2
1975	CHI	N	P		25	0- 1
1977	DET	A	P		20	6- 2
1978	DET	A	P		29	13-12
			BRTR	196	197	41-44

WILES, RANDALL E (RANDY)
B.SEPT.10,1951 FORT BELVOIR,VA.

YR	CL	LEA	POS	GP	G	REC
1977	CHI	A	/P		5	1- 1
			BLTL			

WILEY

YR	CL	LEA	POS	GP	G	REC
1884	WAS	U	3-O		1	.000

WILEY, MARK EUGENE
B.FEB.28,1948 NATIONAL CITY,CAL.

YR	CL	LEA	POS	GP	G	REC
1975	MIN	A	P		15	1- 3
1978	SD	N	/P		4	1- 0
	TOR	A	/P		2	0- 0
			BRTR		21	2- 3

WILFONG, ROBERT DONALD (ROB)
B.SEPT.1,1953 PASADENA,CAL.

YR	CL	LEA	POS	GP	G	REC
1977	MIN	A	2		73	.246
1978	MIN	A	2		92	.266
			BLTR		165	.257

WILHELM, CHARLES ERNEST (SPIDER)
B.MAY 23,1929 BALTIMORE,MD.

YR	CL	LEA	POS	GP	G	REC
1953	PHI	A	S		7	.286
			BRTR			

WILHELM, HARRY LESTER
B.APR.7,1874 UNIONTOWN,PA.
D.FEB.20,1944 REPUBLIC,PA.

YR	CL	LEA	POS	GP	G	REC
1899	LOU	N	P		4	1- 1
			BRTR			

WILHELM, IRVIN KEY (KAISER)
B.JAN.26,1874 WOOSTER,OHIO
D.MAY 21,1936 ROCHESTER,N.Y.

YR	CL	LEA	POS	GP	G	REC
1903	PIT	N	P		15	5- 3
1904	BOS	N	P		39	15-21
1905	BOS	N	P	34	38	4-25
1908	BRO	N	P		42	16-22
1909	BRO	N	P		22	3-13
1910	BRO	N	P		15	3- 7
1914	BAL	F	P		47	12-17
1915	BAL	F	P		1	0- 0
1921	PHI	N	M-P		4	0- 0
			BRTR	217	221	58-108

NON-PLAYING MANAGER PHI[N] 1922

WILHELM, JAMES HOYT (HOYT)
B.JULY 26,1923 HUNTSVILLE,N.C.

YR	CL	LEA	POS	GP	G	REC
1952	NY	N	P		71	15- 3
1953	NY	N	P		68	7- 8
1954	NY	N	P		57	12- 4
1955	NY	N	P		59	4- 1
1956	NY	N	P		64	4- 9
1957	STL	N	P		40	1- 4
	CLE	A	P		2	1- 0
1958	CLE	A	P		30	2- 7
	BAL	A	P		9	1- 3
1959	BAL	A	P		32	15-11
1960	BAL	A	P		41	11- 8
1961	BAL	A	P		51	9- 7
1962	BAL	A	P		52	7-10
1963	CHI	A	P		55	5- 8
1964	CHI	A	P		73	12- 9
1965	CHI	A	P		66	7- 7
1966	CHI	A	P		46	5- 2
1967	CHI	A	P		49	8- 3
1968	CHI	A	P		72	4- 4
1969	CAL	A	P		44	5- 7
	ATL	N	/P		8	2- 0
1970	ATL	N	P		50	6- 4
	CHI	N	/P		3	0- 1
1971	ATL	N	/P		3	0- 0
	CHI	N	/P		9	0- 1
1972	LA	N	P		16	0- 1
			BRTR		1070	143-122

WILHELM, JAMES WEBSTER (JIM)
B.SEPT.20,1952 GREENBRAE,CAL.

YR	CL	LEA	POS	GP	G	REC
1978	SD	N	O		10	.368
			BRTR			

WILHOIT, JOSEPH WILLIAM
B.DEC.20,1891 HIAWATHA,KAN.
D.SEPT.25,1930 SANTA BARBARA,CAL.

YR	CL	LEA	POS	GP	G	REC
1916	BOS	N	O		116	.230
1917	BOS	N	O		54	.280
	PIT	N	O		9	.200
	NY	N	O		34	.320
1918	NY	N	O		64	.274
1919	BOS	A	O		6	.333
			BLTR		283	.257

WILIE, DENNIS ERNEST (DENNEY)
B.SEPT.22,1890 MT.CALM,TEX.
D.JUNE 20,1966 HAYWARD,CAL.

YR	CL	LEA	POS	GP	G	REC
1911	STL	N	O		15	.235
1912	STL	N	O		30	.229
1915	CLE	A	O		45	.252
			BLTL		90	.243

WILKE, HENRY JOSEPH (HARRY)
B.DEC.14,1900 CINCINNATI,OHIO

YR	CL	LEA	POS	GP	G	REC
1927	CHI	N	3		3	.000
			BRTR			

WILKES, IGNACIO ALFREDO [JAVIER]
[SEE IGNACIO ALFREDO JAVIER]

WILKIE, ALDON JAY (LEFTY)
B.OCT.30,1914 ZEALANDIA,SASK.,CANADA

YR	CL	LEA	POS	GP	G	REC
1941	PIT	N	P		26	2- 4
1942	PIT	N	P	35	36	6- 7
1946	PIT	N	P		7	0- 0
			BLTL	68	69	8-11

WILKINS, ROBERT LINWOOD
B.AUG.11,1922 DENTON,N.C.

YR	CL	LEA	POS	GP	G	REC
1944	PHI	A	S		24	.240
1945	PHI	A	S-O		62	.260
			BRTR		86	.257

WILKINSON, EDWARD E.
B.1890 SAN FRANCISCO,CAL.

YR	CL	LEA	POS	GP	G	REC
1911	NY	A	O		10	.231
			BRTR			

YR	CL LEA POS	GP	G	REC

WILKINSON, ROY HAMILTON
B.MAY 9,1894 CANANDAIGUA,N.Y.
```
1918 CLE A P        1  0- 0
1919 CHI A P        4  1- 1
1920 CHI A P       34  7- 9
1921 CHI A P       36  4-19
1922 CHI A P        4  0- 1
        BRTR       79 12-30
```

WILKS, THEODORE (TED) OR (CORK)
B.NOV.13,1915 FULTON,N.Y.
```
1944 STL N P       36 17- 4
1945 STL N P       18  4- 7
1946 STL N P       40  8- 0
1947 STL N P       37  4- 0
1948 STL N P       57  6- 6
1949 STL N P       59 10- 3
1950 STL N P       18  2- 0
1951 STL N P       17  0- 0
     PIT N         48  3- 5
1952 PIT N P       44  5- 5
     CLE A P        7  0- 0
1953 CLE A P        4  0- 0
        BRTR      385 59-30
```

WILL, ROBERT LEE (BOB) OR (BUTCH)
B.JULY 15,1931 BERWYN,ILL.
```
1957 CHI N  O      70  .223
1958 CHI N  O       6  .250
1960 CHI N  O     138  .255
1961 CHI N  1-O    86  .257
1962 CHI N  O      87  .239
1963 CHI N  1      23  .174
        BLTL      410  .247
```

WILLETT, ROBERT EDGAR (ED)
B.MAR.7,1884 NORFOLK,VA.
D.MAY 10,1934 WELLINGTON,KAN.
```
1906 DET A P        4     0- 3
1907 DET A P        9     1- 5
1908 DET A P       30    15- 9
1909 DET A P    40 41    22- 9
1910 DET A P       38    16-11
1911 DET A P       39    13-14
1912 DET A P       37    17-15
1913 DET A P    33 34    13-14
1914 STL F P       27     4-16
1915 STL F P       17     2- 3
        BRTR      274 276 103-99
```

WILLEY, CARLTON FRANCIS (CARL)
B.JUNE 6,1931 CHERRYFIELD,ME.
```
1958 MIL N P       23  9- 7
1959 MIL N P       26  5- 9
1960 MIL N P       28  6- 7
1961 MIL N P       35  6-12
1962 MIL N P       30  2- 5
1963 NY  N P       30  9-14
1964 NY  N P       14  0- 2
1965 NY  N P       13  1- 2
        BRTR      199 38-58
```

WILLHITE, JON NICHOLAS (NICK)
B.JAN.27,1941 TULSA,OKLA.
```
1963 LA  N P        8  2- 3
1964 LA  N P       10  2- 4
1965 WAS A /P       5  0- 0
     LA  N P       15  2- 2
1966 LA  N /P       6  0- 0
1967 CAL A P       10  0- 2
     NY  N /P       4  0- 1
        BLTL       58  6-12
```

WILLIAMS, ALMON EDWARD
B.MAY 11,1914 VALHERMOSA
SPRINGS,ALA.
D.JULY 19,1949 GROVES,TEX.
```
1937 PHI A P       16  4- 1
1938 PHI A P       30  0- 7
        BRTR       46  4- 8
```

WILLIAMS, ALVA MITCHEL (RIP)
B.JAN.31,1882 CARTHAGE,ILL.
D.JULY 23,1933 KEOKUK,IOWA
```
1911 BOS A C-1     95  .239
1912 WAS A C       56  .318
1913 WAS A C       64  .283
1914 WAS A C       81  .278
1915 WAS A C-1     91  .244
1916 WAS A C       76  .267
1918 CLE A 1       28  .239
        BRTR      491  .265
```

WILLIAMS, ARTHUR FRANKLIN
B.AUG.26,1877 SOMERVILLE,MASS.
D.MAY 16,1941 ARLINGTON,VA.
```
1902 CHI N 1-O     49  .232
        TR
```

WILLIAMS, AUGUST JOSEPH (GLOOMY GUS)
B.MAY 7,1888 OMAHA,NEB.
D.APR.16,1964 STERLING,ILL.
```
1911 STL A  O       9  .269
1912 STL A  O      64  .290
1913 STL A  O     149  .273
1914 STL A  O     143  .253
1915 STL A  O      45  .202
        BLTL      410  .263
```

WILLIAMS, AUGUSTINE H.
B.1870 NEW YORK,N.Y.
D.OCT.4,1890 NEW YORK,N.Y.
```
1890 BRO AA P       2  1- 1
```

WILLIAMS, BERNARD (BERNIE)
B.OCT.8,1948 ALAMEDA,CAL.
```
1970 SF  N /O       7  .313
1971 SF  N  O      35  .178
1972 SF  N  O      46  .191
1974 SD  N /O      14  .133
        BRTR      102  .192
```

WILLIAMS, BILLY LEO
B.JUNE 15,1938 WHISTLER,ALA.
```
1959 CHI N  O      18  .152
1960 CHI N  O      12  .277
1961 CHI N  O     146  .278
1962 CHI N  O     159  .298
1963 CHI N  O     161  .286
1964 CHI N  O     162  .312
1965 CHI N *O     164  .315
1966 CHI N  O     162  .276
1967 CHI N *O     162  .278
1968 CHI N  O     163  .288
1969 CHI N *O     163  .293
1970 CHI N *O     161  .322
1971 CHI N  O     157  .301
1972 CHI N *O/1   150  .333
1973 CHI N *O-1   156  .288
1974 CHI N  1-O   117  .280
1975 OAK A *O/1   155  .244
1976 OAK A *O/D   120  .211
        BLTR     2488  .290
```

WILLIAMS, CHARLES PROSEK (CHARLIE)
B.OCT.11,1947 FLUSHING,N.Y.
```
1971 NY  N P       31  5- 6
1972 SF  N /P       3  0- 2
1973 SF  N  P      12  3- 0
1974 SF  N  P      39  1- 3
1975 SF  N  P      59  3- 3
1976 SF  N  P      48  2- 0
1977 SF  N  P      55  6- 5
1978 SF  N  P      25  1- 3
        BRTR      268 23-22
```

WILLIAMS, CLAUDE PRESTON
B.MAR.9,1893 AURORA,MO.
D.NOV.4,1959 LAGUNA BEACH,CAL.
```
1913 DET A P        4  0- 1
1914 DET A P        3  0- 0
1916 CHI A P       43 13- 7
1917 CHI A P       45 17- 8
1918 CHI A P       15  6- 4
1919 CHI A P       41 23-11
1920 CHI A P       39 22-14
        BRTL      190 81-45
```

WILLIAMS, DAVID CARLOUS (DAVEY)
B.NOV.2,1927 DALLAS,TEX.
```
1949 NY  N  2      13  .240
1951 NY  N  2      30  .266
1952 NY  N  2     138  .254
1953 NY  N  2     112  .297
1954 NY  N  2     142  .222
1955 NY  N  2      82  .251
        BRTR      517  .252
```

WILLIAMS, DAVID CARTER (MUTT)
B.JULY 31,1891 OZARK,ARK.
D.MAR.30,1962 FAYETTEVILLE,ARK.
```
1913 WAS A P        1  0- 0
1914 WAS A P        5  1- 0
        BRTR        6  1- 0
```

WILLIAMS, DAVID OWEN
B.SCRANTON,PA.
```
1902 BOS A P        3  0- 0
        TL
```

WILLIAMS, DEWEY EDGAR (DEE)
B.FEB.5,1916 DURHAM,N.C.
```
1944 CHI N  C      79  .240
1945 CHI N  C      59  .240
1946 CHI N  C       4  .200
1947 CHI N  C       3  .000
1948 CIN N  C      48  .168
        BRTR      193  .233
```

WILLIAMS, DONALD FRED (DON)
B.SEPT.14,1931 FLOYD,VA.
```
1958 PIT N P        2  0- 0
1959 PIT N P        6  0- 0
1962 KC  A P        3  0- 0
        BRTR       11  0- 0
```

**WILLIAMS, DONALD REID
(DON) OR (DINO)**
B.SEP.2,1935 LOS ANGELES,CAL.
```
1963 MIN A P        3  0- 0
        BRTR
```

WILLIAMS, EARL BAXTER
B.JAN.27,1903 CUMBERLAND GAP,TENN.
D.MAR.10,1958 KNOXVILLE,TNNN.
```
1928 BOS N C        3  .000
        BRTR
```

WILLIAMS, EARL CRAIG
B.JULY 14,1948 NEWARK,N.J.
```
1970 ATL N /1-3    10  .368
1971 ATL N  C-3-1 145  .260
1972 ATL N *C-3-1 151  .258
1973 BAL A  C-1   132  .237
1974 BAL A  C-1   118  .254
1975 ATL N  1-C   111  .240
1976 ATL N  C-1    61  .212
     MON N  1-C    61  .237
1977 OAK A  D-C-1 100  .241
        BRTR      889  .247
```

WILLIAMS, EDWIN DIBRELL (DIB)
B.JAN.19,1910 GREENBRIER,ARK.
```
1930 PHI A  2-S    67  .262
1931 PHI A  2-S    86  .269
1932 PHI A  2      62  .251
1933 PHI A  2-S   115  .289
1934 PHI A  2      66  .273
1935 PHI A  2-S     4  .100
     BOS A  2-S-3  75  .211
        BRTR      475  .267
```

WILLIAMS, ELISHA ALPHONSO (DALE)
B.OCT.6,1855 LUDLOW,KY.
D.OCT.22,1939 COVINGTON,KY.
```
1876 CIN N  P       9  1- 8
        BRTR
```

WILLIAMS, EVON DANIEL (DENNY)
B.DEC.13,1899 PORTLAND,ORE.
D.MAR.24,1929 LOS ANGELES,CAL.
```
1921 CIN N  O      10  .000
1924 BOS A  O      25  .365
1925 BOS A  O      68  .229
1928 BOS A  O      16  .222
        BLTR      119  .259
```

WILLIAMS, FRANK C.
[SEE FRANK C. SELMAN]

WILLIAMS, FRED (CY)
B.DEC.21,1887 WADENA,IND.
D.APR.23,1974 EAGLE RIVER,WIS.
```
1912 CHI N  O      28  .242
1913 CHI N  O      49  .224
1914 CHI N  O      55  .202
1915 CHI N  O     151  .257
1916 CHI N  O     118  .279
1917 CHI N  O     138  .241
1918 PHI N  O      94  .276
1919 PHI N  O     109  .278
1920 PHI N  O     148  .325
1921 PHI N  O     146  .320
1922 PHI N  O     151  .308
1923 PHI N  O     136  .293
1924 PHI N  O     148  .328
1925 PHI N  O     107  .331
1926 PHI N  O     107  .345
1927 PHI N  O     111  .274
1928 PHI N  O      99  .256
1929 PHI N  O      66  .292
1930 PHI N  O      21  .471
        BLTL     2002  .292
```

WILLIAMS, FRED (PAPA)
B.JULY 17,1913 MERIDIAN,MISS.
```
1945 CLE A  1      19  .211
        BRTR
```

WILLIAMS, GEORGE
B.OCT.23,1939 DETROIT,MICH.
```
1961 PHI N  2        17  .250
1962 HOU N  2         5  .375
1964 KC  A  2-S-3-O  37  .209
        BRTR         59  .230
```

WILLIAMS, HARRY PETER
B.JUNE 23,1890 OMAHA,NEB.
D.DEC.21,1963 HUNTINGTON PARK,CAL.
```
1913 NY  A  1      27  .256
        BRTR
```

WILLIAMS, JAMES A.
B.JAN.3,1848 COLUMBUS,OHIO
D.OCT.2,1918 N.HEMPSTEAD,N.Y.
NON-PLAYING MANAGER
STL[AA] 1884; CLE[AA] 1887-88

WILLIAMS, JAMES ALFRED (JIM)
B.APR.29,1947 ZACHARY,LA.
```
1969 SD  N /O      13  .280
1970 SD  N /O      11  .286
        BRTR       24  .282
```

WILLIAMS, JAMES FRANCIS (JIM)
B.OCT.4,1943 SANTA MARIA,CAL.
```
1966 STL N /S-2    13  .273
1967 STL N /S       1  .000
        BRTR       14  .231
```

WILLIAMS, JAMES THOMAS (JIMMY)
B.DEC.20,1876 ST.LOUIS,MO.
D.JAN.16,1965 ST.PETERSBURG,FLA

YR	CL	LEA	POS	GP	G	REC
1899	PIT	N	3		153	.352
1900	PIT	N	3		106	.266
1901	BAL	A	2		131	.321
1902	BAL	A	1-2-3		125	.311
1903	NY	A	2		132	.281
1904	NY	A	2		146	.259
1905	NY	A	2		129	.228
1906	NY	A	2		139	.277
1907	NY	A	2		139	.270
1908	STL	A	2		148	.236
1909	STL	A	2		110	.195
	BRTR				1458	.276

WILLIAMS, JOHN BRODIE (HONOLULU JOHNNIE)
B.JULY 16,1889 HONOLULU,HAWAII
D.SEPT.6,1963 LONG BEACH,CAL.

YR	CL	LEA	POS	GP	G	REC
1914	DET	A	P		4	0- 3
	BRTR					

WILLIAMS, KENNETH ROY (KEN)
B.JUNE 28,1890 GRANTS PASS,ORE.
D.JAN.22,1959 GRANTS PASS,ORE.

YR	CL	LEA	POS	GP	G	REC
1915	CIN	N	O		71	.242
1916	CIN	N	O		10	.111
1918	STL	A	O		2	.000
1919	STL	A	O		65	.300
1920	STL	A	O		141	.307
1921	STL	A	O		146	.347
1922	STL	A	O		153	.332
1923	STL	A	O		147	.357
1924	STL	A	O		114	.324
1925	STL	A	O		102	.331
1926	STL	A	O		108	.280
1927	STL	A	O		131	.323
1928	BOS	A	O		133	.303
1929	BOS	A	O		74	.346
	BLTR				1397	.319

WILLIAMS, LEON THEO (LEFTY)
B.DEC.2,1905 MACON,GA.

YR	CL	LEA	POS	GP	G	REC
1926	BRO	N	P	8	12	0- 0
	BLTL					

WILLIAMS, MARK WESTLEY
B.JULY 28,1953 ELMIRA,N.Y.

YR	CL	LEA	POS	GP	G	REC
1977	OAK	A	/O		3	.000
	BLTR					

WILLIAMS, MARSHALL MC DIARMID (MARSH) OR (CAP)
B.FEB.21,1893 FAISON,N.C.
D.FEB.22,1935 TUCSON,ARIZ.

YR	CL	LEA	POS	GP	G	REC
1916	PHI	A	P		10	0- 6
	BRTR					

WILLIAMS, OTTO GEORGE
B.NOV.2,1877 NEWARK,N.J.
D.MAR.19,1937 OMAHA,NEB.

YR	CL	LEA	POS	GP	G	REC
1902	STL	N	S		2	.400
1903	STL	N	S		53	.203
	CHI	N	S		37	.223
1904	CHI	N	1-O		54	.200
1906	WAS	A	2		20	.137
	BRTR				166	.202

WILLIAMS, REES GEPHARDT (STEAMBOAT)
B.JAN.31,1892 CASCADE,MONT.

YR	CL	LEA	POS	GP	G	REC
1914	STL	N	P		6	0- 1
1916	STL	N	P		36	6- 7
	BRTR				42	6- 8

WILLIAMS, RICHARD ALLEN (RICK)
B.NOV.9,1952 MERCED,CAL.

YR	CL	LEA	POS	GP	G	REC
1978	HOU	N	P		17	1- 2
	BRTR					

WILLIAMS, RICHARD HIRSCHFELD (DICK)
B.MAY 7,1928 ST.LOUIS,MO.

YR	CL	LEA	POS	GP	G	REC
1951	BRO	N	O		23	.200
1952	BRO	N	1-3-O		36	.309
1953	BRO	N	O		30	.218
1954	BRO	N	O		16	.147
1956	BRO	N	H		7	.286
	BAL	A	1-2-3-O		87	.286
1957	BAL	A	1-3-O		47	.234
	CLE	A	3-O		67	.283
1958	BAL	A	1-2-3-O		128	.276
1959	KC	A	1-2-3-O		130	.266
1960	KC	A	1-3-O		127	.288
1961	BAL	A	1-3-O		103	.206
1962	BAL	A	1-3-O		82	.247
1963	BOS	A	1-3-O		79	.257
1964	BOS	A	1-3-O		61	.159
	BRTR				1023	.260

NON-PLAYING MANAGER
BOS(A) 1967-69, OAK(A) 1971-73,
CAL(A) 1974-76, MON(N) 1977-78

WILLIAMS, RINALDO LEWIS
B.DEC.18,1893 SANTA CRUZ,CAL.
D.APR.24,1966 COTTONWOOD,ARIZ.

YR	CL	LEA	POS	GP	G	REC
1914	BRO	F	3		4	.207
	BLTR					

WILLIAMS, ROBERT ELIAS
B.APR.27,1884 MONDAY,OHIO
D.AUG.6,1962 NELSONVILLE,OHIO

YR	CL	LEA	POS	GP	G	REC
1911	NY	A	C		20	.191
1912	NY	A	C		20	.136
1913	NY	A	C		6	.158
1914	NY	A	1		59	.163
	BRTR				105	.163

WILLIAMS, ROBERT FULTON (ACE)
B.MAR.18,1917 MONTCLAIR,N.J.

YR	CL	LEA	POS	GP	G	REC
1940	BOS	N	P		5	0- 0
1946	BOS	N	P		1	0- 0
	BRTL				6	0- 0

WILLIAMS, STANLEY WILSON (STAN)
B.SEP.14,1936 ENFIELD,N.H.

YR	CL	LEA	POS	GP	G	REC
1958	LA	N	P		27	9- 7
1959	LA	N	P		35	5- 5
1960	LA	N	P		38	14-10
1961	LA	N	P		41	15-12
1962	LA	N	P		40	14-12
1963	NY	A	P		29	9- 8
1964	NY	A	P	21	22	1- 5
1965	CLE	A	/P		3	0- 0
1967	CLE	A	P		16	6- 4
1968	CLE	A	P		44	13-11
1969	CLE	A	P		61	6-14
1970	MIN	A	P		68	10- 1
1971	MIN	A	P		46	4- 5
	STL	N	P		10	3- 0
1972	BOS	A	/P		3	0- 0
	BRTR			482	483	109-94

WILLIAMS, THEODORE SAMUEL (TED) (THE KID), (THE THUMPER) OR (THE SPLENDID SPLINTER)
B.AUG.30,1918 SAN DIEGO,CAL.

YR	CL	LEA	POS	GP	G	REC
1939	BOS	A	O		149	.327
1940	BOS	A	P-O	1	144	0- 0
						.344
1941	BOS	A	O		143	.406
1942	BOS	A	O		150	.356
1946	BOS	A	O		150	.342
1947	BOS	A	O		156	.343
1948	BOS	A	O		137	.369
1949	BOS	A	O		155	.343
1950	BOS	A	O		89	.317
1951	BOS	A	O		148	.318
1952	BOS	A	O		6	.400
1953	BOS	A	O		37	.407
1954	BOS	A	O		117	.345
1955	BOS	A	O		98	.356
1956	BOS	A	O		136	.345
1957	BOS	A	O		132	.388
1958	BOS	A	O		129	.328
1959	BOS	A	O		103	.254
1960	BOS	A	O		113	.316
	BRTR			1	2292	0- 0
						.344

NON-PLAYING MANAGER
WAS(A) 1969-71, TEX(A) 1972

WILLIAMS, THOMAS C.
B.AUG.19,1870 MINERSVILLE,OHIO
D.JULY 27,1940 COLUMBUS,OHIO

YR	CL	LEA	POS	GP	G	REC
1892	CLE	N	P		3	1- 0
1893	CLE	N	P		8	1- 1
					11	2- 1

WILLIAMS, WALTER ALLEN (WALT) OR (NO-NECK)
B.DEC.19,1943 BROWNWOOD,TEX.

YR	CL	LEA	POS	GP	G	REC
1964	HOU	N	O		10	.000
1967	CHI	A	O		104	.240
1968	CHI	A	O		63	.241
1969	CHI	A	*O		135	.304
1970	CHI	A	O		110	.251
1971	CHI	A	O/3		114	.294
1972	CHI	A	O/3		77	.249
1973	CLE	A	O		104	.289
1974	NY	A	O		43	.113
1975	NY	A	O-D/2		82	.281
	BRTR				842	.270

WILLIAMS, WALTER MERRILL (POP)
B.MAY 19,1874 BOWDOINHAM,ME.
D.AUG.4,1959 TOPSHAM,MAINE

YR	CL	LEA	POS	GP	G	REC
1898	WAS	N	P		2	0- 2
1902	CHI	N	P-O	31	32	11-16
						.194
1903	CHI	N	P		2	0- 1
	PHI	N	P		3	1- 2
	BOS	N	P		14	4- 5
	BLTL			52	53	16-25
						.217

WILLIAMS, WASHINGTON J.
B.PHILADELPHIA,PA.
D.AUG.9,1892

YR	CL	LEA	POS	GP	G	REC
1884	RIC	AA	O		2	.250
1885	CHI	N	P-O		1	0- 0
						.250
				1	3	0- 0
						.250

WILLIAMS, WILLIAM (BILLY)
B.JUNE 13,1933 NEWBERRY,S.C.

YR	CL	LEA	POS	GP	G	REC
1969	SEA	A	/O		4	.000
	BLTR					

WILLIAMS, WOODROW WILSON (WOODY)
B.AUG.22,1912 PAMPLIN,VA.

YR	CL	LEA	POS	GP	G	REC
1938	BRO	N	S		20	.333
1943	CIN	N	2-S-3		30	.377
1944	CIN	N	2		155	.240
1945	CIN	N	2		133	.237
	BRTR				338	.250

WILLIAMSON, EDWARD NAGLE (NED)
B.OCT.24,1857 PHILADELPHIA,PA.
D.MAR.3,1894 WILLOW SPRINGS,ARK

YR	CL	LEA	POS	GP	G	REC
1878	IND	N	3		60	.223
1879	CHI	N	3		77	.299
1880	CHI	N	C-2-3		74	.255
1881	CHI	N	P-2-S-3	1	82	0- 1
						.266
1882	CHI	N	P-3	1	82	0- 0
						.281
1883	CHI	N	P-C-3	1	98	0- 0
						.276
1884	CHI	N	P-C-3	1	106	0- 0
						.276
1885	CHI	N	P-C-3	2	112	0- 0
						.238
1886	CHI	N	S		121	.216
1887	CHI	N	S		127	.371
1888	CHI	N	S		132	.250
1889	CHI	N	S		47	.237
1890	CHI	N	P-S-3		73	.204
	BRTR			6	1191	0- 1
						.267

WILLIAMSON, NATHANIEL HOWARD (HOWIE)
B.DEC.23,1904 LITTLE ROCK,ARK.

YR	CL	LEA	POS	GP	G	REC
1928	STL	N	H		10	.222
	BLTL					

WILLIAMSON, SILAS ALBERT (AL)
B.FEB.20,1900 BUCKSVILLE,ARK.

YR	CL	LEA	POS	GP	G	REC
1928	CHI	A	P		1	0- 0
	BRTR					

WILLIGROD, JULIUS
B.CALIFORNIA

YR	CL	LEA	POS	GP	G	REC
1882	DET	N	S-O		2	.286
	CLE	N	O		8	.114
					10	.143

WILLINGHAM, THOMAS HUGH (HUGH)
B.MAY 30,1908 DALHART,TEX.

YR	CL	LEA	POS	GP	G	REC
1930	CHI	A	2		3	.250
1931	PHI	N	1-S-3		23	.257
1932	PHI	N	H		4	.000
1933	PHI	N	H		1	.000
	BRTR				31	.233

WILLIS, CHARLES WILLIAM (LEFTY)
B.NOV.4,1905 LEETOWN,W.VA.
D.MAY 10,1962 BETHESDA,MD.

YR	CL	LEA	POS	GP	G	REC
1925	PHI	A	P		3	0- 0
1926	PHI	A	P		13	0- 0
1927	PHI	A	P		14	3- 1
	BLTL				30	3- 1

WILLIS, DALE JEROME
B.MAY 29,1938 CALHOUN,GA.

YR	CL	LEA	POS	GP	G	REC
1963	KC	A	P	25	26	0- 2
	BRTR					

WILLIS, JAMES GLADDEN
B.MAR.20,1927 DOYLINE,LA.

YR	CL	LEA	POS	GP	G	REC
1953	CHI	N	P		13	2- 1
1954	CHI	N	P		14	0- 1
	BLTR				27	2- 2

WILLIS, JOSEPH DENK
B.APR.9,1890 COAL GROVE,OHIO
D.DEC.4,1966 IRONTON,OHIO

YR	CL	LEA	POS	GP	G	REC
1911	STL	A	P		1	0- 0
	STL	N	P		2	0- 1
1912	STL	N	P		31	4- 9
1913	STL	N	P		2	0- 0
	BRTL				36	4-10

WILLIS, LESTER EVANS (LES) (WIMPY) OR (LEFTY)
B.JAN.17,1908 NACOGDOCHES,TEX.

YR	CL	LEA	POS	GP	G	REC
1947	CLE	A	P		22	0- 2
	BLTL					

WILLIS, MICHAEL HENRY (MIKE)
B.DEC.26,1956 OKLAHOMA CITY,OKLA

YR	CL	LEA	POS	GP	G	REC
1977	TOR	A	P		43	2- 6
1978	TOR	A	P		44	3- 7
	BLTR				87	5-13

YR	CL	LEA	POS	GP	G	REC

WILLIS, RONALD EARL (RON)
B.JULY 12,1943 WILLISVILLE,TENN.
D.NOV.21,1977 MEMPHIS,TENN.

YR	CL	LEA	POS	GP	G	REC
1966	STL	N	/P		4	0- 0
1967	STL	N	P	65	6- 5
1968	STL	N	P	48	2- 3
1969	STL	N	P	26	1- 2
	HOU	N	/P	3	0- 0
1970	SD	N	P	42	2- 2
		BRTR		188	11-12

WILLIS, VICTOR GAZAWAY (VIC)
B.APR.12,1876 WILMINGTON,DEL.
D.AUG.3,1947 ELKTON,MD.

1898	BOS	N	P	38	23-12
1899	BOS	N	P	38	40	27- 9
1900	BOS	N	P	28	9-16
1901	BOS	N	P	36	18-17
1902	BOS	N	P	51	27-19
1903	BOS	N	P	33	39	12-19
1904	BOS	N	P	43	49	18-25
1905	BOS	N	P	41	10-29
1906	PIT	N	P	41	23-13
1907	PIT	N	P	39	21-11
1908	PIT	N	P	41	23-11
1909	PIT	N	P	39	22-11
1910	STL	N	P	33	9-12
		BRTR		501	515	242-204

**WILLOUGHBY, CLAUDE WILLIAM
(FLUNKY) OR (WEEPING WILLIE)**
B.NOV.14,1898 FREDONIA,KAN.
D.AUG.14,1973 MC PHERSON,KAN.

1925	PHI	N	P	3	2- 1
1926	PHI	N	P	47	8-12
1927	PHI	N	P	35	3- 7
1928	PHI	N	P	35	6- 5
1929	PHI	N	P	49	15-14
1930	PHI	N	P	41	4-17
1931	PIT	N	P	9	0- 2
		BRTR		219	38-58

WILLOUGHBY, JAMES ARTHUR (JIM)
B.JAN.31,1949 SALINAS,CAL.

1971	SF	N	/P	2	0- 1
1972	SF	N	P	11	6- 4
1973	SF	N	P	39	4- 5
1974	SF	N	P	18	20	1- 4
1975	BOS	A	P	24	5- 2
1976	BOS	A	P	54	3-12
1977	BOS	A	P	31	6- 2
1978	CHI	A	P	59	1- 6
		BRTR		238	242	26-36

WILLS

1884	WAS	AA	O	4	.133
	KC	U	O	5	.150
				9	.143

WILLS, DAVIS BOWLES (DAVE)
B.JAN.26,1877 CHARLOTTESVILLE,VA.
D.OCT.12,1959 WASHINGTON,D.C.

1899	LOU	N	1	24	.255
		BLTL			

WILLS, ELLIOTT TAYLOR (BUMP)
B.JULY 27,1952 WASHINGTON,D.C.

1977	TEX	A	*2/S-1	152	.287
1978	TEX	A	*2	157	.250
		BBTR		309	.269

WILLS, MAURICE MORNING (MAURY)
B.OCT.2,1932 WASHINGTON,D.C.

1959	LA	N	S	83	.260
1960	LA	N	S	148	.295
1961	LA	N	S	148	.282
1962	LA	N	S	165	.299
1963	LA	N	S-3	134	.302
1964	LA	N	S-3	158	.275
1965	LA	N	*S	158	.286
1966	LA	N	*S/3	143	.273
1967	PIT	N	*3/S	149	.302
1968	PIT	N	*3-S	153	.278
1969	MON	N	S/2	47	.222
	LA	N	S/2	104	.297
1970	LA	N	*S/3	132	.270
1971	LA	N	*S/3	149	.281
1972	LA	N	S-3	71	.129
		BBTR		1942	.281

WILLS, THEODORE CARL (TED)
B.FEB.9,1934 FRESNO,CAL.

1959	BOS	A	P	9	2- 6
1960	BOS	A	P	15	16	1- 1
1961	BOS	A	P	17	3- 2
1962	BOS	A	P	1	0- 0
	CIN	N	P	26	0- 2
1965	CHI	A	P	15	2- 0
		BLTL		83	84	8-11

WILLSON, FRANK HOXIE (KID)
B.NOV.3,1895 BLOOMINGTON,NEB.
D.APR.17,1964 UNION GAP,WASH.

1918	CHI	A	H	4	.000
1927	CHI	A	O	7	.100
		BLTL		11	.091

WILMOT, WALTER ROBERT
B.OCT.18,1863 PLOVER,WIS.
D.FEB.1,1929 CHICAGO,ILL.

1888	WAS	N	O	119	.224
1889	WAS	N	O	107	.301
1890	CHI	N	O	139	.278
1891	CHI	N	O	120	.285
1892	CHI	N	O	92	.220
1893	CHI	N	O	93	.318
1894	CHI	N	O	135	.331
1895	CHI	N	O	108	.299
1897	NY	N	O	13	.242
1898	NY	N	O	34	.246
		BBTR		960	.282

WILSHERE, VERNON SPRAGUE (WHITEY)
B.AUG.3,1912 POPLAR RIDGE,N.Y.

1934	PHI	A	P	9	0- 1
1935	PHI	A	P	27	9- 9
1936	PHI	A	P	5	1- 2
		BLTL		41	10-12

WILSHUSEN, TERRY WAYNE
B.MAR.22,1949 ATASCADERO,CAL.

1973	CAL	A	/P	1	0- 0
		BRTR			

WILSON, ARCHIE CLIFTON
B.NOV.25,1923 LOS ANGELES,CAL.

1951	NY	A	O	4	.000
1952	NY	A	H	3	.500
	WAS	A	O	26	.208
	BOS	A	O	18	.263
		BRTR		51	.221

WILSON, ARTHUR EARL (DUTCH)
B.DEC.11,1885 MACON,ILL.
D.JUNE 12,1960 CHICAGO,ILL.

1908	NY	N	C	1	.000
1909	NY	N	C	17	.238
1910	NY	N	C	26	.269
1911	NY	N	C	64	.302
1912	NY	N	C	65	.289
1913	NY	N	C	54	.190
1914	CHI	F	C	138	.287
1915	CHI	F	C	96	.309
1916	PIT	N	C	53	.258
	CHI	N	C	36	.193
1917	CHI	N	C	81	.213
1918	BOS	N	C	89	.211
1919	BOS	N	C-1	71	.257
1920	BOS	N	C	16	.053
1921	CLE	A	C	2	.000
		BRTR		809	.258

**WILSON, CHARLES WOODROW
(CHARLIE) OR (SWAMP BABY)**
B.JAN.13,1905 CLINTON,S.C.
D.DEC.19,1970 ROCHESTER,N.Y.

1931	BOS	N	3	16	.190
1932	STL	N	S	24	.198
1933	STL	N	3	1	.000
1935	STL	N	3	16	.323
		BBTR		57	.215

WILSON, DONALD EDWARD (DON)
B.FEB.12,1945 MONROE,LA.
D.JAN.5,1975 HOUSTON,TEX.

1966	HOU	N	/P	1	1- 0
1967	HOU	N	P	31	10- 9
1968	HOU	N	P	33	34	13-16
1969	HOU	N	P	34	16-12
1970	HOU	N	P	29	30	11- 6
1971	HOU	N	P	35	16-10
1972	HOU	N	P	33	15-10
1973	HOU	N	P	37	11-16
1974	HOU	N	P	33	11-13
		BRTR		266	268	104-92

WILSON, DUANE LEWIS
B.JUNE 29,1934 WICHITA,KAN.

1958	BOS	A	P	2	0- 0
		BLTL			

**WILSON, EARL LAWRENCE
(PLAYED UNDER NAME OF
ROBERT EARL WILSON)**

WILSON, EDWARD FRANCIS
B.SEPT.7,1909 HAMDEN,CONN.

1936	BRO	N	O	52	.347
1937	BRO	N	O	36	.222
		BLTL		88	.317

WILSON, FINIS ELBERT
B.DEC.9,1889 EAST FORK,KY.
D.MAR.9,1959 CORAL GABLES,FLA.

1914	BRO	F	P	2	0- 1
1915	BRO	F	P	18	1- 8
		BLTL		20	1- 9

**WILSON, FRANCIS EDWARD
(FRANK) OR (SQUASH)**
B.APR.20,1901 MALDEN,MASS.
D.NOV.25,1974 LEICESTER,MASS.

1924	BOS	N	O	61	.237
1925	BOS	N	O	12	.419
1926	BOS	N	O	87	.237
1928	CLE	A	H	2	.000
	STL	A	O	6	.000
		BLTR		168	.246

WILSON, FRANK EALTON (ZEKE)
B.DEC.24,1869 BENTON,ALA.
D.APR.26,1928 MONTGOMERY,ALA.

1895	BOS	N	P	6	2- 4
	CLE	N	P	11	5- 2
1896	CLE	N	P	29	17-10
1897	CLE	N	P	29	35	14-14
1898	CLE	N	P	32	34	13-18
1899	STL	N	P	5	1- 1
				112	120	52-49

WILSON, GEORGE ARCHIBALD (HICKIE)
B.BROOKLYN,N.Y.

1884	BRO	AA	C-O	24	.214

WILSON, GEORGE FRANCIS (SQUANTO)
B.MAR.29,1889 OLD TOWN,ME.
D.MAR.26,1967 WINTHROP,MAINE

1911	DET	A	C	6	.187
1914	BOS	A	1	1	.000
		BBTR		6	.187

WILSON, GEORGE PEACOCK (ICEHOUSE)
B.SEPT.14,1912 MARICOPA,CAL.
D.OCT.13,1973 MORAGA,CAL.

1934	DET	A	H	1	.000
		BRTR			

WILSON, GEORGE PEPPER (KITTEN)
[SEE GEORGE PEPPER PRENTISS]

WILSON, GEORGE WASHINGTON (TEDDY)
B.AUG.30,1925 CHERRYVILLE,N.C.
D.OCT.29,1974 GASTONIA,N.C.

1952	CHI	A	O	8	.111
	NY	N	1-O	62	.241
1953	NY	N	H	11	.125
1956	NY	N	O	53	.132
	NY	A	O	11	.167
		BLTR		145	.191

WILSON, GOMER RUSSELL (TEX)
B.JULY 8,1901 TRENTON,TEX.
D.SEPT.15,1946 SULPHUR SPRINGS,TEX.

1924	BRO	N	P	2	0- 0
		BRTL			

WILSON, GRADY HERBERT
B.NOV.23,1922 COLUMBUS,GA.

1948	PIT	N	S	12	.100
		BRTR			

WILSON, HENRY C.
B.BALTIMORE,MD.

1898	BAL	N	C	1	.000

WILSON, HOWARD P. (HIGHBALL)
B.PHILADELPHIA,PA.

1899	CLE	N	P	1	0- 1
1902	PHI	A	P	13	7- 4
1903	WAS	A	P	31	32	8-18
1904	WAS	A	P	3	4	0- 3
		TR		48	50	15-26

WILSON, HOWARD WILLIAM (CHINK)

1906	WAS	A	P	1	0- 1

WILSON, JAMES (JIMMY) OR (ACE)
B.JULY 23,1900 PHILADELPHIA,PA.
D.MAY 31,1947 BRADENTON,FLA.

1923	PHI	N	C-O	85	.262
1924	PHI	N	C-1-O	95	.279
1925	PHI	N	C-O	108	.328
1926	PHI	N	C	90	.305
1927	PHI	N	C	128	.275
1928	PHI	N	C	21	.300
	STL	N	C	120	.258
1929	STL	N	C	120	.325
1930	STL	N	C	107	.318
1931	STL	N	C	115	.274
1932	STL	N	C	92	.248
1933	STL	N	C	113	.255
1934	PHI	N	M-C	91	.292
1935	PHI	N	M-C-2	93	.279
1936	PHI	N	M-C	85	.278
1937	PHI	N	M-C	39	.276
1938	PHI	N	M-C	3	.000
1939	CIN	N	C	4	.333
1940	CIN	N	C	16	.243
		BRTR		1525	.284
NON-PLAYING MANAGER CHI(N) 1941-44

WILSON, JAMES ALGER (JIM)
B.FEB.20,1922 SAN DIEGO,CAL.

YR	CL	LEA	POS	GP	G	REC
1945	BOS	A	P	23	25	6- 8
1946	BOS	A	P		1	0- 0
1948	STL	A	P		4	0- 0
1949	PHI	A	P		2	0- 0
1951	BOS	N	P		20	7- 7
1952	BOS	N	P		33	12-14
1953	MIL	N	P		20	4- 9
1954	MIL	N	P		27	8- 2
1955	BAL	A	P		34	12-18
1956	BAL	A	P		7	4- 2
	CHI	A	P		28	9-12
1957	CHI	A	P	30	31	15- 8
1958	CHI	A	P		28	9- 9
			BRTR	257	260	86-89

WILSON, JAMES GARRETT (GARY)
B.JAN.12,1877 BALTIMORE,MD.
D.MAY 1,1969 RANDALLSTOWN,MD.

YR	CL	LEA	POS	GP	G	REC
1902	BOS	A	2		3	.181
			BRTR			

WILSON, JOHN FRANCIS
(JACK) OR (BLACK JACK)
B.APR.12,1912 PORTLAND,ORE.

YR	CL	LEA	POS	GP	G	REC
1934	PHI	A	P		2	0- 1
1935	BOS	A	P		23	3- 4
1936	BOS	A	P	43	44	6- 8
1937	BOS	A	P		51	16-10
1938	BOS	A	P		37	15-15
1939	BOS	A	P	36	37	11-11
1940	BOS	A	P		41	12- 6
1941	BOS	A	P		27	4-13
1942	WAS	A	P		12	1- 4
	DET	A	P		9	0- 0
			BRTR	281	283	68-72

WILSON, JOHN NICODEMUS
B.JUNE 15,1890 BOONSBORO,MD.
D.SEPT.23,1954 ANNAPOLIS,MD.

YR	CL	LEA	POS	GP	G	REC
1913	WAS	A	P		3	0- 0
			BRTL			

WILSON, JOHN OWEN (CHIEF)
B.AUG.21,1883 AUSTIN,TEX.
D.FEB.22,1954 BERTRAM,TEX.

YR	CL	LEA	POS	GP	G	REC
1908	PIT	N	O		144	.227
1909	PIT	N	O		154	.273
1910	PIT	N	O		146	.276
1911	PIT	N	O		146	.300
1912	PIT	N	O		152	.300
1913	PIT	N	O		155	.266
1914	STL	N	O		154	.259
1915	STL	N	O		107	.276
1916	STL	N	O		120	.239
			BLTR		1278	.268

WILSON, JOHN SAMUEL
B.APR.25,1905 COAL CITY,ALA.

YR	CL	LEA	POS	GP	G	REC
1927	BOS	A	P		5	0- 2
1928	BOS	A	P		2	0- 0
			BRTR		7	0- 2

WILSON, LESTER WILBUR (LES) OR (TUG)
B.JULY 15,1885 GRATIOT COUNTY,MICH.
D.APR.4,1969 EDMONDS,WASH.

YR	CL	LEA	POS	GP	G	REC
1911	BOS	A	O		4	.000
			BLTR			

WILSON, LEWIS ROBERT (HACK)
B.APR.26,1900 ELLWOOD CITY,PA.
D.NOV.23,1948 BALTIMORE,MD.

YR	CL	LEA	POS	GP	G	REC
1923	NY	N	O		3	.200
1924	NY	N	O		107	.295
1925	NY	N	O		62	.239
1926	CHI	N	O		142	.321
1927	CHI	N	O		146	.318
1928	CHI	N	O		145	.313
1929	CHI	N	O		150	.345
1930	CHI	N	O		155	.356
1931	CHI	N	O		112	.261
1932	BRO	N	O		135	.297
1933	BRO	N	2-O		117	.267
1934	BRO	N	O		67	.262
	PHI	N	O		7	.100
			BRTR		1348	.307

WILSON, MAX
B.JUNE 3,1916 HAW RIVER,N.C.
D.JAN.2,1977 GREENSBORO,N.C.

YR	CL	LEA	POS	GP	G	REC
1940	PHI	N	P		3	0- 0
1946	WAS	A	P		9	0- 1
			BLTL		12	0- 1

WILSON, PARKE ASEL
B.OCT.26,1867 KEITHSBURG,ILL.
D.DEC.20,1934 HERMOSA BEACH,CAL

YR	CL	LEA	POS	GP	G	REC
1893	NY	N	C		29	.280
1894	NY	N	C		45	.329
1895	NY	N	C		62	.243
1896	NY	N	C		69	.230
1897	NY	N	C		44	.310
1898	NY	N	O		1	.000
1899	NY	N	C-1		93	.268
			BRTR		343	.270

WILSON, PETER ALEX (PETE)
B.OCT.9,1885 SPRINGFIELD,MASS.
D.JUNE 5,1957 ST.PETERSBURG,FLA

YR	CL	LEA	POS	GP	G	REC
1908	NY	A	P		7	3- 3
1909	NY	A	P		14	5- 6
			TL		21	8- 9

WILSON, ROBERT
B.FEB.22,1928 DALLAS,TEX.

YR	CL	LEA	POS	GP	G	REC
1958	LA	N	O		3	.200
			BRTR			

WILSON, ROBERT EARL (EARL)
[NAME CHANGED FROM
WILSON, EARL LAWRENCE]
B.OCT.2,1934 PONCHATOULA,LA.

YR	CL	LEA	POS	GP	G	REC
1959	BOS	A	P		9	1- 1
1960	BOS	A	P	13	15	3- 2
1962	BOS	A	P	31	35	12- 8
1963	BOS	A	P	37	38	11-16
1964	BOS	A	P	33	54	11-12
1965	BOS	A	P	36	47	13-14
1966	BOS	A	P	15	18	5- 5
	DET	A	P	23	27	13- 6
1967	DET	A	P	39	52	22-11
1968	DET	A	P	34	40	13-12
1969	DET	A	P	35	37	12-10
1970	DET	A	P		18	4- 6
	SD	N	P		15	1- 6
			BRTR	338	405	121-109

WILSON, ROBERT JAMES (RED)
B.MAR.7,1929 MILWAUKEE,WIS.

YR	CL	LEA	POS	GP	G	REC
1951	CHI	A	C		4	.273
1952	CHI	A	C		2	.000
1953	CHI	A	C		71	.250
1954	CHI	A	C		8	.200
	DET	A	C		54	.282
1955	DET	A	C		78	.220
1956	DET	A	C		78	.289
1957	DET	A	C		59	.242
1958	DET	A	C		103	.299
1959	DET	A	C		67	.263
1960	DET	A	C		45	.216
	CLE	A	C		32	.216
			BRTR		601	.258

WILSON, ROY EDWARD (ROY) OR (LEFTY)
B.SEPT.13,1896 FOSTER,IOWA
D.DEC.3,1969 CLARION,IOWA

YR	CL	LEA	POS	GP	G	REC
1928	CHI	A	P		1	0- 0
			BLTL			

WILSON, SAMUEL MARSHALL (MIKE)
B.DEC.2,1896 EDGE HILL,PA.
D.MAY 16,1978 BOYNTON BEACH,FLA

YR	CL	LEA	POS	GP	G	REC
1921	PIT	N	C		5	.000
			BRTR			

WILSON, SAMUEL O NEIL
B.JUNE 14,1935 LEXINGTON,TENN.

YR	CL	LEA	POS	GP	G	REC
1960	SF	N	C		6	.000
			BLTR			

WILSON, THOMAS C.
B.1889

YR	CL	LEA	POS	GP	G	REC
1914	WAS	A	C		1	.000
			BRTR			

WILSON, WALTER WOOD
B.NOV.24,1913 GLENN,GA.

YR	CL	LEA	POS	GP	G	REC
1945	DET	A	P		25	1- 3
			BLTR			

WILSON, WILLIAM
B.OCT.28,1867 HANNIBAL,MO.

YR	CL	LEA	POS	GP	G	REC
1890	PIT	N	C-1-O		83	.213
1897	LOU	N	C		106	.218
1898	LOU	N	C		30	.182
					219	.211

WILSON, WILLIAM CLARENCE
(MUTT) OR (LANK)
B.JULY 20,1896 KISER,N.C.
D.AUG.31,1962 WILDWOOD,FLA.

YR	CL	LEA	POS	GP	G	REC
1920	DET	A	P		3	1- 1
			BRTR			

WILSON, WILLIAM DONALD (BILL)
B.NOV.6,1928 CENTRAL CITY,NEB.

YR	CL	LEA	POS	GP	G	REC
1950	CHI	A	O		3	.000
1953	CHI	A	O		9	.059
1954	CHI	A	O		20	.171
	PHI	A	O		94	.238
1955	KC	A	P-O	1	98	0- 0
						.223
			BRTR	1	224	0- 0
						.222

WILSON, WILLIAM HARLAN (BILL)
B.SEP.21,1942 POMEROY,OHIO

YR	CL	LEA	POS	GP	G	REC
1969	PHI	N	P		37	2- 5
1970	PHI	N	P		37	1- 0
1971	PHI	N	P/3		38	4- 6
						.100
1972	PHI	N	P		23	1- 1
1973	PHI	N	P		44	1- 3
			BRTR		179	9-15
						.083

WILSON, WILLIE JAMES
B.JULY 9,1955 MONTGOMERY,ALA.

YR	CL	LEA	POS	GP	G	REC
1976	KC	A	/O		12	.167
1977	KC	A	/O		13	.324
1978	KC	A	*O		127	.217
			BBTR		152	.231
			BR 1976			

WILSONHOLM

YR	CL	LEA	POS	GP	G	REC
1883	PHI	N	C-O		3	.091

WILTSE, GEORGE LEROY (HOOKS)
B.SEPT.7,1880 HAMILTON,N.Y.
D.JAN.21,1959 LONG BEACH,N.Y.

YR	CL	LEA	POS	GP	G	REC
1904	NY	N	P		25	13- 3
1905	NY	N	P	32	33	14- 7
1906	NY	N	P	38	40	16-11
1907	NY	N	P	33	34	13-12
1908	NY	N	P		44	23-14
1909	NY	N	P		37	20-11
1910	NY	N	P		36	14-12
1911	NY	N	P		30	12- 9
1912	NY	N	P		28	9- 6
1913	NY	N	P	17	20	0- 0
1914	NY	N	P	20	21	1- 1
1915	BRO	F	P	18	19	3- 5
			BRTL	358	367	138-91

WILTSE, HAROLD JAMES
(HAL) OR (WHITEY)
B.AUG.6,1903 CLAY CITY,ILL.

YR	CL	LEA	POS	GP	G	REC
1926	BOS	A	P		37	8-15
1927	BOS	A	P		36	10-18
1928	BOS	A	P		2	0- 2
	STL	A	P		26	2- 5
1931	PHI	N	P		1	0- 0
			BLTL		102	20-40

WILTSE, LEWIS DE WITT (SNAKE)
B.DEC.5,1871 BOUCKVILLE,N.Y.
D.AUG.25,1928 HARRISBURG,PA.

YR	CL	LEA	POS	GP	G	REC
1901	PIT	N	P		7	1- 4
	PHI	A	P		19	14- 5
1902	PHI	A	P		20	8- 8
	BAL	A	P-1-	16	35	7- 9
			2-O			.296
1903	NY	A	P		4	0- 3
			BRTL	66	85	30-29
						.276

WINCENIAK, EDWARD JOSEPH (ED)
B.APR.16,1929 CHICAGO,ILL.

YR	CL	LEA	POS	GP	G	REC
1956	CHI	N	2-3		15	.118
1957	CHI	N	2-S-3		17	.240
			BRTR		32	.209

WINCHELL, FREDERICK RUSSELL
[REAL NAME FREDERICK COOK]
B.JAN.23,1882 ARLINGTON,MASS.
D.AUG.8,1958 TORONTO,ONT.,CAN.

YR	CL	LEA	POS	GP	G	REC
1909	CLE	A	P		4	0- 3

WINDHORN, GORDON RAY (GORDIE)
B.DEC.19,1933 WATSEKA,ILL.

YR	CL	LEA	POS	GP	G	REC
1959	NY	A	O		7	.000
1961	LA	N	O		34	.242
1962	KC	A	O		14	.158
	LA	A	O		40	.178
			BRTR		95	.176

WINDLE, WILLIS BREWER (BILL)
B.DEC.13,1904 GALENA,KAN.

YR	CL	LEA	POS	GP	G	REC
1928	PIT	N	1		1	1.000
1929	PIT	N	1		2	.000
			BLTL		3	.500

WINE, ROBERT PAUL (BOBBY)
B.SEP.17,1938 NEW YORK,N.Y.

YR	CL	LEA	POS	GP	G	REC
1960	PHI	N	S		4	.143
1962	PHI	N	S-3		112	.244
1963	PHI	N	S-3		142	.215
1964	PHI	N	S-3		126	.212
1965	PHI	N	*S/1		139	.228
1966	PHI	N	S/O		46	.236
1967	PHI	N	*S/1		135	.190
1968	PHI	N	S/3		27	.169
1969	MON	N	*S/1-3		121	.200
1970	MON	N	*S		159	.232
1971	MON	N	*S		119	.200
1972	MON	N	3/S-2		34	.222
			BRTR		1164	.215

WINEAPPLE, EDWARD (LEFTY)
B.AUG.10,1906 BOSTON,MASS.

YR	CL	LEA	POS	GP	G	REC
1929	WAS	A	P		1	0- 0
			BLTL			

WINEGARNER, RALPH LEE
B.OCT.29,1909 BENTON,KAN.

YR	CL	LEA	POS	GP	G	REC
1930	CLE	A	3		5	.455
1932	CLE	A	P	5	7	1- 0
1934	CLE	A	P-O	22	32	5- 4
						.196
1935	CLE	A	P-1-	25	65	2- 2
			3-O			.310
1936	CLE	A	P	9	18	0- 0
1949	STL	A	P		9	0- 0
			BRTR	70	136	8- 6
						.276

```
YR  CL LEA POS    GP    G   REC
```

WINFIELD, DAVID MARK (DAVE)
B.OCT.3,1951 ST.PAUL,MINN.
```
1973 SD  N  O/1          56   .277
1974 SD  N *O           145   .265
1975 SD  N *O           143   .267
1976 SD  N *O           137   .283
1977 SD  N *O           157   .275
1978 SD  N *O/1         158   .308
         BRTR           796   .280
```

WINFORD, JAMES HEAD (COWBOY)
B.OCT.9,1909 SHELBYVILLE,TENN.
D.DEC.16,1970 MIAMI,OKLA.
```
1932 STL N  P            4   1- 1
1934 STL N  P            5   0- 2
1935 STL N  P            2   0- 0
1936 STL N  P           39  11-10
1937 STL N  P           16   2- 4
1938 BRO N  P            2   0- 1
         BRTR           68  14-18
```

WINGARD, ERNEST JAMES (JIM)
B.OCT.1,1900 PRATTVILLE,ALA.
D.JAN.17,1977 PRATTVILLE,ALA.
```
1924 STL A  P     36  37  13-12
1925 STL A  P-O   32  34   9-10
                          .288
1926 STL A  P     39  42   5- 8
1927 STL A  P     38  42   2-13
         BLTL    145 155  29-43
                          .232
```

WINGFIELD, FREDERICK DAVIS (TED)
B.AUG.7,1899 BEDFORD,VA.
D.JULY 18,1975 JOHNSON CITY,TENN.
```
1923 WAS A  P            1   0- 0
1924 WAS A  P            4   0- 0
         BOS A  P        4   0- 2
1925 BOS A  P           41  12-19
1926 BOS A  P           43  11-16
1927 BOS A  P     20  22   1- 7
         BRTR    113 115  24-44
```

WINGO, ABSALOM HOLBROOK
(AL) OR (RED)
B.MAY 6,1898 NORCROSS,GA.
D.OCT.9,1964 DETROIT,MICH.
```
1919 PHI A  O           15   .305
1924 DET A  O           78   .287
1925 DET A  O          130   .370
1926 DET A  O          108   .282
1927 DET A  O           75   .234
1928 DET A  O           87   .285
         BLTR          493   .308
```

WINGO, EDMOND ARMAND
[REAL NAME EDMOND ARMAND LA RIVIERE]
B.OCT.8,1895 ST.ANNE DE
BELLEVUE,QUE.,CANADA
D.DEC.5,1964 LACHINE,QUE.,CAN.
```
1920 PHI A  C            1   .250
         BRTR
```

WINGO, IVEY BROWN
B.JULY 8,1890 GAINESVILLE,GA.
D.MAR.1,1941 NORCROSS,GA.
```
1911 STL N  C           18   .211
1912 STL N  C          100   .265
1913 STL N  C          112   .254
1914 STL N  C           80   .300
1915 CIN N  C-O        119   .221
1916 CIN N  M-C        119   .245
1917 CIN N  C          121   .266
1918 CIN N  C          100   .254
1919 CIN N  C           76   .273
1920 CIN N  C-2        108   .264
1921 CIN N  C           97   .268
1922 CIN N  C           80   .284
1923 CIN N  C           61   .263
1924 CIN N  C-1         66   .286
1925 CIN N  C           55   .205
1926 CIN N  C            7   .200
1929 CIN N  C            1   .000
         BLTR         1320   .260
```

WINHAM, LAFAYETTE SHARKEY
(LAVE) OR (LEFTY)
B.OCT.23,1881 BROOKLYN,N.Y.
D.SEPT.12,1951 BROOKLYN,N.Y.
```
1902 BRO N  P            1   0- 0
1903 PIT N  P            5   3- 1
         BLTL            6   3- 1
```

WINKELMAN
```
1886 WAS N  P            1   0- 1
         BLTL
```

WINKELMAN, GEORGE EDWARD
B.JUNE 14,1861 PHILADELPHIA,PA.
```
1883 LOU AA O            4   .000
```

WINKLES, BOBBY BROOKS
B.MAR.11,1930 TUCKERMAN,ARK.
NON-PLAYING MANAGER
CAL[A] 1973-74, OAK[A] 1977-78

WINN, GEORGE BENJAMIN (GEORGE)
(BREEZY) OR (LEFTY)
B.OCT.26,1897 PERRY,GA.
D.NOV.1,1969 ROBERTA,GA.
```
1919 BOS A  P            3   0- 0
1922 CLE A  P            8   1- 2
1923 CLE A  P            1   0- 0
         BLTL           12   1- 2
```

WINSETT, JOHN THOMAS (LONG TOM)
B.NOV.24,1909 MC KENZIE,TENN.
```
1930 BOS A  H            1   .000
1931 BOS A  O           64   .198
1933 BOS A  O            6   .083
1935 STL N  O            7   .500
1936 BRO N  O           22   .235
1937 BRO N  P-O    1  118   .237
1938 BRO N  O           12   .300
         BLTR      1  230   0- 0
                          .237
```

WINSTON, HENRY RUDOLPH (HANK)
B.JUNE 15,1904 YOUNGVILLE,N.C.
D.FEB.4,1974 JACKSONVILLE,FLA.
```
1933 PHI A  P            1   0- 0
1936 BRO N  P           14   1- 3
         BLTR           15   1- 3
```

WINTER, GEORGE LOVINGTON (SASSAFRAS)
B.APR.27,1878 NEW PROVIDENCE,PA
D.MAY 26,1951 RAMSEY,N.J.
```
1901 BOS A  P           28  17-10
1902 BOS A  P           20  11- 9
1903 BOS A  P           23  10- 8
1904 BOS A  P           20   8- 4
1905 BOS A  P           34  14-16
1906 BOS A  P           29   6-18
1907 BOS A  P           35  12-15
1908 BOS A  P           22   3-14
         DET A  P        7   2- 5
         TR            218  83-99
```

WINTERS, CLARENCE JOHN
B.SEPT.7,1898 DETROIT,MICH.
D.JUNE 29,1945 DETROIT,MICH.
```
1924 BOS A  P            4   0- 1
```

WINTERS, JESSE FRANKLIN (JESSE)
(BUCK) OR (T-BONE)
B.DEC.22,1893 STEPHENVILLE,TEX.
```
1919 NY  N  P           16   1- 2
1920 NY  N  P           21   0- 0
1921 PHI N  P           18   5-10
1922 PHI N  P           34   6- 6
1923 PHI N  P           21   1- 6
         BRTR          110  13-24
```

WIRTH, ALAN LEE
B.DEC.8,1956 MESA,ARIZ.
```
1978 OAK A  P           16   5- 6
         BRTR
```

WIRTS, ELWOOD VERNON (KETTLE)
B.OCT.31,1897 CONSUMNES,CAL.
D.JULY 22,1968 SACRAMENTO,CAL.
```
1921 CHI N  C            7   .182
1922 CHI N  C           31   .172
1923 CHI N  C            5   .200
1924 CHI N  C            5   .083
         BRTR           48   .165
```

WISE, ARCHIBALD EDWIN
B.JULY 31,1912 WAXAHACHIE,TEX.
D.FEB.2,1978 DALLAS,TEX.
```
1932 CHI A  P            3   0- 0
         BRTR
```

WISE, HUGH EDWARD
B.MAR.9,1906 CAMPBELLSVILLE,KY.
```
1930 DET A  C            2   .333
         BBTR
```

WISE, KENDALL COLE (CASEY)
B.SEPT.8,1932 LAFAYETTE,IND.
```
1957 CHI N  2-S         43   .179
1958 MIL N  2-S-3       31   .197
1959 MIL N  2-S         22   .171
1960 DET A  2-S-3       30   .147
         BBTR          126   .175
```

WISE, NICHOLAS JOSEPH
B.JUNE 15,1866 BOSTON,MASS.
D.JAN.15,1923 BOSTON,MASS.
```
1888 BOS N  C            1   .000
         BRTR
```

WISE, RICHARD CHARLES (RICK)
B.SEP.13,1945 JACKSON,MICH.
```
1964 PHI N  P           25   5- 3
1966 PHI N  P     22  23   5- 6
1967 PHI N  P           36  11-11
1968 PHI N  P           30   9-15
1969 PHI N  P           33  15-13
1970 PHI N  P     35  37  13-14
1971 PHI N  P     38  39  17-14
1972 STL N  P           35  16-16
1973 STL N  P           35  16-12
1974 BOS A  /P           9   3- 4
1975 BOS A  P           35  19-12
1976 BOS A  P           34  14-11
1977 BOS A  P           26  11- 5
1978 CLE A  P           33   9-19
         BRTR    426 430 163-155
```

WISE, ROY OGDEN
B.NOV.18,1924 SPRINGFIELD,ILL.
```
1944 PIT N  P            2   0- 0
         BBTR
```

WISE, SAMUEL WASHINGTON (MODOC)
B.AUG.18,1857 AKRON,OHIO
D.JAN.22,1910 AKRON,OHIO
```
1881 DET N  3            1   .500
1882 BOS N  S-3         77   .225
1883 BOS N  S           95   .270
1884 BOS N  2-S        109   .220
1885 BOS N  2-S-O      107   .283
1886 BOS N  1-2-S       96   .289
1887 BOS N  S-O        104   .386
1888 BOS N  S          104   .239
1889 WAS N  2-S        120   .250
1890 BUF P  2          119   .295
1891 BAL AA 2          103   .250
1893 BAL AA 2-3        121   .317
         TR           1162   .285
```

WISE, WILLIAM E.
B.MAR.15,1861 WASHINGTON,D.C.
D.MAY 5,1940 WASHINGTON,D.C.
```
1882 BAL AA P-O    3   5   1- 1
                          .156
1884 WAS U  P-O   44  78  23-20
                          .233
1886 WAS N  P            1   0- 1
                  48  84  24-22
                          .224
```

WISNER, JOHN HENRY
B.NOV.5,1899 GRAND RAPIDS,MICH.
```
1919 PIT N  P            4   1- 0
1920 PIT N  P           17   1- 3
1925 NY  N  P           24   0- 0
1926 NY  N  P            5   2- 2
         BRTR           50   4- 5
```

WISNER, PHILIP N.
B.WASHINGTON,D.C.
```
1895 WAS N  S            1   .000
         TR
```

WISSLER, LEWIS
[PLAYED UNDER NAME OF
LEWIS WHISTLER]

WISSMAN, DAVID ALVIN (DAVE)
B.FEB.17,1941 GREENFIELD,MASS.
```
1964 PIT N  O           16   .148
         BLTR
```

WISTERT, FRANCIS MICHAEL (WHITEY)
B.FEB.20,1912 CHICAGO,ILL.
```
1934 CIN N  P      2   3   0- 1
         BRTR
```

WISTERZIL, GEORGE J. (TEX)
B.MAR.7,1891 DETROIT,MICH.
D.JUNE 27,1964 SAN ANTONIO,TEX.
```
1914 BRO F  3          149   .253
1915 BRO F  3           36   .311
         CHI F  3        7   .250
         STL F  3       50   .240
         TR            242   .258
```

WITEK, NICHOLAS JOSEPH (MICKEY)
B.DEC.19,1915 LUZERNE,PA.
```
1940 NY  N  2-S        119   .256
1941 NY  N  2           26   .362
1942 NY  N  2          148   .260
1943 NY  N  2          153   .314
1946 NY  N  2-3         82   .264
1947 NY  N  2           51   .219
1949 NY  A  H            1  1.000
         BRTR          580   .277
```

WITHERUP, FOSTER LEROY (ROY)
B.JULY 26,1886 N.WASHINGTON,PA.
D.DEC.23,1941 NEW BETHLEHEM,PA.
```
1906 BOS N  P            8   0- 3
1908 WAS A  P            6   2- 4
1909 WAS A  P           12   2- 6
                        26   4-13
```

```
YR  CL LEA POS    GP   G   REC
```

WITHROW, FRANK BLAINE (KID)
B.JUNE 14,1891 GREENWOOD,MO.
D.SEPT.5,1966 OMAHA,NEB.
```
1920 PHI N C           48  .182
1922 PHI N C           10  .333
     BRTR              58  .208
```

WITHROW, RAYMOND WALLACE (CORKY)
B.NOV.28,1937 HIGH COAL,W.VA.
```
1963 STL N O            6  .000
     BRTR
```

WITT, GEORGE ADRIAN (RED)
B.NOV.9,1933 LONG BEACH,CAL.
```
1957 PIT N P            1   0- 1
1958 PIT N P           18   9- 2
1959 PIT N P           15   0- 7
1960 PIT N P           10   1- 2
1961 PIT N P            9   0- 1
1962 LA  A P            5   1- 1
     HOU N P            8   0- 2
     BRTR              66  11-16
```

WITT, LAWTON WALTER (WHITEY)
[REAL NAME
LADISLAW WALDEMAR WITTKOWSKI]
B.SEPT.28,1895 ORANGE,MASS.
```
1916 PHI A S          143  .245
1917 PHI A S          128  .252
1919 PHI A 2-O        122  .267
1920 PHI A O           65  .321
1921 PHI A O          154  .315
1922 NY  A O          140  .297
1923 NY  A O          146  .314
1924 NY  A O          147  .297
1925 NY  A O           31  .200
1926 BRO N O           63  .259
     BLTR            1139  .287
```

WITTE, JEROME CHARLES (JERRY)
B.JULY 30,1915 ST.LOUIS,MO.
```
1946 STL A 1           18  .192
1947 STL A 1           34  .141
     BRTR              52  .159
```

WITTIG, JOHN CARL
(JOHNNIE) OR (HANS)
B.JUNE 16,1914 BALTIMORE,MD.
```
1938 NY  N P           13   2- 3
1939 NY  N P            5   0- 2
1941 NY  N P           25   3- 5
1943 NY  N P           40   5-15
1949 BOS A P            1   0- 0
     BRTR              84  10-25
```

WITTKOWSKI, LADISLAW WALDEMAR
[PLAYED UNDER NAME OF
LAWTON WALTER WITT]

WOCKENFUSS, JOHNNY BILTON (JOHN)
B.FEB.27,1949 WELCH,W.VA.
```
1974 DET A C           13  .138
1975 DET A C           35  .229
1976 DET A C           60  .222
1977 DET A /O          53  .274
1978 DET A C/O         71  .283
     BRTR             232  .251
```

WOEHR, ANDREW EMIL
B.FEB.4,1896 FORT WAYNE,IND.
```
1923 PHI N 3           13  3341
1924 PHI N 2-3         50  .217
     BRTR              63  .244
```

WOERLIN
B.ST.LOUIS,MO.
```
1895 WAS N S            1  .333
```

WOHLFORD, JAMES EUGENE (JIM)
B.FEB.28,1951 VISALIA,CAL.
```
1972 KC  A /2          15  .240
1973 KC  A D-O         45  .266
1974 KC  A *O         143  .271
1975 KC  A *O         116  .255
1976 KC  A O/2        107  .249
1977 MIL A *O/2       129  .248
1978 MIL A  O          46  .297
     BRTR             601  .260
```

WOJCIK, JOHN JOSEPH
B.APR.6,1942 OLEAN,N.Y.
```
1962 KC  A O           16  .302
1963 KC  A O           19  .186
1964 KC  A O            6  .136
     BLTR              41  .218
```

WOJEY, PETER PAUL (PETE)
B.DEC.1,1919 STOWE,PA.
```
1954 BRO N P           14   1- 1
1956 DET A P            2   0- 0
1957 DET A P            2   0- 0
     BRTR              18   1- 1
```

WOLF, ERNEST A.
B.FEB.2,1889 NEWARK,N.J.
D.MAY 23,1944 ATLANTIC
HIGHLANDS,N.J.
```
1912 CLE A P            1   0- 0
     BRTR
```

WOLF, RAYMOND BERNARD (GRANDPA)
B.JULY 15,1904 CHICAGO,ILL.
```
1927 CIN N 1            1  .000
     BRTR
```

WOLF, WALTER BECK (WALLY)
B.JAN.5,1942 SOUTH GATE,CAL.
```
1969 CAL A /P           2   0- 0
1970 CAL A /P           4   0- 0
     BRTR               6   0- 0
```

WOLF, WALTER FRANCIS (LEFTY)
B.JUNE 10,1900 HARTFORD,CONN.
D.SEPT.25,1971 NEW ORLEANS,LA.
```
1921 PHI A P            9   0- 0
     BRTL
```

WOLF, WILLIAM VAN WINKLE (CHICKEN)
B.MAY 12,1862 LOUISVILLE,KY.
D.MAY 16,1903 LOUISVILLE,KY.
```
1882 LOU AA P-1-    1   78   0- 0
           S-3-O             .294
1883 LOU AA C-2-S-O    88  .250
1884 LOU AA C-O       112  .303
1885 LOU AA O         113  .288
1886 LOU AA O         129  .274
1887 LOU AA O         137  .324
1888 LOU AA S-O       127  .298
1889 LOU AA M-O       130  .291
1890 LOU AA M-O       134  .366
1891 LOU AA M-O       136  .250
1892 STL N M-O          4  .220
        BR       1 1188   0- 0
                          .296
```

WOLFE, CHARLES HUNT (CHUCK)
B.FEB.15,1897 WOLFSBURG,PA.
D.NOV.27,1957 SCHELLSBURG,PA.
```
1923 PHI A P            3   0- 0
     BLTR
```

WOLFE, EDWARD ANTHONY
B.JAN.2,1929 LOS ANGELES,CAL.
```
1952 PIT N P            3   0- 0
     BRTR
```

WOLFE, HARRY
B.JULY 7,1893 CLEVELAND,OHIO
```
1917 CHI N S            5  .333
     PIT N 2            2  .000
     BRTR               7  .200
```

WOLFE, LAURENCE MARCY (LARRY)
B.MAR.2,1953 MELBOURNE,FLA.
```
1977 MIN A /3           8  .240
1978 MIN A  3/S        88  .234
     BRTR              96  .235
```

WOLFE, ROY CHAMBERLAIN (POLLY)
B.SEPT.1,1888 KNOXVILLE,ILL.
D.NOV.21,1938 MORRIS,ILL.
```
1912 CHI A O            1  .000
1914 CHI A O            8  .214
     BLTR               9  .207
```

WOLFE, WILLIAM
B.JERSEY CITY,N.J.
```
1902 PHI N P            1   0- 1
```

WOLFE, WILLIAM O.
B.JAN.7,1876 INDEPENDENCE,PA.
D.FEB.27,1953 GIBSONTOWN,PA.
```
1903 NY  A P           20   6- 9
1904 NY  A P            7   0- 3
     WAS A P           18   6- 9
1905 WAS A P           27   9-14
1906 WAS A P            4   0- 3
     BRTR              76  21-38
```

WOLFF, ROGER FRANCIS
B.APR.10,1911 EVANSVILLE,ILL.
```
1941 PHI A P            2   0- 2
1942 PHI A P           32  12-15
1943 PHI A P           41  10-15
1944 WAS A P           33   4-15
1945 WAS A P           33  20-10
1946 WAS A P           21   5- 8
1947 CHI A P            7   0- 0
     PIT N P           13   1- 4
     BRTR             182  52-69
```

WOLFGANG, MELDON JOHN (MELLIE)
B.MAR.20,1890 ALBANY,N.Y.
D.JUNE 30,1947 ALBANY,N.Y.
```
1914 CHI A P           24   9- 5
1915 CHI A P           17   2- 2
1916 CHI A P           28   4- 6
1917 CHI A P            5   0- 0
1918 CHI A P            5   0- 1
     BRTR              79  15-14
```

WOLTER, HARRY MEIGS
B.JULY 11,1884 MONTEREY,CAL.
D.JULY 7,1970 PALO ALTO,CAL.
```
1907 CIN N O            4  .133
     PIT N P            1   0- 0
     STL N P       3   12   0- 0
1909 BOS A P-1    10   54   4- 3
                           .244
1910 NY  A O          135  .267
1911 NY  A O          122  .304
1912 NY  A O           11  .393
1913 NY  A O          127  .256
1917 CHI N O          117  .249
     BLTL        14  583   4- 3
                           .270
```

WOLTERS, REINDERS ALBERTIS (RINIE)
B.DEC.18,1842 U.S.A.
D.JAN.3,1917
```
1871 MUT NA P          32  15-16
1872 CLE NA P-O    8   15   2- 6
                           .221
1873 RES NA P     41   48  17-23
                            -
```

WOLVERTON, HARRY STERLING
(FIGHTING HARRY)
B.DEC.6,1873 MT.VERNON,OHIO
D.FEB.4,1937 OAKLAND,CAL.
```
1898 CHI N 3           13  .327
1899 CHI N 3           99  .295
1900 CHI N 3            3  .182
     PHI N 3           98  .280
1901 PHI N 3           92  .308
1902 WAS A 3           59  .297
     PHI N 3           34  .284
1903 PHI N 3          123  .308
1904 PHI N 3          102  .266
1905 BOS N 3          122  .225
1912 NY  A M-O         33  .300
     TR              778  .279
```

WOMACK, HORACE GUY (DOOLEY)
B.AUG.25,1939 COLUMBIA,S.C.
```
1966 NY  A P           42   7- 3
1967 NY  A P           65   5- 6
1968 NY  A P           45   3- 7
1969 HOU N P           30   2- 1
     SEA A /P           9   2- 1
1970 OAK A /P           2   0- 0
     BLTR             193  19-18
```

WOMACK, SIDNEY KIRK (TEX)
B.OCT.2,1896 GREENSBURG,LA.
D.AUG.6,1958 JACKSON,MISS.
```
1926 BOS N C            1  .000
     BRTR
```

WOOD, CHARLES ASHER (SPADES)
B.JAN.13,1909 SPARTANBURG,S.C.
```
1930 PIT N P            9   4- 3
1931 PIT N P           15   2- 6
     BLTL              24   6- 9
```

WOOD, CHARLES SPENCER (DOC)
B.FEB.28,1900 BATESVILLE,MISS.
D.NOV.3,1974 NEW ORLEANS,LA.
```
1923 PHI A S            3  .333
     BRTR
```

WOOD, FRED S.
B.1863 HAMILTON,ONT.,CANADA
D.AUG.23,1933 NEW YORK,N.Y.
```
1884 DET N P-C-    1   28   0- 1
           S-O              .221
1885 BUF N C            1      .250
                   1   29   0- 1
                            .222
```

WOOD, GEORGE A. (DANDY)
B.NOV.9,1858 BOSTON,MASS.
D.APR.4,1924 HARRISBURG,PA.
```
1880 WOR N 1-O         79  .243
1881 DET N O           80  .296
1882 DET N O           81  .263
1883 DET N P-O     1   96   0- 0
                           .295
1884 DET N 3-O        112  .251
1885 DET N P-S-    1   82   0- 0
           3-O             .295
1886 PHI N O          106  .273
1887 PHI N O          113  .342
1888 PHI N O          105  .230
1889 PHI N O           97  .251
     BAL AA O           3  .200
1890 PHI N O          132  .304
1891 ATH AA M-O       131  .302
1892 BAL N O           20  .183
     CIN N O           30  .210
     BLTR         2 1267   0- 0
                           .278
```

WOOD, HARRY
B.BALTIMORE,MD.
```
1903 CIN N O            2  .000
     BLTR
```

YR	CL LEA POS	GP	G	REC

WOOD, JACOB (JAKE)
B.JUNE 22,1937 ELIZABETH,N.J.

1961	DET A 2		162	.258
1962	DET A 2		111	.226
1963	DET A 2-3		85	.271
1964	DET A 1-2-3-0		64	.232
1965	DET A 2/1-S-3		58	.288
1966	DET A 2/3-1		98	.252
1967	DET A /1-2		14	.050
	CIN N /O		16	.118
	BRTR		608	.250

WOOD, JAMES BURR
B.DEC.1,1844 BROOKLYN,N.Y.
D.NOV.30,1886

1871	CHI NA 2		28	-
1872	TRO NA M-2		25	.322
	PHI NA 2		7	.176
1873	PHI NA 2		41	-
1874	BAL NA 2		1	.000
			102	-

NON-PLAYING MANAGER CHI[NA] 1874-75

WOOD, JOHN B.

1896	STL N P		1	0- 0

WOOD, JOSEPH (SMOKEY JOE)
B.OCT.25,1889 KANSAS CITY,MO.

1908	BOS A P		6	1- 1
1909	BOS A P		24	11- 7
1910	BOS A P		35	12-13
1911	BOS A P		44	23-17
1912	BOS A P		43	34- 5
1913	BOS A P	22	23	11- 5
1914	BOS A P	18	20	9- 3
1915	BOS A P	25	29	14- 5
1917	CLE A P	5	10	0- 1
1918	CLE A 2-0		119	.296
1919	CLE A P-O	1	72	0- 0
				.255
1920	CLE A P-O	1	61	0- 0
				.270
1921	CLE A O		66	.366
1922	CLE A O		142	.297
	BRTR	224	694	115-57
				.284

WOOD, JOSEPH FRANK
B.MAY 20,1916 SHOHOLA,PA.

1944	BOS A P		3	0- 1
	BRTR			

WOOD, JOSEPH PERRY
B.OCT.3,1919 HOUSTON,TEX.

1943	DET A 2-3		60	.323
	BRTR			

WOOD, KENNETH LANIER (KEN)
B.JULY 1,1924 LINCOLNTON,N.C.

1948	STL A O		10	.083
1949	STL A O		7	.000
1950	STL A O		128	.225
1951	STL A O		109	.237
1952	BOS A O		15	.100
	WAS A O		61	.238
1953	WAS A O		12	.212
	BRTR		342	.224

WOOD, PETER BURKE
B.FEB.1,1857 HAMILTON,ONT.,CAN.
D.MAR.15,1923 CHICAGO,ILL.

1885	BUF N P-1	23	28	8-15
	O			.212
	O		3	1- 1
1889	PHI N P		31	9-16
	TR	26		.205

WOOD, ROBERT LYNN
B.JULY 28,1865 THORN HILL,OHIO
D.MAY 22,1943 CHURCHILL,OHIO

1898	CIN N C		30	.280
1899	CIN N C		58	.317
1900	CIN N C-3		34	.264
1901	CLE A C		96	.289
1902	CLE A C-1-2-3-0		81	.286
1904	DET A C		49	.244
1905	DET A C		8	.125
	BRTR		356	2280

WOOD, ROY WINTON (ROY) OR (WOODY)
B.AUG.29,1892 MONTICELLO,ARK.
D.APR.6,1974 FAYETTEVILLE,ARK.

1913	PIT N O		14	.285
1914	CLE A 1-O		72	.236
1915	CLE A 1		33	.193
	BRTR		119	.231

WOOD, WILBUR FORRESTER
B.OCT.22,1941 CAMBRIDGE,MASS.

1961	BOS A P		6	0- 0
1962	BOS A P		1	0- 0
1963	BOS A P		25	0- 5
1964	BOS A P		4	0- 0
	PIT N P		3	0- 2
1965	PIT N P		34	1- 1
1967	CHI A P		51	4- 2
1968	CHI A P		88	13-12
1969	CHI A P		76	10-11
1970	CHI A P		77	9-13
1971	CHI A P		44	22-13
1972	CHI A P		49	24-17
1973	CHI A P		49	24-20
1974	CHI A P		42	20-19
1975	CHI A P		43	16-20
1976	CHI A /P		7	4- 3
1977	CHI A P		24	7- 8
1978	CHI A P		28	10-10
	BRTL		651	164-156

WOODALL, CHARLES LAWRENCE (LARRY)
B.JULY 26,1894 STAUNTON,VA.
D.MAY 6,1963 BOSTON,MASS.

1920	DET A C		18	.245
1921	DET A C		46	.363
1922	DET A C		50	.344
1923	DET A C		71	.277
1924	DET A C		67	.309
1925	DET A C		75	.205
1926	DET A C		67	.233
1927	DET A C		88	.280
1928	DET A C		65	.210
1929	DET A H		1	.000
	BRTR		548	.268

WOODARD, DARRELL LEE
B.DEC.10,1956 WILMA,ARK.

1978	OAK A 2/3		33	.000
	BRTR			

WOODBURN, EUGENE STEWART
B.AUG.20,1886 BELLAIRE,OHIO
D.JAN.18,1961 SANDUSKY,OHIO

1911	STL N P		11	1- 5
1912	STL N P		20	1- 4
	BRTR		31	2- 9

WOODCOCK, FRED WAYLAND
B.MAY 17,1868 WINCHENDON,MASS.
D.AUG.11,1943 ASHBURNHAM,MASS.

1892	PIT N P		7	1- 3
	BLTL			

WOODEND, GEORGE ANTHONY
B.DEC.9,1917 HARTFORD,CONN.

1944	BOS N P		3	0- 0
	BRTR			

WOODESHICK, HAROLD JOSEPH (HAL)
B.AUG.24,1932 WILKES-BARRE,PA.

1956	DET A P		2	0- 2
1958	CLE A P		14	6- 6
1959	WAS A P	31	32	2- 4
1960	WAS A P		41	4- 5
1961	WAS A P		7	3- 2
	DET A P		12	1- 1
1962	HOU N P		31	5-16
1963	HOU N P		55	11- 9
1964	HOU N P		61	2- 9
1965	HOU N P		27	3- 4
	STL N P		51	3- 2
1966	STL N P		59	2- 1
1967	STL N P		36	2- 1
	BRTL	427	428	44-62

WOODHEAD, JAMES (RED)
B.JULY 1851 CHELSEA,MASS.
D.SEPT.7,1881 BOSTON,MASS.

1873	MAR NA S		1	.000
1879	SYR N 3		34	.169
			35	.168

WOODLING, EUGENE RICHARD (GENE)
B.AUG.16,1922 AKRON,OHIO

1943	CLE A O		8	.320
1946	CLE A O		61	.188
1947	PIT N O		22	.266
1949	NY A O		112	.270
1950	NY A O		122	.283
1951	NY A O		120	.281
1952	NY A O		122	.309
1953	NY A O		125	.306
1954	NY A O		97	.250
1955	BAL A O		47	.221
	CLE A O		79	.278
1956	CLE A O		100	.262
1957	CLE A O		133	.321
1958	BAL A O		133	.276
1959	BAL A O		140	.300
1960	BAL A O		140	.283
1961	WAS A O		110	.313
1962	WAS A O		44	.280
	NY N O		81	.274
	BLTR		1796	.284

WOODMAN, DANIEL COURTENAY (COCOA)
B.JULY 8,1893 DANVERS,MASS.
D.DEC.14,1962 DANVERS,MASS.

1914	BUF F P		13	0- 0
1915	BUF F P		6	0- 0
	BRTR		19	0- 0

WOODRUFF, ORVILLE FRANCIS (SAM)
B.DEC.27,1876 CHILO,OHIO
D.JULY 22,1937 CINCINNATI,OHIO

1899	NY N O		20	.246
1901	CLE A O		1	.250
1904	CIN N 2-3		87	.190
1910	CIN N 3		21	.148
	BRTR		129	.192

WOODS, ALVIS (AL)
B.AUG.8,1953 OAKLAND,CAL.

1977	TOR A *O		122	.284
1978	TOR A O		62	.241
	BLTL		184	.270

WOODS, CLARENCE COFIELD
B.JUNE 11,1892 WOODS RIDGE,
OHIO COUNTY,IND.
D.JULY 2,1969 RISING SUN,IND.

1914	IND F P		2	0- 0
	BRTR			

WOODS, GARY LEE
B.JULY 20,1954 SANTA BARBARA,CAL

1976	OAK A /O		6	.125
1977	TOR A O		60	.216
1978	TOR A /O		8	.158
	BRTR		74	.209

WOODS, GEORGE ROWLAND (PINKY)
B.MAY 22,1915 WATERBURY,CONN.

1943	BOS A P		23	5- 6
1944	BOS A P		38	4- 8
1945	BOS A P		24	4- 7
	BRTR		85	13-21

WOODS, JAMES JEROME (JIM) OR (WOODY)
B.SEPT.17,1939 CHICAGO,ILL.

1957	CHI N H		2	.000
1960	PHI N 3		11	.176
1961	PHI N 3		23	.229
	BRTR		36	.207

WOODS, JOHN FULTON (ABE)
B.JAN.18,1898 PRINCETON,W.VA.
D.OCT.4,1946 NORFOLK,VA.

1924	BOS A P		1	0- 0
	BRTR			

WOODS, RONALD LAWRENCE (RON)
B.FEB.1,1943 HAMILTON,OHIO

1969	DET A /O		17	.267
	NY A O		72	.175
1970	NY A O		95	.227
1971	NY A /O		25	.250
	MON N O		51	.297
1972	MON N O		97	.258
1973	MON N *O		135	.230
1974	MON N O		90	.205
	BRTR		582	.233

WOODS, WALTER SYDNEY
B.APR.28,1875 RYE,N.H.
D.OCT.30,1951 PORTSMOUTH,N.H.

1898	CHI N P		22	41	9-13
1899	LOU N P		22	40	8-13
1900	PIT N P		1	0- 0
	TR		45	82	17-26

WOODSON, RICHARD LEE (DICK)
B.MAR.30,1945 OELWEIN,IOWA

1969	MIN A P		44	7- 5
1970	MIN A P		21	1- 2
1972	MIN A P		36	14-14
1973	MIN A P		23	10- 8
1974	MIN A /P		5	1- 1
	NY A /P		8	1- 2
	BRTR		137	34-32

WOODWARD, FRANK RUSSELL
B.MAY 17,1894 NEW HAVEN,CONN.
D.JUNE 11,1961 NEW HAVEN,CONN.

1918	PHI N P		2	0- 0
1919	PHI N P		17	6- 9
	STL N P		17	3- 5
1921	WAS A P		3	0- 0
1922	WAS A P		1	0- 0
1923	CHI A P		2	0- 1
	BRTR		42	9-15

YR CL LEA POS GP G REC

WOODWARD, WILLIAM FREDERICK (WOODY)
B.SEP.23,1942 MIAMI,FLA.
1963 MIL N S 10 .000
1964 MIL N 1-2-S-3 77 .209
1965 MIL N *S/2 112 .208
1966 ATL N 2-S 144 .264
1967 ATL N *2-S 136 .226
1968 ATL N /S-3-2 12 .167
CIN N S/2-1 56 .244
1969 CIN N S/2 97 .261
1970 CIN N S-3-2/1 100 .223
1971 CIN N S-3/2 136 .242
BRTR 880 .236

WOOLDRIDGE, FLOYD LEWIS
B.AUG.25,1928 JERICO SPRINGS,MO
1955 STL N P 18 2- 4
BRTR

WOOTEN, EARL HAZWELL (JUNIOR)
B.JAN.16,1924 PELZER,S.C.
1947 WAS A O 6 .083
1948 WAS A P-1- 1 88 0- 0
O .256
BRTL 1 94 0- 0
.241

WORDEN, FRED
1914 PHI A P 1 0- 0
TR

WORDSWORTH, FAVEL PERRY
B.JAN.1851 NEW YORK,N.Y.
D.AUG.2,1888
1873 RES NA S 10 -

WORKMAN, CHARLES THOMAS (CHUCK)
B.JAN.6,1915 LEETON,MO.
D.JAN.3,1953 KANSAS CITY,MO.
1938 CLE A O 2 .400
1941 CLE A H 9 .000
1943 BOS N 1-3-O 153 .249
1944 BOS N 3-O 140 .208
1945 BOS N 3-O 139 .274
1946 BOS N O 25 .167
PIT N 3-O 58 .221
BLTR 526 .242

WORKMAN, HARRY HALL (HOGE)
B.SEPT.25,1899 HUNTINGTON,W.VA.
D.MAY 20,1972 FT.MYERS,FLA.
1924 BOS A P 11 0- 0
BRTR

WORKMAN, HENRY KILGARIFF (HANK)
B.FEB.5,1926 LOS ANGELES,CAL.
1950 NY A 1 2 .200
BLTR

WORKS, RALPH TALMADGE (JUDGE)
B.MAR.16,1888 PAYSON,ILL.
D.AUG.8,1941 PASADENA,CAL.
1909 DET A P 16 3- 1
1910 DET A P 18 3- 6
1911 DET A P 31 11- 5
1912 DET A P 27 5-10
CIN N P 3 1- 1
1913 CIN N P 4 0- 1
BLTR 99 23-24

WORTH, HERBERT
1872 ATL NA O 1 .167

WORTHAM, RICHARD COOPER (RICH)
B.OCT.22,1953 ODESSA,TEX.
1978 CHI A /P 8 3- 2
BRTL

WORTHINGTON, ALLAN FULTON
(AL) OR (RED)
B.FEB.5,1929 BIRMINGHAM,ALA.
1953 NY N P 20 4- 8
1954 NY N P 10 0- 2
1956 NY N P 28 7-14
1957 NY N P 55 8-11
1958 SF N P 54 11- 7
1959 SF N P 42 2- 3
1960 BOS A P 6 0- 1
CHI A P 4 1- 1
1963 CIN N P 50 4- 4
1964 CIN N P 6 1- 0
MIN A P 41 5- 6
1965 MIN A P 62 10- 7
1966 MIN A P 65 6- 3
1967 MIN A P 59 8- 9
1968 MIN A P 54 4- 5
1969 MIN A P 46 4- 1
BRTR 602 75-82

WORTHINGTON, ROBERT LEE (RED)
B.APR.24,1906 ALHAMBRA,CAL.
D.DEC.8,1963 SEPULVEDA,CAL.
1931 BOS N O 128 .291
1932 BOS N O 105 .303
1933 BOS N O 17 .156
1934 BOS N O 41 .246
STL N H 1 .000
BRTR 292 .287

YR CL LEA POS GP G REC

WORTMAN, WILLIAM LEWIS (CHUCK)
B.JAN.5,1892 BALTIMORE,MD.
D.AUG.19,1977 LAS VEGAS,NEV.
1916 CHI N S 69 .201
1917 CHI N S 75 .174
1918 CHI N 2-S 17 .118
BRTR 161 .163

WOULFE, JAMES JOSEPH
B.NOV.25,1859 NEW ORLEANS,LA.
D.DEC.20,1924 NEW ORLEANS,LA.
1884 CIN AA 3-O 8 .118
PIT AA O 16 .127
TR 24 .124

WRIGHT, ALBERT EDGAR (A-1)
B.NOV.11,1912 SAN FRANCISCO,CAL
1933 BOS N 2 4 1.000
BRTR

WRIGHT, ALBERT OWEN (AB)
B.NOV.16,1905 TERLTON,OKLA.
1935 CLE A O 67 .238
1944 BOS N O 71 .256
BRTR 138 .248

WRIGHT, ALFRED L. H.
B.MAR.30,1842 CEDAR GROVE,N.J.
D.APR.20,1905
NON-PLAYING MANAGER ATH[N] 1876

WRIGHT, CLARENCE EUGENE
B.DEC.11,1878 CLEVELAND,OHIO
D.OCT.29,1930 BARBERTON,OHIO
1901 BRO N P 1 1- 0
1902 CLE A P-1 22 24 7- 9
.143
1903 CLE A P 15 2- 7
STL A P 8 2- 4
1904 STL A P 1 0- 1
BRTR 47 49 12-21
.165

WRIGHT, CLYDE
B.FEB.20,1941 JEFFERSON CITY,TENN.
1966 CAL A P 20 24 4- 7
1967 CAL A P 20 23 5- 5
1968 CAL A P 41 51 10- 6
1969 CAL A P 37 40 1- 8
1970 CAL A P 39 47 22-12
1971 CAL A P 37 40 16-17
1972 CAL A P 35 18-11
1973 CAL A P 37 11-19
1974 MIL A P 38 9-20
1975 TEX A P 25 4- 6
BRTL 329 360 100-111

WRIGHT, DAVID WILLIAM
B.AUG.27,1875 DENNISON,OHIO
D.JAN.18,1946 DENNISON,OHIO
1895 PIT N P 1 0- 0
1897 CHI N P 1 1- 0
BRTR 2 1- 0

WRIGHT, EDWARD YATMAN (CEYLON)
1916 CHI A S 8 .000
BLTR

WRIGHT, FOREST GLENN
(GLENN) OR (BUCKSHOT)
B.FEB.6,1901 ARCHIE,MO.
1924 PIT N S 153 .287
1925 PIT N S-3 153 .308
1926 PIT N S 119 .308
1927 PIT N S 143 .281
1928 PIT N S 108 .310
1929 BRO N S 24 .200
1930 BRO N S 135 .321
1931 BRO N S 77 .284
1932 BRO N S 127 .274
1933 BRO N 1-S-3 71 .255
1935 CHI A 2 9 .120
BRTR 1119 .294

WRIGHT, GEORGE
B.JAN.28,1847 YONKERS,N.Y.
D.AUG.21,1937 BOSTON,MASS.
1871 BOS NA 1-S 17 .387
1872 BOS NA S 48 .336
1873 BOS NA S 59 .378
1874 BOS NA S 60 .344
1875 BOS NA S 79 .337
1876 BOS N S 70 .292
1877 BOS N 2-S 61 .276
1878 BOS N S 59 .224
1879 PRO N M-S 84 .281
1880 BOS N S 1 .250
1881 BOS N S 7 .179
1882 PRO N S 45 .162
BRTR 590 .303

WRIGHT, HENDERSON EDWARD (ED)
B.MAY 15,1919 DYERSBURG,TENN.
1945 BOS N P 15 8- 3
1946 BOS N P 36 12- 9
1947 BOS N P 23 3- 3
1948 BOS N P 3 0- 0
1952 PHI A P 24 2- 1
BRTR 101 25-16

YR CL LEA POS GP G REC

WRIGHT, JAMES (JIGGS)
B.SEPT.19,1900 HYDE,ENGLAND
D.APR.10,1963 OAKLAND,CAL.
1927 STL A P 2 1- 0
1928 STL A P 2 0- 0
BRTR 4 1- 0

WRIGHT, JAMES CLIFTON (JIM)
B.DEC.21,1950 REED CITY,MICH.
1978 BOS A P 24 8- 4
BRTR

WRIGHT, JOSEPH
B.PITTSBURGH,PA.
1895 LOU N O 59 .289
1896 LOU N O 2 .143
PIT N O 15 .308
BL 76 .279

WRIGHT, KENNETH WARREN (KEN)
B.SEP.4,1946 PENSACOLA,FLA.
1970 KC A P 47 1- 2
1971 KC A P 21 3- 6
1972 KC A P 17 1- 2
1973 KC A P 25 6- 5
1974 NY A /P 3 0- 0
BRTR 113 11-15

WRIGHT, MELVIN JAMES (MEL)
B.MAY 11,1928 MANILA,ARK.
1954 STL N P 9 0- 0
1955 STL N P 29 2- 2
1960 CHI N P 9 0- 1
1961 CHI N P 11 0- 1
BRTR 58 2- 4

WRIGHT, PATRICK W.
B.JULY 5,1868 POTTSVILLE,PA.
1890 CHI N 2 1 .000
1893 BAL N 2 1 .500
2 .250

WRIGHT, ROBERT CASSIUS
B.DEC.13,1891 GREENSBURG,IND.
1915 CHI N P 2 0- 0
BRTR

WRIGHT, ROY EARL
B.SEPT.26,1933 BUCHTEL,OHIO
1956 NY N P 1 0- 1
BRTR

WRIGHT, SAMUEL
B.NOV.25,1848 NEW YORK,N.Y.
D.MAY 6,1928 BOSTON,MASS.
1875 NH NA S 33 -
1876 BOS N S 2 .125
1880 CIN N S 9 .058
1881 BOS N S 1 .250
45 -

WRIGHT, TAFT SHEDRON (TAFFY)
B.AUG.10,1911 TABOR CITY,N.C.
1938 WAS A O 100 .350
1939 WAS A O 129 .309
1940 CHI A O 147 .337
1941 CHI A O 136 .322
1942 CHI A O 85 .333
1946 CHI A O 115 .275
1947 CHI A O 124 .324
1948 CHI A O 134 .279
1949 PHI A O 59 .235
BLTR 1029 .311

WRIGHT, THOMAS EVERETTE (TOM)
B.SEPT.22,1923 SHELBY,N.C.
1948 BOS A H 3 .500
1949 BOS A H 5 .250
1950 BOS A O 54 .318
1951 BOS A O 28 .222
1952 STL A O 29 .242
CHI A O 60 .258
1953 CHI A O 77 .250
1954 WAS A O 76 .246
1955 WAS A H 7 .000
1956 WAS A H 2 .000
BLTR 341 .255

WRIGHT, WAYNE BROMLEY (RASTY)
B.NOV.5,1895 CEREDO,W.VA.
D.JUNE 12,1948 COLUMBUS,OHIO
1917 STL A P 16 0- 0
1918 STL A P 18 8- 2
1919 STL A P 24 0- 5
1922 STL A P 31 9- 7
1923 STL A P 20 7- 4
BRTR 109 24-18

WRIGHT, WILLIAM H.
1887 WAS N C 1 .667

```
YR  CL LEA POS     GP   G   REC

WRIGHT, WILLIAM HENRY (HARRY)
B.JAN.1C,1835 SHEFFIELD,ENGLAND
D.OCT.3,1895 ATLANTIC CITY,N.J.
1871 BOS NA M-S-O        33  .300
1872 BOS NA M-P-    2   48   2- 0
          O                  .261
1873 BOS NA M-P-    3   58   2- 1
          O                  .260
1874 BOS NA M-C-O       41   .310
1875 BOS NA M-O          1   .250
1876 BOS N  M-O          1   .000
1877 BOS N  M-O          1   .000
1878 BOS N  M-O          1   .000
       BRTR    5  184   4- 1
                             .278
NON-PLAYING MANAGER
BOS[N] 1879-81, PRO[N] 1882-83,
PHI[N] 1884-93

WRIGHT, WILLIAM JAMES (DICK)
B.MAY 5,1890 WORCESTER,N.Y.
D.JAN.24,1952 BETHLEHEM,PA.
1915 BRO F  C            4   .000
       TR

WRIGHT, WILLIAM S. (RASTY)
B.JAN.31,1863 BIRMINGHAM,MICH.
D.OCT.14,1922 DULUTH,MINN.
1890 SYR AA O           89   .285
     CLE N  O           13   .106
                       102   .265

WRIGHT, WILLIAM SIMMONS (LUCKY)
(WILLIAM THE RED) OR (DEACON)
B.FEB.21,1880 TONTOGANY,OHIO
D.JULY 6,1941 TONTOGANY,OHIO
1909 CLE A  P            5   0- 4
       BRTR

WRIGHTSTONE, RUSSELL GUY (RUSS)
B.MAR.18,1893 BOWMANSDALE,PA.
D.FEB.25,1969 HARRISBURG,PA.
1920 PHI N  3           76   .262
1921 PHI N  3-O        109   .296
1922 PHI N  1-S-3       99   .305
1923 PHI N  2-S-3      119   .273
1924 PHI N  2-S-3-O    118   .307
1925 PHI N  1-2-S-3-O   92   .346
1926 PHI N  1-2-3      112   .307
1927 PHI N  1          141   .306
1928 PHI N  O           33   .209
     NY  N  H           30   .160
       BLTR           929   .297

WRIGLEY, GEORGE WATSON (ZEKE)
B.JAN.18,1874 PHILADELPHIA,PA.
D.SEPT.28,1952 PHILADELPHIA,PA.
1896 WAS N  2            5   .100
1897 WAS N  S-3-O      102   .284
1898 WAS N  S          111   .245
1899 NY  N  3            4   .133
     BRO N  S           15   .229
                       237   .258

WUESTLING, GEORGE (YATS)
B.OCT.18,1903 ST.LOUIS,MO.
D.APR.26,1970 ST.LOUIS,MO.
1929 DET A  S           54   .200
1930 DET A  S            4   .000
     NY  A  S           25   .190
       BRTR            83   .189

WURM, FRANK JAMES
B.APR.27,1924 CAMBRIDGE,N.Y.
1944 BRO N  P            1   0- 0
       BBTL

WYATT, JOHN THOMAS
B.APR.9,1935 CHICAGO,ILL.
1961 KC  A  P            5   0- 0
1962 KC  A  P           59  10- 7
1963 KC  A  P           63   6- 4
1964 KC  A  P           81   9- 8
1965 KC  A  P           65   2- 6
1966 KC  A  P           19   0- 3
     BOS A  P           42   3- 4
1967 BOS A  P           60  10- 7
1968 BOS A /P            8   1- 2
     NY  A /P            7   0- 2
     DET A  P           22   1- 0
1969 OAK A /P            4   0- 1
       BRTR          435  42-44
```

```
YR  CL LEA POS     GP   G   REC

WYATT, JOHN WHITLOW (WHIT)
B.SEPT.27,1907 KENSINGTON,GA.
1929 DET A  P            4   0- 1
1930 DET A  P      21   22   4- 5
1931 DET A  P            4   0- 2
1932 DET A  P           43   9-13
1933 DET A  P           10   0- 1
     CHI A  P           26   3- 4
1934 CHI A  P           23   4-11
1935 CHI A  P           30   4- 3
1936 CHI A  P            3   0- 0
1937 CLE A  P           29   2- 3
1939 BRO N  P           16   8- 3
1940 BRO N  P           37  15-14
1941 BRO N  P      38   40  22-10
1942 BRO N  P           31  19- 7
1943 BRO N  P      26   27  14- 5
1944 BRO N  P       9   11   2- 6
1945 PHI N  P           10   0- 7
       BRTR    360  366 106-95

WYATT, LORAL JOHN (JOE)
B.APR.6,1900 PETERSBURG,IND.
D.DEC.5,1970 OBLONG,ILL.
1924 CLE A  O            4   .166
       BRTR

WYCKOFF, JOHN WELDON
B.FEB.19,1892 WILLIAMSPORT,PA.
D.MAY 8,1961 SHEBOYGAN FALLS,WIS.
1913 PHI A  P           17   3- 4
1914 PHI A  P           32  11- 8
1915 PHI A  P      43   45  10-22
1916 PHI A  P            8   0- 1
     BOS A  P            8   0- 0
1917 BOS A  P            1   0- 0
1918 BOS A  P            1   0- 0
       BRTR    110  112  24-35

WYLIE, JAMES RENWICK (REN)
B.DEC.14,1861 ELIZABETH,PA.
D.AUG.17,1951 WILKINSBURG,PA.
1882 PIT AA O            1   .000

WYMAN, FRANK C.
B.MAY 10,1862 HAVERHILL,MASS.
1884 KC  U  P-1-    3   30   0- 2
            3-O              .203
     CHI U  1            2   .375
                    3   32   0- 2
                             .214

WYNEGAR, HAROLD DELANO (BUTCH)
B.MAR.14,1956 YORK,PA.
1976 MIN A  *C         149   .260
1977 MIN A  *C/3       144   .261
1978 MIN A  *C/3       135   .229
       BBTR           428   .251

WYNN, EARLY (EARLY) OR (GUS)
B.JAN.6,1920 HARTFORD,ALA.
1939 WAS A  P            3   0- 2
1941 WAS A  P            5   3- 1
1942 WAS A  P           30  10-16
1943 WAS A  P      37   38  18-12
1944 WAS A  P      33   43   8-17
1946 WAS A  P      17   25   8- 5
1947 WAS A  P      33   54  17-15
1948 WAS A  P      33   73   8-19
1949 CLE A  P      26   35  11- 7
1950 CLE A  P      32   39  18- 8
1951 CLE A  P      37   41  20-13
1952 CLE A  P      42   44  23-12
1953 CLE A  P      36   37  17-12
1954 CLE A  P           40  23-11
1955 CLE A  P      32   34  17-11
1956 CLE A  P           38  20- 9
1957 CLE A  P           40  14-17
1958 CHI A  P           40  14-16
1959 CHI A  P           37  22-10
1960 CHI A  P           36  13-12
1961 CHI A  P           17   8- 2
1962 CHI A  P           27   7-15
1963 CLE A  P           20   1- 2
       BBTR    691  796 300-244
       BR 1941-44

WYNN, JAMES SHERMAN (JIM)
B.MAR.12,1942 HAMILTON,OHIO
1963 HOU N  S-3-O       70   .244
1964 HOU N  O           67   .224
1965 HOU N  *O         157   .275
1966 HOU N  *O         105   .256
1967 HOU N  *O         158   .249
1968 HOU N  *O         156   .269
1969 HOU N  *O         149   .269
1970 HOU N  *O         157   .282
1971 HOU N  *O         123   .203
1972 HOU N  *O         145   .273
1973 HOU N  *O         139   .220
1974 LA  N  *O         150   .271
1975 LA  N  *O         130   .248
1976 ATL N  *O         148   .207
1977 NY  A  D/O         30   .143
     MIL A  D-O         36   .197
       BRTR          1920   .250
```

```
YR  CL LEA POS.    GP   G   REC

WYNNE, BILLY VERNON
B.JULY 31,1943 WILLIAMSTON,N.C.
1967 NY  N /P            6   0- 0
1968 CHI A /P            1   0- 0
1969 CHI A  P           20   7- 7
1970 CHI A  P           12   1- 4
1971 CAL A /P            3   0- 0
       BLTR            42   8-11

WYNNE, WILLIAM ANDREW
B.MAR.27,1869 NEUSE,N.C.
D.AUG.7,1951 RALEIGH,N.C.
1894 WAS N  P            1   0- 1

WYROSTEK, JOHN BARNEY (JOHNNY)
B.JULY 12,1919 FAIRMONT CITY,ILL.
1942 PIT N  O            9   .114
1943 PIT N  1-2-3-O     51   .152
1946 PHI N  O          145   .281
1947 PHI N  O          128   .273
1948 CIN N  O          136   .273
1949 CIN N  O          134   .249
1950 CIN N  1-O        131   .285
1951 CIN N  O          142   .311
1952 CIN N  1-O         30   .236
     PHI N  O           98   .274
1953 PHI N  O          125   .271
1954 PHI N  1-O         92   .239
       BLTR          1221   .271

WYSE, HENRY WASHINGTON
(HANK) OR (HOOKS)
B.MAR.1,1918 LUNSFORD,ARK.
1942 CHI N  P            4   2- 1
1943 CHI N  P      38   40   9- 7
1944 CHI N  P           41  16-15
1945 CHI N  P           38  22-10
1946 CHI N  P           40  14-12
1947 CHI N  P           37   6- 9
1950 PHI N  P           41   9-14
1951 PHI N  P            9   1- 2
     WAS A  P            3   0- 0
       BRTR    251  253  79-70

WYSHNER, PETER
[PLAYED UNDER NAME OF PETER J. GRAY]

WYSONG, HARLAN (BIFF)
B.APR.13,1905 CLARKSVILLE,OHIO
D.AUG.8,1951 XENIA,OHIO
1930 CIN N  P            1   0- 1
1931 CIN N  P           12   0- 2
1932 CIN N  P            7   1- 0
       BLTL            20   1- 3

YAIK, HENRY
B.DETROIT,MICH.
1888 PIT N  O            2   .333

YALE, WILLIAM M. (AD)
B.APR.17,1870 BRISTOL,CONN.
D.APR.27,1948 BRIDGEPORT,CONN.
1905 BRO N  1            4   .076

YANCY, HUGH
B.OCT.16,1950 SARASOTA,FLA.
1972 CHI A /3            3   .111
1974 CHI A /H            1   .000
1976 CHI A /2            3   .100
       BRTR             7   .105

YANKOWSKI, GEORGE EDWARD
B.NOV.19,1922 CAMBRIDGE,MASS.
1942 PHI A  C            6   .154
1949 PHI A  C           12   .167
       BRTR            18   .161

YANTZ, GEORGE WEBB
B.JULY 27,1886 LOUISVILLE,KY.
D.FEB.26,1967 LOUISVILLE,KY.
1912 CHI N  C            1  1.000
       BRTR

YAPP, FREDERICK FRANCIS
[PLAYED UNDER NAME OF
FREDERICK FRANCIS MITCHELL]

YARNELL, WALDO WILLIAM (RUSTY)
B.OCT.22,1902 CHICAGO,ILL.
1926 PHI N  P            1   0- 0

YARRISON, BYRON WARDSWORTH (RUBE)
B.MAR.9,1896 MONTGOMERY,PA.
1922 PHI A  P           18   1- 2
1924 BRO N  P            3   0- 2
       BRTR            21   1- 4

YARYAN, CLARENCE EVERETT (YAM)
B.NOV.5,1892 KNOWLTON,IOWA
D.NOV.16,1964 BIRMINGHAM,ALA.
1921 CHI A  C           45   .304
1922 CHI A  C           36   .197
       BRTR            81   .260
```

YR	CL	LEA	POS	GP	G	REC

YASTRZEMSKI, CARL MICHAEL (CARL) OR (YAZ)
B.AUG.22,1939 SOUTHAMPTON,N.Y.

YR	CL	LEA	POS	GP	G	REC
1961	BOS	A	O		148	.266
1962	BOS	A	O		160	.296
1963	BOS	A	O		151	.321
1964	BOS	A	3-O		151	.289
1965	BOS	A	*O		133	.312
1966	BOS	A	*O		160	.278
1967	BOS	A	*O		161	.326
1968	BOS	A	*O/1		157	.301
1969	BOS	A	*O-1		162	.255
1970	BOS	A	1-O		161	.329
1971	BOS	A	*O		148	.254
1972	BOS	A	O-1		125	.264
1973	BOS	A	*1-3-O		152	.296
1974	BOS	A	*1-O		148	.301
1975	BOS	A	*1/O		149	.269
1976	BOS	A	1-O-O		155	.267
1977	BOS	A	*O/1		150	.296
1978	BOS	A	O-1-O		144	.277
		BLTR			2715	.289

YATES, ALBERT ARTHUR (AL)
B.MAY 26,1945 JERSEY CITY,N.J.

1971	MIL	A	O		24	.277
		BRTR				

YOE, EMIL OGDEN
B.JAN.28,1900 GREAT LAKES,ILL.
D.DEC.4,1968 LEESBURG,FLA.

1924	PIT	N	P	33	50	16- 3
1925	PIT	N	P	33	47	17- 9
1926	PIT	N	P	37	43	8- 7
1927	PIT	N	P	9	23	1- 3
1929	DET	A	P	29	46	7- 3
		BBTL		141	209	49-25

YEABSLEY, ROBERT WATKINS (BERT)
B.DEC.17,1893 PHILADELPHIA,PA.
D.FEB.8,1961 PHILADELPHIA,PA.

1919	PHI	N	H		2	.000
		TR				

YEAGER, GEORGE C. (ABE)
B.JUNE 4,1873 CINCINNATI,OHIO
D.OCT.16,1923

1896	BOS	N	1		2	.167
1897	BOS	N	C		26	.239
1898	BOS	N	C		57	.263
1899	BOS	N	C		2	.000
1901	CLE	A	C		39	.226
	PIT	N	C		24	.267
1902	NY	N	C-1-O		29	.194
	BAL	A	C		11	.184
		TR			190	.236

YEAGER, JOSEPH F. (LITTLE JOE)
B.AUG.28,1875 PHILADELPHIA,PA.
D.JULY 2,1937 DETROIT,MICH.

1898	BRO	N	P	33	36	13-20
1899	BRO	N	P	10	15	3- 2
1900	BKJ	N	P-3	2	3	1- 1
						.333
1901	DET	A	P	26	37	12-12
1902	DET	A	P-2-3	19	48	5-12
			S-3-O			.231
1903	DET	A	3		109	.259
1905	NY	A	S-3		115	.267
1906	NY	A	S		57	.301
1907	STL	A	2-3		123	.239
1908	STL	A	2		10	.150
		TR		90	553	34-47
						.254

YEAGER, STEPHEN WAYNE (STEVE)
B.NOV.24,1948 HUNTINGTON,W.VA.

1972	LA	N	C		35	.274
1973	LA	N	C		54	.254
1974	LA	N	C		94	.266
1975	LA	N	*C		135	.228
1976	LA	N	*C		117	.214
1977	LA	N	*C		125	.256
1978	LA	N	C		94	.193
		BRTR			654	.237

YEARGIN, JAMES ALMOND (AL)
B.OCT.16,1901 MAULDIN,S.C.
D.MAY 8,1937 GREENVILLE,S.C.

1922	BOS	N	P		1	0- 1
1924	BOS	N	P		32	1-11
		BRTR			33	1-12

YEATMAN, WILLIAM SUTER
B.1859 ALEXANDRIA,VA.
D.APR.20,1901 YORK,PA.

1872	NAT	NA	O		1	.000

YELLE, ARCHIE JOSEPH
B.JUNE 11,1892 SAGINAW,MICH.

1917	DET	A	C		25	.137
1918	DET	A	C		56	.174
1919	DET	A	C		6	.000
		BRTR			87	.166

YELLEN, LAWRENCE ALAN (LARRY)
B.JAN.4,1943 BROOKLYN,N.Y.

1963	HOU	N	P		1	0- 0
1964	HOU	N	P		13	0- 0
		BRTR			14	0- 0

YELLOWHORSE, MOSES J. (CHIEF)
B.JAN.28,1898 PAWNEE,OKLA.
D.APR.10,1964 PAWNEE,OKLA.

1921	PIT	N	P		10	5- 3
1922	PIT	N	P		28	3- 1
		BRTR			38	8- 4

YERKES, CHARLES CARROLL (CARROLL) OR (LEFTY)
B.JUNE 13,1903 MC SHERRYSTOWN,PA.
D.DEC.20,1950 OAKLAND,CAL.

1927	PHI	A	P		1	0- 0
1928	PHI	A	P		2	0- 1
1929	PHI	A	P		19	1- 0
1932	CHI	N	P		2	0- 0
1933	CHI	N	P		1	0- 0
		BRTL			25	1- 1

YERKES, STANLEY LEWIS (YANK)
B.NOV.28,1874 CHELTENHAM,PA.
D.JULY 28,1940 BOSTON,MASS.

1901	BAL	A	P		1	0- 1
	STL	N	P		4	3- 1
1902	STL	N	P		36	12-21
1903	STL	N	P		1	0- 1
					42	15-24

YERKES, STEPHEN DOUGLAS
B.MAY 15,1888 HATBORO,PA.
D.JAN.31,1971 LANSDALE,PA.

1909	BOS	A	S		5	.286
1911	BOS	A	S		142	.279
1912	BOS	A	2		131	.252
1913	BOS	A	2		137	.267
1914	BOS	A	2		92	.218
	PIT	F	S		39	.333
1915	PIT	F	2		121	.286
1916	CHI	N	2		44	.263
		BRTR			711	.267

YERRICK, WILLIAM JOHN
[PLAYED UNDER NAME OF
WILLIAM JOHN BANKS]

YEWCIC, THOMAS J. (TOM) OR (KIBBY)
B.MAY 9,1932 CONEMAUGH,PA.

1957	DET	A	C		1	.000
		BRTR				

YEWELL, EDWIN LEONARD
B.AUG.22,1862 WASHINGTON,D.C.
D.SEPT.15,1940 WASHINGTON,D.C.

1884	WAS	AA	2-3		35	.258
	WAS	U	3		1	.000
					36	.247

YINGLING, EARL HERSHEY (CHINK)
B.OCT.29,1888 CHILLICOTHE,OHIO
D.OCT.2,1962 COLUMBUS,OHIO

1911	CLE	A	P		6	2- 1
1912	BRO	N	P		25	6-11
1913	BRO	N	P	26	40	8- 8
1914	CIN	N	P	34	61	9-13
1918	WAS	A	P		8	1- 2
		BLTL		99	140	26-35

YINGLING, JOSEPH
B.1864 BALTIMORE,MD.

1886	WAS	N	P		1	0- 1
1894	PHI	N	S		1	.333
				1	2	0- 1
						.200

YNOCENCIO, JOSE [SOSA]
[PLAYED UNDER NAME OF
JOSE YNOCENCIO SOSA]

YOCHIM, LEONARD JOSEPH (LEN)
B.OCT.16,1928 NEW ORLEANS,LA.

1951	PIT	N	P		2	1- 1
1954	PIT	N	P		10	0- 1
		BLTL			12	1- 2

YOCHIM, RAYMOND AUSTIN ALOYSIUS (RAY)
B.JULY 19,1922 NEW ORLEANS,LA.

1948	STL	N	P		1	0- 0
1949	STL	N	P		3	0- 0
		BRTR			4	0- 0

YOHE, WILLIAM F.
B.SEPT.2,1879 MATOON,ILL.

1909	WAS	A	3		21	.208
		TR				

YORK, ANTHONY BATTON
B.NOV.27,1912 IRENE,TEX.
D.APR.18,1970 HILLSBORO,TEX.

1944	CHI	N	S-3		28	.235
		BRTR				

YORK, JAMES E. (LEFTY)
B.NOV.1,1895 TUSKEGEE,ALA.
D.APR.9,1961 YORK,PA.

1919	PHI	A	P		2	0- 2
1921	CHI	N	P		40	5- 9
		BRTL			42	5-11

YORK, JAMES HARLAN (JIM)
B.AUG.27,1947 MAYWOOD,CAL.

1970	KC	A	/P		4	1- 1
1971	KC	A	P		53	5- 5
1972	HOU	N	P		26	0- 1
1973	HOU	N	P		41	3- 4
1974	HOU	N	P		28	2- 2
1975	HOU	N	P		19	4- 4
1976	NY	A	/P		3	1- 0
		BRTR			174	16-17

YORK, PRESTON RUDOLPH (RUDY)
B.AUG.17,1913 RAGLAND,ALA.
D.FEB.5,1970 ROME,GA.

1934	DET	A	C		3	.167
1937	DET	A	C-3		104	.307
1938	DET	A	C-O		135	.298
1939	DET	A	C-1		102	.307
1940	DET	A	1		155	.316
1941	DET	A	1		155	.259
1942	DET	A	1		153	.260
1943	DET	A	1		155	.271
1944	DET	A	1		151	.276
1945	DET	A	1		155	.264
1946	BOS	A	1		154	.276
1947	BOS	A	1		48	.212
	CHI	A	1		102	.243
1948	PHI	A	1		31	.157
		BRTR			1603	.275

NON-PLAYING MANAGER
BOS(A) 1959 [INTERIM]

YORK, THOMAS J.
B.JULY 13,1851 BROOKLYN,N.Y.
D.FEB.17,1936 NEW YORK,N.Y.

1871	TRO	NA	O		29	.218
1872	BAL	NA	O		49	.269
1873	BAL	NA	P-O	1	57	1- 0
1874	PHI	NA	O		50	-
1875	HAR	NA	O		85	-
1876	HAR	NA	O		67	.249
1877	HAR	N	O		56	.283
1878	PRO	N	O		60	.302
1879	PRO	N	O		80	.307
1880	PRO	N	O		50	.211
1881	PRO	N	O		84	.304
1882	PRO	N	O		81	.267
1883	CLE	N	O		97	.255
1884	BAL	AA	O		84	.228
1885	BAL	AA	O		22	.271
		BL		1	951	1- 0

YOST, EDWARD FREDERICK JOSEPH (EDDIE) OR (THE WALKING MAN)
B.OCT.13,1926 BROOKLYN,N.Y.

1944	WAS	A	S-3		7	.143
1946	WAS	A	3		8	.080
1947	WAS	A	3		115	.238
1948	WAS	A	3		145	.249
1949	WAS	A	3		124	.253
1950	WAS	A	3		155	.295
1951	WAS	A	3-O		154	.283
1952	WAS	A	3		157	.233
1953	WAS	A	3		152	.272
1954	WAS	A	3		155	.256
1955	WAS	A	3		122	.243
1956	WAS	A	3-O		152	.231
1957	WAS	A	3		110	.251
1958	WAS	A	1-2-3-O		134	.224
1959	DET	A	2-3		148	.278
1960	DET	A	3		143	.260
1961	LA	A	3		76	.202
1962	LA	A	1-3		52	.240
		BRTR			2109	.254

YOST, GUS
B.TORONTO,ONTARIO,CANADA
D.OCT.16,1895 TORONTO,ONT.,CAN.

1893	CHI	N	P		1	1- 0

YOTER, ELMER ELSWORTH
B.JUNE 26,1900 PLAINFIELD,PA.
D.JULY 26,1966 CAMP HILL,PA.

1921	PHI	A	H		2	.000
1924	CLE	A	3		19	.273
1927	CHI	N	3		13	.222
1928	CHI	N	3		1	.000
		BRTR			35	.245

YOUNG, CHARLES V.
B.1894 TRENTON,N.J.

1915	BAL	F	P		9	2- 3
		BBTR				

YOUNG, DAVID
B.OCT.6,1872 PHILADELPHIA,PA.
D.OCT.25,1924

1895	STL	N	3		1	.400

YR	CL LEA POS	GP	G	REC

YOUNG, DELMER EDWARD (DEL)
B.MAR.11,1912 CLEVELAND,OHIO

YR	CL LEA POS	GP	G	REC
1937	PHI N 2	109		.194
1938	PHI N 2-S	108		.229
1939	PHI N 2-S	77		.263
1940	PHI N 2-S	15		.242
	BBTR	309		.224

YOUNG, DELMER JOHN
B.DEC.24,1885 MACON CITY,MO.
D.DEC.17,1959 CLEVELAND,OHIO

1909	CIN N O	2		.286
1914	BUF F O	79		.278
1915	BUF F O	12		.133
	BLTR	93		.268

YOUNG, DENTON TRUE (CY)
B.MAR.29,1867 GILMORE,OHIO
D.NOV.4,1955 NEWCOMERSTOWN,OHIO

1890	CLE N P	17		9- 7
1891	CLE N P	50		28-20
1892	CLE N P	49		36-11
1893	CLE N P	51		34-17
1894	CLE N P	47	48	25-21
1895	CLE N P	45	46	33-10
1896	CLE N P	47	48	29-14
1897	CLE N P	40	45	21-18
1898	CLE N P	41	44	24-15
1899	STL N P	42	43	26-14
1900	STL N P		39	20-16
1901	BOS A P	42	43	31-10
1902	BOS A P		45	32-11
1903	BOS A P	40	41	28- 9
1904	BOS A P		43	26-16
1905	BOS A P		38	16-18
1906	BOS A P	39	40	13-21
1907	BOS A P	44	43	22-15
1908	BOS A P		36	21-11
1909	CLE A P		34	19-15
1910	CLE A P		21	7-10
1911	CLE A P		7	3- 4
	BOS N P	10	11	4- 5
	BRTR	867	906	507-308

YOUNG, DONALD WAYNE (DON)
B.OCT.18,1945 HOUSTON,TEX.

1965	CHI N O	11		.057
1969	CHI N *O	101		.239
	BRTR	112		.218

YOUNG, GEORGE JOSEPH
B.APR.1,1890 BROOKLYN,N.Y.
D.MAR.13,1950 BRIGHTWATERS,N.Y.

1913	CLE A H	2		.000
	BLTR			

YOUNG, GEORGE W.
NON-PLAYING MANAGER PHI[NA] 1873, 75

YOUNG, HARLEY E.
(HARLEY) OR (CY THE THIRD)
B.KANSAS

1908	PIT N P	8		0- 2
	BOS N P	6		0- 1
	TR	14		0- 3

YOUNG, HERMAN JOHN
B.APR.14,1886 BOSTON,MASS.
D.DEC.13,1966 IPSWICH,MASS.

1911	BOS N S-3	9		.230
	BRTR			

YOUNG, IRVING MELROSE
(YOUNG CY) OR (CY THE SECOND)
B.JULY 21,1877 COLUMBIA FALLS,MAINE
D.JAN.14,1935 BREWER,MAINE

1905	BOS N P	43		20-21
1906	BOS N P	43		16-25
1907	BOS N P	40		10-23
1908	BOS N P	16		4- 9
	PIT N P	16		4- 3
1910	CHI A P	27		4- 8
1911	CHI A P	24		5- 6
	BLTL	209		63-95

YOUNG, J. D.
B.MT.CARMEL,PA.

1892	STL N P	1		0- 0

YOUNG, JOHN THOMAS
B.FEB.9,1949 LOS ANGELES,CAL.

1971	DET A /1	2		.500
	BLTL			

YOUNG, KIP LANE
B.OCT.29,1954 GEORGETOWN,OHIO

1978	DET A P	14		6- 7
	BRTR			

YOUNG, LEMUEL FLOYD (PEP)
B.AUG.29,1907 JAMESTOWN,N.C.
D.JAN.14,1962 JAMESTOWN,N.C.

1933	PIT N 2-S	25		.300
1934	PIT N 2-S	19		.235
1935	PIT N 2-S-3-O	128		.265
1936	PIT N 2	125		.248
1937	PIT N 2-S-3	113		.260
1938	PIT N 2	149		.278
1939	PIT N 2	84		.276
1940	PIT N 2-S-3	54		.250
1941	CIN N 3	4		.167
	STL N H	2		.000
1945	STL N 2-S-3	27		.149
	BRTR	730		.262

YOUNG, NICHOLAS EPHRAIM
B.SEPT.12,1840 AMSTERDAM,N.Y.
D.OCT.31,1916 WASHINGTON,D.C.
NON-PLAYING MANAGER
OLY[NA] 1871-72, NAT[NA] 1873

YOUNG, NORMAN ROBERT (BABE)
B.JULY 1,1915 ASTORIA,N.Y.

1936	NY N 1	1		.000
1939	NY N 1	22		.307
1940	NY N 1	149		.286
1941	NY N 1	152		.265
1942	NY N 1-O	101		.279
1946	NY N 1-O	104		.290
1947	NY N H	14		.071
	CIN N 1	95		.283
1948	CIN N 1-O	49		.231
	STL N 1	41		.243
	BLTL	728		.274

YOUNG, RALPH STUART
B.SEPT.19,1889 PHILADELPHIA,PA.
D.JAN.24,1965 PHILADELPHIA,PA.

1913	NY A S	7		.067
1915	DET A 2	123		.244
1916	DET A 2	153		.263
1917	DET A 2	141		.231
1918	DET A 2	91		.188
1919	DET A 2	125		.210
1920	DET A 2	150		.291
1921	DET A 2	107		.299
1922	PHI A 2	125		.223
	BBTR	1022		.247

YOUNG, RICHARD ENNIS (DICK)
B.JUNE 3,1928 SEATTLE,WASH.

1951	PHI N 2	15		.235
1952	PHI N 2	5		.222
	BBTR	20		.234
	BL 1951			

YOUNG, ROBERT GEORGE (BOBBY)
B.JAN.22,1925 GRANITE,MD.

1948	STL N 3	3		.000
1951	STL A 2	147		.260
1952	STL A 2	149		.247
1953	STL A 2	148		.258
1954	BAL A 2	130		.245
1955	BAL A 2	59		.199
	CLE A 2-3	18		.311
1956	CLE A H	1		.000
1958	PHI N 2	32		.233
	BLTR	687		.249

YOUNG, RUSSELL CHARLES
B.SEPT.15,1902 BRYAN,OHIO

1931	STL A 2	16		.118
	BBTR			

YOUNGBLOOD, ALBERT CLYDE (CHIEF)
B.JUNE 13,1900 HILLSBORO,TEX.
D.JULY 6,1968 AMARILLO,TEX.

1922	WAS A P	2		0- 0
	BLTR			

YOUNGBLOOD, JOEL RANDOLPH
B.AUG.28,1951 HOUSTON,TEX.

1976	CIN N /O-3-C-2	55		.193
1977	STL N O/3	25		.185
	NY N 2-O-3	70		.253
1978	NY N O-2/3-S	113		.252
	BRTR	263		.242

YOUNGMAN, HENRY
B.1865 INDIANA,PA.
D.JAN.24,1936 PITTSBURGH,PA.

1890	PIT N 2-3	13		.167

YOUNGS, ROSS MIDDLEBROOK
(ROSS) OR (PEP)
[REAL NAME ROYCE MIDDLEBROOK YOUNGS]
B.APR.10,1897 SHINER,TEX.
D.OCT.22,1927 SAN ANTONIO,TEX.

1917	NY N O	7		.346
1918	NY N 2-O	121		.302
1919	NY N O	130		.311
1920	NY N O	153		.351
1921	NY N O	141		.327
1922	NY N O	149		.330
1923	NY N O	152		.336
1924	NY N 2-O	133		.355
1925	NY N 2-O	130		.264
1926	NY N O	95		.306
	BLTR	1211		.322

YOUNGS, ROYCE MIDDLEBROOK
[PLAYED UNDER NAME OF
ROSS MIDDLEBROOK YOUNGS]

YOUNT, FLOYD EDWIN (EDDIE)
B.DEC.19,1916 NEWTON,N.C.
D.OCT.26,1973 NEWTON,N.C.

1937	PHI A H	4		.286
1939	PIT N O	2		.000
	BRTR	6		.222

YOUNT, HERBERT MACON
(DUCKY) OR (HUB)
B.DEC.7,1885 IREDELL CO.,N.C.
D.MAY 9,1970 WINSTON-SALEM,N.C.

1914	BAL F P	14		1- 1

YOUNT, LAWRENCE KING (LARRY)
B.FEB.15,1950 HOUSTON,TEX.

1971	HOU N /P	1		0- 0
	BRTR			

YOUNT, ROBIN R
B.SEPT.16,1955 DANVILLE,ILL.

1974	MIL A *S	107		.250
1975	MIL A *S	147		.267
1976	MIL A *S/O	161		.252
1977	MIL A *S	154		.288
1978	MIL A *S	127		.293
	BRTR	696		.271

YOWELL, CARL COLUMBUS (SUNDOWN)
B.DEC.20,1902 MADISON VA.

1924	CLE A P	4		1- 1
1925	CLE A P	12		2- 3
	BLTL	16		3- 4

YUHAS, JOHN EDWARD (EDDIE)
B.AUG.5,1924 YOUNGSTOWN,OHIO

1952	STL N P	54		12- 2
1953	STL N P	2		0- 0
	BRTR	56		12- 2

YURAK, JEFFREY LYNN (JEFF)
B.FEB.26,1954 PASADENA,CAL.

1978	MIL A /O	5		.000
	BBTR			

YVARS, SALVADOR ANTHONY (SAL)
B.FEB.20,1924 NEW YORK,N.Y.

1947	NY N C	1		.200
1948	NY N C	15		.211
1949	NY N C	3		.000
1950	NY N C	9		.143
1951	NY N C	25		.317
1952	NY N C	66		.245
1953	NY N C	23		.277
	STL N C	30		.246
1954	STL N C	38		.246
	BRTR	210		.244

ZABALA, ADRIAN [RODRIGUEZ]
B.AUG.26,1916 SAN ANTONIO
DE LOS BANOS,CUBA

1945	NY N P	11		2- 4
1949	NY N P	15		2- 3
	BLTL	26		4- 7

ZABEL, GEORGE WASHINGTON (ZIP)
B.FEB.18,1891 WETMORE,KAN.
D.MAY 31,1970 BELOIT,WIS.

1913	CHI N P	1		1- 0
1914	CHI N P	29		4- 4
1915	CHI N P	36	37	7-10
	BRTR	66	67	12-14

ZACHARY, ALBERT MYRON (CHINK)
B.OCT.19,1917 BROOKLYN,N.Y.

1944	BRO N P	4		0- 0
	BRTR			

ZACHARY, JONATHAN THOMPSON WALTON (TOM)
(PLAYED UNDER NAME OF ZACH WALTON IN 1918)
B.MAY 7,1896 GRAHAM,N.C.
D.JAN.24,1969 BURLINGTON,N.C.

YR	CL	LEA	POS	GP	G	REC
1918	PHI	A	P		2	2- 0
1919	WAS	A	P		17	1- 5
1920	WAS	A	P	44	51	15-16
1921	WAS	A	P		38	18-16
1922	WAS	A	P		32	15-10
1923	WAS	A	P		35	10-16
1924	WAS	A	P		32	15- 9
1925	WAS	A	P		38	12-15
1926	STL	A	P		34	14-15
1927	STL	A	P		13	4- 6
	WAS	A	P		15	4- 7
1928	WAS	A	P		20	6- 9
	NY	A	P		7	3- 3
1929	NY	A	P		26	12- 0
1930	NY	A	P		3	1- 1
	BOS	N	P	24	25	11- 5
1931	BOS	N	P		33	11-15
1932	BOS	N	P	32	33	12-11
1933	BOS	N	P	26	27	7- 9
1934	BOS	N	P		5	1- 2
	BRO	N	P	22	24	5- 6
1935	BRO	N	P		25	7-12
1936	BRO	N	P		1	0- 0
	PHI	N	P	7	8	0- 3
	BLTL			531	544	186-191

ZACHARY, WILLIAM CHRISTOPHER (CHRIS)
B.FEB.19,1944 KNOXVILLE,TENN.

YR	CL	LEA	POS	GP	G	REC
1963	HOU	N	P		22	2- 2
1964	HOU	N	P		0	0- 1
1965	HOU	N	/P		4	0- 2
1966	HOU	N	P		10	3- 5
1967	HOU	N	/P	9	10	1- 6
1969	KC	A	/P		8	0- 1
1971	STL	N	P	23	24	3-10
1972	DET	A	P		23	1- 1
1973	PIT	N	/P		6	0- 1
	BLTR			108	110	10-29

ZACHER, ELMER HENRY (SILVER)
B.SEPT.17,1883 BUFFALO,N.Y.
D.DEC.20,1944 BUFFALO,N.Y.

YR	CL	LEA	POS	GP	G	REC
1910	NY	N	O		1	.000
	STL	N	O		38	.212
	BRTR				39	.212

ZACHRY, PATRICK PAUL (PAT)
B.APR.24,1952 RICHMOND,TEX.

YR	CL	LEA	POS	GP	G	REC
1976	CIN	N	P		38	14- 7
1977	CIN	N	P		12	3- 7
	NY	N	P		19	7- 6
1978	NY	N	P		21	10- 6
	BRTR				90	34-26

ZACKERT, GEORGE CARL
B.DEC.24,1884 BUCHANAN CO.,MO.
D.FEB.18,1977 BURLINGTON,IOWA

YR	CL	LEA	POS	GP	G	REC
1911	STL	N	P		4	0- 2
1912	STL	N	P		1	0- 0
	BLTL				5	0- 2

ZAHN, GEOFFREY CLAYTON (JEFF)
B.DEC.19,1945 BALTIMORE,MD.

YR	CL	LEA	POS	GP	G	REC
1973	LA	N	/P		6	1- 0
1974	LA	N	P		21	3- 5
1975	LA	N	/P		2	0- 1
	CHI	N	P		16	2- 7
1976	CHI	N	/P		3	0- 1
1977	MIN	A	P		34	12-14
1978	MIN	A	P		35	14-14
	BLTL				117	32-42

ZAHNISER, FREDERICK JOSEPH
B.JUNE 5,1870 LOUISVILLE,KY.
D.JULY 24,1900 LOUISVILLE,KY.

YR	CL	LEA	POS	GP	G	REC
1894	LOU	N	C		14	.204
1895	LOU	N	C		18	.234
					32	.218

ZAHNISER, PAUL VERNON
B.SEPT.6,1896 SAC CITY,IOWA
D.SEPT.26,1964 KLAMATH FALLS,ORE.

YR	CL	LEA	POS	GP	G	REC
1923	WAS	A	P		33	9-10
1924	WAS	A	P		25	5- 7
1925	BOS	A	P		38	5-12
1926	BOS	A	P		30	6-18
1929	CIN	N	P		1	0- 0
	BRTR				125	25-47

ZAK, FRANK THOMAS
B.FEB.22,1922 PASSAIC,N.J.
D.FEB.6,1972 PASSAIC,N.J.

YR	CL	LEA	POS	GP	G	REC
1944	PIT	N	S		87	.300
1945	PIT	N	2-S		15	.143
1946	PIT	N	S		21	.200
	BRTR				123	.269

ZALUSKY, JOHN FRANCIS
B.JUNE 22,1879 MINNEAPOLIS,MINN
D.AUG.11,1935 MINNEAPOLIS,MINN.

YR	CL	LEA	POS	GP	G	REC
1903	NY	A	C		6	.267
	BRTR					

ZAMLOCH, CARL EUGENE
B.OCT.6,1889 OAKLAND,CAL.
D.AUG.19,1963 SANTA BARBARA,CAL

YR	CL	LEA	POS	GP	G	REC
1913	DET	A	P		17	1- 6
	BRTR					

ZAMORA, OSCAR JOSE [SOSA]
B.SEPT.23,1944 CAMAGUEY,CUBA

YR	CL	LEA	POS	GP	G	REC
1974	CHI	N	P		56	3- 9
1975	CHI	N	P		52	5- 2
1976	CHI	N	P		40	5- 3
1978	HOU	N	P		10	0- 0
	BRTR				158	13-14

ZANNI, DOMINICK THOMAS (DOM)
B.MAR.1,1932 BRONX,N.Y.

YR	CL	LEA	POS	GP	G	REC
1958	SF	N	P		1	1- 0
1959	SF	N	P		9	0- 0
1961	SF	N	P		8	1- 0
1962	CHI	A	P		44	6- 5
1963	CHI	A	P		5	0- 0
	CIN	N	P		31	1- 1
1965	CIN	N	/P		8	0- 0
1966	CIN	N	/P		5	0- 0
	BRTR				111	9- 6

ZAPUSTAS, JOSEPH JOHN
B.JULY 25,1907 BOSTON,MASS.

YR	CL	LEA	POS	GP	G	REC
1933	PHI	A	O		2	.200
	BRTR					

ZARDON, JOSE ANTONIO [SANCHEZ] (GUINEO)
B.MAY 20,1923 HAVANA,CUBA

YR	CL	LEA	POS	GP	G	REC
1945	WAS	A	O		54	.290
	BRTR					

ZARILLA, ALLEN LEE (ZEKE)
B.MAY 1,1919 LOS ANGELES,CAL.

YR	CL	LEA	POS	GP	G	REC
1943	STL	A	O		70	.254
1944	STL	A	O		100	.299
1946	STL	A	O		125	.259
1947	STL	A	O		127	.224
1948	STL	A	O		144	.329
1949	STL	A	O		15	.250
	BOS	A	O		124	.285
1950	BOS	A	O		130	.325
1951	CHI	A	O		120	.257
1952	CHI	A	O		39	.232
	STL	A	O		48	.238
	BOS	A	O		21	.183
1953	BOS	A	O		57	.194
	BLTR				1120	.277

ZAUCHIN, NORBERT HENRY (NORM)
B.NOV.17,1929 ROYAL OAK,MICH.

YR	CL	LEA	POS	GP	G	REC
1951	BOS	A	1		5	.167
1955	BOS	A	1		130	.239
1956	BOS	A	1		44	.214
1957	BOS	A	1		52	.264
1958	WAS	A	1		96	.228
1959	WAS	A	1		19	.211
	BRTR				346	.233

ZAY

YR	CL	LEA	POS	GP	G	REC
1886	BAL	AA	P		1	0- 1

ZDEB, JOSEPH EDMUND (JOE)
B.JUNE 27,1953 COMPTON,ILL.

YR	CL	LEA	POS	GP	G	REC
1977	KC	A	O/3		105	.297
1978	KC	A	O/2-3		60	.252
	BRTR				165	.280

ZEARFOSS, DAVID WILLIAM TILDEN
B.JAN.1,1868 SCHENECTADY,N.Y.
D.SEPT.12,1945 WILMINGTON,DEL.

YR	CL	LEA	POS	GP	G	REC
1896	NY	N	C		16	.220
1897	NY	N	C		5	.363
1898	NY	N	C		1	1.000
1904	STL	N	C		23	.213
1905	STL	N	C		19	.197
	TR				66	.208

ZEBER, GEORGE WILLIAM
B.AUG.29,1950 ELLWOOD CITY,PA.

YR	CL	LEA	POS	GP	G	REC
1977	NY	A	2/S-3		25	.323
1978	NY	A	/2		3	.000
	BBTR				28	.296

ZEIDER, ROLLIE HUBERT (BUNIONS)
B.NOV.16,1883 AUBURN,IND.
D.SEPT.12,1967 GARRETT,IND.

YR	CL	LEA	POS	GP	G	REC
1910	CHI	A	2-S		136	.217
1911	CHI	A	1-S		73	.254
1912	CHI	A	1-3		129	.245
1913	CHI	A	2		15	.438
	NY	A	2-S		46	.227
1914	CHI	F	2		120	.263
1915	CHI	F	2-S-3		130	.233
1916	CHI	N	2-3		98	.235
1917	CHI	N	2-S-3		108	.243
1918	CHI	N	1-2-3		82	.223
	BRTR				937	.239

ZEISER, MATTHEW J.
B.SEPT.25,1888 CHICAGO,ILL.

YR	CL	LEA	POS	GP	G	REC
1914	BOS	A	P		2	0- 0
	BRTR					

ZELLER, BARTON WALLACE (BART)
B.JULY 22,1941 CHICAGO HEIGHTS,ILL.

YR	CL	LEA	POS	GP	G	REC
1970	STL	N	/C		1	.000
	BRTR					

ZEPP, WILLIAM CLINTON (BILL)
B.JULY 22,1946 DETROIT,MICH.

YR	CL	LEA	POS	GP	G	REC
1969	MIN	A	/P		4	0- 0
1970	MIN	A	P		43	9- 4
1971	DET	A	P		16	1- 1
	BRTR				63	10- 5

ZERNIAL, GUS EDWARD (OZARK IKE)
B.JUNE 27,1923 BEAUMONT,TEX.

YR	CL	LEA	POS	GP	G	REC
1949	CHI	A	O		73	.318
1950	CHI	A	O		143	.280
1951	CHI	A	O		4	.105
	PHI	A	O		139	.274
1952	PHI	A	O		143	.262
1953	PHI	A	O		147	.284
1954	PHI	A	1-O		97	.250
1955	KC	A	1-O		120	.254
1956	KC	A	1-O		109	.224
1957	KC	A	1-O		131	.236
1958	DET	A	O		66	.323
1959	DET	A	1-O		60	.227
	BRTR				1234	.265

ZETTLEIN, GEORGE (CHARMER)
B.JULY 18,1844 BROOKLYN,N.Y.
D.MAY 23,1905 PATCHOGUE,N.Y.

YR	CL	LEA	POS	GP	G	REC
1871	CHI	NA	P-O	24	25	17- 7
						0- 1
	MUT	NA	P		1	0- 1
	CHI	NA	P		3	1- 2
1872	TRO	NA	P-O	22	25	14- 8
						.248
	ECK	NA	P-O	8	9	1- 7
						.059
1873	PHI	NA	P		49	35-14
1874	CHI	NA	P		57	27-30
1875	CHI	NA	P		33	18-15
	PHI	NA	P		20	21 11- 9
1876	ATH	N	P-1	25	32	4-19
						.211
	BRTR			242	255	128-112

ZICK, ROBERT GEORGE
B.APR.26,1927 CHICAGO,ILL.

YR	CL	LEA	POS	GP	G	REC
1954	CHI	N	P		10	0- 0
	BLTR					

ZIEBER, HARRY
[SEE EDWARD C. WHITING]

ZIEGLER, CHARLES W.
B.FEB.2,1875 CANTON,OHIO
D.MAR.16,1904 CANTON,OHIO

YR	CL	LEA	POS	GP	G	REC
1899	CLE	N	2-S		2	.250
1900	PHI	N	3		3	.273
					5	.263

ZIEGLER, GEORGE J.
B.1872 CHICAGO,ILL.
D.JULY 22,1916 KANKAKEE,ILL.

YR	CL	LEA	POS	GP	G	REC
1890	PIT	N	P		1	0- 0

ZIENTARA, BENEDICT JOSEPH
B.JUNE 14,1920 CHICAGO,ILL.

YR	CL	LEA	POS	GP	G	REC
1941	CIN	N	2		9	.286
1946	CIN	N	2-3		78	.289
1947	CIN	N	2-3		117	.258
1948	CIN	N	2-S-3		74	.187
	BRTR				278	.254

ZIES, WILLIAM

YR	CL	LEA	POS	GP	G	REC
1891	STL	AA	C		1	.000

ZIMMER, CHARLES LOUIS (CHIEF)
B.NOV.23,1860 MARIETTA,OHIO
D.AUG.22,1949 CLEVELAND,OHIO

YR	CL	LEA	POS	GP	G	REC
1884	DET	N	C-O		8	.071
1886	MET	AA	C		5	.187
1887	CLE	AA	C		14	.321
1888	CLE	AA	C		63	.250
1889	CLE	N	C		80	.258
1890	CLE	N	C		125	.214
1891	CLE	N	C		116	.261
1892	CLE	N	C		111	.268
1893	CLE	N	C		55	.309
1894	CLE	N	C		88	.285
1895	CLE	N	C		83	.336
1896	CLE	N	C		89	.273
1897	CLE	N	C		81	.314
1898	CLE	N	C		18	.250
1899	CLE	N	C		20	.342
	LOU	N	C		74	.299
1900	PIT	N	C		80	.298
1901	PIT	N	C		67	.222
1902	PIT	N	C-1		40	.268
1903	PHI	N	M-C		35	.220
	BRTR				1252	.272

YR	CL	LEA	POS	GP	G	REC		YR	CL	LEA	POS	GP	G	REC		YR	CL	LEA	POS	GP	G	REC

ZIMMER, DONALD WILLIAM (DON)
B.JAN.17,1931 CINCINNATI,OHIO

YR	CL	LEA	POS	G	REC
1954	BRO	N	S	24	.182
1955	BRO	N	2-S-3	88	.239
1956	BRO	N	2-S-3	17	.300
1957	BRO	N	2-S-3	84	.219
1958	LA	N	2-S-3	127	.262
1959	LA	N	2-S-3	97	.165
1960	CHI	N	2-S-3-O	132	.258
1961	CHI	N	2-3-O	128	.252
1962	NY	N	3	14	.077
	CIN	N	2-S-3	63	.250
1963	LA	N	2-S-3	22	.217
	WAS	A	2-3	83	.248
1964	WAS	A	C-2-3-O	121	.246
1965	WAS	A	C-3-2	95	.199
			BRTR	1095	.235

NON-PLAYING MANAGER
SD[N] 1972-73, BOS[A] 1976-78

ZIMMERMAN, EDWARD DESMOND
B.JAN.4,1883 OCEANIC,N.J.
D.MAY 6,1945 EMMAUS,PA.

YR	CL	LEA	POS	G	REC
1906	STL	N	3	5	.213
1911	BRO	N	3	122	.185
			BRTR	127	.186

ZIMMERMAN, GERALD ROBERT (JERRY)
B.SEP.21,1934 OMAHA,NEB.

YR	CL	LEA	POS	G	REC
1961	CIN	N	C	76	.206
1962	MIN	A	C	34	.274
1963	MIN	A	C	39	.232
1964	MIN	A	C	63	.200
1965	MIN	A	C	83	.214
1966	MIN	A	C	60	.252
1967	MIN	A	*C	104	.167
1968	MIN	A	C	24	.111
			BRTR	483	.204

ZIMMERMAN, HENRY (HEINIE)
B.FEB.9,1887 NEW YORK,N.Y.
D.MAR.14,1969 NEW YORK,N.Y.

YR	CL	LEA	POS	G	REC
1907	CHI	N	2	3	.142
1908	CHI	N	2	30	.292
1909	CHI	N	2	47	.273
1910	CHI	N	2-S-3	86	.284
1911	CHI	N	2-3	139	.307
1912	CHI	N	1-3	145	.372
1913	CHI	N	3	127	.313
1914	CHI	N	S-3	146	.296
1915	CHI	N	2-3	139	.265
1916	CHI	N	2-3	107	.294
	NY	N	2-3	40	.265
1917	NY	N	3	150	.297
1918	NY	N	1-3	121	.272
1919	NY	N	3	123	.255
			BRTR	1403	.295

ZIMMERMAN, ROY FRANKLIN
B.SEPT.13,1916 PINE GROVE,PA.

YR	CL	LEA	POS	G	REC
1945	NY	N	1-O	27	.276
			BLTL		

ZIMMERMAN, WILLIAM H.
B.JAN.20,1889 KENGEN,GERMANY
D.OCT.4,1952 NEWARK,N.J.

YR	CL	LEA	POS	G	REC
1915	BRO	N	O	22	.281
			BRTR		

ZINK, WALTER NOBLE
B.NOV.21,1899 PITTSFIELD,MASS.
D.JUNE 12,1964 QUINCY,MASS.

YR	CL	LEA	POS	G	REC
1921	NY	N	P	2	0- 0
			BRTR		

ZINN, FRANK
B.1865 PHILADELPHIA,PA.

YR	CL	LEA	POS	G	REC
1888	ATH	AA	C	2	.000

ZINN, GUY
B.FEB.13,1887 HALLBROOK,W.VA.
B.OCT.6,1949 CLARKSBURG,W.VA.

YR	CL	LEA	POS	G	REC
1911	NY	A	O	9	.148
1912	NY	A	O	106	.264
1913	BOS	N	O	36	.297
1914	BAL	F	O	61	.277
1915	BAL	F	O	100	.269
			BLTR	312	.270

ZINN, JAMES EDWARD
B.JAN.21,1895 BENTON,ARK.

YR	CL	LEA	POS	GP	G	REC
1919	PHI	A	P	5	10	1- 3
1920	PIT	N	P	6	8	1- 1
1921	PIT	N	P	32	33	7- 6
1922	PIT	N	P		5	0- 0
1929	CLE	A	P	18	20	4- 6
			BLTR	66	76	13-16

ZINSER, WILLIAM FRANCIS
B.JAN.6,1918 ASTORIA,N.Y.

YR	CL	LEA	POS	G	REC
1944	WAS	A	P	2	0- 0
			BRTR		

ZIPFEL, MARION SYLVESTER (BUD)
B.NOV.18,1938 BELLEVILLE,ILL.

YR	CL	LEA	POS	G	REC
1961	WAS	A	1	50	.200
1962	WAS	A	1-O	68	.239
			BLTR	118	.220

ZISK, RICHARD WALTER (RICHIE)
B.FEB.6,1949 BROOKLYN,N.Y.

YR	CL	LEA	POS	G	REC
1971	PIT	N	/O	7	.200
1972	PIT	N	O	17	.189
1973	PIT	N	O	103	.324
1974	PIT	N	*O	149	.313
1975	PIT	N	*O	147	.290
1976	PIT	N	*O	155	.289
1977	CHI	A	*O-O	141	.290
1978	TEX	A	O-D	140	.262
			BRTR	859	.291

ZITZMANN, WILLIAM ARTHUR
B.NOV.19,1897 LONG ISLAND CITY,N.Y.

YR	CL	LEA	POS	G	REC
1919	PIT	N	O	11	.192
	CIN	N	O	2	.000
1925	CIN	N	S-O	104	.252
1926	CIN	N	O	53	.245
1927	CIN	N	S-3-O	88	.284
1928	CIN	N	O	101	.297
1929	CIN	N	1-O	47	.226
			BRTR	406	.267

ZMICH, EDWARD ALBERT
B.OCT.1,1884 CLEVELAND,OHIO
D.AUG.20,1950 CLEVELAND,OHIO

YR	CL	LEA	POS	G	REC
1910	STL	N	P	9	0- 5
1911	STL	N	P	4	1- 0
			BLTL	13	1- 5

ZOLDAK, SAMUEL WALTER (SAD SAM)
B.DEC.8,1918 BROOKLYN,N.Y.
D.AUG.25,1966 NEW HYDE PARK,N.Y

YR	CL	LEA	POS	GP	G	REC
1944	STL	A	P		18	0- 0
1945	STL	A	P	26	27	3- 2
1946	STL	A	P		35	9-11
1947	STL	A	P		35	9-10
1948	STL	A	P		11	2- 4
	CLE	A	P		23	9- 6
1949	CLE	A	P		27	1- 2
1950	CLE	A	P		33	4- 2
1951	PHI	A	P		26	6-10
1952	PHI	A	P		16	0- 6
			BLTL	250	291	43-53

ZUBER, WILLIAM HENRY
(BILL) OR (GOOBER)
B.MAR.26,1913 MIDDLE AMANA,IOWA

YR	CL	LEA	POS	G	REC
1936	CLE	A	P	2	1- 1
1938	CLE	A	P	15	0- 3
1939	CLE	A	P	16	2- 0
1940	CLE	A	P	17	1- 1
1941	WAS	A	P	36	6- 4
1942	WAS	A	P	37	9- 9
1943	NY	A	P	20	8- 4
1944	NY	A	P	22	5- 7
1945	NY	A	P	21	5-11
1946	NY	A	P	3	0- 1
	BOS	A	P	15	5- 1
1947	BOS	A	P	20	1- 0
			BRTR	224	43-42

ZUPO, FRANK JOSEPH
(FRANK) OR (NOODLES)
B.AUG.29,1939 SAN FRANCISCO,CAL

YR	CL	LEA	POS	G	REC
1957	BAL	A	C	10	.083
1958	BAL	A	C	1	.000
1961	BAL	A	C	5	.500
			BLTR	16	.167

ZUVERINK, GEORGE
B.AUG.20,1924 HOLLAND,MICH.

YR	CL	LEA	POS	GP	G	REC
1951	CLE	A	P		16	0- 0
1952	CLE	A	P	1	2	0- 0
1954	CIN	N	P		2	0- 0
	DET	A	P		35	9-13
1955	DET	A	P		14	0- 5
	BAL	A	P		28	4- 3
1956	BAL	A	P		62	7- 6
1957	BAL	A	P		56	10- 6
1958	BAL	A	P		45	2- 2
1959	BAL	A	P		6	0- 1
			BRTR	265	266	32-36

ZWILLING, EDWARD HARRISON (DUTCH)
B.NOV.2,1888 ST.LOUIS,MO.
D.MAR.27,1978 LA CRESCENTA,CAL.

YR	CL	LEA	POS	G	REC
1910	CHI	A	O	27	.184
1914	CHI	F	O	155	.308
1915	CHI	F	O	150	.291
1916	CHI	N	O	35	.113
			BLTR	367	.284

THE LAST OF HIS KIND

Connie Mack, baseball's most revered figure, died February 8, 1956, in German-town, Pa., at the age of 93. His career spanned two centuries as player, manager and clubowner, and for the first 50 years of the American League he was the Philadelphia Athletics' only manager. In 1886 (left) the thin New England shoe factory hand started as a catcher with Washington of the National League. This is how he looked (right), 70 years later, only three months before he was to die.

IV WORLD SERIES

America's most discussed and popular sporting event is the World Series which annually pits the championship teams of the two major leagues against each other.

The Series is a logical, lucrative and legendary climax to every baseball season. After five months of campaigning, each club strictly within its own league, two teams survive as the fittest. What better than a post-season play-off to determine a single undisputed champion? Yet the World Series did not always extend in an unbroken skein through professional baseball history. League snobbishness of one sort or another has kept pennant winners apart in certain years rather than let the question of league superiority be settled on the ball field.

In those seasons when the majors consisted of only one league, no World Series was necessary. Still, it is interesting to note that the craving for some sort of post-season playoff was so strong that for several years there was an artificial "championship" set played each Autumn between the first and second place finishers for the Temple Cup.

Herewith are the highlights, scoring summary, winning and losing pitchers, homers and attendance figures of all past World Series games:

1882

At the end of the American Association's first season, the champion Cincinnati club challenged Chicago's NL winners. Bespectacled Will White blanked Chicago in the opener. Larry Corcoran retaliated in the next game. With honors all even, the series came to an untimely end. AA president Denny McKnight, enraged at player raids and other shabby treatment during the season from the NL, wired the Reds that they would be expelled if they continued the series. Cincinnati was ready to defy McKnight, but Chicago player-manager Cap Anson decided to abandon further play for the best interest of all concerned.

Result: Chicago NL won 1; Cincinnati AA, 1.

1st Game, at Cincinnati, Oct 6				R.	H.	E.
Chicago (NL)	000	000	000	---	0	7	3
Cincinnati (AA)	000	004	00x	---	4	10	2

Pitchers--GOLDSMITH vs. WHITE. Attendance--2,700.

2nd Game, at Cincinnati, Oct. 7				R.	H.	E.
Chicago (NL)	200	000	000	---	2	4	0
Cincinnati (AA)	000	000	000	---	0	3	3

Pitchers--CORCORAN vs. WHITE. Attendance--4,500.

1884

With league quarrels ironed out by now, the pennant winners met in a fully sanctioned playoff. Hardly tired after pitching 60 victories for Providence in NL competition, Old Hoss Radbourn went on to conquer New York's Mets, pride of the AA, three times in as many days. He topped Tim Keefe's fine flinging the first two games. Keefe turned umpire for the third game, and when it began to turn into a rout he mercifully called a halt because of alleged darkness at the end of six innings.

Result: Providence NL won 3; Mets AA, 0.

1st Game, at New York, Oct. 23				R.	H.	E.
Metropolitan(AA)	000	000	000	---	0	2	1
Providence (NL)	201	000	30x	---	6	5	3

Pitchers--KEEFE vs. RADBOURN. Attend.--1,800.

2nd Game, at New York, Oct. 24			R.	H.	E.
Providence (NL)	000	030	0	---	3	5	3
Metropolitan(AA)	000	010	0	---	1	3	0

(called, end of seventh: darkness)
Pitchers -- RADBOURN vs. KEEFE. Homer -- Denny (Pro.). Attendance--1,000.

3rd Game, at New York, Oct. 25			R.	H.	E.
Providence (NL)	120	144	---	12	13	4
Metropolitan(AA)	000	011	---	2	5	2

(called, end of sixth: darkness)
Pitchers--RADBOURN vs. BECANNON. Att.--300.

1885

In the sixth inning of the second game of this bitter rivalry, manager-captain-first baseman Charlie Comiskey pulled his St. Louis AA club off the field in protest against a decision by umpire Dan Sullivan. The game was declared forfeit to Chicago NL, but the Browns won a moral victory since Sullivan did not officiate thereafter. Animosity lingered long after the series, which ended in a tie. St. Louis counted itself the champion, insisting that the forfeited second game should not count in the records. Most people agreed with Cap Anson that his White Stockings were co-champions. Anson hit safely in every game, batting .423. Comiskey, first to field his position away from first base, was outstanding on defense during an erratic series which totaled more errors than hits.

Result: Chicago NL won 3; St. Louis AA, 3; 1 tie.

```
1st Game, at Chicago, Oct. 14          R.  H.  E.
St. Louis (AA)  010  400  00    ---    5   7   4
Chicago (NL)    000  100  04    ---    5   6  11
        (called, end of 8th: darkness)
   Pitchers -- Caruthers vs. Clarkson. Homer -- Pfeffer
(Chi.). Attendance -- 3,000.

2nd Game, at St. Louis, Oct. 15
Chicago (NL)    110  003       ---    5   6   5
St. Louis (AA)  300  10x       ---    4   2   4
        (Game forfeited to Chicago, 9-0)
   Pitchers--McCORMICK vs. FOUTZ. Attendance--2,000.

3rd Game, at St. Louis, Oct. 16
Chicago (NL)    111  000  001   ---   4   8  12
St. Louis (AA)  500  002  00x   ---   7   8   4
   Pitchers--CLARKSON vs. CARUTHERS. Att.--3,000.

4th Game, at St. Louis, Oct. 17
Chicago (NL)    000  020  000   ---   2   8   3
St. Louis (AA)  001  000  02x   ---   3   6   7
   Pitchers--McCORMICK vs. FOUTZ. Homer--Dalrymple
(Chi.). Attendance--3,000.

5th Game, at Pittsburgh, Oct. 22
Chicago (NL)    400  110  3     ---   9   7   1
St. Louis (AA)  010  000  1     ---   2   4   7
        (called, end of 7th: darkness)
   Pitchers--CLARKSON vs. FOUTZ. Attendance--500.

6th Game, at Cincinnati, Oct. 23
Chicago (NL)    200  111  040   ---   9  11  10
St. Louis (AA)  002  000  000   ---   2   2   7
   Pitchers--McCORMICK vs. CARUTHERS. Att.--1,500.

7th Game, at Cincinnati, Oct. 24
Chicago (NL)    200  020  00    ---   4   9  17
St. Louis (AA)  004  621  0x    ---  13  12  10
        (called in 8th: darkness)
   Pitchers--McCORMICK vs. FOUTZ. Attend.--1,200.
```

1886

Renewing their feud of the previous Fall, the Browns and White Stockings met on a winner-take-all basis. St. Louis won only one of the first three games in Chicago, but swept all three at home to make their colorful club-owner, Chris Von der Ahe, gloat over "my poys, champeens of the world." The series ended on a dramatic note. Curt Welch, Brown centerfielder, was on third base in the 10th inning of the last game when King Kelly signaled for a pitchout. Welch daringly streaked for home and made it when Kelly momentarily bobbled the pitch in his mitt. This play was dubbed "Welch's fifteen thousand dollar slide," as a rough estimate of how much it meant to the winners.

Result: St. Louis AA won 4; Chicago NL, 2.

```
1st Game, at Chicago, Oct. 18          R.  H.  E.
St. Louis (AA)  000  000  000   ---    0   5   7
Chicago (NL)    200  001  03x   ---    6  10   5
   Pitchers--FOUTZ vs. CLARKSON. Attend.--6,000.

2nd Game, at Chicago, Oct. 19
St. Louis (AA)  200  230  50    ---  12  13   5
Chicago (NL)    000  000  00    ---   0   2  13
        (called, end of 8th: darkness)
   Pitchers--CARUTHERS vs. McCORMICK. Homers --
O'Neill (St. L.) 2. Attendance--5,000.

3rd Game, at Chicago, Oct. 20
St. Louis (AA)  200  112  32    ---  11  11   7
Chicago (NL)    010  002  01    ---   4   9   7
        (called, end of 8th: darkness)
   Pitchers--CLARKSON, Williamson (8) vs. CARUTHERS.
Homers--Kelly (Chi.), Gore (Chi.). Attendance--6,000.

4th Game, at St. Louis, Oct. 21
Chicago (NL)    300  002  0     ---   5   6   4
St. Louis (AA)  011  033  x     ---   8   7   4
        (called in 7th: darkness)
   Pitchers--CLARKSON vs. FOUTZ. Attendance--8,000.

5th Game, at St. Louis, Oct. 22
Chicago (NL)    011  100  00    ---   3   3   3
St. Louis (AA)  214  003  0x    ---  10  11   3
        (called in 8th: darkness)
   Pitchers--WILLIAMSON, Ryan (2) vs. HUDSON. At-
tendance--10,000.

6th Game, at St. Louis, Oct. 23
Chicago (NL)    010  101  000  0   ---  3   6   2
St. Louis (AA)  000  000  030  1   ---  4   5   3
   Pitchers--CLARKSON vs. CARUTHERS. Homer--
Pfeffer (Chi.). Attendance--8,000.
```

1887

Behind its famed "Big Four" of Dan Brouthers, Deacon White, Hardy Richardson and Jack Rowe, Detroit NL trounced St. Louis AA in a 15-game traveling circus played in 10 different cities. Pitchers Charles Getzein and Lady Baldwin each won four for the new champions, while Ned Hanlon gained a reputation for

his fine field direction from center-field. Arlie Latham stole a dozen bases for the losers, acted as pivot-man in a triple play and hit .333.

Result: Detroit NL won 10; St. Louis AA, 5.

```
1st Game, at St. Louis, Oct. 10       R.  H.  E.
St. Louis (AA)  200 040 000  ---      6  16  0
Detroit (NL)    000 000 001  ---      1   5  5
 Pitchers--CARUTHERS vs. GETZEIN. Attend.--4,208.

2nd Game, at St. Louis, Oct. 11
Detroit (NL)    022 000 100  ---      5  12  2
St. Louis (AA)  000 000 120  ---      3  10  7
 Pitchers--CONWAY vs. FOUTZ. Attendance--6,408.

3rd Game, at Detroit, Oct. 12
St. Louis (AA)  010 000 000 000 0 --- 1  13  7
Detroit (NL)    000 000 010 000 1 --- 2   7  1
 Pitchers--CARUTHERS vs. GETZEIN. Attend.--4,509.

4th Game, at Pittsburgh, Oct. 13
Detroit (NL)    410 012 000  ---      8  12  1
St. Louis (AA)  000 000 000  ---      0   5  6
 Pitchers--BALDWIN vs. KING. Attendance--2,447.

5th Game, at Brooklyn, Oct. 14
St. Louis (AA)  200 002 100  ---      5   7  4
Detroit (NL)    000 020 000  ---      2   8  5
 Pitchers--CARUTHERS vs. CONWAY. Att.--6,796.

6th Game, at New York, Oct. 15
Detroit (NL)    330 000 003  ---      9  15  1
St. Louis (AA)  000 000 000  ---      0   5  8
 Pitchers--GETZEIN vs. FOUTZ. Attendance--5,797.

7th Game, at Philadelphia, Oct. 17
St. Louis (AA)  000 000 001  ---      1  10  1
Detroit (NL)    030 000 00x  ---      3   7  2
 Pitchers--CARUTHERS vs. BALDWIN. Homer--O'Neill
(St. L.). Attendance--6,478.

8th Game, at Boston, Oct. 18
Detroit (NL)    031 003 200  ---      9  17  2
St. Louis (AA)  100 001 000  ---      2  12  5
 Pitchers -- GETZEIN vs. CARUTHERS. Homers --
Thompson (Det.) 2. Attendance--2,891.

9th Game, at Philadelphia, Oct. 19
St. Louis (AA)  000 101 000  ---      2   9  2
Detroit (NL)    000 100 21x  ---      4   6  3
 Pitchers--KING vs. CONWAY. Attendance--2,389.

10th Game, at Washington, Oct. 21 (AM)
Detroit (NL)    200 010 001  ---      4   9  3
St. Louis (AA)  200 031 41x  ---     11  19  5
 Pitchers--GETZEIN vs. CARUTHERS. Homers--Latham
(St. L.), Welch (St. L.), Richardson (Det.). Attendance--
1,261.

11th Game, at Baltimore, Oct. 21 (PM)
St. Louis (AA)  110 010 000  ---      3  13  7
Detroit (NL)    100 344 10x  ---     13  18  7
 Pitchers -- FOUTZ vs. BALDWIN. Homer -- Twitchell
(Det.). Attendance--2,707.

12th Game, at Brooklyn, Oct. 22
Detroit (NL)    000 010  0   ---      1   5  3
St. Louis (AA)  410 000  x   ---      5  10  2
 (called in 7th: darkness)
 Pitchers--CONWAY vs. KING. Attendance--1,138.

13th Game, at Detroit, Oct. 24
Detroit (NL)    020 100 120  ---      6  14  3
St. Louis (AA)  100 010 001  ---      3   5  5
 Pitchers--BALDWIN vs. CARUTHERS. Attend.--3,389.

14th Game, at Chicago, Oct. 25
St. Louis (AA)  000 002 100  ---      3  10  5
Detroit (NL)    300 010 00x  ---      4   4  4
 Pitchers--KING vs. GETZEIN. Attendance--378.

15th Game, at St. Louis, Oct. 26
St. Louis (AA)  340 110      ---      9  11  4
Detroit (NL)    011 000      ---      2  10  7
 (called, end of 6th: cold)
 Pitchers--CARUTHERS vs. BALDWIN. Att.--659.
```

1888

Though St. Louis sold five regulars after losing the previous series, the Browns won the AA pennant for the fourth straight year... only to lose to their NL rivals again. It was decided to play a best-six-out-of-ten series. The New York Giants clinched it in eight games, then tossed away the last two by sending home their big stars: Tim Keefe, Buck Ewing and John Montgomery Ward. Keefe fast-balled four victories. Ewing hit hard and, in an era of stolen bases and passed balls galore, stood out as the colossus of catchers. Ward was such a superb all-around player that one newspaperman wrote that the Browns would have won the series if Ward had shortstopped for them instead.

Result: New York NL won 6; St. Louis AA, 4.

```
1st Game, at New York, Oct. 16       R.  H.  E.
St. Louis (AA)  001 000 000  ---      1   3  5
New York (NL)   011 000 00x  ---      2   3  4
 Pitchers--KING vs. KEEFE. Attendance--4,876.

2nd Game, at New York, Oct. 17
St. Louis (AA)  010 000 002  ---      3   7  4
New York (NL)   000 000 000  ---      0   6  1
 Pitchers--CHAMBERLAIN vs. WELCH. Att.--5,575.

3rd Game, at New York, Oct. 18
St. Louis (AA)  000 000 011  ---      2   5  5
New York (NL)   200 100 10x  ---      4   5  2
 Pitchers--KING vs. KEEFE. Attendance--5,780.

4th Game, at Brooklyn, Oct. 19
New York (NL)   104 010 000  ---      6   8  2
St. Louis (AA)  001 000 020  ---      3   6  4
 Pitchers--CRANE vs. CHAMBERLAIN. Att.--3,062.

5th Game, at New York, Oct. 20
St. Louis (AA)  003 001 00   ---      4   5  5
New York (NL)   100 000 05   ---      6   9  2
 (called, end of 8th: darkness)
 Pitchers--KING vs. KEEFE. Attendance--9,124.

6th Game, at Philadelphia, Oct. 22
New York (NL)   000 103 35   ---     12  13  5
St. Louis (AA)  301 000 01   ---      5   3  7
 (called, end of 8th: darkness)
 Pitchers--WELCH vs. CHAMBERLAIN. Att.--3,281.

7th Game, at St. Louis, Oct. 24
New York (NL)   030 002 00   ---      5  11  3
St. Louis (AA)  000 300 04   ---      7   8  3
 (called, end of 8th: darkness)
 Pitchers--CRANE vs. KING. Attendance--4,624.

8th Game, at St. Louis, Oct. 25
New York (NL)   103 100 006  ---     11  12  2
St. Louis (AA)  000 100 110  ---      3   5  6
 Pitchers--KEEFE vs. CHAMBERLAIN. Homers--Ewing
(N.Y.), Tiernan (N.Y.). Attendance--4,865.

9th Game, at St. Louis, Oct. 26
St. Louis (AA)  140 020 202 3 ---    14  15  4
New York (NL)   035 000 120 0 ---    11  14  5
 Pitchers--King, DEVLIN (4) vs. GEORGE. Homer--
O'Neill (St. L.). Attendance--711.

10th Game, at St. Louis, Oct. 27
St. Louis (AA)  010 505 421  ---     18  17  3
New York (NL)   011 300 008  ---      7  13  8
 Pitchers--CHAMBERLAIN vs. TITCOMB. Hatfield (5).
Homers--George (N.Y.), O'Neill (St. L.), McCarthy (St. L.)
Attendance--412.
```

1889

Manager Jim Mutrie wore his stovepipe hat with regal pride when his Giants repeated as world champions. Cannonball Ed Crane won four games and Hank O'Day, later a famous umpire, won two others. John Ward hit .417 and shortstopped wonderfully. Brooklyn won three of the first four games, only to lose the next five straight.

Result: New York NL won 6; Brooklyn AA, 3.

```
1st Game, at New York, Oct. 18              R.   H.   E.
New York (NL)    020  210  50    ---    10   11   3
Brooklyn (AA)    510  000  24    ---    12   14   6
               (called, end of 8th: darkness)
   Pitchers--KEEFE vs. TERRY. Homer--Collins (Bklyn.).
Attendance--8,848.

2nd Game, at Brooklyn, Oct. 19
New York (NL)    111  120  000   ---    6    9    4
Brooklyn (AA)    110  000  001   ---    2    3    8
   Pitchers--CRANE vs. CARUTHERS. Attend.--16,172.

3rd Game, at New York, Oct. 22
New York (NL)    200  032  00    ---    7    15   2
Brooklyn (AA)    023  120  00    ---    8    11   3
               (called, end of 8th: darkness)
   Pitchers--WELCH, O'Day (6) vs. HUGHES, Caruthers (8).
Homers--Corkhill (Bklyn.), O'Rourke (N.Y.). Attendance--
5,181.

4th Game, at Brooklyn, Oct. 23
New York (NL)    001  105    ---    7    9    8
Brooklyn (AA)    202  033    ---   10    7    1
              (called end of sixth: darkness)
   Pitchers--CRANE vs. TERRY. Homer--Burns (Bklyn.).
Attendance--3,045.

5th Game, at Brooklyn, Oct. 24
New York (NL)    004  040  021   ---   11   12   2
Brooklyn (AA)    000  111  000   ---    3    8    2
   Pitchers--CRANE vs. CARUTHERS. Homers--Brown
(N.Y.), Richardson (N.Y.), Crane (N.Y.). Attendance--2,901.

6th Game, at New York, Oct. 25
Brooklyn (AA)    010  000  000  00  ---   1    6    4
New York (NL)    000  000  001  01  ---   2    6    1
   Pitchers--TERRY vs O'DAY. Attendance--2,556.

7th Game, at New York, Oct. 26
Brooklyn (AA)    004  030  000   ---    7    5    3
New York (NL)    180  001  10x   ---   11   14   4
   Pitchers--LOVETT, Caruthers (4) vs. CRANE, Keefe
(5). Homers--Richardson (N.Y.), O'Rourke (N.Y.). Attend-
ance--3,312.

8th Game, at Brooklyn, Oct. 28
New York (NL)    541  203  001   ---   16   15   4
Brooklyn (AA)    200  000  023   ---    7    5    4
   Pitchers--CRANE vs. TERRY, Fouts (5). Homers--
Foutz (Bklyn.), Tiernan (N.Y.). Attendance--2,584.

9th Game, at New York, Oct. 29
Brooklyn (AA)    200  000  000   ---    2    4    2
New York (NL)    100  001  10x   ---    3    8    5
   Pitchers--TERRY vs. O'DAY. Attendance--3,067.
```

1890

Brooklyn's AA kingpins of 1889 jumped to the NL in 1890 and won the pennant. In the AA, Louisville rose from last to first in one season. However, much of the top talent had switched to the Players League, so the public couldn't cotton to the alleged ''world championship'' playoff between the NL and AA leaders. Miserable weather further plagued the series. After seven games, the whole thing was called off. By then, each team had won three and one was tied, so, appropriately enough, there was no clear-cut champion.

Result: Brooklyn NL won 3; Louisville AA, 3; 1 tie.

```
1st Game, at Louisville, Oct. 17           R.   H.   E.
Brooklyn (NL)    300  030  30    ---    9   11   1
Louisville (AA)  000  000  00    ---    0    2    6
               (called, end of 8th: darkness)
   Pitchers--TERRY vs. STRATTON. Attendance--5,600.

2nd Game, at Louisville, Oct. 18
Brooklyn (NL)    020  201  000   ---    5    5    3
Louisville (AA)  101  000  001   ---    3    6    5
   Pitchers--LOVETT vs. DAILY. Attendance--2,860.

3rd Game, at Louisville, Oct. 20
Brooklyn (NL)    020  130  10    ---    7    10   2
Louisville (AA)  001  102  03    ---    7    11   3
               (called, end of 8th: darkness)
   Pitchers--Terry vs Stratton, Meakim (4). Attendance
--2,500.

4th Game, at Louisville, Oct. 21
Brooklyn (NL)    031  000  000   ---    4    7    2
Louisville (AA)  301  000  10x   ---    5    9    2
   Pitchers--LOVETT vs. EHRET. Attendance--1,050.

5th Game, at Brooklyn, Oct. 25
Louisville (AA)  010  010  000   ---    2    5    6
Brooklyn (NL)    210  200  20x   ---    7    7    0
   Pitchers--DAILY vs. LOVETT. Homer--Burns (Bklyn.).
Attendance--1,000.

6th Game, at Brooklyn, Oct. 27
Louisville (AA)  012  101  220   ---    9   13   3
Brooklyn (NL)    100  004  030   ---    8   12   3
   Pitchers--STRATTON, Ehret (7) vs. TERRY. Attend-
ance--600.

7th Game, at Brooklyn, Oct. 28
Louisville (AA)  103  000  020   ---    6    8    3
Brooklyn (NL)    200  000  000   ---    2    4    1
   Pitchers--EHRET vs. LOVETT. Attendance--300.
```

1892

Interleague bitterness over player raids prevented an AA-NL playoff in 1891. By the next year, the majors had amalgamated into one league, the 12-club NL. They used an artificial ''split season'' to create a ''world series,'' but the experiment was dropped after one trial. Cleveland's Spiders won the first-half pennant.

Boston won the second-half, and also had the best full-season record. The opening playoff game was a memorable 11-inning scoreless tie between two pitchers now in the Hall of Fame, Cy Young and Kid Nichols. Boston won the next five straight. No line scores are listed for this spurious World Series, nor for the similar Temple Cup games of the '90s.

Result: Boston NL won 5, Cleveland NL, 0; 1 tie.

1894

William C. Temple, a Pittsburgh sportsman, donated an expensive cup as prize for a post-season series between the NL champion and runner-up. Ned Hanlon's colorful, scrappy Baltimore Orioles refused to take this series seriously after winning the pennant. They didn't bother keeping in shape, and fell easy prey to the second place Giants.

Result: New York NL won 4; Baltimore NL, 0.

1895

Ned Hanlon's Orioles, still regarding the Temple Cub play as post-season exhibition games, bowed again as the runnerup Spiders cleaned up in five games.

Result: Cleveland NL won 4; Baltimore NL, 1.

1896

Stung by taunts of fans who wouldn't let them forget two straight playoff beatings, the Orioles captured their third straight pennant and then entered the Temple Cup set with calculated fury. Third baseman John McGraw and the rest of Baltimore's champions worked into tiptop shape for the October series. They perfected new strategy, including the notable cutoff play. Then they tore into Cleveland for vengeful 7-1, 7-2, 6-2 and 5-0 trouncings.

Result: Baltimore NL won 4; Cleveland NL, 0.

1897

Baltimore barely lost to Boston in the regular season, but the Orioles proved too strong in post-season play, with 54 runs in five games. Since the Temple Cup was one-sided for the fourth straight year, the event lost its flavor, so the league returned the cup to its donor with thanks and ended the unprofitable playoffs.

Result: Baltimore NL won 4; Boston NL, 1.

1903

Marking the end of AL-NL warfare, presidents of the pennant-winning clubs arranged a best five-out-of-nine Series. Pittsburgh had just won its third straight NL flag, but untimely injuries reduced the Pirate pitching staff to one effective operator, Deacon Phillippe. The Deacon pitched 44 innings and won three games, but couldn't carry the load alone. Boston lost three of the first four games, then won four straight to bring the crown to the new league. Bill Dinneen pitched three victories and Cy Young two for Boston.

Result: Boston AL won 5; Pittsburgh NL, 3.

1st Game, at Boston, Oct. 1					R.	H.	E.
Pittsburgh (NL)	401	100	100	---	7	12	2
Boston (AL)	000	000	201	---	3	6	4

Pitchers -- PHILLIPPE vs. YOUNG. Homer -- Sebring (Pitt.). Attendance--16,242.

2nd Game, at Boston, Oct. 2					R.	H.	E.
Pittsburgh (NL)	000	000	000	---	0	3	2
Boston (AL)	200	001	00x	---	3	9	0

Pitchers--LEEVER, Vail (2) vs. DINNEEN. Homers--Dougherty (Bos.) 2. Attendance--9,415.

3rd Game, at Boston, Oct. 3					R.	H.	E.
Pittsburgh (NL)	012	000	010	---	4	7	0
Boston (AL)	100	000	010	---	2	4	2

Pitchers--PHILLIPPE vs. HUGHES, Young (3). Attendance--18,801.

4th Game, at Pittsburgh, Oct. 6					R.	H.	E.
Boston (AL)	000	010	003	---	4	9	1
Pittsburgh (NL)	100	010	30x	---	5	12	1

Pitchers--DINNEEN vs. PHILLIPPE. Attend.--7,600.

5th Game, at Pittsburgh, Oct. 7					R.	H.	E.
Boston (AL)	000	006	410	---	11	14	2
Pittsburgh (NL)	000	000	020	---	2	6	4

Pitchers--YOUNG vs. KENNEDY, Thompson (8). Attendance--12,322.

6th Game, at Pittsburgh, Oct. 8
```
Boston (AL)     003  020  100    ---    6  10  1
Pittsburgh (NL) 000  000  300    --     3  10  3
```
Pitchers--DINEEN vs. LEEVER. Attendance--11,556.

7th Game, at Pittsburgh, Oct. 10
```
Boston (AL)     200  202  010    ---    7  11  4
Pittsburgh (NL) 000  101  001    ---    3  10  3
```
Pitchers--YOUNG vs. PHILLIPPE. Attend.--17,038.

8th Game, at Boston, Oct. 13
```
Pittsburgh (NL) 000  000  000    ---    0  4  3
Boston (AL)     000  201  00x    ---    3  8  0
```
Pitchers--PHILLIPPE vs. DINEEN. Attend.--7,455.

1905

Owner John T. Brush and manager John J. McGraw of the Giants felt such personal bitterness toward the "upstart" American League that they refused to let their 1904 NL champions meet Boston's repeating AL winners. Giant players petitioned in vain to have the series played. However, fans and writers criticized Brush so severely that he later drew up the Brush Rules to govern annual post-season playoffs. These regulations are the same ones that are used today, with few exceptions. Brush's Giants happened to repeat in 1905, so they became the first NL team to play under the modern code. Connie Mack's Athletics furnished poor opposition, since Rube Waddell was sidelined with a lame arm. All five games ended in shutouts, with young Christy Mathewson wielding three of them.

Result: New York NL won 4; Philadelphia AL, 1.

1st Game, at Philadelphia, Oct. 9
```
                                 R.  H.  E.
New York (NL)    000  020  001    ---    3  10  1
Philadelphia(AL) 000  000  000    ---    0  4  0
```
Pitchers--MATHEWSON vs. PLANK. Attend.--17,955.

2nd Game, at New York, Oct. 10
```
Philadelphia(AL) 001  000  020    ---    3  6  2
New York (NL)    000  000  000    ---    0  4  2
```
Pitchers--BENDER vs. McGINNITY, Ames (9). Attendance--24,922.

3rd Game, at Philadelphia, Oct. 12
```
New York (NL)    200  050  002    ---    9  9  1
Philadelphia(AL) 000  000  000    ---    0  4  5
```
Pitchers--MATHEWSON vs. COAKLEY. Att.--10,991.

4th Game, at New York, Oct. 13
```
Philadelphia(AL) 000  000  000    ---    0  5  2
New York (NL)    000  100  00x    ---    1  4  1
```
Pitchers--PLANK vs. McGINNITY. Att.--13,598.

5th Game, at New York, Oct. 14
```
Philadelphia (AL)000  000  000    ---    0  6  0
New York (NL)    000  010  01x    ---    2  5  1
```
Pitchers--BENDER vs. MATHEWSON. Attend.--24,187.

1906

No upset in World Series history ever matched the one in this first intracity battle. The Cubs were favored after having won a record number of 116 games that gave them the NL flag by a margin of 20 games. The White Sox, mired in the second division at midseason, finished first only by virtue of a 19-game winning streak in the last month. The "Hitless Wonders" owned a season batting average of .228, ranking next to last in the majors. Yet outfielder-manager Fielder Jones' White Sox won the series in six games. A lowly substitute named George Rohe decided two games for them with triples, and hit .333. Ed Reulbach pitched a one-hitter and Three-Fingered Brown a two-hitter for the only Cub victories.

Result: Chicago AL won 4; Chicago NL, 2.

1st Game, at West Side Park, Chi., Oct. 9
```
                                 R.  H.  E.
Chicago (AL)    000  011  000    ---    2  4  1
Chicago (NL)    000  001  000    ---    1  4  2
```
Pitchers--ALTROCK vs. BROWN. Attendance--12,693.

2nd Game, at Comiskey Park, Chi., Oct. 10
```
Chicago (NL)    031  001  020    ---    7  10  2
Chicago (AL)    000  010  000    ---    1  1  2
```
Pitchers--REULBACH vs. WHITE, Owen. Att.--12,595.

3rd Game, at West Side Park, Chi., Oct. 11
```
Chicago (AL)    000  003  000    ---    3  4  1
Chicago (NL)    000  000  000    ---    0  2  2
```
Pitchers--WALSH vs. PFEISTER. Attendance--13,750.

4th Game, at Comiskey Park, Chi., Oct. 12
```
Chicago (NL)    000  000  100    ---    1  7  1
Chicago (AL)    000  000  000    ---    0  2  1
```
Pitchers--BROWN vs. ALTROCK. Attendance--18,385.

5th Game, at West Side Park, Chi., Oct. 13
```
Chicago (AL)    102  401  000    ---    8  12  6
Chicago (NL)    300  102  000    ---    6  6  0
```
Pitchers--WALSH, White (7) vs. Reulbach, PFEISTER (3), Overall (4). Attendance--23,257.

6th Game, at Comiskey Park, Chi., Oct. 14
```
Chicago (NL)    100  010  001    ---    3  7  0
Chicago (AL)    340  000  01x    ---    8  14  3
```
Pitchers--BROWN, Overall (2) vs. WHITE. Att.--19,249.

1907

Though a 20-year-old thunderbolt named Ty Cobb had just won his first of a dozen batting crowns, he was a .200 bust in the series, and his Tiger teammates collapsed with him. Hit-

ting hero with a .470 average was Harry Steinfeldt, underrated third baseman of the Cubs' legendary Tinker-Evers-Chance double play combination. Detroit would have won the opener if catcher Charley Schmidt hadn't muffed a third strike with two out in the ninth. Chicago capitalized with the two tying runs, and the game ended in a 12-inning deadlock. The Cubs easily bagged the next four games.

Result: Chicago NL won 4; Detroit AL, 0; 1 tie.

1st Game, at Chicago, Oct. 8
```
                                    R.  H.  E.
Detroit (AL)   000  000  030  000  ---   3   9   3
Chicago (NL)   000  100  002  000  ---   3  10   5
          (called, end of 12th: darkness)
  Pitchers--Donovan vs. Overall, Reulbach (10). Attend-
ance--24,377.
```

2nd Game, at Chicago, Oct. 9
```
Detroit (AL)   010  000  000   ---   1   9   1
Chicago (NL)   010  200  00x   ---   3   9   1
  Pitchers--MULLIN vs. PFEISTER. Attend.--21,901.
```

3rd Game, at Chicago, Oct. 10
```
Detroit (AL)   000  001  000   ---   1   6   1
Chicago (NL)   010  310  00x   ---   5  10   1
  Pitchers--SIEVER, Killian (5) vs. REULBACH. Attend-
ance--13,114.
```

4th Game, at Detroit, Oct. 11
```
Chicago (NL)   000  020  301   ---   6   7   2
Detroit (AL)   000  100  000   ---   1   5   2
  Pitchers--OVERALL vs. DONOVAN. Attend.--11,306.
```

5th Game, at Detroit, Oct. 12
```
Chicago (NL)   110  000  000   ---   2   7   1
Detroit (AL)   000  000  000   ---   0   7   2
  Pitchers--BROWN vs. MULLIN. Attendance--7,370.
```

1908

After winning the pennant on the last day of the season, the Tigers ran into their series nemesis and lost again in five games. Manager-first baseman Frank Chance, whose Cubs clinched the pennant in a playoff of the "Merkle Boner" game with the Giants, led his team with a .421 batting average and five stolen bases. Orvie Overall and Three-Fingered Brown each pitched a shutout and won one other decision.

Result: Chicago NL won 4; Detroit AL, 1.

1st Game, at Detroit, Oct. 10
```
                                    R.  H.  E.
Chicago (NL)   004  000  105   ---  10  14   2
Detroit (AL)   100  000  320   ---   6  10   4
  Pitchers--Reulbach, Overall (7), BROWN (8) vs. Killian,
SUMMERS (3). Attendance--10,812.
```

2nd Game, at Chicago, Oct. 11
```
Detroit (AL)   000  000  001   ---   1   4   1
Chicago (NL)   000  000  06x   ---   6   7   1
  Pitchers--DONOVAN vs. OVERALL. Homer--Tinker
(Chi.). Attendance--17,760.
```

3rd Game, at Chicago, Oct. 12
```
Detroit (AL)   100  005  020   ---   8  11   4
Chicago (NL)   000  300  000   ---   3   7   2
  Pitchers--MULLIN vs. PFEISTER, Reulbach (9). Attend-
ance--14,543.
```

4th Game, at Detroit, Oct. 13
```
Chicago (NL)   002  000  001   ---   3  10   0
Detroit (AL)   000  000  000   ---   0   4   1
  Pitchers--BROWN vs. SUMMERS, Winter (9). Attend-
ance--12,907.
```

5th Game, at Detroit, Oct. 14
```
Chicago (NL)   100  010  000   ---   2  10   0
Detroit (AL)   000  000  000   ---   0   3   0
  Pitchers--OVERALL vs. DONOVAN. Attend.--6,210.
```

1909

After winning 66 games for Pittsburgh in the regular season, Howie Camnitz, Vic Willis and Lefty Leifield failed to take a series game. But freshman righthander Charles (Babe) Adams whipped the Tigers three times. In the only direct offensive duel between those diamond immortals, Honus Wagner of Pittsburgh surpassed Ty Cobb. Wagner hit .333 stole six bases. Cobb hit only .231 and stole one base, a daring dash home which helped win the second game.

Result: Pittsburgh NL won 4; Detroit AL, 3.

1st Game, at Pittsburgh, Oct. 8
```
                                  R.  H.  E.
Detroit (AL)     100  000  000  ---   1   6   4
Pittsburgh (NL)  000  120  00x  ---   4   5   0
  Pitchers--MULLIN vs. ADAMS. Homer--Clarke (Pitt.).
Attendance--29,264.
```

2nd Game, at Pittsburgh, Oct. 9
```
Detroit (AL)     023  020  000  ---   7   9   3
Pittsburgh (NL)  200  000  000  ---   2   5   1
  Pitchers--DONOVAN vs. CAMNITZ, Willis (3). Attend-
ance--30,915.
```

3rd Game, at Detroit, Oct. 11
```
Pittsburgh (NL)  510  000  002  ---   8  10   3
Detroit (AL)     000  000  402  ---   6  10   5
  Pitchers--MADDOX vs. SUMMERS, Willett (1), Works
(8). Attendance--18,277.
```

4th Game, at Detroit, Oct. 12
```
Pittsburgh (NL)  000  000  000  ---   0   5   6
Detroit (AL)     020  300  00x  ---   5   8   0
  Pitchers--LEIFIELD, Phillippe (5) vs. MULLIN. At-
tendance--17,036.
```

5th Game, at Pittsburgh, Oct 13
```
Detroit (AL)     100  002  010  ---   4   6   1
Pittsburgh (NL)  111  000  41x  ---   8  10   2
  Pitchers--SUMMERS, Willett (8) vs. ADAMS. Homers--
D. Jones (Det.), Crawford (Det.), Clarke (Pitts.). Attend-
ance--21,706.
```

6th Game, at Detroit, Oct. 14
```
Pittsburgh (NL)  300  000  001  ---   4   7   3
Detroit (AL)     100  211  00x  ---   5  10   3
  Pitchers--WILLIS, Camnitz (6), Phillippe (7) vs. MUL-
LIN. Attendance--10,535.
```

7th Game, at Detroit, Oct. 16
```
Pittsburgh (NL)  020  203  010  ---   8   7   0
Detroit (AL)     000  000  000  ---   0   6   3
  Pitchers--ADAMS vs. DONOVAN, Mullin (4). Attend-
ance--17,562.
```

1910

After winning the pennant for the fourth time in five years, the veteran Cubs ran into a series ambush by the young Athletics and were thrashed in five games. Philadelphia averaged seven runs a game and feasted on Cub hurling for a .317 average. Jack Coombs posted three victories and Eddie Collins hit .429.

Result: Philadelphia AL won 4; Chicago NL, 1.

1st Game, at Philadelphia, Oct. 17					R.	H.	E.
Chicago (NL)	000	000	001	---	1	3	1
Philadelphia(AL)	021	000	01x	---	4	7	2

Pitchers--OVERALL, McIntire (4) vs. BENDER. Attendance--26,891.

2nd Game, at Philadelphia, Oct. 18							
Chicago (NL)	100	000	101	---	3	8	3
Philadelphia(AL)	002	010	60x	---	9	14	4

Pitchers--BROWN, Richie (8) vs. COOMBS. Attendance--24,597.

3rd Game, at Chicago, Oct. 20							
Philadelphia(AL)	125	000	400	---	12	15	1
Chicago (NL)	120	000	020	---	5	6	5

Pitchers -- COOMBS vs. Reulbach, McINTIRE (3), Pfeister (3). Homer -- Murphy (Phila.). Attend.--26,210.

4th Game, at Chicago, Oct. 22							
Philadelphia(AL)	001	200	000	0	---	3	11	3
Chicago (NL)	100	100	001	1	---	4	9	1

Pitchers--BENDER vs. Cole, BROWN (9). Attendance--19,150.

5th Game, at Chicago, Oct. 23							
Philadelphia(AL)	100	010	050	---	7	9	1
Chicago (NL)	010	000	010	---	2	9	2

Pitchers--COOMBS vs. BROWN. Attendance--27,374.

1911

John Franklin Baker, third baseman for the A's, earned the nickname "Home Run" in this series. His four-base blasts beat Rube Marquard in the second game and Christy Mathewson in the third. Though the Giants had stolen 347 bases from NL rivals, they took no such liberties against A's catching. Every game was a pitching duel till the finale, when the A's hammered three hurlers for 13 hits and 13 runs that brought Chief Bender an easy decision. Giant cleanup hitter Jack Murray went 21-for-0 at the plate.

Result: Philadelphia AL won 4; New York NL, 2.

1st Game, at New York, Oct. 14					R.	H.	E.
Philadelphia(AL)	010	000	000	---	1	6	2
New York (NL)	000	100	10x	---	2	5	0

Pitchers--BENDER vs. MATHEWSON. Att.--38,281.

2nd Game, at Philadelphia, Oct. 16							
New York (NL)	010	000	000	---	1	5	3
Philadelphia(AL)	100	002	00x	---	3	4	0

Pitchers--MARQUARD, Crandall (8) vs. PLANK. Homer--Baker (Phil.). Attendance--26,286.

3rd Game, at Philadelphia, Oct. 17							
Philadelphia(AL)	000	000	001	02	---	3	9	2
New York (NL)	001	000	000	01	---	2	3	5

Pitchers--COOMBS vs. MATHEWSON. Homer--Baker (Phil.). Attendance--37,216.

4th Game, at Philadelphia, Oct. 24							
New York (NL)	200	000	000	---	2	7	3
Philadelphia(AL)	000	310	00x	---	4	11	1

Pitchers--MATHEWSON, Wiltse (8) vs. BENDER. Attendance--24,355.

5th Game, at New York, Oct. 25							
Philadelphia(AL)	000	000	000	0	---	3	7	1
New York (NL)	000	000	102	1	---	4	9	2

Pitchers--Coombs, PLANK (10) vs. Marquard, Ames (4), CRANDALL (8). Homer--Oldring (Phil.). Attendance--33,228.

6th Game, at Philadelphia, Oct. 26							
New York (NL)	100	000	001	---	2	4	3
Philadelphia(AL)	001	401	70x	---	13	13	5

Pitchers--AMES, Wiltse (5), Marquard (7) vs. BENDER. Attendance--20,485.

1912

Behind, three games to one, the Giants rallied to win the next two and practically clinched the title with a 2-1 lead behind Matty in the 10th inning of the last game. In the fateful last half, outfielder Fred Snodgrass muffed a lazy fly by Clyde Engle, Red Sox pinch hitter. On the next play, Snodgrass speared Harry Hooper's deep drive. Steve Yerkes walked. Tris Speaker's simple foul fell between Chief Meyers and Fred Merkle, though either could have caught the ball while shaking hands with the other. Speaker then lined a single to score Engle with the tying run. Duffy Lewis was passed intentionally, and Larry Gardner flied to Josh Devore in deep right, Yerkes scoring after the catch for the winning tally. This marked the third victory of the series for Smoky Joe Wood, who had posted a phenomenal 34-5 season mark for the Sox.

Result: Boston AL won 4; New York NL, 3; 1 tie.

1st Game, at New York, Oct. 8					R.	H.	E.
Boston (AL)	000	001	300	---	4	6	1
New York (NL)	002	000	001	---	3	8	1

Pitchers--WOOD vs. TESREAU, Crandall (8). Attendance--35,730.

2nd Game, at Boston, Oct. 9
New York (NL) 010 100 030 10 --- 6 11 5
Boston (AL)   300 010 010 10 --- 6 10 1
(called, end of 11th: darkness)
Pitchers--Mathewson vs. Collins, Hall (8). Bedient (11). Attendance--30,148.

3rd Game, at Boston, Oct. 10
New York (NL) 010 010 000 --- 2 7 1
Boston (AL)   000 000 001 --- 1 7 0
Pitchers--MARQUARD vs. O'BRIEN, Bedient (9). Attendance--36,624.

4th Game, at New York, Oct. 11
Boston (AL)   010 100 001 --- 3 8 1
New York (NL) 000 000 100 --- 1 9 2
Pitchers--WOOD vs. TESREAU, Ames (8). Attendance --36,502.

5th Game, at Boston, Oct. 12
New York (NL) 000 000 100 --- 1 3 1
Boston (AL)   002 000 00x --- 2 5 1
Pitchers--MATHEWSON vs. BEDIENT. Att.--34,683.

6th Game, at New York, Oct. 14
Boston (AL)   020 000 000 --- 2 7 2
New York (NL) 500 000 00x --- 5 11 2
Pitchers--O'BRIEN, Collins (2) vs. MARQUARD. Attendance--30,622.

7th Game, at Boston, Oct. 15
New York (NL) 610 002 101 --- 11 16 4
Boston (AL)   010 000 210 --- 4 9 3
Pitchers--TESREAU vs. WOOD, Hall (2). Homers--Doyle (N. Y.), Gardner (Bos.). Attendance--32,694.

8th Game, at Boston, Oct. 16
New York (NL) 001 000 000 1 --- 2 9 2
Boston (AL)   000 000 100 2 --- 3 8 5
Pitchers--MATHEWSON vs. Bedient, WOOD (8). Attendance--17,034.

1913

A series of injuries ruined Giant chances. Their only victory was a 10-inning shutout by Mathewson. The A's really romped, with another home run for Baker, who hit .450, plus a .421 average for Eddie Collins. Chief Bender won two; Eddie Plank pitched a two-hitter to top his rival of college days, Matty, and 20-year-old Bullet Joe Bush won his only start handily.

Result: Philadelphia AL won 4; New York NL, 1.

1st Game, at New York, Oct. 7   R. H. E.
Philadelphia(AL) 000 320 010 --- 6 11 1
New York (NL)   001 030 000 --- 4 11 0
Pitchers--BENDER vs. MARQUARD, Crandall (6), Tesreau (8). Homer--Baker (Phil.). Attend.--36,291.

2nd Game, at Philadelphia, Oct. 8
New York (NL)   000 000 000 3 --- 3 7 2
Philadelphia(AL) 000 000 000 0 --- 0 8 2
Pitchers--MATHEWSON vs. PLANK. Attend.--20,563.

3rd Game, at New York, Oct. 9
Philadelphia(AL) 320 000 210 --- 8 12 1
New York (NL)   000 010 100 --- 2 5 1
Pitchers--BUSH vs. TESREAU, Crandall (7). Homer--Schang (Phil.). Attendance--36,896.

4th Game, at Philadelphia, Oct. 10
New York (NL)   000 000 320 --- 5 8 2
Philadelphia(AL) 010 320 00x --- 6 9 0
Pitchers--MARQUARD vs. BENDER. Homer--Merkle (N. Y.). Attendance--20,568.

5th Game, at Philadelphia, Oct. 11
Philadelphia(AL) 102 000 000 --- 3 6 1
New York (NL)   000 010 000 --- 1 2 2
Pitchers--PLANK vs. MATHEWSON. Attend.--36,682.

1914

Rising from the cellar in mid-July to the pennant in September, the Boston Braves "Miracle Team" kept their magic touch through the Fall classic. They swept the vaunted A's, $100,000 infield and all. Connie Mack was so shocked that he broke up his star-studded squad the next season. Boston's dependable mound trio of Dick Rudolph, Bill James and George Tyler held the A's to a collective BA of .172. Hank Gowdy went on a .545 hitting rampage for Boston with five walks, a single, three doubles, a triple and homer.

Result: Boston NL won 4; Philadelphia AL, 0.

1st Game, at Philadelphia, Oct. 9   R. H. E.
Boston (NL)   020 013 010 --- 7 11 2
Philadelphia(AL) 010 000 000 --- 1 5 0
Pitchers--RUDOLPH vs. BENDER, Wyckoff (6). Attendance--20,562.

2nd Game, at Philadelphia, Oct. 10
Boston (NL)   000 000 001 --- 1 7 1
Philadelphia(AL) 000 000 000 --- 0 2 1
Pitchers--JAMES vs. PLANK. Attendance--20,562.

3rd Game, at Boston, Oct. 12
Philadelphia(AL) 100 100 000 200 --- 4 8 2
Boston (NL)   010 100 000 201 --- 5 9 1
Pitchers--BUSH vs. Tyler, JAMES (11). Homer--Gowdy (Bos.). Attendance--35,520.

4th Game, at Boston, Oct. 13
Philadelphia(AL) 000 010 000 --- 1 7 0
Boston (NL)   000 120 .00x --- 3 6 0
Pitchers--SHAWKEY, Pennock (6) vs. RUDOLPH. Attend. --34,365.

1915

Grover Alexander's 31 victories earned the Phils their first pennant. Alex proceeded to shade Ernie Shore of the Red Sox in the series opener. But Boston bounced back to win the next four, each by one run. Woodrow Wilson, first U. S. President to attend a World Series, threw out the first ball in the second game. A rookie named George Herman Ruth had led the AL with a won-lost of 18-6, but manager Bill Carrigan wouldn't risk him in series competition beyond one unsuccessful pinch-hitting appearance.

Result: Boston AL won 4; Philadelphia NL, 1.

1st Game, at Philadelphia, Oct. 8   R.   H.   E.
Boston (AL)   000   000   010   ---   1   8   1
Philadelphia(NL) 000   100   02x   ---   3   5   1
    Pitchers--SHORE vs. ALEXANDER. Attend.--19,343.

2nd Game, at Philadelphia, Oct. 9
Boston (AL)   100   000   001   ---   2   10   0
Philadelphia(NL) 000   010   000   ---   1   3   1
    Pitchers--FOSTER vs. MAYER. Attendance--20,306.

3rd Game, at Boston, Oct. 11
Philadelphia(NL) 001   000   000   ---   1   3   0
Boston (AL)   000   100   001   ---   2   6   1
    Pitchers--ALEXANDER vs. LEONARD. Att.--42,300.

4th Game, at Boston, Oct. 12
Philadelphia(NL) 000   000   010   ---   1   7   0
Boston (AL)   001   001   00x   ---   2   8   1
    Pitchers--CHALMERS vs. SHORE. Attendance--41,096.

5th Game, at Philadelphia, Oct. 13
Boston (AL)   011   000   021   ---   5   10   1
Philadelphia(NL) 200   200   000   ---   4   9   1
    Pitchers--FOSTER vs. Mayer, RIXEY (3). Homers--
Hooper (Bos.) 2, Lewis (Bos.), Luderus (Phil.). At.--20,306.

1916

Brooklyn's plan to beat the Red Sox with southpaws failed. The only Dodger victory was notched by Jack Coombs, the old AL castoff, who thereby won his fifth series game while never being beaten. Duffy Lewis led the Boston batters and Casey Stengel was Brooklyn's hardest hitter. The second game turned out to be the longest in series history, 14 innings, with Babe Ruth blanking the Brooks after a first-inning homer by Hi Myers. Babe drove in the tying run two innings later. Boston won in the 14th when pinch-runner Mike McNally scored from first on a pinch double by Del Gainer.

Result: Boston AL won 4; Brooklyn NL, 1.

1st Game, at Boston, Oct. 7   R.   H.   E.
Brooklyn (NL)   000   100   004   ---   5   10   4
Boston (AL)   001   010   31x   ---   6   8   1
    Pitchers--MARQUARD, Pfeffer (8) vs. SHORE, Mays (9).
Attendance--36,117.

2nd Game, at Boston, Oct. 9
Brooklyn (NL)   100   000   000 000 00 --   1   6   2
Boston (AL)   001   000   000 000 01 --   2   7   1
    Pitchers--SMITH vs. RUTH. Homer--H. Myers (Bklyn.).
Attendance--41,373.

3rd Game, at Brooklyn, Oct. 10
Boston (AL)   000   002   100   ---   3   7   1
Brooklyn (NL)   001   120   00x   ---   4   10   0
    Pitchers--MAYS, Foster (6) vs. COOMBS, Pfeffer (7).
Homer--Gardner (Bos.). Attendance--21,087.

4th Game, at Brooklyn, Oct. 11
Boston (AL)   030   110   100   ---   6   10   1
Brooklyn (NL)   200   000   000   ---   2   5   4
    Pitchers--LEONARD vs. MARQUARD, Cheney (5),
Rucker (9). Homer--Gardner (Bos.). Attendance--21,662.

5th Game, at Boston, Oct. 12
Brooklyn (NL)   010   000   000   ---   1   3   3
Boston (AL)   012   010   00x   ---   4   7   2
    Pitchers--PFEFFER, Dell (8) vs. SHORE. Attendance--
42,620.

1917

This was a series of heroes and goats. Sometimes the same man was cheered and jeered. Urban Faber tried to steal second base with the bag already occupied, yet more than compensated for the boner by beating the Giants three times. Dave Robertson made a costly muff in the last game, yet the Giant right fielder led both teams with 11 for 22, or an even .500 batting average. Ferdie Schupp, knocked out of the box by the White Sox in less than two innings of the second game, came back to hurl a shutout in the fourth. Third baseman Heinie Zimmerman of the Giants was unjustly ridiculed for chasing Eddie Collins home with the deciding run of the last game, but the real goats were the catcher and first baseman, who had left the plate uncovered in the rundown play. Collins led the victorious Sox with a BA of .409.

Result: Chicago AL won 4; New York NL, 2.

1st Game, at Chicago, Oct. 6   R.   H.   E.
New York (NL)   000   010   000   ---   1   7   1
Chicago (AL)   001   100   00x   ---   2   7   1
    Pitchers -- SALLEE vs. CICOTTE. Homer -- Felsch
(Chi.). Attendance--32,000.

2nd Game, at Chicago, Oct. 7
New York (NL)   020   000   000   ---   2   8   1
Chicago (AL)   020   500   00x   ---   7   14   1
    Pitchers--Schupp, ANDERSON (2), Perritt (4), Tesreau
(8) vs. FABER. Attendance--32,000.

3rd Game, at New York, Oct. 10
Chicago (AL)   000   000   000   ---   0   5   3
New York (NL)   000   200   00x   ---   2   8   0
    Pitchers--CICOTTE vs. BENTON. Attendance--33,616.

4th Game, at New York, Oct. 11
Chicago (AL)   000   000   000   ---   0   7   0
New York (NL)   000   110   12x   ---   5   10   1
    Pitchers--FABER, Danforth (8) vs. SCHUPP. Homers--
Kauff (N.Y.) 2. Attendance--27,746.

5th Game, at Chicago, Oct. 13
New York (NL)   200   200   100   ---   5   12   3
Chicago (AL)   001   001   33x   ---   8   14   6
    Pitchers--SALLEE, Perritt (8) vs. Russell, Cicotte (1),
Williams (7), FABER (8). Attendance--27,323.

6th Game, at New York, Oct. 15
Chicago (AL)   000   300   001   ---   4   7   1
New York (NL)   000   020   000   ---   2   6   3
    Pitchers--FABER vs. BENTON, Perritt (6). Attendance
--33,969.

1918

In this war-curtailed season, the World Series continued only through special permission from the government. Many topnotch stars were in

the Service. George Whiteman, a wartime replacement, helped the Red Sox beat Chicago with five timely hits and several crucial catches. Babe Ruth and Carl Mays each won twice, with Babe extending his streak to an all-time record that still stands—29 consecutive scoreless innings. Ruth was held to only one hit in the series, but it was a triple that drove in two runs of a 3-2 decision in the fourth game. The start of the fifth game was delayed an hour by an unsuccessful player "strike" for a higher share of the receipts.

Result: Boston AL won 4; Chicago NL, 2.

```
1st Game, at Chicago, Sept. 5           R.  H.  E.
Boston (AL)     000  100  000   ---     1   5   0
Chicago (NL)    000  000  000   ---     0   6   0
  Pitchers--RUTH vs. VAUGHN. Attendance--19,274.

2nd Game, at Chicago, Sept. 6
Boston (AL)     000  000  001   ---     1   6   1
Chicago (NL)    030  000  00x   ---     3   7   1
  Pitchers--BUSH vs. TYLER. Attendance--20,040.

3rd Game, at Chicago, Sept. 7
Boston (AL)     000  200  000   ---     2   7   0
Chicago (NL)    000  010  000   ---     1   7   1
  Pitchers--MAYS vs. VAUGHN. Attendance--27,054.

4th Game, at Boston, Sept. 9
Chicago (NL)    000  000  020   ---     2   7   1
Boston (AL)     000  200  01x   ---     3   4   0
  Pitchers--Tyler, DOUGLASS (8) vs. RUTH, Bush (9).
Attendance--22,183.

5th Game, at Boston, Sept. 10
Chicago (NL)    001  000  002   ---     3   7   0
Boston (AL)     000  000  000   ---     0   5   0
  Pitchers--VAUGHN vs. JONES. Attendance--24,694.

6th Game, at Boston, Sept. 11
Chicago (NL)    000  100  000   ---     1   3   2
Boston (AL)     002  000  00x   ---     2   5   0
  Pitchers--TYLER, Hendrix (8) vs. MAYS. Attendance--
15,238.
```

1919

Post-war interest in baseball was so high that the series was stretched to best-five-out-of-nine. Chicago's White Sox and the Cincinnati Reds had outclassed their league rivals completely. What should have been a memorable struggle between champions turned out to be one of the most shameful events in sports history, because eight players of the favored Sox "sold out" to gamblers. Ed Cicotte, one of the notorious "Black Sox" later dropped by organized baseball, was knocked out of the box in the opening game. Little Dickie

Kerr bravely tried to hold off the Reds and won twice. But Chicago was ruined by the conspirators and lost in eight games. Strangely, Shoeless Joe Jackson led his team with a .375 average even though he was in on the shady deal. Earle (Greasy) Neale, later a famous football coach, led the Reds with .357.

Result: Cincinnati NL won 5; Chicago AL, 3.

```
1st Game, at Cincinnati, Oct. 1         R.  H.  E.
Chicago (AL)    010  000  000   ---     1   6   1
Cincinnati (NL) 100  500  21x   ---     9  14   1
  Pitchers--CICOTTE, Wilkinson (4), Lowdermilk (8) vs.
RUETHER. Attendance--30,511.

2nd Game, at Cincinnati, Oct. 2
Chicago (AL)    000  000  200   ---     2  10   1
Cincinnati (NL) 000  301  00x   ---     4   4   2
  Pitchers--WILLIAMS vs. SALLEE. Attend.--29,690.

3rd Game, at Chicago, Oct. 3
Cincinnati (NL) 000  000  000   ---     0   3   1
Chicago (AL)    020  100  00x   ---     3   7   0
  Pitchers--FISHER, Luque (8) vs. KERR. Att.--29,126.

4th Game, at Chicago, Oct. 4
Cincinnati (NL) 000  020  000   ---     2   5   2
Chicago (AL)    000  000  000   ---     0   3   2
  Pitchers--RING vs. CICOTTE. Attendance--34,363.

5th Game, at Chicago, Oct. 6
Cincinnati (NL) 000  004  001   ---     5   4   0
Chicago (AL)    000  000  000   ---     0   3   3
  Pitchers--ELLER vs. WILLIAMS, Mayer (9). Attend-
ance--34,379.

6th Game, at Cincinnati, Oct. 7
Chicago (AL)    000  013  000  1 ---    5  10   3
Cincinnati (NL) 002  200  000  0 ---    4  11   0
  Pitchers--KERR vs. Ruether, RING (6). Att.--32,006.

7th Game, at Cincinnati, Oct. 8
Chicago (AL)    101  020  000   ---     4  10   1
Cincinnati (NL) 000  001  000   ---     1   7   4
  Pitchers--CICOTTE vs. SALLEE, Fisher (5), Luque (6).
Attendance--13,923.

8th Game, at Chicago, Oct. 9
Cincinnati (NL) 410  013  010   ---    10  16   2
Chicago (AL)    001  000  040   ---     5  10   1
  Pitchers--ELLER vs. WILLIAMS, James (1), Wilkinson
(6). Homer--Jackson (Chi.). Attendance--32,930.
```

1920

Player-manager Tris Speaker reached his greatest glory by leading the Indians to the world championship over the Dodgers. Cleveland's conquest was featured by that sturdy battery of former coal miners from Pennsylvania: spitball pitcher Stanley Coveleski, who pitched three complete-game victories and allowed exactly five hits each time, and catcher Steve O'Neill, who hit .333. Walter Mails, a Dodger castoff, hurled a three-hitter to shade Brooklyn's ace, Sherry Smith, 1-0. In the weird fifth

game, Brooklyn outhit Cleveland, yet lost, 8-1; Elmer Smith hit a grand slam homer, and Indian second baseman Bill Wambsganns executed an unassisted triple play.

Result: Cleveland AL won 5; Brooklyn NL, 2.

1st Game, at Brooklyn, Oct. 5   R. H. E.
Cleveland (AL) 020 100 000 --- 3 5 0
Brooklyn (NL)   000 000 100 --- 1 5 1
  Pitchers--COVELESKI vs. MARQUARD, Mamaux (7). Cadore (9). Attendance--23,573.

2nd Game, at Brooklyn, Oct. 6
Cleveland (AL) 000 000 000 --- 0 7 1
Brooklyn (NL)   101 010 00x --- 3 7 0
  Pitchers--BAGBY, Uhle (7) vs. GRIMES. Att.--22,559.

3rd Game, at Brooklyn, Oct. 7
Cleveland (AL) 000 100 000 --- 1 3 1
Brooklyn (NL)   200 000 00x --- 2 6 1
  Pitchers--CALDWELL, Mails (1), Uhle (8) vs. SMITH. Attendance--25,088.

4th Game, at Cleveland, Oct. 9
Brooklyn (NL)   000 100 000 --- 1 5 1
Cleveland (AL) 202 001 00x --- 5 12 2
  Pitchers--CADORE, Mamaux (2), Marquard (3), Pfeffer (6) vs. COVELESKI. Attendance--25,734.

5th Game, at Cleveland, Oct. 10
Brooklyn (NL)   000 000 001 --- 1 13 1
Cleveland (AL) 400 310 00x --- 8 12 2
  Pitchers--GRIMES, Mitchell (4) vs BAGBY. Homers--E. Smith (Clev.), Bagby (Clev.). Attendance--26,884.

6th Game, at Cleveland, Oct. 11
Brooklyn (NL)   000 000 000 --- 0 3 0
Cleveland (AL) 000 001 00x --- 1 7 3
  Pitchers--SMITH vs. MAILS. Attendance--27,194.

7th Game, at Cleveland, Oct. 12
Brooklyn (NL)   000 000 000 --- 0 5 2
Cleveland (AL) 000 110 10x --- 3 7 3
  Pitchers--GRIMES, Mamaux (8) vs. COVELESKI. Attendance--27,525.

1921

The Yankees, later to dominate the World Series scene, won their first league title but failed to beat the Giants in an all-New York series. Successive shutouts by Carl Mays and Waite Hoyt gave the Yankees a two-game edge. Then the Giants found their batting eye and evened up the series. Hoyt won the fifth game, too, but Babe Ruth wrenched his knee and was lost to the Yanks. The Giants rallied to capture the next three games and the title. Hoyt, who hurled 27 innings in this series without an earned run, lost a 1-0 duel with Art Nehf in the finale.

Result: New York NL won 5; New York AL, 3.

1st Game, at Polo Grounds, N. Y., Oct. 5   R. H. E.
New York (AL)   100 010 000 --- 3 7 0
New York (NL)   000 000 000 --- 0 5 0
  Pitchers--MAYS vs. DOUGLAS, Barnes (9). Attendance --30,202.

2nd Game, at Polo Grounds, N. Y., Oct. 6
New York (NL)   000 000 000 --- 0 2 3
New York (AL)   000 100 02x --- 3 3 0
  Pitchers--NEHF vs. HOYT. Attendance--34,939.

3rd Game, at Polo Grounds, N. Y., Oct. 7
New York (AL)   004 000 010 --- 5 8 0
New York (NL)   004 000 81x --- 13 20 0
  Pitchers--Shawkey, QUINN (3), Collins (7), Rogers (8) vs. Toney, BARNES (3). Attendance--36,509.

4th Game, at Polo Grounds, N. Y., Oct. 9
New York (NL)   000 000 031 --- 4 9 1
New York (AL)   000 010 001 --- 2 7 1
  Pitchers--DOUGLAS vs. MAYS. Homer--Ruth (AL). Attendance--36,372.

5th Game, at Polo Grounds, N. Y., Oct. 10
New York (AL)   001 200 000 --- 3 6 1
New York (NL)   100 000 000 --- 1 10 1
  Pitchers--HOYT vs. NEHF. Attendance--35,758.

6th Game, at Polo Grounds, N. Y., Oct. 11
New York (NL)   030 401 000 --- 8 13 0
New York (AL)   320 000 000 --- 5 7 2
  Pitchers--Toney, BARNES (1) vs. Harper, SHAWKEY (2), Piercy (9). Homers--E. Meusel (NL), Snyder (NL), Fewster (AL). Attendance--34,283.

7th Game, at Polo Grounds, N. Y., Oct. 12
New York (AL)   010 000 000 --- 1 8 1
New York (NL)   000 100 10x --- 2 6 0
  Pitchers--MAYS vs. DOUGLAS. Attendance--36,503.

8th Game, at Polo Grounds, N. Y., Oct. 13
New York (NL)   100 000 000 --- 1 6 0
New York (AL)   000 000 000 --_ 0 4 1
  Pitchers--NEHF vs. HOYT. Attendance--25,410.

1922

Giant pitchers held the Yankees to a .203 batting average, Babe Ruth himself being shackled at .118. Poor baserunning further hampered the Yanks, and the best they could do was tie one game. The second match was called at 3-3 after 10 innings because of "darkness." Since there was still half an hour of daylight left, fans booed the game's untimely ending so heavily that Commissioner Landis ordered the gate receipts that day, about $120,000, turned over to charity. Heavy Giant hitting was paced by Heinie Groh's .474 and Frankie Frisch's .471.

Result: New York NL won 4; New York AL, 0; 1 tie.

1st Game, at Polo Grounds, N. Y., Oct. 4   R. H. E.
New York (AL)   000 001 100 --- 2 7 0
New York (NL)   000 000 03x --- 3 11 3
  Pitchers--BUSH, Hoyt (8) vs. Nehf, RYAN (8). Attendance--36,514.

2nd Game, at Polo Grounds, N. Y., Oct. 5
New York (NL)   300 000 000 0 --- 3 8 1
New York (AL)   100 100 010 0 --- 3 8 0
  (called, end of 10th; darkness)
  Pitchers--Barnes vs. Shawkey. Homers--E. Meusel (NL), Ward (AL). Attendance--37,020.

3rd Game, at Polo Grounds, N. Y., Oct. 6
New York (AL)   000 000 000 --- 0 4 1
New York (NL)   002 000 10x --- 3 12 1
  Pitchers--HOYT, Jones (8) vs. J. SCOTT. Att.--37,620.

4th Game, at Polo Grounds, N. Y., Oct. 7
New York (NL) 000 040 000   --- "4   9   1
New York (AL) 200 000 100   ---   3   8   0
  Pitchers--McQUILLAN vs. MAYS, Jones (9). Homer--
Ward (AL). Attendance--36,242.

5th Game, at Polo Grounds, N. Y., Oct. 8
New York (AL) 100 010 100   ---   3   5   0
New York (NL) 020 000 03x   ---   5 10   0
  Pitchers--BUSH vs. NEHF. Attendance--38,551.

1923

The same rivals met for the third straight Fall, but this time there was a new setting and a different result. The Yankees now had their own Stadium and proceeded to bring it their first world championship banner. Outfielder Casey Stengel of the Giants, destined for fame as manager of Yankee champions more than a quarter century later, accounted for the only two NL victories with timely homers. Herb Pennock pitched two complete game victories and saved another for the Yanks in relief. Babe Ruth featured this first million-dollar Series with three homers, a triple, a double, three singles and eight walks.

Result: New York AL won 4; New York NL, 2.

1st Game, at Yankee Stadium, N. Y., Oct. 10 R. H. E.
New York (NL) 004 000 001   ---   5   8   0
New York (AL) 120 000 100   ---   4 12   1
  Pitchers--Watson, RYAN (3) vs. Hoyt, BUSH (3). Homer
--Stengel (NL). Attendance--55,307.

2nd Game, at Polo Grounds, N. Y., Oct. 11
New York (AL) 010 210 000   ---   4 10   0
New York (NL) 010 001 000   ---   2   9   2
  Pitchers -- PENNOCK vs. McQUILLAN, Bentley (4).
Homers--Ward (AL), E. Meusel (NL), Ruth (AL) 2. Attend-
ance--40,402.

3rd Game, at Yankee Stadium, N. Y., Oct. 12
New York (NL) 000 000 100   ---   1   4   0
New York (AL) 000 000 000   ---   0   6   1
  Pitchers--NEHF vs. JONES, Bush (8). Homer--Stengel
(NL). Attendance--62,430.

4th Game, at Polo Grounds, N. Y., Oct. 13
New York (AL) 061 100 000   ---   8 13   1
New York (NL) 000 000 031   ---   4 13   1
  Pitchers--SHAWKEY, Pennock (8) vs. J. SCOTT, Ryan
(2), McQuillan (3), Jonnard (8), Barnes (9). Homer--Youngs
(NL). Attendance--46,302.

5th Game, at Yankee Stadium, N. Y., Oct. 14
New York (NL) 010 000 000   ---   1   3   2
New York (AL) 340 100 00x   ---   8 14   0
  Pitchers--BENTLEY, J. Scott (2), Barnes (8) vs. BUSH.
Homer--Dugan (AL). Attendance--62,817.

6th Game, at Polo Grounds, N. Y., Oct. 15
New York (AL) 100 000 050   ---   6   5   0
New York (NL) 100 111 000   ---   4 10   1
  Pitchers--PENNOCK, Jones (8) vs. NEHF, Ryan (8),
Homers--Ruth (AL), Snyder (NL). Attendance--34,172.

1924

Second baseman Bucky Harris was only 27, and in his first year as manager, when he brought Washington its first flag. In the Series he conquered John McGraw's last pennant club by the barest margin. The opener went to the Giants, 4-3, with old Walter Johnson bowing to Art Nehf in 12 innings. The seventh and deciding game also was a 12-inning, 4-3 affair, but this time Johnson, appearing in his first World Series after 18 seasons with the Senators, was the winner. The last game saw the Giants suffer three bad breaks: in the eighth, Harris' grounder took a sudden hop over the head of the substitute third baseman Fred Lindstrom, allowing the two tying runs to score; in the 12th, Giant catcher Hank Gowdy dropped a foul fly when he accidentally stepped on his mask, and on the last play of the series Earl McNeely's grounder took a sharp bounce over Lindstrom's head to send in the winning run.

Result: Washington AL won 4; New York NL, 3.

1st Game, at Washington, Oct. 4   R. H. E.
New York (NL)   010 100 000 002 ---   4 14   1
Washington (AL) 001 001 001 001 ---   3 10   1
  Pitchers--NEHF vs. JOHNSON. Homers--Kelly (N.Y.),
Terry (N.Y.). Attendance--35,760.

2nd Game, at Washington, Oct. 5
New York (NL)   000 000 102   ---   3   6   0
Washington (AL) 200 010 001   ---   4   6   1
  Pitchers--BENTLEY vs. ZACHARY, Marberry (9). Hom-
ers--Gosslin (Wash.), Harris (Wash.). Attend.--35,922.

3rd Game, at New York, Oct. 6
Washington (AL) 000 200 011   ---   4   9   2
New York (NL)   021 101 01x   ---   6 12   0

  Pitchers - - MARBERRY, Russell (4),
Martina (7), Speece (8) vs. McQuillan, RYAN
(4), Jonnard (9), Watson (9). Homer - -
Ryan (N.Y.). Attendance - - 47,608.

4th Game, at New York, Oct. 7
Washington (AL) 003 020 020   ---   7 13   3
New York (NL)   100 001 011   ---   4   6   1
  Pitchers--MOGRIDGE, Marberry (8) vs. BARNES, Bald-
win (6), Dean (8). Homer--Goslin (Wash.). Att.--49,243.

5th Game, at New York, Oct. 8
Washington (AL) 000 100 010   ---   2   9   1
New York (NL)   001 020 03x   ---   6 13   0
  Pitchers--JOHNSON vs. BENTLEY. Homers--Goslin (Wash.),
ers--Bentley (N.Y.), Goslin (Wash.). Attend.--49,211.

6th Game, at Washington, Oct. 9
New York (NL)   100 000 000   ---   1   7   1
Washington (AL) 000 020 00x   ---   2   4   0
  Pitchers--NEHF, Ryan (8) vs. ZACHARY. Attendance
--34,254.

7th Game, at Washington, Oct. 10
New York (NL)   000 003 100 000   ---   3   8   3
Washington (AL) 000 100' 020 001   ---   4 10   4
  Pitchers--Barnes, McQuillan (8), Nehf (10), BENTLEY
(11) vs. Ogden, Mogridge (1), Marberry (6), JOHNSON (9).
Homer--Harris (Wash.). Attendance--31,667.

1925

On the verge of extinction several times, Pittsburgh rallied to upset Washington in seven games. Walter Johnson won the opener. His shutout in the fourth gave the Senators a 3-1 edge. But Pittsburgh swept the next three, with Johnson the subject of a sad form reversal in the finale. The gallant righthander couldn't put his usual stuff on the wet ball, this final rainy afternoon, so that the seven Senator runs were not enough. Kiki Cuyler doubled off him with bases loaded in the eighth to drive in the tying and winning runs. Roger Peckinpaugh was the Washington "goat" with eight errors.

Result: Pittsburgh NL won 4; Washington AL, 3.

```
1st Game, at Pittsburgh, Oct. 7          R.  H.  E.
Washington (AL) 010  020  001   ---      4   8   1
Pittsburgh (NL) 000  010  000   ---      1   5   0
  Pitchers--JOHNSON vs. MEADOWS, Morrison (9). Hom-
ers--J. Harris (Wash.), Traynor (Pitt.). Att.--41,723.

2nd Game, at Pittsburgh, Oct. 8
Washington (AL) 010  000  001   ---      2   8   2
Pittsburgh (NL) 000  100  02x   ---      3   7   0
  Pitchers -- COVELESKIE vs. ALDRIDGE. Homers --
Judge (Wash.), Wright (Pitt.), Cuyler (Pitt.). Att.--43,364.

3rd Game, at Washington, Oct. 10
Pittsburgh (NL) 010  101  000   ---      3   8   3
Washington (AL) 001  001  20x   ---      4  10   1
  Pitchers -- KREMER vs. FERGUSON, Marberry (8).
Homer--Goslin (Wash.). Attendance--36,495.

4th Game, at Washington, Oct. 11
Pittsburgh (NL) 000  000  000   ---      0   6   1
Washington (AL) 004  000  00x   ---      4  12   0
  Pitchers--YDE, Morrison (3) Adams (8) vs. JOHNSON.
Homers--Goslin (Wash.), J. Harris (Wash.). Att.--38,701.

5th Game, at Washington, Oct. 12
Pittsburgh (NL) 002  000  211   ---      6  13   0
Washington (AL) 100  100  100   ---      3   8   1
  Pitchers--ALDRIDGE vs. COVELESKIE, Ballou (7),
Zachary (8), Marberry (9). Homer--J. Harris (Wash.). At-
tendance--35,899.

6th Game, at Pittsburgh, Oct. 13
Washington (AL) 110  000  000   ---      2   6   2
Pittsburgh (NL) 002  010  00x   ---      3   7   1
  Pitchers--FERGUSON, Ballou (8) vs. KREMER. Homers
--Goslin (Wash.), Moore (Pitt.). Attendance--43,810.

7th Game, at Pittsburgh, Oct. 15
Washington (AL) 400  200  010   ---      7   7   2
Pittsburgh (NL) 003  010  23x   ---      9  15   2
  Pitchers--JOHNSON vs. Aldridge, Morrison (1) KREMER
(5), Oldham (9). Homer--Peckinpaugh (Wash.). Attendance--
42,856.
```

1926

Led by Rogers Hornsby, St. Louis won its first NL pennant and upset the Yankees in the Series. Babe Ruth blasted four homers, three of them in one game, but 39-year-old Grover Alexander emerged as the legendary hero of this battle. Alex won the second and sixth games, then ambled out of the bullpen in the seventh inning of the seventh game to strike out Tony Lazzeri with bases loaded. He added two more hitless innings to seal the triumph.

Result: St. Louis NL won 4; New York AL, 3.

```
1st Game at New York, Oct. 2            R.  H.  E.
St. Louis (NL)  100  000  000   ---     1   3   1
New York (AL)   100  001  00x   ---     2   6   0
  Pitchers--SHERDEL, Haines (8) vs. PENNOCK. At-
tendance--61,658.

2nd Game, at New York, Oct. 3
St. Louis (NL)  002  000  301   ---     6  12   1
New York (AL)   020  000  000   ---     2   4   0
  Pitchers--ALEXANDER vs. SHOCKER, Shawkey (8),
Jones (9). Homers--Southworth (St. L.), Thevenow (St. L.).
Attendance--63,600.

3rd Game, at St. Louis, Oct. 5
New York (AL)   000  000  000   ---     0   5   1
St. Louis (NL)  000  310  00x   ---     4   8   0
  Pitchers--RUETHER, Shawkey (5), Thomas (8) vs.
HAINES. Homer--Haines (St. L.). Attendance--37,708.

4th Game, at St. Louis, Oct. 6
New York (AL)   101  142  100   ---    10  14   1
St. Louis (NL)  100  300  000   ---     5  14   0
  Pitchers--HOYT vs. Rhem, REINHART (5), H. Bell (5),
Hallahan (9), Keen (9). Homers--Ruth (N.Y.)3. Attendance--
38,825.

5th Game, at St. Louis, Oct. 7
New York (AL)   000  001  001  1 ---    3   9   1
St. Louis (NL)  000  100  100  0 ---    2   7   1
  Pitchers--PENNOCK vs. SHERDEL. Att.--39,552.

6th Game, at New York, Oct. 9
St. Louis (NL)  300  010  501   ---    10  13   2
New York (AL)   000  100  100   ---     2   8   1
  Pitchers--ALEXANDER vs. SHAWKEY, Shocker (7),
Thomas (8). Homer--L. Bell (St. L.). Attend.--48,615.

7th Game, at New York, Oct. 10
St. Louis (NL)  000  300  000   ---     3   8   0
New York (AL)   001  001  000   ---     2   8   3
  Pitchers--HAINES, Alexander (7) vs. HOYT, Pennock
(7). Homer--Ruth (N.Y.). Attendance--38,093.
```

1927

Regarded by many experts as the greatest team of all time, the 1927 Yankees set a league record with 110 victories and went on to sink the Pirates in four straight. Ruth added two Series homers to his season's bag of 60. Relief specialist Cy Moore started the last game for the Yanks and won when John Miljus wild-pitched home the winning run with two out in the ninth. Though he had hit .309 in the regular season, Kiki Cuyler, hero of the 1925 series, was kept on the Pirate bench throughout

452   THE OFFICIAL ENCYCLOPEDIA OF BASEBALL

these four games because of a grudge held by manager Donie Bush.

Result: New York AL won 4; Pittsburgh NL, 0.

1st Game, at Pittsburgh, Oct 5				R.	H.	E.
New York (AL)	103	010	000	---	5	6	1
Pittsburgh (NL)	101	010	010	---	4	9	2

Pitchers--HOYT, Moore (8) vs. KREMER, Miljus (6). Attendance--41,567.

2nd Game, at Pittsburgh, Oct. 6						
New York (AL)	003	000	030	---	6	11	0
Pittsburgh (NL)	100	000	010	---	2	7	2

Pitchers--PIPGRAS vs. ALDRIDGE, Cvengros (8), Dawson (9). Attendance--41,634.

3rd Game, at New York, Oct. 7						
Pittsburgh (NL)	000	000	010	---	1	3	1
New York (AL)	200	000	60x	---	8	9	0

Pitchers -- MEADOWS, Cvengros (7) vs. PENNOCK. Homer--Ruth (N.Y.). Attendance--60,695.

4th Game, at New York, Oct. 8						
Pittsburgh (NL)	100	000	200	---	3	10	1
New York (AL)	100	020	001	---	4	12	2

Pitchers--Hill, MILJUS (7) vs. MOORE. Homer--Ruth (N.Y.). Attendance--57,909.

1928

Though riddled by injuries to four regulars, the Yankees revenged their 1926 upset by mowing down the Cardinals in four straight. Ruth, lame ankle and all, murdered St. Louis pitching for a .625 average, highest in series history. He topped off the fourth game with three homers. Waite Hoyt won the first and last games. Lou Gehrig, middle man in the Yankee "Murderers' Row", had six passes and six hits for the four games, including four homers.

Result: New York AL won 4; St. Louis NL, 0.

1st Game at New York, Oct. 4				R.	H.	E.
St. Louis (NL)	000	000	100	---	1	3	1
New York (AL)	100	000	01x	---	4	7	0

Pitchers--SHERDEL, Johnson (8) vs. HOYT. Homers--Meusel (N.Y.), Bottomley (St. L.). Attendance--61,425.

2nd Game at New York, Oct. 5						
St. Louis (NL)	030	000	000	---	3	4	1
New york (AL)	314	000	10x	---	9	8	2

Pitchers--ALEXANDER, Mitchell (3) vs. PIPGRAS. Homer--Gehrig (N.Y.). Attendance--60,714.

3rd Game, at St. Louis, Oct. 7						
New York (AL)	010	203	100	---	7	7	2
St. Louis (NL)	200	010	000	---	3	9	3

Pitchers--ZACHARY vs. HAINES, Johnson (7), Rhem (8). Homers--Gehrig (N.Y.) 2. Attendance--39,602.

4th Game, at St. Louis, Oct. 9						
New York (AL)	000	100	420	---	7	15	2
St. Louis (NL)	001	000	001	---	3	11	0

Pitchers--HOYT vs. SHERDEL, Alexander (7). Homers--Ruth (NY.) 3, Durst (N.Y.), Gehrig (N.Y.). Att.--37,331.

1929

The A's trounced the Cubs by unleashing two of the greatest sur-

prises in World Series history. Connie Mack's pitching choice in the opener was aged Howard Ehmke, who had worked only 55 innings in the regular season. The sidearmer struck out 13, a new Series record, to trim Cub ace Charlie Root. The next thunderbolt came in the seventh inning of the fourth game. With Chicago leading, 8-0, Philadelphia suddenly tore into four pitchers with a record 10-run rally. The ill-starred Cubs had a 2-0 lead in the last inning of the fifth game, with one out and bases empty, when the A's exploded for three runs that wound up the Series.

Result: Philadelphia AL won 4; Chicago NL, 1.

1st Game, at Chicago, Oct. 8				R.	H.	E.
Philadelphia(AL)	000	000	102	---	3	6	1
Chicago (NL)	000	000	001	---	1	8	2

Pitchers--EHMKE vs. ROOT, Bush (8). Homer--Foxx (Phil.). Attendance--50,740.

2nd Game, at Chicago, Oct. 9						
Philadelphia(AL)	003	300	120	---	9	12	0
Chicago (NL)	000	030	000	---	3	11	1

Pitchers--EARNSHAW, Grove (5) vs. MALONE, Blake (4), Carlson (6), Nehf (9). Homers--Simmons (Phil.), Foxx (Phil.). Attendance--49,987.

3rd Game, at Philadelphia, Oct. 11						
Chicago (NL)	000	003	000	---	3	6	1
Philadelphia(AL)	000	010	000	---	1	9	1

Pitchers--BUSH vs. EARNSHAW. Attendance--29,991.

4th Game, at Philadelphia, Oct. 12						
Chicago (NL)	000	205	100	---	8	10	2
Philadelphia(AL)	000	000	(10)0x	---	10	15	2

Pitchers--Root, Nehf (7), BLAKE (7), Malone (7), Carlson (8) vs. Quinn, Walberg (6), ROMMEL (7), Grove (8). Homers--Grimm (Chi.), Haas (Phil.), Simmons (Phil.). Attandance--29,991.

5th Game, at Philadelphia, Oct. 14						
Chicago (NL)	002	000	000	---	2	8	1
Philadelphia(AL)	000	000	003	---	3	6	0

Pitchers--MALONE vs. Ehmke, WALBERG(4). Homer--Haas (Phil.). Attendance--29,991.

1930

Connie Mack piloted his fifth world championship team, his A's trumping the Cards in a well-pitched Series. Philadelphia won the first two at home and lost the next two in St. Louis. The fifth game was a scoreless tie until the ninth inning, when Jimmy Foxx cracked a two-run homer off Burleigh Grimes. George Earnshaw notched his second complete-game victory in the sixth game to end the struggle.

Result: Philadelphia AL won 4; St. Louis NL, 2.

1st Game, at Philadelphia, Oct. 1   R. H. E.
St. Louis (NL) 002 000 000 --- 2 9 0
Philadelphia(AL) 010 101 11x --- 5 5 0
    Pitchers -- GRIMES vs. GROVE. Homers -- Cochrane (Phil.), Simmons (Phil.). Attendance--32,295.

2nd Game, at Philadelphia, Oct. 2
St. Louis (NL) 010 000 000 --- 1 6 2
Philadelphia(AL) 202 −200 00x --- 6 7 2
    Pitchers--RHEM, Lindsey (4), Johnson (7) vs. EARNSHAW. Homers--Cochrane (Phil.), Watkins (St. L.). Attendance--32,295.

3rd Game, at St. Louis, Oct. 4
Philadelphia(AL) 000 000 000 --- 0 7 0
St. Louis (NL) 000 110 21x --- 5 10 0
    Pitchers--WALBERG, Shores (5), Quinn (7) vs. HALLAHAN. Homer--Douthit (St. L.). Attendance--36,944.

4th Game, at St. Louis, Oct. 5
Philadelphia(AL) 100 000 000 --- 1 4 1
St. Louis (NL) 001 200 00x --- 3 5 1
    Pitchers--GROVE vs. HAINES. Attendance--39,946.

5th Game, at St. Louis, Oct. 6
Philadelphia(AL) 000 000 002 --- 2 5 0
St. Louis (NL) 000 000 000 --- 0 3 1
    Pitchers--Earnshaw, GROVE (8) vs. GRIMES. Homer--Foxx (Phil.). Attendance--38,844.

6th Game, at Philadelphia, Oct. 8
St. Louis (NL) 000 000 001 --- 1 5 1
Philadelphia(AL) 201 211 00x --- 7 7 0
    Pitchers--HALLAHAN, Johnson (3), Lindsey (6), Bell (8) vs. EARNSHAW. Homers -- Dykes (Phil.), Simmons (Phil.). Attendance--32,295.

1931

Pepper Martin, a brash rookie, ran wild for the Cardinals to thwart a star-studded A's team. Martin batted .500, with a homer, four doubles, seven singles, five runs scored and five runs batted in. Hardboiled Burleigh Grimes and lefthander Bill Hallahan each won a pair. Hallahan beat Earnshaw with a shutout in the second game, yielded only one run while beating Waite Hoyt in the fifth and came back in the seventh and last game to save Grimes' victory by stifling a ninth-inning rally.

Result: St. Louis NL won 4; Philadelphia AL, 3.

1st Game, at St. Louis, Oct. 1   R. H. E.
Philadelphia(AL) 004 000 200 --- 6 11 0
St. Louis (NL) 200 000 000 --- 2 12 0
    Pitchers--GROVE vs. DERRINGER, Johnson (8). Homer--Simmons (Phil.). Attendance--38,529.

2nd Game, at St. Louis, Oct. 2
Philadelphia(AL) 000 000 000 --- 0 3 0
St. Louis (NL) 010 000 10x --- 2 6 1
    Pitchers--EARNSHAW vs. HALLAHAN. Att.--35,947.

3rd Game, at Philadelphia, Oct. 5
St. Louis (NL) 020 200 001 --- 5 12 0
Philadelphia(AL) 000 000 002 --- 2 2 0
    Pitchers--GRIMES vs. GROVE, Mahaffey (9). Homer--Simmons (Phil.). Attendance--32,295.

4th Game, at Philadelphia, Oct. 6
St. Louis (NL) 000 000 000 --- 0 2 1
Philadelphia(AL) 100 000 00x --- 3 10 0
    Pitchers--JOHNSON, Lindsey (6) vs. EARNSHAW. Homer--Foxx (Phil.). Attendance--32,295.

5th Game, at Philadelphia, Oct. 7   R. H. E.
St. Louis (NL) 100 002 011 --- 5 12 0
Philadelphia(AL) 000 000 100 --- 1 9 0
    Pitchers--HALLAHAN vs. HOYT, Walberg (7), Rommel (9). Homers--Martin (St. L.), Watkins (St. L.). Attendance--32,295.

6th Game, at St. Louis, Oct. 9
Philadelphia(AL) 000 040 400 --- 8 8 1
St. Louis (NL) 000 001 000 --- 1 5 2
    Pitchers--GROVE vs. DERRINGER, Johnson (5), Lindsey (7), Rhem (9). Attendance--39,401.

7th Game, at St. Louis, Oct. 10
Philadelphia(AL) 000 000 002 --- 2 7 1
St. Louis (NL) 202 000 00x --- 4 5 0
    Pitchers--EARNSHAW, Walberg (8) vs. GRIMES, Hallahan (9). Attendance--20,805.

1932

The old Yankee habit of winning in four straight victimized the Cubs this time. It was sweet revenge for Yank manager Joe McCarthy, who had been fired as Cub manager two years earlier. Playing in his last World Series, Ruth poled two homers, including his blast into the bleachers right after fabulously pointing there. Though less dramatic than Babe, Gehrig was even more effective with three homers, a double, five singles, two passes, nine runs scored and eight runs batted in.

Result: New York AL won 4; Chicago NL, 0.

1st Game, at New York, Sept. 28   R. H. E.
Chicago (NL) 200 000 220 --- 6 10 1
New York (AL) 000 305 31x --- 12 8 2
    Pitchers--BUSH, Grimes (6), Smith (8) vs. RUFFING. Homer--Gehrig (N.Y.). Attendance--41,459.

2nd Game, at New York, Sept. 29
Chicago (NL) 101 000 000 --- 2 9 0
New York (AL) 202 010 00x --- 5 10 1
    Pitchers--WARNEKE vs. GOMEZ. Attendance--50,709.

3rd Game, at Chicago, Oct. 1
New York (AL) 301 020 001 --- 7 8 1
Chicago (NL) 102 100 001 --- 5 9 4
    Pitchers--PIPGRAS, Pennock (9) vs. ROOT, Malone (5), May (7), Tinning (9). Homers--Ruth (N.Y.) 2, Gehrig (N.Y.) 2, Cuyler (Chi.), Hartnett (Chi.). Attendance--49,986.

4th Game, at Chicago, Oct. 2
New York (AL) 102 002 404 --- 13 19 4
Chicago (NL) 400 001 001 --- 6 9 1
    Pitchers--Allen, MOORE (1), Pennock (7) vs. Bush, Warneke (1), MAY (4), Tinning (7), Grimes (9). Homers--Demaree (Chi.), Lazzeri (N.Y.), Combs (N.Y.). Attendance--49,844.

1933

Player-manager Bill Terry's strategy, sterling Giant pitching and strong stickwork by Mel Ott repulsed the Senators in five games. Earl

Whitehill prevented a sweep by blanking the Giants in the third game. Carl Hubbell won twice, including an 11-inning struggle in the fourth game. The fifth game also went into extra innings. Ott homered in the 10th, and Dolph Luque stemmed a Senator surge in the last half to end the Series.

Result: New York NL won 4; Washington AL, 1.

1st Game, at New York, Oct. 3					R.	H.	E.
Washington (AL)	000	100	001	---	2	5	3
New York (NL)	202	000	00x	---	4	10	2

Pitchers--STEWART, Russell (3), Thomas (8) vs. HUBBELL. Homer--Ott (N.Y.). Attendance--46,672.

2nd Game, at New York, Oct. 4							
Washington (AL)	001	000	000	---	1	5	0
New York (NL)	000	006	00x	---	6	10	0

Pitchers--CROWDER, Thomas (6), McColl (7) vs. SCHUMACHER. Homer--Goslin (Wash.). Attend.--35,461.

3rd Game, at Washington, Oct. 5							
New York (NL)	000	000	000	---	0	5	0
Washington (AL)	210	000	10x	---	4	9	1

Pitchers--FITZSIMMONS, Bell (8) vs. WHITEHILL. Attendance-25,727.

4th Game, at Washington, Oct. 6							
New York (NL)	000	100	000	01	---	2	11	1
Washington (AL)	000	000	100	00	---	1	8	0

Pitchers--HUBBELL vs. WEAVER, Russell (11). Homer--Terry (N.Y.). Attendance--27,762.

5th Game, at Washington, Oct. 7							
New York (NL)	020	001	000	1	---	4	11	1
Washington (AL)	000	003	000	0	---	3	10	0

Pitchers--Schumacher, LUQUE (6) vs. Crowder, RUSSELL (6). Homers--Schulte (Wash.), Ott (N.Y.). Attendance--28,454.

1934

Coming from behind to capture the NL flag on the last day of the season, the swashbuckling Gashouse Gang then tamed the Tigers. Dizzy Dean, with 30 victories in the regular season, stole the spotlight with two more against Detroit. Brother Paul (nicknamed Daffy) also won a pair. Dizzy was beaned while pinch running in the fourth game, and had to be carried off the field, yet returned to pitch the next day. The roisterous seventh game was an 11-0 triumph for Dizzy, who contributed two of the 17 hits off half a dozen Detroit pitchers. St. Louis slugging star Ducky Medwick bowled over third baseman Owen with a slashing slide in the seventh inning of the finale. When Medwick went to his position in left field, the fans showered him with fruit, vegetables and assorted missiles, so

Commissioner Landis ordered Medwick benched to end the ruckus.

Result: St. Louis NL won 4; Detroit AL, 3.

1st Game, at Detroit, Oct. 3					R.	H.	E.
St. Louis (NL)	021	014	000	---	8	13	2
Detroit (AL)	001	001	010	---	3	8	5

Pitchers--J. DEAN vs. CROWDER, Marberry (6) Hogsett (6). Homers--Medwick (St. L.), Greenberg (Det.). Attendance--42,505.

2nd Game, at Detroit, Oct. 4							
St. Louis (NL)	011	000	000	000	---	2	7	3
Detroit (AL)	000	100	001	001	---	3	7	0

Pitchers--Hallahan, W. WALKER (9) vs. ROWE. Attendance--43,451.

3rd Game, at St. Louis, Oct. 5							
Detroit (AL)	000	000	001	---	1	8	2
St. Louis (NL)	110	020	00x	---	4	9	1

Pitchers--BRIDGES, Hogsett (5) vs. P. DEAN. Attendance--34,073.

4th Game, at St. Louis, Oct. 6							
Detroit (AL)	003	100	150	---	10	13	1
St. Louis (NL)	011	200	000	---	4	10	5

Pitchers--AUKER vs. Carleton, Vance (3), W. WALKER (5), Haines (8), Mooney (9). Attendance--37,492.

5th Game, at St. Louis, Oct. 7							
Detroit (AL)	010	002	000	---	3	7	0
St. Louis (NL)	000	000	100	---	1	7	1

Pitchers--BRIDGES vs. J. DEAN, Carleton (9). Homers--Gehringer (Det.), Delancey (St. L.). Attendance--38,536.

6th Game, at Detroit, Oct. 8							
St. Louis (NL)	100	020	100	---	4	10	2
Detroit (AL)	001	002	000	---	3	7	1

Pitchers--P. DEAN vs. ROWE. Attendance--44,551.

7th Game, at Detroit, Oct. 9							
St. Louis (NL)	007	002	200	---	11	17	1
Detroit (AL)	000	000	000	---	0	6	3

Pitchers--J. DEAN vs. AUKER, Rowe (3), Hogsett (3), Bridges (4), Marberry (8), Crowder (9). Attendance--40,-902.

1935

Detroit lost its heavy hitting first baseman, Hank Greenberg, with a broken wrist in the third game, but still managed to stop the Cubs in six games. Tommy Bridges curve-balled two decisions for Detroit and Lon Warneke won Chicago's pair. With the score tied in the last inning of the sixth game, and the Cubs needing a victory to square the series, Stan Hack led off for them with a triple. However, he was stranded as Bridges retired the next three batters. In the Tiger half, catcher-manager Mickey Cochrane singled, advanced on an infield out and scored the deciding run on Goose Goslin's single.

Result: Detroit AL won 4; Chicago NL, 2.

1st Game, at Detroit, Oct. 2				R.	H.	E.
Chicago (NL)	200	000	001	---	3	7	0
Detroit (AL)	000	000	000	---	0	4	3

Pitchers -- WARNEKE vs. ROWE. Homer -- Demaree (Chi.). Attendance--47,391.

2nd Game, at Detroit, Oct. 3
Chicago (NL)   000   010   200   ---   3   6   1
Detroit (AL)   400   300   10x   ---   8   9   2
Pitchers--ROOT, Henshaw (1) Kowalik (4) vs. BRIDGES.
Homer--Greenberg (Det.). Attendance--46,742.

3rd Game, at Chicago, Oct. 4
Detroit (AL)   000   001   040   01   ---   6   12   2
Chicago (NL)   020   010   002   00   ---   5   10   3
Pitchers--Auker, Hogsett (7), ROWE (8) vs. Lee, War-
neke (8), FRENCH (10). Homer--Demaree. Attendance--
45,532.

4th Game, at Chicago, Oct. 5
Detroit (AL)   001   001   000   ---   2   7   0
Chicago (NL)   010   000   000   ---   1   5   2
Pitchers--CROWDER vs. CARLETON, Root (8). Homer
--Hartnett (Chi.). Attendance--49,350.

5th Game, at Chicago, Oct. 6
Detroit (AL)   000   000   001   ---   1   7   1
Chicago (NL)   002   000   10x   ---   3   8   0
Pitchers--ROWE vs. WARNEKE, Lee (7). Homer--Klein
(Chi.). Attendance--49,237.

6th Game, at Detroit, Oct. 7
Chicago (NL)   001   020   000   ---   3   12   0
Detroit (AL)   100   101   001   ---   4   12   1
Pitchers -- FRENCH vs. BRIDGES. Homer -- Herman
(Chi.). Attendance--48,420.

1936

Carl Hubbell closed the NL season
with 16 straight victories and opened
the Series with a 6-1 triumph for the
Giants. But the Yanks bounced back to
bag four of the next five. Lefty Gomez
was winning pitcher in a record 18-4
drubbing and a 13-5 whipping that
each featured a seven-run inning.
Contrasted with his ignoble bases-
loaded strikeout of 1926, Tony Lazzeri cleaned the sacks with a homer
in the second game. Leading Yank
sluggers included Jake Powell (.455),
Red Rolfe and rookie Joe DiMaggio.
Result: New York AL won 4; New
York NL, 2.

1st Game, at Polo Grounds, N. Y., Sept. 30   R.   H.   E.
New York (AL)   001   000   000   ---   1   7   2
New York (NL)   000   011   04x   ---   6   9   1
Pitchers--RUFFING vs. HUBBELL. Homers--Bartell
(NL), Selkirk (AL). Attendance--39,419.

2nd Game, at Polo Grounds, N. Y., Oct. 2
New York (AL)   207   001   206   ---   18   17   0
New York (NL)   010   300   000   ---   4   6   1
Pitchers--GOMEZ vs. SCHUMACHER, Coff-
man (3), Gabler (5), Gumbert (9). Homers--Dickey (AL),
Lazzeri (AL). Attendance--43,543.

3rd Game, at Yankee Stadium, N. Y., Oct. 3
New York (NL)   000   010   000   ---   1   11   0
New York (AL)   010   000   01x   ---   2   4   0
Pitchers--FITZSIMMONS vs. HADLEY, Malone (9).
Homers--Gehrig (AL), Ripple (NL). Attendance--64,842.

4th Game, at Yankee Stadium, N. Y., Oct. 4
New York (NL)   000   100   010   ---   2   7   1
New York (AL)   013   000   01x   ---   5   10   1
Pitchers--HUBBELL, Gabler (8) vs. PEARSON. Homer
--Gehrig (AL). Attendance--66,669.

5th Game, at Yankee Stadium, N. Y., Oct. 5
New York (NL)   300   001   000   1   ---   5   8   3
New York (AL)   011   000   000   0   ---   4   10   1
Pitchers--SCHUMACHER vs. Ruffing, MALONE (7).
Homer--Selkirk (AL). Attendance--50,024.

6th Game, at Polo Grounds, N. Y., Oct. 6
New York (AL)   021   200   017   ---   13   17   2
New York (NL)   200   010   110   ---   5   9   1
Pitchers--GOMEZ, Murphy (7) vs. FITZSIMMONS, Cas-
tleman (4), Coffman (8), Gumbert (9). Homers--Moore (NL),
Ott (NL), Powell (AL). Attendance--38,427.

1937

Interrupted only by Hubbell's victory in the fourth game, the Yanks
easily drove through the Giants. Hubbell was the opening-game victim of
a typical Yank "big inning" as the
AL sluggers scored seven runs in the
sixth inning. Lazzeri hit safely in
every game and led the batters with
.400. Gomez again won twice.
Result: New York AL won 4; New
York NL, 1.

1st Game, at Yankee Stadium, N. Y., Oct. 6   R.   H.   E.
New York (NL)   000   010   000   ---   1   6   2
New York (AL)   000   007   01x   ---   8   7   0
Pitchers--HUBBELL, Gumbert (6), Coffman (6), Smith
(8) vs. GOMEZ. Homer--Lazzeri (AL). Attend.--60,573.

2nd Game, at Yankee Stadium, N. Y., Oct. 7
New York (NL)   100   000   000   ---   1   7   0
New York (AL)   000   024   20x   ---   8   12   0
Pitchers--MELTON, Gumbert (5), Coffman (6) vs. RUF-
FING. Attendance--57,675.

3rd Game, at Polo Grounds, N. Y., Oct. 8
New York (AL)   012   110   000   ---   5   9   0
New York (NL)   000   000   100   ---   1   5   4
Pitchers--PEARSON, Murphy (9) vs. SCHUMACHER,
Melton (7), Brennan (9). Attendance--37,395.

4th Game, at Polo Grounds, N. Y., Oct. 9
New York (AL)   101   000   001   ---   3   6   0
New York (NL)   060   000   10x   ---   7   12   3
Pitchers--HADLEY, Andrews (2), Wicker (8) vs. HUB-
BELL. Homer--Gehrig (AL). Attendance--44,293.

5th Game, at Polo Grounds, N. Y., Oct. 10
New York (AL)   011   020   000   ---   4   8   0
New York (NL)   002   000   000   ---   2   10   0
Pitchers--GOMEZ vs. MELTON, Smith (6), Brennan (8).
Homers--DiMaggio (AL), Hoag (AL), Ott (NL). Att.--38,-
216.

1938

Manager Joe McCarthy again beat
his former Cub club in four straight
games. Big Bill Lee, who won 22
while leading Chicago to the pennant,
lost both his starts to the Yanks.
Dizzy Dean's fireball was gone, but
his slick, sidearm stuff stopped the
Bombers for seven innings. Diz lost
when Frank Crosetti and Joe Di-
Maggio poked two-run homers in the
last two innings. Veteran catcher
Bill Dickey and rookie infielder Joe
Gordon each hit .400 for the Yanks.
Result: New York AL won 4; Chicago NL, 0.

1st Game, at Chicago, Oct. 5   R. H. E.
```
New York (AL)  020  000  100  ---  3  12  1
Chicago (NL)   001  000  000  ---  1   9  1
```
Pitchers--RUFFING vs. LEE, Russell (9). Attendance
--43,642.

2nd Game, at Chicago, Oct. 6
```
New York (AL)  020  000  022  ---  6   7  2
Chicago (NL)   102  000  000  ---  3  11  0
```
Pitchers--GOMEZ, Murphy (8) vs. J. DEAN, French (9).
Homers--Crosetti (N.Y.), DiMaggio (N.Y.). Att.--42,108.

3rd Game, at New York, Oct. 8
```
Chicago (NL)   000  010  010  ---  2  5  1
New York (AL)  000  022  01x  ---  5  7  2
```
Pitchers--BRYANT, Russell (6), French (7) vs. PEAR-
SON. Homers--Dickey (N.Y.), Gordon (N.Y.), Marty (Chi.).
Attendance--55,236.

4th Game, at New York, Oct. 9
```
Chicago (NL)   000  100  020  ---  3  8  1
New York (AL)  030  100  04x  ---  8  11  1
```
Pitchers--LEE, Root (4), Page (7), French (8), Carleton
(8), Dean (8) vs. RUFFING. Homers--Henrich (N.Y.), O'Dea
(Chi.). Attendance--59,847.

1939

Alert and able to cash in on every break, the Yankees snuffed out the Reds in four straight games to become the first team to win four straight world championships. Monte Pearson's two-hitter in the second game was backed by the timely hitting of Babe Dahlgren, who filled in at first base for non-playing captain Lou Gehrig. Yankee rookie Charlie Keller hit hardest in the Series. Enjoying a 4-2 lead in the ninth inning of the fourth game, the Reds suddenly snapped their Series streak of error-less ball with four costly bobbles in two innings, including catcher Ernie Lombardi's famous "snooze" at home plate (when he was understandably stunned in a collision with King Kong Keller).

Result: New York AL won 4; Cincinnati NL, 0.

1st Game, at New York, Oct. 4   R. H. E.
```
Cincinnati (NL)  000  100  000  ---  1  4  0
New York (AL)    000  010  001  ---  2  6  0
```
Pitchers--DERRINGER vs. RUFFING. Attend.--58,541.

2nd Game, at New York, Oct. 5
```
Cincinnati (NL)  000  000  000  ---  0  2  0
New York (AL)    003  100  00x  ---  4  9  0
```
Pitchers--WALTERS vs. PEARSON. Homer--Dahlgren
(N.Y.). Attendance--59,791.

3rd Game, at Cincinnati, Oct. 7
```
New York (AL)    202  030  000  ---  7  5  1
Cincinnati (NL)  120  000  000  ---  3  10  0
```
Pitchers--Gomez, HADLEY (2) vs. THOMPSON, Gris-
som (5), Moore (7). Homers--Keller (N.Y.) 2, DiMaggio
(N.Y.), Dickey (N.Y.). Attendance--32,723.

4th Game, at Cincinnati, Oct. 8
```
New York (AL)    000  000  202  3  ---  7  7  1
Cincinnati (NL)  000  000  310  0  ---  4  11  4
```
Pitchers--Hildebrand, Sundra (5), MURPHY (7) vs.
Derringer, WALTERS (8). Homers--Keller (N.Y.), Dickey
(N.Y.). Attendance--32,794.

1940

No longer having to face the terrifying Yankees, the NL returned to the peak. Cincinnati nipped Detroit's team of oldsters in an airtight series. Bobo Newsom won the opener, but his father, up from South Carolina to watch him, died of a heart attack several hours after the game. Newsom pitched a shutout "for dad" in his next start. Newsom's two decisions were matched by each of two Reds, Bucky Walters and Paul Derringer. Derringer beat Newsom in the finale, when each yielded only seven hits, as slow fielding by Detroit enabled Cincy to score an extra run. Forty-year-old Jimmy Wilson, filling in behind the bat for lame Ernie Lombardi in six games, hit .353 and stole the only base of the Series.

Result: Cincinnati NL won 4; Detroit AL, 3.

1st Game, at Cincinnati, Oct. 2 R. H E.
```
Detroit (AL)     050  020  000  ---  7  10  1
Cincinnati (NL)  000  100  010  ---  2  8  3
```
Pitchers--NEWSOM vs. DERRINGER, Moore (2), Riddle
(9). Homer--Campbell (Det.). Attendance--31,793.

2nd Game, at Cincinnati, Oct. 3
```
Detroit (AL)     200  001  000  ---  3  3  1
Cincinnati (NL)  022  100  00x  ---  5  9  0
```
Pitchers--ROWE, Gorsica (4) vs. WALTERS. Homer--
Ripple (Cin.). Attendance--30,640.

3rd Game, at Detroit, Oct. 4
```
Cincinnati (NL)  100  000  012  ---  4  10  1
Detroit (AL)     000  100  42x  ---  7  13  1
```
Pitchers--TURNER, Moore (7), Beggs (8) vs. BRIDGES.
Homers--York (Det.), Higgins (Det.). Attend.--52,877.

4th Game, at Detroit, Oct. 5
```
Cincinnati (NL)  201  100  010  ---  5  11  1
Detroit (AL)     001  001  000  ---  2  5  1
```
Pitchers--DERRINGER vs. TROUT, Smith (3), McKain
(7). Attendance--54,093.

5th Game, at Detroit, Oct. 6
```
Cincinnati (NL)  000  000  000  ---  0  3  0
Detroit (AL)     003  400  01x  ---  8  13  0
```
Pitchers--THOMPSON, Moore (4), Vander Meer (5),
Hutchings (8), vs. NEWSOM. Homer--Greenberg (Det.).
Attendance--55,189.

6th Game, at Cincinnati, Oct. 7
```
Detroit (AL)     000  000  000  ---  0  5  0
Cincinnati (NL)  200  001  01x  ---  4  10  2
```
Pitchers--ROWE, Gorsica (1), Hutchinson (8) vs. WAL-
TERS. Homer--Walters (Cin.). Attendance--30,481.

7th Game, at Cincinnati, Oct. 8
```
Detroit (AL)     001  000  000  ---  1  7  0
Cincinnati (NL)  000  000  20x  ---  2  7  1
```
Pitchers--NEWSOM vs. DERRINGER. Att.--26,854.

1941

Brooklyn bowed to the Yankees in five games that had some bizarre highlights. Joe Gordon, who hit an

even .500, backed Red Ruffing's pitching with the deciding runs in the opener. This marked 10 consecutive Series games won by the Bronx Bombers. Whitlow Wyatt severed the proud streak the next day. Fred Fitzsimmon was locked in a scoreless hill duel with Marius Russo in the third game when Russo lined a seventh-inning drive off Fitz kneecap, sending him to the hospital. Sloppy fielding by relief pitcher Hugh Casey opened the gate for the two crucial Yank runs in the eighth. Next day, Casey struck out Tom Henrich for what should have been the last out of the game. But catcher Mickey Owen muffed the pitch too. Henrich raced to first to ignite a four-run rally that won for the Yanks, 7-4.

Result: New York AL won 4; Brooklyn NL, 1.

```
1st Game, at New York, Oct. 1              R.  H.  E.
Brooklyn (NL)    000  010  100   ---       2   6   0
New York (AL)    010  101  00x   ---       3   6   1
   Pitchers--DAVIS, Casey (6), Allen (7) vs. RUFFING.
Homer--Gordon (N.Y.). Attendance--68,540.

2nd Game, at New York, Oct. 2
Brooklyn (NL)    000  021  000   ---       3   6   2
New York (AL)    011  000  000   ---       2   9   1
   Pitchers--WYATT vs. CHANDLER, Murphy (6). At-
tendance--66,248.

3rd Game, at Brooklyn, Oct. 4
New York (AL)    000  000  020   ---       2   8   0
Brooklyn (NL)    000  000  010   ---       1   4   0
   Pitchers--RUSSO vs. Fitzsimmons, CASEY (8), French
(8), Allen (9). Attendance--33,100.

4th Game, at Brooklyn, Oct. 5
New York (AL)    100  200  004   ---       7  12   0
Brooklyn (NL)    000  220  000   ---       4   9   1
   Pitchers--Donald, Breuer (5), MURPHY (8) vs. Higbe,
French (4), Allen (5), CASEY (5). Homer--Reiser (Bklyn.).
Attendance--33,813.

5th Game, Brooklyn, Oct. 6
New York (AL)    020  010  000   ---       3   6   0
Brooklyn (NL)    001  000  000   ---       1   4   1
   Pitchers -- BONHAM vs. WYATT. Homer -- Henrich
(N.Y.). Attendance--34,072.
```

1942

A youthful, speedy and nervy Cardinal crew exploded a baseball bombshell by winning the pennant after trailing the Dodgers by 10 1/2 games in August. The Redbirds followed with even a more astounding assault, beating the awesome Yankees four straight after dropping the Series opener to Red Ruffing. St. Louis went winging with such freshman phenoms

as third baseman Whitey Kurowski, pitcher John Beazley and outfielder Stan Musial. Kurowski's triple in the eighth inning of the second game and last-inning homer in the finale brought victory to Beazley each time. Rival centerfielders Terry Moore and Joe DiMaggio dazzled on defense.

Result: St. Louis NL won 4; New York AL, 1.

```
1st Game, at St. Louis, Sept. 30         R.  H.  E.
New York (AL)    000  110  032   ---      7  11   0
St. Louis (NL)   000  000  004   ---      4   7   4
   Pitchers--RUFFING, Chandler (9) vs. M. COOPER,
Gumbert (8), Lanier (9). Attendance--34,385.

2nd Game, at St. Louis, Oct. 1
New York (AL)    000  000  030   ---      3  10   2
St. Louis (NL)   200  000  110   ---      4   6   0
   Pitchers -- BONHAM vs. BEAZLEY. Homer -- Keller
(N.Y.). Attendance--34,255.

3rd Game, at New York, Oct. 2
St. Louis (NL)   001  000  001   ---      2   5   1
New York (AL)    000  000  000   ---      0   6   1
   Pitchers--WHITE vs. CHANDLER, Breuer (9), Turner
(9). Attendance--69,123.

4th Game, at New York, Oct. 4
St. Louis (NL)   000  600  201   ---      9  12   1
New York (AL)    100  005  000   ---      6  10   1
   Pitchers--M. Cooper, Gumbert (6), Pollet (6), LANIER
(7) vs. Borowy, DONALD (4), Bonham (7). Homer--Keller
(N.Y.). Attendance--69,902.

5th Game, at New York, Oct. 5
St. Louis (NL)   000  100  002   ---      4   9   4
New York (AL)    100  100  000   ---      2   7   1
   Pitchers--BEAZLEY vs. RUFFING. Homers--Rizzuto
(N.Y.), Slaughter (St. L.), Kurowski (St. L.). Att.--69,052.
```

1943

This one was a reverse of 1942, with the Yanks whipping the Cards in five games. Spud Chandler won the opener and closer. Though his father died the morning of the second game, Morton Cooper pitched to brother Walker, and they brought St. Louis its only decision. Two Card errors in the eighth inning of the third game opened the gates for the winning four-run rally. Marius Russo pitched and batted his way to a 2-1 victory in the next game. Bill Dickey's homer with one aboard accounted for all the runs in the finale, which also saw Cooper strike out the first five Yank batters.

Result: New York AL won 4; St. Louis NL, 1.

```
1st Game, at New York, Oct. 5            R.  H.  E.
St. Louis (NL)   010  010  000   ---      2   7   2
New York (AL)    000  202  00x   ---      4   8   2
   Pitchers--LANIER vs. CHANDLER. Homer--Gordon
(N.Y.). Attendance--68,676.
```

2nd Game, at New York, Oct. 6

					R.	H.	E.
St. Louis (NL)	001	300	000	---	4	7	2
New York (AL)	000	100	002	---	3	6	0

Pitchers--M. COOPER vs. BONHAM, Murphy (9). Homers--Marion (St. L.), Sanders (St. L.). Att.--68,578.

3rd Game at New York, Oct. 7

St. Louis (NL)	000	200	000	---	2	6	4
New York (AL)	000	001	05x	---	6	8	0

Pitchers--BRAZLE, Krist (8), Brecheen (8) vs. BOROWY, Murphy (9). Attendance--69,990.

4th Game at St. Louis, Oct. 10

New York (AL)	000	100	010	---	2	6	2
St. Louis (NL)	000	000	100	---	1	7	1

Pitchers--RUSSO vs. Lanier, BRECHEEN (8). Attendance--36,196.

5th Game at St. Louis, Oct. 11

New York (AL)	000	002	000	---	2	7	1
St. Louis (NL)	000	000	000	---	0	10	1

Pitchers--CHANDLER vs. M. COOPER, Lanier (8), Dickson (9). Homer--Dickey (N.Y.). Attendance--33,872.

1944

The city of St. Louis enjoyed a "Trolley Series," with the NL entry twice coming from behind to beat the only Brownie team ever to win the AL flag. Of 10 Brown errors, seven came in scoring innings. Mort Cooper lost the opener despite a two-hitter, as George McQuinn blasted a two-run homer. Ken O'Dea's pinch single in the 10th won the next for the Cards. Jack Kramer tamed the Cards the next day, but they snapped back with three straight pitching gems to capture the crown.

Result: St. Louis NL won 4; St. Louis AL, 2.

1st Game, at Sportsman's Park, Oct. 4

					R.	H.	E.
St. Louis (AL)	000	200	000	---	2	2	0
St. Louis (NL)	000	000	001	---	1	7	0

Pitchers--GALEHOUSE vs. M. COOPER, Donnelly (8). Homer--McQuinn (AL). Attendance--33,242.

2nd Game, at Sportsman's Park, Oct. 5

St. Louis (AL)	000	002	000	0 ---	2	7	4
St. Louis (NL)	001	100	000	1 ---	3	7	0

Pitchers--Potter, MUNCRIEF (7) vs. Lanier, DONNELLY (8). Attendance--35,076.

3rd Game, at Sportsman's Park, Oct. 6

St. Louis (NL)	100	000	100	---	2	7	0
St. Louis (AL)	004	000	20x	---	6	8	2

Pitchers--WILKS, Schmidt (3), Jurisich (7), Byerly (7) vs. KRAMER. Attendance--34,737.

4th Game, at Sportsman's Park, Oct. 7

St. Louis (NL)	202	001	000	---	5	12	0
St. Louis (AL)	000	000	010	---	1	9	1

Pitchers--BRECHEEN vs. JAKUCKI, Hollingsworth (4), Shirley (8). Homer--Musial (NL). Attendance--35,455.

5th Game, at Sportsman's Park, Oct. 8

St. Louis (NL)	000	001	010	---	2	6	1
St. Louis (AL)	000	000	000	---	0	7	1

Pitchers--M. COOPER vs. GALEHOUSE. Homers--Sanders (NL), Litwhiler (NL). Attendance--36,568.

6th Game, at Sportsman's Park, Oct. 9

St. Louis (AL)	010	000	000	---	1	3	2
St. Louis (NL)	000	300	00x	---	3	10	0

Pitchers--POTTER, Muncrief (4), Kramer (7) vs. LANIER, Wilks (6). Attendance--31,630.

1945

Returned from war service in midseason, Hank Greenberg hit a grandslam homer on the last day of the season to put Detroit into the Series. He continued his timely hitting to help beat the Cubs, though he couldn't match the 11 hits each by Doc Cramer, Stan Hack and Phil Cavarretta. Hank Borowy, waived out of the AL in midseason, blanked Detroit in the opener. Only 10 days out of the Navy, Virgil Trucks cuffed the Cubs in the next. Then came Claude Passeau's historic one-hitter, fine flinging jobs by Detroit's Dizzy Trout and Hal Newhouser and a weird overtime Cub victory. That put it up to Newhouser vs. Borowy in the finale, and lefty Hal won decisively as he extended his strikeout total for the Series to 22, a new record.

Result: Detroit AL won 4; Chicago NL, 3.

1st Game, at Detroit, Oct. 3

					R.	H.	E.
Chicago (NL)	403	000	200	---	9	13	1
Detroit (AL)	000	000	000	---	0	6	0

Pitchers--BOROWY vs. NEWHOUSER, Benton (3), Tobin (5), Mueller (8). Homer--Cavarretta (Chi.). Attendance--54,637.

2nd Game, at Detroit, Oct. 4

Chicago (NL)	000	100	000	---	1	7	0
Detroit (AL)	000	040	00x	---	4	7	0

Pitchers--WYSE, Erickson (7) vs. TRUCKS. Homer--Greenberg (Det.). Attendance--53,636.

3rd Game, at Detroit, Oct. 5

Chicago (NL)	000	200	100	---	3	8	0
Detroit (AL)	000	000	000	---	0	1	2

Pitchers--PASSEAU vs. OVERMIRE, Benton (7). Attendance--55,500.

4th Game, at Chicago, Oct. 6

Detroit (AL)	000	400	000	---	4	7	1
Chicago (NL)	000	001	000	---	1	5	1

Pitchers--TROUT vs. PRIM, Derringer (4), Vandenberg (6), Erickson (8). Attendance--42,923.

5th Game, at Chicago, Oct. 7

Detroit (AL)	001	004	102	---	8	11	0
Chicago (NL)	001	000	201	---	4	7	2

Pitchers--NEWHOUSER vs. BOROWY, Vandenberg (6), Chipman (6), Derringer (7), Erickson (9). Attend.--43,463.

6th Game, at Chicago, Oct. 8

Detroit (AL)	010	000	240	000	---	7	13	1
Chicago (NL)	000	041	200	001	---	8	15	3

Pitchers--Trucks, Caster (5), Bridges (6), Benton (7), TROUT (8) vs. Passeau, Wyse (7), Prim (8), BOROWY (9). Homer--Greenberg (Det.). Attendance--41,708.

7th Game, at Chicago, Oct. 10

Detroit (AL)	510	000	120	---	9	9	1
Chicago (NL)	100	100	010	---	3	10	0

Pitchers--NEWHOUSER vs. BOROWY, Derringer (1), Vandenberg (2), Erickson (6), Passeau (8), Wyse (9). Attendance--41,590.

1946

Freshman manager Eddie Dyer guided the Cards to victory in the

first pennant playoff in major league history, to break a tie with Brooklyn. Then his underdog team went on to topple the mighty Red Sox in the Series. Hero laurels went to Harry Brecheen for his three victories. Ted Williams earned the "goat horns" for figuratively beating his head against the stonewall "Boudreau defense" throughout the Series. Only once did he deliberately slice a bunt against the overshifted defense, and he reached base easily. Otherwise he pulled as hard as ever and collected only four other hits, all singles, for a .200 average. With two out and the score tied in the eighth inning of the last game, Enos Slaughter scored all the way from first on Harry Walker's hit over the shortstop's head.

Result: St. Louis NL won 4; Boston AL, 3.

```
1st Game, at St. Louis, Oct. 6         R.  H.  E.
Boston (AL)   010  000  001  1 ---    3   9   2
St. Louis (NL) 000  001  010  0 ---    2   7   0
  Pitchers--Hughson, JOHNSON (9) vs. POLLET. Homer
--York (Bos.). Attendance--36,218.

2nd Game, at St. Louis, Oct. 7
Boston (AL)    000  000  000  ---   0   4   1
St. Louis (NL) 001  020  00x  ---   3   6   0
  Pitchers--HARRIS, Dobson (8) vs. BRECHEEN. Attend-
ance--35,815.

3rd Game, at Boston, Oct. 9
St. Louis (NL) 000  000  000  ---   0   6   1
Boston (AL)    300  000  01x  ---   4   8   0
  Pitchers--DICKSON, Wilks (8) vs. FERRISS. Homer--
York (Bos.). Attendance--34,500.

4th Game, at Boston, Oct. 10
St. Louis (NL) 033  010  104  ---  12  20   1
Boston (AL)    000  100  020  ---   3   9   4
  Pitchers--MUNGER vs. HUGHSON, Bagby (3), Zuber
(6), Brown (8), Ryba (9), Dreisewerd (9). Homers--Slaughter
(St. L.), Doerr (Bos.). Attendance--35,645.

5th Game, at Boston, Oct. 11
St. Louis (NL) 010  000  002  ---   3   4   1
Boston (AL)    110  001  30x  ---   6  11   3
  Pitchers--Pollet, BRAZLE (1), Beazley (8) vs DOBSON.
Homer--Culberson (Bos.). Attendance--35,982.

6th Game, at St. Louis, Oct. 13
Boston (AL)    000  000  100  ---   1   7   0
St. Louis (NL) 003  000  01x  ---   4   8   0
  Pitchers--HARRIS, Hughson (3), Johnson (8) vs. BRE-
CHEEN. Attendance--35,768.

7th Game, at St. Louis, Oct. 15
Boston (AL)    100  000  020  ---   3   8   0
St. Louis (NL) 010  020  01x  ---   4   9   1
  Pitchers--Ferriss, Dobson (5), KLINGER (8), Johnson
(8) vs. Dickson, BRECHEEN (8). Attendance--36,143.
```

1947

Despite the lack of a single route-going pitcher, the Dodgers forced the Yanks to the full seven games before

bowing. This two-million-dollar series was a duel between two of the greatest relief artists in history, with Joe Page surpassing Hugh Casey. In the memorable fourth game, Bill Bevens was one out away from an unprecedented no-hitter when pinch hitter Cookie Lavagetto suddenly doubled home the tying and winning runs for Brooklyn. The sixth game was a three-hour, 19-minute marathon highlighted by Al Gionfriddo's miraculous stab of Joe DiMaggio's 415-foot drive to the bullpen gate. Page pitched five scoreless innings of relief to sew up the finale.

Result: New York AL won 4; Brooklyn NL, 3.

```
1st Game, at New York, Sept. 30        R.  H.  E.
Brooklyn (NL) 100  001  100  ---   3   6   0
New York (AL) 000  050  00x  ---   5   4   0
  Pitchers--BRANCA, Behrman (5), Casey (7) vs. SHEA,
Page (6). Attendance--73,365.

2nd Game, at New York, Oct. 1
Brooklyn (NL) 001  100  001  ---   3   9   2
New York (AL) 101  121  40x  ---  10  15   1
  Pitchers--LOMBARDI, Gregg (5), Behrman (7), Barney
(7) vs. REYNOLDS. Homers--Walker (Bklyn.), Henrich
(N.Y.). Attendance--69,865.

3rd Game, at Brooklyn, Oct. 2
New York (AL) 002  221  100  ---   8  13   0
Brooklyn (NL) 061  200  00x  ---   9  13   1
  Pitchers--NEWSOM, Raschi (2), Drews (3), Chandler
(4), Page (6), vs. Hatten, Branca (5), CASEY (7), Homers--
DiMaggio (N.Y.), Berra (N.Y.). Attendance--33,098.

4th Game, at Brooklyn, Oct. 3
New York (AL) 100  100  000  ---   2   8   1
Brooklyn (NL) 000  010  002  ---   3   1   3
  Pitchers--BEVENS vs. Taylor, Gregg (1), Behrman
(8), CASEY (9). Attendance--33,443.

5th Game, at Brooklyn, Oct. 4
New York (AL) 000  110  000  ---   2   5   0
Brooklyn (NL) 000  001  000  ---   1   4   1
  Pitchers--SHEA vs. BARNEY, Hatten (5), Behrman (7),
Casey (8). Homer--DiMaggio (N.Y.). Attendance--34,379.

6th Game, at New York, Oct. 5
Brooklyn (NL) 202  004  000  ---   8  12   1
New York (AL) 004  100  001  ---   6  15   2
  Pitchers--Lombardi, BRANCA (3), Hatten (6), Casey
(9) vs. Reynolds, Drews (3), PAGE (5), Newsom (6), Raschi
(7), Wensloff (8). Attendance--74,065.

7th Game, at New York, Oct. 6
Brooklyn (NL) 020  000  000  ---   2   7   0
New York (AL) 010  201  10x  ---   5   7   0
  Pitchers--GREGG, Behrman (4), Hatten (6), Barney (6),
Casey (7) vs. Shea, Bevens (2), PAGE (5). Att.--71,548.
```

1948

Player-manager Lou Boudreau cracked four-for-four to beat Boston for Cleveland in the first playoff in AL annals. But Gene Bearden, a wounded war veteran, was the hurling hero of that extra game, and the

rookie southpaw proved the main difference in the Series, too. Bob Feller lost the opener to the Braves despite a two-hitter. Bob Lemon, a converted outfielder; Bearden, via shutout, and second-stringer Steve Gromek pitched the Indians to victory in the next three games. Boston won an 11-5 slugfest before the largest crowd in baseball history: 86,288 paid. Lemon started folding late in the sixth game, so tireless Bearden came out of the bullpen for a relief job that clinched the championship.

Result: Cleveland AL won 4; Boston NL, 2.

1st Game, at Boston, Oct. 6				R.	H.	E.
Cleveland (AL)	000	000	000	---	0	4	0
Boston (NL)	000	000	01x	---	1	2	2

Pitchers--FELLER vs. SAIN. Attendance--40,135.

2nd Game, at Boston, Oct. 7				R.	H.	E.
Cleveland (AL)	000	210	001	---	4	8	1
Boston (NL)	100	000	000	---	1	8	3

Pitchers--LEMON vs. SPAHN, Barrett (5), Potter (8). Attendance--39,633.

3rd Game, at Cleveland, Oct. 8				R.	H.	E.
Boston (NL)	000	000	000	---	0	5	1
Cleveland (AL)	001	100	00x	---	2	5	0

Pitchers--BICKFORD, Voiselle (4), Barrett (8) vs. BEARDEN. Attendance--70,306.

4th Game, at Cleveland, Oct. 9				R.	H.	E.
Boston (NL)	000	000	100	---	1	7	0
Cleveland (AL)	101	000	00x	---	2	5	0

Pitchers--SAIN vs. GROMEK. Homers--Doby (Cle.), Rickert (Bost.). Attendance--81,897.

5th Game, at Cleveland, Oct. 10				R.	H.	E.
Boston (NL)	301	001	600	---	11	12	0
Cleveland (AL)	100	400	000	---	5	6	2

Pitchers--Potter, SPAHN (4) vs. FELLER, Klieman (7), Christopher (7), Paige (7), Muncrief (8). Homers--Elliott (Bost.) 2, Mitchell (Cle.), Hegan (Cle.), Salkeld (Bost.). Attendance--86,288.

6th Game, at Boston, Oct. 11				R.	H.	E.
Cleveland (AL)	001	002	010	---	4	10	0
Boston (NL)	000	100	020	---	3	9	0

Pitchers--LEMON, Bearden (8) vs. VOISELLE, Spahn (8). Homer--Gordon (Cle.). Attendance--40,103.

1949

Conquering the Dodgers for the third time in less than a decade, the Yankees kept coming up with the right man in the right spot to win in five games. Don Newcombe struck out 11 Yanks in eight innings, only to lose his first game scoreless duel with Allie Reynolds as Tom Henrich opened the home ninth with a homer. Preacher Roe evened it up with a 1-0 job the next day. However, Brooklyn was ruined in the three remaining games by an old nemesis, Bobby

Brown, a part-time third baseman and medical student. Brown blasted six hits in those three games and accounted for the deciding margin in all three. Fireman Joe Page contributed more of his incomparable relief to seal the Yankee triumph.

Result: New York AL won 4; Brooklyn NL, 1.

1st Game, at New York, Oct. 5				R.	H.	E.
Brooklyn (NL)	000	000	000	---	0	2	0
New York (AL)	000	000	001	---	1	5	1

Pitchers -- NEWCOMBE vs. REYNOLDS. Homer -- Henrich (N.Y.). Attendance--66,224.

2nd Game, at New York, Oct. 6				R.	H.	E.
Brooklyn (NL)	010	000	000	---	1	7	2
New York (AL)	000	000	000	---	0	6	1

Pitchers--ROE vs. RASCHI. Attendance--70,053.

3rd Game, at Brooklyn, Oct. 7				R.	H.	E.
New York (AL)	001	000	003	---	4	5	0
Brooklyn (NL)	000	100	002	---	3	5	0

Pitchers--Byrne, PAGE (4) vs. BRANCA, Banta (9). Homers--Reese (Bklyn.), Olmo (Bklyn.), Campanella (Bklyn.). Attendance--32,788.

4th Game, at Brooklyn, Oct. 8				R.	H.	E.
New York (AL)	000	330	000	---	6	10	0
Brooklyn (NL)	000	004	000	---	4	9	1

Pitchers--LOPAT, Reynolds (6) vs. NEWCOMBE, Hatten (4), Erskine (6), Banta (7). Attendance--33,934.

5th Game, at Brooklyn, Oct. 9				R.	H.	E.
New York (AL)	203	113	000	---	10	11	1
Brooklyn (NL)	001	001	400	---	6	11	2

Pitchers--RASCHI, Page (7) vs. BARNEY, Banta (3), Erskine (6), Hatten (6), Palica (7), Minner (9). Homers--DiMaggio (N.Y.), Hodges (Bklyn.). Attendance--33,711.

1950

After winning the pennant in the 10th inning of the last day of the season, the Philadelphia "Whiz Kids" suffered a severe letdown in the World Series, losing four straight to the Yankees. A daring gamble almost paid off for the NL entry. Manager Ed Sawyer named Jim Konstanty to open the Series, though the bullpen denizen had broken the all-time season record with 74 relief appearances (and no starts!). Konstanty dropped a 1-0 duel to Vic Raschi, who spun a two-hitter. Locked in a .222 batting slump, the Yankees relied on further fine pitching by Allie Reynolds, Ed Lopat, Tom Ferrick and rookie Ed Ford to sweep the rest of the series for their 13th title. Joe DiMaggio blasted a 10th-inning homer into the upper deck of Shibe Park to win the second game.

Result: New York AL won 4; Philadelphia NL, 0.

1st Game, at Philadelphia, Oct. 4
| | | | R. | H. | E. |
New York (AL)   000   100   000   ---   1   5   0
Philadelphia(NL) 000   000   000   ---   0   2   1
Pitchers--RASCHI vs. KONSTANTY, Meyer (9). Attendance--30,746.

2nd Game, at Philadelphia, Oct. 5
New York (AL)   010   000   000   1   ---   2   10   0
Philadelphia(NL) 000   010   000   0   ---   1   7   0
Pitchers--REYNOLDS vs. ROBERTS. Homer--DiMaggio (N.Y.). Attendance--32,660.

3rd Game, at New York, Oct. 6
Philadelphia(NL) 000   001   100   ---   2   10   2
New York (AL)   001   000   011   ---   3   7   0
Pitchers--Heintzelman, Konstanty (8), MEYER (9) vs. Lopat, FERRICK (9). Attendance--64,505.

4th Game, at NewYork, Oct. 7
Philadelphia(NL) 000   000   002   ---   2   7   1
New York (AL)   200   003   00x   ---   5   8   2
Pitchers--MILLER, Konstanty (1), Roberts (8) vs. FORD, Reynolds (9). Homer--Berra (N.Y.). Att.--68,098.

1951

The red-hot New York Giants, who had made a sensational late season drive to haul in the NL pennant, were cooled off in the series by a rainy day and resurgent Yankee bats. The Giants had taken a 2-1 lead in games when rain postponed the fourth contest and gave Yankee pitching ace Allie Reynolds an additional day of rest. The Giants were unable to win a game after play resumed. Monte Irvin's theft of home—first in fall competition since 1928—and lefty Dave Koslo's strong hurling job got the Giants off in front in the opener. After Lopat whipped the Giants in the second clash Jim Hearn put the NL one-up the following day. Then came the rain which washed out the Giant chances. McDougald's bases-loaded homer in the fourth battle, Lopat's second win in the fifth and Bob Kuzava's strong relief bit and Hank Bauer's game-saving catch in the sixth game featured the Yankees' next three victories. Irvin slammed 11 hits to tie a record for most safeties in a six-game set, and paced all series hitters with a .458 figure. The series also was marked by the famous "drop kick" incident when Ed Stanky kicked the ball from Phil Rizzuto's hand as the Yankee shortstop was about to tag out the fiery Giant infielder who was attempting to slide into second base on a hit and run play which backfired. Rizzuto dropped the ball and the Giants went on to score five runs in the inning, a vital factor in their third game triumph.

Result: New York AL won 4; New York NL, 2.

1st Game, at Yankee Stadium, N.Y., Oct. 4
| | | | R. | H. | E. |
New York (NL)   200   003   000   ---   5   10   1
New York (AL)   010   000   000   ---   1   7   1
Pitchers--KOSLO vs. REYNOLDS, Hogue (7), Morgan (8). Homer--Dark (NL). Attendance--65,673.

2nd Game, at Yankee Stadium, N.Y., Oct. 5
New York (NL)   000   000   100   ---   1   5   1
New York (AL)   110   000   01x   ---   3   6   0
Pitchers--JANSEN, Spencer (7) vs. LOPAT. Homer--Collins (AL). Attendance--66,018.

3rd Game, at Polo Grounds, N.Y., Oct. 6
New York (AL)   000   000   011   ---   2   5   2
New York (NL)   010   050   00x   ---   6   7   2
Pitchers--RASCHI, Hogue (5), Ostrowski (7) vs. HEARN, Jones (8). Homers--Lockman (NL), Woodling (AL). Attendance--52,035.

4th Game, at Polo Grounds, N.Y., Oct. 8
New York (AL)   010   120   200   ---   6   12   0
New York (NL)   100   000   001   ---   2   8   2
Pitchers--REYNOLDS vs. MAGLIE, Jones (6), Kennedy (9). Homer--DiMaggio (AL). Attendance--49,010.

5th Game, at Polo Grounds, N.Y., Oct. 9
New York (AL)   005   202   400   ---   13   12   1
New York (NL)   100   000   000   ---   1   5   3
Pitchers--LOPAT vs. JANSEN, Kennedy (4), Spencer (6), Corwin (7), Konikowski (9). Homers--McDougald (AL), Rizzuto (AL). Attendance--47,530.

6th Game, at Yankee Stadium, N.Y., Oct. 10
New York (NL)   000   010   002   ---   3   11   1
New York (AL)   100   003   00x   ---   4   7   0
Pitchers--KOSLO, Hearn (7), Jansen (8) vs. RASCHI, Sain (7), Kuzava (9). Attendance--61,711.

1952

Casey Stengel tied the world's championship record of four straight titles as he guided the Yankees through a successful seven-game set against the Brooklyn Dodgers. It equaled the mark established by the Bombers of Joe McCarthy vintage who nailed down titles in 1936, '37, '38 and '39. The Yankees did it the hard way, coming from behind to defeat the Dodgers in the last two games played at the National Leaguers' park. Dodger manager Charley Dressen started ace relief artist Joe Black in the opening game and the big right hander responded with a 4-2 victory. It was the first series pitching triumph ever turned in by a Negro. The teams alternated in winning the next four games before the Yankees thundered back to take the last two. Perhaps the most exciting game of the set was the 11-inning thriller won by Brooklyn, 6-5, which gave the Dodgers their three-two edge. Carl Erskine pitched

the distance for the Dodgers, allowing all Yankee runs in the fifth inning. The most dramatic moment of the series was reserved for the seventh inning of the final game. Jackie Robinson popped up a wind-blown fly ball with two out and bases-loaded. With all the runners dashing plateward, second baseman Billy Martin circled for the catch. When it appeared as if the ball would drop safely, he just managed to grab it with a last second lunge. Duke Snider slammed four homers for the Dodgers.

Result: New York AL won 4; Brooklyn NL, 3.

1st Game, at Brooklyn, Oct. 1

				R.	H.	E.
New York (AL)	010	000	010	---	2	6	2
Broklyn (NL)	010	002	01x	---	4	6	0

Pitchers--REYNOLDS, Scarborough (8) vs. BLACK. Homers--Robinson (Bklyn.), Snider (Bklyn.), Reese (Bklyn.), McDougald (N.Y.). Attendance--34,861.

2nd Game, at Brooklyn, Oct. 2

New York (AL)	000	115	000	---	7	10	0
Brooklyn (NL)	001	000	000	---	1	3	1

Pitchers--RASCHI vs. ERSKINE, Loes (6), Lehman (8). Homer--Martin (N.Y.). Attendance--33,792.

3rd Game, at New York, Oct. 3

Brooklyn (NL)	001	010	012	---	5	11	0
New York (AL)	010	000	011	---	3	6	2

Pitchers--ROE vs. LOPAT, Gorman (9). Homers--Berra (N.Y.), Mize (N.Y.). Attendance--66,698.

4th Game, at New York, Oct. 4

Brooklyn (NL)	000	000	000	---	0	4	1
New York (AL)	000	100	01x	---	2	4	1

Pitchers -- BLACK, Rutherford (8) vs. REYNOLDS. Homer--Mize (N.Y.). Attendance--71,787.

5th Game, at New York, Oct. 5

Brooklyn (NL)	010	030	100	01	---	6	10	0
New York (AL)	000	050	000	00	---	5	5	1

Pitchers--ERSKINE vs. Blackwell, SAIN (6). Homers--Snider (Bklyn.), Mize (N.Y.). Attendance--70,536.

6th Game, at Brooklyn, Oct. 6

New York (AL)	000	000	210	---	3	9	0
Brooklyn (NL)	000	001	010	---	2	8	1

Pitchers--RASCHI, Reynolds (8) vs. LOES, Roe (9). Homers--Snider (Bklyn.) 2, Berra (N.Y.), Mantle (N.Y.). Attendance--30,037.

7th Game, at Brooklyn, Oct. 7

New York (AL)	000	111	100	---	4	10	4
Brooklyn (NL)	000	110	000	---	2	8	1

Pitchers--Lopat, REYNOLDS (4), Raschi (7), Kuzava (7) vs. BLACK, Roe (6), Erskine (8). Homers--Woodling (N.Y.), Mantle (N.Y.). Attendance--33,195.

1953

The Yankees became the first team in history to win five straight world championships as they again tamed Brooklyn, this time in six games. The Yankees won the first two games; the Dodgers rallied to cop the next two but the Yankees, with Mickey Mantle driving a grandslammer in the third inning of game No. 5, took the next two clashes. Erskine es-

tablished an all-time series mark by striking out 14 batters to give Brooklyn its first victory, a brilliant 3-2 effort which wasn't decided until catcher Roy Campanella clouted an eighth inning home run. Billy Loes got Brooklyn even the following day with a nine-hit triumph before the Yankees recovered to sail through the next two games. Carl Furillo's two-on ninth-inning homer tied the score in the sixth game but Billy Martin, brilliant at bat and in the field throughout, delivered the payoff poke, a game-winning single in the Bombers' half. It was Martin's 12th hit—a new record for a six game series—and he wound up with a .500 batting average.

Result: New York AL won 4; Brooklyn NL, 2.

1st Game, at New York, Sept. 30

				R.	H.	E.
Brooklyn (NL)	000	013	100	---	5	12	2
New York (AL)	400	010	13x	---	9	12	0

Pitchers--Erskine, Hughes (2), LABINE (6), Wade (8) vs. Reynolds, SAIN (6). Homers--Gilliam (Bklyn.), Hodges (Bklyn.), Shuba (Bklyn.), Berra (N.Y.), Collins (N.Y.). Attendance--69,374.

2nd Game, at New York, Oct. 1

Brooklyn (NL)	000	200	000	---	2	9	1
New York (AL)	100	000	12x	---	4	5	0

Pitchers--ROE vs. LOPAT. Homers -- Martin (N.Y.), Mantle (N.Y.). Attendance--66,786.

3rd Game, at Brooklyn, Oct. 2

New York (AL)	000	010	010	---	2	6	0
Brooklyn (NL)	000	011	.01x	---	3	9	0

Pitchers--RASCHI vs. ERSKINE. Homer--Campanella (Bklyn.). Attendance--35,270.

4th Game, at Brooklyn, Oct. 3

New York (AL)	000	020	001	---	3	9	0
Brooklyn (NL)	300	102	10x	---	7	12	0

Pitchers--FORD, Gorman (2), Sain (5), Schallock (7) vs. LOES, Labine (9). Homers--McDougald (N.Y.), Snider (Bklyn.). Attendance--36,775.

5th Game, at Brooklyn, Oct. 4

New York (AL)	105	000	311	---	11	11	1
Brooklyn (NL)	010	010	041	---	7	14	1

Pitchers--MCDONALD, Kuzava (8), Reynolds (9), vs. PODRES, Meyer (3), Wade (8), Black (9). Homers--Woodling (N.Y.), Mantle (N.Y.), Martin (N.Y.), McDougald (N.Y.), Cox (Bklyn.), Gilliam (Bklyn.). Attendance--36,665.

6th Game, at New York, Oct. 5

Brooklyn (NL)	000	001	002	---	3	8	3
New York (AL)	210	000	001	---	4	13	0

Pitchers--Erskine, Milliken (5), LABINE (7) vs. Ford, REYNOLDS (8). Homer--Furillo (Bklyn.). Attendance--62,370.

1954

The irrepressible Giants waved their magic wand known as Dusty Rhodes to blot out Cleveland four straight times and smash a seven-year monopoly held by the AL in

post-season conflict. It was the first time since 1946 that the AL had lost a series and only the second time in the history of the classic that the NL had swept a series, the miracle Boston Braves first performing the trick on the Philadelphia Athletics in 1914. A Cleveland team which had established a new standard for league victories with 111 was no match for Leo Durocher's surprises after the first two games. The Indians seemed on their way to victory in the eighth inning of the opener only to see outfielder Willie Mays snatch it from their grasp at the base of the centerfield wall. His incredible catch of Vic Wertz' long bid for a triple with two aboard will remain as one of the series' most historic fielding plays. It prevented the Tribe from nailing down the verdict and allowed Rhodes, pinch hitter extraordinary, to drive a three-run, game-winning homer which barely reached the right field stands in the 10th inning. Pitcher Early Wynn failed the following day, as his opponent, Johnny Antonelli, drove in what proved to be the winning tally and Rhodes once again belted a home run. Cleveland's famed hurling staff came apart in the third and fourth frays and the Giants didn't have to resort to heroics to clinch victories in both of them. Rhodes, in six official times at bat, drove in seven runs; Al Dark hit .412 to top the New York batters; Giant third baseman Hank Thompson coaxed seven bases on balls, a new record for a four-game series. But Wertz, the bald-headed outfielder-first baseman, hit for a .500 average to lead both clubs.

Result: New York NL won 4; Cleveland AL, 0.

1st Game, at New York, Sept. 29
					R.	H.	E.
Cleveland (AL)	200	000	000	0 ---	2	8	0
New York (NL)	002	000	000	3 ---	5	9	0
Pitchers--LEMON vs. Maglie, Liddle (8), GRISSOM (8). Homer--Rhodes (N.Y.). Attendance--52,751

2nd Game, at New York, Sept. 30
					R.	H.	E.
Cleveland (AL)	100	000	000	---	1	8	0
New York (NL)	000	020	10x	---	3	4	0
Pitchers--WYNN, Mossi (8) vs. ANTONELLI. Homers--Smith (Cleve), Rhodes (N.Y.). Attendance--49,099.

3rd Game, at Cleveland, Oct. 1
					R.	H.	E.
New York (NL)	103	011	000	---	6	10	1
Cleveland (AL)	000	000	110	---	2	4	2
Pitchers--GOMEZ, Wilhelm (7) vs. GARCIA, Houtteman (4), Narleski (6), Mossi (9). Homer --Wertz (Cleve). Attendance--71,555.

4th Game, at Cleveland, Oct. 2
					R.	H.	E.
New York (NL)	021	040	000	---	7	10	3
Cleveland (AL)	000	030	100	---	4	6	2
Pitchers -- LIDDLE, Wilhelm (7), Antonelli (8) vs. LEMON, Newhouser (5), Narleski (5), Mossi (6), Garcia (8). Homer--Majeski (Cleve.). Attendance--78,102.

1955

This became the "next year" Brooklyn fans had waited for since their American Association champs of 1889 began the habit of losing post-season series. Fittingly enough, the Dodgers, who made a complete shambles of the NL race, victimized the Yankees, a team which had thwarted their last five series bids. Moreover, Walter Alston's boys broke an old series jinx by becoming the first club to take a seven-game set after losing the first two games. Hero of the victory was a 23-year old southpaw, Johnny Podres, who twice befuddled the Yankee sluggers with his tantalizing change-up, winning the third game, 8-3, and then taking the decisive seventh contest, 2-0. In that last one, Gil Hodges, goat of so many past Dodger series setbacks, batted in both runs with a single and a sacrifice fly, while Sandy Amoros made a game-saving catch on Yogi Berra's slice down the left field line and turned it into a double play to kill the Yanks' sixth inning rally. Casey Stengel had defied the "no-southpaws-against-Brooklyn" tradition to win the first two games at Yankee Stadium behind Whitey Ford and Tommy Byrne, the pitchers who had enabled New York to win a close AL pennant race from Cleveland, Chicago and Boston. But the Dodgers came back to take three at Ebbets Field on the pitching of Podres and Clem Labine and the home runs of Duke Snider and Roy Campanella. Alston passed up 20-game winner Don Newcombe to start rookie Karl Spooner in the sixth game, but he was blasted in a five-run first inning, featuring Bill Skowron's three-run homer, and Ford had his first complete game series win. This left it to Podres and Byrne in the finale, with the young southpaw from up-

state New York edging the hero of 1955's biggest baseball comeback story. Snider's four homers raised his NL series record to nine, one back of Lou Gehrig, six behind Babe Ruth.

Result: Brooklyn NL won 4; New York AL, 3.

1st game, at New York, Sept. 28

					R.	H.	E.
Brooklyn (NL)	021	000	020	---	5	10	0
New York (AL)	021	102	00x	---	6	9	1

Pitchers--NEWCOMBE, Bessent (6), Labine (8) vs. FORD, Grim (9). Homers--Furillo (Bklyn), Snider (Bklyn), Howard (N.Y.), Collins (N.Y.) 2. Attendance--63,869.

2nd game, at New York, Sept. 29

Brooklyn (NL)	000	110	000	---	2	5	2
New York (AL)	000	400	00x	---	4	8	0

Pitchers--LOES, Bessent (4), Spooner (5), Labine (8) vs BYRNE. Attendance--64,707.

3rd game, at Brooklyn, Sept. 30

New York (AL)	020	000	100	---	3	7	0
Brooklyn (NL)	220	200	20x	---	8	11	1

Pitchers--TURLEY, Morgan (2), Kucks (5), Sturdivant (7) vs PODRES. Homers--Campanella (Bklyn), Mantle (N.Y.). Attendance--34,209.

4th game, at Brooklyn, Oct. 1

New York (AL)	110	102	000	---	5	9	0
Brooklyn (NL)	001	330	10x	---	8	14	0

Pitchers--LARSEN, Kucks (5), R. Coleman (6), Morgan (7), Sturdivant (8) vs Erskine, Bessent (4), LABINE (5). Homers--McDougald (N.Y.), Campanella (Bklyn), Hodges (Bklyn), Snider (Bklyn). Attendance--36,242.

5th game, at Brooklyn, Oct. 2

New York (AL)	000	100	110	---	3	6	0
Brooklyn (NL)	021	010	01x	---	5	9	2

Pitchers--GRIM, Turley (7) vs CRAIG, Labine (7). Homers--Cerv (N.Y.), Berra (N.Y.), Amoros (Bklyn), Snider (Bklyn). Attendance--36,796.

6th game, at New York, Oct. 3

Brooklyn (NL)	000	100	000	---	1	4	1
New York (AL)	500	000	00x	---	5	8	0

Pitchers--SPOONER, Meyer (1), Roebuck (7) vs FORD. Homer--Skowron (N.Y.). Attendance--64,022.

7th game, at New York, Oct. 4

Brooklyn (NL)	000	101	000	---	2	5	0
New York (AL)	000	000	000	---	0	8	1

Pitchers--PODRES vs BYRNE, Grim (6), Turley (8). Attendance--62,465.

Pitcher Don Larsen is greeted jubilantly by Catcher Yogi Berra after final out of the fifth game in the 1956 World Series. Larsen retired 27 Dodgers in order for the first perfectly pitched game in Series history. (Wide World Photo)

1956

Don Larsen, who in 1954 had lost 21 games while pitching for Baltimore, made history by pitching the only perfect game (27 batters retired consecutively) in Series history when he turned back the Dodgers in the fifth game, 2-0. Form took a complete reversal of the Series played between these two clubs the previous year. This time the Dodgers started fast with victories in the first two games, only to see the Yankees sweep the next three. Clem Labine then outdueled Bob Turley in a 10-inning, 1-0 duel to tie the set at three games apiece before the Yankees blasted Don Newcombe in the decisive contest, 9-0, behind the three-hit pitching of Johnny Kucks. Yogi Berra slammed two homers in the finale and his .360 average was tops for the classic. The Yankee catcher established a new Series mark when he drove in ten runs. Duke Snider's tenth homer put him in a second-place tie with Lou Gehrig for most homers in Series competition. The Yankees established two undistinguished records for futility in the second game when they (1) paraded seven pitchers to the mound (2) who issued a total of 11 bases on balls. But the next five Yankee starters went the distance as the American Leaguers won their 17th title and sixth over their most persistent post-season challengers. Larsen's perfect game, in which Mickey Mantle's homer and Hank Bauer's sacrifice fly accounted for both Yank runs, and Labine's sixth game shutout were the top pitching performances of the Series. Jackie Robinson's left field single tied up the Series in game No. 6.

Result: New York AL won 4; Brooklyn NL, 3.

1st Game, at Brooklyn, Oct. 3

					R.	H.	E.
New York (AL)	200	100	000	---	3	9	1
Brooklyn (NL)	023	100	00x	---	6	9	0

Pitchers--FORD, Kucks (4), Morgan (6) vs. MAGLIE. Homers--Mantle (N.Y.), Robinson (Bklyn.), Hodges (Bklyn.). Martin (N.Y.). Attendance--34,479.

2nd Game, at Brooklyn, Oct. 5

New York (AL)	150	100	001	---	8	12	2
Brooklyn (NL)	061	220	02x	---	13	12	0

Pitchers--Larsen, Kucks (2), Byrne (2), Sturdivant (3), MORGAN (3), Turley (5), McDermott (6) vs. Newcombe, Roebuck (2), BESSENT (3). Homers--Berra (N.Y.), Snider (Bklyn.). Attendance--36,217.

3rd Game, at New York, Oct. 6

Brooklyn (NL)	010	001	100	---	3	8	1
New York (AL)	010	003	01x	---	5	8	1

Pitchers-- CRAIG, Labine (7) vs. FORD   Homers--Martin (N.Y.). Slaughter (N.Y.). Attendance--73,977.

4th Game, at New York, Oct. 7

Brooklyn (NL)	000	100	100	---	2	6	0
New York (AL)	100	201	20x	---	6	7	2

Pitchers--ERSKINE, Roebuck (5), Drysdale (7) vs. STURDIVANT. Homers--Mantle (N.Y.). Bauer (N.Y.). Attendance--69,705.

5th Game, at New York, Oct. 8

Brooklyn (NL)	000	000	000	---	0	0	0
New York (AL)	000	101	00x	---	2	5	0

Pitchers--MAGLIE vs. LARSEN. Homer -- Mantle (N.Y.). Attendance--64,519.

6th Game, at Brooklyn, Oct. 9

New York (AL)	000	000	000	0----	0	7	0
Brooklyn (NL)	000	000	000	1----	1	4	0

Pitchers--TURLEY vs. LABINE. Attendance--33,224.

7th Game, at Brooklyn, Oct. 10

New York (AL)	202	000	400	---	9	10	0
Brooklyn (NL)	000	000	000	---	0	3	1

Pitchers--KUCKS vs. NEWCOMBE. Bessent (4). Craig (7), Roebuck (7), Erskine (9). Homers--Berra (N.Y.) 2, Howard (N.Y.). Skowron (N.Y.). Attendance--33,782.

1957

Lew Burdette, who was brought up to the big leagues by the Yankees, turned on his old mates with the most superb one-man pitching performance since Christy Mathewson of the Giants shut out the Philadelphia Athletics three times in the 1905 Series. The tall righthander who had been suspected—but never convicted—of firing the outlawed spit ball during the season, turned in three complete game triumphs as Milwaukee won its first post-season classic. Warren Spahn, the lefthander who hooked up with Burdette to pace the Braves to the pennant, was the other winner—a 10-inning, 7—5 thriller which Eddie Mathews decided with a one-on homer. Burdette began his mastery of the Yankees in the second game, and concluded the Series with a second shutout, 5-0, at Yankee Stadium. Whitey Ford, Don Larsen and Bob Turley were the winning Yankee hurlers. Milwaukee's Hank Aaron hit safely in every game and his .393 average led both clubs. The Yankees were below par physically due to Mickey Mantle's

leg injury and Bill Skowron's back injury. The Braves played without Bill Bruton, their regular center-fielder. The Series established two historic records—most attendance (394,712) and total receipts ($5,475,-978.94). The net gate receipts were $2,475,978.94 but an additional three million dollars from a new TV-radio contract was added to the kitty to help establish a new financial high.

Result: Milwaukee NL won 4; New York AL, 3.

```
1st Game, at New York, Oct. 2           R.  H.  E.
Milwaukee (NL)  000  000  100   ---      1   5   0
New York (AL)   000  012  00x   ---      3   9   1
    Pitchers--SPAHN, Johnson (6), McMahon (7) vs. FORD.
Attendance--69,476.
```

```
2nd Game, at New York, Oct. 3
Milwaukee (NL)  011  200  000   ---      4   8   0
New York (AL)   011  000  000   ---      2   7   2
    Pitchers--BURDETTE vs. SHANTZ, Ditmar (4), Grim
(8). Homers -- Logan (Mil.), Bauer (N.Y.). Attendance--
65,202.
```

```
3rd Game, at Milwaukee, Oct. 5
New York (AL)   302  200  500   ---     12   9   0
Milwaukee (NL)  010  020  000   ---      3   8   1
    Pitchers--Turley, LARSEN (2) vs. BUHL, Pizarro (1),
Conley (3), Johnson (5), Trowbridge (7), McMahon (8).
Homers -- Kubek (N.Y.) 2, Mantle (N.Y.), Aaron (Mil.).
Attendance--45,804.
```

```
4th Game, at Milwaukee, Oct. 6
New York (AL)   100  000  003  1 ---     5  11   0
Milwaukee (NL)  000  400  000  3 ---     7   7   0
    Pitchers -- Sturdivant, Shantz (5), Kucks (8), Byrne (8),
GRIM (10) vs. SPAHN. Homers--Aaron (Mil.), Torre (Mil.),
Howard (N.Y.), Mathews (Mil.). Attendance--45,804.
```

```
5th Game, at Milwaukee, Oct. 7
New York (AL)   000  000  000   ---      0   7   0
Milwaukee (NL)  000  001  00x   ---      1   6   1
    Pitchers--FORD, Turley (8) vs. BURDETTE. Attend-
ance--45,811.
```

```
6th Game, at New York, Oct. 9
Milwaukee (NL)  000  010  100   ---      2   4   0
New York (AL)   002  000  10x   ---      3   7   0
    Pitchers--Buhl, JOHNSON (3), McMahon (8) vs.
TURLEY. Homers -- Berra (N.Y.), Torre (Mil.), Aaron
(Mil.), Bauer (N.Y.). Attendance--61,408.
```

```
7th Game, at New York, Oct. 10
Milwaukee (NL)  004  000  010   ---      5   9   1
New York (AL)   000  000  000   ---      0   7   3
    Pitchers--BURDETTE vs. LARSEN, Shantz (3), Ditmar
(4), Sturdivant (6), Byrne (8). Homer--Crandall (Mil.). At-
tendance--61,207.
```

1958

The New York Yankees, down three games to one, staged a magnificent comeback to whip the Milwaukee Braves in the fourth straight Series to go the legal limit of seven games.

Only once before—when Pittsburgh upset Washington in 1925—had a team come from so far behind to take the classic. It was the 18th championship for the Yankees in 24 attempts and their seventh in nine tries under the guidance of Casey Stengel who settled his personal score with Milwaukee manager Fred Haney. The Braves, behind Warren Spahn and Lew Burdette, took the first two games at Milwaukee. Don Larsen and Ryne Duren combined to halt the Braves in the third contest but Spahn's sparkling two-hit shutout in the fourth game gave the National Leaguers a commanding 3-1 lead and almost assured them of their second straight title. However, the Yankees, with brilliant pitching, refused to fold. Bob Turley hurled a five-hit shutout in the fifth game and stout relief pitching by Art Ditmar, Dúren and Turley overcame Spahn's heroic effort in the 4-3 sixth contest which went ten innings. Larsen and Burdette started the decisive battle but big Don left in the third inning after the Yanks had taken a 2-1 lead. Del Crandall's sixth-inning homer tied the game and it was 2-2 as the eighth inning started. After Burdette retired the first two batters, the American Leaguers exploded. Yogi Berra doubled to right and scored on Elston Howard's single through the middle. Andy Carey then beat out an infield hit and Bill Skowron delivered the clincher with a three-run homer. It was the end of the road for Burdette and the Braves. Hank Bauer tied a Series record with four home runs. Milwaukee's Ed Mathews established a new individual mark for futility with eleven strikeouts.

Result: New York AL won 4; Milwaukee NL, 3.

```
1st Game, at Milwaukee, Oct. 1          R.  H.  E.
New York (AL)   000  120  000  0 ---     3   8   1
Milwaukee (NL)  000  200  010  1 ---     4  10   0
    Pitchers -- Ford, DUREN (8) vs. SPAHN. Homers--
Skowron (N.Y.), Bauer (N.Y.). Attendance--46,367.
```

```
2nd Game, at Milwaukee, Oct. 2
New York (AL)   100  100  003   ---      5   7   0
Milwaukee (NL)  710  000  23x   ---     13  15   1
    Pitchers -- TURLEY, Maas (1), Kucks (1), Dickson (5),
Monroe (8) vs. BURDETTE. Homers--Bruton (Mil.), Bur-
dette (Mil.), Mantle (N.Y.) 2, Bauer (N.Y.). Attendance--
46,367.
```

3rd Game, at New York, Oct. 4

Milwaukee (NL)	000	000	000	---	0	6	0
New York (AL)	000	020	20x	---	4	4	0

Pitchers--RUSH, McMahon (7) vs. LARSEN, Duren (8).
Homer--Bauer (N.Y.). Attendance--71,599.

4th Game, at New York, Oct. 5

Milwaukee (NL)	000	001	110	---	3	9	0
New York (AL)	000	000	000	---.	0	2	0

Pitchers--SPAHN vs. FORD, Kucks (8), Dickson (9).
Attendance--71,563.

5th Game, at New York, Oct. 6

Milwaukee (NL)	000	000	000	---	0	5	0
New York (AL)	001	006	00x	---	7	10	0

Pitchers-- BURDETTE, Pizarro (6), Willey (8) vs.
TURLEY. Homer--McDougald (N.Y.). Attendance--65,279.

6th Game, at Milwaukee, Oct. 8

New York (AL)	100	001	000	2	---	4	10	1
Milwaukee (NL)	110	000	000	1	---	3	10	4

Pitchers--Ford, Ditmar (2), DUREN (6), Turley (10) vs.
SPAHN, McMahon (10). Homers--Bauer (N.Y.), McDougald
(N.Y.). Attendance--46,367.

7th Game, at Milwaukee, Oct. 9

New York (AL)	020	000	040	---	6	8	0
Milwaukee (NL)	100	001	000	---	2	5	2

Pitchers-- Larsen, TURLEY (3) vs. BURDETTE,
McMahon (8). Homers--Crandall (Mil.), Skowron (N.Y.).
Attendance--46,367.

1959

After eight failures in nine attempts, the rejuvenated Dodgers, now transplanted to the West Coast, beat Al Lopez' Chicago White Sox, in six games in the fifty-sixth fall classic. For attendance, receipts and size of players' shares, the series broke all existing records thanks to the enormous seating capacity of the Los Angeles Memorial Coliseum. The three games at Los Angeles drew 92,394; 92,650, and 92,706 respectively. Including the TV and radio rights the receipts totaled $5,628,809.44. Each winning Dodger received $11,231.18 while the losing White Sox each received $7,275.17, also a record. Opening the Series in Chicago Early Wynn, mainstay of the White Sox staff, had little trouble in white-washing the Dodgers 11-0. The Dodgers played badly with Duke Snider booting two chances in the same inning for a Series record. In the third inning the Dodgers collapsed completely when the Go-Go Sox scored seven runs climaxed by Ted Kluszewski's first homer with two aboard. Big Klu repeated with another powerful clout with Landis aboard in the fourth. The Dodgers eked out a victory in the second game on two homers by Charley Neal and another by pinch-hitter Chuck Essegian. Larry Sherry, coming to the aid of Johnny Podres, did a masterful relief job. In the third game the Sox lacked the punch and scored only one run although they got 12 hits, 4 walks, and Billy Goodman was hit by a pitched ball. Don Drysdale gained the victory, although Larry Sherry again had to be called in from the bull pen. The fourth game was a different story to Wynn who gave up 8 hits in 2-2/3 innings and had to give way to Turk Lown when the Dodgers jumped on him in the third for five hits and four runs. The Sox came to life in the seventh and tied the score when Sherm Lollar hammered one over the left field screen scoring Fox and Big Klu, who had singled. Gil Hodges homer in the eighth was the deciding blow as the Dodgers picked up the marbles 5-4. The fifth game was a thriller as Shaw and Donovan stifled the Dodger bats and allowed only one extra-base hit, a triple, by Hodges. In the seventh inning Rivera went to right field and made a sensational running catch of Neal's hard drive with runners on second and third. Fox scored the only run of the game when he led off the fourth inning with a single, advanced to third on Landis' one-bagger, and scored when Lollar hit into a double play. The Dodgers made 13 hits including homers by Snider, Moon, and Essegian to smother the Sox 9-3 in the sixth and deciding game. Wynn, making his third start, was the victim of the savage Dodger attack and left the game in the fourth when the Dodgers scored six runs to put the game and the series on ice.

Result: Los Angeles NL won 4: Chicago AL, 2.

```
    1st Game, at Chicago, Oct. 1st        R   H   E
Los Angeles (NL) 000  000  000    ---    0   8   3
Chicago (AL)     207  200  00X    ---   11  11   0
    Pitchers—CRAIG, Churn (3), Labine (4), Koufax (5),
Klippstein (2) vs. WYNN, Staley (8). Homers—Kluszewski
(Chi.) 2. Attendance—48,013.
```

```
    2nd Game, at Chicago, Oct. 2nd        R   H   E
Los Angeles (NL) 000  010  300    ---    4   9   1
Chicago (AL)     200  000  010    ---    3   8   0
    Pitchers—PODRES, Sherry (7) vs. SHAW, Lown (7).
Homers—Neal (LA) 2, Essegian (LA). Attendance—47,368.
```

```
    3rd Game, at Los Angeles, Oct. 4th    R   H   E
Chicago (AL )    000  000  010    ---    1  12   0
Los Angeles (NL) 000  000  21X    --•    3   5   0
    Pitchers—DONOVAN, Staley (7) vs. DRYSDALE,
Sherry (8). Attendance—92,394.
```

```
    4th Game, at Los Angeles, Oct. 5th    R   H   E
Chicago, (AL)    000  000  400    ---    4  10   3
Los Angeles (NL) 004  000  01X    ---    5   9   0
    Pitchers—Wynn, Lown (3), Pierce (4), STALEY (7) vs.
Craig, SHERRY (8). Homers—Lollar, (Chi), Hodges (LA).
Attendance—92,650.
```

```
    5th Game, at Los Angeles, Oct. 6th    R   H   E
Chicago (AL)     000  100  000    ---    1   5   0
Los Angeles (NL) 000  000  000    ---    0   9   0
    Pitchers—SHAW, Pierce (7), Donovan (8) vs. KOUFAX,
Williams (8). Attendance—92,706.
```

```
    6th Game, at Chicago, Oct. 8th        R   H   E
Los Angeles (NL) 002  600  001    ---    9  13   0
Chicago (AL)     000  300  000    ---    3   6   1
    Pitchers—Podres, SHERRY (4) vs. WYNN, Donovan
(4), Staley (5), Pierce (8), Moore (9). Homers—Snider
(LA), Moon (LA), Kluszewski (Chi), Essegian (LA).
Attendance—47,653.
```

1960

The 57th World Series was most peculiar due to the fact that the New York Yankees set many amazing records but were defeated by the Pirates four games to three. Among the World Series records set by the Yanks were: highest batting average (.338), most runs (55), most hits (91), most total bases (142) and most runs batted in (54). The Pirates' ability to come from behind was demonstrated in the first game when Maris homered with two out in the first inning. In their half, the Pirates bounced back with three runs and managed to stay ahead for the rest of the game with Bill Mazeroski, who later clouted the homer that beat the Yanks in the final game, weighing in with his first four-bagger. The second game was a breeze for the Yanks who belted six Pirate pitchers for 16 runs on 19 hits including two homers by Mickey Mantle for a 16-3 win behind Bullet Bob Turley. Resuming the series in Yankee Stadium on Oct. 8th, the Yanks again powdered the ball, winning 10-0 on 16 hits and Whitey Ford's fine four-hit pitching perform-ance. In this game, Bobby Richardson, Yank second-sacker who hit only one home run during the entire season, hit a grand-slam homer in the first inning and batted in a record-breaking six runs during the game. In the fourth game Vern Law and Elroy Face combined to stifle the Yankee bats aided by a remarkable circus catch by Bill Virdon of a liner off Bob Cerv's bat. From that point Face went on to save a 3-2 decision for Law. The Yankee drouth continued into the fifth game despite Maris' second home run of the series. They could do little with Harvey Haddix and when they did threaten the Pirate's lead in the seventh, Face again put out the fire in his accustomed fashion. The sixth game was almost a repetition of the fourth with Whitey Ford returning to the mound. He allowed only seven hits and one walk, shutting out the Pirates by a 12-0 score. In this game the Yank bats again exploded for 17 hits including two triples by Richardson. With the series all even at three games apiece the do-or-die Pirates went to work on Turley and Stafford by scoring four times in the first two innings. Skowron's homer in the fifth gave the Yanks their first run. They scored four more in the sixth which was featured by Yogi Berra's three-run homer. They went ahead 7-4 by continuing the assault on reliefer Elroy Face. Com-ing to bat in their half of the eighth with their backs to the wall, the Pirates

found themselves in familiar surroundings and proceeded to blast out five runs capped by catcher Hal Smith's mighty three-run homer over the left field wall giving them a 9-7 lead. Murtaugh then sent Friend in to protect the 2-run lead but the Yanks tied it all up at 9-9 on three singles and a force. Mazeroski, the lead-off batter for the Pirates in the bottom of the ninth, clobbered Ralph Terry's second pitch over the left field wall and the Corsairs wrapped up their first World Championship since 1925.

Result: Pittsburgh NL won 4; New York AL, 3.

1960

1st Game, at Pittsburgh, Oct. 5th				R	H	E
New York (AL)	100	100	002	---	4	13	2
Pittsburgh (NL)	300	201	00X	---	6	8	0

Pitchers—DITMAR, Coates (1), Maas (5), Duren (7) vs. LAW, Face (8). Homers—Maris (NY), Mazeroski (Pit), Howard (NY). Attendance—36,676.

2nd Game, at Pittsburgh, Oct. 6th				R	H	E
New York (AL)	002	127	301	---	16	19	1
Pittsburgh (NL)	000	100	002	---	3	13	1

Pitchers - - TURLEY, Shantz (9) vs. FRIEND, Green (5), Labine (6), Witt (6), Gibbon (7), Cheney (9). Homers - - Mantle (NY) 2. Attendance - - 37,308.

3rd Game, at New York, Oct. 8th				R	H	E
Pittsburgh (NL)	000	000	000	---	0	4	0
New York (AL)	600	400	00X	---	10	16	1

Pitchers—MIZELL, Labine (1), Green (1), Witt (4), Cheney (6), Gibbon (8) vs. FORD. Homers—Richardson (NY), Mantle (NY). Attendance—70,001.

4th Game, at New York, Oct. 9th				R	H	E
Pittsburgh (NL)	000	030	000	---	3	7	0
New York (AL)	000	100	100	---	2	8	0

Pitchers—LAW, Face (7), vs. TERRY, Shantz (7), Coates (8). Homers—Skowron (NY). Attendance—67,812.

5th Game, at New York, Oct. 10th				R	H	E
Pittsburgh (NL)	031	000	001	---	5	10	2
New York (AL)	011	000	000	---	2	5	2

Pitchers—HADDIX, Face (7), vs. DITMAR, Arroyo (2), Stafford (3), Duren (8). Homers—Maris (NY). Attendance—62,753.

6th Game, at Pittsburgh, Oct. 12th				R	H	E
New York (AL)	015	002	220	---	12	17	1
Pittsburgh (NL)	000	000	000	---	0	7	1

Pitchers—FORD vs. FRIEND, Cheney (3), Mizell (4), Green (6), Labine (6), Witt (9). Attendance--38,580.

7th Game, at Pittsburgh, Oct. 13th				R	H	E
New York (AL)	000	014	022	---	9	13	1
Pittsburgh (NL)	220	000	051	---	10	11	0

Pitchers—Turley, Stafford (2), Shantz (3), Coates (8), TERRY (8) vs. Law, Face (6), Friend (9), HADDIX (9). Homers—Nelson (Pit), Skowron (NY), Berra (NY), Smith (Pit), Mazeroski (Pit). Attendance—36,683.

1961

The Yankees returned to their winning ways in the 1961 series, having no trouble in disposing of the jittery Cincinnati Reds in five games. In the first game, the peerless Whitey Ford set the Reds down on two measley singles for a 2-0 shutout, striking out six and allowing only one base on balls. Elston Howard and Bill Skowron supplied the punch—each with a homer. Bobby Richardson, batting star of the 1960 series, smacked three singles in four trips to the plate. The Reds turned the tables in the second game, thanks to Joey Jay's 4-hit pitching, and beat the Yanks by a score of 6-2. Scoring two runs in the fourth on an error by Boyer followed by Gordon Coleman's homer, they scored one in each the fifth and sixth and added a couple more in the eighth for good measure. The third game in Cincinnati was a thriller featured by a Yankee attack in the last three innings which overcame a two-run deficit. Roger Maris, who had gone hitless until he came up in the ninth, supplied the clincher when he homered off Bob Purkey. It was all Whitey Ford in the fourth game when he handed out another string of goose-eggs to the Reds allowing only five singles until he retired in the sixth with an ankle injury suffered earlier in the game. In pitching five scoreless frames Ford broke Babe Ruth's record of 29-2/3 consecutive scoreless inning which had stood since 1918. Richardson was again a thorn

in the Reds side as he made three more hits. The fifth game resulted in a complete rout of the Reds, the Yanks scoring 13 runs of eight Red pitchers. It set a new record for the number of pitchers used in one World Series game. The Yanks lost no time when nine batters paraded to the plate in the first inning—five of them scoring. Another 5-run blast in the fourth topped by Hector Lopez' homer over the center field fence put the game entirely out of reach of the hapless Reds.

Result: New York AL won 4; Cincinnati NL, 1.

1st Game, at New York, Oct. 4th

					R	H	E
Cincinnati (NL)	000	000	000	---	0	2	0
New York (AL)	000	101	00X	---	2	6	0

Pitchers—O'TOOLE, Brosnan (8), vs. FORD. Homers—Howard (NY), Skowron (NY). Attendance—62,397.

2nd Game, at New York, Oct. 5th

					R	H	E
Cincinnati (NL)	000	211	020	---	6	9	0
New York (AL)	000	200	000	---	2	4	3

Pitchers—JAY vs. TERRY, Arroyo (8). Homers—Coleman (Cin.), Berra (NY). Attendance—63,083.

3rd Game, at Cincinnati, Oct. 7th

					R	H	E
New York (AL)	000	000	111	---	3	6	1
Cincinnati (NL)	001	000	100	---	2	8	0

Pitchers—Stafford, Daley (7), ARROYO (8) vs. PURKEY. Homers—Blanchard (NY), Maris (NY). Attendance—32,589.

4th Game, at Cincinnati, Oct. 8th

					R	H	E
New York (AL)	000	112	300	---	7	11	0
Cincinnati (NL)	000	000	000	---	0	5	1

Pitchers—FORD, Coates (6), vs. O'TOOLE, Brosnan (6), Henry (9). Attendance—32,589.

5th Game, at Cincinnati, Oct. 9th

					R	H	E
New York (AL)	510	502	000	---	13	15	1
Cincinnati (NL)	003	020	000	---	5	11	3

Pitchers—Terry, DALEY (3), vs. JAY, Maloney (1), K. Johnson (2), Henry (3), Jones (4), Purkey (5), Brosnan (7), Hunt (9). Homers—Blanchard (NY), Robinson (Cin.), Lopez (NY), Post (Cin.). Attendance—32,589.

1962

Rainstorms, first in New York and then in San Francisco, produced the most elongated World Series in history. Beginning in New York, the first game was played on October 4th and the final or 7th game finally was completed on October 16th. As usual, the Yankee ace, Whitey Ford, got the Yanks off to a flying start by setting the Giants down by a score of 6 to 2. It was his fifth consecutive victory in World Series play and his 10th World Series win. The game was even at 2-2 until the Yanks finally broke through with one run in the 7th, two in the 8th and another one for good measure in the ninth. Clete Boyer really iced the game in the 7th when he clouted a homer over the left field fence. The Giants evened it up in the second game with a classy 3-hit performance by Jack Sanford who throttled the Yanks completely, shutting them out by a score of 2-0. Sanford allowed only one extra base hit to Mickey Mantle in pitching his masterpiece. Willie McCovey hit a tremendous homer over the right field barrier for the insurance run. The see-saw action continued in the third game when Roger Maris singled sharply to right-center driving in Tresh and Mantle who had singles before him. Ed Bailey's two-run homer in the ninth was the Giants only scoring threat. The game was well pitched on both sides with Stafford and Pierce in a scoreless duel until the 7th. Pierce allowed the Yanks 5 hits to Stafford's 4 for the Giants. The Giants evened it up again in game Number 4. The go-ahead runs were produced by Chuck Hiller's grand slam homer in the seventh inning. It was the first grand-slammer ever hit by a National League player in a World Series. The Giants used four pitchers in this game and the Yanks three. Whitey Ford was going along with a 2-2 tie when he was lifted for Jim Coates in the seventh. Coates had walked Jim Davenport and Haller had struck out when Matty Alou, batting for Pagan doubled to left. Houk then sent in Bridges and with two down, Hiller lined his homer into the right field seats. As in the previous game, game Number 5 was all tied up at 2-2 in the eighth when Rookie Tom Tresh connected with one of Jack Sanford's serves and the Yankees went ahead to stay. Moving to San

Francisco after the 5th game, the series was delayed five days by rain and it was not until October 15th that the sixth game was played. This time it was all Billy Pierce. Bouncing back after his loss in game Number 3, Billy was master of the situation all the way allowing the powerful Yanks only 3 hits and winning by a score of 5-2. With the Giants ahead 3-0, Roger Maris hammered one over the right field fence. The only other extra base blow was Clete Boyer's double in the eighth. However the Yanks were not to be denied and in the final game they rallied behind Ralph Terry's 4-hit shutout to eke out a narrow 1-0 victory and the series. It was a heart-breaker for Jack Sanford who allowed the Yanks only 7 hits. The lone run was scored in the 5th when Bill Skowron and Clete Boyer singled, Terry walked when Sanford temporarily lost control and Skowron scored as Kubek bounced into a double play. The pitching in the series on the part of both clubs was out-standing especially the Giants corps which held the vaunted power of the Yanks to a meager team average of .199.

Result: New York AL won 4; San Francisco NL, 3.

1962

1st Game, at San Francisco, Oct. 4th					R	H	E
New York (AL)	200	000	121	---	6	11	0
San Francisco							
(NL)	011	000	000	---	2	10	0

Pitchers—FORD vs. O'DELL, Larson (7), Miller (1). Homer—Boyer (NY). Attendance—43,852.

2nd Game, at San Francisco, Oct. 5th					R	H	E
New York (AL)	000	000	000	---	0	3	1
San Francisco							
(NL)	100	000	10X	---	2	6	0

Pitchers—TERRY, Daley (8) vs. SANFORD. Homer—McCovey (SF) Attendance—43,910.

3rd Game, at New York, Oct. 7th					R	H	E
San Francisco							
(NL)	000	000	002	---	2	4	3
New York (AL)	000	000	30X	---	3	5	1

Pitchers—PIERCE, Larsen (8), Bolin (8) vs. STAFFORD. Homer—Bailey (SF). Attendance—71,434.

4th Game, at New York, Oct. 8th					R	H	E
San Francisco							
(NL)	020	000	401	---	7	9	1
New York (AL)	000	002	001	---	3	9	1

Pitchers—Marichal, Bolin (5), LARSEN (6), O'Dell (7) vs. Ford, COATES (7), Bridges (7). Homers—Haller (SF), Hiller (SF). Attendance—66,607.

5th Game, at New York, Oct. 10th					R	H	E
San Francisco							
(NL)	001	010	001	---	3	8	2
New York (AL)	000	101	03X	---	5	6	0

Pitchers—SANFORD, Miller (8) vs. TERRY. Homers—Pagan (SF), Tresh (NY). Attendance—63,165.

6th Game, at San Francisco, Oct. 15th					R	H	E
New York (AL)	000	010	010	---	2	3	2
San Francisco							
(NL)	000	320	00X	---	5	10	1

Pitchers—FORD, Coates (5), Bridges (8) vs. PIERCE. Homer—Maris (NY). Attendance—43,948.

7th Game, at San Francisco, Oct. 16th					R	H	E
New York (AL)	000	010	000	---	1	7	0
San Francisco							
(NL)	000	000	000	---	0	4	1

Pitchers—TERRY vs. SANFORD, O'Dell (8). Attendance—43,948.

1963

Stung by the caustic remarks of their followers when they booted away the 1962 pennant to their arch-rivals, the Giants, in a play-off, the surprising Dodgers performed the incredible feat of whipping the vaunted Yanks four straight games to win the Series in 1963. It was the first time that the Yanks had been shut out in a World Series since the Giants turned the trick in 1922.

MVP Sandy Koufax was the big gun of the Series when he won the opener 5-2 and repeated in the fourth game by a score of 2-1. Money pitcher Johnny Podres did his usual excellent pressure job in the second game with a little help from ace reliever Ron Perranoski. The pitching gem of the Series, however, was Don Drysdale's 1-0 victory in the third game. In his three-hit masterpiece, Big Don mowed down the Yanks with monotonous regularity, facing only the minimum three batters per inning in six of the nine innings.

Whitey Ford turned in a fine 2-hit performance in the fourth and final game but had the misfortune to run into Koufax again. This game was a nip and tuck affair

with a 1-1 tie due to homers by Frank Howard and Mickey Mantle when an error by Joe Pepitone on a throw by third baseman Clete Boyer gave a life to Jim Gilliam who raced all the way to third and scored the deciding run on a fly to deep center by Willie Davis. It was a dramatic victory for the Dodgers and one of the greatest upsets in World Series history.

Result: Los Angeles NL won 4; New York AL, 0.

1st Game, at New York, Oct. 2nd	R	H	E
Los Angeles (NL) 041 000 000	5	9	0
New York (AL) 000 000 020	2	6	0

Pitchers—KOUFAX vs. FORD, Williams (6), Hamilton (9). Homers—Roseboro (LA) Tresh (NY). Attendance—69,000.

2nd Game, at New York, Oct. 3rd	R	H	E
Los Angeles (NL) 200 100 010	4	10	1
New York (AL) 000 000 001	1	7	0

Pitchers—PODRES, Perranoski (9) vs. DOWNING, Terry (6), Reniff (9). Homer—Skowron (LA). Attendance—66,455.

3rd Game, at Los Angeles, Oct. 5th	R	H	E
New York (AL) 000 000 000	0	3	0
Los Angeles (NL) 100 000 00x	1	4	1

Pitchers—BOUTON, Reniff (8) vs. DRYSDALE. Attendance—55,912.

4th Game, at Los Angeles, Oct. 6th	R	H	E
New York (AL) 000 000 100	1	6	1
Los Angeles (NL) 000 010 10x	2	2	1

Pitchers—FORD, Reniff (8) vs. KOUFAX. Homers—F. Howard (LA), Mantle (NY). Attendance—55,912.

1964

The Cardinals, who finished fast to win the National League pennant on the final day, continued their winning ways by defeating the Yankees in the World Series, four games to three. It marked the first time since 1921-22 that the Bronx Bombers lost two consecutive Series. Surprisingly, the Bombers had most of the batting and pitching stars. Mickey Mantle unloaded three prodigious home runs to raise his record total to 18, and set several other marks besides. Bobby Richardson broke another Series record by collecting 13 hits and Joe Pepitone hit a grand slam home run, still something of a Series rarity. In pitching, Jim Bouton posted two victories and youthful Mel Stottlemyre one, although he did well enough to have won more often. The Cards roared into the Series by taking the opener, 9-5, overcoming a 4-2 deficit to do it. The Yanks squared it the next day, 8-3, behind Stottlemyre, who tossed a 7-hitter. Card ace Bob Gibson was the loser, no less. Mantle's dramatic ninth-inning homer off reliever Barney Schultz provided the Bombers with the third game, 2-1. Bouton held the Redbirds to six hits and the Yankees managed only four off St. Louis starter Curt Simmons through eight. Ken Boyer's fifth-inning bases-filled homer accounted for all the runs in the Cards' 4-3 triumph in Game No. 4. The Yanks chased 20-game winner Ray Sadecki in the first, scoring three runs on five hits, but Roger Craig and Ron Taylor limited them to one safety the rest of the way. Another home run, this one by catcher Tim McCarver in the 10th inning, decided the fifth game in St. Louis' favor, 5-2. Gibson, who struck out 13, appeared headed for a 2-0 victory, but Tom Tresh's two-run circuit in the ninth tied it. McCarver's clout came with two aboard. New York had the big bats in the sixth game as Roger Maris and Mantle stroked back-to-back homers on consecutive pitches and Pepitone hit his 'slam' for an 8-3 verdict. Gibson came back in the seventh game for St. Louis and, although he was touched for homers by Mantle, Clete Boyer and Phil Linz, was around at the finish which saw a 7-5 Cardinal victory. Gibson eclipsed a Series mark with 31 strikeouts and was generally considered to be the Classic's most valuable player.

Result: St. Louis NL won 4; New York AL, 3.

1st Game, at St. Louis, Oct. 7th	R	H	E
New York (AL) 030 010 010	5	12	2
St. Louis (NL) 110 004 03x	9	12	0

Pitchers—FORD, Downing (6), Sheldon (8), Mikkelsen (9) vs. SADECKI, Schultz (7). Homers—Tresh (NY), Shannon (St. L.). Attendance—30,805.

2nd Game, at St. Louis, Oct. 8th	R	H	E
New York (AL) 000 101 204	8	12	0
St. Louis (NL) 001 000 011	3	7	0

Pitchers—STOTTLEMYRE vs. GIBSON, Schultz (9), Richardson (9), Craig (9). Homer—Linz (NY). Attendance—30,805.

3rd Game, at New York, Oct. 10th	R	H	E
St. Louis (NL) 000 000 000	1	6	0
New York (AL) 010 000 001	2	5	2

Pitchers—Simmons, SCHULTZ (9) vs. BOUTON. Homer—Mantle (NY). Attendance—67,101.

4th Game, at New York, Oct. 11th	R	H	E
St. Louis (NL) 000 004 000	4	6	1
New York (AL) 300 000 000	3	6	1

Pitchers—Sadecki, CRAIG (1), Taylor (6) vs. DOWNING, Mikkelsen (7), Terry (8). Homer—K. Boyer (St. L.). Attendance—66,312.

5th Game, at New York, Oct. 12th	R	H	E
St. Louis (NL) 000 020 003	5	10	1
New York (AL) 000 000 002 0	2	6	2

Pitchers—GIBSON vs. Stottlemyre, Reniff (8), MIKKELSEN (8). Homers—Tresh (NY), McCarver (St. L.). Attendance—65,633.

6th Game, at St. Louis, Oct. 14th	R	H	E
New York (AL) 000 012 050	8	10	0
St. Louis (NL) 100 000 011	3	10	1

Pitchers—BOUTON, Hamilton (9) vs. SIMMONS, Taylor (7), Schultz (8), Richardson (8), Humphreys (9). Homers—Maris (NY), Mantle (NY), Pepitone (NY). Attendance—30,805.

```
7th Game, at St. Louis, Oct. 15th    R   H   E
New York (AL)   000  003  002  ......  5   9   2
St. Louis (NL)  000  330  10x  ......  7  10   1
    Pitchers—STOTTLEMYRE, Downing (5), Shel-
don (5), Hamilton (7), Mikkelsen (8) vs. GIBSON.
Homers—Brock (St. L.), Mantle (NY), K. Boyer
(St. L.), C. Boyer (NY), Linz (NY). Attendance—
30,346.
```

1965

The National League triumphed for the eighth time in 12 years and won its third straight as Los Angeles defeated Minnesota in a seven-game thriller. Again, it was the superior Dodger pitching that told the story. The great Sandy Koufax, who lost his initial start although surrendering only one earned run, came back with shutouts in the fifth and seventh games to give the Dodgers their fourth world title. And both Don Drysdale and Claude Osteen pitched creditably. The Twins, however, chased Drysdale in the opener with a six-run third inning and went on to an 8-2 triumph. Zoilo Versalles and Don Mincher hit round-trippers for Minnesota, which had often used the home run to advantage during the regular season. The Twins took a 2-0 lead in the classic by defeating Koufax, 5-1, as Jim Kaat checked the Dodgers on 7 hits. Leftfielder Bob Allison made a brilliant catch of Jim Lefebvre's sinking liner in the fifth to prevent a Dodger run. The Series shifted to Dodger Stadium for Game Three, and the Dodgers did an about-face, taking the next three games. Osteen, who had been obtained from the lowly Washington Senators in the off-season, got them started with a nifty 5-hit, 4-0 win. Drysdale followed with another 5-hitter and a 7-2 triumph as Los Angeles squared the Series. There were four homers in the game, two by each side, but two Twin errors helped to put the win in the Dodger column. Koufax scattered four singles in Game Five as L.A. rolled to a 7-0 decision. He was helped by Maury Wills' record-tying four hits. The Twins weren't through, though, as Jim (Mudcat) Grant pitched and batted them to a Series-tying 5-1 win. Grant allowed six hits and smashed a three-run homer in the sixth inning. But the invincible Koufax came back with a sparkling 2-0 three-hitter in the decisive seventh game. Sandy struck out 10, giving him 29 for three games. Lou Johnson, minor league retread, gave him all the runs he needed when he led off the fourth inning with his second homer of the Series.

Result: Los Angeles NL won 4; Minnesota AL, 3.

```
1st Game, at Minnesota, Oct. 6th    R   H   E
Los Angeles (NL) 010  000  001  ...... 2  10   1
Minnesota (AL)   016  001  00x  ...... 8  10   0
    Pitchers—DRYSDALE, Reed (3), Brewer (5),
Perranoski (7) vs. GRANT. Homers—Fairly (LA),
Mincher (M), Versalles (M). Attendance—47,797.

2nd Game, at Minnesota, Oct. 7th    R   H   E
Los Angeles (NL) 000  000  100  ...... 1   7   3
Minnesota (AL)   000  002  12x  ...... 5   9   0
    Pitchers—KOUFAX, Perranoski (7), Miller (8)
vs. KAAT. Attendance—48,700.

3rd Game, at Los Angeles, Oct. 9th   R   H   E
Minnesota (AL)   000  000  000  ...... 0   5   0
Los Angeles (NL) 000  211  00x  ...... 4  10   1
    Pitchers—PASCUAL, Merritt (6), Klippstein (8)
vs. OSTEEN. Attendance—55,934.

4th Game, at Los Angeles, Oct. 10th  R   H   E
Minnesota (AL)   000  101  000  ...... 2   5   2
Los Angeles (NL) 110  103  01x  ...... 7  10   0
    Pitchers—GRANT, Worthington (6), Pleis (8) vs.
DRYSDALE. Homers—Killebrew (M), Parker (LA),
Oliva (M), Johnson (LA). Attendance—55,920.

5th Game, at Los Angeles, Oct. 11th  R   H   E
Minnesota (AL)   000  000  000  ...... 0   4   1
Los Angeles (NL) 202  100  20x  ...... 7  14   0
    Pitchers—KAAT, Boswell (3), Perry (6) vs.
KOUFAX. Attendance—55,801.

6th Game, at Minnesota, Oct. 13th    R   H   E
Los Angeles (NL) 000  000  100  ...... 1   6   1
Minnesota (AL)   000  203  00x  ...... 5   6   1
    Pitchers—OSTEEN, Reed (6), Miller (8) vs.
GRANT. Homers—Allison (M), Grant (M), Fairly
(LA). Attendance—49,578.

7th Game, at Minnesota, Oct. 14th    R   H   E
Los Angeles (NL) 000  200  000  ...... 2   7   0
Minnesota (AL)   000  000  000  ...... 0   3   1
    Pitchers—KOUFAX vs. KAAT, Worthington (4),
Klippstein (6), Merritt (7), Perry (9). Homer—
Johnson (LA). Attendance—50,596.
```

1966

The Dodgers set new lows for futility as Baltimore rolled to a four-game sweep. The Orioles pitching, suspect during the season, held Los Angeles to two runs and 17 hits for a .142 batting average climaxed by 33 consecutive scoreless innings. One would have to go back to 1905, when the Giants blanked Philadelphia for 28 straight innings, to find something comparable. Never before had the Dodgers, either in

Brooklyn or Los Angeles, been swept in a World Series; never before had Baltimore even participated in one. The Baltimore heroes were, naturally, its pitchers: Jim Palmer, 20, Wally Bunker, 21, Dave McNally, 23, and Moe Drabowsky, a 31-year-old castoff. Drabowski relieved McNally in the third inning of the opener and proceeded to hurl 6⅔ innings of one-hit, 11-strikeout relief as the Orioles posted a 5-2 triumph. Six of his strikeouts were consecutive, tying Hod Eller's mark with the 1919 Cincinnati Reds. The Robinsons, Frank and Brooks, unloaded successive home runs, the former with one man on, off Dodger starter Don Drysdale in the first inning for a quick 3-0 lead. Jim Lefebvre's homer in the second and a bases-filled walk to Jim Gilliam — and by Drabowsky, no less — in the third produced the only Dodger runs of the game — and Series. Palmer's 4-hit pitching combined with a faulty Dodger defense gave the second game to Baltimore, 4-0. Dodger star Sandy Koufax was the victim of five miscues, including three on two successive plays by center-fielder Willie Davis in the fifth when the Orioles scored three times. There was a sixth Dodger error in the eighth as Baltimore scored twice. Bunker dazzled the Dodgers on six hits in Game Three at Baltimore in outdueling Claude Osteen, 1-0. Osteen permitted only three hits, but one was a home run by Paul Blair, and that was all the Orioles needed. Baltimore completed the sweep the next day, 1-0, behind the 4-hit twirling of McNally. Drysdale pitched well this time, also giving up four hits, but, as in Osteen's case, one was a homer. Frank Robinson was the culprit. Boog Powell, whose .357 average led both teams, had a potential home run taken away by Davis' brilliant leaping catch in dead center in the sixth. Except for the first game, the Los Angeles pitching was nearly as effective as the Orioles' holding the American League champs to a .200 average.

Result: Baltimore AL won 4; Los Angeles NL, 0.

1st Game, at Los Angeles, Oct. 5th

			R	H	E
Baltimore (AL)	310 100	000	5	9	0
Los Angeles (NL)	011 000	000	2	3	0

Pitchers - - McNally, DRABOWSKY (3) vs. DRYSDALE, Moeller (3), Miller (5), Perranoski (8). Homers - - F. Robinson (B), B. Robinson (B), Lefebvre (LA). Attendance - - 55,941.

2nd Game, at Los Angeles, Oct. 6th

			R	H	E
Baltimore (AL)	000 031	020	6	8	0
Los Angeles (NL)	000 000	000	0	4	6

Pitchers—PALMER vs. KOUFAX, Perranoski (7), Regan (8), Brewer (9). Attendance—55,947.

3rd Game, at Baltimore, Oct. 8th

			R	H	E
Los Angeles (NL)	000 000	000	0	6	0
Baltimore (AL)	000 010	000	1	3	0

Pitchers—OSTEEN, Regan (8) vs. BUNKER. Homer—Blair (B). Attendance—54,445.

4th Game, at Baltimore, Oct. 9th

			R	H	E
Los Angeles (NL)	000 000	000	0	4	0
Baltimore (AL)	000 100	000	1	4	0

Pitchers—DRYSDALE vs. McNALLY. Homer—F. Robinson (B). Attendance—54,458.

1967

The 64th World Series almost was a case of Bob Gibson vs. Jim Lonborg. Gibson, the Cardinal fireballer, tied a record last equalled by Lew Burdette in 1957 by winning three games, including the decisive seventh. Lonborg, 22-game winner of the surprising Boston Red Sox, who won the American League flag on the final day, breezed to two triumphs before being shelled in the finale after coming back with only two days rest. St. Louis, long the National League's best in these autumn classics, won its eighth World Series in 11 tries with some slugging help from veteran Roger Maris and some record base-stealing by fleet Lou Brock. Maris batted in seven runs, high for both sides, and hit .385, second to Brock's .414. The latter's 12 hits came within one of tying a record, but his seven stolen bases eclipsed by one Honus Wagner's record in the 1909 classic. Boston's Triple Crown Winner, Carl Yastrzemski, also enjoyed a fine Series with three home runs and a .400 batting average. St. Louis took the opener, 2-1, behind Gibson's 6-hit pitching and the four hits of Brock, who became the 32nd player to achieve this feat. Boston's run was supplied by losing pitcher Jose Santiago, who homered in the third inning. Lonborg pitched a masterly 1-hitter — a two-out double by Julian Javier in the eighth — as Boston squared the Series with a 5-0 win. Gentleman Jim had a perfect game going for 6⅔ innings. Yastrzemski provided the punch with two round-trippers, good for four RBIs. The third game went to St. Louis, 5-2, behind the steady 7-hit pitching of Nelson Briles, and the Cards went two up, 6-0, as Gibson shackled the Bosox on 5 hits in Game Four. It was up to Lonborg to keep the Sox in the Series, and he responded with a 3-hit, 3-1 victory. Maris' homer in the ninth deprived him of his second straight shutout. A home run barrage, including a record three in the fourth inning, put the sixth game

in the Boston win column, 8-4, and evened the Series again. Shortstop Rico Petrocelli smashed two and Yastrzemski and rookie Reggie Smith one apiece. This left it up to Gibson and Lonborg in the seventh game, but the latter, who had pitched just two days previously, was tired and wasn't his old self. St. Louis cuffed him for all of its 10 hits and seven runs the first six innings and coasted to a 7-2 triumph behind Gibson's 3-hitter. Gibson even homered in the fifth and Javier supplied the death blow with a three-run wallop in the sixth. Brock swiped three bases in the finale to break Wagner's record.

Result: St. Louis NL won 4; Boston AL, 3.

1st Game, at Boston, Oct. 4th   R   H   E
St. Louis (NL)   001 000 100   2 10   0
Boston (AL)   001 000 000   1   6   0
Pitchers—GIBSON vs. SANTIAGO, Wyatt (8).
Homer—Santiago (B). Attendance—34,796.

2nd Game, at Boston, Oct. 5th   R   H   E
St. Louis (NL)   000 000 000   0   1   1
Boston (AL)   000 101 30x   5   9   0
Pitchers—HUGHES, Willis (6), Hoerner (7), Lamabe (7) vs. LONBORG. Home runs—Yastrzemski (B) 2. Attendance—35,188.

3rd Game, at St. Louis, Oct. 7th   R   H   E
Boston (AL)   000 001 100   2   7   1
St. Louis (NL)   120 001 01x   5 10   0
Pitchers—BELL, Waslewski (3), Stange (6), Osinski (8) vs. BRILES. Home runs—Shannon (St. L.), Smith (B). Attendance—54,575.

4th Game, at St. Louis, Oct. 8th   R   H   E
Boston (AL)   000 000 000   0   5   0
St. Louis (NL)   402 000 00x   6   9   0
Pitchers—SANTIAGO, Bell (1), Stephenson (3), Morehead (5), Brett (8) vs. GIBSON. Attendance—54,575.

5th Game, at St. Louis, Oct. 9th   R   H   E
Boston (AL)   001 000 002   3   6   1
St. Louis (NL)   000 000 001   1   3   2
Pitchers—**LONBORG** vs. CARLTON, Washburn (7), Willis (9), Lamabe (9). Home runs—Maris (St. L.). Attendance—54,575.

6th Game, at Boston, Oct. 11th   R   H   E
St. Louis (NL)   002 000 200   4   8   0
Boston (AL)   010 300 40x   8 12   1
Pitchers—Hughes, Willis (4), Briles (5)., LAMABE (7), Hoerner (7), Jaster (7), Washburn (7), Woodeshick (8) vs. Waslewski, WYATT (6), Bell (8). Home runs—Petrocelli (B) 2, Yastrzemski (B), Smith (B), Brock (St. L.). Attendance—35,188.

7th Game, at Boston, Oct. 12th   R   H   E
St. Louis (NL)   002 023 000   7 10   1
Boston (AL)   000 010 010   2   3   1
Pitchers—GIBSON vs. LONBORG, Santiago (7), Morehead (9), Osinski (9), Brett (9). Home runs—Gibson (St. L.), Javier (St. L.). Attendance—35,188.

1968

Mickey Lolich, a portly lefthander, equalled the World Series record by pitching three complete-game victories as Detroit overcame the Cardinals' 3–1 edge in games to post its first Series triumph since 1945. Bob Gibson, St. Louis' brilliant righthander, won two games, which gave him seven career victories in these fall classics, but dropped the decisive seventh game to Lolich, 4–1. Bob set a Series record of 17 strikeouts in the opener as he handcuffed the Motor City team on five hits, 4–0. Detroit bounced back the next day, 8–1, on Lolich's 6-hitter, and Mickey was one of three Tigers to crash home runs. But St. Louis took the next two for a commanding 3–1 lead. The Cards collected 13 hits en route to a 7–3 win in Game Four and Gibson and swift Lou Brock combined talents in a 10–1 Redbird rout in Game Five. Bob scattered five hits as he became the first pitcher to win seven Series games in a row; his fourth-inning homer made him the only hurler with two Series round-trippers. Brock homered, tripled and doubled and stole his seventh base—which tied his own one-Series record established the previous year. His career total of 14 SBs tied Eddie Collins' long-standing mark. But it was Detroit the rest of the way. Lolich survived St. Louis' three-run outburst in the first inning of Game Five for a 5–3 win and Denny McLain, a 31-game winner during the season but twice a loser in the classic, squared things in the sixth contest with a one-sided 13–1 decision. The Tigers put it away early by scoring 10 runs in the third inning, the big blow being Jim Northrup's grand-slam homer. For the third time in five years, the Cards left it up to Gibson in the finale. Bob blanked the Tigers for six innings, but the Bengals erupted for three runs in the seventh, two of them scoring on Northrup's triple which was misplayed by centerfielder Curt Flood. The Tigers added another tally in the ninth as Lolich responded with a 5-hit, 4–1 victory. Mike Shannon's homer in the ninth spoiled his shutout but little else.

Result: Detroit AL won 4; St. Louis NL, 3.

1st Game, at St. Louis, Oct. 2   R H E
Detroit (AL)   000 000 000   0 5 3
St. Louis (NL)   000 300 10x   4 6 0
  Pitchers—McLAIN, Dobson (6), McMahon
(8) vs. GIBSON. Homers—Brock (St. L.). At-
tendance—54,692.

2nd Game, at St. Louis, Oct. 3   R H E
Detroit (AL)   011 003 102   8 13 1
St. Louis (NL)   000 001 000   1 6 1
  Pitchers—LOLICH vs. BRILES, Carlton (6),
Willis (7), Hoerner (9). Homers—Horton
(D), Lolich (D), Cash (D). Attendance—
54,692.

3rd Game, at Detroit, Oct. 5   R H E
St. Louis (NL)   000 040 300   7 13 0
Detroit (AL)   002 010 000   3 4 0
  Pitchers—WASHBURN, Hoerner (6) vs.
WILSON, Dobson (5), McMahon (6), Patter-
son (7), Hiller (8). Homers—Kaline (D), Mc-
Carver (St. L.), McAuliffe (D), Cepeda (St.
L.). Attendance—53,634.

4th Game, at Detroit, Oct. 6   R H E
St. Louis (NL)   202 200 040   10 13 0
Detroit (AL)   000 100 000   1 5 4
  Pitchers—GIBSON vs. McLAIN, Sparma (3),
Patterson (4), Lasher (6), Hiller (8), Dob-
son (8). Homers—Brock (St. L.), Gibson (St.
L.), Northrup (D). Attendance—53,634.

5th Game, at Detroit, Oct. 7   R H E
St. Louis (NL)   300 000 000   3 9 0
Detroit (AL)   000 200 30x   5 9 1
  Pitchers—Briles, HOERNER (7), Willis (7)
vs. LOLICH. Homers—Cepeda (St. L.). At-
tendance—53,634.

6th Game, at St. Louis, Oct. 9   R H E
Detroit (AL)   02 10 010 000   13 12 1
St. Louis (NL)   00 0 000 001   1 9 1
  Pitchers—McLAIN vs. WASHBURN, Jaster
(3), Willis (3), Hughes (3), Carlton (4),
Granger (7), Nelson (9). Homers—Northrup
(D), Kaline (D). Attendance—54,692.

7th Game, at St. Louis, Oct. 10   R H E
Detroit (AL)   000 000 301   4 8 1
St. Louis (NL)   000 000 001   1 5 0
  Pitchers—LOLICH vs. GIBSON. Homers—
Shannon (St. L.). Attendance—54,692.

1969

This was the year of the cinderella club. The New York Mets, after having languished in ninth and tenth place for the first eight years of its existence, finally reached the pinacle. Winning four consecutive games after losing the opener to the American League champion Baltimore Orioles was a feat last performed in 1942. Baltimore took the opener in the fifth consecutive post-season success after eliminating the Los Angeles Dodgers in the 1966 Series by four games and the Minnesota Twins in three games in the American League playoff to qualify for the 1969 Series. The single run by the NL champs in the seventh inning of the first game broke a streak of 39 consecutive Series shutout innings by the Orioles. Don Buford's home run·gave him the distinction of being the eighth player to hit for the circuit on his first trip to the plate in World Series competition. In the same inning, Brooks Robinson made a spectacular third base play bare-handed to stop the Mets most serious threat of the day. Oriole pitcher Mike Cuellar, in winning his six-hitter, became the second Cuban to win a Series game. In the second game of the Series, Jerry Koosman, N.Y. pitcher, achieved a brilliant two-hitter that even spotlight fielding from both teams could not diminish. The third game was exceptional for Met outfielder Tommie Agee with fingertip catches. The National League champs again triumphed in ten innings of the fourth game by a throwing error. Pinch hitter J. C. Martin of the Mets was struck on the wrist after Oriole pitcher Pete Richert picked up Martin's bunt and threw toward first base. The ball struck Martin and lurched toward second, bringing in the winning run standing up. It wasn't until the sixth inning of the fifth game before the Mets got on the scoreboard. The Orioles were enjoying a 3–0 lead when Cleon Jones, New York outfielder, jumped to get out of the way of a low pitched curve. A black

smudge of shoe polish proved Jones was struck, as he had claimed, and was waved on first. Donn Clendenon slammed a scorcher to the scoreboard making the score 3–2. That homer was No. 3 for Clendenon in the Series. Al Weis drove the tying run home over the 371-foot mark in left field. Weis' homer brought his batting average for the Series to .455 for eleven trips to the plate. Cleon Jones scored the go-ahead run when Ron Swoboda lined to left field. Swoboda scored the fifth and final run with a bobbled ball and error.

Result: New York NL won 4; Baltimore AL, 1.

```
1st Game, at Baltimore, Oct. 11th    R  H  E
New York (NL)       000 000 100      1  6  1
Baltimore (AL)      100 300 00x      4  6  0
  Pitchers -SEAVER Cardwell (6), Taylor (7)
vs. CUELLAR. Home runs—Buford (Bal.).
Attendance—50,429.
```

```
2nd Game, at Baltimore, Oct. 12th    R  H  E
New York (NL)       000 100 001      2  6  0
Baltimore (AL)      000 000 100      1  2  0
  Pitchers—KOOSMAN,  Taylor   (9)  vs.
McNALLY. Home runs—Clendenon (N.Y.).
Attendance—50,850.
```

```
3rd Game, at New York, Oct. 14th    R  H  E
Baltimore (AL)      000 000 000      0  4  1
New York (NL)       120 001 01x      5  6  0
  Pitchers—PALMER, Leonhard (7) vs.
GENTRY, Ryan (7). Home runs—Agee
(N.Y.),  Kranepool  (N.Y.).  Attendance—
56,335.
```

```
4th Game, at New York, Oct. 15th    R  H  E
Baltimore (AL)      000 000 001 0    1  6  1
New York (NL)       010 000 000 1    2 10  1
  Pitchers - - Cuellar, Watt (8), HALL (10),
Richert (10) vs. SEAVER. Homer - - Clende-
non (N.Y.). Attendance - - 57,367.
```

```
5th Game, at New York, Oct. 16th    R  H  E
Baltimore (AL)      003 000 000      3  5  2
New York (NL)       000 002 12x      5  7  0
  Pitchers—McNally, WATT (8) vs. KOOS-
MAN. Home runs—McNally (Bal.), F. Robin-
son (Bal.), Clendenon (N.Y.), Weis (N.Y.).
Attendance—57,397.
```

1970

The Baltimore Orioles easily whipped the Cincinnati Reds, four games to one. Brooks Robinson led the Orioles to their triumph, although many players contributed to the balanced attack which featured superior hitting, fielding and pitching. Brooks slugged at an .810 clip and handled 23 chances in the field, coming up with fine plays time after time. The Reds were weakened by injuries to their pitching staff. Reliever Clay Carroll hurled eight shutout innings in four games and saved the only contest Cincinnati could win. Lee May was the lone Red regular to hit well, slugging at a .833 rate. The Orioles repeatedly came from behind to win, rallying from 3–0 deficits in the first, second and fifth games. These comebacks were often sparked by home runs. Three circuit clouts decided the first game, a two-run job by Boog Powell and solo blasts by Elrod Hendricks and Brooks Robinson. Brooks contributed a defensive gem off May in the 6th inning. Later that inning Bernie Carbo was called out at home in a disputed play when he unexpectedly attempted to score on a chopper in front of the plate. Photos afterwards showed that Carbo had been safe. The Birds won 4–3. Hendricks stroked a key double to lead the Baltimore team to their second game rally and a 6–5 victory. The third game was won easily 9–3, as pitcher Dave McNally slugged a grand slam home run. Cincinnati's only win came next by a 6–5 score, as May clouted a three-run homer in the 8th to overcome a 5–3 Oriole lead. Carroll fashioned 3⅔ innings of scoreless relief. Baltimore stormed back quickly in the fifth game to take the series. The 9–3 victory was sparked by Frank Robinson's two-run homer in the first and Paul Blair struck the eventual winning blow, a single in the second. Mike Cuellar allowed only two hits and no runs after the first inning to pick up the win.

Result: Baltimore AL won 4; Cincinnati NL, 1.

1st Game, at Cincinnati, Oct. 10th　R　H　E
Baltimore (AL)　　000 210 100　　4　7　2
Cincinnati (NL)　　102 000 000　　3　5　0
　Pitchers - - PALMER, Richert (9) vs. NOLAN, Carroll (7). Home runs - - May (Cin), Powell (Bal), Hendricks (Bal), B. Robinson (Bal). Attendance - - 51,531.

2nd Game, at Cincinnati, Oct. 11th　R　H　E
Baltimore (AL)　　000 150 000　　6　10　2
Cincinnati (NL)　　301 001 000　　5　7　0
　Pitchers—Cuellar, PHOEBUS (3), Drabowsky (5), Lopez (7), Hall (7) vs. McGlothlin, WILCOX (5), Carroll (5), Gullett (8). Home runs—Tolan (Cin), Powell (Bal), Bench (Cin). Attendance—51,531.

3rd Game, at Baltimore, Oct. 13th　R　H　E
Cincinnati (NL)　　010 000 000　　3　9　0
Baltimore (AL)　　201 014 10x　　9　10　1
　Pitchers—CLONINGER, Granger (6), Gullett (7) vs. McNALLY. Home runs—F. Robinson (Bal), Buford (Bal), McNally (Bal). Attendance—51,773.

4th Game, at Baltimore, Oct. 14th　R　H　E
Cincinnati (NL)　　011 010 030　　6　8　3
Baltimore (AL)　　013 001 000　　5　8　0
　Pitchers—Nolan, Gullett (3), CARROLL (6) vs. Palmer, WATT (8), Drabowsky (9). Home runs—B. Robinson (Bal), Rose (Cin), May (Cin). Attendance—53,007.

5th Game, at Baltimore, Oct. 15th　R　H　E
Cincinnati (NL)　　500 000 000　　3　6　0
Baltimore (AL)　　222 010 02x　　9　15　0
　Pitchers—MERRITT, Granger (2), Wilcox (3), Cloninger (5), Washburn (7), Carroll (8) vs. CUELLAR. Home runs—F. Robinson (Bal), Rettenmund (Bal). Attendance—45,341.

1971

　Roberto Clemente excelled as the Pittsburgh Pirates took a close decision from the Baltimore Orioles in seven games. Clemente topped all hitters with a .414 mark, hit safely in every game and played superb right field. Steve Blass won his two starts, allowing only seven hits and two runs. The Orioles won the first two games rather easily. After a shaky defense gave the Pirates three unearned runs, the Birds came back with three homers—solo blasts by Frank Robinson and Don Buford sandwiched around a three-run shot by Merv Rettenmund. Dave McNally threw a three-hitter as the Orioles won, 5–3. The Bucs next fell 11–3, as Brooks Robinson drove in three runs and got on base five times. Blass started the Pirate comeback in Game Three, firing a three-hitter. Bob Robertson supplied the power with a three-run homer after missing a bunt sign. The pivotal fourth game went to Pittsburgh, 4–3. Young Bruce Kison slammed the door on the Birds, relieving after a three-run first and allowing the Pirates to get back into the game. Al Oliver drove in two runs and then Milt May delivered a tie-breaking pinch single. Nelson Briles weaved a two-hit shutout in the next game, a 4–0 verdict which gave Pittsburgh the series lead for the first time. Hustle by Frank Robinson capped the Orioles' 3–2 squeaker in ten innings in Game Six. Frank walked in the tenth, sped to third on Rettenmund's single and scored on a short sacrifice fly by Brooks. This set the stage for the dramatic seventh game. Clemente had an early homer, but the deciding blow was a double by Jose Pagan to score Willie Stargell in the 8th. Blass allowed only four hits and was at his best in the bottom of the 8th when Baltimore made their final bid. With runners on second and third and only one out, Steve escaped with a single run being scored, winning 2–1.

　Result: Pittsburgh NL won 4; Baltimore AL, 3.

1st Game, at Baltimore, Oct. 9th   R H E
Pittsburgh (NL)   030 000 000   3   3   0
Baltimore (AL)   013 010 00x   5 10   3
    Pitchers—ELLIS, Moose (3), Miller (7) vs. McNALLY. Home runs—F. Robinson (Bal), Rettenmund (Bal), Buford (Bal). Attendance —53,229.

2nd Game, at Baltimore, Oct. 11th   R H E
Pittsburgh (NL)   000 000 030   3   8   1
Baltimore (AL)   010 361 00x   11 14   1
    Pitchers - - R. JOHNSON, Kison (4), Moose (4), Veale (5), Miller (6), Giusti (8) vs. PALMER, Hall (9). Homerun - - Hebner (Pit). Attendance - - 53,239.

3rd Game, at Pittsburgh, Oct. 12th   R H E
Baltimore (AL)   000 000 100   1   3   3
Pittsburgh (NL)   100 001 30x   5   7   0
    Pitchers—CUELLAR, Dukes (7), Watt (8) vs. BLASS. Home runs—F. Robinson (Bal), Robertson (Pit). Attendance—50,403.

4th Game, at Pittsburgh, Oct. 13th   R H E
Baltimore (AL)   300 000 000   3   4   1
Pittsburgh (NL)   201 000 10x   4 14   0
    Pitchers—Dobson, Jackson (6), WATT (7), Richert (8) vs. Walker, KISON (1), Giusti (8). Attendance—51,378.

5th Game, at Pittsburgh, Oct. 14th   R H E
Baltimore (AL)   000 000 000   0   2   1
Pittsburgh (NL)   021 010 00x   4   9   0
    Pitchers—McNALLY, Leonard (5), Dukes (6) vs. BRILES. Home run—Robertson (Pit). Attendance—51,377.

6th Game, at Baltimore, Oct. 16th   R H E
Pittsburgh (NL)   011 000 000 0   2   9   1
Baltimore (AL)   000 001 100 1   3   8   0
    Pitchers—Moose, R. Johnson (6), Giusti (7), MILLER (10) vs. Palmer, Dobson (10), McNALLY (10). Home runs—Clemente (Pit), Buford (Bal). Attendance—44,174.

7th Game, at Baltimore, Oct. 17th   R H E
Pittsburgh (NL)   000 100 010   2   6   1
Baltimore (AL)   000 000 010   1   4   0
    Pitchers—BLASS vs. CUELLAR, Dobson (9), McNally (9). Home run—Clemente (Pit). Attendance—47,291

1972

The Oakland A's edged the big red machine from Cincinnati in the closest series ever. All but one of the seven games were decided by a single run. The hero was unquestionably Gene Tenace, who had hit only .225 as a utility man for the A's during the season. He banged out four homers, drove in nine runs, hit .348 and slugged .913 in the series. Tenace hit home runs his first two times up in Game One, knocking in all runs for a 3–2 triumph. He also had a key hit in a rally that won the fourth game, clouted a three-run homer in a losing cause in the fifth contest, and contributed an important double in the final game. A's pilot Dick Williams and Reds' skipper Sparky Anderson used innumerable pinch hitters, pinch runners, and relief pitchers throughout the series. Rollie Fingers appeared in six games for Oakland, winning one and saving two, while Tom Hall hurled 8⅓ shutout innings for the Reds in four games. Ross Grimsley picked up two wins in relief for Cincinnati. Jim Hunter won two games for the Athletics and Jack Billingham did not allow an earned run for the Reds in 13⅔ innings. Joe Rudi led the A's to a 2–1 win in the second game, whacking a homer to break a 1–1 tie and making a game-saving miraculous catch in the ninth. Billingham shut out Oakland in Game Three, 1–0, as Cesar Geronimo drove in the only run. The A's took the apparent series-tieing game out of the Reds' hands in the last inning of game number four. Three pinch hits were sandwiched around Tenace's single, as Angel Mangual scored Gene with the winning run, 3–2. The Cincinnati club rallied to win the next two games, one on a ninth-inning tie-breaking outburst sparked by Pete Rose and the next in the only runaway game in the series, 8–1, truly a team effort. The final game reverted to the nip-and-tuck pattern, as the A's triumphed 3–2. Tenace's double knocked across the second run. His pinch runner, Allan Lewis, who was

used in six of the seven games, scored the winner on a double by Sal Bando.
Result: Oakland AL won 4; Cincinnati NL, 3.

1st Game, at Cincinnati, Oct. 14th　R　H　E
Oakland (AL)　　　0 2 0 0 1 0 0 0 0　3　4　0
Cincinnati (NL)　　0 1 0 1 0 0 0 0 0　2　7　0
Pitchers—HOLTZMAN, Fingers (6), Blue
(7) vs. NOLAN, Borbon (7), Carroll (8).
Homers—Tenace (Oak) 2. Attendance—52,918.

2nd Game, at Cincinnati, Oct. 15th　R　H　E
Oakland (AL)　　　0 1 1 0 0 0 0 0 0　2　9　2
Cincinnati (NL)　　0 0 0 0 0 0 0 0 1　1　6　0
Pitchers—HUNTER, Fingers (9) vs. GRIMS-
LEY, Borbon (6), Hall (8). Homer—Rudi
(Oak). Attendance—53,224.

3rd Game, at Oakland, Oct. 18th　R　H　E
Cincinnati (NL)　　0 0 0 0 0 0 1 0 0　1　4　2
Oakland (AL)　　　0 0 0 0 0 0 0 0 0　0　3　2
Pitchers—BILLINGHAM, Carroll (9) vs.
ODOM, Blue (8), Fingers (8). Attendance—
49,410.

4th Game, at Oakland, Oct. 19th　R　H　E
Cincinnati (NL)　　0 0 0 0 0 0 0 2 0　2　7　1
Oakland (AL)　　　0 0 0 0 1 0 0 0 2　3 10　1
Pitchers—Gullett, Borbon (8), CARROLL
(9) vs. Holtzman, Blue (8), FINGERS (9).
Homer—Tenace (Oak). Attendance—49,410.

5th Game, at Oakland, Oct. 20th　R　H　E
Cincinnati (NL)　　1 0 0 1 1 0 0 1 1　5　8　0
Oakland (AL)　　　0 3 0 1 0 0 0 0 0　4　7　2
Pitchers—McGlothlin, Borbon (4), Hall (5),
Carroll (7), GRIMSLEY (8), Billingham (9)
vs. Hunter, FINGERS (5), Hamilton (9).
Homers—Rose (Cin), Tenace (Oak), Menke
(Cin). Attendance—49,410.

6th Game, at Cincinnati, Oct. 21st　R　H　E
Oakland (AL)　　　0 0 0 0 1 0 0 0 0　1　7　1
Cincinnati (NL)　　0 0 0 1 1 1 5 0 x　8 10　0
Pitchers—BLUE, Locker (6), Hamilton (7),
Horlen (7) vs. Nolan, GRIMSLEY (5), Borbon
(6), Hall (7). Homer—Bench (Cin). Atten-
dance—52,737.

7th Game, at Cincinnati, Oct. 22nd　R　H　E
Oakland (AL)　　　1 0 0 0 0 2 0 0 0　3　6　1
Cincinnati (NL)　　0 0 0 0 1 0 0 1 0　2　4　2
Pitchers—Odom, HUNTER (5), Holtzman
(8), Fingers (8) vs. Billingham, BORBON (6),
Carroll (6), Grimsley (7), Hall (8). Atten-
dance—56,040.

1973

Oakland nipped the amazing New York Mets in seven games in what had
to be the most hectic series in history. On and off field developments vied for
the limelight daily. There were many heroes. Reggie Jackson was the key man
in the A's rally which gave them the final two games. Darold Knowles appeared in all seven games and saved two, while Rollie Fingers matched the
two saves in one less game. Ken Holtzman won the first and last games. Bert
Campaneris and Joe Rudi sparkled both at the plate and in the field. The
Mets were led by Rusty Staub, who gave a marvelous performance. With a
shoulder so sore he could barely throw, Rusty led all hitters with a .423
mark. Jon Matlack allowed no earned runs in his first two starts and reliever
Tug McGraw appeared in five games, winning one and saving one. Bud Harrelson excelled at shortstop. Holtzman pitched the A's to the first game win,
2–1. He also rapped a doubled which keyed the two-run third, as Felix Millan
made a damaging error that inning. The second game was a wild 10–7 victory
for the Mets in 12 innings. Willie Mays drove in the lead run for the New
Yorkers and Oakland's Mike Andrews made two errors that led to three more
runs. The A's, who had rallied to score two in the 9th for a 6–6 tie, came back
with one in the bottom of the 12th. After the game, Andrews was placed on
the disabled list by owner Finley, resulting in a revolt by the Oakland players. Leaders were Sal Bando and Jackson, who asked to be traded. Commissioner Kuhn ordered Andrews reinstated and Mike received a standing ova-
tion from the Met fans when he appeared in Game Four. Manager Dick Williams, who had been opposed to Finley's action, announced to his players
that he would resign after the series, a fact that later leaked out and was con-

firmed before the seventh game had begun. Oakland settled down to win the third game, 3–2, also in extra innings. Campaneris scored the tieing run in the 8th and knocked in the winner in the 10th. In the only runaway game of the series, the Mets evened things up in the fourth game, 6–1. Staub banged out four hits and drove in five runs to back fine pitching by Matlack. The Mets won again the following day, 2–0, as runs were knocked in by John Milner and Don Hahn. Jerry Koosman and McGraw combined for the whitewash. Then Jackson took over, twice doubling in runs and later scoring the third to help Hunter to a 3–1 verdict, and matching Campaneris with a two-run homer in the 5–2 finale. The last out was made with the Mets having the tieing run at the plate. After the series, Jackson revealed that a threat had been made on his life and that he had been under FBI guard since the final weeks of the season.

Result: Oakland AL won 4, New York NL, 3.

1st Game, at Oakland, Oct. 13th
			R	H	E
New York (NL)	000 100 000		1	7	2
Oakland (AL)	002 000 00x		2	4	0

Pitchers—MATLACK, McGraw (7) vs. HOLTZMAN, Fingers (6), Knowles, (9). Attendance–46,021.

2nd Game, at Oakland, Oct. 14th
		R	H	E
New York (NL)	011 004 000 004	10	15	1
Oakland (AL)	210 000 102 001	7	13	5

Pitchers—Koosman, Sadecki (3), Parker (5), McGRAW (6), Stone (12) vs. Blue, Pina (6), Knowles (6), Odom (8), FINGERS (10), Lindblad (12). Homers—Jones (NY), Garrett (NY). Attendance–49,151.

3rd Game, at New York, Oct. 16th
		R	H	E
Oakland (AL)	000 001 010 01	3	10	1
New York (NL)	200 000 000 00	2	10	2

Pitchers—Hunter, Knowles (7), LINDBLAD (9), Fingers (11) vs. Seaver, Sadecki (9), McGraw (9), PARKER (11). Homer—Garrett (NY). Attendance–54,817.

4th Game, at New York, Oct. 17th
			R	H	E
Oakland (AL)	000 100 000		1	5	1
New York (NL)	300 300 00x		6	13	1

Pitchers—HOLTZMAN, Odom (1), Knowles (4), Pina (5), Lindblad (8) vs. MATLACK, Sadecki (9). Homer—Staub (NY). Attendance–54,817.

5th Game, at New York, Oct. 18th
		R	H	E
Oakland (AL)	000 000 000	0	3	1
New York (NL)	010 001 00x	2	7	1

Pitchers—BLUE, Knowles (6), Fingers (7) vs. KOOSMAN, McGraw (7). Attendance–54,817.

6th Game, at Oakland, Oct. 20th
		R	H	E
New York (NL)	000 000 010	1	6	2
Oakland (AL)	101 000 01x	3	7	0

Pitchers—SEAVER, McGraw (8) vs. HUNTER, Knowles (8), Fingers (8). Attendance–49,333.

7th Game, at Oakland, Oct. 21st
		R	H	E
New York (NL)	000 001 001	2	8	1
Oakland (AL)	004 010 00x	5	9	1

Pitchers—MATLACK, Parker (3), Sadecki (5), Stone (7) vs. HOLTZMAN, Fingers (6), Knowles (9). Homers—Campaneris (Oak), Jackson (Oak). Attendance–49,333.

1974

Oakland won their third straight series, beating Los Angeles in five games. This was the first time since 1953 that any team had managed this feat, and it was the third longest streak in history. As in recent years, the games were close, with four of the five being decided by 3-2 scores. A major contributor for the A's was Ken Holtzman, who pitched four scoreless innings and smacked a double in the first game, which Oakland won, 3-2. He also hit a homer and got credit for the win in Game Four. Steve Garvey was the top Dodger, hitting .381 in the series. Joe Ferguson, who had made a fine throw from the outfield

in the first game, clubbed a two-run homer in Game Two, as the Dodgers came back to win, 3-2, behind Don Sutton. Bert Campaneris, who scored the winning run in the first game, drove in the deciding marker in the A's 3-2 victory in Game Three. Campy hit .353 overall. It looked like the Dodgers were on their way to tieing the series in Game Four, building a 2-1 lead on Bill Russell's two-run triple. But Oakland turned the series around with a four-run rally in the sixth. After the A's had tied the score, pinch-hitter Jim Holt cracked out a two-run single which led to a 5-2 win. The final game was another nip-and-tuck affair. Los Angeles came back to cancel a two-run Oakland lead in the sixth. But in the next inning, after a six-minute delay to remove debris thrown on the field for no apparent reason by the A's fans, Oakland struck again. Joe Rudi, a .333 hitter for the series, clouted Mike Marshall's first pitch into the left field seats. The game ended with no further scoring. Bill Buckner led off the eighth with a single for the Dodgers, and went to second as the ball got by the outfield. But when he tried to go all the way to third, he was thrown out by a fine relay from Reggie Jackson to Dick Green to Sal Bando. Green, who went hitless in the series, was still a factor due to his superior fielding throughout. Rollie Fingers, who had picked up a win in the first game, preserved Athletic victories in the final three games.

Result: Oakland AL won 4; Los Angeles NL, 1.

1st Game, at Los Angeles, Oct. 12th R H E
Oakland (AL)   010 010 010   3 6 2
Los Angeles (NL)   000 010 001 2 11 1
Pitchers—Holtzman, FINGERS (5), Hunter (9) vs. MESSERSMITH, Marshall (9). Homers—Jackson (Oak), Wynn (LA). Attendance—55,974.

2nd Game, at Los Angeles, Oct. 13 R H E
Oakland (AL)   000 000 002   2 6 0
Los Angeles (NL)   010 002 00x 3 6 1
Pitchers—BLUE, Odom (8) vs. SUTTON, Marshall (9). Homer—Ferguson (LA). Attendance—55,989.

3rd Game at Oakland, Oct. 15th   R H E
Los Angeles (NL)   000 000 011 2 7 2
Oakland (AL)   002 100 00x 3 5 2
Pitchers—DOWNING, Brewer (4), Hough (5), Marshall (7) vs. HUNTER, Fingers (8). Homers—Buckner (LA), Crawford (LA). Attendance—49,347.

4th Game, at Oakland, Oct. 16th   R H E
Los Angeles (NL)   000 200 000 2 7 1
Oakland (AL)   001 004 00x 5 7 0
Pitchers—MESSERSMITH, Marshall (7) vs. HOLTZMAN, Fingers (8). Homer—Holtzman (Oak). Atttendance—49,347.

5th Game, at Oakland, Oct. 17th   R H E
Los Angeles (NL)   000 002 000 2 5 1
Oakland (AL)   110 000 10x 3 6 1
Pitchers—Sutton, MARSHALL (6) vs. Blue, ODOM (7), Fingers (8). Homers—Fosse (Oak), Rudi (Oak). Attendance—49,347.

1975

The Cincinnati Reds outlasted the Boston Red Sox in seven games in a series whose sixth game was one of the classics in history. Virtually every player on both teams contributed a key play during the series. Pete Rose, who hit .370, led the Reds, along with young reliever Rawly Eastwick, who won two games

and saved a third. Luis Tiant, who won two games for Boston, started the series with a masterful five-hit shutout. All runs were scored in a six-run seventh-inning rally by the Sox, sparked by a two-run single by Rico Petrocelli. Cincinnati came back to win Game Two, 3-2, with a two-out ninth inning rally. Dave Concepcion sent a perfectly-placed bouncer up the middle to score Johnny Bench with the tieing run, then stole second and came home on Ken Griffey's double. The third game also went to the Reds with a last-inning rally, this time in the tenth on a controversial play. Boston had come from a 5-1 deficit to tie the score, thanks to homers by Bernie Carbo and Dwight Evans. Cesar Geronimo started the tenth with a single and Ed Armbrister attempted to bunt him along. Sox catcher Carlton Fisk collided with Armbrister while fielding the ball, and then made a hurried throw past second. This gave the Reds runners on second and third with none out. Boston argued that interference had taken place, but were denied. Joe Morgan's single then won the game. Tiant came back in Game Four to win 5-4, as the Sox scored five in the fourth, keyed by Evans' two-run triple. Cincinnati went ahead in the series, winning the fifth game 6-2, as Tony Perez hit two home runs good for four runs. Boston then won the sixth game in truly dramatic fashion. Super rookie Fred Lynn gave the Sox an early lead with a three-run homer in the first, but the Reds came back to tie in the fifth with a three-run rally. A double by George Foster and homer by Cesar Geronimo gave Cincinnati a 6-3 lead off Tiant going into the last of the eighth. But Bernie Carbo struck a towering homer to center with two on to tie the score. The Sox loaded the bases with none out in the ninth, but were unable to score, as Foster made a fine catch and throw which resulted in a double play at the plate. Then in the eleventh, it looked like the Reds' turn, as Morgan sent a screaming liner to right with Griffey on first. But Evans came up with a terrific catch to save the game, doubling up Griffey. Carlton Fisk then won the game with a smash off the foul pole in the twelfth. The seventh game was an anti-climax, as both clubs seemed spent. Boston got an early 3-0 lead thanks to Cincinnati wildness, but the Reds picked away and finally won in the top of the ninth, 4-3, on a bloop single by Joe Morgan.

Result: Cincinnati NL won 4; Boston AL 3.

1st Game, at Boston, Oct. 11th

	R	H	E
Cincinnati (NL) 000 000 000	0	5	0
Boston (AL) 000 000 60x	6	12	0

Pitchers—GULLETT, Carroll (7), McEnaney (7) vs. TIANT. Attendance—35,205.

2nd Game, at Boston, Oct 12th

	R	H	E
Cincinnati (NL) 000 100 002	3	7	1
Boston (AL) 100 001 000	2	7	0

Pitchers—Billingham, Borbon (6), McEnaney (7), EASTWICK (8) vs. Lee, DRAGO (9). Attendance—35,205.

3rd Game, at Cincinnati, Oct. 14th

	R	H	E
Boston (AL) 010 001 1020	5	10	2
Cincinnati (NL) 000 230 0001	6	7	0

Pitchers—Wise, Burton (5), Cleveland (5), WILLOUGHBY (7), Moret (10) vs. Nolan, Darcy (5), Carroll (7), McEnaney (7), EASTWICK (9). Homers—Fisk (Bos), Bench (Cin), Concepcion (Cin), Geronimo (Cin), Carbo (Bos), Evans (Bos). Attendance—55,392.

4th Game, at Cincinnati, Oct. 15th R H E
Boston (AL)   000 500 000 5 11 1
Cincinnati (NL)   200 200 000 4 9 1
Pitchers——TIANT vs. NORMAN, Borbon
(4), Carroll (5), Eastwick (7). Attendance—
55,667.

5th Game, at Cincinnati, Oct. 16th R H E
Boston (AL)   100 000 001 2 5 0
Cincinnati (NL)   000 113 01x 6 8 0
Pitchers—CLEVELAND, Willoughby (6),
Pole (8), Segui (8) vs. GULLETT, Eastwick
(9). Homers—Perez (Cin) 2. Attendance—
56,393.

6th Game, at Boston, Oct. 21st   R H E
Cincinnati (NL)   000 030 210 000   6 14 0
Boston (AL)   300 000 030 001   7 10 1
Pitchers—Nolan, Norman (3), Billingham
(3), Carroll (5), Borbon (6), Eastwick (8),
McEnaney (9), DARCY (10) vs. Tiant, Moret
(8), Drago (9), WISE (12). Homers—Lynn
(Bos), Geronimo (Cin), Carbo (Bos), Fisk
(Bos). Attendance—35, 205.

7th Game, at Boston, Oct. 22nd   R H E
Cincinnati (NL)   000 002 101   4 9 0
Boston (AL)   003 000 000   3 5 2
Pitchers—Gullett, Billingham (5), CAR-
ROLL (7), McEnaney (9) vs. Lee, Moret
(7), Willoughby (7), BURTON (9), Cleve-
land (9). Homer—Perez (Cin). Attendance—
35,205.

1976

The Cincinati Reds swept aside the New York Yankees in four straight games, thus becoming the first NL club since 1922 to win back-to-back championships. The Reds trailed only for three innings at the start of the third game and became the first team to win seven post-season games in a row. Johnny Bench, who had been hampered with injuries during the regular season, batted .533 in the series and drove in six runs with seventeen total bases in fifteen at bats. Six other Reds went over the .300 mark, including George Foster at .429, and the club as a unit compiled a .313 mark. The AL's designated hitter rule was in force in the series for the first time. Cincinnati's Dan Driessen hit .357, while a combination of Yankee DH's managed an anemic .063. The first game went to the Reds 5–1, but starter Don Gullett dislocated his ankle and was lost for the rest of the series. The Yankees' only threat towards a victory came in the next game, as Catfish Hunter settled down after allowing three runs in the second and the New Yorkers pecked away to tie. The Reds rose to the challenge, however, with Tony Perez driving in the winning run in the last of the ninth. Game Three was another clear Cincinnati victory. Bench nailed the coffin shut in the final game, clouting two home runs. The first was a two-run blast in the fourth that gave the Reds the lead and the second went for three runs in the ninth. Roy White made a gallant effort to keep the ball out of the stands. The Reds' superb relief crew was led by Will McEnaney with two saves. A tower of strength for New York was Thurman Munson, who batted .529, after a .435 mark in the championship series. Chris Chambliss, whose dramatic homer won the final game with Kansas City, hit .524 in that set and .313 in the World Series.

Result: Cincinnati NL won 4; New York AL, 0.

1st Game, at Cincinnati, Oct. 16th R H E
New York (AL)   010 000 000   1 5 1
Cincinnati (NL)   101 001 20x   5 10 1
Pitchers—ALEXANDER, Lyle (7), vs. GUL-
LETT, Borbon (8). Homers—Morgan (Cin).
Attendance—54,826.

2nd Game, at Cincinnati, Oct. 17th R H E
New York (AL)   000 100 200   3 9 1
Cincinnati (NL)   030 000 001   4 10 0
Pitchers—HUNTER vs. Norman, BILL-
INGHAM (7). Attendance—54,816.

3rd Game, at New York, Oct. 19th. R H E
Cincinnati (NL)   030 100 020   6 13 2
New York (AL)   000 100 100   2 8 0
Pitchers—ZACHRY, McEnaney (7) vs. EL-
LIS, Jackson (4), Tidrow (8). Homers—
Driessen (Cin), Mason (NY). Attendance—
56,667.

4th Game, at New York, Oct. 21st. R H E
Cincinnati (NL)   000 300 004   7 9 2
New York (AL)   100 010 000   2 8 0
Pitchers—NOLAN, McEnaney (7) vs. FI-
GUEROA, Tidrow (9), Lyle (9). Homers—
Bench (Cin) 2. Attendance—56,700.

1977

Reggie Jackson performed the incredible feat of hitting three consecutive pitches out of the park to propel the Yankees to an 8-4 victory in the final game and win the series from their longtime Dodger foes. Jackson, obtained in the free-agent draft, batted .450 and slugged five homers altogether, giving him eight runs batted in and 25 total bases in 20 at-bats. The Yankees started slowly, taking twelve innings to win the first game 4-3, on a double by Willie Randolph and a single by Paul Blair. Los Angeles came back to tie as they blasted sore-armed Catfish Hunter for three homers and went on to win 6-1, behind Burt Hooton. Mike Torrez, who had two complete game victories in the series, won the third game 5-3. The Yankees also took Game Four, as Ron Guidry allowed only four hits. The Dodgers then pummelled the Yanks' other free-agent sore-armed pitcher, Don Gullett, 10-4, as Steve Yeager drove in four runs. But in the eighth inning, Thurman Munson and Jackson hit consecutive homers, apparently meaningless at the time, but perhaps foreshadowing the Dodger downfall in the next game. Torrez allowed Los Angeles two runs in the first, but Chris Chambliss tied the score with a homer in the second, driving in Jackson, who had walked. Reggie hit his first blast in the fourth, putting the Yanks ahead 4-3. His next made it 6-3 in the fifth, and the final one was a 450-foot shot in the eighth, which was a fitting climax to an amazing performance.

Result: New York AL won 4; Los Angeles NL, 2.

1st Game, at New York, Oct. 11th   R H E
Los Angeles (NL) 2 0 0 0 0 0 0 0 1 0 0 0   3 6 0
New York (AL)   1 0 0 0 0 1 0 1 0 0 0 1   4 11 0
Pitchers—Sutton, Rautzhan (8), Sosa (8), Garman (9), RHODEN (12) vs. Gullett, LYLE (9). Homer—Randolph (NY). Attendance—56,668.

2nd Game, at New York, Oct. 12th   R H E
Los Angeles (NL) 2 1 2 0 0 0 0 0 1   6 9 0
New York (AL)   0 0 0 1 0 0 0 0 0   1 5 0
Pitchers—HOOTON vs. HUNTER, Tidrow (3), Clay (6), Lyle (9). Homers—Cey (LA), Yeager (LA), Smith (LA), Garvey (LA). Attendance—56,691.

3rd Game, at Los Angeles, Oct. 14th   R H E
New York (AL)   3 0 0 1 1 0 0 0 0   5 10 0
Los Angeles (NL) 0 0 3 0 0 0 0 0 0   3 7 1
Pitchers—TORREZ vs. JOHN, Hough (7). Homer—Baker (LA). Attendance—55,992.

4th Game, at Los Angeles, Oct. 15th   R H E
New York (AL)   0 3 0 0 0 1 0 0 0   4 7 0
Los Angeles (NL) 0 0 2 0 0 0 0 0 0   2 4 0
Pitchers—GUIDRY vs. RAU, Rhoden (2), Garman (9). Homers—Lopes (LA), Jackson (NY). Attendance—55,995.

5th Game, at Los Angeles, Oct. 16th   R H E
New York (AL)   0 0 0 0 0 0 2 2 0   4 9 2
Los Angeles (NL) 1 0 0 4 3 2 0 0 x 10 13 0
Pitchers—GULLETT, Clay (5), Tidrow (6). Hunter (7) vs. SUTTON. Homers—Yeager (LA), Smith (LA), Munson (NY), Jackson (NY). Attendance—55,995.

6th Game, at New York, Oct. 18th   R H E
Los Angeles (NL) 2 0 1 0 0 0 0 0 1   4 9 0
New York (AL)   0 2 0 3 2 0 0 1 x   8 8 1
Pitchers—HOOTON, Sosa (4), Rau (5), Hough (7) vs. TORREZ. Homers—Chambliss (NY), Smith (LA), Jackson (NY) 3. Attendance—56,407.

1978

The Yankees took the Dodgers once again, repeating their six-game triumph of the previous year, but their method was quite different. They spotted Los Angeles two games and then came on to win four straight, led by Bucky Dent (.417), their least-famous regular and Brian Doyle (.438), who was playing only because Willie Randolph was injured. Reggie Jackson was in the middle of the action as usual, hitting .391 with two homers, but his most important contribution came in an unusual way at the turning point of the series in the fourth game. The Dodgers won Game One 11-5, behind two homers by Davey

Lopes and hung on to win the next contest, as Ron Cey drove in all four runs and rookie Bob Welch struck out Jackson to seal a 4–3 verdict. New York took the third game 5–1, thanks mainly to four fine fielding plays by Graig Nettles, cutting off potential Dodger rallies. The key play occurred in the sixth inning of Game Four, with Los Angeles ahead 3 to 1. Shortstop Bill Russell appeared to intentionally drop Lou Piniella's line drive to try for a double play, forcing Jackson at second. But his throw to first glanced off Reggie, allowing Thurman Munson, who was on second, to score a crucial run. It seemed that Jackson had purposely leaned into the throw, but no violation was called. Piniella drove in the winning run in the tenth to even the series at two games apiece. New York mauled the Dodgers 12–2 in the next game behind Jim Beattie and then took the sixth game 7–2. Doyle and Dent had three hits apiece in each of the final pair of games. Free agent Rich Gossage was super in relief, allowing only one hit and no runs in six innings spread out over three games.

Result: New York AL won 4; Los Angeles NL, 2.

1st Game, at Los Angeles, Oct. 10th R H E
New York (AL) 000 000 320 5 9 1
Los Angeles (NL) 030 310 31x 11 15 2
Pitchers—FIGUEROA, Clay (2), Lindblad (5), Tidrow (7) vs. JOHN, Forster (8). Homers—Baker (LA), Lopes (LA) 2, Jackson (NY). Attendance—55,997.

2nd Game, at Los Angeles, Oct. 11th R H E
New York (AL) 002 000 100 3 11 0
Los Angeles (NL) 000 103 00x 4 7 0
Pitchers—HUNTER, Gossage (7) vs. HOOTON, Forster (7), Welch (9). Homer—Cev (LA). Attendance—55,982.

3rd Game, at New York, Oct. 13th R H E
Los Angeles (NL) 001 000 000 1 8 0
New York (AL) 100 000 30x 5 10 1
Pitchers—SUTTON, Rautzhan (7), Hough (8) vs. GUIDRY. Homer—White (NY). Attendance—56,447.

4th Game, at New York. Oct. 14th R H E
Los Angeles (NL) 000 030 000 0 3 6 1
New York (AL) 000 002 010 1 4 9 0
Pitchers—John, Forster (8), WELCH (8) vs. Figueroa, Tidrow (6), GOSSAGE (9). Homer—Smith (LA). Attendance—56,445.

5th Game, at New York, Oct. 15th R H E
Los Angeles (LA) 101 000 000 2 9 3
New York (AL) 004 300 41x 12 18 0
Pitchers—HOOTON, Rautzhan (3), Hough (4) vs. BEATTIE. Attendance—56,448.

6th Game at Los Angeles, Oct. 17th R H E
New York (AL) 030 002 200 7 11 0
Los Angeles (NL) 101 000 000 2 7 1
Pitchers—HUNTER, Gossage (8) vs. SUTTON, Welch (7), Rau (8). Homers—Lopes (LA), Jackson (NY). Attendance—55,985.

Year	National League	American League (or AA).	Games W-L	Attendance	Receipts	Winning Player's Share	Losing Player's Share
1882	Chicago	Cincinnati(AA)	1-1	7,200	$ 2,000.00	$ 0	$ 0
1884	*Providence	Metropolitans(AA)	3-0	3,100	850.00	100.00	0
1885	Chicago	St. Louis(AA)	3-3a	14,200	3,000.00	0	0
1886	Chicago	*St. Louis(AA)	2-4	43,000	14,000.00	855.00	0
1887	*Detroit	St. Louis(AA)	10-5	51,455	41,050.00	500.00	0
1888	*New York	St. Louis(AA)	6-4	42,270	24,362.10	450.00	0
1889	*New York	Brooklyn (AA)	6-3	47,256	24,262.10	380.15	389.29
1890	Brooklyn	Louisville (AA)	3-3a	13,910	6,000.00	100.00	100.00
1903	Pittsburgh	*Boston	3-5	100,429	55,500.00	1,316.25	1,182.00
1905	*New York	Philadelphia	4-1	91,723	68,437.00	1,142.00	833.75
1906	Chicago	*Chicago	2-4	99,845	106,550.00	1,874.63	439.50
1907	*Chicago	Detroit	4-0a	78,068	101,728.50	2,142.85	1,945.96
1908	*Chicago	Detroit	4-1	62,232	94,975.50	1,317.58	870.00
1909	*Pittsburgh	Detroit	4-3	145,295	188,302.50	1,825.22	1,274.76
1910	Chicago	*Philadelphia	1-4	124,222	173,980.00	2,062.79	1,375.16
1911	New York	*Philadelphia	2-4	179,851	342,164.50	3,654.58	2,436.39
1912	New York	*Boston	3-4a	252,037	490,449.00	4,024.68	2,566.47
1913	New York	*Philadelphia	1-4	151,000	325,980.00	3,246.36	2,164.22
1914	*Boston	Philadelphia	4-0	111,009	225,739.00	2,812.28	2,031.65
1915	Philadelphia	*Boston	1-4	143,351	320,361.50	3,780.25	2,520.17
1916	Brooklyn	*Boston	1-4	162,859	385,590.50	3,910.26	2,834.82
1917	New York	*Chicago	2-4	186,654	425,878.00	3,669.32	2,442.61
1918	Chicago	*Boston	2-4	128,483	179,619.00	1,102.51	671.09
1919	*Cincinnati	Chicago	5-3	236,928	722,414.00	5,207.01	3,254.36
1920	Brooklyn	*Cleveland	2-5	178,737	564,800.00	4,168.00	2,419.60
1921	*New York	New York	5-3	269,976	900,233.00	5,265.00	3,510.00
1922	*New York	New York	4-0a	185,947	605,475.00	4,470.00	3,225.00
1923	New York	*New York	2-4	301,430	1,063,815.00	6,143.49	4,112.89
1924	New York	*Washington	3-4	283,665	1,093,104.00	5,969.64	3,820.29
1925	*Pittsburgh	Washington	4-3	282,848	1,182,854.00	5,332.72	3,734.60
1926	*St. Louis	New York	4-3	328,051	1,207,864.00	5,584.51	3,417.75
1927	Pittsburgh	*New York	0-4	201,705	783,217.00	5,592.17	3,728.10
1928	St. Louis	*New York	0-4	199,072	777,290.00	5,531.91	4,197.37
1929	Chicago	*Philadelphia	1-4	190,490	859,494.00	5,620.57	3,782.01
1930	St. Louis	*Philadelphia	2-4	212,619	953,772.00	5,785.00	3,875.00
1931	*St. Louis	Philadelphia	4-3	231,567	1,030,723.00	4,467.59	3,032.09
1932	Chicago	*New York	0-4	191,998	713,377.00	5,231.77	4,244.60
1933	*New York	Washington	4-1	163,076	679,365.00	4,256.72	3,019.86
1934	*St. Louis	Detroit	4-3	281,510	1,031,341.00	5,389.57	3,354.57
1935	Chicago	*Detroit	2-4	286,672	1,073,794.00	6,544.76	4,198.53
1936	New York	*New York	2-4	302,924	1,204,399.00	6,430.55	4,655.58
1937	New York	*New York	1-4	238,142	985,994.00	6,471.10	4,489.05
1938	Chicago	*New York	0-4	200,833	851,166.00	5,782.76	4,674.87
1939	Cincinnati	*New York	0-4	183,849	745,329.00	5,614.26	4,282.58
1940	*Cincinnati	Detroit	4-3	281,927	1,222,328.21	5,803.62	3,531.81
1941	Brooklyn	*New York	1-4	235,773	1,007,762.00	5,943.31	4,829.40
1942	*St. Louis	New York	4-1	277,101	1,105,249.00	5,573.78	3,018.77
1943	St. Louis	*New York	1-4	277,312	1,105,784.00	6,139.46	4,321.96
1944	*St. Louis	St. Louis	4-2	206,708	906,122.00	4,626.01	2,743.79
1945	Chicago	*Detroit	3-4	333,457	1,492,454.00	6,443.34	3,930.22
1946	*St. Louis	Boston	4-3	250,071	1,052,900.00	3,742.34	2,140.89
1947	Brooklyn	*New York	3-4	389,763	1,781,348.92	5,830.03	4,081.19
1948	Boston	*Cleveland	2-4	358,362	1,633,685.56	6,772.05	4,651.51
1949	Brooklyn	*New York	1-4	236,710	1,129,627.88	5,665.54	4,272.73
1950	Philadelphia	*New York	0-4	196,009	953,669.03	5,737.95	4,081.34
1951	New York	*New York	2-4	341,977	1,633,457.47	6,446.09	4,951.03
1952	Brooklyn	*New York	3-4	340,906	1,622,753.01	5,982.65	4,200.64
1953	Brooklyn	*New York	2-4	307,350	1,779,269.44	8,280.68	6,178.42
1954	*New York	Cleveland	4-0	251,507	1,566,203.38	11,147.90	6,712.50
1955	*Brooklyn	New York	4-3	362,310	2,337,515.34	9,768.00	5,598.00
1956	Brooklyn	*New York	3-4	345,903	2,183,254.59	8,714.76	6,934.34
1957	*Milwaukee	New York	4-3	394,712	2,475,978.94	8,924.36	5,606.06
1958	Milwaukee	*New York	3-4	393,909	2,397,223.03	8,759.10	5,896.09

Year	National League	American League	Games W-L	Attendance	Receipts	Winning Player's Share	Losing Player's Share
1959	*Los Angeles	Chicago	4-2	420,784	2,628,809.44	11,231.18	7,257,17
1960	*Pittsburgh	New York	4-3	349,813	2,230,627.88	8,417.94	5,214.64
1961	Cincinnati	*New York	1-4	223,247	1,480,059.95	7,389.13	5,356.37
1962	San Francisco	*New York	3-4	376,864	2,878,891.11	9,882.74	7,291.49
1963	*Los Angeles	New York	4-0	247,279	1,995,189.09	12,794.00	7,874.32
1964	*St. Louis	New York	4-3	321,807	2,243,187.96	8,622.19	5,309.29
1965	*Los Angeles	Minnesota	4-3	364,326	2,975,041.60	10,297.43	6,634.36
1966	Los Angeles	*Baltimore	0-4	220,791	2,047,142.46	11,683.04	8,189.36
1967	*St. Louis	Boston	4-3	304,085	2,350,607.10	8,314.81	5,115.23
1968	St. Louis	*Detroit	3-4	379,670	3,018,113.40	10,936.66	7,078.71
1969	*New York	Baltimore	4-1	272,378	2,857,782.78	18,338.18	14,904.21
1970	Cincinnati	*Baltimore	1-4	253,183	2,599,170.26	18,215.78	13,687.59
1971	*Pittsburgh	Baltimore	4-3	351,091	3,049,803.46	18,164.58	13,906.46
1972	Cincinnati	*Oakland	3-4	363,149	3,954,542.99	20,705.01	15,080.25
1973	New York	*Oakland	3-4	358,289	3,923,968.37	24,617.57	14,950.17
1974	Los Angeles	*Oakland	1-4	260,004	3,007,194.00	22,219.09	15,703.97
1975	*Cincinnati	Boston	4-3	308,272	3,380,579.61	19,060.46	13,325.87
1976	*Cincinnati	New York	4-0	223,009	2,498,416.53	26,366.68	19,935.48
1977	Los Angeles	*New York	2-4	337,708	3,978,825.33	27,758.04	20,899.05
1978	Los Angeles	*New York	2-4	337,304	4,667,542.57	31,237.00	25,483.21

Note: Player's shares for 1969 to date include League Championship Series

* indicates winning team
a indicates one game tied

TEAM RECAPITULATION (1903-1975)

(Figure after team indicates number of Series participated in; figures in parentheses indicate number of Series won and lost; figures following parentheses indicate number of Series games won and lost.)

NATIONAL LEAGUE
Boston, 2 (1-1) 6-4
Brooklyn, 9 (1-8) 20-36
Chicago, 10 (2-8) 19-33
Cincinnati, 8 (4-4) 22-25
Los Angeles, 7 (3-4) 17-21
Milwaukee, 2 (1-1) 7-7
Philadelphia, 2 (0-2) 1-8
Pittsburgh, 6 (4-2) 19-21
New York Giants, 14 (5-9) 39-41
New York Mets, 2 (1-1) 7-5
San Francisco, 1 (0-1) 3-4
St. Louis, 12 (8-4) 38-37

AMERICAN LEAGUE
Baltimore, 4 (2-2) 12-9
Boston, 8 (5-3) 30-22
Chicago, 4 (2-2) 13-13
Cleveland, 3 (2-1) 9-8
Detroit, 8 (3-5) 22-28
Minnesota, 1 (0-1) 3-4
New York, 32 (22-10) 107-73
Oakland, 3 (3-0) 12-7
Philadelphia, 8 (5-3) 24-19
St. Louis, 1 (0-1) 2-4
Washington, 3 (1-2) 8-11

YR	CL LEA POS	GP	G	REC
AARON, HENRY LOUIS				
1957 MIL N O			7	.393
1958 MIL N O			7	.333
			14	.364
ABBATICCHIO, EDWARD JAMES				
1909 PIT N H			1	.000
ABSTEIN, WILLIAM HENRY				
1909 PIT N 1			7	.231
ADAIR, KENNETH JERRY				
1967 BOS A 2			5	.125
ADAMS, CHARLES BENJAMIN				
1909 PIT N P			3	3-0
1925 PIT N P			1	0-0
			4	3-0
ADAMS, EARL JOHN				
1930 STL N 3			6	.143
1931 STL N 3			2	.250
			8	.160
ADAMS, SPENCER DEWEY				
1925 WAS A 2			2	.000
1926 NY A H			2	.000
			4	.000
ADCOCK, JOSEPH WILBUR				
1957 MIL N 1			5	.200
1958 MIL N 1			4	.308
			9	.250
AGEE, TOMMIE LEE				
1969 NY N O			5	.167
AGNEW, SAMUEL LESTER				
1918 BOS A C			4	.000
ALDRIDGE, VICTOR EDDINGTON				
1925 PIT N P			3	2-0
1927 PIT N P			1	0-1
			4	2-1
ALEXANDER, DOYLE LAFAYETTE				
1976 NY A P			1	0-1
ALEXANDER, GROVER CLEVELAND				
1915 PHI N P			2	1-1
1926 STL N P			3	2-0
1928 STL N P			2	0-1
			7	3-2
ALLEN, JOHN THOMAS				
1932 NY A P			1	0-0
1941 BRO N P			3	0-0
			4	0-0
ALLEY, LEONARD EUGENE				
1971 PIT N S			2	.000
ALLISON, WILLIAM ROBERT				
1965 MIN A O			5	.125
ALOU, FELIPE ROJAS				
1962 SF N O			7	.269
ALOU, JESUS MARIA ROJAS				
1973 OAK A O			7	.158
1974 OAK A H			1	.000
			8	.150
ALOU, MATEO ROJAS				
1962 SF N O			6	.333
1972 OAK A O			7	.042
			13	.139
ALTROCK, NICHOLAS				
1906 CHI A P			2	1-1
AMES, LEON KESSLING				
1905 NY N P			1	0-0
1911 NY N P			2	0-1
1912 NY N P			1	0-0
			4	0-1
AMOROS, EDMUNDO ISASI				
1952 BRO N H			1	.000
1955 BRO N O			5	.333
1956 BRO N O			6	.053
			12	.161
ANDERSON, JOHN FREDERICK				
1917 NY N P			1	0-1
ANDREWS, IVY PAUL				
1937 NY A P			1	0-0
ANDREWS, MICHAEL JAY				
1967 BOS A 2			5	.308
1973 OAK A 2			2	.000
			7	.250
ANTONELLI, JOHN AUGUST				
1954 NY N P			2	1-0
APARICIO, LUIS ERNESTO				
1959 CHI A S			6	.308
1966 BAL A S			4	.250
			10	.286
ARCHER, JAMES PATRICK				
1907 CHI A C			1	.000
1910 CHI N C-1			3	.182
			4	.143
ARMBRISTER, EDISON ROSANDA				
1975 CIN N H			4	.000
ARNOVICH, MORRIS				
1940 CIN N O			1	.000
ARROYO, LUIS ENRIQUE				
1960 NY A P			1	0-0
1961 NY A P			2	1-0
			3	1-0
ASHBURN, DON RICHIE				
1950 PHI N O			4	.176
AUERBACH, FREDERICK STEVEN				
1974 LA N R			1	.000
AUKER, ELDON LEROY				
1934 DET A P			2	1-1
1935 DET A P			1	0-0
			3	1-1
AVERILL, HOWARD EARL				
1940 DET A H			3	.000
AVILA, ROBERTO FRANCISCO				
1954 CLE A 2			4	.133
BAGBY, JAMES CHARLES JACOB JR.				
1946 BOS A P			1	0-0
BAGBY, JAMES CHARLES JACOB SR.				
1920 CLE A P			2	1-1
BAILEY, LONAS EDGAR				
1962 SF N C			6	.071
BAKER, EUGENE WALTER				
1960 PIT N H			3	.000
BAKER, FLOYD WILSON				
1944 STL A 2			2	.000
BAKER, JOHN FRANKLIN				
1910 PHI A 3			5	.409
1911 PHI A 3			6	.375
1913 PHI A 3			5	.450
1914 PHI A 3			4	.250
1921 NY A 3			4	.250
1922 NY A H			1	.000
			25	.363
BAKER, JOHNNIE B				
1977 LA N O			6	.292
1978 LA N O			6	.238
			12	.267
BAKER, WILLIAM PRESLEY				
1940 CIN N C			3	.250
BALDWIN, HOWARD EDWARD				
1924 NY N P			1	0-0
BALL, CORNELIUS				
1912 BOS A H			1	.000
BALLOU, NOBLE WINFIELD				
1925 WAS A P			2	0-0
BANCROFT, DAVID JAMES				
1915 PHI N S			5	.294
1921 NY N S			8	.152
1922 NY N S			5	.211
1923 NY N S			6	.083
			24	.172
BANDO, SALVATORE LEONARD				
1972 OAK A 3			7	.269
1973 OAK A 3			7	.231
1974 OAK A 3			5	.063
			19	.206
BANKHEAD, DANIEL ROBERT				
1947 BRO N R			1	.000
BANTA, JOHN KAY				
1949 BRO N P			3	0-0
BARBER, TYRUS TURNER				
1918 CHI N H			3	.000
BARBIERI, JAMES PATRICK				
1966 LA N H			1	.000
BARNES, JESSE LAWRENCE				
1921 NY N P			3	2-0
1922 NY N P			1	0-0
			4	2-0
BARNES, VIRGIL JENNINGS				
1923 NY N P			2	0-0
1924 NY N P			2	0-1
			4	0-1
BARNEY, REX EDWARD				
1947 BRO N P			3	0-1
1949 BRO N P			1	0-1
			4	0-2
BARNHART, CLYDE LEE				
1925 PIT N O			7	.250
1927 PIT N O			4	.313
			11	.273
BARRETT, CHARLES HENRY				
1948 BOS N P			2	0-0
BARRY, JOHN JOSEPH				
1910 PHI A S			5	.235
1911 PHI A S			6	.368
1913 PHI A S			5	.300
1914 PHI A S			4	.071
1915 BOS A 2			5	.176
			25	.241
BARTELL, RICHARD WILLIAM				
1936 NY N S			6	.381
1937 NY N S			5	.238
1940 DET A S			7	.269
			18	.294
BATTEY, EARL JESSE				
1965 MIN A C			7	.120
BAUER, HENRY ALBERT				
1949 NY A O			3	.167
1950 NY A O			4	.133
1951 NY A O			6	.167
1952 NY A O			7	.056
1953 NY A O			6	.261
1955 NY A O			6	.429
1956 NY A O			7	.281
1957 NY A O			7	.258
1958 NY A O			7	.323
			53	.245
BEARDEN, HENRY EUGENE				
1948 CLE A P			2	1-0
BEATTIE, JAMES LOUIS				
1978 NY A P			1	1-0
BEAUCHAMP, JAMES EDWARD				
1973 NY N H			4	.000
BEAUMONT, CLARENCE HOWETH				
1903 PIT N O			8	.265
1910 CHI N H			3	.000
			11	.250
BEAZLEY, JOHN ANDREW				
1942 STL N P			2	2-0
1946 STL N P			1	0-0
			3	2-0
BECKER, DAVID BEALS				
1911 NY N H			3	.000
1912 NY N O			2	.000
1915 PHI N O			2	.000
			7	.000
BECKER, HEINZ REINHARD				
1945 CHI N H			3	.500
BEDIENT, HUGH CARPENTER				
1912 BOS A P			4	1-0
BEGGS, JOSEPH STANLEY				
1940 CIN N P			1	0-0
BEHRMAN, HENRY BERNARD				
1947 BRO N P			5	0-0
BELANGER, MARK HENRY				
1969 BAL A S			5	.200
1970 BAL A S			5	.105
1971 BAL A S			7	.238
			17	.182
BELARDI, CARROLL WAYNE				
1953 BRO N H			2	.000
BELL, DAVID RUSSELL				
1961 CIN N H			3	.000
BELL, GARY				
1967 BOS A P			3	0-1
BELL, HERMAN S				
1926 STL N P			1	0-0
1930 STL N P			1	0-0
1933 NY N P			1	0-0
			3	0-0
BELL, LESTER ROWLAND				
1926 STL N 3			7	.259

YR	CL	LEA	POS	GP	G	REC
BENCH, JOHNNY LEE						
1970	CIN	N	C		5	.211
1972	CIN	N	C		7	.261
1975	CIN	N	C		7	.207
1976	CIN	N	C		4	.533
					23	.279
BENDER, CHARLES ALBERT						
1905	PHI	A	P		2	1- 1
1910	PHI	A	P		2	1- 1
1911	PHI	A	P		3	2- 1
1913	PHI	A	P		2	2- 0
1914	PHI	A	P		1	0- 1
					10	6- 4
BENGOUGH, BERNARD OLIVER						
1927	NY	A	C		2	.000
1928	NY	A	C		4	.231
					6	.176
BENIQUEZ, JUAN JOSE						
1975	BOS	A	O		3	.125
BENTLEY, JOHN NEEDLES						
1923	NY	N	P	2	5	0- 1
1924	NY	N	P	3	5	1- 2
				5	10	1- 3
BENTON, JOHN ALTON						
1945	DET	A	P		3	0- 0
BENTON, JOHN CLEBON						
1917	NY	N	P		2	1- 1
BERGAMO, AUGUST SAMUEL						
1944	STL	N	O		3	.000
BERGER, WALTER ANTONE						
1937	NY	N	H		3	.000
1939	CIN	N	O		4	.000
					7	.000
BERRA, LAWRENCE PETER						
1947	NY	A	C-O		6	.158
1949	NY	A	C		4	.063
1950	NY	A	C		4	.200
1951	NY	A	C		6	.261
1952	NY	A	C		7	.214
1953	NY	A	C		6	.429
1955	NY	A	C		7	.417
1956	NY	A	C		7	.360
1957	NY	A	C		7	.320
1958	NY	A	C		7	.222
1960	NY	A	C-O		7	.318
1961	NY	A	O		4	.273
1962	NY	A	C		2	.000
1963	NY	A	H		1	.000
					75	.274
BESSENT, FRED DONALD						
1955	BRO	N	P		3	0- 0
1956	BRO	N	P		2	1- 0
					5	1- 0
BEVENS, FLOYD CLIFFORD						
1947	NY	A	P		2	0- 1
BICKFORD, VERNON EDGELL						
1948	BOS	N	P		1	0- 1
BIGBEE, CARSON LEE						
1925	PIT	N	O		4	.333
BILLINGHAM, JOHN EUGENE						
1972	CIN	N	P		3	1- 0
1975	CIN	N	P		3	0- 0
1976	CIN	N	P		1	1- 0
					7	2- 0
BISHOP, MAX FREDERICK						
1929	PHI	A	2		5	.190
1930	PHI	A	2		6	.222
1931	PHI	A	2		7	.148
					18	.182
BLACK, JOSEPH						
1952	BRO	N	P		3	1- 2
1953	BRO	N	P		1	0- 0
					4	1- 2
BLACKWELL, EWELL						
1952	NY	A	P		1	0- 0
BLADES, FRANCIS RAYMOND						
1928	STL	N	H		1	.000
1930	STL	N	O		5	.111
1931	STL	N	H		2	.000
					8	.083
BLAIR, CLARENCE VICK						
1929	CHI	N	H		1	.000
BLAIR, PAUL L D						
1966	BAL	A	O		4	.167
1969	BAL	A	O		5	.100
1970	BAL	A	O		5	.474
1971	BAL	A	O		4	.333
1977	NY	A	O		4	.250
1978	NY	A	O		6	.375
					28	.288
BLAKE, JOHN FREDERICK						
1929	CHI	N	P		2	0- 1
BLANCHARD, JOHN EDWIN						
1960	NY	A	C		5	.455
1961	NY	A	O		4	.400
1962	NY	A	H		1	.060
1963	NY	A	H		1	.000
1964	NY	A	H		4	.250
					15	.345
BLASINGAME, DON LEE						
1961	CIN	N	2		3	.143
BLASS, STEPHEN ROBERT						
1971	PIT	N	P		2	2- 0
BLEFARY, CURTIS LEROY						
1966	BAL	A	O		4	.077
BLOCK, SEYMOUR						
1945	CHI	N	R		1	.000
BLOODWORTH, JAMES HENRY						
1950	PHI	N	2		1	.000
BLUE, VIDA ROCHELLE						
1972	OAK	A	P		4	0- 1
1973	OAK	A	P		2	0- 1
1974	OAK	A	P		2	0- 1
					8	0- 3
BLUEGE, OSWALD LOUIS						
1924	WAS	A	S-3		7	.192
1925	WAS	A	3		5	.278
1933	WAS	A	3		5	.125
					17	.200
BOLEY, JOHN PETER						
1929	PHI	A	S		5	.235
1930	PHI	A	S		6	.095
1931	PHI	A	H		1	.000
					12	.154
BOLIN, BOBBY DONALD						
1962	SF	N	P		2	0- 0
BOLLWEG, DONALD RAYMOND						
1953	NY	A	1		3	.000
BOLTON, WILLIAM CLIFTON						
1933	WAS	A	H		2	.000
BONGIOVANNI, ANTHONY THOMAS						
1939	CIN	N	H		1	.000
BONHAM, ERNEST EDWARD						
1941	NY	A	P		1	1- 0
1942	NY	A	P		2	0- 1
1943	NY	A	P		1	0- 1
					4	1- 2
BOONE, RAYMOND OTIS						
1948	CLE	A	H		1	.000
BORBON, PEDRO						
1972	CIN	N	P		6	0 -1
1975	CIN	N	P		3	0- 0
1976	CIN	N	P		1	0- 0
					10	0- 1
BOKDAGARAY, STANLEY GEORGE						
1939	CIN	N	R		2	.000
1941	NY	A	R		1	.000
					3	.000
BOROM, EDWARD JONES						
1945	DET	A	H		2	.000
BOROWY, HENRY LUDWIG						
1942	NY	A	P		1	0- 0
1943	NY	A	P		1	1- 0
1945	CHI	N	P		4	2- 2
					6	3- 2
BOSWELL, DAVID WILSON						
1965	MIN	A	P		1	1- 0
BOSWELL, KENNETH GEORGE						
1969	NY	N	2		1	.333
1973	NY	N	H		3	1.000
					4	.667
BOTTOMLEY, JAMES LEROY						
1926	STL	N	1		7	.345
1928	STL	N	1		4	.214
1930	STL	N	1		6	.045
1931	STL	N	1		7	.160
					24	.200
BOUDREAU, LOUIS						
1948	CLE	A	S		6	.273
BOURQUE, PATRICK DANIEL						
1973	OAK	A	1		2	.500
BOUTON, JAMES ALAN						
1963	NY	A	P		1	0- 1
1964	NY	A	P		2	2- 0
BOWMAN, ERNEST FERRELL						
1962	SF	N	S		2	.000
BOYER, CLETIS LEROY						
1960	NY	A	S-3		4	.250
1961	NY	A	3		5	.267
1962	NY	A	3		7	.318
1963	NY	A	3		4	.077
1964	NY	A	3		7	.208
					27	.233
BOYER, KENTON LLOYD						
1964	STL	N	3		7	.222
BRAGAN, ROBERT RANDALL						
1947	BRO	N	H		1	1.000
BRANCA, RALPH THEODORE JOSEPH						
1947	BRO	N	P		3	1- 1
1949	BRO	N	P		1	0- 1
					4	1- 2
BRANSFIELD, WILLIAM EDWARD						
1903	PIT	N	1		8	.207
BRAVO, ANGEL ALFONSO						
1970	CIN	N	H		4	.000
BRAZLE, ALPHA EUGENE						
1943	STL	N	P		1	0- 1
1946	STL	N	P		1	0- 1
					2	0- 2
BRECHEEN, HARRY DAVID						
1943	STL	N	P		3	0- 1
1944	STL	N	P		1	1- 0
1946	STL	N	P		3	3- 0
					7	4- 1
BRENNAN, JAMES DONALD						
1937	NY	N	P		2	0- 0
BRESNAHAN, ROGER PHILIP						
1905	NY	N	C		5	.313
BRESSOUD, EDWARD FRANCIS						
1967	STL	N	S		2	.000
BRETT, KENNETH ALVEN						
1967	BOS	A	P		2	0- 1
BREUER, MARVIN HOWARD						
1941	NY	A	P		1	0- 0
1942	NY	A	P		1	0- 0
					2	0- 0
BREWER, JAMES THOMAS						
1965	LA	N	P		1	0- 0
1966	LA	N	P		1	0- 0
1974	LA	N	P		1	0- 0
					3	0- 0
BRICKELL, GEORGE FREDERICK						
1927	PIT	N	H		2	.000
BRIDGES, MARSHALL						
1962	NY	A	P		2	0- 0
BRIDGES, THOMAS JEFFERSON DAVIS						
1934	DET	A	P		3	1- 1
1935	DET	A	P		2	2- 0
1940	DET	A	P		1	1- 0
1945	DET	A	P		1	0- 0
					7	4- 1
BRIGHT, HARRY JAMES						
1963	NY	A	H		2	.000
BRILES, NELSON KELLEY						
1967	STL	N	P		2	1- 0
1968	STL	N	P		2	0- 1
1971	PIT	N	P		1	1- 0
					5	2- 1
BROCK, LOUIS CLARK						
1964	STL	N	O		7	.300
1967	STL	N	C		7	.414
1968	STL	N	O		7	.464
					21	.391
BROSNAN, JAMES PATRICK						
1961	CIN	N	P			0- 0
BROWN, JAMES ROBERSON						
1942	STL	N	2		5	.300

YR	CL	LEA	POS	GP	G	REC

BROWN, MACE STANLEY
| 1946 | BOS | A | P | | 1 | 0- 0 |

BROWN, MORDECAI PETER CENTENNIAL
1906	CHI	N	P		3	1- 2
1907	CHI	N	P		1	1- 0
1908	CHI	N	P		2	2- 0
1910	CHI	N	P		3	1- 2
					9	5- 4

BROWN, ROBERT WILLIAM
1947	NY	A	H		4	1.000
1949	NY	A	3		4	.500
1950	NY	A	3		4	.333
1951	NY	A	3		5	.357
					17	.439

BROWN, THOMAS MICHAEL
| 1949 | BRO | N | P | | 2 | .000 |

BROWN, WILLIAM JAMES
| 1968 | DET | A | H | | 1 | .000 |

BROWNE, GEORGE EDWARD
| 1905 | NY | N | O | | 5 | .182 |

BRUTON, WILLIAM HARON
| 1958 | MIL | N | O | | 7 | .412 |

BRYANT, CLAIBORNE HENRY
| 1938 | CHI | N | P | | 1 | 0- 1 |

BUCHEK, GERALD PETER
| 1964 | STL | N | 2 | | 4 | 1.000 |

BUCKNER, WILLIAM JOSEPH
| 1974 | LA | N | O | | 5 | .250 |

BUFORD, DONALD ALVIN
1969	BAL	A	O		5	.100
1970	BAL	A	O		4	.267
1971	BAL	A	O		6	.261
					15	.207

BUHL, ROBERT RAY
| 1957 | MIL | N | P | | 2 | 0- 1 |

BUNKER, WALLACE EDWARD
| 1966 | BAL | A | P | | 1 | 1- 0 |

BURDETTE, SELVA LEWIS
1957	MIL	N	P		3	3- 0
1958	MIL	N	P		3	1- 2
					6	4- 2

BURGESS, FORREST HARRILL
| 1960 | PIT | N | C | | 5 | .333 |

BURKE, GLENN LAWRENCE
| 1977 | LA | N | O | | 3 | .200 |

BURLESON, RICHARD PAUL
| 1975 | BOS | A | S | | 7 | .292 |

BURNS, EDWARD JAMES
| 1915 | PHI | N | C | | 5 | .188 |

BURNS, GEORGE HENRY
1920	CLE	A	1		5	.300
1929	PHI	A	H		1	.000
					6	.250

BURNS, GEORGE JOSEPH
1913	NY	N	O		5	.158
1917	NY	N	O		6	.227
1921	NY	N	O		8	.333
					19	.257

BURTON, JIM SCOTT
| 1975 | BOS | A | P | | 2 | 0- 1 |

BUSH, GUY TERRELL
1929	CHI	N	P		2	1- 0
1932	CHI	N	P		2	0- 1
					4	1- 1

BUSH, LESLIE AMBROSE
1913	PHI	A	P		1	1- 0
1914	PHI	A	P		1	0- 1
1918	BOS	A	P		2	0- 1
1922	NY	A	P		2	0- 2
1923	NY	A	P	3	4	1- 1
				9	10	2- 5

BUSH, OWEN JOSEPH
| 1909 | DET | A | S | | 7 | .261 |

BYERLY, ELDRED WILLIAM
| 1944 | STL | N | P | | 1 | 0- 0 |

BYRD, SAMUEL DEWEY
| 1932 | NY | A | O | | 1 | .000 |

BYRNE, ROBERT MATTHEW
1909	PIT	N	3		7	.250
1915	PHI	N	H		1	.000
					8	.240

BYRNE, THOMAS JOSEPH
1949	NY	A	P		1	0- 0
1955	NY	A	P	2	3	1- 1
1956	NY	A	P	1	2	0- 0
1957	NY	A	P		2	0- 0
				6	8	1- 1

BYRNES, MILTON JOHN
| 1944 | STL | A | H | | 3 | .000 |

CABALLERO, RALPH JOSEPH
| 1950 | PHI | N | H | | 3 | .000 |

CADORE, LEON JOSEPH
| 1920 | BRO | N | P | | 2 | 0- 1 |

CADY, FORREST LEROY
1912	BOS	A	C		7	.136
1915	BOS	A	C		4	.333
1916	BOS	A	C		2	.250
					13	.188

CALDWELL, RAYMOND BENJAMIN
| 1920 | CLE | A | P | | 1 | 0- 1 |

CAMILLI, ADOLPH LOUIS
| 1941 | BRO | N | 1 | | 5 | .167 |

CAMNITZ, SAMUEL HOWARD
| 1909 | PIT | N | P | | 2 | 0- 1 |

CAMPANELLA, ROY
1949	BRO	N	C		5	.267
1952	BRO	N	C		7	.214
1953	BRO	N	C		6	.273
1955	BRO	N	C		7	.259
1956	BRO	N	C		7	.182
					32	.237

CAMPANERIS, DAGBERTO
1972	OAK	A	S		7	.179
1973	OAK	A	S		7	.290
1974	OAK	A	S		5	.353
					19	.263

CAMPBELL, BRUCE DOUGLAS
| 1940 | DET | A | O | | 7 | .360 |

CAMPBELL, PAUL MC LAUGHLIN
| 1946 | BOS | A | R | | 1 | .000 |

CARBO, BERNARDO
1970	CIN	N	O		4	.000
1975	BOS	A	O		4	.429
					8	.200

CARDENAS, LEONARDO LAZARO
| 1961 | CIN | N | H | | 3 | .333 |

CARDWELL, DONALD EUGENE
| 1969 | NY | N | P | | 1 | 0- 0 |

CAREY, ANDREW ARTHUR
1955	NY	A	H		2	.500
1956	NY	A	3		7	.158
1957	NY	A	3		2	.286
1958	NY	A	3		5	.083
					16	.175

CAREY, MAX GEORGE
| 1925 | PIT | N | O | | 7 | .458 |

CARLETON, JAMES OTTO
1934	STL	N	P		2	0- 0
1935	CHI	N	P		1	0- 1
1938	CHI	N	P		1	0- 0
					4	0- 1

CARLSON, HAROLD GUST
| 1929 | CHI | N | P | | 2 | 0- 0 |

CARLTON, STEVEN NORMAN
1967	STL	N	P		1	0- 1
1968	STL	N	P		2	0- 0
					3	0- 1

CARRIGAN, WILLIAM FRANCIS
1912	BOS	A	C		2	.000
1915	BOS	A	C		1	.000
1916	BOS	A	C		1	.667
					4	.167

CARROLL, CLAY PALMER
1970	CIN	N	P		4	1- 0
1972	CIN	N	P		5	0- 1
1975	CIN	N	P		5	1- 0
					14	2- 1

CARROLL, THOMAS EDWARD
| 1955 | NY | A | R | | 2 | .000 |

CASEY, HUGH THOMAS
1941	BRO	N	P		3	0- 2
1947	BRO	N	P		6	2- 0
					9	2- 2

CASH, DAVID
| 1971 | PIT | N | 2 | | 7 | .133 |

CASH, NORMAN DALTON
1959	CHI	A	H		4	.000
1968	DET	A	1		7	.385
					11	.333

CASTER, GEORGE JASPER
| 1945 | DET | A | P | | 1 | 0- 0 |

CASTLEMAN, CLYDELL
| 1936 | NY | N | P | | 1 | 0- 0 |

CATHER, THEODORE P
| 1914 | BOS | N | O | | 1 | .000 |

CAVARETTA, PHILIP JOSEPH
1935	CHI	N	1		6	.125
1938	CHI	N	O		4	.462
1945	CHI	N	1		7	.423
					17	.317

CEPEDA, ORLANDO MANUEL
1962	SF	N	1		5	.158
1967	STL	N	1		7	.103
1968	STL	N	1		7	.250
					19	.171

CERV, ROBERT HENRY
1955	NY	A	C		5	.125
1956	NY	A	H		1	1.000
1960	NY	A	O		4	.357
					10	.258

CEY, RONALD CHARLES
1974	LA	N	3		5	.176
1977	LA	N	3		6	.190
1978	LA	N	3		6	.286
					17	.220

CHACON, ELIO
| 1961 | CIN | N | 2 | | 4 | .250 |

CHALMERS, GEORGE W.
| 1915 | PHI | N | P | | 1 | 0- 1 |

CHAMBLISS, CARROLL CHRISTOPHER
1976	NY	A	1		4	.313
1977	NY	A	1		6	.292
1978	NY	A	1		3	.182
					13	.275

CHANCE, FRANK LEROY
1906	CHI	N	1		6	.238
1907	CHI	N	1		4	.214
1908	CHI	N	1		5	.421
1910	CHI	N	1		5	.353
					20	.310

CHANDLER, SPURGEON FERDINAND
1941	NY	A	P		1	0- 1
1942	NY	A	P		2	0- 1
1943	NY	A	P		2	2- 0
1947	NY	A	P		1	0- 0
					6	2- 2

CHANEY, DARREL LEE
1970	CIN	N	S		3	.000
1972	CIN	N	S		4	.000
1975	CIN	N	H		2	.000
					9	.000

CHAPMAN, WILLIAM BENJAMIN
| 1932 | NY | A | C | | 4 | .294 |

CHARLES, EDWIN DOUGLAS
| 1969 | NY | N | 3 | | 4 | .133 |

CHARTAK, MICHAEL GEORGE
| 1944 | STL | A | H | | 2 | .000 |

CHENEY, LAURANCE RUSSELL
| 1916 | BRO | N | P | | 1 | 0- 0 |

CHENEY, THOMAS EDGAR
| 1960 | PIT | N | P | | 3 | 0- 0 |

CHIOZZA, LOUIS PEO
| 1937 | NY | N | O | | 2 | .286 |

CHIPMAN, ROBERT HOWARD
| 1945 | CHI | N | P | | 1 | 0- 0 |

CHRISTMAN, MARQUETTE JOSEPH
| 1944 | STL | A | 3 | | 6 | .091 |

CHRISTOPHER, JOSEPH O#NEAL
| 1960 | PIT | N | H | | 3 | .000 |

CHRISTOPHER, RUSSELL ORMAND
| 1948 | CLE | A | P | | 1 | 0- 0 |

CHURN, CLARENCE NOTTINGHAM
| 1959 | LA | N | P | | 1 | 0- 0 |

YR	CL	LEA	POS	GP	G	REC
CICOTTE, EDWARD VICTOR						
1917	CHI	A	P		3	1-1
1919	CHI	A	P		3	1-2
					6	2-3
CIMOLI, GINO NICHOLAS						
1956	BRO	N	O		1	.000
1960	PIT	N	O		7	.250
					8	.250
CLARK, ALFRED ALOYSIUS						
1947	NY	A	O		3	.500
1948	CLE	A	O		1	.000
					4	.200
CLARKE, FRED CLIFFORD						
1903	PIT	N	O		8	.265
1909	PIT	N	O		7	.211
					15	.245
CLARY, ELLIS						
1944	STL	A	H		1	.000
CLAY, KENNETH EARL						
1977	NY	A	P		2	0-0
1978	NY	A	P		1	0-0
					3	0-0
CLEMENTE ROBERTO						
1960	PIT	N	O		7	.310
1971	PIT	N	O		7	.414
					14	.362
CLENDENON, DONN ALVIN						
1969	NY	N	1		4	.357
CLEVELAND, REGINALD LESLIE						
1975	BOS	A	P		3	0-1
CLIFTON, HERMAN EARL						
1935	DET	A	3		4	.000
CLINE, TYRONE ALEXANDER						
1970	CIN	N	H		3	.333
CLINES, EUGENE ANTHONY						
1971	PIT	N	O		3	.091
CLONINGER, TONY LEE						
1970	CIN	N	P		2	0-1
COAKLEY, ANDREW JAMES						
1905	PHI	A	P		1	0-1
COATES, JAMES ALTON						*
1960	NY	A	P		3	0-0
1961	NY	A	P		1	0-0
1962	NY	A	P		2	0-1
					6	0-1
COBB, TYRUS RAYMOND						
1907	DET	A	O		5	.200
1908	DET	A	O		5	.368
1909	DET	A	O		7	.231
					17	.262
COCHRANE, GORDON STANLEY						
1929	PHI	A	C		5	.400
1930	PHI	A	C		6	.222
1931	PHI	A	C		7	.160
1934	DET	A	C		7	.214
1935	DET	A	C		6	.292
					31	.245
COFFMAN, SAMUEL RICHARD						
1936	NY	N	P		2	0-0
1937	NY	N	P		2	0-0
					4	0-0
COLE, LEONARD LESLIE						
1910	CHI	N	P		1	0-0
COLEMAN, GERALD FRANCIS						
1949	NY	A	2		5	.250
1950	NY	A	2		4	.286
1951	NY	A	2		5	.250
1955	NY	A	S		3	.000
1956	NY	A	2		2	.000
1957	NY	A	2		7	.364
					26	.275
COLEMAN, GORDON CALVIN						
1961	CIN	N	1		5	.250
COLEMAN, WALTER GARY						
1955	NY	A	P		1	0-0
COLLINS, EDWARD TROWBRIDGE						
1910	PHI	A	2		5	.429
1911	PHI	A	2		6	.286
1913	PHI	A	2		5	.421
1914	PHI	A	2		4	.214
1917	CHI	A	2		6	.409
1919	CHI	A	2		8	.226
					34	.328
COLLINS, HARRY WARREN						
1921	NY	A	P		1	0-0
COLLINS, JAMES ANTHONY						
1931	STL	N	1		2	.000
1934	STL	N	1		7	.367
1938	CHI	N	1		4	.133
					13	.277
COLLINS, JAMES JOSEPH						
1903	BOS	A	3		8	.250
COLLINS, JOHN FRANCIS						
1917	CHI	A	O		6	.286
1919	CHI	A	O		4	.250
					10	.270
COLLINS, JOSEPH EDWARD						
1950	NY	A	1		1	.000
1951	NY	A	1-O		6	.222
1952	NY	A	1		6	.000
1953	NY	A	1		6	.167
1955	NY	A	1-O		5	.167
1956	NY	A	1		6	.238
1957	NY	A	1		6	.000
					36	.163
COLLINS, RAYMOND WILLISTON						
1912	BOS	A	P		2	0-0
COLLINS, THARON PATRICK						
1926	NY	A	C		3	.000
1927	NY	A	C		2	.600
1928	NY	A	C		1	1.000
					6	.500
COMBS, EARLE BRYAN						
1926	NY	A	O		7	.357
1927	NY	A	O		4	.313
1928	NY	A	H		1	.000
1932	NY	A	O		4	.375
					16	.350
COMER, HARRY WAYNE						
1968	DET	A	H		1	1.000
CONATSER, CLINTON ASTOR						
1948	BOS	N	O		2	.000
CONCEPCION, DAVID ISMAEL						
1970	CIN	N	S		3	.333
1972	CIN	N	S		6	.308
1975	CIN	N	S		7	.179
1976	CIN	N	S		4	.357
					20	.266
CONIGLIARO, WILLIAM MICHAEL						
1973	OAK	A	H		3	.000
CONLEY, DONALD EUGENE						
1957	MIL	N	P		1	0-0
CONNOLLY, JOSEPH ALOYSIUS						
1914	BOS	N	O		3	.111
COOMBS, JOHN WESLEY						
1910	PHI	A	P		3	3-0
1911	PHI	A	P		2	1-0
1916	BRO	N	P		1	1-0
					6	5-0
COOPER, CECIL CELESTER						
1975	BOS	A	1		5	.053
COOPER, CLAUDE WILLIAM						
1913	NY	N	R		2	.000
COOPER, MORTON CECIL						
1942	STL	N	P		2	0-1
1943	STL	N	P		2	1-1
1944	STL	N	P		2	1-1
					6	2-3
COOPER, WILLIAM WALKER						
1942	STL	N	C		5	.286
1943	STL	N	C		5	.294
1944	STL	N	C		6	.318
					16	.300
CORRALES, PATRICK						
1970	CIN	N	H		1	.000
CORWIN, ELMER NATHAN						
1951	NY	N	P		1	0-0
COSCARART, PETER JOSEPH						
1941	BRO	N	2		3	.000
COUGHLIN, WILLIAM PAUL						
1907	DET	A	3		5	.250
1908	DET	A	3		3	.125
					8	.214
COVELESKI, STANLEY ANTHONY						
1920	CLE	A	P		3	3-0
1925	WAS	A	P		2	0-2
					5	3-2
COVINGTON, JOHN WESLEY						
1957	MIL	N	O		7	.208
1958	MIL	N	O		7	.269
1966	LA	N	H		1	.000
					15	.235
COX, WILLIAM RICHARD						
1949	BRO	N	3		2	.333
1952	BRO	N	3		7	.296
1953	BRO	N	3		6	.304
					15	.302
CRAFT, HARRY FRANCIS						
1939	CIN	N	O		4	.091
1940	CIN	N	H		1	.000
					5	.083
CRAIG, ROGER LEE						
1955	BRO	N	P		1	1-0
1956	BRO	N	P		2	0-1
1959	LA	N	P		2	0-1
1964	STL	N	P		2	1-0
					7	2-2
CRAMER, ROGER MAXWELL						
1931	PHI	A	H		2	.500
1945	DET	A	O		7	.379
					9	.387
CRANDALL, DELMAR WESLEY						
1957	MIL	N	C		6	.211
1958	MIL	N	C		7	.240
					13	.227
CRANDALL, JAMES OTIS						
1911	NY	N	P	2	3	1-0
1912	NY	N	P		1	0-0
1913	NY	N	P	2	4	0-0
				5	8	1-0
CRAVATH, CLIFFORD CARLTON						
1915	PHI	N	O		5	.125
CRAWFORD, CLIFFORD RANKIN						
1934	STL	N	H		3	.000
CRAWFORD, SAMUEL EARL						
1907	DET	A	O		5	.238
1908	DET	A	O		5	.238
1909	DET	A	1-O		7	.250
					17	.243
CRAWFORD, WILLIE MURPHY						
1965	LA	N	H		2	.500
1974	LA	N	O		3	.333
					5	.375
CRESPI, FRANK ANGELO JOSEPH						
1942	STL	N	R		1	.000
CRIGER, LOUIS						
1903	BOS	A	C		8	.231
CRITZ, HUGH MELVILLE						
1933	NY	N	2		5	.136
CRONIN, JOSEPH EDWARD						
1933	WAS	A	S		5	.318
CROSETTI, FRANK PETER JOSEPH						
1932	NY	A	S		4	.133
1936	NY	A	S		6	.269
1937	NY	A	S		5	.048
1938	NY	A	S		4	.250
1939	NY	A	S		4	.063
1942	NY	A	3		1	.000
1943	NY	A	S		5	.278
					29	.174
CROSS, LAFAYETTE NAPOLEON						
1905	PHI	A	3		5	.105
CROSS, MONTFORD MONTGOMERY						
1905	PHI	A	S		5	.176
CROUCHER, FRANK DONALD						
1940	DET	A	S		1	.000
CROWDER, ALVIN FLOYD						
1933	WAS	A	P		2	0-1
1934	DET	A	P		2	0-1
1935	DET	A	P		1	1-0
					5	1-2
CROWLEY, TERRENCE MICHAEL						
1970	BAL	A	H		1	.000
1975	CIN	N	H		2	.500
					3	.333
CUELLAR, MIGUEL ANGEL						
1969	BAL	A	P		2	1-0
1970	BAL	A	P		2	1-0
1971	BAL	A	P		2	0-2
					6	2-2
CULBERSON, DELBERT LEON						
1946	BOS	A	O		5	.222

YR	CL LEA POS	GP	G	REC
CULLENBINE, ROY JOSEPH				
1942 NY A O			5	.263
1945 DET A O			7	.227
			12	.244
CUNNINGHAM, WILLIAM ALOYSIUS				
1922 NY N O			4	.200
1923 NY N O			4	.143
			8	.176
CUTSHAW, GEORGE WILLIAM				
1916 BRO N 2			5	.105
CUYLER, HAZEN SHIRLEY				
1925 PIT N O			7	.269
1929 CHI N O			5	.300
1932 CHI N O			4	.278
			16	.281
CVENGROS, MICHAEL JOHN				
1927 PIT N P			2	0- 0
DAHLEN, WILLIAM FREDERICK				
1905 NY N S			5	.000
DAHLGREN, ELLSWORTH TENNEY				
1939 NY A 1			4	.214
DALEY, LEAVITT LEO				
1961 NY A P			2	1- 0
1962 NY A P			1	0- 0
			3	1- 0
DALRYMPLE, CLAYTON ERROL				
1969 BAL A H			2	1.000
DANFORTH, DAVID CHARLES				
1917 CHI A P			1	0- 0
DANNING, HARRY				
1936 NY N C			2	.000
1937 NY N C			3	.250
			5	.214
DARCY, PATRICK LEONARD				
1975 CIN N P			2	0- 1
DARK, ALVIN RALPH				
1948 BOS N S			6	.167
1951 NY N S			6	.417
1954 NY N S			4	.412
			16	.323
DAUBERT, JACOB ELLSWORTH				
1916 BRO N 1			4	.176
1919 CIN N 1			8	.241
			12	.217
DAVALILLO, VICTOR JOSE				
1971 PIT N O			3	.333
1973 OAK A 1-O			6	.091
1977 LA N H			3	.333
1978 LA N O			2	.333
			14	.200
DAVENPORT, JAMES HOUSTON				
1962 SF N 3			7	.136
DAVIS, CURTIS BENTON				
1941 BRO N P			1	0- 1
DAVIS, GEORGE STACEY				
1906 CHI A S			3	.308
DAVIS, GEORGE WILLIS				
1933 NY N O			5	.368
1936 NY N H			4	.500
			9	.381
DAVIS, HARRY H				
1905 PHI A 1			5	.200
1910 PHI A 1			5	.353
1911 PHI A 1			6	.208
			16	.246
DAVIS, HERMAN THOMAS				
1963 LA N O			4	.400
1966 LA N O			4	.250
			8	.348
DAVIS, RONALD EVERETTE				
1968 STL N O			2	.000
DAVIS, VIRGIL LAWRENCE				
1934 STL N H			2	1.000
DAVIS, WILLIAM HENRY				
1963 LA N O			4	.167
1965 LA N O			7	.231
1966 LA N O			4	.063
			15	.167
DAWSON, RALPH FENTON				
1927 PIT N P			1	0- 0
DEAL, CHARLES ALBERT				
1914 BOS N 3			4	.125
1918 CHI N 3			6	.176
			10	.152

YR	CL LEA POS	GP	G	REC
DEAN, JAY HANNA				
1934 STL N P	3	4	2- 1
1938 CHI N P	2	0- 1
	5	6	2- 2
DEAN, PAUL DEE				
1934 STL N P		2	2- 0
DEAN, WAYLAND OGDEN				
1924 NY N P		1	0- 0
DELAHANTY, JAMES CHRISTOPHER				
1909 DET A 2		7	.346
DE LANCEY, WILLIAM PINKNEY				
1934 STL N C		7	.172
DELL, WILLIAM GEORGE				
1916 BRO N P		1	0- 0
DE MAESTRI, JOSEPH PAUL				
1960 NY A S		4	.500
DEMAREE, ALBERT WENTWORTH				
1913 NY N P		1	0- 1
DEMAREE, JOSEPH FRANKLIN				
1932 CHI N O		2	.286
1935 CHI N O		6	.250
1938 CHI N O		3	.100
1943 STL N H		1	.000
		12	.214
DE MERIT, JOHN STEPHEN				
1957 MIL N R		1	.000
DEMETER, DONALD LEE				
1959 LA N O		6	.250
DENT, RUSSELL EARL				
1977 NY A S		6	.263
1978 NY A S		6	.417
		12	.349
DENTE, SAMUEL JOSEPH				
1954 CLE A S		3	.000
DERRINGER, SAMUEL PAUL				
1931 STL N P	3	0- 2
1939 CIN N P	2	0- 1
1940 CIN N P	3	2- 1
1945 CHI N P	3	0- 0
	11	2- 4
DEVLIN, ARTHUR MC ARTHUR				
1905 NY N 3		5	.250
DEVORE, JOSHUA D.				
1911 NY N O	6	.167
1912 NY N O	7	.250
1914 BOS N H	1	.000
	14	.204
DE VORMER, ALBERT E.				
1921 NY A C		2	.000
DICKEY, WILLIAM MALCOLM				
1932 NY A C	4	.438
1936 NY A C	6	.120
1937 NY A C	5	.211
1938 NY A C	4	.400
1939 NY A C	4	.267
1941 NY A C	5	.167
1942 NY A C	5	.263
1943 NY A C	5	.278
	38	.255
DICKSON, MURRY MONROE				
1943 STL N P	1	0- 0
1946 STL N P	2	0- 1
1958 NY A P	2	0- 0
	5	0- 1
DI MAGGIO, DOMINIC PAUL				
1946 BOS A O		7	.259
DI MAGGIO, JOSEPH PAUL				
1936 NY A O	6	.346
1937 NY A O	5	.273
1938 NY A O	4	.267
1939 NY A O	4	.313
1941 NY A O	5	.263
1942 NY A O	5	.333
1947 NY A O	7	.231
1949 NY A O	5	.111
1950 NY A O	4	.308
1951 NY A O	6	.261
	51	.271
DINNEEN, WILLIAM HENRY				
1903 BOS A P		4	3- 1
DITMAR, ARTHUR JOHN				
1957 NY A P	2	0- 0
1958 NY A P	1	0- 0
1960 NY A P	2	0- 2
	5	0- 2

YR	CL LEA POS	GP	G	REC
DOBSON, JOSEPH GORDON				
1946 BOS A P		3	1- 0
DOBSON, PATRICK EDWARD				
1968 DET A P		3	0- 0
1971 BAL A P		3	0- 0
		6	0- 0
DOBY, LAWRENCE EUGENE				
1948 CLE A O		6	.318
1954 CLE A O		4	.125
		10	.237
DOERR, ROBERT PERSHING				
1946 BOS A 2		6	.409
DOLJACK, FRANK JOSEPH				
1934 DET A O		2	.000
DONAHUE, JOHN AUGUSTUS				
1906 CHI A 1		6	.333
DONALD, RICHARD ATLEY				
1941 NY A P		1	0- 0
1942 NY A P		1	0- 1
		2	0- 1
DONLIN, MICHAEL JOSEPH				
1905 NY N O		5	.263
DONNELLY, SYLVESTER URBAN				
1944 STL N P		2	1- 0
DONOVAN, RICHARD EDWARD				
1959 CHI A P		3	0- 1
DONOVAN, WILLIAM EDWARD				
1907 DET A P		2	0- 1
1908 DET A P		2	0- 2
1909 DET A P		2	1- 1
		6	1- 4
DOUGHERTY, PATRICK HENRY				
1903 BOS A O		8	.235
1906 CHI A O		6	.100
		14	.185
DOUGLAS, PHILLIP BROOKS				
1918 CHI N P		1	0- 1
1921 NY N P		3	2- 1
		4	2- 2
DOUTHIT, TAYLOR LEE				
1926 STL N O		4	.267
1928 STL N O		3	.091
1930 STL N O		6	.083
		13	.140
DOWNING, ALPHONSO ERWIN				
1963 NY A P		1	0- 1
1964 NY A P		3	0- 1
1974 LA N P		1	0- 1
		5	0- 3
DOWNS, JEROME WILLIS				
1908 DET A 2		2	.167
DOYLE, BRIAN REED				
1978 NY A 2		6	.438
DOYLE, LAWRENCE JOSEPH				
1911 NY N 2		6	.304
1912 NY N 2		8	.242
1913 NY N 2		5	.150
		19	.237
DOYLE, ROBERT DENNIS				
1975 BOS A 2		7	.267
DRABOWSKY, MYRON WALTER				
1966 BAL A P		1	1- 0
1970 BAL A P		2	0- 0
		3	1- 0
DRAGO, RICHARD ANTHONY				
1975 BOS A P		2	0- 1
DREISEWERD, CLEMENT JOHN				
1946 BOS A P		1	0- 0
DREWS, KARL AUGUST				
1947 NY A P		2	0- 0
DRIESSEN, DANIEL				
1975 CIN N H		2	.000
1976 CIN N O		4	.357
		6	.312
DRYSDALE, DONALD SCOTT				
1956 BRO N P		1	0- 0
1959 LA N P		1	1- 0
1963 LA N P		1	1- 0
1965 LA N P	2	3	1- 1
1966 LA N P		2	0- 2
	7	8	3- 3

YR	CL LEA POS	GP	G	REC

DUBUC, JEAN JOSEPH OCTAVE ARTHUR
| 1918 BOS A H | | 1 | .000 |

DUGAN JOSEPH ANTHONY
1922 NY A 3	5	.250
1923 NY A 3	6	.280
1926 NY A 3	7	.333
1927 NY A 3	4	.200
1928 NY A 3	3	.167
	25	.267

DUGEY, OSCAR JOSEPH
| 1915 PHI N R | 2 | .000 |

DUKES, THOMAS EARL
| 1971 BAL A P | 2 | 0- 0 |

DUNCAN, DAVID EDWIN
| 1972 OAK A C | 3 | .200 |

DUNCAN, LOUIS BAIRD
| 1919 CIN N O | 8 | .269 |

DUREN, RINOLD GEORGE
1958 NY A P	3	1- 1
1960 NY A P	2	0- 0
	5	1- 1

DUROCHER, LEO ERNEST
1928 NY A 2	4	.000
1934 STL N S	7	.259
	11	.241

DURST, CEDRIC MONTGOMERY
1927 NY A H	1	.000
1928 NY A O	4	.375
	5	.333

DUSAK, ERVIN FRANK
| 1946 STL N O | 4 | .250 |

DYER, DON ROBERT
| 1969 NY N H | 1 | .000 |

DYKES, JAMES JOSEPH
1929 PHI A 3	5	.421
1930 PHI A 3	6	.222
1931 PHI A 3	7	.227
	18	.288

EARNSHAW, GEORGE LIVINGSTON
1929 PHI A P	2	1- 1
1930 PHI A P	3	2- 0
1931 PHI A P	3	1- 2
	8	4- 3

EASTWICK, RAWLINS JACKSON
| 1975 CIN N P | 5 | 2- 0 |

EATON, ZEBULON VANCE
| 1945 DET A H | 1 | .000 |

EDWARDS, CHARLES BRUCE
1947 BRO N C	7	.222
1949 BRO N H	2	.500
	9	.241

EDWARDS, JOHN ALBAN
1961 CIN N C	3	.364
1968 STL N H	1	.000
	4	.333

EHMKE, HOWARD JONATHAN
| 1929 PHI A P | 2 | 1- 0 |

ELLER, HORACE OWEN
| 1919 CIN N P | 2 | 2- 0 |

ELLIOTT, ROBERT IRVING
| 1948 BOS N 3 | 6 | .333 |

ELLIS, DOCK PHILLIP
1971 PIT N P	1	0- 1
1976 NY A P	1	0- 1
	2	0- 2

ENGLE, ARTHUR CLYDE
| 1912 BOS A H | 3 | .333 |

ENGLISH, ELWOOD GEORGE
1929 CHI N S	5	.190
1932 CHI N 3	4	.176
	9	.184

ENNIS, DELMER
| 1950 PHI N O | 4 | .143 |

EPSTEIN, MICHAEL PETER
| 1972 OAK A 1 | 6 | .000 |

ERICKSON PAUL WALFORD
| 1945 CHI N P | 4 | 0- 0 |

ERSKINE, CARL DANIEL
1949 BRO N P	2	0- 0
1952 BRO N P	3	1- 1
1953 BRO N P	3	1- 0
1955 BRO N P	1	0- 0
1956 BRO N P	2	0- 1
	11	2- 2

ESPOSITO, SAMUEL
| 1959 CHI A 3 | 2 | .000 |

ESSEGIAN, CHARLES ABRAHAM
| 1959 LA N H | 4 | .667 |

ETCHEBARREN, ANDREW AUGUSTE
1966 BAL A C	4	.083
1969 BAL A C	2	.000
1970 BAL A C	2	.143
1971 BAL A C	1	.000
	9	.075

ETTEN, NICHOLAS RAYMOND THOMAS
| 1943 NY A 1 | 5 | .105 |

EVANS, DWIGHT MICHAEL
| 1975 BOS A O | 7 | .292 |

EVANS, JOSEPH PATTON
| 1920 CLE A O | 4 | .308 |

EVERS, JOHN JOSEPH
1906 CHI N 2	6	.150
1907 CHI N 2-S	5	.350
1908 CHI N 2	5	.350
1914 BOS N 2	4	.438
	20	.316

FABER, URBAN CHARLES
| 1917 CHI A P | 4 | 3- 1 |

FACE, ELROY LEON
| 1960 PIT N P | 4 | 0- 0 |

FAIRLY, RONALD RAY
1959 LA N O	6	.000
1963 LA N O	4	.000
1965 LA N O	7	.379
1966 LA N 1-O	3	.143
	20	.300

FALLON, GEORGE DECATUR
| 1944 STL N 2 | 2 | .000 |

FARRELL, CHARLES ANDREW
| 1903 BOS A H | 2 | .000 |

FELLER, ROBERT WILLIAM ANDREW
| 1948 CLE A P | 2 | 0- 2 |

FELSCH, OSCAR EMIL
1917 CHI A O	6	.273
1919 CHI A O	8	.192
	14	.229

FERGUSON, JAMES ALEXANDER
| 1925 WAS A P | 2 | 1- 1 |

FERGUSON, JOSEPH VANCE
1974 LA N C-O	5	.125
1978 LA N C	2	.500
	7	.200

FERRARA, ALFRED JOHN
| 1966 LA N H | 1 | 1.000 |

FERRICK, THOMAS JEROME
| 1950 NY A P | 1 | 1- 0 |

FERRIS, ALBERT SAYLES
| 1903 BOS A 2 | 8 | .290 |

FERRISS, DAVID MEADOW
| 1946 BOS A P | 2 | 1- 0 |

FEWSTER, WILSON LLOYD
| 1921 NY A O | 4 | .200 |

FIGUEROA, EDUARDO
1976 NY A P	1	0- 1
1978 NY A P	2	0- 1
	3	0- 2

FINGERS, ROLAND GLEN
1972 OAK A P	6	1- 1
1973 OAK A P	6	0- 1
1974 OAK A P	4	1- 0
	16	2- 2

FISHER, GEORGE ALOYS
| 1930 STL N H | 2 | .500 |

FISHER, RAYMOND LYLE
| 1919 CIN N P | 2 | 0- 1 |

FISK, CARLTON ERNEST
| 1975 BOS A C | 7 | .240 |

FITZSIMMONS, FREDERICK LANDIS
1933 NY N P	1	0- 1
1936 NY N P	2	0- 2
1941 BRO N P	1	0- 0
	4	0- 3

FLACK, MAX JOHN
| 1918 CHI N O | 6 | .263 |

FLETCHER, ARTHUR
1911 NY N S	6	.130
1912 NY N S	8	.179
1913 NY N S	5	.278
1917 NY N S	6	.200
	25	.191

FLOOD, CURTIS CHARLES
1964 STL N O	7	.200
1967 STL N O	7	.179
1968 STL N O	7	.286
	21	.221

FLOWERS, D#ARCY RAYMOND
1926 STL N H	3	.000
1931 STL N 3	5	.091
	8	.071

FORD, EDWARD CHARLES
1950 NY A P	1	1- 0
1953 NY A P	2	0- 1
1955 NY A P	2	2- 0
1956 NY A P	2	1- 1
1957 NY A P	2	1- 1
1958 NY A P	3	0- 1
1960 NY A P	2	2- 0
1961 NY A P	2	2- 0
1962 NY A P	3	1- 1
1963 NY A P	2	0- 2
1964 NY A P	1	0- 1
	22	10- 8

FORSTER, TERRY JAY
| 1978 LA N P | 3 | 0- 0 |

FOSSE, RAYMOND EARL
1973 OAK A C	7	.156
1974 OAK A C	5	.143
	12	.152

FOSTER, GEORGE
1915 BOS A P	2	2- 0
1916 BOS A P	1	0- 0
	3	2- 0

FOSTER, GEORGE ARTHUR
1972 CIN N O	2	.000
1975 CIN N O	7	.276
1976 CIN N O	4	.429
	13	.326

FOX, ERVIN
1934 DET A O	7	.286
1935 DET A O	6	.385
1940 DET A H	1	.000
	14	.327

FOX, JACOB NELSON
| 1959 CHI A 2 | 6 | .375 |

FOXX, JAMES EMORY
1929 PHI A 1	5	.350
1930 PHI A 1	6	.333
1931 PHI A 1	7	.348
	18	.344

FOY, JOSEPH ANTHONY
| 1967 BOS A 3 | 6 | .133 |

FRANKS, HERMAN LOUIS
| 1941 BRO N C | 1 | .000 |

FREEHAN, WILLIAM ASHLEY
| 1968 DET A C | 7 | .083 |

FREEMAN, JOHN FRANCIS
| 1903 BOS A O | 8 | .281 |

FREESE, EUGENE LEWIS
| 1961 CIN N 3 | 5 | .063 |

FRENCH, LAWRENCE HERBERT
1935 CHI N P	2	0- 2
1938 CHI N P	3	0- 0
1941 BRO N P	2	0- 0
	7	0- 2

FRENCH, WALTER EDWARD
| 1929 PHI A H | 1 | .000 |

FREY, LINUS REINHARD
1939 CIN N 2	4	.000
1940 CIN N H	3	.000
1947 NY A H	1	.000
	8	.000

FRIEND, ROBERT BARTMESS
| 1960 PIT N P | 3 | 0- 2 |

YR	CL	LEA	POS	GP	G	REC

FRISCH, FRANK FRANCIS
1921	NY	N	3		8	.300
1922	NY	N	2		5	.471
1923	NY	N	2		6	.400
1924	NY	N	2-3		7	.333
1928	STL	N	2		4	.231
1930	STL	N	2		6	.208
1931	STL	N	2		7	.259
1934	STL	N	2		7	.194
					50	.294

FULLIS, CHARLES PHILIP
| 1934 | STL | N | O | | 3 | .400 |

FURILLO, CARL ANTHONY
1947	BRO	N	O		6	.353
1949	BRO	N	O		3	.125
1952	BRO	N	O		7	.174
1953	BRO	N	O		6	.333
1955	BRO	N	O		7	.296
1956	BRO	N	O		7	.240
1959	LA	N	O		4	.250
					40	.266

GABLER, FRANK HAROLD
| 1936 | NY | N | P | | 2 | 0- 0 |

GAGLIANO, PHILIP JOSEPH
1967	STL	N	H		1	.000
1968	STL	N	H		3	.000
					4	.000

GAINER, DELLOS CLINTON
1915	BOS	A	1		1	.333
1916	BOS	A	H		1	1.000
					2	.500

GALAN, AUGUST JOHN
1935	CHI	N	O		6	.160
1938	CHI	N	H		2	.000
1941	BRO	N	H		2	.000
					10	.138

GALEHOUSE, DENNIS WARD
| 1944 | STL | A | P | | 2 | 1- 1 |

GAMBLE, LEE JESSE
| 1939 | CIN | N | H | | 1 | .000 |

GAMBLE, OSCAR CHARLES
| 1976 | NY | A | O | | 3 | .125 |

GANDIL, CHARLES ARNOLD
1917	CHI	A	1		6	.261
1919	CHI	A	1		8	.233
					14	.245

GARAGIOLA, JOSEPH HENRY
| 1946 | STL | N | C | | 5 | .316 |

GARCIA, EDWARD MIGUEL
| 1954 | CLE | A | P | | 2 | 0- 1 |

GARDNER, WILLIAM FREDERICK
| 1961 | NY | A | H | | 1 | .000 |

GARDNER, WILLIAM LAWRENCE
1912	BOS	A	3		8	.179
1915	BOS	A	3		5	.235
1916	BOS	A	3		5	.176
1920	CLE	A	3		7	.208
					25	.198

GARMAN, MICHAEL DOUGLAS
| 1977 | LA | N | P | | 2 | 0- 0 |

GARMS, DEBS C.
1943	STL	N	O		2	.000
1944	STL	N	H		2	.000
					4	.000

GARRETT, RONALD WAYNE
1969	NY	N	3		2	.000
1973	NY	N	3		7	.167
					9	.161

GARVEY, STEVEN PATRICK
1974	LA	N	1		5	.381
1977	LA	N	1		6	.375
1978	LA	N	1		6	.208
					17	.319

GASPAR, RODNEY EARL
| 1969 | NY | N | O | | 3 | .000 |

GAZELLA, MICHAEL
| 1926 | NY | A | 3 | | 1 | .000 |

GEARIN, DENNIS JOHN
| 1923 | NY | N | R | | 1 | .000 |

GEHRIG, HENRY LOUIS
1926	NY	A	1		7	.348
1927	NY	A	1		4	.308
1928	NY	A	1		4	.545
1932	NY	A	1		4	.529
1936	NY	A	1		6	.292
1937	NY	A	1		5	.294
1938	NY	A	1		4	.286
					34	.361

GEHRINGER, CHARLES LEONARD
1934	DET	A	2		7	.379
1935	DET	A	2		6	.375
1940	DET	A	2		7	.214
					20	.321

GELBERT, CHARLES MAGNUS
1930	STL	N	S		6	.353
1931	STL	N	S		7	.261
					13	.300

GENTRY, GARY EDWARD
| 1969 | NY | N | P | | 1 | 1- 0 |

GERNERT, RICHARD EDWARD
| 1961 | CIN | N | H | | 4 | .000 |

GERONIMO, CESAR FRANCISCO
1972	CIN	N	O		7	.158
1975	CIN	N	O		7	.280
1976	CIN	N	O		4	.308
					18	.246

GESSLER, HARRY HOMER
| 1906 | CHI | N | H | | 2 | .000 |

GETZ, GUSTAVE
| 1916 | BRO | N | H | | 1 | .000 |

GIBBON, JOSEPH CHARLES
| 1960 | PIT | N | P | | 2 | 0- 0 |

GIBSON, GEORGE C.
| 1909 | PIT | N | C | | 7 | .240 |

GIBSON, JOHN RUSSELL
| 1967 | BOS | A | C | | 2 | .000 |

GIBSON, ROBERT
1964	STL	N	P		3	2- 1
1967	STL	N	P		3	3- 0
1968	STL	N	P		3	2- 1
					9	7- 2

GILBERT, LAWRENCE WILLIAM
| 1914 | BOS | N | H | | 1 | .000 |

GILBERT, WILLIAM OLIVER
| 1905 | NY | N | 2 | | 5 | .235 |

GILLESPIE, PAUL ALLEN
| 1945 | CHI | N | C | | 3 | .000 |

GILLIAM, JAMES WILLIAM
1953	BRO	N	2		6	.296
1955	BRO	N	2-O		7	.292
1956	BRO	N	2-O		7	.083
1959	LA	N	3		6	.240
1963	LA	N	3		4	.154
1965	LA	N	3		7	.214
1966	LA	N	3		2	.000
					39	.211

GIONFRIDDO, ALBERT FRANCIS
| 1947 | BRO | N | O | | 4 | .000 |

GIUSTI, DAVID JOHN
| 1971 | PIT | N | P | | 3 | 0- 0 |

GLYNN, WILLIAM VINCENT
| 1954 | CLE | A | 1 | | 2 | .500 |

GOLIAT, MIKE MITCHEL
| 1950 | PHI | N | 2 | | 4 | .214 |

GOMEZ, RUBEN
| 1954 | NY | N | P | | 1 | 1- 0 |

GOMEZ, VERNON LOUIS
1932	NY	A	P		1	1- 0
1936	NY	A	P		2	2- 0
1937	NY	A	P		2	2- 0
1938	NY	A	P		1	1- 0
1939	NY	A	P		1	0- 0
					7	6- 0

GONZALEZ, MIGUEL ANGEL
| 1929 | CHI | N | C | | 2 | .000 |

GONZALEZ, PEDRO
| 1964 | NY | A | 3 | | 3 | .000 |

GOOCH, JOHN BEVERLEY
1925	PIT	N	C		3	.000
1927	PIT	N	C		3	.000
					6	.000

GOODMAN, IVAL RICHARD
1939	CIN	N	O		4	.333
1940	CIN	N	O		7	.276
					11	.295

GOODMAN, WILLIAM DALE
| 1959 | CHI | A | 3 | | 5 | .231 |

GOODSON, JAMES EDWARD
| 1977 | LA | N | H | | 1 | .000 |

GORDON, JOSEPH LOWELL
1938	NY	A	2		4	.400
1939	NY	A	2		4	.143
1941	NY	A	2		5	.500
1942	NY	A	2		5	.095
1943	NY	A	2		5	.235
1948	CLE	A	2		6	.182
					29	.243

GORMAN, THOMAS ALOYSIUS
1952	NY	A	P		1	0- 0
1953	NY	A	P		1	0- 0
					2	0- 0

GORSICA, JOHN JOSEPH PERRY
| 1940 | DET | A | P | | 2 | 0- 0 |

GOSLIN, LEON ALLEN
1924	WAS	A	O		7	.344
1925	WAS	A	O		7	.308
1933	WAS	A	O		5	.250
1934	DET	A	O		7	.241
1935	DET	A	O		6	.273
					32	.287

GOSSAGE, RICHARD MICHAEL
| 1978 | NY | A | P | | 3 | 1- 0 |

GOWDY, HENRY MORGAN
1914	BOS	N	C		4	.545
1923	NY	N	C		3	.000
1924	NY	N	C		7	.259
					14	.310

GRABOWSKI, JOHN PATRICK
| 1927 | NY | A | C | | 1 | .000 |

GRANEY, JOHN GLADSTONE
| 1920 | CLE | A | O | | 3 | .000 |

GRANGER, WAYNE ALLAN
1968	STL	N	P		1	0- 0
1970	CIN	N	P		2	0- 0
					3	0- 0

GRANT, EDWARD LESLIE
| 1913 | NY | N | H | | 2 | .000 |

GRANT, JAMES TIMOTHY
| 1965 | MIN | A | P | | 3 | 2- 1 |

GRANTHAM, GEORGE FARLEY
1925	PIT	N	2		5	.133
1927	PIT	N	2		3	.364
					8	.231

GRASSO, NEWTON MICHAEL
| 1954 | CLE | A | C | | 1 | .000 |

GRBA, ELI
| 1960 | NY | A | R | | 1 | .000 |

GREEN, FRED ALLEN
| 1960 | PIT | N | P | | 3 | 0- 0 |

GREEN, RICHARD LARRY
1972	OAK	A	2		7	.333
1973	OAK	A	2		7	.063
1974	OAK	A	2		5	.000
					19	.149

GREENBERG, HENRY BENJAMIN
1934	DET	A	1		7	.321
1935	DET	A	1		2	.167
1940	DET	A	O		7	.357
1945	DET	A	O		7	.304
					23	.318

GREGG, HAROLD DANA
| 1947 | BRO | N | P | | 3 | 0- 1 |

GRIFFEY, GEORGE KENNETH
1975	CIN	N	O		7	.269
1976	CIN	N	O		4	.059
					11	.186

GRIFFIN, DOUGLAS LEE
| 1975 | BOS | A | H | | 1 | .000 |

GRIFFITH, THOMAS HERMAN
| 1920 | BRO | N | O | | 7 | .190 |

GRIM, ROBERT ANTON
1955	NY	A	P		3	0- 1
1957	NY	A	P		2	0- 1
					5	0- 2

YR	CL	LEA	POS	GP	G	REC
GRIMES, BURLEIGH ARLAND						
1920	BRO	N	P		3	1- 2
1930	STL	N	P		2	0- 2
1931	STL	N	P		2	2- 0
1932	CHI	N	P		2	0- 0
					9	3- 4
GRIMM, CHARLES JOHN						
1929	CHI	N	1		5	.389
1932	CHI	N	1		4	.333
					9	.364
GRIMSLEY, ROSS ALBERT II						
1972	CIN	N	P		4	2- 1
GRISSOM, LEE THEO						
1939	CIN	N	P		1	0- 0
GRISSOM, MARVIN EDWARD						
1954	NY	N	P		1	1- 0
GROAT, RICHARD MORROW						
1960	PIT	N	S		7	.214
1964	STL	N	S		7	.192
					14	.204
GROH, HENRY KNIGHT						
1919	CIN	N	3		8	.172
1922	NY	N	3		5	.474
1923	NY	N	3		6	.182
1924	NY	N	H		1	1.000
1927	PIT	N	H		1	.000
					21	.264
GROMEK, STEPHEN JOSEPH						
1948	CLE	A	P		1	1- 0
GROTE, GERALD WAYNE						
1969	NY	N	C		5	.211
1973	NY	N	C		7	.267
1977	LA	N	C		1	.000
1978	LA	N	C		2	.000
					15	.240
GROVE, ROBERT MOSES						
1929	PHI	A	P		2	0- 0
1930	PHI	A	P		3	2- 1
1931	PHI	A	P		3	2- 1
					8	4- 2
GUDAT, MARVIN JOHN						
1932	CHI	N	H		2	.000
GUIDRY, RONALD AMES						
1977	NY	A	P		1	1- 0
1978	NY	A	P		1	1- 0
					2	2- 0
GULLETT, DONALD EDWARD						
1970	CIN	N	P		3	0- 0
1972	CIN	N	P		1	0- 0
1975	CIN	N	P		3	1- 1
1976	CIN	N	P		1	1- 0
1977	NY	A	P		2	0- 1
					10	2- 2
GUMBERT, HARRY EDWARD						
1936	NY	N	P		2	0- 0
1937	NY	N	P		2	0- 0
1942	STL	N	P		2	0- 0
					6	0- 0
GUTTERIDGE, DONALD JOSEPH						
1944	STL	A	2		6	.143
1946	BOS	A	2		3	.400
					9	.192
HAAS, GEORGE WILLIAM						
1929	PHI	A	O		5	.238
1930	PHI	A	O		6	.111
1931	PHI	A	O		7	.130
					18	.161
HACK, STANLEY CAMFIELD						
1932	CHI	N	H		1	.000
1935	CHI	N	S-3		6	.227
1938	CHI	N	3		4	.471
1945	CHI	N	3		7	.367
					18	.348
HADDIX, HARVEY						
1960	PIT	N	P		2	2- 0
HADLEY, IRVING DARIUS						
1936	NY	A	P		1	1- 0
1937	NY	A	P		1	0- 1
1939	NY	A	P		1	1- 0
					3	2- 1
HAFEY, CHARLES JAMES						
1926	STL	N	O		7	.185
1928	STL	N	O		4	.200
1930	STL	N	O		6	.273
1931	STL	N	O		6	.167
					23	.205

YR	CL	LEA	POS	GP	G	REC
HAGUE, JOE CLARENCE						
1972	CIN	N	O		3	.000
HAHN, DONALD ANTONE						
1973	NY	N	O		7	.241
HAHN, WILLIAM EDGAR						
1906	CHI	A	O		6	.273
HAINES, HENRY LUTHER						
1923	NY	A	O		2	.000
HAINES, JESSE JOSEPH						
1926	STL	N	P		3	2- 0
1928	STL	N	P		1	0- 1
1930	STL	N	P		1	1- 0
1934	STL	N	P		1	0- 0
					6	3- 1
HALL, CHARLES LOUIS						
1912	BOS	A	P		2	0- 0
HALL, JIMMIE RANDOLPH						
1965	MIN	A	O		2	.143
HALL, RICHARD WALLACE						
1969	BAL	A	P		1	0- 1
1970	BAL	A	P		1	0- 0
1971	BAL	A	P		1	0- 0
					3	0- 1
HALL, TOM EDWARD						
1972	CIN	N	P		4	0- 0
HALLAHAN, WILLIAM ANTHONY						
1926	STL	N	P		1	0- 0
1930	STL	N	P		2	1- 1
1931	STL	N	P		3	2- 0
1934	STL	N	P		1	0- 0
					7	3- 1
HALLER, THOMAS FRANK						
1962	SF	N	C		4	.286
HAMILTON, DAVID EDWARD						
1972	OAK	A	P		2	0- 0
HAMILTON, STEVEN ABSHER						
1963	NY	A	P		1	0- 0
1964	NY	A	P		2	0- 0
					3	0- 0
HAMNER, GRANVILLE WILBUR						
1950	PHI	N	S		4	.429
HANEBRINK, HARRY ALOYSIUS						
1958	MIL	N	H		2	.000
HANEY, WALLACE LARRY						
1974	OAK	A	C		2	.000
HARPER, GEORGE WASHINGTON						
1928	STL	N	O		3	.111
HARPER, HARRY CLAYTON						
1921	NY	A	P		1	0- 0
HARRELSON, DERREL MC KINLEY						
1969	NY	N	S		5	.176
1973	NY	N	S		7	.250
					12	.220
HARRELSON, KENNETH SMITH						
1967	BOS	A	H		4	.077
HARRIS, DAVID STANLEY						
1933	WAS	A	O		3	.000
HARRIS, JOSEPH						
1925	WAS	A	O		7	.440
1927	PIT	N	1		4	.200
					11	.350
HARRIS, MAURICE CHARLES						
1946	BOS	A	P		2	0- 2
HARRIS, STANLEY RAYMOND						
1924	WAS	A	2		7	.333
1925	WAS	A	2		7	.087
					14	.232
HARTNETT, CHARLES LEO						
1929	CHI	N	H		3	.000
1932	CHI	N	C		4	.313
1935	CHI	N	C		6	.292
1938	CHI	N	C		3	.091
					16	.241
HARTSEL, TULLY FREDERICK						
1905	PHI	A	O		5	.294
1910	PHI	A	O		1	.200
					6	.273
HARTUNG, CLINTON CLARENCE						
1951	NY	N	O		2	.000

YR	CL	LEA	POS	GP	G	REC
HASSETT, JOHN ALOYSIUS						
1942	NY	A	1		3	.333
HATTEN, JOSEPH HILARIAN						
1947	BRO	N	P		4	0- 0
1949	BRO	N	P		2	0- 0
					6	0- 0
HAYWORTH, MYRON CLAUDE						
1944	STL	A	C		6	.118
HAYWORTH, RAYMOND HALL						
1934	DET	A	C		1	.000
HAZLE, ROBERT SIDNEY						
1957	MIL	N	O		4	.154
HEARN, JAMES TOLBERT						
1951	NY	N	P		2	1- 0
HEATH, MICHAEL THOMAS						
1978	NY	A	C		1	.000
HEATHCOTE, CLIFTON EARL						
1929	CHI	N	H		2	.000
HEBNER, RICHARD JOSEPH						
1971	PIT	N	3		3	.167
HEGAN, JAMES EDWARD						
1948	CLE	A	C		6	.211
1954	CLE	A	C		4	.154
					10	.188
HEGAN, JAMES MICHAEL						
1964	NY	A	H		3	.000
1972	OAK	A	1		6	.200
					9	.167
HEINTZELMAN, KENNETH ALPHONSE						
1950	PHI	N	P		1	0- 0
HELMS, TOMMY VANN						
1970	CIN	N	2		5	.222
HEMSLEY, RALSTON BURDETT						
1932	CHI	N	C		3	.000
HENDRICK, GEORGE ANDREW						
1972	OAK	A	O		5	.133
HENDRICK, HARVEY LEE						
1923	NY	A	H		1	.000
HENDRICKS, ELROD JEROME						
1969	BAL	A	C		3	.100
1970	BAL	A	C		3	.364
1971	BAL	A	C		6	.263
1976	NY	A	H		2	.000
					14	.238
HENDRIX, CLAUDE RAYMOND						
1918	CHI	N	P	1	2	0- 0
HENRICH, THOMAS DAVID						
1938	NY	A	O		4	.250
1941	NY	A	O		5	.167
1947	NY	A	O		7	.323
1949	NY	A	1		5	.263
					21	.262
HENRICKSEN, OLAF						
1912	BOS	A	H		2	1.000
1915	BOS	A	H		2	.000
1916	BOS	A	H		1	.000
					5	.333
HENRY, WILLIAM RODMAN						
1961	CIN	N	P		2	0- 0
HENSHAW, ROY K.						
1935	CHI	N	P		1	0- 0
HERMAN, WILLIAM JENNINGS BRYAN						
1932	CHI	N	2		4	.222
1935	CHI	N	2		6	.333
1938	CHI	N	2		4	.188
1941	BRO	N	2		4	.125
					18	.242
HERMANSKI, EUGENE VICTOR						
1947	BRO	N	O		7	.158
1949	BRO	N	O		4	.308
					11	.219
HERNANDEZ, JACINTO						
1971	PIT	N	S		7	.222
HERSHBERGER, WILLARD MC KEE						
1939	CIN	N	C		3	.500
HERZOG, CHARLES LINCOLN						
1911	NY	N	3		6	.190
1912	NY	N	3		8	.400
1913	NY	N	3		5	.053
1917	NY	N	2		6	.250
					25	.245

YR CL LEA POS	GP	G	REC

HEVING, JOHN ALOYSIUS
1931 PHI A H   1 .000

HIGBE, WALTER KIRBY
1941 BRO N P   1 0- 0

HIGGINS, MICHAEL FRANCIS
1940 DET A 3   7 .333
1946 BOS A 3   7 .208
               14 .271

HIGH, ANDREW AIRD
1928 STL N 3   4 .294
1930 STL N 3   1 .500
1931 STL N 3   4 .267
                9 .294

HILDEBRAND, ORAL CLYDE
1939 NY A P   1 0- 0

HILL, CARMEN PROCTOR
1927 PIT N P   1 0- 0

HILLER, CHARLES JOSEPH
1962 SF N 2   7 .269

HILLER, JOHN FREDERICK
1968 DET A P   2 0- 0

HOAG, MYRIL OLIVER
1932 NY A H   1 .000
1937 NY A O   5 .300
1938 NY A O   2 .400
                8 .320

HOAK, DONALD ALBERT
1955 BRO N 3   3 .333
1960 PIT N 3   7 .217
               10 .231

HOBLITZEL, RICHARD CARLETON
1915 BOS A 1   5 .313
1916 BOS A 1   5 .235
               10 .273

HODGES, GILBERT RAYMOND
1947 BRO N H   1 .000
1949 BRO N 1   5 .235
1952 BRO N 1   7 .000
1953 BRO N 1   6 .364
1955 BRO N 1   7 .292
1956 BRO N 1   7 .304
1959 LA N 1   6 .391
               39 .267

HODGES, RONALD WRAY
1973 NY N H   1 .000

HOERNER, JOSEPH WALTER
1967 STL N P   2 0- 0
1968 STL N P   3 0- 1
                5 0- 1

HOFFMAN, DANIEL JOHN
1905 PHI A H   1 .000

HOFMAN, ARTHUR FREDERICK
1906 CHI N O   6 .304
1908 CHI N O   5 .316
1910 CHI N O   5 .267
               16 .298

HOFFMANN, FRED
1923 NY A H   2 .000

HOGSETT, ELON CHESTER
1934 DET A P   3 0- 0
1935 DET A P   1 0- 0
                4 0- 0

HOGUE, ROBERT CLINTON
1951 NY A P   2 0- 0

HOLKE, WALTER HENRY
1917 NY N 1   6 .266

HOLLINGSWORTH, ALBERT WAYNE
1944 STL A P   1 0- 0

HOLLOCHER, CHARLES JACOB
1918 CHI N S   6 .190

HOLM, ROSCOE ALBERT
1926 STL N O   5 .125
1928 STL N O   3 .167
                8 .136

HOLMES, THOMAS FRANCIS
1948 BOS N O   6 .192
1952 BRO N O   3 .000
                9 .185

HOLT, JAMES WILLIAM
1974 OAK A 1   4 .667

HOLTZMAN, KENNETH DALE
1972 OAK A P   3 1- 0
1973 OAK A P   3 2- 1
1974 OAK A P   2 1- 0
                8 4- 1

HOOPER, HARRY BARTHOLOMEW
1912 BOS A O   8 .290
1915 BOS A O   5 .350
1916 BOS A O   5 .333
1918 BOS A O   6 .200
               24 .293

HOOTON, BURT CARLTON
1977 LA N P   2 1- 1
1978 LA N P   2 1- 1
                4 2- 2

HOOVER, ROBERT JOSEPH
1945 DET A S   1 .333

HOPP, JOHN LEONARD
1942 STL N 1   5 .176
1943 STL N O   1 .000
1944 STL N O   6 .185
1950 NY A 1   3 .000
1951 NY A H   1 .000
               16 .160

HORLEN, JOEL EDWARD
1972 OAK A P   1 0- 0

HORNSBY, ROGERS
1926 STL N 2   7 .250
1929 CHI N 2   5 .238
               12 .245

HORTON, WILLIAM WATTERSON
1968 DET A O   7 .304

HOSTETLER, CHARLES CLOYD
1945 DET A H   3 .000

HOUGH, CHARLES OLIVER
1974 LA N P   1 0- 0
1977 LA N P   2 0- 0
1978 LA N P   2 0- 0
                5 0- 0

HOUK, RALPH GEORGE
1947 NY A H   1 1.000
1952 NY A H   1 .500
                2 .500

HOUTTEMAN, ARTHUR JOSEPH
1954 CLE A P   1 0- 0

HOWARD, ELSTON GENE
1955 NY A O   7 .192
1956 NY A O   1 .400
1957 NY A 1   6 .273
1958 NY A O   6 .222
1960 NY A C   5 .462
1961 NY A C   5 .250
1962 NY A C   6 .143
1963 NY A C   4 .333
1964 NY A C   7 .292
1967 BOS A C   7 .111
               54 .246

HOWARD, FRANK OLIVER
1963 LA N O   3 .300

HOWARD, GEORGE ELMER
1907 CHI N 1   2 .200
1908 CHI N H   1 .000
                3 .167

HOYT, WAITE CHARLES
1921 NY A P   3 2- 1
1922 NY A P   2 0- 1
1923 NY A P   1 0- 0
1926 NY A P   2 1- 1
1927 NY A P   1 1- 0
1928 NY A P   2 2- 0
1931 PHI A P   1 0- 1
               12 6- 4

HUBBELL, CARL OWEN
1933 NY N P   2 2- 0
1936 NY N P   2 1- 1
1937 NY N P   2 1- 1
                6 4- 2

HUGHES, JAMES ROBERT
1953 BRO N P   1 0- 0

HUGHES, RICHARD HENRY
1967 STL N P   2 0- 1
1968 STL N P   1 0- 0
                3 0- 1

HUGHES, ROY JOHN
1945 CHI N S   6 .294

HUGHES, THOMAS JAMES
1903 BOS A P   1 0- 1

HUGHSON, CECIL CARLTON
1946 BOS A P   3 0- 1

HUMPHREYS, ROBERT WILLIAM
1964 STL N P   1 0- 0

HUNT, KENNETH RAYMOND
1961 CIN N P   1 0- 0

HUNTER, JAMES AUGUSTUS
1972 OAK A P   3 2- 0
1973 OAK A P   2 1- 0
1974 OAK A P   2 1- 0
1976 NY A P   1 0- 1
1977 NY A P   2 0- 1
1978 NY A P   2 1- 1
               12 5- 3

HUTCHINGS, JOHN RICHARD JOSEPH
1940 CIN N P   1 0- 0

HUTCHINSON, FREDERICK CHARLES
1940 DET A P   1 0- 0

HYATT, ROBERT HAMILTON
1909 PIT N O   2 .000

IRVIN, MONFORD
1951 NY N O   6 .458
1954 NY N O   4 .222
               10 .394

ISBELL WILLIAM FRANK
1906 CHI A 2   6 .308

JACKSON, GRANT DWIGHT
1971 BAL A P   1 0- 0
1976 NY A P   1 0- 0
                2 0- 0

JACKSON, JOSEPH JEFFERSON
1917 CHI A O   6 .304
1919 CHI A O   8 .375
               14 .345

JACKSON, RANSOM JOSEPH
1956 BRO N H   3 .000

JACKSON, REGINALD MARTINEZ
1973 OAK A O   7 .310
1974 OAK A O   5 .286
1977 NY A O   6 .450
1978 NY A O   6 .391
               24 .360

JACKSON, TRAVIS CALVIN
1923 NY N H   1 .000
1924 NY N S   7 .074
1933 NY N 3   5 .222
1936 NY N 3   6 .190
               19 .149

JAKUCKI, SIGMUND
1944 STL A P   1 0- 1

JAMES, CHARLES WESLEY
1964 STL N H   3 .000

JAMES, WILLIAM HENRY
1919 CHI A P   1 0- 0

JAMES, WILLIAM LAWRENCE
1914 BOS N P   2 2- 0

JAMIESON, CHARLES DEVINE
1920 CLE A O   6 .333

JANSEN, LAWRENCE JOSEPH
1951 NY N P   3 0- 2

JANVRIN, HAROLD CHANDLER
1915 BOS A S   1 .000
1916 BOS A 2   5 .217
                6 .208

JASTER, LARRY EDWARD
1967 STL N P   1 0- 0
1968 STL N P   1 0- 0
                2 0- 0

JAVIER, MANUEL JULIAN
1964 STL N 2   1 .000
1967 STL N 2   7 .360
1968 STL N 2   7 .333
1972 CIN N H   4 .000
               19 .333

JAY, JOSEPH RICHARD
1961 CIN N P   2 1- 1

JENSEN, JACK EUGENE
1950 NY A R   1 .000

JOHN, THOMAS EDWARD
1977 LA N P   1 0- 1
1978 LA N P   2 1- 0
                3 1- 1

YR CL LEA POS   GP   G   REC   YR CL LEA POS   GP   G   REC   YR CL LEA POS   GP   G   REC

JOHNSON, CLIFFORD
1977 NY A C	2	.000
1978 NY A H	2	.000
	4	.000

JOHNSON, DARRELL DEAN
| 1961 CIN N C | 2 | .500 |

JOHNSON, DAVID ALLEN
1966 BAL A 2	4	.286
1969 BAL A 2	5	.063
1970 BAL A 2	5	.313
1971 BAL A 2	7	.148
	21	.192

JOHNSON, DERON ROGER
| 1973 OAK A 1 | 6 | .300 |

JOHNSON, DONALD SPORE
| 1945 CHI N 2 | 7 | .172 |

JOHNSON, EARL DOUGLAS
| 1946 BOS A P | 3 | 1- 0 |

JOHNSON, ERNEST RUDOLPH
| 1923 NY A S | 2 | .000 |

JOHNSON, ERNEST THORWALD
| 1957 MIL N P | 3 | 0- 1 |

JOHNSON, KENNETH TRAVIS
| 1961 CIN N P | 1 | 0- 0 |

JOHNSON, KENNETH WANDERSEE
| 1950 PHI N R | 1 | .000 |

JOHNSON, LOUIS BROWN
1965 LA N O	7	.296
1966 LA N O	4	.267
	11	.286

JOHNSON, ROBERT DALE
| 1971 PIT N P | 2 | 0- 1 |

JOHNSON, ROY CLEVELAND
| 1936 NY A H | 2 | .000 |

JOHNSON, SYLVESTER W.
1928 STL N P	2	0- 0
1930 STL N P	2	0- 0
1931 STL N P	3	0- 1
	7	0- 1

JOHNSON, WALTER PERRY
1924 WAS A P	3	1- 2
1925 WAS A P	3	2- 1
	6	3- 3

JOHNSON, WILLIAM RUSSELL
1943 NY A 3	5	.300
1947 NY A 3	7	.269
1949 NY A 3	2	.143
1950 NY A 3	4	.000
	18	.237

JOHNSTON, JAMES HARLE
1916 BRO N O	3	.300
1920 BRO N 3	4	.214
	7	.250

JOHNSTON, WHEELER ROGER
| 1920 CLE A 1 | 5 | .273 |

JOHNSTONE, JOHN WILLIAM
| 1978 NY A O | 2 | .000 |

JONES, CLEON JOSEPH
1969 NY N O	5	.158
1973 NY N O	7	.286
	12	.234

JONES, DAVID JEFFERSON
1907 DET A O	5	.353
1908 DET A H	3	.000
1909 DET A O	7	.233
	15	.265

JONES, FIELDER ALLISON
| 1906 CHI A O | 6 | .095 |

JONES, JAMES DALTON
| 1967 BOS A 3 | 6 | .389 |

JONES, SAMUEL POND
1918 BOS A P	1	0- 1
1922 NY A P	2	0- 0
1923 NY A P	2	0- 1
1926 NY A P	1	0- 0
	6	0- 2

JONES, SHELDON LESLIE
| 1951 NY N P | 2 | 0- 0 |

JONES, SHERMAN JARVIS
| 1961 CIN N P | 1 | 0- 0 |

JONES, THOMAS
| 1909 DET A 1 | 7 | .250 |

JONES, VERNAL LEROY
1946 STL N H	1	.000
1957 MIL N H	3	.000
	4	.000

JONES, WILLIE EDWARD
| 1950 PHI N 3 | 4 | .286 |

JONNARD, CLAUDE ALFRED
1923 NY N P	2	0- 0
1924 NY N P	1	0- 0
	3	0- 0

JOOST, EDWIN DAVID
| 1940 CIN N 2 | 7 | .200 |

JORGENSEN, JOHN DONALD
1947 BRO N 3	7	.200
1949 BRO N 3	4	.182
	11	.194

JOSHUA, VON EVERETT
| 1974 LA N H | 4 | .000 |

JUDGE, JOSEPH IGNATIUS
1924 WAS A 1	7	.385
1925 WAS A 1	7	.174
	14	.286

JUDNICH, WALTER FRANKLIN
| 1948 CLE A O | 4 | .077 |

JURGES, WILLIAM FREDERICK
1932 CHI N S	3	.364
1935 CHI N S	6	.250
1938 CHI N S	4	.231
	13	.275

JURISICH, ALVIN JOSEPH
| 1944 STL N P | 1 | 0- 0 |

KAAT, JAMES LEE
| 1965 MIN A P | 3 | 1- 2 |

KALINE, ALBERT WILLIAM
| 1968 DET A O | 7 | .379 |

KANE, JOHN FRANCIS
| 1910 CHI N R | 1 | .000 |

KASKO, EDWARD MICHAEL
| 1961 CIN N S | 5 | .318 |

KAUFF, BENJAMIN MICHAEL
| 1917 NY N O | 6 | .160 |

KEEN, HOWARD VICTOR
| 1926 STL N P | 1 | 0- 0 |

KELLER, CHARLES ERNEST
1939 NY A O	4	.438
1941 NY A O	5	.389
1942 NY A O	5	.200
1943 NY A O	5	.222
	19	.306

KELLERT, FRANK WILLIAM
| 1955 BRO N H | 3 | .333 |

KELLY, GEORGE LANGE
1921 NY N 1	8	.233
1922 NY N 1	5	.278
1923 NY N 1	6	.182
1924 NY N 1-2-0	7	.290
	26	.248

KELTNER, KENNETH FREDERICK
| 1948 CLE A 3 | 6 | .095 |

KENNEDY, JOHN EDWARD
1965 LA N 3	4	.000
1966 LA N 3	2	.200
	6	.167

KENNEDY, MONTIA CALVIN
| 1951 NY N P | 2 | 0- 0 |

KENNEDY, ROBERT DANIEL
| 1948 CLE A O | 3 | .500 |

KENNEDY, WILLIAM P.
| 1903 PIT N P | 1 | 0- 1 |

KERR, JOHN FRANCIS
| 1933 WAS A R | 1 | .000 |

KERR, RICHARD HENRY
| 1919 CHI A P | 2 | 2- 0 |

KILDUFF, PETER JOHN
| 1920 BRO N 2 | 7 | .095 |

KILLEBREW, HARMON CLAYTON
| 1965 MIN A 3 | 7 | .286 |

KILLEFER, WILLIAM LAVIER
1915 PHI N H	1	.000
1918 PHI N C	6	.118
	7	.111

KILLIAN, EDWIN HENRY
1907 DET A P	1	0- 0
1908 DET A P	1	0- 0
	2	0- 0

KING, EDWARD LEE
| 1922 NY N O | 2 | 1.000 |

KISON, BRUCE EUGENE
| 1971 PIT N P | 2 | 1- 0 |

KLEIN, CHARLES HERBERT
| 1935 CHI N O | 5 | .333 |

KLEIN, LOUIS FRANK
| 1943 STL N 2 | 5 | .136 |

KLIEMAN, EDWARD FREDERICK
| 1948 CLE A P | 1 | 0- 0 |

KLING, JOHN GRADWOHL
1906 CHI N C	6	.176
1907 CHI N C	5	.211
1908 CHI N C	5	.250
1910 CHI N C	5	.077
	21	.185

KLINGER, ROBERT HAROLD
| 1940 BOS A P | 1 | 0- 1 |

KLIPPSTEIN, JOHN CALVIN
1959 LA N P	1	0- 0
1965 MIN A P	2	0- 0
	3	0- 0

KLUSZEWSKI, THEODORE BERNARD
| 1959 CHI A 1 | 6 | .391 |

KNOWLES, DAROLD DUANE
| 1973 OAK A P | 7 | 0- 0 |

KOENIG, MARK ANTHONY
1926 NY A S	7	.125
1927 NY A S	4	.500
1928 NY A S	4	.158
1932 CHI N S	2	.250
1936 NY N 2	3	.333
	20	.237

KONETCHY, EDWARD JOSEPH
| 1920 BRO N 1 | 7 | .174 |

KONIKOWSKI, ALEXANDER JAMES
| 1951 NY N P | 1 | 0- 0 |

KONSTANTY, CASIMIR JAMES
| 1950 PHI N P | 3 | 0- 1 |

KOOSMAN, JEROME MARTIN
1969 NY N P	2	2- 0
1973 NY N P	2	1- 0
	4	3- 0

KOPF, WILLIAM LORENZ
| 1919 CIN N S | 8 | .222 |

KOSLO, GEORGE BERNARD
| 1951 NY N P | 2 | 1- 1 |

KOUFAX, SANFORD
1959 LA N P	2	0- 1
1963 LA N P	2	0- 0
1965 LA N P	3	2- 1
1966 LA N P	1	0- 1
	8	4- 3

KOWALIK, FABIAN LORENZ
| 1935 CHI N P | 1 | 0- 0 |

KRAMER, JOHN HENRY
| 1944 STL A P | 2 | 1- 0 |

KRANEPOOL, EDWARD EMIL
1969 NY N 1	1	.250
1973 NY N H	4	.000
	5	.143

KREEVICH, MICHAEL ANDREAS
| 1944 STL A O | 6 | .231 |

KREMER, REMY PETER
1925 PIT N P	3	2- 1
1927 PIT N P	1	0- 1
	4	2- 2

KRIST, HOWARD WILBUR
| 1943 STL N P | 1 | 0- 0 |

KRUEGER, ERNEST GEORGE
| 1920 BRO N C | 4 | .167 |

```
YR   CL LEA POS    GP    G    REC        YR   CL LEA POS    GP    G    REC        YR   CL LEA POS    GP    G    REC

KUBEK, ANTHONY CHRISTOPHER               LAZZERI, ANTHONY MICHAEL                 LINZ, PHILIP FRANCIS
1957 NY  A  3-O          7   .286        1926 NY  A  2            7   .192         1963 NY  A  H            3   .333
1958 NY  A  S           7   .048         1927 NY  A  2            4   .267         1964 NY  A  S           7   .226
1960 NY  A  S-O          7   .333        1928 NY  A  2            4   .250                                10   .235
1961 NY  A  S           5   .227         1932 NY  A  2            4   .294
1962 NY  A  S           7   .276         1936 NY  A  2            6   .250        LITWHILER, DANIEL WEBSTER
1963 NY  A  S           4   .188         1937 NY  A  2            5   .400         1943 STL N  O            5   .267
                       37   .240         1938 CHI N  H            2   .000         1944 STL N  O           5   .200
                                                                32   .262                                 10   .229
KUBIAK, THEODORE RODGER
1972 OAK A  2           4   .333         LEACH, THOMAS WILLIAM                    LIVINGSTON, THOMPSON ORVILLE
1973 OAK A  2           4   .000         1903 PIT N  3            8   .273         1945 CHI N  C            6   .364
                        8   .167         1909 PIT N  3-O          7   .320
                                                                15   .293        LOCKER, ROBERT AWTRY
KUCKS, JOHN CHARLES                                                               1972 OAK A  P            1   0- 0
1955 NY  A  P           2   0- 0         LEE, WILLIAM CRUTCHER
1956 NY  A  P           3   1- 0         1935 CHI N  P            2   0- 0        LOCKMAN, CARROLL WALTER
1957 NY  A  P           1   0- 0         1938 CHI N  P            2   0- 2         1951 NY  N  1            6   .240
1958 NY  A  P           2   0- 0                                 4   0- 2         1954 NY  N  1           4   .111
                        8   1- 0                                                                          10   .186
                                         LEE, WILLIAM FRANCIS
KUENN, HARVEY EDWARD                      1975 BOS A  P            2   0- 0        LOES, WILLIAM
1962 SF  N  O           4   .063                                                  1952 BRO N  P            2   0- 1
                                         LEEVER, SAMUEL                           1953 BRO N  P           1   1- 0
KUHEL, JOSEPH ANTHONY                     1903 PIT N  P            2   0- 2        1955 BRO N  P           1   0- 1
1933 WAS A  1           5   .150                                                                           4   1- 2
                                         LEFEBVRE, JAMES KENNETH
KUROWSKI, GEORGE JOHN                     1965 LA  N  2            3   .400        LOGAN, JOHN
1942 STL N  3           5   .267         1966 LA  N  2           4   .167         1957 MIL N  S            7   .185
1943 STL N  3           5   .222                                 7   .273         1958 MIL N  S           7   .120
1944 STL N  3           6   .217                                                                          14   .154
1946 STL N  3           7   .296         LEHMAN, KENNETH KARL
                       23   .253         1952 BRO N  P            1   0- 0        LOHRKE, JACK WAYNE
                                                                                  1951 NY  N  H            2   .000
KUZAVA, ROBERT LEROY                     LEIBER, HENRY EDWARD
1951 NY  A  P           1   0- 0         1936 NY  N  O            2   .000        LOLICH, MICHAEL STEVEN
1952 NY  A  P           1   0- 0         1937 NY  N  O           3   .364         1968 DET A  P            3   3- 0
1953 NY  A  P           1   0- 0                                 5   .235
                        3   0- 0                                                  LOLLAR, JOHN SHERMAN
                                         LEIBOLD, HARRY LORAN                      1947 NY  A  C            2   .750
LAABS, CHESTER PETER                      1917 CHI A  O            2   .400        1959 CHI A  C           6   .227
1944 STL A  O           5   .200         1919 CHI A  O           5   .056                                  8   .306
                                         1924 WAS A  O           3   .167
LABINE, CLEMENT WALTER                    1925 WAS A  H           3   .500        LOMBARDI, ERNESTO NATALI
1953 BRO N  P           3   0- 2                                13   .161         1939 CIN N  C            4   .214
1955 BRO N  P           4   1- 0                                                  1940 CIN N  C           2   .333
1956 BRO N  P           2   1- 0         LEIFIELD, ALBERT PETER                                            6   .235
1959 LA  N  P           1   0- 0         1909 PIT N  P            1   0- 1
1960 PIT N  P           3   0- 0                                                  LOMBARDI, VICTOR ALVIN
                       13   2- 2         LE JOHN, DONALD EVERETT                   1947 BRO N  P    2      3   0- 1
                                         1965 LA  N  H            1   .000
LA CHANCE, GEORGE JOSEPH                                                          LONBORG, JAMES REYNOLD
1903 BOS A  1           8   .222         LEMON, ROBERT GRANVILLE                   1967 BOS A  P            3   2- 1
                                         1948 CLE A  P            2   2- 0
LACY, LEONDAUS                            1954 CLE A  P    2      3   0- 2        LONG, RICHARD DALE
1974 LA  N  H           1   .000                          4      5   2- 2         1960 NY  A  H            3   .333
1977 LA  N  O           4   .429                                                  1962 NY  A  1           2   .200
1978 LA  N  O           4   .143         LEONARD, HUBERT BENJAMIN                                          5   .250
                        9   .227         1915 BOS A  P            1   1- 0
                                         1916 BOS A  P           1   1- 0        LOPAT, EDMUND WALTER
LAMABE, JOHN ALEXANDER                                           2   2- 0         1949 NY  A  P            1   1- 0
1967 STL N  P           3   0- 1                                                  1950 NY  A  P           1   0- 0
                                         LEONHARD, DAVID PAUL                      1951 NY  A  P           2   2- 0
LAMAR, WILLIAM HARMONG                    1969 BAL A  P            1   0- 0        1952 NY  A  P           2   0- 1
1920 BRO N  H           3   .000         1971 BAL A  P           1   0- 0         1953 NY  A  P           1   1- 0
                                                                2   0- 0                                   7   4- 1
LANDESTOY, RAFAEL SILVIALDO
1977 LA  N  R           1   .000         LESLIE, SAMUEL ANDREW                    LOPATA, STANLEY EDWARD
                                         1936 NY  N  H            3   .667         1950 PHI N  C            2   .000
LANDIS, JAMES HENRY                       1937 NY  N  H           2   .000
1959 CHI A  O           6   .292                                 5   .500        LOPES, DAVID EARL
                                                                                  1974 LA  N  2            5   .111
LANIER, HUBERT MAX                        LEWIS, ALLAN SYDNEY                      1977 LA  N  2           6   .167
1942 STL N  P           2   1- 0         1972 OAK A  R            6   .000        1978 LA  N  2           6   .308
1943 STL N  P           3   0- 1         1973 OAK A  R           3   .000                                 17   .206
1944 STL N  P           2   1- 0                                 9   .000
                        7   2- 1                                                  LOPEZ, HECTOR HEADLEY
                                         LEWIS, GEORGE EDWARD                      1960 NY  A  O            3   .429
LAPP, JOHN WALKER                         1912 BOS A  O            8   .156        1961 NY  A  O           4   .333
1910 PHI A  C           1   .250         1915 BOS A  O           5   .444         1962 NY  A  H           2   .000
1911 PHI A  C           2   .250         1916 BOS A  O           5   .353         1963 NY  A  O           3   .250
1913 PHI A  C           1   .250                                18   .284         1964 NY  A  O           3   .000
1914 PHI A  C           1   .000                                                                          15   .286
                        5   .235         LIDDLE, DONALD EUGENE
                                         1954 NY  N  P            2   1- 0        LOPEZ, MARCELINO PONS
LARKER, NORMAN HOWARD JOHN                                                        1970 BAL A  P            1   0- 0
1959 LA  N  O           6   .188         LINDBLAD, PAUL AARON
                                         1973 OAK A  P            3   1- 0        LORD, BRISTOL ROBOTHAM
LARSEN, DONALD JAMES                      1974 OAK A  P           1   0- 0         1905 PHI A  O            5   .100
1955 NY  A  P           1   0- 1                                 4   1- 0         1910 PHI A  O           5   .182
1956 NY  A  P           2   1- 0                                                  1911 PHI A  O           6   .185
1957 NY  A  P           2   1- 1                                                                          16   .159
1958 NY  A  P           2   1- 0         LINDELL, JOHN HARLAN
1962 SF  N  P           3   1- 0         1943 NY  A  O            4   .111        LOWDERMILK, GROVER CLEVELAND
                       10   4- 2         1947 NY  A  O           6   .500         1919 CHI A  P            1   0- 0
                                         1949 NY  A  O           2   .143
LASHER, FREDERICK WALTER                                        12   .324        LOWN, OMAR JOSEPH
1968 DET A  P           1   0- 0                                                  1959 CHI N  P            3   0- 0
                                         LINDSEY, JAMES KENDRICK
LAVAGETTO, HARRY ARTHUR                   1930 STL N  P            2   0- 0        LOWREY, HARRY LEE
1941 BRO N  3           3   .100         1931 STL N  P           2   0- 0         1945 CHI N  O            7   .310
1947 BRO N  3           5   .143                                 4   0- 0
                        8   .118                                                  LUDERUS, FREDERICK WILLIAM
                                         LINDSTROM, FREDERICK CHARLES              1915 PHI N  1            5   .438
LAW, VERNON SANDERS                       1924 NY  N  3            7   .333
1960 PIT N  P           3   2- 0         1935 CHI N  3-O         4   .200        LUMPE, JERRY DEAN
                                                                11   .289         1957 NY  A  3            6   .286
                                                                                  1958 NY  A  S-3         6   .167
                                                                                                          12   .231
```

YR	CL	LEA	POS	GP	G	REC
LUNTE, HARRY AUGUST						
1920	CLE	A	2		1	.000
LUQUE, ADOLFO						
1919	CIN	N	P		2	0- 0
1933	NY	N	P		1	1- 0
					3	1- 0
LYLE, ALBERT WALTER						
1976	NY	A	P		2	0- 0
1977	NY	A	P		2	1- 0
					4	1- 0
LYNCH, GERALD THOMAS						
1961	CIN	N	H		4	.000
LYNN, BYRD						
1917	CHI	A	H		1	.000
1919	CHI	A	C		1	.000
					2	.000
LYNN, FREDRIC MICHAEL						
1975	BOS	A	O		7	.280
MAAS, DUANE FREDRICK						
1958	NY	A	P		1	0- 0
1960	NY	A	P		1	0- 0
					2	0- 0
MADDOX, ELLIOTT						
1976	NY	A	O-O		2	.200
MADDOX, NICHOLAS						
1909	PIT	N	P		1	1- 0
MAGEE, SHERWOOD ROBERT						
1919	CIN	N	H		2	.500
MAGLIE, SALVATORE ANTHONY						
1951	NY	N	P		1	0- 1
1954	NY	N	P		1	0- 0
1956	BRO	N	P		2	1- 1
					4	1- 2
MAGUIRE, FREDERICK EDWARD						
1923	NY	N	R		2	.000
MAHAFFEY, LEE ROY						
1931	PHI	A	P		1	0- 0
MAIER, ROBERT PHILLIP						
1945	DET	A	H		1	1.000
MAILS, JOHN WALTER						
1920	CLE	A	P		2	1- 0
MAJESKI, HENRY						
1954	CLE	A	3		4	.167
MALONE, PERCE LEIGH						
1929	CHI	N	P		3	0- 2
1932	CHI	N	P		1	0- 0
1936	NY	A	P		2	0- 1
					6	0- 3
MALONEY, JAMES WILLIAM						
1961	CIN	N	P		1	0- 0
MAMAUX, ALBERT LEON						
1920	BRO	N	P		3	0- 0
MANCUSO, AUGUST RODNEY						
1930	STL	N	C		2	.286
1931	STL	N	C		2	.000
1933	NY	N	C		5	.118
1936	NY	N	C		6	.263
1937	NY	N	C		3	.000
					18	.173
MANCUSO, FRANK OCTAVIUS						
1944	STL	A	C		2	.667
MANGUAL, ANGEL LUIS						
1972	OAK	A	O		4	.300
1973	OAK	A	O		5	.000
1974	OAK	A	H		1	.000
					10	.176
MANN, LESLIE						
1914	BOS	N	O		3	.286
1918	CHI	N	O		6	.227
					9	.241
MANTILLA, FELIX						
1957	MIL	N	2		4	.000
1958	MIL	N	S		4	.000
					8	.000

YR	CL	LEA	POS	GP	G	REC
MANTLE, MICKEY CHARLES						
1951	NY	A	O		2	.200
1952	NY	A	O		7	.345
1953	NY	A	O		6	.208
1955	NY	A	O		3	.200
1956	NY	A	O		7	.250
1957	NY	A	O		6	.263
1958	NY	A	O		7	.250
1960	NY	A	O		7	.400
1961	NY	A	O		2	.167
1962	NY	A	O		7	.120
1963	NY	A	O		4	.133
1964	NY	A	O		7	.333
					65	.257
MANUSH, HENRY EMMETT						
1933	WAS	A	O		5	.111
MAPES, CLIFFORD FRANKLIN						
1949	NY	A	O		4	.100
1950	NY	A	O		1	.000
					5	.071
MARANVILLE, WALTER JAMES VINCENT						
1914	BOS	N	S		4	.308
1928	STL	N	S		4	.308
					8	.308
MARBERRY, FREDRICK						
1924	WAS	A	P		4	0- 1
1925	WAS	A	P		2	0- 0
1934	DET	A	P		2	0- 0
					8	0- 1
MARICHAL, JUAN ANTONIO						
1962	SF	N	P		1	0- 0
MARION, MARTIN WHITFORD						
1942	STL	N	S		5	.111
1943	STL	N	S		5	.357
1944	STL	N	S		6	.227
1946	STL	N	S		7	.250
					23	.231
MARIS, ROGER EUGENE						
1960	NY	A	O		7	.267
1961	NY	A	O		5	.105
1962	NY	A	O		7	.174
1963	NY	A	O		2	.000
1964	NY	A	O		7	.200
1967	STL	N	O		7	.385
1968	STL	N	O		6	.158
					41	.217
MARQUARD, RICHARD WILLIAM						
1911	NY	N	P		3	0- 1
1912	NY	N	P		2	2- 0
1913	NY	N	P		2	0- 1
1916	BRO	N	P		2	0- 2
1920	BRO	N	P		2	0- 1
					11	2- 5
MARQUEZ, GONZALO ENRIQUE						
1972	OAK	A	H		5	.600
MARSHALL, MICHAEL GRANT						
1974	LA	N	P		5	0- 1
MARTIN, ALFRED MANUEL						
1951	NY	A	R		1	.000
1952	NY	A	2		7	.217
1953	NY	A	2		6	.500
1955	NY	A	2		7	.320
1956	NY	A	2-3		7	.296
					28	.333
MARTIN, JOHN LEONARD ROOSEVELT						
1928	STL	N	R		1	.000
1931	STL	N	O		7	.500
1934	STL	N	3		7	.355
					15	.418
MARTIN, JOSEPH CLIFTON						
1969	NY	N	H		1	.000
MARTINA, JOSEPH JOHN						
1924	WAS	A	P		1	0- 0
MARTINEZ, TEODORO NOEL						
1973	NY	N	R		2	.000
MARTY, JOSEPH ANTON						
1938	CHI	N	O		3	.500
MASI, PHILIP SAMUEL						
1948	BOS	N	C		5	.125
MASON, JAMES PERCY						
1976	NY	A	S		3	1.000
MATCHICK, JOHN THOMAS						
1968	DET	A	H		3	.000
MATHEWS, EDWIN LEE						
1957	MIL	N	3		7	.227
1958	MIL	N	3		7	.160
1968	DET	A	3		2	.333
					16	.200

YR	CL	LEA	POS	GP	G	REC
MATHEWSON, CHRISTOPHER						
1905	NY	N	P		3	3- 0
1911	NY	N	P		3	1- 2
1912	NY	N	P		3	0- 2
1913	NY	N	P		2	1- 1
					11	5- 5
MATLACK, JONATHAN TRUMPBOUR						
1973	NY	N	P		3	1- 2
MAXVILL, CHARLES DALLAN						
1964	STL	N	2		7	.200
1967	STL	N	S		7	.158
1968	STL	N	S		7	.000
1974	OAK	A	2		2	.000
					23	.115
MAY, CARLOS						
1976	NY	A	D		4	.000
MAY, DAVID LA FRANCE						
1969	BAL	A	H		2	.000
MAY, FRANK SPRUIELL						
1932	CHI	N	P		2	0- 1
MAY, LEE ANDREW						
1970	CIN	N	1		5	.389
MAY, MILTON SCOTT						
1971	PIT	N	H		2	.500
MAYER, ERSKINE JOHN						
1915	PHI	N	P		2	0- 1
1919	CHI	A	P		1	0- 0
					3	0- 1
MAYO, EDWARD JOSEPH						
1936	NY	N	3		1	.000
1945	DET	A	2		7	.250
					8	.241
MAYO, JOHN LEWIS						
1950	PHI	N	O		3	.000
MAYS, CARL WILLIAM						
1916	BOS	A	P		2	0- 1
1918	BOS	A	P		2	2- 0
1921	NY	A	P		3	1- 2
1922	NY	A	P		1	0- 1
					8	3- 4
MAYS, WILLIE HOWARD						
1951	NY	N	O		6	.182
1954	NY	N	O		4	.286
1962	SF	N	O		7	.250
1973	NY	N	O		3	.286
					20	.239
MAZEROSKI, WILLIAM STANLEY						
1960	PIT	N	2		7	.320
1971	PIT	N	H		1	.000
					8	.308
MC ANANY, JAMES						
1959	CHI	A	O		3	.000
MC AULIFFE, RICHARD JOHN						
1968	DET	A	2		7	.222
MC BRIDE, THOMAS RAYMOND						
1946	BOS	A	O		5	.167
MC CABE, WILLIAM FRANCIS						
1918	CHI	N	H		3	.000
1920	BRO	N	R		1	.000
					4	.000
MC CARTHY, JOHN JOSEPH						
1937	NY	N	1		5	.211
MC CARTY, GEORGE LEWIS						
1917	NY	N	C		3	.400
MC CARVER, JAMES TIMOTHY						
1964	STL	N	C		7	.478
1967	STL	N	C		7	.125
1968	STL	N	C		7	.333
					21	.311
MC COLL, ALEXANDER BOYD						
1933	WAS	A	P		1	0- 0
MC CORMICK, FRANK ANDREW						
1939	CIN	N	1		4	.400
1940	CIN	N	1		7	.214
1948	BOS	N	1		3	.200
					14	.271
MC CORMICK, HARRY ELWOOD						
1912	NY	N	H		5	.250
1913	NY	N	H		2	.500
					7	.333
MC CORMICK, MYRON WINTHROP						
1940	CIN	N	O		7	.310
1948	BOS	N	O		6	.261
1949	BRO	N	O		1	.000
					14	.286

YR	CL	LEA	POS	GP	G	REC

MC COSKY, WILLIAM BARNEY
| 1940 | DET | A | O | | 7 | .304 |

MC COVEY, WILLIE LEE
| 1962 | SF | N | 1-O | | 4 | .200 |

MC CULLOUGH, CLYDE EDWARD
| 1945 | CHI | N | H | | 1 | .000 |

MC DERMOTT, MAURICE JOSEPH
| 1956 | NY | A | P | | 1 | 0- 0 |

MC DONALD, JIMMIE LE ROY
| 1953 | NY | A | P | | 1 | 1- 0 |

MC DOUGALD, GILBERT JAMES
1951	NY	A	2-3		6	.261
1952	NY	A	3		7	.200
1953	NY	A	3		6	.167
1955	NY	A	3		7	.259
1956	NY	A	S		7	.143
1957	NY	A	S		7	.250
1958	NY	A	2		7	.321
1960	NY	A	3		6	.278
					53	.237

MC ENANEY, WILLIAM HENRY
1975	CIN	N	P		5	0- 0
1976	CIN	N	P		2	0- 0
					7	0- 0

MC FARLAND, EDWARD WILLIAM
| 1906 | CHI | A | H | | 1 | .000 |

MC GANN, DENNIS LAWRENCE
| 1905 | NY | N | 1 | | 5 | .235 |

MC GINNITY, JOSEPH JEROME
| 1905 | NY | N | P | | 2 | 1- 1 |

MC GLOTHLIN, JAMES MILTON
1970	CIN	N	P		1	0- 0
1972	CIN	N	P		1	0- 0
					2	0- 0

MC GRAW, FRANK EDWIN
| 1973 | NY | N | P | | 5 | 1- 0 |

MC HALE, JOHN JOSEPH
| 1945 | DET | A | H | | 3 | .000 |

MC INNIS, JOHN PHALEN
1911	PHI	A	1		1	.000
1913	PHI	A	1		5	.118
1914	PHI	A	1		4	.143
1918	BOS	A	1		6	.250
1925	PIT	N	1		4	.286
					20	.260

MC INTIRE, JOHN REID
| 1910 | CHI | N | P | | 2 | 0- 1 |

MC INTYRE, MATTHEW W.
1908	DET	A	O		5	.222
1909	DET	A	O		4	.000
					9	.190

MC KAIN, ARCHIE RICHARD
| 1940 | DET | A | P | | 1 | 0- 0 |

MC LAIN, DENNIS DALE
| 1968 | DET | A | P | | 3 | 1- 2 |

MC LEAN, JOHN BANNERMAN
| 1913 | NY | N | C | | 5 | .500 |

MC MAHON, DONALD JOHN
1957	MIL	N	P		3	0- 0
1958	MIL	N	P		3	0- 0
1968	DET	A	P		2	0- 0
					8	0- 0

MC MILLAN, NORMAN ALEXIS
1922	NY	A	O		1	.000
1929	CHI	N	3		5	.100
					6	.091

MC MULLIN, FREDERICK WILLIAM
1917	CHI	A	3		6	.125
1919	CHI	A	H		2	.500
					8	.154

MC NAIR, DONALD ERIC
1930	PHI	A	1		1	.000
1931	PHI	A	2		2	.000
					3	.000

NC NALLY, DAVID ARTHUR
1966	BAL	A	P		2	1- 0
1969	BAL	A	P		2	0- 1
1970	BAL	A	P		1	1- 0
1971	BAL	A	P		4	2- 1
					9	4- 2

MC NALLY, MICHAEL JOSEPH
1916	BOS	A	H		1	.000
1921	NY	A	3		7	.000
1922	NY	A	2		1	.000
					9	.200

MC NEELY, GEORGE EARL
1924	WAS	A	O		7	.222
1925	WAS	A	O		4	.000
					11	.222

MC QUILLAN, HUGH A.
1922	NY	N	P		1	1- 0
1923	NY	N	P		2	0- 1
1924	NY	N	P		3	0- 0
					6	1- 1

MC QUINN, GEORGE HARTLEY
1944	STL	A	1		6	.438
1947	NY	A	1		7	.130
					13	.256

MC RAE, HAROLD ABRAHAM
1970	CIN	N	O		3	.455
1972	CIN	N	O		5	.444
					8	.450

MEADOWS, HENRY LEE
1925	PIT	N	P		1	0- 1
1927	PIT	N	P		1	0- 1
					2	0- 2

MEDWICK, JOSEPH MICHAEL
1934	STL	N	O		7	.379
1941	BRO	N	O		5	.235
					12	.326

MELTON, CLIFFORD GEORGE
| 1937 | NY | N | P | | 3 | 0- 2 |

MENKE, DENIS JOHN
| 1972 | CIN | N | 3 | | 7 | .083 |

MERKLE, FREDERICK CHARLES
1911	NY	N	1		6	.150
1912	NY	N	1		8	.273
1913	NY	N	1		4	.231
1916	BRO	N	1		3	.250
1918	CHI	N	1		6	.278
					27	.239

MERRITT, JAMES JOSEPH
1965	MIN	A	P		2	0- 0
1970	CIN	N	P		1	0- 1
					3	0- 1

MERTES, SAMUEL BLAIR
| 1905 | NY | N | O | | 5 | .176 |

MERULLO, LEONARD RICHARD
| 1945 | CHI | N | S | | 3 | .000 |

MESSERSMITH, JOHN ALEXANDER
| 1974 | LA | N | P | | 2 | 0- 2 |

METHENY, ARTHUR BEAUREGARD
| 1943 | NY | A | O | | 2 | .125 |

METKOVICH, GEORGE MICHAEL
| 1946 | BOS | A | H | | 2 | .500 |

MEUSEL, EMIL FREDERICK
1921	NY	N	O		8	.345
1922	NY	N	O		5	.250
1923	NY	N	O		6	.280
1924	NY	N	O		4	.154
					23	.276

MEUSEL, ROBERT WILLIAM
1921	NY	A	O		8	.200
1922	NY	A	O		5	.300
1923	NY	A	O		6	.269
1926	NY	A	O		7	.238
1927	NY	A	O		4	.118
1928	NY	A	O		4	.200
					34	.225

MEYER, RUSSELL CHARLES
1950	PHI	N	P		2	0- 1
1953	BRO	N	P		1	0- 0
1955	BRO	N	P		1	0- 0
					4	0- 1

MEYERS, JOHN TORTES
1911	NY	N	C		6	.300
1912	NY	N	C		8	.357
1913	NY	N	C		1	.000
1916	BRO	N	C		3	.200
					18	.290

MIERKOWICZ, EDWARD FRANK
| 1945 | DET | A | O | | 1 | .000 |

MIKKELSEN, PETER JAMES
| 1964 | NY | A | P | | 4 | 0- 1 |

MIKSIS, EDWARD THOMAS
1947	BRO	N	2-O		5	.250
1949	BRO	N	3		3	.286
					8	.273

MILJUS, JOHN KENNETH
| 1927 | PIT | N | P | | 2 | 0- 1 |

MILLAN, FELIX BERNARDO
| 1973 | NY | N | 2 | | 7 | .187 |

MILLER, EDMUND JOHN
1929	PHI	A	O		5	.368
1930	PHI	A	O		6	.143
1931	PHI	A	O		7	.269
					18	.258

MILLER, ELMER
| 1921 | NY | A | O | | 8 | .161 |

MILLER, JOHN BARNEY
| 1909 | PIT | N | 2 | | 7 | .250 |

MILLER, LAWRENCE H.
| 1918 | BOS | A | H | | 1 | .000 |

MILLER, LOWELL OTTO
1916	BRO	N	C		2	.125
1920	BRO	N	C		6	.143
					8	.136

MILLER, RALPH JOSEPH
| 1924 | WAS | A | 3 | | 4 | .182 |

MILLER, RICHARD ALAN
| 1975 | BOS | A | O | | 3 | .000 |

MILLER, ROBERT JOHN
| 1950 | PHI | N | P | | 1 | 0- 1 |

MILLER, ROBERT LANE
1965	LA	N	P		2	0- 0
1966	LA	N	P		1	0- 0
1971	PIT	N	P		3	0- 1
					6	0- 1

MILLER, STUART LEONARD
| 1962 | SF | N | P | | 2 | 0- 0 |

MILLIKEN, ROBERT FOGLE
| 1953 | BRO | N | P | | 1 | 0- 0 |

MILNER, JOHN DAVID
| 1973 | NY | N | 1 | | 7 | .296 |

MINCHER, DONALD RAY
1965	MIN	A	1		7	.130
1972	OAK	A	H		3	1.000
					10	.167

MINNER, PAUL EDISON
| 1949 | BRO | N | P | | 1 | 0- 0 |

MITCHELL, CLARENCE ELMER
1920	BRO	N	P	1	2	0- 0
1928	STL	N	P		1	0- 0
				2	3	0- 0

MITCHELL, LOREN DALE
1948	CLE	A	O		6	.174
1954	CLE	A	H		3	.000
1956	BRO	N	H		4	.000
					13	.138

MIZE, JOHN ROBERT
1949	NY	A	H		2	1.000
1950	NY	A	1		4	.133
1951	NY	A	1		4	.286
1952	NY	A	1		5	.400
1953	NY	A	H		3	.000
					18	.286

MIZELL, WILMER DAVID
| 1960 | PIT | N | P | | 2 | 0- 1 |

MOELLER, JOSEPH DOUGLAS
| 1966 | LA | N | P | | 1 | 0- 0 |

MOGRIDGE, GEORGE ANTHONY
| 1924 | WAS | A | P | | 2 | 1- 0 |

MONDAY, ROBERT JAMES
1977	LA	N	O		4	.167
1978	LA	N	O-D		5	.154
					9	.160

MONROE, ZACHARY CHARLES
| 1958 | NY | A | P | | 1 | 0- 0 |

MONTGOMERY, ROBERT EDWARD
| 1975 | BOS | A | H | | 1 | .000 |

MOON, WALLACE WADE
1959	LA	N	O		6	.261
1965	LA	N	H		2	.000
					8	.240

MOONEY, JIM IRVING
| 1934 | STL | N | P | | 1 | 0- 0 |

MOORE, EUGENE JR.
| 1944 | STL | N | O | | 6 | .182 |

MOORE, GRAHAM EDWARD
| 1925 | PIT | N | 2 | | 7 | .231 |

YR	CL	LEA	POS	GP	G	REC
MOORE, JAMES WILLIAM						
1930	PHI	A	O		3	.333
1931	PHI	A	O		2	.333
					5	.333
MOORE, JOHN FRANCIS						
1932	CHI	N	O		2	.000
MOORE, JOSEPH GREGG						
1933	NY	N	O		5	.227
1936	NY	N	O		6	.214
1937	NY	N	O		5	.391
					16	.274
MOORE, LLOYD ALBERT						
1939	CIN	N	P		1	0- 0
1940	CIN	N	P		3	0- 0
					4	0- 0
MOORE, RAYMOND LEROY						
1959	CHI	A	P		1	0- 0
MOORE, TERRY BLUFORD						
1942	STL	N	O		5	.294
1946	STL	N	O		7	.148
					12	.205
MOORE, WILLIAM WILCY						
1927	NY	A	P		2	1- 0
1932	NY	A	P		1	1- 0
					3	2- 0
MOOSE, ROBERT RALPH						
1971	PIT	N	P		3	0- 0
MORAN, JOHN HERBERT						
1914	BOS	N	O		3	.077
MORAN, PATRICK JOSEPH						
1906	CHI	N	H		2	.060
1907	CHI	N	H		1	.000
					3	.000
MOREHEAD, DAVID MICHAEL						
1967	BOS	A	P		2	0- 0
MORET, ROGELIO						
1975	BOS	A	P		3	0- 0
MORGAN, JOE LEONARD						
1972	CIN	N	2		7	.125
1975	CIN	N	2		7	.259
1976	CIN	N	2		4	.333
					18	.227
MORGAN, ROBERT MORRIS						
1952	BRO	N	3		2	.000
1953	BRO	N	H		1	.000
					3	.000
MORGAN, TOM STEPHEN						
1951	NY	A	P		1	0- 0
1955	NY	A	P		2	0- 0
1956	NY	A	P		2	0- 1
					5	0- 1
MORIARTY, GEORGE JOSEPH						
1909	DET	A	3		7	.273
MORRISON, JOHN DEWEY						
1925	PIT	N	P		3	0- 0
MOSES, WALLACE						
1946	BOS	A	O		4	.417
MOSSI, DONALD LOUIS						
1954	CLE	A	P		3	0- 0
MOTA, MANUEL RAFAEL						
1977	LA	N	H		3	.000
1978	LA	N	H		1	.000
					4	.000
MOTTON, CURTELL HOWARD						
1969	BAL	A	H		1	.000
MOWERY, HARRY HARLAN						
1916	BRO	N	3		5	.176
MUELLER, DONALD FREDERICK						
1954	NY	N	O		4	.389
MUELLER, LESLIE CLYDE						
1945	DET	A	P		1	0- 0
MULLIN, GEORGE JOSEPH						
1907	DET	A	P		2	0- 2
1908	DET	A	P		1	1- 0
1909	DET	A	P	4	6	2- 1
				7	9	3- 3
MUNCRIEF, ROBERT CLEVELAND						
1944	STL	A	P		2	0- 1
1948	CLE	A	P		1	0- 0
					3	0- 1
MUNGER, GEORGE DAVID						
1946	STL	N	P		1	1- 0
MUNSON, THURMAN LEE						
1976	NY	A	C		4	.529
1977	NY	A	C		6	.320
1978	NY	A	C		6	.320
					16	.373
MURPHY, DANIEL FRANCIS						
1905	PHI	A	2		5	.188
1910	PHI	A	O		5	.350
1911	PHI	A	O		6	.304
					16	.288
MURPHY, JOHN EDWARD						
1913	PHI	A	O		5	.227
1914	PHI	A	O		4	.188
1919	CHI	A	H		3	.000
					12	.200
MURPHY, JOHN JOSEPH						
1936	NY	A	P		1	0- 0
1937	NY	A	P		1	0- 0
1938	NY	A	P		1	0- 0
1939	NY	A	P		1	1- 0
1941	NY	A	P		2	1- 0
1943	NY	A	P		2	0- 0
					8	2- 0
MURRAY, JOHN JOSEPH						
1911	NY	N	O		6	.000
1912	NY	N	O		8	.323
1913	NY	N	O		5	.250
					19	.206
MUSIAL, STANLEY FRANK						
1942	STL	N	O		5	.222
1943	STL	N	O		5	.278
1944	STL	N	O		6	.304
1946	STL	N	1		7	.222
					23	.256
MYER, CHARLES SOLOMON						
1925	WAS	A	3		3	.250
1933	WAS	A	2		5	.300
					8	.286
MYERS, HENRY HARRISON						
1916	BRO	N	O		5	.182
1920	BRO	N	O		7	.231
					12	.208
MYERS, WILLIAM HARRISON						
1939	CIN	N	S		4	.333
1940	CIN	N	S		7	.130
					11	.200
NARAGON, HAROLD RICHARD						
1954	CLE	A	C		1	.000
NARLESKI, RAYMOND EDMOND						
1954	CLE	A	P		2	0- 0
NARRON, SAMUEL						
1943	STL	N	H		1	.000
NEAL, CHARLES LENARD						
1956	BRO	N	2		1	.000
1959	LA	N	2		6	.370
					7	.323
NEALE, ALFRED EARLE						
1919	CIN	N	O		8	.357
NEEDHAM, THOMAS J.						
1910	CHI	N	H		1	.000
NEHF, ARTHUR NEUKOM						
1921	NY	N	P		3	1- 2
1922	NY	N	P		2	1- 0
1923	NY	N	P		2	1- 1
1924	NY	N	P		3	1- 1
1929	CHI	N	P		2	0- 0
					12	4- 4
NEIS, BERNARD EDMUND						
1920	BRO	N	O		4	.000
NELSON, GLENN RICHARD						
1952	BRO	N	H		4	.000
1960	PIT	N	1		4	.333
					8	.250
NELSON, MELVIN FREDERICK						
1968	STL	N	P		1	0- 0
NETTLES, GRAIG						
1976	NY	A	3		4	.250
1977	NY	A	3		6	.190
1978	NY	A	3		6	.160
					16	.190
NEWCOMBE, DONALD						
1949	BRO	N	P		2	0- 2
1955	BRO	N	P		1	0- 1
1956	BRO	N	P		2	0- 1
					5	0- 4
NEWHOUSER, HAROLD						
1945	DET	A	P		3	2- 1
1954	CLE	A	P		1	0- 0
					4	2- 1
NEWSOM, LOUIS NORMAN						
1940	DET	A	P		3	2- 1
1947	NY	A	P		2	0- 1
					5	2- 2
NIARHOS, CONSTANTINE GREGORY						
1949	NY	A	C		1	.000
NICHOLSON, WILLIAM BECK						
1945	CHI	N	O		7	.214
NIEHOFF, JOHN ALBERT						
1915	PHI	N	2		5	.063
NIEMAN, ROBERT CHARLES						
1962	SF	N	H		1	.000
NOBLE, RAFAEL MIGUEL						
1951	NY	N	C		2	.000
NOLAN, GARY LYNN						
1970	CIN	N	P		2	0- 1
1972	CIN	N	P		2	0- 1
1975	CIN	N	P		2	0- 0
1976	CIN	N	P		1	1- 0
					7	1- 2
NOREN, IRVING ARNOLD						
1952	NY	A	O		4	.300
1953	NY	A	H		2	.000
1955	NY	A	O		5	.063
					11	.148
NORMAN, FREDIE HUBERT						
1975	CIN	N	P		2	0- 1
1976	CIN	N	P		1	0- 0
					3	0- 1
NORTH, WILLIAM ALEX						
1974	OAK	A	O		5	.059
1978	LA	N	O		4	.125
					9	.080
NORTHRUP, JAMES THOMAS						
1968	DET	A	O		7	.250
NOSSEK, JOSEPH RUDOLPH						
1965	MIN	A	O		6	.200
NUNAMAKER, LESLIE GRANT						
1920	CLE	A	C		2	.500
OATES, JOHNNY LANE						
1977	LA	N	C		1	.000
1978	LA	N	C		1	1.000
					2	.500
O'BRIEN, JOHN JOSEPH						
1903	BOS	A	H		2	.000
O'BRIEN, THOMAS JOSEPH						
1912	BOS	A	P		2	0- 2
O'CONNELL, JAMES JOSEPH						
1923	NY	N	H		2	.000
O'CONNOR, PATRICK FRANCIS						
1909	PIT	N	H		1	.000
O'DEA, JAMES KENNETH						
1935	CHI	N	C		1	1.000
1938	CHI	N	C		3	.200
1942	STL	N	C		1	1.000
1943	STL	N	C		2	.667
1944	STL	N	C		3	.333
					10	.462
O'DELL, WILLIAM OLIVER						
1962	SF	N	P		3	0- 1
ODOM, JOHNNY LEE						
1972	OAK	A	P	2	4	0- 1
1973	OAK	A	P	2	3	0- 0
1974	OAK	A	P	2	2	1- 0
				6	9	1- 1
O'DOUL, FRANCIS JOSEPH						
1933	NY	N	H		1	1.000
O'FARRELL, ROBERT ARTHUR						
1918	CHI	N	C		3	.000
1926	STL	N	C		7	.304
					10	.269
OGDEN, WARREN HARVEY						
1924	WAS	A	P		1	0- 0
OLDHAM, JOHN CYRUS						
1925	PIT	N	P		1	0- 0
OLDIS, ROBERT CARL						
1960	PIT	N	C		2	.000

```
YR  CL LEA POS    GP   G   REC

OLDRING REUBEN HENRY
1911 PHI A  O          6   .200
1913 PHI A  O          5   .273
1914 PHI A  O          4   .067
                      15   .194

O*LEARY, CHARLES TIMOTHY
1907 DET A  S          5   .059
1908 DET A  S          5   .158
1909 DET A  3          1   .000
                      11   .103

OLIVA, PEDRO
1965 MIN A  O          7   .192

OLIVER, ALBERT
1971 PIT N  O          5   .211

OLIVER, NATHANIEL
1966 LA  N  R          1   .000

OLMO, LUIS FRANCISCO
1949 BRO N  O          4   .273

OLSON, IVAN MASSIE
1916 BRO N  S          5   .250
1920 BRO N  S          7   .520
                      12   .293

O*MARA, OLIVER EDWARD
1916 BRO N  H          1   .000

O*NEILL, STEPHEN FRANCIS
1920 CLE A  C          7   .333

O*NEILL, WILLIAM JOHN
1906 CHI A  O          1   .000

ORSATTI, ERNEST RALPH
1928 STL N  O          4   .286
1930 STL N  H          1   .000
1931 STL N  O          1   .000
1934 STL N  O          7   .318
                      13   .273

ORSINO, JOHN JOSEPH
1962 SF  N  C          1   .000

OSINSKI, DANIEL
1967 BOS A  P          2   0- 0

OSTEEN, CLAUDE WILSON
1965 LA  N  P          2   1- 1
1966 LA  N  P          1   0- 1
                       3   1- 2

OSTROWSKI, JOSEPH PAUL
1951 NY  A  P          1   0- 0

O*TOOLE, JAMES JEROME
1961 CIN N  P          2   0- 2

OTT, MELVIN THOMAS
1933 NY  N  O          5   .389
1936 NY  N  O          6   .304
1937 NY  N  3          5   .200
                      16   .295

OUTLAW, JAMES PAULUS
1945 DET A  3          7   .179

OVERALL, ORVAL
1906 CHI N  P          2   0- 0
1907 CHI N  P          2   1- 0
1908 CHI N  P          3   2- 0
1910 CHI N  P          1   0- 1
                       8   3- 1

OVERMIRE, FRANK
1945 DET A  P          1   0- 1

OWEN, ARNOLD MALCOLM
1941 BRO N  C          5   .167

OWEN, FRANK MALCOLM
1906 CHI A  P          1   0- 0

OWEN, MARVIN JAMES
1934 DET A  3          7   .069
1935 DET A  1-3        6   .050
                      13   .061

OYLER, RAYMOND FRANCIS
1968 DET A  S          4   .000

PACIOREK, THOMAS MARIAN
1974 LA  N  H          3   .500

PAFKO, ANDREW
1945 CHI N  O          7   .214
1952 BRO N  O          7   .190
1957 MIL N  O          6   .214
1958 MIL N  O          4   .333
                      24   .222

PAGAN, JOSE ANTONIO
1962 SF  N  S          7   .368
1971 PIT N  3          4   .267
                      11   .324


PAGE, JOSEPH FRANCIS
1947 NY  A  P          4   1- 1
1949 NY  A  P          3   1- 0
                       7   2- 1

PAGE, VANCE LINWOOD
1938 CHI N  P          1   0- 0

PAIGE, LEROY ROBERT
1948 CLE A  P          1   0- 0

PALICA, ERWIN MARTIN
1949 BRO N  P          1   0- 0

PALMER, JAMES ALVIN
1966 BAL A  P          1   1- 0
1969 BAL A  P          1   0- 1
1970 BAL A  P          2   1- 0
1971 BAL A  P          2   1- 0
                       6   3- 1

PARENT, FREDERICK ALFRED
1903 BOS A  S          8   .281

PARKER, HARRY WILLIAM
1973 NY  N  P          3   0- 1

PARKER, MAURICE WESLEY
1965 LA  N  1          7   .304
1966 LA  N  1          4   .231
                      11   .278

PARTEE, ROY ROBERT
1946 BOS A  C          5   .100

PASCHAL, BENJAMIN EDWIN
1926 NY  A  H          5   .250
1928 NY  A  O          3   .200
                       8   .214

PASCUAL, CAMILO ALBERTO
1965 MIN A  P          1   0- 1

PASKERT, GEORGE HENRY
1915 PHI N  O          5   .158
1918 CHI N  O          6   .190
                      11   .175

PASSEAU, CLAUDE WILLIAM
1945 CHI N  P          3   1- 0

PATTERSON, DARYL ALAN
1968 DET A  P          2   0- 0

PAYNE, FREDERICK THOMAS
1907 DET A  C          2   .250

PEARSON, MONTGOMERY MARCELLUS
1936 NY  A  P          1   1- 0
1937 NY  A  P          1   1- 0
1938 NY  A  P          1   1- 0
1939 NY  A  P          1   1- 0
                       4   4- 0

PECK, HAROLD ARTHUR
1944 CLE A  O          1   .000

PECKINPAUGH, ROGER THORPE
1921 NY  A  S          8   .179
1924 WAS A  S          4   .417
1925 WAS A  S          7   .250
                      19   .250

PEEL, HOMER HEFNER
1933 NY  N  O          2   .500

PENNOCK, HERBERT JEFFERIS
1914 PHI A  P          1   0- 0
1923 NY  A  P          3   2- 0
1926 NY  A  P          3   2- 0
1927 NY  A  P          1   1- 0
1932 NY  A  P          2   0- 0
                      10   5- 0

PEPITONE, JOSEPH ANTHONY
1963 NY  A  1          4   .154
1964 NY  A  1          7   .154
                      11   .154

PEREZ, ATANACIO
1970 CIN N  3          5   .056
1972 CIN N  1          7   .435
1975 CIN N  1          7   .179
1976 CIN N  1          4   .313
                      23   .247

PERRANOSKI, RONALD PETER
1963 LA  N  P          1   0- 0
1965 LA  N  P          2   0- 0
1966 LA  N  P          2   0- 0
                       5   0- 0

PERRITT, WILLIAM DAYTON
1917 NY  N  P          3   0- 0

PERRY, JAMES EVAN
1965 MIN A  P          2   0- 0


PESKY, JOHN MICHAEL
1946 BOS A  S          7   .233

PETROCELLI, AMERICO PETER
1967 BOS A  S          7   .200
1975 BOS A  3          7   .308
                      14   .261

PFEFFER, EDWARD JOSEPH
1916 BRO N  P      3   4   0- 1
1920 BRO N  P          1   0- 0
                   4   5   0- 1

PFIESTER, JOHN ALBERT
1906 CHI N  P          2   0- 2
1907 CHI N  P          1   1- 0
1908 CHI N  P          1   0- 1
1910 CHI N  P          1   0- 0
                       5   1- 3

PHELPS, EDWARD JAYKILL
1903 PIT N  C          8   .231

PHILLEY, DAVID EARL
1954 CLE A  O          4   .125

PHILLIPPE, CHARLES LOUIS
1903 PIT N  P          5   3- 2
1909 PIT N  P          2   0- 0
                       7   3- 2

PHILLIPS, JACK DORN
1947 NY  A  1          2   .000

PHILLIPS, JOHN MELVIN
1959 CHI A  3-O        3   .300

PHOEBUS, THOMAS HAROLD
1970 BAL A  P          1   1- 0

PICK, CHARLES THOMAS
1918 CHI N  2          6   .389

PIERCE, WALTER WILLIAM
1959 CHI A  P          3   0- 0
1962 SF  N  P          2   1- 1
                       5   1- 1

PIERCY, WILLIAM BENTON
1921 NY  A  P          1   0- 0

PIGNATANO, JOSEPH BENJAMIN
1959 LA  N  C          1   .000

PINA, HORACIO
1973 OAK A  P          2   0- 0

PINIELLA, LOUIS VICTOR
1976 NY  A  O-D        4   .333
1977 NY  A  O          6   .273
1978 NY  A  O          6   .280
                      16   .286

PINSON, VADA EDWARD
1961 CIN N  O          5   .091

PIPGRAS, GEORGE WILLIAM
1927 NY  A  P          1   1- 0
1928 NY  A  P          1   1- 0
1932 NY  A  P          1   1- 0
                       3   3- 0

PIPP, WALTER CLEMENT
1921 NY  A  1          8   .154
1922 NY  A  1          5   .286
1923 NY  A  1          6   .250
                      19   .224

PIZARRO, JUAN RAMON
1957 MIL N  P          1   0- 0
1958 MIL N  P          1   0- 0
                       2   0- 0

PLANK, EDWARD STEWART
1905 PHI A  P          2   0- 2
1911 PHI A  P          2   1- 1
1913 PHI A  P          2   1- 1
1914 PHI A  P          1   0- 1
                       7   2- 5

PLEIS, WILLIAM
1965 MIN A  P          1   0- 0

PODRES, JOHN JOSEPH
1953 BRO N  P          1   0- 1
1955 BRO N  P          2   2- 0
1959 LA  N  P      2   3   1- 0
1963 LA  N  P          1   1- 0
                   6   7   4- 1

POLE, RICHARD HENRY
1975 BOS A  P          1   0- 0

POLLET, HOWARD JOSEPH
1942 STL N  P          1   0- 1
1946 STL N  P          2   0- 1
                       3   0- 1
```

YR	CL	LEA	POS	GP	G	REC

POPE, DAVID
| 1954 | CLE | A | O | | 3 | .000 |

POST, WALTER CHARLES
| 1961 | CIN | N | O | | 5 | .333 |

POTTER, NELSON THOMAS
1944	STL	A	P		2	0- 1
1948	BOS	N	P		2	0- 0
					4	0- 1

POWELL, ALVIN JACOB
1936	NY	A	O		6	.455
1937	NY	A	H		1	.000
1938	NY	A	O		1	.000
					8	.435

POWELL, JOHN WESLEY
1966	BAL	A	1		4	.357
1969	BAL	A	1		5	.263
1970	BAL	A	1		5	.294
1971	BAL	A	1		7	.111
					21	.234

POWERS, MICHAEL RILEY
| 1905 | PHI | A | C | | 3 | .143 |

PRICE, JIMMIE WILLIAM
| 1968 | DET | A | H | | 2 | .000 |

PRIDDY, GERALD EDWARD
| 1942 | NY | A | 1-3 | | 3 | .100 |

PRIM, RAYMOND LEE
| 1945 | CHI | N | P | | 2 | 0- 1 |

PUCCINELLI, GEORGE LAWRENCE
| 1930 | STL | N | H | | 1 | .000 |

PURKEY, ROBERT THOMAS
| 1961 | CIN | N | P | | 2 | 0- 1 |

QUILICI, FRANCIS RALPH
| 1965 | MIN | A | 2 | | 7 | .2CO |

QUINN, JOHN PICUS
1921	NY	A	P		1	0- 1
1929	PHI	A	P		1	0- 0
1930	PHI	A	P		1	0- 0
					3	0- 1

RACKLEY, MARVIN EUGENE
| 1949 | BRO | N | O | | 2 | .000 |

RANDOLPH, WILLIAM LARRY
1976	NY	A	2		4	.071
1977	NY	A	2		6	.160
					10	.128

RARIDEN, WILLIAM ANGEL
1917	NY	N	C		5	.385
1919	CIN	N	C		5	.211
					10	.281

RASCHI, VICTOR JOHN ANGELO
1947	NY	A	P		2	0- 0
1949	NY	A	P		2	1- 1
1950	NY	A	P		1	1- 0
1951	NY	A	P		2	1- 1
1952	NY	A	P		3	2- 0
1953	NY	A	P		1	0- 1
					11	5- 3

RATH, MORRIS CHARLES
| 1919 | CIN | N | 2 | | 8 | .226 |

RAU, DOUGLAS JAMES
1977	LA	N	P		2	0- 1
1978	LA	N	P		1	0- 0
					3	0- 1

RAUTZHAN, CLARENCE GEORGE
1977	LA	N	P		1	0- 0
1978	LA	N	P		2	0- 0
					3	0- 0

RAWLINGS, JOHN WILLIAM
| 1921 | NY | N | 2 | | 8 | .333 |

REED, HOWARD DEAN
| 1965 | LA | N | P | | 2 | 0- 0 |

REED, JOHN BURWELL
| 1961 | NY | A | O | | 3 | .000 |

REESE, HAROLD HENRY
1941	BRO	N	S		5	.200
1947	BRO	N	S		7	.304
1949	BRO	N	S		5	.316
1952	BRO	N	S		7	.345
1953	BRO	N	S		6	.208
1955	BRO	N	S		7	.296
1956	BRO	N	S		7	.222
					44	.272

REGALADO, RUDOLPH VALENTINO
| 1954 | CLE | A | H | | 4 | .333 |

REGAN, PHILIP RAYMOND
| 1966 | LA | N | P | | 2 | 0- 0 |

REINHART, ARTHUR CONRAD
| 1926 | STL | N | P | | 1 | 0- 1 |

REISER, HAROLD PATRICK
1941	BRO	N	O		5	.200
1947	BRO	N	O		5	.250
					10	.214

RENIFF, HAROLD EUGENE
1963	NY	A	P		3	0- 0
1964	NY	A	P		1	0- 0
					4	0- 0

REPULSKI, ELDON JOHN
| 1959 | LA | N | O | | 1 | .000 |

RETTENMUND, MERVIN WELDON
1969	BAL	A	R		1	.000
1970	BAL	A	O		2	.400
1971	BAL	A	O		7	.185
1975	CIN	N	H		3	.000
					13	.200

REULBACH, EDWARD MARVIN
1906	CHI	N	P		2	1- 0
1907	CHI	N	P		2	1- 0
1908	CHI	N	P		2	0- 0
1910	CHI	N	P		1	0- 0
					7	2- 0

REYNOLDS, ALLIE PIERCE
1947	NY	A	P		2	1- 0
1949	NY	A	P		2	1- 0
1950	NY	A	P		2	1- 0
1951	NY	A	P		2	1- 1
1952	NY	A	P		4	2- 1
1953	NY	A	P		3	1- 0
					15	7- 2

REYNOLDS, CARL NETTLES
| 1938 | CHI | N | O | | 4 | .000 |

RHEM, CHARLES FLINT
1926	STL	N	P		1	0- 0
1928	STL	N	P		1	0- 0
1930	STL	N	P		1	0- 1
1931	STL	N	P		1	0- 0
					4	0- 1

RHODEN, RICHARD ALAN
| 1977 | LA | N | P | | 2 | 0- 1 |

RHODES, JAMES LAMAR
| 1954 | NY | N | O | | 3 | .667 |

RHYNE, HAROLD J.
| 1927 | PIT | N | 2 | | 1 | .000 |

RICE, DELBERT W
1946	STL	N	P		3	.500
1957	MIL	N	C		2	.167
					5	.333

RICE, EDGAR CHARLES
1924	WAS	A	O		7	.207
1925	WAS	A	O		7	.364
1933	WAS	A	H		1	1.000
					15	.302

RICHARDS, PAUL RAPIER
| 1945 | DET | A | C | | 7 | .211 |

RICHARDSON, GORDON CLARK
| 1964 | STL | N | P | | 2 | 0- 0 |

RICHARDSON, ROBERT CLINTON
1957	NY	A	2		2	.000
1958	NY	A	3		4	.000
1960	NY	A	2		7	.367
1961	NY	A	2		5	.391
1962	NY	A	2		7	.148
1963	NY	A	2		4	.214
1964	NY	A	2		7	.406
					36	.305

RICHERT, PETER GERARD
1969	BAL	A	P		1	0- 0
1970	BAL	A	P		1	0- 0
1971	BAL	A	P		1	0- 0
					3	0- 0

RICHIE, LEWIS A.
| 1910 | CHI | N | P | | 1 | 0- 0 |

RICKERT, MARVIN AUGUST
| 1948 | BOS | N | O | | 5 | .211 |

RICKETTS, DAVID WILLIAM
1967	STL	N	H		3	.000
1968	STL	N	H		1	1.000
					4	.250

RIDDLE, ELMER RAY
| 1940 | CIN | N | P | | 1 | 0- 0 |

RIGGS, LEWIS SIDNEY
1940	CIN	N	H		3	.000
1941	BRO	N	3		3	.250
					6	.182

RIGNEY, WILLIAM JOSEPH
| 1951 | NY | N | H | | 4 | .250 |

RING, JAMES JOSEPH
| 1919 | CIN | N | P | | 2 | 1- 1 |

RIPPLE, JAMES ALBERT
1936	NY	N	O		5	.333
1937	NY	N	O		5	.294
1940	CIN	N	O		7	.333
					17	.320

RISBERG, CHARLES AUGUST
1917	CHI	A	H		2	.500
1919	CHI	A	S		8	.080
					10	.111

RITCHEY, CLAUDE CASSIUS
| 1903 | PIT | N | 2 | | 8 | .111 |

RIVERA, MANUEL JOSEPH
| 1959 | CHI | A | O | | 5 | .000 |

RIVERS, JOHN MILTON
1976	NY	A	O		4	.167
1977	NY	A	O		6	.222
1978	NY	A	O		5	.333
					15	.238

RIXEY, EPPA
| 1915 | PHI | N | P | | 1 | 0- 1 |

RIZZUTO, PHILIP FRANCIS
1941	NY	A	S		5	.111
1942	NY	A	S		5	.381
1947	NY	A	S		7	.308
1949	NY	A	S		4	.167
1950	NY	A	S		4	.143
1951	NY	A	S		6	.320
1952	NY	A	S		7	.148
1953	NY	A	S		6	.316
1955	NY	A	S		7	.267
					52	.246

ROBERTS, ROBIN EVAN
| 1950 | PHI | N | P | | 2 | 0- 1 |

ROBERTSON, DAVIS AYDELOTTE
| 1917 | NY | N | O | | 6 | .500 |

ROBERTSON, EUGENE EDWARD
| 1928 | NY | A | 3 | | 3 | .125 |

ROBERTSON, ROBERT EUGENE
| 1971 | PIT | N | 1 | | 7 | .240 |

ROBINSON, AARON ANDREW
| 1947 | NY | A | C | | 3 | .200 |

ROBINSON, BROOKS CALBERT
1966	BAL	A	3		4	.214
1969	BAL	A	3		5	.053
1970	BAL	A	3		5	.429
1971	BAL	A	3		7	.318
					21	.263

ROBINSON, FRANK
1961	CIN	N	O		5	.200
1966	BAL	A	O		4	.286
1969	BAL	A	O		5	.188
1970	BAL	A	O		5	.273
1971	BAL	A	O		7	.280
					26	.250

ROBINSON, JACK ROOSEVELT
1947	BRO	N	1		7	.259
1949	BRO	N	2		5	.188
1952	BRO	N	2		7	.174
1953	BRO	N	O		6	.320
1955	BRO	N	3		6	.182
1956	BRO	N	3		7	.250
					38	.234

ROBINSON, WILLIAM EDWARD
1948	CLE	A	1		6	.300
1955	NY	A	1		4	.667
					10	.348

ROE, ELWIN CHARLES
1949	BRO	N	P		1	1- 0
1952	BRO	N	P		3	1- 0
1953	BRO	N	P		1	0- 1
					5	2- 1

ROEBUCK, EDWARD JACK
1955	BRO	N	P		1	0- 0
1956	BRO	N	P		3	0- 0
					4	0- 0

ROETTGER, WALTER HENRY
| 1931 | STL | N | O | | 3 | .286 |

YR	CL	LEA	POS	GP	G	REC

ROGELL, WILLIAM GEORGE

YR	CL	LEA	POS	GP	G	REC
1934	DET	A	S		7	.276
1935	DET	A	S		6	.292
					13	.283

ROGERS, THOMAS ANDREW

1921	NY	A	P		1	0- 0

ROHE, GEORGE ANTHONY

1906	CHI	A	3		6	.333

ROLFE, ROBERT ABAIL

1936	NY	A	3		6	.400
1937	NY	A	3		5	.300
1938	NY	A	3		4	.167
1939	NY	A	3		4	.125
1941	NY	A	3		5	.300
1942	NY	A	3		4	.353
					28	.284

ROLLINS, RICHARD JOHN

1965	MIN	A	H		3	.000

ROMANO, JOHN ANTHONY

1959	CHI	A	H		1	.000

ROMMEL, EDWIN AMERICUS

1929	PHI	A	P		1	1- 0
1931	PHI	A	P		1	0- 0
					2	1- 0

ROOT, CHARLES HENRY

1929	CHI	N	P		2	0- 1
1932	CHI	N	P		1	0- 1
1935	CHI	N	P		2	0- 1
1938	CHI	N	P		1	0- 0
					6	0- 3

ROSAR, WARREN VINCENT

1941	NY	A	H		1	.000
1942	NY	A	H		1	1.000
					2	1.000

ROSE, PETER EDWARD

1970	CIN	N	O		5	.250
1972	CIN	N	O		7	.214
1975	CIN	N	3		7	.370
1976	CIN	N	3		4	.188
					23	.264

ROSEBORO, JOHN

1959	LA	N	C		6	.095
1963	LA	N	C		4	.143
1965	LA	N	C		7	.286
1966	LA	N	C		4	.071
					21	.157

ROSEN, ALBERT LEONARD

1948	CLE	A	H		1	.000
1954	CLE	A	3		3	.250
					4	.231

ROSSMAN, CLAUDE R.

1907	DET	A	1		5	.400
1908	DET	A	1		5	.211
					10	.308

ROTHROCK, JOHN HOUSTON

1934	STL	N	O		7	.233

ROUSH, EDD J

1919	CIN	N	O		8	.214

ROWE, LYNWOOD THOMAS

1934	DET	A	P		3	1- 1
1935	DET	A	P		3	1- 2
1940	DET	A	P		2	0- 2
					8	2- 5

RUCKER, GEORGE NAPOLEON

1916	BRO	N	P		1	0- 0

RUDI, JOSEPH ODEN

1972	OAK	A	O		7	.240
1973	OAK	A	O		7	.333
1974	OAK	A	O		5	.333
					19	.300

RUDOLPH, RICHARD

1914	BOS	N	P		2	2- 0

RUEL, HEROLD DOMINIC

1924	WAS	A	C		7	.095
1925	WAS	A	C		7	.316
					14	.200

RUETHER, WALTER HENRY

1919	CIN	N	P	2	3	1- 0
1925	WAS	A	H		1	.000
1926	NY	A	P	1	3	0- 1
				3	7	1- 1
						.364

RUFFING, CHARLES HERBERT

1932	NY	A	P	1	2	1- 0
1936	NY	A	P	2	3	0- 1
1937	NY	A	P		1	1- 0
1938	NY	A	P		2	2- 0
1939	NY	A	P		1	1- 0
1941	NY	A	P		1	1- 0
1942	NY	A	P	2	4	1- 1
				10	14	7- 2

RUSH, ROBERT RANSOM

1958	MIL	N	P		1	0- 1

RUSSELL, ALLAN E.

1924	WAS	A	P		1	0- 0

RUSSELL, EWELL ALBERT

1917	CHI	A	P		1	0- 0

RUSSELL, GLEN DAVID

1946	BOS	A	3		2	1.000

RUSSELL, JACK ERWIN

1933	WAS	A	P		3	0- 1
1938	CHI	N	P		2	0- 0
					5	0- 1

RUSSELL, WILLIAM ELLIS

1974	LA	N	S		5	.222
1977	LA	N	S		6	.154
1978	LA	N	S		6	.423
					17	.271

RUSSO, MARIUS UGO

1941	NY	A	P		1	1- 0
1943	NY	A	P		1	1- 0
					2	2- 0

RUTH, GEORGE HERMAN

1915	BOS	A	H		1	.000
1916	BOS	A	P		1	1- 0
1918	BOS	A	P-O	2	3	2- 0
						.200
1921	NY	A	O		6	.313
1922	NY	A	O		5	.118
1923	NY	A	1-O		6	.368
1926	NY	A	O		7	.300
1927	NY	A	O		4	.400
1928	NY	A	O		4	.625
1932	NY	A	O		4	.333
				3	41	3- 0
						.326

RUTHERFORD, JOHN WILLIAM

1952	BRO	N	P		1	0- 0

RYAN, CORNELIUS JOSEPH

1948	BOS	N	H		2	.000

RYAN, JOHN COLLINS

1933	NY	N	H		5	.278
1937	NY	N	H		1	.000
					6	.263

RYAN, LYNN NOLAN

1969	NY	N	P		1	0- 0

RYAN, MICHAEL JAMES

1967	BOS	A	C		1	.000

RYAN, WILFRED PATRICK DOLAN

1922	NY	N	P		1	1- 0
1923	NY	N	P		3	1- 0
1924	NY	N	P		2	1- 0
					6	3- 0

RYBA, DOMINIC JOSEPH

1946	BOS	A	P		1	0- 0

SADECKI, RAYMOND MICHAEL

1964	STL	N	P		2	1- 0
1973	NY	N	P		4	0- 0
					6	1- 0

SAIN, JOHN FRANKLIN

1948	BOS	N	P		2	1- 1
1951	NY	A	P		1	0- 0
1952	NY	A	P	1	2	0- 1
1953	NY	A	P		2	1- 0
				6	7	2- 2

SALKELD, WILLIAM FRANKLIN

1948	BOS	N	C		5	.222

SALLEE, HARRY FRANKLIN

1917	NY	N	P		2	0- 2
1919	CIN	N	P		2	1- 1
					4	1- 3

SALMON, RUTHFORD EDUARDO

1969	BAL	A	R		2	.000
1970	BAL	A	H		1	1.000
					3	1.000

SANDERS, RAYMOND FLOYD

1942	STL	N	H		2	.000
1943	STL	N	1		5	.294
1944	STL	N	1		6	.286
1948	BOS	N	H		1	.000
					14	.275

SANDS, CHARLES DUANE

1971	PIT	N	H		1	.000

SANFORD, JOHN STANLEY

1962	SF	N	P		3	1- 2

SANGUILLEN, MANUEL DE JESUS

1971	PIT	N	C		7	.379

SANTIAGO, JOSE RAFAEL

1967	BOS	A	P		3	0- 2

SAUER, EDWARD

1945	CHI	N	H		2	.000

SAWATSKI, CARL ERNEST

1957	MIL	N	H		2	.000

SCARBOROUGH, RAY WILSON

1952	NY	A	P		1	0- 0

SCHAEFER, HERMAN A.

1907	DET	A	2		5	.143
1908	DET	A	2-3		5	.125
					10	.135

SCHALK, RAYMOND WILLIAM

1917	CHI	A	C		6	.263
1919	CHI	A	C		8	.304
					14	.286

SCHALLOCK, ARTHUR LAWRENCE

1953	NY	A	P		1	0- 0

SCHANG, WALTER HENRY

1913	PHI	A	C		4	.357
1914	PHI	A	C		4	.167
1918	BOS	A	C		5	.444
1921	NY	A	C		8	.286
1922	NY	A	C		5	.188
1923	NY	A	C		6	.318
					32	.287

SCHENZ, HENRY LEONARD

1951	NY	N	R		1	.000

SCHMANDT, RAYMOND HENRY

1920	BRO	N	P		1	.000

SCHMIDT, CHARLES

1907	DET	A	C		4	.167
1908	DET	A	C		4	.071
1909	DET	A	C		6	.222
					14	.159

SCHMIDT, CHARLES JOHN

1914	BOS	N	1		4	.294

SCHMIDT, FREDERICK ALBERT

1944	STL	N	P		1	0- 0

SCHOENDIENST, ALBERT FRED

1946	STL	N	2		7	.233
1957	MIL	N	2		5	.278
1958	MIL	N	2		7	.300
					19	.269

SCHOFIELD, JOHN RICHARD

1960	PIT	N	S		3	.333
1968	STL	N	S		2	.000
					5	.333

SCHRECKENGOST, OSSEE FREEMAN

1905	PHI	A	C		3	.222

SCHULTE, FRANK M.

1906	CHI	N	O		6	.269
1907	CHI	N	O		5	.250
1908	CHI	N	O		5	.389
1910	CHI	N	O		5	.353
					21	.309

SCHULTE, FRED WILLIAM

1933	WAS	A	O		5	.333

SCHULTZ, GEORGE WARREN

1964	STL	N	P		4	0- 1

SCHUMACHER, HAROLD HENRY

1933	NY	N	P		2	1- 0
1936	NY	N	P		2	1- 1
1937	NY	N	P		1	0- 1
					5	2- 2

SCHUPP, FERDINAND MAURICE

1917	NY	N	P		2	1- 0

SCHUSTER, WILLIAM CHARLES

1945	CHI	N	S		2	.000

YR	CL	LEA	POS	GP	G	REC
SCOTT, GEORGE CHARLES						
1967	BOS	A	1		7	.231
SCOTT, JOHN WILLIAM						
1922	NY	N	P		1	1- 0
1923	NY	N	P		2	0- 1
					3	1- 1
SCOTT, LEWIS EVERETT						
1915	BOS	A	S		5	.056
1916	BOS	A	S		5	.125
1918	BOS	A	S		6	.095
1922	NY	A	S		5	.143
1923	NY	A	S		6	.318
					27	.156
SEAVER, GEORGE THOMAS						
1969	NY	N	P		2	1- 1
1973	NY	N	P		2	0- 1
					4	1- 2
SEBRING, JAMES DENNISON						
1903	PIT	N	O		8	.367
SECORY, FRANK EDWARD						
1945	CHI	N	H		5	.400
SEEDS, ROBERT IRA						
1936	NY	A	R		1	.000
SEGUI, DIEGO PABLO						
1975	BOS	A	P		1	0- 0
SELKIRK, GEORGE ALEXANDER						
1936	NY	A	O		6	.333
1937	NY	A	O		5	.263
1938	NY	A	O		3	.200
1939	NY	A	O		4	.167
1941	NY	A	H		2	.500
1942	NY	A	H		1	.000
					21	.265
SEMINICK, ANDREW WASIL						
1950	PHI	N	C		4	.182
SEVEREID, HENRY LEVAI						
1925	WAS	A	C		1	.333
1926	NY	A	C		7	.273
					8	.280
SEWELL, JAMES LUTHER						
1933	WAS	A	C		5	.176
SEWELL, JOSEPH WHEELER						
1920	CLE	A	S		7	.174
1932	NY	A	3		4	.333
					11	.237
SEYBOLD, RALPH ORLANDO						
1905	PHI	A	O		5	.125
SHAFER, ARTHUR JOSEPH						
1912	NY	N	S		3	.000
1913	NY	N	3-O		5	.158
					8	.158
SHAMSKY, ARTHUR LOUIS						
1969	NY	N	O		3	.000
SHANNON, THOMAS MICHAEL						
1964	STL	N	O		7	.214
1967	STL	N	3		7	.208
1968	STL	N	3		7	.276
					21	.235
SHANTZ, ROBERT CLAYTON						
1957	NY	A	P		3	0- 1
1960	NY	A	P		3	0- 0
					6	0- 1
SHAW, ROBERT JOHN						
1959	CHI	A	P		2	1- 1
SHAWKEY, JAMES ROBERT						
1914	PHI	A	P		1	0- 1
1921	NY	A	P		2	0- 1
1922	NY	A	P		1	0- 0
1923	NY	A	P		1	1- 0
1926	NY	A	P		3	0- 1
					8	1- 3
SHEA, FRANCIS JOSEPH						
1947	NY	A	P		3	2- 0
SHEAN, DAVID WILLIAM						
1918	BOS	A	2		6	.211
SHECKARD, SAMUEL JAMES TILDEN						
1906	CHI	N	O		6	.000
1907	CHI	N	O		5	.238
1908	CHI	N	O		5	.238
1910	CHI	N	O		5	.286
					21	.182
SHEEHAN, JOHN THOMAS						
1920	BRO	N	3		3	.182

YR	CL	LEA	POS	GP	G	REC
SHELDON, ROLAND FRANK						
1964	NY	A	P		2	0- 0
SHERDEL, WILLIAM HENRY						
1926	STL	N	P		2	0- 2
1928	STL	N	P		2	0- 2
					4	0- 4
SHERRY, LAWRENCE						
1959	LA	N	P	4	5	2- 0
SHIRLEY, ALVIS NEWMAN						
1944	STL	A	P		2	0- 0
SHIRLEY, ERNEST RAEFORD						
1924	WAS	A	H		3	.500
SHOCKER, URBAN JAMES						
1926	NY	A	P		2	0- 1
SHOPAY, THOMAS MICHAEL						
1971	BAL	A	H		5	.000
SHORE, ERNEST GRADY						
1915	BOS	A	P		2	1- 1
1916	BOS	A	P		2	2- 0
					4	3- 1
SHORES, WILLIAM DAVID						
1930	PHI	A	P		1	0- 0
SHORTEN, CHARLES HENRY						
1916	BOS	A	O		2	.571
SHUBA, GEORGE THOMAS						
1952	BRO	N	O		4	.300
1953	BRO	N	H		2	1.000
1955	BRO	N	H		1	.000
					7	.333
SIEBERN, NORMAN LEROY						
1956	NY	A	H		1	.000
1958	NY	A	O		3	.125
1967	BOS	A	O		3	.333
					7	.167
SIEVER, EDWARD T.						
1907	DET	A	P		1	0- 1
SILVERA, CHARLES ANTHONY RYAN						
1949	NY	A	C		1	.000
SILVESTRI, KENNETH JOSEPH						
1950	PHI	N	C		1	.000
SIMMONS, ALOYSIUS HARRY						
1929	PHI	A	O		5	.300
1930	PHI	A	O		6	.364
1931	PHI	A	O		7	.333
1939	CIN	N	O		1	.250
					19	.329
SIMMONS, CURTIS THOMAS						
1964	STL	N	P		2	0- 1
SIMPSON, HARRY LEON						
1957	NY	A	1		5	.083
SISLER, RICHARD ALLAN						
1946	STL	N	H		2	.000
1950	PHI	N	O		4	.059
					6	.053
SISTI, SEBASTIAN DANIEL						
1948	BOS	N	2		2	.000
SKINNER, ROBERT RALPH						
1960	PIT	N	O		2	.200
1964	STL	N	H		4	.667
					6	.375
SKOWRON, WILLIAM JOSEPH						
1955	NY	A	1		5	.333
1956	NY	A	1		3	.100
1957	NY	A	1		2	.000
1958	NY	A	1		7	.259
1960	NY	A	1		7	.375
1961	NY	A	1		5	.353
1962	NY	A	1		6	.222
1963	LA	N	1		4	.385
					39	.293
SLAGLE, JAMES FRANKLIN						
1907	CHI	N	O		5	.273
SLAUGHTER, ENOS BRADSHEAR						
1942	STL	N	O		5	.263
1946	STL	N	O		7	.320
1956	NY	A	O		6	.350
1957	NY	A	O		5	.250
1958	NY	A	H		4	.000
					27	.291
SMITH, ALFRED JOHN						
1936	NY	N	P		1	0- 0
1937	NY	N	P		2	0- 0
					3	0- 0

YR	CL	LEA	POS	GP	G	REC
SMITH, ALPHONSE EUGENE						
1954	CLE	A	O		4	.214
1959	CHI	A	O		6	.250
					10	.235
SMITH, CARL REGINALD						
1967	BOS	A	O		7	.250
1977	LA	N	O		6	.273
1978	LA	N	O		6	.200
					19	.239
SMITH, CLAY JAMIESON						
1940	DET	A	P		1	0- 0
SMITH, EARL SUTTON						
1921	NY	N	C		3	.000
1922	NY	N	C		4	.143
1925	PIT	N	C		6	.350
1927	PIT	N	C		3	.000
1928	STL	N	C		1	.750
					17	.239
SMITH, ELMER JOHN						
1920	CLE	A	O		5	308
1922	NY	A	H		2	.000
					7	.267
SMITH, HAROLD WAYNE						
1960	PIT	N	C		3	.375
SMITH, HARRY THOMAS						
1903	PIT	N	C		1	.000
SMITH, JAMES LAWRENCE						
1919	CIN	N	R		1	.000
SMITH, ROBERT ELDRIDGE						
1932	CHI	N	P		1	0- 0
SMITH, SHERROD MALONE						
1916	BRO	N	P		1	0- 1
1920	BRO	N	P		2	1- 1
					3	1- 2
SNIDER, EDWIN DONALD						
1949	BRO	N	O		5	.143
1952	BRO	N	O		7	.345
1953	BRO	N	O		6	.320
1955	BRO	N	O		7	.320
1956	BRO	N	O		7	.304
1959	LA	N	O		4	.200
					36	.286
SNODGRASS, FREDERICK CARLISLE						
1911	NY	N	O		6	.105
1912	NY	N	O		8	.212
1913	NY	N	1-O		2	.333
					16	.182
SNYDER, FRANK ELTON						
1921	NY	N	C		7	.364
1922	NY	N	C		4	.333
1923	NY	N	C		5	.118
1924	NY	N	H		1	.000
					17	.273
SNYDER, RUSSELL HENRY						
1966	BAL	A	O		3	.167
SOSA, ELIAS						
1977	LA	N	P		2	0- 0
SOUTHWORTH, WILLIAM HARRISON						
1924	NY	N	O		5	.000
1926	STL	N	O		7	.345
					12	.333
SPAHN, WARREN EDWARD						
1948	BOS	N	P		3	1- 1
1957	MIL	N	P		2	1- 1
1958	MIL	N	P		3	2- 1
					8	4- 3
SPARMA, JOSEPH BLASE						
1968	DET	A	P		1	0- 0
SPEAKER, TRISTRAM E						
1912	BOS	A	O		8	.300
1915	BOS	A	O		5	.294
1920	CLE	A	O		7	.320
					20	.306
SPEECE, BYRON FRANKLIN						
1924	WAS	A	P		1	0- 0
SPENCER, GEORGE ELWELL						
1951	NY	N	P		2	0- 0
SPENCER, JAMES LLOYD						
1978	NY	A	1		4	.167
SPENCER, ROY HAMPTON						
1927	PIT	N	C		1	.000
SPIEZIO, EDWARD WAYNE						
1967	STL	N	H		1	.000
1968	STL	N	H		1	1.000
					2	.500

YR	CL	LEA	POS	GP	G	REC

SPOONER, KARL BENJAMIN
| 1955 | BRO | N | P | | 2 | 0- 1 |

STAFFORD, WILLIAM CHARLES
1960	NY	A	P		2	0- 0
1961	NY	A	P		1	0- 0
1962	NY	A	P		1	1- 0
					4	1- 0

STAHL, CHARLES SYLVESTER
| 1903 | BOS | A | O | | 8 | .303 |

STAHL, GARLAND
| 1912 | BOS | A | 1 | | 8 | .281 |

STAINBACK, GEORGE TUCKER
1942	NY	A	H		2	.000
1943	NY	A	O		5	.176
					7	.176

STALEY, GERALD LEE
| 1959 | CHI | A | P | | 4 | 0- 1 |

STANAGE, OSCAR HARLAND
| 1909 | DET | A | C | | 2 | .200 |

STANGE, ALBERT LEE
| 1967 | BOS | A | P | | 1 | 0- 0 |

STANKY, EDWARD RAYMOND
1947	BRO	N	2		7	.240
1948	BOS	N	2		6	.286
1951	NY	N	2		6	.136
					19	.213

STANLEY, FREDERICK BLAIR
1976	NY	A	S		4	.167
1977	NY	A	S		1	.000
1978	NY	A	2		3	.240
					8	.182

STANLEY, MITCHELL JACK
| 1968 | DET | A | S-O | | 7 | .214 |

STARGELL, WILVER DORNEL
| 1971 | PIT | N | O | | 7 | .208 |

STAUB, DANIEL JOSEPH
| 1973 | NY | N | O | | 7 | .423 |

STEINFELDT, HARRY M.
1906	CHI	N	3		6	.250
1907	CHI	N	3		5	.471
1908	CHI	N	3		5	.250
1910	CHI	N	3		5	.100
					21	.260

STENGEL, CHARLES DILLON
1916	BRO	N	O		4	.364
1922	NY	N	O		2	.400
1923	NY	N	O		6	.417
					12	.393

STEPHENS, VERNON DECATUR
| 1944 | STL | A | S | | 6 | .227 |

STEPHENSON, JACKSON RIGGS
1929	CHI	N	O		5	.316
1932	CHI	N	O		4	.444
					9	.378

STEPHENSON, JERRY JOSEPH
| 1967 | BOS | A | P | | 1 | 0- 0 |

STEPHENSON, WALTER MC QUEEN
| 1935 | CHI | N | H | | 1 | .000 |

STEWART, JAMES FRANKLIN
| 1970 | CIN | N | H | | 2 | .000 |

STEWART, WALTER CLEVELAND
| 1933 | WAS | A | P | | 1 | 0- 1 |

STIRNWEISS, GEORGE HENRY
1943	NY	A	H		1	.000
1947	NY	A	2		7	.259
1949	NY	A	H		1	.000
					9	.250

STOCK, MILTON JOSEPH
| 1915 | PHI | N | 3 | | 5 | .118 |

STONE, GEORGE HEARD
| 1973 | NY | N | P | | 2 | 0- 0 |

STOTTLEMYRE, MELVIN LEON
| 1964 | NY | A | P | | 3 | 1- 1 |

STRANG, SAMUEL NICKLIN
| 1905 | NY | N | H | | 1 | .000 |

STRICKLAND, GEORGE BEVAN
| 1954 | CLE | A | S | | 3 | .000 |

STRUNK, AMOS AARON
1910	PHI	A	O		4	.278
1911	PHI	A	H		1	.000
1913	PHI	A	O		5	.118
1914	PHI	A	O		2	.286
1918	BOS	A	O		6	.174
					18	.200

STUART, RICHARD LEE
1960	PIT	N	1		5	.150
1966	LA	N	H		2	.000
					7	.136

STURDIVANT, THOMAS VIRGIL
1955	NY	A	P		2	0- 0
1956	NY	A	P		2	1- 0
1957	NY	A	P		2	0- 0
					6	1- 0

STURM, JOHN PETER JOSEPH
| 1941 | NY | A | 1 | | 5 | .286 |

SULLIVAN, WILLIAM JOSEPH JR.
| 1940 | DET | A | C | | 5 | .154 |

SULLIVAN, WILLIAM JOSEPH SR.
| 1906 | CHI | A | C | | 6 | .000 |

SUMMA, HOMER WAYNE
| 1929 | PHI | A | H | | 1 | .000 |

SUMMERS, ORON EDGAR
1908	DET	A	P		2	0- 2
1909	DET	A	P		2	0- 2
					4	0- 4

SUNDRA, STEPHEN RICHARD
| 1939 | NY | A | P | | 1 | 0- 0 |

SUTTON, DONALD HOWARD
1974	LA	N	P		2	1- 0
1977	LA	N	P		2	1- 0
1978	LA	N	P		2	0- 2
					6	2- 2

SWIFT, ROBERT VIRGIL
| 1945 | DET | A | C | | 3 | .250 |

SWOBODA, RONALD ALAN
| 1969 | NY | N | O | | 4 | .400 |

TANNEHILL, LEE FORD
| 1906 | CHI | A | S | | 3 | .111 |

TARTABULL, JOSE MILAGES
| 1967 | BOS | A | O | | 7 | .154 |

TATE, HENRY BENNETT
| 1924 | WAS | A | H | | 3 | .000 |

TAYLOR, JAMES HARRY
| 1947 | BRO | N | P | | 1 | 0- 0 |

TAYLOR, JAMES WREN
| 1929 | CHI | N | C | | 5 | .176 |

TAYLOR, RONALD WESLEY
1964	STL	N	P		2	0- 0
1969	NY	N	P		2	0- 0
					4	0- 0

TAYLOR, THOMAS LIVINGSTONE CARLTON
| 1924 | WAS | A | 3 | | 3 | .000 |

TEBBETTS, GEORGE ROBERT
| 1940 | DET | A | C | | 4 | .000 |

TENACE, FURY GENE
1972	OAK	A	C-1		7	.348
1973	OAK	A	C-1		7	.158
1974	OAK	A	1		5	.222
					19	.255

TERRY, RALPH WILLARD
1960	NY	A	P		2	0- 2
1961	NY	A	P		2	0- 1
1962	NY	A	P		3	2- 1
1963	NY	A	P		1	0- 0
1964	NY	A	P		1	0- 0
					9	2- 4

TERRY, WILLIAM HAROLD
1924	NY	N	1		5	.429
1933	NY	N	1		5	.273
1936	NY	N	1		6	.240
					16	.295

TESREAU, CHARLES MONROE
1912	NY	N	P		3	1- 2
1913	NY	N	P		2	0- 1
1917	NY	N	P		1	0- 0
					6	1- 3

THEODORE, GEORGE BASIL
| 1973 | NY | N | O | | 2 | .000 |

THEVENOW, THOMAS JOSEPH
1926	STL	N	S		7	.417
1928	STL	N	S		1	.000
					8	.417

THOMAS, ALPHONSE
| 1933 | WAS | A | P | | 2 | 0- 0 |

THOMAS, CHESTER DAVID
1915	BOS	A	C		2	.200
1916	BOS	A	C		3	.143
1920	CLE	A	C		1	.000
					6	.167

THOMAS, FREDERICK HARVEY
| 1918 | BOS | A | 3 | | 6 | .125 |

THOMAS, GEORGE EDWARD
| 1967 | BOS | A | O | | 2 | .000 |

THOMAS, IRA FELIX
1908	DET	A	C		2	.500
1910	PHI	A	C		4	.250
1911	PHI	A	C		4	.083
					10	.214

THOMAS, MYLES LEWIS
| 1926 | NY | A | P | | 2 | 0- 0 |

THOMASSON, GARY LEAH
| 1978 | NY | A | O | | 3 | .250 |

THOMPSON, DONALD NEWLIN
| 1953 | BRO | N | O | | 2 | .000 |

THOMPSON, EUGENE EARL
1939	CIN	N	P		1	0- 1
1940	CIN	N	P		1	0- 1
					2	0- 2

THOMPSON, HENRY CURTIS
1951	NY	N	O		5	.143
1954	NY	N	3		4	.364
					9	.240

THOMPSON, JOHN GUSTAV
| 1903 | PIT | N | P | | 1 | 0- 0 |

THOMSON, ROBERT BROWN
| 1951 | NY | N | 3 | | 6 | .237 |

THORPE, JAMES FRANCIS
| 1917 | NY | N | O | | 1 | .000 |

THRONEBERRY, MARVIN EUGENE
| 1958 | NY | A | H | | 1 | .000 |

TIANT, LUIS CLEMENTE
| 1975 | BOS | A | P | | 3 | 2- 0 |

TIDROW, RICHARD WILLIAM
1976	NY	A	P		2	0- 0
1977	NY	A	P		2	0- 0
1978	NY	A	P		2	0- 0
					6	0- 0

TINKER, JOSEPH BERT
1906	CHI	N	S		6	.167
1907	CHI	N	S		5	.154
1908	CHI	N	S		5	.263
1910	CHI	N	S		5	.333
					21	.235

TINNING, LYLE FORREST
| 1932 | CHI | N | P | | 2 | 0- 0 |

TIPTON, JOE HICKS
| 1948 | CLE | A | H | | 1 | .000 |

TOBIN, JAMES ANTHONY
| 1945 | DET | A | P | | 1 | 0- 0 |

TODT, PHILIP JULIUS
| 1931 | PHI | A | H | | 1 | .000 |

TOLAN, ROBERT
1967	STL	N	H		3	.000
1968	STL	N	H		1	.000
1970	CIN	N	O		5	.211
1972	CIN	N	O		7	.269
					16	.229

TOLSON, CHARLES JULIUS
| 1929 | CHI | N | H | | 1 | .000 |

TONEY, FREDERICK ARTHUR
| 1921 | NY | N | P | | 2 | 0- 0 |

TORPORCER, GEORGE
| 1926 | STL | N | H | | 1 | .000 |

TORGESON, CLIFFORD EARL
1948	BOS	N	1		5	.389
1959	CHI	A	1		3	.000
					8	.368

YR	CL	LEA	POS	GP	G	REC
TORRE, FRANK JOSEPH						
1957 MIL	N	1			7	.300
1958 MIL	N	1			7	.176
					14	.222
TORREZ, MICHAEL AUGUSTINE						
1977 NY	A	P			2	2-0
TOWNE, JAY KING						
1906 CHI	A	H			1	.000
TRACEWSKI, RICHARD JOSEPH						
1963 LA	N	2			4	.154
1965 LA	N	2			6	.118
1968 DET	A	3			2	.000
					12	.133
TRAYNOR, HAROLD JOSEPH						
1925 PIT	N	3			7	.346
1927 PIT	N	3			4	.200
					11	.293
TRESH, THOMAS MICHAEL						
1962 NY	A	O			7	.321
1963 NY	A	O			4	.200
1964 NY	A	O			7	.273
					18	.277
TROUT, PAUL HOWARD						
1940 DET	A	P			1	0-1
1945 DET	A	P			2	1-1
					3	1-2
TROWBRIDGE, ROBERT						
1957 MIL	N	P			1	0-0
TRUCKS, VIRGIL OLIVER						
1945 DET	A	P			2	1-0
TUCKER, THURMAN LOWELL						
1948 CLE	A	O			1	.333
TURLEY, ROBERT LEE						
1955 NY	A	P			3	0-1
1956 NY	A	P			3	0-1
1957 NY	A	P			3	1-0
1958 NY	A	P			4	2-1
1960 NY	A	P			2	1-0
					15	4-3
TURNER, JAMES RILEY						
1940 CIN	N	P			1	0-1
1942 NY	A	P			1	0-0
					2	0-1
TURNER, THOMAS RICHARD						
1944 STL	A	H			1	.000
TYLER, GEORGE ALBERT						
1914 BOS	N	P			1	0-0
1918 CHI	N	P			3	1-1
					4	1-1
UHLAENDER, THEODORE OTTO						
1972 CIN	N	H			4	.250
UHLE, GEORGE ERNEST						
1920 CLE	A	P			2	0-0
VALDESPINO, HILARIO						
1965 MIN	A	O			5	.273
VANCE, CLARENCE ARTHUR						
1934 STL	N	P			1	0-0
VANDENBERG, HAROLD HARRIS						
1945 CHI	N	P			3	0-0
VANDER MEER, JOHN SAMUEL						
1940 CIN	N	P			1	0-0
VAUGHAN, JOSEPH FLOYD						
1947 BRO	N	H			3	.500
VAUGHN, JAMES LESLIE						
1918 CHI	N	P			3	1-2
VEACH, ROBERT HAYES						
1925 WAS	A	H			2	.000
VEALE, ROBERT ANDREW						
1971 PIT	N	P			1	0-0
VEIL, FREDERICK WILLIAM						
1903 PIT	N	P			1	0-0
VELEZ, OTONIEL						
1976 NY	A	H			3	.000
VERBAN, EMIL MATTHEW						
1944 STL	N	2			6	.412
VERSALLES, ZOILO CASANOVA						
1965 MIN	A	S			7	.286
VIRDON, WILLIAM CHARLES						
1960 PIT	N	O			7	.241
VOISELLE, WILLIAM SYMMES						
1948 BOS	N	P			2	0-1
WADE, BENJAMIN STYRON						
1953 BRO	N	P			2	0-0
WAGNER, CHARLES F.						
1912 BOS	A	S			8	.167
WAGNER, HAROLD EDWARD						
1946 BOS	A	C			5	.000
WAGNER, JOHN PETER						
1903 PIT	N	S			8	.222
1909 PIT	N	S			7	.333
					15	.275
WAITKUS, EDWARD STEPHEN						
1950 PHI	N	1			4	.267
WALBERG, GEORGE ELVIN						
1929 PHI	A	P			2	1-0
1930 PHI	A	P			1	0-1
1931 PHI	A	P			2	0-0
					5	1-1
WALKER, ALFRED BLUFORD						
1956 BRO	N	H			2	.000
WALKER, CLARENCE WILLIAM						
1916 BOS	A	O			3	.273
WALKER, FRED						
1941 BRO	N	O			5	.222
1947 BKO	N	O			7	.222
					12	.222
WALKER, GERALD HOLMES						
1934 DET	A	H			3	.333
1935 DET	A	O			3	.250
					6	.286
WALKER, HARRY WILLIAM						
1942 STL	N	H			1	.000
1943 STL	N	O			5	.167
1946 STL	N	O			7	.412
					13	.278
WALKER, HARVEY WILLOS						
1945 DET	A	H			2	.500
WALKER, JAMES LUKE						
1971 PIT	N	P			1	0-0
WALKER, WILLIAM HENRY						
1934 STL	N	P			2	0-2
WALSH, EDWARD AUGUSTINE						
1906 CHI	A	P			2	2-0
WALSH, JAMES CHARLES						
1914 PHI	A	O			3	.333
1916 BOS	A	O			1	.000
					4	.222
WALTERS, WILLIAM HENRY						
1939 CIN	N	P			2	0-2
1940 CIN	N	P			2	2-0
					4	2-2
WAMBGANSS, WILLIAM ADOLPH						
1920 CLE	A	2			7	.154
WANER, LLOYD JAMES						
1927 PIT	N	O			4	.400
WANER, PAUL GLEE						
1927 PIT	N	O			4	.333
WARD, AARON LEE						
1921 NY	A	2			8	.231
1922 NY	A	2			5	.154
1923 NY	A	2			6	.417
					19	.286
WARNEKE, LONNIE						
1932 CHI	N	P			2	0-1
1935 CHI	N	P			3	2-0
					5	2-1
WARWICK, CARL WAYNE						
1964 STL	N	H			5	.750
WASDELL, JAMES CHARLES						
1941 BRO	N	O			3	.200
WASHBURN, RAY CLARK						
1967 STL	N	P			2	0-0
1968 STL	N	P			2	1-1
1970 CIN	N	P			1	0-0
					5	1-1
WASHINGTON, CLAUDELL						
1974 OAK	A	O			5	.571
WASHINGTON, HERBERT LEE						
1974 OAK	A	R			3	.000
WASLEWSKI, GARY LEE						
1967 BOS	A	P			2	0-0
WATKINS, GEORGE ARCHIBALD						
1930 STL	N	O			4	.167
1931 STL	N	O			5	.266
					9	.231
WATSON, JOHN REEVES						
1923 NY	N	P			1	0-0
1924 NY	N	P			1	0-0
					2	0-0
WATT, EDWARD DEAN						
1969 BAL	A	P			2	0-1
1970 BAL	A	P			1	0-1
1971 BAL	A	P			2	0-1
					5	0-3
WEATHERLY, CYRIL ROY						
1943 NY	A	H			1	.000
WEAVER, GEORGE DAVIS						
1917 CHI	A	S			6	.333
1919 CHI	A	S			8	.324
					14	.327
WEAVER, MONTGOMERY MORTON						
1933 WAS	A	P			1	0-1
WEBB, JAMES LAVERNE						
1945 DET	A	S			7	.185
WEIS, ALBERT JOHN						
1969 NY	N	2			5	.455
WELCH, ROBERT LYNN						
1978 LA	N	P			3	0-1
WENSLOFF, CHARLES WILLIAM						
1947 NY	A	P			1	0-0
WERBER, WILLIAM MURRAY						
1939 CIN	N	3			4	.250
1940 CIN	N	3			7	.370
					11	.326
WERT, DONALD RALPH						
1968 DET	A	3			6	.118
WERTZ, VICTOR WOODROW						
1954 CLE	A	1			4	.500
WESTLAKE, WALDON THOMAS						
1954 CLE	A	O			2	.143
WESTRUM, WESLEY NOREEN						
1951 NY	N	C			6	.235
1954 NY	N	C			4	.273
					10	.250
WHEAT, ZACHARY DAVIS						
1916 BRO	N	O			5	.211
1920 BRO	N	O			7	.333
					12	.283
WHITE, ERNEST DANIEL						
1942 STL	N	P			1	1-0
1943 STL	N	R		1	1	0-0
				1	2	1-0
						.000
WHITE, GUY HARRIS						
1906 CHI	A	P			3	1-1
WHITE, JOYNER CLIFFORD						
1934 DET	A	O			7	.130
1935 DET	A	O			5	.263
					12	.190
WHITE, ROY HILTON						
1976 NY	A	O			4	.133
1977 NY	A	H			2	.000
1978 NY	A	O			6	.333
					12	.244
WHITE, WILLIAM DEKOVA						
1964 STL	N	1			7	.111
WHITEHEAD, BURGESS URQUHART						
1934 STL	N	S			1	.000
1936 NY	N	2			6	.048
1937 NY	N	2			5	.250
					12	.135
WHITEHILL, EARL OLIVER						
1933 WAS	A	P			1	1-0
WHITEMAN, GEORGE						
1918 BOS	A	H			6	.250
WHITMAN, DICK CORWIN						
1949 BRO	N	H			1	.000
1950 PHI	N	H			3	.000
					4	.000

YR	CL	LEA	POS	GP	G	REC
WHITTED, GEORGE BOSTIC						
1914	BOS	N	O		4	.214
1915	PHI	N	1-O		5	.067
					9	.138
WICKER, KEMP CASWELL						
1937	NY	A	P		1	0- 0
WILCOX, MILTON EDWARD						
1970	CIN	N	P		2	0- 1
WILHELM, JAMES HOYT						
1954	NY	N	P		2	G- 0
WILHOIT, JOSEPH WILLIAM						
1917	NY	N	H		2	.000
WILKINSON, ROY HAMILTON						
1919	CHI	A	P		2	0- 0
WILKS, THEODORE						
1944	STL	N	P		2	0- 1
1946	STL	N	P		1	0- 0
					3	0- 1
WILLETT, ROBERT EDGAR						
1909	DET	A	P		2	0- 0
WILLEY, CARLTON FRANCIS						
1958	MIL	N	P		1	0- 0
WILLIAMS, CLAUDE PRESTON						
1917	CHI	A	P		1	0- 0
1919	CHI	A	P		3	0- 3
					4	0- 3
WILLIAMS, DAVID CARLOUS						
1951	NY	N	H		2	.000
1954	NY	N	2		4	.000
					6	.000
WILLIAMS, DEWEY EDGAR						
1945	CHI	N	C		2	.000
WILLIAMS, EDWIN DIBRELL						
1931	PHI	A	S		7	.320
WILLIAMS, RICHARD HIRSCHFELD						
1953	BRO	N	H		3	.500
WILLIAMS, STANLEY WILSON						
1959	LA	N	P		1	0- 0
1963	NY	A	P		1	0- 0
					2	0- 0
WILLIAMS, THEODORE SAMUEL						
1946	BOS	A	O		7	.200
WILLIS, RONALD EARL						
1967	STL	N	P		3	0- 0
1968	STL	N	P		3	0- 0
					6	0- 0
WILLIS, VICTOR GAZAWAY						
1909	PIT	N	P		2	0- 1
WILLOUGHBY, JAMES ARTHUR						
1975	BOS	A	P		3	0- 1
WILLS, MAURICE MORNING						
1959	LA	N	S		6	.250
1963	LA	N	S		4	.133
1965	LA	N	S		7	.367
1966	LA	N	S		4	.077
					21	.244
WILSON, ARTHUR EARL						
1911	NY	N	C		1	.000
1912	NY	N	C		2	1.000
1913	NY	N	C		3	.000
					6	.200
WILSON, GEORGE WASHINGTON						
1956	NY	A	H		1	.000
WILSON, JAMES						
1928	STL	N	C		3	.091
1930	STL	N	C		4	.267
1931	STL	N	C		7	.217
1940	CIN	N	C		6	.353
					20	.242
WILSON, JOHN OWEN						
1909	PIT	N	O		7	.154
WILSON, LEWIS ROBERT						
1924	NY	N	O		7	.233
1929	CHI	N	O		5	.471
					12	.319
WILSON, ROBERT EARL						
1968	DET	A	P		1	0- 1
WILTSE, GEORGE LEROY						
1911	NY	N	P		2	G- 0
1913	NY	N	1		2	.000
				2	4	0- 0
						.000
WINGO, IVEY BROWN						
1919	CIN	N	C		3	.571
WINTER, GEORGE LOVINGTON						
1908	DET	A	P	1	2	0- 0
WISE, KENDALL COLE						
1958	MIL	N	H		2	.000
WISE, RICHARD CHARLES						
1975	BOS	A	P		2	1- 0
WITT, GEORGE ADRIAN						
1960	PIT	N	P		3	0- 0
WITT, LAWTON WALTER						
1922	NY	A	O		5	.222
1923	NY	A	O		6	.240
					11	.233
WOOD, JOSEPH						
1912	BOS	A	P		4	3- 1
1920	CLE	A	O		4	.200
				4	8	3- 1
						.235
WOODESHICK, HAROLD JOSEPH						
1967	STL	N	P		1	0- 0
WOODLING, EUGENE RICHARD						
1949	NY	A	O		3	.400
1950	NY	A	O		4	.429
1951	NY	A	O		6	.167
1952	NY	A	O		7	.348
1953	NY	A	O		6	.300
					26	.318
WOODWARD, WILLIAM FREDERICK						
1970	CIN	N	S		4	.200
WORKS, RALPH TALMADGE						
1909	DET	A	P		1	0- 0
WORTHINGTON, ALLAN FULTON						
1965	MIN	A	P		2	0- 0
WORTMAN, WILLIAM LEWIS						
1918	CHI	N	2		1	.000
WRIGHT, FORREST GLENN						
1925	PIT	N	S		7	.185
1927	PIT	N	S		4	.154
					11	.175
WYATT, JOHN THOMAS						
1967	BOS	A	P		2	1- 0
WYATT, JOHN WHITLOW						
1941	BRO	N	P		2	1- 1
WYCKOFF, JOHN WELDON						
1914	PHI	A	P		1	0- 0
WYNN, EARLY						
1954	CLE	A	P		1	0- 1
1959	CHI	A	P		3	1- 1
					4	1- 2
WYNN, JAMES SHERMAN						
1974	LA	N	O		5	.188
WYSE, HENRY WASHINGTON						
1945	CHI	N	P		3	0- 1
YASTRZEMSKI, CARL MICHAEL						
1967	BOS	A	O		7	.400
1975	BOS	A	1-O		7	.310
					14	.352
YDE, EMIL OGDEN						
1925	PIT	N	P	1	2	0- 1
1927	PIT	N	R		1	.000
				1	3	0- 1
						.000
YEAGER, STEPHEN WAYNE						
1974	LA	N	C		4	.364
1977	LA	N	C		6	.316
1978	LA	N	C		5	.231
					15	.302
YERKES, STEPHEN DOUGLAS						
1912	BOS	A	2		8	.250
YORK, PRESTON RUDOLPH						
1940	DET	A	1		7	.231
1945	DET	A	1		7	.179
1946	DET	A	1		7	.261
					21	.221
YOUNG, DENTON TRUE						
1903	BOS	A	P		4	2- 1
YOUNG, ROSS MIDDLEBROOK						
1921	NY	N	O		8	.280
1922	NY	N	O		5	.375
1923	NY	N	O		6	.348
1924	NY	N	O		7	.185
					26	.285
YVARS, SALVADOR ANTHONY						
1951	NY	N	H		1	.000
ZACHARY, JONATHAN THOMPSON WALTON						
1924	WAS	A	P		2	2- 0
1925	WAS	A	P		1	0- 0
1928	NY	A	P		1	1- 0
					4	3- 0
ZACHRY, PATRICK PAUL						
1976	CIN	N	P		1	1- 0
ZARILLA, ALLEN LEE						
1944	STL	N	O		4	.100
ZEBER, GEORGE WILLIAM						
1977	NY	A	H		2	.000
ZEIDER, ROLLIE HUBERT						
1918	CHI	N	3		2	.000
ZIMMER, DONALD WILLIAM						
1955	BRO	N	2		4	.222
1959	LA	N	S		1	.000
					5	.200
ZIMMERMAN, GERALD ROBERT						
1961	CIN	N	C		2	.000
1965	MIN	A	C		2	.000
					4	.000
ZIMMERMAN, HENRY						
1907	CHI	N	2		1	.000
1910	CHI	N	2		5	.235
1917	NY	N	3		6	.120
					12	.163
ZUBER, WILLIAM HENRY						
1946	BOS	A	P		1	0- 0

V BEST LIFETIME MARKS

MANAGERIAL LEADERS
(Top Five in Each Classification)

SEASONS MANAGED —Connie Mack 53, John McGraw 34, Bucky Harris 29,
Bill McKechnie 25, Casey Stengel 25.

PENNANTS WON —McGraw 10, Stengel 10, Mack 9,
Joe McCarthy 9, Walter Alston 7, Miller Huggins 6,
Harry Wright 6.

WORLD SERIES WON—McCarthy 7, Stengel 7, Mack 5, Alston 4, McGraw 3,
Huggins 3.

THREE THOUSAND HITTERS
(Players Who Have Amassed 3,000 or More Hits in the Majors)

	YEARS	GAMES	HITS		YEARS	GAMES	HITS
Ty Cobb	24	3,033	4,191	Willie Mays	22	2,992	3,283
Hank Aaron	23	3,298	3,771	Nap Lajoie	21	2,475	3,251
Stan Musial	21	3,026	3,630	Paul Waner	20	2,549	3,152
Cap Anson	27	2,509	3,516	Al Kaline	22	2,834	3,007
Tris Speaker	22	2,789	3,515	Roberto			
Honus Wagner	21	2,785	3,430	Clemente	18	2,433	3,000
Eddie Collins	25	2,826	3,313	Pete Rose	16	2,505	3,164

THREE HUNDRED VICTORIES
(Pitchers Who Have Won 300 or More Games in the Majors)

	Years	Games Pitched	Won		Years	Games Pitched	Won
Cy Young	22	867	507	Tim Keefe	14	588	345
Walter Johnson	21	802	416	John Clarkson	12	523	327
Grover Alexander	20	696	373	Eddie Plank	17	623	326
Christy Mathewson	17	632	373	Mike Welch	13	540	315
Warren Spahn	21	750	363	Hoss Radbourn	11	514	306
Jim Galvin	15	682	362	Lefty Grove	17	616	300
Kid Nichols	15	597	361	Early Wynn	23	691	300

FIFTY HOMERS A SEASON
(Players Who Have Hit 50 or More Homers in a Season)

	YEAR	HOMERS		YEAR	HOMERS
Roger Maris	1961	61	Mickey Mantle	1961	54
Babe Ruth	1927	60	Ralph Kiner	1949	54
Babe Ruth	1921	59	Mickey Mantle	1956	52
Hank Greenberg	1938	58	Willie Mays	1965	52
Jimmy Foxx	1932	58	George Foster	1977	52
Hack Wilson	1930	56	Ralph Kiner	1947	51
Babe Ruth	1920	54	Willie Mays	1955	51
Babe Ruth	1928	54	Johnny Mize	1947	51
			Jimmy Foxx	1938	50

FOUR HUNDRED HOMER HITTERS
(Players Who Have Hit 400 or More Homers in the Majors)

	YEARS	HOMERS		YEARS	HOMERS
Hank Aaron	23	755	Eddie Mathews	17	512
Babe Ruth	22	714	Ernie Banks	19	512
Willie Mays	22	660	Mel Ott	22	511
Frank Robinson	21	586	Willie McCovey	20	505
Harmon Killebrew	22	573	Lou Gehrig	17	493
Mickey Mantle	18	536	Stan Musial	22	475
Jimmy Foxx	20	534	Willie Stargell	17	429
Ted Williams	19	521	Billy Williams	18	426
			Duke Snider	18	407

TRIPLE PLAY UNASSISTED

Neal Ball (shortstop), Cleveland AL vs. Boston, July 19, 1909.
George H. Burns (first base), Boston AL vs. Cleveland, Sept. 14, 1923.
Ernest K. Padgett (shortstop), Boston NL vs. Philadelphia, Oct. 6, 1923.
Forest Glenn Wright (shortstop), Pittsburgh NL vs. St. Louis, May 7, 1925.
James E. Cooney (shortstop), Chicago NL at Pittsburgh, May 30, 1927.
John H. Neun (first base), Detroit AL vs. Cleveland, May 31, 1927.
Ronald L. Hansen (shortstop), Washington AL at Cleveland, July 30, 1968

NOTE: William A. Wambganss (second base), Cleveland AL vs. Brooklyn NL, Oct. 10, 1920 (World Series).

FOUR HUNDRED BATTERS
(Players Who Have Hit .400 or More per Season, at Least 100 Games)

	YEAR	B.A.		YEAR	B.A.
Hugh Duffy	1894	.438	Tip O'Neill	1887	.492
Willie Keeler	1897	.432	Pete Browning	1887	.471
Rogers Hornsby	1924	.424	Denny Lyons	1887	.469
Jesse Burkett	1895	.423	YankRobinson	1887	.426
Nap Lajoie	1901	.422	Cap Anson	1887	.421
Ty Cobb	1911	.420	Dan Brouthers	1887	.419
George Sisler	1922	.420	Reddy Mack	1887	.410
Jesse Burkett	1896	.410	Sam Thompson	1887	.406
Ty Cobb	1912	.410	Paul Radford	1887	.404
Dude Esterbrook	1884	.408	Harry Stovey	1887	.402
Ed Delahanty	1899	.408	Tom Burns	1887	.401
Joe Jackson	1911	.408			
George Sisler	1920	.407	NOTE: In 1887, Walks counted as		
Fred Clarke	1897	.406	Hits; if walks were not		
Ted Williams	1941	.406	counted as hits, only three		
Harry Stovey	1884	.404	players would have hit over		
Sam Thompson	1894	.403	.400		
Harry Heilmann	1923	.403			
Rogers Hornsby	1925	.403	Tip O'Neill	1887	.442
Jesse Burkett	1899	.402	Denny Lyons	1887	.425
Ty Cobb	1922	.401	Pete Browning	1887	.418
Rogers Hornsby	1922	.401			
Bill Terry	1930	.401			
Ed Delahanty	1894	.400			

HIGHEST LIFETIME BATTERS
(Players Whose Lifetime Average is .340 or Better)

	YEARS	B.A.		YEARS	B.A.
Ty Cobb	24	.367	Tris Speaker	22	.344
Rogers Hornsby	23	.358	Ted Williams	19	.344
Joe Jackson	13	.356	Babe Ruth	22	.342
Pete Browning	13	.355	Jesse Burkett	16	.342
Lefty O'Doul	11	.349	Harry Heilmann	17	.342
Dan Brouthers	19	.348	Bill Terry	14	.341
Ed Delahanty	16	.346	George Sisler	15	.340
Willie Keeler	19	.345	Lou Gehrig	17	.340
Billy Hamilton	14	.344			

SEVEN HUNDRED SLUGGERS
(Players who have Slugged .700 or more per Season, at least 100 Games,
Slugging Percentage equals Total Bases divided by At Bats)

	YEAR	S.A.		YEAR	S.A.
Babe Ruth	1920	.847	Hack Wilson	1930	.723
Babe Ruth	1921	.846	Rogers Hornsby	1922	.722
Babe Ruth	1927	.772	Lou Gehrig	1930	.721
Lou Gehrig	1927	.765	Babe Ruth	1928	.709
Babe Ruth	1923	.764	Al Simmons	1930	.708
Rogers Hornsby	1925	.756	Lou Gehrig	1934	.706
Jimmie Foxx	1932	.749	Mickey Mantle	1956	.705
Babe Ruth	1924	.739	Jimmie Foxx	1938	.704
Babe Ruth	1926	.737	Jimmie Foxx	1933	.703
Ted Williams	1941	.735	Stan Musial	1948	.702
Babe Ruth	1930	.732	Babe Ruth	1931	.700
Ted Williams	1957	.731			

HIGHEST LIFETIME SLUGGERS
(Players whose Lifetime Slugging Average is .520 or better)

	YEARS	S.A.		YEARS	S.A.
Babe Ruth	22	.690	Dick Allen	14	.539
Ted Williams	19	.634	Frank Robinson	21	.537
Lou Gehrig	17	.632	Al Simmons	20	.535
Jimmie Foxx	20	.609	Mel Ott	22	.533
Hank Greenberg	13	.605	Earl Averill	13	.533
Joe DiMaggio	13	.579	Babe Herman	15	.532
Rogers Hornsby	23	.577	Ken Williams	14	.531
Johnny Mize	15	.562	Willie Stargell	17	.531
Stan Musial	22	.559	Chick Hafey	13	.526
Willie Mays	22	.557	Dan Brouthers	19	.525
Mickey Mantle	18	.557	Willie McCovey	20	.523
Hank Aaron	23	.555	Hal Trosky	11	.522
Ralph Kiner	10	.548	Wally Berger	11	.522
Hack Wilson	12	.545	Harry Heilmann	17	.520
Chuck Klein	17	.543			
Duke Snider	18	.540			

HIGHEST SEASON ON-BASE AVERAGE
(Players with .490 or better On-Base Average per season, at least 100 games, On-Base Average counts walks and hit-by-pitch as base hits)

	YEAR	OBA		YEAR	OBA
Ted Williams	1941	.551	Joe Kelley	1894	.501
John McGraw	1899	.545	Hugh Duffy	1894	.500
Babe Ruth	1923	.545	Ted Williams	1942	.499
Babe Ruth	1920	.530	Ted Williams	1947	.499
Ted Williams	1957	.528	Rogers Hornsby	1928	.498
Billy Hamilton	1894	.516	Ted Williams	1946	.497
Ted Williams	1954	.516	Ed Delahanty	1895	.496
Babe Ruth	1926	.516	Billy Hamilton	1896	.494
Mickey Mantle	1957	.515	Babe Ruth	1931	.494
Babe Ruth	1924	.513	Babe Ruth	1930	.493
Babe Ruth	1921	.512	Arky Vaughan	1935	.492
Rogers Hornsby	1924	.507	Tip O'Neill	1887	.492

HIGHEST LIFETIME ON-BASE AVERAGE
(Players whose Lifetime On-Base Average is .410 or better)

	YEARS	OBA		YEARS	OBA
Ted Williams	19	.483	Mickey Mantle	18	.423
Babe Ruth	22	.474	Clarence Childs	13	.421
John McGraw	16	.464	Denny Lyons	13	.419
Billy Hamilton	14	.457	Mickey Cochrane	13	.419
Lou Gehrig	17	.447	Stan Musial	22	.418
Rogers Hornsby	23	.434	Jesse Burkett	16	.418
Ty Cobb	24	.433	Mel Ott	22	.414
Jimmie Foxx	20	.430	Ed Delahanty	16	.412
Tris Speaker	22	.427	Hank Greenberg	13	.412
Ferris Fain	9	.425	Roy Thomas	13	.411
Dan Brouthers	19	.424	Charley Keller	13	.410
Eddie Collins	25	.424	Eddie Stanky	11	.410
Joe Jackson	13	.423	Jackie Robinson	10	.410
Max Bishop	12	.423	Harry Heilmann	17	.410

CONSECUTIVE RECORD STREAKS

(1) CLUB CONSECUTIVE MARKS

World Series Won—
  5, New York AL (1949–53)
  4, New York AL (1936–39)
  3, Oakland AL (1972–74)

Pennants Won—
  5, New York AL (1949–53)
  5, New York AL (1960–64)
  4, Boston NA (1872–75)
  4, St. Louis AA (1885–88)
  4, New York NL (1921–24)
  4, New York AL (1936–39)
  4, New York AL (1955–58)

Games Won—
  26, New York NL (1916)
  26, Boston NA (1875)
  21, Chicago NL (1880)
  21, Chicago NL (1935)
  20, St. Louis UA (1884)
  20, Providence NL (1884)
  19, Chicago AL (1906)
  19, New York AL (1947)

Games Lost—
  26, Louisville AA (1889)
  24, Cleveland NL (1899)
  23, Philadelphia NL (1961)
  23, Pittsburgh NL (1890)
  22, Philadelphia AA (1890)
  20, Boston AL (1906)
  20, Philadelphia AL (1916)
  20, Philadelphia AL (1943)
  20, Louisville NL (1894)
  20, Montreal NL (1969)

Games without being shut out—
  308, New York AL (1931–33)
  196, Athletics AA (1886–88)
  182, Philadelphia NL (1893–95)

Innings shut out opponents—
  56, Pittsburgh NL (1903)
  47, Cleveland AL (1948)

Innings shut out by opponents—
  48, Philadelphia AL (1906)
  48, Chicago NL (1968)

Games in which homers were hit—
25, New York AL (1941)
24, Brooklyn NL (1953)

Errorless games—
15, Cincinnati NL (1975)
12, Detroit AL (1963)

(2) BATTING STREAKS
Games played—
2,130 H. L. Gehrig AL (1925–39)
1,117 B. L. Williams NL (1963–70)

Games scoring runs—
24, W. R. Hamilton NL (1894)
18, R. A. Rolfe AL (1939)
17, T. B. Kluszewski NL (1954)

Games hit safely—
56, J. P. DiMaggio AL (1941)
44, W. H. Keeler NL (1897)
44, P. E. Rose NL (1978)

Games hit homer—
8, R. D. Long NL (1956)
6, K. R. Williams AL (1922)
6, H. L. Gehrig AL (1931)
6, R. E. Sievers AL (1957)
6, R. E. Maris AL (1961)
6, F. O. Howard AL (1968)
6, R. M. Jackson AL (1976)
Hits—
12, M. F. Higgins AL (1938)
12, W. Dropo AL (1952)
10, E. J. Delahanty NL (1897)
10, J. J.Gettman NL (1897)
10, E. J. Konetchy NL (1919)
10, H. S. Cuyler NL (1925)
10, C. J. Hafey NL (1929)
10, J. M. Medwick NL (1936)
10, W. W. Williams NL (1943)

Bases on balls—
7, W. G. Rogell AL (1938)
7, M. T. Ott NL (1943)
7, E. R. Stanky NL (1950)

Strikeouts—
14, W. A. Hands NL (1968)
13, J. J. Hannan AL (1968)

(3) FIELDING STREAKS
Games caught—
312, F. W. Hayes AL (1943–46)
233, R. C. Mueller NL (1943–46)

Catcher's chances without error—
950, L. P. Berra AL (1957–59)
805, J. A. Edwards NL (1970–71)

Catcher's games without error—
148, L. P. Berra AL (1957–59)
138, J. A. Edwards NL (1970–71)

Pitcher's chances without error—
273, C. W. Passeau NL (1941–46)
159, T. A. Lyons AL (1934–38)

Pitcher's games without error—
385, P. A. Lindblad AL (1966–74)
225, L. D. McDaniel NL (1964–68)

First baseman's chances without error—
1625, J. P. McInnis AL (1921–22)
1337, F. A. McCormick NL (1945–46)

First baseman's games without error—
178, J. M. Hegan AL (1970–73)
(Note: Hegan was used as a late-inning defensive replacement in many of the 178 games)
163, J. P. McInnis AL (1921–22)
138, F. A. McCormick NL (1945–46)

Second baseman's chances without error—
458, K. J. Adair AL (1964–65)
418, K. D. Hubbs NL (1962)

Second baseman's games without error—
91, J. L. Morgan NL (1977–78)
89, K. J. Adair AL (1964–65)

Shortstop's chances without error—
383, J. J. Kerr NL (1946–47)
331, E. A. Brinkman AL (1972)

Shortstop's games without error—
72, E. A. Brinkman AL (1972)
68, J. J. Kerr NL (1946–47)

Third baseman's chances without error—
261, D. W. Money AL (1973–74)
209, J. H. Davenport NL (1966–68)

Third baseman's games without error—
97, J. H. Davenport NL (1966–68)
88, D. W. Money AL (1973–74)

Outfielder's chances without error—
568, C. C. Flood NL (1965–67)
439, L. E. Doby AL (1954–55)

Outfielder's games without error—
266, D. L. Demeter NL-AL (1962–65)
242, A. W. Kaline AL (1970–72)
226, C. C. Flood NL (1965–67)

(4) PITCHING STREAKS
Innings without relief—
1727, J. W. Taylor NL (1901–06)
337, W.H. Dineen AL (1904)

Games won—
24, C. O. Hubbell NL (1936–37)
24, A. G. Spalding NA (1875)
19, T. J. Keefe NL (1888)
19, R. W. Marquard NL (1912)
17, J. T. Allen AL (1936–37)
17, D. A. McNally AL (1968–69)
16, W. P. Johnson AL (1912)
16, J. Wood AL (1912)
16, R. M. Grove AL (1931)
16, L. T. Rowe AL (1934)

Games lost—
23, C. G. Curtis NL (1910–11)
19, R. Groom AL (1909)
19, J. H. Nabors AL (1916)
18, C. G. Curtis NL (1910)
18, R. L. Craig NL (1963)

Shut out games—
6, D. S. Drysdale NL (1968)
5, G. H. White AL (1904)

Shut out innings—
58 2/3, D. S. Drysdale NL (1968)
56, W. P. Johnson AL (1913)

Strikeouts—
10, G. T. Seaver NL (1970)
9, M. F. Welch NL (1884)
8, C. G. Buffington NL (1885)
8, E. L. Cushman AA (1885)
8, M. G. Surkont NL (1953)
8, J. J. Podres NL (1962)
8, J. W. Maloney NL (1963)
8, D. E. Wilson NL (1968)
8, L. N. Ryan AL (1972, 1973)

Bases on balls—
7, W. D. Gray AL (1909)
6, W. H. Kennedy NL (1900)

Innings without base on balls—
84 1/3, W. C. Fischer AL (1962)
68, C. Mathewson NL (1913)
68, R. L. Jones NL (1976)

LIFETIME MARKS
Season, Game, Inning

ML—Major Leagues, NL—National League, MNL—Modern National League (1900 to date), AL—American League, AA—American Association, PL—Players League, UA—Union Association

INDIVIDUAL BATTING RECORDS

Seasons
27 Anson, A. C., ML
26 McGuire, J. T., ML
25 Collins, E. T., AL
25 Wallace, R. J., ML
24 Cobb, T. R., AL
23 Maranville, W. J., NL
23 Hornsby, R., ML
23 Aaron, H. L., ML
23 Robinson, B. C., AL

Games—Lifetime
3298 Aaron, H. L., ML
3033 Cobb, T. R., AL
3026 Musial, S. F., NL
2992 Mays, W. H., NL
2896 Robinson, B. C., AL
(3076 Aaron, H. L., NL)

Season (162-game schedule)
165 Wills, M. M., NL (1962)
165 Tovar, C. L., AL (1967)

Season (154-game schedule)
162 Barrett, J. E., AL (1904)
160 Groh, H. K., NL (1915)
    Griffith, T. H., NL (1915)

At bats—Lifetime
12364 Aaron, H. L., ML
11429 Cobb, T. R., AL
10972 Musial, S. F., NL
10881 Mays, W. H., NL
10654 Robinson, B. C., AL
(11628 Aaron, H. L., NL)

Season (162-game schedule)
699 Cash, D., NL (1975)
692 Richardson, R. C., AL (1962)

Season (154-game schedule)
696 Jensen, F. D., NL (1936)
679 Kuenn, H. E., AL (1953)

Game (extra innings)
11 Many, NL/AL

Game (nine innings)
8 Many, NL
7 Many, MNL/AL

Inning
3 Many, NL/AL

Runs—Lifetime
2244 Cobb, T. R., AL
2174 Ruth, G. H., ML
2174 Aaron, H. L., ML
2062 Mays, W. H., NL
1969 Anson, A. C., ML
(2107 Aaron, H. L., NL)

Season
196 Hamilton, W. R., NL (1894)
177 Ruth, G. H., AL (1921)
158 Klein, C. H., MNL (1930)

Game
7 Hecker, G. J., AA (1886)
6 Pesky, J. M., AL (1946)
6 Many, NL
6 Ott, M. T., MNL (1934 and 1944)
    Torre, F. J., (1957)

Inning
3 Burns, T. E., NL (1883)
    Williamson, E. N., NL (1883)
3 White, S. C., AL (1953)
2 Many, MNL

Hits—Lifetime
4191 Cobb, T. R., AL
3771 Aaron, H. L., ML
3630 Musial, S. F., NL
3516 Anson, A. C., ML
3515 Speaker, T. E., AL

Season
257 Sisler, G. H., AL (1920)
254 O'Doul, F. J., NL (1929)
    Terry, W. H., NL (1930)

Game (extra innings)
9 Burnett, J. H., AL (1932)

Game (nine innings)
7 Robinson, W., NL (1892)
7 Stennett, R. A. NL (1975)
6 Many, AL

Inning
3 Burns, T. E., NL (1883)
    Williamson, E. N., NL (1883)
3 Stephens, G. E., AL (1953)
2 Many, MNL

Total Bases—Lifetime
6856 Aaron, H. L., ML
6134 Musial, S. F., NL
6066 Mays, W. H., NL
5863 Cobb, T. R., AL
5793 Ruth, G. H., ML
(6591 Aaron, H. L., NL)

Season
457 Ruth, G. H., AL (1921)
450 Hornsby, R., NL (1922)

Game (nine innings)
18 Adcock, J. W., NL (1954)
16 Cobb, T. R., AL (1925)
    Gehrig, H. L., AL (1932)
    Colavito, R. D., AL (1959)
    Lynn, F. M., AL (1975)

Game (extra innings)
16 Seerey, J. P., AL (1948)
    Foxx, J. E., AL (1932)

Inning
8 Many, NL/AL

Times on Base—Lifetime
5531 Cobb, T. R., AL
5282 Musial, S. F., NL
5107 Aaron, H. L., ML
4998 Speaker, T. E., AL
4971 Ruth, G. H., ML

Season
379 Ruth, G. H., AL (1923)
358 Hamilton, W. R., NL (1894)
334 O'Doul, F. J., MNL (1929)

Singles—Lifetime
3052 Cobb, T. R., AL
2650 Anson, A. C., ML
2641 Collins, E. T., AL

2534 Keeler, W. H., ML
2426 Wagner, J. P., NL
(2253 Musial, S. F., MNL)

Season
202 Keeler, W. H., NL (1898)
198 Waner, L. J., MNL (1927)
182 Rice, E. C., AL (1925)
Game (extra innings)
7 Burnett, J. H., AL (1932)
Game (nine innings)
6 Many, NL/AL
Inning
2 Many, NL/AL

Doubles—Lifetime
793 Speaker, T. E., AL
725 Musial, S. F., NL
724 Cobb, T. R., AL
651 Wagner, J. P., NL
650 Lajoie, N., ML
Season
67 Webb, E. W., AL (1931)
64 Medwick, J. M., NL (1936)
Game
4 Larkin, H. E., AA (1885)
Milligan, J., AA (1886)
4 O'Rourke, J., NL (1880)
Anson, A. C., NL (1883)
Dalrymple, A. F., NL (1883)
Tucker, T. J., NL (1893)
Bonner, F. J., NL (1894)
Kelley, J. J., NL (1894)
Delahanty, E. J., NL (1899)
Cravath, C. C., NL (1915)
Sothern, D. E., NL (1930)
Waner, P. G., NL (1932)
Bartell, R. W., NL (1933)
Lombardi, E. N., NL (1935)
Medwick, J. M., NL (1937)
Werber, W. M., NL (1940)
Jones, W. E., NL (1949)
Greengrass, J. R., NL (1954)
Williams, B. L., NL (1969)
4 Dillon, F. E., AL (1901)
Werber, W. M., AL (1935)
Hayes, F. W., AL (1936)
Kreevich, M. A., AL (1937)
Owen, M. J., AL (1939)
Lindell, J. H., AL (1944)
Boudreau, L., AL (1946)
Zarilla, A. L., AL (1950)
Wertz, V. W., AL (1956)
Lau, C. R., AL (1962)
Bruton, W. H., AL (1963)
Cepeda, O. M., AL (1973)
Mason, J. P., AL (1974)
Duncan, D. E., AL (1975)
Inning
2 Many, NL/AL

Triples—Lifetime
312 Crawford, S. E., ML
297 Cobb, T. R., AL
252 Wagner, J. P., NL
246 Beckley, J. P., ML
227 Connor, R., ML
(231 Wagner, J. P., MNL)
Season
36 Wilson, J. O., NL (1912)
26 Jackson, J. J., AL (1912)
Crawford, S. E., AL (1914)

Game
4 Strief, G. A., AA (1885)
4 Joyce, W. M., NL (1897)

3 Wolverton, H. S., MNL (1900)
Sheckard, J. T., MNL (1901)
Donlin, M. J., MNL (1903)
Huggins, M. J., MNL (1904)
Brain, D. L., MNL (1905 twice)
Moran, P. J., MNL (1905)
Wilson, J. O., MNL (1911)
Youngs, R. M., MNL (1920)
Powell, R. R., MNL (1921)
Hollocher, C. J., MNL (1922)
Bottomley, J. L., MNL (1923 and 1927)
Bell, L. R., MNL (1926)
Richbourg, L. C., MNL (1929)
Bernier, C. R., MNL (1953)
O'Connell, D. F., MNL (1956)
Clemente, R. W., MNL (1958)
Mays, W. H., MNL (1960)
Banks, E., MNL (1966)
3 Flick, E. H., AL (1902)
Bradley, W. J., AL (1903)
Dougherty, P. H., AL (1903)
Lush, W. L., AL (1903)
Lajoie, N., AL (1904)
Chase, H. H., AL (1906)
Jackson, J. J., AL (1912)
Williams, A. R., AL (1913)
Jacobson, W. C., AL (1922)
Judge, J. I., AL (1921)
Tavener, J. A., AL (1925)
Combs, E. B., AL (1927)
Gehringer, C. L., AL (1929)
Kuhel, J. A., AL (1937)
DiMaggio, J. P., AL (1938)
Chapman, W. B., AL (1939)
Campaneris, D. B., AL (1967)
Bumbry, A. B., AL (1973)

Inning
2 Wheeler, H. E., AA (1882)
Stovey, H. D., AA (1884)
2 Hornung, M. J., NL (1882)
Pietz, H. C., NL (1895)
Freeman, J. B., NL (1900)
Dahlen, W. F., NL (1900)
Walker, W. C., NL (1926)
2 Zarilla, A. L., AL (1946)
Coan, G. F., AL (1951)

Home Runs—Lifetime
755 Aaron, H. L., ML
714 Ruth, G. H., ML
660 Mays, W. H., NL
586 Robinson, F., ML
573 Killebrew, H. C., AL
(733 Aaron, H. L., NL)
(708 Ruth, G. H., AL)
Season (162-game schedule)
61 Maris, R. E., AL (1961)
Season (154-game schedule)
60 Ruth, G. H., AL (1927)
56 Wilson, L. R., NL (1930)
Game (extra innings)
4 Seerey, J. P., AL (1948)
4 Klein, C. H., NL (1936)
Game (nine innings)
4 Lowe, R. L., NL (1894)
Delahanty, E. J., NL (1896)

Hodges, G. R., NL (1950)
Adcock, J. W., NL (1954)
Mays, W. H., NL (1961)
  Schmidt, M. J., NL (1976)
4 Gehrig, H. L., AL (1932)
  Colavito, R. D., AL (1959)
Inning
  2 Many, NL/AL

Runs Batted In—Lifetime
  2297 Aaron, H. L., ML
  2205 Ruth, G. H., ML
  1990 Gehrig, H. L., AL
  1954 Cobb, T. R., AL
  1951 Musial, S. F., NL
  (2202 Aaron, H. L., NL)
  (2193 Ruth, G. H., AL)
Season
  190 Wilson, L. R., NL (1930)
  184 Gehrig, H. L., AL (1931)
Game
  12 Bottomley, J. L., NL (1924)
  11 Lazzeri, A. M., AL (1936)
Inning
  7 Cartwright, E. H., AA (1890)
  6 Many, NL/AL

Batting Average—Lifetime
  .367 Cobb, T. R., AL
  .358 Hornsby, R., ML
  .356 Jackson, J. J., AL
  .355 Browning, L. R., ML
  .349 O'Doul, F. J., ML
  (.359 Hornsby, R., NL)
Season
  .438 Duffy, H., NL (1894)
  .424 Hornsby, R., MNL (1924)
  .422 Lajoie, N., AL (1901)

Slugging Average—Lifetime
  .690 Ruth, G. H., ML
  .634 Williams, T. S., AL
  .632 Gehrig, H. L., AL
  .609 Foxx, J. E., ML
  .605 Greenberg, H. B., AL
  (.692 Ruth, G. H., AL)
  .578 Hornsby, R., NL)
Season
  .847 Ruth, G. H., AL (1920)
  .756 Hornsby, R., NL (1925)

On-Base Average—Lifetime
  .483 Williams, T.S., AL
  .474 Ruth, G. H., ML
  .464 McGraw, J. J., NL
  .457 Hamilton, W. R., ML
  .447 Gehrig, H. L., AL
  (.434 Hornsby, R., MNL)
Season
  .551 Williams, T. S., AL (1941)
  .545 McGraw, J. J., NL (1899)
  .507 Hornsby, R., MNL (1924)

Bases on Balls—Lifetime
  2057 Ruth, G. H., ML
  2018 Williams, T. S., AL
  1734 Mantle, M. C., AL
  1708 Ott, M. T., NL
  1614 Yost, E. F., AL
  (2036 Ruth, G. H., AL)
Season (154-game schedule)
  170 Ruth, G. H., AL (1923)
  148 Stanky, E. R., NL (1945)

Season (162-game schedule)
  148 Wynn, J. S., NL (1969)
Game
  6 Wilmot, W. R., NL (1891)
  6 Foxx, J. E., AL (1938)
  5 Many, MNL
Inning
  2 Many, NL/AL

Strikeouts—Lifetime
  1746 Stargell, W. D., NL
  1710 Mantle, M. C., AL
  1699 Killebrew, H. C., AL
  1687 Brock, L. C., NL
  1556 Allen, R. A., ML
Season (162-game schedule)
  189 Bonds, B. L., NL (1970)
  175 Nicholson, D. L., AL (1963)
Season (154-game schedule)
  138 Lemon, J. R., AL (1956)
  136 Herrera, J. F., NL (1960)
Game (extra innings)
  6 Many, NL/AL
Game (nine innings)
  5 Many, NL/AL
Inning
  2 Many, NL/AL

Hit by Pitch—Lifetime (1887–date)
  260 Jennings, H. A., ML
  250 Tucker, T. J., ML
  243 Hunt, R. K., ML
  198 Robinson, F., ML
  192 Minoso, O. A., ML
  (250 Jennings, H. A., NL
  189 Minoso, O. A., AL)
Season
  51 Jennings, H. A., NL (1896)
  50 Hunt, R. K., MNL (1971)
  25 Elberfeld, N. A., AL (1911)
Game
  3 Many, NL/AL
Inning
  2 Schmidt, W. R., NL (1959)
    Thomas, F. J., NL (1959)
  1 Many, AL

Note: Hit by pitch first in effect 1887.

Sacrifice Hits—Lifetime (1894–date)
  511 Collins, E. T., AL
  392 Daubert, J. E., NL
  383 McInnis, J. P., ML
  372 Keeler, W. H., ML
  340 Chapman, R. J., AL
Season (including sacrifice flies)
  67 Chapman, R. J., AL (1917)
  46 Sheckard, J. T., NL (1909)
Season (no sacrifice flies)
  46 Bradley, W. J., AL (1907)
  43 Gleason, W. J., NL (1905)
Game
  4 Killefer, W. H., AL (1910)
    Barry, J. J., AL (1916)
    Chapman, R. J., AL (1919)
  4 Daubert, J. E., NL (1914)
Inning
  2 Benton, J. A., AL (1941)
  1 Many, NL

Note: Sacrifice hits were first recorded in 1889. They were credited to batters for advancing runners on any out and at-bats were charged. In 1894 the rule was changed so that only bunts were counted as sacrifices with no at-bats charged. A sacrifice fly was tabulated with no time at bat for scoring a runner with a fly ball out from 1908 to 1930, 1939 and 1954 to the present. In addition from 1926–1930 a sacrifice fly was counted for advancing any runner with a fly ball out.

Stolen Bases—Lifetime (1886–date)
937 Hamilton, W. R., ML
917 Brock, L. C., NL
892 Cobb, T. R., AL
791 Latham, W. A., ML
744 Stovey, H. D., ML
Season (162-game schedule)
118 Brock, L. C., NL (1974)
Season (154-game schedule)
156 Stovey, H. D., AA (1888)
115 Hamilton, W. R., NL (1891)
96 Cobb, T. R., AL (1915)
80 Bescher, R. H., MNL (1911)
Game
7 Gore, G. F., NL (1881)
Hamilton, W. R., NL (1894)
6 Collins, E. T., AL (1912 twice)
5 McGann, D. L., MNL (1904)
Lopes, D. E., MNL (1974)

Inning
3 Many, NL/AL

Note: Stolen bases were first recorded in 1886. They were credited to runners for any extra bases taken on pitches or hits. In 1898 the rule was changed so that only bases stolen on pitches without errors were counted as stolen bases. Gore's game record in 1881 was established before official tabulation but was documented in newspaper accounts.

INDIVIDUAL PITCHING RECORDS

Seasons
23 Quinn, J. P., ML
23 Wynn, E., AL
22 Young, D. T., ML
22 Pennock, H. J., AL
22 Jones, S. P., AL
22 Ruffing, C. H., AL
(21 Spahn, W. E., NL
21 Rixey, E., NL)

Games—Lifetime
1070 Wilhelm, J. H., ML
987 McDaniel, L. D., ML
867 Young, D. T., ML
874 McMahon, D. J., ML
848 Face, E. L., ML
(846 Face, E. L., NL
805 Johnson, W. P., AL)
Season (162-game schedule)
106 Marshall, M. G., NL (1974)
88 Wood, W. F., AL (1968)

Season (154-game schedule)
75 White, W. H., NL (1879)
74 Konstanty, C. J., MNL (1950)
70 Fornieles, J. M., AL (1960)

Innings Pitched—Lifetime
7377 Young, D. T., ML
5959 Galvin, J. F., ML
5924 Johnson, W. P., AL
5246 Spahn, W. E., NL
5189 Alexander, G. C., NL
Season
683 White, W. H., NL (1879)
464 Walsh, E. A., AL (1908)
434 McGinnity, J. J., MNL (1903)
Game (extra innings)
26 Oeschger, J. C., NL (1920)
Cadore, L. L., NL (1920)
24 Coombs, J. W., AL (1906)
Harris, J. W., AL (1906)

Complete Games—Lifetime
751 Young, D. T., ML
639 Galvin, J. F., ML
555 Keefe, T. J., ML
531 Johnson, W. P., AL
530 Nichols, C. A., NL
(560 Galvin, J. F., NL
437 Alexander, G. C., MNL)
Season
74 White, W. H., NL (1879)
48 Chesbro, J. D., AL (1904)
45 Willis, V. G., MNL (1902)

Games Won—Lifetime
507 Young, D. T., ML
414 Johnson, W. P., AL
373 Mathewson, C., NL
373 Alexander, G. C., NL
363 Spahn, W. E., NL
Season
60 Radbourn, C. G., NL (1884)
41 Chesbro, J. D., AL (1904)
40 Walsh, E. A., AL (1908)
37 Mathewson, C., MNL (1908)

Games Lost—Lifetime
308 Galvin, J. F., ML
308 Young, D. T., ML
281 Johnson, W. P., AL
253 Powell, J. J., ML
251 Rixey, E., NL
Season
48 Coleman, J. F., NL (1883)
29 Willis, V. G., MNL (1905)
27 Townsend, J., AL (1904)

Shutouts—Lifetime
113 Johnson, W. P., AL
90 Alexander, G. C., NL
83 Mathewson, C., NL
77 Young, D. T., ML
70 Plank, E. S., ML
Season
16 Bradley, G. W., NL (1876)
Alexander, G. C., NL (1916)
13 Coombs, J. W., AL (1910)

Runs Allowed—Lifetime
3168 Young, D. T., ML
2117 Ruffing, C. H., AL
2033 Grimes, B. A., MNL

Season
544 Coleman, J. F., NL (1883)
211 McGinnity, J. J., AL (1901)
196 Pittinger, C. R., MNL (1903)
Game
35 Rowe, D. E., NL (1882)
24 Travers, A. J., AL (1912)
21 Parker, H. P., MNL (1901)
Inning
16 Mullane, A. J., NL (1894)
13 O'Doul, F. J., AL (1923)
12 Kelleher, H. J., MNL (1938)

Hits Allowed—Lifetime
7078 Young, D. T., ML
6334 Galvin, J. F., ML
4920 Johnson, W. P., AL
4868 Alexander. G. C.. MNL
4854 Nichols, C A., NL
(5490 Galvin, J. F., NL)
Season
809 Coleman, J. F., NL (1883)
401 McGinnity, J. J., AL (1901)
393 Pittinger, C. R., MNL (1903)
Game
36 Wadsworth, W. J., NL (1894)
26 Lisenbee, H. M., AL (1936)
26 Parker, H. P., MNL (1901)
Inning
13 Weidman, G. E., NL (1883)
12 Adkins, M. T., AL (1902)
11 Grabowski, R. J., MNL (1934)

Strikeouts—Lifetime
3508 Johnson, W. P., AL
3117 Gibson, R. NL
3001 Perry, G. J., ML
2855 Bunning, J. P., ML
2819 Young, D. T., ML
Season (162-game schedule)
383 Ryan, L. N., AL (1973)
382 Koufax, S., MNL (1965)
Season (154-game schedule)
505 Kilroy, M. A., AA (1886)
411 Radbourn, C. G., NL (1884)
349 Waddell, G. E., AL (1904)
269 Koufax, S., MNL (1961)
Game (extra innings)
21 Cheney, T. E., AL (1962)
Game (nine innings)
19 Sweeney, C. J., NL (1884)
Carlton, S. N., NL (1969)
Seaver, G. T., NL (1970)
19 Daly, H. I., UA (1884)
19 Ryan, L. N., AL (1974)
Inning
4 Many, NL/AL
Bases on Balls—Lifetime
1775 Wynn, E., AL
1637 Rusie, A. W., NL
1434 Spahn, W. E., MNL
Season
276 Rusie, A. W., NL (1890)
208 Feller, R. W. A., AL (1938)
185 Jones, S., MNL (1955)
Game
16 George, W. M., NL (1887)
VanHaltren, G. E., NL (1887)
16 Gruber, H. J., PL (1890)
16 Haas, B. P., AL (1915)
14 Mathewson, H., MNL (1906)

Inning
8 Gray, W. D., AL (1909)
7 Mullane, A. J., NL (1894)
Ewing, G. L., NL (1902)

Hit Batsmen (1887–date)
217 Fraser, C. C., ML
206 Johnson, W. P., AL
205 Hawley, E. P., ML
(195 Hawley, E. P., NL
154 Drysdale, D. S., MNL)
Season
54 Knell, P. H., AA (1891)
41 McGinnity, J. J., NL (1900)
32 Fraser, C. C., AL (1901)
Game
6 Knouff, E., AA (1887)
5 Shaw, S., NL (1893)
Hawley, E. P., NL (1896)
Bates, F. C., NL (1899)
4 Many, MNL/AL
Inning
3 Many, NL/AL

Homers Allowed—Lifetime
502 Roberts, R. E., ML
434 Spahn, W. E., NL
359 Hunter, J. A., AL
Season
56 Roberts, R. E., NL (1956)
43 Ramos, P., AL (1957)
Game
6 Benton, L. J., NL (1930)
Thurston, H. J., NL (1932)
Kerksieck, W. W., NL (1939)
6 Thomas, A. T., AL (1936)
Caster, G. J., AL (1940)
Inning
4 Many, NL/AL

Wild Pitches
Season
64 Stemmeyer, W., NL (1886)
30 Ames, L. K., MNL (1905)
21 Johnson, W. P., AL (1910)
Wilson, R. E., AL (1963)
Game
10 Ryan, J. J., NL (1876)
5 Wheatley, C., AL (1912)
5 Cheney, L. D., MNL (1918)
Inning
6 Cunningham, E. E., PL (1890)
4 Johnson, W. P., AL (1914)
3 Many, NL
Balks
Season
8 Shaw, R. J., NL (1963)
Bonham, W. G., NL (1974)
Tanana, F. D., AL (1978)

Game
5 Shaw, R. J., NL (1963)
4 Raschi, V. A., AL (1950)
Inning
3 Shoffner, M. J., AL (1930)
3 Shaw, R. J., NL (1963)
Owens, J. P., NL (1963)

Earned Run Average (Lowest)
Season
1.01 Leonard, H. B., AL (1914)

1.12 Gibson, R., NL (1968)

Note: Earned run average first recorded in 1912 for the NL and 1913 for the AL.

TEAM BATTING RECORDS

At Bats
Season (162-game schedule)
  5767 Cincinnati, NL (1968)
  5705 New York, AL (1964)
Season (154-game schedule)
  5667 Philadelphia, NL (1930)
  5646 Cleveland, AL (1936)
Game (extra innings)
  85 New York, AL (1962)
  89 New York, NL (1974)
Game (nine innings)
  66 Chicago, NL (1883)
  58 New York, MNL (1925 and 1931)
  56 New York, AL (1939)
Batters faced pitcher—inning
  23 Chicago, NL (1883)
  23 Boston, AL (1953)
  21 Brooklyn, MNL (1952)

Runs
Season
  1221 Boston, NL (1894)
  1067 New York, AL (1931)
  1004 St. Louis, MNL (1930)
Game
  36 Chicago, NL (1897)
  29 Boston, AL (1950)
     Chicago, AL (1955)
  28 St. Louis, MNL (1929)
Inning
  18 Chicago, NL (1883)
  17 Boston, AL (1953)
  15 Brooklyn, MNL (1952)

Hits
Season
  1783 Philadelphia, NL (1930)
  1724 Detroit, AL (1921)
Game (extra innings)
  33 Cleveland, AL (1932)
Game (nine innings)
  36 Philadelphia, NL (1894)
  31 New York, MNL (1901)
  30 New York, AL (1923)
Inning
  18 Chicago, NL (1883)
  14 Boston, AL (1953)
  12 St. Louis, MNL (1925)

Total bases
Season
  2703 New York, AL (1936)
  2684 Chicago, NL (1930)
Game
  60 Boston, AL (1950)
  55 Cincinnati, NL (1893)
  50 San Francisco, MNL (1958)
Inning
  29 Chicago, NL (1883)
  27 San Francisco, MNL (1961)
  25 Boston, AL (1940)

Batting Average
Season
  .343 Philadelphia, NL (1894)
  .319 New York, MNL (1930)
  .316 Detroit, AL (1921)

Note: In 1887 when walks counted as hits, Detroit NL hit .347.

Singles
Season
  1338 Philadelphia, NL (1894)
  1298 Detroit, AL (1921)
  1297 Pittsburgh, MNL (1922)
Game
  28 Philadelphia, NL (1894)
     Boston, NL (1896)
  28 Cleveland, AL (1928)
     Boston, AL (1953)
  23 New York, MNL (1931)
Inning
  11 St. Louis, NL (1925)
  11 Boston, AL (1953)

Doubles
Season
  373 St. Louis, NL (1930)
  358 Cleveland, AL (1930)
Game
  14 Chicago, NL (1883)
  13 St. Louis, MNL (1931)
  11 Detroit, AL (1934)
Inning
  7 Boston, NL (1936)
  6 Washington, AL (1934)

Triples
Season
  153 Baltimore, NL (1894)
  129 Pittsburgh, MNL (1912)
  112 Baltimore, AL (1901)
     Boston, AL (1903)
Game
  9 Baltimore, NL (1894)
  8 Pittsburgh, MNL (1925)
  6 Chicago, AL (1901 and 1920)
    Detroit, AL (1922)
Inning
  5 Chicago, AL (1901)
  4 Boston, NL (1882)
    Baltimore, NL (1892)
    St. Louis, NL (1895)
    Chicago, NL (1899)
    Brooklyn, NL (1902)
    Cincinnati, NL (1926)
    New York, NL (1936)

Homers
Season (162-game schedule)
  240 New York, AL (1961)
Season (154-game schedule)
  221 New York, NL (1947)
     Cincinnati, NL (1956)
  193 New York AL (1960)
Game
  8 New York, AL (1939)
    Minnesota, AL (1963)
  8 Milwaukee, NL (1953)
    Cincinnati, NL (1956)
    San Francisco, NL (1961)

Inning
5 New York, NL (1939)
Philadelphia, NL (1949)
San Francisco, NL (1961)
5 Minnesota, AL (1966)

Bases on Balls
Season
835 Boston, AL (1949)
732 Brooklyn, NL (1947)
Game (extra innings)
20 Boston, AL (1920)
Game (nine innings)
19 Louisville, AA (1887)
18 Detroit, AL (1916)
Cleveland, AL (1948)
17 Chicago, NL (1887)
Brooklyn, NL (1903)
New York, NL (1944)
Inning
11 New York, AL (1949)
9 Cincinnati, NL (1957)

Strikeouts
Season (162-game schedule)
1203 New York, NL (1968)
1125 Washington, AL (1965)
Season (154-game schedule)
1054 Philadelphia, NL (1960)
883 Washington, AL (1960)
Game (extra innings)
26 California, AL (1971)
22 New York, NL (1964)
Cincinnati, NL (1972)
Game (nine innings)
19 Boston, NL (1884)
New York, NL (1969)
San Diego, NL (1970)
19 Boston, UA (1884)
19 Detroit, AL (1966)
Inning
4 Many, NL/AL

Hit Batsmen
Season (162-game schedule)
78 Montreal, MNL (1971)
Season (154-game schedule)
151 Baltimore, NL (1898)
80 Washington, AL (1911)
78 St. Louis, MNL (1910)
Game
6 Brooklyn, AA (1887)
6 New York, NL (1893)
6 New York, AL (1913)
5 Atlanta, MNL (1969)
Inning
3 Many, MNL/AL

Sacrifice Hits (1894–date)
Season (including sacrifice flies)
310 Boston, AL (1917)
270 Chicago, NL (1908)
Season (no sacrifice flies)
231 Chicago, NL (1906)
207 Chicago, AL (1906)
Game
8 New York, AL (1918)
Chicago, AL (1927)
St. Louis, AL (1928)
8 Cincinnati, NL (1926)

Inning
3 Cleveland, AL (1949)
Detroit, AL (1970)
3 Chicago, NL (1962)
Philadelphia, NL (1967)
Los Angeles, NL (1972)

Stolen Bases (1886–date)
Season
638 Philadelphia, AA (1887)
426 New York, NL (1893)
347 New York, MNL (1911)
341 Oakland AL (1976)
Game
19 Philadelphia, AA (1890)
17 New York, NL (1890)
15 New York, AL (1911)
11 New York, MNL (1912)
St. Louis, MNL (1916)

Left on Base
Season (162-game schedule)
1328 Cincinnati NL (1976)
Season (154-game schedule)
1334 St. Louis, AL (1941)
1278 Brooklyn, NL (1947)
Game (extra innings)
27 Atlanta, NL (1973)
24 Cleveland, AL (1932)
Game (nine innings)
20 New York, AL (1956)
18 Baltimore, AA (1891)
18 Many, NL

Runs scored at home
Season
625 Boston, AL (1950)
543 Philadelphia, NL (1930)

Runs scored on road
Season
591 New York, AL (1930)
492 Chicago, NL (1929)

Runs allowed at home
Season
644 Philadelphia, NL (1930)
561 St. Louis, AL (1939)

Runs allowed on road
Season
555 Philadelphia, NL (1930)
523 Philadelphia, AL (1940)

TEAM FIELDING RECORDS

Putouts
Season (162-game schedule)
4520 New York, AL (1964)
4473 Los Angeles, NL (1973)
Season (154-game schedule)
4396 Cleveland, AL (1910)
4359 Philadelphia, NL (1913)

Assists
Season
2446 Chicago, AL (1907)
2293 St. Louis, NL (1917)
Game (extra innings)
41 Boston, NL (1920)

38 Detroit, AL (1945)
  Washington, AL (1967)
Game (nine innings)
  28 Pittsburgh, NL (1911)
  27 St. Louis, AL (1919)
Inning
  10 Cleveland, AL, 1921)
     Boston, AL (1952)
   8 Boston, NL (1911)

Errors
Season
  867 Washington, NL (1886)
  425 Detroit, AL (1901)
  408 Brooklyn, MNL (1905)
Game
  24 Boston, NL (1876)
  12 Detroit, AL (1901)
     Chicago, AL (1903)
  11 St. Louis, MNL (1902 and 1909)
     Boston, MNL (1906)
Inning
   7 Cleveland, AL (1905)
   6 Pittsburgh, MNL (1903)

Double Plays
Season (162-game schedule)
  215 Pittsburgh, NL (1966)
Season (154-game schedule)
  217 Philadelphia, AL (1949)
  198 Los Angeles, NL (1958)
Game
   7 New York, AL (1942)
   7 Houston, NL (1969)

Triple Plays
Season
   3 Cincinnati, AA (1882)
     Rochester, AA (1890)
   3 Detroit, AL (1911)
     Boston, AL (1924)
   3 Philadelphia, NL (1964)
     Chicago, NL (1965)

Fielding Average
Season
  .9847 Baltimore, AL (1964)
  .9837 Cincinnati NL (1975)

GENERAL TEAM RECORDS

World Series Won
  20 New York, AL
   8 St Louis, NL
Pennants Won
  29 New York, AL
  17 New York Giants, NL
  16 New York Giants, MNL
  Note: The Giants also won one pennant in
  San Francisco.

Games Won —Season
  116 Chicago, NL (1906)
  111 Cleveland, AL (1954)
Games Lost
Season (162-game schedule)
  120 New York, MNL (1962)
Season (154-game schedule)
  134 Cleveland, NL (1899)
  117 Philadelphia, AL (1916)
  115 Boston, MNL (1935)
Shutouts Won—Season
  32 Chicago, NL (1907 and 1909)
  30 Chicago, AL (1906)
Shutouts Lost—Season
  33 St. Louis, NL (1908)
  29 Washington, AL (1909)
Longest Game (innings)
  26 Bro. vs. Bos., NL (1920)
  24 Phi. vs. Bos., AL (1906)
     Det. vs. Phi., AL (1945)
Longest Game (time) extra innings
  7:23 S.F. vs. N.Y., NL (1964)
  7:00 N.Y., vs. Det., AL (1962)
Longest Game (time) nine innings
  4:18 L.A. vs. S.F., NL (1962)
  3:54 Det. vs. K.C., AL (1961)
Shortest Game (time) nine innings
  0:51 N.Y. vs. Phi., NL (1919)
  0:55 St.L. vs. N.Y., AL (1926)
Players Used
Season (162-game schedule)
  54 New York, NL (1967)
Season (154-game schedule)
  56 Philadelphia, AL (1915)
  53 Brooklyn, NL (1944)
Game (extra innings)
  30 Oakland, AL (1972)
  27 Philadelphia NL (1974)
     Chicago NL (1978)
Game (nine innings)
  27 Kansas City, AL (1969)
  25 St. Louis, NL (1959)
     Milwaukee, NL (1964)
Pitchers Used
Season (162-game schedule)
  27 New York, NL (1967)
Season (154-game schedule)
  27 Philadelphia, AL (1915)
     Kansas City, AL (1955)
  24 Cincinnati, NL (1912)
     Philadelphia, NL (1946)
Game (extra innings)
   9 Los Angeles, AL (1963)
     Minnesota, AL (1964)
     Washington, AL (1971)
     Cleveland, AL (1971)
   9 Cincinnati, NL (1962)
Game (nine innings)
   9 St. Louis, AL (1949)
   8 Many, NL

VI LEAGUE LEADERS

YEAR	LG	BATTING		RUNS		HITS		DOUBLES		TRIPLES	
1876	N	BARNES CHI	.404	BARNES CHI	126	BARNES CHI	138	BARNES CHI	23	HALL,ATH PIKE,STL	12
1877	N	J.WHITE BOS	.387	J.WHITE BOS	39	O'ROURKE BOS	89	ANSON CHI	20	JONES CIN	10
1878	N	DALRYMPLE MIL	.356	HIGHAM,PRO START,CHI	58	START CHI	97	BURDOCK BOS	17	HIGHAM PRO	16
1879	N	ANSON CHI	.407	JONES BOS	85	HINES PRO	145	EDEN CLE	26	DICKERSON CIN	14
1880	N	GORE CHI	.365	DALRYMPLE CHI	90	DALRYMPLE CHI	123	WILLIAMSON CHI	29	STOVEY WOR	13
1881	N	ANSON CHI	.399	GORE CHI	86	ANSON CHI	137	KELLY CHI	27	ROWE BUF	11
1882	N	BROUTHERS BUF	.367	GORE CHI	99	BROUTHERS BUF	129	KELLY CHI	34	CONNOR TRO	17
	AA	BROWNING LOU	.382	SWARTWOOD PIT	93	CARPENTER CIN	125	BROWNING LOU	18	TAYLOR PIT	12
1883	N	BROUTHERS BUF	.371	HORNUNG BOS	106	BROUTHERS BUF	156	WILLIAMSON CHI	50	BROUTHERS BUF	11
	AA	SWARTWOOD PIT	.369	STOVEY ATH	110	SWARTWOOD PIT	149	STOVEY ATH	30	SMITH COL	18
1884	N	O'ROURKE BUF	.350	KELLY CHI	120	DALRYMPLE CHI	160	HINES PRO	34	EWING NY	18
	AA	ESTERBROOK MET	.408	STOVEY ATH	126	ESTERBROOK MET	185	BARKLEY TOL	39	STOVEY ATH	25
	U	DUNLAP STL	.420	DUNLAP STL	157	DUNLAP STL	178	SHAFFER STL	38	ROWE STL	13
1885	N	CONNOR NY	.371	KELLY CHI	124	CONNOR NY	169	ANSON CHI	35	O'ROURKE NY	16
	AA	BROWNING LOU	.367	STOVEY ATH	128	BROWNING LOU	176	LARKIN ATH	40	KUEHNE PIT	20
1886	N	KELLY CHI	.388	KELLY CHI	155	RICHARDSON DET	189	BROUTHERS DET	38	CONNOR NY	20
	AA	ORR MET	.346	LATHAM STL	153	ORR MET	196	LARKIN ATH	34	ORR MET	33
1887	N	ANSON CHI	.421	BROUTHERS DET	153	BROUTHERS DET	239	BROUTHERS DET	33	CONNOR NY	24
	AA	O'NEILL STL	.492	O'NEILL STL	170	LYONS ATH	284	O'NEILL STL	46	O'NEILL STL	24
1888	N	ANSON CHI	.343	BROUTHERS DET	118	RYAN CHI	182	RYAN CHI	36	CONNOR NY	17
	AA	O'NEILL STL	.332	PINCKNEY BRO	133	O'NEILL STL	176	REILLY CIN	33	STOVEY ATH	21
1889	N	BROUTHERS BOS	.373	TIERNAN NY	146	GLASSCOCK IND	209	KELLY BOS	40	WILMOT WAS	18
	AA	TUCKER BAL	.375	STOVEY ATH	154	TUCKER BAL	198	WELCH ATH	38	HAMILTON KC	15
1890	N	GLASSCOCK NY	.336	COLLINS BRO	148	GLASSCOCK,NY THOMPSON,PH	172	THOMPSON PHI	38	REILLY CIN	26
	AA	WOLF LOU	.366	MC CARTHY STL	134	WOLF LOU	200	CHILDS SYR	32	JOHNSON,COL WERDEN,TOL	19
	P	BROWNING CLE	.391	DUFFY CHI	161	DUFFY CHI	194	BROWNING,CLE BECKLEY,PIT	41	SHINDLE PHI	25
1891	N	HAMILTON PHI	.338	HAMILTON PHI	142	HAMILTON PHI	179	GRIFFIN BRO	44	STOVEY BOS	22
	AA	BROUTHERS BOS	.352	BROWN BOS	170	BROUTHERS BOS	160	BROWN BOS	35	BROWN BOS	22
1892	N	CHILDS CLE	.335	CHILDS CLE	135	BROUTHERS BRO	197	CONNOR PHI	29	SHINDLE BAL	14
1893	N	DUFFY BOS	.378	LONG,BOS DUFFY,BOS	149	THOMPSON PHI	220	THOMPSON PHI	38	WERDEN STL	28
1894	N	DUFFY BOS	.438	HAMILTON PHI	196	DUFFY BOS	236	DUFFY BOS	46	THOMPSON,PHI REITZ,BAL	28
1895	N	BURKETT CLE	.423	HAMILTON PHI	166	BURKETT CLE	235	DELAHANTY PHI	49	THOMPSON,PHI COOLEY,STL	21
1896	N	BURKETT CLE	.410	BURKETT CLE	159	BURKETT CLE	240	MILLER CIN	35	DAHLEN CHI	21

HOME RUNS	RUNS BATTED IN	STOLEN BASES	STRIKEOUTS	WON-LOST PCT.	EARNED RUN AVE.	
HALL ATH 5			SPALDING CHI 115	SPALDING CHI 46-14		76
PIKE CIN 4			BOND BOS 123	BOND BOS 40-17		77
MC KELVY IND 9			BOND BOS 177	BOND BOS 40-19		78
JONES BOS 9			WARD PRO 271	WARD PRO 44-18		79
O'ROURKE,BOS STOVEY,WOR 6			GOLDSMITH CHI 178	GOLDSMITH CHI 22-3		80
BROUTHERS BUF 8			CORCORAN CHI 252	CORCORAN CHI 31-14		81
WOOD DET 7			KEEFE TRO 289	CORCORAN CHI 27-13		82
WALKER STL 7			MULLANE LOU 281	WHITE CIN 40-12		
EWING NY 9			WHITNEY BOS 308	MC CORMICK CLE 27-13		83
STOVEY ATH 14			KEEFE MET 360	MATHEWS ATH 30-14		
WILLIAMSON CHI 27			RADBOURN PRO 411	RADBOURN PRO 60-12		84
STOVEY,ATH REILLY,CIN 11			HECKER LOU 368	LYNCH MET 39-14		
DUNLAP,STL CRANE,BOS 13			DALY CHI-PIT 464	TAYLOR STL 24-2		
DALRYMPLE CHI 11			CLARKSON CHI 333	WELCH NY 47-11		85
STOVEY ATH 13			MORRIS PIT 303	CARUTHERS STL 40-13		
RICHARDSON DET 11		ANDREWS PHI 56	BALDWIN DET 340	FLYNN CHI 24-6		86
MC PHEE CIN 8		STOVEY ATH 96	KILROY BAL 505	FOUTZ STL 41-16		
W.O'BRIEN WAS 19		WARD NY 111	CLARKSON CHI 227	GETZEIN DET 29-13		87
O'NEILL STL 13		STOVEY ATH 143	RAMSEY LOU 348	CARUTHERS STL 29-9		
RYAN CHI 16		HOY WAS 82	KEEFE NY 334	KEEFE NY 35-12		88
REILLY CIN 12		STOVEY ATH 156	SEWARD ATH 219	HUDSON STL 26-10		
THOMPSON,PHI DENNY,IND 17		FOGARTY PHI 99	CLARKSON BOS 292	CLARKSON BOS 48-19		89
HOLLIDAY,CIN STOVEY,ATH 19		HAMILTON KC 117	BALDWIN COL 368	CARUTHERS BRO 40-12		
TIERNAN NY 14		HAMILTON PHI 102	RUSIE NY 345	LOVETT BRO 31-11		90
CAMPAU STL 9		WELCH ATH-BAL 95	RAMSEY STL 234	STRATTON LOU 34-15		
RICHARDSON,BOS CONNOR,NY 13		BROWN BOS 87	BALDWIN CHI 200	GUMBERT BOS 22-9		
STOVEY,BOS TIERNAN,NY 16		HAMILTON PHI 115	RUSIE NY 321	HUTCHINSON CHI 43-19		91
FARRELL BOS 12		BROWN BOS 110	STIVETTS STL 232	BUFFINGTON BOS 27-9 / HADDOCK BOS 33-11		
HOLLIDAY CIN 9		WARD BRO 94	RUSIE NY 303	YOUNG CLE 36-11		92
DELAHANTY PHI 19		WARD NY 72	RUSIE NY 208	GASTRIGHT PIT-BOS 15-6		93
DUFFY BOS 18		HAMILTON PHI 99	RUSIE NY 204	MEEKIN NY 36-10		94
THOMPSON PHI 18		HAMILTON PHI 95	RUSIE NY 199	HOFFER BAL 29-8		95
DELAHANTY PHI 13		LANGE CHI 100	YOUNG CLE 137	HOFFER BAL 26-7		96

YEAR	LG	BATTING		RUNS		HITS		DOUBLES		TRIPLES	
1897	N	KEELER BAL	.432	HAMILTON BOS	153	KEELER BAL	243	BECKLEY CIN	38	DAVIS PIT	28
1898	N	KEELER BAL	.379	MC GRAW BAL	142	BURKETT CLE	215	LAJOIE PHI	43	ANDERSON BRO	20
1899	N	DELAHANTY PHI	.408	KEELER BRO	141	DELAHANTY PHI	234	DELAHANTY PHI	56	WILLIAMS PIT	27
1900	N	WAGNER PIT	.381	THOMAS PHI	131	VAN HALTREN NY	181	WAGNER PIT	45	WAGNER PIT	22
1901	N	BURKETT STL	.382	BURKETT STL	139	BURKETT STL	228	BECKLEY CIN	39	SHECKARD BRO	21
	A	LAJOIE PHI	.422	LAJOIE PHI	145	LAJOIE PHI	229	LAJOIE PHI	48	WILLIAMS BAL	22
1902	N	BEAUMONT PIT	.357	WAGNER PIT	105	BEAUMONT PIT	194	WAGNER PIT	32	CRAWFORD CIN	23
	A	DELAHANTY WAS	.376	FULTZ PHI	110	HICKMAN CLE	194	DAVIS PHI	43	WILLIAMS BAL	23
1903	N	WAGNER PIT	.355	BEAUMONT PIT	137	BEAUMONT PIT	209	STEINFELDT,CIN CLARKE,PIT MERTES,NY	32	WAGNER PIT	19
	A	LAJOIE CLE	.355	DOUGHERTY BOS	108	DOUGHERTY BOS	195	SEYBOLD PHI	43	CRAWFORD DET	25
1904	N	WAGNER PIT	.349	BROWNE NY	99	BECKLEY STL	179	WAGNER PIT	44	LUMLEY BRO	18
	A	LAJOIE CLE	.381	DOUGHERTY BOS-NY	113	LAJOIE CLE	211	LAJOIE CLE	50	STAHL BOS	22
1905	N	SEYMOUR CIN	.377	DONLIN NY	124	SEYMOUR CIN	219	SEYMOUR CIN	40	SEYMOUR CIN	21
	A	FLICK CLE	.306	DAVIS PHI	92	STONE STL	187	DAVIS PHI	47	FLICK CLE	19
1906	N	WAGNER PIT	.339	CHANCE,CHI WAGNER,PIT	103	STEINFELDT CHI	176	WAGNER PIT	38	CLARKE,PIT SCHULTE,CHI	13
	A	STONE STL	.358	FLICK CLE	98	LAJOIE CLE	214	LAJOIE CLE	49	FLICK CLE	22
1907	N	WAGNER PIT	.350	SHANNON NY	104	BEAUMONT BOS	187	WAGNER PIT	38	ALPERMAN,BRO GANZEL,CIN	16
	A	COBB DET	.350	CRAWFORD DET	102	COBB DET	212	DAVIS PHI	37	FLICK CLE	18
1908	N	WAGNER PIT	.354	TENNEY NY	101	WAGNER PIT	201	WAGNER PIT	39	WAGNER PIT	19
	A	COBB DET	.324	MC INTYRE DET	105	COBB DET	188	COBB DET	36	COBB DET	20
1909	N	WAGNER PIT	.339	LEACH PIT	126	DOYLE NY	172	WAGNER PIT	39	MITCHELL CIN	17
	A	COBB DET	.377	COBB DET	116	COBB DET	216	CRAWFORD DET	35	BAKER PHI	19
1910	N	MAGEE PHI	.331	MAGEE PHI	110	BYRNE,PIT WAGNER,PIT	178	BYRNE PIT	43	MITCHELL CIN	18
	A	COBB DET	.385	COBB DET	106	LAJOIE CLE	227	LAJOIE CLE	51	CRAWFORD DET	19
1911	N	WAGNER PIT	.334	SHECKARD CHI	121	MILLER BOS	192	KONETCHY STL	38	DOYLE NY	25
	A	COBB DET	.420	COBB DET	147	COBB DET	248	COBB DET	47	COBB DET	24
1912	N	ZIMMERMAN CHI	.372	BESCHER CIN	120	ZIMMERMAN CHI	207	ZIMMERMAN CHI	41	WILSON PIT	36
	A	COBB DET	.410	COLLINS PHI	137	COBB DET	227	SPEAKER BOS	53	JACKSON CLE	26
1913	N	DAUBERT BRO	.350	CAREY,PIT LEACH,PIT	99	CRAVATH PHI	179	SMITH BRO	40	SAIER CHI	21
	A	COBB DET	.390	COLLINS PHI	125	JACKSON CLE	197	JACKSON CLE	39	CRAWFORD DET	23
1914	N	DAUBERT BRO	.329	BURNS NY	100	MAGEE PHI	171	MAGEE PHI	39	CAREY PIT	17
	A	COBB DET	.368	COLLINS PHI	122	SPEAKER BOS	193	SPEAKER BOS	46	CRAWFORD DET	26
	F	KAUFF IND	.366	KAUFF IND	118	KAUFF IND	210	KAUFF IND	45	EVANS BRO	15

HOME RUNS	RUNS BATTED IN	STOLEN BASES	STRIKEOUTS	WON-LOST PCT.	EARNED RUN AVE.	
DELAHANTY PHI 29		LANGE CHI 83	MC JAMES WAS 161	RUSIE NY 28- 8		97
COLLINS BOS 15		F.CLARKE LOU 66	SEYMOUR NY 249	LEWIS BOS 25- 8		98
FREEMAN WAS 25		SHECKARD BAL 78	HAHN CIN 147	HUGHES BRO 25- 5		99
LONG BOS 12		BARRETT CIN 46	WADDELL PIT 133	MC GINNITY BRO 29- 9		00
CRAWFORD CIN 16		WAGNER PIT 48	HAHN CIN 237	CHESBRO PIT 21- 9		01
LAJOIE PHI 13		ISBELL CHI 48	YOUNG BOS 163	YOUNG BOS 31-10		
LEACH PIT 6		WAGNER PIT 43	WILLIS BOS 219	CHESBRO PIT 27- 6		02
SEYBOLD PHI 16		HARTSEL PHI 54	WADDELL PHI 210	WADDELL PHI 24- 7		
SHECKARD BRO 9		SHECKARD,BRO CHANCE,CHI 67	MATHEWSON NY 267	LEEVER PIT 25- 7		03
FREEMAN BOS 13		BAY CLE 46	WADDELL PHI 301	MOORE CLE 22- 7		
LUMLEY BRO 9		WAGNER PIT 53	MATHEWSON NY 212	MC GINNITY NY 35- 8		04
DAVIS PHI 10		FLICK CLE 42	WADDELL PHI 349	CHESBRO NY 41-13		
ODWELL CIN 9		MALONEY,CHI DEVLIN,NY 59	MATHEWSON NY 206	MATHEWSON NY 32- 8		05
DAVIS PHI 8		HOFFMAN PHI 46	WADDELL PHI 286	COAKLEY PHI 20- 8		
JORDAN BRO 12		CHANCE CHI 57	BEEBE CHI-STL 171	REULBACH CHI 19- 4		06
DAVIS PHI 12		ANDERSON,WAS FLICK,CLE 39	WADDELL PHI 203	PLANK PHI 19- 6		
BRAIN BOS 10	WAGNER PIT 91	WAGNER PIT 61	MATHEWSON NY 178	REULBACH CHI 17- 4		07
DAVIS PHI 8	COBB DET 116	COBB DET 49	WADDELL PHI 226	DONOVAN DET 25- 4		
JORDAN BRO 12	WAGNER PIT 106	WAGNER PIT 53	MATHEWSON NY 259	REULBACH CHI 24- 7		08
CRAWFORD DET 7	COBB DET 101	DOUGHERTY CHI 47	WALSH CHI 269	WALSH CHI 40-15		
MURRAY NY 7	WAGNER PIT 102	BESCHER CIN 54	OVERALL CHI 205	MATHEWSON,NY S.CAMNITZ 25- 6 PIT		09
COBB DET 9	COBB DET 115	COBB DET 76	SMITH CHI 177	MULLIN DET 29- 8		
BECK,BOS SCHULTE,CHI 10	MAGEE PHI 116	BESCHER CIN 70	MOORE PHI 185	COLE CHI 20- 4		10
STAHL BOS 10	CRAWFORD DET 115	COLLINS PHI 81	JOHNSON WAS 313	BENDER PHI 23- 5		
SCHULTE CHI 21	SCHULTE CHI 121	BESCHER CIN 80	MARQUARD NY 237	MARQUARD NY 24- 7		11
BAKER PHI 9	COBB DET 144	COBB DET 83	WALSH CHI 255	BENDER PHI 17- 5		
ZIMMERMAN CHI 14	ZIMMERMAN CHI 106	BESCHER CIN 67	ALEXANDER PHI 195	HENDRIX PIT 24- 9	TESREAU NY 1.96	12
BAKER PHI 10	BAKER PHI 133	MILAN WAS 88	JOHNSON WAS 303	WOOD BOS 34- 5		
CRAVATH PHI 19	CRAVATH PHI 129	CAREY PIT 61	SEATON PHI 168	HUMPHERIES CHI 16- 4	MATHEWSON NY 2.06	13
BAKER PHI 12	BAKER PHI 126	MILAN WAS 74	JOHNSON WAS 243	JOHNSON WAS 36- 7	JOHNSON WAS 1.09	
CRAVATH PHI 19	MAGEE PHI 101	BURNS NY 62	ALEXANDER PHI 214	JAMES BOS 26- 7	DOAK STL 1.72	14
CRAWFORD,DET BAKER,PHI 8	CRAWFORD DET 112	MAISEL NY 74	JOHNSON WAS 225	BENDER PHI 17- 3	LEONARD BOS 1.01	
ZWILLING CHI 16		KAUFF IND 75	FALKENBERG IND 245	FORD BUF 21- 6	KRAPP BUF 1.19	

YEAR	LG	BATTING	RUNS	HITS	DOUBLES	TRIPLES
1915	N	DOYLE NY .320	CRAVATH PHI 89	DOYLE NY 189	DOYLE NY 40	LONG STL 25
	A	COBB DET .370	COBB DET 144	COBB DET 208	VEACH DET 40	CRAWFORD DET 19
	F	KAUFF BRO .344	BORTON STL 99	TOBIN STL 186	CHASE BUF 33	KELLY,PIT MANN,CHI 19
1916	N	CHASE CIN .339	BURNS NY 105	CHASE CIN 184	NIEHOFF PHI 42	HINCHMAN PIT 16
	A	SPEAKER CLE .386	COBB DET 113	SPEAKER CLE 211	GRANEY,CLE SPEAKER,CLE 41	JACKSON CHI 21
1917	N	ROUSH CIN .341	BURNS NY 103	GROH CIN 182	GROH CIN 39	HORNSBY STL 17
	A	COBB DET .383	BUSH DET 112	COBB DET 225	COBB DET 44	COBB DET 23
1918	N	WHEAT BRO .335	GROH CIN 88	HOLLOCHER CHI 161	GROH CIN 28	DAUBERT BRO 15
	A	COBB DET .382	CHAPMAN CLE 84	BURNS PHI 178	SPEAKER CLE 33	COBB DET 14
1919	N	ROUSH CIN .321	BURNS NY 86	OLSON BRO 164	YOUNGS NY 31	SOUTHWORTH,PIT MYERS,BRO 14
	A	COBB DET .384	RUTH BOS 103	COBB,DET VEACH,DET 191	VEACH DET 45	VEACH DET 17
1920	N	HORNSBY STL .370	BURNS NY 115	HORNSBY STL 218	HORNSBY STL 44	MYERS BRO 22
	A	SISLER STL .407	RUTH NY 158	SISLER STL 257	SPEAKER CLE 50	JACKSON CHI 20
1921	N	HORNSBY STL .397	HORNSBY STL 131	HORNSBY STL 235	HORNSBY STL 44	HORNSBY,STL POWELL,BOS 18
	A	HEILMANN DET .394	RUTH NY 177	HEILMANN DET 237	SPEAKER CLE 52	SHANKS WAS 19
1922	N	HORNSBY STL .401	HORNSBY STL 141	HORNSBY STL 250	HORNSBY STL 46	DAUBERT CIN 22
	A	SISLER STL .420	SISLER STL 134	SISLER STL 246	SPEAKER CLE 48	SISLER STL 18
1923	N	HORNSBY STL .384	YOUNGS NY 121	FRISCH NY 223	ROUSH CIN 41	TRAYNOR,PIT CAREY,PIT 19
	A	HEILMANN DET .403	RUTH NY 151	JAMIESON CLE 222	SPEAKER CLE 59	GOSLIN,WAS RICE,WAS 18
1924	N	HORNSBY STL .424	HORNSBY,STL FRISCH,NY 121	HORNSBY STL 227	HORNSBY STL 43	ROUSH CIN 21
	A	RUTH NY .378	RUTH NY 143	RICE WAS 216	HEILMANN,DET J.SEWELL CLE 43	PIPP NY 19
1925	N	HORNSBY STL .403	CUYLER PIT 144	BOTTOMLEY STL 227	BOTTOMLEY STL 44	CUYLER PIT 26
	A	HEILMANN DET .393	MOSTIL CHI 135	SIMMONS PHI 253	MC MANUS STL 44	GOSLIN WAS 20
1926	N	HARGRAVE CIN .353	CUYLER PIT 113	BROWN BOS 201	BOTTOMLEY STL 40	P.WANER PIT 22
	A	MANUSH DET .378	RUTH NY 139	BURNS,CLE RICE,WAS 216	BURNS CLE 64	GEHRIG NY 20
1927	N	P.WANER PIT .380	L.WANER,PIT HORNSBY,NY 133	P.WANER PIT 237	STEPHENSON CHI 46	P.WANER PIT 17
	A	HEILMANN DET .398	RUTH NY 158	COMBS NY 231	GEHRIG NY 52	COMBS NY 23
1928	N	HORNSBY BOS .387	P.WANER PIT 142	LINDSTROM NY 231	P.WANER PIT 50	BOTTOMLEY STL 20
	A	GOSLIN WAS .379	RUTH NY 163	MANUSH STL 241	MANUSH,STL GEHRIG,NY 47	COMBS NY 21
1929	N	O'DOUL PHI .398	HORNSBY CHI 156	O'DOUL PHI 254	FREDERICK BRO 52	L.WANER PIT 20
	A	FONSECA CLE .369	GEHRINGER DET 131	ALEXANDER,DET GEHRINGER 215 DET	GEHRINGER,DET MANUSH,STL 45 JOHNSON,DET	GEHRINGER DET 19
1930	N	TERRY NY .401	KLEIN PHI 158	TERRY NY 254	KLEIN PHI 59	COMOROSKY PIT 23
	A	SIMMONS PHI .381	SIMMONS PHI 152	HODAPP CLE 225	HODAPP CLE 51	COMBS NY 22

HOME RUNS		RUNS BATTED IN		STOLEN BASES		STRIKEOUTS		WON-LOST PCT.		EARNED RUN AVE.		
CRAVATH PHI	24	CRAVATH PHI	118	CAREY PIT	36	ALEXANDER PHI	241	ALEXANDER PHI	31-10	ALEXANDER PHI	1.22	15
ROTH CHI-CLE	7	CRAWFORD DET	116	COBB DET	96	JOHNSON WAS	203	MC CONNELL CHI	25-10	WOOD BOS	1.49	
CHASE BUF	17			KAUFF BRO	54	DAVENPORT STL	228			PLANK STL	2.01	16
ROBERTSON,NY WILLIAMS,CH	12	CHASE CIN	84	CAREY PIT	63	ALEXANDER PHI	167	HUGHES BOS	16- 3	ALEXANDER PHI	1.55	
PIPP NY	12	PIPP NY	99	COBB DET	68	JOHNSON WAS	228	CICOTTE CHI	15- 7	RUTH BOS	1.75	17
ROBERTSON,NY CRAVATH,PHI	12	ZIMMERMAN	100	CAREY PIT	46	ALEXANDER PHI	201	SCHUPP NY	21- 7	ALEXANDER PHI	1.85	
PIPP NY	9	VEACH DET	115	COBB DET	55	JOHNSON WAS	185	RUSSELL CHI	15- 5	CICOTTE CHI	1.53	18
CRAVATH PHI	8	MERKLE CHI	71	CAREY PIT	58	VAUGHN CHI	148	HENDRIX CHI	20- 7	VAUGHN CHI	1.74	
RUTH,BOS WALKER,PHI	11	BURNS,PHI VEACH,DET	74	SISLER STL	45	JOHNSON WAS	162	JONES BOS	16- 5	JOHNSON WAS	1.28	19
CRAVATH PHI	12	MYERS BRO	72	BURNS NY	40	VAUGHN CHI	141	RUETHER CIN	19- 6	ALEXANDER PHI	1.72	
RUTH BOS	29	RUTH BOS	112	E.COLLINS CHI	33	JOHNSON WAS	147	CICOTTE CHI	29- 7	JOHNSON WAS	1.49	20
WILLIAMS PHI	15	HORNSBY,STL KELLY,NY	94	CAREY PIT	52	ALEXANDER CHI	173	GRIMES BRO	23-11	ALEXANDER CHI	1.91	
RUTH NY	54	RUTH NY	137	RICE WAS	62	COVELESKI CLE	133	BAGBY CLE	31-12	SHAWKEY NY	2.46	21
KELLY NY	23	HORNSBY STL	126	FRISCH NY	49	GRIMES BRO	136	DOAK STL	15- 6	DOAK STL	2.58	
RUTH NY	59	RUTH NY	171	SISLER STL	35	JOHNSON WAS	143	MAYS NY	27- 9	FABER CHI	2.48	22
HORNSBY STL	42	HORNSBY STL	152	CAREY PIT	51	VANCE BRO	134	DONOHUE CIN	18- 9	RYAN NY	3.00	
WILLIAMS STL	39	WILLIAMS STL	155	SISLER STL	51	SHOCKER STL	149	BUSH NY	26- 7	FABER CHI	2.81	23
WILLIAMS PHI	41	MEUSEL NY	125	CAREY PIT	51	VANCE BRO	197	LUQUE CIN	27- 8	LUQUE CIN	1.93	
RUTH NY	41	RUTH NY	131	COLLINS CHI	49	JOHNSON WAS	126	PENNOCK NY *	19- 6	COVELESKI CLE	2.76	24
FOURNIER BRO	27	KELLY NY	136	CAREY PIT	49	VANCE BRO	262	YDE PIT	16- 3	VANCE BRO	2.16	
RUTH NY	46	GOSLIN WAS	129	COLLINS CHI	42	JOHNSON WAS	158	JOHNSON WAS	23- 7	JOHNSON WAS	2.72	
HORNSBY STL	39	HORNSBY STL	143	CAREY PIT	46	VANCE BRO	221	SHERDEL STL	15- 6	LUQUE CIN	2.63	25
MEUSEL NY	33	MEUSEL NY	138	MOSTIL CHI	43	GROVE PHI	116	COVELESKI WAS	20- 5	COVELESKI WAS	2.84	
WILSON CHI	21	BOTTOMLEY STL	120	CUYLER PIT	35	VANCE BRO	140	KREMER PIT	20- 6	KREMER PIT	2.61	26
RUTH NY	47	RUTH NY	145	MOSTIL CHI	35	GROVE PHI	194	UHLE CLE	27-11	GROVE PHI	2.51	
WILLIAMS,PHI WILSON,CHI	30	P.WANER PIT	131	FRISCH STL	48	VANCE BRO	184	BENTON BOS	17- 7	KREMER PIT	2.47	27
RUTH NY	60	GEHRIG NY	175	SISLER STL	27	GROVE PHI	174	HOYT NY	22- 7	MOORE NY	2.28	
BOTTOMLEY,STL WILSON,CHI	31	BOTTOMLEY STL	136	CUYLER CHI	37	VANCE BRO	200	BENTON NY	25- 9	VANCE BRO	2.09	28
RUTH NY	54	GEHRIG,NY RUTH,NY	142	MYER BOS	30	GROVE PHI	183	CROWDER STL	21- 5	BRAXTON WAS	2.52	
KLEIN PHI	43	WILSON CHI	159	CUYLER CHI	43	MALONE CHI	166	ROOT CHI	19- 6	WALKER NY	3.08	29
RUTH NY	46	SIMMONS PHI	157	GEHRINGER DET	27	GROVE PHI	170	GROVE PHI	20- 6	ZACHARY NY	2.47	
WILSON CHI	56	WILSON CHI	190	CUYLER CHI	37	HALLAHAN STL	177	FITZSIMMONS NY	19- 7	VANCE BRO	2.61	30
RUTH NY	49	GEHRIG NY	174	MC MANUS DET	23	GROVE PHI	209	GROVE PHI	28- 5	GROVE PHI	2.54 *	

YEAR	LG	BATTING		RUNS		HITS		DOUBLES		TRIPLES	
1931	N	HAFEY STL	.349	KLEIN,PHI TERRY,NY	121	L.WANER PIT	214	ADAMS STL	46	TERRY NY	20
	A	SIMMONS PHI	.390	GEHRIG NY	163	GEHRIG NY	211	WEBB BOS	67	JOHNSON DET	19
1932	N	O'DOUL BRO	.368	KLEIN PHI	152	KLEIN PHI	226	P.WANER PIT	62	HERMAN CIN	19
	A	ALEXANDER DET-BOS	.367	FOXX PHI	151	SIMMONS PHI	216	MC NAIR PHI	47	CRONIN WAS	18
1933	N	KLEIN PHI	.368	MARTIN STL	122	KLEIN PHI	223	KLEIN PHI	44	VAUGHAN PIT	19
	A	FOXX PHI	.356	GEHRIG NY	138	MANUSH WAS	221	CRONIN WAS	45	MANUSH WAS	17
1934	N	P.WANER PIT	.362	P.WANER PIT	122	P.WANER PIT	217	CUYLER,CHI ALLEN,PHI	42	MEDWICK STL	18
	A	GEHRIG NY	.363	GEHRINGER DET	134	GEHRINGER DET	214	GREENBERG DET	63	CHAPMAN NY	13
1935	N	VAUGHAN PIT	.385	GALAN CHI	133	HERMAN CHI	227	HERMAN CHI	57	GOODMAN CIN	18
	A	MYER WAS	.349	GEHRIG NY	125	VOSMIK CLE	216	VOSMIK CLE	47	VOSMIK CLE	20
1936	N	P.WANER PIT	.373	VAUGHAN PIT	122	MEDWICK STL	223	MEDWICK STL	64	GOODMAN CIN	14
	A	APPLING CHI	.388	GEHRIG NY	167	AVERILL CLE	232	GEHRINGER DET	60	DI MAGGIO,NY ROLFE,NY AVERILL,CLE	15
1937	N	MEDWICK STL	.374	MEDWICK STL	111	MEDWICK STL	237	MEDWICK STL	56	VAUGHAN PIT	17
	A	GEHRINGER DET	.371	DI MAGGIO NY	151	BELL STL	218	BELL STL	51	KREEVICH,CHI WALKER,CHI	16
1938	N	LOMBARDI CIN	.342	OTT NY	116	MC CORMICK CIN	209	MEDWICK STL	47	MIZE STL	16
	A	FOXX BOS	.349	GREENBERG DET	144	VOSMIK BOS	201	CRONIN BOS	51	HEATH CLE	18
1939	N	MIZE STL	.349	WERBER CIN	115	MC CORMICK CIN	209	SLAUGHTER STL	52	HERMAN CHI	18
	A	DI MAGGIO NY	.381	ROLFE NY	139	ROLFE NY	213	ROLFE NY	46	LEWIS WAS	16
1940	N	GARMS PIT	.355	VAUGHAN PIT	113	MC CORMICK,CIN HACK,CHI	191	F.MC CORMICK CIN	44	VAUGHAN PIT	15
	A	DI MAGGIO NY	.352	WILLIAMS BOS	134	MC COSKY,DET CRAMER,BOS 200 RADCLIFF,STL		GREENBERG DET	50	MC COSKY DET	19
1941	N	REISER BRO	.343	REISER BRO	117	HACK CHI	186	REISER,BRO MIZE,STL	39	REISER BRO	17
	A	WILLIAMS BOS	.406	WILLIAMS BOS	135	TRAVIS WAS	218	BOUDREAU CLE	45	HEATH CLE	20
1942	N	LOMBARDI BOS	.330	OTT NY	118	SLAUGHTER STL	188	MARION STL	38	SLAUGHTER STL	17
	A	WILLIAMS BOS	.356	WILLIAMS BOS	141	PESKY BOS	205	KOLLOWAY CHI	40	SPENCE WAS	15
1943	N	MUSIAL STL	.357	VAUGHAN BRO	112	MUSIAL STL	220	MUSIAL STL	48	MUSIAL STL	20
	A	APPLING CHI	.328	CASE WAS	102	WAKEFIELD DET	200	WAKEFIELD DET	38	LINDELL,NY MOSES,CHI	12
1944	N	WALKER BRO	.357	NICHOLSON CHI	116	CAVARETTA,CHI MUSIAL,STL	197	MUSIAL STL	51	BARRETT PIT	19
	A	BOUDREAU CLE	.327	STIRNWEISS NY	125	STIRNWEISS NY	205	BOUDREAU CLE	45	STIRNWEISS,NY LINDELL,NY	16
1945	N	CAVARETTA CHI	.355	STANKY BRO	128	HOLMES BOS	224	HOLMES BOS	47	OLMO BRO	13
	A	STIRNWEISS NY	.309	STIRNWEISS NY	107	STIRNWEISS NY	195	MOSES CHI	35	STIRNWEISS NY	22
1946	N	MUSIAL STL	.365	MUSIAL STL	124	MUSIAL STL	228	MUSIAL STL	50	MUSIAL STL	20
	A	VERNON WAS	.353	WILLIAMS BOS	142	PESKY BOS	208	VERNON WAS	51	EDWARDS CLE	16

HOME RUNS	RUNS BATTED IN	STOLEN BASES	STRIKEOUTS	WON-LOST PCT.	EARNED RUN AVE.	
KLEIN PHI 31	KLEIN PHI 121	FRISCH STL 28	HALLAHAN STL 159	DERRINGER STL 18-8	WALKER NY 2.26	31
GEHRIG,NY RUTH,NY 46	GEHRIG NY 184	CHAPMAN NY 61	GROVE PHI 175	GROVE PHI 31-4	GROVE PHI 2.05	
KLEIN,PHI OTT,NY 38	HURST PHI 143	KLEIN PHI 20	DEAN STL 191	WARNEKE CHI 22-6	WARNEKE CHI 2.37	32
FOXX PHI 58	FOXX PHI 169	CHAPMAN NY 38	RUFFING NY 190	ALLEN NY 17-4	GROVE PHI 2.84	
KLEIN PHI 28	KLEIN PHI 120	MARTIN STL 26	DEAN STL 199	CANTWELL BOS 20-10	HUBBELL NY 1.66	33
FOXX PHI 48	FOXX PHI 163	CHAPMAN NY 27	GOMEZ NY 163	GROVE PHI 24-8	PEARSON CLE 2.35	
COLLINS,STL OTT,NY 35	OTT NY 135	MARTIN STL 23	J.DEAN STL 195	J.DEAN STL 30-7	HUBBELL NY 2.30	34
GEHRIG NY 49	GEHRIG NY 165	WERBER BOS 40	GOMEZ NY 158	GOMEZ NY 26-5	GOMEZ NY 2.33	
BERGER BOS 34	BERGER BOS 130	GALAN CHI 22	J.DEAN STL 182	LEE CHI 20-6	BLANTON PIT 2.59	35
GREENBERG,DET FOXX,PHI 36	GREENBERG DET 170	WERBER BOS 29	BRIDGES DET 163	AUKER DET 18-7	GROVE BOS 2.70	
OTT NY 33	MEDWICK STL 138	J.MARTIN STL 23	MUNGO BRO 238	HUBBELL NY 26-6	HUBBELL NY 2.31	36
GEHRIG NY 49	TROSKY CLE 162	LARY STL 37	BRIDGES DET 175	PEARSON NY 19-7	GROVE BOS 2.81	
MEDWICK,STL OTT,NY 31	MEDWICK STL 154	GALAN CHI 23	HUBBELL NY 159	HUBBELL NY 22-8	TURNER BOS 2.38	37
DI MAGGIO NY 46	GREENBERG DET 183	CHAPMAN,WAS-BOS WERBER,PHI 35	GOMEZ NY 194	ALLEN CLE 15-1	GOMEZ NY 2.33	
OTT NY 36	MEDWICK STL 122	HACK CHI 16	BRYANT CHI 135	LEE CHI 22-9	LEE CHI 2.66	38
GREENBERG DET 58	FOXX BOS 175	CROSETTI NY 27	FELLER CLE 240	RUFFING NY 21-7	GROVE BOS 3.07	
MIZE STL 28	MC CORMICK CIN 128	HANDLEY,PIT HACK,CHI 17	PASSEAU,PHI-CHI WALTERS,CIN 137	DERRINGER CIN 25-7	WALTERS CIN 2.29	39
FOXX BOS 35	WILLIAMS BOS 145	CASE WAS 51	FELLER CLE 246	GROVE BOS 15-4	GROVE BOS 2.54	
MIZE STL 43	MIZE STL 137	FREY CIN 22	HIGBE PHI 137	FITZSIMMONS BRO 16-2	WALTERS CIN 2.48	40
GREENBERG DET 41	GREENBERG DET 150	CASE WAS 35	FELLER CLE 261	ROWE DET 16-3	FELLER CLE 2.62	
CAMILLI BRO 34	CAMILLI BRO 120	MURTAUGH PHI 18	VANDER MEER CIN 202	E.RIDDLE CIN 19-4	E.RIDDLE CIN 2.24	41
WILLIAMS BOS 37	DI MAGGIO NY 125	CASE WAS 33	FELLER CLE 260	GOMEZ NY 15-5	LEE CHI 2.37	
OTT NY 30	MIZE NY 110	REISER BRO 20	VANDER MEER CIN 186	FRENCH BRO 15-4	M.COOPER STL 1.77	42
WILLIAMS BOS 36	WILLIAMS BOS 137	CASE WAS 44	HUGHSON,BOS NEWSOM,WAS 113	BONHAM NY 21-5	LYONS CHI 2.10	
NICHOLSON CHI 29	NICHOLSON CHI 128	VAUGHAN BRO 20	VANDER MEER CIN 174	M.COOPER STL 21-8	POLLET STL 1.75	43
YORK DET 34	YORK DET 118	CASE WAS 61	REYNOLDS CLE 151	CHANDLER NY 20-4	CHANDLER NY 1.64	
NICHOLSON CHI 33	NICHOLSON CHI 122	BARRETT PIT 28	VOISELLE NY 161	WILKS STL 17-4	HEUSSER CIN 2.38	44
ETTEN NY 22	STEPHENS STL 109	STIRNWEISS NY 55	NEWHOUSER DET 187	HUGHSON BOS 18-5	TROUT DET 2.12	
HOLMES BOS 28	WALKER BRO 124	SCHOENDIENST STL 26	ROE PIT 148	BRECHEEN STL 15-4	BOROWY CHI 2.14	45
STEPHENS STL 24	ETTEN NY 111	STIRNWEISS NY 33	NEWHOUSER DET 212	NEWHOUSER DET 25-9	NEWHOUSER DET 1.81	
KINER PIT 23	SLAUGHTER STL 130	REISER BRO 34	SCHMITZ CHI 135	DICKSON STL 15-6	POLLET STL 2.10	46
GREENBERG DET 44	GREENBERG DET 127	CASE CLE 28	FELLER CLE 348	FERRISS BOS 25-6	NEWHOUSER DET 1.94	

YEAR	LG	BATTING			RUNS			HITS			DOUBLES			TRIPLES		
1947	N	WALKER	STL-PHI	.363	MIZE	NY	137	HOLMES	BOS	191	MILLER	CIN	38	WALKER	STL-PHI	16
	A	WILLIAMS	BOS	.343	WILLIAMS	BOS	125	PESKY	BOS	207	BOUDREAU	CLE	45	HENRICH	NY	13
1948	N	MUSIAL	STL	.376	MUSIAL	STL	135	MUSIAL	STL	230	MUSIAL	STL	46	MUSIAL	STL	18
	A	WILLIAMS	BOS	.369	HENRICH	NY	138	DILLINGER	STL	207	WILLIAMS	BOS	44	HENRICH	NY	14
1949	N	ROBINSON	BRO	.342	REESE	BRO	132	MUSIAL	STL	207	MUSIAL	STL	41	SLAUGHTER,STL MUSIAL,STL		13
	A	KELL	DET	.343	WILLIAMS	BOS	150	MITCHELL	CLE	203	WILLIAMS	BOS	39	MITCHELL	CLE	23
1950	N	MUSIAL	STL	.346	TORGESON	BOS	120	SNIDER	BRO	199	SCHOENDIENST	STL	43	ASHBURN	PHI	14
	A	GOODMAN	BOS	.354	DI MAGGIO	BOS	131	KELL	DET	218	KELL	DET	56	DI MAGGIO,BOS DOERR,BOS EVERS,DET		11
1951	N	MUSIAL	STL	.355	MUSIAL,STL KINER,PIT		124	ASHBURN	PHI	221	DARK	NY	41	MUSIAL,STL BELL,PIT		12
	A	FAIN	PHI	.344	DI MAGGIO	BOS	113	KELL	DET	191	KELL,DET MELE,WAS YOST,WAS		48	MINOSO	CLE-CHI	14
1952	N	MUSIAL	STL	.336	MUSIAL,STL HEMUS,STL		105	MUSIAL	STL	194	MUSIAL	STL	42	THOMSON	NY	14
	A	FAIN	PHI	.327	DOBY	CLE	104	FOX	CHI	192	FAIN	PHI	43	AVILA	CLE	11
1953	N	FURILLO	BRO	.344	SNIDER	BRO	132	ASHBURN	PHI	205	MUSIAL	STL	53	GILLIAM	BRO	17
	A	VERNON	WAS	.337	ROSEN	CLE	115	KUENN	DET	209	VERNON	WAS	43	RIVERA	CHI	16
1954	N	MAYS	NY	.345	MUSIAL,STL SNIDER,BRO		120	MUELLER	NY	212	MUSIAL	STL	41	MAYS	NY	13
	A	AVILA	CLE	.341	MANTLE	NY	129	KUENN,DET FOX,CHI		201	VERNON	WAS	33	MINOSO	CHI	18
1955	N	ASHBURN	PHI	.338	SNIDER	BRO	126	KLUSZEWSKI	CIN	192	LOGAN,MIL AARON,MIL		37	MAYS,NY LONG,PIT		13
	A	KALINE	DET	.340	SMITH	CLE	123	KALINE	DET	200	KUENN	DET	38	MANTLE,NY CAREY,NY		11
1956	N	AARON	MIL	.328	ROBINSON	CIN	122	AARON	MIL	200	AARON	MIL	34	BRUTON	MIL	15
	A	MANTLE	NY	.353	MANTLE	NY	132	KUENN	DET	196	PIERSALL	BOS	40	JENSEN,BOS LEMON,WAS MINOSO,CHI SIMPSON,KC		11
1957	N	MUSIAL	STL	.351	AARON	MIL	118	SCHOENDIENST	NY-MIL	200	HOAK	CIN	39	MAYS	NY	20
	A	WILLIAMS	BOS	.388	MANTLE	NY	121	FOX	CHI	196	GARDNER,BAL MINOSO,CHI		36	MC DOUGALD,NY BAUER,NY SIMPSON KC-NY		9
1958	N	ASHBURN	PHI	.350	MAYS	SF	121	ASHBURN	PHI	215	CEPEDA	SF	38	ASHBURN	PHI	13
	A	WILLIAMS	BOS	.328	MANTLE	NY	127	FOX	CHI	187	KUENN	DET	39	POWER	KC-CLE	10
1959	N	AARON	MIL	.355	PINSON	CIN	131	AARON	MIL	223	PINSON	CIN	47	MOON,LA NEAL,LA		11
	A	KUENN	DET	.353	YOST	DET	115	KUENN	DET	198	KUENN	DET	42	ALLISON	WAS	9
1960	N	GROAT	PIT	.325	BRUTON	MIL	112	MAYS	SF	190	PINSON	CIN	37	BRUTON	MIL	13
	A	RUNNELS	BOS	.320	MANTLE	NY	119	MINOSO	CHI	184	FRANCONA	CLE	36	FOX	CHI	10
1961	N	CLEMENTE	PIT	.351	MAYS	SF	129	PINSON	CIN	208	AARON	MIL	39	ALTMAN	CHI	12
	A	CASH	DET	.361	MANTLE,NY MARIS,NY		132	CASH	DET	193	KALINE	DET	41	WOOD	DET	14

HOME RUNS	RUNS BATTED IN	STOLEN BASES	STRIKEOUTS	WON-LOST PCT.	EARNED RUN AVE.	
KINER,PIT MIZE,NY 51	MIZE NY 138	ROBINSON BRO 29	BLACKWELL CIN 193	JANSEN NY 21- 5	SPAHN BOS 2.33	47
WILLIAMS BOS 32	WILLIAMS BOS 114	DILLINGER STL 34	FELLER CLE 196	REYNOLDS NY 19- 8	HAYNES CHI 2.42	
KINER,PIT MIZE,NY 40	MUSIAL STL 131	ASHBURN PHI 32	BRECHEEN STL 149	BRECHEEN STL 20- 7	BRECHEEN STL 2.24	48
DI MAGGIO NY 39	DI MAGGIO NY 155	DILLINGER STL 28	FELLER CLE 164	KRAMER BOS 18- 5	BEARDEN CLE 2.43	
KINER PIT 54	KINER PIT 127	ROBINSON BRO 37	SPAHN BOS 151	ROE BRO 15- 6	KOSLO NY 2.50	49
WILLIAMS BOS 43	STEPHENS,BOS WILLIAMS,BO 159	DILLINGER STL 20	TRUCKS DET 153	KINDER BOS 23- 6	PARNELL BOS 2.78	
KINER PIT 47	ENNIS PHI 126	JETHROE BOS 35	SPAHN BOS 191	MAGLIE NY 18- 4	HEARN STL-NY 2.49	50
ROSEN CLE 37	STEPHENS,BOS DROPO,BOS 144	DI MAGGIO BOS 15	LEMON CLE 170	RASCHI NY 21- 8	WYNN CLE 3.20	
KINER PIT 42	IRVIN NY 121	JETHROE BOS 35	NEWCOMBE,BRO SPAHN,BOS 164	ROE BRO 22- 3	NICHOLS BOS 2.88	51
ZERNIAL CHI-PHI 33	ZERNIAL CHI-PHI 129	MINOSO CLE-CHI 31	RASCHI NY 164	FELLER CLE 22- 8	ROGOVIN DET-CHI 2.78	
KINER,PIT SAUER,CHI 37	SAUER CHI 121	REESE BRO 30	SPAHN BOS 183	WILHELM NY 15- 3	WILHELM NY 2.43	52
DOBY CLE 32	ROSEN CLE 105	MINOSO CHI 22	REYNOLDS NY 160	SHANTZ PHI 24- 7	REYNOLDS NY 2.07	
MATHEWS MIL 47	CAMPANELLA BRO 142	BRUTON MIL 26	ROBERTS PHI 198	ERSKINE BRO 20- 6	SPAHN MIL 2.10	53
ROSEN CLE 43	ROSEN CLE 145	MINOSO CHI 25	PIERCE CHI 186	LOPAT NY 16- 4	LOPAT NY 2.43	
KLUSZEWSKI CIN 49	KLUSZEWSKI CIN 141	BRUTON MIL 34	ROBERTS PHI 185	ANTONELLI NY 21- 7	ANTONELLI NY 2.29	54
DOBY CLE 32	DOBY CLE 126	JENSEN BOS 22	TURLEY BAL 185	CONSUEGRA CHI 16- 3	GARCIA CLE 2.64	
MAYS NY 51	SNIDER BRO 136	BRUTON MIL 25	JONES CHI 198	NEWCOMBE BRO 20- 5	FRIEND PIT 2.84	55
MANTLE NY 37	JENSEN,BOS BOONE,DET 116	RIVERA CHI 25	SCORE CLE 245	BYRNE NY 16- 5	PIERCE CHI 1.97	
SNIDER BRO 43	MUSIAL STL 109	MAYS NY 40	JONES CHI 176	NEWCOMBE BRO 27- 7	BURDETTE MIL 2.71	56
MANTLE NY 52	MANTLE NY 130	APARICIO CHI 21	SCORE CLE 263	FORD NY 19- 6	FORD NY 2.46	
AARON MIL 44	AARON MIL 132	MAYS SF 38	SANFORD PHI 188	BUHL MIL 18- 7	PODRES BRO 2.66	57
STIEVERS WAS 42	SIEVERS WAS 114	APARICIO CHI 28	WYNN CLE 184	STURDIVANT,NY DONOVAN CHI 16- 6	SHANTZ NY 2.45	
BANKS CHI 47	BANKS CHI 129	MAYS SF 31	JONES STL 225	BURDETTE MIL 20-10 SPAHN MIL 22-11	MILLER SF 2.47	58
MANTLE NY 42	JENSEN BOS 122	APARICIO CHI 29	WYNN CHI 179	TURLEY NY 21- 7	FORD NY 2.01	
MATHEWS MIL 46	BANKS CHI 143	MAYS SF 27	DRYSDALE LA 242	FACE PIT 18- 1	JONES SF 2.82	59
KILLEBREW,WAS COLAVITO CLE 42	JENSEN BOS 112	APARICIO CHI 56	BUNNING DET 201	WYNN CHI 22-10	WILHELM BAL 2.19	
BANKS CHI 41	AARON MIL 126	WILLS LA 50	DRYSDALE LA 246	BROGLIO STL 21- 9	MC CORMICK SF 2.70	60
MANTLE NY 40	MARIS NY 112	APARICIO CHI 51	BUNNING DET 201	J.PERRY CLE 18-10	BAUMANN CHI 2.68	
CEPEDA SF 46	CEPEDA SF 142	WILLS LA 35	KOUFAX LA 269	PODRES LA 18- 5	SPAHN MIL 3.01	61
MARIS NY 61	MARIS NY 142	APARICIO CHI 53	PASCUAL MIN 221	FORD NY 25- 4	DONOVAN WAS 2.40	

YEAR	LG	BATTING		RUNS		HITS		DOUBLES		TRIPLES	
1962	N	H.DAVIS BRO	.346	ROBINSON CIN	134	H.DAVIS BRO	230	ROBINSON CIN	51	CALLISON,PHI WILLS,LA W.DAVIS,LA VIRDON,PIT	10
	A	RUNNELS BOS	.326	PEARSON LA	115	RICHARDSON NY	209	F.ROBINSON CHI	45	CIMOLI KC	15
1963	N	H.DAVIS BRO	.326	H.AARON MIL	121	PINSON CIN	204	GROAT STL	43	PINSON CIN	14
	A	YASTRZEMSKI BOS	.321	ALLISON MIN	99	YASTRZEMSKI BOS	183	YASTRZEMSKI BOS	40	VERSALLES MIN	13
1964	N	CLEMENTE PIT	.339	ALLEN PHI	125	CLEMENTE,PIT FLOOD,STL	211	MAYE MIL	44	ALLEN,PHI SANTO,CHI	13
	A	OLIVA MIN	.323	OLIVA MIN	109	OLIVA MIN	217	OLIVA MIN	43	ROLLINS,MINN VERSALLES MIN	10
1965	N	CLEMENTE PIT	.329	HARPER CIN	126	ROSE CIN	209	H.AARON MIL	40	CALLISON PHI	16
	A	OLIVA MIN	.321	VERSALLES MIN	126	OLIVA MIN	185	YASTRZEMSKI,BOS VERSALLES MIN	45	CAMPANERIS,KC VERSALLES MIN	12
1966	N	M.ALOU PIT	.342	F.ALOU ATL	122	F.ALOU ATL	218	CALLISON PHI	40	MC CARVER STL	13
	A	F.ROBINSON BAL	.326	F.ROBINSON BAL	122	OLIVA MIN	191	YASTRZEMSKI BOS	39	KNOOP CAL	11
1967	N	CLEMENTE PIT	.357	AARON,ATL BROCK,STL	113	CLEMENTE PIT	209	STAUB HOU	44	PINSON CIN	13
	A	YASTRZEMSKI BOS	.326	YASTRZEMSKI BOS	112	YASTRZEMSKI BOS	189	OLIVA MIN	34	BLAIR BAL	12
1968	N	ROSE CIN	.335	BECKERT CHI	98	F.ALOU,ATL ROSE,CIN	210	BROCK STL	46	BROCK STL	14
	A	YASTRZEMSKI BOS	.301	MC AULIFFE DET	95	CAMPANERIS OAK	177	SMITH BOS	37	FREGOSI CAL	13
1969	N	ROSE CIN	.348	ROSE,CIN BONDS,SF	120	M.ALOU PIT	231	M.ALOU PIT	41	CLEMENTE PIT	12
	A	CAREW MIN	.332	JACKSON OAK	123	OLIVA MIN	197	OLIVA MIN	39	UNSER WAS	8
1970	N	CARTY ATL	.366	WILLIAMS CHI	137	WILLIAMS,CHI ROSE,CIN	205	PARKER LA	47	DAVIS LA	16
	A	JOHNSON CAL	.329	YASTRZEMSKI BOS	125	OLIVA MIN	204	OLIVA,MIN OTIS,KC TOVAR,MINN	36	TOVAR MIN	13
1971	N	TORRE STL	.363	BROCK STL	126	TORRE STL	230	CEDENO HOU	40	METZGER,HOU MORGAN,HOU	11
	A	OLIVA MIN	.337	BUFORD BAL	99	TOVAR MIN	204	SMITH BOS	33	PATEK KC	11
1972	N	WILLIAMS CHI	.333	MORGAN CIN	122	ROSE CIN	198	MONTANEZ,PHI CEDENO,HOU	39	BOWA PHI	13
	A	CAREW MIN	.318	MURCER NY	102	RUDI OAK	181	PINIELLA KC	33	FISK,BOS RUDI,OAK	9
1973	N	ROSE CIN	.338	BONDS SF	131	ROSE CIN	230	STARGELL PIT	43	METZGER HOU	14
	A	CAREW MIN	.350	JACKSON OAK	99	CAREW MIN	203	BANDO,OAK GARCIA,MIL	32	BUMBRY,BAL CAREW,MIN	11
1974	N	GARR ATL	.353	ROSE CIN	110	GARR ATL	214	ROSE CIN	45	GARR ATL	17
	A	CAREW MIN	.364	YASTRZEMSKI BOS	93	CAREW MIN	218	RUDI OAK	39	RIVERS CAL	11
1975	N	MADLOCK CHI	.354	ROSE CIN	112	CASH PHI	213	ROSE CIN	47	GARR ATL	11
	A	CAREW MIN	.359	LYNN BOS	103	BRETT KC	195	LYNN BOS	47	RIVERS,CAL BRETT,KC	13
1976	N	MADLOCK CHI	.339	ROSE CIN	130	ROSE CIN	215	ROSE CIN	42	CASH PHI	12
	A	BRETT KC	.333	WHITE NY	104	BRETT KC	215	OTIS KC	40	BRETT KC	14

HOME RUNS	RUNS BATTED IN	STOLEN BASES	STRIKEOUTS	WON-LOST PCT.	EARNED RUN AVE.	
MAYS SF 49	H.DAVIS LA 153	WILLS LA 104	DRYSDALE LA 232	PURKEY CIN 23-5	KOUFAX LA 2.54	62
KILLEBREW MIN 48	KILLEBREW MIN 126	APARICIO CHI 31	PASCUAL MIN 206	HERBERT CHI 20-9	AGUIRRE DET 2.21	
MC COVEY,SF H.AARON,MIL 44	H.AARON MIL 130	WILLS LA 40	KOUFAX LA 306	PERRANOSKI LA 16-3	KOUFAX LA 1.88	63
KILLEBREW MIN 45	STUART BOS 118	APARICIO BAL 40	PASCUAL MIN 202	FORD NY 24-7	PETERS CHI 2.33	
MAYS SF 47	BOYER STL 119	WILLS LA 53	VEALE PIT 250	KOUFAX LA 19-5	KOUFAX LA 1.74	64
KILLEBREW MIN 49	B.ROBINSON BAL 118	APARICIO BAL 57	DOWNING NY 217	BUNKER BAL 19-5	CHANCE LA 1.65	
MAYS SF 52	JOHNSON CIN 130	WILLS LA 94	KOUFAX LA 382	KOUFAX LA 26-8	KOUFAX LA 2.04	65
CONIGLIARO BOS 32	COLAVITO CLE 108	CAMPANERIS LC 51	MC DOWELL CLE 325	GRANT MIN 21-7	MC DOWELL CLE 2.18	
H.AARON ATL 44	H.AARON ATL 127	BROCK STL 74	KOUFAX LA 317	MARICHAL SF 25-6	KOUFAX LA 1.73	66
F.ROBINSON BAL 49	F.ROBINSON BAL 122	CAMPANERIS KC 52	MC DOWELL CLE 225	SIEBERT CLE 16-8	PETERS CHI 1.98	
H.AARON ATL 39	CEPEDA SF 111	BROCK STL 52	BUNNING PHI 253	HUGHES STL 16-6	P.NIEKRO ATL 1.87	67
YASTRZEMSKI,BOS KILLEBREW,MIN 44	YASTRZEMSKI BOS 121	CAMPANERIS KC 55	LONBORG BOS 246	HORLEN CHI 19-7	HORLEN CHI 2.06	
MC COVEY SF 36	MC COVEY SF 105	BROCK STL 62	GIBSON STL 268	BLASS PIT 18-6	GIBSON STL 1.12	68
HOWARD WAS 44	HARRELSON BOS 109	CAMPANERIS OAK 62	MC DOWELL CLE 283	MC LAIN DET 31-6	TIANT CLE 1.60	
MC COVEY SF 45	MC COVEY SF 126	BROCK STL 53	JENKINS CHI 273	SEAVER NY 25-7	MARICHAL SF 2.10	69
KILLEBREW MIN 49	KILLEBREW MIN 140	HARPER SEA 73	MC DOWELL CLE 279	PALMER BAL 16-4	BOSMAN WAS 2.19	
BENCH CIN 45	BENCH CIN 148	TOLAN CIN 57	SEAVER NY 283	GIBSON STL 23-7	SEAVER NY 2.81	70
HOWARD WAS 44	HOWARD WAS 126	CAMPANERIS OAK 42	MC DOWELL CLE 304	CUELLAR BAL 24-8	SEGUI OAK 2.56	
STARGELL PIT 48	TORRE STL 137	BROCK STL 64	SEAVER NY 289	GULLETT CIN 16-6	SEAVER NY 1.76	71
MELTON CHI 33	KILLEBREW MIN 119	OTIS KC 52	LOLICH DET 308	MC NALLY BAL 21-5	BLUE OAK 1.82	
BENCH CIN 40	BENCH CIN 125	BROCK STL 63	CARLTON PHI 310	NOLAN CIN 15-5	CARLTON PHI 1.98	72
R.ALLEN CHI 37	R.ALLEN CHI 113	CAMPANERIS OAK 52	RYAN CAL 329	HUNTER OAK 21-7	TIANT BOS 1.91	
STARGELL PIT 44	STARGELL PIT 119	BROCK STL 70	SEAVER NY 251	JOHN LA 16-7	SEAVER NY 2.08	73
JACKSON OAK 32	JACKSON OAK 117	HARPER BOS 54	RYAN CAL 383	HUNTER OAK 21-5	PALMER BAL 2.40	
SCHMIDT PHI 36	BENCH CIN 129	BROCK STL 118	CARLTON PHI 240	MESSERSMITH LA 20-6	CAPRA ATL 2.28	74
ALLEN CHI 32	BURROUGHS TEX 118	NORTH OAK 54	RYAN CAL 367	CUELLAR BAL 22-10	HUNTER OAK 2.49	
SCHMIDT PHI 38	LUZINSKI PHI 120	LOPES LA 77	SEAVER NY 243	GULLETT CIN 15-4	JONES SD 2.24	75
JACKSON,OAK SCOTT,MIL 36	SCOTT MIL 109	RIVERS CAL 70	TANANA CAL 269	TORREZ BAL 20-9	PALMER BAL 2.09	
SCHMIDT PHI 38	FOSTER CIN 121	LOPES LA 63	SEAVER NY 235	CARLTON PHI 20-7	DENNY STL 2.52	76
NETTLES NY 32	MAY BAL 109	NORTH OAK 75	RYAN CAL 327	CAMPBELL MIN 17-5	FIDRYCH DET 2.34	

YEAR	LG	BATTING		RUNS		HITS		DOUBLES		TRIPLES	
1977	N	PARKER PIT	.338	FOSTER CIN	124	PARKER PIT	215	PARKER PIT	44	TEMPLETON STL	18
	A	CAREW MIN	.388	CAREW MIN	128	CAREW MIN	239	MC RAE KC	54	CAREW MIN	16
1978	N	PARKER PIT	.334	DE JESUS CHI	104	GARVEY LA	202	ROSE CIN	51	TEMPLETON STL	13
	A	CAREW MIN	.333	LE FLORE DET	126	RICE BOS	213	BRETT KC	45	RICE BOS	15

HOME RUNS		RUNS BATTED IN		STOLEN BASES		STRIKEOUTS		WON-LOST PCT.		EARNED RUN AVE.		
FOSTER CIN	52	FOSTER CIN	149	TAVERAS PIT	70	P.NIEKRO ATL	262	CANDELARIA PIT	20- 5	CANDELARIA PIT	2.34	77
RICE BOS	39	HISLE MIN	119	PATEK KC	53	RYAN CAL	341	SPLITTORFF KC	16- 6	TANANA CAL	2.54	
FOSTER CIN	40	FOSTER CIN	120	MORENO PIT	71	RICHARD HOU	303	G.PERRY SD	21- 6	SWAN NY	2.43	78
RICE BOS	46	RICE BOS	139	LE FLORE DET	68	RYAN CAL	260	GUIDRY NY	25- 3	GUIDRY NY	1.74	

CLUB LEADERS—INDIVIDUAL LIFETIME

AMERICAN ASSOCIATION

CLUB	BATTING	REC.	PITCHING	W–L	REC.
Athletics	Dennis Lyons (1887)	.469	Bob Matthews (1883)	30–14	.682
Baltimore	Tommy Burns (1887)	.401	Mat Kilroy (1887)	46–20	.697
Boston	Dan Brouthers (1891)	.352	Charles Buffinton (1891)	27–9	.750
			George Haddock (1891)	33–11	.750
Brooklyn	Jim McTamany (1887)	.354	Bob Caruthers (1889)	40–12	.769
Cincinnati	Frank Fennelly (1887)	.368	Will White (1882)	40–12	.769
Cleveland	Pete Hotaling (1887)	.367	Ed Bakely (1888)	25–33	.417
Columbus	John Johnson (1890)	.354	Ed Morris (1884)	35–13	.729
Indianapolis	Jim Keenan (1884)	.305	Larry McKeon (1884)	18–41	.305
Kansas City	Jim Burns (1889)	.303	Jim Conway (1889)	18–19	.486
Louisville	Pete Browning (1887)	.471	Guy Hecker (1884)	52–20	.722
Metropolitans	Dude Esterbrook (1884)	.408	John Lynch (1884)	39–14	.736
Milwaukee	Harry Vaughn (1891)	.330	Frank Killen (1891)	8–3	.727
Pittsburgh	Cy Swartwood (1883)	.369	Ed Morris (1886)	41–20	.672
Richmond	Mike Mansell (1884)	.301	Pete Meegan (1884)	7–12	.368
Rochester	Sandy Griffin (1890)	.305	Bill Calihan (1890)	18–13	.581
St. Louis	Tip O'Neill (1887)	.492	Silver King (1887)	34–11	.756
Syracuse	Cupid Childs (1890)	.344	Ed Mars (1890)	9–6	.600
Toledo	Cy Swartwood (1890)	.309	Tony Mullane (1884)	36–26	.581
Washington	Jim McGuire (1891)	.296	Frank Foreman (1891)	22–22	.500

AMERICAN LEAGUE

CLUB	BATTING	REC.	PITCHING	W–L	REC.
Baltimore					
1901–02	Mike Donlin (1901)	.340	Joe McGinnity (1901)	26–19	.578
1954–	Bob Nieman (1956)	.322	Dave McNally (1971)	21–5	.808
Boston	Ted Williams (1941)	.406	Bob Stanley (1978)	15–2	.882
California	Alex Johnson (1970)	.329	Dean Chance (1964)	20–9	.690
Chicago	Luke Appling (1936)	.388	Sandy Consuegra (1954)	16–3	.842
Cleveland	Joe Jackson (1911)	.408	Johnny Allen (1937)	15–1	.938
Detroit	Ty Cobb (1911)	.420	Bill Donovan (1907)	25–4	.862
Kansas City					
1955–67	Vic Power (1955)	.319	Bud Daley (1959)	16–13	.522
1969–	George Brett (1976	.333	Paul Splittorff (1977)	16–6	.727
Milwaukee					
1901	John Anderson (1901)	.339	Bill Reidy (1901)	15–18	.455
1970–	George Scott (1973)	.306	Mike Caldwell (1978)	22–9	.710
Minnesota	Rod Carew (1977)	.388	Bill Campbell (1976)	17–5	.773
New York	Babe Ruth (1923)	.393	Ron Guidry (1978)	25–3	.893
Oakland	Joe Rudi (1970)	.309	Jim Hunter (1973)	21–5	.808
Philadelphia	Nap Lajoie (1901)	.422	Lefty Grove (1931)	31–4	.886
St. Louis	George Sisler (1922)	.420	General Crowder (1928)	21–5	.808
Seattle					
1969	Tommy Davis (1969)	.271	Diego Segui (1969)	12–6	.667
1977–	Leon Roberts (1978)	.301	Henry Romo (1978)	11–7	.611
Texas	Al Oliver (1978)	.324	Ferguson Jenkins (1974)	25–12	.676
Toronto	Bob Bailor (1977)	.310	Jim Clancy (1978)	10–12	.455
Washington					
1901–60	Goose Goslin (1928)	.379	Walter Johnson (1913)	36–7	.837
1961–71	Chuck Hinton (1962)	.3100	Dick Bosman (1970)	16–12	.571

FEDERAL LEAGUE

CLUB	BATTING	REC.	PITCHING	W–L	REC.
Baltimore	Steve Evans (1915)	.319	Jack Quinn (1914)	26–14	.650
Brooklyn	Steve Evans (1914)	.355	Tom Seaton (1914)	25–14	.641
Buffalo	Hal Chase (1914)	.354	Russ Ford (1914)	21–6	.778
Chicago	Bill Fischer (1915)	.326	Claude Hendrix (1914)	29–10	.744
Indianapolis	Bennie Kauff (1914)	.366	George Kaiserling (1914)	17–10	.630
Kansas City	Ted Easterly (1914)	.331	Nick Cullop (1915)	22–11	.667
Newark	Vin Campbell (1915)	.314	Ed Reulbach (1915)	21–10	.677
Pittsburgh	Eggie Lennox (1914)	.317	Frank Allen (1915)	23–13	.639
St. Louis	Doc Crandall (1914)	.312	Mordecai Brown (1914)	11–5	.684

NATIONAL ASSOCIATION

Due to the fact that the records of this first major league are largely incomplete and that some box scores are missing, it is therefore impossible to compute the club leaders in batting and pitching for the National Association.

NATIONAL LEAGUE (1876–1899)

CLUB	BATTING	REC.	PITCHING	W–L	REC.
Athletics	George Hall (1876)	.355	Lon Knight (1876)	10–23	.303
Baltimore	Willie Keeler (1897)	.432	Bill Hoffer (1896)	26–7	.788
Boston	Hugh Duffy (1894)	.438	Fred Klobedanz (1897)	25–8	.758
			Parson Lewis (1898)	25–8	.758
Brooklyn	Willie Keeler (1899)	.376	Jim Hughes (1899)	25–5	.833
Buffalo	Dan Brouthers (1883)	.371	Jim Galvin (1884)	46–21	.687
Chicago	Cap Anson (1887)	.421	Fred Goldsmith (1880)	22–3	.880
Cincinnati	Bug Holliday (1894)	.383	Noodles Hahn (1899)	23–8	.742
Cleveland	Jess Burkett (1895)	.423	Cy Young (1895)	33–10	.767
Detroit	Dan Brouthers (1887)	.419	Lady Baldwin (1886)	31–11	.764
Hartford	John Cassidy (1877)	.378	Tommy Bond (1876)	32–13	.711
Indianapolis	Otto Shomberg (1887)	.389	Bill Burdick (1888)	10–10	.500
			Amos Rusie (1889)	11–11	.500
Kansas City	Al Myers (1886)	.276	Grasshopper Whitney (1886)	12–32	.273
Louisville	Fred Clarke (1897)	.406	Ellsworth Cunningham (1898)	28–15	.651
Milwaukee	Abner Dalrymple (1878)	.356	Sam Weaver (1878)	12–30	.286
Mutuals	Jim Hallinan (1876)	.277	Bob Mathews (1876)	21–34	.382
New York	Roger Connor (1887)	.382	Mickey Welch (1885)	47–11	.810
Philadelphia	Ed Delahanty (1899)	.408	Al Orth (1899)	13–3	.813
Pittsburgh	Jake Stenzel (1895)	.384	Adonis Terry (1892)	20–7	.741
Providence	Paul Hines (1879)	.357	Hoss Radbourn (1884)	60–12	.833
St. Louis	Jess Burkett (1899)	.402	George Bradley (1876)	45–19	.703
Syracuse	John Farrell (1879)	.304	Pat McCormick (1879)	11–13	.458
Troy	Roger Connor (1880)	.332	Mickey Welch (1880)	34–30	.531
Washington	Paul Hines (1887)	.370	Al Maul (1895)	11–6	.647
Worcester	Lewis Dickerson (1881)	.316	Fred Corey (1880)	9–8	.529

NATIONAL LEAGUE (1900–1973)

CLUB	BATTING	REC.	PITCHING	W–L	REC.
Atlanta	Rico Carty (1970)	.366	Ron Reed (1969)	18–8	.643
Boston	Rogers Hornsby (1928)	.387	Tom Hughes (1916)	16–3	.842
Brooklyn	Babe Herman (1930)	.393	Fred Fitzsimmons (1940)	16–2	.889
Chicago	Rogers Hornsby (1929)	.380	King Cole (1910)	20–4	.833
Cincinnati	Cy Seymour (1905)	.377	Elmer Riddle (1941)	19–4	.826
Houston	Rusty Staub (1967)	.333	Larry Dierker (1972)	15–8	.652
Los Angeles	Tommy Davis (1962)	.346	Ron Perranoski (1963)	16–3	.842
Milwaukee	Hank Aaron (1959)	.355	Warren Spahn (1953, 63)	23–7	.767
Montreal	Rusty Staub (1971)	.311	Mike Torrez (1974)	15–8	.652
			Dale Murray (1975)	15–8	.652
N. Y. Giants	Bill Terry (1930)	.401	Hoyt Wilhelm (1952)	15–3	.833
N. Y. Mets	Cleon Jones (1969)	.340	Tom Seaver (1969)	25–7	.781
Philadelphia	Lefty O'Doul (1929)	.398	Robin Roberts (1952)	28–7	.800
Pittsburgh	Arky Vaughan (1935)	.385	Elroy Face (1959)	18–1	.947
St. Louis	Rogers Hornsby (1924)	.424	Dizzy Dean (1934)	30–7	.811
San Diego	Clarence Gaston (1970)	.318	Gaylord Perry (1978)	21–6	.778
San Francisco	Willie Mays (1958)	.347	Juan Marichal (1966)	25–6	.806

PLAYER'S LEAGUE

CLUB	BATTING	REC.	PITCHING	W–L	REC.
Boston	Dan Brouthers (1890)	.345	Ad Gumbert (1890)	22–9	.710
Brooklyn	Dave Orr (1890)	.387	Gus Weyhing (1890)	31–15	.674
Buffalo	Ed Beecher (1890)	.357	Bert Cunningham (1890)	10–15	.400
Chicago	Jimmy Ryan (1890)	.330	Silver King (1890)	33–20	.623
Cleveland	Pete Browning (1890)	.391	Billy McGill (1890)	11–9	.550
New York	Roger Connor (1890)	.372	Tim Keefe (1890)	17–8	.680
Philadelphia	George Wood (1890)	.304	Philip Knell (1890)	20–11	.645
Pittsburgh	Jake Beckley (1890)	.325	Al Maul (1890)	17–11	.607

UNION ASSOCIATION

CLUB	BATTING	REC.	PITCHING	W–L	REC.
Altoona	Germany Smith (1884)	.307	Connie Murphy (1884)	4–6	.400
Baltimore	John Seery (1884)	.309	Bill Sweeney (1884)	40–21	.656
Boston	Ed Crane (1884)	.304	Dupee Shaw (1884)	22–15	.595
Chicago	Lew Shoenick (1884)	.315	One-Arm Daly (1884)	22–25	.468
Cincinnati	Dick Burns (1884)	.315	Jim McCormick (1884)	22–4	.846
Kansas City	Jack Gorman (1884)	.275	Ernest Hickman (1884)	3–13	.188
Keystone	Bill Hoover (1884)	.355	Enoch Bakely (1884)	14–24	.368
Milwaukee	Al Myers (1884)	.326	Ed Cushman (1884)	4–0	1.000
Pittsburgh	Lew Shoenick (1884)	.276	One-Arm Daly (1884)	5–4	.556
St. Louis	Fred Dunlap (1884)	.420	Charles Hodnet (1884)	12–1	.923
			Bill Taylor (1884)	24–2	.923
St. Paul	Jimmy Brown (1884)	.313	Bill O'Brien (1884)	1–1	.500
Washington	Harry Moore (1884)	.337	Charles Gagus (1884)	11–9	.550
Wilmington	Tom Lynch (1884)	.281	Dan Casey (1884)	1–1	.500

SPECIAL AWARDS

(Chosen by Baseball Writers' Association)

MOST VALUABLE PLAYER

*unanimous selection

AMERICAN LEAGUE	NATIONAL LEAGUE
Year Player Club	Player Club
1931—Robert Grove, Philadelphia, p	Frank Frisch, St. Louis, 2b
1932—James Foxx, Philadelphia, 1b	Charles Klein, Philadelphia, of
1933—James Foxx, Philadelphia, 1b	Carl Hubbell, New York, p
1934—Gordon Cochrane, Detroit, c	Jerome Dean, St. Louis, p
1935—Henry Greenberg, Detroit, 1b*	Charles Hartnett, Chicago, c
1936—H. Louis Gehrig, New York, 1b.	Carl Hubbell, New York, p
1937—Charles Gehringer, Detroit, 2b	Joseph Medwick, St. Louis, of
1938—James Foxx, Boston, 1b	Ernest Lombardi, Cinncinnati, c
1939—Joseph DiMaggio, N. York, of	William Walters, Cincinnati, p
1940—Henry Greenberg, Detroit, of	Frank McCormick, Cincinnati, 1b
1941—Joseph DiMaggio, N. York, of	Adolph Camilli, Brooklyn, 1b
1942—Joseph Gordon, New York, 2b	Morton Cooper, St. Louis, p
1943—Spurgeon Chandler, N. Y., p	Stanley Musial, St. Louis, of
1944—Harold Newhouser, Detroit, p	Martin Marion, St. Louis, ss
1945—Harold Newhouser, Detroit, p	Philip Cavarretta, Chicago, 1b
1946—Theodore Williams, Boston, of	Stanley Musial, St. Louis, 1b
1947—Joseph DiMaggio, N. York, of	Robert Elliott, Boston, 3b
1948—Louis Boudreau, Cleveland, ss	Stanley Musial, St. Louis, of
1949—Theodore Williams, Boston, of	Jack Robinson, Brooklyn, 2b
1950—Philip Rizzuto, New York, ss	C. James Konstanty, Philadelphia, p
1951—Lawrence Berra, New York, c	Roy Campanella, Brooklyn, c
1952—Robert Shantz, Philadelphia, p	Henry Sauer, Chicago, of
1953—Albert Rosen, Cleveland, 3b*	Roy Campanella, Brooklyn, c
1954—Lawrence Berra, New York, c	Willie Mays, New York, of
1955—Lawrence Berra, New York, c	Roy Campanella, Brooklyn, c
1956—Mickey Mantle, New York, of*	Donald Newcombe, Brooklyn, p
1957—Mickey Mantle, New York, of	Henry Aaron, Milwaukee, of
1958—Jack Jensen, Boston, of	Ernest Banks, Chicago, ss
1959—J. Nelson Fox, Chicago, 2b	Ernest Banks, Chicago, ss
1960—Roger Maris, New York, of	Richard Groat, Pittsburgh, ss
1961—Roger Maris, New York, of	Frank Robinson, Cincinnati, of
1962—Mickey Mantle, New York, of	Maurice Wills, Los Angeles, ss
1963—Elston Howard, New York, c	Sanford Koufax, Los Angeles, p
1964—Brooks Robinson, Baltimore, 3b	Kenton Boyer, St. Louis, 3b
1965—Zoilo Versalles, Minn., ss	Willie Mays, San Francisco, of
1966—Frank Robinson, Baltimore, of*	Roberto Clemente, Pittsburgh, of
1967—Carl Yastrzemski, Boston, of	Orlando Cepeda, St. Louis, 1b*
1968—Dennis McLain, Detroit, p*	Robert Gibson, St. Louis, p
1969—Harmon Killebrew, Minn., 1-3b	Willie McCovey, San Francisco, 1b
1970—John Powell, Baltimore, 1b	Johnny Bench, Cincinnati, c
1971—Vida Blue, Oakland, p	Joe Torre, St. Louis, 1-c
1972—Richard Allen, Chicago 1b	Johnny Bench, Cincinnati, c
1973—Reginald Jackson, Oakland, of	Peter Rose, Cincinnati, of
1974—Jeffrey Burroughs, Texas, of	Steven Garvey, Los Angeles, 1b
1975—Fredric Lynn, Boston, of	Joseph Morgan, Cincinnati, 2b
1976—Thurman Munson, New York, c	Joseph Morgan, Cincinnati, 2b
1977—Rodney Carew, Minnesota, 1b	George Foster, Cincinnati, of
1978—James Rice, Boston, of	David Parker, Pittsburgh, of

ROOKIE OF THE YEAR

1947—Combined selection—Jack Robinson, Brooklyn, 1b
1948—Combined selection—Alvin Dark, Boston, N. L., ss

AMERICAN LEAGUE	NATIONAL LEAGUE
Year Player Club	Player Club
1949—Roy Sievers, St. Louis, of	Donald Newcombe, Brooklyn, p
1950—Walter Dropo, Boston, 1b	Samuel Jethroe, Boston, of
1951—Gilbert McDougald, N. Y., 3b	Willie Mays, New York, of
1952—Harry Byrd, Philadelphia, p	Joseph Black, Brooklyn, p
1953—Harvey Kuenn, Detroit, ss	James Gilliam, Brooklyn, 2b
1954—Robert Grim, New York, p	Wallace Moon, St. Louis, of
1955—Herbert Score, Cleveland, p	William Virdon, St. Louis, of
1956—Louis Aparicio, Chicago, ss	Frank Robinson, Cincinnati, of*
1957—Anthony Kubek, N. Y., inf.-of	John Sanford, Philadelphia, p
1958—Albert Pearson, Washington, of	Orlando Cepeda, San Francisco, 1b*
1959—W. Robert Allison, Wash., of	Willie McCovey, San Francisco, 1b*
1960—Ronald Hansen, Baltimore, ss	Frank Howard, Los Angeles, of
1961—Donald Schwall, Boston, p	Billy Williams, Chicago, of
1962—Thomas Tresh, New York, of-ss	Kenneth Hubbs, Chicago, 2b
1963—Gary Peters, Chicago, p	Peter Rose, Cincinnati, 2b
1964—Pedro (Tony) Oliva, Minn., of	Richard Allen, Philadelphia, 3b
1965—Curtis Blefary, Baltimore, of	James Lefebvre, Los Angeles, 2b
1966—Tommie Agee, Chicago, of	Tommy Helms, Cincinnati, 3b
1967—Rod Carew, Minnesota, 2b	Tom Seaver, New York, p
1968—Stan Bahnsen, New York, p	Johnny Bench, Cincinnati, c
1969—Lou Piniella, Kansas City, of	Ted Sizemore, Los Angeles, 2b
1970—Thurman Munson, New York, c	Carl Morton, Montreal, p
1971—Chris Chambliss, Cleveland, 1b	Earl Williams, Atlanta, 3b
1972—Carlton Fisk, Boston, c	Jonathan Matlack, New York, p
1973—Alonza Bumbry, Baltimore, of	Gary Matthews, San Francisco, of
1974—D. Michael Hargrove, Texas, 1b	Arnold McBride, St. Louis, of
1975—Fredric Lynn, Boston, of	John Montefusco, San Francisco, p
1976—Mark Fidrych, Detroit, p	Clarence Metzger, San Diego, p (tie)
	Patrick Zachry, Cincinnati, p (tie)
1977—Eddie Murray, Baltimore, 1b	Andre Dawson, Montreal, of
1978—Lou Whitaker, Detroit, 2b	J. Robert Horner, Atlanta, 3b

CY YOUNG MEMORIAL AWARD

Year   Pitcher   Club
1956—Donald Newcombe, Brooklyn
1957—Warren Spahn, Milwaukee
1958—Robert Turley, N. Y., A. L.
1959—Early Wynn, Chicago, A. L.
1960—Vernon Law, Pittsburgh
1961—Edward Ford, N. Y., A. L.
1962—Donald Drysdale, L. A., N. L.
1963—Sanford Koufax, L. A., N. L.*
1964—Dean Chance, L. A., A. L.
1965—Sanford Koutax, L. A., N. L.*
1966—Sanford Koufax, L. A., N. L.*
1967—A. L.—Jim Lonborg, Boston
        N. L.—Michael McCormick, San Francisco
1968—A. L.—Dennis McLain, Detroit*
        N. L.—Bob Gibson, St Louis*
1969—A. L.—Dennis McLain, Detroit
            Mike Cuellar, Baltimore
        N. L.—Tom Seaver, New York
1970—A. L.—Jim Perry, Minn.
        N. L.—Bob Gibson, St. Louis
1971—A. L.—Vida Blue, Oakland
        N. L.—Ferguson Jenkins, Chicago
1972—A. L.—Gaylord Perry, Cleveland
        N. L.—Steven Carlton, Philadelphia*
1973—A. L.—James Palmer, Baltimore
        N. L.—G. Thomas Seaver, New York

1974—A. L.—James Hunter, Oakland
     N. L.—Michael Marshall, Los Angeles
1975—A. L.—James Palmer, Baltimore
     N. L.—G. Thomas Seaver, New York
1976—A. L.—James Palmer, Baltimore
     N. L.—Randall Jones, San Diego
1977—A. L.—Albert (Sparky) Lyle, New York
     N. L.—Steven Carlton, Philadelphia
1978—A. L.—Ronald Guidry, New York*
     N. L.—Gaylord Perry, San Diego

VII SPECIAL RECORDS

VANDY'S DOUBLE
NO-HITTER
In 1938 a 23-year-old Cincinnati lefthander put together baseball's most unusual pitching feat—no-hit, no-run games back-to-back.

Johnny Vander Meer earned the distinction of being called "Double No-Hitter" by pitching 18 consecutive hitless inning in two complete games, perhaps the most phenomenal of all single season pitching records.

Vandy was in his second season in the National League when lightning struck twice for him. It started on June 11 at Cincinnati where the southpaw whipped the Boston Bees, 3-0. Losing pitcher Danny MacFayden allowed only six hits but gave up a run in the fourth inning and a one-on home run to Ernie Lombardi in the sixth. Vandy's initial no-hitter was fashioned in one hour and 48 minutes, and only his three passes prevented a perfect performance.

On June 15, four days after he became a national figure, Vandy turned in his second successive no-hit, no-run job under more dramatic circumstances. The game marked the first night contest at Brooklyn's Ebbets Field and a capacity crowd watched the Reds' lefty blank the Dodgers, 6-0. Losing pitcher Max Butcher, Tot Pressnell, Luke Hamlin and Vito Tamulis were the Brooklyn hurlers but the center of attraction was the visitors' moundsman.

Four runs in the third inning all but assured Cincinnati of victory but the fans stayed to watch Vander Meer's bid for his double no-hitter. When he recorded the 27th out—his 54th straight without a hit—he had established a personal pitching record which may never be equaled in baseball history.

GIANTS'
RECORD
STREAKS
The New York Giants of 1916 ran off a remarkable winning streak of 26 games, modern baseball's longest victory string. However, unlike other teams which used long winning runs to make their push for a pennant a bit easier, the Giants of that year finished no higher than fourth.

The streaky Giants actually played that 1916 season in two parts: the first one being another victory string of 17 straight, the second a run of 26. Of the 86 games won by the New Yorkers that season, 43 were accomplished in unusual fashion. The 17 straight victories were all made while the Giants were the visiting club; the streak of 26 was compiled in the last month of the season, all at the Polo Grounds, home grounds for the Giants.

Here are the dates and scores of the two streaks:

ABROAD (17 straight)

May 9:	13—Pittsburgh 5.
May 10:	7—Pittsburgh 1.
May 11:	3—Pittsburgh 2.
May 12:	3—Pittsburgh 2.
May 14:	6—Chicago 4.
May 15:	3—Chicago 2.
May 17:	9—St. Louis 3.
May 18:	3—St. Louis 0.
May 19:	5—St. Louis 4.
May 20:	4—St. Louis 1.
May 21:	11—Cincinnati 1.
May 23:	4—Cincinnati 3.
May 24:	6—Cincinnati 1.
May 26:	12—Boston 1.
May 27:	4—Boston 3.
May 27:	2—Boston 1.
May 29:	3—Boston 0.

HOME (26 straight)

September 7:	4—Brooklyn 1.
September 8:	9—Philadelphia 3.
September 9:	3—Philadelphia 1.
September 9:	3—Philadelphia 0.
September 10:	9—Philadelphia 4.
September 12:	3—Cincinnati 2.
September 13:	3—Cincinnati 0.
September 13:	6—Cincinnati 4.
September 14:	3—Cincinnati 1.
September 16:	8—Pittsburgh 2.
September 16:	4—Pittsburgh 3.
September 18:	2—Pittsburgh 0.
September 18:	1—Pittsburgh 1 (tie)
September 19:	9—Pittsburgh 2.
September 19:	5—Pittsburgh 1.
September 20:	4—Chicago 2.
September 21:	4—Chicago 0.
September 22:	5—Chicago 0.
September 23:	6—St. Louis 1.
September 23:	3—St. Louis 0.
September 25:	1—St. Louis 0.
September 25:	6—St. Louis 2.
September 26:	6—St. Louis 1.
September 27:	3—St. Louis 2.
September 28:	2—Boston 0.
September 28:	6—Boston 0.
September 30:	4—Boston 0.

DIMAGGIO'S 56

Baseball's most amazing single season hitting streak is the one performed by Joe DiMaggio in 1941 when he hit safely in 56 straight games. The graceful New York Yankee outfielder started his incredible string on May 15 and continued it through July 16, a two-month period during which he hit for a .408 average.

On his way to this all-time standard DiMag early passed the National League mark of 33 made by Rogers Hornsby and eclipsed the then existing American League record of 41 set by George Sisler. Three games later, the previous record run of 44 established by Willie Keeler in 1897 was by the boards.

Here is the statistical story of the DiMaggio streak, from start to finish:

Date		Club—Pitchers	AB	R	H	2B	3B	HR	RBI
May	15	Chi—Smith	4	—	1	—	-	—	1
	16	Chi—Lee	4	2	2	—	1	1	1
	17	Chi—Rigney	3	1	1	—	-	—	—
	18	St. L—Harris (2 hits), Niggeling (1)	3	3	3	1	-	—	1
	19	St. L—Galehouse	3	—	1	1	-	—	—
	20	St. L—Auker	5	1	1	—	-	—	1
	21	Det—Rowe (1), Benton (1)	5	—	2	—	-	—	1
	22	Det—McKain	4	—	1	—	-	—	1
	23	Bos—Newsom	5	—	1	—	-	—	2
	24	Bos—Johnson	4	2	1	—	-	—	2
	25	Bos—Grove	4	—	1	—	-	—	—
	27	Was—Chase (1), Anderson (2), Carrasquel (1)	5	3	4	—	-	1	3
(Night)	28	Was—Hudson	4	1	1	—	1	—	—
	29	Was—Sundra	3	1	1	—	-	—	—
	30	Bos—Johnson	2	1	1	—	-	—	—
	30	Bos—Harris	3	—	1	1	-	—	—
June	1	Cle—Milnar	4	1	1	—	-	—	—
	1	Cle—Harder	4	—	1	—	-	—	—
	2	Cle—Feller	4	2	2	1	-	—	—
	3	Det—Trout	4	1	1	—	-	1	1
	5	Det—Newhouser	5	1	1	—	1	—	1
	7	St. L—Muncrief (1), Allen (1), Caster (1)	5	2	3	—	-	—	1
	8	St. L—Auker	4	3	2	—	-	2	4
	8	St. L—Caster (1), Kramer (1)	4	1	2	1	-	1	3
	10	Chi—Rigney	5	1	1	—	-	—	—
(Night)	12	Chi—Lee	4	1	2	—	-	1	1
	14	Cle—Feller	2	—	1	1	-	—	1
	15	Cle—Bagby	3	1	1	—	-	1	1
	16	Cle—Milnar	5	—	1	1	-	—	—
	17	Chi—Rigney	4	1	1	—	-	—	—
	18	Chi—Lee	3	—	1	—	-	—	—
	19	Chi—Smith (1), Ross (2)	3	2	3	—	-	1	2
	20	Det—Newsom (2), McKain (2)	5	3	4	1	-	—	1
	21	Det—Trout	4	—	1	—	-	—	1
	22	Det—Newhouser (1), Newsom (1)	5	1	2	1	-	1	2
	24	St. L—Muncrief	4	1	1	—	-	—	—
	25	St. L—Galehouse	4	1	1	—	-	1	3
	26	St. L—Auker	4	—	1	1	-	—	1
	27	Phi—Dean	3	1	2	—	-	1	2
	28	Phi—Babich (1), Harris (1)	5	1	2	1	-	—	—
	29	Was—Leonard	4	1	1	1	-	—	—
	29	Was—Anderson	5	1	1	—	-	—	1
July	1	Bos—Harris (1), Ryba (1)	4	—	2	—	-	—	1
	1	Bos—Wilson	3	1	1	—	-	—	1
	2	Bos—Newsom	5	1	1	—	-	1	3
	5	Phi—Marchildon	4	2	1	—	-	1	2
	6	Phi—Babich (1), Hadley (3)	5	2	4	1	-	—	2
	6	Phi—Knott	4	—	2	—	1	—	2
(Night)	10	St. L—Niggeling	2	—	1	—	-	—	—
	11	St. L—Harris (3), Kramer (1)	5	1	4	—	-	1	2
	12	St. L—Auker (1), Muncrief (1)	5	1	2	1	-	—	1
	13	Chi—Lyons (2), Hallett (1)	4	2	3	—	-	—	—
	13	Chi—Lee	4	—	1	—	-	—	—
	14	Chi—Rigney	3	—	1	—	-	—	—
	15	Chi—Smith	4	1	2	1	-	—	2
	16	Cle—Milnar (2), Krakauskas (1)	4	3	3	1	-	—	—

Totals for 56 games.................................... 223 56 91 16 4 15 55

Streak stopped in Cleveland night game, July 17, by Smith and Bagby. Batting average for this streak, .408.

Numbers in parenthesis indicate number of hits off each pitcher if there was more than one in game.

RUTH'S 60 Quick, now! Which is baseball's most remembered number? Why 60, of course, the total number of home runs hit by Babe Ruth in 1927.

It's true that when Ruth reached the magic figure of 60 in 1927 a ball which bounced from the field into the stands was scored as a home run. Under today's rules, this is scored as a two base hit. However, those fortunate enough to see Ruth in all his majesty cannot recall when any of the home runs he drove in his record-making year first struck the playing field before bouncing into the stands.

The Babe, who was the creator of all the home run standards in the ledgers of baseball, hit his 60th homer in the last game of the season. Previous record-holder? Babe Ruth, with 59 in 1921.

The Significant Sixty smashed by Ruth, only 28 of which were hit at his home grounds, the Yankee Stadium.

HR No.	Game No. Date	Opposing Pitcher and Club	Where Made
	April		
1.	4	15--Ehmke, (R), Phi	N.Y.
2.	11	23--Walberg, (L), Phi	Phi.
3.	12	24--Thurston, (R), Was	Was.
4.	14	29--Harriss, (R), Bos	Bos.
	May		
5.	16	1--Quinn, (R), Phi	N.Y.
6.	16	1--Walberg, (L), Phi	N.Y.
7.	24	10--Gaston, (R), St. L	St.L.
8.	25	11--Nevers, (R), St.L	St.L.
9.	29	17--Collins, (R), Det.	Det.
10.	33	22--Karr, (R), Cle	Cle.
11.	34	23--Thurston, (R), Was	Was.
12.	37	28--Thurston, (R), Was	N.Y.
13.	39	29--MacFayden, (R), Bos	N.Y.
14.	41	30--Walberg, (L), Phi	Phi.
15.	42	31--Ehmke, (R), Phi	Phi.
16.	43	31--Quinn, (R), Phi	Phi.
	June		
17.	47	5--Whitehill, (L), Det	N.Y.
18.	48	7--Thomas, (R), Chi	N.Y.
19.	52	11--Buckeye, (L), Cle	N.Y.
20.	52	11--Buckeye, (L), Cle	N.Y.
21.	53	12--Uhle, (R), Cle	N.Y.
22.	55	16--Zachary, (L), St.L	N.Y.
23.	60	22--Wiltse, (L), Bos	Bos.
24.	60	22--Wiltse, (L), Bos	Bos.
25.	70	30--Harriss, (R), Bos	N.Y.
	July		
26.	73	3--Lisenbee, (R), Was	Was.
27.	78	8--Whitehill, (L), Det	Det.
28.	79	9--Holloway, (R), Det	Det.
29.	79	9--Holloway, (R), Det	Det.
30.	83	12--Shaute, (L), Cle	Cle.
31.	94	24--Thomas, (R), Chi	Chi.
32.	95	26--Gaston, (R), St. L	N.Y.
33.	95	26--Gaston, (R), St. L	N.Y.
34.	98	28--Stewart, (L), St. L	N.Y.
	August		
35.	106	5--G. Smith, (R), Det	N.Y.
36.	110	10--Zachary, (L), Was	Was.
37.	114	16--Thomas, (R), Chi	Chi.
38.	115	17--Connally, (R), Chi	Chi.
39.	118	20--Miller, (L), Cle	Cle.
40.	120	22--Shaute, (L), Cle	Cle.
41.	124	27--Nevers, (R), St.L	St.L.
42.	125	28--Wingard, (L), St. L	St.L.
43.	127	31--Welzer, (R), Bos	N.Y.
	September		
44.	128	2--Walberg, (L), Phi	Phi.
45.	132	6--Welzer, (R), Bos	Bos.
46.	132	6--Welzer, (R), Bos	Bos.
47.	133	6--Russell, (R), Bos	Bos.
48.	134	7--MacFayden, (R), Bos.	Bos.
49.	134	7--Harriss, (R), Bos	Bos.
50.	138	11--Gaston, (R), St. L	N.Y.
51.	139	13--Hudlin, (R), Cle	N.Y.
52.	140	13--Shaute, (L), Cle	N.Y.
53.	143	16--Blankenship, (R), Chi	N.Y.
54.	147	18--Lyons, (R), Chi	N.Y.
55.	148	21--Gibson, (R), Det	N.Y.
56.	149	22--Holloway, (R), Det	N.Y.
57.	152	27--Grove, (L), Phi	N.Y.
58.	153	29--Lisenbee, (R), Was	N.Y.
59.	153	29--Hopkins, (R), Was	N.Y.
60.	154	30--Zachary, (L), Was	N.Y.

MARIS' 61 Ever since Babe Ruth hit his 60 home runs in 1927 fans have argued about the chances of his record being broken. These arguments were revived in 1930 when Hack Wilson of the Chicago Cubs walloped 56, and again in 1932 and 1938 when first Jimmy Foxx and then Hammerin' Hank Greenberg smacked 58. It took an elongated season of 162 games and Roger Maris' booming bat to best the Babe's record. Like the Babe, Roger socked his record-breaking homer in the last game of the season. Maris, however, hit 30 homers at the Yankee Stadium whereas Babe hit only 28 on his home grounds.

HR No.	Game No.	Date	Opposing Pitcher and Club	Where Made
		April		
1.	10	26	Foytack, (R), Det	Det.
		May		
2.	16	3	Ramos, (R), Min	Min.
3.	19	6	Grba, (R), L.A	L.A.
4.	28	17	Burnside (L), Was	N.Y.
5.	29	19	Perry (R), Cle	Cle.
6.	30	20	Bell, (R), Cle	Cle.
7.	31	21	Estrada, (R), Bal	N.Y.
8.	34	24	Conley (R), Bos	N.Y.
9.	37	28	McLish, (R), Chi	N.Y.
10.	39	30	Conley (R), Bos	Bos.
11.	39	30	Fornieles (R), Bos	Bos.
12.	40	31	Muffett (R), Bos	Bos.
		June		
13.	42	2	McLish (R), Chi	Chi.
14.	43	3	Shaw (R), Chi	Chi.
15.	44	4	Kemmerer (R), Chi	Chi.
16.	47	6	Palmquist, (R), Min	N.Y.
17.	48	7	Ramos, (R), Min	N.Y.
18.	51	9	Herbert, (R), K.C	N.Y.
19.	54	11	Grba, (R), L.A	N.Y.
20.	54	11	James, (R), L.A	N.Y.
21.	56	13	Perry, (R), Cle	Cle.
22.	57	14	Bell, (R), Cle	Cle.
23.	60	17	Mossi, (L), Det	Det.
24.	61	18	Casale, (R), Det	Det.
25.	62	19	Archer, (L), K.C	K.C.
26.	63	20	Nuxhall, (L), K.C	K.C.
27.	65	22	Bass, (R), K.C	K.C.
		July		
28.	73	1	Sisler, (R), Was	N.Y.
29.	74	2	Burnside, (L), Was	N.Y.
30.	74	2	Klippstein, (R), Was	N.Y.
31.	76	4	Lary, (R), Det	N.Y.
32.	77	5	Funk, (R), Cle	N.Y.
33.	81	9	Monbouquette, (R), Bos	N.Y.
34.	83	13	Wynn, (R), Chi	Chi.

HR No.	Game No.	Date	Opposing Pitcher and Club	Where Made
		July		
35.	85	15	Herbert, (R), Chi	Chi.
36.	91	21	Monbouquette, (R), Bos.	Bos.
37.	94	25	Baumann, (L), Chi	N.Y.
38.	94	25	Larsen, (R), Chi	N.Y.
39.	95	25	Kemmerer, (R), Chi	N.Y.
40.	95	25	Hacker, (R), Chi	N.Y.
		August		
41.	105	4	Pascual, (R), Min	N.Y.
42.	113	11	Burnside, (L), Was	Was.
43.	114	12	Donovan, (R), Was	Was.
44.	115	13	Daniels, (R), Was	Was.
45.	116	13	Kutyna, (R), Was	Was.
46.	117	15	Pizarro, (L), Chi	N.Y.
47.	118	16	Pierce, (L), Chi	N.Y.
48.	118	16	Pierce, (L), Chi	N.Y.
49.	122	20	Perry, (R), Cle	Cle.
50.	124	22	McBride, (R), L.A	L.A.
51.	128	26	Walker, (R), K.C	K.C.
		September		
52.	134	2	Lary, (R), Det	N.Y.
53.	134	2	Aguirre, (L), Det	N.Y.
54.	139	6	Cheney, (R), Was	N.Y.
55.	140	7	Stigman, (L), Cle	N.Y.
56.	142	9	Grant, (R), Cle	N.Y.
57.	150	16	Lary, (R), Det	Det.
58.	151	17	Fox, (R), Det	Det.
59.	154	20	Pappas, (R), Bal	Bal.
60.	158	26	Fisher, (R), Bal	N.Y.
		October		
61.	162	1	Stallard, (R), Bos	N.Y.

19 STRAIGHT WINS

Two more remarkable pitching performances were those recorded by two New York Giants under different pitching standards. Tim Keefe and Rube Marquard each pitched 19 straight victories, Keefe's coming in 1888 when the pitching distance to the plate was a mere 50 feet. Lefthander Marquard managed his record in 1912 under present day pitching requirements. The victory-by-victory tables of baseball's best season winning streaks:

TIM KEEFE, NEW YORK, N. L., 1888

50 feet; 5½ × 4 Box. High or Low Ball abolished.

DATE	OPPOSING CLUB	DATE	OPPOSING CLUB
June 23 -- Keefe, 7;	Philadelphia, 6	July 20 -- Keefe, 7;	Philadelphia, 6
June 26 -- Keefe, 4;	Philadelphia, 1	July 23 -- Keefe, 2;	Boston, 0
June 29 -- Keefe, 8;	Washington, 3	July 25 -- Keefe, 5;	Boston, 1
July 2 -- Keefe, 6;	Washington, 2	July 28 -- Keefe, 4;	Philadelphia, 2
July 4 -- Keefe, 4;	Detroit, 1	Aug. 1 -- Keefe, 5;	Washington, 4
July 7 -- Keefe, 6;	Pittsburgh, 4	Aug. 3 -- Keefe, 9;	Boston, 6
July 11 -- Keefe, 5;	Indianapolis, 2	Aug. 6 -- Keefe, 3;	Indianapolis, 2
July 13 -- Keefe, 4;	Indianapolis, 0	Aug. 8 -- Keefe, 4;	Indianapolis, 1
July 16 -- Keefe, 12;	Chicago, 4	Aug. 10 -- Keefe, 2;	Pittsburgh, 1
July 17 -- Keefe, 7;	Chicago, 4		

RUBE MARQUARD, NEW YORK, N. L., 1912

60 feet, 5 inches: 24-inch Slab; One Step.

DATE	OPPOSING CLUB	DATE	OPPOSING CLUB
April 11 -- Marquard, 18;	Brooklyn, 3	June 3 -- Marquard, 8;	St. Louis, 3
April 16 -- Marquard, 8;	Boston, 2	June 8 -- Marquard, 6;	Cincinnati, 2
April 24 -- Marquard, 11;	Philadelphia, 4	June 12 -- Marquard, 3;	Chicago, 2
May 1 -- Marquard, 11;	Philadelphia, 4	June 17 -- Marquard, 5;	Pittsburgh, 4
May 7 -- Marquard, 6;	St. Louis, 2	June 19 -- Marquard, 6;	Boston, 5
May 11 -- Marquard, 10;	Chicago, 3	June 21 -- Marquard, 5;	Boston, 2
May 16 -- Marquard, 4;	Pittsburgh, 1	June 25 -- Marquard, 2;	Philadelphia, 1
May 20 -- Marquard, 3;	Cincinnati, 0	June 29 -- Marquard, 8;	Boston, 6
May 24 -- Marquard, 6;	Brooklyn, 3	July 3 — Marquard, 2;	Brooklyn, 1
May 30 -- Marquard, 7;	Philadelphia, 1		

VIII   HONORED PLAYERS

HALL OF FAME   Baseball has produced giants in all departments of play since the National Association was born in 1871, and it was inevitable that the deeds of these greats would someday be enshrined in a permanent vault which would make imperishable their all-time credentials.

Thirty-two years before the National Baseball Hall of Fame was established in Cooperstown, New York, on June 12, 1939 the administrators of baseball had set into motion the machinery which was to result in the recognition of this small central New York State village as the cradle of the game.

A special investigating committee appointed by Albert G. Spalding was entrusted with the historical task of discovering the original spot on which baseball was played in America. This committee, headed by A. G. Mills, a former National League president, reported on December 30, 1907 that "the first scheme for playing baseball, according to best obtainable evidence, was devised by Abner Doubleday at Cooperstown, New York, in 1839."

No committee was ever so far from the facts. Doubleday, who may have played at some form of baseball, and in the very village which borders picturesque Lake Otsego, was a student at West Point in the very year he was supposed to have "devised his scheme." Evidently Mills and his committee never bothered to investigate the authenticity of a report which in later years was proved to be without any circumstantial foundation by recognized historians.

But baseball deserves a shrine, and since the natives of Cooperstown have provided a mecca worthy of the pastime just where and when the game was started no longer is an issue of bitter and major controversy. Now at last the game was granted its own permanent museum and display case and dedication came on June 12, 1939. The Museum, Hall of Fame and Doubleday Field, which used to be Farmer Phinney's pasture when Doubleday, later to become a Union Major General in the Civil War, romped as a schoolboy, were all officially launched in impressive ceremonies, the most dramatic of which was the spectacle of the game's greatest heroes taking their appointed places with immortality.

In the National Baseball Museum is housed the world's most complete collection of the game's memorabilia: the largest baseball library in the world; priceless relics such as the first catcher's mitt and the bat with which Ruth clouted his 60th homer in 1927; sculptures, paintings, photographs and drawings that form a classic and graphic history of the colorful long-ago.

Enshrined in The Hall of Fame wing of the Museum are the bronze plaques of the pastime's immortals, placed there by a vote of outstanding experts who have been selected to choose the greats of the diamond. The method of selection is simple: A special committee of baseball officials, picked because of their deep knowledge and service to the game, is entrusted with the honor of choosing players who performed more than a quarter of century ago. All players whose careers began 30 years before and ended five years prior to the election are eligible to gain entrance into the Hall of Fame by a ballot system. Only members of the Baseball Writers' Association of America for at

least ten years are eligible to vote, and the successful player must receive at least 75 percent of all votes cast to gain admission.

Since the first group was chosen in 1936 the annual balloting system has been frequently under attack by those who claim sectional and personal favoritism occasionally is the basis for a writer's ballot. However few will deny the qualities of the giants who have been so honored. Their selection has met with an almost unanimous approval from the fans.

A special committee also votes on candidates for Veterans Hall of Fame plaque awards. To be eligible for admission an oldtime player must be retired for at least 30 years prior to election; managers and umpires, retired from their capacities for at least five years, are also eligible.

THE SELECT FIVE

To start its huge family in 1936 the baseball writers of that era chose five players whose performances have stamped them as the greatest of them all by more people than any others. The Select Five to acquire more than 75 percent on the first balloting for Hall of Fame entrance consisted of Ty Cobb, Babe Ruth, Christy Mathewson, Honus Wagner and Walter Johnson, all selected in that order.

It's only fitting that the man to establish more records than any other spiked hero would receive the greatest number of votes. That would be Cobb, the Georgia Peach, son of an educator, who in 24 years in the American League played 3,033 games as if each one was the final clash of a World Series.

What qualities did Cobb possess which made him the first of a heroic group? What abilities did this comet from the South bring to the diamond which enabled him to create records which will forever withstand assault?

TY COBB

First, and always, in the trigger-mind of Cobb was the idea that in competition there must be a loser, and he wanted to be in that role as seldom as possible. Cobb made himself learn to beat his opponent through the simple method of studying his every move and habit. He punished himself to the point of perfection, creating new tricks and ideas which would always keep him far removed, and above, from the rest. He knew the habits of every player he faced, their weaknesses and strengths, and he learned to strike at their most vulnerable points with a fiery spirit, constant study and an unquenchable desire for victory. His education paid off handsomely. He stole 892 bases, compiled 4,191 hits, scored 2,244 runs and amassed a batting average of .367—the most imposing individual lifetime marks ever established in the majors.

Cobb just didn't play at baseball, he lived it—on and off the field. For 12 seasons he paced the league in batting, nine of them in a row. He batted .400 or better three times, and belted .420 in 1911 and .410 the following season.

A lefthanded hitter who gripped his bat with his left hand four inches above his right, Cobb subscribed to the theory that this was the best method with which to strike at a pitched ball. Although the unorthodox grip nullified some of his power, Ty could belt them long when the situation called for it. However, he proved that this grip was adaptable to the drag bunt, at which he was a master, and perfect to pull a pitch to right field, slice it to left or smash straight through the middle of the diamond.

A centerfielder by choice Ty also played the other outfield positions, filled in at second and first base and even pitched. For 24 years he was baseball's dominant figure, the scourge of rival pitchers and opponents' stratagems. Just once did he fail to reach the .300 level—in his freshman season in 1905 when he was an 18-year-old stripling.

Ty was the game's fiercest competitor. He baited rivals, umpires and teammates—but always for a purpose. He claimed, and the records bear him out, that all of this was calculated psychology designed to upset the opposition and inspire his teammates. Cobb's methods must have been successful, his name leads all others in the Hall of Fame.

Cobb helped the Tigers to three pennants; he managed Detroit from 1921 to 1926 and closed out his career with the Philadelphia Athletics, batting .323 in his final season when he was 41 years old. He was truly the game's most dynamic competitor.

BABE
RUTH

If Ty Cobb was the most dynamic figure in the history of baseball then George Herman Ruth must have been the most fabulous. Babe Ruth, a snub-nosed, moon-faced man captured the imagination of a nation with a mincing walk, a pair of pipe-stem legs and the most explosive bat ever carried. For 20 years he held the interest of millions merely by swinging a 42-ounce bat which propelled 714 home runs, more than any player in history.

No other sports figure fired the emotion as did the Babe. Whatever he did—slam a home run or strike out—was accomplished with dramatic overtones. He was a giant of a figure who did everything with gargantuan effects.

Ruth's early boyhood was passed in a Baltimore orphanage while his father eked out a livelihood as a bartender in one of the city's less swanky districts. It was in such a setting that one of America's most legendary sports figures began an education which would elevate him to a position befitting presidents, kings and emperors.

It was as a pitcher that Ruth started his diamond career, and in that role he made his first entrance into the record books. The Boston Red Sox purchased his contract from the Baltimore Orioles of the International League and baseball's most amazing Odyssey was about to be written.

Babe became an outstanding hurler with the Sox, leading the league on two occasions in earned run averages. He also established a World Series record for consecutive scoreless innings by stringing together 29 in the 1916 and 1918 classics. Ruth was quite a pitcher but he was already evidencing prowess at the plate and his manager, Ed Barrow, decided that Ruth as an everyday performer would be more valuable than as an occasional pitcher.

In 1919, playing the outfield when he wasn't occupied on the mound, Ruth shattered all previous home run marks with an insignificant total of 29. The following winter he was sold to the New York Yankees in baseball's biggest deal, the Red Sox receiving $125,000 for their slugging pitcher-outfielder, and an additional $350,000 loan to pay off debts. Ruth's pitching days were now at an end, except for an occasional chore at season's end.

Recognizing the gate attraction of the Bambino's homeric slams, the magnates quickly agreed to introduce the lively ball. It brought fame and fortune to Ruth who crashed 59 homers in 1921 and bettered this standard with an output of 60 in 1927.

His booming bat brought showmanship and busy turnstiles to the game and helped the Yankees erect the Yankee Stadium in 1923, referred to as The House That Ruth Built. The Babe was baseball and he demanded, and received, top dollar for his achievements which included record salaries of

$85,000 in 1930 and 1931, years which will be recalled as the peak of a severe depression.

Ruth was more than just a home run slugger. It was said that he never made a bad play. As a pitcher, he constantly kept the hitters guessing; as an outfielder, he was invariably in the proper position and runners seldom dared to take liberties with one of the game's most powerful and accurate throwing arms; as a base runner, he knew exactly when to try for an extra base.

The Babe retired in 1935 but, like the true showman, reserved one of his most spectacular hitting performances for his last appearance. He slammed three homers in this farewell to baseball at Pittsburgh's spacious Forbes Field, one of which is still regarded as the longest blow ever struck in that city. So closed 22 years by the game's greatest power hitter.

Everything the Babe did was majestic. He commanded the largest tax-free baseball salary, hit the most homers, drew the biggest fine ($5,000) and brought baseball its most lush period. Even in death the Bambino played to an SRO crowd. Thousands filed past to view the idol of millions as his body lay in kingly state in, appropriately enough, The House that He Had Built.

There will always be controversy as to who was better, Cobb or Ruth. Each was superb in his field—Cobb for hitting and base running and aggressive play, Ruth for power, pitching and crowd appeal.

CHRISTY MATHEWSON

Perhaps the first prototype of the All-American boy to enter the majors was Christopher Mathewson, Bucknell University football hero who pitched 373 victories in the National League from 1900 to 1916, a 20th century all-time yearly high average of 23 triumphs.

Matty was cut from a slightly different mold than most of the players of his era and this quality plus his amazing World Series performance in 1905 was to make him the idol of the sports world. Although a member of the New York Giants, one of baseball's most truculent teams of the time, Matty managed to remain above the rest of a hurly-burly cast. His gentle manner and casual aloofness stamped him as an individual who definitely didn't fit in with the pattern of his era.

Mathewson was a model of perfection in all departments. He was more than a pitcher, and frequently served as a fill-in in the outfield and first base replacement, and occasionally was called upon as a pinch-hitter. But Matty was essentially a pitcher, perhaps the finest in the modern annals of the National League and certainly a champion performer in crucial contests.

Perhaps his most sensational stint was the World Series of 1905 when he hurled three victories, all shutouts. He helped the Giants defeat the Philadelphia Athletics by yielding a total of 14 hits in his three shutout triumphs, an unparalleled performance. This was Matty's greatest pitching hour.

Before he concluded his career as manager of the Cincinnati Reds, Matty was to win 30 or more games for three seasons and 20 or more for 12 straight years. He was the greatest exponent of control in the game, and in 1908 walked but 42 batters in 416 innings with a pitch known as the fadeaway. today's version of the screwball. He didn't require the normal four days' rest between assignments and was always ready to pitch an important contest.

Matty was anathema to most of the hitters in the league, but to the weak-hitting Joe Tinker he was just another pitcher. It was the Chicago shortstop who assaulted Matty for the game-winning blows in the memorable 1908 "playoff" contest which gave the pennant to the Cubs.

The loosely-written amateur rules of Matty's day enabled him to embark on a major league career almost immediately after leaving college. While at Bucknell he pitched in the New England League, and was soon moved to the Virginia League where he won 21 games for Norfolk. This earned him a chance with the Giants in 1900 but, after losing three games, he was sent back to the minors. Cincinnati drafted him for the 1901 season, but traded him to the Giants before the opening game. Matty's freshman year was a success and he won 20 games, one of which was a no-hitter. He was to lead New York to four pennants and strike out 2,499, an all-time league standard, in 17 seasons.

Big Six, as he was called, after a famous New York fire engine, had his career—and life—curtailed as a result of World War I. He was gassed while on active duty and fought a losing battle with tuberculosis. When he died in 1925, Matty was president of the Boston Braves.

Beneath the centerfield stands of New York's Polo Grounds a bronze tablet was erected to the memory of Christopher Mathewson. The walk which leads to the campus of Bucknell University also reveres Matty's memory. Baseball, too, hasn't forgotten --and justifiably so. Matty was touched with immortality, enough of it to qualify for The Select Five.

HONUS WAGNER

John McGraw, the famed New York Giant manager, and Ed Barrow, who helped create the New York Yankee dynasty, were regarded as the shrewdest judges of diamond talent of their day. Whenever they were asked to name the best all-around player either ever saw, the answer would always be the same: Honus Wagner.

John Peter Wagner was more than a myth, he was baseball's best shortstop, his league's best hitter, one of its fleetest runners and his league's top record maker. An ungainly man who carried most of his 200 pounds on a ponderous chest and in his gorilla-like arms, Wagner had sheer power and an eagerness for competition which clearly placed him in a class by himself.

His brute strength also lay in a huge pair of hands which were as deft and certain as any that ever pounced on a ground ball. Wagner just didn't scoop up ground balls, he excavated them, digging up large portions of loose dirt and stones. His throws were swift and powerful, and somehow the first baseman could always pluck the ball from the hail of debris aimed at him by Wagner. Very few hits skipped by Honus, and very few runners took their time getting down to first base when he cocked his muscular arm to throw.

Honus' first hero was his brother Al who was something of a semipro star, but it was young John who got to the majors first. However, Honus couldn't quite make up his mind as to whether he was a pitcher, outfielder or infielder, and it wasn't until 1901, his fifth National League season, that he was shifted to shortstop on a permanent basis. It didn't make too much difference where he played, as long as he was allowed to get up to the plate. Honus was at home immediately in his freshman year at Louisville where he carved out a .344 figure. He was to hit better than .300 for the next 16 seasons, play every position but catcher, and finish a brilliant 21-year career with a .329 lifetime average, most of it compiled against a ball as lively as a spool of cotton. After three seasons at Louisville, Wagner was to spend the rest of a remarkable span in Pittsburgh.

Ed Barrow was chiefly responsible for getting Honus started on his baseball career, but only because Ed was out scouting brother Al. Barrow was told he could find the elder Wagner around the railroad tracks outside of Mansfield, Ohio, "throwing stones." So Barrow headed for the tracks. A bowlegged, broad-shouldered youngster was tossing stones faster—and far-

ther—than the others and Barrow was immediately impressed by the boy's marksmanship and strength. It was the wrong Wagner, but Barrow made no mistake. Two seasons of minor league ball and the Flying Dutchman was ready for a career which would see him lead the league eight times in batting, appear in 2,785 games and get 3,430 hits.

In death as in the record-making department, Wagner has proved to be second best and about as imperishable. Matty, Walter Johnson and Babe Ruth preceded the Flying Dutchman to Valhalla. Cobb remained the last stubborn holdout to the inevitable.

WALTER JOHNSON

Of all the nicknames bestowed upon ball players since Adrian Constantine (Cap) Anson came down the pike, perhaps none was more appropriate than the tag placed on Walter Perry (Barney) Johnson. The Big Train he was called, and he was the fastest express of them all.

Johnson was a man, and a pitcher, completely without guile. Born on a farm in Humboldt, Kansas, he never attempted to act the part of a sophisticated cavalier. On the mound, he remained in character. Speed was his forte, and he never resorted to other artful devices to deceive the batter. Johnson was completely honest at all times—a simple, sincere man; a pitcher of enormous strength who made the ball whistle past the plate like bird shot. It is said that his announced appearance on the mound created more sick cases than the common cold, batters suddenly becoming indisposed when Johnson began his pregame warmup session. But he never took advantage of his exalted position, and none who ever batted against him can recall Johnson deliberately using his tremendous speed to drive batters away from the plate.

From the day he began a fabled career with Washington in 1907, until 1927, when he pitched the last of his 416 victories for the Senators, Walter wasn't heavily blessed with diamond fortune. During his finest years when his arm was strong and his fast ball resembled a blue darter, Washington bore slight resemblance to a baseball team. But in the mid-twenties, when the Senators were chronic challengers and two-time pennant winners, The Big Train was about to be shunted on to a siding.

Johnson's total victories are more than any ever put together in the modern era. His strikeouts (3,508), innings pitched (5,924), complete games (531) and shutouts (113) are other all-time modern marks which are far beyond the grasp of any current competitor. And all of these incredible figures were achieved while he was surrounded by mediocrity and lack of talent. Yet Barney never complained of his lot. He was happy in Washington, and Washington was more than pleased with Walter.

Johnson may never have scaled the peak of pitching pinnacles if it wasn't for the persistence of a cigar salesman who saw him pitch a semipro game in 1906 in Weiser, Idaho. The salesman saw in Walter a potential star, but Joe Cantillon, Washington manager, paid no heed when the salesman wrote him of his Idaho discovery. More letters came to Cantillon, so detailed, that Cantillon no longer could ignore them. Finally Cantillon dispatched an aide to look over Johnson, who reported that everything the salesman said was true.

After three mediocre seasons, Johnson finally caught fire, but not before he blanked the New York Highlanders three times in four days in 1908. Walter's first big season was 1910 when he won 25 games; he was to win 20 or more 11 more times, and twice went over the 30-won mark. During this span he averaged fewer than 2.00 earned runs per season 6 times; won 16

straight in 1912; 14 straight in 1913 and 13 in 1914. In 1913 he pitched 56 consecutive scoreless innings.

Walter, so rich in talent as a pitcher, closed his major league career as an unsuccessful manager. He led his beloved Senators from 1929 through '32 and piloted Cleveland from 1933 to '35. However, these lack-lustre campaigns as a field leader never dulled his brilliant playing record, the finest ever assembled by a pitcher, after the turn of the century.

Gentle in spirit, indomitable in competition, Walter Perry Johnson made baseball much richer by his performances.

HALL OF FAME MEMBERS

Pilgrimages to Cooperstown always reach the Hall of Fame wing of the Museum. Here are enshrined the real immortals of the game, titans all. With an eminently qualified Hall of Fame Committee selecting a core of oldtimers, and baseball writers of at least 10 years' standing choosing the modern players (by 75% vote), a true cross-section of the sport's greats has been elected. Plaques with suitable inscriptions hang in the Hall of Fame honoring the following:

Members	Year Elected	Members	Year Elected
GROVER CLEVELAND ALEXANDER	1938	ED. DELAHANTY	1945
ADRIAN CONSTANTINE ANSON	1939	WILLIAM DICKEY	1954
LUCIUS APPLING	1964	MARTIN DIHIGO	1977
H. EARL AVERILL	1975	JOSEPH P. DiMAGGIO	1955
J. FRANKLIN (HOME RUN) BAKER	1955	HUGH DUFFY	1945
DAVID J. BANCROFT	1971	WILLIAM G. EVANS	1973
ERNEST BANKS	1977	JOHN JOSEPH EVERS	1946
EDWARD G. BARROW	1953	WM. B. (BUCK) EWING	1939
JACOB P. BECKLEY	1971	URBAN C. FABER	1964
JAMES (COOL PAPA) BELL	1974	ROBERT W. FELLER	1962
CHARLES (CHIEF) BENDER	1953	ELMER H. FLICK	1963
LAWRENCE P. (YOGI) BERRA	1972	EDWARD C. (WHITEY) FORD	1974
JAMES L. BOTTOMLEY	1974	JAMES E. FOXX	1951
LOUIS BOUDREAU	1970	FORD FRICK	1970
ROGER BRESNAHAN	1945	FRANK FRISCH	1947
DAN BROUTHERS	1945	JAMES F. GALVIN	1965
MORDECAI PETER BROWN	1949	HENRY LOUIS GEHRIG	1939
HON. MORGAN G. BULKELEY	1937	CHARLES GEHRINGER	1949
JESSE C. BURKETT	1946	JOSHUA GIBSON	1972
ROY CAMPANELLA	1969	VERNON L. (LEFTY) GOMEZ	1972
MAX G. CAREY	1961	HENRY GREENBERG	1956
ALEXANDER JOY CARTWRIGHT, JR.	1938	CLARK C. GRIFFITH	1946
HENRY CHADWICK	1938	LEON A. GOSLIN	1968
FRANK LEROY CHANCE	1946	BURLEIGH A. GRIMES	1964
OSCAR CHARLESTON	1976	ROBERT MOSES GROVE	1947
JOHN DWIGHT CHESBRO	1946	CHARLES J. (CHIC) HAFEY	1971
FRED CLARKE	1945	JESSE J. HAINES	1970
JOHN G. CLARKSON	1963	WILLIAM R. HAMILTON	1961
ROBERTO W. CLEMENTE	1973	WILLIAM HARRIDGE	1972
TYRUS RAYMOND COBB	1936	STANLEY R. (BUCKY) HARRIS	1975
GORDON (MICKEY) COCHRANE	1947	CHARLES LEO (GABBY) HARTNETT	1955
EDWARD TROWBRIDGE COLLINS	1939	HARRY HEILMANN	1952
JAMES COLLINS	1945	WILLIAM J. B. HERMAN	1975
EARLE B. COMBS	1970	HARRY B. HOOPER	1971
CHARLES A. COMISKEY	1939	ROGERS HORNSBY	1942
JOHN B. (JOCKO) CONLAN	1974	WAITE C. HOYT	1969
THOMAS H. CONNOLLY	1953	R. CAL HUBBARD	1976
ROGER CONNOR	1976	CARL HUBBELL	1947
STANLEY A. COVELESKI	1969	MILLER J. HUGGINS	1964
SAM CRAWFORD	1957	MONFORD M. IRVIN	1973
JOSEPH CRONIN	1956	HUGHIE JENNINGS	1945
W. A. (CANDY) CUMMINGS	1939	BYRON BANCROFT JOHNSON	1937
HAZEN S. CUYLER	1968	WALTER PERRY JOHNSON	1936
JAY HANNA (DIZZY) DEAN	1953	WILLIAM J. (JUDY) JOHNSON	1975

Members	Year Elected	Members	Year Elected
ADRIAN JOSS	1978	EDGAR C. RICE	1963
TIMOTHY J. KEEFE	1964	WESLEY BRANCH RICKEY	1967
WILLIE KEELER	1939	EPPA RIXEY	1963
JOSEPH JAMES KELLEY	1971	ROBIN E. ROBERTS	1976
GEORGE L. KELLY	1973	WILBERT ROBINSON	1945
MIKE J. (KING) KELLY	1945	JACK ROBINSON	1962
RALPH M. KINER	1975	EDD J. ROUSH	1962
WILLIAM J. KLEM	1953	CHARLES H. RUFFING	1967
SANFORD KOUFAX	1972	AMOS W. RUSIE	1977
NAPOLEON (LARRY) LAJOIE	1937	GEORGE HERMAN (BABE) RUTH	1936
KENESAW MOUNTAIN LANDIS	1944	RAY SCHALK	1955
ROBERT G. LEMON	1976	JOSEPH W. SEWELL	1977
WALTER F. (BUCK) LEONARD	1972	AL SIMMONS	1953
FREDERICK C. LINDSTROM	1976	GEORGE HAROLD SISLER	1939
JOHN HENRY LLOYD	1977	WARREN E. SPAHN	1973
ALFONSO R. LOPEZ	1977	ALBERT GOODWILL SPALDING	1939
THEODORE LYONS	1955	TRISTRAM E. (TRIS) SPEAKER	1937
CONNIE MACK	1937	CHARLES D. STENGEL	1966
LELAND S. MacPHAIL	1978	WILLIAM H. TERRY	1954
MICKEY C. MANTLE	1974	SAMUEL L. THOMPSON	1974
HENRY E. MANUSH	1964	JOSEPH B. TINKER	1946
WALTER (RABBIT) MARANVILLE	1954	HAROLD J. (PIE) TRAYNOR	1948
RICHARD W. (RUBE) MARQUARD	1971	C. ARTHUR (DAZZY) VANCE	1955
EDWIN L. MATHEWS	1978	GEORGE EDWARD WADDELL	1946
CHRISTY MATHEWSON	1936	HONUS WAGNER	1936
JOSEPH V. McCARTHY	1957	RODERICK (BOBBY) WALLACE	1953
THOMAS F. McCARTHY	1946	EDWARD ARTHUR WALSH	1946
JOSEPH JEROME McGINNITY	1946	LLOYD J. WANER	1967
JOHN J. McGRAW	1937	PAUL WANER	1952
WILLIAM B. MC KECHNIE	1962	JOHN MONTGOMERY WARD	1964
JOSEPH M. MEDWICK	1968	GEORGE M. WEISS	1971
STANLEY F. MUSIAL	1969	MICHAEL F. WELCH	1973
CHARLES A. (KID) NICHOLS	1949	ZACK WHEAT	1959
JAMES H. O'ROURKE	1945	THEODORE S. WIIILIAMS	1966
MELVIN T. OTT	1951	GEORGE WRIGHT	1937
LEROY R. (SATCHEL) PAIGE	1971	HARRY WRIGHT	1953
HERBERT J. PENNOCK	1948	EARLY WYNN	1972
EDWARD S. PLANK	1946	DENTON T. (CY) YOUNG	1937
CHARLIE RADBOURN	1939	ROSS M. YOUNGS	1972

NO-HIT GAMES

Quite distinct from baseball's Hall of Fame is its "hall of fame." The capital difference comes down to this—meritorious service for a long period of years leads to candidacy for an actual plaque in Cooperstown's honored corridors, whereas anybody can make the lower-case "hall of fame" simply by pitching a no-hit game.

Many mediocrities have found the magic formula for one unhittable afternoon, pitchers who landed back in the minors a scant year or two after their headline-making masterpiece. "It's like catching lightning in a bottle," says one veteran manager. Though this simile exaggerates the factor of luck involved, still it can't be a matter of sheer skill, speed and stamina, because fully half the pitchers in the upper-strata, upper-case Hall of Fame never notched no-hitters.

When no batter can reach base—whether by hit, walk, error, hit-by-pitched-ball or plain black magic—then the pitcher has earned a "perfect game." Seven such paragons adorn the no-hit roster, though some statistical purists still challenge Ernie Shore's right to rank up there.

On June 23, 1917, Shore shuffled out of the Red Sox bullpen to relieve Babe Ruth, who had just been ordered out of the game for squawking too boisterously after pitching a fourth ball to the first Washington batter, Ray Morgan. With Shore on the mound, Morgan was thrown out trying to steal second base. Shore proceeded to retire the remaining 26 batters in order.

Far more controversial than Shore's game are two other entries on the all-time no-hit honor roll, which made the grade only when the official scorer changed his mind after having announced a "hit" earlier in the game. Some record books also omit the early no-hitters, because all pitching was underhand until 1884, while the pitching distance was only 45 feet until 1881, 50 feet until 1893 and 60½ feet thereafter.

Here is the complete chronological collection of major league no-hit performances over the first nine innings of a game. An asterisk (*) marks "perfect game." Each line shows the date, pitcher, his club and league, opposing club and final score. All games were played in the home park of the no-hit hurler, except when "at" appears just before the name of the victimized club.

July 28, 1875 - Joseph E. Borden, Philadelphia NA vs. Chicago........	4-0
July 15, 1876 - George W. Bradley, St. Louis NL vs. Hartford..........	2-0
June 12, 1880 - John L. Richmond, Worcester NL vs. Cleveland........	1-0*
June 17, 1880 - John M. Ward, Providence NL vs. Buffalo (AM).......	5-0*
Aug. 19, 1880 - Lawrence J. Corcoran, Chicago NL vs. Boston........	6-0
Aug. 20, 1880 - James F. Galvin, Buffalo NL at Worcester.............	1-0
Sept. 11, 1882 - Antoine J. Mullane, Louisville AA at Cincinnati........	2-0
Sept. 19, 1882 - Guy J. Hecker, Louisville AA at Pittsburgh.............	3-1
Sept. 20, 1882 - Lawrence J. Corcoran, Chicago NL at Worcester....	5-0
July 25, 1883 - Charles G. Radbourn, Providence NL at Cleveland....	8-0
Sept. 13, 1883 - Hugh I. Daly, Cleveland NL at Philadelphia.............	1-0
May 24, 1884 - Albert W. Atkisson, Philadelphia AA at Pittsburgh....	10-1
May 29, 1884 - Edward Morris, Columbus AA at Pittsburgh............	5-0
June 5, 1884 - Frank H. Mountain, Columbus AA at Washington.......	12-0
June 27, 1884 - Lawrence J. Corcoran, Chicago NL vs. Providence...	6-0
Aug. 4, 1884 - James F. Galvin, Buffalo NL at Detroit....................	18-0
Aug. 26, 1884 - Richard S. Burns, Cincinnati UA at Kansas City........	3-1
Sept. 28, 1884 - Edward L. Cushman, Milwaukee UA vs. Washington...	5-0
Oct. 4, 1884 - Samuel J. Kimber, Brooklyn AA at Toledo (10 innings)................	0-0
July 27, 1885 - John G. Clarkson, Chicago NL at Providence...........	4-0
Aug. 29, 1885 - Charles J. Ferguson, Philadelphia NL vs. Providence	1-0
May 1, 1886 - Albert W. Atkisson, Philadelphia AA vs. New York ...	3-2
July 24, 1886 - William J. Terry, Brooklyn AA vs. St. Louis...........	1-0
Oct. 6, 1886 - Matthew A. Kilroy, Baltimore AA at Pittsburgh........	6-0
May 27, 1888 - William J. Terry, Brooklyn AA vs. Louisville..........	4-0
June 6, 1888 - Henry Porter, Kansas City AA at Baltimore............	4-0
July 26, 1888 - Edward W. Seward, Philadelphia AA vs. Cincinnati ...	12-2
July 31, 1888 - August P. Weyhing, Philadelphia AA vs. Kansas City	4-0
Sept. 15, 1890 - Ledell Titcomb, Rochester AA vs. Syracuse............	7-0
June 22, 1891 - Thomas J. Lovett, Brooklyn NL vs. New York.........	4-0
July 31, 1891 - Amos W. Rusie, New York NL vs. Brooklyn............	6-0
Oct. 4, 1891 - Theodore P. Breitenstein, St. Louis AA vs. Louisville	8-0
Aug. 6, 1892 - John C. Stivetts, Boston NL at Brooklyn.................	11-0
Aug. 22, 1892 - Alexander B. Sanders, Louisville NL vs. Baltimore...	6-2
Oct. 15, 1892 - Charles L. Jones, Cincinnati NL vs. Pittsburgh........	7-1
Aug. 16, 1893 - William V. Hawke, Baltimore NL at Washington........	5-0
Sept. 18, 1897 - Denton T. Young, Cleveland NL vs. Cincinnati..........	6-0
Apr. 22, 1898 - Theodore P. Breitenstein, Cincinnati NL vs. Pittsburgh..................	11-0
Apr. 22, 1898 - James J. Hughes, Baltimore NL vs. Boston.............	8-0

July 8, 1898 - Francis R. Donahue, Philadelphia NL vs. Boston.......	5-0
Aug. 21, 1898 - Walter M. Thornton, Chicago NL vs. Brooklyn..........	2-0
May 25, 1899 - Charles L. Phillippe, Louisville NL vs. New York.....	7-0
Aug. 7, 1899 - Victor G. Willis, Boston NL vs. Washington.............	7-1
July 12, 1900 - Frank G. Hahn, Cincinnati NL vs. Philadelphia.........	4-0
May 9, 1901 - Earl L. Moore, Cleveland AL vs. Chicago (9 innings, lost 10th).....................................	2-4
July 15, 1901 - Christopher Mathewson, New York NL at St. Louis....	5-0
Sept. 20, 1902 - James J. Callahan, Chicago AL vs. Detroit (1st game)	3-0
Sept. 18, 1903 - Charles C. Fraser, Philadelphia NL at Chicago.......	10-0
May 5, 1904 - Denton T. Young, Boston AL vs. Philadelphia...........	3-0*
June 11, 1904 - Robert K. Wicker, Chicago NL vs. New York (9 innings, won in 12th).....................................	1-0
Aug. 17, 1904 - Jesse N. Tannehill, Boston AL at Chicago...............	6-0
June 13, 1905 - Christopher Mathewson, New York NL at Chicago......	1-0
July 22, 1905 - Weldon Henley, Philadelphia AL at St. Louis (1st game)	6-0
Sept. 6, 1905 - Frank E. Smith, Chicago AL at Detroit (2nd game)....	15-0
Sept. 27, 1905 - William H. Dinneen, Boston AL vs. Chicago (1st game)	2-0
May 1, 1906 - John C. Lush, Philadelphia NL at Brooklyn..............	1-0
July 20, 1906 - Malcolm W. Eason, Brooklyn NL at St. Louis...........	2-0
Aug. 1, 1906 - Harry M. McIntire, Brooklyn NL vs. Pittsburgh (10 innings, lost in 13th)..........................	0-1
May 8, 1907 - Francis X. Pfeffer, Boston NL vs. Cincinnati..........	6-0
Sept. 20, 1907 - Nicholas Maddox, Pittsburgh NL vs. Brooklyn..........	2-1
June 30, 1908 - Denton T. Young, Boston AL at New York	8-0
July 4, 1908 - George L. Wiltse, New York NL vs. Philadelphia (10 innings) (AM).....................................	1-0
Sept. 5, 1908 - George N. Rucker, Brooklyn NL vs. Boston (2nd game).....................................	6-0
Sept. 18, 1908 - Robert B. Rhoades, Cleveland AL vs. Boston...........	2-1
Sept. 20, 1908 - Frank E. Smith, Chicago AL vs. Philadelphia..........	1-0
Oct. 2, 1908 - Adrian C. Joss, Cleveland AL vs. Chicago..............	1-0*
Apr. 15, 1909 - Leon K. Ames, New York NL vs. Brooklyn (9 innings, lost in 13th).....................................	0-3
Apr. 20, 1910 - Adrian C. Joss, Cleveland AL at Chicago...............	1-0
May 12, 1910 - Charles A. Bender, Philadelphia AL vs. Cleveland....	4-0
Aug. 30, 1910 - Thomas L. Hughes, New York AL vs. Cleveland (9 innings, lost in 11th)	0-5
July 29, 1911 - Joe Wood, Boston AL vs. St. Louis (1st game)..........	5-0
Aug. 27, 1911 - Edward A. Walsh, Chicago AL vs. Boston...............	5-0
July 4, 1912 - George E. Mullin, Detroit AL vs. St. Louis (PM).......	7-0
Aug. 30, 1912 - Earl A. Hamilton, St. Louis AL at Detroit.............	5-1
Sept. 6, 1912 - Charles M. Tesreau, New York NL at Philadelphia (1st game).....................................	3-0
May 14, 1914 - James Scott, Chicago AL at Washington (9 innings, lost in 10th).....................................	0-1
May 31, 1914 - Joseph L. Benz, Chicago AL vs. Cleveland	6-1
Sept. 9, 1914 - George A. Davis, Boston NL vs. Philadelphia (2nd game).....................................	7-0
Sept. 19, 1914 - Edward F. LaFitte, Brooklyn FL vs. Kansas City (1st game).....................................	6-2
Apr. 15, 1915 - Richard W. Marquard, New York NL vs. Brooklyn	2-0
Apr. 24, 1915 - Frank L. Allen, Pittsburgh FL at St. Louis..............	2-0
May 15, 1915 - Claude R. Hendrix, Chicago FL at Pittsburgh...........	10-0

Aug. 16, 1915 - Miles G. Main, Kansas City FL at Buffalo................   5-0
Aug. 31, 1915 - James S. Lavender, Chicago NL at New York (1st
               game)...   2-0
Sept. 7, 1915 - Arthur D. Davenport, St. Louis FL vs. Chicago (1st
               game)...   3-0
June 16, 1916 - Thomas L. Hughes, Boston NL vs. Pittsburgh...........   2-0
June 21, 1916 - George Foster, Boston AL vs. New York   2-0
Aug. 26, 1916 - Leslie J. Bush, Philadelphia AL vs. Cleveland.........   5-0
Aug. 30, 1916 - Hubert B. Leonard, Boston AL vs. St. Louis.............   4-0
Apr. 14, 1917 - Edward V. Cicotte, Chicago AL at St. Louis   11-0
Apr. 24, 1917 - George A. Mogridge, New York AL at Boston   2-1
May   2, 1917 - Frederick A. Toney, Cincinnati NL at Chicago (10
               innings)   1-0
May   2, 1917 - James L. Vaughn, Chicago NL vs. Cincinnati (9 in-
               nings, lost in 10th)   0-1
May   5, 1917 - Ernest G. Koob, St. Louis AL vs. Chicago...............   1-0
May   6, 1917 - Robert Groom, St. Louis AL vs. Chicago (2nd game)..   3-0
June 23, 1917 - Ernest G. Shore, Boston· AL vs. Washington (1st
               game)...   4-0*
June 3, 1918 - Hubert B. Leonard, Boston AL at Detroit   5-0
May 11, 1919 - Horace O. Eller, Cincinnati NL vs. St. Louis............   6-0
Sept. 10, 1919 - Raymond B. Caldwell, Cleveland AL at New York
               (1st game)........   3-0
July 1, 1920 - Walter P. Johnson, Washington AL at Boston............   1-0
Apr. 30, 1922 - Charles C. Robertson, Chicago AL at Detroit 2-0*
May   7, 1922 - Jesse L. Barnes, New York NL vs. Philadelphia......   6-0
Sept. 4, 1923 - Samuel P. Jones, New York AL at Philadelphia........   2-0
Sept. 7, 1923 - Howard J. Ehmke, Boston AL at Philadelphia...........   4-0
July 17, 1924 - Jesse J. Haines, St. Louis NL vs. Boston   5-0
Sept. 13, 1925 - Arthur C. Vance, Brooklyn NL vs. Philadelphia (1st
               game)...   10-1
Aug. 21, 1926 - Theodore A. Lyons, Chicago AL at Boston   6-0
May   8, 1929 - Carl O. Hubbell, New York NL vs. Pittsburgh...........   11-0
Apr. 29, 1931 - Wesley C. Ferrell, Cleveland AL vs. St. Louis.........   9-0
Aug. 8, 1931 - Robert J. Burke, Washington AL vs. Boston   5-0
Sept. 18, 1934 - Louis N. Newsom, St. Louis AL vs. Boston (9 in-
               nings, lost in 10th)..   1-2
Sept. 21, 1934 - Paul D. Dean, St. Louis NL at Brooklyn (2nd game)...   3-0
Aug. 31, 1935 - Lloyd V. Kennedy, Chicago AL vs. Cleveland............   5-0
June 1, 1937 - William J. Dietrich, Chicago AL vs. St. Louis.........   8-0
June 11, 1938 - John S. Vander Meer, Cincinnati NL vs. Boston........   3-0
June 15, 1938 - John S. Vander Meer, Cincinnati NL vs. Brooklyn
               (night)...   6-0
Aug. 27, 1938 - Marcellus M. Pearson, New York AL vs. Cleveland
               (2nd game)...   13-0
Apr. 16, 1940 - Robert W. Feller, Cleveland AL at Chicago.............   1-0
Apr. 30, 1940 - James O. Carleton, Brooklyn NL at Cincinnati.........   3-0
Aug. 30, 1941 - Lonnie Warneke, St. Louis NL at Cincinnati   2-0
Apr. 27, 1944 - James A. Tobin, Boston NL vs. Brooklyn   2-0
May 15, 1944 - Clyde M. Shoun, Cincinnati NL vs. Boston   1-0
Sept. 9, 1945 - Richard J. Fowler, Philadelphia AL vs. St. Louis
               (2nd game)..   1-0
Apr. 23, 1946 - Edward M. Head, Brooklyn NL vs. Boston................   5-0

Apr. 30, 1946	- Robert W. Feller, Cleveland AL at New York	1-0
June 18, 1947	- Ewell Blackwell, Cincinnati NL vs. Boston (night).....	6-0
July 10, 1947	- Donald P. Black, Cleveland AL vs. Philadelphia (twilight)	3-0
Sept. 3, 1947	- William G. McCahan, Philadelphia AL vs. Washington	3-0
June 30, 1948	- Robert G. Lemon, Cleveland AL at Detroit (night).....	2-0
Sept. 9, 1948	- Rex E. Barney, Brooklyn NL at New York (night)......	2-0
Aug. 11, 1950	- Vernon E. Bickford, Boston NL vs. Brooklyn (night)..	7-0
May 6, 1951	- Clifford D. Chambers, Pittsburgh NL at Boston (2nd game)...	3-0
July 1, 1951	- Robert W. Feller, Cleveland AL vs. Detroit (1st game)...	2-1
July 12, 1951	- Allie P. Reynolds, New York AL at Cleveland (night)	1-0
Sept. 28, 1951	- Allie P. Reynolds, New York AL vs. Boston (1st game)...	8-0
May 15, 1952	- Virgil O. Trucks, Detroit AL vs. Washington	1-0
June 19, 1952	- Carl D. Erskine, Brooklyn NL vs. Chicago	5-0
Aug. 25, 1952	- Virgil O. Trucks, Detroit AL at New York	1-0
May 6, 1953	- Alva L. Holloman, St. Louis AL vs. Philadelphia (night)	6-0
June 12, 1954	- James A. Wilson, Milwaukee NL vs. Philadelphia	2-0
May 12, 1955	- Sam Jones, Chicago NL vs. Pittsburgh	4-0
May 12, 1956	- Carl D. Erskine, Brooklyn NL vs. New York	· 3-0
July 14, 1956	- Melvin L. Parnell, Boston AL vs. Chicago	4-0
Sept. 25, 1956	- Salvatore A. Maglie, Brooklyn NL vs. Philadelphia ...	5-0
Oct. 8, 1956	- Donald J. Larsen, New York AL vs. Brooklyn NL (World Series)	2-0*
Aug. 20, 1957	- Robert C. Keegan, Chicago AL vs. Washington (2nd game, night)	6-0
July 20, 1958	- James Bunning, Detroit AL at Boston (1st game)	3-0
Sept. 20, 1958	- Hoyt Wilhelm, Baltimore AL vs. New York	1-0
May 26, 1959	- Harvey Haddix, Pittsburgh NL at Milwaukee (night)	0-1
May 15, 1960	- Donald Cardwell, Chicago NL vs. St. Louis (2nd game)	4-0
Aug. 18, 1960	- S. Lewis Burdette, Milwaukee NL vs. Philadelphia (night)	1-0
Sept. 16, 1960	- Warren E. Spahn, Milwaukee NL vs. Philadelphia (night)	4-0
April 28, 1961	- Warren E. Spahn, Milwaukee NL vs. San Francisco (night)	1-0
May 5, 1962	- Robert Belinsky, Los Angeles AL vs. Baltimore (night)	2-0
June 26, 1962	- Earl L. Wilson, Boston AL vs. Los Angeles (night) ..	2-0
June 30, 1962	- Sandy Koufax, Los Angeles NL vs. New York (night) ..	5-0
Aug. 1, 1962	- William Monbouquette, Boston AL at Chicago (night)	1-0
Aug. 26, 1962	- Jack Kralick, Minnesota AL vs. Kansas City	1-0
May 11, 1963	- Sandy Koufax, Los Angeles NL vs. San Francisco (night)	8-0
May 17, 1963	- Donald Nottebart, Houston NL vs. Philadelphia (night)	4-1
June 15, 1963	- Juan Marichal, San Francisco NL vs. Houston	1-0
April 23, 1964	- Kenneth T. Johnson, Houston NL vs. Cincinnati (night)	0-1
June 4, 1964	- Sandy Koufax, Los Angeles NL at Philadelphia (night)	3-0
June 21, 1964	- James Bunning, Philadelphia NL at New York (1st game)	6-0*
June 14, 1965	- James W. Maloney, Cincinnati NL vs. New York (night) (10 innings, lost in 11th)	0-1
Aug. 19, 1965	- James W. Maloney, Cincinnati NL at Chicago (1st game, 10 innings)	1-0
Sept. 9, 1965	- Sandy Koufax, Los Angeles NL vs. Chicago (night) ..	1-0*
Sept. 16, 1965	- David M. Morehead, Boston AL vs. Cleveland	2-0
June 10, 1966	- Wilfred C. Siebert, Cleveland AL vs. Washington (night)	3-0
June 18, 1967	- Donald E. Wilson, Houston NL vs. Atlanta	2-0
Aug. 25, 1967	- W. Dean Chance, Minnesota AL at Cleveland (2nd game, night)	2-1

Sept. 10, 1967—Joel E. Horlen, Chicago AL vs. Detroit (1st game) ...   6-0
April 27, 1968—Thomas H. Phoebus, Baltimore AL vs. Boston   6-0
May   8, 1968—James A. Hunter, Oakland AL at Minnesota (night) ..   4-0*
July 29, 1968—George R. Culver, Cincinnati NL at Philadelphia (2nd
                game, night)   6-1
Sept. 17, 1968—Gaylord Perry, San Francisco NL vs. St. Louis (night) .   1-0
Sept. 18, 1968—Ray C. Washburn, St. Louis NL at San Francisco   2-0
April 17, 1969—William H. Stoneman, Montreal NL at Philadelphia
                (night)   7-0
April 30, 1969—James W. Maloney, Cincinnati NL vs. Houston (night)   10-0
May   1, 1969—Donald E. Wilson, Houston NL at Cincinnati (night)   4-0
Aug. 13, 1969—James A. Palmer, Baltimore AL vs. Oakland (night) ..   8-0
Aug. 19, 1969—Kenneth Holtzman, Chicago NL vs. Atlanta   3-0
Sept. 20, 1969—Robert R. Moose, Pittsburgh NL at New York   4-0
June 12, 1970—Dock Ellis, Pittsburgh NL at San Diego (1st game) ..   2-0
July   3, 1970—Clyde Wright, California AL vs. Oakland (night)   4-0
July 20, 1970—William Singer, Los Angeles NL vs. Philadelphia   5-0
Sept. 21, 1970—Vida Blue, Oakland AL vs. Minnesota (night)   6-0
June   3, 1971—Kenneth Holtzman, Chicago NL at Cincinnati (night) ..   1-0
June 23, 1971—Richard Wise, Philadelphia NL at Cincinnati (night) ..   4-0
Aug. 14, 1971—Robert Gibson, St. Louis NL at Pittsburgh (night)   11-0
April 16, 1972—Burt Hooton, Chicago NL vs. Philadelphia   4-0
Sept. 2, 1972—Milton Pappas, Chicago NL vs. San Diego   8-0
Oct.   2, 1972—William Stoneman, Montreal NL vs. New York (1st game,
                twilight)   7-0
April 27, 1973—Steven Busby, Kansas City AL at Detroit (night)   3-0
May   15, 1973—L. Nolan Ryan, California AL at Kansas City (night)   3-0
July 15, 1973—L. Nolan Ryan, California AL at Detroit   6-0
July 30, 1973—James Bibby, Texas AL at Oakland (night)   6-0
Aug.   5, 1973—Philip Niekro, Atlanta NL vs. San Diego   9-0
June 19, 1974—Steven Busby, Kansas City AL at Milwaukee (night)   2-0
July 19, 1974—Richard Bosman, Cleveland AL vs. Oakland (night)   4-0
Sept. 28, 1974—L. Nolan Ryan, California AL vs. Minnesota (night) ..   4-0
June   1, 1975—L. Nolan Ryan, California AL vs. Baltimore   1-0
Aug. 24, 1975—Edward Halicki, San Francisco NL vs. New York (2nd g)   6-0
July   9, 1976—Lawrence Dierker, Houston NL vs. Montreal (night) ..   6-0
Aug.   9, 1976—John Candelaria, Pittsburgh NL vs. Los Angeles (night) ..   2-0
Sept. 29, 1976—John Montefusco, San Francisco NL at Atlanta (night) ..   9-0
May   14, 1977—James W. Colborn, Kansas City AL vs. Texas (night) ..   6-0
May   30, 1977—Dennis L. Eckersley, Cleveland AL vs. California (night)   1-0
Sept. 22, 1977—Rik A. Blyleven, Texas AL at California (night)   6-0
Apr. 16, 1978—Robert H. Forsch, St. Louis NL vs. Philadelphia   5-0

ALL-STAR GAMES

For sheer spectacle, the All-Star Game is perhaps baseball's greatest one-day show for the fans. The idea, conceived by the late Arch Ward, sports editor of the *Chicago Tribune*, was originally planned to add a baseball flavor to the Chicago Century of Progress exposition in 1933. However, the success of the initial contest made Ward envision an annual affair between the two leagues in which the best players from each circuit would play.

For a time the fans selected the makeup of the two teams through the use of ballots. However, baseball decided that it would be the best judge of playing talent, and the squads were chosen by the rival managers. When the fans expressed nation-wide dissatisfaction with this system, the game was placed back into their hands. Only the pitchers are now chosen by the rival managers, who qualify for their posts by virtue of winning the pennant in the previous season.

HIGHLIGHTS, THROUGH THE YEARS: 1933, Babe Ruth's line drive homer with one aboard brought the AL triumph. Two of baseball's most famous managers were selected to guide their respective leagues, Connie Mack and John McGraw. . . . 1934, Carl Hubbell, although pitching for the losing NL, gained immortality by striking out Babe Ruth, Lou Gehrig, Jimmy Foxx, Al Simmons and Joe Cronin in succession with his incredible screwball. . . . 1935, Lefty Gomez and Mel Harder hurled flawlessly for the winning AL. . . . 1936, Joe DiMaggio, baseball's highly-touted rookie, played poorly as Augie Galan's foul-pole homer gave NL its first triumph. . . . 1937, President Roosevelt watched Dizzy Dean receive a broken toe which was to hasten the end of his meteoric career. . . . 1938, Double no-hit hero Johnny Vander Meer hurled NL to victory. . . . 1939, Bob Feller, in relief role, helped Yankee-dominated AL. . . . 1940, Max West's first inning homer with two aboard clinched triumph for NL. . . . 1941, Ted Williams drove circuit over right field roof with two on and two out in ninth inning to give AL dramatic come-from-behind verdict. . . . 1942, Twilight game marked by pair of first inning AL homers. . . . 1943, Bobby Doerr drove in three runs for victorious AL. . . . 1944, NL coasted as Phil Cavarretta reached base five times. . . . 1945, Game suspended in order to comply with war-time restrictions on travel curtailment. . . . 1946, Two homers by Ted Williams gave AL its most one-sided triumph. . . . 1947, Pitching dominated in slickly-played AL verdict. . . . 1948, Underdog AL, riddled by injuries, prevailed. . . . 1949, Hitters held sway as AL won slugfest. . . . 1950, Red Schoendienst's 14th inning homer gave NL victory behind brilliant pitching. . . . 1951, Four homers helped NL. . . . 1952, Rain-curtailed contest decided by NL circuit clouts. . . . 1953, Strong NL pitching kept AL hitters at bay. . . . 1954, Nellie Fox's eighth-inning bloop single gave AL decision in homer-punctuated thriller. . . . 1955, Stan Musial cracked game-winning homer in 12th inning as NL overcame five-run deficit. . . . 1956, Timely hitting and sparkling third-base play by Ken Boyer helped NL to victory. . . . 1957, Early AL lead barely held off late NL rally. . . . 1958, Superb relief hurling by Billy O'Dell featured AL triumph. . . . 1959, Increased to two games to increase player's pension fund. A pitching duel climaxed by Willie Mays' triple enabled the Nationals to win 5-4. The AL won the second tilt 5-3. The big blows were a homer by Berra, two errors and a single by Nellie Fox. . . . 1960, Again a double feature with NL winning both games. Mays' triple and Banks' homer featured the NL attack in the first game. The second game featured four home runs by Mathews, Mays, Musial and Boyer; the Nationals winning 6-0. . . . 1961, Two games again featured the 1961 All-Star games. The Nationals won the first game and the second ended in a 1-1 tie. Most of the action in the first game was concentrated in the 9th

and 10th innings when the Giants relief artist, little Stu Miller was almost blown off the mound for a costly balk from the gales blowing in Candlestick Park. The gale was also responsible for the 7 errors committed in the game. George Altman of the Cubs entered the game as a pinch hitter in the 8th inning and slammed a home run. The second game marked the first tie game in All-Star history when the rains washed it out after nine innings of play. Rocky Colavito of the Tigers connected with one of Bob Purkey's pitches for a homer in the first inning and the Nationals tied it up in the sixth, filling the bases and then scoring the lone run on an infield hit by Bill White. . . . 1962, In the first game played in Washington's new park Maury Wills of the Dodgers put on a base-running exhibition by stealing second as a pinch runner for Stan Musial who had singled and again in the eighth, this time on his own, he thrilled the crowd by stealing third on a single to left when Colavito momentarily held the ball and then scoring on a short fly to right field. The Nationals triumphed 3–1 to win their fifth victory in seven games and to come within one game of tying the Americans. However the American League recovered to take the second game which was played in Wrigley Field, Chicago by a score of 9 to 4. The AL won this one by relying on their old weapon, the home run. Pete Runnels, Leon Wagner and Rocky Colavito slammed the round-trippers for the Americans. The game was also featured by the excellent pitching of the White Sox' Ray Herbert who entered the game in the third and faced only 10 batters until relieved by Hank Aguirre of the Tigers at the start of the sixth inning. . . . 1963—Reverting to the single All-Star Game for the first time since 1958, the NL won the 34th game of the All-Star Classic by a score of 5–3. Willie Mays was the outstanding star of this one when he stole two bases and played his usual brilliant game in the field. Tommy Davis scored the deciding run. . . . 1964—Johnny Callison's dramatic three-run homer in the bottom of the ninth provided the NL with a 7–4 victory in the 35th game. Billy Williams and Ken Boyer also cracked round-trippers for the Nationals, who squared the series at 17 games apiece with one tie. . . . 1965—Mays, who has made the All-Star game his private showcase, homered, walked twice, scored the deciding run and starred afield as the NL posted a 6–5 triumph and took the lead in the series for the first time, 18 to 17. Joe Torre and Willie Stargell also connected for the senior circuit while Dick McAuliffe and Harmon Killebrew poled circuits for the AL. . . . 1966—The 37th All-Star game was the fourth to go into extra innings, and for the third time a member of the St. Louis Cardinals scored the winning run. Redbird catcher Tim McCarver opened the 10th with a sharp single, moved to second on Ron Hunts' perfect sacrifice bunt and tallied on Maury Wills' single to short right, the NL prevailing by a 2–1 count. Brooks Robinson, Baltimore's crack third baseman, punched out three hits, scored the Americans' only run and set a record for third sackers by handling eight chances, several of an eye-catching nature. . . . 1967—Home runs accounted for all the scoring and, as has become the habit in recent games, the NL had the edge. Richie Allen connected in the second inning and Tony Perez hit one out in the 15th to win the 38th classic, 2–1. Brooks Robinson homered in the sixth for the AL. . . . 1968—The NL extended its winning streak to six and its over-all advantage to 21–17 with a narrow 1–0 victory in Houston's Astrodome. Pitchers stole the spotlight as the winning NL managed only five hits, the losing AL three. Willie Mays scored the lone run on a double play. . . . 1969—The hitters finally broke loose, after three pitching-dominated games, with the NL romping to a 9–3 win for its seventh straight triumph. San Francisco's Willie McCovey slammed a pair of homers and Cincinnati catcher John Bench hit one to lead the Nationals' on-slaught. Frank Howard and Bill Freehan tagged solo homers for the AL.

. . . 1970—After 13 years, balloting for players was again given to the fans. The NL won their eighth straight game, 5–4 in 12 innings. Jim Hickman singled in Pete Rose, who bowled over catcher Ray Fosse, with the winning run. The NL had rallied from a 4–1 deficit to tie the game in the ninth. . . . 1971—The AL won their first game in nine years, thanks to two-run homers by Frank Robinson, Reggie Jackson, and Harmon Killebrew. All runs for both teams in the 6–4 triumph resulted from the record-tying six home runs. . . . 1972—Joe Morgan scored Nate Colbert from second in the last of the tenth to give the NL a 4–3 verdict. The Nationals had to come from behind in the ninth to tie after Hank Aaron and Cookie Rojas exchanged two-run homers earlier. . . . 1973—Bobby Bonds cracked out a double and two-run homer to lead the NL to a 7–1 romp. Johnny Bench and Willie Davis also homered for the Nationals, who now stand 25–18 in 44 games. Willie Mays tied Stan Musial's mark of 24 games played. . . . 1974—Steve Garvey contributed a double, single and a key defensive play as the NL took another victory, 7–2. Reggie Smith added a homer. . . . 1975— The National League took advantage of sloppy fielding to score three runs in the 9th, giving them a 6–3 win, their 12th in the last 13 games, and 27 of 45 overall. Carl Yastrzemski had previously cancelled an early NL lead with a pinch 3-run homer in the 6th. Hank Aaron played in his 24th game, tying Musial and Mays. . . . 1976—George Foster led the National League to still another All-Star win, driving in three runs. Foster was one of five Cincinnati players voted into the starting lineup. . . . 1977—NL jumped on Jim Palmer for two homers in the first inning and then hung on for another victory. . . . 1978—Rod Carew's two triples were wasted as Jim Palmer's control failed, allowing the NL to tie in the third. Steve Garvey tripled and scored the winning run in the eighth. The National League has now won 15 of the last 16 games and leads 30–18 overall.

1st game, at Chicago (AL), July 6, 1933

					R.	H.	E.
National	000	002	000	---	2	8	0
American	012	001	00x	---	4	9	1

Pitchers--HALLAHAN, Warneke (3), Hubbell (7) vs. GOMEZ, Crowder (4), Grove (7). Homers--Ruth (AL), Frisch (NL). Attendance--49,200. Receipts--$56,378.50.

2nd game, at New York (NL), July 10, 1934

American	000	261	000	---	9	14	1
National	103	030	000	---	7	8	1

Pitchers--Gomez, Ruffing (4), HARDER (5) vs. Hubbell, Warneke (4), MUNGO (5), J. Dean (6), Frankhouse (8). Homers--Frisch (NL), Medwick (NL). Attendance--48,363. Receipts--$52,982.

3rd game, at Cleveland (AL), July 8, 1935

National	000	100	000	---	1	4	1
American	210	010	00x	---	4	8	0

Pitchers--WALKER, Schumacher (3), Derringer (7), J. Dean (8) vs. GOMEZ, Harder (7). Homer--Foxx (AL). Attendance- 69,812. Receipts--$82,179.12.

4th game, at Boston (NL), July 7, 1936

American	000	000	300	---	3	7	1
National	020	020	00x	---	4	9	0

Pitchers--GROVE, Rowe (4), Harder (7) vs. J. DEAN, Hubbell (4), C. Davis (7), Warneke (7). Homers--Gehrig (AL), Galan (NL). Attendance--25,534. Receipts--$24,588.-80.

5th game, at Washington (AL), July 7, 1937

National	000	111	000	---	3	13	0
American	002	312	00x	---	8	13	2

Pitchers--J. DEAN, Hubbell (4), Blanton (5), Grissom (5), Mungo (6), Walters (8) vs. GOMEZ, Bridges (4), Harder (7). Homer--Gehrig (AL). Attendance--31,391. Receipts--$28,475.18.

6th game, at Cincinnati (NL), July 6, 1938

American	000	000	001	---	1	7	4
National	100	100	20x	---	4	8	0

Pitchers--GOMEZ, Allen (4), Grove (7) vs. VANDER MEER, Lee (4), Brown (7). Homers--None. Attendance--27,607. Receipts--$38,469.05.

7th game, at New York (AL), July 11, 1939

National	001	000	000	---	1	7	1
American	000	210	00x	---	3	6	1

Pitchers--Derringer, LEE (4), Fette (7) vs. Ruffing, BRIDGES (4), Feller (6). Homer--J. DiMaggio (AL). Attendance--62,892. Receipts--$75,701.

8th game, at St. Louis (NL), July 9, 1940

American	000	000	000	---	0	3	1
National	300	000	01x	---	4	7	0

Pitchers--RUFFING, Newsom (4), Feller (7) vs. DER-RINGER, Walters (3), Wyatt (5), French (7), Hubbell (9). Homer--West (NL). Attendance--32,373. Receipts--$36,-723.03.

9th game, at Detroit (AL), July 8, 1941

National	000	001	220	---	5	10	2
American	000	101	014	---	7	11	3

Pitchers--Wyatt, Derringer (3), Walters (5), PASSEAU (7) vs. Feller, Lee (4), Hudson (7), SMITH (8). Homers--Vaughan (NL) 2, Williams (AL). Attendance--54,675. Receipts--$63,267.06.

10th game, at New York (NL), July 6, 1942

American	300	000	000	---	3	7	0
National	000	000	010	---	1	6	1

Pitchers--CHANDLER, Benton (5), vs. M. COOPER, Vander Meer (4), Passeau (7), Walters (9). Homers--Boudreau (AL), York (AL), Owen (NL). Attendance--33,694. Receipts--$86,102.98.

11th game, at Philadelphia (AL), July 13, 1943

National	100	000	101	---	3	10	1
American	031	010	00x	---	5	8	2

Pitchers--M. COOPER, Vander Meer (3), Sewell (6), Javery (7) vs. LEONARD, Newhouser (4), Hughson (7). Homers--Doerr (AL), V. DiMaggio (NL). Attendance--31,938. Receipts--$65,674.

12th game, at Pittsburgh (NL), July 11, 1944

American	010	000	000	---	1	6	3
National	000	040	21x	---	7	12	1

Pitchers--Borowy, HUGHSON (4), Muncrief (5), Newhouser (7), Newsom (8) vs. Walters, RAFFENSBERGER (4), Sewell (6), Tobin (9). Homers--None. Attendance--29,589. Receipts--$81,275.

(NO GAME IN 1945) R. H. E.

13th game, at Boston (AL), July 9, 1946

National	000	000	000	---	0	3	0
American	200	130	24x	---	12	14	1

Pitchers--PASSEAU, Higbe (4), Blackwell (5), Sewell (8) vs. FELLER, Newhouser (4), Kramer (7). Homers- Williams (AL) 2, Keller (AL). Attendance--34,906. Receipts--$89,071.

14th game, at Chicago (NL), July 8, 1947

American	000	001	100	---	2	8	0
National	000	100	000	---	1	5	1

Pitchers--Newhouser, SHEA (4), Masterson (7), Page (8) vs. Blackwell, Brecheen (4), SAIN (7), Spahn (8). Homer Mize (NL). Attendance--41,123. Receipts--$105,314.90.

15th game, at St. Louis (AL), July 13, 1948

National	200	000	000	---	2	8	0
American	011	300	00x	---	5	6	0

Pitchers--Branca, SCHMITZ (4), Sain (4), Blackwell (6) vs. Masterson, RASCHI (4), Coleman (7). Homers--Musial (NL), Evers (AL). Attendance--34,009. Receipts--$93,447.07.

16th game, at Brooklyn (NL), July 12, 1949

American	400	202	300	---	11	13	1
National	212	002	000	---	7	12	5

Pitchers--Parnell, TRUCKS (2), Brissie (4), Raschi (7) vs. Spahn, NEWCOMBE (2), Munger (6), Bickford (6), Pollet (7), Blackwell (8), Roe (9). Homers- Musial (NL), Kiner (NL). Attendance--32,577. Receipts--$79,225.02.

17th game, at Chicago (AL), July 11, 1950

National	020	000	001 000 01	--	4	10	0
American	001	020	000 000 00	--	3	8	1

Pitchers--Roberts, Newcombe (4), Konstanty (6), Jansen (7), BLACKWELL (12) vs. Raschi, Lemon (4), Houtteman (7), Reynolds (10), GRAY (13), Feller (14). Homers--Kiner (NL), Schoendienst (NL). Attendance- 46,127. Receipts--$126,179.51.

18th game, at Detroit (AL), July 10, 1951

National	100	302	110	---	8	12	1
American	010	110	000	---	3	10	2

Pitchers--Roberts, MAGLIE (3), Newcombe (6), Blackwell (9) vs. Garver, LOPAT (4), Hutchinson (5), Parnell (8), Lemon (9). Homers--Musial (NL), Elliott (NL), Hodges (NL), Kiner (NL), Wertz (AL), Kell (AL). Attendance--52,075. Receipts--$124,294.07.

19th game, at Philadelphia (NL), July 8, 1952

American	000	20	---	2	5	0
National	100	20	---	3	3	0

Pitchers--Raschi, LEMON (3), Shantz (5) vs. Simmons, RUSH (4). Homers--Robinson (NL), Sauer (NL). Attendance--32,785. Receipts--$108,762.40.

20th game, at Cincinnati (NL), July 14, 1953

American	000	000	001	---	1	5	0
National	000	020	12x	---	5	10	0

Pitchers--Pierce, REYNOLDS (4), Garcia (6), Paige (8) vs. Roberts, SPAHN (4), Simmons (6), Dickson (8). Attendance--30,846. Receipts--$155,654.

21st game, at Cleveland (AL), July 13, 1954

National	000	520	020	---	9	14	0
American	004	121	03x	---	11	17	1

Roberts, Antonelli (4) Spahn (6), Grissom (6), CONLEY (8), Erskin (8) vs. Ford, Consuegra (4), Lemon (4), Porterfield (5), Keegan (8), STONE (8), Trucks (9). Homers--Rosen (AL) 2, Boone (AL), Doby (AL), Kluszewski (NL), Bell (NL). Attendance--68,751. Receipts--$292,678.

22nd game, at Milwaukee (NL), July 12, 1955

American	400	001	000	---	5	10	2
National	000	000	230 001	---	6	13	1

Pierce, Wynn (4), Ford (7), SULLIVAN (8) vs. Roberts, Haddix (4), Newcombe (7), Jones (8), Nuxhall (8), CONLEY (12). Homers--Mantle (AL), Musial (NL). Attendance--45,314. Receipts--$179,545.50.

23rd Game, at Washington (AL), July 10, 1956
```
National   001 211 200   ---   7 11 0
American   000 003 000   ---   3 11 0
```
FRIEND, Spahn (4), Antonelli (6) vs. PIERCE, Ford (4), Wilson (5), Brewer (6), Score (8), Wynn (9). Homers--Mays (NL), Musial (NL), Williams (AL), Mantle (AL). Attendance--28,843. Receipts--$105,928.50.

24th game, at St. Louis (NL), July 9, 1957
```
American   020 001 003   ---   6 10 0
National   000 000 203   ---   5  9 1
```
BUNNING, Loes (4), Wynn (7), Pierce (7), Moss (9), Grim (9) vs. SIMMONS, Burdette (2), Sanford (6), Jackson (7), Labine (9). Attendance--30,693. Receipts--$122,027.

25th game, at Baltimore (AL), July 8, 1958
```
National   210 000 000   ---   3 4 2
American   011 011 00x   ---   4 9 2
```
Spahn, FRIEND (4), Jackson (6), Farrell (7) vs. Turley, Nirleski (2), WYNN (6), O'Dell (7). Attendance--48,829. Receipts--$202,492.

26th game, at Pittsburgh (NL), July 7, 1959 (1st game)
```
American   000 100 030   ---   4 8 4
National   100 000 22X   ---   5 9 1
```
Pitchers--Wynn, Duren (4), Bunning (7), FORD (8), Daley (8) vs Drysdale, Burdette (4), Face (7), ANTONELLI (8), Elston (9). Homers--Mathews (NL), Kaline (AL). Attendance--35,277. Receipts--$229,636.

27th game, at Los Angeles (NL), August 3, 1959 (2nd game)
```
American   012 000 110   ---   5 6 0
National   100 010 100   ---   3 6 3
```
Pitchers--WALKER, Wynn (4), Wilhelm (6), O'Dell (7), McLish (8) vs DRYSDALE, Conley (4), Jones (6), Face (8). Homers--Malzone (AL), Berra (AL), Robinson (NL), Gilliam (8), Colavito (AL). Attendance--55,105. Receipts--$283,120.

28th game, at Kansas City (AL), July 11, 1960 (1st game)
```
National   311 000 000   ---   5 12 4
American   000 001 020   ---   3  6 1
```
Pitchers--FRIEND, McCormick (4), Face (6), Buhl (8), Law (9) vs MONBOUQUETTE, Estrada (3), Coates (4), Bell (6), Lary (8), Daley (9). Homers--Banks (NL), Crandall (NL), Kaline (AL) 2, Fox (AL). Attendance--30,619. Receipts--$151,238.38 (net).

29th game, at New York (AL), July 13, 1960 (2nd game)
```
National   021 000 102   ---   6 10 0
American   000 000 000   ---   0  8 0
```
Pitchers--LAW, Podres (3), S. Williams (5), Jackson (7), Henry (8), McDaniel (9) vs FORD, Wynn (4), Staley (6), Lary (8), Bell (9). Homers--Mathews (NL), Mays (NL), Musial (NL), Boyer (NL). Attendance--38,362. Receipts--$177,688.57 (net).

30th game, at San Francisco (NL), July 11, 1961 (1st game)
```
American   000 001 002 1   ....   4 4 2
National   010 100 010 2   ....   5 11 5
```
Pitchers--Ford, Lary (4), Donovan (4), Bunning (6), Fornieles (8), WILHELM (8) vs Spahn, Purkey (4), McCormick (6), Face (9), Koufax (9), MILLER (9). Homers--Killebrew (AL), Altman (NL). Attendance--44,115. Receipts--$259,230.81 (net).

31st game, at Boston (AL), July 31, 1961 (2nd game)
```
National   000 001 000   ---   1 5 1
American   100 000 000   ---   1 4 0
```
Pitchers--Bunning, Schwall (4), Pascual (7) vs Purkey, Mahaffey (3), Koufax (5), Miller (7). Homer--Colavito (AL). Attendance--31,851. Receipts--$172,298.19 (net).

32nd Game, at Washington (AL), July 10, 1962 (1st Game)
```
                             R. H. E.
National   000 002 010   ---   3 8 0
American   000 001 000   ---   1 4 0
```
Pitchers--Bunning, PASCUAL (4), Donovan (7), Pappas (9) vs Drysdale, MARICHAL (4), Purkey (6), Shaw (8). Attendance--45,480. Receipts--$228,082.21.

33rd game, at Chicago (NL), July 30, 1962 (2nd game)
```
American   001 201 302   ---   9 10 0
National   010 000 111   ---   4 10 4
```
Pitchers--Stenhouse, HERBERT (3), Aguirre (6), Pappas (9) vs Podres, MAHAFFEY (3), Gibson (5), Farrell (7), Marichal (8). Homers--Runnels (AL), Wagner (AL), Colavito (AL), Roseboro (NL). Attendance--38,359. Receipts--$216,908.71.

34th game, at Cleveland (AL) July 9, 1963
```
American   012 000 000   ---   3 11 1
National   012 010 010   ---   5  6 0
```
Pitchers--O'Toole, JACKSON (3), Culp (5), Woodeshick (6), Drysdale (8) vs. McBride, BUNNING (4), Bouton (6), Pizarro (7), Radatz (8). Attendance--44,160. Receipts--$250,384.59 (net)

35th game, at New York (NL) July 7, 1964
```
American   100 002 100   ....   4 9 1
National   000 210 004   ......   7 8 0
```
Pitchers--Chance, Wyatt (4), Pascual (5), RADATZ (7) vs. Drysdale, Bunning (4), Short (6), Farrell (7), MARICHAL (9). Homers--Williams (NL), Boyer (NL), Callison (NL). Attendance--50,850. Receipts--$215,801.85 (net).

36th game, at Minnesota (AL) July 13, 1965
```
American   000 140 000   ....   5 6 1
National   320 000 100   ......   6 11 0
```
Pitchers--Marichal, Maloney (4), Drysdale (5), KOUFAX (6), Farrell (7), Gibson (8) vs. Pappas, Grant (2), Richert (4), McDOWELL (6), Fisher (8). Homers--Mays (NL), Torre (NL), Stargell (NL), McAuliffe (AL), Killebrew (AL). Attendance-- 46,-706. Receipts--$284,949.31 (net).

37th game, at St. Louis (N) July 12, 1966
```
American   010 000 000 0   ....   1 6 0
National   000 100 000 1   ....   2 6 0
```
Pitchers--McLain, Kaat (4), Stottlemyre (6), Siebert (8), RICHERT (10) vs. Koufax, Bunning (4), Marichal (6), PERRY (9). Attendance--49,936. Receipts--$284,949.31 (net).

38th game, at California (A) July 11, 1967
```
National   010 000 000 000 001   ....   2 9 0
American   000 001 000 000 000   ....   1 8 0
```
Pitchers--Marichal, Jenkins (4), Gibson (7), Short (9), Cuellar (11), DRYSDALE (8), Seaver (15) vs. Chance, McGlothlin (4), Peters (6), Downing (9), HUNTER (11). Homers--Allen (NL). B. Robinson (AL), Perez (NL). Attendance--46,309. Receipts--$324,428 (gross).

39th game, at Houston (N) July 9, 1968
```
American   000 000 000   ....   0 3 1
National   100 000 00x   ....   1 5 0
```
Pitchers--TIANT, Odom (3), McLain (5), McDowell (7), Stottlemyre (8), John (8) vs. DRYSDALE, Marichal (4), Carlton (6), Seaver (7), Reed (9), Koosman (9). Attendance--48,321.

40th game, at Washington (AL) July 23, 1969
```
National   125 100 000   ....   9 11 0
American   011 100 000   ....   3  6 2
```
Pitchers--CARLTON, Gibson (4), Singer (5), Koosman (7), Dierker (8), P. Niekro (9) vs. STOTTLEMYRE, Odom (3), Knowles (3), McLain (4), McNally (6), McDowell (7), Culp (9). Homers--Bench (NL), Howard (AL), McCovey 2 (NL), Freehan (AL). Attendance--45,259.

41st Game, at Cincinnati (NL), July 14, 1970
                              R. H. E.
American   000 001 120 000— 4 12 0
National   000 000 103 001— 5 10 0
Pitchers—Palmer, McDowell (4), J. Perry
(7), Hunter (9), Peterson (9), Stottlemyre
(9), WRIGHT (11) vs. Seaver, Merritt (4),
G. Perry (6), Gibson (8), OSTEEN (10).
Homer—Dietz (NL). Attendance—51,838.

42nd Game, at Detroit (AL), July 13, 1971
                              R. H. E.
National   021   000   010 — 4 5 0
American   004   002   00X— 6 7 0
Pitcher—ELLIS, Marichal (4), Cuellar
(6), Lolich (8). Homers—Bench (NL), Aaron
(NL), Jackson (AL), F. Robinson (AL),
Killebrew (AL), Clemente (NL). Attendance
—53,559.

43rd Game, at Atlanta (NL), July 25, 1972
                              R H E
American   001 000 020 0—3 6 0
National   000 002 001 1—4 10 0
Pitchers—Palmer, Lolich (4), G. Perry (6),
Wood (8), McNALLY (10) vs. Gibson, Blass
(3), Sutton (4), Carlton (6), Stoneman (7),
McGRAW (9). Homers—Aaron (NL), Rojas
(AL). Attendance—53,107.

44th Game, at Kansas City (AL), July 24, 1973
                              R H E
National   002 122 000—7 10 0
American   010 000 000—1 5 0
Pitchers—WISE, Osteen (3), Sutton (5),
Twitchell (6), Giusti (7), Seaver (8), Brewer
(9) vs. Hunter, Holtzman (2), BLYLEVEN
(3), Singer (4), Ryan (6), Lyle (8), Fingers
(9). Homers—Bench (NL), Bonds (NL), W.
Davis (NL). Attendance—40,849.

45th Game, at Pittsburgh (NL), July 23, 1974
                              R. H. E.
American   002 000 000—2 4 1
National   010 210 12x—7 10 1
Pitchers—Perry, TIANT (4), Hunter (6),
Fingers (8) vs. Messersmith, BRETT (4),
Matlack (6), McGlothen (7), Marshall (8).
Homer—Smith (NL). Attendance—50,706.

46th Game, at Milwaukee (AL), July 15, 1975
                              R. H. E.
National   021 000 003—6 13 1
American   000 003 000—3 10 1
Pitchers—Reuss, Sutton (4), Seaver (6),
MATLACK (7), Jones (9) vs. Blue, Busby
(3), Kaat (5), HUNTER (7), Gossage (9).
Homers—Garvey (NL), Wynn (NL), Yastr-
zemski (AL). Attendance—51,480.

47th Game, at Philadelphia (NL), July 13, 1976
                              R H E
American   000 100 000—1 5 0
National   202 000 03x—7 10 0
Pitchers—FIDRYCH, Hunter (3), Tiant
(5), Tanana (7) vs. JONES, Seaver (4),
Montefusco (6), Rhoden (8), Forsch (9),
Homers—Foster (NL), Lynn (AL), Cedeno
(NL). Attendance—63,974.

48th Game at New York (AL), July 19, 1977
                              R H E
National   401 000 020—7 9 1
American   000 002 102—5 8 0
Pitchers—SUTTON, Lavelle (4), Seaver (6),
R. Reuschel (8), Gossage (9) vs. PALMER,
Kern (3), Eckersley (4), LaRoche (6), Camp-
bell (7), Lyle (8). Homers—Morgan (NL), Lu-
zinski (NL), Garvey (NL), Scott (AL). At-
tendance—56,683.

49th Game at San Diego (NL), July 11, 1978
                              R H E
American   201 000 000—3 8 1
National   003 000 04x—7 10 0
Pitchers—Palmer, Keough (3), Sorenson (4),
Kern (7), Guidry (7), GOSSAGE (8) vs. Blue,
Rogers (4), Fingers (6), SUTTER (8), Niekro
(9). Homers—None. Attendance—51,549.

IX UMPIRES

"Please Do Not Shoot the Umpire; he is Doing the Best he Can."
This was the inspiring prose which greeted the durable man in blue who umpired a game during the 1886 National League season in the Kansas City park. On the outfield barrier, for all to see, was this ode to the umpire which was not too far removed from the emotion of the day's fan and player.

Between baseball's earliest days and his present-day standing of absolute autocracy on the field of play, the umpire passed through one of the diamond's roughest and rowdiest eras. He could do no right in the eyes of the fan, the player, the owner, the press; he was wrong, blind, lame, incompetent and crooked, accusations which were hurled ceaselessly and shamefully. But in the long history of the sport it is interesting to note that the umpire—not the player—has been far removed from suspicion. Only one umpire has been expelled because of dishonesty: Richard Higham, in 1882, who committed the unpardonable sin of announcing to certain people the probable winners of games in which he was to officiate. But Higham's offense never may have occurred if the owners had the foresight to hire extra umpires and spread their work a bit more around the rest of the league.

Higham's high-handed tactics were suspected by William G. Thompson, president of the Detroit team, who thought his club was losing too many games in which Higham served as arbiter. Higham officiated 26 of the first 29 games played by Detroit, and private detectives learned the umpire's work was not always beyond reproach. They produced evidence in the form of a letter Higham allegedly had written in which he tipped off eventual winners of games in which he was to work, enough to expel baseball's only dishonest umpire.

In baseball's earliest days, before the start of the major leagues, the position of the umpire was dignified. He donned a Prince Albert coat, silk hat and cane. Stationed just outside the foul line between home and first, he was given a stool on which to rest one foot as he viewed the game. In those days of long-flowing whiskers, he gave his decisions deliberately.

Between the patriarchal overseer of the early 19th century and the nimble, forceful man-in-blue of the present, the umpiring profession has weathered many storms. "Kill the umpire! " once was more than a euphemism. Clarence (Brick) Owens got his nickname from the object thrown at him in a game. Minor league umpires have been tarred and feathered. Police protection used to be standard equipment for a long time even in the big leagues.

Founding fathers of professional baseball recognized the need for investing the umpire with real authority. For that reason they stated in the first set of pro rules, 1871, that there can be no appeal from a decision involving the umpire's judgment (fair or foul, safe or out, etc.). Protests can be based only on interpretation of the rules. This fundamental principle has not been changed since.

Hoping to insure the integrity of the umpire, league officials forbade any pay for working the game. The visiting club would submit three names as prospective umpires for the game, and the home team would select one. The system sagged so badly, the day's umpire often had to be picked from a volunteer in the stands.

Back in the pioneering National Association, a part-time prize fighter from

Philadelphia, William B. McLean, quickly established himself as "King of Umpires." He ran the games so competently that clubs gladly paid his expenses for road trips, and he became the first umpire to officiate in every city.

McLean was responsible for another innovation. He commanded a fee of $5 a game. In the first two years of the National League, rules-makers tried to stick to the amateur tradition, but by 1878 it became obvious that capable officials could be obtained only by proper pav, and the McLean standard of $5 a game was written into the rules.

At first, the visiting club was required to pay the $5, while the home club paid all other expenses. Later, the home club became responsible for all umpiring costs.

In 1883, the American Association decided to pay the umpires out of the league treasury at the rate of $140 per month "plus traveling expenses and hotel bills, not to exceed $3 a day." Umpires by now were technically members of the league staff. They no longer could be removed in the middle of a game merely by agreement of the rival captains. Yet league headquarters still failed to back up the umpires in disputes with players. Fines didn't stick. Suspensions were easily rescinded.

Until the end of the 19th century, and well into the 20th, league games were handled by a single umpire. While the harassed official behind the plate ran part of the way down the baseline to judge a drive near the foul line in right field, baserunners would cut inside second base en route from first to third. In the boisterous 90's, fights often broke out because the third baseman would slyly grab the belt of the baserunner and restrain him while the lone umpire was busy watching the relay from the outfield.

In the early 1900's, a second umpire finally came into general use. It wasn't till 1910 that the rules spoke of an Umpire-in-Chief (plate umpire) and Field Umpire (for baseline decisions). Thirty years later, a third umpire became a regular sight. By now, it is taken for granted that there will be four umpires at all important games, with six being used at the World Series (one for each base, and one at each foul pole to decide between home runs and foul balls).

Leagues have always tried various stratagems to bolster the respect of umpires. The old AA ruled that no umpire while in uniform could enter a poolroom or saloon, under penalty of fine by the league president. They also halted the "undignified practice" of allowing the umpire to take testimony from spectators in case of doubt over whether a ball had left the field fair or foul, or whether a fair catch had been made in the outfield. The National League in the 1890's even wrote into the rules that the players must address him as "Mr. Umpire!"

Yet all these dodges to compel respect for the umpires faded when the belligerent players were allowed to intimidate the officials without reprisal from the league's top echelon. One of the main reasons the American League became soundly established at the start of this century was that its founder, Byron Bancroft (Ban) Johnson, removed rowdyism from the game by carefully selecting a staff of umpires and by completely backing every one of their field rulings, a wise move which put to an end the endless debates between the umpires and outraged players.

John McGraw, bred in the boisterous Old Oriole days, found himself practically manacled in the new AL, so he jumped into the NL.

For a few years, McGraw had a picnic with the arbiters. Then he crossed the path of a spunky little newcomer named Bill Klem. Ordered out of a game by Klem, the Little Napoleon raged, "I'll have your job for this!"

"If it's possible for you to take my job," answered Klem coldly, "then I don't want it."

Largely through the insistence of Klem, who was to earn an immortal niche as "The Old Arbitrator," the NL began raising its umpiring standards to meet the Americans. Through Klem's campaigning, World Series pay rose from $400 to $2,500. Umpires were provided with a separate clubhouse, so they no longer had to retreat to an old peanut shed or storage bin after a game, to use a sponge and fire bucket to swab the day's dust from their body.

Klem umpired in 18 World Series, a record. He brought dignity, respect and authority to the job. In 1949, the fans honored him with a special "Day" at the Polo Grounds. Sports writers awarded him a plaque for meritorious service to baseball over a long period of years, and in his brief but dramatic acceptance speech he announced his credo, "Baseball is more than a game to me—it's a religion!"

Klem started the practice of "getting on the ball" by crouching to judge each pitch from right over the catcher's shoulder. Cy Rigler was the one who started the sensible custom of raising the right arm to denote a strike. There are some 60,000 in the umpiring population of the United States, counting high school and sandlot games. The leagues have an elaborate scouting system to bring up the best. They look for a man with keen eyesight, knowledge of the rules, ability to get into the right position quickly, poise, decisiveness, impartiality (meaning an imperviousness to the hoots of a home crowd, which tries to sway decisions toward the home team), psychology of handling men and a flair for the game.

For his salary of about $20,000 to cover the six-month season, the big league umpire is a lonely man. He may not fraternize with the players on the field, nor can he travel in the same train or stay at the same hotel as the players. His future assignments are never made more than a week ahead, so his family life is practically nil during the season.

Umpires have a host of duties, besides the obvious ball-and-strike decisions (more than 200 of these a game for the plate umpire), safe-or-out and fair-or-foul. He administers rules as to equipment, conditions of the grounds, etc. He is the sole judge over whether to end a game because of climatic conditions or other circumstances.

Still, there are many decisions which an umpire is not allowed to make unless there is a direct protest. These are "appeal plays," and include declaring a runner out for failing to tag a bag. Klem once admitted that the deciding run of the fifth game of the 1911 World Series was scored by Larry Doyle, who slid half a foot wide of the plate to avoid a tag that never was made. Doyle brushed himself off, trotted to the clubhouse and Klem had no way of declaring him out, since the catcher also walked away.

Besides the aforementioned McLean, Rigler and Klem, there have been many famous umpires of long service, like Honest John Kelly, John Gaffney, Hank O'Day, Silk O'Loughlin, Tom Connolly, Bill Dinneen, Charles Moran, Billy Evans and many others. Bill McGowan set the Iron man mark by umpiring 2,541 consecutive AL games in 16½ seasons without missing an inning.

John K. Tener, who later became Governor of the state of Pennsylvania, umpired one season in the NL. On June 26, 1897 in Washington, Thomas J. Lynch umpired the first Giant game and John A. Heydler umpired the second. Lynch and Heydler later became presidents of the league.

Baseball management was confronted with an umpire strike threat in the spring of 1969 by the newly formed Association of Major League Umpires. Umpires of both leagues formed one union on September 30, 1968, and at that time agreed to stage a general strike the following spring unless umpires Al Salerno and Bill Valentine were reinstated by American League President Joe Cronin.

Both Valentine and Salerno had been released by Cronin for imcompetence and their contracts not renewed for the 1969 season. A charge of unfair labor practice was brought against the American League by Salerno and Valentine as they insisted they were fired because of their activities in unionizing their fellow A.L. umpires. Attorney Jack Reynolds, administrator and league counsel for the N.L. umpires, began bargaining procedures with Cronin. Eventually an economic agreement was announced with umpires in both leagues advised to sign their contracts. The law suit would be handled separately.

The Salerno and Valentine case was dismissed by the National Labor Relations Board on July 13, 1970, for lack of sufficient evidence. Attorneys for the umpires appealed to higher courts, even the Supreme Court in January, 1971, with the same verdict. The case was then returned to the NLRB in Washington for final arbitration. The umpires charges were finally dismissed on April 2, 1972.

A one-day strike on Oct. 3, 1970, prompted re-opening of contract negotiations between baseball commissioner Bowie Kuhn, league presidents Chub Feeney and Joe Cronin, and Jack Reynolds, attorney for the Association of Major League Umpires. The playoffs proceeded as usual using minor league umps. Agreement provided increased wages for senior umpires along with new pension benefits and championship playoffs, World Series and All-Star Games raises.

There was another one-day strike on August 25, 1978, the umpires claiming the three-year contract they had signed previous season was not valid. The major leagues obtained a temporary restraining order against the strike immediately, and most of the umpires were back on the job the following day. Their places had been taken by local umpires recruited by the individual clubs.

ALL-TIME REGISTER

NATIONAL LEAGUE

Abbey, Charles S., 1897
Abbot, 1905
Adams, James, 1897
Allen, Hezekiah, 1876
Anderson, William, 1890
Andrews, George E., 1889, 1893, 1895, 1898–99
Arundel, John T., 1888
Ayers, 1876
Baker, Charles, 1884
Baker, Philip, 1889
Baker, William P., 1957
Baldwin, Marcus E., 1892
Ballafant, Edward L., 1936–57
Bannon, James H., 1894
Barker, Alfred L., 1876, 1880–81
Barlick, Albert J., 1940–43, 46–55, 58–71
Barnie, William S., 1882, 1892
Barr, George M., 1931–49
Barton, 1876
Bates, 1877
Battin, Joseph V., 1882, 1889, 1891, 1895–96
Bausewine, George, 1908
Beard, Oliver P., 1894
Becannon, James M., 1885
Beck, Erwin T., 1902
Beckley, Jacob P., 1906
Beebe, Fred L., 1907
Behle, Frank, 1895–96, 1901
Berger, Frederick, 1886
Berger, John H., 1891
Betts, William G., 1893–96, 1898–99
Bigelow, 1877
Bittman, Henry, 1892–95, 1897
Blakiston, Robert J., 1884
Blodgett, C. W., 1876
Boggess, Lynton, 1944–48, 50–62
Boles, Charles, 1877
Bond, Thomas H., 1883, 1885
Bonner, Frank J., 1894
Boston, K. K., 1878
Boyle, Henry J., 1886
Boyle, John A., 1892, 1897
Bradley, George H., 1877, 1879–83
Brady, 1877
Brady, Jackson, 1887
Bransfield, William E., 1917
Bredburg, George W., 1877, 1879
Breitenstein, Theodore P., 1900
Brennan, John E., 1887, 1899
Brennan, William T., 1909, 1913, 1921
Brjody, Charles F., 1882
Brockway, John, 1887, 1879
Brown, Samuel W., 1907
Brown, Thomas T., 1891, 1898–99, 1901–02
Brunton, Thomas H., 1879
Buckenberger, Alfred C., 1890
Budding, 1877
Buelow, Frederick W., 1901

Buffinton, Charles G., 1883, 1888–89, 1892
Bullymore, Charles L., 1882
Bunce, Joshua, 1877
Burke, 1892
Burkhart, Kenneth William, 1957–73
Burlingame, Frank A., 1878
Burnham, George W., 1883, 1886–87, 1889, 1893, 1895
Burns, John S., 1884
Burns, Thomas E., 1892
Burns, Thomas P., 1895, 1899
Burtis, D. W., 1876–77
Bush, Garner C., 1911–12
Bushong, Albert J., 1880, 1890
Butler, Richard H., 1897
Byron, William J., 1913–19
Callahan, Edward J., 1881
Campbell, Al., 1886
Campbell, Daniel, 1893–97
Campbell, William M., 1939–40
Cantillon, Joseph D., 1902
Carey, S., 1870
Carey, Thomas J., 1881–82
Carpenter, William B., 1897, 1904, 1906–07
Carrick, William M., 1900
Carroll, Frederick H., 1887
Carsey, Wilfred, 1894, 1896, 1901
Caruthers, Robert L., 1886, 1891, 1893
Casey, Daniel M., 1888
Caskin, Edward J., 1884
Cassidy, John P., 1882
Chamberlain, Elton P., 1894
Chance, Frank L., 1902
Chandler, Moses E., 1877
Chaplin, Harry, 1886
Chapman, John C., 1876, 1880, 1882–83, 1885
Chapman, John, 1880
Chill, Oliver P., 1916
Chipper, 1876
Clack, Robert H., 1876, 1897
Clark, Arthur F., 1890
Clarke, Robert M., 1930–31
Clarke, William J., 1893–94, 1896
Clarkson, Arthur H., 1892–96
Clarkson, John G., 1888, 1892–93
Cockill, George W., 1915
Cohen, 1893
Coleman, John F., 1884
Colgan, Harry W., 1899, 1901, 1903
Collins, Daniel T., 1876
Colosi, Nicholas, 1968–
Cone, J. F., 1876–77
Conlan, John, 1941–64
Connell, Terence G., 1885, 1887
Connolly, John M., 1886–87, 1892–93
Connolly, Thomas H., 1898–1900
Conahan, 1896
Conway, John H., 1906
Coogan, Daniel G., 1895

Crandall, Robert, 1876–78
Crane, Edward N., 1892–93
Crane, Samuel N., 1886–87, 1890
Crawford, Gerald J., 1977–
Crawford, Henry C., 1956–75
Cray, 1893
Crolius, Frederick J., 1901
Cronin, John J., 1902–03
Cross, John A., 1876, 1878–79
Cross, Lafayette N., 1892
Cunningham, Elmer E., 1896–97, 1900–01
Cuppy, George M., 1894
Curren, Peter, 1876
Curry, Wesley, 1885–86, 1889–90, 1898
Cusack, Stephen P., 1909
Cushman, Carles H., 1884–85, 1894, 1898
Cusick, Andrew, 1886–87
Daily, Cornelius F., 1886, 1891, 1894, 1896
Dailey, John J., 1882
Dale, Jerry P., 1970–
Daly, Thomas P., 1901
Daniels, Charles F., 1876–80, 1887–88
Darling, Dell C., 1887
Dascoli, Frank, 1948–62
Davidson, David L., 1969–
Davis, C. E., 1880
Day, 1879
Dealey, Patrick E., 1886
Deane, Henry C., 1876, 1878
Decker, Stewart M., 1883–85, 1888
Delmore, Victor, 1956–59
Devinney, Daniel, 1876–77
Dexter, Charles D., 1896–97
Dezelan, Frank J., 1966–70
Dixon, Hal, 1953–59
Donahue, Francis R., 1897
Donahue, Timothy C., 1895–96
Donatelli, August J., 1950–73
Donlin, Michael J., 1900
Donnelly, Charles H., 1931–32
Donnelly, James B., 1896
Donohue, Michael R., 1930
Donovan, Timothy H., 1882
Donovan, William E., 1902
Dooin, Charles S., 1904
Doscher, John H., 1879–82, 1887
Douglass, William B., 1903
Dowse, Thomas J., 1890
Doyle, John J., 1911
Draper, John H., 1877
Ducharme, 1876–77
Duggleby, William J., 1905
Dunlap, Frederick C., 1879
Dunn, John, 1879
Dunn, Thomas P., 1939–46
Dunnigan, Joseph, 1881–82
Dwyer, John F., 1889, 1893–97, 1899, 1901
Dyler, John F., 1892, 1897
Eagan, John J., 1878, 1886
Earle, William M., 1892, 1894

Eason, Malcolm W., 1901–02, 1910–15
Ehret, Philip S., 1892, 1895–97
Ellick, Joseph J., 1886
Emslie, Robert D., 1891–1924
Engel, Robert A., 1965–
Engeln, William R., 1952–56
English, John W., 1876
Evans, Jacob, 1886
Farrell, Charles A., 1901–02
Feber, Fred W., 1879
Fenno, Norman, 1876
Ferguson, Robert V., 1879, 1884–85
Fessenden, Wallace C., 1889–90
Finch, R. B., 1880
Finneran, William E., 1911–12
Fisher, William C., 1876
Flaherty, Patrick J., 1904–1907
Flynn, John A., 1893
Force, David W., 1881
Foreman, Frank I., 1895
Foreman, John D., 1896
Forman, Allen, 1962–65
Foster, Clarence F., 1900
Fountain, Edward G., 1879
Fouser, William C., 1876
Frary, Robert, 1911
Freeman, John F., 1900
Froemming, Bruce N., 1971–
Fulmer, Charles J., 1881, 1886
Furlong, William E., 1877–80, 1882–84, 1888
Gaffney, John H., 1884–95
Galvin, James F., 1886–87, 1889, 1893, 1895
Ganzel, Charles W., 1901
Gardner, James A., 1899
Geer, William H., 1879
George, William M., 1889
German, Lester S., 1895
Getzein, Charles N., 1890
Gifford, James H., 1881
Gill, Thomas H., 1886
Gillean, Thomas, 1879–81
Gleason, John D., 1877
Gleason, William G., 1877
Gleason, William J., 1890, 1892
Glenn, John W., 1880
Goetz, Lawrence J., 1936–57
Goldsmith, Frederick E., 1886
Gore, Arthur J., 1947–56
Gorman, Thomas D., 1951–76
Grady, Michael W., 1895
Graves, Frank M., 1886, 1895
Gregg, Eric E., 1977–
Griffith, Clark C., 1894
Grimm, John H., 1892, 1895–96
Gross, Edward M., 1881
Gruber, Henry J., 1889
Guglielmo, Angelo, 1952
Guinney, Daniel, 1882–83
Gumbert, Addison C., 1892–1895
Gunning, Thomas F., 1884–85, 1887
Gunson, Joseph B., 1892
Guthrie, William J., 1913–1915
Hackett, Merton M., 1886
Haddock, George S., 1889
Haley, Ed., 1876
Halliman, William W., 1903
Hanlon, Edward H., 1892
Hardie, Louis W., 1887

Harrison, Peter A., 1916–20
Hart, Eugene F., 1920–29
Hart, William F., 1896–97, 1914–15
Hartley, John, 1894
Harvey, H. Douglas, 1962–
Hastings, Winfield S., 1877
Hatfield, Gilbert, 1889
Hatfield, John V. B., 1876
Hawes, William A., 1881–82
Healy, John J., 1887
Hegeman, William H., 1881
Hemming, George E., 1895–96
Henderson, James H., 1895–96
Hengle, Edward S., 1887
Henline, Walter J., 1945–48
Hernon, Thomas H., 1894
Heuble, George A., 1876
Heydler, John A., 1895–98
Hickey, James L., 1882
Higham, Richard, 1881–82
Hiller, George J., 1881
Hines, Michael P., 1884
Hoagland, Willard A., 1894
Hodges, A. D., 1876–77, 1879
Hoffer, William L., 1896
Hogan, 1897
Hogriever, George C., 1893
Holland, John A., 1887
Holliday, James W., 1897, 1903
Hornung, Joseph M., 1892–93, 1896
Houtz, Charles, 1876, 1879
Howard, C. F., 1884
Howe, John, 1890
Hunt, John T., 1893, 1895, 1898–99
Hurst, Timothy C., 1891–98, 1900, 1903–04
Hyatt, Robert H., 1912
Irwin, Arthur A., 1881, 1902
Jacklitsch, Fred L., 1901
Jackowski, William, 1952–68
Jeffers, W. W., 1881
Jennings, Hugh A., 1893, 1900
Jevne, Frederick, 1892–95
Johnson, Harry S., 1914
Johnstone, James E., 1903–12
Jones, Henry M., 1890
Jorda, Louis D., 1927–31, 1940–52
Jose, 1889
Joyce, C. E., 1879
Julian, Joseph O., 1878
Kahle, 1905
Kane, Stephen J., 1906, 1909–10
Karger, Edwin, 1906
Kecher, W. H., 1910
Keefe, Timothy J., 1880, 1882–85, 1887, 1892–96
Keenan, James W., 1881, 1890, 1893
Kelley, Joseph J., 1892, 1904
Kelley, W. W., 1877
Kellum, Winford A., 1905
Kelly, John O., 1882, 1884–85, 1888, 1897
Kelly, Michael J., 1893
Kelly, S., 1880
Kennedy, Charles, 1904
Kennedy, Michael J., 1884
Kenney, John, 1876–77
Kerins, John A., 1888

Kibler, John W., 1963–
Killen, Frank B., 1896–97
Kinslow, Thomas F., 1892
Kipp, Eden, 1881
Kitson, Frank R., 1902
Klem, William J., 1905–41
Kling, John G., 1901
Klusman, William F., 1892–93
Knell, Philip H., 1895
Knight, Alonzo P., 1876, 1888–89
Knowles, James, 1892
Krieg, William F., 1887
Lally, Daniel J., 1891–94, 1896
Landes, Stanley A., 1955–72
Lane, Frank, 1883
Laney, B., 1884
Lanigan, Charles, 1908
Latham, Walter A., 1899–1900, 1902
Laughlin, 1876
Lavers, George W., 1882
Lawler, Michael H., 1882
Leever, Samuel W., 1900, 1904
Libby, Stephen A., 1880
Lincoln, Frederick H., 1914, 1917
Lindeman, Vivian A., 1907
Long, William H., 1893, 1895, 1897
Lowell, William, 1882
Lundgren, Carl L., 1905–06
Lynch, J. T., 1880
Lynch, Thomas J., 1888–99, 1902
Macullar, John F., 1892
Maddox, Charles, 1882
Magee, Sherwood R., 1928
Magerkurth, George L., 1929–47
Mahoney, Michael J., 1892
Malone, Ferguson G., 1884, 1892
Maloney, William A., 1902
Manassau, Alfred S., 1899
Manning, James H., 1886, 1893
Mapledoram, Blake A., 1886
Martin, Alphonse C., 1876
Mason, Charles E., 1876
Mathews, Robert T., 1876, 1880, 1882
Mathewson, Christopher, 1901, 1907
Mayer, 1893
McAllister, Louis W., 1899
McCaffrey, Harry, 1885, 1886
McCarthy, Thomas F. M., 1896
McCauley, Patrick M., 1896
McCauley, Allen B., 1890
McCormick, James, 1885
McCormick, William J., 1919–29
McCrum, 1892
McDermott, Michael J., 1890, 1897
McDonald, James F., 1895, 1897–99
McDowell, 1893
McElwee, Harvey, 1877
McFarland, Edward W., 1896
McFarland, Horace, 1896–97
McGann, Dennis L., 1903
McGarr, James B., 1895, 1899

McGee, 1876
McGinnis, 1910
McGinnity, Joseph J., 1900
McGinty, 1897
McGrew, Harry T., 1930–31, 1933–34
McGuire, James T., 1886–87, 1894, 1896–97, 1901
McGunnigle, Edward, 1888
McLaughlin, Edward J., 1929
McLaughlin, Michael, 1893
McLaughlin, Peter J., 1924–26
McLean, William B., 1876–80, 1882–84
McLeod, 1895
McMahon, John H., 1893
McMater, 1877
McMullen, John F., 1876
McQuaid, John H., 1889–95
McSherry, John P., 1971–
Meagher, John, 1877
Mears, Charles W., 1894
Medart, William, 1876–77
Meekin, Jouette, 1895–96
Megrue, Cliff, 1876
Mertes, Samuel B., 1903–05
Miller, George E., 1879
Miller, George F., 1893, 1896
Miller, Joseph H., 1884
Mills, Abraham G., 1877
Mitchell, Charles, 1892
Montague, 1877
Montague, Edward M., 1976–
Moran, 1894
Moran, August, 1903–04, 1910–11, 1918
Moran, Charles B., 1917–39
Moran, Patrick J., 1901
Morrill, John F., 1891, 1896
Morris, Edward, 1895, 1897
Morris, John S., 1876
Muir, Thomas, 1876
Mullane, Anthony J., 1893, 1897
Mullen, Peter C., 1893
Mullin, John, 1909
Mulvey, Joseph H., 1895
Murnane, Timothy H., 1886
Murphy, Henry, 1880
Murphy, Morgan E., 1893, 1896, 1898
Murphy, Martin W., 1886
Murphy, William H., 1895, 1897
Murray, Jeremiah J., 1893–95, 1900, 1905, 1910
Myers, George D., 1886
Myers, Henry C., 1890
Nash, William M., 1901
Needham, Thomas J., 1904, 1907
Newton, Eustace J., 1902
Nichols, Charles A., 1900–01
Nickerson, S. W., 1880
Nicol, Hugh N., 1894
Nolan, Edward S., 1881
Noonan, Peter J., 1906–07
O'Brien, John F., 1889
O'Brien, William, 1876
O'Connor, Arthur, 1914
O'Connor, John J., 1893–1901
O'Day, Henry F., 1888–89, 1893, 1895–1911, 1913, 1915–27

Odlin, Albert F., 1883
O'Hara, 1915
O'Leary, Daniel, 1879
Olsen, Andrew H., 1968–
O'Neill, Michael J., 1904
O'Rourke, James H., 1893–94
Orth, Albert L., 1901, 1912–17
Osborne, William, 1876
O'Sullivan, John J., 1922
Overall, Orval, 1905, 1910
Owens, Clarence B., 1908, 1912–13
Paparella, Joseph J., 1946–65
Parker, George L., 1936–38
Pearce, Grayson S., 1886–87, 1892
Pearce, Richard J., 1878, 1882
Pears, Frank, 1897
Peitz, Henry C., 1901, 1906
Pelekoudas, Chris G., 1960–75
Pfeffer, Nathaniel F., 1897
Pfirman, Charles H., 1922–36
Phelan, 1896
Phelps, Edward J., 1912
Phillippe, Charles L., 1903
Pierce, 1893
Pike, Lipman E., 1890
Pinelli, Ralph A., 1935–56
Powell, Jack, 1923–24, 1933
Power, Charles B., 1893, 1895, 1902
Power, Thomas E., 1887–88, 1894–95
Powers, James T., 1895
Powers, Philip J., 1881, 1886–91
Pratt, Albert G., 1879–80, 1887
Pratt, Thomas J., 1886
Pryor, J. Paul, 1961–
Pulli, Frank V., 1972–
Quest, Joseph L., 1886–87
Quick, James E., 1976–
Quigley, Ernest C., 1913–37
Quinn, Joseph C., 1881–82
Quinn, Joseph J., 1889, 1894, 1896
Quinn, P. J., 1876
Quinn, William H., 1887
Reardon, John E., 1926–49
Redheffer, 1893, 1895
Reid, William A., 1882
Reilly, Charles T., 1892–95
Reilly, William, 1880
Reitz, Henry P., 1895
Remsen, John J., 1880
Rennert, Lawrence H., 1973–
Rhines, William P., 1891, 1896
Rhodes, Eugene A., 1887
Richardson, Arthur H., 1887, 1892
Richmond, John L., 1883
Rigler, Charles, 1905–22, 1924–35
Riley, William J., 1880
Ritchie, F., 1876
Robb, Douglas W., 1948–52
Roberts, Lew, 1953–55
Robinson, Wilbert, 1898
Rocap, Adam, 1876
Roll, 1876
Rudderham, Francis F., 1907
Rudderham, John E., 1908
Runge, Paul E., 1973–
Ryan, James E., 1892

Ryan, Walter, 1946
Sanders, Alexander B., 1889
Schew, Augustus, 1880–81
Schmidt, Henry M., 1903
Schofield, J. W., 1880
Schriver, William F., 1901
Schurer, 1896
Scott, James, 1930–31
Sears, John W., 1943–45
Secory, Frank, 1952–70
Sentelle, Leopold T., 1922–23
Serad, William T., 1884
Seward, Edward W., 1892–93
Seward, George E., 1876–79
Sheridan, John F., 1892–93, 1896–97
Simons, J., 1876
Skinner, S. A., 1886
Smith, 1876
Smith, Charles M., 1881–82
Smith, Edward E., 1890
Smith, George H., 1901
Smith, Vincent, 1957–65
Smith, William E., 1886
Smith, William W., 1898–99
Sneeden, 1895
Snyder, Charles N., 1892–95, 1898, 1901
Sommers, Joseph A., 1889, 1893
Stafford, John H., 1906
Stage, Charles W., 1893—95
Staley, Harry E., 1892, 1895
Stambaugh, Calvin G., 1876–79
Stark, Albert D., 1928–35, 1937–39, 1942
Stearns, Daniel E., 1880–81
Stein, Edward F., 1890, 1894, 1896
Steiner, Melvin J., 1961–72
Steinfeldt, Henry M., 1905
Stello, Richard J., 1968–
Sternburg, 1909
Stewart, William J., 1933–54
Stivetts, John C., 1894
Stockdale, M. J., 1915
Stocksdale, Otis H., 1895
Stricker, John A., 1892
Stricklett, Elmer E., 1970
Strief, George A., 1889–90
Sudol, Edward L., 1957–77
Sugden, Joseph, 1887
Sullivan, David F., 1880–83, 1885, 1888
Sullivan, Dennis J., 1881
Sullivan, James E., 1896
Sullivan, Jeremiah, 1887
Sullivan, John R., 1882
Sullivan, Martin J., 1889
Sullivan, Michael J., 1897
Summer, James G., 1876–77, 1879
Supple, 1906
Sutcliffe, Elmer E., 1889, 1892
Sutton, Ezra B., 1876
Swartwood, Cyrus E., 1894–1900
Sweasy, Charles J., 1879
Sweeney, James M., 1924–26
Tannehill, Jesse N., 1897, 1901–02
Tata, Terry A., 1973–
Tate, Edward F., 1888
Taylor, John B., 1899
Taylor, John W., 1901, 1905

AMERICAN LEAGUE

Springstead, Martin J., 1965–
Stafford, John H., 1907
Stevens, John W., 1948–71
Stewart, Ernest D., 1941–45
Stewart, Robert W., 1959–70
Summers, William R., 1933–59

Tabacchi, Frank, 1956–59
Umont, Frank W., 1954–73
Valentine, William, 1963–68
Van Graflan, Roy, 1927–33
Voltaggio, Vito H., 1977–
Wallace, Roderick J., 1915–16

Walsh, Edward A., 1922
Weafer, Harold L., 1943–47
Westervelt, Frederick E., 1911–12
Wilson, Frank, 1921–22

X BASEBALL ADMINISTRATION

Baseball's first professional league, the National Association, folded because its forthright player-president, Bob Ferguson, had a blustering type of ballfield leadership that did not carry over into sorely needed executive diplomacy. NA directors ignored his roars for sorely needed reform. Suave, magnetic and dynamic William A. Hulbert proved perfect for establishing the National League on a permanent basis.

Col. A. G. Mills, an uncompromising administrator in the Hulbert mold, ruled the NL for two years before the iron-handed "Bismarck of Baseball" resigned when the league refused his demand to crack down on players who had jumped to the "outlaw" Union Association in 1884.

That brought kindly, honest and conciliatory Nicholas E. Young into power in 1885. Uncle Nick was so unaggressive that clubowners' cliques virtually ruled the sprawling 12-club NL in the Gay Nineties. Umpires were kicked and choked. The rowdy Baltimore Orioles were a law unto themselves. Young's timidity gave reign to excesses that eventually wrecked his administration and led to the establishment of the AL.

After two years of ruinous war between the leagues, genial and expansive Garry Herrmann, president of the Cincinnati Reds, engineered peace in January, 1903. For his valuable services, Herrmann was rewarded with the chairmanship of a new three-man National Commission which was to rule baseball for almost two full decades. The other Commission members were the league presidents, Ban Johnson and Harry Pulliam.

Baseball's triumvirate started disintegrating in the wake of the Browns vs. Pirates battle over title to George Sisler. When Herrmann cast the deciding vote with the AL club, Barney Dreyfuss of the Pirates howled at Herrmann's "treason" to his own league. He accused Herrmann of being under the influence of his old friend, AL president Johnson. Dreyfuss had pamphlets printed which intended to discredit Herrmann's decision. This insurrection died down, but the three-man Commission had lost face, and Dreyfuss at least succeeded in starting a snowballing drive to name a single Commissioner with no stake in baseball.

Johnson had trouble in his own league. The Yankees overruled him with a court injunction on the Carl Mays case, then drew support from the Red Sox and White Sox in a secession move aimed at switching to the NL. Meanwhile, NL president John A. Heydler felt the pressure of anti-Herrmann propaganda, and refused to vote to return the Reds' chief to the Commission in 1920. Since Johnson and Heydler couldn't agree on Herrmann's successor, baseball was without an actual chief in 1920, leaving the two presidents to settle their own league controversies.

On September 28, the Black Sox scandal exploded in a Chicago courtroom. Eight Chicago players were exposed as having agreed to lose the 1919 World Series to Cincinnati. The sports world was especially bitter that this crisis in baseball history should come at a time when there was no real governing head. In the nation's press, on the floor of Congress and from pulpits came cries to clean up the game for its very salvation.

Commissioner's Office

Against this turbulent backdrop, Federal Judge K. M. Landis was ushered into baseball's throne room. The white-maned jurist had earned the gratitude of organized ball in 1915 by his deft handling of the dangerous lawsuit brought by the "outlaw" Federal League. He also had a reputation as a racket-buster, having fined Standard Oil Company $29,240,000 in a rebate case in 1907.

Though Landis was earning only $7,500 on the Federal bench, he didn't indicate immediate enthusiasm at baseball's offer of a seven-year contract at $50,000 per. He demanded and immediately was granted carte blanche in any matter he deemed "detrimental to baseball." Under this sweeping provision he wielded the big stick, often autocratically, yet with such crusading zeal that he restored the good name of the game.

The new Czar risked his crown that very first year when he fined Babe Ruth and suspended him for breaking the post-season barnstorming rule of 1921. Babe's immeasurable popularity caused the public to grumble over the drastic decree; but the complaints were tinged with a growing respect for this inflexible disciple of law and order.

In a quarter century as administrator, Landis became known as the "ballplayer's friend." He fought for extension of the annual draft to all minor leagues. He regarded the "farm system" as a similar stratagem to cover up capable players in the bushes, and in two earthquaking edicts the Great Emancipator freed 127 Cardinal farmhands in 1938 and 91 Tiger chattels in 1940. Other player petitions resulted in free agency for Tommy Henrich, Rick Ferrell, Phil Todt, Claude Jonnard and dozens of others.

Landis never compromised with even the slightest tint of gambling or dishonesty. He forced Giant owner Charles Stoneham and manager John McGraw to sell their interests in the Havana racetrack. He expelled Bill Cox, president of the Phillies, for betting on a game. Though the courts failed to convict the Black Sox, Landis blacklisted them from baseball for life: Joe Jackson, Ed Cicotte, Chick Gandil, Swede Risberg, Happy Felsch, Buck Weaver, Claude Williams and Fred McMullin. He also threw his dreaded black book in later years at players Benny Kauff, Cozy Dolan, Phil Douglas and Jim O'Connell. However, he exonerated Ty Cobb and Tris Speaker after Hubert (Dutch) Leonard had charged them in 1926 with collusion on a 1919 game.

Judge Landis died November 25, 1944. His assistant, Leslie O'Connor, took charge of affairs until U. S. Senator Albert Benjamin (Happy) Chandler was elected on April 24, 1945 for a seven-year term at $50,000 a year (later raised to $65,000). The former Class D ballplayer headed the game through its most prosperous years, but he met his share of administrative headaches.

Early in 1946, the free-spending Mexican League raided the majors. Chandler stemmed the tide by announcing a five-year ban against jumping players. Three years later, after the Jorge Pasquel-bankrolled league collapsed, Chandler declared general amnesty. However, Danny Gardella, former outfielder who had broken only the reserve clause of his Giant contract to take the "Mexican holiday" pressed a lawsuit against organized baseball's alleged monopoly. When this case received a favorable vote in the New York State Supreme Court, Chandler suddenly effected an out-of-court settlement with Gardella who, incidentally, was represented by Chandler's former classmate at Harvard Law School, Frederic A. Johnson.

In 1947, Chandler suspended Dodger manager Lippy Leo Durocher for a year, citing an accumulation of "incidents." Lippy took his medicine and returned the next year.

The Commissioner's vigilant administration of the rule against signing high school players brought him into head-on battle with Leslie O'Conner, former Acting Commissioner, who was fined as White Sox general manager for signing a schoolboy. O'Connor claimed Chandler was overstepping his authority, and even threatened to go to court. Chandler held firm. Sox owners finally paid the fine and released O'Connor.

Seeking a renewal of his contract in December, 1950, Chandler received a majority vote, but not the required two-thirds. Clubowners then decided on a committee to select a new Commissioner "as soon as practicable." Chandler, whose contract ran to April, 1952, was voted out of office before his contract expired.

Ford C. Frick, who had advanced to the presidency of the National League after serving as a sportswriter on a New York newspaper, radio sportscaster and manager of the National League Service Bureau, became baseball's third commissioner on September 20, 1951. He signed a seven-year contract at a salary of $65,000 per year. In 1957, Frick signed his second seven-year contract.

Financially, the Commissioner's office is supported solely by the World Series. Fifteen percent of all net receipts of each game are set aside for the expenses (salaries, travel and overhead) involved in conducting the normal business of the office.

Frick announced his intentions to retire in 1965 and finally, on November 17, after a year-long search, William Dole Eckert, a retired Air Force lieutenant-general, was named the game's fourth commissioner. Eckert, 56, was elected to a seven-year term with an annual salary of $65,000, the same as Frick received.

Most fans and even the news media were surprised at Eckert's selection. He had had, for example, no previous connection with baseball. Although his name appeared among the original 156 nominees, it was never mentioned publicly. He was not included when the list was reduced to 15 in July, but was subsequently restored to the list and reportly was the only man to whom the job was offered.

William Eckert resigned as Commissioner of Baseball on the final day of the winter meeting in San Francisco of 1968, effective with the appointment of his successor. Removal from office, after serving only three years of his seven-year contract, was urged by owners who wanted reconstruction of the game to combat upcoming professional football.

By the end of December there were four candidates named. Deadlocked meetings brought about a compromise candidate; a Wall Street lawyer active in baseball legislation since 1950. Bowie Kuhn was selected protem commissioner by unanimous consent of the Executive Committee in February, 1969, and then given a firm seven-year contract shortly thereafter.

One of his first acts as Commissioner was the settlement of a pension dispute between club owners and the Major League Baseball Players' Association to prevent baseball's first general player strike. Major league players were threatening a boycott of spring training unless a satisfactory method was found of splitting the revenue from games in the playoff system about to be established for the World Series.

Kuhn faced many crises as his term progressed. He ironed out retirement problems with Donn Clendenon and Ken Harrelson in 1969, Tony Conigliaro and Clete Boyer in 1971 and Vida Blue in 1972. He dealt suspensions to Denny McLain in 1969 and 1970. He was sued by Curt Flood in 1969 in a test of the reserve clause. Flood's final appeal was denied by the Supreme Court in 1972. He chastised Jim Bouton about his writings in 1970. He was unable to avert the 1972 player strike, which resulted in one week of unplayed games and an improved pension plan for the players. He ruled that Charley Finley had to

reinstate Mike Andrews during the 1973 World Series and later fined Finley $7000 and placed him on probation for his conduct in the matter.

Finley and Kuhn clashed again in 1976. Faced with the likely defection of his stars after the season, Charley peddled Vida Blue to the Yankees for $1.5 million, and Joe Rudi and Rollie Fingers to the Red Sox for $1 million each in June. However, Kuhn voided the sales, stating that they were not in the best interests of baseball.

League Agreements

Organized Baseball has five main documents: Major League Agreement, Major League Rules, Major-Minor League Agreements, Major-Minor League Rules and the National Association Rules.

Top man is the Commissioner. As specified in the Major League Agreement, and underwritten in the Major-Minor pact, his functions may be summarized as follows:

(a) To investigate any act detrimental to baseball.

(b) To decide on punitive action.

(c) To decide any interleague dispute brought to him by either league president.

(d) To determine any dispute involving a player.

(e) To formulate rules of procedure in cases under his control.

In case "detrimental conduct" originates outside of organized baseball, Article I, Section 4 says he "may pursue appropriate legal remedies, advocate remedial legislation and take such other steps as he may deem necessary and proper to the interests and morale of the players and the honor of the game."

Another important article in the Major League Agreement stipulates that all contracts between clubs and their officers, players and other employers shall contain a clause binding the parties to submit to the discipline of the Commissioner.

Baseball's legislative arm is the joint meeting of major leagues. In interleague affairs, majority rules within each circuit, and then each league votes as a unit. In case of a tie, the Commissioner casts the deciding vote.

In the interim between league meetings, the majors are guided by an Executive Council. It consists of the Commissioner, both league presidents and one member elected by each of the leagues. However, in matters dealing with players' grievances, two active players are added to this Council, with majority to rule and all decisions binding and final.

Except in cases of critical clashes, the Major League Agreement is not as important as the Major League Rules. The latter is a lengthy covenant completely regulating league, club, player and umpire rights and responsibilities. The Commissioner is obliged to enforce these rules, and has no power to abrogate any of them on "detrimental to baseball" grounds. Any amendment passed by the majors, which affect the Major-Minor Agreement, must be submitted to a mail vote of all the minor leagues.

The Major-Minor League Agreement places the minors under jurisdiction of the Commissioner either in cases of "detrimental conduct" or in major-minor disputes. It also sets up a Major-Minor Executive Council for interim rule, and fixes the scale of payments in the annual player draft.

Major-Minor League Rules deal with protection of franchises, player limits, reserve lists, drafting, optional agreements, stock ownership, etc. As for the fifth charter of baseball's government, the National Association Agreement details a method of operation for the minors.

XI BASEBALL AUXILIARIES

It is true that the vast popularity of baseball is due to its national, year-round publicity in the form of box scores, daily reports, feature stories, notes, columns, etc., all dutifully reported in every newspaper in the land.

The morning-after straight result story of the game is eagerly absorbed by the fan for information and discussion with his neighbor and fellow-worker. The box score is as important a way of life as the normal functions of the day. The afternoon paper carries the whys and hows of the previous day's game and the "confidential" information on how it was won or lost. This is called a "p.m." story and is usually composed from a so-called "angle" in which the writer is permitted more latitude of expression than his colleague on a morning paper. However, both types of stories have their vast audiences who, because of business and family duties, are forced to follow their favorites only through the words of an on-the-scene observer.

Writers

Baseball writing is probably as old as baseball playing. Ex-Senator William Cauldwell, editor of the *New York Mercury*, wrote baseball news in his paper as far back as 1853. Three years later, British-born Henry Chadwick became the first professional baseball writer. This is the same "Father Chadwick" who guided the development of official rules, edited annuals, crusaded for fundamental baseball reforms and served as the sport's "Chief Justice" for half a century.

Then came a string of other famous chroniclers of the sport: Charles Peverelly, who wrote the first history of the game; Mike Kelly, who introduced the short-hand system of scoring in 1861; the Rankin brothers of New York, W. M. Spink of St. Louis and many more. Among the earliest baseball scribes was Walt Whitman of the *Brooklyn Eagle*, whose stilted reporting ("Mr. Johnson struck the ball well in the seventh innings.") gave no portent of his classic poetry to come.

After the 1887 season, major league baseball writers banded into the first national organization, with George Munson of St. Louis as president. It was called the National Base Ball Reporters' Association and had a short but useful life. This group suggested a number of changes in the playing and scoring rules which were subsequently adopted. However, it broke up in 1890, when the Brotherhood war split baseball into two hostile camps.

The second attempt at a scribes' association grew out of the 1908 World Series, which climaxed endless hardships and indignities suffered by the working press. In Detroit, the press box could be reached only by climbing a rickety ladder. In Chicago, the press box was as wide open as a Barbary saloon, "crashed" by assorted actors, politicians, jockeys and pals of the club officials.

When Hugh Fullerton reached his press seat in the Cub ballpark, he found it already occupied by Louis Mann, the famous actor. Mann refused to vacate. So Fullerton plunked himself down in Mann's lap and covered the entire World Series game from that bizarre perch.

That did it. On October 10, 1908, the writers formed a temporary organization. A permanent union was formed two months later in New York, with 125 members, and Joe Jackson of Detroit as president. The first constitution

of the Base Ball Writers' Association of America set up its objectives as (1) Better accommodations in press boxes, (2) More uniformity in scoring, and (3) Conferences with the majors' rules committee regarding playing rules.

The BBWAA has made great strides since that humble beginning. It now controls every major league press box, and even the clubowner is not allowed to enter his press box without permission of the scribes. It has been woven into the fabric of the big leagues to the extent of handling the official scoring for all games, picking the Most Valuable Players as well as Rookie for the Year, naming players to the Hall of Fame and serving on the joint major leagues' committee on playing rules.

Radio and Television

Modern electronics have brought baseball its greatest popularity in history. Through the magic lantern of the television tube and the all-reaching sound of radio, a major league game can be seen and/or heard by just about everyone in the country. Whether this is good for the future profit growth of the game is something the clubowners must still decide.

The daily chatter of the radio play-by-play announcer and the casual flick of a TV dial can bring a major league contest into any room in an American home. The game is no longer isolated to its point of origin and the characteristics, performances and personal statistics of all the players are known to millions who have yet to see a "live" major league game.

Over the years, these lusty and lucrative wireless media have converted countless millions of new fans to baseball . . . brought over a hundred million dollars from sponsors into the coffers of the clubs . . . and, in a vital service that is too easily overlooked, brightened the lives of hospitalized veterans and other shut-ins.

It all started back in 1921, when Graham McNamee sat in front of a pie-sized microphone at the Polo Grounds and broadcast the eight games of the Yank-Giant World Series. Subsequent Series were aired, too, but it was not until 1934 that a sponsor moved in: Henry Ford signed a four-year contract at $100,000 per. Eventually the All-Star Game came into radio "gravy" too.

It was a big step from broadcasting special events to transmitting every game in the regular season. The first station to venture into daily baseball broadcasts directly from the ballpark was Chicago's WMAQ, with Hal Totten describing the games in 1924. This custom eventually blanketed practically every club in organized ball.

By 1959, more than a thousand radio stations were saturating the country with play-by-play, costing sponsors about $40,000,000. The Mutual Broadcasting System sent a "live" account of its cooperatively-sponsored Game of the Day through about 500 stations all over the nation. Television, too, with two major networks beaming big league baseball into non-major league areas, was on a coast-to-coast weekly schedule and creating vast problems for those minor league teams which played games in those cities where the fans could stay at home and watch a major league game via television.

A major headache arose when minor league clubs claimed that "invasion" of their territory by big league broadcasts was ruining their gate. The majors were eager to help, but feared placing any restraint on the all-engulfing networks lest organized baseball be hauled into court and sued on the touchy issue of "monopolistic practice in interstate commerce." As a compromise a 50-mile area of protection was set up to screen minor league games, but this couldn't

be enforced, and the leagues had to set up special committees to handle radio and TV problems.

Television cameras were focussed on major league teams in action for the first time at Ebbets Field on August 26, 1939, at a Dodger-Red doubleheader. Though only a handful of TV sets existed in the entire metropolitan area at the time, National Broadcasting Company engineers moved their experimental equipment into Ebbets Field. Walter L. (Red) Barber, already famous as a radio broadcaster, gave this pioneering effort the full treatment by announcing the plays. Between games, Barber brought Bucky Walters and Dolph Camilli to the field cameras, for closeups that showed how Bucky gripped the ball for a curve and how Dolph kept his hand in the first baseman's mitt. The telecast went out over station W2XBS, atop the Empire State Building.

Bold and imaginative Larry MacPhail, Dodger president, encouraged the telecasters, and through 1940–41 on the average of one game a week was screened at Ebbets Field. The war put a quietus on TV activity, but when MacPhail headed the Yankees in 1946, he sold the first commercial rights. Metropolitan New York had fewer than 500 sets at the time, but Dumont paid $75,000 for season rights to Yankee games.

Video fees multiplied so rapidly that by 1950 Dumont was able to pay sportscaster Dizzy Dean $30,000, or more than he had ever gotten as a star pitcher with the Cards and Cubs. Since then the number one telecaster in areas like New York and Chicago has been handsomely rewarded by the sponsors and the ball clubs. In 1950 Commissioner A. B. Chandler closed a deal bringing baseball $6,000,000 for the TV rights alone to the World Series covering 1951–56. An even juicier deal for World Series TV-radio privileges was made with the start of the 1957 World Series. The sponsors (The Gillette Safety Razor Company) paid $3,000,000 annually for the exclusive TV-radio rights, or approximately $15,000,000 for the period from 1957 through 1962. This bonanza just about guaranteed the success of the costly ballplayers' pension fund.

Most of the outstanding sportscasters like Barber, Russ Hodges, Mel Allen, Jim Britt, Bob Elson, etc., cut their eyeteeth in this profession. However, there are many former major league ballplayers who stepped right into sportscasting and made an instant hit.

With the increasing coverage of baseball by television and radio, many of the sportscasters became household names and their faces and voices became as familiar as those of the players.

In May of 1971, the Major Leagues signed a new 4-year contract with NBC increasing the number of night games, especially in 1972. The World Series had one night game, with plans for three games in 1972. The financial details were not made public due to the Major League Players Association pact with the major league teams concerning property rights for its pension fund.

Sources indicated that the contract was worth around $70 million for 1972 through 1975. Divided between 24 teams, it would amount to over two million dollars plus what each team receives from local radio-tv packages, an average of $1 million more.

Statisticians

Baseball statisticians are a breed apart. Strange but admirable, they pursue Truth in the shape of cold, hard numbers. Never compromising, never relaxing, these busy beavers compile the totals and averages that form the only possible unbiased evaluation of a ballplayer.

Most amateur statisticians are like Thomas Gray's "Many a flower is born

to blush unseen, and waste its sweetness on the desert air." Notable exception is John A. Heydler, a Washington linotype operator who kept exhaustive baseball records as a hobby. When Harry Pulliam became National League president in 1903 and found the league statistics in terrible shape, he hired Heydler as secretary and statistician. Honest John soon became the league's secretary-treasurer and eventually president.

Newspaper, wire service and radio/TV demand nowadays for quick, accurate daily statistics during the season would put too great a strain on the league offices, so the figure-tending is farmed out to pros: Elias Sports Bureau (New York City) for the NL, Sports Information Center (Boston) for the AL. The American League went to a computerized system of record-keeping in 1973. Daily score sheets are sent across phone lines and up-to-date figures are returned to each club in time for the next game. The Howe News Bureau (Chicago), which previously handled the AL work, and William J. Weiss (San Mateo, California) do most of the minor league work and derive further income from club officials who want complete up-to-the-minute averages of the minor leagues— either to check on their farmhands' progress or to scout other prospects.

During the baseball season, the Howe and Elias offices employ a dozen or more figure filberts for such jobs as entering data in a master ledger from the official score sheets (which are large, detailed pages sent in by newspapermen designated by the league as official scorers) ; figuring out the five leading players in each department, for use in daily newspaper "boxes"; compiling full league averages for use in weekend editions; writing "leads," or short descriptive articles, to interpret and accompany the averages issued to papers and radio or TV stations; filing, mimeographing, checking, etc.

Someone once figured out that of the myriad statistics issued all season long, these bureaus err about once in every 3,500 figures. However, after some 7,057,600 "live" figures on file are quadruple-checked for official release each winter, they prove to be 99.9996 correct!

Irwin Howe founded his bureau in 1911, and Al Munro Elias started his a few years later. These baseball mills are now run respectively by John Phillips and Seymour Siwoff, who also edits the oldest and most famous annual of "best" records, *The Little Red Book,* which was first compiled by Charlie White and John B. Foster.

Both bureaus are antedated by the Heilbroner Baseball Bureau, founded in 1909 at Fort Wayne, Indiana, by ex-St. Louis Cardinal manager Louis Heilbroner. The HBB, a service bureau for all pro baseball, keeps personal cards and transaction records to cover every organized league. Ever since 1910, it has issued the annual Baseball Blue Book, the most complete and authentic directory of the game. Earle Halstead is the Heilbroner chief.

The tremendous burden of daily, up-to-the game statistical information has placed greater emphasis on the figure filbert. Many clubs now carry full-time statisticians to record the inning-by-inning report of all games. Radio and TV announcers have added a season-long statistician to their staffs to prepare the latest in figures for their audiences.

Concessionaires

"The hot dog is king," a Chicago Club official once explained. "For every dollar we get in paid admissions, our total cost of operating the club is $1.06. If we didn't have extra income from concessions in the ballpark, we'd have to lock our gates."

To save all the headaches that go with the catering business, practically all ball clubs lease the food-and-drink privileges at their park to established concessionaires like the Stevens family, Blake Harper, Jacobs Brothers, etc. The result is substantial revenue and no risk. Vending rights can prove quite lucrative, as when the all-time record was set at a Chicago White Sox doubleheader in 1950, averaging $1.05 spent per fan.

The royal family of sports caterers is the Stevens clan. Operating under the corporate title of Harry Mosley Stevens, Inc., the founder's four sons and several grandsons boomed the business beyond even the fabulous pace of old Harry M., who died a multi-millionaire 55 years after arriving here in 1879 from England, down to his last pound ($5). The Stevens concession empire embraces ballparks and racetracks stretching, as their letterhead proudly boasts, "From the Hudson to the Rio Grande."

"Columbus, 1492" may be the famous date for schoolboys, but "Columbus, 1887" is the memorable milestone in concession history. On a summer day in 1887, Harry M. Stevens went to a ballgame in Columbus, Ohio. He bought a scorecard, but couldn't decipher its garbled list of players. Soon after the last putout, he was in the club's front office, offering $700 for the privilege of printing and selling a decent scorecard in the park. Improving the design and selling space on his scorecard, Harry quickly recouped his initial investment and started operating in the black. To this day, the Stevens brothers still publish scorecards for the several ballparks in which they have catering rights.

Shortly after his scorecard success, Harry M. branched into the peanuts-and soda-pop line. He reached the big leagues for good in 1894, moving into the Polo Grounds. A few years later, at a cold and windy Giant game, he noticed his soft drinks sales lagging. So he rushed his vendors to buy up all the frankfurters and rolls in the neighborhood. He boiled the franks, split the rolls to form a natural bed for them and sold them to the chilled spectators, with the slogan that still rings up sales to this very day, "Get 'em while they're hot!"

Frankfurter sales proved popular from the first. Sports cartoonist Tad Dorgan liked to caricature the dachshund-shaped delicacy as animated dogs, but despite the whimsical "libel" on the beef ingredients, customers consumed the "hot dogs" in ever increasing numbers. Soon the item became world famous.

The Stevens business kept growing until now it employs almost 3,500 people on an average summer day. The Jacobs Brothers and other baseball concessionaires hire thousands of others.

The vendor in the ballpark is paid on salary plus commission. He (or she, since some concessionaires employ women to sell) usually has a minimum guarantee of $3 per day and averages from $16 to $20 daily, if the attendance is of normal size. A top vendor can make as much as $50 at a capacity crowd.

In the average big league ballpark, the total yearly consumption by fans includes 700,000 bottles of pop, 800,000 hot dogs, 500,000 slabs of ice cream and 400,000 bags of peanuts.

Fans

Professional implies "for pay." Pay means money, money comes from the cash customer . . . and so, quite obviously, the most important factor in professional baseball is the fan. Everybody connected with sports recognizes this axiom. In fact, even the caustic newspaperman is treated graciously by the ball club, only because he represents a link with the thousands (or millions) of fans who read his story daily.

Rabid fans, who worship the baseball headliner, aren't adverse to making headlines themselves. There was the Dodger fan who shot a Giant rooter to death for making cynical cracks. En route to the electric chair, the murderer asked the chaplain, "Did the Bums beat the Giants today?" Then there was the Cleveland flagpole sitter who vowed not to leave his perch till the Indians returned to first place . . . the fan who climbed out of the Ebbets Field grandstand to assault umpire George Magerkurth . . . and the psychotic girl who shot Eddie Waitkus to prove her intense love for the Philly first baseman.

In the "old faithful" class, Arthur Felsch of Milwaukee rates notice because every year he parks outside the bleacher entrance about a week before the start of the World Series, and lives in a cardboard crate . . . just so he can have the honor of being the first one admitted to the park. However, the long-term rooters are usually more reserved and rarely make even a single line in the papers all their lives. In this latter category are such veterans as George Doerzbach, who saw 55 consecutive season opening games at Cleveland; Lou Schulte, who missed only seven Cincinnati home games in 24 years, and Hyman Pearlstone, who made at least one road trip a season with the defunct Philadelphia Athletics for 44 years.

Every ballpark abounds in favorite grandstand "characters." St. Louis had Mary Ott for many years, distracting enemy players with her penetrating whinny; Pittsburgh had a coal dealer who barked like a wounded seal; Cincinnati had Harry Thobe, retired bricklayer, who danced on the dugout roof while holding a red umbrella and wearing a red-banded straw hat. The "daffy Dodgers", as might be expected, always led the way in quaint customers: the late Shorty Laurice and his catch-as-catch-can Sym-phoney Band; Hilda Chester and her cowbell; Eddie Bettan with his tin whistle and explorer's helmet; Jack Pearce and his gas-filled balloons, etc.

The Hollywood influence has invaded baseball in recent years, and "fan clubs" seem to be the rage, numbering most of its membership among teenage girls.

Brooklyn still recalls Abie the Iceman, who would hitch his ice wagon just outside Ebbets Field every afternoon and go in to jeer at the Dodgers. "Ya bums, ya!" he'd rasp. One day, manager Wilbert Robinson came up to Abie and said, "Wouldn't you like a season pass, so you can see the games free instead of having to pay every day? Here, take this. Just stop yelling at my boys. You make them nervous."

Abie accepted the pass joyfully. But a week later he knocked on the clubhouse door, came up to Uncle Robbie and said, "I can't stand it any more. Here's back your pass. I gotta yell—'cause they ARE bums!"

Patsy O'Toole, a Navin Field and then Briggs Stadium fixture, was Detroit's most prominent rooter. He would roar "you're a faker!" at opposing players and his bellow could be heard throughout the stands.

Cleveland once honored one of its patrons with a Special Fan's Night, showering the lucky fan with a number of gifts for his loyalty to the Indians.

XII FEATURES

Famous Families

When a man wants his son to inherit his money, he writes a will. But all the penmanship and planning in the world cannot guarantee that a boy will inherit the skill, the strength or the spiritual drive of his father. Baseball immortals like Ty Cobb and Walter Johnson were frustrated when their sons showed no special aptitude or preference for the sport. Yet there are enough examples of father-and-son or brothers who made the majors to conclude that playing talent can run in a family.

Of all the great baseball clans, none could match the six Cleveland-born sons of Irish immigrants James Delahanty and Bridget Croke. Five of their boys made the majors. A sixth, Willie, starred in the minors and was drafted by the Dodgers—but before he could report for National League duty, he was hit in the head by a pitched ball at Waterbury, Connecticut, and he had to give up the game soon afterward.

Big Ed Delahanty, eldest of the baseball tribe, is the only person ever to lead both the National and American Leagues in batting, with .408 for Philadelphia NL in 1899 and .376 for Washington AL in 1902. A prodigious slugger, he once hit four homers in one game and added a single for good measure. Jim Delahanty led the World Series hitters of 1909 with an average of .346. Brother Joe was the main prop for St. Louis NL at one time. Tom and Frank both played for Cleveland.

Another clan of shillelagh swingers de luxe was the O'Neill quartet of brothers, Mike, Steve, Jack and Jim. Brother trios include the families Allen, Alou, Boyer, Clarkson, Cross, Cruz, DiMaggio, High, Mansell, Reccius, Sadowski, Sewell, Sowders and Wright.

Here is a comprehensive list of the major leagues' famous families:

Father and Son

ADAMS—Robert H., R. Michael
ARAGON—Angel, Angel Jr.
AVERILL—Howard E., Earl D.
BAGBY—James C., James C., Jr.
BARNHART—Clyde L., Victor D.
BEAMON—Charles A., Charles A., Jr.
BELL—David R., David G.
BERRA—Lawrence P., Dale A.
BERRY—Charles J., Charles F.
BERRY—Joseph H., Joseph H., Jr.
BOONE—Raymond O., Robert R.
BRICKELL—Frederick B., Fritz D.
BRUCKER—Earle F., Earle F., Jr.
CAMILLI—Adolph L., Douglas J.
CAMPANIS—Alexander S., James A.
COLEMAN—Joseph P., Joseph H.
COLLINS—Edward T., Edward T., Jr.
CONNOLLY—Edward J., Edward J., Jr.

COONEY—James J., James E.
& John W.
CORRIDEN—John M., John M., Jr.
CROUCH—William H., William E.
DOSCHER—John H., John H., Jr.
ESCHEN—James G., Lawrence E.
GABRIELSON—Leonard H.,
Leonard G.
GANZEL—Charles W., Foster P.
GILBERT—Lawrence W., Charles M.
& Harold J.
GRAHAM—George F., John B.
GRIMES—Oscar R., Oscar R., Jr.
GRIMSLEY—Ross A., Ross A., II
HAIRSTON—Samuel, John L. & Jerry
HEGAN—James E., James M.
HEINTZELMAN—Kenneth A.,
Thomas K.

591

HOOD—Wallace J., Wallace J., Jr.
JOHNSON—Adam R., Adam R., Jr.
JOHNSON—Edward W., James B.
JOHNSON—Ernest R., Donald S.
KENNEDY—Robert D., Terrence E.
KEOUGH—R. Martin, Matthew L.
KRAUSSE—Lewis B., Lewis B., Jr.
LANIER—Hubert M., Harold C.
LEE—Thornton S., Donald E.
LERCHEN—Bertram R., George E.
LIEBHARDT—Glenn J., Glenn I.
LINDSTROM—Frederick C.,
   Charles W.
LIVELY—Henry E., Everett A.
MACK—Cornelius, Earle T.
MAGGERT—Harl V., Harl W.
MALAY—Charles F., Joseph C.
MARTIN—Barnes R., Jerry L.
MATTICK—Walter J., Robert J.
MAY—Merrill G., Milton S.
MEINKE—Frank L., Robert B.
MILLS—William G., Arthur G.
MONTEAGUDO—Rene M.,
   Aurelio F.
MOORE—Eugene, Eugene Jr.
MORTON—Guy, Guy Jr.
MUELLER—Walter J., Donald F.
NARLESKI—William E., Raymond E.
NICHOLS—Chester R., Chester R., Jr.
NORTHEY—Ronald J., Scott R.
OKRIE—Frank A., Leonard J.
O'ROURKE—James H., James S.

O'ROURKE—Joseph P., Joseph L.
OSBORNE—Ernest P., Lawrence S.
PARTENHEIMER—Harold P.,
   Stanwood W.
PILLETTE—Herman P., Duane X.
QUEEN—Melvin J., Melvin D.
RIPLEY—Walter F., Allen S.
SAVIDGE—Ralph A., Donald S.
SCHULTZ—Joseph C., Joseph C., Jr.
SHEELY—Earl H., Hollis K.
SIEBERT—Richard W., Paul E.
SISLER—George H., David M.
   & Richard A.
SMALLEY—Roy F., Roy F., Jr.
STEPHENSON—Joseph C., Jerry J.
SULLIVAN—William J., William J.,
   Jr.
SUSCE—George C. M., George D.
TORRES—Ricardo J., Don G.
TRESH—Michael, Thomas Michael
TROSKY—Harold A., Harold A., Jr.
TROUT—Paul H., Steven R.
UNSER—Albert B., Delbert B.
WAKEFIELD—Howard J., Richard C.
WALKER—Ewart G., Fred
   & Harry W.
WALSH—Edward A., Edward A., Jr.
WHITE—Joyner C., Joyner M.
WILLS—Maurice M., Elliott T.
WISE—Hugh E., Kendall C.
WOOD—Joseph, Joseph F.
YOUNG—Delmar J., Delmar E.

Brothers

AARON—Henry L., Tommie L.
ACOSTA—Balmadero M., Jose
ADAMS—Richard L., Robert H.
ALLEN—(3) Harold A., Richard A.,
   & Ronald F.
ALLISON—Arthur A., Douglass L.
ALOU—Felipe R., Mateo R., Jesus M.
ANDREWS—Michael J., Robert P.
ASPROMONTE—Kenneth J.,
   Robert T.
BAILEY—James H., Lonas E.
BANNON—James H., Thomas E.
BARNES—Jesse L., Virgil J.
BAXES—Dimitrios S., Michael
BELL—Charles C., Frank G.
BENNETT—David H., Dennis J.

BERGEN—Martin, William A.
BIGBEE—Carson L., Lyle R.
BLANKENSHIP—Homer, Theodore
BLUEGE—Oswald L., Otto A.
BOLLING—Frank E., Milton J.
BOONE—Isaac M., James A.
BOYER—(3) Cletus L., Cloyd V.
   & Kenton L.
BOYLE—Edward J., John A.
BOYLE—James J., Ralph F.
BRASHEAR—Robert N., Roy P.
BREEDEN—Danny R., Harold N.
BRETT—George H., Kenneth A.
BRINKMAN—Charles, Edwin A.
BROWN—Jackie G., Paul
BROWN—Larry L., Richard E.

BROWN—Ollie L., Oscar L.
CAMNITZ—R. Harry, Samuel H.
CAMP—Llewellyn R., Winfield S.
CAMPBELL—Hugh, Michael
CANTWELL—Michael J., Thomas A.
CARLYLE—Hiram C., Roy E.
CASEY—Daniel M., Dennis P.
CHAPMAN—Calvin L., Edwin V.
CHIOZZA—Dino J., Louis P.
CHRISTOPHER—Loyd E., Russell O.
CLAPP—Aaron B., John E.
CLARKE—Fred C., Joshua B.
CLARKE—Rufus R., Sumpter E.
CLARKSON—(3) Arthur H., John G.
 & Walter H.
COFFMAN—George D., Samuel R.
COHEN—Andrew H., Sydney H.
CONIGLIARO—Anthony R.,
 William M.
CONNELL—Eugene J., Joseph B.
CONNOR—Joseph F., Roger
CONWAY—James P., Peter J.
CONWAY—Richard B., William F.
COONEY—James E., John W.
COOPER—Morton C., William W.
CORCORAN—Lawrence J., M.
COSCARART—Joseph M., Peter J.
COVELESKI—Harry F., Stanley A.
COVINGTON—Clarence C.,
 William W.
CROSS—(3) Amos C., Frank A.
 & Lafayette N.
CRUZ—(3) Cirilo, Hector, Jose
CUCCINELLO—Alfred E.,
 Anthony F.
DAILY—Cornelius F., Edward M.
DALY—Joseph J., Thomas P.
DANNING—Harry, Ike
DARINGER—Clifford C., Rolla H.
DAVALILLO—Pompeyo R., Victor J.
DAVENPORT—Arthur D., Claude E.
DEAN—Jay H., Paul D.
DEASLEY—James, Thomas H.
DELAHANTY—(5) Edward J., Frank
 G., James C., Joseph N., Thomas J.
DeMONTREVILLE—Eugene N.,
 Leon
DICKEY—George W., William M.
DiMAGGIO—(3) Dominic P., Joseph
 P. & Vincent P.
DONAHUE—John A., Patrick W.
DONOVAN—Jeremiah F., Thomas J.
DORGAN—Jeremiah F., Michael C.

DOYLE—Brian R., R. Dennis
DOYLE—Cornelius J., John J.
DRAKE—Samuel H., Solomon L.
DUGAN—Edward J., William E.
EDWARDS—David L., Michael L.
EGGLER—David D., John
ENS—Anton, Jewel W.
ERAUTT—Edward L. S., Joseph M.
EVERS—John J., Joseph F.
EWING—John, William
FALK—Bibb A., Chester E.
FERRELL—Richard B., Wesley C.
FERRY—Alfred J., John F.
FINNEY—Harold W., Louis K.
FISHER—Chauncey B., Thomas C.
FISHER—Newton, Robert T.
FOGARTY—James G., Joseph J.
FOLEY—Thomas J., William B.
FORD—Eugene W., Russell W.
FOREMAN—Francis I., John D.
FORSCH—Kenneth R., Robert H.
FREESE—Eugene L., George W.
FRIEL—Patrick H., William E.
FULLER—Henry W., William B.
GAGLIANO—Philip J., Ralph M.
GARRETT—Henry A., Ronald W.
GALVIN—James F., Louis
GANZEL—Charles W., John H.
GARBARK—Nathaniel M.,
 Robert M.
GARDELLA—Alfred S., Daniel L.
GASTON—Alexander N.,
 Nathaniel M.
GETTINGER—Charles H.,
 Thomas L.
GILBERT—Charles M., Harold J.
GILBERT—Harry, John G.
GLEASON—Harry G., William J.
GLEASON—John D., William G.
GRABOWSKI—Albert F., Reginald J.
GRAVES—Joseph E., Samuel S.
GREGG—David C., Sylveanus A.
GRIMES—(Twins) Oscar R., Roy A.
GRISSOM—Leo T., Marvin E.
GROH—Henry K., Lewis C.
GUMBERT—Addison C., William S.
HACKETT—Mortimer M., Walter H.
HAFEY—Daniel A., Thomas F.
HAIRSTON—Jerry, John L.
HALL—George W., James
HAMNER—Granville W., Wesley G.
HANDLEY—Eugene L., Lee E.
HARGARVE—Eugene F., William M.

HARRINGTON—Andrew F.,
  Joseph C.
HATFIELD—Gilbert, John V.
HAYWORTH—Myron C.,
  Raymond H.
HEMPHILL—Charles J., Frank V.
HENGLE—Edward S., Emory J.
HEVING—John A., Joseph W.
HIGH—(3) Andrew A., Charles E.
  & Hugh J.
HILL—Hugh E., William C.
HINCHMAN—Harry S., William W.
HITCHCOCK—James F., William C.
HOVLIK—Edward C., Joseph
HOWARD—George E., Ivan C.
HUGHES—Edward H., Thomas J.
HUGHES—James J., Michael F.
HUNTER—(Twins) George H.,
  William E.
IORG—Dane C., Garth R.
IRWIN—Arhur A., John
JEFFCOAT—George E., Harold B.
JIMENEZ—Felix E., Manuel E.
JOHNSON—Chester L., Earl D.
JOHNSON—Robert L., Roy C.
JOHNSTON—James H., Wheeler R.
JONES—Gary H., Steven H.
JONNARD—(Twins) Clarence J.,
  Claude A.
JORGENS—Arndt L., Orville E.
KAPPEL—Henry, Joseph
KELL—Everett L., George C.
KELLER—Charles E., Howard K.
KELLNER—Alexander R., Walter J.
KELLY—George L., Reynolds C.
KENNEDY—James E., Junior R.
KEOUGH—Richard M., Joseph
KILLEFER—Wade H., William L.
KILROY—Matthew A., Michael J.
KING—Marshall N., Stephen F.
KLAUS—William J., Robert F.
KLING—John G., William
KNODE—Kenneth T., Robert T.
KNOTHE—George B., Wilfred E.
KOPF—William L., Walter H.
KRSNICH—Michael, Rocco P.
LACHEMANN—Marcel E., Rene G.
LARY—Alfred A., Frank S.
LELIVELT—John F., William J.
LILLARD—Robert E., William B.
LOBERT—Frank J., John B.
LOOK—Dean Z., Bruce M.
LOWDERMILK—Grover C., Louis B.

LUSH—Ernest B., William L.
MAHER—F., Thomas
MAISEL—Frederick C., George J.
MANCUSO—August R., Frank O.
MANGUAL—Angel L., Jose M.
MANSELL—(3) John, Michael R.
  & Thomas E.
MANUSH—Frank B., Henry E.
MARION—John W., Martin W.
MASKREY—Harry H., Samuel L.
MATHEWSON—Christopher, Henry
MATTOX—Cloy M., James P.
MAY—Carlos, Lee A.
MAYER—James E., Samuel F.
McDANIEL—Lyndall D., Max V.
McFARLAN—Alexander S.,
  Anderson D.
McFARLAND—Charles E., Lamont A.
McGEEHAN—Cornelius B., Daniel D.
McLAUGHLIN—Bernard, Francis M.
MEUSEL—Emil F., Robert W.
MILAN—Horace R., Jesse C.
MILLER—Edmund J., Ralph H.
MILLER—Russell L., Walter J.
MOFFET—Joseph W., Samuel R.
MORIARTY—George J., William J.
MORRISON—John D., Philip M.
MORRISSEY—John H., Thomas J.
MUELLER—Clarence F., Walter J.
MYERS—Lynn, William H.
NETTLES—Graig, James W.
NIEKRO—Joseph, Philip H.
O'BRIEN—(Twins) Edward J.,
  John T.
OGDEN—John M., Warren H.
OLIVO—Diomedes Antonio,
  Fred Emilio
O'NEILL—(4) James L., John J.,
  Stephen F., Michael J.
ONSLOW—Edward J., John J.
O'ROURKE—James H., John
ORTIZ—Oliverio N., Roberto G.
O'TOOLE—Dennis J., James
PACIOREK—John F., Thomas M.
PARKER—Harley P., Jay
PARROTT—Thomas W., Walter E.
PASCUAL—Camilo A., Carlos L.
PATTERSON—Hamilton, William
  J. B.
PEITZ—Henry C., Joseph
PEPLOSKI—Henry S., Joseph A.
PERRY—Gaylord J., James E.

PFEFFER—Edward J., Francis X.
PIERSON—Donald P., Edmund D.
PIKE—J., Lipman E.
PIPGRAS—Edward J., George W.
POTTER—Maryland D., Squire
RECCIUS—(3) J. William, (Twins)
  Philip, John
REUSCHEL—Paul R., Rickey E.
RICKETTS—David W., Richard J.
RIDDLE—Elmer R., John L.
ROBINSON—Frederic H., Wilbert
ROETTGER—Oscar F., Walter H.

ROSENBERG—Harry, Louis
ROTH—Frank C., Robert F.
ROWE—David E., John C.
ROY—Charles R., Luther F.
RUSSELL—Allen E., Clarence D.
SADOWSKI—Edward R., Robert,
  Theodore
SAUER—Edward, Henry J.
SAY—James I., Lewis I.
SCANLAN—Frank A., William D.
SCHAFFER—George, Taylor
SCHANG—Robert M., Walter H.
SCHAREIN—Arthur O., George A.
SCHMIDT—Charles, Walter J.
SCHULTE—Herman J., Leonard W.
SEWELL—(3) James L., Joseph W.
  & Thomas W.
SHAFFER—(3) Frank, George, Taylor
SHANNON—(Twins) Joseph A.,
  Maurice
SHANTZ—Robert C., Wilmer E.
SHERLOCK—John C., Vincent T.
SHERRY—Lawrence, Norman B.
SISLER—David M., Richard A.
SMITH—Charles E., Frederick V.
SNYDER—James, Joshua
SOWDERS—(3) John, Leonard,
  & William J.
STAFFORD—James J., John J.

STAHL—Charles S., Garland
STANLEY—John L., Joseph B.
STOVALL—George T., Jesse C.
SUTHERLAND—Darrell W., Gary L.
TANNEHILL—Jesse N., Lee F.
TEBEAU—George E., Oliver W.
THIELMAN—Henry J., John P.
THOMAS—Roy A., William M.
THOMPSON—Homer, Thomas C.
THRONEBERRY—Marvin E.,
  Maynard F.
TOBIN—James A., John P.
TORRE—Frank J., Joseph P.
TRAFFLEY—John, William F.
TREACEY—Frederick, P.
TWOMBLY—Clarence E., George F.
TYLER—Frederick F., George A.
TYRONE—James V., O. Wayne
UPTON—Thomas H., William R.
VAN CUYK—Christian G., John H.
WADE—Benjamin S., Jacob F.
WAGNER—Albert, John P.
WALKER—Ernest R., Ewart G.
WALKER—Fred, Harry W.
WALKER—Gerald H., Harvey W.
WALKER—Moses F., Welday W.
WANER—Lloyd J., Paul G.
WATT—Albert B., Frank M.
WEILAND—Edwin N., Robert G.
WESTLAKE—James P., Waldon T.
WEYHING—August, John
WHEAT—McKinley D., Zachary D.
WHITE—James L., William H.
WHITNEY—Arthur W., Frank T.
WILLIAMS—August R., Harry P.
WILTSE—George L., Lewis D.
WINGO—Absalom H., Ivy B.
WOOD—Fred S., Peter B.
WRIGHT—(3) George, Samuel,
  & William H.
YOCHIM—Leonard J., Raymond A.
YOUNT—Lawrence K., Robin R.

Grandfather and Grandson

COLLINS—John F., and **GALLAGHER**, Robert C.
HERRMANN—Martin J., Edward M.
SPENCER—L. Benjamin, James L.

Night Baseball

There's nothing new under the sun—nor under electric lights either. Though night baseball has been called the saviour of the modern game, it actually dates back to September, 1880. Two amateur teams tangled at Nantasket Beach, Massachusetts, and with the aid of arclights strung along the field they were able to complete nine full innings between 8 and 9:30 P.M.

The next night game of record was June 2, 1883, when the Quincys of Illinois beat a picked team of home players at Fort Wayne, Indiana, 19–11. Other 19th-century games at night were strictly exhibitions, too. Baltimore played at Hartford, Connecticut, on July 23, 1890. Manager Ed Barrow arranged a game for his Paterson, New Jersey, team (boasting Honus Wagner at shortstop) on the night of July 4, 1896 at Wilmington, Delaware.

E. Lee Keyser boldly announced at the National Association meeting in the winter of 1929 that his Des Moines club would be the first in organized baseball to play a league game at night. However, Des Moines opened the season on the road, and Keyser, after having spent $19,000 to install lights, was robbed of the distinction when promoters at Independence, Kansas—a rival club in the Western Association—hastily posted some arclights and played against Muskogee on the night of April 28, 1930. Four days afterward, Des Moines staged its gala arclight affair.

Two seasons later, Larry MacPhail, as general manager of the Columbus Redbirds of the American Association, installed high-level lighting in his stadium. In 1935, as leader of Cincinnati, he introduced night ball to the majors, with President Roosevelt in the White House pressing a button that first turned on the Crosley Field lights. Later, as president of the Dodgers and Yanks, MacPhail put lights in Ebbets Field and Yankee Stadium. Now every team in the majors except Chicago's Wrigley Field NL has lights at home.

Originally, the big leagues limited each team to seven home night games a season. In 1942, ostensibly to cater to the defense worker, the limit was raised to 14, with Washington insisting on 21. Since the summer sun makes a blast furnace of the Kansas City, Los Angeles, Washington and St. Louis ballparks at mid-day, these cities now play practically all their mid-season games in the cooler evening air.

Introduced into organized ball strictly as a novelty, night baseball proved such an immediate success that it saved dozens of minor leagues in the depression years of the 1930's. It also wrought financial miracles for poorer major league clubs.

Modern engineering has made night baseball enjoyable for the players as well as fans. Boston's Fenway Park, for instance, is bathed in 10 times as much light as the average person gets while reading under his living room lamp. Scientific angling of the individual floodlights—and even specialized styles of mowing the grass—add up to optimum visibility. The owners don't stint, either, for Tiger Stadium's 1,386 floodlights are 1,500 watts each . . . enough power to light a city of 10,000 people!

In 1971, the fourth game of the World Series came under the lights for the first time. With an estimated 61,000,000 TV-viewing audience, all weekday games were played at night, starting in 1972. In 1976, the Sunday game was played at night.

Spring Training

With scattered exceptions, 19th-century ballplayers trained at home. They would report to their home park a week or two before the season started, then shiver through a crude training period. In case of rain or snow, they would pitch, catch, bunt and run under the stands.

Today every team travels to a tropical clime for leisurely and luxurious spring training. Why? Certainly not in chase of the almighty dollar. The hard fact is that practically every club loses money in the venture . . . as much as $30,000 each spring. Yet they all indulge, for two compelling reasons:

(1) Conditioning. After five months of loafing, players would strain many more tendons and muscles if they had to work into regular season form in a chilly week or two.

(2) Publicity. When big league heroes cavort under the palms of Florida, and California, a full contingent of newspapermen, sportscasters and photographers are on hand to report daily progress to the baseball-hungry fans at home.

Whetting the customers' appetite by furnishing accounts of spring training, instead of letting the fans watch it first hand, is such valid psychology that even the minor league clubs of Southern cities train at distant bases. Clubowners have found it better salesmanship to bring in their club, fresh and unseen, for the opening of the championship season.

Once the teams got the spring wanderlust, even this country's boundaries couldn't contain them. The Yanks of 1911 were the first to leave the U. S. They trained on Bermuda's coral strand. The touring custom has become so prevalent in recent years that New York fans hardly batted an eye in 1947 when their three home teams trained and played spring exhibitions in such faraway places as Puerto Rico, Venezuela, Cuba, Panama and Hawaii.

As far back as 1884, the Boston Nationals played some spring games in New Orleans. However, the inaugural year of spring training is generally accepted as 1886, when Harry Wright brought his Phillies to Charleston, South Carolina, and Cap Anson took a dozen of his Chicago regulars for conditioning at Hot Springs, Arkansas.

These early "luxury" trips were hardly joyrides. Connie Mack tells of going South with the Washington club in '88: "It took us three nights and two days to reach Jacksonville, Florida. At night we'd travel Pullman, with two players sleeping in each berth, and by day we'd switch to coaches. The first hotel we tried wouldn't even register us. Manager Ted Sullivan scoured the town before he finally found us lodgings—though the hotel clerk made the strict stipulation that the ballplayers would not mingle with the other guests or eat in the same dining room."

By contrast, even the swankiest hotels nowadays vie for patronage by the ball clubs. Many a Chamber of Commerce lies awake nights thinking up ways to lure big league teams to their town as a training base, mindful of the priceless publicity and lucrative business that accrues.

Nicknames

Americans dote on nicknames. This habit is so ingrained, that in time a person's real name becomes obscured. Not many baseball fans, for instance, know the correct first names of Babe Ruth, Jake Flowers, Kiki Cuyler, Honus Wagner, Ping Bodie, Zack Taylor or Arky Vaughan. (Answers: George, D'Arcy, Hazen, John, Frank, James and Joseph) .

A minor victim of this custom was Jeff Tesreau. While he was coaching Dartmouth's baseball team, townsfolk persuaded him to run for public office. He lost the race . . . only because local rules specified that a man's legal name must be written on the ballot in order for it to be valid. To the baseball public, which means most of America, the former Giant pitching hero was always "Jeff." Few ever knew him as Charles Monroe Tesreau!

Baseball players often resort to the direct approach, either by tagging someone for the color of his hair (Whitey Lockman, Red Ruffing, Blondy Ryan) or for some other obvious physical characteristic: Lefty Grove, Slim Sallee, Stubby Overmire, Fatty Fothergill, etc. On the other hand, they sometimes become whimsical, calling big fellows "Babe" (Phelps) or "Tiny" (Bonham).

No stick-in-the-muds, baseball folks keep 'em guessing by applying the same nickname for different reasons. Harold Reese is "Pee Wee" because he once was a champion at marbles (which are also known as "pee wees") ; Peewee Wanninger, on the other hand simply was a little fellow. Spec Meadows, for his specs (spectacles) ; Spec Shea, because he's freckled . . . speckled.

Odell Hale was "Bad News" in tribute to his troubling enemy pitchers. However, Jim Galloway had the same nickname for another reason. The star infielder was a telegrapher before he came into pro ball. In order to break away from work for semipro games, he'd have a crony in another office fake a message to him that some relative was sick and had to see him. So many of these "bad news" wires came during the season that he soon acquired that nickname.

Among other appelations serving double duty are Birdie (Tebbetts, because he chirps like a bird; Cree, because he once played under the assumed name of Burdee) . . . Zack (Taylor, because of a famous general by that name; Wheat, because his first name is Zachary) . . . Spud (Chandler, to abbreviate his first name, Spurgeon; Davis, because he liked "spuds," or potatoes) . . . Crab (Burkett, because of his crabby disposition; Evers, because of the sure way he clawed the ball) . . . Cy (Young, shorted from "cyclone"; Williams, a rustic appelation for the hayseed-looking rookie).

Baseball dips heavily into the animal kingdom for nicknames indicating a resemblance: Ducky Medwick, Rabbit Maranville, Skeeter Newsome, Goose Goslin, Moose McCormick, Old Hoss Radbourn, Flea Clifton, Spider Jorgenson, Bullfrog Dietrich, Mule Haas, Ox Eckhardt, Hippo Vaughn, Monk Dubiel, Harry (The Cat) Brecheen, etc.

Loquaciousness is never overlooked. Hence Lippy Durocher, Gabby Hartnett, Dizzy Dean, Goofy Gomez, Buzzy Wares, Orator O'Rourke, Foghorn Kennedy.

Since comic strips have always been among the favorite reading matter of ballplayers, many nicknames are derived from that source, including Wimpy Quinn, Flash Gordon, Bing Miller, Skinny Shaner, Boob McNair, Li'l Abner Erickson, Nemo Liebold, Muggsy McGraw, Pinky Whitney, Dusty Rhodes, Buster Brown, Moon Mullen, Stinky Davis, Jeep Handley, Tarzan Parmelee, Popeye Mahaffey, Available Jones. Hack Wilson was tagged in honor of his physique, which resembled the great wrestler, Hackenschmidt; Firpo Marberry and Jeff Tesreau were nicknamed after the famous heavyweights, and Packy Rogers earned his tag for being as scrappy as Packy McFarland.

Since Mickey Cochrane was such a great catcher, subsequent receivers of any promise were called Mickey, too, even though their correct names happened to be Arnold Owen, Thompson Livingston and Newton Grasso. The ironic part of it all is that Mickey isn't even Cochrane's legitimate tag. His first name is Gordon, and he was called Mickey only because Bostonians thought he had a real Irish face, and "Mickey" is the catch-name for Irishmen, the way "Hans"

is used for a German or "Ivan" for a Russian.

Some players are stuck with infant mispronunciations. When Harold Gilbert at the age of 2 said "Tookie" instead of rookie, the family never let him live it down. Players who had difficulty in saying "brother" as tots, wound up in the majors as Bubba Harris, Boo Ferriss and Bruz Hammer.

Predilections for certain foods got these fellows their nicknames: Nap Rucker, Pie Traynor, Salty Parker, Lemons Solters, Pretzels Pezzullo, Candy Cummings. Geographical handles include Dixie Walker, Tex Carleton, Bama Rowell and Arky Vaughan, the last two coming from Alabama and Arkansas.

Nationalities enter the picture, too, as in the cases of Greek George, Frenchy Bordagaray, Swede Hansen, Dutch Leonard, Jap Barbeau, Chink Mattick. Dapper dressers included Broadway Smith, Dude Esterbrook, Beau Bell and Count Mullane. Staid, sedate fellows earned appropriate soubriquets: Deacon Phillippe, Parson Nicholson and Preacher Roe.

Other interesting derivations: Casey Stengel, because he comes from Kansas City (KC); Grandma Murphy, for his rocking-chair motion when winding up; Satchel Paige, whose feet seemed as big as suitcases; Bruno Betzel, from the name of the dog that was his inseparable pal in boyhood; Beauty Bancroft, for yelling that word invariably when a teammate made a nice play; Wish Egan, shortened from his baptismal name of Aloysius; Suitcase Seeds, always seemed en route from one club to another; Pants Rowland, once tore his trousers sliding home; Cracker Schalk, whose rear view was square and small like a cracker when he squatted behind the plate.

More recent players have continued the tradition of having colorful nicknames. Yogi Berra reversed the normal procedure by having a cartoon character named after him. Hair color gave Whitey Ford, Red Schoendienst and Rusty Staub their nicknames. Boog Powell's name was the result of a childhood word for one that gets into mischief. The Oakland Athletics at one time had a pitching staff that included Mudcat Grant, Blue Moon Odom and Catfish Hunter (Jim, John, and Jim respectively).

FAMOUS FIRSTS

1845—First code of playing rules, by A. J. Cartwright.

1846—First match game, N.Y. Knickerbockers losing to New York Club, 23-1.

1849—First playing uniform, Knickerbockers' blue and white.

1853—First box score appeared in N.Y. *Clipper*.

1856—First regular baseball reporter, Henry Chadwick.

1857—First official rulebook published and edited by Chadwick...First baseball league: National Association of Baseball Players.

1858—First admission charged, 50 cents, All-Star N. Y. vs. Brooklyn, at Fashion Race Course, L. I.

1859—First college game, Amherst beat Williams.

1862—First enclosed ballpark, Union Grounds, Brooklyn.

1863—First calling of balls and strikes.

1864—First professional player, A. J. Reach, paid $1,000 for season by Philadelphia.

1865—First stolen base, Ed Cuthbert of Keystones.

1866—First slide to steal a base, Bob Addy of Rockford; Dicky Pearce of Atlantics first to lay down bunt.

1867—First prominent use of curve ball, W. A. Cummings.

1869—First salaried team, Cincinnati Red Stockings, who were also first team to wear short trousers.

1870—First demonstration at Brooklyn by Fred Goldsmith (Aug. 16) that a baseball really curves.

1871—First professional league, NA.

1873—First time two games played in one day. Resolutes at Boston, July 4.

1874—First foreign tour, Athletics and Boston to England.

1875—First mask, worn by Jim Tyng as invented by Harvard teammate Fred Thayer . . . . First glove, by Charles Waite.... First major league 1-0 game, Chicago beating St. Louis.

1876—First year of NL... First major team to play twice in one day, Cincinnati.

1877—First minor league organized, International Association.

1878—First turnstiles.

1879—First use of reserve clause in player contract.

1882—First salaried staff of umpires paid by league, AA, and adopted by NL the next year. . . First interleague playoff (World Series). . . First doubleheader Sept. 25 (Providence vs. Worcester) NL.

1884—First organization of a third "major league", UA.

1885—First use of chest protectors for catchers and umpires.

1886—First use of two umpires in one game, World Series. . . First Players' union recognized, "Brotherhood of Ball Players"...First spring training trip, Chicago NL at Hot Springs, Ark.

1887—First catcher to work continuously behind bat, Charles Zimmer.

1888—First round-the-world tour by baseball teams.

1892—First Sunday games permitted in NL.

1894—First player to hit four homers in one game, Bobby Lowe.

1901—First American League game, Chicago vs. Cleveland.

1902—First organization of minor leagues, National Association.

1903—First NL-AL World Series.

1907—First shin guards for catcher introduced by Roger Bresnahan.

1909—First unassisted triple play in majors, Neal Ball... First U.S. President at opening game, W. H. Taft.

1910—First use of cork center in baseball.

1913—First round-world tour by two major league teams, Giants and White Sox.

1919—First Sunday game allowed in New York.

1921—First baseball commissioner takes office, K. M. Landis. . First radio broadcast of World Series.

1926—First amplifiers used, Polo Grounds.

1933—First All-Star Game.

1935—First major league night game, at Cincinnati. . . First major league team to fly, Cincinnati.

1936—First players elected to Hall of Fame: Cobb, Ruth, Mathewson, Wagner and Johnson.

1939—First use of yellow baseball, Pittsburgh vs. Brooklyn. . . First telecast of game, in Brooklyn.

1941—First team to wear helmets at bat, Brooklyn.

1946—First Negro player in modern pro ball, Jackie Robinson at Montreal. . . First playoff in NL, St. Louis beating Brooklyn in two straight games.

1947—First Negro player in NL, Robinson; first in AL, Larry Doby.

1953—First franchise shift of modern times, Boston NL moves to Milwaukee.

1956—First World Series no-hitter and perfect game, Don Larsen, New York AL vs. Brooklyn.

1958—First major league franchises on West Coast, Brooklyn NL and New York NL shift to Los Angeles and San Francisco, respectively.

1961—First expansion of modern times, American League adds Los Angeles and Washington (with former Washington club shifting to Minnesota).

1962—First Negro elected to Hall of Fame, Jackie Robinson.

1965—First domed stadium, the "Astrodome" in Houston, also first stadium with artificial turf.

1968—First expansion of NL to cross international borders, awarding Montreal along with San Diego franchises to begin participation in 1969.

1971—First night World Series game played.

1973—First permanent pinch-hitter for pitcher—American League designated hitter.

1975—First black manager—Frank Robinson, Cleveland AL

THE AMERICAN LEAGUE
DESIGNATED HITTER FOR THE PITCHER

A hitter may be designated to bat for the starting pitcher and all subsequent pitchers in any game without otherwise affecting the status of the pitcher(s) in the game. A Designated Hitter for the pitcher must be selected prior to the game and must be included in the lineup cards presented to the umpire-in-chief.

It is not mandatory that a club designate a hitter for the pitcher, but failure to do so prior to the game precludes the use of a Designated Hitter for that game.

Pinch hitters for a Designated Hitter may be used. Any substitute hitter for a Designated Hitter himself becomes a Designated Hitter. A replaced Designated Hitter shall not re-enter the game in any capacity.

The Designated Hitter may be used defensively, continuing to bat in the same position in the batting order, but the pitcher must then bat in the place of the substituted defensive player, unless more than one substitution is made, and the manager then must designate their spots in the batting order.

A runner may be substituted for the Designated Hitter and the runner assumes the role of Designated Hitter.

A Designated Hitter is "locked" into the batting order. No multiple substitutions may be made that will alter the batting rotation of the Designated Hitter.

Once the game pitcher is switched from the mound to a defensive position this move shall terminate the Designated Hitter role for the remainder of the game.

Once a pinch hitter bats for any player in the batting order and then enters the game to pitch, this move shall terminate the Designated Hitter role for the remainder of the game.

Once the game pitcher bats for the Designated Hitter this move shall terminate the Designated Hitter role for the remainder of the game. (The game pitcher may only pinch-hit for the Designated Hitter.)

Once a Designated Hitter assumes a defensive position this move shall terminate the Designated Hitter role for the remainder of the game.

ONE-DAY MAJOR LEAGUERS

Every young man who has ever played high school or college baseball harbors dreams of someday becoming a major leaguer. Such vision rarely becomes reality but Ty Cobb, unwittingly, made it so for eight awe-struck St. Joseph's (Philadelphia) College players on May 18, 1912.

The truculent Detroit Tigers came to Philadelphia on that date to play a scheduled game with the world champion Athletics, but Cobb was not allowed to play. A fracas in New York three days before when he climbed into the stands to chase down a heckler resulted in a suspension for the fiery Georgia Peach, league action by president Ban Johnson which the Tiger players considered unjust.

His teammates stood by Cobb. "If Ty doesn't play," they agreed, "neither do we. We'll strike." Reminded by manager Hugh Jennings that a forfeiture would result in a $5,000 fine, the players still remained adamant.

Athletics' manager Connie Mack, informed of the Tiger players' stand, approached Jennings and suggested he hire, for the one game, a group of collegians. Mack's idea made sense to Jennings who was worried lest he would be unable to place a team on the field. The Tiger pilot wasted no time. He had contracts drawn up and they were signed by Jack Coffey, Aloysius Travers, Pat Meany, Hap Ward, Billy Maharg, Jim McGarr, Dan McGarvey and Bill Leinhauser. The dream was realized for eight St. Joseph's collegians—they were to be Kings for a Day! Ed Irwin, a sandlotter, also was added to the day's Detroit roster.

The game itself was a travesty, but Detroit saved $5,000. Travers, later to be ordained a Catholic priest, pitched for the Tigers and established an all-time single game mark which still stands—most runs allowed in one game. The 20-year-old Travers was belted by 24-2, nine errors by his mates allowing 10 unearned runs.

Of the four hits collected by the Tigers two were obtained by the sandlotter, Irwin. He cracked two triples in three times at bat for a lifetime batting average of .667.

Of the nine one-day fill-ins only Maharg, later to become a professional boxer, was to play again. Four years later he appeared in the outfield of the Philadelphia Phillies, another one-day stand.

Perhaps the proudest of the collegians was Leinhauser, the wearer of Cobb's uniform. Eventually it was through Leinhauser, who was to become a Philadelphia police officer, that S. C. Thompson, co-author of THE OFFICIAL ENCYCLOPEDIA OF BASEBALL, was able to track down the full names and birth data on the one-shot big leaguers who saved the Detroit club $5,000.

Moses F. Walker, 1884 Toledo A.A. (Courtesy of Ralph Lin Weber, Baseball Research Bureau.)

Negro Players

Cap Anson, the giant of his day and one of the pillars of organized baseball, may have been one of the factors which mitigated against the Negro player in the early days of the majors. During the first 73 years of the majors only two Negro players managed to get into a big league box score before Jackie Robinson.

In 1884 the Walker brothers—Welday and Moses—played for Toledo of the American Association, a recognized major league at the time. Both quickly faded into oblivion although Moses was above average as a catcher.

Anson indicated his sentiments toward the Negro player when he brought his Chicago White Stockings to Newark, New Jersey in 1884 for an exhibition game with the local minor leaguers. George Stovey, artful Negro hurler, was scheduled to pitch against the big leaguers. When Anson discovered that his team would face the fast slants of a Negro, he refused to have his men play the Newark club unless Stovey was removed from the lineup. So the management kept Stovey out of the game.

Anson continued to crusade against the entrance of Negro players into the National League, because of their color not their ability.

Between the Walkers' brief tenure at Toledo, and Jackie Robinson's epochal entrance into Brooklyn in 1947, there were several Negro players in organized ball—all of them in the 19th century minor leagues. They included such standouts as shortstop Clarence Matthews, second baseman Frank Grant, first baseman Charles Kelly and second baseman J. W. (Bud) Fowler.

The first team of paid Negro players was a group of fellow waiters Frank Thompson recruited in 1885 at the Argyle Hotel, Babylon, Long Island. They played 10 games that summer against white teams on Long Island, then went on tour billed as the Cuban Giants. Thompson hoped to ease the social barriers by passing his team off as Cubans, and a few players furthered the illusion by chattering in a rapid Spanish-sounding gibberish on the field. Thompson

added the nickname Giants because it was a popular team in the majors at that time. It remained a good tag, and later Negro teams were known as the Lincoln Giants, Chicago American Giants, Bacharach Giants, Brooklyn Royal Giants, etc.

None of these troupes could establish a stable league setup till 1920, when the Negro National League was formed in Kansas City. The next year a Negro Eastern League arose, and they started a regular World Series in 1924.

These leagues collapsed in the depression depths of 1932. Several years later, the Negro American and National Leagues opened shop, followed by a host of lesser leagues in the South. Player incomes were rounded out by winter ball in Mexico, Cuba and Venezuela, which had no color lines.

Between World Wars I and II, Negro baseball boasted such legendary heroes as shortstop John Henry Lloyd, catcher Josh Gibson, pitchers Cyclone Joe Williams and Cannonball Dick Redding, outfielder Oscar Charleston, etc. Only one of the fabled figures of this lost chapter in baseball history managed to benefit through modern emancipation: Leroy (Satchel) Paige, though well past 40 at the time, joined the Indians and helped pitch them to the pennant in 1948.

A special committee was set up in 1971 to enshrine the best players from the Negro Leagues in the Hall of Fame.

Spitball Pitchers

The spitball pitcher—legally—is as extinct as the American buffalo. When Burleigh Grimes tossed his last dewy pitch in 1934, it marked the end of a hurling breed which was declared null and void as far back as 1920 when the game's administrators outlawed the pitch.

The 17 pitchers in the majors at the time the pitch was outlawed were permitted to continue their salivary trade, but no other hurler was allowed to introduce it if it wasn't already part of his mound repertoire.

There are still occasional squawks from the batters that they have been slipped a spitball every now and then, but the umpires are vigilant and have instructions to eject from the game any pitcher they detect resorting to the outlawed pitch.

Here is the list of spitball hurlers in action at the time the 1920 ban was imposed (showing first and last season of major league action) :

NATIONAL	AMERICAN
Bill Doak (1912–29)	Yancey Ayers (1913–21)
Phil Douglas (1912–22)	Ray Caldwell (1910–21)
Dana Fillingim (1915–25)	Stan Coveleskie (1912–28)
Ray Fisher (1910–20)	Urban Faber (1914–33)
Marvin Goodwin (1916–25)	Hub Leonard (1913–25)
Burleigh Grimes (1916–34)	Jack Quinn (1909–33)
Clarence Mitchell (1911–32)	Allan Russell (1915–25)
Dick Rudolph (1910–27)	Urban Shocker (1916–28)
	Allen Sothoron (1914–26)

Handicaps

The bespectacled major league no longer is a novelty, and the nickname "specs," first applied to a player who wore glasses, has long since passed into limbo. However, baseball has known players who have played creditably despite the handicap of the loss of a leg, arm or eye.

A one-legged player was Bert Shepard, who lost his right limb as the result of an Army crash. Shepard had been a fair minor league prospect and was determined to make the majors, finally realizing his ambition in 1945 when he hurled for the Washington Senators.

Perhaps the most remarkable of all physically handicapped ball players was a pitcher, Hugh (One-Arm) Daly, who won 72 games in his career. Daly, who also played second base and shortstop, recorded a no-hit, no-run triumph and struck out 19 players in a game, still the all-time mark.

A handicap worked in favor of Mordecai Brown, the famous Chicago Cub pitcher of the early century, who didn't possess all the fingers on his pitching hand. The crippled digits on Brown's hand enabled him to grip the ball in such a manner that his curve was actually more effective.

Pete Gray, who had one arm, played the outfield for the 1945 St. Louis Browns and the loss of several toes didn't hamper pitcher Charley Ruffing and outfielder Hal Peck.

Harry Jasper lost the sight of an eye when hit by a batted ball, but he played several seasons of major league ball after the accident. Few knew Tom Sunkel's left eye was blinded by a cataract throughout his big league career. Still another one-eyed pitcher was Bill Irwin of the old Cincinnati club.

So much for one-eyed players. How about the "four-eyes" . . . the eyeglass brigade? A bespectacled player used to be a rare spectacle indeed, with Will White of Cincinnati the lone lens wearer in the first 44 years of organized baseball. But recent generations produced dozens of examples to refute the saying, "Baseball doesn't make passes at players who wear glasses."

Trying to explain the eyeglass evolution, veteran Arlie Latham always insisted, "Back in the '80s, the diamond was laid out east to west, from batter to pitcher, so that the afternoon sun shone only in the batter's eyes. Nowadays the fields are turned around so that the sinking sun slants steadily into the fielders' faces. That's what ruins the players' eyes and that's why so many of them have to wear glasses."

A more likely explanation is that common sense has replaced common vanity. When people need glasses to correct their vision nowadays, they wear them.

Foreign Tours

The Boston and Athletics teams, only ones to win pennants in the old National Association, made the first foreign baseball trip in 1874. They played in 14 baseball games and seven cricket matches in England and Ireland. Five years later Frank Bancroft took a barnstorming team to Havana, but it was a financial failure. The A's and Phillies had better results when they visited Cuba in 1886.

The first globe-circling ambassadors of the game were the 20 players headed by A. G. Spalding, who made a notable tour in 1888–89. The Chicago NL team played a picked club of league rivals, tagged the All-American nine, in such places as Auckland, New Zealand; Sydney and Melbourne, Australia; Ceylon; Egypt; Rome, Naples and Florence, Italy; Paris, several English cities and Dublin, Ireland. Though expenses ran to $50,000, the trip proved profitable.

The Reach All-America team toured Japan in 1908, and a year later the University of Wisconsin played a series of games there. But the first big league teams to show as units in that baseball-loving land were the Giants and White Sox, who toured the world in 1913–14 under the guidance of John McGraw and Charlie Comiskey. From here, the teams went on to play in Shanghai, Hong Kong, Manila, Australia, Ceylon, Egypt, Italy, France and Great Britain . . . 31 games in all, with Bill Klem as umpire.

McGraw and Comiskey planned a similar tour in 1924, but had to quit after playing in England, Ireland and France. The reason: poor attendances. However, baseball was at fever pitch in Japan, and a 1922 tour by major league barnstormers was quite successful. Herb Hunter, who organized the 1922 trip, rounded up another with the help of sportswriter Fred Lieb in 1931, using many World Series players. Four games in Tokyo drew 250,000! Soon after this, the Japanese developed professional teams for the first time.

Lefty O'Doul, one of the players on that 1931 junket to Japan, returned to that isle five times in later years, and became the second greatest sports idol over there. Lefty was overshadowed only by the immortal Babe Ruth, who headed Connie Mack's team of American Leaguers that whipped the best available Japanese competition in an 18-game series in 1934.

Since 1953, a major league club has visited Japan every few years. In 1962 an agreement was reached between the respective commissioners—Ford Frick and Yushi Uchimura concerning the honoring of each other's player contracts. Approximately twenty players from the U. S. play in the Japanese leagues each season, many of them ex-major leaguers.

Baseball Ballads

Since every game is a new adventure, every season a new saga, baseball lends itself well to song and story. Even daily newspaper sportswriters sometimes attempt Homeric prose in praise of their latest hero. Sentiment runs so high, baseball odes don't have to be epics to capture popular appeal. Still, the game has inspired some gusty classics . . . like "Casey At The Bat," which, even if it doesn't rate as full-blown literature, must be accorded everlasting tribute for rescuing the horde of fading vaudevillians who recited "Casey" as a last prop against unemployment.

Back in 1869, when Cincinnati's Red Stockings were riding high through an unbeaten season, the players had their own theme song. It was written to the tune of "Bonnie Blue Flag." Just before each game, the mustachioed Reds would line up near home plate, hat in hand, to serenade the grandstand with:

We are a band of baseball players
    From Cincinnati city.
We come to toss the ball around
    And sing to you our ditty.

And if you listen to our song
    We are about to sing,
We'll tell you all about baseball
    And make the welkin ring.

Hurrah, hurrah,
    For the noble game, hurrah.
Red Stockings all will toss the ball
    And shout our loud hurrah.

Baseball polkas and poems turned up as frequently as pennant winners in those early years. Yet none of the 19th-century compositions had the flair and flavor of that fictional opus written in 1888, and popularized by the masterful recitations of De Wolf Hopper, to wit:

CASEY AT THE BAT
By Ernest L. Thayer

The outlook wasn't brilliant for the Mudville nine that day;
The score stood four to two with but one inning more to play.
And then when Cooney died at first, and Barrows did the same,
A sickly silence fell upon the patrons of the game.

A straggling few got up to go in deep despair. The rest
Clung to that hope which springs eternal in the human breast.
They thought if only Casey could but get a whack at that—
We'd put up even money now with Casey at the bat.

But Flynn preceded Casey, as did also Jimmy Blake,
And the former was a lulu and the latter was a cake;
So upon the stricken multitude grim melancholy sat,
For there seemed but little chance of Casey's getting to the bat.

But Flynn let drive a single, to the wonderment of all,
And Blake, the much despised, tore the cover off the ball;
And when the dust had lifted and the men saw what had occurred,
There was Johnny safe at second and Flynn a-hugging third.

Then from 5,000 throats and more there rose a lusty yell;
It rambled through the valley, it rattled in the dell;
It knocked upon the mountain and recoiled upon the flat,
For Casey, mighty Casey, was advancing to the bat.

There was ease in Casey's manner as he stepped into his place;
There was pride in Casey's bearing and a smile on Casey's face.
And when, responding to the cheers, he lightly doffed his hat,
No stranger in the crowd could doubt 'twas Casey at the bat.

Ten thousand eyes were on him as he rubbed his hands with dirt;
Five thousand tongues applauded when he wiped them on his shirt.
Then while the writhing pitcher ground the ball into his hip,
Defiance gleamed in Casey's eye, a sneer curled Casey's lip.

And now the leather-covered sphere came hurtling through the air,
And Casey stood a-watching it in haughty grandeur there.
Close by the sturdy batsman the ball unheeded sped—
"That ain't my style," said Casey. "Strike one," the umpire said.

From the benches, black with people, there went up a muffled roar,
Like the beating of the storm waves on a stern and distant shore.
"Kill him! Kill the umpire!" shouted some one in the stand,
And it's likely they'd have killed him had not Casey raised his hand.

608 THE OFFICIAL ENCYCLOPEDIA OF BASEBALL

With a smile of Christian charity great Casey's visage shone;
He stilled the rising tumult, he bade the game go on;
He signaled to the pitcher, and once more the spheroid flew;
But Casey still ignored it, and the umpire said, "Strike two."

"Fraud!" cried the maddened thousands, and the echo answered "Fraud!"
But one scornful look from Casey and the audience was awed.
They saw his face grow stern and cold, they saw his muscles strain,
And they knew that Casey wouldn't let that ball go by again.

The sneer is gone from Casey's lip, his teeth are clenched in hate;
He pounds with cruel violence his bat upon the plate.
And now the pitcher holds the ball, and now he lets it go,
And now the air is shattered by the force of Casey's blow.

Oh! somewhere in this favored land the sun is shining bright;
The band is playing somewhere, and somewhere hearts are light.
And somewhere men are laughing, and somewhere children shout;
But there is no joy in Mudville—mighty Casey has struck out.

———

But the American public, notorious in its constant clamor for a "winner," wouldn't settle for a discredited Casey. In the very nature of baseball's campaign, "there is always another game tomorrow," so mighty Casey had to have his revenge. It remained for a proud young Southerner to redeem the fallen hero by composing this ode in 1906:

———

CASEY'S REVENGE
By Grantland Rice

There were saddened hearts in Mudville for a week or even more;
There were mutterd oaths and curses—every fan in town was sore.
"Just think," said one, "how soft it looked with Casey at the bat,
And to think he'd go and spring a bush league trick like that."

All his past fame was forgotten—he was now a hopeless "shine"—
They called him "Strike-out Casey" from the Mayor down the line;
And as he came to bat each day his bosom heaved a sigh,
While a look of hopeless fury shone in Casey's eye.

He soon began to sulk and loaf—his batting eye went lame;
No home runs on the score card now were chalked against his name.
The fans without exception gave the manager no peace,
For one and all kept clamoring for Casey's quick release.

The lane is long, some one has said, that never turns again,
And Fate, though fickle, often gives another chance to men;
And Casey smiled—his rugged face no longer wore a frown—
The pitcher who had started all the trouble came to town.

All Mudville had assembled—ten thousand fans had come
To see the twirler who had put big Casey on the bum;
And when he stepped into the box the multitude went wild.
He doffed his cap in proud disdain—but Casey only smiled.

"Play ball!" the umpire's voice rang out—and then the game began;
But in that throng of thousands there was not a single fan
Who thought that Mudville had a chance, and with the setting sun
Their hopes sank low—the rival team was leading "four to one."

The last half of the ninth came round with no change in the score,
But when the first man up hit safe the crowd began to roar;
The din increased—the echo of ten thousand shouts was heard
When the pitcher hit the second and gave "four balls" to the third.

Three men on base—nobody out—three runs to tie the game!
A triple meant the highest niche in Mudville's hall of fame;
But here the rally ended and the gloom was deep as night,
When the fourth one "fouled to catcher" and the fifth "flew out to right."

A dismal, groaning chorus came—a scowl was on each face—
When Casey walked up, bat in hand, and slowly took his place.
His bloodshot eyes in fury gleamed—his teeth were clenched in hate;
He gave his cap a vicious hook and pounded on the plate.

The pitcher smiled and cut one loose—across the plate it sped—
Another hiss—another groan—"Strike one," the umpire said.
Zip! Like a shot the second curve broke just below his knee—
"Strike two!" the umpire roared aloud—but Casey made no plea.

No roasting for the umpire now—his was an easy lot;
But here the pitcher whirled again—was that a rifle shot?
A whack—a crack—and out through space the leather pellet flew:
A blot against the distant sky—a speck against the blue.

Above the fence in centre field in rapid whirling flight
The sphere sailed on—the blot grew dim and then was lost to sight;
Ten thousand hats were thrown in air—ten thousand threw a fit—
But no one ever found the ball that mighty Casey hit.

Oh! somewhere in this favored land dark clouds may hide the sun,
And somewhere bands no longer play and children have no fun;
And somewhere over blighted loves there hangs a heavy pall;
But Mudville hearts are happy now—for Casey hit the ball.

———————

Around this same period, Jack Norworth and Albert Von Tilzer wrote a song that is destined to live as long as the game itself, "Take Me Out To The Ball Game." Norworth sang it in the Follies with his wife, the beauteous Nora Bayes. Almost overnight, it became the game's national anthem, and today it's as popular as ever.

Another lilting rhythm that became baseball legend was "Tinker to Evers to Chance," an eight-line lament penned by Franklin P. Adams of the old *New York Evening Mail*. Though this double play combination of the Cubs was not the greatest of all time, it was the most dreaded of its day. As F.P.A. versified:

These are the saddest of possible words:
"Tinker to Evers to Chance."
Trio of bear Cubs and fleeter than birds,
"Tinker to Evers to Chance."
Ruthlessly pricking our gonfalon bubble,
Making a Giant hit into a double—
Words that are heavy with nothing but trouble:
"Tinker to Evers to Chance."

But baseball isn't all romance and poetry. The characters and situations rife in the sport are ripe material for literate wits; so it's no wonder that a sports-minded genius like Ring Lardner was able to weave such classic comedy as his "You Know Me Al" series. First a comic strip and later a series of short stories, this literary effort excels all the plays, books and movies written about the national pastime.

In recent years, baseball's best ballads have evolved from the writers' annual winter banquets held in the big cities. With tabs ranging up to $25 per plate, and guests numbering 1,500, they serve tender steaks . . . but not half so tender as the "hams", meaning the baseball writers disporting on the stage in hour-long topical revues. If the acting is sometimes punk, the lyrics never are. The scribes really outdo themselves with songs ranging from sentimental ballads to pungent parodies.

Manufacture of a Bat

Bats are made of ash, hackberry and hickory, but ash is preferred because of superior resiliency or "drive." The best white ash comes from Northeastern United States. Special bat timber experts determine which trees are suitable, and these are felled, cut into logs about 40 inches long and hauled to the timber mill. There they are sawed into either square or round billets before being sent to the bat factory.

Upon arrival at the yards of the factory, the billets are inspected, graded and then stacked loosely—so that air can circulate freely—for 10 to 18 months of seasoning. More than 3,000,000 billets are in the process of drying this way at any one time.

Billets which have split during seasoning are thrown out and the others hauled to the factory to go through a turning process that brings them into the approximate shape of a bat. They are then weighed and graded to see for which models they will best be suitable. The bat is then placed on a lathe alongside the original model and cut down to the same shape. The turner weighs and measures for fractional accuracy, then sands the embryo bat, which is finally stained and branded.

Manufacture of a Baseball

Harassed pitchers may swear there's a live jackrabbit inside the ball, but according to A. G. Spalding Bros. Inc.—which manufactures all the official American and National League baseballs in its plant at Chicopee, Massachusetts —actually the core consists of a cork composition containing a small percentage of rubber. This core is 13/16 of an inch in diameter.

Two black rubber shells, each approximately 5/32 of an inch thick, are wrapped around the core with a thin cushion of red rubber between the edges of the hemispherical black rubber shells. Next comes a red rubber wrapping 3/32 of an inch thick. The entire "pill" is molded perfectly round to 4 1/8 inches circumference.

Wool is wound around the pill under precise humidity and tension control in three operations: first application, 121 yards of four-ply gray woolen yarn, brings size to 7 3/4 inches circumference; second winding, 45 yards of three-ply white woolen yarn, increases it to 8 3/16 inches circumference; third winding, 53 yards of three-ply gray woolen yarn, makes size of ball 8 3/4 inches circumference. Next comes 150 yards of fine cotton winding, coated with a layer of latex (rubber cement) to prevent unraveling. By now the overall circumference is 8 7/8 inches.

The covers, of selected horsehide leather between .050–.055 of an inch thick, are cut on a machine into the pattern of "a swollen figure 8," with 108 stitch-holes bordering each cover. Two such pieces are used to cover a baseball. After dampening the horsehide to make it pliable, the covers are hand-stitched with red cotton thread. Any pinching that occurs when the cover shrinks back tight is eliminated by rolling the balls. By now the circumference is the regulation 9–9 1/4 inches circumference and weighs between 5–5 1/4 ounces.

All the balls head for either of two stamping machines. One, for American League baseball, stamps the "Reach" trademark plus the AL president's autograph on the cover. The other, for official NL balls, registers the "Spalding" symbol as well as the league president's signature. Aside from the printing on the cover, the balls of both leagues are absolutely identical.

Manufacture of a Glove

Leather for baseball gloves comes from hides of native cows. Animals slaughtered in late May and early November (called Summer Hides) are preferred. The tanned leather is then taken to die-cutting machines.

Next step is stamping. This is done by applying heat and pressure while the glove palm is laid out flat. Fielders' gloves are then sewn inside out with finest quality cotton thread. More expensive gloves have an extra row of stitches around the thumb, sewed with wax linen thread. After sewing, gloves are turned and then stretched over a form heated to about 210 degrees Fahrenheit. They remain there long enough to set the shape, the operation ironing all the seams evenly and giving the glove a well-tailored appearance.

Sewed linings are then inserted, followed by binding, wrist eyeletting and lacing. The gloves are then oiled, with warm oil rubbed in by hand. This water-proofs the leather and gives the glove a good feel and fine color.

The gloves are then "laid off" over another hot form. This consists of pulling the heel into position, ironing all wrinkles out of the lining, forming the pocket and putting a further set in the leather. One more inspection, and then they're ready for shipment.

Care of Equipment

Bats—Hit with the "label up," since batting against the grain invites breakage. Never hit the bat against sole of the shoe to dislodge mud or dirt, as chipping may result. Bats should not be left in dew-covered grass. In the offseason, rub the bat with linseed oil or tung oil, or with any good lubricant, like vaseline. Keep the bat in a dry place, but not near any excessive heat, lest it dry out. Many players advise bone-rubbing the bat as a further preservative.

Baseballs—Even a single broken stitch should be repaired immediately. Covers should be cleaned and kept dry.

Gloves—High temperatures and excessive moisture are the most common sources of trouble. In order to prevent green mold rot, keep the glove in a cool dry place. When wet, dry the glove immediately, but the action should not be forced. It should be dried at normal room temperature without use of artificial heat. If repeated wetting occurs, harshness in the leather may develop, but this can be counter-acted by applying neat's-foot oil or light paraffin (mineral) oil. Leather that has become soiled should be cleaned with saddle soap only. Use a moist cloth to work up a cream by rubbing over the soap. Rub the cloth over the leather until the lather works loose the dirt. Dirty lather should then be wiped off with a clean cloth, and the leather briskly rubbed with a clean cloth.

Shoes—Oil or other lubricant should be used often on uppers to maintain softness and strength. Since night games causes shoes to be soaked in dew, use treatment recommended in preceding paragraph for repeated wetting of gloves.

XIII PLAYING HINTS

HOW TO HIT BY TY COBB

The first item in scientific hitting is selection of bat. For a swing hitter (one who starts his bat far back and completes his swing with a full follow-through) I suggest a bat with the feel on the light side. For the one with a shorter, more compact swing, the bat should feel slightly heavy.

Next comes position. Never copy a batter with an exaggerated crouch. The best hitters stand up and have the look of a good hitter. In case your normal stance becomes uncomfortable while awaiting the delivery, breaking of the knees (a dip or slight squat) will relieve this. But of course you must always come back to the position first assumed.

The space between feet should be measured by how well balanced you feel. This will measure about 14 inches for players of average height. But don't think of this kind of thing in inches. Just stand so you feel balanced, and can step either into the pitch or away.

If you are able to put a little extra weight on the front foot and still feel balanced to step either way, so much the better. The ability to do this will assure proper stride and, when swinging, will bring the body and arms up to the ball more automatically. I emphasize the value of proper striding because over-striding is fatal. It causes uppercutting and fly balls, upsets coordination and costs freedom to step in or out.

A righthanded batter attempting to hit the ball to right, or opposite (from normal), field should use the closed stance. That means the left foot is about 4 inches closer to the plate than the right. Hitting to left field, his front foot is about 4 inches further away, or in open stance. The straightaway hitter lines up both feet with the line of the pitch.

I always had trouble hitting lefthanded pitching, especially curve ballers, until I went to the back line of the batter's box. That gave me the benefit of the extra inches from the pitcher, and the split-second extra time in which to judge the pitch.

Keep your arms, particularly the elbows, away from the body. This insures freedom of swing. I also recommend the elbow nearer the pitcher be raised and exaggerated. This, plus a slight bending of the body from the waist up, will give you better body balance, insures automatically hitting the ball out in front and brings your eyes in better focusing position.

Do all your "fixing" as to grip and stance before delivery, then forget about your swing. Watch the pitcher's every move and never let your eye leave the ball. Many batters are thrown out by a half-step, so once you've hit the ball, run with all the speed you have, no matter where the ball goes.

(*Condensed from "Famous Slugger Year Book," Copyright* 1950 *by Hillerich & Bradsby Co., Louisville, Ky.*)

HOW TO PITCH BY CARL HUBBELL

Pitching is the most important single factor in any game . . . as much as 70%, according to some deep thinkers. I would like to offer these "ten commandments" for pitching aspirants:

1: A limber arm. 2: A rugged physique, or, as an alternative, wiriness.
3: A repertoire, meaning a fast ball and at least one breaking ball, preferably

a curve. 4: Control. 5: Competitive courage. 6: Endurance. 7: Intelligence. 8: The ability to size up a hitter. 9: Confidence. 10: Fielding skill.

Note that the list emphasizes developed skills over natural endowment. Development of these "extras" will give a pitcher the advantage over those relying entirely on physical assets.

Of course, the arm must be the primary consideration. Unless a boy can throw hard, or a "live" ball with reasonable speed, his pitching future can only be limited. Tricky deliveries may succeed on the sandlots, but as a pitcher moves into faster company, conditions eventually demand that he overpower a good hitter.

Pitching mechanics are important, too. A smooth, easy delivery, perfected by attention to detail, is an aid to control. Faulty form beats pitchers more often than opposing hitters, and often explains arm ailments.

The pitching delivery can be broken down and analyzed to reveal six distinct actions: Windup, Stretch, Leg Lift, Stride, Body Pivot and Follow Through.

The Windup promotes rhythm, so each pitcher can best judge his own style. It's usual to start with hands brought forward and then upward over the head. The Stretch brings the pitching arm behind the head. The Leg Lift gets drive into the motion, while the Stride is an important element for control. Most young pitchers tend to over-stride, thereby losing power and accuracy.

The weight shifts from rear to front foot in the Body Pivot. Follow Through enables the pitcher to get his body into the pitch and is also a control element. A pitcher constantly throwing the ball too high generally is failing to follow through properly.

To deliver a fast ball, the pitcher should grip it tightly, with index and middle fingers on top of the ball, and the thumb underneath. The fingers are usually placed across the seams, but if along them, then at the place where the seams are closest together. When pitched, the ball rolls from under the fingers. This reverse rotation gives the ball back-spin, causing it to "hop."

The grip for the curve is the same as for the fast ball. With the pitch, the ball rolls over the fingers as the wrist is snapped sharply to provide forward spin for the ball. The thumb does its work as it comes over with the wrist snap. The wrist snap should be sharp...the sharper the snap, the sharper the curve. All curves should be thrown low to a batter. The ball takes more spin that way, breaks away from the batter and is harder to hit.

The change of pace differs from the fast ball only in the manner in which it is held. Where the fast ball is gripped tightly, the change of pace is only lightly held by the fingers on top. Some pitchers lift these guiding fingers slightly as they let the ball go.

(Condensed from "Playing the Giants Game," Copyright 1949 by National Exhibition Co., New York)

HOW TO CATCH
BY BILL DICKEY

Since a catcher's job requires endurance, he should be sturdy rather than fast afoot. Yet he has to be nimble to pounce on bunts and waste no time or steps chasing pop fouls. He must also have a good arm.

Brain-power must come with stamina in this job. The catcher mentally catalogues the batting strength and weakness of every player in the league. He needs fine judgment to mix up the pitches he calls for, in such a way as to pace the pitcher and baffle the hitter. He must decide when to call for a pitchout, when to throw to a base, and also directs the throw of teammates who field bunts or slow rollers with men on base.

To give signals, the catcher squats on his haunches, feet comfortably apart about six inches, with the weight balanced on the ball of each foot. Signs come from the fingers of the right hand, which is held well up the thigh. The mitt helps shield the fingered signal from enemy coaches.

Just before the delivery, the catcher shifts into a quarter-crouch, with the left foot slightly forward and the legs slightly farther apart. The full face of his mitt is presented toward the pitcher, making a good target. By playing as close as possible to the batter, the catcher is less likely to miss foul tips, gets best position to throw on steals, is best situated to catch low pitches in the strike zone and is poised to break for a bunt.

The right hand should be relaxed, while awaiting the pitch, with fingers loosely closed around the thumb. This avoids broken fingers on foul tips. As the ball thuds into the mitt, the mitt hand rolls over and traps the ball in the pocket, fingers automatically encircling the ball in correct throwing position.

If the pitch is above the belt, catch it with the fingers of the mitt pointed upward; if below, hold the fingers down. Don't just reach for a wide pitch—step in that direction, too. If the pitch is too low, drop your knees into the dirt to block it with a man on base.

Immediately after receiving the pitch, snap into a good throwing position by pivoting with the weight on the right foot, striding forward with the left, and throwing the ball overhand...especially for basestealers. The weight shifts from right foot to left as the throw is made, thus putting body and shoulders behind it. To nab a base-stealer, throw in a low trajectory. Bluff throws to keep runners close to the bag.

In fielding a bunt, use one hand only if the ball has stopped dead. If the bunt is rolling, place your mitt in front of it and scoop the ball into the mitt with your bare hand. Never take your eye off the ball, or try to throw it, before you actually have it.

Other tips: On pop fouls, flip off your mask immediately and toss it in opposite direction from ball...Tag with both hands when possible...With a man on first, hurry to cover third on a sacrifice bunt...Back up throws to first with none on...Practice exhaustively on catching high fouls, because the ball has terrific spin as it hits the mitt...Keep the mitt in a flat plane when catching pop-ups.

HOW TO PLAY FIRST BASE
BY GEORGE SISLER

Everything else being equal, the tall left-hander has the edge as a first baseman. He can reach farther for high, wide or late throws, and he can throw more easily to the other bases. However, there have been smaller righthanded fielders who were good on defense.

When fielding a ball hit to him, the first baseman should, as the pitch is made, have his weight come over on the ball of each foot. Don't ever be back on your heels. If possible, advance toward the ball, judging the hop as it comes. A good fielder is one who can judge a bounce well. A long hop or short pickup is easiest to catch. The long pickup (sometimes called a short hop) is hardest, and should be avoided if possible. Catch the ball in front of you and "give" with the catch. Keep your eye on the grounder from the time it leaves the bat. Never be caught with your chin up in the air.

When not guarding the bag to keep the runner from taking too big a lead, the first baseman should play 20 to 25 feet back of the base and as far away from the foul line as the type of hitter would justify. On the hit to another infielder, go quickly to first base and find the bag with your left foot. Then turn to take the throw, shifting feet if necessary. I am against straddling the bag and kicking back to tag the base as the catch is made, because the first

baseman would not have time for these actions if he were playing at his maximum depth to start with.

Here are some important tips on first base play:

(1) When the play is close and the ball is thrown into the runner, the left-handed first baseman must keep his left foot on the base, right foot forward, and make a one-handed, backhand catch of the ball.

(2) On close plays, stretch forward as far as possible to catch the ball as soon as possible. The last portion of the foot to touch the bag is the toe, and not the heel, because if you try to stretch with only the heel on the bag, it certainly will come off.

(3) Catch the ball with two hands if possible.

(4) Make long throws to third base overhanded.

(5) If the throw to you is bad, and you see you will not be able to stick on the bag while reaching the ball, then by all means leave the bag and make the catch. That will prevent the runner from taking an extra base.

(6) Shifting should be done with a little natural hop from side to side. Practice this a lot.

(7) Do not reach for a runner in tagging Make him come to you. Be able to cover every portion of the bag with your tagging hand.

(8) If you are no longer needed at first base, move around and back up bases or go out for relays. Make yourself generally useful. Learn your role for cut-off plays.

(9) Catch all pop flies that are in your territory.

(10) When fielding a ball in such a way that the pitcher has to cover first, throw the ball to him underhanded and while moving toward him. Aim the toss chest-high and never conceal the ball from him.

HOW TO PLAY SECOND BASE
BY ROGERS HORNSBY

The second baseman has many responsibilities that require not only skill but mental alertness. There are many things to do besides field ground balls and throw to first base... but as he has to field and throw many times in an average game, it is important that he reach the highest point of efficiency in these departments. That means hours and hours of practice.

Be set to make a quick start either to the left or right for a grounder. Be prepared to dash in for a slow, dribbling grounder or to turn around and run back for a short fly into the shallow outfield.

Do not overlook your training in mastering the art of catching a pop fly.

Proper position on the diamond is not fixed. Shift according to whether the batter is left or right handed, whether he is a notorious pull hitter or straight-away or slicer. Play the left handed pull hitter a bit deeper, say on the edge of the outfield grass, and closer to first than usual. If he is a very fast runner, however, you can't afford to play him quite that deep.

When expecting a sacrifice bunt, play closer to the batter and far enough toward first so you can cover that bag should the first baseman go in for a bunt. Be sure, however, not to leave your position too soon, or the batter may double-cross you by hitting through the vacant spot, or by dragging a bunt in that direction.

Also be alert in case the ball is bunted past the pitcher. In this case you have to field it and try for the putout at first.

When a double play is hoped for, then, regardless of whether a right or left-handed batter is at the plate, you must move toward second base so as to be in position to cover that bag in time for the double play. In order to pivot

correctly, always try to touch the bag with your right foot, then step with the left foot in toward the pitcher's mound and make the throw to first.

In running to cover second, it is wise to straddle the bag, so that in case of a wide throw you can touch the bag with either foot for a forceout.

When runners on first and third try a double steal, the second baseman is important in breaking it up. In case of a pitchout, the second baseman runs to a spot 10 feet in front of the bag while the shortstop goes right to the bag. If the runner on third starts for home, the second baseman should cut off the throw from the catcher and return the ball to the plate. When the double steal is attempted without a pitchout, the bag is covered as in the usual manner with only a man on first, and the man who takes the throw at second base never waits for the tag but instead fires the ball right back to the catcher.

When a ball is hit to right or right center for extra bases, the second baseman should run out to take the relay throw. Make up your mind as you dash out whether the ball will be good for three bases or a homer, and you'll know where to relay the ball. If the ball should not be good for more than a double, then the second baseman should break for second to be in position for the throw. With the ball hit to left field, the shortstop takes the throw at second, with the second baseman backing him up in case of a wild throw.

(*Condensed from "How to Play," Copyright* 1951 *by The Sporting News, St. Louis*)

HOW TO PLAY SHORTSTOP
BY HONUS WAGNER

A shortstop must have a good arm as the prime requisite. Next, he must be fast, able to shift his feet and ready to move in any direction. Keep trying. Don't be afraid of making an error. Seek the advice of older players, the coaches and manager. Above all, never lose sight of the ball.

Always keep in mind the number of outs, which bases are occupied and the score. Study each hitter. On a fast runner, you must handle the ball cleanly and hurry the throw. Shift for each batter, according to where he is most likely to hit.

Think out each play before it happens. If you boot the ball, think where you're going to throw it even before you pick it up, so no time is lost.

The hardest play for a shortstop to make is going to his right for a deep hit ball. Set yourself when you get your hands on the ball, and be in a position to throw to first. Another tough play is the slowly hit ball coming right at you, especially with a fast batter. Play this on your barehanded side so as to get the ball away quickly, picking the ball up and throwing it without hesitation in virtually a single motion.

In starting a double play, remember it is wiser to make sure of one out than lose two. Grab the ball and feed it to the second baseman letter-high. If the ball goes to your right, or deep, put something on the throw to second. If it's a grounder near second, flip it underhand to the second baseman.

When pivoting in a double play, be in motion when receiving the ball, step on second base with the right foot and remain on balance by stepping forward with the left before finally throwing to first.

With a runner on first, the shortstop covers second on a bunt. With runners on first and second, keep the runner as close to second as possible by feinting him back. To pick a runner off second, stand about five feet behind the line and slowly work your way up close behind him. Break for the bag when the runner is leaning toward the next base, so as to catch him off balance.

The shortstop takes most of the relays on long hits to the outfield; otherwise, he directs the player who does take the relay, as to where the throw should go.

With a runner on first and a hit to right field, the shortstop stands about 25 feet in front of third base, on the grass, awaiting and guiding the throw from the outfielder. If there is a chance for the third baseman to catch the runner coming from first, he yells to the shortstop, "Let it go!" The shortstop bluffs the catch, to discourage the batter from advancing during the ensuing play, but lets the ball go through to the third baseman.

Other tips: Shortstop gets pitching signs from catcher and relays them to outfielders by hand or voice signal...Whether short or second baseman covers base on attempted steal depends on batter and type of pitch. . .Tag a runner with almost the same motion you get the ball, then get rid of the ball as fast as you can. . . Size up a pop fly and yell for it as soon as you feel sure you can get it; otherwise yell for either the left or center fielder to take it.

(Condensed from "How to Play Shortstop," by Honus Wagner, in April 13, 1949 issue of The Sporting News, St. Louis)

HOW TO PLAY THIRD BASE BY PIE TRAYNOR

Like any other player on the field, the third baseman must always make up his mind—before each pitch—exactly what to do with the ball if it is hit to him. The number of men on base, the score, the inning, the number of outs, the speed afoot of batter and baserunners. . . all figure in the decision. But, like a woman's mind and the cost of living, that decision is subject to change without notice. A reckless baserunner may break, or a grounder may take a bad hop and the "correct" play becomes something entirely different from the preconceived strategy. Split-second thinking in such situations is not completely a matter of intuition. Experience counts!

Position play depends on the tactical situation of the game and the type of hitter. In general it is best to play behind the line. Move up against a lefthanded batter or notorious bunter. In any case, the third baseman must have a trained reflex to spring toward the plate, the moment a bunt develops. When the batter snaps into the flatfooted, square-facing bunt posture, the third baseman should be charging in even before the pitch reaches the plate.

Hard-hit balls are the true test of a third baseman. If he can't field them, or at least block them, extra-base hits result. It takes more courage than skill to stop those smashes.

The swinging bunt, or topped dribbler by a batter taking full cut, is really tough. Since he can't get the jump on such a play, the third baseman reaches the ball late. To make up for lost time, the baseman must charge in, while keeping his eyes glued to the ball, scoop it up barehanded and make the throw to first with the same motion.

Many hard smashes reach the third baseman before the hitter has broken out of the batter's box. That leaves plenty of time for the throw. The baseman should straighten his body, take aim, cock his arm and coordinate his throw with the stride.

Many valuable putouts are made even when the third baseman can only knock down the ball. A quick recovery and immediate throw will turn the trick. The baseman should practice throwing from any position, since he must get rid of the ball as soon as possible, and he should cock his arm only for throws on which he has plenty of time.

Other hints for third basemen:

Straddle the bag to receive a throw. If the play is not close, leave the bag to take the throw.

Practice exhaustively on catching high pop fouls.

Range as far as possible on grounders to your left.

When fielding a grounder with less than two out and men on first and second, make the double play relay via second base. Never start the play be stepping on third, unless the act of fielding the ball brings you toward the bag.

Handle squeeze bunts with a barehanded scoop-up and underhand throw.

Never let the runner on third take a long lead. Feint him back.

If the pitcher fields a bunt with a man on base, direct his throw and hurry back to cover third base.

HOW TO PLAY THE OUTFIELD
BY JOE DiMAGGIO

To be an outfielder in the majors today, a player must be a good, consistent hitter, exceptionally fast if he isn't a long-ball hitter, and a first-rate flychaser and thrower. A team is far better off with an outfielder who piles up errors trying for hard catches than with one who handles perfectly every ball hit to him but doesn't go after the tough ones.

Before every play, size up the possibilities. Know the hitter and where he is likely to hit certain types of pitches. Get the sign from the shortstop as to what type of pitch is coming, so you will know in which direction to break "with the crack of the bat." Curve balls are more likely to be pulled than fast balls. Pre-game practice will familiarize you with ground conditions (whether the bounce is likely to be hard or soft), wind, background, fences, etc. However, wind currents are tricky, so check occasionally with flags flying around the stands.

Make every catch in the best possible position from which to throw. I prefer to take fly balls with my hands above my head, left foot toward the plate, so as to save time making the throw. On ground balls, there is rarely any choice; when you catch up with it, the ball is usually hugging the ground. If it happens to be a bouncing ball, charge it in order to field it at the top of the hop, leaving you in good throwing position.

It is easier to catch a ball when standing still than on the dead run. Still, an outfielder who has a good jump on the ball may slow down in order to take the ball deliberately on the run to increase the force of his throw to beat a runner to the plate.

With a man on base, make up your mind in advance where you will throw, but be ready to react instantly to any change in circumstances. The safest rule to follow is: throw ahead of the runner. On throws to all bases, it is better to throw on one hop than on the fly. A bounding throw is more accurate and easier for a fielder to handle. Also, low throws set up cutoffs plays. Exception to the bounce-throw rule is when the ground is soft because of recent rain, and only when the outfielder is close enough to reach the base on the fly.

All outfielders should wear sunglasses. Never stare into the sun. Even with sunglasses, no outfielder can take a ball coming out of the sun. The sun-fielder should try to gauge the ball by getting a sidewise glimpse and shielding his eyes with his glove.

No outfielder is a real workman unless he can turn his back on the ball, run his legs off and take the catch over his shoulder. Practice this play till you are sure of it. Backpedalling outfielders get nowhere.

Other outfielding tips: Never gamble with a shoestring or diving catch unless a single would send in the tying or winning run. . .Use both hands for a catch, except where extra reach is necessary. . .Remember that balls hit wide of the centerfielder tend to swerve toward the nearer foul line. . .There are some advantages to playing shallow, but in these days of the lively ball it is dangerous

. . .Outfielders should back each other up and also back up the infield whenever possible. A "bluff catch" of a Texas Leaguer often keeps a runner from advancing an extra base.

(Condensed from "Baseball for Everyone," Copyright 1948 by Whittlesey House, N.Y.)

HOW TO UMPIRE
BY BILLY EVANS

Umpiring is a mixture of good physique, good eyes, plenty of courage, pride in your work, a knowledge of the rules, getting the right angle, a respect for the ability of others—managers, players and umpires—plus plenty of common sense. There is no greater asset than common sense properly applied.

Anticipation is an umpire's greatest trouble-maker. It is invariably the source of calling plays too quickly. Instead of anticipating the play, let it happen, follow it intently to its completion before reaching a decision.

There is considerably more to umpiring than the mere calling of ball or strike—out or safe—fair or foul. True, they are six basic operations in the life of an umpire, but many other things are equally important.

Umpires are human—all opinions to the contrary—hence, they err. In all the 25 years that I umpired, I have never tried to prove infallibility. Rather, I have very forcefully stated that I called the play as I saw it, and that made the decision arrived at "official." Even when positive I had not erred. I always regarded it as diplomacy to listen to the player's side of the argument. It is far easier to reason with the player who has let off steam rather than one who is burning up over an adverse decision and finds no one willing to listen. It is then that he goes berserk.

Never try to alibi your error. That makes two mistakes out of one. Umpires dislike ball players who alibi. In like manner, ball players have no particular use for the umpire who always has an alibi.

Don't work your thumb overtime, pointing the way to the clubhouse. Baseball is played on the field, not under the showers. Eject players from the game only as a last resort. Constantly work for some other solution. However, there are times when nothing but a nice cold shower will cool off a protesting player.

"Run your ball game, but don't overrun it."

Umpiring is largely a matter of angles. There is a best angle or spot for every play. Be in the right spot and you reduce the chances to err to a minimum.

The right way on the bases is always to be on top of the play. If you are over the play and miss it, you are far more liable to get away with an incorrect ruling than if you rendered the same decision fifteen or twenty feet away from the play. Ball players like umpires who hustle.

In getting over a play, I think it helps the umpire's judgment if he comes to a stop as he focuses on the play rather than rendering the decision while on the run.

Never lose sight of the ball. If you know where the ball is at all times, it will keep you out of a lot of trouble. Nothing shows up an umpire more than not to see the hidden ball trick. It makes the umpire look far worse than the player who was trapped.

Keep your eye on the ball to the completion of every play. Never turn your head or run by a play after you have given a decision. A lot of things can happen to the ball while you are looking in some other direction after making final ruling.

(Condensed from "Umpiring from the Inside," Copyright 1947 by Wm. G. Evans.)

BALL PARKS
American League

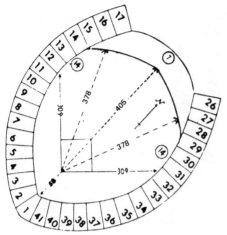

MEMORIAL STADIUM
Home of:
Baltimore Orioles AL
Seating Capacity: 52,860

MEMORIAL STADIUM

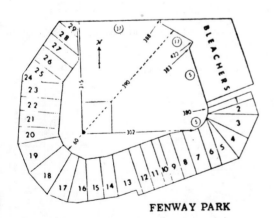

FENWAY PARK
Home of:
Boston Red Sox AL
Seating Capacity: 33,502

FENWAY PARK

622

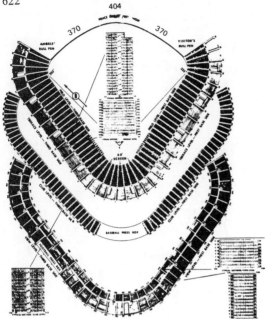

ANAHEIM STADIUM

Home of:
  California Angels AL
Seating Capacity: 43,250

COMISKEY PARK
Home of:
  Chicago White Sox AL
Seating Capacity: 44,492

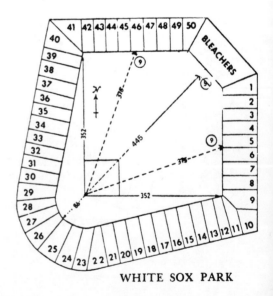

WHITE SOX PARK

623

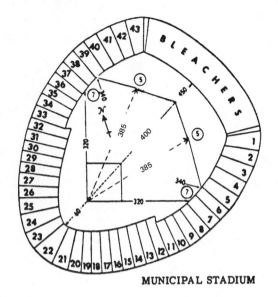

CLEVELAND STADIUM

Home of:
  Cleveland Indians AL
Seating Capacity, 76,713

MUNICIPAL STADIUM

TIGER STADIUM

  Home of:
    Detroit Tigers AL
  Seating Capacity: 53,676

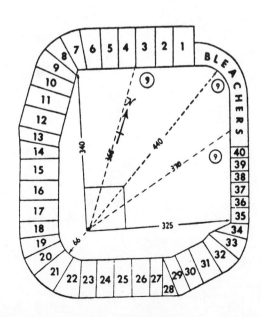

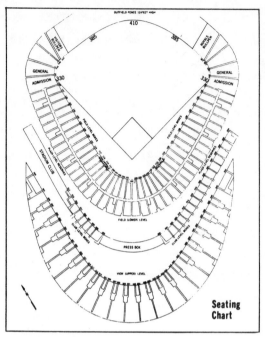

ROYALS STADIUM
Home of:
  Kansas City Royals A
Seating Capacity: 40,762

Seating
Chart

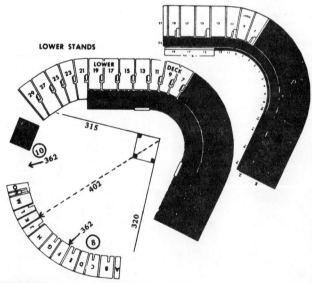

COUNTY STADIUM
Home of:
  Milwaukee Brewers AL
Seating Capacity: 54,187

625

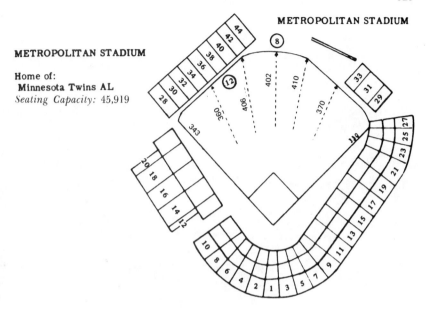

METROPOLITAN STADIUM

METROPOLITAN STADIUM

Home of:
 Minnesota Twins AL
Seating Capacity: 45,919

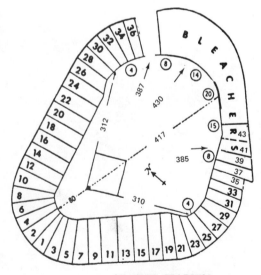

YANKEE STADIUM
Home of:
 New York Yankees AL
Seating Capacity: 57,545

YANKEE STADIUM

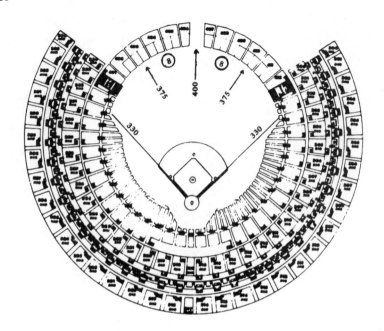

OAKLAND-ALAMEDA COUNTY STADIUM

Home of:
Oakland Athletics AL
Seating Capacity: 50,000

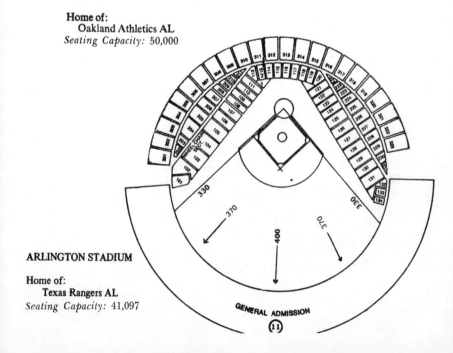

ARLINGTON STADIUM

Home of:
Texas Rangers AL
Seating Capacity: 41,097

EXHIBITION STADIUM
Home of:
   Toronto Blue Jays
Seating Capacity: 43,737

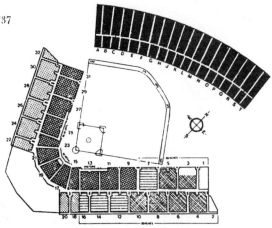

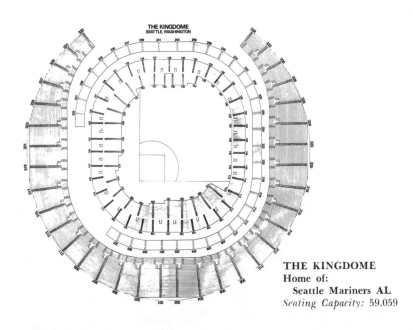

THE KINGDOME
Home of:
   Seattle Mariners AL
Seating Capacity: 59,059

ATLANTA STADIUM

Home of:
Atlanta Braves NL
Seating Capacity: 52,194

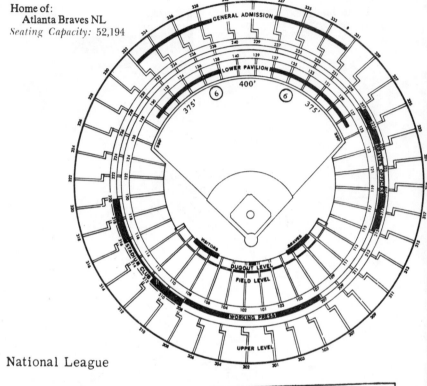

National League

WRIGLEY FIELD
Home of:
Chicago Cubs NL
Seating Capacity: 37,741

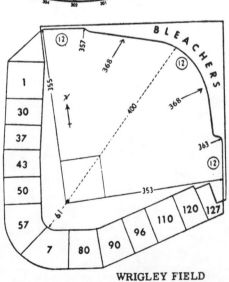

WRIGLEY FIELD

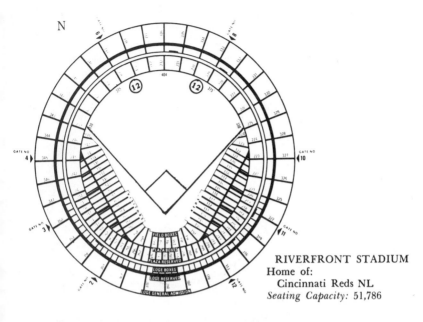

N

RIVERFRONT STADIUM
Home of:
  Cincinnati Reds NL
Seating Capacity: 51,786

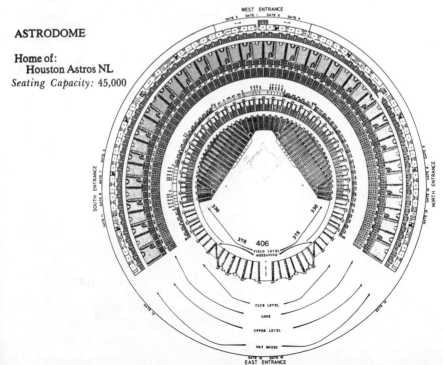

ASTRODOME

Home of:
  Houston Astros NL
Seating Capacity: 45,000

630

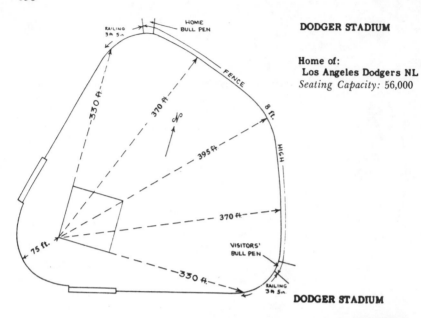

DODGER STADIUM

Home of:
Los Angeles Dodgers NL
Seating Capacity: 56,000

DODGER STADIUM

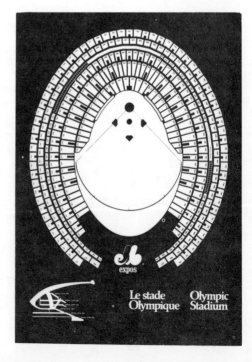

OLYMPIC STADIUM
Home of:
Montreal Expos
Seating Capacity: 59,512

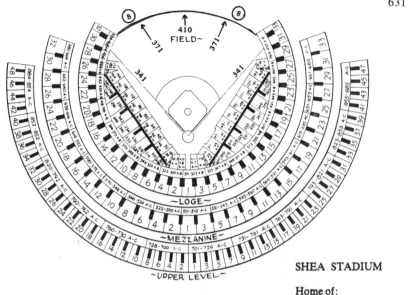

SHEA STADIUM

Home of:
New York Mets NL
Seating Capacity: 55,300

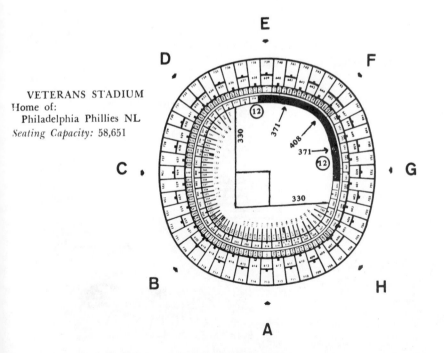

VETERANS STADIUM
Home of:
Philadelphia Phillies NL
Seating Capacity: 58,651

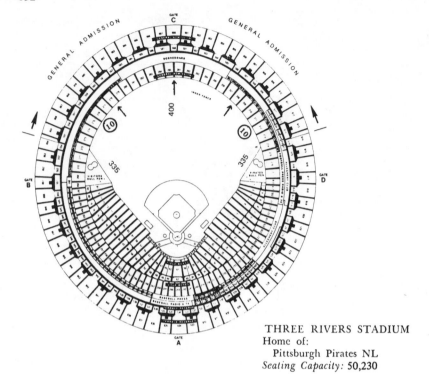

THREE RIVERS STADIUM
Home of:
    Pittsburgh Pirates NL
Seating Capacity: **50,230**

BUSCH MEMORIAL STADIUM

Home of:
    St. Louis Cardinals NL
Seating Capacity: 50,222

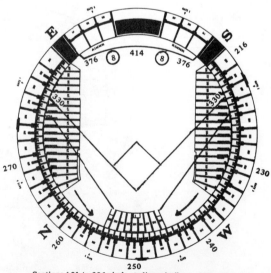

Sections 301 to 396 circle stadium similar to 200 series.

SAN DIEGO STADIUM
Home of
San Diego Padres NL
Seating Capacity: 48,443

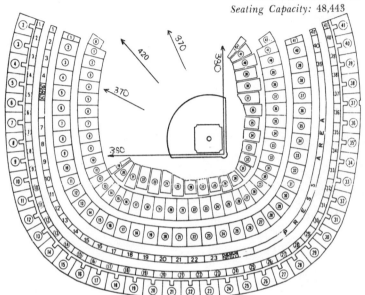

CANDLESTICK PARK

Home of:
San Francisco Giants NL
Seating Capacity: 58,000

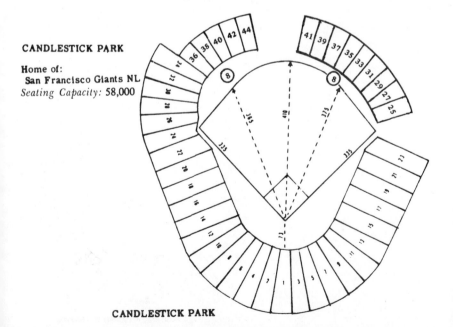

CANDLESTICK PARK